October 19-23, 2015
Melbourne, Australia

AF765860

Association for Computing Machinery

Advancing Computing as a Science & Profession

CIKM'15

Proceedings of the 24th ACM International Conference on Information and Knowledge Management

Sponsored by:

ACM SIGIR and ACM SIGWEB

Supported by:

Microsoft Research, Sportsbet, Google, City of Melbourne, Professor Ram Kumar Memorial Foundation, Yahoo! Labs, Deakin University, RMIT University, and The University of Melbourne

Association for
Computing Machinery

Advancing Computing as a Science & Profession

The Association for Computing Machinery
2 Penn Plaza, Suite 701
New York, New York 10121-0701

Copyright © 2015 by the Association for Computing Machinery, Inc. (ACM). Permission to make digital or hard copies of portions of this work for personal or classroom use is granted without fee provided that copies are not made or distributed for profit or commercial advantage and that copies bear this notice and the full citation on the first page. Copyright for components of this work owned by others than ACM must be honored. Abstracting with credit is permitted. To copy otherwise, to republish, to post on servers or to redistribute to lists, requires prior specific permission and/or a fee. Request permission to republish from: permissions@acm.org or Fax +1 (212) 869-0481.

For other copying of articles that carry a code at the bottom of the first or last page, copying is permitted provided that the per-copy fee indicated in the code is paid through www.copyright.com.

Notice to Past Authors of ACM-Published Articles
ACM intends to create a complete electronic archive of all articles and/or other material previously published by ACM. If you have written a work that has been previously published by ACM in any journal or conference proceedings prior to 1978, or any SIG Newsletter at any time, and you do NOT want this work to appear in the ACM Digital Library, please inform permissions@acm.org, stating the title of the work, the author(s), and where and when published.

ISBN: 978-1-4503-3794-6 (Digital)

ISBN: 978-1-4503-4116-5 (Print)

Additional copies may be ordered prepaid from:

ACM Order Department
PO Box 30777
New York, NY 10087-0777, USA

Phone: 1-800-342-6626 (USA and Canada)
+1-212-626-0500 (Global)
Fax: +1-212-944-1318
E-mail: acmhelp@acm.org
Hours of Operation: 8:30 am – 4:30 pm ET

Printed in the USA

General Chairs' Preface

It is our great pleasure to welcome you to the 24th ACM International Conference on Information and Knowledge Management (CIKM 2015). CIKM is a top-tier ACM conference in the areas of databases, information retrieval, and knowledge management. It has successfully brought together leading researchers and developers from these three communities since 1992, with the purpose of identifying challenging problems facing the development of advanced knowledge and information systems, and shaping future research directions through the publication of high-quality applied and theoretical research findings. The 24th edition of CIKM continues this tradition, placing particular emphasis on the utility of data science across structured and semi-structured data.

We are delighted to present three outstanding keynote speakers: Jaime Teevan, from Microsoft; Andrew Tomkins, from Google; and Xiaofang Zhou, from the University of Queensland. We are also honored to host six distinguished invited speakers for the conference's Industry Track: Hang Li (Huawei Noah's Ark), Wei-Ying Ma (Microsoft Research Asia), Sofus A. Macskassy (Facebook), Igor Perisic (LinkedIn), Amy Shi-Nash (SingTel DataSpark), and Andrew Tomkins (Google).

We are indebted to the many authors who submitted their work to the CIKM technical program, and to the team of people who evaluated them. The Program Committee was expertly led by six PC Chairs: Timos Sellis and Jeffrey Xu Yu (Database Track); Maarten de Rijke and Vanessa Murdock (Information Retrieval Track); and Charu Aggarwal and Ravi Kumar (Knowledge Management Track). The review process was supported by the Microsoft CMT system. A report on the paper selection process appears in the PC Chairs' Preface.

We also thank the other chairs in the organization team: Shonali Krishnaswamy and Marc Najork (Industry Track); Wei Wang and Grace Hui Yang (Tutorials); Shane Culpepper and Chee Yong Chan (Workshops); and Yun Sing Koh (Publicity). CIKM 2015 includes a machine learning competition, sponsored by Sportsbet, with participants tackling the challenge of predicting the outcomes of the Australian Rules Football Finals. A substantial prize will be awarded to the best-performing system on the third day of the conference.

Running a conference the scale of CIKM is a serious undertaking and we are grateful to our local organization team for their effective and efficient handling of logistics. In particular, the Local Arrangements Chairs Tony Wirth and Rui Zhang provided extensive support, as did the team of student volunteers that Tony and Rui helped recruit and manage.

We gratefully acknowledge the support of our sponsors for the conference: Microsoft as Gold Sponsor; Sportsbet as Silver Sponsor; Google, The City of Melbourne, The Professor Ram Kumar Memorial Foundation, and Yahoo Labs, as Bronze sponsors; and The University of Melbourne, RMIT University, and Deakin University, as Academic Sponsors. We also received support from the CIKM Steering Committee, and from the Association for Computing Machinery and their special interest groups SIGIR and SIGWEB.

ICMS Australasia provided expert assistance with the logistics of the event, and we thank them for their professional advice and guidance. We also benefited greatly from the support provided by the Melbourne Convention Bureau during the early stages of our planning; and from the knowledge and skills of the many expert staff at the Melbourne Convention and Exhibition Center, the venue for CIKM 2015.

We trust that you enjoy the conference, and also the other activities you are able to fit in during your visit to Melbourne. Indeed, there are many things to see and enjoy in Victoria and in the whole Australasian region at this time of year, and we hope that you will be able to combine business and pleasure in to a memorable experience while you are here. Finally, CIKM 2016 will be in Indianapolis, in the USA, and we hope to see you again there.

James Bailey and Alistair Moffat
The University of Melbourne

August 2015.

CIKM2015
19–23 October 2015 Melbourne Australia

PC Chairs' Preface

We are delighted to welcome you to the 24th ACM International Conference on Information and Knowledge Management (CIKM 2015), held in Melbourne from October 19–23, 2015. CIKM is now well-established as a leading venue for bringing together researchers from across the Database, Information Retrieval, and Knowledge Management communities.

Continuing the pattern of previous years, we received a large number of high-quality submissions in all three tracks, in both full- and short-paper categories. As a result, we are confident that CIKM 2015 has succeeded in creating an outstanding technical program including research paper presentations; short-paper presentations during the poster session; plenary talks; and an engaging Industry Track arranged by the Industry Track Chairs. In total, we received 646 full-paper (10-page) submissions and 276 short-paper (4-page) submissions, which were reviewed and discussed by 88 area chairs, 471 program committee members, and a further 145 expert external reviewers.

We accepted 165 full papers (26%) and 69 short papers (25%). The acceptance statistics per track were as follows: Databases, 35/129 full papers and 6/37 short papers; Information Retrieval, 43/171 full papers and 27/101 short papers; and Knowledge Management, 87/346 papers and 36/138 short papers. Two of the Knowledge Management short papers were withdrawn by their authors prior to the proceedings being finalized. Our work was greatly eased by the support provided by the Microsoft CMT service, and we thank the CMT team for their assistance.

We are grateful to the many people who helped with the process of bringing this program together. We would in particular like to recognize the immense efforts of the area chairs, program committee members, and external reviewers, who each volunteered many hours of time, and contributed their deep expertise in order to allow the selection of the work that you can see in this volume. Most importantly of all, we thank the authors who submitted contributions for consideration. Without the drive and energy of the several thousand researchers and students who prepared manuscripts and carried out evaluations, the conference would be doomed to failure; but with that drive and energy, we have been able to achieve the success that you see here. We hope that participants in the conference in Melbourne, as well as subsequent readers of the proceedings, will find the technical program of CIKM 2015 to be both inspiring and rewarding.

Charu C. Aggarwal, IBM
Maarten de Rijke, University of Amsterdam
Ravi Kumar, Google
Vanessa Murdock, Microsoft
Timos Sellis, RMIT University
Jeffrey Xu Yu, Chinese University of Hong Kong

August 2015.

CIKM2015
19–23 October 2015 Melbourne Australia

Table of Contents

CIKM 2015 Conference Organization xxiv

CIKM 2015 Sponsors and Supporters xxxiii

Keynote Address I
Session Chair: Alistair Moffat *(The University of Melbourne)*

- **Slow Search: Improving Information Retrieval Using Human Assistance** 1
  Jaime Teevan *(Microsoft Research)*

Session 1A: Scalability
Session Chair: Rui Zhang *(The University of Melbourne)*

- **External Data Access and Indexing in AsterixDB** 3
  Abdullah Alamoudi, Raman Grover, Michael J. Carey, Vinayak Borkar *(University of California, Irvine)*
- **Dynamic Resource Management in a Massively Parallel Stream Processing Engine** 13
  Kasper Grud Skat Madsen, Yongluan Zhou *(University of Southern Denmark)*
- **A Parallel GPU-Based Approach to Clustering Very Fast Data Streams** 23
  Pengtao Huang, Xiu Li, Bo Yuan *(Tsinghua University)*
- **Scalable Clustering Algorithm via a Triangle Folding Processing for Complex Networks** 33
  Ying Kang *(Institute of Information Engineering, Chinese Academy of Sciences & University of Chinese Academy of Sciences)*,
  Xiaoyan Gu, Weiping Wang, Dan Meng *(Institute of Information Engineering, Chinese Academy of Sciences)*

Session 1B: Personal Search
Session Chair: Peter Bailey *(Microsoft)*

- **Understanding the Impact of the Role Factor in Collaborative Information Retrieval** 43
  Lynda Tamine, Laure Soulier *(Université de Toulouse UPS IRIT)*
- **Experiments with a Venue-Centric Model for Personalised and Time-Aware Venue Suggestion** 53
  Romain Deveaud, M-Dyaa Albakour, Craig Macdonald, Iadh Ounis *(University of Glasgow)*
- **Search Result Diversification Based on Hierarchical Intents** 63
  Sha Hu *(Beijing Key Laboratory of Big Data Management and Analysis Methods and Renmin University of China)*,
  Zhicheng Dou, Xiaojie Wang
  (Key Laboratory of Data Engineering and Knowledge Engineering, MOE and Renmin University of China),
  Tetsuya Sakai *(Waseda University)*,
  Ji-Rong Wen *(Beijing Key Laboratory of Big Data Management and Analysis Methods and Renmin University of China)*
- **Category-Driven Approach for Local Related Business Recommendations** 73
  Yonathan Perez *(Stanford University)*,
  Michael Schueppert, Matthew Lawlor, Shaunak Kishore *(Google)*

Session 1C: Learning
Session Chair: Leif Azzopardi *(University of Glasgow)*

- **A Soft Computing Approach for Learning to Aggregate Rankings** 83
  Javier A. Vargas, Ricardo da S. Torres *(University of Campinas)*,
  Marcos André Gonçalves *(Universidade Federal de Minas Gerais)*
- **Approximate String Matching by End-Users using Active Learning** 93
  Lutz Büch, Artur Andrzejak *(Heidelberg University, Germany)*

- **A Unified Posterior Regularized Topic Model with Maximum Margin for Learning-to-Rank** 103
  Shoaib Jameel *(Cardiff University)*, Wai Lam *(The Chinese University of Hong Kong)*,
  Steven Schockaert *(Cardiff University)*, Lidong Bing *(Carnegie Mellon University)*
- **Collaborating between Local and Global Learning for Distributed Online Multiple Tasks** 113
  Xin Jin *(Chinese Academy of Sciences, Huawei Technologies Co. Ltd.)*,
  Ping Luo, Fuzhen Zhuang *(Chinese Academy of Sciences)*,
  Jia He *(Chinese Academy of Sciences & Huawei Technologies Co. Ltd.)*,
  Qing He *(Chinese Academy of Sciences)*

Session 1D: Text Processing

Session Chair: Tim Baldwin *(The University of Melbourne)*

- **Lifespan-based Partitioning of Index Structures for Time-travel Text Search** 123
  Animesh Nandi, Suriya Subramanian, Sriram Lakshminarasimhan, Prasad M. Deshpande,
  Sriram Raghavan *(IBM Research)*
- **Contextual Text Understanding in Distributional Semantic Space** 133
  Jianpeng Cheng *(Microsoft Research Asia, University of Oxford)*,
  Zhongyuan Wang *(Renmin University of China, Microsoft Research Asia)*,
  Ji-Rong Wen *(Renmin University of China)*, Jun Yan, Zheng Chen *(Microsoft Research Asia)*
- **External Knowledge and Query Strategies in Active Learning: a Study in Clinical Information Extraction** 143
  Mahnoosh Kholghi *(Queensland University of Technology & The Australian e-Health Research Centre)*,
  Laurianne Sitbon, Guido Zuccon *(Queensland University of Technology)*,
  Anthony Nguyen *(The Australian e-Health Research Centre, CSIRO)*
- **Ranking Deep Web Text Collections for Scalable Information Extraction** 153
  Pablo Barrio, Luis Gravano *(Columbia University)*, Chris Develder *(Ghent University - iMinds)*

Session 1E: Applications

Session Chair: Huizhi (Elly) Liang *(The University of Melbourne)*

- **Forming Online Support Groups for Internet and Behavior Related Addictions** 163
  Chih-Ya Shen *(Academia Sinica)*, Hong-Han Shuai *(National Taiwan University)*,
  De-Nian Yang *(Academia Sinica)*, Yi-Feng Lan *(Tamkang University)*,
  Wang-Chien Lee *(The Pennsylvania State University)*,
  Philip S. Yu *(University of Illinois at Chicago & Tsinghua University)*,
  Ming-Syan Chen *(National Taiwan University)*
- **Concept-Based Relevance Models for Medical and Semantic Information Retrieval** 173
  Chunye Wang, Ramakrishna Akella *(University of California Santa Cruz)*
- **PlateClick: Bootstrapping Food Preferences Through an Adaptive Visual Interface** 183
  Longqi Yang, Yin Cui, Fan Zhang *(Cornell University & Cornell Tech)*,
  John P. Pollak *(Cornell University)*,
  Serge Belongie, Deborah Estrin *(Cornell University & Cornell Tech)*
- **Data Driven Water Pipe Failure Prediction: A Bayesian Nonparametric Approach** 193
  Peng Lin *(NICTA & UNSW)*, Bang Zhang *(NICTA)*, Yi Wang *(NICTA & UNSW)*,
  Zhidong Li, Bin Li, Yang Wang *(NICTA)*, Fang Chen *(NICTA & UNSW)*

Session 1F: Social Media 1

Session Chair: Lynda Tamine *(IRIT/CNRS France)*

- **Tumblr Blog Recommendation with Boosted Inductive Matrix Completion** 203
  Donghyuk Shin *(University of Texas at Austin)*, Suleyman Cetintas, Kuang-Chih Lee *(Yahoo Labs)*,
  Inderjit S. Dhillon *(University of Texas at Austin)*
- **BiasWatch: A Lightweight System for Discovering and Tracking Topic-Sensitive Opinion Bias in Social Media** 213
  Haokai Lu, James Caverlee, Wei Niu *(Texas A&M University)*

- **Knowlywood: Mining Activity Knowledge From Hollywood Narratives** 223
  Niket Tandon *(Max Planck Institute for Informatics)*, Gerard de Melo *(Tsinghua University)*,
  Abir De *(IIT Kharagpur)*, Gerhard Weikum *(Max Planck Institute for Informatics)*
- **Entity and Aspect Extraction for Organizing News Comments** 233
  Radityo Eko Prasojo, Mouna Kacimi, Werner Nutt *(Free University of Bozen-Bolzano)*

Session 2A: Graphs

Session Chair: Sourav S. Bhowmick *(Nanyang Technological University)*

- **HDRF: Stream-Based Partitioning for Power-Law Graphs** 243
  Fabio Petroni, Leonardo Querzoni *(Sapienza University of Rome)*,
  Khuzaima Daudjee, Shahin Kamali *(University of Waterloo)*, Giorgio Iacoboni *(Sapienza University of Rome)*
- **Towards Scale-out Capability on Social Graphs** 253
  Haichuan Shang *(National Institute of Information and Communications Technology and University of Tokyo)*,
  Xiang Zhao *(National University of Defense Technology)*,
  Uday Kiran *(National Institute of Information and Communications Technology and University of Tokyo)*,
  Masaru Kitsuregawa *(National Institute of Informatics and University of Tokyo)*
- **Identifying Top-k Structural Hole Spanners in Large-Scale Social Networks** 263
  Mojtaba Rezvani, Weifa Liang *(Australian National University)*,
  Wenzheng Xu *(Australian National University & Sichuan University)*,
  Chengfei Liu *(Swinburne University of Technology)*
- **Scalable Facility Location for Massive Graphs on Pregel-like Systems** 273
  Kiran Garimella, Gianmarco De Francisci Morales, Aristides Gionis *(Aalto University)*,
  Mauro Sozio *(Télécom ParisTech & CNRS LTCI)*

Session 2B: Retrieval Algorithms

Session Chair: Guido Zuccon *(Queensland University of Technology)*

- **Rank by Time or by Relevance? Revisiting Email Search** 283
  David Carmel, Guy Halawi, Liane Lewin-Eytan, Yoelle Maarek, Ariel Raviv *(Yahoo Labs)*
- **On the Cost of Extracting Proximity Features for Term-Dependency Models** 293
  Xiaolu Lu *(RMIT University)*, Alistair Moffat *(The University of Melbourne)*,
  J. Shane Culpepper *(RMIT University)*
- **An Optimization Framework for Merging Multiple Result Lists** 303
  Chia-Jung Lee, Qingyao Ai, W. Bruce Croft, Daniel Sheldon *(University of Massachusetts Amherst)*
- **Searching and Stopping: An Analysis of Stopping Rules and Strategies** 313
  David Maxwell, Leif Azzopardi *(University of Glasgow)*,
  Kalervo Järvelin, Heikki Keskustalo *(University of Tampere)*

Session 2C: Text Analysis

Session Chair: Krisztian Balog *(University Of Stavanger)*

- **Automated News Suggestions for Populating Wikipedia Entity Pages** 323
  Besnik Fetahu *(Leibniz University of Hannover)*, Katja Markert *(Leibniz University of Hannover & University of Leeds)*, Avishek Anand *(Leibniz University of Hannover)*
- **Mining Coordinated Intent Representation for Entity Search and Recommendation** 333
  Huizhong Duan *(Walmart Labs)*, ChengXiang Zhai *(University of Illinois at Urbana-Champaign)*
- **Sentiment Extraction by Leveraging Aspect-Opinion Association Structure** 343
  Li Zhao, Minlie Huang *(Tsinghua National Laboratory for Information Science and Technology)*,
  Jiashen Sun, Hengliang Luo *(Samsung R&D Institute of China - Beijing)*,
  Xiankai Yang, Xiaoyan Zhu *(Tsinghua National Laboratory for Information Science and Technology)*
- **Leveraging Joint Interactions for Credibility Analysis in News Communities** 353
  Subhabrata Mukherjee, Gerhard Weikum *(Max Planck Institute for Informatics)*

Session 2D: Clustering

Session Chair: Ravi Kumar *(Google)*

- **Clustering-based Active Learning on Sensor Type Classification in Buildings** 363
  Dezhi Hong, Hongning Wang, Kamin Whitehouse *(University of Virginia)*
- **gSparsify: Graph Motif Based Sparsification for Graph Clustering** 373
  Peixiang Zhao *(Florida State University)*
- **Incomplete Multi-view Clustering via Subspace Learning** 383
  Qiyue Yin, Shu Wu, Liang Wang *(Institute of Automation, Chinese Academy of Sciences)*
- **Robust Subspace Clustering via Tighter Rank Approximation** 393
  Zhao Kang, Chong Peng, Qiang Cheng *(Southern Illinois University)*

Session 2E: Users and Predictions

Session Chair: James Caverlee *(Texas A&M University)*

- **Interactive User Group Analysis** 403
  Behrooz Omidvar-Tehrani, Sihem Amer-Yahia *(Université Grenoble Alpes - LIG, CNRS)*,
  Alexandre Termier *(University of Rennes 1, IRISA/INRIA)*
- **Viewability Prediction for Online Display Ads** 413
  Chong Wang *(New Jersey Institute of Technology)*, Achir Kalra *(Forbes Media)*,
  Cristian Borcea, Yi Chen *(New Jersey Institute of Technology)*
- **10 Bits of Surprise: Detecting Malicious Users with Minimum Information** 423
  Reza Zafarani *(Syracuse University)*, Huan Liu *(Arizona State University)*
- **MAPer: A Multi-scale Adaptive Personalized Model for Temporal Human Behavior Prediction** 433
  Sarah Masud Preum, John A. Stankovic, Yanjun Qi *(University of Virginia)*

Session 2F: Heterogeneous Networks

Session Chair: Michael Quan Z. Sheng *(The University of Adelaide)*

- **Classification with Active Learning and Meta-Paths in Heterogeneous Information Networks** 443
  Chang Wan, Xiang Li, Ben Kao *(The University of Hong Kong)*,
  Xiao Yu, Quanquan Gu *(University of Illinois at Urbana-Champaign)*,
  David Cheung *(The University of Hong Kong)*, Jiawei Han *(University of Illinois at Urbana-Champaign)*
- **Semantic Path based Personalized Recommendation on Weighted Heterogeneous Information Networks** 453
  Chuan Shi, Zhiqiang Zhang *(Beijing University of Posts and Telecommunications)*,
  Ping Luo *(Institute of Computing Technology, CAS)*, Philip S. Yu *(University of Illinois at Chicago)*,
  Yading Yue *(Tencent Corporation)*, Bin Wu *(Beijing University of Posts and Telecommunications)*
- **A Graph-based Recommendation across Heterogeneous Domains** 463
  Deqing Yang *(Fudan University)*, Jingrui He *(Arizona State University)*,
  Huazheng Qin, Yanghua Xiao, Wei Wang *(Fudan University)*
- **Query Relaxation across Heterogeneous Data Sources** 473
  Verena Kantere *(University of Geneva)*, George Orfanoudakis *(National Technical University of Athens)*,
  Anastasios Kementsietsidis *(Google Inc.)*, Timos Sellis *(RMIT University)*

Session 3A: Veracity

Session Chair: Laure Berti-Équille *(Qatar Computing Research Institute)*

- **Approximated Summarization of Data Provenance** 483
  Eleanor Ainy *(Tel Aviv University)*, Pierre Bourhis *(CNRS CRIsTAL UMR 9189)*,
  Susan B. Davidson *(University of Pennsylvania)*, Daniel Deutch, Tova Milo *(Tel Aviv University)*
- **An Integrated Bayesian Approach for Effective Multi-Truth Discovery** 493
  Xianzhi Wang, Quan Z. Sheng, Xiu Susie Fang, Lina Yao *(The University of Adelaide)*,
  Xiaofei Xu *(Harbin Institute of Technology)*, Xue Li *(The University of Queensland)*
- **Approximate Truth Discovery via Problem Scale Reduction** 503
  Xianzhi Wang, Quan Z. Sheng, Xiu Susie Fang *(The University of Adelaide)*,
  Xue Li *(The University of Queensland)*, Xiaofei Xu *(Harbin Institute of Technology)*,
  Lina Yao *(The University of Adelaide)*

Session 3B: Social Networks 1

Session Chair: Niloy Ganguly *(Indian Institute of Technology Kharagpur)*

- **Organic or Organized? Exploring URL Sharing Behavior** 513
  Cheng Cao, James Caverlee *(Texas A&M University)*, Kyumin Lee *(Utah State University)*, Hancheng Ge *(Texas A&M University)*, Jinwook Chung *(Utah State University)*
- **Mining Brokers in Dynamic Social Networks** 523
  Chonggang Song, Wynne Hsu, Mong Li Lee *(National University of Singapore)*
- **Who Will You "@"?** 533
  Yeyun Gong, Qi Zhang, Xuyang Sun, Xuanjing Huang *(Fudan University)*

Session 3C: Query Completion

Session Chair: Maarten de Rijke *(University of Amsterdam)*

- **Characterizing and Predicting Voice Query Reformulation** 543
  Ahmed Hassan Awadallah, Ranjitha Gurunath Kulkarni, Umut Ozertem, Rosie Jones *(Microsoft)*
- **A Hierarchical Recurrent Encoder-Decoder for Generative Context-Aware Query Suggestion** 553
  Alessandro Sordoni, Yoshua Bengio *(Université de Montréal)*, Hossein Vahabi *(Yahoo ! Labs)*, Christina Lioma, Jakob Grue Simonsen *(University of Copenhagen)*, Jian-Yun Nie *(Université de Montréal)*
- **A Network-Aware Approach for Searching As-You-Type in Social Media** 563
  Paul Lagrée, Bogdan Cautis *(Inria Saclay and Université Paris-Sud)*, Hossein Vahabi *(Yahoo Labs)*

Session 3D: Microblogs

Session Chair: Antoine Doucet *(Université de La Rochelle)*

- **Improving Microblog Retrieval with Feedback Entity Model** 573
  Feifan Fan, Runwei Qiang, Chao Lv, Jianwu Yang *(Peking University)*
- **Extracting Situational Information from Microblogs during Disaster Events: A Classification-Summarization Approach** 583
  Koustav Rudra, Subham Ghosh, Niloy Ganguly, Pawan Goyal *(Indian Institute of Technology)*, Saptarshi Ghosh *(MPI-SWS, IIEST Shibpur)*
- **Profession-Based Person Search in Microblogs: Using Seed Sets to Find Journalists** 593
  Mossaab Bagdouri, Douglas W. Oard *(University of Maryland)*

Session 3E: Graph-Based Analysis

Session Chair: Lina Yao *(The University of Adelaide)*

- **Learning Entity Types from Query Logs via Graph-Based Modeling** 603
  Jingyuan Zhang *(University of Illinois at Chicago)*, Luo Jie, Altaf Rahman *(Yahoo! Labs)*, Sihong Xie *(University of Illinois at Chicago)*, Yi Chang *(Yahoo! Labs)*, Philip S. Yu *(University of Illinois at Chicago & Tsinghua University)*
- **Collaborative Prediction for Multi-entity Interaction with Hierarchical Representation** 613
  Qiang Liu, Shu Wu, Liang Wang *(Chinese Academy of Sciences)*
- **Learning to Represent Knowledge Graphs with Gaussian Embedding** 623
  Shizhu He, Kang Liu, Guoliang Ji, Jun Zhao *(Chinese Academy of Sciences)*

Session 3F: Classification 1

Session Chair: Alexandra Uitdenbogerd *(RMIT University)*

- **Associative Classification with Statistically Significant Positive and Negative Rules** 633
  Jundong Li, Osmar Zaiane *(University of Alberta)*
- **A Min-Max Optimization Framework for Online Graph Classification** 643
  Peng Yang, Peilin Zhao *(Institute for Infocomm Research, A*STAR)*
- **An Inference Approach to Basic Level of Categorization** 653
  Zhongyuan Wang *(Renmin University of China & Microsoft Research)*, Haixun Wang *(Facebook)*, Ji-Rong Wen *(Renmin University of China)*, Yanghua Xiao *(Fudan University)*

Keynote Address II
Session Chair: James Bailey *(The University of Melbourne)*

- **Making Sense of Spatial Trajectories** 671
  Xiaofang Zhou (Keynote speaker), presenting work by
  Xiaofang Zhou , Kai Zheng *(The University of Queensland & Soochow University)*,
  Hoyoung Jueng *(SAP Innovation Center Network)*, Jiajie Xu *(Soochow University)*,
  Shazia Sadiq *(The University of Queensland)*

Session 4A: Location-Based Services
Session Chair: Timos Sellis *(RMIT University)*

- **ReverseCloak: Protecting Multi-level Location Privacy over Road Networks** 673
  Chao Li, Balaji Palanisamy *(University of Pittsburgh)*
- **GLUE: a Parameter-Tuning-Free Map Updating System** 683
  Hao Wu, Chuanchuan Tu, Weiwei Sun *(Fudan University)*, Baihua Zheng *(Singapore Management University)*,
  Hao Su, Wei Wang *(Fudan University)*
- **A Cost-based Method for Location-Aware Publish/Subscribe Services** 693
  Minghe Yu, Guoliang Li, Jianhua Feng *(Tsinghua University)*
- **Probabilistic Forecasts of Bike-Sharing Systems for Journey Planning** 703
  Nicolas Gast *(INRIA Grenoble)*, Guillaume Massonnet *(INRIA University Grenoble Alpes)*,
  Daniel Reijsbergen *(University of Edinburgh)*, Mirco Tribastone *(IMT - Institute for Advanced Studies Lucca)*

Session 4B: Query Explanation
Session Chair: Sebastian Link *(The University of Auckland)*

- **Efficient Computation of Polynomial Explanations of Why-Not Questions** 713
  Nicole Bidoit *(Université Paris Sud / Inria)*, Melanie Herschel *(Universität Stuttgart)*,
  Aikaterini Tzompanaki *(Université Paris Sud / Inria)*
- **Interruption-Sensitive Empty Result Feedback: Rethinking the Visual Query Feedback Paradigm for Semistructured Data** 723
  Sourav S Bhowmick *(Nanyang Technological University)*, Curtis Dyreson *(Utah State University)*,
  Byron Choi *(Hong Kong Baptist University)*, Min-Hwee Ang *(Nanyang Technological University)*
- **Implementing Query Completeness Reasoning** 733
  Werner Nutt *(Free University of Bozen-Bolzano)*, Sergey Paramonov *(Katholieke Universiteit Leuven)*,
  Ognjen Savković *(Free University of Bozen-Bolzano)*
- **Towards Scalable and Complete Query Explanation with OWL 2 EL Ontologies** 743
  Zhe Wang, Mahsa Chitsaz, Kewen Wang *(Griffith University)*,
  Jianfeng Du *(Guangdong University of Foreign Studies)*

Session 4C: Crowds
Session Chair: Falk Scholer *(RMIT University)*

- **Crowdsourcing Pareto-Optimal Object Finding by Pairwise Comparisons** 753
  Abolfazl Asudeh, Gensheng Zhang, Naeemul Hassan, Chengkai Li,
  Gergely V. Zaruba *(The University of Texas at Arlington)*
- **Practical Aspects of Sensitivity in Online Experimentation with User Engagement Metrics** 763
  Alexey Drutsa, Anna Ufliand, Gleb Gusev *(Yandex)*
- **Generalized Team Draft Interleaving** 773
  Eugene Kharitonov *(Yandex & University of Glasgow)*, Craig Macdonald *(University of Glasgow)*,
  Pavel Serdyukov *(Yandex)*, Iadh Ounis *(University of Glasgow)*
- **Exploiting Document Content for Efficient Aggregation of Crowdsourcing Votes** 783
  Martin Davtyan, Carsten Eickhoff, Thomas Hofmann *(ETH Zurich)*

Session 4D: Optimization

Session Chair: Xuan Vinh Nguyen *(The University of Melbourne)*

- **L2Knng: Fast Exact K-Nearest Neighbor Graph Construction with L2-Norm Pruning** 791
  David C. Anastasiu, George Karypis *(University of Minnesota, Twin Cities)*
- **Lingo: Linearized Grassmannian Optimization for Nuclear Norm Minimization** 801
  Qian Li, Wenjia Niu *(Chinese Academy of Sciences)*, Gang Li *(Deakin University)*,
  Yanan Cao, Jianlong Tan, Li Guo *(Chinese Academy of Sciences)*
- **Deep Collaborative Filtering via Marginalized Denoising Auto-encoder** 811
  Sheng Li *(Northeastern University)*, Jaya Kawale *(Adobe Research)*, Yun Fu *(Northeastern University)*
- **Improving Latent Factor Models via Personalized Feature Projection for One Class Recommendation** 821
  Tong Zhao *(Shenzhen Research Institute, The Chinese University of Hong Kong)*,
  Julian McAuley *(University of California, San Diego)*,
  Irwin King *(Shenzhen Research Institute, The Chinese University of Hong Kong)*

Session 4E: Social Networks 2

Session Chair: Hongzhi Yin *(The University of Queensland)*

- **Node Immunization over Infectious Period** 831
  Chonggang Song, Wynne Hsu Mong Li Lee *(National University of Singapore)*
- **Enterprise Social Link Recommendation** 841
  Jiawei Zhang *(University of Illinois at Chicago)*, Yuanhua Lv *(Microsoft Research)*,
  Philip Yu *(University of Illinois at Chicago)*
- **Exploiting Game Theoretic Analysis for Link Recommendation in Social Networks** 851
  Tong Zhao *(The Chinese University of Hong Kong)*, H.Vicky Zhao *(University of Alberta)*,
  Irwin King *(The Chinese University of Hong Kong)*
- **Extracting Interest Tags for Non-famous Users in Social Network** 861
  Wei He *(Renmin University of China)*, Hongyan Liu *(Tsinghua University)*,
  Jun He, Shu Tang, Xiaoyong Du *(Renmin University of China)*

Session 4F: Matrix Factorization

Session Chair: Jeffrey Chan *(RMIT University)*

- **Robust Capped Norm Nonnegative Matrix Factorization: Capped Norm NMF** 871
  Hongchang Gao, Feiping Nie *(University of Texas at Arlington)*, Weidong Cai *(University of Sydney)*,
  Heng Huang *(University of Texas at Arlington)*
- **MF-Tree: Matrix Factorization Tree for Large Multi-Class Learning** 881
  Lei Liu *(Hewlett Packard Laboratories)*, Pang-Ning Tan, Xi Liu *(Michigan State University)*
- **GraRep: Learning Graph Representations with Global Structural Information** 891
  Shaosheng Cao *(Xidian University)*, Wei Lu *(Singapore University of Technology and Design)*,
  Qiongkai Xu *(IBM Research, China, Australian National University)*
- **Context-Adaptive Matrix Factorization for Multi-Context Recommendation** 901
  Tong Man, Huawei Shen *(Institute of Computing Technology, Chinese Academy of Sciences)*,
  Junming Huang *(University of Electronic Science and Technology of China)*,
  Xueqi Cheng *(Institute of Computing Technology, Chinese Academy of Sciences)*

Session 5A: Trips and Trajectories

Session Chair: Iadh Ounis *(University of Glasgow)*

- **Personalized Trip Recommendation with POI Availability and Uncertain Traveling Time** 911
  Chenyi Zhang *(Zhejiang University, Simon Fraser University)*,
  Hongwei Liang, Ke Wang *(Simon Fraser University)*, Jianling Sun *(Zhejiang University)*
- **Range Search on Uncertain Trajectories** 921
  Liming Zhan *(The University of New South Wales)*, Ying Zhang *(The University of Technology, Sydney)*,
  Wenjie Zhang, Xiaoyang Wang, Xuemin Lin *(The University of New South Wales)*

- **Efficient Computation of Trips with Friends and Families** 931
  Tanzima Hashem, Sukarna Barua, Mohammed Eunus Ali *(Bangladesh University of Engineering and Technology)*, Lars Kulik, Egemen Tanin *(University of Melbourne)*
- **Sampling Big Trajectory Data** 941
  Yanhua Li *(Worcester Polytechnic Institute)*, Chi-Yin Chow *(City University of Hong Kong)*, Ke Deng *(RMIT University)*, Mingxuan Yuan *(Noah's Ark Lab)*, Jia Zeng *(Soochow University, Novel Software Technology and Industrialization, Noah's Ark Lab)*, Jia-Dong Zhang *(City University of Hong Kong)*, Qiang Yang *(Hong Kong University of Science and Technology)*, Zhi-Li Zhang *(University of Minnesota, Twin Cities)*

Session 5B: Retrieval Enhancements 1

Session Chair: J. Shane Culpepper *(RMIT University)*

- **EsdRank: Connecting Query and Documents through External Semi-Structured Data** ... 951
  Chenyan Xiong, Jamie Callan *(Carnegie Mellon University)*
- **A Probabilistic Framework for Temporal User Modeling on Microblogs** 961
  Jitao Sang *(Chinese Academy of Sciences, China-Singapore Institute of Digital Media)*, Dongyuan Lu *(University of International Business and Economics)*, Changsheng Xu *(Chinese Academy of Sciences, China-Singapore Institute of Digital Media)*
- **Deriving Intensional Descriptions for Web Services** 971
  Maria Koutraki *(University of Versailles)*, Dan Vodislav *(University of Cergy-Pontoise)*, Nicoleta Preda *(University of Versailles)*
- **An Optimization Framework for Propagation of Query-Document Features by Query Similarity Functions** 981
  Maxim Zhukovskiy, Tsimafei Khatkevich, Gleb Gusev, Pavel Serdyukov *(Yandex)*

Session 5C: Privacy

Session Chair: James Thom *(RMIT University)*

- **Rank Consistency based Multi-View Learning: A Privacy-Preserving Approach** 991
  Han-Jia Ye, De-Chuan Zhan, Yuan Miao, Yuan Jiang, Zhi-Hua Zhou *(Nanjing University)*
- **Differentially Private Histogram Publication for Dynamic Datasets: An Adaptive Sampling Approach** 1001
  Haoran Li, Li Xiong *(Emory University)*, Xiaoqian Jiang *(University of California, San Diego)*, Jinfei Liu *(Emory University)*
- **WaveCluster with Differential Privacy** 1011
  Ling Chen *(North Carolina State University)*, Ting Yu *(North Carolina State University, Qatar Computing Research Institute)*, Rada Chirkova *(North Carolina State University)*
- **Process-Driven Data Privacy** 1021
  Weiyi Xia Xia *(Vanderbilt University)*, Murat Kantarcioglu *(University of Texas at Dallas)*, Zhiyu Wan, Raymond Heatherly, Yevgeniy Vorobeychik, Bradley Malin *(Vanderbilt University)*

Session 5D: Data Streams

Session Chair: Anthony Wirth *(The University of Melbourne)*

- **Unsupervised Feature Selection on Data Streams** 1031
  Hao Huang *(GE Global Research)*, Shinjae Yoo *(Computational Science Center, Brookhaven National Laboratory)*, Shiva Prasad Kasiviswanathan *(Samsung Research America)*
- **Unsupervised Streaming Feature Selection in Social Media** 1041
  Jundong Li *(Arizona State University)*, Xia Hu *(Texas A&M University)*, Jiliang Tang *(Yahoo! Labs)*, Huan Liu *(Arizona State University)*
- **Weighted Similarity Estimation in Data Streams** 1051
  Konstantin Kutzkov, Mohamed Ahmed, Sofia Nikitaki *(NEC Laboratories Europe)*
- **Private Analysis of Infinite Data Streams via Retroactive Grouping** 1061
  Rui Chen, Yilin Shen, Hongxia Jin *(Samsung Research America)*

Session 5E: Classification 2

Session Chair: Ping Luo *(Chinese Academy of Sciences)*

- **Parallel Lazy Semi-Naive Bayes Strategies for Effective and Efficient Document Classification** 1071
  Felipe Viegas, Marcos André Gonçalves *(Universidade Federal de Minas Gerais)*,
  Wellington Martins *(Universidade Federal de Goiás)*,
  Leonardo Rocha *(Universidade Federal de São João Del Rei)*
- **A Novel Class Noise Estimation Method and Application in Classification** 1081
  Lin Gui *(Harbin Institute of Technology)*, Qin Lu *(Hong Kong Polytechnic University)*,
  Ruifeng Xu *(Harbin Institute of Technology)*, Minglei Li *(Hong Kong Polytechnic University)*,
  Qikang Wei *(Harbin Institute of Technology)*
- **Learning Task Grouping using Supervised Task Space Partitioning in Lifelong Multitask Learning** 1091
  Meenakshi Mishra, Jun Huan *(University of Kansas)*
- **KSGM: Keynode-driven Scalable Graph Matching** 1101
  Xilun Chen, K. Selçuk Candan *(Arizona State University)*, Maria Luisa Sapino *(University of Torino)*,
  Paulo Shakarian *(Arizona State University)*

Session 5F: Sentiment and Content Analysis

Session Chair: Ke Deng *(RMIT University)*

- **Protecting Your Children from Inappropriate Content in Mobile Apps: An Automatic Maturity Rating Framework** 1111
  Bing Hu *(Samsung Research America)*, Bin Liu *(Rutgers University)*,
  Neil Zhenqiang Gong *(Iowa State University)*, Deguang Kong, Hongxia Jin *(Samsung Research America)*
- **The Role of Query Sessions in Interpreting Compound Noun Phrases** 1121
  Marius Pasca *(Google Inc.)*
- **Deep Semantic Frame-based Deceptive Opinion Spam Analysis** 1131
  Seongsoon Kim, Hyeokyoon Chang, Seongwoon Lee, Minhwan Yu, Jaewoo Kang *(Korea University)*
- **Topic Modeling in Semantic Space with Keywords** 1141
  Xiaojia Pu *(Nanjing University)*, Rong Jin *(Michigan State University & Alibaba Group)*,
  Gangshan Wu *(Nanjing University)*, Dingyi Han, Gui-Rong Xue *(Alibaba Group)*

Session 6A: Time Series and Streams

Session Chair: Jenny Xuizhen Zhang *(RMIT University)*

- **F1: Accelerating the Optimization of Aggregate Continuous Queries** 1151
  Anatoli U. Shein, Panos K. Chrysanthis, Alexandros Labrinidis *(University of Pittsburgh)*
- **Fast Distributed Correlation Discovery Over Streaming Time-Series Data** 1161
  Tian Guo *(École Polytechnique Fédérale de Lausanne)*, Saket Sathe *(IBM Research)*,
  Karl Aberer *(École Polytechnique Fédérale de Lausanne)*
- **Time Series Analysis of Nursing Notes for Mortality Prediction via a State Transition Topic Model** 1171
  Yohan Jo, Natasha Loghmanpour, Carolyn Penstein Rosé *(Carnegie Mellon University)*

Session 6B: Adaptive Learning

Session Chair: Damiano Spina *(RMIT University)*

- **Learning Relative Similarity from Data Streams: Active Online Learning Approaches** .. 1181
  Shuji Hao *(Interdisciplinary Graduate School, Nanyang Technological University)*,
  Peilin Zhao *(Institute for Infocomm Research, A*STAR)*,
  Steven C.H. Hoi *(Singapore Management University)*, Chunyan Miao *(Nanyang Technological University)*
- **Ad Hoc Monitoring of Vocabulary Shifts over Time** 1191
  Tom Kenter *(University of Amsterdam)*, Melvin Wevers, Pim Huijnen *(University of Utrecht)*,
  Maarten de Rijke *(University of Amsterdam)*
- **Balancing Novelty and Salience: Adaptive Learning to Rank Entities for Timeline Summarization of High-impact Events** 1201
  Tuan Tran, Claudia Niederée, Nattiya Kanhabua, Ujwal Gadiraju, Avishek Anand *(Leibniz University Hannover)*

Session 6C: Points-of-Interest

Session Chair: Egemen Tanin *(The University of Melbourne)*

- **Location-Based Influence Maximization in Social Networks** 1211
  Tao Zhou, Jiuxin Cao, Bo Liu, Shuai Xu, Ziqing Zhu, Junzhou Luo *(Southeast University)*
- **Location and Time Aware Social Collaborative Retrieval for New Successive Point-of-Interest Recommendation** 1221
  Wei Zhang *(Tsinghua University)*, Jianyong Wang *(Tsinghua University, Jiangsu Normal University)*
- **Where you Instagram? Associating Your Instagram Photos with Points of Interest** 1231
  Xutao Li, Tuan-Anh Nguyen Pham, Gao Cong, Quan Yuan *(Nanyang Technological University)*, Xiao-Li Li, Shonali Krishnaswamy *(Institute for Infocomm Research, A*STAR)*

Session 6D: Matrices

Session Chair: Weidong Cai *(The University of Sydney)*

- **Gradient-based Signatures for Efficient Similarity Search in Large-scale Multimedia Databases** 1241
  Christian Beecks, Merih Seran Uysal, Judith Hermanns, Thomas Seidl *(RWTH Aachen University)*
- **Cross-Modal Similarity Learning: A Low Rank Bilinear Formulation** 1251
  Cuicui Kang, Shengcai Liao, Yonghao Hem, Jian Wang, Wenjia Niu, Shiming Xiang, Chunhong Pan *(Chinese Academy of Sciences)*
- **Efficient Sparse Matrix Multiplication on GPU for Large Social Network Analysis** 1261
  Yong-Yeon Jo, Sang-Wook Kim, Duck-Ho Bae *(Hanyang University)*

Session 6E: Citation Networks

Session Chair: Zhifeng Bao *(RMIT University)*

- **The Role of Citation Context in Predicting Long-Term Citation Profiles: An Experimental Study Based on A Massive Bibliographic Text Dataset** 1271
  Mayank Singh, Vikas Patidar, Suhansanu Kumar, Tanmoy Chakraborty, Animesh Mukherjee, Pawan Goyal *(Indian Institute of Technology, Kharagpur)*
- **Discovering Canonical Correlations between Topical and Topological Information in Document Networks** 1281
  Yuan He, Cheng Wang, Changjun Jiang *(Tongji University)*
- **Chronological Citation Recommendation with Information-Need Shifting** 1291
  Zhuoren Jiang *(Peking University & Dalian Maritime University)*, Xiaozhong Liu *(Indiana University Bloomington)*, Liangcai Gao *(Peking University)*

Session 6F: Knowledge Bases

Session Chair: Vanessa Murdock *(Microsoft)*

- **Answering Questions with Complex Semantic Constraints on Open Knowledge Bases** 1301
  Pengcheng Yin *(The University of Hong Kong)*, Nan Duan *(Microsoft Research Asia)*, Ben Kao *(The University of Hong Kong)*, Junwei Bao *(Harbin Institute of Technology)*, Ming Zhou *(Microsoft Research Asia)*
- **Inducing Space Dirichlet Process Mixture Large-Margin Entity Relationship Inference in Knowledge Bases** 1311
  Sotirios P. Chatzis *(Cyprus University of Technology)*
- **Semi-Automated Exploration of Data Warehouses** 1321
  Thibault Sellam *(CWI)*, Emmanuel Müller *(KIT)*, Martin Kersten *(CWI)*
- **Large-scale Knowledge Base Completion: Inferring via Grounding Network Sampling over Selected Instances** 1331
  Zhuoyu Wei, Jun Zhao, Kang Liu, Zhenyu Qi, Zhengya Sun, Guanhua Tian *(Chinese Academy of Sciences)*

Keynote Address III
Session Chair: Shonali Krishnaswamy *(Institute for Infocomm Research)*

- **Large-Scale Analysis of Dynamics of Choice Among Discrete Alternatives** 1349
  Andrew Tomkins *(Google, Inc.)*

Session 7A: Database Optimization
Session Chair: Sven Helmer *(Free University of Bozen-Bolzano)*

- **On Gapped Set Intersection Size Estimation** 1351
  Chen Chen, Jianbin Qin, Wei Wang *(University of New South Wales)*
- **Inclusion Dependencies Reloaded** 1361
  Henning Köhler *(Massey University)*, Sebastian Link *(The University of Auckland)*
- **Comprehensible Models for Reconfiguring Enterprise Relational Databases to Avoid Incidents** 1371
  Ioana Giurgiu, Mirela Madalina Botezatu, Dorothea Wiesmann *(IBM Research - Zurich)*
- **An Optimal Online Algorithm for Retrieving Heavily Perturbed Statistical Databases in the Low-Dimensional Querying Model** 1381
  Krzysztof Choromanski, Afshin Rostamizadeh, Umar Syed *(Google Research)*

Session 7B: Retrieval Enhancements 2
Session Chair: Mark Sanderson *(RMIT University)*

- **Aggregation of Crowdsourced Ordinal Assessments and Integration with Learning to Rank: a Latent Trait Model** 1391
  Pavel Metrikov, Virgil Pavlu, Javed A. Aslam *(Northeastern University)*
- **Weakly Supervised Natural Language Processing Framework for Abstractive Multi-Document Summarization** 1401
  Peng Li *(University of Texas at Arlington)*, Weidong Cai *(University of Sydney)*, Heng Huang *(University of Texas at Arlington)*
- **Short Text Similarity with Word Embeddings** 1411
  Tom Kenter, Maarten de Rijke *(University of Amsterdam)*
- **Building Representative Composite Items** 1421
  Vincent Leroy, Sihem Amer-Yahia, Eric Gaussier, Hamid Mirisaee *(Université Grenoble Alpes - LIG, CNRS)*

Session 7C: Search Mechanisms
Session Chair: Justin Zobel *(The University of Melbourne)*

- **More Accurate Question Answering on Freebase** 1431
  Hannah Bast, Elmar Haussmann *(University of Freiburg)*
- **Improving Ranking Consistency for Web Search by Leveraging a Knowledge Base and Search Logs** 1441
  Jyun-Yu Jiang *(National Taiwan University)*, Jing Liu, Chin-Yew Lin *(Microsoft Research)*, Pu-Jen Cheng *(National Taiwan University)*
- **Assessing the Impact of Syntactic and Semantic Structures for Answer Passages Reranking** 1451
  Kateryna Tymoshenko *(University of Trento)*, Alessandro Moschitti *(Qatar Computing Research Institute)*
- **Ranking Entities for Web Queries Through Text and Knowledge** 1461
  Michael Schuhmacher, Laura Dietz, Simone Paolo Ponzetto *(University of Mannheim)*

Session 7D: Social Networks 3
Session Chair: Carsten Eickhoff *(ETH Zurich)*

- **What Is a Network Community? A Novel Quality Function and Detection Algorithms** 1471
  Atsushi Miyauchi, Yasushi Kawase *(Tokyo Institute of Technology)*
- **DifRec: A Social-Diffusion-aware Recommender System** 1481
  Hossein Vahabi *(Yahoo Labs)*, Iordanis Koutsopoulos *(AUEB and CERTH)*, Francesco Gullo *(Yahoo Labs)*, Maria Halkidi *(University of Piraeus)*

- **Who With Whom and How? - Extracting Large Social Networks Using Search Engines** 1491
  Stefan Siersdorfer, Philipp Kemkes, Hanno Ackermann, Sergej Zerr *(L3S Research Center)*
- **Modeling Individual-Level Infection Dynamics Using Social Network Information** 1501
  Suppawong Tuarob *(Mahidol University)*,
  Conrad S. Tucker, Marcel Salathe, Nilam Ram *(The Pennsylvania State University)*

Session 8A: Query Evaluation

Session Chair: Yiqun Liu *(Tsinghua University)*

- **Finding Probabilistic k-Skyline Sets on Uncertain Data** 1511
  Jinfei Liu, Haoyu Zhang, Li Xiong, Haoran Li *(Emory University)*, Jun Luo *(Lenovo; CAS)*
- **Ordering Selection Operators Under Partial Ignorance** 1521
  Khaled H. Alyoubi *(Birkbeck, University of London)*, Sven Helmer *(Free University of Bozen-Bolzano)*,
  Peter T. Wood *(Birkbeck, University of London)*
- **Querying Temporal Drifts at Multiple Granularities** 1531
  Sofia Kleisarchaki *(LIG)*, Sihem Amer-Yahia *(CNRS, LIG)*, Ahlame Douzal-Chouakria *(LIG)*,
  Vassilis Christophides *(CSD, UoC, Greece & INRIA)*
- **Efficient Incremental Evaluation of Succinct Regular Expressions** 1541
  Henrik Björklund *(Umeå University)*, Wim Martens, Thomas Timm *(Universität Bayreuth)*

Session 8B: Web Search

Session Chair: David Hawking *(Microsoft)*

- **Struggling and Success in Web Search** 1551
  Daan Odijk *(University of Amsterdam)*,
  Ryen W. White, Ahmed Hassan Awadallah, Susan T. Dumais *(Microsoft Research)*
- **Behavioral Dynamics from the SERP's Perspective: What are Failed SERPs and How to Fix Them?** 1561
  Julia Kiseleva *(Eindhoven University of Technology)*, Jaap Kamps *(University of Amsterdam)*,
  Vadim Nikulin, Nikita Makarov *(Yandex)*
- **What Users Ask a Search Engine: Analyzing One Billion Russian Question Queries** 1571
  Michael Völske *(Bauhaus-Universität Weimar)*, Pavel Braslavski *(Ural Federal University)*,
  Matthias Hagen *(Bauhaus-Universität Weimar)*, Galina Lezina *(Ural Federal University)*,
  Benno Stein *(Bauhaus-Universität Weimar)*
- **Does Vertical Bring more Satisfaction? Predicting Search Satisfaction in a Heterogeneous Environment** 1581
  Ye Chen, Yiqun Liu *(Tsinghua University)*, Ke Zhou *(Yahoo Labs)*,
  Meng Wang *(HeFei University of Technology)*, Min Zhang, Shaoping Ma *(Tsinghua University)*

Session 8C: Social Media 2

Session Chair: Karin Verspoor *(The University of Melbourne)*

- **Characterizing and Predicting Viral-and-Popular Video Content** 1591
  David Vallet *(NICTA)*, Shlomo Berkovsky *(CSIRO)*,
  Sebastien Ardon, Anirban Mahanti, Mohamed Ali Kafaar *(NICTA)*
- **Social Spammer and Spam Message Co-Detection in Microblogging with Social Context Regularization** 1601
  Fangzhao Wu *(Tsinghua University)*, Jinyun Shu *(Beijing University of Posts and Telecommunications)*,
  Yongfeng Huang, Zhigang Yuan *(Tsinghua University)*
- **Central Topic Model for Event-oriented Topics Mining in Microblog Stream** 1611
  Min Peng, Jiahui Zhu, Xuhui Li, Jiajia Huang *(Wuhan University)*,
  Hua Wang, Yanchun Zhang *(Victoria University)*
- **Video Popularity Prediction by Sentiment Propagation via Implicit Network** 1621
  Wanying Ding, Yue Shang *(Drexel University)*, Lifan Guo *(TCL Research American)*,
  Xiaohua Hu *(Drexel University)*, Rui Yan, Tingting He *(Central China Normal University)*

Session 8D: Recommendation

Session Chair: Gangshan Wu *(Nanjing University)*

- **Joint Modeling of User Check-in Behaviors for Point-of-Interest Recommendation** 1631
  Hongzhi Yin *(The University of Queensland)*,
  Xiaofang Zhou *(The University of Queensland, Soochow University)*,
  Yingxia Shao *(Peking University)*, Hao Wang *(Chinese Academy of Sciences)*,
  Shazia Sadiq *(The University of Queensland)*
- **ORec: An Opinion-Based Point-of-Interest Recommendation Framework** 1641
  Jia-Dong Zhang, Chi-Yin Chow *(City University of Hong Kong)*, Yu Zheng *(Microsoft Research)*
- **Toward Dual Roles of Users in Recommender Systems** 1651
  Suhang Wang *(Arizona State University)*, Jiliang Tang *(Yahoo Labs)*, Huan Liu *(Arizona State University)*
- **TriRank: Review-aware Explainable Recommendation by Modeling Aspects** 1661
  Xiangnan He, Tao Chen, Min-Yen Kan *(National University of Singapore)*,
  Xiao Chen *(Chinese Academy of Sciences)*

Short Papers: Databases

- **RoadRank: Traffic Diffusion and Influence Estimation in Dynamic Urban Road Networks** 1671
  Tarique Anwar *(Swinburne University of Technology, NICTA)*,
  Chengfei Liu, Hai L. Vu, Md. Saiful Islam *(Swinburne University of Technology)*
- **On Query-Update Independence for SPARQL** 1675
  Nicola Guido, Pierre Genevès, Nabil Layaïda, Cécile Roisin *(University Grenoble-Alpes)*
- **A Structured Query Model for the Deep Relational Web** 1679
  Hasan M. Jamil *(University of Idaho)*, Hosagrahar V. Jagadish *(University of Michigan)*
- **A Flash-aware Buffering Scheme using On-the-fly Redo** 1683
  Kyosung Jeong, Sang-Wook Kim *(Hanyang University)*, Sungchae Lim *(Dongduk Women's University)*
- **Defragging Subgraph Features for Graph Classification** 1687
  Haishuai Wang, Peng Zhan, Ivor Tsang, Ling Chen, Chengqi Zhang *(University of Technology, Sydney)*
- **Structural Constraints for Multipartite Entity Resolution with Markov Logic Network** 1691
  Tengyuan Ye *(Zhejiang University)*, Hady W. Lauw *(Singapore Management University)*

Short Papers: Information Retrieval

- **Know Your Onions: Understanding the User Experience with the Knowledge Module in Web Search** 1695
  Ioannis Arapakis *(Yahoo Labs)*, Luis A. Leiva *(PRHLT, UPV)*, B. Barla Cambazoglu *(Yahoo Labs)*
- **Personalized Federated Search at LinkedIn** 1699
  Dhruv Arya, Viet Ha-Thuc, Shakti Sinha *(LinkedIn)*
- **Balancing Exploration and Exploitation: Empirical Parameterization of Exploratory Search Systems** 1703
  Kumaripaba Ahukorala, Alan Medlar, Kalle Ilves, Dorota Glowacka *(University of Helsinki)*
- **On Predicting Deletions of Microblog Posts** 1707
  Mossaab Bagdouri, Douglas W. Oard *(University of Maryland)*
- **Semi-Automated Text Classification for Sensitivity Identification** 1711
  Giacomo Berardi, Andrea Esuli *(Consiglio Nazionale delle Ricerche)*,
  Craig Macdonald, Iadh Ounis *(University of Glasgow)*, Fabrizio Sebastiani *(Hamad bin Khalifa University)*
- **Identification of Microblogs Prominent Users during Events by Learning Temporal Sequences of Features** 1715
  Imen Bizid, Nibal Nayef *(L3i, University of La Rochelle)*, Patrice Boursier *(IUMW)*,
  Sami Faiz *(LTSIRS, University of Tunis)*, Antoine Doucet *(L3i, University of La Rochelle)*
- **A Real-Time Eye Tracking Based Query Expansion Approach via Latent Topic Modeling** 1719
  Yongqiang Chen, Peng Zhang *(Tianjin University)*, Dawei Song *(Tianjin University, The Open University)*,
  Benyou Wang *(Tianjin University)*

- **Clustered Semi-Supervised Relevance Feedback** 1723
  Kripabandhu Ghosh, Swapan Kumar Parui *(Indian Statistical Institute, Kolkata)*
- **On the Effect of "Stupid" Search Components on User Interaction with Search Engines** 1727
  Lidia Grauer, Aleksandra Lomakina *(Yandex LLC)*
- **Social-Relational Topic Model for Social Networks** 1731
  Weiyu Guo *(Chinese Academy of Sciences, University of Chinese Academy of Sciences)*,
  Shu Wu, Liang Wang, Tieniu Tan *(Chinese Academy of Sciences)*
- **Building Effective Query Classifiers: A Case Study in Self-harm Intent Detection** 1735
  Ashiqur R. KhudaBukhsh *(Carnegie Mellon University)*, Paul N. Bennett, Ryen W. White *(Microsoft Research)*
- **Modelling the Usefulness of Document Collections for Query Expansion in Patient Search** 1739
  Nut Limsopatham *(University of Cambridge)*, Craig Macdonald, Iadh Ounis *(University of Glasgow)*
- **A Convolutional Click Prediction Model** 1743
  Qiang Liu, Feng Yu, Shu Wu, Liang Wang *(Chinese Academy of Sciences)*
- **A Study of Query Length Heuristics in Information Retrieval** 1747
  Yuanhua Lv *(Microsoft Research)*
- **Detect Rumors Using Time Series of Social Context Information on Microblogging Websites** 1751
  Jing Ma *(Beijing University of Posts and Telecommunications & The Chinese University of Hong Kong)*,
  Wei Gao *(Hamad Bin Khalifa University)*, Zhongyu Wei *(The University of Texas at Dallas)*,
  Yueming Lu *(Beijing University of Posts and Telecommunications)*,
  Kam-Fai Wong *(The Chinese University of Hong Kong, MoE Key Laboratory of High Confidence Software Technologies)*
- **Query Auto-Completion for Rare Prefixes** 1755
  Bhaskar Mitra, Nick Craswell *(Microsoft)*
- **Pooled Evaluation Over Query Variations: Users are as Diverse as Systems** 1759
  Alistair Moffat *(The University of Melbourne)*, Falk Scholer *(RMIT University)*, Paul Thomas *(CSIRO)*,
  Peter Bailey *(Microsoft)*
- **The Influence of Pre-processing on the Estimation of Readability of Web Documents** 1763
  João Palotti *(Vienna University of Technology)*, Guido Zuccon *(Queensland University of Technology)*,
  Allan Hanbury *(Vienna University of Technology)*
- **Atypical Queries in eCommerce** 1767
  Neeraj Pradhan, Vinay Deolalikar, Kang Li *(Search and Data Mining Groupon)*
- **Bottom-up Faceted Search: Creating Search Neighbourhoods with Datacube Cells** 1771
  Mark Sifer *(University of Wollongong)*
- **Personalized Recommendation Meets Your Next Favorite** 1775
  Qiang Song, Jian Cheng, Ting Yuan, Hanqing Lu *(Chinese Academy of Sciences)*
- **Recommending Short-lived Dynamic Packages for Golf Booking Services** 1779
  Robin M.E. Swezey, Young-joo Chung *(Rakuten Institute of Technology)*
- **Large-Scale Question Answering with Joint Embedding and Proof Tree Decoding** 1783
  Zhenghao Wang, Shengquan Yan, Huaming Wang, Xuedong Huang *(Microsoft Corporation)*
- **Query Length, Retrievability Bias and Performance** 1787
  Colin Wilkie, Leif Azzopardi *(University of Glasgow)*
- **Gauging Correct Relative Rankings for Similarity Search** 1791
  Weiren Yu, Julie A. McCann *(Imperial College London)*
- **Learning User Preferences for Topically Similar Documents** 1795
  Mustafa Zengin, Ben Carterette *(University of Delaware)*
- **Modeling Parameter Interactions in Ranking SVM** 1799
  Yaogong Zhang *(Nankai University)*, Jun Xu, Yanyan Lan, Jiafeng Guo *(Chinese Academy of Sciences)*,
  Maoqiang Xie, Yalou Huang *(Nankai University)*, Xueqi Cheng *(Chinese Academy of Sciences)*

Short Papers: Knowledge Management

- **Best First Over-Sampling for Multilabel Classification** ... 1803
  Xusheng Ai, Jian Wu *(Soochow University)*, Victor S. Sheng *(University of Central Arkansas)*, Yufeng Yao, Pengpeng Zhao, Zhiming Cui *(Soochow University)*
- **Co-clustering Document-term Matrices by Direct Maximization of Graph Modularity** ... 1807
  Melissa Ailem, François Role, Mohamed Nadif *(LIPADE - Paris Descartes University)*
- **A Data-Driven Approach to Distinguish Cyber-Attacks from Physical Faults in a Smart Grid** ... 1811
  Adnan Anwar, Abdun Naser Mahmood, Zubair Shah *(UNSW Australia)*
- **Improving Event Detection by Automatically Assessing Validity of Event Occurrence in Text** ... 1815
  Andrea Ceroni, Ujwal Kumar Gadiraju, Marco Fisichella *(Leibniz Universität Hannover)*
- **DAAV: Dynamic API Authority Vectors for Detecting Software Theft** ... 1819
  Dong-Kyu Chae, Sang-Wook Kim *(Hanyang University)*, Seong-Je Cho, Yesol Kim *(Dankook University)*
- **Towards Multi-level Provenance Reconstruction of Information Diffusion on Social Media** ... 1823
  Tom De Nies *(Ghent University - iMinds - Multimedia Lab)*, Io Taxidou *(University of Freiburg)*, Anastasia Dimou, Ruben Verborgh *(Ghent University - iMinds - Multimedia Lab)*, Peter M. Fischer *(University of Freiburg)*, Erik Mannens, Rik Van de Walle *(Ghent University - iMinds - Multimedia Lab)*
- **Profiling Pedestrian Distribution and Anomaly Detection in a Dynamic Environment** ... 1827
  Minh Tuan Doan, Sutharshan Rajasegarar, Mahsa Salehi, Masud Moshtaghi, Christopher Leckie *(The University of Melbourne)*
- **A Clustering-based Approach to Detect Probable Outcomes of Lawsuits** ... 1831
  Daniel Lemes Gribel *(Pontifical Catholic University of Rio de Janeiro)*, Maira Gatti de Bayser, Leonardo Guerreiro Azevedo *(IBM Research Brazil)*
- **Detecting Check-worthy Factual Claims in Presidential Debates** ... 1835
  Naeemul Hassan, Chengkai Li, Mark Tremayne *(University of Texas at Arlington)*
- **Where You Go Reveals Who You Know: Analyzing Social Ties from Millions of Footprints** ... 1839
  Hsun-Ping Hsieh *(National Taiwan University)*, Rui Yan *(Baidu Inc.)*, Cheng-Te Li *(Academia Sinica)*
- **Message Clustering based Matrix Factorization Model for Retweeting Behavior Prediction** ... 1843
  Bo Jiang, Jiguang Liang, Ying Sha, Lihong Wang *(Chinese Academy of Sciences)*
- **Heterogeneous Multi-task Semantic Feature Learning for Classification** ... 1847
  Xin Jin *(Chinese Academy of Sciences, Huawei Technologies)*, Fuzhen Zhuang *(Chinese Academy of Sciences)*, Sinno Jialin Pan *(Nanyang Technological University)*, Changying Du, Ping Luo, Qing He *(Chinese Academy of Sciences)*
- **Top-k Reliable Edge Colors in Uncertain Graphs** ... 1851
  Arijit Khan *(ETH Zurich)*, Francesco Gullo *(Yahoo! Labs)*, Thomas Wohler *(ETH Zurich)*, Francesco Bonchi *(Yahoo! Labs)*
- **Probabilistic Non-negative Inconsistent-resolution Matrices Factorization** ... 1855
  Masahiro Kohjima, Tatsushi Matsubayashi, Hiroshi Sawada *(NTT Corporation)*
- **Identifying Attractive News Headlines for Social Media** ... 1859
  Sawa Kourogi, Hiroyuki Fujishiro *(Hosei University)*, Akisato Kimura *(NTT Corporation)*, Hitoshi Nishikawa *(Tokyo Institute of Technology)*
- **A Probabilistic Rating Auto-encoder for Personalized Recommender Systems** ... 1863
  Huizhi Liang, Timothy Baldwin *(The University of Melbourne)*
- **Real-time Rumor Debunking on Twitter** ... 1867
  Xiaomo Liu, Armineh Nourbakhsh, Quanzhi Li, Rui Fang, Sameena Shah *(Thomson Reuters)*
- **Fraud Transaction Recognition: A Money Flow Network Approach** ... 1871
  Renxin Mao, Zhao Li, Jinhua Fu *(Alibaba Group)*

- **Identifying Top-k Consistent News-Casters on Twitter** 1875
  Sahisnu Mazumder *(Indian Institute of Technology - Roorkee)*, Sameep Mehta *(IBM Research Lab - India)*, Dhaval Patel *(Indian Institute of Technology - Roorkee)*
- **Mining the Minds of Customers from Online Chat Logs** 1879
  Kunwoo Park, Jaewoo Kim, Jaram Park, Meeyoung Cha *(Korea Advanced Institute of Science and Technology)*, Jiin Nam, Seunghyun Yoon, Eunhee Rhim *(Samsung Electronics)*
- **A Fast k-Nearest Neighbor Search Using Query-Specific Signature Selection** 1883
  Youngki Park *(Seoul National University)*, Heasoo Hwang *(University of Seoul)*, Sang-goo Lee *(Seoul National University)*
- **Core-Sets for Canonical Correlation Analysis** 1887
  Saurabh Paul *(Rensselaer Polytechnic Institute)*
- **DeepCamera: A Unified Framework for Recognizing Places-of-Interest based on Deep ConvNets** 1891
  Pai Peng, Hongxiang Chen, Lidan Shou, Ke Chen, Gang Chen, Chang Xu *(Zhejiang University)*
- **Structured Sparse Regression for Recommender Systems** 1895
  Mingjie Qian *(University of Illinois at Urbana-Champaign)*, Liangjie Hong, Yue Shi, Suju Rajan *(Yahoo Labs)*
- **Analyzing Document Intensive Business Processes Using Ontology** 1899
  Suman Roychoudhury, Vinay Kulkarni, Nikhil Bellarykar *(Tata Consultancy Services)*
- **Transductive Domain Adaptation with Affinity Learning** 1903
  Le Shu, Longin Jan Latecki *(Temple University)*
- **Update Summarization using Semi-Supervised Learning Based on Hellinger Distance** 1907
  Dingding Wang, Sahar Sohangir *(Florida Atlantic University)*, Tao Li *(Florida International University)*
- **Multi-view Clustering via Structured Low-rank Representation** 1911
  Dong Wang, Qiyue Yin, Ran He, Liang Wang, Tieniu Tan *(Chinese Academy of Sciences)*
- **Partially Labeled Data Tuple Can Optimize Multivariate Performance Measures** 1915
  Jim Jing-Yan Wang, Xin Gao *(King Abdullah University of Science and Technology)*
- **Modeling Infinite Topics on Social Behavior Data with Spatio-temporal Dependence** 1919
  Peng Wang *(Chinese Academy of Sciences & Alibaba Group)*, Peng Zhang *(QCIS, University of Technology Sydney)*, Chuan Zhou *(Chinese Academy of Sciences)*, Zhao Li *(Alibaba Group)*, Guo Li *(Chinese Academy of Sciences)*
- **ASEM: Mining Aspects and Sentiment of Events from Microblog** 1923
  Ruhui Wang, Weijing Huang, Wei Chen, Tengjiao Wang, Kai Lei *(Peking University)*
- **Enhanced Word Embeddings from a Hierarchical Neural Language Model** 1927
  Xun Wang, Katsuhoto Sudoh, Masaaki Nagata *(NTT Communication Science Laboratories)*
- **Improving Label Quality in Crowdsourcing Using Noise Correction** 1931
  Jing Zhang *(Nanjing University of Science and Technology)*, Victor S. Sheng *(University of Central Arkansas)*, Jian Wu *(Soochow University)*, Xiaoqin Fu *(University of Central Arkansas)*, Xindong Wu *(Hefei University of Technology)*
- **Improving Collaborative Filtering via Hidden Structured Constraint** 1935
  Qing Zhang, Houfeng Wang *(Peking University)*

Workshop Reports

- **DOLAP 2015 Workshop Summary** 1939
  Carlos Garcia-Alvarado *(Pivotal Software Inc.)*, Carlos Ordonez *(University of Houston)*, Il-Yeol Song *(Drexel University)*
- **DTMBIO 2015: International Workshop on Data and Text Mining in Biomedical Informatics** 1941
  Min Song *(Yonsei University)*, Doheon Lee *(Korea Advanced Institute of Science and Technology)*, Karin Verspoor *(The University of Melbourne)*

- **ECol 2015: First international workshop on the Evaluation on Collaborative Information Seeking and Retrieval** 1943
  Leif Azzopardi *(University of Glasgow)*,
  Jeremy Pickens *(Catalyst Repository Systems)*, Tetsuya Sakai *(Waseda University)*,
  Laure Soulier, Lynda Tamine *(Université de Toulouse UPS IRIT)*
- **Eighth Workshop on Exploiting Semantic Annotations in Information Retrieval (ESAIR'15)** 1945
  Krisztian Balog *(University of Stavanger)*, Jeffrey Dalton *(Google Research)*,
  Antoine Doucet *(University of La Rochelle)*, Yusra Ibrahim *(Max Planck Institute for Informatics)*
- **LSDS-IR'15: 2015 Workshop on Large-Scale and Distributed Systems for Information Retrieval** 1947
  Ismail Sengor Altingovde *(Middle East Technical University)*, B. Barla Cambazoglu *(Yahoo Labs)*,
  Nicola Tonellotto *(ISTI-CNR)*
- **NWSearch 2015 - International Workshop on Novel Web Search Interfaces and Systems** 1949
  Davood Rafiei *(University of Alberta)*, Katsumi Tanaka *(Kyoto University)*
- **PIKM 2015: The 8th ACM Workshop for Ph.D. Students in Information and Knowledge Management** 1951
  Mouna Kacimi *(Free University of Bozen-Bolzano)*, Nicoleta Preda *(Versailles University)*,
  Maya Ramanath *(Indian Institute of Technology – Delhi)*
- **TM 2015 -- Topic Models: Post-Processing and Applications Workshop** 1953
  Nikolaos Aletras *(University College London)*, Jey Han Lau *(King's College London)*,
  Timothy Baldwin *(The University of Melbourne)*, Mark Stevenson *(University of Sheffield)*
- **UCUI'15: The 1st International Workshop on Understanding the City with Urban Informatics** 1955
  Yashar Moshfeghi, Iadh Ounis, Craig Macdonald, Joemon M. Jose, Peter Triantafillou, Mark Livingston,
  Piyushimita Thakuriah *(University of Glasgow)*

Author Index 1957

Conference Organization

General Chairs

James Bailey (*The University of Melbourne*)
Alistair Moffat (*The University of Melbourne*)

Program Committee Chairs

Charu C. Aggarwal (*IBM*)
Maarten de Rijke (*University of Amsterdam*)
Ravi Kumar (*Google*)
Vanessa Murdock (*Microsoft*)
Timos Sellis (*RMIT University*)
Jeffrey Xu Yu (*Chinese University of Hong Kong*)

Industry Track Chairs

Shonali Krishnaswamy (*Institute for Infocomm Research*)
Marc Najork (*Google*)

Tutorial Chairs

Wei Wang (*University of New South Wales*)
Grace Hui Yang (*Georgetown University*)

Workshop Chairs

Chee Yong Chan (*National University of Singapore*)
Shane Culpepper (*RMIT University*)

Local Arrangements Chairs

Tony Wirth (*The University of Melbourne*)
Rui Zhang (*The University of Melbourne*)

Publicity Chair

Yin Sing Koh (*The University of Auckland*)

Best Papers Chair

Ramamohanarao Kotagiri (*The University of Melbourne*)

Principal Conference Organizers

ICMS Australasia (`http://icmsaust.com.au`)

Program Committee and Referees

Database Track Senior Program Committee Members

Klaus Berberich (*Max Planck Institut*)
Selcuk Candan (*Arizona State U.*)
Lei Chen (*Hong Kong U. Sc. Tech.*)
Minos Garofalakis (*Tech. U. Crete*)
Wook-Shin Han (*PosTech*)
Nick Koudas (*U. Toronto*)
Laks Lakshmanan (*U. British Columbia*)
Huan Liu (*Arizona State U.*)
Vivek Narasayya (*Microsoft Research*)
Tamer Ozsu (*U. Waterloo*)
Kian-Lee Tan (*National U. Singapore*)
Yufei Tao (*Chinese U. Hong Kong*)
X. Sean Wang (*Fudan U.*)
Jun Yang (*Duke U.*)
Haruo Yokota (*Tokyo Institute Tech.*)
Wenjie Zhang (*U. New South Wales*)
Xiaofang Zhou (*U. Queensland*)

Information Retrieval Track Senior Program Committee Members

Eugene Agichtein (*Emory U.*)
James Allan (*U. Massachusetts Amherst*)
Omar Alonso (*Microsoft*)
Jaime Arguello (*U. North Carolina*)
Javed Aslam (*Northeastern U.*)
Leif Azzopardi (*U. Glasgow*)
Peter Bailey (*Microsoft*)
Krisztian Balog (*U. Stavanger*)
Michael Bendersky (*Google*)
Klaus Berberich (*Max Planck Institut*)
Roi Blanco (*Yahoo Labs*)
Jamie Callan (*Carnegie Mellon U.*)
David Carmel (*Yahoo Labs*)
Ben Carterette (*U. Delaware*)
Carlos Castillo (*QCRI*)
James Caverlee (*Texas A&M U.*)
Charles L.A. Clarke (*U. Waterloo*)
Nick Craswell (*Microsoft*)
Fabio Crestani (*U. Lugano*)
Bruce Croft (*U. Massachusetts Amherst*)
Shane Culpepper (*RMIT U.*)
Brian Davison (*Lehigh U.*)
Franciska de Jong (*U. Twente*)
Gianluca Demartini (*U. Sheffield*)
Fernando Diaz (*Microsoft*)
Debora Donato (*StumbleUpon*)
Shlomo Geva (*Queensland U. Tech.*)
Aristides Gionis (*Aalto U.*)
Claudia Hauff (*TU Delft*)
Ben He (*Chinese Academy Sc.*)
Qi He (*LinkedIn*)
Hideo Joho (*U. Tsukuba*)
Gareth Jones (*Dublin City U.*)
Jaap Kamps (*U. Amsterdam*)
Evangelos Kanoulas (*U. Amsterdam*)
Jussi Karlgren (*Gavagai & KTH*)
Gabriella Kazai (*Lumi*)
Diane Kelly (*U. North Carolina Chapel Hill*)
Oren Kurland (*Technion*)
Mounia Lalmas (*Yahoo Labs*)
Matthew Lease (*U. Texas Austin*)
Yoelle Maarek (*Yahoo Labs*)
Craig Macdonald (*U. Glasgow*)
Donald Metzler (*Google*)
Gonzalo Navarro (*U. Chile*)
Filip Radlinski (*Microsoft*)
Tetsuya Sakai (*Waseda U.*)
Mark Sanderson (*RMIT U.*)
Pavel Serdyukov (*Yandex*)
Ian Soboroff (*NIST*)
Ryen W. White (*Microsoft*)
Emine Yilmaz (*U. College London*)

Knowledge Management Track Senior Program Committee Members

Deepak Agarwal (*LinkedIn*)
Diego Calvanese (*Free U. Bozen-Bolzano*)
Anirban Dasgupta (*IIT Gandhinagar*)
Evgeniy Gabrilovich (*Google*)
Sreenivas Gollapudi (*Google*)
Murat Kantarcioglu (*U. Texas Dallas*)
Yan Liu (*USC*)
Nikos Mamoulis (*U. Hong Kong*)
Qiaozhu Mei (*U. Michigan*)
Wen-Chih Peng (*NTU*)
B. Aditya Prakash (*Virginia Tech.*)
Kunal Punera (*Bento Labs*)
Guojun Qi (*U. Central Florida*)
Sujith Ravi (*Google*)
Chandan Reddy (*Wayne State U.*)
Joerg Sander (*U. Alberta*)
Jimeng Sun (*Georgia Tech*)
Evimaria Terzi (*Boston U.*)
Hanghang Tong (*City U. New York*)
Wei Wang (*UCLA*)

Database Track Program Committee Members

Ashraf Aboulnaga (*QCRI*)
Periklis Andritsos (*U. Toronto*)
Walid Aref (*Purdue U.*)
Spiros Bakiras (*City U. New York*)
Zhifeng Bao (*RMIT U.*)
Spyros Blanas (*Ohio State U.*)
Panagiotis Bouros (*HU-Berlin*)
Bogdan Cautis (*U. Paris-Sud*)
Lijun Chang (*U. New South Wales*)
Muhammad Cheema (*Monash U.*)
Hong Cheng (*Chinese U. Hong Kong*)
Reynold Cheng (*U. Hong Kong*)
Gao Cong (*Nanyang Tech. U.*)
Alfredo Cuzzocrea (*ICAR-CNR & U. Calabria*)
Ke Deng (*RMIT U.*)
Prasad Deshpande (*IBM India*)
Gill Dobbie (*U. Auckland*)
Josep Domingo-Ferrer (*U. Rovira i Virgili*)
Markus Endres (*U. Augsburg*)
Csilla Farkas (*U. South Carolina*)
Ada Fu (*Chinese U. Hong Kong*)
Ariel Fuxman (*Google*)
Floris Geerts (*U. Antwerp*)
Dimitrios Gunopulos (*U. Athens*)
Yeye He (*Microsoft Research*)
Seung-won Hwang (*PosTech*)
Stratos Idreos (*Harvard U.*)
Yoshiharu Ishikawa (*Nagoya U.*)
Mizuho Iwaihara (*Waseda U.*)
Lili Jiang (*Max Planck Institut*)
Anastasios Kementsietsidis (*Google*)
Yannis Kotidis (*AUEB Greece*)
Julien Leblay (*AIST*)
Justin Levandoski (*Microsoft Research*)
Chengkai Li (*U. Texas Arlington*)
Guoliang Li (*Tsinghua U.*)
Chengfei Liu (*Swinburne U. Tech.*)
Mengchi Liu (*Carleton U.*)
Lei Liu (*HP Labs*)
Hua Lu (*Aalborg U.*)
Jiebo Luo (*U. Rochester*)
Balaji Palanisamy (*U. Pittsburgh*)
Ippokratis Pandis (*Cloudera*)
Stavros Papadopoulos (*Intel and MIT*)
Milan Petkovic (*Eindhoven U. Tech.*)
Weining Qian (*East China Normal U.*)
Lu Qin (*UTS*)
Matthias Renz (*U. Munich*)
Senjuti Roy (*U. Washington Tacoma*)
Pierangela Samarati (*U. Milan*)
Rusty Sears (*Pure Storage*)
Mohamed Sharaf (*U. Queensland*)
Fabian Suchanek (*Télécom ParisTech U.*)
Dimitri Theodoratos (*New Jersey Inst. Tech.*)
Yannis Theodoridis (*U. Piraeus*)
Aibo Tian (*LinkedIn*)
Pinar Tozun (*IBM Almaden*)
Goce Trajcevski (*Northwestern U.*)
Stratis Viglas (*U. Edinburgh*)
Chi Wang (*Microsoft*)
Jianyong Wang (*Tsinghua U.*)
Wei Wang (*U. New South Wales*)
Raymond Chi-Wing Wong (*Hong Kong U. Sc. Tech.*)
Yinghui Wu (*UCSB*)
Xiaokui Xiao (*Nanyang Tech. U.*)
Yanghua Xiao (*Fudan U.*)
De-Nian Yang (*Academia Sinica*)

Xiaochun Yang (*Northeastern U.*)
Mi-Yen Yeh (*Academia Sinica*)
Man Lung Yiu (*Hong Kong Polytechnic U.*)
Hwanjo Yu (*Pohang U. Sc. Tech.*)
Ji Zhang (*U. Southern Queensland*)
Ying Zhang (*UTS*)
Kevin Zheng (*U. Queensland*)
Yongluan Zhou (*U. Southern Denmark*)
Lei Zou (*Peking U.*)

Information Retrieval Track Program Committee Members

Pal Aditya (*IBM*)
Dirk Ahlers (*NTNU*)
M-Dyaa Albakour (*U. Glasgow*)
Ismail Altingovde (*Middle East Tech. U.*)
Gianni Amati (*Fondazione Ugo Bordoni*)
Linda Andersson (*Vienna U. Tech.*)
Akash Anil (*IIT Guwahati*)
Avi Arampatzis (*Democritus U. Thrace*)
Ioannis Arapakis (*Yahoo Labs*)
Olga Arkhipova (*Yandex*)
Diego Arroyuelo (*U. Técn. Federico Santa María*)
Paul Baecke (*Microsoft Research Cambridge*)
Niranjan Balasubramanian (*U. Washington*)
Andras Benczur (*Hungarian Acad. Sc.*)
Bodo Billerbeck (*Microsoft*)
Ilaria Bordino (*Yahoo Labs*)
Gloria Bordogna (*CNR Italy*)
Pavel Braslavski (*Ural Federal U.*)
Marc Bron (*Yahoo Labs*)
Eric Brown (*IBM Research*)
Fei Cai (*U. Amsterdam*)
Rui Cai (*Microsoft Research*)
B. Barla Cambazoglu (*Yahoo Labs*)
Bin Cao (*Microsoft Research Asia*)
Mark Carman (*Monash U.*)
Marc-Allen Cartright (*Google*)
Pablo Castells (*U. Autónoma Madrid*)
Suleyman Cetintas (*Yahoo Labs*)
Sunandan Chakraborty (*New York U.*)
Praveen Chandar (*U. Delaware*)
Yi Chang (*Yahoo Labs*)
Francine Chen (*FX Palo Alto Laboratory*)
Lin Chen (*U. Illinois Chicago*)
Wei Chen (*Microsoft Research*)
Aleksandr Chuklin (*U. Amsterdam*)
Francisco Claude (*U. Diego Portales*)
Paul Clough (*U. Sheffield*)
Michael Cole (*Rutgers U.*)
Gordon V. Cormack (*U. Waterloo*)
Peng Cui (*Tsinghua U.*)
Ronan Cummins (*U. Greenwich*)
Sally Jo Cunningham (*U. Waikato*)
Mahashweta Das (*HP Labs*)
Gianmarco De Francisci Morales (*Yahoo Labs*)
Alexey Drutsa (*Yandex*)
Sergio Duarte (*U. Twente*)
Thanh Tran Duc (*San Jose State U.*)
Sourav Dutta (*Max Planck Institut*)
Carsten Eickhoff (*ETH Zurich*)
Andrea Esuli (*ISTI-CNR*)
Henry Feild (*Endicott College*)
Dan Feldman (*MIT*)
Nicola Ferro (*U. Padova*)
Luanne Freund (*U. British Columbia*)
Ingo Frommholz (*U. Bedfordshire*)
Bin Gao (*Microsoft Research Asia*)
Judith Gelernter (*Carnegie Mellon U.*)
Lorraine Goeuriot ()
Simon Gog (*Karlsruhe Inst. Tech.*)
Marcos Goncalves (*UFMG*)
Julio Gonzalo (*UNED*)
David Graus (*U. Amsterdam*)
Artem Grotov (*U. Amsterdam*)
Fan Guo (*Carnegie Mellon U.*)
Qi Guo (*Microsoft*)
Manish Gupta (*Microsoft*)
Gleb Gusev (*Yandex*)
Ido Guy (*Yahoo Labs*)
Martin Halvey (*U. Strathclyde*)
Donna Harman (*NIST*)
Jiyin He (*CWI*)
Bruce Hedin (*H5*)
Tomi Heimonen (*U. Tampere*)
Katja Hofmann (*Microsoft*)
Frank Hopfgartner (*U. Glasgow*)
Winston Hsu (*National Taiwan U.*)
Samuel Huston (*U. Massachusetts Amherst*)
Ichiro Ide (*Nagoya U.*)
Adam Jatowt (*Kyoto U.*)
Jiepu Jiang (*U. Massachussetts*)
Noriko Kando (*National Institute of Informatics*)
Nattiya Kanhabua (*L3S Research Center*)

Sarvnaz Karimi (*CSIRO*)
Mostafa Keikha (*U. Massachusetts Amherst*)
Liadh Kelly (*Trinity College Dublin*)
Tom Kenter (*U. Amsterdam*)
Sadegh Kharazmi (*RMIT U.*)
Eugene Kharitonov (*Yandex*)
Yubin Kim (*Carnegie Mellon U.*)
Akisato Kimura (*NTT Japan*)
Irwin King (*Chinese U. Hong Kong*)
Julia Kiseleva (*Eindhoven U. Tech.*)
Pranam Kolari (*Walmart Labs*)
Bevan Koopman (*CSIRO*)
Yehuda Koren (*Google*)
Udo Kruschwitz (*U. Essex*)
Séamus Lawless (*Trinity College Dublin*)
Chia-Jung Lee (*U. Massachusetts Amherst*)
Kyumin Lee (*Utah State U.*)
Teerapong Leelanupab (*KMITL Thailand*)
Jochen Leidner (*Thomson Reuters*)
Johannes Leveling (*Dublin City U.*)
David D. Lewis (*David D. Lewis Consulting*)
Lei Li (*Florida International U.*)
Shangsong Liang (*U. Amsterdam*)
Daniel Liebling (*Microsoft Research*)
Ee-Peng Lim (*Singapore Management U.*)
Nut Limsopatham (*U. Glasgow*)
Christina Lioma (*U. Copenhagen*)
Suzanne Little (*Dublin City U.*)
Claudio Lucchese (*ISTI-CNR*)
Roger Jie Luo (*Yahoo Labs*)
Yuan Luo (*IBM & MIT*)
Mihai Lupu (*Vienna U. Tech.*)
Yuanhua Lv (*Microsoft*)
Dimitrios Lymberopoulos (*Microsoft Research*)
Andrew MacFarlane (*City U. London*)
Walid Magdy (*QCRI*)
Stephane Marchand-Maillet (*U. Geneva*)
Miguel Martinez Alvarez (*Signal*)
Flavio Martins (*U. Nova de Lisboa*)
Maarten Marx (*U. Amsterdam*)
Yosi Mass (*IBM*)
Richard McCreadie (*U. Glasgow*)
Paul McNamee (*JHU*)
Edgar Meij (*Yahoo Labs*)
Yelena Mejova (*QCRI*)
Marcelo Mendoza (*Yahoo Labs*)
Thomas Mensink (*U. Amsterdam*)
Peter Mika (*Yahoo Labs*)
Natasa Milic-Frayling (*Microsoft Research*)
Bhaskar Mitra (*Microsoft*)
Prasenjit Mitra (*Pennsylvania State U.*)
Marie-Francine Moens (*Katholieke U. Leuven*)
Samaneh Moghaddam (*eBay*)
Yashar Moshfeghi (*U. Glasgow*)
Josiane Mothe (*IRIT U. Toulouse*)
Isabelle Moulinier (*Thomson Reuters*)
Hidetsugu Nanba (*Hiroshima U.*)
Franco Maria Nardini (*ISTI-CNR*)
Wolfgang Nejdl (*L3S Research Center*)
Vincent Ng (*U. Texas Dallas*)
Dong Nguyen (*Twente U.*)
Quoc Viet Hung Nguyen (*EPFL*)
Tu Nguyen (*L3S Research Center*)
Feiping Nie (*UT Arlington*)
Jian-Yun Nie (*U. Montreal*)
Alexandros Ntoulas (*Microsoft Research*)
Neil O'Hare (*Yahoo Labs*)
Daan Odijk (*U. Amsterdam*)
Denis Parra (*PUC Chile*)
Gabriella Pasi (*U. Milano-Bicocca*)
Virgil Pavlu (*Northeastern U.*)
Raffaele Perego (*ISTI-CNR*)
Alvaro Pereira Jr (*Federal U. Ouro Preto*)
Barbara Poblete (*U. Chile*)
John Prager (*IBM Research*)
Mu Qiao (*IBM Research*)
Tao Qin (*Microsoft*)
Edie Rasmussen (*U. British Columbia*)
Mohammad Raza (*Microsoft Cambridge*)
Yongli Ren (*RMIT U.*)
Zhaochun Ren (*U. Amsterdam*)
Haggai Roitman (*IBM Research Haifa*)
Stevan Rudinac (*U. Amsterdam*)
Stefan Rüger (*The Open U.*)
Egor Samosvat (*Yandex*)
Jose San Pedro (*Telefonica Research*)
Rodrygo Santos (*U. Federal de Minas Gerais*)
Shin'ichi Satoh (*NII Japan*)
Klaus Schoeffmann (*Klagenfurt U.*)
Anne Schuth (*U. Amsterdam*)
Satoshi Sekine (*New York U.*)
Jangwon Seo (*Google*)
Jialie Shen (*Singapore Management U.*)
Xiaolin Shi (*Microsoft*)
Milad Shokouhi (*Microsoft*)
Edleno Silva de Moura (*Federal U. Amazonas*)
Fabrizio Silvestri (*Yahoo Labs*)
Marc Sloan (*U. College London*)

Yang Song (*Microsoft Research*)
Hanna Suominen (*NICTA & ANU*)
Idan Szpektor (*Yahoo Labs*)
James Thom (*RMIT U.*)
Paul Thomas (*CSIRO*)
Xinmei Tian (*U. Sc. Tech. China*)
Gabriele Tolomei (*Yahoo Labs*)
Elaine Toms (*U. Sheffield*)
Nicola Tonellotto (*ISTI-CNR*)
Dolf Trieschnigg (*U. Twente*)
Andrew Trotman (*eBay*)
Manos Tsagkias (*904Labs*)
Theodora Tsikrika (*CERTH*)
Julián Urbano (*U. Pompeu Fabra*)
Christophe Van Gysel (*U. Amsterdam*)
Suzan Verberne (*Radboud U. Nijmegen*)
Changhu Wang (*Microsoft Research China*)
Hongning Wang (*U. Virginia*)
Lidan Wang (*U. Maryland College Park*)
Meng Wang (*Hefei U. Tech.*)
Shuaiqiang Wang (*U. Jyväskylä*)
William Webber (*Willaim Webber Consulting*)
Wouter Weerkamp (*904Labs*)
Xing Wei (*Inmobi*)
Jerome White (*New York U.*)
Xiaobing Xue (*Twitter*)
Grace Hui Yang (*Georgetown U.*)
Kuiyuan Yang (*Microsoft Research*)
Liu Yang (*U. Massachusetts Amherst*)
Xuchen Yao (*Johns Hopkins U.*)
Jie Yin (*CSIRO*)
Muhammad Bilal Zafar (*Max Planck Institut*)
Duo Zhang (*Twitter*)
Jianwen Zhang (*Microsoft Research Asia*)
Lanbo Zhang (*Twitter*)
Yongfeng Zhang (*Tsinghua U.*)
Zhiwei Zhang (*Purdue U.*)
Ke Zhou (*Yahoo Labs*)
Imed Zitouni (*Microsoft*)
Guido Zuccon (*Queensland U. Tech.*)

Knowledge Management Track Program Committee Members

Gail-Joon Ahn (*Arizona State U.*)
Mohammad AlHassan (*IUPUI*)
David Anastasiu (*U. Minnesota*)
Azin Ashkan (*Technicolor*)
Bahman Bahmani (*Stanford U.*)
Gustavo Batista (*U. Sao Paulo*)
Srikanta Bedathur (*IBM Research India*)
Kanishka Bhaduri (*Netflix*)
Arnab Bhattacharya (*IIT Kanpur*)
Albert Bifet (*U. Waikato*)
Petko Bogdanov (*SUNY Albany*)
Klemens Böhm (*Karlsruhe Institut Tech.*)
Mohamed Bouguessa (*U. Quebec*)
Christos Boutsidis (*Yahoo Labs*)
Andrea Cali (*Birkbeck College London*)
Ricardo Campello (*U. São Paulo*)
Huiping Cao (*New Mexico State U.*)
Jeffrey Chan (*U. Melbourne*)
Varun Chandola (*U. Buffalo*)
Michael Chau (*U. Hong Kong*)
Nitesh Chawla (*Notre Dame*)
Ye Chen (*Microsoft*)
Zhiyuan Chen (*U. Illinois Chicago*)
Jaegul Choo (*Korea U.*)
Vassilis Christophides (*U. Crete*)
Kun-Ta Chuang (*National Cheng Kung U.*)
James Cook (*Google*)
Bernardo Cuenca-Grau (*U. Oxford*)
Alfredo Cuzzocrea (*U. Calabria*)
Na Dai (*Google*)
Theodore Dalamagas (*Athena Research Greeve*)
Abhimanyu Das (*Google*)
Antonios Deligiannakis (*Tech. U. Crete*)
Christos Doulkeridis (*U. Piraeus*)
Dora Erdos (*Boston U.*)
Alex Fabrikant (*Google*)
Elena Ferrari (*U. Insubria*)
Avrilia Floratou (*IBM Almaden*)
Esther Galbrun (*Boston U.*)
Jing Gao (*SUNY Buffalo*)
Dinesh Garg (*IBM India Research Lab*)
Chiara Ghidini (*FBK Trento*)
Nikos Giatrakos (*Tech. U. Crete*)
Kasneci Gjergji (*Hasso Plattner Institut*)
Aris Gkoulalas-Divanis (*IBM*)
Bart Goethals (*U. Antwerp*)
Manuel Gomez Rodriguez (*MPI*)
Amit Goyal (*Yahoo Labs*)
Francesco Gullo (*Yahoo Labs*)
Stephan Günnemann (*Carnegie Mellon U.*)
Sunil Gupta (*Deakin*)
Maxim Gurevich (*Bento Labs*)

Claudio Gutierrez (*Universidad De Chile*)
Maria Halkidi (*U. Piraeus*)
Jingrui He (*Arizona State U.*)
Raquel Hill (*Indiana U.*)
Thanh Lam Hoang (*IBM Research Dublin*)
Bing Hu (*Samsung*)
Luke Huan (*U. Kansas*)
Ekaterini Ioannou (*Tech. U. Crete*)
Yunliang Jiang (*Thumbtack*)
James Joshi (*U. Pittsburg*)
Panos Kalnis (*KAUST*)
Bhargav Kanagal (*Google*)
Ramakrishnan Kannan (*Georgia Tech*)
Ben Kao (*U. Hong Kong*)
Panagiotis Karras (*Skoltech*)
Daniel Keren (*U. Haifa*)
Arijit Khan (*ETH Zurich*)
Latifur Khan (*U. Texas Dallas*)
Xiangnan Kong (*WPI*)
Ioannis Konstantinou (*NTUA*)
Georgia Koutrika (*HP Labs*)
Zornitsa Kozareva (*Yahoo Labs*)
Tim Kraska (*Brown U.*)
Ashish Kundu (*IBM Research*)
Ni Lao (*Google*)
Theodoros Lappas (*Stevens Inst. Tech.*)
Silvio Lattanzi (*Google*)
Hady Lauw (*Singapore Management U.*)
Wang-Chien Lee (*Pennsylvania State U.*)
Yang Li (*Google*)
Zhenhui Li (*Pennsylvania State U.*)
Lei Liu (*HP Labs*)
Claudio Lucchese (*ISTI-CNR*)
Michael Mathioudakis (*Helsinki U. Tech.*)
Julian McAuley (*UCSD*)
Sebastian Michel (*TU Kaiserslautern*)
Pauli Miettinen (*Max Planck Institut*)
Marco Montali (*Free U. Bozen-Bolzano*)
Abdullah Mueen (*UMN*)
Emmanuel Müller (*Karlsruhe Inst. Tech.*)
Ndapa Nakashole (*Carnegie Mellon U.*)
Xia Ning (*IUPUI*)
Eirini Ntoutsi (*LMU*)
Werner Nutt (*Free U. Bozen-Bolzano*)
Gaurav Pandey (*Mount Sinai School of Medicine*)
Spiros Papadimitriou (*Rutgers U.*)
Apostolos Papadopoulos (*Aristotle U. Thessaloniki*)
Evangelos Papalexakis (*Carnegie Mellon U.*)
Odysseas Papapetrou (*Tech. U. Crete*)
Panagiotis Papapetrou (*Stockholm U.*)
Stott Parker (*UCLA*)
Konstantinos Pelechrinis (*U. Pittsburgh*)
Peter Pietzuch (*Imperial College*)
Ali Pinar (*Sandia National Labs*)
Dimitris Plexousakis (*U. Crete*)
Davood Rafiei (*U. Alberta*)
Santu Rana (*Deakin U.*)
Huzefa Rangwala (*George Mason U.*)
Chotirat Ann Ratanamahatana (*Chulalongkorn U.*)
Chiara Renso (*CNR*)
Matteo Riondato (*Brown U.*)
Dimitris Sacharidis (*Vienna U. Tech.*)
Barna Saha (*U. Massachusetts Amherst*)
Vasilis Samoladas (*Tech. U. Crete*)
Mohamed Sarwat (*U. Minnesota*)
Saket Sathe (*IBM*)
Ralf Schenkel (*U. Passau*)
Erich Schubert (*LMU Munich*)
Matthias Schubert (*LMU Munich*)
Thomas Seidl (*RWTH Aachen U.*)
Nisheeth Shrivastava (*Amazon*)
Alkis Simitsis (*HP Labs*)
Yannis Sismanis (*Google*)
Sucheta Soundarajan (*Rutgers U.*)
Anna Squicciarini (*Pennsylvania State U.*)
Kostas Stefanidis (*FORTH-ICS Greece*)
Karthik Subbian (*Facebook*)
Fabian Suchanek (*Télécom ParisTech U.*)
Yizhou Sun (*NEU*)
Pang-Ning Tan (*Michigan State U.*)
Jiliang Tang (*Yahoo Labs*)
Liang Tang (*LinkedIn*)
Sandeep Tata (*Google*)
Shirish Tatikonda (*IBM Almaden*)
Manolis Terrovitis (*IMIS Athena*)
Brian Thompson (*U.S. Army Research Lab*)
Srikanta Tirthapura (*Iowa State U.*)
Truyen Tran (*Deakin U.*)
Panayiotis Tsaparas (*U. Ioannina*)
Charalampos Tsourakakis (*Brown U.*)
Deepak Turaga (*IBM*)
Leong Hou U (*U. Macau*)
Antti Ukkonen (*Helsinki U. Tech.*)
Aparna Varde (*Montclair State U.*)
Vasilis Vassalos (*AUEB Greece*)
Panos Vassiliadis (*U. Ioannina*)

Akrivi Vlachou (*AUEB Greece*)
Anil Vullikanti (*Virginia Tech*)
Dong Wang (*U. Notre Dame*)
Jason Wang (*New Jersey Inst. Tech.*)
Shengrui Wang (*U. Sherbrooke*)
William Yang Wang (*Carnegie Mellon U.*)
Yue Wang (*U. Michigan*)
Tim Weninger (*Notre Dame*)
Anthony Wirth (*U. Melbourne*)
Dingming Wu (*U. Hong Kong*)
Donghui Wu (*Lexis Nexis*)
Zhaoming Wu (*Georgia Tech*)
Rongjing Xiang (*Google*)
Li Xiong (*Emory U.*)
Shengqi Yang (*Facebook*)
Yuan Yao (*Nanjing U.*)
Ke Yiping (*Nanyang Tech. U.*)
Philip S. Yu (*U. Illinois Chicago*)
Wenchao Yu (*UCLA*)
Reza Zafarani (*Arizona State U.*)
Hessam Zakerzadeh (*U. Calgary*)
Ce Zhang (*U. Wisconsin Madison*)
Jiawei Zhang (*UIC*)
Qin Zhang (*Indiana*)
Ruofei Zhang (*Microsoft*)
Yuchen Zhao (*AppDynamics*)
Zhe Zhao (*U. Michigan*)
Dmitriy Zheleznyakov (*U. Oxford*)
Arthur Zimek (*LMU Munich*)
Andreas Zuefle (*LMU Munich*)

Additional Referees

Karam Abdulahhad (*CNRS Grenoble*)
Tenindra Abeywickrama (*Monash U.*)
Cem Aksoy (*New Jersey Inst. Tech.*)
Daniel Alejandro Garcia Ulloa (*Emory U.*)
Akhil Arora (*Xerox Research Bangalore*)
Besim Avci (*Northwestern U.*)
Alexander Beloborodov (*Ural Federal U.*)
Rafael Berlanga Llavori (*U. Jaume I Castellon*)
Nikos Bikakis (*Athena Research Greece*)
Fei Bi (*U. New South Wales*)
Dritan Bleco (*AUEB Greece*)
Luca Bonomi (*Emory U.*)
Matteo Catena (*ISTI-CNR*)
Kai Ho Chan (*Hong Kong U. Sc. Tech.*)
Anveshi Charuvaka (*George Mason U.*)
Abon Chaudhuri (*Walmart Labs*)
Jiecao Chen (*Indiana U. Bloomington*)
Lisi Chen (*Nanyang Tech. U.*)
Liu Chen (*Wuhan U.*)
Xu Chu (*U. Waterloo*)
David Corney (*Signal*)
Ananya Dass (*New Jersey Inst. Tech.*)
Sabrina De Capitani di Vimercati (*U. degli Studi di Milano*)
Alberto De Francesco (*ISTI-CNR*)
Amra Delic (*Tech. U. Wien*)
Aggeliki Dimitriou (*National Tech. U. Athens*)
Daniel Ditursi (*SUNY Albany*)
Vasilis Efthymiou (*FORTH-ICS Greece*)
Pavlos Fafalios (*FORTH-ICS Greece*)
Xing Feng (*U. New South Wales*)
Ioanna Filippidou (*AUEB Greece*)
Christian Frey (*Ludwig Maximilians U.*)
Debasis Ganguly (*Dublin City U.*)
Cheng Gao (*U. Kansas*)
Konstantinos Georgoulas (*AUEB Greece*)
Giorgos Giannopoulos (*Athena Research Greece*)
Benoit Groz (*U. Paris Sud*)
Kshiteesh Hegde (*Rensselaer Polytechnic Inst.*)
Zhenying He (*Fudan U.*)
Chuan Hu (*New Mexico State U.*)
Mas-ud Hussain (*Northwestern U.*)
Go Irie (*NTT Japan*)
Saiful Islam (*Swinburne U. Tech.*)
Alankar Jain (*IBM Research India*)
Nandish Jayaram (*U. Texas Austin*)
Meng Jiang (*Tsinghua U.*)
Minhao Jiang (*Hong Kong U. Sc. Tech.*)
Salil Joshi (*IBM Research India*)
Gregor Josse (*Ludwig Maximilians U.*)
Ilias Kanellos (*Athena Research Greece*)
Maria Karanasou (*U. Piraeus*)
Enkelejda Kasneci (*U. Tuebingen*)
Akshar Kaul (*IBM Research India*)
Evgeny Kharlamov (*U. Oxford*)
Roberto Konow (*U. Chile*)
Egor Kostylev (*U. Oxford*)
Jitin Krishnan (*George Mason U.*)
Anastasia Krithara (*IIT Demokritos Greece*)
Alexander Krumpholz (*CSIRO*)
Durgesh Kumar (*IIT Guwahati*)
Christina Lantzaki (*FORTH-ICS Greece*)

Chao Lan (*U. Kansas*)
Léa Laporte (*INSA Lyon*)
Haoran Li (*Emory U.*)
Jianxin Li (*RMIT U.*)
Lei Li (*Hefei U. Tech.*)
Wei Li (*Google*)
Xiaoli Li (*U. Kansas*)
Yuchen Li (*National U. Singapore*)
Zechao Li (*Nanjing U. Sc. Tech.*)
Kewen Liao (*U. Melbourne*)
Aldo Lipani (*Tech. U. Vienna*)
Ruifeng Liu (*Chinese U. Hong Kong*)
Yubao Liu (*Sun Yat Sen U.*)
Cheng Long (*Hong Kong U. Sc. Tech.*)
Xin Lu (*Pennsylvania State U.*)
Nantia Makrynioti (*AUEB Greece*)
Sebastian Mattheis (*BMW Car IT*)
Nianzu Ma (*U. Illinois Chicago*)
Meenakshi Mishra (*U. Kansas*)
Cristina Muntean (*ISTI-CNR*)
Nikhil Muralidhar (*George Mason U.*)
Masaya Murata (*NTT Japan*)
Bin Mu (*City U. New York*)
Azad Naik (*George Mason U.*)
Julia Neidhardt (*Tech. U. Wien*)
Konstantinos Nikolopoulos (*City U. New York*)
Koninika Pal (*Tech. U. Kaiserslautern*)
Panayiotis Papadakos (*FORTH-ICS Greece*)
Theodore Patkos (*FORTH-ICS Greece*)
Kostas Patroumpas (*National Tech. U. Athens*)
Nikos Pelekis (*U. Piraeus*)
Gerardo Pelosi (*Politecnico di Milano*)
Wei Pengfei (*Nanyang Tech. U.*)
Matthias Petri (*U. Melbourne*)
Trang T.M. Pham (*Deakin U.*)
Tuan Anh Nguyen Pham (*Nanyang Tech. U.*)
Layla Pournajaf (*Emory U.*)
Bo Qin (*Hong Kong U. Sc. Tech.*)
Jianbin Qin (*U. New South Wales*)
Ridho Reinanda (*U. Amsterdam*)
Navid Rekabsaz (*Tech. U. Vienna*)
Zhiyun Ren (*George Mason U.*)
Bryan Reynaert (*Akori S.A.*)
Klaus Schmid (*Ludwig Maximilians U.*)
Baoxu Shi (*U. Notre Dame*)
Vasilis Spyropoulos (*AUEB Greece*)
Joseph St.Amand (*U. Kansas*)
Li Su (*U. Southern Denmark*)
Dan Suciu (*U. Washington*)
Yifang Sun (*U. New South Wales*)
Mack Sweeney (*George Mason U.*)
Natasha Tagasovska (*U. Lausanne*)
Aditya Telang (*IBM Research India*)
Camilo Thorne (*U. Mannheim*)
Salvatore Trani (*ISTI-CNR*)
Erald Troja (*City U. New York*)
Yannis Tzitzikas (*FORTH-ICS Greece*)
Utkarsh Upadhyay (*Max Planck Institut*)
Tassos Venetis (*AUEB Greece*)
Thanasis Vergoulis (*Athena Research Greece*)
Hongjian Wang (*Pennsylvania State U.*)
Shuai Wang (*U. Illinois Chicago*)
Xiang Wang (*U. New South Wales*)
Xiaoyang Wang (*U. New South Wales*)
Victor Junqiu Wei (*Hong Kong U. Sc. Tech.*)
Udi Weinsberg (*Facebook*)
Buwen Wu (*U. Southern Denmark*)
Fei Wu (*Pennsylvania State U.*)
Xiaoying Wu (*Wuhan U.*)
Yingjun Wu (*National U. Singapore*)
Xike Xie (*Aalborg U.*)
Xiaofeng Xu (*Emory U.*)
Bin Yang (*Aalborg U.*)
Shiyu Yang (*U. New South Wales*)
Yang Yang (*U. Electronic Sc. Tech. China*)
Zhengwei Yang (*Chinese U. Hong Kong*)
Peifeng Yin (*IBM*)
Quan Yuan (*U. Illinois Urbana-Champaign*)
Ting Yu (*Wuhan U.*)
Shuangfei Zhai (*SUNY Binghamton*)
Bing Zhang (*Northwestern U.*)
Jingyuan Zhang (*U. Illinois Chicago*)
Xu Zhiqiang (*Institute Infocomm Research*)
Rui Zhou (*Victoria U.*)

Sponsors and Supporters

Sponsors

SIGIR
Special Interest Group
on Information Retrieval

sig web

Gold Supporter

Microsoft®
Research

Silver Supporter

sportsbet
.com.au

Bronze Supporters

Academic Supporters

Making Sense of Spatial Trajectories

Xiaofang Zhou [1,2] , Kai Zheng [1,2], Hoyoung Jueng [3], Jiajie Xu [2], Shazia Sadiq [1]
[1]School of Information Technology and Electrical Engineering, The University of Queensland, QLD 4072, Australia
[2]School of Computer Science and Technology, Soochow University, China
[3]SAP Innovation Center Network, Brisbane, Australia
[1]{zxf, kevinz, shazia}@itee.uq.edu.au [2]xujj@suda.edu.cn [3]hoyoung.jeung@sap.com

ABSTRACT

Spatial trajectory data is widely available today. Over a sustained period of time, trajectory data has been collected from numerous GPS devices, smartphones, sensors and social media applications. Daily increases of real-time trajectory data have also been phenomenal in recent years. More and more new applications have emerged to derive business values from both trajectory data warehouses and real-time trajectory data. Due to their very large volumes, their nature of streaming, their highly variable levels of data quality, as well as many possible links with other types of data, making sense of spatial trajectory data becomes one of the crucial areas for big data analytics. In this paper we will present a review of the extensive work in spatiotemporal data management and trajectory mining, and discuss new challenges and new opportunities in the context of new applications, focusing on recent advances in trajectory data management and trajectory mining from their foundations to high performance processing with modern computing infrastructure.

Categories and Subject Descriptors

H.2.8 [**Database Management**]: Database Applications – *Data mining, Spatial databases and GIS*

Keywords

Trajectory data management; trajectory mining

1. EXTENDED ABSTRACT

A spatial trajectory is the trace of an object moving in a geographical space, typically represented by a sequence of locations with timestamps[20]. One common type of trajectory data is recordings from GPS-equipped vehicles. There are many other types of trajectory data, collected from smart phones, user check-ins and geo-tagged messages and photos in social networking applications. Trajectory data can also be collected without user's active participation, through, for example, mobile phone cell tower IDs, WiFi connections, the use of public transport cards and many location-based services. Trajectory data can also be derived from RFID readers, video cameras and remote sensing data.

Permission to make digital or hard copies of part or all of this work for personal or classroom use is granted without fee provided that copies are not made or distributed for profit or commercial advantage and that copies bear this notice and the full citation on the first page. Copyrights for third-party components of this work must be honored. For all other uses, contact the Owner/Author(s). Copyright is held by the owner/author(s).
CIKM'15, October 19–23, 2015, Melbourne, Australia.
ACM 978-1-4503-3794-6/15/10.
DOI: http://dx.doi.org/10.1145/2806416.2806418.

The amount of trajectory data is mounting up rapidly. It is common to see trajectory data repositories with billions of trajectories. Depending on the applications, a trajectory can last for a few minutes to a few days, and the number of moving objects can range from tens of thousands for a transport company to millions for a navigation company or an Internet service provider. The sampling rates also vary widely, from every a few seconds for navigation services to hours even days for some social network applications. As trajectory data can represent how people, vehicles, animals and natural phenomena (e.g., hurricanes, flooding and bushfires) move with real and precise spatial and temporal information, they become a foundation to support many applications, including intelligent transport systems, transport engineering, urban management and planning, transport and logistics, environment protection, emergency services, location-based services, social networks and recommendation systems.

It is highly challenging to manage and process trajectory data. Raw trajectory data can have many data quality problems, including *inaccuracy* caused by problems with location capturing devices, location estimation methods and sometime the physical environment for moving objects, *incompleteness* caused by unrecorded origin and destination information and missing data for a period of time or for a region, *inconsistency* as the same trajectory could be recorded in many different ways due to location update strategies used, data inaccuracy and changing context data such as maps, and *redundancy* as some parts of a trajectory can be derived. To this end, an extensive range of methods have been developed, such as map matching [2], trajectory calibration[16], trajectory simplifications and compression[6, 13], uncertainty resolution [17], points-of-interest detection [19].

Trajectory data management has its root in spatial and spatiotemporal databases. There are only a few database research prototypes dedicated to trajectory data[7], in spite of the importance of trajectory data and the need for general purpose trajectory database systems. Traditional database systems are not suitable for trajectory data, which have vastly variable length, high level redundancy, spatiotemporally localized operations as well as per-trajectory operations, unbounded temporal dimension, and often to be used with contextual data such as maps and data capturing parameters. They are often managed in file systems or using spatial databases, for flexibility and efficiency at the cost of general database functionality. However, there are a substantial amount of research on trajectory databases focusing on specific aspects, such as trajectory query languages[1], indexing[15] and query processing[5]. Similarity measure is another area of active research, mainly because it is often hard and sometimes subjective to define trajectory similarity, which can be closely coupled with applications and indexing methods[16, 3]. Many similarity measures have been proposed by adapting similarity measures from computational geometry, time series and string processing with or without added temporal considerations. In recent years, trajectory data mining and predication have received extensive attention from both academia and industry. Some representative work include co–traveller pattern mining[9, 12], trajectory clustering[11], and discovery of frequent travel patterns, popular routes and significant locations and events[8, 4, 19, 14].

The focus of trajectory data management and mining has now been changed to addressing the problem of deriving values from trajectory data in a holistic approach. We need to deal with not only very large volume of historical trajectory data but also for streaming location data in the context of rich links with other types of information such as business data, social media data and environment data. It is the time to revisit every step in trajectory data management and mining, from data capturing, cleaning, calibration, compression, storage, management to query processing and knowledge discovery. The hierarchical nature of trajectory data has to be considered systematically[10], so different levels of representation from raw trajectories, calibrated data to semantic annotations that serve different purposes can be managed and queried in one database. Extensive and sometimes on-demand links from trajectory data to other type of information based on the ubiquitous attributes of location and time of trajectory data hold the key to making values of trajectory data. They should also be supported for extracting, maintaining and using such links. Modern application can also have an extremely high level of concurrency, for example, with tens of thousands of concurrent shortest path queries using real-time traffic information for smart phone users. That demands a rethinking of the ways to index and process trajectory data to support data and query caching and parallel processing. To make commercial use of trajectory data, benchmarking, data archiving, privacy and crowd sousing also need to be addressed. How to make effective use of modern computing infrastructure, such as column stores, NoSQL databases and distributed file systems, in-memory databases and large computer clusters, also needs urgent attention[18].

Trajectory data becomes a fundamental type of data with unlimited potentials. We need to develop a general-purpose and scalable trajectory data management system to manage. It is necessary to combine effort from different and previously often disconnected communities, including geographical information systems, intelligent transport systems, database management and data mining, to work with the industry to address real problems and to derive values.

2. ACKNOWLEDGEMENT

The work presented in this paper is partially supported by the Australian Research Council (LP130100164, DP120102829 and DP110103423) and the National Natural Science Foundation of China (61232006, 61402312 and 61472263).

3. REFERENCES

[1] V. Bogorny, B. Kuijpers, and L. O. Alvares. ST-DMQL: a semantic trajectory data mining query language. *International Journal of Geographical Information Science*, 23(10):1245–1276, 2009.

[2] S. Brakatsoulas, D. Pfoser, R. Salas, and C. Wenk. On map-matching vehicle tracking data. In *VLDB*, pages 853–864. VLDB Endowment, 2005.

[3] L. Chen, M. T. Özsu, and V. Oria. Robust and fast similarity search for moving object trajectories. In *SIGMOD*, pages 491–502. ACM, 2005.

[4] Z. Chen, H. T. Shen, and X. Zhou. Discovering popular routes from trajectories. In *ICDE*, pages 900–911. IEEE, 2011.

[5] Z. Chen, H. T. Shen, X. Zhou, Y. Zheng, and X. Xie. Searching trajectories by locations: an efficiency study. In *SIGMOD*, pages 255–266. ACM, 2010.

[6] D. H. Douglas and T. K. Peucker. Algorithms for the reduction of the number of points required to represent a digitized line or its caricature. *Cartographica: The International Journal for Geographic Information and Geovisualization*, 10(2):112–122, 1973.

[7] F. Giannotti, M. Nanni, D. Pedreschi, F. Pinelli, C. Renso, S. Rinzivillo, and R. Trasarti. Unveiling the complexity of human mobility by querying and mining massive trajectory data. *The VLDB Journal*, 20(5):695–719, 2011.

[8] F. Giannotti, M. Nanni, F. Pinelli, and D. Pedreschi. Trajectory pattern mining. In *SIGKDD*, pages 330–339. ACM, 2007.

[9] H. Jeung, M. L. Yiu, X. Zhou, C. S. Jensen, and H. T. Shen. Discovery of convoys in trajectory databases. *VLDB*, 1(1):1068–1080, 2008.

[10] B. Kuipers. The spatial semantic hierarchy. *Artificial Intelligence*, 119:191–233, 1999.

[11] J.-G. Lee, J. Han, and K.-Y. Whang. Trajectory clustering: a partition-and-group framework. In *SIGMOD*, pages 593–604. ACM, 2007.

[12] Z. Li, B. Ding, J. Han, and R. Kays. Swarm: Mining relaxed temporal moving object clusters. *VLDB*, 3(1-2):723–734, 2010.

[13] N. Meratnia and A. Rolf. Spatiotemporal compression techniques for moving point objects. In *EDBT*, pages 765–782. Springer, 2004.

[14] A. T. Palma, V. Bogorny, B. Kuijpers, and L. O. Alvares. A clustering-based approach for discovering interesting places in trajectories. In *Proceedings of the 2008 ACM symposium on Applied Computing*, pages 863–868. ACM, 2008.

[15] D. Pfoser, C. S. Jensen, Y. Theodoridis, et al. Novel approaches to the indexing of moving object trajectories. In *VLDB*, pages 395–406, 2000.

[16] H. Su, K. Zheng, H. Wang, J. Huang, and X. Zhou. Calibrating trajectory data for similarity-based analysis. In *SIGMOD*, pages 833–844. ACM, 2013.

[17] G. Trajcevski, O. Wolfson, K. Hinrichs, and S. Chamberlain. Managing uncertainty in moving objects databases. *ACM Transactions on Database Systems (TODS)*, 29(3):463–507, 2004.

[18] H. Wang, K. Zheng, X. Zhou, and S. W. Sadiq. SharkDB: An in-memory storage system for massive trajectory data. In *SIGMOD*, pages 1099–1104, 2015.

[19] Y. Zheng, L. Zhang, X. Xie, and W.-Y. Ma. Mining interesting locations and travel sequences from GPS trajectories. In *Proceedings of the 18th international conference on World Wide Web*, pages 791–800. ACM, 2009.

[20] Y. Zheng and X. Zhou. *Computing with Spatial Trajectories*. Springer, November 2011.

ReverseCloak: Protecting Multi-level Location Privacy over Road Networks

Chao Li
School of Information Sciences
University of Pittsburgh
Pittsburgh, PA, USA
chl205@pitt.edu

Balaji Palanisamy
School of Information Sciences
University of Pittsburgh
Pittsburgh, PA, USA
bpalan@pitt.edu

ABSTRACT

With advances in sensing and positioning technology, fueled by the ubiquitous deployment of wireless networks, location-aware computing has become a fundamental model for offering a wide range of life enhancing services. However, the ability to locate users and mobile objects opens doors for new threats - the intrusion of location privacy. Location anonymization refers to the process of perturbing the exact location of users as a cloaking region such that a user's location becomes indistinguishable from the location of a set of other users. A fundamental limitation of existing location anonymization techniques is that location information once perturbed to provide a certain anonymity level cannot be reversed to reduce anonymity or the degree of perturbation. This is especially a serious limiting factor in multi-level privacy-controlled scenarios where different users of the location information have different levels of access. This paper presents ReverseCloak, a new class of reversible location cloaking mechanisms that effectively support multi-level location privacy, allowing selective de-anonymization of the cloaking region to reduce the granularity of the perturbed location when suitable access credentials are provided. We evaluate the ReverseCloak techniques through extensive experiments on realistic road network traces generated by GT-MobiSim. Our experiments show that the proposed techniques are efficient, scalable and provide the required level of privacy.

Categories and Subject Descriptors

H.2.7 [**Database Management**]: Database Administration—*Security, integrity, and protection*; H.2.8 [**Database Management**]: Database Applications—*Spatial databases and GIS*

General Terms

Algorithms, Design.

Permission to make digital or hard copies of all or part of this work for personal or classroom use is granted without fee provided that copies are not made or distributed for profit or commercial advantage and that copies bear this notice and the full citation on the first page. Copyrights for components of this work owned by others than ACM must be honored. Abstracting with credit is permitted. To copy otherwise, or republish, to post on servers or to redistribute to lists, requires prior specific permission and/or a fee. Request permissions from Permissions@acm.org.
CIKM'15, October 19–23, 2015, Melbourne, Australia.
© 2015 ACM. ISBN 978-1-4503-3794-6/15/10 ...$15.00.
DOI: http://dx.doi.org/10.1145/2806416.2806437.

Keywords

Location privacy, multilevel privacy, reversible cloaking algorithm, k-anonymity, road network.

1. INTRODUCTION

The proliferation of low-cost GPS-enabled mobile devices and the ubiquitous deployment of wireless networks drive the rapid emergence of mobile technology to satisfy the growing demands for location-based service applications. Examples of location-based applications include searching nearest points of interest *("where is the nearest gas station to my current location?")*, spatial alerts *("Remind me when I drive close to the grocery store.")*, location-based social networking *("Tell my friends where I am.")*. The market of location-based systems is predicted to be $3.3 billion in 2013 [23] and is expected to grow further to sustain the growth in LBS and mobile applications markets [18]. While location-based services find numerous potential benefits, they also open new doors for privacy threats. For example, through statistical analysis of usual haunts of the users, an attacker can speculate about user's private information, such as hobbies, living habits, health status and so on. In the worst cases, disclosure of location information can be even life-threatening [25]. Such privacy threats directly affect people's attitude towards location-based applications as people become more conscious and aware of the potential privacy risks associated with it [16].

Location privacy is a system-level capability of location-based systems, which controls the access to location information at different spatial and temporal granularity instead of completely stopping access. Location anonymization refers to the process of perturbing user location information such that it masks the exact location of the user using a cloaked region. A subject is said to be location k-anonymous if her location information is indistinguishable from that of $k-1$ other users . However, a fundamental limitation of all existing location privacy protection schemes is that location information once perturbed to provide a certain anonymity level cannot be reversed to reduce anonymity or the degree of perturbation. This is especially a serious limiting factor in multi-level privacy controlled scenarios where different users of the location information have different levels of access on the exposed location. For instance if Alice is concerned of her location privacy, she might decide to expose her location with a certain privacy level with one location-based service provider. However, she may wish to give some other location-based service providers access to a reduced anonymity level as she may trust those providers more than the others. Also, Alice may want to give access to her exact location to some providers who are most trustworthy. In existing schemes, location information once lost during perturbation cannot be restored and therefore, becomes unavailable when more privileged users try to access finer information, resulting in a loss of utility.

There are several location anonymization techniques [3, 10, 11, 14, 19, 28] proposed in the literature to tackle the location privacy problem. Most of these techniques are developed as unidirectional location perturbation schemes that can only perturb in an irreversible manner without being able to de-anonymize when users with higher privilege have access to more fine granular information. This paper presents ReverseCloak, a new class of reversible location cloaking mechanisms that allows selective de-anonymization of the cloaking area when suitable access credentials are provided. A key objective of our work is to support multilevel location privacy requirements that allow different users to infer different levels of information from the same exposed location based on their access credentials and the access privilege levels entitled to them. Our proposed approaches transform the raw point location of a user into a cloaked location region such that finer location information can be obtained through careful de-anonymization using a shared secret anonymization key. However, without the secret key, the cloaked region preserves strong privacy properties, allowing no additional information to be inferred. To the best of our knowledge, the techniques proposed in this paper are the first set of location privacy protection schemes aimed at supporting multi-level privacy/utility controls through novel development of secure reversible location cloaking techniques.

The rest of the paper is organized as follows: Section 2 provides a background and an overview of the multi-level reversible location anonymization problem. In Section 3, we discuss two reversible multi-level location anonymization schemes namely reversible global expansion and reversible pre-assignment-based local expansion techniques that support multi-level location privacy. In Section 4, we present the analysis of our experiments on realistic road network traces generated using GTMobiSim. We discuss related work in Section 5 and we conclude in Section 6.

2. CONCEPTS AND MODELS

In this section, we first describe the road network model used to capture the mobility features of mobile users and then introduce the concept of location cloaking. After that, we define the multilevel reversible location privacy problem and discuss two effective attack models used to evaluate the attack resilience of the proposed solutions.

2.1 Road network model

We model the road network as a graph $G = (V_G, E_G)$, where V_G represents the set of junctions and E_G represents the set of road segments. An example is shown in Figure 1, which consists of 23 junctions and 33 road segments. A junction is defined as the crossover point of any two roads or the end of a road. A road segment is defined as the direct road connecting any two adjacent junctions. Each segment is uniquely determined by the two junctions associated with it while each junction is associated with one or more adjacent road segments. The number of segments adjacent to a road junction, j_i defines the degree of the junction, denoted by $d(j_i)$. Based on that, each junction

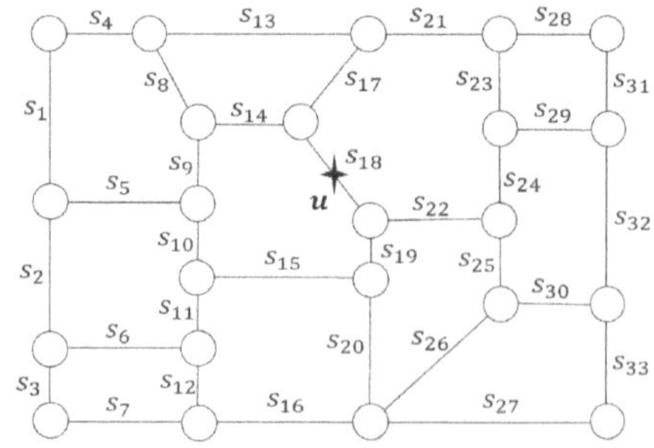

Figure 1: Road network model

can be classified into three categories namely an intersection junction ($d \geqslant 3$), an intermediate junction ($d = 2$) and an end junction ($d = 1$). In the road network, each mobile user is assumed to move along the segments and change direction only at junctions. A user interested in sharing her anonymized location information forwards her true location with the anonymization requirements and spatial information to a trusted anonymization which then transforms this raw point location into a perturbed spatial region that meets the required privacy levels.

2.2 Location anonymization

We consider the key privacy requirement arising in a road network namely *location k-anonymity*, which ensures that the exposed location of a user is indistinguishable from a set of other users on the road network.

Definition 1 (*Location k-anonymity*). *The location information of a user is said to be k-anonymous if the location information is indistinguishable from the location information of at least k-1 other users.*

In a personalized location privacy model, for each location anonymization request, the level of k-anonymity is decided by the user in a customizable manner. Also, in order to bound the size of the cloaking region that has a direct influence on the performance of the anonymous query processing technique [19, 27], a customizable maximum spatial resolution level, denoted by σ_s is specified. These two parameters together define the user-defined privacy profile: (δ_k, σ_s). In the past, several cloaking models have been proposed for location anonymization. In this paper, we discuss two broad class of techniques namely (i) random sampling and (ii) road-network-based expansion as candidate approaches for location cloaking over road networks.

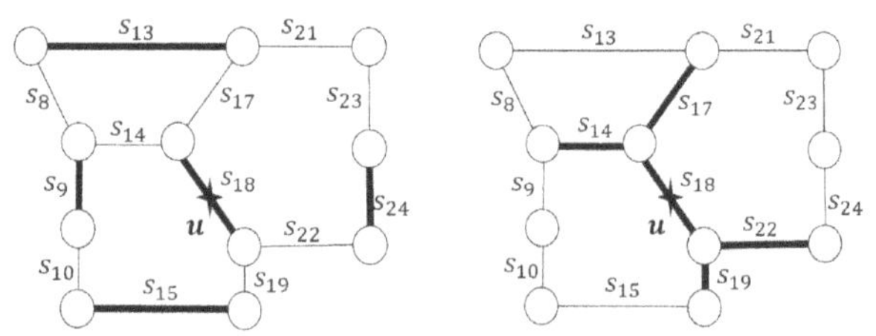

(a) Random sampling (b) Road network expansion

Figure 2: Two typical anonymizatioin models

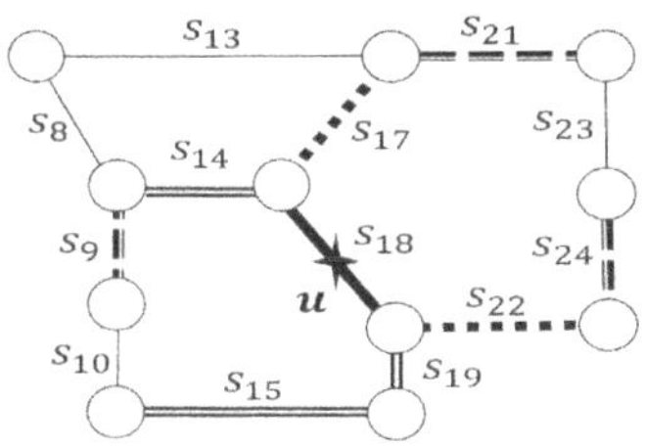

Figure 3: Multilevel reversible location anonymization

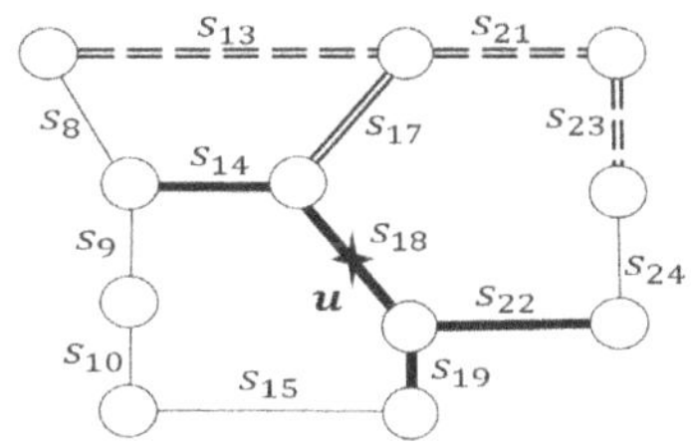

Figure 4: Replay attack

Random sampling: Given the anonymization request and the user-defined profile, the random sampling approach first chooses the road segment containing the actual user. It then randomly adds segments within the bounded area restricted by σ_s into the cloaking region until the requirements of δ_k is met. In the example shown in Figure 2(a), we find that the entire region is a part of the road network shown in Figure 1. It represents the region restricted by the spatial tolerance level σ_s. To meet the requirement of δ_k, in addition to the segment containing the actual user, the algorithm randomly adds four additional segments to form the cloaked region. While the random sampling approach attempts to ensure higher randomness in the cloaking process, it is however shown that it is not desirable from an anonymous query processing perspective as the discrete segments added in the random sampling process are not amenable for scalable and efficient query processing [27]. From a query processing perspective, a well-connected cloaked region over the network is more efficient as the query processing complexity is simplified. This motivates us to the road-network-based expansion techniques, which are described next.

Road-network-based expansion: In the road-network-based expansion approach, instead of randomly choosing segments from the bounded region in a discrete manner, the segments are chosen continuously based on an expansion scheme. The expansion begins from the segment containing the actual user and randomly expands such that each newly added segment is adjacent to at least one other segment in the currently formed cloaking region. Figure 2(b) shows an example of a road-network-based cloaking where the chosen segments, satisfying δ_k, form a tightly connected structure than the one generated by random sampling. Several road network-based cloaking schemes have been proposed in the past [27, 29] and they vary in terms of how randomly the expansion process proceeds to reach the required anonymity levels.

As it can be noted, most existing work on location privacy have focused on achieving variations of location k-anonymity and in such schemes, anonymity level once achieved in the cloaked region cannot be reduced when users with higher privileges need to access fine granular information. Therefore, in multi-level access controlled scenarios, such irreversible approaches can protect location privacy at at-most one privacy/utility level.

2.3 Multilevel reversible location privacy

The focus in this paper is developing a new class of reversible cloaking techniques, which can support multi-level location privacy in access controlled scenarios. In such cases, the location privacy of users is protected under multiple privacy levels, with higher anonymity levels for users with lower privileges and lower privacy levels for users with higher privileges.

In the multi-level reversible location privacy framework, a trusted anonymizer obtains the raw location information from the mobile clients with the user-defined profile. However, with the multi-level privacy model, the user-defined profile consists of the privacy requirements for each privacy level, L^i, except L^0 referring to a cloaking region with only the segment of actual user. Accordingly, the user-defined privacy profile is represented by (δ_k^i, σ_s^i), where $1 \leq i \leq N-1$ and N denotes the number of privacy levels. In addition, each privacy level, L^i is associated with a shared secret key, Key^i, which is used to drive anonymization process for that privacy level. Therefore, with access to the anonymization key of a particular privacy level, users of the cloaked location can selectively de-anonymize the cloaked region to reduce privacy levels to obtain finer location information. A detailed example of a four level case is shown in Figure 3. The segment s_{18} contains the actual user belongs to level, L^0. Using the anonymization key Key^1, $\{s_{17}, s_{22}\}$ are added to reach the privacy level, δ_k^1 of L^1. Then, Key^2 is used further to extend the cloaking region to meet δ_k^2 of level L^2 by adding segments $\{s_{14}, s_{15}, s_{19}\}$. Finally, $\{s_9, s_{21}, s_{24}\}$ are added using the anonymization key, Key^3 to reach the highest privacy level, L^3.

Later, when the cloaked location information needs to be reduced in privacy levels, it can be done using the anonymization keys. For instance, for accessing the information at the lower privilege level, L^2, Key^3 can be used to exactly identify and remove the segments $\{s_9, s_{21}, s_{24}\}$ from the cloaking region to reduce to the cloaked region corresponding to level, L^2. Similarly, using both Key^3 and Key^2, the segments $\{s_9, s_{21}, s_{24}, s_{14}, s_{15}, s_{19}\}$ can be identified and removed from the cloaking region to reduce to level, L^1. Therefore, by merely managing the shared anonymization keys among the location users at different privilege levels, the whole process protects location privacy under multiple discrete levels as customized in the user-defined privacy profile.

2.4 Replay attack

The security and privacy strength of any location privacy mechanism comes from the attacker's inability to infer the exact user location within the cloaked location. Specifically, the attacker is interested in analyzing the associativity of the actual user with each road segment in the cloaked location. Therefore, a segment with higher associativity is more likely to be the segment of the actual user. From the attacker's perspective, the attack is most ineffective when the associativity for the segments follows a uniform distribution. This leads to the highest uncertainty in identifying the true location of the user. In this paper, we use the replay attack

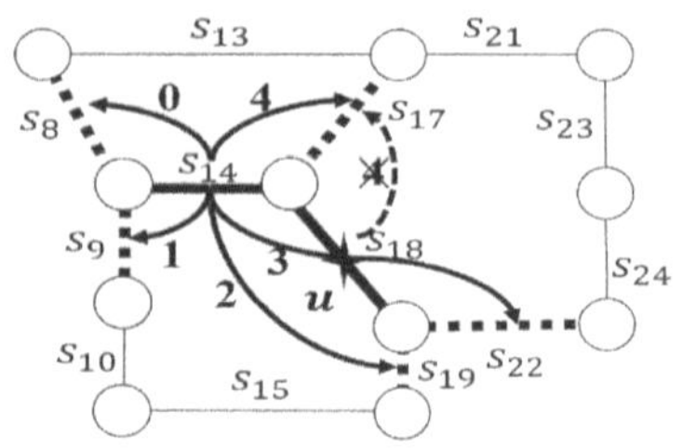

Figure 5: Forward transition collision

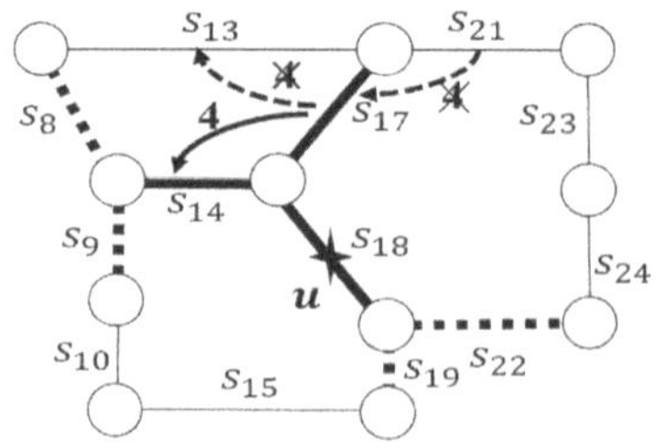

Figure 6: Backward transition collision

to evaluate the attack-resilience of the proposed cloaking schemes. Similar to the adversary models in [3, 19, 27], we primarily focus on snapshot exposure of location information for supporting snapshot location-based queries. For continuous location-based queries, with the additional ability to combine and correlate information from the location exposure of multiple snapshot instances, the adversary's chances of inferring the true location can be increased [9, 22]. While addressing such query-correlation attacks is a promising direction of future work, the scope of the replay attack model considered in our work is limited to snapshot queries.

In the replay attack, each segment within the cloaking region is iteratively considered to be the segment of the actual user to compute the associativity for all the segments. If the number of segments shared by the replayed cloaking region generated from a segment, s_i, and the real cloaking region generated from the real start segment is N_i, which is 1, (s_{17}), in the example of Figure 4. The associativity, A_i of s_i, can be calculated as $A_i = \frac{N_i}{\sum N_i}$. After obtaining A_i for all the segments within the cloaking region, the uncertainty of the attacker can be quantified by Entropy [24] measured as $E = -\sum A_i \log A_i$. The Entropy is a measure of the amount of information required to break the anonymity provided by the system. Therefore, the larger is the entropy, the higher is the uncertainty of the attacker and the scheme is more attack-resilient.

In the next section, we present our proposed reversible cloaking mechanisms that support efficient multi-level location privacy over road networks.

3. REVERSIBLE LOCATION CLOAKING

In this section, we present the proposed ReverseCloak cloaking mechanisms that support efficient multi-level location privacy over road networks. Before we present the details of the proposed approach, we discuss why conventional location cloaking techniques that perform road network-based expansion are not amenable for reversibility. We then discuss the key ideas behind the proposed reversible cloaking approach and discuss the challenges and the solution techniques for achieving reversible location cloaking over road networks.

In road network-based location cloaking schemes, a road segment is considered as the basic unit of expansion. At any point in the expansion process, the set of road segments selected to be part of the cloaking region forms the cloaking set. Therefore, in the beginning of the expansion process, the cloaking set contains only the segment containing the actual user. As the expansion process proceeds, the segments are added to the cloaking set until the required privacy levels are met. In the de-anonymization process, upon providing the anonymization key, the segments in the cloaking set are removed in the reverse order to reduce the anonymity level. At the end of the process, the segment containing the actual user is obtained.

The conventional road-network-based expansion cloaking mechanisms are designed to expand either randomly or semi-randomly based on additional factors such as network distance and the number of users present in the added segment. For example, in Figure 5, we find that the actual user who sends query is located in segment s_{18} and together with the second chosen segment s_{14} form the current cloaking region. At this phase of the cloaking process, the five segments, denoted with dotted lines are the candidates of the next segment to be added to the cloaking region. Since these segments are adjacent to at least one segment within the current cloaking region, these five segments form the candidate set.

For conventional expansion-based cloaking algorithms, the newly added segment within the candidate set may be selected either randomly or semi-randomly based on additional factors. However, in both the cases, we note that it is impossible for the privileged users to de-anonymize it as the cloaking region inherently protects against such de-anonymization attempts by the adversary due to the randomness. In order to support effective multi-level privacy protection, an ideal situation is when the cloaked region provides the highest uncertainty to an attacker attempting to de-anonymize it but has no uncertainty to users who possess the privileges to de-anonymize it. We achieve this property by devising our road network-based expansion process to be driven through an anonymization key to handle the randomness. In our approach, the cloaking process expands in a pseudo-random fashion by adding road segments into the cloaking region until the privacy requirements are met.

We refer to each addition of a new segment in anonymization process as a forward transition from a segment within the current cloaking set to a segment in the current candidate set. Similarly, during the de-anonymization process, the removal of each segment in the cloaked region represents a backward transition, which is essentially an inversion of the forward transition in the anonymization process. In this way, the relationships between any two successively selected segments are established. Therefore, the anonymization and de-anonymization can be considered as a series of forward and backward transitions respectively. For two segments s_i and s_j, the forward transition from s_i to s_j is denoted by $ft\{s_i \rightarrow s_j\}$ and the backward transition from s_j to s_i is denoted by $bt\{s_j \rightarrow s_i\}$. They together form a transition pair. To reverse the anonymization process, the goal is to make the transition chain reversible so that the forward and backward transitions in pair are correlated one by one. In the proposed approach, we use a secret key to generate the transition chain in a pseudo-random manner. Specifically, the anonymization process generates a stream of pseudo-random numbers using the anonymization key as the seed value. In each expansion step, the candidate set contains a certain number of candidate segments and each of them corresponds to a candidate forward transition pointing to them from the segment selected in the last expansion step. Then, each of them is assigned a unique transition value to be used for this step. Among these possible candidate forward transitions, the algorithm pseudo-randomly picks a unique transition based on a *pick value*, determined by the pseudo-random integer and the size of the candidate set. This pick value enables to choose a unique candidate forward transition based on the transition value. In the example shown in Figure 5, the candidate expansion region contains 5 segments and the transition values 0 to 4 are assigned to the five possible transitions. Here the pick value is generated as $R_i mod\ 5$, where R_i is the ith pseudo-random number in the stream. The pick value uniquely selects the transition with a matched transition value.

In contrast, in the de-anonymization process, uniquely identifying the exact backward transition is more challenging. Even though the pick value of every step can be calculated using the secret key in the de-anonymization process, the assignment of transition values for forward and backward transitions should be done very carefully. Otherwise collision of transition values may occur for either forward transitions (Figure 5) or backward transitions (Figure 6), which may result in incorrect selection of backward transitions. In the example shown in Figure 5, we find that when s_{17} is removed in the de-anonymization process, the transition values from the segments within the cloaking region to segment, s_{17} should be checked. If the pick value here is 4, for instance, we find that the transition corresponding to $ft\{s_{14} \rightarrow s_{17}\}$ matches the pick value, 4. While this indicates that s_{14} is a potential previous segment, we notice that a collision may happen if another transition such as value of $ft\{s_{18} \rightarrow s_{17}\}$ also has a transition value matching the pick value, 4, in this case. Therefore, the de-anonymization can no longer uniquely identify the backward transitions and de-anonymize the cloaked location.

In general, there are two ways to handle collisions in a reversible cloaking scheme. A simple and straight-forward approach is to simply record information about the collisions as additional metadata which can then be used to aid the de-anonymization process to enable skipping the corresponding colliding transitions [17]. However, from a location cloaking mechanism design standpoint, it is more desirable to have a collision-free anonymization approach that guarantees that the de-anonymization process is collision-free. Such a scheme can operate without any additional metadata. In this paper, we devise collision-free reversible cloaking mechanisms based on two different approaches. In the first approach, collisions are prevented by carefully assigning the transition values to the forward transitions $ft\{s_i \rightarrow s_j\}$ in a dynamic on-the-fly manner during anonymization. We propose the reversible dynamic global expansion scheme based on this (Section 3.1). In the second approach, both the backward and forward transitions are assigned transition values and we ensure that all backward and forward transition values are unique. In the example shown in Figure 6, the backward transitions are also assigned unique transition values. Since the pick values for a transition pair are same, we need to ensure that their transition values are also the same. Therefore, for instance if the pick value is 4 and if the transition value of $bt\{s_{17} \rightarrow s_{14}\}$ is also 4, then de-anonymization can proceed successfully without collision as only s_{14} matches the backward transition value uniquely. However, since 4 is uniquely assigned among the backward transitions from s_{17} and the transition values for a transition pair are same, we note here the same transition value, 4 in this example, cannot be assigned to any other forward transitions to s_{17} or backward transitions from s_{17} (denoted by the dotted arrow lines). Therefore, to determine the transition value for a certain transition, the restrictions from other transitions need be carefully taken into account. We also note that this assignment of unique forward and backward transitions can be done *apriori* for the entire road network in a statically pre-assigned manner. We develop reversible pre-assigned local expansion scheme (Section 3.2) based on this approach.

3.1 Reversible global expansion

The goal of the reversible global expansion cloaking mechanism is to perturb the raw point location of the actual user into a cloaked location region on the road network in a reversible manner such that the key privacy requirement namely location k-anonymity is met. The cloaking algorithm starts from the segment containing the actual user. For each transition, a transition matrix, containing transition values for all possible transitions between the current cloaking region and the candidate expansion region are generated. These transition values are carefully assigned to make sure that there are no repeated values in each row and column so that no collisions occur during de-anonymization. For each forward transition in the anonymization process, a pick value generated by the pseudo-random number uniquely determines the forward transition.. During de-anonymization, the same pick value can be used to find the forward transition uniquely.

Next, we introduce the mechanism to assign the transition values in a collision-free manner using the notion of n-hop neighboring segment on a road network.

Definition 2 *(n-hop neighboring segment). Two segments on a road network are n-hop neighboring segments of each other if there is a path between them on the road network passing through n junctions. Therefore, their topological distance on the road network is n hops.*

The proximity between road segments is defined based on their topological distance and therefore all n-hop neighboring segments of a segment form its n-hop neighboring set. Since there may be multiple road network paths between two segments, a segment may belong to multiple n-hop neighboring sets of another segment. The n-hop neighboring set for a single segment s_i is represented as N_i^n and the n-hop neighboring set for a cloaking segment set $C = \{s_a, s_b, s_c\}$ is defined as the n-hop global neighboring set, represented as $G_C^n = \{s_i \mid s_i \in N_a^n \bigcup N_b^n \bigcup N_c^n,\ s_i \notin C\}$. Therefore, the transition matrix used in this algorithm is formed by C and its global neighboring set G_C^n. Segments from global neighboring set with fewer hops are put into the global neighboring set in order until the number of segments in the global neighboring set is same as that of C, $|G_C^n| = |C|$. For each transition, a matrix $\mathbb{M}$ with X columns and Y rows is built,

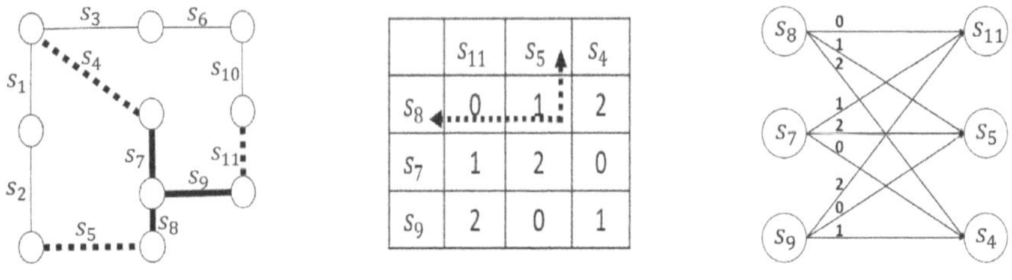

(a) Model (b) Transition matrix (c) Transition graph

Figure 7: Reversible global expansion

where $X = |G_C^n|$ and $Y = |C|$. Based on the segment length, the elements of G_C^n and C are sorted and mapped to columns and rows respectively. Here, if the first column and first row of $\mathbb{M}$ are numbered zero, then transition values can be calculated by $\mathbb{M}(x, y) = (x + y) \ mod \ X$, where x and y are the number of columns and rows respectively. Once the transition matrix is dynamically formed, the pick value, denoted by p, (calculated as $p = R \ mod \ X$, where R stands for the pseudo-random number), uniquely picks the forward transition among the set of candidate transitions for the currently formed cloaking region.

An example of the global expansion scheme is presented in Figure 7(a). We assume that the actual user asks for three privacy levels with (δ_k^1) and (δ_k^2) for L^1 and L^2 respectively. For this example, we assume that the currently formed cloaking region is $C = \{s_7, s_8, s_9\}$ and it is close to (δ_k^1), with $G_C^n = \{s_4, s_5, s_{11}\}$. The size of G_C^n can be larger for large n, but we just need the first three in this case to guarantee $|G_C^n| = |C|$. To select the next segment from G_C^n with the pick value generated using the key for level 1, L^1, a transition matrix is built as discussed above. The transition matrix is shown in Figure 7(b) and the corresponding transition graph is shown in Figure 7(c), where the arrow lines stand for forward transitions and the values represent the transition values. For this example, if the last selected segment is s_8, since $X = 3$ and $y = 0$, the pick value will be computed as $p = (R \ mod \ 3)$ and for $R = 7$, we will get $p = 1$. Therefore, based on the graph, the transition from s_8 with value 1 points to s_5. After adding the segment corresponding to this forward transition, the privacy requirement for L^1 may be met, however, the privacy requirements for L^2 may require adding more segments. In this case, the anonymization process changes the anonymization key to Key^2 and the process continues to pseudo-randomly expand until (δ_k^2) is met. In the de-anonymization process, it is straight-forward to see that users can de-anonymize the cloaking region if they have access to Key^2 in order to access the location information entitled to users at level, L^1. By removing the last selected segment from the current cloaking region, the remaining cloaking region can be used to build the same transition matrix and transition graph and since no collision exists in this approach, the backward transition can be uniquely determined by finding the forward transition that shares the same transition value as the generated pick value.

3.2 Reversible pre-assignment-based local expansion

Similar to the global expansion scheme, the reversible pre-assignment-based local expansion algorithm also starts the expansion from the segment containing the actual user. It keeps adding new segments until the privacy requirements of the user-defined profile is satisfied. As mentioned before, the transition values in the pre-assignment-based approach are assigned to both forward and backward transitions. However, unlike the reversible global expansion algorithm, where the forward transitions represent segments within the currently formed cloaking region to segments within the candidate expansion region, the forward transitions in the pre-assignment-based approach represent transitions from the previously added segment to a set of candidate segments for expansion. The candidate segments for expansion in the global scheme are neighboring segments of the entire currently formed cloaking region, however, the candidates for the local expansion scheme include only the neighboring segments of the previously added segment in the cloaking area.

The transition pre-assignment algorithm first determines the number of candidate transition segments for each transition. The algorithm ensures that for all the forward and backward transitions, this number is the same in order to ensure that the overall number of forward transitions is equal to that of backward transitions. For example, if the number of candidate transition segments is chosen as 3, the required transition values assigned to candidates should be 0, 1 and 2. Therefore, for each segment within the map, the three transition values need be carefully assigned to avoid collisions as discussed before. To build the transition graph, the algorithm establishes three tables namely a neighboring table, an encoding table and a decoding table. The encoding and decoding tables contain the transition values for the forward and backward transitions and the neighboring table contains the road network adjacency information for all the segments in the road network. For each segment s_i, its neighboring segments are recorded as a row in the order of topological distance. That is, the entries start from N_i^1 and end to N_i^m where m is the allowed maximum number of hops in a single expansion step. In this algorithm, the encoding table and decoding table are established together progressively to guarantee collision-free transitions for both forward and backward transitions. Concretely, the encoding and decoding tables are built by following three rules: (i) the candidates for each transition can be selected in a flexible manner, however, if a neighboring segment of s_i cannot be added into its encoding table due to collisions, the next neighboring segment should be considered. Given that the neighboring segment set is built based on the n-hop neighboring segment sets, the encoding and decoding tables bounded by the number of candidates can be always fully established, (ii) the transition values of any transition pair

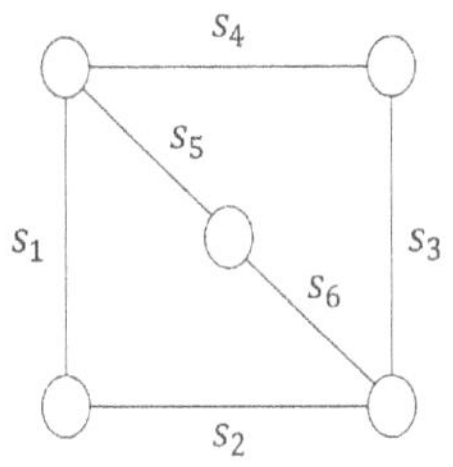

(a) Model

Seg	Next Seg		
	0	1	2
s_1	s_2	s_4	s_5
s_2	s_1	s_3	s_6
s_3	s_4	s_2	s_2s_1
s_4	s_3	s_1	s_1s_2
s_5	s_6	$s_1s_2s_6$	s_4
s_6	s_5	$s_2s_1s_5$	s_3

(b) Encoding table

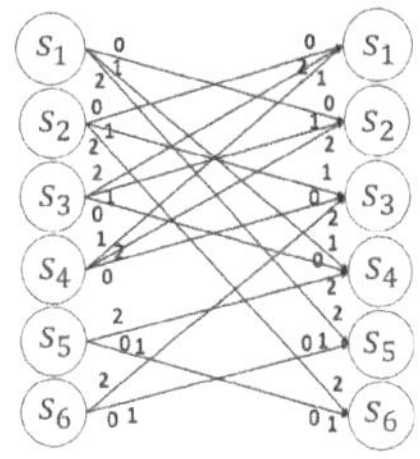

(c) Transition graph

Figure 8: Reversible pre-assignment-based local expansion

should be equal. For example, if s_j is added into the encoding table of s_i, then the transition value of $ft\{s_i \rightarrow s_j\}$, which is 0, should be same for s_i as well in the decoding table of s_j in order to guarantee that the transition value of $bt\{s_j \rightarrow s_i\}$ is 0. (iii) Once a certain transition value, v is assigned to $bt\{s_j \rightarrow s_i\}$, all the forward transitions from other segments except s_i to s_j cannot be assigned the same transition value, v. The encoding and decoding tables are gradually filled, for each neighboring segment, the encoding table shows a set of the remaining positions, denoted by E, and the decoding table also provides a set of remaining positions, denoted by D. Only if $E \cap D \neq \emptyset$, the neighboring segments are chosen to update the two tables.

An example with 6 segments is shown in Figure 8(a) where the number of candidates for each transition is set to 3. The corresponding encoding table is shown in Figure 8(b), which can be used to easily deduce the decoding table as the decoding table is a matrix transposition of the encoding table. Here, the candidate with one segment belongs to one-hop neighboring set N_i^1 while the candidates with two and three segments belong to N_i^2 and N_i^3 respectively. The final transition graph generated from the encoding and decoding tables is shown in Figure 8(c) where the transition values on the left stand for the forward transitions and the ones on the right represent the backward transition values. Once the pre-assigned transition graph is established, for any future cloaking requests, the algorithm proceeds to generate pick values pseudo-randomly and chooses the transitions that are guaranteed to be collision-free based on pre-assignment. Similarly, the de-anonymization process becomes straightforward, involving the removal of the road segments based on the backward transitions from this pre-assigned collision-free transition graph.

4. EXPERIMENTAL EVALUATION

In this section, we experimentally evaluate the performance and privacy offered by the proposed ReverseCloak algorithms. Before reporting our results, we first briefly describe the experimental setup.

4.1 Experimental setup

To simulate and compare different anonymization schemes, we use GTMobiSim mobile trace generator for road network [13]. Our experiments were designed based on a real road network map of northwest part of Atlanta, involving 6979 junctions and 9187 segments, obtained from maps of National Mapping Division of the USGS. There are 10,000 cars randomly generated along the roads based on Gaussian distribution. Once a car is generated, the associated destination is also randomly chosen and the route selection is based on shortest path routing.

In our experiments, four different anonymization schemes are implemented: Random Sampling (RS), Star-based road-network expansion (SE)[27], a candidate representative of existing road network-based expansion schemes, Reversible Global Expansion (RGE) and Reversible Pre-assignment-based Local Expansion (RPLE). The first two algorithms (RS and SE) are irreversible while the two ReverseCloak algorithms proposed in this paper (RGE and RPLE) are reversible and support multi-level privacy control. All the schemes are implemented in Java with the help of GTMobiSim.

4.2 Experimental results

Our experimental evaluation consists of three parts. First, we evaluate the performance of the selected cloaking algorithms by measuring anonymization time, de-anonymization time, relative spatial resolution and success rate. We collect and compare the results by varying user-defined parameters, δ_k and σ_s. Then, we evaluate the performance of the algorithms under multilevel privacy scenarios. Finally, we evaluate the effectiveness of these algorithms in terms of resilience to replay attack by measuring entropy towards varying δ_k and σ_s. Our results show that the proposed algorithms have good resilience towards replay attacks and effectively support multilevel privacy requirements while still maintaining good performance and efficiency.

4.2.1 *Varying User-defined k-anonymity*

This set of experiments evaluates the performance of the algorithms by varying the anonymity level δ_k as

$$\delta_k = 10i \; for \; i = 1, 2...10$$

Here, the spatial tolerance, d, is set as a function of the anonymity level, δ_k such that

$$d = 400\sqrt{i} \; for \; i = 1, 2...10$$

where the unit is meter(m). Therefore, the maximum allowable special region is a circular region with the user's actual location as the center and the spatial tolerance, d as the radius. We also set 5% standard deviation for each d. For this experiment, we consider only two privacy levels and for the multi-level reversible techniques, this privacy requirement represents the privacy levels of the least and most privileged users.

We compare the average anonymization time for the various approaches in Figure 9(a). In Figure 9(a), we find that RPLE is fastest in the anonymization phase among all the compared techniques. The reason is that the assignment of

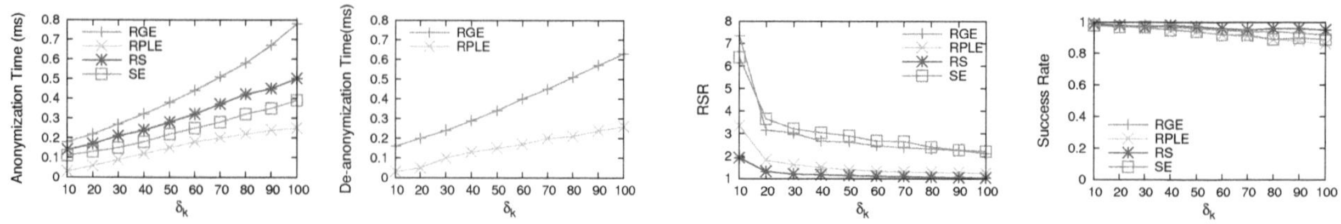

(a) Anonymization Time (b) De-anonymization Time (c) Relative Spatial Resolution (d) Success Rate

Figure 9: Performance with Varying Anonymity Level

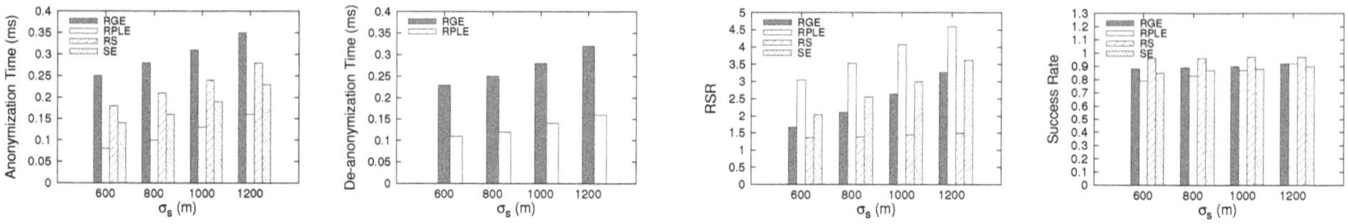

(a) Anonymization Time (b) De-anonymization Time (c) Relative Spatial Resolution (d) Success Rate

Figure 10: Performance with Varying Spatial Tolerance

transition values in the RPLE scheme has been done *apriori* and at the time location cloaking, the transition graph is directly looked up as compared to dynamically computing it on the fly in the RGE approach. Also, for all the algorithms, the anonymization time is longer for larger δ_k as stricter privacy requirements result in cloaking areas with more segments and it therefore requires addition of more segments into the cloaking area.

Figure 9(b) shows the impact of varying δ_k on the de-anonymization time. Since only ReverseCloak algorithms can perform de-anonymization of the cloaked region, RS and SE are not considered for this experiment. For both RGE and RPLE, the variation trends of de-anonymization time are similar as the anonymization time in Figure 9(a) as the computational complexity of the de-anonymization process is similar to that of the anonymization process. In both anonymization and de-anonymization phases, RPLE is faster than RGE because RPLE prevents collision in a *apriori* manner through its intelligent pre-assignment of forward and backward transitions while RGE prevents collision by dynamically assigning the transition values during location cloaking.

Figure 9(c) displays the impact of changing the anonymity level, δ_k on relative spatial resolution (RSR) which is defined the ratio of the size of the obtained cloaking area to size of the maximum allowable spatial area, specified by the spatial tolerance level, *d*. Here, RS has the lowest relative spatial resolution (RSR) as its candidate expansion region covers all the segments within the maximum allowable spatial area, thus making the size of the cloaking area close to the maximum spatial area even when δ_k is small. We also find that the relative spatial resolution of SE and RGE is larger than RPLE as the cloaking segments in SE and RGE are selected from a global neighboring segment set, providing a tighter structure as compared to a local neighboring set in the RPLE approach.

In Figure 9(d), we compare the success rate of anonymization process with varying δ_k value. The success rate represents the fraction of the cases where the cloaking algorithm is able to provide a cloaking region meeting the privacy requirements in terms of δ_k. We find that all the algorithms have a high success rate indicating that most of the anonymization requests are cloaked successfully to meet the privacy requirements. We also find that for all the schemes, the success rate decreases slowly when δ_k becomes very large. This is because a larger δ_k requires a larger cloaking area, which is harder to be satisfied by a given spatial tolerance. However, we note that even for higher anonymity levels, such as $\delta_k = 100$, the success rates of both RGE and RPLE are high and are close to 90%. RS keeps the highest success rate here as its failure occurs only when the total number of users within the maximum spatial area is smaller than δ_k. In fact, the success rate of the RS scheme defines the theoretical maximum success rate of the cloaking process for the given anonymization requests. We also note that SE and RGE have slightly higher success rate than RPLE as their cloaking regions have higher density and smaller size, thus being easier to meet the spatial tolerance requirement.

4.2.2 Varying User-defined Spatial Tolerance

To test the impact of spatial tolerance, the anonymity level δ_k is set to be 30 with standard deviation of 10. The spatial tolerance values, σ_s, are chosen as 600m, 800m, 1000m and 1200m as the mean values with 5% standard deviation.

Figure 10(a) shows that all the algorithms experience an increase in cloaking time as σ_s increases. With an increase in the maximum spatial region size, the expansion process in the cloaking schemes have more candidate segments for expansion, causing an increase in the anonymization time. Figure 10(b) indicates that the de-anonymization time for the reversible algorithms follow a similar trend as the anonymization time. In Figure 10(c), we find that all techniques except RS have higher relative spatial resolution as the RS scheme attempts to distribute the cloaking segments throughout the entire maximum spatial cloaking area. In Figure 10(d), we measure the influence of spatial tolerance on the obtained success rate. We find that the success rate of all the algo-

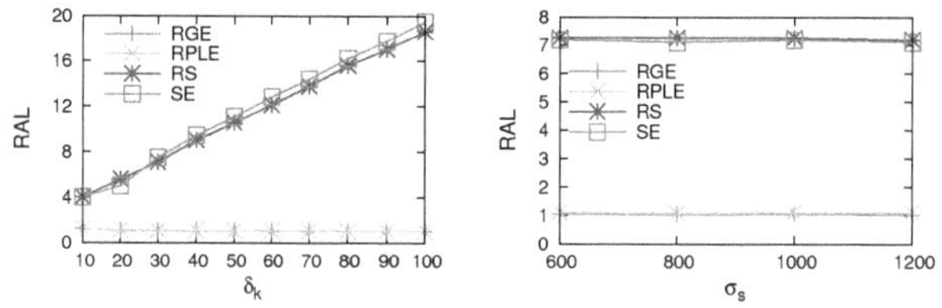

(a) RAL - δ_k (b) RAL - σ_s

Figure 11: Multilevel Privacy Protection

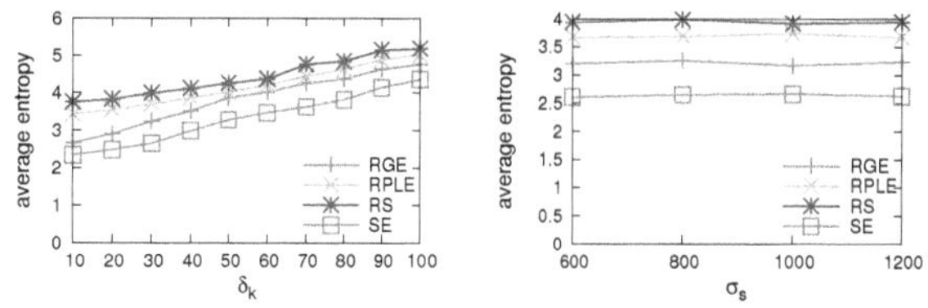

(a) Resilience of Varying δ_k (b) Resilience of Varying σ_s

Figure 12: Repaly Attack

rithms grows with increase in σ_s. The increments for RS and RGE are not very significant as their initial success rate for 600m spatial tolerance itself is higher. We again note here that the success rate of the RS approach is a theoretical maximum as the RS scheme would fail only when there are less than δ_k users within the maximum allowable spatial region. However, for the other approaches, we find that an increase in spatial tolerance has a slight increase in the success rate. Higher spatial tolerance provides a larger candidate expansion region and permits larger cloaking area, so the privacy requirements of a query is much easier to be achieved. Besides that, since the failures mostly occur where the density of mobile users is low, with higher spatial tolerance, part of the request that were dropped with lower spatial tolerance may now become successful.

4.2.3 Multilevel Privacy Protection

To evaluate the multilevel location privacy performance, relative anonymity level (RAL) is measured. The relative anonymity in a multi-level privacy scenario refers to the ratio of the obtained anonymity to the anonymity level entitled to a given access privilege level. Figure 11(a) and Figure 11(b) show the average relative anonymity of the cloaking techniques with respect to δ_k and σ_s . In Figure 11(b), the requirement of δ_k is set as 30. In both Figure 11(a) and Figure 11(b), we assume that there are six access privilege levels with uniformly distributed requirement of δ_k. The users with lowest privilege have access to the cloaking region with the maximum δ_k while users with the highest privilege have access to the location with the lowest anonymity. A good cloaking algorithm should ensure that the RAL is close to one for all access privilege levels, thereby providing exactly the anonymity level required for that level. We notice that existing irreversible algorithms result in very large RAL due to their lack of reversibility. In contrast, ReverseCloak algorithms achieves a RAL close to one for all privilege levels ensuring that users in each privilege level obtain the information at the level of anonynmity and accuracy entitled to them, thus protecting the multilevel privacy successfully.

4.2.4 Attack Resilience

This set of experiments evaluate the effectiveness of the algorithms in terms of their resilience to replay attacks. For replay attack, average information entropy is calculated as the metric to evaluate the uncertainty of the attacker: $E = -\sum A_i \log A_i$, where A_i is the associativity for each segment. Here, higher entropy means higher randomness and higher uncertainty for the attacker in inferring the true location of the user, thus leaking out less information and providing better privacy protection. Figure 12(a) shows average entropy of the replay attack with varying δ_k. Here, RS keeps the highest entropy for the whole range as its cloaking process is completely random and is therefore the most resilient to replay attacks. We also find that the entropy of SE is high as the road network expansion has a good degree of randomness, however, both RGE and RPLE provide even higher entropy, indicating that the randomness of the expansion process in RGE and RPLE is much higher than that of the SE approach. In the RGE and RPLE schemes, the randomness of both these schemes are only a little lower than the RS scheme. Figure 12(b) shows the average entropy with varying σ_s. Here, the anonymity requirement, δ_k is set as 30. Compared with the previous case, the entropy for all the algorithms is nearly constant suggesting that larger spatial tolerance does not have impact on the attacker's uncertainty. Our final observation here is that in general, higher δ_k provide higher entropy for all the algorithms, illustrating that a cloaking area with more segments provides better protection.

5. RELATED WORK

Location privacy has been an active area of research in the past. Broadly, location privacy protection mechanism can be classified into policy-based protection techniques and inference prevention-based techniques. Policy-based schemes give users permission to define privacy rules according to the service request, thus getting users' active participation. The inference-prevention schemes are more focused on prevention by protectively processing and perturbing the location information prior to disclosure. The latter can be further broken down into location data perturbation techniques represented by [1, 10, 19, 28] and trajectory inference prevention techniques represented by [5, 4, 21, 22, 20]. Location data perturbation schemes consists of perturbation through dummies [15], spatial location cloaking [3, 7, 10, 11, 14, 19, 28] and encryption-based techniques [1]. Recent work has studied the location privacy problem by perturbing the location information based on differential privacy constraints prior to disclosure [2, 6]. By replacing the real location information with dummies, location privacy can be protected, but the safety and service quality is dependent on the distance between the two positions. Encryption-based techniques provide strong confidentiality properties, however, an encrypted location has very little utility compared to a perturbed location which can be effectively used for query processing. In the past, there has been many works related to spatial location cloaking. To proactively protect user's location privacy, k-anonymity, which was proposed for sensitive data protection [26], was applied to protect location privacy in the context of location-aware systems [12]. Since then, the techniques related to spatial cloaking has been developing rapidly. *CliqueCloak* algorithm proposed in 2004 considered the individual user's personalized privacy requirement for the first time [10]. A grid-based cloaking framework, *Casper* further extended this model with a privacy-aware query processor [19]. Subsequently, a directed-graph based cloaking algorithm was proposed to improve the success rate of anonymization [28] and the Hilbert Cloak algorithm uses a Hilbert curve to fill the whole area and track users [11]. While these techniques were designed for mobile users traveling on Euclidean space, recent work has considered the location cloaking problem under a constrained road network model [8, 27, 30]. As we can observe, most existing location privacy protection mechanisms have focused on developing unidirectional location perturbation approaches that does not allow fine granular information to be inferred even when some users have the privileges to access it. The approach presented in [17] introduces a de-anonymizable location perturbation scheme by recording some additional information as metadata during the anonymization process. However, such an approach requires the overhead of maintaining and managing the additional metadata, without which, the perturbed data cannot be reduced in privacy levels. In comparison, to the best of our knowledge, the work presented in this paper is the first comprehensive set of location privacy protection mechanisms aimed at providing a multi-level reversible location privacy model to support privacy-preserving exposure of location information in access controlled environments.

6. CONCLUSION

In this paper, we presented ReverseCloak, a new class of reversible location privacy protection mechanisms for supporting multi-level privacy requirements in access controlled environments. We argue that conventional location privacy protection techniques are not inherently designed to support reversible privacy and we proposed two reversible location cloaking mechanisms namely (i) reversible dynamic global expansion scheme and (ii) reversible pre-assignment-based local expansion technique that effectively support multi-level privacy, allowing users with higher privileges to obtain finer information through reduced anonymity levels. Extensive experiments conducted on GTMobiSim show that the proposed techniques are efficient, scalable and achieve the multilevel functionality through their reversibility property. Our ongoing work is focused on applying the principles and techniques developed in this work to protect multi-level privacy for continuous location-based services that require continuous exposure of location information as compared to one-time exposure in the case of snapshot queries.

7. REFERENCES

[1] S.I. Ahamed, M.M. Haque, and C.S. Hasan. A novel location privacy framework without trusted third party based on location anonymity prediction. *ACM SIGAPP Applied Computing Review*, 12(1):24–34, 2012.

[2] M.E. Andres, N.E. Bordenabe, K. Chatzikokolakis, et al. Geo-indistinguishability: differential privacy for location-based systems. In *20th ACM SIGSAC conference on Computer and communications security*, pages 901–914, 2014.

[3] B. Bamba, L. Liu, P. Pesti, et al. Supporting anonymous location queries in mobile environments with privacygrid. In *17th international conference on World Wide Web*, pages 237–246, 2008.

[4] A. Beresford and S. Frank. Mix zones: User privacy in location-aware services. 2004.

[5] A. Beresford and F. Stajano. Location privacy in pervasive computing. In *Pervasive Computing*, pages 46–55, 2003.

[6] N.E. Bordenabe, K. Chatzikokolakis, and C. Palamidessi. Optimal geo-indistinguishable mechanisms for location privacy. In *21th ACM SIGSAC Conference on Computer and Communications Security*, pages 251–262, 2014.

[7] R. Cheng, Y. Zhang, E. Bertino, et al. Preserving user location privacy in mobile data management infrastructures. In *Privacy Enhancing Technologies*, pages 393–412, 2006.

[8] H.J. Cho, S.J. Kwon, R. Jin, et al. A privacy-aware monitoring algorithm for moving k-nearest neighbor queries in road networks. *Distributed and Parallel Databases*, pages 1–34, 2014.

[9] C.F. Chow and M.F. Mokbel. Enabling private continuous queries for revealed user locations. *Advances in Spatial and Temporal Databases*, pages 258–275, 2007.

[10] B. Gedik and L. Liu. A customizable k-anonymity model for protecting location privacy. 2004.

[11] G. Ghinita, P. Kalnis, and S. Skiadopoulos. Prive: anonymous location-based queries in distributed mobile systems. In *16th international conference on World Wide Web*, pages 371–380, 2007.

[12] M. Gruteser, D. Grunwald, and X. Liu. Anonymous usage of location-based services through spatial and temporal cloaking. In *1st international conference on Mobile systems, applications and services*, pages 31–42, 2003.

[13] GTMobiSim. `https://code.google.com/p/gt-mobisim/`.

[14] P. Kalnis, G. Ghinita, K. Mouratidis, et al. Preventing location-based identity inference in anonymous spatial queries. *IEEE Transactions on Knowledge and Data Engineering*, 19(12):1719–1733, 2007.

[15] H. Kido, Y. Yanagisawa, and T. Satoh. Protection of location privacy using dummies for location-based services. In *25th International Conference on Distributed Computing Systems*, pages 1248–1248, 2005.

[16] J. Krumm. A survey of computational location privacy. *Personal and Ubiquitous Computing*, 13(6):391–399, 2009.

[17] C. Li and B. Palanisamy. De-anonymizable location cloaking for privacy-controlled mobile systems. In *9th International Conference on Network and System Security*, 2015, in press.

[18] Marketsandmarkets. Location based services market worldwide forecasts and analysis (2014 - 2019). 2014.

[19] M.F. Mokbel, C.Y. Chow, and W.G. Aref. The new casper:query processing for location services without compromising privacy. *VLDB Endowment*, pages 763–774, 2006.

[20] B. Palanisamy and L. Liu. Mobimix: Protecting location privacy with mix-zones over road networks. In *27th International Conference on Data Engineering*, pages 494–505, 2011.

[21] B. Palanisamy and L. Liu. Attack-resilient mix-zones over road networks: architecture and algorithms. *IEEE Transactions on Mobile Computing*, 14(3):495–508, 2014.

[22] B. Palanisamy, L. Liu, K. Lee, et al. Anonymizing continuous queries with delay-tolerant mix-zones on road networks. *Distributed and Parallel Databases*, 32(1):91–118, 2014.

[23] ABI Research. Location-based mobile social networking. 2008.

[24] R. Shokri, G. Theodorakopoulos, J.Y. Le Boudec, et al. Quantifying location privacy. In *32nd IEEE Symposium on Security and Privacy*, pages 247–262, 2011.

[25] K.O. Stalker. Victims should check for GPS. *Associated Press*, 2003.

[26] L. Sweeney. A model for protecting privacy. In *International Journal of Uncertainty, Fuzziness and Knowledge-Based Systems*, pages 557–570, 2002.

[27] T. Wang, L. Liu, and P. Pesti. Privacy-aware mobile services over road networks. *VLDB Endowment*, 2(1):1042–1053, 2009.

[28] Z. Xiao, X. Meng, and J. Xu. Quality aware privacy protection for location-based services. *Advances in Databases: Concepts, Systems and Applications*, pages 434–446, 2007.

[29] J. Xue, X. Liu, X. Yang, et al. Protecting location privacy using cloaking subgraphs on road network. In *11th Web Information Systems and Applications Conference*, pages 65–68, 2010.

[30] B. Ying and D. Makrakis. Protecting location privacy with clustering anonymization in vehicular networks. In *Computer Communications Workshops*, pages 305–310, 2014.

GLUE: a Parameter-Tuning-Free Map Updating System

Hao Wu*† Chuanchuan Tu*† Weiwei Sun*† Baihua Zheng‡ Hao Su*† Wei Wang*†
*School of Computer Science, Fudan University, Shanghai, China
†Shanghai Key Laboratory of Data Science, Fudan University, Shanghai, China
‡Singapore Management University, Singapore
{wuhao5688, tucc, wwsun, haosu12, weiwang1}@fudan.edu.cn,
bhzheng@smu.edu.sg

ABSTRACT

Map data are widely used in mobile services, but most maps might not be complete. Updating a map automatically is an important problem because road networks are frequently changed with the development of the city. This paper studies the problem of recovering missing road segments via GPS trajectories, especially low sampled data. Our approach takes the GPS measurement error into consideration and proposes an effective self-adaptive algorithm. Our work is similar as many existing works in this field as they all rely on many parameters. However, we propose theoretical models behind all the important parameters to enable self-adaptive parameter setting. To the best of our knowledge, this is the first work that addresses the parameter setting issue successfully so our approach is free of parameter-tuning. In addition, we also propose a quantitative evaluation method for map updating problem. The result shows our algorithm has a much better performance than the existing approaches.

Categories and Subject Descriptors

H.2.8 [**Database Management**]: Database Applications—*Spatial databases and GIS*

Keywords

Map Updating; Map Inference; Trajectory Mining

1. INTRODUCTION

Research and markets predict that Global Digital Map market will grow at a compound annual growth rate of 9.37% over the period 2013-2018. Most, if not all, mobile users enjoy the great convenience of having digital maps available in mobile devices (e.g., smart phones). Meanwhile, we are also aware of the potential danger caused by inaccurate map data, as illustrated by a few example news reported by media. A 67 year old Belgian woman traveling to Brussels, 38 miles from her home, trustingly followed incorrect GPS directions on a detour of more than 800 miles, arriving two days later in Zagreb, Croatia. A woman followed her GPS past a "Do Not Enter" sign and down the wrong way on a divided highway near Scranton, Pennsylvania, causing a head-on collision. To name but a few.

On the other hand, the road network keeps changing, although the frequency might not be very high. For example, all the governments invest in transport infrastructure every year and part of the budget is for upgrading the road network. Beijing's xinhuanet.com reported that 11,000 kilometers (7,000 miles) of new freeways were built in China in 2012, which is about 1.5 times as long as the freeway mileage in California, US. More than 30,000 miles of roads were built in Brazilian Amazon in 3 years, from 2004 to 2007.

Given the fact that digital map becomes more and more important and the map data do change from time to time, how to accurately gather real-time map data is critical. A large number of map providers update their maps by investigating the real roads manually. This approach is expensive and it is hard to update the map timely. Some map providers employ some automatic approaches, clustered as *map inference technology*, to generate maps based on satellite images. However, the high cost of equipments and the fact that it can only find out the major roads make it hard to be put into practice widely. Instead of generating the whole map automatically as map inference technology aims to achieve, we propose a solution based on *map updating* in this paper. To be more specific, we assume a base map that captures a majority of roads in a real road network is available and we use massive GPS trajectories to automatically fine-tune the map by adding missing roads.

We want to highlight that our approach is doable as a large collections of GPS trajectories are becoming widely available, thanks for the fast deployment of GPS devices in mobile platforms. According to the "Transportation Statistics Annual Report-2007" released by Department of Transportation (DOT), there were estimated 254.4 million registered passenger vehicles in the United States; according to National Household Travel Survey 2009, each vehicle travels 38.4 miles daily. If we assume 1% of the vehicles are equipped with GPS devices, the GPS trajectories reported by the vehicles in the United States travel 2.93 billion miles in total within a month, which is about 1.82×10^4 times of the total length of its National Highway System. In other words, it is practical to update the map automatically by leveraging massive GPS trajectories. Meanwhile, digital maps are also widely available if we can bear the inaccuracy of map data to certain degree. Map updating fully utilizes all the available map resources to cut down the total

Permission to make digital or hard copies of all or part of this work for personal or classroom use is granted without fee provided that copies are not made or distributed for profit or commercial advantage and that copies bear this notice and the full citation on the first page. Copyrights for components of this work owned by others than ACM must be honored. Abstracting with credit is permitted. To copy otherwise, or republish, to post on servers or to redistribute to lists, requires prior specific permission and/or a fee. Request permissions from Permissions@acm.org.
CIKM'15, October 19–23, 2015, Melbourne, Australia.
© 2015 ACM. ISBN 978-1-4503-3794-6/15/10 ...$15.00.
DOI: http://dx.doi.org/10.1145/2806416.2806425.

cost. However, we also want to highlight that map updating problem is very challenging, as explained below.

First, most trajectory data are collected in a low sampling rate, for sake of power consumption and storage. According to [19], only 34% trajectories of more than 10,000 Beijing taxis have a sampling rate higher than 1 point per minute. Existing works have poor performance in low sampling rate situations because they are mainly based on trajectory clustering which highly depends on the sampling rate of trajectory data [2, 5, 9, 15, 18]. The sparse-sampled data has lost lots of information which make it difficult to obtain the road information directly. We need to think of ways to dig useful information out from those low-sampled trajectories to recover the roads.

Second, there are many noisy GPS points, those with large measurement error, in the collection. Measurement error occurs by many reasons, such as weather and buildings nearby. The noise points lead to wrong roads generated and influence the performance of our approach. Although there are several existing outlier detection methods to detect the noises [6, 17], they either need a fixed threshold working as a filter, e.g. global proximity-based approaches, or is not suitable for road-like distribution, such as clustering-based approaches and mixture model-based approach. However, in the case of map updating, the density of points in different roads may have a great difference and the distribution of the points is complex which challenges those methods. Note that although a relative density outlier detection method utilizing the Local Outlier Factor (LOF) technique can handle the different density problem, parameter selection is difficult, which is not suitable for application with data having different properties [17].

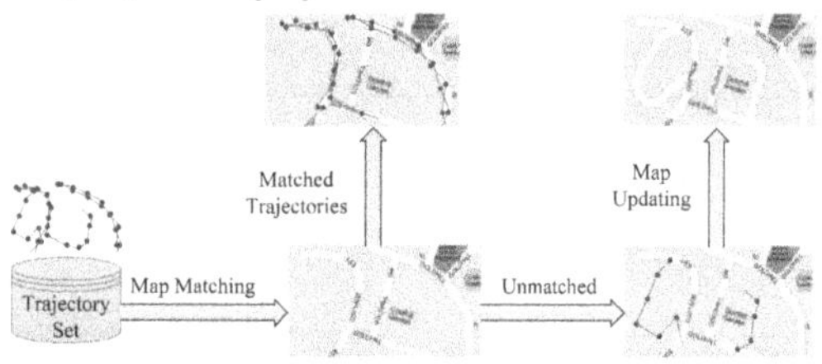

Figure 1: GLUE: GPS Trajectories (Low-Sampling rate) Based Map Updating Engine

By considering the challenges mentioned above, we propose a *GPS Trajectories (Low-sampling rate) based Map Update Engine (GLUE)* that can support auto map updates based on massive low-sampled GPS trajectories, with its main components shown in Fig. 1. It takes the trajectories set that captures the movement of moving objects on a real road network as input, and maps all the trajectories to a given map[1]. Map matching technique classifies the trajectory set into two parts, those matched and those un-matched. Our map updating is based on all the *unmatched* trajectories as they imply those roads they should be matched to are missing. Ideally, map updating can locate the missing roads and then make corresponding changes to the map.

As a summary, the major contributions of this paper are five-fold. First, we propose an effective direction clustering based approach on GLUE that is based on low sampling rate trajectory data. No existing work achieves good performance using low sampling rate data, although most trajectory data are sparsely-sampled. To the best of our knowledge, GLUE is the first attempt to utilize low-sampled GPS trajectory data for auto map updating. Second, we take GPS measurement error into consideration and propose an effective denoising algorithm. It is a self-adaptive and heuristic-based algorithm that can deal with regions of different point density. Third, we propose analytical models to select proper values for parameters in GLUE. The effectiveness of our parameter auto-tuning algorithms is demonstrated by the comprehensive experiments. Fourth, we design a quantitative evaluation method to evaluate the performance of map updating algorithms. Last but not least, we use massive *real data* to conduct the experiment and complement the Singapore map of OpenStreetMap. Trajectories of more than 15,000 Singapore taxis are used in our experiment. Result shows that our approach outperforms the existing work on low sampling rate trajectory data (sampling interval longer than 30 seconds).

[1]We employ existing *map matching* algorithms to perform this step, and related work on map matching will be reviewed in Section 2.

2. RELATED WORK

In this section, we review existing work related to GLUE, including map updating, map inference, and map matching. Map updating and map inference both are based on GPS trajectories while the former is to update an existing map and the latter is to generate the whole map from scratch. Map matching is to map a given trajectory set into roads of an existing map and it is employed to pre-process GPS trajectories before map updating in GLUE.

As introduced in Section 1, map updating approach is to update a given map (e.g., inserting new roads) based on massive GPS trajectories. CrowdAtlas, proposed in [18], is the only piece of existing work. It directly clusters unmatched trajectories according to the Hausdorff distance. During the clustering process, the size of each cluster increases as more and more unmatched trajectories are clustered. Once the size of one cluster reaches a predefined threshold, a new road will be generated from the trajectories within that cluster. Note the generation of one new road triggers a new iteration. In a new iteration, unmatched trajectories are re-matched and re-clustered as some of them might be mapped to the newly added road.

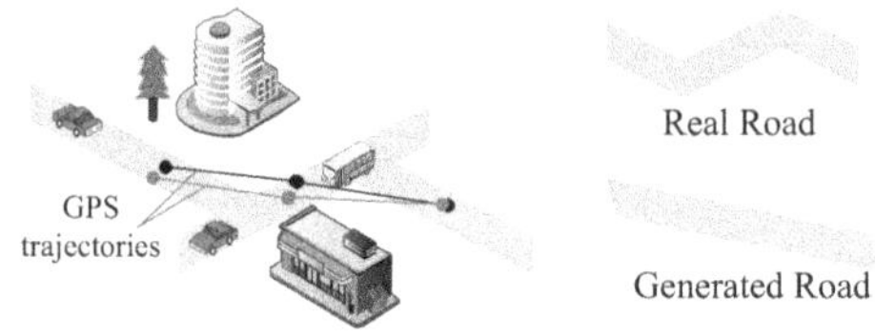

Figure 2: Incorrect road generation with low sampling rate trajectories

This algorithm performs well in high sampling rate data (e.g., 1 point per five seconds). However, in reality, sampling rate of most trajectory data is much lower. In many cases, the shape of a trajectory cannot capture the real moving path well and hence it may result in generating wrong roads. An example is plotted in Fig. 2 where two GPS trajectories are shown on a road network that is missing. Obviously, these two trajectories, together with other potential similar trajectories, lead to the generation of a new straight road that is wrong. In addition, we have to highlight that low sampling rate trajectories make clustering based on Hausdorff distance difficult, since it only considers the longest distance between two trajectories and might not be able to find some roads.

Map inference is a technology to generate the whole map automatically, which attracts wide attention both in industry and research. It mainly relies on satellite images and/or trajectory data. In other words, map inference has to employ image processing technology to generate map from images [11] and it has to use data mining technology to process the trajectory data [2, 3, 5, 9, 15]. For performance evaluation, it employs *recall* and *precision* as the metrics to quantify the effectiveness of a map inference algorithm [8, 20]. Recall refers to the ratio of the roads successfully generated by the algorithm to all the available roads in the map region; precision stands for the ratio of correctly generated roads to all roads generated by the algorithm. Map inference technology provides a solution to map updating problem by regenerating the whole map. As studied in [8], approach TC1 [9] performs the best among all the existing map inference approaches and it is selected as the representative map inference approach in our experimental study.

Map matching approach is used in our framework in the pre-processing step. Existing map matching technologies can be clustered into three groups, one based on the geometry of each road [14, 20], one based on the topology of the road network [12, 13], and the other based on probability [10, 16, 19, 21]. As the algorithm proposed in [19] has a good performance and is also adopted in the only existing map updating approach CrowdAtlas, we select it to perform map matching in GLUE.

3. GLUE

Without loss of generality, we assume a trajectory consists of a series of two-dimensional points (x_i, y_i) with corresponding time stamps t_i, denoted as $T = ((x_1, y_1, t_1), (x_2, y_2, t_2), \ldots, (x_n, y_n, t_n))$. A road network (digital map) is modelled as a directional graph $G(V, E)$ where V refers to the set of vertexes and E refers to the set of edges (i.e., roads). A road $r \in E$ has two endpoints represented as $r.s \rightarrow r.e$. In this paper, GLUE is based on an incomplete road network G'. It takes all the unmatched sparse-sampled GPS trajectories as input and tries to recover and then complement the missing road segments to G'. To be more specific, it consists of six steps, as shown in Fig. 3. In the following, we first present the main objective and detailed process of each step, and then propose analytical models to select proper values for key parameters used in GLUE.

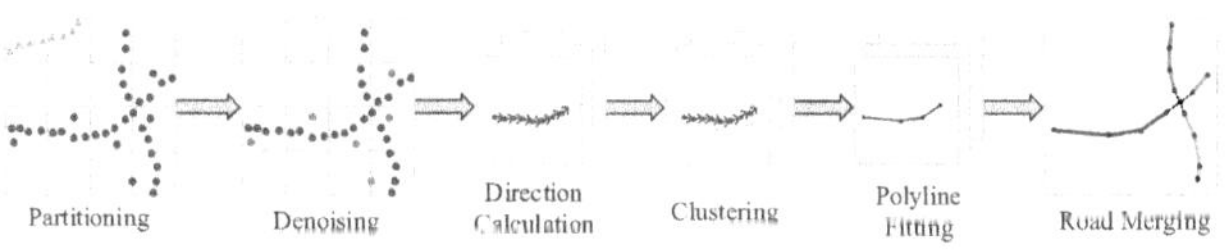

Figure 3: Flow of GLUE

3.1 Key steps of GLUE

Partitioning. The first step, partitioning, is a preprocessing step. We observe that GPS points far from each other in most cases belong to different roads. Potentially, we can separate and parallel the processing of multiple roads in order to improve the performance, and grid-based clustering offers a way to separate those far away points [17].

The main idea of grid clustering is to create a set of grid cells, to locate each GPS point to the corresponding grid cell, and then to merge adjacent grid cells together as well as to eliminate empty cells. The output of this step is a set of disjoint partitions, with each partition P_i formed by a set of connected non-empty grid cells. Due to space limitation, we use an example to illustrate the main idea. As depicted in Fig. 4, all the non-empty grid cells form two partitions, P_i on the left and P_j on the right.

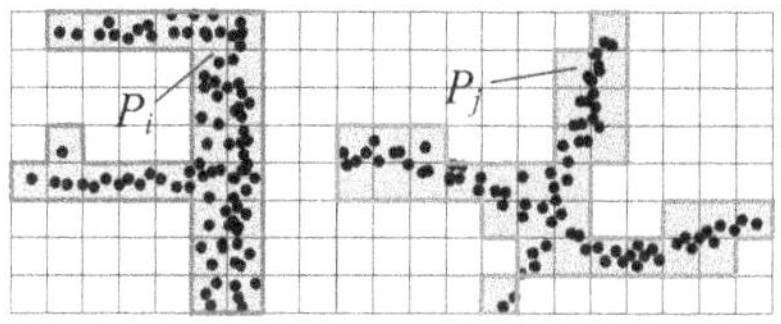

Figure 4: Example grids P_i and P_j formed by partitioning step

Denoising. The second step denoising is mainly to filter out points that do not contribute to the formation of any road, e.g., points reported by GPS errors. It is a common observation that GPS points with large GPS errors are very likely to be far away from other points. Thus we use a kNN-based approach to detect the noise. Specifically, we denote the distance between a point p to its kth nearest neighbor as $p.d_k$. The larger $p.d_k$ is, the more likely that p is a noise. In our work, we introduce a threshold γ and all the points p with $p.d_k > \gamma$ are filtered out. Note that given the GPS points located in grid cells, we can invoke a range query to find the number of GPS points located within the circle centered at p with γ as radius to decide whether $p.d_k > \gamma$. This approach looks simple but is not trivial in practice since γ should not be fixed and its setting has to consider density of GPS points. It is obvious that how to find a proper γ is critical. We develop a heuristic-based approach to automatically select proper γ values for regions with different GPS points distributions, as presented in Section 3.2.

Direction Calculation. After the denoising step, we have a set of partitions with each containing GPS points that can contribute to the formation of certain missing road segments. If we can cluster points that are on the same road together, we can adopt methods of fitting points to a polyline [7] to form a road segment. In this way, as long as there are abundant GPS points scattered on the road segment, the centerline of the road can be extracted which is relevant to the sampling rate.

In order to find points on the same road, we need information other than the position. One important information we want to consider is the heading direction of vehicles. Unfortunately, we cannot decide the heading direction of a vehicle based on the direction formed by the two consequent points with *low* sampling rate trajectory data as the example shown in Fig. 2.

Given a GPS point p, intuitively, the direction of p shall align nicely with the road segment. In other words, nearby GPS points that capture the trajectories passing by the same road segment shall have same or very close direction. Motivated by this observation, we count the number of GPS points that fall within different small rectangles formed by p along various directions. The one containing the maximum number of GPS points can help determine the direction of p, denoted as $p.\omega$. Note that a direction is a relative angle to the baseline (e.g. a horizontal line) and $p.\omega \in [0, \pi)$, formally defined in Definition 1. The intuition is that, given a fixed shaped rectangle formed by p, when the rectangle is located along the correct direction of p, it shall cover the maximum number of GPS points. We assume the average cost of range query is proportional to $r_l \times r_w$, i.e, the size of rectangle used in this step. We traverse angles in $[0, \pi)$ with a step of θ_{step} ($1/24\pi$ in our experiment). Thus, the computational cost of the direction calculation for each point is $O(r_w \cdot r_l \cdot \frac{\pi}{\theta_{step}})$. As both r_l and r_w have a direct impact on the determination of direction and the computational cost, they are not selected randomly. We have developed a scheme to select the optimal values of r_l and r_w, as to be presented in Section 3.2.

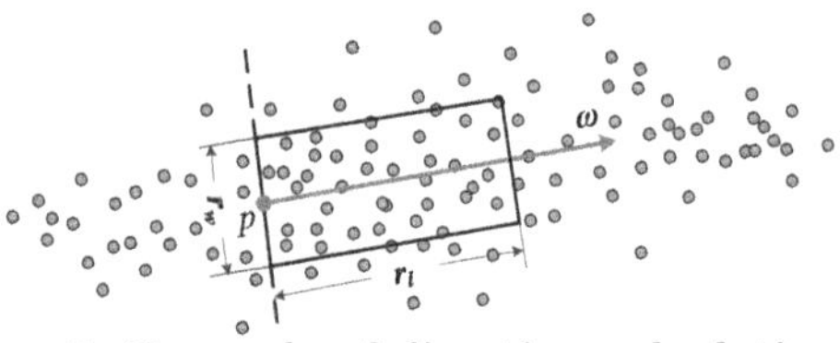

Figure 5: Example of direction calculation step

Definition 1. **Point Direction**: Given a point p, two parameters r_l and r_w and a direction ω, $count(p, \omega, r_l, r_w)$ is a function that counts the number of GPS points fallen within a $r_l \times r_w$ rectangle formed by p and ω, as illustrated in Fig. 5. *The direction of* p, denoted as $p.\omega$, is the direction ω such that $count(p, \omega, r_l, r_w)$ is maximized, i.e.,

$$p_0.\omega = \text{argmax}_{\omega \in [0,\pi)}(count(p, \omega, r_l, r_w))$$

Clustering. After calculating all points' directions, we cluster them and prepare for the polyline fitting step. The aim of this step is to group points on *the same road* together. A point p has three fields $(p.x, p.y, p.\omega)$, referring to spatial coordinates and direction. Traditional clustering methods, such as k-means, DBSCAN and SNN [6, 17], are not directly applicable in our case, for reasons including i) the shape of cluster is linear which makes k-means unworkable and ii) clusters are attached to each other which makes density-based clustering methods falsely cluster several clusters together. Instead, we propose a greedy based linkage clustering algorithm as a solution.

Our algorithm is based on an intuition that points on the same part of the road always have a relatively similar direction, and they are close to each other. In order to evaluate the proximity from a point p to a cluster that is represented by a set of points C, we use the distance from p to its nearest neighbor within C as the distance from p to C, as formally defined in Definition 2.

Algorithm 1 lists the pseudo code of our clustering algorithm. It takes the set of GPS points, and two thresholds th_{dis} and th_{dir} as inputs, and outputs a set of cluster C_i generated. It first randomly picks a point $p \in P$ that has not yet been clustered to form a new cluster C_i, and then inserts all the points $p' \in P$ with $d(p', C_i) \leq th_{dis}$ and $|p'.\omega - C_i.\omega| \leq th_{dir}$ into the newly formed cluster C_i. Note, we use the average direction of all the points currently clustered in cluster C_i as the direction of C_i, denoted as $C_i.\omega$. The above process repeats until all the points in P have been clustered. Note that clusters with very few points will be ignored in the following steps.

Fig. 6 depicts an example. Assume all the points shown in Fig. 6 form the input point set P, and we randomly pick a point to form a new cluster C_i, as shown in Fig. 6(a). Thereafter, we gradually add points to C_i, as shown in Fig. 6(b) and Fig. 6(c), until none of existing points can be added. Similarly, we form another cluster C_j for the rest of the points, as shown in Fig. 6(d).

Definition 2. **Distance to Cluster**: Given a point p and a cluster represented by a point set C, let $p' \in C$ be the point that is nearest to p in C, i.e., $\forall p'' \in C$, $d(p, p') \leq d(p, p'')$. *The distance from* p *to cluster* C, denoted as $d(p, C)$, is equivalent to $d(p, p')$, i.e., $d(p, C) = \min_{p' \in C} d(p, p')$, where $d(p_i, p_j)$ returns the Euclidean distance between p_i and p_j;

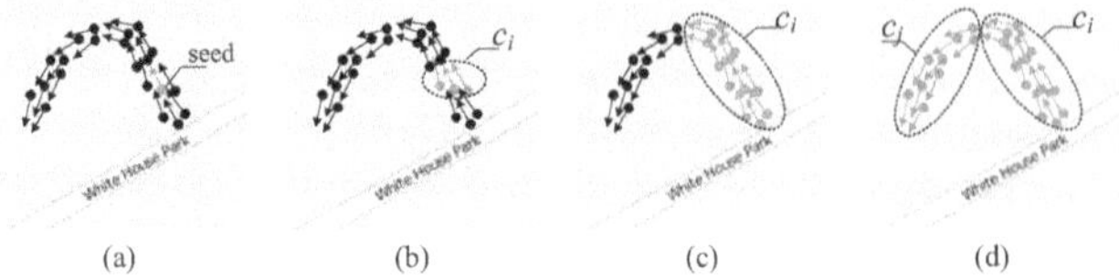

Figure 6: Example of clustering step

Algorithm 1 Clustering

Input: GPS points set P, thresholds th_{dis} and th_{dir}
Output: generated clusters
Procedure:

```
i = 0;
while P is not empty do
    randomly select a point p from P;
    new cluster C_i = {p}, i++;
    for each p' ∈ P accessed based on ascending order for their distance to p do
        if d(p', C_i) < th_dis && |p'.ω − C_i.ω| ≤ th_dir then
            C_i += {p'}, P −= {p'}
return C_is;
```

Polyline Fitting. After we cluster the points, we fit points within one cluster into a polyline $poly_i$ via algorithm proposed in [7] and then compute its direction, denoted as $poly_i.\omega$, following Definition 3. If $|poly_i.\omega - C_i.\omega| > th_{dir}$ and $|poly_i.\omega - C_i.\omega| < \pi - th_{dir}$, $poly_i$ will be ignored as C_i may not be a cluster on a missing road or $poly_i$ is wrongly generated. Due to space limitation, we skip the detail of this step.

Definition 3. **Polyline Direction**: A polyline $poly_i$ can be presented as a sequence of points $(p_1, p_2, ..., p_m)$. Its direction is defined as the length-weighted average of the segment direction, i.e., $poly_i.\omega = \frac{\sum_{i=2}^{m} d(p_{i-1}, p_i) \times \vec{v}_{p_{i-1}, p_i}.\omega}{\sum_{i=2}^{m} d(p_{i-1}, p_i)}$. $\vec{v}_{p_{i-1}, p_i}$ is the vector from p_{i-1} to p_i, and $\vec{v}_{p_{i-1}, p_i}.\omega$ is the direction of this vector.

Road Merging. After generating the polylines, we can attach the road segments to the map in this step, based on following three criteria as defined in Definition 4, 5, and 6. To be more specific, *trajectory-reachable* ensures the confidence provided by the trajectory data; *point-reachable* is weaker but more robust than trajectory-reachable criterion under the low-sampling condition, as it is very rare for low-sampling rate trajectories to have two adjacent points located on two adjacent roads. Note that there is no need to satisfy both trajectory-reachable and point-reachable criteria. The decision on which one should be adopted is based on the property of the data. Furthermore, the *reasonable* criterion prevents generating the redundant topological relationship of the roads. Although there are some parameters introduced in the criteria, setting these parameters is empirical, based on the property of the data. That is to say, the better the quality of data, the stricter the criteria. Besides, since the merging process does not affect the generation of the roads which is the main object of GLUE, we do not take these parameters into consideration.

The merging process is incremental. Everytime, we tend to select a generated road near to an intersection of G_c and attach it to G_c, after which G_c is updated. The process continues until all the roads are attached to G_c. We skip the determination of road direction as it is straightforward with the help of trajectory-reachable and our space is limited.

Definition 4. **Trajectory-Reachable**: Given two road segments r_1, r_2 and a trajectory set T, if there are η trajectories satisfying that each trajectory has two adjacent points p_{pre} and p_{succ} where $d(p_{pre}, r_1) < \varepsilon$ and $d(p_{succ}, r_2) < \varepsilon$, we call r_1 and r_2 are *trajectory-reachable*. $d(p, r)$ denotes the vertical distance from point p to road segment r.

Definition 5. **Point-Reachable**: Given two road segments r_1, r_2, and a trajectory points set P, we construct the graph as following. $\forall p_i, p_j \in P$, if $d(p_i, p_j) < \lambda$, p_i and p_j are connected via an edge. If $r_1.e$ and $r_2.s$ belong to the same connected component, r_1 and r_2 are *point-reachable*.

Definition 6. **Reasonable**: Given two road segments r_1, r_2, and a road network G_c, if $\frac{d_{G_c}(r_1.e, r_2.s)}{d(r_1.e, r_2.s)} > \zeta$, connecting r_1 to r_2 is *reasonable*, where $d_{G_c}(p_i, p_j)$ denotes the distance between vertexes p_i, p_j on the road network G_c. Note that $d_{G_c}(r_1.e, r_2.s) = \infty$ if r_1 and r_2 is unreachable on G_c.

3.2 Parameter Inference

Our GLUE framework relies on some parameters to process the GPS points. Because of space limitation, we in the following explain how to decide five most important parameters, including i) parameter γ used in our first filtering step; ii) parameters r_w and r_l used in direction calculation step; and iii) parameters th_{dis} and th_{dir} used in clustering step.

Selection of γ. In our filtering step, if the majority of the error points can be successfully filtered out, it can significantly improve the performance of following steps. How to determine the value of γ? In our work, we utilize a common property of all the correct GPS points to derive the value of γ. Given a road segment s, we represent it using a center line with width $2L_d$. Here, L_d denotes the average width of the roads (10.79m in our experiments). If $S(T)$ represents a set of trajectories T that can be successfully mapped to s, the vertical distance δ from a GPS point $p \in T$ to s follows the Gaussian distribution [4], i.e., $p(\delta) = e^{-\frac{(\delta-\mu)^2}{2\sigma^2}}/\sqrt{2\pi}\sigma$. Without loss of generality, we assume $\mu = 0$ and GPS points mapped to different road segments share a common σ value. Consequently, we can use all the GPS trajectories that are successfully mapped to existing road network (i.e., those trajectories not considered by our work) to derive σ value (e.g., 15.4307 in our experiments).

For better description, we define the coordinate axes as shown in Fig. 7. We denote $N(p, \varphi)$ as the number of GPS points that have their distances to a given point p bounded by φ, as shown in Eq. 1 .

$$N(p, \varphi) = \rho \iint_{(x-p.x)^2+(y-p.y)^2 \leq \varphi^2} p(x)dxdy \qquad (1)$$

$$\rho = \frac{N(s)}{\int_0^{L_s}\int_{-\infty}^{+\infty} p(x)dxdy} = \frac{N(s)}{L_s}$$

Note, ρ here is the density. As presented in denosing step, we re-express the denoising criteria in a perspective of k. Given γ fixed, all the GPS points p with $N(p, \gamma) < k$ shall be filtered as the distance to their k^{th} nearest neighbor $p.d^k$ is definitely larger than γ. Since noisy points are all far away from the centerline of the road, filtering the noise is equivalent to filtering out the points whose vertical distance to r is larger than δ_M, say $1.5L_d$ in our experiment. Note that Eq. 1 is monotonous with $d(p, s)$, i.e., $|p.x|$. Thus, we aim to find a proper γ to satisfy the critical stated, that is to say, $N(p, \gamma) = k$ where $d(p, s) = \delta_M$. By solving this function (using square to approximate the circle integral domain can achieve a simple analytic solution which can greatly save time for the solving process), we can get γ.

The only problem remained is how to get the density ρ. We notice that the distribution of points in different areas could be very different. Thus, ρ should be changed with the change of points' distribution rather than set to a fixed value. Consequently, we propose a way to estimate ρ of the region near p. With the help of grids generated in the first step, we first find all the non-empty grids g near p, e.g. less than 100m. The area covered by these girds are denoted as $area(g)$. We use $area(g)/2L_d$ (2 is for the sake of bi-direction roads) to approximate the length of road segments near p. Thereafter, the density ρ corresponding to the region near p can be approximated by $\frac{N(g)}{area(g)} \times 2L_d$, where $N(g)$ is the number of points in g.

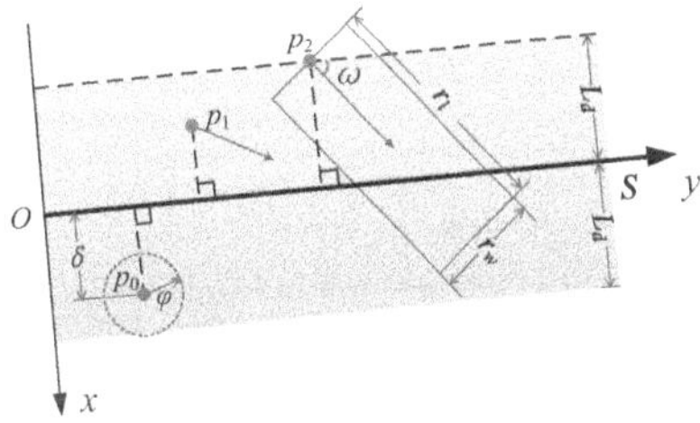

Figure 7: Example of a road segment model

Selection of r_w, r_l, th_{dis} and th_{dir}. Recall that our direction calculation of point p relies on two parameters r_w and r_l which are inputs for the function $count(p, \omega, r_w, r_l)$, and our clustering algorithm relies on two threshold th_{dis} and th_{dir}. We explain the settings of those four parameters together as their values are correlated. We need r_w and r_l to derive the direction of p, so that we can assign p to the cluster C it belongs to. In the clustering process, only a point p with $|p.\omega - C.\omega| \leq th_{dir}$ might be clustered into C. For simplicity, we use $C.\omega$ as the baseline of direction, i.e., $C.\omega = 0$, such that $p.\omega \leq th_{dir} \Leftrightarrow |p.\omega - C.\omega| \leq th_{dir}$.

Intuitively, the density of points close to s is higher than that of points far away from s. In other words, for a point p_b located on the boundary (p_2 in Fig. 7) of a road segment s (i.e., points that have the largest distance to s considered in our filtering step), $p_b.\omega$ is larger, compared with other points closer to s (p_1 in Fig. 7). Consequently, the setting of r_w and r_l is to serve the boundary points p_b to make sure $|p_b.\omega| \leq th_{dir}$. As the calculation of $p_b.\omega$ depends on function $count(p, \omega, r_w, r_l)$, we try to estimate $count(p_b, \omega, r_w, r_l)$ based on Eq. 2.

$$count(p, \omega, r_w, r_l) = \rho \iint_{rect(p,\omega,r_w,r_l)} p(x)dxdy \qquad (2)$$

Note, here ρ is the density, introduced when we explain how to determine the value of γ, and $p(x)$ is a Gaussian probability distribution function. The larger the $count(p_b, \omega, r_w, r_l)$ value, the smaller the direction. Therefore, we take the derivative with respect to ω and set it to zero to get $p_b.\omega$, i.e., $p_b.\omega = \omega_0$ where $\frac{\partial}{\partial\omega}count(p_b, \omega, r_w, r_l)\big|_{\omega=\omega_0} = 0$. In our experiments, we fix r_w to L_d to ensure most area of the rectangle can cover the points. Then, we plot $\frac{\partial}{\partial\omega}count(p_b, \omega, r_w, r_l)$ as a function of (ω, r_l). As marked contour shown in Fig. 8, there are a set of (ω, r_l) pairs where $\frac{\partial}{\partial\omega}count(p_b, \omega, r_l) = 0$, which infers that for a point p_b, the maximum direction of a boundary point is $\omega^{(i)}$ given $r_l^{(i)}$. Consequently, we rely on experimental results of our clustering algorithm to select a good threshold th_{dir} for the direction (e.g., 25° in our experiments) and this experiment will be conducted only once. All the (ω, r_l) pairs with $\omega < th_{dir}$ are feasible. Recall that the computational cost of direction calculation is proportional to r_l and this step is the most time-consuming part in GLUE, which means we prefer a smaller r_l. From Fig. 8, we can infer that when $\omega = 25°$, r_l achieves its minimum as highlighted in the figure. Last but not least, to ensure p_b can be added into the cluster, we set th_{dis} to L_d as well.

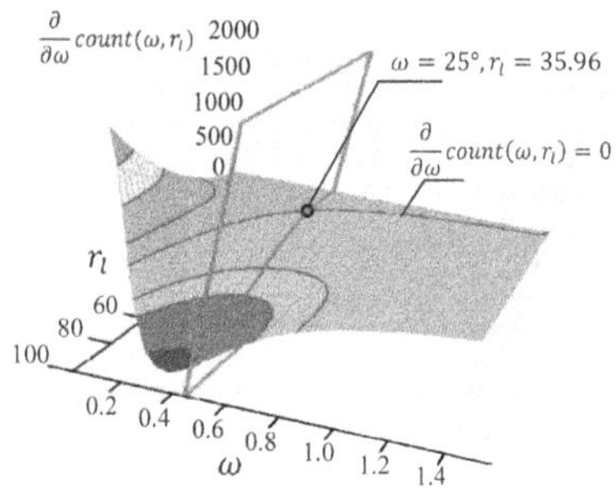

Figure 8: Visualization of $\frac{\partial}{\partial\omega}count(\omega, r_l)$

4. EXPERIMENT

In this section, we first introduce a robust quantitative evaluation method for map updating approaches since the existing work relies on manual approaches to evaluating the generated roads [18]. Thereafter, we study the impact of different parameters on the performance of GLUE and then compare our approach with other state-of-the-art approaches based on newly developed evaluation approach. Finally, we demonstrate how GLUE can update the roads in real applications.

4.1 Quantitative Evaluation Method

As mentioned before, existing work relies mainly on manual efforts to evaluate the quality of generated road segments. Although it is easy to implement, it has lots of limitations, e.g., the lack of scalability and the relatively high error rate of manual evaluation. Consequently, we want to propose a method of evaluating map updating algorithm quantitatively. In order to achieve this objective, we need a method to judge whether a road is correctly generated or not which requires a ground-truth map. In an ideal case, a ground-truth map is a map that contains all the roads in the real world, which might not be available in many cases. In the following, we explain how to construct a ground-truth map based on existing map.

First, we match all the trajectory data to a given map using map matching algorithm proposed in [19]. A map with relatively good quality (e.g., covering many parts of the road network) is highly recommended as it serves as our ground-truth map. For all the trajectories that cannot be matched to the given map, they are excluded from our evaluation in this step. The reason is that some of them are sampled from the real missing roads that are not present in the ground-truth map and the roads generated from those data will be reported as false. In other words, we exclude those trajectories that cannot be matched to the original map because we do not have the ground-truth to verify whether the roads generated from those trajectories are correct. Thereafter, we randomly delete some road segments from the ground-truth map, and try to recover those removed road segments using our approach.

Definition 7. **Correctly Recovered Segment**: Given a segment s_m which is part of a missing road (e.g., s_1 and s_3 in Fig. 9), let road r_g (e.g., *Generated road* in Fig. 9) be the one that is nearest to s_m, among all the generated roads. We then project both endpoints of s_m to r_g and get the projected segment s_g (e.g., s_2 and s_4 in Fig. 9). If both of the projection distance do not exceed a distance threshold δ_0, and the angle between $\vec{s_m}$ and $\vec{s_g}$ is less than an angle threshold α_0, we consider the missing segment s_m is *correctly recovered*. In our experiment, we set δ as the average width of all roads in map (i.e., 10 m) and α_0 as the angle threshold used in our clustering step (25°).

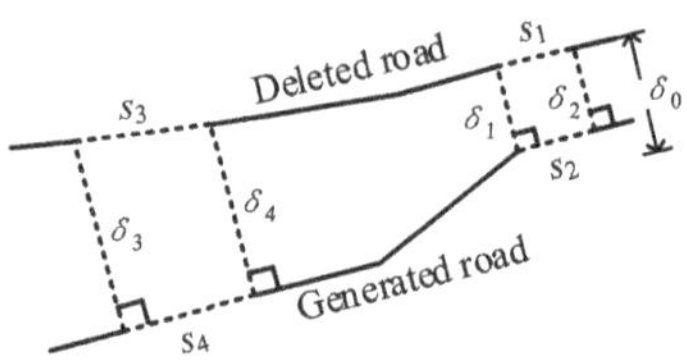

Figure 9: Example of a correctly recovered segment

We partition the removed road into small segments with equal length (20m in our experiments). We then introduce the concept of *correctly recovered segment*, formally presented in Definition 7. For example in Fig. 9, s_1 is correctly recovered and s_3 is not since δ_3 and δ_4 exceed the threshold δ_0. All correctly generated segments are collected and we rely on *the total length* of correctly generated segments to evaluate the performance of different map-updating algorithms via *recall* and *precision*, as defined in Eq. 3 and Eq. 4 respectively. Here, recall rate measures how complete the updated map is and the precision rate indicates how accurately the algorithm generates roads. R_m refers to the set of missing roads that we purposely delete from our ground-truth map and R_g is the set of generated roads. $I[condition]$ is an indicator function which returns 1 if the *condition* is true and 0 otherwise. We use r to indicate a road and s refers to a segment of a road, and the function $len(r)$ is to return the length of r.

$$recall = \frac{\sum_{r_m \in R_m} \sum_{s \in r_m} I[s\ is\ correctly\ recovered] \cdot len(s)}{\sum_{r_m \in R_m} len(r_m)} \quad (3)$$

$$precision = \frac{\sum_{r_m \in R_m} \sum_{s \in r_m} I[s\ is\ correctly\ recovered] \cdot len(s)}{\sum_{r_g \in R_g} len(r_g)} \quad (4)$$

In addition to the recall and precision, we also introduce the metric of *F-score*. It tries to integrate both recall and precision, as defined in Eq. 5.

$$F\_score = \frac{2 \times precision \times recall}{precision + recall} \quad (5)$$

In our study, we download the Singapore map from OpenStreetMap[2] and choose three representative regions. Regions with low trajectory density are ignored as we prefer high trajectory density. Each of the selected regions covers roughly 20% of Singapore. We delete randomly road segments from the map, in total 106.33 km. Fig. 10 shows a small region of our experiment as an example. Roads within the circles (i.e., those in red) are the ones randomly deleted. The experiments are based on real trajectory data from one of the largest taxi companies in Singapore. Each taxi has GPS installed, and it reports its location regularly. In our studies, we use the trajectories reported from 1 January 2011 to 15 January 2011, in total 225,000 trajectories generated by about 15,000 taxis and the average sampling rate is about 30s. Please refer to [1] for a detailed description of the dataset.

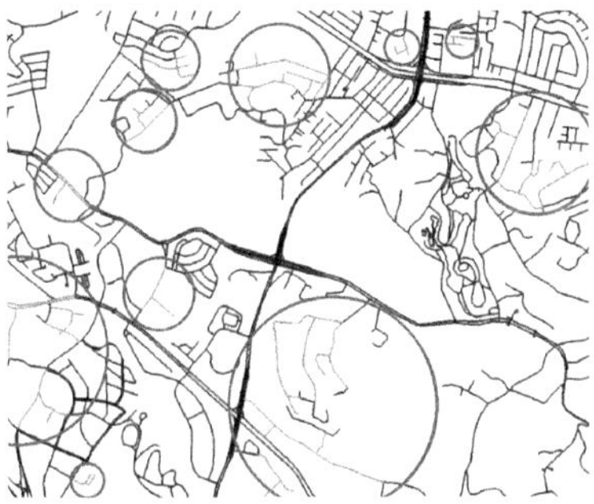

Figure 10: A sample region with deleted roads

4.2 Parameter Experiments

Table 1 lists the most important parameters introduced in GLUE. We have explained how to decide the values of γ, r_w, r_l, th_{dis} and th_{dir}. Here, we conduct experiments to study the impacts of different parameters on GLUE and to demonstrate the effectiveness of our parameter inference approach.

Table 1: Parameters introduced in GLUE

Notation	Description
γ	denoise threshold
r_w	width of the rectangle
r_l	height of the rectangle
th_{dis}	distance threshold in clustering step
th_{dir}	angle threshold in clustering step

Parameter γ. First, we perform the denoising step in a region with different point densities to demonstrate the effectiveness of our heuristic-based auto-tuning method. Fig. 11 visualizes the result of the denoising process under different γ. Fig. 11(a) plots all the points in the area. When γ is set to a small value, GLUE performs well around the high density areas, as shown in Fig. 11(d). However, points on the low density areas are filtered out. On the other hand, when γ is set to a big value, the denoising process is not so strict that the non-noise points on the low density areas are preserved but noises in the high density areas are hardly filtered out, as shown in Fig. 11(c). Result of our auto parameter tuning approach is shown in Fig. 11(b). As observed, it works very well in both dense areas and sparse

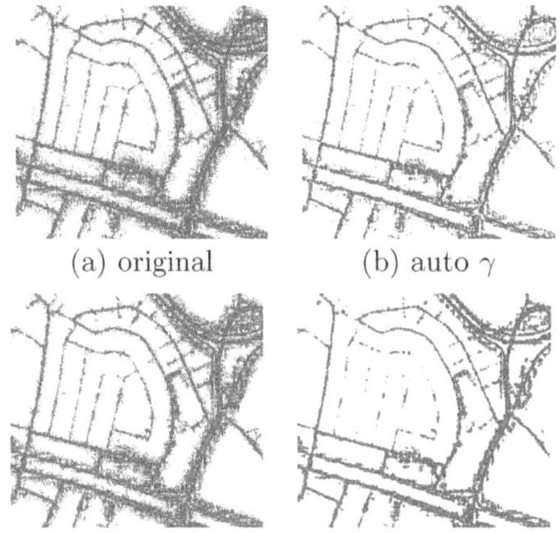

(a) original (b) auto γ

(c) large γ (d) small γ

Figure 11: Performance of denoising process

areas since it can automatically adjust γ by estimating the density.

Parameter $r_w$and r_l. Next, we conduct the experiments to study the impacts of parameters r_w and r_l. As discussed in Section 3.2, we set r_w to 10m and then see how r_l effects the performance of GLUE, with the efficiency in terms of time taken and accuracy of GLUE shown in Fig. 12. As r_l increases its value, the cost of direction calculation increases accordingly although the performance (i.e., recall, precision, and F-score) also improves. When r_l exceeds 30m, the performance has an obvious enhancement. This is in accordance with our conclusion in Section 3.2, i.e., when r_l exceeds 35.96m, the difference between the direction of the points located on the edge of the road ($p_b.\omega$) and the direction of the cluster ($C.\omega$) will not be larger than th_{dir}, which means all the points on the road will be clustered in the same cluster. A larger r_l triggers a scanning of more points which directly increases the computation cost and this step is the most time-consuming step as shown in Fig. 12(a), and hence in practice r_l should be as small as possible. This experiments also demonstrate the effectiveness of our analytic method of calculating the minimum of r_l.

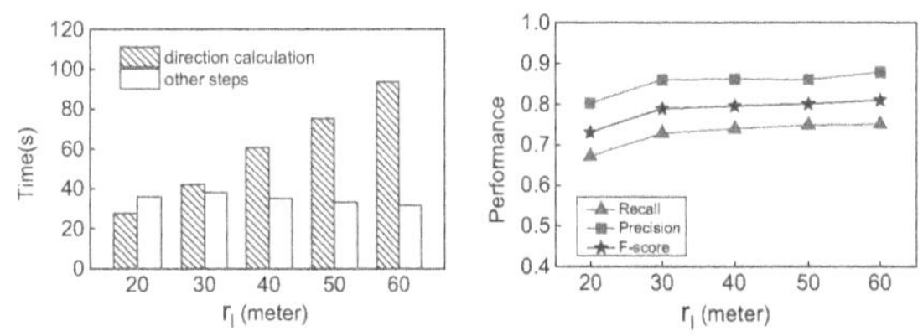

(a) time cost (b) GLUE performance

Figure 12: Performance vs. r_l

Parameter th_{dir}. We next conduct the experiment to study the impact of direction threshold th_{dir} introduced in the clustering step. Fig. 13(a) shows the result. When th_{dir} increases, it is easier for a cluster to retrieve the points near it. Thus, by absorbing those points which have different directions, many wrong clusters might be formed. Recall that when we fit a polyline for a cluster, we also check the average direction of the points within the cluster and the direction of the polyline to eliminate those wrongly generated clusters. As a result, with the increase of th_{dir}, more wrongly generated clusters are eliminated which explains the high precision value (85%+) but dropped recall value. Note that

[2]http://www.openstreetmap.org/

when th_{dir} is too small (e.g., $5°$), clustering becomes harder which directly affects the recall. Based on F-score, we conclude that the ideal value of th_{dir} is between $10°$ and $40°$, which explains why we set th_{dir} to $25°$ ($(10° + 40°)/2$) in Section 3.2.

Parameter th_{dis}. Finally, we investigate the impact of th_{dis}. According to Fig. 13(b), the performance of GLUE drops when th_{dis} exceeds 20m. This is because points on the different road may be clustered together, similar as the reason we list above for th_{dir}. Note that the precision reduces, which is different from the results on th_{dir}. The reason is that varying th_{dis} will not trigger the elimination of those clusters with wrong directions thus the precision drops. In addition, the smaller number of eliminated roads explains why the recall in th_{dis} declines in a slower pace than that in th_{dir}. On the other hand, when th_{dis} is smaller than 10m, the performance also drops. It is resulted by the failure of clustering, which means points on one road may be clustered into several tiny parts and some of them may be eliminated. According to F-score, th_{dir} should be set between 10m and 20m (i.e., the average width of the roads), which justifies our selection of th_{dir} to be the average width of the roads is reasonable.

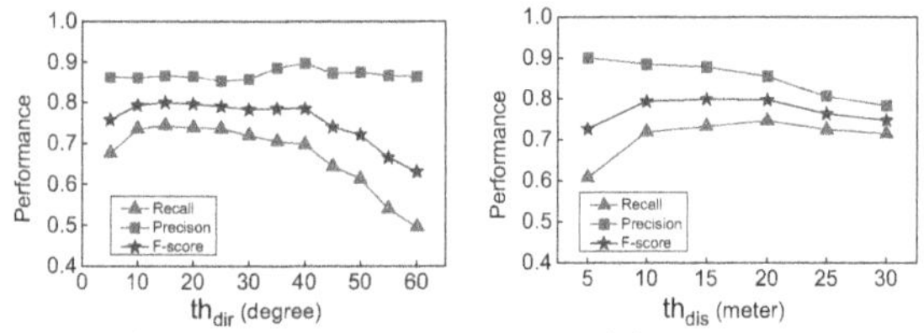

(a) vs. th_{dir} (b) vs. th_{dis}

Figure 13: Performance vs. thresholds

4.3 Comparison Experiments

In this section, we compare the performance of GLUE with two competitors, including a map updating algorithm CrowdAtlas [18] and a map inference algorithm TC1 [9]. As presented in Section 2, CrowdAtlas and TC1 represent the state-of-the-art techniques to the best of our knowledge. They are the latest proposed methods in map updating and map inference problems and have best performances.

First, we report the recall rate of three algorithms under different sampling rate trajectory data in Fig. 14(a). It is observed that the recall rate of all algorithms drops as the sampling interval increases, and our algorithm GLUE performs consistently much better than the other two. Algorithm GLUE is able to achieve a much higher recall rate, and it is also much more resilient to the sampling rate. On average, GLUE can achieve a recall rate that is about 1.7 times and 6 times better than that of CrowdAtlas and TC1, respectively.

Second, we investigate the precision of different algorithms, with the results again under different sampling rates plotted in Fig. 14(c). All methods have relatively high precision (e.g., 85%), when the sampling rate is at 30 seconds per point. With the increases of sampling intervals, precision of both TC1 and GLUE increases a little bit but that of CrowdAtlas drops. CrowdAtlas and TC1 actually share very similar ideas on clustering trajectories and generating roads, but TC1 has a much higher precision than CrowdAtlas. The reason is that TC1 implements a pruning step. In the pruning step, trajectories are divided into small segments and those in turning corners are pruned away. With the

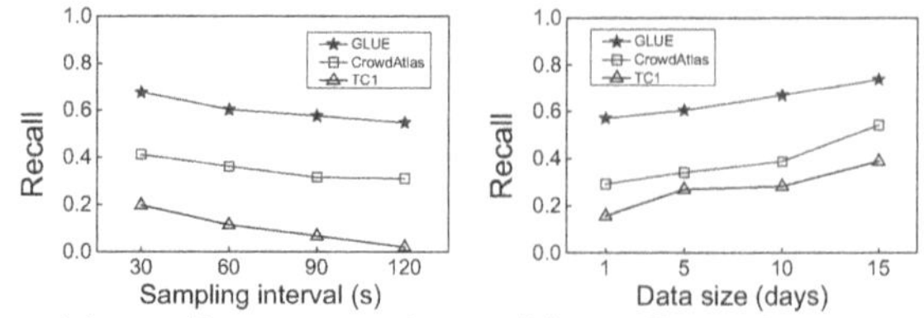

(a) recall vs. interval (b) recall vs. data size

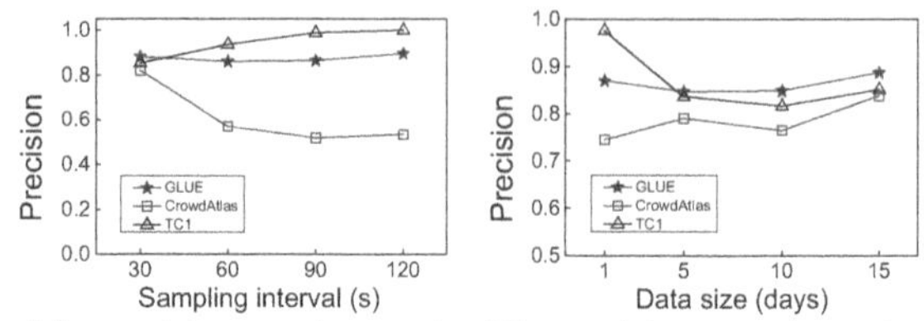

(c) precision vs. interval (d) precision vs. data size

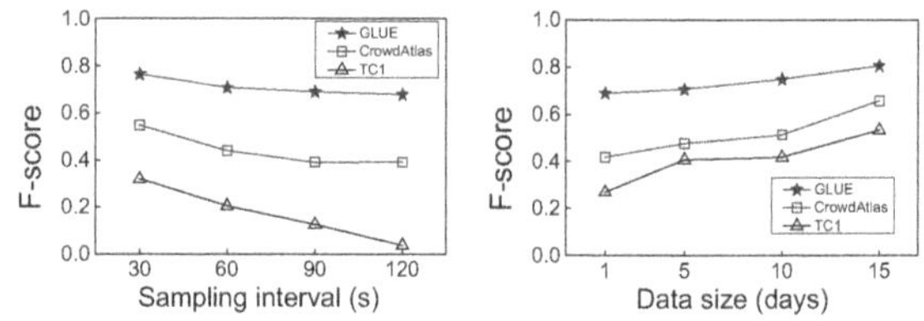

(e) F-score vs. interval (f) F-score vs. data size

Figure 14: The results of comparison experiments

increases of sampling intervals, more segments are pruned away and only those on straight roads remain, which improves the accuracy of clustering step. However, because of the same reason, TC1 has a very low recall rate as this pruning step brushes off too many trajectories and it only can generate long straight roads. On the other hand, CrowdAtlas utilizes all the trajectories as input and clusters them to generate roads. Without implementing any filtering step to filter out error GPS points, CrowdAtlas always generates many roads with many of them not correct. This explains why CrowdAtlas has a high recall rate but a low precision.

Third, we examine the F-score of all three algorithms, with their performance under different sampling intervals shown in Fig. 14(e). Recall that F-score is synthesised by recall and precision using Eq. 5. We observe that as the sampling interval increases, less GPS points are available for road generation and F-score of all three algorithms drops. We also want to highlight that GLUE performs significantly better than the other two in all cases. To be more specific, GLUE achieves a F-score that is about 1.6 times higher than that of CrowdAtlas and 4 times higher than that of TC1 in average.

Last but not least, we also report the average performance of three approaches in Fig. 14(b), 14(d) and 14(f), by using the GPS data collected in different durations ranging from 1 day to 15 days. It is observed that the recall rate of all the algorithms increases as the duration extends. GLUE has the highest recall rate consistently, almost 1.5 times better than that of CrowdAtlas and 2 times better than that of TC1. As for precision, all three algorithms have high precision although GLUE in most cases performs the best. We also notice that TC1 has the highest precision when we consider only one-day's data. As explained before, TC1 prunes away lots of GPS points and it only generates long and straight road segment. This explains why it has a very high precision but a low recall rate.

4.4 Confidence Test

In map updating, we need to decide whether we should accept all the roads generated by GLUE. Here, we propose a function to evaluate the confidence of a generated road. Intuitively, a longer road which has more existing trajectories located on it tends to have a higher chance to be real. Thus, we take the length l and the density ρ into consideration. ρ is the density of the GPS points introduced in Section 3.2. Moreover, a road with a smoother shape should have a higher confidence than a tortuous road. Thus, we also take the angle in the shape of the road into account. Besides, under the observation that the distribution of the points located on a correctly generated road should follow Gaussian, we consider bias of the distribution as well. Accordingly, the confidence evaluation function for a generated road $\hat{r}$ is defined below.

$$C(\hat{r}) = \frac{\mathcal{N}\left(\bar{\delta}\,|0,\sigma^2\right)}{\mathcal{N}\left(0\,|0,\sigma^2\right)} L\left(\rho\,|k_1,\rho_0\right) L\left(l\,|k_2,l_0\right) \prod_{\theta} L\left(\theta\,\middle|k_3,\frac{\pi}{2}\right)$$

The first factor $\mathcal{N}\left(\bar{\delta}\,|0,\sigma^2\right)/\mathcal{N}\left(0\,|0,\sigma^2\right)$ evaluates the distribution of the points, where $\bar{\delta}$ is the average distance from points near $\hat{r}$ to $\hat{r}$ and $\mathcal{N}\left(0\,|0,\sigma^2\right)$ is a normalization coefficient. Before we introduce the next tree factors, we first introduce the logistic function $L(\cdot)$. A logistic function is commonly used as a threshold function with smoothing:

$$L(x\,|k,x_0) = (1 + e^{(-k(x-x_0))})^{-1},$$

where k and x_0 are the parameters controlling L. In detail, k controls the steepness of the curve and x_0 is the x-value of the midpoint of the curve which also can be regarded as the threshold. Once x is larger than x_0, $L(x)$ will become much closer to 1 and when x is smaller than x_0, $L(x)$ will suddenly drop down to 0. Fig. 15(a) shows how k and x_0 effect the shape of L. The second and the third factors evaluate the density and length of $\hat{r}$ correspondingly. ρ_0 and l_0 are the threshold set by the user according to different situations. The last factor $\prod_\theta L\left(\theta\,|k_3,\frac{\pi}{2}\right)$ evaluates the shape of the generated road. θ iterates the angles formed by adjacent segments in a polyline ($\hat{r}$). A road with some acute angles will be penalized through the logistic function with threshold setting to $\pi/2$. Note that k_1, k_2, k_3, ρ_0 and l_0 are set by user according to different needs. A higher k will exert a severer penalization to those roads failing to meet the threshold, which enlarges the importance of the corresponding feature. In our experiment, we set $k_1 = 2, k_2 = 0.02, k_3 = 6, \rho_0 = 1$ and $l_0 = 100$ under the 15 days' dataset.

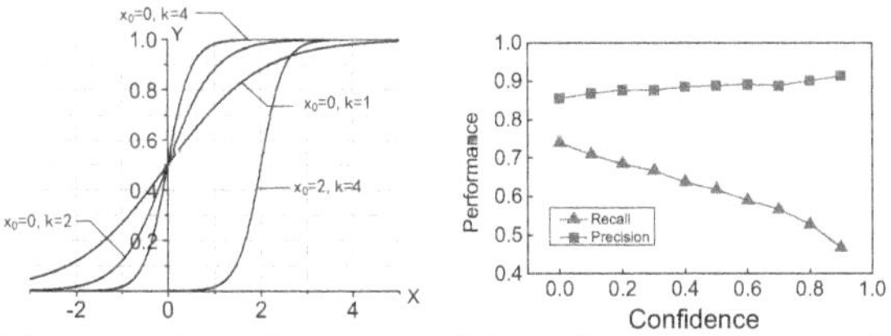

(a) example of logistic function (b) performance vs. confidence

Figure 15: Example and result for confidence test

Fig. 15(b) shows the performance using different confidence thresholds th_c to reject some generated roads. Note, when threshold set to 0, all roads will be accepted. With the increase of th_c, the precision increases and the recall drops, which is consistent with our expectation. As more roads are filtered by th_c, recall drops. On the other hand, roads with low precision are eliminated. Consequently, wrong generated roads are rejected and precision arises. We can conclude that roads with confidence over 0.8 can achieve over 90% precision; from the fact that recall drops from 0.73 to 0.52, we can infer that most roads generated by GLUE have a relatively high confidence. Note that th_c could be tuned based on how important the precision is, as compared with the recall.

4.5 Real Cases

The experiments conducted above are all based on the randomly deleted roads. Here, we focus on finding out the missing roads in a real application. Fig. 16(a) visualizes the generated roads on top of the satellite map downloaded from OpenStreetMap (OSM)in 2012, based on the Singapore Taxi trajectories collected in 2011. Points in the same color belong to the same cluster except that those in gray are the noise detected by our denosing algorithm. This further shows the ability of our denoising algorithm to handle points with different density automatically. Our approach successfully generates almost all the missing roads which existed in 2011 and correctly recovers the topological relations of the roads. Fig. 16(c) and Fig. 16(e) show the map of the same region downloaded from OpenStreetMap and Google Map recently. We can see although some roads existed 4 years ago (i.e., those inside the marked rectangles), they have not yet been updated as they are still missing in maps.

Fig. 16(b) shows the generated road from the trajectories collected by the Geolife project. Detail of this dataset can be found in [22]. We endeavor to repeat all the quantitative experiments presented above using this dataset but unfortunately it is very hard, mainly because the volume of this dataset is very small (1/250 of Singapore's dataset, per unit area) and it only covers a very small portion of Beijing's road network. As a result, we can hardly find enough points located on most randomly deleted roads to support the updating. Therefore, we only conduct one experiment to generate missing roads. The dataset is generated in 2009 but we do not have 2009 Beijing map. Hence, we plot our results on top of the map downloaded from OpenStreetMap in 2014, as shown in Fig. 16(b). Again, we compare our results with the maps available online. Consistent with observations made based on Singapore taxi datasets, we notice some of the roads in Beijing successfully generated by GLUE still do not exist in maps available in OpenStreetMap and Google Map today, shown in Fig. 16(d) and 16(f) respectively. Roads in red in Fig. 16(b) are the roads with low confidence, showing that our confidence evaluation method is able to eliminate some wrong roads. Even though the data quality is quite low, GLUE can still detect the roads correctly. This area shows some small roads in a hospital with roads in this estate having not been updated, which means the map updating approach is necessary.

5. CONCLUSION AND FUTURE WORK

In this paper, we investigate the problem of map updating using low sampling rate trajectory data. The main challenges of map updating include low sampling rates and lots of noises.

We propose an effective approach to address all the challenges by direction clustering and de-nosing. In order to

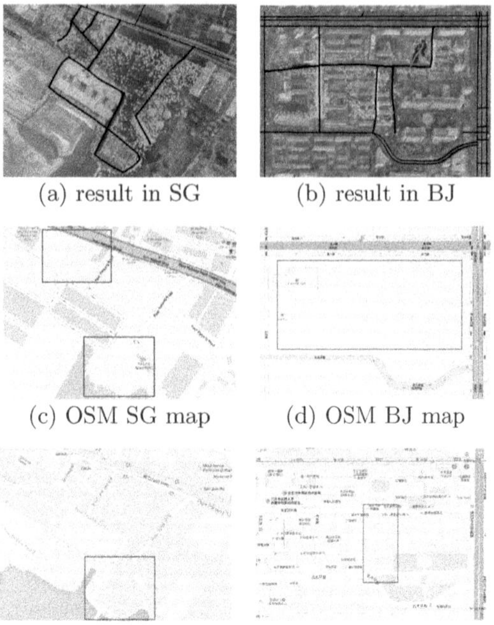

(a) result in SG (b) result in BJ

(c) OSM SG map (d) OSM BJ map

(e) Google SG map (f) Google BJ map

Figure 16: Results of updating the roads of two regions in real cases

evaluate the performance of a map updating approach, we also design a robust quantitative evaluation method and compare our approach with another two state-of-the-art methods using the newly proposed evaluation method. With roughly 15-days' real GPS trajectories from around 15,000 taxis in Singapore, the evaluation result demonstrates that our approach significantly outperforms the existing ones. Besides, we also conduct experiments to demonstrate GLUE does not require manual efforts to decide the values of key parameters. The property of parameter-tuning-free is very desirable in many applications.

In this paper, we only focus on the real roads that are missing in the current map. However, we also observe that some roads in map are actually unavailable in reality, e.g., some closed road segments. In the near future, we plan to find those unavailable roads based on GPS trajectory data. Our ultimate goal is to develop an on-line map updating system that can automatically recover all the missing roads and meanwhile remove all the outdated road segments using low sampled GPS trajectories.

6. ACKNOWLEDGMENTS

This research is supported in part by National Natural Science Foundation of China (NSFC) under grant 61073001, Shanghai Natural Science Foundation under grant 14ZR1403100, and Shanghai Science and Technology Development Funds under grant 13dz2260200 and grant 13511504300. Zheng Baihua was funded through a research grant (14-C220-SMU-001) from MOEŠs AcRF Tier 1 funding support through SMU.

7. REFERENCES

[1] R. K. Balan, K. X. Nguyen, and L. Jiang. Real-time trip information service for a large taxi fleet. In *MobiSys'11*, pages 99–112, 2011.

[2] L. Cao and J. Krumm. From gps traces to a routable road map. In *GIS'09*, pages 3–12, 2009.

[3] J. Davics, A. R. Beresford, and A. Hopper. Scalable, distributed, real-time map generation. *Pervasive Computing*, 5(4):47–54, 2006.

[4] F. V. Diggelen. System design & test-gnss accuracy-lies, damn lies, and statistics. *GPS World*, 18(1):26–33, 2007.

[5] S. Edelkamp and S. Schrödl. Route planning and map inference with global positioning traces. In *Computer Science in Perspective*, pages 128–151. 2003.

[6] J. Han and M. Kamber. *Data mining: concepts and techniques*. 2001.

[7] B. Kégl, A. Krzyzak, T. Linder, and K. Zeger. Learning and design of principal curves. *TPAMI*, 22(3):281–297, 2000.

[8] X. Liu, J. Biagioni, J. Eriksson, Y. Wang, G. Forman, and Y. Zhu. Mining large-scale, sparse gps traces for map inference: comparison of approaches. In *KDD'12*, pages 669–677, 2012.

[9] X. Liu, Y. Zhu, Y. Wang, G. Forman, L. M. Ni, Y. Fang, and M. Li. Road recognition using coarse-grained vehicular traces. *HP Labs2012*, 2012.

[10] Y. Lou, C. Zhang, Y. Zheng, X. Xie, W. Wang, and Y. Huang. Map-matching for low-sampling-rate gps trajectories. In *GIS'09*, pages 352–361, 2009.

[11] M. Mokhtarzade and M. Zoej. Road detection from high-resolution satellite images using artificial neural networks. *JAG*, 9(1):32–40, 2007.

[12] P. Newson and J. Krumm. Hidden markov map matching through noise and sparseness. In *GIS'09*, pages 336–343, 2009.

[13] W. Y. Ochieng, M. Quddus, and R. B. Noland. Map-matching in complex urban road networks. *Revista Brasileira de Cartografia*, 2(55), 2009.

[14] B. P. Phuyal. Method and use of aggregated dead reckoning sensor and gps data for map matching. In *GNSS'01*, pages 430–437, 2001.

[15] S. Schroedl, K. Wagstaff, S. Rogers, P. Langley, and C. Wilson. Mining gps traces for map refinement. *DMKD*, 9(1):59–87, 2004.

[16] R. Song, W. Lu, W. Sun, Y. Huang, and C. Chen. Quick map matching using multi-core cpus. In *GIS'12*, pages 605–608, 2012.

[17] P.-N. Tan, M. Steinbach, V. Kumar, et al. *Introduction to data mining*, volume 1. 2006.

[18] Y. Wang, X. Liu, H. Wei, G. Forman, C. Chen, and Y. Zhu. Crowdatlas: Self-updating maps for cloud and personal use. In *Mobisys'13*, pages 27–40, 2013.

[19] H. Wei, Y. Wang, G. Forman, Y. Zhu, and H. Guan. Fast viterbi map matching with tunable weight functions. In *GIS'12*, pages 613–616, 2012.

[20] C. E. White, D. Bernstein, and A. L. Kornhauser. Some map matching algorithms for personal navigation assistants. *Transportation Research Part C: Emerging Technologies*, 8(1):91–108, 2000.

[21] J. Yuan, Y. Zheng, C. Zhang, X. Xie, and G.-Z. Sun. An interactive-voting based map matching algorithm. In *MDM'10*, pages 43–52, 2010.

[22] Y. Zheng, Q. Li, Y. Chen, X. Xie, and W. Ma. Understanding mobility based on GPS data. In *UbiComp'08*, pages 312–321, 2008.

A Cost-based Method for Location-Aware Publish/Subscribe Services

Minghe Yu Guoliang Li Jianhua Feng
Department of Computer Science and Technology, Tsinghua University, Beijing 100084, China.
yumh12@mails.tsinghua.edu.cn, liguoliang@tsinghua.edu.cn, fengjh@tsinghua.edu.cn

ABSTRACT

Location-based services have attracted significant attentions from both industry and academia, thanks to modern smartphones and mobile Internet. To provide users with gratifications, location-aware publish/subscribe has been recently proposed, which delivers spatio-textual messages of publishers to subscribers whose registered spatio-textual subscriptions are relevant to the messages. Since there could be large numbers of subscriptions, it is necessary to devise an efficient location-aware publish/subscribe system to enable instant message filtering. To this end, in this paper we propose two novel indexing structures, MBRTrie and PT-Quadtree. Using the indexes, we devise two filtering algorithms to support fast message filtering. We analyze the complexities of the two filtering algorithms and develop a cost-based model to judiciously select the best filtering algorithm for different scenarios. The experimental results show that our method achieves high performance and significantly outperforms the baseline approaches.

1. INTRODUCTION

Location-based services (LBS) such as Foursquare[1] and Yelp[2] have been extensively deployed in many systems and widely accepted by the Internet users. LBS includes two important models: user-initiated model and server-initiated model. The former, aka location-aware keyword search, returns the relevant answers for each user-initiated spatio-textual query (which includes the query location and query keywords) [7, 5]. For example, considering a user who wants to find a hotel nearby, she issues a spatio-textual query with her current location and keywords "`hotel two-beds room`" to an LBS system, which returns relevant answers by considering the spatial proximity and textual relevancy. The latter, aka location-aware publish/subscribe, delivers the spatio-textual messages of publishers to relevant subscribers.

In this paper, we focus on location-aware publish/subscribe. The subscribers register spatio-textual subscriptions. When a publisher posts a spatio-textual message, the system instantly delivers the message to the subscribers whose registered subscriptions are relevant to the message. To evaluate the relevancy between spatio-textual messages and subscriptions, we need to combine spatial proximity and textual relevancy (see Section 2 for more details).

There are many real-world applications that require the location-aware publish/subscribe services. For example, consider a Groupon system. The subscribers (e.g., Groupon customers) register their spatio-textual subscriptions (e.g., "`The Avengers`" at `Melbourne University`) to the system. For each message posted by the publisher (e.g., a Groupon message about movie "`The Avengers: Age of Ultron`", at Melbourne Downtown), the system delivers the message to relevant subscribers. Location-aware publish/subscribe has many other real applications, e.g., location-aware news delivery, location-aware advertisements, and location-aware market analysis [14, 3].

A publish/subscribe system requires to support large numbers of subscriptions and a big challenge is to enable instant message filtering [14, 3, 24]. Although Li et al. [14] proposes an R^t-tree based method, which adds some selected tokens from spatio-textual subscriptions into R-tree nodes and uses the R^t-tree to filter messages, it cannot meet the high-performance requirement, because it has low pruning power on the textual part, especially for upper-level R^t-tree nodes that contain too many selected tokens.

To address this challenge, we propose two novel spatio-textual index structures, MBRTrie and PT-Quadtree. MBRTrie constructs a trie structure based on the textual description and integrates spatial information into trie nodes while PT-Quadtree utilizes a quadtree to index spatial information and adds the textual descriptions into the quadtree nodes. Using the indexes, we devise two efficient filtering algorithms. MBRTrie and PT-Quadtree have their own superiorities: MBRTrie is efficient for the messages with a small number of tokens while PT-Quadtree is efficient for messages with small spatial regions. To achieve high performance for various settings, we analyze the complexities of the two algorithms and develop a cost-based model to judiciously select the best filtering algorithm for various scenarios.

To summarize, we make the following contributions.

(1) We propose two spatio-textual index structures, MBRTrie and PT-Quadtree. Based on the two index structures, we propose two efficient filtering algorithm.

(2) We analyze the complexities of the two filtering algo-

[1]http://foursquare.com
[2]http://www.yelp.com/

Permission to make digital or hard copies of all or part of this work for personal or classroom use is granted without fee provided that copies are not made or distributed for profit or commercial advantage and that copies bear this notice and the full citation on the first page. Copyrights for components of this work owned by others than ACM must be honored. Abstracting with credit is permitted. To copy otherwise, or republish, to post on servers or to redistribute to lists, requires prior specific permission and/or a fee. Request permissions from Permissions@acm.org.
CIKM'15, October 19–23, 2015, Melbourne, Australia.
© 2015 ACM. ISBN 978-1-4503-3794-6/15/10 ...$15.00.
DOI: http://dx.doi.org/10.1145/2806416.2806427.

rithms and develop a cost-based model that selects the best algorithm to filter a message.

(3) Based on the cost model, we develop a new filtering algorithm and develop several pruning techniques.

(4) We have implemented our method. The experimental results on real datasets show our method achieves high performance and significantly outperforms existing approaches.

The rest of this paper is organized as follows. In Section 2, we formulate the problem and review related works. We present an MBRTrie index and develop a filter-verification framework in Section 3 while PT-Quadtree index structure is proposed in Section 4. Then we devise a cost-based algorithm in Section 5. The experimental results are shown in Section 6. And finally we conclude in Section 7.

2. PRELIMINARIES

We first formalize the location-aware publish/subscribe problem and then review related works.

2.1 Problem Formulation

In a location-aware publish/subscribe system, publishers post spatio-textual messages and subscribers register subscriptions to capture their interests. A subscription s includes a textual description $s.T$ and spatial information $s.R$, denoted by $s = \langle T, R \rangle$. The spatial information is used to capture a subscriber's most interested region. In this paper we use the well-known minimum bounding rectangle (MBR) to denote a region $s.R$. We use the bottom-left corner and top-right corner to describe an MBR, denoted by $s.R = \langle (x_{bl}, y_{bl}), (x_{tr}, y_{tr}) \rangle$. Especially if $x_{bl} = x_{tr}$ and $y_{bl} = y_{tr}$, the region is reduced to a point. The textual description is used to capture a subscriber's content interests, denoted by a set of tokens $s.T = \langle t_1, t_2, \cdots, t_{|s.T|} \rangle$.

A message m is denoted by $m = \langle T, R \rangle$ in which $m.T$ and $m.R$ have the same meaning as those of subscriptions. If the spatial information of a message is a point, we call it *point message*; otherwise it is called a *range message*.

Given a subscription s and a message m, s could be an answer of m if s and m have spatial overlap and all the tokens in s are contained in m[3], i.e. they satisfy

(1) *Spatial constraint*: $m.R \cap s.R \neq \phi$ and;

(2) *Textual constraint*: $m.T \supseteq s.T$.

Based on the notations, we formalize the location-aware publish/subscribe problem.

DEFINITION 1 (LOCATION-AWARE PUBLISH/SUBSCRIBE). *Given a set of subscriptions $\mathcal{S} = \{s_1, s_2, \cdots, s_{|\mathcal{S}|}\}$ and a message m, a location-aware publish/subscribe system delivers m to $s_i \in \mathcal{S}$ if $m.R \cap s_i.R \neq \phi$ and $m.T \supseteq s_i.T$.*

For example, consider the twelve subscriptions in Figure 1. For a point message $m_p = (\{b, c, d, e, f\}, (26, 14))$, subscription $s_4 = (\{b, c, d\}, \langle (20, 10), (28, 18) \rangle)$ is an answer of m_p. $s_3 = (\{b, c, d\}, \langle (20, 32), (35, 35) \rangle)$ is not an answer as it does not contain the point of m_p. $s_1 = (\{a, b, c\}, \langle (25, 0), (30, 20) \rangle)$ is also not an answer as it has a token "a" which does not appear in m_p. We deliver subscriptions s_4, s_7, s_{10} to message m_p. For a range message $m_r = (\{a, c, d, e\}, \langle (10, 10), (40, 40) \rangle)$, we deliver the subscriptions s_2, s_{10}, s_{11} to m_r.

[3]Our method can efficiently support other metrics, and due to space constraints, we omit the details.

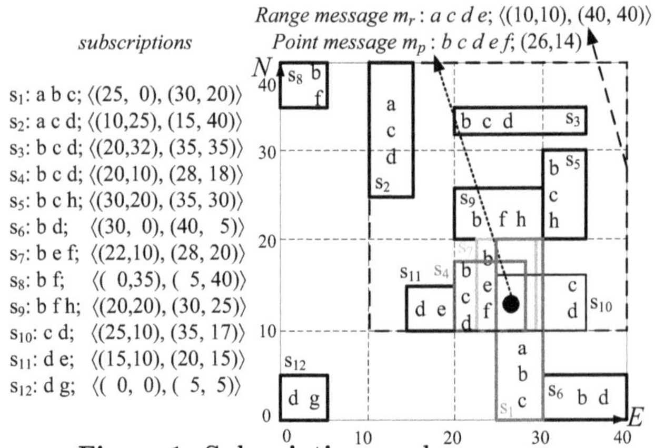

Figure 1: Subscriptions and messages

2.2 Related Work

Location-Aware Publish/Subscribe. Li et al. [14] proposed the R^t-tree to support location-aware publish/subscribe, which extended the R-Tree by selecting some representative tokens from subscriptions and adding them into R-tree nodes to enable textual pruning. However, for upper-level nodes, there are many tokens and thus it has low pruning power on textual part. We have compared with this approach and our method significantly outperformed it (see Section 6).

Hu et al. [11] studied the parameterized location-aware publish/subscribe, which requires subscribers to specify parameters to enable personalize filtering. Chen et al. [3] studied the problem of matching boolean range continuous queries to streaming objects. Guo et al. [9] studied on filtering dynamic streams for continuous moving boolean subscriptions. Obviously they are different from our problem. Wang et al. [19] proposed a cost-based method to support spatial keyword queries using a tree structure. Different from our works, they utilized keyword partition and space partition in one tree structure when constructing index for queries based on expected matching cost. And they computed the cost based on the number of queries associated to each partition and the probability that whether the partition is explored during object matching, instead of the complexity of filter and verification steps.

Location-Aware Keyword Search: There are several studies on location-aware keyword search [7, 25, 13, 2, 16, 12]. Felipe et al. [7] proposed IR^2-Tree which combines an R-tree with text signatures to find top-k answers. Cong et al. [2] presented a location-aware textual search model based on integrating R-tree and inverted files. Lu et al. [16] studied on supporting reverse spatial textual search. All these works designed algorithms to find answers based on the given location and keywords. For the region-based keyword search problem, Jin et al. [12] proposed a hybrid model to return objects that contain related keywords within a given region. Zhou et al. [25] and Hariharan et al. [10] proposed different strategies for combining R^*-tree and inverted lists.

In addition, location-aware keyword search has been applied into different scenarios. For example, Yao et al. [23] presented a model to answer similarity string queries in spatial databases. Chen et al. [4] studied on query processing in geographic search engines based on spatial keyword search. Roy and Chakrabarti [17] designed a location-aware type ahead search. Wu et al. [20] studied on processing continuously moving spatial keywords queries.

Different from location-aware keyword search, location-aware publish/subscribe services adopt a push model which delivers message to relevant subscribers.

Traditional Publish/Subscribe Services: Foltz and Dumais [8, 21, 22] studied on selecting textual information under space model from IR perspective. Fabret et al. [6] designed a "processor cache conscious" algorithm for matching subscriptions. Liu et al. [15] utilized synopses to construct an index to support the publish/subscribe problem.

3. MBRTRIE BASED METHOD

In this section, we first propose an index MBRTrie in Section 3.1, and devise a filtering framework in Section 3.2. Then we develop efficient filtering algorithms in Section 3.3.

3.1 MBRTrie Index Structure

Before index construction, we first fix a global order for tokens in subscriptions, e.g., the alphabetical order. Then for each subscription, we sort its tokens based on this order. Given a sorted token set $T = \langle t_1, t_2, \cdots, t_{|T|}\rangle$, $\langle t_1, t_2, \cdots, t_i\rangle$ is called a prefix of $\langle t_1, t_2, \cdots, t_j\rangle$ if $i \le j \le |T|$. A token set $\langle t_1, t_2, \cdots, t_x\rangle$ is smaller than token set $\langle t'_1, t'_2, \cdots, t'_y\rangle$ if $t_i < t'_i$ and $t_j = t'_j$ for $j < i$. We also sort the subscriptions based on their token-set order, and associate each subscription with a subscription ID.

We construct an MBRTrie for subscriptions as follows. For each subscription, we utilize its token set to build a unique path from the root to a leaf in which each trie node is associated with a token. The root and leaf have an empty token ϵ. For simplicity, a trie node is interchangeably used with its corresponding token in this paper. Based on this structure, the subscriptions with a common prefix of token sets share the same ancestors. And children of a node are sorted by the corresponding token. Each leaf has an inverted list of subscriptions' IDs which contains the corresponding token set. As subscriptions are sorted by the token-set order, we associate each node n with a subscription ID range $[n_l, n_u]$, where n_l and n_u respectively denote the minimum and maximal IDs of subscriptions under this node (which are subscriptions on the inverted lists of its leaf descendants).

For each node n, we also associate it with a *node MBR*, which is the minimum bounding rectangle of MBRs of subscriptions under node n, denoted by n_{mbr}. And if the MBR of a message m has no overlap with n_{mbr}, the subtrie rooted at node n can be pruned since all the subscriptions under it have no spatial overlap with m.

For example, Figure 2 gives an MBRTrie of subscriptions in Figure 1 with alphabetical order. The MBR of node 1 is $\langle(10, 0), (30, 40)\rangle$, which is the minimum bounding rectangle of MBRs of subscriptions under node 1, i.e., s_1 and s_2. Node 8 has a subscription range $[s_3, s_9]$. That means subscriptions s_3 to s_9 are under this node. In other words, subscriptions with token "b" (node 8) as the first token must be in $[s_3, s_9]$.

Space Complexity: Suppose the average token number of subscriptions is $\mathcal{S}_{avg}$, which is usually very small, e.g., 3. The number of nodes in the MBRTrie is at most $\mathcal{S}_{avg} \times |\mathcal{S}|$. As many token sets share prefix, the real number is smaller than it. Thus with the total length of inverted lists $|\mathcal{S}|$, the space complexity of MBRTrie is $\mathcal{O}(\mathcal{S}_{avg} \times |\mathcal{S}|)$.

Updates: For a new subscription, we only need to insert it into MBRTrie and update the MBRs and subscription ranges of the nodes on the path from the root to the new inserted leaf. As subscription IDs are sorted in order, we can reserve some IDs for accommodating future insertions. For deletions, we can use a special mark to denote the deletions.

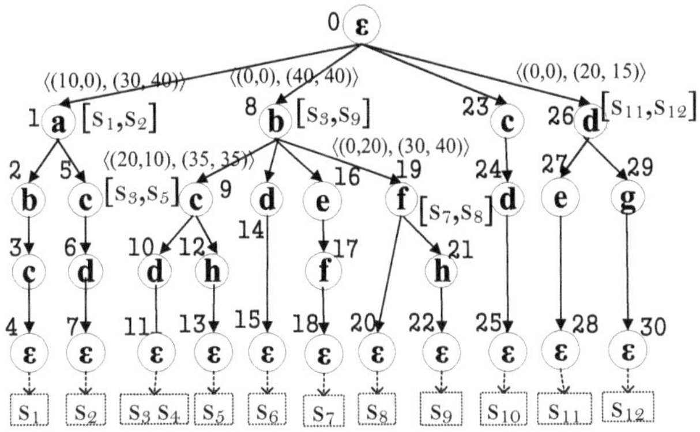

Figure 2: MBRTrie index by an alphabetical order

3.2 A Filtering Framework

To achieve high performance, we want to only visit a small number of relevant trie nodes. Thus in this subsection, we will discuss how to filter MBRTrie nodes.

When traversing MBRTrie, we only need to visit the nodes having leaf descendants which contain subscriptions as results of message. However an MBRTrie node may have a lot of leaf descendants and checking whether it satisfies this condition is expensive. Therefore we propose a filter-and-verification framework. The first step identifies a set of candidate nodes (there is an answer under the node) and the second step verifies the subscriptions on the inverted lists of leaf descendants of these candidate nodes.

Step 1 - Filter: For a trie node n, we prune node n, if

(1) MBR Filter: $n_{mbr} \cap m.R = \phi$, which means any subscriptions under node n have no spatial overlap with m; or

(2) Token Filter: $n \notin m.T$ (The token of n is not in $m.T$). As all subscriptions under node n containing this token which does not appear in m, it invalidates the textual constraint.

Step 2 - Verification: For each leaf node surviving in the filter step, the subscriptions on its inverted list are candidate answers of message m. All of them must already satisfy the textual constraint since all the tokens in their ancestors appear in the message (otherwise this node should be pruned). However the subscriptions may not satisfy the spatial constraint because the node MBR contains some regions that have no overlap with the subscriptions in its leaf descendants. Therefore we need a verification step to do spatial checking for the subscriptions.

In the verification step, we examine all subscriptions on the inverted lists of leaf candidate nodes. And time complexity is $\mathcal{O}(\sum_l |\mathcal{I}_l|)$, where l denotes a leaf candidate node and $\mathcal{I}_l$ is the inverted list of l. In the filter step, we traverse MBRTrie to find candidate nodes. Given a node, the MBR filter checks whether its node MBR has spatial overlap with the message with complexity $\mathcal{O}(1)$. For token filter, we find all the trie nodes which appear in the message. Next we introduce several algorithms to efficiently find such nodes.

3.3 Filtering Algorithms

Given a message m, we first sort the tokens in message m based on a global order (e.g., alphabetical order) and remove the duplicates. Let $T = \langle t_1, t_2, \cdots, t_N\rangle$ denote the sorted token set of m. Next we propose three algorithms to implement the token filter.

ProbeTokenSet - Use trie nodes to probe token sets: The first method traverses MBRTrie in pre-order. For each node n, we check whether it satisfies two filters. If not, we prune node n; otherwise we access its children. Iteratively, we can find all leaf candidate nodes.

As tokens in T are sorted, we can do a binary search to check whether a node n appears in T. The time complexity for checking is $\mathcal{O}(\log N)$, where N is the number of tokens in T. In the worst case, we need to enumerate all trie nodes, thus the worst-case complexity is $\mathcal{O}(M \times \log N)$, where M is the number of nodes in MBRTrie. Next we analyze the average-case complexity.

Suppose there are totally D distinct tokens which are independent. That is given a node, any token has the same probability to appear as a child of it, which is $\frac{1}{D}$. Suppose there are L_i nodes in the i-th level (the level of the root is 0). For the root, the probability to visit its children in the first level is 1. As there are L_1 nodes in the first level, the time complexity for the first-level nodes is $\mathcal{O}(L_1 \times \log N)$. Each node in this level has $\frac{N}{D}$ probability to appear in T, which means the probability to access nodes in the second level is $\frac{N}{D}$. As there are L_2 nodes in the second level, the average-case complexity for the second-level nodes is $\mathcal{O}(L_2 \times \frac{N}{D} \times \log N)$. Similarly the average-case time complexity for the i-th level nodes is $\mathcal{O}(L_i \times (\frac{N}{D})^{i-1} \times \log N)$. Thus the average-case time complexity for all nodes is

$$\mathcal{O}\big(\log N \times \sum_{i=1}^{H_t}(L_i \times (\tfrac{N}{D})^{i-1})\big),$$

where H_t is the height of MBRTrie.

In practice, $N \ll D$, and for $i \geq 3$, $L_i \times (\frac{N}{D})^{i-1} \times \log N$ is close to 0. The average-case time complexity can reduce to

$$\mathcal{O}\big((L_1 + \tfrac{L_2 \times N}{D}) \times \log N\big).$$

ProbeTrie - Use the tokens to probe trie nodes: The second method visits tokens in T in order. For each token $t_i \in T$, it checks whether the root has a child with token t_i and has spatial overlap with m. If there is no such node, it breaks and visits the next token t_{i+1}; otherwise, it locates the node with token t_i, and as tokens in T are sorted in order, next we repeat this step for each token after t_i in T. Iteratively, it can find all leaf candidate nodes.

To check whether a trie node has a child with token t_i, we can do a binary search among all the children of this node. Suppose the average fanout of a node is F. The complexity to do the checking is $\mathcal{O}(\log F)$. In the worst case for each combination of tokens in T, we need to do a binary search on the trie, thus the worst-case complexity is

$$\mathcal{O}\Big(\textstyle\sum_{i=1}^{N}\binom{N}{i} \times \log F = 2^N \times \log F\Big).$$

Next we give the average-case complexity. The fanout of the root is L_1. Thus the average-case time complexity for the first-level nodes is $\mathcal{O}(N \times \log L_1)$. Considering the i-th level nodes, their parents are in $(i-1)$-th level and have $(\frac{N}{D})^{i-1}$ probability in T. The average fan-out of $(i-1)$-th level nodes is $F_{i-1} = \frac{L_i}{L_{i-1}}$. The average-case time complexity for the i-th level nodes is $\mathcal{O}\Big(logF_{i-1} \times L_{i-1} \times (\frac{N}{D})^{i-1}\Big)$. So the average-case complexity is

$$\mathcal{O}\Big(N \times \textstyle\sum_{i=1}^{H_t}\big(\log F_{i-1} \times L_{i-1} \times (\frac{N}{D})^{i-1}\big)\Big).$$

In practice, for $i \geq 3$, $\log F_{i-1} \times L_{i-1} \times (\frac{N}{D})^{i-1}$ is close to 0. Thus the average-case time complexity can reduce to

$$\mathcal{O}\big(N \times \log L_1 + N \times \log F_1 \times L_1 \times \tfrac{N}{D}\big).$$

Algorithm 1: MBRTrie ($\mathcal{S}, m$)

Input: $\mathcal{S}$: The subscription set; m: A message
Output: $\mathcal{R}$: Answers of m

begin
  Fix a global token order ;
  Build an MBRTrie with root r ;
  $T \leftarrow$ sorted distinct token set of m ;
  Initialize a candidate node set $\mathcal{CN}$;
  if $r_{mbr} \cap m.R \neq \phi$ **then**
    MBRTrie-Filter (r, $m.T$ m, $\mathcal{CN}$) ;
    $\mathcal{R}$ = MBRTrie-Verify ($m, \mathcal{CN}$) ;
end

Function MBRTrie-Filter(n, T_n, m, $\mathcal{CN}$)

Input: n: A trie node; T_n: Token set; m: A message $\mathcal{CN}$: Candidate leaf node set

begin
  if *n is a leaf node* **then** $\mathcal{CN} \leftarrow n$;
  $\mathcal{P}$ = SelectPair (n, T_n, m) ;
  for *each pair* $\langle c, T_c \rangle \in \mathcal{P}$ **do**
    MBRTrie-Filter (c, T_c, m, $\mathcal{CN}$);
end

Function SelectPair(n, T_n, m)

Input: n: A trie node; T_n: Token set; m: A message
Output: $\mathcal{P}$: Candidate node set

begin
  if $|T_n| \times \log |n| < |n| \times \log |T_n|$ **then**
    for *each token t of T_n* **do**
      Use t to do a binary search on n's children;
      if *child c with label t & $c_{mbr} \cap m.R = \phi$* **then**
        $\mathcal{P} \cup = \langle c, T_c \rangle$; //$T_c$: tokens after c in T_n
  else
    for *each child c of n & $c_{mbr} \cap m.R = \phi$* **do**
      Use c to do a binary search on T_n;
      if $c \in T_n$ **then**
        $\mathcal{P} \cup = \langle c, T_c \rangle$; //$T_c$: tokens after c in T_n
end

Function MBRTrie-Verify(m, $\mathcal{CN}$)

Input: m: A message; $\mathcal{CN}$: Leaf candidate node set
Output: $\mathcal{R}$: Answers of m

begin
  for *each node* $n \in \mathcal{CN}$ **do**
    for *each subscription* $s \in \mathcal{I}_n$ **do**
      if $s.R \cap m.R \neq \phi$ **then** $\mathcal{R} \leftarrow s$;
end

Figure 3: MBRTrie algorithm

A Cost-based Method: Notice that upper-level nodes usually have many children, thus it is efficient to use tokens to do a binary search on the trie structure. On the contrary, it is more efficient to use trie nodes to probe tokens in message on the lower-level trie nodes which have few children. Based on this observation, we propose a cost-based method.

Consider a candidate node n. There exists one and only one token in T that matches n (as tokens in T are distinct).

Suppose it is t_i. Let $T_n = \{t_{i+1} \cdots t_N\}$. We call $\langle n, T_n \rangle$ a candidate pair if n satisfies the spatial constraint. If $\langle n, T_n \rangle$ is a candidate pair, we try to find candidate pairs from n's children. As tokens in T are sorted, n's children can only match tokens in T_n. Based on this observation, we propose an extension-based method to find candidate pairs. Let $\mathcal{P}$ denotes the candidate-pair set for n's children, $|n|$ denotes the number of n's children. We compute $\mathcal{P}$ as follows.

(1) If $|T_n| \times \log |n| < |n| \times \log |T_n|$, we use each token $t_j \in T_n$ to probe n's children. If a child c matches t_j and $c_{mbr} \cap m.R \neq \phi$, $\langle c, T_c = \langle t_{j+1}, \cdots, t_N \rangle \rangle$ is a candidate pair and added into $\mathcal{P}$.

(2) Otherwise, we use each child of n to probe token set T_n. For a child c, if c matches a token $t_j \in T_n$ and $c_{mbr} \cap m.R \neq \phi$, $\langle c, T_c = \langle t_{j+1}, \cdots, t_N \rangle \rangle$ is a candidate pair and added to $\mathcal{P}$.

Next we repeat the above steps for pairs in $\mathcal{P}$. Iteratively we can find all candidate pairs. And based on the candidate pairs, we can find the leaf candidate nodes.

Figure 3 illustrates the MBRTRIE algorithm. It first fixes a global token order and constructs an MBRTrie (line 2- 3). Then it calls function MBRTRIE-FILTER to find candidate nodes (line 7). Finally it verifies the candidates and gets the answers by calling function MBRTRIE-VERIFY (line 8).

MBRTRIE-FILTER first checks whether the node in a candidate pair is a leaf node. If yes, we select it into leaf candidate node set (line 2). Next MBRTRIE-FILTER adaptively selects a better method to find candidate pairs by calling function SELECTPAIR (line 3). If MBRTRIE-FILTER finds a candidate pair, it recursively finds candidate pairs based on the current pair (line 5).

Time Complexity: As we select a better method to find trie nodes, the average-case complexity of the filter step is

$$\mathsf{Cost}_T^{\mathcal{F}} = \mathcal{O}\Big(\sum_{i=1}^{H_t} \min\big(\log N \times L_i, N \times \log F_{i-1} \times L_{i-1}\big) \times \big(\frac{N}{D}\big)^{i-1}\Big). \quad (1)$$

Suppose there are cand_T candidate nodes and the inverted lists of leaf nodes are $\mathcal{I}_1, \mathcal{I}_2, \cdots, \mathcal{I}_{\mathsf{cand}_T}$. In the verification step, the time complexity is

$$\mathsf{Cost}_T^{\mathcal{V}} = \mathcal{O}\Big(\sum_{i=1}^{\mathsf{cand}_T} |\mathcal{I}_i|\Big). \quad (2)$$

An algorithm should satisfy (1) completeness: any subscription satisfying the spatial constraint and the textual constraint must be found by the algorithm; and (2) correctness: any subscription found by the algorithm must satisfy the spatial constraint and the textual constraint. The MBRTrie satisfies the two properties as formalized in Theorem 1.

THEOREM 1. *The MBRTrie algorithm satisfies completeness and correctness.*[4]

For example, consider message $m_p = (\{b, c, d, e, f\}, (26, 14))$ and the MBRTrie in Figure 2. As there are 5 tokens in the message and the root has 4 children, we use trie nodes to probe the token set and find three candidate nodes 1, 8, 23. Node 26 is pruned as its MBR does not contain the message point. For node 1, we find an answer s_1 in its child node 2. For node 8, we select its children 9, 16 and prune nodes 14 and 19. Iteratively we can find all answers for the message m_p. Here we prune sixteen nodes and only visit fifteen nodes in MBRTrie, and the visisted nodes are nodes 0∼4, 8∼11, 16∼18, and 23∼25.

[4]We omit proofs of Lemmas and Theorems due to space constraints.

4. PT-QUADTREE BASED METHOD

The node MBRs of the upper-level nodes in the MBRTrie cover large numbers of subscription MBRs and may involve many unnecessary regions. Thus they may have low spatial pruning power. To address this issue, we propose a quadtree-based index structure in Section 4.1, and then introduce efficient filtering algorithms in Section 4.2.

4.1 Pivotal-Token Quadtree

To facilitate spatial pruning, we construct a qudatree for MBRs of subscriptions. Firstly we generate a minimal region to cover all subscription MBRs and select the center of the region as root node, and then divide the region into four subregions. Recursively, we divide each subregion into four small regions. For each region, we terminate its division and take it as a leaf node if (1) the number of subscription MBRs that have overlap with the region is smaller than a threshold τ_{num}; or (2) the area of the region is smaller than a threshold τ_{area}. For each leaf node, we maintain an inverted list of sorted IDs of subscriptions whose MBRs have overlap with the region.

If many MBRs have overlaps, they may appear in many inverted lists of leaf nodes. To address this issue, we can use the MX-CIF quadtree implementation [18], which associates each MBR with the quadtree node corresponding to the smallest region that contains the MBR. In other words, the subscription IDs can be associated with both leaf and non-leaf nodes, and each subscription ID appears in one and only one inverted list. Moreover, given an extra space buffer, we can select some regions and push down the subscription IDs in these regions to their leaf descendant regions.

To support textual pruning in the quadtree, we integrate textual description into nodes. A straightforward method associates a node with all the distinct tokens of subscriptions that have overlap with it. Based on this method, given a message m, we traverse the quadtree from root. For each node, if it has overlap with $m.R$ and there exists a token associated with the node appearing in $m.T$, we access the node. Otherwise we prune the node, as it does not satisfy the spatial or textual constraint.

For example, consider the quadtree in Figure 4. Subscriptions s_3, s_5, s_9 are in node 1. The token set associated with node 1 should be the union of their token sets, i.e., $\{b, c, d, f, h\}$. For range message $m_r = (\{a, c, d, e\}; \langle (10, 10), (40, 40) \rangle)$ in Figure 1, as node 1 has spatial overlap with m_r and contains a token "c" that appears in the token set, we need to access the node.

In the straightforward method, the number of tokens associated with a node is very large and the pruning power is low. For instance, in the last example we should prune node 1, because although node 1 shares token "c" with message m_r, all subscriptions under this node contain another token "b" which does not appear in the message. This is not achieved when we access node 1. To address this issue, we propose a pivotal-token quadtree to reduce the number of tokens associated with nodes. Next we discuss how to select and associate pivotal tokens with each node.

For a leaf node, we generate its pivotal-token set by selecting *a single token* from each subscription on its inverted list to represent it. For an internal node, its pivotal-token set is the union of its children's pivotal-token sets. Obviously if the

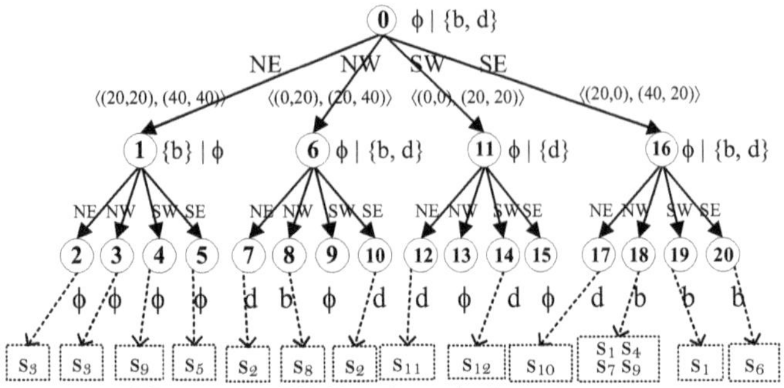

Figure 4: PT-Quadtree index structure

pivotal-token set has no common token with the message, we can prune the node, as stated in Lemma 1.

LEMMA 1. *Given a quadtree node n and a message m, if n's pivotal-token set has no common token with m.T, we can prune the node.*

To save the space and improve the performance, we want to minimize the pivotal-token set. However like the minimum hitting set problem, this is an NP-hard problem [1]. Thus we propose a greedy algorithm. First we select the largest df token into the pivotal-token set and remove the subscriptions contain it. Then the largest df token in the rest of subscriptions is put into pivotal-token set. Iteratively we can generate the pivotal-token set for leaf nodes until no subscription left. For each internal node, its pivotal-token set is generated by computing the union of its children's sets.

We can further remove tokens for internal nodes as follows. Given a node n, if all its children contain a token t, we will keep t in n, and remove it from all four children. In this way, when checking whether t is contained in the message, we just do it for parent and not repeat for its descendants. Utilizing this idea, we keep two pivotal-token sets for a quadtree node: a cover set and a non-cover set. In the cover set, we keep the token appearing in all four children. For the no common tokens are kept in non-cover set, and they are not removed from children. We call such a quadtree Pivotal-Token Quadtree (PT-Quadtree).

For example, the subscriptions in Figure 1 can be constructed as a PT-Quadtree shown in Figure 4. Consider leaf nodes 2, 3, 4, 5 with subscriptions s_3, s_3, s_9, s_5. As the four nodes contain token "b", we select token "b" as their pivotal tokens. Obviously token "b" should be kept in their parent's cover set, i.e., node 1. For nodes 17, 18, 19, 20, we respectively select pivotal tokens d, b, b, b. As their pivotal-token token is not the same, the cover set of their parent (node 16) is ϕ and the non-cover set is $\{b, d\}$.

Space Complexity: Suppose the height of PT-Quadtree is H_q and there are N_q nodes in the quadtree. If we use the MX-CIF Quadtree [18], each subscription is stored only at the node corresponding to the smallest region that contains the subscription MBR, and the sum of lengths of all inverted lists is $|\mathcal{S}|$. To achieve high performance, we want to keep inverted lists only for leaf nodes, and the inverted-list size is $\alpha \times |\mathcal{S}|$, where α is a parameter and depends on datasets. There are at most $|\mathcal{S}|$ pivotal tokens in leaf nodes, and each token is at most stored H_q times. Thus the maximal size of pivotal-token sets is $\mathcal{O}(|\mathcal{S}| \times H_q)$. In practice, as many subscriptions share tokens, the size is much smaller. Thus the overall space complexity is $\mathcal{O}(N_q + \alpha \times |\mathcal{S}| + |\mathcal{S}| \times H_q)$.

Updates: For a new subscription, we insert into PT-Quadtree and select a pivotal token to insert into the non-cover set of nodes on the path from root to the leaf (if the non-cover set does not contain the token). For deletions, we can use a special mark to denote the deletions.

Algorithm 2: PT-QUADTREE $(\mathcal{S}, m)$

```
Input: S: The subscription set; m: A message
Output: R: Answers of m
begin
    Build an PT-Quadtree with root r;
    Initialize a candidate node set CN;
    PT-QUADTREE-FILTER (r, m, CN) ;
    R = PT-QUADTREE-VERIFY (m, CN);
end
```

Function PT-QUADTREE-FILTER$(n, m, \mathcal{CN})$

```
Input: n: An PT-Quadtree node; m: A message
       CN: Leaf candidate node set
begin
    if n ∩ m.R == ϕ then return CN;
    if n.CSet ∩ m.T ≠ ϕ then
        Traverse the subtree rooted at n, and add the
        leaf nodes that have overlaps with m.R to CN;
        return CN ;
    if n.NSet ∩ m.T ≠ ϕ then
        for each child c of n do
            PT-QUADTREE-FILTER (c, m, CN);
end
```

Function PT-QUADTREE-VERIFY$(m, \mathcal{CN})$

```
Input: m: A message; CN: leaf candidate node set
Output: R: Answers of m
begin
    for each node n ∈ CN do
        for each subscription s ∈ I_n do
            if s.T ⊆ m.T&s.R ∩ m.R ≠ ϕ then R ← s;
end
```

Figure 5: PT-Quadtree algorithm

4.2 Filtering Algorithms

For the PT-Quadtree, we introduce a filter-and-verification framework. In the filter step, we generate a set of leaf candidate nodes. Then we verify the subscriptions on the inverted lists of leaf candidate nodes in the verification step.

Step 1 - Filter: We traverse PT-Quadtree in a depth-first order. For each PT-Quadtree node n, let $n.CSet$ and $n.NSet$ respectively denote n's cover set and non-cover set.

(1) If $n \cap m.R = \phi$, we prune node n based on spatial constraint;

(2) If $n.CSet \cap m.T = \phi$ and $n.NSet \cap m.T = \phi$, we prune the node as it invalidates textual constraint;

(3) If $n \cap m.R \neq \phi$, $n.CSet \cap m.T = \phi$, and $n.NSet \cap m.T \neq \phi$, n is a candidate. We repeat the filter steps for its children.

(4) Otherwise $n \cap m.R \neq \phi$ and $n.CSet \cap m.T \neq \phi$, subscriptions on the inverted lists of n's leaf descendants share a common token with m. Thus we only check whether the descendants of n satisfy the spatial constraint. If yes, these leaf nodes are candidate nodes; otherwise we prune them.

Step 2 - Verification: Given a leaf candidate node, as subscriptions on its inverted list may not satisfy both constraints, we need a verification step to examine the subscriptions to get the final answers.

Next we devise an PT-Quadtree based algorithm as shown in Figure 5. First we construct a PT-Quadtree (line 2). Then for the message m, we call function PT-QUADTREE-FILTER to find candidate nodes from the root (line 4). Consider a candidate node n. PT-QUADTREE-FILTER first checks whether node n has an overlap with $m.R$. If not, we prune it (line 2); otherwise, we check whether it satisfies the textual constraint as follows. First if $n.CSet \cap m.T \neq \phi$, we need to access all of n's descendants (line 3, 4); otherwise, we check whether $n.NSet \cap m.T \neq \phi$ (line 6). If yes we need to visit n's children (line 8); otherwise, we prune the node. Iteratively we can get all leaf candidate nodes. Theorem 2 formalizes the correctness of our algorithm.

THEOREM 2. *The* PT-QUADTREE *algorithm satisfies completeness and correctness.*

For example, consider PT-Quadtree in Figure 4. For range message m_r in Figure 1. As the non-cover set of root contains token "*d*" which appears in $m_r.T$, we need to visit its children. Node 1 is pruned as its pivotal-token set has no overlap with the token set of m_r. We can also prune nodes 14, 19, and 20 as they have no spatial overlap with m_r. Thus the leaf candidate nodes are 7, 10, 12, 17. Next we verify the subscriptions s_2, s_{11}, and s_{10} on their inverted lists.

Time Complexity: We can check whether $m.T \cap n.CSet \neq \phi (m.T \cap n.NSet \neq \phi)$ using the cost model in Section 3.3. The time complexity is $\mathcal{O}(\min(\log N \times |n.CSet|, \log |n.CSet| \times N))$, where N is the number of tokens in $m.T$. Suppose there are cand_Q leaf candidate nodes and the height of PT-Quadtree is H_q. The complexity of the filter step is

$$\text{Cost}_Q^{\mathcal{F}} = \mathcal{O}(H_q \times \text{cand}_Q \times \min(\log N \times Avg_{RT}, \log Avg_{RT} \times N)), \quad (3)$$

where Avg_{RT} is the average size of pivotal-token sets.

Note that each subscription of candidate nodes may not have overlap with the message. To find the final answers that satisfy both two constraint, we can use each token in $s.T$ to do a binary search on $m.T$ and the complexity is $\mathcal{O}(|s.T| \times \log N)$. Suppose there are cand_Q candidate leaf nodes, the inverted lists of them are $\mathcal{I}_1, \cdots, \mathcal{I}_{\text{cand}_Q}$, and the average token size of the subscriptions is $\mathcal{S}_{avg}$. The time complexity of the verification step is

$$\text{Cost}_Q^{\mathcal{V}} = \mathcal{O}(\sum_{i=1}^{\text{cand}_Q} |\mathcal{I}_i| \times \mathcal{S}_{avg} \times \log N). \quad (4)$$

5. COST-BASED ALGORITHMS

In this section, we first compare MBRTrie and PT-Quadtree algorithms in Section 5.1. Then we propose a pruning technique in Section 5.2 and give a cost-based model in Section 5.3. Finally, we propose an algorithm in Section 5.4.

5.1 Comparison of MBRTrie and PT-Quadtree

In the verification step, MBRTrie only verifies the spatial constraint (Section 3.3) and PT-Quadtree needs to verify both spatial constraint and textual constraint (Section 4.2), thus MBRTrie has lower complexity than PT-Quadtree in verification. Next we consider the filter step of two methods.

Let $\text{Cost}_T^{\mathcal{F}}$ and $\text{Cost}_T^{\mathcal{V}}$ respectively denote the cost of the filter step and the verification step of MBRTrie which can be computed by Equations 1 and 2, and the cost of filter and verifications steps of PT-Quadtree are denoted by $\text{Cost}_Q^{\mathcal{F}}$ and $\text{Cost}_Q^{\mathcal{V}}$, respectively. They can be computed by Equations 3 and 4. We consider the following two cases.

Case 1: $\text{Cost}_Q^{\mathcal{F}} > \text{Cost}_T^{\mathcal{F}}$. This happens when the message's MBR is large, for example. $\text{Cost}_Q^{\mathcal{F}}$ will be very large. Moreover MBRTrie is very efficient to verify the candidates in the verification step, thus we employ the MBRTrie algorithm.

Case 2: $\text{Cost}_Q^{\mathcal{F}} \leq \text{Cost}_T^{\mathcal{F}}$. In this case, we employ the PT-Quadtree algorithm in the filter step since PT-Quadtree is more efficient than MBRTrie in the filter step. For example, for a point message, as PT-Quadtree only accesses a single quadtree node in each level, $\text{Cost}_Q^{\mathcal{F}}$ is very small. And in the verification step $\text{Cost}_Q^{\mathcal{V}}$ is expensive, we have two strategies to verify candidates. The first verifies results as discussed in PT-Quadtree algorithm directly. The second utilizes MBRTrie algorithm to do further pruning by their inverted lists after generating leaf candidate nodes by PT-Quadtree. The detail of this method is described in the next subsection.

5.2 List Pruning

In the MBRTrie, subscriptions are sorted in the token-set order. Therefore subscriptions under node n must be in a range $[n_l, n_u]$ which means all the ID of subscriptions in the inverted list of n's leaf nodes are between n_l and n_u. Based on these ranges we can integrate MBRTrie and PT-Quadtree to filter a message. First we consider a point message.

For a leaf candidate node found by PT-Quadtree for the point message, there are two strategies to find answers from its inverted list $\mathcal{I}$. The first is to directly verify the subscriptions in $\mathcal{I}$. The second is to utilize MBRTrie and $\mathcal{I}$ to do further filtering as follows.

When we traverse MBRTrie, for a trie node n with subscription range $[n_l, n_u]$, we check whether $\mathcal{I}$ contains a subscription in $[n_l, n_u]$. We prune node n if there is no such subscription, as any subscription under it will not satisfy the spatial constraint. We call this technique *list pruning* which can prune many unnecessary subscriptions.

We utilize a binary search to check whether $\mathcal{I}$ has overlap with $[n_l, n_u]$. If $\mathcal{I}$ has no subscription within $[n_l, n_u]$, we prune node n. Otherwise, suppose the smallest ID not smaller than n_l is n_{min} and n_{max} is the largest ID that no larger than n_u. We generate a sublist $\mathcal{I}_n$ of $\mathcal{I}$ by selecting the subscriptions in $[n_{min}, n_{max}]$. Thus subscriptions under node n that satisfy the spatial constraint must be in $\mathcal{I}_n$. Next we use $\mathcal{I}_n$ to do pruning for n's children. Interactively we can find a set of leaf nodes $\mathcal{L}$. For each leaf node $l \in \mathcal{L}$, suppose its new list is $\mathcal{I}_l$. Each subscriptions in $\mathcal{I}_l$ must satisfy the textual constraint and the sum of number of subscriptions in the inverted list of leaf nodes in $\mathcal{L}$ is smaller than that of $\mathcal{I}$ ($\sum_{l \in \mathcal{L}} |\mathcal{I}_l| \leq |\mathcal{I}|$). Therefore we only verify subscriptions in $\mathcal{I}_l$ for spatial constraint and this complexity on new lists is smaller than that on the original list $\mathcal{I}$.

For example, consider PT-Quadtree in Figure 4. For point message m_p in Figure 1, we can generate the inverted list $\mathcal{I} = \{s_1, s_4, s_7, s_9\}$. Then we traverse MBRTrie in Figure 2. For the children of the root, we prune node 26 as $\mathcal{I}$ has no subscription in range ($[s_{11}, s_{12}]$) of node 26. For node 8 with range $[s_3, s_9]$, it generate a sublist $\mathcal{I}_n = \{s_4, s_7, s_9\}$. We can easily extend our method to support range messages.

5.3 Cost-based Model

Selecting an algorithm in the filter step: As discussing in Section 5.1. We select the filter algorithm based on the cost of $\text{Cost}_Q^{\mathcal{F}}$ and $\text{Cost}_T^{\mathcal{F}}$ as shown in Equation 1 and 3, respectively. $\text{Cost}_T^{\mathcal{F}}$ can be easily computed based on the MBR-Trie structure and the message m. For $\text{Cost}_Q^{\mathcal{F}}$, we only need to estimate cand_Q and other parameters can be gotten from the PT-Quadtree structure. For a point message $\text{cand}_Q = 1$. Next we discuss how to estimate cand_Q for a range message. We can use the k-th level PT-Quadtree nodes to estimate the number of candidates. For each PT-Quadtree node n_i in the k-th level, suppose it has $|\texttt{leaves}(n_i)|$ leaf descendants. Obviously, the larger the spatial overlap $||n_i \cap m.R||$ is, the more leaf nodes have overlap with m under node n_i, where $||n_i \cap m.R||$ is the overlap area between node n_i and $m.R$. Thus we use the following equation to estimate the number, $\text{cand}_Q = \sum_{n_i} |\texttt{leaves}(n_i)| \times \frac{||n_i \cap m.R||}{||n_i||}$.

If $\text{Cost}_Q^{\mathcal{F}} > \text{Cost}_T^{\mathcal{F}}$, we use MBRTrie algorithm in both the filter and verification steps; otherwise, in the filter step we select PT-Quadtree algorithm. Next we discuss how to select an algorithm for the verification step in this situation.

Selecting an algorithm in the verification step: Given a trie node n in the i-th level and a list $\mathcal{I}_n$, suppose n matches the j-th token t_j in message token set T. As discussed in Section 3.3, we estimate the complexity to find n's descendants with tokens in $T_n = \{t_{j+1}, \cdots, t_N\}$ as below.

$$\mathcal{C}_F = \mathcal{O}\Big(\min\big(L_{i+1} \times \log|T_n| + L_{i+2} \times \frac{|T_n|}{D} \times \log|T_n|,$$
$$\log L_{i+1} \times |T_n| + \log L_{i+2} \times \frac{|T_n|}{D} \times |T_n|\big)\Big).$$

For n's leaf descendants, we verify subscriptions on their lists with the complexity $\mathcal{O}(\mathcal{I}_n)$. As we need to use the range of n to probe $\mathcal{I}_n$ with complexity $\mathcal{O}(\log|\mathcal{I}_n|)$, the total complexity of the list-pruning technique is

$$\mathcal{C}_L = \mathcal{C}_F + \log|\mathcal{I}_n| + \mathcal{I}_n. \quad (5)$$

The time complexity to directly verify the list is

$$\mathcal{C}_V = \mathcal{O}(|\mathcal{I}_n| \times \mathcal{S}_{avg} \times \log|T_n|), \quad (6)$$

where $\mathcal{S}_{avg}$ is the average token number of subscriptions.

Initially we consider the root node and the inverted list gotten by PT-Quadtree. If $\mathcal{C}_L > \mathcal{C}_V$, we directly verify the list; otherwise we traverse MBRTrie using list-pruning technique. Iteratively, we always select a better verification model for each accessed node.

For multiple inverted lists, $\mathcal{C}_L = \mathcal{O}(\mathcal{C}_F + \sum_{\mathcal{I}\in\Phi_{\mathcal{I}}}(\log|\mathcal{I}| + \mathcal{I}))$ and $\mathcal{C}_V = \mathcal{O}(\sum_{\mathcal{I}\in\Phi_{\mathcal{I}}}|\mathcal{I}| \times \mathcal{S}_{avg} \times \log|T_n|)$, where $\Phi_{\mathcal{I}}$ is the set of inverted lists generated by PT-Quadtree.

5.4 LFilter Algorithm

In this section, we devise an efficient location-based filtering algorithm, LFilter, asillustrated in Figure 6.

In LFilter, we first construct an PT-Quadtree (line 2) and an MBRTrie (line 3). If $\text{Cost}_Q^{\mathcal{F}} > \text{Cost}_T^{\mathcal{F}}$, LFilter calls MBRTrie algorithm (line 5); otherwise it calls function PT-Quadtree-Filter to generate the candidate nodes based on PT-Quadtree (line 7). Then based on the inverted-list set $\Phi_{\mathcal{I}}$, LFilter calls function HybridPrune to filter the message using a cost model (line 9).

For each trie node n, if n is a leaf node, we check whether subscriptions on its inverted list satisfy spatial constraint (line 3). Next we select a better verification strategy for the inverted lists. If $\mathcal{C}_L > \mathcal{C}_V$, we directly verify whether the subscriptions on the inverted lists on it satisfy both two constraints (line 6); otherwise we use *list pruning* technique on

Algorithm 3: LFilter $(\mathcal{S}, m)$

```
   Input: S: The subscription set; m: A message
   Output: R : Answers of m
1  begin
2      Build an PT-Quadtree with root r_q;
3      Build an MBRTrie with root r_t ;
4      if Cost_Q^F > Cost_T^F then
5          R = MBRTrie (S, m) ;
6      else
7          PT-Quadtree-Filter (r_q, m, CN) ;
8          Compute inverted-list set Φ_I of nodes in CN;
9          HybridPrune (r_t, m, Φ_I, R) ;
10 end
```

Function HybridPrune$(n, T_n, \Phi_{\mathcal{I}}, \mathcal{R})$

```
   Input: n: A trie node; m: A message
          Φ_I: A set of inverted lists; R: Answers of m
1  begin
2      if n is a leaf node then
3          R∪ = MBRTrie-Verify (m, {n});
4      if C_L > C_V then
5          for I ∈ Φ_I do
6              R∪ = PT-Quadtree-Verify (m,I);
7              //verify the subscriptions on the list I
8      else
9          P = SelectPair (n, T_n, m) ;
10         for each pair ⟨c, T_c⟩ ∈ P do
11             Φ'_I = ListPruning (c, Φ_I); //∀I ∈ Φ_I,
               compute sublist of I in range [c_l, c_u], I_c
12             HybridPrune (c, T_c, Φ'_I, R);
13 end
```

Figure 6: LFilter algorithm

n's children (line 9), update the inverted lists using its children' ranges (line 11), and recursively check whether access its children (line 12). Iteratively we can find the answers and Theorem 3 guarantees the correctness and completeness.

Theorem 3. *The* LFilter *algorithm satisfies complexness and correctness.*

6. EXPERIMENTAL STUDY

We compared with state-of-the-art location-aware publish/subscribe method R^{t++}-Tree [14] and location-aware keyword search method IRTree [5][5].

We used two datasets. The first one was a real dataset Twitter. We collected 60 million tweets and selected 10 million tweets with region information as subscriptions and used others as messages. Each subscription contained an MBR and had 1-5 frequent tokens selected from tweets. The average token number of subscriptions was 3. The second dataset was a synthetic dataset by combing Point of Interests (POIs) in USA and publications in DBLP. The USA dataset contained 17 million POIs and DBLP had 1.5 million publications. We generated MBRs from the POIs by selecting a POI as the center and extending a random width

[5]We extended it to support our problem by checking whether IR-tree nodes can be pruned with our filters.

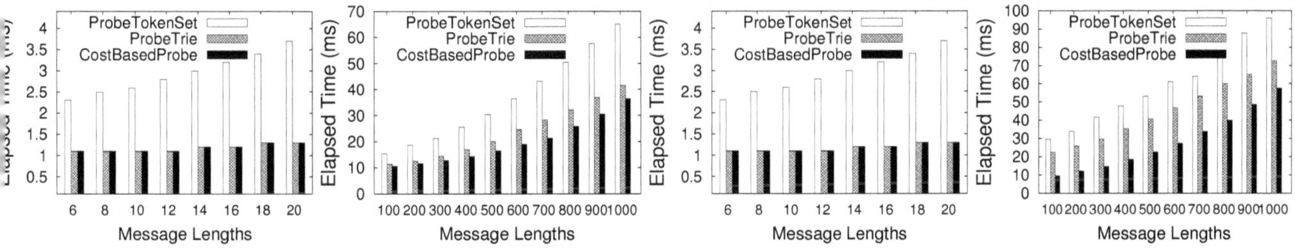

(a) Short Point Messages (b) Long Point Messages (c) Short Range Messages (d) Long Range Messages

Figure 7: Evaluating probing strategies in MBRTrie algorithm on the Twitter dataset (using idf order)

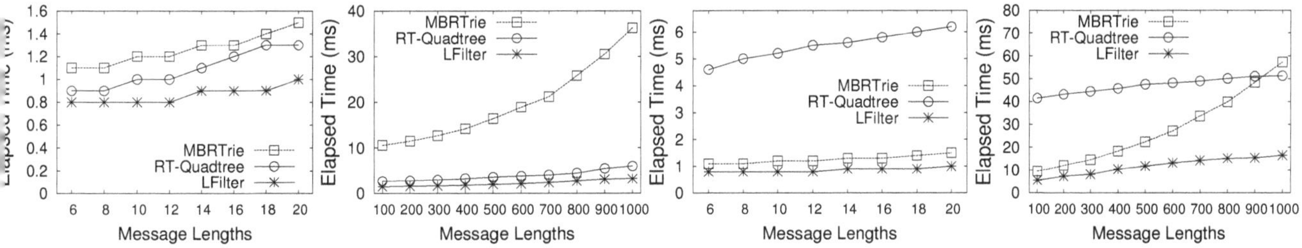

(a) Short Point Messages (b) Long Point Messages (c) Short Range Messages (d) Long Range Messages

Figure 8: Comparison of MBRTrie, PT-Quadtree and LFilter on the Twitter dataset

and height. Each subscription was generated by selecting an MBR and 1-6 tokens from DBLP. Each message was generated by selecting an MBR and a publication.

To evaluate different algorithms, we generated four groups of messages for both datasets by considering the number of tokens and a point location or an region. For the length of messages, the short and long messages contained 6-20 and 100-1000 tokens, respectively. And each group contained 10, 000 messages. We computed the average elapsed time. Table 1 showed datasets and index sizes, where subscription length represents the number of tokens in a subscription. Due to space constraints, the results on USA dataset were only shown in Section 6.3 to compare with existing methods.

All the algorithms were implemented in C++. All the experiments were run on a machine running Ubuntu with a 3.0GHz CPU and 8 GB memory.

Table 1: Dataset statistics.

	Twitter	USA
Subscription number	10 million	10 million
Subscription length	1-5	1-6
Avg Subscription length	3	3.5
Subscription size	542 MB	654 MB
MBRTrie size	1.33 GB	1.45 GB
PT-Quadtree size	1.28 GB	1.37 GB

6.1 Evaluating MBRTrie Algorithm

We evaluated the MBRTrie algorithm by varying different probe strategies: ProbeTokenSet, ProbeTrie, and CostBasedProbe, as discussed in Section 3.3. Figure 7 shows the results. We can see that CostBasedProbe achieved the best performance as it adaptively selected a better probing strategy. For upper-level nodes which had large numbers of children, CostBasedProbe used messages to probe trie structures; when the nodes in the lower-level had small number, it used the trie nodes to probe messages. For instance, in Figure 7(d), for messages with 1000 tokens, ProbeTrie took 98 milliseconds, ProbeTokenSet took 72 milliseconds, and CostBasedProbe only took 56 milliseconds.

6.2 Comparison of MBRTrie, PT-Quadtree, LFILTER

We compared our three algorithms, MBRTrie, PT-Quadtree, and LFILTER by varying the message lengths. The results are shown in Figure 8. LFILTER significantly outperformed other two algorithms as it used a cost-based model to select a better strategy to deal with any types of messages. PT-Quadtree was better than MBRTrie for point messages, since it only accessed one node in each level (see Figure 8(a) and 8(b)). However, for range messages, MBRTrie achieved higher performance than PT-Quadtree, as PT-Quadtree was very expensive in the verification step (see Figures 8(c) and 8(d)). For example, in Figure 8(d), for messages with 1000 tokens, LFILTER took 16 milliseconds and MBRTrie and PT-Quadtree took more than 50 milliseconds.

6.3 Comparison with Existing Methods

We compared our LFILTER with existing methods, R^{t++}-Tree [14] and IRTree [5]. Figures 9 and 10 showed the results on Twitter and USA respectively.

We can see that LFILTER outperformed R^{t++}-Tree, which in turn was better than IRTree. The reason is that the two existing methods had low pruning power on the textual part. For each R-tree node, if the node contained a token in the message, their method had to visit its children. Thus it accessed huge number of unnecessary nodes. So IRTree and R^{t++}-Tree were not efficient for the location-aware filtering problem. Our algorithm always achieved the highest performance for any types of messages utilizing its cost-based model to select a better filtering strategy for both filtering and verification. For example, in Figure 9(b), IRTree took more than 15 milliseconds, R^{t++}-Tree decreased to 10 milliseconds, and LFILTER only took 2-4 milliseconds.

6.4 Scalability

Figure 11 showed the results of the scalability of our method by varying the numbers of subscriptions. We can see that our method scaled very well, and with increasing the numbers of subscriptions, the elapsed time increased almost linearly. For example, for messages with 600 tokens, the performance was 6 milliseconds for 2 million subscriptions and the elapsed time for 10 million subscriptions was only 16 milliseconds. This is because even if the number of subscriptions increased, our index structures can pruned a large number of unnecessary subscriptions.

7. CONCLUSION

In this paper we have studied the location-aware publish/subscribe problem. We propose two new index struc-

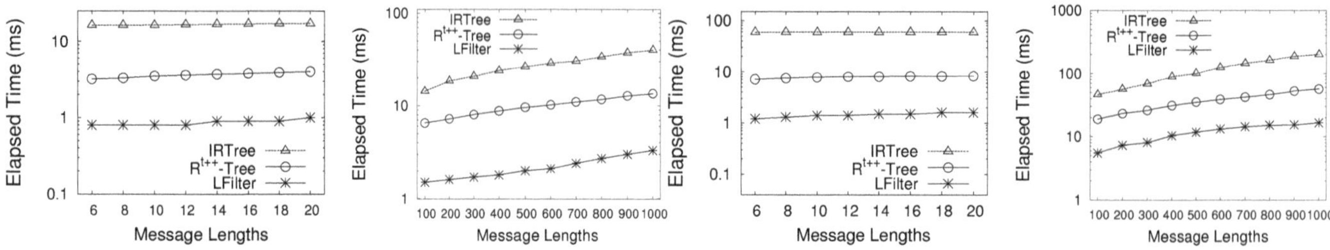

(a) Short Point Messages (b) Long Point Messages (c) Short Range Messages (d) Long Range Messages

Figure 9: Comparison with existing studies on the Twitter dataset

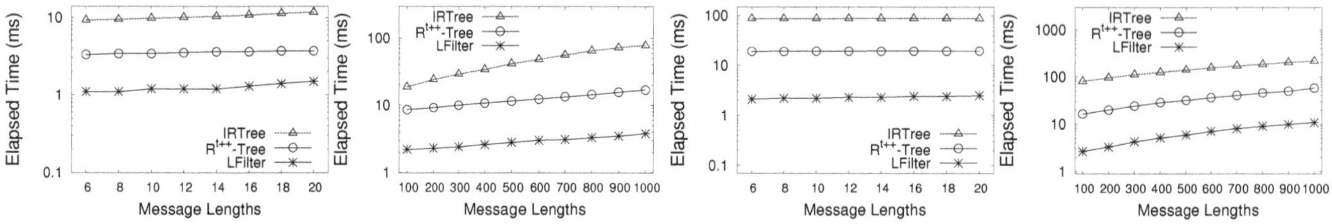

(a) Short Point Messages (b) Long Point Messages (c) Short Range Messages (d) Long Range Messages

Figure 10: Comparison with existing studies on the USA dataset

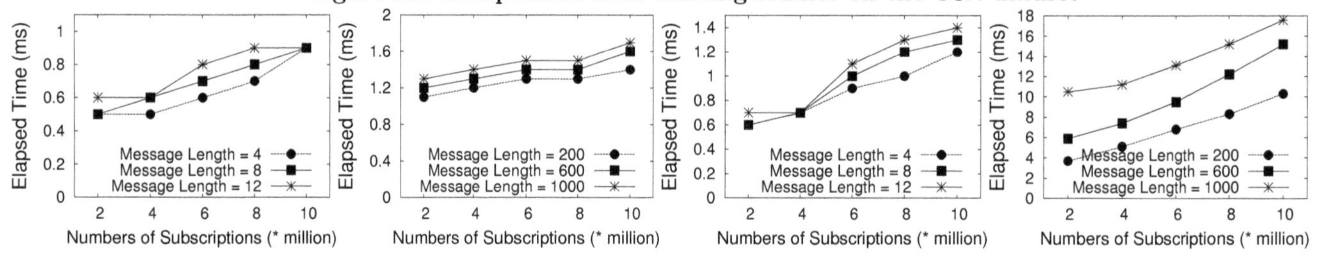

(a) Short Point Messages (b) Long Point Messages (c) Short Range Messages (d) Long Range Messages

Figure 11: Scalability on the Twitter dataset

tures MBRTrie and PT-Quadtree to address this problem. MBRTrie is efficient for the messages with a small number of tokens and PT-Quadtree achieves high performance for messages with small regions. We also develop a cost-based model LFILTER to select the best filtering strategy to achieve high performance for any types of messages. Experimental results show that our method achieves high performance and significantly outperforms existing approaches.

Acknowledgement. This work was supported by 973 Program of China (2015CB358700), and NSF of China (61272090, 61373024), Beijing Higher Education Young Elite Teacher Project (YETP0105), Tencent, SAP, Huawei, the "NExT Research Center" funded by MDA, Singapore (WBS:R-252-300-001-490), and FDCT/106/2012/A3.

8. REFERENCES

[1] G. Ausiello, A. D'Atri, and M. Protasi. Structure preserving reductions among convex optimization problems. *J. Comput. Syst. Sci.*, 21(1):136–153, 1980.

[2] X. Cao, G. Cong, and C. S. Jensen. Retrieving top-k prestige-based relevant spatial web objects. *PVLDB*, 3(1):373–384, 2010.

[3] L. Chen, G. Cong, and X. Cao. An efficient query indexing mechanism for filtering geo-textual data. In *SIGMOD Conference*, pages 749–760, 2013.

[4] Y.-Y. Chen, T. Suel, and A. Markowetz. Efficient query processing in geographic web search engines. In *SIGMOD Conference*, pages 277–288, 2006.

[5] G. Cong, C. S. Jensen, and D. Wu. Efficient retrieval of the top-k most relevant spatial web objects. *PVLDB*, 2009.

[6] F. Fabret, H.-A. Jacobsen, F. Llirbat, J. Pereira, K. A. Ross, and D. Shasha. Filtering algorithms and implementation for very fast publish/subscribe. In *SIGMOD*, pages 115–126, 2001.

[7] I. D. Felipe, V. Hristidis, and N. Rishe. Keyword search on spatial databases. In *ICDE*, 2008.

[8] P. W. Foltz and S. T. Dumais. Personalized information delivery: An analysis of information filtering methods. *Commun. ACM*, 35(12):51–60, 1992.

[9] L. Guo, D. Zhang, G. Li, K. lee Tan, and Z. Bao. Location-aware pub/sub system: When continuous moving queries meet dynamic event streams. In *SIGMOD*, 2015.

[10] R. Hariharan, B. Hore, C. Li, and S. Mehrotra. Processing spatial-keyword (SK) queries in geographic information retrieval (GIR) systems. In *SSDBM*, 2007.

[11] H. Hu, G. Li, Y. Liu, J. Feng, and K.-L. Tan. A location-aware publish/subscribe framework for parameterized spatio-textual subscriptions. In *ICDE*, 2015.

[12] P. Jin, H. Chen, S. Lin, X. Zhao, and L. Yue. Hybrid index structures for temporal-textual web search. In *APWeb*, pages 271–277, 2011.

[13] G. Li, J. Feng, and J. Xu. DESKS: direction-aware spatial keyword search. In *ICDE*, pages 474–485, 2012.

[14] G. Li, Y. Wang, T. Wang, and J. Feng. Location-aware publish/subscribe. In *KDD*, pages 802–810, 2013.

[15] X. Liu, L. Chen, and C. Wan. LINQ: A framework for location-aware indexing and query processing. *IEEE Trans. Knowl. Data Eng.*, 27(5):1288–1300, 2015.

[16] J. Lu, Y. Lu, and G. Cong. Reverse spatial and textual k nearest neighbor search. In *SIGMOD Conference*, pages 349–360, 2011.

[17] S. B. Roy and K. Chakrabarti. Location-aware type ahead search on spatial databases: semantics and efficiency. In *SIGMOD*, pages 361–372, 2011.

[18] H. Samet. *Foundations of Multidimensional and Metric Data Structure.* 2006.

[19] X. Wang, Y. Zhang, W. Zhang, X. Lin, and W. Wang. Ap-tree: Efficiently support continuous spatial-keyword queries over stream. In *ICDE 2015*, pages 1107–1118, 2015.

[20] D. Wu, M. L. Yiu, C. S. Jensen, and G. Cong. Efficient continuously moving top-k spatial keyword query processing. In *ICDE*, pages 541–552, 2011.

[21] T. W. Yan and H. Garcia-Molina. Index structures for information filtering under the vector space model. In *ICDE*, pages 337–347, 1994.

[22] T. W. Yan and H. Garcia-Molina. The sift information dissemination system. *ACM Trans. Database Syst.*, 24(4):529–565, 1999.

[23] B. Yao, F. Li, M. Hadjieleftheriou, and K. Hou. Approximate string search in spatial databases. In *ICDE*, 2010.

[24] M. Yu, G. Li, T. Wang, J. Feng, and Z. Gong. Efficient filtering algorithms for location-aware publish/subscribe. *IEEE Trans. Knowl. Data Eng.*, 27(4):950–963, 2015.

[25] Y. Zhou, X. Xie, C. Wang, Y. Gong, and W.-Y. Ma. Hybrid index structures for location-based web search. In *CIKM*, 2005.

Probabilistic Forecasts of Bike-Sharing Systems for Journey Planning

Nicolas Gast
Inria
Univ. Grenoble Alpes
CNRS, LIG, F-38000
Grenoble, France
nicolas.gast@inria.fr

Guillaume Massonnet
Inria
Univ. Grenoble Alpes
CNRS, LIG, F-38000
Grenoble, France
guillaume.massonnet@inria.fr

Daniël Reijsbergen
LFCS
University of Edinburgh
dreijsbe@inf.ed.ac.uk

Mirco Tribastone
IMT - Institute for Advanced
Studies Lucca
mirco.tribastone@imtlucca.it

ABSTRACT

We study the problem of making forecasts about the future availability of bicycles in stations of a bike-sharing system (BSS). This is relevant in order to make recommendations guaranteeing that the probability that a user will be able to make a journey is sufficiently high. To do this we use probabilistic predictions obtained from a queuing theoretical time-inhomogeneous model of a BSS. The model is parametrized and successfully validated using historical data from the *Vélib'* BSS of the City of Paris.

We develop a critique of the standard root-mean-square-error (RMSE), commonly adopted in the bike-sharing research as an index of the prediction accuracy, because it does not account for the stochasticity inherent in the real system. Instead we introduce a new metric based on scoring rules. We evaluate the average score of our model against classical predictors used in the literature. We show that these are outperformed by our model for prediction horizons of up to a few hours. We also discuss that, in general, measuring the current number of available bikes is only relevant for prediction horizons of up to few hours.

1. INTRODUCTION

In recent years, bicycle sharing systems (BSS) have proven to be very successful in several major cities and are now spreading all across the world [4, 5]. Nowadays, there exist more than 700 such systems that operate on five continents. The benefits for cities are multiple: from a greener image due to more eco-friendly means of transportation to the reduction of traffic congestion, noise and air pollution, they provide an alternative to private motorized vehicles, especially for short-distance trips. From the user's perspective, they offer an affordable and efficient transport alternative with several benefits over the use of a personal bicycle with respect to maintenance, theft or storage issues.

A BSS is composed of a number of stations where a limited number of bikes can be parked. The dynamics is simple. A user arrives at a station to pick up a bike. The ride ends when she returns the bike to any station. User experience and provider revenue can be hampered when the origin station is empty, which forces the user to either resort to another means of transport or try to find an available bike in another station. Similarly, if the destination station is full, the user must either wait until one bike is picked up, or return the bike to another station with at least one parking spot available.

BSS providers publish, typically through their websites, live data about the availability of bikes and empty parking spots at BSS stations, as a means of helping users plan their journey. This has caught the attention of many researchers, who used this data to study user behavior and mobility patterns [3, 6, 14]. Some notable effort has been put on the development of predictive models for BSS, which can be calibrated using the real available datasets [9, 12, 13, 15]. Having a predictive model can benefit both the user and the BSS provider. The user can employ it as a journey advisor [15], for instance identifying likely origin/destination stations for which the trip can be successfully made. BSS providers can run the model to discover usage trends, and proactively adopt countermeasures to potentially adverse situations, such as performing a rebalancing to put more bikes in stations that will likely be emptied.

The first contribution of this paper is a predictive model of availability in BSS based on queuing theory. We model a BSS station as a queue which is subject to two stochastic events: an arrival process for the bikes that are returned, and a departure process for the bikes that are checked out by users wishing to start a journey. Thus each station is modeled in isolation, but the effects from the overall BSS are incorporated into these aggregate processes. For instance, the arrival process subsumes all journeys started from any BSS station, while the departure process accounts for pick-ups by users who had not found an available bike elsewhere.

Modeling a station in isolation simplifies the analysis and the parameter fitting. This approximation is justified by the-

Permission to make digital or hard copies of all or part of this work for personal or classroom use is granted without fee provided that copies are not made or distributed for profit or commercial advantage and that copies bear this notice and the full citation on the first page. Copyrights for components of this work owned by others than the author(s) must be honored. Abstracting with credit is permitted. To copy otherwise, or republish, to post on servers or to redistribute to lists, requires prior specific permission and/or a fee. Request permissions from Permissions@acm.org.
CIKM'15, October 19–23, 2015, Melbourne, Australia.
Copyright is held by the owner/author(s). Publication rights licensed to ACM.
ACM 978-1-4503-3794-6/15/10 ...$15.00.
DOI: http://dx.doi.org/10.1145/2806416.2806569.

oretical results stating that in the asymptotic regime of the number of stations going to infinity, under mild assumptions the stations can be viewed as independent of each other [7, 8]. Furthermore, this approximation is also used in more empirical related works which use Bayesian classifiers [9] and time-series analysis [13]. Differently from these, our model is *explanatory* in that the dynamics is explicitly given. Using real data from the *Vélib'* system of the City of Paris, we actually validate that the real dynamics can be accurately captured by time-inhomogenous Poisson arrival and departure processes. To the best of our knowledge, such a validation of a theoretical model of BSS has not been done before. In contrast, Kaltenbrunner *et al.* adopt a deterministic time series [13], while in [9] stochasticity is encoded as a hidden node in the Bayesian network through a Gaussian variable learned from the data. Our model also improves on two other aspects. First, being time-inhomogeneous, it naturally accounts for non-stationary behavior (a limitation of the auto-regressive moving-average model of [13] that was pointed out in [15]). Second, it can predict the whole probability distribution of the number of bikes at a BSS station, instead of a coarser Bayesian classification into occupation ranges as in [9]. Models that take into account the state of neighbouring stations have also been proposed. A time-series model is presented in [15], which encodes stochasticity through an exogenous normally distributed noise term, to be fitted from the data. However, the empirical results do not show significant improvements over neighborhood-unaware predictive models. Guenther and Bradley [12] consider both a time-inhomogeneous population continuous-time Markov chain model and a model that uses regression analysis and errors fitted to a time series. The population model has the same probabilistic behaviour as the queuing model considered in this paper. They use a fluid approximation approach to obtain point estimators for bike availability in each station of the system, whereas we focus on the entire probability distribution for a single station. Furthermore, we validate the core assumptions of the approach, *i.e.*, Poisson arrivals.

The ability to make probabilistic forecasts can improve the usability of the models by both users and providers. A group of users wishing to ride together may obtain an estimate for the probability of finding no fewer bikes than the group size at the origin station [15]. BSS providers, on the other hand, may rank critical stations according to the probabilities of them being empty (or full) at a given time. Unfortunately, all the aforementioned approaches [9, 13, 15, 12] only focus on point estimators.

Acknowledging the stochastic nature of a BSS also has an important implication on the methodology used to measure and compare the accuracy of its predictors. In the bike-sharing literature, the most important accuracy index used so far has been the well-known root mean square error (RMSE) between the point predictor and the actual observed outcome. This is also the metric used in an ongoing initiative aimed at comparing predictive models of BSS [1]. Our second main contribution, of a methodological nature, is to challenge the use of this metric by putting forward two arguments. First, we claim that it does not properly account for the inherent stochasticity in the system. In the ideal case, an RMSE of zero would indicate a perfect predictor; larger values can be used to rank the accuracy of different predictors. Instead in this paper we show an analysis concluding that, when applied to a BSS, even a point predictor with perfect information about the dynamical evolution of the system *cannot* yield zero RMSE. Second, we observe that the point predictors available so far may not always be informative for practical applications such as the deployment of a recommendation system. In this case, for instance, the user is not interested in the actual number of bikes available at some point in the future; rather, she is interested in being able to pick up a bike with high probability. This information cannot be recovered directly from point estimators.

To overcome these difficulties, we propose new metrics for BSS based on scoring rules, known to be appropriate to evaluate the accuracy of probabilistic predictors and to relatively compare them [11]. We use classical scoring rules to evaluate our ability to predict the number of available bikes. We propose a new scoring rule to evaluate our ability to recommend the feasibility of a journey based on a tuneable threshold on the probability of finding at least one bike at the origin station. We apply this new methodology to evaluate the accuracy of our queuing model using a real dataset from *Vélib'*. We show that for prediction horizons up to 5 hours, it significantly outperforms other predictors such as the Last-Value predictor (where the prediction is equal to the last observed value) and the Historic-Trend predictor (where the prediction equals the historical averages).

Contributions. To summarize, this paper makes the following contributions.

- We discuss an explanatory time-inhomogeneous queuing theoretic model of a BSS station and successfully validate it through fitting of the arrival and departure processes to Poisson distributions using real data from the *Vélib'* BSS of the City of Paris.
- We show that RMSE is not an appropriate metric for journey planning. Instead, we propose new metrics based on scoring rules which can capture provider-related measures (e.g., estimating the number of bikes at a station) as well as user-oriented ones (e.g., estimating the probability that the origin station of a journey is not empty).
- We evaluate our predictor on data from *Vélib'*, showing that it outperforms other point predictors for prediction horizons of 2 to 5 hours, thus advocating its use as a probabilistic recommendation system for BSS.

Paper structure. We discuss the queuing model in Section 2, and validate the model against historic data in Section 3. We show that RMSE in not relevant for our metric in Section 4. We introduce a new metric based on scoring rules in Section 5. We conclude in Section 6.

2. MATHEMATICAL MODEL AND DATASET

2.1 Predicting Trips Feasibility

We focus on a BSS that consists of N stations located in different areas of a city. Each station $i = 1, \dots, N$ has a fixed *capacity* κ_i, which corresponds to the maximum number of bikes that can be parked at this station. The number of bikes that are available for rental at station i at time t is denoted by $X_i(t) \in \{0, \dots \kappa_i\}$ and the occupancy of all stations at t is represented by a vector $\mathbf{X}(t) = (X_1(t), \ldots, X_N(t))$. Two types of events modify the state $X_i(t)$: If $X_i(t) > 0$, a bike can be picked up at station i (this modifies $X_i(t)$ into $X_i(t) - 1$); and if $X_i(t) < \kappa_i$, a bike can be returned at the station (therefore increasing $X_i(t)$ by one). It should be clear that $\mathbf{X}$ is a complex stochastic process: these events are influenced not only by external factors like weather and traffic conditions, but also by endogenous variables such as the occupancy of other stations in the network.

Now assume that at time t, a user decides that she wants to start a trip at time $t+h$ from station i to go to station j. If she had a perfect knowledge of the occupancy of the stations at any time, her decision to use the system would only depend on whether there are enough resources available to complete the trip successfully. That is, she is interested in knowing if station i is non-empty at the time of departure and station j is non-full at the time of arrival. If τ_{ij} is the travel time from i to j, the trip is *successful* if the conditions $X_i(t+h) > 0$ and $X_j(t+h+\tau_{ij}) < \kappa_j$ are satisfied. In practice, the user has only access to the information up to time t, denoted by $\mathcal{F}_t$. Given the stochastic nature of the evolution of $\mathbf{X}$, the problem from the user's perspective therefore reduces to estimate the following probability:

$$\mathbb{P}\left(X_i(t+h) > 0 \wedge X_j(t+h+\tau_{ij}) < \kappa_j \mid \mathcal{F}_t\right). \qquad (1)$$

In what follows, we aim to define a method to provide the user with a reliable prediction for the feasibility of her trip. We rely on a stochastic model introduced in the next section.

2.2 A Queuing Model for a Single Station

Throughout this paper, we focus on the behavior of one station is isolation. We consider the following Markovian model for a station's behavior: Users arrive at station i to pick up bikes according to a time-inhomogeneous Poisson process[1] of intensity $\mu_i(t)$, and bikes are returned to station i according to a time-inhomogeneous Poisson process of intensity $\lambda_i(t)$. Using Kendal's notation for queuing networks [2], one station is modeled as a time-inhomogeneous $M/M/1/\kappa_i$ queue, represented in Figure 1.

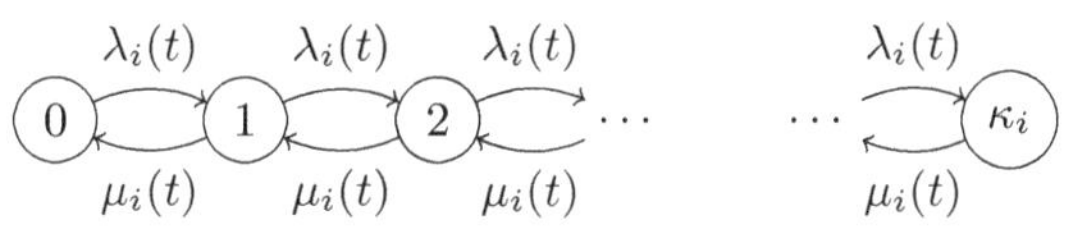

Figure 1: Time-inhomogeneous Markovian model of a station i.

This model makes two approximations. The first one is that the transitions of our system are memory-less and that the arrival processes of users and bikes can be represented as a Poisson process. While this might seem restrictive, we will see in Section 3.2 that this behavior is close to what happens in reality. Moreover, Markovian models have been successfully used to model bike-sharing systems, for example in [7, 10, 12]. The second assumption is that the state of a particular station does not depend on the state of the other ones. Again, this is not true in practice since when a station is empty, no bike can depart from it, therefore reducing the arrival rate at other stations. An alternative, more realistic assumption, would be to consider a process for each trip from an origin i to a destination j, with departure and arrival intensities $\lambda_{ij}(t)$ and $\mu_{ij}(t)$ for each process. However this greatly complicates the model and the parameter fitting for little gain. Moreover, the great number of stations usually involved in BSS such as *Vélib'* allows us to apply the asymptotic analysis techniques introduced in [8], which argue that the isolation approximation becomes exact as the number of stations goes to infinity. Therefore in this paper, we restrict ourselves to a model in which each station behaves as an independent $M/M/1/\kappa$ queue.

Under this assumption, the probability (1) simplifies into the independent computation of $\mathbb{P}\left(X_i(t+h) > 0 | X_i(t)\right)$ and $\mathbb{P}\left(X_j(t+h+\tau_{ij}) < \kappa_j | X_j(t)\right)$. The problem is symmetric between the departure (number of bikes available) and the arrival (number of free parking stands) stations. Hence, in the remainder of this paper, we focus on predicting the non-empty probability.

2.3 Deterministic and Probabilistic Predictors

In this section, we describe the predictors that we will compare later. A probabilistic predictor issued at a time $t \in \mathcal{T}$ for a time $t+h \geq t$ is a guess about the probability distribution of $\mathbb{P}\left(X_i(t+h) = y \mid X_i(t) = x\right)$, and can be written as $p_i(y|x,t,h)$. Here, $y \in \{0, \ldots, \kappa_i\}$, $p_i(y|x,t,h) \in [0,1]$ $\forall y$ and $\sum_y p_i(y|x,t,h) = 1$. In words, $p_i(y|x,t,h)$ is the estimated probability that there are y bicycles at station i at time $t+h$, knowing that there are x bicycles at time t.

We will now discuss some commonly chosen predictors.

Last-value (LVP). The last-value predictor assigns all probability mass to the number of bicycles in the last observation:

$$p_i(y|x,t,h) = \begin{cases} 1 & \text{if } y = x, \\ 0 & \text{otherwise.} \end{cases}$$

This predictor depends on the time t at which the prediction is issued but not on the prediction horizon h.

The "historical" predictor (HP). The historical predictor uses statistical information about the past. We decompose each day into intervals of 15min. Our dataset is composed of measurements $x_i(d,s)$, where i is a station, $d \in D$ is one day in the set of days for which we have measurements and $s \in S$ represents a time interval. Let $|D|$ denote the number of elements in D. The historical predictor is then given by

$$p_i(y|x,t,h) = \frac{1}{|D|}\#\{x_i(d, \text{time of day}(t+h)) = y\}.$$

This predictor does not depends on t directly. It only depends on which time-interval of the day $t+h$ belongs to. The current state x of the station does not influence this predictor.

The "queuing model" predictor (QMP). As we discussed in Section 2.2, we model the behavior of each station i as an M/M/1/κ_i queue with varying arrival or departure rate. If we know these two parameters, we can compute the probability that a station is full or empty at a given time in the future. Indeed, the transition kernel of the Markov chain for

[1]A time-inhomogeneous Poisson process of intensity $\lambda(t)$ is defined by two properties. First, for any $t_1 < t_2$, the number of events A_{t_1,t_2} a time interval $[t_1, t_2]$, follows a Poisson distribution of parameters $\int_{t_1}^{t_2} \lambda(s)ds$. Second, when $t_1 < t_2 < t_3 < t_4$, then A_{t_1,t_2} and A_{t_3,t_4} are independent

the station i is $Q(\lambda_i(t), \mu_i(t))$, where $Q(\lambda, \mu)$ is the following matrix:

$$Q(\lambda,\mu) = \begin{pmatrix} -\mu & \mu & & & \\ \lambda & -(\lambda+\mu) & \mu & & \\ & \ddots & \ddots & \ddots & \\ & & \lambda & -(\lambda+\mu) & \mu \\ & & & \lambda & -\lambda \end{pmatrix}. \quad (2)$$

Note that to simplify the notation, we often denote by $Q_i(t)$ the quantity $Q_i(t) = Q(\lambda_i(t), \mu_i(t))$.

By using the Kolmogorov equation, the probability that the station has y bikes at time $t + h$ given that this station has x bikes at time t is:

$$p_i(y|x, t, h) = \exp\left(\int_0^h Q(t+s)ds\right)_{x,y},$$

where $\exp(M)$ is the matrix exponential of M and $\exp(M)_{x,y}$ is its term at row x and column y. In Section 3.1, we discuss how to estimate $\lambda_i(t)$ and $\mu_i(t)$ using the historical dataset.

"Always go" predictor. The "always go" predictor predicts that the station will be non-empty. That is, it returns a probability distribution for the occupancy of the station such that for all x, t, h, $p_i(0|x, t, h) = 0$. It disregards any information about the system and is independent of t and h. It models a situation in which the user plans to use the system but has no *a priori* knowledge about the system.

2.4 Dataset

In all numerical evaluation, we use historical data from the *Vélib'* system in Paris collected between 1 October 2013 and 31 December 2014 provided by the operator of *Vélib'*. Our dataset contains two types of data, one describing the availability at all the stations of the system and the other containing the individual trip information. The station measurements are made every minute and specify the number of available bikes and free slots in each station. In the other dataset each bike move is recorded with an indication of the reason for the move (bike rental by a user, maintenance or reallocation), the stations of origin and destination as well as the departure and arrival dates and times. We use this information to compute a historical predictor and estimate the (bike) departure and arrival rates, for each minute of a typical working day or weekend day (see the details in the next section).

In the numerical evaluations, we issue a new forecast each day of the week at $t \in \{7\text{am}, 11\text{am}, 3\text{pm}, 6\text{pm}\}$ for prediction horizons from 5min to 10 hours. To simplify notation, in Sections 4 and 5, we write that we issue forecast at a time $t \in \mathcal{T}$. In fact, each element of the set $\mathcal{T}$ corresponds to a prediction issued for one particular station, at one of the times (7am, 11am, 3pm or 6pm) of a particular day. What we call the average performance of a predictor is the average over these $|\mathcal{T}| \approx 2 \cdot 10^6$ values.

3. MODEL VALIDATION

3.1 Parameter Estimation

We estimate the intensities $\lambda_i(t)$ and $\mu_i(t)$ defined in Section 2 by using the dataset. As written in Section 2.3, each measurement can be written as $x_i(d, s)$, where $d \in D$ is a day and $s \in \mathbb{N}$ represents the time of day. The set D of days

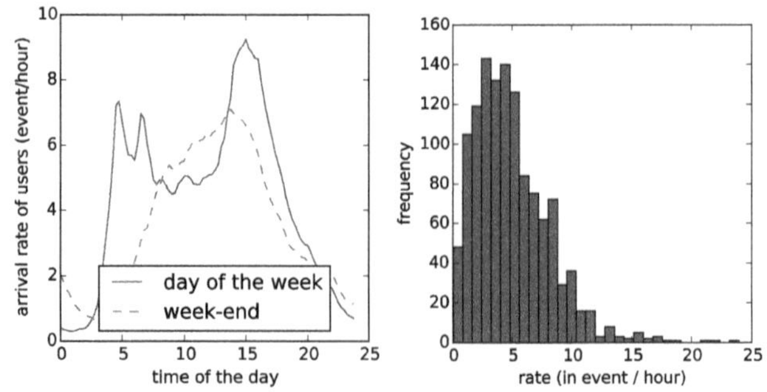

Figure 2: Station use intensities: arrival of users as a function of the time of the day (left) and histogram of arrivals between 10am and 12am (right).

is such that the intensities are assumed to be the same (e.g., all weekdays and roughly in the same season).

So far, we have not imposed any requirements on $\lambda_i(t)$ and $\mu_i(t)$. We consider that intensities are *piecewise constant* (also called *step functions*) and depend only on the time of day and whether this day is during the weekend or not. For one day, the function $\lambda_i : [0, 24h] \to \mathbb{R}$ is piecewise constant with n steps/pieces on $\mathbb{R}$ if there exist times $t_1, \dots, t_{n-1}$ and step heights $l_{i1}, \dots, l_{in}$ such that

$$\lambda_i(x) = l_{ij} \quad \text{if} \quad t_{j-1} < x < t_j,$$

with $t_0 = 0$ and $t_n = 24h$, and t_j, $l_{ij} \in \mathbb{R}\ \forall j$. Similarly, μ_i is piecewise constant if

$$\mu_i(x) = m_{ij} \quad \text{if} \quad t_{j-1} < x < t_j,$$

with $m_{ij} \in \mathbb{R}\ \forall j$. We consider that the times $t_1, \dots, t_{n-1}$ are evenly distributed (all intervals have the same duration) and we estimate the step heights from the dataset. A naive estimator for l_{ij} (in seconds) based on the $|D|$ days observed would be to count the number of observed arrivals in the $|D|$ corresponding intervals and divide this by $(t_j - t_{j-1})|D|$. This, however, ignores the fact that we do not observe arrivals that take place when the station is full. We say that a second during the observation $x_i(s, d)$ is 'valid' for the purpose of estimating arrival intensities if station i is non-full; the resulting estimator for the arrival rate is

$$\hat{l}_{ij} = \frac{\sum_{d\in D} \#\{\text{arrivals on } [t_{j-1}, t_j] \text{ on day } d\}}{\sum_{d\in D} \#\{\text{'valid' seconds on } [t_{j-1}, t_j] \text{ on day } d\}}. \quad (3)$$

A similar argument holds for $\hat{m}_j$, departures and seconds during which the station is non-empty.

The estimated intensities l_{ij} and m_{ij} vary to a considerable degree among the 1225 stations in the dataset. For example, the variation in terms of arrival intensities is displayed in the right-hand figure of Figure 2. Still, some meaningful trends can be observed, especially if the measurements are partitioned into a 'weekday' and a 'weekend' part. This can be seen in the left-hand figure of Figure 2. In particular, the weekdays have two rush-hour peaks whereas the weekends have a single peak in the afternoon.

Figure 3 displays how the choice of the number of steps impacts the estimated intensities. When there are many steps (*e.g.*, $t_i - t_{i-1} = 5$min as in the top-left figure), the estimates have considerable variance: given a dataset of a fixed size, more windows mean fewer observations per win-

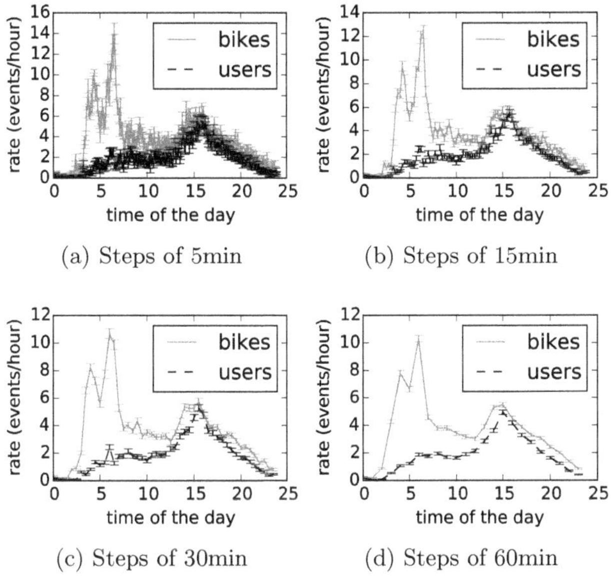

(a) Steps of 5min (b) Steps of 15min

(c) Steps of 30min (d) Steps of 60min

Figure 3: Estimated intensities using different time granularities for the "Pecqueur" station. The error bars show the 95% confidence interval of the estimated parameter of the Poisson distribution.

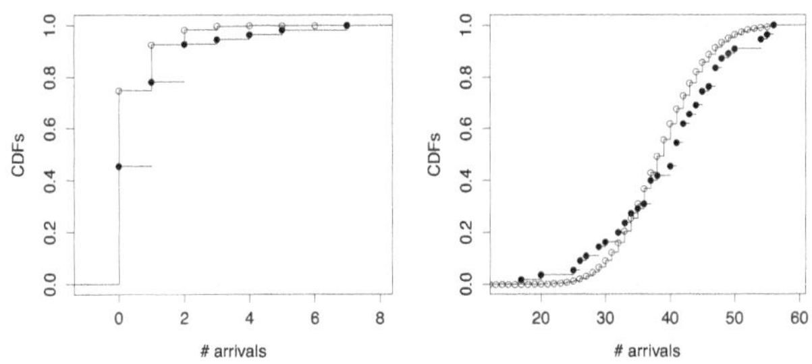

(a) Station "Pecqueur" (b) Station "Gare du Nord"

Figure 4: Comparisons between the theoretical (white dots) and empirical (black dots) CDFs for bike arrivals at two stations, in time window 6. The K-S test statistic is the maximum (vertical) distance between a pair of white and black dots in the graphs. The station on the left has a higher K-S test statistic ($K = 0.3815$) than the one on the right ($K = 0.1633$). There were 53 total arrivals at Pecqueur in this time window throughout the observation period, and 2186 at Gare du Nord (2187 if we account for a brief period of station fullness).

dow, which in turn means more variance. However, if the windows are very large (as in the bottom-right figure, where there are only 24 windows per day), too much information may be lost. For example, the fact that the morning rush hour seems to have two peaks is less clear in the bottom-right panel of Figure 3. In the numerical evaluation, we divided a day in 96 intervals of 15min and we focus only on week-days.

3.2 Model Validation

Alongside parameter estimation, we use the data to validate the assumptions underlying the queuing model. The central assumption underlying the choice to model each station as a time-inhomogeneous $M/M/1/\kappa$ queue is that the bicycle arrivals and departures form Poisson processes. There are several ways to validate this. For example, one could verify whether inter-event times are exponentially distributed and uncorrelated. In this paper, we check whether on each time interval on which the arrival and departure rates are constant, the distribution of arrivals/departure follows a Poisson distribution. Let

$$A_j = \#\{\text{arrivals during } [t_{j-1}, t_j]\}, \quad x, y \in \mathbb{R},$$

and let D_j be similarly defined for the departure process. Then if $\lambda(t) = \lambda \ \forall t \in [t_{j-1}, t_j]$ for some $\lambda \in (0, \infty)$, it should hold that

$$\begin{aligned} F_{A_j}(x) &= \mathbb{P}(A_j \leq x) \\ &= \sum_{z=0}^{x} e^{-\lambda(t_{j-1}-t_j)} \frac{(\lambda(t_{j-1}-t_j))^z}{z!}. \end{aligned} \quad (4)$$

Again, this is analogous for D_j and a constant μ. If we partition the entire time period of interest into n pieces as discussed in Section 3.1, then we would obtain for all j one measurement a_j of A_j per day. Again, this assumption is invalid if there are parts of the day where the bicycle station is full (for arrivals) or empty (for departures). There are two remedies: we can discard days when the station becomes full/empty, or we can assume that if the station is non-full/non-empty some fraction p of the time, we rescale the measurements by p (so if we observe x arrivals in window j on some day and the station is full half the time, we would record $2x$ measurements). The latter choice will have an impact on the confidence levels of related statistical tests; still, this is what we will use in this paper.

Having obtained measurements $(a_{j,d})_{d \subset D}$ of the arrivals during time window j on day d, the question is whether the resulting empirical CDF given by

$$\hat{F}_{A_j}(m) = \frac{1}{\#D} \#\{a_{j,d} \leq m\}$$

is 'sufficiently' close to $F_{A_j}(m)$ as defined in (4). Several measures of the distance between F_{A_j} and $\hat{F}_{A_j}$ — called 'goodness-of-fit' measures — exist, including the Cramér-von Mises criterion and the Kolmogorov-Smirnov (K-S) test statistic. We focus on the latter, given by

$$K = \max\left\{|\hat{F}_{A_j}(m) - F_{A_j}(m)|, m \in \mathbb{N}\right\}.$$

A statistical test for the null hypothesis that $F_{A_j}(m)$ is the distribution underlying $\hat{F}_{A_j}(m)$ can be performed based on K. This test is implemented for discrete distributions in the `dgof` package of the statistical package R. Note that we do not actually conduct the K-S test in this paper; we just use its criterion as an indicator for prediction accuracy.

The K-S test statistic is illustrated in Figure 4. For two stations, both the empirical and Poisson distribution functions have been displayed. The K-S test statistic is the maximum difference between the two functions. As can be seen, the K-S test statistic has a lower value (*i.e.*, a better fit) for the station on the right than for the station on the left.

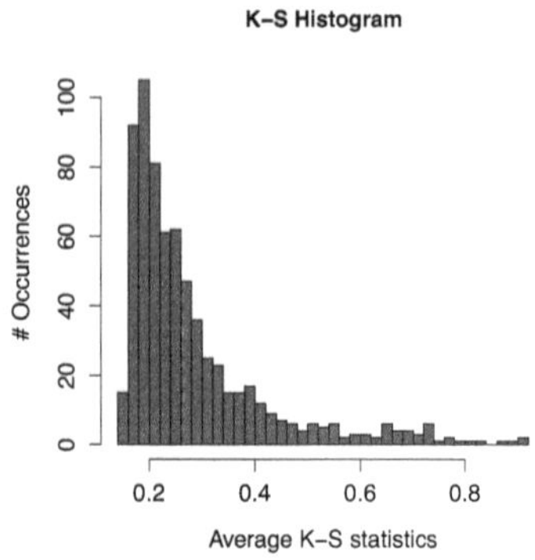

Figure 5: Histogram of the values of the average K-S statistics for the bike arrivals during the one-hour time windows between 5AM and 8PM.

In general, stations for which we have many observations have a better fit with the Poisson distribution. Computation of K-S test statistics, or even an average of K-S statistics over all (or just the daytime) time windows for a station gives an indication of how well the prediction algorithm is going to perform. An example of this is Figure 5, which is a histogram of the average K-S statistics for the bike arrival processes during the one-hour time windows between 5AM and 7PM. The stations for which our approach can be expected to do best will be those stations corresponding to the peak on the left. To mitigate seasonal effects, we only considered observations between 1 December 2013 and 28 February 2014. Stations for which there was at least one one-hour window without arrivals between 5AM and 8PM throughout the entire observation period, or for which the station was full or empty for a whole hour during this period, were discarded, leaving 692 stations.

The median K-S statistic in Figure 5 is 0.23579 (see Figure 4 for a visual interpretation of the K-S statistics). Bearing in mind that even small weather effects would violate the assumption of Poisson distributions, we can conclude that the model assumptions are valid to a reasonable degree.

4. A CRITIQUE OF DETERMINISTIC FORECASTS AND RMSE

Most of the work dealing with prediction for bike-sharing systems, *e.g.*, [9, 12, 13, 15], focuses on providing a single value for $X_i(t)$, whose performance is generally evaluated using the root-mean-square-error (RMSE). The recently initiated bike-sharing prediction challenge [1], also uses this metric: Participants are expected to submit a deterministic time series that represents the estimated number of bikes at a given station in the future. In this section, we show that regardless of their quality, the RMSE of such predictors will always be large due to the stochastic nature of bike-sharing systems. For instance, we present evidence that the best RMSE one can expect from a single-valued estimator for a prediction 2 hours in advance will lie between 10% and 20% of the capacity of a station.

4.1 Deterministic Prediction and RMSE

Assume we want to determine the occupancy of the stations h hours in advance, using all the information available up to now. A deterministic prediction of the vector $\mathbf{X}$ issued at t for the time $t+h$ is a vector $\mathbf{Y}^t(t+h)$, where for all $i = 1, \ldots, N$, $\mathbf{Y}_i^t(t+h) \in [0; \kappa_i]$ is a single real-valued number that corresponds to the predicted number of bikes at time $t+h$ for the station i.

A classical way to evaluate the performance of a deterministic prediction [1, 9, 12, 13, 15] is to compute the root-mean-square-error (RMSE) of a predictor, defined as

$$RMSE(\mathbf{Y}, h) = \sqrt{\frac{1}{|\mathcal{T}|}\sum_{t\in\mathcal{T}} \|\mathbf{X}(t+h) - \mathbf{Y}^t(t+h)\|_2^2},$$

where $\|\mathbf{X}-\mathbf{Y}\|_2^2 = \sum_i (X_i - Y_i)^2$ and $\mathcal{T}$ is the set of time steps at which predictions are made. Note that the RMSE depends on the predictor used ($\mathbf{Y}$) and on the time horizon of the prediction, h.

4.2 A Lower Bound on the RMSE

The smaller the RMSE, the closer our prediction is to the true value. It is tempting to say that the best predictor should have an RMSE of 0. However, we have seen in Section 2 that bike-sharing systems exhibit a stochastic behavior. We now show that this stochasticity implies that the best predictor will have an RMSE of 1 bike at 5min and 3 bikes at 1h for typical parameter values, even if we have perfect knowledge of the parameters of our model (see Figure 6a). Note that these values are consistent with the ones found in [15, Table I] in which the authors show that all their predictors have this performance. Note that we also obtain similar figures for the Paris dataset (see Figure 6b).

We consider a simple scenario with one station for which $\lambda(t) = \lambda$ and $\mu(t) = \mu$ are constant in time. The quantity $X(t)$ behaves as a time-homogeneous continuous time Markov chain of transition kernel $Q = Q(\lambda, \mu)$, as defined in Equation (2). In particular, we have

$$\mathbb{P}(X(t+h) = j \mid X(t) = i) = \exp(Qh)_{ij}$$

In this case, the deterministic predictor $\mathbf{Y}^t_{\text{best}}(h)$ that minimizes the RMSE is $\mathbf{Y}^t_{\text{best}}(h) = \sum_{i=0}^{\kappa}(\exp(Qh)_{X(t),i})i$.

In Figure 6a, we plot the RMSE of the best predictor. We consider two scenarios, in which the capacity of the station is $\kappa = 20$ bikes and such that at the time $t \in \mathcal{T}$ when the predictions are made, $X(t) = 10$ bikes. In the first scenario, the flow at the station is balanced: $\lambda = \mu = 5$ bikes/hour while in the second scenario: $\lambda = 5$ bikes/hour and $\mu = 2\lambda$.

We draw two observations from these figures. First, for both scenarios, the RMSE are around 0.9 or 1.1 for a prediction at horizon $h =$ 5min and around 3.5 for a prediction at horizon $h =$ 1h. This implies that even someone who has perfect knowledge of the parameters λ and μ of the system cannot predict the number of bikes in $1h$ with a RMSE less than 3.5 bikes. In particular, this shows that the predictors presented in [15] all produce values that are close to the best that can be achieved. The second remark is that the RMSE is not sufficient to provide the users with a precise indication on whether a trip is feasible. In particular, a user who wants to depart from a station is interested in knowing if there will be 0 or at least 1 bike but has little interest in the real value. These numbers are hard to guess from deterministic predictors. For example, in the unbalanced scenario, the predictions at $1h$ are $\mathbf{Y}_{\text{best}}(2h) = 2.50$ which suggest that the trip would be possible. Another tentative approach would be to use a linear predictor $\mathbf{Y}^t_{\text{linear}}(h) = ((X(t)+(\lambda-\mu)h)\vee 0)\wedge\kappa$,

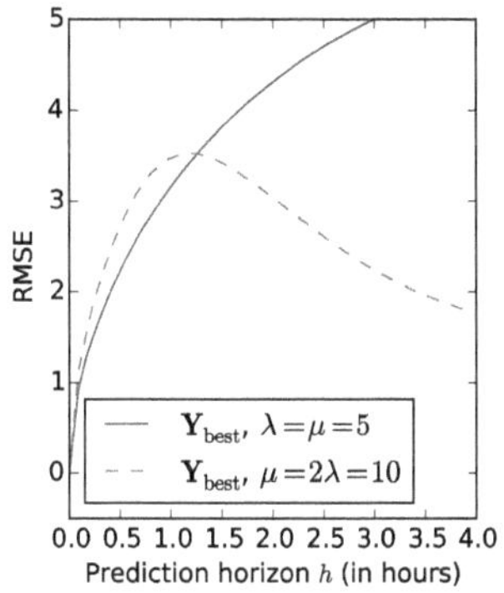

(a) Artificial model

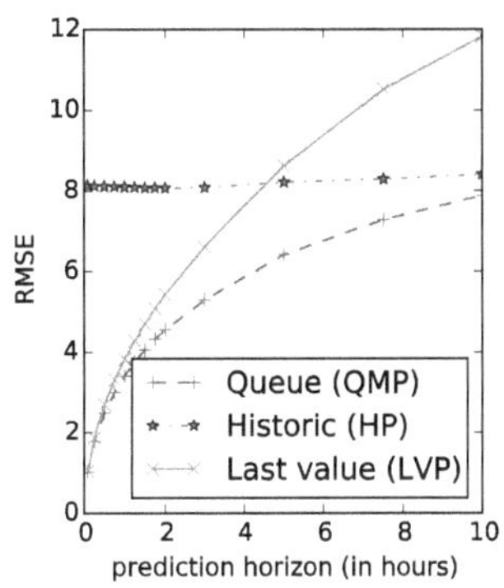

(b) Paris dataset

Figure 6: RMSE for the best-predictors on an artificial model (left) and on the Paris dataset (right).

which corresponds to a linear evolution of the number of bikes truncated at 0 or κ when the capacity is exceeded. This would give $\mathbf{Y}_{\text{linear}}(2h) = 0$ and suggest that the trip is not feasible. A true calculation shows that the probability of empty is 0.34, but neither the two predictors proposed above is able to provide this crucial information.

4.3 RMSE on the *Vélib'* data

In Figure 6b, we compare the RMSE of the deterministic predictors based on the queuing model introduced in Section 2.2, as well as the ones based on historical data and the last-value. The deterministic queuing model predictor is $Y^t(t+h) = \sum_{i=0}^{\kappa}(\exp(Qh)_{X(t),i})i$ and the historic is the average number of bikes observed is the past at hour $t+h$.

For all prediction horizons h, our queuing model provides the best RMSE and converges to the RMSE of the historic model as h increases. Last-value outperforms the predictor from historic data up to $h = 5$ hours but it deteriorates significantly as the horizon grows, reaching values worse by up to 50% for a large prediction horizon. In fact, we will see in Section 5 that when one wants to assess the feasibility of a trip, last-value is beaten by historic as soon as the prediction horizon exceeds $h = 1$ hour. This again reflects the fact that the RMSE is not an appropriate metric when the objective is to determine whether a trip will be successful: LVP has a much smaller RMSE than HP for a time horizon of 2h but is worse at predicting successful trips (Figure 9) because in the latter case, knowing if there will be exactly 10 or 15 bikes in a station is less important whereas knowing if there will be 0 or 1 is critical. As we will see in the next section, we need a different metric to easily express these estimations and measure probabilistic forecasts.

5. PROBABILISTIC FORECASTS AND SCORING RULES

Bike-sharing systems exhibit stochastic behavior. Hence, an alternative to using a deterministic predictor is to forecast the probability distribution of the number of available bikes at the station in the future. In this section, we first show how to evaluate probabilistic predictors by using proper scoring rules. We then develop two scoring rules to assess the performance of QMP in terms of its probabilistic predictions.

5.1 Proper Scoring Rules

A probabilistic forecast for a value X can be represented by a probability distribution $\mathbf{P}$. A probabilistic forecast contains information about the value that we think X will take but also a measure of confidence in this forecast. A natural way to evaluate a forecast is to use proper scoring rules. We now recall briefly the mathematical definition of a proper scoring rule; see [11] for a more complete exposition.

Assume that we want to forecast a random variable X that takes values in a set $\mathcal{X}$. A scoring rule is a function $S(\mathbf{P}, .) : \mathcal{X} \to \overline{\mathbb{R}}$ that associates to each $i \in \mathcal{X}$ a score $S(\mathbf{P}, i) \in \mathbb{R} \cup \{-\infty\}$. The score of a forecast $\mathbf{P}$ is defined by its average score $\mathbb{E}(S(\mathbf{P}, X))$. A scoring rule is said to be proper if, when X is generated according to a probability distribution $\mathbf{Q}$, the score is maximized by the distribution $\mathbf{Q}$. In other word, we have for any distribution $\mathbf{P}$ on $\mathcal{X}$:

$$\mathbb{E}(S(\mathbf{Q}, X)) \geq \mathbb{E}(S(\mathbf{P}, X)). \quad (5)$$

It is strictly proper if $\mathbf{Q}$ is the only maximizer of (5). Note that scoring rules are defined without a priori knowledge on the distribution $\mathbf{Q}$: it is not necessary to know $\mathbf{Q}$ to define a proper scoring rule and to compute the score $S(\mathbf{P}, X)$. This is important as in practice the distribution $\mathbf{Q}$ is unknown (it is the one we try to forecast).

A proper scoring rule encourages honesty: a forecaster knowing the true distribution $\mathbf{Q}$ of $\mathcal{X}$ should issue a forecast $\mathbf{P} = \mathbf{Q}$. If one is very confident that $X \approx x$, then the issued predictor $\mathbf{P}$ will be concentrated on a single value x. In that case, the score $S(\mathbf{P}, X)$ will be high when $X \approx x$ but very low when X is far from x. On the other hand, when one has a low confidence in the prediction, $\mathbf{P}$ will give weight to many values and $S(\mathbf{P}, X)$ will be neither high nor low regardless of the actual value of X.

Skill score. When evaluated over a trace of measurement, the performance of a probabilistic forecast is measured in terms of average score over all forecasts and realizations:

$$\text{Score}(\mathbf{P}, h) = \frac{1}{|\mathcal{T}|} \sum_{t \in \mathcal{T}} S(\mathbf{P}^t(t+h), \mathbf{X}(t+h)). \quad (6)$$

The higher the score, the better the forecast.

5.2 Scoring for the Number of Available Bikes

The predictors described in Section 2.3 provide a deterministic or probabilistic estimation of the number of bikes in a station in the future. Each predictor is a probability distribution over a finite set $\{0, 1 \ldots, \kappa_i\}$, where κ_i is the capacity of the station i considered. Note that a deterministic predictor is a degenerated probabilistic predictor that assigns all the probability mass to a single value. We evaluate numerically these predictors on the Paris dataset by using classical scoring rules. The results are reported in Figure 7.

The most classical scoring rules are Brier score, the spherical score and the logarithmic score. Given a forecast $\mathbf{P}$ and a realization i, Brier score assigns a score $S(\mathbf{P}, i) = 2p_i - \sum_j p_j^2 - 1$, the spherical score assigns $S(\mathbf{P}, i) = p_i/(\sum_j p_j^2)^{1/2}$ and the logarithmic score assigns $S(\mathbf{P}, i) = -\log p_i$ to $\mathbf{P}$, respectively. In Figure 7, we report the average score of the three predictors defined in Section 2.3 as a function of the prediction horizon for Brier and the spherical score. We choose not to report the performance of the logarithmic score for two reasons: First, because the performance of the QMP

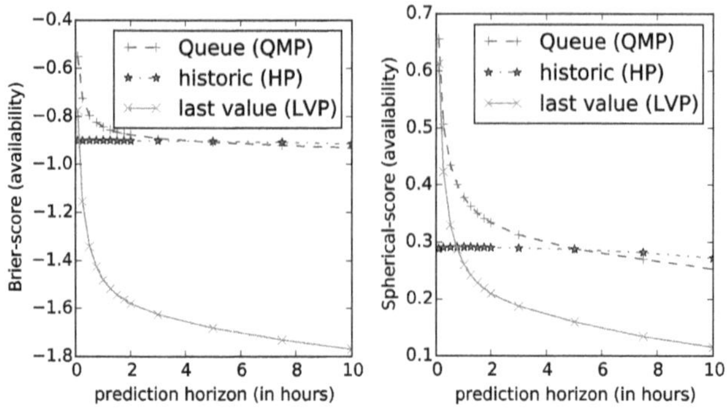

(a) Brier score (b) Spherical score

Figure 7: Average Brier score and spherical score when predicting the number of bikes available (the higher the score, the better is the predictor).

and of HP exhibit the same trend, and second because the average score of LVP is always $-\infty$ with this score (LVP is a deterministic predictor, so when the actual number of bikes is not exactly equal to the prediction, the score is $-\infty$).

For both scoring rules, the shape of the curves are similar: the QMP has the best score for a prediction up to $h = 5$ hours in advance. After 5 hours, HP becomes slightly better. This seems to indicate that knowing the current number of bikes in a station is only important for prediction up to 2 to 3 hours in advance. Moreover, for both scoring rules, LVP quickly has the worst score (for prediction horizons larger than 10min (Brier) or 45min (spherical)). This comes from the deterministic nature of LVP, leading to an over-confidence in wrong predictions that tend to be heavily penalized by these scoring rules.

5.3 Scoring for the Availability of One Bike

Predicting the number of available bikes is important from the system operator's point of view, for example when she decides how to redistribute bikes in the system. However, this metric is less useful from a user's point of view: A user who wants to take a bike from a station is only interested in knowing if there is at least 1 bike available but is less interested in knowing, *e.g.*, if there are 5 or 15 bikes. In this section, we design a scoring rule to evaluate a user-centered prediction, which aims at predicting if there will be "no bikes" or if there will be "1 or more bikes" available at a given station at a given time in the future.

To construct our scoring rule, we assume that a user has preferences that can be modeled by a utility function. If a user decides to go to a station and finds a bike available, she gets a utility $U(\text{Go}, \text{OK})$ greater than $U(\text{Go}, \emptyset)$, the score she would get if she goes and the station is empty. If she decides not to go, her utility is $U(\text{No go}, \emptyset) \geq U(\text{No go}, \text{OK})$, indicating that she can be frustrated by knowing that in fact her trip was possible. If the user knows the probability p for a station to be non-empty, she will decide to go to the station to see if there is a bike if $p \geq p^*$, where p^* is equal to:

$$p^* = \frac{S(\text{Go}, \emptyset) - S(\text{No go}, \emptyset)}{S(\text{Go}, \emptyset) + S(\text{No go}, \text{OK}) - S(\text{Go}, \text{OK}) - S(\text{No go}, \emptyset)}.$$

Theorem 2 of and Section 3.2 of [11] show that for any utility U such that $U(\text{Go}, \text{OK}) \geq U(\text{Go}, \emptyset)$ and $U(\text{No go}, \emptyset) \geq$

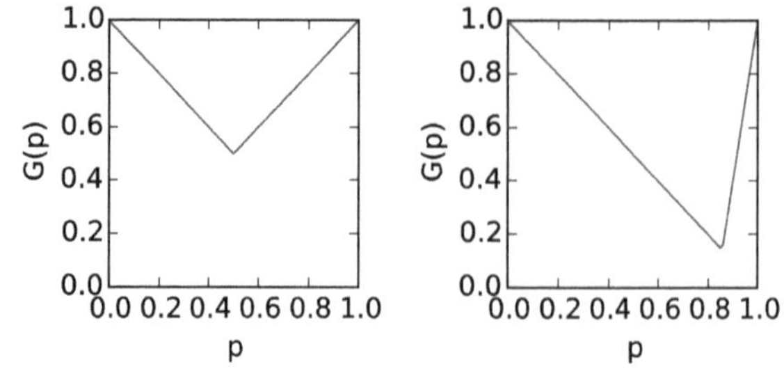

(a) $U(\text{Go}, \emptyset)$=0 (p^*=0.5) (b) $U(\text{Go}, \emptyset)$=−5 (p^*≈0.86)

Figure 8: Example of functions G of Equation (8) that correspond to the scores given by Equation (7).

$U(\text{No go}, \text{OK})$ the following score is a proper scoring rule:

$$S(p, i) = \begin{cases} U(\text{Go}, i) & \text{if } p \geq p^* \\ U(\text{No go}, i) & \text{if } p < p^* \end{cases} \tag{7}$$

More generally, if $G : [0, 1] \to \overline{\mathbb{R}}$ is a convex function, then a scoring rule that assigns the following scores is proper:

$$S(p, \text{OK}) = G(p) + (1 - p)G'(p) \tag{8}$$

$$S(p, \emptyset) = G(p) - pG'(p). \tag{9}$$

Conversely, any proper scoring rules have the form (8)-(9). The function G corresponding to the score (7) is represented in Figure 8 for the parameters $U(\text{Go}, \text{OK}) = U(\text{No go}, \emptyset) = 1$, $U(\text{No go}, \text{OK}) = 0$ and two possible values of $U(\text{Go}, \emptyset)$.

We evaluate numerically the average score on the Paris dataset for the three predictors given in Section 2.3 and the scoring rule (7). We plot the average score of the different predictors as a function of the prediction horizon in Figure 9. We set the parameters $U(\text{Go}, \text{OK}) = U(\text{No go}, \emptyset) = 1$ to normalize the values at 1: a perfect predictor will get a average score of 1. Moreover, we set $U(\text{No go}, \text{OK}) = 0$ and we examine three possible values of $U(\text{Go}, \emptyset) \in \{0, -5, -10\}$. These may indicate increasing degrees of "conservativeness" of a recommendation system, which more heavily penalizes false positives. In practice, we believe that it is reasonable to assume that $U(Go, \emptyset)$ is closer to -10 than 0 to capture that a user is more frustrated by going at a station and not finding a bike than deciding to not go to this station and realizing later that there was in fact a bike available.

First, we remark that in Figure 9, the performance of HP and of the always-go policy depends on the prediction horizon. This comes from the fact the plotted values are averages over predictions issued at 7am, 11am, 3pm and 6pm. Hence, a value at prediction horizon of 10h is the average over values at 5pm, 9pm, 1am and 4am which is different from the average over values at 7am, 11am, 3pm and 6pm. Figure 9a indicates that, on average, a user is more likely to find a bike in the former case.

We note that when $U(\text{Go}, \emptyset) = 0$ (Figure 9a), the score obtained by a predictor corresponds to the proportion of accurate information it gives to the user. Thus, from the score the always-go predictor we can see that, on average, the stations were non-empty 89% of the time.

For a short horizon (5-15min), both LVP and QMP make relatively accurate predictions compared to the other predictors. However the performance of LVP significantly decreases with the prediction horizon, while QMP remains

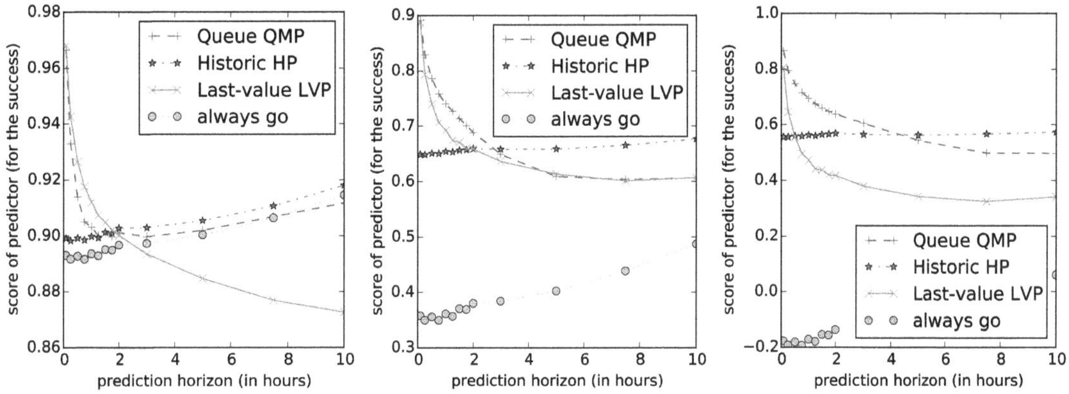

(a) $U(\text{Go}, \emptyset)=0$ (b) $U(\text{Go}, \emptyset)=-5$ (c) $U(\text{Go}, \emptyset)=-10$

Figure 9: Average score (defined in Equation (7)) for measuring the ability of a predictor to predict the feasibility of a trip as a function of the prediction horizon (higher scores mean better predictors).

competitive. In particular in the case $U(\text{Go}, \emptyset) = 0$, notice how QMP separates from LVP and catches up with the better middle and long-term predictors when the horizon becomes large. In the latter case (*i.e.* more than 3 hours), HP is sufficient to give an accurate prediction to the user. This emphasizes how the main source of information used by a predictor influences its "optimal" length of the prediction horizon: The more heavily it relies on the current state of the system (cf. LVP), the more appropriate it will be for short-term predictions. Instead a predictor based on the average behavior of a station such as HP will exhibit better performance for large prediction horizons, because the future availability becomes independent of the current occupancy.

While QMP only slightly outperforms LVP and is comparable to HP in their respective optimal prediction windows, it clearly stands out when it comes to middle-term predictions, *i.e.* for horizons between 15 minutes and 3 hours. In particular, by comparing the accuracy of QMP as a function of $U(\text{Go}, \emptyset)$ indicates that it is better suited than the other predictors for more conservative recommendation systems. This is also confirmed by the analysis of the next section, which looks at the probability that the user makes the wrong decision based on a tuneable probability threshold.

5.4 Computing the Probability of Making Wrong Decisions

In the previous section, we showed that the user's utility function $U(\cdot,\cdot)$ induces a unique threshold p^* that completely defines her "Go/No go" policy, namely:

$$\begin{cases} \text{Go} & \text{if } \mathbb{P}(\text{OK}) \geq p^* \\ \text{No go} & \text{otherwise} \end{cases}$$

In this section, we study the reverse question: given a threshold, what is the proportion of the time that a user decides to go to a station but does not find a bike: $(\text{Go}, \emptyset)$; and what is the proportion of the time that a user decides not to go to a station while there was in fact a bike available: $(\text{No go}, \text{OK})$. For instance, the policy (*i.e.* threshold) $p^* = 0$ corresponds to the "always go" behavior, whereas a policy $p^* = 1$ will always lead to a "No go" decision. We are now interested in how often the different predictors are misleading from the user's perspective, depending on her threshold policy.

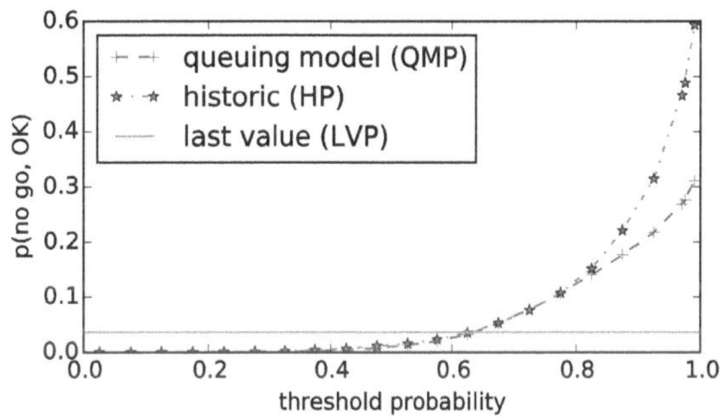

(a) Probability of $(\text{No go}, \text{OK})$

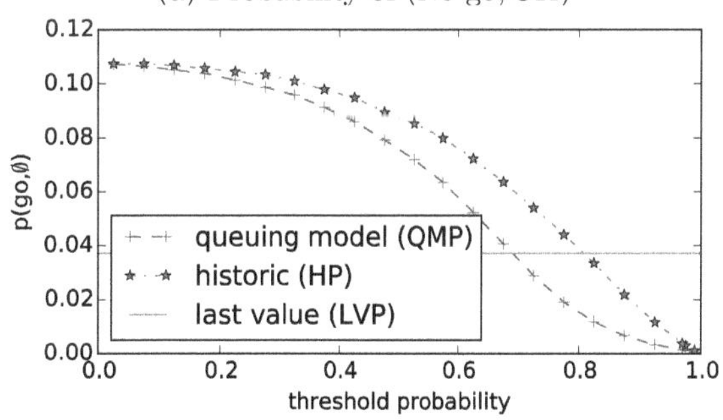

(b) Probability of $(\text{Go}, \emptyset)$

Figure 10: False positive and false negative probabilities as functions of the threshold probability p^* for a prediction horizon of $h = 30$min (lower is better).

In Figure 10 we plot the proportion of bad decisions (wrong "go" decisions or wrong "no go" decisions) for a prediction horizon of 30 minutes as a function of the parameter p^*. When this threshold is set to 0, the proportion of wrong "go" decisions is 11%. This proportion corresponds to the proportion of wrong decisions of an "always go" policy. It is consistent with the value 89% of Figure 9a. For both HP and QMP, the proportion of wrong "go" decisions decreases as the threshold p^* increases while the proportion of wrong "no go" decisions increases. This is due to the fact that, as p^*

increases, the user less often decides to go to the station and therefore misses more opportunities. The situation is different for LVP: In this case, for any threshold $p^* \in (0, 1)$, the decisions taken by a user using LVP are policy-independent since LVP returns a deterministic value (LVP returns either "the trip is feasible with probability 1" or "the trip is feasible with probability 0"). This shows an advantage of informing the user of the probability of the trip feasibility rather than just a recommendation to go/not go: A user can set her own risk-level and decide to go as a function of this level.

6. CONCLUSIONS

We presented an approach to make forecasts of availability in bike sharing systems (BSS). Our approach uses a queuing theoretic model. Unlike previous techniques based on time-series analysis, our model is explanatory in the sense that it provides an explicit (time-inhomogeneous) dynamics, which is successfully validated across an entire one-year dataset of all stations' activity in *Vélib'*, the BSS of the City of Paris.

The model naturally allows one to make *probabilistic* forecasts, *i.e.*, predictions of the probability distribution of the state of a station, whereas previous work has focused on point estimators only. Shifting to this setting requires us to revisit the notion of accuracy of a predictor, which until now was measured by the root mean square error between the estimate and the actual observation. In this paper, we challenged this view and proposed instead new scoring rules for BSS predictors.

We believe that the possibility of making probabilistic forecasts has significant added value, since it may broaden the scope of the applicability of predictive models. For instance, it more directly provides user-centric quantities of interest, useful for journey planning, such as the probability of finding a bike at the origin station (and dually, of finding an empty slot at the destination station). Furthermore, it can be used in more sophisticated recommendation systems that rank stations not only on their expected number of available bikes, but also on higher-order moments (e.g., the standard deviation), to favour those that exhibit less variability.

The extensive model validation conducted in this paper suggests that our model can in general be used in these applications with high accuracy for prediction horizons up to 2-3 hours. For longer time horizons, we see on average no significant gain of a model that takes into account the current number of bikes parked at a station compared to just using the historical trend. In future work, we plan to examine the prediction accuracy in specific "critical" circumstances, for instance during peak times in popular stations that tend to be either completely empty or full.

A limitation of our model is the implicit assumption of independence which allowed us to consider a station as an isolated queuing system. Future work will aim to relax this, by incorporating the BSS network structure in order to improve the prediction accuracy. Furthermore, we will test the generality of the approach by validating the model against other public datasets of availability in BSS.

7. ACKNOWLEDGMENTS

This work is supported by the EU project QUANTICOL, 600708. The authors would also like to thank JCDecaux for providing the access to the data of the *Vélib'* system.

8. REFERENCES

[1] MoReBikeS: Model reuse with bike rental station data. `http://reframe-d2k.org/Challenge` and `http://www.ecmlpkdd2015.org/discovery-challenges`. Accessed 17/04/2015.

[2] G. Bolch, S. Greiner, H. de Meer, and K. Trivedi. *Queueing networks and Markov chains: modeling and performance evaluation with computer science applications.* Wiley, 2005.

[3] P. Borgnat, P. Abry, C. Robardet, J.-B. Rouquier, and E. Fleury. Shared bicycles in a city: A signal processing and data analysis perspective. *Advances in Complex Systems*, 14(3):415–438, 2011.

[4] P. DeMaio. Bike-sharing: Its history, models of provision, and future. In *Velo-city Conference*, 2009.

[5] E. Fishman. Bikeshare: A review of recent literature. *Transport Reviews*, pages 1–22, 2015.

[6] I. Frade and A. Ribeiro. Bicycle sharing systems demand. *Transportation: Can We Do More with Less Resources? - 16th Meeting of the Euro Working Group on Transportation - Porto 2013*, 111:518–527, 2014.

[7] C. Fricker and N. Gast. Incentives and redistribution in homogenous bike-sharing systems with stations of finite capacity. *EURO J. Transp. Logist.*, 2014.

[8] C. Fricker, N. Gast, and A. Mohamed. Mean field analysis for inhomogeneous bike sharing systems. In *Aofa 2012, International Meeting on Probabilistic, Combinatorial and Asymptotic Methods for the Analysis of Algorithms*, 2012.

[9] J. Froehlich, J. Neumann, and N. Oliver. Sensing and predicting the pulse of the city through shared bicycling. In *IJCAI*, volume 9, pages 1420–1426, 2009.

[10] D. George and C. Xia. Fleet-sizing and service availability for a vehicle rental system via closed queueing networks. *European Journal of Operational Research*, 211(1):198–207, 2011.

[11] T. Gneiting and A. E. Raftery. Strictly proper scoring rules, prediction, and estimation. *Journal of the American Statistical Association*, 102(477):359–378, 2007.

[12] M. C. Guenther and J. T. Bradley. Journey data based arrival forecasting for bicycle hire schemes. In *Analytical and Stochastic Modeling Techniques and Applications*, pages 214–231. Springer, 2013.

[13] A. Kaltenbrunner, R. Meza, J. Grivolla, J. Codina, and R. Banchs. Urban cycles and mobility patterns: Exploring and predicting trends in a bicycle-based public transport system. *Pervasive and Mobile Computing*, 6(4):455–466, 2010.

[14] R. Nair, E. Miller-Hooks, R. Hampshire, and A. Bušić. Large-scale vehicular sharing systems: analysis of Vélib'. *International Journal of Sustainable Transportation*, 7(1):85–106, 2013.

[15] J. W. Yoon, F. Pinelli, and F. Calabrese. Cityride: a predictive bike sharing journey advisor. In *Mobile Data Management (MDM), 2012 IEEE 13th International Conference on*, pages 306–311. IEEE, 2012.

Efficient Computation of Polynomial Explanations of Why-Not Questions

Nicole Bidoit
Université Paris Sud / Inria
91405 Orsay Cedex, France
nicole.bidoit@lri.fr

Melanie Herschel
Universität Stuttgart
70569 Stuttgart, Germany
melanie.herschel@ipvs.uni-stuttgart.de

Aikaterini Tzompanaki
Université Paris Sud / Inria
91405 Orsay Cedex, France
katerina.tzompanaki@lri.fr

ABSTRACT

Answering a Why-Not question consists in explaining why a query result does not contain some expected data, called missing answers. This paper focuses on processing Why-Not questions in a query-based approach that identifies the culprit query components. Our first contribution is a general definition of a Why-Not explanation by means of a polynomial. Intuitively, the polynomial provides all possible explanations to explore in order to recover the missing answers, together with an estimation of the number of recoverable answers. Moreover, this formalism allows us to represent Why-Not explanations in a unified way for extended relational models with probabilistic or bag semantics. We further present an algorithm to efficiently compute the polynomial for a given Why-Not question. An experimental evaluation demonstrates the practicality of the solution both in terms of efficiency and explanation quality, compared to existing algorithms.

Categories and Subject Descriptors

H.4 [**Information Systems Applications**]: Miscellaneous

General Terms

Algorithms

Keywords

Why-Not question, explanation, provenance

1. INTRODUCTION

The increasing load of data produced nowadays is coupled with an increasing need for complex data transformations that developers design to process these data in every-day tasks. These transformations, commonly specified declaratively, may result in unexpected outcomes. For instance, given the sample query and data of Fig. 1 on airlines and destination countries, a developer (or traveller) may wonder why Emirates does not appear in the result. Traditionally, she would repeatedly manually analyze the query to identify a possible reason, fix it, and test it to check whether the *missing answer* is now present or if other problems need to be fixed.

Permission to make digital or hard copies of all or part of this work for personal or classroom use is granted without fee provided that copies are not made or distributed for profit or commercial advantage and that copies bear this notice and the full citation on the first page. Copyrights for components of this work owned by others than ACM must be honored. Abstracting with credit is permitted. To copy otherwise, or republish, to post on servers or to redistribute to lists, requires prior specific permission and/or a fee. Request permissions from Permissions@acm.org.
CIKM'15, October 19–23, 2015, Melbourne, Australia.
© 2015 ACM. ISBN 978-1-4503-3794-6/15/10 ...$15.00.
DOI: http://dx.doi.org/10.1145/2806416.2806426.

```
SELECT airline,
       country
FROM Airline A,
     Country C
WHERE ccode = code
AND year < 1985
```

Airline

airline	year	ccode
KLM	1919	1
Qatar	1993	1
Aegean	1987	2
Emirates	1985	3

Country

code	country
1	*Australia*
2	*France*

Figure 1: Example query and data

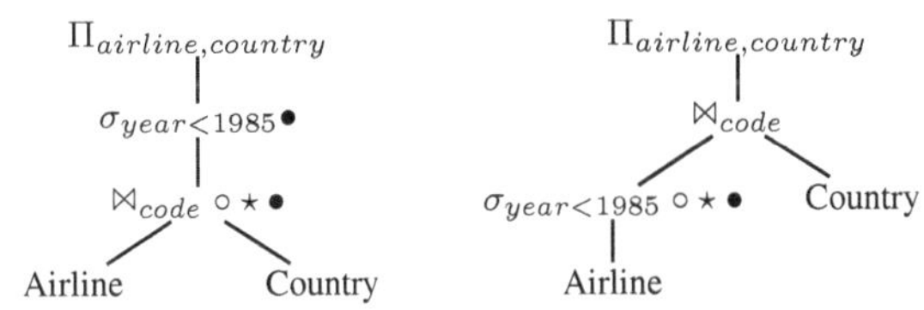

Figure 2: Reordered query trees for the query of Fig. 1 and algorithm results (Why-Not ○, NedExplain ⋆, Conseil •)

Answering such *Why-Not questions*, that is, understanding why some data are *not* part of the result, is valuable in a series of applications, such as query debugging and refinement, data verification or what-if analysis. To help developers *explain missing answers*, different algorithms have recently been proposed for relational and SQL queries and other types of queries (top-k, reverse skyline).

For relational queries, Why-Not questions can be answered for example based on the data (instance-based explanations), the query (query-based explanations), or both (hybrid explanations). We focus on solutions producing query-based explanations, as these are generally more efficient while providing sufficient information for query analysis and debugging. Essentially, a query-based explanation is a set of query conditions that are responsible for pruning out data relevant to the missing answers. Existing methods producing query-based explanations are not satisfactory as they are designed over query trees, making the explanations depending on the topology of a given tree. Consequently, they return different explanations for the same SQL query and may miss explanations.

EXAMPLE 1.1. *Consider again the SQL query and data of Fig. 1 and assume that a developer wants an explanation for the absence of Emirates from the query result. Fig. 2 shows two possible query trees. It also shows the tree operators that Why-Not [7] (○) and NedExplain [3] (⋆) return as query-based explanations as well as the tree operators returned as part of hybrid explanations by Conseil [13, 14] (•). Each algorithm returns a different result for each of the two query trees, and in most cases, it is only a partial result as the true explanation of the missing answer is that* both *the selection is too strict for the tuple* $(Emirates, 1985, 3)$ *from table* $Airline$ *and this tuple does not find join partners in table* $Country$.

The above example clearly shows the shortcomings of existing algorithms. Indeed, the developer first has to understand and reason at the level of query trees instead of reasoning at the level of the declarative SQL query she is familiar with. Second, she always has to wonder whether the explanation is complete, or if there are other explanations that she could consider instead. In this paper, we make the following contributions:

Extended formalization of Why-Not explanation polynomial. We have recently introduced polynomials as Why-Not explanations in the context of the relational model under set semantics [2]. A polynomial provides a complete explanation and is independent of a specific query tree representation, solving the problems illustrated by Ex. 1.1. We now extend Why-Not explanations to the relational model under bag and probabilistic semantics. This confirms the robustness of the chosen polynomial representation, making it a good fit for a unified framework for representing Why-Not explanations. In parallel, we considerably simplify our initial framework by eliminating the formerly used notion of query tableaux.

Efficient *Ted++* algorithm. We show that a naive algorithm computing Why-Not explanations, as presented in [2], is impractical. We thus propose a novel algorithm, *Ted++*, capable of efficiently computing the Why-Not explanation polynomial, based on techniques like schema and data partitioning (allowing for a distributed computation) and advantageous replacement of expensive database evaluations by mathematical calculations.

Experimental validation. We validate our solutions both in terms of efficiency and effectiveness. Our experiments include a comparative evaluation to existing algorithms computing query-based explanations for SQL queries (or sub-languages thereof) as well as a thorough study of *Ted++* performance w.r.t. different parameters. Note that such an evaluation was missing from [2].

The remainder of this paper is structured as follows. Sec. 2 covers related work. Sec. 3 defines in detail our problem setting and the Why-Not explanation polynomials. Next, we discuss the *Ted++* algorithm in Sec 4. Finally, we present our experimental setup and evaluation in Sec. 5 and conclude in Sec. 6.

2. RELATED WORK

The work presented in this paper falls in the category of data provenance research and specifically on explaining missing answers from query results. Due to the lack of space, we focus here on this sub-problem, thus on algorithms answering Why-Not questions, summarized in Tab. 1. This table classifies the algorithms according to the type of explanation they generate and reports the class of query and Why-Not question (simple or complex)[1] they support.

Table 1: Algorithms for answering Why-Not questions

Algorithm	Why-Not question	Explanation format	Query
Query-based explanations			
Why-Not [7]	simple	query operators	SPJU
NedExplain [3]	simple	query operators	SPJUA
Ted [2]	complex	polynomial	conj. queries with inequalities
Hybrid explanations			
Conseil [13, 14]	simple	source table edits + query operators	SPJAN
Instance-based explanations			
MA [16]	simple	source table edits	SPJ
Artemis [15]	complex	source table edits	SPJUA
Meliou *et. al.* [19]	simple	causes (tuples) and responsibility	conjunctive queries
Calvanese *et. al.* [5]	simple	additions to ABox	instance & conj. queries over DL-Lite ontology
Ontology-based explanations			
Cate *et. al.* [6]	simple	tuples concepts	conj. queries with comparisons
Refinement-based explanations			
ConQueR [20] TALOS [21]	complex	refined query	SPJA SPJ
FlexIQ [17]	simple	refined query & Why-Not question	SPJ
Zhang *et. al.* [12]	simple	refined query	Top-k query
Islam *et. al.* [18]	simple	refined query & Why-Not question	Reverse skyline query
WQRTQ [9]	simple	refined query & Why-Not question	Reverse Top-k query
Chen *et. al.* [8]	simple	refined query	Spatial keyword Top-k query

Query-based and hybrid explanations. Why-Not [7] takes as input a simple Why-Not question and a selection, projection, join, and union (SPJU) query and returns the erroneous query operators as query-based explanations. Similarly, NedExplain [3] considers selection, projection, join, and aggregation and unions thereof (SPJUA queries) and simple Why-Not questions as well. The common drawback of the two algorithms is that their design is dependent on a specific query tree representation, thus the explanations proposed are tied to this tree. Moreover, the generated explanations are incomplete. To address this problem, Ted [2] proposes explanations in the form of a polynomial. The shortcomings of this work have already been presented in Sec. 1.

Conseil [13, 14] produces hybrid explanations that include an instance-based and a query-based component. The latter consists in a set of picky query operators. However, as Conseil considers both the data to be possibly incomplete and the query to be possibly faulty, the set of picky query operators associated to a hybrid explanation depends on the set of source edits of the same hybrid explanation.

Instance-based explanations. Missing-Answers (MA) [16] and Artemis [15] compute explanations in the form of source table edits for SPJ queries and SPJUA queries respectively. Meliou *et. al.* [19] study the concepts of causality and responsibility of instance-based explanations for data present or missing in a conjunctive query result. Calvanese *et. al.* [5] compute instance-based explanations on data represented by a DL-Lite ontology.

Ontology-based explanations. Cate *et. al.* [6] have recently introduced this type of explanation that is based on external or data-workload generated ontologies. However, they are completely independent of the query to be analyzed.

Refinement-based explanations. Another approach to answering Why-Not questions is by directly proposing queries that include in their result the missing answers. Several algorithms follow this direction for different types of queries, like relational, Top-K, reverse skyline queries, etc, as listed in Tab. 1. Although these approaches are generally very interesting, they do not focus on pinpointing the erroneous parts of the query. Indeed, the refined queries may contain changes that are not necessarily tied to an erroneous part of the query. Moreover, the changes are based on the database values and do not take into account any semantics or domain knowledge that could render a refinement meaningful for the user.

3. WHY-NOT EXPLANATION POLYNOMIAL

This section introduces a polynomial formalization of query-based Why-Not explanations. We assume the reader familiar with the relational model [1], and we only briefly revisit some relevant notions in Sec. 3.1 while we formalize Why-Not questions. In Sec. 3.2, we define the explanation of a Why-Not question as a polynomial. In Sec. 3.3 we provide a unified general framework for Why-Not explanations in the context of set, bag, and probabilistic semantics databases.

[1]A *simple* Why-Not question involves conditions that impact one relation only, otherwise it is *complex* (see Sec. 3).

R

A	B	R.Id
1	3	Id_1
2	4	Id_2
4	5	Id_3
8	9	Id_4

S

D	E	S.Id
4	8	Id_5
5	3	Id_6
3	9	Id_7

T

B	C	D	T.Id
3	4	5	Id_8
3	8	1	Id_9
5	3	3	Id_{10}
5	9	4	Id_{11}

(a) Sample Instance $\mathcal{I}$

$\mathcal{S} = \{R, S, T\}$

$\Gamma = \{R.B, S.D, T.C\}$

$C = \{c_1, c_2, c_3, c_4, c_5\}$

C

c_1	$R.A > 3$
c_2	$R.B = T.B$
c_3	$T.C \geq 8$
c_4	$T.D = S.D$
c_5	$S.E \geq 3$

(b) query $Q = (\mathcal{S}, \Gamma, C)$ and naming of conditions

$\{R.B{<}S.D, T.C \leq 9\}$

(c) Why-Not question WN

Figure 3: Running example

3.1 Preliminaries

For the moment, we limit our discussion to relational databases under set semantics. A database schema $\mathcal{S}$ is a set of relation schemas. A relation schema R is a set of attributes. We assume each attribute of R qualified, i.e., of the form $R.A$ and for the sake of simplicity we assume a unique domain Dom. $\mathcal{I}$ denotes a database instance over $\mathcal{S}$ and $\mathcal{I}_{|R}$ denotes the instance of a relation $R \in \mathcal{S}$. We assume that each database relation R has a special attribute $R.Id$, which is used as identifier for the tuples in $\mathcal{I}_{|R}$. For any object O (relational or database schema, condition etc), $\mathcal{A}(O)$ denotes the set of attributes occurring in O. Finally, a condition c over $\mathcal{S}$ is defined as an expression of the form $R.A\ \theta\ a$ where $a \in Dom$ or of the form $R.A\ \theta\ S.B$, where $R.A, S.B \in \mathcal{A}(\mathcal{S})$, and $\theta \in \{=, \neq, <, \leq\}$. A condition over two relations is *complex*, otherwise it is *simple*. In this article, we consider conjunctive queries with inequalities. Note that in our approach, the database schema $\mathcal{S}$ denotes the query input schema. In an SQL-like approach, each time we need an instance of a relation, we refer to it by a different name. In this way, we are able to correctly define Why-Not questions in case of self-joins as well.

DEFINITION 3.1 (QUERY Q). *A query Q is specified by the triple $(\mathcal{S}, \Gamma, C)$, where $\mathcal{S}$ is a database schema, $\Gamma \subseteq \mathcal{A}(\mathcal{S})$ is the projection attribute set, and C is a set of conditions over $\mathcal{A}(\mathcal{S})$. The semantics of Q are given by the relational algebra expression $\pi_\Gamma[\sigma_{\bigwedge_{c \in C} c}[\times_{R \in \mathcal{S}}[R]]]$.*

The result of Q over $\mathcal{I}$ is denoted by $Q[\mathcal{I}]$. Note here that we are not concerned about the evaluation/optimization of Q and that any equivalent rewriting of the algebraic expression given in Def. 3.1 is a candidate for evaluating Q.

EXAMPLE 3.1. *Fig. 3 describes our running example. Fig. 3(a) displays an instance $\mathcal{I}$ over $\mathcal{S}=\{R, S, T\}$. Fig. 3(b) displays a query Q over $\mathcal{S}$, whose conditions have been named for convenience. $R.B=T.B$ and $T.D=S.D$ are complex whereas the others are simple conditions. Moreover, $Q[\mathcal{I}]=\{(R.B{:}5, S.D{:}4, T.C{:}9)\}$.*

In our framework, a Why-Not question specifies missing tuples from the result of a query Q through a conjunctive set of conditions. A Why-Not question is related to the result of Q and so its conditions are restricted to the attributes of the output schema of Q.

DEFINITION 3.2 (WHY-NOT QUESTION). *A Why-Not question WN w.r.t. Q is defined as a set of conditions over Γ.*

The notion of complex and simple conditions is extended to complex and simple Why-Not questions in a straightforward manner. Due to lack of space, we do not provide here more real-world examples of Why-Not questions and refer the reader to scenarios in [4].

As we said, a Why-Not question WN summarizes a set of (missing) tuples that the user expected to find in the query result. To be able to obtain these missing tuples as query results, data from the input relation instances that satisfy WN need to be combined by the query. The candidate data combinations are what we call *compatible* tuples and can be computed using WN as in Def. 3.3.

DEFINITION 3.3 (COMPATIBLE TUPLES). *Consider the query $Q_{WN}=(\mathcal{S}, \mathcal{A}(\mathcal{S}), WN)$, where $\mathcal{S}$ is also the input schema of Q. The set CT of compatible tuples is the result of the query Q_{WN} over $\mathcal{I}$.*

We further introduce the notion of a *well founded* Why-Not question. Intuitively, a Why-Not question can be answered under a query-based approach, only if some data in $\mathcal{I}$ match the Why-Not question (otherwise instance-based explanations should be sought for). Moreover, a Why-Not question is meaningful if it tracks data not already returned by the query.

DEFINITION 3.4 (WELL FOUNDED WHY-NOT QUESTION). *A Why-Not question WN is said to be well founded if $CT \neq \emptyset$ and $\pi_\Gamma[CT] \cap Q[\mathcal{I}]=\emptyset$.*

EXAMPLE 3.2. *Continuing Ex. 3.1, we may wonder why there is not a tuple for which $R.B{<}S.D$ and $T.C \leq 9$. According to Def. 3.2, this Why-Not question can be seen as the conjunction of the conditions $R.B{<}S.D \wedge T.C \leq 9$ (Fig. 3(c)). Since $R.B{<}S.D$ is a complex condition, WN is a complex Why-Not question. The compatible tuples set CT is the result of the query $Q_{WN}=\sigma_{R.B<S.D \wedge T.C \leq 9}[R \times S \times T]$, which contains 12 tuples. For example, one compatible tuple is $\tau_1=(R.Id{:}1, R.A{:}1, R.B{:}3, S.Id{:}5, S.D{:}4, S.E{:}8, T.Id{:}8, T.B{:}3, T.C{:}4, T.D{:}5)$.*

Each tuple in CT could have led to a missing tuple, if it was not eliminated by some of the query conditions. Thus, explaining WN amounts to identifying these blocking query conditions.

3.2 Why-Not Explanation

To build the query based explanation of WN, we start by specifying what explains that a compatible tuple τ did not lead to an answer. Intuitively, the explanation consists of the query conditions pruning out τ.

DEFINITION 3.5 (EXPLANATION FOR τ). *Let $\tau \in CT$ be a compatible tuple w.r.t. WN, given Q. Then, the explanation for τ is the set of conditions $\mathcal{E}_\tau=\{c | c \in C$ and $\tau \not\models c\}$.*

EXAMPLE 3.3. *Consider the compatible tuple τ_1 in Ex. 3.2. The conditions of Q (see Ex. 3.1), not satisfied by τ_1 are: c_1, c_3, and c_4. So, the explanation for τ_1 is $\mathcal{E}_{\tau_1}=\{c_1, c_3, c_4\}$.*

Having defined the explanation w.r.t. one compatible tuple, the explanation for WN is obtained by simply summing up the expression $\sum_{\tau \in CT} \prod_{c \in \mathcal{E}_\tau} c$. We justify modelling the explanation of τ with a product (meaning conjunction) of conditions by the fact that in order for τ to 'survive' the query conditions and give rise to a missing tuple, every single condition in the explanation must be 'repaired'. The sum (meaning disjunction) of the products for each $\tau \in CT$ means that if any explanation is 'correctly repaired', the associated τ will produce a missing tuple.

Of course, several compatible tuples can share the same explanation. Thus, the final Why-Not explanation is a polynomial having as variables the query conditions and as integer coefficients the number of compatible tuples sharing an explanation.

DEFINITION 3.6 (WHY-NOT EXPLANATION). *With the same assumption as before, the Why-Not explanation for WN is defined as the polynomial*

$$\text{PEX} = \sum_{\mathcal{E}\in E} coef_{\mathcal{E}} \prod_{c\in\mathcal{E}} c$$

where $E = 2^C$ and $coef_{\mathcal{E}} \in \{0, \ldots, |CT|\}$.

Intuitively, E contains all potential explanations, and each of these explanations prunes from zero to at most $|CT|$ compatible tuples. Moreover, an important property of *PEX* is the fact that $coef_{\mathcal{E}} = |\{\tau \in CT | \mathcal{E}$ is the explanation for $\tau\}|$, meaning that $coef_{\mathcal{E}}$ equals the number of compatible tuples with the same explanation.

Each term of the polynomial provides an alternative explanation to be explored by the user who wishes to recover some missing tuples. Additionally, the polynomial offers, through its coefficients, some useful hints to users interested in the *number* of recoverable tuples. More precisely, by choosing an explanation $\mathcal{E}$ to repair, we obtain an upper bound for the number of compatible tuples that can be recovered. The upper bound is the sum of the coefficients of all the explanations that are sub-sets of (the set of conditions of) $\mathcal{E}$. Consequently, the coefficients could be used to answer Why-Not questions of the form *Why-Not $x missing tuples?*.

EXAMPLE 3.4. *In Ex. 3.3 we found the explanation $\{c_1, c_3, c_4\}$, which is translated to the polynomial term $c_1 * c_3 * c_4$. Taking into consideration all the 12 compatible tuples of our example, we obtain the following* PEX *polynomial: $2*c_1*c_4 + 2*c_1*c_3*c_4 + 4*c_1*c_2*c_4 + 2*c_1*c_2*c_3 + 2*c_1*c_2*c_3*c_4$. In the polynomial, each addend, composed by a coefficient and an explanation, captures a way to obtain missing tuples. For instance, the explanation $c_1 * c_2 * c_4$ indicates that we may recover some missing answers if c_1 and c_2 and c_4 are changed. Then, the sum of its coefficient 4 and the coefficient 2 of the explanation $c_1 * c_4$ ($\{c_1, c_4\} \subseteq \{c_1, c_2, c_4\}$) indicates that we can recover from 0 to 6 tuples.*

As the visualization of the polynomial per se may be cumbersome and thus not easy for a user to manipulate, some post-processing steps could be applied. Depending on the application or needs, only a subset of the explanations could be returned like for instance minimum explanations (i.e., for which no sub-explanations exist), or explanations giving the opportunity to recover a specific number of tuples, or have specific condition types etc.

3.3 Extension: Bag & Probabilistic Semantics

So far, we have considered databases under *set* semantics only. In this section, we discuss how the definition of Why-Not explanation (Def. 3.6) extends to settings with conjunctive queries over bag and probabilistic semantics.

K-relations, as introduced in [10], capture in a unified manner relations under set, bag, and probabilistic semantics. Briefly, tuples in a K-relation are annotated with elements in K. In our case, we consider that K is a set of unique tuple identifiers, similar to our special attribute $R.Id$ in Sec. 3.1.

In what follows, we use the notion of *how*-provenance of tuples in the result of a query Q. The how-provenance of $t \in Q(\mathcal{I})$ is modelled as the polynomial obtained by the positive algebra on K-relations, proposed in [10]. Briefly, each t is annotated with a polynomial where variables are tuple identifiers and coefficients are natural numbers. Roughly, if t results from a selection operator on t_1 annotated with Id_1, then t is also annotated with Id_1. If t is the result of the join of t_1 and t_2, then t is annotated with $Id_1 Id_2$.

We compute the *generalized* Why-Not explanation polynomial PEX_{gen} as follows. Firstly, we compute the how-provenance for compatible tuples in CT by evaluation of the query Q_{WN} (Def. 3.3) w.r.t. the algebra in [10]. Recall that Q_{WN} contains only selection and join operators. Thus, each compatible tuple τ in CT is annotated with its how-provenance polynomial, denoted by η_τ.

Then, we associate the expressions of *how* and *why-not* provenance. In order to do this, for each compatible tuple τ in CT, we combine its how-provenance polynomial η_τ with its explanation $\mathcal{E}_\tau$ (Def. 3.5). So, each τ is associated with the expression $\eta_\tau \mathcal{E}_\tau$.

Finally, we sum the combined expressions for all compatible tuples, which leads to the expression $\sum_{\tau \in CT} \eta_\tau \mathcal{E}_\tau$.

We now briefly comment on how PEX_{gen} is instantiated to deal either with the set, bag, or probabilistic semantics. Indeed, the 'specialization' of PEX_{gen} relies on the interpretation of the elements in K, that is on a function $Eval$ from K to some set L. For the set semantics, each tuple in a relation occurs only once. This results in choosing L to be the singleton $\{1\}$ and mapping each tuple identifier to 1. It is then quite obvious to note, for the set semantics, that $PEX_{gen} = PEX$ (Def. 3.6). In the same spirit, for bag semantics, L is chosen as the set of natural numbers $\mathbb{N}$ and each tuple identifier is mapped to its number of occurences. Finally, for probabilistic databases, L is chosen as the interval $[0, 1]$ and each tuple identifier is mapped to its occurrence probability.

Thus, the generalized definition of Why-Not explanation is parametrized by the mapping $Eval$ of the annotations (elements in K) in the set L.

DEFINITION 3.7. *(Generalized Why-Not explanation polynomial) Given a query Q over a database schema $\mathcal{S}$ of K-relations, the generalized Why-Not explanation polynomial for WN is*

$$\text{PEX}_{gen} = \sum_{\mathcal{E}\in E} \Big(\sum_{\tau \in CT s.t.\ \mathcal{E}_\tau = \mathcal{E}} Eval(\eta_\tau)\Big)\mathcal{E}$$

where $E = 2^C$, η_τ is the how-provenance of τ, and $Eval{:}K \to L$ maps the elements of K to values in L.

4. TED++ ALGORITHM

The naive Ted algorithm [2] implements the definitions of [2] for Why-Not explanations in a straightforward manner. Essentially, Ted first enumerates the set of compatible tuples. Then, it computes the explanation for each compatible tuple, leading to the computation of the final Why-Not explanation. However, both of these steps make Ted computationally prohibitive. Not only is the computation of the set of compatible tuples time and space consuming as it often requires cross product executions, but the same holds for the iteration over this (potentially very large) set. Ted's time complexity is $O(n^{|\mathcal{S}|})$, $n = max(\{|\mathcal{I}_R|\})$, $R \in \mathcal{S}$. As experiments in Sec. 5 confirm, this complexity renders Ted impractical.

To overcome Ted's poor performance, we propose *Ted++*. The main feature of *Ted++* is to completely avoid enumerating and iterating over the set CT, thus it significantly reduces both space and time consumption. Instead, *Ted++* opts for (i) iterating over the space of possible explanations, which is expected to be much smaller, (ii) computing *partial* sets of *passing* compatible tuples, and (iii) computing the *number* of *eliminated* compatible tuples for each explanation. Intuitively, passing tuples w.r.t. an explanation are tuples satisfying the conditions of the explanation. Finally, we compute the polynomial based on mathematical calculations.

Alg. 1 provides an outline of *Ted++*. The input includes the query $Q = (\mathcal{S}, \Gamma, C)$, the Why-Not question WN and the input instance $\mathcal{I}$. Firstly in Alg. 1, line 1, all potential explanations (combinations of the conditions in C) are enumerated ($E = 2^C$). The remaining steps, discussed in the next subsections, aim at computing the coefficient of each explanation. To illustrate the concepts

Algorithm 1: *Ted++*

Input: $Q{=}(\mathcal{S},\Gamma,C), \mathcal{I}, WN$
Output: *PEX*
1 $E \leftarrow$ powerset(C);
2 $\mathcal{P} \leftarrow$validPartitioning($\mathcal{S}$, WN); * Def. 4.1 *
3 **for** $Part$ *in* $\mathcal{P}$ **do**
4 $\quad CT_{|Part} \leftarrow (Part, \mathcal{A}(Part), WN_{|Part})[\mathcal{I}_{|Part}]$;
5 coefficientEstimation(E, $Partition$);
6 *PEX* $\leftarrow$post-processing(); * Eq. (F) *
7 **return** PEX;

introduced in the detailed discussions, we will rely on our running example, for which Fig. 4 shows all relevant intermediate results. It should be read bottom-up. For convenience, in our examples, we use subscript i instead of c_i.

The subsequent discussion on *Ted++* can be considered as a proof sketch of the following theorem.

THEOREM 4.1. *Given a query Q, a Why-Not question WN and an input instance $\mathcal{I}$, Ted++ computes exactly* PEX.

4.1 Partial Compatible Tuples Computation

Using the conditions in WN, *Ted++* partitions the schema $\mathcal{S}$ (Alg. 1, line 2) into components of relations connected by the conditions in WN (Def. 4.1).

DEFINITION 4.1. *(Valid Partitioning of $\mathcal{S}$). Given WN, the partitioning of a database schema $\mathcal{S}$ into k partitions, denoted $\mathcal{P} = \{Part_1, \ldots, Part_k\}$, is* valid *if each $Part_i$, $i{\in}\{1,\ldots,k\}$ is minimal w.r.t. the following property:*
if $R{\in}Part_i$ and $R'{\in}\mathcal{S}$ s.t. $\exists c{\in}WN$ with $\mathcal{A}(c){\cap}\mathcal{A}(R'){\neq}\emptyset$ and $\mathcal{A}(c){\cap}\mathcal{A}(R){\neq}\emptyset$ then $R'{\in}Part_i$.

The partitioning of $\mathcal{S}$ allows for handling compatible tuples more efficiently, by 'cutting' them in distinct meaningful 'chunks'. We refer to chunks of compatible tuples as *partial* compatible tuples and group them in sets depending on the partition they belong to.

The set $CT_{|Part}$, where $Part{\in}\mathcal{P}$ is obtained by evaluating the query $Q_{Part}{=}(Part, \mathcal{A}(Part),\ WN_{|Part})$ over $\mathcal{I}_{|Part}$ (Alg. 1, line 4). $WN_{|Part}$ and $\mathcal{I}_{|Part}$ denote the restriction of WN and $\mathcal{I}$ over the relations in $Part$, respectively.

EXAMPLE 4.1. *The valid partitioning of $\mathcal{S}$ is $Part_1{=}\{R,S\}$ (because of the condition $R.B{<}S.D$) and $Part_2{=}\{T\}$. The sets of partial compatible tuples $CT_{|Part_1}$ and $CT_{|Part_2}$ are given in the bottom line of Fig. 4.*

It is easy to prove that the valid partitioning of $\mathcal{S}$ is unique and that the set CT can be computed from the sets $CT_{|Part}$.

LEMMA 4.1. *Let $\mathcal{P}$ be the valid partitioning of $\mathcal{S}$. Then, $CT{=} \times_{Part\in\mathcal{P}} [CT_{|Part}]$.*

Lemma. 4.1 makes it clear how to compute CT from partial compatible tuples. Our algorithm is designed in a way that avoids computing CT and relies on the computation of $CT_{|Part}$ only.

Next, we compute the number of compatible tuples pruned by each potential explanation, using the partial compatible tuple sets. In this way we calculate the coefficient of the terms in the polynomial. Since from this point on we are only handling compatible tuples, we omit the word 'compatible' to lighten the discussion.

Algorithm 2: coefficientEstimation

Input: E explanations space, $\mathcal{P}$ valid partitioning of $\mathcal{S}$
1 **for** $\mathcal{E}{\in}E$ **access in ascending size order** **do**
2 $\quad$ Compute $part_{\mathcal{E}}$;
3 $\quad$ **if** $|\ \mathcal{E}\ | = 1$ **then**
4 $\quad\quad$ materialize $V_{\mathcal{E}}$;
5 $\quad\quad$ $\beta_{\mathcal{E}} \leftarrow$ Eq. (B);
6 $\quad$ **else**
7 $\quad\quad$ **if** $\alpha_{subcombination\ of\ \mathcal{E}} \neq 0$ **then**
8 $\quad\quad\quad$ $\{\mathcal{E}1,\mathcal{E}2\} \leftarrow$ subCombinationsOf($\mathcal{E}$);
9 $\quad\quad\quad$ $\Gamma_{12} \leftarrow \Gamma_1 \cap \Gamma_2$; *$\Gamma_i$ is the output schema of $V_{\mathcal{E}i}$*
10 $\quad\quad\quad$ **if** $\Gamma_{12} \neq \emptyset$ **then**
11 $\quad\quad\quad\quad$ $V_{\mathcal{E}} \leftarrow V_{\mathcal{E}1} \bowtie_{\Gamma_{12}} V_{\mathcal{E}2}$;
12 $\quad\quad\quad\quad$ materialize $V_{\mathcal{E}}$;
13 $\quad\quad\quad$ **else**
14 $\quad\quad\quad\quad$ $|\ V_{\mathcal{E}}\ | \leftarrow |\ V_{\mathcal{E}1}\ | * |\ V_{\mathcal{E}2}\ |$;
15 $\quad\quad$ **else**
16 $\quad\quad\quad$ $|\ V_{\mathcal{E}}\ | \leftarrow |\ V_{\mathcal{E}1}\ | * |\ V_{\mathcal{E}2}\ |$;
17 $\quad\quad$ $\beta_{\mathcal{E}} \leftarrow \prod_{Part\in part_{\mathcal{E}}} |CT_{|Part}| - |\ (\bigcup_{i=1}^{n} V_{ci})^{ext}\ |$; * Eq. (E) *
18 $\quad$ $\alpha_{\mathcal{E}} \leftarrow$ Eq. (A);

4.2 Polynomial Coefficient Estimation

Each set $\mathcal{E}$ in the powerset E is in fact a potential explanation that is further processed. This process is meant to associate with $\mathcal{E}$ (i) the set of partitions $part_{\mathcal{E}}$ on which $\mathcal{E}$ is defined, (ii) the view definition $V_{\mathcal{E}}$ meant to store the passing partial tuples w.r.t. $\mathcal{E}$[2], and (iii) the number $\alpha_{\mathcal{E}}$ of tuples eliminated by $\mathcal{E}$.

Alg. 2 describes how we process E in ascending order of explanation size. This enables us to reuse results obtained for sub-explanations and in combination with mathematics, avoid cross product computations.

We first determine the set of partitions for an explanation $\mathcal{E}$ as $part_{\mathcal{E}}{=}\cup_{c\in\mathcal{E}}\{Part_c\}$, where $Part_c$ contains at least one relation over which c is specified.

EXAMPLE 4.2. *Consider $\mathcal{E}_1{=}\{c_1\}$ and $\mathcal{E}_2{=}\{c_2\}$. From Fig. 3(b) and the partitions in Fig. 4, we can see that c_1 impacts only $Part_1$, whereas c_2 spans over $Part_1$ and $Part_2$. Hence, $part_{\mathcal{E}_1}{=}\{Part_1\}$ and $part_{\mathcal{E}_2}{=}\{Part_1, Part_2\}$. Then, $\mathcal{E}{=}\{c_1,c_2\}$ is impacted by the union of $part_{\mathcal{E}_1}$ and $part_{\mathcal{E}_2}$, thus $part_{\mathcal{E}}{=}\{Part_1, Part_2\}$.*

We use Eq. (A) to calculate the number $\alpha_{\mathcal{E}}$ of eliminated tuples, using the number $\beta_{\mathcal{E}}$ of eliminated *partial* tuples and the cardinality of the partitions not in $part_{\mathcal{E}}$. Intuitively, this formula extends the partial tuples to "full" tuples over CT's schema.

$$\alpha_{\mathcal{E}} = \beta_{\mathcal{E}} * \prod_{Part\in\overline{part_{\mathcal{E}}}} |CT_{|Part}|, \qquad \text{(A)}$$

where $\overline{part_{\mathcal{E}}}{=}\mathcal{P}\setminus part_{\mathcal{E}}$. Note that when $\overline{part_{\mathcal{E}}}$ is empty, we abusively consider that $\prod_{\emptyset}{=}1$.

The presentation now focuses on calculating $\beta_{\mathcal{E}}$. Two cases arise depending on the size of $\mathcal{E}$.

Atomic explanations. We start with atomic explanations $\mathcal{E}$ containing only one condition c (Algorithm 2 lines 3-5). We firstly compute the set of *passing* partial tuples w.r.t. c, i.e., the tuples that satisfy c, which we store in the view V_c:

$$V_c = \begin{cases} \pi_{\{R\_id|R\in Part\}}(\sigma_c[CT_{|Part}]) \text{ if } part_{\mathcal{E}}{=}\{Part\} \\ \pi_{\{R\_id|R\in Part_1\cup Part_2\}}([CT_{|Part_1}] \bowtie_c [CT_{|Part_2}]) \\ \qquad\qquad \text{if } part_{\mathcal{E}}{=}\{Part_1, Part_2\} \end{cases}$$

[2]We choose to store passing rather than eliminated tuples as they are usually less numerous. In an optimized version this decision could be made dynamically based on view cardinality estimation.

Then, the number of eliminated partial tuples by $\mathcal{E}$ is

$$\beta_{\mathcal{E}} = \prod_{Part \in part_{\mathcal{E}}} |CT_{|Part}| - |V_c| \qquad \text{(B)}$$

EXAMPLE 4.3. *For* c_2*, we have* $part_{c_2}=\{Part_1, Part_2\}$*, so* $V_{c2}=\pi_{R\_Id,S\_Id,T\_Id}([CT_{|Part_1}]\bowtie_{R.B=T.B}[CT_{|Part_2}])$*. This results in* $|V_{c_2}|=4$*, and by Eq. (B) we obtain* $\beta_{c2}=|CT_{|Part1}| * |CT_{|Part2}|-|V_{c2}|=3*4-4=8$*. Since all partitions of* $\mathcal{P}$ *are in* $part_{c2}$*, applying Equ. (A) results in* $\alpha_{c2}=\beta_{c2}=8$*. For* c_3*,* $\beta_{c3}=|CT_{|Part_2}|-V_{c3}=4-2=2$*, so* $\alpha_{c3}=3*2=6$*. Fig. 4 (second level) displays the process for all atomic explanations.*

Non atomic explanations. Now, assume that $\mathcal{E}=\{c_1,\ldots,c_n\}$, $n>1$ (Alg. 2, lines 6-16). For the moment, we assume that the conditions in $\mathcal{E}$ share the same schema, so the intersection and union of V_{ci} for $i=1,\ldots,n$ are well-defined. Firstly, we compute the view $V_{\mathcal{E}}$ of passing partial tuples w.r.t. $\mathcal{E}$ as $V_{\mathcal{E}}=V_{c1}\cap\ldots\cap V_{cn}$. To compute the number of partial tuples pruned out by $\mathcal{E}$, we need to find the number of partial tuples pruned out by c_1 and ... and c_n, i.e., $\beta_{\mathcal{E}}=|\overline{V_{c1}}\cap\cdots\cap\overline{V_{cn}}|$. By the well-known *DeMorgan law* [22], we have $\beta_{\mathcal{E}}=|\overline{V_{c1}\cup\cdots\cup V_{cn}}|$, which spares us from computing the complements of V_{ci}.

To compute the cardinality of the union of the V_{ci}, we rely on the *Principle of Inclusion and Exclusion for counting* [11]:

$$|\bigcup_{i=1}^{n} V_{c_i}| = \sum_{\emptyset\neq J\subseteq[n]} (-1)^{|J|+1} |\bigcap_{j\in J} V_{cj}|$$

We further rewrite the previous formula to reuse results obtained for sub-combinations of $\mathcal{E}$, obtaining Eq. (C).

$$|\bigcup_{i=1}^{n} V_{ci}| = |\bigcup_{i=1}^{n-1} V_{ci}| + |V_{cn}| + \sum_{\emptyset\neq J\subseteq[n-1]} (-1)^{|J|} |\bigcap_{j\in J} V_{cj}\cap V_{cn}| \qquad \text{(C)}$$

At this point, we can compute $\beta_{\mathcal{E}}$. However, so far we assumed that the conditions in $\mathcal{E}$ have the same schema. In the general case, this does not hold and we have to "extend" the schema of a view V_c to the one of $V_{\mathcal{E}}$, in order to ensure set operations to be well-defined. The cardinality of an extended V_c^{ext} is given by Eq. (D).

$$|V_c^{ext}| = \prod_{Part\in part_{\mathcal{E}}\setminus part_c} |CT_{Part}| * |V_c| \qquad \text{(D)}$$

Based on Eq. (D) we obtain Eq. (E) that generalizes Eq. (C).

$$|(\bigcup_{i=1}^{n} V_{ci})^{ext}| = |(\bigcup_{i=1}^{n-1} V_{ci})^{ext}| + |V_{cn}^{ext}| + \sum_{\emptyset\neq J\subseteq[n-1]} (-1)^{|J|} |((\bowtie V_{cj})_{j\in J}\bowtie V_{cn})^{ext}| \qquad \text{(E)}$$

In Eq. (E) we have replaced the intersection with natural join. The cardinalities of the views $V_{\mathcal{E}'}=(\bowtie V_{cj})_{j\in J}\bowtie V_{cn}$ associated with $\mathcal{E}'$ for $|J|<n-1$, have already been computed by previous steps and have only to be extended to the schema of $V_{\mathcal{E}}$. When $|J|=n-1$, then $V_{\mathcal{E}'}=V_{\mathcal{E}}$. A detailed discussion on how and when we materialize the view $V_{\mathcal{E}}$ is given shortly after.

Now, we trivially compute the number $\beta_{\mathcal{E}}$ of eliminated partial tuples as the complement of $|(\bigcup_{i=1}^{n} V_{ci})^{ext}|$ (Alg. 2, line 17). The number of 'full' eliminated tuples is then calculated by Eq. (A).

EXAMPLE 4.4. *To illustrate the concepts introduced above, please follow on Fig. 4 below discussion.*

For the explanation c_2c_3*, Eq. (E) gives:* $|(V_2\cup V_3)^{ext}|=|V_2^{ext}|+|V_3^{ext}|-|(V_2\bowtie V_3)^{ext}|$*. The schema of* $part_{23}=\{Part_1, Part_2\}$ *is* $\Gamma_{23}=\{R\_Id, S\_Id, T\_Id\}$*. The view* V_2 *has already a matching schema, thus* $|V_2^{ext}|=|V_2|=4$*. For* V_3*,* $\Gamma_3=\{T\_Id\}$*, we thus apply Eq. (D) and obtain* $|V_3^{ext}|=|V_{Part_1}|*|V_3|=3*2=6$*. Still,* $|V_{23}|=|(V_2\bowtie V_3)^{ext}|$ *remains to be calculated. Intuitively, because* V_2 *and* V_3 *target schemas share attribute* T_Id*,* $V_{23}=V_2\bowtie_{T\_Id}V_3$*. The view* V_{23} *is materialized and contains 2 tuples (as shown in Fig. 4). So, finally, from Eq. (E) we obtain* $|(V_2\cup V_3)^{ext}|=4+6-2=8$*. Since* $|Part_1|*|Part_2|=12$ *then* $\beta_{23}=12-8=4$*, and by Eq. (A)* $\alpha_{23}=4$*.*

We now focus on the explanation c_3c_5*. The schemas of* V_3 *and* V_5 *are disjoint and intuitively* $V_{35}=V_3 X V_5$*. Here,* V_{35} *is not materialized, we simply calculate* $|V_{35}|=|V_3|*|V_5|=6$*. Then,* $|\beta_{35}|=12-(12+6-6)=0$*. As we will see later, these steps are never performed in our algorithm. The fact that* c_5 *does not eliminate any tuple (see* $\alpha_5=0$ *in Fig. 4) implies that neither do any of its super-combinations. Thus, a priori we know that* $\alpha_{35}=\alpha_{235}=\ldots=0$*.*

Finally, we illustrate the case of a bigger size combination, for example $c_2c_3c_4$ *of size 3. Eq. (E) yields* $|(V_2\cup V_3\cup V_4)^{ext}|=|(V_2\cup V_4)^{ext}|+|V_3^{ext}|-|(V_2\bowtie V_3)^{ext}|-|(V_4\bowtie V_3)^{ext}|+|(V_2\bowtie V_3\bowtie V_4)^{ext}|$*. All terms of the right side of the equation are available from previous iterations, except for* $|(V_2\bowtie V_3\bowtie V_4)^{ext}|$*. As before, we check the common attributes of the views and obtain* $V_{234}=V_{24}\bowtie_{R\_Id,S\_Id,T\_Id}V_3$*. So,* $|(V_2\cup V_3\cup V_4)^{ext}|=6+6-2-1+0=9$ *and* $\beta_{234}=\alpha_{234}=12-9=3$*. In the same way, we compute all the possible explanations until* $c_1c_2c_3c_4c_5$*.*

View Materialization: when and how. To decide when and how to materialize the views for the explanations, we partition the set of the views associated with the conditions in $\mathcal{E}$. Consider the relation $\sim$ defined over these views by $V_i\sim V_j$ if the target schemas of V_i and V_j have at least one common attribute. Consider the transitive closure $\sim^*$ of $\sim$ and the induced partitioning of $\mathcal{V}_{\mathcal{E}}$ through $\sim^*$.

When this partitioning is a singleton, $V_{\mathcal{E}}$ needs to be materialized (Alg. 2, line 9). The materialization of $V_{\mathcal{E}}$ is specified by joining the views associated with the sub-conditions, which may be done in more than one way, as usual. For example, for the combination $c_2c_3c_4$, V_{234} can either be computed through $V_{23}\bowtie V_4$ or $V_{24}\bowtie V_3$ or $V_{34}\bowtie V_2$ or $V_2\bowtie V_3\bowtie V_4$... because all these views are known from previous iterations. The choice of the query used to materialize $V_{\mathcal{E}}$ is done based on a cost function. This function gives priority to materializing $V_{\mathcal{E}}$ by means of one join, which is always possible: because $V_{\mathcal{E}}$ needs to be materialized, we know that at least one view associated with a sub-combination of size $n-1$ has been materialized. In other words, priority is given to using at least one materialized view associated with one of the largest sub-combinations. For our example, it means that either $V_{23}\bowtie V_4$ or $V_{24}\bowtie V_3$ or $V_{34}\bowtie V_2$ is considered. In order to choose among the one-join queries computing $V_{\mathcal{E}}$, we favour a one-join query $V_i\bowtie V_j$ minimal w.r.t. $|V_i|+|V_j|$. For the example, and considering also Fig. 4 we find that $|V_2|+|V_{34}|=|V_4|+|V_{23}|=5$ and $|V_3|+|V_{24}|=3$. So, the query used for the materialization is $V_3\bowtie V_{24}$ (its result being empty in our example). Nevertheless, we avoid the materialization of $V_{\mathcal{E}}$ if the partitioning is a singleton (Alg. 2, line 9

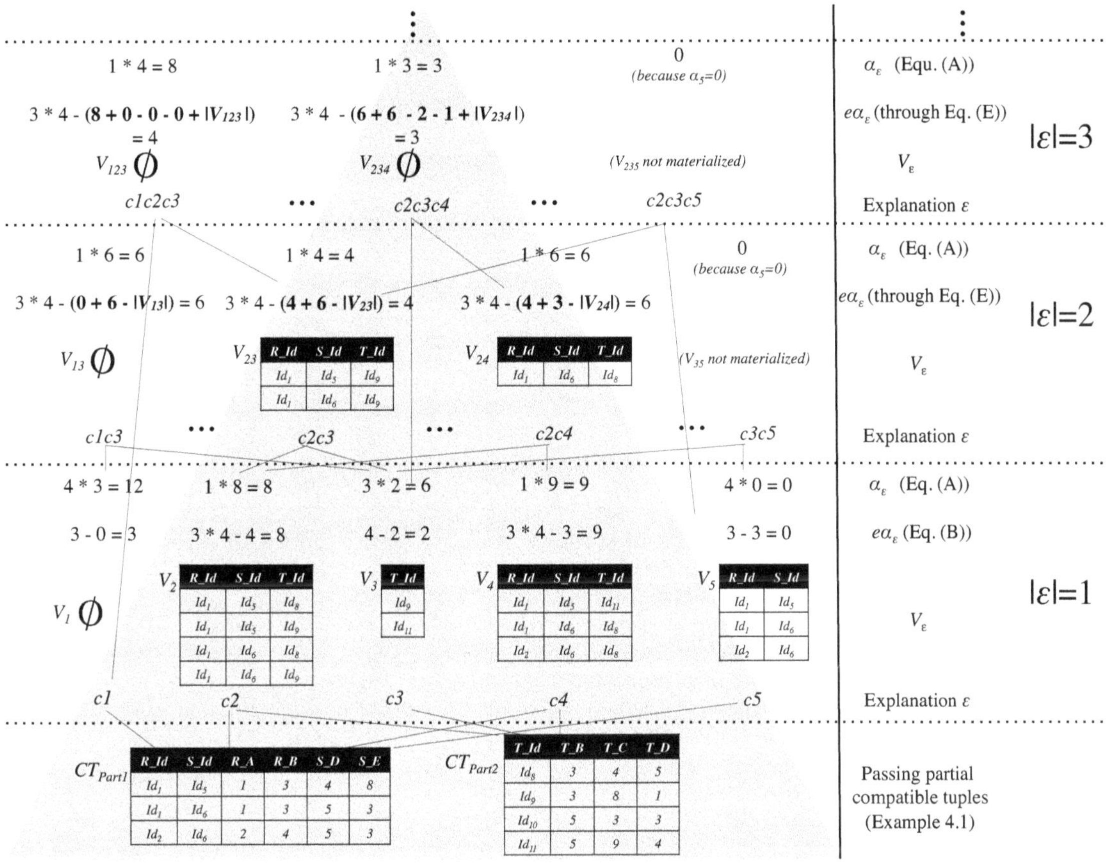

R_Id	S_Id	T_Id
Id_1	Id_5	Id_9
Id_1	Id_6	Id_9

R_Id	S_Id	T_Id
Id_1	Id_6	Id_8

R_Id	S_Id	T_Id
Id_1	Id_5	Id_8
Id_1	Id_5	Id_9
Id_1	Id_6	Id_8
Id_1	Id_6	Id_9

T_Id
Id_9
Id_{11}

R_Id	S_Id	T_Id
Id_1	Id_5	Id_{11}
Id_1	Id_6	Id_8
Id_2	Id_6	Id_8

R_Id	S_Id
Id_1	Id_5
Id_1	Id_6
Id_2	Id_6

R_Id	S_Id	R_A	R_B	S_D	S_E
Id_1	Id_5	1	3	4	8
Id_1	Id_6	1	3	5	3
Id_2	Id_6	2	4	5	3

T_Id	T_B	T_C	T_D
Id_8	3	4	5
Id_9	3	8	1
Id_{10}	5	3	3
Id_{11}	5	9	4

Figure 4: Running example with the different steps of *Ted++* (up to explanations of size 3) in Alg. 1 and Alg. 2

& 16), when for some sub-combination $\mathcal{E}'$ of $\mathcal{E}$ it was computed that $\alpha_{\mathcal{E}'}$=0. In that case, we know a priori that $\alpha_{\mathcal{E}}$=0 (see Ex. 4.4).

If the partitioning is not a singleton, $V_{\mathcal{E}}$ is not materialized (Alg. 2, line 14). For example, the partitioning for c_3c_5 is not a singleton and so the size $|V_{35}|=|V_3|\times|V_5|=6$.

Post-processing. In Alg. 2 we associated with each possible explanation $\mathcal{E}$ the number of eliminated tuples $\alpha_{\mathcal{E}}$. However, $\alpha_{\mathcal{E}}$s includes any tuple eliminated by $\mathcal{E}$, even though the same tuples may be eliminated by some super-combinations of $\mathcal{E}$ (see Ex. 4.5). This means that for some tuples, multiple explanations have been assigned. To make things even, the last step of *Ted++* (Alg. 1, line 6) is about calculating the coefficient of $\mathcal{E}$ by subtracting the coefficients of its super-combinations from $\alpha_{\mathcal{E}}$:

$$coef_{\mathcal{E}} = \alpha_{\mathcal{E}} - \left(\sum_{\mathcal{E}\subseteq\mathcal{E}'} coef_{\mathcal{E}'}\right) \qquad \text{(F)}$$

EXAMPLE 4.5. *Consider known $coef_{1234}$=2 and $coef_{123}$=2. We have found in Ex. 4.4 that α_{23}=4. With Eq. (F), $coef_{23}$=4−2−2=0. In the same way $coef_2$=4−0−2−2=0. The algorithm leads to the expected Why-Not explanation polynomial already provided in Ex. 3.4.*

4.3 Complexity Analysis

In the pseudo-code provided by Alg. 1, we can see that *Ted++* divides into the phases of (i) partitioning $\mathcal{S}$, (ii) materializing a view for each partition, (iii) computing the explanations, and (iv) computing the exact coefficients. When computing the explanations, according to Alg. 2, *Ted++* iterates through $2^{|C|}$ condition combinations and for each, it decides upon view materialization (again through partitioning) before materializing it, or simply calculates $|V_{\mathcal{E}}|$ before applying equations to compute $\alpha_{\mathcal{E}}$. Overall, we consider that all mathematical computations are negligible so, the worst case complexities of steps (i) through (iv) sum up to $O(|\mathcal{S}|+|WN|)+O(|\mathcal{S}|)+O(2^{|C|}(|\mathcal{S}|+|C|))+O(2^{|C|})$. For sufficiently large queries, we can assume that $|\mathcal{S}|+|C|<<2^{|C|}$, in which case the complexity simplifies to $O(2^{|C|})$.

The complexity analysis above does not take into account the cost of actually materializing views; in its simplified form, it only considers how many views need to be materialized in the worst case. Assume that $n=max(\{|\mathcal{I}_R||R\in\mathcal{S}\})$. The materialization of any view is bound by the cost of materializing a cross product over the relations involved in the view - in the worst case $O(n^{|\mathcal{S}|})$. This yields a combined complexity of $O(2^{|C|}n^{|\mathcal{S}|})$. However, *Ted++* in the general case (more than one induced partitions), has a tighter upper bound: $O(n^{k_{\mathcal{E}1}}+n^{k_{\mathcal{E}2}}+\cdots+n^{k_{\mathcal{E}N}})$, where $k_{\mathcal{E}}=|part_{\mathcal{E}}|$, for all combinations $\mathcal{E}$ and $N=2^{|C|}$.

5. EXPERIMENTAL EVALUATION

We perform an experimental evaluation of *Ted++* on real and synthetic datasets. In Sec. 5.1, we compare *Ted++* to Ted [2], NedExplain [3], and Why-Not [7]. Sec. 5.2 studies the runtime of *Ted++* w.r.t. various parameters that we vary in a controlled manner. All Java implementations of the algorithms ran on MAC OS X 10.9.5 with 1.8 GHz Intel Core i5, 4GB memory, and 120GB SSD. PostgreSQL 9.3 was used as database system.

Table 2: Queries for the scenarios in Table 3

Query	Expression
Q1	$C \bowtie_{sector} W \bowtie_{witnessName} S \bowtie_{hair,clothes} P$
Q2	$\sigma_{C.sector>99}[C] \bowtie_{sector} W \bowtie_{witnessName} S \bowtie_{hair,clothes} P$
Q3	$W \bowtie_{sector2} C2 \bowtie_{sector1} \sigma_{C.type=Aiding}[C]$
Q4	$P2 \bowtie_{!name,hair} \sigma_{P1.name<B}[P1]$
Q5	$L \bowtie_{movieId} \sigma_{M.year>2009}[M] \bowtie_{name} \sigma_{R.rating\geq 8}[R]$
Q6	$\sigma_{AA.party=Republican}[AA] \bowtie_{id} \sigma_{Co.Byear>1970}[Co]$
Q7	$E \bowtie_{eId} \sigma_{ES.sub=Sen.\ Com.}[ES] \bowtie_{id} \sigma_{SPO.party=Rep.}[SPO]$
Q_{s3}	$\sigma_{type=Aiding}[Q2]$
Q_{s4}	$\sigma_{witnessname>S}[Q_{s3}]$
Q_j	$C \bowtie_{sector} \sigma_{name>S}[W]$
Q_{j2}	$Q_j \bowtie_{witnessname} S$
Q_{j3}	$Q_{j2} \bowtie_{clothes} P$
Q_{j4}	$Q_{j3} \bowtie_{hair} P$
Q_c	$L1 \bowtie_{lid} L2 \bowtie_{M2.mid=L2.mid} M2 \bowtie_{year,!mid} \sigma_{year=1980}[M1]$
Q_{tpch}	$C \bowtie_{ckey} \sigma_{odate<1998-07-21}[O] \bowtie_{okey} \sigma_{sdate>1998-07-21}[L]$

Table 3: Scenarios

Scenario	Query	Why-Not question
crime1	Q1	{P.Name=Hank,C.Type=Car theft}
crime2	Q1	{P.Name=Roger,C.Type=Car theft}
crime3	Q2	{P.Name=Roger,C.Type=Car theft}
crime4	Q2	{P.Name=Hank,C.Type=Car theft}
crime5	Q2	{P.Name=Hank}
crime6	Q3	{C2.Type=kidnapping}
crime7	Q3	{W.Name=Susan,C2.Type=kidnapping}
crime8	Q4	{P2.Name=Audrey}
imdb1	Q5	{name=Avatar}
imdb2	Q5	{name=Christmas Story,L.locationId=USANew York}
gov1	Q6	{Co.firstname=Christopher}
gov2	Q6	{Co.firstname=Christopher,Co.lastname=MURPHY}
gov3	Q6	{Co.firstname=Christopher,Co.lastname=GIBSON}
gov4	Q7	{sponsorId=467}
gov5	Q7	{SPO.sponsorln=Lugar,E.camount>=1000}
$crime_s-crime_{s4}$	Q1,Q2, Q_{s3},Q_{s4}	{P.Name=Hank,C.Type=Car theft}
$crime_j-crime_{j4}$	Q_j-Q_{j4},	{W.name=Jane, C.type=Car theft}
$imdb_c$	Q_{c4}	{L2.locationid=L1.locationid, M1.mid=L2.mid, L1.year>L2.year,M1.name=Duck Soup}
$imdb_{c2}$	Q_{c4}	({L2.locationid=L1.locationid, M1.mid=L2.mid, L1.year>L2.year}
$crime_{5c2}$	Q2	{P.Name=Hank, C.type=Car theft}
$crime_{5c3}$	Q2	{P.Name=Hank, C.type=Car theft, S.witness=Aphrodite}
$crime_{5c4}$	Q2	({P.Name=Hank ,C.type=Car theft, S.witness=Aphrodite, W.sector =34}
$crime_{5c5}$	Q2	{P.Name=Hank ,C.type=Car theft, S.witness=Aphrodite, W.sector =34,S.hair=green}
$imdb_{cc}$	Q_c	{M.year>M2.year}
$tpch_s$	Q_{tpch}	{L.extprice>50000,O.odate<1996-01-01}
$tpch_c$	Q_{tpch}	{L.extprice>100000, O.odate=L.cdate, C.nkey=4}

5.1 Comparative Evaluation

The comparative evaluation to Why-Not and NedExplain considers both efficiency (runtime) and effectiveness (explanation quality). When considering efficiency, we also include Ted in the comparison (Ted producing the same Why-Not explanation as *Ted++*).

For the experiments we have used data from three databases named *crime*, *imdb*, and *gov*. The *crime* database (available at http://infolab.stanford.edu/trio/) is a synthetic database about crimes and involved persons (suspects and witnesses). The *imdb* database contains real-world movie data from IMDB (http://www.imdb.com). Finally, the *gov* database contains information about US congressmen and financial activities (data from http://bioguide.congress.gov, http://usaspending.gov, and http://earmarks.omb.gov).

For each dataset, we have created a series of scenarios (crime1-gov5 in Tab. 3 - ignore remaining scenarios for now). Each scenario consists of a query further defined in Tab. 2 (Q1-Q7) and a simple Why-Not question, as Why-Not and NedExplain support only this type of Why-Not question. We have designed queries with a small set of conditions (Q6) or a larger one (Q1, Q3, Q5, Q7), containing self-joins (Q3, Q4), having empty intermediate results (Q2), as well as containing inequalities (Q2, Q4, Q5, Q6).

5.1.1 Why-Not Explanation Evaluation

Tab. 1 states that the explanations returned by Why-Not and NedExplain consist of sets of query conditions, whereas *Ted++* returns a polynomial of query conditions. For comparison purposes, we trivially map *Ted++*'s Why-Not explanation to sets of conditions, e.g., $3c_3 * c_4 + 2c_3 * c_6$ maps to $\{\{c_3, c_4\}, \{c_3, c_6\}\}$. For conciseness, we abbreviate condition sets, e.g., to c_{34}, c_{36}.

Tab. 4 summarizes the Why-Not explanations of the three algorithms. These scenarios make apparent that the explanations by NedExplain or Why-Not are incomplete, in two senses. First, they produce only a subset of the possible explanations, failing to provide alternatives that could be useful to the user when she tries to fix the query. Second, even the explanation they provide may lack parts, which can drive the user to fruitless fixing attempts. On the contrary, *Ted++* produces all the possible, complete explanations.

For the first argument, consider the scenario $gov2$. Why-Not and NedExplain return c_1 and c_3 respectively, but they both fail to indicate that both the explanations are valid, as opposed to *Ted++*. Then, consider $crime8$. NedExplain returns the join c_2 ($S \bowtie_{hair} P$) - Why-Not does not produce any explanations. *Ted++* indicates that except for this join, the selection c_3 ($\sigma_{name<'B'}[P]$) for instance is also an explanation. From a developer's perspective, selections are typically easier or more reasonable to change. So, having the complete set of explanations potentially provides the developer with useful alternatives.

For the second argument consider $crime5$. NedExplain returns c_1 ($C \bowtie_{sector} W$). The explanation of *Ted++* does not contain the atomic explanation c_1, but there exist combinations including c_1 as a part, like c_{15}. This means that the explanation by NedExplain is incomplete; a repair attempt of c_1 alone will never yield the desired results. Similarly, $crime7$ illustrates a case, when the Why-Not algorithm produces an explanation (c_3) that misses some parts. Then, in gov3 NedExplain and Why-Not both return c_2. However, let us now assume the developer prefers to not change this condition. Keeping in mind that those algorithms' answers may change when changing the query tree, she may start trying different trees to possibly obtain a Why-Not explanation without c_2. Knowing the explanation of *Ted++* prevents her from spending any effort on this, as it shows that all explanations contain c_2 as a part.

By mapping the explanation of *Ted++* to sets of explanations, the usefulness of the coefficients of the polynomial has been neglected. For example, the Why-Not explanation polynomial of $crime8$ is $2384 * c_{23} + 20 * c_3 + 4 * c_1 + 8 * c_2$. Assume that the developer would like to recover at least 5 missing tuples, by changing as few conditions as possible. The polynomial implies to change either c_3 or c_2: they both require one condition change and provide the possibility of obtaining up to 20 and 8 missing tuples, respectively. c_1 can recover up to 4 tuples, whereas c_2c_3 require two condition changes. Clearly, the results of NedExplain or Why-Not are not informative enough for such a discussion.

5.1.2 Runtime Evaluation

***Ted++* vs. NedExplain and Why-Not.** Fig. 5 shows the runtimes in logarithmic scale for each algorithm and scenario. We observe that *Ted++* and NedExplain are comparable and that in some cases,*Ted++* is significantly faster than Why-Not.

Why-Not traces compatible tuples based on tuple lineage stored in Trio. As already stated in [3, 7], this design choice slows down Why-Not. On the contrary, both NedExplain and *Ted++* compute

Table 4: *Ted++*, Why-Not, NedExplain answers per scenario

Scenario	*Ted++*	Why-Not	NedExplain
crime1	$c_{1234}, \ldots, c_{12}, c_3, c_2, c_1$		c_1
crime2	$c_{1234}, c_{34}, c_{13}, \ldots, c_3$	c_{34}	c_{34}, c_1
crime3	$c_{12345}, \ldots, c_{145}, c_{345}, c_{35}$	c_{34}, c_5	c_5, c_{34}
crime4	$c_{12345}, \ldots, c_{25}, c_{15}$	c_5	c_1, c_5
crime5	$c_{12345}, \ldots, c_{15}, c_5$	c_5	c_1
crime6	$c_{123}, c_{31}, c_{23}, c_{12}, c_3, c_2, c_1$	c_3	c_2
crime7	$c_{123}, c_{13}, c_{12}, c_1$	c_3	c_2, c_1
crime8	c_{23}, c_3, c_2, c_1		c_2
imdb1	$c_{123}, c_{13}, c_{23}, c_3$	c_3	c_3, c_2
imdb2	c_{13}		c_1, c_3
gov1	$c_{123}, c_{13}, c_{23}, c_{12}, c_3, c_2, c_1$	c_3	c_2, c_3
gov2	c_{13}, c_3, c_1	c_1	c_3
gov3	c_{123}, c_{23}, c_2	c_2	c_2
gov4	c_{123}, c_{23}, c_2	c_3	c_3, c_2
gov5	$c_{124}, c_{14}, c_{24}, c_{12}, c_4, c_2, c_1$	c_1	c_1

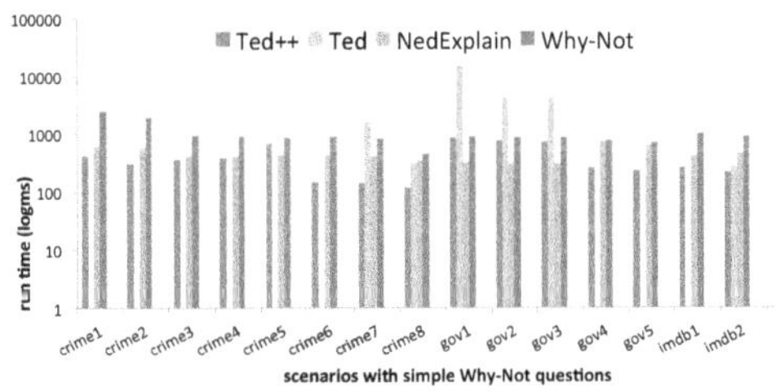

Figure 5: Runtime for *Ted++*, Ted, NedExplain, and Why-Not

compatible data more efficiently. We claim that a better implementation choice for tuple tracing in Why-Not would yield a runtime comparable to NedExplain, a claim backed up by their comparable runtime complexities. Another problem of NedExplain and Why-Not lies in the choice to trace compatible data w.r.t. tuples from the input relations but not necessarily compatible ones.

Let us see what happens when *Ted++* is slower than - but still comparable to - NedExplain, for example in $gov1$-$gov3$. In NedExplain all compatible tuples are pruned out by conditions very close to the leaf level of the query tree, so the bottom-up traversal of the tree can stop very early. *Ted++* always "checks" all conditions so cannot benefit from such an early termination. However, this runtime improvement of NedExplain often comes at the price of incomplete explanations (e.g., $gov1$).

***Ted++* vs. Ted.** Fig. 5 reports runtimes for Ted on 6 out of 15 scenarios as for the others, Ted runs out of time. To examine this behavior, we compare the time distribution in Ted and *Ted++*(Fig. 6). The algorithms are divided in four common phases. Note that in scenarios $crime7$, $gov1 - gov3$ the diagram bars for Ted are not totally displayed as the execution time is much higher compared to the other scenarios and to the runtime of *Ted++* (the runtime of the coefficientEstimation phase is the label on the respective bars) .

As said in Sec. 4, Ted's main issue is its dependence on the number of compatible tuples. This is experimentally observed in Fig. 6: with the growth of the set of compatible tuples, the time dedicated to coefficientEstimation also grows (the scenarios are reported in an ascending order of number of compatible tuples). The number of compatible tuples affects *Ted++* too, but not as much. This can be seen in $crime8$ and $crime7$, or $gov3$ and $gov1$; while the number of tuples grows, *Ted++*'s runtime remains roughly steady.

5.2 Ted++ Analysis

We now study *Ted++*'s behavior w.r.t. the following parameters: (i) the type (simple or complex) of the input query Q and the number of Q's conditions, (ii) the type of the Why-Not question (simple

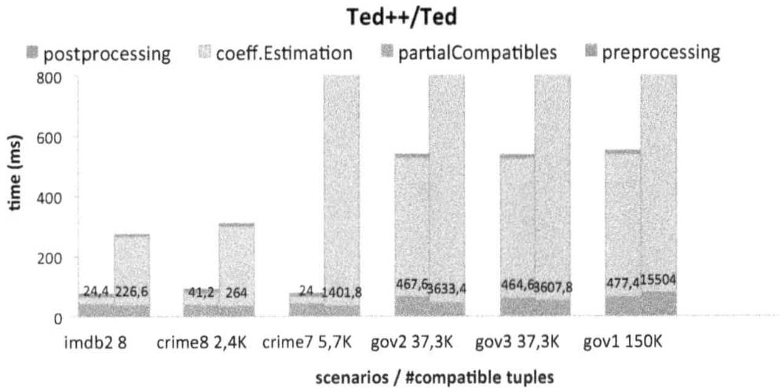

Figure 6: *Ted++* and Ted runtime distribution

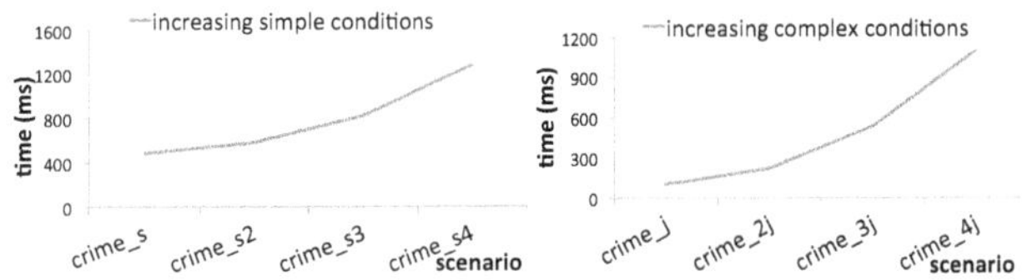

(a) simple conditions (b) complex conditions

Figure 7: *Ted++* runtime w.r.t. number of conditions in Q

or complex) and the number and selectivity of conditions the Why-Not question involves, and (iii) the size of the database instance $\mathcal{I}$. Note that (ii) and (iii) are tightly connected with the number of compatible tuples, which is one of the main parameters influencing the performance. Another important factor is the selectivity of the query conditions over the compatible data.

For the parameter variations (i) and (ii), we use again the *crime*, *imdb*, and *gov* databases. To adjust the database instance size for case (iii), we use data produced by the TPC-H benchmark data generator (http://www.tpc.org/tpch/). We have generated instances of 1GB and 10GB and further produced smaller data sets of 10MB and 100MB to obtain a series of datasets whose size differs by a factor of 10. In this paper, we report results for the original query Q3 of the TPC-H set of queries. It includes two complex and three simple conditions, two of which are inequality conditions. Since the original TPC-H query Q3 is an aggregation query, we have changed the projection condition. The queries used in this section are Q_s-Q_{tpch} (Tab. 2) and the scenarios are $crime_s$-$tpch_c$ (Tab. 3).

Adjusting the query. Given a fixed database instance and Why-Not question, we start from query Q1 and gradually add simple conditions, yielding the series of queries Q1, Q2, Q_{s3}, Q_{s4}. The evolution of *Ted++* runtime for these queries is shown in Fig. 7 (a). Similarly, starting from query Q_j, we introduce step by step complex conditions, yielding Q_j-Q_{j4}. Corresponding runtime results are reported in Fig. 7 (b).

As expected, in both cases, increasing the number of query conditions (either complex or simple) results in increasing runtime. The incline of the curve depends on the selectivity of the introduced condition; the less selective the condition the steeper the line becomes. This is easy to explain, as the view for the explanations involving a low selective condition contains more tuples (=passing partial tuples). This, leaves space for further optimization by dynamically deciding on passing vs eliminated tuples materialization.

Adjusting the Why-Not question. The scenarios considered for Fig. 8 (a) have as starting point the simple Why-Not question of $crime5$ (see Tab. 3). Keeping the same input instance and query, we add attibute-constant comparisons (i.e., simple conditions) to WN, resulting in fewer tuples in each step. As expected, the more conditions (the less tuples) the faster the Why-Not explanation is returned, until we reach a certain point (here from $crime5_{c3}$ on).

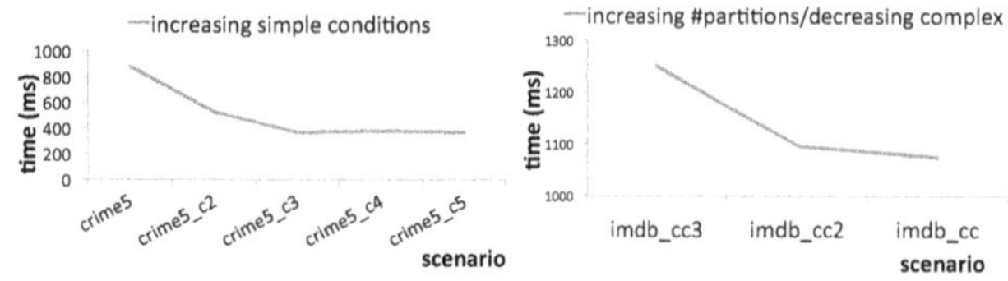

(a) simple conditions (b) complex conditions

Figure 8: *Ted++* runtime w.r.t. number of conditions in WN

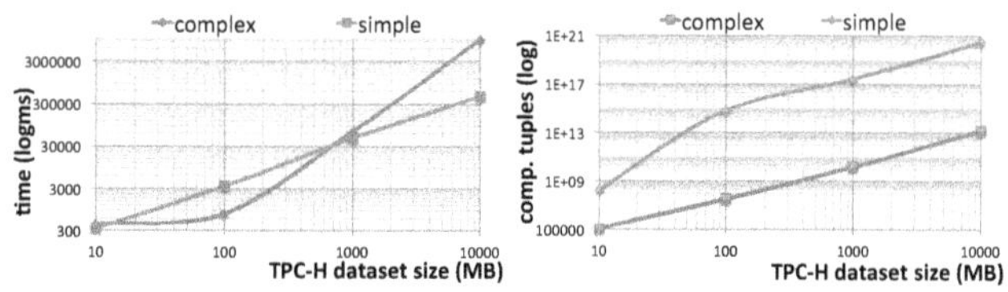

(a) runtime (b) # compatible tuples

Figure 9: *Ted++* behavior for varying database size

From this point, the runtime is dominated by the time to communicate with the database that is constant over all scenarios.

In Fig. 8 (b) we examine complex Why-Not questions. As we add complex conditions in a Why-Not question, the number of generated partitions (potentially) drops as more relations are included in a same partition. To study the impact of the induced number of partitions in isolation, we *keep the number of the compatible tuples constant* in our series of complex scenarios ($imdb_{cc}$-$imdb_{cc3}$). The number of partitions entailed by $imdb_{cc}$, $imdb_{cc2}$, and $imdb_{cc3}$ are 3, 2, and 1, respectively. The results of Fig. 8 (b) confirm our theoretical complexity discussion, i.e., as the number of partitions decreases, the time needed to produce the Why-Not explanation increases.

Increasing size of input instance. Now we increase the database size for scenarios with one simple or one complex Why-Not question WN, over the same query Q_{tpch}. The simple WN includes two inequality conditions, in order to be able to compute a reasonable number of compatible tuples. The complex WN contains one complex condition, one inequality simple condition and one equality simple condition. It thus represents an average complex Why-Not question, creating two partitions over three relations.

Fig. 9 (a) shows the runtimes for both scenarios. The increasing runtime is tightly coupled to the fact that the number of computed tuples is augmenting proportionally to the database size, as shown in Fig. 9 (b). We observe that for small datasets (<500MB) in the complex scenario *Ted++*'s performance decreases with a low rate, whereas the rate is higher for larger datasets. For the simple scenario, runtime deteriorates in a steady pace. This behavior is aligned with the theoretical study; when the number of partitions is decreasing the complexity rises.

In summary, our experiments have shown that *Ted++* generates a more useful and complete Why-Not explanation than the state of the art. Moreover, *Ted++* is competitive in terms of runtime. The dedicated experimental evaluation on *Ted++* verifies that it can be used in a large variety of scenarios with different parameters. Finally, the fact that the experiments were conducted on an ordinary laptop supports *Ted++*'s feasibility.

6. CONCLUSION AND OUTLOOK

This paper provides a framework for Why-Not explanations based on polynomials, which enables to consider relational databases under set, bag and probabilistic semantics in a unified way. To efficiently compute the Why-Not explanation polynomial under set semantics we have designed a new algorithm *Ted++*, whose main feature is to completely avoid enumerating and iterating over the set of compatible tuples, thus significantly reducing both space and time consumption. Our experimental evaluation showed that *Ted++* is at least as efficient as existing algorithms while providing useful insights in its Why-Not explanation for a developer. Also, we show that *Ted++* scales well w.r.t various parameters, making it a practical solution.

Why-Not explanation polynomials are easy to extend for unions of conjunctive queries, whereas an extension for aggregation queries is subject to future work. Currently, we have been working on exploiting the Why-Not explanation polynomial to efficiently rewrite a query in order to include the missing answers in its result set. As there are many rewriting possibilities, we plan to select the most promising ones based on a cost function, built with the polynomial. For instance, we may rank higher rewritings with minimum condition changes (i.e., small combinations), minimum side-effects (i.e., small coefficients), etc.

7. REFERENCES

[1] S. Abiteboul, R. Hull, and V. Vianu. *Foundations of Databases*. Addison-Wesley, 1995.

[2] N. Bidoit, M. Herschel, and K. Tzompanaki. Immutably answering why-not questions for equivalent conjunctive queries. In *Workshop on Theory and Practice of Provenance (TAPP)*, 2014.

[3] N. Bidoit, M. Herschel, and K. Tzompanaki. Query-based why-not provenance with NedExplain. In *International Conference on Extending Database Technology (EDBT)*, 2014.

[4] N. Bidoit, M. Herschel, and K. Tzompanaki. EFQ: Why-not answer polynomials in action. *Proceedings of the VLDB Endowment (PVLDB)*, 2015.

[5] D. Calvanese, M. Ortiz, M. Simkus, and G. Stefanoni. Reasoning about explanations for negative query answers in DL-Lite. *Journal on Artificial Intelligence Research (JAIR)*, 2013.

[6] B. t. Cate, C. Civili, E. Sherkhonov, and W.-C. Tan. High-level why-not explanations using ontologies. In *Principles of Database Systems (PODS)*, 2015.

[7] A. Chapman and H. V. Jagadish. Why not? In *International Conference on the Management of Data (SIGMOD)*, 2009.

[8] L. Chen, X. Lin, C. S. Jensen, and J. Xu. Answering why-not questions on spatial keyword top-k queries. In *International Conference on Data Engineering (ICDE)*, 2015.

[9] Y. Gao, Q. Liu, G. Chen, B. Zheng, and L. Zhou. Answering why-not questions on reverse top-k queries. *PVLDB*, 8(7):738–749, 2015.

[10] T. J. Green, G. Karvounarakis, and V. Tannen. Provenance semirings. In *Principles of Database Systems (PODS)*, 2007.

[11] M. Hall. *Combinatorial theory*, volume 71. John Wiley & Sons, 1998.

[12] Z. He and E. Lo. Answering why-not questions on top-k queries. In *International Conference on Data Engineering (ICDE)*, 2012.

[13] M. Herschel. Wondering why data are missing from query results? ask Conseil Why-Not. In *International Conference on Information and Knowledge Management (CIKM)*, 2013.

[14] M. Herschel. A hybrid approach to answering why-not questions on relational query results. *Journal on Data Information and Quality*, 5(3):10:1–10:29, 2015.

[15] M. Herschel and M. A. Hernández. Explaining missing answers to SPJUA queries. *Proceedings of the VLDB Endowment (PVLDB)*, 3(1), 2010.

[16] J. Huang, T. Chen, A. Doan, and J. F. Naughton. On the provenance of non-answers to queries over extracted data. *Proceedings of the VLDB Endowment (PVLDB)*, 1(1), 2008.

[17] M. S. Islam, C. Liu, and R. Zhou. Flexiq: A flexible interactive querying framework by exploiting the skyline operator. *Journal of Systems and Software*, 97:97–117, 2014.

[18] M. S. Islam, R. Zhou, and C. Liu. On answering why-not questions in reverse skyline queries. In *International Conference on Data Engineering (ICDE)*, 2013.

[19] A. Meliou, W. Gatterbauer, K. F. Moore, and D. Suciu. The complexity of causality and responsibility for query answers and non-answers. *Proceedings of the VLDB Endowment (PVLDB)*, 2011.

[20] Q. T. Tran and C.-Y. Chan. How to ConQueR why-not questions. In *International Conference on the Management of Data (SIGMOD)*, 2010.

[21] Q. T. Tran, C.-Y. Chan, and S. Parthasarathy. Query reverse engineering. *The VLDB Journal*, 23(5):721–746, 2014.

[22] R. Vaught. *Set Theory An Introduction*. Birkhaeuser, 2001.

Interruption-Sensitive Empty Result Feedback: Rethinking the Visual Query Feedback Paradigm for Semistructured Data

Sourav S Bhowmick
School of Computer Engg.
Nanyang Technological University, Singapore
assourav@ntu.edu.sg

Curtis Dyreson
Department of Computer Sc.
Utah State University, USA
curtis.dyreson@usu.edu

Byron Choi
Department of Computer Sc.
Hong Kong Baptist University, Hong Kong, China
choi@hkbu.edu.hk

Min-Hwee Ang
School of Computer Engg.
Nanyang Technological University, Singapore
Y070005@e.ntu.edu.sg

ABSTRACT

The usability of visual querying schemes for tree and graph-structured data can be greatly enhanced by providing feedback during query construction, but feedback at inopportune times can hamper query construction. In this paper, we rethink the traditional way of providing feedback. We describe a novel vision of *interruption-sensitive* query feedback where relevant notifications are delivered *quickly but at an appropriate moment* when the mental workload of the user is low. Though we focus on one class of query feedback, namely *empty result detection*, where a user is notified when a partially constructed visual query yields an empty result, our new paradigm is applicable to other kinds of feedback. We present a framework called *i*SERF that bridges the classical database problem of empty-result detection with intelligent notification management from the domains of HCI and psychology. Instead of immediate notification, *i*SERF considers the structure of query formulation tasks and *breakpoints* when reasoning about when to notify the user. We present an HCI-inspired model to quantify the performance bounds that *i*SERF must abide by for checking for an empty result in order to ensure interruption-sensitive notification at *optimal* breakpoints. We implement this framework in the context of visual XML query formulation and highlight its effectiveness empirically.

Categories and Subject Descriptors

H.2.4 [**Database Management**]: Systems - Query processing

General Terms

Algorithms, Experimentation, Human Factors, Performance

Permission to make digital or hard copies of all or part of this work for personal or classroom use is granted without fee provided that copies are not made or distributed for profit or commercial advantage and that copies bear this notice and the full citation on the first page. Copyrights for components of this work owned by others than ACM must be honored. Abstracting with credit is permitted. To copy otherwise, or republish, to post on servers or to redistribute to lists, requires prior specific permission and/or a fee. Request permissions from Permissions@acm.org.

CIKM'15, October 19–23, 2015, Melbourne, Australia.
© 2015 ACM. ISBN 978-1-4503-3794-6/15/10 ...$15.00.
DOI: http://dx.doi.org/10.1145/2806416.2806432.

Keywords

Visual querying; query formulation; graphs; XML; query feedback; empty result detection; interruption; notifications; breakpoints

1. INTRODUCTION

Formulating queries over semistructured databases (*e.g.,* XML, JSON, graphs) using database query languages (*e.g.,* XQuery, SPARQL, Cypher) often demands considerable cognitive effort from users and requires "programming" skill that is at least comparable to SQL. Providing a visual query interface (GUI) is a popular approach to making query construction user-friendly [1, 6, 7, 10, 30]. Typically, these interfaces enable visual query formulation involving a sequence of tasks ranging from *primitive* operations such as pointing and clicking a mouse button to higher-level tasks such as selection of a menu item.

1.1 Interactive Visual Query Feedback

A user-friendly visual query system is expected to interactively guide users into constructing correct queries. A non-exhaustive list of the kinds of guidance such a system may employ is given below.

- *Syntactic and semantic help.* A visual query system can detect and notify users when there is a syntax or semantic problem in a query (*e.g.,* a missing quote on a string or a wrong type passed to a function). A system could even suggest better alternative syntax. These techniques can greatly enhance users' ability to formulate syntactically correct queries visually without resorting to memorizing various syntactic flavors of a query language.
- *Empty result feedback.* When a user specifies *"Leningrad"* instead of *"St. Petersburg"* (Leningrad is the former name of St. Petersburg) as a value predicate on an attribute `city` in a query on the *Mondial* dataset[1], the query returns an empty result. It is important to detect such scenarios during query construction and alert a user in a timely fashion so that she can undertake appropriate remedial action(s).
- *Long-running query feedback.* A recent study [29] shows that a graph query that runs fast may slow down significantly after a slight modification to the query's structure. Unexpected query behaviors like this can confuse and annoy users

[1] http://datahub.io/dataset/mondial.

of visual query systems, especially in the context of exploratory search. It would be better if the system could warn a user about a potentially long-running query fragment during query formulation.

- *Query fragments suggestion.* Given a partially-constructed visual XML or subgraph query, it is useful to suggest top-k possible query fragments that the user may potentially add to her query in the subsequent step. Such suggestions can enhance user experience by greatly reducing the query formulation time.

There are two common threads in the above scenarios. First, without the aid of a visual query feedback mechanism, users would be unaware of these cases, since each case requires comprehensive knowledge of the underlying data or query language. Feedback about various problems encountered during query construction as well as possible solutions is critical to enhancing the usability of a visual querying system. Second, as query conditions in a visual querying environment are typically constructed iteratively, it is often critical to detect and notify the aforementioned issues *opportunely*. It is ineffective to provide feedback at the *end* of query formulation. For instance, consider the empty result problem. It is ineffective to provide feedback *after* the query formulation as a user may have wasted her time and effort in formulating additional query conditions. Similarly, it is ineffective if the visual querying scheme fails to alert the user opportunely when a "long-running" query fragment is detected. Such opportune notification is also important in the context of query fragment suggestion as it is not beneficial if suggestions are made after the query has been visually constructed.

1.2 Importance of Intelligent Notifications

Feedback during visual query construction can be intuitively modeled as an alert or notification for a secondary task (*e.g.*, handling the empty result problem) when a user is working on a primary task (query formulation). It is desirable to build an *intelligent notification system* that can efficiently *detect* issues and *notify* users effectively. Such notification systems play a pivotal role in visual query systems, as well as in many software systems. Research in HCI demonstrates that there are numerous benefits of notifications such as quick availability of important and relevant information (*e.g.*, long-running query fragment, empty answer) as well as access to nearly instantaneous communication [18].

A notification can be *intrusive* or *non-intrusive* [19]. *Non-intrusive* notifications are usually less disruptive to user activities as they are often presented in the periphery of a user's attention. In general, non-urgent information can be presented to a user in a non-intrusive fashion. *Intrusive* notifications are for urgent messages. They demand immediate action from the user and hence they need to grab a user's attention. For instance, an empty result problem that arises during visual query formulation might generate an intrusive notification since an immediate response is needed by the user.

1.3 Interruption - The Other Side of the Coin

Notifications, however, come with a cost: they *interrupt* a primary task (*i.e.*, query formulation). This is because notifications divert attention [15, 25]. Intuitively, an *interruption* is a distraction that causes one to stop a scheduled task to respond to a stimulus. Many studies in the cognitive psychology and HCI communities have reported that interrupting users engaged in tasks by delivering notifications inopportunely can negatively impact task completion time, lead to more errors, and increase user frustration [3, 5, 9, 12, 15, 16, 21, 22]. In summary, three key findings are reported in these studies. First, interruptions slow and degrade performance on the primary task. In particular, interruptions lead to *resumption lag*, which is the additional time needed to resume the primary task after interruption [22]. Second, the timing of the interruptions can adversely impact performance. It has been observed that notifications occurring at points of higher mental workload are more disruptive in nature compared to those that occur during lower mental workload [3, 9, 15, 16]. The former may lead not only to larger resumption lags but also increase frustration. Third, interruptions with similar content with the main task could be quite disruptive even if they are very short [12].

For instance, suppose a user is notified intrusively (*e.g.*, invoking a pop-up dialog box, highlighting a condition) of an empty result (due to previously formulated condition) when she is dragging an attribute from one panel and preparing to drop it in to another panel to construct a new condition. This interruption may frustrate her as mental resources allocated for the current task are disrupted. Such inopportune, intrusive feedback adversely affects the usability of the system.

It is worth noting that recent research [28] in the HCI community has demonstrated that *acceptability* of a notification is essentially a tradeoff between the cost of interrupting the user's activities and the value of receiving the notification message. Specifically, acceptability of low-urgency and medium-urgency messages (*e.g.*, query fragment suggestions) improves when presented in a non-intrusive manner. This is because this type of notification is expected to be less disruptive of the primary task (*e.g.*, visual query formulation) in comparison to its intrusive counterpart. Furthermore, recent research has suggested that users typically delay processing of a non-intrusive interruption, when it is sent to them at points of higher mental workload, until they have reached a point of lower mental workload [26]. On the other hand, acceptability of high-urgency messages (*e.g.*, empty results, syntax error) is expected to be low when presented non-intrusively as immediate user response is expected for such notifications. In other words, *a user would typically like to see urgent messages in an immediate and intrusive way* (*e.g.*, modal boxes, highlighting query conditions).

1.4 Interruption-sensitive Query Feedback

Classical visual query feedback strategies are "interruption-insensitive". These strategies have historically focused on speed and scalability, often devoting very little attention to the cognitive aspect of a solution. Hence, we need to make our visual query feedback mechanism "cognitive-aware" by devising models and techniques to deliver a notification (especially an intrusive one) *quickly but at an appropriate moment* when the mental workload of the user is minimal. Detecting such an opportune moment should be transparent to the user and must not seek explicit input from her.

In this paper, we rethink the classical interruption-insensitive query feedback paradigm and lay down the vision of *interruption-sensitive* visual query feedback by taking the first step to mitigate the problem of inopportune interruptions made by *intrusive*[2] query feedback notifications. Specifically, we focus on *one class of visual query feedback problem* to illustrate this novel paradigm, namely ***empty result* (ER) *feedback***[3], where a user is notified when a partially constructed visual query yields an empty result. Note that an empty result is not always undesirable to an end user especially in an exploratory querying environment. However, whenever a visual query fragment returns an empty result, it is particularly important to notify the user about[4] the following: (a) The ER problem re-

[2]We focus on intrusive notification in this paper as this type of notification delivers messages that are important to the user and requires immediate attention.

[3]We chose the ER feedback as a representative problem as it has consistently received attention from the database community over decades [8, 17, 20, 23].

[4]The notification can be a single message.

sulted from the constructed query fragment *opportunely* so that she can avoid wasting time and effort in continuing constructing new conditions; (b) Identify the constructed query condition(s) that is responsible for an empty result; and (c) Optionally, suggest a query modification to mitigate the ER problem.

Hence our proposed paradigm *bridges the classical visual query feedback problem with intelligent notification management from the domains of* HCI *and cognitive psychology*. We propose a novel psychology and HCI-inspired model for delivering intrusive notification of an empty result for visual queries, the theory based on this model, and a framework for detecting empty results efficiently and delivering notifications at opportune times. Although as we shall see later, our proposed paradigm can be realized on visual query interfaces for tree or graph-structured databases, to demonstrate its effectiveness we realize it on top of a visual XML query formulation framework. Specifically, we make the following contributions.

- We present a psychology-inspired notification scheme that exploits a *defer-to-breakpoint* strategy [14–16] for the effective delivery of intrusive notification to the user when a visual query fragment returns an empty result (Section 3).
- We present an HCI-inspired extensible quantitative model for estimating the *optimal notification time* available for empty-result detection so that the defer-to-breakpoint notification scheme can be effectively realized. The model takes into consideration the time to undertake various actions in order to construct a visual query condition (Section 4).
- We propose a novel and generic framework called *i*SERF (**I**nterruption-**S**ensitive **E**mpty **R**esults noti**F**ication), grounded on well-founded principles from HCI and cognitive psychology, to efficiently detect an empty result during visual query formulation and intrusively notify users along with the query condition(s) that is responsible for this problem. Note that here we do not focus on providing to the user suggestions on how to modify or relax the visual query to get a non-empty result as it is orthogonal to our framework (we shall elaborate on it further in Section 6). Additionally, *i*SERF is *not* designed with the explicit aim to minimize query construction time, which is an orthogonal problem. Instead, the broad goal of *i*SERF is to *improve each user's experience during visual query formulation by reducing the adverse effects of intrusive notifications* (Section 5).
- We implement *i*SERF on a visual XML querying environment to demonstrate its effectiveness in realizing the interruption-sensitive visual query feedback paradigm (Section 6).
- We conduct an empirical study on real XML data with real users to demonstrate the effectiveness of *i*SERF (Section 7).

2. BACKGROUND

We begin by laying out the generic structure of a visual query interface for tree or graph-structured data. Then, we formally define the *empty result feedback* problem. Lastly, we discuss related research in this arena.

2.1 Visual Query Interfaces for Trees or Graphs

Most visual query interfaces for tree or graph-structured data are comprised of *at least* three key panels: (a) a *Schema Panel* to display the structural summary (*e.g.,* XML schema or *DataGuide* [13]) or distinct set of node and edge labels of the underlying tree or graph data, respectively, (b) a *Query Panel* for iteratively constructing the query conditions (value and structural constraints) graphically, and (c) a *Results Panel* (Panel 4) that displays the query results.

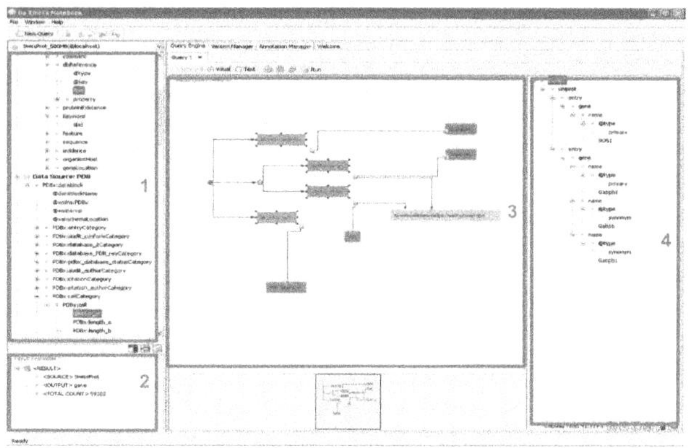

Figure 1: A visual interface for formulating XML queries.

EXAMPLE 1. Figure 1 depicts a screen dump of a visual interface for querying XML data [31]. Observe that Panels 1, 3, and 4 in this GUI correspond to the *Schema*, *Query*, and *Results* Panel, respectively. In addition it has an *Output Panel* (Panel 2) that displays the item(s) to be returned by the query. Note that this panel may not appear in other interfaces for querying XML data as different interfaces may visually specify the result nodes differently. A new XML query can be formulated using the interface as follows.

1. Specify the output item(s) by dragging selected item(s) from Panel 1 and dropping it to Panel 2.
2. Move the mouse pointer to Panel 1.
3. Scan and select an item in Panel 1.
4. Drag the item to Panel 3 and drop it. Each such action represents formulation of a non-join predicate (condition).
5. A *Dialog Box* will automatically appear for users to fill (optionally) in the value predicates, comparison operators, aggregate functions, etc.
6. Combine two or more conditions in Panel 3 using AND/OR connectives. Note that in this step one may also build join predicates if necessary.
7. Repeat Steps 2–6 for each new condition.
8. Execute the query by clicking on the Run icon. Panel 4 displays the query results.

Very similar visual query interfaces for graph queries are described elsewhere [6, 30]. Hence we treat tree and graph query interfaces as the same for the purposes of this paper. □

2.2 Empty Result (ER) Feedback Problem

Given a visual query Q (tree or graph query), we denote the result set of Q as $R(Q)$. A visual query fragment Q' of Q consists of a subset of conditions $C' \subseteq C$ of Q. Then the result set satisfying C' is denoted as $R(C')$. A visual query fragment Q' (query Q) returns an *empty result iff* $R(C') = \emptyset$ ($R(Q) = \emptyset$). In this paper, we present a framework for (a) *detecting* if $R(C') = \emptyset$ for a partially-constructed visual query Q'; (b) identifying the condition(s) in Q' responsible for an empty result, and (c) notifying the user intrusively at an *opportune time* so that the "interruption cost" is minimized. Observe that traditional ER feedback techniques typically focus on (a) and (b) but not (c).

2.3 Related Work

To the best of our knowledge, none of the state-of-the-art visual querying schemes [1,6,7,10,30] are interruption-sensitive. In [17], an empty-result detection method is proposed for SQL queries. The key idea is to reuse the evaluation results from prior empty-result queries by leveraging *lowest-level* query fragments from the query plans that lead to an empty result. In our proposed paradigm, we operate in a visual querying environment where the entire query is available only at the end of query formulation. Hence, the aforementioned technique is inapplicable here. Importantly, *i*SERF supports interruption-sensitive notification which is absent from [17].

Research in non-interactive [8] and interactive [20, 23] query relaxation solutions propose solutions to the empty-result problem. However, none of these efforts focus on opportune notification delivery of the relaxation solutions. In fact, the work reported in this paper complements these efforts as it automatically determines the opportune time to notify users about relaxation suggestions.

Research in cognitive psychology and HCI has investigated intelligent notification management [5, 9, 15, 21, 24], focusing on visual tasks such as document editing, diagram editing, image manipulation, and programming. However, prior to our work, it has not been studied in the context of database query feedback.

3. DEFER-TO-BREAKPOINT-BASED INTRUSIVE NOTIFICATION

The HCI community has shown that the negative effects of interruption (recall from Section 1.3) can be mitigated by deferring interruptions until more opportune moments in a task sequence [5, 15, 16]. The argument being that when a user completes a task, mental resources allocated to perform the task are released, momentarily reducing workload before the cycle of allocation and deallocation occurs again in the next task. One particular approach for deferring interruptions is to schedule them at *breakpoints*.

Defer-to-breakpoint strategy. A *breakpoint* represents the moment of transition between two observable, meaningful units of task execution, and reflects a change in perception or action [24]. Recent research in the HCI community identified three granularities (types) of breakpoints during interactive tasks - *Coarse*, *Medium*, and *Fine* [14]. Coarse exists between the largest units while Fine exists between the smallest. For example, consider the task of editing documents. Fine may be switching paragraphs, Medium may be switching documents, and Coarse may be switching to an activity other than editing (*e.g.,* checking emails).

Iqbal and Bailey have recently shown that the best moment to interrupt a user is on breakpoints between tasks [15]. That is, to defer the notification to appear at the next breakpoint detected in the user's task-sequence. *We shall adopt this defer-to-breakpoint-based strategy for interrupting query formulation tasks.*

Our decision to choose the above strategy is bolstered by the following interesting results demonstrated by the HCI community [5, 15]. First, the *interruption cost* is reduced and users are less frustrated when intrusive notifications are scheduled to occur at breakpoints rather than when delivered immediately. Second, users prefer having notifications scheduled at breakpoints and they react faster to notifications that were scheduled at breakpoints. Third, applications that generate notifications that are relevant to the user's ongoing activity should request that they be delivered at Medium or Fine breakpoints. This ensures that notifications are delivered when they have most utility, and are least disruptive. In contrast, notifications of general interest should be delivered at Coarse breakpoints.

Generic Breakpoints in Visual Query Formulation. Reconsider the generic structure of the GUIs for tree or graph query construction tasks as described in Section 2.1. The different types of breakpoints for these tasks are shown in Table 1. Observe that for each of the tasks related to Medium and Fine breakpoints, mental resources allocated to perform the task are released at the end of the task, thus momentarily reducing the workload. For instance,

Type	Tasks for Tree Queries	Tasks for Graph Queries
Coarse	**CB1:** User switch to another application (*e.g.*, email); **CB2:** Minimize query window.	Same as tree queries.
Medium	**MB1:** Clicking a menu item to initiate creation of a new query; **MB2:** Switching to another query.	Same as tree queries.
Fine	**FB1:** Move mouse to *Schema Panel* to search items; **FB2:** Selection of an item in the *Schema Panel*; **FB3:** Dragging an item from *Schema Panel* to *Query Panel*; **FB4:** Combining/joining query conditions; **FB5:** Clicking OK on any Dialog box related to predicates;**FB6:** Click on the Run icon.	**FB1:** Move mouse to *Schema Panel* to search node labels; **FB2:** Selection of a label in the *Schema Panel*; **FB3:** Dragging a label from *Schema Panel* to *Query Panel* for query node creation, **FB4:** Connecting two nodes with an edge; **FB5:** Clicking OK any Dialog box for node/edge predicates; **FB6:** Click on the Run icon.

Table 1: Breakpoints for visual query formulation.

consider the task of selecting an item or node label in the *Schema Panel*. The mental resource of a user is allocated to scanning it and selecting an item/label. Upon completion the resource is released which reduces the mental workload. The mental resource allocation cycle begins again when the subsequent task of dragging the selected item/label to the *Query Panel* begins.

EXAMPLE 2. Reconsider the steps for formulating XML queries using the GUI in Example 1. The Fine breakpoints according to Table 1 are at the end of Steps 2, 3, 4, 5, 6, and 8. In addition, there is another Fine breakpoint at the end of Step 1, which is specific to this interface. □

Observe that for a given query there is only one Medium breakpoint. Hence, in the subsequent sections we shall combine Medium and Fine breakpoints as a single type of breakpoint. Specifically, *our objective is to ensure delivery of intrusive notifications at Fine breakpoints.*

4. MODELING NOTIFICATION TIME

We now present a quantitative model for estimating the *optimal notification time* (ONT) so that the defer-to-breakpoint notification scheme can be effectively realized for the query feedback problem. We first discuss it w.r.t the ER problem and then highlight how it can also be used to model other types of query feedback.

4.1 Optimal Notification Time

Let C' be a non-empty set of currently constructed conditions representing a twig pattern or a subgraph pattern and $R(C') \neq \emptyset$. Let C_{new} be a new condition (*i.e.,* a new edge in a subgraph query fragment, a new XPath condition in an XQuery fragment) drawn by a user (drawn after the construction of C'). For each C_{new}, our proposed framework takes two key steps. First, it checks whether $R(C' \cup C_{new}) = \emptyset$. If so then the query formulated thus far does not produce any results and the next available breakpoint to deliver the empty-result notification is found. Clearly, efficient checking for an empty result is pivotal as breakpoint selection can only proceed after detection. Consequently, inefficient execution of the first step can result in inopportune notification delivery, which may increase user frustration. Ideally, we should be able to deliver empty-result notification *before* the construction of the succeeding condition C_{next} (*e.g.,* the next edge in a subgraph query fragment) is finished. In this situation, a user does not need to waste her time and effort in constructing additional conditions before realizing that the query produces an empty result. Hence, notifications should be delivered at fine breakpoints FB1 and FB2 (Table 1). We refer to these breakpoints as *optimal breakpoints*. Observe that construction of C_{next} is already completed after FB3.

Given the most recent constructed condition C_{new} and a set of previously constructed conditions C', the ONT, denoted as T_{ont}, refers to the amount of time available for checking if $R(C_{new} \cup C') = \emptyset$, so that notification can be delivered at optimal breakpoints. We now present an HCI-inspired quantitative model to estimate this time.

Given C', adding a new condition C_{new} in a tree or graph query involves tasks related to the breakpoints FB1-FB5 in Table 1. Let us now refer to the times taken to complete tasks that end with fine breakpoints FB1, FB2, and FB3 as *movement time* (denoted by T_m), *selection time* (T_s), and *drag time* (T_d), respectively. Then, T_{ont} can be bounded by the following equation.

$$0 < T_{ont} < T_m + T_s \tag{1}$$

That is, as long as the check for an empty result of $(C' \cup C_{new})$ can be finished before the breakpoint FB2 of C_{next}, notification can be easily delivered at an optimal breakpoint. Observe that we did not include T_d in the right-hand side of the above equation. When a user starts dragging a selected item or label, C_{next} is in the process of materialization. Hence, the notification related to the conditions $(C' \cup C_{new})$ will be displayed only when she drops C_{next} on the *Query Panel* (breakpoint FB3). This may confuse the user as the notification related to C_{new} appears only after the creation of C_{next}. Additionally, she may have wasted her time in constructing C_{new}. Hence, Equation 1 enforces a tighter bound on T_{ont}. Note that the values of T_m and T_s vary with end users. For a given GUI, how can we theoretically quantify $(T_m + T_s)$? We now address this question.

4.2 Estimating Movement and Selection Times

Estimating movement time T_m. Reconsider the task ending with breakpoint FB1. It involves acquisition of a target from the *Schema Panel* at a distance D from the mouse cursor which is in the *Query Panel*. Note that typically the *Schema Panel* is a rectangular two-dimensional target. Consequently, the item selection is constrained by both the width and height of the panel and the cursor must travel along a two-dimensional vector to it. Hence, we adopt the model proposed by Accot and Zhai [2] that focuses on acquiring targets having rectangular, square, or circular shapes. The movement time T_m is quantified as follows.

$$T_m = a + b\log_2\left(\sqrt{\left(\frac{D}{W}\right)^2 + \eta\left(\frac{D}{H}\right)^2} + 1\right) \tag{2}$$

where D is the *Schema Panel*'s distance to the cursor, H and W denote *Schema Panel*'s height and width, respectively. The parameter a varies approximately in the range of [-50, 200], b in [100, 170], and η in [1/7, 1/3]. Note that η allows the model to weight the effect of the height differently from the effect of the width.

Estimating selection time T_s. The above model for computing T_m can only be applied if the mouse movement is one-directional and involves a single target which is rectangular, square, or circular in shape. Consequently, selection of a label or item cannot be modeled using it. Observe that searching for a label involves moving the cursor over multiple targets to select an item. In fact, the *Schema Panel* is similar to a hierarchical menu and one needs to select an item during query formulation by navigating the cursor through the hierarchy using predominately vertical movements to select the desired label.

Note that we assume the labels or items are organized vertically and hence ignore horizontal movements in this panel as the horizontal width is negligible here. Furthermore, we assume that they are organized in a specific order (*e.g.,* lexicographically ordered). Hence, a user can move to the direction of the target item rapidly using an "open loop" movement. Consequently, we adopt the following *logarithmic* model proposed by Ahlström [4] for modeling selection time of an item, which integrates both the time to find the item and the time to move to the target.

$$T_s = m + n \times (\log_2(p + 1)) \tag{3}$$

where p is the *position number* of the target item, and m and n are empirically-determined constants. For XML or graph data, p can be computed as the total number of items below or above the item selected in the preceding condition.

Remark. Observe that Equation 1 demands empty result check should consume less than $(T_m + T_s)$ time. Although, as we shall see in Section 7, it is possible to realize this for a variety of queries, certain framework may possibly take more than $(T_m + T_s)$ time for certain scenario. Can our proposed model be easily extended to handle such scenario? We posit that it is indeed the case as additional times (*e.g.,* T_d) to complete tasks related to breakpoints FB3, FB4, etc. can easily be added to the right hand side of Equation 1 and notifications can then be delivered during corresponding breakpoints. Although such delivery is not at optimal breakpoints, it is still delivered opportunely when the mental workload is low.

4.3 Applicability to Other Feedback Problems

Equation 1 can also be used to model other kinds of query feedback problems (discussed in Section 1.1). We answer to this question affirmatively for the following reason. Consider the long-running query feedback or the query fragment suggestions problem. Given C' and C_{new} already constructed in the GUI, the long-running query feedback problem aims to detect if this query fragment will take a long time to run and notify the user opportunely. Similarly, the query fragment suggestions problem aims to provide top-k suggestions based on conditions C' and C_{new} constructed by the user. Observe that these notifications must be delivered to the user before the construction of C_{next} for reasons identical to the ER problem. For instance, it is ineffective to provide suggestions when the user has already constructed C_{next}. Hence, similar to the ER problem, notifications for these problems must also be delivered at breakpoints FB1 and FB2. That is, Equation 1 is applicable for these scenarios as well. This is also the case for the query syntax feedback problem. Hence, *our proposed model is applicable for a variety of interruption-sensitive query feedback problems.*

5. THE ISERF FRAMEWORK

We now present the *i*SERF framework to efficiently detect the empty-result (ER) phenomenon during query construction and to effectively deliver appropriate notification by realizing our defer-to-breakpoint-based notification scheme. It is comprised of two key modules, which are described below.

Empty results detection module. The goal of this module is to efficiently detect if the partially constructed query fragment returns an empty result. If it does, then the *interruption-sensitive notification* module is invoked to deliver intrusive notification at an opportune time. Specifically, there are two scenarios for empty result. *Scenario 1:* a newly constructed condition C_{new} does not have any match in the underlying database (*i.e.,* $R(C_{new}) = \emptyset$). *Scenario 2:* the constructed conditions are connected by AND connectives and each has a non-empty result match but there does not exist any data instance that satisfies *all* constructed conditions (*i.e.,* $R(C') = \emptyset$ and $\forall C_i \in C', R(C_i) \neq \emptyset$). Observe that efficient implementation of this module depends on the type of database (graphs or XML).

Interruption-sensitive notification module. Algorithm 1 outlines a generic implementation framework of this module. It takes as input parameters *nullCond* and *allCond* (output from the above module representing Scenarios 1 and 2 of empty-result queries, respectively) and are set to `true` if the query returns an empty result.

The reason we use two separate parameters to represent the two scenarios is because we intend to deliver two different notifications with different content to explain these scenarios. The values of the remaining input parameters a, b, m, n, and η (Equations 2 and 3) are empirically determined. The *hasCoarseBreakpoint* procedure in Line 3 detects Coarse breakpoints (Table 1). Lines 4 - 21 are executed if there are no Coarse breakpoints. The *getCursorDirection* procedure checks if the user is moving the cursor towards the *Schema Panel* (Panel 1). One approach to determine this movement is to use the following heuristic. Consider Figure 2(a). Let the cursor be at point A in the *Query Panel* and the rectangular box represents the *Schema Panel* with height H. Let the perpendicular distance from the cursor to the *Schema Panel* be Z. Then,

$$\theta_1 + \theta_2 = \arctan\left(\frac{\tan(\theta_1) + \tan(\theta_2)}{1 - \tan(\theta_1)\tan(\theta_2)}\right) \quad (4)$$

where $\tan(\theta_1) = \frac{H_1}{Z}$, $\tan(\theta_2) = \frac{H_2}{Z}$, and $H_1 + H_2 = H$.

Let the angle of motion of the mouse be β. Then, as long as the direction of motion of the mouse is on the left of A and β is within $(\theta_1 + \theta_2)$, the cursor is moving towards the *Schema Panel*. That is, given the angle of movement β, we can determine whether the cursor is moving towards the *Schema Panel* using $(\theta_1 + \theta_2)$.

If the mouse pointer is moving towards the *Schema Panel*, the movement time T_m is computed using Equation 2 (Line 6) and the notification delivery is suspended by T_m time (Line 7) to allow the cursor to move to the *Schema Panel*. Note that T_m is not constant for a given query as the distance D varies with each constructed condition. A keen reader may observe that we estimate T_m to determine the waiting time instead of waiting until the cursor reaches the *Schema Panel*. This is due to two key reasons. First, the theoretical estimate of T_m has been proven to have high real-world accuracy [2] and as a result it simulates the time to reach the *Schema Panel* with high degree of accuracy. Second, the mouse movement may be disrupted or stalled half way as a user may be distracted with other non-query activities (*e.g.*, phone call, discussion with a colleague). Consequently, it will prevent the notification to be delivered to the user even when she has stalled query formulation temporarily.

Lines 10 - 17 capture the case when the mouse pointer is already in the *Schema Panel* searching for an item. The selection time T_s is computed in Line 13. The notification delivery is suspended by T_s time (Line 14) to allow the item to be selected (for reasons justified above). Finally, Lines 22 - 26 display appropriate notification message identifying condition(s) $C_\varnothing$ responsible for empty result.

Observe that the above strategy delivers interruption-sensitive notifications by considering only optimal breakpoints (FB1 or FB2). However, as remarked in Section 4.2, it can be easily augmented to deliver such notifications when empty result checking time exceeds $(T_m + T_s)$ by simply adding the wait times associated with tasks related to FB3, FB4, etc.

Generality of the framework. Observe the two notable features of the *i*SERF framework. First, it is orthogonal to the expressiveness of the GUI as well as the underlying query processor. Hence, *i*SERF can easily be built on top of any XML or graph query processor. Furthermore, it does not impact query evaluation time as it is only invoked during query formulation. Second, the interruption-sensitive notification module is not tightly coupled to the ER detection module. Hence, it can be easily incorporated to support other types of interruption-sensitive query feedback problem.

6. ISERF FOR XML QUERY FORMULATION

In the preceding section we have presented the generic implementation of *i*SERF on tree or graph-structured data. To demonstrate its effectiveness, we have implemented it on top of XBLEND [27,31],

Algorithm 1: INTERRUPTION-SENSITIVE NOTIFICATION MODULE

```
Input: nullCond, allCond, C∅, a, b, m, n, η.
Output: Notification N
1  Initialize canInterrupt = false;
2  while canInterrupt is false do
3      if !HASCOURSEBREAKPOINT() then
4          moveDir ← GETCURSORDIRECTION() ;
5          if moveDir is true then
6              Tm ← MOVEMENTTIME(D, W, H, a, b, η) /* Equation 2 */;
7              WAIT(Tm) ;
8              canInterrupt = true;
9          else
10             if cursor is in Schema Panel then
11                 if an item is not dragged then
12                     p ← getPosition();
13                     Ts ← SELECTIONTIME(m, n, p) /*Equation 3 */;
14                     WAIT(Ts) ;
15                     canInterrupt = true;
16                 else
17                     canInterrupt = false;
18         if cursor is in Query Panel and selected item is dropped then
19             canInterrupt = true;
20     else
21         canInterrupt = false;
22 if NullCond is true then
23     Display N = "The condition C∅ will return an empty result.";
24 else
25     if NullCond is false ∧ AllCond is true then
26         Display N = "The conditions C∅ will return an empty result.";
```

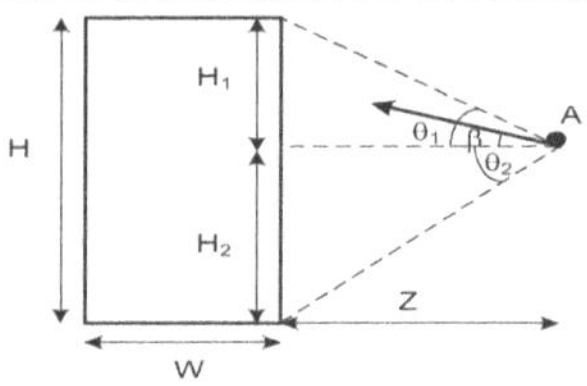

(a) β

Source	Size	No. of files	No. of Attributes	No. of Elements
UniProt	1.5GB	1	38,380,645	20,836,316
Interpro	69MB	1	1,427,234	988,079
PDB	287MB	30	692,583	5,578,498

(b) Datasets.

Figure 2: (a) Computing movement angle; (b) Datasets.

a visual XML query processor built on top of a relational framework. XBLEND interleaves visual query construction and query processing to prune false results and prefetch partial query results by exploiting the latency offered by the GUI-based query formulation. Note that we chose XBLEND as it supports materialization of intermediate *results synopsis* during visual query construction, which we leverage for realizing the *i*SERF framework. However, the techniques we develop in the rest of the paper are largely independent of this choice, and we can replace XBLEND with another visual querying system that supports such a query processing paradigm.

Next, we introduce the visual XML query model that we use to demonstrate the *i*SERF framework. Then, we briefly elaborate on the XBLEND GUI for formulating visual queries. We propose a data structure called a *condition-results tree* (CR-tree) to support efficient detection of the ER phenomenon in XBLEND. Lastly, we present the algorithm for realizing *i*SERF.

6.1 A Visual XML Query Model

For ease of presentation, we primarily focus on a special type of visual XML query prevalent in many applications. Specifically, it can be textually represented by an XQuery query $Q = (\mathcal{F}, \mathcal{W}, \mathcal{R})$ where $\mathcal{F}$ is a set of `for` clause items, $\mathcal{W}$ is a set of predicates logically connected by AND or OR operators in the `where` clause, and $\mathcal{R}$ contains the *output expression* specified in the `return` clause. The predicates in $\mathcal{W}$ can be categorized into two types, namely *join expressions* and *non-join expressions*. A *join expression* captures value-based join between elements (attributes) of single or multiple data sources. On the other hand, a *non-join expression* expresses a non-join filtering condition on a single data source. In the sequel, we refer to each expression in the `where` clause as a *condition*. We denote a set of conditions as C. Finally, the `return` clause has a single *output expression* r representing the *output node*.

Remark. The above query model can easily be extended to support a wider variety of features such as different location steps[5] and qualifiers (*e.g.*, position predicate, not-predicate) as long as the underlying XML database engine can support their evaluation. For instance, if a user visually specifies a condition c involving a path expression containing `descendant` and `preceding` axis at a particular formulation step, then this visual action will be translated to a corresponding textual query and forwarded to the underlying query engine for execution. The result set of c is then used by *i*SERF to detect whether the partially-constructed query yields an empty result. Having said this, it is paramount to balance expressiveness and usability in a visual querying environment as a wide variety of XML queries (*e.g.*, queries with nested `for`s) are not easy to formulate even visually as it requires a deep understanding of the language which many end-users do not possess [7]. Nevertheless, as we shall see later, *our strategy to realize the* iSERF *framework on an* XML *querying system is orthogonal to the expressiveness of its visual querying environment.*

6.2 Visual Query Interface of XBLEND

A visual XML query interface can be classified into two types, namely, *node-based* and *path-based*. In a *node-based* interface an XML query is constructed by taking a node-at-a-time approach. On the other hand, in a *path-based* interface, a query is formulated by taking a path-at-a-time strategy. The visual interface of XBLEND belongs to the latter type. Figure 1 depicts a screen dump of the XBLEND visual interface. Specifically, the DataGuide [13] is adopted to construct the structural summary of an XML document in Panel 1. When a user drags a vertex from Panel 1, the path expression corresponding to this vertex is automatically built. To formulate a query, a user takes the steps described in Section 2.1.

6.3 Condition-Results Tree (CR-Tree)

A *condition-results tree* (CR-tree), denoted as U, describes the set of currently constructed conditions that are connected by AND or OR connectives and corresponding sets of intermediate results that satisfy these conditions. Specifically, each internal node of U represents an AND or OR connective. Each leaf node of U contains a set of non-join conditions that are processed together[6] and the *vertex identifier set* M in which the prefetched vertices[7] satisfying the conditions are stored. Figure 3 depicts examples of CR-trees. Note that we only materialize the vertex identifiers of an XML document $\mathbb{D}$ in M instead of entire content of XML subtrees because it is more space-efficient. Furthermore, the identifier scheme is not tightly coupled to any specific system as any numbering scheme that can uniquely identify vertices in an XML tree can be deployed.

DEFINITION 1. *The condition-results tree (*CR*-tree) is a 2-tuple* $U = (\mathcal{V}_u, \mathcal{E}_u)$, *where* $\mathcal{V}_u$ *is a set of nodes in U and* $\mathcal{E}_u$ *is a set of edges. A leaf node* $v \in \mathcal{V}_u$ *is a 2-tuple* $v = (C_{nj}, M)$, *where* C_{nj} *is a set of non-join conditions that are processed together and M is the vertex identifier set that stores the prefetched data satisfying* C_{nj}. *If* $v_i \in \mathcal{V}_u$ *is an internal node then* $label(v_i) \in \{AND, OR\}$. □

[5] We consider `parent-child` (/) and `attribute` (/@) location steps due to the availability of structural summaries of underlying XML data in the GUI (Panel 1 in Figure 1).

[6] The set of conditions that need to be processed together is determined by XBLEND [31].

[7] For clarity, we distinguish between a node in a CR-tree and a node in an XML document or structural summary by using the terms "node" and "vertex", respectively.

Algorithm 2: *i*SERF on XBLEND

Input: Actions on the *Query Panel*, set of vertex identifiers R_o satisfying the output expression r.
Output: Notification N
1 Initialize *nullCond* and *allCond* to `false` ;
2 Initialize CR-tree U;
3 Initialize set of conditions $C = \emptyset$;
4 Set parameters a, b, m, n, η ;
5 $\mathcal{A} \leftarrow$ GETGUIACTION();
6 **while** ($\mathcal{A} \neq$ "Run" *or* $\mathcal{A} \neq$ "Abort") **do**
7 **if** ($\mathcal{A}$ == "Add") **then**
8   /* *Thread 1* */;
9   C_{new} is the new condition and C_t is the drop target;
10   $R_{new} \leftarrow$ PREFETCH(C_{new}, C_t, C, R_o) //XBLEND ;
11   C.INSERT(C_{new});
12   U.INSERT(C_{new}, R_{new});
13   $(nullCond, allCond, C_{\emptyset}) \leftarrow$ CHECKEMPTY(U, $nullCond$, $allCond$);
14   Lines 1–21 in Algorithm 1 /* *Thread 2* */;
15   **if** *nullCond is* `true` $\vee$ *allCond is* `true` **then**
16    $N \leftarrow$ Lines 22– 26 in Algorithm 1 ;
17   **return** N;
18 $\mathcal{A} \leftarrow$ GETGUIACTION();

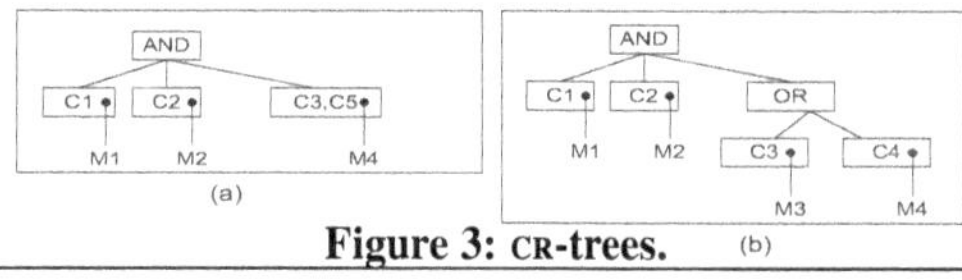

Figure 3: CR-trees.

Note that for practical cases the number of leaf nodes in a CR-tree is small as users typically do not formulate a large number of conditions using a visual interface. Furthermore, each leaf node is associated with an identifier set and not a set of XML subtrees. Hence, a CR-tree can easily fit in the main memory of a modern commodity desktop machine.

Observe that the CR-tree can be leveraged to efficiently detect the two scenarios of empty results (recall from Section 5). Consider the CR-tree with an AND node in Figure 3(a) and the vertex identifier sets M_1, M_2, and M_4. Here, $M_1 = R(C_1)$, $M_2 = R(C_2)$, and $M_4 = R(C_3, C_5)$. Let C_1 be the most recent condition constructed by a user. Then, the query represented by this CT-tree returns empty result if any one of the following conditions is satisfied: (a) *Scenario 1*: $M_1 = \emptyset$; (b) *Scenario 2*: $M_1 \neq \emptyset$, $M_2 \neq \emptyset$, $M_3 \neq \emptyset$, and $M_1 \cap M_2 \cap M_4 = \emptyset$. On the other hand, when the subtree root is an OR node, all vertex identifier sets associated with its leaf nodes have to be empty to qualify as an empty result. These conditions for AND and OR nodes of a CR-tree can be combined to determine whether a query fragment returns an empty result.

6.4 iSERF on XBLEND

Algorithm 2 outlines the implementation of *i*SERF on top of XBLEND. Since XBLEND uses a path-based visual interface that leverages structural summaries, we assume that the path expression in each formulated condition has at least one match in the XML document $\mathbb{D}$. R_o represents the set of vertex identifiers matching the output expression (generated by XBLEND) which is specified in Step 1 during query formulation (Section 2.1).

The variable $\mathcal{A}$ represents the query condition formulation action in the *Query Panel*. When a user drags a new query condition C_{new} and drop it on an existing condition C_t (Line 7), Lines 7–14 are executed in two concurrent threads. In the first thread, the algorithm invokes the prefetching technique of XBLEND [27, 31] (Line 10) to materialize the vertex identifiers in R_o that satisfy C_{new} in a temporary relation T_{new}. Details of this technique, which is orthogonal to this work, can be found in [27]. Next, it adds C_{new} and the vertex identifiers in T_{new} into the CR-tree U (Line 12). Then, the algorithm invokes the *checkEmpty* procedure which detects if

Algorithm 3: CHECKEMPTY

Input: CR-tree U, boolean flags *allCond*, *nullCond*.
Output: *nullCond*, *allCond*, Condition set $C_{\emptyset}$.

1 (*IdSet*, *nullCond*) $\leftarrow$ U.TRAVERSE(C_{new}, *nullCond*) ;
2 **if** *IdSet* = $\emptyset$ **then**
3   *allCond* = `true`;
4   Find conditions $C_{\emptyset}$ in U responsible for unsatisfiability;
5 **return** *allCond*, *nullCond*, $C_{\emptyset}$

Id	Queries	Result Size
Q1	for $entry in doc('UNIPROT.BIOXML')/uniprot/entry, $interpro in doc('INTERPRO.BIOXML')/interprodb/interpro, $cellCategory in doc('PDB.BIOXML')/PDBx:datablock/PDBx:cellCategory where $intepro/pub_list/publication/year > "1950" {C2} and $entry/keyword = "3D-structure"{C1} and $interpro/@id = $entry/dbReference/@id {J2} and $PDBx:cellCategory/PDBx:cell/@entry_id = $entry/dbReference/@id {J3} return $entry/name;	8
Q2	for $entry in doc('UNIPROT.BIOXML')/uniprot/entry, $interpro in doc('INTERPRO.BIOXML')/interprodb/interpro, $publication in $entry/pub_list/publication where $publication/journal = "Structure" {C3} and $publication/year = "2002" {C4} and $entry/@created[contains(., "2001")] {C1} and $entry/organism/name = "Human" {C2} and $interpro/@id = $entry/dbReference/@id {J3} return $entry/name;	23
Q3	$interpro in doc('INTERPRO.BIOXML')/interprodb where $interpro/name[contains(., "hydrolase")] {C1} and $interpro/name[contains(., "subfamily")] {C2} return $interpro/pub_list/publication/journal	35
Q4	for $entry in doc('UNIPROT.BIOXML')/uniprot/entry, $interpro in doc('INTERPRO.BIOXML')/interprodb/interpro where $interpro/abstract/reaction[contains(., "H2O")] {C2} and $entry/keyword[contains(., "3D-structure")] {C1} and $interpro/@id = $entry/dbReference/@id {J2} return $entry/gene	5
Q5	for $entry in doc('UNIPROT.BIOXML')/uniprot/entry, $interpro in doc('INTERPRO.BIOXML')/interprodb/interpro, $classification in $interpro/class_list/classification where $classification/category/category = "Molecular Function" {C2} and $entry/keyword[contains (., "3D-structure")] {C1} and $classification/description[contains(., "binding")] {C3} $interpro/@id = $entry/dbReference/@id {J2} return $entry/gene;	2776

Figure 4: Query set.

the query fragment returns an empty result. Concurrently, in the second thread Lines 1–21 of Algorithm 1 are executed to determine the breakpoint for notifications. If the query result is empty (Line 16), then Lines 22–26 of Algorithm 1 are executed to deliver interruption-sensitive notification at an opportune time.

checkEmpty procedure. This procedure (Algorithm 3) encapsulates the checking of Scenarios 1 and 2. Note that our goal is to check both these scenarios efficiently so that for practical cases T_{ont} satisfies the bounds in Equation 1. Hence, we take several optimization strategies towards this goal. We first check if R_{new} in U is empty (before traversing to other nodes) and it is not connected by the OR operator with other existing conditions. If it is then Scenario 1 is satisfied. Consequently, *nullCond* is set to `true`, $C_{\emptyset}$ is set to C_{new}, and the algorithm terminates early (all these steps are encapsulated in Line 1). Otherwise, an empty result is only possible due to Scenario 2. Hence, it traverses U in a depth-first fashion. If an internal node is an "`AND`" node, then the vertex identifier sets associated with its child nodes are intersected to determine if some vertices are shared by all, indicating a non-empty result for the constructed query fragment. Otherwise, the vertex identifiers are combined (union). We use the adaptive set-intersection algorithm in [11] which aims to use a number of comparisons as close as possible to the minimum number of comparisons ideally required to establish the intersection. After traversing U, the set of vertex identifiers *idSet* that are shared by M_{new} and rest of the identifier sets is returned. Lastly, *allCond* is set to `true` if Scenario 2 is satisfied (Lines 2-3). Additionally, the conditions $C_{\emptyset}$ which are responsible for an empty result are identified and returned as well.

6.5 Extensibility

A keen reader may observe the three notable features of the *i*SERF framework on XML. First, the interruption-sensitive empty-result detection and notification scheme is orthogonal to the underlying visual XML query processor. Hence, *it can easily be built on top of any* XML *query processor that supports such incremental query processing paradigm.* Second, the solution is not limited to the visual XML query model in Section 6.1, but can be applied to richer variety of XML queries. To elaborate further, reconsider the steps for visual query formulation in Section 2.1. Now suppose that the visual interface enables us to formulate richer variety of queries by enabling specification of various XPath axis, qualifiers, `order-by` clause, aggregation functions, etc. Then the visual construction of these features in a query condition(s) will often take place during Steps 4 or 5 (*after* the selection of an attribute or element). For instance, if a user wishes to specify a `descendant` axis then she may do it on the dropped condition after Step 4 or in the *Dialog Box* that appears in Step 5. Once formulated, *the time to detect an empty result for such a query condition is still bounded by Equation 1.* Hence, as long as the underlying XML query processor is efficient to evaluate these complex conditions, the *i*SERF framework is amenable to richer variety of queries. Third, the *i*SERF framework *can easily incorporate more advanced features related to the* ER *problem* such as top-k query modification or relaxation suggestions [20,23] as the latter is orthogonal to the framework. Note that such suggestions also need to be delivered to the user (along with the empty results problem) using intrusive notifications at opportune times.

7. PERFORMANCE STUDY

*i*SERF is implemented in Java JDK 1.7. In this section, we investigate its performance in the context of visual XML query formulation using XBLEND (Section 6). The experiments were conducted on an Intel Core 2 Quad 2.66GHz processor and 3GB RAM. The operating system was Windows XP Professional SP3. A Logitech Mouse was used and its acceleration was set to its default settings (acceleration: 2/1). We compare *i*SERF (denoted by ISF) against XBLEND (denoted by XB), which is interruption-insensitive.

Specifically, we investigate the following issues. (a) Can the empty-result check be efficiently realized in a visual querying framework like XBLEND? (b) Is the defer-to-breakpoint notification scheme the most effective strategy for notification in *i*SERF? (c) Can *i*SERF deliver notification at optimal breakpoints (Equation 1) in most practical cases? (d) What is the impact of interruption-sensitive notifications on the *query formulation time*?

7.1 Experimental Setup

Data and Query Sets. We use the XML representations of UNIPROT, PDB, and INTERPRO downloaded from their official websites. The features of these datasets are given in Figure 2(b). We chose the representative queries in Figure 4 that join up to three data sources. Although our approach can support conditions which are connected by AND/OR connectives, here we chose queries with AND connectives as they are more likely to generate empty answers. The numbers with labels in curly braces in the `where` clause represent the default sequence of steps for formulation of conditions. Note that if a join (denoted by J_i) and a non-join condition (denoted by C_k) have same subscript then it means that the join condition is formulated immediately after its non-join counterpart[8]. For instance, the join condition $J2$ in $Q1$ and the non-join condition $C2$ share same subscript. That is, $J2$ is specified immediately after the formulation of $C2$. Unless mentioned otherwise, we shall be using the default query formulation sequence.

Observe that we did not choose XQuery queries that are too complex as it is observed by Augurusa *et al.* that a visual XQuery interface is useful when it serves the needs of the majority of the users in expressing their queries, which are typically simple [1].

Furthermore, observe that the above queries return a non-empty result. Hence, we create *modified* versions of these *original* queries

[8]They are evaluated together by XBLEND to create a single temporary relation. XBLEND can automatically detect the need for a join condition across multiple data sources during query formulation.

Id	Modifications	Id	Modifications
Q1[C1]	$entry/keyword = "3-D structure"	Q3[C2]	$interpro/name[contains(., "sub-family")]
Q1[C2]	$interpro/pub_list/publication/year >2050	Q4[C1]	$entry/keyword[contains(., "3-Dim-structure")]
Q2[C1]	$entry/@created[contains(., "2050")]	Q4[C2]	$interpro/abstract/reaction[contains(., "H3O")]
Q2[C2]	$entry/organism/name = "Human being"	Q5[C1]	$entry/keyword[contains(., "luminiscence")]
Q2[C3]	$publication/journal = "Chemistry"	Q5[C2]	$classification/category/category = "Mol. Function"
Q3[C1]	$interpro/name[contains(., "lipoprotein")]		

Figure 5: Modifications for creating empty-result queries.

to generate 11 empty-result queries. Each original query is modified one condition-at-a-time and is identified by $Qi[Cj]$ indicating that it is created by modifying condition Cj in Qi (*e.g.*, $Q1[C1]$ means that the condition $C1$ of $Q1$ is modified to make $Q1$ return an empty result). The set of actual modifications to the conditions is given in Figure 5.

Participants Profile. Ten unpaid volunteers with varying degrees of familiarity with XML participated in the experiments to formulate visual queries. At the start, participants were trained to use the GUI. For every query the participants were given some time to determine the steps that are needed to formulate it visually. This is to ensure that the effect of thinking time is minimized during query formulation. Note that if a user quickly formulates a query, less time is available for delivering notification at optimal breakpoints. The participants were given one query at a time. If an error was committed by a participant then that particular formulation effort is ignored and he had to start afresh.

Query formulation by participants. The participants were asked to formulate two categories of queries. (a) *Empty-result queries:* Each participant first formulates the modified queries (Figure 5) without being aware of the fact that these queries return empty result. For example, a participant constructs the modified condition $Q_1[C_1]$ instead of C_1 while formulating Q_1. Note that when he/she formulates a condition that results in empty result (*e.g.*, $Q_1[C_1]$), the ER problem is notified and suggestion to the participant is provided to modify the query by incorporating the original condition (*e.g.*, the condition C_1 in Figure 4). The participant then modifies the query and continues constructing remaining conditions in the query until completion. (b) *Nonempty-result queries:* After formulating all the modified queries, each participant formulates the original queries in Figure 4. Each query was formulated five times by each participant.

Values of Parameters a, b, m, n, and η. In order to empirically determine the parameter values of Equations 2 and 3, the participants were tasked to formulate three queries ($Q1$, $Q3$, $Q4$) according to the above setup. The movement and selection times (T_m and T_s) were recorded for all participants and for all trials. Then, the average movement time $\overline{T}_m = 1071.2ms$ with $\sigma = 7.17$. Hence, we use $\overline{T}_m$ as movement time for the XBLEND GUI. We set $\eta = 0.33$ according to [2]. Then, we compute a and b that best fits this movement time using Equation 2. It turns out that for $a = -30$ and $b = 106$, $T_m = 1061.8ms$. Similarly, the average selection time $\overline{T}_s = 1802ms$ with $\sigma = 52.12$. Note that high σ is expected as some users may be unfamiliar with the structural summaries and might expand and collapse the subtrees several times before selecting a vertex. Using these values and Equation 3, $m = 586$ and $n = 140$ give us selection time that is closest to $\overline{T}_s$ ($T_s = 1846ms$).

7.2 Experimental Results

Effect of Empty Result Check. Before we investigate the impact of interruption-sensitive notification during query formulation, we would like to investigate the cost of accommodating a query feedback technique (in our case, empty-result check) in a visual querying framework like XBLEND. Specifically, we compare the execution cost of Lines 10-11 (XB [27]) and Lines 10-13 (ISF) in

Query	System	Step 1	Step 2	Step 3	Step 4
Q1	XB	0.26 (6123)	1.39 (156172)	0.38 (9)	
	ISF	0.36	1.47	0.46	
Q2	XB	0.32 (5850)	0.42 (9595)	7.21 (30294)	1.14 (4317)
	ISF	0.39	0.5	7.29	1.23
Q3	XB	0.08 (710)	0.11 (35)		
	ISF	0.15	0.19		
Q4	XB	0.22 (5601)	0.66 (166)		
	ISF	0.31	0.76		
Q5	XB	0.15 (5601)	1.21(130318)	1.01 (70327)	
	ISF	0.22	1.29	1.09	

Figure 6: Effect of an empty-result check (in sec.).

Algorithm 2. Note that Line 13 is not executed if the visual querying framework does not support the check for an empty-result (*e.g.*, XBLEND). Also, in this set of experiments Lines 14 and 16 are not executed as we use the original queries in Figure 4. We shall study the impact of the notification service later.

Figure 6 shows the execution times for prefetching (XB) and (additionally) checking an empty result (ISF). Each column labeled Step*i* represents the running time associated with corresponding query condition C_i in a query. The values in parenthesis represent the size of the materialized relations (vertex identifier set). Note that here we do not report times taken by XB to retrieve the final query results as it is orthogonal to the problem. It is evident that the cost of accommodating an empty result check is sufficiently low as execution time of each step is not significantly increased for all queries. Also, it is robust to large size of intermediate results (*e.g.*, Step 2 of $Q1$ and $Q5$) as ISF only retrieves vertex identifiers. In other words, the *checkEmpty* procedure is efficiently realized by ISF.

Justification for Defer-to-Breakpoint Notification Scheme. Next, we design a user study to justify the defer-to-breakpoint notification scheme realized by ISF and its impact on users. All participants were tasked to formulate any four empty-result queries (Figure 5). Measurements were taken on frustration level of the participants at the timing of notification (interruption). The rating was made using a 7-point Likert scale, ranging from 1 being very pleasing to 7 being very frustrating. Three types of notification schemes were presented to participants to experience, namely, *"Immediate notification"*, *"Fixed duration notification"* and our proposed *"Defer-to-breakpoint-based notification"*. Note that the *"Immediate notification"* scheme delivers notification as soon as a query is detected to generate an empty result. In the *"Fixed duration notification"* scheme, the notification is triggered after a fixed 2 seconds delay. Figure 7(a) reports the results. Clearly, participants find our proposed approach most effective. On the other hand, they found the *"Fixed duration notification"* scheme most annoying.

Optimal Notification Time (ONT). Given the superiority of defer-to-breakpoint notification strategy, we now investigate whether notifications can be delivered at optimal breakpoints (Equation 1). Specifically, we study whether ONT satisfies the upper bound in Equation 1 in practice. In our experiments, $T_m = 1061.8ms$ and $T_s = 1846ms$ (see Section 7.1). Hence, $0 < T_{ont} < 2907.8$.

Figure 7(b) reports the execution times for checking for an empty result for Scenario 1 cases. We plot the execution times (Lines 10-13 in Algorithm 2) of the original condition Ci in the nonempty-result query Qi (denoted by ISF) and the modified condition in the empty-result query $Qi[Ci]$. Observe that the *time taken to execute these steps is less when the condition does not have a match* in the dataset. This is beneficial as necessity to deliver notification at optimal breakpoints only arises when the query returns empty answer. Note that the execution times *include* the prefetching times for partial matches in XB.

Figure 7(c) reports the performance due to Scenario 2 for queries $Q3[C1]$ and $Q5[C1]$. Note that in both these modified queries each condition has non-empty result matches ($R(C_i) \neq \emptyset$) but together they return an empty result. For each modified query, we plot the

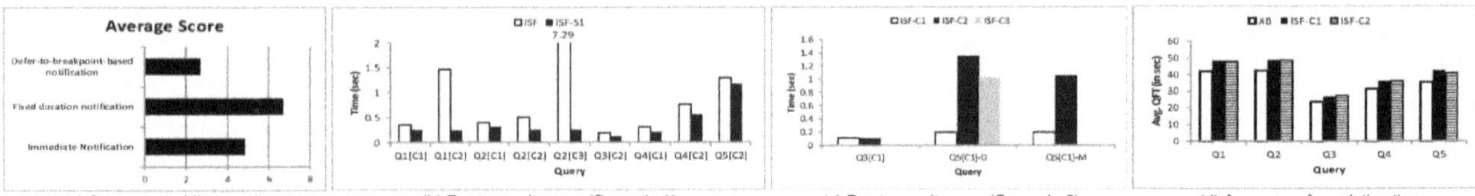

(a) Avg score in Likert scale (b) Empty-result query (Scenario 1) (c) Empty-result query (Scenario 2) (d) Avg. query formulation time

Figure 7: Performance results.

time for checking for an empty result after formulation of each condition (denoted by ISF-*ci*). For $Q5[C1]$, we create two variants; one with the original query formulation sequence C1-C2-C3 (denoted by $Q5[C1] - D$) and the other following the sequence: C1-C3-C2 (denoted by $Q5[C1] - M$). Note that the former becomes empty after formulation of the three conditions whereas the latter becomes empty after formulating the second condition $C3$. In all cases, the empty-result check can be completed within a second or less.

Importantly, *the time taken to prefetch partial results in* XB *(Line 10) and check for an empty result (Lines 11-13) is significantly less than* $(T_m + T_s)$. This is highly desirable as *notifications can be delivered at optimal breakpoints (FB1 and FB2 in Table 1)*. Note that the movement and selection times may vary with different users, *i.e.*, users familiar with the GUI and structural summary may move their mouse faster than others. Observe that $T_{ont} < 0.5(T_m + T_s)$ for all modified conditions. That is, even if a user moves twice as fast as normal users, the notification will still be delivered at optimal breakpoints. Only, when the speed of movement is less than $0.4(T_m + T_s)$, the notification has to be suspended until the construction of the next condition. However, such speed is highly unlikely from typical end users as seen in Section 7.1.

Effect on Query Formulation Times. Lastly, we study the impact of interruption-sensitive notifications on the *query formulation time* (QFT), which is the time taken to formulate each query. Each query is formulated by all participants in its original and modified forms. Specifically, the QFT of a modified query *includes time to acknowledge the notification and continue formulation of all remaining conditions* (if any). Figure 7(d) plots the average QFT of the original query (denoted by XB) and its modified versions (denoted by ISF-*ci* for queries generated by modifying *Ci*). Obviously, modified queries require higher QFTs than the original ones due to resumption lag (recall from Section 1.3). However, the increase is very modest primarily due to the deferred notification scheme and the time users take to acknowledge notifications. Since the notifications are delivered only at breakpoints, the participants react faster to notifications as reported in several HCI studies such as [15].

8. CONCLUSIONS

There is increasing interest in enhancing the usability of database systems. This paper improves usability by contributing a novel paradigm of interruption-sensitive visual query feedback. Specifically, we present a framework called *i*SERF for detecting and scheduling notifications of empty-result queries at breakpoints in a visual environment. A key feature of our framework is its multidisciplinary flavor, integrating principles from HCI and cognitive psychology with data management. First, we drew upon the literature in cognitive psychology to establish that *i*SERF needs to consider the structure of visual query formulation tasks and breakpoints when reasoning about when to notify the user. Second, we leveraged work in HCI to quantitatively model the time available to *i*SERF to detect empty-result queries in order to ensure notification delivery at optimal breakpoints that lower the interruption cost. Lastly, we showed the usefulness and effectiveness of *i*SERF in efficiently checking for an empty result and delivering notification at optimal breakpoints in a visual XML querying environment.

Acknowledgement: Sourav S Bhowmick is supported by the Singapore-MOE AcRF Tier-1 Grant RG24/12. Byron Choi is partially supported by the Hong Kong RGC GRF12201315.

9. REFERENCES

[1] E. Augurusa, D. Braga, A. Campi, S. Ceri. Design and Implementation of a Graphical Interface to XQuery. In *ACM SAC*, 2003.
[2] J. Accot, S. Zhai. Refining Fitts' Law Models for Bivariate Pointing. *In ACM SIGCHI*, 2003.
[3] P. D. Adamczyk, B. P. Bailey. If not now, when? The effects of interruptions at different moments within task execution. In *CHI*, 2004.
[4] D. Ahlstrom. Modeling and Improving Selection in Cascading Pull-Down Menus Using Fitt's Law, the Steering Law, and Force Fields. *In CHI*, 2005.
[5] B. P. Bailey, J. A. Konstan. On the Need for Attention Aware Systems: Measuring Effects of Interruption on Task Performance, Error Rate, and Affective State. *In Journal of Computers in Human Behavior*, 22(4), 2006.
[6] S. S. Bhowmick, B. Choi, S. Zhou. VOGUE: Towards a Visual Interaction-aware Graph Query Processing Framework. In *CIDR*, 2013.
[7] D. Braga, A. Campi, S. Ceri. XQBE (XQuery By Example): A Visual Interface to the Standard XML Query Language. In *TODS*, 30(2), 2005.
[8] S. Chaudhuri. Generalization and a framework for query modification. *In ICDE*, 1990.
[9] E. Cutrell, et al. Notification, Disruption, and Memory: Effects of Messaging Interruptions on Memory and Performance. *In IFIP Int Conf on HCI*, 2001.
[10] S. Comai, E. Damiani, P. Fraternali. Computing Graphical Queries Over XML Data. *In ACM TOIS*, 19(4): 371–430, 2001.
[11] E. D. Demaine, et al. Experiments on Adaptive Set Intersections for Text Retrieval Systems. *In ALENEX*, 2001.
[12] T. Gillie, D. Broadbent. What makes Interruption Disruptive? A Study of Length, Similarity and Complexity. *Psychological Research*, 50(4), 1989.
[13] R. Goldman, J. Widom. Dataguides: Enabling query formulation and optimization in semistructured databases. In *VLDB*, 1997.
[14] S. T. Iqbal, B. P. Bailey. Understanding and Developing Models for Detecting and Differentiating Breakpoints during Interactive Tasks. *In CHI*, 2007.
[15] S. T. Iqbal, B. P. Bailey. Effects of Intelligent Notification Management on Users and Their Tasks. *In CHI*, 2008.
[16] S. T. Iqbal, B. P. Bailey. Investigating the effectiveness of mental workload as a predictor of opportune moments for interruption. *In CHI*, 2005.
[17] G. Luo. Automatic Detection of Empty-result Queries. *In VLDB*, 2006.
[18] D. S. McCrickard, et al. Introduction: design and evaluation of notification user interfaces. *Int. J. Human-Computer Studies*, 58, 2003.
[19] D. S. McCrickard, C. M. Chewar. Attuning notification design to user goals and attention costs. *CACM*, 46(3), 2003.
[20] C. Mishra, N. Koudas. Interactive query refinement. *In EDBT*, 2009.
[21] C. A. Monk, D. A. Boehm-Davis, J. G. Trafton. The Attentional Costs of Interrupting Task Performance at Various Stages. *In Proc of the Human Factors and Ergonomics Society*, 2002.
[22] C. A. Monk, J. G. Trafton, D. A. Boehm-Davis. The effect of interruption duration and demand on resuming suspended goals. *J. of Experimental Psychology: Applied*, 14, 2008.
[23] D. Mottin, et al. A Probabilistic Optimization Framework for the Empty-Answer Problem. *In PVLDB*, 6(14), 2013.
[24] D. Newtson. Attribution and the Unit of Perception of Ongoing Behavior. *In J. of Personality and Social Psychology*, 28(1), 1973.
[25] P. Palanque, M. Winckler, et al. A Formal Approach Supporting the Comparative Predictive Assessment of the Interruption-Tolerance of Interactive Systems. *In ACM EICS*, 2009.
[26] D. D. Salvucci, P. Bogunovich. Multitasking and Monotasking: The Effects of Mental Workload on Deferred Task Interruptions. *In CHI*, 2010.
[27] B. Q. Truong, et al. MUSTBLEND: Blending Visual Multi-Source Twig Query Formulation and Query Processing RDBMS. *In DASFAA*, 2013.
[28] M. H. Vastenburg, D. V. Keyson, H. de Ridder. Considerate home notification systems: A user study of acceptability of notifications in a living-room laboratory. *In Int. J of Human Computer Studies*, 67, 2009.
[29] X. Xie, et al. PIGEON: Progress Indicator for Subgraph Queries. *ICDE*, 2015.
[30] S. Yang, et al. SLQ: A User-friendly Graph Querying System. *In SIGMOD*, 2014.
[31] Y. Zhou, et al. XBLEND: Visual XML Query Formulation Meets Query Processing. *In ICDE*, 2009.

Implementing Query Completeness Reasoning

Werner Nutt
Free Univ. of Bozen-Bolzano
Bozen, Italy
werner.nutt@unibz.it

Sergey Paramonov
KU Leuven
Leuven, Belgium
sergey.paramonov@kuleuven.be

Ognjen Savković
Free Univ. of Bozen-Bolzano
Bozen, Italy
ognjen.savkovic@unibz.it

ABSTRACT

Data completeness is commonly regarded as one of the key aspects of data quality. With this paper we make two main contributions: (i) we develop techniques to reason about the completeness of a query answer over a partially complete database, taking into account constraints that hold over the database, and (ii) we implement them by an encoding into logic programming paradigms. As constraints we consider primary and foreign keys as well as finite domain constraints. In this way we can identify more situations in which a query is complete than was possible with previous work. For each combination of constraints, we establish characterizations of the completeness reasoning and we show how to translate them into logic programs. As a proof of concept we ran our encodings against test cases that capture characteristics of a real-world scenario.

Categories and Subject Descriptors

H.2.7 [**Database Management**]: Database Administration—*Repository, Data warehouse, Security, integrity, and protection*

Keywords

Data Quality; Data Completeness; Answer Set Programming

1. INTRODUCTION

In database applications such as information integration and decision support, one is interested in data sets that are complete, in the sense that the data represent all relevant facts that hold in the real world. In many situations, though, it is only possible to guarantee partial completeness of the data, which means that for certain aspects of the application domain the data are complete, but not for others. In such a situation, one would like to know at least whether the available data are sufficient to answer a given query completely, that is, whether the answers to the query over the available data are the same as if the data set were complete [5,6,8,9].

School Information System. A typical scenario is the management of administrative data that are contributed by people. An example is the management of school data in the province of Bolzano, which motivated the work reported here. Data in the school information system of the province are often incomplete because each school is individually responsible for inserting its data into the system and because for certain kinds of data the contribution is optional. Decision makers, however, need to know whether or not the statistics on which they base the allocation of resources to schools are derived from complete data. As often some parts of the data are complete, one would like to automatically provide guarantees that some query answers are guarantees and hint at those that need further checks.

Example. Consider the following example of a partially complete school database. Among other data, the database contains facts about pupils and classes, e.g., "John belongs to class *a1* at Newton school", $pupil(john, a1, newton)$, or "Class *a1* at Newton school is at level 1 and it belongs to the science branch", $class(a1, newton, 1, sci)$.

Assume we know that we have all pupils from class *a1* and all pupils from class *b2* at Newton school. Thus, the query that asks for "all pupils in class *a1* at Newton school", $Q_{a1n}(N) \leftarrow pupil(N, a1, newton)$, has a complete answer. However, if we consider the query that asks for "all science pupils at Newton school", $Q_{sn}(N) \leftarrow pupil(N, C, newton), class(C, newton, L, sci)$, then under the completeness assumptions above we cannot say whether the query answer of Q_{sn} is complete. Note that, in principle, there can be other classes different from *a1* and *b2*.

Databases typically come with integrity constraints such as primary and foreign keys. But there can be also other kinds of constraints that restrict the domains of attributes.

Example (cont'd). Continuing the example, assume that there is a constraint on the *class* relation, saying that "if a class at Newton school belongs to the science branch then that class has a class code among *a1* and *b2*", expressed with $class\{school = newton, branch = sci\}[ccode] = \{a1, b2\}$. We call this a conditional finite domain constraint.

Now we can reason in the following way. The query Q_{sn} selects Newton pupils from the science branch. Since the above constraint holds for the *class* relation, and *pupil* is joined with *class*, pupils in Q_{sn} must be either from class *a1* or *b2*. Considering that we are complete for *a1* and *b2*, as assumed above, we conclude that we are complete for all pupils selected by Q_{sn}. Assume further that there exists a foreign key from *pupil* to *class* in our database, $pupil[ccode, sname] \subseteq class[ccode, sname]$. Then we have all records of *class* that can be joined with *pupil*, i.e. we have all *class* records selected by Q_{sn}. Overall, assuming the constraint and the foreign key, we can conclude that the answer to Q_{sn} is complete.

Related Work. Motro [17] was the first to formalize incomplete databases and completeness of queries. Levy [15], in addition, in-

Permission to make digital or hard copies of all or part of this work for personal or classroom use is granted without fee provided that copies are not made or distributed for profit or commercial advantage and that copies bear this notice and the full citation on the first page. Copyrights for components of this work owned by others than ACM must be honored. Abstracting with credit is permitted. To copy otherwise, or republish, to post on servers or to redistribute to lists, requires prior specific permission and/or a fee. Request permissions from Permissions@acm.org.
CIKM'15, October 19–23, 2015, Melbourne, Australia.
© 2015 ACM. ISBN 978-1-4503-3794-6/15/10 ...$15.00.
DOI: http://dx.doi.org/10.1145/2806416.2806439.

troduced a format for assertions that say which parts of a relational database are complete. We call these assertions *table completeness* or *TC* statements. He raised the problem to determine whether a set of such TC statements imply that some given query can be answered completely. Razniewski and Nutt [20] showed how to reduce this *completeness reasoning problem* to containment of conjunctive queries [4] and gave a comprehensive analysis of its complexity, considering several variants of queries and assertions. In particular, they showed that for the most expressive queries and assertions they considered, completeness reasoning is Π_2^P-complete. Such a degree of difficulty is reached, for instance, if queries and assertions are expressed by conjunctive queries and if finite-domain constraints hold over the database.

Contributions. In this work, we consider databases that are incomplete in that entire tuples are missing. We address the problem of completeness reasoning for conjunctive queries and for TC statements in the presence of constraints. We generalize the previously investigated problem by taking into consideration two kinds of constraints. The first are primary and foreign key constraints, the second one are a new kind of constraints, that we call *conditional finite domain constraints* (CFDCs), which restrict the domain of relation attributes depending on the values of other attributes. CFDCs are more expressive than classical *finite domains constraints* (FDCs). On the other hand, if we have a database instance at disposal, reasoning about completeness with a database instance is typically intractable [20], and therefore not feasible for large instances in realistic scenarios. In this respect, we expect that CFDCs offer a good trade-off that allows for feasible running times while still carrying more information than FDCs.

Further, we provide a new approach to completeness reasoning which gives rise to an implementation technique of the problem that was not obvious from previous work [19]. A demonstrator system, MAGIK, which realizes our approach and which is publicly accessible on the Web[1] has been implemented based on the techniques in this paper and was presented in [21] and [22].

Our approach consists of two steps. First, we develop theorems that provide a syntactic characterization of the reasoning tasks for each combination of constraints. Based on these, we develop encodings of the problems into logic programming formalisms, where disjunction occurs in the head of the rules that encode CFDCs. One can run such encodings using Answer Set Programming (ASP) solvers (or Prolog engines if there are no CFDCs) such that the resulting program under cautious reasoning entails a test fact if and only if the original problem has the answer "yes". While logic programming is conceptually close to the characterizations, they can in principle also be used to establish encodings into other paradigms.

In the paper we present some of the proofs. For more technical ones we only provide the intuition, due to the space limitations. Complete proofs can be found in [18].

We tested our encoding using two state-of-the-art ASP solvers, `dlv`[2] [14] and `clingo`[3] [10], and one Prolog implementation, `swi`[4]. The obtained results show that our encoding is able to process inputs that mirror the requirements of real world systems.

The remainder of the paper is organized as follows. In Section 2, we recall basic definitions from database theory and fix our notation. Section 3 formally introduces completeness reasoning. In Section 4, we characterize completeness reasoning in the absence of constraints and present our encoding for this case. Characterization and encoding are generalized in Section 5 to take account of key and foreign key constraints, and in Section 6 to conditional finite domain constraints into account, while the combination of both is studied in Section 7. Section 8 investigates the problem of finding a complete generalization of an incomplete query. Section 9 reports on our experiments and Section 10 concludes.

[1] `http://magik-demo.inf.unibz.it`

[2] `http://www.dlvsystem.com`

[3] `http://potassco.sourceforge.net`

[4] `http://www.swi-prolog.org`

2. PRELIMINARIES

Relational Databases and Conjunctive Queries. We assume an infinite set of constants, *dom*, and a database schema, Σ, with an infinite set of relations. Each relation is identified by a relation name, e.g., R, and a list of attributes, $att(R)$. We use $ary(R)$ to denote the arity of R. In the following, we assume the schema to be fixed. For a relation R with arity n, an *atom* is an expression $R(t_1,\ldots,t_n)$, where $t_1 \ldots t_n$ are either elements of *dom* or variables. We denote constants with lower-case and variables with upper-case letters. A database *instance* D is a finite set of ground atoms, that is, atoms that contain only constants. We sometimes refer to the atoms in an instance as facts. For a relation R, we denote as $R(D)$ the set $\{\bar{t} \mid R(\bar{t}) \in D\}$ of all tuples occurring in an R-atom in D. A *condition* is a set of atoms.

A *conjunctive query* is written as $Q(\bar{X}) \leftarrow B$, where B is a condition and $\bar{X}$ is a tuple of variables, each of which occurs also in B. We call B the *body* of Q, the variables in $\bar{X}$ the *distinguished variables* and the other variables in B the *nondistinguished variables*. Given a conjunctive query $Q(\bar{X}) \leftarrow B$ and an instance D, an answer to Q is a tuple $\alpha\bar{X}$, where α is an assignment of domain values to variables such that $\alpha B \subseteq D$. The *set* of all answers to Q over D is written as $Q^s(D)$. Similarly, we define $Q^b(D)$ as the *bag* of answers that contains as many copies of a tuple as there are assignments returning it. We say that Q is evaluated under *set* or *bag semantics*, respectively, if we refer to the set or bag of answers.

Constraints. Database systems allow one to formulate conditions, so-called (integrity) constraints, that all instances of a database have to satisfy. Many of them can be captured in logic and allow for more inferences when reasoning about instances and queries. In this paper, we consider key constraints, foreign key constraints, and conditional finite domain constraints.

A *primary key* (PK) constraint has the form $Key(R,A)$, where R is a relation symbol and A is a sublist of $att(R)$. A *foreign key* (FK) constraint has the form $R[A] \subseteq S[B]$, where R, S, are relations, A is a sublist of $att(R)$, and B is from $Key(S,B)$. Satisfaction of PK and FK constraints are defined as usual (cf. [1]).

In this paper, we also consider *weakly acyclic* sets of FK constraints, which have been introduced by Fagin et al. For the definition, we refer to their paper [7].

A *conditional finite domain* (CFD) constraint has the form $R\{A = \bar{v}\}[a] = W$, where R is a relation, A is a sublist of $att(R)$, $\bar{v}$ is a list of constants of the same length as A, a is an attribute from $att(R)$ that is not in A, and W is a set of constants. An instance D satisfies such a constraint if for every fact $R(\bar{t}) \in D$ we have that if $R(\bar{t})[A] = \bar{v}$ then $R(\bar{t})[a] \in W$, where $R(\bar{t})[A]$ is the projection of the values of $R(\bar{t})$ at the attribute places from A and $R(\bar{t})[a] \in W$ is defined similarly. Alternatively, if $A = a_1,\ldots,a_n$ and $\bar{v} = v_1,\ldots,v_n$, we write the condition $A = \bar{v}$ as a list of equalities, $a_1 = v_1,\ldots,a_n = v_n$. For example, the CFD constraint that states "a class at Newton school from the science branch has as code either *a1* or *b2*", is expressed as $class\{school = newton, branch = sci\}[ccode] = \{a1, b2\}$. If A and $\bar{v}$ are empty in a CFD constraint, we simply write $R[a] = W$ and call this a *finite domain* (FD) constraint.

We will use $\mathcal{K}$ and $\mathcal{F}$ generically to denote sets of FK, and CFD constraints, respectively.

Logic Programming. A *disjunctive rule* has the form

$$A_1 \mid \ldots \mid A_k \leftarrow B_1, \ldots, B_n,$$

where the A's and B's are atoms (see [11]). If $k = 1$, that is, the head consists of a single atom, we say that the rule is a *Horn* rule. A *fact* is a Horn rule with empty body (we omit "$\leftarrow$"). A rule with empty head (the empty disjunction) is a *denial*. (We avoid the common term "integrity constraint" in this paper to avoid confusion with integrity constraints over databases.) An *answer-set program* is a finite set of disjunctive rules. For the theory of answer set programs we refer to [23] and [3]. A *positive logic program* contains only Horn rules. Positive logic programs can be executed under SLD resolution as implemented in Prolog [2].

3. DATA COMPLETENESS

Running Example. Our examples build upon a toy schema from the school world with the three relations

$$pupil(\underline{name}, ccode, sname),$$
$$class(\underline{ccode}, \underline{sname}, level, branch),$$
$$takes(\underline{name}, \underline{activity}).$$

Here, $pupil(fred, a1, newton)$ means that Fred is a pupil of class $a1$ at Newton school; $class(a1, newton, 1, sci)$ means that class $a1$ at Newton school is a 1st level class that belongs to the science branch; and $takes(fred, chess)$ means that Fred is taking chess as an extracurricular activity.

Underlined attributes indicate the primary key, which in our notation can be expressed as the key constraints $Key(pupil, \{name\})$, $Key(class, \{ccode, sname\})$, and $Key(takes, \{name, activity\})$. We also consider two FK constraints, which say that every class, identified by class code and school name, referred to by a *pupil* tuple occurs in the *class* relation, and every pupil name referred to by a *takes* tuple occurs in the *pupil* relation. Formally, this is expressed as $pupil[ccode, sname] \subseteq class[ccode, sname]$ and $takes[name] \subseteq pupil[name]$. Finally, we consider a CFD constraint that restricts classes at Newton school to belong either to the science or the humanities branch, expressed as $class\{sname = newton\}[branch] = \{sci, hum\}$.

The conjunctive query Q_{s1n}, defined by the rule

$$Q_{s1n}(N) \leftarrow pupil(N, C, newton), class(C, newton, 1, sci) \quad (1)$$

asks for "the names of all pupils from Newton school of the 1st level that attend a class from the science branch".

Query and Table Completeness. When stating that data is incomplete, one must have a conceptual complete reference. We model an *incomplete database* in the style of [17] as a pair of database instances $\mathcal{D} = (D^i, D^a)$, where $D^a \subseteq D^i$. Here, D^i is called the *ideal* state and D^a the *available* state. In an application, the state stored in a DBMS is the available state, which often represents only a part of the facts that hold in reality. The facts holding in reality constitute the ideal state, which however is unknown. (Later on we will introduce table completeness statements as a way to express meta-information about the extent to which the available state captures the ideal state.)

Data are accessed by posing queries. We would like to know whether a database has sufficient information to answer a query completely, that is, whether the query is *complete*. If we can infer from meta-information that a query is complete, we know that the answer we receive over the available database is the same as the one we would get over the (hypothetical) ideal database.

We write $Compl^s(Q)$ and $Compl^b(Q)$, respectively, to indicate that Q is complete under set or bag semantics. The first statement is satisfied by an incomplete database $\mathcal{D} = (D^i, D^a)$, written $\mathcal{D} \models Compl^s(Q)$, if $Q^s(D^i) = Q^s(D^a)$. Analogously, the second is satisfied if $Q^b(D^i) = Q^b(D^a)$.

With *table completeness* (TC) statements we specify that parts of a table are complete. A TC statement, written $Compl(R(\bar{s}); G)$, has two components, a relational atom $R(\bar{s})$ and a condition G. In the sequel, we will denote a TC statement generically as C. As an example, consider

$$C_{sci} = Compl(pupil(N, C, S); class(C, S, L, sci)) \quad (2)$$
$$C_{lev1} = Compl(class(C, S, 1, B); true). \quad (3)$$

The first statement asserts that the table *pupil* contains all records of pupils from science classes, while the second asserts that the table *class* contains all records of classes at level 1.

To define the semantics of a TC statement C, we associate a query $Q_C(\bar{s}) \leftarrow R(\bar{s}), G$ to it. Then C is satisfied by $\mathcal{D} = (D^i, D^a)$, written $\mathcal{D} \models Compl(R(\bar{s}); G)$, if $Q_C(D^i) \subseteq R(D^a)$. This means that the ideal instance D^i is used to determine those tuples in the ideal version $R(D^i)$ that satisfy G, and that the statement C is satisfied if these tuples are present in the available version $R(D^a)$. We refer to the query associated to C as Q_C. For instance, the query associated to C_{sci} is $Q_{C_{sci}}(N, C, S) \leftarrow pupil(N, C, S), class(C, S, L, sci)$.

To reason about completeness, we define for every set $\mathcal{C}$ of TC statements the operator $T_{\mathcal{C}}$ that maps database instances to database instances. If C is a TC statement about R, then we define $T_C(D) := \{R(\bar{t}) \mid \bar{t} \in Q_C(D)\}$. For $\mathcal{C}$ we define

$$T_{\mathcal{C}}(D) := \textstyle\bigcup_{C \in \mathcal{C}} T_C(D). \quad (4)$$

The operator $T_{\mathcal{C}}$ is monotonic, and for every instance D, the pair $(D, T_{\mathcal{C}}(D))$ is an incomplete database satisfying $\mathcal{C}$, and $T_{\mathcal{C}}(D)$ is the smallest set (wrt set inclusion) for which this holds. We formalize this with the following claim that we need for the proofs later on.

PROPOSITION 1 ([20]). *Let $\mathcal{C}$ be a set of TC statements. Then*

a) $T_{\mathcal{C}}(D) \subseteq D$, *for all database instances D;*

b) $(D^i, D^a) \models \mathcal{C}$ *iff* $T_{\mathcal{C}}(D^i) \subseteq D^a$, *for all* $D^a \subseteq D^i$.

We say that $\mathcal{C}$ entails the completeness of Q with respect to set semantics, written $\mathcal{C} \models Compl^s(Q)$, if every incomplete database $\mathcal{D}$ that satisfies the statements in $\mathcal{C}$, also satisfies $Compl^s(Q)$. The meaning of "$\mathcal{C} \models Compl^b(Q)$" is defined analogously.

The *completeness reasoning problem* is to check, given $\mathcal{C}$ and Q, whether the entailments above hold. An instance of this problem for set semantics is to check whether $\{C_{sci}, C_{lev1}\} \models Compl^s(Q_{s1n})$ (which intuitively holds and which we prove to hold in Section 4).

Let $\mathcal{F}$ be a set of CFD constraints and $\mathcal{K}$ be a set of key and FK constraints. We say that $\mathcal{D} = (D^i, D^a)$ *satisfies* $\mathcal{F}$ (resp., $\mathcal{K}$) if D^i satisfies $\mathcal{F}$ (resp., $\mathcal{K}$). Note that, due to $D^a \subseteq D^i$, this implies that also D^a satisfies $\mathcal{F}$ and that D^a satisfies the key constraints in $\mathcal{K}$. We say that $\mathcal{K}$ is *enforced* over $\mathcal{D}$ if both D^i and D^a satisfy $\mathcal{K}$. If $\mathcal{D}$ satisfies $\mathcal{K}$, this means that in the real world, represented by the ideal database, the FK constraints hold. If $\mathcal{K}$ is enforced over $\mathcal{D}$, then the constraints of $\mathcal{K}$ hold also over the available database. For instance, we may know that all pupils at our school belong to a class (because there are no external pupils), but the information about the levels and branches of classes contained in the relation class has not been entered into the available database. In that case, $\mathcal{D}$ satisfies $pupil[ccode, sname] \subseteq class[ccode, sname]$, but the constraint is not enforced.

We say that $\mathcal{C}$ entails the completeness of Q wrt $\mathcal{F}$, and write $\mathcal{C} \models_{\mathcal{F}} Compl^s(Q)$, if every $\mathcal{D}$ that satisfies both $\mathcal{C}$ and $\mathcal{F}$, also satisfies $Compl^s(Q)$. Analogously, we define "$\models_{\mathcal{K}}$", while "$\models^e_{\mathcal{K}}$" means that only such $\mathcal{D}$'s are considered where $\mathcal{K}$ is enforced.

From [20] we know that the completeness reasoning problem, both for set and bag semantics, can be reduced to query containment (cf. [4] and [13]). Reasoning in the presence of FD constraints can be reduced to containment with respect to FD constraints [19].

4. PLAIN COMPLETENESS REASONING

In previous work, Razniewski and Nutt reduced completeness reasoning to query containment by which they readily obtained complexity results [20]. However, the reduction did not give rise to an implementation technique. In this paper, we will reduce completeness checking to the question whether a test query returns a specific result over a test database. We will then use these characterizations to translate completeness checks into logic programs that can be executed by ASP or Prolog engines.

In the rest of the paper, we always consider a set of TC statements $\mathcal{C}$ and a conjunctive query Q defined by the rule $Q(\bar{X}) \leftarrow R_1(\bar{t}_1), \ldots, R_n(\bar{t}_n)$.

Characterizing Completeness Reasoning. While developing our approach, we illustrate it with an example. Consider the query Q_{s1n} in (1) and the set $\mathcal{C}_{\text{sci,lev1}} = \{C_{\text{sci}}, C_{\text{lev1}}\}$ comprising the TC statements in (2) and (3). Suppose $\mathcal{D} = (D^i, D^a)$ satisfies $\mathcal{C}_{\text{sci,lev1}}$. Consider an answer, say n', returned by Q_{s1n} over the ideal instance D^i. Then D^i contains two atoms of the form $pupil(n', c', newton)$ and $class(c', newton, 1, sci)$. Now, due to C_{sci}, also D^a contains $pupil(n', c', newton)$, and due to C_{lev1}, the atom $class(c', newton, 1, sci)$ is in D^a, too. Consequently, Q_{s1n} returns n' also over D^a. Since D^i and D^a were arbitrary, this shows that $\mathcal{C}_{\text{sci,lev1}} \models Compl^s(Q_{\text{s1n}})$.

Using the $T_{\mathcal{C}}$ transformation in (4), we can generalize this approach to a completeness test. We define the set of facts D_Q, which we call the *canonical database* of Q, obtained by freezing the atoms in the body of Q. ("Freezing" variables is a well-known concept in logic programming and database theory, which allows one to treat a variable like a constant.) Thus,

$$D_Q = \{R_1(\theta\bar{t}_1), \ldots, R_n(\theta\bar{t}_n)\},$$

where θ is the substitution that maps each variable X to the "frozen version" θX of X.

To check whether Q is complete we apply $T_{\mathcal{C}}$ to D_Q and check whether Q can retrieve the frozen tuple of distinguished variables.

THEOREM 2 (CHARACTERIZATION SET SEMANTICS). *Let $\mathcal{C}$ be a set of TC statements, and $Q(\bar{X}) \leftarrow B$ be a conjunctive query. Then*

$$\mathcal{C} \models Compl^s(Q) \iff \theta\bar{X} \in Q(T_{\mathcal{C}}(D_Q)).$$

PROOF. ($\Rightarrow$) Suppose that $\mathcal{C} \models Compl^s(Q)$. To show that $\theta\bar{X} \in Q(T_{\mathcal{C}}(D_Q))$, we construct the pair $\mathcal{D}_Q = (D_Q, T_{\mathcal{C}}(D_Q))$, which is an incomplete database according to Proposition 1 a). Obviously, it holds that $T_{\mathcal{C}}(D_Q) \subseteq T_{\mathcal{C}}(D_Q)$, and thus from Proposition 1 b) we conclude that $\mathcal{D}_Q \models \mathcal{C}$. Hence, $\mathcal{D}_Q \models Compl^s(Q)$ and $Q(D_Q) = Q(T_{\mathcal{C}}(D_Q))$. Further, D_Q is the frozen version of the body of Q, where the output variables $\bar{X}$ have been substituted with $\theta\bar{X}$. Thus $\theta\bar{X} \in Q(D_Q)$, and it follows that $\theta\bar{X} \in Q(T_{\mathcal{C}}(D_Q))$.

($\Leftarrow$) Suppose that $\theta\bar{X} \in Q(T_{\mathcal{C}}(D_Q))$. We want to show that $\mathcal{C} \models Compl^s(Q)$. To this end let $\mathcal{D} = (D^i, D^a)$ be an incomplete database such that $\mathcal{D} \models \mathcal{C}$. Suppose that $\bar{c} \in Q(D^i)$. We show that $\bar{c} \in Q(D^a)$. Let α be an assignment satisfying Q over D^i that retrieves $\bar{c}$. Then $\alpha\bar{X} = \bar{c}$ and $\alpha B \subseteq D^i$, where B is the body of Q. Since $\mathcal{C} \models Compl^s(Q)$, it follows that $T_{\mathcal{C}}(\alpha B) \subseteq D^a$. Now, let β be a satisfying assignment for Q over $T_{\mathcal{C}}(D_Q)$ that retrieves $\theta\bar{X}$. Then $\beta\bar{X} = \theta\bar{X}$ and $\beta B \subseteq T_{\mathcal{C}}(D_Q) = T_{\mathcal{C}}(\theta B)$. Consider the composed assignment $\alpha\theta^{-1}\beta$. Because of the inclusion just derived, it holds that $\alpha\theta^{-1}\beta B \subseteq \alpha\theta^{-1}T_{\mathcal{C}}(\theta B)$. It also holds that $\alpha\theta^{-1}T_{\mathcal{C}}(\theta B) \subseteq T_{\mathcal{C}}(\alpha\theta^{-1}\theta B)$, since α may map a variable to a constant appearing in $\mathcal{C}$, or may map distinct variables to the same constant, thus enabling more TC statements in $\mathcal{C}$ to be applied. Moreover, we have that $T_{\mathcal{C}}(\alpha\theta^{-1}\theta B) = T_{\mathcal{C}}(\alpha B) \subseteq D^a$, where the last inclusion has been derived above. In summary, we have shown that $\alpha\theta^{-1}\beta$ satisfies Q over D^a. We verify that $\bar{c} = \alpha\bar{X} = \alpha\theta^{-1}\theta\bar{X} = \alpha\theta^{-1}\beta\bar{X}$, which implies that $\bar{c}$ is the result retrieved by Q over D^a with the assignment $\alpha\theta^{-1}\beta$, so that $\bar{c} \in Q(D^a)$. □

Encoding Completeness Reasoning. For any Q and $\mathcal{C}$, the check whether $\theta\bar{X} \in Q(T_{\mathcal{C}}(D_Q))$ can be encoded into a positive logic program. As a set of facts, the program contains the atoms in D_Q. Then we extend our signature by two additional relation symbols R^i and R^a for every R in Σ, to be able to reason about the ideal and available instances. We also introduce a *copy rule* r_R: $R^i(\bar{X}) \leftarrow R(\bar{X})$ for every relation and denote the set of all such copy rules as P_Σ. Thus, any model of D_Q and P_Σ contains an "ideal" copy of D_Q.

Next, to capture the reasoning with TC statements, we introduce for each $C \in \mathcal{C}$, $C = Compl(R(\bar{s}); G)$, the rule r_C, defined as:

$$R^a(\bar{s}) \leftarrow R^i(\bar{s}), G^i,$$

where the i in G^i indicates that all relation symbols are replaced by their ideal version. For example, $r_{C_{\text{sci}}}$ is the rule $pupil^a(N, C, S) \leftarrow pupil^i(N, C, S), class^i(C, S, L, sci)$ and $r_{C_{\text{lev1}}}$ the rule $class^a(C, S, 1, B) \leftarrow class^i(C, S, 1, B)$. The set of all rules for statements in $\mathcal{C}$ is

$$P_{\mathcal{C}} = \{r_C \mid C \in \mathcal{C}\}.$$

Intuitively, D_Q is a prototypical instance where Q returns an answer, namely, the prototypical answer $\theta\bar{X}$. Applying the copy rules in P_Σ turns D_Q into an ideal database D^i_Q. In the following, we use $ideal(D)$ or D^i (resp., $avail(D)$ or D^a) to denote the ideal copy (resp., the available copy) of the instance D. The application of the statement rules in $P_{\mathcal{C}}$ then amounts to computing the available instance $avail(T_{\mathcal{C}}(D^i_Q))$. It remains to check whether Q returns the answer $\theta\bar{X}$ also over $avail(T_{\mathcal{C}}(D^i_Q))$.

To this end, we introduce the boolean *test query* Q^s, which is obtained from Q by replacing each relation symbol by its available version and freezing the *distinguished* variables. Formally, Q^s is defined by the rule $r_{Q^s} = Q^s \leftarrow R^a_1(\theta\bar{t}_1), \ldots, R^a_n(\theta\bar{t}_n)$, where θ is the substitution that maps every *distinguished* variable to its frozen version. In our example, the test query is $Q^s_{\text{s1n}} \leftarrow pupil^a(n', C, newton), class^a(C, newton, 1, sci)$.

In addition to the program $P_{\mathcal{C}}$, encoding $\mathcal{C}$, we define $P^s_Q := D_Q \cup P_\Sigma \cup \{r_{Q^s}\}$, as the program encoding Q.

THEOREM 3 (SET ENCODING). *Let Q be a conjunctive query and $\mathcal{C}$ be a set of TC statements. Then $\mathcal{C} \models Compl^s(Q)$ iff*

1. *the atom Q^s is in the answer set of $P_{\mathcal{C}} \cup P^s_Q$, or*
2. *the goal Q^s succeeds with $P_{\mathcal{C}} \cup P^s_Q$ under SLD resolution.*

PROOF. 1. To prove the claim it is sufficient to show that $\theta\bar{X} \in Q(T_{\mathcal{C}}(D_Q))$ if and only if the atom Q^s is in the answer set of $P_{\mathcal{C}} \cup P^s_Q$. From this and Theorem 2 the claim follows directly. Since $P_{\mathcal{C}} \cup P^s_Q$ is a positive program, it has a unique answer set that corresponds to the least fixed point (LFP) of the program. By the program definition, the LFP of the program is consists of the facts in

(i) D_Q, (ii) the ideal copy D^i_Q produced by $\mathcal{P}_\Sigma$, (iii) the available version $avail(T_\mathcal{C}(D_Q))$ of $T_\mathcal{C}(D_Q)$, obtained by applying the program $\mathcal{P}_\mathcal{C}$ on D^i_Q, and (iv) possibly the ground atom Q_s that can be produced by the rule r_{Q^s} over the facts from $avail(T_\mathcal{C}(D_Q))$. Thus, we have that Q^s is in the LFP of the encoding program if and only if $\theta\bar{X} \in Q(T_\mathcal{C}(D_Q))$.

2. For SLD resolution it holds that each SLD-provable ground atom of a program belongs to the least Herbrand model (LHM) of the program. Since, in our case, the LFP of the answer set program is the same as the LHM of the Prolog program, the claim follows from Case 1. □

Recall that in the definition of the test query, we *freeze* the distinguished variables because we want to test whether Q returns $\theta\bar{X}$, and we do *not freeze* the non-distinguished variables because we do not want to impose constraints on *how* $\theta\bar{X}$ is retrieved. To see why this definition works, consider the query

$$Q_{\text{cht}}(N) \leftarrow takes(N, chess), takes(N, A), \quad (5)$$

which asks for "all pupils that take chess, which in addition take some activity" (which may be chess). Suppose, our data are complete for all pupils that take chess, expressed by the TC statement C_{ch}, that has rule form $takes^a(N, chess) \leftarrow takes^i(N, chess)$. The ideal copy of the canonical database $D_{Q_{\text{cht}}}$ is $D^i_{Q_{\text{cht}}} = \{takes^i(n', chess), takes^i(n', a')\}$. With our TC rule, we can derive the fact $takes^a(n', chess)$, but not $takes^a(n', a')$. Still, this is enough to succeed for our test query $Q^s_{\text{cht}} \leftarrow takes^a(n', chess), takes^a(c', A)$, since the variable A can be bound to *chess*. Thus, the check in Theorem 3 returns the intuitively expected answer "yes".

Completeness Under Bag Semantics. Under bag semantics, a query returns an answer tuple as many times as there are satisfying assignments for that tuple. Thus, a set $\mathcal{C}$ may entail completeness of Q under set, but not under bag semantics. The query Q_{cht} in (5) returns each pupil that takes chess as many times as there are activities taken by that pupil. Thus, under bag semantics the additional atom $takes(N, A)$ makes sense, as it does not change the answers as such, but the multiplicity with which they appear. The query now asks, "How many activities does each chess taker take?"

For reasoning under bag semantics, it no longer suffices to check whether each answer of Q over D^i is also an answer over D^a, but whether each *satisfying assignment* for Q over D^i is retained over D^a. Intuitively, the freezing assignment θ is a prototypical satisfying assignment for Q over the prototypical ideal database D_Q. The minimal available database that, together with D_Q, satisfies $\mathcal{C}$, is $T_\mathcal{C}(D_Q)$. To test whether θ is also a satisfying assignment over $T_\mathcal{C}(D_Q)$, we simply check whether $D_Q \subseteq T_\mathcal{C}(D_Q)$.

THEOREM 4 (CHARACTERIZATION BAG SEMANTICS). *Let $\mathcal{C}$ be a set of TC statements, and Q be a conjunctive query. Then*

$$\mathcal{C} \models Compl^b(Q) \iff D_Q \subseteq T_\mathcal{C}(D_Q).$$

PROOF. ($\Rightarrow$) As in the proof of Theorem 2, we observe that $(D_Q, T_\mathcal{C}(D_Q)) \models \mathcal{C}$. Hence, $(D_Q, T_\mathcal{C}(D_Q)) \models Compl^b(Q)$, that is, the number of times a tuple occurs as an answer of Q over $T_\mathcal{C}(D_Q)$ is the same it occurs over D_Q. Since $T_\mathcal{C}(D_Q) \subseteq D_Q$, this is only possible if every assignment that satisfies Q over D_Q also satisfies Q over $T_\mathcal{C}(D_Q)$. In particular, the freezing mapping θ is an assignment that satisfies Q over $D_Q = \theta B$ where B is the body of Q. By the argument above, θ also satisfies Q over $T_\mathcal{C}(D_Q)$, and hence $\theta B \subseteq T_\mathcal{C}(D_Q)$, that is, $D_Q \subseteq T_\mathcal{C}(D_Q)$.

($\Leftarrow$) Suppose $D_Q \subseteq T_\mathcal{C}(D_Q)$. Let $\mathcal{D} = (D^i, D^a) \models \mathcal{C}$ for an incomplete database $\mathcal{D}$ and let $\bar{c} \in Q(D^i)$. We show that $\bar{c}$ appears the same number of times as answer to Q over D^a as it does over D^i. Since $D^a \subseteq D^i$, it suffices to show that each assignment α returning $\bar{c}$ over D^i also returns $\bar{c}$ over D^a. Similar to the proof for the case of set semantics, one can show that $T_\mathcal{C}(\alpha B) \subseteq D^a$. Further, from $D_Q \subseteq T_\mathcal{C}(D_Q)$ it follows that $\alpha\theta^{-1}(\theta B) \subseteq \alpha\theta^{-1}T_\mathcal{C}(\theta B)$. Next, $\alpha\theta^{-1}T_\mathcal{C}(\theta B) \subseteq T_\mathcal{C}(\alpha\theta^{-1}\theta B) = T_\mathcal{C}(\alpha B)$ for the same reasons as in the proof of Theorem 2. Altogether, $\alpha B \subseteq T_\mathcal{C}(\alpha B)$. Then, from $\alpha B \subseteq T_\mathcal{C}(\alpha B) \subseteq D^a$ we conclude $\alpha B \subseteq D^a$. This implies that α is also a satisfying assignment for Q over D^a, which returns $\bar{c}$. □

This characterization can be readily encoded into a logic program. Instead of freezing only the *distinguished* variables of Q, we freeze *all* variables in Q. We thus define Q^b by the rule $r_{Q^b} = Q^b \leftarrow R^a_1(\theta\bar{t}_1), \ldots, R^a_n(\theta\bar{t}_n)$, where now θ is the substitution that maps *every* variable to its frozen version. The encoding of Q is now $P^b_Q := D_Q \cup P_\Sigma \cup \{r_{Q^b}\}$.

THEOREM 5 (BAG ENCODING). *Let Q be a conjunctive query and $\mathcal{C}$ be a set of TC statements. Then $\mathcal{C} \models Compl^b(Q)$ iff*

1. *the atom Q^b is in the answer set of $P_\mathcal{C} \cup P^b_Q$, or*
2. *the goal Q^b succeeds with $P_\mathcal{C} \cup P^b_Q$ under SLD resolution.*

PROOF SKETCH. 1. Due to Theorem 4, it suffices to prove that the atom Q^b is in the answer set of $P_\mathcal{C} \cup P^b_Q$ iff $D_Q \subseteq T_\mathcal{C}(D_Q)$. Similarly to the case of set semantics, this can be proved by showing that the test $D_Q \subseteq T_\mathcal{C}(D_Q)$ succeeds if and only if the rule r_{Q^b} fires.

2. As for Theorem 3, the claim follows from the fact that a ground atom can be SLD-resolved iff it belongs to the least Herbrand model (LHM) of the program. In our encoding, the LHM corresponds to least fixed point of the program. Thus, the claim follows from Claim 1. □

The tests in Theorems 2 and 4 can be performed in nondeterministic polynomial time, which complies with the overall complexity of the problems, which are NP-complete.

5. REASONING UNDER FOREIGN KEYS

Foreign keys can help us draw additional conclusions about query completeness. We provide an example for both the effects of unenforced and enforced FKs.

Example. Consider the query $Q_\text{n}(N) \leftarrow pupil(N, C, newton)$. Recall that for each class, identified by its code and the name of its school, the relation *class* records the level and branch of that class. Assume that our database is "complete for those pupils at Newton school that attend a class that belongs to some level and branch," expressed as $Compl(pupil(N, C, newton); class(C, newton, L, B))$. If there may exist classes at Newton school present in the *pupil* relation but not in *class* relation, then the completeness of Q_n does not follow. However, if we know that every class in the application domain has a level and belongs to a branch, we can express this by stating that the FK $pupil[ccode, sname] \subseteq class[ccode, sname]$ holds (without being enforced). In this case, for every pupil record there exists a corresponding class record in the ideal database, hence the above TC statement is enough to guarantee the completeness of Q_n.

However, if we ask for all pupils attending a class of the science branch at Newton school, $Q_\text{sn}(N) \leftarrow pupil(N, C, newton), class(C, newton, L, sci)$, then the non-enforced FK does not guarantee completeness, since then for every *pupil* record a corresponding *class* record exists in the ideal database, representing the state of the real world, but such *class* records may not be present in the available database so that we cannot identify classes of the science branch. If the FK holds *and* is enforced, then all such records must be present, and the completeness of Q_{sn} is ensured.

We will characterize query completeness in the presence of key and weakly acyclic FK constraints, both for non-enforced and enforced semantics. We assume that the bodies of the conjunctive queries to be checked for completeness satisfy the key constraints, that is, if A is the list of key attributes of R and if $R(\bar{s})$ and $R(\bar{t})$ are two atoms in R such that $R(\bar{s})[A] = R(\bar{t})[A]$, then $\bar{s} = \bar{t}$. Satisfaction of key constraints can be achieved efficiently by chasing the body with the key constraints (see [12]).

The conceptual tool needed for foreign key reasoning is the chase with inclusion dependencies (IDs), which generalize foreign-key constraints. Johnson and Klug defined two versions, the *oblivious* chase, which introduces a new atom whenever an ID is "applicable," and the *restricted* or *standard* chase, which only introduces a new atom for an applicable ID if the ID is not yet satisfied [12]. We will use an intermediate chase version, introduced by Marnette [16], the *oblivious Skolem chase*, which generates atoms with Skolem terms whenever an ID is applicable, and the atom to be generated does not exist yet. The oblivious Skolem chase bears some similarity with the restricted chase in that a chase step is blocked if the corresponding ID is satisfied by an atom with Skolem terms.

To apply this chase, IDs are translated into rules with Skolem terms in the head. For instance, the foreign key from pupil to class is translated into the rule

$$class(C,S,f_{class,level}(C,S),f_{class,branch}(C,S)) \leftarrow pupil(N,C,S), \quad (6)$$

which introduces a new class atom for every pupil atom, with a new level and branch generated by two Skolem functions that take the keys of the class atom as arguments. Let $\mathcal{K}$ be a set of FKs. We denote the result of chasing a set of (ground) atoms D with the rules obtained from $\mathcal{K}$ as $Ch_{\mathcal{K}}(D)$. If $\mathcal{K}$ is clear from the context, we drop the subscript and write $Ch(D)$. In general, chase termination is not guaranteed for FKs.

From now on, we consider only weakly acyclic sets of FKs [7]. Weakly acyclic tuple generating dependencies (which are more general constraints than FKs) have been introduced in the context of data exchange as syntactic class that ensures termination of the restricted chase for every instance [7]. Marnette extended this result to the oblivious Skolem chase [16]. Under this assumption, $Ch_{\mathcal{K}}(D)$ is always finite for a finite D.

Now, we can formulate a result for non-enforced FKs that generalizes Theorems 2 and 4 by replacing the prototypical database D_Q with the chase of D_Q.

THEOREM 6 (CHARACTERIZATION NON-ENFORCED FKS). *Let $\mathcal{C}$ be a set of TC statements, $\mathcal{K}$ be a weakly acyclic set of FKs, and Q be a conjunctive query. Then*

1. $\mathcal{C} \models_{\mathcal{K}} Compl^s(Q) \iff \theta\bar{X} \in Q(T_{\mathcal{C}}(Ch_{\mathcal{K}}(D_Q)))$
2. $\mathcal{C} \models_{\mathcal{K}} Compl^b(Q) \iff D_Q \subseteq T_{\mathcal{C}}(Ch_{\mathcal{K}}(D_Q))$.

PROOF IDEA. 1. ($\Rightarrow$) The proof is based on a similar construction as the one for Theorem 2. In this case we take $\mathcal{D}_Q = (Ch(D_Q), T_{\mathcal{C}}(Ch(D_Q)))$ as an incomplete database.

($\Leftarrow$) This direction is more involved. We have to cope with the difficulty that applying our chase to a database instance that satisfies the key constraints in $\mathcal{K}$ may result in an instance that no more satisfies the keys because of additional atoms with Skolem terms. For instance, chasing $\{pupil(fred,a1,newton), class(a1,newton,1,sci)\}$ with rule (6) adds the atom $class(a1,newton,f_{class,level}(a1,newton),f_{class,branch}(a1,newton))$, so that the key constraint for *class* is violated.

We compensate this proliferation of atoms by introducing for $\mathcal{K}$ a new set inclusion relation $\subseteq_{\mathcal{K}}$ (and based on that an equivalence relation $\equiv_{\mathcal{K}}$) that regards atoms as identical if the keys implies they are the same. With respect to this inclusion relation, the operator $Ch_{\mathcal{K}}()$ is idempotent and monotonic. Moreover, for any constant tuple $\bar{c}$, query Q, and database instances D, D', possibly with Skolem terms, we have that $\bar{c} \in Q(D)$ implies $\bar{c} \in Q(D)$, whenever $D \subseteq_{\mathcal{K}} D'$. Then the proof of Theorem 2 can be generalized to the new setting, replacing set inclusion and equality with $\subseteq_{\mathcal{K}}$ and $\equiv_{\mathcal{K}}$.

2. Can be shown in the similar way as Claim 1 by generalizing the ideas in the proof of Theorem 2. □

If the FKs are enforced, we also need to extend the available database obtained by applying $T_{\mathcal{C}}$ to the chase of D_Q to satisfy $\mathcal{K}$. However, this cannot be done by chasing this result a second time. To see this, consider the query Q_{sn} from above and the TC statement $C_p = Compl(pupil(N,C,S); true)$, which states that the table *pupil* is complete. Together with the enforced FK from *pupil* to *class* this implies completeness of Q_{sn}, since then any available database must contain (i) all pupils and (ii) the class of each pupil. Let us try to reach this consequence by reasoning about the prototypical database for Q_{sn}. Clearly, $D_{Q_{sn}} = \{pupil(n,c,newton), class(c,newton,l,sci)\}$ and $Ch_{\mathcal{K}}(D_{Q_{sn}}) = D_{Q_{sn}}$, since there is already a class for the pupil in $D_{Q_{sn}}$. Applying $T_{\mathcal{C}}$ yields $T_{\mathcal{C}}(Ch_{\mathcal{K}}(D_{Q_{sn}})) = \{pupil(n,c,newton)\}$, since we are complete for *pupil*, but not for *class*. The chase would add a new *class* atom, say, $class(c,newton,l',b')$. However, Q_{sn} will not retrieve the pupil n over the database $\{pupil(n,c,newton), class(c,newton,l',b')\}$, because it looks for pupils in a science class.

Clearly, instead of generating a new *class* atom, we should have copied the atom $class(c,newton,l,sci)$ from the ideal db to satisfy the FK. To achieve this, we define the chase operator $Ch^a_{\mathcal{K}}(\cdot)$, which, given an incomplete database (D^i, D^a) where D^i satisfies $\mathcal{K}$, extends D^a to satisfy $\mathcal{K}$ by copying atoms from D^i. Formally, if $R(\bar{s}) \in D^a$ and if $R[A] \subseteq S[B] \in \mathcal{K}$, we add *all* atoms $S(\bar{t}) \in D^i$ to D^a where $S(\bar{t})[B] = R(\bar{s})[A]$. The result is denoted as $Ch^a_{\mathcal{K}}(D^i, D^a)$.

To formalize the reasoning performed in the previous example, we combine the two chase operators and the $T_{\mathcal{C}}$ operator to a new operator $\mathcal{K}_{\mathcal{C}}$, defined as $\mathcal{K}_{\mathcal{C}}(D) = Ch^a_{\mathcal{K}}(Ch(D), T_{\mathcal{C}}(Ch(D)))$. This means that (i) we chase D to obtain an ideal db that satisfies the foreign keys in $\mathcal{K}$, (ii) apply $T_{\mathcal{C}}$, and (iii) extend the result by copying atoms from $Ch_{\mathcal{K}}(D)$.

THEOREM 7 (CHARACTERIZATION ENFORCED FKS). *Let $\mathcal{C}$ be a set of TC statements, $\mathcal{K}$ be a weakly acyclic set of FKs, and Q be a conjunctive query. Then*

1. $\mathcal{C} \models^e_{\mathcal{K}} Compl^s(Q) \iff \theta\bar{X} \in Q(\mathcal{K}_{\mathcal{C}}(D_Q))$
2. $\mathcal{C} \models^e_{\mathcal{K}} Compl^b(Q) \iff D_Q \subseteq \mathcal{K}_{\mathcal{C}}(D_Q)$.

The proof generalizes the techniques for showing Theorem 6.

Now we extend our encoding so that it supports reasoning under FKs. Since a partial database satisfies an FK constraint if the ideal database satisfies it, we introduce for every FK constraint a rule like the one in (6), albeit for the ideal version of the relations involved. For instance, instead of (6), we introduce the rule $class^i(C,S,f_{class,level}(C,S),f_{class,branch}(C,S)) \leftarrow pupil^i(N,C,S)$. We denote the set of all FK rules obtained from $\mathcal{K}$ as $P^i_{\mathcal{K}}$, where $\cdot^i$ indicates that the rules create atoms for the ideal instance.

Finally, to model reasoning about enforced foreign keys, we introduce rules that copy foreign key atoms from the ideal to the available database. For example, the rule for the FK from *pupil* to *class* is

$$class^a(C,S,L,B) \leftarrow pupil^a(N,C,S), class^i(C,S,L,B).$$

We denote the set of all such rules obtained from $\mathcal{K}$ as $P^e_{\mathcal{K}}$, where $\cdot^e$ indicates enforcement.

We are now ready to state the encoding theorems for reasoning about FKs, whose proofs are consequences of the Characterization Theorems 6 and 7.

THEOREM 8 (SET ENCODING FOR NON-ENFORCED FKS). *Let Q and $\mathcal{C}$ be as previously. Let $\mathcal{K}$ be a weakly acyclic set of FK constraints. Then $\mathcal{C} \models_{\mathcal{K}} Compl^s(Q)$ iff*

1. *the atom Q^s is in the answer set of $P_{\mathcal{C}} \cup P^i_{\mathcal{K}} \cup P^s_Q$, or*

2. *Q^s succeeds with $P_{\mathcal{C}} \cup P^i_{\mathcal{K}} \cup P^s_Q$ under SLD resolution.*

Similar Encoding Theorems hold for any combination of set/bag semantics and non-enforced/enforced semantics. For bag semantics, we have to replace the rule set P^s_Q by P^b_Q and for enforced semantics we have to add the rule set $P^e_{\mathcal{K}}$.

6. REASONING UNDER CONDITIONAL FINITE DOMAIN CONSTRAINTS

Finite domain constraints make it necessary to reason by cases.

Example. We take up again the example from the introduction, with the query

$$Q_{\text{sn}}(N) \leftarrow pupil(N,C,newton), class(C,newton,L,sci),$$

asking for the pupils from the science branch at Newton school, the CFDC $F_{\text{sn}} = class\{school = newton, branch = sci\}[ccode] = \{a1, b2\}$, stating that the only science classes at Newton school are $a1$ and $b2$, and the TC statements $C_{\text{a1n}} = Compl(pupil(N, a1, newton); true)$ and $C_{\text{b2n}} = Compl(pupil(N, b2, newton); true)$, stating completeness for the pupils of classes $a1$ and $b2$. The TC statements alone do not entail completeness of Q_{sn}, because in principle there could be other science classes. However, together with the CFDC, they do imply completeness.

The characterization in Theorem 2, though, does not apply here because the operators $T_{C_{\text{a1n}}}$ and $T_{C_{\text{b2n}}}$ map the frozen body of Q_{sn} to the empty set. They transfer *pupil* atoms where the class code is $a1$ or $b2$. Therefore, a reasoning procedure has to instantiate the codes in all ways permitted by the CFDC before applying the $T_{\mathcal{C}}$ operator. If the test of Theorem 2 succeeds for all such instantiations, then we can conclude completeness.

In the following, we develop concepts that allow us to characterize completeness wrt CFDCs and then provide an encoding of the characterizing condition. Since CFDCs are essentially disjunctive, we encode reasoning only into answer set programming, which supports disjunctive rules, while Prolog does not.

Let $\mathcal{F}$ be a fixed set of CFDCs. Suppose B is a conjunction of atoms. Let γ be a substitution that maps each variable Y of B either to a constant occurring in $\mathcal{F}$ (a *proper* constant) or to the frozen version of Y. We say that γ *satisfies B and $\mathcal{F}$* if the instance γB satisfies $\mathcal{F}$. We say that a substitution γ' is *at least as general* as γ, written $\gamma' \succ \gamma$, if for all variables Y in B and all proper constants c we have that $\gamma' Y = c$ implies $\gamma Y = c$. We say that γ is an *$\mathcal{F}$-case of C* if γ is maximally general among all substitutions satisfying B and $\mathcal{F}$. For instance, the body of the query Q_{sn} has two $\{F_{\text{sn}}\}$-cases, γ_{a1}, which substitutes the variable C with $a1$ and freezes all other variables, and γ_{b2}, which is analogously defined. By $\Gamma_{\mathcal{F},B}$ we denote the set of all $\mathcal{F}$-cases of B.

We remark that by a reduction of the 3-colorability problem one can construct a set $\mathcal{F}_{3\text{col}}$ of CFDCs such that it is NP-hard to decide whether $\Gamma_{\mathcal{F}_{3\text{col}},B} \neq \emptyset$ for a conjunction B. It is also not difficult to see that in polynomial time one can verify whether a substitution is an $\mathcal{F}$-case of B. Thus, checking whether $\Gamma_{\mathcal{F},B} \neq \emptyset$ is NP-complete. We now generalize Theorem 2 to CFD constraints. We drop the analogous generalization of Theorem 4 due to the limited space.

THEOREM 9 (CHARACTERIZATION CFD CONSTRAINTS). *Let $\mathcal{C}$ be a set of TC statements, $\mathcal{F}$ be a set of CFD constraints, and $Q(\bar{X}) \leftarrow B$ be a conjunctive query. Then*

$$\mathcal{C} \models_{\mathcal{F}} Compl^s(Q) \iff \gamma\bar{X} \in Q(T_{\mathcal{C}}(\gamma B)) \text{ for every case } \gamma \text{ in } \Gamma_{\mathcal{F},B}. \quad (7)$$

PROOF IDEA. For $\gamma \in \Gamma_{\mathcal{F},B}$ we define the substitution $\tilde{\gamma}$ as $\tilde{\gamma}Y = \gamma Y$ if γY is a constant, and $\tilde{\gamma}Y = Y$ otherwise. That is, $\tilde{\gamma}$ substitutes variables that are subject to a CFD constraint by one of the possible values and leaves the other variables as they are. The proof then exploits the fact that over any database satisfying $\mathcal{F}$, a query $Q(\bar{X}) \leftarrow B$ is equivalent to the union of conjunctive queries $\bigcup_{\gamma \in \Gamma_{\mathcal{F},B}} Q_\gamma$, where each Q_γ is defined as $Q_\gamma(\tilde{\gamma}\bar{X}) \leftarrow \tilde{\gamma}B$. □

Condition (7) stipulates a test comprising the following steps: (i) Instantiate the query body B in all possible ways permitted by the CFD constraints. This amounts to considering all possible ways in which an answer to Q can be retrieved. (ii) For each such instantiation γB, compute $T_{\mathcal{C}}(\gamma B)$, the set of atoms that must be present in any available database if the ideal database contains γB. (iii) Evaluate Q over $T_{\mathcal{C}}(\gamma B)$ and check whether the result contains $\gamma\bar{X}$, the prototypical answer to Q over γB. We now show how to encode (i) $\mathcal{F}$-cases, (ii) the operator $T_{\mathcal{C}}$, and (iii) the final test into disjunctive rules.

The starting point is again the canonical database D_Q. Since D_Q consists of ground atoms, which cannot be instantiated, we have to mimic the instantiation by cases. To this end, we introduce a new binary predicate *val*, where intuitively $val(t, v)$ indicates that the term t is instantiated by the value v. To achieve modularity, we keep the encodings of Q, $\mathcal{F}$, and $\mathcal{C}$ independent from each other. Therefore, no information as to which variable can be instantiated by which value should influence the encoding of Q. We achieve this by introducing $val(t,t)$ for each term in D_Q both for original constants and for frozen variables. The set of all such facts is denoted as Val_Q. Then we require that every term can have at most one *val*-value other than itself, which can be seen as a requirement for *val* to be functional. This can be expressed by the denial r_{fun}:

$$\leftarrow val(X,Y), val(X,Z), X \neq Y, X \neq Z, Y \neq Z.$$

To mimic the instantiation of the query body by cases, we introduce for each CFD constraint $F = R\{a_1 = v_1, \dots, a_n = v_n\}[a] = \{w_1, \dots, w_m\}$ the disjunctive rule r_F as

$$val(X_a, w_1) \mid \cdots \mid val(X_a, w_m) \leftarrow$$
$$R^i(X_1, \dots, X_a, \dots X_n), val(X_{a_1}, v_1), \dots, val(X_{a_n}, v_n),$$

which nondeterministically binds the term in attribute position a to one of the values in $\{w_1, \dots, w_m\}$, provided the attribute positions $a_1, \dots, a_n$ are bound to $v_1, \dots, v_n$, respectively. Thus, the CFD constraint F_{sn} is translated into the rule $val(C, a1) \mid val(C, b2) \leftarrow class(C,S,L,B), val(S,newton), val(B,sci)$. We collect the rules encoding $\mathcal{F}$ into the program $P_{\mathcal{F}} := \{r_F \mid F \in \mathcal{F}\} \cup \{r_{\text{fun}}\}$.

We keep the rules P_Σ that copy D_Q into the ideal database D^i_Q. However, to make the TC rules applicable to facts with *val*-bindings, we need to unfold them. For an atom $A = R(t_1, \dots, t_n)$, the *unfolding* consists of the atom $A^u = R(Y_1, \dots, Y_n)$, where each argument is replaced by a fresh variable, and the set of *val*-bindings $U^A = \{val(Y_1, t_1), \dots, val(Y_n, t_n)\}$. Earlier, we have shown how to translate a TC statement C into the rule r_C: $R^a(t_1,\dots,t_n) \leftarrow R^i(t_1,\dots,t_n), G^i$. The *unfolded rule* for C is then

$$r^u_C: \quad R^a(Y_1,\dots,Y_n) \leftarrow R^i(Y_1,\dots,Y_n), U^{R^i(t_1,\dots,t_n)}, (G^i)^u, U^{G^i},$$

where the unfolding $(G^i)^u$ of the condition G^i and the set of value atoms U^{G^i} are defined analogously to the case of single atoms. For example the rule $r^u_{C_{\rm sci}}$ for $C_{\rm sci}$ in (2) is

$$pupil^a(N_1,C_1,S_1) \leftarrow$$
$$pupil^i(N_1,C_1,S_1), val(N_1,N), val(C_1,C), val(S_1,S),$$
$$class^i(C_2,S_2,L_2,B_2), val(C_2,C), val(S_2,S), val(L_2,L), val(B_2,sci).$$

The program consisting of the unfolded rules is denoted as $P^u_{\mathcal{C}} = \{r^u_C \mid C \in \mathcal{C}\}$.

Let $Q(X_1,\dots,X_n) \leftarrow B$ be the query which we want to check for completeness. We have to modify the test query in two ways, first by unfolding, and second by adding *val*-atoms to encode the check whether Q returns $\gamma\bar{X}$ over $T_{\mathcal{C}}(\gamma B)$. Thus, the rule $r_{Q^u_s}$ for the test query Q^u_s is

$$Q^u_s \leftarrow (B^a)^u, U^{B^a}, val(x_1,X_1),\dots,val(x_n,X_n),$$

where the x_j are the frozen versions of the X_j. For example, the test query for $Q_{\rm sn}$ in (7) is

$$Q^u_{\rm sn} \leftarrow pupil^a(N_1,C_1,S_1), class^a(C_2,S_2,L_2,B_2), val(N_1,N), val(n',N), val(C_1,C), val(S_1,newton), val(C_2,C), val(S_2,newton), val(L_2,L), val(B_2,sci),$$

where n' is the frozen version of N. Let $P^{s,u}_Q := D^i_Q \cup Val_Q \cup \{r_{Q^u_s}\}$ be the set of rules about Q.

THEOREM 10 (ASP ENCODING OF CFDCS). *Let Q be a conjunctive query, $\mathcal{C}$ a set of TC statements, and $\mathcal{F}$ a set of CFD constraints. Then*

$$\mathcal{C} \models_{\mathcal{F}} Compl^s(Q) \iff$$
$$Q^u_s \text{ is in every answer set of } P^u_{\mathcal{C}} \cup P_{\mathcal{F}} \cup P^{s,u}_Q.$$

As in Theorem 5, we obtain an analogous encoding of bag completeness checks by modifying the rule for the test query. In order to ensure that no assignment is lost, we add to the body of the rule for Q^u_b for every variable Y in Q an atom $val(y,Y)$ with the frozen version y of Y.

7. FOREIGN KEYS AND CFDCS

Foreign keys, in particular combined with conditional finite domains, allow for a larger set of inferences.

Example. Consider $Q_{\rm n}(N) \leftarrow pupil(N,C,newton)$, which asks for the names of all pupils at Newton school, and assume the FK and CFD constraints from our running example hold. Consider as well the TC statement $C_{\rm sci}$ in (2) and an analogous statement $C_{\rm hum}$, which asserts completeness for pupils in humanities classes. Now, $Q_{\rm n}$ is complete because every pupil of Newton school belongs to a class of some branch (by the FKs), the only possible branches are *sci* and *hum* (by the CFDCs), and we are complete for each by $C_{\rm sci}$ and $C_{\rm hum}$. Note that we arrived at this conclusion without assuming that the FKs are enforced.

We now sketch how the constructions in Sections 5 and 6 can be combined to reasoning about CFDCs and FKs in conjunction. First we provide a characterization of completeness under set semantics. The difference with respect to Theorem 9 is now that we have to consider all cases of the chase of the body B of Q instead of B alone. One can show that it still does not matter which version of the chase is used.

THEOREM 11 (CHARACTERIZATION). *Let $\mathcal{C}$ be a set of TC statements, $\mathcal{K}$ be a weakly acyclic set of FKs, $\mathcal{F}$ be a set of CFDCs, and $Q(\bar{X}) \leftarrow B$ be a conjunctive query. Then*

$$\mathcal{C} \models_{\mathcal{K},\mathcal{F}} Compl^s(Q) \iff$$
$$\gamma\bar{X} \in Q(T_{\mathcal{C}}(\gamma(Ch_{\mathcal{K}}(B)))) \text{ for every case } \gamma \text{ in } \Gamma_{\mathcal{F},Ch_{\mathcal{K}}(B)}.$$

The characterization theorem for enforced FKs is a modification of Theorem 7 where Ch^a is to be applied to $(\gamma(Ch_{\mathcal{K}}(B)), T_{\mathcal{C}}(\gamma(Ch_{\mathcal{K}}(B))))$ for every γ in $\Gamma_{\mathcal{F},Ch_{\mathcal{K}}(B)}$.

For the encoding, there are now two modifications with respect to the case of plain FKs. The first is that every new term that is created by a chase rule must be a value of itself. The second is that the copy rules for enforced semantics need to be unfolded. For example, for the FK from *pupil* to *class*, we have to add the rule

$$val(f_{class,level}(C,S), f_{class,level}(C,S)) \leftarrow pupil^i(N,C,S),$$

which makes every new level term a value of itself. A similar rule is also needed for the branch of a class.

Let $\mathcal{K}$ be a set of FKs. We denote the extension of $P_{\mathcal{K}}$ by these rules as $P^u_{\mathcal{K}}$. Similarly, we denote the set of unfolded versions of the copy rules as $P^{e,u}_{\mathcal{K}}$. With these rules we can now encode completeness reasoning that considers both FKs and CFDCs into answer set programming.

THEOREM 12 (ASP ENCODING). *Let Q, $\mathcal{C}$, and $\mathcal{F}$ as before and let $\mathcal{K}$ be a weakly acyclic set FK constraints. Then*

1. $\mathcal{C} \models_{\mathcal{F},\mathcal{K}} Compl^s(Q) \iff$ Q^u_s *is in every answer set of* $P^u_{\mathcal{C}} \cup P_{\mathcal{F}} \cup P^{i,u}_{\mathcal{K}} \cup P^{s,u}_Q$;
2. $\mathcal{C} \models^e_{\mathcal{F},\mathcal{K}} Compl^s(Q) \iff$ Q^u_s *is in every answer set of* $P^u_{\mathcal{C}} \cup P_{\mathcal{F}} \cup P^{i,u}_{\mathcal{K}} \cup P^{e,u}_{\mathcal{K}} \cup P^{s,u}_Q$.

An analogous result holds for bag semantics.

8. EXPERIMENTS

We performed experiments to find out what is the maximal size of problems that can be solved with our encodings on standard Prolog and Answer Set Programming (ASP) platforms and how the running time depends on the input. Since we expect that in applications there are many constraints that are not relevant to a reasoning problem, we also explored how the performance is influenced by irrelevant information.

We performed four tests and ran them on two state-of-the-art ASP reasoners, `dlv` and `clingo`. We also ran the first test on the `swi` Prolog implementation. The experiments were executed on a desktop machine with an Intel i5 3.40GHz CPU and 8GB memory. Each experiment was repeated ten times and since the time measurements were close, we show here average running times.

For the tests, we extended our schema with two relations: *school*(<u>*sname*</u>, *scluster*, *type*) and *schoolcluster*(<u>*scluster*</u>, *district*, *status*), which model that every school belongs to some school cluster and is of a certain type, e.g., *school*(*newton*, *cluster5*, *middle*), and that each school cluster is in some district and has the status public or private, e.g., *schoolcluster*(*cluster5*, *north*, *pub*).

Test 1. We studied the cost of reasoning with FKs with the query

$$Q_{1\text{pub}}(N) \leftarrow pupil(N,C,S), class(C,S,1,B), \\ school(S,SC,T), schoolcluster(SC,D,pub),$$

which asks for "all 1st level pupils from public clusters." We asserted that we are complete for pupils, expressed by $pupil^a(N,C,S) \leftarrow pupil^i(N,C,S)$, and that we enforced the FKs $pupil[ccode, sname] \subseteq class[ccode, sname]$, $class[sname] \subseteq school[sname]$, and $school[scluster] \subseteq schoolcluster[scluster]$. So, $Q_{1\text{pub}}$ is complete under these assertions.

To simulate reasoning in the presence of irrelevant information, we added TC statements of the form

$$pupil^a(N,\$c,\$s) \leftarrow pupil^i(N,\$c,\$s),$$

where $\$c$ ranged over $\{1, 10, 10^2\}$ and $\$s$ ranged over $\{1, 10, \ldots, 10^5\}$, which gave rise to 8 test cases with 10^0 to 10^7 irrelevant TC statements.

The results in Figure 1 show that all systems could deal with sets of up to 10^6 TC statements. While `swi` Prolog could deal also with the largest input, the ASP reasoners timed out after 30 minutes. Moreover, for small and large sets of TC statements, `swi` was one order of magnitude faster than the ASP reasoners.

Test 2. We wanted to assess the cost of reasoning with CFDCs. We ran this test only on ASP reasoners, since implementing CFD reasoning in Prolog requires the usage of meta-programming predicates to cope with disjunctive rules. We reasoned about the query

$$Q_{\text{high}}(N) \leftarrow pupil(N,C,S), class(C,S,L,B), \\ school(S,SC,high),$$

which asks for "all pupils from a class at a high school."

We enumerated all possible schools, class levels, and class branches with FDCS of the form $class\{\}[sname] = \{s_1, \ldots, s_k\}$, $class\{\}[level] = \{l_1, \ldots, l_m\}$, and $class\{\}[branch] = \{b_1, \ldots, b_n\}$. In addition, we asserted that we have complete information about all schools, $Compl(school(S,SC,T); true)$, all school classes, $Compl(class(C,\$S,L,B); true)$, and all pupils in all classes, $Compl(pupil(N,C,\$S); class(C,\$S,\$L,\$B))$, where $\$S$, $\$L$, and $\$B$ range over all school names, class levels, and branches, resp. The combination of the CFD constraints and the TC statements entail that Q_{high} is complete. To conclude completeness, all possible cases combining school name, class level, and branch must be explored. We varied the sizes of these three domains in such a way that the number of cases (and the number of TC statements for class) ranged from 1 to 10^6.

From the results in Figure 2 we observe that for both `clingo` and `dlv` the running times were linear in the size of the input. Both reasoners could cope with up to 1 mio cases. The fastest reasoner, `dlv`, could process 10^4 cases within less than 1 second, which we deem acceptable.

Test 3. We wanted to check whether the running time observed in Test 2 depended on the size of the input or on the number of cases. We constructed an extreme setup where we had a small input, but a large number of cases, and where completeness of the query followed already from few TC statements, while the case analysis was not needed to conclude completeness. We reasoned about the query

$$Q_{\text{pub}}(N) \leftarrow pupil(N,C,S), class(C,S,L,B), \\ school(S,SC,T), schoolcluster(SC,D,pub),$$

which asks for "all pupils from public clusters," in the presence of TC statements that assert the completeness of each of the relations

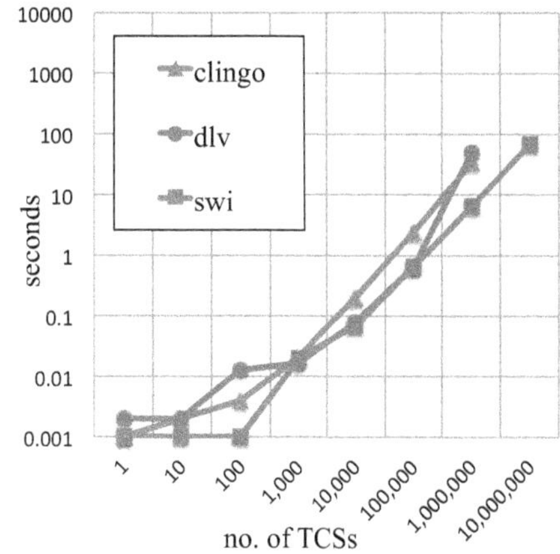

Figure 1: Test 1

in the query, such as $Compl(pupil(N,C,S); true)$, etc. Together, these TCSs guaranteed the completeness of Q_{pub}.

Additionally, we asserted a chain of CFDCs that did not contribute to the completeness of Q_{pub}, but made the reasoning more complicated. Specifically, we stated that there are i different districts, $schoolcluster[district] = \{d_1, \ldots, d_i\}$, that for every such district d there are j different public school clusters, $schoolcluster\{district = d, status = pub\}[scluster] = \{sc_1, \ldots, sc_j\}$, and that for each such cluster there are m different schools, while for each school, there are n different levels.

We varied the parameters i, j, m, n and k to be 1 or 10 (i could be also 100) to obtain different sizes of CFDCs, which gave rise to problems with 10^p answer sets, where $p = 0, \ldots, 6$.

Figure 3 displays the running times as depending on the number of answer sets, instead on the input size, which is logarithmically smaller. We observed running times linear in the number of answer sets, which correspond to the number of possible cases, but exponential in the size of the input. The running time, measured in this way, is approximately 10 times faster, than in Test 2, where the case analysis was actually needed. We conclude that reasoning about irrelevant cases takes time, but less than about relevant cases.

Test 4. We wanted to assess the cost of reasoning jointly about FKs and CFDCs. To this end, we slightly modified the setup of Test 3: (i) we dropped the TC statement asserting the completeness of *class*, and (ii) added the enforced FK constraint $pupil[ccode, sname] \subseteq class[ccode, sname]$, which ensures the presence of all class information needed for the query.

The results in Figure 4 show that the number of answer sets that reasoners could cope with before the 30 minutes timeout dropped from 10^6 to 10^4 and that the running time was no more linear in the number of cases.

In summary, our encoding of completeness reasoning allows for efficient reasoning with foreign keys in the presence of large numbers of TC statements, while reasoning about CFDCs depends in the first place on the number of cases covered by a set of CFDCs, rather than the input size. For combinations of FKs and CFDCs, the performance is not yet fully satisfactory.

9. CONCLUSION

We presented techniques to reason about query completeness over partially complete databases satisfying primary and foreign key constraints as well as conditional finite domain constraints. This generalizes previous work on query completeness and allows

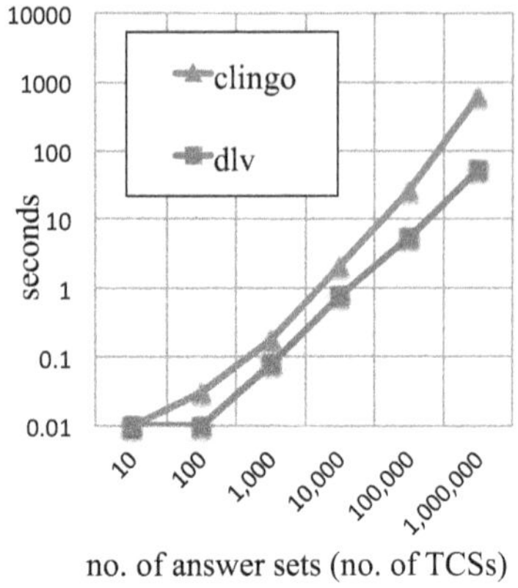

Figure 2: Test 2

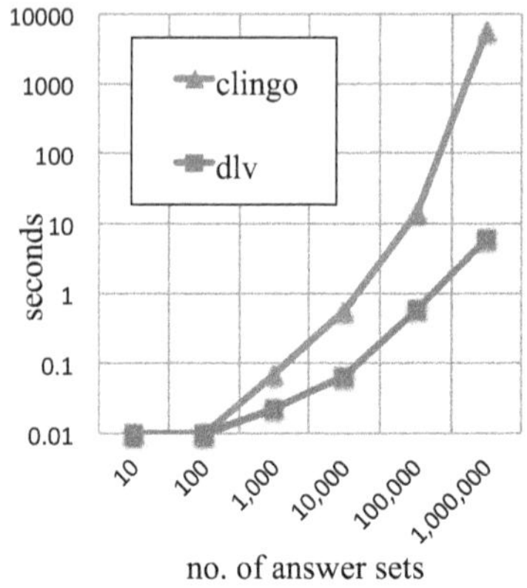

Figure 3: Test 3

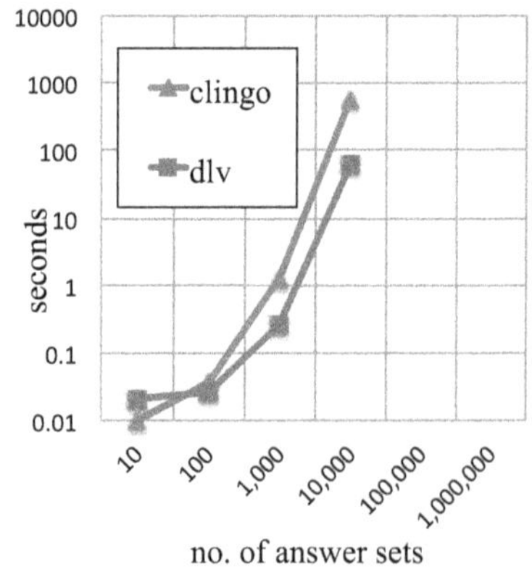

Figure 4: Test 4

one to identify more situations in which queries are complete than was possible before. Our approach also provides a basis for the implementation of these reasoning techniques. We provided syntactic characterizations of completeness reasoning tasks which are independent of any implementation. In a second step, we used them to develop provably correct encodings into logic programming, with and without disjunctive rules, depending on the constraints involed. The encodings can be executed immediately by Prolog engines or ASP solvers.

As a proof of concept, we tested these encodings in a scenario that reflects the requirements of an administrative information system. The results suggest that the encodings are adequate for medium-sized data sets, as they may occur in the administration of a cluster of schools or a university. Currently, we are working on the integration of completeness management into the research information system of a university.

Acknowledgments. This work was partially supported by the project "Managing Completeness of Data (MAGIC)", funded by the province of Bolzano, and the project "Completeness-Aware Querying and Navigation on the Web of Data (CANDy), funded by the Free University of Bozen-Bolzano." We thank the anonymous reviewers for their helpful comments.

10. REFERENCES

[1] S. Abiteboul, R. Hull, and V. Vianu. *Foundations of Databases*. Addison-Wesley, 1995.

[2] K. Apt and M. van Emden. Contributions to the theory of logic programming. *J. ACM*, 29(3):841–862, 1982.

[3] C. Baral. *Knowledge Representation, Reasoning, and Declarative Problem Solving*. Cambridge University Press, New York, NY, USA, 2003.

[4] A. Chandra and P. Merlin. Optimal implementation of conjunctive queries in relational databases. In *Proc. 9th STOC*, 1977.

[5] A. Cortés-Calabuig, M. Denecker, O. Arieli, and M. Bruynooghe. Approximate query answering in locally closed databases. In *AAAI*, pages 397–402, 2007.

[6] A. Cortés-Calabuig, M. Denecker, O. Arieli, and M. Bruynooghe. Accuracy and efficiency of fixpoint methods for approximate query answering in locally complete databases. In *KR*, pages 81–91, 2008.

[7] R. Fagin, P. G. Kolaitis, R. J. Miller, and L. Popa. Data exchange: Semantics and query answering. In *ICDT 2003*, pages 207–224, 2003.

[8] W. Fan and F. Geerts. Relative information completeness. In *PODS*, pages 97–106, 2009.

[9] W. Fan and F. Geerts. Capturing missing tuples and missing values. In *PODS*, pages 169–178, 2010.

[10] M. Gebser, B. Kaufmann, A. Neumann, and T. Schaub. clasp: A conflict-driven answer set solver. In *In LPNMR '07*, pages 260–265. Springer, 2007.

[11] M. Gelfond and V. Lifschitz. Classical negation in logic programs and disjunctive databases. *New Generation Computing*, 9:365–385, 1991.

[12] D. S. Johnson and A. C. Klug. Testing containment of conjunctive queries under functional and inclusion dependencies. In *PODS*, pages 164–169, 1982.

[13] A. Klug. On conjunctive queries containing inequalities. *J. ACM*, 35(1):146–160, 1988.

[14] N. Leone, G. Pfeifer, W. Faber, T. Eiter, G. Gottlob, S. Perri, and F. Scarcello. The DLV system for knowledge representation and reasoning. *ACM Trans. Comput. Log.*, 7(3):499–562, 2006.

[15] A. Levy. Obtaining complete answers from incomplete databases. In *Proc. VLDB*, pages 402–412, 1996.

[16] B. Marnette. Generalized schema-mappings: from termination to tractability. In *PODS*, pages 13–22, 2009.

[17] A. Motro. Integrity = Validity + Completeness. *ACM TODS*, 14(4):480–502, 1989.

[18] S. Paramonov. Query completeness—A logic programming approach. Technical Report KRDB13-2, KRDB Research Center, Free Univ. Bozen-Bolzano, 2013. http://www.inf.unibz.it/krdb/pub/tech-rep.php.

[19] S. Razniewski and W. Nutt. Checking query completeness over incomplete data. Technical Report KRDB11-2, KRDB Research Center, Free University of Bozen-Bolzano, 2011.

[20] S. Razniewski and W. Nutt. Completeness of queries over incomplete databases. In *VLDB*, 2011.

[21] O. Savković, M. Paramita, S. Paramonov, and W. Nutt. MAGIK: Managing completeness of data. In *CIKM*, pages 2725–2727, 2012.

[22] O. Savković, M. Paramita, A. Tomasi, and W. Nutt. Complete approximations of incomplete queries. *PVLDB*, 6(12):1378–1381, 2013.

[23] P. Simons, I. Niemelá, and T. Soininen. Extending and implementing the stable model semantics. *Artif. Intell.*, 138(1-2):181–234, June 2002.

Towards Scalable and Complete Query Explanation with OWL 2 EL Ontologies

Zhe Wang
School of Info. & Comm. Tech.
Griffith University, Australia
zhe.wang@griffith.edu.au

Mahsa Chitsaz
School of Info. & Comm. Tech.
Griffith University, Australia
mahsa.chitsaz@griffithuni.edu.au

Kewen Wang
School of Info. & Comm. Tech.
Griffith University, Australia
k.wang@griffith.edu.au

Jianfeng Du
Cisco School of Informatics
Guangdong University of Foreign Studies, China
jfdu@mail.gdufs.edu.cn

ABSTRACT

Ontology-mediated data access and management systems are rapidly emerging. Besides standard query answering, there is also a need for such systems to be coupled with explanation facilities, in particular to explain missing query answers (i.e. desired answers of a query which are not derivable from the given ontology and data). This support is highly demanded for debugging and maintenance of big data, and both theoretical results and algorithms proposed. However, existing query explanation algorithms either cannot scale over relative large data sets or are not guaranteed to compute all desired explanations. To the best of our knowledge, no existing algorithm can efficiently and completely explain conjunctive queries (CQs) w.r.t. $\mathcal{ELH}_\bot$ ontologies. In this paper, we present a hybrid approach to achieve this. An implementation of the proposed query explanation algorithm has been developed using an off-the-shelf Prolog engine and a datalog engine. Finally, the system is evaluated over practical ontologies. Experimental results show that our system scales over large data sets.

Categories and Subject Descriptors

I.2.4 [**Artificial Intelligence**]: Knowledge Representation Formalisms and Methods—*Representations*; H.4.0 [**Information Systems Applications**]: General

Keywords

Abductive reasoning; description logics; conjunctive query.

Permission to make digital or hard copies of all or part of this work for personal or classroom use is granted without fee provided that copies are not made or distributed for profit or commercial advantage and that copies bear this notice and the full citation on the first page. Copyrights for components of this work owned by others than ACM must be honored. Abstracting with credit is permitted. To copy otherwise, or republish, to post on servers or to redistribute to lists, requires prior specific permission and/or a fee. Request permissions from Permissions@acm.org.

CIKM'15, October 19–23, 2015, Melbourne, Australia.
© 2015 ACM. ISBN 978-1-4503-3794-6/15/10 ...$15.00.
DOI: http://dx.doi.org/10.1145/2806416.2806547.

1. INTRODUCTION

One promising solution to the effective access and management of the ever-growing sea of digital information has been to use computers in setting up databases of information, completed with ontologies that assist in organization and access. In such an ontology-mediated data access framework, ontologies are used as virtual schemas over data sets to enrich query answering with ontological knowledge through logical reasoning, while making use of practical database management systems to scale over very large data sets. The standardised web ontology language OWL 2 and its three profiles, EL, QL and RL[1], are based on description logics (DLs), and conjunctive queries (CQs) are used as a vital querying tool.

Besides standard query answering, explanation services are often required by end-users to understand why certain answers are derived or missing. For instance, suppose ontology $\mathcal{O}$ specifies that a PhD student is a student, i.e., $\mathsf{PhD} \sqsubseteq \mathsf{Student}$, each PhD student has some supervisor, i.e., $\mathsf{PhD} \sqsubseteq \exists \mathsf{hasSupervisor.Person}$, Tom is a PhD student and Mary is a student, i.e., $\mathsf{PhD(Tom)}$ and $\mathsf{Student(Mary)}$. For the query to retrieve those individuals who have supervisors, which can be expressed as $\mathcal{Q}(x) = \exists y.\mathsf{hasSupervisor}(x, y)$, "Tom" is an answer whereas "Mary" is not. One explanation for "Mary" being missing is that $\mathsf{PhD(Mary)}$ is absent. Such explanation services are critical for knowledge management to identify specific pieces of the knowledge that need to be revised. For example, the observation that Mary should have a supervisor indicates that the current knowledge is incomplete and $\mathsf{PhD(Mary)}$ could be added.

On the other hand, however, the implementation of existing OWL reasoners does not support such an explanation mechanism even through tracing the execution of query answering. For this reason, extensive efforts have been devoted to equip ontology-based systems with various explanation facilities [22, 23, 4, 15, 24, 6]. While early research was mainly on explaining derived answers (a.k.a. positive answers, like "Tom" in the above example), explaining missing answers (a.k.a. negative answers, like "Mary") has attracted much attention lately [3, 6]. Such an explanation facility is essential to understand why the ontology-based system fails

[1] `http://www.w3.org/TR/owl2-profiles/`

to derive certain desired answers, and to enrich incomplete data according to user observations. Such a query explanation problem is usually formalised as a problem of abduction in AI, called *query abduction.*

Existing research efforts showed that query abduction is challenging. First, while ontology-based reasoning empowers query answering, it also complicates query abduction. The computational complexity of query abduction is indeed higher than query answering [6]. Also, efficiency of abduction implementation has not been a central concern in AI but it is essential for ontology-based systems, and it is highly non-trivial to develop a scalable algorithm for query abduction. Furthermore, existing query abduction approaches are either incapable to scale over large data sets or incomplete in explaining CQs (i.e., they may fail to compute certain explanations, see a detailed discussion in Section 2). In this paper, we demonstrate that *it is possible to achieve both scalability and completeness in one framework*, by presenting a complete and scalable query abduction method for $\mathcal{ELH}_\bot$ontologies. We choose $\mathcal{ELH}_\bot$because it underlies the OWL 2 EL profile, is expressive enough for many practical ontologies such as SNOMED CT, and is a core fragment of most expressive DLs. CQ answering for $\mathcal{ELH}_\bot$ ontologies has attracted intensive interest lately [19, 26].

The main contributions of the paper include: (1) We reduce a query abduction problem in $\mathcal{ELH}_\bot$ to an equivalent one in datalog, and prove the soundness and completeness. (2) We introduce a method to extract (often very small) modules of the data through data summarisation, and we introduce an advanced pruning strategy to couple the basic backward chaining procedure in the search for solutions. (3) We implemented a prototype system that integrates highly optimised Prolog and datalog engines, and our evaluation shows that the algorithm is capable of handling query abduction involving around 10 million facts.

2. RELATED WORKS

Several approaches to query abduction have been proposed, which vary according to their underlying DLs and types of observations. Some of these focused on expressive DLs and observations formulated by simple atomic queries or ground CQs [17, 14, 21, 9]. These approaches typically use tableau-based methods, which however, could rarely scale over relative large data sets. One exception is the approach by Du et al. [9], which we will discuss in detail later.

Query abduction for CQs with existentially quantified variables, which will be referred to as *general CQs*, has been investigated only for light-weight DLs underlying OWL 2 RL and QL profiles. Borgida et al. [3] are among the first who advocated to study the explanation of negative answers, and they focused on OWL 2 QL. Du et al. [10] have proposed a practical approach in OWL 2 RL, and an OWL 2 RL ontology can be directly translated into a datalog program. Calvanese et al. [6] investigated the computational complexity of query abduction in OWL 2 QL. To the best of our knowledge, we are the first to study query abduction for general CQs in OWL 2 EL.

Du et al. [9, 8] were among the first to tackle the scalability issue, yet those approaches still suffer from some shortcomings. The method proposed in [9] is incomplete for general CQs, that is, their method is unable to compute all minimal explanations for some general CQs. This is mainly due to the ontology transformation adopted in that approach, which discard rules with existentially quantified variables in the head. Such rules will be referred to as *genuine existential rules.* For example, consider the ontology $\mathcal{O}$ in Section 1, the algorithm developed in [9] discards the axiom $\mathsf{PhD} \sqsubseteq \exists \mathsf{hasSupervisor.Person}$ and thus cannot obtain the explanation $\mathsf{PhD(Mary)}$. Also, the system developed in [9] still has difficulty in processing large data sets (see Section 5 for details). In [8], a notion of a representative explanation is introduced, which is informally a schema of multiple explanations. While a scalable algorithm is developed, the approach works only for first-order (FO) rewritable ontologies, and ontologies expressed in popular ontology languages, such as OWL 2 EL which we look into, may not be FO rewritable. It is challenging to efficiently compute representative explanations for ontologies that may not be FO rewritable. To see this, consider an ontology consisting of one axiom $\exists R.A \sqsubseteq A$. For the observation $A(a)$, there would an infinite number of representative explanations of the form $\{R(a,u_1), R(u_1,u_2), \ldots, R(u_{n-1},u_n), A(u_n)\}$.

In summary, compared to existing query abduction approaches, our approach is the only one that enjoys all the following three properties: (1) In contrast to [17, 14, 21], our approach scales over large data sets. (2) In contrast to [9], our approach is complete for general CQs in a sense that all (minimal) explanations can be computed. (3) In contrast to [3, 10, 6, 8], our approach applies to $\mathcal{ELH}_\bot$ ontologies that are not necessarily FO rewritable.

3. PRELIMINARIES

We use standard notions of first-order (FO) constants, variables, terms, substitutions, predicates, atoms, (ground) formulae, and sentences. All atoms and formulae considered in the paper are function free. A *fact* is a ground atom. For a formula ϕ, with $\phi(\vec{x})$ we denote that $\vec{x}$ are the free variables in ϕ. For a (set of) formula(e) ϕ, $\mathit{pred}(\phi)$, $\mathit{term}(\phi)$, $\mathit{const}(\phi)$ denote the set of predicates, terms, and constants occurring in ϕ. First-order entailment are defined as usual. For convenience, we sometimes treat a conjunction of atoms as a set consisting of the atoms.

3.1 Description Logic and Query Answering

Consider countably infinite and mutually disjoint sets N_C, N_R, N_I, and N_V of concept names (i.e., unary predicates), role names (i.e. binary predicates), individuals (i.e. constants), and variables respectively. In $\mathcal{ELH}_\bot$, a *concept description* (or simply *concept*) C is defined inductively using the following constructors:

$$C := \top \mid \bot \mid A \mid C_1 \sqcap C_2 \mid \exists R.C,$$

where $A \in N_C$, $R \in N_R$, and C_1 and C_2 are concepts. A *TBox* is a finite set of axioms of the forms $C \sqsubseteq D$, and $R \sqsubseteq S$, where C, D are both concepts and $R, S \in N_R$. An *ABox* is a finite set of facts of the forms $A(a)$ and $R(a,b)$, where $A \in N_C$, $R \in N_R$ and $a, b \in N_I$. A *knowledge base* (KB) $\mathcal{K} = (\mathcal{T}, \mathcal{A})$ consists of a TBox $\mathcal{T}$ and an ABox $\mathcal{A}$. The semantics of $\mathcal{ELH}_\bot$ is defined as usual in terms of an interpretation $\mathcal{I} = (\Delta^\mathcal{I}, \cdot^\mathcal{I})$, and we refer to [1] for details.

An $\mathcal{ELH}_\bot$ TBox is *normalized* if it consists of only axioms of the forms $A \sqsubseteq B$, $A_1 \sqcap \cdots \sqcap A_n \sqsubseteq A$, $A_1 \sqsubseteq \exists R.A$, $\exists R.A_1 \sqsubseteq A$, and $R \sqsubseteq S$, where $A_{(i)} \in N_C \cup \{\top\}$, $B \in N_C \cup \{\top, \bot\}$, and $R, S \in N_R$. An $\mathcal{ELH}_\bot$ TBox can be transformed in polynomial time to a normalized TBox that is equivalent to the TBox [1]. Without loss of generality, we consider only TBoxes in normal form.

An *FO query* $\mathcal{Q}(\vec{x})$ is a first-order formula (with free variables $\vec{x}$, we will sometimes write $\mathcal{Q}$ for simplicity). It is called *boolean* if $\vec{x}$ is empty. For a tuple of constants $\vec{a}$ with the same arity as $\vec{x}$, we write $\mathcal{Q}(\vec{a})$ to denote the Boolean FO query obtained from $\mathcal{Q}(\vec{x})$ by substituting the variables $\vec{x}$ with constants $\vec{a}$. For a TBox $\mathcal{T}$, an ABox $\mathcal{A}$, and a FO query $\mathcal{Q}(\vec{x})$, a tuple of constants $\vec{a}$ is a *certain answer* (or simply an *answer*) to $\mathcal{Q}(\vec{x})$ over $\mathcal{T}$ and $\mathcal{A}$, if the arity of $\vec{a}$ agrees with that of $\vec{x}$ and $\mathcal{T} \cup \mathcal{A} \models \mathcal{Q}(\vec{a})$. Otherwise, if $\mathcal{T} \cup \mathcal{A} \not\models \mathcal{Q}(\vec{a})$ then $\vec{a}$ is a *negative answer*.

A conjunctive query (CQ) $\mathcal{Q}(\vec{x})$ is of the form $\exists \vec{y}.\phi(\vec{x}, \vec{y})$, where ϕ is a conjunction of atoms with predicates and terms from $N_C \cup N_R$ and $N_I \cup N_V$, respectively. Variables $\vec{x}$ are *answer variables* and $\vec{y}$ are *quantified variables*. A *ground CQ* is a CQ where $\vec{y}$ is empty, and an *atomic query* is a ground CQ where $\phi(\vec{x}, \vec{y})$ consists of a single atom.

3.2 Query Abduction

We consider the *query abduction problem (QAP)* where a CQ and an answer tuple are given as the *observation* and a solution to the problem (or equivalently an explanation to the query answer) is a set of facts [6]. Formally, given a background ontology consisting of a TBox $\mathcal{T}$ and an ABox $\mathcal{A}$, taking an instantiated CQ (or a BCQ) $\mathcal{Q}(\vec{a})$ as the *observation*, a solution to the query abduction problem is a (possibly empty) set $\mathcal{E}$ of facts such that $\mathcal{E}$ is consistent with $\mathcal{T} \cup \mathcal{A}$ and $\vec{a}$ is an answer to $\mathcal{Q}(\vec{x})$ over $\mathcal{T} \cup \mathcal{A}$ (only) together with $\mathcal{E}$. In classical abduction setting, to reduce the search space and retrieve only relevant solutions, the predicates allowed in the solutions are often pre-specified, which are called *abducibles*. Furthermore, for the ease of understanding, solutions should be as succinct as possible, and the minimal solutions (w.r.t. set containment) are desired. The formal definition of QAP and a solution to the QAP is given as follows.

Definition 1 (QAP). *An instance of a query abduction problem (QAP) is a five tuple $\mathcal{P} = \langle \mathcal{T}, \mathcal{A}, \mathcal{Q}(\vec{a}), \Sigma, \Delta \rangle$, where $\mathcal{T}$ is an $\mathcal{ELH}_\bot$ TBox, $\mathcal{A}$ is an $\mathcal{ELH}_\bot$ ABox, $\mathcal{Q}(\vec{x})$ is a CQ, $\vec{a}$ a tuple of constants with the same arity as $\vec{x}$, $\Sigma \subseteq N_C \cup N_R$ is a finite set of predicates, and Δ is a finite set of constants. BCQ $\mathcal{Q}(\vec{a})$ is the* observation, *Σ is the set of* abducibles, *and Δ is the* domain.

A solution $\mathcal{E}$ to the QAP $\mathcal{P}$ is a set of facts such that

1. *$pred(\mathcal{E}) \subseteq \Sigma$ and $const(\mathcal{E}) \subseteq \Delta$;*
2. *$\mathcal{T} \cup \mathcal{A} \cup \mathcal{E} \models Q(\vec{a})$;*
3. *$\mathcal{T} \cup \mathcal{A} \cup \mathcal{E} \not\models \bot$; and*
4. *$\mathcal{E} \not\models \mathcal{Q}(\vec{a})$;*

Conditions 3 and 4 are called non-triviality *conditions for a solution. Let $\mathsf{sol}(\mathcal{P})$ be the set of solutions to $\mathcal{P}$. Moreover, $\mathcal{E}$ is* minimal *if there is no solution $\mathcal{E}' \in \mathsf{sol}(\mathcal{P})$ s.t. $\mathcal{E}' \subset \mathcal{E}$.*

In contrast to the definitions in [6, 8], the above definition has a finite domain Δ as an additional attribute, and Δ contains all the constants occurring in a solution. In [6, 8], a solution can contain any constants, including arbitrarily many fresh constants not present in the initial ABox. In this case infinitely many (minimal) solutions often exist for a QAP, and hence it is impossible to compute all the (minimal) solutions. Even if *representative solutions* are considered [8], which ignore renaming of fresh constants and are minimal up to substitution, still infinitely many such representative solutions may exist in general, as shown in Section 2. On the other hand, allowing uncontrolled introduction of fresh constants to QAP solutions is arguably of mere theoretical interest. In query explanation, a finite number of constants are often sufficient. Hence, we assume a finite domain Δ in a QAP, which can either be specified by the user, or by default set to be the set of all the constants in the initial ABox $\mathcal{A}$ and/or the constants in the observation Q. Given that the predicates and constants allowed in a solution are both finite and pre-specified, the total number of solutions to a QAP is always finite (even for ontologies that are not FO rewritable).

3.3 Existential Rules

Since our new approach translates a QAP for $\mathcal{ELH}_\bot$ into a problem of abduction in programs of existential rules, we recall some basics of existential rules in this subsection. Formally, an *existential rule* [5, 2] is a sentence of the form

$$\forall \vec{x}.\forall \vec{y}.[\phi(\vec{x}, \vec{y}) \rightarrow \exists \vec{z}.\psi(\vec{x}, \vec{z})]$$

where $\phi(\vec{x}, \vec{y})$ and $\psi(\vec{x}, \vec{z})$ are conjunctions of function-free atoms and $\vec{x}$, $\vec{y}$ and $\vec{z}$ are pairwise disjoint. For convenience of presentation, universal quantifiers are often omitted. Formula ϕ is the *body* and formula ψ is the *head* of the rule. It is shown in [5] that $\mathcal{ELH}_\bot$ can be captured by existential rules. In particular, given an $\mathcal{ELH}_\bot$ TBox $\mathcal{T}$, $\mathcal{T}$ can be transformed into an existential program $\mathcal{R}_\mathcal{T}$ that is semantically equivalent to $\mathcal{T}$ in first-order logic. Query answering and query abduction in programs of existential rules are defined in the same way as in $\mathcal{ELH}_\bot$, and for query abduction of existential rules, we extend the definition QAP to allow $\mathcal{Q}$ in observations to be a FO query.

A *datalog* rule is an existential rule whose head $\psi(\vec{x}, \vec{z})$ consists of a single atom and $\vec{z}$ is empty. In logic programming, the semantics of a datalog program $\mathcal{D}$ is given by the least Herbrand model. For a datalog program $\mathcal{D}$, let $\mathcal{M}$ be the least Herbrand model of $\mathcal{D} \cup \mathcal{F}$, it is well known that for a tuple $\vec{a}$, $\mathcal{D} \cup \mathcal{F} \models \mathcal{Q}(\vec{a})$ if and only if $\mathcal{M}$ satisfies $\mathcal{Q}(\vec{a})$.

Answering CQs w.r.t. a datalog program can also be achieved through a backward chaining procedure based on SLD-resolution (with *tabling*, a technique to control cycles and to guarantee termination), which we formally present as follows. A *goal* is a conjunction of atoms $\alpha_1 \wedge \ldots \wedge \alpha_m$. The *SLD-resolution rule* takes as premises a goal and a datalog rule, and it produces a new goal as follows

$$\frac{\alpha_1 \wedge \ldots \wedge \alpha_m, \quad \phi \rightarrow \beta}{\sigma(\alpha_2) \wedge \ldots \wedge \sigma(\alpha_m) \wedge \sigma(\phi)}$$

where σ is the most general unifier of α_1 and β. An *SLD-proof* of a goal G_0 w.r.t. a datalog program $\mathcal{D}$ and a set $\mathcal{F}$ of facts is a sequence of goals $G_0, \ldots, G_n$, where $G_n \subseteq \mathcal{F}$ and each G_{i+1} is obtained from G_i by a single SLD-resolution. SLD-resolution is sound and complete for datalog: for a datalog program $\mathcal{D}$, a set $\mathcal{F}$ of fact, a CQ $\mathcal{Q}(\vec{x}) = \exists \vec{y}.\phi(\vec{x}, \vec{y})$ and a tuple $\vec{a}$ of constants, $\mathcal{D} \cup \mathcal{F} \models Q(\vec{a})$ iff there exists an SLD-proof of the goal $\phi(\vec{a}, \vec{y})$ w.r.t. $\mathcal{D}$ and $\mathcal{F}$. In this case, we call it an SLD-proof of $\mathcal{Q}(\vec{a})$ *w.r.t.* $\mathcal{D}$ and $\mathcal{F}$. For a rule $r \in \mathcal{D}$, denote $r \in SLD(\mathcal{Q}, \mathcal{D}, \mathcal{F})$ if r is involved in an SLD-proof of $\mathcal{Q}$ *w.r.t.* $\mathcal{D}$ and $\mathcal{F}$; and for a fact α, denote

$\alpha \in SLD(\mathcal{Q}, \mathcal{D}, \mathcal{F})$ if there exists an SLD-proof $G_0, \ldots, G_n$ of $\mathcal{Q}(\vec{a})$ such that $\alpha \in G_n$.

4. OUR APPROACH

In our query abduction setting, observations may contain existentially quantified variables and ontologies may have genuine existential rules. It is well observed in query answering and abduction literature that the sophisticated interaction between general CQs and genuine existential rules often post great challenges to computation. Our approach to address the scalability and completeness issues in query abduction combines several novel techniques for ontology transformation, query rewriting, data summarisation and module extraction, and our system integrates a datalog engine, a Prolog engine and an RDBMS. The key feature of our approach is that it reduces ontological query abduction in $\mathcal{ELH}_\bot$ to rule-based reasoning and thus can make use of off-the-shelf rule-based systems (instead of less scalable OWL reasoners). Also, it is sound and complete in computing all the minimal solutions, and at the same time scales over large data sets.

4.1 Overview

In a nutshell, given a QAP $\mathcal{P} = \langle \mathcal{T}, \mathcal{A}, \mathcal{Q}, \Sigma, \Delta \rangle$ in $\mathcal{ELH}_\bot$ our approach computes all its minimal solutions in the following steps.

Ontology transformation and observation rewriting: Our first step is to compute a datalog approximation $\mathcal{D}_\mathcal{T}$ of the initial TBox $\mathcal{T}$ and a rewriting $\mathcal{Q}^*$ of the initial observation. In the construction of $\mathcal{D}_\mathcal{T}$, instead of eliminating all the axioms in $\mathcal{T}$ that cannot be equivalently translated into datalog, we replace the existentially quantified variables with fresh constants. For approximated reasoning, we could replace $\mathcal{T}$ with $\mathcal{D}_\mathcal{T}$ and compute solutions for the new QAP using a resolution-based procedure. However, the approximation may introduce incorrect solutions, and hence $\mathcal{Q}^*$ is constructed by adding filtering conditions to $\mathcal{Q}$, which will invalidate certain resolution proofs and hence filter out the corresponding (spurious) solutions.

Module Extraction: In the second step, we extract (small) modules of each component (except for the observation) of the QAP that are used for query abduction, and we achieve this through data summarisation. First, we obtain a compact summary $\delta(A)$ of the initial ABox $\mathcal{A}$ by grouping and merging individuals in $\mathcal{A}$. Then, using $\delta(A)$ together with $\mathcal{D}_\mathcal{T}$ and $\mathcal{Q}^*$, we extract modules of $\mathcal{D}_\mathcal{T}$, $\mathcal{A}$, Σ and Δ that are relevant to the query abduction. For example, two (small) modules $\mathcal{A}_\mathcal{Q}$ and $\mathcal{A}_\bot$ of $\mathcal{A}$ are extracted, one for solution generation and one for solution verification. The module $\mathcal{A}_\mathcal{Q}$ is obtained through a resolution-based procedure and by tracking the facts in $\delta(A)$ that participate in some resolution proof of $\mathcal{Q}$.

Solution generation and verification with pruning: In the final step, we use the modules extracted in the previous step to generate and verify solution candidates. We employ a Prolog engine in this step and the previous step to perform resolution, by encoding the corresponding QAPs in Prolog. Besides a systematic search for solutions via resolution, an advanced pruning strategy is also applied. That is, once a solution $\mathcal{E}$ is computed, we exploit it further to generate other candidates $\mathcal{E}'$, by applying hierarchical knowledge from the TBox $\mathcal{T}$. In this the resolution proof for constructing $\mathcal{E}'$ is often pruned. Verifications of solution candidates are performed with a datalog engine. Hence, our approach consists of a combination of backward chaining (for solution generation) and forward chaining (for verification).

4.2 Ontology Transformation

For an $\mathcal{ELH}_\bot$ KB $\mathcal{K} = (\mathcal{T}, \mathcal{A})$ with a normalized TBox, we will first transform $\mathcal{T}$ into a datalog program $\mathcal{D}_\mathcal{T}$ in a way similar to [26]. In particular, $\mathcal{D}_\mathcal{T}$ consists of the rules in Table 1, plus one rule $A(x) \to \top(x)$ for each concept name A occurring in $\mathcal{T}$ and two rules $R(x,y) \to \top(x)$ and $R(x,y) \to \top(y)$ for each role name R occurring in $\mathcal{T}$, where we use $\top$ as a special unary predicate in datalog. These datalog rules capture the semantics of $\top$ in $\mathcal{ELH}_\bot$.

$\mathcal{ELH}_\bot$ axiom		datalog rule
$A \sqsubseteq \bot$	$\rightsquigarrow$	$A(x) \to \bot(x)$ $\bot$ is a unary predicate.
$A_1 \sqsubseteq A$	$\rightsquigarrow$	$A_1(x) \to A(x)$
$A_1 \sqcap A_2 \sqsubseteq A$	$\rightsquigarrow$	$A_1(x) \wedge A_2(x) \to A(x)$
$A_1 \sqsubseteq \exists R.A$	$\rightsquigarrow$	$A_1(x) \to R(x, c_{R,A})$ $A_1(x) \to A(c_{R,A})$ $c_{R,A}$ is a fresh constant.
$\exists R.A_1 \sqsubseteq A$	$\rightsquigarrow$	$R(x,y) \wedge A_1(y) \to A(x)$
$R \sqsubseteq S$	$\rightsquigarrow$	$R(x,y) \to S(x,y)$

Table 1: Transformation from $\mathcal{ELH}_\bot$ to datalog.

The following example illustrates the transformations.

EXAMPLE 1. *Let TBox $\mathcal{T}$ consist of the following three axioms:*

T1) $\mathsf{RA} \sqsubseteq \mathsf{Person} \sqcap \exists \mathsf{works}.\mathsf{RG}$
T2) $\mathsf{Student} \sqsubseteq \mathsf{Person} \sqcap \exists \mathsf{takes}.\mathsf{Course}$
T3) $\mathsf{Person} \sqcap \exists \mathsf{takes}.\mathsf{Course} \sqsubseteq \mathsf{Student}$

*Axiom T1 says that a research assistant (*RA*) is a person and she works in some research group (*RG*), and axioms T2 and T3 say that a student is a person who takes some courses.*

The corresponding existential program $\mathcal{R}_\mathcal{T}$ has five rules R1–R5:

R1) $\mathsf{RA}(x) \to \mathsf{Person}(x)$
R2) $\mathsf{RA}(x) \to \exists y.(\mathsf{works}(x,y) \wedge \mathsf{RG}(y))$
R3) $\mathsf{Student}(x) \to \mathsf{Person}(x)$
R4) $\mathsf{Student}(x) \to \exists y.(\mathsf{takes}(x,y) \wedge \mathsf{Course}(y))$
R5) $\mathsf{Person}(x) \wedge \mathsf{takes}(x,y) \wedge \mathsf{Course}(y) \to \mathsf{Student}(x)$

where R5 is an abbreviation of two rules and the auxiliary concept introduced via normalization is omitted for brevity.

Then, $\mathcal{R}_\mathcal{T}$ is transformed into the datalog program $\mathcal{D}_\mathcal{T}$ containing R1, R3, R5, and the following datalog rules S1–S4:

S1) $\mathsf{RA}(x) \to \mathsf{works}(x, c_1)$ *S2)* $\mathsf{RA}(x) \to \mathsf{RG}(c_1)$
S3) $\mathsf{Student}(x) \to \mathsf{takes}(x, c_2)$
S4) $\mathsf{Student}(x) \to \mathsf{Course}(c_2)$

where c_1, c_2 are fresh constants, S1 and S2 are transformed from R2, and S3 and S4 from R4.

The following result states that the datalog approximation of each KB is complete for query abduction. That is, each solution to the QAP *w.r.t.* KB $\mathcal{T} \cup \mathcal{A}$ is a solution to the corresponding QAP *w.r.t.* datalog program $\mathcal{D}_\mathcal{T} \cup \mathcal{A}$.

PROPOSITION 1. *Let $\mathcal{P} = \langle \mathcal{T}, \mathcal{A}, \mathcal{Q}(\vec{a}), \Sigma, \Delta\rangle$ be a QAP in $\mathcal{ELH}_\bot$, and $\mathcal{P}'$ be the QAP obtained from $\mathcal{P}$ by replacing $\mathcal{T}$ with $\mathcal{D}_\mathcal{T}$. Then, $\mathsf{sol}(\mathcal{P}) \subseteq \{\mathcal{E} \in \mathsf{sol}(\mathcal{P}') \mid \mathcal{D}_\mathcal{T} \cup \mathcal{A} \cup \mathcal{E} \not\models \exists x.\bot(x)\}$.*

However, the converse of Proposition 1 may not hold, that is, the transformation is not necessarily sound, and the following example illustrates it.

EXAMPLE 2. *Let TBox $\mathcal{T} = \{A \sqsubseteq \exists R.A\}$. Then, the datalog program $\mathcal{D}_\mathcal{T}$ contains the following datalog rules $A(x) \to R(x,c)$ and $A(x) \to A(c)$. Take $\Sigma = \{A\}$ and $\Delta = \{a,b\}$.*

1. *Consider CQ $\mathcal{Q}_1(x,y) = \exists z.[R(x,z) \wedge R(y,z)]$ and QAP $\mathcal{P}_1 = \langle \mathcal{T}, \emptyset, \mathcal{Q}_1(a,b), \Sigma, \Delta\rangle$. Then, the QAP has no solution, i.e., $\mathsf{sol}(\mathcal{P}_1)$ is empty. However, let $\mathcal{P}_1'$ be the QAP obtained from $\mathcal{P}_1$ by replacing $\mathcal{T}$ with $\mathcal{D}_\mathcal{T}$. Then, $\{A(a), A(b)\}$ is a solution to $\mathcal{P}_1'$.*
2. *Consider CQ $\mathcal{Q}_2(x) = \exists y.[R(x,y) \wedge R(y,y)]$ and QAP $\mathcal{P}_2 = \langle \mathcal{T}, \emptyset, \mathcal{Q}_2(a), \Sigma, \Delta\rangle$. Again, $\mathsf{sol}(\mathcal{P}_2)$ is empty. Yet for $\mathcal{P}_2'$ the QAP obtained from $\mathcal{P}_2$ by replacing $\mathcal{T}$ with $\mathcal{D}_\mathcal{T}$, $\{A(a)\}$ is a solution to $\mathcal{P}_2'$.*

The cause of incorrect solutions is that the above transformation from a TBox to a datalog program enforces fork-shaped and cyclic structures in the models by unifying the instantiation of existentially quantified variables in each rule.

4.3 Observation Rewriting

To retain the soundness of our TBox transformation, we rewrite observations to filter out spurious solutions. In particular, we rewrite a CQ $\mathcal{Q}(\vec{x})$ into a FO query $\mathcal{Q}^*(\vec{x})$ such that for any observation $\mathcal{Q}(\vec{a})$, the solutions to a QAP $\mathcal{P}$ are exactly those to the QAP $\mathcal{P}'$ obtained by replacing the TBox $\mathcal{T}$ in $\mathcal{P}$ with $\mathcal{D}_\mathcal{T}$. Our rewriting approach is adapted from [20], where a rewriting method is used to filter out spurious query matching. While the rewriting in [20] is shown to be sufficient for query answering, it was unknown whether it works for abduction. Also, it is worth noting that our rewriting is simpler than that of [20], as we use a different program transformation from theirs. In what follows, we show that the rewriting technique can be used in abduction and in particular, our transformation-based procedure and the adapted observation rewriting form a sound and complete algorithm for query abduction in $\mathcal{ELH}_\bot$.

We first introduce unary predicates Ind and Aux to assert respectively the individuals occurring in the initial ABox and the auxiliary constants (i.e., those fresh constants generated in the approximation phase shown in Table 1). Then, to prevent spurious solutions introduced by fork-shaped or cyclic structures in the least Herbrand model of $\mathcal{D}_\mathcal{T}$ (but not in models of $\mathcal{T}$), for a CQ $\mathcal{Q}$, we define the equivalence relation $\sim$ over the terms (i.e., variables and constants) in $\mathcal{Q}$ as in [20]. Formally, $\sim \subseteq term(\mathcal{Q}) \times term(\mathcal{Q})$ is the smallest reflexive, symmetric and transitive relation that satisfies the following condition:

(*) if $R_1(s,t), R_2(s',t') \in \mathcal{Q}$ with $t \sim t'$ then $s \sim s'$.

Intuitively, the relation $\sim$ will be used to guarantee that if an instantiation of the query is satisfied by the least Herbrand model of $\mathcal{D}_\mathcal{T}$, then the instantiation does not contain a fork or cycle introduced by auxiliary constants (e.g., as in Example 2). For each equivalent class ξ of $\sim$, a representative $t_\xi \in \xi$ is chosen.

For a CQ $\mathcal{Q}$, the following notions help us to identify substructures in $\mathcal{Q}$ that can possibly lead to spurious solutions, as their instantiations may contain forks and cycles:

- **Fork** is the set of pairs $(pre(\xi), \xi)$ with ξ being an equivalence class of $\sim$, $pre(\xi) = \{t \in term(\mathcal{Q}) \mid \exists R \in N_R, \exists t' \in \xi$ such that $R(t,t') \in \mathcal{Q}\}$, and $|pre(\xi)| \geq 2$.
- **Cyc** is the set of quantified variables v such that there are $R_0(t_0,t_0'), \cdots, R_m(t_m,t_m'), \cdots, R_n(t_n,t_n') \in \mathcal{Q}$ $(n,m \geq 0)$, with $v \sim t_i$ for some $0 \leq i \leq n$, $t_i' \sim t_{i+1}$ for all $i < n$, and $t_n' \sim t_m$.

Fork and **Cyc** can be also computed in time polynomial to the size of $\mathcal{Q}$ [20].

Now, we introduce the rewriting of observations. Let CQ $\mathcal{Q}(\vec{x}) = \exists \vec{y}.\phi(\vec{x},\vec{y})$, its *rewriting* $\mathcal{Q}^*(\vec{x})$ is the FO query $\exists \vec{y}.[\phi \wedge \phi_1 \wedge \phi_2]$ where

$$\phi_1 := \bigwedge_{(\{t_1,\cdots,t_k\},\xi)\in\textbf{Fork}} (Aux(t_\xi) \to \bigwedge_{1\leq i<k} t_i = t_{i+1})$$

$$\phi_2 := \bigwedge_{v\in\textbf{Cyc}} Ind(v).$$

Intuitively, filter ϕ_1 says that fork-shaped substructures in $\mathcal{Q}$ should be instantiated in a way that all the legs merge into one, and ϕ_2 says that a cyclic substructure in $\mathcal{Q}$ can only be instantiated with individuals (not auxiliary constants).

EXAMPLE 3 (CONT'D EXAMPLE 1). *There are two equivalence classes $\{x,y\}$ and $\{z\}$ with respect to the relation $\sim$ in $\mathcal{Q}_1(x,y)$, and the rewriting of CQ $\mathcal{Q}_1(x,y)$ is*

$$\mathcal{Q}_1^*(x,y) = \exists z.[R(x,z) \wedge R(y,z) \wedge (Aux(z) \to x = y)].$$

Let $\mathcal{P}_1''$ be obtained from $\mathcal{P}_1'$ by replacing $\mathcal{Q}_1(a,b)$ with $\mathcal{Q}_1^*(a,b)$, then $\{A(a), A(b)\}$ is not a solution to $\mathcal{P}_1''$. Indeed, $\mathcal{P}_1''$ has no solution just as $\mathcal{P}_1$.

There is only one equivalence classes $\{x,y\}$ with respect to the relation $\sim$ in $\mathcal{Q}_2(x)$, and the rewriting of CQ $\mathcal{Q}_2(x)$ is

$$\mathcal{Q}_2^*(x) = \exists y.[R(x,y) \wedge R(y,y) \wedge (Aux(y) \to x = y) \wedge Ind(y)].$$

Let $\mathcal{P}_2''$ be obtained from $\mathcal{P}_2'$ by replacing $\mathcal{Q}_2(a)$ with $\mathcal{Q}_2^*(a)$, then $\{A(a)\}$ is not a solution to $\mathcal{P}_2''$, and no solution exists to $\mathcal{P}_2''$.

Note that our rewriting is simpler than that of [20], largely due to the datalog transformation we adopt in the paper, which provides a tighter approximation on the models. For example, given an axiom $A \sqsubseteq \exists R.B \sqcap \exists S.B$, it is transformed into four datalog rules $A(x) \to R(x, c_{R,B})$, $A(x) \to B(c_{R,B})$, $A(x) \to S(x, c_{S,B})$, and $A(x) \to B(c_{S,B})$. In an approximated model in [20], however informally, $c_{R,B}$ and $c_{S,B}$ are not distinguished. Thus, it is not hard to see that we do not need the filter queries related to $\textbf{Fork}_{\neq}$ and $\textbf{Fork}_{\mathcal{H}}$ in [20].

The following theorem states that the ontology transformation combined with observation rewriting is sound and complete in $\mathcal{ELH}_\bot$.

THEOREM 1. *Let $\mathcal{P} = \langle \mathcal{T}, \mathcal{A}, \mathcal{Q}(\vec{a}), \Sigma, \Delta\rangle$ be a QAP in $\mathcal{ELH}_\bot$ and $\mathcal{P}' = \langle \mathcal{D}_\mathcal{T}, \mathcal{A}, \mathcal{Q}^*(\vec{a}), \Sigma, \Delta\rangle$. Then, $\mathsf{sol}(\mathcal{P}) = \{\mathcal{E} \in \mathsf{sol}(\mathcal{P}') \mid \mathcal{D}_\mathcal{T} \cup \mathcal{A} \cup \mathcal{E} \not\models \exists x.\bot(x)\}$.*

Reducing a QAP in $\mathcal{ELH}_\bot$ to an equivalent one in datalog allows us to use a resolution-based procedure, like SLD-resolution, to generate solution candidates $\mathcal{E}$. Let Λ be the set of all facts constructed from the predicates in Σ and the constants in Δ. Then, all the candidates for minimal solutions can be generated by enumerating the SLD-proofs of goal $\mathcal{Q}(\vec{a})$ *w.r.t.* $\mathcal{D}_{\mathcal{T}}$ and $\mathcal{A} \cup \Lambda$. We will speak informally about (SLD-)resolution proofs of $\mathcal{Q}^*(\vec{a})$, which are SLD-proofs of $\mathcal{Q}(\vec{a})$ validated against the additional filtering conditions in $\mathcal{Q}^*(\vec{a})$. Practically, $\mathcal{Q}^*(\vec{a})$ can be encoded in Prolog, and hence it makes sense to talk about resolution proofs of $\mathcal{Q}^*(\vec{a})$ and the solution candidates generated from them. We will omit $\vec{a}$ in the (rewritten) observation for simplicity.

To verify the non-triviality of a solution $\mathcal{E}$, existing query abduction algorithms [10] often use an OWL reasoner like HermiT or Pellet. Theorem 1 shows that we can use a datalog engine for such verifications, which is often more efficient than an OWL reasoner.

4.4 Module Extraction

Although reducing a QAP in $\mathcal{ELH}_\bot$ to a QAP in datalog allows us to apply rule-based reasoning and highly efficient rule-based systems to compute solutions, a resolution procedure can still be computationally very expensive, especially when handling a large number of facts. In such cases, even if there are a small number of datalog rules, a resolution procedure may suffer from a significant computational overhead when it attempts to find out valid substitutions for a large number of constants. This is illustrated with the following example.

EXAMPLE 4. *Consider the BCQ* $\mathcal{Q} = \exists x.[A(x) \wedge B(x) \wedge C(x)]$, *datalog program* $\mathcal{D} = \{R(x,y) \wedge D(y) \rightarrow B(x), E(x) \rightarrow F(x)\}$, *and ABox* $\mathcal{A} = \{A(a), C(a), D(b), A(c_1), \ldots, A(c_m), E(d_1), \ldots, E(d_n)\}$. *Let* $\Sigma = \{R\}$ *and* Δ *consist of all the individuals in* $\mathcal{A}$. *Then the QAP* $\mathcal{P} = \langle \mathcal{D}, \mathcal{A}, \mathcal{Q}, \Sigma, \Delta \rangle$ *has a single solution* $\{R(a,b)\}$. *Yet in the computation of (all minimal) solutions, a resolution procedure will attempt to resolve* $A(x)$ *with each* $A(c_i)$ $(1 \leq i \leq m)$. *Then, after resolving* $B(c_i)$ *to* $R(c_i, y) \wedge D(y)$ *via the rule* $R(x,y) \wedge D(y) \rightarrow B(x)$, *it will attempt to resolve* y *in* $R(c_i, y)$ *with all the individuals including all the* d_j*'s* $(1 \leq j \leq n)$. *Such an effort only fails eventually when trying to resolve say* $D(d_j)$ *and* $C(c_i)$.[2]

When the ABox is large, a huge number of similar unfortunate attempts may occur, and as a result the computation suffers.

Hence, we want to reduce the number of input facts by extracting modules of the initial QAP components that are sufficient for the query abduction. Using ABox modules can effectively reduce the search spaces for resolution. We achieve this through data summarisation, a technique used in query answering [7, 11, 27]. Yet instead of using the result of summarisation directly for reasoning, we apply a novel method to extract modules of the initial QAP components. A data summarisation method groups the individuals in the ABox according to their occurrences in the ABox and merges individuals within the same group. In the result of summarisation, only one representative individual remains for each group. Individuals are grouped according to their *types* in the ABox. For an ABox $\mathcal{A}$ and an individual a in $\mathcal{A}$, the *type* of a in $\mathcal{A}$ is $\tau = \{A \mid A(a) \in \mathcal{A}, A \in N_C\}$, i.e., a type is a finite set of concept names an individual is asserted to be a member in the ABox. Then, an ABox summary is defined as follows.

DEFINITION 2. *Given an ABox* $\mathcal{A}$, *for each type* τ *of an individual in* $\mathcal{A}$, *assign a distinct fresh individual* c_τ *to* τ. *Let* δ *map each individual* a *in* $\mathcal{A}$ *to* c_τ *where* τ *is the type of* a *in* $\mathcal{A}$. *Then,* $\delta(\mathcal{A})$ *is the ABox obtained by replacing each individual* a *in* $\mathcal{A}$ *with* $\delta(a)$, *and is referred to as the* summary *of* $\mathcal{A}$.

In practice, the number of types of individuals in a dataset is often much smaller than the number of individuals. As individuals with the same type tend to behave in a similar way in reasoning, merging them in data summarisation often leads to a compact and tight approximation of the initial ABox.

For a QAP $\mathcal{P}' = \langle \mathcal{D}_{\mathcal{T}}, \mathcal{A}, \mathcal{Q}^*, \Sigma, \Delta \rangle$, we first show how to use the ABox summary to extract two modules of the ABox $\mathcal{A}$, one for generating QAP solutions and the other for verifying non-triviality. After that, we will show how to extract modules of other components of the QAP. For convenience, we regard δ as a mapping defined on the set of individuals in Δ by defining $\delta(a) = a$ for each a not occurring $\mathcal{A}$. Given an ABox summary, we are able to define two modules as follows. Recall that Λ is the set of all facts over the predicates in Σ and the constants in Δ.

$$\mathcal{A}_{\mathcal{Q}} = \{\alpha \in \mathcal{A} \mid \delta(\alpha) \in SLD(\delta(\mathcal{Q}^*), \mathcal{D}_{\mathcal{T}}, \delta(\mathcal{A} \cup \Lambda))\},$$
$$\mathcal{A}_\bot = \{\alpha \in \mathcal{A} \mid \delta(\alpha) \in SLD(\exists x.\bot(x), \mathcal{D}_{\mathcal{T}}, \delta(\mathcal{A} \cup \Lambda))\}.$$

Module $\mathcal{A}_{\mathcal{Q}}$ is for generating candidate solutions, whereas module $\mathcal{A}_\bot$ is for verifying non-triviality. To extract $\mathcal{A}_{\mathcal{Q}}$, we start with QAP $\mathcal{P}'' = \langle \mathcal{D}_{\mathcal{T}}, \delta(\mathcal{A}), \delta(\mathcal{Q}^*), \Sigma, \delta(\Delta) \rangle$, and generate solution candidates to $\mathcal{P}''$ with a resolution-based procedure. Note that using ABox summary $\delta(\mathcal{A})$ instead of $\mathcal{A}$ can largely reduce the number of input facts. In the process of generating solution candidates, we keep track of the facts in $\delta(\mathcal{A})$ that are involved in the resolution. Finally, the corresponding facts in $\mathcal{A}$ are extracted to form the module $\mathcal{A}_{\mathcal{Q}}$. Module $\mathcal{A}_\bot$ is extracted analogously.

In the same resolution and solution generation processes, we can also extract modules for other components of the QAP. In particular, define

$$\mathcal{D}_{\mathcal{Q}} = \{r \in \mathcal{D}_{\mathcal{T}} \mid r \in SLD(\delta(\mathcal{Q}^*), \mathcal{D}_{\mathcal{T}}, \delta(\mathcal{A} \cup \Lambda))\},$$
$$\mathcal{D}_\bot = \{r \in \mathcal{D}_{\mathcal{T}} \mid r \in SLD(\exists x.\bot(x), \mathcal{D}_{\mathcal{T}}, \delta(\mathcal{A} \cup \Lambda))\},$$
$$\Sigma_{\mathcal{Q}} = \{P \in \Sigma \mid \text{a fact } \alpha \text{ containing } P \text{ exists s.t. } \alpha \in SLD(\delta(\mathcal{Q}^*), \mathcal{D}_{\mathcal{T}}, \delta(\mathcal{A} \cup \Lambda))\},$$
$$\Delta_{\mathcal{Q}} = \{a \in \Delta \mid \text{a fact } \alpha \text{ containing } \delta(a) \text{ exists s.t. } \alpha \in SLD(\delta(\mathcal{Q}^*), \mathcal{D}_{\mathcal{T}}, \delta(\mathcal{A} \cup \Lambda))\}.$$

Note that $\mathcal{A}_{\mathcal{Q}}$, $\mathcal{D}_{\mathcal{Q}}$, $\Sigma_{\mathcal{Q}}$ and $\Delta_{\mathcal{Q}}$ can be extracted in one go via the resolution of $\delta(\mathcal{Q}^*)$, and $\mathcal{A}_\bot$ and $\mathcal{D}_\bot$ can be extracted via the resolution of $\exists x.\bot(x)$.

EXAMPLE 5 (CONT'D EXAMPLE 4). *There are four types in* $\mathcal{A}$: $\{A, C\}$ *for* a, $\{D\}$ *for* b, $\{C\}$ *for each* c_i $(1 \leq i \leq m)$, *and* $\{E\}$ *for each* d_j $(1 \leq j \leq n)$. *Using* a *and* b *themselves as representatives, and* c *and* d *as representatives for* c_i*'s and* d_j*'s, respectively,* $\delta(\mathcal{A}) = \{A(a), C(a), D(b), A(c), E(d)\}$. *Then,* $\mathcal{A}_{\mathcal{Q}} = \{A(a), C(a), D(b)\}$, $\mathcal{A}_\bot = \emptyset$, $\mathcal{D}_{\mathcal{Q}} = \{R(x,y) \wedge D(y) \rightarrow B(x)\}$, $\mathcal{D}_\bot = \emptyset$, $\Sigma_{\mathcal{Q}} = \{R\}$, $\Delta_{\mathcal{Q}} = \{a, b\}$.

[2]We assume the resolution proceeds from left to right as implemented in most Prolog engines, which may not be the case for every resolution procedure. Indeed, certain optimisation with ordering could help in this specific example, yet the example is to demonstrate a general issue not necessarily tied to ordering.

The following theorem shows that the above modules are sufficient for query abduction.

THEOREM 2. *Let* $\mathcal{P} = \langle \mathcal{T}, \mathcal{A}, \mathcal{Q}, \Sigma, \Delta \rangle$ *be a QAP in* $\mathcal{ELH}_\bot$. *Then,* $\mathcal{E}$ *is a minimal solution in* $\mathsf{sol}(\mathcal{P})$ *iff the following conditions hold:*

1. $pred(\mathcal{E}) \subseteq \Sigma_\mathcal{Q}$ *and* $const(\mathcal{E}) \subseteq \Delta_Q$;
2. $\mathcal{D}_\mathcal{Q} \cup \mathcal{A}_\mathcal{Q} \cup \mathcal{E} \models \mathcal{Q}^*$;
3. $\mathcal{D}_\bot \cup \mathcal{A}_\bot \cup \mathcal{E} \not\models \exists x.\bot(x)$;
4. $\mathcal{E} \not\models \mathcal{Q}$; *and*
5. *no* $\mathcal{E}' \subset \mathcal{E}$ *exists satisfying conditions 1–4.*

In Exampe 5, $\mathcal{E} = \{R(a,b)\}$, which is the only ABox that satisfies the conditions in Theorem 2. $\mathcal{E}$ can be obtained via a SLD-proof of $\mathcal{Q}$ (the same as $\mathcal{Q}^*$) *w.r.t.* $\mathcal{D}_\mathcal{Q}$ and $\mathcal{A}_\mathcal{Q} \cup \Lambda_\mathcal{Q}$, where $\Lambda_\mathcal{Q}$ is the set of all facts over $\Sigma_\mathcal{Q}$ and $\Delta_\mathcal{Q}$. Then, $\mathcal{E}$ is verified against non-triviality conditions $\mathcal{D}_\bot \cup \mathcal{A}_\bot \cup \mathcal{E} \not\models \exists x.\bot(x)$ and $\mathcal{E} \not\models \mathcal{Q}$, and is returned as a solution.

4.5 Solution Search with Pruning

After preprocessing of the initial QAP, we obtain a datalog QAP of relatively small size. Our basic approach systematically searches for solution candidates using a resolution-based procedure (with tabling to guarantee termination), verifies each candidate using a datalog engine, and keeps only the minimal solutions. Besides systematically enumerating the resolution proofs, the search for solutions can largely benefit from advanced pruning methods. In particular, when a solution $\mathcal{E}$ is computed, instead of discarding $\mathcal{E}$ and constructing a new resolution proof, a pruning method further exploits $\mathcal{E}$ to generate another candidate solution $\mathcal{E}'$. When $\mathcal{E}'$ is verified to be a solution, the resolution proofs for $\mathcal{E}'$ and those for its supersets are pruned. Various heuristics can be applied in pruning. In [9], a pruning strategy that exploits the subsets $\mathcal{E}'$ of $\mathcal{E}$ is proposed, which allows the minimality of a solution to be checked immediately after its generation. Although such a pruning strategy for query abduction may require a larger number of verifications than the basic approach, such verifications are often less expensive than resolution. Given that the candidates $\mathcal{E}'$ obtained from $\mathcal{E}$ are close enough to valid solutions and can be enumerated efficiently, a search with pruning can largely outperform a basic one.

Once a minimal solution $\mathcal{E}$ is computed, we propose a new pruning strategy for solution search that exploits $\mathcal{E}$ and the hierarchical knowledge from the TBox. A *hierarchical axiom* in $\mathcal{ELH}_\bot$ is of the form $A \sqsubseteq B$ or $R \sqsubseteq S$. Such hierarchical axioms often constitute a large portion of practical ontology axioms, and can cause computation difficulty in resolution. This is illustrated in the following example.

EXAMPLE 6. *Consider the BCQ* $Q = A_1(a_1) \wedge \ldots \wedge A_1(a_m)$ *and the datalog program* $\mathcal{D} = \{A_{i+1}(x) \rightarrow A_i(x) \mid 1 \leq i \leq n\}$. *Let* $\mathcal{A} = \emptyset$, $\Sigma = \{A_1, \ldots, A_n\}$, *and* $\Delta = \{a_1, \ldots, a_m\}$. *The QAP* $\mathcal{P} = \langle \mathcal{D}, \mathcal{A}, Q, \Sigma, \Delta \rangle$ *has* n^m *minimal solutions of the form* $\{A_{j_1}(a_1), \ldots, A_{j_m}(a_m) \mid 1 \leq j_1, \ldots, j_m \leq n\}$.

Constructing a resolution proof for each of the minimal solution is a tedious job and involves a large amount of repetition. However, from one minimal solution $\{\ldots, A_j(a_i), \ldots\}$, *it is convenient to directly construct another minimal solution* $\{\ldots, A_{j+1}(a_i), \ldots\}$ *using hierarchical rule* $A_{j+1}(x) \rightarrow A_j(x)$.

Based on this observation, we propose the following pruning technique that makes use of the hierarchical knowledge on concept names and role names in the TBox. Consider the QAP $\mathcal{P}' = \langle \mathcal{D}_\mathcal{T}, \mathcal{A}, \mathcal{Q}^*, \Sigma, \Delta \rangle$ and the modules of its components $\mathcal{D}_\mathcal{Q}$, $\mathcal{A}_\mathcal{Q}$, $\Sigma_\mathcal{Q}$, and $\Delta_\mathcal{Q}$. For a solution $\mathcal{E} \in \mathsf{sol}(\mathcal{P})$, a *weakening* of $\mathcal{E}$ is obtained by replacing some $A(a) \in \mathcal{E}$ with $B(a)$ such that $B \in \Sigma_\mathcal{Q}$ and $\mathcal{T} \models A \sqsubseteq B$, or by replacing some $R(a,b) \in E$ with $S(a,b)$ such that $S \in \Sigma_\mathcal{Q}$ and $\mathcal{T} \models R \sqsubseteq S$; a *strengthening* of $\mathcal{E}$ is obtained by replacing some $A(a) \in \mathcal{E}$ with $B(a)$ such that $B \in \Sigma_\mathcal{Q}$ and $\mathcal{T} \models B \sqsubseteq A$, or by replacing some $R(a,b) \in E$ with $S(a,b)$ such that $S \in \Sigma_\mathcal{Q}$ and $\mathcal{T} \models S \sqsubseteq R$. $\mathcal{E}_\uparrow$ and $\mathcal{E}_\downarrow$ denote a weakening and a strengthening of $\mathcal{E}$, respectively.

PROPOSITION 2. *Let* $\mathcal{P} = \langle \mathcal{T}, \mathcal{A}, \mathcal{Q}, \Sigma, \Delta \rangle$ *be a QAP in* $\mathcal{ELH}_\bot$. *For a solution* $\mathcal{E} \in \mathsf{sol}(\mathcal{P})$, *the following conditions hold:*

- $\mathcal{E}_\uparrow \in \mathsf{sol}(\mathcal{P})$ *iff* $\mathcal{D}_\mathcal{Q} \cup \mathcal{A}_\mathcal{Q} \cup \mathcal{E}_\uparrow \models \mathcal{Q}^*$ *and* $\mathcal{E}_\uparrow \not\models \mathcal{Q}$; *and* $\mathcal{E}_\uparrow$ *is minimal if* $\mathcal{E}$ *is minimal.*
- $\mathcal{E}_\downarrow \in \mathsf{sol}(\mathcal{P})$ *iff* $\mathcal{D}_\bot \cup \mathcal{A}_\bot \cup \mathcal{E}_\downarrow \not\models \exists x.\bot(x)$ *and* $\mathcal{E}_\downarrow \not\models \mathcal{Q}$; *and* $\mathcal{E}_\downarrow$ *is minimal only if* $\mathcal{E}$ *is minimal.*

Note that in the second condition, the minimality of $\mathcal{E}_\downarrow$ is not guaranteed by the second half of the condition. For example, let $\mathcal{Q} = D(a)$, $\mathcal{D}_\mathcal{Q} = \{B(x) \rightarrow A(x), A(x) \wedge C(x) \rightarrow D(x), B(x) \rightarrow D(x)\}$, $\Sigma_\mathcal{Q} = \{A, B, C\}$, $\Delta_\mathcal{Q} = \{a\}$, and $\mathcal{D}_\bot$ and $\mathcal{A}_\mathcal{Q} \cup \mathcal{A}_\bot$ are both empty. Then, a minimal solution is $\mathcal{E} = \{A(a), C(a)\}$, whereas $\mathcal{E}_\downarrow = \{B(a), C(a)\}$ is a solution but not minimal.

Once a solution $\mathcal{E}$ is computed, our pruning method checks the minimality of $\mathcal{E}$ as in [9]. If $\mathcal{E}$ is minimal, the method enumerates and verifies whether each $\mathcal{E}_\uparrow$ and each $\mathcal{E}_\downarrow$ is a minimal solution. $\mathcal{E}_\uparrow$ and $\mathcal{E}_\downarrow$ are enumerated using the concept and role hierarchies pre-computed from $\mathcal{T}$ using an OWL reasoner. Verifications of $\mathcal{E}_\uparrow$ and $\mathcal{E}_\downarrow$ are performed efficiently using a datalog engine.

5. EXPERIMENTS

Based on the approach proposed in Section 4, we have implemented a prototype system called ABEL (ABduction for EL). Our experiments show that ABEL is efficient and can be used to compute minimal explanations for large ontologies and data sets in $\mathcal{ELH}_\bot$.

ABEL is implemented in Java. In our system, the KARMA system [26] is used for ontology transformation, Prolog engine XSB 3.4 [25] is used for generating solution candidates, and OWL reasoner Pellet[3] as well as datalog engine RDFox[4] is used for verifying solution candidates. We have evaluated our system on three suites of ontology benchmarks and under different settings. All the experiments were performed on a PC with an Intel Xenon 2.8 GHz processor and 16 GB RAM. The system and testing data are available at `http://www.ict.griffith.edu.au/~kewen/AbductionEL/`.

5.1 Test Cases

In our experiments, we have employed ontologies that are widely used for benchmarking ontology-based CQ answering and for abduction [19, 26, 9]. The ontologies, corresponding data sets and queries are described as follows. To generate observations, we instantiated each query by substituting

[3] `clarkparsia.com/pellet`
[4] `www.cs.ox.ac.uk/isg/tools/RDFox`

their query variables with randomly chosen constants from the corresponding data set and verified that each instantiation indeed formed a negative answer to the query.

VICODI: The VICODI ontology[5] describes European history and contains no genuine existential rules. This benchmark has a moderate-sized data set, has been widely used for evaluating atomic queries, and hence is useful for comparing our system with DuQAP, a system developed by Du et al. [9], since it allows only atomic queries. We generated 40 atomic queries for this benchmark with a random set of atomic concepts and roles.

SEMINTEC: The SEMINTEC ontology[6] for modelling financial processes contains genuine existential rules and is coupled with a moderate-sized data set. We used it in comparing our system with DuQAP, and we generated 40 atomic queries for this benchmark as above.

LSTW: The LSTW ontology [19] extends the Lehigh University benchmark LUBM [13] with many genuine existential rules. Corresponding data sets can be automatically generated in a range of sizes using EUGen [19]. LSTW(n) denotes the variant with a data set of n universities. Besides using this benchmark for comparison, with 40 atomic queries generated as above, we also used it in the scalability evaluation, with 120 CQs generated using the query generator SyGENiA [16][7].

Table 2 shows some statistics on the aforementioned ontologies: the numbers of their concept names (#C), role names (#R), TBox axioms ($|\mathcal{T}|$), genuine existential rules (#E), ABox facts ($|\mathcal{A}|$), and individuals (#I).

Table 2: Benchmark statistics.

Ontology	#C	#R	$\|\mathcal{T}\|$	#E	$\|\mathcal{A}\|$	#I
VICODI	194	10	214	0	116,181	32,238
SEMINTEC	60	16	207	8	65,244	17,945
LSTW(n)	132	32	223	29	$\approx 10^5 n$	$\approx 10^4 n$

We evaluated ABEL in three different configurations.

ABEL-N is the naive version of ABEL without pruning nor module extraction, and was used for comparison with DuQAP. In order to have a fair comparison, database techniques were not employed in ABEL-N. Also, Pellet was used instead of a datalog engine for reasoning tasks such as solution verification.

ABEL-P uses MySQL database system to store data and enables the pruning optimisation. Also, datalog engine RDFox was employed for solution verification. However, module extraction was disabled in order to study its effect on performance.

ABEL-M is the optimised version of ABEL-P using the module extraction technique. It is tested in the scalability evaluation with large data sets.

5.2 Comparison

In the first set of experiments, we compared our system with DuQAP. DuQAP accepts as input expressive ontologies in $\mathcal{SHIOQ}$ but only allows observations formulated in atomic queries. For each of our testing ontologies, we generated 40 observations by instantiating the corresponding 40 atomic queries. We included all concepts in the ontology as abducibles, and the domain includes all constants in the corresponding data set. Roles were not included in the abducibles, since DuQAP ran out of memory in those cases.

Table 3 shows the comparison results: the average numbers of minimal solutions (#$\mathcal{E}$, averaged over 40 observations)[8], and the average times (in seconds) for computing all the minimal solutions. DuQAP could not handle LSTW(10) or beyond due to running out of memory. It is worth noting that ABEL-N already outperformed DuQAP, and this superiority is largely enhanced with other optimisations like pruning (with the time reduced by at least 90%).

Table 3: Comparison of DuQAP and ABEL.

Ontology	#$\mathcal{E}$	DuQAP	ABEL-N	ABEL-P
VICODI	12.4	9.5	5.8	0.1
SEMINTEC	0.4	3.4	1.0	0.1
LSTW(1)	8.6	7.8	5.1	0.4
LSTW(5)	8.6	46.9	24.8	1.1
LSTW(10)	8.6	N/A	85.9	5.2

5.3 Scalability Evaluation

To evaluate the scalability of our system with observations formulated in general CQs that can interact with genuine existential rules in a complex manner, we evaluated ABEL-P and ABEL-M with the 120 generated CQs, a large portion of which are general CQs. One observation is generated for each query. Since LSTW contains no disjointness axiom, to enforce non-triviality checks, we added 5 disjointness axioms to the LSTW ontology. We increased the scope of abducibles so that all the concepts and all the roles in the ontology are included, and each domain is of size 5 (with constants in the observation plus possibly some from the data set). We set a 10 minutes' time bound for each QAP instance, and a QAP instance is considered to be successfully processed only if all its minimal solutions are computed in the time bound.

ABEL-P was able to handle all the 120 observations for moderate-sized LSTW(1), and the average computation time was 19.2 seconds. Table 4 shows the results for large-sized LSTW(10), LSTW(50) and LSTW(100): the number of observations successfully processed (#), the times for computing all the minimal solutions and for extracting modules (t_c and t_m, in seconds, both averaged over the successfully processed observations), and the sizes of modules divided by the sizes of the initial data set $\mathcal{A}$ ($|\mathcal{A}_\mathcal{Q}|$ and $|\mathcal{A}_\perp|$, in percentage, both averaged over the successfully processed observations).

ABEL-P was able to successfully process most of the observations (105, that is 88%) for LSTW(10), and nearly half of them (55, that is 46%) for each of LSTW(50) and LSTW(100). ABEL-M could handle all the observations successfully processed by ABEL-P, and the advantage of ABEL-M (in particular, the module extraction optimisation) becomes more obvious when the data sets get larger. In

[5] `http://www.vicodi.org`

[6] `http://www.cs.put.poznan.pl/alawrynowicz/semintec.htm`

[7] As SyGENiA failed to terminate in some cases on LSTW, we set a bound on the chase algorithm of SyGENiA to generate CQs with up to three atoms.

[8] The numbers were the same for both ABEL(-N and -P) and DuQAP.

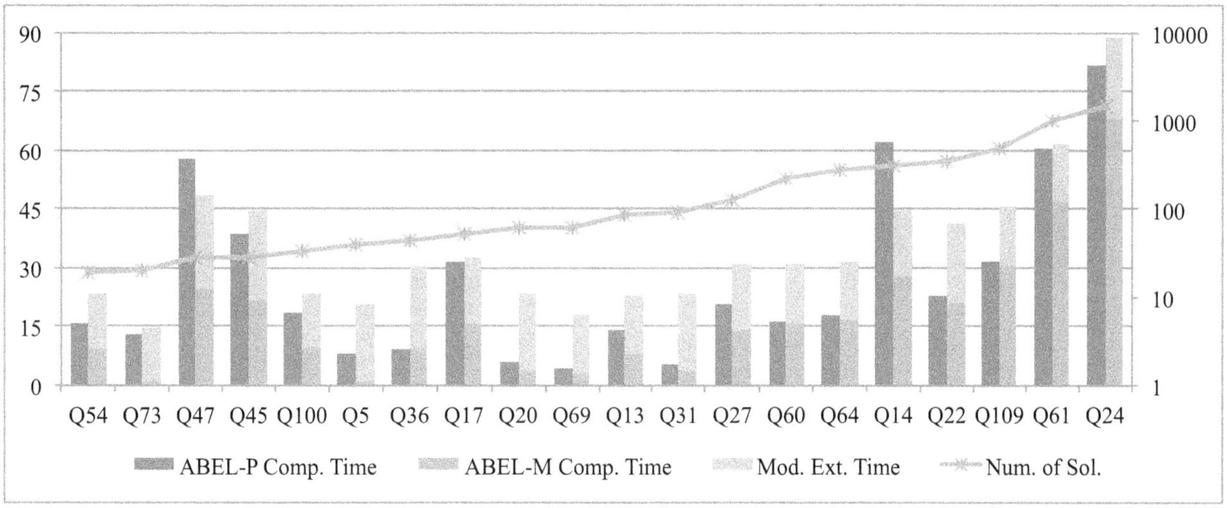

Figure 1: Scalability evaluation on LSTW(50).

Table 4: Scalability evaluation on generated queries.

LSTW	ABEL-P		ABEL-M				
(n)	#	t_c	#	t_c	t_m	$\lvert\mathcal{A}_\mathcal{Q}\rvert$	$\lvert\mathcal{A}_\bot\rvert$
10	105	39.2	106	25.6	15.4	3.4%	10.7%
50	55	23.6	83	41.1	26.2	3.7%	8.5%
100	55	43.7	82	31.5	31.4	0.3%	1.8%

particular, for LSTW(50) and LSTW(100), ABEL-M could process 28 and 27 observations respectively, on which ABEL-P failed. Moreover, for all the observations over LSTW(50), ABEL-M could compute at least some minimal solutions, and failed to output any solutions for only two observations in the case of LSTW(100). These two difficult observations are both associated with recursive rules in the ontology.

Figure 1 shows the reasoning times and the numbers of solutions computed by ABEL-P and ABEL-M, on 20 selected observations over LSTW(50). These 20 observations are the most challenging ones among those successfully processed by both ABEL-P and ABEL-M. The column chart shows the computation and module extraction times of ABEL-P and ABEL-M (the left vertical axis, in seconds). The line chart shows the total numbers of minimal solutions (the right vertical axis, in logarithm scale).

Figure 1 demonstrates the efficiency gain as well as the overhead for module extraction in ABEL-M (compared to ABEL-P). On the observations that could be easily processed by ABEL-P, the efficiency gain from module extraction was often not significant enough to override its overhead. The efficient gain was significant however, on observations that were hard for ABEL-P, such as Q14, Q17, Q45, and Q47, where the computation times were reduced by half because of module extraction. On hard observations where ABEL-P failed to process, the advantage of module extraction became very significant, as shown in Table 4. Hence, in general, for query explanation over large data sets, it would be a good strategy to first attempt to generate explanations with ABEL-P, and to employ module extraction (ABEL-M) only when ABEL-P fails in the time bound.

6. CONCLUSION

We have developed a scalable and complete system for query abduction w.r.t. observations formulated in BCQs and background ontologies in $\mathcal{ELH}_\bot$. Our approach involves transforming an $\mathcal{ELH}_\bot$ ontologies to a datalog program and rewriting the observation. While the ontology transformations and rewriting techniques have been intensively studied for query answering, our work initiates to adapt such techniques from standard query answering to query abduction. Indeed, by adapting these techniques, we provide, to the best of our knowledge, the first sound and complete algorithm for query abduction that supports both general CQs and ontologies with genuine existential rules. Moreover, we introduced a novel method for module extraction in query abduction, by applying data summarisation techniques, and we developed a pruning strategy that largely enhances the efficiency of solution generation. Finally, the potential of using our algorithm to handle practical ontologies and large data sets in practice is corroborated through our evaluation.

Interesting future work includes, firstly, extending the current approach to other ontology languages, including Horn DLs and existential rules. The approach in [18] can be a starting point. For more expressive Horn DLs and existential rules, an interesting research problem is to decide which fragments or which ontologies/queries are *combined rewritable*, that is, an ontology transformation and an observation rewriting exist that are sound and complete for query abduction. The study on combined rewritability of existential rules regarding query answering in presented in [12], and would shed light on this research direction. Moreover, although the observation rewriting explores the structures of the CQs to some extent, we believe a more fine-grained analysis of query structures and possibly specific structures of some ontology axioms will allow us to apply advanced heuristics in solution construction.

7. ACKNOWLEDGMENTS

This work was partially supported by Australian Research Council (ARC) under grants DP110101042 and DP130102302. Jianfeng Du is partially supported by NSFC (61375056) and Guangdong Natural Science Foundation (S2013010012928).

8. REFERENCES

[1] F. Baader, S. Brandt, and C. Lutz. Pushing the $\mathcal{EL}$ Envelope. In *Proceedings of the 19th International Joint Conference on Artificial Intelligence*, pages 364–369, 2005.

[2] J.-F. Baget, M. Leclère, M.-L. Mugnier, and E. Salvat. On rules with existential variables: Walking the decidability line. *Artificial Intelligence*, 175(9-10):1620–1654, 2011.

[3] A. Borgida, D. Calvanese, and M. Rodriguez-Muro. Explanation in the DL-Lite family of description logics. In *On the Move to Meaningful Internet Systems: OTM*, pages 1440–1457. 2008.

[4] A. Borgida, E. Franconi, I. Horrocks, D. L. McGuinness, and P. F. Patel-Schneider. Explaining $\mathcal{ALC}$ subsumption. In *Proceedings of the 14th European Conference on Artificial Intelligence*, pages 209–213, 2000.

[5] A. Calì, G. Gottlob, T. Lukasiewicz, and A. Pieris. Datalog+/-: A family of languages for ontology querying. In *Datalog Reloaded - First International Workshop*, pages 351–368, 2010.

[6] D. Calvanese, M. Ortiz, M. Šimkus, and G. Stefanoni. Reasoning about explanations for negative query answers in DL-Lite. *Journal of Artificial Intelligence Research*, 48:635–669, 2013.

[7] J. Dolby, A. Fokoue, A. Kalyanpur, E. Schonberg, and K. Srinivas. Scalable highly expressive reasoner SHER. *Journal of Web Semantics*, 7(4):357–361, 2009.

[8] J. Du and Y.-D. S. Kewen Wang. Tractable approach to ABox abduction over description logic ontologies. In *Proceedings of the 28th AAAI Conference on Artificial Intelligence*, 2014.

[9] J. Du, G. Qi, Y. Shen, and J. Z. Pan. Towards practical ABox abduction in large description logic ontologies. *International Journal on Semantic Web and Information Systems*, 8(2):1–33, 2012.

[10] J. Du, S. Wang, G. Qi, J. Z. Pan, and Y. Hu. A new matchmaking approach based on abductive conjunctive query answering. In *Proceedings of the Joint International Semantic Technology Conference*, pages 144–159, 2011.

[11] B. Glimm, Y. Kazakov, T. Liebig, T. Tran, and V. Vialard. Abstraction refinement for ontology materialization. In *Proceedings of the 13th International Semantic Web Conference* , pages 180–195, 2014.

[12] G. Gottlob, M. Manna, and A. Pieris. Polynomial combined rewritings for existential rules. In *Proceedings of the 14th International Conference on Principles of Knowledge Representation and Reasoning*, 2014.

[13] Y. Guo, Z. Pan, and J. Heflin. LUBM: A benchmark for OWL knowledge base systems. *Web Semantics: Science, Services and Agents on the World Wide Web*, 3(2-3):158 – 182, 2005.

[14] K. Halland and K. Britz. ABox abduction in $\mathcal{ALC}$ using a DL tableau. In *Proceedings of the South African Institute for Computer Scientists and Information Technologists Conference*, pages 51–58, 2012.

[15] M. Horridge, B. Parsia, and U. Sattler. Laconic and precise justifications in OWL. In *Proceedings of the 7th International Semantic Web Conference*, pages 323–338, 2008.

[16] M. Imprialou, G. Stoilos, and B. C. Grau. Benchmarking ontology-based query rewriting systems. In *Proceedings of the 26th AAAI Conference on Artificial Intelligence*, 2012.

[17] S. Klarman, U. Endriss, and S. Schlobach. ABox abduction in the description logic $\mathcal{ALC}$. *Journal of Automated Reasoning*, 46(1):43–80, 2011.

[18] R. Kontchakov, C. Lutz, D. Toman, F. Wolter, and M. Zakharyaschev. The combined approach to query answering in DL-Lite. In *Proceedings of the 12th International Conference on Principles of Knowledge Representation and Reasoning*, 2010.

[19] C. Lutz, n. Seylan, D. Toman, and F. Wolter. The combined approach to OBDA: Taming role hierarchies using filters. In *Proceedings of the 12th International Semantic Web Conference*, pages 314–330. 2013.

[20] C. Lutz, D. Toman, and F. Wolter. Conjunctive query answering in the description logic $\mathcal{EL}$ using a relational database system. In *Proceedings of the 20th International Joint Conference on Artificial Intelligence*, 2009.

[21] Y. Ma, T. Gu, B. Xu, and L. Chang. An ABox abduction algorithm for the description logic $\mathcal{ALCI}$. In *Intelligent Information Processing*, pages 125–130, 2012.

[22] D. L. McGuinness and A. T. Borgida. Explaining subsumption in description logics. In *Proceedings of the 14th International Joint Conference on Artificial Intelligence*, pages 816–821, 1995.

[23] D. L. McGuinness and P. F. Patel-Schneider. Usability issues in knowledge representation systems. In *Proceedings of the 15th AAAI Conference on Artificial Intelligence*, pages 608–614, 1998.

[24] R. Peñaloza and B. Sertkaya. Complexity of axiom pinpointing in the DL-Lite family of description logics. In *Proceedings of the 19th European Conference on Artificial Intelligence*, pages 29–34, 2010.

[25] P. Rao, K. Sagonas, T. Swift, D. Warren, and J. Freire. XSB: A system for efficiently computing well-founded semantics. In *Logic Programming And Nonmonotonic Reasoning*, volume 1265 of *Lecture Notes in Computer Science*, pages 430–440. Springer Berlin Heidelberg, 1997.

[26] G. Stefanoni, B. Motik, and I. Horrocks. Introducing nominals to the combined query answering approaches for $\mathcal{EL}$. In *Proceedings of the 27th AAAI Conference on Artificial Intelligence*, 2013.

[27] Y. Zhou, Y. Nenov, B. C. Grau, and I. Horrocks. Pay-as-you-go OWL query answering using a triple store. In *Proceedings of the 28th AAAI Conference on Artificial Intelligence*, pages 1142–1148, 2014.

Crowdsourcing Pareto-Optimal Object Finding by Pairwise Comparisons

Abolfazl Asudeh, Gensheng Zhang, Naeemul Hassan, Chengkai Li, Gergely V. Zaruba
Department of Computer Science and Engineering, The University of Texas at Arlington
{ab.asudeh,gensheng.zhang,naeemul.hassan}@mavs.uta.edu
{cli,zaruba}@uta.edu

ABSTRACT

This is the first study of crowdsourcing Pareto-optimal object finding over partial orders and by pairwise comparisons, which has applications in public opinion collection, group decision making, and information exploration. Departing from prior studies on crowdsourcing skyline and ranking queries, it considers the case where objects do not have explicit attributes and preference relations on objects are strict partial orders. The partial orders are derived by aggregating crowdsourcers' responses to pairwise comparison questions. The goal is to find all Pareto-optimal objects by the fewest possible questions. It employs an iterative question-selection framework. Guided by the principle of eagerly identifying non-Pareto optimal objects, the framework only chooses candidate questions which must satisfy three conditions. This design is both sufficient and efficient, as it is proven to find a short terminal question sequence. The framework is further steered by two ideas—macro-ordering and micro-ordering. By different micro-ordering heuristics, the framework is instantiated into several algorithms with varying power in pruning questions. Experiment results using both real crowdsourcing marketplace and simulations exhibited not only orders of magnitude reductions in questions when compared with a brute-force approach, but also close-to-optimal performance from the most efficient instantiation.

1. INTRODUCTION

The growth of user engagement and functionality in crowdsourcing platforms has made computationally challenging tasks unprecedentedly convenient. The subject of our study is one such task—crowdsourcing *Pareto-optimal object finding*. Consider a set of objects O and a set of criteria C for comparing the objects. An object $\mathsf{x}{\in}O$ is *Pareto-optimal* if and only if x is not dominated by any other object. Object y dominates x (denoted $\mathsf{y}{\succ}\mathsf{x}$) if and only if x is not better than y by any criterion and y is better than x by at least one criterion, i.e., $\forall c{\in}C : \mathsf{x}{\not\succ_c}\mathsf{y}$ and $\exists c{\in}C : \mathsf{y} \succ_c \mathsf{x}$. If x and y do not dominate each other (i.e., $\mathsf{x}{\not\succ}\mathsf{y}$ and $\mathsf{y}{\not\succ}\mathsf{x}$), we denote it by $\mathsf{x}{\sim}\mathsf{y}$. The *preference (better-than) relation* P_c (also denoted $\succ_c$) for each $c{\in}C$ is a binary relation subsumed by $O{\times}O$, in which a tuple $(\mathsf{x},\mathsf{y}){\in}P_c$ (also denoted $\mathsf{x}{\succ_c}\mathsf{y}$) is interpreted as "x is better than (preferred over) y with regard to criterion c". Hence, if $(\mathsf{x},\mathsf{y}){\notin}P_c$ (also denoted $\mathsf{x}{\not\succ_c}\mathsf{y}$), x is not better than y by criterion c. We say x and y are *indifferent* regarding c (denoted $\mathsf{x}{\sim_c}\mathsf{y}$), if $(\mathsf{x},\mathsf{y}){\notin}P_c \wedge (\mathsf{y},\mathsf{x}){\notin}P_c$. We consider the setting where each P_c is a *strict partial order*, i.e., P_c is irreflexive ($\forall\mathsf{x} : (\mathsf{x},\mathsf{x}) \notin P_c$) and transitive ($\forall\mathsf{x},\mathsf{y} : (\mathsf{x},\mathsf{y}){\in}P_c{\wedge}(\mathsf{y},\mathsf{z}){\in}P_c{\Rightarrow}(\mathsf{x},\mathsf{z}){\in}P_c$), which together imply asymmetry ($\forall\mathsf{x},\mathsf{y} : (\mathsf{x},\mathsf{y}){\in}P_c \Rightarrow (\mathsf{y},\mathsf{x}){\notin}P_c$). We note that such definition of better-than relation has been widely used in modeling preferences (e.g., [20, 13, 28]), and the definition of Pareto-optimal objects follows the concept of *Pareto composition* of preference relations in [13].

Permission to make digital or hard copies of all or part of this work for personal or classroom use is granted without fee provided that copies are not made or distributed for profit or commercial advantage and that copies bear this notice and the full citation on the first page. Copyrights for components of this work owned by others than the author(s) must be honored. Abstracting with credit is permitted. To copy otherwise, or republish, to post on servers or to redistribute to lists, requires prior specific permission and/or a fee. Request permissions from Permissions@acm.org.
CIKM'15 October 19 - 23, 2015, Melbourne, VIC, Australia
Copyright is held by the owner/author(s). Publication rights licensed to ACM.
ACM 978-1-4503-3794-6/15/10 ...$15.00
DOI: http://dx.doi.org/10.1145/2806416.2806451.

Novelty Pareto-optimal queries resembles *skyline* queries [5]. However, except for [23, 4, 17], previous studies on preference and skyline queries do not use the crowd; they focus on query processing on *existing* data. On the contrary, we examine how to obtain sufficient data from the crowd for determining Pareto-optimal objects. Furthermore, our work differs in several radical ways, as summarized in Table 1 and explained below.

- The preference relation for a criterion is *not* governed by explicit scores or values on object attributes (e.g., sizes of houses, prices of hotels), while prior studies (except [4, 17]) assumed explicit attribute representation. For many comparison criteria, it is difficult to model objects by explicit attributes, not to mention asking people to provide such values or scores; people's preferences are rather based on complex, subtle perceptions, as Examples 1 and 2 shall demonstrate. The concept definitions deliberately do not admit notations for attribute or object equivalence.
- Due to the above reason, we request crowdsourcers to perform pairwise comparisons instead of directly providing attribute values or scores. On the contrary, [23] assumes explicit attribute representation and thereby answers skyline queries by asking the crowd to provide missing attribute values. Pairwise comparison is extensively studied in social choice and welfare, preferences, and voting. It is known that people are more comfortable and confident with comparing objects than directly scoring them, since it is easier, faster, and less error-prone [30].
- The crowd's preference relations are modeled as strict partial orders, as opposed to total orders. This is not only a direct effect of using pairwise comparisons instead of numeric scores or explicit attribute values, but also a reflection of the psychological nature of human's preferences [20, 13], since it is not always natural to enforce a total order. Most studies on skyline queries assume total orders, except for [11, 28, 29, 32] which consider partial orders.

Several recent studies used crowdsourcing to compare objects for answering ranking, top-k and group-by queries. Crowd-BT [12] ranks objects by crowdsourcing pairwise object comparisons. Polychronopoulos et al. [25] find top-k items in an itemset by asking human workers to rank small subsets of items. Davidson et al. [15] evaluate top-k and group-by queries by asking the crowd to answer

	Task	Question type	Multiple attributes	Order among objects (on each attribute)	Explicit attribute representation
[12]	full ranking	pairwise comparison	no	total order	no
[25]	top-k ranking	rank subsets of objects	no	total order	no
[15]	top-k ranking and grouping	pairwise comparison	no	total order	no
[23]	skyline/Pareto-optimal queries	missing value inquiry	yes	total order	yes
[17]	skyline/Pareto-optimal queries	pairwise comparison	yes	total order	no
[4], this work	skyline/Pareto-optimal queries	pairwise comparison	yes	strict partial order	no

Table 1: Related work comparison.

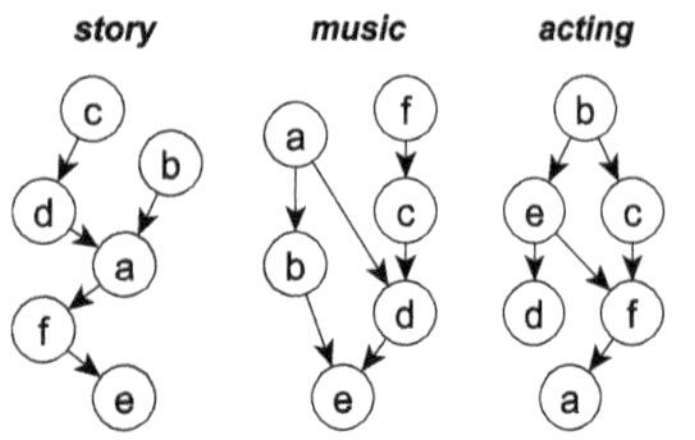

(a) Preference relations (i.e., strict partial orders) on three criteria.

QUESTION	ANSWER $\succ$	ANSWER $\sim$	ANSWER $\prec$	OUTCOME
$a?_sb$	1	0	4	$b\succ_s a$
$a?_sc$	0	0	5	$c\succ_s a$
$a?_sd$	0	2	3	$d\succ_s a$
$a?_se$	4	0	1	$a\succ_s e$
$a?_sf$	3	1	1	$a\succ_s f$
$b?_sc$	1	2	2	$b\sim_s c$
$b?_sd$	1	3	1	$b\sim_s d$
$b?_se$	5	0	0	$b\succ_s e$
$b?_sf$	4	1	0	$b\succ_s f$
$c?_sd$	3	2	0	$c\succ_s d$
$c?_se$	4	0	1	$c\succ_s e$
$c?_sf$	3	1	1	$c\succ_s f$
$d?_se$	3	0	2	$d\succ_s e$
$d?_sf$	3	2	0	$d\succ_s f$
$e?_sf$	1	1	3	$f\succ_s e$

(b) Deriving the preference relation for criterion *story* by pairwise comparisons. Each comparison is performed by 5 workers. $\theta = 60\%$.

Figure 1: Finding Pareto-optimal movies by *story*, *music*, *acting*.

type questions (whether two objects belong to the same group) and *value* questions (ordering two objects). They do not consider multiple attributes in modeling objects, while skyline and Pareto-optimal objects are def ned in a space of multiple attributes. They assume total orders instead of partial orders.

To recap, ours is so far the only work on crowdsourcing Pareto-optimal object f nding over partial orders, and we reported in the extended version of this paper [4] the f rst study of crowdsourcing Pareto-optimal queries by pairwise comparisons and without explicit attribute representation.

Motivating Applications Pareto-optimal object f nding lends itself to applications in several areas, including public opinion collection, group decision making, and information exploration, exemplif ed by the following motivating examples.

Example 1 (Collecting Public Opinion and Group Decision Making). Consider a set of movies O={a,b,c,d,e,f} and a set of criteria C={*story, music, acting*} (denoted by s, m, a in the ensuing discussion). Fig.1a shows the individual preference relations (i.e., strict partial orders), one per criterion. Each strict partial order is graphically represented as a directed acyclic graph (DAG), more specif cally a Hasse diagram. The existence of a simple path from x to y in the DAG means x is better than (preferred to) y by the corresponding criterion. For example, $(a, e)\in P_m$ ($a\succ_m e$), i.e., a is better than e by *music*. $(b, d)\notin P_s$ and $(d, b)\notin P_s$; hence $b\sim_s d$. The partial orders def ne the dominance relation between objects. For instance, movie c dominates d ($c\succ d$), because c is preferred than d on *story* and *music* and they are indifferent on *acting*, i.e., $c\succ_s d$, $c\succ_m d$, and $c\sim_a d$; a and b do not dominate each other ($a\sim b$), since $b\succ_s a$, $a\succ_m b$ and $b\succ_a a$. Based on the three partial orders, b is the only Pareto-optimal object, since no other objects dominate it and every other object is dominated by some object.

Note that tasks such as the above one may be used in both understanding the public's preference (i.e., the preference relations are collected from a large, anonymous crowd) and making decisions for a target group (i.e., the preference relations are from a small group of people). □

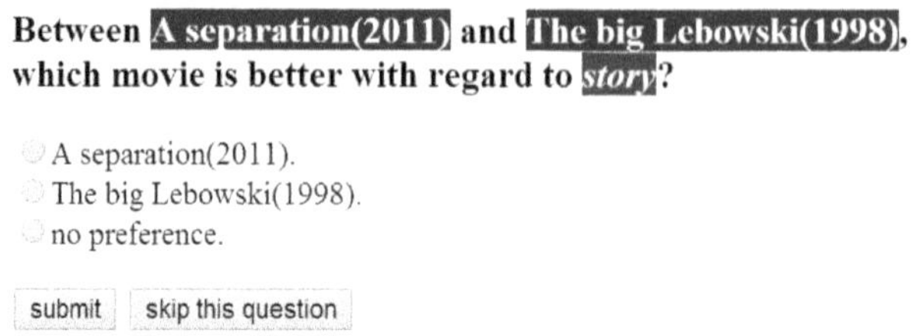

Figure 2: A question that asks to compare two movies by *story*.

Example 2 (Information Exploration). Consider a photography enthusiast, *Amy*, who is drown in a large number of photos she has taken and wants to select a subset of the better ones. She resorts to crowdsourcing for the task, as it has been exploited by many for similar tasks such as photo tagging, location/face identif cation, sorting photos by (guessed) date, and so on. Particularly, she would like to choose Pareto-optimal photos with regard to *color*, *sharpness* and *landscape*. □

By def nition, the crux of f nding Pareto-optimal objects lies in obtaining the preference relations, i.e., the strict partial orders on individual criteria. Through crowdsourcing, the preference relations are derived by aggregating the crowd's responses to *pairwise comparison* tasks. Each such comparison between objects x and y by criterion c is a question, denoted $x?_cy$, which has three possible outcomes—$x\succ_c y$, $y\succ_c x$, and $x\sim_c y$, based on the crowd's answers. An example is as follows.

Example 3 (Deriving Preference Relations from Pairwise Comparisons by the Crowd). Fig.1b shows the hypothetical results of all 15 pairwise comparisons between the 6 movies in Example 1, by criterion s=*story*. The outcomes of all comparisons form the crowd's preference relation on *story* (the leftmost DAG in Fig.1a). Fig.2 is the screenshot of a question form designed for one such comparison. A crowdsourcer, when facing this question, would make a choice among the three possible answers or skip a question if they do not have enough conf dence or knowledge to answer it. Fig.1b shows how many crowdsourcers have selected each answer. For instance, for question $a?_sf$, three people preferred movie a, one person preferred f, and one person is indifferent. By aggregating these answers, it is derived that a is better than f with regard to *story*, since 60% of the crowdsourcers who responded to the question chose this answer. For question $\mathsf{b}?_s\mathsf{c}$, the result is $\mathsf{b}\sim_s\mathsf{c}$, since neither $\mathsf{b}\succ_s\mathsf{c}$ nor $\mathsf{b}\prec_s\mathsf{c}$ received enough votes. (Assuming a threshold θ=60%, i.e., either $\mathsf{b}\succ_s\mathsf{c}$ or $\mathsf{b}\prec_s\mathsf{c}$ should have at least 60% of votes, in order to not declare $\mathsf{b}\sim_s\mathsf{c}$.) □

It is important to point out that, in the aforementioned applications, there is an intrinsic lack of the notion of "ground truth". Since objects are not explicitly represented by attribute values, the partial orders are purely ref ections of crowdsourcers' opinions. For this reason, we shall not investigate if crowdsourcers can obtain answers close to "ground truth", which does not exist. This also means that our techniques may get different answers when using different crowdsourcers or even the same crowdsourcers at different times, because people's opinions alter.

Algorithmic Framework Our goal is to f nd all Pareto-optimal objects with as few questions as possible. A brute-force approach will obtain complete preference relations via pairwise comparisons of all object pairs by every criterion. However, without such exhaustive comparisons, incomplete knowledge collected from a small set of questions may suff ce in discerning all Pareto-optimal objects. Toward this end, it may appear that we can take advantage of the transitivity of object dominance—a cost-saving property often exploited in skyline query algorithms (e.g., [5]) to exclude dominated objects from participating in any future comparison once they are detected. But, as also discussed in [13], object dominance in our case is *not* transitive (Property 1), due to the lack of explicit attribute representation. Hence, the aforementioned cost-saving technique is inapplicable.

Aiming at Pareto-optimal object f nding by a short sequence of questions, we introduce a general, iterative algorithm framework (Sec.3). Each iteration goes through four steps—*question selection*, *outcome derivation*, *contradiction resolution*, and *termination test*. In the i-th iteration, a question q_i=$\mathsf{x}?_c\mathsf{y}$ is selected and its outcome is determined based on crowdsourcers' answers. On unusual occasions, if the outcome presents a contradiction to the obtained outcomes of other questions, it is changed to the closest outcome such that the contradiction is resolved. Based on the transitive closure of the outcomes to the questions so far, the objects O are partitioned into three sets—$O_{\surd}$ (objects that must be Pareto-optimal), $O_{\times}$ (objects that must be non-Pareto optimal), and $O_?$ (objects whose Pareto-optimality cannot be fully discerned by the incomplete knowledge so far). When $O_?$ becomes empty, $O_{\surd}$ contains all Pareto-optimal objects and the algorithm terminates. The question sequence so far is thus a *terminal sequence*.

There are a vast number of terminal sequences. Our goal is to f nd one that is as short as possible. We observe that, for a non-Pareto optimal object, knowing that it is dominated by at least one object is suff cient, and we do not need to f nd all its dominating objects. It follows that we do not really care about the dominance relation between non-Pareto optimal objects and we can skip their comparisons. Hence, the overriding principle of our question selection strategy is to identify non-Pareto optimal objects as early as possible. Guided by this principle, the framework only chooses from *candidate questions* which must satisfy three conditions (Sec.3.1). This design is suff cient, as we prove that an empty candidate question set implies a terminal sequence, and vice versa (Property 2). The design is also eff cient, as we further prove that, if a question sequence contains non-candidate questions, there exists a shorter or equally long sequence with only candidate questions that produces the same $O_{\times}$, matching the principle of eagerly f nding non-Pareto optimal objects (Theorem 1). Moreover, by the aforementioned principle, the framework selects in every iteration such a candidate question $\mathsf{x}?_c\mathsf{y}$ that x is more likely to be dominated by y. The selection is steered by two ideas—*macro-ordering* and *micro-ordering*. By using different micro-ordering heuristics, the framework is instantiated into several algorithms with varying power in pruning questions (Sec.4). We also derive a lower bound on the number of questions required for f nding all Pareto-optimal objects (Theorem 2).

In summary, this paper makes the following contributions:

- This is the f rst work on crowdsourcing Pareto-optimal object f nding over partial orders and by pairwise comparisons. We def ne preference relations based on pairwise comparisons and we aim to f nd all Pareto-optimal objects by fewest possible comparisons.
- We propose a general, iterative algorithm framework (Sec.3) which follows the strategy of choosing only candidate questions that must satisfy three conditions. We prove important properties that establish the advantage of the strategy (Sec.3.1).
- We design macro-ordering and micro-ordering heuristics for f nding a short terminal question sequence. Based on the heuristics, the generic framework is instantiated into several algorithms (RandomQ, RandomP, FRQ) with varying eff ciency. We also derive a non-trivial lower bound on the number of required pairwise comparison questions. (Sec.4)
- We carried out experiments using both simulations and real crowdsourcing marketplace to compare the amount of comparisons by different instantiations of the framework under varying problem sizes. The results demonstrate the effectiveness of selecting only candidate questions, macro-ordering, and micro-ordering. When these ideas are stacked together, they use orders of magnitude less comparisons than a brute-force approach. The results reveal that FRQ is nearly optimal and the lower bound is practically tight, since FRQ gets very close to the lower bound. (Sec.5)

2. RELATED WORK

Besides [12], there were multiple studies on ranking objects by pairwise comparisons, which date back to decades ago as aggregating the preferences of multiple agents has always been a fundamental problem in social choice and welfare [14, 3]. The more recent studies can be categorized into three types: **1)** Approaches such as [21, 26, 31] predict users' object ranking by completing a user-object scoring matrix. Their predictions take into account users' similarities in pairwise comparisons, resembling *collaborative f ltering* [16]. They thus do not consider explicit attribute representation for objects. **2)** Approaches such as [7, 9, 8] infer query-specif c (instead of user-specif c) ranked results to web search queries. Following the paradigm of *learning-to-rank* [22], they rank a query's result documents according to pairwise result comparisons of other queries. The documents are modeled by explicit ranking features. **3)** Approaches such as [6, 19, 1, 2, 24] are similar to [12] as they use pairwise comparisons to infer a single ranked list that is neither user-specif c nor query-specif c. Among them, [19] is special in that it also applies learning-to-rank and requires explicit feature representation. Different from our work, none of these studies is about Pareto-optimal objects, since they all assume a total order among objects; those using learning-to-rank require explicit feature representation, while the rest do not consider multiple attributes. Moreover, except [19, 1, 2], they all assume comparison results are already obtained before their algorithms kick in. In contrast, we aim at minimizing the pairwise comparison questions to ask in f nding Pareto-optimal objects.

3. GENERAL FRAMEWORK

By the def nition of Pareto-optimal objects, the key to f nding such objects is to obtain the preference relations, i.e., the strict partial orders on individual criteria. Toward this end, the most basic operation is to perform *pairwise comparison*—given a pair of objects x and y and a criterion c, determine whether one is better than the other (i.e., $(\mathsf{x},\mathsf{y}) \in P_c$ or $(\mathsf{y},\mathsf{x}) \in P_c$) or they are indifferent (i.e., $(\mathsf{x},\mathsf{y}) \notin P_c \wedge (\mathsf{y},\mathsf{x}) \notin P_c$).

The problem of crowdsourcing Pareto-optimal object f nding is thus essentially crowdsourcing pairwise comparisons. Each comparison task between x and y by criterion c is presented to the crowd as a question q (denoted $\mathsf{x}?_c\mathsf{y}$). The outcome to the question (denoted $rlt(q)$) is aggregated from the crowd's answers. Given a set of questions, the outcomes thus contain an (incomplete) knowledge of the crowd's preference relations for various criteria. Fig.2 illustrates the screenshot of one such question (comparing two movies by *story*) used in our empirical evaluation. We note that there are other viable designs of question, e.g., only allowing the f rst two choices ($\mathsf{x}\succ_c\mathsf{y}$ and $\mathsf{y}\succ_c\mathsf{x}$). Our work is agnostic to the specif c question design.

Given n objects and r criteria, a brute-force approach will perform pairwise comparisons on all object pairs by every criterion, which leads to $r{\cdot}n{\cdot}(n-1)/2$ comparisons. The corresponding question outcomes amount to the complete underlying preference relations. The quadratic nature of the brute-force approach renders it wasteful. The bad news is that, in the worst case, we cannot do better than it. To understand this, consider the scenario where all objects are indifferent by every criterion. If any comparison $\mathsf{x}?_c\mathsf{y}$ is skipped, we cannot determine if x and y are indifferent or if one dominates another.

In practice, though, the outlook is much brighter. Since we look for only Pareto-optimal objects, it is an overkill to obtain complete preference relations. Specif cally, for a Pareto-optimal object, knowing it is not dominated by any object is suff cient, and we do not need to f nd all the objects dominated by it; for a non-Pareto optimal object, knowing it is dominated by at least one object is suff cient, and we do not need to f nd all its dominating objects. Hence, without exhausting all possible comparisons, incomplete knowledge on preference relations collected from a set of questions may suff ce in fully discerning all Pareto-optimal objects.

Our objective is to f nd all Pareto-optimal objects with as few questions as possible. By pursuing this goal, we are applying a very simple cost model—the cost of a solution only depends on its number of questions. Although the cost of a task in a crowdsourcing environment may depend on monetary cost, latency and other factors, the number of questions is a generic, platform-independent cost measure and arguably proportionally correlates with the real cost. Therefore, we assume a sequential execution model which asks the crowd an ordered sequence of questions $Q = \langle q_1, ..., q_n\rangle$—it only asks q_{i+1} after $rlt(q_i)$ is obtained. Thereby, we do not consider asking multiple questions concurrently. In practice, such a parallel-execution framework will lead to shorter latency but more questions (which may imply higher monetary cost) than our sequential-execution framework. One interesting direction of future work is to adapt our algorithms to a parallel framework and investigate the tradeoffs between latency and cost. Furthermore, in discussion of our approach, the focus shall be on how to f nd a short question sequence instead of the algorithms' complexity, since the time taken by crowdsourcers to answer questions will dominate the algorithms' execution time.

To f nd a short sequence, we design a general algorithm framework, as displayed in Fig.3. Alg.1 shows the framework's pseudocode. Its execution is iterative. Each iteration goes through four steps—*question selection, outcome derivation, contradiction resolution*, and *termination test*. In the i-th iteration, a question $q_i{=}\mathsf{x}?_c\mathsf{y}$ is selected and presented to the crowd. The question outcome $rlt(q_i)$ is derived from the crowd's aggregated answers. On unusual occasions, if the outcome presents a contradiction to the obtained outcomes of other questions so far, it is changed to the closest outcome to resolve contradiction. By computing $R^+(Q_i)$, the *transitive closure* of $R(Q_i)$—the obtained outcomes to questions so far $\langle q_1, \ldots, q_i\rangle$, the outcomes to certain questions are derived and such questions will never be asked. Based on $R^+(Q_i)$, if every object is determined to be either Pareto-optimal or non-Pareto optimal without uncertainty, the algorithm terminates.

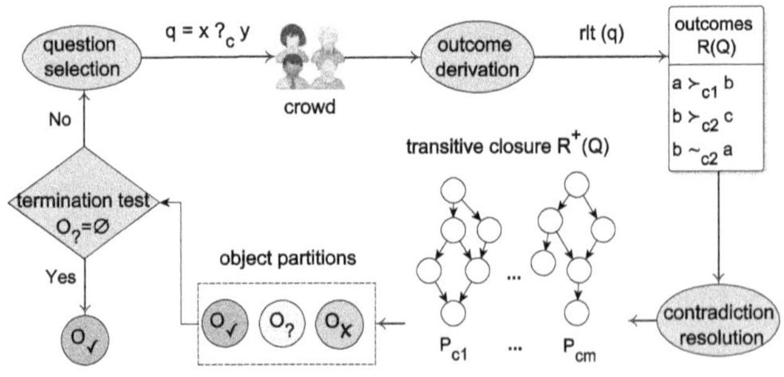

Figure 3: The general framework.

Algorithm 1: The general framework

Input: O : the set of objects
Output: $O_{\surd}$: Pareto-optimal objects of O

```
R(Q) ← ∅;                                       /* question outcomes */
repeat
    x?_c y ← question selection;
    rlt(x?_c y) ← outcome derivation;           /* resolve conf ict, if any */
    R(Q) ← R(Q) ∪ {rlt(x?_c y)};
    (O_√, O_×, O_?) ← partitioning objects based on R+(Q);
    /* R+(Q) is the transitive closure of R(Q) */
until O_? = {};
return O_√;
```

Below, we discuss outcome derivation and termination test. Sec.3.1 examines the framework's key step—question selection, and Sec.3.2 discusses contradiction resolution.

Outcome derivation Given a question $\mathsf{x}?_c\mathsf{y}$, its outcome $rlt(\mathsf{x}?_c\mathsf{y})$ must be aggregated from multiple crowdsourcers, in order to reach a reliable result with conf dence. Particularly, one of three mutually-exclusive outcomes is determined based on k crowdsourcers' answers to the question:

$$rlt(\mathsf{x}?_c\mathsf{y}) = \begin{cases} \mathsf{x} \succ_c \mathsf{y} & \text{if } \frac{\#\mathsf{x}}{k} \geq \theta \\ \mathsf{y} \succ_c \mathsf{x} & \text{if } \frac{\#\mathsf{y}}{k} \geq \theta \\ \mathsf{x} \sim_c \mathsf{y}\ (\mathsf{x} \not\succ_c \mathsf{y} \wedge \mathsf{y} \not\succ_c \mathsf{x}) & \text{otherwise} \end{cases} \quad (1)$$

where θ is such a predef ned threshold that $\theta{>}50\%$, $\#\mathsf{x}$ is the number of crowdsourcers (out of k) preferring x over y on criterion c, and $\#\mathsf{y}$ is the number of crowdsourcers preferring y over x on c. Fig.1b shows the outcomes of all 15 questions according to Equation (1) for comparing movies by *story* using $k{=}5$ and $\theta{=}60\%$. Other conceivable def nitions may be used in determining the outcome of $\mathsf{x}?_c\mathsf{y}$. For example, the outcome may be def ned as the choice (out of the three possible choices) that receives the most votes from the crowd. The ensuing discussion is agnostic to the specif c def nition.

The current framework does not consider different levels of conf dence on question outcomes. The conf dence on the outcome of a question may be represented as a probability value based on the distribution of crowdsourcers' responses. An interesting direction for future work is to f nd Pareto-optimal objects in probabilistic sense. The conf dence may also ref ect the crowdsourcers' quality and credibility [18].

Termination test In each iteration, Alg.1 partitions the objects into three sets by their Pareto-optimality based on the transitive closure of question outcomes so far. If every object's Pareto-optimality has been determined without uncertainty, the algorithm terminates. Details are as follows.

Definition 1 (Transitive Closure of Outcomes). Given a set of questions $Q{=}\langle q_1, ..., q_n\rangle$, the transitive closure of their outcomes $R(Q){=}\{rlt(q_1), ..., rlt(q_n)\}$ is $R^+(Q){=}\{\mathsf{x}{\sim_c}\mathsf{y} \mid \mathsf{x}{\sim_c}\mathsf{y} \in R(Q)\} \bigcup \{\mathsf{x}{\succ_c}\mathsf{y} \mid (\mathsf{x}{\succ_c}\mathsf{y} \in R(Q)) \vee (\exists\, \mathsf{w}_1,\mathsf{w}_2,...,\mathsf{w}_m : \mathsf{w}_1{=}\mathsf{x}, \mathsf{w}_m{=}\mathsf{y} \wedge (\forall 0{<}i{<}m : \mathsf{w}_i \succ_c \mathsf{w}_{i+1} \in R(Q)))\}$. □

In essence, the transitive closure dictates $\mathsf{x}{\succ_c}\mathsf{z}$ without asking the question $\mathsf{x}?_c\mathsf{z}$, if the existing outcomes $R(Q)$ (and recursively the transitive closure $R^+(Q)$) contains both $\mathsf{x}{\succ_c}\mathsf{y}$ and $\mathsf{y}{\succ_c}\mathsf{z}$. Based on $R^+(Q)$, the objects O can be partitioned into three sets:

$O_{\surd} = \{\mathsf{x} \in O \mid \forall \mathsf{y} \in O : (\exists c \in C : \mathsf{x}{\succ_c}\mathsf{y} \in R^+(Q)) \vee (\forall c \in C : \mathsf{x}{\sim_c}\mathsf{y} \in R^+(Q))\}$;

$O_{\times} = \{\mathsf{x} \in O \mid \exists \mathsf{y} \in O : (\forall c \in C : \mathsf{y}{\succ_c}\mathsf{x} \in R^+(Q) \vee \mathsf{x}{\sim_c}\mathsf{y} \in R^+(Q)) \wedge (\exists c \in C : \mathsf{y}{\succ_c}\mathsf{x} \in R^+(Q))\}$;

$O_? = O \backslash (O_{\surd} \cup O_{\times})$.

$O_{\surd}$ contains objects that must be Pareto-optimal, $O_{\times}$ contains objects that cannot possibly be Pareto-optimal, and $O_?$ contains objects for which the incomplete knowledge $R^+(Q)$ is insufficient for discerning their Pareto-optimality. The objects in $O_?$ may turn out to be Pareto-optimal after more comparison questions. If the set $O_?$ for a question sequence Q is empty, $O_{\surd}$ contains all Pareto-optimal objects and the algorithm terminates. We call such a Q a *terminal sequence*, defined below.

Definition 2 (Terminal Sequence). A question sequence Q is a terminal sequence if and only if, based on $R^+(Q)$, $O_?{=}\varnothing$.

3.1 Question Selection

Given objects O and criteria C, there can be a huge number of terminal sequences. Our goal is to find a sequence as short as possible. As Fig.3 and Alg.1 show, the framework is an iterative procedure of object partitioning based on question outcomes. It can also be viewed as the process of moving objects from $O_?$ to $O_{\surd}$ and $O_{\times}$. Once an object is moved to $O_{\surd}$ or $O_{\times}$, it cannot be moved again. With regard to this process, we make two important observations, as follows.

- *In order to declare an object* x *not Pareto-optimal, it is sufficient to just know* x *is dominated by another object.* It immediately follows that we do not really care about the dominance relationship between objects in $O_{\times}$ and thus can skip the comparisons between such objects. Once we know $\mathsf{x}{\in}O_?$ is dominated by another object, it cannot be Pareto-optimal and is immediately moved to $O_{\times}$. Quickly moving objects into $O_{\times}$ can allow us skipping many comparisons between objects in $O_{\times}$.
- *In order to declare an object* x *Pareto-optimal, it is necessary to know that no object can dominate* x. This means we may need to compare x with all other objects including non Pareto-optimal objects. As an extreme example, x may be dominated by only a non-Pareto optimal object y but not by any other object (not even the objects dominating y). This is because object dominance based on preference relations is intransitive, which is formally stated in Property 1. The intransitivity of preference relation formed by Pareto composition of strict partial orders was discussed in [13].

Property 1 (Intransitivity of Object Dominance). Object dominance based on the preference relations over a set of criteria is not transitive. Specifically, if $\mathsf{x}{\succ}\mathsf{y}$ and $\mathsf{y}{\succ}\mathsf{z}$, it is not necessarily true that $\mathsf{x}{\succ}\mathsf{z}$. In other words, it is possible that $\mathsf{x}{\sim}\mathsf{z}$ or even $\mathsf{z}{\succ}\mathsf{x}$. □

We show the intransitivity of object dominance by an example. Consider objects $O{=}\{\mathsf{x,y,z}\}$, criteria $C{=}\{c_1, c_2, c_3\}$, and the preference relations in Fig.4. Three dominance relationships violate transitivity: (i) $\mathsf{x}{\succ}\mathsf{y}$ (based on $\mathsf{x}{\succ_{c_1}}\mathsf{y}$, $\mathsf{x}{\sim_{c_2}}\mathsf{y}$, $\mathsf{x}{\sim_{c_3}}\mathsf{y}$), (ii) $\mathsf{y}{\succ}\mathsf{z}$ (based on $\mathsf{y}{\sim_{c_1}}\mathsf{z}$, $\mathsf{y}{\succ_{c_2}}\mathsf{z}$, $\mathsf{y}{\sim_{c_3}}\mathsf{z}$), and (iii) $\mathsf{z}{\succ}\mathsf{x}$ (based on $\mathsf{z}{\sim_{c_1}}\mathsf{x}$, $\mathsf{z}{\sim_{c_2}}\mathsf{x}$, $\mathsf{z}{\succ_{c_3}}\mathsf{x}$). As another example, in Fig.1a, $\mathsf{b}{\succ}\mathsf{c}$ (since $\mathsf{b}{\sim_s}\mathsf{c}$, $\mathsf{b}{\sim_m}\mathsf{c}$, $\mathsf{b}{\succ_a}\mathsf{c}$, where $s{=}$*story*, $m{=}$*music*, $a{=}$*acting*) and $\mathsf{c}{\succ}\mathsf{a}$ (since $\mathsf{c}{\succ_s}\mathsf{a}$, $\mathsf{c}{\sim_m}\mathsf{a}$, $\mathsf{c}{\succ_a}\mathsf{a}$), but $\mathsf{a}{\sim}\mathsf{b}$ (since $\mathsf{b}{\succ_s}\mathsf{a}$, $\mathsf{a}{\succ_m}\mathsf{b}$, $\mathsf{b}{\succ_a}\mathsf{a}$) where transitivity does not hold.

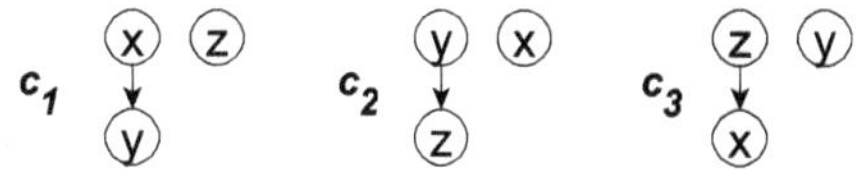

Figure 4: Intransitivity of object dominance: $\mathsf{x}{\succ}\mathsf{y}$, $\mathsf{y}{\succ}\mathsf{z}$, $\mathsf{z}{\succ}\mathsf{x}$.

Differently, transitivity of object dominance holds in skyline analysis [5]. The contradiction is due to the lack of explicit attribute representation—in our case two objects may be considered equally good on a criterion if they are indifferent, while in skyline analysis they are equally good regarding an attribute if they bear identical values. Skyline query algorithms exploit the transitivity of object dominance to reduce execution cost, because an object can be immediately excluded from further comparison once it is found dominated by any other object. However, due to Property 1, we cannot leverage such pruning anymore.

Based on these observations, the overriding principle of our question selection strategy (Alg.2) is to identify non-Pareto optimal objects as early as possible. At every iteration of the framework (Alg.1), we choose to compare x and y by criterion c (i.e., ask question $\mathsf{x}?_c\mathsf{y}$) where $\mathsf{x}?_c\mathsf{y}$ belongs to *candidate questions*. Such candidate questions must satisfy three conditions (Definition 3). There can be many candidate questions. In choosing the next question, by the aforementioned principle, we select such $\mathsf{x}?_c\mathsf{y}$ that x is more likely to be dominated by y. More specifically, we design two ordering heuristics—*macro-ordering* and *micro-ordering*. Given the three object partitions $O_{\surd}$, $O_{\times}$ and $O_?$, the macro-ordering idea is simply that we choose x from $O_?$ (required by one of the conditions on candidate questions) and y from $O_{\surd} \cup O_?$ (if possible) or $O_{\times}$ (otherwise). The reason is that it is less likely for an object in $O_{\times}$ to dominate x. Micro-ordering further orders all candidate questions satisfying the macro-ordering heuristic. In Sec.4, we instantiate the framework into a variety of solutions with varying power in pruning questions, by using different micro-ordering heuristics.

Definition 3 (Candidate Question). Given Q, the set of asked questions so far, $\mathsf{x}?_c\mathsf{y}$ is a *candidate question* if and only if it satisfies the following conditions:

(i) The outcome of $\mathsf{x}?_c\mathsf{y}$ is unknown yet, i.e., $rlt(\mathsf{x}?_c\mathsf{y}) \notin R^+(Q)$;

(ii) x must belong to $O_?$;

(iii) Based on $R^+(Q)$, the possibility of $\mathsf{y}{\succ}\mathsf{x}$ must not be ruled out yet, i.e., $\nexists c' \in C : \mathsf{x} \succ_{c'} \mathsf{y} \in R^+(Q)$.

Algorithm 2: Question selection

Input: $R^+(Q_i), O_{\surd}(Q_i), O_?(Q_i), O_{\times}(Q_i)$
Output: Q^1_{can} or Q^2_{can}

$Q_{can} \leftarrow \{\mathsf{x}?_c\mathsf{y} \mid rlt(\mathsf{x}?_c\mathsf{y}) \notin R^+(Q_i) \wedge \mathsf{x} \in O_?(Q_i) \wedge (\nexists c' \in C : \mathsf{x} \succ_{c'} \mathsf{y} \in R^+(Q_i))\}$;
$Q^1_{can} \leftarrow \{\mathsf{x}?_c\mathsf{y} \mid \mathsf{x}?_c\mathsf{y} \in Q_{can}, \mathsf{y} \notin O_{\times}(Q_i)\}$;
$Q^2_{can} \leftarrow \{\mathsf{x}?_c\mathsf{y} \mid \mathsf{x}?_c\mathsf{y} \in Q_{can}, \mathsf{y} \in O_{\times}(Q_i)\}$;
/* *Macro-ordering: consider* Q^1_{can} *before* Q^2_{can}. */
if $Q^1_{can} \neq \varnothing$ **then**
  return *micro-ordering*(Q^1_{can});
else if $Q^2_{can} \neq \varnothing$ **then**
  return *micro-ordering*(Q^2_{can});

We denote the set of candidate questions by Q_{can}. Thus, $Q_{can} = \{x?_c y \mid rlt(x?_c y) \notin R^+(Q) \wedge x \in O_? \wedge (\nexists c' \in C : x \succ_{c'} y \in R^+(Q))\}$. □

If no candidate question exists, the question sequence Q is a terminal sequence. The reverse statement is also true, i.e., upon a terminal sequence, there is no candidate question left. This is formalized in the following property.

Property 2. $Q_{can} = \varnothing$ if and only if $O_? = \varnothing$.

Proof. The proof is omitted due to space limitations and can be found in the technical report [4]. □

Questions violating the three conditions may also lead to terminal sequences. However, choosing only candidate questions matches our objective of quickly identifying non-Pareto optimal objects. Below we justify the conditions.

Condition (i): This is straightforward. If $R(Q)$ or its transitive closure already contains the outcome of $x?_c y$, we do not ask the same question again.

Condition (ii): This condition essentially dictates that at least one of the two objects in comparison is from $O_?$. (If only one of them belongs to $O_?$, we make it x.) Given a pair x and y, if neither is from $O_?$, there are three scenarios—(1) $x \in O_\surd, y \in O_\surd$, (2) $x \in O_\surd, y \in O_\times$ or $x \in O_\times, y \in O_\surd$, (3) $x \in O_\times, y \in O_\times$. Once we know an object is in $O_\surd$ or $O_\times$, its membership in such a set will never change. Hence, we are not interested in knowing the dominance relationship between objects from $O_\surd$ and $O_\times$ only. In all these three scenarios, comparing x and y is only useful for indirectly determining (by transitive closure) the outcome of comparing other objects. Intuitively speaking, such indirect pruning is not as efficient as direct pruning.

Condition (iii): This condition requires that, when $x?_c y$ is chosen, we cannot rule out the possibility of y dominating x. Otherwise, if y cannot possibly dominate x, the outcome of $x?_c y$ cannot help prune x. Note that, in such a case, comparing x and y by c may help prune y, if y still belongs to $O_?$ and x may dominate y. Such possibility is not neglected and is covered by a different representation of the same question—$y?_c x$, i.e., swapping the positions of x and y in checking the three conditions. If it is determined x and y cannot dominate each other, then their further comparison is only useful for indirectly determining the outcome of comparing other objects. Due to the same reason explained for condition (ii), such indirect pruning is less efficient.

The following simple Property 3 helps to determine whether $y \succ x$ is possible: If x is better than y by any criterion, then we can already rule out the possibility of $y \succ x$, without knowing the outcome of their comparison by every criterion. This allows us to skip further comparisons between them. Its correctness is straightforward based on the definition of object dominance.

Property 3 (Non-Dominance Property). At any given moment, suppose the set of asked questions is Q. Consider two objects x and y for which the comparison outcome is not known for every criterion, i.e., $\exists c$ such that $rlt(x?_c y) \notin R^+(Q)$. It can be determined that $y \not\succ x$ if $\exists c \in C$ such that $x \succ_c y \in R^+(Q)$. □

In justifying the three conditions in defining candidate questions, we intuitively explained that indirect pruning is less efficient—if it is known that x does not belong to $O_?$ or y cannot possibly dominate x, we will not ask question $x?_c y$. We now justify this strategy theoretically and precisely. Consider a question sequence $Q = \langle q_1, \ldots, q_n \rangle$. We use $O_\surd(Q)$, $O_?(Q)$, $O_\times(Q)$ to denote object partitions according to $R^+(Q)$. For any question q_i, the subsequence comprised of its preceding questions is denoted $Q_{i-1} = \langle q_1, \ldots, q_{i-1} \rangle$. If q_i was not a candidate question when it was chosen (i.e., after $R(Q_{i-1})$ was obtained), we say it is a *non-candidate*. The following Theorem 1 states that, if a question sequence contains non-candidate questions, we can replace it by a shorter or equally long sequence without non-candidate questions that produces the same set of dominated objects $O_\times$. Recall that the key to our framework is to recognize dominated objects and move them into $O_\times$ as early as possible. Hence, the new sequence will likely lead to less cost when the algorithm terminates.

Theorem 1. If Q contains non-candidate questions, there exists a question sequence Q' without non-candidate questions such that $|Q'| \leq |Q|$ and $O_\times(Q') = O_\times(Q)$.

Proof. We prove by demonstrating how to transform Q into such a Q'. Given any non-candidate question $q_i = x?_c y$ in Q, we remove it and, when necessary, replace several questions. The decisions and choices are partitioned into three mutually exclusive scenarios, which correspond to violations of the three conditions in Definition 3. The detailed proof is omitted due to space limitations and can be found in the technical report [4]. □

3.2 Resolving Unusual Contradictions in Question Outcomes

A preference relation can be more accurately derived, if more input is collected from the crowd. However, under practical constraints on budget and time, the limited responses from the crowd (k answers per question) may present two types of contradicting preferences.

(i) Suppose $rlt(x?_c y) = x \succ_c y$ and $rlt(y?_c z) = y \succ_c z$ have been derived, i.e., they belong to $R(Q)$. They together imply $x \succ_c z$, since a preference relation must be transitive. Therefore the question $x?_c z$ will not be asked. If the crowd is nevertheless asked to further compare x and z, the result $rlt(x?_c z)$ might be possibly $z \succ_c x$, which presents a contradiction.

(ii) Suppose $rlt(x?_c y) = x \sim_c y$ and $rlt(y?_c z) = y \succ_c z$ have been derived from the crowd. If the crowd is asked to further compare x and z, the result $rlt(x?_c z)$ might be possibly $z \succ_c x$. The outcomes $y \succ_c z$ and $z \succ_c x$ together imply $y \succ_c x$, which contradicts with $x \sim_c y$. (A symmetric case is $rlt(x?_c y) = x \sim_c y$, $rlt(y?_c z) = z \succ_c y$, and the crowd might respond with $rlt(x?_c z) = x \succ_c z$, which also leads to contradiction with $x \sim_c y$. The following discussion applies to this symmetric case, which is thus not mentioned again.)

In practice, such contradictions are uncommon. This is easy to understand intuitively—as long as the underlying preference relation is transitive, collective wisdom of the crowds will reflect it. We can find evidence of it in [27, 10], which confirmed that preference judgments of relevance in document retrieval are transitive.

Nevertheless, contradictions still occur. Type (i) contradictions can be prevented by enforcing the following simple Rule 1 to assume transitivity and thus skip certain questions. They will never get into the derived preference relations. In fact, in calculating transitive closure (Definition 1) and defining candidate questions (Sec.3.1), we already apply this rule.

Rule 1 (Contradiction Prevention by Skipping Questions). Given objects x, y, z and a criterion c, if $rlt(x?_c y) = x \succ_c y$ and $rlt(y?_c z) = y \succ_c z$, we assume $rlt(x?_c z) = x \succ_c z$ and thus will not ask the crowd to further compare x and z by criterion c. □

To resolve type (ii) contradictions, we enforce the following simple Rule 2.

Rule 2 (Contradiction Resolution by Choosing Outcomes). Consider objects x, y, z and a criterion c. Suppose $rlt(x?_c y) = x \sim_c y$ and $rlt(y?_c z) = y \succ_c z$ are obtained from the crowd. If $rlt(x?_c z) = z \succ_c x$ is obtained from the crowd afterwards, we replace the outcome of this question by $x \sim_c z$. (Note that we do not replace it by $x \succ_c z$, since $z \succ_c x$ is closer to $x \sim_c z$.) □

i	$rlt(q_i)$	Derived Results	$O_{\checkmark}$	$O_?$	$O_\times$
1-9	$b \succ_m \underline{e}$, $\underline{c} \sim_a d$, $\underline{a} \sim_m c$, $\underline{c} \succ_s e$, $\underline{b} \sim_s d$, $b \succ_a \underline{a}$, $\underline{d} \succ_m e$, $\underline{b} \sim_m d$, $\underline{b} \succ_s f$		$\varnothing$	{a,b,c,d,e,f}	$\varnothing$
10	$\underline{a} \succ_m d$	$a \succ_m e$			
11	$c \succ_a \underline{a}$				
12	$\underline{b} \sim_s c$				
13	$c \succ_m \underline{d}$	$c \succ_m e$			
14-19	$d \succ_s \underline{e}$, $\underline{e} \sim_a c$, $\underline{d} \sim_a f$, $\underline{a} \sim_a d$, $f \succ_a \underline{a}$, $\underline{b} \succ_a e$				
20	$b \succ_a \underline{d}$	$b \succ d$	$\varnothing$	{a,b,c,e,f}	{d}
21-23	$c \succ_s \underline{f}$, $a \succ_s \underline{e}$, $\underline{f} \sim_m b$				
24	$a \succ_s \underline{f}$	$a \sim f$			
25	$\underline{e} \succ_a f$	$b \succ_a f$, $b \succ_a a$, $e \succ_a a$, $b \succ f$	$\varnothing$	{a,b,c,e}	{d,f}
26	$\underline{b} \succ_a c$				
27	$a \succ_m \underline{b}$				
28	$b \succ_s \underline{e}$	$b \succ e$	$\varnothing$	{a,b,c}	{d,e,f}
29	$\underline{c} \succ_s a$	$c \succ_s e$, $c \succ a$	$\varnothing$	{b,c}	{a,d,e,f}
30	$\underline{b} \sim_m c$	$b \succ c$	{b}	$\varnothing$	{a,c,d,e,f}

Table 2: RandomQ on Example 1.

i	$rlt(q_i)$	Derived Results	$O_{\checkmark}$	$O_?$	$O_\times$
1	$c \succ_s \underline{f}$		$\varnothing$	{a,b,c,d,e,f}	$\varnothing$
2	$\underline{f} \succ_m c$	$f \sim c$			
3 – 4	$\underline{a} \succ_s e$, $\underline{a} \succ_m e$				
5	$e \succ_a \underline{a}$	$a \sim e$			
6 – 7	$c \succ_s \underline{e}$, $c \succ_m \underline{e}$				
8	$\underline{e} \sim_a c$	$c \succ e$	$\varnothing$	{a,b,c,d,f}	{e}
9	$\underline{b} \succ_s a$	$b \succ_s e$			
10	$a \succ_m \underline{b}$	$a \sim b$			
11	$\underline{d} \succ_s f$				
12	$f \succ_m \underline{d}$	$f \sim d$			
13	$d \succ_s \underline{a}$	$d \succ_s e$			
14	$\underline{a} \succ_m d$	$a \sim d$			
15 – 16	$\underline{b} \sim_s c$, $\underline{b} \sim_m c$				
17	$\underline{b} \succ_a c$	$b \succ c$	$\varnothing$	{a,b,d,f}	{c,e}
18 – 19	$\underline{d} \sim_s b$, $\underline{d} \sim_m b$				
20	$b \succ_a \underline{d}$	$b \succ d$	$\varnothing$	{a,b,f}	{c,d,e}
21	$\underline{a} \succ_s f$	$b \succ_s f$			
22	$\underline{a} \sim_m f$				
23	$f \succ_a \underline{a}$	$a \sim f$			
24	$b \sim_m \underline{f}$				
25	$b \succ_a \underline{f}$	$b \succ_a a$, $b \succ f$	{b}	{a}	{c,d,e,f}
26 – 27	$c \succ_s \underline{a}$, $\underline{a} \sim_m c$				
28	$c \succ_a \underline{a}$	$c \succ a$	{b}	$\varnothing$	{a,c,d,e,f}

Table 3: RandomP on Example 1.

4. MICRO-ORDERING IN QUESTION SELECTION

At every iteration of Alg.1, we choose a question $x?_c y$ from the set of candidate questions. By macro-ordering, when available, the question selection strategy (Alg.2) chooses a candidate question in which $y \notin O_\times$, i.e., it chooses from Q^1_{can}. Otherwise, it chooses from Q^2_{can}. The size of Q^1_{can} and Q^2_{can} can be large. Micro-ordering is for choosing from the many candidates. As discussed in Sec.3, in order to find a short question sequence, the overriding principle of our question selection strategy is to identify non-Pareto optimal objects as early as possible. Guided by this principle, this section discusses several micro-ordering strategies. Since the strategies are the same for Q^1_{can} and Q^2_{can}, we will simply use the term "candidate questions" without distinction between Q^1_{can} and Q^2_{can}.

4.1 Random Question (RandomQ)

RandomQ, as its name suggests, simply selects a random candidate question. Table 2 shows an execution of the general framework under RandomQ for Example 1. For each iteration i, the table shows the question outcome $rlt(q_i)$. Following the question form $x?_c y$ in Definition 3, the object "x" in a question is underlined when we present the question outcome. The column "derived results" displays derived question outcomes by transitive closure (e.g., $a \succ_m e$ based on $rlt(q_7)=d \succ_m e$ and $rlt(q_{10})=a \succ_m d$) and derived object dominance (e.g., $b \succ d$ after q_{20}). The table also shows the object partitions ($O_{\checkmark}$, $O_?$ and $O_\times$) when the execution starts and when the partitions are changed after an iteration. Multiple iterations may be presented together if other columns are the same for them.

As Table 2 shows, this particular execution under RandomQ requires 30 questions. When the execution terminates, it finds the only Pareto optimal object b. This simplest micro-ordering strategy already avoids many questions in the brute-force approach. The example clearly demonstrates the benefits of choosing candidate questions only and applying macro-strategy.

4.2 Random Pair (RandomP)

RandomP randomly selects a pair of objects x and y and keeps asking questions to compare them ($x?_c y$ or $y?_c x$) until no such candidate question remains, upon which it randomly picks another pair of objects. This strategy echoes our principle of eagerly identifying non-Pareto optimal objects. To declare an object x non-Pareto optimal, we must identify another object y such that y dominates x. If we directly compare x and y, it requires comparing them by every criterion in C in order to make sure $y \succ x$. By skipping questions according to transitive closure, we do not need to directly compare them by every criterion. However, Property 4 below states that we still need at least $|C|$ questions involving x—some are direct comparisons with y, others are comparisons with other objects which indirectly lead to outcomes of comparisons with y. When there is a candidate question $x?_c y$, it means y may dominate x. The fewer criteria remain for comparing them, the more likely y will dominate x. Hence, by keeping comparing the same object pair, RandomP aims at finding more non-Pareto objects by less questions.

Property 4. Given a set of criteria C and an object $x \in O$, at least $|C|$ pairwise comparison questions involving x are required in order to find another object y such that $y \succ x$.

Proof. The proof is omitted due to space limitations and can be found in the technical report [4]. □

Table 3 illustrates an execution of RandomP for Example 1. The initial two questions are between c and f. Afterwards, it is concluded that $c \sim f$ by Property 3. Therefore, RandomP moves on to ask 3 questions between a and e. In total, the execution requires 28 questions. Although it is shorter than Table 2 by only 2 questions due to the small size of the example, it clearly moves objects into $O_\times$ more quickly. (In Table 2, $O_\times$ is empty until the 20th question. In Table 3, $O_\times$ already has 3 objects after 20 questions.) The experiment results in Sec.5 exhibit significant performance gain of RandomP over RandomQ on larger data.

4.3 Pair with Fewest Remaining Questions (FRQ)

Similar to RandomP, once a pair of objects x and y are chosen, FRQ keeps asking questions between x and y until there is no such candidate questions. Different from RandomP, instead of randomly picking a pair of objects, FRQ always chooses a pair with the fewest remaining questions. There may be multiple such pairs. To break ties, FRQ chooses such a pair that x has dominated the fewest other objects and y has dominated the most other objects. Furthermore, in comparing x and y, FRQ orders their remaining questions (and thus criteria) by how likely x is worse than y on the criteria. Below we explain this strategy in more detail.

Selecting Object Pair Consider a question sequence Q_i so far and FRQ is to select the next question Q_{i+1}. We use $C_{x,y}$ to denote the set of criteria c such that $\mathsf{x}?_c\mathsf{y}$ is a candidate question, i.e., $C_{\mathsf{x,y}}=\{c\in C \mid \mathsf{x}?_c\mathsf{y}\in Q^1_{can}\}$. (We assume Q^1_{can} is not empty. Otherwise, FRQ chooses from Q^2_{can} in the same way; cf. Alg.2.) By Definition 3, the outcomes of these questions are unknown, i.e., $\forall c\in C_{\mathsf{x,y}}: rlt(\mathsf{x}?_c\mathsf{y})\notin R^+(Q_i)$. Furthermore, if any remaining question (whose outcome is unknown) between x and y is a candidate question, then all remaining questions between them are candidate questions. FRQ chooses a pair with the fewest remaining candidate questions, i.e., a pair belonging to $S_1=\arg\min_{(\mathsf{x,y})}|C_{\mathsf{x,y}}|$.

The reason to choose such a pair is intuitive. It requires at least $|C_{\mathsf{x,y}}|$ candidate questions to determine $\mathsf{y}\succ\mathsf{x}$. (The proof would be similar to that of Property 4.) Therefore, $\min_{(\mathsf{x,y})}|C_{\mathsf{x,y}}|$ is the minimum number of candidate questions to further ask, in order to determine that an object is dominated, i.e., non-Pareto optimal. Thus, a pair in S_1 may lead to a dominated object by the fewest questions, matching our goal of identifying non-Pareto optimal objects as soon as possible.

We further justify this strategy in a probabilistic sense. For $\mathsf{y}\succ\mathsf{x}$ to be realized, it is necessary that none of the remaining questions has an outcome $\mathsf{x}\succ_c\mathsf{y}$, i.e., $\forall c\in C_{\mathsf{x,y}}: rlt(\mathsf{x}?_c\mathsf{y})\neq\mathsf{x}\succ_c\mathsf{y}$. Make the simplistic assumption that every question $\mathsf{x}?_c\mathsf{y}$ has an equal probability p of not having outcome $\mathsf{x}\succ_c\mathsf{y}$, i.e., $\forall\mathsf{x}?_c\mathsf{y}\in Q^1_{can}$, $P(rlt(\mathsf{x}?_c\mathsf{y})\neq\mathsf{x}\succ_c\mathsf{y})=p$. Further assuming independence of question outcomes, the probability of satisfying the aforementioned necessary condition is $p^{|C_{\mathsf{x,y}}|}$. By taking a pair belonging to S_1, we have the largest probability of finding a dominated object. We note that, for $\mathsf{y}\succ\mathsf{x}$ to be realized, in addition to the above necessary condition, another condition must be satisfied—if $\nexists c$ such that $\mathsf{y}\succ_c\mathsf{x}\in R^+(Q_i)$, the outcome of at least one remaining question should be $\mathsf{y}\succ_c\mathsf{x}$, i.e., $\exists c\in C_{\mathsf{x,y}}: rlt(\mathsf{x}?_c\mathsf{y})=\mathsf{y}\succ_c\mathsf{x}$. Our informal probability-based analysis does not consider this extra requirement.

Breaking Ties There can be multiple object pairs with the fewest remaining questions, i.e., $|S_1|>1$. To break ties, FRQ chooses such an x that has dominated the fewest other objects, since it is more likely to be dominated. If there are still ties, FRQ further chooses such a y that has dominated the most other objects, since it is more likely to dominate x. More formally, FRQ chooses a pair belonging to $S_2=\{(\mathsf{x,y})\in S_1 \mid \nexists(\mathsf{x',y'})\in S_1$ such that $d(\mathsf{x'})>d(\mathsf{x})\vee(d(\mathsf{x'})=d(\mathsf{x})\wedge d(\mathsf{y'})>d(\mathsf{y}))\}$, where the function $d(\cdot)$ returns the number of objects so far dominated by an object, i.e., $\forall\mathsf{x}, d(\mathsf{x}) = |\{\mathsf{y}|\mathsf{x}\succ\mathsf{y}$ based on $R^+(Q_i)\}|$. This heuristic follows the principle of detecting non-Pareto optimal objects as early as possible. Note that S_2 may still contain multiple object pairs. In such a case, FRQ chooses an arbitrary pair.

Selecting Comparison Criterion Once a pair (x,y) is chosen, FRQ has to select a criterion for the next question. FRQ orders the remaining criteria $C_{\mathsf{x,y}}$ based on the heuristic that the sooner it understands $\mathsf{y}\succ\mathsf{x}$ will not happen, the lower cost it pays. As discussed before, $|C_{\mathsf{x,y}}|$ questions are required in order to conclude that $\mathsf{y}\succ\mathsf{x}$; on the other hand, only one question (if asked first) can be enough for ruling it out. Consider the case that x is better than y by only one remaining criterion, i.e., $\exists c\in C_{\mathsf{x,y}}: rlt(\mathsf{x}?_c\mathsf{y})=\mathsf{x}\succ_c\mathsf{y}$ and $\forall c'\in C_{\mathsf{x,y}}, c'\neq c: rlt(\mathsf{x}?_{c'}\mathsf{y})=\mathsf{x}\nsucc_{c'}\mathsf{y}$. If FRQ asks $\mathsf{x}?_c\mathsf{y}$ after all other remaining questions, it takes $|C_{\mathsf{x,y}}|$ questions to understand y does not dominate x; but if $\mathsf{x}?_c\mathsf{y}$ is asked first, no more questions are necessary, because there will be no more candidate questions in the form of $\mathsf{x}?_c\mathsf{y}$.

Therefore, FRQ orders the criteria $C_{\mathsf{x,y}}$ by a scoring function that reflects the likelihood of x's superiority than y by the corresponding criteria. More specifically, for each $c\in C_{\mathsf{x,y}}$, its score is $r_c(\mathsf{x,y}) = r_c(\mathsf{y})+r'_c(\mathsf{y})-r''_c(\mathsf{y})-(r_c(\mathsf{x})+r'_c(\mathsf{x})-r''_c(\mathsf{x}))$ where $r_c(\mathsf{y}) = |\{\mathsf{z} \mid \mathsf{z}\succ_c\mathsf{y}\in R^+(Q_i)\}|$, $r'_c(\mathsf{y})=|\{\mathsf{z} \mid \mathsf{y}\sim_c\mathsf{z}\in R^+(Q_i)\}|$,

i	$rlt(q_i)$	Derived Results	(x,y), $C_{\mathsf{x,y}}$	$O_{\checkmark}$	$O_?$	$O_\times$
			(a,b), $\{s, m, a\}$	$\varnothing$	{a,b,c,d,e,f}	$\varnothing$
1	$\mathsf{b}\succ_s\underline{\mathsf{a}}$		(a,b), $\{m, a\}$			
2	$\underline{\mathsf{a}}\succ_m\mathsf{b}$	a∼b	(a,c), $\{s, a, m\}$			
3	$\mathsf{c}\succ_s\underline{\mathsf{a}}$		(a,c), $\{a, m\}$			
4	$\mathsf{c}\sim_a\underline{\mathsf{a}}$		(a,c), $\{m\}$			
5	$\mathsf{c}\succ_m\underline{\mathsf{a}}$	c≻a	(b,c), $\{a, s, m\}$	$\varnothing$	{b,c,d,e,f}	{a}
6	$\underline{\mathsf{b}}\sim_a\mathsf{c}$		(b,c), $\{s, m\}$			
7	$\underline{\mathsf{b}}\sim_s\mathsf{c}$		(b,c), $\{m\}$			
8	$\underline{\mathsf{b}}\succ_m\mathsf{c}$	$\mathsf{b}\succ_m\mathsf{a}$, b≻c	(d,b), $\{a, s, m\}$	$\varnothing$	{b,d,e,f}	{a,c}
9	$\mathsf{b}\sim_a\underline{\mathsf{d}}$		(d,b), $\{s, m\}$			
10	$\mathsf{b}\sim_s\underline{\mathsf{d}}$		(d,b), $\{m\}$			
11	$\mathsf{b}\succ_m\underline{\mathsf{d}}$	b≻d	(e,b), $\{a, s, m\}$	$\varnothing$	{b,e,f}	{a,c,d}
12	$\mathsf{b}\succ_a\underline{\mathsf{e}}$		(e,b), $\{s, m\}$			
13	$\mathsf{b}\succ_s\underline{\mathsf{e}}$		(e,b), $\{m\}$			
14	$\mathsf{b}\succ_m\underline{\mathsf{e}}$	$\mathsf{a}\succ_m\mathsf{e}$, b≻e	(f,b), $\{a, s, m\}$	$\varnothing$	{b,f}	{a,c,d,e}
15	$\mathsf{b}\succ_a\underline{\mathsf{f}}$		(f,b), $\{s, m\}$			
16	$\mathsf{b}\succ_s\underline{\mathsf{f}}$		(f,b), $\{m\}$			
17	$\mathsf{b}\succ_m\underline{\mathsf{f}}$	b≻f		{b}	$\varnothing$	{a,c,d,e,f}

Table 4: FRQ on Example 1.

and $r''_c(\mathsf{y})=|\{\mathsf{z} \mid \mathsf{y}\succ_c\mathsf{z}\in R^+(Q_i)\}|$. In this scoring function, $r_c(\mathsf{y})$ is the number of objects preferred over y by criterion c, $r'_c(\mathsf{y})$ is the number of objects equally good (or bad) as y by c, and $r''_c(\mathsf{y})$ is the number of objects to which y is preferred with regard to c. FRQ asks the remaining questions in decreasing order of the corresponding criteria's scores. This way, it may find such a question that $rlt(\mathsf{x}?_c\mathsf{y})=\mathsf{x}\succ_c\mathsf{y}$ earlier than later.

Table 4 presents the framework's execution for Example 1, by applying the FRQ policy. In addition to the same columns in Tables 2 and 3, Table 4 also includes an extra column to show, at each iteration, the chosen object pair for the next question (x,y) and the set of remaining comparison criteria between them ($C_{\mathsf{x,y}}$). The criteria in $C_{\mathsf{x,y}}$ are ordered by the aforementioned ranking function $r(\cdot)$. At the beginning of the execution, the object pair is arbitrarily chosen and the criteria are arbitrarily ordered. In the example, we assume $\mathsf{a}?_s\mathsf{b}$ is chosen as the first question. After q_2, FRQ can derive that a∼b. Hence, there is no more candidate question between them and FRQ chooses the next pair (a,c). Three questions are asked for comparing them. At the end of q_5, multiple object pairs have the fewest remaining questions. By breaking ties, (b,c) is chosen as the next pair, since only c has dominated any object so far. The remaining criteria $C_{\mathsf{b,c}}$ are ordered as $\{a, s, m\}$, because $r_a(\mathsf{b,c})>r_s(\mathsf{b,c})$ and $r_a(\mathsf{b,c})>r_m(\mathsf{b,c})$. The execution sequence terminates after 17 questions, much shorter than the 30 and 28 questions by RandomQ and RandomP, respectively.

To conclude the discussion on micro-ordering, we derive a lower bound on the number of questions required for finding all Pareto-optimal objects (Theorem 2). The experiment results in Sec.5 reveal that FRQ is nearly optimal and the lower bound is practically tight, since the number of questions used by FRQ is very close to the lower bound.

Theorem 2. Given objects O and criteria C, to find all Pareto-optimal objects in O, at least $(|O|-k)\times|C|+(k-1)\times 2$ pairwise comparison questions are necessary, where k is the number of Pareto-optimal objects in O.

Proof. The proof is omitted due to space limitations and can be found in the technical report [4]. □

5. EXPERIMENTS

We designed and conducted experiments to compare the efficiency of different instantiations of the general framework under varying problem sizes. Our experiments used both a real crowdsourcing marketplace and simulations based on a real dataset.

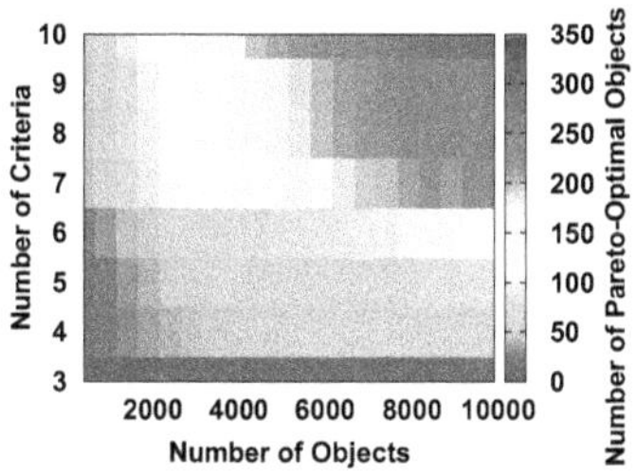

Figure 5: No. of Pareto-optimal objects. Varying $|O|$ and $|C|$.

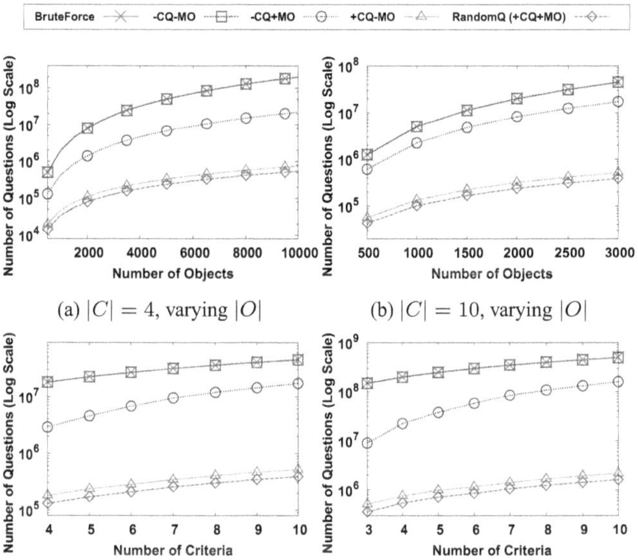

(a) $|C| = 4$, varying $|O|$ (b) $|C| = 10$, varying $|O|$

(c) $|O| = 3,000$, varying $|C|$ (d) $|O| = 10,000$, varying $|C|$

Figure 6: No. of questions by BruteForce and basic methods.

5.1 Efficiency and Scalability

We studied the efficiency and scalability of various instantiations of the general framework. Given the large number of questions required for such a study, we cannot afford using a real crowdsourcing marketplace. Hence, we performed the following simulation. Each object is an NBA player in a particular year. The objects are compared by 10 criteria, i.e., performance categories such as *points*, *rebounds*, *assists*, etc. We simulated the corresponding 10 preference relations based on the players' real performance in individual years, as follows. Consider a performance category c and two objects x=(player1, year1) and y=(player2, year2). x.c is player1's per-game performance on category c in year1 (similarly for y.c). Values in each category c are normalized into the range $[0, 1]$, where 0 and 1 correspond to the minimal and maximal values in c, respectively. Suppose x.c>y.c. We generated a uniform random number v in $[0, 1]$. If $v<1 - e^{-(x.c-y.c)}$, we set $x \succ_c y$, otherwise we set $x \sim_c y$. This way, we introduced a perturbation into the preference relations in order to make sure they are partial orders, as opposed to directly using real performance statistics (which would imply total orders). Fig.5 shows that the number of Pareto-optimal objects increases by the sizes of both object set O (objects are randomly selected) and criteria set C (the first $|C|$ criteria of the aforementioned 10 criteria).

Effectiveness of candidate questions and macro-ordering

To verify the effectiveness of candidate questions and macro-ordering, we compared five methods—BruteForce, –CQ–MO, –CQ+MO, +CQ–MO, and +CQ+MO. The notation +/– before CQ and MO indicates whether a method only selects candidate questions (CQ) and whether it applies the macro-ordering strategy (MO), respectively. In all these five methods, qualifying questions are randomly selected, i.e., no particular micro-ordering heuristics are applied. For instance, +CQ+MO selects only candidate questions and applies macro-ordering. Hence, it is equivalent to RandomQ. Fig.6 shows the numbers of required pairwise comparisons (in logarithmic scale) for each method, varying by object set size ($|O|$ from 500 to $10,000$ for $|C|$=4 and $|C|$=10) and criterion set size ($|C|$ from 3 to 10 for $|O|$=3, 000 and $|O|$=10, 000). The figure clearly demonstrates the effectiveness of both CQ and MO, as taking out either feature leads to significantly worse performance than RandomQ. Particularly, the gap between +CQ–MO and –CQ+MO suggests that choosing only candidate questions has more fundamental impact than macro-ordering. If neither is applied (i.e., –CQ–MO), the performance is equally poor as that of BruteForce. (–CQ–MO uses slightly less questions than BruteForce, since it can terminate before exhausting all questions. However, the difference is negligible for practical purpose, as their curves overlap under logarithmic scale.)

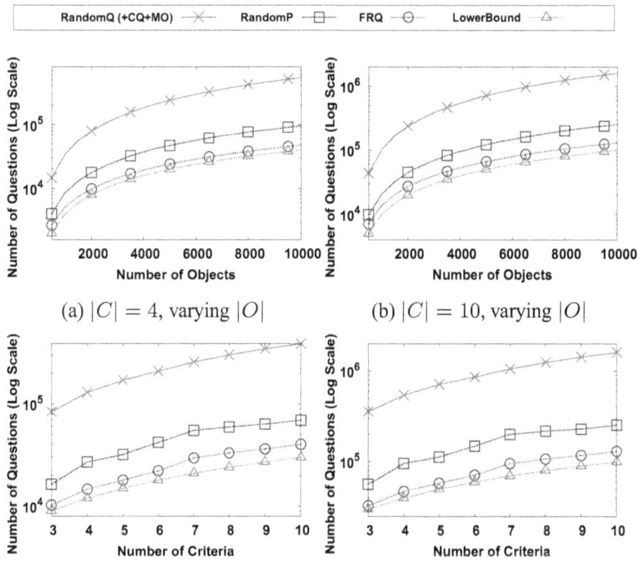

(a) $|C| = 4$, varying $|O|$ (b) $|C| = 10$, varying $|O|$

(c) $|O| = 3,000$, varying $|C|$ (d) $|O| = 10,000$, varying $|C|$

Figure 7: No. of questions by different micro-ordering heuristics.

Effectiveness of micro-ordering

Fig.7 presents the numbers of pairwise comparisons required by different micro-ordering heuristics (RandomQ, i.e., +CQ+MO, RandomP, FRQ) and LowerBound (cf. Theorem 2) under varying sizes of the object set ($|O|$ from 500 to $10,000$ for $|C|$=4 and $|C|$=10) and the criteria set ($|C|$ from 3 to 10 for $|O|$=3, 000 and $|O|$=10, 000). In all these instantiations of the general framework, CQ and MO are applied. The results are averaged across 30 executions. All these methods outperformed BruteForce by orders of magnitude. (BruteForce is not shown in Fig.7 since it is off scale, but its number can be calculated by equation $|C|\times|O|\times(|O|-1)/2$.) For instance, for $5,000$ objects and 4 criteria, the ratio of pairwise comparisons required by even the naive RandomQ to that used by BruteForce is already as low as 0.0048. This clearly shows the effectiveness of CQ and MO, as discussed for Fig.6. The ratios for RandomP and FRQ are further several times smaller (0.00094 and 0.00048, respectively). The big gain by FRQ justifies the strategy of choosing object pairs with the fewest remaining questions. Especially, FRQ has nearly optimal performance, because it gets very close to LowerBound in Fig.7. The small

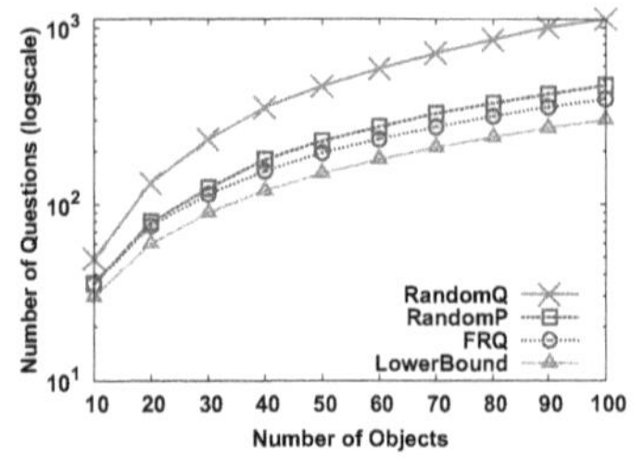

Figure 8: No. of questions by different micro-ordering heuristics. $|C| = 3$, varying $|O|$.

gap between FRQ and LowerBound also indicates that the lower bound is practically tight. The f gure further suggests excellent scalability of FRQ as its number of questions grows almost linearly by both $|C|$ and $|O|$.

5.2 Experiments Using a Real Crowdsourcing Marketplace

We also studied the performance of the proposed algorithms using the popular crowdsourcing marketplace Amazon Mechanical Turk (AMT). The task is to compare 100 photos of our institution with regard to *color*, *sharpness* and *landscape*. To obtain the ground-truth data, all $14,850$ possible pairwise questions were partitioned into $1,650$ tasks, each containing 9 questions on a criterion. An AMT crowdsourcer is allowed to perform a task only if they have responded to at least 100 HITs (Human Intelligence Tasks) before with at least 90% approval rate. Furthermore, we implemented basic quality control by including 2 additional validation questions in each task that expect certain answers. For instance, one such question asks the crowd to compare a colorful photo and a dull photo by criterion *color*. A crowdsourcer's responses in a task are discarded if their response to a validation question deviates from our expectation. (236 crowdsourcers failed on this.) The parameters in Equation (1) were set to be k=5 and θ=0.6. Hence, in total $(1,650 \times 5+236) \times (9+2) = 93,346$ pairwise comparisons were performed by AMT crowdsourcers. We paid 1 cent for each comparison and therefore spent close to $1,000 in total.

The responses to all possible questions provide the ground-truth data. An algorithm execution only needs the responses to a subset of the questions. We randomly selected a subset of photos O ($|O|$ from 10 to 100) and applied various algorithms to f nd Pareto-optimal photos. Figure 8 shows, for varying $|O|$, the number of questions (in logarithmic scale) required by each micro-ordering strategy. To account for the randomness in RandomP and RandomQ, we repeated these two algorithms, respectively, 30 times, and we reported the average numbers of questions. Conf rming the results in Figure 7, FRQ was close to the theoretical lower bound, performing better than the other two methods, and RandomP outperformed RandomQ.

6. CONCLUSIONS

This is the f rst study on using crowdsourcing to f nd Pareto-optimal objects when objects do not have explicit attributes and preference relations are strict partial orders. The partial orders are obtained by pairwise comparison questions to the crowd. It introduces an iterative question-selection framework that is instantiated into different methods by exploiting the ideas of candidate questions, macro-ordering and micro-ordering. Experiment were conducted by simulations on large object sets and by using a real crowdsourcing marketplace. The results exhibited not only orders of magnitude reductions in questions against a brute-force approach, but also close-to-optimal performance from the most eff cient method.

7. REFERENCES

[1] N. Ailon. Active learning ranking from pairwise preferences with almost optimal query complexity. In *NIPS*, pages 810–818, 2011.

[2] N. Ailon. An active learning algorithm for ranking from pairwise preferences with an almost optimal query complexity. *Journal of Machine Learning Research*, 13(1):137–164, Jan. 2012.

[3] K. J. Arrow. *Social choice and individual values*. Yale University Press, 1951.

[4] A. Asudeh, G. Zhang, N. Hassan, C. Li, and G. V. Zaruba. Crowdsourcing Pareto-Optimal Object Finding by Pairwise Comparisons. *ArXiv e-prints 1409.4161*, Sept. 2014.

[5] S. Borzsony, D. Kossmann, and K. Stocker. The skyline operator. In *ICDE*, pages 421–430, 2001.

[6] M. Braverman and E. Mossel. Noisy sorting without resampling. In *SODA*, pages 268–276, 2008.

[7] C. Burges, T. Shaked, E. Renshaw, A. Lazier, M. Deeds, N. Hamilton, and G. Hullender. Learning to rank using gradient descent. In *ICML*, pages 89–96, 2005.

[8] C. J. C. Burges, R. Ragno, and Q. V. Le. Learning to Rank with Nonsmooth Cost Functions. In *NIPS*, pages 193–200, 2006.

[9] Y. Cao, J. Xu, T.-Y. Liu, H. Li, Y. Huang, and H.-W. Hon. Adapting ranking SVM to document retrieval. In *SIGIR*, pages 186–193, 2006.

[10] B. Carterette, P. N. Bennett, D. M. Chickering, and S. T. Dumais. Here or there: Preference judgments for relevance. In *ECIR*, 2008.

[11] C.-Y. Chan, P.-K. Eng, and K.-L. Tan. Stratif ed computation of skylines with partially-ordered domains. In *SIGMOD*, 2005.

[12] X. Chen, P. N. Bennett, K. Collins-Thompson, and E. Horvitz. Pairwise ranking aggregation in a crowdsourced setting. In *WSDM*, pages 193–202, 2013.

[13] J. Chomicki. Preference formulas in relational queries. *TODS*, 2003.

[14] M. d. Condorcet. Essay on the application of analysis to the probability of majority decisions. *Paris: Imprimerie Royale*, 1785.

[15] S. B. Davidson, S. Khanna, T. Milo, and S. Roy. Using the crowd for top-k and group-by queries. In *ICDT*, pages 225–236, 2013.

[16] D. Goldberg, D. Nichols, B. M. Oki, and D. Terry. Using collaborative f ltering to weave an information tapestry. *CACM*, 1992.

[17] B. Groz and T. Milo. Skyline queries with noisy comparisons. In *PODS*, pages 185–198, 2015.

[18] P. G. Ipeirotis, F. Provost, and J. Wang. Quality management on amazon mechanical turk. In *HCOMP*, pages 64–67, 2010.

[19] K. G. Jamieson and R. D. Nowak. Active ranking using pairwise comparisons. In *NIPS*, pages 2240–2248, 2011.

[20] W. Kießling. Foundations of preferences in database systems. In *VLDB*, pages 311–322, 2002.

[21] N. N. Liu, M. Zhao, and Q. Yang. Probabilistic latent preference analysis for collaborative f ltering. In *CIKM*, pages 759–766, 2009.

[22] T.-Y. Liu. Learning to rank for information retrieval. *Foundations and Trends in Information Retrieval*, 3(3):225–331, Mar. 2009.

[23] C. Lof, K. El Maarry, and W.-T. Balke. Skyline queries in crowd-enabled databases. In *EDBT*, pages 465–476, 2013.

[24] S. Negahban, S. Oh, and D. Shah. Iterative ranking from pair-wise comparisons. In *NIPS*, pages 2483–2491, 2012.

[25] V. Polychronopoulos, L. de Alfaro, J. Davis, H. Garcia-Molina, and N. Polyzotis. Human-powered top-k lists. In *WebDB*, 2013.

[26] S. Rendle, C. Freudenthaler, Z. Gantner, and L. Schmidt-Thieme. BPR: Bayesian personalized ranking from implicit feedback. In *UAI*, pages 452–461, 2009.

[27] M. E. Rorvig. The simple scalability of documents. *Journal of the American Society for Information Science*, 41(8):590–598, 1990.

[28] D. Sacharidis, S. Papadopoulos, and D. Papadias. Topologically sorted skylines for partially ordered domains. In *ICDE*, 2009.

[29] N. Sarkas, G. Das, N. Koudas, and A. K. Tung. Categorical skylines for streaming data. In *SIGMOD*, pages 239–250, 2008.

[30] L. L. Thurstone. A law of comparative judgment. *Psychological Review*, 34:273–286, 1927.

[31] J. Yi, R. Jin, S. Jain, and A. K. Jain. Inferring users' preferences from crowdsourced pairwise comparisons: A matrix completion approach. In *HCOMP*, 2013.

[32] S. Zhang, N. Mamoulis, D. W. Cheung, and B. Kao. Eff cient skyline evaluation over partially ordered domains. In *VLDB*, 2010.

Practical Aspects of Sensitivity in Online Experimentation with User Engagement Metrics

Alexey Drutsa
Yandex
Moscow, Russia
adrutsa@yandex.ru

Anna Ufliand
Yandex
St.Petersburg, Russia
anna.uflyand@gmail.com

Gleb Gusev
Yandex
Moscow, Russia
gleb57@yandex-team.ru

ABSTRACT

Online controlled experiments, e.g., A/B testing, is the state-of-the-art approach used by modern Internet companies to improve their services based on data-driven decisions. The most challenging problem is to define an appropriate online metric of user behavior, so-called Overall Evaluation Criterion (OEC), which is both interpretable and sensitive. A typical OEC consists of a key metric and an evaluation statistic. Sensitivity of an OEC to the treatment effect of an A/B test is measured by a statistical significance test. We introduce the notion of Overall Acceptance Criterion (OAC) that includes both the components of an OEC and a statistical significance test. While existing studies on A/B tests are mostly concentrated on the first component of an OAC, its key metric, we widely study the two latter ones by comparison of several statistics and several statistical tests with respect to user engagement metrics on hundreds of A/B experiments run on real users of Yandex. We discovered that the application of the state-of-the-art Student's t-tests to several main user engagement metrics may lead to an underestimation of the false-positive rate by an order of magnitude. We investigate both well-known and novel techniques to overcome this issue in practical settings. At last, we propose the entropy and the quantiles as novel OECs that reflect the diversity and extreme cases of user engagement.

Categories and Subject Descriptions: H.1.2 [User/Machine Systems]: Human information processing; H.5.2 [User interface]: Evaluation/methodology

General Terms: Measurement, Experimentation

Keywords: User engagement; online controlled experiment; Overall Acceptance Criterion; A/B test; sensitivity; quality metrics; evaluation statistic; significance level; p-value

1. INTRODUCTION

Nowadays, online controlled experiments, e.g., A/B testing, is the state-of-the-art approach utilized by modern Internet companies (such as web search engines [35, 6, 5], social networks [1], etc.) to improve their services based on data-driven decisions [21]. An A/B test compares two variants of a service at a time, usually its current version (control) and a new one (treatment), by exposing them to two groups of users. The aim of controlled experiments is to detect the causal effect of service updates on its performance relying on an *Overall Evaluation Criterion (OEC)* [22], a user behavior metric that is assumed to correlate with the quality of the service, i.e., the value of the OEC must have a clear *interpretation*. When the treatment effect exists, the OEC has to detect the difference of the two versions of the service at a high level of statistical significance in order to distinguish the treatment effect from the noise observed when the effect does not exist. This property is referred to as the *sensitivity* of the OEC [22].

A common OEC consists of two main components [22]: (a) a *key metric* (e.g., the number of sessions, the number of queries, etc.), calculated for each event (entity, *experimental unit*) of a certain type observed in the behavioral data (e.g., a query, a user, a session, etc); and (b) the *evaluation statistic* of the key metric over the experimental units (e.g., the average value, the median, etc.). A third (c) component of any A/B test is the *statistical significance test* (e.g., t-test, bootstrap, etc.), which examines weather the evaluation statistic of the key metric over the two groups of users coincide. We refer to these three components (a)–(c) as an *Overall Acceptance Criterion (OAC)*.

The first two components (i.e., the OEC) are responsible for the interpretation of the OAC, and all of them directly affect its sensitivity. On the one hand, one important part of existing studies on interpretation of an OEC concerns only development or improvement of key metrics that correlate with different aspects of the system quality [12, 33, 10]. On the other hand, the large set of studies devoted to the sensitivity of an OEC relates either to experimental units (e.g., increasing of the experiment duration or of the user population participated in the experiment [22, 35, 5]) or to the key metric as well (e.g., variation reduction techniques [22, 7, 6], metric transformation [21, 11]). At the same time, to the best of our knowledge, the statistical significance test and the statistic used in an OAC are understudied areas in online evaluation of web services.

In the current study, we focus on the impact of the statistics and statistical tests chosen for an OAC on the sensitivity of different key metrics. First, we show that a key metric is most effective in combination with an appropriate statistical test, which is individual for each key metric. Utilization of the usual t-test with a default p-value threshold may lead to

Permission to make digital or hard copies of all or part of this work for personal or classroom use is granted without fee provided that copies are not made or distributed for profit or commercial advantage and that copies bear this notice and the full citation on the first page. Copyrights for components of this work owned by others than ACM must be honored. Abstracting with credit is permitted. To copy otherwise, or republish, to post on servers or to redistribute to lists, requires prior specific permission and/or a fee. Request permissions from Permissions@acm.org.
CIKM'15, October 19–23, 2015, Melbourne, Australia.
© 2015 ACM. ISBN 978-1-4503-3794-6/15/10 ...$15.00.
DOI: http://dx.doi.org/10.1145/2806416.2806496.

wrong conclusions on the performance of some state-of-the-art key metrics. Second, we show that each combination of a key metric and a statistical test requires its individual p-value threshold to control the false-positive rate at a predefined level.

We conduct our study for the case of user engagement metrics, since they are often considered to be most appropriate for online evaluation. User engagement reflects how often the user solves her needs (e.g., to search something) by means of the considered service (e.g., a search engine). On the one hand, these metrics are measurable in the short-term experiment period, and, on the other hand, they are predictive of the long-term success of the company [19, 20, 21, 27]. In this study, we pay special attention to the metrics that reflect the loyalty aspect of engagement: the state-of-the-art *number of sessions per user* metric [19, 33] (which is accepted as the "North-star" for A/B testing evaluation in major search engine companies like Bing [20, 21]) and the recently proposed *absence time* metric [12].

The state-of-the-art evaluation statistic of the key metric over experimental units is the average value, which is used in vast majority of studies on A/B testing [4, 18, 35, 19, 33, 20, 21, 5, 10, 11]. Nonetheless, there are other statistics that have intelligible interpretation for user engagement metrics. The *median* is a popular statistic within statistical tests [34, 31] and it measures engagement of a typical user of the web service. Other *quantiles* quantify the extreme cases [14]: users whose behaviors are far from the mean (e.g., they are able to describe users that are engaged with the service less or more than an average user) [24, 16]. *Entropy* [30] measures the *diversity* of users against their engagement with a web service. Hence, these statistics could be utilized to detect the treatment effect in an evaluated update for such user behavior aspects as well[1]. We consider all these statistics in our OACs and compare them in terms of sensitivity. We found that each of the described above evaluation statistics noticeably outperforms the state-of-the-art mean statistic for some metrics in terms of the treatment detection rate with a fixed false-positive rate.

The widely applicable statistical significance test is the unpaired Student's t-test [7, 33, 6, 10, 11]. However, a key metric may not follow assumptions underlying this test (such as the normality of the metric's distribution or the independence of experimental units). This makes the statistical test inappropriate for such key metrics, and its utilization may lead to an underestimate of the false-positive rate. In our study, we show that application of the t-test to several different user engagement key metrics leads to the underestimation of this rate by an order of magnitude. Moreover, we demonstrate practical efficiency of both well-known and novel techniques (Bootstrapping, p-value adjustment, and others) to overcome this issue.

Different statistical significance tests were widely studied and compared in offline evaluation of information retrieval (IR) systems [28, 31, 38, 32, 2, 36, 29]. Unfortunately, statistical tests in offline evaluation are almost always paired. Hence, the results presented in these studies could not be straightforwardly applied to the case of A/B testing. In our study, we compare 5 statistical significance tests (Student's t-test, Bootstrapping, Mann Whitney U test, Tarone-Ware test, and Logrank test) and show how their application to different user engagement metrics results in different sensitivity of the OECs.

Despite the largest web services have designed special experimental platforms that allow them to run A/B tests at large scale (e.g., hundreds of concurrent experiments per day) [35, 20], to the best of our knowledge, the existing studies on A/B testing evaluate their approaches on dozens real online experiment runs (e.g., the largest numbers are 21 A/B tests in [3], 32 A/B tests and 18 A/A tests in [11]). In our study, we conduct our experimental analysis on 169 A/B experiments and 98 A/A ones run on real users of Yandex (www.yandex.com) with duration from one to several weeks. This should make the results of our study more valuable for practical use in modern web companies.

To sum up, our study considers the problem, which coincides with the *emerging Internet companies' needs*: to use more sensitive and interpretable OECs in online controlled experiments and to get their results on a proper false-positive level. Specifically, the major contributions of our work include:

- The practical comparison of 5 statistical significance tests (Student's t-test, Bootstrapping, Mann Whitney U test, Tarone-Ware test, and Logrank test) w.r.t. 16 commonly used engagement metrics and finding the most effective combinations of them.
- Investigation of the entropy and the quantiles as novel OECs that quantify the diversity and extreme cases of user engagement.
- Practical refinement and validation of several existing observations and pitfalls on the basis of hundreds of large-scale A/B tests run on real users of Yandex.

The rest of the paper is organized as follows. In Section 2, the related work on A/B testing and user engagement is discussed. In Section 3, A/B testing background is described and our key metrics, evaluation statistics and statistical significance tests are presented. In Section 4, we show and discuss the results of applying OACs to the set of A/B experiments. In Section 5, the study's conclusions and our plans for the future work are presented.

2. RELATED WORK

We compare our research with other studies in three aspects. The first one relates to the common methodology of conducting online controlled experiments. The second one concerns user engagement metrics used in web services and, particularly, search engines. The third one relates to statistical tests used to measure significance level in information retrieval evaluation.

Online controlled experiment studies. The theoretical details of the online controlled experiment methodology were widely described in the existing works [26, 22], and we conduct our experiments in accordance with them. A number of practical lessons learned from the applications of this methodology to different evaluation cases in many web companies was recently described in [18, 35, 20]. These studies concern, inter alia, experiments with different components of a web service (e.g., the user interface [18, 10, 25] and ranking algorithms [33, 10, 25]), large-scale experimental infrastructure [35, 20], different aspects of user behavior and interaction with a web service (clicks [19, 21], speed [21], abandonment [21], periodicity [10, 9]), and so on. These experiments show that system updates of different types may

[1]Some similar statistics were utilized in risk-sensitive optimization and offline evaluation of retrieval systems [37, 8].

affect various key metrics differently. Some of the existing works focused on the study of the trustworthiness of the results of an A/B test. Various pitfalls and puzzling outcomes of online controlled experimentation were shared in [4, 19] and several "rules of thumb" were discussed in [21].

Some other studies focused on sensitivity improvement techniques for an online controlled experiment. The simplest ones [22] include increasing of the experimental time period or expanding the user population participating in the experiment; investigation of evaluation metric with lower variance [10, 9]; and elimination of users who were not affected by the service change in the treatment group [33]. More sophisticated sensitivity improvement techniques include the stratification and the usage of control variates that are defined on the basis of pre-experiment data [7]; the reduction of skewness of the evaluation metric [21] (e.g., transformation of the metric or capping its values); the sensitivity improvement for two-stage online controlled experiments [6]; the future user behavior prediction approach [11]; and diluted treatment effect estimation for trigger analysis [5]. To the best of our knowledge, the existing studies on A/B testing evaluated their approaches on dozens real online experiment runs (e.g., maximal are 21 A/B tests in [3], 32 A/B tests and 18 A/A tests in [11]). In our study, we experiment with a diverse and huge set of system changes: 169 large-scale A/B tests and 98 A/A experiments based on actual interactions of hundreds of thousands of real users (we use no artificially simulated data).

This allowed our study to produce more essential results on the relative sensitivity of different metrics. We believe, these results are more valuable in practice than the previous studies did, since the largest modern web companies run up to hundreds of concurrent A/B tests per day [35, 20].

Evaluation metrics. *User engagement metrics* are popular in A/B testing practice of many companies, because user engagement reflects how often the user solves her needs (e.g., to search something) by means of the considered service (e.g., a search engine) [19, 20, 21]. Hence, on the one hand, these metrics are measurable in the short-term experiment period, and, on the other hand, they are predictive of long-term goals of the company [19, 20, 21]. The most well-known metrics of loyalty aspect of user engagement are the state-of-the-art *number of sessions per user* [33] and the *absence time* [12] metrics. There are also several widely used metrics of activity aspect of user engagement like the number of clicks per user, shows per user, queries per user [22, 7], etc. All these metrics were utilized to evaluate different changes in search engines [3, 10, 11, 9]. However, to the best of our knowledge, these metrics were not thoroughly compared on the same data: e.g., the number of sessions and the absence time were studied together in [11], but their absence time is a measure over users as experimental units, while its original definition [12] considers it as a measure over periods of absence between consecutive sessions of a user (as in [3]). In our work, we compare sensitivity of these and other main user engagement metrics (as in [33, 12, 3, 11]) in Overall Acceptance Criteria (OACs) with different statistics (the mean, the median, etc.) and statistical tests (T-test, bootstrap, etc.).

Statistical tests in information retrieval. Different statistical significance tests were widely studied and compared in *offline evaluation* of information retrieval (IR) systems [28, 31, 38, 32, 2, 36, 29]. Unfortunately, statistical tests in offline evaluation are almost always paired, since the systems are compared using the same test data set. Hence, the results presented in these studies could not be straightforwardly adopted to the case of A/B testing, where two systems are compared using *different* sets of users, and thus unpaired tests are needed. Our study addresses this understudied area of *online evaluation* of web services w.r.t. user engagement metrics. We compare the Student's t-test, which is the state-of-the-art in A/B testing [7, 33, 6, 10, 11]; Mann Whitney U, Tarone-Ware, Logrank tests, which are widely used in survival analysis [34]; and Bootstrapping whose different variants (including unpaired ones) were shown to be very useful for both evaluation of IR systems and for comparing the sensitivity of IR metrics (like nDCG or Q-measure) [28, 31, 32, 36]. Bootstrapping was applied to A/B tests in [1] and was also mentioned in [4, 21] as a method to estimate the variance, when the key metric in A/B testing is very skewed or its experimental unit does not coincide with the randomization one.

Table 1: User engagement metrics and corresponding experimental units used in our study.

UE metric	Exp. unit	Description
Sessions		
S	user	the number of sessions of a user
sS	"user-2"	the number of sessions of a user
Absence time		
AT	absence	the duration of an absence in seconds
logAT	absence	the logarithm of the duration of an absence
ATpA	"user-2"	the average duration of a user's absences
log(ATpA)	"user-2"	the log. of the aver. duration of a user's absences
log(AT)pA	"user-2"	the average log. of duration of a user's absences
Queries		
Q	user	the number of queries of a user
logQ	user	the logarithm of the number of queries of a user
Clicks		
C	user	the number of clicks of a user
logC	user	the logarithm of the clicks of a user
Clicks per query		
CpQ	user	the average number of clicks of a user's queries
Presence time		
PT	session	the duration of a session in seconds
logPT	session	the logarithm of the duration of a session
sumPT	user	the sum of durations of a user's sessions
logsumPT	user	the logarithm of the presence time of a user

3. FRAMEWORK

3.1 A/B testing background

In A/B testing, users participated in an experiment, are randomly exposed to one of the two variants of a service (the control (A) and the treatment (B), e.g., the current production version of the service and its update) in order to compare their performance [22, 19, 21]. The difference between the variants is quantitatively measured by an *Overall Evaluation Criterion* ξ (*OEC*, also known as the evaluation metric, the online service quality metric, etc. [22]). In the classical methodology of A/B testing, this OEC is usually an *evaluation statistic* $\xi = \xi_\Omega(\mathtt{X})$ (e.g., *the average value*) of a *key metric* $\mathtt{X}(\omega)$ over the *events* (*entities*) $\omega \in \Omega$. More precisely, for each user group $v \in \{A, B\}$, we have the observations of the metric X over the experimental units Ω_v. Then, the evaluation statistics $\xi_v = \xi_{\Omega_v}(\mathtt{X})$, $v \in \{A, B\}$, are

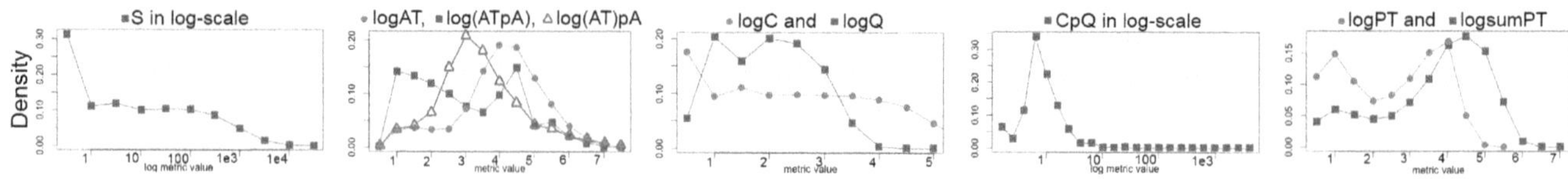

Figure 1: The distributions of 9 representative key metrics over their experimental units.

used as OEC, and their difference $\Delta = \xi_B - \xi_A$ is calculated to quantify the sign and the magnitude of the change in the OEC.

Nonetheless, the quantity Δ could not serve itself as an indicator of positive or negative consequences of the evaluated changes of the service. The difference between the evaluation metrics over groups should be controlled by a statistical significance test (e.g., Student's t-test) that calculates the probability (also known as *p-value*) to observe the difference under *the null hypothesis*, which assumes that the observed difference is caused by random fluctuations, and the variants of the system are not actually different in terms of user experience. If the p-value is lower than the threshold $p_{\text{val}} \leq \alpha$ ($\alpha = 0.05$ is commonly used [22, 19, 7, 33, 21, 10, 11]), then the test rejects the null hypothesis, and the difference Δ is accepted as statistically significant. We refer to the triplet (a key metric, an evaluation statistic, a statistical test) as an *Overall Acceptance Criterion* (*OAC*). The additional details of the A/B testing framework could be found in the survey and practical guide [22]. All key metrics, evaluation statistics, and statistical significance tests studied in this paper are specified further in the next subsections.

3.2 User engagement metrics

In this work, we study several popular engagement metrics and their modifications, which are calculated based on actions of users[2] of Yandex, one of the most popular global search engines. Following common practice [15, 19, 12, 33, 3, 10, 11], we define a *session* as a sequence of user actions whose *dwell times*[3] are less than 30 minutes. The *number of sessions* `S` (as in [33, 10, 11]) for each user in an A/B experiment is our first metric. In our study, we also consider this metric for the reduced set of users that have at least 2 sessions during the experiment (such experimental unit is referred to as "user-2"). The time between two consecutive user sessions (i.e., the duration of an absence) is the *absence time* (as in [12, 3]), which is referred to as `AT` and is calculated for each pair of consecutive sessions of each user. The experimental unit for `AT` is the *period of absence* between a pair of sessions, and, in order to match absence time to a user (as an experimental unit), we also consider the average duration of user's absences `ATpA` for each "user-2"[4]. We logarithmically transform[5] these metrics and obtain `logAT`, `log(ATpA)`, and `log(AT)pA`.

All above described metrics represent the *loyalty aspect* of user engagement, whereas, further, we present metrics that are associated with the *user activity* [27]. They are: the number of queries `Q` [10, 11], the number of clicks `C` [10, 11], and the number of clicks per query `CpQ` (i.e., the CTR of the search engine result pages [11]) for each user. The presence time is considered both for each user's session (i.e., its duration `PT` in seconds) and for each user (i.e., the sum of the durations of her sessions `sumPT` [10, 11]). We logarithmically transform these metrics and obtain `logQ`, `logC`, `logPT`, and `logsumPT`. Thereby, we study 16 key user engagement metrics in total, whose descriptions and corresponding experimentation units are summarized in Table 1. The shape of distributions of 9 representative key metrics over their experimental units are shown in Fig. 1 (their values are given in arbitrary units for confidentiality reasons). Short analysis of their persistence across time and relationships between almost all of them are studied in [10, 11].

3.3 Evaluation statistics

Mean and standard deviation. The average value[6] (AVG) is the state-of-the-art evaluation statistic of the key metric over experimental units. The vast majority of studies on A/B testing [4, 18, 35, 19, 33, 20, 21, 5, 10, 11, 9] utilize it, including the fact that the mean describes the typical behavior of a web service user (an "average" user). The second commonly used statistic in probability theory is the standard deviation (SD). It measures how the key metric `X` vary across the experimental units Ω. In many studies on A/B testing [4, 7, 5], the standard deviation is assumed to be equal for the control variant and the treatment one, when a statistical test is applied. We consider this statistic in our analysis and show that this statement is not valid for some metrics (see Section 4).

Median and quantiles. The *γ-quantile* (also known as the γ-th population quantile [14]) is defined as the value q_γ such that $\mathbb{P}(\mathtt{X} \leq q_\gamma) \geq \gamma$ and $\mathbb{P}(\mathtt{X} > q_\gamma) \leq 1 - \gamma$, $\gamma \in [0, 1]$, where $\mathbb{P}(\mathtt{X})$ is the distribution of the key metric `X` over the experimental units Ω. For a finite sample of observations of the key metric, we use the traditional estimator of the γ-quantile, presented in the equation (1) in [14][7]. In our work, we have considered 19 different γ-quantiles with $\gamma = 0.05i$, $i = 1, \ldots, 19$, but, due to the space constraints, we present the results only for the 5 most representative ones. Their γ are 0.5 (*the median*), 0.25 (the first quantile), 0.75 (the third quantile), 0.05, and 0.95.

The median is one of the popular statistics: its meaning is similar to the one of the mean value AVG, but the median is better suited for skewed distributions to quantify behavior of a typical user since it is much more robust and sensible (the mean value is highly influenced by outliers). There are a lot of paired [31] and unpaired [34] statistical tests specialized on the median as well. Contrariwise, a quantile with $|\gamma - 0.5| \gg 0$ could be useful in measuring the extreme cases [24, 16]: it quantifies user behaviors that are far from the mean.

[2]Users are identified by means of Cookie IDs [22] as done in other studies on user engagement [12, 23, 33, 10, 11, 9].

[3]i.e., times between two consecutive actions of a user [10]

[4]A user with only 1 session has no absence times `AT` by the definition above.

[5]It should increase the power of OACs if the key metric has a skewed distribution [17].

[6]A "rate" OEC, which is a percent of experimental units with some properties over all experimental units (e.g., the percent of users who click on a link) could be formalized via averaging as well [4].

[7]Subtler estimators (like in [14]) could be also considered, we left it for the future work.

Table 2: **Comparison of OACs w.r.t. the number of A/B and A/A experiments with detected treatment effect with the constant threshold $\alpha = 0.05$.**

$\alpha =$ 0.05	Success rate | False-positive rate [# of the 169 A/B tests] | [# of the 98 A/A tests]				
Stat.test:	T-test	BS-AVG	MW test	TW test	LR test
S	18 | 2	23 | 2	15 | 5	21 | 3	24 | 2
sS	20 | 2	20 | 2	17 | 2	19 | 1	22 | 2
AT	63 | 20	20 | 8	74 | 27	77 | 27	76 | 24
logAT	72 | 26	19 | 9	74 | 27	77 | 27	76 | 24
ATpA	11 | 4	16 | 5	24 | 3	24 | 3	20 | 4
log(ATpA)	20 | 3	**28** | 3	24 | 3	24 | 3	20 | 4
log(AT)pA	22 | 8	29 | 7	29 | 6	26 | 9	26 | 9
Q	34 | 3	41 | 4	35 | 4	39 | 5	38 | 2
logQ	34 | 5	39 | 4	35 | 4	39 | 5	38 | 2
C	52 | 3	**58** | 3	46 | 3	54 | 3	57 | 2
logC	49 | 3	53 | 3	46 | 3	54 | 3	57 | 2
CpQ	80 | 9	81 | 9	96 | 10	94 | 8	90 | 8
PT	70 | 22	27 | 3	82 | 26	80 | 23	79 | 24
logPT	80 | 24	50 | 5	82 | 26	80 | 23	79 | 24
sumPT	26 | 3	34 | 3	30 | 3	34 | 1	36 | 1
logsumPT	27 | 2	27 | 3	30 | 3	34 | 1	36 | 1

Table 3: **Comparison of OACs w.r.t. the number of A/B and A/A experiments with detected treatment effect with the constant threshold $\alpha = 0.01$.**

$\alpha =$ 0.01	Success rate | False-positive rate [# of the 169 A/B tests] | [# of the 98 A/A tests]				
Stat.test:	T-test	BS-AVG	MW test	TW test	LR test
S	11 | 0	**18** | 0	8 | 0	14 | 0	15 | 0
sS	**18** | 0	16 | 0	12 | 0	13 | 0	17 | 0
AT	43 | 12	9 | 0	49 | 14	55 | 15	56 | 15
logAT	51 | 14	10 | 2	49 | 14	55 | 15	56 | 15
ATpA	6 | 0	11 | 1	13 | 0	13 | 0	13 | 0
log(ATpA)	8 | 0	15 | 0	13 | 0	13 | 0	13 | 0
log(AT)pA	8 | 0	14 | 2	13 | 0	14 | 0	13 | 0
Q	19 | 0	27 | 1	20 | 1	24 | 0	28 | 0
logQ	19 | 0	20 | 0	20 | 1	24 | 0	28 | 0
C	35 | 0	38 | 0	38 | 0	44 | 0	**49** | 0
logC	37 | 0	41 | 0	38 | 0	44 | 0	**49** | 0
CpQ	73 | 3	73 | 2	78 | 2	77 | 4	80 | 4
PT	53 | 14	13 | 1	70 | 13	63 | 11	61 | 15
logPT	69 | 13	32 | 2	70 | 13	63 | 11	61 | 15
sumPT	12 | 1	20 | 1	16 | 0	18 | 0	19 | 0
logsumPT	21 | 1	21 | 0	16 | 0	18 | 0	19 | 0

Hence, such quantile may help a web service to detect the treatment effect of an evaluated update on users either with lower, or higher engagement than an "average" user (e.g., the 0.25-quantile of the number of sessions S describes users that use the service rarely, while the 0.75-quantile of it quantifies frequent users). This may be definitely important for web companies that fight for new, rare users in a competitive environment or choose to preserve and increase engagement of loyal, regular users. The γ-quantile is referred to as Q-γ.

Entropy. The *entropy* statistic (also known as the Shannon entropy) is defined as the expectation $\mathrm{E}(\mathtt{X}) = \mathbb{E}(\mathrm{I}(\mathtt{X}))$ of the information $\mathrm{I}(\mathtt{X}) = -\ln \mathbb{P}(\mathtt{X})$ [30]. Entropy is a measure of "chaos" or unpredictability of information content. In our case, entropy is a measure of *diversity* of user engagement with a web service w.r.t. the metric X over Ω (e.g., it quantifies the diversity of users w.r.t. their number of sessions for X = S). Hence, the entropy statistic may help the web service to detect the treatment effect of an evaluated update in terms of such diversity: whether the update increases or decreases the variety of different types of user behavior. *We propose to use the entropy as a novel OEC in A/B testing.*

3.4 Statistical significance tests

Unpaired two-sample Student's t-test. The *Student's t-test* (T-test) is the most popular statistical test for comparing the mean values of unpaired data samples, and, hence, it is the widely used one in A/B testing [7, 33, 6, 10, 11]. Its popularity could be explained, first, by its computational costs. Indeed, this test is based on *t-statistic*:

$$\frac{\mathrm{AVG}_B(\mathtt{X}) - \mathrm{AVG}_A(\mathtt{X})}{\sqrt{\mathrm{SD}_A^2(\mathtt{X}) \cdot |\Omega_A|^{-1} + \mathrm{SD}_B^2(\mathtt{X}) \cdot |\Omega_B|^{-1}}}$$

whose calculation takes $3n + o(n)$ arithmetic operations, where $n = \max\{|\Omega_A|, |\Omega_B|\}$. Second, despite the normality of the key metric's distribution is one of the assumptions underlying the test, it may be applicable in practice to some key metrics that do not follow a normal distribution even approximately. Further in our study, our experimental results confirm applicability of the statistical test in the case of such metrics. On the other hand, we show that violation of independence of experimental units (which is another assumption underlying the test) results in inapplicability of the T-test due to underestimation of its false-positive rate.

Mann–Whitney, Tarone–Ware, and Logrank tests. This family of rank-based statistical tests is widely used in survival analysis [34] and is based on the χ^2_{FH} statistic:

$$\chi^2_{FH} = \frac{\left(\sum_{j=1}^{K} \omega_j (d_{j,B} r_j - r_{j,B} d_j) r_j^{-1}\right)^2}{\sum_{j=1}^{K} \omega_j^2 r_{j,B} r_{j,A} d_j (r_j - d_j) r_j^{-2} (r_j - 1)^{-1}},$$

where the values of $r_{j,A}, r_{j,B}, r_j, d_{j,A}, d_{j,B}, d_j$, and K are calculated in the following way. Given two samples of the key metrics $\{X_\omega\}_{\omega \in \Omega_v}$, $v = A, B$, we merge them into one increasing sequence of values. Among these values, there are K unique: $y_1 < \ldots < y_K$, $K \leq |\Omega_A| + |\Omega_B|$. Then, for each value $j = 1, \ldots, K$, the following values are computed: $d_{j,v}$ is the number of observations equal to y_j, and $r_{j,v}$ is the number of observations not less than y_j in the sample $v = A, B$. The values d_j and r_j are defined analogously using the union of the two samples.

For $\omega_j = r_j$, we get the Gehan tests, which is equal to the *Mann-Whitney U test* (MW test), also known as the *Wilcoxon rank-sum test*; for $\omega_j = \sqrt{r_j}$, we get the *Tarone-Ware test* (TW test); and, for $\omega_j = 1$, we get the *Logrank test*[8] (LR test). Calculation of χ^2_{FH} usually takes $O(n \log n)$ operations, since one needs to sort the samples Ω_A and Ω_B by the values of the key metric. These tests could be considered as tests of medians with the additional assumption that the distributions for the samples have the same shape.

Bootstrapping. As opposed to the previous ones, this test can be applied to any evaluation statistic ξ. Therefore, the *Bootstrap test* is referred to as BS-ξ with the statistic ξ whose null hypothesis is tested (e.g., BS-AVG means that the Bootstrap test is applied to the mean values of the samples). We use the Bootstrap test as described in [13,

[8]The Logrank test is one of the main statistical tests used [34] in the Cox Model, which was applied to the absence time metric in [12].

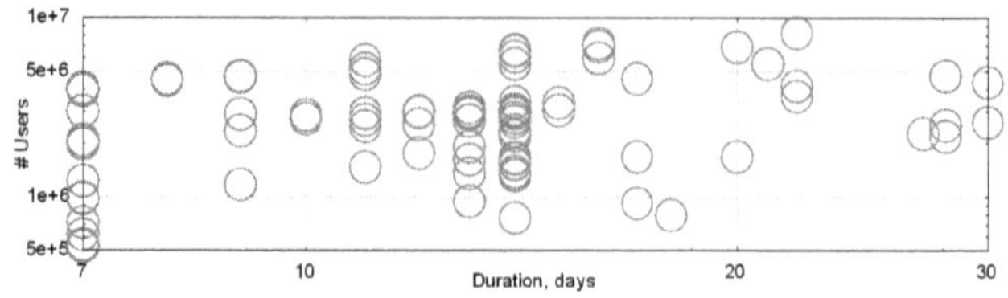

Figure 2: The distribution of 169 A/B tests w.r.t. their duration and the size of their sample of users.

Alg. 16.1] with *resampling of users*[9]. This statistical test is the most computational expensive among test we consider, since it takes $O(NB)$ operations, where N is the number of operations needed to calculate the statistic ξ (e.g., $N = O(n)$ for the mean) and B is the number of bootstrap iterations. In our study, $B = 1000$ as in [28, 25].

Summarizing, *we study 16 key user engagement metrics and apply* 26 *evaluation-statistic–statistical-test pairs: 2 statistical tests (T-test and BS) for AVG, 4 tests (MW test, TW test, LR test, and BS) for Q-0.5 (the median), 1 test (BS) for all other considered statistics.*

4. EXPERIMENTATION

4.1 Set of our A/B tests

In our paper, we consider 169 large-scale A/B experiments conducted on *real users* of Yandex with duration from 7 to 30 days. The user samples used in our A/B tests are all uniformly randomly selected, and the control and the treatment groups are of approximately the same size (at least, hundreds of thousands of users). The distribution of these 169 A/B tests w.r.t. their duration and the size of their sample of users is presented in Figure 2. Each experiment evaluates a change in one of the main components of the search engine (including the ranking algorithm, the user interface, the server efficiency, etc). Each of these changes is either an artificial deterioration of a component[10] [20], or its update, which is evaluated before being shipped. In our experimentation, we also consider 98 control experiments: 70 1-week and 28 2-week so-called A/A tests that compare the same versions of the service [22, 4]. Both A/B and A/A tests were conducted during the period from January, 2013 to November, 2014.

Additionally, we generate several thousands of synthetic A/A experiments (like in [1, 7]) by randomly splitting users from one of our control experiments. We find that the results for these synthetic A/A experiments (p-value distributions, false-positive rares, etc.) are similar to the ones for real A/A experiments. Therefore, due to the space constraints, we present the results only for our 98 real control experiments.

4.2 Success and false-positive rates

The straightforward way to compare sensitivity of OACs is to apply them to a series of A/B experiments and compare the number of A/B tests whose treatment effect is detected by each OAC for a selected p-value threshold $p_{\text{val}} \leq \alpha$ (as in [10, 11, 9, 25]). This number is also referred to as the *success rate* in IR offline evaluation [36]. The threshold $\alpha = 0.05$ is commonly used in existing studies on A/B testing [22, 19, 7, 33, 21, 10, 11]. However, smaller thresholds are also considered (e.g., $\alpha = 0.01, 0.001, 0.0001$) in order to focus on strong signals [20], since this is aligned with emerging needs of modern web companies to be more confident in the effect of evaluated updates on the quality of their services. But this is a double-edged sword for OAC comparison as well, since the lower the threshold α (i.e., the lower the false-positive rate), the lower the success rate. We expect that comparison of OACs at different p-value thresholds may lead to different results. Hence, in order to reveal it, we present our results both for the state-of-the-art threshold $\alpha = 0.05$, and for the stronger one $\alpha = 0.01$.

[9]Thus, we correctly bootstrap dependent data when the experimental unit of a considered key metric is not a user [1], e.g., in the case of PT, two sessions in a sample can be of the same user, and, thus, their durations are dependent.

[10]like the swap of the second and the fourth results in the ranked list formed by the current ranking [10, 25].

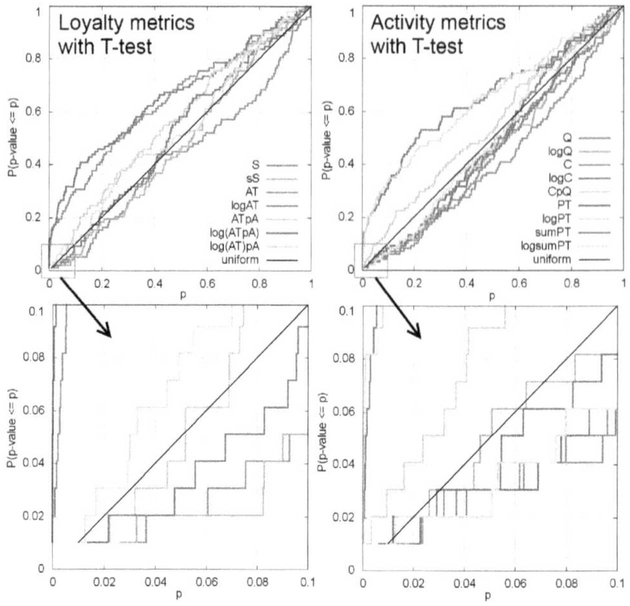

Figure 3: The CDFs of the p-value of the T-test for all loyalty and activity metrics over 98 A/A tests.

We compare all studied key metrics (7 loyalty and 9 activity ones) applied with 5 main statistical tests (T-test, Bootstrap test for AVG, MW test, TW test, and LR test) with respect to the success rate of their OACs in Table 2 and Table 3 (the first number in a cell) for the *constant threshold* $\alpha = 0.05$ and 0.01 respectively. We see that the success rates of the key metrics `AT` and `logAT`[11] with the Tarone–Ware test for $\alpha = 0.05$ (77 detected treatments in 169 A/B tests, i.e., 46%) and with the Logrank test (33%) for $\alpha = 0.01$ are the highest ones among all loyalty OACs, moreover, the success rates of the OACs of these metrics with T-test, MW test, TW test, and LR test dominate among other loyalty OACs by a large margin. The activity metrics `CpQ`, `PT`, and `logPT` (applied with almost all presented statistical tests) dominate other OACs w.r.t. the success rate both for $\alpha = 0.05$ and 0.01 (with the success rates up to 57% and 47% respectively).

In A/B testing, correctness of an experimentation is verified by control experiments (i.e., A/A tests) [22, 4]. Each of them compares two identical versions of the service and

[11]Note that logarithmic transformation is monotone, and, hence, the p-value results for the non-transformed and log-transformed variants of the same key metric for one of MW, TW, and LR tests are the same.

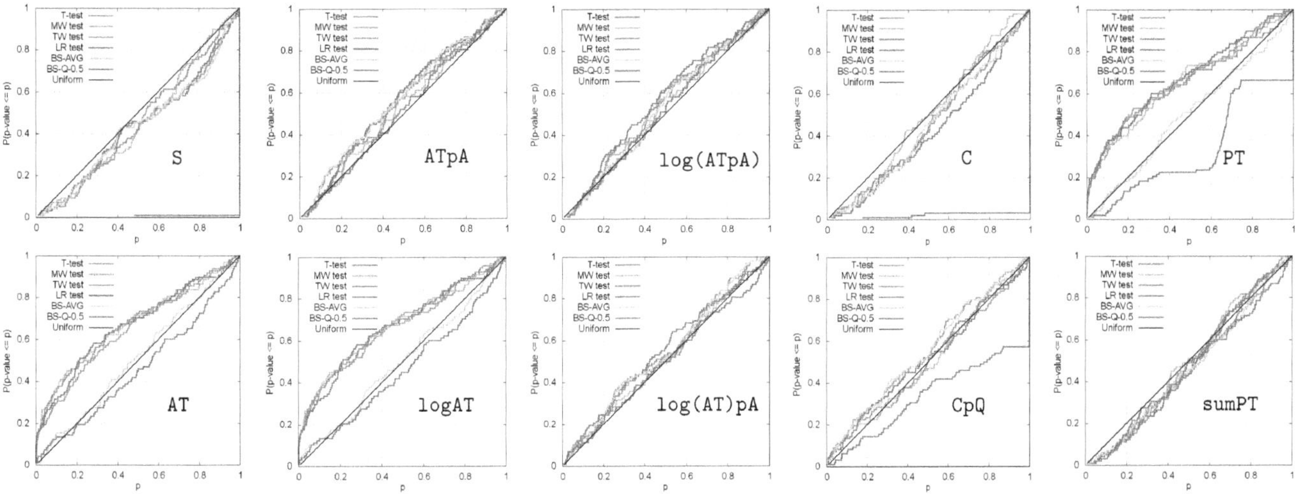

Figure 4: Comparison of the CDFs of the p-value for different statistical test of the mean and the median values over 98 A/A tests.

should be failed (i.e, the treatment effect is wrongly detected) in not more than $\alpha \cdot 100\%$ of cases (e.g., 5% for $\alpha = 0.05$), if the experimentation platform is correct and the OAC is valid. The number of failed A/A tests is referred to as the *false-positive rate* (also known as the type I error) and is reported as the second number in the cell for each OACs in Tables 2, 3. The cells of OACs that have inappropriate false-positive rates (> 4 and > 0 for $\alpha = 0.05$ and 0.01, respectively) are highlighted in red color. Such OACs should be rejected in the classical approach, since their statistical tests underestimate the standard deviation of their OEC [4]. According to this, all the previously top-rated key metrics `AT`, `logAT`, `CpQ`, `PT`, and `logPT` are rejected. Hence, *we conclude that the metrics* `log(ATpA)` *and* `C` *for $\alpha = 0.05$ (*`S`*,* `sS`*,* `C` *and* `logC` *for $\alpha = 0.01$) with suitable statistical tests (their cells are highlighted in* **boldface***) are the best ones w.r.t. the success rate among OACs with a valid false-positive rate.*

4.3 P-value distributions

In order to understand the dramatic underestimation of the false-positive rate of several OACs by their p-values (see the previous subsection), we consider the empirical Cumulative Distribution Function (CDF) of the p-value of an OAC over the 98 A/A experiments. If a key metric's distribution satisfies the assumptions that underlay a statistical test, then the p-value of this OAC should be uniformly distributed over [0, 1] [22, 4].

We present the empirical CDFs of the p-value of the T-test for all loyalty and activity metrics in Fig. 3. We see that only the CDFs of the key metrics `AT`, `logAT`, `PT`, and `logPT` are noticeably higher than the uniform CDF, and this becomes even more apparent near 0, where commonly used p-value thresholds ($\alpha = 0.01$ and 0.05) are situated (see also Tables 2 and 3). These metrics are united by the fact that their experimental units do not coincide with the randomization one, i.e., a user (see Table 1). This finding is in line with the observations made in [4, 35], where Boostrapping and Delta methods are suggested to estimate the variance of non-per-user metrics.

We compare the CDFs of the p-value of the 6 statistical tests (T-test, MW test, TW test, LR test, BS-AVG, and BS-Q-0.5) that are utilized for the mean and the median of some representative engagement metrics[12] over 98 A/A experiments (see Fig. 4). We see that the observation made above for the metrics with non-user experimental units holds for all considered statistical tests except for the Bootstrapping for the mean value (BS-AVG), whose CDF is approximately uniform for all these metrics. Note that their analogs that are mapped to a user (i.e., the metrics `ATpA`, `log(ATpA)`, `log(AT)pA`, `sumPT`, and `logsumPT`) do not have such convexity in their CDFs, and this results in noticeably lower false-positive rates of their OACs (see Tables 2 and 3). Therefore, we conclude that, *for a non-per-user metric, its transformation to a per-user one or utilization of the Bootstrap test noticeably reduce the dramatic underestimation of the false-positive rate (up to the correct estimation).*

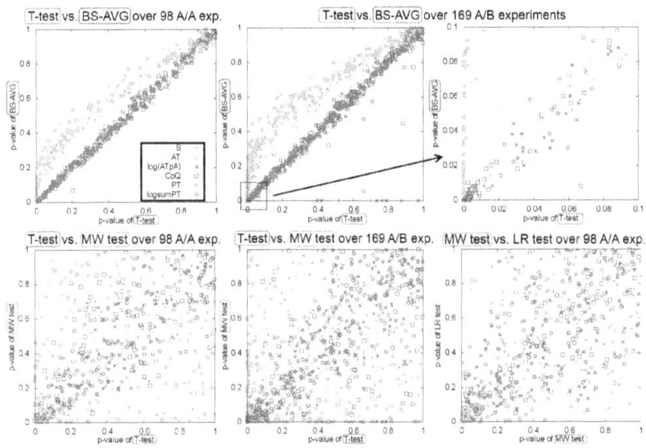

Figure 5: The joint distributions of our A/A and A/B experiments w.r.t. the pairs of the p-values of two statistical tests for some representative engagement metrics.

From Fig.3 and 4, we also make an interesting observation: the metrics `S`, `sS`, `Q`, `C`, `sumPT`, and `logsumPT` have a noticeable overestimation of false-positive rate. This observation prompts that their real success rates for the real

[12]From here on in this paper, due to the space constraints, we present results only for the best or representative metrics, statistics, and statistical tests, and we pay more attention to the loyalty aspect of user engagement.

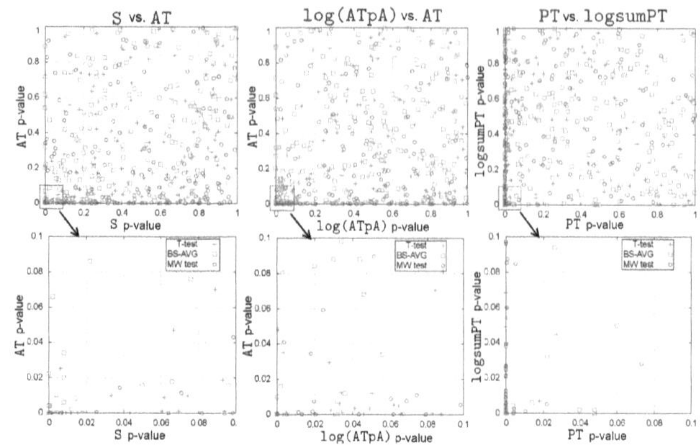

Figure 6: The joint distributions of our A/B experiments w.r.t. the pairs of the p-values of statistical tests for two engagement metrics.

false-positive rates of 5% or 1% are greater than the ones presented in Tables 2 and 3 (see the next subsection).

We also find that there is a strong relationship between the p-values of the Student's t-test and the Bootstrap test for the mean (BS-AVG) for all metrics, including the metrics with significantly skewed CDFs like AT or PT. The relationship of the tests is not linear for such metrics and is linear for the other metrics (see the top of Fig. 5). The similarity between the Student's t-test and bootstrapping is also observed for IR metrics in [32, 36]. The relation for each of other pairs of statistical tests (see examples of joint distributions in the bottom of Fig. 5) is noticeably more chaotic than the ones described above. There is no relation between the p-value of the same test applied to different metrics as well (e.g., see Fig. 6). The relation of T-test and BS-AVG infers that the false-positive level of an OAC could be improved by utilization of the latter one instead of the former one if the metric is skewed, since the Bootstrapping has approximately uniform distribution of its p-value for such metrics.

4.4 P-value adjustment

Motivated by the observations made in the previous subsection, we estimate the p-value threshold α for each OAC individually, such that its real false-positive rate is 5 failed A/A tests of the 98 ones from our set of experiments. This estimator equals to the 5-th smaller p-value from the observations. It is the traditional estimator of the 5/98-quantile, presented in the equation (1) in [14]. The subtler estimators from this study could also be considered, but we left it for the future work. The obtained estimations of p-value thresholds are referred to as $\alpha_{5:98} = \alpha_{5:98}(\text{OAC})$ and are presented in Table 4. The highest values for each row are highlighted in **boldface**, the lowest ones are underlined, the highest and the lowest values for each column both for loyalty and activity metrics are highlighted in green color and blue color, respectively. For instance, we see that the Mann–Whitney U test is the frequent one, whose false-positive rate has the worst underestimation, while the Logrank test (from the same family as MW test), contrariwise, frequently shows the highest overestimation for the activity metrics.

We utilize the individually adjusted thresholds $\alpha = \alpha_{5:98}$ to get the success rates of our OACs, that are presented in Table 5. Comparing these results with the ones from Table 2, we see that, on the one hand, the previously top-rated absence-time metrics (e.g., AT and ATpA) have now moderate success rates (similar to or lower than the ones of other loyalty metrics). On the other hand, the metrics S and sS, whose false-positive rates have been overestimated, demonstrate now higher success rates and the best ones among the loyalty metrics (for all statistical tests except the MW one). For activity metrics, we observe decay in the success rates of PT and logPT, while CpQ remains the leadership. Hence, we conclude that *the adjustment of the p-value threshold to a desired false-positive rate could significantly change the state of affairs in evaluation of Overall Acceptance Criteria: the success rates of ones can noticeably increase, other OACs can become usable in evaluation of a web service, since their false-positive rates reduce to an acceptable level.*

Table 4: The thresholds $\alpha = \alpha_{5:98}$ for each OAC.

Stat.test:	T-test	BS-AVG	MW test	TW test	LR test
S	0.1439	0.126	0.0726	0.1007	0.1144
sS	0.1004	0.098	0.0747	0.1025	**0.1105**
AT	0.0029	**0.04**	0.0002	0.0003	0.0005
logAT	0.0002	0.022	0.0002	0.0003	0.0005
ATpA	0.0519	0.05	0.0791	0.0729	0.0702
log(ATpA)	**0.0828**	0.082	0.0791	0.0729	0.0702
log(AT)pA	0.033	0.03	**0.0498**	0.0362	0.0333
Q	0.0993	0.06	0.0537	0.0503	0.138
logQ	0.0508	0.062	0.0537	0.0503	0.138
C	0.0961	0.108	0.0724	0.0839	**0.127**
logC	0.0632	0.058	0.0724	0.0839	**0.127**
CpQ	**0.0322**	0.026	0.0223	0.0304	0.0193
PT	0.0017	**0.066**	0.0009	0.0017	0.0028
logPT	0.0008	**0.058**	0.0009	0.0017	0.0028
sumPT	0.089	0.102	0.0784	0.1004	**0.1234**
logsumPT	0.0796	0.09	0.0784	0.1004	**0.1234**

Table 5: Comparison of OACs w.r.t. the number of A/B and A/A experiments with detected treatment effect with the adjusted threshold $\alpha = \alpha_{5:98}$.

<table>
<tr><td>$\alpha =$
$\alpha_{5:98}$</td><td colspan="5">Success rate | False-positive rate
[# of the 169 A/B tests] | [# of the 98 A/A tests]</td></tr>
<tr><td>Stat.test:</td><td>T-test</td><td>BS-AVG</td><td>MW test</td><td>TW test</td><td>LR test</td></tr>
<tr><td>S</td><td>37 | 5</td><td>41 | 5</td><td>19 | 5</td><td>35 | 5</td><td>35 | 5</td></tr>
<tr><td>sS</td><td>33 | 5</td><td>34 | 5</td><td>20 | 5</td><td>26 | 5</td><td>33 | 5</td></tr>
<tr><td>AT</td><td>29 | 5</td><td>20 | 5</td><td>27 | 5</td><td>31 | 5</td><td>33 | 5</td></tr>
<tr><td>logAT</td><td>23 | 5</td><td>10 | 5</td><td>27 | 5</td><td>31 | 5</td><td>33 | 5</td></tr>
<tr><td>ATpA</td><td>11 | 5</td><td>16 | 5</td><td>33 | 5</td><td>29 | 5</td><td>24 | 5</td></tr>
<tr><td>log(ATpA)</td><td>27 | 5</td><td>32 | 5</td><td>33 | 5</td><td>29 | 5</td><td>24 | 5</td></tr>
<tr><td>log(AT)pA</td><td>14 | 5</td><td>20 | 5</td><td>29 | 5</td><td>24 | 5</td><td>20 | 5</td></tr>
<tr><td>Q</td><td>39 | 5</td><td>43 | 5</td><td>35 | 5</td><td>39 | 5</td><td>53 | 5</td></tr>
<tr><td>logQ</td><td>35 | 5</td><td>41 | 5</td><td>35 | 5</td><td>39 | 5</td><td>53 | 5</td></tr>
<tr><td>C</td><td>60 | 5</td><td>65 | 5</td><td>53 | 5</td><td>61 | 5</td><td>67 | 5</td></tr>
<tr><td>logC</td><td>51 | 5</td><td>54 | 5</td><td>53 | 5</td><td>61 | 5</td><td>67 | 5</td></tr>
<tr><td>CpQ</td><td>79 | 5</td><td>80 | 5</td><td>85 | 5</td><td>88 | 5</td><td>83 | 5</td></tr>
<tr><td>PT</td><td>39 | 5</td><td>29 | 5</td><td>54 | 5</td><td>55 | 5</td><td>48 | 5</td></tr>
<tr><td>logPT</td><td>52 | 5</td><td>51 | 5</td><td>54 | 5</td><td>55 | 5</td><td>48 | 5</td></tr>
<tr><td>sumPT</td><td>31 | 5</td><td>39 | 5</td><td>34 | 5</td><td>43 | 5</td><td>47 | 5</td></tr>
<tr><td>logsumPT</td><td>36 | 5</td><td>37 | 5</td><td>34 | 5</td><td>43 | 5</td><td>47 | 5</td></tr>
</table>

4.5 Other evaluation statistics

In order to compare different evaluation statistics (considered in Sec. 3.3), we select 6 most representative key metrics and present the success and false-positive rates in Table 6 for their OACs. These rates are calculated both for the *constant* threshold $\alpha = 0.05$ and for the *adjusted* one $\alpha = \alpha_{5:98}$ (the rates are highlighted as in the previous subsections).

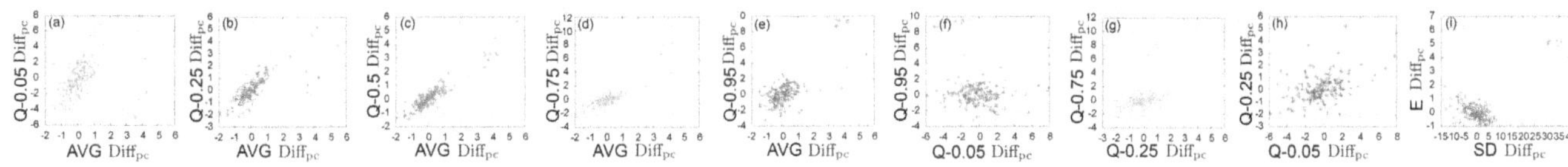

Figure 7: The distributions of A/B tests w.r.t. Diff_{pc} of some pairs of evaluation statistics for `log(ATpA)`.

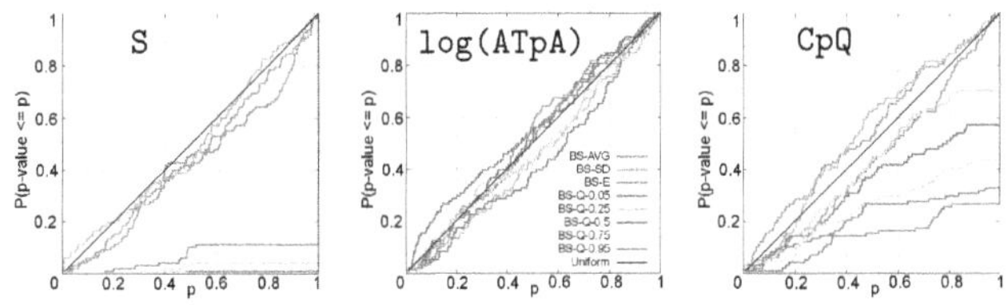

Figure 8: The CDFs of the p-values for all statistics for the metrics `S`, `log(ATpA)`, and `CpQ` obtained from the Bootstrap test over 98 A/A experiments.

Since the considered statistics have different meaning w.r.t. user behavior (see Sec. 3.3), we group OACs in such a way that their statistics have similar meaning and their key metrics have the same type of engagement (activity or loyalty). The highest success rate in each group is highlighted in blue color. In Fig. 8, we compare different statistics w.r.t. the CDFs of the p-values for several metrics.

In order to compare the meaning of our statistics, we calculate the scaled relative difference $\text{Diff}_{\text{pc}} = \varkappa\Delta/\xi_A$[13] of them for each of 169 A/B experiments. In Fig. 7, we plot joint distributions of these experiments w.r.t. Diff_{pc} of some pairs of OECs for the metric `log(ATpA)`, whose OACs demonstrate the most consistent CDFs for different evaluation statistics (see Fig. 8). First, the joint distribution for the mean and the median (the plot (c) in Fig. 7) reveals that they have similar meaning. Therefore, we conclude that *both the mean-aware and the median-aware statistical tests could be rivals in the area of typical user behavior evaluation.*

Second, the mean value also coincides with the γ-quantile (in terms of Diff_{pc}) for $|\gamma - 0.5| \approx 0$, and this correlation reduces while the quantile becomes far from the median (i.e., $|\gamma - 0.5| \gg 0$). We demonstrate it by the joint distributions for the mean and the γ-quantile, $\gamma = 0.05$, 0.25, 0.75, and 0.95, in Fig. 7 (the plots (a), (b), (d), and (e) respectively). The correlation between two quantiles (in terms of Diff_{pc}) also depends on how far the values of their γ are (see in Fig. 7). Therefore, we conclude that *quantiles correspond to really independent components of user engagement that represent different extreme cases of user behavior.* Note that the distributions of the metrics `S`, `Q`, and `C` are discrete, and a significant fraction of users has the same metric value (e.g., several percents of users have 1 session during an experiment). Hence, quantiles of these metrics do not change during most A/B experiments, and the p-values for the corresponding OACs have very skewed distributions (see Fig. 8 and Table 6).

Third, we see that the entropy statistic (E) has a weak correlation with the standard deviation (SD), whose meaning seems similar to diversity. Hence, we conclude that *entropy could be considered as a very promising statistic since it encodes a novel independent feature of engagement (diversity) in case of A/B testing, and OACs with entropy have very high sensitivity level (see Table 6).* Finally, note that the standard deviations (SD) for the control and the treatment variants of the service are significantly different for a noticeable number of A/B experiments (see the success rates for SD in Table 6). Therefore, we conclude that *the assumption on equality of SD for the variants A and B (as in [4, 7, 5]) should be used carefully and should be regularly validated for each OEC.*

[13]The factor $\varkappa$ is randomly chosen once in our study in order to hide real values for confidentiality reasons.

5. CONCLUSIONS AND FUTURE WORK

In our work, we considered a huge set of hundreds of large-scale A/B tests. We focused on the impact of different statistics and statistical tests of an OAC on the sensitivity of different key metrics. We utilized our set of experiments to evaluate dozens of key metrics of user engagement with dozens of statistical tests. First, we demonstrated that a key metric is most effective in combination with an appropriate statistical test, which is individual for each key metric. We found that utilization of the common Student's t-test with a default p-value may lead to wrong conclusions on the performance of some state-of-the-art key metrics. Second, we shown that each combination of a key metric and a statistical test requires its individual p-value threshold to control the false-positive rate at a predefined level. Third, we also proposed the entropy and the quantiles as novel OECs that quantify the diversity and extreme cases of user engagement.

Future work. First, we can extend the set of evaluation statistics or statistical tests by investigating more sophisticated ones. Second, we can improve the technique of adjusting the p-value threshold by utilizing more precise statistics. Third, we can study the sign of the treatment effect and the confidence interval for each of our OACs.

6. ACKNOWLEDGMENTS

The authors would like to thank Nikita Povarov and Pavel Serdyukov for useful discussions.

7. REFERENCES

[1] E. Bakshy and D. Eckles. Uncertainty in online experiments with dependent data: An evaluation of bootstrap methods. In *KDD'2013*, pages 1303–1311, 2013.

[2] B. A. Carterette. Multiple testing in statistical analysis of systems-based information retrieval experiments. *ACM Transactions on Information Systems (TOIS)*, 30(1):4, 2012.

[3] S. Chakraborty, F. Radlinski, M. Shokouhi, and P. Baecke. On correlation of absence time and search effectiveness. In *SIGIR'2014*, pages 1163–1166, 2014.

[4] T. Crook, B. Frasca, R. Kohavi, and R. Longbotham. Seven pitfalls to avoid when running controlled experiments on the web. In *KDD'2009*, pages 1105–1114, 2009.

[5] A. Deng and V. Hu. Diluted treatment effect estimation for trigger analysis in online controlled experiments. In *WSDM'2015*, pages 349–358, 2015.

[6] A. Deng, T. Li, and Y. Guo. Statistical inference in two-stage online controlled experiments with treatment selection and validation. In *WWW'2014*, pages 609–618, 2014.

Table 6: **Comparison of statistics w.r.t. the number of A/B and A/A experiments with detected treatment effect with the constant threshold $\alpha = 0.05$ and the adjusted threshold $\alpha = \alpha_{5:98}$.**

$\alpha = 0.05$	**Success rate** [# of the 169 A/B tests] | **False-positive rate** [# of the 98 A/A tests]											
Statistic:	Average		0.5-Quantile (Q-0.5) / Median				Q-0.05	Q-0.25	Q-0.75	Q-0.95	Entropy	St. Dev.
Stat.test:	T-test	BS	MW test	TW test	LR test	BS (Bootstrap)						
S	18 | 2	23 | 2	15 | 5	21 | 3	24 | 2	0 | 0	0 | 0	0 | 0	0 | 0	8 | 0	23 | 3	27 | 8
log(ATpA)	20 | 3	28 | 3	24 | 3	24 | 3	20 | 4	17 | 2	13 | 2	17 | 1	19 | 5	19 | 12	16 | 3	16 | 2
Q	34 | 3	41 | 4	35 | 4	39 | 5	38 | 2	2 | 0	0 | 0	0 | 0	1 | 0	12 | 0	37 | 2	2 | 5
C	52 | 3	58 | 3	46 | 3	54 | 3	57 | 2	1 | 0	1 | 0	0 | 0	8 | 0	31 | 1	57 | 2	6 | 1
CpQ	80 | 9	81 | 9	96 | 10	94 | 8	90 | 8	62 | 3	13 | 2	70 | 2	54 | 4	7 | 0	46 | 3	6 | 4
logsumPT	27 | 2	27 | 3	30 | 3	34 | 1	36 | 1	18 | 1	0 | 0	13 | 5	25 | 3	24 | 2	32 | 2	39 | 6
$\alpha = \alpha_{5:98}$	**Success rate** [# of the 169 A/B tests] | **False-positive rate** [# of the 98 A/A tests]											
S	37 | 5	41 | 5	19 | 5	35 | 5	35 | 5	2 | 5	0 | 5	0 | 5	9 | 5	13 | 5	33 | 5	14 | 5
log(ATpA)	27 | 5	32 | 5	33 | 5	29 | 5	24 | 5	23 | 5	20 | 5	19 | 5	19 | 5	13 | 5	29 | 5	19 | 5
Q	39 | 5	43 | 5	35 | 5	39 | 5	53 | 5	4 | 5	0 | 5	1 | 5	6 | 5	26 | 5	41 | 5	1 | 5
C	60 | 5	65 | 5	53 | 5	61 | 5	67 | 5	11 | 5	5 | 5	3 | 5	24 | 5	41 | 5	63 | 5	14 | 5
CpQ	79 | 5	80 | 5	85 | 5	88 | 5	83 | 5	66 | 5	18 | 5	76 | 5	62 | 5	9 | 5	54 | 5	6 | 5
logsumPT	36 | 5	37 | 5	34 | 5	43 | 5	47 | 5	31 | 5	11 | 5	10 | 5	33 | 5	34 | 5	37 | 5	31 | 5

[7] A. Deng, Y. Xu, R. Kohavi, and T. Walker. Improving the sensitivity of online controlled experiments by utilizing pre-experiment data. In *WSDM'2013*, 2013.

[8] B. T. Dinçer, C. Macdonald, and I. Ounis. Hypothesis testing for the risk-sensitive evaluation of retrieval systems. In *SIGIR'2014*, pages 23–32, 2014.

[9] A. Drutsa. Sign-aware periodicity metrics of user engagement for online search quality evaluation. In *SIGIR'2015*, 2015.

[10] A. Drutsa, G. Gusev, and P. Serdyukov. Engagement periodicity in search engine usage: Analysis and its application to search quality evaluation. In *WSDM'2015*, pages 27–36, 2015.

[11] A. Drutsa, G. Gusev, and P. Serdyukov. Future user engagement prediction and its application to improve the sensitivity of online experiments. In *WWW'2015*, pages 256–266, 2015.

[12] G. Dupret and M. Lalmas. Absence time and user engagement: evaluating ranking functions. In *WSDM'2013*, pages 173–182, 2013.

[13] B. Efron and R. J. Tibshirani. *An introduction to the bootstrap.* CRC press, 1994.

[14] F. E. Harrell and C. Davis. A new distribution-free quantile estimator. *Biometrika*, 69(3):635–640, 1982.

[15] B. J. Jansen, A. Spink, and V. Kathuria. How to define searching sessions on web search engines. In *Advances in Web Mining and Web Usage Analysis*, pages 92–109. Springer, 2007.

[16] H. Kashima. Risk-sensitive learning via expected shortfall minimization. In *SDM*, pages 529–533. SIAM, 2006.

[17] L. Keele, C. McConnaughy, and I. White. Statistical inference for experiments. *Unpublished manuscript*, 2008.

[18] R. Kohavi, T. Crook, R. Longbotham, B. Frasca, R. Henne, J. L. Ferres, and T. Melamed. Online experimentation at microsoft. *Data Mining Case Studies*, page 11, 2009.

[19] R. Kohavi, A. Deng, B. Frasca, R. Longbotham, T. Walker, and Y. Xu. Trustworthy online controlled experiments: Five puzzling outcomes explained. In *KDD'2012*, pages 786–794, 2012.

[20] R. Kohavi, A. Deng, B. Frasca, T. Walker, Y. Xu, and N. Pohlmann. Online controlled experiments at large scale. In *KDD'2013*, pages 1168–1176, 2013.

[21] R. Kohavi, A. Deng, R. Longbotham, and Y. Xu. Seven rules of thumb for web site experimenters. In *KDD'2014*, 2014.

[22] R. Kohavi, R. Longbotham, D. Sommerfield, and R. M. Henne. Controlled experiments on the web: survey and practical guide. *Data Min. Knowl. Discov.*, 18(1):140–181, 2009.

[23] J. Lehmann, M. Lalmas, G. Dupret, and R. Baeza-Yates. Online multitasking and user engagement. In *CIKM'2013*, pages 519–528, 2013.

[24] H. Mausser and D. Rosen. Beyond var: From measuring risk to managing risk. In *CIFEr'1999*, pages 163–178. IEEE, 1999.

[25] K. Nikolaev, A. Drutsa, E. Gladkikh, A. Ulianov, G. Gusev, and P. Serdyukov. Extreme states distribution decomposition method for search engine online evaluation. In *KDD'2015*, 2015.

[26] E. T. Peterson. *Web analytics demystified: a marketer's guide to understanding how your web site affects your business.* Ingram, 2004.

[27] K. Rodden, H. Hutchinson, and X. Fu. Measuring the user experience on a large scale: user-centered metrics for web applications. In *CHI'2010*, pages 2395–2398, 2010.

[28] T. Sakai. Evaluating evaluation metrics based on the bootstrap. In *SIGIR'2006*, pages 525–532, 2006.

[29] T. Sakai. Statistical reform in information retrieval? In *ACM SIGIR Forum*, volume 48, pages 3–12, 2014.

[30] C. E. Shannon. A mathematical theory of communication. *ACM SIGMOBILE Mobile Computing and Communications Review*, 5(1):3–55, 2001.

[31] M. D. Smucker, J. Allan, and B. Carterette. A comparison of statistical significance tests for information retrieval evaluation. In *CIKM'2007*, pages 623–632, 2007.

[32] M. D. Smucker, J. Allan, and B. Carterette. Agreement among statistical significance tests for information retrieval evaluation at varying sample sizes. In *SIGIR'2009*, pages 630–631, 2009.

[33] Y. Song, X. Shi, and X. Fu. Evaluating and predicting user engagement change with degraded search relevance. In *WWW'2013*, pages 1213–1224, 2013.

[34] G. P. Suciu, S. Lemeshow, and M. Moeschberger. Statistical tests of the equality of survival curves: reconsidering the options. *Handbook of Statistics*, 23:251–262, 2004.

[35] D. Tang, A. Agarwal, D. O'Brien, and M. Meyer. Overlapping experiment infrastructure: More, better, faster experimentation. In *KDD'2010*, pages 17–26, 2010.

[36] J. Urbano, M. Marrero, and D. Martín. A comparison of the optimality of statistical significance tests for information retrieval evaluation. In *SIGIR'2013*, pages 925–928, 2013.

[37] L. Wang, P. N. Bennett, and K. Collins-Thompson. Robust ranking models via risk-sensitive optimization. In *SIGIR'2012*, pages 761–770, 2012.

[38] W. Webber, A. Moffat, and J. Zobel. Statistical power in retrieval experimentation. In *CIKM'2008*, pages 571–580, 2008.

Generalized Team Draft Interleaving

Eugene Kharitonov[1,2], Craig Macdonald[2], Pavel Serdyukov[1], Iadh Ounis[2]
[1]Yandex, Russia
[2]University of Glasgow, UK
[1]{kharitonov, pavser}@yandex-team.ru
[2]{craig.macdonald, iadh.ounis}@glasgow.ac.uk

ABSTRACT

Interleaving is an online evaluation method that compares two ranking functions by mixing their results and interpreting the users' click feedback. An important property of an interleaving method is its sensitivity, i.e. the ability to obtain reliable comparison outcomes with few user interactions. Several methods have been proposed so far to improve interleaving sensitivity, which can be roughly divided into two areas: (a) methods that optimize the credit assignment function (how the click feedback is interpreted), and (b) methods that achieve higher sensitivity by controlling the interleaving policy (how often a particular interleaved result page is shown).

In this paper, we propose an interleaving framework that generalizes the previously studied interleaving methods in two aspects. First, it achieves a higher sensitivity by performing a joint data-driven optimization of the credit assignment function and the interleaving policy. Second, we formulate the framework to be general w.r.t. the search domain where the interleaving experiment is deployed, so that it can be applied in domains with grid-based presentation, such as image search. In order to simplify the optimization, we additionally introduce a stratified estimate of the experiment outcome. This stratification is also useful on its own, as it reduces the variance of the outcome and thus increases the interleaving sensitivity.

We perform an extensive experimental study using large-scale document and image search datasets obtained from a commercial search engine. The experiments show that our proposed framework achieves marked improvements in sensitivity over effective baselines on both datasets.

Categories and Subject Descriptors: H.3.3 [Information Storage & Retrieval]: Information Search & Retrieval
Keywords: interleaving; online evaluation

1. INTRODUCTION

Online evaluation approaches, such A/B testing and interleaving, are crucial tools in modern search engine evaluation [2, 5, 7, 11, 12, 13]. These approaches leverage the implicit feedback of the real users to evaluate changes to the search engine and can be applied even when the offline evaluation approaches might be impractical [19].

Since the online evaluation approaches rely on the noisy user feedback, a considerable number of observations is needed before a statistically significant conclusion can be made [2, 12]. Usually, an A/B testing experiment is deployed for a week or two [12]. A typical length of an interleaving experiment used in the literature is up to five days [2]. Such a long duration of the online experiments considerably limits their usefulness, and bounds the rate of the search engine's evolution.

Another concern is that a considerable fraction of the changes evaluated online turn out to actually degrade the user's search experience [12]. When evaluated in an online experiment during a period of a week, such a change increases the users' frustration with the results and might even force them to switch to another search engine.

These observations support the need to increase the speed of online evaluation experiments. When comparing two web document search ranking functions, interleaving is faster to obtain the comparison outcome than an A/B test [2, Section 7]. A variety of methods were proposed to further reduce the duration of interleaving experiments by improving the interleaving sensitivity. Roughly, this research can be divided into two areas: optimization of the credit assignment [2, 14, 20]; and optimization of the probability of showing of the interleaved result pages (interleaving policy) [10, 15]. In both areas, only document search has been studied so far. Furthermore, the current research in the interleaving policy optimization explicitly relies on a user model that is specific to the list-based representation.

In this paper we propose an interleaving framework that generalizes the existing research in two aspects. First, we consider both the interleaving policy and the credit assignment function as optimized parameters in our framework. As a result, our framework has a higher flexibility that can be used to achieve a higher sensitivity. Second, we formulate our framework to be general w.r.t. the actual presentation of the result pages, so that it can be applied for the domains such as image search, where grid-based presentation is used.

In order to simplify the parameter optimization procedure, we propose to use a stratified estimate of the interleaving experiment outcome, where the stratification is performed according to the teams of the results on the result pages shown. We demonstrate that our proposed stratification approach is also useful on its own, as in some cases it considerably increases the interleaving sensitivity.

Overall, the contributions of our work are three-fold:

- We propose a principled, data-driven framework to develop sensitive interleaving that combines the stratification, the interleaving policy optimization, and the

Permission to make digital or hard copies of all or part of this work for personal or classroom use is granted without fee provided that copies are not made or distributed for profit or commercial advantage and that copies bear this notice and the full citation on the first page. Copyrights for components of this work owned by others than ACM must be honored. Abstracting with credit is permitted. To copy otherwise, or republish, to post on servers or to redistribute to lists, requires prior specific permission and/or a fee. Request permissions from Permissions@acm.org.
CIKM'15, October 19–23, 2015, Melbourne, Australia.
© 2015 ACM. ISBN 978-1-4503-3794-6/15/10 ...$15.00.
DOI: http://dx.doi.org/10.1145/2806416.2806477.

credit function learning in a single framework that can be applied in domains with the list-based and the grid-based result presentations;

- We propose sufficient conditions that the click feature representation and the interleaving policy need to satisfy so that the resulting interleaving method remains unbiased;
- We perform a large-scale evaluation study of the proposed framework, using two datasets that contain document and image search online experiments.

The remainder of this paper is organised as follows. In Section 2 we discuss the related work. In Section 3 we define our interleaving framework and discuss its details in Section 4. Our proposed stratification technique, and how to optimize the interleaving parameters, is discussed in Sections 5 and 6, respectively. In Section 8 we describe the instantiations of our framework for the web document search and for the image search domains. The datasets and the evaluation scenario we use are described in Section 7 and 9, respectively. We discuss our obtained results in Section 10. We conclude this paper and discuss future work in Section 11.

2. RELATED WORK

Since the introduction of the first interleaving method, Balanced Interleaving [7, 8], several other interleaving methods were proposed, including Team Draft [16], Probabilistic Interleaving [6], Optimized Interleaving [15]. An important characteristic of an interleaving method is its sensitivity, i.e. ability to obtain a reliable experiment outcome with as few user interactions as possible. The problem of increasing the sensitivity of an interleaving method has attracted a considerable attention from the research community, and below we review the most relevant work in this area.

Yue et al. [20] proposed a method to learn a more sensitive credit assignment function for the Team Draft interleaving experiments. Later, this approach was also discussed by Chapelle et al. [2]. Informally, the core idea of [20] is to learn how to weight user clicks in the interleaving comparisons so that the confidence in the already performed experiments is maximized. As a result, new interleaving experiments will achieve the required level of confidence in their outcomes with fewer user interactions, i.e. the interleaving method will have a higher sensitivity. Yue et al. refer to this learning problem to as an "inverse" hypothesis test: given user interaction data for the comparisons with known outcomes, one learns a credit assignment function that maximizes the power of the test statistic in these comparisons.

Our work is based on the ideas of Yue et al. [20], and aims to overcome some of the shortcomings of their approach. First, it is not straightforwardly clear what kind of features and weighting functions are allowed so that no biases are introduced when learning the credit assignment function. It is possible to build an example of the click feature representation that make the credit function learning process prone to biases (Section 4). In our work, we propose a formal unbiasedness requirement that ensures that a feature-based credit assignment function is not biased. Moreover, we propose a restricted family of the click features that allow us to make this requirement easy to operate in practice.

In their work, Yue et al. assume that the interleaving policy (the probabilities of showing of the different interleaved result pages) is fixed. We propose to optimize both the interleaving policy and the credit assignment function jointly, and this results in a higher interleaving sensitivity.

Radlinski and Craswell [15] proposed the Optimized Interleaving framework, which specifies a set of requirements that an interleaving method has to meet so that (a) its results are not biased, (b) it is sensitive, and (c) the users are not too frustrated by the interleaved results pages. Our framework is based on Optimized Interleaving, but it also has significant differences from it. First, Optimized Interleaving is formulated specifically with a particular web document search user model in mind, and the interleaving policy optimization it performs is formulated with respect to a click model that is specific for the list-based result presentation. This hinders extending the interleaving approaches to other domains. In contrast, we propose a generalized unbiasedness requirement, that can be applied for the grid-based result pages. Second, we perform a joint data-driven optimization of the interleaving policy and the credit assignment function. In contrast, in Optimized Interleaving, the credit assignment function is fixed; and the interleaving policy is optimized with respect to a randomly clicking user, in a data-free manner. Moreover, the interleaving policy optimization considered by Radlinski and Craswell is performed on a per-query basis. This makes the evaluation runtime system more sophisticated, as this optimization must be performed each time a long-tail query is submitted. Finally, due to using a large set of possible interleaved result pages that is different from the result pages generated by Team Draft and Balanced Interleaving, it is hard to perform a representative evaluation study of this method without actually implementing it and deploying a large set of real-life experiments. Unlike Optimized Interleaving, our proposed framework has the same interleaving policy for all queries and experiments which is fixed once learned, thus it imposes little implementation costs over the standard Team Draft interleaving. Further, its performance can be evaluated using a set of historical experiments, available to each search engine that uses Team Draft-based interleaving experiments.

While studying a different problem of the document search multileaving, Schuth et al. [18] used the variance of the outcome as a proxy for the interleaving sensitivity. This approach can be considered as a hybrid between approaches in [20] and [15]: the optimization is performed w.r.t. to a randomly clicking user, as in [15]; the optimization objective is close to z-score used in [20], as the latter favours a lower variance, too. We believe this approach can be suboptimal in comparison to the data-driven optimization used by Yue et al. [20] and our framework. Indeed, in the case of the sufficiently large dataset, the parameters can be optimized based on the real-life data, without relying on a model of a randomly clicking user.

Kharitonov et al. [10] addressed the problem of improving the interleaving sensitivity by predicting the future user clicks using the historical click data. Their approach explicitly relies on the document search click models, thus it is hard to generalize to other domains. Moreover, [10] requires the search engine to store per-query click models in runtime, and use them when interleaving the result pages. It is not clear how practical this requirement can be in the presence of the long-tail queries that form a considerable part of the query stream. Further, as it can be applied only for the head queries with click data available, it is not clear if any additional biases can occur due to increased sensitivity to the changes in the top queries. In contrast, our framework does not requires significant changes in the search engine's experimentation infrastructure and can be applied for the domains with the grid-based presentation of the results.

In their work [3], Chuklin et al. proposed an interleaving method that goes beyond the classic "ten blue links" web document presentation and deals with the vertical results (e.g. News, Images, Finance) incorporated in the main web search result page. However, the challenges that Chuklin et al. address (e.g., ensuring that in the interleaved result page vertical results are still grouped) are quite different from the problems faced when developing an interleaving mechanism for a new domain. In the latter case, one needs to decide how to specify the credit assignment function, how to select the interleaving policy, etc. To the best of our knowledge, our work is the first to address the problem of interleaving in a domain with the grid-based result presentation.

One of the approaches to improve the interleaving sensitivity we discuss is stratification, a simple yet effective technique that has its roots in the Monte-Carlo stratified sampling methods [1, 17]. Previously, its application for online A/B tests was studied by Deng et al. [4], but it was never considered in the context of interleaving.

Overall, our framework finds a solid foundation in the research discussed above, but it also addresses several shortcomings of the earlier approaches. In the next section we formally introduce it.

3. FRAMEWORK DEFINITION

First, we informally outline how interleaving experiments are performed. Suppose, that we need to compare a changed system B to the production system A using an interleaving experiment. To do that, a random subset of the users is selected to take part in the experiment. When a query is submitted, both results from A and B are retrieved. Further, the interleaving policy is used to determine which of the possible mixed (interleaved) result pages to show to the user. Next, the users' clicks on the interleaved result page are observed, and the credit assignment function is used to infer the credits of the alternatives. After the experiment is stopped, the aggregated credits of the alternatives are compared. If B has a statistically significantly higher credit, it is accepted that B outperformed A.

The works of Yue et al. [20] and Radlinski and Craswell [15] lay the foundation for our framework. However, our framework has significant differences from [20] and [15]. Specifically, our proposed framework performs a joint optimization of the interleaving policy and the credit assignment function, while Yue et al. and Radlinski and Craswell optimize only one of these parameters. Further, our framework can be applied for search domains with grid-based result pages. Below, we provide a formal requirement that a feature-based credit assignment function, the click feature representation, and the interleaving policy have to meet for the interleaving to be unbiased. In contrast, Yue et al. do not discuss possible biases that can emerge due to feature-based learning, and Radlinski and Craswell only discuss simple, feature-less credit assignment rules. By addressing the above discussed gaps, we build a sensitive interleaving framework that generalizes approaches proposed by Yue et al. [20] and Radlinski and Craswell [15].

In our framework, we consider the result pages that are obtained by applying the Team Draft mixing algorithm [16] to the lists of the results of the underlying rankers A and B, sorted according to their relevance. The exact mapping of the sorted result list into a result page is domain-specific (the list-based for document search, or the grid-based for image search). Assuming that under this mapping the results ranked higher in the ranked list are mapped into positions with higher examination probability, mixing the sorted result lists of the rankers A and B according to Team Draft will result in a result page that cannot be more frustrating for the users than both the result pages generated from outputs of A and B. Due to this assumption we avoid the necessity of specifying the mixing algorithm for each possible domain-specific presentation, and can work with the underlying ranker output, which is always list-wise in practice. Apart from that, relying on the Team Draft-based result pages allows us to re-use a large-scale dataset of the experiments collected by a search engine for our evaluation study (Section 10).

The Team Draft mixing algorithm builds the interleaved result list in steps. At each step, both teams contribute one result each to the combined list. Each team contributes the result that it ranks highest among those that are not in the combined list. However, the team that contributes first at each step is decided by a coin toss. For instance, as there are usually 10 results on a document search result page, 5 coin tosses are required to build it. Thus, there are exactly $2^5 = 32$ different distributions of the result teams on a result page[1].

Now we can define the first component of our framework:

F1. The set $\{(L_i, T_i)\}_{i=1}^{l}$ of the pairs of the interleaved result pages $L_i \in \mathbb{L}$ and their corresponding distributions of the result teams $T_i \in \mathbb{T}$. The result pages $\mathbb{L}$ are obtained by applying the Team Draft [16] mixing algorithm to the sorted outputs of the rankers A and B, and further domain-specific presentation of the ranked list. We define $T_i(p)$ to be equal to 1 (-1) if the team of the result on position p of the interleaved list that produced L_i is B (A);

It is possible that some pairs (L_i, T_i) contain identical result pages L_i, despite that the team distributions T_i associated with them are different (e.g. if A and B produce identical result lists). We consider such pairs to be different.

Further, following [15] we explicitly define the interleaving policy as a parameter of the framework:

F2. An interleaving policy π, $\pi \in \mathbb{R}^l$ determines the probability of using a particular team distribution when building an interleaved result page: $\pi_i = P(T_i)$;

Under our framework, the interleaving policy is the same for all queries and interleaving experiments. Informally, it can be considered as a distribution over the random seeds that can be used to "initialize" the coin used in Team Draft.

From [20] we adopt the feature representation of the user's click $\phi(\cdot)$ and the form of the credit assignment function S:

F3. A function $\phi(\cdot)$ that maps a user click c on an interleaved result page to its feature representation $\phi(c) \in \mathbb{R}^n$. We also define an auxiliary indicator $T(c)$ that equates to 1 (-1) if the team of the clicked result is B (A);

F4. A scoring rule, $S = S(q; w) = \sum_{c \in q} T(c) \cdot w^T \phi(c)$ that maps a sequence of clicks in the interaction q to the score of the alternative B. The vector w is a parameter, $w \in \mathbb{R}^n$.

After running an experiment e, the score statistic $\Delta(e)$ can be calculated:

$$\Delta(e) = \frac{1}{|Q|} \sum_{q \in Q} S(q; w) \qquad (1)$$

[1] They can be enumerated as *ababababab*, *abababab ba*, *ababab baab*, ..., *bababababa*.

where Q is a set of the user interactions in the experiment e. If $\Delta(e)$ is statistically significantly above zero, it is concluded that B outperforms A in the experiment e.

To ensure that the interleaving is unbiased, Radlinski and Craswell [15] suggested the following criterion for the document search scenario: a randomly clicking user should not create any preference between A and B. To formalize this idea, they considered a user who (a) samples the number of the considered top results k randomly and (b) clicks uniformly at random on η results from the top-k results. This formulation explicitly relies on a list-based presentation. Furthermore, in our case the formalization is even more challenging as the credit $S(q; w)$ is a function itself, since some feature representations might be prone to biases (we discuss this further in Section 4). We propose the following generalization of unbiasedness criterion from [15]:

R1. For any fixed sequence of clicks, the expectation of the total credit over the all pairs (L_i, T_i) of the interleaved pages L_i and distributions of teams T_i should be zero. Denoting the length of the sequence as J, the positions clicked as $p_1, p_2, ..., p_J$, and their corresponding click features as $\phi_1, \phi_2, ..., \phi_J$ we formalize this requirement as follows:

$$\forall J,\ \forall \{(p_j, \phi_j)\}_{j=1}^{J}\ \sum_i \pi_i \cdot \sum_j T_i(p_j) \cdot w^T \phi_j = 0$$

Due to the linearity of the expectation, R1 is sufficient to guarantee the absence of the preferences for any randomized combination of the click sequences, too. Informally, this guarantees that a user who specifies an arbitrary interaction scenario that does not depend on the presented documents (e.g., "click on the first position, sample the dwell time uniformly from [0, 30], click on the third result, ...") will not create any preference for A or B in expectation.

Next, we require the policy π to be a valid distribution:

R2. $\forall i\ \ \pi_i \geq 0;\ \ \sum_i \pi_i = 1$

Among all of the possible combinations of $\{\pi, w\}$ that satisfy R1 and R2, we want to select the combination that maximizes the interleaving sensitivity. Based on [20], we use a *dissimilarity* measure D between compared alternatives in a set of historical experiments E as a proxy for the sensitivity in future experiments. Indeed, the more dissimilar the alternatives are, the easier it is to differentiate them.

O1. The optimal combination of parameters π and w should maximize the dissimilarity D over a set of experiments E:

$$\hat{\pi}, \hat{w} = \arg\max_{\pi, w} D(E, \pi, w)$$

This ends the framework description. In the next section, we discuss the requirement R1 in more detail.

4. UNBIASEDNESS REQUIREMENT

The motivation behind R1 is to ensure that a user who clicks according to a fixed pattern that does not depend on the results shown would not provide any preference for A or B. Clearly, if R1 is not satisfied, a certain bias towards one of the alternatives might appear.

To illustrate how such a bias might arise, let us consider the following "toy" example. Let us assume that the feature representation vector $\phi(c)$ is a two dimensional vector, with its first component $\phi_0(c)$ being equal to 1 if the clicked result is from A, and zero otherwise. Similarly, $\phi_1(c)$ is equal to 1 if click c is performed on a result from B. Suppose we fix the interleaving policy to be uniform, and learn the vector of weights w based on the dataset of experiments. It is possible that, as a result of the learning, the weights of the features will obtain different values, e.g. if the learning dataset has more experiments with A winning. This results in poor generalization capabilities and biased interleaving. By considering a user who always clicks on the first position, we notice that in our toy example R1 requires w_1 to be equal to w_2.

In this work we simplify R1 by using a restricted family of features. Namely, we use click features that do not depend on the result page[2] L_i. By restricting the set of possible features, we achieve an intuitive *symmetry* property: after swapping A and B ("renaming" A to B, and B to A), the experiment outcome $\Delta(e)$ will only change its sign, but not its absolute value (which is violated in our toy example). Furthermore, the following Lemma 1 shows the conditions that are sufficient to satisfy R1 if we restrict the used features:

LEMMA 1. *For a feature representation ϕ, and a policy π to satisfy R1, it is sufficient that:*

- *ϕ is independent from L_i;*
- *For each position p on the result page, the probability of observing a result from A must be equal to the probability of observing a result from B: $\forall p\ \sum_i \pi_i \cdot T_i(p) = 0$.*

PROOF. First, using the independence of ϕ from L_i, we re-write R1 as follows:

$$\sum_j w^T \phi_j \cdot \sum_i \pi_i \cdot T_i(p_j) = 0 \qquad (2)$$

An obvious way to satisfy Equation (2) is to select π such that for any click position the expectation of T_i is zero for every position:

$$\forall p \sum_i \pi_i \cdot T_i(p) = 0 \qquad (3)$$

□

Lemma 1 provides us with a convenient approach to satisfy R1 while optimizing the interleaving parameters. Indeed, once we use only the features that are independent from the particular interleaved result pages shown, whether R1 is satisfied or not depends only on the interleaving policy. In that case, R1 reduces to the following equality constraint:

$$R\pi = 0 \qquad (4)$$

where $R \in \mathbb{R}^{m \times l}$ is a matrix with its element R_{ji} equal to the team $T_i(j)$ (1 or -1) of the result shown on jth position of the interleaved result page L_i.

Equation (4) gives an intuition how the optimization of the interleaving policy can be performed: the number of independent[3] equality constraints grows linearly as $m/2$ with the number of positions m, but the number of different team

[2]The features cannot depend on the clicked result, its team, and its position in A and B. In contrast, the features can depend on the properties of the clicks itself (e.g. the position of the click, its dwell time) and the total number of clicks.

[3]As discussed in F1, our framework relies on the Team Draft mixing algorithm. Due to its specifics, if Equation (3) holds for a position $2k$ and a policy π, it also holds for the position $2k+1$ and π.

distributions $\mathbb{T}$ and thus the dimensionality of the policy vector π grows exponentially as $2^{m/2}$. As a result, some "degrees of freedom" appear that can be used to find a sensitive yet unbiased policy. This intuition is similar to the one behind the optimization in Optimized Interleaving [15].

5. STRATIFIED SCORING

In Section 3, the experiment outcome is calculated as a sample mean of the scores of the individual interactions $\Delta(e)$, Equation (1). This approach is similar to the one used previously [2, 8, 15, 16]. We propose to use a stratified estimate $\Delta_s(e)$, where the stratification is performed according to the distribution of the teams (*ababababab*, ...) on the result pages shown to the users. Further, by Q_i we denote the set of the user interactions where the distribution of the teams on the result page shown is T_i. Using this notation, our proposed stratified estimate can be estimated as follows:

$$\Delta_s(e) = \sum_i \pi_i \cdot \frac{1}{|Q_i|} \sum_{q \in Q_i} S(q; w) \tag{5}$$

Both the stratified estimate $\Delta_s(e)$ and the sample mean $\Delta(e)$ have the same expected values, but the variance of $\Delta_s(e)$ can be lower and, consequently, it has higher sensitivity. Indeed, denoting the number of interactions in the experiment e as N, the variance and the expectation of the interaction score S among the sessions in the ith stratum as $var_i[S]$ and $\mathbb{E}_i[S]$, and applying the law of total variance, we obtain:

$$\begin{aligned} var\left[\Delta(e)\right] &= \frac{\sum_i \pi_i \cdot var_i[S] + \sum_i \pi_i(\mathbb{E}_i[S] - \sum_i \pi_i \cdot \mathbb{E}_i[S])^2}{N} \\ &\geq \frac{1}{N} \sum_i \pi_i \cdot var_i[S] = var\left[\Delta_s(e)\right] \end{aligned} \tag{6}$$

Since the frequency of T_i is determined by π_i, the probability of each stratum is known and fixed before starting an interleaving experiment.

As can be seen from Equation (6), the stratification reduces the variance only when the inner-strata means $\mathbb{E}_i[S]$ are different from the overall mean $\sum_i \pi_i \cdot \mathbb{E}_i[S]$. In our proposed approach of Equation (5), the stratification is performed according to the teams of the results on a result page T_i. In the case of the document search, T_i is a strong indicator of the outcome of a single comparison, as it specifies, for instance, if the click on the first result is counted in favour of A or B.

The stratification alone can considerably improve the sensitivity of the interleaving experiments in some cases (Section 10). Moreover, as we discuss in Section 6, the use of the stratified outcome Δ_e considerably simplifies the optimization of the interleaving parameters.

6. OPTIMIZATION OF THE PARAMETERS

To specify an instantiation of our proposed interleaving framework, we need to specify the interleaving policy π, the feature representation $\phi(c)$, and the vector of weights w. The feature representation is domain-specific. However, our proposed approach to determine the vector of weights w and the interleaving policy π are the same irrespective of the domain. We adopt a data-centric approach [20] to select π and w and select them maximize the sensitivity on the previously collected data.

We assume that a dataset E of interleaving experiments is available, so that for each experiment in this dataset the user interactions are recorded, and the experiment outcome is known. Such a dataset can be obtained from running interleaving experiments by a search engine (e.g., Team Draft-based experiments) and selecting the experiments with a high confidence in the outcome [2, 20] or by deploying "data collection" experiments where B is obtained by manually degrading A, and all possible combinations of the result lists and the team distributions are shown to the users with the uniform policy. We discuss these two approaches in more detail in Section 8.

To simplify the notation, without any loss in generality, we further assume that in all experiments $e \in E$ the alternative B outperformed A so that $\Delta_s(e)$ is positive. If it is not the case in a particular experiment, A and B can be swapped for that experiment.

As stated in the sensitivity optimization objective $O1$, we want to find the values of parameters π and w that maximize the dissimilarity between A and B over the available experiments and satisfy constraints $R1$ and $R2$. Since the sensitivity of the interleaving does not depend on the scaling of w, to make the optimization problem well-posed, we additionally constrain w to have the unit norm. Overall, this results in a general optimization problem of the following form:

$$\hat{\pi}, \hat{w} = \arg\max_{\pi, w} D(E, \pi, w) \;\; s.t. \; R1, R2, \; w^T w = 1$$

Further, we discuss two ways to specify the idea of dissimilarity, proposed by Yue et al. [20]: the *mean score* and the *z-score* dissimilarities.

Mean score We start with the simplest case, when dissimilarity is calculated as the mean value of the stratified score:

$$D_m(E, \pi, S) = \frac{1}{|E|} \sum_{e \in E} \sum_i \pi_i \frac{1}{|Q_{e,i}|} \sum_{c \in q, q \in Q_{e,i}} T(c) \cdot w^T \phi(c) \tag{7}$$

where $Q_{e,i}$ is the set of user interactions with the team distribution T_i demonstrated.

Further, we introduce a matrix X with its columns corresponding to the individual features, and rows corresponding to the strata, so that the element X_{kr} is equal to the mean value of the rth feature ϕ_r in the kth stratum:

$$X_{kr} = \frac{1}{|E|} \sum_{e \in E} \frac{1}{|Q_{e,k}|} \sum_{c \in q, q \in Q_{e,k}} T(c) \cdot \phi_r(c)$$

Using the introduced notation, the optimization objective can be re-written as follows:

$$D_m(E, \pi, w) = \pi^T X w$$

Thus, we are looking for π, w that maximize (8):

$$\begin{aligned} &\hat{\pi}, \hat{w} = \arg\max\nolimits_{\pi, w} \left[\pi^T X w\right] \\ &s.t. \; R1, R2, \; w^T w = 1 \end{aligned} \tag{8}$$

Finally, we notice that if we set π to be the uniform policy, the solution of the optimization problem (8) becomes similar to the solution of the corresponding case in Yue et al. [20]: w lies on the unit sphere $w^T w = 1$ and maximizes the dot product $\pi^T X \cdot w$, so $\hat{w} = \frac{\pi^T X}{||\pi^T X||_2}$. The difference is in the way X is calculated, as the scores are stratified in our case.

Z-score The second way to specify the level of dissimilarity between A and B proposed by Yue et al. [20] is to measure the z-score statistic. Informally, this measures how the distance between A and B is far from zero in terms of the variance of this distance.

Following Yue et al., we simplify the optimization by combining the set of experiments E into a single artificial experiment $\bar{e}$. In that case, the z-score can be calculated as follows:

$$D_z(E, \pi, w) = \frac{\Delta_s(\bar{e})}{\sqrt{var\left[\Delta_s(\bar{e})\right]}} \quad (9)$$

As earlier, we introduce a matrix X with its elements equal to the per-stratum means of the individual features:

$$X_{kr} = \frac{1}{|Q_{\bar{e},k}|} \sum_{c \in q, q \in Q_{\bar{e},k}} T(c) \cdot \phi_r(c)$$

Again, the score $\Delta_s(\bar{e})$ can be found as $\pi^T X w$. Due to the stratified representation of the score, the variance of $\Delta_s(\bar{e})$ breaks down to a weighted sum of the per-stratum variances:

$$var\left[\Delta_s(\bar{e})\right] = \frac{1}{N} \sum_i \pi_i \cdot var_i\left[S\right] = \frac{1}{N} \sum_i \pi_i \cdot w^T Z_i w$$

where N is the number of interactions in $\bar{e}$, and Z_i is the covariance matrix of the interaction scores $\sum_{c \in q} T(c) \cdot \phi(c)$ for the ith stratum:

$$Z_i = \sum_{q \in Q_{\bar{e},i}} \frac{1}{|Q_{\bar{e},i}|} \left(\sum_{c \in q} T(c)\phi(c) - \bar{\phi}_i \right) \left(\sum_{c \in q} T(c)\phi(c) - \bar{\phi}_i \right)^T$$

and $\bar{\phi}_i$ is the mean feature vector for the ith stratum:

$$\bar{\phi}_i = \frac{1}{|Q_{\bar{e},i}|} \sum_{c \in q, q \in Q_{\bar{e},i}} T(c) \cdot \phi(c)$$

Overall, we obtain the following optimization problem:

$$\hat{\pi}, \hat{w} = \arg\max_{\pi, w} \frac{\pi^T X w}{\sqrt{w^T \left(\sum_i \pi_i \cdot Z_i\right) w}} \quad s.t.\ R1, R2,\ w^T w = 1 \quad (10)$$

The use of stratification considerably simplifies the form of the optimization problem (10). Indeed, to calculate the variance of $\Delta_s(e)$ in the denominator of Equation (9) we used the right part of the inequality (6). In the non-stratified case, the variance is represented by the left part of (6). The latter case is harder for the optimization due to additional mutual dependencies of the variables (e.g. the variance becomes a third-order polynomial w.r.t. π, while it is linear in the stratified case).

In contrast to the case considered by Yue et al., there is no closed-form solution to the problems (8) and (10) (due to the additional variable π and requirements R1 and R2). Instead, we optimize (8) and (10) numerically[4]. As an initial approximation, we use the uniform policy and the solution of the corresponding problem in [20].

7. DATASETS

In our evaluation study we use two datasets: a dataset of Team Draft-based document search online experiments performed by a commercial search engine, and a dataset of preliminary interleaving experiments performed on the image search service. We discuss them in more detail below.

Document search We build the dataset of the Team Draft-based online experiments as follows. First, we randomly sample a subset of interleaving experiments performed

[4]Using the SLSQP routine implemented in scipy [9].

Table 1: Datasets statistics.

Domain	# exp.	B > A	mean/median # sessions	mean/median # days
Document	67	30	840K/620K	9.8/8.0
Image	5	0	38K / 34K	4.0/4.0

by the search engine in the period from January to November, 2014. These experiments test changes in the search ranking algorithm that were developed as a part of the search engine's evolution. The experiments also differ by country, and geographical region they are deployed on. We select the experiments where the winner (A or B) is determined with a high level of confidence, $p \leq 0.005$ (binomial sign test, deduped click weighting scheme [2]).

Image search In contrast to the web document search case, a representative set of online interleaving experiments is not available to us. Instead, we take five "data collection" experiments. In each of these experiments, the evaluated ranker B is obtained by degrading A in a controlled manner. After that, the corresponding "comparison" of A and B is deployed. In these "experiments" the interleaved result pages are obtained by interleaving the ranked lists returned by A and B, as discussed in Section 3, and showing them with the uniform policy (i.e. applying Team Draft). The following modifications of the production ranker to generate the alternative system B were used:

- swapping the results ranked as 1..15 with the results ranked 16..30;
- random permutation of the top-ranked results;
- promoting results with a low resolution;
- setting an important subset of the ranking features to zero;
- randomly ignoring some subsets of the search index.

As a result, we obtained a dataset of experiments, which can be used to adjust the interleaving parameters w and π, as discussed in Section 6. Once the number of organic evaluation experiments have grown, the optimization procedure we propose can be repeated on a more representative dataset.

We provide descriptive statistics of the datasets in Table 1.

8. INSTANTIATION

As discussed above, what changes for different domains is the feature representation of the clicks ($\phi(c)$). Further we describe what features we use in our experimental study. All features we use are independent from the result page demonstrated, so they meet the requirements of Lemma 1.

Document search features For each click in a user interaction, we calculate a set of 24 features, split into four families: Rank-based, Dwell time-based, Order-based, and Linear score-based features. We report these features along with their descriptions in Table 2.

Image search features The click features we use for image search interleaving are similar to the features used for document search. We exclude some rank-based features, as they are not meaningful for the two-dimensional result presentation (e.g. feature #11 assumes that the users tend to examine results in a rank-wise order). The full list of features used for the image search click representation is provided in Table 3.

Stratification In the document search scenario, we stratify the estimate of the experiment outcome according to the teams of the results on the first result page. This gives us $2^{10/2} = 32$ strata. The same strata are used for the policy optimization: the policy specifies the probability of using a specific team distribution to generate the first interleaved

Table 2: Click features for document search.

Feature family	id	Description
Rank-based		Transformations of the click's rank, normalized by the number of clicks
	1-10	position indicators, $f_i = \mathbb{I}\{rank = i\}$
	11	rank
	12	$\sqrt{rank}$
	13	$log(rank)$
	14	$\mathbb{I}\{rank > 4\}$
	15	$\mathbb{I}\{rank > d\}$, where d is the number of identical results in the tops of A and B
Dwell time-based		Indicators of the dwell time (seconds), normalized by the number of clicks
	16	$\mathbb{I}\{dwell \leq 30\}$
	17	$\mathbb{I}\{dwell \in (30, 60]\}$
	18	$\mathbb{I}\{dwell \in (60, 90]\}$
	19	$\mathbb{I}\{dwell \in (90, 120]\}$
	20	$\mathbb{I}\{dwell > 120\}$
Order-based		Indicators of the click's position in the interaction
	21	is the click first
	22	is the click last
Linear score-based		after applying the scoring rule F4, these features represent the (normalized) number of clicks the results from B received
	23	$f_{23} = 1$
	24	$f_{24} = 1/n$, where n is the total number of clicks

result page. The remaining pages are generated using the standard Team Draft procedure, and it can be shown that the interleaving is unbiased in terms of R1 in that case.

In the case of image search, the stratification is less straightforward. Indeed, the stratification according to the teams of the top 30 results on the first result page, will yield $2^{30/2} = 32768$ strata. On one hand, according to Equation (6), using more fine-grained strata results in equal or lower variance. On the other hand, to run the optimization discussed in Section 6, we need to estimate per-stratum means and covariances of the features. This results in a trade-off between an increased sensitivity due to more fine-grained stratification and a higher error of the optimization with unreliable parameters. Thus we performed the search for the optimal number of top results to be used in stratification as a part of the training process, as discussed in Section 9.3.

9. EVALUATION

In our evaluation study, we aim to answer the following research questions: (RQ1) is our framework more sensitive than the baselines on the document and image search data, and (RQ2) if yes, then what aspects of the sensitivity optimization (stratification, credit assignment and policy optimization) contribute to the increased sensitivity?

To answer these questions, we firstly describe the baselines we use in Section 9.1. After that, we introduce the metric we use in Section 9.2. Finally, we describe the evaluation methodology in Section 9.3.

9.1 Baselines

In our study, we compare the sensitivity of our proposed framework to the Team Draft algorithm with the credit assignment functions varied. We consider credit assignment functions of two types: the heuristic click weighting schemes that are applicable for Team Draft and considered in [2], and the learned scoring functions trained according to the approach of Yue et al. [20]. All these baselines are non-stratified.

Linear In the simplest scoring scheme, we calculate the difference in the number of clicks on the results from A and B:

$$S(q; w) = \sum_{c \in q} T(c)$$

Normalized Linear In the *Normalized Linear* scheme, the score of B in a particular interaction is normalised by the number of clicks in this interaction:

$$S(q; w) = \frac{1}{|q|} \sum_{c \in q} T(c)$$

Binary Another approach to aggregate clicks in a single impression is to assign a unit credit to the alternative that received more clicks:

$$S(q; w) = sign\left(\sum_{c \in q} T(c)\right)$$

Deduped Binary In the web document search scenario, it is often assumed that the users examine result lists from top to bottom. In that case, if the top k documents are identical both in A and B, all the interleaved lists have the same top k results, too. Thus, clicks on these top k results add a zero mean additive noise to the difference between the number of clicks A and B receive. A useful trick is to ignore such clicks. We combine this approach with the binary aggregation scheme:

$$S(q; w) = sign\left(\sum_{c \in q} T_d(c)\right)$$

where $T_d(\cdot)$ is a modified team indicator function, equal to zero if the click is performed on one of the top results, identical for A and B, and equal to $T(\cdot)$ otherwise. The deduped binary scheme is one of the most sensitive schemes [2].

Learned-mean, Learned-z In contrast to the above discussed credit assignment functions that are based on intuitive considerations, *Learned-mean* and *Learned-z* are machine-learned credit assignment functions that based on the approach of Yue et al. [20]. These baselines use the same feature representations as our proposed interleaving framework. However, the optimization of the interleaving policy is not performed, and it is fixed to be constant and uniform (as in Team Draft). *Learned-mean* selects the vector of weights w such that the differences between A and B are maximized, and *Learned-z* maximizes the z-score objective. These objectives are close to the objectives we use in Section 6, but they assume a non-stratified experiment outcome and the uniform policy.

It would be interesting to compare our framework to the Optimized Interleaving framework [15]. However, Optimized Interleaving relies on considerably larger sets of interleaved result pages, thus the datasets of Team Draft-based interleaving experiments cannot be re-used to evaluate its performance. An alternative approach is to leverage the natural variation of the search engine's rankings as a source of the result pages, as used in [15]. However, in this case, the evaluation is performed on a query level, and it is restricted to be based on the head queries only. Overall, this might lead to a less representative study.

9.2 Metric

In this work, we use the *z-score* metric that is used to measure the interleaving sensitivity on the historical data [2, 10]. *z-score* indicates the confidence of the evaluated method in the experiment outcome, thus it serves as a proxy to measure

Table 3: Click features for image search.

Feature family	id	Description
Rank-based		position indicators
	1-30	$f_i = \mathbb{I}\{rank = i\}$
	31	$\mathbb{I}\{rank > d\}$, where d is the number of identical results in the tops of A and B
Dwell time-based		Indicators of the dwell time (seconds), normalized by the number of clicks
	32	$\mathbb{I}\{dwell \leq 30\}$
	33	$\mathbb{I}\{dwell \in (30, 60]\}$
	34	$\mathbb{I}\{dwell \in (60, 90]\}$
	35	$\mathbb{I}\{dwell \in (90, 120]\}$
	36	$\mathbb{I}\{dwell > 120\}$
Order-based		Indicators of the click's position in the interaction
	37	is the click first
	38	is the click last
Linear score-based		after applying the scoring rule F4, these features represent the (normalized) number of clicks the results from B received
	39	$f_{48} = 1$
	40	$f_{49} = 1/n$, where n is the total number of clicks

the sensitivity of the method: a higher confidence indicates a higher sensitivity.

Assuming that $\Delta_s(e)$ is normally distributed[5] and using the notation introduced above, we define the *z-score* statistic on the data of the experiment e as follows:

$$Z = \frac{\Delta_s(e)}{\sqrt{var[\Delta_s(e)]}} = \frac{\Delta_s(e)}{\sqrt{\sum_i \pi_i \cdot var_i[S]}}\sqrt{N} \quad (11)$$

To calculate the z-score statistic for an interleaving method with a non-uniform policy on data obtained from an experiment with the uniform policy, we use the per-stratum sample estimates of the expectation $\mathbb{E}_i[S]$ and the variance $var_i[S]$ (Equation (6)), calculated on the experimental data, and the policy specified by the interleaving method.

The value of (11) indicates how far the score $\Delta_s(e)$ deviates from zero in the standard normal distribution. Thus it indicates the confidence level of the experiment outcome and can be mapped into p-value (under the null hypothesis the true value of $\Delta_s(e)$ is 0). For instance, Z of 1.96 (2.58) corresponds to the two-sided p-value of 0.05 (0.01).

In the case of the non-stratified estimate $\Delta(e)$, z-score is calculated similarly:

$$Z = \frac{\Delta(e)}{\sqrt{var[\Delta(e)]}} = \frac{\Delta(e)}{\sqrt{var[S]}}\sqrt{N} \quad (12)$$

For each interleaving experiment, we calculated the relative z-score by dividing the outcome's z-score by the z-score of the Team Draft method with the linear click weighting scheme. The relative z-score z_e has an intuitive interpretation [2]: the corresponding interleaving method needs z_e^2 less interactions in the same experiment e than the Team Draft algorithm with the linear weighting scheme to achieve the same level of confidence.

9.3 Procedure

In our evaluation on the document search dataset, we use 10-fold cross-validation: in each split, 90% of the interleaving experiments are used for optimization, and 10% are used to evaluate the resulting sensitivity. The same splits are used for all the approaches that run optimization (our proposed framework with two types of dissimilarity, and *Learned-mean* and *Learned-z* baselines). In each split, we measure the relative z-scores of an interleaving method on the experiments in the test set. For each interleaving method, we report the overall mean and the median relative z-scores collected across all folds. We use the paired t-test on the absolute values of the non-normalized z-scores when testing the statistical significance of the performance differences.

In the case of image search, due to the smaller dataset, we replace the 10-fold cross-valuation with the leave-one-out procedure: one experiment is used for evaluation, while the others are used for training. Further, within a training step, we additionally run a nested 2-fold cross-validation procedure on the training set to find the optimal number of the result teams to be considered in stratification: for k in $3, ..., 15$ we evaluate the performance of our proposed method when teams of the top $2k$ are used for the stratification. The search is stopped when the performance degrades. In most folds the optimal k is found to be equal to 3 (i.e., the top 6 results are used for the stratification).

[5]This assumption holds when $\pi_i \cdot N$ is large enough for all i with $\pi_i > 0$, as $\Delta_s(e)$ is a sum of approximately normally distributed per-stratum sample means, thus it is normally distributed.

10. RESULTS AND DISCUSSION

In this section, we use the following notation. Linear, Normalized Linear, Binary, and Deduped Binary weighting schemes correspond to *Linear, NLinear, Binary,* and *Deduped*, respectively. L_m and L_z indicate the Learned-mean and Learned-z baselines. The instantiations of our proposed framework are referred to as F_m and F_z, when the optimization is performed to maximize the mean difference (8) and the z-score (10) objectives, respectively.

As we are interested in evaluating the effects of the stratification and the effects of the joint optimization individually, we additionally measure the performance of the baselines when the stratified outcome $\Delta_s(e)$ is calculated. The stratified modifications of the interleaving methods L_m and L_z are denoted as L_m^s and L_z^m. L_m^s and L_z^s use the stratified objectives we proposed in Section 6, and correspond to our framework with the interleaving policy fixed to be uniform.

In our experiments on both document and image search datasets, all of the studied interleaving methods correctly determined the preference for A or B.

10.1 Document Search

In Table 4 we report the results of the evaluation procedure discussed in Section 9.3 applied for the web document search data. In the left part of Table 4 (*Non-stratified* column), we report the mean and median relative z-scores for the baselines with no stratification applied. In the right part (*Stratified* column), we report the performance of our proposed framework as well as for the baselines with the stratification applied.

On analysing the results of the non-stratified baselines, reported in the left part of Table 4, we notice that their relative performance is generally in line with the results reported in [2]. Indeed, the deduped binary scheme with its median relative z-score of 1.59 considerably outperforms other considered heuristic schemes: Linear (1.0), Normalized Linear (0.93), and Binary (0.98); similarly, L_z outperforms L_m.

On comparing the relative z-scores of Linear, NLinear, Binary, and Deduped with and without the stratification applied (left vs right parts of Table 4), we observe that in some cases the stratification greatly increases the interleaving sensitivity. For instance, the mean and the median relative z-scores of Binary grow from 1.10 and 0.98 to 1.22 and

Table 4: **Relative confidence levels of the interleaving outcomes, document search. The scores of the interleaving method with the highest sensitivity ($p < 0.01$) are denoted by $^\diamond$.**

	Non-stratified						Stratified							
	Linear	NLinear	Binary	Deduped	L_m	L_z	Linear	NLinear	Binary	Deduped	L^s_m	L^s_z	F_m	F_z
Mean	1.00	1.03	1.10	1.88	1.34	2.14	1.06	1.16	1.22	1.88	1.39	2.28	1.38	**2.45**$^\diamond$
Median	1.00	0.93	0.98	1.59	1.20	1.80	1.04	1.03	1.10	1.60	1.24	1.96	1.23	**2.05**$^\diamond$

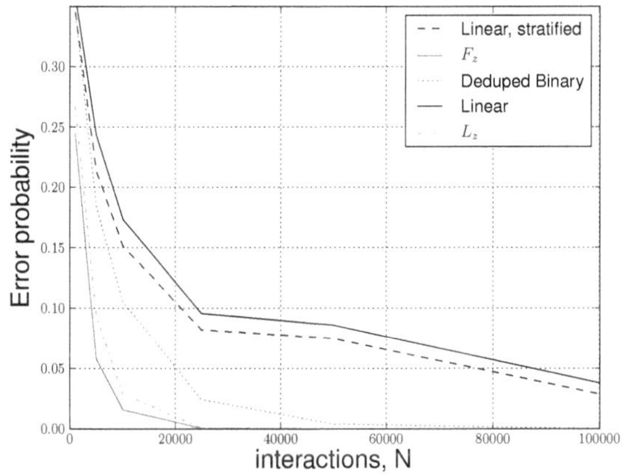

Figure 1: The probability that an interleaving method disagrees with the true preference, depending on the size of the sample.

1.10, respectively. Noticeable improvements are obtained for all of the considered baseline schemes, except for Deduped, where the improvement is small. Interestingly, a considerable improvement is also observed for L_z: its stratified modification L^s_z exhibits a median relative z-score of 1.96, while L_z has a median z-score of 1.80. This level of improvement is roughly comparable to the difference between the best heuristic baseline (Deduped, median relative z-score 1.59) and the best machine-learned baseline (L_z, median relative z-score 1.80) in the non-stratified case.

In all cases, the credit assignment function that optimizes the mean difference between A and B performs worse the credit assignment functions learned to maximize the z-score. For instance, L^s_z demonstrates considerably higher median relative confidence than L^s_m (1.96 vs 1.24).

By additionally performing the interleaving policy optimization, F_z achieves a considerable sensitivity gain in comparison with the stratified L^s_z (F_z, 2.05 vs L_z, 1.96). This gain is roughly similar to the difference between performance obtained by performing stratification (L_z, 1.80 vs L^s_z, 1.96). F_z also achieves the highest overall sensitivity, with the median relative z-score of 2.05 and the mean z-score of 2.45. This implies that an interleaving experiment that uses the interleaving method F_z requires $2.05^2 = 4.20$ times less user interactions (in median) than the non-stratified Team Draft with the linear scoring to achieve the same level of confidence. In comparison with the best performing baseline, L_z, it requires $(\frac{2.05}{1.80})^2 = 1.30$ times less data to achieve the same level of confidence (in median).

Visualization We illustrate the relative performance of the studied interleaving methods on the document search dataset using the following procedure. We randomly select one experiment to be used as a test experiment, and use the remaining experiments to optimize the interleaving parameters. Further, we estimate the probability that an interleaving method disagrees with the ground truth preference in the test experiment by obtaining 10,000 samples of N user interactions. We varied N in $(10^3, ..., 10^5)$. For the baseline methods, N interactions are obtained by sampling from the experiment's interactions with replacement (bootstrap sampling). For F_z, the sample is obtained by firstly allocating N interactions to the strata according to multinomial distribution specified by the policy π, and further sampling from the individual strata (with replacement). The outcome is calculated using the stratified estimate Δ_e. This sampling process simulates the case of policy π to be applied in a real-life scenario. The stratified modification of *Linear* differs from *Linear* only by using the stratified estimate of the outcome, Δ_s instead of the sample mean Δ. A higher error probability indicates lower sensitivity and it is related to the outcome's p-value under the bootstrap test.

In Figure 1, we report the obtained error probabilities. From Figure 1 we observe that the optimization-based methods (F_z and L_z) dramatically increase the interleaving sensitivity and outperform *Linear*, stratified *Linear*, and *Deduped* by a considerable margin. For instance, the probability error of 0.05 is achieved by F_z with less than 10,000 interactions, but *Linear* requires about 90,000 interactions to achieve the same level of error. Among the methods that use optimization, F_z consistently demonstrates lower probability of error than L_z. For instance, when 5,000 interactions is used, F_z has the probability of error below 0.06, while L_z makes an error in more than 0.09 of the samples. Further, we observe that the performance of *Linear* is noticeably improved by adding stratification. Overall, these observations are in line with results reported in Table 4. However, this illustration is also important as it does not rely on the z-score statistic.

10.2 Image Search

In Table 5 we report the results of the evaluation for the case of image search. Generally, we observe the results similar to the document search case. The machine-learned interleaving methods that optimize the z-score objective (L_z, L^s_m, L^s_z, and F_z) outperform both the methods with the heuristic credit assignment (*Linear*, *NLinear*, *Binary*, and *Deduped*) and the methods that optimize the mean difference.

In contrast to the document search experiments, the sensitivity gains due to stratification are less noticeable on the image search data. A possible explanation is that the differences of the means of the strata are smaller than in the case of the document search. Indeed, if the users tend to examine most of the results (which is easier for images than for document snippets) and click more, then the teams of the first results is not such a strong indicator of the total credit in an interaction, as in the case of document search. Interestingly, *Deduped* is sensitive in image search, too.

The overall highest performance ($p < 0.05$) is achieved by our proposed framework with the z-score-based optimization objective (F_z, mean relative z-score 1.21, median 1.18). This value of the metric implies that our proposed framework requires $1.18^2 = 1.39$ less data (median) than the *Linear* baseline to achieve the same level of confidence. In comparison to the best-performing baseline L_z, the corresponding de-

Table 5: Relative confidence levels of the interleaving outcomes, image search. The scores of the interleaving method with the highest sensitivity ($p < 0.05$) are denoted by $^\diamond$.

	Non-stratified						Stratified							
	Linear	NLinear	Binary	Deduped	L_m	L_z	Linear	NLinear	Binary	Deduped	L^s_m	L^s_z	F_m	F_z
Mean	1.00	1.03	1.05	1.17	1.11	1.17	1.00	1.03	1.05	1.17	1.11	1.18	1.14	**1.21**$^\diamond$
Median	1.00	0.98	1.02	1.11	1.08	1.16	1.00	0.98	1.03	1.11	1.08	1.16	1.14	**1.18**$^\diamond$

crease is $(\frac{1.18}{1.16})^2 = 1.03$ in median. However, the difference of the means is higher (L_z, 1.18 vs F_z, 1.21). A possible explanation for the smaller improvements is that the degradations used in our image search dataset are relatively strong and easy to detect, thus it is harder achieve a high level of improvement over the baselines.

Summary Our evaluation study allows us to answer the research questions we stated in Section 9. Our proposed framework achieves the highest sensitivity on both the document search and the image search datasets (RQ1). On the document search data, each of the proposed sensitivity optimization aspects contributes to the increased performance the credit optimization. Indeed, the non-stratified optimized interleaving method L_z (median, 1.80) outperforms best of the non-learned baselines (*Deduped Binary*, 1.59). In turn, the stratified method L^s_z has even higher performance (1.96). Further, our proposed F_z additionally performs the policy optimization and achieves the highest median relative confidence level (2.05). In contrast, on the image search data the contribution of the stratification is small. However, gains in the sensitivity are still obtained by the credit assignment learning (L_z, 1.16 vs *Deduped*, 1.11) and the policy optimization (F_z, 1.18 vs L^s_z, 1.16). These observations answer RQ2: the credit assignment and the policy optimization increase the interleaving sensitivity on both datasets; our proposed stratification has higher impact on the interleaving sensitivity in the document search than in the image search domain.

11. CONCLUSION

In this work we address an important problem of improving of the interleaving sensitivity. We proposed an interleaving framework that generalizes the existing research in two aspects. First, it achieves an increased sensitivity by performing a joint optimization of the credit assignment function and the interleaving policy. Second, it is formulated to be general with respect to the way the results are presented, thus it can be applied in the domains with the grid-based representation, such as image search. Further, to simplify the optimization procedure, we proposed to use a stratified estimate of the experiment outcome. This stratification is useful on its own, as in some cases it reduces the variance of the experiment outcome and thus increases the sensitivity. Finally, we proposed a generalized unbiasedness requirement that the feature-based credit assignment and the interleaving policy have to meet for the interleaving to be unbiased.

In our evaluation study, we used two datasets of the Team Draft-based experiments obtained from a commercial search engine. The first dataset contains 67 interleaving experiments performed in the document search domain, and the second dataset contains 5 "data collection" experiments deployed for image search. In our study, we demonstrated that our proposed framework achieves the highest sensitivity on both datasets. Specifically, we observe that our framework requires up to 1.30 times (median) less data than the top-performing baseline on the document search dataset, and up to 1.03 times (median) less data on the image search dataset.

An interesting direction of future work is to apply our framework to other domains such as video search, and to incorporate a non-linear credit assignment function in our proposed framework.

Acknowledgements We thank Aleksandr Vorobev for his feedback on a draft of this paper.

12. REFERENCES

[1] S. Asmussen and P. W. Glynn. *Stochastic simulation: Algorithms and analysis*, volume 57. Springer Science & Business Media, 2007.

[2] O. Chapelle, T. Joachims, F. Radlinski, and Y. Yue. Large-scale validation and analysis of interleaved search evaluation. *ACM TOIS*, 30(1):6, 2012.

[3] A. Chuklin, A. Schuth, K. Hofmann, P. Serdyukov, and M. de Rijke. Evaluating aggregated search using interleaving. In *CIKM 2013*.

[4] A. Deng, Y. Xu, R. Kohavi, and T. Walker. Improving the sensitivity of online controlled experiments by utilizing pre-experiment data. In *WSDM 2013*.

[5] G. Dupret and M. Lalmas. Absence time and user engagement: evaluating ranking functions. In *WSDM 2013*.

[6] K. Hofmann, S. Whiteson, and M. de Rijke. A probabilistic method for inferring preferences from clicks. In *CIKM 2011*.

[7] T. Joachims. Optimizing search engines using clickthrough data. In *KDD 2002*.

[8] T. Joachims. Evaluating retrieval performance using clickthrough data. In J. Franke, G. Nakhaeizadeh, and I. Renz, editors, *Text Mining*. Physica/Springer Verlag, 2003.

[9] E. Jones, T. Oliphant, P. Peterson, et al. SciPy: Open source scientific tools for Python, 2001–.

[10] E. Kharitonov, C. Macdonald, P. Serdyukov, and I. Ounis. Using historical click data to increase interleaving sensitivity. In *CIKM 2013*.

[11] R. Kohavi, T. Crook, R. Longbotham, B. Frasca, R. Henne, J. L. Ferres, and T. Melamed. Online experimentation at microsoft. *Data Mining Case Studies*, page 11, 2009.

[12] R. Kohavi, A. Deng, B. Frasca, T. Walker, Y. Xu, and N. Pohlmann. Online controlled experiments at large scale. In *KDD 2013*.

[13] R. Kohavi, R. Longbotham, D. Sommerfield, and R. M. Henne. Controlled experiments on the web: survey and practical guide. *Data Mining and Knowledge Discovery*, 18(1), 2009.

[14] F. Radlinski and N. Craswell. Comparing the sensitivity of information retrieval metrics. In *SIGIR 2010*.

[15] F. Radlinski and N. Craswell. Optimized interleaving for online retrieval evaluation. In *WSDM 2013*.

[16] F. Radlinski, M. Kurup, and T. Joachims. How does clickthrough data reflect retrieval quality? In *CIKM 2008*.

[17] C. Robert and G. Casella. *Introducing Monte Carlo Methods with R*. Springer Science & Business Media, 2009.

[18] A. Schuth, F. Sietsma, S. Whiteson, D. Lefortier, and M. de Rijke. Multileaved comparisons for fast online evaluation. In *CIKM 2014*.

[19] E. Voorhees. The philosophy of information retrieval evaluation. In *Evaluation of Cross-Language Information Retrieval Systems*, LNCS, pages 355–370. 2002.

[20] Y. Yue, Y. Gao, O. Chapelle, Y. Zhang, and T. Joachims. Learning more powerful test statistics for click-based retrieval evaluation. In *SIGIR 2010*.

Exploiting Document Content for Efficient Aggregation of Crowdsourcing Votes

Martin Davtyan
Dept. of Computer Science
ETH Zurich, Switzerland
martin.davtyan@gmail.com

Carsten Eickhoff
Dept. of Computer Science
ETH Zurich, Switzerland
ecarsten@inf.ethz.ch

Thomas Hofmann
Dept. of Computer Science
ETH Zurich, Switzerland
thomas.hofmann@inf.ethz.ch

ABSTRACT

The use of crowdsourcing for document relevance assessment has been found to be a viable alternative to corpus annotation by highly trained experts. The question of quality control is a recurring challenge that is often addressed by aggregating multiple individual assessments of the same topic-document pair from independent workers. In the past, such aggregation schemes have been weighted or filtered by estimates of worker reliability based on a multitude of behavioural features. In this paper, we propose an alternative approach by relying on document information. Inspired by the clustering hypothesis of information retrieval, we assume textually similar documents to show similar degrees of relevance towards a given topic. Following up on this intuition, we propagate crowd-generated relevance judgments to similar documents, effectively smoothing the distribution of relevance labels across the similarity space.

Our experiments are based on TREC Crowdsourcing Track data and show that even simple aggregation methods utilizing document similarity information significantly improve over majority voting in terms of accuracy as well as cost efficiency.

Categories and Subject Descriptors

H.5 [**Information Retrieval**]: Evaluation of retrieval results—*Relevance assessment*;
H.4 [**World Wide Web**]: Web applications—*Crowdsourcing*

General Terms

Theory, Experimentation

Keywords

Crowdsourcing, Clustering Hypothesis, Relevance Assessment

Permission to make digital or hard copies of all or part of this work for personal or classroom use is granted without fee provided that copies are not made or distributed for profit or commercial advantage and that copies bear this notice and the full citation on the first page. Copyrights for components of this work owned by others than ACM must be honored. Abstracting with credit is permitted. To copy otherwise, or republish, to post on servers or to redistribute to lists, requires prior specific permission and/or a fee. Request permissions from Permissions@acm.org.

CIKM'15, October 19 - 23, 2015, Melbourne, VIC, Australia.
© 2015 ACM. ISBN 978-1-4503-3794-6/15/10 ...$15.00.
DOI: http://dx.doi.org/10.1145/2806416.2806460.

1. INTRODUCTION

Evaluation of retrieval performance is a crucial step in the overall IR system design process. In order to ensure frequent repeatability of tests, many researchers and practitioners rely on static test collections with known relevance judgments for pairs of topics and documents. The creation of such resources, especially at large scale, can require considerable amounts of time and money as an expensive group of trained domain experts carefully judges the relevance of individual pairs [29].

Crowdsourcing is defined as the practice of obtaining content from a large (typically, online) community, rather than from traditional employees. There are many ways in which individuals can be incentivized to offer their work force on crowd markets. While altruistic motives [3], community credibility [33], and entertainment [11] form valid motivating factors, paid crowd labour tends to be one of the most broadly applicable schemes. Crowdsourcing platforms such as CrowdFlower or Amazon's Mechanical Turk take the role of intermediaries between *requesters* and *workers*. Assignments are typically given out and paid for in the form of small, atomic units, so-called *Human Intelligence Tasks* (HITs). In the case of our IR evaluation scenario, making a single binary relevance assessment between a topic and a document can be considered a HIT.

Quality control is a traditional challenge that crowdsourcing requesters have to address when drawing from the considerable power of the crowd. While most workers attempt to truthfully complete tasks, there are frequent reports of workers showing sloppy or random judging behaviour in order to increase their time efficiency [10]. A widely accepted way of overcoming this obstacle is to present the same HIT to multiple workers and subsequently aggregate their submissions. To continue with our IR test collection creation example, each query-document pair is presented to multiple workers and its final relevance label is determined by means of an aggregation method such as interpolation or majority voting. For many tasks, including document relevance assessment, this practice has effects that go beyond mere filtering of spam submissions but can also account for subjective differences in judgments across workers.

Instead of uniformly merging raw votes, much work has been dedicated into estimating worker reliability based on their past accuracy, judging behaviour, or topic affinity. Subsequently, this form of worker information can be used to bias the aggregation process towards the most reliable workers or to empower active learning schemes in which the most suitable worker for each task is to be selected. There is, how-

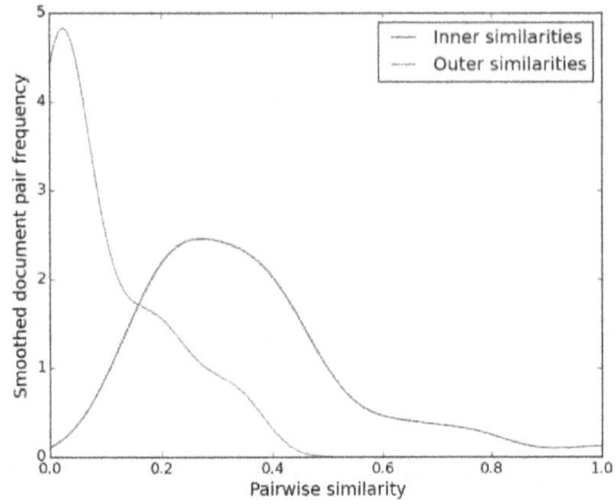

Figure 1: Gaussian kernel density estimate of the document similarity distribution for topic 20542

ever, another, largely untapped source of information, the document's content. For example, one could exploit similarities between documents to aggregate worker votes in an efficient manner.

Consider a cosine similarity between the tf–idf representations of documents. Figure 1 shows the distribution of similarities a) between relevant documents (inner similarities) and b) between relevant and irrelevant documents (outer similarities) for topic 20542 of the TREC Crowdsourcing Track 2011. We can clearly observe how relevant documents share much stronger commonalities than irrelevant ones. In this paper, we exploit this well-known *Clustering Hypothesis* by propagating relevance assessments to "nearby" neighbours for the purpose of vote aggregation.

The novel contributions of this paper are threefold: 1) We present a systematic overview of the spread of crowdsourced relevance labels across a textual similarity space, supporting the validity of the clustering hypothesis for label aggregation. 2) We introduce three content-aware vote aggregation methods. Beginning with light and moderate modifications to the standard majority voting approach, we finally describe the use of Gaussian process classification models for this purpose. 3) In a set of experiments based on historic submissions to the TREC 2011 Crowdsourcing Track, we demonstrate the merit of our methods in terms of cost-efficiency and accuracy in comparison to content agnostic methods.

The remainder of this paper is structured as follows: Section 2 gives an overview of related work dedicated to crowdsourced relevance assessments and quality control mechanisms. Section 3 formally introduces our methods and discusses relevant technical considerations. Our experimental setup and results are described in Section 4, before Section 5 concludes our investigation with a brief discussion of practical implications as well as future directions inspired by our findings.

2. RELATED WORK

Ever since the introduction of the Cranfield experiments [28], test collections have been one of the pillars of IR system evaluation. Traditionally, such collections are created by trained professionals in controlled lab environments. In the IR community, the Text REtrieval Conference (TREC) [29] supports one of the most widely known efforts to creating such collections. In the face of constantly growing demands in terms of test collection diversity and scale, there have been numerous attempts at reducing the considerable cost involved in corpus creation and annotation. Most notably, previous work proposes designing more robust performance measures [4], selecting the right subset of documents for evaluation [6] and inferring implicit judgments from user interaction logs [16].

With the rise of crowdsourcing, there has been an extensive line of research dedicated to using this new channel for the creation and annotation of IR test collections. An early set of experiments [21, 1, 20, 12] find that aggregated labels of multiple untrained crowd workers can reach a quality comparable to that of a single highly trained NIST assessor.

While this alternative labour market has been shown to be time and cost efficient [11], researchers have less control over the way in which relevance judgments are created. Traditionally, inaccurate judgments as well as spam submissions have been a major challenge in the crowdsourcing process. There are many effective quality control schemes, ranging from aggregating the results of independent workers to the use of honey pot questions [13, 15, 10]. Marshall et al. [24] highlight the importance of engaging HIT design on result quality. Active learning techniques have been demonstrated to greatly improve the worker-task allocation step [32].

Significant effort has been made into estimating worker reliability based on various behavioural and demographic traits. Tang and Lease [26] introduce a semi-supervised method for reliability estimation based both on labeled as well as unlabeled examples. Kazai et al. [18, 19] group workers into 5 different classes and study their respective judgment reliability and behaviour. Based on social media profiles, Difallah et al. [9] model worker topic affinities, enabling them to assign tasks to workers with matching interest, resulting in significantly improved result quality. Karger et al. [17] propose a joint model for iteratively learning worker reliability and aggregating votes by means of approximate belief propagation. Blanco et al. [2] investigate the robustness of crowdsourced relevance assessments over time, finding that repeated labeling efforts produce stable results even as longer periods of time elapse.

Another prominent source of evidence can be found in the analysis of systematic judgment behaviour. Following Dawid and Skene [8], who investigated disagreements between diagnoses posed by multiple individual medical doctors, there have been several successful attempts at harnessing similar methods for crowdsourcing quality assurance [30, 14]. In this way, reliable workers that make occasional mistakes can be accurately separated from spammers that select answers at random or follow other, more sophisticated, cheating strategies.

Several scientific workshops have been dedicated to pursuing how to use crowdsourcing effectively and efficiently [7, 23]. Most notably, TREC 2011 for the first time offered a dedicated crowdsourcing track [22], addressing the crowdsourced collection of document relevance assessments.

While previous approaches have been successfully using worker demographics and behaviour in order to predict judgment accuracy, in this paper, we propose to investigate the content of the documents being judged. Inspired by the clustering hypothesis of information retrieval [27], we assume similar documents to show similar degrees of relevance towards a given topic. Our experiments show significantly improved label aggregation performance at lower overall cost, when relying on this source of evidence.

3. METHODOLOGY

In this section, we formally introduce the problem statement alongside our proposed method. For each topic, there is a set documents D, that each require relevance labels. For every document $d_i \in D$, we can, via a crowdsourcing platform, request binary relevance judgments (votes) v_{ij}. Individual votes are encoded such, that $v_{ij} = 1$ denotes "relevance" and $v_{ij} = 0$ denotes "non-relevance" of the given topic-document pair. To account for errors or worker subjectivity in the creation of individual votes, a final processing step specifies vote aggregation methods to produce overall relevance labels $r_i \in \{0, 1\}$ on the basis of the the collected raw votes. For practical reasons, suppose that we can query the crowd for a worker vote on any document d_i at any given time. Crowdsourcing can then be represented as a process of iterative requesting of votes, where relevance labels can be aggregated at every step:

Algorithm 1 CROWDSOURCED RELEVANCE ASSESSMENT

```
for k ← 1...K do
    d_i ← PickDocument(ω)
    V_i ← V_i ∪ RequestVote(d_i)
    R ← AggregateVotes(ω, D)
end for
```

Where K delimits the number of iterations, taking the role of a budget parameter. V_i denotes the set of all raw votes v_{ij} requested for document d_i, ω is the super set of all currently requested votes across D and R is the set of all final relevance labels. There are three fundamental components to the generalized crowdsourcing-based relevance assessment process described in Algorithm 1. PICKDOCUMENT selects the next document to request a vote for. To this end, we randomly sample among those documents that currently received the lowest overall number of votes ($d_i = D(\arg\min(V_i))$), effectively introducing a weighted round robin scheduling. REQUESTVOTE details the exact procedure under which a new vote is requested (e.g., crowdsourcing platform, interface, gold standard, etc.). In this work, we rely on a large set of existing votes collected for the TREC 2011 Crowdsourcing Track [22] from which we randomly sample with replacement in order to obtain an infinite supply of votes.

Since the focus of our work resides on content-aware vote aggregation methods, we do not alter the remaining components in the course of our experiments. Please refer to Section 5 for a discussion of future work on content-aware active learning schemes that may indeed want to introduce alternative realizations of PICKDOCUMENT and REQUESTVOTE.

3.1 Tie Breaking

As stated earlier, we require aggregation methods to produce relevance labels for *all* documents at *every* iteration. As a consequence, there can be ties when:

- Some documents have not been judged by workers, leaving us without explicit evidence of relevance.
- The aggregation method received both positive and negative votes on document relevance, and is unable to decide. In case of standard majority voting, this can occur simply when the numbers of "relevant" and "non-relevant" votes for a document are equal.

These cases can be handled similarly for all proposed aggregation methods. In this work, we resolve ties by *selecting between "relevance" and "non-relevance" by tossing a fair coin.* Ideally, we would want to toss a biased coin informed by the underlying probability of relevance in the collection, but for the sake of realism, we assume the aggregation method to only have access to the subset of votes currently yielded by the crowdsourcing process. Since this assumption affects all proposed methods and baselines equally, we do not expect it to introduce any systematic bias towards favoring either of the methods. In fact, as we will see in Section 4, our experimental collection shows a near-uniform distribution of relevant and irrelevant documents.

3.2 Baseline: Majority Voting

As an intuitive performance baseline, we rely on the *de facto* standard in crowdsourcing vote aggregation [10], majority voting. Let us consider the set of votes V_i received for document d_i as a realization of a sequence of Bernoulli trials. If we denote the amount of "relevant" votes received for the topic-document pair as N_i,

$$N_i \sim Binomial(|V_i|, p_i)$$

Therefore p_i can be estimated as:

$$\widehat{p_i} = \frac{N_i}{|V_i|} = \overline{V_i}$$

Here we use a vertical bar to denote the arithmetic mean across all votes in the set. We can now present a Majority Vote aggregation function in an algorithmic form, see Algorithm 2.

Algorithm 2 MAJORITYVOTE

```
for all i ∈ I do
    if |V_i| = 0 then
        p̂_i ← 0.5
    else
        p̂_i ← mean(V_i)
    end if
end for
```

3.3 Document similarity

As stated earlier, the novel methods introduced in this work are based on the notion of similarity between textual documents. To this end, we represent each document d_i by its tf–idf vector $T(d_i)$ and define pairwise similarity between two documents d_a and d_b in terms of *cosine similarity* ρ between their vector representations:

$$\rho(d_a, d_b) = \frac{T(d_a) \cdot T(d_b)}{|T(d_a)||T(d_b)|},$$

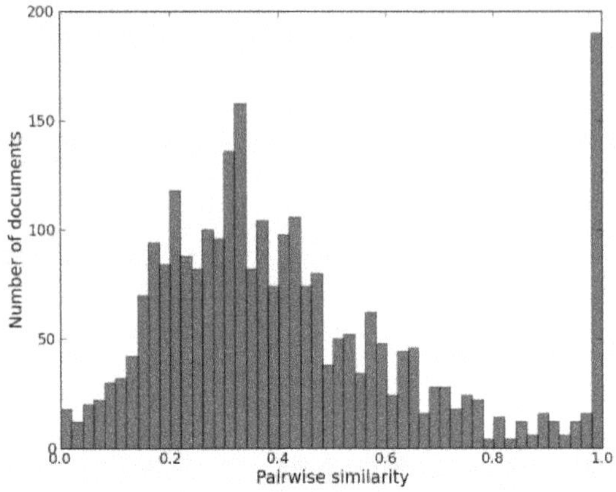

Figure 2: (Inner) Similarity between relevant documents averaged across queries.

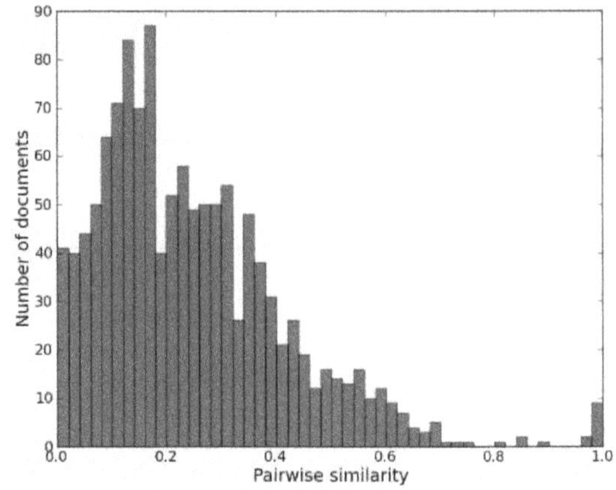

Figure 3: (Outer) Similarity between relevant and irrelevant documents averaged across queries.

where $|\cdot|$ denotes the Euclidean norm of a vector. Documents are processed as they are, without any form of vocabulary pruning, stop word removal, stemming etc. To validate our choice of distance metric for the task of separating relevant documents from irrelevant ones, let us first test the clustering hypothesis. We apply the method which was originally proposed by van Rijsbergen and Spärck Jones [27] for identifying document collections for which retrieval could yield meaningful results. We consider a set $D_r \subset D$ of documents which are relevant to a particular topic and compute two sets of pairwise similarities:

1. "Inner" similarities $S_I = \{\rho(d_u, d_v)|d_u, d_v \in D_r\}$ - similarities between relevant documents.
2. "Outer" similarities $S_O = \{\rho(d_u, d_v)|d_u \in D_r, d_v \notin D_r\}$ - similarities between relevant documents and irrelevant ones.

Our investigation is based on the ClueWeb09-T11Crowd collection, a subset of the full ClueWeb09 dataset [5], and uses NIST-created TREC 2011 Crowdsourcing Track topics and relevance judgments. We join these respective sets across all queries in the document collection and produce two histograms, where inner and outer similarities are plotted against their relative frequency in corresponding joined sets. The results are shown in Figures 2 and 3.

The separation between the two histograms supports the clustering hypothesis and justifies our choice of document similarity metric. In Figure 2 one can see the spike indicating there is a relatively high number of document pairs with similarities close to 1. Manual inspection of some randomly selected pairs hints that these could be Wikipedia pages redirecting to one common page, which differ only in the "Redirected from" header. The presence of such near duplicates in the dataset may pose problems in performance estimation. The aggregation methods we propose attempt to use relevance judgments from similar documents when aggregating final estimates. For pairs of documents which are very similar to each other this strategy is likely to be very successful. Hence, the fact that the dataset contains a significant amount of document pairs that are near duplicates means that the accuracy gain may be *overestimated*.

To investigate the effect of such document pairs with artificially high similarity scores, we manually inspect their distribution across the data. Queries "20694" and "20584" show the highest number of pairs close to a similarity of 1. One could argue that such topics are outliers and should be disregarded. However, even after removing these topics, there is no noticeable change to the spiking behaviour or the overall pattern. Hence, we do not consider these topics outliers, rather, having a number of near-duplicate documents appears to be a specific population property of a sizeable Web document collection.

3.4 Aggregation Methods

In the following, we will introduce three content-aware aggregation methods that serve as alternative realizations of the AGGREGATEVOTES component in Algorithm 1.

Majority Voting with Nearest Neighbor

Our first candidate method, Majority Voting with Nearest Neighbor (MVNN), is a straightforward extension of the baseline method that draws evidence from the single closest neighbor in tf-idf space. Consider a permutation $O^i = \{o^i(1) \ldots o^i(|I|)\}$ which sorts all documents by decreasing similarity to document d_i:

$$a, b \in I : a < b \rightarrow \rho(d_{o^i(b)}, d_i) \leq \rho(d_{o^i(a)}, d_i)$$

While $o^i(1) = i$ refers to the document itself, $o^i(2)$ is the index of the *closest neighbor* of document d_i. We then define a similarity threshold parameter $\rho_s \in [0, 1]$ to control for topical drift. Algorithm 3 details the aggregation algorithm that for every document d_i merges votes V_i with all votes $V_{o^i(2)}$ requested for its single nearest neighbor $d_{o^i(2)}$ if that neighbor's similarity to d_i is greater than ρ_s. In this way, we locally smooth relevance labels across the tf–idf space.

Merging Enough Votes

As an extension to the previous method, we would like to use evidence from multiple neighbors instead of just one. For example, such an extension could define the number of neighbors to consider as an additional parameter. Additionally, we may even want to vary the amount of neighbors

Algorithm 3 MAJORITYVOTEWITHNEARESTNEIGHBOR

```
Parameters: similarity threshold ρ_s
for all i ∈ I do
    if |V_i| = 0 then
        p̂_i ← 0.5
    else
        if ρ(d_i, d_{o^i(2)}) > ρ_s then
            p̂_i ← mean(V_i ∪ V_{o^i(2)})
        else
            p̂_i ← mean(V_i)
        end if
    end if
end for
```

employed in the aggregation for a particular document depending on the number of votes already requested. For documents which did not yet receive many votes, we rely more heavily on votes in the neighborhood. We formalize this intuition by requiring a desired overall amount of votes per document rather than explicitly fixing the number of neighbors as a parameter. If the document has less votes than required, we merge votes with the closest neighbors until the required vote count is reached. This Merge Enough Votes (MEV) strategy is preferable since it ensures comparable amounts of information to be used in the label aggregation of each document, even if this requires relying on a wider neighborhood. See Algorithm 4:

Algorithm 4 MERGEENOUGHVOTES

```
Parameters: votes per document required C
for all i ∈ I do
    U_i ← V_i
    if |U_i| < C then
        for k = 2...|I| do
            U_i ← U_i ∪ V_{o^i(k)}
            if |U_i| ≥ C then
                break
            end if
        end for
    end if
    p̂_i ← mean(U_i)
end for
```

Gaussian Process Aggregation

In this work, we aim to improve the aggregation of crowdsourced relevance votes by utilizing the similarity between documents in content space. The previously proposed heuristic methods (MVNN and MEV) achieve this by incorporating votes from a number of highly similar neighboring documents.

Gaussian process classification [31] is a well-known discriminative method, in which labels are inferred by modeling "similarity" of points in a feature space. We use this method to utilize votes available for *all* documents, as opposed to just immediate neighbors. To consider the GP classification method a formal extension of the proposed heuristics, we rely on the same notion of similarity, Cosine similarity between the tf–idf vectors becomes our *linear* covariance function in tf–idf space.

We specify the Gaussian process with a constant mean function and a linear covariance function:

$$m(x) = c,$$

$$k(x, x') = x \cdot x',$$

where $\cdot$ denotes a scalar product. We train a GP classifier on a set P of all available (document, vote) pairs, where the tf–idf representation of a document $T(d_i)$ becomes our feature vector, with the raw binary vote $v \in \{0, 1\}$ as the class label. We then retrieve posterior probabilities of relevance $\widehat{p_i}$ for all documents in a topic. Algorithm 5 illustrates this process. The exact inference for the posterior Gaussian Process is not feasible, hence an approximate solution is found using an expectation propagation algorithm [25] with cumulative Gaussian likelihood function. The only calculated hyperparameter is the constant mean c.

Algorithm 5 GAUSSIANPROCESSAGGREGATION

```
P ← ∅
for all i ∈ I do
    for all v ∈ V_i do
        P ← P ∪ (T(d_i), v)
    end for
end for
GPClassifier.train(P)
for all i ∈ I do
    p̂_i ← GPClassifier.posterior(T(d_i))
end for
```

4. EXPERIMENTS

In this section, we describe our experimental collection alongside the evaluation strategy and compare the performance of the individual methods. We show that content-aware aggregation methods attain the goal of outperforming content-agnostic approaches such as majority voting.

4.1 Data

The TREC Crowdsourcing Track [22], hosted between 2011 and 2013, is dedicated to investigating the use of crowdsourcing for search engine evaluation. In 2011, participating teams were offered two tasks:

1. *Assessment*, in which participants are to gather individual relevance judgments through a crowdsourcing platform.
2. *Consensus*, in which teams have to perform *label aggregation* over a set of individual worker judgments to produce a final overall relevance label.

The consensus task is highly relevant to the vote aggregation problem addressed here. In 2012 and 2013 tracks, there was no explicit separation between assessment and aggregation. Therefore, in this paper, we adopt the data and evaluation procedure from the Crowdsourcing Track 2011 and focus on the problem setting of the consensus task. The ClueWeb09-T11Crowd collection is a subset of the full ClueWeb09 dataset [5]. Every document in the collection is a uniquely identified Web page represented by the page

URL, the full page text, comparable to what a user would see when opening the page in a browser, the HTML code of the page alongside the HTML header. Out of this information, we only use the full page text. Although structural information contained in the HTML code could be potentially useful in the future, that sort of application would require a different choice of similarity metric.

We use the original *relevance judgments* submitted by TREC 2011 participants. They were given for 30 different topics, such as "free email directory" or "growing tomatoes". For every topic, there is a set of approximately 100 documents. For every document there are on average 15 relevance judgments from individual workers, although some topic-document pairs have fewer affiliated judgments. For two topics (20644 and 20922) there were documents with as few as one single vote. Since such singleton "pools" of votes are very brittle and make for a poor representation of human knowledge, we exclude these two outlier topics from our investigation, leaving us with 28 functional ones.

In the 2011 Crowdsourcing Track evaluation was based on two benchmark annotations, expert judgments from NIST assessors as well as aggregated consensus labels gathered across all participating teams. In this work, we solely rely on data from the NIST assessors as ground truth. It consists of 395 relevance judgments and most topics contain ten to twenty documents with such ground truth labels. After the track participants submitted the aggregated judgments they were evaluated using the benchmark sets. For every submission precision, recall, accuracy and specificity were measured. For the available ground truth labels, both relevance classes have similar orders of magnitude – 68% of 395 labels are "relevant". While the "relevant" class is larger across all topics, there is only one case in which it represents as much as 80% of labels. We therefore concentrate on accuracy as a performance measure, since, in our case, it is expressive of the classifier's performance.

The average differences between the ground truth judgment and the majority vote estimate for a document vary from topic to topic. Averaged across topics the difference is 0.15 (on a scale from -1 to 1). Intuitively, this indicates that the worker judgments aggregated with majority voting are a reasonable estimate of the true relevance and indeed provide a meaningful baseline for our methods. Nevertheless, for four topics the average difference exceeds 0.30, for one of them (20922) reaching the value of 0.55. For these topics it appears less likely to attain a reasonable accuracy with any aggregation method due to the low overall agreement between crowd and experts.

4.2 Results

Our experimental setup is based on the general iterative crowdsourcing procedure presented in Algorithm 1. At each step, one of the documents with the least amount of votes is sampled at random and a vote is requested. Since we work with a stale collection of votes, we sample with replacement from the pool of raw votes submitted for document d_i to prevent running out of votes in case of sparsely-annotated topics. We measure accuracy of aggregated relevance estimates at every step. Optimal settings of MVNN ($C = 0.5$) and MEV($\rho_s = 1.0$) parameters were determined empirically in a dedicated set of experiments while Gaussian process hyperparameter c is determined within each learning iteration. Figure 4 displays aggregation performance as a function of the number of votes per document within a given topic. Each plotted performance measurement represents the mean accuracy across 50 sampling randomizations of the crowdsourcing process. Within each randomized run, the individual methods are evaluated on the exact same realizations of the various sampling processes in order to ensure comparability of our findings.

There are several interesting trends to be observed. MVNN closely follows the performance curve of the majority voting baseline. While less than 2 votes per document are requested, the neighborhood information introduces a slight performance gain that levels out and is eventually reversed as more document-specific votes are procured. GP and MEV start at a significant performance offset, yielding significant improvements when only few votes are requested. With every additional requested vote,we can note the relative advantage of both methods shrinking. While MEV maintains a narrow lead, GP performance eventually dwindles. At approximately three votes per document, all methods reach a stable accuracy level of approximately 0.75 which is not significantly improved by further votes. This finding is in line with previous observations, made, e.g., by Vuurens et al. [30], who find that requesting more than three votes on average does not improve labelling performance. We believe that the observed method ranking stems from the particular scope at which neighborhood information is considered by the individual methods. MV shows the steepest performance increase, drawing new information from every new vote. MVNN has an initial advantage by using the single closest neighbor for smoothing. As sufficiently many local votes are available, this smoothing effect, however, begins to turn into noise. Gaussian processes use the widest neighborhood range, drawing from *all* available labels which results in a very strong early performance, but serves for noisy labels later on. MEV offers a good trade-off between strong early performance and good noise robustness since it effectively defaults back to local majority voting as soon as more local votes are available.

In this work, we focus especially on the extremely low-budget scenario in which aggregation effectiveness is subjected to tight cost-efficiency bounds. Settings like these are frequently encountered when large-scale problems are studied. To get a better impression of the relative comparison between the four methods as votes are scarce, Table 1 investigates aggregation performance per topic at a cut-off of 1 vote per document. It should be noted that in this particular case, majority voting (MV) defaults to the case where the single requested crowd label is believed to be true for every document. Statistically significant improvements over the content-agnostic baseline MV are denoted by an asterisk character. Methods that outperform *all* competitors at significance level are indicated by a hash symbol. Statistical significance was tested using a Wilcoxon signed rank at $\alpha < 0.05$-level. Again, all presented results are mean values across 50 randomizations.

We can note that in the extremely resource-constrained setting, the wide-coverage neighborhood model used by GP performs best. Out of 28 topics, the method yields the highest overall accuracy in 18 cases, often significantly outperforming all competing methods. MEV is the runner-up with 8 overall best accuracies. MVNN typically introduces only mild improvements over the majority voting baseline, few of which turn out to be statistically significant.

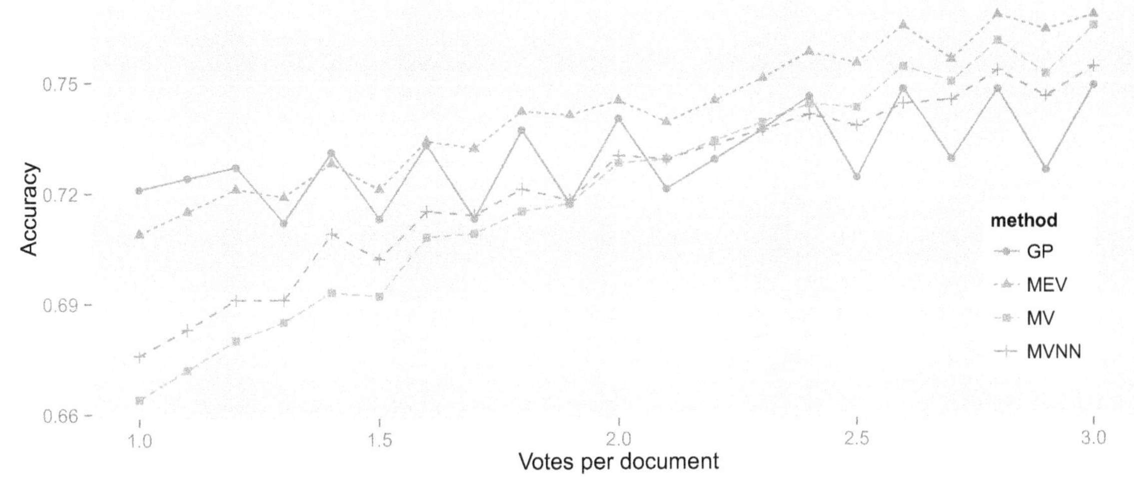

Figure 4: Aggregation performance across topics

Table 1: Performance comparison in terms of accuracy at 1 vote per document for each topic.

Topic	MV	MVNN(0.5)	MEV(1)	GP
20424	0.594	0.608	0.602	**0.702**$^{\#}$
20488	0.667	0.722	0.744*	**0.792**$^{\#}$
20542	0.676	0.673	0.707	**0.720***
20584	0.689	0.761*	0.793*	**0.856**$^{\#}$
20636	0.716	0.774*	**0.784**$^{\#}$	0.712
20642	0.693	0.756*	0.789*	**0.877**$^{\#}$
20686	**0.693**	0.639	0.665	0.688
20690	0.703	0.744*	0.766*	**0.830**$^{\#}$
20694	0.726	0.746	0.783*	**0.801***
20696	0.562	0.622*	0.634*	**0.734**$^{\#}$
20704	0.670	0.790*	0.804*	**0.942**$^{\#}$
20714	0.808	0.818	0.868*	**0.884***
20764	**0.676**	0.600	**0.676**	0.448
20766	0.796	0.794	**0.852***	0.846*
20778	0.652	0.662	0.654	**0.694**
20780	0.641	0.732*	0.761*	**0.771***
20812	0.688	0.695	**0.740***	0.727*
20814	0.792	0.770	0.858*	**0.906**$^{\#}$
20832	0.630	0.642	**0.658**	0.656
20910	0.661	0.643	**0.707**$^{\#}$	0.681
20916	0.650	0.638	0.628	**0.706**$^{\#}$
20932	0.576	0.540	0.577	**0.696**$^{\#}$
20956	0.616	0.646	0.666*	**0.824**$^{\#}$
20958	0.610	0.556	0.636	**0.638**
20962	0.552	0.610*	0.596*	**0.622***
20972	0.668	0.632	**0.692**	0.492
20976	0.632	0.620	**0.676**$^{\#}$	0.616
20996	**0.542**	0.504	0.534	0.326
Overall	0.664	0.676	0.709*	**0.721***

5. DISCUSSION & CONCLUSION

In this paper, we demonstrated the use of document similarity information for aggregating crowdsourced relevance assessments. Following the intuition that textually similar documents should show similar degrees of relevance towards a given query, we propagate crowdsourced relevance judgements across documents in order to infer the relevance of those documents that have not yet received (enough) explicit votes. In a series of experiments based on the data and guidelines of the TREC 2011 Crowdsourcing Track, we show that even straight-forward methods informed by document similarity estimates significantly outperform commonly used majority voting schemes in terms of both label accuracy as well as cost efficiency.

We investigated three novel aggregation schemes relying on varying scopes of neighborhood information. Gaussian process classification considers the full available set of all votes, resulting in competitive performance in cold-start scenarios with very few available votes. The two heuristics MVNN and MEV are more conservative in their use of neighborhood information, relying on fewer, highly similar neighbors, making them suitable for resource-rich scenarios in which many raw votes are available for every document.

A particular caveat when using methods like these lies in the danger of biasing the created labels too strongly towards the same intuition underlying common retrieval systems (i.e., tf–idf locality of relevant documents). While this is a valid concern, we believe that it can easily be controlled for by making only careful use of local neighborhood information instead of long-distance propagation of relevance labels.

There are several exciting directions for future work. In this paper, we rely solely on document information, ignoring evidence of worker reliability. In the future it would be interesting to investigate to which degree these orthogonal sources of information can be joined to increase overall performance. Currently, our method does not include any active selection of documents to request votes for next. It would be interesting to holistically model all documents to be evaluated for a given topic and carefully select which concrete documents to require judgements for in an active learning scheme such that the entire system is benefitted most.

6. REFERENCES

[1] Omar Alonso, Daniel E Rose, and Benjamin Stewart. Crowdsourcing for relevance evaluation. In *ACM SigIR Forum*, volume 42, pages 9–15. ACM, 2008.

[2] Roi Blanco, Harry Halpin, Daniel M Herzig, Peter Mika, Jeffrey Pound, Henry S Thompson, and Thanh Tran Duc. Repeatable and reliable search system evaluation using crowdsourcing. In *Proceedings of the 34th international ACM SIGIR conference on Research and development in Information Retrieval*, pages 923–932. ACM, 2011.

[3] Daren C Brabham. Moving the crowd at threadless: Motivations for participation in a crowdsourcing application. *Information, Communication & Society*, 13(8):1122–1145, 2010.

[4] Chris Buckley and Ellen M Voorhees. Retrieval evaluation with incomplete information. In *Proceedings of the 27th annual international ACM SIGIR conference on Research and development in information retrieval*, pages 25–32. ACM, 2004.

[5] Jamie Callan, Mark Hoy, Changkuk Yoo, and Le Zhao. Clueweb09 data set, 2009.

[6] Ben Carterette, James Allan, and Ramesh Sitaraman. Minimal test collections for retrieval evaluation. In *Proceedings of the 29th annual international ACM SIGIR conference on Research and development in information retrieval*, pages 268–275. ACM, 2006.

[7] Vitor R Carvalho, Matthew Lease, and Emine Yilmaz. Crowdsourcing for search evaluation. In *ACM Sigir forum*, volume 44, pages 17–22. ACM, 2011.

[8] Alexander Philip Dawid and Allan M Skene. Maximum likelihood estimation of observer error-rates using the em algorithm. *Applied statistics*, pages 20–28, 1979.

[9] Djellel Eddine Difallah, Gianluca Demartini, and Philippe Cudré-Mauroux. Pick-a-crowd: tell me what you like, and i'll tell you what to do. In *Proceedings of the 22nd international conference on World Wide Web*, pages 367–374. International World Wide Web Conferences Steering Committee, 2013.

[10] Carsten Eickhoff and Arjen P de Vries. Increasing cheat robustness of crowdsourcing tasks. *Information retrieval*, 16(2):121–137, 2013.

[11] Carsten Eickhoff, Christopher G Harris, Arjen P de Vries, and Padmini Srinivasan. Quality through flow and immersion: gamifying crowdsourced relevance assessments. In *Proceedings of the 35th international ACM SIGIR conference on Research and development in information retrieval*, pages 871–880. ACM, 2012.

[12] Catherine Grady and Matthew Lease. Crowdsourcing document relevance assessment with mechanical turk. In *Proceedings of the NAACL HLT 2010 workshop on creating speech and language data with Amazon's mechanical turk*, pages 172–179. Association for Computational Linguistics, 2010.

[13] Matthias Hirth, Tobias Hoßfeld, and Phuoc Tran-Gia. Cheat-detection mechanisms for crowdsourcing. *University of Würzburg, Tech. Rep*, 4, 2010.

[14] Mehdi Hosseini, Ingemar J Cox, Nataša Milić-Frayling, Gabriella Kazai, and Vishwa Vinay. On aggregating labels from multiple crowd workers to infer relevance of documents. In *Advances in information retrieval*, pages 182–194. Springer, 2012.

[15] Panos Ipeirotis. Crowdsourcing using mechanical turk: quality management and scalability. In *Proceedings of the 8th International Workshop on Information Integration on the Web: in conjunction with WWW 2011*, page 1. ACM, 2011.

[16] Thorsten Joachims. Optimizing search engines using clickthrough data. In *Proceedings of the eighth ACM SIGKDD international conference on Knowledge discovery and data mining*, pages 133–142. ACM, 2002.

[17] David R Karger, Sewoong Oh, and Devavrat Shah. Budget-optimal task allocation for reliable crowdsourcing systems. *Operations Research*, 62(1):1–24, 2014.

[18] Gabriella Kazai, Jaap Kamps, and Natasa Milic-Frayling. Worker types and personality traits in crowdsourcing relevance labels. In *Proceedings of the 20th ACM international conference on Information and knowledge management*, pages 1941–1944. ACM, 2011.

[19] Gabriella Kazai, Jaap Kamps, and Natasa Milic-Frayling. An analysis of human factors and label accuracy in crowdsourcing relevance judgments. *Information retrieval*, 16(2):138–178, 2013.

[20] Gabriella Kazai and Natasa Milic-Frayling. On the evaluation of the quality of relevance assessments collected through crowdsourcing. In *SIGIR 2009 Workshop on the Future of IR Evaluation*, page 21, 2009.

[21] Aniket Kittur, Ed H Chi, and Bongwon Suh. Crowdsourcing user studies with mechanical turk. In *Proceedings of the SIGCHI conference on human factors in computing systems*, pages 453–456. ACM, 2008.

[22] Matthew Lease and Gabriella Kazai. Overview of the trec 2011 crowdsourcing track. In *Proceedings of the text retrieval conference (TREC)*, 2011.

[23] Matthew Lease and Emine Yilmaz. Crowdsourcing for information retrieval. In *ACM SIGIR Forum*, volume 45, pages 66–75. ACM, 2012.

[24] Catherine C Marshall and Frank M Shipman. The ownership and reuse of visual media. In *Proceedings of the 11th annual international ACM/IEEE joint conference on Digital libraries*, pages 157–166. ACM, 2011.

[25] Thomas P. Minka. Expectation propagation for approximate bayesian inference. In *Proceedings of the Seventeenth Conference on Uncertainty in Artificial Intelligence*, UAI'01, pages 362–369, San Francisco, CA, USA, 2001. Morgan Kaufmann Publishers Inc.

[26] Wei Tang and Matthew Lease. Semi-supervised consensus labeling for crowdsourcing. In *SIGIR 2011 workshop on crowdsourcing for information retrieval (CIR)*, 2011.

[27] Cornelis J van Rijsbergen and Karen Spärck Jones. A test for the separation of relevant and non-relevant documents in experimental retrieval collections. *Journal of Documentation*, 29(3):251–257, 1973.

[28] Ellen M Voorhees. The philosophy of information retrieval evaluation. In *Evaluation of cross-language information retrieval systems*, pages 355–370. Springer, 2002.

[29] Ellen M Voorhees, Donna K Harman, et al. *TREC: Experiment and evaluation in information retrieval*, volume 1. MIT press Cambridge, 2005.

[30] Jeroen Vuurens, Arjen P de Vries, and Carsten Eickhoff. How much spam can you take? an analysis of crowdsourcing results to increase accuracy. In *Proc. ACM SIGIR Workshop on Crowdsourcing for Information Retrieval (CIR'11)*, pages 21–26, 2011.

[31] Christopher KI Williams and Carl Edward Rasmussen. Gaussian processes for machine learning. *the MIT Press*, 2(3):4, 2006.

[32] Yan Yan, Glenn M Fung, Rómer Rosales, and Jennifer G Dy. Active learning from crowds. In *Proceedings of the 28th international conference on machine learning (ICML-11)*, pages 1161–1168, 2011.

[33] Yu Zhang and Mihaela van der Schaar. Reputation-based incentive protocols in crowdsourcing applications. In *INFOCOM, 2012 Proceedings IEEE*, pages 2140–2148. IEEE, 2012.

L2Knng: Fast Exact K-Nearest Neighbor Graph Construction with L2-Norm Pruning

David C. Anastasiu
University of Minnesota, Twin Cities
Minneapolis, USA
dragos@cs.umn.edu

George Karypis
University of Minnesota, Twin Cities
Minneapolis, USA
karypis@cs.umn.edu

ABSTRACT

The k-nearest neighbor graph is often used as a building block in information retrieval, clustering, online advertising, and recommender systems algorithms. The complexity of constructing the exact k-nearest neighbor graph is quadratic on the number of objects that are compared, and most existing methods solve the problem approximately. We present L2Knng, an efficient algorithm that finds the exact cosine similarity k-nearest neighbor graph for a set of sparse high-dimensional objects. Our algorithm quickly builds an approximate solution to the problem, identifying many of the most similar neighbors, and then uses theoretic bounds on the similarity of two vectors, based on the ℓ^2-norm of part of the vectors, to find each object's exact k-neighborhood. We perform an extensive evaluation of our algorithm, comparing against both exact and approximate baselines, and demonstrate the efficiency of our method across a variety of real-world datasets and neighborhood sizes. Our approximate and exact L2Knng variants compute the k-nearest neighbor graph up to an order of magnitude faster than their respective baselines.

Keywords

k nearest neighbor graph, similarity search, top-k, cosine similarity

1. INTRODUCTION

Computing the k-nearest neighbor graph (k-NNG) for a set of objects is a common task in fields such as information retrieval, clustering, recommender systems, and online advertising. For example, item-based nearest neighbor collaborative filtering algorithms recommend items (e.g., books or movies) to a user based on the k most similar items to each of the user's preferred items [16].

The task of computing the k-NNG is computationally expensive, requiring $O(n^2)$ similarity comparisons, given a set of n objects. As a result, current methods that tackle the problem focus on either pruning the similarity search space, or solving the problem approximately. Exact methods either rely on efficient index structures to limit computation to only those object pairs with non-zero similarities (e.g., *IDX* [21], *BMM* [9]) or on effective pruning techniques that enable efficient discovery of all object pairs with similarity above a threshold t, which is iteratively lowered until all objects have at least k neighbors (e.g., *SIM* [21]). Approximate methods employ heuristic strategies that aim to return a neighborhood that contains the majority of the *true neighbors*, i.e., those that would be found by an exhaustive search. These strategies include focusing on object pairs that share high-weight features (e.g., *Greedy Filtering* [21]) and iterative improvement of an initial random k-NNG by considering neighbors' neighbors as potential neighbors (e.g., *NN-Descent* [11]).

Permission to make digital or hard copies of all or part of this work for personal or classroom use is granted without fee provided that copies are not made or distributed for profit or commercial advantage and that copies bear this notice and the full citation on the first page. Copyrights for components of this work owned by others than ACM must be honored. Abstracting with credit is permitted. To copy otherwise, or republish, to post on servers or to redistribute to lists, requires prior specific permission and/or a fee. Request permissions from Permissions@acm.org.
CIKM'15, October 19–23, 2015, Melbourne, Australia.
© 2015 ACM. ISBN 978-1-4503-3794-6/15/10 ...$15.00.
DOI: http://dx.doi.org/10.1145/2806416.2806534.

Despite this extensive body of work, each of these two classes of methods have their limitations. Exact methods either do not rely on pruning, use computationally expensive pruning estimates, or repeat many similarity estimations in the search for the true minimum neighborhood similarity threshold across all neighborhoods. Approximate methods use candidate selection and comparison strategies that can lead to unnecessary similarity computations.

In this work, we introduce L2Knng, which solves the *exact* cosine similarity k-NNG construction problem efficiently by effectively pruning much of the similarity search space. We focus on input objects that are encoded by *sparse high-dimensional non-negative vectors*. Some examples include Web pages, and user/item profiles in a recommender system. In this context, *cosine similarity* has long been a standard comparison measure, especially in the fields of information retrieval [19] and text mining [14]. To solve the k-NNG construction problem, L2Knng first obtains an initial approximate solution by considering, for each query object, a set of candidates that are likely to be part of the final k-NNG. Then, using the approximate graph as a guide to prune the search space, L2Knng executes a neighbor search for each input object. We introduce several filtering methods specific to the problem at hand that successfully prune most objects that will not be part of the final k-NNG, resulting in few objects having their similarity to a query object computed in full. We evaluate our methods experimentally on a variety of real-world datasets and neighborhood sizes, against both exact and approximate baselines. We find that L2Knng can provide over an order of magnitude performance improvement over baselines.

The remainder of the paper is organized as follows. Section 2 introduces the problem and notation used throughout the paper. Section 3 summarizes existing approaches to solving the k-NNG construction problem. Section 4 introduces our methods for constructing the exact and approximate k-NNG. We describe our evaluation methodology in Section 5 and analyze experimental results in Section 6, and Section 7 concludes the paper.

2. DEFINITION & NOTATIONS

Let $D = \{d_1, d_2, \dots, d_n\}$ be a set of objects such that each object d_i is a (sparse) vector in an m dimensional feature space. We will use d_i to indicate the ith object, $\boldsymbol{d}_i$ to indicate the feature vector associated with the ith object, and $d_{i,j}$ to indicate the value (or weight) of the jth feature of object d_i.

We use the *cosine function* to measure vector similarity. To simplify the presentation of the algorithms, we assume that all vectors have been scaled to be of unit length ($||\boldsymbol{d}_i|| = 1, \forall d_i \in D$). Given that, the cosine between two vectors $\boldsymbol{d}_i$ and $\boldsymbol{d}_j$ is simply their dot-product, which we denote by $\text{dot}(\boldsymbol{d}_i, \boldsymbol{d}_j)$.

Given object d_i, its k nearest neighbors in D, denoted by N_{d_i}, is the set of objects in $D \setminus \{d_i\}$ whose similarity with d_i is the highest among all objects in $D \setminus \{d_i\}$. The k-NNG of D is a directed graph $G = (V, E)$ where vertices correspond to the objects and an edge (v_i, v_j) indicates that the jth object is among the k nearest neighbors of the ith object. An approximate k-NNG is one in which the k neighbors of each vertex do not necessarily correspond to the k most similar objects.

During its execution, our method keeps track of up to k neighbors in each object's neighborhood. We denote by the *minimum (neighborhood) similarity* σ_{d_i} the minimum similarity between object d_i and one of its current k neighbors. We say that a neighborhood is *improved* when its minimum similarity σ_{d_i} increases in value, and it is *complete* once all true neighbors that belong to a neighborhood have been added to it. Note that subsequently processed objects that have σ_{d_i} similarity with the query object will not be added to the neighborhood as they do not improve it.

An *inverted index* representation of D is a set of m lists, $\mathcal{I} = \{I_1, I_2, \ldots, I_m\}$, one for each feature. List I_j contains pairs $(d_i, d_{i,j})$, also called postings, where d_i is an indexed object that has a non-zero value for feature j and $d_{i,j}$ is that value. Postings may store additional information, such as the position of the feature in the given document or other statistics.

Given a vector $\boldsymbol{d}_i$ and a dimension p, we will denote by $\boldsymbol{d}_i^{\leq p}$ the vector $\langle d_{i,1}, \ldots, d_{i,p}, 0, \ldots, 0\rangle$, obtained by keeping the p leading dimensions in $\boldsymbol{d}_i$, which we call the *prefix* (vector) of $\boldsymbol{d}_i$. Similarly, we refer to $\boldsymbol{d}_i^{>p} = \langle 0, \ldots, 0, d_{i,p+1}, \ldots, d_{i,m}\rangle$ as the *suffix* of $\boldsymbol{d}_i$, obtained by setting the first p dimensions of $\boldsymbol{d}_i$ to 0. One can then verify that

$$\boldsymbol{d}_i = \boldsymbol{d}_i^{\leq p} + \boldsymbol{d}_i^{>p}, \text{ and}$$
$$\text{dot}(\boldsymbol{d}_i, \boldsymbol{d}_j) = \text{dot}(\boldsymbol{d}_i, \boldsymbol{d}_j^{\leq p}) + \text{dot}(\boldsymbol{d}_i, \boldsymbol{d}_j^{>p}).$$

Table 1 provides a summary of notation used in this work.

Table 1: Notation used throughout the work

	Description
D	set of objects
k	size of desired neighborhoods
$\boldsymbol{d}_i$	vector representing object d_i
$d_{i,j}$	value for jth feature in $\boldsymbol{d}_i$
$\boldsymbol{d}_i^{\leq p}, \boldsymbol{d}_i^{>p}$	prefix and suffix of $\boldsymbol{d}_i$ at dimension p
N_{d_i}	neighborhood for object d_i
σ_{d_i}	smallest similarity value in N_{d_i}
t_{d_j}	similarity threshold used when indexing d_i
$\mathcal{N}$	set of neighborhoods
$\hat{\mathcal{N}}$	set of initial approximate neighborhoods
$\mathcal{I}$	inverted index
it	minimum indexing threshold for indexed objects
μ	candidate list sizes
γ	number of neighborhood enhancement updates
δ	early neighborhood enhancement termination
ν	number of completion blocks

3. RELATED WORK

Relatively few k-NNG construction algorithms have been designed to address cosine similarity. Park et al. [21] describe *Greedy Filtering*, an approximate filtering-based approach which prioritizes computing similarities between objects with high weight features in common. After first reordering the dimensions of each vector based on their weight, in decreasing weight order, the algorithm builds a partial inverted index, which it uses to find candidates for each object. Candidates for an object d_i are those objects in the inverted index lists associated with the leading dimensions in $\boldsymbol{d}_i$, i.e., the prefix of $\boldsymbol{d}_i$. *Greedy Filtering* indexes enough of each vector's prefix as to lead to at least μ candidates for each object. After all prefixes are identified and the partial inverted index is constructed, *Greedy Filtering* computes pairwise similarities of objects in each inverted index list, which can lead to much more than μ similarity computations for each object, and repeated computations for pairs of objects with two or more common features in their prefixes.

In *NN-Descent*, Dong et al. [11] follow an iterative neighborhood improvement strategy based on the intuition that similar objects are likely to be found among the neighborhoods of objects in a query object's neighborhood. Starting with a randomly chosen initial k-NNG, they iteratively improve the graph by computing, for each object d_i, via a *local join*, pairwise similarities between d_i, objects in its neighborhood, and those objects that contain d_i in their neighborhoods. The neighborhoods of both objects participating in a similarity computation are updated with the result. They avoid duplication of effort between iterations by only allowing an object to participate in the local join if it has been added to some neighborhood in the last update. Sampling and early termination parameters provide a way to control the compromise between algorithm runtime and recall. However, *NN-Descent* computes $O(n \times k^2)$ object similarities in its first iteration. Furthermore, the algorithm does not provide a way to filter out candidates that are unlikely to improve the query object's neighborhood.

A number of k-NNG construction algorithms have been proposed for *metric spaces*, where we seek the k objects with the smallest metric distance from the query. Tree-based data structures are often used to facilitate partitioning the search space, allowing neighbor searches to be prioritized within grids close to the one the query object is in [5]. These types of methods have been shown effective in low dimensional spaces, but do not scale well as dimensionality increases.

Top-k document retrieval is a related problem from information retrieval, which has had many proposed solutions over the years. Most methods in this class have been designed for very large document collections, focused on minimizing and/or parallelizing operations needed to quickly answer fairly short input queries. Result sets are in most cases inexact. Some recent works use an in-memory inverted index and pruning, called *safe early termination*, to return the same result set as an exhaustive search [6, 9, 10, 22, 23]. One could then solve the exact k-NNG problem by executing n top-k queries with one of these methods, one for each of the input objects. In their Block-Max WAND (*BMW*) method [10], Ding and Suel use an augmented index structure, called a Block-Max index, which stores inverted lists as compressed blocks of postings, along with the maximum score that could be achieved given the values in the block postings. By using the block maximum scores for early termination, many blocks can be skipped, resulting in improved execution. Dimopoulos et al. [9] extended the work of Ding and Suel and designed several methods that take advantage of Block-Max type indexes. Among them, docID-oriented Block-Max Maxscore with variable block sizes (*BMM*) has been shown to outperform the others and several baselines (including *BMW*) for long queries. The method partitions the postings in each inverted list into blocks of equally-sized ID ranges, allowing fast look-up for the block a document's posting may be found in. Block sizes vary based on the number of postings in each list. For each block, *BMM* also keeps track of the maximum document ID and maximum score for any of the postings in the block. The *Maxscore* [24] algorithm described by Turtle and Flood is then adapted to use block maximum scores for early termination.

Locality Sensitive Hashing (LSH) [13,15] uses families of functions that hash *signatures* of similar objects to the same bucket with high probability. The objects in the buckets that a query object hashes to can be considered its neighbors. The similarity with a neighbor can then either be estimated by comparing the object signatures or computed exactly. Created initially to solve the top-k retrieval problem, LSH has been shown effective at solving the nearest-neighbor problem (1-NNG), but suffers from low recall as the required neighborhood size increases [10]. In this work, we specifically focus on results with high recall (at least 95%). Some recent LSH variations have tackled the k-NNG problem specifically (e.g., E2LSH [2] and DSH [12]), but focus on metric distance functions between objects, such as the Euclidean distance.

Another related problem is All-Pairs Similarity Search (APSS), or *similarity join*, which returns all object pairs in D with a similarity value of at least some threshold t. Bayardo et al. [4] proposed an initial algorithm to solve APSS which employed several strategies to prune the search space, based on a predefined object processing order. The majority of subsequently developed APSS methods [1,3,17] use the same framework as in their work. In the context of cosine similarity, Anastasiu and Karypis recently introduced *L2AP* [1], which has been shown to outperform all previous APSS methods by introducing tighter pruning bounds in each phase of the framework.

There have been a large number of top-k retrieval and approximate k-NN search methods designed for distributed or parallel architectures, which can be used to search Web-scale datasets. The focus in these methods are query objects outside the input set. In contrast, `L2Knng` is an in-memory serial method designed for the efficient construction of a k-NNG from the input set of objects. We leave parallel and distributed extensions as future work.

4. METHODS

The `L2Knng` algorithm consists of two distinct steps. In the first step, it uses a fast method that identifies, for each object, k similar objects that may not necessarily be the k nearest neighbors. In the second step, it scans over all the objects and progressively updates the k most similar objects of each object. Specifically, while processing an object d_i, which we call the *query*, `L2Knng` updates the k nearest neighbors of all previously processed objects by taking into account their similarity to the query object. At the same time, it updates the k most similar objects of the query object by considering its similarity to the preceding objects. Since the second step potentially considers all pairs of objects, the final set of the k most similar objects for each object are guaranteed to be their k nearest neighbors.

The key to `L2Knng`'s efficiency stems from the following: (i) It uses an index data structure that enables it to quickly find potential neighbors, while pruning some that do not have enough features in common with the object being indexed. (ii) When searching for neighbors, it uses several vector similarity theoretic bounds to filter out many of the potential neighbors found by traversing the index. (iii) It uses a block processing strategy, which leads to efficient traversal of the inverted index lists and additionally improves the effectiveness of the pruning bounds. (iv) Finally, the initial approximate k-NNG built in its first step is instrumental towards effective indexing and pruning in `L2Knng`.

4.1 Approximate graph construction

`L2KnngApprox` is the inexact k-NNG construction method used by `L2Knng` to build an initial approximate graph. It consists of two steps. First, it builds a set of initial neighborhoods, relying on the idea that *high-weight features count heavily towards the similarity of two vectors* [7,21]. Then, given that *an object's neighbor's neighbor is also likely their neighbor* [11,20], it iteratively enhances the k-NNG by looking for new candidates in each neighbor's neighborhood.

The first step is achieved as follows. For each object d_i, `L2KnngApprox` builds a list of up to μ ($\mu \geq k$) candidates, choosing among those objects that have features in common with d_i until there are no more features to check or μ candidates were found. It then computes the exact similarities of all candidates with d_i and adds the objects with the top k values to d_i's initial neighborhood.

The choice of candidate objects is crucial to obtaining an approximate graph that is close to the exact k-NNG. `L2KnngApprox` uses an inverted index to identify candidate objects with common features with d_i. As a heuristic way to prioritize high-weight common features, it sorts the features in each vector in decreasing weight order, and sorts each of the lists in the inverted index in decreasing order of feature weights. `L2KnngApprox` then traverses two index lists at a time, in decreasing order of their associated weights in $\boldsymbol{d}_i$. From the two lists, it chooses the candidate d_c with the higher prefix dot product, which is more likely to be a true neighbor.

In the second step, `L2KnngApprox` executes up to γ iterative neighborhood enhancement updates, in which, for each object d_i, its k neighbors are updated by taking into account its similarity to some of the objects that are neighbors of its neighbors. This is done as follows. For each object d_i, it traverses its neighborhood in decreasing order of d_i's neighbor similarities. Given some neighbor d_j, it then traverses its neighborhood, in decreasing order of d_j's neighbor similarities, to identify potential neighbors for d_i. Avoiding objects that are already in d_i's neighborhood or have d_i in their neighborhood, `L2KnngApprox` greedily chooses as candidates only those neighbor's neighbors d_k with a similarity value greater or equal than that between the query vector and its neighbor, $\text{sim}(\boldsymbol{d}_j, \boldsymbol{d}_k) \geq \text{sim}(\boldsymbol{d}_i, \boldsymbol{d}_j)$, and limits the size of the candidate list to be μ. `L2KnngApprox` then computes similarities between $\boldsymbol{d}_i$ and candidates, updating both relevant neighborhoods with the results. We use δ as an early termination parameter, stopping iterations early if less than $\delta \times k \times |D|$ neighborhood changes occurred in an update.

Our strategy for choosing candidates in the first step improves upon the work of Park et al. [21] by limiting, for each object, the number of computed similarities. High quality candidates are greedily chosen from few inverted index lists. The neighborhood enhancement step improves upon the work of Dong et al. [11] in two ways. First, it ensures an upper bound on the number of similarity computations and prioritizes those candidates more likely to improve the neighborhood. Second, the enhancement steps will probably converge faster and to higher recall, as the input neighbors likely have higher similarity values than the randomly chosen neighbors in their method.

4.2 Indexing

`L2Knng` uses information in the approximate k-NNG to prune some object pairs by indexing only a subset of the features in each object. In each iteration, `L2Knng` needs to identify among the previously processed objects those whose neighborhoods can be updated by including the *query* object d_i. In order to do this efficiently, it builds an inverted index incrementally, delaying the indexing of d_i until after its processing. However, future potential neighbors can only improve d_i's neighborhood if their similarity with d_i is higher than the minimum similarity in d_i's neighborhood, σ_{d_i}. In a similar context, Chaudhuri et al. [8] noted that, given a predefined feature order, one can stop indexing features in $\boldsymbol{d}_i$ as soon as they can ensure d_i will be found when processing future objects that have a greater similarity with d_i than σ_{d_i}. By indexing only the leading features of the query object, its prefix, those future objects with common features with d_i only in its suffix, which will not be able to improve its neighborhood, will not be encountered when traversing the index and will thus be automatically pruned.

L2Knng indexes objects until their suffix ℓ^2-norm falls below the minimum neighborhood similarity σ_{d_i}. Given that all vectors in the dataset have unit length, based on the Cauchy-Schwarz inequality, the suffix ℓ^2-norm of d_i is an upper bound of the similarity of d_i's suffix with any other object [1], including unprocessed objects in the set,

$$\text{dot}(\boldsymbol{d}_i^{>j}, \cdot) \leq ||\boldsymbol{d}_i^{>j}|| \times ||\cdot|| = ||\boldsymbol{d}_i^{>j}||.$$

Once the suffix norm $||\boldsymbol{d}_i^{>j}||$ falls below σ_{d_i}, if no common features were found between d_i and some object d_c within d_i's indexed prefix, then d_c cannot improve d_i's neighborhood, since,

$$\text{dot}(\boldsymbol{d}_i, \boldsymbol{d}_c) = \text{dot}(\boldsymbol{d}_i^{\leq j}, \boldsymbol{d}_c) + \text{dot}(\boldsymbol{d}_i^{>j}, \boldsymbol{d}_c) < 0 + \sigma_{d_i}.$$

The query object d_i must also be identified when processing future objects if d_i can improve their neighborhoods. Let t_{d_i} be the minimum neighborhood similarity for object d_i at the time of its indexing (*indexing threshold*), which later may be different than σ_{d_i}. Consider indexing an object d_i at a threshold t_{d_i} and then processing an object d_j with a smaller minimum neighborhood similarity. If $\sigma_{d_j} \leq \text{sim}(\boldsymbol{d}_i, \boldsymbol{d}_j) < t_{d_i}$, then d_i is no longer guaranteed to be found when processing d_j, and d_j's neighborhood may be inexact at the end of the algorithm execution. Therefore, to ensure correctness, objects must be indexed in a strictly non-decreasing indexing threshold order. L2Knng thus fixes the object processing order based on the minimum similarities in the initial approximate k-NNG it builds before processing objects.

Algorithm 1 Indexing in L2Knng

1: **function** INDEX($\boldsymbol{d}_i, \mathcal{I}, se, t_{d_i}$)
2: $\quad b \leftarrow 1$
3: $\quad$**for each** $j = 1, \ldots, m$, s.t. $d_{i,j} > 0$ **and** $\sqrt{b} \geq t_{d_i}$ **do**
4: $\quad\quad b \leftarrow b - d_{i,j} \times d_{i,j}$
5: $\quad\quad I_j \leftarrow I_j \cup \{(d_i, d_{i,j}, ||\boldsymbol{d}_i^{>j}||)\}$
6: $\quad$**end for**
7: $\quad se[d_i] \leftarrow ||\boldsymbol{d}_i^{>j}||$

Algorithm 1 details the indexing procedure in L2Knng. The prefix of a vector $\boldsymbol{d}_i$ is indexed while its suffix ℓ^2-norm, computed in b, is above or equal to our threshold t_{d_i} (lines 3-6). The suffix ℓ^2-norm at each indexed feature (line 5) and the suffix ℓ^2-norm of the un-indexed portion of $\boldsymbol{d}_i$ (*suffix estimate*, line 7) are also stored, to be used in other stages of the algorithm. We denote by $\boldsymbol{d}_i^{\leq}$ the indexed prefix of object d_i and by $\boldsymbol{d}_i^{>}$ its un-indexed suffix.

4.3 Pruning the search space

L2Knng searches for neighbors of an object in two stages. During the *candidate generation* stage, L2Knng computes prefix similarities by traversing the index, using an accumulator [19] to keep track of partial dot-products between the query and encountered objects. An accumulator is a map based data structure that accumulates values for given keys. Each object with non-zero accumulated value becomes a *candidate* and is added to a candidate list. Then, during *candidate verification*, L2Knng traverses the list of candidates and finalizes their similarity computations with the query, accumulating suffix similarities for each candidate. In the end, the accumulator will contain the exact similarity with each un-pruned candidate.

A computed similarity can only improve the neighborhood of a query object d_i if it is above σ_{d_i}. Furthermore, it can only improve neighborhoods of already processed objects if it is greater than the minimum of all neighborhood similarities of indexed objects. To keep track of this value, L2Knng could update a heap data structure each time the neighborhood of an indexed object is improved, but we have found this affects overall efficiency. Instead, L2Knng approximates this value by the minimum indexing threshold among all indexed objects, denoted by it, which is strictly smaller than the current minimum of all indexed objects' neighborhood similarities. Using a similar idea as during indexing, L2Knng only starts accumulating for an object d_c while the query suffix ℓ^2-norm is above the lower of these two bounds, $\min(it, \sigma_{d_i})$. Once the suffix ℓ^2-norm falls below this threshold, only index values for objects with non-zero accumulated partial dot-products are processed. Additionally, L2Knng uses the initial approximate k-NNG and the current version of the k-NNG to bypass already computed similarities.

During both the candidate generation and verification stages, there is a further opportunity for pruning when a common feature j is encountered between the query and candidate vectors. To be useful, the final similarity value should improve the neighborhoods of either the query or candidate objects. The accumulator contains the exact similarity of the two prefix vectors, and the similarity of the suffix vectors can be estimated, based on the Cauchy-Schwarz inequality, as upper bounded by the product of their suffix ℓ^2-norms [1]. Thus, a candidate can be pruned if

$$A[d_c] + ||\boldsymbol{d}_i^{>j}|| \times ||\boldsymbol{d}_c^{>j}|| < \min(\sigma_{d_i}, \sigma_{d_c}).$$

L2Knng employs one additional pruning strategy during the candidate verification stage. The $se[d_c]$ suffix estimate value that was stored when indexing the candidate d_c estimates the dot-product between the un-indexed portion of d_c and any other vector in the dataset, $\text{sim}(\boldsymbol{d}_c^{>}, \cdot)$. We use this value here as an estimate for the similarity between the query and candidate suffix, $\text{dot}(\boldsymbol{d}_i, \boldsymbol{d}_c^{>})$. If the sum of the accumulated score and the estimate falls below $\min(\sigma_{d_i}, \sigma_{d_c})$, the candidate is discarded.

Having presented the different pruning bounds used in L2Knng, note that their effectiveness would be greatly reduced without first computing the initial approximate k-NNG. First, indexing thresholds for unprocessed objects would be unknown, and L2Knng would have to index all object features, missing an important pruning opportunity. Similarly, during a search, the algorithm would have to consider all possible candidates with common features, as the minimum indexing threshold it would be 0. Finally, the minimum neighborhood similarities of previously processed objects would likely be smaller, leading to less object pairs being pruned and more neighborhood updates. While L2Knng does not require the initial approximate graph to be computed by L2KnngApprox, an initial graph with high recall will lead to more effective pruning and higher efficiency in constructing the exact graph.

Algorithm 2 delineates the procedure used to find neighbors in L2Knng. The variable r computes the suffix ℓ^2-norm of the query vector, which is used to prevent accumulating similarity for objects that cannot improve neighborhoods (line 6) in the candidate generation stage. At the end of the verification stage, the accumulator contains the exact similarity between the query and objects that survive pruning. These objects are added to the candidate or query neighborhoods if they can improve them.

4.4 Block processing

Algorithm 3 gives an overview of L2Knng. The initial approximate graph k-NNG ($\hat{\mathcal{N}}$, line 2) bootstraps the search framework, providing the necessary processing order for the main loop. As suggested by Bayardo et al. [4], we reorder dimensions in all vectors

Algorithm 2 Searching for neighbors in L2Knng

function FINDNEIGHBORS($\boldsymbol{d}_i, \mathcal{I}, se, it, \hat{\mathcal{N}}, \mathcal{N}$)
$r \leftarrow 1$; $A \leftarrow \varnothing$ ▷ accumulator
$A[d_c] \leftarrow \emptyset$ for neighbors d_c in $\hat{\mathcal{N}}$ and $\mathcal{N}$
for each $j = 1, \ldots, m$, s.t. $d_{i,j} > 0$ **do** ▷ candidate generation
for each $(d_c, d_{c,j}, ||\boldsymbol{d}_c^{\geq j}||) \in I_j$ **do**
if $A[d_c] > 0$ **or** $[A[d_c] \neq \emptyset$ **and** $\sqrt{r} \geq \min(it, \sigma_{d_i})]$ **then**
$A[d_c] \leftarrow A[d_c] + d_{i,j} \times d_{c,j}$
if $A[d_c] + ||\boldsymbol{d}_i^{>j}|| \times ||\boldsymbol{d}_c^{>j}|| < \min(\sigma_{d_i}, \sigma_{d_c})$ **then**
$A[d_c] \leftarrow \emptyset$
end if
end if
end for
$r \leftarrow r - d_{i,j} \times d_{i,j}$
end for
for each d_c s.t. $A[d_c] > 0$ **do** ▷ candidate verification
next d_c **if** $A[d_c] + se[d_c] < \min(\sigma_{d_i}, \sigma_{d_c})$
for each j s.t. $d_{c,j}^{>} > 0 \wedge d_{i,j} > 0$ **do**
$A[d_c] \leftarrow A[d_c] + d_{i,j} \times d_{c,j}$
if $A[d_c] + ||\boldsymbol{d}_i^{>j}|| \times ||\boldsymbol{d}_c^{>j}|| < \min(\sigma_{d_i}, \sigma_{d_c})$ **then**
next d_c
end if
end for
$N_{d_c} \leftarrow N_{d_c} \cup \{(d_i, A[d_c])\}$ **if** $A[d_c] > \sigma_{d_c}$
$N_{d_i} \leftarrow N_{d_i} \cup \{(d_c, A[d_c])\}$ **if** $A[d_c] > \sigma_{d_i}$
end for

Algorithm 3 The L2Knng Algorithm

function L2KNNG(D, k, μ, γ, δ, ν)
$\hat{\mathcal{N}} \leftarrow$`L2KnngApprox` ($D$, k, μ, γ, δ)
Reorder dimensions in non-decreasing object frequency order
$\mathcal{N} \leftarrow \hat{\mathcal{N}}$; $t_{d_i} \leftarrow \sigma_{d_i}$, $it \leftarrow \min(it, t_{d_i})$, **for** $i = 1, \ldots, n$
$I_j \leftarrow \varnothing$, $\mathcal{I} \leftarrow \mathcal{I} \cup I_j$, **for** $j = 1, \ldots, m$
for each $i = 1, 2, \ldots, n$ **s.t.** $t_{d_i} \leq t_{d_j}$, $\forall j > i$ **do**
FindNeighbors($\boldsymbol{d}_i, \mathcal{I}, se, it, \hat{\mathcal{N}}, \mathcal{N}$)
Index($\boldsymbol{d}_i, \mathcal{I}, se, t_{d_i}$)
$it \leftarrow$ CompleteBlock(i, $\mathcal{I}$, se, $\hat{\mathcal{N}}$, $\mathcal{N}$, ν) **if** $i \% \frac{|D|}{\nu} = 0$
end for
return $\mathcal{N}$

in non-decreasing object frequency order as a heuristic way to minimize the inverted index size.

The index keeps growing as more and more objects are processed. The minimum indexing threshold it defined by the initial k-NNG is likely very small, causing the majority of objects in the index to become candidates for each subsequent query. While many candidates will later be eliminated based on pruning bounds that take advantage of continuously updated neighborhood similarities, the delayed pruning can lead to slower execution. `L2Knng` improves the indexing threshold by periodically "flushing" the index. After completing the k-NNG construction for the already indexed objects, the index can be discarded, speeding up future candidate generation and providing an improved minimum indexing threshold it. Neighborhood construction can be finalized for a block of objects by executing *FindNeighbors* for all un-processed vectors, without indexing them. `L2Knng` then uses the updated minimum neighborhood similarities of unprocessed objects to define a new processing order. Given a number of blocks parameter ν, `L2Knng` finalizes a block of indexed objects after processing every $|D|/\nu$ objects.

4.5 L2Knng comparison with APSS

Many of the pruning schemes used by `L2Knng` are similar in nature with corresponding schemes that were developed to solve the all pairs similarity search (APSS) problem. However, there are a number of key differences between the solutions to the two problems. First, APSS seeks to prune object pairs with a similarity below a threshold t, while `L2Knng` filters those pairs that cannot improve k-neighborhoods. These distinct goals lead to very different pruning bounds in the two methods. The threshold t is an input to the APSS problem. In our problem, t could be chosen to be the minimum neighborhood similarity σ_{d_i} among all objects in the true k-NNG, which is unknown and would nonetheless be a sub-optimal choice for the k-NNG construction problem. Instead, we devise better thresholds, detailed in Sections 4.2 and 4.3, that can be used in each stage of the method to *safely* prune object pairs that cannot be a part of the true k-NNG. Second, the APSS solutions define an object processing order based on feature weights in each vector, which is not possible in our problem due to the absence of a common indexing threshold for all objects. `L2Knng` instead processes objects based on the minimum neighborhood similarities of an initial approximate graph, which ensures correctness and leads to higher pruning performance. Finally, we further improve performance by periodically finalizing a set of neighborhoods, which provides better pruning for unprocessed objects.

5. EXPERIMENTAL METHODOLOGY

In this section, we describe the datasets, baseline algorithms, and performance measures used in our experiments.

5.1 Datasets

Table 2: Dataset Statistics

Dataset	n	m	nnz	mrl	mcl
RCV1	804414	45669	62e6	76.5	1347.3
RCV1-400k	400000	45669	31e6	76.5	670.3
RCV1-100k	100000	45669	8e6	78.2	187.4
WW200	1017531	663419	437e6	429.9	659.4
WW500	243223	660600	202e6	830.3	305.7
WW200-250k	250000	663410	108e6	430.3	163.7

For each dataset, n is the number of vectors (rows), m is the number of features (columns), nnz is the number of non-zero values, and mrl and mcl are the mean row and column lengths (number of non-zeros).

We use six text-based datasets to evaluate each method. They represent some real-world and benchmark text corpora often used in text-categorization research. Their characteristics, including number of rows (n), columns (m), and non-zeros (nnz), and mean row/column length (mrl/mcl), are detailed in Table 2. Standard pre-processing, including tokenization, lemmatization, and *tf-idf* weighting, were used to encode text documents as vectors. We present additional details below.

- **RCV1** is a standard benchmark corpus containing over 800,000 newswire stories provided by Reuters, Ltd. for research purposes, made available by Lewis et al. [18].
- **RCV1-100k** and **RCV1-400k** are random subsets of 100,000 and 400,000 documents, respectively, from RCV1.
- **WW500** contains documents with at least 500 distinct features, extracted from the October 2014 article dump of the English Wikipedia[1] (Wiki dump).
- **WW200** contains documents from the Wiki dump with at least 200 distinct features.
- **WW200-250k** is a random subset of size 250,000 from WW200.

5.2 Baseline approaches

We compare our methods against the following baselines.

[1] http://download.wikimedia.org

- kIdxJoin is a straight-forward baseline similar to *IDX* in [21] that first builds a full inverted index. Then, without performing any pruning, it uses the index to compute exactly, via accumulation, the similarity of each object with all other objects in the set, returning the top-k matches for each query object.
- kL2AP solves the k-NNG problem by executing similarity searches using *L2AP* [1]. We modified *L2AP* to allow specifying a set of input query vectors. Then, as we iteratively reduce the search threshold t, we provide as input only those objects with incomplete neighborhoods.
- *BMM* refers to the docID-oriented with variable block sizes version of the Block-Max Maxscore method by Dimopoulos et al. [9]. The method splits inverted lists into blocks and uses maximum scores for postings in each block to prune the similarity search space. We adapted the method for cosine similarity ranking and chose the same block sizes as in their paper. Blocks were stored in compressed form, using PForDelta compression [25].
- *Maxscore* is an in-memory implementation of the *max_score* information retrieval algorithm [24], as described by Dimopoulos et al. in [9], adapted to rank based on cosine similarity.
- *Greedy Filtering* is a state-of-the-art approach for solving the approximate k-NNG construction problem applied to sparse weighted vectors, proposed by Park et al. [21].
- *NN-Descent* was designed by Dong et al. [11] to work with generic similarity measures and has been shown effective at solving the approximate k-NNG construction problem in both sparse and dense datasets.

While LSH has been a popular method for top-k search, it does not perform well in the k-NNG construction setting. Both *Greedy Filtering* and *NN-Descent* have been shown to outperform LSH when applied to this problem, for k typically ≥ 10. Additionally, *L2AP* outperformed LSH in the related APSS problem. As we will show in Section 6, L2Knng significantly outperforms kL2AP, the k-NNG method based on *L2AP*, as well as *Greedy Filtering* and *NN-Descent*. As a result, we have chosen not to compare against LSH in this work.

5.3 Performance measures

When comparing approximate k-NNG construction methods, we use average recall to measure the accuracy of the returned result. We obtain the true k-NNG via a brute-force search, then compute the average recall as,

$$R = \frac{1}{|D|} \sum_{d_i \in D} \frac{\#\,\text{true neighbors in } N_{d_i}}{|N_{d_i}|}.$$

We follow others in using the number of full similarity computations as an architecture and programming language independent way to measure k-NNG construction cost [11, 21]. However, we use a slightly different normalization constant, $NC = |D|(|D|-1)$, as our kIdxJoin baseline does not take advantage of symmetry in similarity computations, and thus may compute up to $n-1$ similarity values for each vector in the dataset. We report, for all algorithms, *scan rate* $=$ *# similarity evaluations*$/NC$, and *candidate rate* $=$ *# candidates*$/NC$.

An important characteristic in our experiments is CPU runtime, which is measured in seconds. Between a method A and a baseline method B, we report speedup as the ratio of B's execution time and that of A's.

5.4 Execution environment

Our method and all baselines are single-threaded, serial programs. A C++ based library implementing *NN-Descent* can be found at http://www.kgraph.org/. A C based implementation of *L2AP* can be found at http://cs.umn.edu/~dragos/l2ap. We implemented[2] kIdxJoin, kL2AP, *Greedy Filtering*[3], *Maxscore*, *BMM*, L2Knng, and L2KnngApprox in C and compiled our program using gcc 4.4.7 with -O3 optimization. Each method was executed on its own node in a cluster of HP ProLiant BL280c G6 blade servers, each with 2.8 GHz Intel Xeon processors and 24 Gb RAM.

We executed each method for $k \in \{1, 5, 10, 25, 50, 75, 100\}$ and tuned parameters to achieve balanced high recall and efficient execution. For all L2Knng and L2KnngApprox experiments, we set the parameter $\delta = 0.0001$. We tested kL2AP by decreasing the threshold t in steps of 0.1, 0.25, and 0.5, and report the best results among the step choices. For the *NN-Descent* library[4], we set $\rho = 1$, $S = 20$, and indexing $K = \mu$ (the candidate list size $\mu \geq k$). For all stochastic methods, we executed a minimum of 5 tries for each set of parameter values and we report averages of all tries.

6. RESULTS & DISCUSSION

We now present our experiment results, along several directions. First, we test L2KnngApprox against approximate baselines. We then evaluate the effectiveness of our exact k-NNG building strategies. We measure the influence of the initial approximate graph quality on L2Knng's efficiency and the pruning effectiveness of different stages in the L2Knng filtering framework. Finally, we evaluate the runtime and memory scalability of L2Knng as the number of input objects increases, and its efficiency as opposed to exact baselines.

6.1 Evaluation of L2KnngApprox

6.1.1 Candidate pool size parameter analysis

The efficiency of all the approximate methods under consideration are dependent on the number of candidates they are allowed to consider for each object, μ. The larger the candidate pool is, the more likely the true neighborhood is found among the objects in the pool. We compare the recall and execution time of L2KnngApprox with other approximate baselines, given the same candidate list and neighborhood size parameters, μ and k. We tested each method, without changing any other parameters, given $\mu = k, 2 \times k, \ldots, 10 \times k$, on the RCV1-400k and WW200-250k datasets. We tested L2KnngApprox with $\gamma = 0$ (L2KnngApprox_0), which does not execute any iterative neighborhood updates, and with $\gamma = 3$ (L2KnngApprox_3).

Figure 1 plots recall versus execution time for our experiment results. For all methods, results for $\mu = k$ are marked with a "-" label, and those for $\mu = 10 \times k$ with a "+" label. The best results are those points in the lower-right corner of each quadrant in the figure, achieving high recall in a short amount of time. Due to lack of space, we include only results for $k \in \{50, 100\}$. Results for other k values exhibit similar trends.

Methods generally exhibit higher recall and higher execution time for larger μ values. L2KnngApprox_0 takes much less time to execute than *Greedy Filtering* and, given large enough

[2] Source code available at http://cs.umn.edu/~dragos/l2knng.

[3] The authors of *Greedy Filtering* kindly provided a Java-based implementation of their algorithm for comparison. On average, our C implementation achieved 1.13x speedup over the Java one.

[4] We thank Wei Dong for his invaluable assistance with using the KGraph library and finding *NN-Descent* evaluation parameters.

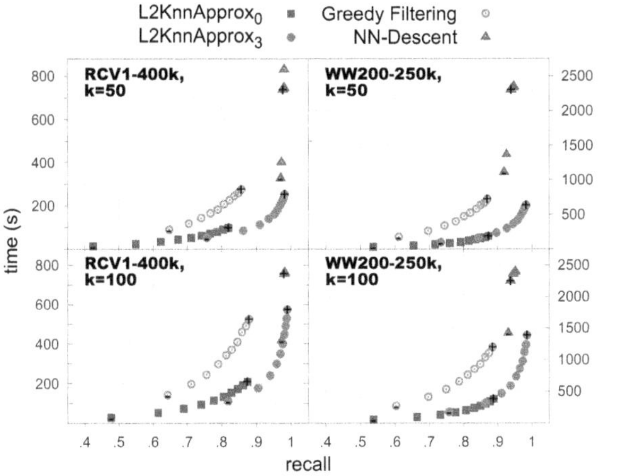

Figure 1: Recall and execution time of approximate methods given increasing candidate pool sizes.

μ, can achieve similar or higher recall. Both `L2KnngApprox` and *Greedy Filtering* require larger μ values than *NN-Descent* to achieve high recall. Yet, *NN-Descent* does not improve much as μ increases. $\texttt{L2KnngApprox}_3$ is able to outperform both competitors, with regards to both time and recall, for large enough μ.

6.1.2 *L2KnngApprox efficiency*

In this work, we focused on building the exact k-NNG. While approximate methods cannot easily achieve perfect recall, we compared their efficiency when seeking a close approximation of the true k-NNG. We executed each approximate method under a wide range of parameters and report the smallest time for which a minimum recall value of 0.95 was achieved. Figure 2 presents execution times for the approximate methods, for four of the datasets. Results for the other datasets are similar and we omit them here due to lack of space. We also include the times for our exact variant, `L2Knng`, as comparison. Note that execution times are log-scaled. Lower values are preferred. The *NN-Descent* result is not included for the WW200 dataset, as we could not obtain high enough recall (the highest recall for $k = 1$ was 0.8854, even with $\mu = 850$).

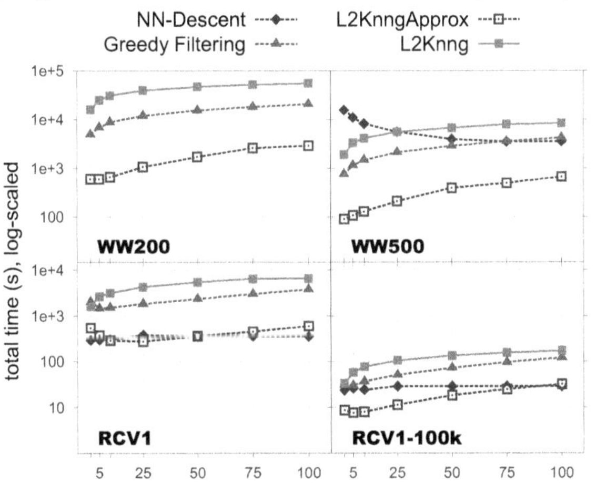

Figure 2: Approximate k-NNG construction efficiency.

`L2KnngApprox` was more efficient than *Greedy Filtering* in all cases and than *NN-Descent* in most cases, while achieving an order of magnitude improvement over our exact solution. For problems where perfect recall is not needed, `L2KnngApprox` can provide a close approximation in much less time. Even though *NN-Descent* had similar execution times as `L2KnngApprox` for some neighborhood sizes of the RCV1 datasets, it performed poorly on the WW datasets. This may be explained by the much higher dimensionality and mean row length of the WW datasets as compared to the RCV1 datasets, which can lead to repeated inclusion of objects in computationally expensive *NN-Descent* local joins. In contrast, `L2KnngApprox` uses several strategies that limit the number of computed dot-products. It builds a higher quality initial graph than *NN-Descent*, prioritizes candidate inclusion, and sets a hard limit on the candidate list size in each iterative update.

6.2 Evaluation of L2Knng

6.2.1 *Initial graph influence*

While the final recall for an `L2Knng` execution is 1.0, our method uses an initial approximate graph $\hat{\mathcal{N}}$ as a guide in its k-NN search. A graph $\hat{\mathcal{N}}$ with high recall provides `L2Knng` with higher minimum neighborhood similarity values, which translate into tighter pruning bounds and leads to fewer full vector dot-products being computed (smaller scan rate) and faster runtime. We tested the influence of the initial graph quality in three scenarios on the RCV1-400k and WW200-250k datasets. In the first scenario (*random*), we generated an initial graph by randomly picking k neighbors for each object from the set of objects with which they shared at least one feature in common. In the second scenario (*fast*), we chose parameters that ensure fast execution, without guaranteeing high recall ($\mu = k$, $\gamma = 1$). We executed the search using 10 completion blocks in both scenarios ($\nu = 10$). Finally, we include for comparison the best results we achieved after a parameter search (*best*).

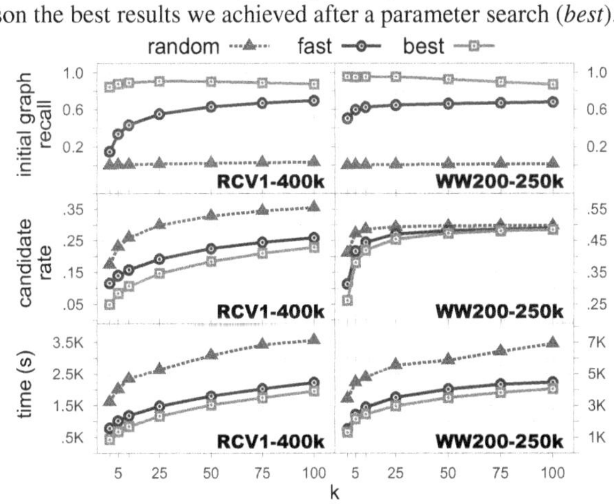

Figure 3: Initial graph influence over `L2Knng` efficiency.

Figure 3 presents our experiment results. The top of the figure shows, for each k value, the recall of the initial graph for the two tested datasets. The middle and bottom of the figure show, for each k value, the candidate rate and execution time after completing the *exact* k NNG construction. The results emphasize the importance of the initial graph quality in `L2Knng`. The initial graph $\hat{\mathcal{N}}$ for the *random* test case had recall 0.018 and 0.009 on average across all k values for the RCV1-400k and WW200-250k datasets, respectively. The recall was 0.496 and 0.628 in the *fast* and 0.883 and 0.929 in the *best* test cases. These better initial graphs translate into both lower candidate rates and smaller execution times. The *fast* case performed similarly to the *best* case, showing that `L2Knng` can be used with reasonable parameter values and does not require extensive parameter tuning.

6.2.2 *Parameter sensitivity*

The parameters μ, γ, and ν can influence the effectiveness and efficiency of our exact and approximate algorithms. Larger values for μ increase the number of candidates considered for building the initial graph and will likely lead to increased recall for this stage. Similarly, higher γ values translate to more iterations of initial neighborhood enhancement, at the cost of more similarity computations. Increasing ν values can lead to improved candidate generation pruning and faster index traversal, at the cost of reading vectors in unprocessed blocks several times to find similarities with indexed vectors. There is a trade-off between the benefit of more efficacious pruning bounds and the time taken to achieve them.

We executed parameter sensitivity experiments on the RCV1-400k and WW200-250k datasets, for $k \in \{25, 50, 75, 100\}$. In each experiment, we fixed two of the parameters and varied the third. In the first experiment, given $\gamma = 0$, and $\nu = 10$, we varied μ between 100 and 1000. In the second experiment, given $\mu = 300$, and $\nu = 10$, we varied γ between 0 (no initial neighborhood enhancement) and 10. Finally, to verify the sensitivity of the number of blocks parameter, ν, given $\mu = 300$, and $\gamma = 1$, we varied ν between 1 and 500. Due to lack of space, we include here only a summary of the parameter study results. As expected, we found recall improves when either μ or γ are increased. While the rise is sharp at first, it levels off quickly as the parameter values get larger, showing that the most benefit is gained from checking a relatively small number of initial candidates and executing few neighborhood enhancement rounds. In general, the best results we obtained after parameter tuning were executed with $1 \leq \gamma \leq 3$ and $300 \leq \mu \leq 500$. The execution time was not greatly affected as we increased the values of μ or γ, showing that `L2Knng` is not very sensitive to these parameter choices. We found that increasing the number of blocks ν initially leads to improved performance for all k values. While the improvement is more drastic at first, ν values greater than 50 do not improve the results much, and can eventually lead to decreased efficiency.

6.2.3 *Pruning effectiveness*

`L2Knng` works by pruning the majority of the candidates that are not true neighbors. Candidates can be pruned while checking the suffix ℓ^2-norm at a common feature during the candidate generation stage (*cg*), during the candidate verification stage (*cv*), or after checking the suffix estimate score (*ses*). Since a partial dot-product is accumulated for each candidate before being pruned, it is important that candidates be pruned as early as possible. In an experiment in which we used fast defaults for all parameters ($\mu = k$, $\gamma = 1$, $\nu = 10$), we counted the number of candidates that were pruned in each stage of the algorithm. Additionally, we display the number of candidates that survived all pruning and had full dot-products computed (*dps*). Figure 4 shows the results of this experiment for the RCV1-400k and WW200-250k datasets, as stacked bar charts showing the number of candidates for each category.

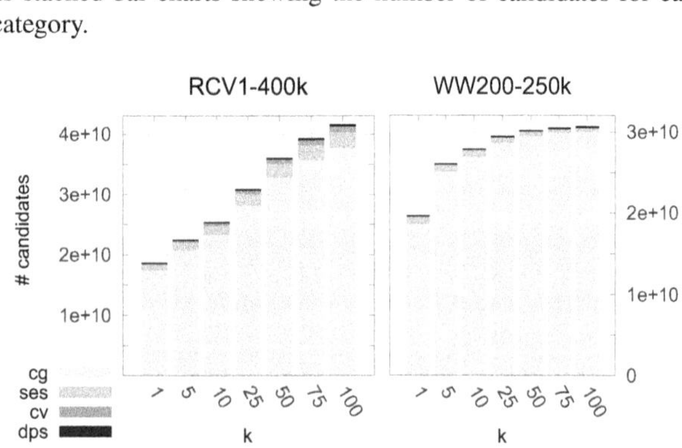

Figure 4: Candidate pruning in `L2Knng`.

Table 3: Execution time and memory scalability.

Mean search time (ms)			`L2Knng`				`L2KnngApprox`			
dataset	# rows	Δ_{sz}	$k = 25$	50	75	100	25	50	75	100
WW200-250k	250000	1.00	12.0	14.0	15.2	16.2	0.7	1.3	1.6	1.9
WW200	1017531	4.07	38.9	46.5	50.9	54.1	1.1	1.7	2.6	2.9
RCV1-100k	100000	1.00	1.0	1.3	1.5	1.7	0.1	0.2	0.2	0.3
RCV1-400k	400000	4.00	2.9	3.8	4.4	4.9	0.3	0.4	0.5	0.6
RCV1	804414	8.04	5.3	6.8	8.0	8.1	0.3	0.4	0.6	0.7

Memory usage (Gb)			`L2Knng`				`L2KnngApprox`			
dataset	# rows	Δ_{sz}	$k = 25$	50	75	100	25	50	75	100
WW200-250k	250000	1.00	8.9	9.5	10.0	10.6	7.2	7.8	8.4	9.0
WW200	1017531	4.07	35.9	38.2	40.5	42.8	29.1	31.7	34.0	36.4
RCV1-100k	100000	1.00	0.9	1.1	1.4	1.6	0.7	1.0	1.2	1.4
RCV1-400k	400000	4.00	3.5	4.4	5.3	6.2	2.9	3.8	4.7	5.6
RCV1	804414	8.04	7.0	8.8	10.6	12.4	5.8	7.7	9.5	11.3

Results show that the majority of objects are pruned soon after becoming candidates, in the candidate generation stage (*cg*). Of the remainder, most are pruned by the suffix estimate bound (*ses*), which is checked once, at the beginning of the candidate verification stage, and by additional pruning in the candidate verification stage (*cv*). On average, across all k values, 0.15% and 0.02% of candidates survived all pruning for the RCV1-400k and WW200-250k datasets, respectively. A large number of objects never become candidates in `L2Knng`, as a result of either the ℓ^2-norm based candidate acceptance bound in the candidate generation stage of the algorithm, or due to the prefix-filtering based index reduction. On average across all k values, only 38.17% and 88.66% of all potential candidates actually became candidates for the RCV1-400k and WW200-250k datasets.

6.2.4 *Scalability testing*

As the dataset size increases, the exact k-NNG problem will take longer to solve, as each object has more potential neighbors that have to be vetted. As a way to verify scalability, we tested our methods on three subsets of the RCV1 and two subsets of the WW200 datasets. For each data subset, Table 3 reports, for $k \in \{25, 50, 75, 100\}$, the mean per-vector search time (top) and the maximum amount of memory used (bottom) for `L2Knng` and `L2KnngApprox`. The Δ_{sz} column shows the relative dataset size increase. Parameters were tuned to achieve efficient execution, and, in the case of `L2KnngApprox`, high recall (95%).

The results show that the performance of both methods scales linearly compared to the dataset size. As the dataset size increases, our two methods perform better than they did for the smaller datasets (e.g., it takes much less than 8.04x the time of searching RCV1-100k to search RCV1 for 100 neighbors), while using memory directly proportional to the number of objects in the set.

6.3 Comparison with other methods

The primary goal of this work is the efficient construction of the exact k-NNG. Figure 5 presents execution times for the exact methods, for all six of the tested datasets. We also include the times for our approximate algorithm, `L2KnngApprox`, as comparison. Note that execution times are log-scaled, and lower values are preferred. The *Maxscore* and *BMM* experiments on the WW200 and WW500 datasets were terminated early, after executing for 5 days, which is more than twice the execution time of `kIdxJoin` for these datasets. Additionally, Table 4 shows the average speedup, across all k values, of our algorithms against the best time achieved by competing approximate (left) and exact (right) methods.

`L2Knng` performed best among all exact methods, achieving over an order of magnitude improvement versus `kIdxJoin` for small values of k. The speedup is less pronounced as the value of k increases. This may be partially due to an increased number of neigh-

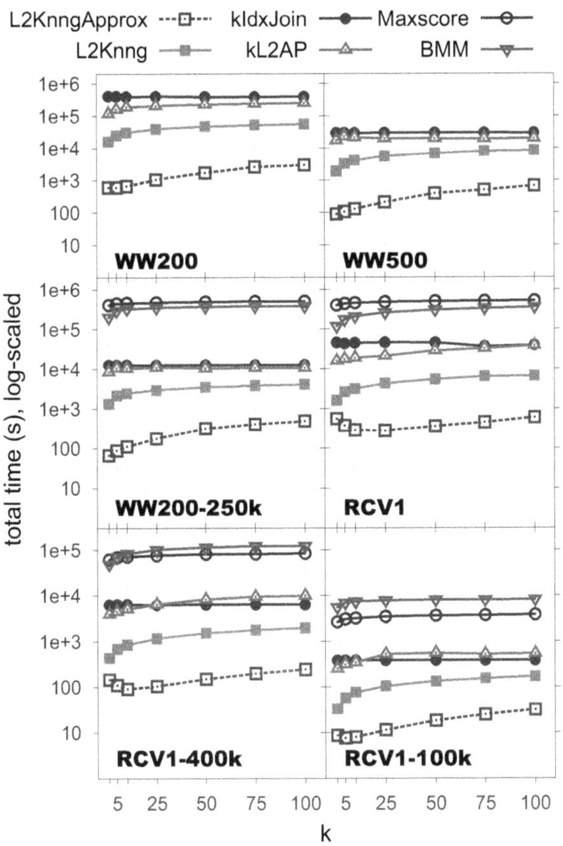

Figure 5: Exact k-NNG construction efficiency comparison.

Table 4: Average speedup of L2Knng and L2KnngApprox over best competing method.

	versus approx		versus exact	
dataset / method	L2Knng	L2KnngApprox	L2Knng	L2KnngApprox
WW200	0.32	9.60	5.57	178.01
WW200-250k	0.41	6.01	3.94	69.08
WW500	0.40	8.68	4.58	110.98
RCV1	0.09	0.87	6.18	61.79
RCV1-100k	0.33	2.19	4.11	27.86
RCV1-400k	0.17	1.19	5.41	40.24

borhood updates during the search, which, in our implementation, incur the cost of heapifying neighborhood data structures.

While using a similar filtering framework as `L2Knng`, `kL2AP` performs poorly, at times taking longer to execute even than `kIdxJoin`, which is equivalent to a brute-force search. This may be due to repeated indexing in `kL2AP` and the size of its final index. As t nears 0, even if we are only interested in finalizing a few neighborhoods, the inverted index lists will contain the majority of values in the dataset, and traversing it will produce many candidates. In contrast, `L2Knng` indexes each vector only once and uses *block completion* as an effective strategy to improve pruning.

Maxscore and *BMM* performed worst among all exact methods, which may be explained by the length of the query vectors used in solving the k-NNG problem. The methods were designed for short queries. They perform a sorting operation with each query and simultaneously traverse as many inverted lists as the number of features in the query vector, which can lead to loosing cache locality. In contrast, our method traverses one inverted list at a time and updates an accumulator in increasing index order, which is much more cache friendly for long queries.

Table 5 presents timing and scan rate results for the three top performing exact and approximate methods. As in Section 6.1.2, we report the smallest time for which a minimum recall value of 0.95 was achieved for all approximate methods. Duc to lack of space, we only include results for the WW500 and RCV1 experiments and $k \in \{1, 25, 100\}$. We use bold font to highlight the best result among approximate (top) and exact (bottom) methods, which are separated in the table by a dashed line. `L2Knng` and `L2KnngApprox` achieve most of the lowest scan rates among the competing methods, highlighting the ability of `L2KnngApprox` to find a quality approximate solution using few similarity comparisons and the pruning ability of the `L2Knng` filtering framework. For the RCV1 datasets, *NN-Descent* achieves similar execution times as `L2KnngApprox` while having much higher scan rates. *NN-Descent* does not use accumulation and can take advantage of cache locality afforded by the short vector sizes in the RCV1 datasets. However, much longer vectors, combined with high scan rates, lead to poor *NN-Descent* performance on the WW datasets.

7. CONCLUSIONS AND FUTURE WORK

We presented `L2Knng`, our *exact* filtering-based solution to the cosine similarity k-NNG construction problem. `L2Knng` uses an initial approximate solution graph as a guide to find the desired true neighborhoods, through a modified similarity search framework. We introduced several new pruning bounds specific to this problem, which leverage the Cauchy-Schwarz inequality in partial vector dot-products at each stage in the framework to prevent full similarity computation for most object pairs. `L2Knng` achieves an order of magnitude improvement against exact baselines. Our inexact k-NNG construction method, `L2KnngApprox`, achieves high recall in less time than competing approximate methods, and is an order of magnitude faster than our approximate baselines.

In this paper, we have focused on the *cosine similarity* function for building the k-NNG. It would be interesting to evaluate the efficiency of ℓ^2-norm filtering in the context of other similarity functions, such as the Dice and Tanimoto similarities. Another avenue of research involves scaling up the number of threads and processors used to solve the problem, which in turn will scale the size of the problem that can be efficiently solved.

Acknowledgment

This work was supported in part by NSF (IIS-0905220, OCI-1048018, CNS-1162405, IIS-1247632, IIP-1414153, IIS-1447788), Army Research Office (W911NF-14-1-0316), Intel Software and Services Group, and the Digital Technology Center at the University of Minnesota. Access to research and computing facilities was provided by the Digital Technology Center and the Minnesota Supercomputing Institute. We thank the reviewers for their helpful comments.

Table 5: Execution time and scan rate for competing algorithms. Best results are emphasized in bold.

		WW500			RCV1		
result	method / k	1	25	100	1	25	100
time:	*Greedy Filtering*	766.3	2135.5	4239.3	2039.9	1846.0	3809.8
	NN-Descent	15586.8	5562.9	3547.1	**289.6**	377.9	**350.0**
	L2KnngApprox	**90.0**	**209.9**	**667.3**	550.1	**275.1**	596.3
	kIdxJoin	29389.8	29412.7	29243.9	45456.7	45585.6	38914.4
	kL2AP	17201.7	19626.5	19588.1	15823.6	21067.7	37705.9
	L2Knng	**1923.2**	**5543.6**	**8340.0**	**1614.8**	**4280.5**	**6550.6**
scan rate:	*Greedy Filtering*	0.0017	0.0045	0.0086	0.0046	0.0034	0.0049
	NN-Descent	1.2913	0.1071	0.8568	0.6805	0.8402	0.6914
	L2KnngApprox	**0.0005**	**0.0014**	**0.0045**	**0.0022**	**0.0010**	**0.0018**
	kIdxJoin	1.0000	1.0000	1.0000	0.8951	0.8951	0.8951
	kL2AP	0.0407	0.4981	0.5003	**0.0003**	0.0249	0.0017
	L2Knng	**0.0005**	**0.0011**	**0.0036**	0.0004	**0.0012**	**0.0013**

8. REFERENCES

[1] David C. Anastasiu and George Karypis. L2ap: Fast cosine similarity search with prefix l-2 norm bounds. In *30th IEEE International Conference on Data Engineering*, ICDE '14, 2014.

[2] Alexandr Andoni and Piotr Indyk. Near-optimal hashing algorithms for approximate nearest neighbor in high dimensions. *Commun. ACM*, 51(1):117–122, January 2008.

[3] Amit Awekar and Nagiza F. Samatova. Fast matching for all pairs similarity search. In *Proceedings of the 2009 IEEE/WIC/ACM International Joint Conference on Web Intelligence and Intelligent Agent Technology - Volume 01*, WI-IAT '09, pages 295–300, Washington, DC, USA, 2009. IEEE Computer Society.

[4] Roberto J. Bayardo, Yiming Ma, and Ramakrishnan Srikant. Scaling up all pairs similarity search. In *Proceedings of the 16th International Conference on World Wide Web*, WWW '07, pages 131–140, New York, NY, USA, 2007. ACM.

[5] Alina Beygelzimer, Sham Kakade, and John Langford. Cover trees for nearest neighbor. In *Proceedings of the 23rd International Conference on Machine Learning*, ICML '06, pages 97–104, New York, NY, USA, 2006. ACM.

[6] Andrei Z. Broder, David Carmel, Michael Herscovici, Aya Soffer, and Jason Zien. Efficient query evaluation using a two-level retrieval process. In *Proceedings of the Twelfth International Conference on Information and Knowledge Management*, CIKM '03, pages 426–434, New York, NY, USA, 2003. ACM.

[7] Chris Buckley and Alan F. Lewit. Optimization of inverted vector searches. In *Proceedings of the 8th Annual International ACM SIGIR Conference on Research and Development in Information Retrieval*, SIGIR '85, pages 97–110, New York, NY, USA, 1985. ACM.

[8] Surajit Chaudhuri, Venkatesh Ganti, and Raghav Kaushik. A primitive operator for similarity joins in data cleaning. In *Proceedings of the 22nd International Conference on Data Engineering*, ICDE '06, pages 5–, Washington, DC, USA, 2006. IEEE Computer Society.

[9] Constantinos Dimopoulos, Sergey Nepomnyachiy, and Torsten Suel. Optimizing top-k document retrieval strategies for block-max indexes. In *Proceedings of the Sixth ACM International Conference on Web Search and Data Mining*, WSDM '13, pages 113–122, New York, NY, USA, 2013. ACM.

[10] Shuai Ding and Torsten Suel. Faster top-k document retrieval using block-max indexes. In *Proceedings of the 34th International ACM SIGIR Conference on Research and Development in Information Retrieval*, SIGIR '11, pages 993–1002, New York, NY, USA, 2011. ACM.

[11] Wei Dong, Charikar Moses, and Kai Li. Efficient k-nearest neighbor graph construction for generic similarity measures. In *Proceedings of the 20th International Conference on World Wide Web*, WWW '11, pages 577–586, New York, NY, USA, 2011. ACM.

[12] Jinyang Gao, Hosagrahar Visvesvaraya Jagadish, Wei Lu, and Beng Chin Ooi. Dsh: Data sensitive hashing for high-dimensional k-nnsearch. In *Proceedings of the 2014 ACM SIGMOD International Conference on Management of Data*, SIGMOD '14, pages 1127–1138, New York, NY, USA, 2014. ACM.

[13] Aristides Gionis, Piotr Indyk, and Rajeev Motwani. Similarity search in high dimensions via hashing. In *Proceedings of the 25th International Conference on Very Large Data Bases*, VLDB '99, pages 518–529, San Francisco, CA, USA, 1999. Morgan Kaufmann Publishers.

[14] Andreas Hotho, Andreas Nürnberger, and Gerhard Paaß. A brief survey of text mining. *LDV Forum - GLDV Journal for Computational Linguistics and Language Technology*, 2005.

[15] Piotr Indyk and Rajeev Motwani. Approximate nearest neighbors: towards removing the curse of dimensionality. In *Proceedings of the thirtieth annual ACM symposium on Theory of computing*, STOC '98, pages 604–613, New York, NY, USA, 1998. ACM.

[16] George Karypis. Evaluation of item-based top-n recommendation algorithms. In *Proceedings of the Tenth International Conference on Information and Knowledge Management*, CIKM '01, pages 247–254, New York, NY, USA, 2001. ACM.

[17] Dongjoo Lee, Jaehui Park, Junho Shim, and Sang-goo Lee. An efficient similarity join algorithm with cosine similarity predicate. In *Proceedings of the 21st International Conference on Database and Expert Systems Applications: Part II*, DEXA'10, pages 422–436, Berlin, Heidelberg, 2010. Springer-Verlag.

[18] David D. Lewis, Yiming Yang, Tony G. Rose, and Fan Li. Rcv1: A new benchmark collection for text categorization research. *J. Mach. Learn. Res.*, 5:361–397, December 2004.

[19] Christopher D. Manning, Prabhakar Raghavan, and Hinrich Schütze. *Introduction to Information Retrieval*. Cambridge University Press, New York, NY, USA, 2008.

[20] Rodrigo Paredes, Edgar Chávez, Karina Figueroa, and Gonzalo Navarro. Practical construction of k-nearest neighbor graphs in metric spaces. In *Proceedings of the 5th International Conference on Experimental Algorithms*, WEA'06, pages 85–97, Berlin, Heidelberg, 2006. Springer-Verlag.

[21] Youngki Park, Sungchan Park, Sang-goo Lee, and Woosung Jung. Greedy filtering: A scalable algorithm for k-nearest neighbor graph construction. In *Database Systems for Advanced Applications*, volume 8421 of *Lecture Notes in Computer Science*, pages 327–341. Springer-Verlag, 2014.

[22] Cristian Rossi, Edleno S. de Moura, Andre L. Carvalho, and Altigran S. da Silva. Fast document-at-a-time query processing using two-tier indexes. In *Proceedings of the 36th International ACM SIGIR Conference on Research and Development in Information Retrieval*, SIGIR '13, pages 183–192, New York, NY, USA, 2013. ACM.

[23] Trevor Strohman and W. Bruce Croft. Efficient document retrieval in main memory. In *Proceedings of the 30th Annual International ACM SIGIR Conference on Research and Development in Information Retrieval*, SIGIR '07, pages 175–182, New York, NY, USA, 2007. ACM.

[24] Howard Turtle and James Flood. Query evaluation: Strategies and optimizations. *Inf. Process. Manage.*, 31(6):831–850, November 1995.

[25] Marcin Zukowski, Sandor Heman, Niels Nes, and Peter Boncz. Super-scalar ram-cpu cache compression. In *Proceedings of the 22Nd International Conference on Data Engineering*, ICDE '06, pages 59–, Washington, DC, USA, 2006. IEEE Computer Society.

Lingo: Linearized Grassmannian Optimization for Nuclear Norm Minimization

Qian Li
Institute of Information Engineering
Chinese Academy of Sciences
Beijing, China
qianli.charlene@gmail.com

Wenjia Niu*
Institute of Information Engineering
Chinese Academy of Sciences
Beijing, China
niuwenjia@iie.ac.cn

Gang Li†
School of Information Technology
Deakin University
Australia
gangli@gmail.com

Yanan Cao
Institute of Information Engineering
Chinese Academy of Sciences
Beijing, China
caoyanan@iie.ac.cn

Jianlong Tan
Institute of Information Engineering
Chinese Academy of Sciences
Beijing, China
tanjianlong@iie.ac.cn

Li Guo
Institute of Information Engineering
Chinese Academy of Sciences
Beijing, China
guoli@iie.ac.cn

ABSTRACT

As a popular heuristic to the matrix rank minimization problem, *nuclear norm minimization* attracts intensive research attentions. *Matrix factorization* based algorithms can reduce the expensive computation cost of SVD for *nuclear norm minimization*. However, most *matrix factorization* based algorithms fail to provide the theoretical guarantee for convergence caused by their non-unique factorizations. This paper proposes an efficient and accurate *Linearized Grassmannian Optimization* (Lingo) algorithm, which adopts matrix factorization and *Grassmann* manifold structure to alternatively minimize the subproblems. More specially, linearization strategy makes the auxiliary variables unnecessary and guarantees the close-form solution for low per-iteration complexity. Lingo then converts linearized objective function into a nuclear norm minimization over *Grassmannian manifold*, which could remedy the non-unique of solution for the low-rank matrix factorization. Extensive comparison experiments demonstrate the accuracy and efficiency of Lingo algorithm. The global convergence of Lingo is guaranteed with theoretical proof, which also verifies the effectiveness of Lingo.

Categories and Subject Descriptors

G.1.6 [**Mathematics of Computing**]: Optimization; H.2.8 [**Database Management**]: Database Applications—*Data Mining*

*Corresponding author.
†Corresponding author.

Permission to make digital or hard copies of all or part of this work for personal or classroom use is granted without fee provided that copies are not made or distributed for profit or commercial advantage and that copies bear this notice and the full citation on the first page. Copyrights for components of this work owned by others than ACM must be honored. Abstracting with credit is permitted. To copy otherwise, or republish, to post on servers or to redistribute to lists, requires prior specific permission and/or a fee. Request permissions from Permissions@acm.org.
CIKM'15, October 19–23, 2015, Melbourne, VIC, Australia.
© 2015 ACM. ISBN 978-1-4503-3794-6/15/10$15.00.
DOI: http://dx.doi.org/10.1145/2806416.2806532.

Keywords

Low-rank; nuclear norm; matrix completion; Grassmannian

1. INTRODUCTION

In the past few years, *matrix rank minimization* has received considerable attention from machine learning, computer vision, recommender systems, and a wide range of problems can be represented under this framework [7,11,14]. However, minimizing the rank of a matrix subject to a convex constraint is NP-hard, and no polynomial time algorithm yields exact solution for most practical problems. A popular heuristic that is widely used to solve the *matrix rank minimization* problem, is to relax the objective function by minimize the *nuclear norm*

$$\min_{X \in R^{m \times n}} f(X) + \lambda \|X\|_* \tag{1.1}$$

where $f(X)$ is any smooth convex function, the *nuclear norm* $\|X\|_*$ can be also represented by the sum the singular values of X, and $\lambda > 0$ is a given regularization parameter. Theoretic research also confirms that the *nuclear norm minimization* leads to the exact solution to *matrix rank minimization* when certain conditions are satisfied [8,9].

Despite its strong theoretical guarantee, the *nuclear norm minimization* has been found incapable to handle large-scale problems in real world applications. For example, the rating matrix in *Netflix* usually has more than 10^8 entries [5], and existing *nuclear norm minimization* solvers are usually not efficient enough.

Existing attempts in scalable and practical nuclear norm minimization solutions can be categorized as rank minimization and matrix factorization. *Semidefinite Program* (SDP) solvers [14] and *First-order methods* (FOMs) [4,15,19] are two representatives in rank minimization. Among them, the SDP solvers such as *Interior-point method* (IPM) require the second order information that is usually unavailable in large-scale problems [14], while FOMs require only the first-order information, and hence are usually preferable for large-scale problems [15,17]. Nevertheless, FOMs's soft-thresholding operator still requires computing the SVD, for which the speed is still an issue in many real applications. Instead of directly minimizing the rank, *Riemannian Optimization*, such as OptSpace [18], GROUSE [3] and SET [10], factorizes the matrix and explores their geometric structures, so that the searching space is limited to manifold. However, although SET reduces the higher-dimensional search space caused by jointly minimization in OptSpace, it has been reported as unstable as more than one solution can be generated [6]. GROUSE [3] empirically outperforms OptSpace and SET, which however is not guaranteed with theoretical convergence. Although most existing *Riemannian Optimization* based algorithms have superior performance than classical heuristics (e.g.,SDP and FOMs) with numerical experiments, they lack the theoretical analysis to prove the stability of their superior performance. Consequently, how to develop an efficient and accurate *Riemannian Optimization* method with theoretical convergence guarantee remains an open issue.

In this paper, we attempt to develop an efficient and accurate *Linearized Grassmannian Optimization* (Lingo) algorithm for a general *nuclear norm minimization* (1.1). The main contributions of this paper are in the following three aspects:

- To achieve the efficient computation, Lingo adopts matrix factorization and fully explores the underlying quotient *Grassmann* nature of the factor matrices. Lingo designs the gradient-based optimization to alternatively minimize the subproblems with *Grassmann* manifold structure, which could remedy the non-unique of solution for the low-rank matrix factorization.

- Linearization strategy is applied and can reduce the extra constraints, hence it avoids updating the unnecessary auxiliary variables and further speeds up the convergence.

- Numerical experiments compared with some state-of-the art methods demonstrate the superior performance of the proposed Lingo. Moreover, theoretical analysis from the differential geometry further confirms the convergence and the efficiency of the Lingo algorithm.

2. BACKGROUNDS

Nuclear norm minimization aims to find the low rank matrix solution via replacing the rank with the nuclear norm, and then to construct a tractable convex problem in (1.1) over the affine subset. The smooth convex functions $f(X)$ is usually referred to as the penalty term to characterize specific applications, such as *Multivariate Regression*, *Multi-task Learning* and *Matrix Completion*.

Multivariate Regression Given an observation data matrix A, and an output matrix Y in which each row represents the label to an input data in A. We can compute the regression model X by solving (1.1) with $f(X) = \|AX - Y\|_F^2$, where a low rank X is usually preferred for multivariate regression [16].

Multi-task Learning Finds the low-dimensional representation shared across a set of multiple related tasks by letting $f(X) = \sum_j(\sum_i L(x_i^T z_i^j, y_i^j))$ [13], where (z_i^j, y_i^j) is the jth sample in ith task and $X = [x_1, ..., x_n]$ refers to the weight or parameter matrix.

Matrix Completion Given a partially low rank matrix A with observed samples in Ω, we can recover a low rank matrix X by letting $f(X) = \|P_\Omega(A - X)\|_F^2$, where P_Ω is a sample projector.

According to the strategies in modeling the low-rank prior, existing approaches to *nuclear norm minimization* can be categories into *rank minimization* and *matrix factorization*.

A straightforward approach to the *nuclear norm minimization* is to directly minimize the nuclear norm in (1.1). Representative methods include *interior-point method* (IPM) and *First-order method* (FOMs). Among them, IPM can achieve exact solution but inefficient for large-scale problems, because of its dependency on the second-order information [14]. IPM's high computation cost has inspired an efficient method FOMs that requires only the first-order information of the matrix. One FOMs algorithm is the *Iterative soft-thresholding* algorithm (IST), which has been shown to be a slow but with asymptotic convergence rate [4]. *Accelerated Proximal Gradient* (APG) algorithm is then proposed to reduce the number of iterations in IST [17]. Although the convergence rate has been improved in APG compared with IPM and IST, APG produces an approximate solution [19]. To achieve exact optimal solution while maintaining a satisfying convergence rate, *Exact Augmented Lagrangian method* (EALM) is proposed, which improves the convergence rate from the sub-linear in APG to Q-linear [19]. It is worthy to mention that both APG and EALM need to use the full *singular value decomposition*. *Inexact Augmented Lagrangian method* (IALM) adopts partial SVD by calculating only the dominated singular values [19]. No matter for full or partial SVD, *singular value decomposition* at each iteration leads to extensive computation cost especially for the large-scale problems.

Matrix factorization is another category of approach to the *nuclear norm minimization*, which factorizes matrix X in problem (1.1) into smaller factor matrices to reduce the computation burden. As one representative method in this category, LMaFit [24] adopts the alternating strategy for each factor matrix and integrates a nonlinear successive over-relaxation scheme to accelerate the convergence. *Riemannian Optimization* is also based on low-rank matrix factorization approach by constraining the searching space over manifolds, such as OptSpace [18], GROUSE [3] and SET [10]. Both OptSpace and SET utilize some special structural properties of the low-rank matrices. OptSpace iteratively estimates the factor matrices and updates them simultaneously by gradient descent over the Grassmannian, so this further introduces numerical and analytical difficulties for theoretical guarantees. Substantially differs from simultaneous updating in OptSpace, SET minimizes over only one space (the column or the row space) but requires a priori on the rank of the matrix $\|X\|_*$, which is sometimes unreliable via rank estimation thus affects the performance of SET. GROUSE is an on-line incremental gradient descent algorithm on the Grassmannian, which accelerates OptSpace and SET. Yet, the convergence of GROUSE is not theoretical guaranteed.

To alleviate those issues mentioned above, this paper proposes an efficient and robust method for the *nuclear norm minimization* in (1.1) with less computational cost and stable accuracy.

3. LINGO ALGORITHM

In this section, we propose the *Linearized Grassmannian Optimization* (Lingo) algorithm to solve the *nuclear norm minimization* via Grassmann optimization, and will also prove that *Lingo* algorithm can converge with low complexity.

3.1 Linearized Grassmann Minimization

Manifolds can be considered as low dimensional smooth "surfaces" embedded in a higher dimensional Euclidean space. *Stiefel manifold* and *Grassmann manifold* are two differentiable manifolds that have been widely used in computer vision [12, 23] and signal processing [21]. Among them, *Stiefel manifold* refers to an embedded sub-manifold in $\mathbb{R}^{n\times r}$, which defines the set of $n \times r$ semi-orthogonal matrices, $\mathcal{S}_{n,r} =: \{U \in \mathbb{R}^{n\times r} : U^T U = I_r\}$; while *Grassmann manifold* refers to a matrix quotient space of *Stiefel manifold* with respect to the orthogonal transformation, $\mathcal{G}_{n,r} \simeq \mathcal{S}_{n,r}/\mathcal{O}(r) = \{span(U) : U \in \mathcal{S}_{n,r}\}$, where $\mathcal{O}(r)$ defines a set of the orthogonal matrices.

In order to obtain Grassmann geometries of the resulting search space, SVD decomposes matrix X in (1.1) and get: $X = USV^T$. However, such SVD decomposition is not unique, since the X remains unchanged under the following transformation.

$$X = USV^T = (UO)(O^T SO)VO)^T$$

where $U \in \mathcal{S}_{m,r}$ and $V \in \mathcal{S}_{n,r}$. Consequently, the optimal matrix X, when rotated by matrix $Q \in \mathcal{O}(r)$, can form a set of equivalent class:

$$[X] = [(U, S, V)] = \left\{(UQ, Q^T SQ, VQ) : Q \in \mathcal{O}(r)\right\} \quad (3.1)$$

Let $[U] = \{UQ : UQ \in \mathcal{S}_{m,r}\}$ and $[V] = \{VQ : VQ \in \mathcal{S}_{n,r}\}$ construct two equivalent classes over *Stiefel manifold*. As $\mathcal{G}_{m,r} \simeq \mathcal{S}_{m,r}/\mathcal{O}(r)$, these equivalent classes satisfy $[U] \in \mathcal{G}_{m,r}$ and $[V] \in \mathcal{G}_{n,r}$. The quotient geometry of *Grassmann manifold* in Lingo algorithm guarantees the uniqueness of matrix factorization. Since $X = USV^T$, from the definition of *nuclear norm*, we have $\|X\|_* = \|S\|_*$.

Based on the discussion above, we can reformulate the general *nuclear norm minimization* (1.1), into a non-convex problem as follows, by applying SVD to solve U and V over the *Grassmann manifold* searching space.

$$\begin{aligned} &\min_{U,S,V} f(USV^T) + \lambda Tr(S) \\ &s.t. : [U] \in \mathcal{G}_{m,r}, S \in R^{r\times r}, [V] \in \mathcal{G}_{n,r} \end{aligned} \quad (3.2)$$

In general, solving U, S and V simultaneously is very time consuming, so *alternating direction method* (ADM) can be adopted to split the optimization objective function (3.2) into several subproblems with respect to each variable. However, some subproblems may have no closed-form solution in ADM [20]. Moreover, the ADM constraints related to quadratic penalty involve unnecessary auxiliary variables, and this usually results in inefficiency for ADM.

Through linearizing the optimization objective $f(USV^T)$ at iterate $X_j = U_j S_j V_j^T$ by adding a proximal term, the optimization objective can be approximated as:

$$\begin{aligned} \min_{U,S,V} f(U_j S_j V_j^T) + \langle\nabla f(U_j S_j V_j^T), USV^T - U_j S_j V_j^T\rangle + \\ \frac{\gamma}{2}\|USV^T - U_j S_j V_j^T\|_F^2 + \lambda Tr(S) \end{aligned} \quad (3.3)$$

where γ is a proximal parameter, $\langle,\rangle$ is the inner product.

After expanding $\|USV^T - U_j S_j V_j^T\|_F^2$, the optimization objective can be further simplified as the quadratic form:

$$\begin{aligned} &\min_{U,S,V} F(U, S, V) := \frac{\gamma}{2}\|USV^T - P_j\|_F^2 + \lambda Tr(S) \\ &s.t. : [U] \in \mathcal{G}_{m,r}, S \in R^{r\times r}, [V] \in \mathcal{G}_{n,r} \end{aligned} \quad (3.4)$$

where $P_j = USV^T - \frac{1}{\gamma}\nabla f(U_j S_j V_j^T)$.

This minimization problem can then be decomposed to three subproblems about U, V and S, respectively:

$$\begin{cases} U_{j+1} &= \underset{[U]\in G_{m,r}}{argmin} \frac{1}{2}\|US_j V_j^T - P_j\|_F^2 \\ V_{j+1} &= \underset{[V]\in G_{n,r}}{argmin} \frac{1}{2}\|U_j S_j V^T - P_j\|_F^2 \\ S_{j+1} &= \underset{S\in R^{r\times r}}{argmin} \frac{1}{2\gamma}\|U_{j+1} S V_{j+1}^T - P_j\|_F^2 + \lambda Tr(S) \end{cases} \quad (3.5)$$

In conclusion, the nuclear norm minimization can be addressed by solving three subproblems in (3.2), where U and V is iteratively updated over the *Grassmann mainifold* by gradient decent algorithm, S can be obtained with close-form solution after linearization strategy. In the following, we discuss how to solve (3.5) in detail.

3.2 Subproblem Optimization

We adopt ADM to alternatively solve each subproblem while fixing the other two variables. Specifically, U and V can be obtained by iteratively minimizing the subproblem on *Grassmann manifold* with gradient descent and S can achieve close-form solution with the guarantees from linearized (3.4). The following part describes the updating processes for U, V and S respectively.

3.2.1 Updating U and V

The updating processes for U and V are similar, since they have similar corresponding subproblem, which can be solved by optimizing on *Grassmann manifold*. In the following, we will explain the updating on U.

- **Gradient Projection** *Grassmann gradient* of F in (3.4) defines the unique tangent vector of $T_U\mathcal{G}_{n,r}$ with respect to the steepest descent direction of $F(U)$ on *tangent space*; i.e., grad $F(U)$. grad $F(U)$ is achieved by projecting the *Euclidean gradient* of F with operator $P_{T_U\mathcal{G}_{n,r}}$ as follows.

$$P_{T_U\mathcal{G}_{n,r}} : Z \to (I - UU^T)Z \quad (3.6)$$

Let Z be the *Euclidean gradient*

$$\nabla F(U) - 2S_j V_j^T \|US_j V_j^T - P_j\|_F$$

it follows that

$$\text{grad}\, F(U) = P_{T_U\mathcal{G}_{n,r}}(\nabla F(U)) \quad (3.7)$$

- **Retraction** *Retraction* operator $R_{\mathcal{G}_{n,r}}$ maps the point $Y \in T_U\mathcal{G}_{n,r}$ onto the manifold $\mathcal{G}_{n,r}$; i.e.,

$$R_{\mathcal{G}_{n,r}} : Y \to \text{qf}(Y) \quad (3.8)$$

where qf$(\cdot)$ defines the QR decomposition and $Y = U + \alpha\text{grad}\, F(U)$ defines a new point by decreasing a step size α along with the descent direction grad $F(x)$. The descent step size is obtained by Armijo condition that guarantees a sufficient degree of accuracy.

Based on the analysis above, the solution for U_{j+1} is

$$U_{j+1} = \text{qf}(U_j + \alpha_j \text{grad}\, F(U_{j+1})) \tag{3.9}$$

Similarly, the solution for V_{j+1} is

$$V_{j+1} = \text{qf}(V_j + \alpha_j \text{grad}\, F(V_{j+1})) \tag{3.10}$$

3.2.2 Updating S

Before discussing how to update S, we first introduce a useful theorem mentioned in [8].

THEOREM 1. *Consider the SVD of a matrix $X = U\Sigma V^T$, for each $\tau \geq 0$ and $Y \in R^{m\times n}$, the singular value shrinkage operator of Y satisfies that*

$$\mathcal{D}_\tau(Y) = \underset{X}{argmin} \frac{1}{2}\|X - Y\|_F^2 + \tau\|X\|_* \tag{3.11}$$

where $\mathcal{D}_\tau(X) = U\mathcal{D}_\tau(\Sigma)V^T, \mathcal{D}_\tau(\Sigma) = diag(max(\sigma - \tau), 0))$.

When U and V are fixed, the optimal S should be updated by minimizing the subproblems:

$$\min_{[S]\in R^{r\times r}} \frac{1}{2\gamma}\|U_{j+1}SV_{j+1}^T - P_j\|_F^2 + \lambda Tr(S) \tag{3.12}$$

where $P_j = U_jS_jV_j^T - \frac{1}{\gamma}\nabla f(U_jS_jV_j^T)$.

According to Theorem 1, the solution of S at $j+1$ iterate for (3.12) can be yielded by the *singular value shrinkage* operator:

$$\begin{aligned} S_{j+1} &= \mathcal{D}_{\frac{\lambda}{\gamma}}(U^T P_j V) = G\mathcal{D}_{\frac{\lambda}{\gamma}}(\Sigma)H^T \\ \mathcal{D}_{\frac{\lambda}{\gamma}}(\Sigma) &= \text{diag}(\max(0, \sigma_i - \frac{\lambda}{\gamma})) \end{aligned} \tag{3.13}$$

where $G\Sigma H^T$ is the SVD of $U^T P_j V$, $\mathcal{D}_{\frac{\lambda}{\gamma}}(\Sigma)$ shrinks the singular values σ below the threshold $\frac{\lambda}{\gamma}$.

Since S is small-scale $r \times r$ matrix, the SVD in above shrinkage operator has significantly low complexity. Consequently, Lingo can update S efficiently and obtains the close-form solution.

4. COMPLEXITY ANALYSIS

Following the above analysis, the pseudo code of Lingo algorithm can be summarized in Alg. 1. The numerical complexity of Lingo algorithm is mainly determined by the computational costs of QR decomposition for solving U and V, the SVD decomposition on small scale matrices $r \times r$ for solving R. The total complexity is $O((n+m)r^2 + r^3)$, where $O(n+m)r^2$ is the time complexity of QR decomposition, $O(r^3)$ is the time complexity by SVD.

5. CONVERGENCE ANALYSIS

Although most existing *Riemannian Optimization* algorithms can achieve satisfactory accuracy in numerical experiments, many have no theoretical guarantee in convergence. In this section, a complete convergence proof is given to provide theoretical guarantee for Lingo to achieve high accuracy.

THEOREM 2. *The accumulation point of $\{U_j, S_j, V_j\}$ produced by Alg. 1 is represented as (U_*, S_*, V_*), which is the stationary point for F in (3.4).*

Algorithm 1 Lingo:Linearized Grassmannian Optimization for Nuclear Norm Minimization

Require: The tolerance parameter err, the rank r, the total number of iterations n and the parameters λ and γ.

Initialize: $(U_0, S_0, V_0) = SVD(X_0)$
while $\|X_{j+1} - X_j\|_F < err$ and $j <= n$ **do**
1) Calculate the Riemannian gradient at U_j and V_j
$\text{grad}\, F(U_j) = (I - U_jU_j^T)\nabla F(U_j)$
$\text{grad}\, F(V_j) = (I - V_jV_j^T)\nabla F(V_j)$
2) Perform Armijo rule to find α_j and compute U_{j+1} and V_{j+1} based on (3.9) and (3.10)
$U_{j+1} = \text{qf}(U_j + \alpha_j \text{grad}\, F(U_{j+1}))$
$V_{j+1} = \text{qf}(V_j + \alpha_j \text{grad}\, F(V_{j+1}))$
3) Compute the temporary variable P_{j+1}
$P_{j+1} = U_{j+1}S_jV_{j+1}^T - \frac{1}{\gamma}\nabla f(U_{j+1}S_jV_{j+1}^T)$
5) Compute S_{j+1} based on (3.13)
end while
Output: $X = USV^T$

PROOF. Let us assume the contrary statement: there is a subsequence $\{U_{j'}\}_{j'\in\mathcal{J}}$ converging to the stationary point U_{j+1} with $\text{grad}F(U_{j+1}) \neq 0$.

According to U_{j+1} calculated by (3.9), the step size starts at $\bar{\alpha}$ and decreases by Armijo Rule. There exists a update $\frac{\alpha_j}{\beta}$ satisfying

$$F(U_j) - F(\text{qf}(U_j + \frac{\alpha_j}{\beta}\sigma_j)) < -c\frac{\alpha_j}{\beta}\langle \text{grad}\, F(U_j), \sigma_j\rangle \tag{5.1}$$

Let $\tilde{\sigma_j} = \frac{\sigma_j}{\|\sigma_j\|}$ and $\tilde{\alpha_j} = \frac{\alpha_j\|\sigma_j\|}{\beta}$, (5.1) is further reformulated as

$$\frac{\hat{F}_{U_j}(0) - \hat{F}_{U_j}(\tilde{\alpha_j}\sigma_j)}{\tilde{\alpha_j}} < -c\langle \text{grad}\, F(U_j), \tilde{\sigma_j}\rangle \tag{5.2}$$

where $\hat{F_U}$ is a real-valued function on the tangent space.

Let $\nabla_{\tilde{\sigma}_j}\hat{F}_{U_j}$ be the directional derivative in the direction of $\tilde{\sigma}_j$, then

$$-\nabla_{\tilde{\sigma}_j}\hat{F}_{U_j}(t\tilde{\sigma_j}) < -c\langle \text{grad}\, F(U_j), \tilde{\sigma}_j\rangle,\ t \in (0, \tilde{\alpha}_j) \tag{5.3}$$

Because F in (3.4) is non-increasing, we have $F(U_j) - F(U_{j+1}) \to 0$ and $\{\alpha_j\} \to 0$. Consequently, according to $t \in (0, \tilde{\alpha}_j)$, we have $t \to 0$. Hence, (5.3) can be reformulated as (5.4)

$$-\nabla_{\tilde{\sigma}_j}\hat{F}_{U_j}(0) < -c\langle \text{grad}\, F(U_j), \tilde{\sigma}_j\rangle, \tag{5.4}$$

Based on the local rigidity property in *Retraction*, (5.2) can be reformulated as

$$-\langle \text{grad}\, F(U_j), \tilde{\sigma}_j\rangle < -c\langle \text{grad}\, F(U_j), \tilde{\sigma}_j\rangle \tag{5.5}$$

When f converges to iterate U_{j+1} and the compact set $\{\tilde{\sigma}_j\}_{\mathcal{J}\subseteq J}$ achieves the accumulation point $\tilde{\sigma}_*$, (5.5) can be reformulated as

$$-\langle \text{grad}\, F(U_{j+1}), \tilde{\sigma}_*\rangle \leq -c\langle \text{grad}\, F(U_{j+1}), \tilde{\sigma}_*\rangle$$

Considering the condition $c < 1$, it can be concluded that $\langle \text{grad}\, F(U_{j+1}), \tilde{\sigma}_*\rangle \geq 0$. Since $\langle \text{grad}\, F(U_{j+1}), \tilde{\sigma}_*\rangle \leq 0$, a contradiction $\langle \text{grad}\, F(U_{j+1}), \tilde{\sigma}_*\rangle \geq 0$ is obtained. Consequently, the *Grassmann gradient* $\text{grad}\, F(U_{j+1}) = 0$ is true. Similar conclusion can also be obtained for $\text{grad}\, F(V_{j+1}) = 0$. According to (3.13), the closed-form solution S_{j+1} is optimal, so we have $\text{grad}\, F(S_{j+1}) \ni 0$.

Consequently, $\text{grad} F(U_{j+1}) = 0$, $\text{grad} F(V_{j+1}) = 0$ and $\text{grad} F(S_{j+1}) \ni 0$, these make $\{U_*, S_*, V_*\}$ the stationary point for optimization problem (3.4). □

THEOREM 3. *Let $G = f(USV^T) + \lambda Tr(S)$ denote the objective function in (3.2). Then the stationary point for F in (3.4) is also the stationary point for G.*

PROOF. The first-order optimality conditions of F with respect to U_{j+1}, V_{j+1} and S_{j+1} are

$$\nabla F(U_{j+1}) = (U_{j+1}S_{j+1}V_{j+1}^T - U_jS_jV_j^T + \frac{1}{\gamma}\nabla f(X_j))V_{j+1}S_{j+1}^T = 0 \tag{5.6}$$

$$\nabla F(V_{j+1}) = S_{j+1}^T U_{j+1}(U_{j+1}S_{j+1}V_{j+1}^T - U_jS_jV_j^T + \frac{1}{\gamma}\nabla f(X_j)) = 0 \tag{5.7}$$

$$\nabla F(S_{j+1}) = U_{j+1}^T(U_{j+1}S_{j+1}V_{j+1}^T - U_jS_jV_j^T + \frac{1}{\gamma}\nabla f(X_j))V_{j+1} + \lambda I \ni 0 \tag{5.8}$$

According to Theorem 3, the sequence $\{U_j, S_j, V_j\}$ converges to (U_*, S_*, V_*). Thus we have

$$X_{j+1} - X_j = U_{j+1}S_{j+1}V_{j+1}^T - U_j^T S_j V_j^T = 0$$

. Then (5.6), (5.6) and (5.8) can be reformulated as

$$\nabla f(X_j)V_{j+1}S_{j+1}^T = 0 \tag{5.9}$$

$$S_{j+1}^T U_{j+1}\nabla f(X_j) = 0 \tag{5.10}$$

$$U_{j+1}^T \nabla f(X_j)V_{j+1} + \lambda I \ni 0 \tag{5.11}$$

which are the first-order optimality condition of G with respect to U_{j+1}, V_{j+1} and S_{j+1} respectively. When $j \to \infty$, then $\{U_*, S_*, V_*\}$ is the stationary point for the original problem (3.2). □

6. EXPERIMENTS ON MATRIX COMPLETION

Matrix completion has attracted significant recent attention [10,19,24], which satisfies the form of the *nuclear norm minimization* in (1.1). Matrix completion (MC) recovers the low rank matrices with missing elements and can be addressed by our Lingo algorithm. In this section, we evaluate both the effectiveness and efficiency of Lingo algorithm for solving a collection of matrix completion problems, such as image restoration, denoising and collaborative filtering.

6.1 Experimental Settings

For a systematic comparison, we compare the proposed Lingo model with three state-of-the-art matrix completion algorithms, including IALM [19], OptSpace [18] and LMaFit [24]. All algorithms were implemented in *Matlab* and tested on a desktop computer with a 3.20 GHz CPU and 4.00 GB of memory.

IALM *Inexact Augmented Lagrange Multiplier Method* [19], accelerates the full SVD through adopting a partial SVD. It is also reported that IALM outperforms both SVT [8] and APGL [22] for low-rank matrices recovery.

OptSpace [18] correctly estimates the rank of the original matrix from a partially revealed matrix under some conditions, so that local optimization can reconstruct the original matrix with high probability.

LMaFit [24] Through applying the matrix factorization, and a nonlinear *successive over-relaxation* (SOR) scheme that requires solving a linear least squares problem per iteration, LMaFit can achieve efficient convergence for *nuclear norm minimization* algorithms.

Lingo The algorithm proposed in this paper, linearized the optimization objective function and alternatively optimizes the factor matrices on *Grassmann manifold* via descent gradient algorithm.

6.2 Results on Synthetic Data

We first compare the Lingo algorithm with state-of-the-art matrix completion algorithms on synthetic data. The datasets are synthesized in the following way: We randomly sample a few entries from the synthetic matrices and compare the recovery results. A set of ground-truth $m \times n$ matrices $X_0 = U_0S_0V_0^T$ of rank r are randomly generated, where U_0 and V_0 are two orthonormal matrices with $m \times r$ and $n \times r$, S is a diagonal matrix with size $r \times r$. m and n are both assigned with 5000 and rank r adopts two values with 5 and 10. The sampling ratios s defining percentage of uniformly observed entries are set with 1.5% and 5%.

We use *Root Mean Squared Error* (RMSE) to measure the matrix recovery accuracy:

$$\text{RMSE} = \frac{1}{\sqrt{mn}}\|X - X_0\|_F$$

, where X_0 refers to the ground-truth matrix and X is reconstructed matrix by the matrix completion algorithms.

Fig. 1 shows RMSE versus computation time for IALM, OptSpace, LMaFit and Lingo. It is observed that the reconstructed errors of all algorithms decrease as their computation time increases. Noted that, our Lingo obtains faster convergence speed as well as faster decreasing of RMSE under all four scenarios in Fig. 1. OptSpace performs the worst under the same settings, since the requirement of iteratively computing the SVD of the trimmed matrix leads to the deteriorated performance. IALM achieves a relatively similar RMSE as OptSpace but converges much faster than OptSpace. Although LMaFit obtains lower RMSE within less time, it still performs worse than Lingo.

Note that the performance of matrix algorithms often depends on two significant factors: the rank and the sampling ratio. We further test parameter sensitivity of Lingo when varying the rank or sampling ratio and their influences to RMSE. Fig. 2(b) plots the RMSE obtained by four methods for varying rank r from 5 to 10 with fixed sampling ratio $s = 1\%$ (i.e. 99% of entries are missing). Apparently, Lingo algorithm still performs substantially better in RMSE than IALM, OptSpace, LMaFit. Moreover, when the rank is fixed as 5 in 2(a), the RMSE from Lingo algorithm is still much lower than compared algorithms. Note that here again IALM performs similar to OptSpace and is worse than LMaFit and Lingo, as shown in Fig. 2(a) and Fig. 2(b).

6.3 Image Restoration

A popular application of matrix completion is image restoration. Here we conduct the task of recovering images from

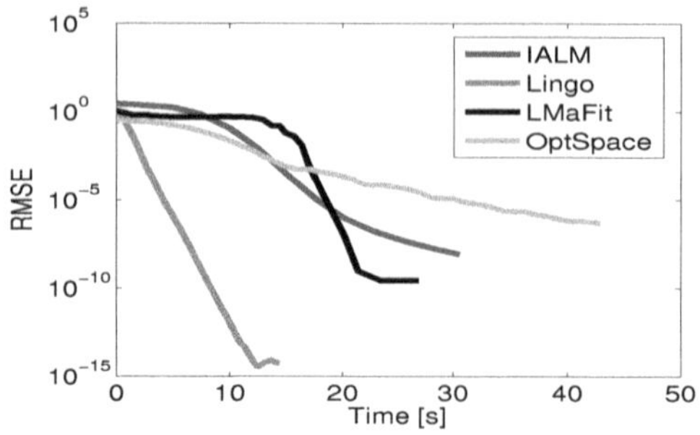

(a) rank $r = 5$, sampling ratio $s = 1.5\%$

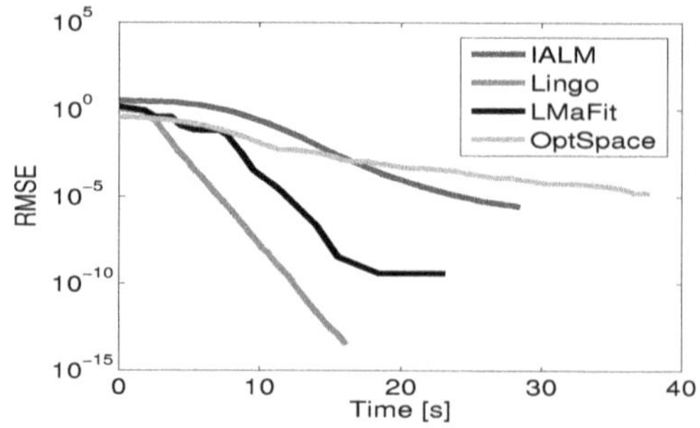

(b) rank $r = 10$, sampling ratio $s = 1.5\%$

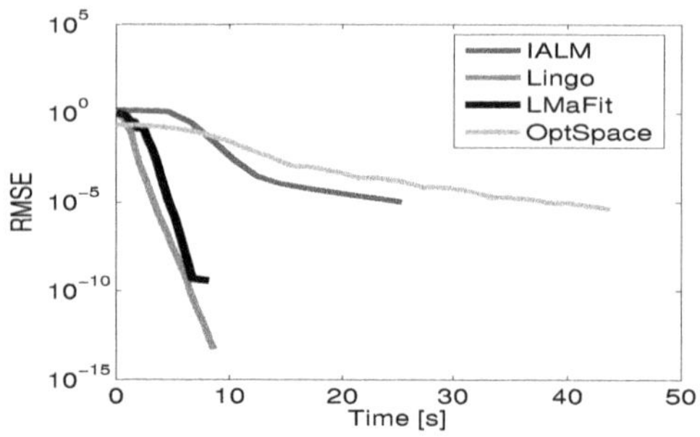

(c) rank $r = 5$, sampling ratio $s = 5\%$

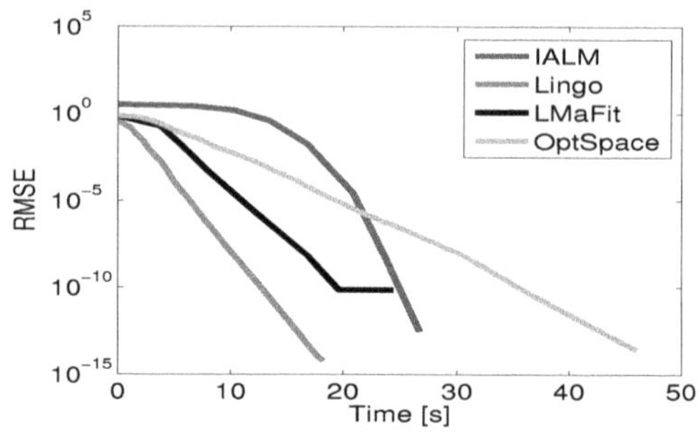

(d) rank $r = 10$, sampling ratio $s = 5\%$

Figure 1: The RMSE versus computation time

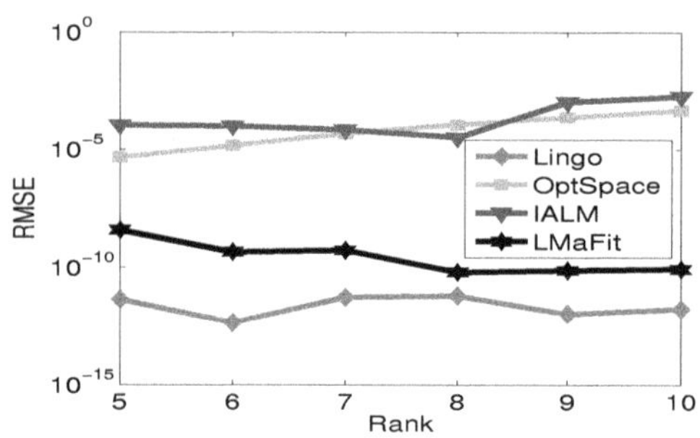

(a) sampling ratio $s = 1\%$

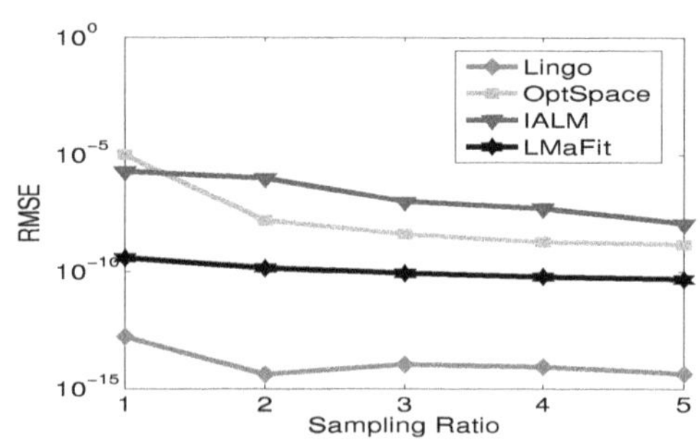

(b) rank $r = 5$

Figure 2: (a) RMSE vesus rank with sampling ratio $s = 1\%$. (b) RMSE vesus sampling ratio with rank $r = 5$

random incomplete observations, and investigate the recovery performance of IALM, OptSpace, LMaFit and Lingo. Four 512 × 512 images are corrupted by randomly removing 50% of pixels. Specifically, IALM, OptSpace, LMaFit and Lingo are required to fill in the missing pixel values to reconstruct the images. We present both the visual reconstructed results and the numerical *Peak Signal-to-Noise Ratio* (PSNR) for all compared algorithms.

PSNR	IALM	OptSpace	LMaFit	Lingo
Image (a)	24.82	23.26	22.35	26.06
Image (b)	25.34	24.12	23.31	27.86
Image (c)	24.36	22.49	25.32	27.79
Image (d)	24.36	22.79	24.14	26.19

Table 1: The PSNR values corresponding to four images in Fig 3.

Fig. 3 shows the recovered images from the IALM, OptSpace, LMaFit and Lingo, along with the masked images. We test all possible rank values from 5 to 20 and choose the best as their results in Fig. 3. By visually inspection, we can see that our Lingo algorithm yields the most visually pleasant recovery results. LMaFit recovers most parts of images with good visual results except that the left parts of these images remain corrupted in some sense. OptSpace and IALM can merely recover the shapes of the objects in corrupted images, which both fails to reconstruct the detailed pixels.

Table 1 qualifies the visual quality using PSNR, from which we further verify the superior visual results of Lingo with the highest PSNR values among all compared algorithms.

Figure 3: From the first row to fourth row are the masked images and recovery results of image (a), image (b), image (c) and image (d) respectively.

When compared with IALM, LMaFit can recover the corrupted images with more clear visualized results, but their PNSR are close, since the left part of LMaFit degrades the overall recover quality. On the contrary, OptSpace has the lowest PSNR value, and this is consistent with the visual results in Fig. 3. Consequently, both the visual results and PSNR results verify that our Lingo can better capture the structure of low rank matrices, and is more robust to noise.

6.4 Image Denoising

In many applications, it is desired to reconstruct the corrupted parts of an image caused by texts or logos. Image denoising task aims to remove the noises from an image, by assuming that the corrupted regions might be unknown. We further conduct image denoising task to test our Lingo algorithm. There are 4 ground-truth images with size 300×300, which are all masked by some text. In the following, we try all possible rank values (i.e., from 5 to 20) to choose the best as their results.

Fig. 4 shows the recovered results of four images indexed as image (e) to image (h), which also demonstrates the satisfying visualized results of Lingo algorithm. OptSpace produces some black blocks at the position of the text, as evident in the recovered image (e) and image (f). IALM somehow improves the OptSpace, but it still produce some black blosks especially in recovered image (f). Moreover, the visual quality of recovery by LMaFit is comparable to Lingo algorithm. To verify the performance, we further quantize these visual quality and takes the computation time into consideration.

Table 6.4 shows the PSNR and the computation time of IALM, OptSpace, LMaFit and Lingo to recover the four images shown in Fig. 4. Lingo can achieve comparable PSNR values with other algorithms, and this is consistent with the visualized results in Fig. 4. Noted that, Lingo consumes much less computation time to achieve the comparable PSNR as LMaFit. Based analysis above, Lingo algorithm is more preferable than other three methods because of the satisfying recovery visual quality as well as the convergence speed.

6.5 Collaborative Filtering

Collaborative filtering aims to predict users' preferences on various items based on existing ratings, and it can be considered as a matrix completion application. The datasets applied in this experiment are two common benchmarks for collaborative filtering: the *Jester joke* dataset [1] and the *MovieLens* dataset [2]. Among them, the *Jester-all* data set contains all 4.1×10^6 rating matrices for 100 jokes from 73421 users; and the *MovieLens* dataset contains three subsets, from which we select *movie-1M* characterized by 1 million rating matrices for 3900 movies by 6040 users. In this experiment, we randomly select about 50% of known entries in the corresponding M_{ij} of *Jester-all* or *movie-1M* dataset as the test set Ω.

The experiment results are evaluated by the *Normalized Mean Absolute Error* (NMAE) [22,24]:

$$\mathrm{NMAE} = \frac{1}{(r_{max} - r_{min})|\Omega|} \sum_{i,j \in \Omega} |X_0 - \hat{X}| \qquad (6.1)$$

Figure 4: From the first row to fourth row are the masked images and recovery results of image (e), image (f), image (g) and image (h) respectively.

Table 2: The PSNR values and computation time corresponding to four images in Fig. 4

	IALM		OptSpace		LMaFit		Lingo	
	PSNR	Time	PSNR	Time	PSNR	Time	PSNR	Time
Image (e)	28.32	13.62	27.70	25.33	29.46	4.07	30.20	3.11
Image (f)	29.31	14.16	28.75	24.66	30.20	5.10	30.18	4.63
Image (g)	29.18	14.80	28.60	28.41	29.27	4.84	30.26	3.99
Image (h)	31.15	13.78	30.18	26.41	31.86	5.26	31.92	4.17

where X_0 refers to the rating matrix, $\hat{X}$ is the reconstructed matrix, $r_{\max}$ and $r_{\min}$ are the upper and the lower bounds for the ratings. For the *jester*-all dataset, we have $r_{\max} = 10$ and $r_{\min} = -10$; while for the *movie*-1M dataset, we have $r_{\max} = 5$ and $r_{\min} = 1$.

We run the compared algorithms with rank =5 and rank=10 on both data sets. The experiments repeated 20 times over the test data Ω for each algorithm, the parameters of the baselines are tuned for the best averaged performance shown in Table 6.5. It is evident that Lingo algorithm generates most often the better or comparable NMAE values, when compared with IALM, OptSpace and LMaFit. More specifically, when we take the computation time into consideration, Lingo algorithm is much more superior to other three methods with less computation time. In contrast, it takes the most computation time for OptSpace algorithm to generate the comparable NMAE values with Lingo. The slow convergence of OptSpace might be caused by the repeated larg-scale SVD. These results indicate that Lingo algorithm provides a computational efficient solution to collaborative filtering with high accuracy.

7. CONCLUSIONS

Various algorithms have been proposed for *nuclear norm minimization*, but most rank minimization based algorithms depend on large-scale SVDs which results in extra computational burden. To alleviate this issue, *matrix factorization* factors the larger matrix into small factor matrices and scales the searching space to reduce the computational burden. Through this measure, most *matrix factorization* algorithms achieve satisfying accuracy, but without theoretical convergence guarantee, and it might be very slow to achieve satisfactory accuracy.

In this work, we propose an efficient and accurate *Linearized Grassmannian Optimization* (Lingo) algorithm with theoretical convergence guarantee. Lingo adopts matrix factorization and fully explores the underlying quotient *Grassmann* nature of the factor matrices. By constraining the search space over manifolds, Lingo designs the gradient-based optimization to alternatively minimize the subproblems with *Grassmann* manifold structure. Moreover, to guarantee the close-form solution with low complexity in each iteration, Lingo adopts linearization to the objective

Settings		IALM		OptSpace		LMaFit		Lingo	
Dataset	Rank	Time	NMAE	Time	NMAE	Time	NMAE	Time	NMAE
jester-all	5	48.53	0.108	1048.9	0.158	21.41	0.156	16.99	0.153
	10	50.57	0.187	1646.8	0.162	26.35	0.153	38.34	0.148
movie-1M	5	21.16	0.310	780	0.321	29.62	0.177	7.14	0.176
	10	29.28	0.321	1238	0.212	35.47	0.173	11.08	0.190

Table 3: Computation time and NMAE on collaborate filtering

function. The convergence of Lingo is guaranteed with theoretical proof, and the effectiveness is validated in extensive comparison experiments with state-of-art algorithms.

8. ACKNOWLEDGMENTS

This research is partially supported by the Strategic Priority Research Program of the Chinese Academy of Sciences Grant (XDA06030200), Beijing Key Lab of Intelligent Telecommunication Software and Multimedia (ITSM201502), Guangxi Key Laboratory of Trusted Software (KX201418), the National Natural Science Foundation of China (No.61403369).

9. REFERENCES

[1] Jester jokes. http://eigentaste.berkeley.edu/user/index.php.

[2] Movielens. http://www.movielens.org.

[3] Laura Balzano, Robert Nowak, and Benjamin Recht. Online identification and tracking of subspaces from highly incomplete information. In *Communication, Control, and Computing (Allerton), 2010 48th Annual Allerton Conference on*, pages 704–711. IEEE, 2010.

[4] Amir Beck and Marc Teboulle. A fast iterative shrinkage-thresholding algorithm for linear inverse problems. *SIAM Journal on Imaging Sciences*, 2(1):183–202, 2009.

[5] James Bennett and Stan Lanning. The netflix prize. In *Proceedings of KDD cup and workshop*, volume 2007, page 35, 2007.

[6] Nicolas Boumal and Pierre-antoine Absil. Rtrmc: A riemannian trust-region method for low-rank matrix completion. In *Advances in neural information processing systems*, pages 406–414, 2011.

[7] Christos Boutsidis, Petros Drineas, and Malik Magdon-Ismail. Near-optimal column-based matrix reconstruction. *SIAM Journal on Computing*, 43(2):687–717, 2014.

[8] Jian-Feng Cai, Emmanuel J Candès, and Zuowei Shen. A singular value thresholding algorithm for matrix completion. *SIAM Journal on Optimization*, 20(4):1956–1982, 2010.

[9] Emmanuel J Candès and Benjamin Recht. Exact matrix completion via convex optimization. *Foundations of Computational mathematics*, 9(6):717–772, 2009.

[10] Wei Dai, Olgica Milenkovic, and Ely Kerman. Subspace evolution and transfer (set) for low-rank matrix completion. *Signal Processing, IEEE Transactions on*, 59(7):3120–3132, 2011.

[11] Petros Drineas, Alan M Frieze, Ravi Kannan, Santosh Vempala, and V Vinay. Clustering in large graphs and matrices. In *SODA*, volume 99, pages 291–299. Citeseer, 1999.

[12] Alan Edelman, Tomás A Arias, and Steven T Smith. The geometry of algorithms with orthogonality constraints. *SIAM journal on Matrix Analysis and Applications*, 20(2):303–353, 1998.

[13] A Evgeniou and Massimiliano Pontil. Multi-task feature learning. *Advances in neural information processing systems*, 19:41, 2007.

[14] Maryam Fazel. *Matrix rank minimization with applications.* PhD thesis, PhD thesis, Stanford University, 2002.

[15] Massimo Fornasier and Holger Rauhut. Iterative thresholding algorithms. *Applied and Computational Harmonic Analysis*, 25(2):187–208, 2008.

[16] AJ Izenman. *Modern multivariate statistical techniques*, volume 1. Springer, 2008.

[17] Shuiwang Ji and Jieping Ye. An accelerated gradient method for trace norm minimization. In *Proceedings of the 26th Annual International Conference on Machine Learning*, pages 457–464. ACM, 2009.

[18] Raghunandan H Keshavan and Sewoong Oh. A gradient descent algorithm on the grassman manifold for matrix completion. *arXiv preprint arXiv:0910.5260*, 2009.

[19] Zhouchen Lin, Minming Chen, and Yi Ma. The augmented lagrange multiplier method for exact recovery of corrupted low-rank matrices. *arXiv preprint arXiv:1009.5055*, 2010.

[20] Zhouchen Lin, Risheng Liu, and Zhixun Su. Linearized alternating direction method with adaptive penalty for low-rank representation. In *Advances in neural information processing systems*, pages 612–620, 2011.

[21] Jonathan H Manton. Optimization algorithms exploiting unitary constraints. *Signal Processing, IEEE Transactions on*, 50(3):635–650, 2002.

[22] Kim-Chuan Toh and Sangwoon Yun. An accelerated proximal gradient algorithm for nuclear norm regularized linear least squares problems. *Pacific Journal of Optimization*, 6(615-640):15, 2010.

[23] Pavan Turaga, Ashok Veeraraghavan, and Rama Chellappa. Statistical analysis on stiefel and grassmann manifolds with applications in computer vision. In *Computer Vision and Pattern Recognition, 2008. CVPR 2008. IEEE Conference on*, pages 1–8. IEEE, 2008.

[24] Zaiwen Wen, Wotao Yin, and Yin Zhang. Solving a low-rank factorization model for matrix completion by a nonlinear successive over-relaxation algorithm. *Mathematical Programming Computation*, 4(4):333–361, 2012.

Deep Collaborative Filtering via Marginalized Denoising Auto-encoder

Sheng Li*
Northeastern University
Boston, MA, USA
shengli@ece.neu.edu

Jaya Kawale
Adobe Research
San Jose, CA, USA
kawale@adobe.com

Yun Fu
Northeastern University
Boston, MA, USA
yunfu@ece.neu.edu

ABSTRACT

Collaborative filtering (CF) has been widely employed within recommender systems to solve many real-world problems. Learning effective latent factors plays the most important role in collaborative filtering. Traditional CF methods based upon matrix factorization techniques learn the latent factors from the user-item ratings and suffer from the cold start problem as well as the sparsity problem. Some improved CF methods enrich the priors on the latent factors by incorporating side information as regularization. However, the learned latent factors may not be very effective due to the sparse nature of the ratings and the side information. To tackle this problem, we learn effective latent representations via deep learning. Deep learning models have emerged as very appealing in learning effective representations in many applications. In particular, we propose a general deep architecture for CF by integrating matrix factorization with deep feature learning. We provide a natural instantiations of our architecture by combining probabilistic matrix factorization with marginalized denoising stacked auto-encoders. The combined framework leads to a parsimonious fit over the latent features as indicated by its improved performance in comparison to prior state-of-art models over four large datasets for the tasks of movie/book recommendation and response prediction.

Categories and Subject Descriptors

H.2.8 [**Database Management**]: Data Mining; H.3.3 [**Information Search Retrieval**]: Information Filtering

Keywords

Collaborative filtering; matrix factorization; deep learning; denoising auto-encoder

1. INTRODUCTION

Recommendation is a fundamental problem that has gained utmost importance in the modern era of information overload. The goal of recommendation is to help users find the item that they maybe potentially interested in from a large repository of items. Recommender systems are widely used by websites (e.g., Amazon, Google News, Netflix, and Last.fm) in various contexts to target customers and provide them with useful information. A widely used setting of recommendation system is to predict how a user would rate an item (such as a movie) if only given the past rating history of the users. Many classical recommendation methods have been proposed during the last decade. The two broad categories of recommendation systems are content filtering approaches and collaborative filtering (CF) based methods. The CF based methods have attracted more attention due to their impressive performance [1]. Among various CF methods, matrix factorization has emerged as a powerful tool to perform recommendations in large datasets [2, 3].

Learning effective latent factors plays the most important role in matrix factorization based CF methods. Traditional matrix factorization methods for CF directly learn the latent factors from the user-item rating matrix [2, 4]. One of the main challenges faced by these systems is to provide a rating when a new user/item arrives in the system, which is also known as the *cold start* scenario. The cold start problem is circular in nature as - the system will not recommend an item unless it has some ratings for it and unless the system recommends it will not get ratings for it. Another practical challenge is learning the appropriate latent factors when the rating matrix is sparse, which is often the case in many real world scenarios. In order to overcome these challenges, researchers have suggested to incorporate additional sources of information about the users or items, also known as the *side information*. This side information could be obtained from the user/item profiles, for example, demographics of a user, genre of a movie, etc. The user demographics could be used to infer the relationships between the users and similarly the item similarity can be used to automatically assign ratings to new items. The use of side information to aid matrix factorization has been successfully applied by various prior work, for example [5, 6, 7]. These methods, however, only utilize the side information as regularizations in the model, and the learned latent factors may not be very effective due to the sparse nature of the ratings and the side information. In order to make matrix factorization based methods effective in such a setting, it is highly desirable to learn and extract discriminative features from the datasets.

One of the powerful approaches to capture feature interactions and complex relations that has emerged in the recent past is deep learning [8, 9]. Deep learning has attracted a lot of attention because of its promising performance to learn representations on various tasks. Deep neural networks have been shown to achieve state-of-the-art results in computer vision, speech recognition and machine translation. The application of deep learning in recommen-

*Part of the work is completed during Sheng Li's internship at Adobe Research.

Permission to make digital or hard copies of all or part of this work for personal or classroom use is granted without fee provided that copies are not made or distributed for profit or commercial advantage and that copies bear this notice and the full citation on the first page. Copyrights for components of this work owned by others than ACM must be honored. Abstracting with credit is permitted. To copy otherwise, or republish, to post on servers or to redistribute to lists, requires prior specific permission and/or a fee. Request permissions from Permissions@acm.org.
CIKM'15, October 19–23, 2015, Melbourne, Australia.
© 2015 ACM. ISBN 978-1-4503-3794-6/15/10 ...$15.00.
DOI: http://dx.doi.org/10.1145/2806416.2806527.

dation systems, however, is very recent. With large-scale data and rich-side information available, it is now practicable to learn latent factors through deep architectures. Researchers have invested in modifying deep learning algorithms like Restricted Botzmann Machines or Convolutional Neural Networks or Deep Belief Networks directly for the task of collaborative filtering [10, 11, 12, 13, 14]. However, there are no prior work that bridge together matrix factorization with deep learning methods with the notable exception of [15]. In this paper, we present a deep learning model for collaborative filtering that tightly couples matrix factorization based collaborative filtering with deep learning algorithm namely marginalized denoising auto-encoders (mDA) [16]. Unlike [15] which integrates collaborative topic regression and bayesian stacked denoising auto-encoders and requires learning of a large number of hyper parameters using an EM style algorithm, our approach uses a much more efficient architecture based upon mDA and stochastic gradient descent and is thus computationally efficient and highly scalable. This paper makes the following contributions:

- We propose a general deep architecture named deep collaborative filtering (DCF), which integrates matrix factorization and deep feature learning. It models the mappings between the latent factors used in CF and the latent layers in deep models.
- We present a practical instantiation (i.e., mDA-CF and mSDA-CF) of the proposed architecture, by utilizing the probabilistic matrix factorization and mDA. The scalability and low computational cost of the mDA makes it a highly attractive deep learning tool, which is unlike the prior work [15].
- We evaluate the performance of our model on three real-world applications, movie recommendation, book recommendation and response prediction. Our model outperforms conventional CF methods.

2. RELATED WORK

In general, our work is closely related to the following topics: matrix factorization based collaborative filtering, and deep learning based collaborative filtering. We will discuss the two in the following subsections.

2.1 Matrix Factorization for Collaborative Filtering

The importance of accurate recommendation techniques motivated by wide ranging applications has fuelled a great amount of academic as well as industrial research in this area [17]. Recommender systems are most often based on collaborative filtering and there are typically two approaches that are widely used. In *neighborhood methods*, the similarity between users based on the content they have consumed and rated is the basis of a new recommendation. A related but intrinsically more powerful approach has been the use of *latent factor models*. Matrix factorization (MF) is the most popular technique to derive latent factor models and their success at the Netflix competition have highlighted their strength [18, 2]. For example, the given matrix $X \in \mathbb{R}^{N\times M}$ consisting of the item preferences of the users can be decomposed as a product of two low dimensional matrices U and V. The decomposition can be carried out by a variety of methods ranging from SVD based approaches [19] to the relatively new non-negative matrix factorization approach [20]. One classical MF method is probabilistic matrix factorization (PMF) [4]. The underlying assumption behind this method is that the prior probability distribution of the latent factors and the probability of the observed ratings given the latent factors follows a Gaussian distribution. Many algorithms have been developed to enhance the performance of PMF, by designing the Bayesian versions [21, 22, 23], or incorporating side information, such as social relationships [24, 5, 25].

Although promising, matrix factorization methods suffer from the problem of cold-start, i.e. what recommendations to make when a new user/item arrives in the system. Another problem often presented in many real world applications is data sparsity or reduced coverage. Incorporating side information has shown promising performance in collaborative filtering in such scenarios. Porteous *et al.* proposed a Bayesian matrix factorization (BMF) approach with side information and Dirichlet process mixtures [26]. A variational BMF method and a hierarchical BMF method that utilizes side information were also proposed in [27] and [28], respectively. Hu *et al.* proposed a cross-domain triadic factorization (CDTF) method [29], which leverages the information from other domains. The methods discussed above are proposed for addressing recommendation problems. Recently, MF based collaborative filtering is also applied to response prediction [30, 31]. The afore-mentioned approaches can alleviate the problem of cold start and data sparsity but might still suffer when the side information is sparse. Learning effective features is critical in matrix factorization. Recently, deep learning based methods have emerged as a powerful tool for learning representation and are widely used in many applications ranging from computer vision to speech recognition and machine translation. In this paper, our goal is to combine deep learning based methods with matrix factorization for collaborative filtering. In the next subsection, we survey the application of deep learning based methods for collaborative filtering.

2.2 Deep Learning for Collaborative Filtering

The application of deep learning models to the task of collaborative filtering is very new and there are not much attempts in this direction. Salakhutdinov *et al.* [10] were the first to apply deep learning to the task of collaborative filtering. They modified the restricted Boltzmann machines as a two-layer undirected graphical model consisting of binary hidden units and softmax visible units for the task of collaborative filtering. They designed an efficient learning procedure called the Contrastive Divergence (CD) to maximize an approximation to the true likelihood function. They also proposed a conditional RBM model and inference procedures. They tested the performance of the model on the Netflix dataset for movie recommendation and showed that their model performs well as compared to the baseline methods.

Truyen *et al.* [14] proposed ordinal Boltzmann machines for collaborative filtering. They studied the parameterizations for handling the ordinal nature of ratings, and presented the integration of multiple Boltzmann machines for user-based and item-based processes.

Recently, some deep learning models learn latent factors from content information such as raw features of audio or articles [32, 33]. Wang *et al.* [12] utilized deep belief nets (DBN) for music recommendation, which unifies feature extraction and recommendation of songs in a joint framework. They assumed that a user has a feature vector β_u drawn from a Gaussian prior and the songs have a feature vector x_v. They automatically learned the feature vectors of the songs using a deep belief network which is a generative probabilistic graphical model with hidden nodes and observation. It has millions of parameters to be learned from the training data. The authors used stacked layers of Restricted Boltzmann Machines for pretraining in an unsupervised fashion, and then employed the Maximum Likelihood Estimation (MLE) for supervised learning.

Oord *et al.* [13] addressed the music recommendation problem using the convolutional neural networks. They first conducted a weighted matrix factorization to handle implicit feedback and obtained latent factors for all songs. After that they used deep learning to map audio content to those latent factors. In particular, they extracted local features from audio signals and aggregated them into a bag-of-words representation. Finally, the deep convolutional network was employed to map this feature representation to the latent factors. They tested their algorithm on the Million song dataset and showed that their model improved the recommendation performance by augmenting the audio signals.

All the previously mentioned approaches mainly modify the deep learning algorithms for the task of collaborative filtering and do not directly couple matrix factorization with deep learning models. Most recently, Wang *et al.* [15] proposed a hierarchical Bayesian model called collaborative deep learning (CDL) which tightly couples stacked denoising auto-encoders (SDA) and collaborative topic regression (CTR). This work is the closest to our work but differs from ours in many significant ways as follows - (i) CDL utilized a Bayesian formulation of SDA. The generative process of CDL consists of drawing samples for CDL uses an EM-style algorithm for obtaining the MAP estimates of Bayesian SDA, and thus it has to learn a large number of parameters. Our model employs a more efficient architecture, marginalized SDA (mSDA), which computes the parameters in closed form and is thus highly efficient and scalable. (ii) CDL only extracts deep features for items, whereas our model learns deep features for both items and users.

3. PRELIMINARIES

Before we describe our general framework, we discuss the preliminaries as follows.

3.1 Matrix Factorization

Matrix Factorization (MF) is the most effective collaborative filtering approach. It allows us to discover the latent factors of user-item interactions by factorizing the interactions matrix into a joint latent space of user and item features respectively. It proceeds by decomposing the original rating matrix $R \in \mathbb{R}^{m \times n}$ consisting of ratings by m users for n items into two low-rank matrices $U \in \mathbb{R}^{m \times d}$ and $V \in \mathbb{R}^{n \times d}$ consisting of the user and item features respectively of rank d.

The system learns the latent factors by minimizing the following objective function -

$$\arg\min_{U,V} l(R,U,V) + \beta(\|U\|_{\mathrm{F}}^2 + \|V\|_{\mathrm{F}}^2), \quad (1)$$

where $l(R,U,V)$ is the loss function of predicting rating using the latent factors U and V and the last two terms are the regularizations used to avoid overfitting. $\|\cdot\|_{\mathrm{F}}$ denotes the Frobenius norm.

Many MF-based methods have been proposed, by designing a sophisticated loss function $l(R,U,V)$. Existing works usually pose some assumptions on the latent factors U and V in (1). Probabilistic matrix factorization (PMF) [4] provides a probabilistic foundation by assuming a probabilistic linear model with Gaussian observation noise and Gaussian priors on the latent factors.

$$p(R|U,V,\sigma^2) = \prod_{i=1}^{M}\prod_{j=1}^{N} \mathcal{N}(R_{ij}|U_i^T V_j, \sigma^2)^{I_{ij}} \quad (2)$$

$$p(U|\sigma_u^2) = \prod_{i=1}^{M} \mathcal{N}(U_i|0,\sigma_u^2)\ ; p(V|\sigma_v^2) = \prod_{j=1}^{N} \mathcal{N}(V_j|0,\sigma_v^2). \quad (3)$$

The model is fitted by finding a MAP estimate of the parameters. Maximizing the log posterior leads to the following objective function that can be solved using stochastic gradient descent (SGD):

$$\arg\min_{U,V} E = \|R - UV^\top\|_{\mathrm{F}}^2 + \beta(\|U\|_{\mathrm{F}}^2 + \|V\|_{\mathrm{F}}^2).$$

To improve the recommendation performance of PMF, Bayesian probabilistic matrix factorization method (BPMF) [34] considers a full Bayesian treatment of the parameter space instead of a point estimate used in PMF. In the weighted matrix factorization (WMF), $l(R,U,V) = \|C \odot (R - UV^\top)\|_{\mathrm{F}}^2$, where C is the weight matrix [35]. Our model is based upon the probabilistic matrix factorization approach as it has shown to have a very good performance on several datasets and at the same time is computationally more efficient as compared to BPMF.

When side information are available, some MF methods make use of these additional information via regression to predict the ratings [28].

3.2 Marginalized Denoising Auto-encoder (mDA)

As a specific form of neural network, an autoencoder takes a given input and maps it (*encodes*) to a hidden representation via a deterministic mapping. Denoising autoencoders reconstruct the input from a corrupted version of the data with the motivation of learning a more robust mapping from the data. Various types of autoencoders have been developed in the literature and have shown promising results in several domains [36, 37]. Moreover, denoising autoencoders can be stacked to construct a deep network also known as stacked denoising autoencoder (SDA) which allows learning higher level representations [38]. Despite their state-of-the-art performance, one of the main drawbacks of SDA is the high computational cost of training, as they rely upon the iterative and numerical optimization techniques to learn a large amount of model parameters.

Marginalized denoising auto-encoder (mDA) [16] is a variant of SDA that avoids the high computational cost by marginalizing out the random feature corruption and thus has a closed-form solution to learn model parameters. Therefore, mDA is highly scalable and faster than SDA. It proceeds as follows:

Given a sample set $X = [x_1, \cdots, x_k]$, mDA considers multiple passes (e.g., c-times) of random corruptions over X to obtain $\widetilde{X}$. It then reconstructs the input with a mapping W that minimizes the squared loss as follows:

$$\mathcal{L}(W) = \frac{1}{2ck}\sum_{j=1}^{c}\sum_{i=1}^{k} \|x_i - W\tilde{x}_{ij}\|^2, \quad (4)$$

where $\tilde{x}_{ij}$ represents the jth corrupted version of the original input x_i and W represents the mapping that is expected to minimizes the loss function.

The above objective can be rewritten in the matrix form as

$$\mathcal{L}(W) = \|\bar{X} - W\widetilde{X}\|_{\mathrm{F}}^2, \quad (5)$$

where $\bar{X} = [X, \cdots, X]$ is the c-times repeated version of X, and $\tilde{X}$ is the corresponding corrupted version. This problem is similar to the ordinary least squares problem and has the analytical solution as given by $W = SQ^{-1}$, where $S = \tilde{X}\tilde{X}^T$, $Q = \bar{X}\tilde{X}^T$ When $c \to \infty$ in (4), we can derive the expectations of Q and P, and obtain the closed form solution of the mDA [16]. Further, multiple mDAs can be stacked to form a deep architecture, marginalized stacked denoising auto-encoder (mSDA). mSDA usually enhances the performance of mDA. Most recently, a nonlinear version of mDA is presented [39].

Table 1: Summary of notations.

Notation	Description
m	Number of users
n	Number of items
d	Dimension of latent factors
p	Dimension of user features
q	Dimension of item features
$R \in \mathbb{R}^{m \times n}$	Rating matrix
$U \in \mathbb{R}^{m \times d}$	Latent factors of users
$V \in \mathbb{R}^{n \times d}$	Latent factors of items
$X \in \mathbb{R}^{p \times m}$	Side information of users
$Y \in \mathbb{R}^{q \times n}$	Side information of items
$W_1 \in \mathbb{R}^{p \times p}$	Mapping function for X in auto-encoder
$P_1 \in \mathbb{R}^{p \times d}$	Projection matrix for U

4. OUR APPROACH

As we noted earlier, deep learning models have been proven to be very effective in extracting high-level representations from the raw input data in several learning tasks. The learned features represent high-level knowledge. In the collaborative filtering problem, we face a similar challenge of inferring effective latent and high-level knowledge on user preferences from the raw inputs, including the rating matrix and related features. MF based CF methods are able to capture the implicit relationship between the users and the items successfully, but they suffer from the cold start and data sparsity problems. Therefore, it is reasonable to draw strength from the deep models to assist the collaborative filtering process.

Table 1 summarizes the symbols used in our approach. Next, we describe a general framework that integrates matrix factorization and deep feature learning.

4.1 Deep Collaborative Filtering (DCF): A General Framework

In this section, we introduce the proposed deep collaborative filtering (DCF) framework which unifies the deep learning models with MF based collaborative filtering. Fig. 1 illustrates the idea of our DCF framework. DCF is a *hybrid* model, which makes use of both rating matrix and side information and bridges together matrix factorization and feature learning.

Given a user-item rating matrix R, the user side information X and the item side information Y, DCF jointly decomposes R and learns latent factors (i.e., U, V) from ratings and side information (i.e., X and Y) through the following formulation:

$$\arg\min_{U,V} \; l(R,U,V) + \beta(\|U\|_F^2 + \|V\|_F^2) + \gamma\mathcal{L}(X,U) + \delta\mathcal{L}(Y,V), \tag{6}$$

where β, γ and δ are the trade-off parameters.

There are two key components in the DCF framework: (i) the function $l(R,U,V)$ for decomposing the rating matrix R into the two latent matrices; (ii) the functions $\mathcal{L}(X,U)$ and $\mathcal{L}(Y,V)$ that connect the user/item contextual features with the latent factors. The first component derived through matrix factorization extracts latent knowledge from the rating matrix. The second component devised using deep learning models establishes connections of the side information with the latent factors.

4.2 DCF using PMF + mDA

A natural instantiation of DCF is combining probabilistic matrix factorization (PMF) with marginalized denoising auto-encoders (mDA). PMF is a widely applied CF approach with excellent performance, and mDA is a powerful tool in extracting high-level features from raw inputs. The combination of the two leverages their benefits for learning even richer models.

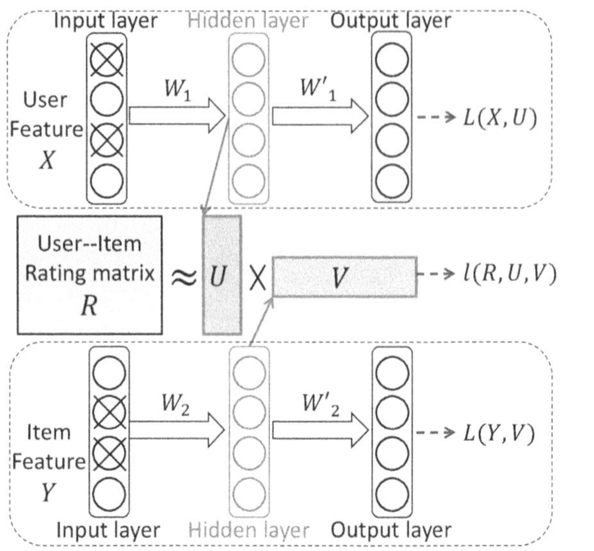

Figure 1: Illustration of DCF framework. The inputs are user-item rating matrix R, the user feature set X and the item feature set Y. Our approach jointly decomposes R and learns latent factors (i.e., U, V) from ratings and side information (i.e., X and Y). In particular, the latent factors are extracted from the hidden layer of deep networks.

4.2.1 mDA based Collaborative Filtering (mDA-CF)

Let $\bar{X} \in \mathbb{R}^{p \times cm}$ and $\bar{Y} \in \mathbb{R}^{q \times cn}$ denote the c-times repeated versions of X and Y respectively and let $\tilde{X}$ and $\tilde{Y}$ denote their corrupted versions. As discussed before, we utilize the loss function of PMF to decompose rating matrix R, i.e., $l(R,U,V) = \|A \odot (R - UV^\top)\|_F^2$, where A is the indicator matrix indicating the non-empty entries in R and $\odot$ denotes the Hadamard or point-wise product. The objective function of mDA-CF is formulated as follows:

$$\begin{aligned}\arg \min_{\substack{U,V,W_1,\\W_2,P_1,P_2}} \; & \mathcal{L}_U(W_1,P_1,U) + \mathcal{L}_V(W_2,P_2,V) + \\ & \alpha\|A \odot (R - UV^\top)\|_F^2 + \beta(\|U\|_F^2 + \|V\|_F^2),\end{aligned} \tag{7}$$

where

$$\mathcal{L}_U(W_1,P_1,U) = \|\bar{X} - W_1\tilde{X}\|_F^2 + \lambda\|P_1U^\top - W_1X\|_F^2,$$

$$\mathcal{L}_V(W_2,P_2,V) = \|\bar{Y} - W_2\tilde{Y}\|_F^2 + \lambda\|P_2V^\top - W_2Y\|_F^2,$$

$W_1 \in \mathbb{R}^{p \times p}$ and $W_2 \in \mathbb{R}^{q \times q}$ are reconstructive mappings, $P_1 \in \mathbb{R}^{p \times d}$ and $P_2 \in \mathbb{R}^{q \times d}$ are projection matrices, α, β and λ are trade-off parameters. Note that, we set γ and δ in (6) to 1 for simplicity.

The first term in $\mathcal{L}_U(W_1,P_1,U)$ denotes the learning process in marginalized denoising auto-encoder. It measures the reconstruction error between input user features $\bar{X}$ and the mapped features of corrupted inputs, i.e., $W_1\tilde{X}$. W_1 is the learned mapping that is expected to minimize the loss. The second term connects the hidden layer feature W_1X and the latent factor U. Generally, the latent factor has much lower dimension than the raw features. Therefore, we add a low-dimensional projection P_1 that maps latent factor to the feature space.

Optimization

Although the optimization problem in (7) is not jointly convex in all the variables, it is convex to each of them when fixing the others. Hence, we can alternately optimize for each of the variables in (7). The detailed procedures are provided below.

First, we derive a solution to solve W_1 and W_2 using [16]. By ignoring the variables irrelevant to W_1, the objective (7) can be rewritten as

$$\arg\min_{W_1} \quad \|\bar{X} - W_1\tilde{X}\|_F^2 + \lambda\|P_1U^\top - W_1X\|_F^2. \tag{8}$$

Inspired by mDA, we consider the infinitely many copies of noisy data, and obtain the optimal solution

$$W_1 = E[S_1]E[Q_1]^{-1}, \tag{9}$$

where $S_1 = \bar{X}\tilde{X}^\top + \lambda P_1U^\top X^\top$ and $Q_1 = \tilde{X}\tilde{X}^\top + \lambda XX^\top$. An efficient solver for calculating the expectations $E[S_1]$ and $E[Q_1]$ is provided in [16].

Similarly, we can derive the closed-form solution to W_2

$$W_2 = E[S_2]E[Q_2]^{-1}, \tag{10}$$

where $S_2 = \bar{Y}\tilde{Y}^\top + \lambda P_2V^\top Y^\top$ and $Q_2 = \tilde{Y}\tilde{Y}^\top + \lambda YY^\top$.

Next, by dropping the irrelevant variables w.r.t. P_1, the objective function becomes

$$\arg\min_{P_1} \quad \lambda\|P_1U^\top - W_1X\|_F^2. \tag{11}$$

We can obtain the closed-form solution as

$$P_1 = W_1XU(U^\top U)^{-1}. \tag{12}$$

Similarly, the optimal solution of P_2 is

$$P_2 = W_2YV(V^\top V)^{-1}. \tag{13}$$

To solve for the latent factors U and V, we use the popular stochastic gradient descent (SGD) algorithm. In particular, when other variables irrelevant to U and V are fixed, we use $f(U,V)$ to denote the objective in (7). The update rules are:

$$\begin{aligned} u_i &= u_i - \eta\frac{\partial}{\partial u_i}f(U,V), \\ v_j &= v_j - \eta\frac{\partial}{\partial v_j}f(U,V), \end{aligned} \tag{14}$$

where η is the learning rate , and the detailed derivatives are defined as

$$\begin{aligned} \tfrac{\partial f(U,V)}{\partial u_i} =& \lambda(P_1^\top(P_1u_i - (W_1X)_i)) + \beta u_i \\ & - \alpha\sum_{(i,j)\in\mathcal{A}}(R_{i,j} - u_iv_j^\top)v_j. \end{aligned} \tag{15}$$

$$\begin{aligned} \tfrac{\partial f(U,V)}{\partial v_j} =& \lambda(P_2^\top(P_2v_j - (W_2Y)_j)) + \beta v_j \\ & - \alpha\sum_{(i,j)\in\mathcal{A}}(R_{i,j} - u_iv_j^\top)u_i. \end{aligned} \tag{16}$$

The above steps are repeated until convergence. Finally, we obtain the latent factors U and V.

Algorithm Complexity

The steps of our mDA-CF approach are summarized in *Algorithm 1*. The learned latent factors U and V can be used to predict missing entries in the rating matrix. In *Algorithm 1*, we have analytical solutions of Steps 3-6 which are efficient to compute. The matrix multiplication and inversion used in Step 5 and Step 6 cost $\mathcal{O}(p^2m + pmd + d^3)$ and $\mathcal{O}(q^2n + qnd + d^3)$, respectively. The Steps 8-9 are implemented in a batch-learning fashion, and cost

Algorithm 1. mDA-CF Algorithm

Input: Rating matrix R, user features X, item features Y, parameters λ, α, β.
Output: Latent factors U, V
1: Initialize U, V, P_1 and P_2;
2: ***while*** validation error decreases, ***do***
3: Update W_1 using (9);
4: Update W_2 using (10);
5: Update P_1 using (12);
6: Update P_2 using (13);
7: ***for*** each observed R_{ij}, ***do***
8: Update u_i using (14);
9: Update v_j using (14);
10: ***end for***
11: ***end while***

$\mathcal{O}(tN)$ to evaluate the gradients, where t is the number of iterations and N is the number of training ratings/responses in R. Considering that $N \gg \max\{m,n,d\}$, the time complexity of *Algorithm 1* is mainly determined by $\mathcal{O}(tN)$. Hence, our approach owns a good scalability. We discuss the settings of the parameters in the experimental section. To further reduce the computational cost, some advanced distributed optimization algorithms could be applied to our model [40].

4.2.2 *Stacked mDA based Collaborative Filtering (mSDA-CF)*

Existing literature show that stacking multiple deep learning layers together can usually generate rich features in the form of hidden layers, and therefore results in better performance for various learning tasks. Inspired by the marginalized stacked denoising auto-encoders (mSDA) [16], we stack multiple mDA together, and present the mSDA-CF approach.

We assume that only one hidden layer should be close to the latent factor. The reasons are two-fold. First, latent factors are high-level representations, which should correspond to the deeper layers in deep models. Secondly, latent factors should be unique, but different hidden layers have various representations. Therefore, enforcing the similarity between multiple hidden layers and latent factors is unreasonable.

In our mSDA-CF model, we assume that the latent factors are generated from the $\lfloor\frac{l+1}{2}\rfloor$ layer, given the total number of layers is l. When we train the model for the rest layers, the parameters λ, α and β are simply set to 0. In particular, if $i \neq \lfloor\frac{l+1}{2}\rfloor$, we only need to update W_1^i and W_2^i and ignore the other steps, where W_1^i and W_2^i denote the mappings in the i-th layer. One benefit of such setting is the time efficiency, as we do not increase too much computational burden when adding multiple layers.

Another interesting problem is how to set the number of layers. The number of layers implies the model complexity, which is usually related to the learning task and the size of training data. In the experiments we will discuss the influence of different number of layers. The detailed procedures of mSDA-CF are summarized in *Algorithm 2*.

4.3 Discussion

We notice that most existing deep learning based collaborative filtering methods can be unified in our DCF framework. For example, Oord *et al.* [13] use deep convolutional neural networks (CNN) to predict latent factors from music audio using the following ob-

Algorithm 2. mSDA-CF Algorithm

Input: Rating matrix R, user features X, item features Y λ, α, β, layers l.

Output: Latent factors U, V

1: ***for*** i 1 : l, ***do***

2: ***if*** $i = \lfloor \frac{l+1}{2} \rfloor$, ***do***

3: Update U and V using *Algorithm 1*, by setting valid values to λ, α and β;

4: ***otherwise***

5: Update W_1^i and W_2^i using *Algorithm 1*, by setting $\lambda = 0$, $\alpha = 0$ and $\beta = 0$;

6: ***end if***

7: ***end for***

jective function:

$$\min_{\theta} \sum_{u,i} c_{u,i}(p_{u,i} - x_u^\top y_i')^2, \tag{17}$$

where x_u, the latent factor of user, is estimated from weighted matrix factorization beforehand, and y_i', the latent factors of audio, are learned from CNN, i.e., $y_i' = \text{CNN}(f_v, \Omega)$. Here, f_v denotes audio contents, and Ω denotes the model parameters in CNN. Eqn (17) can be interpreted in our DCF formulation (i.e., Eqn (6)). First, it utilizes the weighted matrix factorization as the loss function $l(\cdot)$. Secondly, the regularization function $\mathcal{L}(Y, V)$ is implemented by CNN.

Wang *et al.* [12] utilize deep belief networks (DBN) to build a hybrid model for collaborative filtering. The objective function is

$$\begin{aligned} L_{\text{Hybrid}} = & \sum_{u,v \in I} (r_{uv} - \beta_u' x_v - r_u' y_v)^2 + \lambda_\beta \|\beta - \mu\|_F^2 \\ & + \lambda_\gamma \|\gamma\|_F^2 + \lambda_y \|y\|_F^2. \end{aligned} \tag{18}$$

where x_v, the latent factor of item, is obtained from DBN, i.e., $x_v = \text{DBN}(f_v, \Omega)$.

Also, we can interpret model (18) in our DCF framework. First, loss function $l(\cdot)$ is implemented in a hybrid way, i.e., rating r_{uv} is predicted by the sum of the CF part $r_u' y_v$ and the content part $\beta_u' x_v$. Secondly, DBN is employed to map the content features f_v and latent factor x_v, which can be formulated by $\mathcal{L}(Y, V)$ in DCF framework. Meanwhile, γ in (6) is set to 0.

Wang *et al.* [15] propose a model with Bayesian stacked denoising auto-encoders (SDAE) and collaborative topic regression are integrated. The objective function is

$$\begin{aligned} L = & -\sum_{i,j} \frac{c_{ij}}{2}(r_{ij} - u_i^\top v_j)^2 - \frac{\lambda_n}{2} \sum_j \|f_r(X_{0,j*}, W^+) - X_{c,j*}\|_2^2 \\ & - \frac{\lambda_v}{2} \sum_j \|v_j - f_e(X_{0,j*}, W^+)^\top\|_2^2 - f_{reg}, \end{aligned} \tag{19}$$

where $f_e(\cdot)$ and $f_r(\cdot)$ denote the encoding and decoding functions in SDAE, λ_n and λ_v denote the trade-off parameters, and f_{reg} denote the regularization terms that prevent overfitting.

Obviously, the model (19) can also be interpreted in the DCF framework. The loss function for decomposing rating matrix in (19) is in the standard matrix factorization fashion. Further, the second and the third terms in (19) infer the item latent factor using SDAE, which can be abstracted as $\mathcal{L}(Y, V)$ in DCF.

In summary, the existing deep collaborative filtering methods [13, 12, 15] can be unified in a common framework, DCF. We also notice that the existing models only infer latent factors of items using deep models, whereas the latent factors of users are generated in traditional ways. Compared to existing works, our DCF framework provides a more flexible way to explore effective latent factors for users and/or items via deep models.

5. EXPERIMENTS

We evaluate the performance of our mDA-CF and mSDA-CF approaches on three challenging tasks that are movie recommendation, book recommendation and response prediction.

5.1 Movie Recommendation

For movie recommendation, we conduct experiments on two benchmark datasets MovieLens-100K and MovieLens-1M [1], which are commonly used for evaluating collaborative filtering algorithms.

The MovieLens-100K dataset contains 100K ratings of 943 users and 1682 movies, and the MovieLens-1M dataset consists of about 1 million ratings of 6040 users and 3706 movies. Each rating is an integer between 1 (worst) and 5 (best). The ratings are highly sparse. Table 2 summarizes the statistics of datasets. We extract the features from side information of users and movies to construct X and Y. To summarize, the user information which consists of the user's age, gender and occupation were encoded into a binary valued vector of length 28. Similarly, the item feature information which consists of the 18 category of movie genre were encoded into a binary valued vector of length 18. Ratings were normalized to be zero-mean.

As our model (7) is an extension of the representative collaborative filtering method PMF, we mainly compare our approach with PMF and its several variants, such as the Biased PMF [41] and sparse covariance matrix factorization (SCMF) [23]. PMF and Biased PMF are special cases of our approach mDA-CF. For example, by adding zero weight to the first two terms in (7), mDA-CF degrades to PMF. Further, since our approach takes advantage of the side information of users and movies, we also compare our approach with the collaborative filtering method that incorporates side information, such as the Bayesian matrix factorization with side information (BMFSI) [26].

We employ the root mean squared error (RMSE) as the evaluation metric. RMSE is defined as:

$$\text{RMSE} = \sqrt{\frac{1}{N} \sum_{i,j} Z_{ij}^P (R_{ij} - \hat{R}_{ij})^2}, \tag{20}$$

where R_{ij} is the ground-truth rating of user i for item j, $\hat{R}_{ij}$ denotes the corresponding predicted rating, N is the total number of ratings in the test set, and Z_{ij}^P is a binary matrix that indicates test ratings.

For all the compared methods, we set the regularization parameters (e.g., λ, α and β) via 5-fold cross validation. Following the experimental settings in [23], we train each compared method with different percentages (50%, 80%, and 99%) of ratings. The training data are randomly chosen from each dataset, and the remaining data are used for testing. This process is repeated five times, and we report the average RMSE.

For the MovieLens-100K dataset, the parameters α, β and λ are set to 0.7, 0.004 and 0.2, respectively. The learning rate used in SGD is set to 0.002. Table 3 shows the average RMSE (with standard deviations) of baselines PMF, Biased PMF, BMFSI, SCMF and our approaches, mDA-CF and mSDA-CF, on the MovieLens-100K dataset. For each method, we have two settings for the dimensions of latent factors, including $d = 10$ and $d = 20$. We can observe from Table 3 that

(a) Our approaches (mDA-CF and mSDA-CF) achieve much better performance than PMF and Biased PMF, which are special cases of our approach. It demonstrates the effectiveness of incorporating side information and deep architectures.

[1] http://grouplens.org/datasets/movielens/

Table 2: Statistics of datasets used in our experiments.

Dataset	#Users	#Items	Sparsity	User Features	Item Features
MovieLens-100K	943	1682	93.7%	Age, gender, and occupation	Genres
MovieLens-1M	6040	3706	95.8%	Age, gender, and occupation	Genres
Book-Crossing	278858	271379	99.9%	Age, country, city, etc.	Title, year, publisher, etc.
Advertising	448158	737	99.7%	Age, geolocation, domain, etc.	Ad size, advertisor, etc.

Table 3: Average RMSE (with standard deviation) of compared methods with different percentages of training data on MovieLens-100K dataset.

Method	99%		80%		50%	
	d=10	d=20	d=10	d=20	d=10	d=20
PMF [4]	0.9184±0.0265	0.9164±0.0261	0.9223±0.0056	0.9190±0.0052	0.9524±0.0023	0.9506±0.0024
Biased PMF [41]	0.8953±0.0189	0.8923±0.0150	0.9135±0.0039	0.9087±0.0030	0.9388±0.0029	0.9337±0.0020
BMFSI [26]	0.8912±0.0127	0.8905±0.0154	0.9114±0.0031	0.9065±0.0029	0.9371±0.0023	0.9335±0.0025SS
SCMF [23]	0.8891±0.0146	0.8896±0.0198	0.9092±0.0033	0.9068±0.0036	0.9334±0.0025	0.9331±0.0021
mDA-CF (Ours)	0.8874±0.0142	0.8861±0.0153	0.9043±0.0043	0.9040±0.0045	0.9312±0.0026	0.9311±0.0025
mSDA-CF (Ours)	**0.8852±0.0135**	**0.8849±0.0167**	**0.9035±0.0028**	**0.9024±0.0030**	**0.9309±0.0026**	**0.9308±0.0028**

(b) BMFSI is a Bayesian matrix factorization method that utilizes side information, so it performs better than PMF and Biased PMF that ignore such information. Our approach outperforms BMFSI, which validates the strengths of the latent factors learned by marginalized denoising auto-encoders.

(c) Usually, deep models with multiple layers lead to better performance. Our mSDA-CF slightly enhances the performance of mDA-CF. We will show the influence of different number of layers in the next section.

(d) Note that the basic component in our approach is PMF. Actually, DCF is a general framework for collaborative filtering. When we implement $l(R, U, V)$ in (6) as some advanced MF methods (e.g., weighted matrix factorization), the results could be further improved.

For the MovieLens-1M dataset, the parameters α, β and λ are set to 0.8, 0.003 and 0.3, respectively. Table 4 shows the average RMSE (with standard deviations) of our approach and compared methods on the MovieLens-1M dataset. Basically, Table 4 shows similar phenomenon to that we observed from Table 3. The proposed mDA-CF and mSDA-CF approaches consistently achieve lower RMSE than compared methods. As before, we evaluate each method in two settings with different dimension of latent factors. Usually, $d = 20$ generates better results than $d = 10$ on the two MovieLens datasets.

In addition, we compare our approaches with the state-of-the-art deep learning based collaborative filtering method, a joint user-item based restricted Boltzmann machine (UI-RBM) [11]. To conduct fair comparisons with UI-RBM, we adopt the mean absolute error (MAE) used in [11] as evaluation metric. The MAE is defined as follows

$$\text{MAE} = \frac{\sum_{i}^{L} |g_i - p_i|}{L}, \tag{21}$$

where g_i is the ground truth rating, p_i is the predicted rating, and L is the total number of ratings.

We follow the experimental settings in [11], and conduct 5-fold cross-validations. The dimension of latent factors is set to 20. Table 5 shows the average MAE of compared methods on the MovieLens-100K dataset. U-RBM and I-RBM denote the user-based model and item-based model, respectively. They are the baselines used in [11]. Table 5 shows that UI-RBM achieves much better performance than traditional methods like PMF, as it takes advantage of the deep feature learning. Our mDA-CF and mSDA-CF approaches obtain lower MAE than UI-RBM, demonstrating the effectiveness of our DCF framework compared to the RBM based deep learning models.

Table 5: MAE of compared methods on MovieLens-100K dataset.

Method	MAE
PMF [4]	0.793
U-RBM [11]	0.779
I-RBM [11]	0.775
I-RBM+INB [11]	0.699
UI-RBM [11]	0.690
mDA-CF (Ours)	0.683
mSDA-CF (Ours)	**0.680**

5.2 Book Recommendation

For book recommendation, we utilize the Book-Crossing dataset [2], which contains 1149780 ratings for 271379 books from 278858 users. The rating scale is from 0 to 10 with the higher score indicating the more preference. Some attributes of users and books are also provided in this dataset. These attributes are encoded to binary vectors, which form the feature sets for users and books. Table 2 shows some statistics of this dataset.

We follow the settings in [43], and conduct 5-fold cross-validation. The baselines include PMF, the implicit social matrix factorization (ISMF) [42] and the coupled item-based matrix factorization (CIMF) [43]. ISMF incorporates the implicit social relationships

[2] http://www2.informatik.uni-freiburg.de/~cziegler/BX/

Table 4: Average RMSE (with standard deviation) of compared methods with different percentages of training data on MovieLens-1M dataset.

Method	99%		80%		50%	
	d=10	d=20	d=10	d=20	d=10	d=20
PMF [4]	0.8424±0.0071	0.8388±0.0059	0.8559±0.0022	0.8512±0.0017	0.8790±0.0009	0.8745±0.0011
Biased PMF [41]	0.8408±0.0070	0.8367±0.0067	0.8531±0.0019	0.8493±0.0020	0.8766±0.0015	0.8722±0.0012
BMFSI [26]	0.8391±0.0067	0.8340±0.0069	0.8503±0.0017	0.8478±0.0019	0.8742±0.0016	0.8703±0.0010
SCMF [23]	0.8364±0.0065	0.8323±0.0065	0.8496±0.0019	0.8465±0.0018	0.8707±0.0013	0.8678±0.0007
mDA-CF (Ours)	0.8335±0.0064	0.8317±0.0062	0.8449±0.0015	0.8429±0.0013	0.8655±0.0007	0.8645±0.0006
mSDA-CF (Ours)	**0.8320±0.0063**	**0.8304±0.0057**	**0.8416±0.0014**	**0.8407±0.0011**	**0.8628±0.0005**	**0.8613±0.0006**

Table 6: RMSE of compared methods on Book-Crossing data.

Method	RMSE (d = 10)	RMSE (d = 50)
PMF [4]	3.7483	3.7452
ISMF [42]	3.7440	3.7415
CIMF [43]	3.7398	3.7372
mDA-CF (Ours)	3.6610	3.6528
mSDA-CF (Ours)	**3.6592**	**3.6513**

between users and between items. CIMF makes use of the attributes of books in the model.

Table 6 shows the RMSE of all compared methods. We can observe that ISMF and CIMF obtain better results than the conventional PMF method, as they incorporate side information to their models. Our approaches obtain much lower RMSE than PMF, ISMF and CIMF in different settings. mSDA-CF achieves the best results among all competitors.

5.3 Response Prediction

Response prediction is another interesting application of collaborative filtering [30]. In particular, we consider a specific type of response prediction, which is click prediction. Given an online advertisement, our task is to predict whether a given user will click it or not in the near future.

Previous research works have proved that collaborative filtering (CF) methods are suitable for addressing the click prediction problem. Unfortunately, there are few datasets available for evaluating the click prediction performance of CF models. To evaluate the performance of our model in real-world applications, we collected an advertising dataset at a large software company. The dataset is collected from its website, which contains the click responses for advertisements over 3 million users. For our purpose, we analyze the data from a 2-month period, from October 1, 2013 to November 30, 2013.

The dataset used in our experiments contains 737 ads and 448,158 users. It also has the impression and click data of the advertisements. For each click event, we have the *user ID*, *day*, *ad ID*, *page ID*, *country*, *browser*, *advertiser ID*, and *size of ad*. Each record can be uniquely identified by a *(user, ad, day)* triplet. In addition, we have information about the user profiles. For each user, we have some attributes such as country, domain, etc. Apart from the user information, our dataset contains the meta-information of the ads such as ad size. In the experiments, we encode the demographic information (e.g., country, state, domain) into a binary valued vector for each user. The attributes of ads (e.g., advertiser, ad size) are also encoded into binary vectors. Some statistics of this dataset can be found in Table 2.

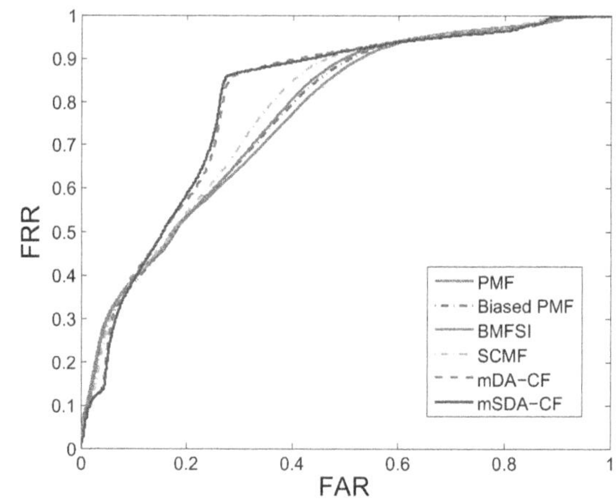

Figure 2: ROC curves of our approach and compared methods on Advertising dataset (d=10).

The advertising dataset used in our experiments is very sparse, which contains 880,569 click responses (density: 0.27%). We use the first 50% click responses for training, and the remaining data for testing. Following [44], we use the receiver operating characteristic (ROC) curve and the area under ROC (AUC-ROC) as our evaluation metrics. The true positive rate (TPR) and false positive rate (FPR) used for generating ROC curves are defined as follows:

$$TPR = \frac{TP}{TP+FN}, \quad FPR = \frac{FP}{FP+TN}, \tag{22}$$

where TP represents the true positives, FN represents the false negatives, TN represents the true negatives, and FP represents the false positives.

We evaluate the performance of each compared method on the Advertising dataset. The major parameters α, β and λ are set to 0.8, 0.02 and 0.12, respectively. Two settings are utilized, by setting the latent factor dimension to 10 and 20, respectively. Fig. 2 shows the ROC curves of PMF, Biased PMF, BMFSI, SCMF, mDA-CF and mSDA-CF. Table 7 shows the corresponding AUC of all compared methods. We can observe that our approaches obtain higher AUC than other methods, which demonstrates the effectiveness of our framework.

5.4 Discussion

So far, we have seen that our approach outperforms the existing approaches on the different datasets. We also analyze the convergence property and parameter settings of our approach on the

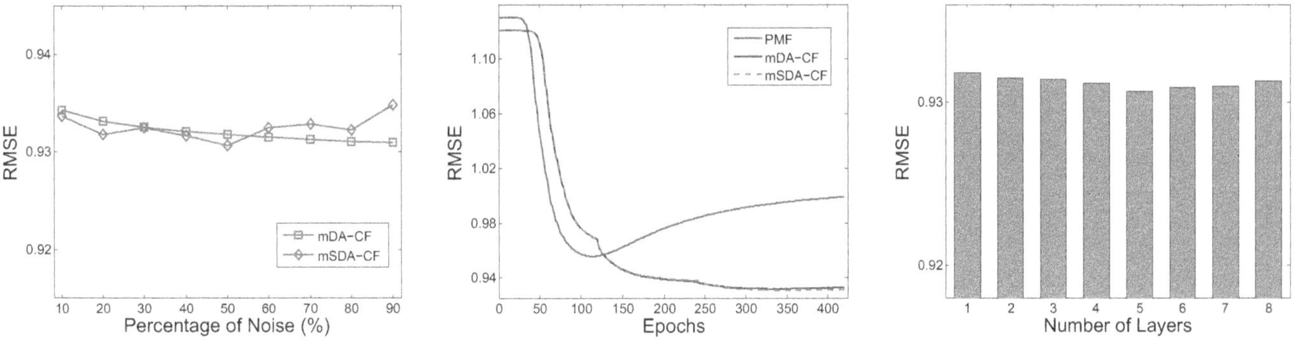

(a) (b) (c)

Figure 3: Experimental analysis on MovieLens-100K dataset: (a) RMSE with different level of noise; (b) RMSE with epochs; (c) RMSE of mSDA-CF with different number of layers.

Table 7: AUC of compared methods on Advertising dataset.

Method	AUC ($d = 10$)	AUC ($d = 20$)
PMF [4]	0.7651	0.7716
Biased PMF [41]	0.7692	0.7724
BMFSI [26]	0.7720	0.7805
SCMF [23]	0.7782	0.7866
mDA-CF (Ours)	0.7961	0.8023
mSDA-CF (Ours)	**0.8057**	**0.8115**

MovieLens-100K dataset. In Fig. 3(a), we show the RMSE of mDA-CF and mSDA-CF with different levels of noise. We observe an interesting phenomena that the RMSE of mDA-CF slightly decreases when increasing the noise level for input samples at first; mSDA-CF achieves the best performance when adding 50% noise. However, when the percentage of noise is larger than 50%, mDA-CF outperforms mSDA-CF. It shows that the latent factors learned from multi-layer models might be unreliable if there are too much noise contained in the input samples.

Fig. 3(b) shows the RMSE in different iterations of PMF and our approaches. We see that PMF overfits the data after 100 epochs. Although our approaches have larger RMSE from epoch 40 to epoch 120, they keep reducing the RMSE even after 400 epochs. It shows that our approach enjoys better stability. Also, by incorporating the side information of users and items, the learned model has a good generalization ability.

Another important property in our approach is the setting of stacked layers. Fig. 3(c) shows the RMSE of mSDA-CF with different number of layers. In general, stacking multiple auto-encoder will lead to better performance. But Fig. 3(c) shows that the improvement becomes marginal when there are more than 5 layers. The reasons are two-fold. First, the model capacity is related to the size of training data. In the experiments, training a very complicated deep model (with many layers) with the employed datasets may be unreasonable. Secondly, accessing rich features of users is always a challenging issue in reality. In our model, these features are the inputs of deep models. Our model achieves better performance than existing works by using these features. However, the features are not extensive enough to train deep models. In a word, this parameter should be carefully tuned in practice.

6. CONCLUSIONS

In this paper, we propose a deep collaborative filtering (DCF) framework, which bridges matrix factorization and deep feature learning. DCF is a hybrid collaborative filtering model, as it learns effective latent factors from both user-item ratings and side information. Using this framework, we present the mDA-CF and mSDA-CF approaches by incorporating the probabilistic matrix factorization and marginalized denoising auto-encoders. We also design efficient optimization algorithms to solve the models. Extensive experimental results on the MovieLens-100K, MovieLens-1M, Book-Crossing and Advertising datasets demonstrate the effectiveness of the latent factors learned by our model. Our mDA-CF and mSDA-CF approaches outperform related methods on the tasks of movie recommendation, book recommendation and response prediction. They also achieve better performance than the existing deep learning based collaborative filtering method such as UI-RBM. In addition, the convergence property and parameter settings of our model are discussed in the experiments.

A part of the future work is to extend other deep learning and matrix factorization methods using our DCF framework and evaluate their performance for collaborative filtering. Another future direction is to apply the distributed optimization algorithms to further reduce the computational costs of our algorithms.

Acknowledgements

This research is supported in part by the National Science Foundation (NSF) CNS award 1314484, Office of Naval Research (ONR) award N00014-12-1-1028, ONR Young Investigator Award N00014-14-1-0484, Naval Postgraduate School (NPS) award N00244-15-1-0041 and U.S. Army Research Office Young Investigator Award W911NF-14-1-0218.

7. REFERENCES

[1] Xiaoyuan Su and Taghi M. Khoshgoftaar. A survey of collaborative filtering techniques. *Adv. Artificial Intellegence*, 2009.

[2] Yehuda Koren, Robert M. Bell, and Chris Volinsky. Matrix factorization techniques for recommender systems. *IEEE Computer*, 42(8):30–37, 2009.

[3] Sotirios Chatzis. Nonparametric bayesian multitask collaborative filtering. In *CIKM*, pages 2149–2158, 2013.

[4] Ruslan Salakhutdinov and Andriy Mnih. Probabilistic matrix factorization. In *NIPS*, 2007.

[5] Hao Ma, Dengyong Zhou, Chao Liu, Michael R. Lyu, and Irwin King. Recommender systems with social regularization. In *WSDM*, pages 287–296, 2011.

[6] Ajit Paul Singh and Geoffrey J. Gordon. Relational learning via collective matrix factorization. In *KDD*, pages 650–658, 2008.

[7] Ajit Paul Singh and Geoffrey J. Gordon. A bayesian matrix factorization model for relational data. *CoRR*, abs/1203.3517, 2012.

[8] Geoffrey E Hinton and Ruslan R Salakhutdinov. Reducing the dimensionality of data with neural networks. *Science*, 313(5786):504–507, 2006.

[9] Geoffrey Hinton, Simon Osindero, and Yee-Whye Teh. A fast learning algorithm for deep belief nets. *Neural computation*, 18(7):1527–1554, 2006.

[10] Ruslan Salakhutdinov, Andriy Mnih, and Geoffrey E. Hinton. Restricted boltzmann machines for collaborative filtering. In *ICML*, pages 791–798, 2007.

[11] Kostadin Georgiev and Preslav Nakov. A non-iid framework for collaborative filtering with restricted boltzmann machines. In *ICML*, pages 1148–1156, 2013.

[12] Xinxi Wang and Ye Wang. Improving content-based and hybrid music recommendation using deep learning. In *ACM MM*, pages 627–636, 2014.

[13] Aäron Van Den Oord, Sander Dieleman, and Benjamin Schrauwen. Deep content-based music recommendation. In *NIPS*, pages 2643–2651, 2013.

[14] Tran The Truyen, Dinh Q. Phung, and Svetha Venkatesh. Ordinal boltzmann machines for collaborative filtering. In *UAI*, pages 548–556, 2009.

[15] Hao Wang, Naiyan Wang, and Dit-Yan Yeung. Collaborative deep learning for recommender systems. *CoRR*, abs/1409.2944, 2014.

[16] Minmin Chen, Zhixiang Eddie Xu, Kilian Q. Weinberger, and Fei Sha. Marginalized denoising autoencoders for domain adaptation. In *ICML*, 2012.

[17] Francesco Ricci, Lior Rokach, Bracha Shapira, and Paul B Kantor. *Recommender systems handbook*, volume 1. Springer, 2011.

[18] James Bennett and Stan Lanning. The netflix prize. In *Proceedings of KDD cup and workshop*, page 35, 2007.

[19] Rahul Mazumder, Trevor Hastie, and Robert Tibshirani. Spectral regularization algorithms for learning large incomplete matrices. *The Journal of Machine Learning Research*, 11:2287–2322, 2010.

[20] Daniel D Lee and H Sebastian Seung. Algorithms for non-negative matrix factorization. In *NIPS*, pages 556–562, 2001.

[21] Ruslan Salakhutdinov and Andriy Mnih. Bayesian probabilistic matrix factorization using markov chain monte carlo. In *ICML*, pages 880–887, 2008.

[22] Minjie Xu, Jun Zhu, and Bo Zhang. Fast max-margin matrix factorization with data augmentation. *ICML*, 2013.

[23] Jianping Shi, Naiyan Wang, Yang Xia, Dit-Yan Yeung, Irwin King, and Jiaya Jia. SCMF: sparse covariance matrix factorization for collaborative filtering. In *IJCAI*, 2013.

[24] Ryan Prescott Adams, George E. Dahl, and Iain Murray. Incorporating side information in probabilistic matrix factorization with gaussian processes. In *UAI*, pages 1–9, 2010.

[25] Tong Zhao, Julian J. McAuley, and Irwin King. Leveraging social connections to improve personalized ranking for collaborative filtering. In *CIKM*, pages 261–270, 2014.

[26] Ian Porteous, Arthur U. Asuncion, and Max Welling. Bayesian matrix factorization with side information and dirichlet process mixtures. In *AAAI*, 2010.

[27] Yong-Deok Kim and Seungjin Choi. Scalable variational bayesian matrix factorization with side information. In *AISTATS*, pages 493–502, 2014.

[28] Sunho Park, Yong-Deok Kim, and Seungjin Choi. Hierarchical bayesian matrix factorization with side information. In *IJCAI*, 2013.

[29] Liang Hu, Jian Cao, Guandong Xu, Longbing Cao, Zhiping Gu, and Can Zhu. Personalized recommendation via cross-domain triadic factorization. In *WWW*, pages 595–606, 2013.

[30] Aditya Krishna Menon, Krishna Prasad Chitrapura, Sachin Garg, Deepak Agarwal, and Nagaraj Kota. Response prediction using collaborative filtering with hierarchies and side-information. In *KDD*, pages 141–149, 2011.

[31] Sheng Li, Jaya Kawale, and Yun Fu. Predicting user behavior in display advertising via dynamic collective matrix factorization. In *SIGIR*, 2015.

[32] Liang Hu, Jian Cao, Guandong Xu, Longbing Cao, Zhiping Gu, and Wei Cao. Deep modeling of group preferences for group-based recommendation. In *AAAI*, pages 1861–1867, 2014.

[33] Yuanxin Ouyang, Wenqi Liu, Wenge Rong, and Zhang Xiong. Autoencoder-based collaborative filtering. In *ICONIP*, pages 284–291, 2014.

[34] Ruslan Salakhutdinov and Andriy Mnih. Bayesian probabilistic matrix factorization using markov chain monte carlo. In *ICML*, pages 880–887. ACM, 2008.

[35] Yifan Hu, Yehuda Koren, and Chris Volinsky. Collaborative filtering for implicit feedback datasets. In *ICDM*, pages 263–272, 2008.

[36] Koray Kavukcuoglu, MarcâĂŹAurelio Ranzato, Rob Fergus, and Yann Le-Cun. Learning invariant features through topographic filter maps. In *CVPR*, pages 1605–1612. IEEE, 2009.

[37] Honglak Lee, Peter Pham, Yan Largman, and Andrew Y Ng. Unsupervised feature learning for audio classification using convolutional deep belief networks. In *NIPS*, pages 1096–1104, 2009.

[38] Pascal Vincent, Hugo Larochelle, Yoshua Bengio, and Pierre-Antoine Manzagol. Extracting and composing robust features with denoising autoencoders. In *ICML*, pages 1096–1103. ACM, 2008.

[39] Minmin Chen, Kilian Q. Weinberger, Fei Sha, and Yoshua Bengio. Marginalized denoising auto-encoders for nonlinear representations. In *ICML*, pages 1476–1484, 2014.

[40] Zhi-Qin Yu, Xing-Jian Shi, Ling Yan, and Wu-Jun Li. Distributed stochastic ADMM for matrix factorization. In *CIKM*, pages 1259–1268, 2014.

[41] Yehuda Koren. Factorization meets the neighborhood: a multifaceted collaborative filtering model. In *KDD*, pages 426–434, 2008.

[42] Hao Ma. An experimental study on implicit social recommendation. In *SIGIR*, pages 73–82, 2013.

[43] Fangfang Li, Guandong Xu, and Longbing Cao. Coupled item-based matrix factorization. In *WISE*, pages 1–14, 2014.

[44] Amr Ahmed, Abhimanyu Das, and Alexander J. Smola. Scalable hierarchical multitask learning algorithms for conversion optimization in display advertising. In *WSDM*, pages 153–162, 2014.

Improving Latent Factor Models via Personalized Feature Projection for One Class Recommendation

Tong Zhao[1,2], Julian McAuley[3], Irwin King[1,2]
[1]Shenzhen Key Laboratory of Rich Media Big Data Analytics and Applications, Shenzhen Research Institute, The Chinese University of Hong Kong, Shenzhen, China
[2]Department of Computer Science and Engineering, The Chinese University of Hong Kong, Shatin, N.T., Hong Kong
[3]Department of Computer Science and Engineering, UC San Diego, La Jolla, CA, USA
{tzhao, king}@cse.cuhk.edu.hk, julian.mcauley@gmail.com

ABSTRACT

Latent Factor models, which transform both users and items into the same latent feature space, are one of the most successful and ubiquitous models in recommender systems. Most existing models in this paradigm define both users' and items' latent factors to be of the same size and use an inner product to represent a user's 'compatibility' with an item. Intuitively, users' factors encode 'preferences' while item factors encode 'properties', so that the inner product encodes how well an item matches a user's preferences. However, a user's opinion of an item may be more complex, for example each dimension of each user's opinion may depend on a combination of multiple item factors simultaneously. Thus it may be better to view each dimension of a user's preference as a personalized projection of an item's properties so that the preference model can capture complex relationships between items' properties and users' preferences.

Therefore, in this paper we propose a novel *personalized feature projection* method to model users' preferences over items. Specifically, for each user, we define a personalized projection matrix, which takes the place of user-specific factors from existing models. This matrix describes a mapping between items' factors and users' preferences in order to build personalized preference models for each user and item. The proposed personalized feature projection method is quite general and existing latent factor models, for example, can be cast as a special case. We present three objective functions to optimize predictions in the form of ranked lists of users' preferences over items, and demonstrate how each can be used to improve one-class recommendation performance. Experiments are conducted on four real-world datasets and our results show that our personalized feature projection method outperforms several state-of-the-art methods on various evaluation metrics.

Categories and Subject Descriptors

H.4 [**Information Systems Applications**]: Miscellaneous

Permission to make digital or hard copies of all or part of this work for personal or classroom use is granted without fee provided that copies are not made or distributed for profit or commercial advantage and that copies bear this notice and the full citation on the first page. Copyrights for components of this work owned by others than ACM must be honored. Abstracting with credit is permitted. To copy otherwise, or republish, to post on servers or to redistribute to lists, requires prior specific permission and/or a fee. Request permissions from Permissions@acm.org.
CIKM'15, October 19–23, 2015, Melbourne, Australia.
© 2015 ACM. ISBN 978-1-4503-3794-6/15/10 ...$15.00.
DOI: http://dx.doi.org/10.1145/2806416.2806511.

General Terms

Algorithms, Experimentation, Performance

Keywords

Collaborative filtering; Personalized feature projection; One-class recommendation

1. INTRODUCTION

Modeling people's opinions and identifying which items are relevant to each person plays a critical role in the online marketplace, and is the basic task of a *recommender system*. A major and ongoing thrust of research on recommender systems is concerned with improving the performance of personalized recommendation. For example, a significant amount of research has been proposed that aims to improve the performance of Latent Factor (LF) models [10, 27, 28, 29], one of the most successful and ubiquitous approaches in recommender systems. Latent factor models assume that each user and each item is associated with some K-dimensional latent factor vector, such that the inner product of a user's and an item's latent factors represents the preference score or compatability between the user and the item.

Given a user-item matrix consisting of the rating scores that users give to items, latent factor models essentially consist of identifying the low-dimensional structure in this matrix. The goal is to identify K-dimensional embeddings of users and items such that their product best recovers this rating matrix in terms of the mean-squared error (MSE). Besides fitting rating values, some works [8, 32, 37, 39] also adapt latent factor models to optimize a ranking loss with the intuition that higher scoring user-item pairs should have larger inner products than lower-scoring items for the given user, e.g., for a user u, their inner product with a 5-star item should be higher than that of a 2-star item, though only the *relative* rather than the exact ratings are modeled.

Another popular research direction using latent factor models is so-called one-class recommendation, which is the focus of this paper. In many real applications, explicit numerical ratings might not be available and one must instead try to model some form of implicit feedback from users, such as the media they consume, the pages they browse, the music they listen to, or whom they befriend [6, 42]. This setting is called "one-class" recommendation and a variety of solutions have been proposed to solve it by directly modeling relative preferences, or *rankings*, of items for personalized recommendation [13, 19, 26, 43]. However, most existing works are still using an inner product of the latent factor vectors to predict users' preferences on items, which essentially assumes that each dimension of a user's preferences is associated with one and only one of an item's factors.

In this paper, we generalize this linear structure and assign a projection matrix to each user instead of a latent factor vector. Intuitively, traditional latent factor models can be interpreted as assuming that a user's latent factors represent how the user thinks about the latent features of an item and more restrictively, that each dimension of their opinion is related to a single latent factor of a product. However, a more expressive model would allow each dimension of a user's opinion to be a function of a *combination* of an item's latent factors. Therefore, it is better to learn a projection between user preferences and item properties so that the model is capable of expressing complex relationships between the two. Moreover since in latent factor models, the inner product of a user's and an item's latent feature vectors is always used to represent the user's preference toward the item, a user's preference on an item is modeled only by a real number, a one-dimensional value, and thus only numerical preference modeling can be used to design objective functions. As we argued above, each dimension of a user's preference is related to a *combination* of their tastes toward an item's properties, so a simple inner product may not be enough. To address the drawbacks mentioned above, we propose a *personalized feature projection* (PFP) method that learns users' latent features as a personalized projection matrix instead of a vector. Figure 1 depicts the idea of our PFP method. Based on items' latent feature vectors and users' projection matrices, our PFP method models users' preferences over items in terms of projected latent feature vectors instead of a real number. Thus, we can leverage metric learning methods to design the objective function for one-class recommendation. In addition, vector-based (rather than numerical) objectives, can be formulated, which provides more flexible structures to describe users' preferences.

The most similar work to our PFP method is the method called *max interest latent factors* [39], which also proposes to model multiple user latent vectors to enrich users' preference representations. In [39], the predicted preference between a user and an item is given by the *maximum* match between the user vectors and the item vector, and omits other tastes of the user. Different from their work, when modeling user's preference on items, the proposed PFP method tries to consider all tastes of the user simultaneously by employing a matrix projection approach.

We summarize our contributions as follows:

1. We develop Personalized Feature Projection methods, that employ users' projection matrices and items' factors to solve one-class recommendation problems using three different optimization criteria.

2. We evaluate the proposed method on four real-world datasets. Empirical results show that the proposed model can significantly improve one-class recommendation performance compared to state-of-the-art alternatives.

3. We conduct a detailed analysis of the effect that various model parameters have on the performance of our method.

The remainder of this paper is organized as follows. Section 2 describes preliminary and related work; Section 3 details the proposed PFP methods and introduces three criteria used to optimize them; Section 4 shows experimental results and verifies the improvements of PFP methods for one-class recommendation problems; Finally, Section 5 concludes the paper.

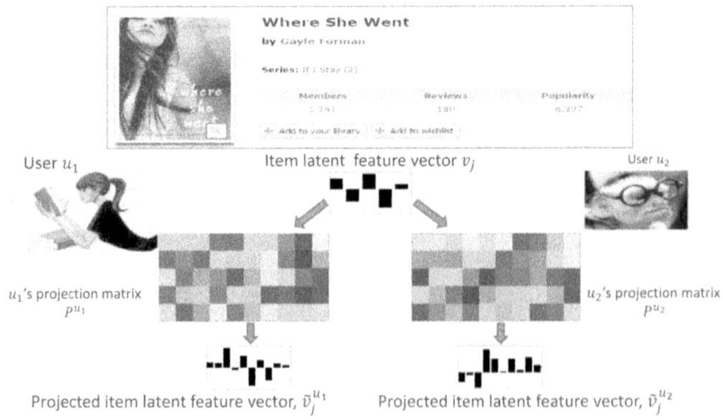

Figure 1: Illustration of the key idea behind the PFP method. Unlike traditional latent factor models, we use a more flexible transform that associates each item's latent factor with a combination of users' latent factors. The above figure is based on a model trained on our *LibraryThing* dataset. Here we set the number of item latent factors to 5 and fit user projection matrices of size 5×10. In this case, the preferences of different users toward the item can be represented by a set of 10-dimensional personalized projection vectors.

2. PRELIMINARY AND RELATED WORK

We consider the *one-class recommendation problem*, where the model is trained on implicit feedback (e.g., a set of items a user purchased), rather than explicit rating scores. Before presenting our *Personalized Feature Projection* method, we first give an overview of existing latent factor models and describe how they can be applied to solve one-class recommendation problems.

2.1 Latent Factor Models for One-class Recommendation

Latent Factor models can be described in terms of matrix factorization. Matrix factorization aims to decompose a matrix into two (or more) low-rank terms whose product reconstructs or approximates the original matrix as closely as possible. Typically, we are given a matrix $R \in \mathbb{R}^{M \times N}$ representing the observed feedback (say, in the form of numeric ratings) from M users and N items.

This feedback matrix can then be factorized into one user-specific matrix $U \in \mathbb{R}^{M \times K}$ and one item-specific matrix $V \in \mathbb{R}^{N \times K}$:

$$R \approx UV^T, \tag{1}$$

where K is the dimensionality of the latent factor vector which characterizes the features of a user or an item. Accordingly, $U_u V_i^T$ captures user u's preference toward item i.

For 'one-class' recommendation problems, there is no numeric feedback matrix R, but rather for each user we observe two signals in the form of *positive feedback* and *negative feedback*:

Positive feedback: positive feedback $D_u = \{i\}$ is defined as the set of items i toward which user u explicitly shows positive feedback (e.g., products they purchased, pages they viewed, etc.).

Negative feedback: negative feedback is denoted by a set of user-item pairs $N_u = \{j\}$, which includes those items j toward which user u has not shown positive feedback.

Then, in lieu of an explicit rating score, we follow the assumption of [24] that users' preferences toward positive feedback items should be higher than those of negative feedback items, which is captured by the following objective function:

$$\max \sum_{u,i,j} \ln \sigma(u_u \cdot v_i - u_u \cdot v_j), \quad (2)$$

where $\sigma(\cdot)$ is the logistic (sigmoid) function, $i \in D_u$, and $j \in N_u$. Here $u_u \cdot v_i$ and $u_u \cdot v_j$ represent user u's preferences towards items i and j modeled by a latent factor model. Eq. (2) can be optimized by using stochastic gradient ascent, which iteratively updates the sampled user-specific latent factors U_u and the sampled positive (and negative) feedback-specific latent factors V_i and V_j.

2.2 Existing Methods for One-Class Recommendation

Several works have studied one-class collaborative filtering and can be mainly divided into two branches: pointwise methods [7, 19, 21] and pairwise methods [22, 24, 25, 26, 36, 40, 43].

Pointwise methods aim to fit a numeric value associated with each evaluated item. These methods model positive feedback as high preference scores and use several strategies to sample negative feedback as low preference scores. Then existing matrix factorization methods can be used to fit the preference scores. Pan et al. [19] solve the one-class recommendation problem in two ways: negative example *weighting* and negative example *sampling*. Hu et al. [7] introduced a novel concept called a "confidence level," associated with positive and negative feedback, and propose an efficient optimization method for confidence-based matrix factorization.

Different from pointwise methods, pairwise methods focus on modeling the order, or ranking of the feedback. Pairwise methods always consider implicit feedback as relative relationships indicating that users show higher preference on positive feedback than on negative feedback items. In [24], Rendle et al. propose a Bayesian personalized ranking (*BPR*) framework. Following this, various ideas have been proposed that incorporate different types of contextual information into the *BPR* framework. [13] extends the *BPR* framework to model both users' feedback on items and on their social relations. In [26], Rendle et al. extend the *BPR* framework from matrix factorization to tensor factorization for tag recommendation. Pan et al. [20] aggregate the features of a group of related users to reduce the uncertainty of the selected training instances. Du et al. [3] improve one-class recommendation performance by incorporating a social regularization term into the *BPR* framework. Zhao et al. [45] leverage social connections to improve the performance of one-class recommendation. In [8], Kabbur et al. use an item-based method for generating top-N recommendations that learns the item-item similarity matrix as the product of two low dimensional latent factor matrices. All of these existing pairwise methods for one-class recommendation use a numerical value to model user preferences, while our model generalizes this setting and describes each user's preferences toward items as a personalized projection vector.

2.3 Metric Learning

Since the method proposed in the following section also relates to metric learning problems with pairwise constraints [2, 11, 12, 23, 31, 35, 41], here we briefly review existing works in this field. Metric learning, whose goal is to model the similarity/dissimilarity between instances, is one of the most fundamental problems of machine learning and has been widely used for clustering and classification. [33] learns a Mahalanobis metric to study the semantic similarity between music songs. In [23], the authors propose a metric learning algorithm to improve the prediction performance for multi-task learning by learning one metric that is shared amongst all the tasks and one specific metric unique to each task. Kusner et al. [15] uses distance metric learning to improve the efficiency and accuracy of k-nearest neighbor (kNN) classification. Yue et al. [44] proposes a personalized collaborative clustering algorithm that leverages the idea of metric learning to investigate how existing users cluster or group items in order to predict similarity models for other users' clustering tasks. Lee et al. [17] assumes the observed user-item feedback matrix is locally low-rank within certain neighborhoods of the metric space defined by some anchor (user, item) pairs and employs the Epanechnikov kernel function to measure the local metric. However, most of the existing work on metric learning problems focus on solving clustering-related problems and few works consider the issue of personalized one-class recommendation.

Table 1: Notation.

Symbol	Discription
M	number of users
N	number of items
K	number of latent factors
K^*	number of projected user latent factors
$C_u, C_i \in \mathbb{R}$	projection constraint in PFP model
$\{\alpha_i\}$	parameters used in WARP-loss function
$U \in \mathbb{R}^{M \times K}$	user latent factor matrix in LF models
$V \in \mathbb{R}^{N \times K}$	item latent factor matrix
$P^u \in \mathbb{R}^{K \times K^*}$	projection matrix of user u in PFP model
$u_u \in \mathbb{R}^K$	u_{th} row vector in U
$v_j \in \mathbb{R}^K$	j_{th} row vector in V
$p_f^u \in \mathbb{R}^K$	f_{th} column vector in P^u

2.4 Non-linear Latent Factorization

Another line of latent factor models are called non-linear latent factor models [16, 30, 39], which break the mold of scoring each item by a linear embedding of users' and items' latent factor vectors. The authors of [16] proposed a nonlinear LF approach with Gaussian processes. The authors of [30] proposed a Restricted Boltzmann machine-based method for collaborative filtering. Baltrunas et al. [1] splits user profiles into several sub-profiles and models each sub-profile in a particular context. In [39], the authors propose a *MaxMF* method that models a user with multiple latent factor vectors representing their different latent tastes and associate each item with a single latent feature vector. The preference score between a user and a given item is then defined as the maximum match between the user tastes and the given item. This work is the most similar one compared to our method. However, there are explicit differences between their method and ours: our proposed PFP method utilizes all latent factor vectors of the user and models the user's preference on the item as a projected vector rather than the maximum inner product in [39].

3. PERSONALIZED FEATURE PROJECTION

We first introduce our *Personalized Feature Projection* (PFP) method. The proposed method inherits the benefits of both metric learning and latent factor models. Then, in Section 3.2 we show how this method can be trained to optimize three different evaluation criteria. Our notation is shown in Table 1.

3.1 Personalized Feature Projection and Preference Modeling

In the PFP method, for each item j, we use a vector v_j to represent its latent features, much as is done using existing latent factor models. However, for each user u, we employ a matrix P^u to represent their latent features. Specifically, let K be the number of latent factors (for each item) and let K^* be the number of *projected* user factors. Then we have the following definition:

Personalized Projection Matrix : for each user u, we define a personalized projection matrix $P^u = \mathbb{R}^{K\times K^*}$. The column vector $p_f^u = \mathbb{R}^K$ represents column f in matrix P^u.

Based on the Personalized Projection Matrix, we can use the following formula to personalize items' latent feature vectors and obtain the projected item-feature vector.

Personalized Feature Projection : for a specific user u, item j's feature vector v_j can be projected by multiplying u's personalized projection matrix. In this way, the projected feature vector of item j, $\widetilde{v}_j^u$ ($\widetilde{v}_j$ for simplicity), can be represented as

$$\widetilde{v}_j = v_j P^u. \tag{3}$$

One can easily check that, when $K^* = 1$, the personalized projection matrix for each user reduces to a latent feature vector of size K, which is equivalent to the user latent feature vector in a latent factor model so that the projected item-feature vector reduces to the dot product of users' and items' latent factors. In this way, we can say that the latent factor model is a special case of the personalized feature projection method. When $K^* > 1$, the projected item-feature vector provides a more flexible way to model users' complex preferences.

Preference Modeling : Based on the personalized projection matrix, we propose a factorized model to describe users' preferences by summarizing all the projected feature vectors from their positive feedback. In particular, for an item j, we consider the preference model as

$$f_u(j) = \frac{1}{|D_u|}\sum_{i\in D_u}\widetilde{v}_i\widetilde{v}_j^T = \frac{1}{|D_u|}\sum_{i\in D_u} v_i P^u (P^u)^T v_j^T, \tag{4}$$

where D_u represents user u's positive feedback. Actually, if we normalize both $\widetilde{v}_i$ and $\widetilde{v}_j$ to be unit vectors, the above equation represents the average cosine similarity of the projected feature vectors between item j and the user's positive feedback items. Compared with [8] and [10], instead of using only item latent vectors, this formula incorporates user's personalized projection matrix into preference modeling, thus, for different users, Eq. (4) can model his/her personalized preference on items. Based on Eq. (4), we propose an assumption to derive the optimization criterion for personalized ranking that is based on pairs of items: for an item i that has been viewed by user u, the preference score of it calculated by Eq. (4) should be larger than other unviewed items j, $f_u(i) \succ f_u(j)$. Actually, the proposed assumption indicates that the projected feature vectors of users' positive feedback items should be closer to users' average taste than are the negative feedback items. Similar assumptions are commonly used in various pairwise-based recommendation methods ([24], [26], [20], [13]). However, unlike existing works, the personalized feature projection method models users' preferences toward items as a projected vector rather than as an inner product, which provides flexible structure for preference representation. Another advantage of our approach is that it summarizes all the projected vectors from users' positive feedback items to reduce the uncertainty caused by training instance selection. More specifically, when we uniformly sample a positive feedback item from a user, the average similarity of Eq. (4) makes the approach insensitive to the choice of which positive feedback items should be selected. $P^u(P^u)^T$ here can be viewed as the personalized metric used to measure the preference difference between items.

3.2 PFP for One-class Recommendation

According to the pairwise assumption proposed above, we will introduce how the PFP model can be trained to optimize three different evaluation criteria to solve the one-class recommendation problem.

3.2.1 *AUC-loss*

In this section, we choose the area under the ROC curve (AUC) as the ranking statistic and explain how to extend the Bayesian Personalized Ranking [24] framework to incorporate our personalized feature projection matrix for recommendation.

The AUC per user is usually defined as

$$AUC(u) = \frac{1}{|D_u||N_u|}\sum_{i\in D_u}\sum_{j\in N_u} I(f_u(i) > f_u(j)), \tag{5}$$

where $I(\cdot)$ is an indicator function. Following [24], maximizing the AUC value can be approximated by maximizing the following likelihood function:

$$\ln\prod_u AUC(u) = \ln \prod_{(u,i,j)\in U\times I\times I} P(f_u(i) > f_u(j))^{i\in D_u \wedge j\in N_u} \\ (1 - P(f_u(i) > f_u(j)))^{j\in D_u\wedge i\in N_u}. \tag{6}$$

Due to the totality and antisymmetry of a pair-wise ordering scheme as in [24], the objective function for a particular user u can be simplified to

$$AUC(u) = \frac{1}{|D_u||N_u|}\sum_{i\in D_u}\sum_{j\in N_u} P(f_u(i) > f_u(j)). \tag{7}$$

By incorporating Eq. (4), the above objective can be rewritten as:

$$\begin{aligned} AUC(u) &= \frac{1}{|D_u||N_u|}\sum_{i\in D_u}\sum_{j\in N_u}\ln\sigma(f_u(i) - f_u(j)) \\ &= \frac{1}{|D_u||N_u|}\sum_{i\in D_u}\sum_{j\in N_u}\ln\sigma(\frac{1}{|D_u|}\sum_{i'\in D_u}\widetilde{v}_{i'}(\widetilde{v}_i - \widetilde{v}_j)^T), \end{aligned} \tag{8}$$

where σ is the logistic (sigmoid) function: $\sigma(x) = \frac{1}{1+e^{-x}}$. We use the gradient-based algorithm to optimize the objective function as Eq. (8). The main process is to randomly pick a (positive, negative) feedback pair and iteratively update parameters based on the sampled feedback pairs.

3.2.2 *WARP-Loss*

In this subsection, we describe how to adapt our projected feature representation to design a WARP-Loss (Weighted Approximated Ranking Pairwise Loss) function.

Based on Eq. (4), we can calculate users' preferences for each item $j \in N$ and the *Weighted Approximate-Rank Pairwise* (WARP) Loss function [38, 39, 40] can be defined as

$$L_{WARP}(f_u, D_u) = \sum_{i\in D_u}\Theta(rank_i(f_u)), \tag{9}$$

where $rank_i(f_u)$ is the margin-based rank of item i, i.e.,

$$rank_i(f_u) = \sum_{j \notin D_u} I(f_u(j) \geq f_u(i)), \quad (10)$$

where $I(.)$ is the indicator function. $\Theta(.)$ is a loss function, which transforms the predicted rank of an item into a loss value,

$$\Theta(k) = \sum_{t=1}^{k} \alpha_t, \alpha_1 \geq \alpha_2 \geq \cdots \geq 0. \quad (11)$$

Different settings of α_t allow the loss function to optimize different objectives. Minimizing Θ with $\alpha_t = \frac{1}{N}$ would optimize the mean rank and minimizing Θ with $\alpha_t > \alpha_{t+1}$ would assign higher importance to the top-ranked items.

In this paper, we use a hinge loss to replace the indicator function so that a margin can be added and stochastic gradient descent (SGD) can be adopted to learn the parameters. Thus, the loss function for a specific item $i \in D_u$ in Eq. (9) can be approximated by Eq. (12) as

$$\begin{aligned} \overline{\Theta}(rank_i(f_u)) &= \sum_{j \notin D_u} \Theta(rank_i(f_u)) \frac{I(f_u(j) \geq f_u(i))}{rank_i(f_u)} \\ &\approx \sum_{j \notin D_u} \Theta(rank_i(f_u)) \frac{|1 - f_u(i) + f_u(j)|_+}{rank_i(f_u)}, \end{aligned} \quad (12)$$

where $|q|_+$ represents the positive part of q.

To minimize Eq. (12), we first uniformly sample a positive training instance $i \in D_u$. Then we need to calculate the margin rank of the item i among all items. However, exactly computing the rank of the item i is highly time-consuming when the number of items is very large. Therefore, following [38], at each iteration, we uniformly sample a negative feedback instance $j \notin D_u$ until a pairwise violation is found, that is, until $1 - f_u(i) + f_u(j) > 0$. If Q steps are required to find such a pairwise violation, then the rank of item i can be approximated as

$$rank_i(f_u) \approx \lfloor \frac{N-1}{Q} \rfloor. \quad (13)$$

Now the loss from the chosen item pair $\{f_u(.), i, j\}$ becomes

$$L_{WARP}(f_u, i, j) = \Theta(\lfloor \frac{N-1}{Q} \rfloor)|1 - f_u(i) + f_u(j)|_+. \quad (14)$$

To optimize Eq. (14), we can simply use gradient descent to perform updates, i.e.,

$$\theta_{t+1} = \theta_t - \eta \frac{\partial L_{WARP}(f_u, i, j)}{\partial \theta_t}, \quad (15)$$

where η is the learning rate.

3.2.3 Vector-based Objective Function

Since most existing latent factor models use the inner product of users' and items' latent factors to represent a user's preference or compatibility toward an item, only numerical loss functions can be used to optimize the ranking objective. However, only a one-dimensional number cannot precisely describe user's complex preference on the item, and moreover, numerical loss functions seem to be too arbitrary when comparing users' preferences on different items. Therefore, we propose to model users' preferences on items via a projected vector and propose a method that measures users' preference differences on items in vector space. Here, we describe how to model users' preferences by directly using the projected vectors. Recalling our *AUC* and *WARP*-Loss objective functions, we find that the basic idea behind them is to let the projected feature vectors of positive instances be 'more similar' to users' average preferences than are negative instances. Therefore, we can follow this intuition and directly model it via vector similarity. Actually, there are various proposed similarity measures that are applicable to compare two vectors to solve classification, clustering and retrieval problems. For example, Sørensen distance [34] uses the L_1 norm to measure similarity, *Wave Hedges* [5] uses an intersection-based measure to model similarity, and the *KL-divergence* [14] measures the similarity based on Shannon's concept of probabilistic uncertainty. In this work, we build our objective function based on the *KL-divergence*, which is a popular similarity measure in machine learning and data mining. The *KL-divergence* between two vectors can be represented as

$$d_{KL}(T, W) = \sum_{q=1}^{K^*} W(q) \ln \frac{W(q)}{T(q)}, \quad (16)$$

where T and W are vectors with size K^* and $W(q)$ represents the qth entry in vector W.

Based on Eq. (16), for a particular user u, our goal is to maximize the *KL-divergence* between the projected vectors from users' positive and negative instances. More specifically, when given a positive instance $i \in D_u$ and a negative instance $j \in N_u$, the objective function can be defined in terms of maximizing

$$\begin{aligned} \mathcal{O}_u(i, j) &= \sum_{f}^{K^*} (\widetilde{v}_j(f) \ln \frac{\widetilde{v}_j(f)}{\widetilde{v}_i(f)}) \\ &= \sum_{f}^{K^*} ((v_j P^u)(f) \ln \frac{(v_j P^u)(f)}{(v_i P^u)(f)}) \\ &= \sum_{f}^{K^*} ((v_j p_f^u) \ln \frac{v_j p_f^u}{v_i p_f^u}). \end{aligned} \quad (17)$$

To maximize Eq. (17), we uniformly sample a positive instance $i \in D_u$ and a negative instance $j \in N_u$. Then we can simply perform updates via gradient ascent. This process is repeated until the model converges. Specifically, the detailed gradients of the corresponding latent variables in the matrix factorization are as follows:

$$\begin{aligned} \frac{\partial \mathcal{O}_u(i, j)}{\partial P_{kf}^u} &= v_{jk}(1 + \ln \frac{v_j p_f^u}{v_i p_f^u}) - v_{ik} \frac{v_j p_f^u}{v_i p_f^u}, \\ \frac{\partial \mathcal{O}_u(i, j)}{\partial v_{ik}} &= \sum_{f}^{K^*} [-\frac{v_j p_f^u}{v_i p_f^u} p_{kf}^u], \\ \frac{\partial \mathcal{O}_u(i, j)}{\partial v_{jk}} &= \sum_{f}^{K^*} [(\ln \frac{v_j p_f^u}{v_i p_f^u} + v_i p_f^u) p_{kf}^u], \end{aligned} \quad (18)$$

where P_{kf}^u and p_f^u are as defined above. To avoid overfitting, we also constrain the parameters using the following inequalities and project the parameters back on the constraints when they violate the constraints at each step:

$$\begin{aligned} \|P^u\|_2 &\leq C_u, u \in 1, 2, ..., M, \\ \|v_j\|_2 &\leq C_i, j \in 1, 2, ..., N, \end{aligned} \quad (19)$$

where C_u and C_i are called projection constraint terms.

We note that although KL-divergence is asymmetric, due to the experimental results, this asymmetry has little impact on model performance. Thus, we just define the objective function as Eq. 17. Our proposed personalized feature projection method is quite general and can be easily extended to other vector similarity measures

Table 2: Statistics of the Datasets.

	Ciao	BeerAdvocate	Ratebeer	Lthing
#Users	1,705	33,387	29,264	73,882
#Item	12,252	63,324	107,381	337,561
#Feedback	22,839	1,424,957	2,578,594	979,053
#Avg. feedback	13	42.67	88.11	13.25
Sparsity	0.11%	0.06%	0.082%	0.004%

to define new objective functions. We do not discuss other similarity measures further, since the focus of this paper is to illustrate how to we can model users' preferences as a personalized projected vector rather than as an inner product.

3.3 Complexity Analysis

The computational complexity for *PFP* (KL) method is $\mathcal{O}(M \cdot N \cdot K \cdot K^*)$. Since we apply stochastic gradient descent methods for optimization, the complexity for each iteration is $\mathcal{O}(K \cdot K^*)$. One solution to scale this algorithm is to alternatively optimize the parameters based on multi-threading and parallelization: fist optimize item-latent factor vectors, then train users' projection matrices. In fact, our proposed method has the same complexity as *MaxMF* [39], therefore, we could use similar MapReduce algorithms to train all user parameters in parallel: when a training triple is sampled, the mapper collects and emits each column vector of the user's projection matrix and the item's latent vector, and the reducer calculates the dot product of each column vector and the item's vector independently. The reducer would then emit the results to build up a final projection vector for training.

4. EXPERIMENTAL RESULTS

In this section, we conduct experiments on the real-world datasets to evaluate the effectiveness of the proposed methods.

4.1 Experimental Setup

4.1.1 Datasets and Evaluation Metrics

The data sets [45] used in this paper are collected from four popular web sites: Ciao, BeerAdvocate, Ratebeer and LibraryThing (Lthing). Statistics of the four datasets are summarized in Table 2. Since this paper focuses on solving the one-class recommendation problem, we filter out explicit negative feedback (rating scores below 4 out of 5 stars) and use the remaining instances as positive feedback for model learning. All are available online.[1] [2]

For each dataset, we randomly split it into a training part, used for model training, and a test part, used for model evaluation. For each user u, we randomly select 90% of their observed feedback items as D_u and leave the remainder as T_u for testing. Grid search is applied to find projection constraint terms and learning rate is set as 0.01.

Our experiments are intended to address the following questions:

1. How does our approach compare with related personalized ranking methods for item recommendation?
2. Can vector-based recommendation models outperform traditional numerical models?
3. How does the number of projected factors affect the results?

[1]http://www.public.asu.edu/jtang20/datasetcode/truststudy.htm
[2]http://cseweb.ucsd.edu/~jmcauley/

We use two popular metrics, *NDCG* (Normalized Discounted Cumulative Gain) and *Area Under the Curve* (AUC), to measure the recommendation quality of our proposed approach in comparison to baseline methods. The average AUC statistic is defined as

$$AUC = \frac{1}{M}\sum_{u \in M}\frac{1}{|E(u)|}\sum_{(i,j)\in E(u)}\delta(x_{ui} > x_{uj}), \tag{20}$$

where $E(u) = \{(i,j)|(u,i) \in T_u \wedge (u,j) \notin (D_u \cup T_u)\}$.

$DCG@X$ considers the ranking of the recommended items by discounting the importance and is defined as

$$DCG@X = \sum_{i=1}^{X}\frac{2^{rel_i}-1}{\log_2(i+1)}, \tag{21}$$

where rel_i represents the relevance score of the item i (we use a binary value for this quantity). *NDCG* is the ratio of the *DCG* value to the ideal *DCG* value for that user. The ideal value of *DCG* comes from the best ranking function for the user. Here we set $X = N - D_u$ where N is the total number of items.

4.1.2 Comparison Methods

In order to demonstrate the benefits of our approach, we compare our model with the following methods for item recommendation. Since the problem we solve in this paper is one-class recommendation (without rating scores), it is unsuitable to compare our methods with rating estimation methods. Instead, we consider some state-of-the-art one-class recommendation methods as baselines.

- **CofiRank:** This method [37] is an extension of Maximum Margin Matrix Factorization for item recommendation optimized by a soft hinge ranking loss.
- **WRMF:** The weighted matrix factorization method is proposed by [19], which uses a point-wise strategy for solving one-class recommendation problems.
- **BPR-MF:** This method [24] proposes a pairwise assumption for item ranking and it is a well-known method for one-class recommendation.
- **GBPR:** This work [20] relaxes *BPR*'s assumption to a group pairwise preference assumption in order to smooth the individual positive feedback model and increase the confidence for pairwise classification. Here we fix the number of grouped users to 5 by cross-validation.
- **FISM-AUC:** This work [8] uses an item-based method for generating top-N recommendations. Since our work solves the one-class recommendation problem, here we choose their AUC-based loss function for comparison.
- **MaxMF:** This method is proposed in [39]. It is a non-linear matrix factorization method we introduced in Section 2.4. Note that *MaxMF* has the same number of parameters as PFP methods in all experiments.
- **PFP (WARP):** This method is proposed in Section 3.2.2 and uses the WARP-loss as an objective function.
- **PFP (KL):** This method is proposed in Section 3.2.3 and the KL-diversity is used for optimization.

Most of the above baseline methods can be found in [4].

Table 3: Recommendation performance of different methods on four real-world datasets. The last column shows the improvement of the proposed method compared with the best baseline method.

Dataset	Metrics	CofiRank	WRMF	BPR	GBPR	FISM-AUC	MaxMF	PFP-WARP	PFP-KL	Improv.
Ciao	NDCG	0.1692	**0.1881**	0.1672	0.1683	0.1570	0.1589	0.1865	0.1831	-0.85%
	AUC	0.6079	0.6948	0.5894	0.5909	0.5446	0.5669	0.6587	**0.7212**	+3.77%
Lthing	NDCG	0.1255	0.1665	0.1220	0.1322	0.1107	0.1132	0.1689	**0.1774**	+6.54%
	AUC	0.6035	0.7255	0.5816	0.6904	0.5926	0.6244	0.6587	**0.7880**	+8.61%
BeerAdvocate	NDCG	0.2180	0.2207	0.2390	0.2449	0.1888	0.1874	0.2354	**0.2501**	+2.12%
	AUC	0.8544	0.8523	0.8389	0.8649	0.7523	0.7812	0.8589	**0.8893**	+2.82%
RateBeer	NDCG	0.2600	0.2708	0.2715	0.2801	0.1728	0.2123	0.2614	**0.2877**	+2.71%
	AUC	0.8879	0.8758	0.8785	0.8881	0.7734	0.8120	0.8364	**0.9048**	+1.88%

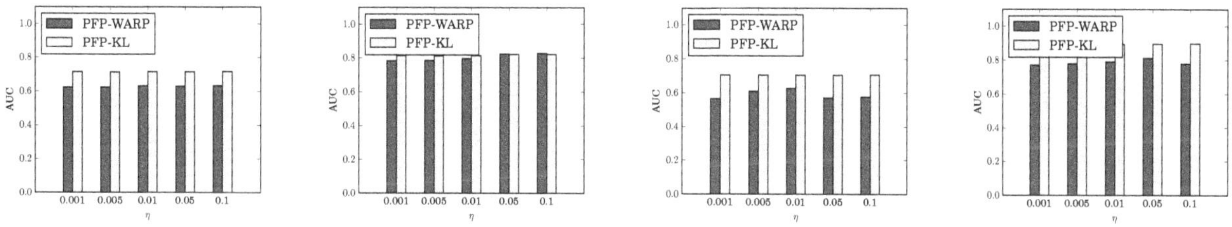

(a) Ciao (b) BeerAdvocate (c) Lthing (d) Ratebeer

Figure 2: Impact of learning rate η.

4.2 Performance Comparison

Results in terms of the AUC and NDCG are shown in Table 3. Although we can assign different values to the number of latent factors and the number of projected factors, here we just report the results by setting the same value for both parameters and leave the discussion of different parameter settings to Section 4.3.

On most datasets, we find that PFP methods outperform baselines. In particular, three observations can be drawn from the results: First, the proposed PFP methods achieve the best performance in most cases; from Table 2, we observe that users in these two datasets have more positive feedback items compared to other datasets (the average RateBeer user reviews close to *ninety* beers in their lifetime as a reviewer). These results corroborate that PFP can better describe users' preferences when we have sufficiently many positive feedback items.

Second, compared to BPR and GBPR, where the AUC is optimized via maximizing the difference of two inner products, PFP (KL) succeeds in enhancing the ranking performance by directly optimizing the difference between two projected vectors. As also can be seen from the results, FISM-AUC performs worse than other AUC-based methods (BPR, GBPR, PFP (WARP) and PFP (KL)) in most datasets. The reason might be that the objective function used in FISM-AUC ignores the influence of user bias for personalized ranking though it should be noted that FISM-AUC is designed for datasets with rating information such that it may be not be suitable for scenarios in which we have only binary feedback. The MaxMF method also uses multiple user latent factors to model users' preferences and this method has the same amounts of parameters as our proposed methods. The better performance of our method validates that modeling users' preferences by a combination of multiple item factors is more accurate than just using a maximal value as MaxMF does.

Third, from Table 3, we find that PFP (KL) always performs better than PFP (WARP). The improvements suggest that vector-based optimization criteria (such as the one used by PFP (KL)) are more plausible to model users' preferences and that modeling users' preferences in terms of a single value may be insufficient.

Note that when setting α_t as a constant in the WARP-Loss function, PFP (WARP) is equivalent to optimizing the AUC loss; moreover, from the results, we find that the proposed method based on the WARP-Loss always achieves similar results with that on the AUC loss, therefore, we omit AUC-based results from Table 3.

4.3 Parameter Analysis

Projection Factor Analysis. Different from existing latent factor models, PFP models require us to set not only the number of latent factors per item, but also the number of users' projection factors as hyperparameters. Therefore in this section, we experimentally investigate how different settings of the two parameter values influence the performance of PFP models. To make the results clear, we also show the performance of the most similar baseline method, MaxMF for comparison. The results are shown in Figure 3 and 4.

We find that in most cases, our proposed methods show better performance than MaxMF. Since MaxMF has the same number of parameters as our proposed methods, these results clearly verify that employing user's all tastes for preference modeling is better than only considering his/her maximum preference score. Moreover, we can also observe that even when PFP methods has a smaller value of K than MaxMF, the former's performance is still better than latter. This fact verifies our assumption that a user's opinion of an item may be complex and taking more parameters for modeling users' latent factors is more effective to improve the recommendation accuracy. As introduced before, K and K^* are two important parameters in PFP methods, we also give some detailed analysis about them below.

First, we examine the case where the number of item latent factors matches the number of users' projection factors. Results are

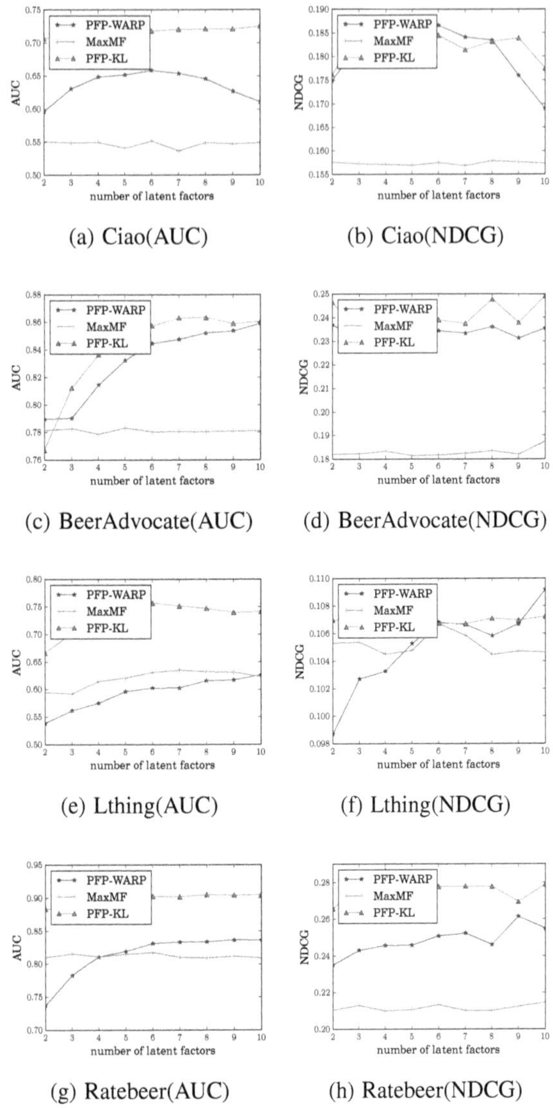

(a) Ciao(AUC) (b) Ciao(NDCG)

(c) BeerAdvocate(AUC) (d) BeerAdvocate(NDCG)

(e) Lthing(AUC) (f) Lthing(NDCG)

(g) Ratebeer(AUC) (h) Ratebeer(NDCG)

Figure 3: Impact of #latent factors, k (here we set the number of projected factors value, k^* as same as k).

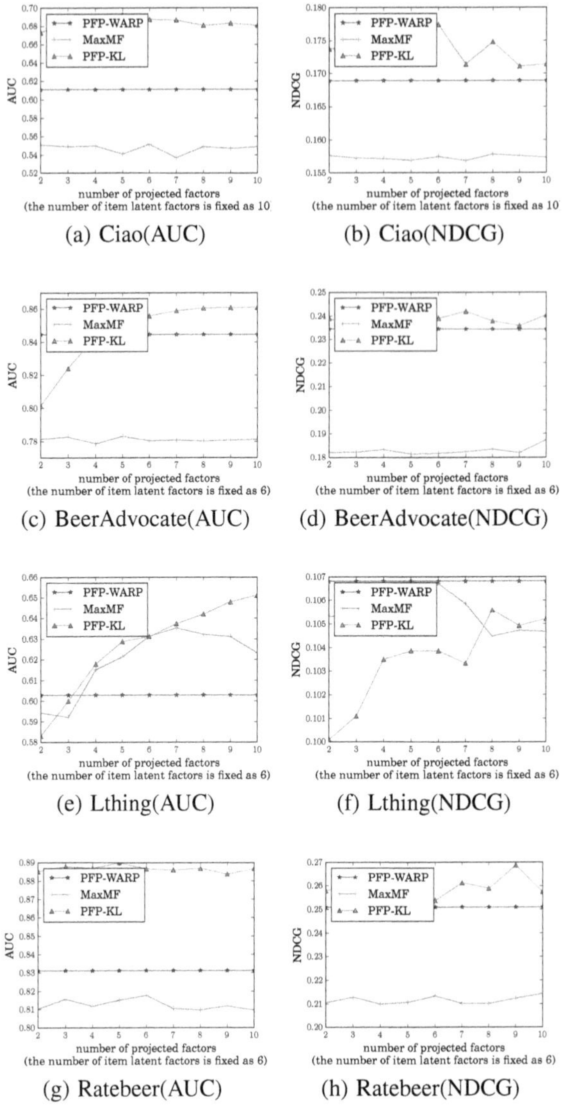

(a) Ciao(AUC) (b) Ciao(NDCG)

(c) BeerAdvocate(AUC) (d) BeerAdvocate(NDCG)

(e) Lthing(AUC) (f) Lthing(NDCG)

(g) Ratebeer(AUC) (h) Ratebeer(NDCG)

Figure 4: Impact of #projected factors.

shown in Figure 3. We vary K from 2 to 10 and compare the performance of PFP (KL) with PFP (WARP). AUC and NDCG are used as evaluation metrics. We find that in all datasets, PFP (KL) always performs better than PFP (WARP). In particular, compared with NDCG results, PFP (KL)'s AUC performance shows stable improvement as the number of latent factors increases. On the Ciao dataset, the NDCG performance of both methods show poor performance when $K = K^* = 10$. The reason we for this might be that when the number of positive feedback items per user is limited for training, a model with many parameters may suffer from overfitting. This conclusion is verified by our results on the Ratebeer dataset. Since Ratebeer contains sufficient positive feedback items for each user in the training set, the models' performance improves as we increase the number of latent factors in most cases.

We also conduct experiments to show how PFP methods perform when setting different values of K and K^*. Figure 4 illustrates the behavior of PFP models on different datasets. We find that different settings of the two parameters lead to varying results. On the Ciao dataset, fixing K to 10 and varying K^* from 2 to 10, PFP (KL) always achieves better performance than PFP (WARP). While on the BeerAdvocate dataset, we find that when we fix K to 6 and gradually increase K^* from 2 to 10, the performance of PFP (KL) improves significantly. This result indicates that when K^* is small, PFP (KL) cannot make use of such a low-dimensional projection space to describe users' preferences, and this also validates our motivation to model a user's preference toward an item as a combination of multiple item factors simultaneously. Similar results can be found on most other datasets. We also find an interesting result on Lthing: although PFP (KL)'s AUC outperforms PFP (WARP) when K^* is larger than 3, its NDCG performance is always unsatisfactory. One reason may be that when $K = 6$, PFP (KL) cannot project items' latent factors properly and moreover, the optimization criterion used in PFP (KL) does not focus on top-N ranking compared with the WARP-loss used in PFP (WARP). Based on the experimental results, we conclude that when we have sufficiently enough observed feedback for training, we can assign a large projection number for better user taste modeling, while when

C_u \ C_i	0.1	1	10	50	100	200
0.1	0.537	0.537	0.536	0.536	0.546	0.537
1	0.537	0.566	0.573	0.572	0.584	0.580
10	0.537	0.672	0.724	**0.725**	0.724	0.722
50	0.537	0.647	0.681	0.681	0.680	0.683
100	0.537	0.633	0.674	0.677	0.677	0.675
200	0.537	0.634	0.670	0.675	0.675	0.682

Table 4: Impact of projection constraints terms on Ciao dataset (AUC metric).

C_u \ C_i	0.1	1	10	50	100	200
0.1	0.503	0.503	0.503	0.503	0.503	0.503
1	0.503	0.878	0.868	0.870	0.867	0.871
10	0.503	0.531	**0.916**	0.909	0.907	0.906
50	0.503	0.871	0.888	0.882	0.881	0.881
100	0.503	0.871	0.887	0.884	0.881	0.880
200	0.503	0.869	0.886	0.883	0.882	0.881

Table 5: Impact of projection constraints terms on BeerAdvocate dataset. (AUC metric).

C_u \ C_i	0.1	1	10	50	100	200
0.1	0.486	0.486	0.486	0.486	0.486	0.486
1	0.486	0.884	0.877	0.874	0.871	0.876
10	0.486	0.351	**0.905**	0.897	0.892	0.891
50	0.486	0.858	0.891	0.885	0.884	0.885
100	0.486	0.856	0.891	0.888	0.886	0.883
200	0.486	0.856	0.892	0.886	0.886	0.885

Table 6: Impact of projection constraints terms on Ratebeer dataset (AUC metric).

C_u \ C_i	0.1	1	10	50	100	200
0.1	0.763	0.763	0.763	0.763	0.763	0.763
1	0.763	0.769	0.741	0.742	0.739	0.738
10	0.763	0.456	0.740	0.744	0.738	0.739
50	0.763	0.611	**0.788**	0.784	0.781	0.780
100	0.763	0.608	0.787	0.782	0.780	0.779
200	0.763	0.608	**0.788**	0.780	0.780	0.778

Table 7: Impact of projection constraints terms on Lthing dataset (AUC metric).

we have limited training data, we may decrease the projection number and use a simple model to avoid overfitting. When K^* is set to 1, the projected preference vector will degenerate to a dot product, as used in existing methods [8, 32, 37, 39].

Projection Constraint Analysis. In order to avoid overfitting, we constrain the parameters C_u and C_i using Eq. (19). Here we analyze the impact of constraint terms on model performance. The experimental results are shown in Tables 4 to 7. These results provide many hints about how to find the proper projection constraint terms for better modeling. On all datasets, we fix $K = K^* = 10$. In particular, we find that when $C_u = 10$ and $C_i = 50$, PFP (KL) exhibits the best performance on the Ciao dataset. Such results indicate that in order to avoid overfitting, we have to constrict the constraint of user's projection matrix, especially when the number of items is not particularly large (less than 20K). On the Lthing dataset, we obtain the best performance when C_u is above 50 and C_i is 10. Such results suggest that when the number of candidate items is large, it is better to reduce the constraint on users' projection matrices so that the model can describe the subtleties of users' preferences. On the BeerAdvocate and Ratebeer datasets, since the average number of positive feedback instances per user is large, the observed information is enough to model users' preferences toward items, so that the projection constraint terms do not affect the model performance on these two datasets as significantly as on the others. The best performance on both BeerAdvocate and Ratebeer datasets occur when setting $C_u = 10$ and $C_i = 10$.

Impact of η. We also perform experiments to investigate the impact of the learning rate η. The results are shown in Figure 2. We consider $\eta \in \{0.001, 0.005, 0.01, 0.05, 0.1\}$ and find that PFP models are insensitive to the value of η. Therefore, we conclude that selecting proper values for K and K^* are much more important to obtain good performance than adjusting the learning rate when training. These results also indicate that we could use relatively large learning rates to improve the convergence time of the model.

5. CONCLUSION AND FUTURE WORK

In this paper, we proposed a *Personalized Feature Projection* method in order to improve recommendation accuracy on one-class recommendation problems. Our model learns a projection matrix for each user that is able to capture the complexities of their preferences towards certain items over others. In contrast to existing methods that assume a one-to-one relationship between users' preferences and item properties, we assume that each dimension of a user's preference is related to a combination of item factors simultaneously. We formulated three optimization criteria for one-class recommendation, and performed experiments on four real-world datasets, finding that our method effectively improves the recommendation accuracy for one-class recommendation problems.

For future work, we are interested in extending PFP method in three ways: (1) Investigating how to incorporate social network information into the PFP model, in order to model the similarity between users' and their friends' preferences via the PFP method. Possible alternatives include modeling the similarity between projection matrices, or modeling the similarity between projected vectors. (2) Employing contextual information (such as text) in order to understand the meaning behind each projected latent factor; similar to [9, 18], we might allow text or time to explain the particular meanings of projected factors. (3) Exploring how to set the number of projected latent factors automatically.

6. ACKNOWLEDGEMENTS

This research was in part supported by grants from the National Grand Fundamental Research 973 Program of China (No. 2014-CB340405), the Research Grants Council of the Hong Kong Special Administrative Region, China (Project No. CUHK 413213), and Microsoft Research Asia Regional Seed Fund in Big Data Research (Grant No. FY13-RES-SPONSOR-036).

References

[1] L. Baltrunas and X. Amatriain. Towards time-dependant recommendation based on implicit feedback. *In Workshop on context-aware recommender systems*, 2009.

[2] J. Davis, B. Kulis, P. Jain, S. Sra, and I. Dhillon. Information-theoretic metric learning. *In Proceedings of ICML*, 2007.

[3] L. Du, X. Li, and Y.-D. Shen. User graph regularized pairwise matrix factorization for item recommendation. *In Proceedings of ADMA*, pages 372–385, 2011.

[4] Z. Gantner, S. Rendle, C. Freudenthaler, and L. Schmidt-Thieme. Mymedialite: a free recommender system library. *In Proceedings of RecSys*, pages 305–308, 2011.

[5] Hedges. An empirical modication to linear wave theory. *In Proceedings of ICE*, pages 575 –579, 1976.

[6] L. Hong, R. Bekkerman, J. Adler, and B. D. Davison. Learning to rank social update streams. *In Proceedings of SIGIR*, 2012.

[7] Y. Hu, Y. Koren, and C. Volin-sky. Collaborative filtering for implicit feedback datasets. *In Proceedings of ICDM*, pages 263–272, 2008.

[8] S. Kabbur, X. Ning, and G. Karypis. Fism: factored item similarity models for top-n recommender systems. *In Proceedings of KDD*, pages 659–667, 2013.

[9] A. Karatzoglou, X. Amatriain, N. Oliver, and L. Baltrunas. Multiverse recommendation: n-dimensional tensor factorization for context-aware collaborative filtering. *In Proceedings of RecSys*, 2010.

[10] Y. Koren and R. Bell. Advances in collaborative filtering. *In Recommender Systems Handbook*, pages 145–186, 2011.

[11] W. K.Q. *Metric Learning with Convex Optimization*. PhD thesis, University of Pennsylvania, July 2007.

[12] W. K.Q. and L. Saul. Distance metric learning for large margin nearest neighbor classification. *The Journal of Machine Learning Research*, 10:207–244, 2009.

[13] A. Krohn-Grimberghe, L. Drumond, C. Freudenthaler, and L. Schmidt-Thieme. Multi-relational matrix factorization us-ing bayesian personalized ranking for social network data. *In Proceedings of WSDM*, pages 173–182, 2012.

[14] S. Kullback and R. Leibler. On info rmation and sufficiency. *Ann. Math.Statist*, pages 79 –86, 1951.

[15] M. Kusner, S. Tyree, K. Q. Weinberger, and K. Agrawal. Stochastic neighbor compression. *In Proceedings of ICML*, 2014.

[16] N. D. Lawrence and R. Urtasun. Non-linear matrix factorization with gaussian processes. *In Proceedings of ICML*, 2009.

[17] J. Lee, S. Bengio, S. Kim, G. Lebanon, and Y. Singer. Local collaborative ranking. *In Proceedings of WWW*, 2014.

[18] J. McAuley and J. Leskovec. Hidden factors and hidden topics: understanding rating dimensions with review text. *In Proceedings of RecSys*, 2013.

[19] R. Pan, Y. Zhou, B. Cao, N. N. Liu, R. Lukose, M. Scholz, and Q. Yang. One-class collaborative filtering. *In Proceedings of ICDM*, pages 502–511, 2008.

[20] W. Pan and L. Chen. Gbpr: Group preference based bayesian personalized ranking for one-class collaborative filtering. *In Proceedings of IJCAI*, 2013.

[21] N. Pappas and A. Popescu-Belis. Sentiment analysis of user comments for one-class collaborative filtering over ted talks. *In Proceedings of SIGIR*, 2013.

[22] U. Paquet and N. Koenigstein. One-class collaborative filtering with random graphs. *In Proceedings of WWW*, pages 999–1008, 2013.

[23] S. Parameswaran and K. Weinberger. Large margin multi-task metric learning. *In Proceedings of NIPS*, 2010.

[24] S. Rendle, C. Freuden-thaler, Z. Gantner, and L. Schmidt-Thieme. Bpr:bayesian personalized ranking from implicit feedback. *In Proceedings of UAI*, pages 452–461, 2009.

[25] S. Rendle, C. Freuden-thaler, and L. S. Thieme. Factorizing personalized markov chains for next-basket recommendation. *In Proceedings of WWW*, pages 811–820, 2010.

[26] S. Rendle and L. Schmidt-Thieme. Pairwise interaction tensor factorization for personalized tag recommendation. *In Proceedings of WSDM*, pages 81–90, 2010.

[27] J. D. M. Rennie and N.Srebro. Fast maximum margin matrix factorization for collaborative prediction. *In Proceedings of ICML*, 2005.

[28] R.Salakhutdinov and A.Mnih. Bayesian probabilistic matrix factorization using markov chain monte carlo. *In Proceedings of ICML*, 2008.

[29] R.Salakhutdinov and A.Mnih. Probabilistic matrix factorization. *In Proceedings of NIPS*, 2008.

[30] R. Salakhutdinov, A. Mnih, and G. Hinton. Restricted boltzmann machines for collaborative filtering. *In Proceedings of ICML*, 2007.

[31] M. Schultz and T. Joachims. Learning a distance metric from relative comparisons. *In Proceedings of NIPS*, 2003.

[32] Y. Shi, A. Karatzoglou, L. Baltrunas, M. Larson, and A. Hanjalic. Climf: Learning to maximize reciprocal rank with collaborative less-is-more filtering. *In Proceedings of RecSys*, 2012.

[33] M. Slaney, K. Weinberger, and W. White. Learning a metric for music similarity. *In Proceedings of ISMIR*, 2008.

[34] Srensen. A method of establishing groups of equal amplitude in plant sociology based on similarity of species and its application to analyses of the vegetation on danish commons. *Kongelige Danske Videnskabernes Selskab*, pages 1–34, 1948.

[35] K. Wagstaff and C. Cardie. Clustering with instance-level constraints. *In Proceedings of AAAI*, 2000.

[36] H. Wang, X. He, M.-W. Chang, Y. Song, R. W. White, and W. Chu. Personalized ranking model adaptation for web search. *In Proceedings of SIGIR*, 2013.

[37] M. Weimer, A. Karatzoglou, and A. Smola. Improving maximum margin matrix factorization. *Machine Learning Journal*, 2008.

[38] J. Weston, S. Bengio, and N. Usunier. Large scale image annotation: learning to rank with joint word-image embeddings. *In Proceedings of Machine Learning*, 2010.

[39] J. Weston, R. J. Weiss, and H. Yee. Nonlinear latent factorization by embedding multiple user interests. *In Proceedings of RecSys*, 2013.

[40] J. Weston, H. Yee, and R. J. Weiss. Learning to rank recommendations with the k-order statistic loss. *In Proceedings of RecSys*, pages 245–248, 2013.

[41] E. Xing, A. Ng, M. Jordan, and S. Russell. Distance metric learning, with application to clustering with side-information. *In Proceedings of NIPS*, 2002.

[42] S.-H. Yang, B. Long, A. Smola, N. Sadagopan, Z. Zheng, and H. Zha. Like like alike: joint friendship and interest propagation in social networks. *In Proceedings of WWW*, 2011.

[43] S.-H. Yang, B. Long, A. J. Smola, H. Zha, and Z. Zheng. Collaborative competitive filtering: learning recommender using context of user choice. *In Proceedings of SIGIR*, pages 295–304, 2011.

[44] Y. Yue, C. Wang, K. El-Arini, and C. Guestrin. Personalized collaborative clustering. *In Proceedings of WWW*, 2014.

[45] T. Zhao, J. McAuley, and I. King. Leveraging social connections to improve personalized ranking for collaborative filtering. *In Proceedings of CIKM*, 2014.

Node Immunization over Infectious Period

Chonggang Song
School of Computing
National University of Singapore
a0095629@nus.edu.sg

Wynne Hsu
School of Computing
National University of Singapore
whsu@comp.nus.edu.sg

Mong Li Lee
School of Computing
National University of Singapore
leeml@comp.nus.edu.sg

ABSTRACT

Locating nodes to immunize in computer/social networks to control the spread of virus or rumors has become an important problem. In real world contagions, nodes may get infected by external sources when the propagation is underway. While most studies formalize the problem in a setting where contagion starts at one time point, we model a more realistic situation where there are likely to be many breakouts of contagions over a time window. We call this the *node immunization over infectious period* (NIIP) problem. We show that the NIIP problem is NP-hard and remains so even in directed acyclic graphs. We propose a NIIP algorithm to select k nodes to immunize over a time period. Simulation is performed to estimate a good distribution of k over the time period. For each time point, the NIIP algorithm will make decisions which nodes to immunize given the estimated value of k for that time point. Experiments show that the proposed NIIP algorithm outperform the state-of-the-art algorithms in terms of both effectiveness and efficiency.

1. INTRODUCTION

With the advent of the Internet, everyone is connected. This enables the data generated by any user to be easily accessed by other users all over the world. Despite the convenience and ease in sharing information, this has also led to the fast propagation of virus in computer networks as well as rumors in the information networks. For example, when the Malaysia Airlines Flight 370 was reported missing on the morning of March 8th 2014, millions of messages flooded the social network. A message saying "Flight MH370 has resurfaced and landed safely in Nanming, China." received millions of shares before it was proven to be a rumor. This is not only a waste of resources in information dissemination, but also causes confusions as well as panics in a very short time. In order to reduce the impact brought about by such epidemics, researchers study the problem of node immunization: Given a graph, which nodes should we immunize so that the maximum number of nodes will remain *healthy* under attacks? In computer networks, a computer is healthy if it is not infected with some malware and in social networks, a user is said to be healthy if he/she does not share/re-tweet any rumor message. In the former case, immunizing a node may mean the shutting down of certain host servers, while in the latter case, this could mean the suspension of a user's account.

Existing works have mostly focused on immunizing nodes *before* the virus/rumor starts spreading [8, 18, 19]. Recently, the realization is that it is more practical and meaningful to identify nodes to immunize *while* the attack is underway. Zhang et al. [20] investigated the problem of node immunization with the awareness of infected nodes. They present a polynomial-time heuristic algorithm called DAVA that constructs a *dominator tree*. They aggregate the infected nodes into one node as the root and examine the paths from the root to each node. A node u is a child of node v if every path from the root must traverse v to reach u. Thus, with the dominator tree, we can say that any descendant of node u in the tree will be healthy if u is immunized. Given this observation, they iteratively select the node that maximizes the expected number of saved descendant nodes. Once selected, this node and its descendants are removed and a new dominator tree is constructed and the process is repeated to select the next node for immunization.

However, we recognize that when an attack happens in the real world, there is a time period where multiple independent sources may actively infect different nodes [15]. This infectious period is often observed in the early stage of a contagion [3]. For example, mendacious messages about MH370's safe landing in Nanming were posted by many users independently, citing different websites, in the first six hours of its attack. This will create a problem when the resources available for immunization are limited.

We will illustrate this issue with an example shown in Figure 1(a) where u_1 is the initial infected node (marked in red). Suppose the infectious period is 2 time points and u_8 becomes infected at the second time point. We also assume we only have enough resources to immunize 2 nodes. Looking at time point 1, we would choose u_2 and u_3 and save the nodes colored in green (Figure 1(b)). However, when u_8 becomes infected at time point 2, we have no resource to immunize additional nodes, as a result, the saved nodes are once again infected, leaving us with only 2 healthy nodes (Figure 1(c)). On the other hand, if we immunize only u_3 at time point 1 and then immunize u_7 at time point 2, we would have 4 healthy nodes at the end as shown in Figure 1(d). This shows that a good immunization strategy should consider the entire infectious period on the whole when making decision as to which nodes to immunize.

In this work, we formalize the problem of node immunization over an infectious period. We show that our problem is NP-hard and present the NIIP algorithm. Our assumption is that the resources available for immunization are limited, that is, we only have resources to immunize k nodes. Hence, we propose a simulation-based approach to estimate how k should be distributed over the infectious period. At the same time, we design a scoring func-

Permission to make digital or hard copies of all or part of this work for personal or classroom use is granted without fee provided that copies are not made or distributed for profit or commercial advantage and that copies bear this notice and the full citation on the first page. Copyrights for components of this work owned by others than ACM must be honored. Abstracting with credit is permitted. To copy otherwise, or republish, to post on servers or to redistribute to lists, requires prior specific permission and/or a fee. Request permissions from Permissions@acm.org.

CIKM 15, October 19-23, 2015, Melbourne, VIC, Australia
ACM 978-1-4503-3794-6/15/10 ...$15.00.
DOI: http://dx.doi.org/10.1145/2806416.2806522 .

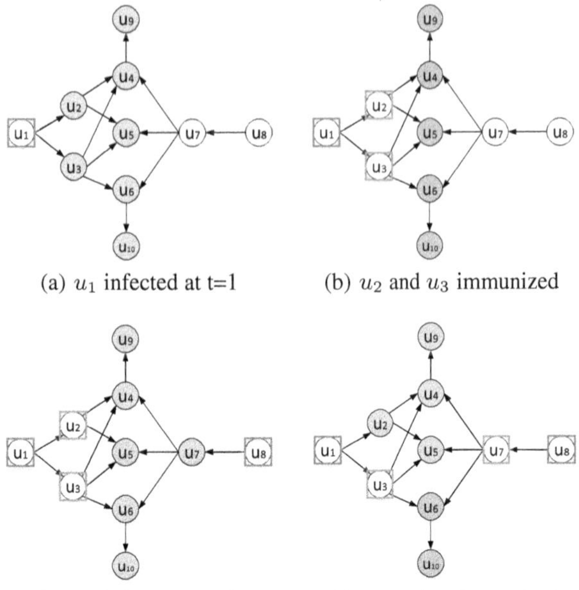

(a) u_1 infected at t=1
(b) u_2 and u_3 immunized
(c) u_8 infected at t=2
(d) u_3 and u_7 immunized

Figure 1: Example network.

tion to model a node's immunization ability in the network. Based on the estimated value of k at time point t, denoted as k_t, we select k_t nodes with the highest scores for immunization at time point t. After immunizing these nodes, we consider the new infected nodes and update the scores of all the affected nodes. The process repeats until we have selected k nodes to immunize. We conduct extensive experiments on several real world datasets covering computer networks, information networks and social networks to demonstrate the efficiency and effectiveness of the proposed NIIP algorithm. Our experimental results show that NIIP clearly outperforms the state-of-the-art DAVA algorithm.

The contributions of this work can be summarized as follows:

- We consider the time window where nodes in a network may get infected from multiple sources independently. We formalize the problem of node immunization over infectious period and show that this problem is NP-hard.
- We propose a simulation-based approach to derive a good allocation scheme that distribute the limited resources k over the time period.
- We design an effective heuristic algorithm S-NIIP to select k_t nodes for immunization at a single time point t. The algorithm takes into account the joint immunization effect of multiple nodes and computes the immunization ability of the node to the rest of the network. The top k_t nodes with the highest immunization ability are selected for immunization.
- We develop the NIIP algorithm that selects k nodes for immunization over a time period. As the number of infected nodes increases within a time window, NIIP algorithm focuses on modeling only the direct immunization ability to reduce the number of updates needed.

2. PRELIMINARIES

In this section, we define the node immunization over infectious period (NIIP) problem and provide an analysis of the problem.

We consider a directed, weighted graph $G = (V, E)$ as the input graph. For each edge $(u, v) \in E$, there is a probability p_{uv} representing the probability that u passes infection to v. Apart from getting infected via network connections, healthy nodes have a probability of getting infected from external sources during the infectious period, and newly infected nodes can, in turn, infect their neighbors and propagate the contagion. To model this, we introduce two parameters α and τ, where α denotes the probability that a healthy node gets infected by some external sources, and τ denote the number of time points where a healthy node can be infected by some external sources and $1 \leq t \leq \tau$. Our goal is to find a set of nodes to immunize such that the expected number of healthy nodes at the end of the propagation is maximized.

DEFINITION 1. ***NIIP problem.*** *Let $G = (V, E)$ be an input network where V is the set of nodes and E is the set of edges. Each edge $(u, v) \in E$ has an infection probability p_{uv}. Let $I_t \subset V$ be a set of infected nodes at time point t where $1 \leq t \leq \tau$, and α be the probability that a healthy node is infected by an external source. We define $\Phi(A_1, A_2, \cdots, A_\tau)$ to be the number of nodes that remain healthy if the nodes in A_t are immunized at time point t. Our goal is to find τ sets of nodes, $A_1, A_2, \cdots, A_\tau$, such that $\sum_i |A_i| = k$ and $\Phi(A_1, A_2, \cdots, A_\tau)$ is maximized.*

Note that the Data-Aware Vaccination (DAV) problem defined in [20] is a special case of the NIIP problem with $\tau = 1$ and $\alpha = 0$. Table 1 summarizes the notations used in this paper.

Table 1: Summary of Notations

Symbol	Description
$G = (V, E)$	directed graph G with set of nodes V and set of edges E
p_{uv}	the infection probability from u to v
k	number of nodes that can be immunized
τ	number of time points where external infection can occur
I_t	the set of infected node at time point t
α	probability of nodes getting infected by external sources
A_t	the set of nodes to be immunized at time point t
$\Phi()$	the expected number of healthy nodes at the end of propagation
$parent(u)$	the set of nodes that point to node u
$child(u)$	the set of nodes that node u points to

2.1 Problem Analysis

Next, we show that the NIIP problem is NP-hard, and even when we restrict the problem to directed acylic graphs (DAG), the problem remains NP-hard.

THEOREM 1. *The NIIP problem in Definition 1 is NP-hard.*

PROOF. (Sketch.) Zhang et al. [20] has shown that the Data-Aware Vaccination (DAV) problem is NP-hard. Since the DAV problem is a special NIIP problem with $\tau = 1$, we see that if there is a polynomial time solution to NIIP problem, we can set $\tau = 1$ and solve the DAV problem in polynomial time. In other words, the NIIP problem is NP-hard. □

THEOREM 2. *The NIIP problem restricted to a directed acyclic graph is NP-hard.*

PROOF. We show that the base case of NIIP problem on a directed acyclic graph with $p_{uv} = 1$ for any $(u, v) \in E$, $\tau = 1$ and $\alpha = 0$ is NP-hard. If the base case is NP-hard, then the general NIIP problem on directed acyclic graph must be NP-hard. To prove that the base case NIIP problem is NP-hard, we first show that the decision version of the problem can be reduced from its function version in polynomial time and then we prove the decision version of the problem is NP-hard.

The decision version is stated as follows: Is there a subset of nodes A in a DAG where $|A| = k$ such that $\Phi(A)$ in Definition 1 is greater than a given value? Clearly, given a directed acyclic graph with n nodes and the infected nodes are I_1, there are at most $|V| - |I_1|$ possible values for $\Phi(A)$. If we can solve the decision version in polynomial time, then the solution to our problem is the set of nodes that gives the largest $\Phi(A)$ value.

Next, we show that the decision problem on a DAG is NP-hard by reducing it from the *k-densest subgraph* problem, namely, determining a k-node subgraph with at least p edges in a given graph [2]. Given an instance $G = (V, E), k, p$ of the k-densest subgraph problem, let $n = |V|$ and $m = |E|$. We can construct a directed acyclic graph $G' = (V', E')$ of $(1 + n + m)$ nodes and $2m$ edges as follows. We first create a source node s in G'. For each node u in G, we create a corresponding node u' in G' and connect s to u'. For each edge $e(u, v)$ in G, let u' and v' be the corresponding nodes of u and v respectively. We create a node e' in G' and connect u' and v' to e'. Let $Y_1 = \{u'_1, \cdots, u'_n\}$ and $Y_2 = \{e'_1, \cdots, e'_m\}$. Then $V' = Y'_1 \cup Y'_2 \cup \{s\}$.

Figure 2 shows an example of the construction from graph G to G'. It is clear that the construction can be done in polynomial time.

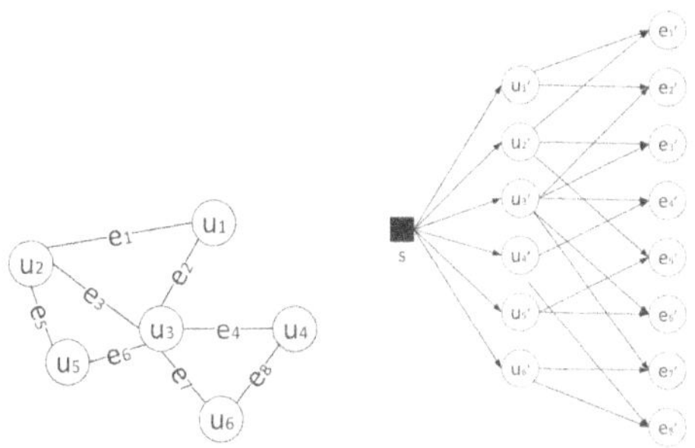

(a) G (b) G'

Figure 2: Construction of G' from G.

Next, we prove that the k-densest subgraph instance is satisfiable *if and only if* there exists a subset $A \subset Y_1$ where $|A| = k$ such that $\Phi(A) \geq (k + p)$.

For the *only if* direction, suppose the k-densest subgraph instance is satisfiable, that is we have a subgraph with k nodes and at least p edges among them in G. Let $A \subset Y_1$ be the set of nodes in G' that corresponds to these k nodes. When we remove the nodes in A from G', there are at least p nodes in Y_2 in G' that become isolated from s. These p isolated nodes correspond to the p edges in the k-densest subgraph solution. Thus, by immunizing the k nodes in A, we have made p nodes healthy. Hence $\Phi(A) = (k + p)$.

For the *if* direction, suppose the NIIP problem is satisfiable, i.e., $\exists A \subset V'$ such that $\Phi(A) \geq (k + p)$. Assume $|A \cap Y_1| = l$ and $|A \cap Y_2| = (k - l)$. Nodes in Y_1 can possibly immunize nodes in Y_2 while immunizing nodes in Y_2 can only immunize themselves. This means the nodes in $A \cap Y_1$ immunize $(k + p) - (k - l) = (p + l)$ nodes in Y_2 in order for A to immunize $(k + p)$ nodes in total. These $p + l$ nodes in Y_2 correspond to the edges in G whose both end points are in $A \cap Y_1$. Thus we have found a subgraph in G with $l \leq k$ nodes and at least p edges among them. In other words, the k-densest subgraph instance I is satisfiable. $\square$

3. ALGORITHMS

Given that the NIIP problem is NP-hard, we use a combination of simulation-based and greedy approach to solve the problem. Figure 3 shows an overview of the main steps in our proposed approach.

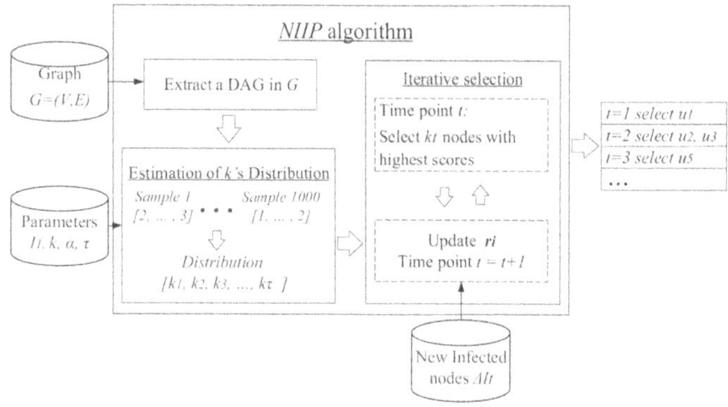

Figure 3: Overview of proposed approach.

Given a network graph, we first extract a maximum DAG from the graph. We then perform a Monte Carlo simulation to estimate the distribution of k over each time point t in τ given the probability α of a healthy node being infected. Next, for each time point t in τ, we compute a score for each node that reflects the node's immunization ability. Suppose the estimated distribution of k at time point t is k_t, this implies that at time point t, we need to select k_t nodes to be immunized. Hence, the top k_t nodes with the highest scores are selected and the scores of the affected nodes are updated. We repeat this process for each t in τ.

The details of each step are given in the following subsections. We first discuss how to select the best k_t nodes at a given time point t. Then we describe how to perform simulation to estimate the distribution of k over the τ time points. Based on this estimated distribution of k, we design a scalable NIIP algorithm to select τ sets of nodes to immunize at each time point t.

3.1 Single time point NIIP

Different nodes have different immunization abilities depending on the network structure and the infected nodes. The DAVA algorithm models this with a dominator tree. Figure 4 shows the dominator tree constructed for Figure 4(a) given u_1 is infected.

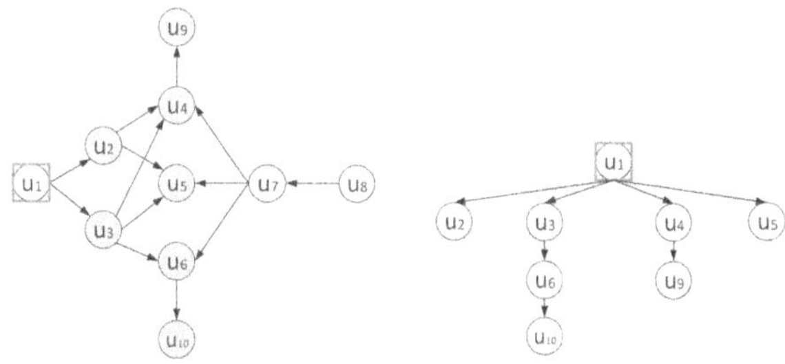

(a) Example network (b) Dominator tree

Figure 4: DAVA algorithm for the example network.

Based on the dominator tree, if we can only immunize 2 nodes, the DAVA algorithm will choose u_3 and u_4 instead of the preferred choice u_2 and u_3. This is because the dominator tree does not capture the joint effect when two or more nodes are immunized. If only u_2 is immunized, none of the nodes can be saved. However, immunizing both u_2 and u_3 will result in the saving of 5 nodes. To model this joint effect, we introduce the concept of immunization ability of a node.

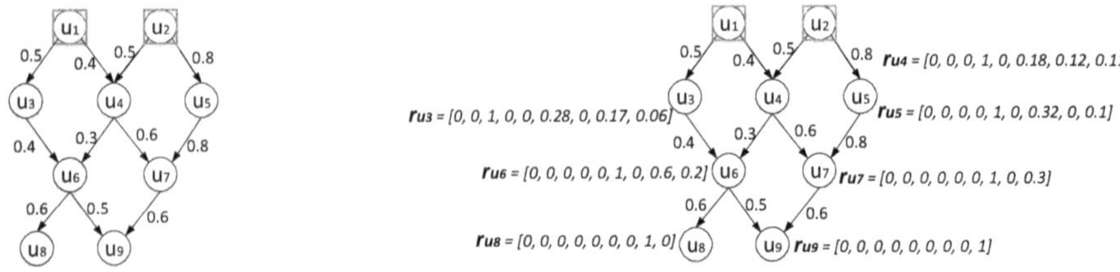

(a) Example network. (b) Computation of $\mathbf{r_u}$ for each node.

Figure 5: Illustration of computing $\mathbf{r_u}$.

Consider the example in Figure 5(a), where each edge (u, v) is labeled with the probability of node u infecting v, denoted as p_{uv}. We see that u_9 has two parents u_6 and u_7. If we immunize u_6 only, u_9 can still be infected by u_7 or via some external source. To measure the protection gain to u_9 by immunizing u_6, we first compute the probability that u_9 does not get its infection from either u_6 or u_7. This is given by $\prod_{v\in\{u_6,u_7\}}(1-p_{vu_9}) = (1-0.5)(1-0.6) = 0.2$. The probability that u_9 is not infected by u_7 is $1 - 0.6 = 0.4$. Hence, the gain by immunizing u_6 is $0.4 - 0.2 = 0.2$. We term this the immunization ability of u_6 over u_9.

Let $parent(u)$ denote the set of parents of a node u and $child(u)$ denote the set of children of u. We model the immunization ability of u over the rest of the nodes as a vector $\mathbf{r_u}$. The vth entry in $\mathbf{r_u}$, denoted as m_{uv}, represents the immunization ability of u over v. m_{uv} is given as:

$$m_{uv} = \begin{cases} \prod\limits_{\substack{w\in parent(u)\\ w\neq u}} - p_{wv} - \prod\limits_{w\in parent(u)} - p_{wv}\ , & u \in parent\ v \\ \sum\limits_{w\in child(u)} m_{uw} \times m_{wv}\ , & u \notin parent\ v \end{cases} \quad (1)$$

Intuitively, this makes sense because when node v has many parents, even though u is immunized, all the other parents of v could still pass the infection to v. Hence, in this case, the m_{uv} value should be small. On the other hand, if node v has only two parents, when u is immunized, the probability of v getting infected is much lower. In other words, m_{uv} value should be large. Note that when v has only one parent u, $m_{uv} = 1 - (1 - p_{uv}) = p_{uv}$. Also, for any node u, $m_{uu} = 1$. Note that when we compute m_{uv}, we do not need to know whether there is a path from u to v. If there is no path from u to v, m_{uv} will be 0 since v cannot pass its immunization ability along its ancestors to u via the computation.

For each node u, we compute the immunization ability of node u over the rest of the nodes in a vector, i.e. $\mathbf{r_u}$, as follows:

$$\mathbf{r_u} = \sum_{v\in child(u)} m_{uv} \cdot \mathbf{r_v} + \mathbf{e_u} \quad (2)$$

where $\mathbf{e_u}$ is a unit vector with its component corresponding to u being one and elsewhere being zeros.

Figure 5(b) illustrates the computation of $\mathbf{r_u}$ vector for each node. Assume u_1 and u_2 are the infected nodes. The susecptible nodes are $[u_3, \cdots, u_8, u_9]$. Traversing this in the reverse order, we start with u_9. Since u_9 has no children, $\mathbf{r_{u_9}}$ has a "1" on the 9th column and zeros elsewhere. Similarly for $\mathbf{r_{u_8}}$ with a "1" on the 8th column. Next, we come to u_7. The immunization ability of u_7 over u_9 is $m_{u_7u_9} = (1-0.5)-(1-0.5)\times(1-0.6) = 0.3$, thus we have $\mathbf{r_{u_7}} = 0.3 \times \mathbf{r_{u_9}} + \mathbf{e_{u_7}}$, as shown in Figure 5(b). Similarly, we compute $m_{u_6u_9} = (1 - 0.6) - (1 - 0.5) \times (1 - 0.6) = 0.2$. Note that $m_{u_7u_9} > m_{u_6u_9}$ makes sense since $p_{u_7u_9} > p_{u_6u_9}$. This implies that the gain obtained by immunizing u_7 is greater than immunizing u_6.

With this, we can now compute the score for each node u:

$$score(u) = \sum_{j=1,\cdots,|V|} \mathbf{r_u}[j] \quad (3)$$

Algorithm 1: S-NIIP algorithm

input : 1. Graph G V, E
2. Number of nodes to immunize k_t
3. Infected node set I_t
output: Top-k nodes for immunization

Initialize $UpdateList$ $\emptyset$, S $\emptyset$;
foreach $u \in I$ **do**
  Peform DFS from u and insert visited nodes into S;
Apply ACYCLIC on S to generate a DAG;
Find a topological sorting σ in the DAG;
foreach *node v in the reverse order of σ* **do**
  foreach $u, v \in E$ **do**
    $parent\ v$ $parent\ v \cup \{u\}$;
    $child\ u$ $child\ u \cup \{v\}$;
  Compute $_\mathbf{v}$ with Equation 2;
  Compute $score\ v$ with Equation 3;
repeat
  Return node u with highest $score\ u$;
  Call $Immunize\ u$;
  Call $ProcessUpdate\ UpdateList$;
until *k nodes are selected*;
Function *Immunize(u)*
  $score\ u$, S $S - \{u\}$;
  foreach $v \in child\ u$ **do**
    if $parent\ v$ $\{u\}$ **then**
      Call $Immunize\ v$;
    else
      $parent\ v$ $parent\ v - \{u\}$;
      $UpdateList$ $UpdateList \cup parent\ v \cap S$;
Function *ProcessUpdate(UpdateList)*
  foreach $u \in UpdateList$ **do**
    Compute $_\mathbf{u}$ with Equation 2 and $score\ u$ with Equation 3;
    $UpdateList$ $UpdateList \cup parent\ u \cap S$;
    $UpdateList$ $UpdateList - \{u\}$;
Return top-k_t nodes for immunization.

Given a graph G and the set of infected nodes I_t, our goal is to select the top k_t nodes with the greatest scores. We first obtain the set of susceptible nodes S by performing depth first search starting with each node in I_t. Then we apply the ACYCLIC algorithm [9] to find the maximum directed acyclic graph (DAG) in S. In this process, some edges may be removed. The edges that are removed would be the outgoing edges of the nodes that point to some earlier nodes in the DAG. These earlier nodes would have already been infected and hence the removal of such edges hardly impacts the analysis. With the DAG, we fix a topological order σ where nodes are ordered such that each edge in the graph originates from an earlier node to a latter node in σ. We traverse each node and compute its score in the reverse order of σ. This guarantees we will compute the score of a child node before computing the score of its parent. The node with the highest score is marked as *immunized*. The scores of its parent nodes need to be updated as they have one less child whom they can potentially infect, and hence, their immunizing ability is reduced. In addition, the descendants of u will be affected. For a node $v \in child(u)$, if u is v's only parent, we mark v as *immunized* since the only infection path to v is from u which has been immunized. For those nodes $w \in child(u)$ with more than one parents, their parents' scores need to be updated too.

The details of S-NIIP algorithm is given in Algorithm 1. Given the set of infected nodes I_t, we first obtain the set of susceptible nodes S and find the maximum DAG (Lines 2-4). Next, we compute the vectors as well as the scores of the nodes in S in a reverse topological order (Lines 5-11). We select the node with the highest score and call the function $Immunize(u)$ to mark u as "immunized" and place the the parents of u into the $UpdateList$ (Lines 12-16). For each node in the $UpdateList$, we call $ProcessUpdate$ to recompute the score for the node and propagate the effect to the parent nodes if they are susceptible (Lines 25-29). The process is repeated till k_t nodes have been immunized.

Consider the example in Figure 5(a). The infected nodes are u_1 and u_2, i.e. $I_1 = \{u_1, u_2\}$. The set of susceptible nodes is $S = \{u_3, u_4, u_5, u_6, u_7, u_8, u_9\}$. We compute the vectors as well as the scores for the nodes in S and select the node with the highest score, i.e. u_6 for immunization (See Figure 5(b)). After immunization, u_6's parents u_3 and u_4 lose one child and we put u_3 and u_4 into $UpdateList$. Its child u_8 is "immunized" as well since u_8 has only one parent u_6. Its child u_9 has not been "immunized" because it still has u_7 as a parent. Since u_7 becomes the only parent of u_9, it is also placed in $UpdateList$ for updates. Now $UpdateList = \{u_3, u_4, u_7\}$. We first update $\mathbf{r_{u_7}}$ and we notice u_7's parent $u_5 \in S$ is not in $UpdateList$, hence we insert u_5 into $UpdateList$. We then update $\mathbf{r_{u_4}}$ and remove u_4 from $UpdateList$. Since u_4's parents u_1 and u_2 are not in S, we do not put u_1 or u_2 in $UpdateList$. Similarly for u_3, we update $\mathbf{r_{u_3}}$ and remove u_3 from $UpdateList$. This process causes $\mathbf{r_{u_3}}$, $\mathbf{r_{u_4}}$, $\mathbf{r_{u_5}}$ and $\mathbf{r_{u_7}}$ to be updated as marked in red in Figure 6.

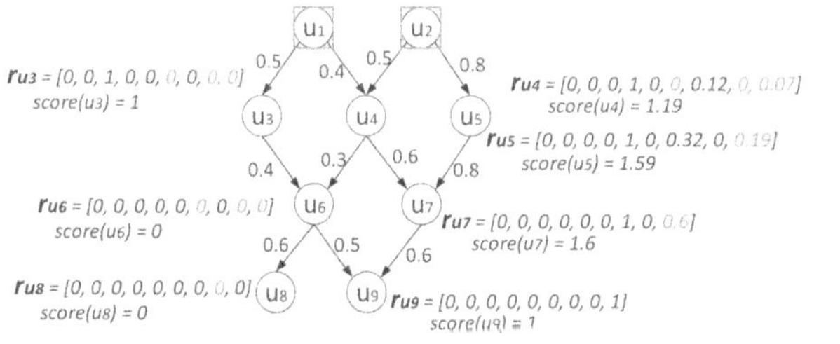

Figure 6: Updated $\mathbf{r_u}$ and scores after u_6 is immunized.

3.2 Estimation of k's distribution over τ

When an infection happens over a time period, putting all the available resources at the start of the infection is not a good strategy as shown in Section 1. We note that the number of nodes we should choose to immunize at each time point is influenced by the initial set of infected nodes I_1 and the rate of infection from external sources α. Given a large I_1 set, we would want to select more nodes to be immunized earlier on so as to prevent the spread of infection from I_1. On the other hand, when we have a large α value, we would want to reserve more quota to later time points.

We perform a Monte Carlo simulation to decide how to distribute the limited resources k over the time point t in τ. We generate τ lists $\{I_1, I_2, \cdots, I_\tau\}$ of randomly infected nodes where $I_{t+1} = I_t \cup$ {new infected nodes by I_{t-1} and by external sources with probability α}. Then we apply the S-NIIP algorithm to get the top k nodes for each list of infected nodes. We process these lists in increasing time order, i.e. from I_1 to I_τ. When all the lists have been processed, we examine each node in the top k results corresponding to time point τ. If the node has appeared in the top k results of an earlier time point, we tag the node with the earlier time point label. The number of the nodes that are tagged with time points $T_1, T_2, \cdots, T_\tau$ forms an instance of the distribution of k over τ. We repeat the process 1000 times and take the average to obtain an estimated distribution of k over τ.

Figure 7 shows the estimation process with $k = 4$ and $\tau = 3$. When $t = 1$, we retrieve the top 4 nodes based on the infected node list I_1 and tag them with T_1. At the next time point, we produce a new top-4 list regarding to I_2. Here node u_2 is selected for immunization and we mark u_2 with T_2. Note that if the same node appears in multiple time points, we mark it with the earliest time point. Similarly in time point $t = 3$, we mark u_4 with T_3. Afterwards, we select the last set of top-k nodes and count the number of markings for each time point. In this example, 2 nodes are selected in time point 1 while one node is selected in time point 2 and 3 respetively. This creates a sample of $[2, 1, 1]$. We repeat the process 1000 times and choose the average number of nodes appearing in each time point as an estimated distribution of k over τ.

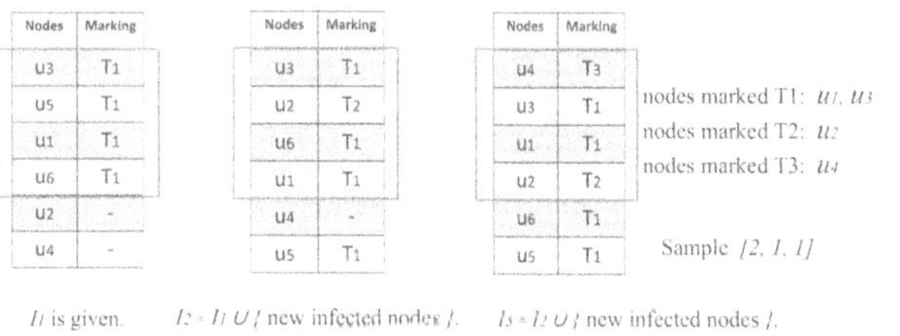

(a) $t = 1$ (b) $t = 2$ (c) $t = 3$

Figure 7: Estimating Distribution of k. k , τ .

3.3 NIIP over time period

With the estimated distribution of k over τ, we extend the S-NIIP algorithm to allow for the selection of k nodes to immunize over a time period. A naive extension is to call the S-NIIP algorithm repeatedly for each time point in τ with a different k_t corresponding to the estimated k at time point t. However, this is not scalable as the number of nodes whose scores need to be updated increases significantly when the number of infected nodes grows.

A careful study reveals that the immunization ability is greatest when it is from a parent to its immediate child. To reduce the number of updates needed, we model only the direct immunization ability between a parent node and its children nodes. We divide the children of node u, $child(u)$, into two sets, $C1$ and $C2$ such that the nodes in $C1$ have only u as their sole parent, while the nodes in $C2$ have multiple parents besides u. The direct immunization ability of node u, denoted as $\mathbf{r'_u}$, is computed as follows:

$$\mathbf{r'_u} = \sum_{v \in C1} p_{uv} \cdot \mathbf{r'_v} + \sum_{v \in C2} m_{uv} \cdot \mathbf{e_v} + \mathbf{e_u} \quad (4)$$

where $\mathbf{e_u}$ is a unit vector with its component corresponding to u being one and elsewhere being zeros.

Let us illustrate the computation of $\mathbf{r'_u}$ with the same example network in Figure 5(a). Vectors for u_6, u_7, u_8 and u_9 are the same because they have no grandchildren in the network. When we compute $\mathbf{r'_{u_3}}$, since u_3 is one of the parents of u_6, u_6 contribute $m_{u_3u_6} \cdot \mathbf{e_{u_6}}$ to $\mathbf{r_{u_4}}$. However, u_3 no longer has immunization ability over u_8 or u_9 as they are not the direct children of u_3 and their direct parent u_6 has multiple parents besides u_3. Hence we compute $\mathbf{r_{u_3}} = m_{u_3u_6} \cdot \mathbf{r_{u_6}} + \mathbf{e_{u_3}}$. The final direct immunization vectors are shown in Figure 8(a).

Algorithm 2: NIIP algorithm

input : 1. Graph G V, E
2. Number of nodes to immunize k
3. Time period τ
4. Infected node set I_1
5. Infection rate α

output: Top-k nodes for immunization

1 Call $EstimateDistribution$ G, I_1, α, k ;
2 Apply ACYCLIC on G to generate a DAG;
3 Find a topological sorting σ in the DAG;
4 Initialize $UpdateList$ $\emptyset, t$, S $\emptyset$;
5 **foreach** $u \in I_1$ **do**
6 Peform DFS from u and insert visited nodes into S;
7 **foreach** *node* $v \in S$ *in the reverse order of* σ **do**
8 Call $ComputeVector$ v ;
9 **repeat**
10 Let ΔI_t be the new infected nodes by I_{t-1} or by external sources with probability α;
11 I_t $I_{t-1} \cup \Delta I_t$;
12 **foreach** $u \in \Delta I_t$ **do**
13 $score$ u ;
14 $UpdateList$ $UpdateList \cup$ $parent$ u $\cap S$;
15 Perform DFS from u, insert visited node v in S;
16 Call $ComputeVector$ v ;
17 Call $ProcessUpdate'$ $UpdateList$;
18 **repeat**
19 Return node u with the highest $score$ u ;
20 Call $Immunize$ u in Algorithm 1;
21 Call $ProcessUpdate'$ $UpdateList$;
22 **until** k_t *nodes are selected*;
23 t t ;
24 **until** t τ;
25 **Function** *ComputeVector(v)*
26 **foreach** w, v $\in E$ **do**
27 $parent$ v $parent$ v $\cup \{w\}$;
28 **if** $|parent$ v $|$ **then**
29 **foreach** $w \in parent$ v **do**
30 C C $\cup \{v\}$
31 **else**
32 **foreach** $w \in parent$ v **do**
33 C C $\cup \{v\}$
34 Compute $'_v$ with Equation 4;
35 Compute $score$ v with Equation 3;
36 **Function** *ProcessUpdate'(UpdateList)*
37 **foreach** $u \in UpdateList$ **do**
38 Compute $'_u$ with Equation 4 and $score$ u with Equation 3;
39 **if** $parent$ u $\{w\}$ *and* $w \in S$ **then**
40 $UpdateList$ $UpdateList \cup \{w\}$;
41 $UpdateList$ $UpdateList - \{u\}$;

Algorithm 2 details how we incorporate the direct immunization vector computation to select the top k nodes over τ time points. We first estimate the distribution of k in Line 1. We then apply ACYCLIC algorithm to extract a maximum DAG in G and find a topological sorting σ in Lines 2 and 3. We find the susceptible nodes in Lines 5 and 6 with depth-first search algorithms and compute their direct immunization vectors in the reverse order of σ (Lines 7 and 8). The $ComputeVector()$ function is given in Lines 25-35. When we reach each node, we update its parent set as well as its parents' children set (Lines 26-33). We then compute the vector following Equation 4 and the score following Equation 3. At each time point, Lines 10-17 take in the newly infected nodes and set their scores to zero. Line 14 puts their parents in $UpdateList$ as they loses a direct child as well as their corresponding immunization ability. Line 16 computes the score for nodes that newly become susceptible. Function $ProcessUpdate'()$ processes the nodes whose vectors need updates (Lines 36-41). Since we merely consider direct immunization, we propagate the change only when a node has a single parent as indicated in Line 39. This enables the $ProcessUpdate'()$ function to end much faster compared to $ProcessUpdate()$ in S-NIIP algorithm. Lines 18-22 select k_t nodes at time point t and we repeat the process for τ times.

Consider the example in Figure 8(a). Initially u_1 and u_2 are infected i.e. $I_1 = \{u_1, u_2\}$. The set of susceptible nodes are $S = \{u_3, u_4, u_5, u_6, u_7, u_8, u_9\}$. We compute the scores for the nodes in S and select the node with the highest score, i.e. u_6 for immunization. Its parents u_3 and u_4 lose one child and we put u_3 and u_4 into $UpdateList$. Since u_7 gains more immunization ability from u_9 because of the immunization of u_6, we insert u_7 into $UpdateList$ for updates. Now $UpdateList = \{u_3, u_4, u_7\}$. Note that all nodes in $UpdateList$ do not need to propagate their updates to the parents because they have multiple parents. Hence only three vectors are changed as marked in red in Figure 8(b). Note that $\mathbf{r_{u_5}}$ is not updated in this case while it is updated in Figure 6. This is because u_7 is not the only child of u_5 and does not propagate the update. The updated vectors are illustrated in Figure 8(b).

Assume in the next time point, we realize u_7 is also infected as illustrated in Figure 8(c). We update S as the set of nodes that are susceptible as $S = \{u_3, u_4, u_5, u_9\}$. For nodes in $parent(u_7) \cap S$, i.e. u_4 and u_5, they lose the immunization ability over u_7 and hence we put u_4 and u_5 into $UpdateList$ to re-compute their vectors with Equation 4. The updated scores are shown in red in Figure 8(c).

Complexity analysis. In S-NIIP, we first perform a DFS traversal of the nodes in $O(|V| + |E|)$ time and find a DAG with the largest number of edges maintained in $O(|E| \cdot log(|V|))$. When a node is immunized, we trace back to all the ancesters of the affected nodes and update their corresponding vectors. In the worst case, we update each vector of every node and hence its time complexity is $O(k_t \cdot (|V| + |E|))$ if we select k_t nodes. In NIIP algorithm, the initialization takes the same time complexity as S-NIIP, i.e. $O(|V| + |E|)$ for DFS traversal and $O(|E| \cdot log(|V|))$ for DAG extraction. When a node is immunized, we update the vector of its parents and propagate the change if the parents only have one parent. This process costs $O(|V|)$ in the worst case. Similarly when new nodes get infected, the propagation of updates is dealt with in $O(|V|)$. In practice, a node with only one parent is likely to be a leaf node and will not be chosen for immunization as it only immunizes itself. Hence on average, the propagation of updates in NIIP can finish rather quickly as shown in the experiments in Section 4.

4. PERFORMANCE STUDY

In this section, we perform comparative experimental evaluation of the various methods for node immunization problem using real world datasets covering both computer networks and information networks.We implemented the algorithms in Python 2.7. The ex-

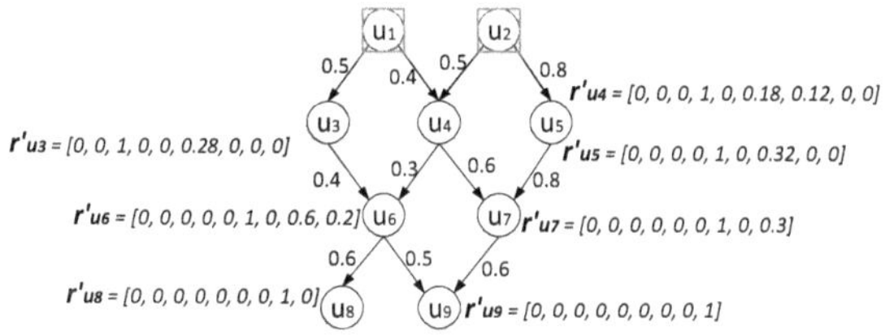

(a) Initial network with $\mathbf{r}'$

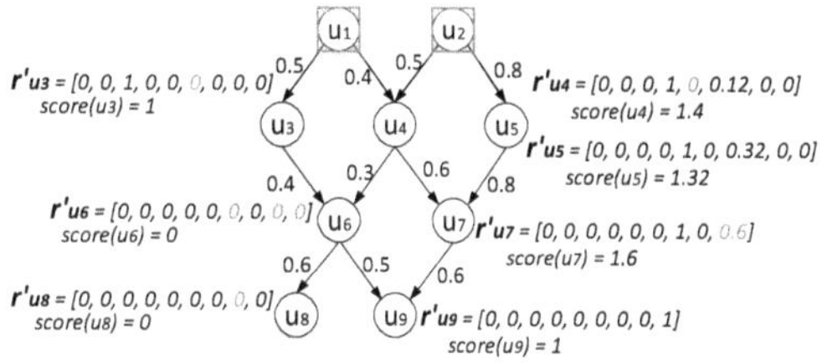

(b) u_6 being immunized

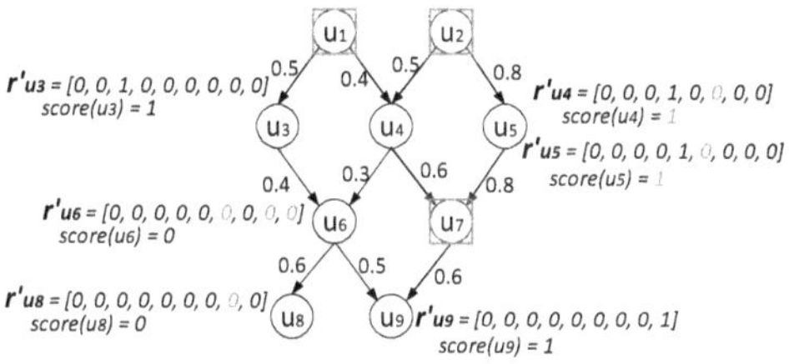

(c) u_7 gets infected

Figure 8: Illustration of NIIP algorithm.

periments are carried out on a 2 Xeon E5440 2.83 GHz CPU with 16 GB RAM.

4.1 Experimental Setting

Datasets. We conduct experiments on the following real world datasets. Table 2 summarizes the datasets used.

- MemeTracker[13][1] This dataset contains the hyperlinks between 96 million news sites, ranging from news distributors to personal blogs. Contagion could be false informtaion published on some news sites. Since the original dataset is very large, we select 2 phrases that has been popularly diffused by various news sites, namely "lipstick on a pig" (Pig) and "american economy is in danger"(Economy). Each phrase initiates a cascade of sites reporting this news and hence captures the propogation in real world web sites.
- Oregon[2] This dataset is the Oregon AS router graph collected from the Oregon router views. The contagion could possibly be malware and viruses.
- Twitter[12][3] This dataset contains the users and their follow relationship in twitter. This dataset is large, containing 41 million users. We prune out the inactive users who never post any tweets and select a connected component for our experiment.
- MH370 This dataset contains the users' tweets that contains the hashtag #MH370 after the Malaysian Airlines MH370 flight went missing on March 8th. Retweet relationships form the edges in the graph. Contagion could be rumors about the MH370 flight.

All networks follow a power law distribution of degrees. The nodes in Twitter tend to have higher degrees due to the ease of following a user in Twitter with more than 80% of them having 20 edges or more. The nodes in Pig, Economy, and Oregon have smaller degrees with more than 60% of the nodes having degree 1.

[1]http://snap.stanford.edu/data/memetracker9.html
[2]http://topology.eecs.umich.edu/data.html
[3]http://an.kaist.ac.kr/traces/www2010.html

Table 2: Dataset Summary

Dataset	Nodes	Edges	#Nodes	#Edges
Pig	web sites	hyperlink	8,727	30,309
Economy	web sites	hyperlink	39,639	156,781
Oregon	routers	peering	6,461	21,530
Twitter	users	follow	542,798	9.8 million
MH370	users	retweet	1.4 million	4.9 million

In the MH370 dataset, the edges are formed by retweeting behavior and hence the nodes' degrees are small (80 % of the nodes have degree less than or equal to 2). The CDFs of the two large datasets Twitter and MH370 are given in Figure 9. In our experiments, we randomly select 100 users in Pig, Oregon and Economy and 1000 users in Twitter and MH370 to form the initial infected nodes I_1.

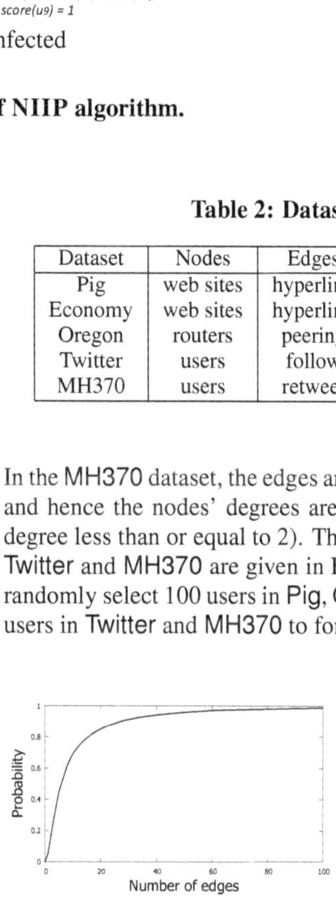

(a) Twitter

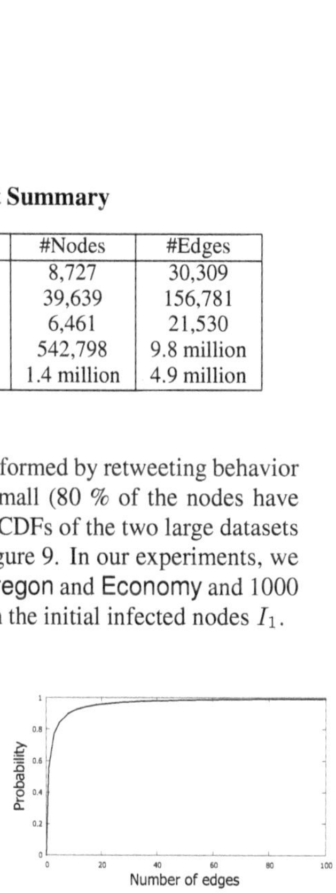

(b) MH370

Figure 9: CDFs of Twitter and MH370.

Parameters. τ is the number of steps that we are allowed to assign our immunization nodes. α is a small probability that decides the fraction of healthy nodes getting infected by independent sources. We set $\tau = 10$ and $\alpha = 0.05$ in all our experiments. In our experiment, we set a uniform propagation probability 0.6 [21]. On each dataset, we conduct our experiment 1000 times and take the average.

Evaluation Metric. We measure the effectiveness of the various methods by defining a metric called *Save Ratio* (SR) which gives the ratio between the reduction in infected nodes when k nodes are immunized over the number of infected nodes with no immunized nodes. We denote the set of infected nodes when nodes in A are immunized as $Immunized(A)$.

$$SR(A) = \frac{|Immunized(\emptyset)| - |Immunized(A)|}{|Immunized(\emptyset)|} \quad (5)$$

Note that the value of SR directly correspond to our objective function $\Phi(A)$, i.e. higher $SR(A)$ represents a higher $\Phi(A)$ value. However, the value of SR will fall in $[0, 1]$ where 1 indicates a full immunization of all healthy nodes while $\Phi(A)$ value is not bounded.

Comparison Methods. We compare the performance of the following methods:

- S-NIIP: our proposed approach to select k nodes in one single time point;
- NIIP: our proposed approach to handle node immunization over τ time points
- BETWEENNESS[10]: this algorithm returns the top k nodes that carry the largest number of shortest paths;
- PAGERANK[16]: this algorithm returns the top k nodes with the highest PageRank scores;
- NETSHIELD [18]: this method pre-emptively immunize the network to minimize the epidemic threshold of the graph;
- DAVA[20]: this algorithm aims to identify the top k nodes in presence of already infected nodes;

4.2 Effectiveness Experiments

In this section, we show the effectiveness of the proposed methods on node immunization tasks.

Results when $\tau = 1$ and $\alpha = 0$. In this set of experiments, we set the time period to one ($\tau = 1$) and assume there is no external source of infection ($\alpha = 0$). This setting reduces our problem to the DAV problem proposed in [20]. Figure 10 shows the performances of the various algorithms. In all datasets, S-NIIP gives the best performance while NIIP is a close runner-up. The narrow gap between these two algorithms demonstrates that it is sufficient to model the immunization ability based only on the direct parent-child relationships. We also observe that both NIIP and S-NIIP outperform DAVA. This shows clearly that it is advantageous to take into account the joint immunization effect of multiple nodes. In general, algorithms which take into account the infected nodes (namely, S-NIIP, NIIP, DAVA) perform better than those which pre-emptively choose nodes for immunization confirming that it is good to perform immunization while an attack is underway.

In the Pig and the Oregon graphs, S-NIIP and NIIP outperform the state-of-the-art methods by more than 20% when k is large. We note that for these two datasets, they have a small number of nodes with high out-degrees. These nodes are good candidates for immunization. As a result, when k is small, all the algorithms pick this small set of nodes to immunize and their performances are similar. However, as k increases, S-NIIP and NIIP rapidly outperform the other methods.

In the three larger datasets, S-NIIP and NIIP manage to outperform all the other algorithms even when k is small. We observe that in these datasets, the networks are composed of multiple clusters and the positions of the infected nodes are critical to the selection of immunization nodes. Pre-emptive methods like NETSHIELD, BETWEENNESS and PAGERANK could not effectively utilize such information and hence perform poorly. As for the DAVA algorithm, it constructs a dominator tree from the infected nodes. If a node has multiple parents, the DAVA algorithm will link this node directly to the ancestors of its parents and therefore ignore the immunization ability of its parents. As a result, the performance of Dava suffers. We observe that S-NIIP outperforms DAVA by 45% in Twitter and 27% in the MH370 dataset.

Results when $\tau = 10$, $\alpha = 0.05$. In this set of experiments, we perform node immunization over 10 time points. For pre-emptive methods PAGERANK, BETWEENNESS and NETSHIELD, we simply run them with the given network structure as they do not consider the set of infected nodes as input. For the DAVA algorithm, we give the final set of infected nodes I_τ as input. This allows the DAVA algorithm to have the complete picture of infection nodes before making its selection of k nodes. Figure 11 gives the results. We see that the overall SR value is less compared to the graph in Figure 10. This is because introducing an infectious period implies we have a much larger set of infected nodes. Hence even if we increase the number of nodes for immunization, the overall performance decreases. As expected, pre-emptive methods give the worst performance; while the NIIP algorithm is the clear winner and outperforms all the other methods significantly (+30%) in all datasets. This shows that the immunization strategy adopted by NIIP is the most effective in immunizing the nodes that lead to the largest number of healthy nodes in the network.

Effect of distributions of k. In this set of experiments, we examine how the distributions of k affect our results. We compare three strategies for assigning k:

- NIIP-ESTIMATED: we follow the learned distribution of k to select k_t nodes at each time point;
- NIIP-UNIFORM: we uniformly select $\frac{k}{\tau}$ nodes for immunization at each time point;
- NIIP-AFTER: we wait until time point τ to select the k nodes all at once.

Results are shown in two datasets, Economy and MH370. Figure 12 demonstrates that while the estimated distribution of k has the best performance, uniform decision also achieves good results in Economy dataset. However in MH370, the NIIP-UNIFORM is clearly not as good as NIIP-ESTIMATED. In both datasets, choosing the k nodes after τ time points hugely impact the performance, indicating it is an effective method to prevent propagation of infection by immunizing nodes as soon as we observe infections in the network.

4.3 Efficiency

In this section, we report the runtime of the algorithms on the larger datasets. Table 3 shows the running time for S-NIIP, NIIP, DAVA and NETSHIELD on the three larger datasets in the case of $\tau = 1, \alpha = 0$. We see that NIIP can produce outputs within the shortest time. In the smaller graph Economy, DAVA performs faster than S-NIIP but as the graphs grow larger, DAVA runs slower. This is because DAVA needs to re-generate the dominator tree when each node is selected which requires a near-linear time algorithm. For S-NIIP, it requires near-linear pre-processing time while the worst case for updating the scores is in linear time.

5. RELATED WORK

There is vast amount of literature on node immunization problem to prevent the spread of virus/rumors. Most of the existing

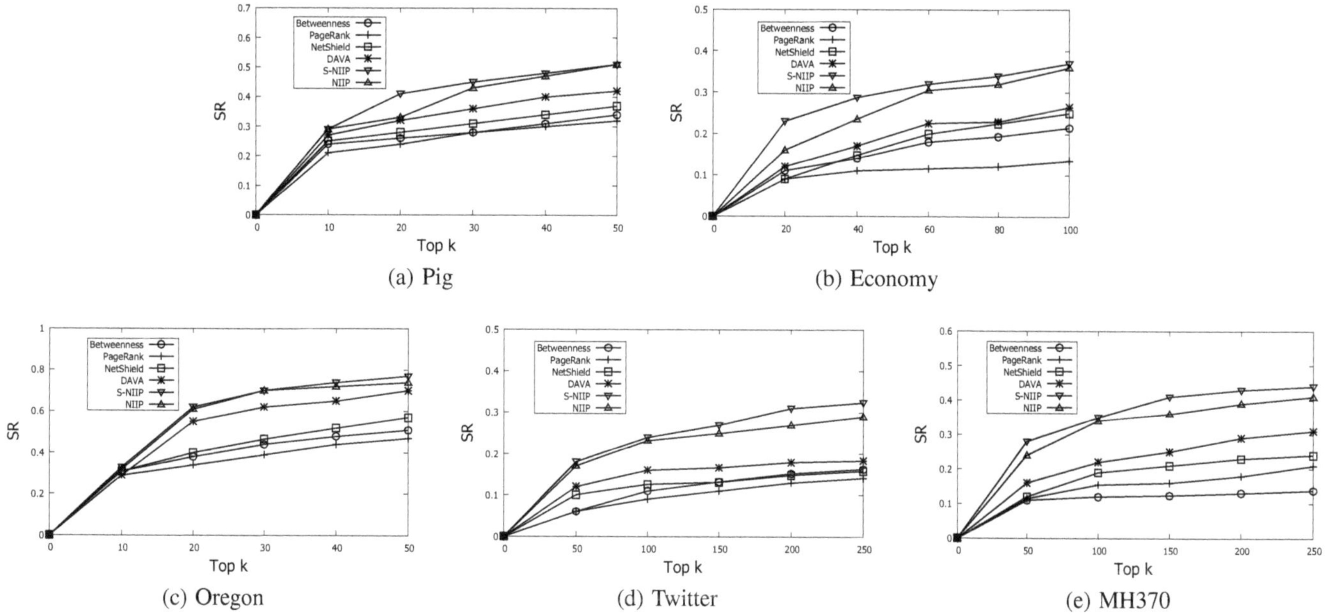

Figure 10: Performance of different algorithms. τ and α .

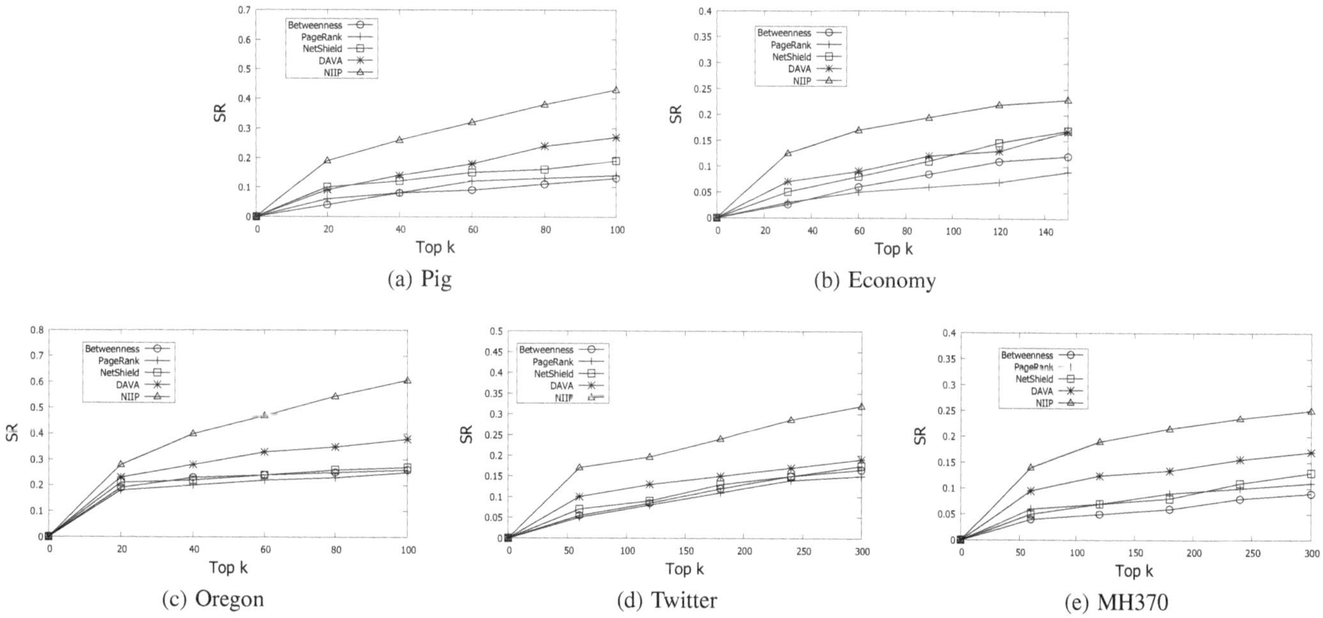

Figure 11: Performance of different algorithms. τ and α . .

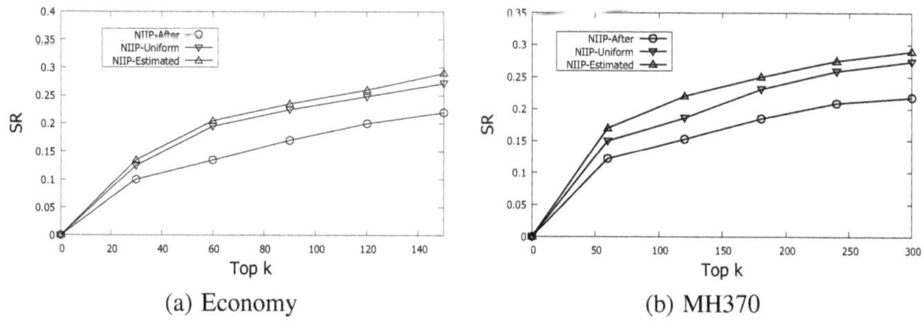

Figure 12: Performance of NIIP given different distribution of k. τ and α . .

Table 3: Execution time (sec.) k , τ and α .

	S-NIIP	NIIP	DAVA	NETSHIELD
Economy	98.5	**23.3**	72.9	63.7
Twitter	5651.4	**574.1**	10566.7	3553.4
MH370	21175.2	**6121.8**	61407.6	14915.6

strategies select nodes to immunize *before* the start of an epidemic [4, 7, 8, 14]. Abbassi and Heidari [1] consider nodes with high degrees and betweenness values tend to be good candidate for immunization. Tong et al. [17, 18] and Wang et al. [6, 19] analyze the topology of an arbitrary graph and found the larger the first eigenvalue of the graph is, the easier for the virus to propogate. Hence, they identify the nodes and edges whose removal would minimize the largest eigenvalue of the graph. They show that their methods are more effective than centrality-based methods. Cohen et al. [8] propose a heuristic *acquaintance immunization* strategy, which is further studied in [4]. They select the random acquaintances of random nodes, in which case high degree nodes will be more likely to be selected. Experiments show that their strategy can greatly reduce the immunization threshold from 80% to 40%. All these works propose pre-emptive strategies for immunization without the awareness of infected nodes.

The work in [20] points out that taking into account the infected nodes to make decision about whom to immunize is more practical and meaningful. They formalize the problem of Data-Aware Vaccination problem given the initial set of infected nodes and propose the DAVA algorithm to select k nodes to immunize. The DAVA algorithm integrates the infected nodes into one source node and generates a *dominator tree* of the graph starting from the source node. It then exams the children of the source node and see which child has the largest number of expected nodes to be infected under the *Susceptible-Infected-Recovered* model [11]. The algorithm greedily chooses one node at a time but it ignores the joint immunization ability of multiple nodes.

Tong et al. further extend their work in [21] by considering the probability of infected nodes not being detected and propose a sample based algorithm to handle uncertain data. They utilize the DAVA algorithm to find the nodes for immunization. Note that our method can be directly utilized in place of DAVA under such an uncertain setting. A related work that also aim to limit the spread of misinformation in social networks given the contagion source is in [5]. Instead of choosing nodes for immunization, they assume the nodes they choose can propagate the truth such that any node which has received the truth will no longer believe in the rumor. Their strategy is to choose the nodes that can reach the largest number of people. Although these works consider the initial infected sources of either rumor or virus, they do not consider the possibility of nodes getting infected independently during a certain period. Our work is the first to address the node immunization problem over an infectious period.

6. CONCLUSIONS

In this paper, we have modeled a realistic situation in real world contagions where healthy nodes have a certain chance of getting infected from sources outside the network and proposed the problem of node immunization over infectious period. We have shown that this problem is NP-hard in both arbitrary graphs and directed acyclic graphs. The S-NIIP algorithm has been developed to take into consideration the joint immunization effect of multiple nodes. We have also presented the NIIP algorithm that strategically immunizes k nodes over a time period. Extensive experiments have been conducted and demonstrated conclusively that our algorithms outperform state-of-the-art algorithms significantly. Future work includes applications to real-time control of rumor propagation in Twitter or extending our model to consider users' credibility and trustworthiness.

7. REFERENCES

[1] Z. Abbassi and H. Heidari. Toward optimal vaccination strategies for probabilistic models. In *WWW*, 2011.

[2] Y. Asahiro, R. Hassin, and K. Iwama. Complexity of finding dense subgraphs. *Discrete Appl. Math.*, 121(1-3), Sept. 2002.

[3] R. Bandari, S. Asur, and B. A. Huberman. The pulse of news in social media: Forecasting popularity. *CoRR*, 2012.

[4] L. Briesemeister, P. Lincoln, and P. Porras. Epidemic profiles and defense of scale-free networks. In *WORM*, 2003.

[5] C. Budak, D. Agrawal, and A. El Abbadi. Limiting the spread of misinformation in social networks. In *WWW*, 2011.

[6] D. Chakrabarti, Y. Wang, C. Wang, J. Leskovec, and C. Faloutsos. Epidemic thresholds in real networks. *ACM Trans. Inf. Syst. Secur.*, 10(4), Jan. 2008.

[7] P.-A. Chen, M. David, and D. Kempe. Better vaccination strategies for better people. In *EC*, 2010.

[8] R. Cohen, S. Havlin, and D. ben Avraham. Efficient immunization strategies for computer networks and populations. *Phys. Rev. Lett.*, 2003.

[9] D. Erdös, V. Ishakian, A. Lapets, E. Terzi, and A. Bestavros. The filter-placement problem and its application to minimizing information multiplicity. *Proc. VLDB Endow.*, Jan. 2012.

[10] M. Haghir Chehreghani. An efficient algorithm for approximate betweenness centrality computation. In *CIKM*, 2013.

[11] H. W. Hethcote. The mathematics of infectious diseases. *SIAM Rev.*, Dec. 2000.

[12] H. Kwak, C. Lee, H. Park, and S. Moon. What is twitter, a social network or a news media? In *WWW*, 2010.

[13] J. Leskovec, L. Backstrom, and J. Kleinberg. Meme-tracking and the dynamics of the news cycle. In *KDD*, 2009.

[14] N. Madar, T. Kalisky, R. Cohen, D. ben Avraham, and S. Havlin. Immunization and epidemic dynamics in complex networks. *Eur. Phys. J. B*, 2004.

[15] S. A. Myers, C. Zhu, and J. Leskovec. Information diffusion and external influence in networks. In *KDD*, 2012.

[16] L. Page, S. Brin, R. Motwani, and T. Winograd. The pagerank citation ranking: Bringing order to the web. In *WWW*, 1998.

[17] H. Tong, B. A. Prakash, T. Eliassi-Rad, M. Faloutsos, and C. Faloutsos. Gelling, and melting, large graphs by edge manipulation. In *CIKM*, 2012.

[18] H. Tong, B. A. Prakash, C. Tsourakakis, T. Eliassi-Rad, C. Faloutsos, and D. H. Chau. On the vulnerability of large graphs. In *ICDM*, 2010.

[19] Y. Wang, D. Chakrabarti, C. Wang, and C. Faloutsos. Epidemic spreading in real networks: An eigenvalue viewpoint. In *In SRDS*, 2003.

[20] Y. Zhang and B. A. Prakash. Dava: Distributing vaccines over networks under prior information. In *SDM*, 2014.

[21] Y. Zhang and B. A. Prakash. Scalable vaccine distribution in large graphs given uncertain data. In *CIKM*, 2014.

Enterprise Social Link Recommendation

Jiawei Zhang*
University of Illinois at Chicago
Chicago, IL, USA
jzhan9@uic.edu

Yuanhua Lv
Microsoft Research
Redmond, WA, USA
yuanhual@microsoft.com

Philip S. Yu
University of Illinois at Chicago
Chicago, IL, USA
Institute for Data Science
Tsinghua University, China
psyu@cs.uic.edu

ABSTRACT

Many companies have started to use Enterprise Social Networks (ESNs), such as Yammer, to facilitate collaboration and communication among their employees in the business context. Social link recommendation, which finds and suggests whom one wants to connect with in a company, is crucial for ESNs to promote their usages. Although link recommendation has been studied extensively in external social networks (e.g., Facebook and Twitter), it has not been addressed in ESNs. In this paper, we study this novel problem. Social link recommendation in ESNs is significantly different from that in external social networks, and also has unique challenges: (1) people usually socialize differently in enterprise than in their personal life, but users' social behaviors in enterprise have not been well explored, and (2) there is important business information available in ESNs under the enterprise context, e.g., a company's organizational chart, but how to exploit it for link recommendation is still an open problem. To this end, we mine not only the social graph and user-generated content in ESNs, but also the company's organizational chart, to model enterprise user social behaviors. We develop a supervised link recommendation algorithm using a large scale ESN based on Yammer (with over 100k users), which shows that the proposed techniques perform effectively. Moreover, we find that social graph and organizational chart are complementary to each other for link recommendation in ESNs.

Categories and Subject Descriptors

H.2.8 [**Database Management**]: Database Applications-Data Mining

Keywords

Link Recommendation; Enterprise Social Networks; Data Mining

*This work was done when the first author was on a summer internship at Microsoft Research.

Permission to make digital or hard copies of all or part of this work for personal or classroom use is granted without fee provided that copies are not made or distributed for profit or commercial advantage and that copies bear this notice and the full citation on the first page. Copyrights for components of this work owned by others than ACM must be honored. Abstracting with credit is permitted. To copy otherwise, or republish, to post on servers or to redistribute to lists, requires prior specific permission and/or a fee. Request permissions from Permissions@acm.org.
CIKM'15, October 19-23, 2015, Melbourne, VIC, Australia
©2015 ACM. ISBN 978-1-4503-3794-6/15/10 ...$15.00.
DOI: http://dx.doi.org/10.1145/2806416.2806549.

1. INTRODUCTION

Traditional social networks, e.g., Facebook and Twitter, usually provide services to help people deal with their personal life issues. Recently, to facilitate the collaboration and communication among employees in companies, a new family of online social networks has been adopted inside the firewalls of many corporations. These social networks are called *Enterprise Social Networks* (ESNs) [34]. ESNs can potentially bring significant benefits to both employees and companies. For example, ESNs can help employees meet new colleagues [5], follow internal news and industry trends [32], identify experts [6] and form teams [20], etc.; ESNs can also bridge the generational gaps among employees with more communication [5]. One of the most popular ESNs is Yammer[1]. Over $500,000$ businesses around the world are using Yammer, including 85% of the Fortune 500[2].

Arguably, social links/connections between people inside the company are key to ESNs. First, many services provided by ESNs are based on social connections. Taking Yammer as an example, one needs to follow another user in order to automatically receive relevant contents from the user. Second, as reported in [19], well-established connections among users can attract them to use the network more frequently. Thus, enterprise social link recommendation, which finds *whom one wants to connect with in the company*, is crucial for ESNs to promote their usages. Although link recommendation or link prediction has been studied extensively in external social networks (e.g., Facebook and Twitter) [21, 13, 35], it has not been addressed in ESNs to the best of our knowledge.

Social link recommendation in ESNs is significantly different from that in external social networks, and also has unique challenges:

- People usually socialize differently in workspace than in their personal life because of the professional context [28], but social behaviors in enterprise have not been well explored. As a result, methods proposed for external social networks, e.g., [21, 13, 35, 31], may not work well for ESNs. To support such a claim, we will compare the link prediction method SCAN proposed from external social networks [31] with the model introduced in this paper in the experiment section.

- There is important and unique business information available in ESNs under the enterprise context, e.g.,

[1]https://www.yammer.com/
[2]https://about.yammer.com/why-yammer/

the company's organizational chart [34]. The organizational chart is a diagram (usually a rooted tree) showing organizational relations (e.g., managers to sub-workers, directors to managers, etc.) between people within an organization. An example of organizational chart is shown in Figure 1. Intuitively, the organizational relations are related to enterprise social relations. For example, we observe that about 23.4% employees connect with his/her managers in our data, which is an important factor that should be utilized in building the models. However, how to exploit the organizational chart and organizational relations for recommending social links is an open problem.

In this paper, we study this novel problem of Enterprise Social Link Recommendation. We mine not only the social graph and user-generated content in ESNs, but also the company's organizational chart, to model enterprise user social behaviors.

- We first propose different methods to measure social affinity, organizational affinity, social-organizational affinity and geographic affinity for any given user pairs, based on the intuition that closer users tend more likely to connect to each other in ESNs.
- Furthermore, observing that different users may have different social behaviors in ESNs (e.g., one user may like to connect to high-level management people, while another user may mostly like to connect his/her collaborators), we also capture users' personal preferences in multiple dimensions.
- In addition, we further exploit the user-generated content to investigate if it can also help link recommendation in ESNs, since intuitively a user may like to connect to another user who has published high-quality contents.

We develop a supervised link recommendation algorithm based on a large-scale ESN (i.e., Yammer with over 100k users), that can leverage all the proposed measures and heuristics. Our experiments show that the proposed techniques perform effectively, achieving a NDCG score of over 0.61 at the first recommendation position. Moreover, we find that the social graph and the organizational chart are complementary to each other for link recommendation in ESNs.

The rest of this paper is organized as follows. In Section 2, we will briefly describe and analyze the Yammer network as well as giving the terminology definitions and problem formulation. Detailed information about the methods will be introduced in Section 3. In Section 4, we show the experiment results. Finally, in Sections 5-6, we introduce the related works and conclude this paper.

2. ENTERPRISE SOCIAL LINK RECOMMENDATION

We use Yammer [34] in this paper to study the enterprise social link recommendation problem. Yammer provides users with various social services to facilitate their daily workloads, such as following other users, watching their posts and activities, creating/joining groups of their interests, initiating conversations and writing posts, uploading and sharing files, sending online/offline messages to other users, etc. Yammer can be represented as a heterogeneous information network [26].

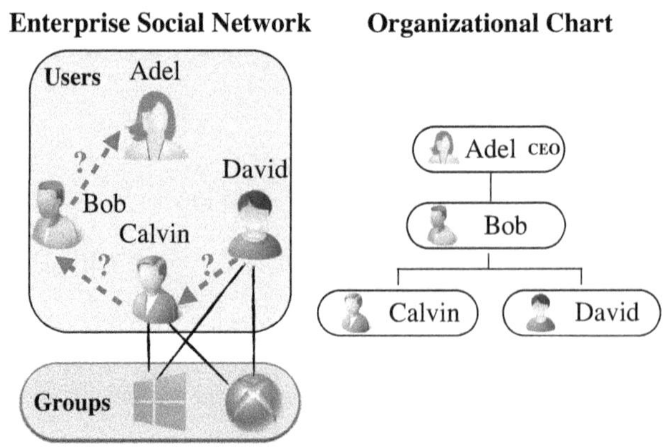

Figure 1: ESN and Organizational Chart (faked examples).

Definition 1. (Enterprise Social Networks): An enterprise social network can be represented as a heterogeneous information network $G = (\mathcal{V}, \mathcal{E})$, where $\mathcal{V} = \cup_i \mathcal{V}_i$ and $\mathcal{E} = \cup_j \mathcal{E}_j$ are the sets of different kinds of nodes and links in the enterprise social network. For example, the Yammer can be represented as $G = (\mathcal{V}, \mathcal{E})$, where $\mathcal{V} = \mathcal{U} \cup \mathcal{G} \cup \mathcal{C} \cup \mathcal{P}$ contains the nodes of users, groups, conversations and posts, and $\mathcal{E} = \mathcal{E}_{u \to u} \cup \mathcal{E}_{u \to g} \cup \mathcal{E}_{u \to c} \cup \mathcal{E}_{u\ write\ p} \cup \mathcal{E}_{u\ like\ p}$ contains the social links among users, group membership links between users and groups, conversation initiation links between users and conversations, write links and like links between users and posts.

Are the social links between users in Yammer usually professional links that connect users in the same department? To answer this question, we compare the social links from Yammer and the organizational links from the organizational chart. The *organizational chart* [34] denotes a diagram that outlines the internal hierarchic structure of a company and is the common visual depiction of how an organization is structured. In most companies, managers can supervise many subordinates simultaneously, but each subordinate only needs to report to one manager. As a result, the organizational charts are mostly tree-structure diagrams with the CEO at the root. The formal definition of *organizational chart* is given as follows:

Definition 2. (Organizational Chart): The *organizational chart* of a company can be represented as a *rooted tree* (i.e., a tree in which one node has been designated as the root) $T = (\mathcal{N}, \mathcal{L}, root)$, where $\mathcal{N}$ and $\mathcal{L}$ are the sets of nodes and links of T. The *root* of tree T represents the CEO of the company.

By designating the root of the *organizational chart* T, all the links in T will have a natural orientation, i.e., *toward* or *away* from the root. The *tree order* of nodes u, v (i.e., $u \leq v$ iff there is one unique path from the root to v via u) denotes that u is a manager of v. In addition, nodes in $\mathcal{N}$ can be associated with certain attributes (i.e., the business profile information of employees), which include the *department*, *job title* and *working location*, etc., of the employees.

We examine the social links in Yammer that have an overlap with the organizational links, i.e., one user in a social link is the direct manager, subordinates, or peer of the other user. We observe that, on average, the probabilities for users to follow their direct manager, subordinates and peers are 23.4%, 11.2% and 9.5% respectively. Interestingly, we also observe that subordinates are more likely to follow their managers than managers to follow their subordinates.

On the one hand, this analysis result shows that organizational chart could help enterprise social link recommendation. For example, in Figure 1, we give an example of ESN and organizational chart. In the ESN, we have 4 users, among whom 3 potential links are to be recommended (i.e., the red dashed lines). Considering the scenario of linking Calvin → Bob: merely based on the information in the social network, "Bob" and "Calvin" have nothing in common, neither "common friends" nor "common groups". However, according to their relationship in the organizational chart, we observe that "Bob" is actually the *direct manager* of "Calvin", who should thus be among the recommendation results. On the other hand, organizational chart alone is still not enough and social links among users in ESN are different from organizational links. By analyzing the ESN and organizational chart, we observe the overlap between the organizational links and social links is very small, which accounts for only 13% of the total social links.

Finally, the enterprise social link recommendation problem can be formally defined as follows:

Definition 3. (Enterprise Social Link Recommendation): For the given enterprise social network G and organizational chart T, the sets of users and existing social links among users in the enterprise social network G can be represented as $\mathcal{U}$ and $\mathcal{E}_{u \to u}$ respectively. The set of candidate social links to be recommended can be represented as $\mathcal{E}_{rec} = \mathcal{U} \times \mathcal{U} \setminus \mathcal{E}_{u \to u}$. In the enterprise social link recommendation problem, we use the existing links in $\mathcal{E}_{u \to u}$ and information about these links in both network G and organizational chart T to build a model, which can score and rank the candidate links in $\mathcal{E}_{rec}$. Candidate links that receive higher scores are expected to be more likely actually formed in the ESN.

3. METHODS

In this section, we introduce the Supervised ENterprise SOcial Recommendation (SENSOR) method in details. We will explore both the enterprise social network and the organizational chart to understand and model whom an employee wants to connect with in the company from three dimensions: (1) user-user affinity, (2) user characteristics, and (3) user-generated content.

3.1 User-User Affinity

In social science, "birds of a feather flock together" [23]. "Homophily" [1] is an important principle in social science and that also structures the social ties among users greatly: close users are more likely to follow each other [27] in online social networks. In this paper, the social closeness among users is measured by the user-user *affinity*, which can be computed based on various information sources, e.g., online social behaviors, offline organizational relationships and geographical user distributions.

Heterogeneous social activities from ESN can often capture the social affinity among some users well. However, there are some inactive users and users who just join ESN for a very short period of time. Their sparse information in ESN would be inadequate to calculate their affinity to other users. In this case, fortunately, large amount of information from the offline workplace, e.g., organizational chart, can be exploited to bridge the gap by computing organizational affinity among users. Social affinity and organizational affinity employ information in ESN and organizational chart independently, but do not take advantage of the deep knowledge that can only be obtained by aligning online ESN and offline organizational chart [34]. To remedy such a problem, a set of social-organizational affinity features will be introduced. In addition, the user-user affinity may also be computed based on user geographical distributions, such as country, timezone and even office location, etc., which will be also explored in this section.

3.1.1 Social Affinity

In *enterprise social networks*, users are connected, either directly or indirectly, by various types of connections, such as follow links, shared groups, etc., which could imply social affinity among users. We propose several novel methods to compute social affinity, such as weighted meta path and weighted group membership, inspired by the term weighting techniques in information retrieval [17].

- **Reciprocal Social Link**: Reciprocal links [36] denote the mutual links between two users. The existence of reciprocal links between users is an intuitively important clue indicating the affinity between them. For example, if we want to predict whether link (u_i, u_j) exists or not, then the existence of its *reciprocal link* (u_j, u_i) could boost our confidence of the existence of the link (u_i, u_j). By analyzing the data, we observe that the ratio of reciprocal link number to the total number of links is about 33% in our enterprise social networks, suggesting it is a good source of evidence for social affinity.
- **Weighted Social Meta Path**: Besides the direct social links, user u_i and u_j can often be "connected" by sequences of indirect links, i.e., meta paths as proposed in [26]. In ESN, the meta paths of length 2 only consisting of user nodes include:

$$MP_1 : U \to U \to U, \text{Follower of Follower},$$
$$MP_2 : U \leftarrow U \leftarrow U, \text{Followee of Followee},$$
$$MP_3 : U \leftarrow U \to U, \text{Common Follower},$$
$$MP_4 : U \to U \leftarrow U, \text{Common Followee}.$$

In this paper, we only consider the above four types of meta paths. Based on these meta paths, a straightforward way of modeling social affinity for potential link (u_i, u_j) is to count the number of meta path instances existing in the network between u_i and u_j [35, 26] formally,

$$|\{p | p \in MP_k\}|, k \in \{1, 2, 3, 4\},$$

where $p \in MP_k$ denotes that p is an instance of meta path MP_k in the network. For instance, based on

MP_1, such feature extracted for link (u_i, u_j) can also be represented as $|\{u_i \rightarrow u \rightarrow u_j | u \in \mathcal{U}\}|$.

However, simply counting meta path instances may suffer from some problems: u_i and u_j can be connected by large number of meta path instances merely because of the large out degrees of either u_i, u_j or the intermediate nodes between them, but the affinity between u_i and u_j is not high. For example, given two users u_i and u_j indirectly connected via MP_4 (i.e., $u_i \rightarrow u_k \leftarrow u_j$), if the common followee u_k is very popular (such as the CEO in a company), then any two users in the network may be connected by u_k and the existence of path $u_i \rightarrow u_k \leftarrow u_j$ may not indicate the affinity between u_i and u_j. To address this problem, we propose to use weighted social meta path to measure social affinity as follows.

For meta paths MP_1 and MP_2: the probabilities of random walking from u_i to u_j (and from u_j to u_i) based on meta paths MP_1 (and MP_2), could intuitively be a better affinity measure than the simple number of path instances. The reason is that the probabilities have been naturally normalized to penalize popular users. The probability of random walking from u_i to u_j, based on meta paths MP_1 can be represented as

(1) $P(MP_1(u_i, u_j))$

$$= \sum_{u_k \in \Gamma_{out}(u_i) \cap \Gamma_{in}(u_j)} P(u_i \rightarrow u_k) P(u_k \rightarrow u_j)$$

$$= \sum_{u_k \in \Gamma_{out}(u_i) \cap \Gamma_{in}(u_j)} \frac{1}{|\Gamma_{out}(u_i)|} \frac{1}{|\Gamma_{out}(u_k)|}.$$

Similarly, we can define the probability of reaching u_i from u_j based on meta paths MP_2 as follows

(2) $$P(MP_2(u_i, u_j)) = \sum_{u_k \in \Gamma_{in}(u_i) \cap \Gamma_{out}(u_j)} \frac{1}{|\Gamma_{out}(u_k)|} \frac{1}{|\Gamma_{out}(u_j)|},$$

where$\Gamma_{out}(u)$ and$\Gamma_{in}(u)$ denote the set of users that u follows and users who follow u respectively, and $p(u_i \rightarrow u_k)$ represents the probability of random walking from u_i to u_k based on social links.

For meta paths MP3 and MP4: the *common followee* and *common follower* of u_i and u_j should also be weighted appropriately to penalize those popular common followees and common followers. To reward/penalize the importance of different common followees (and common followers), we propose to weight them by both an idf-like measure and the pointwise mutual information [24]:

(3) $$\text{idf}(MP_3(u_i, u_j)) = \sum_{u_k \in \Gamma_{in}(u_i) \cap \Gamma_{in}(u_j)} \log \frac{|\mathcal{U}|}{|\Gamma_{out}(u_k)|},$$

(4) $$\text{idf}(MP_4(u_i, u_j)) = \sum_{u_k \in \Gamma_{out}(u_i) \cap \Gamma_{out}(u_j)} \log \frac{|\mathcal{U}|}{|\Gamma_{in}(u_k)|},$$

(5) $mi(MP_3(u_i, u_j))$

$$= \frac{|\Gamma_{in}(u_i) \cap \Gamma_{in}(u_j)|}{|\mathcal{U}|} \log \frac{\frac{|\Gamma_{in}(u_i) \cap \Gamma_{in}(u_j)|}{|\mathcal{U}|}}{\frac{|\Gamma_{in}(u_i)|}{|\mathcal{U}|} \cdot \frac{|\Gamma_{in}(u_j)|}{|\mathcal{U}|}},$$

(6) $mi(MP_4(u_i, u_j))$

$$= \frac{|\Gamma_{out}(u_i) \cap \Gamma_{out}(u_j)|}{|\mathcal{U}|} \log \frac{\frac{|\Gamma_{out}(u_i) \cap \Gamma_{out}(u_j)|}{|\mathcal{U}|}}{\frac{|\Gamma_{out}(u_i)|}{|\mathcal{U}|} \cdot \frac{|\Gamma_{out}(u_j)|}{|\mathcal{U}|}},$$

where $\mathcal{U}$ is the set of all users in the network.

These 6 proposed measures consider not only the meta path instances between u_i and u_j but also the weight of each meta path and are named weighted meta path based social affinities in this paper.

- **Common Group Membership**: Besides social connections, users can also join groups in enterprise social networks. These groups are created either for professional techniques (e.g., C#, Machine learning, Cloud computing, etc.) or just for users' personal interests (e.g., jogging, swimming, etc.). Intuitively, sharing more groups often suggests that two users have more common interests.

  However, different groups may have different discrimination power. For two users sharing group "Cornell 2013 Alumni" (a small-sized group) are more likely to link to each other than users who share group "Employee News Events" (a large group posting internal news). In order to capture the discrimination of different groups, we propose a concept called "Inverse Membership Frequency" (IMF), inspired by the widely-used IDF [17] in information retrieval. Specifically, if we regard a group as a word and a user as a document. Each user can join many groups, corresponding to that a document is comprised of many words. Specifically, the IMF of group g can be represented as

$$IMF(g) = \log \frac{|\mathcal{U}|}{|\Gamma(g)|},$$

  where $\Gamma(g)$ represents the set of users joining group g. And for any two users u_i and u_j sharing common groups$\Gamma_g(u_i) \cap \Gamma_g(u_j)$, where$\Gamma_g(u)$ denotes the set of groups that u joins, the common-group membership affinity between u_i and u_j can be computed as

$$\sum_{g \in \Gamma_g(u_i) \cap \Gamma_g(u_j)} IMF(g) = \sum_{g \in \Gamma_g(u_i) \cap \Gamma_g(u_j)} \log \frac{|\mathcal{U}|}{|\Gamma(g)|}.$$

3.1.2 *Organizational affinity*

For inactive and new users, the above introduced social affinity measures would not be very useful due to their sparse activity information in ESNs. However, in the enterprise context, useful alternative information about these users can be obtained, in particular, the organizational chart. We next introduce the organizational affinity, a set of affinity measures among users calculated based on the organizational chart.

Company organizational chart is a tree structured diagram outlining the relationships among users, where users are connected by sequences of "management" links between managers and their subordinates. Given any two users, an intuitive idea to represent their affinity is using the number of required steps to walk to each other along the links in the organizational chart. Colleagues in the same department need less steps to connect from one to another than those in different departments. Based on such an observation, we propose a novel affinity measure "*organizational distance*"

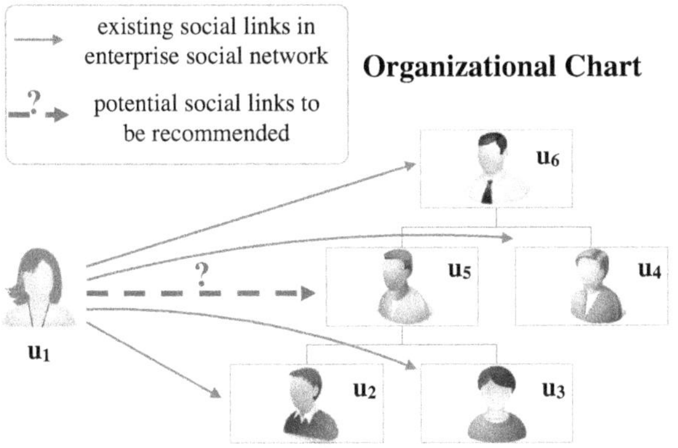

Figure 2: Example of affinity measure extraction across hybrid aligned enterprise graphs

for link (u_i, u_j): the number of steps required to walking from u_i to u_j via the links in the the organizational chart.

However, as mentioned in Section 2, users are more interested in connecting to their managers than their subordinates. As a result, the organizational distance should be asymmetric. Specifically, if we let the *organizational distance* from a user to any of his subordinates be 1, then the *organizational distance* from a user to his direct manager should be $\alpha < 1$. Our preliminary results show that $\alpha = 0.7$ works very well, which is also used throughout our experiments. For instance, based on the organizational chart in Figure 1, the organizational distance from "Calvin" to "Bob" is α, but that from "Adel" to "Bob" is 1.

Besides the links, in the organizational chart, the employees are associated with a set of attributes, which include their departments and job titles. Intuitively, people in the same department have a higher chance to know each other, and people with the same job title are more likely to work together and connect to each other (e.g., software engineer likes to connect to software engineer, while statistician likes to connect to statistician). In addition to the "*organizational distance*", features denoting whether u_i and u_j (1) are in the same department, and (2) share the same title or not are extracted as another two affinity measures from the organizational chart.

3.1.3 Social-Organizational Affinity

The above two categories of affinity measures are extracted from the enterprise social network and the organizational chart *independently*. However, aligning the enterprise social network and organizational chart together [18, 33], many other interesting signals (which were not observable when using either the ESN or the organizational chart alone) arise that could capture the affinity among users from different perspectives.

To illustrate, in Figure 2, we show part of the *organizational chart* involving $\{u_2, u_3, u_4, u_5, u_6\}$ as well as the existing social links between u_1 and u_2, u_3, u_4 and u_6. We observe that the users u_1 follows in ESNs, i.e., u_2, u_3, u_4 and u_6, are all closely working together with u_5. We define the "*groupmates*" concept in this paper to represent such relationship between u_5 and $\{u_2, u_3, u_4, u_6\}$. "Groupmates" is essentially a union set of the user's "*direct manager*", "*peers*" and "*direct subordinates*". For example, based on organizational chart fragment in Figure 2, we can find u_5's "*groupmates*" to be $\{u_2, u_3, u_4, u_6\}$, where u_2 and u_3 are the subordinates of u_5, and u_4 and u_6 are u_5's peer and direct manager respectively.

Then, when predicting the social link (u_i, u_j) in ESNs, if we observe that u_i has followed a large number/proportion of "*groupmates*" of u_j, then u_i is likely to be familiar with u_j's group, and has a high probability to follow u_j as well. For the example in Figure 2, we observe that u_1 has followed 4 of u_5's *groupmates*, then u_1 is likely to follow u_5. Following this intuition, we propose to compute (1) the number of u_j's groupmates followed by u_i, and (2) the percentage of u_j's groupmates followed by u_i as two social-organizational affinity measures across both ESN and organizational chart.

3.1.4 Geographical Affinity

Users who are in the same geo-location tend to have a higher chance to know each other, which thus may also be a possible signal for user-user affinity. We propose to also exploit information about users' working locations, e.g., timezone, country, and longitude/latitude. In this paper, we compute several such geo-affinity features including (1) whether u_i and u_j are in the same timezone, (2) whether u_i and u_j are in the same country, and (3) the geo-distance between u_i and u_j's working locations based on the longitude/latitude coordinate information.

3.2 User Characteristics

To provide personalized recommendations so as to improve user experience, users' personal characteristics play an important role. By analyzing the data, we observe that different users have quite different characteristics. For example, (1) some users like to follow users who have followed them but some other users seldom do so, (2) some users like to follow their managers but some other users like to follow their peers and subordinates, (3) some users like to follow their *groupmates* but some others like to follow employees in other divisions or departments.

To capture users' characteristics and preferences when recommending link (u_i, u_j), a set of user characteristics features are designed for u_i and u_j, which includes: (1) the *reciprocal rate* of users u_i and u_j: $\frac{|\Gamma_{out}(u_i) \cap \Gamma_{in}(u_i)|}{|\Gamma_{in}(u_i)|}$ and $\frac{|\Gamma_{out}(u_j) \cap \Gamma_{in}(u_j)|}{|\Gamma_{in}(u_j)|}$, (2) the probabilities that u_i follows his *managers, peers*, and *subordinates* based on u_i's existing follow links, (3) the sum and average of the *organizational distance* between u_i (u_j), and users that u_i (u_j) follows, (4) the number of users that $u_i(u_j)$ follows and number of followers that $u_i(u_j)$ has, (5) the average number of followers of users that u_i follows, and the average number of followers of users who follow u_j: $\frac{1}{|\Gamma_{out}(u_i)|} \sum_{u_k \in \Gamma_{out}(u_i)} |\Gamma_{in}(u_k)|$ as well as $\frac{1}{|\Gamma_{in}(u_j)|} \sum_{u_k \in \Gamma_{in}(u_j)} |\Gamma_{in}(u_k)|$, and (6) the number of employees that u_i and u_j manage.

3.3 User-Generated Content

User-generated content can reveal important information about users, e.g., the *activeness* and *popularity*. Various types of content can be generated by users via their social activities in enterprise social networks, e.g., writing posts, initiating conversations, posting comments in the conversations, and "*liking*" other users' posts, etc. Based on these user-generated contents, we compute a set of related features for (u_i, u_j), which include: (1) numbers of posts written by u_i and u_j, (2) numbers of conversations initiated by u_i and u_j, (3) the total and average numbers of "*likes*" that u_i (u_j) receives from other users, and (4) the total and average numbers of comments posted in the conversations initiated by u_i (and u_j).

3.4 Supervised Link Recommendation based on Multiple Additive Regression Tree

Link recommendation (or friend recommendation) services provided by online social networks aim at providing a ranked list of suggested social links (i.e., friends) for users. The setting of the standard link prediction problem [13, 27], essentially does point-wise prediction [3] of the existence of individual links. However, point-wise prediction has been shown ineffective for ranking problem. Besides, there are often much more negative links than positive links in the training data, and pointwise classification-based link prediction suffers from class imbalance problem [14]. Motivated by the effectiveness of the pairwise learning algorithms for learning to rank [22], we solve the link recommendation as a ranking problem rather than a pointwise prediction problem. Our later experiments also justify empirically our choice.

For a certain given user (corresponding query) u_i, our link recommendation model aims at returning a set of friend candidates in the decreasing order of their likelihood that u_i wants to follow a user. The query user u_i together with his potential followees, e.g., u_j, returned by link recommendation model, can be represented as pair (u_i, u_j). In the link recommendation problem, a set of features that depict either the relationships or the characteristics of users u_i and u_j are extracted from the network, which can be represented as vector $\mathbf{x}_{i,j}$. Besides the features, pair (u_i, u_j) is labeled with the relevance scores between the query user u_i and his potential followee u_j, which can be represented as $y_{i,j}$ ($y_{i,j} = 1$ if (u_i, u_j) is connected and 0 otherwise).

Formally, both the positive and negative pairs in the training set $\mathcal{T}$ can be represented as $\mathcal{D} = \{(\mathbf{x}_{i,j}, y_{i,j})\}, (u_i, u_j) \in \mathcal{T}$, where $\mathbf{x}_{i,j} \in \mathbb{R}^k$ of length k is the feature vector extracted for pair (u_i, u_j) and $y_{i,j}$ denotes the correlation between u_i and u_j. Link recommendation can be formalized as building a regression function $h : \mathbb{R}^k \to \mathbb{R}$, such that $h(\mathbf{x}_{i,j}) \approx y_{i,j}$. The regression model will be applied to users in the test set and can return the predicted existence confidence scores $\{h(\mathbf{x}_{i,j})\}$ for pairs consisting of the query user u_i and potential followees u_j in the test set.

We use a state-of-the-art pairwise based regression algorithm, namely MART (Multiple Additive Regression Trees) [29], to develop a regression function. MART is based on the stochastic gradient boosting approach described in [7, 8] which performs gradient descent optimization in the functional space. In our experiments, we used the log-likelihood as the loss function, steepest-descent (gradient descent) as the optimization technique, and binary decision trees as the fitting function.

4. EXPERIMENTS

To evaluate the proposed techniques for enterprise social link recommendation, we conduct extensive experiments on a real-world enterprise social network Yammer used in a large IT company and its organizational chart.

4.1 Dataset

We crawl all the Microsoft employees' information from Yammer and obtain the complete organizational chart involving all these employees in Microsoft during June, 2014 [34]. The social network data covers all the user-generated content (such as posts, replies, topics, etc.) and social graphs (such as user-user following links, user-group memberships, user-topic following links, etc.) by then that are set to be public. In summary, it includes more than $100k$ Microsoft employees, and millions of user-generated posts published and the social links.[3]

The social network data contains the complete information of all users till June 20, 2014. We treat the data before May 17, 2014 as the existing graph, which will be purely used to extract features. Users registered before May 17, 2014 are "*old users*" and users registered during May 17, 2014 - June 20, 2014 are "*new users*". Links formed during May 17, 2014 - June 20, 2014 are used as the positive links and randomly split into training, validation and test sets according to a $3:1:1$ ratio. All the non-existing links for each user (both "*old*" and "*new*" users) are used as the negative links (compared with the existing links). The positive training set together with all the negative link set are used to build the model. Parameters of the MART algorithm, such as tree depth, tree number and iteration numbers, etc., are selected with the validation set. The built model will be applied to the test set, the results of which are used in our comparison.

4.2 Experiment Settings

To evaluate the effectiveness of the proposed techniques in recommending social links for users in enterprise social networks, we compare our techniques with several representative baseline methods, including both supervised and unsupervised methods proposed in existing works for link prediction in *external* social networks [31]. Now, we summarize all the comparison methods as follows:

- *Enterprise Social Network + Organizational Chart*: We can use information of users in both enterprise social networks and the company internal organizational chart all about the same company to recommend social links. Our method is a general method and can be potentially applied to the enterprise social networks of other companies.
- *Enterprise Social Network Only*: To examine whether employees' information in the company internal organizational chart is helpful for improving link recommendation results. We introduce a baseline method called SENSOR-N (SENSOR Network), which uses information purely from the enterprise social network.
- *Organizational Chart Only*: One may wonder whether organizational chart alone is enough to predict employees' social links in an enterprise social network? To answer this question, we compare SENSOR with another baseline SENSOR-C (SENSOR Chart), which only utilizes information from the organizational chart.
- *Classification Based Link Prediction*: Existing supervised link prediction methods all use point-wise regression/classification algorithms, which do prediction for

[3] We are not able to reveal the actual numbers here and throughout the paper for commercial reasons.

each candidate link one by one. As discussed before, we hypothesize that pair-wise learning to rank algorithms would work better, observing their effectiveness in Web search [29]. To verify this hypothesis, we also compare our method with SCAN [31]. SCAN is a representative point-wise supervised learning method which use SVM for training the model. We use SCAN to develop a baseline link recommendation based on the same set of features (including those from both enterprise social networks and organizational chart).

- *Unsupervised Methods*: All the above methods are supervised link recommendation methods. For completeness, in the experiments, some traditional unsupervised link prediction methods are also used as the unsupervised baseline methods, which include "Common Neighbor" (CN), "Jaccard's Coefficient" (JC), "Adamic Adar" (AA). More detailed descriptions about these unsupervised predictors are available in [14].

We use the widely-accepted Normalized Discounted Cumulative Gain (NDCG) [16] to compare different methods. NDCG is a common evaluation metric to measure the performance of ranking methods. NDCG@1, NDCG@2, NDCG@3, NDCG@4 are used in our experiments, since the accuracy of top results is more important in a recommendation scenario like this.

4.3 Experiment Results

The comparison results are given in Figure 3, where Subfigures 3(a)-3(d) show the performance of all the comparison methods measured respectively by NDCG@1, NDCG@2, NDCG@3, and NDCG@4.

According to the results shown in Figure 3, SENSOR which utilizes information from both enterprise social network and the organizational chart performs the best among all the comparison methods across all metrics. First, SENSOR achieves NDCG scores higher than SENSOR-N by 16.8%, and SENSOR-C by 13.7% at different ranking positions 1, 2, 3, and 4 respectively. Recall that SENSOR-N only uses information from ESN. This suggests that incorporating information from organizational chart can improve the link recommendation results significantly. Meanwhile, SENSOR-C recommends social links merely based on information in organizational chart. This shows that social links are still different from those professional and business links implied by the organizational chart, and organizational chart alone is not enough. Furthermore, SENSOR performs much better than SCAN, which uses the same feature set but is using a point-wise learning algorithm instead. Possible reasons are (1) SCAN is a point-wise prediction algorithm, which has been shown less effective than pairwise prediction algorithm like MART [7] for ranking; and (2) SCAN suffers from class imbalance problem, while in real world applications like in our case, there tend to always be much more negative labels than positive labels. In addition, SENSOR can also achieve dramatically better performance than traditional unsupervised link prediction methods CN, JC and AA.

4.4 Feature Ablation Analysis

Different dimensions of features have been extracted from the network, e.g., user affinity, user personal preference, and the quality of user-generated content. To investigate the effectiveness of different kinds of features, we also do a feature ablation analysis. We remove one category of features while keeping all other categories each time, and the results achieved are given in Table 1.

First, we check the user affinity features. By comparing the results achieved by SENSOR with features "*All*", and "*All - affinity features*" (including "*All - social affinity*", "*All - org affinity*", "*All - hybrid affinity*" and "*All - geo affinity*"), we observe that, as expected, by using "*All*" the features, SENSOR performs the best. When excluding the "*social affinity*", "*org affinity*" and "*hybrid affinity*" features, the performance of SENSOR will degrade a lot. For example, with "*All*" features, SENSOR can achieve 0.611 NDCG@1 but when excluding "*social affinity*", "*org affinity*" and "*hybrid affinity*" features, the performance will drop 38.9%, 10.3% and 4.1% respectively. This suggests that the user affinity implied by social networks and organizational chart are both useful, and, what is more, they complement to each other. However, when excluding the "*geo-affinity*" features, the performance of SENSOR does not decrease much. This shows that enterprise social connections are not closely related to users' geographical locations.

Second, we look into the "*user characteristics*" features. As shown in Table 1, when excluding the *user characteristics* features, SENSOR's performance will degrade a lot. For example, Its NDCG@1 is 24.5% lower than that achieved by SENSOR with "*All*" features. This confirms that users in enterprise social networks do have different personal preferences, which significantly influences their decisions of who to connect with in company.

Third, we examine the features based on user-generated content. When excluding this set of features, SENSOR performs almost the same as when using "All" features, which shows that *user generated content* does not help recommend social links in enterprise social networks. One possible reason is that the links in ESN are mostly social links rather than content-based links: a user may not always follow another user who has published high-quality content.

4.5 Link Recommendation for New Users

It has been shown that new users often suffer from the cold start problem, since we do not have data for new users [25]. Does the cold start problem also exist in enterprise social link recommendation? In Figure 4, we give the recommendation results of SENSOR and SENSOR-N (which does not use the organizational chart) in recommending social links for "*new*" users and "*old*" users. The x axis of the figure denotes the number of existing links users have and users with zero existing links are "*new*" users while users with existing links represent "*old*" users. First of all, we see that SENSOR performs better than SENSOR-N consistently for users with different numbers of existing following links. This confirms again that the organizational chart helps link recommendation. Specifically, for users with fewer existing links, SENSOR performs even better than SENSOR-N, which suggests that the organizational chart information is more important in recommending links for "*new*" users. As users become "old" and have more existing links, the advantages of SENSOR over SENSOR-N will decrease steadily. In other words, for "*old*" users who have already had much information in the enterprise social network, organizational chart may not help much.

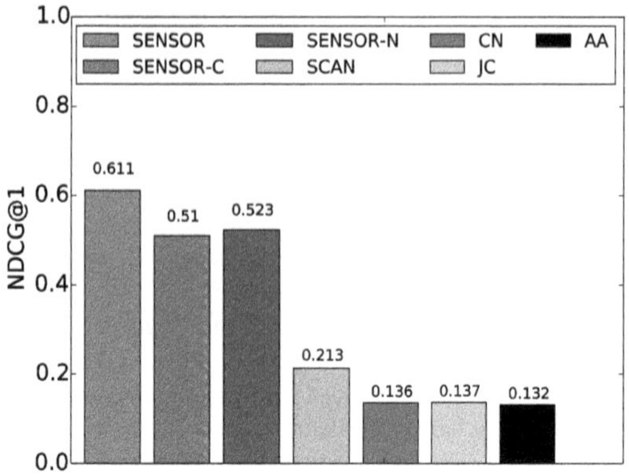

(a) NDCG@1

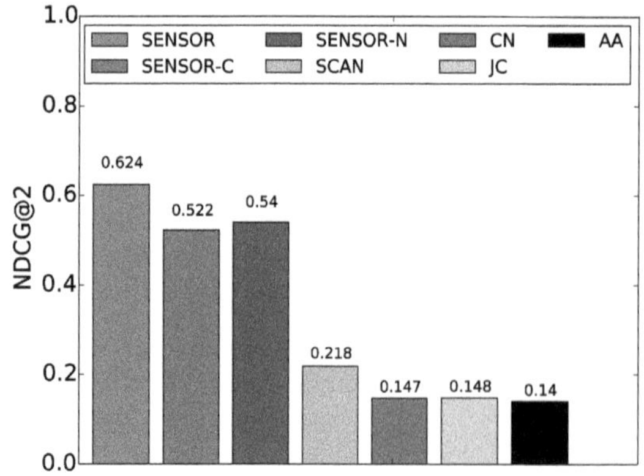

(b) NDCG@2

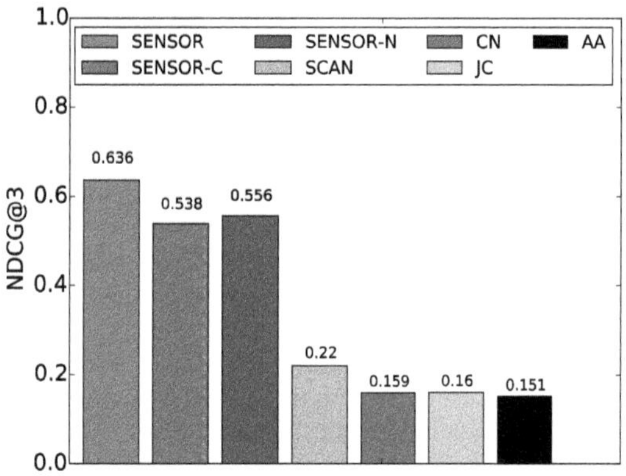

(c) NDCG@3

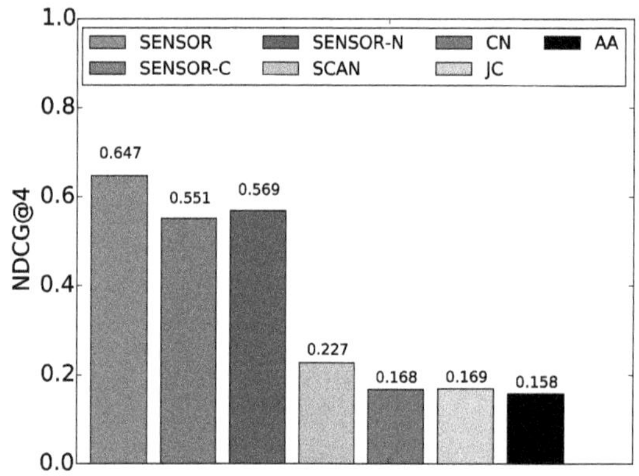

(d) NDCG@4

Figure 3: Link recommendation results. The improvements of SENSOR over SENSOR-n, SENSOR-c, SCAN, CN, JC, AA are all statistically significant at the 0.01 level using Wilcoxon non-directional test.

One possible reason is that *"new" users* tend to first connect with employees in the same group or department, and then connect with friends beyond the organizational boundaries. This would also lead the link recommendation problem for "new" users to be relatively easier than for "old" users. This has also been confirmed by the results in Figure 4, which shows that we can even achieve higher NDCG for new users. In summary, there is no "cold start" (but a "hot start" instead) for new users in enterprise social link recommendation, thanks to the knowledge from the organizational chart.

4.6 Interesting Findings

We summarize some interesting findings we have observed:

- Organizational chart is useful.
- Users tend to first connect with colleagues within the same group and then to employees beyond the organizational boundaries.
- Social affinity and organizational affinity are both useful, but geo-affinity is useless.
- User-generated content does not help, suggesting social links rather than content links.

5. RELATED WORK

Enterprise social networks [34] can help employees in companies get reliable information [30, 6, 12]. Yarosh et al. [30] explore the importance of different types of information in expert searching based on a small-sized questionnaire dataset and useful information is used to improve the usefulness of supporting systems. Ehrlich et al. [6] propose to search for experts in enterprise with both text and social network analysis techniques. They propose to examine the users' dynamic profile information and get the social distance to the expert before deciding how to initiate the contact. Meanwhile, Enterprise social networks can lead to other benefits to companies and DiMicco et al. [5] study the motivations for social networking at work. Users in enterprise social networks will connect and learn from each other through personal and professional sharing. DiMicco et al. [4] propose to study people sensemaking and relation building on an enterprise social network site. Based on the heterogeneous information in enterprise social networks, Zhang et

Table 1: **Feature ablation analysis**

	All	All - social affinity	All - org affinity	All - hybrid affinity	All - geo affinity	All - user characteristics	All - user generated content
NDCG@1	0.611	0.373	0.548	0.586	0.605	0.461	0.614
NDCG@2	0.624	0.382	0.561	0.600	0.619	0.486	0.621
NDCG@3	0.636	0.395	0.580	0.616	0.631	0.504	0.636
NDCG@4	0.647	0.408	0.594	0.628	0.641	0.517	0.645

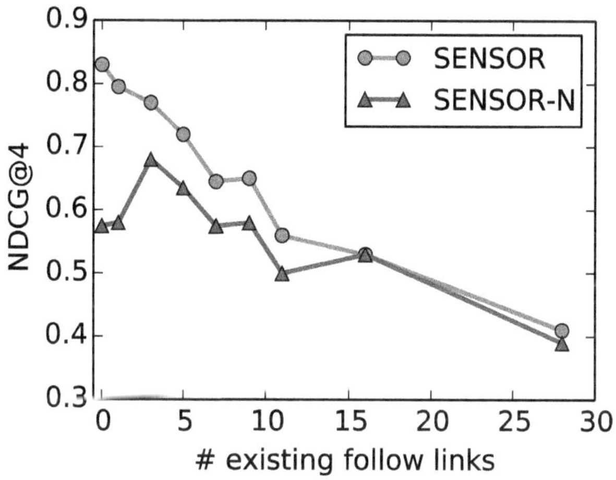

Figure 4: Link recommendation for new users and old users

al. propose to infer the complete organizational chart based on an unsupervised learning framework CREATE in [34].

Social connections among users in enterprise social networks usually have multiple facets. Wu et al. [28] study the multiplexity of social connections among users in enterprise social networks, which include both professional and personal closeness. Zhang et al. [32] give a case study about the early adoption and use of micro-blogging in 500 companies, and attempt to understand how knowledge workers are likely to use micro-bolgging in the enterprise. Hsieh et al. [15] study the problem of computing edge affinity between two users on a social network. Some friend recommendation works have been done either on small-sized enterprise social networks, like Beehive [2], or survey based dataset [11, 2, 10, 9]. Chen et al. [2] study people recommendations designed to help users find known, offline contacts and discover new friends on social networking sites. They evaluated four recommender algorithms in an enterprise social networking site using a personalized survey of 500 users and a field study of 3,000 users. Guy et al. explore the personalized recommendation of social software items [11], close friends [9] and even strangers [10] based on user studies involving less than 500 users in enterprises. Different from these works, we are doing link recommendation using a real-world large-scale ESN.

Link prediction in online social networks first proposed by Liben-Nowell et al. [21] has become an important research topic in recent years. In [21], Liben-Nowell et al. propose various unsupervised link predictors to calculate the existence scores of potential links. Meanwhile, Hasan et al. [13] propose a supervised learning framework to predict potential links in online social networks. These works are all based on one single homogeneous networks. Sun et al. [26] propose a meta path based prediction model to predict co-author relationships in the heterogeneous bibliographic network.

Nowadays, link prediction in multiple heterogeneous social networks simultaneously has attracted much attention. Kong et al. [18] notice that users nowadays are usually involved in multiple social networks at the same time to enjoy specific social services provided by different networks. Zhang et al. [35] study the social link recommendations in multiple partially aligned social networks simultaneously.

6. CONCLUSION

In this paper, we study a new problem of enterprise social link recommendation. To understand and model whom an employee wants to connect with in the company, new techniques are introduced to explore both enterprise social network and organizational chart from three dimensions: (1) user-user affinity, (2) user characteristics, and (3) user generated content. A supervised machine-learned recommendation algorithm, SENSOR, is developed. Evaluation using a real-world large-scale enterprise social network shows that the proposed techniques perform effectively in recommending social links for enterprise social networks.

We plan to further investigate the relationship between ESN and organizational chart. To name a few, e.g., organizational chart inference based on ESN as well as hybrid information diffusion across ESN and organizational chart, will be studied in the future.

7. ACKNOWLEDGEMENT

We thank Ariel Fuxman and Panayiotis Tsaparas for their useful discussions. We also thank Dhyanesh Narayanan, John Pigeon and Chris Slemp for helping crawl the data.

8. REFERENCES

[1] L. Aiello, A. Barrat, R. Schifanella, C. Cattuto, B. Markines, and F. Menczer. Friendship prediction and homophily in social media. *ACM TWEB*, 2012.

[2] J. Chen, W. Geyer, C. Dugan, M. Muller, and I. Guy. Make new friends, but keep the old: Recommending people on social networking sites. In *CHI*, 2009.

[3] W. Chen, T. Liu, Y. Lan, Z. Ma, and H. Li. Ranking Measures and Loss Functions in Learning to Rank. In Y. Bengio, D. Schuurmans, J. Lafferty, C. Williams, and A. Culotta, editors, *Advances in Neural Information Processing Systems 22*. 2009.

[4] J. DiMicco, W. Geyer, D. Millen, C. Dugan, and B. Brownholtz. People sensemaking and relationship building on an enterprise social network site. In *HICSS*, 2009.

[5] J. DiMicco, D. Millen, W. Geyer, C. Dugan, B. Brownholtz, and M. Muller. Motivations for social networking at work. In *CSCW*, 2008.
[6] K. Ehrlich, C. Lin, and V. Griffiths-Fisher. Searching for experts in the enterprise: Combining text and social network analysis. In *GROUP*, 2007.
[7] J. Friedman. Greedy function approximation: A gradient boosting machine. *Annals of Statistics*, 2000.
[8] J. Friedman. Stochastic gradient boosting. *Comput. Stat. Data Anal.*, 2002.
[9] I. Guy, I. Ronen, and E. Wilcox. Do you know?: Recommending people to invite into your social network. In *IUI*, 2009.
[10] I. Guy, S. Ur, I. Ronen, A. Perer, and M. Jacovi. Do you want to know?: Recommending strangers in the enterprise. In *CSCW*, 2011.
[11] I. Guy, N. Zwerdling, D. Carmel, I. Ronen, E. Uziel, S. Yogev, and S. Ofek-Koifman. Personalized recommendation of social software items based on social relations. In *RecSys*, 2009.
[12] S. Han, D. He, J. Jiang, and Z. Yue. Supporting exploratory people search: A study of factor transparency and user control. In *CIKM*, 2013.
[13] M. Hasan, V. Chaoji, S. Salem, and M. Zaki. Link prediction using supervised learning. In *SDM*, 2006.
[14] M. Hasan and M. Zaki. A survey of link prediction in social networks. In C. Aggarwal, editor, *Social Network Data Analytics*. 2011.
[15] C. Hsieh, M. Tiwari, D. Agarwal, X. Huang, and S. Shah. Organizational overlap on social networks and its applications. In *WWW*, 2013.
[16] K. Järvelin and J. Kekäläinen. Cumulated gain-based evaluation of ir techniques. *ACM Transactions on Information Systems*, 2002.
[17] T. Joachims. A probabilistic analysis of the rocchio algorithm with tfidf for text categorization. In *ICML*, 1997.
[18] X. Kong, J. Zhang, and P. Yu. Inferring anchor links across multiple heterogeneous social networks. In *CIKM*, 2013.
[19] H. Kwak, C. Lee, H. Park, and S. Moon. What is twitter, a social network or a news media? In *WWW*, 2010.
[20] T. Lappas, K. Liu, and E. Terzi. Finding a team of experts in social networks. In *KDD*, 2009.
[21] D. Liben-Nowell and J. Kleinberg. The link prediction problem for social networks. In *CIKM*, 2003.
[22] T. Liu. *Learning to Rank for Information Retrieval*. Springer, 2011.
[23] M. McPherson, L. Lovin, and J. Cook. Birds of a Feather: Homophily in Social Networks. *Annual Review of Sociology*, 2001.
[24] L. Paninski. Estimation of entropy and mutual information. *Neural Computation*, 15(6), 2003.
[25] A. Schein, A. Popescul, L. Ungar, and D. Pennock. Methods and metrics for cold-start recommendations. In *SIGIR*, 2002.
[26] Y. Sun, R. Barber, M. Gupta, C. Aggarwal, and J. Han. Co-author relationship prediction in heterogeneous bibliographic networks. In *ASONAM*, 2011.
[27] J. Tang, H. Gao, X. Hu, and H. Liu. Exploiting homophily effect for trust prediction. In *WSDM*, 2013.
[28] A. Wu, J. DiMicco, and D. Millen. Detecting professional versus personal closeness using an enterprise social network site. In *CHI*, 2010.
[29] Q. Wu, C. Burges, K. Svore, and J. Gao. Adapting boosting for information retrieval measures. *Information Retrieval*, 2010.
[30] S. Yarosh, T. Matthews, and M. Zhou. Asking the right person: Supporting expertise selection in the enterprise. In *CHI*, 2012.
[31] J. Zhang, X. Kong, and P. Yu. Transfer heterogeneous links across location-based social networks. In *WSDM*, 2014.
[32] J. Zhang, Y. Qu, J. Cody, and Y. Wu. A case study of micro-blogging in the enterprise: User, value, and related issues. In *CHI*, 2010.
[33] J. Zhang and P. Yu. Integrated anchor and social link predictions across partially aligned social networks. In *IJCAI*, 2015.
[34] J. Zhang, P. Yu, and Y. Lv. Organizational chart inference. In *KDD*, 2015.
[35] J. Zhang, P. Yu, and Z. Zhou. Meta-path based multi-network collective link prediction. In *KDD*, 2014.
[36] Y. Zhu, X. Zhang, G. Sun, M. Tang, T. Zhou, and Z. Zhang. Influence of reciprocal links in social networks. *PLoS ONE*, 9(7), 2014.

Exploiting Game Theoretic Analysis for Link Recommendation in Social Networks

Tong Zhao[1,2], H. Vicky Zhao[3], Irwin King[1,2]
[1]Shenzhen Key Laboratory of Rich Media Big Data Analytics and Applications, Shenzhen Research Institute,
The Chinese University of Hong Kong, Shenzhen, China
[2]Department of Computer Science and Engineering,
The Chinese University of Hong Kong, Shatin, N.T., Hong Kong
[3]Electrical and Computer Engineering Department, University of Alberta, Edmonton, AB Canada
{tzhao, king}@cse.cuhk.edu.hk, vzhao@ece.ualberta.ca

ABSTRACT

The popularity of Online Social Networks (OSNs) has attracted great research interests in different fields. In Economics, researchers use game theory to analyze the mechanism of network formation, which is called Network Formation Game. While in Computer Science, much effort has been done in building machine learning models to predict future or missing links. However, there are few works considering how to combine game theoretic analysis and machine learning models. Therefore, in this paper, we study the problem of Exploiting Game Theoretic Analysis for Link Recommendation in Social Networks. Our goal is to improve link recommendation accuracy via leveraging the power of Network Formation Games into machine learning models. We present two different approaches to solve this problem. First, we propose a three-phase method that straightforwardly combines game theoretic analysis with machine learning models. Second, we develop a unified model, *BPRLGT*, that incorporates Network Formation Game into a Bayesian ranking framework for link recommendation. Specifically, *BPRLGT* takes advantage of network topology and we design a game theoretic sampling approach to improve its training process. The experiments are conducted on four real world datasets and the results on all datasets demonstrate that both our proposed three-phase method and the unified ranking model outperform the baseline methods.

Categories and Subject Descriptors

H.4 [**Information Systems Applications**]: Miscellaneous

General Terms

Algorithms, Experimentation, Performance

Keywords

Game Theory; Network Formation Game; Link Prediction

Permission to make digital or hard copies of all or part of this work for personal or classroom use is granted without fee provided that copies are not made or distributed for profit or commercial advantage and that copies bear this notice and the full citation on the first page. Copyrights for components of this work owned by others than ACM must be honored. Abstracting with credit is permitted. To copy otherwise, or republish, to post on servers or to redistribute to lists, requires prior specific permission and/or a fee. Request permissions from Permissions@acm.org.
CIKM'15, October 19–23, 2015, Melbourne, Australia.
© 2015 ACM. ISBN 978-1-4503-3794-6/15/10 ...$15.00.
DOI: http://dx.doi.org/10.1145/2806416.2806510.

1. INTRODUCTION

Online social networks (OSNs) play an important role for people to satisfy their social needs and seek novel information on Internet. As shown by recent studies, there are over 5.7 billion users on the world's top 21 social networks and 72% of all Internet users are active on social media for sharing feelings, posting pictures and most importantly, making friends. Such popularity has attracted great research interests from different fields.

In Economics, a popular research direction is to use game theory to study the mechanism of the formation of social networks, which refers to *Network Formation Game* (NFG). Typically, in NFG models, utility functions are defined to represent how much utility people can gain from their connected neighbors and the models assume that people build social links in order to maximize their utility. Here utility represents the benefit or profit for people. Based on NFG, economic researchers try to investigate the following problems: 1) given a specific social network, how to find the particular utility functions that can explain why people form such a network; 2) how different definitions of utility function can trigger people to form different social networks in order to maximize their utility. To answer these questions, several possible modeling approaches are proposed, including simultaneous move modeling, pairwise-stability modeling [16], bargaining for network formation [8], dynamic modeling [31], farsighted network formation modeling [11], etc.. However, most of these works focus on explaining the formation of current network and cannot be directly used for link prediction.

While in Computer Science, much effort has also been done for social network analysis, especially in predicting new links for people. Many methods are proposed to solve this problem. Several atomic propagation models are proposed in [12] such as direct propagation, co-citation propagation, transpose propagation and coupling propagation for trust link prediction. Leskovec et al. [21] leverage the topological feature of a social network to predict the trust and distrust relations among users. Tang et al. propose a method for link prediction by capturing the evolution of trust in [34]. Guha et al. propose a framework for modeling trust propagation [12]. Dong et al. [10] design a factor graph method to predict trust links between users across heterogeneous networks. While the existing methods can learn the network and predict links to users, none of them consider how users' utility change when building the recommended links.

Therefore, in this paper, we study the problem of *Exploiting Game Theoretic Analysis for Link Recommendation in Social Networks*. The goal is to improve link recommendation (link prediction) accuracy via leveraging the power of Network Formation Games (NFG). However, there are several challenges when combining game theoretic models and link prediction models. First, most of the NFG models focus on explaining the formation of current networks and assume that no users can further improve their utility through building new links. This assumption conflicts the goal of link prediction models. Second, the goals of NFG analysis and link prediction models are different. NFG models aim to maximize users' utility value while the goal of link prediction models is to maximize the accuracy of link recommendation. To our best knowledge, there is no work investigating the connections between the two goals. Third, no existing link prediction models consider the utility analysis when training, how to integrate utility analysis into model training is a challenging problem.

To address these challenges, in this paper, we first conduct an empirical study to investigate how well NFG models describe the formation mechanism of real networks. Then we propose a three-phase approach that leverages the power of game theory into link prediction models. Given a social network G, the first phase employs NGF models to calculate an original utility value of each user in G; at the second phase, link prediction models are used to find the candidate links; after adding the candidate links to G, the third phase then calculates users' utility via NFG models again and uses the utility difference based on the current and original utility as a criterion to help re-rank the candidate links. In particular, the links which are highly-ranked by link prediction models but cannot improve the utility of connected users will be re-ranked to a lower priority for final recommendation.

Although the three-phase method provides a simple way to combine NFG models and machine learning models, it processes the knowledge from NFG models and machine learning models in separated steps. In particular, NFG models have no contribution when training machine learning models and no utility information is considered when generating candidate links.

To alleviate these problems and better integrate NFG models into machine learning models, we further propose a novel unified pairwise ranking model, namely, *BPRLGT* (*Bayesian Personalized Ranking for Link recommendation with Game Theory*), integrating NFG models into a Bayesian ranking model for link recommendation. Our model is built based on Bayesian Personalized Ranking framework (BPR) [27], which always requires sampling technique to select training data. In BPRLGT, we emphasize on designing a game theoretic sampling approach to improve model training. More specifically, different from uniformly sampling and other heuristic sampling approaches [29] such as popularity-based sampling, etc., the proposed game theoretic sampling approach considers users' utility and helps the model punish the links that cannot increase users' utility but with high-rank. Moreover, BPRLGT model also takes network topology into account, which makes BPRLGT more suitable for link prediction.

We conduct experiments on four real world social network datasets and the results show that our proposed three-phase method and the unified model consistently outperform other state-of-the-art methods.

Organization. In Section 2, we discuss the related work. In Section 3, we provide the background and then formulate the problem ; Section 4 details the proposed three-phase method and the unified ranking model with the game theoretic sampling technique. Section 5 demonstrates the experimental results and verifies the contribution of integrating game theoretical analysis into link prediction problems. Finally, Section 6 concludes the paper.

2. RELATED WORK

In this section we review the related work, regarding the Network Formation Game, link prediction in social network, as well as one-class recommendation problem.

Network Formation Game. Recent years, Game Theory [5, 17, 18, 22] has been used to investigate people's behaviors and social relations in social networks. Typically, a utility function is defined to represent people's utility in a social network. By analyzing parameters in utility function and the network structure, researchers try to explain the mechanism of the network formation. We refer readers to [14] and [15] for a detailed survey of models in Network Formation Games. Xiao et al. [35] formulate the wireless security problem as an indirect reciprocity game, and propose a method that applies the indirect reciprocity principle to suppress attacks in wireless networks. In [16], the authors study the stability and efficiency of social and economic networks. Bramoulle et al. [7] provide a general network analysis to a wide class of games, including strategic innovation, public goods and social interactions. Mele [23] analyzes the network formation by a dynamic meeting protocol and Badev [2] further extends the model. Paula et al. [26] provide a framework to learn parameters of utility function in network formation models.

Link Prediction. A large number of studies about link prediction [9, 36, 32, 1, 34] have been proposed based on either similarity analysis or propagation analysis. Siegler et al. point out that there is a strong and significant correlation between trust link and similarity [39] and then use the similarity for link prediction. Guha et al. propose a framework for modeling trust propagation [12]. Leskovec et al. utilize the topological feature of a social network to predict the trust and distrust relations among users[21]. Tang [32] et al. exploit homophily effect for link prediction. Lee et al. [20] develop an integer programming problem for the link prediction problem. Besides the machine learning models, some game theory-based methods are also proposed for link prediction, but they all need some additional information, such as users' rating or tagging behavior on items, to help define the game parameters. Zappella et al. [37] present a Graph Transduction Game for link prediction and Beigi et al. [6] also employ a game theoretic approach for community detection and link prediction. Few work considers to integrate game theory models into machine learning models to improve the accuracy on link prediction.

One-class Recommendation. One-class recommendation focus on solving recommendation problems when one can only observe some forms of users' implicit feedback from data, typically binary feedback, such as the webpages they browse, the music they listen to, the link they click or whom they make friend with. We view users' observed feedback as positive feedback and others as negative feedback. In this paper, we cast link prediction as an one-class recommendation problem since we can only observe users' positive feedback (existing links) and aim at predicting missing or future links. Several works have studied one-class recommendation and can be mainly divided into two branches: pointwise methods [13, 25] and pairwise methods [27, 30]. Pointwise methods aim to fit a numeric value associated with each evaluated item, while pairwise methods focus on modeling the order, or ranking of the feedback. Pairwise methods always consider implicit feedback as relative relationships indicating that users show higher preference on positive feedback than on negative feedback. In [27], Rendle et al. propose a bayesian personalized ranking (*BPR*) framework. Following this, various ideas have been proposed that incorporate different types of contextual information into the *BPR* framework. [19] extends the *BPR* framework to model both users' feedback on items and on their social relations. In [38], Zhao et al. leverage social connections to improve item recommendations by building a new preference system. Since the learning method used in most related works is stochastic gradient descent (SGD), how to select the training instances has great impact on model performance. In [29], the authors propose two strategies to sample negative feedback and also design an efficient implementation to improve the convergence of the learning algorithm.

Summary. Our proposed methods differentiate themselves from all these existing methods in that the study of incorporating game theoretic analysis into machine learning models is unexplored in previous work.

3. BACKGROUND AND PROBLEM DEFINITION

In this section, we first present several notations and definitions used in the paper and then detail two Network Formation models, Co-author model and Linear Best Reply model, which will be used in our proposed methods. We analyze the property of Network Formation models and then formally define the problem of *Exploiting Game Theoretic Analysis to Improve Link Recommendation in Social Networks.*

3.1 Definitions and Notations

Let $G = (V, E)$ denote the social network, where V is a set of $|V| = M$ users and $E \subset V \times V$ is a set of links between users. G can be either directed or undirected. N_i represents the directed neighbors of user i in graph G. $e_{ij} \in E(G)$ means there is a direct link between user i and j in G and $e_{ij} \notin E(G)$ represents that there is no direct link between the two users. Given a network G and $e_{ij} \notin E$, let $G + e_{ij}$ denote the network formed by adding the link e_{ij} to the network G, and G/e_{ij} denote the network formed by deleting the link e_{ij} from the network G. $\mathbf{I}$ denotes the identity matrix, $\mathbf{1}$ denotes a vector of ones, A^T denotes the transpose of matrix A and $det(A)$ represents the determinant of matrix A. We also have the following concept definitions.

Definition 1. **Action**: Actions in this paper are defined as user's behaviors to build social relations with others. In particular, given G, each user i's action can be represented as $x_i \in \mathbb{R}^M$, where the j_{th} entry in x_i equals to 1 if $e_{ij} \in E$ and 0 otherwise. Let $\mathbf{x} = \langle x_1, x_2, ..., x_M \rangle$ denote the action vector for all users and $\mathbf{x}_{-i} = \langle x_1, x_2, ..., x_{i-1}, x_{i+1}, ..., x_M \rangle$ denote the action vector of all users other than i.

Definition 2. **Individual utility**: The individual utility represents the profit, quantity or "utility" in result of user's actions. Typically, it can be constructed as the value of a utility function, $U(\cdot)$. In this paper, we assume that users' utility will change only when G changes and only building new links or deleting existing links will affect users' utility. Let $U(x_i; \mathbf{x}_{-i}, G)$ denote the utility function to calculate user i's utility value in network G since G is formed by action vector $\mathbf{x}$. For simplicity, we use $U_i(G)$ or U_i to represent user i's utility value in social network G.

Definition 3. **Utility difference**: Utility difference of user i, Δ_i, describes the difference when user i builds some new links. Specifically, given G and a set of recommended links, $\{e_{ij}\} \notin E(G)$, $\Delta_i = U_i(G + \{e_{ij}\}) - U_i(G)$. If $\Delta_i \geq 0$, we conclude that e_{ij} is a *beneficial link* for user i. In particular, for a recommended link $e_{ij} \notin E(G)$, if $\Delta_i \geq 0$ and $\Delta_j \geq 0$, we call e_{ij} a *mutual consent link*.

Table 1: Statistics of the Datasets after filtering.

	Ciao	Epinions	COL	FB
#Users	2342	9049	40421	63732
#Edges	51789	320150	316246	1071968
#Avg.Edges	22	35	8	17
Density	9.4×10^{-3}	3.9×10^{-3}	1.9×10^{-4}	2.6×10^{-4}

In game theory, the most important concept is Nash Equilibrium, which describes a solution concept of a Network Formation Game such that no player in the game can gain more by changing only their own actions. Here we also introduce the Nash Equilibrium concept used in Network Formation Games.

Definition 4. **Nash Equilibrium**: An action vector $\mathbf{x}$ is a Nash Equilibrium if and only if for all users i,

$$U_i(x_i; \mathbf{x}_{-i}, G) \geq U_i(x_i'; \mathbf{x}_{-i}, G).$$

This definition shows that for user i, his/her utility cannot increase by changing his/her action from x_i to x_i'. In fact, Nash Equilibrium describes the optimal utility that users can gain in network G. Based on the definition of action, we can see that the network G is the result of users' actions and given a network G, we can calculate users' utility based on $U(\cdot)$. In this paper, we aim to improve link recommendation accuracy by considering the utility that users will gain from building the recommended links. Specifically, given a network G and a set of recommended links $\{e_{ij}\}$, we first assume that both G and $G + \{e_{ij}\}$ reach Nash Equilibrium, then we can obtain the optimal utilities, $U_i(G)$ and $U_i(G + \{e_{ij}\})$, for each user i on G and $G + \{e_{ij}\}$. More importantly, we can then judge whether $\{e_{ij}\}$ should be recommended to people based on $\Delta_i = U_i(G + \{e_{ij}\}) - U_i(G)$: if $\Delta_i \geq 0$ for user i, then we conclude that $\{e_{ij}\}$ should be recommended; otherwise, we should not recommend them to people since people cannot increase their utilities by building them.

3.2 Network Formation Games

In this section, we first formally define the Network Formation Game and then present several utility functions that are widely used in NFG. Following that, we analyze their properties when reaching Nash Equilibrium.

A Network Formation Game (NFG) in game theory is always used to analyze user's discretion when they build links in social network and it can be represented by a triple (G, $\mathbf{U}$, $U(\cdot)$), where $\mathbf{U} = \langle U_1(G), ..., U_i(G), ..., U_M(G) \rangle \in \mathbb{R}^M$ records users' utilities in G and $U(\cdot)$ is the utility function which defines how utilities are allocated across the users when they build a particular network. The key component of NFG is to find a proper utility function and ensure that it could explain why users build such a particular network. Specifically, the utility function describes the utilities that users directly receive, taking both benefit and cost of maintaining their social links into account. Different utility functions lead to different models in NFG and also motivate users to set up different network structures. The goal of NFG is to analyze users' utilities when assuming the given network G reach a Nash Equilibrium. In the following subsection, we will introduce two popular NFG models, Co-author model and Linear Best-Response model in details.

3.2.1 Models in Network Formation Games

The Co-author Model. The Co-author model [16] is firstly proposed to describe the collaboration relationship between researchers. Each user in this model is assumed to own a fixed

Input: A network $G = (V, E)$ and δ
Output: Effort vector $\mathbf{U}(G)$
$\mathbf{U}_S(G) = \mathbf{0}$;
repeat
  Select a subset of users, $S \subseteq V$;
  Construct $G_S(G)$ and G_{V-S};
  if *det(I* $+ \delta G_S$*) equals to 0* **then**
    Continue;
  end
  $\mathbf{U}_S(G) = (\mathbf{I} + \delta G_S)^{-1}\mathbf{1}$;
until $\mathbf{U}_S(G) \geq 0$ *and* $\delta G_{V-S}\mathbf{U}_S(G) \geq \mathbf{1}$;
Return $\mathbf{U}_S(G)$.

Algorithm 1: Utility calculation in LBR. G_S denotes the subgraph of G connecting the selected users S and G_{V-S} denotes the graph of links connecting users S to the rest users. $\mathbf{U}_S(G)$ denotes the utility vector when users S are selected to estimate the Nash Equilibrium in network G.

amount of time to spend or pay, so the time user i spends on each collaboration is inversely related to the number of links he/she has, say $n_i = |N_i|$. The utility of user i is represented by

$$U_i(G) = \sum_{j:e_{ij} \in E(G)} \left(\frac{1}{n_i} + \frac{1}{n_j} + \frac{1}{n_i n_j}\right). \quad (1)$$

Here we can see that the more links user i has, the lower synergy he/she could gain from this link. Note that there is no direct cost modeling, but the diluted gains reflect the cost when user builds too many links with others. Given G, users' utilities can be directly calculated from Eq (1). In this way, when considering to build new links, user i needs to think about the utility difference after they constructing these links. Specifically, when user i considers to make friends with user k, the utility difference can be estimated as

$$\begin{aligned}\Delta_i =& \frac{1}{n_k} + \frac{1}{n_k(n_i+1)} + \left(1 + \frac{1}{n_i+1}\right) \sum_{j:e_{ij} \in E(G)} \frac{1}{n_j} \\ &- \left(1 + \frac{1}{n_i}\right) \sum_{j:e_{ij} \in E(G)} \frac{1}{n_j}, \\ =& \frac{1}{n_k} + \frac{1}{n_k(n_i+1)} - \frac{1}{n_i(n_i+1)} \sum_{j:e_{ij} \in E(G)} \frac{1}{n_j}.\end{aligned} \quad (2)$$

If $\Delta_i \geq 0$, we conclude e_{ik} as a beneficial link to user i since it could increase i's utility.

The Linear Best-Response Model. In Linear Best Response (LBR) model [7], vector $\mathbf{U}$ is used to represent users' effort on network G, $\overline{u}$ is the required efforts that each user needs take in isolation; for each user i, his/her effort can be calculated as following,

$$U_i(G) = \begin{cases} \overline{u} - \delta \sum_{e_{ij} \in E(G)} U_j(G) & \text{if} \quad \overline{u} > \delta \sum_{e_{ij} \in E(G)} U_j(G) \\ 0 & \text{if} \quad \overline{u} \leq \delta \sum_{e_{ij} \in E(G)} U_j(G), \end{cases} \quad (3)$$

where δ is a measure of how much user i's directed neighbors affect his/her efforts. Thus, user i achieves his/her required efforts $\overline{u}$ through combining his/her own effort and his/her friends' efforts. From this definition, we find that the more efforts user i's neighbors could offer, the less effort user i herself would take. In LBR model, each user wants to minimize his/her own efforts while reaching the required $\overline{u}$ by others.

LBR model captures the property of several exemplary games including network formation game. For example, researchers benefit from the results of experiments done by their collaborators, which explains the formation of academic collaboration networks; people in Facebook learn more by the sharings of their friends, which explains the formation of social networks.

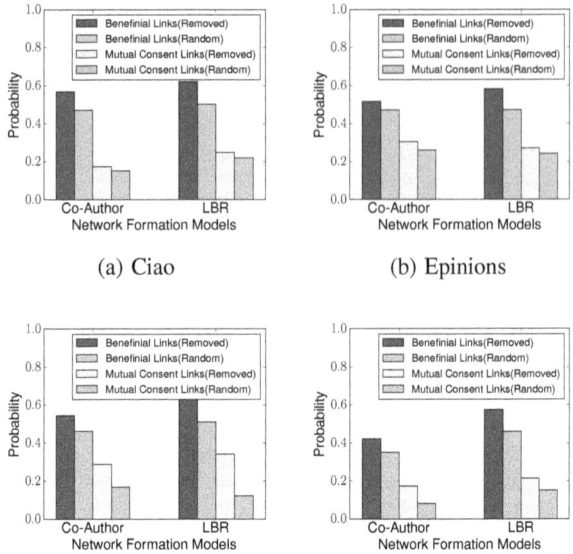

(a) Ciao (b) Epinions

(c) Collaboration (d) Facebook

Figure 1: Empirical analysis of Network Formation Models. We investigate how much different network formation models can capture the real network evolution from benefit perspective. We include a random setting for clear comparison. Y-axis represents the probability that Network Formation Game models precisely capture the beneficial links.

Accordingly, user i's utility function then can be equivalently represented as

$$U(x_i; \mathbf{x}_{-i}, \delta, G) = -\frac{1}{2}U_i^2 - \delta \sum_{e_{ij} \in E(G)} U_i U_j + \overline{u} U_i. \quad (4)$$

Equation (3) can be obtained by calculating the derivation of Eq (4). However, one can see that from Eq (4), utility value cannot be directly calculated since Eq (4) contains both U_i and U_j. Therefore, we need to borrow the concept of Nash Equilibrium to obtain the final utility of each user. Several works are done for the analysis of Nash Equilibrium of LBR model [3, 4]. According Proposition 1 in [7], we can obtain the utility of each user via Algorithm 1.

Similar to Co-author model, here we also use the utility difference as criteria to identify beneficial and mutual consent links. Specifically, when user i considers to make friends with user k, the utility difference can be estimated as $\Delta_i = -(U_i(G + e_{ik}) - U_i(G))$. If $\Delta_i \geq 0$, we say e_{ik} a beneficial link to user i since it could decrease i's effort.

3.2.2 Empirical Analysis on Real Networks

As we discussed in Section 1, though the above game theoretic models show their strength on analyzing the formation mechanism of a static network from theory perspective, an important issue still remains: could these model capture the mechanism of evolution of real networks? In particular, we are interested in understanding: **Q1**, if we exactly know the links users will build and apply NFG models to estimate their utilities before and after they setting up these links, whether their utilities would increase accordingly? **Q2**, how precise the models can achieve in identifying beneficial or mutual consent links? **Q3**, could users gain more utility by adding arbitrary links?

To answer questions **Q1** to Q3, we conduct an empirical analysis on four real-world datasets, Ciao, Epinions[1], Collaboration Network (COL)[2] and Facebook[3]. The statistics of these datasets are shown in Table 1 and we will introduce the datasets in detail in Section 5. To answer these questions, we first remove X% links $\{e_{ij} \in E(G)\}$ as $\mathcal{N}$ from network G and note the network with the rest links as $G_{removed}$, then we utilize the models of NFG to calculate the utilities of each user in $G_{removed}$, say $\mathbf{U}(G_{removed})$; following that, we add the removed links back and again calculate the utilities of each user, say $\mathbf{U}(G)$; thus, for each user i who has link changes, we calculate Δ_i. Based on the description in *Definition 3*, we can then count the number of beneficial links and further obtain the number of mutual consent links. The more a NFG model can identify beneficial and mutual consent links, the better this model will be when using it to model real network evolution. In addition, we also calculate users' utility difference by randomly adding links to $G_{removed}$ for answering **Q3**. The number of randomly added links is same as removed links. We test X as 10, 20 and 30. Since the performance are similar, here we just report the result of X=20.

By cross validation, we find the best performance of each models as Figure 1. Here we set $\delta = 0.25$ and $\overline{u} = 1$ in LBR model. We summarize the results by following observations:

- On all datasets, NFG models achieve almost 60% precision on average for capturing beneficial links;
- Co-author model estimates most of the removed links as beneficial links. LBR model always achieves better performance on capturing mutual consent link.
- Compared with the random setting, NFG models have higher probability to model *removed links* as beneficial and mutual consent links than randomly added links. Since the *removed links* are the real links users would like to build, this result verifies NFG models' effectiveness on explaining users' actions in social networks: users are more likely to build new links such that they can increase their utility from them.

In summary, these results indicate that NFG models can partially describe the evolution of real networks from utility perspective, which motivates us to consider an approach to leverage NFG models to help improve the recommendation performance of link prediction methods. In the following section, we will first introduce a three-phase method. Furthermore, we present a unified model that incorporates Network Formation Game into a Bayesian ranking model for link recommendation.

3.3 Problem Formulation

Given the definitions and empirical analysis above, now we can formally define the problem solved in this paper.

Problem 1. **Exploiting Game Theoretic Analysis for Link Recommendation in Social Networks**: Given a network G, a utility function $U(\cdot)$, the goal is to learn a predictive model from $e_{ij} \in E(G)$ and $U(\cdot)$ such that the model can recommend new links to each user as accurate as possible.

[1]Ciao and Epinions datasets can be found from [33]'s first author webpage

[2]http://www-personal.umich.edu/ mejn/netdata/

[3]http://konect.uni-koblenz.de/networks/facebook-wosn-links

Input: Recommended link number T, a social network $G = (V, E)$, link prediction model $\mathcal{L}$ and a utility function $U(.)$
Output: A set of recommended links $e_{ij} \notin G$
Calculate the utility of each user i via $U_i(G)$.
Learning the link prediction model, $\mathcal{L}$, on G.
Rank the probability of the links $e_{ij} \notin G$ based on $\mathcal{L}$.
Adding links with top-$2T$ highest probability, $\{e_{ij}\}$, to G.
Calculate the utility of each user i via $U_i(G + \{e_{ij}\})$.
for *each link $e_{ij} \notin E(G)$ from the top on the ranking list* **do**
  if $\Delta_i \le 0$ *and* $\Delta_j \le 0$ **then**
    Replace the probability of link e_{ij} with the closest following link $e_{i'j'}$, satisfying $\Delta_{i'} \ge 0$ and $\Delta_{j'} \ge 0$.
  end
end
Re-rank the probability of links.
Return Top-T links.

Algorithm 2: A game theoretic framework for link prediction.

4. PROPOSED METHODS

In this section, we first introduce a three-phase method that employs NFG models to improve link recommendation performance. The proposed framework is quite general and the idea here is straightforward that by using NFG models to calculate the utility difference when adding links to the network, the links which are highly-recommended by link prediction models but cannot improve the utility of connected users will be re-ranked to a lower priority for final recommendation. Besides this three-phase approach, we also propose a novel unified pairwise ranking model, namely, *BPRLGT*, integrating NFG models into a Bayesian ranking model for link recommendation. Our model is built based on Bayesian Personalized Ranking framework (BPR) [27], which always requires sampling technique to select training data. In BPRLGT, we extend the preference assumption of BPR by considering network topology and further propose a game theoretic sampling approach to improve model training.

4.1 A Three-phase Game Theoretic Method for Link Prediction

In this section, we introduce the proposed method that leverages the power of game theory to improve the accuracy of link recommendation in social networks.

Given a network graph G, a utility function $U(\cdot)$, a link prediction model $\mathcal{L}$, our goal is to recommend T links for users. The proposed method includes three phases. At first phase, we utilize $U(\cdot)$ to calculate the current utility of each user i, as $U_i(G)$ on network G. Then a link prediction method $\mathcal{L}$ is trained on G and suggests a list of new links $\{e_{ij}\}$ for users. After getting the recommended links from $\mathcal{L}$, at the beginning of third phase, we add them to G and form a new graph, $G + \{e_{ij}\}$. Based on this new graph, we can compute a new utility of each user by calling $U(\cdot)$ again, say $U_i(G + \{ij\})$. By comparing $\Delta_i = U_i(G + \{ij\}) - U_i(G)$ with 0, we can identify the beneficial links and further adjust the ranking of suggested links. In particular, we can decrease the ranking of those non-beneficial links. Thus, after the third phase, the links in the top ranking positions are approved by both machine learning method and NFG model. In other words, these recommended links not only have high probability to be set up but also are beneficial links once they could be set up. The algorithm for this framework is shown as Algorithm 2.

Although the proposed framework provides a straightforward way to combine NFG models and machine learning models, and it can improve the recommendation performance as we will show in Section 5, we notice that the framework processes the knowledge from NFG models and machine learning models in separated steps, which makes NFG models insufficient in improving machine learning models directly. To better integrate NFG models into machine learning models, we therefore develop a unified Bayesian ranking model with game theoretic sampling techniques for link recommendation.

4.2 A Unified Game Theoretic Ranking Model for Link Recommendation

Since the observed network data only contains binary feedback between two users (1 for an observed link, 0 for no link), the link recommendation problem then can be cast as a one-class recommendation problem, as we introduced in Section 2. Thus, we propose a pairwise ranking method, *BPRLGT* (Bayesian Personalized Ranking for Link recommendation with Game Theory), to solve this problem. Our proposed model is built upon Bayesian Personalized Ranking framework, BPR [27], which requires sampling technique to select pairwise data for Stochastic Gradient Descent (SGD) training. In BPRLGT, we emphasize on designing a game theoretic sampling approach to improve model training. Moreover, BPRLGT model also takes network topology into account, which makes BPRLGT more suitable for link prediction than BPR.

Model Assumption. We first introduce the basic assumption used in BPR [27] in a link recommendation scenario as following,

$$p_{ui} \succeq p_{uj}, for\ e_{ui} \in E(G)\ and\ e_{uj} \notin E(G), \tag{5}$$

where p_{ui} represents a user u's preference on building a link with user i and the assumption requires that p_{ui} should be larger than p_{uj}, $p_{ui} \succeq p_{uj}$, when user u has a direct link with user i rather than j in G. This assumption models the preference order of users when building links with others and are commonly used in one-class recommendation problems.

However, different from existing works [27, 28, 30, 19], here network topology provides us more reliable auxiliary knowledge to solve link prediction problems. Based on the point that people are more likely to make friends with the friends of their friends, we extend the original assumption to a topology-based preference assumption consisting two pairwise preference comparisons,

$$\begin{aligned} &p_{ui} \succeq p_{uj}, p_{uk} \succeq p_{uj}, \\ &for\ e_{ui}\ and\ e_{ik} \in E(G),\ e_{uj}\ and\ e_{uk} \notin E(G). \end{aligned} \tag{6}$$

Compared this with Eq (5), here we further assume that user u prefer to make friends with k other than j since user u and i are friends and k is the friend of i.

Model Formulation. Based on the assumption, we propose an optimization criterion for each user. In particular, the inequality in Eq (6) can be used to maximize the value of the Area Under the ROC Curve (AUC) which is widely used in ranking problems. We utilize a matrix factorization framework to estimate the link preference between users. Specifically, $H \in \mathbb{R}^{M\times k}$ is a low-rank representation with $k \ll M$ for users, thus, the preference value of p_{ui} can be estimated as $H_u H_i^T + b_i$, where H_u is the u_{th} row vector in H representing the user u's latent factors, $b_i \in \mathbb{R}$ is a biased term for user i. Then, for each user u, our goal is to maximize the likelihood of his/her all assumed preference order as Eq (6) shows, which is equivalent to maximize Eq (7):

$$\begin{aligned} &\sum_{e_{ui}\in E(G),\ e_{uj}\notin E(G)} \ln \mathcal{P}(p_{ui} \succeq p_{uj}) \\ &+ \sum_{\substack{e_{ui}\ and\ e_{ik}\in E(G)\\ e_{uj}\ and\ e_{uk}\notin E(G)}} \ln \mathcal{P}(p_{uk} \succeq p_{uj}). \end{aligned} \tag{7}$$

Input: A social network $G = (U, E)$
Output: Parameters $\Theta = \{H \in \mathbb{R}^{M\times k}, b \in \mathbb{R}^M\}$
Initialization:
Initialize H and b
Training:
for *iterations* **do**
  Sample user u from V uniformly;
  Sample user i and k uniformly according to $e_{ui}, e_{ik} \in E(G)$ and $e_{uk} \notin E(G)$;
  Calculate $h_u = H_u H^T + b$ and sort the entries in descending order;
  Scan from the top of h_u, find the first j satisfying $\Delta_u = U_u(G + e_{uh_u(v)}) - U_u(G) \leq 0$;
  for *#training sample* **do**
    Calculate $\frac{\partial \mathcal{O}(\Theta)}{\Theta_{u,i,k,j}}$;
    Update H_u, H_i, H_k, H_j, b according to Eq (9);
  end
end

Algorithm 3: Bayesian Personalized Ranking for Link recommendation with Game Theory.

When optimizing for the AUC, it is common practice to work with a differentiable function, such as a sigmoid function which has the form $\sigma(x) = \frac{1}{1+e^{-x}}$, to approximate the function $\mathcal{P}(.)$, so that the objective function is differentiable. Based on this trick, our goal is to maximize the following objective function,

$$\begin{aligned} \mathcal{O}_u(\Theta) = \sum_{u\in V}[&\sum_{\substack{e_{ui}\in E(G)\\ e_{uj}\notin E(G)}} \ln(\sigma(p_{ui} - p_{uj})) \\ + &\sum_{\substack{e_{ui}\ and\ e_{ik}\in E(G)\\ e_{uj}\ and\ e_{uk}\notin E(G)}} \ln(\sigma(p_{uk} - p_{uj}))] \\ - &\ regularization, \end{aligned} \tag{8}$$

where a regularization term is used to avoid overfitting in the learning process, $p_{ui} = H_u H_i^T + b_i$, $p_{uk} = H_u H_k^T + b_k$ and $p_{uj} = H_u H_j^T + b_j$. We adopt ℓ_2-norm regularization terms for model parameters $\Theta = \{H, b\}$.

Model Learning. We employ the widely used stochastic gradient descent (SGD) algorithm to optimize the objective function in Eq (8). The main process of SGD is to sample a training instance. Here we first randomly select a user u, then we pick a triple of users i,j,k such that $e_{ui}, e_{ik} \in E(G)$ and $e_{uk}, e_{uj} \notin E(G)$. Specifically, for each selected instance, we calculate the derivative and update the corresponding parameters Θ by walking along the ascending gradient direction,

$$\Theta^{t+1} = \Theta^t + \eta \times \frac{\partial \mathcal{O}_u(\Theta)}{\partial \Theta}. \tag{9}$$

Game Theoretic Sampling Strategy. Since the learning method we use in this paper is stochastic gradient descent (SGD), the selected training instances might have great impact on the recommendation performance. Here we adopt the utility analysis in Network Formation Game to develop a game theoretic sampling strategy for model training. In each iteration, the model needs to sample a tuple of users $\{u, i, j, k\}$. First, a user u is uniformly sampled from V, then i and k are sampled uniformly according to $e_{ui}\ and\ e_{ik} \in E(G),\ and\ e_{uk} \notin E(G)$. Then we calculate a preference vector $h_u = H_u H^T + b \in \mathbb{R}^M$ for user u based on current estimation of H. We rank the elements in h_u in descending order and let $h_u(v)$ be the user who has the v_{th} largest value in h_u. Then the game theoretic sampling strategy can be described as follows: scan from the top of h_u, find the first $h_u(v)$ satisfying $\Delta_u = U_u(G + e_{uh_u(v)}) - U_u(G) \leq 0$, set $j = h_u(v)$.

The key point of the sampling strategy is to select effective training instances by examining users' utility difference. In particular, we check the candidate j from the user with highest preference score of u, which is estimated by current model parameters. The idea is that if a user j is strongly recommended to u by current parameters but adding edge e_{uj} cannot improve u's utility, we need to punish the model preference on j by maximizing the preference difference between p_{ui} and p_{uj}. In this way, BPRLGT not only maximize the likelihood of observed preference order but also consider the utility of each user during the learning process. The detailed algorithm is shown in Algorithm 3.

5. EXPERIMENTAL EVALUATION

In this section, we conduct several experiments to evaluate the performance of the proposed three-phase method and the unified ranking method. We demonstrate the recommendation accuracy, analyze the parameters and the convergence of the proposed methods. The results show that link recommendation performance can be improved under the help of game theoretic analysis.

5.1 Experimental Setup

First, we introduce the datasets we use in Section 3.2.2. We use four real world datasets to validate the performance of the proposed methods, namely, Ciao, Epinions, COL and Facebook. Ciao and Epinions are online product review websites. Both websites allow users to build their social connections with others in order to share their experience and knowledge on the products. COL describes a scientific collaboration network between authors submitting papers to *www.arxiv.org*. Facebook is one of the most popular social networking websites that users can make friends with others on it. The statistics of the four datasets are shown in Table. 1. The datasets are preprocessed by eliminating users with less than three neighbors. For each dataset, we randomly split it into a training part, used for model training, and a test part, used for model evaluation. Similar to [24], for each user u, we select 80% of their observed social links as P_u and leave the remainder as T_u for testing. Cross-validation is applied to find best parameters in the proposed methods, δ in LBR model is set as 0.25, k is set as 10 and learning rate, η, of each link prediction model is set as 0.01.

Our experiments are intended to answer the following questions:

1. Can the proposed three-phase method and unified ranking model improve the performance of existing link prediction methods?
2. Whether the proposed game theoretic sampling strategy help improve recommendation performance?
3. How does the value of k in *BPRLGT* affect model performance?

We use four popular metrics, *Recall@K* (R@K), *NDCG* (Normalized Discounted Cumulative Gain), Accuracy and *Area under the curve* (AUC), to measure the recommendation quality of our proposed approach in comparison to baseline methods.

The average AUC statistic is defined as

$$AUC = \frac{1}{M}\sum_{u\in M}\frac{1}{|E(u)|}\sum_{(i,j)\in E(u)}\mathbf{1}(x_{ui} > x_{uj}), \qquad (10)$$

where $E(u) = \{(i,j)|(u,i) \in T_u \wedge (u,j) \notin (P_u \cup T_u)\}$ and $\mathbf{1}(\cdot)$ is an indicator function.

For each user u, $DCG@K$ considers the ranking of the recommended users by discounting the importance and is defined as

$$DCG@K = \sum_{i=1}^{K}\frac{2^{rel_i} - 1}{\log_2(i+1)}, \qquad (11)$$

where rel_i represents the preference score of user i (we use a binary value for this quantity, if $e_{ui} \in T_u$, $rel_i = 1$; otherwise, 0). $NDCG$ is the ratio of the DCG value to the ideal DCG value for that user. The ideal value of DCG comes from the best ranking function for the user. Here we set $K = M - |P_u|$ where M is the total number of users.

Following [32], we also use the prediction accuracy metric to measure the recommendation quality of link prediction. Specifically, the method ranks candidate links in decreasing order of confidence and we take the first $|T_u|$ candidates as the set of predicted links, denoted as C, for recommendation. Then the prediction accuracy (Accuracy) can be calculated as,

$$Accuracy = \frac{|C \cap T_u|}{|T_u|} \qquad (12)$$

where $|\cdot|$ is the size of a set.

5.2 Comparison Methods

In order to demonstrate the benefits of our methods, we adopt several link prediction methods as baselines and compare their performance for link recommendation.

- **Common Neighbor (CN):** This is a basic heuristic method for link prediction which counts the number of common neighbors for link prediction.
- **Adamic-Adar (AA):** This method is an extension of common neighbor count method, where the link confidence score is computed as following,

$$AA(i,j) = \sum_{k:ik,jk\in E(G)}\frac{1}{\log deg(k)} \qquad (13)$$

  where $deg(k)$ is the degree of node k in graph.
- **BPR:** This method [27] proposes a pairwise assumption for item ranking and it is a well-known method for one-class recommendation. Here we employ it as a baseline method to compare with our proposed pairwise ranking method.
- **hTrust:** This method [32] is one of the state-of-the-art method for link prediction by exploiting homophily effect between users.
- **FactLog:** This method [24] also exploits matrix factorization framework for link prediction. Here we use log-loss with sigmoid function as the objective function with the code provided at *http://cseweb.ucsd.edu/ akmenon/code/*.
- **BPRLGT:** This is the proposed Bayesian ranking method, which extends the pairwise assumption by considering topological structure of networks and arms with a game theoretic sampling strategy.

The experimental results are shown in Table 2. In this table, for a specific method **B**, the column **B** demonstrates its performance without the help of proposed framework while **B*** describes the performance of method **B** when a NFG model is used to adjust the ranking results. The results here are achieved when LBR model is used in the framework and *BPRLGT*.

Table 2: **Recommendation performance of different methods on four real-world datasets. For a specific method B, the column B demonstrates its performance without the help of proposed framework while B* describes the performance of method B when a NFG model is used to adjust the ranking results. The results here are achieved when *LBR* model is used.**

Dataset	Metrics	AA	AA*	CN	CN*	BPR	BPR*	hTrust	hTrust*	FactLog	FactLog*	BPRLGT
Ciao	R@5	0.010	0.0104	0.003	0.0037	0.007	0.0076	0.0186	0.0192	0.0275	0.0281	**0.0545**
	R@10	0.015	0.0159	0.011	0.01125	0.0122	0.0127	0.0375	0.0377	0.0621	0.0627	**0.1044**
	NDCG	0.2094	0.2099	0.1834	0.1855	0.2082	0.2090	0.2201	0.2236	0.2088	0.2092	**0.3101**
	Accuracy	0.081	0.086	0.032	0.034	0.134	0.148	0.172	0.179	0.159	0.163	**0.1831**
	AUC	0.562	0.568	0.546	0.551	0.6663	0.6703	0.6452	0.6477	0.6882	0.6884	**0.9021**
Epinions	R@5	0.0127	0.0129	0.0083	0.0091	0.0311	0.0323	0.0356	0.0359	0.0323	0.0330	**0.040**
	R@10	0.0231	0.0238	0.0162	0.0175	0.0443	0.0452	0.0547	0.0551	0.0521	0.0522	**0.0620**
	NDCG	0.1365	0.1373	0.124	0.1266	0.2241	0.2268	0.2378	0.2381	0.2314	0.2322	**0.2485**
	Accuracy	0.079	0.088	0.074	0.082	0.168	0.175	0.217	0.2202	0.1819	0.1842	**0.2380**
	AUC	0.5724	0.5766	0.5421	0.5508	0.8011	0.8042	0.833	0.8341	0.8211	0.8227	**0.8562**
COL	R@5	0.043	0.045	0.0034	0.0041	0.0012	0.0014	0.03924	0.04	0.05924	0.05930	**0.0715**
	R@10	0.0833	0.0841	0.0062	0.0067	0.0021	0.0025	0.08734	0.0882	0.09234	0.0928	**0.1006**
	NDCG	0.0853	0.0860	0.061	0.0618	0.0573	0.0582	0.1288	0.1300	0.1433	0.1444	**0.1491**
	Accuracy	0.0966	0.098	0.0391	0.0421	0.088	0.0894	0.118	0.121	0.1392	0.1397	**0.1481**
	AUC	0.761	0.7682	0.6233	0.6313	0.6174	0.6188	0.7323	0.7355	0.8232	0.8244	**0.8440**
Facebook	R@5	0.0032	0.00326	0.0017	0.00174	0.0025	0.0256	0.0275	0.0278	0.0321	0.0323	**0.0370**
	R@10	0.0048	0.0051	0.00246	0.00251	0.0044	0.0048	0.0532	0.0538	0.055	0.0562	**0.0618**
	NDCG	0.2214	0.2218	0.1832	0.1838	0.2191	0.2199	0.2934	0.2945	0.3341	0.3352	**0.3740**
	Accuracy	0.0126	0.0132	0.0042	0.0051	0.009	0.0093	0.0623	0.0643	0.0681	0.0683	**0.0769**
	AUC	0.6682	0.6685	0.5823	0.5848	0.6461	0.6488	0.7245	0.7248	0.7823	0.7844	**0.9642**

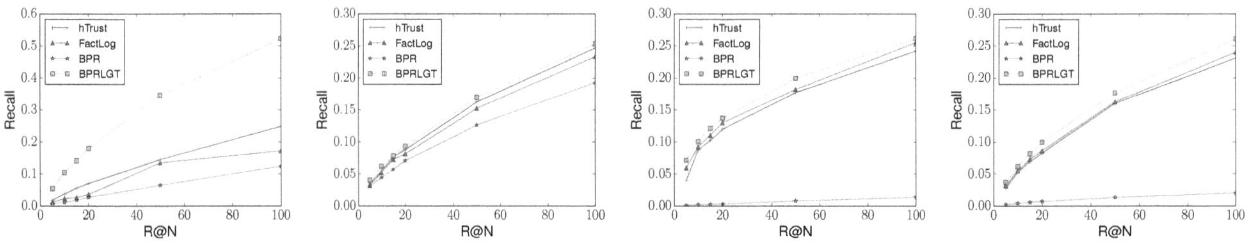

(a) Ciao (b) Epinions (c) COL (d) Facebook

Figure 2: Recommendation performance comparisons (Recall@N) on four datasets.

5.3 Summary of Experimental Results

Performance Comparison. Based on the results in Table 2, we can see that the proposed unified model clearly outperforms the comparison methods. *CN* and *AA* are two static scoring methods using only local network structure information for link prediction, which often lead to suboptimal performance. *BPR* is a popular pairwise ranking method for one-class recommendation problem and here we use it to model users' preference order when building links. However, it does not perform well because it misses network topology and just uses a uniform sampling strategy for model training. *hTrust* is a state-of-the-art point wise method for link prediction, incorporating low-rank matrix factorization and homophily regularization terms. *FactLog* also exploits matrix factorization framework for link prediction and also take advantage of network topology as explicit feature for model learning. Although both *hTrust* and *FactLog* methods improve the performance of link prediction compared with *BPR* and other heuristic methods, they still cannot beat the proposed *BPRLGT* model. *BPRLGT* carries on the merits of *BPR* and further extends *BPR*'s assumption by directly modeling users' preference on their second-degree friends. Moreover, when learning the model, the proposed game theoretic sampling strategy allows *BPRLGT* to consider users' utility difference for effective training instance selection. Based on these, *BPRLGT* obtains significant improvements over all baseline methods on all datasets.

Detailed results for *Recall@N* can be found in Figure 2. We can see that on Ciao dataset, *BPRLGT* achieves clearly better performance than other methods. For other datasets, although the curves of different methods seem to be close to each other, *BPRLGT* consistently outperform baselines on different *Recall@N* measure points. We also find that compared with *BPRLGT*, *BPR* always performs bad, especially in COL dataset. The reason we consider is that *BPR* samples training instances via uniform sampling and do not consider network topology information. Since users' observed links are always very limited and there are huge number of unobserved links acting as candidate links to be recommended, thus the original assumption of *BPR*, Eq (5), cannot correctly capture users' preference on building links. This also indicates the necessity of proposing new pairwise preference assumption for link prediction, as *BPRLGT* does.

We also take experiments to evaluate the performance of the proposed framework. For a specific method **B**, the column **B** demonstrates its performance without the help of proposed framework while **B*** describes the performance of method **B** when a NFG model is used to adjust the ranking results. The results here are achieved when *LBR* model is used since *LBR* performs better in

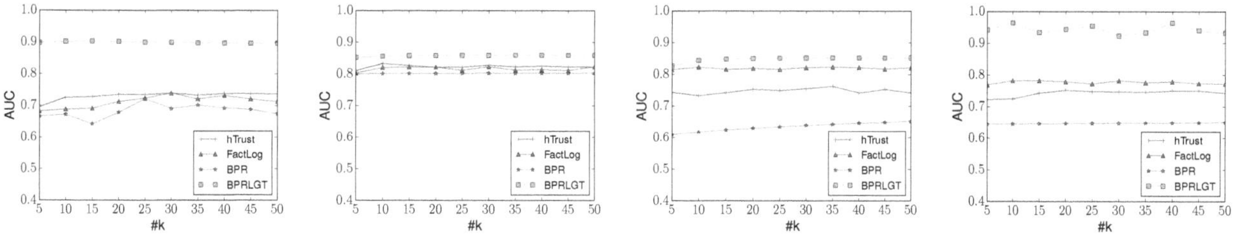

(a) Ciao (b) Epinions (c) COL (d) Facebook

Figure 3: Effects of latent factor number.

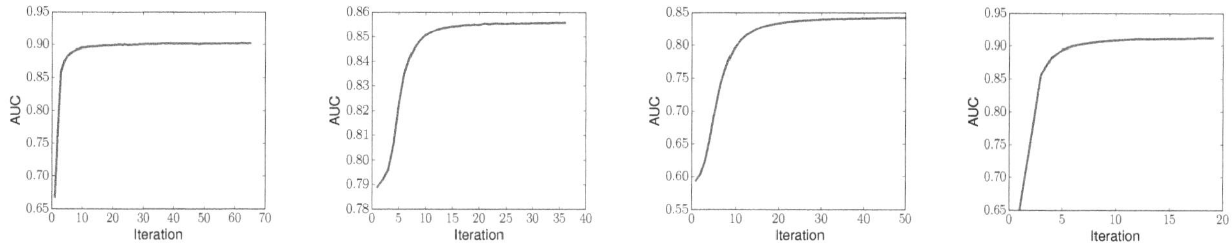

(a) Ciao (b) Epinions (c) COL (d) Facebook

Figure 4: Convergence analysis.

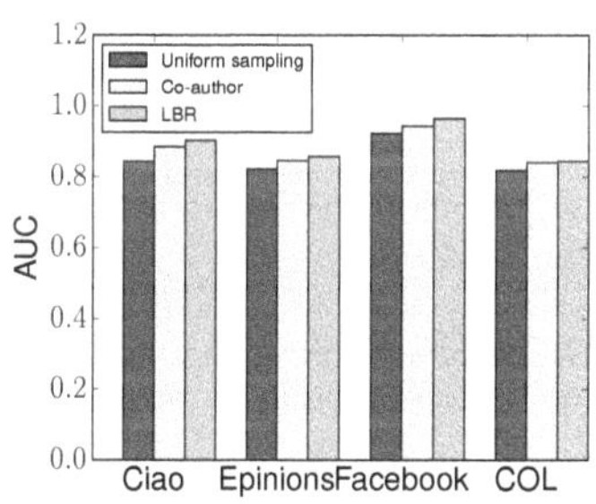

Figure 5: Effects of sampling strategies.

Sec 3.2.2. From the results, on all datasets, we find that exploiting game theoretic analysis can improve prediction performance for all link prediction methods. By exchanging the positions of lower-ranked but beneficial links with those higher-ranked but non-beneficial links, our proposed framework can help link prediction methods achieve better performance, which verifies the contribution of Network Formation Game. In summary, with the help of game theoretic analysis, both the proposed framework and the unified ranking model can always improve the performance of baseline methods.

5.4 Analysis and Discussion

Impact of k. Since *BPRLGT* is built upon matrix factorization framework, which requires us to predefine the number of latent factors in advance, here we take experiments to investigate the impact of the number of latent factor k on recommendation performance. The results are shown in Figure 3. We use AUC as evaluation metric and vary the value of k from 5 to 50. We find that on all datasets, all comparison methods perform stable with different values of k and *BPRLGT* always achieves best and stable performance. The results verify the significant contribution of the extended preference assumption as Eq (6) and game theoretic sampling strategy. Moreover, we also notice that on COL and Facebook datasets, *BPR* shows clearly poor performance than other methods. The reasons we consider are that the observed feedback in these datasets is too sparse and *BPR* does not consider network topology to help select effective instances for better learning.

Impact of Game Theoretic Sampling Strategy. In this subsection, we compare the performance when we use different Network Formation Game models in *BPRLGT*. The results are shown in Figure 5. We find that on all datasets, *BPRLGT* with game theoretic sampling strategy achieves better performance over uniformly sampling strategy. Moreover, by using *LBR* model, it achieves best performance over Co-author models. Through cross validation, δ and $\overline{x}$ here are set as 0.25 and 1 in *LBR*, respectively. This results verify the simulation results in Section 3.2.2 and also demonstrate the advantages of incorporating game theoretic analysis into machine learning models for link prediction.

Convergence Analysis. We further investigate the convergence of *BPRLGT*. Figure 4 shows the convergence analysis of *BPRLGT* model on different datasets. We see that our method always converges within 30 iterations on all datasets, since *BPRLGT* incorporates network topology into the model assumption and also benefits from utility analysis from NFG models, making it learn more effective knowledge in each iteration. The fast convergence ensures its ability to scale up to huge data.

6. CONCLUSION

In this paper, we study the problem of exploiting game theoretic analysis for link recommendation in social networks. We first propose a three-phase game theoretic framework combining the models in Network Formation Game with the machine learning models.

Besides this framework, we also develop a unified model by incorporating Network Formation Game into a Bayesian ranking model for link recommendation. Specifically, we design a game theoretic sampling approach to improve the model training process. Experiments on four real datasets validate the effectiveness of the proposed methods for link recommendation.

The idea and methods proposed in this paper represents a novel and interesting research direction. There are several potential directions for future work. One straightforward extending is to study the performance when other Network Formation models are incorporated into the proposed framework and ranking model. Moreover, it is also interesting to investigate how to combine contextual knowledge with Network Formation models for link recommendation. Furthermore, integrating game theory with other machine learning models, such as Markov Decision Process, should also be an intriguing direction for future research.

7. ACKNOWLEDGEMENTS

This research was in part supported by grants from the National Grand Fundamental Research 973 Program of China (No. 2014CB340405), the Research Grants Council of the Hong Kong Special Administrative Region, China (Project No. CUHK 413213), and Microsoft Research Asia Regional Seed Fund in Big Data Research (Grant No. FY13-RES-SPONSOR-036).

8. REFERENCES

[1] R. Andersen, C. Borgs, J. Chayes, U. Feige, A. Flaxman, A. Kalai, V. Mirrokni, and M. Tennenholtz. Trust-based recommendation systems: an axiomatic approach. *In WWW.*, 2008.

[2] A. I. Badev. Social networks and the stepping stone effect: The case of tobacco and marijuana. *working paper*, 2014.

[3] Ballester, Coralio, and A. CalvU-Armengol. Moderate interactions in games with induced complementarities. 2007.

[4] Ballester, Coralio, A. CalvU-Armengol, and Y. Zenou. Who's who in networks. wanted: the key player. *Econometrica*, 2006.

[5] M. Bayati, C. Borgs, J. Chayes, Y. Kanoria, and A. Montanari. Bargaining dynamics in exchange networks. 2010.

[6] G. Beigi, H. Alvari, M. Jalili, and G. Sukthankar. Leveraging community detection for accurate trust prediction. *ASE ICSC*, 2014.

[7] Y. Bramoulle, R. Kranton, and M. DiAmours. Strategic interaction and networks. *CIRPEE Working Paper*, 2011.

[8] S. Currarini and M. Morelli. Network formation with sequential demands. *Review of Economic Design*, 2010.

[9] L.-N. David and K. Jon. The link prediction problem for social networks. *CIKM*, 2003.

[10] Y. Dong, J. Tang, S. Wu, J. Tian, N. Chawla, J. Rao, and H. Cao. Link prediction and recommendation across heterogenous social networks. *In ICDM*, 2012.

[11] B. Dutta, S. Ghosal, and D. Ray. Farsighted network formation. *Journal of Economic Theory*, 2005.

[12] R. Guha, R. Kumar, P. Raghavan, and A. Tomkins. Propagation of trust and distrust. *In WWW*, 2004.

[13] Y. Hu, Y. Koren, and C. Volin-sky. Collaborative filtering for implicit feedback datasets. *In ICDM*, pages 263–272, 2008.

[14] M. Jackson and Y. Zenou. Games on networks. *Handbook of Game Theory*, 2012.

[15] M. O. Jackson. A survey of models of network formation: Stability and efficiency. *Group Formation in Economics. Networks, Clubs and Coalitions*, 2004.

[16] M. O. Jackson and A. Wolinsky. A strategic model of social and economic networks. *Journal of Economic Theory*, pages 44–74, 1996.

[17] P. Kohli, Y. Bachrach, T. Graepel, G. Smyth, M. Armstrong, D. Stillwell, and M. Kearns. Behavioral game theory on online social networks: Colonel blotto is on facebook. 2011.

[18] P. Kohli, Y. Bachrach, D. Stillwell, M. Kearns, and R. Herbrich. Colonel blotto on facebook: The effect of social relations on strategic interaction. *Proceedings of the 3rd Annual ACM Web Science Conference*, 2012.

[19] A. Krohn-Grimberghe, L. Drumond, C. Freudenthaler, and L. Schmidt-Thieme. Multi-relational matrix factorization using bayesian personalized ranking for social network data. *In WSDM*, pages 173–182, 2012.

[20] C. Lee, M. Pham, N. Kim, M. K. Jeong, D. K. Lin, and W. A. Chavalitwongse. A novel link prediction approach for scale free networks. *In WWW*, 2014.

[21] J. Leskovec, D. Huttenlocher, and J. Kleinberg. Predicting positive and negative links in online social networks. *In WWW*, 2010.

[22] W. S. Lin, H. V. Zhao, and K.J.RayLiu. Game-theoretic strategies and equilibriums in multimedia fingerprinting social networks. *IEEE TRANSACTIONS ON MULTIMEDIA*, 2011.

[23] A. Mele. A structural model of segregation in social networks. *working paper*, 2010.

[24] A. K. Menon and C. Elkan. Link prediction via matrix factorization. *In ECML/PKDD.*, 2011.

[25] R. Pan, Y. Zhou, B. Cao, N. N. Liu, R. Lukose, M. Scholz, and Q. Yang. One-class collaborative filtering. *In ICDM*, pages 502–511, 2008.

[26] A. D. Paula, S. Richards-Shubik, and E. Tamer. Identification of preferences in network formation games. 2015.

[27] S. Rendle, C. Freuden-thaler, Z. Gantner, and L. Schmidt-Thieme. Bpr:bayesian personalized ranking from implicit feedback. *In UAI*, pages 452–461, 2009.

[28] S. Rendle, C. Freuden-thaler, and L. S. Thieme. Factorizing personalized markov chains for next-basket recommendation. *In WWW*, pages 811–820, 2010.

[29] S. Rendle and C. Freudenthaler. Improving pairwise learning for item recommendation from implicit feedback. *In WSDM*, 2014.

[30] S. Rendle and L. Schmidt-Thieme. Pairwise interaction tensor factorization for personalized tag recommendation. *In WSDM*, pages 81–90, 2010.

[31] B. Skyrms and Pemantle. A dynamic model of social network formation. *National Academy of Sciences*, 2000.

[32] J. Tang, H. Gao, X. Hu, and H. Liu. Exploiting homophily effect for trust prediction. *In WSDM*, 2013.

[33] J. Tang, H. Gao, and H. Liu. mtrust: Discerning multi-faceted trust in a connected world. *In WSDM*, 2012.

[34] J. Tang, H. Gao, H. Liu, and A. D. Sarma. etrust: Understanding trust evolution in an online world. *In KDD.*, 2012.

[35] L. Xiao, Y. Chen, W. S. Lin, and K. J. R. Liu. Indirect reciprocity security game for large-scale wireless networks. *IEEE Transactions on Information Forensics and Security*, 2012.

[36] Y. Yao, H. Tong, X. Yan, F. Xu, and J. Lu. Matri a multi-aspect and transitive trust inference model. *In WWW*, 2013.

[37] G. Zappella, A. Karatzoglou, and L. Baltrunas. Games of friends: A game-theoretical approach for link prediction in online social networks. *Workshop in AAAI*, 2013.

[38] T. Zhao, J. J. McAuley, and I. King. Leveraging social connections to improve personalized ranking for collaborative filtering. In *In CIKM*, 2014.

[39] C. Ziegler and J. Golbeck. Investigating interactions of trust and interest similarity. *Decision Support Systems.*, 2007.

Extracting Interest Tags for Non-famous Users in Social Network

Wei He
Renmin University of China
Beijing, China
heweihust@126.com

Hongyan Liu
Tsinghua University
Beijing, China
hyliu@tsinghua.edu.cn

Jun He
Renmin University of China
Beijing, China
hejun@ruc.edu.cn

Shu Tang
Renmin University of China
Beijing, China
tangshu615@ruc.edu.cn

Xiaoyong Du
Renmin University of China
Beijing, China
duyong@ruc.edu.cn

ABSTRACT

Inferring interests of users in social network is important for many applications such as personalized search, recommender systems and online advertising. Most previous studies inferred users' interests based on text posted in social network, which is usually not related to their interests. In this paper, we propose a modified topic model, *Bi-Labeled LDA* with a term weighting scheme, to extract interest tags for users in social network. The proposed model utilize only users' relationship information without requirement for text information, and incorporates supervision into traditional LDA. Specifically, we introduce method to extract tags for non-famous user through their relationship with famous users in Twitter, and study why a non-famous user follows famous users simultaneously. Comparison with state-of-the-art methods on real dataset shows that our method is far more superior in terms of precision and recall of the extracted tag set, and also more applicable for many personalized applications. Besides, we find that a reasonable term weighting scheme can actually improve the performance further.

Categories and Subject Descriptors

J.4 [**Computer Applications**]: Social and behavioral sciences

General Terms

Algorithms, Experimentation

Keywords

Tag extraction; topic model; Twitter; user interests

Permission to make digital or hard copies of all or part of this work for personal or classroom use is granted without fee provided that copies are not made or distributed for profit or commercial advantage and that copies bear this notice and the full citation on the first page. Copyrights for components of this work owned by others than ACM must be honored. Abstracting with credit is permitted. To copy otherwise, or republish, to post on servers or to redistribute to lists, requires prior specific permission and/or a fee. Request permissions from Permissions@acm.org.

CIKM'15, October 19–23, 2015, Melbourne, Australia.
© 2015 ACM. ISBN 978-1-4503-3794-6/15/10 ...$15.00.
DOI: http://dx.doi.org/10.1145/2806416.2806514.

1. INTRODUCTION

All kinds of social networks such as Twitter are increasingly being used to discover topics of users' interests. Users' interests are very useful for many applications such as personalized search, recommender systems and online advertising. In this paper, we focus on extracting interest tags for non-famous users[1] in Twitter.

A key challenge of this problem is how to accurately infer the topics of interest for a Twitter user u. Most prior studies attempted to infer the topics of interest from the tweet content posted or retweeted by user u [7, 8, 10, 13, 16, 17], mainly using topic models (e.g., Labeled Latent Dirichlet Allocation [11], a supervised version of LDA). To the best of our knowledge, Labeled LDA is one of the most competitive models for solving this problem using tweet content information [1, 8]. Some other approaches used both the tweet content and the social relationship information, mining users' topics of interest from tweets and re-ranking users' interests based on underlying social network using technique such as Random Walk [10, 16]. However, Twitter users often post interest-unrelated tweets about their lives or have conversation with their friends [3, 15, 17], and 82.2% Twitter users post less than 100 tweets per year [5], which both make it difficult to infer meaningful interests from tweets.

To address this problem, Bhattacharya et al. [1] first deduced the topical expertise of famous Twitter users based on their Twitter Lists features, and then transitively inferred the interests of the users who follow them. Although their approach is very effective for deducing the topical expertise of famous users, it doesn't perform well for non-famous users. Our experiments show that it always recommends some common tags such as "celeb", "news", "media", etc. Ding et al. [3] extracted interest tags from Twitter user biographies, which heavily depends on the availability of users' biographies. Lappas et al. [5] inferred the famous aspects of popular Twitter users using traditional LDA to model non-famous users' followings, but they ignored the similarities between famous users, treating every famous user as a unique id.

In this paper, we extract interest tags for non-famous users based on the underlying social network, without using text

[1] We define users who are followed by less than 2000 users as non-famous users, and users who are followed by at least 2000 users as famous users [4, 5].

content information. In particular, taking Twitter as the social network, we first deduce the topical expertise of famous Twitter users based on their Twitter List features, represented by a bag of tags. And then extract interest tags for non-famous users using a modified LDA model, *Bi-Labeled LDA* with a term weighting scheme. People usually follow a famous user for personal interest reason, while follow a non-famous user usually not for personal interest reason but because they are friends, families, etc. or just following each other back [19]. Based on this observation, we design the supervised topic model, Bi-Labeled LDA to model **why a non-famous user follows famous users**, and ultimately infer a set of tags to decribe a user's interests.

The major contributions we make in this paper are as follows:

- We propose a new topic model, *Bi-Labeled LDA*, which restricts both the document topic distribution and the word topic distribution. Using this model, we model why a non-famous user follows famous users, and infer tags (users' interest topics) for them effectively. Comparing to existing model, it not only takes the similarity between famous users into consideration, but also incorporates more supervision information into traditional LDA model.
- Our methodology has no requirement for users' publishing text information, i.e. it can be used to extract interest tags for any user who follows a few famous users in social network.
- We compare the interest tags extracted by our method with those extracted by existing state-of-the-art approaches. We find that interest tags extracted by our method are far superior to others either in accuracy or recall, and our method is more applicable for many personalized applications.

The rest of the paper is organized as follows. In section 2, related work is discussed. The method to deduce the topical expertise of famous users is introduced in section 3. And, the proposed supervised LDA model to extract interest tags for non-famous users is presented in section 4. In section 5, Experiment setup and results are described. Finally, conclusions are drawn in section 6.

2. RELATED WORK

In this section, we briefly review some closely related work and point out the differences compared to our own work, as well as the details of our comparative methods.

Most prior studies attempted to mine the interests of users from the tweets posted or retweeted by users [7, 8, 10, 13, 16, 17], mainly using topic models such as LDA. Xu et al. [17] proposed a modified author-topic model named twitter-user model to discover users' topics of interest on Twitter by filtering out interest-unrelated tweets from the aggregated user tweets. For each tweet they introduced a latent variable to indicate whether it is related to its author's interests. Zhao et al. [20] developed a new topic model named Twitter-LDA to improve the quality of topics by restricting each tweet to one topic and a common background topic. Quercia et al. [9] inferred users' topics of interest with a supervised topic model, Labeled Latent Dirichlet Allocation (*Labeled LDA*) and showed it to be more effective than other LDA. Specifically, *Labeled LDA* uses the same underlying mechanisms as traditional LDA, but each topic is seeded with a label (i.e. a word chosen by the researcher), to help anchor the topic extraction process. Quercia et al. labeled each Twitter user using some text classification APIs, while Ottoni et al. [8] selected the 300 most common hash-tags from all the tweets as topic labels. Besides, Bhattacharya et al. [1] used Labeled LDA as the most competitive baseline to show the efficacy of their method to infer user interests in Twitter. Some other approaches used both tweets and network information, mining users' topics of interest from tweets and then re-ranking users' interests based on underlying social network based on techniques such as Random Walk [10, 16]. Si et al. [13] proposed a topic model called *tag-LDA* to model the generative process of words and tags of a labeled document at the same time. After all, all the methods above rely on the tweet content. However, Twitter users often post noisy tweets about their daily lives or have conversation with their friends, which are usually not related to their interests [3, 15, 17], and 82.2% Twitter users post less than 100 tweets per year [5], which both make it difficult to infer meaningful interests from tweets.

To address this problem, most prior studies focused on users' other features, such as biographies and network information, and incorporated extra information such as Wikipedia and human effort [1, 3, 5, 6]. Bhattacharya et al. [1] first deduced the topical expertise of famous Twitter users based on their Twitter Lists features, and then transitively inferred the interests of the users who follow them. Although their approach is very effective for deducing the topical expertise of famous users, it doesn't perform well for non-famous users. Our experiments show that it always recommends some famous common tags such as "celeb", "news", "media", etc. to non-famous users. Ding et al. [3] extracted interest tags from Twitter user biographies, with a sequential labeling model based on automatically constructed labeled data. However, their approach heavily depends on the availability of users' biographies, actually only 22% of Twitter users have a biography on their profile [1] and Ding et al. revealed that only 28.8% of biographies contain meaningful interest tags. Then even in the most ideal case, they are only able to recommend interest tags for 6.336% users in Twitter. Lappas et al. [5] inferred the famous aspects of popular Twitter users using two standard LDA models to respectively model the generative process of non-famous users' followings and famous users' tweets as well as other related text (such as, search results with their names as queries). The problem of their approach is that they do not consider the similarities between famous users, treating every famous user as a unique id.

Our proposed model, *Bi-Labeled LDA*, extracts interest tags for non-famous users based on the underlying social network, without using text content information. In addition, by mapping each famous user with a tag set, it takes the similarities between famous users into consideration.

3. EXTRACTING TOPICAL EXPERTISE OF FAMOUS TWITTER USERS

In Twitter, List is introduced to help users organize their followings. A user can create a List, specify a List name and an optional description, and then add some of its followings to this List. Usually, a famous Twitter user is a member of many Lists. For instance, Barack Obama is a member of

Lists such as "politics", "government", "celeb", "leader" and etc.

Bhattacharya et al. [1] proposed a methodology to discover the topical expertise of famous Twitter users utilizing Twitter List names and descriptions. Based on their method, to determine the topical expertise of a popular Twitter user v, we first collect all the Lists which have v as a member, and then extract frequently occurring terms (unigrams and bigrams which are identified as nouns or adjectives) from the List names and descriptions. For each term, we count its frequency, the number of times it occurs in the list names or descriptions. In particular, if term t has frequency no less than 10, we identify v as an expert on a topic t, and we regard t as a tag of user v. As a result, each famous user is temporarily tagged by the set of terms selected.

After we extract tags for each famous user, for each distinct tag, we count the number of users who have the tag. We find out that there are a lot of meaningless or misspelled low-frequency tags such as "guest", "support", "page", "stat-up", etc. Therefore, we only retain those tags which occur in more than 1% users' tags. We also translate all the high-frequency non-English tags into English, such as "nieuws" (Dutch) to "news", "esporte" (Portuguese) to "sports", etc . and merge all the tags with the identical meaning, such as "famous people" and "celebrity", "gaming" and "game". After this step, we get 159 meaningful and qualified tags, and we keep only these tags as all users' candidate tag set. Through this method, 64.2% of famous users who have at least 5000 followers in our dataset have at least tag. We will show that there is no need for every famous user to have tags later.

4. INFERRING TAGS FOR NON-FAMOUS TWITTER USERS

After extracting the topical expertise of famous Twitter users, we know that which aspects a famous Twitter user is an expert at or famous in, and we aggregate all the tags of famous users a non-famous user u follows as u's tag set, which is considered as candidate aspects u may be interested in. To refine the tag set for each user, we need to know why a non-famous user follows a famous user, since a famous user is usually famous in several aspects, and more famous in one aspect than in any other aspects. For instance, Lance Armstrong[2] is more famous as a world-class cyclist than as a cancer survivor. When a user follows Lance Armstrong, he may be interested in cycling, or he may also be a cancer survivor and interested in charity.

In order to figure out **why a non-famous user u follows a famous user v?** We suppose that each famous user v is expert at or famous in several aspects, and in each aspect a non-famous user u who follows v has interest of different level. For example, when a user follows Lance Armstrong, he may be more interested in cycling than in charity with 70% to 30%. Here are our intuitions:

1. If a non-famous user u follows more users who are famous in aspect a than the ones who are famous in aspect b, u follows a user v who is famous both in aspect a and b more because of interest in aspect a than in b.
2. If a famous user v is followed by more non-famous users with interest in aspect a than b, then v is followed by a non-famous user u more due to u's interest in aspect a than in b.

Lappas et al. [5] inferred the famous aspects of popular Twitter users using two standard LDA to respectively model the generative process of non-famous users' followings and famous users' tweets as well as other related text (such as, search results with their names as queries). The problem of their approach is that they do not consider the similarities between famous Twitter users, treating every famous user as a unique id. Usually in every aspect, there are many famous Twitter users, so when two different non-famous users follow two different set of famous users in the same aspect, the two non-famous users should have the same interest in the aspect, but the approach of Lappas et al. fails to find it out because they treat each famous people differently. Hence, we need to take the similarities between famous users into consideration. Based on our above-mentioned discussions, we propose a modified LDA model, *Bi-Labeled LDA*, together with a term weighting scheme to model the generative process of non-famous users' followings, taking not only the above two intuitions but also the similarities between famous users into consideration.

As we mentioned above, since people usually follow a famous user for personal interest reason, while follow a non-famous user usually not for personal interest reason but because they are friends, families, etc. or just following each other back [19], we remove all the non-famous users from users' followings, and use *Bi-Labeled LDA* to model why a non-famous user follows famous users.

4.1 Bi-Labeled LDA

Bi-Labeled LDA is a probabilistic graphical model that describes a process for generating a labeled document collection. Like *Latent Dirichlet Allocation* [2], *Bi-Labeled LDA* models each document as a mixture of latent topics and generates each word from one topic. Specifically, each non-famous user u is regarded as a document, consisting of a set of famous users who are followed by user u. Hence, each followed famous user corresponds to a word of the document. For simplicity, famous users followed by a user u is called u's followings.

In other words, all the followings of a non-famous user u constitute a document, and every famous user v in followings is a word. Informally, to generate a document, a non-famous user u first picks an aspect (topic) from its personal distribution of interests, and then pick a famous user in that aspect based on the aspect's distribution over all the famous users. Formally, let U denote the set of non-famous users who follow famous users from the set V. Let the set $K = \{t_1, t_2, \ldots, t_{|K|}\}$ be the set of topics (tags) extracted for famous users based on methods described in the last section. Each famous user v's tag set is denoted by a vector $T^{(v)} = (T_1^{(v)}, T_2^{(v)}, \ldots, T_{|K|}^{(v)})$, where each $T_k^{(v)} \in \{0,1\}$, $T_k^{(v)} = 1$ if user v has tag t_k, otherwise $T_k^{(v)} = 0$. Let a non-famous user u be represented as a bag of famous users u follows, $V^{(u)} = (V_1^{(u)}, V_2^{(u)}, \ldots, V_{N_u}^{(u)})$ and a binary presence/absence indicators of u's candidate tag set, $\Lambda^{(u)} = (\Lambda_1^{(u)}, \Lambda_2^{(u)}, \ldots, \Lambda_{|K|}^{(u)})$ where each $V_i^{(u)} \in V$ and each $\Lambda_k^{(u)} \in \{0,1\}$, $\Lambda_k^{(u)} = 1$ if tag t_k is a tag of user $v \in V^{(u)}$,

[2]https://twitter.com/lancearmstrong

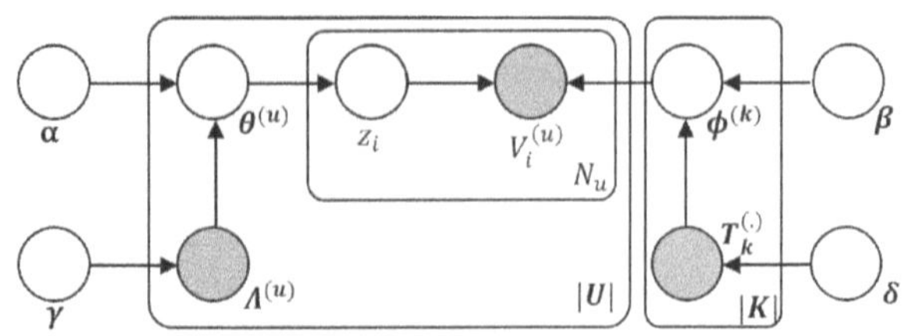

Figure 1: Graphical model of *Bi-Labeled LDA*

otherwise, $\Lambda_k^{(u)} = 0$. Here N_u is the number of famous users in u's followings.

The graphical model of *Bi-Labeled LDA* is illustrated in Figure 1. Notice that the top part of the graphical model is the same as the standard LDA. What is different is the lower part. We think a user u's topics correspond to its followings' tags. Therefore, a user's topic distribution is restricted by a label prior γ. Similarly, for each topic t_k, its word distribution is restricted by a label prior δ. Specifically, user u's topic distribution is restricted to be only over user u's tag set (while each tag is regarded as a possible latent topic), and the word distribution of a topic t_k is restricted to be only over those famous users who have this topic (i.e., the famous user has tag t_k).

In other words, unlike traditional LDA, *Bi-Labeled LDA* defines a one-to-one correspondence between latent topics and tags. Every document is restricted to those topics that correspond to its tag set. Meanwhile every word is restricted to be generated from those topics that correspond to its tag set, i.e., every topic can only generate words which have its corresponding tag. By this way, we not only incorporate supervision into traditional LDA, but also consider the similarities between famous users (words). As if two users are famous in the same topic, they will share the same tag.

In addition, as mentioned in Section 3, some famous users end up with no tags extracted with the methodology introduced in Section 3. Using *Bi-Labeled LDA* we can mine tags for them. Since we restrict a non-famous user u's topics to its followings' tags, in turn we restrict the tags of every famous user that u follows to u's tags. For those famous users without any tags extracted, their corresponding tags are decided by their followers, since they are followed based on users' topic vectors. Therefore, our model does not require tags for all the famous users.

Let $\alpha = \{\alpha_1, \alpha_2, \ldots, \alpha_{|K|}\}^T$ and $\beta = \{\beta_1, \beta_2, \ldots, \beta_{|V|}\}^T$ be the Dirichlet smoothing parameters for topics and words respectively, $\delta = \{\delta_1, \delta_2, \ldots, \delta_{|K|}\}^T$ and $\gamma = \{\gamma_1, \gamma_2, \ldots, \gamma_{|K|}\}^T$ are the label priors for topic t_k, $\theta^{(u)} : \{\theta_k^{(u)} = p(t_k|u), \forall t_k \in K\}$ be a non-famous user u's topic vector, $\phi^{(k)} : \{\phi_v^{(k)} = p(v|t_k), \forall v \in V\}$ be the topic t_k distribution over famous users. $L^{(u)}$ and $M^{(k)}$ are two matrices used to constrain the topics user u could have and the topics v could belong to respectively.

In order to restrict $\theta^{(u)}$ to be defined only over the topics that correspond to u's indicator of its tag set, $\Lambda^{(u)}$, we define a tag projection matrix $L^{(u)}$ of size $|K| \times |K|$ for each non-famous user u. For each row $i \in \{1, \ldots, |K|\}$ and column $j \in \{1, \ldots, |K|\}$:

$$L_{ij}^{(u)} = \begin{cases} \Lambda_i^{(u)} & \text{if } i = j; \\ 0 & \text{otherwise.} \end{cases} \tag{1}$$

Table 1: Generative process for Bi-Labeled LDA

- For each famous user v:
  - For each topic $t_k \in K$:
    - Generate $T_k^{(v)} \in \{0, 1\} \sim Bernoulli(\delta_k)$
- For each topic $t_k \in K$:
  - Generate $\beta^{(k)} = M^{(k)} \times \beta$
  - Generate $\phi^{(k)} \sim Dir(\beta^{(k)})$
- For each user $u \in U$:
  - For each topic $t_k \in K$:
    - Generate $\Lambda_k^{(u)} \in \{0, 1\} \sim Bernoulli(\gamma_k)$
  - Generate $\alpha^{(u)} = L^{(u)} \times \alpha$
  - Generate $\theta(u) \sim Dir(\alpha^{(u)})$
  - For each user u's following user i:
    - Generate $z_i \sim Mult(\theta^{(u)})$
    - Generate $V_i^{(u)} \sim Mult(\phi^{(z_i)})$

$$\alpha^{(u)} = L^{(u)} \times \alpha = (\alpha_1^{(u)}, \ldots, \alpha_{|K|}^{(u)})^T \tag{2}$$

In other words, $\alpha_k^{(u)}$ is equal to α_k if and only if $\Lambda_k^{(u)}$ is 1, and 0 otherwise. Clearly, the topics of user u are constrained to its tag set. For example, suppose $|K| = 4$, a non-famous user u's indicator of its tag set is $\Lambda^{(u)} = (1, 0, 0, 1)$, then $L^{(u)}$ would be:

$$L^{(u)} = \begin{pmatrix} 1 & 0 & 0 & 0 \\ 0 & 0 & 0 & 0 \\ 0 & 0 & 0 & 0 \\ 0 & 0 & 0 & 1 \end{pmatrix}$$

Then, $\alpha^{(u)} = L^{(u)} \times \alpha = \{\alpha_1, 0, 0, \alpha_4\}^T$.

Similarly, we define a matrix $M^{(k)}$ of size $|V| \times |V|$ for each topic t_k. For each row $i \in \{1, \ldots, |V|\}$ and column $j \in \{1, \ldots, |V|\}$:

$$M_{ij}^{(k)} = \begin{cases} T_k^{(i)} & \text{if } i = j; \\ 0 & \text{otherwise.} \end{cases} \tag{3}$$

$$\beta^{(k)} = M^{(k)} \times \beta = (\beta_1^{(k)}, \ldots, \beta_{|V|}^{(k)})^T \tag{4}$$

In other words, $\beta_i^{(k)}$ is equal to β_i if $T_k^{(i)}$ is 1 (i.e. famous user i can belong to topic t_k), and 0 otherwise. Clearly, the topics a famous user can belong to are constrained to its tag set. The generative process for *Bi-Labeled LDA* is shown in Table 1.

4.2 Learning and Inference

Since *Bi-Labeled LDA* is the same as standard LDA, except the topic prior $\alpha^{(u)}$ is restricted to u's tag set and the word prior $\beta^{(k)}$ is restricted to famous users who have tag t_k. Therefore, we can learn $\theta^{(u)}$ and $\phi^{(k)}$ using collapsed Gibbs sampling [12]. The final sampling update equation for picking a topic to explain why user u follows user v is as follows:

$$\begin{aligned} & p(z_i = t_k | z_{\neg i}, V, \alpha^{(u)}, \beta^{(k)}) \\ \propto\ & p(z_i = t_k, v_i = v | z_{\neg i}, V_{\neg i}, \alpha^{(u)}, \beta^{(k)} = \widehat{\theta_{k,\neg i}^{(u)}} \cdot \widehat{\phi_{v,\neg i}^{(k)}} \\ =\ & \frac{n_{k,\neg i}^{(u)} + \alpha_k^{(u)}}{\sum_{k=1}^{|K|}(n_{k,\neg i}^{(u)} + \alpha_k^{(u)})} \cdot \frac{n_{v,\neg i}^{(k)} + \beta_v^{(k)}}{\sum_{v=1}^{|V|}(n_{v,\neg i}^{(k)} + \beta_v^{(k)})} \end{aligned} \tag{5}$$

$$\widehat{\theta_k^{(u)}} = \frac{n_k^{(u)} + \alpha_k^{(u)}}{\sum_{k=1}^{|K|}(n_k^{(u)} + \alpha_k^{(u)})} \tag{6}$$

$$\widehat{\phi_v^{(k)}} = \frac{n_v^{(k)} + \beta_v^{(k)}}{\sum_{v=1}^{|V|}(n_v^{(k)} + \beta_v^{(k)})} \tag{7}$$

Where $n_{k,\neg i}^{(u)}$ is the number of u's followings who is assigned to topic t_k, and $n_{v,\neg i}^{(k)}$ is the times of famous user v assigned to topic t_k, and $\neg i$ means not including the current topic assignment z_i, $\widehat{\theta_k^{(u)}}$ is the estimated value of $\theta_k^{(u)}$, $\widehat{\phi_v^{(k)}}$ is the estimated value of $\phi_v^{(k)}$.

Although the equations above look almost the same as that of traditional LDA, our topic prior $\alpha^{(u)}$ is document-specific, and our word prior $\beta^{(k)}$ is topic-specific. Besides, it reflects our intuitions very well as explained below.

1. If a non-famous user u follows more users who are famous in aspect a than the ones who are famous in aspect b, then $n_a^{(u)} > n_b^{(u)} \rightarrow \widehat{\theta_a^{(u)}} > \widehat{\theta_b^{(u)}}$, i.e. u follows a user v who is famous both in aspect a and b more because of interest in aspect a than in b.
2. If a famous user v is followed by more non-famous users with interest in aspect a than that in b, then $n_v^{(a)} > n_v^{(b)} \rightarrow \widehat{\phi_v^{(a)}} > \widehat{\phi_v^{(b)}}$, i.e. v is followed by a non-famous user u more due to u's interest in aspect a than in b.

After the learning and inferring step, we obtained $\theta^{(u)}$ and $\phi^{(k)}$, which indicate a non-famous users u's topic distribution and the topic t_k's distribution over famous users respectively. Since we map every topic to a tag, we then recommend the top ranked tags to a non-famous user according to their probability scores in $\theta^{(u)}$. As a result, each non-famous user u is recommended a tag set, and we record each tag as a pair (*tag, probability score*), i.e. (t_k, $\theta_k^{(u)}$).

4.3 Term Weighting Schemes for Bi-Labeled LDA

In order to answer why a non-famous user u follows a famous user v more precisely, it is reasonable that different famous users in u's followings should be different as a indicator of u's interests, hence we propose three term weighting schemes.

Based on a famous user v's followers[3]

Should all the famous users in the followings get the same weight as an indicator of a user's interests? Intuitively, if a famous user is followed by less users, it should get more weight. In particular, if the more famous a user v is, the more likely a user follows v not because of interest but because of v's popularity [5]. So we define a term weight based on v's followers:

$$wf_v = \log(1 + \max_{i \in V}\{Nf_i\}/Nf_v) \tag{8}$$

Where, Nf_v is the number of v's followers.

Based on a famous user v's tag set

As we assume a non-famous user follows a famous user only because of one single aspect, the more tags user v has, the more likely the assumption goes against the reality. In addition, the more aspects v is famous in, the more likely its popularity in some aspect is overestimated. So we define a term weight based on v's tag set as follows:

$$wt_v = \log(1 + \max_{i \in V}\{Nt_i\}/Nt_v) \tag{9}$$

Where, Nt_v is the number of v's corresponding tags.

Based on the popularity of topic t_k

Popularity of different topics (the number of famous users that have t_k in their tag sets) is usually quite different. As shown in Eq. 6, more popular topics usually have bigger $n_k^{(u)}$, which will dominate u's other less popular interests. So we define a term weight based on the popularity of topic t_k as follows:

$$w_k = \log(1 + \max_{i \in K}\{NK_i\}/NK_k) \tag{10}$$

Where, NK_k is the number of famous users that have tag t_k.

Finally, the term weight of a famous user v who is assigned to topic t_k would be combination of the three schemes as shown below.

$$w_{v,k} = \lambda_1 \times wf_v + \lambda_2 \times wt_v + \lambda_3 \times w_k \tag{11}$$

Where $\lambda_1 + \lambda_2 + \lambda_3 = 1$.

Now, we can extend Eq. 5 to obtain a new equation for use with Gibbs sampler:

$$\begin{aligned} & p(z_i = t_k | z_{\neg i}, V, \alpha^{(u)}, \beta^{(k)}) \\ & \propto p(z_i = t_k, v_i = v | z_{\neg i}, V_{\neg i}, \alpha^{(u)}, \beta^{(k)}) \\ = & \frac{w_{v,k} \cdot n_{k,\neg i}^{(u)} + \alpha_k^{(u)}}{\sum_{k=1}^{|K|}(w_{v,k} \cdot n_{k,\neg i}^{(u)} + \alpha_k^{(u)})} \cdot \frac{w_{v,k} \cdot n_{v,\neg i}^{(k)} + \beta_v^{(k)}}{\sum_{v=1}^{|V|}(w_{v,k} \cdot n_{v,\neg i}^{(k)} + \beta_v^{(k)})} \end{aligned} \tag{12}$$

5. EXPERIMENTS

In this section, we illustrate the efficacy of our proposed method through experimental evaluation on real data, comparing with existing state-of-the-art methods. We first show how to extract our experimental dataset and ground truth, and then compare the performance of different term weighting schemes. Finally, we discuss each evaluated experiment in details.

5.1 Dataset

We use the Twitter graph published by Kwak et al. [4] and the tweets published by Yang et al. [18] as our experimental dataset, which contain a snapshot of the entire Twitter network in 2009, and about 20-30% of all public tweets published on Twitter from June 1, 2009 to December 31, 2009. To make sure that other evaluated methods can get enough text data, we first filter out all the users who post less than 100 tweets during the particular time frame. Given that the original data set is huge and we have limited computing resources, we extract a relatively small network based on a breadth first search (BFS) algorithm. The dataset contains 24,599 non-famous users, 15,701 famous users, and all their tweets and followings. The detail of the dataset is shown in Table 2.

[3]Followers of a famous user are all the users who follow the famous user.

[4]The follow relationships only include the cases that a non-famous user follows a famous user.

Table 2: Detail of our experimental dataset

Item	Value
# of non-famous users	26,478
# of famous users	15,701
# of follow relationships[4]	2,771,580
# of tweet vocabulary	23,385
# of tags	159

In particular, we remove from the tweets all the URLs, non-English letters (except the hash-tag, such as "#iran-election"), stop-words, top 100 high-frequency words (such as "good", "love", "time", etc.), and words which occur less than 10 times in all the tweets. In addition, as described in section 3, we get 159 meaningful and qualified tags from famous users' Twitter List features.

To evaluate the quality of these tag sets, we need to compare the inferred interest tags with some ground truth, i.e. known interests for some specific Twitter users. To do that, we select those non-famous users who declare their interests in their bios[5] as test dataset. Ding et al. [3] found that users always use "play + NP", "NP fan", "interested in + NP", "love <topic>" or some similar phrases to describe their interests in their biography, where NP stands for a noun phrase. So we use the *Stanford POS-Tagger* [14] to find out all the users whose biographies contain such phrases. Finally we get 3,242 such users. Further, we randomly select 120 users from them, and manually tag all the users according to their Twitter homepage, biographies, Lists they created and subscribe to. Note that, the reason for manually tagging is that biographies are in free form and ambiguous. For instance, they usually express their interest as someone's fan, such as "Howard Stern fan", "Orlando Magic fan", and etc. Besides, for each selected user, we also classify its interests into several aspects. For example, Jim Harris[6] corresponds to "{sport (Gator, NBA, Orlando Magic, etc.), music, Howard Stern (TV, show, comedy, etc.)}". Hence, as a result we get 120 users with interest tags, which are clustered into several aspects.

5.2 Performance of Term Weighting Schemes

In this section we compare different term weighting schemes in terms of precision and recall. The three weighting schemes and their combinations total seven different weighting ways. We compare these term weighting ways with the original *Bi-Labeled LDA* without term weighting scheme, and we set the coefficients $(\lambda_1, \lambda_2, \lambda_3)$ in Eq. 11 to $(1/3, 1/3, 1/3)$, $(1/2, 1/2, 0)$, $(1/2, 0, 1/2)$, $(0, 1/2, 1/2)$, $(1, 0, 0)$, $(0, 1, 0)$, $(0, 0, 1)$ respectively.

We compute DCG[7] values of the top 10 tags extracted by each setting for a user u as a measure of *precision*, and report the percentage of the aspects of each user's interests reflected in top-n tags ($n \in \{1, 3, 5, 10\}$) as a measure of *recall*. In particular, since it is difficult to decide which aspect a user is more interested in, we only consider whether a tag is relevant to a user's interest or not. In addition, even though there are usually more than one tag relevant to one aspect, these tags are usually not completely the same but slightly different. For example, "book, reading, writer, write, kindle" are all relevant to book, but not completely the same. Given that, we calculate DCG and define the graded relevance in Eq. 13 and Eq. 14 respectively, where tag_i is the tag at position i, rel_i is the graded relevance of tag_i, $tag_i \in k$ means tag_i is related to u's interest in aspect k.

$$DCG_{10} = \frac{\sum_{i=1}^{10} 2^{rel_i} - 1}{\log_2(i+1)} \tag{13}$$

$$rel_i = \begin{cases} 5 & \text{if } tag_i \in k, \text{and } \nexists j < i,\ tag_j \in k \\ 3 & \text{if } tag_i \in k, \text{and } \exists j < i,\ tag_j \in k \\ 0 & \text{otherwise} \end{cases} \tag{14}$$

In other words, when more than one tags in a tag set correspond to the same aspect k, the graded relevance of the first one is 5 and the others are 3. In this way, tag sets with top 10 tags covering all of aspects get the highest score. Specifically, the more aspects a tag set captures and the more tags that reflect different sides of the same aspect, the higher score the tag set will get.

The *precisions* of the seven term weighting schemes and the original Bi-Labeled LDA without weighting schemes are shown in Table 3. Weight based on a famous user's followers (i.e. $(1, 0, 0)$) and weight based on a famous user's tag set (i.e. $(0, 1, 0)$) make an improvement in precision. But, weight based on the popularity of topics (i.e. $(0, 0, 1)$) causes an obvious decrease in precision, because it lowers the weight of popular topics and then lower their rank ordering, but interest topics declared by users usually include some popular topics, such as "sport", "music", "movie", "travel" and etc. And the combination of it with the other two weight schemes (i.e. $(1/2, 0, 1/2)$ and $(0, 1/2, 1/2)$) further lowers the weight of popular topics, and lead to a more obvious decrease in precision.

Table 3: Precision of 7 term weighting schemes compared to *Bi-Labeled LDA* without term weighting

Weighting Scheme	DCG of top 10 tags
No term weighting scheme	45.6585
$(1/3, 1/3, 1/3)$	45.9507
$(1/2, 1/2, 0)$	47.0041
$(1/2, 0, 1/2)$	37.5485
$(0, 1/2, 1/2)$	34.0895
$(1, 0, 0)$	47.1321
$(0, 1, 0)$	46.8259
$(0, 0, 1)$	41.0005

The *recalls* of the seven term weighting schemes minus the recall of the original *Bi-Labeled LDA* without weighting schemes, *relative recalls*, are shown in Figure 2. Only $(1/2, 0, 1/2)$ and $(0, 1/2, 1/2)$ cause a relatively obvious decrease, average -0.06399 and -0.0997 respectively. Since weight based on the popularity of topics (i.e. $(0, 0, 1)$) lowers the weight of very popular topics, weight based on a famous user's followers (i.e. $(1, 0, 0)$) and weight based on a famous user's tag set (i.e. $(0, 1, 0)$) lowers the weight of very popular users, the combinations further lower the weight of very popular topics and remove them out of top 10, while users' declared topics usually include some very popular topics.

[5]Bio is a short self-introduction in free form, written by a user in its account profile.

[6]https://twitter.com/jabberjim, Bio: Gator Fan, Howard Stern, Orlando Magic, Random Stupidity, Wannabe Superhero, Paranormal, Horror, Crying, Singing, Piano Playing, bla bla

[7]http://en.wikipedia.org/wiki/Discounted_cumulative_gain

On average, $(1/2, 1/2, 0)$, $(1, 0, 0)$ and $(0, 1, 0)$ cause a slight increase, all the others cause a certain degree of decline.

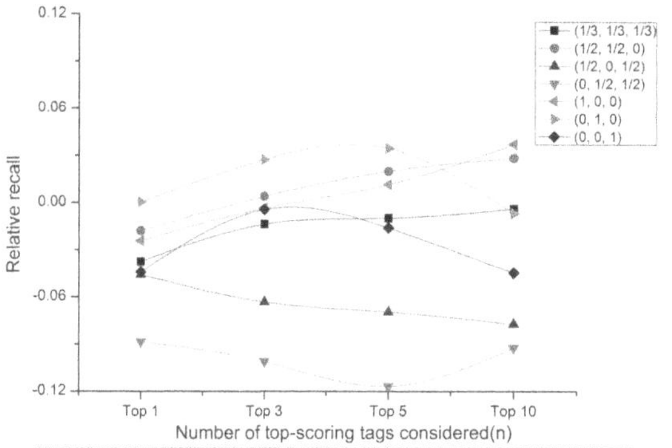

Average relative recall						
(1/3, 1/3, 1/3)	(1/2, 1/2, 0)	(1/2, 0, 1/2)	(0, 1/2, 1/2)	(1, 0, 0)	(0, 1, 0)	(0, 0, 1)
-0.01621	0.00865	-0.06399	-0.0997	0.00521	0.01387	-0.02727

Figure 2: Recall of 7 term weighting schemes relative to *Bi-Labeled LDA* without term weighting

Overall, our results show that weight based on a famous user's followers and tags can improve the precision of *Bi-Labeled LDA*, and cause a slight increase in recall (on average for all values of n). But note that even though weight based on the popularity of topics cause a decrease both in precision and recall, it may be very useful for finding more specific interests for users in social networks, which is one of our future works. We finally set the coefficients $(\lambda_1, \lambda_2, \lambda_3)$ as $(1/2, 1/2, 0)$.

5.3 Evaluated Approaches

In this section we briefly introduce approaches to be compared with our proposed methods, and more details can be found in related work.

- *Bi-Labeled LDA*: This refers to our own approach.
- *List-Based*: This baseline refers to the method proposed by Bhattacharya et al. [1]
- *Labeled LDA*: This baseline refers to the approach in [8]. We select the same tag set extracted from famous users' List features as topic labels.
- *Labeled LDA-Follow*: This baseline is the same as Labeled LDA, but it models the generative process of user's tweets and followings at the same time.
- *Tag-LDA-Follow*: This baseline is proposed to model the generative process of words and tags of a labeled document at the same time [13]. Different from *Labeled LDA*, it has no restriction on the topics a document can have.
- *Tag-LDA-Tag*: For this baseline, it is the same with *Tag-LDA-Follow*, but we replace users' followings with famous users' tag set.

For all the topic models using tweet content listed above, after learning and inference, we also get $\theta^{(u)}$ and $\phi^{(k)}$, which indicate a non-famous user u's topic distribution and the topic k's distribution over terms respectively. We recommend a term t to user u via use of Information Gain measure as shown in [5]:

$$\begin{aligned} p(t|u) = IG(t|u) = -p(u)\log p(u) \\ +p(t)[p(u|t)\log p(u|t) + p(\neg u|t)\log p(\neg u|t)] \\ +p(\neg t)[p(u|\neg t)\log p(u|\neg t) + p(\neg u|\neg t)\log p(\neg u|\neg t)] \end{aligned} \quad (15)$$

The equation measures the reduction in the entropy associated with user u, incurred by the presence or absence of term t.

Where, $p(u) = 1/(|U|)$ is assumed to be the same for all users, and we compute $p(t)$ and $p(u|t)$ as follows:

$$\begin{aligned} p(t) &= \sum_{u=1}^{|U|} p(t|u)p(u) \\ &= \sum_{u=1}^{|U|}\sum_{k=1}^{|K|} p(u)p(t|z=k)p(z=k|u) \\ &= \sum_{u=1}^{|U|}\sum_{k=1}^{|K|} p(u)\phi_t^{(k)}\theta_k^{(u)} \end{aligned} \quad (16)$$

$$\begin{aligned} p(u|t) &= p(u,t)/p(t) \\ &= \sum_{k=1}^{|K|} p(u)p(t|z=k)p(z=k|u) \;/\; p(t) \\ &= \sum_{k=1}^{|K|} p(u)\phi_t^{(k)}\theta_k^{(u)} \;/\; p(t) \end{aligned} \quad (17)$$

After computing the information gain scores, we recommend top-scoring terms to users. In addition, we tried several other mechanisms, but this one performs best.

5.4 Case Study

In this section, we showcase the experimental results with several typical cases, which can help you understand the subsequent experiments better. Due to limitation of space, we only show part of the results.

Table 4 shows the declared interests for some non-famous users (as given in their bio) and the top 10 tags recommended by the four different methods. The tags in bold score 5 in terms of relevance and ones in italic score 3, all the others score 0. Among the tags in bold, those in underline are ones that cannot find from their bios. It is evident that the tag sets recommended by our method *Bi-Labeled LDA* are more precise and capture a larger fraction of users' interests declared in their bios. For instance, Lisa is a photographer and a fan of several musicians, loves music and hockey. We infer her interests such as "musician", "photographer" and "sport", while List-Based method recommends "media", "business" and "news", and tags extracted by *Labeled LDA* and *Tag-LDA-Follow* are hot topics or meaningless words. Even though *List-Based* method can cover many aspects of users' interests, it always ranks very famous tags in the top of its tag set, such as "news", "movie", "media", "tech", etc. *Labeled LDA* and *Tag-LDA-Follow* which are based on tweet content usually either capture only one aspect of users' interest, or recommend tags related to their daily life, recent events or globally popular topics (e.g. "iranelection" and "fb"). Moreover, tags recommended by tweet-based methods are not generalized enough. For example, "bike" and "ride" could be generalized to "cycling", "redsox" and "sox" could be generalized to "hockey". In this sense, the tags recommended by *Bi-Labeled LDA* and *List-Based* method are more generalized and more applicable for all kinds of personalized applications.

In addition, a few interests undeclared in their bios can be inferred too. For instance, we recommend foody to Kelli

Table 4: Top-10 tags inferred by four methods.

User with its bio	The tag sets extracted by different methods			
	Bi-Labeled LDA	*List-Based*	*Labeled LDA*	*Tag-LDA-Follow*
Connie Laubenthal: Cycling fan, amateur musician (voice), professional laboratorian (medical), Catholic, full time RVer	**cycling**, **politics**, blogger, science, media, government, **travel**, *fitness*, **food**, *health*	news, media, sport, world, **cycling**, pro, **politics**, stuff, celeb, blogger	#fb, **bike**, *health*, run, *ride*, cancer, marathon, *miles*, *race*, #militarymon	**bike**, *health*, *ride*, portland, cancer, care, *riding*, **medical**, *tour*, *bikes*
Marty Burian: Husband, Dog Lover, Badger, IT Professional, Pilot, Runner, Curler, Beer Brewer, Personal Trainer, Rock Climber, Scuba Diver	**tech**, **entrepreneur**, seo, media, **beer**, travel, **fitness**, love, lover, **developer**	media, **business**, news, **tech**, social media, marketing, web, **entrepreneur**, blogger, world	**run**, bike, ride, *race*, *miles*, cycling, *marathon*, weekend, *ran*, *running*	**run**, *running*, *miles*, *gym*, **training**, *marathon*, *ran*, *race*, *mile*, *workout*
Kelli Masilun: Creative-minded marketer, Kentucky alumni/fan, mother of 3, hopelessly opinionated.	**foody**, pro, **marketer**, lover, *media*, *expert*, *market*, *pr*, group, football	media, news, social media, business, **marketing**, tech, peep, world, *pr*, *seo*	kids, **coffee**, daughter, baby, family, hubby, husband, child, lunch, #fb	kids, **coffee**, baby, daughter, family, #fb, son, husband, mom, hubby
Lisa: Photography, music, hockey. Jeff Buckley, Jimmy Gnecco, Ours, Serena Ryder, WIM. Boston Bruins fan. @NYCCountryMusic Photographer.	**musician**, media, writer, **photographer**, coach, humor, food, **sport**, event, business	media, business, news, social media, tech, marketing, **music**, peep, entertainment, writer	#fb, coffee, **#redsox**, design, obama, totally, app, *sox*, #tcot, nyc	yay, totally, sigh, #fb, heh, omg, guess, stuff, kinda, hahaha
Alex Williams: What can I say: Unique, magickal, artist, photographer find me on rebelmouse	**news**, **photography**, **app**, community, *tech*, usa, info, love, content, government	**news**, media, tech, business, social media, world, marketing, web, stuff, politics	iranelection, iran, iran, ranElection, ran, tehran, ranelection, iranian, gr88, neda	iranelection, iran, iran, ranElection, tehran, ran, ranelection, iranian, gr88, neda

Masilun[8], and it turns out that Kelli Masilun only subscribes to a list, which includes 49 users related to food&drink. In the same way, we find Conni Laubenthal is actually interested in politics, travel and food. Actually all the tags in underline in Table 4 are interests undeclared in their bios, but inferred by our method, which suggests that using users' bios alone may not be sufficient and interest tags extracted by our method can provide supplementary information for those users with qualified bios.

5.5 Comparing with Existing Methods

5.5.1 Evaluation via Manually Labeling

In this section we adopt the same evaluation method presented in [5] to evaluate the quality of the tag sets extracted by the different approaches. In order to evaluate how all the approaches perform for users of different activeness (number of tweets), we separate the non-famous users into 3 groups with different number of tweets $[100, 500)$, $[500, 1000)$ and $[1000, \infty)$, posted from June 1 2009 to December 31 2009. We then randomly select 40 users in each group, and show them to two annotators, along with the anonymous tag sets extracted by each approach. Each tag set contains the top 10 tags recommended by corresponding approach. For each user, the annotators were asked to pick the approach with the best tag set, and they could also pick multiple winners or no winners at all. Then we report the average fraction of wins for each approach. We also compute the average Kappa statistic of agreement between each pair of annotators on the wins for each approach. This value was 0.85, which signifies a robust agreement between annotators.

The fraction of wins of each approaches are shown in Figure 3. As can be seen, our approach consistently outperforms all others in all three ranges, and actually the achieved score of our method is more than double that of the second best. We found out that tweet-based methods always recommend tags which either relate to daily life, recent events, globally popular topics, or relate to only one aspect. Even though *List-Based* method can cover many aspects of users' interests, it always ranks famous tags such as "news", "movie", "media", "tech", etc. in the top of its tag set. In addition, even though we incorporate the network information to *Labeled LDA* and *Tag-LDA*, it didn't make any remarkable improvement, even a little decline. It can be seen that the number of tweets users post in each aspect is not necessarily proportional to the number of famous users they follow in each aspect, and tweets posted by users may be not related to their interests.

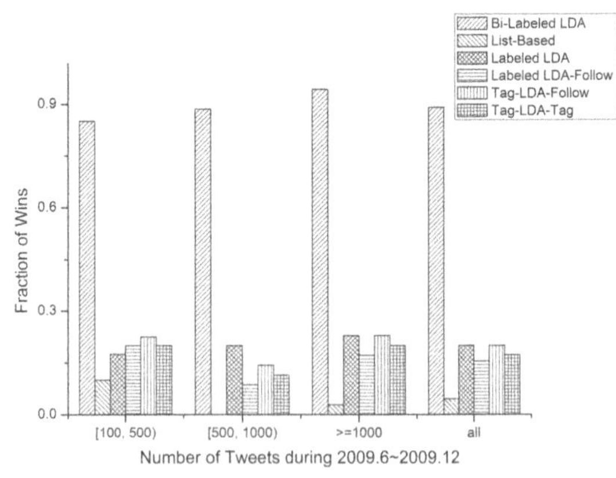

Figure 3: Fraction of wins for each approach in each group

[8]https://twitter.com/kkmaz/lists

5.5.2 *Evaluation with Ground Truth*

To determine the quality of a tag set inferred for a user, *precision* (how correct the extracted interests are) and *recall* (whether a large fraction of the user's interests could be inferred) are both important aspects.

Based on our *ground truth*, the results of *precision* and *recall* are shown in Table 5 and Figure 4 respectively. As we can see, our method are superior to all other methods both in terms of *precision* and *recall* (for all values of n). Note that, it is very difficult to predict the self-declared interests, and there are about 4.83 interests on average for each user. *List-Based* method is the worst one with respect to precision, but the second best with respect to recall in Top 10 and Top 5. As we discussed above, *List-Based* method always ranks some common tags in the top of its extracted tag set, which results in a low DCG, but it can infer more aspects in which a user has an interest in, which leads to a relatively high recall. For *tweet-based* methods, we find out that even though users usually post many interest-unrelated tweets, sometimes they also tweet a lot about one of their daily interests or want to show their professions, such as "sport", "food", "god", "marketer", "IT" and etc. After all, *tweet-based* methods usually can only capture no more than one aspect of users' interests. Besides, we actually are very tolerant of the tags recommended by tweet-based methods, which are usually not precise enough. For example, tags recommended by them for users who are interested in "politics" are usually "government", "iranelection", "health care" and etc, tags recommended by them for users who are interested in "baseball" may be "redsox" (an American professional baseball team), even "sox" and etc. Even though these tags recommended by tweet-based methods are not directly applicable for personalized applications, we still treat them as related to users' interests in order to avoid the deviation of artificial evaluation. In this sense, the tags recommended by our method is more applicable for many personalized applications.

Table 5: Comparison of different methods on precision

Methods	DCG of top 10 tags
Bi-Labeled LDA	47.0041
List-Based	27.9974
Labeled LDA	32.9850
Labeled LDA-Follow	29.4253
Tag-LDA-Follow	31.5904
Tag-LDA-Tag	31.6807

6. CONCLUSIONS

In this work, we proposed a modified topic model, *Bi-Labeled LDA* with a term weighting scheme, to extract interest tags for non-famous users in social network based on the underlying relationship network, without using text content information. In particular, we first deduced the topical expertise of famous Twitter users based on their Twitter Lists features, represented by a bag of tags, and then extracted interest tags for non-famous users using *Bi-Labeled LDA* to uncover why a non-famous user follows other famous users. Comparison with state-of-the-art methods shows that our method is far more superior in terms of accuracy and completeness (recall) of the extracted tag set, and more applica-

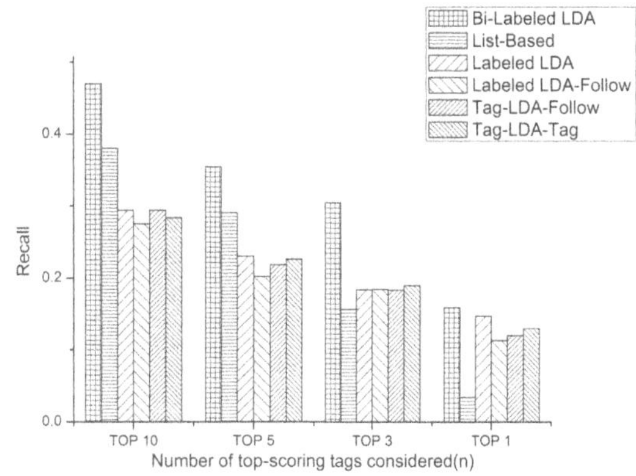

Figure 4: Comparison of different methods in terms of recall

ble. Besides, we also find that a reasonable term weighting scheme can actually improve the performance. In future, we would like to evaluate our extracted tags on tasks, such as personalize recommendation, online advertising and topic sensitive expert finding. In addition, improvements may be further made by clustering all the tags and recommending more specific interest tags.

7. ACKNOWLEDGMENTS

X. Du acknowledges the support from the 973 Project under Grant No. 2012CB316205. J. He acknowledges the support from the Beijing Municipal Natural Science Foundation under No. 4152026 and the NSSFC under Grant No. 13&ZD155. H. Liu acknowledges the support from the NSFC under Grant No. 71272029, 71110107027 and 71490724.

8. REFERENCES

[1] P. Bhattacharya, M. B. Zafar, N. Ganguly, S. Ghosh, and K. P. Gummadi. Inferring user interests in the twitter social network. In *Proceedings of the 8th ACM Conference on Recommender systems*, pages 357–360. ACM, 2014.

[2] D. M. Blei, A. Y. Ng, and M. I. Jordan. Latent dirichlet allocation. *J. Mach. Learn. Res.*, 3:993–1022, Mar. 2003.

[3] Y. Ding and J. Jiang. Extracting interest tags from twitter user biographies. In *Information Retrieval Technology*, pages 268–279. Springer, 2014.

[4] H. Kwak, C. Lee, H. Park, and S. Moon. What is twitter, a social network or a news media? In *Proceedings of the 19th international conference on World wide web*, pages 591–600. ACM, 2010.

[5] T. Lappas, K. Punera, and T. Sarlos. Mining tags using social endorsement networks. In *Proceedings of the 34th international ACM SIGIR conference on Research and development in Information Retrieval*, pages 195–204. ACM, 2011.

[6] K. H. Lim and A. Datta. Interest classification of twitter users using wikipedia. In *Proceedings of the 9th International Symposium on Open Collaboration*, page 22. ACM, 2013.

[7] M. Michelson and S. A. Macskassy. Discovering users' topics of interest on twitter: a first look. In *Proceedings of the fourth workshop on Analytics for noisy unstructured text data*, pages 73–80. ACM, 2010.

[8] R. Ottoni, D. Las Casas, J. P. Pesce, W. Meira Jr, C. Wilson, A. Mislove, and V. Almeida. Of pins and tweets: Investigating how users behave across image-and text-based social networks. *AAAI ICWSM*, 2014.

[9] D. Quercia, H. Askham, and J. Crowcroft. Tweetlda: supervised topic classification and link prediction in twitter. In *Proceedings of the 4th Annual ACM Web Science Conference*, pages 247–250. ACM, 2012.

[10] V. Rakesh, D. Singh, B. Vinzamuri, and C. K. Reddy. Personalized recommendation of twitter lists using content and network information. In *Eighth International AAAI Conference on Weblogs and Social Media*, 2014.

[11] D. Ramage, D. Hall, R. Nallapati, and C. D. Manning. Labeled lda: A supervised topic model for credit attribution in multi-labeled corpora. In *Proceedings of the 2009 Conference on Empirical Methods in Natural Language Processing: Volume 1-Volume 1*, pages 248–256. Association for Computational Linguistics, 2009.

[12] P. Resnik and E. Hardisty. Gibbs sampling for the uninitiated. Technical report, DTIC Document, 2010.

[13] X. Si and M. Sun. Tag-lda for scalable real-time tag recommendation. *Journal of Computational Information Systems*, 6(1):23–31, 2009.

[14] K. Toutanova, D. Klein, C. D. Manning, and Y. Singer. Feature-rich part-of-speech tagging with a cyclic dependency network. In *Proceedings of the 2003 Conference of the North American Chapter of the Association for Computational Linguistics on Human Language Technology - Volume 1*, NAACL '03, pages 173–180, Stroudsburg, PA, USA, 2003. Association for Computational Linguistics.

[15] C. Wagner, V. Liao, P. Pirolli, L. Nelson, and M. Strohmaier. It's not in their tweets: Modeling topical expertise of twitter users. In *Privacy, Security, Risk and Trust (PASSAT), 2012 International Conference on and 2012 International Confernece on Social Computing (SocialCom)*, pages 91–100. IEEE, 2012.

[16] T. Wang, H. Liu, J. He, and X. Du. Mining user interests from information sharing behaviors in social media. In *Advances in Knowledge Discovery and Data Mining*, pages 85–98. Springer, 2013.

[17] Z. Xu, R. Lu, L. Xiang, and Q. Yang. Discovering user interest on twitter with a modified author-topic model. In *Web Intelligence and Intelligent Agent Technology (WI-IAT), 2011 IEEE/WIC/ACM International Conference on*, volume 1, pages 422–429. IEEE, 2011.

[18] J. Yang and J. Leskovec. Patterns of temporal variation in online media. In *Proceedings of the fourth ACM international conference on Web search and data mining*, pages 177–186. ACM, 2011.

[19] D. Zhao and M. B. Rosson. How and why people twitter: the role that micro-blogging plays in informal communication at work. In *Proceedings of the ACM 2009 international conference on Supporting group work*, pages 243–252. ACM, 2009.

[20] X. Zhao and J. Jiang. An empirical comparison of topics in twitter and traditional media. *Singapore Management University School of Information Systems Technical paper series. Retrieved November*, 10:2011, 2011.

Robust Capped Norm Nonnegative Matrix Factorization

Hongchang Gao
Computer Science and Engineering
University of Texas at Arlington
Arlington, TX, 76019
hongchanggao@gmail.com

Feiping Nie
Computer Science and Engineering
University of Texas at Arlington
Arlington, TX, 76019
feipingnie@gmail.com

Weidong Cai
School of Information Technologies
University of Sydney
NSW 2006, Australia
tom.cai@sydney.edu.au

Heng Huang *
Computer Science and Engineering
University of Texas at Arlington
Arlington, TX, 76019
heng@uta.edu

ABSTRACT

As an important matrix factorization model, Nonnegative Matrix Factorization (NMF) has been widely used in information retrieval and data mining research. Standard Nonnegative Matrix Factorization is known to use the Frobenius norm to calculate the residual, making it sensitive to noises and outliers. It is desirable to use robust NMF models for practical applications, in which usually there are many data outliers. It has been studied that the $\ell_{2,1}$-norm or ℓ_1-norm can be used for robust NMF formulations to deal with data outliers. However, these alternatives still suffer from the extreme data outliers. In this paper, we present a novel robust capped norm orthogonal Nonnegative Matrix Factorization model, which utilizes the capped norm for the objective to handle these extreme outliers. Meanwhile, we derive a new efficient optimization algorithm to solve the proposed non-convex non-smooth objective. Extensive experiments on both synthetic and real datasets show our proposed new robust NMF method consistently outperforms related approaches.

Categories and Subject Descriptors

H.2.8 [**Database Management**]: Database Applications-Data Mining

General Terms

Algorithms

*Corresponding author.

Permission to make digital or hard copies of all or part of this work for personal or classroom use is granted without fee provided that copies are not made or distributed for profit or commercial advantage and that copies bear this notice and the full citation on the first page. Copyrights for components of this work owned by others than ACM must be honored. Abstracting with credit is permitted. To copy otherwise, or republish, to post on servers or to redistribute to lists, requires prior specific permission and/or a fee. Request permissions from Permissions@acm.org.
CIKM'15, October 19–23, 2015, Melbourne, Australia.
© 2015 ACM. ISBN 978-1-4503-3794-6/15/10 ...$15.00.
DOI: http://dx.doi.org/10.1145/2806416.2806568.

Keywords

Capped Norm; Robust Nonnegative Matrix Factorization; Robust Clustering

1. INTRODUCTION

Nonnegative Matrix Factorization (NMF) is an important matrix factorization algorithm which deals with a specific class of the nonnegative matrix. It is first used by G. Golub's notes, and further discussed by Paatero [18]. The work of [16] made this matrix factorization algorithm well-known in data mining and information retrieval areas. The original motivation of NMF is to make the factors coherent with the original nonnegative data, making the factorization easy to interpret, as opposed to singular value decomposition (SVD) which has both negative values and positive ones.

Later work [4] showed the connection between NMF and clustering methods. After that, the NMF methods have been widely used as one of the most important clustering methods, and have been applied to a lot of different applications, *e.g.* multimedia data analysis [1], text and document mining [26], protein interaction prediction [23], transfer learning [21], and multi-relational clustering [22, 24].

Driven by such huge amounts of different useful applications, a lot of research has been done to further improve NMF algorithm and its performance. [3] improved the NMF algorithm by adding an orthogonal constraint, proving the equivalence between orthogonal NMF and the relaxed K-Means clustering [13], and also extending it to Nonnegative Matrix Tri-Factorization (NMTF) for co-clustering. [10] explicitly incorporated the notion of sparseness to improve the found decompositions. [25] proposed a large-scale NMF and NMTF algorithms using clustering indicators.

However, most NMF models use the Frobenius norm based objectives, such that these models are sensitive to data outliers. Recently, several robust NMF models have been proposed. [5] proposed to use the correntropy induced metric to make it insensitive to outliers. [9] adopted a hypersurface cost function to make the NMF robust to the outliers. [27] proposed to subtract a sparse outlier matrix from the data matrix to reduce the effect of the outliers. In the other work [14], the authors adopted $\ell_{2,1}$-norm based objective function to weaken the effect of data outliers. [11] further introduced robust NMF formulation with manifold regularization. All of these methods can reduce the effects of data outliers on the NMF calculation. However, they can not remove the effect of the outliers. Therefore, these methods still suffer from the extreme data outliers, which can dominate the residue calculation even with the ℓ_1-norm distance.

To address this problem, in this paper, we propose novel robust capped norm NMF formulations, which can remove the effect of extreme data outliers via the capped norm based residual calculation. Meanwhile, we derive a new efficient optimization algorithm to solve the proposed non-smooth and non-convex objective with rigorous theoretical analysis. Our new algorithm is as efficient as the traditional NMF and $\ell_{2,1}$-norm based NMF. Extensive experiments on both toy data and benchmark datasets show our proposed new robust NMF model's correctness and effectiveness.

Notations: We use $\Re^{m\times n}$ to denote $m \times n$ matrices. For matrix M, its j-th column is denoted by m_j. $||M||_F$ denotes the Frobenius norm.

2. ROBUST CAPPED NORM NONNEGATIVE MATRIX FACTORIZATION

In this section, we will revisit the traditional NMF as well as robust $\ell_{2,1}$-norm NMF, giving the motivation for proposing the capped $\ell_{2,1}$-norm NMF models.

2.1 Revisit NMF

The traditional Nonnegative Matrix Factorization (NMF) is defined as the following:

$$\min_{F,G} ||X - FG^T||_F^2 \quad s.t.\ F \geq 0, G \geq 0\,, \tag{1}$$

where $X \in \Re^{d\times n}$, d is the dimension of features, n is the number of data points. When using NMF to do the clustering, $F \in \Re^{d\times k}$ denotes the k basis factors, where k is the number of classes. $G \in \Re^{n\times k}$ represents the class indicators, indicating the final clustering result.

However, the traditional NMF uses the Frobenius norm to calculate the residual, known to be sensitive to data outliers in practical problems. To address the robustness issue, several robust NMF models have been proposed. The main idea is to use the $\ell_{2,1}$-norm or ℓ_1-norm based objective functions. For example, [14] proposed to use $\ell_{2,1}$-norm to replace the Frobenius norm in objective and solved:

$$\min_{F,G} ||X - FG^T||_{2,1} \quad s.t.\ F \geq 0, G \geq 0\,. \tag{2}$$

Let $X = [x_1, x_2, ..., x_n]$, $G^T = [g_1, g_2, ..., g_n]$. The $\ell_{2,1}$-norm based loss function can be reformulated as following:

$$||X - FG^T||_{2,1} = \sum_{j=1}^{n} ||x_j - Fg_j||_2\,. \tag{3}$$

The above loss function uses the ℓ_2-norm within a data point and the ℓ_1-norm among data points, such that the $\ell_{2,1}$-norm NMF is robust to data outliers (the non-squared residuals reduce the effects of data outliers) [14]. In data mining and information retrieval applications, we usually consider the data outliers exist and trust the feature generation. For example, we trust the instrument which measures the features of data points, but the data outliers are often created during the data collection process. If the noise exists in both data and feature dimensions, we can use the ℓ_1-norm NMF model, which uses the ℓ_1-norm for both data points and features. But, in terms of optimization, there is no big difference between these two types of models.

Although the $\ell_{2,1}$-norm NMF is a robust formulation, it still suffers from the extreme odd points. For example, there exists an extreme odd point x_k whose residual $||x_k - Fg_k||$ is extremely large, which could affect the clustering result significantly. The reason is that the $\ell_{2,1}$-norm based objective just weakens the effect of the outliers, but it still cannot remove the effects of the outliers. Therefore, we hope to design a better robust NMF model to deal with such situation.

2.2 New Robust NMF via Capped Norm

In order to get a more robust clustering model, we propose a novel capped norm NMF method with solving:

$$J(F,G) = \min_{F,G} \sum_{j=1}^{n} \min\{||x_j - Fg_j||_2, \theta\} \quad s.t.\ F \geq 0, G \geq 0\,, \tag{4}$$

where $\theta > 0$ is a thresholding parameter for choosing the extreme data outliers.

In this new objective, if the residual of a data point $||x_i - Fg_i||_2 > \theta$, we consider the data point x_i as extreme outlier and its residual is also capped as θ such that its effect to the whole model is fixed (if we don't cap the residual and x_i is extremely large, it will affect the final result dramatically). For other data points with residual $||x_j - Fg_j||_2 \leq \theta$, our objective will minimize $\sum_{j=1}^{n} ||x_j - Fg_j||_2$, *i.e.* the standard ℓ_1-norm residual minimization, which is robust to regular data outliers. Thus, the proposed capped norm NMF is a more robust model than previous $\ell_{2,1}$-norm NMF.

Note that, in our new model, the extreme data outliers are not heuristically decided based on their magnitude. They are indeed chosen during the nonnegative matrix factorization process, *i.e.* they are the extreme data outliers for the clustering task. When we iteratively optimize the capped norm NMF objective, the selected extreme data outliers can be distinct in different iterations (with the same thresholding parameter θ). When the solution converges, we will find the correct extreme data outliers.

To enhance the performance of the capped norm NMF, we enforce the orthogonal constraint to G, which was used in previous Orthogonal Nonnegative Matrix Factorization (ONMF) method [3]. Thus, our new capped norm orthogonal NMF is to solve:

$$J(F,G) = \min_{F,G} \sum_{j=1}^{n} \min\{||x_j - Fg_j||_2, \theta\} \quad s.t.\ F \geq 0, G \geq 0, G^T G = I\,. \tag{5}$$

The main advantage of orthogonal constraint is that the orthogonality of G guarantees the uniqueness of the solution and makes the clustering results easily to be interpreted. Thus, the capped norm ONMF method is a more robust clustering model. Our new objective function (5) is difficult to solve. In next section, we will propose an efficient optimization algorithm to solve it.

3. OPTIMIZATION ALGORITHM AND THEORETICAL ANALYSIS

In this section, we will propose an efficient optimization algorithm to solve the new objective in Eq. (5), and prove the convergence of our proposed algorithm.

3.1 Optimization Algorithm

We can easily verify that the derivative of Eq. (5) is equivalent to the derivative of the following objective:

$$\begin{aligned}&\min_{F,G} \sum_{j=1}^{n} d_j ||x_j - Fg_j||_2^2 \\ &s.t.\ F \geq 0, G \geq 0, G^T G = I\,,\end{aligned} \tag{6}$$

where

$$d_j = \begin{cases} \frac{1}{2||x_j - Fg_j||_2}, & if\ ||x_j - Fg_j||_2 \leq \theta; \\ 0, & otherwise. \end{cases} \tag{7}$$

We can reformulate Eq. (6) as the following:

$$\begin{aligned}&\min_{F,G} Tr((X - FG^T)D(X - FG^T)^T) \\ &s.t.\ \ F \geq 0, G \geq 0, G^T G = I\,,\end{aligned} \tag{8}$$

where D is a diagonal matrix with the j-th diagonal element $D_{jj} = d_j$.

Such a problem can be solved via the iterative re-weighted optimization strategy. When D is fixed, the objective function in Eq. (8) can be expanded as:

$$\begin{aligned}&\min_{F,G} Tr(FG^T DGF^T) - 2Tr(XDGF^T) \\ &s.t.\ \ F \geq 0, G \geq 0, G^T G = I\,.\end{aligned} \tag{9}$$

Therefore, the updating rules for F and G are:

$$\begin{aligned}F_{ik} &\Leftarrow F_{ik} \frac{(XDG)_{ik}}{(FG^T DG)_{ik}}\,, \\ G_{jk} &\Leftarrow G_{jk} \sqrt{\frac{(DX^T F)_{jk}}{(DGG^T X^T F)_{jk}}}\,.\end{aligned} \tag{10}$$

When F and G are fixed, the updating rule for D is as following:

$$D_{jj} = \begin{cases} \frac{1}{2||x_j - Fg_j||_2}, & if\ ||x_j - Fg_j||_2 \leq \theta \\ 0, & otherwise \end{cases} \tag{11}$$

The detail of our algorithm is summarized in Algorithm 1.

3.2 Theoretical Analysis

In this section, we will prove the convergence of our proposed algorithm.

Theorem 1. *In each iteration, the updating rule for matrix G while fixing F will monotonically decrease the objective value in Eq. (5).*

To make Eq. (5) more compact, we separate all the data points as two subsets and re-write Eq. (5) as:

$$\begin{aligned}&J(F,G) = \min_{F,G} \sum_{j\in\mathcal{A}} ||x_j - Fg_j||_2 + \sum_{j\notin\mathcal{A}} \theta \\ &s.t.\ \ F \geq 0, G \geq 0, G^T G = I\end{aligned} \tag{12}$$

where $\mathcal{A} = \{x_j | ||x_j - Fg_j||_2 \leq \theta\}$.

Algorithm 1 Algorithm to solve the problem in Eq. (5).

Initialize F and G using the traditional k-means method, $F = F_k$ where F_k is the clustering centroid obtained by k-means method, $G = G_k + 0.2$, where G_k is the k-means clustering result. Initialize matrix D as the identity matrix.

repeat

Update F by Eq. (10): $F_{ik} \Leftarrow F_{ik}\frac{(XDG)_{ik}}{(FG^T DG)_{ik}}$

Update G by Eq. (10): $G_{jk} \Leftarrow G_{jk}\sqrt{\frac{(DX^T F)_{jk}}{(DGG^T X^T F)_{jk}}}$

Update D by Eq. (11):

$$D_{jj} = \begin{cases} \frac{1}{2||x_j - Fg_j||_2}, & if\ ||x_j - Fg_j||_2 \leq \theta \\ 0, & otherwise \end{cases}$$

until Converges

We first prove that the updating rule for matrix G while fixing F will monotonically decrease the value of the above $J(F,G)$. In the following proof, we will not count the $||x_j - Fg_j||_2$ when its value is greater than θ. Thus, Eq. (12) is equivalent to the following:

$$\begin{aligned}&\min_{F,G} \sum_{j\in\mathcal{A}} ||x_j - Fg_j||_2 \\ &s.t.\ \ \ F \geq 0, G \geq 0, G^T G = I\,.\end{aligned} \tag{13}$$

We will prove the following inequality after updating G:

$$\sum_{j\in\mathcal{A}} ||x_j - Fg_j^{t+1}||_2 \leq \sum_{j\in\mathcal{A}} ||x_j - Fg_j^t||_2\,. \tag{14}$$

where $G^T G = I$. To prove this inequality, we need the following lemma.

Lemma 1. *Under the updating rule for matrix G in Eq. (10) while fixing matrix F, the following inequality holds:*

$$\sum_{j\in\mathcal{A}} d_j ||x_j - Fg_j^{t+1}||_2^2 \leq \sum_{j\in\mathcal{A}} d_j ||x_j - Fg_j^t||_2^2$$

where $d_j = 1/(2||x_j - Fg_j^t||_2)$, $G^T G = I$.

PROOF. To prove this constrained problem, we need prove the Lagrangian function $J(G) = \sum_{j\in\mathcal{A}} d_j ||x_j - Fg_j||_2^2 + Tr(\Lambda(G^T G - I))$ is monotonically decreasing. Similar to the proof in [16], we use the auxiliary function approach, where if a function $A(G, G')$ satisfies

$$\begin{aligned}J(G) &\leq A(G, G'), \\ A(G, G) &= J(G)\,.\end{aligned} \tag{15}$$

Let's denote $A(G, G')$ as the auxiliary function of $J(G)$. We further define $G^{t+1} = arg\min A(G, G^t)$. As a result, we can get that $J(G^{t+1}) = A(G^{t+1}, G^{t+1}) \leq A(G^{t+1}, G^t) \leq J(G^t)$, which proves that $J(G^t)$ decreases monotonically. Thus, the key point is to find an auxiliary function $J(G)$. Note that the objective function $J(G)$ can be written as:

$$\begin{aligned}J(G) &= Tr(XDX^T - 2XDGF^T) + Tr(G^T DGF^T F) \\ &+ Tr(\Lambda(G^T G - I))\,,\end{aligned} \tag{16}$$

An appropriate auxiliary function is as the following:

$$\begin{aligned}A(G,G') =& Tr(XDX^T - \Lambda) \\ & - 2\sum_{k=1}^{c}\sum_{j\in\mathcal{A}}(DX^TF)_{jk}G'_{jk}(1+log\frac{G_{jk}}{G'_{jk}}) \\ & + \sum_{k=1}^{c}\sum_{j\in\mathcal{A}}\frac{(DG'F^TF+G'\Lambda)_{jk}G^2_{jk}}{G'_{jk}}.\end{aligned} \quad (17)$$

To prove the auxiliary function (17) satisfies equation (15), we need the inequality, $z \geq 1 + log(z)$ for all $z > 0$, and the following inequality derived in [2]:

$$Tr(H^TAHB) \leq \sum_{jk}(AH'B)_{jk}\frac{H^2_{jk}}{H'_{jk}}, \quad (18)$$

where A and B are nonnegative symmetric matrices, H is nonnegative matrix, and the equality holds when $H = H'$. Therefore, we have the following inequality:

$$\begin{aligned}& Tr(G^TDGF^TF) + Tr(\Lambda G^TG) \\ \leq & \sum_{k=1}^{c}\sum_{j\in\mathcal{A}}\frac{(DG'F^TF)_{jk}G^2_{jk}}{G'_{jk}} \\ & + \sum_{k=1}^{c}\sum_{j\in\mathcal{A}}\frac{(G'\Lambda)_{jk}G^2_{jk}}{G'_{jk}} \\ = & \sum_{k=1}^{c}\sum_{j\in\mathcal{A}}\frac{(DG'F^TF+G'\Lambda)_{jk}G^2_{jk}}{G'_{jk}}.\end{aligned} \quad (19)$$

Consequently, the auxiliary function defined in Eq. (17) is a valid auxiliary function. In the next step, we should find the stationary point of $A(G,G')$. Let $f(G) = A(G,G')$, taking the derivative of $f(G)$ with respect to G:

$$\frac{\partial f(G)}{\partial G_{jk}} = -2(DX^TF)_{jk}\frac{G'_{jk}}{G_{jk}} + 2\frac{(DG'F^TF+G'\Lambda)_{jk}G_{jk}}{G'_{jk}}. \quad (20)$$

Setting it to zero and substituting $\Lambda = -G'^TDG'F^TF + G'^TDX^TF$, we can get the stationary point:

$$G_{jk} = G'_{jk}\sqrt{\frac{(DX^TF)_{jk}}{(DG'G'^TX^TF)_{jk}}}. \quad (21)$$

To prove the stationary point is the minimum of $f(G)$, we should check the Hessian matrix whether is a positive semidefinite matrix. Taking the second derivative with respect to G, we get:

$$\frac{\partial^2 f(G)}{\partial G_{jk}\partial G_{il}} = (2(DX^TF)_{jk}\frac{G'_{jk}}{G^2_{jk}} + 2\frac{(DG'F^TF+G'\Lambda)_{jk}}{G'_{jk}})\delta_{ji}\delta_{kl} \quad (22)$$

Obviously, the Hessian matrix is a positive semidefinite matrix, which means $f(G)$ is a convex function, thus the stationary point in Eq. (21) is the unique global minima of $f(G)$. Note that if replacing $G = G^{(t+1)}$ and $G' = G^{(t)}$ for Eq. (21), we will get the updating rule in Eq. (10). Consequently, we complete the proof of lemma 1. □

Now we go back to prove the Theorem 1. We can easily have the following inequality:

$$||u||_2 - \frac{||u||_2^2}{2||u_t||_2} \leq ||u_t||_2 - \frac{||u_t||_2^2}{2||u_t||_2}, \quad (23)$$

where u and u_t are nonzero vectors. We replace the u and u_t with $x_j - Fg_j^{t+1}$ and $x_j - Fg_j^t$, respectively, and have:

$$\begin{aligned}& ||x_j - Fg_j^{t+1}||_2 - \frac{||x_j - Fg_j^{t+1}||_2^2}{2||x_j - Fg_j^t||_2} \\ \leq & ||x_j - Fg_j^t||_2 - \frac{||x_j - Fg_j^t||_2^2}{2||x_j - Fg_j^t||_2},\end{aligned} \quad (24)$$

which is further equivalent to:

$$\begin{aligned}& ||x_j - Fg_j^{t+1}||_2 - ||x_j - Fg_j^t||_2 \\ \leq & \frac{||x_j - Fg_j^{t+1}||_2^2}{2||x_j - Fg_j^t||_2} - \frac{||x_j - Fg_j^t||_2^2}{2||x_j - Fg_j^t||_2}.\end{aligned} \quad (25)$$

Summing all the j together, we will get:

$$\begin{aligned}& \sum_{j\in\mathcal{A}}||x_j - Fg_j^{t+1}||_2 - \sum_{j\in\mathcal{A}}||x_j - Fg_j^t||_2 \\ \leq & \sum_{j\in\mathcal{A}}\frac{||x_j - Fg_j^{t+1}||_2^2}{2||x_j - Fg_j^t||_2} - \sum_{j\in\mathcal{A}}\frac{||x_j - Fg_j^t||_2^2}{2||x_j - Fg_j^t||_2} \\ = & \sum_{j\in\mathcal{A}}d_j||x_j - Fg_j^{t+1}||_2^2 - \sum_{j\in\mathcal{A}}d_j||x_j - Fg_j^t||_2^2,\end{aligned} \quad (26)$$

where $d_j = 1/(2||x_j - Fg_j^t||_2)$. According to the inequality in Lemma 1, $\sum_{j\in\mathcal{A}}d_j||x_j - Fg_j^{t+1}||_2^2 \leq \sum_{j\in\mathcal{A}}d_j||x_j - Fg_j^t||_2^2$. Therefore, the inequality in Eq. (13) is proved, *i.e.* $J(F, G^{t+1}, \mathcal{A}) \leq J(F, G^t, \mathcal{A})$.

Theorem 2. *In each iteration, the updating rule for matrix F while fixing G will monotonically decrease the objective value in Eq. (5).*

The proof of Theorem 2 need prove that the following inequality holds:

$$\sum_{j\in\mathcal{A}}||x_j - F^{t+1}g_j||_2 \leq \sum_{j\in\mathcal{A}}||x_j - F^tg_j||_2.$$

Like the proof of Theorem 1, we need the following lemma:

Lemma 2. *Under the updating rule for matrix G in Eq. (10) while fixing matrix F, the following inequality holds:*

$$\sum_{j\in\mathcal{A}}d_j||x_j - F^{t+1}g_j||_2^2 \leq \sum_{j\in\mathcal{A}}d_j||x_j - F^tg_j||_2^2$$

where $d_j = 1/(2||x_j - F^tg_j||_2)$.

PROOF. We can get the same function for $J(F)$ as Eq. (16):

$$J(F) = Tr(XDX^T - 2XDGF^T) + Tr(F^TFG^TDG) \quad (27)$$

Also, we can get an auxiliary function as Eq. (17):

$$\begin{aligned}& A(F,F') \\ = & Tr(XDX^T - 2XDGF^T) + \sum_{i=1}^{d}\sum_{k=1}^{c}\frac{(F'G^TDG)_{ik}F^2_{ik}}{F'_{ik}}\end{aligned} \quad (28)$$

Similar to prove Lemma 1, we can prove Lemma 2. □

The rest proof of Theorem 2 is also similar to the proof of Theorem 1. We skip them due to limited space.

We should notice that the set $\mathcal{A}$ will be also updated to $\mathcal{A}'$ in our objective of Eq. (5), after F and G are updated. Based on the definition of our objective, we can easily have: $J(F^{t+1}, G^{t+1}, \mathcal{A}') \leq J(F^{t+1}, G^{t+1}, \mathcal{A})$. Based on the above Theorems 1 and 2, we know: $J(F^{t+1}, G^{t+1}, \mathcal{A}) \leq J(F^t, G^{t+1}, \mathcal{A}) \leq J(F^t, G^t, \mathcal{A})$. Thus, $J(F^{t+1}, G^{t+1}, \mathcal{A}') \leq J(F^t, G^t, \mathcal{A})$, *i.e.* our algorithm monotonically decreases the objective function.

After proving the monotonic decrease of the objective function, we need to prove the limit point (F^*, G^*) of the sequence $\{F^k, G^k\}$ generated under the updating rule in Eq. (10) is a stationary point, satisfying the KKT condition.

Theorem 3. *The limit solution G^* satisfies the Karush-Kohn-Tucker (KKT) condition of the constrained optimization theory.*

PROOF. The objective function for G while fixing F is:

$$\begin{aligned} &\min_G \sum_{j\in\mathcal{A}} ||x_j - Fg_j||_2 \\ &s.t. \quad G \geq 0, G^TG = I\,. \end{aligned} \tag{29}$$

According to the standard theory of constrained optimization, we introduce the Lagrangian multipliers C and Λ, and minimize the Lagrangian function:

$$L(G, C, \Lambda) = \sum_{j\in\mathcal{A}} ||x_j - Fg_j||_2 - Tr(C^TG) + Tr(\Lambda(G^TG - I)) \tag{30}$$

According to the KKT condition $\frac{\partial L(G,C,\Lambda)}{\partial G} = 0$ and $C_{jk}G_{jk} = 0$, we can get the following equation:

$$\left(\frac{\partial \sum_{j\in\mathcal{A}} ||x_j - Fg_j||_2}{\partial G_{jk}} + 2(G\Lambda)_{jk}\right)G_{jk} = 0 \tag{31}$$

In the next, we should prove Eq. (31) holds for the limit points G^*. Note that

$$\begin{aligned} &\frac{\partial \sum_{j\in\mathcal{A}} ||x_j - Fg_j||_2}{\partial G_{jk}} = 2\frac{[(X - FG^T)^TF]_{jk}}{2||x_j - Fg_j||_2} \\ &= 2(DX^TF)_{jk} - 2(DGF^TF)_{jk} \end{aligned} \tag{32}$$

where $D_{jj} = 1/(2||x_j - Fg_j||_2)$. Then Eq. (31) becomes:

$$((DX^TF)_{jk} - (DGF^TF)_{jk} + (G\Lambda)_{jk})G_{jk} = 0 \tag{33}$$

According to [3], Eq. (33) has the same fixed point condition with the following equation:

$$((DX^TF)_{jk} - (DGF^TF)_{jk} + (G\Lambda)_{jk})G_{jk}^2 = 0 \tag{34}$$

Following [3], when G converges, it satisfies the following equation according to the updating rule (10):

$$G^*_{jk} = G^*_{jk}\sqrt{\frac{(DX^TF)_{jk}}{(DG^*G^{*T}X^TF)_{jk}}} \tag{35}$$

which exactly satisfies the Eq. (34). Thus, the limit solution G^* satisfies the KKT condition. □

Theorem 4. *The limit solution F^* satisfies the Karush-Kohn-Tucker (KKT) condition of the constrained optimization theory.*

PROOF. The objective function for F while fixing G is:

$$\begin{aligned} &\min \sum_{j\in\mathcal{A}} ||x_j - Fg_j||_2 \\ &s.t. \quad F \geq 0\,. \end{aligned} \tag{36}$$

Similar to the proof for Theorem 3, we also introduce the Lagrangian multiplier Λ which is a matrix and minimize the Lagrangian function:

$$\min L(F, \Lambda) = \sum_{j\in\mathcal{A}} ||x_j - Fg_j||_2 - Tr(\Lambda^TF) \tag{37}$$

According to the KKT condition, we can get $\frac{\partial L(F,\Lambda)}{\partial F} = 0$, $\Lambda_{ik}F_{ik} = 0$ and the following equation:

$$\frac{\partial \sum_{j\in\mathcal{A}} ||x_j - Fg_j||_2}{\partial F_{ik}} F_{ik} = 0 \tag{38}$$

Specifically, the derivation for F_{ik} is as the following:

$$\frac{\partial \sum_{j\in\mathcal{A}} ||x_j - Fg_j||_2}{\partial F_{ik}} \tag{39}$$

$$= \left(\sum_{j\in\mathcal{A}} \frac{(x_j - Fg_j)g_j^T}{||x_j - Fg_j||_2}\right)_{ik} \tag{40}$$

$$= 2(XDG)_{ik} - 2(FG^TDG)_{ik} \tag{41}$$

Therefore, Eq. (38) becomes the following:

$$((XDG)_{ik} - (FG^TDG)_{ik})F_{ik} = 0 \tag{42}$$

Furthermore, the updating rule for the limit solution F^* is:

$$F^*_{ik} = F^*_{ik}\frac{(XDG)_{ik}}{(F^*G^TDG)_{ik}} \tag{43}$$

which is identical to Eq. (42). Thus, the limit solution F^* satisfies the KKT condition. □

3.3 Connection to Capped Norm K-means

The G-orthogonal nonnegative matrix factorization is equivalent to relaxed K-means clustering method [3]. Thus, we can represent the objective function of the K-means with clustering indicator as the following:

$$\min_{W,H\in Ind} ||X - WH||_F^2\,, \tag{44}$$

where $W \in \Re^{d\times k}$ is the cluster centroid matrix, and $H \in \Re^{k\times n}$ is the cluster indicator matrix and each column of H is coded as *1-of-K* scheme. It satisfies $HH^T = I$.

Similarly, we can use capped norm based objective to make K-means robust to outliers as our proposed capped norm orthogonal NMF. This new objective function is defined as following:

$$\min_{W,H\in Ind} \sum_{j=1}^{n} \min\{||x_j - Wh_j||_2, \theta\}\,, \tag{45}$$

where $\theta > 0$ is a thresholding parameter. Apparently, because $HH^T = I$ and $W \geq 0$, hence the relaxed capped norm K-means method is equivalent to our proposed capped norm orthogonal NMF model.

4. EXPERIMENT

In this section, we use both toy data and real-world datasets to show the performance of our proposed capped norm ONMF method.

4.1 Toy Data

Toy Data Setup The toy data is generated according to the equation $X = FG^T$, where the feature dimension of X is 2, the number of samples is 20, and we set $k = 1$. Because

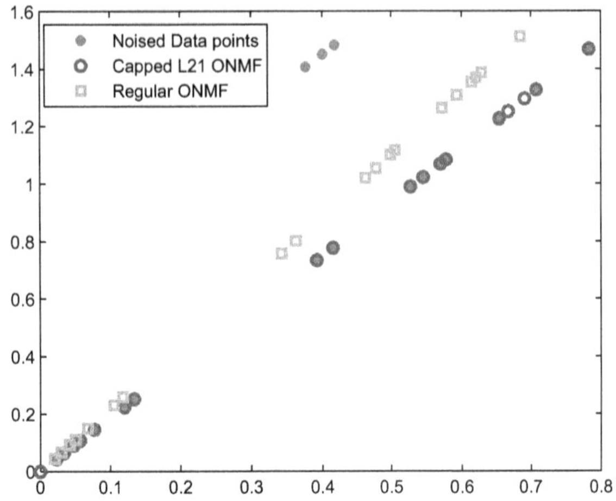

Figure 1: The fitting result from both regular ONMF and our proposed capped norm ONMF in fitting 20 data points with 3 outliers.

we want to show the robustness of our proposed method, three of the generated data samples are corrupted to be the outliers.

Implementation We use the ONMF proposed in [3] to be our comparative. The initialization of F and G for both ONMF and our proposed capped norm ONMF is generated randomly. For each data point, we use Fg_j to fit the original data point. The fitting values from both ONMF and our proposed method are shown in Fig. 1. From Fig. 1 we can see that our method can fit the original data points with much higher accuracy, while the fitting curve of the traditional ONMF deviates a lot from the original one because of the existence of the outliers. Therefore, our proposed method is robust to the outliers.

4.2 Real World Datasets

In this section, we use 10 benchmark real world datasets, including 3 face datasets, 2 handwritten datasets, 1 object image dataset and 4 document datasets, to evaluate our proposed capped norm ONMF.

Data Description The following is the brief description of each dataset, and the detailed information about these 10 datasets are summarized in Table 1.

- **Yale** [20] is a face dataset. It contains 165 images of 15 subjects. Each subject has 11 images, taken with different facial expression and configuration. We crop each image as 32×32 pixels.
- **ORL** [19] dataset contains 40 distinct subjects. Each subject corresponds to 10 different images taken at different times, varying lighting and facial expressions. In our experiment, each image is resized to 28 × 23 pixels.
- **UMIST** [7] is also a face dataset. It consists of 575 images from 20 distinct subjects. Each subject is taken from in a range of poses from profile to frontal views. We resize each image into 28 × 23 pixels.
- **MNIST** [15] is a hand-written digits dataset. It contains 70000 images about different hand-written number 0-9. We randomly select 15 images for each digit and resize each image into 28 × 28 pixels.

Table 1: Description of Benchmark Datasets

Dataset	Number of Instances	Dimensions	Classes
Yale	165	1024	15
ORL	400	644	40
UMIST	575	644	20
MNIST	150	784	10
USPS	9298	256	10
COIL-20	1440	1024	20
BBCNews	2225	9635	5
BBCSport	737	4613	5
WebKB	4199	7770	4
20News	18774	61188	20

- **USPS** [12] is also a hand-written digits dataset. We use the popular subset which contains 9298 images, and each image is 16×16 pixels.
- **COIL-20** [17] is an object image dataset. It contains 20 different objects. Each object is taken images at every angle in a 360 rotation. In our experiment, each image is resized to 32 × 32 pixels.
- **BBCNews** [8] contains 2225 documents from the BBC news website corresponding to five topics, business, entertainment, politics, sport and technique.
- **BBCSport** [8] contains 737 documents from the BBC sport website corresponding to five topics, athletics, cricket, football, rugby and tennis.
- **WebKB** [1] is a document dataset. It contains 504 documents about project topic, 930 documents about course topic, 1124 documents about faculty topic and 1641 documents about student topic.
- **20Newsgroup** [2] contains 18774 documents from 20 different newsgroups corresponding to different topics.

Experiment Setup For the image dataset, we normalize each data point as a vector with unit length. For the document dataset, we apply TF-IDF term weight normalisation to each data point and normalize the TF-IDF vector to unit length.

To evaluate the clustering performance, we adopt the widely used clustering accuracy and normalized mutual information as our metric. The details about the two metrics are described as the following:

- **Clustering Accuracy (ACC)** is a widely used metric to evaluate the clustering performance. It is defined as following:

$$ACC = \frac{\sum_{i=1}^{n} \delta(map(r_i), l_i)}{n} \tag{46}$$

where $\delta(x, y)$ is the delta function that $\delta(x, y) = 1$ if $x = y$, and $\delta(x, y) = 0$ otherwise, r_i and l_i are the clustering label and true label respectively, $map(r_i)$ is

[1] `http://www.cs.cmu.edu/~WebKB/`
[2] `http://people.csail.mit.edu/jrennie/20Newsgroups/`

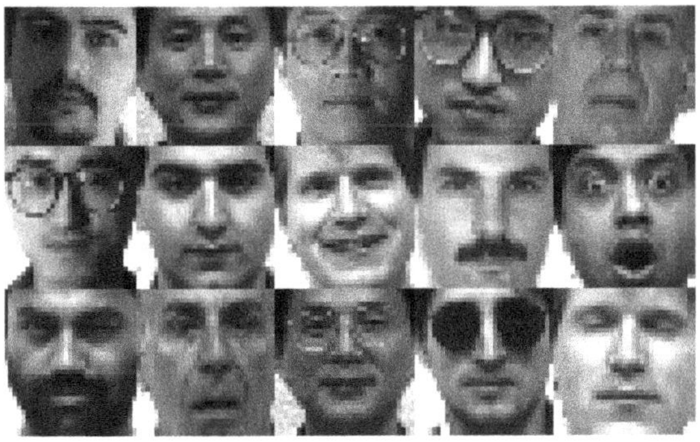

(a) Sample images from Yale dataset

(b) The outliers found by our method

Figure 2: The randomly selected sample images and the outliers found by our method on Yale dataset. The ratio of the outliers is set as 0.05. Most of the outliers have bad illumination.

a mapping function that matches the clustering label to the best true label. A large ACC value indicates a better clustering result.

- **Normalized Mutual Information (NMI)** is another usually used metric, and it is defined as:

$$NMI = \frac{I(S,C)}{(H(S)+H(C))/2} \tag{47}$$

where $I(S,C)$ is the mutual information function between the true class label C and the clustering label S, and $H(.)$ is the entropy function. The larger the NMI value is, the better the clustering result is.

We compare our proposed method with K-Means, standard NMF, traditional ONMF and $\ell_{2,1}$-norm NMF [14]. We run K-Means method for 50 times and choose the best clustering result, corresponding to the lowest objective value, as the K-Means final result. For fairness, we use such best K-Means result to initialize all the NMF methods as described in Algorithm 1. For each dataset, the value k is set to the real number of classes. In our experiment, the value of θ is set according to the ratio of the outliers. For all the datasets, we set the ratio of outliers between 0.03 and 0.05.

Result Analysis The clustering accuracy and normalized mutual information results are shown in Table 2 and Table 3. In Table 2 we can see that our proposed method is very competitive, always better than the other 4 methods. From Table 3 we can also conclude that our proposed method results are better than other 4 methods in all datasets in terms of the normalized mutual information.

To illustrate the effectiveness of our method on outliers, we show the outliers of the Yale face dataset as an example in Fig. 2. In this dataset, each subject is taken pictures under different conditions. In our experiment, we set the ratio of the outliers as 5 percentage. As shown in the Fig. 2, all the outliers have a bad illumination comparing with the other sample images. They are odd compared with the other faces, therefore they are selected as the outliers by our proposed method automatically.

Table 4: The 10 most representative terms of each topic found by our method on BBCSport dataset

athletics	cricket	football	rugby	tennis
olymp	wicket	chelsea	wale	seed
athlet	cricket	arsen	ireland	63
indoor	test	leagu	robinson	open
athen	pakistan	club	england	64
kenteri	seri	unit	nation	76
thanou	bowl	liverpool	franc	australian
greek	india	mourinho	rugbi	roddick
iaaf	south	football	six	75
drug	onedai	manag	scotland	hewitt
race	africa	manchest	itali	beat

To show the correctness of our method on document dataset, we show the 10 most representative terms of each topic found by our method on BBCSport dataset in Table 4. In this dataset, there are five topics, *athletics*, *cricket*, *football*, *rubgy* and *tennis*. In the NMF method, each column of the basis matrix F corresponds to a topic, and the elements in such a column are the representative terms for the corresponding topic. We select the 10 most representative terms for each topic. From Table 4 we can see that the representative terms found by our method can describe the corresponding topic to some extent.

4.3 Real World Datasets with Outliers

To further illustrate the effectiveness our proposed method, we construct a real word dataset with outliers. That is to add two images, which are randomly extracted from Caltech101 [6] dataset, to each class of ORL dataset, just as shown in Fig. 3. Due to the limitation of space, we only show the first ten subjects.

We perform standard NMF, traditional ONMF, $\ell_{2,1}$-norm NMF and our method on this dataset. We reshape the basis factors f_k contained in the matrix $F \in \Re^{d \times k}$ to show the reconstructed confusion face images, just as shown in Fig. 4.

We can conclude that confusion face images produced by our proposed method are more clear than those produced by the other three NMF methods. As examples are the groups in the red rectangle in Fig. 4, the base faces produced by our method is disturbed by the noises less than the other three methods apparently. Specifically, our method can successfully remove the effect from the outlier images, generating the face images rather than the outlier images.

In addition, we show the relationship between the ratio of outliers (determines the value of θ) and the clustering performance in Fig. 5. We perform this experiment on our constructed ORL dataset with outliers as shown in Fig. 3. In this dataset, the ratio of the added outliers is 1/6. As shown in Fig. 5, when we set the ratio of outliers as a small value, some outliers will be remained, impairing the clus-

Table 2: ACC of Real Datasets

Dataset	K-Means	NMF	ONMF	$\ell_{2,1}$ NMF	Ours
Yale	0.4182(±0.0212)	0.3933(±0.0278)	0.4279(±0.0254)	0.3994(±0.0258)	**0.4532**(±0.0301)
ORL	0.6655(±0.0163)	0.5525(±0.0375)	0.6803(±0.0491)	0.5705(±0.0454)	**0.7148**(±0.0465)
UMIST	0.4699(±0.0230)	0.3932(±0.0446)	0.4520(±0.0328)	0.4080(±0.0343)	**0.4856**(±0.0241)
MNIST	0.7973(±0.0298)	0.7800(±0.0665)	0.7987(±0.0478)	0.8087(±0.0371)	**0.8261**(±0.0403)
USPS	0.7704(±0.0008)	0.6259(±0.0954)	0.7440(±0.0399)	0.6424(±0.1099)	**0.7792**(±0.0010)
COIL-20	0.6648(±0.0046)	0.5771(±0.0735)	0.6542(±0.0455)	0.6130(±0.0439)	**0.6942**(±0.0295)
BBCNews	0.9575(±0.0073)	0.9620(±0.0022)	0.9636(±0.0013)	0.9607(±0.0029)	**0.9657**(±0.0037)
BBCSport	0.9516(±0.0327)	0.9469(±0.0329)	0.9571(±0.0347)	0.9455(±0.0324)	**0.9607**(±0.0365)
WebKB	0.6598(±0.0040)	0.6700(±0.0242)	0.6672(±0.0207)	0.6663(±0.0267)	**0.6715**(±0.0211)
20News	0.4738(±0.0209)	0.4948(±0.0120)	0.5228(±0.0155)	0.4828(±0.0214)	**0.5259**(±0.0168)

Table 3: NMI of Real Datasets

Dataset	K-Means	NMF	ONMF	$\ell_{2,1}$ NMF	Ours
Yale	0.4667(±0.0185)	0.4404(±0.0222)	0.4565(±0.0187)	0.4421(±0.0212)	**0.4935**(±0.0190)
ORL	0.8185(±0.0081)	0.7265(±0.0240)	0.8178(±0.0251)	0.7395(±0.0265)	**0.8355**(±0.0174)
UMIST	0.5978(±0.0151)	0.5086(±0.0383)	0.5659(±0.0332)	0.5220(±0.0342)	**0.5983**(±0.0204)
MNIST	0.7539(±0.0201)	0.7444(±0.0505)	0.7530(±0.0383)	0.7552(±0.0313)	**0.7865**(±0.0260)
USPS	0.6652(±0.0009)	0.5341(±0.0652)	0.6331(±0.0309)	0.5493(±0.0747)	**0.6678**(±0.0038)
COIL-20	0.7506(±0.0103)	0.6801(±0.0432)	0.7531(±0.0199)	0.6927(±0.0361)	**0.7556**(±0.0195)
BBCNews	0.8743(±0.0162)	0.8814(±0.0048)	0.8857(±0.0028)	0.8781(±0.0062)	**0.8915**(±0.0103)
BBCSport	0.8839(±0.0345)	0.8571(±0.0340)	0.8855(±0.0399)	0.8538(±0.0304)	**0.8978**(±0.0422)
WebKB	0.3578(±0.0161)	0.3757(±0.0128)	0.3698(±0.0209)	0.3707(±0.0161)	**0.3869**(±0.0190)
20News	0.4891(±0.0211)	0.4748(±0.0075)	0.5002(±0.0130)	0.4661(±0.0170)	**0.5100**(±0.0141)

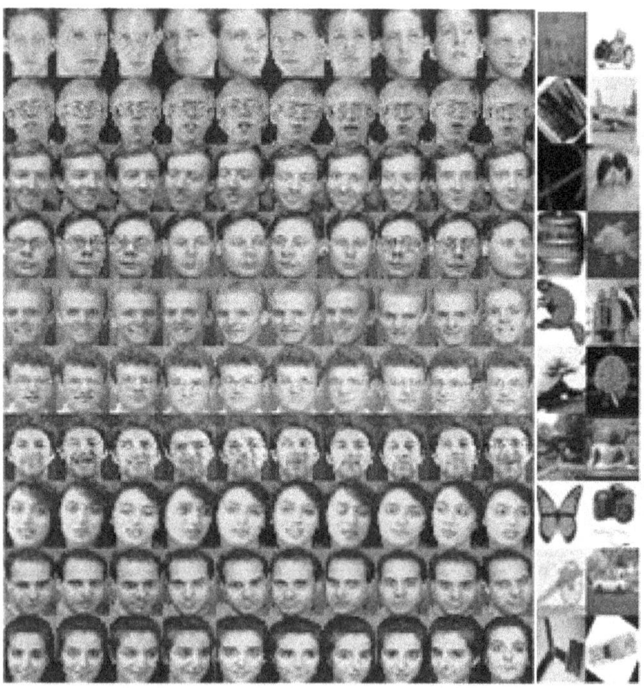

Figure 3: The ORL data set with noise images from Caltech101. Each class has two noise images.

tering performance. When we set it with a larger value, the performance is improved. Specifically, before the setting ratio approaches to 1/6, the performance is improved dramatically. After the setting ratio is greater than 1/6, the performance is improved slightly due to the removement of the outliers.

Based on the experiment result of all the datasets, we can conclude that it is reasonable to use the more robust capped norm orthogonal NMF to deal with practical problems with outliers and noises.

4.4 Convergence Analysis

In Fig. 6, we show the convergence of our proposed algorithm. As we have talked about in the previous part, we normalize each data point to unit length. In addition, the stop criteria for all the NMF methods is defined as following:

$$\frac{|f^{t+1} - f^t|}{f^t} < 10^{-6} \tag{48}$$

where f^t is the objective value in the t-th iteration. We implement our experiment with Matlab 2014 on an ordinary computer, which is configured with 4 Intel i5-4210U (up to 2.60GHz) cores, 8GB RAM and Windows 8.1 operating system.

Due to the limitation of the space, we only show the result of two datasets, ORL and UMIST. In Fig. 6, to make the difference among these four NMF methods clear, we only show the first 200 iterations. In Table 5, we show the iterations and time that each method needs to converge to the optimal solution. We can find that our method needs the least iterations to be converged. Comparing with the other two methods, $\ell_{2,1}$-norm based NMF and our method consume more time due to the re-weight strategy.

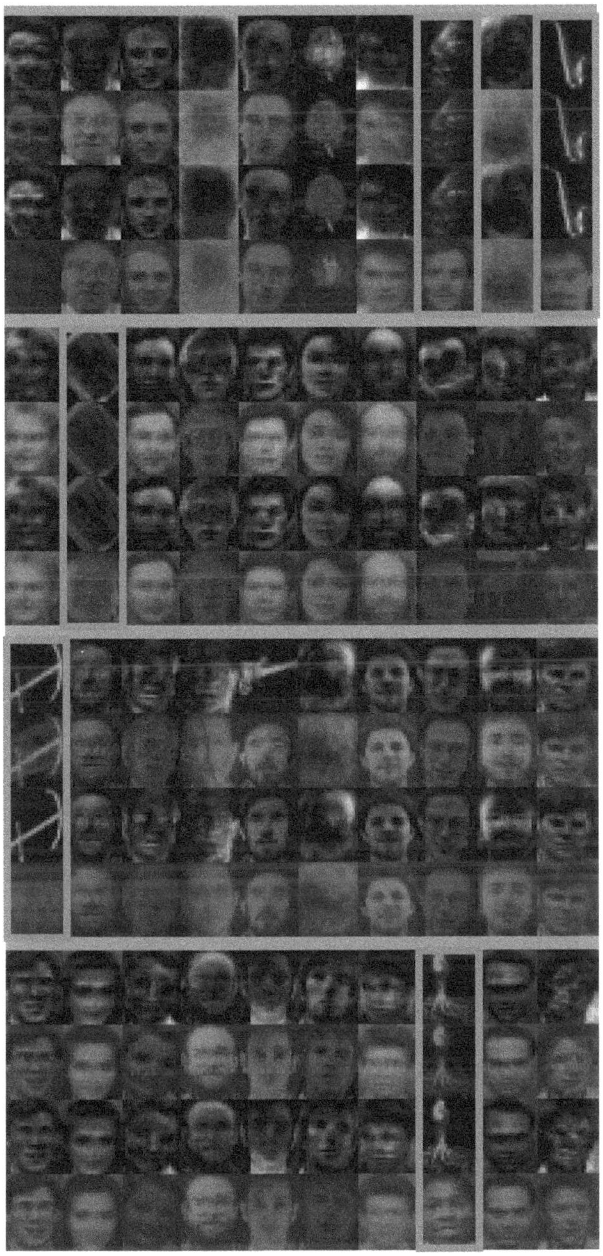

Figure 4: The basis face images obtained by performing standard NMF, ONMF, $\ell_{2,1}$-norm NMF and our method on noise dataset. Four rows constitute a group where each group corresponds to a face. In each group, the first row is standard NMF, the second is ONMF, the third is the $\ell_{2,1}$-norm NMF, and the fourth is our proposed method. Obviously, in the images within the red rectangles, the outliers effect the standard NMF, ONMF and $\ell_{2,1}$-norm NMF calculation. But our method can successfully remove the effect from these outlier images.

5. CONCLUSION

In this paper, we propose a new robust NMF method, which is called capped norm orthogonal NMF, to make the NMF method more robust to the outliers and noises. Although our proposed objective function is difficult to solve, we use the re-weighted strategy to solve it successfully. Furthermore, we prove the convergence and correctness of our proposed method. Extensive experiments for both synthetic and real world data demonstrate the correctness and effectiveness of our method in dealing with the clustering problem.

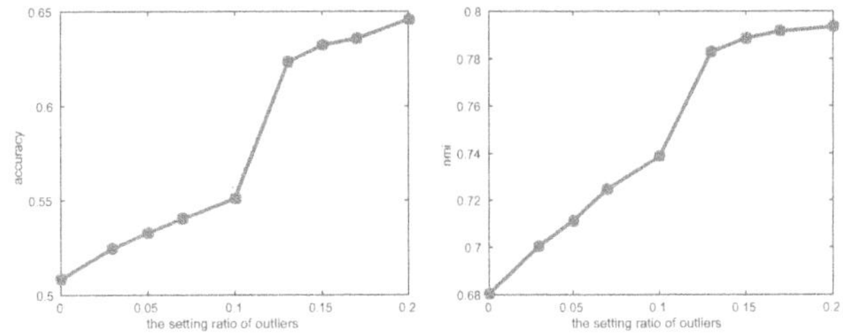

(a) ACC (b) NMI

Figure 5: The relationship between the setting ratio of outliers (determines the value of θ) and clustering performance on our constructed ORL dataset with 1/6 outliers.

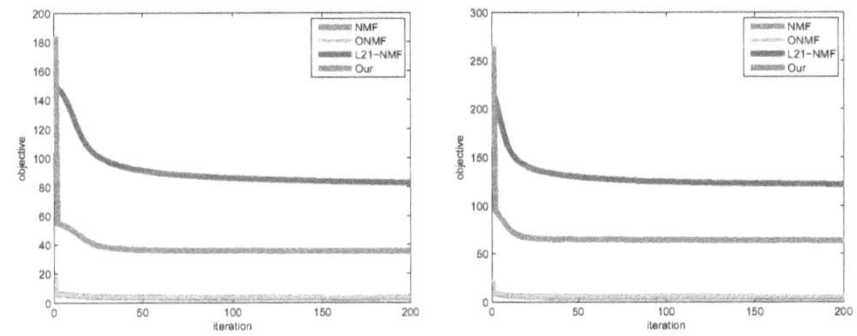

(a) ORL (b) UMIST

Figure 6: The convergence of the four NMF methods on ORL and UMIST datasets.

Table 5: The computational time and iterations of different methods to reach convergence.

Dataset	Metric	NMF	ONMF	$\ell_{2,1}$ NMF	Ours
ORL	Time(sec)	72.9301	56.8457	224.3732	173.4679
	Iterations	5299	2126	6155	1868
UMIST	Time(sec)	86.3794	68.8907	258.2697	255.2915
	Iterations	5154	1693	4324	1635

6. ACKNOWLEDGMENTS

This work was supported in part by Australian Research Council (ARC) grants and U.S. NSF-IIS 1117965, NSF-IIS 1302675, NSF-IIS 1344152, NSF-DBI 1356628.

7. REFERENCES

[1] M. Cooper and J. Foote. Summarizing video using non-negative similarity matrix factorization. In *Multimedia Signal Processing, 2002 IEEE Workshop on*, pages 25–28. IEEE, 2002.

[2] C. Ding, T. Li, and M. I. Jordan. Convex and semi-nonnegative matrix factorizations. *Pattern Analysis and Machine Intelligence, IEEE Transactions on*, 32(1):45–55, 2010.

[3] C. Ding, T. Li, W. Peng, and H. Park. Orthogonal nonnegative matrix t-factorizations for clustering. In *Proceedings of the 12th ACM SIGKDD international conference on Knowledge discovery and data mining*, pages 126–135. ACM, 2006.

[4] C. H. Ding, X. He, and H. D. Simon. On the equivalence of nonnegative matrix factorization and spectral clustering. In *SDM*, volume 5, pages 606–610. SIAM, 2005.

[5] L. Du, X. Li, and Y.-D. Shen. Robust nonnegative matrix factorization via half-quadratic minimization. In *ICDM*, pages 201–210, 2012.

[6] L. Fei-Fei, R. Fergus, and P. Perona. Learning generative visual models from few training examples: An incremental bayesian approach tested on 101 object categories. *Computer Vision and Image Understanding*, 106(1):59–70, 2007.

[7] D. B. Graham and N. M. Allinson. Characterising virtual eigensignatures for general purpose face recognition. In *Face Recognition*, pages 446–456. Springer, 1998.

[8] D. Greene and P. Cunningham. Practical solutions to the problem of diagonal dominance in kernel document clustering. In *Proceedings of the 23rd international conference on Machine learning*, pages 377–384. ACM, 2006.

[9] A. B. Hamza and D. J. Brady. Reconstruction of reflectance spectra using robust nonnegative matrix factorization. *Signal Processing, IEEE Transactions on*, 54(9):3637–3642, 2006.

[10] P. O. Hoyer. Non-negative matrix factorization with sparseness constraints. *The Journal of Machine Learning Research*, 5:1457–1469, 2004.

[11] J. Huang, F. Nie, H. Huang, and C. Ding. Robust manifold non-negative matrix factorization. *ACM Transactions on Knowledge Discovery from Data (TKDD)*, 8(3):11:1–11:21, 2013.

[12] J. J. Hull. A database for handwritten text recognition research. *Pattern Analysis and Machine Intelligence, IEEE Transactions on*, 16(5):550–554, 1994.

[13] T. Kanungo, D. M. Mount, N. S. Netanyahu, C. D. Piatko, R. Silverman, and A. Y. Wu. An efficient k-means clustering algorithm: Analysis and implementation. *Pattern Analysis and Machine Intelligence, IEEE Transactions on*, 24(7):881–892, 2002.

[14] D. Kong, C. Ding, and H. Huang. Robust nonnegative matrix factorization using l21-norm. In *Proceedings of the 20th ACM international conference on Information and knowledge management*, pages 673–682. ACM, 2011.

[15] Y. LeCun, L. Bottou, Y. Bengio, and P. Haffner. Gradient-based learning applied to document recognition. *Proceedings of the IEEE*, 86(11):2278–2324, 1998.

[16] D. D. Lee and H. S. Seung. Algorithms for non-negative matrix factorization. In *Advances in neural information processing systems*, pages 556–562, 2001.

[17] S. A. Nene, S. K. Nayar, H. Murase, et al. Columbia object image library (coil-20). Technical report, Technical Report CUCS-005-96, 1996.

[18] P. Paatero and U. Tapper. Positive matrix factorization: A non-negative factor model with optimal utilization of error estimates of data values. *Environmetrics*, 5(2):111–126, 1994.

[19] F. S. Samaria and A. C. Harter. Parameterisation of a stochastic model for human face identification. In *Applications of Computer Vision, 1994., Proceedings of the Second IEEE Workshop on*, pages 138–142. IEEE, 1994.

[20] T. Sim, S. Baker, and M. Bsat. The cmu pose, illumination, and expression database. *Pattern Analysis and Machine Intelligence, IEEE Transactions on*, 25(12):1615–1618, 2003.

[21] H. Wang, H. Huang, and C. Ding. Cross-language web page classification via joint nonnegative matrix tri-factorization based dyadic knowledge transfer. *Annual ACM SIGIR Conference*, pages 933–942, 2011.

[22] H. Wang, H. Huang, and C. Ding. Simultaneous clustering of multi-type relational data via symmetric nonnegative matrix tri-factorization. *ACM Conference on Information and Knowledge Management (CIKM)*, pages 279–284, 2011.

[23] H. Wang, H. Huang, C. Ding, and F. Nie. Predicting protein-protein interactions from multimodal biological data sources via nonnegative matrix factorization. *The 16th International Conference on Research in Computational Molecular Biology (RECOMB)*, pages 314–325, 2012.

[24] H. Wang, H. Huang, F. Nie, and C. Ding. Nonnegative matrix tri-factorization based simultaneous clustering of large-scale multi-type related data. *IEEE International Conference on Data Mining (ICDM)*, pages 774–783, 2011.

[25] H. Wang, F. Nie, H. Huang, and F. Makedon. Fast nonnegative matrix tri-factorization for large-scale data co-clustering. *International Joint Conferences on Artificial Intelligence (IJCAI)*, pages 1553–1558, 2011.

[26] W. Xu, X. Liu, and Y. Gong. Document clustering based on non-negative matrix factorization. In *Proceedings of the 26th annual international ACM SIGIR conference on Research and development in informaion retrieval*, pages 267–273. ACM, 2003.

[27] L. Zhang, Z. Chen, M. Zheng, and X. He. Robust non-negative matrix factorization. *Frontiers of Electrical and Electronic Engineering in China*, 6(2):192–200, 2011.

MF-Tree: Matrix Factorization Tree for Large Multi-Class Learning

Lei Liu
Hewlett Packard Laboratories,
Palo Alto, CA, USA 94304
lei.liu2@hp.com

Pang-Ning Tan
Michigan State University,
East Lansing, MI, USA 48824
ptan@cse.msu.edu

Xi Liu
Michigan State University,
East Lansing, MI, USA 48824
liuxi4@cse.msu.edu

ABSTRACT

Many big data applications require accurate classification of objects into one of possibly thousands or millions of categories. Such classification tasks are challenging due to issues such as class imbalance, high testing cost, and model interpretability problems. To overcome these challenges, we propose a novel hierarchical learning method known as `MF-Tree` to efficiently classify data sets with large number of classes while simultaneously inducing a taxonomy structure that captures relationships among the classes. Unlike many other existing hierarchical learning methods, our approach is designed to optimize a global objective function. We demonstrate the equivalence between our proposed regularized loss function and the Hilbert-Schmidt Independence Criterion (HSIC). The latter has a nice additive property, which allows us to decompose the multi-class learning problem into hierarchical binary classification tasks. To improve its training efficiency, an approximate algorithm for inducing MF-Tree is also proposed. We performed extensive experiments to compare MF-Tree against several state-of-the-art algorithms and showed both its effectiveness and efficiency when applied to real-world data sets.

1. INTRODUCTION

Multi-class learning is a pervasive problem in the current age of big data, cutting across a broad range of applications, including text categorization [26, 19], image recognition [11, 24, 14], video classification [18, 23], and malware detection [9, 8, 25, 7]. In addition to the massive volume of data that must be handled, the classification tasks in these applications involve thousands or possibly millions of classes. Traditional multi-class learning methods, based on one-versus-one or one-versus-all strategies, require building $O(c)$ or $O(c^2)$ binary classifiers, where c is the number of classes. Such methods are computationally expensive during testing since one must apply a large number of classifiers to predict the class of a test instance.

Hierarchical learning methods [1, 2, 10, 28], which organize the binary classifiers into a tree-like structure, have been developed to overcome this limitation. The advantages to these methods are three-fold. First, they can reduce model testing to sublinear time in c since the test complexity depends on the maximum depth of the tree. Second, they could help alleviate the class imbalanced problem by learning to discriminate groups of related classes instead of individual classes (except at the leaf nodes of the tree). Finally, the hierarchical structure induced by such methods may offer interesting insights into the semantic relationships among the classes.

Numerous hierarchical learning methods have been developed in recent years, from greedy top-down decision tree classifiers that use simple attribute test conditions as internal nodes of the tree, to more advanced methods that employ binary classifiers such as SVM as their internal nodes. Each of these methods has its own pros and cons. While decision tree classifiers are easy to construct, they are susceptible to the class imbalanced and data fragmentation problems. In addition, a class can be assigned to multiple leaf nodes of the tree, resulting in an unnecessarily large and complex tree. This affects both its runtime for testing as well as interpretability of its hierarchical structure as a class taxonomy. Alternative methods, such as filter tree [2] and its variants, impose a random tree structure on the classes and learn a set of binary classifiers to route the classes to their appropriate leaf nodes in the tree. Because of the arbitrariness in which the classes are assigned to the leaf nodes, the resulting tree might be suboptimal and loses descriptive information about the class relationships. More importantly, both types of methods were not designed to optimize a global objective function. To address these limitations, we propose a novel method known as matrix factorization tree (MF-Tree, in short) to organize the classes into a binary tree by solving a global objective function based on a regularized loss function.

We provide a theoretical proof to demonstrate the equivalence between the proposed loss function and the Hilbert-Schmidt Independence Criterion (HSIC) [13][3][30]. HSIC is a recently proposed criterion for taxonomy learning in an unsupervised learning setting. In this paper, we demonstrate how HSIC can be applied to a supervised multi-class learning problem. We also showed the additive property of the objective function, which allows us to decompose the problem into a hierarchical matrix factorization task that can be represented as a binary tree. Since the tree is constructed by partitioning the classes into disjoint subclasses, the resulting tree provides a good representation of a class taxonomy as each class resides in exactly one leaf node of the tree.

For massive classification problems involving thousands of classes or more, factorizing the matrices is computationally expensive especially at the top levels of the tree. To address this problem, we present an approximate algorithm for inducing MF-Tree, where the partitioning of classes at the top level of the hierarchy is performed using a fast method instead of solving a matrix factorization problem involving large number of classes. The more expensive matrix factorization can be applied at the lower levels of the tree when

Permission to make digital or hard copies of all or part of this work for personal or classroom use is granted without fee provided that copies are not made or distributed for profit or commercial advantage and that copies bear this notice and the full citation on the first page. Copyrights for components of this work owned by others than ACM must be honored. Abstracting with credit is permitted. To copy otherwise, or republish, to post on servers or to redistribute to lists, requires prior specific permission and/or a fee. Request permissions from Permissions@acm.org.
CIKM'15, October 19–23, 2015, Melbourne, Australia.
© 2015 ACM. ISBN 978-1-4503-3794-6/15/10 ...$15.00.
DOI: http://dx.doi.org/10.1145/2806416.2806540

there are fewer number of classes and training examples to be dealt with. We showed that the accuracy of the approximate MF-Tree is quite comparable to that of MF-Tree, but with a significant improvement in its training time. In short, the main contributions of this paper are as follows:

- We introduce a novel hierarchical classification method for large multi-class learning problems known as MF-Tree. The tree is designed to optimize a global loss function.
- We provide a theoretical proof showing the equivalence between optimizing our regularized loss function and the Hilbert-Schmidt Independence Criterion (HSIC) by setting appropriate constraints on the latent factors of the factorization. We demonstrate the additive property of HSIC that enables the design of a hierarchical tree learning framework.
- We present an approximate algorithm for learning MF-Tree to speed up the tree induction process.
- We provide extensive experiments to evaluate and compare the performance of MF-Tree against several state-of-the-art baselines.

2. RELATED WORK

Classification with large number of classes is an important but challenging problem, and has received increasing attention in recent years [10][18][12]. Existing methods for multi-class learning employ a collection of binary classifiers, organized either in a non-hierarchical (flat) structure or a hierarchical tree architecture.

Flat (Non-hierarchical) classification methods, including one-versus-all [29], one-versus-one [15], and error-correcting output coding (ECOC) [21], require invocation of all the binary classifiers during testing time in order to determine the final prediction. Both one-versus-one and one-versus-all methods are inefficient when the number of classes is large due to the linear and quadratic number of binary classifiers that must be invoked during testing. The ECOC method assigns a unique m bit codeword to each class label (where $m > \log_2 c$). Given a test instance, we must generate an m-bit vector by applying m binary classifiers and then compute its distance to the codewords of all c classes, which is an expensive operation.

Hierarchical methods [28, 2, 1, 10] help to reduce the number of classifiers that need to be invoked during the testing phase by organizing the classifiers in a hierarchical structure. Their runtime for testing depends on the depth of the structure. For example, the Decision Directed Acyclic Graph (DDAG) [28] approach arranges the one-versus-one classifiers in a rooted binary DAG in order to reduce the runtime complexity from $O(c(c-1)/2)$ to $O(c)$. In fact, it is possible to achieve sublinear complexity (e.g., $O(\log c)$) by assigning each class to a single leaf node of the hierarchy. Such a strategy was adopted by label tree learning methods such as [11, 1, 10], which constructs a linear classifier at each node to assign training instances to their corresponding child nodes. With this approach, only the binary classifiers located along the path from the root node to one of the leaf nodes are invoked when determining the class label of a test instance.

Hierarchical methods vary in terms of how their structure and the associated classes of each leaf node are learned from training data. For example, Bengio et al. [1] developed a label embedding tree approach by training c one-vs-all classifiers to obtain an initial confusion matrix, which is then used as the affinity matrix for applying spectral clustering to partition the classes into smaller subgroups. Deng et al. [10] presented an alternative strategy that simultaneously learns the class partitioning and the weights of the associated linear classifiers by optimizing their joint objective function. However, the approach requires solving an integer programming problem, which is NP-hard. Instead they relaxed the optimization problem into a linear program in order to find a polynomial time solution. Shi et al. [11] also introduced a relaxed hierarchical learning approach for large-scale visual recognition. At each node, the classes are colored into positive and negative labels by a binary classifier while a subset of confusing classes are ignored. The coloring of classes and training of binary classifier is done simultaneously using a max-margin optimization approach. Lei et al. [22] proposed a label tree learning approach that allows for soft partitioning of the classes by minimizing an information theoretic loss function. Unlike other previous works, the leaf node of the tree may contain one or more one-class SVM models to distinguish the instances from different classes. Despite the extensive work, the main drawbacks of existing hierarchical methods is that they either assume the hierarchical structure is given [2] or they allow a class to be assigned to multiple leaf nodes of the tree. As noted in the previous section, the latter produces trees that are larger than necessary and affects its interpretability.

Hierarchical methods have also been widely used for unsupervised learning, starting with classical methods such as agglomerative hierarchical clustering. Kuang et al. [20] developed a hierarchical clustering method based on rank-2 nonnegative matrix factorization. The authors proposed a fast algorithm based on the active set method to solve their optimization problem. Their method also spent considerable amount of time detecting outliers to avoid generating too many leaf nodes with few instances. However, similar to classical hierarchical clustering, there is no global objective function solved by their algorithm. Taxonomy learning is another related area of our work. A family of unsupervised learning algorithms for taxonomy learning [13][3][30][4] have been proposed to cluster data into a hierarchical structure. Our work is inspired by the Hilbert-Schmidt Independence Criterion (HSIC) metric employed by these works. We showed how HSIC is related to our global objective function for matrix factorization, which enables us to decompose the problem into a hierarchical tree learning task.

3. PRELIMINARIES

This section presents a formal definition of the multi-class learning problem. We also introduce the concepts of Hilbert-Schmidt Independence Criterion and the tree-structured covariance matrix. The connections between these concepts and the proposed MF-tree method will be shown in Section 4.

3.1 Problem Definition

Let $\mathcal{D} = \{(\mathbf{x}_1, y_1), (\mathbf{x}_2, y_2), \ldots, (\mathbf{x}_n, y_n)\}$ denote a set of training instances sampled from an unknown distribution P over $\mathcal{X} \times \mathcal{Y}$, where $\mathcal{X} \subseteq \mathcal{R}^d$ is the d-dimensional feature space and $\mathcal{Y} = \{1, 2, \cdots, c\}$ is the set of permissible categories. For large multi-class learning problems, we assume $c >> 2$. The goal of multi-class learning is to infer a target function f that minimizes the expected risk of misclassifying any instance drawn from P, i.e., $\min_f E_{(\mathbf{x},y)\in P}[\mathcal{L}(f(\mathbf{x}), y)]$, where $\mathcal{L}$ is known as the loss function.

A standard approach for multi-class learning is to reduce the problem into multiple binary classification tasks. However, when the number of classes c is too large, applying all the binary classifiers to predict the class of a test instance is computationally infeasible. To overcome this problem, hierarchical labeled tree algorithms have been developed for large multi-class learning problems. A hierarchical labeled tree is a 4-tuple $T =< V, E, \Phi, \Lambda >$, where V is the set of nodes, E is the set of edges connecting parent nodes to their corresponding child nodes, $\Phi = \{f_v(\mathbf{x})|v \in V\}$ is the set of classifiers associated with the internal nodes of T, and $\Lambda = \{y_{\hat{v}}|y_{\hat{v}} \in \mathcal{Y}, \hat{v} \in V\}$ is the set of labels associated with the leaf nodes. In this paper, we restrict our framework to binary rooted trees only, even though, in principle, it is applicable to rooted trees with a branching factor greater than 2. Our objective in this work is to learn an optimal tree T for large, multi-class learning problems.

3.2 Hilbert-Schmidt Independence Criterion (HSIC)

This section introduces the Hilbert-Schmidt Independence Criterion. Our presentation follows closely the definitions given in [13] [30][3]. Let (X, Y) be a pair of random variables drawn from a joint distribution $P_{X,Y}$. The Hilbert-Schmidt Independence Criterion (HSIC)[13] measures the dependence between X and Y by calculating the norm of its cross-covariance operator C_{xy} in Hilbert space. It has been shown that this norm vanishes if and only if X and Y are independent variables. A larger value of HSIC also indicates a stronger dependence between the two variables, with respect to the choice of kernels [30].

Let $\mathcal{F}$ be a Reproducing Kernel Hilbert Space (RKHS) of functions from $\mathcal{X}$ to $\mathcal{R}$ with a feature map ϕ, such that $\langle\phi(x), \phi(x')\rangle_{\mathcal{F}} = k_X(x, x')$, where $k_X : \mathcal{X} \times \mathcal{X} \to \mathcal{R}$ is a positive definite kernel. Likewise, let $\mathcal{G}$ be the RKHS on $\mathcal{Y}$ with a feature map ψ, such that $\langle\psi(y), \psi(y')\rangle_{\mathcal{G}} = k_Y(y, y')$, where $k_Y : \mathcal{Y} \times \mathcal{Y} \to \mathcal{R}$ is the corresponding kernel for the metric space $\mathcal{Y}$. The covariance operator C_{xy} is defined as

$$C_{xy} = E_{x,y}[(\phi(x) - \mu_x) \otimes (\psi(y) - \mu_y)]^2_{HS}$$

where $\mu_x = E[\phi(x)]$, $\psi_y = E[\psi(y)]$ and $\otimes$ denote a tensor product. The Hilbert-Schmidt Independence Criterion is defined as the squared Hilbert-Schmidt norm of the cross-covariance operator C_{xy}, which can be written as follows:

$$\begin{aligned} \text{HSIC}_{X,Y} &= \|C_{xy}\|^2_{HS} \\ &= E_{x,x',y,y'}[k_X(x, x')k_Y(y, y')] \\ &\quad + E_{x,x'}[k_X(x, x')]E_{y,y'}[k_Y(y, y')] \\ &\quad - 2E_{x,y}[E_{x'}[k_X(x, x')]E_{y'}[k_Y(y, y')]] \quad (1) \end{aligned}$$

Let $\{(\mathbf{x}_1, y_1), (\mathbf{x}_2, y_2), \cdots, (\mathbf{x}_n, y_n)\}$ be the set of training instances drawn from Pr_{XY}. HSIC can be empirically estimated from the training data as follows [13, 3]:

$$\text{HSIC} = \frac{1}{(n-1)^2}\mathbf{tr}\left[\mathbf{H}_n\hat{\mathbf{K}}\mathbf{H}_n\mathbf{L}\right] \quad (2)$$

where $\mathbf{tr}[\cdot]$ denote the trace of a matrix, $\mathbf{H}_n = \mathbf{I} - \frac{1}{n}\mathbf{1}_n\mathbf{1}_n^T$ is a centering matrix, $\mathbf{I}$ is the identity matrix, $\mathbf{1}_n$ is a column vector of all ones, $\hat{\mathbf{K}}$ is an $n \times n$ uncentered kernel matrix for $\mathbf{x}$, and $\mathbf{L}$ is an $n \times n$ kernel matrix for the class labels y. The matrix product $\mathbf{H}_n\hat{\mathbf{K}}\mathbf{H}_n$ corresponds to a centered kernel matrix. If $\mathbf{K}$ denote the centered kernel matrix, then the computation of HSIC simplifies to $(n-1)^{-2}\mathbf{tr}[\mathbf{KL}]$.

3.3 Tree-Structured Covariance Matrix

Given a rooted binary tree T on the labeled set $\mathcal{Y}$, we can represent it as a tree-structured covariance matrix [3] as follows.

DEFINITION 1. *(Tree-Structured Covariance Matrix) A matrix* $\mathbf{C} \in \mathcal{R}^{c \times c}$ *is a covariance matrix associated with the label tree structure* T, *where* $\mathbf{C}_{ij}$ *is a measure of similarity between the i-th and j-th classes computed based on the path length from the root node to the closest common ancestor between the leaf nodes for* i *and* j *in* T. *The larger the value of* $\mathbf{C}_{ij}$, *the closer is the relationship between the two classes.*

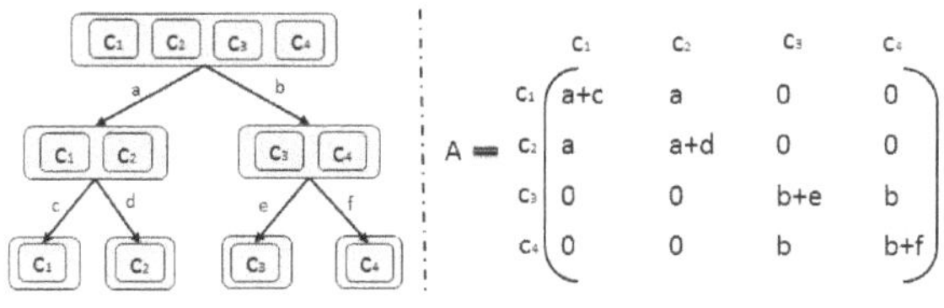

Figure 1: Example Tree Structure with 8 classes

Figure 1 shows an example of a labeled tree structure for 4 classes, c_1, c_2, c_3, and c_4. Let a, b, c, d, e, f denote the edge weights between the nodes. Based on the structure, the tree-structured covariance matrix is a 4×4 matrix shown on the right hand side of the diagram. For example, $C_{1,2} = a$ since the closest common ancestor between the classes has a path length equals to a from the root node. Similarly, $C_{3,3} = b + e$, which is the path length from the root to the leaf node for c_3. Note that the edge weight a, b, c, d, e, f determines the similarity between the different categories. For brevity, the edge weights are assumed to be 1 in the examples presented in the next section.

4. MF-TREE: PROPOSED METHOD

This section presents an overview of the proposed method. We first introduce the global objective function to be optimized by MF-Tree. We then show its connection to the HSIC measure described in the previous section. We also illustrate the additive property of HSIC, which allows us to develop a hierarchical tree-based induction algorithm.

4.1 Global Objective Function of MF-Tree

Let $\mathbf{X}$ denote an $n \times d$ centered design matrix, whose rows correspond to the data instances and columns correspond to the features. An uncentered design matrix $\tilde{\mathbf{X}}$ can always be centered by applying the following operation, $\mathbf{H}_n\tilde{\mathbf{X}}$, where $\mathbf{H}_n$ is the centering matrix defined in Section 3.2.

MF-Tree is designed to minimize the following regularized squared error loss function.

$$\begin{aligned} \mathcal{J} &= \|\mathbf{X} - \mathbf{Z}\mathbf{W}^T\|^2_F + \lambda\mathbf{tr}\left[\mathbf{W}\mathbf{A}\mathbf{W}^T\right] \\ &= \mathbf{tr}\left[\mathbf{X}\mathbf{X}^T - \mathbf{X}\mathbf{W}\mathbf{Z}^T - \mathbf{Z}\mathbf{W}^T\mathbf{X}^T + \mathbf{Z}\mathbf{W}^T\mathbf{W}\mathbf{Z}^T\right] \\ &\quad + \lambda\,\mathbf{tr}\left[\mathbf{W}\mathbf{A}\mathbf{W}^T\right], \quad (3) \end{aligned}$$

where $\mathbf{Z}$ is an $n \times c$ matrix, which represents the class membership of each data instance, $\mathbf{W}$ is a $d \times c$ matrix, which represents the feature vector of each class, $\mathbf{A}$ is a symmetric, positive-definite, $c \times c$ class covariance matrix, and λ is the regularization parameter. $\|\cdot\|_F$ denote the Frobenius norm of a matrix and the superscript T denote the transpose operator. The intuition behind the objective function given in Equation (3) is to factorize the centered design matrix $\mathbf{X}$ into a product of latent factors $\mathbf{Z}$ and $\mathbf{W}$.

4.2 Relationship between Global Objective Function and HSIC

To demonstrate the relationship between the objective function and HSIC, let us take the partial derivative of $\mathcal{J}$ given in Equation

(3) with respect to $\mathbf{W}$ and set it to zero:

$$\begin{aligned}\frac{\partial \mathcal{J}}{\partial \mathbf{W}} &= -2\mathbf{X}^T\mathbf{Z} + 2\mathbf{W}\mathbf{Z}^T\mathbf{Z} + 2\lambda\mathbf{W}\mathbf{A} = 0 \\ \mathbf{W} &= \mathbf{X}^T\mathbf{Z}\Big[\mathbf{Z}^T\mathbf{Z} + \lambda\mathbf{A}\Big]^{-1}\end{aligned}$$

Replacing this back into Equation (3) yields the following:

$$\begin{aligned}\mathcal{J} &= \mathbf{tr}\Big\{\mathbf{X}\mathbf{X}^T - 2\mathbf{X}\mathbf{X}^T\mathbf{Z}\Big[\mathbf{Z}^T\mathbf{Z} + \lambda\mathbf{A}\Big]^{-1}\mathbf{Z}^T \\ &\quad + \mathbf{Z}\Big[\mathbf{Z}^T\mathbf{Z} + \lambda\mathbf{A}\Big]^{-1}\mathbf{Z}^T\mathbf{X}\mathbf{X}^T\mathbf{Z}\Big[\mathbf{Z}^T\mathbf{Z} + \lambda\mathbf{A}\Big]^{-1}\mathbf{Z}^T\Big\} \\ &\quad + \lambda\,\mathbf{tr}\Big\{\mathbf{X}^T\mathbf{Z}\Big[\mathbf{Z}^T\mathbf{Z} + \lambda\mathbf{A}\Big]^{-1}\mathbf{A}\Big[\mathbf{Z}^T\mathbf{Z} + \lambda\mathbf{A}\Big]^{-1}\mathbf{Z}^T\mathbf{X}\Big\} \\ &= \mathbf{tr}\Big\{\mathbf{X}\mathbf{X}^T - \mathbf{X}\mathbf{X}^T\mathbf{Z}\Big[\mathbf{Z}^T\mathbf{Z} + \lambda\mathbf{A}\Big]^{-1}\mathbf{Z}^T\Big\}\end{aligned}$$

Thus, finding a solution for $\mathbf{Z}$ that minimizes $\mathcal{J}$ is equivalent to finding one that maximizes the following objective function:

$$\max_{\mathbf{Z}} \mathbf{tr}\Big\{\mathbf{X}\mathbf{X}^T\mathbf{Z}\Big[\mathbf{Z}^T\mathbf{Z} + \lambda\mathbf{A}\Big]^{-1}\mathbf{Z}^T\Big\}$$

Let $\hat{\mathbf{K}} = \mathbf{X}\mathbf{X}^T$ be the centered kernel matrix associated with the training instances $\mathbf{X}$. During training, we enforce the following constraint:

$$\mathbf{Z}_{\text{train}}\Big[\mathbf{Z}_{\text{train}}^T\mathbf{Z}_{\text{train}} + \lambda\mathbf{A}\Big]^{-1}\mathbf{Z}_{\text{train}}^T = \mathbf{Y}\mathbf{C}\mathbf{Y}^T, \tag{4}$$

where $\mathbf{Y}$ is an $n \times c$ matrix of class labels and $\mathbf{C}$ is the tree-structured covariance matrix. This can be achieved by setting $\mathbf{Z}_{\text{train}} = \mathbf{Y}$ and $\mathbf{C} = \Big[\mathbf{Z}_{\text{train}}^T\mathbf{Z}_{\text{train}} + \lambda\mathbf{A}\Big]^{-1}$.

THEOREM 1. *If $\mathbf{A}$ be a symmetric, positive-definite matrix, and $\lambda > 0$, then $\mathbf{Z}_{train}^T\mathbf{Z}_{train} + \lambda\mathbf{A}$ is also positive-definite.*

PROOF. Given any real vector $\mathbf{v}$, $\mathbf{v}^T\Big[\mathbf{Z}_{\text{train}}^T\mathbf{Z}_{\text{train}} + \lambda\mathbf{A}\Big]\mathbf{v} = \mathbf{v}^T\mathbf{Z}_{\text{train}}^T\mathbf{Z}_{\text{train}}\mathbf{v} + \lambda\mathbf{v}^T\mathbf{A}\mathbf{v} = \|\mathbf{Z}_{\text{train}}\mathbf{v}\|^2 + \lambda\mathbf{v}^T\mathbf{A}\mathbf{v} > 0$ since $\mathbf{A}$ is a positive definite matrix. □

Since $\mathbf{Z}_{\text{train}}^T\mathbf{Z}_{\text{train}} + \lambda\mathbf{A}$ is positive-definite, it is invertible. The equality constraint in Equation (4) ensures that an appropriate λ and $\mathbf{A}$ can be chosen to generate a viable tree, in which the entries of the matrix $\mathbf{C}$ must have a specific structure. Furthermore, let $\mathbf{L} = \mathbf{Y}\mathbf{C}\mathbf{Y}^T$ denote the kernel matrix associated with the class labels. The objective function can now be simplified to:

$$\max_{\mathbf{C}} \mathbf{tr}\Big[\mathbf{K}\mathbf{L}\Big] \quad \text{s.t. } \mathbf{L} = \mathbf{Y}\mathbf{C}\mathbf{Y}^T, \tag{5}$$

which is equivalent to a constrained optimization of HSIC.

4.3 Additive Property of HSIC

In the previous subsection, we have shown that the global objective function for MF-Tree is equivalent to HSIC by setting appropriate constraints on $\mathbf{A}$ and λ. This enables us to define a kernel matrix for the class labels as $\mathbf{L} = \mathbf{Y}\mathbf{C}\mathbf{Y}^T$, where $\mathbf{C}$ is the tree-structured covariance matrix. In this section, we demonstrate the additive property of HSIC, which enables us to decompose the optimization problem into a hierarchical binary classification task.

First, we show that the tree-structured covariance matrix can be written as a sum of block diagonal matrices. We illustrate this with a simple example. Consider the following covariance matrix for a labeled tree that contains 8 leaf nodes (assuming the edge weights are equal to 1):

$$\mathbf{C}_8 = \begin{bmatrix} 3 & 2 & 1 & 1 & 0 & 0 & 0 & 0 \\ 2 & 3 & 1 & 1 & 0 & 0 & 0 & 0 \\ 1 & 1 & 3 & 2 & 0 & 0 & 0 & 0 \\ 1 & 1 & 2 & 3 & 0 & 0 & 0 & 0 \\ 0 & 0 & 0 & 0 & 3 & 2 & 1 & 1 \\ 0 & 0 & 0 & 0 & 2 & 3 & 1 & 1 \\ 0 & 0 & 0 & 0 & 1 & 1 & 3 & 2 \\ 0 & 0 & 0 & 0 & 1 & 1 & 2 & 3 \end{bmatrix} \tag{6}$$

We can rewrite the matrix as follows:

$$\mathbf{C}_8 = \mathbf{I}_2 \otimes \mathbf{1}_4\mathbf{1}_4^T + \mathbf{I}_4 \otimes \mathbf{1}_2\mathbf{1}_2^T + \mathbf{I}_8 \otimes \mathbf{1} \tag{7}$$

where $\otimes$ denote a Kronecker product and

$$\mathbf{I}_2 \otimes \mathbf{1}_4\mathbf{1}_4^T = \begin{bmatrix} 1 & 1 & 1 & 1 & 0 & 0 & 0 & 0 \\ 1 & 1 & 1 & 1 & 0 & 0 & 0 & 0 \\ 1 & 1 & 1 & 1 & 0 & 0 & 0 & 0 \\ 1 & 1 & 1 & 1 & 0 & 0 & 0 & 0 \\ 0 & 0 & 0 & 0 & 1 & 1 & 1 & 1 \\ 0 & 0 & 0 & 0 & 1 & 1 & 1 & 1 \\ 0 & 0 & 0 & 0 & 1 & 1 & 1 & 1 \\ 0 & 0 & 0 & 0 & 1 & 1 & 1 & 1 \end{bmatrix}$$

$$\mathbf{I}_4 \otimes \mathbf{1}_2\mathbf{1}_2^T = \begin{bmatrix} 1 & 1 & 0 & 0 & 0 & 0 & 0 & 0 \\ 1 & 1 & 0 & 0 & 0 & 0 & 0 & 0 \\ 0 & 0 & 1 & 1 & 0 & 0 & 0 & 0 \\ 0 & 0 & 1 & 1 & 0 & 0 & 0 & 0 \\ 0 & 0 & 0 & 0 & 1 & 1 & 0 & 0 \\ 0 & 0 & 0 & 0 & 1 & 1 & 0 & 0 \\ 0 & 0 & 0 & 0 & 0 & 0 & 1 & 1 \\ 0 & 0 & 0 & 0 & 0 & 0 & 1 & 1 \end{bmatrix}$$

$$\mathbf{I}_8 \otimes \mathbf{1} = \begin{bmatrix} 1 & 0 & 0 & 0 & 0 & 0 & 0 & 0 \\ 0 & 1 & 0 & 0 & 0 & 0 & 0 & 0 \\ 0 & 0 & 1 & 0 & 0 & 0 & 0 & 0 \\ 0 & 0 & 0 & 1 & 0 & 0 & 0 & 0 \\ 0 & 0 & 0 & 0 & 1 & 0 & 0 & 0 \\ 0 & 0 & 0 & 0 & 0 & 1 & 0 & 0 \\ 0 & 0 & 0 & 0 & 0 & 0 & 1 & 0 \\ 0 & 0 & 0 & 0 & 0 & 0 & 0 & 1 \end{bmatrix}$$

The first term on the right hand side of Equation (7) simply partitions the first 4 rows and columns of the matrix into 1 cluster and the last 4 rows and columns into a second cluster. The second term on the right hand side partitions the first cluster into 2 smaller subclusters, while the third term puts each subcluster as a cluster itself (this is at the leaf node of the tree). In general, we can write

$$\mathbf{C}_{2^m} = \mathbf{B}_2 + \mathbf{B}_4 + \cdots + \mathbf{B}_{2^m}, \tag{8}$$

where $\mathbf{B}_{2^j} = \mathbf{I}_{2^j} \otimes \mathbf{1}_{2^{m-j}}\mathbf{1}_{2^{m-j}}^T$, $\mathbf{1}_{2^0} = 1$, and m is the depth of the binary tree. We can further simplify the decomposition to the following:

$$\begin{aligned}\mathbf{C}_8 &= \mathbf{B}_2 + \mathbf{B}_4 + \mathbf{B}_8 \\ &= \Big[\mathbf{B}_{2,1}\Big] + \begin{bmatrix} \mathbf{B}_{4,1} & \mathbf{0}_{4\times4} \\ \mathbf{0}_{4\times4} & \mathbf{B}_{4,2} \end{bmatrix} + \begin{bmatrix} \mathbf{B}_{8,1} & \mathbf{0}_{2\times2} & \mathbf{0}_{2\times2} & \mathbf{0}_{2\times2} \\ \mathbf{0}_{2\times2} & \mathbf{B}_{8,2} & \mathbf{0}_{2\times2} & \mathbf{0}_{2\times2} \\ \mathbf{0}_{2\times2} & \mathbf{0}_{2\times2} & \mathbf{B}_{8,3} & \mathbf{0}_{2\times2} \\ \mathbf{0}_{2\times2} & \mathbf{0}_{2\times2} & \mathbf{0}_{2\times2} & \mathbf{B}_{8,4} \end{bmatrix}\end{aligned}$$

where each diagonal block has the following form

$$\mathbf{B}_{2^i,j} = \begin{bmatrix} \mathbf{1}\mathbf{1}^T & \mathbf{0} \\ \mathbf{0} & \mathbf{1}\mathbf{1}^T \end{bmatrix} \tag{9}$$

and the dimension for each of the submatrices of **0**s and $\mathbf{1}\mathbf{1}^T$s in $\mathbf{B}_{2^i,j}$ is $2^{m-i} \times 2^{m-i}$. Furthermore, given a block matrix $\mathbf{B}_k$, we have

$$\mathbf{Y}\mathbf{B}_k\mathbf{Y}^T = \mathbf{Y}_1\mathbf{B}_{k,1}\mathbf{Y}_1^T + \mathbf{Y}_2\mathbf{B}_{k,2}\mathbf{Y}_2^T + \cdots + \mathbf{Y}_{k/2}\mathbf{B}_{k,k/2}\mathbf{Y}_{k/2}^T$$

where

$$\mathbf{Y} = \begin{bmatrix}\mathbf{Y}_1 \cdots \mathbf{Y}_j \cdots \mathbf{Y}_{k/2}\end{bmatrix} \quad (10)$$

$$\mathbf{B}_k = \begin{bmatrix} \mathbf{B}_{k,1} & \mathbf{0} & \cdots & \mathbf{0} & \cdots & \mathbf{0} \\ \mathbf{0} & \mathbf{B}_{k,2} & \ddots & \ddots & \ddots & \vdots \\ \vdots & \ddots & \ddots & \ddots & \ddots & \vdots \\ \vdots & \ddots & \ddots & \mathbf{B}_{k,j} & \ddots & \vdots \\ \vdots & \ddots & \ddots & \ddots & \ddots & \vdots \\ \mathbf{0} & \cdots & \cdots & \cdots & \cdots & \mathbf{B}_{k,k/2} \end{bmatrix} \quad (11)$$

$$\mathbf{Y}^T = \begin{bmatrix} \mathbf{Y}_1^T \\ \cdots \\ \mathbf{Y}_j^T \\ \cdots \\ \mathbf{Y}_{k/2}^T \end{bmatrix} \quad (12)$$

As each $\mathbf{B}_{i,j}$ corresponds to a block-diagonal matrix given by Equation (9), we can write

$$\mathbf{Y}\mathbf{C}\mathbf{Y}^T = \sum_{i=1}^{\log_2 k} \mathbf{Y}\mathbf{B}_{2^i}\mathbf{Y}^T = \sum_{i=1}^{\log_2 k}\sum_{j=1}^{2^{i-1}} \mathbf{Y}_j\mathbf{B}_{2^i,j}\mathbf{Y}_j^T$$

This decomposition enables us to solve the optimization problem with a hierarchical tree-like decomposition. The outer sum corresponds to decomposition at each depth of the tree, while the inner sum corresponds to expanding the internal nodes associated with the particular depth. Instead of learning $\mathbf{C}$ directly by maximizing the trace of HSIC (see Equation (5)), we can learn the set of $\mathbf{B}_{2^i,j}$ iteratively, each of which is associated with an internal node in the tree structure.

4.4 MF-Tree construction

To construct the tree, we need to solve the objective function given in (5). Based on the discussion in the previous subsection, the objective function can be simplified as follows:

$$\max_{\{\mathbf{B}\}} \sum_{i,j} \mathbf{tr}\left[\mathbf{K}_{j,j}\mathbf{Y}_j\mathbf{B}_{2^i,j}\mathbf{Y}_j^T\right] \quad (13)$$

This allows us to solve the optimization problem one node at a time. Let $\mathbf{D}_j = \mathbf{Y}_j^T\mathbf{K}_{j,j}\mathbf{Y}_j$, which is simply a $c \times c$ similarity matrix of the classes, computed based on their attributes $\mathbf{X}$ and the known ground truth labels associated with the block $\mathbf{B}_{2^i,j}$. At each node of the tree construction process, we need to find a matrix $\mathbf{B}_{2^i,j}$ that maximizes its alignment with $\mathbf{D}_j$, i.e.:

$$\max_{\mathbf{B}_{2^i,j}} \mathbf{tr}\left[\mathbf{D}_j\mathbf{B}_{2^i,j}\right]$$

For notational convenience, we drop the subscripts i and j in the remainder of the discussion. Note that $\mathbf{B}$ is simply a co-association matrix, whose element

$$[\mathbf{B}]_{p,q} = \begin{cases} 1, & \text{if classes p and q are in the same partition;} \\ 0, & \text{otherwise.} \end{cases}$$

To create binary partitions, let $\mathbf{G}$ be a $c \times 2$ matrix [1], where

$$[\mathbf{G}]_{i,j} = \begin{cases} 1, & \text{if class i belongs to partition j;} \\ 0, & \text{otherwise.} \end{cases}$$

It is easy to show that $\mathbf{B} = \mathbf{G}\mathbf{G}^T$. Thus,

$$\mathbf{tr}\left[\mathbf{D}\mathbf{B}\right] = \mathbf{tr}\left[\mathbf{D}\mathbf{G}\mathbf{G}^T\right] = \mathbf{tr}\left[\mathbf{G}^T\mathbf{D}\mathbf{G}\right].$$

This objective function is equivalent to finding a clustering of the classes in a way that maximizes the within-cluster similarity.

4.5 Optimization

Note that the following optimization problem at each node

$$\max_{\mathbf{G}} \mathbf{tr}\left[\mathbf{G}^T\mathbf{D}\mathbf{G}\right] \quad \text{s.t. } \mathbf{G}^T\mathbf{1}_2 = \mathbf{1}_n$$

is not feasible unless we enforce a non-negative constraint $\mathbf{G} \succeq \mathbf{0}$ [6]. Furthermore, if we relax the condition that elements of $\mathbf{G}$ must be either 0 or 1 and replace it with a constraint that $\mathbf{G}$ must be an orthogonal matrix

$$\max_{\mathbf{G}} \mathbf{tr}\left[\mathbf{G}^T\mathbf{D}\mathbf{G}\right] \quad \text{s.t. } \mathbf{G}^T\mathbf{G} = \mathbf{I}_2$$

we can solve the problem easily by finding the first two eigenvectors corresponding to the largest eigenvalues of $\mathbf{D}$ [27, 17, 5]. Let $\mathbf{G}\mathbf{\Lambda}\mathbf{G}^T$ be the eigendecomposition of matrix $\mathbf{D}$.

By definition, $\mathbf{D} = \mathbf{Y}^T\mathbf{K}\mathbf{Y}$. Following the eigendecomposition of $\mathbf{D}$, we have

$$\mathbf{Y}^T\mathbf{K}\mathbf{Y} = \mathbf{G}\mathbf{\Lambda}\mathbf{G}^T$$

Since $\mathbf{G}^T\mathbf{G} = \mathbf{I}$:

$$\mathbf{G}^T\mathbf{Y}^T\mathbf{K}\mathbf{Y}\mathbf{G} = \mathbf{\Lambda}$$

Let $\mathbf{P} = \mathbf{Y}\mathbf{G}$, which is an $n \times 2$ matrix that determines the assignment of each data instance to the corresponding child nodes. Thus,

$$\mathbf{P}^T\mathbf{K}\mathbf{P} = \mathbf{\Lambda}$$

During the testing phase, let $\hat{\mathbf{k}}$ be an n-dimensional column vector that contains similarity between the test instance to all the training instances. We compute the 2-dimensional partition vector $\hat{\mathbf{p}} \in \Re^2$ as follows:

$$\hat{\mathbf{p}} = \mathbf{G}^T\mathbf{Y}^T\hat{\mathbf{k}} = \mathbf{P}^T\hat{\mathbf{k}}$$

After computing $\hat{\mathbf{p}}$, we assign the test instance to the partition with the larger value, i.e., $\arg\max_i(\mathbf{P}^T\hat{\mathbf{k}})_i$.

4.6 MF-Tree Induction Algorithm

The pseudocode for constructing MF-Tree is summarized in Algorithm 1. Our algorithm recursively partitions each node by calling the `TreeGrowth` function. Each invocation of the function returns a root node for a subtree that partitions the classes and their associated training instances into 2 groups. Each node is assumed to have a complex data structure, with the following fields: (1) $v.index$ contains the indices of the training instances assigned to the node, (2) $v.class$ represents the class label if v is a leaf node, (3) $v.\mathbf{G}$ is the discriminant function if v is an internal node, and (4) $v.left$ and $v.right$ are pointers to its left and right child.

[1] Here, we assume the number of classes associated with the given node is c. As the tree grows deeper, the number of classes also decreases, which in turn, reduces the number of rows in $\mathbf{G}$.

Algorithm 1 MF-Tree Construction

Input: $X_{train} \in \mathbf{R}^{n \times d}$, $Y_{train} \in \mathbf{R}^{n \times k}$
Output: Tree Structure, T
1. $root$ = `TreeGrowth`(X_{train}, Y_{train})
2. Insert $root$ into T
3. **return** T

function `TreeGrowth`(X, Y)
1. v = `createNode()`
2. $v.index$ = getIndex(X)
3. **if** number of classes in $Y < 2$ **then**
4. $\quad v.class$ = `unique`(Y)
5. **else**
6. $\quad (X^{(l)}, Y^{(l)}, X^{(r)}, Y^{(r)}, v.\mathbf{G})$ = `Partition`(X, Y)
7. $\quad v.left$ = `TreeGrowth`$(X^{(l)}, Y^{(l)})$
8. $\quad v.right$ = `TreeGrowth`$(X^{(r)}, Y^{(r)})$
9. **end if**
10. **return** v

function `Partition`(X, Y)
1. Compute the centered kernel $\mathbf{K}$ from X.
2. Compute $\mathbf{D} = Y^T \mathbf{K} Y$
3. Compute the first two eigenvectors $g^{(1)}, g^{(2)}$ of $\mathbf{D}$
4. Let $\mathbf{G} = [g^{(1)}, g^{(2)}]$
5. $(X^{(l)}, Y^{(l)}) = \{(\mathbf{x}_i, y_i) | y_i = k, \arg\max_j \mathbf{G}_{kj} = 1\}$
6. $(X^{(r)}, Y^{(r)}) = \{(\mathbf{x}_i, y_i) | y_i = k, \arg\max_j \mathbf{G}_{kj} = 2\}$
7. **return** $(X^{(l)}, Y^{(l)}, X^{(r)}, Y^{(r)}, \mathbf{G})$

The `Partition` function decides how to partition each class and their training examples into different branches of the tree. The partitioning is done based on the magnitude of matrix $\mathbf{G}$ as described in the previous section. If a class k is assigned to the left child of a node, all the training instances that belong to class k will also be propagated to the left child. The algorithm continues to expand a node until all the training instances associated with the node belong to the same class.

To determine its time complexity, note that at each node v, we need to compute the kernel matrix $\mathbf{K}$, an operation that requires $O(n^2 d)$ time. Computing $\mathbf{D}$ from the kernel matrix $\mathbf{K}$ and class label $\mathbf{Y}$ takes $O(n^2 c + c^2 n)$ time while finding its first two eigenvectors requires, in the worst-case, $O(c^3)$ time. Thus, the computational cost at each node is $O(n^2 c + c^2 n + c^3)$. The cost reduces significantly as the tree grows deeper since the size of matrices $\mathbf{K}$ and $\mathbf{D}$ decreases substantially. Once the tree structure is induced from the training set, we can predict the label for any test instance using the method presented in Algorithm 2.

5. APPROXIMATE MF-TREE

As shown in the previous section, the time complexity for constructing MF-Tree can be quite expensive especially at the top levels of the hierarchy. This is due to the large size of matrices that must be constructed and factorized according to their largest two eigenvalues. However, as we traverse down the tree, the number of classes and training instances to be dealt with decreases considerably, which in turn, helps to speed up the computations. Thus, the bottleneck of our computation lies in the first few iterations of the MF-Tree algorithm. In this section, we present an approach to speed up the tree construction process by learning an approximation for the $\mathbf{G}$ matrix during the first few iterations. Once the matrices become small enough, we can proceed with applying the original `TreeGrowth` function shown in Algorithm 1.

Algorithm 2 Testing with MF-Tree

Input: $X_{test}, X_{train}, Y_{train}, T$
Output: Y_{test}
1. **for each** $\mathbf{x} \in X_{test}$ **do**
2. $\quad v = T.root$
3. $\quad$ **while** $v.class = \emptyset$ **do**
4. $\quad\quad \hat{k}$ = `Similarity`$(\mathbf{x}, X_{train}, v.index)$
5. $\quad\quad \hat{Y}$ = `Subset`$(Y_{train}, v.index)$
6. $\quad\quad \hat{G} = v.\mathbf{G}$
7. $\quad\quad \hat{p} = \hat{G}^T \hat{Y}^T \hat{k}$
8. $\quad\quad v$ = `getChild`$(\hat{p}, v)$
9. $\quad$ **end while**
9. $\quad$ Insert $y = v.class$ into Y_{test}
10. **end for**
11. **return** Y_{test}

Our proposed method attempts to balance the tradeoff between accuracy and efficiency of the labeled tree construction process. While efficiency is a concern at the top levels of the tree, accuracy is an issue at lower levels of the tree. Even if the class partitioning at the top levels is suboptimal, one might still be able to recover good partitions at subsequent iterations when refining the tree. Based on this rationale, we develop the following two-step approach to improve training efficiency. First, we apply a simple method to calculate $\mathbf{G}$ at the top levels of the tree. When the depth of the tree exceeds some threshold τ, we revert back to the original `TreeGrowth` function. We termed this approach as *Approximate MF-Tree*, which is summarized in Algorithm 3.

Consider the root node of the labeled tree. Let n be the number of training instances and c be the number of classes. We first sort the classes in decreasing order of their class size and then assign the largest class (c_1) to the left node of the root and the second largest class (c_2) to the right child. The sorting operations requires only $O(c \log c)$ computations. For the remaining classes, we compute their corresponding mean vectors, an operation that requires $O(nd)$ time. We then assign each class to the left or right child based on their distance to the mean vectors of the first two largest classes. For example, if the mean vector for c_3 is closer to the mean vector for c_1 than c_2, we assign c_3 to the left child of the root node. Otherwise, we assign it to the right child. This process is repeated until depth τ. This reduces the time complexity of each node from $O(c^3)$ to $O(c \log c + nd)$. As will be shown in our experimental results section, substantial improvement in training time can be achieved by setting the depth threshold τ to be 2 or 3 without losing significant accuracy.

6. EXPERIMENTAL EVALUATION

In this section, we compared the performance of our proposed MF-Tree algorithm against several state-of-the-art hierarchical learning algorithms[2], including DAGSVM [28], Discriminative Relaxed Hierarchy Learning (DRHL) [11], confusion matrix based label embedding tree learning approach (CMTL) [1] and Recursive Nonnegative Matrix Factorization (RNMF) [22]. In addition to these methods, we have also implemented a recursive version of HSIC clustering by dependence maximization (RDM) algorithm [30]. In this approach, the data instances are partitioned into p groups at each level of the tree until a stopping criterion is met (when no other classes have more than 5 instances at the leaf node). We con-

[2] Even though the accuracy of non-hierarchical methods such as one-versus-one was comparable to hierarchical methods, they are extremely slow when the number of classes is too large.

Algorithm 3 Approximate MF-Tree

Input: $X_{train} \in \mathbf{R}^{n \times d}$, $Y_{train} \in \mathbf{R}^{n \times k}$, τ
Output: Tree structure T
1. Set depth, $d = 0$
2. $root$ = `TreeGrowthApprox`$(X_{train}, Y_{train}, d, \tau)$
3. Insert $root$ into T
4. **return** T

function `TreeGrowthApprox`(X,Y,d,τ)
1. v = `createNode()`
2. $v.index$ = getIndex(X)
3. **if** $d < \tau$ and number of classes in $Y < 2$
4. $(X^{(l)}, Y^{(l)}, X^{(r)}, Y^{(r)})$= `Partition2`$(X,Y)$
5. $v.left$ = `TreeGrowthApprox`$(X^{(l)}, Y^{(l)}, d+1)$
6. $v.right$ = `TreeGrowthApprox`$(X^{(r)}, Y^{(r)}, d+1)$
7. **else**
8. v = `TreeGrowth`(X, Y)
9. **end if**
10. **return** v

function `Partition2`(X,Y)
1. classes = `Sort`(Y)
2. $(X^{(l)}, Y^{(l)}) = \{(\mathbf{x}_i, y_i) | y_i = c_1$ (largest class) $\}$
3. $(X^{(r)}, Y^{(r)}) = \{(\mathbf{x}_i, y_i) | y_i = c_2$ (second largest class) $\}$
4. meanvectors = `Mean`(X, Y)
5. **for each** remaining class $c \in$ classes **do**
6. m_1 = `distance`(meanvectors, c, c_1)
7. m_2 = `distance`(meanvectors, c, c_2)
8. **if** $m_1 \leq m_2$ **then**
9. $(X^{(l)}, Y^{(l)}) = (X^{(l)}, Y^{(l)}) \cup \{(\mathbf{x}_i, y_i) | y_i = c\}$
10. **else**
11. $(X^{(r)}, Y^{(r)}) = (X^{(r)}, Y^{(r)}) \cup \{(\mathbf{x}_i, y_i) | y_i = c\}$
12. **end if**
13. **end for**
14. **return** $(X^{(l)}, Y^{(l)}, X^{(r)}, Y^{(r)})$

struct a binary classifier at each internal node of the tree as well as 1-class SVM classifiers at the leaf nodes to determine the class labels.

6.1 Experimental Setup

We performed our experiments on two real-world data sets: (1) `Caltech-256`[3], which is a benchmark data set for multi-class learning. The data set contains 30,607 images from 256 classes, with at least 80 images in each class, and (2) `Wiki`, a collection of Wikipedia articles. We generated four variants of the data sets for our experiments and denote them as $\texttt{Wiki}_1$, $\texttt{Wiki}_2$, $\texttt{Caltech}_1$ and $\texttt{Caltech}_2$, respectively. A summary of the characteristics for each data set is shown in Table 1.

$\texttt{Caltech}_1$ and $\texttt{Caltech}_2$ are subsets of image data from the Caltech-256 collection. $\texttt{Caltech}_1$ is generated using the same approach as described in [11], in which 80 images are randomly sampled from each class to create the data set. We use a repeated holdout method to create the training and test sets. Specifically, half of the sampled images were reserved for training while the remaining half for testing. We repeat the sampling process five times to create five versions of the data set. We then applied all the algorithms on the data sets and compute their average F1-score. The F1-score is defined as the harmonic mean of the precision (positive predictive value) and recall (sensitivity) for each class. Results are

[3]http://authors.library.caltech.edu/7694/

Table 1: Summary of data sets used.

Data set	# Classes	# data instances	# features
$\texttt{Caltech}_1$	256	20480	3287
$\texttt{Caltech}_2$	256	30607	4635
$\texttt{Wiki}_1$	214	24378	3705
$\texttt{Wiki}_2$	1618	65156	4238

reported based on the average F1-score for all the classes over all five versions of the data sets. In addition, we created a larger data set called $\texttt{Caltech}_2$ by randomly choosing 40 images from each class for training and use all the remaining images for testing. The sampling process is again repeated five times to generate five versions of $\texttt{Caltech}_2$ for our experiments. In both $\texttt{Caltech}_1$ and $\texttt{Caltech}_2$ data sets, we extracted SIFT (scale-invariant feature transform) features to represent the images.

$\texttt{Wiki}_1$ is a data set generated using the same approach as described in [22]. Here, we choose articles from the 214 largest categories to obtain a data set that contains 24,378 articles. In addition, we also created a larger sample data set from the Wikipedia dump, which covers the largest 1618 categories with 65,156 articles. Similar to $\texttt{Caltech}_1$, half of the sampled data were used for training and the remaining half for testing. The sampling process is also repeated five times to generate five versions of the data sets.

6.2 Experimental Results

This section presents the results of our experiments. We use average F1-score as our measure of accuracy for each algorithm. In addition, we compared the testing time for each algorithm along with the size of the induced hierarchy.

6.2.1 Comparison against Baseline Algorithms

We first compare the performance of MF-Tree against the five baseline algorithms. The results shown in Table 2 suggest that the proposed MF-Tree algorithm consistently outperforms other baseline algorithms both in terms of its F1-score and testing efficiency. The size of the hierarchy generated by MF-Tree is also comparable to some of the best algorithms. Even though RNMF generates a shorter tree than MF-Tree, its test time is higher because the leaf nodes of RNMF contains multiple 1-class SVM classifiers that must be invoked in order to predict the class. In contrast, the leaf nodes of MF-Tree has a single class label, which allows us to predict the class efficiently. Among all the competing methods, DAGSVM creates the largest tree. This is because it eliminates one class at a time at each level of the hierarchy. So the depth of the tree is equal to the number of classes. In the meantime, DRHL and RDM also create larger trees because they both allow a class to be assigned to more than one leaf nodes. This affects the test time of the algorithms.

6.2.2 Effect of Parameter Tuning

Unlike MF-Tree, which is parameter-free, the performance of several baseline algorithms depends on the values of their parameters. For example, the branching factor p in RNMF method determines the structure and depth of the tree. If $p = 1$, this produces a decision stump consisting of c 1-class SVM models. This is equivalent to implementing a one-versus-all approach. If $p = 2$, then it produces a binary tree. Clearly, the choice of p affects the depth of the tree. As depth increases, the test efficiency reduces significantly at the expense of decreasing F1 values. Similarly, tree construction parameters are also needed in other baseline methods. To provide a fair comparison, we vary the parameters for each method based on the suggestion of their original papers. Specifically, for RNMF [22]

Table 2: Experimental Results

$\texttt{Caltech}_1$	F1	Test Time (s)	Depth of Tree
DAGSVM	0.369 ± 0.0019	436.8 ± 10.2	256
RNMF	0.360 ± 0.0022	91.2 ± 6.4	**9**
DRHL	0.375 ± 0.003	312.76 ± 9.6	196
CMTL	0.348 ± 0.006	122.18 ± 10.4	10
RDM	0.331 ± 0.0103	198.2 ± 11.2	18
MF-Tree	$\mathbf{0.3816 \pm 0.03}$	$\mathbf{77.5 \pm 4.5}$	10
$\texttt{Caltech}_2$	F1	Test Time (s)	Depth of Tree
DAGSVM	0.356 ± 0.0017	751.68 ± 11.8	256
RNMF	0.353 ± 0.0017	157.66 ± 7.9	**9**
DRHL	0.365 ± 0.0021	523.7 ± 12.2	196
CMTL	0.343 ± 0.005	192.8 ± 11.2	10
RDM	0.323 ± 0.0098	367.4 ± 10.5	18
MF-Tree	$\mathbf{0.376 \pm 0.029}$	$\mathbf{135.6 \pm 5.6}$	10
$\texttt{Wiki}_1$	F1	Test Time (s)	Depth of Tree
DAGSVM	0.5309 ± 0.002	942.9 ± 17.6	214
RNMF	0.5227 ± 0.0017	188.3 ± 9.3	**5**
DRHL	0.5217 ± 0.0019	457.5 ± 16.9	64
CMTL	0.4826 ± 0.0017	195.5 ± 9.2	10
RDM	0.4229 ± 0.0135	256.6 ± 14.7	33
MF-Tree	$\mathbf{0.5406 \pm 0.0216}$	$\mathbf{152.7 \pm 4.2}$	9
$\texttt{Wiki}_2$	F1	Test Time (s)	Depth of Tree
DAGSVM	0.3106 ± 0.0021	1618.6 ± 17.6	1618
RNMF	0.2998 ± 0.0017	351.8 ± 13.6	**8**
DRHL	0.3089 ± 0.0016	772.5 ± 16.9	116
CMTL	0.2459 ± 0.0029	312.2 ± 11.3	12
RDM	0.2296 ± 0.022	456.6 ± 12.5	52
MF-Tree	$\mathbf{0.3318 \pm 0.016}$	$\mathbf{267.7 \pm 6.9}$	11

and RDM [30], we vary their parameters $p \in \{2,3,4,5\}$ whereas for $DRHL$ [11], we set $\rho \in \{0.5, 0.6, 0.7, 0.8\}$.

We plotted their classification performance in Figure 2, where the horizontal axis corresponds to test time while the vertical axis corresponds to average F1-score. Ideally, we seek for a classifier with lowest test time and highest F1-score (i.e., closest to the upper left corner). As can be seen from these plots, MF-Tree is better than the baseline hierarchical learning methods on all four data sets.

6.2.3 *Comparison of Taxonomy Structure*

In addition to their F1-scores, it is useful to compare the tree generated by the different methods against their ground truth structure. To do this, we need an evaluation measure to compare the similarity between two trees. In this paper, we apply the edit distance measure, which was originally used for string comparison, to compare the ordered labeled trees (see [31] for a review). Ordered labeled trees are trees in which the left-to-right order among siblings is significant. The distance between two trees is computed by considering the optimal mapping between the two trees. Specifically, the distance is given by the minimum cost of elementary operations to convert one tree into the other. An alternative way to map and edit the trees is by using tree alignment [16].

To quantify the difference between two trees based on their pairwise class ordering, we first construct an adjacency matrix A for a tree structure using the formula: $A_{ij} = \frac{1}{num_{hops}(c_i \rightarrow c_j)}$, where A_{ij} is the similarity between classes c_i and c_j and $num_{hops}(c_i \rightarrow c_j)$ is the minimum number of hops required to traverse the tree from class c_i to c_j. To measure the difference between two trees represented by the matrices A and $\hat{A}$, we compute its mean squared error (MSE), which is given by:

$$MSE(A, \hat{A}) = \frac{1}{n^2} \sum_{i,j=1}^{n} (A_{ij} - \hat{A}_{ij})^2$$

To illustrate how the measure works, consider the hypothetical trees shown in Figure 3. Let A be the adjacency matrix for the actual tree while $\hat{A}_{result1}$ and $\hat{A}_{result2}$ are the corresponding adjacency matrices for two competing trees, $result1$ and $result2$. The MSE for $result2$ is 0.01383, which is smaller than the MSE for $result1$, which is 0.03125. This is consistent with our observation since $result2$ resembles the actual tree except for the misplaced class c_2. In contrast, the classes c_2 and c_3 are misplaced in $result1$. For example, $A(c_3, c_4) = 0.5$ in the actual tree as the number of hops from category c_3 to c_4 is equal to two. However, $\hat{A}_{result1}(c_3, c_4) = 0.25$ for $result1$ since class c_3 is 4 hops away from c_4 whereas $\hat{A}_{result2}(c_3, c_4) = 0.5$, which is the same as the distance according to the actual tree.

We compared the MSE score of MF-Tree against the confusion matrix based label embedding tree learning (CMTL) method. We choose this baseline method for two reasons. First, the size of the tree is comparable to MF-Tree. Second, similar to MF-Tree, this approach produces a tree in which each class can only reside in a single leaf node of the tree (whereas other methods allow a class to be assigned to multiple leaf nodes). Trees that restrict each class to a single leaf node are more interpretable as they may be used to define a concept hierarchy for the application domain. The experimental results shown in Figure 4 suggest that MF-Tree produces a tree structure that is closer to the ground truth compared to CMTL. Note that $\texttt{Caltech}_1$ and $\texttt{Caltech}_2$ use the same set of classes for training to construct the taxonomy, so their trees are identical. We report their results together as $\texttt{Caltech}$ in Figure 4.

Figure 5 shows a subset of the tree structure generated by MF-Tree on the $\texttt{Caltech}_1$ data set. Observe that the tree was able to capture the relationships among many of the classes quite well. For example, some of the classes of animals (dog, horse, chimp, bear) was assigned to the same branch. Though there were exceptions and misclassifications (e.g., bats and crabs) but the related classes are often quite close together at the lower levels of the tree.

6.3 Results for Approximate MF-Tree

Despite its lower test time compared to other approaches, training an MF-Tree is still expensive when the number of classes is large. To overcome this problem, we propose an approximate MF-Tree algorithm, which uses an inexpensive partitioning method to assign classes to their child nodes at the top levels of the hierarchy. The algorithm has a parameter τ that determines the maximum depth at which to apply the inexpensive partitioning method.

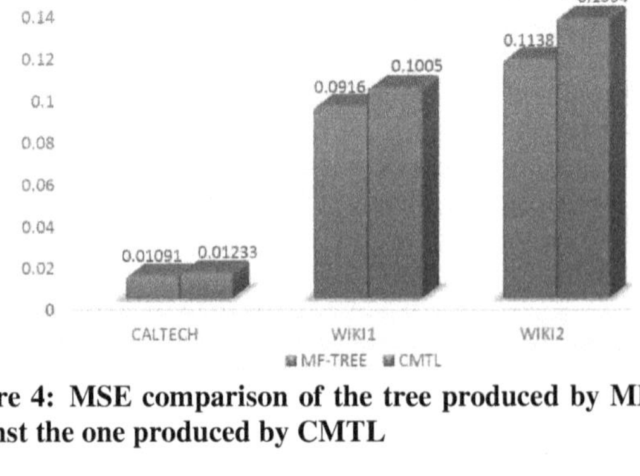

Figure 4: MSE comparison of the tree produced by MF-Tree against the one produced by CMTL

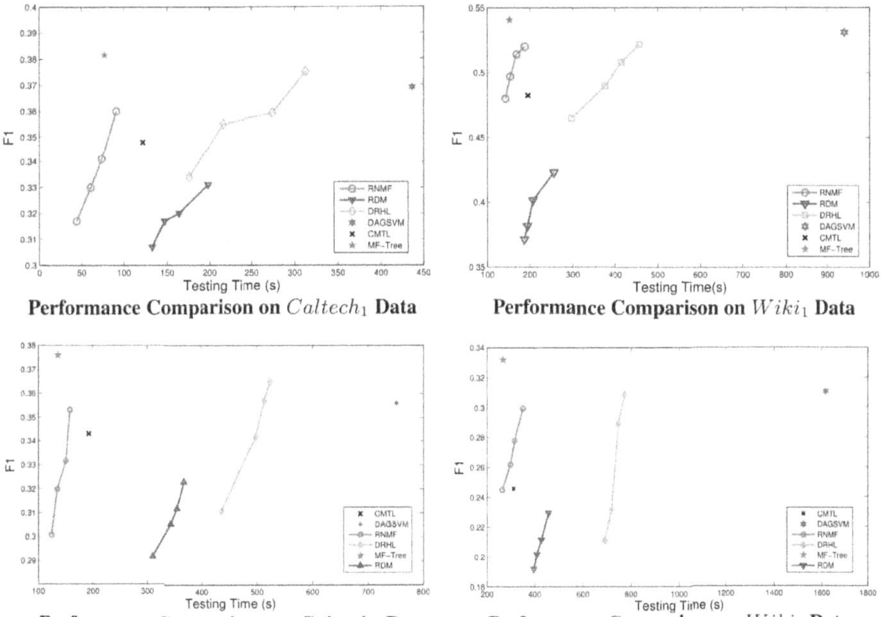

Performance Comparison on $Caltech_1$ Data | Performance Comparison on $Wiki_1$ Data
Performance Comparison on $Caltech_2$ Data | Performance Comparison on $Wiki_2$ Data

Figure 2: Performance Comparison in terms of average F1-score and testing time for MF-Tree against baseline algorithms

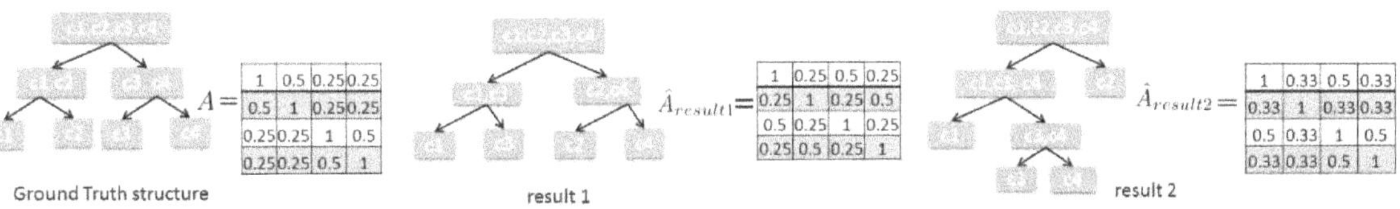

Figure 3: Example of mapping a tree structure to an adjacency matrix representation

To justify the effectiveness of the approximate MF-Tree approach, we perform an experiment on the `Wiki`$_2$ data set. We choose this data set because it has the largest number of classes. For this experiment, we vary τ from 3 to 6 and compare the average F1-score as well as training time of the algorithms. The results are shown in Table 3. Recall that the average F1-score for MF-Tree on the `Wiki`$_2$ data set is 0.3318. When $\tau = 3$, the F1-score reduces slightly to 0.3289. However, there was a 22.6% training time improvement. As τ increases, the F1-score gradually decreases while its training time continues to improve. Note that the size of the tree generated by the original MF-Tree algorithm has a depth equals to 11. When $\tau = 6$, the improvement in training time appears to taper off while its F1-score decreases to 0.2868. This clearly shows a trade-off between accuracy and training time efficiency. In practice, we could set the τ threshold based on the specific needs of the problem. If our priority is lower training speed, we could set a higher τ value. τ can also be set based on the computational resources available. If there is limited memory, τ can be set to a threshold in such a way that the resulting data matrices can fit into the memory available.

Table 3: Approximate MF-Tree on `Wiki`$_2$

Threshold	F1	% improvement in training time
$\tau = 3$	0.3289	22.6%
$\tau = 4$	0.3169	32.3%
$\tau = 5$	0.3034	37.8%
$\tau = 6$	0.2868	39.5%

7. CONCLUSION

In this paper, we proposed a novel hierarchical method for large-scale multi-class learning called MF-Tree. Our proposed algorithm is driven by a global objective function. We demonstrate the equivalence between the global objective function and the HSIC metric and show it has an additive property that can be exploited to design a hierarchical tree learning algorithm. Experimental results comparing the method against five baseline methods demonstrated both the effectiveness and efficiency of our method.

8. REFERENCES

[1] S. Bengio, J. Weston, and D. Grangier. Label embedding trees for large multi-class tasks. In *Advances in Neural Information Processing Systems (NIPS'2010)*, pages 163–171, 2010.

[2] A. Beygelzimer, J. Langford, and P. Ravikumar. Multiclass classification with filter trees. In *Information Theory and Application Workshop (ITA'2007)*, 2007.

[3] M. Blaschko and A. Gretton. Learning taxonomies by dependence maximization. In *Advances in Neural Information (NIPS'2008)*, pages 153–160, 2008.

[4] M. Blaschko, W. Zaremba, and A. Gretton. Taxonomic prediction with tree-structured covariances. In *Proc of the Machine Learning and Knowledge Discovery in Databases-European Conf. (ECML/PKDD'2013)*, pages 304–319.

[5] D. Boley. Principal direction divisive partitioning. *Data Mining and Knowledge Discovery*, 2(4):325–344, 1998.

[6] D. Chen and R. J. Plemmons. Nonnegativity constraints in numerical analysis. In A. Bultheel and R. Cools, editors, *Symposium on the Birth of Numerical Analysis,*, 2010.

[7] P. M. Comar, L. Liu, A. Nucci, S. Saha, and P.-N. Tan. Missing or inapplicable: Treatment of incomplete

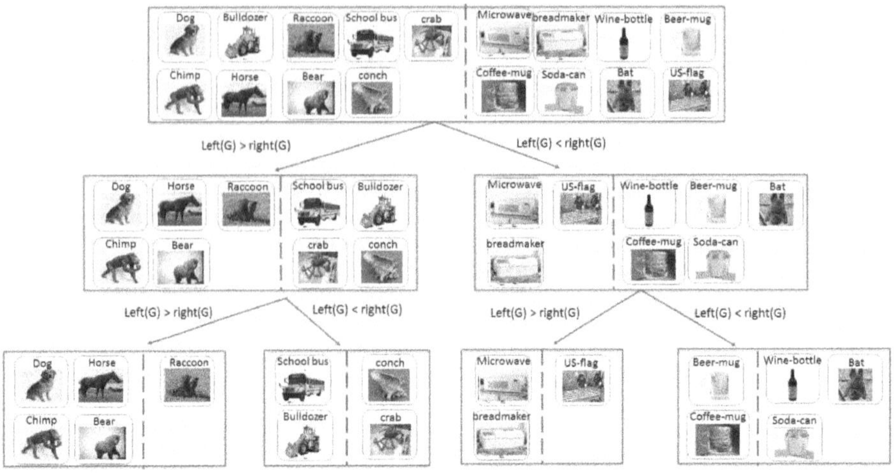

Figure 5: Illustration of tree structure generated by MF-Tree.

continuous-valued features in supervised learning. In *SIAM International Conference on Data Mining*, 2013.

[8] P. M. Comar, L. Liu, S. Saha, A. Nucci, and P.-N. Tan. Weighted linear kernel with tree transformed features for malware detection. In *CIKM'12*, pages 2287–2290, 2012.

[9] P. M. Comar, L. Liu, S. Saha, P.-N. Tan, and A. Nucci. Combining supervised and unsupervised learning for zero-day malware detection. In *Proc of IEEE Int'l Conf. on Computer Communications (INFOCOM'2013)*, pages 2022–2030, 2013.

[10] J. Deng, S. Satheesh, A. C. Berg, and F. F. F. Li. Fast and balanced: Efficient label tree learning for large scale object recognition. In *Advances in Neural Information Processing Systems (NIPS'2011)*, pages 567–575. 2011.

[11] T. Gao and D. Koller. Discriminative learning of relaxed hierarchy for large-scale visual recognition. In *Proc of IEEE Int'l Conf. on Computer Vision*, pages 2072–2079, 2011.

[12] R. Ghani. Using error-correcting codes for efficient text classification with a large number of categories. Masters thesis, Carnegie Mellon University, 2001.

[13] A. Gretton, O. Bousquet, A. Smola, and B. Schölkopf. Measuring statistical dependence with hilbert-schmidt norms. In *Proc of Int'l Conf. on Algorithmic Learning Theory*, pages 63–77, 2005.

[14] J. M. Hailpern, R. Vernica, M. Bullock, U. Chatow, J. Fan, G. Koutrika, J. Liu, L. Liu, S. J. Simske, and S. Wu. To print or not to print: hybrid learning with METIS learning platform. In *Proceedings of the 7th ACM SIGCHI Symposium on Engineering Interactive Computing Systems, EICS 2015*, pages 206–215, 2015.

[15] T. Hastie and R. Tibshirani. Classification by pairwise coupling. In *Advances in Neural Information Processing Systems (NIPS'1997)*, pages 507–513, 1997.

[16] T. Jiang, L. Wang, and K. Zhang. Alignment of trees - an alternative to tree edit. *Theor. Comput. Sci.*, 143(1):137–148, 1995.

[17] W. Jiang and F.-l. Chung. A trace ratio maximization approach to multiple kernel-based dimensionality reduction. *Neural Networks*, 49:96–106, 2014.

[18] A. Karpathy, G. Toderici, S. Shetty, T. Leung, R. Sukthankar, and L. Fei-Fei. Large-scale video classification with convolutional neural networks. In *Proc of Int'l Conf. on Computer Vision and Pattern Recognition*, 2014.

[19] G. Koutrika, L. Liu, and S. Simske. Generating reading orders over document collections. In *31st IEEE International Conference on Data Engineering, ICDE'2015*, pages 507–518, 2015.

[20] D. Kuang and H. Park. Fast rank-2 nonnegative matrix factorization for hierarchical document clustering. In *Proc of the ACM SIGKDD Int'l Conf. on Knowledge Discovery and Data Mining (SIGKDD'2013)*, pages 739–747, 2013.

[21] J. Langford and A. Beygelzimer. Sensitive error correcting output codes. In *Proc of the Conf. on Learning Theory (COLT'2005)*, pages 158–172, 2005.

[22] L. Liu, P. M. Comar, S. Saha, P.-N. Tan, and A. Nucci. Recursive nmf: Efficient label tree learning for large multi-class problems. In *Proc of Int'l Conf. on Pattern Recognition (ICPR'2012)*, pages 2148–2151, 2012.

[23] L. Liu, G. Koutrika, and S. Wu. Learningassistant: A novel learning resource recommendation system. In *31st IEEE International Conference on Data Engineering, ICDE 2015*, pages 1424–1427, 2015.

[24] L. Liu, J. Liu, and S. Wu. Image discovery and insertion for custom publishing. In *The 9th ACM Conference on Recommender System (RecSys 2015)*, 2015.

[25] L. Liu, S. Saha, R. Torres, J. Xu, P.-N. Tan, A. Nucci, and M. Mellia. Detecting malicious clients in isp networks using http connectivity graph and flow information. In *ASONAM'14*, pages 150–157, 2014.

[26] L. Liu and P.-N. Tan. A framework for co-classification of articles and users in wikipedia. In *Web Intelligence'10*, pages 212–215, 2010.

[27] T. Ngo, M. Bellalij, and Y. Saad. The trace ratio optimization problem. *SIAM Review*, 54(3):545–569, 2012.

[28] J. C. Platt, N. Cristianini, and J. Shawe-taylor. Large margin dags for multiclass classification. In *Advances in Neural Information Processing Systems (NIPS'2000)*, pages 547–553, 2000.

[29] R. Ryan and K. Aldebaro. In defense of one-vs-all classification. *Journal of Machine Learning Research*, 5:101–141, December 2004.

[30] L. Song, A. J. Smola, A. Gretton, and K. M. Borgwardt. A dependence maximization view of clustering. In *Proc of Int'l Conf. on Machine Learning*, pages 815–822, 2007.

[31] E. Tanaka and K. Tanaka. The tree-to-tree editing problem. *Journal Pattern Recognition and Artificial Intelligence*, 2(2):221–224, 1988.

GraRep: Learning Graph Representations with Global Structural Information

Shaosheng Cao
Xidian University
shelsoncao@gmail.com

Wei Lu
Singapore University of Technology and Design
luwei@sutd.edu.sg

Qiongkai Xu
IBM Research - China
Australian National University
xuqkai@cn.ibm.com

ABSTRACT

In this paper, we present GraRep, a novel model for learning vertex representations of weighted graphs. This model learns low dimensional vectors to represent vertices appearing in a graph and, unlike existing work, integrates global structural information of the graph into the learning process. We also formally analyze the connections between our work and several previous research efforts, including the DeepWalk model of Perozzi *et al.* [20] as well as the skip-gram model with negative sampling of Mikolov *et al.* [18]

We conduct experiments on a language network, a social network as well as a citation network and show that our learned global representations can be effectively used as features in tasks such as clustering, classification and visualization. Empirical results demonstrate that our representation significantly outperforms other state-of-the-art methods in such tasks.

Categories and Subject Descriptors

I.2.6 [**Artificial Intelligence**]: Learning; H.2.8 [**Database Management**]: Database Applications - Data Mining

General Terms

Algorithms, Experimentation

Keywords

Graph Representation, Matrix Factorization, Feature Learning, Dimension Reduction

1. INTRODUCTION

In many real-world problems, information is often organized using graphs. For example, in social network research, classification of users into meaningful social groups based on social graphs can lead to many useful practical applications such as user search, targeted advertising and recommendations. Therefore, it is essential to accurately learn useful information from the graphs. One strategy is to learn the *graph representations* of a graph: each vertex of the graph is represented with a low-dimensional vector in which meaningful semantic, relational and structural information conveyed by the graph can be accurately captured.

Permission to make digital or hard copies of all or part of this work for personal or classroom use is granted without fee provided that copies are not made or distributed for profit or commercial advantage and that copies bear this notice and the full citation on the first page. Copyrights for components of this work owned by others than ACM must be honored. Abstracting with credit is permitted. To copy otherwise, or republish, to post on servers or to redistribute to lists, requires prior specific permission and/or a fee. Request permissions from Permissions@acm.org.

CIKM'15, October 19–23, 2015, Melbourne, Australia.
© 2015 ACM. ISBN 978-1-4503-3794-6/15/10 ...$15.00.
DOI: http://dx.doi.org/10.1145/2806416.2806512.

Recently, there has been a surge of interest in learning graph representations from data. For example, DeepWalk [20], one recent model, transforms a graph structure into a sample collection of linear sequences consisting of vertices using uniform sampling (which is also called *truncated random walk*). The skip-gram model [18], originally designed for learning word representations from linear sequences, can also be used to learn the representations of vertices from such samples. Although this method is empirically effective, it is not well understood what is the exact loss function defined over the graph involved in their learning process.

In this work, we first present an explicit loss function of the skip-gram model defined over the graph. We show that essentially we can use the skip-gram model to capture the k-step ($k = 1, 2, 3, \dots$) relationship between each vertex and its k-step neighbors in the graph with different values of k. One limitation of the skip-gram model is it projects all such k-step relational information into a common subspace. We argue that such a simple treatment can lead to potential issues. The above limitation is overcome in our proposed model through the preservation of different k-step relational information in distinct subspaces.

Another recently proposed work is LINE [25], which has a loss function to capture both 1-step and 2-step local relational information. To capture certain complex relations in such local information, they also learn non-linear transformations from such data. While their model can not be easily extended to capture k-step (with $k > 2$) relational information for learning their graph representation, one important strategy used to enhance the effectiveness of their model is to consider higher-order neighbors for vertices with small degrees. This strategy implicitly captures certain k-step information into their model to some extent. We believe k-step relational information between different vertices, with different values of k, reveals the useful global structural information associated with the graph, and it is essential to explicitly take full advantage of this when learning a good graph representation.

In this paper, we propose GraRep, a novel model for learning graph representations for knowledge management. The model captures the different k-step relational information with different values of k amongst vertices from the graph directly by manipulating different global transition matrices defined over the graph, without involving slow and complex sampling processes. Unlike existing work, our model defines different loss functions for capturing the different k-step local relational information (*i.e.*, a different k). We optimize each model with matrix factorization techniques, and construct the global representations for each vertex by combining different representations learned from different models. Such learned global representations can be used as features for further processing.

We give a formal treatment of this model, showing the connections between our model and several previous models. We also demonstrate the empirical effectiveness of the learned representations in solving several real-world problems. Specifically, we conducted experiments on a language network clustering task, a social network multi-label classification task, as well as a citation network visualization task. In all such tasks, GraRep outperforms other graph representation methods, and is trivially parallelizable.

Our contributions are as follows:

- We introduce a novel model to learn latent representations of vertices on graphs, which can capture global structural information associated with the graph.
- We provide from a probabilistic prospective an understanding of the uniform sampling method used in DeepWalk for learning graph representations, which translates a graph structure into linear sequences. Furthermore, we explicitly define their loss function over graphs and extend it to support weighted graphs.
- We formally analyze the deficiency associated with the skip-gram model with negative sampling. Our model defines a more accurate loss function that allows non-linear combinations of different local relational information to be integrated.

The organization of this paper is described below. Section 2 discusses related work. Section 3 proposes our loss function and states the optimization method using matrix factorization. Section 4 presents the overall algorithm. Section 5 gives a mathematical explanation to elucidate the rationality of the proposed work and shows its connection to previous work. Section 6 discusses the evaluation data and introduces baseline algorithms. Section 7 presents experiments as well as analysis on the parameter sensitivity. Finally, we conclude in Section 8.

2. RELATED WORK

2.1 Linear Sequence Representation Methods

Natural language corpora, consisting of streams of words, can be regarded as special graph structures, that is, linear chains. Currently, there are two mainstream methods for learning word representations: neural embedding methods and matrix factorization based approaches.

Neural embedding methods employ a fixed slide window capturing context words of current word. Models like skip-gram [18] are proposed, which provide an efficient approach to learning word representations. While these methods may yield good performances on some tasks, they can poorly capture useful information since they use separate local context windows, instead of global co-occurrence counts [19]. On the other hand, the family of matrix factorization methods can utilize global statistics [5]. Previous work include Latent Semantic Analysis (LSA) [15], which decomposes term-document matrix and yields latent semantic representations. Lund et al. [17] put forward Hyperspace Analogue to Language (HAL), factorizing a word-word co-occurrence counts matrix to generate word representations. Levy et al. [4] presented matrix factorization over shifted positive Pointwise Mutual Information (PMI) matrix for learning word representations and showed that the Skip-Gram model with Negative Sampling (SGNS) can be regarded as a model that implicitly such a matrix [16].

2.2 Graph Representation Approaches

There exist several classical approaches to learning low dimensional graph representations, such as multidimensional scaling (MDS) [8], IsoMap [28], LLE [21], and Laplacian Eigenmaps [3]. Recently, Tang et al. [27] presented methods for learning latent representational vectors of the graphs which can then be applied to social network classification. Ahmed et al. [1] proposed a *graph factorization* method, which used stochastic gradient descent to optimize matrices from large graphs. Perozzi et al. [20] presented an approach, which transformed graph structure into several linear vertex sequences by using a truncated random walk algorithm and generated vertex representations by using skip-gram model. This is considered as an equally weighted linear combination of k-step information. Tang et al. [25] later proposed a large-scale information network embedding, which optimizes a loss function where both 1-step and 2-step relational information can be captured in the learning process.

3. GRAREP MODEL

In this section, we define our task and present our loss function for our task, which is then optimized with the matrix factorization method.

3.1 Graphs and Their Representations

Definition 1. (Graph) A *graph* is defined as $G = (V, E)$. $V = \{v_1, v_2, \ldots, v_n\}$ is the set of *vertices* with each V indicating one object while $E = \{e_{i,j}\}$ is the set of *edges* with each E indicating the relationship between two vertices. A *path* is a sequence of edges which connect a sequence of vertices.

We first define *adjacency matrix* S for a graph. For an unweighted graph, we have $S_{i,j} = 1$ if and only if there exists an edge from v_i to v_j, and $S_{i,j} = 0$ otherwise. For a weighted graph, $S_{i,j}$ is a real number called the weight of the edge $e_{i,j}$, which indicates the significance of edge. Although weights can be negative, we only consider non-negative weights in this paper. For notational convenience, we also use w and c to denote vertices throughout this paper.

The following diagonal matrix D is known as the *degree matrix* for a graph with adjacency matrix S:

$$D_{ij} = \begin{cases} \sum_p S_{ip}, & \text{if } i = j \\ 0, & \text{if } i \neq j \end{cases}$$

Assume we would like to capture the transitions from one vertex to another, and assume in the adjacency matrix $S_{i,j}$ is proportional to the transition probability from v_i to v_j, we can define the following *(1-step) probability transition matrix*

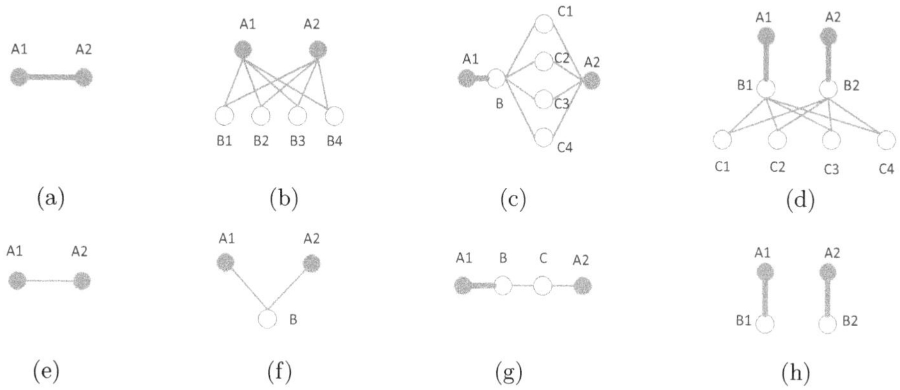

Figure 1: The importance of capturing different k-step information in the graph representations. Here we give examples for $k = 1, 2, 3, 4$.

A:

$$A = D^{-1}S$$

where $A_{i,j}$ is the probability of a transition from v_i to vertex v_j within one step. It can be observed that the A matrix can be regarded as a re-scaled S matrix whose rows are normalized.

Definition 2. (Graph Representations with Global Structural Information) Given a *graph* G, the task of *Learning Graph Representations with Global Structural Information* aims to learn a global representation matrix $W \in \mathbb{R}^{|V| \times d}$ for the complete graph, whose i-th row W_i is a d-dimensional vector representing the vertex v_i in the graph G where the global structural information of the graph can be captured in such vectors.

In this paper, global structural information serves two functions: 1) the capture of long distance relationship between two different vertices and 2) the consideration of distinct connections in terms of different transitional steps. This would be further illustrated later.

As we have discussed earlier, we believe the k-step (with varying k) relational information from the graph needs to be captured when constructing such global graph representations. To validate this point, Figure 1 gives some illustrative examples showing the importance of k-step (for k=1,2,3,4) relational information that needs to be captured between two vertices A_1 and A_2. In the figure, a thick line indicates a strong relation between two vertices, while a thin line indicates a weaker relation. Here, (a) and (e) show the importance of capturing the simple 1-step information between the two vertices which are directly connected to each other, where one has a stronger relation and the other has a weaker relation. In (b) and (f), 2-step information is shown, where in (b) both vertices share many common neighbors, and in (f) only one neighbor is shared between them. Clearly, 2-step information is important in capturing how strong the connection between the two vertices is – the more common neighbors they share, the stronger the relation between them is. In (c) and (g), the importance of 3-step information is illustrated. Specifically, in (g), despite the strong relation between A_1 and B, the relation between A_1 and A_2 can be weakened due to the two weaker edges connecting B and C, as well as C and A_2. In contrast, in (c), the relation between A_1 and A_2 remains strong because of the large number of common neighbors between B and A_2 which strengthened their relation. Clearly such 3-step information is essential to be captured when learning a good graph representation with global structural information. Similarly, the 4-step information can also be crucial in revealing the global structural properties of the graph, as illustrated in (d) and (h). Here, in (d), the relation between A_1 and A_2 is clearly strong, while in (h) the two vertices are unrelated since there does not exist a path from one vertex to the other. In the absence of 4-step relational information, such important distinctions can not be properly captured.

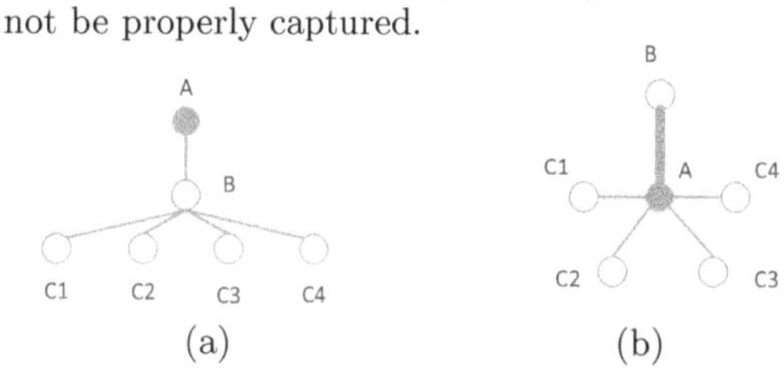

Figure 2: The importance of maintaining different k-step information separately in the graph representations.

We also additionally argue that it is essential to treat different k-step information differently when learning graph representations. We present one simple graph in (a) of Figure 2. Let us focus on learning the representation for the vertex A in the graph. We can see that A receives two types of information when learning its representation: 1-step information from B, as well as 2-step information from all C vertices. We note that if we do not distinguish these two different types of information, we can construct an alternative graph as shown in (b) of Figure 2, where A receives exactly the same information as (a), but has a completely different structure.

In this paper, we propose a novel framework for learning accurate graph representations, integrating various k-step information which together captures the global structural information associated with the graph.

3.2 Loss Function On Graph

We discuss our loss function used for learning the graph representations with global structural information in this section. Assume we are now given a graph with a collection of vertices and edges. Consider a vertex w together with another vertex c. In order for us to learn global representations to capture their relations, we need to understand how strongly these two vertices are connected to each other.

Let us begin with a few questions. Does there exist a path from w to c? If so, if we randomly sample a path starting with w, how likely is it for us to reach c (possibly within a fixed number of steps)? To answer such questions, we first use the term $p_k(c|w)$ to denote the probability for a transition from w to c in exactly k steps. We already know what are the 1-step transition probabilities, to compute the k-step transition probabilities we introduce the following *k-step probability transition matrix*

$$A^k = \underbrace{A \cdots A}_{k}$$

We can observe that $A^k_{i,j}$ exactly refers to the transition probability from vertex i to vertex j where the transition consists of exactly k step(s). This directly leads to:

$$p_k(c|w) = A^k_{w,c}$$

where $A^k_{w,c}$ is the element from w-th row and c-th column of the matrix A^k.

Let us consider a particular k first. Given a graph G, consider the collection of all paths consisting of k steps that can be sampled from the graph which start with w and end with c (here we call w "current vertex", and c "context vertex"). Our objective aims to maximize: 1) the probability that these pairs come from the graph, and 2) the probability that all other pairs do not come from the graph.

Motivated by the skip-gram model by Mikolov et al. [18], we employ *noise contrastive estimation* (NCE), which is proposed by Gutmann et al. [11], to define our objective function. Following a similar discussion presented in [16], we first introduce our k-step loss function defined over the complete graph as follows:

$$L_k = \sum_{w \in V} L_k(w)$$

where

$$L_k(w) = \left(\sum_{c \in V} p_k(c|w) \log \sigma(\vec{w} \cdot \vec{c}) \right) + \lambda \mathbb{E}_{c' \sim p_k(V)}[\log \sigma(-\vec{w} \cdot \vec{c'})]$$

Here $p_k(c|w)$ describes the k-step relationship between w and c (the k-step transition probability from w to c), $\sigma(\cdot)$ is sigmoid function defined as $\sigma(x) = (1 + e^{-x})^{-1}$, λ is a hyper-parameter indicating the number of negative samples, and $p_k(V)$ is the distribution over the vertices in the graph. The term $\mathbb{E}_{c' \sim p_k(V)}[\cdot]$ is the expectation when c' follows the distribution $p_k(V)$, where c' is an instance obtained from *negative sampling*. This term can be explicitly expressed as:

$$\begin{aligned} &\mathbb{E}_{c' \sim p_k(V)}[\log \sigma(-\vec{w} \cdot \vec{c'})] \\ &= p_k(c) \cdot \log \sigma(-\vec{w} \cdot \vec{c}) + \sum_{c' \in V \setminus \{c\}} p_k(c') \cdot \log \sigma(-\vec{w} \cdot \vec{c'}) \end{aligned}$$

This leads to a local loss defined over a specific (w,c):

$$L_k(w,c) = p_k(c|w) \cdot \log \sigma(\vec{w} \cdot \vec{c}) + \lambda \cdot p_k(c) \cdot \log \sigma(-\vec{w} \cdot \vec{c})$$

In this work, we set a maximal length for each path we consider. In other words, we assume $1 \le k \le K$. In fact, when k is large enough, the transition probabilities converge to certain fixed values. The distribution $p_k(c)$ can be computed as follows:

$$p_k(c) = \sum_{w'} q(w') p_k(c|w') = \frac{1}{N} \sum_{w'} A^k_{w',c}$$

Note that here N is the number of vertices in graph G, and $q(w')$ is the probability of selecting w' as the first vertex in the path, which we assume follow a uniform distribution, *i.e.*, $q(w') = 1/N$. This leads to:

$$L_k(w,c) = A^k_{w,c} \cdot \log \sigma(\vec{w} \cdot \vec{c}) + \frac{\lambda}{N} \sum_{w'} A^k_{w',c} \cdot \log \sigma(-\vec{w} \cdot \vec{c})$$

Following [16], we define $e = \vec{w} \cdot \vec{c}$, and setting $\frac{\partial L_k}{\partial e} = 0$. This yields the following:

$$\vec{w} \cdot \vec{c} = \log \left(\frac{A^k_{w,c}}{\sum_{w'} A^k_{w',c}} \right) - \log(\beta)$$

where $\beta = \lambda / N$.

This concludes that we essentially need to factorize the matrix Y into two matrices W and C, where each row of W and each row of C consists of a vector representation for the vertex w and c respectively, and the entries of Y are:

$$Y^k_{i,j} = W^k_i \cdot C^k_j = \log \left(\frac{A^k_{i,j}}{\sum_t A^k_{t,j}} \right) - \log(\beta)$$

Now we have defined our loss function and showed that optimizing the proposed loss essentially involves a matrix factorization problem.

3.3 Optimization with Matrix Factorization

Following the work of Levy et al. [16], to reduce noise, we replace all negative entries in Y^k with 0. This gives us a positive k-step log probabilistic matrix X^k, where

$$X^k_{i,j} = \max(Y^k_{i,j}, 0)$$

While various techniques for matrix factorization exist, in this work we focus on the popular singular value decomposition (SVD) method due to its simplicity. SVD has been shown successful in several matrix factorization tasks [9, 14], and is regarded as one of the important methods that can be used for dimensionality reduction. It was also used in [16].

For the matrix X^k, SVD factorizes it as:

$$X^k = U^k \Sigma^k (V^k)^T$$

where U and V are orthonormal matrices and Σ is a diagonal matrix consisting of an ordered list of singular values.

We can approximate the original matrix X^k with X^k_d:

$$X^k \approx X^k_d = U^k_d \Sigma^k_d (V^k_d)^T$$

where Σ^k_d is the matrix composed by the top d singular values, and U^k_d and V^k_d are first d columns of U^k and V^k, respectively (which are the first d eigenvector of XX^T and X^TX respectively).

This way, we can factorize our matrix X^k as:

$$X^k \approx X^k_d = W^k C^k$$

where

$$W^k = U^k_d (\Sigma^k_d)^{\frac{1}{2}}, \qquad C^k = (\Sigma^k_d)^{\frac{1}{2}} {V^k_d}^T$$

The resulting W^k gives representations of current vertices as its column vectors, and C^k gives the representations of context vertices as its column vectors [6, 5, 30]. The final matrix W^k is returned from the algorithm as the low-d representations of the vertices which capture k-step global structural information in the graph.

In our algorithm we consider all k-step transitions with all $k = 1, 2, \ldots, K$, where K is a pre-selected constant. In our algorithm, we integrate all such k-step information when learning our graph representation, as to be discussed next.

Note that here we are essentially finding a projection from the row space of X^k to the row space of W^k with a lower rank. Thus alternative approaches other than the popular SVD can also be exploited. Examples include incremental SVD [22], independent component analysis (ICA) [7, 13], and deep neural networks [12]. Our focus in this work is on the novel model for learning graph representations, so we do not pursue any alternative methods. In fact, if alternative method such as sparse auto-encoder is used at this step, it becomes relatively harder to justify whether the empirical effectiveness of our representations is due to our novel model, or comes from any non-linearity introduced in this dimensionality reduction step. To maintain the consistency with Levy et al. [16], we only employed SVD in this work.

4. ALGORITHM

We detail our learning algorithm in this section. In general, graph representations are extracted for other applications as features, such as classification and clustering. An effective way to encode k-step representation in practice is to concatenate the k-step representation as a global feature for each vertex, since each different step representation reflects different local information. Table 1 shows the overall algorithm, and we explain the essential steps of our algorithm here.

Step 1. Get k-step transition probability matrix A^k for each $k = 1, 2, \ldots, K$.

As shown in Section 3, given a graph G, we can calculate the k-step transition probability matrix A^k through the product of inverse of degree matrix D and adjacent matrix S. For a weighted graph, S is a real matrix, while for an unweighted graph, S is a binary matrix. Our algorithm is applicable to both cases.

Step 2. Get each k-step representation

We get k-step log probability matrix X^k, then subtract each entry by $\log(\beta)$, and replace the negative entries by zeros. After that, we construct the representational vectors as rows of W^k, where we introduce a solution to factorize the positive log probability matrix X^k using SVD. Finally, we get all k-step representations for each vertex on the graph.

Step 3. Concatenate all k-step representations

We concatenate all k-step representations to form a global representation, which can be used in other tasks as features.

Table 1: Overall Algorithm

GraRep Algorithm
Input
Adjacency matrix S on graph
Maximum transition step K
Log shifted factor β
Dimension of representation vector d
1. Get k-step transition probability matrix A^k
Compute $A = D^{-1}S$
Calculate $A^1, A^2, \ldots, A^K$, respectively
2. Get each k-step representations
For $k = 1$ to K
2.1 Get positive log probability matrix
calculate $\Gamma_1^k, \Gamma_2^k, \ldots, \Gamma_N^k$ ($\Gamma_j^k = \sum_p A_{p,j}^k$) respectively
calculate $\{X_{i,j}^k\}$
$X_{i,j}^k = \log\left(\frac{A_{i,j}^k}{\Gamma_j^k}\right) - \log(\beta)$
assign negative entries of X^k to 0
2.2 Construct the representation vector W^k
$[U^k, \Sigma^k, (V^k)^T] = SVD(X^k)$
$W^k = U_d^k (\Sigma_d^k)^{\frac{1}{2}}$
End for
3. Concatenate all the k-step representations
$W = [W^1, W^2, \ldots, W^K]$
Output
Matrix of the graph representation W

5. SKIP-GRAM MODEL AS A SPECIAL CASE OF GRAREP

GraRep aims to learn representations for graphs where we optimize the loss function based on matrix factorization. On the other hand, SGNS has been shown to be successful in handling linear structures such as natural language sentences. Is there any intrinsic relationship between them? In this section, we provide a view of SGNS as a special case of the GraRep model.

5.1 Explicit Loss of Skip-gram Model on Graph

SGNS aims at representing words in linear sequences, so we need to translate a graph structure into linear structures. Deepwalk reveals an effective way with uniform sampling (*truncated random walk*). This method first samples uniformly a random vertex from the graph, then walks randomly to one of its neighbors and repeats this process. If the length of the vertex sequence reaches a certain preset value, then stop and start generating a new sequence. This procedure can be used to produce a large number of sequences from the graph.

Essentially, for an unweighted graph, this strategy of uniform sampling works, while for a weighted graph, a probabilistic sampling method based on the weights of the edges is needed, which is not employed in DeepWalk. In this paper, we propose an Enhanced SGNS (E-SGNS) method suitable for weighted graphs. We also note that DeepWalk optimizes an alternative loss function (hierarchical softmax) that is different from negative sampling.

First, we consider total K-step loss L on whole graph

$$L = f(L_1, L_2, \ldots, L_K)$$

where $f(\cdot)$ is a linear combination of its arguments defined as follows:

$$f(\varphi_1, \varphi_2, \cdots, \varphi_K) = \varphi_1 + \varphi_2 + \cdots + \varphi_K$$

We focus on the loss of a specific pair (w,c) which are i-th and j-th vertex in the graph. Similar to Section 3.2, we assign partial derivative to 0, and get

$$Y_{i,j}^{E-SGNS} = \log\left(\frac{M_{i,j}}{\sum_t M_{t,j}}\right) - \log(\beta)$$

where M is transition probability matrix within K step(s), and $M_{i,j}$ refers to transition probability from vertex i to vertex j. $Y_{i,j}^{E-SGNS}$ is a factorized matrix for E-SGNS, and

$$M = A^1 + A^2 + \cdots + A^K$$

The difference between E-SGNS and GraRep model is on the definition of $f(\cdot)$. E-SGNS can be considered as a linear combination of K-step loss, and each loss has an equal weight. Our GraRep model does not make such a strong assumption, but allows their (potentially non-linear) relationship to be learned from data in practice. Intuitively, different k-step transition probabilities should have different weights, and linear combination of these may not achieve desirable results for heterogeneous network data.

5.2 Intrinsic Relation Between Sampling and Transition Probabilities

In our approach, we used transition probabilities to measure relationship between vertices. Is this reasonable? In this subsection, we articulate the intrinsic relation between sampling and transition probabilities.

Among the sequences generated by random walk, we assume vertex w occurs total times:

$$\#(w) = \alpha_w \gamma K$$

where γ is the total length of sequences and α_w is the probability of observing the vertex w in such all sequences. We regard vertex w as the current vertex, then the expected number of times that we see c_1 as its direct neighbor (1-step away from w) is:

$$\#(w, c_1) = \alpha_w \gamma K \cdot p_1(c|w)$$

This holds for both uniform sampling for unweighted graphs or our proposed probabilistic sampling for weighted graphs.

Further, we analyze the expected number of times of co-occurrence for w and c of context window size 2,

$$\#(w, c_2) = \alpha_w \gamma K \sum_{c'} p(c_2|c') \cdot p(c'|w) = \alpha_w \gamma K \cdot p_2(c|w)$$

where c' can be any vertex bridging w and c_2. That is, c' is shared neighbor between w and c_2. Similarly, we can derive the equations for $k = 3, 4, \cdots, K$:

$$\#(w, c_3) = \alpha_w \gamma K \cdot p_3(c|w)$$

$$\vdots$$

$$\#(w, c_K) = \alpha_w \gamma K \cdot p_K(c|w)$$

then we add them up and divide both sides by K, leading to:

$$\#(w, c) = \alpha_w \gamma \sum_{k=1}^{K} p_k(c|w)$$

where $\#(w, c)$ is the expected co-occurrence count between w and c within K step(s).

According to definition of $M_{w,c}$, we can get

$$\#(w, c) = \alpha_w \gamma M_{w,c}$$

Now, we can also compute the expected number of times we see c as the context vertex, $\#(c)$:

$$\#(c) = \sum_{w} \alpha_w \gamma M_{w,c}$$

where we consider the transitions from all possible vertices to c. To find the relationship with SGNS model, we consider a special case for α_w here. If we assume α_w follows an uniform distribution, we have $\alpha_w = \frac{1}{N}$. We plug these expected counts into the equation of $Y_{i,j}^{E-SGNS}$, and we arrive at:

$$Y_{w,c}^{E-SGNS} = \log\left(\frac{\#(w,c) \cdot |\mathcal{D}|}{\#(w) \cdot \#(c)}\right) - \log(\lambda)$$

where $\mathcal{D}$ is the collection of all observed pairs in sequences, that is, $|D| = \gamma K$. This matrix Y^{E-SGNS} becomes exactly the same as that of SGNS as described in [16].

This shows SGNS is essentially a special version of our GraRep model that deals with linear sequences which can be sampled from graphs. Our approach has several advantages over the slow and expensive sampling process, which typically involves several parameters to tune, such as maximum length of linear sequence, sampling frequency for each vertex, and so on.

6. EXPERIMENTAL DESIGN

In this section, we assess the effectiveness of our GraRep model through experiments. We conduct experiments on several real-word datasets for several different tasks, and make comparisons with baseline algorithms.

6.1 Datasets and Tasks

In order to demonstrate the performance of GraRep, we conducted the experiments across three different types of graphs – a social network, a language network and a citation network, which include both weighted and unweighted graphs. We conducted experiments across three different types of tasks, including clustering, classification, and visualization. As we mentioned in earlier sections, this work focuses on proposing a novel framework for learning good representation of graph with global structural information, and aims to validate the effectiveness of our proposed model. Thus we do not employ alternative more efficient matrix factorization methods apart from SVD, and focused on the following three real-world datasets in this section.

1. **20-Newsgroup**[1] is a language network, which has approximately 20,000 newsgroup documents and is partitioned by 20 different groups. In this network, each document is represented by a vector with tf-idf scores of each word, and the cosine similarity is used to calculate the similarity between two documents. Based on these similarity scores of each pair of documents, a language network is built. Following [29], in order to show the robustness of our model, we also construct the following 3 graphs built from 3, 6 and 9 different newsgroups respectively (note that NG refers to "Newsgroups"):

3-NG: *comp.graphics, comp.graphics and talk.politics.guns;*
6-NG: *alt.atheism, comp.sys.mac.hardware, rec.motorcycles, rec.sport.hockey, soc.religion.christian and talk.religion.misc;*
9-NG: *talk.politics.mideast, talk.politics.misc, comp.os.ms-windows.misc, sci.crypt, sci.med, sci.space, sci.electronics, misc.forsale, and comp.sys.ibm.pc.hardware*

Besides randomly sampling 200 documents from a topic as described in [29], we also conduct experiment on all documents as comparison. The topic label on each document is considered to be true.

This language network is a fully connected and weighted graph, and we will demonstrate the results of clustering, using graph representation as features.

[1] qwone.com/~jason/20Newsgroups/

2. **Blogcatalog**[2] is a social network, where each vertex indicates one blogger author, and each edge corresponds to the relationship between authors. 39 different types of topic categories are presented by authors as labels.

Blogcatalog is an unweighted graphs, and we test the performance of the learned representations on the multi-label classification task, where we classify each author vertex into a set of labels. The graph representations generated from our model and each baseline algorithm are considered as features.

3. **DBLP Network**[3] is a citation network. We extract author citation network from DBLP, where each vertex indicates one author and the number of references from one author to the other is recorded by the weight of edge between these two authors. Following [26], we totally select 6 different popular conferences and assign them into 3 groups, where WWW and KDD are grouped as *data mining*, NIPS and ICML as *machine learning*, and CVPR and ICCV as *computer vision*. We visualize the learned representations from all systems using a visualisation tool t-SNE [31], which provides both qualitative and quantitative results for the learned representations. We give more details in Section 6.4.3.

To summarize, in this paper we conduct experiments on both weighted and unweighted graphs, and both sparse and dense graphs, where three different types of learning tasks are carried out. More details of the graph we used are shown in Table 2.

6.2 Baseline Algorithms

We use the following methods of graph representation as baseline algorithms.

1. **LINE** [25]. LINE is a recently proposed method for learning graph representations on large-scale information networks. LINE defines a loss function based on 1-step and 2-step relational information between vertices. One strategy to improve the performance of vertices with small degrees is to make graph denser by expanding their neighbors. LINE will get the best performance, if concatenating the representation of 1-step and 2-step relational information and tuning the threshold of maximum number of vertices.

2. **DeepWalk** [20]. DeepWalk is a method that learns the representation of social networks. The original model only works for unweighted graph. For each vertex, truncated random walk is used to translate graph structure into linear sequences. The skip-gram model with hierarchical softmax is used as the loss function.

3. **E-SGNS**. Skip-gram is an efficient model that learns the representation of each word in large corpus [18]. For this enhanced version, we first utilize uniform sampling for unweighted graph and probabilistic sampling proportional to weight of edges for weighted graph, to generate linear vertex sequences, and then introduce SGNS to optimize. This method can be regarded as a special case of our model, where different representational vector of each k-step information is averaged.

4. **Spectral Clustering** [23]. Spectral clustering is a reasonable baseline algorithm, which aims at minimizing Normalized Cut (NCut). Like our method, Spectral clustering also factorize a matrix, but it focuses on a different matrix of the graphs – the *Laplacian Matrix*. Essentially, the difference between spectral clustering and E-SGNS lies on their different loss function.

6.3 Parameter Settings

As suggested in [25], for LINE, we set the mini-batch size of stochastic gradient descent (SGD) as 1, learning rate of starting value as 0.025, the number of negative samples as 5, and the total number of samples as 10 billion. We also concatenate both 1-step and 2-step relational information to form the representations and employ the reconstruction strategy for vertices with small degrees to achieve the optimal performance. As mentioned in [20], for DeepWalk and E-SGNS, we set window size as 10, walk length as 40, walks per vertex as 80. According to [25], LINE yielded better results when the learned graph representations are L2 normalized, while DeepWalk and E-SGNS can achieve optimal performance without normalization. For GraRep, we found the L2 normalization yielded better results. We reported all the results based on these findings for each system accordingly. For a fair comparison, the dimension d of representations is set as 128 for Blogcatalog network and DBLP network as used in [25] and is set as 64 for 20-NewsGroup network as used in [29]. For GraRep, we set $\beta = \frac{1}{N}$ and maximum matrix transition step K=6 for Blogcatalog network and DBLP network and K=3 for 20-NewsGroup network. To demonstrate the advantage of our model which captures global information of the graph, we also conducted experiments under various parameter settings for each baseline systems, which are discussed in detail in the next section.

6.4 Experimental Results

In this section, we present empirical justifications that our GraRep model can integrate different k-step local relational information into a global graph representation for different types of graphs, which can then be effectively used for different tasks. We make the source code of GraRep available at http://shelson.top/.

6.4.1 20-Newsgroup Network

We first conduct an experiment on a language network through a clustering task by employing the learned representations in a k-means algorithm [2].

To assess the quality of the results, we report the averaged Normalized Mutual Information (NMI) score [24] over 10 different runs for each system. To understand the effect of different dimensionality d in the end results, we also show the results when dimension d is set to 192 for DeepWalk, E-SGNS and Spectral Clustering. For LINE, we employ the reconstruction strategy proposed by their work by adding neighbors of neighbors as additional neighbors to improve performance. We set k-max=0, 200, 500, 1000 for experiments, where k-max is a parameter that is used to control how the higher-order neighbors are added to each vertex in the graph.

As shown in Table 3, the highest results are highlighted in bold for each column. We can see that GraRep consistently outperforms other baseline methods for this task. For DeepWalk, E-SGNS and Spectral Clustering, increasing

[2]leitang.net/code/social-dimension/data/blogcatalog.mat
[3]aminer.org/billboard/citation

Table 2: Statistics of the real-world graphs

	Language Network		Social Network	Citation Network
Name	20-NewsGroup (200 samples)	20-NewsGroup (all data)	Blogcatalog	DBLP (author citation)
Type	weighted	weighted	unweighted	weighted
#(V)	600, 1200 and 1800	1,720, 3,224 and 5,141	10,312	7,314
#(E)	Fully connected	Fully connected	333,983	72,927
Avg. degree	—	—	64.78	19.94
#Labels	3, 6 and 9	3, 6 and 9	39	3
Task	Clustering	Clustering	Classification	Visualization

Table 3: Results on 20-NewsGroup

	200 samples			all data		
Algorithm	3NG(200)	6NG(200)	9NG(200)	3NG(all)	6NG(all)	9NG(all)
GraRep	**81.12**	**67.53**	**59.43**	**81.44**	**71.54**	**60.38**
LINE (k-max=0)	80.36	64.88	51.58	80.58	68.35	52.30
LINE (k-max=200)	78.69	66.06	54.14	80.68	68.83	53.53
DeepWalk	65.58	63.66	48.86	65.67	68.38	49.19
DeepWalk (192dim)	60.89	59.89	47.16	59.93	65.68	48.61
E-SGNS	69.98	65.06	48.47	69.04	67.65	50.59
E-SGNS (192dim)	63.55	64.85	48.65	66.64	66.57	49.78
Spectral Clustering	49.04	51.02	46.92	62.41	59.32	51.91
Spectral Clustering (192dim)	28.44	27.80	36.05	44.47	36.98	47.36
Spectral Clustering (16dim)	69.91	60.54	47.39	78.12	68.78	57.87

Table 4: Results on Blogcatalog

Metric	Algorithm	10%	20%	30%	40%	50%	60%	70%	80%	90%
Micro-F1	GraRep	**38.24**	**40.31**	**41.34**	**41.87**	**42.60**	**43.02**	**43.43**	**43.55**	**44.24**
	LINE	37.19	39.82	40.88	41.47	42.19	42.72	43.15	43.36	43.88
	DeepWalk	35.93	38.38	39.50	40.39	40.79	41.28	41.60	41.93	42.17
	E-SGNS	35.71	38.34	39.64	40.39	41.23	41.66	42.01	42.16	42.25
	Spectral Clustering	37.16	39.45	40.22	40.87	41.27	41.50	41.48	41.62	42.12
Macro-F1	GraRep	**23.20**	**25.55**	**26.69**	**27.53**	**28.35**	**28.78**	**29.67**	**29.96**	**30.93**
	LINE	19.63	23.04	24.52	25.70	26.65	27.26	27.94	28.68	29.38
	DeepWalk	21.02	23.81	25.39	26.27	26.85	27.36	27.67	27.96	28.41
	E-SGNS	21.01	24.09	25.61	26.59	27.64	28.08	28.33	28.34	29.26
	Spectral Clustering	19.26	22.24	23.51	24.33	24.83	25.19	25.36	25.52	26.21

(a) Spectral Clustering (b) DeepWalk (c) E-SGNS (d) LINE (e) GraRep

Figure 3: Visualization of author citation network. Each point indicates one author. Green: *Data Mining*, magenta: *computer vision* and blue: *Machine Learning*.

the dimension d of representations does not appear to be effective in improving the performance. We believe this is because a higher dimension does not provide different complementary information to the representations. For LINE, the reconstruction strategy does help, since it can capture additional structural information of the graph beyond 1-step and 2-step local information.

It is worth mentioning that GraRep and LINE can achieve good performance with a small graph. We believe this is because both approaches can capture rich local relational information even when the graph is small. Besides, for tasks with more labels, such as 9NG, GraRep and LINE can provide better performances than other methods, with GraRep providing the best. An interesting finding is that Spectral Clustering arrives at its best performance when setting dimension d to 16. However, for all other algorithms, their best results are obtained when d is set to 64. We show these results in Figure 5 when we assess the sensitivity of parameters.

Due to limited space, we do not report the detailed results with d=128 and d=256 for all baseline methods, as well as k-max=500, 1000 and without reconstruction strategy for LINE, since these results are no better than the results presented in Table 3. In Section 6.5, we will further discuss the issue of parameter sensitivity.

6.4.2 Blogcatalog Network

In this experiment, we focus on a supervised task on a social network. We evaluate the effectiveness of different graph representations through a multi-label classification task by regarding the learned representations as features.

Following [20, 27], we use the LIBLINEAR package [10] to train one-vs-rest logistic regression classifiers, and we run this process for 10 rounds and report the averaged Micro-F1 and Macro-F1 measures. For each round, we randomly sample 10% to 90% of the vertices and use these samples for training, and use the remaining vertices for evaluation. As suggested in [25], we set k-max as 0, 200, 500 and 1000, respectively, and we report the best performance with k-max=500.

Table 4 reports the results of GraRep and each baseline algorithm. The highest performance is highlighted in bold for each column which corresponds to one particular train/test split. Overall, GraRep significantly outperforms other methods, especially under the setting where only 10% of the vertices are used for training. This indicates different types of rich local structural information learned by the GraRep model can be used to complement each other to capture the global structural properties of the graph, which serves

Table 5: **Final KL divergence for the DBLP dataset**

Algorithm	GraRep	LINE	DeepWalk	E-SGNS
KL divergence	1.0070	1.0816	1.1115	1.1009

as a distinctive advantage over existing baseline approaches, especially when the data is relatively scarce.

6.4.3 DBLP Network

In this experiment, we focus on visualizing the learned representations by examining a real citation network – DBLP. We feed the learned graph representations into the standard *t-SNE* tool [31] to lay out the graph, where the authors from the same research area (one of *data mining, machine learning* or *computer vision*, see Section 6.1) share the same color. The graphs are visualized on a 2-dimensional space and the Kullback-Leibler divergence is reported [31], which captures the errors between the input pairwise similarities and their projections in the 2-dimensional map as displayed (a lower KL divergence score indicates a better performance).

Under the help of *t-SNE* toolkit, we set the same parameter configuration and import representations generated by each algorithm. From Figure 3, we can see that the layout using Spectral Clustering is not very informative, since vertices of different colors are mixed with each other. For DeepWalk and E-SGNS, results look much better, as most vertices of the same color appear to form groups. However, vertices still do not appear in clearly separable regions with clear boundaries. For LINE and GraRep, the boundaries of each group become much clearer, with vertices of different colors appearing in clearly distinguishable regions. The results for GraRep appear to be better, with clearer boundaries for each regions as compared to LINE.

Table 5 reports the KL divergence at the end of iterations. Under the same parameter setting, a lower KL divergence indicates a better graph representation. From this result, we also can see that GraRep yields better representations than all other baseline methods.

6.5 Parameter Sensitivity

We discuss the parameter sensitivity in this section. Specifically, we assess the how the different choices of the maximal k-step size K, as well as the dimension d for our representations can affect our results.

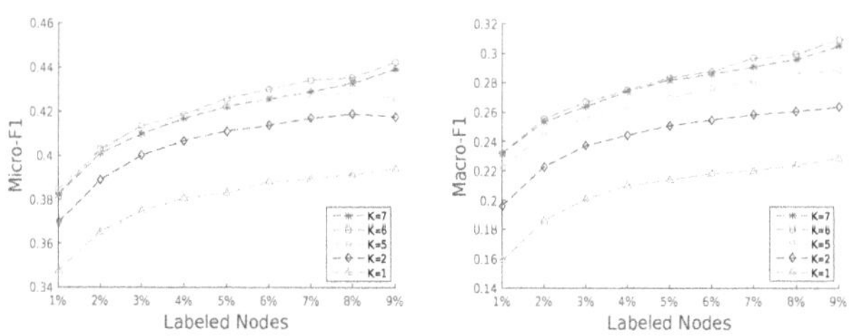

(a) Blogcatalog, Micro-F1 (b) Blogcatalog, Macro-F1

Figure 4: Performance over steps, K

Figure 4 shows the Micro-F1 and Macro-F1 scores over different choices of K on the Blogcatalog data. We can observe that the setting K=2 has a significant improvement over the setting K=1, and K=3 further outperforms K=2. This confirms that different k-step can learn complementary local information. In addition, as mentioned in Section 3, when k is large enough, learned k-step relational information becomes weak and shifts towards a steady distribution. Empirically we can observe that the performance of K=7 is no better than K=6. In this figure, for readability and clarity we only present the results of K=1,2,3,6 and 7. We found the performance of $K = 4$ is slightly better than K=3, while the results for K=5 is comparable to K=4.

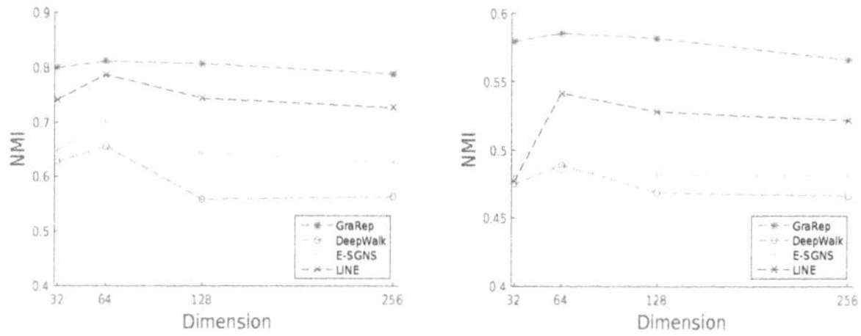

(a) 3NG, NMI (b) 9NG, NMI

Figure 5: Performance over dimensions, d

Figure 5 shows the NMI scores of each algorithm over different settings of the dimension d on 3NG and 9NG data. We can observe that GraRep consistently outperforms other baseline algorithms which learn representations with the same dimension. This set of experiments serves as an additional supplement to Table 3. Interestingly, all algorithms can obtain the optimal performance with $d = 64$. As we increase d from 64 to larger values, it appears that the performances of all the algorithms start to drop. Nevertheless, our GraRep algorithm is still superior to the baseline systems across different d values.

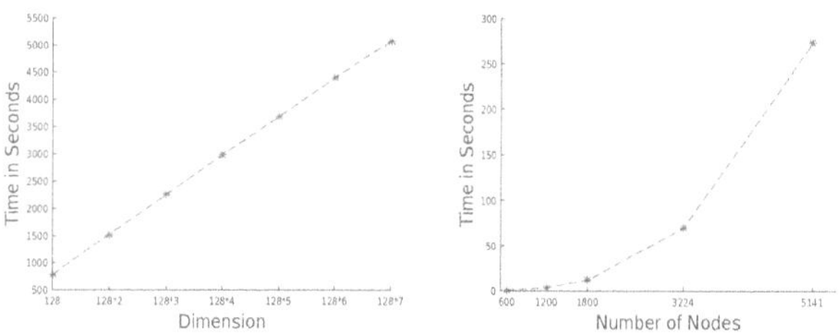

(a) Blogcatalog, running time (b) 20NG, running time

Figure 6: Running time as a function of a) dimension and b) size of graph.

Figure 6 shows the running time over different dimensions as well as over different graph sizes. In Figure 6(a), we set K from 1 to 7 where each complementary feature vector has a dimension of 128. This set of experiments is conducted on the Blogcatalog dataset which contains around 10,000 vertices. It can be seen that the running time increases approximately linearly as the dimension increases. In Figure 6(b), we analyze running time with respect to graph sizes. This set of experiment is conducted on different size of the 20-NewsGroup dataset. The result shows a significant increase of running time as graph size increases. The reason resulting in the large increase in running time is mainly due to high time complexity involved in the computation of the power of a matrix and the SVD procedure.

7. CONCLUSIONS

In this paper, GraRep, a novel model for learning better graph representations is proposed. Our model, with our k-step loss functions defined on graphs which integrate rich local structural information associated with the graph, captures the global structural properties of the graph. We also provide mathematical derivations justifying the model and establish the connections to previous research efforts. Empirically, the learned representations can be effectively used as features in other learning problems such as clustering and classification. This model comes with one limitation: the expensive computation of the power of a matrix and SVD involved in the learning process. Future work would include the investigation of efficient and online methods to approximate matrix algebraic manipulations, as well as investigation of alternative methods by employing deep architectures for learning low-dimensional representations in place of SVD.

8. ACKNOWLEDGMENTS

The authors would like to thank the anonymous reviewers for their helpful comments. The authors would also like to thank Fei Tian, Qingbiao Miao and Jie Liu for their suggestions or help with this work. This paper was done when the first author was an intern at SUTD. This work was supported by SUTD grant ISTD 2013 064 and Temasek Lab project IGDST1403013.

9. REFERENCES

[1] A. Ahmed, N. Shervashidze, S. Narayanamurthy, V. Josifovski, and A. J. Smola. Distributed large-scale natural graph factorization. In *WWW*, pages 37–48. International World Wide Web Conferences Steering Committee, 2013.

[2] D. Arthur and S. Vassilvitskii. k-means++: The advantages of careful seeding. In *SODA*, pages 1027–1035. Society for Industrial and Applied Mathematics, 2007.

[3] M. Belkin and P. Niyogi. Laplacian eigenmaps and spectral techniques for embedding and clustering. In *NIPS*, volume 14, pages 585–591, 2001.

[4] J. A. Bullinaria and J. P. Levy. Extracting semantic representations from word co-occurrence statistics: A computational study. *BRM*, 39(3):510–526, 2007.

[5] J. A. Bullinaria and J. P. Levy. Extracting semantic representations from word co-occurrence statistics: stop-lists, stemming, and svd. *BRM*, 44(3):890–907, 2012.

[6] J. Caron. Experiments with lsa scoring: Optimal rank and basis. In *CIR*, pages 157–169, 2001.

[7] P. Comon. Independent component analysis, a new concept? *Signal processing*, 36(3):287–314, 1994.

[8] T. F. Cox and M. A. Cox. *Multidimensional scaling*. CRC Press, 2000.

[9] C. Eckart and G. Young. The approximation of one matrix by another of lower rank. *Psychometrika*, 1(3):211–218, 1936.

[10] R.-E. Fan, K.-W. Chang, C.-J. Hsieh, X.-R. Wang, and C.-J. Lin. Liblinear: A library for large linear classification. *JMLR*, 9:1871–1874, 2008.

[11] M. U. Gutmann and A. Hyvärinen. Noise-contrastive estimation of unnormalized statistical models, with applications to natural image statistics. *JMLR*, 13(1):307–361, 2012.

[12] G. E. Hinton and R. R. Salakhutdinov. Reducing the dimensionality of data with neural networks. *Science*, 313(5786):504–507, 2006.

[13] C. Jutten and J. Herault. Blind separation of sources, part i: An adaptive algorithm based on neuromimetic architecture. *Signal processing*, 24(1):1–10, 1991.

[14] V. Klema and A. J. Laub. The singular value decomposition: Its computation and some applications. *Automatic Control*, 25(2):164–176, 1980.

[15] T. K. Landauer, P. W. Foltz, and D. Laham. An introduction to latent semantic analysis. *Discourse processes*, 25(2-3):259–284, 1998.

[16] O. Levy and Y. Goldberg. Neural word embedding as implicit matrix factorization. In *NIPS*, pages 2177–2185, 2014.

[17] K. Lund and C. Burgess. Producing high-dimensional semantic spaces from lexical co-occurrence. *BRMIC*, 28(2):203–208, 1996.

[18] T. Mikolov, I. Sutskever, K. Chen, G. S. Corrado, and J. Dean. Distributed representations of words and phrases and their compositionality. In *NIPS*, pages 3111–3119, 2013.

[19] J. Pennington, R. Socher, and C. D. Manning. Glove: Global vectors for word representation. *EMNLP*, 12, 2014.

[20] B. Perozzi, R. Al-Rfou, and S. Skiena. Deepwalk: Online learning of social representations. In *SIGKDD*, pages 701–710. ACM, 2014.

[21] S. T. Roweis and L. K. Saul. Nonlinear dimensionality reduction by locally linear embedding. *Science*, 290(5500):2323–2326, 2000.

[22] B. Sarwar, G. Karypis, J. Konstan, and J. Riedl. Incremental singular value decomposition algorithms for highly scalable recommender systems. In *ICIS*, pages 27–28. Citeseer, 2002.

[23] J. Shi and J. Malik. Normalized cuts and image segmentation. *PAMI*, 22(8):888–905, 2000.

[24] A. Strehl, J. Ghosh, and R. Mooney. Impact of similarity measures on web-page clustering. In *Workshop on Artificial Intelligence for Web Search (AAAI 2000)*, pages 58–64, 2000.

[25] J. Tang, M. Qu, M. Wang, M. Zhang, J. Yan, and Q. Mei. Line: Large-scale information network embedding. In *WWW*. ACM, 2015.

[26] J. Tang, J. Zhang, L. Yao, J. Li, L. Zhang, and Z. Su. Arnetminer: extraction and mining of academic social networks. In *SIGKDD*, pages 990–998. ACM, 2008.

[27] L. Tang and H. Liu. Relational learning via latent social dimensions. In *SIGKDD*, pages 817–826. ACM, 2009.

[28] J. B. Tenenbaum, V. De Silva, and J. C. Langford. A global geometric framework for nonlinear dimensionality reduction. *Science*, 290(5500):2319–2323, 2000.

[29] F. Tian, B. Gao, Q. Cui, E. Chen, and T.-Y. Liu. Learning deep representations for graph clustering. In *AAAI*, 2014.

[30] P. D. Turney. Domain and function: A dual-space model of semantic relations and compositions. *JAIR*, pages 533–585, 2012.

[31] L. Van der Maaten and G. Hinton. Visualizing data using t-sne. *JMLR*, 9(2579-2605):85, 2008.

Context-Adaptive Matrix Factorization for Multi-Context Recommendation

Tong Man[1], Huawei Shen[1], Junming Huang[2*], Xueqi Cheng[1]
[1]CAS Key Lab of Network Data Science and Technology
Institute of Computing Technology, Chinese Academy of Sciences
mantong@software.ict.ac.cn {shenhuawei,cxq}@ict.ac.cn
[2]CompleX Lab, Web Sciences Center
University of Electronic Science and Technology of China, Chengdu 611731, China
mail@junminghuang.com

ABSTRACT

Data sparsity is a long-standing challenge for recommender systems based on collaborative filtering. A promising solution for this problem is multi-context recommendation, i.e., leveraging users' explicit or implicit feedback from multiple contexts. In multi-context recommendation, various types of interactions between entities (users and items) are combined to alleviate data sparsity of a single context in a collective manner. Two issues are crucial for multi-context recommendation: (1) How to differentiate context-specific factors from entity-intrinsic factors shared across contexts? (2) How to capture the salient phenomenon that some entities are insensitive to contexts while others are remarkably context-dependent? Previous methods either do not consider context-specific factors, or assume that a context imposes equal influence on different entities, limiting their capability of combating data sparsity problem by taking full advantage of multiple contexts.

In this paper, we propose a context-adaptive matrix factorization method for multi-context recommendation by simultaneously modeling context-specific factors and entity-intrinsic factors in a unified model. We learn an entity-intrinsic latent factor for every entity, and a context-specific latent factor for every entity in each context. Meanwhile, using a context-entity mixture parameter matrix we explicitly model the extent to which each context imposes influence on each entity. Experiments on two real scenarios demonstrate that our method consistently outperforms previous multi-context recommendation methods on all different sparsity levels. Such a consistent performance promotion forms the unique superiority of our method, enabling it to be a reliable model for multi-context recommendation.

Categories and Subject Descriptors

H.2.8.d [**Information Technology and Systems**]: Database Applications - Data Mining

General Terms

Algorithms, Measurement, Experimentation

Keywords

Recommender System, Collaborative Filtering, Multi-context Recommendation, Data Sparsity

*This work is done when Junming Huang as a PhD candidate in Institute of Computing Technology, Chinese Academy of Sciences.

Permission to make digital or hard copies of all or part of this work for personal or classroom use is granted without fee provided that copies are not made or distributed for profit or commercial advantage and that copies bear this notice and the full citation on the first page. Copyrights for components of this work owned by others than ACM must be honored. Abstracting with credit is permitted. To copy otherwise, or republish, to post on servers or to redistribute to lists, requires prior specific permission and/or a fee. Request permissions from Permissions@acm.org.
CIKM 2015, October 19-23, 2015, Melbourne, Australia.
© 2015 ACM. ISBN 978-1-4503-3794-6/15/10 ...$15.00.
DOI: http://dx.doi.org/10.1145/2806416.2806503.

1. INTRODUCTION

With the increasingly growing amount of information available online, recommender system becomes a necessary tool to help users efficiently find their desired items, e.g., movies [1], music [2], news [3], books [4], online friends [5] and travel packages [6]. Personalized recommender systems gain great success in industry by collecting and analyzing users' explicit or implicit feedback, generally represented as interactions between *users* and *items*. For example, users offer explicit scores to movies they watched or books they read; users listen to their favorite songs multiple times; users frequently browse the products they potentially want to buy. Based on these observed interactions, collaborative filtering is widely used to infer users' preference and to predict items they are likely to interact with. Existing collaborative filtering methods could be classified into neighborhood-based methods [7] and model-based methods [8, 9]. Among those methods, matrix factorization [1] is the mainstream technique in personalized recommender system.

Matrix factorization (MF) formalizes collaborative filtering into a matrix completion problem, recovering an incomplete user-item preference matrix according to observed interactions or ratings between users and items [1]. MF factorizes the preference matrix into two low-rank matrices that represent latent factors for users and items respectively. With the two latent factor matrices, recommendation problem is addressed simply by their inner product. Recommendation accuracy of matrix factorization heavily depends on observed preference matrix. Unfortunately, preference matrix is often highly *sparse* in practical scenarios, forming a hard barrier for most real-world recommender systems [10]. Moreover, preference matrix is *unevenly distributed*, i.e., a majority of inactive users express preference on a small number of items and a majority of unpopular items get few feedbacks. Such a data sparsity problem is particularly severe for newly-joining users and newly-arriving items, forming the so-called cold-start problem. As the number of users and items rapidly grows, the sparsity problem and the cold-start problem become the bottleneck of modern recommender systems in business.

Many efforts have been made to combat the long-standing data sparsity problem. Existing methods could be roughly classified into

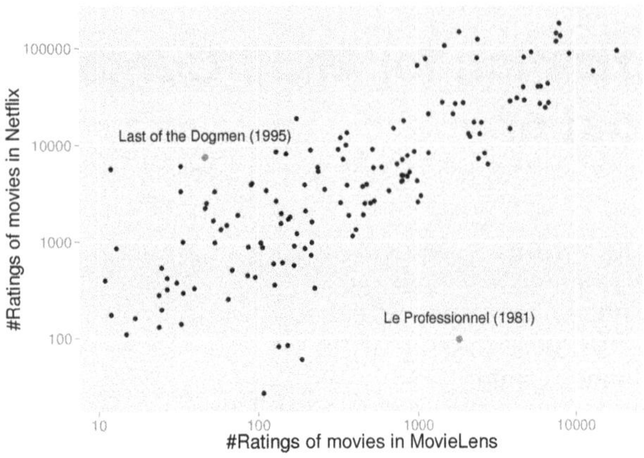

Figure 1: Rating counts in two movie datasets.

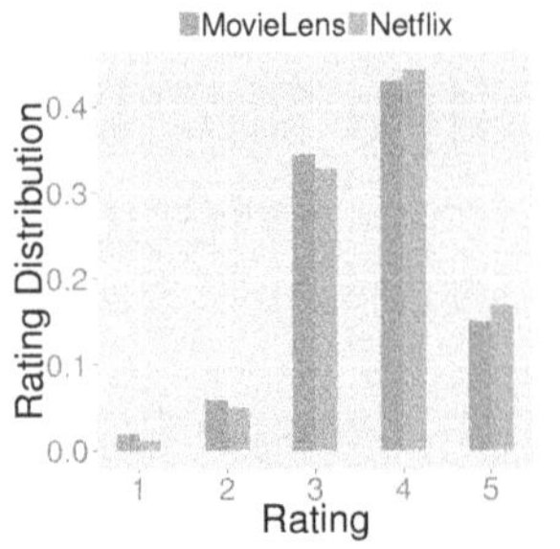

(a) 20,000 Leagues Under the Sea

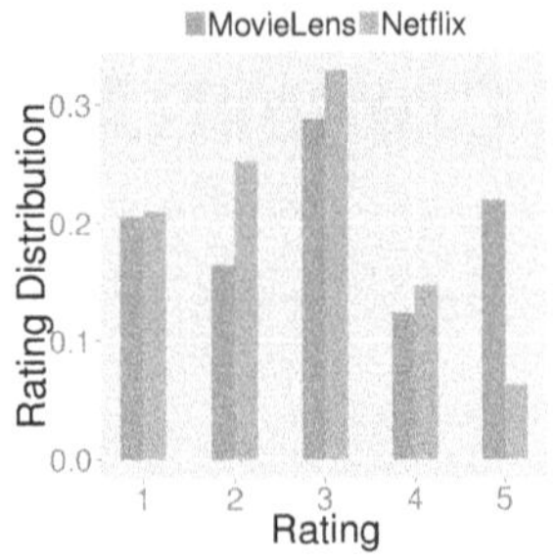

(b) Mad Dog Time

Figure 2: Rating distribution of two movies under two different contexts, i.e., MovieLens and Netflix.

two paradigms. The first focuses on improving recommendation methods or models, dealing with data sparsity problem by introducing appropriate priors or regularization [11]. Although some improvements have been achieved, these methods quickly hit the limit caused by data sparsity of single context. Therefore researchers turn to multi-context recommendation, leveraging feedbacks or ratings from multiple contexts to improve the recommendation accuracy in a particular context [12, 13, 14]. This is motivated by the fact that entities (users or items) are always involved in multiple contexts. For example, one user may express his/her preferences on music at Last.fm and preferences on videos at YouTube; one movie could receive ratings in different movie-rating websites, such as Netflix and MovieLens. Moreover, the degree of data sparsity for a user/item could be quite different across contexts. Figure 1 illustrates the distribution of rating counts for 140 randomly-sampled movies occurring in two different datasets — Netflix and MovieLens. Although the distribution of rating counts in the two datasets as a whole is linearly correlated, several movies have remarkably different rating counts in the two datasets. For example, the French action thriller film '*Le Professionnel*' has only a few ratings in Netflix but gets a lot of ratings in MovieLens, and the western adventure film '*Last of the Dogmen*' is popular in Netflix but cold in MovieLens. For multi-context recommendation, it is expected that users/items that have no or little data in the context of interest may have data in other contexts that could be leveraged to improve the recommendation in the target context.

Collective matrix factorization (CMF) was first proposed to address the multi-context recommendation problem [12]. CMF assumes that *one entity (user or item) shares the same latent factor across different contexts*. The global factor for each entity is learned based on the observed interaction data from all the contexts in which this entity is involved. CMF simply takes the observed interactions in all contexts as being from a single one. Consequently, in CMF, there is a danger that the context with high number of observed interactions could dominate other contexts with few observations. This is problematic for multi-context recommendation because the volume of interactions in different contexts could be remarkably different in real scenario. To address this problem, localized matrix factorization (LMF) [13] and HeteroMF [14] were proposed. In the two models, each entity has two latent factors, i.e., a global latent factor shared across different contexts and a local latent factor specific to each context. Context-specific factors are viewed as being generated from the global one by multiplying it with a context-specific transfer matrix. By modeling context-specific factors and context-independent factors separately, these two models outperform CMF for entities that have spare observations in one context but lots of observations in other contexts. However, their performance is limited by their underlying assumption: the same context exerts the same influence to all entities indiscriminately, reflected by the transfer matrix specific to each context. Indeed, the influence of the same context to different entities could be quite different. Figure 2 depicts the rating distribution of two movies under two contexts. For movie '*20,000 Leagues Under the Sea*', the rating distribution is almost the same in these two contexts, indicating that it is insusceptible to contexts. For movie '*Mad Dog Time*', on the other hand, its rating distribution is highly affected by contexts. Neglecting the difference at the degree to which contexts influence different entities, existing models fail to fully, even improperly, capture the knowledge offered by multi-context observations.

In this paper, we address two critical issues in multi-context recommendation: (1) How to differentiate context-specific factors from entity-intrinsic factors shared across contexts? (2) How to capture such a salient phenomenon: some entities are insensitive to contexts while others are remarkably context-dependent? We propose a context-adaptive matrix factorization (AdaMF) method, addressing the multi-context recommendation problem via simultaneously modeling context-specific factors and entity-intrinsic factors in a unified model. We learn for every entity an entity-intrinsic latent factor shared cross different contexts and a latent factor specific to each context. Meanwhile, using a context-entity mixture parameter matrix we explicitly model the degree to which each context imposes influence on each entity. We develop a Gaussian mixture model to describe the interaction between users' intrinsic factors and users' context-specific factors. Experiments on two real scenarios demonstrate that our method consistently outperforms previous methods for multi-context recommendation on all different sparsity levels.

Our main contributions are summarized as follows:

- We propose a novel AdaMF method for multi-context recommendation, adaptively learning global entity-intrinsic factors shared across different contexts and context-specific factors. Compared with existing models, our model could flexibly distinguish the context-specific interactions and context-independent ones, improving the recommendation performance for multi-context recommendation.
- We apply the AdaMF method in two real scenarios – an item-aligned scenario where movies receive ratings in MovieLens and Netflix, and a user-aligned scenario where users of Douban

give ratings to three types of items, i.e., music, books, and movies. Experimental results demonstrate that our method consistently improves the prediction accuracy in both scenarios on all the sparsity levels.

This paper is organized as follows: we first give some preliminaries about multi-context recommendation. Next, related works are described in Section 3. In Section 4, we propose our model and design an EM framework to train the model. In Section 5, we present our experiments on two multi-context datasets, namely an item-aligned context and a user-aligned context. Section 6 concludes this paper.

2. PRELIMINARY

Let us consider L different contexts, each of which could represent a recommendation application. We use special indexing letters to distinguish users from items: a user set $\mathcal{U}$ with M users and an item set $\mathcal{I}$ with N items. These users and items are embedded in the L contexts. We use $R_{ij}^{(l)}$ to denote the rating that user i gives to item j in context l. All the rating information in context l is stored in a context-specific rating matrix $R^{(l)}$. Typically, $R^{(l)}$ is highly sparse. We denote all rating matrices as $R = \{R^{(1)}, R^{(2)}, ..., R^{(L)}\}$. Then the multi-context recommendation problem could be formalized as:

Multi-Context Recommendation: Observing the rating information R from L different contexts, the user set $\mathcal{U}$ and item set $\mathcal{I}$, for a user-item pair (i, j) and a context l such that $R_{ij}^{(l)}$ is unknown, we predict $R_{ij}^{(l)}$.

In real application, there are two typical scenarios of multi-context recommendation, i.e., user-aligned scenario and item-aligned scenario. For user-aligned scenario, users are involved in multiple contexts. For example, a user may register in multiple online social networks, such as Facebook and Twitter. Even in one network, the user could be involved in multiple contexts, reflecting their different actions or feedbacks. For example, in Twitter, a user involves himself in multiple contexts by following other users or forwarding tweets. The other scenario is item-aligned. Taking movie recommendation as an example, there are many movie rating resources, such as Netflix, MovieLens, and IMDB. With movies' names, release date, actors, directors, and other information, we can identify movies that appear in multiple contexts.

What is a context?

Context is a multi-faceted concept across different research disciplines. For context-aware recommender systems (CARS) [15, 16], the term "context" refers to the contextual information when a user takes an action on an item, e.g., rating a movie. Contextual information can be explicit, like time, location, and mood. CARS aims to incorporate these explicit information into recommendation models.

The context considered in this paper refers to the data source of users' (items') information. In the real world, users' and items' information is decentralized into multiple data sources, which could be considered as a context for the users and items involved. Some related works considered cross-domain recommendation [17, 18], a special scenario for multi-context problem where users are aligned across different contexts and items are heterogenous in different contexts. The definition of multi-context recommendation is more general, since items could be homogenous across different contexts. To summarize, the key point of multi-context recommendation is the method of combining the information from different contexts, where items from different contexts could be heterogenous or homogeneous.

Matrix Factorization

Matrix factorization (MF) is one of the state-of-the-art techniques in collaborative filtering. MF was proposed to make prediction for a single user-item rating matrix under single-context scenario. In MF, each user/item is associated with a low-dimensional latent factor. Users' latent factor vectors are stored in matrix U, where latent factor of user i is the ith column of matrix U, denoted by U_i. The latent factor V_j of item j is the jth column of the item factor matrix V. The rating of user-item pair (i, j) is modeled by a probabilistic model with Gaussian observation noise. The conditional distribution over observed rating matrix R as

$$p(R|U, V, \sigma^2) = \prod_{i=1}^{M} \prod_{j=1}^{N} \left[\mathcal{N}(R_{ij}|U_i^T V_j, \sigma^2)\right]^{I_{ij}}, \quad (1)$$

where $\mathcal{N}(x|\mu, \sigma^2)$ is the probability density function of the Gaussian distribution with mean μ and variance σ^2, and I_{ij} is an indicator function that reflects whether user i rated item j. Generally, spherical Gaussian priors are placed on user and item factor vectors:

$$p(U|\sigma_u^2) = \prod_{i=1}^{M} (U_i|\vec{\mathbf{0}}, \sigma_u^2 \mathbf{I}), \quad (2)$$

$$p(V|\sigma_v^2) = \prod_{j=1}^{N} (V_j|\vec{\mathbf{0}}, \sigma_v^2 \mathbf{I}). \quad (3)$$

Figure 3(a) shows the graphical model of matrix factorization. The latent factors of users and items are inferred in the learning phase using the observed rating matrix. Typically, stochastic gradient descent learning method is used. To predict the rating of user i on item j, the inner product of latent factor vectors U_i and V_j is computed. Our AdaMF model is built on matrix factorization.

3. RELATED WORKS

3.1 Recommendation with Side Information

Former researchers tried to solve data sparsity problem and cold-start problem by involving new information sources such as social relationship and taxonomy information. For example, Ma [19] and Liu [20] included social network information to improve the accuracy of recommender systems. In these works, social information is incorporated into recommendation models as regularization terms, constraining taste difference between a user and his/her friends. Noam [2] and Weng [21] used taxonomy information on the item side. Noam extended the matrix factorization model by incorporating a rich bias model with terms that capture information from the taxonomy of items. Weng modified the similarity measurement with the item taxonomy information, improving the traditional neighborhood-based recommender system.

Recently, some general frameworks are proposed to incorporate multiple kinds of information across multiple contexts. Berkovsky extended the neighborhood-based models into the multi-context scenario [22]. Similarity between users and items are calculated by assembling all the information across all the contexts. Since this work is only an simple extension of neighborhood-based models, the improvement is limited. Chen proposed SVDFeature, a feature-based matrix factorization framework [23]. The feature-based setting allows to build factorization models, incorporating side information like temporal dynamics, neighborhood relationship, and hierarchical information. Xiao solved the recommendation problem in a heterogeneous information network [24]. Using the concept of meta-path to construct many different user-item preference matrices, they built recommendation algorithm based on these matrices separately. The final results are formulated by combining all these preference matrices using a linear model. However, side-information, both from user-side and item-side, is hard to get in many real world applications.

3.2 Transfer Learning

Multi-context recommendation problem could also be done by *transfer learning*, which transfers the knowledge from some auxiliary data source to a target data source [25]. Pan considered a collective factorization model to transfer rating knowledge from some auxiliary data source in binary form to a target numerical rating matrix [26]. Li considered a Codebook transfer (CBT) algorithm under the scenario to transfer rating information across different domains [17]. Auxiliary rating matrix is first compressed into an informative and yet compact cluster-level rating pattern representation referred to as a codebook, and then the target rating matrix is reconstructed by expanding the codebook. However, the hard clustering constraint greatly reduces the expressive power of CBT. A generative model is introduced in [27], relaxing the constraints in CBT from hard clustering to soft clustering using a probabilistic graphical model. In our model, all rating matrices in different contexts are factorized simultaneously, without the need to explicitly distinguish these matrices into auxiliary and target ones. The knowledge is transferred on two directions for all these matrices.

3.3 Collective Matrix Factorization

As discussed before, matrix factorization is proposed for single context, where only one rating matrix is considered. In multi-context recommender system, users (items) will be involved in interactions across multiple contexts. Factorizing the rating matrix in each context separately would not take advantage of any correlation between contexts. We use MF as one of our baseline model in our experiments.

There are some related works of multi-context recommendation based on direct extension of matrix factorization model. Collective matrix factorization (CMF) is proposed by Singh and Gordon [12] to deal with multi-context data. CMF decomposes the rating matrix in each context into a product of two latent factor matrices, representing users' and items' latent interest space respectively. Whenever one entity participates into more than one context, the latent factor for the entity is shared across all contexts. Fig 3(b) shows the probabilistic graphical model of CMF. In this model, latent factors of users and items are shared in all different contexts.

In CMF, the latent factor for an entity is learned based on the observed ratings from the contexts in which the entity participates. However, there is one issue with CMF that objects share the same latent factor across different contexts. This is claimed to be problematic in [13, 14] in two aspects. Firstly, latent factors for objects that are cold in a context will be learned mainly based on the data from other contexts where it is not cold. Consequently, latent factors for the cold objects are not properly learned. Secondly, the latent factors for objects participating in multi-context are learned mainly based on the dominating context and the dominated context has little effect on the learned latent factors. LMF and HeteroMF models are proposed to tackle these problems. In both of these two models, each entity has one global latent factor. For each context, there is a transfer matrix to transfer the global latent factor into the context-specific latent factor. The probabilistic graphical model of HeteroMF is shown in Fig 3(c). Just as the probabilistic graphical model of CMF, there are L contexts, rating for user-item pair (i, j) in the lth context is labeled by $R_{ij}^{(l)}$. For the ith user, the global factor is U_i, and for each item there is a global factor V_j. For each context and the entity (namely, user and item) type, there is a transfer matrix to model the influence of context. The local factor is the result of the interaction between the transfer matrix and the global factor. Taking user-side as an example, the local factor for the ith user in the lth context is generated by the product of the global factor and a transfer matrix M_u^l. Following the notation in the preliminary, the probability distribution of the global and local factors of the ith user are:

$$\begin{aligned} U_i &\sim \mathcal{N}(\vec{\mathbf{0}}, \sigma_u^2 \mathbf{I}), \\ U_i^{(l)} &\sim \mathcal{N}(M_u^l U_i, \sigma_{u,l}^2 \mathbf{I}). \end{aligned} \tag{4}$$

The definition of the global factor and local factor of the items are just the same as the users. The underlying assumption of modeling the context as a transfer matrix is that the effect of one context to all objects in the context is the same. We relax this assumption by directly modeling the context-specific factor of one entity in a given context. The final local factor for one entity is the result of a mixture interaction between the context-specific factor and the global factor. The parameters of the mixture model are adaptively learned from the data.

4. AdaMF

In this section we propose AdaMF, a *context-adaptive matrix factorization* model, to address multi-context recommendation. Consider M users and N items involved in L different contexts. Each context l is associated with a preference matrix $R^{(l)}$, whose element $R_{ij}^{(l)}$ describes the preference (usually a rating) of user i on item j. Our task is to predict the missing value $R_{ij}^{(l)}$.

As shown in Figure 3(d), AdaMF predicts a missing preference $R_{ij}^{(l)}$ based on latent factors representing user i and item j. Different from a standard matrix factorization model that uses one latent factor for each user/item, a sharing-user version of AdaMF uses multiple factors to describe each user, representing her intrinsic preference and context-specific interests respectively, in a scenario where different contexts share an identical set of users. A sharing-item version of AdaMF uses multiple factors to describe each item, representing its intrinsic quality and context-specific quality respectively. Here, as an example, we discuss the sharing-item version of AdaMF without loss of generalization. Specifically, each user i is assigned with a latent factor U_i while each item j is assigned with multiple latent factors, including an *entity-intrinsic factor* V_j related to its inherit property, and a *context-specific factor* $V_j^{(l)}$ associated with each context l. A rating $R_{ij}^{(l)}$ is then drawn from a mixture of two Gaussian distributions, with mean values of $U_i^T V_j$ and $U_i^T V_j^{(l)}$, reflecting the preference of user i on the entity-intrinsic and context-specific part of item j respectively. Those two distributions are mixed with an item-context mixture parameter $\pi_j^{(l)}$, written as

$$\begin{aligned} P(R_{ij}^{(l)} | U_i, V_j, V_j^{(l)}, \pi_j^{(l)}) = \pi_j^{(l)} \mathcal{N}(R_{ij}^{(l)} | U_i^T V_j^{(l)}, {\sigma_l}^2) \\ +(1 - \pi_j^{(l)}) \mathcal{N}(R_{ij}^{(l)} | U_i^T V_j, {\sigma_l}^2). \end{aligned} \tag{5}$$

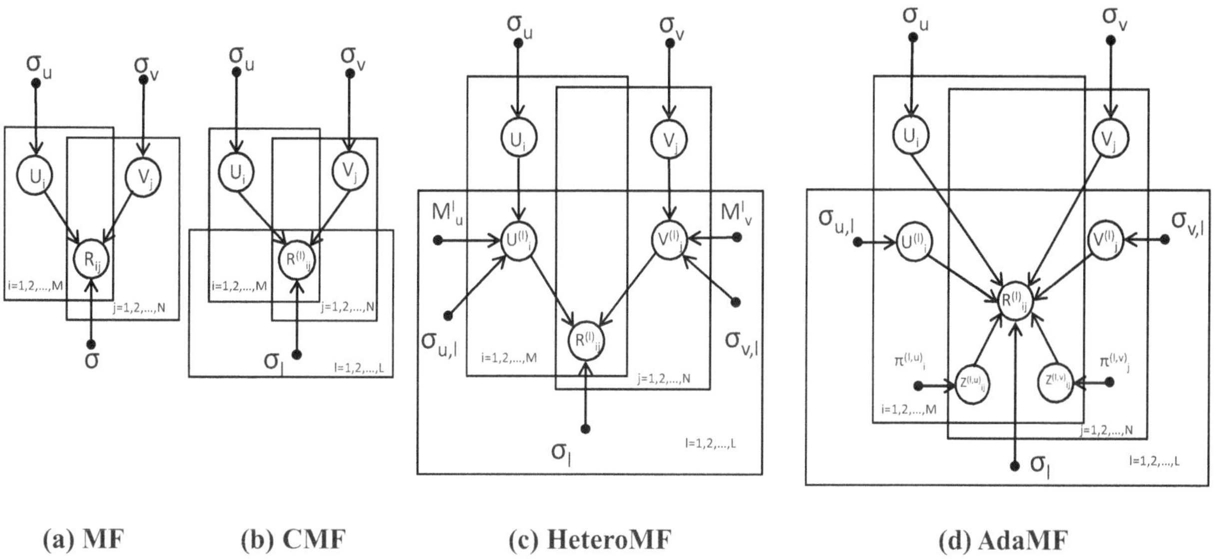

Figure 3: Probabilistic graphical models.

We assume zero-mean spherical Gaussian priors for all latent factors

$$p(U_i|\sigma_u) = \mathcal{N}(U_i|\vec{\mathbf{0}}, \sigma_u^2\mathbf{I}),$$
$$p(V_j^{(l)}|\sigma_{v,l}) = \mathcal{N}(V_j^{(l)}|\vec{\mathbf{0}}, \sigma_{v,l}^2\mathbf{I}),$$
$$p(V_j|\sigma_v) = \mathcal{N}(V_j|\vec{\mathbf{0}}, \sigma_v^2\mathbf{I}),$$

where $\mathbf{I}$ denotes an identity matrix.

We introduce a latent Bernoulli variable $Z_{ij}^{(l)} \sim Bern(\pi_j^{(l)})$. $Z_{ij}^{(l)} = 0$ indicates that the rating $R_{ij}^{(l)}$ is drawn from the distribution based on the entity-intrinsic factor, while $Z_{ij}^{(l)} = 1$ indicates that the context-specific factor is used.

The joint distribution of $R_{ij}^{(l)}$ and $Z_{ij}^{(l)}$ is as follows,

$$P(R_{ij}^{(l)}, Z_{ij}^{(l)}|U_i, V_j^{(l)}, V_j, \pi_j^{(l)})$$
$$= \left(\pi_j^{(l)}\mathcal{N}(R_{ij}^{(l)}|U_i^T V_j^{(l)}, \sigma_l{}^2)\right)^{Z_{ij}^{(l)}}$$
$$\cdot \left((1-\pi_j^{(l)})\mathcal{N}(R_{ij}^{(l)}|U_i^T V_j, \sigma_l^2)\right)^{\left(1-Z_{ij}^{(l)}\right)}.$$

Accordingly, the joint likelihood of observations and latent variables of the whole dataset could be written as

$$P(R, Z, U, V, \bigcup_l V^{(l)}|\pi, \Omega) = \prod_l P(R^{(l)}, Z^{(l)}|U, V, V^{(l)}, \pi^{(l)}, \sigma_l)$$
$$\prod_i P(U_i|\sigma_u)\prod_j P(V_j|\sigma_v)\prod_l\prod_j P(V_j^{(l)}|\sigma_{v,l}),$$

where $R = \{R_{ij}^{(l)}\}$, $Z = \{Z_{ij}^{(l)}\}$, $U = \{U_i\}$, $V = \{V_i\}$, $V^{(l)} = \{V_j^{(l)}\}$, and $\Omega = \{\sigma_u, \sigma_v, \bigcup_l \sigma_{v,l}\}$ is the variance parameter set of the model, $\pi = \{\pi^{(l)}\}$ is a mixture parameter matrix. Here, $\pi^{(l)}$ is the mixture parameter vector of items in context l.

4.1 Inference

We use an expectation maximization (EM) algorithm to infer model parameters and latent factors by maximizing the logarithmic likelihood $\mathcal{L}$ of the whole dataset,

$$\mathcal{L} =$$
$$\sum_l\sum_i\sum_j\left(Z_{ij}^{(l)}\left(\log\pi_j^{(l)} - \frac{1}{2}\left(\frac{\left(R_{ij}^{(l)} - U_i^T V_j^{(l)}\right)^2}{\sigma_l^2} + \log\sigma_l^2\right)\right)\right.$$
$$\left.+\left(1-Z_{ij}^{(l)}\right)\left(\log\left(1-\pi_j^{(l)}\right) - \frac{1}{2}\left(\frac{\left(R_{ij}^{(l)} - U_i^T V_j\right)^2}{\sigma_l^2} + \log\sigma_l^2\right)\right)\right)^{I_{ij}^l}$$
$$-\frac{1}{2}\sum_i\frac{1}{\sigma_u}||U_i||_F^2 - \frac{1}{2}\sum_j\frac{1}{\sigma_v}||V_j||_F^2 - \frac{1}{2}\sum_l\sum_j\frac{1}{\sigma_{v,l}}||V_j^{(l)}||_F^2, \quad (6)$$

where $I_{i,j}^l = 1$ if user i has ratings of item j in context l; $I_{i,j}^l = 0$ otherwise. $||\cdot||_F^2$ denotes the Frobenius norm. In the E-step, we compute the expected logarithmic likelihood with respect to the mixture parameters of items and latent variables. In the M-step, we maximize that expected likelihood of the whole dataset. The two steps are repeated alternately until convergence.

4.1.1 E-step

In the E-step, we use the current mixture parameter values π and latent factors to find the posterior distribution of the latent variables Z. We then use this posterior distribution to find the expectation of the complete-data logarithmic likelihood evaluated according to the mixture parameters and latent factors.

The expected values (responsibility) of $Z_{ij}^{(l)}$ is evaluated as follow,

$$\gamma(Z_{ij}^{(l)}) = E[Z_{ij}^{(l)}]$$
$$= \frac{\pi_j^{(l)}\cdot\mathcal{N}(R_{ij}^{(l)}|U_i^T V_j^{(l)}, \sigma_l^2)}{\pi_j^{(l)}\cdot\mathcal{N}(R_{ij}|U_i^T V_j^{(l)}, \sigma_l^2) + (1-\pi_j^{(l)})\cdot\mathcal{N}(R_{ij}^{(l)}|U_i^T V_j, \sigma_l^2)}$$
$$= \frac{1}{1 + \frac{1-\pi_j^{(l)}}{\pi_j^{(l)}}\cdot\frac{e^{-(R_{ij}^{(l)} - U_i^T V_j)^2/\sigma_l^2}}{e^{-(R_{ij}^{(l)} - U_i^T V_j^{(l)})^2/\sigma_l^2}}}. \quad (7)$$

The expected log-likelihood is computed as follows,

$$
\begin{aligned}
&E_Z[\mathcal{L}] = \\
&\sum_l \sum_i \sum_j \left(\gamma\left(Z_{ij}^{(l)}\right) \log \pi_j^{(l)} + \left(1-\gamma\left(Z_{ij}^{(l)}\right)\right) \log\left(1-\pi_j^{(l)}\right)\right)^{I_{ij}^l} \\
&-\frac{1}{2}\left(\gamma\left(Z_{ij}^{(l)}\right)\left(\frac{1}{\sigma_l^2}\left(R_{ij}^{(l)} - U_i^T V_j^{(l)}\right)^2 + \log \sigma_l^2\right)\right. \\
&\left.+\left(1-\gamma\left(Z_{ij}^{(l)}\right)\right)\left(\frac{1}{\sigma_l^2}\left(R_{ij}^{(l)} - U_i^T V_j\right)^2 + \log\sigma_l^2\right)\right)^{I_{ij}^l} \\
&-\frac{1}{2}\sum_i \frac{1}{\sigma_u}||U_i||_F^2 - \frac{1}{2}\sum_j \frac{1}{\sigma_v}||V_j||_F^2 \\
&-\frac{1}{2}\sum_l \sum_j \frac{1}{\sigma_{v,l}}||V_j^{(l)}||_F^2.
\end{aligned} \tag{8}
$$

4.1.2 M-step

In the M-step, we maximize the expected log-likelihood of the complete dataset. Note that the expected log-likelihood could be divided into two parts. The first part only involves the mixture parameters $\pi_j^{(l)}$, which could be estimated by

$$\pi_j^{(l)} = \frac{\sum_i (\gamma(Z_{ij}^{(l)}))^{I_{ij}^l}}{\sum_i I_{ij}^l}. \tag{9}$$

The second part of the objective function with respect to the latent variables is maximized by the stochastic gradient descent strategy (SGD) with a tiny update step η. Just as what was done in [9], maximizing the second part of the objective function is equivalent to minimizing the sum-of-squared-errors objective function with quadratic regularization terms, written as

$$
\begin{aligned}
E = &\sum_l \sum_i \sum_j I_{ij}^l \{\gamma(Z_{ij}^{(l)})(R_{ij}^{(l)} - U_i^T V_j^{(l)})^2 \\
&+ (1-\gamma(Z_{ij}^{(l)}))(R_{ij}^{(l)} - U_i^T V_j)^2\} \\
&+ \lambda_u \sum_i ||U_i||_F^2 + \lambda_v \sum_j ||V_j||_F^2 \\
&+ \sum_l \lambda_{v,l} \sum_j ||V_j^{(l)}||_F^2 + \mathcal{C}.
\end{aligned} \tag{10}
$$

For simplicity, we set all the σ_l and $\sigma_{v,l}$ as the same for all contexts: so $\lambda_u = \sigma_l^2/\sigma_u^2$, $\lambda_v = \sigma_l^2/\sigma_v^2$, $\lambda_{v,l} = \sigma_l^2/\sigma_{v,l}^2$. We set $\lambda = \{\lambda_u, \lambda_v, \bigcup_l \lambda_{v,l}\}$ as the regularization parameters set, and $\mathcal{C}$ is the constant term.

For each rating in one context $R_{ij}^{(l)}$, we update for U_i, V_j, $V_j^{(l)}$ leveraging gradients,

$$
\begin{aligned}
U_i \leftarrow U_i - \eta \cdot &\left(\gamma(Z_{ij}^{(l)})(U_i^T V_j^{(l)} - R_{ij}^{(l)})V_j^{(l)}\right. \\
&\left.+ (1-\gamma(Z_{ij}^{(l)}))(U_i^T V_j - R_{ij}^{(l)})V_j + \lambda_u U_i\right), \\
V_j \leftarrow V_j - \eta \cdot &\left((1-\gamma(Z_{ij}^{(l)}))(U_i^T V_j - R_{ij}^{(l)})U_i + \lambda_v V_j\right), \\
V_j^{(l)} \leftarrow V_j^{(l)} - \eta \cdot &\left(\gamma(Z_{ij}^{(l)})(U_i^T V_j^{(l)} - R_{ij}^{(l)})U_i + \lambda_{v,l} V_j^{(l)}\right).
\end{aligned} \tag{11}
$$

The framework of the whole algorithm is formalized in Algorithm 1.

After inference, we predict an unobserved rating of user i on item j in context l with its expectation,

$$\hat{R}_{ij}^{(l)} = \pi_j^{(l)} \cdot U_i^T V_j^{(l)} + (1-\pi_j^{(l)}) \cdot U_i^T V_j.$$

Algorithm 1 AdaMF

$[U, V, \bigcup_l V^{(l)}, \pi] = AdaMF(R, \eta, \lambda)$

E-Step:
For all observed user-item pairs (i, j) in all contexts:
Evaluate $P(Z_{ij}^{(l)} | R_{ij}^{(l)}, U_i, V_j, V_j^{(l)}) = \gamma(Z_{ij}^{(l)})$
M-Step:
Maximize $E_Z[\mathcal{L}]$ with respect of $U, V, \bigcup_l V^{(l)}, \pi$
Estimate π by Eq. (9)
SGD used in this step:
For one rating pair in one context (i, j, l), update the latent factors and parameters U_i,V_j,$V_j^{(l)}$ by Eq. (11)
Repeated until convergence.

5. EXPERIMENTS

AdaMF is evaluated with two real-world datasets, compared with mainstream baselines. The MovieLens-Netflix dataset contains users and aligned movies in two contexts corresponding to two public benchmark datasets from Netflix Prize[1] and MovieLens project[2]. $5,871$ movies are aligned by IMDB meta information after data cleaning. Since there are much fewer MovieLens users than Netflix users, we sampled $70,132$ users from Netflix for balancing two contexts. The Douban dataset contains items and aligned users in three contexts, namely books, movies, and music. It is crawled from an online social network Douban[3] where users rate books, movies, and music [28]. We remove inactive users with less than 5 items, and obtain $10,000$ users and their ratings. Statistics of the two datasets are shown in Table 1 and Table 2.

Table 1: Statistics of MovieLens-Netflix dataset

Statistics	MovieLens	Netflix
Num of movies	5,871	5,871
Num of users	69,258	70,132
Num of ratings	7,891,832	11,658,783

Each dataset is split into a 80% training set and a 20% testing set. The dimension of the latent factors are chosen as 20, 50 and 100. In the training phase, we set all regularization parameters as 0.01, although later we empirically find that our model is insensitive to those parameters. The training data is split into 5 parts to do 5-fold cross validation, determining when we stop the learning phase. In the testing phase, we evaluate prediction performance of AdaMF using root mean squared error (RMSE) as,

$$RMSE = \sqrt{\frac{\sum_{R_{ij} \in R_{testing}} (R_{ij} - \hat{R}_{ij})^2}{|R_{testing}|}},$$

where R_{ij} denotes the actual rating that user i posts to item j, $\hat{R}_{ij}$ is the predicted rating, and $R_{testing}$ denotes the ratings in the testing set.

Besides the rating-based metric RMSE, we also considered a ranking-based metric, mean average precision (MAP). Given all the candidate items, we generate a recommendation list L for each user by ranking all the items in a descending order according to the predicted rating score. Then, the top-K average precision (AP@K)

[1]http://www.netflixprize.com/
[2]http://www.movielens.org/
[3]http://www.douban.com/

Table 2: Statistics of Douban dataset

Statistics	Movie	Music	Book
Num of users	10,000	10,000	10,000
Num of items	25,342	78,133	51,204
Num of ratings	2,287,712	1,060,704	832,103

is defined as

$$AP@K(u) = \frac{\sum_{j=1}^{K} P(j)I(L_j)}{\sum_{j=1}^{K} I(L_j)},$$

$P(j)$ is the precision of the recommendation list at position j, $I(L_j)$ is the function to indicate if the jth item in the list is preferred by the user. In our experiments, we set the highest rated item as the preferred items for one user. K is set as 5 in our experiments. We evaluate recommendation method using the mean AP over all users, i.e.,

$$MAP = \frac{\sum_{i=1}^{M} AP@K(i)}{M},$$

where M is the number of users.

Three baseline methods are:

- **Matrix Factorization (MF)**: for each context, latent factors of users and items are learned using standard matrix factorization method with regularization.
- **Collective matrix factorization (CMF)**: each user or item has a context-sharing latent factor.
- **HeteroMF**: each entity has a global latent factor shared across contexts. Context-dependent factor for each entity is generated from the global one by multiplying it with a context-specific transfer matrix. This model assumes that the same context exerts the same influence to all entities indiscriminately.

5.1 Prediction Performance

We first compare our algorithm with baseline methods on the whole dataset. Table 3 and table 4 show the performance of all these methods on the movie-aligned dataset. On the two different movie contexts, our method consistently outperforms all the baselines on all the tested number of dimensions. As the dimension of latent factors increases, the improvement becomes more significant.

Table 5 and table 6 show the performance of all the methods on the user-aligned dataset. As there are three domains of items

Table 3: RMSE on MovieLens-Netflix dataset

D	Models	MovieLens	Netflix
20	MF	0.8051	0.8334
	CMF	0.7986 (-0.81%)	0.8330 (-0.05%)
	HeteroMF	0.7937 (-1.42%)	0.8315 (-0.23%)
	AdaMF	**0.7907* (-1.79%)**	**0.8296* (-0.46%)**
50	MF	0.8023	0.8321
	CMF	0.7957 (-0.81%)	0.8309 (-0.14%)
	HeteroMF	0.7917 (-1.32%)	0.8300 (-0.25%)
	AdaMF	**0.7859** (-2.04%)**	**0.8245** (-0.91%)**
100	MF	0.7990	0.8303
	CMF	0.7928 (-0.78%)	0.8283 (-0.24%)
	HeteroMF	0.7895 (-1.18%)	0.8280 (-0.27%)
	AdaMF	**0.7821** (-2.12%)**	**0.8203** (-1.20%)**

Significantly outperforms HeteroMF at the:
** 0.01 and * 0.05 level, paired t-test

Table 4: MAP on MovieLens-Netflix dataset

D	Models	MovieLens	Netflix
20	MF	0.6247	0.6885
	CMF	0.6290 (+0.68%)	0.6890 (+0.07%)
	HeteroMF	0.6320 (+1.16%)	0.6898 (+0.18%)
	AdaMF	**0.6404** (+2.50%)**	**0.6930** (+0.65%)**
50	MF	0.6279	0.6902
	CMF	0.6331 (+0.82%)	0.6910 (+0.11%)
	HeteroMF	0.6355 (+1.21%)	0.6912 (+0.14%)
	AdaMF	**0.6450** (+2.72%)**	**0.6962** (+0.87%)**
100	MF	0.6299	0.6925
	CMF	0.6352 (+0.84%)	0.6934 (+0.13%)
	HeteroMF	0.6380 (+1.28%)	0.6937 (+0.17%)
	AdaMF	**0.6490** (+3.03%)**	**0.7001** (+1.09%)**

Significantly outperforms HeteroMF at the:
** 0.01 and * 0.05 level, paired t-test

in Douban dataset, we conduct experiments on three scenarios: movie-book, movie-music, and book-music respectively. The results show that our AdaMF model outperforms other baselines on all the three scenarios. However, the improvement of AdaMF is not always significant. For example, the improvement of music recommendation in book-music scenario is not as significant as that in movie-music scenario. This phenomenon may be related to correlation between these domains.

5.2 Against Sparsity

Due to the imbalance problem in observations, users/items with extremely few ratings suffer most severely from data sparsity. The AdaMF model is particularly effective on those sparsity entities. To show this, we categorize movies in the MovieLens-Netflix dataset into three sparsity levels: "cold" movies with 100 or less ratings in a context, "normal" movies with $100 - 1,000$ ratings, and "warm" movies with more than $1,000$ ratings. In this way, a movie can be warm in MovieLens and normal in Netflix. In total, 7 label configurations are observed, leaving two empty zones, since no warm movies in MovieLens are observed cold in Netflix and vice versa. Figure 4(a) reports the RMSE of prediction on MovieLens (target context), leveraging ratings in Netflix (auxiliary context). In most configurations, standard matrix factorization performs the worst. CMF slightly reduces RMSE on movies that are cold (bottom row) and normal (middle row), but performs even worse on movies labeled warm (top row). That might be due to that it does no good to incorporate external ratings for items with sufficient ratings in the target context. HeteroMF outperforms MF and CMF on movies labeled "normal" and "warm" in the target context (middle and right column), but shows modest advantage on movies labeled "cold" in the target context (left column), implying that a fixed form of transfer matrix sharing mechanism as done in HeteroMF does harm to items sparse in the target context. In contrast, AdaMF consistently shows significant advantage on every configuration, demonstrating that AdaMF works well in any sparse level. Figure 4(b) reports prediction RMSE on Netflix, exhibiting similar results.

5.3 Case Analysis

To offer some intuition about why adaMF works well, we present three typical cases in Figure 5. The first movie is '*Love is all there is*' that receives sparse ratings in both contexts forming a cold-cold case. '*Hellfighter*' is sparse in MovieLens but warm in Netflix, forming a cold-warm case. '*Titanic*' receives plenty of ratings in both contexts forming a warm-warm case. From the perspective of model complexity, a simple model works well when few ratings are available, and a complex model captures more detailed information with a large dataset. Therefore, as the simplest model, CMF uses

Table 5: RMSE on Douban dataset

D	Models	Scenario					
		Movie-Music		Movie-Book		Book-Music	
20	MF	0.7219	0.6933	0.7219	0.7630	0.7630	0.6933
	CMF	0.7277 (+0.80%)	0.6868 (-0.94%)	0.7324 (+1.45%)	0.7460 (-2.22%)	0.7531 (-1.30%)	0.6953 (+0.29%)
	HeteroMF	0.7210 (-0.12%)	0.6869 (-0.92%)	0.7215 (-0.05%)	0.7593 (-0.48%)	0.7552 (-1.02%)	0.6943 (+0.14%)
	AdaMF	**0.7199* (-0.28%)**	**0.6860* (-1.05%)**	**0.7210* (-0.12%)**	**0.7455** (-2.29%)**	**0.7466** (-2.15%)**	**0.6871** (-0.90%)**
50	MF	0.7187	0.6902	0.7187	0.7600	0.7600	0.6902
	CMF	0.7252 (+0.90%)	0.6840 (-0.90%)	0.7284 (+1.35%)	**0.7411 (-2.49%)**	0.7495 (-1.38%)	0.6922 (+0.29%)
	HeteroMF	0.7155 (-0.45%)	0.6835 (-0.97%)	0.7182 (-0.07%)	0.7563 (-0.49%)	0.7482 (-1.55%)	0.6910 (+0.12%)
	AdaMF	**0.7130* (-0.79%)**	**0.6807** (-1.38%)**	**0.7167* (-0.28%)**	0.7421** (-2.36%)	**0.7451* (-1.96%)**	**0.6841** (-0.88%)**
100	MF	0.7152	0.6888	0.7152	0.7555	0.7555	0.6888
	CMF	0.7202 (+0.70%)	0.6811 (-1.12%)	0.7254 (+1.42%)	0.7389 (-2.20%)	0.7480 (-1.00%)	0.6917 (+0.42%)
	HeteroMF	0.7135(-0.24%)	0.6806 (-1.19%)	0.7140 (-0.17%)	0.7550 (-0.07%)	0.7471 (-1.11%)	0.6882 (-0.09%)
	AdaMF	**0.7101** (-0.71%)**	**0.6775** (-1.64%)**	**0.7101** (-0.71%)**	**0.7370** (-2.45%)**	**0.7440* (-1.52%)**	**0.6813** (-1.09%)**

Significantly outperforms HeteroMF at the: ** 0.01 and * 0.05 level, paired t-test

Table 6: MAP on Douban dataset

D	Models	Scenario					
		Movie-Music		Movie-Book		Book-Music	
20	MF	0.8026	0.8890	0.8026	0.8840	0.8840	0.8890
	CMF	0.8020 (-0.07%)	0.8910 (+0.22%)	0.8021 (-0.06%)	0.8950 (+1.24%)	0.8889 (+0.55%)	0.8887 (-0.03%)
	HeteroMF	0.8040 (+0.17%)	0.8908 (+0.20%)	0.8011 (-0.19%)	0.8876 (+0.41%)	0.8872 (+0.36%)	0.8889 (-0.01%)
	AdaMF	**0.8075** (+0.61%)**	**0.9054** (+1.84%)**	**0.8058** (+0.40%)**	**0.8990** (+1.70%)**	**0.8942** (+1.15%)**	**0.9011** (+1.36%)**
50	MF	0.8060	0.8908	0.8060	0.8873	0.8873	0.8908
	CMF	0.8050 (-0.12%)	0.8930 (+0.25%)	0.8055 (-0.06%)	0.8989 (+1.31%)	0.8919 (+0.52%)	0.8912 (+0.04%)
	HeteroMF	0.8078 (+0.22%)	0.8947 (+0.44%)	0.8065 (+0.06%)	0.8904 (+0.35%)	0.8907 (+0.38%)	0.8915 (+0.08%)
	AdaMF	**0.8119** (+0.73%)**	**0.9096** (+2.11%)**	**0.8105** (+0.56%)**	**0.8993** (+1.35%)**	**0.8990** (+1.31%)**	**0.9050** (+1.59%)**
100	MF	0.8093	0.8928	0.8093	0.8901	0.8901	0.8928
	CMF	0.8081 (-0.15%)	0.8955 (+0.30%)	0.8075 (-0.22%)	0.9022 (+1.36%)	0.8943 (+0.47%)	0.8930 (+0.02%)
	HeteroMF	0.8092 (-0.01%)	0.8969 (+0.46%)	0.8090 (-0.04%)	0.8915 (+0.16%)	0.8931 (+0.34%)	0.8932 (+0.04%)
	AdaMF	**0.8130** (+0.46%)**	**0.9115** (+2.09%)**	**0.8175** (+1.01%)**	**0.9043** (+1.60%)**	**0.9020** (+1.34%)**	**0.9081** (+1.71%)**

Significantly outperforms HeteroMF at the: ** 0.01 and * 0.05 level, paired t-test

an identical latent factor to represent all occurrences of a movie on different contexts, and not surprisingly outperforms MF and HeteroMF when predicting the first movie and the sparse side of the second movie. On the other hand, HeteroMF builds a complex model to describe specific behaviors of a movie in multiple contexts, and significantly outperforms CMF for the third movie and the rich side of the second movie. Due to the different applicability of simple and complex models, no baseline consistently perform well in all levels of sparsity. Noticeably, with a flexible parameter to adjust the weight of a global latent factor and a context-specific one, our model actually gains the ability to adaptively fit different levels of sparsity, and as a result outperforms baselines on all three typical cases.

5.4 Mixture Parameters

In AdaMF model, context-entity mixture parameter reflects the balance between entity-intrinsic factor and context-specific factor. One interesting question is: what is the distribution of the values of this mixture parameter over all users/items? As shown in Figure 6, for most movies the mixture parameters locate within $[0.4, 0.6]$, indicating that an entity's intrinsic attributes play almost the same important role in producing preference with the context-specific attributes.

Table 7 shows the mixture parameters for the three movies, studied in the aforementioned case analysis. For movie '*Love is all there is*', mixture parameters are small in both contexts. In this case, entity-intrinsic factors are more critical than context-specific factors. For movie '*Hellfighter*', the mixture parameter is small in the "cold" context but large in the "warm" context, indicating that the AdaMF indeed adaptively capture the degree to which context influences rating. For movie '*Titanic*', a "warm-warm" case, the mixture parameter in both contexts is larger than 0.5, indicating that context matters much more. As above, the diversity of mixture parameters reveal the necessity to develop an adaptive method rather than a fixed form as done in HeteroMF.

5.5 Model Complexity

We now discuss the issue of model complexity. To this end, we list the number of effective parameters for all the multi-context recommendation models discussed in this paper. We assume that there are M users, N items, and l contexts. We denote with d the dimension of latent factors. For CMF, the effective number is $(M+N)*d$. For HeteroMF, the effective number is $(M+N)*d+d*d*l$. For our AdaMF, the effective number is $(M+N)*d+(M+N)*d*l$. We can see that HeteroMF and AdaMF are more complex than CMF since the two models attempt to model context-specific factors in different schemas. HeteroMF simply assumes that each context indiscriminately affects all entities, reflected by a transfer matrix. AdaMF aims to adaptively capture the influence of context through a context-entity mixture matrix.

Note that the main superiority of AdaMF over other competing models is its flexibility at adaptively capturing the degree that each context exerts on each entity. As such, AdaMF achieves consistent

Table 7: Mixture parameter learned in the two contexts.

Movie Name	Context	
	MovieLens	Netflix
Love is all there is	0.260	0.330
Hellfighters	0.045	0.821
Titanic	0.601	0.560

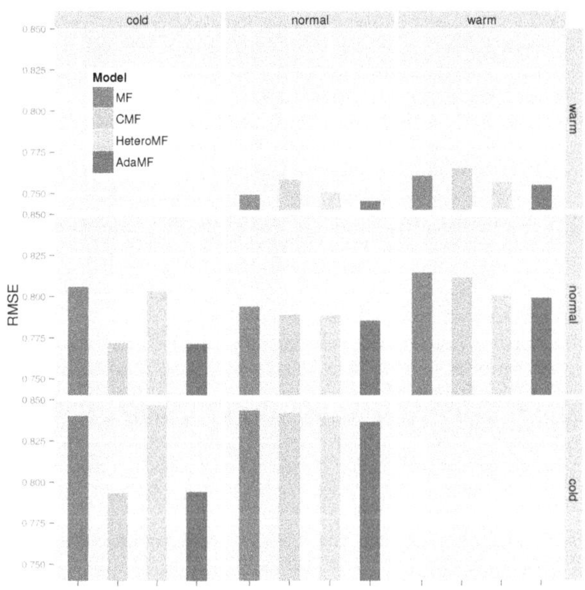

(a) RMSE in MovieLens. X-axis represents the sparsity level in MovieLens, Y-axis represents the sparsity level in Netflix

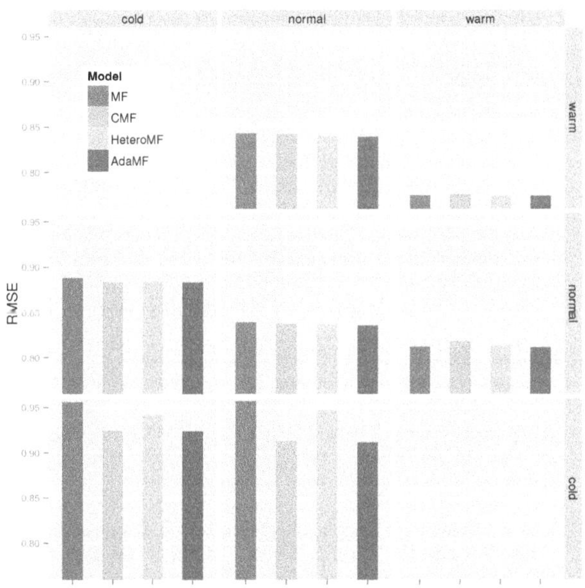

(b) RMSE in Netflix. X-axis represents the sparsity level in Netflix, Y-axis represents the sparsity level in MovieLens

Figure 4: Rating prediction accuracy of movies with different sparse levels.

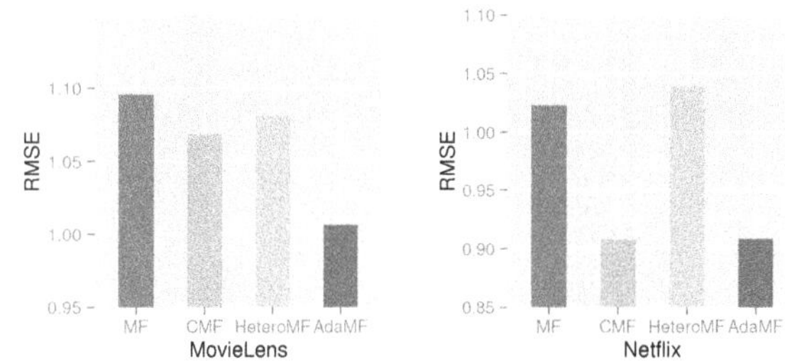

(a) Cold-cold case: *'Love is all there is'*

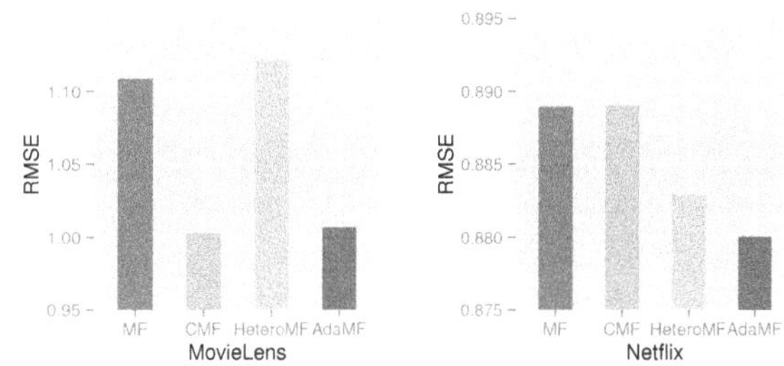

(b) Cold-warm case: *'Hellfighters'*

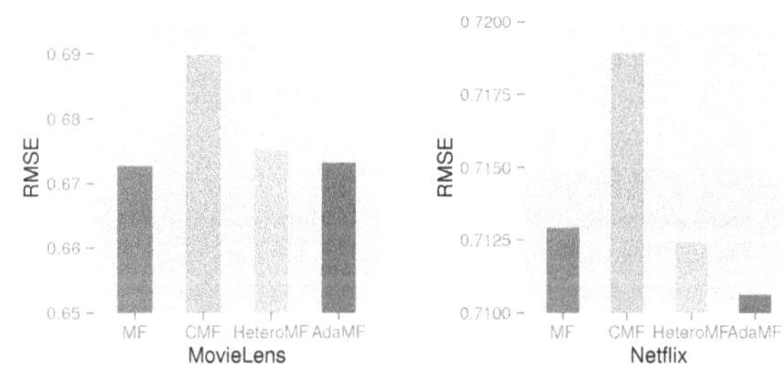

(c) Warm-warm case: *'Titanic'*

Figure 5: Performance in different sparse levels (a) Cold-cold case: movie *'Love is all there is'* has 23 ratings in MovieLens dataset and 32 ratings in Netflix dataset; (b) Cold-warm case: movie *'Hellfighter'* has 16 ratings in MovieLens dataset and 455 ratings in Netflix dataset; (c) Warm-warm case: movie *'Titanic'* has 27550 ratings in MovieLens dataset and 21234 ratings in Netflix dataset.

improvements for entities at all sparsity levels, i.e., cold, normal, and warm (Figure 4). This consistent improvement is particularly important for a real recommender system, since such a system exhibits reliable performance than systems that work better on some cases but worse on others. Perhaps, some people may argue that the improvement of the AdaMF is marginal, compared with HeteroMF. Indeed, the main point of this paper is that AdaMF could consistently improve multi-context recommendation by adaptively balancing the entity-intrinsic factor and context-specific factor. Its gain deserves its cost.

6. CONCLUSIONS AND DISCUSSIONS

Data sparsity is one of the challenges for recommender system. Lack of relevant information for users and items is the key issue for data sparsity problem. In the real world, users (items) are involved in multiple contexts but not isolated. In this paper, we propose a context-adaptive matrix factorization method for multi-context recommendation problem via simultaneously modeling context-specific factors and entity-intrinsic factors in a unified model. We learn for every entity an entity-intrinsic latent factor and a context-specific latent factor in each context. Meanwhile, using a context-entity mixture parameter we explicitly model the degree to which each context imposes influence on each entity. We performed experiments on two real scenarios, an item-aligned movie dataset and a user-aligned online social network, demonstrating that our model

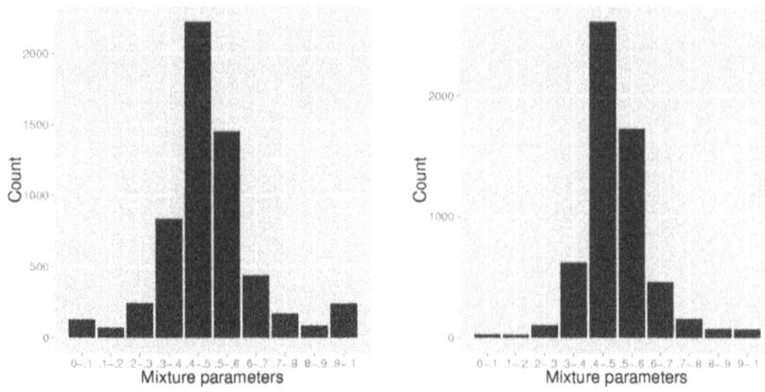

(a) Movies in MovieLens (b) Movies in Netflix

Figure 6: Distribution of mixture parameters.

is better than the baseline models on all sparsity level. As future work, we will extend the AdaMF model to heterogenous networks containing contexts with various types.

Acknowledgments

This work was funded by the National Basic Research Program of China (the 973 program) under grant numbers 2014CB340401 and 2012CB316303, and the National Natural Science Foundation of China with Nos. 61232010, 61472400, 61202215, 61433014. This work is also funded by the National Information Security Program of China (the 242 program) with grant number 2014A137.

7. REFERENCES

[1] Yehuda Koren, Robert Bell, and Chris Volinsky. Matrix factorization techniques for recommender systems. *Computer*, 42(8):30–37, 2009.

[2] Noam Koenigstein, Gideon Dror, and Yehuda Koren. Yahoo! music recommendations: modeling music ratings with temporal dynamics and item taxonomy. In *Proceedings of the fifth ACM conference on Recommender systems*, pages 165–172. ACM, 2011.

[3] Jiahui Liu, Peter Dolan, and Elin Rønby Pedersen. Personalized news recommendation based on click behavior. In *Proceedings of the 15th international conference on Intelligent user interfaces*, pages 31–40. ACM, 2010.

[4] Raymond J Mooney and Loriene Roy. Content-based book recommending using learning for text categorization. In *Proceedings of the fifth ACM conference on Digital libraries*, pages 195–204. ACM, 2000.

[5] Michael Moricz, Yerbolat Dosbayev, and Mikhail Berlyant. Pymk: friend recommendation at myspace. In *Proceedings of the 2010 ACM SIGMOD International Conference on Management of data*, pages 999–1002. ACM, 2010.

[6] Qi Liu, Yong Ge, Zhongmou Li, Enhong Chen, and Hui Xiong. Personalized travel package recommendation. In *Data Mining (ICDM), 2011 IEEE 11th International Conference on*, pages 407–416. IEEE, 2011.

[7] Badrul Sarwar, George Karypis, Joseph Konstan, and John Riedl. Item-based collaborative filtering recommendation algorithms. In *Proceedings of the 10th international conference on World Wide Web*, pages 285–295. ACM, 2001.

[8] Yehuda Koren. Factorization meets the neighborhood: a multifaceted collaborative filtering model. In *Proceedings of the 14th ACM SIGKDD international conference on Knowledge discovery and data mining*, pages 426–434. ACM, 2008.

[9] Andriy Mnih and Ruslan Salakhutdinov. Probabilistic matrix factorization. In *Advances in neural information processing systems*, pages 1257–1264, 2007.

[10] Jonathan L Herlocker, Joseph A Konstan, Loren G Terveen, and John T Riedl. Evaluating collaborative filtering recommender systems. *ACM Transactions on Information Systems (TOIS)*, 22(1):5–53, 2004.

[11] Ruslan Salakhutdinov and Andriy Mnih. Bayesian probabilistic matrix factorization using markov chain monte carlo. In *Proceedings of the 25th international conference on Machine learning*, pages 880–887. ACM, 2008.

[12] Ajit P Singh and Geoffrey J Gordon. Relational learning via collective matrix factorization. In *Proceedings of the 14th ACM SIGKDD international conference on Knowledge discovery and data mining*, pages 650–658. ACM, 2008.

[13] Deepak Agarwal, Bee-Chung Chen, and Bo Long. Localized factor models for multi-context recommendation. In *Proceedings of the 17th ACM SIGKDD international conference on Knowledge discovery and data mining*, pages 609–617. ACM, 2011.

[14] Mohsen Jamali and Laks Lakshmanan. Heteromf: recommendation in heterogeneous information networks using context dependent factor models. In *Proceedings of the 22nd international conference on World Wide Web*, pages 643–654. International World Wide Web Conferences Steering Committee, 2013.

[15] Gediminas Adomavicius and Alexander Tuzhilin. Context-aware recommender systems. In *Recommender systems handbook*, pages 217–253. Springer, 2011.

[16] Steffen Rendle, Zeno Gantner, Christoph Freudenthaler, and Lars Schmidt-Thieme. Fast context-aware recommendations with factorization machines. In *Proceedings of the 34th international ACM SIGIR conference on Research and development in Information Retrieval*, pages 635–644. ACM, 2011.

[17] Bin Li, Qiang Yang, and Xiangyang Xue. Can movies and books collaborate? cross-domain collaborative filtering for sparsity reduction. In *IJCAI*, volume 9, pages 2052–2057, 2009.

[18] Liang Hu, Jian Cao, Guandong Xu, Longbing Cao, Zhiping Gu, and Can Zhu. Personalized recommendation via cross-domain triadic factorization. In *Proceedings of the 22nd international conference on World Wide Web*, pages 595–606. International World Wide Web Conferences Steering Committee, 2013.

[19] Hao Ma, Dengyong Zhou, Chao Liu, Michael R Lyu, and Irwin King. Recommender systems with social regularization. In *Proceedings of the fourth ACM international conference on Web search and data mining*, pages 287–296. ACM, 2011.

[20] Xin Liu and Karl Aberer. Soco: a social network aided context-aware recommender system. In *Proceedings of the 22nd international conference on World Wide Web*, pages 781–802. International World Wide Web Conferences Steering Committee, 2013.

[21] Li-Tung Weng, Yue Xu, Yuefeng Li, and Richi Nayak. Exploiting item taxonomy for solving cold-start problem in recommendation making. In *Tools with Artificial Intelligence, 2008. ICTAI'08. 20th IEEE International Conference on*, volume 2, pages 113–120. IEEE, 2008.

[22] Shlomo Berkovsky, Tsvi Kuflik, and Francesco Ricci. Cross-domain mediation in collaborative filtering. In *User Modeling 2007*, pages 355–359. Springer, 2007.

[23] Tianqi Chen, Weinan Zhang, Qiuxia Lu, Kailong Chen, Zhao Zheng, and Yong Yu. Svdfeature: a toolkit for feature-based collaborative filtering. *The Journal of Machine Learning Research*, 13(1):3619–3622, 2012.

[24] Xiao Yu, Xiang Ren, Yizhou Sun, Quanquan Gu, Bradley Sturt, Urvashi Khandelwal, Brandon Norick, and Jiawei Han. Personalized entity recommendation: a heterogeneous information network approach. In *Proceedings of the 7th ACM international conference on Web search and data mining*, pages 283–292. ACM, 2014.

[25] Sinno Jialin Pan and Qiang Yang. A survey on transfer learning. *Knowledge and Data Engineering, IEEE Transactions on*, 22(10):1345–1359, 2010.

[26] Weike Pan, Evan Wei Xiang, Nathan Nan Liu, and Qiang Yang. Transfer learning in collaborative filtering for sparsity reduction. In *AAAI*, volume 10, pages 230–235, 2010.

[27] Bin Li, Qiang Yang, and Xiangyang Xue. Transfer learning for collaborative filtering via a rating-matrix generative model. In *Proceedings of the 26th Annual International Conference on Machine Learning*, pages 617–624. ACM, 2009.

[28] Junming Huang, Xue-Qi Cheng, Hua-Wei Shen, Tao Zhou, and Xiaolong Jin. Exploring social influence via posterior effect of word-of-mouth recommendations. In *Proceedings of the fifth ACM international conference on Web search and data mining*, pages 573–582. ACM, 2012.

Personalized Trip Recommendation with POI Availability and Uncertain Traveling Time

Chenyi Zhang[#*], Hongwei Liang[*], Ke Wang[*], Jianling Sun[#]
[#] College of Computer Science, Zhejiang University
[*] School of Computing Science, Simon Fraser University
{chenyiz,hongweil,wangk}@sfu.ca, sunjl@zju.edu.cn

ABSTRACT

As location-based social network (LBSN) services become increasingly popular, trip recommendation that recommends a sequence of points of interest (POIs) to visit for a user emerges as one of many important applications of LBSNs. *Personalized* trip recommendation tailors to users' specific tastes by learning from past check-in behaviors of users and their peers. Finding the optimal trip that maximizes user's experiences for a given time budget constraint is an NP hard problem and previous solutions do not consider two practical and important constraints. One constraint is *POI availability* where a POI may be only available during a certain time window. Another constraint is *uncertain traveling time* where the traveling time between two POIs is uncertain. This work presents efficient solutions to personalized trip recommendation by incorporating these constraints to prune the search space. We evaluated the efficiency and effectiveness of our solutions on real life LBSN data sets.

Categories and Subject Descriptors

H.2.8 [**Database Applications**]: Data mining; I.2.8 [**Problem Solving, Control Methods, and Search**]: Scheduling

Keywords

Trip plan; location-based social network; recommender systems

1. INTRODUCTION

With the emerging development of location-based social network (LBSN) services such as Yelp and Foursquare, users are able to "check in" at a certain point of interest (POI), such as restaurant/museum/park, via their mobile devices. A user may rate and make comments after visiting a POI and other users may consider those ratings and comments to select the POIs for their visits at a later time. The availability of such rating data and LBSN services open up an array of new research problems in both academia and industry, such as user behavior analysis, movement pattern study [5, 15], and various real-world applications [6, 32, 34]. Among them, POI recommendation and trip recommendation [14, 28] are hot topics and require a location sensitive solution. For example, recommending a highest rated Chinese restaurant in Beijing to a user who is currently visiting New York City will fail, even if the user loves Chinese food. Recommending a nearby Chinese restaurant with a reasonable rating score makes more sense in this case.

Permission to make digital or hard copies of all or part of this work for personal or classroom use is granted without fee provided that copies are not made or distributed for profit or commercial advantage and that copies bear this notice and the full citation on the first page. Copyrights for components of this work owned by others than the author(s) must be honored. Abstracting with credit is permitted. To copy otherwise, or republish, to post on servers or to redistribute to lists, requires prior specific permission and/or a fee. Request permissions from Permissions@acm.org.
CIKM'15, October 19–23, 2015, Melbourne, VIC, Australia
Copyright is held by the owner/author(s). Publication rights licensed to ACM.
ACM 978-1-4503-3794-6/15/10 ...$15.00
DOI: http://dx.doi.org/10.1145/2806416.2806558

In this paper, we focus on the personalized trip recommendation problem. In this problem, a user travels to a new region (e.g., on a business trip to a new city) and wants to visit several POIs within a limited amount of time. The goal is to recommend a trip route visiting several POIs according to not only the temporal-spatial constraints (more details shortly), but also the user specific preferences on POIs.

1.1 Motivation

The trip recommendation is not trivial because of the following challenges:

- (*Personalization*) First, while a user has its own interests, explicitly soliciting this information does not work in large scale applications because the user often does not know what POIs are available and where they are. Modeling user preferences by learning from historical rating and check-in behaviors of users and their peers to predict the user's preferences on unvisited POIs would be a preferred solution.
- (*Sequence of POIs*) Second, the traditional POI recommendation recommends individual POIs with highest scores, such POIs may not form a feasible trip due to the spatial and time constraints.
- (*POI availability and uncertain traveling time*) Third, the traditional trip recommendation assumes that POIs are always available any time and the traveling time between two POIs are known in advance, but in practice, a POI may be available only at certain times (say, due to opening hours and closing hours) and traveling time is uncertain due to traffic conditions at the time of travel. As a result, whether a POI can be visited will depend on its available time and predictability of the time traveling to the POI. If the timeliness of finishing the trip is important to the user, a trip with a more predictable traveling time would be preferred. For example, the user may give up one more POI to visit in order to ensure a high probability of visiting another more preferred POI or arriving at the specified destination on time.
- (*Large search space*) Finally, the POI availability and uncertain traveling time imply each order of visiting a set of POIs may have a different consequence, thus, a brute-force search of all candidate trips is prohibitive. For example, with 150 POIs in total, the number of trips that consist of 5 POIs can reach billions (i.e., 150!). Most of these candidate trips do not follow the POI availability or match user's preferences, or cannot be finished within a given time limited. A strategy that prunes such infeasible and non-optimal trips based on user preferences, POI availability, traveling time uncertainty is essential for scaling a solution to large applications.

Trip recommendation has been studied recently. [17] analyzed the characteristics of travel packages and proposed a graphical model to extract the topics conditioned on tourists, areas and travel seasons for personalized travel package recommendation. [3] developed a Bayesian learning model to extract travel paths from photos and conducted personalized travel recommendation according to user-specific profiles. All these works, however, adopt probabilistic models to generate a possible travel package or path but do not consider the objective function to maximize the user's happiness under the trip and other constraints.

The recent work [9] formulated the trip recommendation as a constrained objective function and presented a dynamic programming solution. Their assumption is that POIs can be grouped into several types or categories and the user knows the order of visiting POI types and likes to visit POIs of each type exactly once in a pre-determined order. The restriction of visiting each type exactly once in a pre-determined order significantly reduces the search space. For example, for 150 POIs falling into 5 types equally, the original 150! possible routes are reduced to 30^5 if the order is fixed. In real world applications, however, the user may not provide this order either because she does not care about the order or because she is concerned that such a fixed order may restrict her options. In addition, their work does not consider the POI availability and the uncertainty of traveling time.

A detailed review of related work is presented in Section 8.

1.2 Contributions

In this paper, we address the trip recommendation by taking into account the following information and constraints: (1) the user's personalized preferences on POIs; (2) the user's time budget that constrains the total traveling and visiting time; (3) the time window for the POI availability; (4) the uncertainty of traveling time between POIs. We formulate the above requirements in our TripRec problem. The goal of the problem is to find an optimal trip that maximizes user happiness under the constraint that all the POIs in the trip can be visited and the trip can be completed within the user time budget with a probability not less than a user specified threshold. This problem is NP-hard as it is a special case of either the Knapsack problem [11] or the Orienteering problem [25].

We solve this problem by using the information and constraints in (1)-(4) to prune unpromising candidate trips. Our algorithm has an offline step and an online step. In the *offline step*, we apply collaborative filtering adopted to items with features to estimate user's preferences on unvisited POIs based on available check-in data. This step is performed only once as it applies to all users. In the *online step* where the user's time budget constraint and start/destination locations are provided, we search for the optimal trip route under the various constraints discussed above. We present two optimal solutions that guarantee to find the optimal trip if it exists. One is based on a state expansion approach and one is based on a prefix based depth-first search strategy. We also present two heuristic solutions that find "good trips" with a significantly better runtime than the optimal solutions. We evaluated all solutions on two real life LBSN data sets, Yelp and Foursquare, and demonstrated the superiority over previous trip recommendation algorithms.

1.3 The Road Map

The rest of the paper is organized as follows: Section 2 defines the problem. Section 3.1 presents the personalized rating estimation for POIs, which corresponds to the offline step, and Section 3.2-3.3 presents our modeling of POI availability and uncertain traveling time. These are the key factors that distinguish our modeling of trip recommendation from previous ones. Section 4 presents the optimal solution based on the state expansion approach, and the state relaxing strategy which scarifies optimality for efficiency. Section 5 introduces the second optimal solution based on the prefix based depth-first search strategy. We present an efficient heuristic solution in Section 6. Section 7 presents experimental evaluation of all solutions. Section 8 presents a review of related works. Finally, we conclude the paper with a discussion on extension to other scenarios of trip recommendation.

2. PRELIMINARY

This section describes our data model and the trip recommendation problem.

2.1 Data model

POI map: We assume that there are n POIs in a (virtual) complete directed graph $G = (V, E)$. $V = \{1, \cdots, n\}$ is a set of POIs. Each POI $i \in V$ is associated with the following information: a touring time m_i, indicating the typical or average staying time for users, and opening hours $[O_i, C_i]$, indicating that i opens at time O_i and closes at time C_i. Each edge $e_{ij} \in E$ represents the route from i to j, where $i, j \in V$, and associates with a traveling time t_{ij} following a distribution with probability density function $f_{ij}(\cdot)$. We assume that these functions $f_{ij}(\cdot)$ are given and that traveling times for different routes e_{ij} are independent.

Rating matrix: We consider a set of users where a user u may rate a POI i after visiting i. A rating matrix R contains all observed ratings r_{ui}. The rating matrix is usually extremely sparse with most entries undefined since a user may only rate a few POIs. Besides, a user u could leave comments on POI i when rating i, represented by a bag of words B_{ui} (If a user u does not rate a POI i, $B_{ui} = \emptyset$). The "content" of POI i is defined as $B_i = \bigcup_u B_{ui}$. Based on the matrix R and comments, we could estimate a user u's rating for an unvisited POI j, denoted as r^*_{uj}.

A trip route: For a specified source location x and a destination location y, and a departure time T_0, where x and y are not necessarily distinct, a trip route has the form $x \to \cdots i \cdots \to y$, that starts from x at the time T_0, visits each POI i listed in the route in order, and ends at y. We assume that the probability density functions $f_{xi}(\cdot)$ and $f_{iy}(\cdot)$ are known for any POI i, and we set $r^*_{ux} = r^*_{uy} = 0$, $m_x = m_y = 0$, $O_x = O_y = T_0$, $C_x = C_y = +\infty$. Such settings ensure that visiting x and y does not cost time because they serve only as the departure and destination locations for a trip. The score of a trip route $\mathcal{P}$ for a user u is defined by an additive function $F(\mathcal{P}, u) = \sum_{i \in \mathcal{P}} r^*_{ui}$. This function simply sums up the estimated ratings r^*_{ui} for all POIs in the route, which models the happiness of u with respect to the route $\mathcal{P}$.

Constraints on a trip route: *POI availability constraint:* a user is considered to visit a POI i only if the user spends m_i time at i during the opening hours $[O_i, C_i]$. Therefore, if a user arrives at i before O_i, she has to wait until the opening hour, and the user should arrive at i no later than $C_i - m_i$ to gain the happiness score. *Time budget constraint:* the whole trip is completed within a period of time b, including traveling time and touring time at POIs. *Completion probability constraint:* the probability that a trip finishes at the destination y by the time $T_0 + b$ is not less than a user specified threshold $\theta \in [0, 1)$.

2.2 Problem definition

PROBLEM 1 (TRIPREC). *Given a user u with the source x and the destination y, a departure time T_0, a time budget b, and a threshold $\theta \in [0, 1)$, we want to find an optimal trip route $\mathcal{P}$*

that maximizes user happiness $F(\mathcal{P}, u)$ under the following constraints: (1) The route starts at location x and ends at location y. (2) The route satisfies the POI availability constraint, the time budget constraint and the completion probability constraint.

In the rest of the paper, we first model the user's personalized preferences and the trip constraints; then, we present several approaches to search the optimal trip route according to the estimated preferences for TripRec.

3. MODELING PREFERENCES AND CONSTRAINTS

In this section, we discuss our modeling of user preference and trip constraints.

3.1 Estimating user preferences

Most existing POI recommendation methods either consider no content information of POIs or treat content information as side information (more discussion in Section 8). We believe that content information of POIs should play a more central role in user preference in that a user likes a POI because of certain features of the POI. To this end, we adopt the feature-centric collaborative filtering proposed in [33]. Unlike the traditional collaborative filtering on POIs, this approach performs collaborative filtering on the features of POIs and determines the rating on a POI using the predicted ratings on the features of the POI.

First, we transform the original user-POI rating matrix R into a user-feature matrix R', where each row represents a user u and each column represents a feature f in $\bigcup_i B_i$ for POIs i. An entry (u, f) in R' stores the aggregated rating on the feature f over the POIs i such that B_i contains f and i are rated by u:

$$g_{uf} = agg(\{r_{ui} | f \in B_{ui} \text{ and } r_{ui} \text{ is defined}\}) \quad (1)$$

In this work, $agg(X)$ returns the average of the values in X, but other aggregation operations are possible. $agg(X)$ is undefined if X is empty.

Then, we apply matrix factorization [12] to R' to extract the latent user vectors p_u for users u and the latent feature vectors q_f for features f. To predict the rating of user i on a POI i, we aggregate the predicted ratings $p_u^T q_f$ over all the features f in B_i:

$$r_{ui}^* = agg(\{p_u^T q_f | f \in B_i\}) \quad (2)$$

We will use r_{ui}^* as the estimated rating of a user u on a POI i. Thus, if the user is estimated to rate highly most features of a POI, the user is estimated to rate highly the POI. Note that the estimation of user ratings is performed offline and only once.

3.2 Testing time constraints

The basic idea of trip planning is to extend the route $\mathcal{P}$ gradually. Suppose that i is the last POI of $\mathcal{P}$, which satisfies the time budget and POI availability constraints, and π_i is the starting time of visiting i. We may extend the route by adding a new POI j after visiting i. We use the `Sat` function to test if the POI availability and the time budget constraints are satisfied after the extension. $\texttt{Sat}(i, j, \pi_i)$ returns *true* if $\pi_j + m_j \leq C_j$ and $\pi_j + m_j + t_{jy} \leq T_0 + b$, where $\pi_j = \max\{\pi_i + m_i + t_{ij}, O_j\}$ indicates the starting time of visiting j. This testing ensures that the user can get the full service at the POI j and still reach the destination y within the time budget.

3.3 Modeling uncertain traveling time

The above assumes that traveling time t_{ij} for a sub-route $i \rightarrow j$ is deterministic. However, even the traveling time can be estimated from historical data and external resources [20], the real traveling time remains uncertain due to many uncertain factors that could affect the traffic. To model this uncertainty, we shall treat the traveling time t_{ij} as a random variable following a certain distribution with probability density function $f_{ij}(\cdot)$. In this case, the best one can guarantee is that the probability that a trip $\mathcal{P}$ can be finished within a given time budget b is above some specified threshold θ. This probability, called *completion probability*, is denoted by $\psi(\mathcal{P})$ so that $\psi(\mathcal{P}) \geq \theta$.

We can modify the above constraint testing function `Sat` for uncertain traveling time as follows. Let $E[t_{ij}]$ denote the expectation of t_{ij}. $\texttt{Sat}(i, j, \pi_i)$ returns *true* if $\pi_j + m_j \leq C_j$, $\pi_j + m_j + E[t_{jy}] \leq T_0 + b$, and $\psi(\mathcal{P}) \geq \theta$, where $\pi_j = \max\{\pi_i + m_i + E[t_{ij}], O_j\}$ indicates the expected starting time of visiting j.

Let us derive $\psi(\mathcal{P})$ for a route $\mathcal{P}$. Consider a sub-route $i \rightarrow j$, we assume that the probability density function $f_{ij}(\cdot)$ is known. For simplicity, we also assume that t_{ij} are independent for different pairs (i, j). Let χ denote the traveling time of the sub-route. The probability of the traveling time less than t is given as follows:

$$P(\chi < t) = \int_0^t f_{ij}(\delta) d\delta \quad (3)$$

Suppose that we extend $i \rightarrow j$ by a POI k, the probability of traveling time of $i \rightarrow j \rightarrow k$ less than t is given by the multiple integral:

$$P(\chi < t) = \iint_D f_{ij}(\delta) f_{jk}(\gamma) d\delta d\gamma \quad (4)$$

where the domain $D = \{(\delta, \gamma) \in \mathbb{R}_{>0}^2 \ : 0 < \delta + \gamma < t\}$ and $\mathbb{R}_{>0}$ means positive real number. In general, for any route $\mathcal{P} : i \rightarrow j \cdots j' \rightarrow k$ with c sub-routes, the probability of the total traveling time χ less than t is estimated by

$$P(\chi < t) = \iint \cdots \int_D f_{ij}(\delta_1) \cdots f_{j'k}(\delta_c) d\delta_1 d \cdots d\delta_c \quad (5)$$

where $D = \{(\delta_1, \cdots, \delta_c) \in \mathbb{R}_{>0}^c \ : 0 < \delta_1 + \cdots + \delta_c < t\}$. This probability can be computed given all the probability density functions $f_{ij} \cdots f_{j'k}$.

THEOREM 1 (**COMPLETION PROBABILITY BASED PRUNING**). *Let χ be the total traveling time of a route $\mathcal{P} : i \rightarrow \cdots \rightarrow j$ and let χ' be the total traveling time of another route $\mathcal{P}' : i \rightarrow \cdots j \rightarrow k$ obtained by adding a new POI k. Assume that both routes start at i at the same time. $P(\chi' < t) \leq P(\chi < t)$.*

PROOF. For simplicity, we consider a route $i \rightarrow j$ and the extension $i \rightarrow j \rightarrow k$, but the proof for the general case is similar. Due to the independence of traveling time at different sub-routes, $P(\chi' < t) = \iint_D f_{ij}(\delta) f_{jk}(\gamma) d\delta d\gamma$, so $P(\chi' < t) = \int_0^t f_{ij}(\delta) \int_0^{t-\delta} f_{jk}(\gamma) d\gamma d\delta \leq \int_0^t f_{ij}(\delta) \cdot 1 d\delta = P(\chi < t)$. □

In other words, the probability of finishing a route within the time budget is never increased by extending the route with one more POI at the end. This is because adding a POI at the end of a route does not affect the traveling time between the previous POIs of the route, but reduces the chance of completing the route within the time budget due to the additional time of traveling to and visiting the new POI. We shall use this property to prune the trips that have their completion probability below the specified threshold θ.

Various studies and methods have been proposed to estimate travel time distributions in the literature. See [31] for a comparison of these methods. Our method does not depend on the choices of such distribution, provided that the probability $P(\chi < t)$ can be computed for a route $\mathcal{P}$. For concreteness, we adopt the log-normal distribution in [27]. The traveling time t_z on the zth sub-route in a route independently follows the log-normal distribution with parameter μ_z, σ_z, that is, $t_z \sim \mathcal{LN}(\mu_z, \sigma_z^2)$. The expected traveling time $E[t_z]$ is given by $\exp(\mu_z + \sigma_z^2/2)$. The total traveling time χ of a route $\mathcal{P}$ made of multiple sub-routes is the sum of the traveling time t_z of each sub-route, i.e., $\chi = \sum_z t_z$. According to [19], χ can be approximated by another log-normal distribution $\mathcal{LN}(\mu_\chi, \sigma_\chi^2)$ with the following parameters:

$$\begin{aligned} \sigma_\chi^2 &= \log\left(\frac{\sum e^{2\mu_z+\sigma_z^2}(e^{\sigma_z^2}-1)}{(\sum e^{\mu_z+\sigma_z^2/2})^2}+1\right) \\ \mu_\chi &= \log\left(\sum e^{\mu_z+\sigma_z^2/2}\right)-\frac{\sigma_\chi^2}{2} \end{aligned} \quad (6)$$

With this distribution for the total traveling time χ, the probability of completing a trip $\mathcal{P}$ is $\psi(\mathcal{P}) = P(\chi < t)$, where t is the time available for traveling, that is, $t = b - \sum m_j$. For the log-normal distribution,

$$P(\chi < t) = \frac{1}{2}\left[1 + \operatorname{erf}\left(\frac{\ln t - \mu_\chi}{\sigma_\chi\sqrt{2}}\right)\right] \quad (7)$$

where $\operatorname{erf}(t) = \frac{2}{\sqrt{\pi}}\int_0^t e^{-\delta^2} d\delta$ [27].

4. STATE EXPANSION

In this section, we present a state expansion algorithm that guarantees to find an optimal route if it exists. The idea is to consider each partially generated route as a *state* associated with some ending POI i, representing a feasible trip route $x \to \cdots \to i \to y$ that has i as the ending POI before reaching the specified destination y. Each state is labeled by $s = (K, T, H, \rho, i)$, where K is the set of POIs already visited, excluding x and y. T is the starting time of visiting at i (i.e., π_i), H is the overall happiness collected (i.e., $F(K, u)$), ρ is the current route $x \to \cdots \to i$ (without the sub-route $i \to y$) and i is the ending POI. These parameters are denoted as s_K, s_T, s_H, s_ρ and s_i, respectively. Initially, there is only one state $s_0 = (\emptyset, T_0, 0, x, x)$, representing the trip route $x \to y$.

At the κth iteration ($\kappa > 0$), the state expansion algorithm extends each state of size $\kappa - 1$ into a new state of size κ by adding a new POI. Specifically, a state $s = (K, T, H, \rho, i)$ is extended into a new state s' associated with POI $j \notin s_K \cup \{x, y\}$ according to the following rules:

$$\begin{cases} s'_H = s_H + r^*_{uj} \\ s'_K = s_K \cup \{j\} \\ s'_T = \max\{s_T + m_i + E[t_{ij}], O_j\} \\ s'_\rho = s_\rho \to j \end{cases} \quad (8)$$

A new state s' is *feasible* if $\texttt{Sat}(i, j, s_T)$ returns *true*. Intuitively, this means that the partial route of the state can be extended to j and then finished at the destination y within the time budget with the completion probability no less than the threshold θ.

4.1 Dominance of states

It is possible that the same ending POI s_i could be reached by different states s of the same POIs s_K, corresponding to different visiting orders. Not all such states need to be maintained because some do not lead to the optimal solution.

We say that a state s *dominates* a state s' if

$$(s_i = s'_i) \wedge (s_K = s'_K) \wedge (s_T \le s'_T) \wedge (\psi(\bar{s_\rho}) \ge \psi(\bar{s'_\rho})) \quad (9)$$

where $\bar{\cdot}$ forms the complete trip by adding y into the route, say $\bar{\rho} = \rho \to y$. Note that $s_K = s'_K$ implies $s_H = s'_H$, i.e., s and s' give the same user happiness. Intuitively, s dominates s' if all of the following conditions hold: the two states s and s' represent two routes $\rho \to y$ and $\rho' \to y$ containing the same set of POIs, the starting visit time of i in s is no later than that in s', and the completion probability of s is no less than that of s'. We assume that the procedure `Check` tests the dominance: `Check(s, s')` returns *true* if s dominates s' (i.e., Eqn 9) and *false* otherwise.

LEMMA 1. *If a state s dominates a state s' and let s_e and s'_e denote the states obtained from extending s and s' with a new POI j at the end, respectively, then s_e dominates s'_e.*

PROOF. Suppose that s and s' represent the routes $\rho \to y$ and $\rho' \to y$. Then s_e and s'_e represent the routes $\rho \to j \to y$ and $\rho' \to j \to y$. It is easy to see that the first three conditions in Eqn (9) remain true for s_e and s'_e. To see the last condition, since s dominates s', both ρ and ρ' have the same ending POI i. If we regard i as the new source of the following identical trip $i \to j \to y$ for both s_e and s'_e, the completion probability of this trip in s_e is no less than that in s'_e because it starts earlier in s_e. Combined with the previous trip ρ and ρ', this condition still holds. □

By repeatedly applying Lemma 1, we have the next theorem.

THEOREM 2 (**DOMINANCE BASED PRUNING**). *Assume that a state s dominates a state s'. If s' can be extended into an optimal trip by a sequence of POIs, so is s by the same sequence of POIs.*

From the above theorem, it suffices to consider only non-dominated states. We will use this property to remove all dominated states without affecting optimality.

4.2 Algorithm

Algorithm 1 summarizes the state expansion for TripRec. Starting at the initial state $S = \{s_0\}$, the algorithm extends the current set of states, S, by adding one new POI at the end of a route in S. If the states in S have the size κ, the new states in S' have the size $\kappa + 1$. The two **for** loops extend each state in S with an unvisited POI and only feasible states are kept. Meanwhile, **Line** 9-10 conducts the dominance test and removes dominated states. **Line** 12-13 records the optimal route with the maximal user happiness. The time complexity of Algorithm 1 is $\mathcal{O}(n^2 2^n)$, which is exponential but much faster than the brute-force search $\mathcal{O}(n!)$. However, due to the time budget and POI availability constraints, each trip typically consists of only a small fraction of all POIs. If the maximum number of POIs in a trip is τ, where $\tau \ll n$, 2^n is replaced with $C(n, \tau)$ in the above complexity.

4.3 State relaxing

The above dominance based pruning applies only to two states that have exactly the same set of POIs, i.e., $s_K = s'_K$. If we are willing to sacrifice optimality for efficiency, it is possible to have a more aggressive pruning by replacing the condition $s_K = s'_K$ with $|s_K| = |s'_K|$ (i.e., visiting the same number of POIs) and $s_H \ge s'_H$ (i.e., s representing a more preferred route than s'). So the dominance test condition in Eqn (9) is relaxed into

$$(s_i = s'_i) \wedge (|s_K| = |s'_K|) \wedge (s_T \le s'_T) \wedge (s_H \ge s'_H) \wedge (\psi(\bar{s_\rho}) \ge \psi(\bar{s'_\rho})) \quad (10)$$

Intuitively, with this relaxed dominance relationship, the route for s takes less time and generates a higher happiness than the route for s', while reaching the same ending POI i. In other words, the route represented by s gives the user more happiness and more remaining time than the route represented by s', thus, is preferred. We call the pruning based on this relaxed dominance relationship *state relaxing*. State relaxing applies to all states ending at the same

Algorithm 1: State expansion

input : POI map G, user u's specific preferences r^*_{ui} for each POI i, departure time T_0, time budget b
output: optimal TripRec trip route, $\mathcal{P}$

$s_0 \leftarrow (\emptyset, T_0, 0, x, x)$, $s^* \leftarrow s_0$;
$S \leftarrow \{s_0\}$, $S' \leftarrow \emptyset$;
while $S \neq \emptyset$ **do**
  for $s \in S$ **do**
    for $j \in V \setminus s_K$ **do**
      if Sat (i, j, s_T) **then** // $i \equiv s_i$
        $s'_T \leftarrow \max\{s_T + m_i + E[t_{ij}], O_j\}$;
        $s' \leftarrow (s_K \cup \{j\}, s'_T, s_H + r^*_{uj}, s_\rho \to j, j)$;
        if $\exists s'' \in S'$: Check (s', s'') =*true* **then**
          remove s'' from S';
        add s' to S';
        if $s'_H > s^*_H$ **then**
          $s^* \leftarrow s'$;
  $S \leftarrow S'$, $S' \leftarrow \emptyset$;
return $s^*_\rho \to y$ as $\mathcal{P}$

POI through visiting the same number of POIs which significantly reduces the size of the set of states S in Algorithm 1 as each ending POI may only be associated with a few states. So the time complexity is decreased from $\mathcal{O}(n^2 2^n)$ to $\mathcal{O}(cn^2)$ for some constant c.

However, due to the POI availability constraint, state relaxing loses the optimality in some cases. For example, suppose $A \to D \to C$ dominates $A \to B \to C$ according to Eqn (10) (we omit the source x and destination y for simplicity), so the former is kept and the latter is eliminated. Now suppose that B only opens in the morning and D opens until midnight. Then the route $A \to D \to C \to B$ may be infeasible due to the late visit to B while the route $A \to B \to C \to D$ could be the optimal solution, but it cannot be generated because $A \to B \to C$ was pruned. Section 7 will study experimentally the trade-off between efficiency and user happiness for the state relaxing strategy.

5. PREFIX BASED DEPTH-FIRST SEARCH

If the states of size κ are represented by the nodes at level κ in a tree structure (with the root at level 0), Algorithm 1 generates the states in a *breadth-first* manner in that the states at level κ are generated before any state at level $\kappa+1$ is generated. For loose time budget and POI availability constraints, this approach may have to keep many "open" states in memory (i.e., all states of the same size), which imposes a bottleneck on the memory requirement.

5.1 Prefix based depth-first enumeration tree

To address this limitation, we present a prefix based depth-first enumeration of states in which a tree structure representing the states is searched in the *depth-first* manner so that only the current branch at any level is searched at any time. First, for the given user u, we order all POIs i by the estimated rating r^*_{ui}. This order together with our tree enumeration strategy below ensures that POIs with larger ratings are considered before those with smaller ratings in the construction of a route. For presentation, we consider $V = \{A, B, C, D, E\}$ of five POIs, excluding the source x and destination y, and we assume that these POIs are ordered in the descending order of estimated ratings for u. The *prefix* of a POI i refers to the set of POIs that precede i in this order.

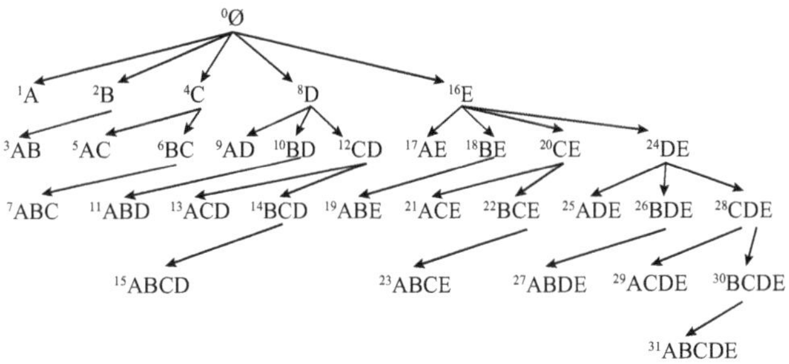

Figure 1: Prefix based depth-first enumeration tree

Figure 1 shows the tree structure for enumerating all the subsets of V with POIs arranged in the above order. The nodes in the tree are generated from left to right in a specific depth-first order, as indicated by the numbers aside the nodes. Each node is labeled by a set of visited POIs arranged in the above order, and the root is labeled by the empty set $\emptyset$. Intuitively, a node with the label K represents all the non-dominated feasible routes that visit exactly all the POIs in K. These routes are divided into $|K|$ groups according to each ending POI in K. To grow the tree, for a node v with a label ending at a POI i, a child node is generated by appending some POI j that precedes i in the above order to the front of the label of v. For example, Node 7 with the label ABC is generated as a child node of Node 6 with label BC by appending A to the front of BC.

Subset first property. An important property of the above depth-first enumeration is that *a label K is always enumerated before any of its supersets*. For example, the proper subsets of ABC are enumerated at Nodes 0-6 and ABC is enumerated at Node 7. This property ensures that, when computing the feasible routes at the node for a label K with the ending POI i, the feasible sub-routes visiting all the POIs in $K \setminus i$ have already been computed at the node with the label $K \setminus i$, so we can retrieve the stored information for such feasible sub-routes to construct the feasible routes at the node for K, by checking the time budget and POI availability constraints and pruning dominated states.

For example, Node 15 with the label $ABCD$ is a child node of Node 14 with the label BCD. There are 4! possible routes at Node 15, but many can be pruned since they either violate the time budget and POI availability constraints, which can be tested by the procedure Sat, or are dominated by other routes, which can be tested by the procedure Check. The feasible routes at Node 15 can be divided into 4 groups corresponding to the ending POIs A, B, C, and D, respectively. The group for the ending POI A can be constructed by retrieving the feasible sub-routes from the already computed Node 14 and appending A to the end by checking the constraints. With the dominance pruning discussed in Section 4 (i.e., Eqn 9), only the non-dominated routes will be kept for this group. The groups for the ending POIs B, C, D can be constructed similarly, by retrieving the feasible sub-routes from the nodes with the labels ACD, ABD, ABC, i.e., Node 13, Node 11, Node 7. Note that these nodes were already computed because their labels are subsets of $ABCD$.

The next theorem lays the foundation for our prefix based depth-first enumeration algorithm for computing the optimal route.

THEOREM 3. *(1) Every non-dominated feasible route stored at a node with the label K and ending POI i must have a prefix that is a non-dominated feasible route stored at the node with the label*

Algorithm 2: `PrefixDFS`(U, K)

1 **for** $j \in U$ *in order* **do**
2 $\quad U^- \leftarrow$ prefix of j in U;
3 $\quad K^+ \leftarrow K \cup \{j\}$;
4 $\quad$ **if** $|K^+| = 1$ **then**
5 $\quad\quad$ **if** $\texttt{Sat}(x, j, T_0) = true$ **then**
6 $\quad\quad\quad \Omega[K^+]_H \leftarrow r^*_{uj}$;
7 $\quad\quad\quad$ add $(j, x \to j, \max\{E[t_{xj}] + T_0, O_j\})$ to $\Omega[K^+]_L$;
8 $\quad\quad\quad$ `PrefixDFS`(U^-, K^+);
9 $\quad$ **else**
10 $\quad\quad$ **for** $k \in K^+$ **do**
11 $\quad\quad\quad K^- \leftarrow K^+ \setminus k$;
12 $\quad\quad\quad$ **if** $\Omega[K^-]$ *is not empty* **then**
13 $\quad\quad\quad\quad$ find $l = (i, \rho, T)$ in $\Omega[K^-]_L$ such that $\texttt{Sat}(i, k, T) = true$ and $\rho \to k$ is non-dominated;
14 $\quad\quad\quad\quad$ **if** l *is found* **then**
15 $\quad\quad\quad\quad\quad T' \leftarrow \max\{T + m_i + E[t_{ik}], O_k\}$
16 $\quad\quad\quad\quad\quad$ **if** $\Omega[K^-]_H + r^*_{uk} > \mathcal{H}$ **then**
17 $\quad\quad\quad\quad\quad\quad$ update $\mathcal{P}$ and $\mathcal{H}$;
18 $\quad\quad\quad\quad\quad \Omega[K^+]_H \leftarrow \Omega[K^-]_H + r^*_{uk}$;
19 $\quad\quad\quad\quad\quad$ add $(k, \rho \to k, T')$ to $\Omega[K^+]_L$;
20 $\quad\quad$ **if** $\Omega[K^+]$ *is not empty* **then**
21 $\quad\quad\quad$ `PrefixDFS`(U^-, K^+);

$K \setminus i$. (2) The node with the label $K \setminus i$ is enumerated prior to the node with the label K.

PROOF. (1) Consider a non-dominated feasible route at a node with the label K, written as $\rho' = \rho \to i$, where ρ is the prefix containing the POIs in $K \setminus i$. From Theorem 1, ρ must satisfy all the constraints, and from Theorem 2, it suffices to consider only non-dominated feasible route ρ at the node with the label $K \setminus i$. This proves Part (1). Part (2) follows from our discussion on the prefix based depth-first enumeration. □

5.2 Implementation

Based on the above discussions, we design a hash map Ω to store the computed results for each node in the tree, whose key is the label K of the corresponding node, and whose value, $\Omega[K]$, contains the information about the non-dominated feasible routes for the node. $\Omega[K]$ has two components, H and L. H is the total happiness for the POIs in K. L is a list $(l_1, l_2, \cdots)$, where each entry l in L has the form (i, ρ, T) and represents a non-dominated feasible route ρ for the node. $i \in K$ is the ending POI of ρ and T is the starting time of visiting i. Essentially, $\Omega[K]$ is a compact representation of all the states that have the same POI set K in Section 4. Let $\Omega[K]_H$ and $\Omega[K]_L$ denote the H and L components of $\Omega[K]$.

We implement the above prefix depth-first search in Algorithm 2 as a recursive procedure `PrefixDFS`(U, K) with a set U of ordered POIs and a node label K as the parameters. Intuitively, `PrefixDFS`(U, K) enumerates the subtree at the node with the label K and U is the set of POIs available for extending the label K within the subtree. The inputs to the algorithm are the POI map G, the departure time T_0, the time budget b and user-specific preferences r^*_{ui}. The output is the optimal route and its happiness, stored in the global variables $\mathcal{P}$ and $\mathcal{H}$. The main algorithm is the call `PrefixDFS`$(V, \emptyset)$ with the set of POIs V in the POI map G.

The algorithm extends the label K by each available POI j in U, creating the child node with the label $K^+ = K \cup \{j\}$ and U^- being the prefix of j in U. If K is empty, **Line** 4-8 adds the route $x \to j \to y$ to the hash entry for K^+ and recursively calls `PrefixDFS`(U^-, K^+). If K is not empty, **Line** 10-19 adds all non-dominated feasible routes having the POI set K^+ to the hash entry for K^+. In particular, for each $k \in K^+$, **Line** 13 searches for the non-dominated feasible route for the POI set K^+ and ending at k. This route consists of a non-dominated feasible route $l = (i, \rho, T)$ for the POI set $K^- = K^+ \setminus k$ and the ending POI k (Theorem 3) such that it satisfies all the constraints, i.e., $\texttt{Sat}(i, k, T) = true$, and the the route $\rho \to k$ is non-dominated (by the conditions in Eqn (9)). From Theorem 3, all non-dominated feasible routes for K^- are stored at the node K^- and were computed already. If there exists such an l, $(k, \rho \to k, T')$ for the extended route $\rho \to k$ is added to $\Omega[K^+]_L$. After considering every $k \in K^+$, if $\Omega[K^+]$ is not empty, the algorithm calls `PrefixDFS`(U^-, K^+) recursively.

Note that the algorithm does not actually materialize the entire enumeration tree; instead, it enumerates the nodes in the tree in the depth-first order. The result at each node is stored in the hash map.

6. HEURISTIC APPROXIMATION

In this section, we propose a simple heuristic algorithm that is essentially linear in the total number of POIs while maintaining the quality of the route. The idea is intuitive: starting with the initial trip route $x \to y$, we insert one POI at a time between two adjacent POIs in the current trip route so that (i) the insertion preserves the satisfaction of all the constraints and (ii) some score of the route is maximized (to be discussed shortly). For example, inserting a POI A into $x \to y$ gives the route $x \to A \to y$, then inserting a POI B before A gives $x \to B \to A \to y$, and so on. To avoid the local optimum, we generate some small number of routes (say 2-3) by applying this method to the set of remaining POIs not contained in the previously generated routes, and we choose the best route from all the routes generated. The time complexity of this algorithm is $\mathcal{O}(cn)$, where n is the number of POI and c is a constant, because each insertion considers at most n unvisited POIs. Note that the length of a route is usually small due to the time budget and POI availability constraints.

A remaining issue is to check whether inserting a POI k between two adjacent POIs i and j (i.e., the sub-route $i \to j$ already exists in the trip) preserves the satisfaction of the time budget constraint, the POI availability constraint and the completion probability constraint. We focus on the POI availability constraint because it is easy to check the other two constraints. We assume $\lambda_{ij} = 1$, that is, a visit to POI i is followed by a visit to POI j. Before the insertion of k, the arrival time at POI j, denoted by a_j, is computed by

$$a_j = \pi_i + m_i + E[t_{ij}] \tag{11}$$

where π_i is the starting time of visiting at POI i. The wait time at POI j, w_j, is computed by

$$w_j = \max\{0, O_j - a_j\} \tag{12}$$

The maximum allowed delay time at i to preserve the satisfaction of constraints, denoted by v_i, is computed by

$$v_i = \min\{C_i - \pi_i - m_i, w_j + v_j\} \tag{13}$$

where $C_i - \pi_i - m_i$ is the maximum allowed delay time to keep the visit to i available (before it closes), and $w_j + v_j$ is the maximum allowed delay time to keep the visit to j available.

For example, if $\pi_i = 10am, C_i = 2pm, m_i = 1h$, the maximum allowed delay time for i itself is $3h$, i.e., the user can at most delay to arrive at $1pm$. However, a delay at i may affect the visit to the next POI j. If $w_j + v_j = 2h$, that is, the visit to j can be delayed at most $2h$, then the maximum allowed delay time at i is $v_i = \min\{3h, 2h\} = 2h$.

The insertion of k between i and j is possible only if the new route satisfies the probability constraint according to Eqn (7) and the extra time caused by the insertion does not exceed the maximum allowed delay time at j, i.e., $w_j + v_j$. The extra time ε_k for inserting POI k is given by

$$\varepsilon_k = E[t_{ik}] + w_k + m_k + E[t_{kj}] - E[t_{ij}] \quad (14)$$

If $\varepsilon_k \leq w_j + v_j$, k can be inserted between i and j and the insertion transforms $i \rightarrow j$ into $i \rightarrow k \rightarrow j$, thus, $\lambda_{ik} = \lambda_{kj} = 1, \lambda_{ij} = 0$.

To determine the score of the insertion of k, we calculate the ratio γ_k as follows:

$$\gamma_k = (r^*_{uk})^2 / \varepsilon_k \quad (15)$$

This ratio measures the gain of happiness per unit of extra time of visiting k. The square of r^*_{uk} places more emphasis on the rating. Since a smaller ε_k has less effect on the feasibility of the whole route, the POI k with a larger ratio γ_k is preferred. We try every adjacent (i, j) in the current route to find the best γ_k.

After each insertion, the arrival time, wait time, and maximum allowed delay time of all affected POIs in the route should be updated according to Eqn (11-13). For example, if k is inserted to form a new route $x \rightarrow i_1 \rightarrow i_2 \cdots \rightarrow k \rightarrow j_1 \rightarrow j_2 \cdots \rightarrow y$, the arrival time, the wait time and the maximum allowed delay time of any POIs after k $(j_1, j_2, \cdots)$ should be updated, and the maximum allowed delay time of any POIs before k $(i_1, i_2, \cdots)$ should be updated. Moreover, the updates must follow the orders imposed by the dependency in Eqn (11-13). For example, Eqn (13) requires first updating a later POI before updating an early POI in a route.

7. EXPERIMENTS

This section presents the empirical evaluation of the proposed methods.

7.1 Experimental setup

We adopt the Yelp[1] and Foursquare[2] data sets in our experiments. Both data sets were previously used for recommendation evaluation in [10]. The Yelp data set contains 45,981 users, 229,906 ratings of 1-5 scales, 11,537 POIs, plus text reviews on POIs. We preprocessed the reviews by removing stop words and infrequent words occurring in $<$ 100 reviews, and using the remaining 8,519 keywords as the features. The feature set or content of a POI, B_i, consists of all keywords contained in the reviews about the POI. The Foursquare data set contains 20,784 users, 153,477 binary 0/1 ratings, 7,711 POIs, and user published tweets when checking-in at a POI. We obtained 1,377 features after preprocessing the tweets.

For each POI i, the touring time m_i is set to 1 hour, and the opening hours were generated from a Gaussian distribution, $(C_i - O_i) \sim \mathcal{N}(\mu, \delta)$ with the mean $\mu = 5$ hours and the standard error $\delta = 1$. The open time O_i was generated using a uniform distribution, $O_i \sim \mathcal{U}(8, 12)$. We set the departure time T_0 to $8am$. The expected traveling time $E[t_{ij}]$ for a pair of POIs (i, j) is estimated using Google Maps[3] with the driving mode. All the experiments were run on a PC with 2.53 GHz Quad-Core CPU and 12G memory.

[1] http://www.yelp.com/dataset_challenge/
[2] https://foursquare.com/
[3] https://www.google.com/maps

7.2 Rating accuracy of individual POIs

First, we evaluate the first step of our approach, that is, the accuracy of estimated ratings of POIs produced by the feature-centric collaborative filtering. For both data sets, we keep 90% rating data for training to conduct matrix factorization and use the remaining 10% rating data for testing the accuracy of estimated ratings. As in the literature [22], we use the standard RMSE (root mean squared error) and MAE (mean absolute error) as the accuracy metrics for POI recommendation. The smaller these values are, the better the result is.

Many POI recommendation approaches are based on topic modeling, for example, STM [10] and LCA [29] predict the probability of visiting a POI, for which the error specific metrics such as RMSE/MAE are incomputable because probabilities are not comparable with ratings. For this reason, we evaluate the following methods.

Probabilistic matrix factorization (denoted PMF): This is the classic matrix factorization on the user-item rating utility matrix [21] where POIs are treated as items. In PMF, matrix factorization is generalized as a probabilistic model where a latent user vector $p_u \sim \mathcal{N}(0, \alpha_p^{-1} I_D)$, a latent item vector $q_i \sim \mathcal{N}(0, \alpha_q^{-1} I_D)$. The predicted user u's rating on item i is given by $r^*_{ui} = p_u^T q_i$. We adopt the default settings in [21] and set $D = 10$, the dimensionality of user and item latent factors.

Collaborative topic regression (denoted CTR): This is the matrix factorization with topic modeling applied to the content of items described in [26]. For our data sets, items are POIs and content of user reviews on POIs. LDA is employed on POI i's content to learn the latent topic vector θ_i, which is incorporated into the PMF framework to confine the search of latent item vectors by setting $q_i \sim \mathcal{N}(\theta_i, \alpha_q^{-1} I_D)$. We adopt the default settings in [26] and set $D = 10$.

Feature centric collaborative filtering (denoted FCF): This is the proposed algorithm in Section 3.1. All the parameter settings are the same as in PMF.

Table 1 shows the results of accuracy of the above three methods. FCF achieves the best performance and has a clear improvement in terms of RMSE/MAE on both data sets. So we believe that the estimated rating by FCF is closer to the true rating. In the rest of the experiments, we study the performance of trip recommendation with the estimated rating r^*_{ui} being generated by FCF.

Table 1: RMSE and MAE. Lower values are better.

	Yelp		Foursquare	
Method	RMSE	MAE	RMSE	MAE
PMF	1.3169	1.0491	0.6197	0.5160
CTR	1.2850	1.0277	0.6000	0.5018
FCF	**1.2152**	**0.9720**	**0.5154**	**0.4402**
improve over PMF	7.7%	7.3%	16.8%	14.7%
improve over CTR	5.4%	5.4%	14.1%	12.2%

7.3 The fixed traveling time model

In this section, we evaluate the trip route $\mathcal{P}$ found by TripRec under the fixed traveling time model where the traveling time t_{ij} for a pair of POIs i and j is fixed, because all the baselines consider fixed traveling time. In this deterministic setting, a feasible route always satisfies the completion probability constraint. The model for uncertain traveling time will be considered in Section 7.4.

We focus on three major cities for trip planning, Phoenix (PX) in Yelp, New York city (NY) and Los Angeles (LA) in Foursquare, and choose Central City, Central Park, and Hollywood as both the source and the destination in these cities respectively. For each city, we randomly pick up 100 users from the testing data, and for each user, we select the top $n = 150$ unvisited POIs, ranked by their estimated ratings, for trip recommendation. This n is a suggested number in [1]. Even with this restriction, the number of trips that consist of 5 POIs can reach billions, which is certainly infeasible for a brute-force search. We compare the following methods in terms of user happiness $F(\mathcal{P}, u)$ and runtime. All the methods adopt the personalized estimated ratings for each POI, learnt by FCF as input.

Greedy algorithm (denoted Greedy): This is the greedy algorithm from the operation research literature [24], which iteratively picks up a POI j with the highest ratio of r_j^*/t_{ij}, where i is the location selected at the last step. Note that we have added the POI availability constraint, which is not considered by [24].

Dynamic programming (denoted DP): This is the dynamic programming approach proposed in [9]. We adapt to the order constraint by setting a "global" type to each POI and fix the visiting order that is from "global" type to "global" type. However, the dynamic programming by filling up a 2-dimensional array [9] still cannot deal with the POI availability constraint.

Heuristic approximation (denoted HA): This is the heuristic algorithm proposed in Section 6. HA is designed for fast approximation and does not guarantee the optimality of solution.

State expansion (denoted SE): This is Algorithm 1 proposed in Section 4. Let SE-SR denote SE with state relaxing. SE guarantees the optimality of solution, but SE-SR does not.

Prefix based depth-first search (denoted PDFS): This is Algorithm 2 in Section 5 that uses the prefix based depth-first enumeration of POIs. PDFS guarantees the optimality of solution.

7.3.1 User happiness

Figure 2 (left column) presents the user happiness score of the trips found by all methods, with y-axis being the happiness score averaged over all testing users and x-axis being the time budget b of a trip (hours). Note that SE and PDFS generate exactly the trips of the same happiness score due to their optimality.

Overall, the number of POIs in the recommended route varies from 3 to 7 depending on the setting of the time budget b. As the time budget increases, the happiness of users generally increases. PDFS/SE is the best performer since they guarantee the global optimum. Interestingly, SE-SR yields a nearly optimal solution as the happiness is only slightly ($< 1\%$) lower than that of the optimal PDFS/SE.

HA performs in the third place and there is an obvious gap between HA and the best two. This is because HA only maintains one route during search, which makes it easy to fall into a local optimum. We will further explain this in the case study below. Greedy performs about 10% worse than HA, as its search strategy is rather simple. DP performs poorly on on all the testing cities, because it cannot deal with the POI availability constraint. In fact, only partial happiness is gained for such routes that some of the POIs are already closed when the user arrives, thus, leading to the low happiness scores for many users. Meanwhile, DP cannot guarantee a better result for a larger time budget.

7.3.2 Runtime

Figure 2 (right column) presents the average runtime per user, with y-axis being the runtime (seconds) and x-axis being the time budget of a trip b (hours). HA and Greedy have a fast and stable runtime because both HA and Greedy only maintain one route, but this feature also overlooks other possible combinations of POIs, thus hardly finding optimal solutions. SE suffers the out of memory

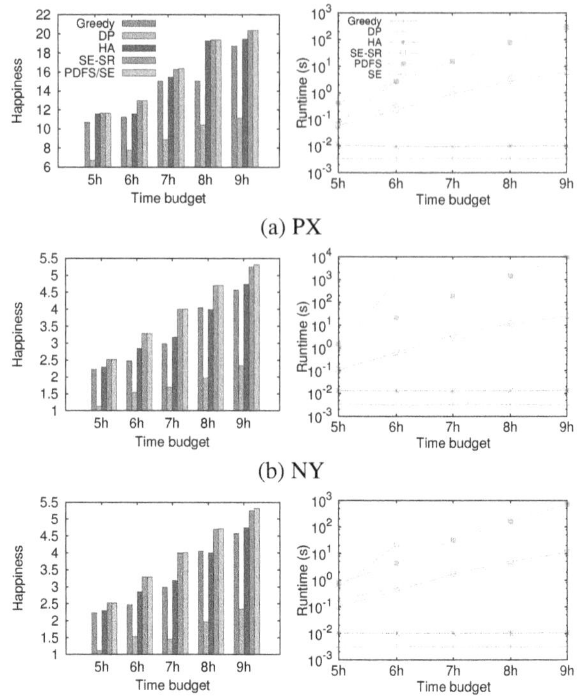

(a) PX (b) NY (c) LA

Figure 2: The fixed traveling time model: (left) happiness of trip routes found (y-axis) vs time budget (x-axis); (right) average runtime (y-axis) vs time budget (x-axis).

problem when the time budget is over 7 hours because there are too many "open" states in each iteration, which exhausts the memory when the time budget is large. PDFS avoids this problem by the prefix based depth-first enumeration. Although it takes the longest time at $b = 5h$, PDFS finds the optimal solution without having the steep increase of runtime encountered by SE. SE-SR takes substantially less time than SE by trading optimality for efficiency.

7.3.3 Case study

For a randomly selected user with $b = 8h$, Figure 3 shows the trip routes designed by PDFS and HA, on the local map of LA, where Location 1 is the source and the destination. The visit follows the increasing order $1 \rightarrow 2 \rightarrow \cdots \rightarrow 1$. PDFS and HA share many POIs in their recommended trip routes (e.g., POIs 2, 3, 6, 7 for PDFS) due to that both methods adopted the personalized preferences. However, HA maintains only one route and easily falls into a local optimum. For example, while POIs 1 and 3 are spatially far away from POIs 2 and 6 in Figure 3(b), HA visits these POIs in the order $1 \rightarrow 2 \rightarrow 3 \rightarrow 6 \rightarrow 1$, in which every sub-route is between two POIs that are far away, thus, too much time is spent on traveling. In contrast, PDFS designs the route in a circle, which reduces the number of sub-routes with long traveling time and allows the user to visit one more POI than HA within the same time budget.

In summary, PDFS finds the optimal solution with less runtime than SE; SE-SR is a very good trade-off for efficiency at a slightly lower happiness than the optimal solution; HA is very efficient but sometime has a significantly lower happiness. Overall, PDFS and SE-SR are two best performers considering both quality and efficiency.

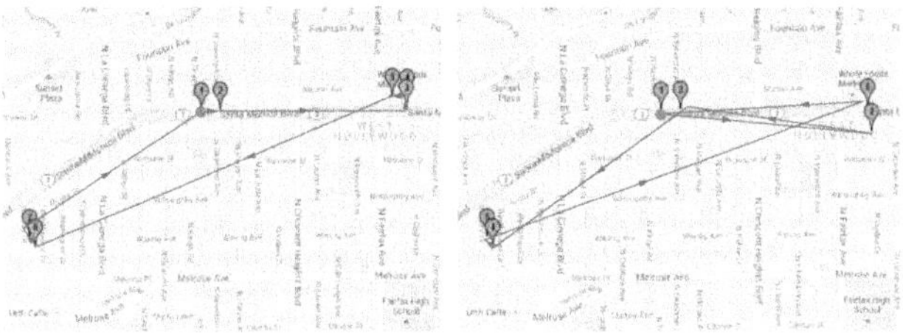

(a) PDFS (5.72) (b) HA (4.89)

Figure 3: Case study of recommended trip routes for LA. The number in bracket is the happiness of the trip.

7.4 The uncertain traveling time model

In this section, we study the effect of the uncertain traveling time on SE-SR and PDFS. For the traveling time distribution of t_{ij} for a sub-route $i \to j$, we adopt the log-normal distribution $t_{ij} \sim \mathcal{LN}(\mu_{ij}, \sigma_{ij}^2)$ in Section 3.3. Note that $E[t_{ij}] = \exp(\mu_{ij} + \sigma_{ij}^2/2)$. σ_{ij} is generated from a uniform distribution to introduce the uncertainty, i.e., $\sigma_{ij} \sim \mathcal{U}(0.5, 2)$.

Figure 4 (left column) presents the happiness scores of SE-SR and PDFS with various threshold θ on completion probability. A color represents a method and a pattern represents a threshold θ on completion probability. Compared to the case for the fixed traveling time in Section 7.3, the happiness of both methods become lower given the same time budget. For example, there is about 20%-40% reduction of happiness from the fixed time cases at $\theta = 0.9$ and $b = 5h$. This is because the route designed in the previous section, although having a higher happiness, may violate the completion probability constraint due to the variance of traveling time, and a more strict constraint (i.e., higher threshold) results in less happiness. In practice, if the user prefers a more reliability of a trip, a route with higher completion probability but a bit less happiness is acceptable.

The uncertain traveling time model also accelerates the runtime of both methods, as shown in Figure 4 (right column). As the completion probability threshold θ increases, there are fewer feasible routes and both methods prune the routes with the probability below the threshold earlier. A cross examination with Figure 2 indicates that at $\theta = 0.7$, the runtime of these methods with modeling uncertain traveling time is close to that with the fixed traveling time model. However, it is almost an order of magnitude less in runtime at $\theta = 0.9$.

8. RELATED WORK

8.1 POI recommendation

Most location-based recommendation falls into this category, which scores each POI individually and recommends top-k POIs to a user. Some examples in this category include [4], [13], which consider no content information, [10], [16], and [29], which consider content as side information. The key difference between trip recommendation and POI recommendation is that POI recommendation considers neither the order of visiting POIs nor the time budget of users and the POI availability constraint. Recommending a visiting order of several POIs to maximize user satisfaction under such time constraints is the main focus of trip recommendation.

8.2 Travel package recommendation

Travel package or itinerary recommendation focuses on a tour of POIs instead of isolated POIs, which is similar to trip recommendation. [14, 30] applied spatio-temporal streams such as tagged photo streams or GPS trajectories to seek for a feasible path by topic modeling or Markov models. [8, 17] developed several probabilistic models to generate possible packages by considering cost, season, area, etc. [1] used user feedback to improve results on interactive tour recommendation. None of these works focus on the objective to maximize user's happiness.

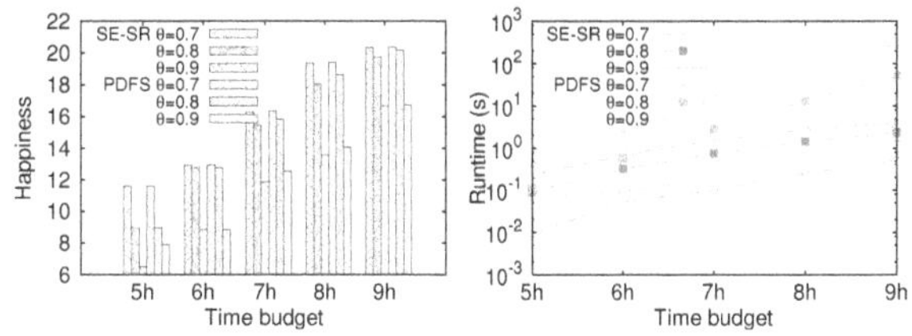

(a) PX

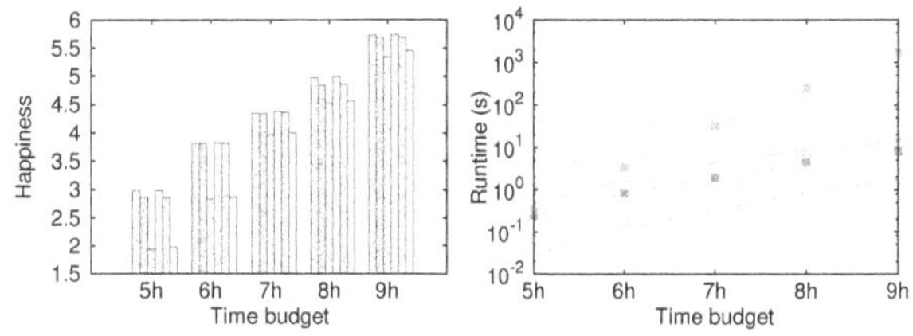

(b) NY

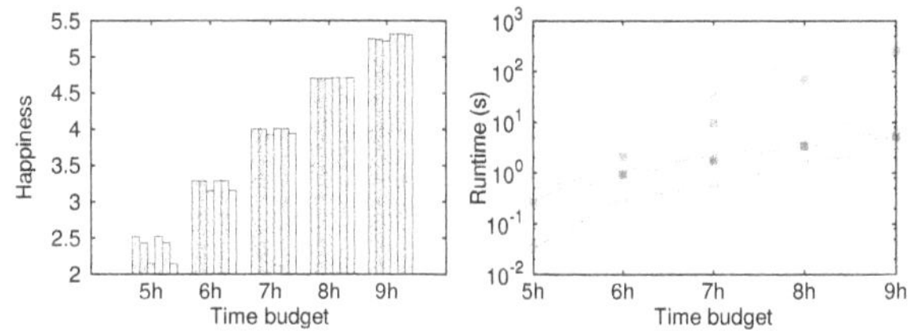

(c) LA

Figure 4: The uncertain traveling time model: (left) happiness of trip routes found (y-axis) by SE-SR and PDFS vs time budget b (x-axis); (right) average runtime (y-axis) vs time budget b (x-axis).

[7, 9, 18] maximized user's happiness in travel recommendation. [9] assumes a fixed order on the types of POIs visited, which is not suitable in the presence of constraints such as opening hours of POIs. The greedy algorithm proposed in [7] cannot guarantee the global optimality. [18] adopted memory-based collaborative filtering to estimate user specific preferences, which are dynamical with time. All these works do not consider the POI availability and probability constraints. The first two works do not consider user specific preferences, thus, generate the same itinerary to all users.

8.3 Operation research and scheduling

The orienteering problem (OP) [25] studied in operation research and theoretical computer science is related to our problem. In OP, a set of vertices is given, each with a score. The goal is to determine a path, limited in length, that visits some vertices and maximizes the sum of the collected scores. However, there are some important differences between trip recommendation and OP. First, OP does not consider personalized user preferences so only a global trip is planned. Second, OP has no touring time for each location, which is an important factor affecting the number of POIs visited. Finally, we consider the uncertain traveling time between POIs through the completion probability constraint, which is absent in OP. While most works on OP focus on heuristic approaches [23, 24] to estimate the global optimum of OP, we present an optimal solution to trip recommendation through a prefix based depth-first search strategy with a focus on efficiency through incremental reconstruction and dominance based pruning of routes.

Other works on real life scheduling problem are related to our modeling of the uncertain traveling time. For example, [2] considered multiple types of transport within a single trip and adopted Monte-Carlo simulation to estimate the probability of catching the trip in non-deterministic transport networks. [27] introduced a Bayesian model to estimate the distribution of ambulance traveling time on the road in a city.

9. CONCLUSION AND EXTENSION

We formulated the personalized trip recommendation problem, which is NP-hard, to retrieve a sequence of POIs that maximizes user's satisfaction according to user's historic activities with various constraints including user's time budget, POI availability and uncertain traveling time. We presented both optimal solutions and heuristic solutions to this problem. Our evaluation on real life data sets suggested that PDFS is the most efficient algorithm for optimal solutions and SE-SR improves efficiency at a slightly lower quality than optimal solutions.

Several variations are possible in the presented trip recommendation model. One variation is to factor the touring time of a POI in the happiness score, that is, it is more important for a POI with a longer staying time to be preferred by the user than a POI with a shorter staying time. We can also factor the completion probability of a trip in the score, in addition to a threshold on the probability. Another variation is adding a financial budget constraint of a user, in addition to the time budget, assuming a cost for traveling and a cost for visiting a POI. If the type of a POI is given and if the diversity of POIs is a desirable goal, we can enforce the specific types of POIs in a trip, or a minimum number of different types in a trip, on a feasible state to prune the search space. These variations or extensions require only a minor modification to our current algorithms.

Acknowledgments. This work is partially supported by a Discovery Grant from Natural Sciences and Engineering Research Council of Canada, and partially supported by China Knowledge Centre for Engineering Sciences and Technology (No. CKCEST-2014-1-5). The work of the third author was partially done during a visit to SA Center for Big Data Research hosted in Renmin University of China. This Center is partially funded by a Chinese National 111 Project "Attracting International Talents in Data Engineering and Knowledge Engineering Research".

10. REFERENCES

[1] S. Basu Roy, G. Das, S. Amer-Yahia, and C. Yu. Interactive itinerary planning. In *ICDE*, pages 15–26, 2011.

[2] A. Botea, E. Nikolova, and M. Berlingerio. Multi-modal journey planning in the presence of uncertainty. In *ICAPS*, 2013.

[3] Y.-Y. Chen, A.-J. Cheng, and W. Hsu. Travel recommendation by mining people attributes and travel group types from community-contributed photos. *IEEE Transactions on Multimedia*, 15(6):1283–1295, Oct 2013.

[4] C. Cheng, H. Yang, I. King, and M. R. Lyu. Fused matrix factorization with geographical and social influence in location-based social networks. In *AAAI*, volume 12, pages 17–23, 2012.

[5] C. Cheng, H. Yang, M. R. Lyu, and I. King. Where you like to go next: Successive point-of-interest recommendation. In *IJCAI*, pages 2605–2611. AAAI Press, 2013.

[6] Z. Cheng, J. Caverlee, K. Y. Kamath, and K. Lee. Toward traffic-driven location-based web search. In *CIKM*, pages 805–814, 2011.

[7] M. De Choudhury, M. Feldman, S. Amer-Yahia, N. Golbandi, R. Lempel, and C. Yu. Automatic construction of travel itineraries using social breadcrumbs. In *Proceedings of the 21st ACM conference on Hypertext and hypermedia*, pages 35–44, 2010.

[8] Y. Ge, Q. Liu, H. Xiong, A. Tuzhilin, and J. Chen. Cost-aware travel tour recommendation. In *KDD*, pages 983–991, 2011.

[9] A. Gionis, T. Lappas, K. Pelechrinis, and E. Terzi. Customized tour recommendations in urban areas. In *WSDM*, pages 313–322, 2014.

[10] B. Hu and M. Ester. Spatial topic modeling in online social media for location recommendation. In *RecSys*, pages 25–32, 2013.

[11] H. Kellerer, U. Pferschy, and D. Pisinger. *Knapsack problems*. Springer, 2004.

[12] Y. Koren, R. Bell, and C. Volinsky. Matrix factorization techniques for recommender systems. *Computer*, pages 30–37, 2009.

[13] T. Kurashima, T. Iwata, T. Hoshide, N. Takaya, and K. Fujimura. Geo topic model: joint modeling of user's activity area and interests for location recommendation. In *WSDM*, pages 375–384, 2013.

[14] T. Kurashima, T. Iwata, G. Irie, and K. Fujimura. Travel route recommendation using geotags in photo sharing sites. In *CIKM*, pages 579–588, 2010.

[15] K. W.-T. Leung, D. L. Lee, and W.-C. Lee. Clr: a collaborative location recommendation framework based on co-clustering. In *SIGIR*, pages 305–314, 2011.

[16] B. Liu, Y. Fu, Z. Yao, and H. Xiong. Learning geographical preferences for point-of-interest recommendation. In *KDD*, pages 1043–1051, 2013.

[17] Q. Liu, Y. Ge, Z. Li, E. Chen, and H. Xiong. Personalized travel package recommendation. In *ICDM*, pages 407–416, 2011.

[18] E. H.-C. Lu, C.-Y. Chen, and V. S. Tseng. Personalized trip recommendation with multiple constraints by mining user check-in behaviors. In *SIGSPATIAL*, pages 209–218, 2012.

[19] N. Marlow. A normal limit theorem for power sums of independent random variables. *Bell System Technical Journal*, 46(9):2081–2089, 1967.

[20] M. Qu, H. Zhu, J. Liu, G. Liu, and H. Xiong. A cost-effective recommender system for taxi drivers. In *KDD*, pages 45–54, 2014.

[21] R. Salakhutdinov and A. Mnih. Probabilistic matrix factorization. *NIPS*, pages 1257–1264, 2008.

[22] G. Shani and A. Gunawardana. Evaluating recommendation systems. In *Recommender systems handbook*, pages 257–297. Springer, 2011.

[23] W. Souffriau, P. Vansteenwegen, J. Vertommen, G. V. Berghe, and D. V. Oudheusden. A personalized tourist trip design algorithm for mobile tourist guides. *Applied Artificial Intelligence*, 22(10):964–985, 2008.

[24] T. Tsiligirides. Heuristic methods applied to orienteering. *Journal of the Operational Research Society*, pages 797–809, 1984.

[25] P. Vansteenwegen, W. Souffriau, and D. V. Oudheusden. The orienteering problem: A survey. *European Journal of Operational Research*, 209(1):1–10, 2011.

[26] C. Wang and D. M. Blei. Collaborative topic modeling for recommending scientific articles. In *KDD*, pages 448–456, 2011.

[27] B. S. Westgate, D. B. Woodard, D. S. Matteson, S. G. Henderson, et al. Travel time estimation for ambulances using bayesian data augmentation. *The Annals of Applied Statistics*, 7(2):1139–1161, 2013.

[28] M. Ye, P. Yin, and W.-C. Lee. Location recommendation for location-based social networks. In *GIS*, pages 458–461, 2010.

[29] H. Yin, Y. Sun, B. Cui, Z. Hu, and L. Chen. Lcars: a location-content-aware recommender system. In *KDD*, pages 221–229, 2013.

[30] H. Yoon, Y. Zheng, X. Xie, and W. Woo. Social itinerary recommendation from user-generated digital trails. *Personal and Ubiquitous Computing*, 16(5):469–484, 2012.

[31] N. B. S. C. Younes Guessousa, Maurice Aron. Estimating travel time distribution under different traffic conditions. *17th Meeting of the EURO Working Group on Transportation, EWGT2014, 2-4 July 2014, Sevilla, Spain*, 2014.

[32] J. Yuan, Y. Zheng, and X. Xie. Discovering regions of different functions in a city using human mobility and pois. In *KDD*, pages 186–194, 2012.

[33] C. Zhang, K. Wang, E.-p. Lim, Q. Xu, J. Sun, and H. Yu. Are features equally representative? a feature-centric recommendation. In *AAAI*, 2015.

[34] Y. Zheng, L. Zhang, Z. Ma, X. Xie, and W.-Y. Ma. Recommending friends and locations based on individual location history. *ACM Transactions on the Web*, 5(1):1–44, 2011.

Range Search on Uncertain Trajectories

†Liming Zhan, ‡Ying Zhang, †Wenjie Zhang, †Xiaoyang Wang, †Xuemin Lin
†The University Of New South Wales ‡The University of Technology, Sydney
zhanl@cse.unsw.edu.au, Ying.Zhang@uts.edu.au
{zhangw, xiaoyangw, lxue}@cse.unsw.edu.au

ABSTRACT

The range search on trajectories is fundamental in a wide spectrum of applications such as environment monitoring and location based services. In practice, a large portion of spatio-temporal data in the above applications is generated with low sampling rate and the uncertainty arises between two subsequent observations of a moving object. To make sense of the uncertain trajectory data, it is critical to properly model the uncertainty of the trajectories and develop efficient range search algorithms on the new model. Assuming uncertain trajectories are modeled by the popular Markov Chains, in this paper we investigate the problem of range search on uncertain trajectories. In particular, we propose a general framework for range search on uncertain trajectories following the filtering-and-refinement paradigm where summaries of uncertain trajectories are constructed to facilitate the filtering process. Moreover, statistics based and partition based filtering techniques are developed to enhance the filtering capabilities. Comprehensive experiments demonstrate the effectiveness and efficiency of our new techniques.

Categories and Subject Descriptors

H.2.4 [**DATABASE MANAGEMENT**]: Systems—*Query processing*

Keywords

Uncertain Trajectory; Range Search

1. INTRODUCTION

With the rapid development of positioning technologies such as radio frequency identification (RFID), wireless sensor networks, smart-phone, radar, satellite and global positioning system (GPS), massive spatio-temporal data has been mounting up. Due to physical and resource limitations of the data collection devices, it is infeasible to continuously capture the location of a moving object (e.g., vehicle, people, animal and iceberg) for each point of time, and hence the uncertainty arises between two subsequent discrete observations. For instance, to save the energy and the communication cost, a taxi may report its location at a low frequency [23]. The time period between two check-in positions might be long in Geo-social applications such as bike routes[1] and tourist routes[2] [13]. Consequently, a large volume of spatio-temporal data with low sampling rate is described by *uncertain trajectories* where the possible locations of a moving object between two subsequent observations are captured by a time-dependent random variable (i.e., a stochastic process).

Permission to make digital or hard copies of all or part of this work for personal or classroom use is granted without fee provided that copies are not made or distributed for profit or commercial advantage and that copies bear this notice and the full citation on the first page. Copyrights for components of this work owned by others than the author(s) must be honored. Abstracting with credit is permitted. To copy otherwise, or republish, to post on servers or to redistribute to lists, requires prior specific permission and/or a fee. Request permissions from Permissions@acm.org.

CIKM'15, October 19–23, 2015, Melbourne, Australia.

Copyright is held by the owner/author(s). Publication rights licensed to ACM.

ACM 978-1-4503-3794-6/15/10 ...$15.00.
DOI: http://dx.doi.org/10.1145/2806416.2806430 .

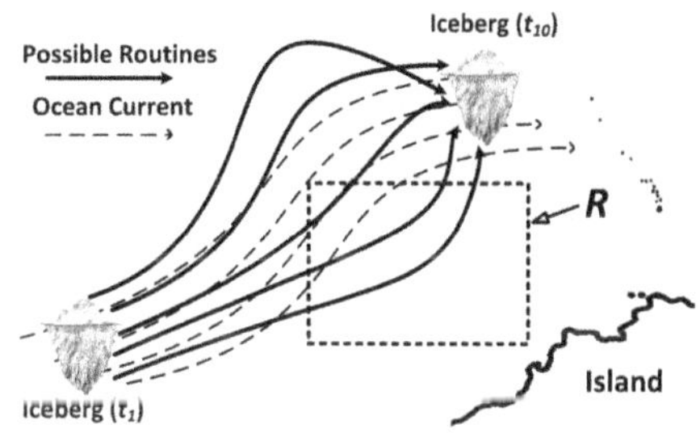

Figure 1: Motivation Example

In this paper, we investigate the problem of *range search* on uncertain trajectories, which is critical to make sense of uncertain trajectories in many key applications such as environment monitoring, location based service, traffic management, and national security. Informally, we aim to retrieve a set of moving objects (trajectories) which consistently appear within a given area with high probabilities during a particular time period. Below are two motivation examples for range search on uncertain trajectories.

Motivation Examples. In Figure 1, an iceberg is observed at times t_1 and t_{10} by satellite or radar systems, while its precise location is unknown at a time $t \in (t_1, t_{10})$ due to the resource limitation. Fortunately, according to the knowledge of nearby ocean currents as well as the historical iceberg trajectory data, an expert can derive possible locations of this iceberg based on Markov Chain model [5]. To choose a particular region for setting up an oil platform or deploying a major military exercises, we may need to evaluate to what degree a region (e.g, R in Figure 1) is affected by icebergs during a certain period in history. Since the location of an iceberg might be uncertain, we can ignore an iceberg at time t if the likelihood of this iceberg falling in the region R is smaller than a given threshold θ ($0 < \theta \leq 1$). Moreover, we may only be interested in the icebergs which consistently (say, at least η times) appear within the region with prob-

[1] `http://www.bikely.com/`
[2] `http://www.everytrail.com/`

ability at least θ. This corresponds to the range search on uncertain trajectories investigated in this paper. Similarly, in the study of wild animal migration, the range search on uncertain trajectories can help scientists to evaluate the importance of a region during a period of time, where locations of a tagged animal can be observed by wireless RFID sensors from time to time.

Challenges. Same as [5, 4, 13, 18], in this paper we assume the uncertain trajectories are described by Markov Chain model because it has solid theoretical foundation and rich applications. A straightforward approach for the problem of range search on uncertain trajectories is to calculate the *appearance probability* of each moving object o at each time within the query time interval, and count the number of times in which o appears within the search region with probability at least θ. Then an object is qualified if the number of accumulated times exceeds a duration threshold η. However, as reported in [4], the computation is still very expensive although efficient algorithm is developed in [5].

Consequently, it is desirable to follow the *filtering-and-refinement* paradigm to significantly reduce the number of candidate trajectories (i.e., moving objects) by exploiting effective filtering techniques. In particular, for any two subsequent observations of a moving object o at times t_i and t_j, denoted by $o(t_i)$ and $o(t_j)$ respectively, we aim to build a summary of the uncertain location distribution of the object. Thus, lower and upper bounds of its appearance probability can be easily derived for any time $t \in (t_i, t_j)$ when a range query is issued. Novel sub-diamonds based filtering technique is proposed in [4] to effectively support range search on uncertain trajectories. However, we observe that its performance is unsatisfactory in our empirical study, because each sub-diamond aims at bounding the appearance probability of the moving object o regarding **all** times between two subsequent observation times t_i and t_j. This motivates us to develop new filtering techniques so that the summary is constructed for a set of time intervals instead of the whole time interval (t_i, t_j) (i.e., partition along the temporal dimension). Specifically, we first introduce a simple filtering technique based on some pre-computed statistics information. Then we further enhance the filtering power by developing partition based approach to approximate the location distribution of a moving object using a set of buckets, which are generated by spatial and temporal partitions. We discuss how to effectively build the partition based summaries following some important observations.

Contributions. Our main contributions can be summarized as follows.

- We formally define the problem of range search on uncertain trajectories.
- We present a general framework for the range search on uncertain trajectories following the filtering-and-refinement paradigm, where summaries of the objects are constructed to facilitate the filtering process.
- A simple and effective filtering technique is proposed based on statistics information of the uncertain trajectories.
- A partition based filtering technique is developed to further enhance the filtering capabilities. Effective summary construction algorithm is proposed based on some important observations.
- Comprehensive experiments on real-life and synthetic datasets demonstrate the effectiveness and efficiency of our techniques.

Roadmap. The rest of the paper is organized as follows. Section 2 presents the related work in the paper. Then we formally define the problem of range search on uncertain trajectories in Section 3. Section 4 introduces a general framework for range search following the filtering and refinement paradigm. Section 5 and Section 6 propose the statistics based and partition based filtering techniques respectively. Experimental results are reported in Section 7, and Section 8 concludes the paper.

2. RELATED WORK

Recent years have witnessed the increasing amount of research on uncertain data modeling and query processing due to their importance in many applications. In this section, we briefly introduce the existing work closely related to the problem studied in this paper.

Uncertain Trajectories Modeling. A variety of models have been proposed to capture the uncertainty of the trajectory data. Early studies on uncertain trajectories employ simple geometric shapes (e.g., cylinders [16] and beads [14]) to approximate the possible locations of a moving object. Despite of its simplicity, this model suffers from an inherent drawback: the probability distribution of an object is not considered and hence cannot appropriately support probabilistic queries. In some recent work (e.g., [22]), the network-constraint model is used where the raw location of a moving object is mapped to a linear range on the road networks. In [2, 11, 17], the uncertain location of an object is captured by an independent probability density function (e.g., Gaussian distribution) at each point of time. As shown in [5, 13], the temporal dependence between two subsequent locations of an object is lost in this model. Recently, a novel evolving density model is proposed in [9] to capture the time-varying uncertainty of the moving objects where the probability density function may change over time. Markov Chain model has been widely used in the literature to capture the temporal dependency of a moving object, and hence is naturally adapted to describe the uncertainty of the trajectory data with low sampling rate in [5, 4, 13, 18]. Moreover, [5, 4] show that the Markov Chain model correctly complies with the classical possible world semantics [3]. In this paper, we employ Markov Chain model to describe the uncertain trajectories.

Range Search on Uncertain Data. Range search on uncertain data has been intensively studied in recent years. A large body of work (e.g., [15, 21]) focus on the range search on a snapshot of uncertain trajectories; that is, each object is described by a probabilistic density function, and objects with appearance probability exceeding a given threshold are retrieved. The problem of range search on uncertain trajectories has been investigated against differerent uncertain models such as cylinder model (e.g., [16]), beads model (e.g., [14]), network-constraint model (e.g., [22]), independent probabilistic density function model (e.g., [2]), evolving density model [9], segments based model [1], as well as the Markov Chain model [5, 4].

As to the best of our knowledge, [5, 4] are only two existing work which study the problem of range search on uncertain trajectories modeled by Markov Chains. Particularly, Emrich *et al.* propose efficient computation algorithm for range search in [5] without the support of indexing technique. In [4], they further improve the performance by utilizing pre-computed sub-diamonds based summaries which can significantly reduce the number of candidate objects for refinement.

Sub-diamonds based Filtering. As shown in [4], all possible valid trajectories within a segment $g(o, t_i, t_j)$ can be bounded by a diamond for each individual dimension if the maximal speed is given. Figure 2 depicts the diamond $\diamond_1$ ($\diamond_1 = \langle o(t_i), a, o(t_j), b \rangle$) where the horizontal axis represents the time and the vertical axis is the dimension D_1. Given a range search query, we may easily *prune* the segment g based on $\diamond_1$. For instance, we have $P(o(t), Q_1) = 0$ for time $t \in [t_i, t_x]$ since the query region Q_1 does not overlap $\diamond_1$ regarding the dimension D_1. Thus, g can be excluded from further computation. Similarly, we can claim $o(t)$ is enclosed by Q_2 for any $t \in [t_i, t_j]$ if Q_2 contains the diamond regarding both D_1 and D_2.

Intuitively, the filtering performance can be further enhanced by maintaining a set of sub-diamonds. For instance, $\diamond_2$ in Figure 2 is a sub-diamond of g where $\diamond_2 = \langle o(t_i), a, o(t_j), c \rangle$, and we know that its associated probability, denoted by $P(\diamond_2)$, is 0.5; that is, with probability at least 0.5, $o(t)$ is bounded by $\diamond_2$ for any $t \in [t_i, t_j]$. Consequently, the segment g can be pruned for search region Q_3 if probability threshold $\theta \geq 0.5$ because Q_3 does not overlap $\diamond_2$. The validation of the segment can be conducted in a similar way. Together with the diamonds and their minimal bounding rectangles, the sub-diamonds of the segments are organized by an R-tree in [4], namely UST-Tree.

The sub-diamonds based filtering technique developed in [4] can significantly reduce the computational cost compared with the diamond based technique. However, as we need to enforce that the object o appears within the sub-diamond $\diamond$ with probability at least $P(\diamond)$ w.r.t **all** $t \in (t_i, t_j)$, this may lead to poor filtering performance. In our empirical study, we observe that the corresponding probability (i.e.,$P(\diamond)$) of the sub-diamonds $\{\diamond\}$ might be rather small, especially when the timespan between t_i and t_j is long. Moreover, sub-diamonds are calculated based on the projected values for each individual dimension separately. As reported in [20], this may lose the spatial correlation of the object location distribution, and hence deteriorates the filtering performance. These problems cannot be addressed by simply increasing the number of sub-diamonds.

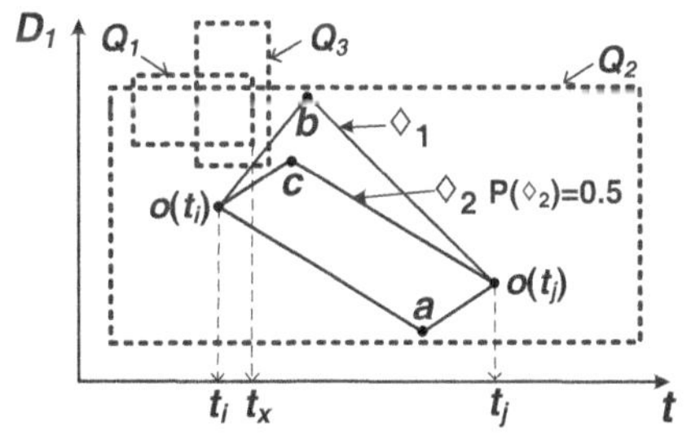

Figure 2: Sub-diamonds based Filtering

3. BACKGROUND

In this section, we formally define the problem of range search on uncertain trajectories. Table 1 summarizes the notations frequently used throughout the paper.

3.1 Capture Uncertainty by Markov Chains

In [5, 4], an uncertain trajectory is modeled as a realization of a stochastic process [10]. Markov Chains can model a discrete spatio-temporal (state-time) space with the assumption that $o(t+1)$ only depends on $o(t)$.

Definition 1 (Markov Chain model). *Given a stochastic process $o(t)$ with $t \in \mathcal{T}$ and a state $s \in \mathcal{S}$, the stochastic process is called Markov Chain iff $P(o(t+1) = s_j | o(0) = s_0, o(1) = s_1, \ldots, o(t) = s_i) = P(o(t+1) = s_j | o(t) = s_i)$.*

Notation	Definition
o ($\mathcal{O}$)	a moving object (a set of moving objects)
$\mathcal{S}$ ($\mathcal{T}$)	discrete space (time) domain
$o(t)$	location (state) of an object o at time t
q	spatio-temporal search region
R	a spatial search region
$[q.s, q.e]$	query time interval
θ	probabilistic threshold
η	duration threshold
$P(o(t), s)$	probability that $o(t)$ is located at sate s
$g(o, t_i, t_j), g$	a segment of an object o with two subsequent observations $o(t_i)$ and $o(t_j)$
$\mathcal{T}(g)$	time interval $[q.s, q.e] \cap [t_i, t_j)$
$\Delta_t(q)(\Delta_t(g))$	duration of a query (segment)
$P(o(t), R)$	probability that $o(t)$ falling in the region R
$d(o, q, \theta), d(o)$	duration (i.e., number of times) that object o satisfies the search region $q.R$
$d^-(o)$ ($d^+(o)$)	lower (upper) bound of $d(o)$
$d(g)$	number of satisfied times of the object o in segment g
$d^-(g)$ ($d^+(g)$)	lower (upper) bound of d(g)
$\mathcal{S}(g)$	partition based summary of segment g
$g.mbr$	minimal bounding rectangle of segment g

Table 1: The summary of notations.

For an object o moving on the space $\mathcal{S}$, we set $P_{i,j}(o) = P(o(t+1) = s_j | o(t) = s_i)$, where $P_{i,j}(o)$ represents the probability of object o moving from state s_i to s_j when the time changes from anytime time $t \in \mathcal{T}$ to its successive time $t+1$. We can store all $P_{i,j}(o)$ in a $n \times n$ matrix $M(o)$ to represent the transition probability of object o from state s_i to s_j at any time t, where n is the number of possible states (locations) and the matrix $M(o)$ is called transition matrix. Then we have $o(t+1) = o(t) \times M(o)$. Recall that $o(t)$ is the distribution vector of an object o at time t where $\sum_{s \in \mathcal{S}} P(o(t), s) = 1$. Similarly, if $M(o)^T$ is defined as a transposed Markov Chain matrix, we have $o(t) = o(t+1) \times M(o)^T$.

Given two subsequent observations $o(t_i)$ and $o(t_j)$, efficient algorithm is proposed in [5] to derive the location distribution $o(t)$ for $t \in (t_i, t_j)$ based on $M(o)$ and $M(o)^T$. Same as [5, 4], we assume objects share the same Markov Chain matrix which can be learned by domain experts in various applications.

3.2 Problem Definition

Following the common assumptions of the existing works (e.g., [5, 4, 13, 18]) which capture the uncertainty of trajectories with Markov Chain model, we assume the space and time are in discrete domain. The space $\mathcal{S}$ consists of n possible states (locations) $\{s_1, \ldots, s_n\}$ in 2-dimensional space. For a state s, $s.D_i$ denotes the coordinate value of s on i-th dimension. We use $\mathcal{T}$ to denote time domain $\{t_1, \ldots, t_m\}$. Consequently, in this paper, the trajectory of a moving object o is represented by a set of m' ($m' \leq m$) tuples $\{t_k, o(t_k)\}$, where $o(t)$ represents the state of o at time t. For a certain trajectory, $o(t)$ is a unique state $s \in \mathcal{S}$. However, it corresponds to a probability distribution when the location of the object is derived from probabilistic models. Following is a formal definition of the uncertain location for an object o at time t.

Definition 2 (Uncertain Location). *Let $P(o(t), s)$ denote the probability that an object o appears on state (loca-*

tion) s at time t. The uncertain location of an object o at time t, denoted by $o(t)$, consists of n' tuples $\{s_i, P(o(t), s_i)\}$ with $P(o(t), s_i) > 0$, where $\sum_{i=1}^{n'} P(o(t), s_i) = 1$.*

Consequently, an **uncertain trajectory** is a trajectory whose location might be uncertain at each point of time. In particular, we assume the location (state) of an object is certain when it is observed (reported), while locations (states) of an object between two subsequent observation times are derived based on the Markov Chain model [4] which is introduced in Section 3.1. Therefore, the uncertain trajectory of an object o consists of a set of **segments** $\{g(o, t_i, t_j)\}$ where t_i and t_j corresponds to two subsequent observations. Each segment g records the location distribution of the object o from time t_i (inclusive) to t_j (exclusive). We use $\Delta_t(g)$ to denote the duration of the segment (a.k.a. observation interval size) where $\Delta_t(g) = t_j - t_i$.

Given a region R, we use $s \in R$ to denote that the location (state) s is within the region R. Then we define the **appearance probability** of o regarding R at time t, denoted by $P(o(t), R)$, to measure the likelihood of the object o falling in the region R at time t.

$$P(o(t), R) = \sum_{s \in R \text{ and } s \in \mathcal{S}} P(o(t), s) \tag{1}$$

Note that we may also interpret the concept of *appearance probability* in terms of *possible world semantics*. In particular, $P(o(t), R)$ denotes the probability mass of the possible worlds at time t in which the object o falls in the region R. This also results in Equation 1.

DEFINITION 3 (SPATIO-TEMPORAL SEARCH REGION (q)). *A spatio-temporal search region q consists of three components $\langle R, s, e\rangle$, where $q.R$ represents the spatial search region, and $q.s(q.e)$ denotes the start (end) time of the query time interval. We use $\Delta_t(q)$ denote the duration of the search region (i.e., $\Delta_t(q) = q.e - q.s + 1$).*

We say an object satisfies the spatio search region $q.R$ with probability at least θ at time t if $P(o(t), q.R) \geq \theta$ for $t \in [q.s, q.e]$. We use $d(o, q, \theta)$ to denote the duration (i.e., the number of times) that a moving object o satisfies $q.R$ with probability at least θ. For presentation simplicity, we use $d(o)$ to represent $d(o, q, \theta)$ whenever there is no ambiguity.

Finally we have the formal definition of the spatio-temporal range search on uncertain trajectories.

Problem Statement. In this paper, we investigate the problem of spatio-temporal range search over uncertain trajectories. Particularly, given a spatio-temporal search region q, a probabilistic threshold θ ($0 < \theta \leq 1$), a duration threshold η ($1 \leq \eta \leq \Delta_t(q)$), and uncertain trajectories of a set $\mathcal{O}$ of moving objects, we aim to identify objects $\{o|\ d(o, q, \theta) \geq \eta\}$ with $o \in \mathcal{O}$; that is, find objects which consistently (at least η times) appear within the spatial search region with probability at least θ.

Range queries on uncertain trajectories with *EXISTS* and *ALL* semantics in [4, 5] are special cases of the problem studied in this paper, which correspond to the range search with $\eta = 1$ and $\eta = \Delta_t(q)$, respectively.

EXAMPLE 1. *In Fig 3(a), $o(t_{10})$ and $o(t_{14})$ are two subsequent observations of object o; a spatio-temporal search region q is given as $\langle R, t_{11}, t_{13}\rangle$ with probabilistic threshold θ and duration threshold η. The snap shots of o are depicted in Fig 3(b) for t_{11}, t_{12} and t_{13}, where the appearance probability for each state is marked. Note that shaded states are contained by $q.R$. Then we have $P(o(t_{11}), q.R) = 0.4$, $P(o(t_{12}), q.R) = 0.5$ and $P(o(t_{13}), q.R) = 0.3$. Given $\eta = 2$, if $\theta \leq 0.4$, o meets the query constraints, otherwise o is not an answer.*

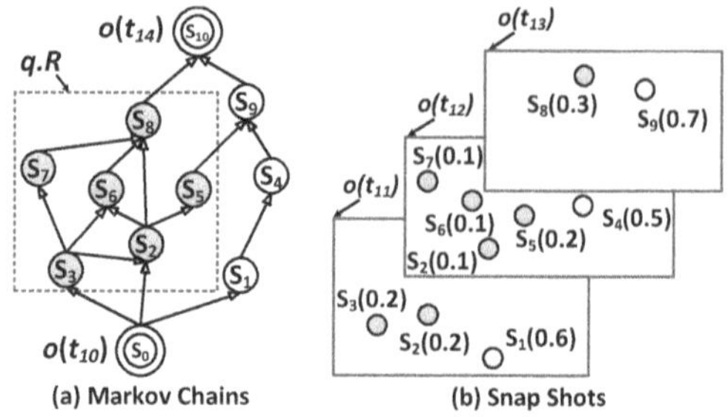

Figure 3: Range Search over Uncertain Trajectories

Thereafter of this paper, the "spatio-temporal range search" is abbreviated to "range search", and "spatio-temporal search region" are abbreviated to "search region" for presentation simplicity. We might use "location" and "state" interchangeably for better understanding of the paper.

4. FRAMEWORK

A straightforward implementation of range search on uncertain trajectories is to calculate $d(o, q, \theta)$ for each individual object $o \in \mathcal{O}$ through Markov Chains based computation technique [5]. However, as shown in [4], this is cost-prohibitive since the *refinement* cost is rather expensive. Therefore, it is desirable to develop effective and efficient *filtering* techniques to **prune** or **validate** objects such that the number of objects involving refinement can be significantly reduced. In particular, suppose we can derive the upper and lower bounds for the duration of an object o regarding the range search, denoted by $d^+(o)$ and $d^-(o)$ respectively. Then an object can be safely pruned if $d^+(o) < \eta$ or validated if $d^-(o) \geq \eta$. Moreover, for each individual time t, we can also derive lower and upper bounds of the appearance probability, denoted by $P^-(o(t), q.R)$ and $P^+(o(t), q.R)$, so we can avoid the computation of $P(o(t), q.R)$ if $P^-(o(t), q.R) \geq \theta$ (*validate*) or $P^+(o(t), q.R) < \theta$ (*prune*).

In this paper, we develop efficient algorithms to support range search on uncertain trajectories following filtering and refinement paradigm. In the sequel, we first introduce a simple minimal bounding box based filtering technique, then present a general framework for range search on uncertain trajectories.

4.1 Minimal Bounding Box Based Filtering

Given two subsequent observations $o(t_i)$ and $o(t_j)$, we may easily come up with a minimal bounding rectangle (MBR) for each segment g, denoted by $g.mbr$, which encloses all possible locations of o during time t_i and t_j if the maximal speed is pre-given. Together with the time dimension, each segment g can be enclosed by a 3-dimensional minimal bounding box (MBB), denoted by $g.mbb$. Clearly, a spatio-temporal search region q is a cube in 3-dimensional space. In this paper, we define three relations between q and $g.mbb$. We say a query q **does not overlap** a segment g if q and $g.mbb$ does not overlap w.r.t spatial or temporal aspects; that is, $q.R \cap g.mbr = \emptyset$, $q.s \geq t_j$ or $q.e < t_i$. Otherwise, we say q **overlaps** g. Particularly, we say q **contains** g if g is contained by q on both spatial and temporal aspects, i.e., $g.mbr \subset q.R$, $q.s \leq t_i$, and $q.e \geq t_j$. Let $d(g)$ denote the contribution of the segment g to $d(o)$ where $0 \le d(g) \le \Delta_t(g)$. It is immediate that we have $d(g) = \Delta_t(g)$ if q contains g, and $d(g) = 0$ if q does not overlap g.

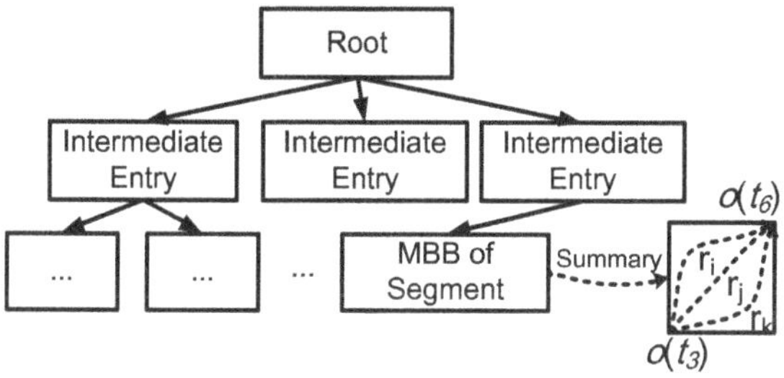

Figure 4: Segments Summaries Tree

4.2 Segments Summaries Tree (STA-tree)

MBB based filtering technique is simple and intuitive, and its filtering capability is rather limited. In Section 5 and Section 6, we introdue advanced filtering techniques based on statistics information and spatio-temporal partitions of the segment respectively where summaries of the segments are pre-computed to facilitate the filtering process.

In this paper, we assume a summary of the segment is constructed for each individual segment w.r.t the filtering technique used (e.g., sub-diamonds based filtering, statistics based filtering and partition based filtering). As shown in Figure 4, MBBs of the segments are organized by a hierarchical spatial index structure (e.g., R-tree [6]). For each segment entry, its corresponding summary is maintained to enhance the filtering performance.

With the same rationale to MBB based filtering in Section 4.1, we can easily come up with three relations between q and an intermediate entry E (i.e., segments enclosed by E). Then an intermediate entry E can be *pruned* or *validated* without further exploring its child entries.

4.3 A General Framework

Assuming the summaries of the segments are organized by an STA-tree, we present a general framework for the range search on uncertain trajectories following the filtering and refinement paradigm, and details are illustrated in Algorithm 1.

In particular, we traverse the entries in a branch and bound fashion. A FIFO queue, denoted by $\mathcal{Q}$, is used to maintain the entries to be visited. In Line 5-13, entries are processed according to their relationships with search region q. Clearly, we do not need to further explore an entry E if it does not overlap q (Line 5), because none of the segments enclosed by E contribute to the final results. On the other hand, if E is *contained* by q, we can immediately *validate* the segments $\{g\}$ enclosed by E; that is, we increase $d^-(o)$ by $\Delta_t(g)$ (Line 8) where g is a segment of the object o. Line 9 validates o if we have $d^-(o) \ge \eta$ where $\mathcal{R}$ is used to keep query results. Otherwise, i.e., E *overlaps* q but is not contained by q, Line 10-13 further explore an entry by expanding its child entries or put its corresponding segment into the set $\mathcal{F}$ which will be further processed by advanced filtering technique at Line 20.

We update $d^+(o)$ by accumulating the durations of its validated segments (Line 14) and unexplored segments, i.e., segments in $\mathcal{F}$ (Line 16). Line 17 retrieves candidate objects which are not validated but have a promising upper bound (i.e., $d^-(o) < \eta$ and $d^+(o) \ge \eta$). Then Line 18-27 further refine the candidate set by exploiting the advanced filtering techniques, in which the summary of segment may derive tighter lower and upper bounds for $d(g)$. Note that Line 21 removes a segment g from candidate segments $\mathcal{F}$ if we have $d^-(g) = \Delta_t(g)$ (i.e., o is qualified at all times $t \in [t_i, t_j)$) or $d^+(g) = 0$ (i.e., o is not qualified at any time $t \in [t_i, t_j)$).

Finally, Line 28-29 refine the remaining candidate objects by exactly computing $d(o, q, \theta)$ for each candidate object o. Note that we only need to compute $d(g)$ for candidate segments $\{g\}$ in $\mathcal{F}$.

As shown in our empirical study, the dominant cost of Algorithm 1 is the refinement cost at Line 29, since it is time consuming to calculate appearance probabilities of objects at different times. This motivates us to develop effective and efficient filtering techniques to significantly reduce the number of survived candidates with reasonable space overhead. In Section 5 and Section 6, we present advanced filtering techniques based on statistics information and spatio-temporal partitions respectively.

Algorithm 1: *Range Search*($\mathcal{O}_T$, q, θ, η)

Input : $\mathcal{O}_T$: Uncertain trajectories of a set $\mathcal{O}$ of objects organized by STA-tree T,
q : range search, θ probabilistic threshold,
η : duration threshold

Output: objects $\{o\}$ with $d(o, q, \theta) \ge \eta$

1 $\mathcal{C} := \emptyset$; $\mathcal{F} := \emptyset$; $\mathcal{R} := \emptyset$;
2 $\mathcal{Q} \leftarrow$ push root of $\mathcal{O}_T$;
3 **while** $\mathcal{Q} \ne \emptyset$ **do**
4 $\quad E :=$ element popped from $\mathcal{Q}$;
5 $\quad$ **if** E *overlaps* q **then**
6 $\quad\quad$ **if** E is *contained* by q **then**
7 $\quad\quad\quad$ **for** each segment $g \in E$ of object o **do**
8 $\quad\quad\quad\quad d^-(o) := d^-(o) + \Delta_t(g)$;
9 $\quad\quad\quad\quad \mathcal{R} := \mathcal{R} \cup o$ **If** $d^-(o) \ge \eta$; // validate
10 $\quad\quad$ **else if** E is an intermediate entry **then**
11 $\quad\quad\quad$ Push child entries of E into $\mathcal{Q}$;
12 $\quad\quad$ **else**
13 $\quad\quad\quad \mathcal{F} := \mathcal{F} \cup$ corresponding segment g;
14 $d^+(o) = d^-(o)$ for all objects with segments in $\mathcal{F}$;
15 **for** each segment g of object o in $\mathcal{F}$ **do**
16 $\quad d^+(o) := d^+(o) + \Delta_t(g)$;
17 $\mathcal{C} \leftarrow$ objects $\{o\}$ if $d^+(o) \ge \eta$ and $o \notin \mathcal{R}$; // prune
18 **for** each candidate object $o \in \mathcal{C}$ **do**
19 $\quad$ **for** each candidate segment g of o in $\mathcal{F}$ **do**
20 $\quad\quad$ Derive $d^-(g)$ and $d^+(g)$ from summary associated with g;
21 $\quad\quad \mathcal{F} := \mathcal{F} \setminus g$ **If** $d^-(g) = \Delta_t(g)$ or $d^+(g) = 0$;
22 $\quad\quad d^-(o) := d^-(o) + d^-(g)$;
23 $\quad\quad d^+(o) := d^+(o) - \Delta_t(g) + d^+(g)$;
24 $\quad$ **if** $d^-(o) \ge \eta$ **then** // validate
25 $\quad\quad \mathcal{R} := \mathcal{R} \cup o$; $\mathcal{C} := \mathcal{C} \setminus o$;
26 $\quad$ **else if** $d^+(o) < \eta$ **then** // prune
27 $\quad\quad \mathcal{C} := \mathcal{C} \setminus o$;
28 **for** each object o in $\mathcal{C}$ **do** // refinement
29 $\quad \mathcal{R} := \mathcal{R} \cup o$ **If** o is verified;
30 **return** $\mathcal{R}$

---

5. STATISTICS BASED APPROACH

In this section, we present the statistics based filtering technique. Section 5.1 introduces the motivation of the technique. Section 5.2 proposes the detailed pruning and validation rules. Performance analysis is conducted in Section 5.3.

5.1 Motivation

In this section, we develop the statistics information based filtering technique. In a nutshell, for each segment $g(o, t_i, t_j)$ we use some simple statistics to capture the uncertain location distribution of the object for each time $t \in (t_i, t_j)$. Then we can derive lower and upper bounds of the appearance probability of o at time t, denoted by $P^-(o(t), q.R)$ and $P^+(o(t), q.R)$ respectively, to *prune* or *validate* the time t. We say a time t is pruned (validated) if $P^+(o(t), q.R) < \theta$ ($P^-(o(t), q.R) \geq \theta$). Furthermore, we can merge the statistics of a set of consecutive times to reduce the summary size.

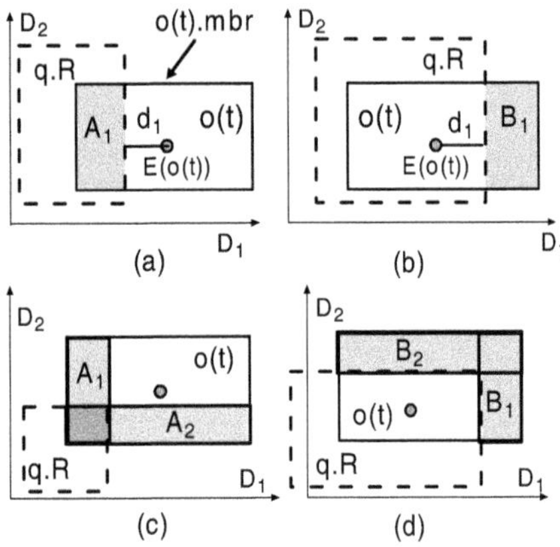

Figure 5: Motivation of Statistics based Filtering

As shown in Figure 5, suppose $o(t)$ is bounded by a minimal bounding rectangle, denoted by $o(t).mbr$. We use $P(A_i)$ ($i = 1, 2$) to denote the probability mass of the states (locations) which are *contained* by $q.R$ along the i-th dimension D_i, and $P(B_i)$ records the probability mass of the states which are *not contained* by $q.R$ along the i-th dimension. In consequence, we have $P(o(t), q.R) = P(A_1)$ in Figure 5(a), since $q.R$ contains $o(t)$ along the dimension D_2. Suppose we can derive an upper bound of $P(A_1)$, denoted by $P^+(A_1)$. Then we can safely prune the time t, if $P^+(A_1) < \theta$. Similarly, t is validated in Figure 5(b) if $1 - P^+(B_1) \geq \theta$, where $P^+(B_1)$ is the upper bound of $P(B_1)$. This observation can be easily extended to the case where the search region overlaps $o(t).mbr$ on both dimensions, e.g., Figure 5(c) and Figure 5(d). In Figure 5(c), we have $P(o(t), q.R) \leq min(P(A_1), P(A_2)) \leq min(P^+(A_1), P^+(A_2))$, and we can prune t if $min(P^+(A_1), P^+(A_2)) < \theta$. With the similar rationale, t is validated if $1 - (P^+(B_1) + P^+(B_2)) \geq \theta$.

EXAMPLE 2. *Suppose we have* $P^+(A_1) = 0.1$, $P^+(B_1) = 0.1$, $P^+(A_2) = 0.2$, *and* $P^+(B_2) = 0.2$ *in Figure 5. Then we have* $P(o(t), q.R) \leq 0.1$ *in Figure 5(a),* $P(o(t), q.R) \geq 0.9$ *in Figure 5(b),* $P(o(t), q.R) \leq min(0.1, 0.2) = 0.1$ *in Figure 5(c), and* $P(o(t), q.R) \geq 1 - (0.1 + 0.2) = 0.7$ *in Figure 5(d).*

In the next subsection, we exploit *Cantelli's inequality* [12] to derive $P^+(A_1)$, $P^+(A_2)$, $P^+(B_1)$, and $P^+(B_2)$ based on the statistics information of $o(t)$.

5.2 Statistics Based Filtering Technique

For presentation simplicity, we use a random variable X to denote the location distribution $o(t)$. Following are formal definitions of the *expectation* and the *variance* of X.

DEFINITION 4. ***Expectation,*** $E(X)$. *We use* $E(X)$ *to denote the expectation of* X, *where* $E(X).D_i = \sum_{s \in \mathcal{S}} s.D_i \times P(X = s)$.

Note that $P(X = s)$ denotes the probability that X resides on the state s, and $s.D_i$ is the i-th coordinate value of the state (location) s.

DEFINITION 5. ***Variance,*** $\sigma^2(X)$. *We use* $\sigma_i^2(X)$ *to denote the variance of* X *on each dimensions; that is,* $\sigma_i^2(X) = \sum_{s \in \mathcal{S}} (s.D_i - E(X).D_i)^2 \times P(X = s)$.

Given two values x and y where $x > 0$ and $y > 0$, we use $\delta(x, y)$ to denote a function where $\delta(x, y) = \frac{1}{1 + \frac{x^2}{y^2}}$. Following is *Cantelli's inequality* introduced in [12], which is demonstrated in Figure 6(a).

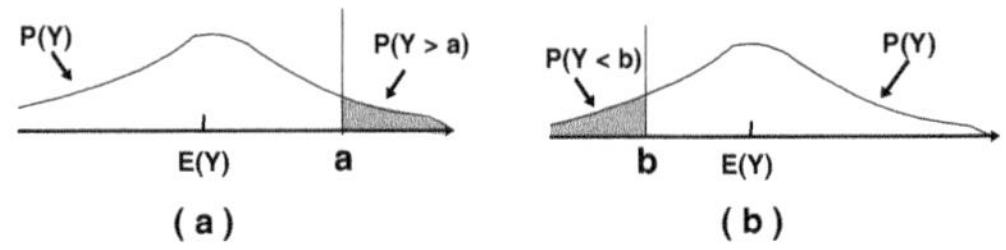

Figure 6: Example for Cantelli's Inequality

LEMMA 1 (CANTELLI'S INEQUALITY [12]). *Suppose that* Y *is a random variable in one dimensional space with expectation* $E(Y)$ *and variance* $\sigma^2(Y)$, $P(Y \geq a) \leq \delta(a - E(Y), \sigma(Y))$ *for any* $a > E(Y)$, *where* $P(Y \geq a)$ *denotes the probability of* $Y \geq a$.

By replacing Y with $2E(Y) - Y$, we have a variant of Lemma 1 which is illustrated in Figure 6(b).

LEMMA 2. *Suppose that* Y *is a random variable in one dimensional space with expectation* $E(Y)$ *and variance* $\sigma^2(Y)$, $P(Y \leq b) \leq \delta(E(Y) - b, \sigma(Y))$ *for any* $b < E(Y)$, *where* $P(Y \leq b)$ *denotes the probability of* $Y \leq b$.

We can come up with $P^+(B_1)$ in Figure 5(b) based on Lemma 1. And Lemma 2 can be used to derive $P^+(A_1)$ in Figure 5(a).

Suppose the expectation and the variance of X (i.e., location distribution $o(t)$) are readily available, we can derive the upper bound of $P(X, q.R)$ for *pruning*.

THEOREM 1. *Suppose that the search region* $q.R$ *overlaps* $X.mbr$ *but does not contain* $E(X)$. *We have* $P^+(A_i) = 1$ *if* $X.mbr$ *is contained by* $q.R$ *on* i*-th dimension, otherwise* $P^+(A_i) = \delta(d_i, \sigma_i(X))$ *where* d_i *denotes the distance between* $q.R$ *and* $E(X)$ *on the* i*-th dimension (e.g.,* d_1 *in Figure 5(a)). Then we have* $P^+(X, q.R) = min(P^+(A_1), P^+(A_2))$.

PROOF. It is immediate that $P^+(A_i) = P(A_i) = 1$ if $X.mbr$ is contained by $q.R$ on i-th dimension according to the definition of $P(A_i)$. Otherwise, suppose $q.R$ is on the left side or bottom of $E(X)$ on i-th dimension (e.g., A_1 in Figure 5(a) and Figure 5(c), and A_2 in Figure 5(c)), then we have $P^+(A_i) = \delta(d_i, \sigma_i(X))$ according to Lemma 2. Similarly, we have $P^+(A_i) = \delta(d_i, \sigma_i(X))$ according to Lemma 1 when $q.R$ is on the right side or top of $E(X)$ on i-th dimension. Then we have $P(X, q.R)) \leq min(P(A_1), P(A_2)) \leq min(P^+(A_1), P^+(A_2))$. Thus, the theorem holds. □

With similar rationale, we have the following theorem which can obtain the lower bound of $P(X, q.R)$ for the *validation* of time t.

THEOREM 2. *Suppose that the search region* $q.R$ *overlaps* $X.mbr$ *and contains* $E(X)$. *We have* $P^+(B_i) = 0$ *if* $X.mbr$ *is contained by* $q.R$ *on* i*-th dimension, otherwise*

$P^+(B_i) = \delta(d_i, \sigma_i(X))$ *where* d_i *denote the distance between* $E(X)$ *and the uncovered area on i-th dimension (e.g.,* d_1 *in Figure 5(b)). Then we have* $P^-(X, q.R) = 1 - (P^+(B_1) + P^+(B_2))$.

Statistics Based Filtering. For a given segment $g(o, t_i, t_j)$, the *expectation* and *variance* information are maintained for each time $t \in (t_i, t_j)$. For a given query q, we can obtain $P^-(o(t), q.R)$ and $P^+(o(t), q.R)$ according to Theorem 1 and Theorem 2. Let $\mathcal{T}(g)$ denote the timestamps within g which satisfy query time constraints, i.e., $\mathcal{T}(g) = [t_i, t_j) \cap [q.s, q.e]$. For each timestamp $t \in \mathcal{T}(g)$, we increase $d^-(g)$ and $d^+(g)$ by one if $P^-(o(t), q.R) \geq \theta$. Otherwise, we increase $d^+(g)$ by one if $P^+(o(t), q.R) \geq \theta$.

Reduce Summary Size. To reduce the space consumption, we may keep the statistics information for a set of consecutive times $\{t_k, t_{k+1}, \ldots, t_l\}$ within a segment. Then instead of keeping the expectation and the variance information for each individual time, we maintain the minimal bounding rectangle of their expectations as well as the maximal variance value on each dimension. Then Theorem 1 and Theorem 2 can be adopted in a conservative way such that any time $t \in \{t_k, t_{k+1}, \ldots, t_l\}$ can be *pruned* or *validated* at the same time. We omit the details due to the space limitation.

5.3 Performance Analysis

Given a segment $g(o, t_i, t_j)$, we assume the location distributions of the objects for time $t \in [t_i, t_j)$ are readily available by applying Markov Chains based techniques in Section 3.1. The construction of the statistics based summary can be finished in $\mathcal{O}(n_s \times \Delta_t(g))$ time where n_s is the average number of tuples in $o(t)$. Regarding the filtering cost, it takes $\mathcal{O}(1)$ time for each time and hence the total cost is $\mathcal{O}(\Delta_t(g))$.

6. PARTITION BASED APPROACH

In this section, we introduce a new filtering approach to build summary for a segment based on both spatial and temporal partitions. Specifically, Section 6.1 introduces the motivation of the partition based filtering approach. Details of the technique are presented in Section 6.2. We discuss how to effectively construct partition based summary in Section 6.3.

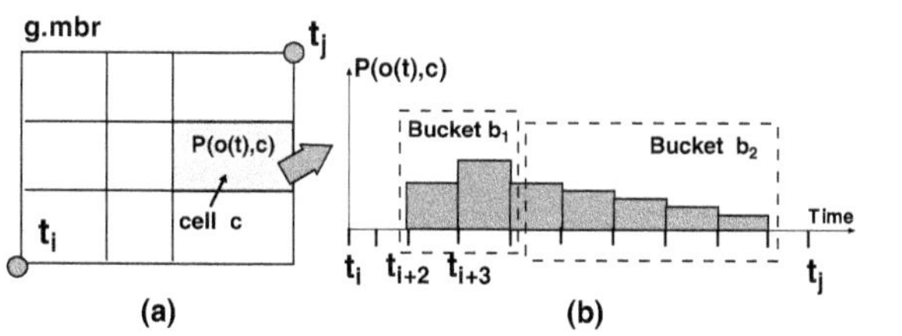

Figure 7: Motivation of Partition based Filtering

6.1 Motivation

Although statistics based filtering technique is simple and effective, a considerable number of segments will still survive from the filtering phase in our empirical study because it is difficult to precisely capture a distribution with a few statistics. This motivates us to develop more sophisticated summary technique by partitioning along both spatial and temporal dimensions, so that the filtering performance can be significantly enhanced with a reasonable space overhead.

As shown in Figure 7(a), we first partition the minimal bounding rectangle of the segment ($g.mbr$) into a set $\mathcal{S}(g)$ of cells. Then for each cell c, Figure 7(b) shows that there is a function $P(o(t), c)$ which presents the appearance probability of the object o within the cell c for times $t \in (t_i, t_j)$. We can immediately derive $P^+(o(t), q.R)$ and $P^-(o(t), q.R)$ as follows.

$$P^-(o(t), q.R) = \sum_{c \in \mathcal{S}(g) \,\wedge\, q.R \text{ contains } c} P(o(t), c) \quad (2)$$

$$P^+(o(t), q.R) = \sum_{c \in \mathcal{S}(g) \,\wedge\, q.R \text{ overlaps } c} P(o(t), c) \quad (3)$$

It is infeasible to explicitly keep $P(o(t), c)$ values for all $t \in (t_i, t_j)$. Consequently, we employ a set of buckets to approximate the appearance probability distribution for each cell c. For instance, in Figure 7(b) we use two buckets $\{b_1, b_2\}$ to represent $P(o(t), c)$ where the time interval size, maximal and minimal appearance probabilities of a bucket b are denoted by $\Delta_t(b)$, $b.p^+$ and $b.p^-$ respectively. In particular, we have $P^-(o(t), c) = b(t, c).p^-$ and $P^+(o(t), c) = b(t, c).p^+$ where $b(t, c)$ is the corresponding bucket of c at time t. Then, we have

$$P^-(o(t), q) = \sum_{c \in \mathcal{S}(g) \,\wedge\, q.R \text{ contains } c} b(t, c).p^- \quad (4)$$

$$P^+(o(t), q) = \sum_{c \in \mathcal{S}(g) \,\wedge\, q.R \text{ overlaps } c} b(t, c).p^+ \quad (5)$$

6.2 Partition Based Filtering

Given a partition based summary of a segment $g(o, t_i, t_j)$, denoted by $\mathcal{S}(g)$, we can come up with an effective computation algorithm to derive lower and upper bounds for $d(g)$ according to Equations 4 and 5. Algorithm 2 illustrates the details. Specifically, we first retrieve cells in $\mathcal{S}(g)$ which are contained by $q.R$ or overlap $q.R$, denoted by $\mathcal{C}_\cap$ and $\mathcal{C}_\cup$, respectively. Then we attempt to *validate* (Line 6-9) or *prune* (Line 11-14) a time $t \in \mathcal{T}(g)$. Line 7 calculates the lower bound of $P(o(t), q.R)$ based on Equation 4, while Line 12 derives the upper bound according to Equation 5. For the given probability threshold θ, we can *validate* a time t if $P^-(o(t), q.R) \geq \theta$ (Line 8). Similarly, t is *pruned* if $P^+(o(t), q.R) < \theta$ (Line 13).

Algorithm 2: Partition based Filter($\mathcal{S}(g)$, q, θ)

```
Input  : S(g) : partition based summary of g,
         q : range search, θ probabilistic threshold
Output: d⁻(g) and d⁺(g)
1  d⁻(g) := 0; d⁺(g) := 0;
2  C∩ ← cells in S(g) which are contained by q.R ;
3  C∪ ← cells in S(g) which overlap q.R ;
4  for each time t ∈ T(g) do
5      P⁻(o(t), q.R) := 0; P⁺(o(t), q.R) := 0;
6      for each cell c in C∩ do
7          P⁻(o(t), q.R) := P⁻(o(t), q.R) + b(t, c).p⁻;
8      if P⁻(o(t), q.R) ≥ θ then                /* validate */
9          d⁻(g) := d⁻(g) + 1; d⁺(g) := d⁺(g) + 1 ;
10     else
11         for each cell c in C∪ do
12             P⁺(o(t), q.R) := P⁺(o(t), q.R) + b(t, c).p⁺;
13         if P⁺(o(t), q.R) ≥ θ then            /* prune */
14             d⁺(g) := d⁺(g) + 1;
15 return d⁻(g) and d⁺(g)
```

Time Complexity. Let C_r denote the cost to retrieve the cells which are contained by $q.R$ or overlaps $q.R$, and there are n_c cells in $\mathcal{C}_\cup$. Then the total filtering cost is $O(C_r + n_c \times \Delta_t(g))$.

6.3 Summary Construction

To effective construct $\mathcal{S}(g)$, we aim to address following three issues in this subsection: *i)* how to generate buckets for a given cell; *ii)* the number of cells assigned for each segment; *iii)* how to generate the cells.

(i) Bucket generation. As discussed in Section 6.1, we cannot afford to keep $P(o(t), c)$ values for all times in $[t_i, t_j)$. Thus, we use B buckets to approximate the probability distribution. Suppose each time t have the same chance to be involved in the filtering phase, the uncertainty introduced by a bucket partition $\mathcal{B}$, denoted by $C(\mathcal{B})$, is as follows.

$$C(\mathcal{B}) = \sum_{t \in (t_i, t_j)} (b(t,c).p^+ - b(t,c).p^-) \quad (6)$$

Recall that $b(t,c)$ is the bucket used for the time t. Similar to V-optimal histogram [8], we come up with the optimal bucket partition $\mathcal{B}^*$ with cost $O(\Delta_t(g)^2 \times B)$ by applying dynamic programming technique.

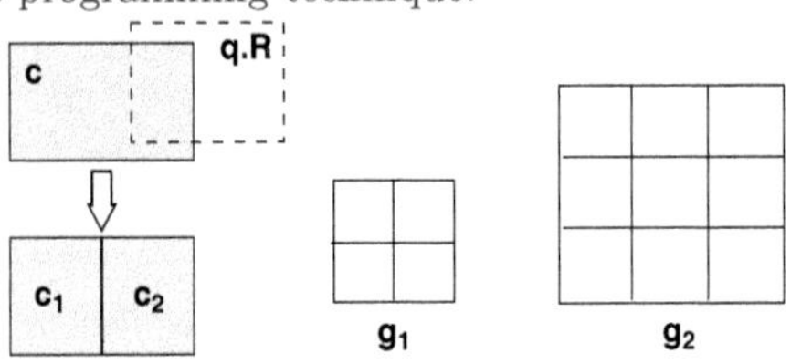

(a) (b)

Figure 8: Motivation of Resource Allocation

In our implementation, the number of buckets for each cell is linear to the duration of the segment; that is, $B = \Delta_t(g)/l$ where l is a pre-given constant.

(ii) Number of cells assigned for each segment. Given two segments g_1 and g_2, we use $Area(g_1)$ ($Area(g_2)$) to denote the area of $g_1.mbr$ ($g_2.mbr$), and n_1 (n_2) denote the number of cells assigned to g_1 (g_2). At the first glance, we may assign a fixed number of cells to each segment (i.e., $n_1 = n_2$) or fix the area of each cell (i.e., $\frac{n_1}{n_2} = \frac{Area(g_1)}{Area(g_2)}$). However, both strategies are not cost-effective according to our observation below.

With similar spirit to [21], we use $P(c) \times W(c)$ to measure the contribution of uncertainty for a cell c, where $P(c)$ is the probability that c overlaps $q.R$ but $q.R$ doesn't contain c, while $W(c)$ denotes the probability mass within the cell (i.e., $W(c) = \sum_{t \in (t_i, t_j)} P(o(t), c)$). As shown in Figure 8(a), we can reduce the uncertainty by evenly partitioning a cell c into two parts c_1 and c_2. Assume the probability mass in c is also evenly distributed, now the overall uncertainty cost becomes $2 \times (\frac{P(c)}{2} \times \frac{W(c)}{2}) = \frac{P(c) \times W(c)}{2}$. In Figure 8(b), we assume $W(g_1) = W(g_2)$ (i.e., two segments have the same duration length), and two cells from the same segment have the same area and probability mass. Intuitive, for a cost-effective resource allocation strategy, each cell should contribute the same amount of uncertainty; that is, $\frac{P(g_1)}{n_1} \times \frac{W(g_1)}{n_1} = \frac{P(g_2)}{n_2} \times \frac{W(g_2)}{n_2}$. Consequently, we have

$$(\frac{n_1}{n_2})^2 = \frac{Area(g_1)}{Area(g_2)} \quad (7)$$

since $\frac{P(g_1)}{P(g_2)} \approx \frac{Area(g_1)}{Area(g_2)}$. For instance, suppose we have $Area(g_1)$ = 10 and $Area(g_2) = 40$ in Figure 8(b), if 4 cells are assigned to g_1, then 8 cells should goes to g_2 because $(\frac{4}{8})^2 = \frac{10}{40}$.

(iii) Cell generation. Now we investigate how to partition the minimal bounding rectangle of a segment g into $m_1 \times m_2$ cells. Following the above argument, the uncertainty cost of a segment g is $\sum_{c \in \mathcal{S}(g)} P(c) \times W(c)$. Because $\sum_{c \in \mathcal{S}(g)} Area(c)$ and $\sum_{c \in \mathcal{S}(g)} W(c)$ are two constants regardless how the cells are generated. This implies that we should have the same $Area(c) \times W(c)$ value for each cell in $\mathcal{S}(g)$ to minimize the uncertainty cost according to Chebyshev Sum Inequality [7]. Nevertheless, it is infeasible to achieve this with a regular grid partition, and hence we resort to a simple heuristic. In particular, for a segment with $m_1 \times m_2$ cells we partition $g.mbr$ into m_i parts with the same probability mass along each dimension i, which can be finished in time $\mathcal{O}(n_s \times \Delta_t(g) + n_s \log(n_s))$ where n_s is the average number of tuples in $o(t)$ for $t \in (t_i, t_j)$.

7. EXPERIMENT

In this section, we present results of a comprehensive performance study to evaluate the efficiency and scalability of the proposed techniques in the paper. Following algorithms are evaluated.

- **UST:** The range search techniques proposed in [4] where sub-diamonds based filtering technique is employed[3].
- **STA:** Algorithm 1 in Section 4 where statistics based filtering technique (Section 5) is employed.
- **GRID:** Algorithm 1 in Section 4 where partition based filtering technique (Section 6) is employed.

In this work, we use techniques proposed in [5] to perform candidate refinement for the above three algorithms.

Datasets. We evaluate our techniques on both synthetic and real datasets using data generator from [4, 13] with following steps. We construct a two dimensions state space, consisting of n states, which are *uniformly* distributed in the domain $[0, 1]^2$. For each state, we randomly choose several neighbors, and then assign random probability to each connection such that the total probability equals to 1. This builds a directed graph where the vertices represent the states and the edges represent the transition probabilities from one state to another. The graph is stored in a matrix as the transition matrix. To create an uncertain trajectory, we randomly choose one state as the start point, and then apply a directed random walk through the non-zero edges of the graph to get a moving sequence with 100 time steps. The size of time domain is set to 1,000, and the start time of an uncertain trajectory is randomly chosen between [1, 900]. The observations of an object are randomly chosen from the moving sequence. In the experiment, we generate 10,000 states with a transition matrix. The number of trajectories N varies from 2,500 to 10,000 with default value 5,000. Two subsequent observations' interval size (i.e., **segment duration**) is randomly chosen from 10 to 15 by default. The probabilistic threshold θ varies from 0.1 to 1.0 with default value 0.5, and the duration threshold η varies from 1 to 10 with default value 6. The real datasets are generated from a set of trajectories of taxis in the city of Beijing [19]. We apply techniques in [13] to get the state set, transition matrix, and trajectories set, and then randomly choose 10,000 state with 583 corresponding trajectories to perform the experiment.

Workload. A workload for the range query consists of 1000 queries in our experiments. The center of a query is uniformly chosen from the domain $[0, 1]^2$, its start time is randomly generated from [1, 990]. The query extent, i.e, search

[3]The range search with *exists* semantics (i.e., $\eta = 1$) is investigated in [4]. Nevertheless, their technique can be easily extended to support range search with $\eta > 1$.

region of a query in each dimension varies from 0.05 to 0.25 with default value 0.1, and the duration of a query ($\Delta_t(q)$) varies from 10 to 25 with default value 10.

Same as [4], the catalog size of the UST-Tree is set to 10 in the experiments. In STA Algorithm, we compress the statistics information for every 3 consecutive times. Regarding GRID Algorithm, suppose one cell is assigned to a unit area with size 0.03×0.03. Then for each segment g with area $Area(g.mbr)$, c_n cells are assigned where $c_n = \lceil\sqrt{\frac{Area(g.mbr)}{0.03\times0.03}}\rceil$ according to Equation 7. Moreover, $\lceil\frac{\Delta_t(g)}{5}\rceil$ buckets are generated for each cell where $\Delta_t(g)$ is the duration of the segment (i.e., observation interval size).

All algorithms proposed in this paper are implemented in standard C++ with STL library and compiled with GNU GCC. Experiments are run on a PC with Intel Xeon 2.40GHz dual CPU and 4G memory running Debian Linux. The disk page size is fixed to 4,096 bytes. As the refinement phase contributes the dominant cost in three algorithms, we evaluate their performance by measuring the average number of candidate segments refined. The average query response time is also recorded to evaluate the efficiency of the algorithms.

Table 2 lists all parameters which may have impacts on our performance study, where default values are in **bold** font. In our experiments, all parameters use default values unless otherwise specified.

Notation	Definition
number of trajectories (N)	2500, **5000**, 7500, 10000
segment duration $\Delta_t(g)$	**[10, 15]**, [15, 20], [20, 25], [25, 30]
probabilistic threshold (θ)	0.1, 0.3, **0.5**, 0.7, 0.9, 1.0
duration threshold (η)	1, 4, **6**, 8, 10
query extent (area of $q.R$)	0.05, **0.1**, 0.15, 0.20, 0.25
query duration $\Delta_t(q)$	**10**, 15, 20, 25

Table 2: Parameter Settings

7.1 Performance Tuning

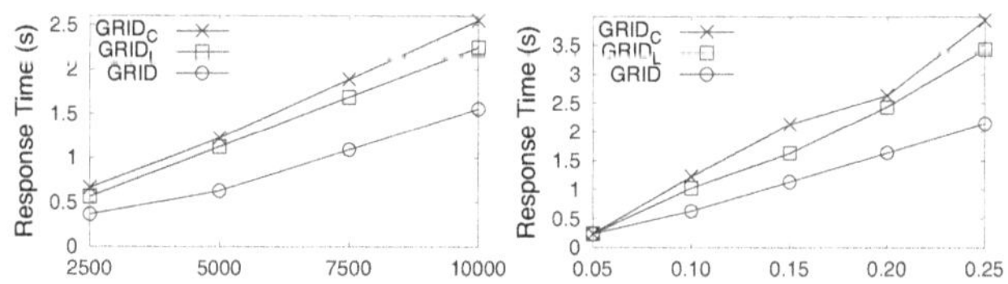

(a) *# Trajectories* (b) *Query Extent*

Figure 9: Performance Tuning

To evaluate effectiveness of the adaptive resource allocation strategy in Section 6.3, we also construct partition based summaries following other two alternative strategies, namely $GRID_C$ and $GRID_L$ respectively. Particularly, $GRID_C$ always allocates 3×3 cells for each segment (i.e., fix the number of cells for each segment), while each cell in $GRID_L$ has the area 0.03×0.03 (i.e., fixed the area of each cell).

Note that summaries constructed in three algorithms have similar summary size under default settings. Nevertheless, Figure 9 shows that GRID always outperforms the other two competitors by varying the number of trajectories and query extent. This confirms the effectiveness of our adaptive resource allocation strategy.

7.2 Performance Evaluation

Impact of the number of trajectories. Figure 10 evaluates the performance of three algorithms on synthetic dataset where the number of trajectories N grows from 2,500 to

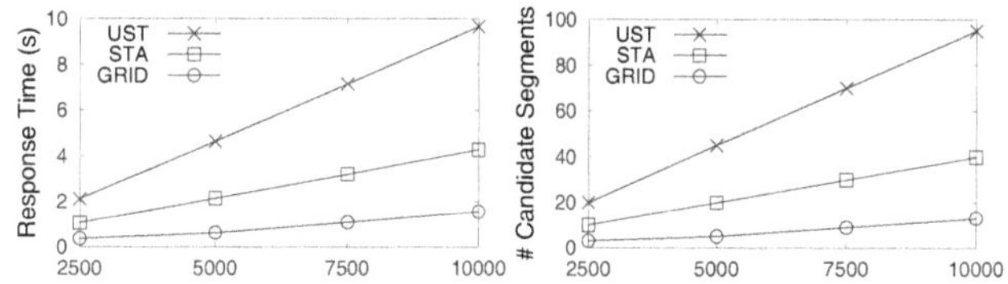

(a) *Response Time* (b) *# Candidate Segments*

Figure 10: Impact of # Trajectories

10,000. With a larger number of trajectories, more trajectories are involved in the computation, thus incurring higher computation cost and more candidate segments. The response time and the number of candidate segments of STA and GRID grow slowly, yet the performance of UST drops more quickly with the growth of the number of trajectories. It is shown that GRID has the best scalability among three algorithms.

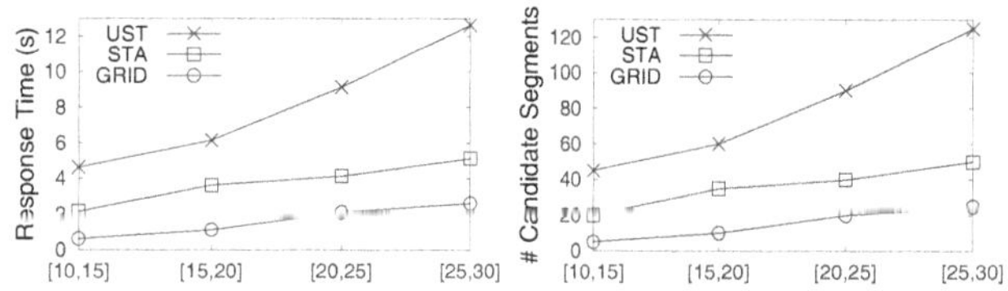

(a) *Response Time* (b) *# Candidate Segments*

Figure 11: Impact of Segment Duration

Impact of segment duration. Figure 11 evaluates the impact of the segment duration $\Delta_t(g)$ on three algorithms where $\Delta_t(g)$ is randomly chosen from each bounded interval. The response time and the number of candidate segments are reported for three algorithms. As expected, the performance of UST degrades quickly because it is difficult to find a proper sub-diamond when the segment duration grows. Recall that a sub-diamond $\diamond$ on a segment $g(o, t_i, t_j)$ need to enforce that the appearance probability of $o(t)$ is bounded by $P(\diamond)$ regarding *all* times $t \in [t_i, t_j)$. On the contrary, STA and GRID are much less sensitive to the growth of the segment duration because of the temporal partition; that is, we build summaries for a set of time intervals in g, instead of the whole time interval.

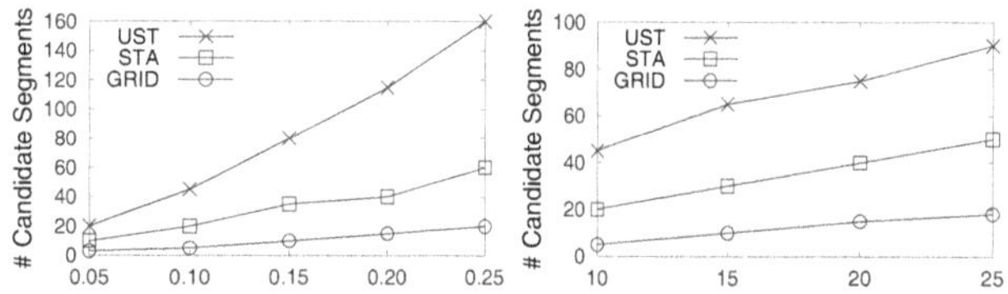

(a) *Diff. Query Extent* (b) *Diff. Query Duration*

Figure 12: Impact of Query Extent and Duration

Impact of query extent and duration. We evaluate the impact of the query extent of $q.R$ as well as the query duration $\Delta_t(q)$ against three algorithms, where the query extent grows from 0.05 to 0.25, and the query duration varies from 10 to 25. With the grow of query extent and query duration, more trajectories are involved in the range search, thus the number of candidate segments increases as expected. Figure 12 shows that GRID has the best filtering capability among three algorithms.

Impact of probabilistic threshold. Figure 13 investigates the performance of three algorithms as a function of the probabilistic threshold θ which varies from 0.1 to 1. The performance of three algorithms is not sensitive to θ. It is

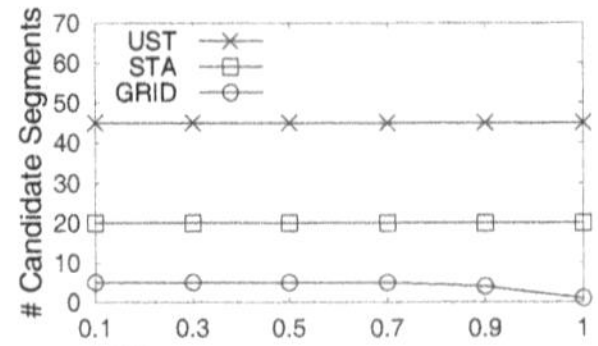

Figure 13: Diff. θ

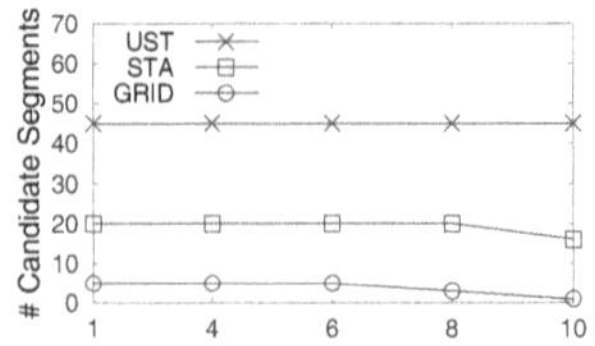

Figure 14: Diff. η

shown that GRID always has the best performance among three algorithms.

Impact of duration threshold. Figure 14 reports the number of candidate segments of the algorithms as a function of the duration threshold η which varies from 1 to 10. It is shown that the growth of η does not noticeablely affect performance of three algorithms, while GRID always achieves the best performance under all settings. Recall that, when η equal 1, the range search exactly corresponds to the range search with *exists* semantics studied in [4].

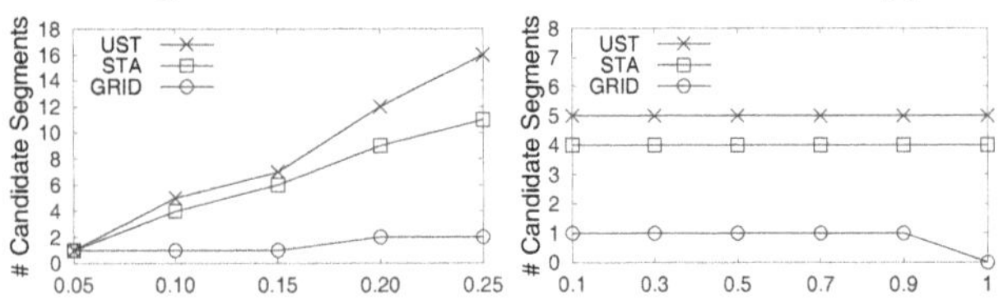

(a) *Query Extent* (b) *Diff. θ*

Figure 15: Experiments on Real Data

Real data. We also perform experiments on the real-life dataset. Figure 15 reports the number of candidate segments against the growth of the query extent and probabilistic threshold θ. Similar trends are observed in Figure 15 compared with the experiments on the synthetic data.

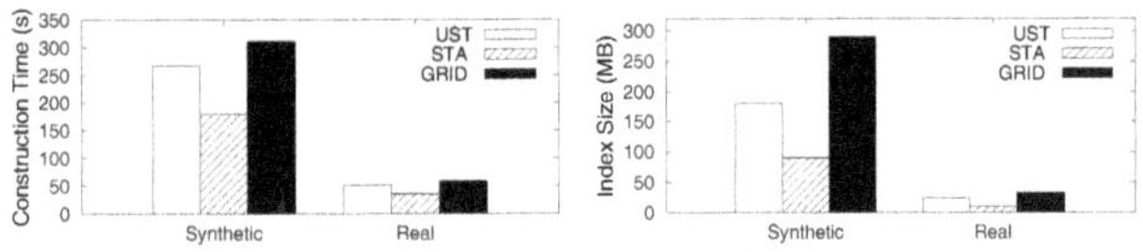

(a) *Construction Time* (b) *Index Size*

Figure 16: Index Construction

Index construction. Figure 16 reports the index construction time and the index size of three algorithms on synthetic data and real-life data. It is interesting that STA outperforms UST in term of query response time, while STA also consumes less index size and index construction time. On the other hand, although GRID has the largest index size and construction time, it is cost effective considering its superior performance compared with other two algorithms.

8. CONCLUSION

To tame the uncertainty of trajectory data collected in a wide spectrum of applications, we have developed effective filtering and query processing techniques to support range search on uncertain trajectories which are modeled by Markov Chains. Particularly, we formally define the problem of range search on uncertain trajectories. Then we introduce an indexing structure where the summaries of the segments are organized by an STA-tree, as well as a general framework to support range search on uncertain trajectories following the filtering and refinement paradigm. To enhance the filtering capabilities, we develop effective statistics based and partition based filtering techniques. Our comprehensive experiments demonstrate the superior performance of our new techniques compared with existing work.

Acknowledgments. Ying Zhang is supported by ARC DE140100679 and DP130103245. Wenjie Zhang is supported by ARC DE120102144 and DP120104168. Xuemin Lin is supported by NSFC61232006, NSFC61021004, ARC DP1201-04168 and DP110102937.

9. REFERENCES

[1] L. Chen, Y. Tang, M. Lv, and G. Chen. Partition-based range query for uncertain trajectories in road networks. *GeoInformatica*, 19(1):61–84, 2015.

[2] R. Cheng, D. V. Kalashnikov, and S. Prabhakar. Querying imprecise data in moving object environments. *IEEE Trans. Knowl. Data Eng.*, 16(9):1112–1127, 2004.

[3] N. N. Dalvi and D. Suciu. Efficient query evaluation on probabilistic databases. *VLDB J.*, 16(4):523–544, 2007.

[4] T. Emrich, H.-P. Kriegel, N. Mamoulis, M. Renz, and A. Züfle. Indexing uncertain spatio-temporal data. In *CIKM*, pages 395–404, 2012.

[5] T. Emrich, H.-P. Kriegel, N. Mamoulis, M. Renz, and A. Züfle. Querying uncertain spatio-temporal data. In *ICDE*, pages 354–365, 2012.

[6] A. Guttman. R-trees: A dynamic index structure for spatial searching. In *SIGMOD Conference*, pages 47–57, 1984.

[7] G. Hardy, J. Littlewood, and G. Pólya. *Inequalities.* Cambridge University Press, 1988.

[8] H. V. Jagadish, N. Koudas, S. Muthukrishnan, V. Poosala, K. C. Sevcik, and T. Suel. Optimal histograms with quality guarantees. In *VLDB*, pages 275–286, 1998.

[9] H. Jeung, H. Lu, S. Sathe, and M. L. Yiu. Managing evolving uncertainty in trajectory databases. *IEEE Trans. Knowl. Data Eng.*, Accppted in 2013.

[10] S. Karlin and H. Taylor. *A First Course in Stochastic Processes.* Academic Press, 1975.

[11] C. Ma, H. Lu, L. Shou, and G. Chen. Ksq: Top-(k) similarity query on uncertain trajectories. *IEEE Trans. Knowl. Data Eng.*, 25(9):2049–2062, 2013.

[12] R. Meester. *A Natural Introduction to Probability Theory.* 2004.

[13] J. Niedermayer, A. Züfle, T. Emrich, M. Renz, N. Mamoulis, L. Chen, and H.-P. Kriegel. Probabilistic nearest neighbor queries on uncertain moving object trajectories. *PVLDB*, 7(3):205–216, 2013.

[14] D. Pfoser and C. S. Jensen. Capturing the uncertainty of moving-object representations. In *SSD*, pages 111–132, 1999.

[15] Y. Tao, X. Xiao, and R. Cheng. Range search on multidimensional uncertain data. *ACM Trans. Database Syst.*, 32(3):15, 2007.

[16] G. Trajcevski, O. Wolfson, K. Hinrichs, and S. Chamberlain. Managing uncertainty in moving objects databases. *ACM Trans. Database Syst.*, 29(3):463–507, 2004.

[17] X. Xie, M. L. Yiu, R. Cheng, and H. Lu. Scalable evaluation of trajectory queries over imprecise location data. *IEEE Trans. Knowl. Data Eng.*, Accppted in 2013.

[18] C. Xu, Y. Gu, L. Chen, J. Qiao, and G. Yu. Interval reverse nearest neighbor queries on uncertain data with markov correlations. In *ICDE*, pages 170–181, 2013.

[19] J. Yuan, Y. Zheng, X. Xie, and G. Sun. Driving with knowledge from the physical world. In *KDD*, pages 316–324, 2011.

[20] Y. Zhang, X. Lin, W. Zhang, J. Wang, and Q. Lin. Effectively indexing the uncertain space. *IEEE Trans. Knowl. Data Eng.*, 22(9):1247–1261, 2010.

[21] Y. Zhang, W. Zhang, Q. Lin, and X. Lin. Effectively indexing the multi-dimensional uncertain objects for range searching. In *EDBT*, pages 504–515, 2012.

[22] K. Zheng, G. Trajcevski, X. Zhou, and P. Scheuermann. Probabilistic range queries for uncertain trajectories on road networks. In *EDBT*, pages 283–294, 2011.

[23] K. Zheng, Y. Zheng, X. Xie, and X. Zhou. Reducing uncertainty of low-sampling-rate trajectories. In *ICDE*, pages 1144–1155, 2012.

Efficient Computation of Trips with Friends and Families

Tanzima Hashem[1], Sukarna Barua[2], Mohammed Eunus Ali[3], Lars Kulik[4], and Egemen Tanin[5]
[1,2,3]Dept of CSE, Bangladesh University of Engineering and Technology, Bangladesh
[4,5]Dept of CIS, University of Melbourne, Australia
{[1]tanzimahashem, [2]sukarnabarua, [3]eunus@cse.buet.ac.bd} {[4]lkulik, [5]etanin@unimelb.edu.au}

ABSTRACT

A group of friends located at their working places may want to plan a trip to visit a shopping center, have dinner at a restaurant, watch a movie at a theater, and then finally return to their homes with the minimum total trip distance. For a group of spatially dispersed users a group trip planning (GTP) query returns points of interests (POIs) of different types such as a shopping center, a restaurant and a movie theater that minimize the aggregate trip distance for the group. The aggregate trip distance could be the sum or maximum of the trip distances of all users in the group, where the users travel from their source locations via the jointly visited POIs to their individual destinations. In this paper, we develop both optimal and approximation algorithms for GTP queries for both *Euclidean space* and *road networks*. Processing GTP queries in real time is a computational challenge as trips involve POIs of multiple types and computation of aggregate trip distances. We develop novel techniques to refine the POI search space for a GTP query based on geometric properties of ellipses, which in turn significantly reduces the number of aggregate trip distance computations. An extensive set of experiments on a real and synthetic datasets shows that our approach outperforms the most competitive approach on an average by three orders of magnitude in terms of processing time.

1 Introduction

The proliferation of social networking sites enables friends and families to remain connected virtually at all times. Since physical meetups are equally important for maintaining and fostering relationships, location-based social networking applications offer a range of services for groups such as finding a nearest meeting place or sending alerts if friends are nearby. In the near future, we envision an application that would enable a group to plan a trip with the minimum aggregate trip distance for visiting multiple types of points of interests (POIs) such as a shopping center, a restaurant and a movie theater. Trip planning for a single user has been studied in the literature [4, 13, 24] due to its wide range of applications. In this paper, we address *group trip planing (GTP) queries and its variants* that allow a group to compute a trip that minimizes the total or maximum travel cost for the group members.

Permission to make digital or hard copies of all or part of this work for personal or classroom use is granted without fee provided that copies are not made or distributed for profit or commercial advantage and that copies bear this notice and the full citation on the first page. Copyrights for components of this work owned by others than ACM must be honored. Abstracting with credit is permitted. To copy otherwise, or republish, to post on servers or to redistribute to lists, requires prior specific permission and/or a fee. Request permissions from Permissions@acm.org.
CIKM '15 October 19-23, 2015, Melbourne, VIC, Australia
© 2015 ACM. ISBN 978-1-4503-3794-6/15/10 ...$15.00.
DOI: http://dx.doi.org/10.1145/2806416.2806433.

Given a set of source-destination pairs for a group of users and their required types of POIs, a GTP query returns a POI for each type that together minimize the aggregate trip distance. The group may specify the order of visiting POI types (e.g., a restaurant after a shopping center) or keep it flexible. A group may be also interested in finding k sets of POIs that provide the k smallest aggregate trip distances in order to select the set based on other parameters such as budget, food or movie preference. In this paper, we develop efficient algorithms for *kGTP* queries that apply to both Euclidean spaces and road networks.

The aggregate trip distance is the sum of the trip distances of all users in the group, where each user's trip starts from the user's source location, goes through POIs one after another, and ends at the user's destination. Figure 1 shows an example of a GTP query for $k = 1$ in a road network, where a group of three users with their source destination pairs $(s_1,d_1),(s_2,d_2),(s_3,d_3)$, finds a trip (shown in blue lines) through two POIs (p and q) of different types, that minimizes the total travel distance. On the other hand, if group members use a shared vehicle to travel the common part of the trip via the POIs, the aggregate trip distance is the sum of the trip distance from the first to the last POI and the trip distances for each individual group member to travel from their source locations to the first POI and from the last POI to their destinations.

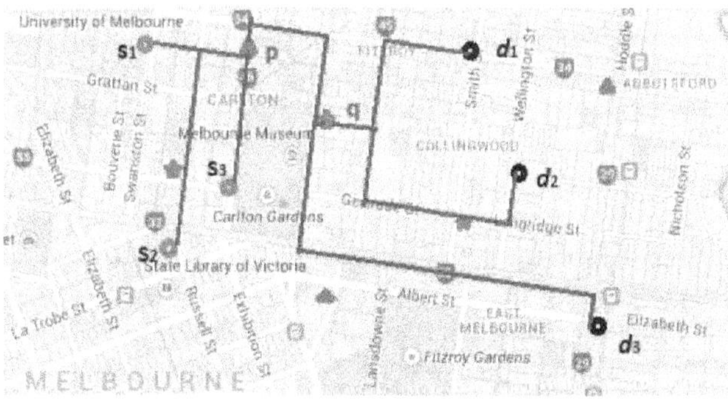

Figure 1: An example of a GTP query for $k = 1$.

Sometimes a group member who is located far away from the other members in the group may need to travel a much longer distance, if the POIs are close to other group members. In such a scenario, instead of minimizing the total travel distance, the group may want to find the set of POIs that minimize the maximum trip distance for the group. Our kGTP algorithms work for all these variants of aggregate functions, i.e., for minimizing both the total and maximum trip distance of a group.

A kGTP query has been introduced in [8], where the authors have developed kGTP algorithms for the *Euclidean space*. However, the developed algorithm in [8] requires significant time (17 minutes on commodity hardware) to find four trips by processing a single

GTP query for *only* three types of POIs and with a group size of 8. Moreover, in a real-life scenario the movement of users is restricted to *road networks* and processing queries in road networks involve complex distance computations. It is not obvious to extend the algorithm in [8] for road networks. To overcome these limitations, we propose efficient algorithms that are one to three orders of magnitudes faster than the algorithm in [8] and can evaluate *k*GTP queries in a few seconds *for both Euclidean space and road networks.*

The major challenge to process *k*GTP queries efficiently depends on identifying POIs from a huge POI database that minimize the aggregate trip distance. The key idea of our approach comes from efficient POI pruning strategies to limit the search space to a smaller elliptical area. We prove that the refined search space can be an elliptical region with foci at two centroids of source and destination locations, respectively, and the major axis of the ellipse is equal to the *average of computed k^{th} smallest total trip distance* for the initial POI set. The smaller search space only requires access to a small number of POIs, which reduces the number of aggregate distance computations and incurs less I/Os and computational cost. Though elliptical properties have been explored in the literature [4, 13, 14, 24, 28] to prune POIs, these pruning techniques are not applicable for *k*GTP queries. We develop a novel pruning technique, which is the base to process *k*GTP queries in real time. Further, we propose an efficient aggregate trip distance computation technique by exploiting an optimal substructure property of trips.

Based on the developed elliptical punning strategies, we propose range-based and incremental algorithms to evaluate *k*GTP queries. The key difference between these two algorithms is in the way they retrieve POIs from the database. The range-based algorithm executes a range query to retrieve POIs within the elliptical search space and finds the optimal *k*GTP query answer from those retrieved candidate POIs. On the other hand, the incremental *k*GTP algorithm retrieves the group nearest POIs with respect to two centroids of source and destination locations and gradually refines the search space. Specifically, with the incremental retrieval of a POI, the aggregate trip distance becomes smaller or remains same, and the elliptical search space whose major axis is equal to the average aggregate trip distance is updated; the search for POIs ends when all POIs within the elliptical region have been retrieved.

Computing the answer for a trip planning query has been shown as an NP-hard problem if the order of visiting POI types is not specified [4, 13, 24]. For a large scale POI set and a large group size, our proposed optimal algorithms cannot compute answers for *non ordered kGTP queries* in a reasonable time. To further minimize the processing overhead in such a case, we propose an approximation algorithm based on our incremental *k*GTP algorithm that can trade accuracy for efficiency. We develop a technique to derive the lower and upper bound of the accuracy for the computed *k*GTP answers. Using our approximation algorithm, the group can set any value for the approximation ratio, where an approximation ratio of 1 represents the exact query answer.

We have conducted extensive experimental study using both real and synthetic datasets. Our solutions outperform our benchmark approach by one to three orders of magnitude in terms of both processing and I/O overhead. Similar to other spatial query types [23], experiments show that our incremental approach performs better than the range based technique for *k*GTP queries.

In summary, the contributions of this paper are as follows:

- We develop an efficient pruning technique that refines the search space to an elliptical area, where the length of the major axis is set as the average trip distance of group members.
- We propose optimal algorithms to evaluate *k*GTP queries with reduced computational overhead.
- For a large scale POI set and a large group size, we propose an approximation algorithm that can process *k*GTP queries efficiently if the order of visiting POIs is not specified.
- We validate the efficiency of our algorithms through extensive experiments using both real and synthetic datasets.

2 Related Work

Query processing in spatial databases has been extensively studied in the forms of nearest neighbor (NN), group nearest neighbor (GNN), route/path planning, and trip planning (TP) queries in both Euclidean space and road networks. Most of these techniques assume that POIs are indexed using *R*-tree [6] or its variant R^*-tree [2]. A *k*NN query [11, 20] and a *k*GNN query [10, 18, 19, 25, 27] return *k* POIs that have the *k* smallest distances with respect to a single user and a group of users, respectively.

A GNN query is different from a GTP query as in a GNN query, group members meet at a single POI and the aggregate distance is measured with respect to the POI and current locations of group members, whereas in a GTP query, group members visit POIs of different types and the aggregate distance is measured with respect to POIs and sets of source and destination locations of group members. The minimum bounding method (MBM) proposed in [19] visits *R*-tree nodes in order of the minimum aggregate distance from all query points and only visits the nodes that may contain candidate POIs. We use MBM for evaluating GNN queries in finding an initial set of POIs in our approach.

Generalized traveling salesman problems, trip and route planning queries have been addressed in the literature [3, 4, 12, 13, 16, 17, 21, 22, 24, 26], where a single user visits POIs of different types with the minimum travel distance. Li et al. [13] have proposed approximation algorithms to find a trip that minimizes the total travel distance. In [24], Sharifzadeh et al. have developed algorithms to find a route with the minimum length passing through a set of POIs in a particular order from the source location of a user. Chen et al. [4] have proposed a multi-rule partial sequenced route (MRPSR) that provides a uniform framework to evaluate both of the above mentioned trip planning variants [13, 24]. All these existing techniques assume *a single user*, and thus are not applicable for a group. Evaluating trips for each group members independently until *k* trips for the group with the *k* smallest aggregate trip distances have been identified would be an exhaustive search on the database and incur extremely high processing overhead.

Recently, Hashem et al. [8] have proposed a method to compute *k*GTP queries in the Euclidean space. However, the proposed algorithm is not scalable and efficient enough to answer *k*GTP queries in real time (e.g., computing four best trips involving two POI types and 16 group members require 16 minutes on commodity hardware!). Another major limitation of their approach is that it uses independent *R*-tree for each POI type, and a real California dataset [1] comprising of 63 categories require 63 different *R*-trees, which is not practical. Moreover, computing *k*GTP queries for a road network involve complex distance computations and thus we cannot extend the algorithm in [8] for road networks as it would make the query processing overhead even worse. In this paper, we propose an efficient solution that can evaluate a *k*GTP query and its variants in a few seconds for both Euclidean space and road networks.

The key idea of our efficient algorithm is the novel search space refinement technique based on geometric properties of ellipses. Though there exist pruning techniques [4, 13, 14, 24] that refine the search space as an elliptical area for other variants of spatial queries, the novelty of our technique is how we set foci and significantly reduce the length of the major axis of the ellipse for processing *k*GTP queries. In [4, 13, 24], the authors simply show that any POI outside an ellipse with foci at the user's source and destination, respectively and the major axis equal to the user's trip distance based on retrieved POIs can be pruned. In [14], the authors refine the search space as an ellipse for GNN queries, where the foci are the locations of any two group members and the major axis equals to the smallest total distance of group members from retrieved POIs. Thus, the length of the major axis (i.e., the area of the ellipse) increases with the increase of the group size. We set the foci of the ellipse at geometric centroid of source and destination locations of group members, respectively and the length of the major axis as the *average* trip distance of group members, which is n (group size) times less than that of the state-of-the-art technique.

3 Problem Formulation

Let O represent a set of POIs in a two-dimensional space, $T = \{t_1, t_2, ..., t_m\}$ represent a set of m POI types, p_{t_i} represent the location of a POI of a type t_i. For two point locations p and q, Function $Dist(p,q)$ returns the distance between p and q, where the distance can be measured in the Euclidean space or road networks. The Euclidean distance is measured as the length of the line connecting p and q. On the other hand, the road network distance is measured as the length of the shortest path between p and q on a given road network $G = (V, E, W)$, where each vertex $v \in V$ represents a road junction, each edge $(u, v) \in E$ represents a direct path connecting u and v, and each weight $w_{u,v} \in W$ represents the length of the direct path represented by the edge (u, v).

Let s_i and d_i represent source and destination locations, respectively, of a user u_i. For a set of POIs of m types, $\{p_{t_1}, p_{t_2}, \ldots, p_{t_m}\}$, the trip distance of a user u_i is computed as $Dist(s_i, p_{t_1}) + \sum_{j=1}^{m-1} Dist(p_{t_j}, p_{t_{j+1}}) + Dist(p_{t_m}, d_i)$. In this paper, we focus on aggregate functions SUM and MAX that minimize total and maximum trip distance of group members, respectively.

For an aggregate function f = SUM, the aggregate trip distance of a group $U = \{u_1, u_2, \ldots, u_n\}$ for a given set of POIs from m types, $\{p_{t_1}, p_{t_2}, \ldots, p_{t_m}\}$, vary depending on whether group members share a vehicle for the common part of the trip or not. If group members travel independently then the aggregate trip distance is computed as $\sum_{i=1}^{n} Dist(s_i, p_{t_1}) + n \times (\sum_{j=1}^{m-1} Dist(p_{t_j}, p_{t_{j+1}})) + \sum_{i=1}^{n} Dist(p_{t_m}, d_i)$. If group members share a vehicle for the common part of the trip then the aggregate trip distance is computed as $\sum_{i=1}^{n} Dist(s_i, p_{t_1}) + \sum_{j=1}^{m-1} Dist(p_{t_j}, p_{t_{j+1}}) + \sum_{i=1}^{n} Dist(p_{t_m}, d_i)$. If some of the group members share a vehicle for the common path or some part of the common path, the computation of the aggregate trip distance can be adjusted accordingly. On the other hand, for f = MAX, the aggregate trip distance is computed as $\max_{i=1}^{n}\{Dist(s_i, p_{t_1}) + \sum_{j=1}^{m-1} Dist(p_{t_j}, p_{t_{j+1}}) + Dist(p_{t_m}, d_i)\}$.

The order of visiting POIs can be specified by the group. If the group fixes the order of visiting POIs, e.g., a shopping center before a restaurant then a movie theater, then the query is called an *ordered GTP query*. If the order of visiting POIs is kept partially or fully flexible, e.g., a shopping center and a restaurant can be visited in any order, then the query is called a *non ordered GTP query*. For the ordered GTP query, the aggregate trip distance for a POI set consisting of a POI from each required type is computed according to the specified order, whereas for the non ordered GTP query, the aggregate trip distance is computed for every possible order of POI types, and the minimum of these aggregate trip distances is considered as the aggregate trip distance for the POI set.

A group may be interested in k trips and selects one based on other factors such as budget, or preference. A kGTP query is formally defined as follows:

DEFINITION 1. *(k **Group Trip Planning (kGTP) Queries**). Given a set of n source locations $S = \{s_1, s_2, ..., s_n\}$, a set of n corresponding destination locations $D = \{d_1, d_2, ..., d_n\}$ of the group members, a set of POI types $T = \{t_1, t_2, ..., t_m\}$, an aggregate function f, and k, the kGTP query returns k sets of POIs that have the k smallest values for aggregate trip distances, where each POI set includes m POIs $\{p_{t_1}, p_{t_2}, \ldots, p_{t_m}\}$, and the group members travel from their source locations via the jointly visited POIs to their individual destinations.*

Note that group members may use transports of varying speed and need different time to travel the same distance. In this paper, we assume that users who arrive earlier at any POI can wait for others and we leave the synchronization of users in terms of time as a future scope of our work.

4 System Overview

We assume a client-server architecture, where the client is the user that acts as a coordinator for the group and the server is the LSP that evaluates kGTP queries. Every group member sends her source and destination locations to the coordinator and the coordinator sends the query along with source and destination locations of the group members to the LSP. The coordinator communicates with the LSP via mobile networks or the Internet. The POIs are indexed using an R^*-tree on the LSP's database. An important benefit of our approach is that it does not need any modification in the existing indexing methods used to process other types of spatial queries. The road network is maintained in a graph structure. The LSP evaluates the query and returns the answer to the coordinator, who forwards the answer to other group members.

5 Our Approaches for kGTP Queries

In this section, we propose optimal and approximation algorithms to process kGTP queries. The key idea comes from the refinement of the search space based on elliptical properties. We present two straightforward techniques (Lemmas 5.1 and 5.2) to refine the search space using multiple ellipses for an aggregate function SUM. The smaller search space causes less POI retrievals from the database and avoids the computation of trips through a large number of POIs, which significantly reduces both I/O and computational overhead. By exploiting geometric properties, we develop a novel and an efficient pruning technique (Lemma 5.4) to refine the search space to a single ellipse, where the foci of the ellipse are the centroids of the source and destination locations, respectively, and the major axis of the ellipse is equal to the *average of kth smallest total trip distance* computed based on current set of retrieved POIs from the database. Based on the proposed refinement of the search space, we develop our range based and incremental algorithms to process kGTP queries in Sections 5.1 and 5.2, respectively.

In our straightforward pruning techniques, the POI search space is refined using an individual or a total trip distance computed based on current set of retrieved POIs from the database. The following two lemmas refine the search space by integrating n individual ellipses:

LEMMA 5.1. *Let $ATDist[k]$ be the kth smallest total trip distance of the group computed based on current set of retrieved POIs from the database, and E_i represent an ellipse with foci at s_i and d_i and the major axis equal to $TDist_i[k]$, where $TDist_i[k]$ is the individual trip distance of user u_i in $ATDist[k]$. A POI or an R^*-tree node can be pruned if it is located outside $\cup_{i=1}^{n} E_i$.*

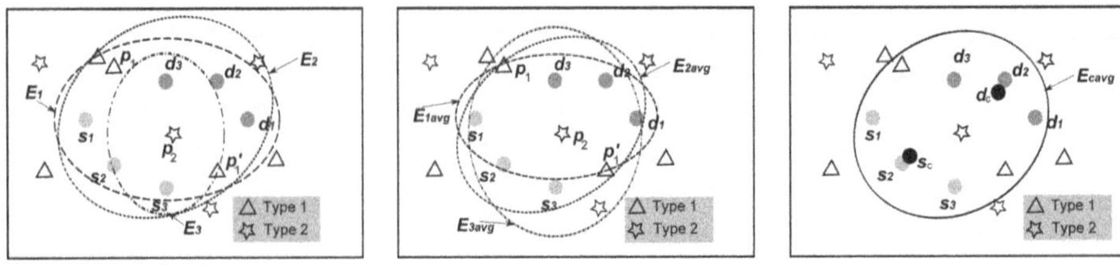

(a) (b) (c)

Figure 2: Refined elliptical search regions obtained by Lemma 5.1 (a), Lemma 5.2 (b), and Lemma 5.4 (c).

PROOF. Let a POI or an R^*-tree node p be located outside $\cup_{i=1}^{n} E_i$. According to elliptical property, since p is located outside E_i, the trip distance of each user u_i via p, i.e., the trip distance from s_i to d_i via p is greater than $TDist_i[k]$. Thus, the total trip distance of a group of n users via p is greater than $\sum_{i=1}^{n} TDist_i[k]$ and we know $ATDist[k] <= \sum_{i=1}^{n} TDist_i[k]$. Thus p located outside $\cup_{i=1}^{n} E_i$ can be pruned as p cannot further minimize $ATDist[k]$. □

LEMMA 5.2. *Let E_{iavg} represent an ellipse with foci at s_i and d_i and the major axis equal to $\frac{ATDist[k]}{n}$, where $ATDist[k]$ is the kth smallest aggregate trip distance of the group computed based on current set of retrieved POIs from the database for $f =$ SUM and n is group size. A POI or an R^*-tree node can be pruned if the POI or the R^*-tree node is located outside $\cup_{i=1}^{n} E_{iavg}$.*

PROOF. Let a POI or an R^*-tree node p be located outside $\cup_{i=1}^{n} E_{iavg}$. According to elliptical property, since p is located outside E_{iavg}, the trip distance of a user u_i via p, i.e., the trip distance from s_i to d_i via p is greater than $\frac{ATDist[k]}{n}$. Thus, the total trip distance of a group of n users via p is greater than $ATDist[k]$ and can be pruned as p cannot further minimize $ATDist[k]$. □

Consider an example scenario for a group size $n = 3$, where $\{s_1, s_2, s_3\}$ represent sources, $\{d_1, d_2, d_3\}$ represent destinations, and $\{p_1, p_1', p_2\}$ represent retrieved POIs from the database. Figures 2 (a) and (b) use Lemmas 5.1 and 5.2, respectively to refine the search space. Any POI that falls outside of $E_1 \cup E_2 \cup E_3$ or $E_{1avg} \cup E_{2avg} \cup E_{3avg}$ can be safely pruned, as it cannot further minimize the current aggregate trip distance for SUM. Note that we use Lemma 5.2 when the distance between every source-destination pair is less than or equal to $ATDist[k]/n$.

Intuitively, if source destinations pairs are spread far away and the overlaps among the ellipses are small, then the integrated area of n ellipses may cover a large portion of the full space. To address this limitation, we develop an efficient technique to bound the search space using a single ellipse. In a straightforward way to refine the search space, we can select any source destination pair as foci and set the major axis length of the ellipse equal to the kth total trip distance computed based on current set of retrieved POIs from the database. In this case, the length of the major axis would increase with the increase of group size and sparse distribution of source destination pairs. In this paper, we reduce the length of the major axis from the kth total trip distance to the average of the kth total trip distance.

We first prove the geometric property stated in Lemma 5.3, and then use this property to give a tight bound for the refined search space in Lemma 5.4.

LEMMA 5.3. *Let $\{l_1, l_2, \ldots, l_n\}$ represent a set of n locations, l_c the geometric centroid of $\{l_1, l_2, \ldots, l_n\}$ in the Euclidean space, p a POI or an R^*-tree node, and $Dist(.,.)$ return the Euclidean distance between two points. Then we have $\sum_{i=1}^{n} Dist(l_i, p) \geq n \times Dist(l_c, p)$.*

PROOF. Let (x_i, y_i) and (x_c, y_c) represent coordinates for a location l_i and l_c, respectively, in the two-dimensional space. Assume

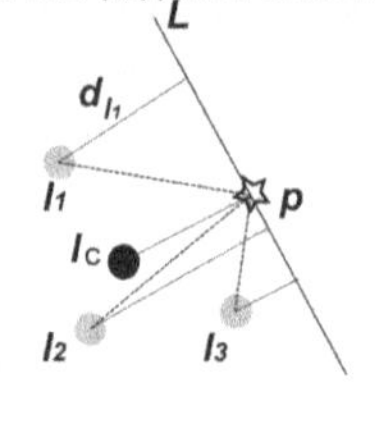

Figure 3: Lemma 5.3 for $\sum_{i=1}^{3} Dist(l_i, p) > 3 \times Dist(l_c, p)$.

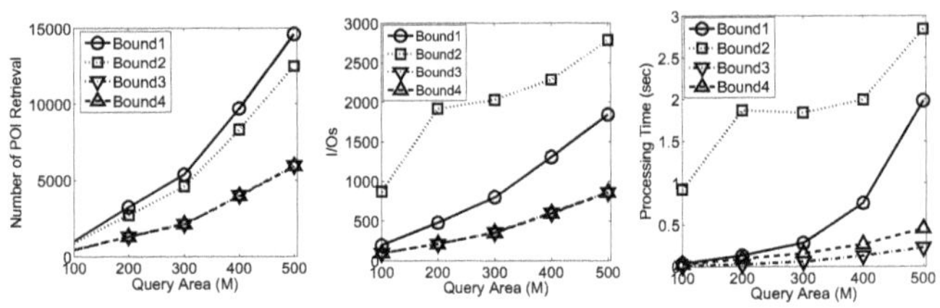

Figure 4: For aggregate function SUM, (a) POIs retrieval, (b) I/O, and (c) processing overhead for different bounds.

that L be a line perpendicular to the line connecting l_c and p and passes through p. Without loss of generality, Figure 3 shows a scenario for $n = 3$. The distance from l_i to L is denoted with d_{l_i}.

Let the equation of the line L be: $ax + by + c = 0$, where a, b, and c are constants. Thus, d_{l_i} can be expressed as follows:

$$d_{l_i} = \frac{1}{\sqrt{(a^2+b^2)}} |ax_i + by_i + c|$$

Since $Dist(l_i, p) \geq d_{l_i}$, when summing up for n distances, we have

$$\Rightarrow \sum_{i=1}^{n} Dist(l_i, p) \geq \frac{1}{\sqrt{(a^2+b^2)}} |a(\sum_{i=1}^{n} x_i) + b(\sum_{i=1}^{n} y_i) + n \times c| \quad (1)$$

Since $x_c = \sum_{i=1}^{n} x_i/n$ and $y_c = \sum_{i=1}^{n} y_i/n$, from Equation 1 we have

$$\sum_{i=1}^{n} Dist(l_i, p) \geq n \times \frac{1}{\sqrt{(a^2+b^2)}} |ax_c + by_c + c| \quad (2)$$

Since $Dist(l_c, p) = \frac{1}{\sqrt{(a^2+b^2)}} |ax_c + by_c + c|$, from Equation 2 we have $\sum_{i=1}^{n} Dist(l_i, p) \geq n \times Dist(l_c, p)$. □

LEMMA 5.4. *Let s_c and d_c represent geometric centroids for sets of source and destination locations $\{s_1, s_2, \ldots, s_n\}$ and $\{d_1, d_2, \ldots, d_n\}$, respectively, in the Euclidean space and $ATDist[k]$ represent k^{th} smallest aggregate trip distance computed based on current set of retrieved POIs from the database for $f =$ SUM. A POI or an R^*-tree node can be pruned if the POI or the R^*-tree node is located outside an ellipse E_{cavg} whose foci are s_c and d_c, and the major axis is equal to $ATDist[k]/n$.*

PROOF. According to Lemma 5.3, for an arbitrary POI or an R^*-tree node p we have $\sum_{i=1}^{n} Dist(s_i, p) \geq n \times Dist(s_c, p)$ and

$\sum_{i=1}^{n} Dist(d_i, p) \geq n \times Dist(d_c, p)$. When summing up, we have

$$\sum_{i=1}^{n} (Dist(s_i, p) + Dist(d_i, p)) \geq n \times (Dist(s_c, p) + Dist(d_c, p)) \quad (3)$$

From elliptical property, we know that the distance between two foci via a point located outside the ellipse is greater than the length of the major axis of the ellipse. Thus for a POI or an R^*-tree node p' located outside of E_{cavg}, we have

$$(Dist(s_c, p') + Dist(d_c, p')) \geq \frac{ATDist[k]}{n} \quad (4)$$

Finally, from Equations 3 and 4, we have

$$\sum_{i=1}^{n} (Dist(s_i, p') + Dist(d_i, p')) \geq ATDist[k] \quad (5)$$

The aggregate trip distance can be measured in both Euclidean space and road networks. Lemma 5.3 assumes that $Dist(.,.)$ function returns Euclidean distance between two points. Thus, for Euclidean space, from Equation 5, we can conclude that a POI or an R^*-tree node p' located outside E_{cavg} can be pruned as the aggregate trip distance via p' is greater than $ATDist[k]$.

For road networks, $ATDist[k]$ is measured in terms of road network distance and the left part of Equation 5 represents Euclidean distance. According to Euclidean distance property, the road network distance between two points is greater or equal to the Euclidean distance of those points. Thus, Equation 5 also holds if $Dist(.,.)$ function returns road network distance between two points and a POI or an R^*-tree node p' located outside E_{cavg} can be pruned as it cannot further minimize $ATDist[k]$. □

In summary, according to Lemma 5.1, all POIs that are inside the boundary computed as the union of n ellipses with foci (s_i, d_i) and major axis $TDist_i[k]$, need to be considered in a kGTP query. According to Lemma 5.2, the POIs that are inside the boundary computed as the union of n ellipses with foci (s_i, d_i) and major axis $ATDist[k]/n$, need to be retrieved for kGTP computation. On the other hand, according to Lemma 5.4, we only need to retrieve POIs that are inside the ellipse with foci (s_c, d_c) and major axis $ATDist[k]/n$. Figure 2(c) uses Lemma 5.4 to refine the search space. Thus, any of the three bounds (Lemma 5.1, Lemma 5.2, and Lemma 5.4) can be considered independently to refine the search region. Alternatively, one can use intersection region of all the three bounds to define the search region for candidate POIs for the answer of a kGTP query.

We have performed an empirical study (Figure 4) on a retrieved POI set and observed that the number of POIs contained in the search region, and the required number of I/Os and time to retrieve these POIs, are much less for Lemma 5.4 (Bound 3) than the other two Bounds (Lemma 5.1-Bound 1 and Lemma 5.2-Bound 2). We have also observed that if we combine all three bounds (i.e., Bound 4), we see that the number of POIs retrieval and I/Os are approximately equal for both Bound 3 and Bound 4 while Bound 4 incurs slightly higher processing overhead. So apparently, we gain no benefit using Bound 4 (all bounds combined) in terms of POIs and I/Os rather incur higher processing overhead. Hence, we use Lemma 5.4 (Bound 3) as our bound to refine the search space.

For $f =$ MAX, Lemma 5.4 can be modified in terms of the length of the major axis, which is set to $ATDist[k]$ instead of $ATDist[k]/n$. From Equation 3, we observe that the average trip distance of group members via any POI p, i.e., $\frac{1}{n} \times \sum_{i=1}^{n} (Dist(s_i, p) + Dist(d_i, p))$ is greater than or equal to $Dist(s_c, p) + Dist(d_c, p)$.

Since for a POI or an R^*-tree node p' located outside E_{cavg}, $(Dist(s_c, p') + Dist(d_c, p')) \geq ATDist[k]$ and the maximum trip distance via p' is greater than or equal to the average trip distance of group members, the maximum trip distance via p' is greater than $ATDist[k]$. Thus, p' can be safely pruned for both Euclidean space and road networks. Note that the kth maximum trip distance represents an individual user's trip distance whereas the kth total trip distance represents the summation of trip distances of group members. Thus, increasing the length of the major axis from the average of the kth smallest total trip distance to the kth smallest maximum trip distance changes the area of the refined search region slightly.

5.1 A Range Based κGTP Algorithm

In our first approach, we propose a range query based optimal kGTP algorithm that works in three steps. First, the algorithm retrieves a set of POIs using a heuristic. Second, based on the initial set of POIs, the algorithm refines the search space and executes a range query to retrieve POIs inside the refined search space. Finally, the algorithm applies a dynamic programming to find the optimal answer for a kGTP query from the reduced set of candidate POIs.

Algorithm 1 shows the steps of our range based algorithm for kGTP queries. The algorithm takes a set of n source locations $S = \{s_1, s_2, \ldots, s_n\}$, n destination locations $D = \{d_1, d_2, \ldots, d_n\}$, a category set $T = \{t_1, t_2, \ldots, t_m\}$, and the number of required smallest trips k. The output of the algorithm is a set $A[1..k]$ of trips with k smallest aggregate trip distances.

The algorithm first finds an initial set of POIs that includes at least k possible trips using Function *FindInitialSet*. For this purpose, any heuristic that retrieves POIs containing the required number of trips can be applied. We use heuristics based on the group nearest neighbors of source and destination locations [8] to retrieve the initial POIs.

After retrieving the initial set IA of POIs, Function *RefineSearch* bounds the search space as a smaller region that includes POIs for k trips with the smallest aggregate trip distances. We use Lemma 5.4 for this purpose. Though for a non ordered kGTP query, *RefineSearch* considers different orders of POI types to determine the current k^{th} smallest aggregate trip distance $ATDist[k]$, intuitively the probability is high that $ATDist[k]$ for a non ordered kGTP query would be smaller than that of an ordered kGTP query. Note that a smaller $ATDist[k]$ represents a smaller POI search space.

After deriving the required search space SA, the algorithm executes a range query by using Function *RangeQuery* and retrieves all POIs of required types specified in $T = \{t_1, t_2, \ldots, t_m\}$ that fall inside the range SA. Finally, the algorithm runs a dynamic programming using Function *RefineAnswer* to find k trips with the k smallest aggregate trip distances from the retrieved set of POIs.

Algorithm 1: Range_kGTP(S, D, T, k)

Input : $S = \{s_1, s_2, \ldots, s_n\}$, $D = \{d_1, d_2, \ldots, d_n\}$, T, and k.
Output: A set of trips with k smallest aggregate trip distances, $A[1..k]$.

$IA \leftarrow FindInitialSet(S, D, T, k)$;
$SA \leftarrow RefineSearch(S, D, k, IA)$;
$CA \leftarrow RangeQuery(SA, T)$;
$A \leftarrow RefineAnswer(S, D, T, k, CA)$;
return A;

RefineAnswer runs a dynamic programming algorithm over the retrieved candidate POIs in CA to determine k POI sets with k smallest aggregate trip distances. For space constraint, we only discuss the dynamic programming algorithm of ordered kGTP queries for $f =$ SUM. A trip distance table M consisting of m columns (for m types) of cells (where each cell represents a POI) is maintained for this purpose. Each table cell $M^j_{t_i}$ stores k optimal partial trip distances starting from source locations, visiting one POI of each type t_l $(1 \leq l < i)$ and ending at the POI $p^j_{t_i}$, the jth POI of type t_i.

For each POI $p^j_{t_1}$, we calculate optimal distances as the sum of distances from all source locations to $p^j_{t_1}$. Then for each POI $p^j_{t_i}$ of intermediate columns, we calculate k optimal distances using stored optimal distances at column t_{i-1} of M and distances of $p^j_{t_i}$ from POIs of type t_{i-1}. We keep k minimum such distances. Finally, for each POI $p^j_{t_m}$ at the last column, we compute k optimal distances using three distances: (i) stored optimal distances at column t_{m-1}, (ii) distances of $p^j_{t_m}$ from POIs of type t_{m-1}, and (iii) distance of $p^j_{t_m}$ from all destination locations. Finally, we select k optimal trip distances among all trip distances of last column POIs.

For non ordered kGTP queries for $f = \text{SUM}$, the above process is repeated for every possible set of order types and thus, cannot compute the answer in reasonable time for a large scale POI dataset and a large group size. To overcome this limitation, we develop an incremental kGTP algorithm that can compute both exact and approximate answers with reduced processing overhead.

5.2 An Incremental kGTP Algorithm

We develop an incremental algorithm to evaluate kGTP queries. The algorithm updates the refined POI search space with the incremental retrieval of POIs until the kGTP query answer has been identified. Since the refined search space continuously decreases or remains same, this incremental approach only accesses necessary POIs that are required to find the optimal answer, whereas, the range based approach may need to access some extra POIs because the required search space is bounded based on an initial POI set. An additional benefit of our incremental algorithm is that it can also approximate kGTP query answers with accuracy guarantee. When POI dataset and group size are large, an approximation algorithm is a good choice for processing non ordered kGTP queries (an NP hard problem) with reduced processing overhead.

The algorithm allows a group to specify the required bound for the accuracy according to the requirement of the group. For example, if users specify that they are happy with a trip taking at most 20% more travel distance than the optimal trip, then the algorithm stops as soon as they satisfy the answer with the required quality specified by the user. We define *accuracy meter* Q as the ratio of upper bound and lower bound of the kth smallest aggregate trip distance. For example, if the optimal aggregate trip distance for a group is 100 and users want the guarantee that their reported answer should not be higher than 150, then they will set Q as 1.5. If $Q = 1$, the algorithm returns optimal kGTP answers.

5.2.1 Lower and Upper Bound Properties

The algorithm incrementally retrieves group nearest POIs with respect to source centroid s_c and destination centroid d_c, where s_c and d_c are computed as $\sum_{i=1}^{n} s_i/n$ and $\sum_{i=1}^{n} d_i/n$, respectively. We compute the kth smallest aggregate trip distance $ATDist[k]$ from the set of *already* retrieved POIs from the database, which act as an upper bound of the kth smallest aggregate trip distance computed on all POIs in the database.

On the other hand, to compute the lower bound of the kth smallest aggregate trip distance, we exploit the available information from the already retrieved group nearest POIs with respect to s_c and d_c. Without loss of generality, assume that at any stage of the execution of the algorithm, j group nearest POIs with respect to s_c and d_c have been retrieved. Assume that E_j represents an ellipse with foci s_c and d_c and the major axis equal to $d_{min}(p)$, i.e., the distance from s_c to d_c via the jth group nearest POI p. At this stage of execution, we know locations of all POIs inside E_j as the distance from s_c to d_c via any POI inside E_j is less than the length of the major axis of E_j and has been already retrieved from the database before p.

According to Lemma 5.4, we can infer that the aggregate trip distance for S and D via any POI outside E_j is greater than $d_{min}(p)$. Thus, $n \times d_{min}(p)$ and $d_{min}(p)$ represent lower bounds of the kth smallest total and maximum trip distance computed on all POIs in the database, respectively. Once the lower bound equals to or greater than the upper bound (i.e., $ATDist[k]$), the optimal answer for the kGTP query has been found.

Algorithm 2: Inc_kGTP(S, D, T, k, Q)

```
Input  : S = {s1, s2, ..., sn}, D = {d1, d2, ..., dn}, T, k, and Q.
Output: A set of k trips, A[1..k], that satisfy Q.
P ← ∅;
end, init ← 0;
A[1..k] ← {∅};
ATDist[1..k] ← {∞};
Enqueue(Qp, root, 0);
while Qp is not empty and end = 0 do
    {p, dmin(p)} ← Dequeue(Qp);
    if dmin(p) ≥ ATDist[k]/(Q×n) then
        end ← 1;
    else if p is a POI and getCategory(p) ∈ T then
        P ← P ∪ p;
        if init = 0 and Include(P, T, k) = 1 then
            init ← 1;
            {A, ATDist} ← CompTrip(S, D, P, T, k);
        else if init = 1 then
            {A, ATDist} ← UpdtTrip(S, D, P, p, T, k);
        if dmin(p) ≥ ATDist[k]/(Q×n) then
            end ← 1;
    else
        for each child node pch of p do
            dmin(pch) ← MinDist(sc, dc, pch);
            if dmin(pch) ≤ ATDist[k]/(Q×n) then
                Enqueue(Qp, pch, dmin(pch));
return A;
```

5.2.2 Algorithm

Algorithm 2 shows the pseudocode for the incremental algorithm for processing kGTP queries for aggregate function $f = \text{SUM}$. The input to the algorithm are a set of n source locations $S = \{s_1, s_2, \ldots, s_n\}$, n destination locations $D = \{d_1, d_2, \ldots, d_n\}$, a type set $T = \{t_1, t_2, \ldots, t_m\}$, the number of required trips k, and an accuracy meter Q. The output of the algorithm is a set of k trips, $A[1..k]$, that satisfy Q. Thus, $A[j]$ stores the set of POIs of required types that provide j^{th} smallest total trip distance equal to or less than $ATDist[j]/Q$, for $1 <= j <= k$.

The algorithm adopts the best-first search technique to incrementally retrieve POIs/R^*-tree nodes in the increasing order of total distance of those POIs/nodes from two centroids s_c and d_c. It maintains a priority queue Q_p that is ordered based on the minimum total distance that is ordered based on $dmin(p)(= Dist(s_c, p) + Dist(d_c, p))$ for a POI/node p from s_c and d_c.

To remind the reader, the distance $d_{min}(p)$, i.e., the aggregate distance of the last retrieved POI/node from Q_p to s_c and d_c, represents the lower bound of the kth smallest aggregate trip distance. The distance $d_{min}(p)$ increases with the retrieval of POIs/nodes from Q_p. Hence, after retrieving every POI/node, $d_{min}(p)$ is updated.

On the other hand the upper bound $ATDist[k]$ is initialized as ∞ and does not change until A includes at least k POIs of a type in T and at least one POI of remaining types in T, which is checked using Function $Include(P,T,k)$. If yes, the algorithm determines trips with k smallest aggregate trip distances using Function $CompTrip$. If $Include(P,T,k)$ returns 0, the algorithm continues the retrieval of new POIs from the database.

Before dequeuing a new POI/node, the algorithm checks whether the current set of trips satisfy the condition for Q, i.e., $d_{min}(p) \geq ATDist[k]/(Q \times n)$. If the condition is true, the algorithm returns those trips as answers, otherwise dequeues a new element from Q_p and updates $d_{min}(p)$. If the dequeued element is a POI, Function $UpdtTrip$ checks whether it is possible to further minimize $ATDist[k]$ by computing new trips via the last dequeued POI. The process repeats until the accuracy of computed trips in A satisfy the required accuracy specified by the group.

For $f = \text{MAX}$, the algorithm works in a similar way to Algorithm 2 except that in Lines 8, 17 and 22, $ATDist[k]/(Q \times n)$ is replaced with $ATDist[k]/Q$.

Since the proof of correctness for our algorithm is similar to the proof of our pruning technique, we omit it for the space constraint.

6 Extensions

Our proposed incremental kGTP algorithm can be adapted to process two other variants: private kGTP queries and moving kGTP queries. We briefly discuss the adaptation procedures of these queries. However, since these problems are orthogonal to our main focus of the paper we leave the detail study as our future scope.

***A Private kGTP Query*:** In a private kGTP query, users do not disclose their source and destination locations to the LSP for privacy reasons [5, 7, 9]. The coordinator of the group sends s_c and d_c instead of actual source and destination locations to the LSP and retrieves a set of group nearest POIs with respect to s_c and d_c, where the set includes at least k POIs of a type in T and at least one POI of remaining types in T. From the retrieved set of POIs, the coordinator computes the lower and upper bounds of kth aggregate trip distance with respect to source and destination locations of group members and checks whether the required quality of identified k trips have been satisfied. If yes, the coordinator forward the kGTP query answer to group members. Otherwise, the coordinator continues retrieving more group nearest POIs from the LSP until k trips with required accuracy have been identified.

***A Moving kGTP Query*:** A moving kGTP query continuously returns k POI sets with k smallest aggregate trip distances for a moving group. A group may request a kGTP query to the LSP with respect to current locations of group members and then the query answer may invalidate when group members start to move due to change of road traffic [15]. A straightforward approach to solve this problem requires reevaluation of a kGTP query for every location update from group members, which will incur high processing overhead. To efficiently process moving kGTP queries, we can exploit one interesting property, i.e., the elliptical bound of the returned POI set, of our incremental approach. Since the coordinator has complete knowledge about all POIs inside this elliptical bound, which we call the known region, for any change of location of group members, the coordinator can validate whether it is possible to update answer from the available POIs. Specifically, as long as the refined search region (Lemma 5.4) with respect to changed locations remain inside the known region, the kGTP query answer can be identified from available POIs without contacting the LSP.

Parameter	Values	Default
Group size (n)	2, 4, 8, 16, 32	8
k	1, 2, 4, 8, 16	4
Number of types (m)	2, 3, 4, 5, 6	3
Query area (M) (in sq. units)	50, 100, 150, 200, 250	100
Quality (Q)	1, 1.25, 1.50, 1.75, 2	1
Dataset size (d_s)	5K, 10K, 15K, 20K	-
Dataset distribution	uniform, Zipfian	-

Table 1: Parameters used in our experiments

7 Experiments

We evaluate the performance of our two proposed kGTP query processing algorithms: (i) range based group trip planning (R-GTP) and (ii) incremental group trip planning (I-GTP). We first compare our approach with the existing hierarchical approach for group trip planning (GTP-HA) [8] in the Euclidian space. Since the GTP-HA approach is not scalable and is not easily adaptable for road networks, we devise a naive approach for group trip planning (N-GTP) and compare our approaches with N-GTP by varying a wide range of parameters.

Instead of using multiple R^*-trees (as used in [8]), we use a single R^*-tree to process kGTP queries using N-GTP. However, we have not applied any pruning technique to refine the search space. After retrieving POIs, for an ordered kGTP query N-GTP computes the distances from every source location to each retrieved POI of first type, distances among intermediary POIs (e.g., distances from each POI of the second type to each POI of the third type), and distances from each POI of the last type to every destination location. In the next step, N-GTP determines the k POI sets with k smallest aggregate trip distances as ordered kGTP query answers by using a dynamic programming algorithm over the retrieved POIs. For a non ordered kGTP query, the above process is repeated for every possible order of POI types and k POI sets that provide k smallest aggregate trip distances are selected as non ordered kGTP query answers.

We have evaluated our algorithms in both Euclidean and road network dataspaces using real and synthetic datasets. For real dataset, we use California [1] datasets. The POI set contains 87635 POIs of 63 different categories. The road network has 21048 nodes and 21693 edges. For synthetic datasets, we generate POIs in the dataspace using uniform and Zipfian distributions. All the dataspaces are normalized into 1000x1000 sq. units. We use an R-tree to index POIs and keep in-memory graph data structure to store the road network.

To evaluate our algorithms for kGTP queries in a wide range of settings, in our experiments, we vary the following parameters: (i) the group size n, (ii) the number of trips k, (iii) the number of POI types m in a trip, and (iii) the query area M, i.e., the minimum bounding rectangle covering the source and destination locations. To evaluate our approximation algorithm for kGTP queries, we vary the quality parameter Q. Table 1 summarizes the parameter names, their ranges, and default values used in our experiments.

In all experiments, we estimate the processing time and I/O to measure the efficiency of our algorithms. In each set of experiments, we run the experiment for 100 trip planning queries and present the average result. We run all experiments using a computer with Intel Core i5 2.30 GHz CPU and 4GB RAM.

7.1 Comparison with GTP-HA

We compare our R-GTP and I-GTP algorithms with the existing GTP-HA in the Euclidian space. Figure 5 shows the I/O cost and processing time of R-GTP, I-GTP, and GTP-HA for aggregate function SUM (a-b) and MAX (c-d) for different group sizes. We ob-

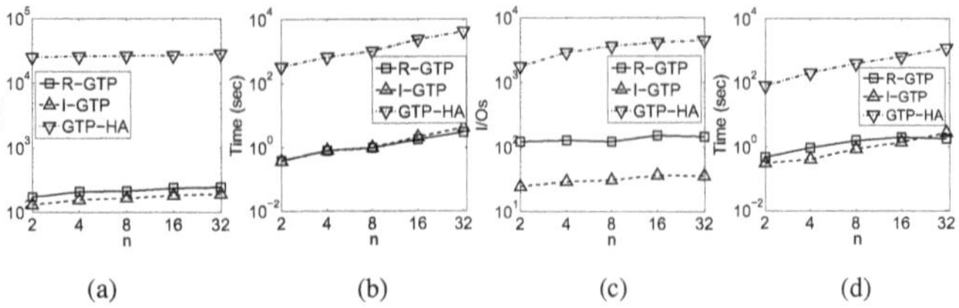

Figure 5: Effect of group size n for SUM (a-b) and MAX (c-d) in Euclidean space using California dataset

serve that for SUM, both of our approaches take less than a second to process a GTP query for any group size. On the other hand GTP-HA takes 5.5 to 39 minutes to process a single GTP query. For MAX, our approaches take 0.3 to 2.7 seconds, whereas GTP-HA takes 1.3 to 20 minutes to process a GTP query. Experimental results show that our approaches are on average three orders of magnitude faster and require two orders of magnitude less I/Os than GTP-HA.

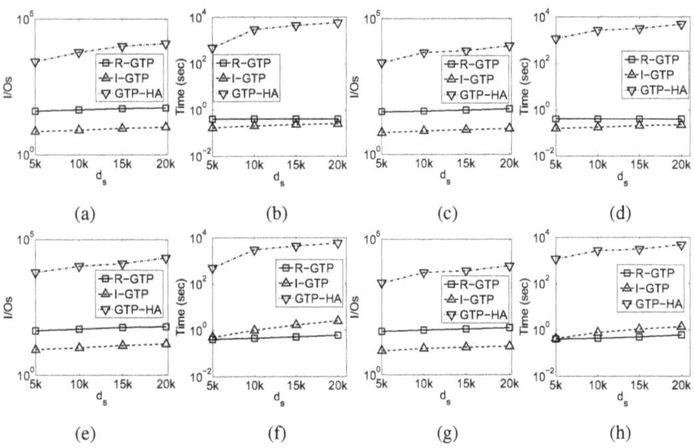

Figure 6: Effect of data set size d_S for SUM with uniform (a-b) and Zipfian (c-d) distributions, and for MAX with uniform (e-f) and Zipfian (g-h) distributions

We also compare our approaches with GTP-HA by varying the dataset sizes for both uniform and Zipfian distributions (Figure 6). Experimental results show that both R-GTP and I-GTP take *less than a second* to process a GTP query for any dataset size. On the other hand, for a dataset size of 5K GTP-HA takes on average 14 minutes to process a single GTP query, and the processing time increases to 90 minutes for the dataset size of 20K.

GTP-HA can only process a GTP query within a reasonable time when the number of POI types is 2. Our experimental results also show that for three POI types, even for a group size of 8, GTP-HA takes 17 minutes to run a single GTP query, which is not practical. Moreover, we could not run GTP-HA for a higher value of m (>3) for prohibitively expensive computational cost. By using synthetic datasets, we have also shown that GTP-HA is not scalable for a large dataset. Therefore, for the next set of experiments, we compare our approach with N-GTP.

7.2 Evaluation of kGTP Queries for SUM

In these sets of experiments, we evaluate our proposed algorithms for processing kGTP queries and compare these with our naive approach N-GTP, in both Euclidean and road network dataspaces.

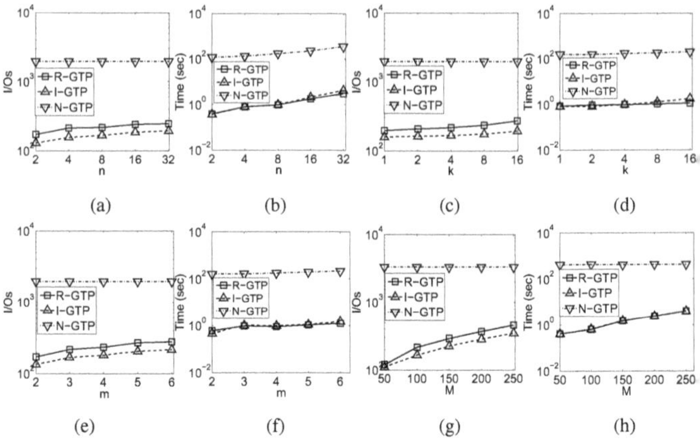

Figure 7: Effect of varying n (a-b), k (c-d), m (e-f), and M (g-h), for kGTP processing in Euclidean space

7.2.1 *Euclidean Space*

Effect of n: In this set of experiments, we vary the number of users n in the group and measure I/O and processing time for processing kGTP queries for R-GTP, I-GTP, and N-GTP algorithms. Figures 7(a) and (b) show I/Os and processing time, respectively, for all three approaches. We observe that N-GTP incurs at least one order of magnitude more I/Os and takes at least two orders of magnitude more processing time than both range based, R-GTP and incremental I-GTP algorithms. This significant performance gain comes from the efficient elliptical pruning strategies of our proposed approaches. We also observe that I-GTP algorithm performs sightly better than R-GTP algorithm as I-GTP only access POIs that are essential for answering kGTP queries, whereas the R-GTP algorithm uses an estimated upper bound to retrieve the POIs.

Effect of k: In this set of experiments, we vary the required answer set size k and compare the performance of our approaches with the naive approach. Figure 7 shows that our approaches significantly outperform N-GTP for all k. Also, we see that I/Os and processing time slightly increase with the increase of k for both R-GTP and I-GTP. Moreover, we observe that R-GTP outperforms I-GTP slightly in terms of processing time as for a large k I-GTP requires more computational steps after every POI retrieval.

Effect of m: Figures 7 (e) and (f) show the performance of our algorithms for varying the number of types m. The results show that for any number of types both of our proposed approaches, R-GTP and I-GTP, outperform N-GTP by at least an order in terms of I/O and two orders in terms of processing time. We observe that both of our approaches are scalable as I/O and processing time grows linearly with the increase of m.

Effect of M: Figures 7 (g) and (h) show the comparison of required I/Os and processing time in all three approaches by varying the query area. We see from the figures that for both R-GTP and I-GTP, I/Os and processing time increase with the increase of query area, as for a larger query area both approaches need to consider more POIs while computing k trips for a GTP query. On the other hand, since N-GTP retrieves all the POIs irrespective of the query area, processing time remains same for any query area. Both of our approaches outperform N-GTP queries significantly for all M.

Effect of dataset size: To show the effect of dataset size, we run experiments using synthetic datasets generated using uniform and Zipfian distributions. Figures 8 (a)-(b) and (c)-(d) show the comparison of required I/Os and processing time in all three approaches by varying the dataset size using uniform and Zipfian distributions, respectively. For both distributions, I/Os and processing time of N-

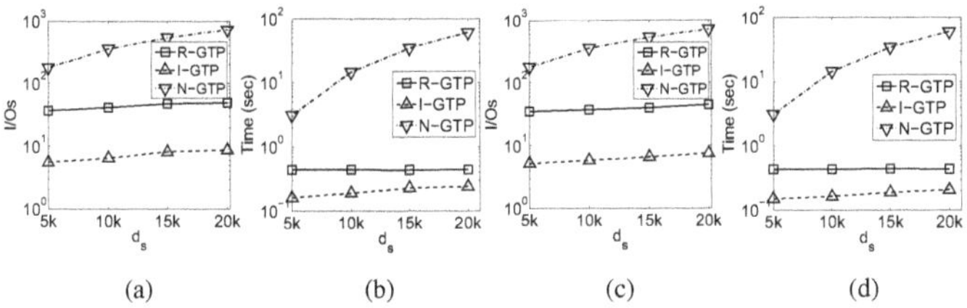

Figure 8: Effect of dataset size using uniform (a-b) and Zipfian (c-d) distributions in Euclidean space

GTP increase sharply with the increase of dataset size, whereas, for both R-GTP and I-GTP, I/Os and processing time increase slightly with the increase of dataset size. Thus, both of our approaches are scalable with respect to dataset size and distributions, and I-GTP takes less I/Os and processing time than that of R-GTP as I-GTP only accesses POIs that are essential for answering *k*GTP queries.

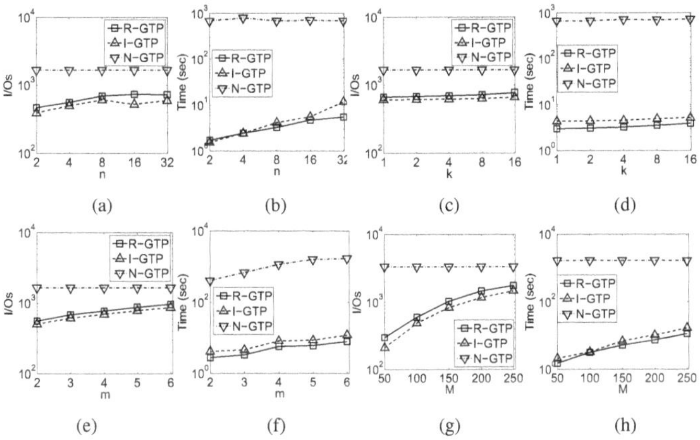

Figure 9: Effect of varying *n* (a-b), *k* (c-d), *m* (e-f), and *M* (g-h), on *k*GTP processing in road networks

7.2.2 Road Networks

In this set of experiments, we evaluate the performance of all three approaches R-GTP, I-GTP, and N-GTP in road networks. Figures 9 (a)-(h) show I/O cost and processing time by varying different parameters. We observe that in all cases the results show similar trends to that of the Euclidean space.

Figures 9 (a) and (b) show that I/Os and processing time of both R-GTP and I-GTP slightly increase with the increase of group size as they need to access more POIs for the *k* trips. We also observe that both R-GTP and I-GTP take at least two orders of magnitude less processing time and incur 5 times less I/O than N-GTP. We see that I-GTP performs slightly better in terms of I/O than R-GTP due to its tighter bound in the incremental retrieval process.

Figures 9 (c) and (d) show the comparison of three approaches in terms of I/Os and processing cost, respectively, by varying *k*. Though I/Os for both R-GTP and I-GTP slightly increase with the increase of *k*, the processing time for all approaches remain almost constant for different values of *k*. Our approaches take at least two orders of magnitude less processing time than the naive approach.

We vary the number of types *m* and present the results in Figures 9 (e) and (f). Though I/O cost increases with the increase of *m*, the overall processing time of both R-GTP and I-GTP is at least two orders of magnitude less than that of N-GTP. Hence, both of our approaches are scalable for a higher value of *m*.

Figures 9 (g) and (h) show I/Os and processing time, respectively, of all approaches for varying query area. We see that for both R-GTP and I-GTP I/O cost increases with the increase of the query space area, and for a large query area they need to retrieve a higher number of POIs. Both of our approaches outperform N-GTP by 1-2 orders of magnitude in terms of overall query processing time.

In summary, we see that I-GTP takes less I/Os than R-GTP, while processing time of R-GTP is slightly better than I-GTP especially when parameter values are large. This is because the incremental updates of I-GTP incur a slightly higher processing overhead.

In Section 3, we see that the aggregate trip distance for SUM depends on whether group members share a vehicle for the common part of the trip or not. In all the above experiments, we assume that group members travel independently. We have also run experiments for the scenario where all group members share a vehicle for the common part of the trip. The results show that for the shared scenario the processing time and I/O are slightly smaller than that of non-shared scenario as in the former trip distance is smaller compared to that of the later case, which results in a smaller search region for the shared query.

7.2.3 Non-ordered *k*GTP Queries

In the above set of experiments, we assume a fixed order of POI types. We have also run experiments for flexible order (i.e., non-ordered) POI types where the group can visit POIs in any order. Due to space constrained, we only show the I/Os and processing time by varying dataset size generated using uniform and Zipfian distributions (Figure 10). Figures show that in all methods, I/Os and processing time are higher than that of ordered *k*GTP queries, which is expected as we need to check different orders of POIs to find the optimal answer. Since our pruning method limits the search region to a smaller area containing a small number of POIs, the query processing time is always within an acceptable limit.

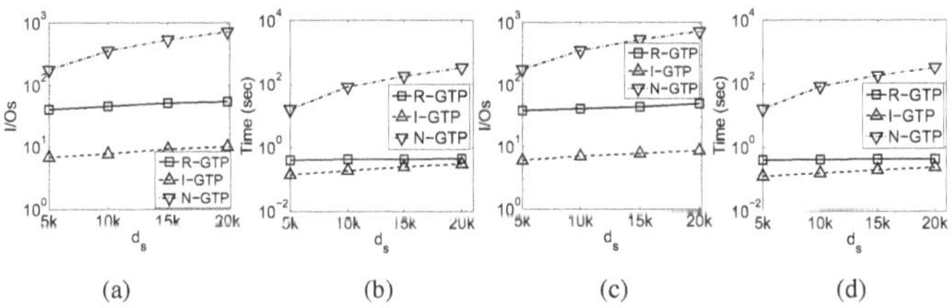

Figure 10: Effect of data set size d_s for SUM with uniform (a-b) and Zipfian (c-d) distributions for non-ordered *k*GTP queries

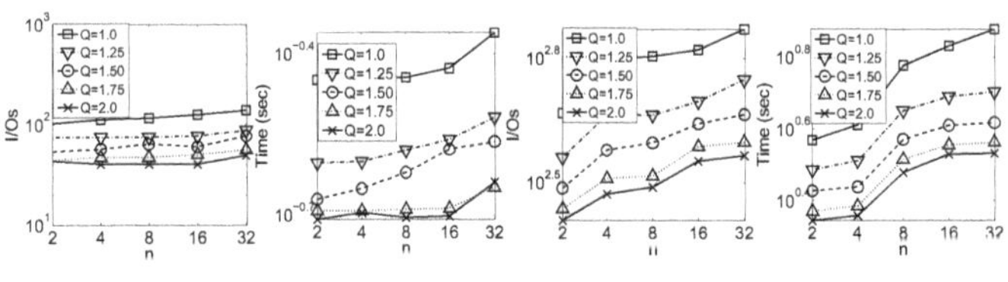

Figure 11: Effect of varying *n* and *Q* for *k*GTP processing in Euclidean space (a-b) and road networks (c-d)

Computing the answer for a non-ordered trip planning query has been shown as an NP-hard problem. Thus, to efficiently process *k*GTP queries for a large data set and for a large group size, we propose an approximation based incremental approach (I-GTP) that can trade efficiency with accuracy. To show the tradeoff between accuracy and efficiency, we vary the quality parameter *Q* as 1.0, 1.25, 1.5, 1.75, and 2.0, where 1.0 represents the exact/optimal answer whereas 2.0 means that the returned trip distance is guaranteed to be not more than twice of the optimal trip.

We run experiments by varying different parameters. For the brevity of the presentation, we show only results of varying the number of users n in the group (Figures 11 (a-b) for Euclidean space and Figures 11 (c-d) for road networks). We see that both I/O cost and the processing time decrease with the increase of Q. We have observed that the processing time for $Q = 2.0$ is approximately 2 times less than the processing time for $Q = 1.0$.

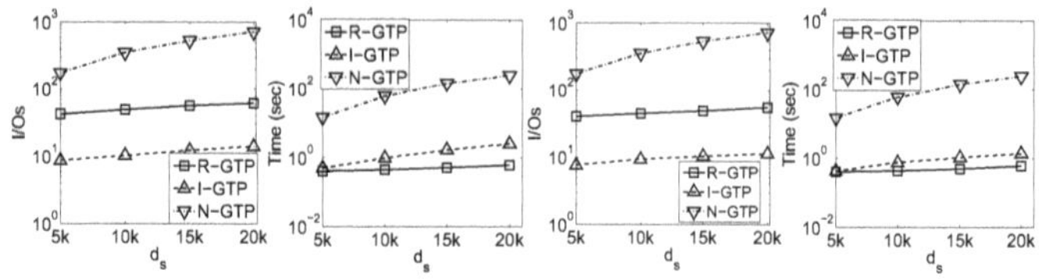

(a) (b) (c) (d)

Figure 12: Effect of dataset size for uniform (a-b) and Zipfian (c-d) distributions for aggregate function MAX

7.3 Evaluation of kGTP Queries for MAX

We have run experiments for aggregate function MAX that minimizes the maximum trip distance of all users. The results show similar trends to that of SUM. For space constraints, we present the results for dataset size variation with uniform and Zipfian distributions, which signify the scalability of our approaches.

Figure 12 shows the comparison of three approaches for processing kGTP queries for aggregate function MAX by varying dataset size. For uniform distribution, Figures 12 (a) and (b) show I/Os and processing time, respectively. We observe that with the increase of dataset size both I/Os and processing time sharply increases for N-GTP, whereas, for both R-GTP and I-GTP, I/Os and processing time slightly increases with increase of dataset size. I-GTP takes less number of I/Os than R-GTP, whereas, I-GTP has higher processing times than R-GTP because of the incremental updates. The results for Zipfian distribution (Figures 12 (c-d)) show similar trends to that of uniform distribution.

8 Conclusion

In this paper, we have proposed efficient solutions for k group trip planning (kGTP) queries and its variants that enable a group of users to plan a trip starting from different source locations, visiting different types of POIs, and ending at different destination locations. Our approach overcomes limitations of the state-of-the-art methods. To solve kGTP queries efficiently, we have developed a novel technique to refine the POI search space, and proposed two algorithms: a range based and an incremental algorithms that both process kGTP queries with reduced computational and I/O overhead. In addition, we have developed an approximation based incremental algorithm that can trade off the efficiency with the accuracy of the answer. Our extensive experiments with real and synthetic datasets show that our approaches outperform the benchmark approach by one to three orders of magnitude in terms of both processing and I/O overhead. In the future, we aim to consider other factors such as cost, POI popularity, user preference in addition to the distance to identify the best trips for the group.

9 References

[1] California road network data: http://www.cs.fsu.edu/~lifeifei/tpq.html.

[2] N. Beckmann, H.-P. Kriegel, R. Schneider, and B. Seeger. The R*-tree: an efficient and robust access method for points and rectangles. *SIGMOD Rec.*, 19(2):322–331, 1990.

[3] I. R. Brilhante, J. A. F. de Macêdo, F. M. Nardini, R. Perego, and C. Renso. Where shall we go today?: planning touristic tours with tripbuilder. In *CIKM*, pages 757–762, 2013.

[4] H. Chen, W. Ku, M. Sun, and R. Zimmermann. The multi-rule partial sequenced route query. In *SIGSpatial*, page 10, 2008.

[5] C.-Y. Chow, M. F. Mokbel, and W. G. Aref. Casper*: Query processing for location services without compromising privacy. *TODS*, 34(4):24:1–24:48, 2009.

[6] A. Guttman. R-trees: a dynamic index structure for spatial searching. In *SIGMOD*, pages 47–57, 1984.

[7] T. Hashem, M. E. Ali, L. Kulik, E. Tanin, and A. Quattrone. Protecting privacy for group nearest neighbor queries with crowdsourced data and computing. In *UbiComp*, pages 559–562, 2013.

[8] T. Hashem, T. Hashem, M. E. Ali, and L. Kulik. Group trip planning queries in spatial databases. In *SSTD*, pages 259–276, 2013.

[9] T. Hashem and L. Kulik. Safeguarding location privacy in wireless ad-hoc networks. In *Ubicomp*, pages 372–390, 2007.

[10] T. Hashem, L. Kulik, and R. Zhang. Privacy preserving group nearest neighbor queries. In *EDBT*, pages 489–500, 2010.

[11] G. R. Hjaltason and H. Samet. Ranking in spatial databases. In *SSD*, pages 83–95, 1995.

[12] R. Levin and Y. Kanza. TARS: traffic-aware route search. *GeoInformatica*, 18(3):461–500, 2014.

[13] F. Li, D. Cheng, M. Hadjieleftheriou, G. Kollios, and S. Teng. On trip planning queries in spatial databases. In *SSTD*, pages 273–290, 2005.

[14] H. Li, H. Lu, B. Huang, and Z. Huang. Two ellipse-based pruning methods for group nearest neighbor queries. In *GIS*, pages 192–199, 2005.

[15] J. Li, M. L. Yiu, and N. Mamoulis. Efficient notification of meeting points for moving groups via independent safe regions. In *ICDE*, pages 422–433, 2013.

[16] X. Ma, S. Shekhar, H. Xiong, and P. Zhang. Exploiting a page-level upper bound for multi-type nearest neighbor queries. In *GIS*, pages 179–186, 2006.

[17] H. Mahmud, A. M. Amin, M. E. Ali, T. Hashem, and S. Nutanong. A group based approach for path queries in road networks. In *SSTD*, pages 367–385, 2013.

[18] S. Namnandorj, H. Chen, K. Furuse, and N. Ohbo. Efficient bounds in finding aggregate nearest neighbors. In *DEXA*, pages 693–700, 2008.

[19] D. Papadias, Q. Shen, Y. Tao, and K. Mouratidis. Group nearest neighbor queries. In *ICDE*, page 301, 2004.

[20] D. Papadias, J. Zhang, N. Mamoulis, and Y. Tao. Query processing in spatial network databases. In *VLDB*, pages 802–813, 2003.

[21] M. N. Rice and V. J. Tsotras. Engineering generalized shortest path queries. In *ICDE*, pages 949–960, 2013.

[22] M. N. Rice and V. J. Tsotras. Parameterized algorithms for generalized traveling salesman problems in road networks. In *SIGSPATIAL*, pages 114–123, 2013.

[23] T. Seidl and H. Kriegel. Optimal multi-step k-nearest neighbor search. In *SIGMOD*, pages 154–165, 1998.

[24] M. Sharifzadeh, M. Kolahdouzan, and C. Shahabi. The optimal sequenced route query. *The VLDB Journal*, 17(4):765–787, 2008.

[25] N. Sultana, T. Hashem, and L. Kulik. Group nearest neighbor queries in the presence of obstacles. In *SIGSPATIAL*, pages 481–484, 2014.

[26] M. Terrovitis, S. Bakiras, D. Papadias, and K. Mouratidis. Constrained shortest path computation. In *SSTD*, pages 181–199, 2005.

[27] M. L. Yiu, N. Mamoulis, and D. Papadias. Aggregate nearest neighbor queries in road networks. *IEEE TKDE*, 17:820–833, 2005.

[28] Y. Zhu and D. Shasha. Warping indexes with envelope transforms for query by humming. In *SIGMOD*, pages 181–192, 2003.

Sampling Big Trajectory Data

Yanhua Li[†], Chi-Yin Chow[#], Ke Deng[*], Mingxuan Yuan[$],
Jia Zeng[♯♮$], Jia-Dong Zhang[#], Qiang Yang[**], and Zhi-Li Zhang[‡]
[†]Worcester Polytechnic Institute, Worcester, MA, [#]City University of Hong Kong, Hong Kong
[*]RMIT University, Australia, [**]Hong Kong University of Science and Technology, Hong Kong
[♯]Soochow University, China, [♮]Novel Software Technology and Industrialization, China
[$]Noah's Ark Lab, Hong Kong, [‡]University of Minnesota, Twin Cities
yli15@wpi.edu

ABSTRACT

The increasing prevalence of sensors and mobile devices has led to an explosive increase of the scale of spatio-temporal data in the form of trajectories. A *trajectory aggregate query*, as a fundamental functionality for measuring trajectory data, aims to retrieve the statistics of trajectories passing a user-specified spatio-temporal region. A large-scale spatio-temporal database with big disk-resident data takes very long time to produce exact answers to such queries. Hence, approximate query processing with a guaranteed error bound is a promising solution in many scenarios with stringent response-time requirements. In this paper, we study the problem of approximate query processing for trajectory aggregate queries. We show that it boils down to the distinct value estimation problem, which has been proven to be very hard with powerful negative results given that no index is built. By utilizing the well-established spatio-temporal index and introducing an inverted index to trajectory data, we are able to design random index sampling (RIS) algorithm to estimate the answers with a guaranteed error bound. To further improve system scalability, we extend RIS algorithm to concurrent random index sampling (CRIS) algorithm to process a number of trajectory aggregate queries arriving concurrently with overlapping spatio-temporal query regions. To demonstrate the efficacy and efficiency of our sampling and estimation methods, we applied them in a real large-scale user trajectory database collected from a cellular service provider in China. Our extensive evaluation results indicate that both RIS and CRIS outperform exhaustive search for single and concurrent trajectory aggregate queries by two orders of magnitude in terms of the query processing time, while preserving a relative error ratio lower than 10%, with only 1% search cost of the exhaustive search method.

Categories and Subject Descriptors

H.2.4 [**Database Management**]: Systems – Query processing; H.4.0 [**Information Systems and Applications**]: General

General Terms

Algorithms, Experimentation.

Permission to make digital or hard copies of all or part of this work for personal or classroom use is granted without fee provided that copies are not made or distributed for profit or commercial advantage and that copies bear this notice and the full citation on the first page. Copyrights for components of this work owned by others than ACM must be honored. Abstracting with credit is permitted. To copy otherwise, or republish, to post on servers or to redistribute to lists, requires prior specific permission and/or a fee. Request permissions from Permissions@acm.org.
CIKM'15, October 19–23, 2015, Melbourne, Australia.
© 2015 ACM. ISBN 978-1-4503-3794-6/15/10 ...$15.00.
DOI: http://dx.doi.org/10.1145/2806416.2806422.

Keywords

Spatio-temporal databases, trajectory aggregate query, sampling, approximate query processing

1. INTRODUCTION

A trajectory stands for a sequential time-stamped geo-locations in a three dimensional spatio-temporal space. In reality, a trajectory may contain a variety of attributes, for example, a taxi GPS trajectory has the instant or average velocity, trajectory length, occupation indicator, etc. [36]; A Flickr user's trajectory may infer users' sequential activities, (e.g., what he/she has done) from the multimedia contents attached to the locations (e.g., text, images and videos). These trajectory data facilitate many emerging applications including urban planning [36, 19], spatio-temporal data mining [21, 15], and various location-based services [33, 20]. *A trajectory aggregate query*, as a fundamental functionality of spatial-temporal databases, aims to retrieve the statistics of distinct trajectories passing a user-specified spatio-temporal region [4, 8]. A typical trajectory aggregate query is "the total number of taxi trajectories with speed greater than 5 miles per hour in New York City during 2013".

The increasing prevalence of sensors and mobile devices, such as GPS set on cars or smart phones carried by people, and the fast development of location-acquisition technologies have led to an explosive increase of the scale of spatio-temporal databases in the form of trajectories, which generates new challenges, namely, how to efficiently process numerous trajectory aggregate queries in large-scale trajectory databases.

Various spatio-temporal indexing techniques, such as augmented R-tree [24], multi-version R-tree [30, 31], and grid-based index [5], have been proposed to divide the spatio-temporal space into indices and facilitate the access to spatio-temporal data. These spatio-temporal indices are of hierarchical structure, namely, multiple adjacent index nodes in a lower level are aggregated to an index node in a higher level. When processing spatio-temporal queries, the index nodes are typically browsed in a top-down manner. Many spatio-temporal aggregate queries, such as counting the total spatio-temporal records, can be answered by aggregating the information maintained in index nodes at the higher levels to avoid accessing the raw spatio-temporal data. However, for a trajectory aggregate query, maintaining the statistical trajectory information on index nodes does not work. The reason is that a trajectory aggregate query aims to find the number of distinct trajectories in a spatio-temporal query region. To determine whether two index nodes contain some trajectories in common, the trajectory IDs must be recorded in every index node. Using such an index structure makes no difference from the brute-forcing. Thus, to produce the exact answer to a trajectory aggregate query, a non-avoidable brute-force search has to be performed, which takes very long time when the spatio-temporal query region covers a large amount of disk-resident data. As a result, approximate query processing becomes a promising solution in many scenarios with stringent response-time requirements, which provides (reasonably accurate) approximate answers.

In this paper, we make the first attempt to investigate the problem of approximate query processing for trajectory aggregate queries. By introducing an inverted index to trajectory data, we design **R**andom **I**ndex **S**ampling (RIS) algorithm to estimate the answers with guaranteed error bounds. To further improve system scalability, we design **C**oncurrent **R**andom **I**ndex **S**ampling (CRIS) algorithm to process a number of trajectory aggregate queries arriving concurrently with overlapping spatio-temporal query regions. We highlight our contributions as follows.

- We show that the approximate query processing for trajectory aggregate queries boils down to the distinct value estimation problem [6], which has been proven to be very hard with powerful negative results given that no index is built. By utilizing the well-established spatio-temporal index and introducing an inverted index to the trajectory data, we develop random index sampling (RIS) algorithm and unbiased estimator to quickly answer the query with bounded estimation error.
- For a large-scale trajectory database management system, a large number of trajectory aggregate queries usually arrive concurrently with overlapping spatio-temporal query regions. Instead of performing RIS algorithm on each individual query, we further extend it to *concurrent random index sampling* (CRIS) algorithm to significantly improve the efficiency of answering concurrent queries, by employing stratified sampling technique and reusing samples collected from the overlapping regions.
- We conduct extensive experiments on a real-world large-scale user trajectory dataset (with 3TB data) collected from a cellular service provider in China to evaluate the efficiency and effectiveness of our sampling and estimation methods. Our experimental results show that both RIS and CRIS outperform an exhaustive search method for single and concurrent trajectory queries by two orders of magnitude in terms of the query processing time, while preserving a relative error ratio lower than 10%, with only 1% search cost of the exhaustive search method.

The remainder of this paper is organized as follows. Section 2 discusses related work. We define our problem in Section 3. In Sections 4 and 5, we present our proposed RIS and CRIS algorithms, respectively. Section 6 analyzes the performance of RIS and CRIS algorithms. Section 7 describes some generalizations of our algorithms. Finally, we conclude this paper in Section 8.

2. RELATED WORK

We make the first attempt to employ sampling techniques to improve the effectiveness in processing trajectory aggregate queries in large-scale spatio-temporal databases, with the aim to significantly reduce the query processing time while preserving certain estimation accuracy. In this section, we discuss three topics that are closely related to our work and highlight the differences from them, including (1) trajectory data management, (2) distinct value estimation, and (3) concurrent query processing.

2.1 Trajectory Data Management

Trajectory queries. As moving object trajectories have been collected in a massive scale due to the advancement of sensor technologies like satellite, RFID, GPS, and mobile cellular networks, the query processing of trajectory databases has been paid much attention. Trajectory queries aim to evaluate various spatio-temporal relationships among spatial data objects, such as regions, points, and trajectories [8]. The trajectory queries can be generally classified into two main categories: range (or window) queries and nearest-neighbor queries. *Range queries* retrieve trajectories passing a given spatio-temporal region [4, 8] or search spatio-temporal regions which are frequently passed by trajectories [16, 18]. *Nearest-neighbor queries* ask for the top-k nearest-neighbor trajectories to a specified point or trajectory [13, 32]. In this paper, we particularly focus on a sub-category of the trajectory range queries, namely, a trajectory aggregate query, which returns the statistics (e.g., counts, sum, or average) of all distinct trajectories in the spatio-temporal query region. Traditional methods to handle trajectory queries are through spatio-temporal indices, as discussed below.

Executing trajectory queries using database indices. It is important to utilize the appropriate indexing techniques for trajectory data to improve the efficiency and effectiveness of processing trajectory queries. The trajectory database has unique requirements to the index techniques because of its spatio-temporal data characteristics [8]. The state-of-the-art trajectory indexing techniques can be grouped into three categories, including augmented R-tree, multi-version R-tree, and grid-based index. (1) An *augmented R-tree* employs R-trees over the 3D spatio-temporal space, e.g., Spatio-Temporal R-tree (STR-tree) and TB-tree (Trajectory Bundle tree) [24]. (2) A *multi-version R-tree* builds multiple structures of R-trees. For each time stamp, an R-tree is created, and R-trees for different time stamps are indexed, e.g., historical R-tree (HR-tree) [30] and multi-version B-trees and 3D R-trees (MV3R-trees) [31]. (3) A *grid-based index* divides the spatial dimension into grids using Quad-trees [9] or KD-trees [1], and then builds a separate temporal index for each grid, e.g., multiple time-split B-tree (MTSB-trees) [37] and Scalable and Efficient Trajectory Index (SETI) [5] to divide the spatio-temporal space into indices and facilitate the spatio-temporal data access.

However, as elaborated in Section 1, to produce the exact answers to a trajectory aggregate query, a non-avoidable brute-force search has to be performed, which takes very long time when the spatio-temporal query region covers a large amount of disk-resident data. As a result, approximate query processing becomes a promising solution for trajectory aggregate queries in many scenarios with stringent response-time requirements. In a spatio-temporal database indexed by one of the index structures, we propose to estimate the answers to the trajectory aggregate queries by sampling a limited number of index leaf nodes. Our proposed random index sampling (RIS) algorithm can significantly reduce the query processing time while preserving certain estimation accuracy. Moreover, RIS algorithm can be applied (and is orthogonal) upon various trajectory indexing methods.

2.2 Distinct Value Estimation

In a column of a large table with each entry filled with a value with no index built, distinct value estimation problem aims to design a scalable approach to generate accurate estimation to the number of distinct values, with limited space or time resources. When time is a major constraint, random sampling is the only approach, which collects samples from the table, and estimates the total number of distinct values. Unfortunately, the existing works

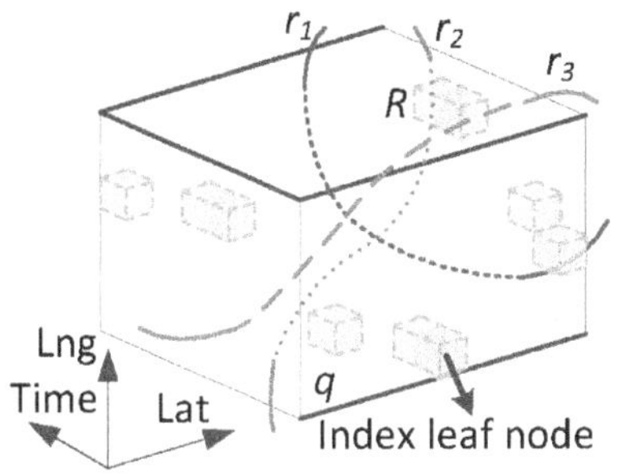

Figure 1: A trajectory aggregate query q returning the number of distinct trajectories in the spatio-temporal query region depicted in the cuboid. r_1, r_2, and r_3 are three trajectories.

show powerful *negative* results [6, 7, 14, 23] that no estimator can guarantee small error across all input distributions, unless it examines a large fraction of the input data. On the other hand, when space is a primary concern, scanning the entire table is allowed, synopses based approaches [2, 12, 17] yield reasonably accurate estimation to the number of distinct values. Our trajectory aggregate query problem boils down to the distinct value estimation problem with stringent time constraint, when sampling is performed upon spatio-temporal points of trajectories, with the trajectory IDs viewed as the "distinct values". To tackle this seemingly unsolvable problem, we in this paper employ spatio-temporal index and inverted index to allow obtaining the probability of each trajectory being collected while sampling, thus enabling the design of unbiased estimator for the number of trajectories with bounded variance and confidence interval.

2.3 Concurrent Query Processing

A database, especially a large-scale spatio-temporal database, usually has to deal with numerous concurrent queries from a large number of users. Thus, it is important and desirable to process these concurrent queries through exploiting a shared execution paradigm to avoid redundant computations and save the computational cost. In general, there are mainly three shared execution paradigms. (1) *Multi-query optimization.* This technique detects and re-uses common sub-expressions among queries by operating on batches of queries only during the optimization phase and materializing shared intermediate results at the cost of memory [27]. (2) *Simultaneous pipelining.* This paradigm extracts identical sub-plans from concurrent queries, executes only one of them and sends the results to the rest simultaneously [25]; however, it is limited to common sub-plans, that is, it is not applicable to the case that two queries have similar sub-plans but with different selection predicates. (3) *Global query plans.* This paradigm utilizes shared operators (with fine granularity) rather than sub-plans (with coarser granularity) to increase sharing opportunities, in which a single shared operator can evaluate two queries sharing a similar plan simultaneously [25]. In this paper, we apply the global query plans paradigm to utilize the sharing opportunities, the key challenge of which is to decompose the operators (i.e., sampling) into shared sub-operators and reconstruct the results for all concurrent trajectory range queries. We employ stratified sampling and sample reuse to solve the problem. (See Section 5 for more details.)

3. PROBLEM STATEMENT

In this section, we clarify key terms used in the paper and formally define the objective of approximate query processing for trajectory aggregate queries. Table 1 provides the notations and terminologies used in this paper.

Table 1: Notations and terminologies

Notation	Description
$Q = \{q_1, \cdots, q_M\}$, $Q_j \subseteq Q$, $1 \le j \le M'$	Q is a set of M concurrent trajectory aggregate queries. Q_j is a subset of concurrent queries in Q.
$Q' = \{q'_1, \cdots, q'_{M'}\}$, $Q'_i \subseteq Q'$, $1 \le i \le M$	Q' is a set of non-overlapping spatio-temporal regions. Q'_i is a subset of spatio-temporal regions in Q'.
q, q_0	q is a trajectory aggregate query. $q_0 = \vee_{q_i \in Q} q_i$ is the union of the spatio-temporal regions of all concurrent queries in Q.
$\mathcal{R}^q = \{R^q_1, \cdots, R^q_n\}$	$\mathcal{R}^q$ is the set of n index leaf nodes that q's spatio-temporal query region covers.
B	B is the sampling budget (i.e., the maximum number of sampled index leaf nodes) for answering q.
$\hat{R}^q_t$, $1 \le t \le B$	$\hat{R}^q_t$ is the t-th sampled index leaf node.
k^q_r	The number of index leaf nodes in $\mathcal{R}^q$ that trajectory r traverses.
N_q, $\hat{N}_q$	N_q is the number of trajectories that match the query constraints of q. $\hat{N}_q$ is the estimator of N_q.

- A **trajectory** is the sequence of spatial points that a moving object follows through space as a function of time. Each point thus consists of an trajectory ID, latitude, longitude, and a time stamp. For example, the GPS points of a vehicle and the spatio-temporal points of a cellphone user are all trajectories.

- **Trajectory attributes:** A trajectory may be associated with a few features describing the properties of the trajectory, e.g., the number of spatio-temporal points, length, average speed, etc.

- **Trajectory data structure:** Trajectory data are usually stored in a database using a spatio-temporal index, such as Quad-tree/R-tree (for spatial indexing) and B/B$^+$-tree (for temporal indexing)[1]. Then, as shown in Figure 1, each *index leaf node* represents a three dimensional subspace, containing spatio-temporal points of trajectories.

- A **trajectory aggregate query** q returns a statistical result of distinct trajectories in a spatio-temporal query region, with or without constraints on trajectories attributes, e.g., ranges on average speed, trajectory length, and etc. Figure 1 illustrates an example of a trajectory aggregate query.

As discussed in Section 1, to produce exact answers to a trajectory aggregate query q, a non-avoidable brute-force search has to be performed, which takes very long time when the spatio-temporal

[1]Note that there are many spatio-temporal index structures in the literature [3, 11], and our random index sampling algorithms can be applied (and is orthogonal) to different indexing methods.

query region covers big disk-resident data. In this paper, we employ sampling methods to perform *approximate query processing* for trajectory aggregate queries with guaranteed error bounds.

Problem definition. Given a trajectory aggregate query q in a large-scale trajectory database, the database returns the total number of distinct trajectories N_q in q's spatio-temporal query region, with certain attribute constraints. Suppose q's query region covers n spatio-temporal index leaf nodes $\mathcal{R}^q = \{R_1^q, \cdots, R_n^q\}$. We aim to sample and search B index leaf nodes (where $B \ll n$), $\{\hat{R}_1^q, \cdots, \hat{R}_B^q\}$ from $\mathcal{R}^q$, based on which we provide an accurate estimator $\hat{N}_q$ that converges to N_q, and for any $\epsilon > 0$ and $0 < \alpha \leq 1$, a certain confidence interval is guaranteed as $Pr(|\hat{N}_q - N_q| > \epsilon) \leq \alpha$.

4. RANDOM INDEX SAMPLING

In this section, we introduce our proposed random index sampling (RIS) algorithm to sample index leaf nodes in the spatio-temporal query region of a trajectory aggregate query q, and design an unbiased estimator to estimate the answer to q, with provable bounds on the confidence interval.

4.1 Model of Random Index Sampling

RIS algorithm works in three stages as follows, inverted indexing stage, sampling stage, and estimating stage.

Inverted indexing stage. An inverted index [38] is an index data structure storing a mapping from content, such as numbers or words, to its locations. We build an inverted index for the trajectory data, where each record represents a trajectory and all index leaf nodes the trajectory traverses (as shown in Figure 2). Given a trajectory aggregate query q, we denote k_r^q as the number of index leaf nodes that a trajectory r goes through in q's spatio-temporal query region. k_r^q can be quickly obtained by checking the record of r in the inverted index. It will be clear shortly that k_r^q governs the probability of a trajectory r being sampled in *sampling stage* and k_r^q is an important variable to design estimator to the answer of q.

Sampling stage. Let B denote the sampling budget, i.e., the maximum number of index leaf nodes allowed to collect. In our analysis, we assume that B is always sufficiently large. We uniformly at random pick up B index leaf nodes from the leaf node set covered by q's spatio-temporal query region, i.e., $\mathcal{R}^q$, with replacement[2]. Thus, each index leaf node in $\mathcal{R}^q$ has an equal probability of $1/n$ being sampled. Then, we scan the sampled index leaf nodes and find the trajectories of our interest, namely, those matching the trajectory attribute constraints of q. If a sampled index leaf node is chosen more than once, we only perform one exhaustive search on it. Hence, as shown in Figure 2, we obtain a list of sampled index leaf nodes, $\{\hat{R}_1^q, \cdots, \hat{R}_B^q\}$, from the population space $\mathcal{R}^q$. Note that a sample $\hat{R}_t^q \in \mathcal{R}^q$ represents both the index leaf node and the trajectory set in it, where we will interchangeably use these two meanings of $\hat{R}_t^q$ in the rest of the paper ($1 \leq t \leq B$).

Various statistics of a sampled index leaf node $\hat{R}_t^q$ can be represented as functions of $\hat{R}_t^q$ ($1 \leq t \leq B$). For instance, the number of distinct trajectories that match the query contraints of q can be viewed as a mapping $g_q : \mathcal{R}^q \rightarrow \mathbb{N}$ from a trajectory set $\hat{R}_t^q \in \mathcal{R}^q$ to a natural number, i.e., $g_q(\hat{R}_t^q)$. Moreover, given a trajectory $r \in \hat{R}_t^q$, the number of index leaf nodes that r traverses in $\mathcal{R}^q$, i.e., k_r^q, is proportional to the probability that the trajectory r being sampled by randomly picking up an index leaf node from $\mathcal{R}^q$. Define a mapping $f_q : \mathcal{R}^q \rightarrow \mathbb{R}^+$ as $N_t^q = f_q(\hat{R}_t^q) = \sum_{r \in \hat{R}_t^q \wedge q}\{1/k_r^q\}$, where $\hat{R}_t^q \wedge q$ represents the trajectory set in $\hat{R}_t^q$ that matches the attribute constraints of q. It is clear that the ground-truth answer for the trajectory aggregate query q, namely, the total number of distinct trajectories in $\mathcal{R}^q$, is $N_q = \sum_{i=1}^n f_q(R_i^q)$. Note that (as shown in Figure 2) after a trajectory r is obtained from $\hat{R}_t^q \in \mathcal{R}^q$, the number of index leaf nodes r traverses in $\mathcal{R}^q$, i.e., k_r^q, can be found by checking the inverted index.

[2]Note that in general q's query region is *much larger* than the index leaf node. Hence, for simplicity, we consider all trajectories in an index leaf node R_i^q traverse q's query region, if q partially or completely covers R_i^q in the spatio-temporal space. On the other hand, when the query region of q is small, exhaustive search can be directly applied to obtain q's exact answer.

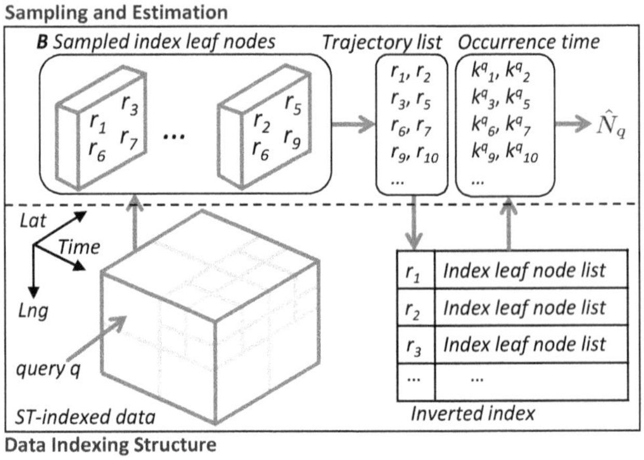

Figure 2: Random index sampling framework

Estimating stage. Using RIS, Theorem 1 presents that the probability of each trajectory being sampled is proportional to the number of index leaf nodes it traverses in $\mathcal{R}^q$.

THEOREM 1 (IMPORTANCE SAMPLING). *The probability $Pr(r)$ of each trajectory $r \in \mathcal{R}^q \wedge q$ being sampled using RIS algorithm is $Pr(r) = k_r^q/n$, where $\mathcal{R}^q = \{R_1^q, \cdots, R_n^q\}$.*

PROOF. Each index leaf node R_i^q ($1 \leq i \leq n$) has an equal probability $Pr(R_i^q) = 1/n$ to be chosen. The conditional probability of each trajectory r being sampled given that R_i^q is sampled is $Pr(r|R_i^q) = 1$, if $r \in R_i^q$; and $Pr(r|R_i^q) = 0$, otherwise. Applying the law of total probability yields the probability of r being sampled as $Pr(r) = \sum_{i=1}^n Pr(R_i^q)Pr(r|R_i^q) = k_r^q/n$. □

In the next subsection, we develop an unbiased estimator to estimate the total number of distinct trajectories that match the query constraints of q, using the samples $\{\hat{R}_q^1, \cdots, \hat{R}_B^q\}$ collected by RIS algorithm.

4.2 Estimator Design

An estimator is a function of a sequence of observations that outputs an estimate of an unknown population parameter. Below, we present an asymptotically unbiased estimator of N_q.

Unbiased estimator. We aim to estimate the total number N_q of distinct trajectories that match the query constraints of q. We define an estimator $\hat{N}_q$ in Theorem 2.

THEOREM 2 (ESTIMATOR TO N_q). *With a sampling budget B, RIS algorithm collects B sampled index leaf nodes $\{\hat{R}_1^q, \cdots, \hat{R}_B^q\}$, with each $\hat{R}_t^q \in \mathcal{R}^q$ for $1 \leq t \leq B$. Then, $\hat{N}_q$ in Equation (1) is the asymptotically unbiased estimator of N_q:*

$$\hat{N}_q = \frac{n}{B}\sum_{t=1}^{B} f_q(\hat{R}_t^q). \quad (1)$$

PROOF. Since each $\hat{R}^q_t$ is chosen uniformly at random from the same population space $\mathcal{R}^q$, $f_q(\hat{R}^q_t)$'s are all independent and follow the same distribution, and thus have the same expectation as $E[f_q(\hat{R}^q_t)] = \mu = \sum_{i=1}^{n} f_q(R^q_i)/n = N_q/n$. Using the linearity of the expectation, $E[\hat{N}_q] = N_q$. □

Sampling Budget Analysis. Under a certain trajectory index structure, such as Quad-tree and B-tree, all the trajectory records and indices are stored as regular files. Thus, the size of an index leaf node is bounded by the file size in the underlying file system. For example, on Hadoop Distributed File System (HDFS), the block file size is 64MB, and when in-block index is built, a smaller memory page size (e.g., 4KB) is used [34]. As a result, given that each trajecotory record takes roughly a constant amount of space, e.g., 100B, the number of distinct trajectories in an index leaf node is bounded, e.g., by $4KB/100B = 40$, and we denote this upper bound as δ. Hence, for a trajectory aggregate query q, $f_q(\hat{R}^q) \leq \delta$ holds. Theorem 3 below determines the sampling budget B needed to achieve a certan estimation accuracy.

THEOREM 3. *The estimator $\hat{N}_q$ (Equation (1)) guarantees that for any $\epsilon > 0$ and $0 < \alpha \leq 1$,*

$$Pr(|\hat{N}_q - N_q| > \epsilon) \leq \alpha, \tag{2}$$

when $B \geq \frac{\ln(2/\alpha)\delta^2 n^2}{2\epsilon^2}$, with δ as the maximium number of trajectories in an index leaf node.

PROOF. Recall that each sample $\hat{R}^q_t \in \mathcal{R}^q$ is drawn uniformly at random from $\mathcal{R}^q$. Hence, random variables $f_q(\hat{R}^q_t)$ are independent and identically distributed, and they follow the same distribution. Given that each $f_q(\hat{R}^q) \leq \delta$ holds, the following bound holds by applying Hoeffding's inequality [28],

$$Pr(|\hat{N}_q - N_q| > \epsilon) \leq 2e^{\frac{-2B\epsilon^2}{n^2\delta^2}}. \tag{3}$$

Then, by letting the right hand side (in Equation (3)) be smaller than or equal to α, we obtain $B \geq \frac{\ln(2/\alpha)\delta^2 n^2}{2\epsilon^2}$ as the minimum budget needed to guarantee the confidence interval in Equation (2). □

It is clear that to achieve a certain confidence interval, governed by ϵ and α, the minimum sampling budget needed satisfies $B \propto \delta^2$ and $B \propto n^2$.

5. CONCURRENT RANDOM INDEX SAMPLING

The proposed RIS algorithm properly deals with a *single* trajectory aggregate query with a guaranteed estimation error bound. However, when it comes to queries in a large-scale trajectory database management system, e.g., user mobility data from carriers in a country with millions of users, a large number of trajectory range queries come concurrently. These queries may overlap in spatio-temporal query regions, as well as ranges of attribute constraints. As illustrated in Figure 3(a), two concurrent queries q_1 and q_2 arrive concurrently and overlap with each other in the spatio-temporal space.

A naive method for handling concurrent queries is to perform RIS algorithm individually for each query. However, by reusing the samples obtained in the overlapping space among queries, the estimation accuracy can be significantly improved. In this section, we extend RIS algorithm to concurrent random index sampling (CRIS) algorithm, that performs *stratified sampling* and *sample reuse* on concurrent trajectory aggregate queries. Our theoretical results show that CRIS algorithm can achieve higher estimation accuracy for each concurrent trajectory aggregate query, with less sampling budget than simply running RIS algorithm for each query. Below, we first formally define the problem of concurrent overlapping queries, and then present our CRIS algorithm.

5.1 Model of Concurrent Random Index Sampling

Two queries q_1 and q_2 are concurrent, if the database system processes them at the same time (i.e., they arrive at the database system or are dispatched from a query buffer at the same moment). Their spatio-temporal query regions may overlap, as well as ranges of trajectory attributes, such as average speed, trajectory length, etc. In the rest of the paper, we will use *concurrent overlapping queries* to represent concurrent queries with overlapping spatio-temporal constraints. Figure 3(a) shows an example of two concurrent overlapping queries. Now, we formally define the problem of concurrent overlapping queries as follows.

Concurrent overlapping queries. Given $M > 1$ concurrent overlapping queries, $Q = \{q_1, \cdots, q_M\}$, with required estimation accuracy guarantees $\epsilon_i > 0$ and $0 < \alpha_i \leq 1$ for $i \in \{1, \cdots, M\}$. The goal is to provide estimations to the numbers of trajectories, $N_{q_1}, \cdots, N_{q_M}$, with guaranteed confidence interval as $Pr(|\hat{N}_{q_i} - N_{q_i}| > \epsilon_i) \leq \alpha_i$. The major challenge is how to reuse the index leaf nodes sampled from overlapping regions of concurrent queries and improve the estimation accuracy over that of running RIS algorithm on each individual query.

Concurrent random index sampling. We propose CRIS algorithm to deal with concurrent overlapping queries. Given M concurrent trajectory aggregate queries, $Q = \{q_1, \cdots, q_M\}$, let $q_0 = q_1 \vee \cdots \vee q_M$ be the entire spatio-temporal region Q covers. Different from RIS algorithm, the basic idea behind CRIS algorithm is that we first divide q_0 into $M' \geq M$ non-overlapping spatio-temporal regions $Q' = \{q'_1, \cdots, q'_{M'}\}$, by the boundaries of all queries q_i's ($1 \leq i \leq M$). Each q'_j corresponds to an intersection of a subset of queries $Q_j \subseteq Q$. Then, CRIS samples index leaf nodes from the leaf node set $\mathcal{R}'_j$ of each q'_j with sampling budget B'_j ($1 < j < M'$), where B'_j is porportionally allocated with respect to the number of index leaf nodes in q'_j. Eventually, for each region q'_j, CRIS algorithm collects B'_j index leaf nodes, denoted as $\hat{\mathcal{R}}'_j = \{\hat{R}^{q'_j}_1, \cdots, \hat{R}^{q'_j}_{B'_j}\}$ for $1 \leq j \leq M'$. These sampled index leaf nodes are exhaustively searched for trajectories matching the attribute constraints of queries in Q. We prove that such design of CRIS reduces the estimation variance and the needed sampling budget over that of running RIS algorithm independently on each query q_i.

5.2 Two Concurrent Overlapping Queries

Now, we use two concurrent overlapping queries to show how CRIS algorithm works. Given two concurrent overlapping queries, q_1 and q_2 as shown in Figure 3(a). The goal is to provide estimations to the numbers of distinct trajectories, N_{q_1} and N_{q_2}, with guaranteed estimation confidence interval, $Pr(|\hat{N}_{q_1} - N_{q_1}| > \epsilon_1) \leq \alpha_1$ and $Pr(|\hat{N}_{q_2} - N_{q_2}| > \epsilon_2) \leq \alpha_2$. CRIS algorithm consists of three stages as follows.

Stratification Stage. The entire spatio-temporal space, defined as $q_0 = q_1 \vee q_2$ is divided into three non-overlapping queries, i.e., $Q' = \{q'_1, q'_2, q'_3\}$, such that $q'_3 := q_1 \wedge q_2$, $q'_1 = q_1 - q_3$, and $q'_2 = q_2 - q_3$. Moreover, we denote $\mathcal{R}'_1$, $\mathcal{R}'_2$, and $\mathcal{R}'_3$ as the corresponding non-overlapping leaf node sets, as illustrated in Figure 3(b). Hence, q_1 (resp. q_2) is divided into two strata, i.e., $q_1 = q'_1 \vee q'_3$ (resp. $q_2 = q'_2 \vee q'_3$).

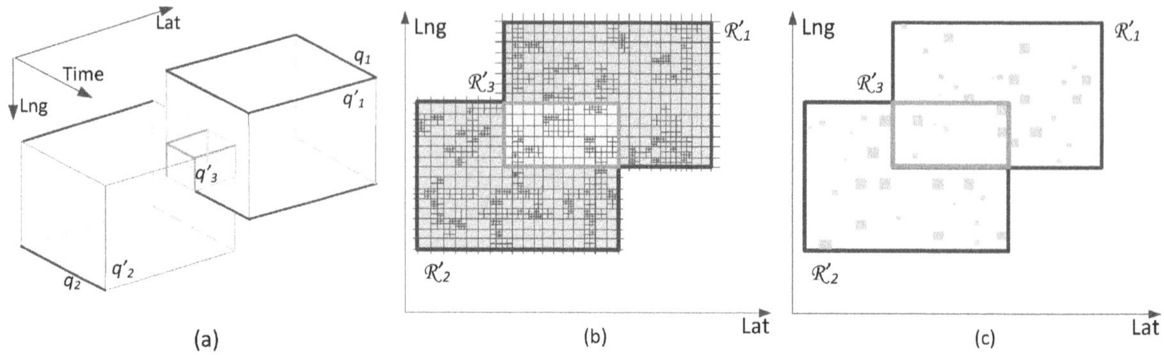

Figure 3: Illustration of CRIS algorithm. (a) Two concurrent overlapping queries q_1 and q_2 are mapped to a three dimensional space. They are divided into non-overlapping regions, q'_1, q'_2, and q'_3. (b) The leaf node sets $\mathcal{R}'_1$, $\mathcal{R}'_2$, and $\mathcal{R}'_3$; (c) Given sampling budgets needed for q_1 and q_2 as $B_1 = B_2 = 28$, q'_1, q'_2, and q'_3 are assigned with budgets $B'_1 = 21$, $B'_2 = 21$, and $B'_3 = 7$ (based on Equation (4)), respectively. Orange boxes represent the sampled index leaf nodes, based on which the numbers of distinct trajectories N_{q_1} and N_{q_2} are estimated by Equations (5) and (6), respectively.

Sampling Stage. Based on Theorem 3, there exist lower bounds B_1 and B_2 on sampling budgets for q_1 and q_2 to guarantee the estimation accuracy, defined by ϵ_1, ϵ_2, α_1, and α_2. Then, each stratum q'_j is sampled individually with a sampling budget B'_j proportional to n'_j as

$$B'_1 = \lceil B_1 n'_1/n_1 \rceil, \quad B'_2 = \lceil B_2 n'_2/n_2 \rceil,$$
$$B'_3 = \max\{\lceil n'_3 B_1/n_1 \rceil, \lceil n'_3 B_2/n_2 \rceil\}. \tag{4}$$

Then, three sample sets, i.e., $\{\hat{R}_1^{q'_j}, \cdots, \hat{R}_{B'_j}^{q'_j}\}$ for $1 \leq j \leq 3$, are drawn uniformly at random from leaf node sets $\mathcal{R}'_1$, $\mathcal{R}'_2$, and $\mathcal{R}'_3$, respectively (See Figure 3(c)).

Estimating Stage. The three sample sets are observations used to estimate N_{q_1} and N_{q_2}. By similar proof for Theorem 2, $\hat{N}_{q_1}$ and $\hat{N}_{q_2}$ in Equation (5) and Equation (6) are proven to be the asymptotically unbiased estimators of N_{q_1} and N_{q_2}.

$$\hat{N}_{q_1}^{CRIS} = \frac{n_1}{B_1}\left(\sum_{t=1}^{\lceil B_1 n'_1/n_1 \rceil} f_{q_1}(\hat{R}_t^{q'_1}) + \sum_{t'=1}^{\lceil B_1 n'_3/n_1 \rceil} f_{q_1}(\hat{R}_{t'}^{q'_3})\right), \tag{5}$$

$$\hat{N}_{q_2}^{CRIS} = \frac{n_2}{B_2}\left(\sum_{t=1}^{\lceil B_2 n'_2/n_2 \rceil} f_{q_2}(\hat{R}_t^{q'_2}) + \sum_{t'=1}^{\lceil B_2 n'_3/n_2 \rceil} f_{q_2}(\hat{R}_{t'}^{q'_3})\right), \tag{6}$$

where $f_q(R) = \sum_{r \in R \vee q} \frac{1}{k_r^q}$.

In next subsection, we prove that for two concurrent overlapping queries, CRIS algorithm outperforms RIS algorithm with smaller estimation variance and less sampling budget.

5.3 Multiple Concurrent Overlapping Queries

Given concurrent queries $Q = \{q_1, \cdots, q_M\}$, the entire spatio-temporal region of those queries is denoted as $q_0 = \vee_{q \in Q} q$. CRIS partitions q_0 into non-overlapping spatio-temporal regions, so each region represents an intersection of a unique subset of queries in Q. Taking the partition as stratification for concurrent queries, we randomly sample index leaf nodes from each region, and reuse the samples to estimate the answers of queries that cover that region. Below we elaborate the details of stratifying q_0 and performing sampling and estimations. The detailed CRIS algorithm is summarized in Algorithm 1.

Stratification. We divide q_0 into $M' \geq M$ non-overlapping queries by the boundaries of q_i's, i.e., $Q' = \{q'_1, \cdots, q'_{M'}\}$, such that $q_0 = \vee_{q' \in Q'} q'$ holds. Let $Q_j \subseteq Q$ be a subset of Q with the size as $1 \leq |Q_j| \leq M$, and $\bar{Q}_j = Q - Q_j$ be the complementary set of Q_j with the size as $|\bar{Q}_j| = M - |Q_j|$. Each $q'_j = \wedge_{q \in Q_j} q - \vee_{q' \in \bar{Q}_j} q'$ with $1 \leq j \leq M'$ corresponds to a region that only covers the intersection of all regions in Q_j, but not any region in $\bar{Q}_j$, as shown in Figure 3(a). Denote the index leaf node set of q'_j as $\mathcal{R}'_j$ with n'_j index leaf nodes. $\mathcal{R}'_j$'s are non-overlapping with each other. Let $Q'_i \subseteq Q'$ with $1 \leq i \leq M$ be a subset of Q' such that $q_i = \vee_{q' \in Q'_i} q'$ holds, namely, each q_i is divided (or stratified) into strata, i.e., Q'_i, which enables us to perform sampling on each q'_j. Note that every index leaf node in the population is assigned to only one stratum and no index leaf node can be excluded.

Algorithm 1 Concurrent random index sampling (CRIS) algorithm

INPUT: Queries $Q = \{q_1, \cdots, q_M\}$, with $\epsilon_i > 0, 0 < \alpha_i \leq 1$.
OUTPUT: Sample Sets $\hat{\mathcal{R}}'_j = \{\hat{R}_1^{q'_j}, \cdots, \hat{R}_{B'_j}^{q'_j}\}, 1 \leq j \leq M'$.
Computer budgets $\{B_1, \cdots, B_M\}$ by Theorem 3.
Generate $\{Q_1, \cdots, Q_{M'}\}$; Each $Q_j \subseteq Q$ and $q'_j = \wedge_{q \in Q_j} q - \vee_{q' \in \bar{Q}_j} q' \neq \phi$.
Keep the non-overlapping region set $Q' = \{q'_1, \cdots, q'_{M'}\}$;
Generate non-overlapping leaf node sets $\{\mathcal{R}'_1, \cdots, \mathcal{R}'_{M'}\}$;
Generate $\{Q'_1, \cdots, Q'_M\}$; Each $Q'_i \subseteq Q'$ and $q_i = \vee_{q' \in Q'_i} q'$.
for $1 \leq j \leq M'$ **do**
  Each sampling budget $B'_j = \max_{q_i \in Q_j} \lceil B_i n'_j/n_i \rceil$;
  Sample leaf nodes from each $\mathcal{R}'_j$ with budget B'_j to obtain $\hat{\mathcal{R}}'_j$;

Sampling on strata. From Theorem 3, the estimation accuracy requirement ϵ_i and α_i, with $1 \leq i \leq M$, determines the sampling budget B_i needed for each q_i. Then, the leaf node set $\mathcal{R}'_j$ of the stratum q'_j is sampled independently with a sampling budget $B'_j \propto n'_j$, namely, proportionate allocation is employed to ensure that the sampling budget fraction in each stratum q'_i is proportional to n'_j. To be precise, for each query q_i, stratum $q'_j \in Q'_i$ is assigned with $B'_j(q_i) = \lceil B_i n'_j/n_i \rceil$ sampling budget. Instead of collecting samples from q'_j repeatedly for each $q_i \in Q_j$, with a total budget of $\tilde{B}'_j = \sum_{q_i \in Q_j} B'_j(q_i)$, we collect only $B'_j = \max_{q_i \in Q_j} B'_j(q_i)$ samples from q'_j and allow sample reuse when performing estimations for different $q_i \in Q_j$. Obviously, $B'_j < \tilde{B}'_j$.

Estimator Design. After the sampling process, a total of M' sample sets are drawn randomly from leaf node sets $\mathcal{R}'_1, \cdots, \mathcal{R}'_{M'}$.

They are expressed as

$$\hat{\mathcal{R}}'_1 = \{\hat{R}_1^{q'_1}, \cdots, \hat{R}_{B'_1}^{q'_1}\}, \cdots, \hat{\mathcal{R}}'_{M'} = \{\hat{R}_1^{q'_{M'}}, \cdots, \hat{R}_{B'_{M'}}^{q'_{M'}}\}.$$

These sample sets are observations for estimating $N_{q_1}, \cdots, N_{q_M}$. Below we first present the asymptotically unbiased estimator of N_{q_i} in Theorem 4. Then, we discuss the corresponding estimation accuracy.

THEOREM 4. *Using CRIS algorithm, $\hat{N}_{q_i}$ in Equation (7) is the asymptotically unbiased estimator of N_{q_i}.*

$$\hat{N}_{q_i}^{CRIS} = \frac{n_i}{B_i} \sum_{q'_j \in Q'_i} \sum_{t=1}^{\lceil B_i n'_j / n_i \rceil} f_{q_i}(\hat{R}_t^{q'_j}), \quad (7)$$

where $f_q(R) = \sum_{r \in R \vee q} \frac{1}{k_r^q}$.

PROOF. Since each $\hat{R}_t^{q'_j}$ is chosen uniformly at random from the same population space $\mathcal{R}'_j$, $f_{q_i}(\hat{R}_t^{q'_j})$'s with $1 \leq t \leq B'_j$ are all independent and follow the same distribution. Thus, they have the same expectation as $E[f_{q_i}(\hat{R}_t^{q'_j})] = \sum_{R \in \mathcal{R}'_j} f_{q_i}(R)/n'_j$. Using the linearity of the expectation, we prove $E[\hat{N}_{q_i}] = N_{q_i}$ for each $1 \leq i \leq M$. □

Performance comparison to RIS algorithm.

THEOREM 5. *For $M > 1$ concurrent overlapping queries, CRIS algorithm achieves lower estimation variance with less sampling budget than RIS algorithm.*

PROOF. Consider M concurrent overlapping queries $Q = \{q_1, \cdots, q_M\}$, with accuracy requirements $\epsilon_i > 0$ and $0 < \alpha_i \leq 1$, $i \in \{1, \cdots, M\}$. Below, we prove (1) CRIS requires less number of samples than individually applying RIS; (2) for the estimation accuracy of each query $q \in Q$, CRIS always outperforms RIS.
(1)*Sampling budget.* By Theorem 3, the sampling budgets $B_1, \cdots, B_M$ of M queries in Q can be obtained. With sample reuse, the total budget spent using CRIS algorithm is $B^{CRIS} = \sum_{j=1}^{M'} B'_j = \sum_{j=1}^{M'} \max_{q_i \in Q_j} \lceil B_i n'_j / n_i \rceil \leq \sum_{j=1}^{M'} \sum_{q_i \in Q_j} \lceil B_i n'_j / n_i \rceil = \sum_{i=1}^{M} B_i = B^{RIS}$.
(2)*Estimation accuracy.* Given a query $q \in Q$, CRIS divides q into $M_q \geq 1$ non-overlapping spatio-temporal regions (strata), q'_j's, with $1 \leq j \leq M_q$, with each q'_j covering n'_j index leaf nodes. Denote $\mathcal{R}^q$ and $\mathcal{R}'_j$ as the index leaf node sets of q and q'_j, respectively. We now prove that given the same sampling budget B, the estimation variances (when using RIS and CRIS algorithms) follow $Var[\hat{N}_q^{CRIS}] \leq Var[\hat{N}_q^{RIS}]$.

Recall that each sample $\hat{R}_t^q \in \mathcal{R}^q$ is drawn uniformly at random from $\mathcal{R}^q$. Hence, for RIS, each random variable $f_q(\hat{R}_t^q)$ follows the same distribution with the expectation $\mu = E[f_q(\hat{R}_t^q)]$ and the variance as $Var[f_q(\hat{R}_t^q)] = \frac{1}{n}\sum_{i=1}^{n}(f_q(R_i^q) - \mu)^2$. Then, the variance of the estimator $\hat{N}_q^{RIS}$ (Equation (1)) is computed as

$$Var[\hat{N}_q^{RIS}] = Var\left[\frac{n}{B}\sum_{t=1}^{B} f_q(\hat{R}_t^q)\right] = \frac{n^2}{B}\left(\frac{S}{n} - \left(\sum_{j=1}^{M_q} \frac{n'_j}{n}\mu_{q'_j}\right)^2\right),$$

where $S = \sum_{i=1}^{n} f_q^2(R_i^q)$ and $\mu_{q'_j} = E[f_q(\hat{R}_t^{q'_j})]$. On the other hand, the variance of $\hat{N}_q^{CRIS}$ (Equation (7)) can be written as

$$Var[\hat{N}_q^{CRIS}] = \frac{n^2}{B^2}\sum_{j=1}^{M_q} B'_j Var[f_q(\hat{R}_t^{q'_j})] = \frac{n^2}{B}\left(\frac{S}{n} - \sum_{j=1}^{M_q} \frac{n'_j}{n}\mu_{q'_j}^2\right).$$

From the above two variances, we obtain

$$Var[\hat{N}_q^{RIS}] - Var[\hat{N}_q^{CRIS}] = \frac{n^2}{B}\left(\left(\sum_{j=1}^{M_q} \frac{n'_j}{n}\mu_{q'_j}\right)^2 - \left(\sum_{j=1}^{M_q} \frac{n'_j}{n}\mu_{q'_j}^2\right)\right) = \frac{n^2}{B} Var[\mu_{q'_j}] \geq 0.$$

Hence, we proved that CRIS always acheives a lower estimation variance than RIS. □

6. EXPERIMENTAL RESULTS

In this section, we conduct extensive experiments to evaluate our RIS and CRIS algorithms in a large-scale user trajectory dataset from a leading cellular network service provider in China. We first introduce our dataset and configurations of the spatio-temporal database system. Then, we provide comprehensive comparison results between our RIS and CRIS algorithms and **E**xhaustive **S**earch (ES) method. The evaluation results demonstrate that RIS and CRIS algorithms can reduce the query processing time by two orders of magnitude, while preserving a relative error ratio lower than 10%, with only 1% search cost of ES method.

6.1 Data and System Descriptions

The trajectory dataset is a collection of mobile broadband (MBB) data in a large city in eastern China, with an urban area of about 400 square miles and three million people. The dataset was collected for eight days at the end of 2010, and it represents trajectories of 109,914 3G users. When a user's 3G service is enabled, the 3G device periodically reports its location by probing the nearby base stations. Moreover, once a user is using 3G data service, e.g., browsing websites or playing online games, the data exchanged with 3G network are also recorded [3]. We consider each user as a single trajectory. Each record in our database is represented as a spatio-temporal point of a user, where in total more than 400 million (407, 040, 083) records were obtained. Each record has four core attributes including *trajectory ID*, *longitude*, *latitude* and *time*. For each user (trajectory), there are eighty-two attributes associated, including the number of spatio-temporal points, time duration (seconds), spatial range (in square miles), activity frequency (number of points per hour), trajectory length (in miles), average speed, total data usage (in Bytes), etc. Figure 4 shows the trajectory distributions over four attributes. In the experiments, we consider a trajectory aggregate query returning the number of distinct trajectories in a spatio-temporal query range, with certain attribute constraints. The dataset takes 3 TB storage space in the database system.

The underlying spatio-temporal data storage system is based on *Clost* [29] and the query system is built on top of Spark [35], a MapReduce-like in-memory cluster computing system. The system runs on a cluster with three machines. Each machine has 24 Intel X5670 2.93GHz processors and 94GB memory. All machines run on Suse Linux Enterprise Server 11. Hadoop 0.20.2-cdh3u6 and Spark-0.7.3 are selected as the running platform.

6.2 Evaluation Results

We perform two sets of experiments for single and concurrent trajectory aggregate queries to evaluate the efficiency of RIS and CRIS algorithms, respectively.

6.2.1 Single Trajectory Aggregate Query

[3]Note that in a 3G network, a user can be located without users' GPS service enabled, since 3G network can locate a user by the signal strength between the device and the nearby base stations.

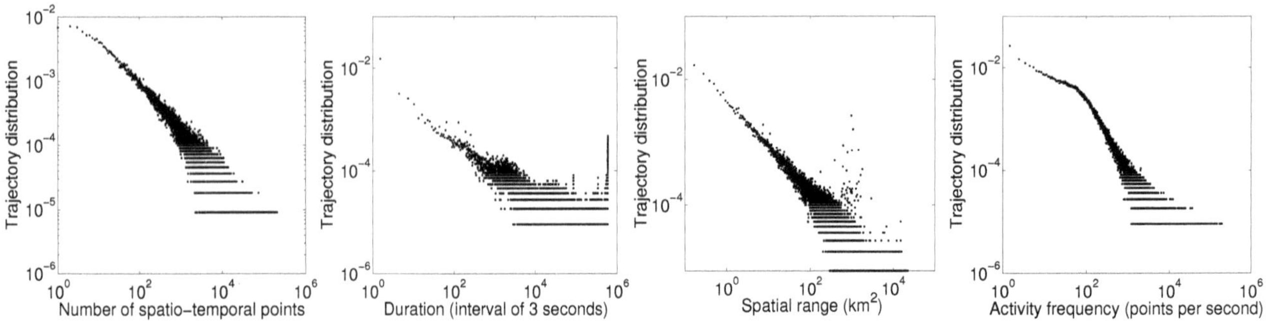

(a) Spatio-temporal points (b) Time duration (c) Spatial range (d) Activity frequency

Figure 4: Trajectory distributions over different attributes

In the experiments, we set the side length of the trajectory aggregate queries as 18 miles, and temporal range as all eight days, and uniformly at random generate 500 trajectory aggregate queries with the same query range size. We use Quad-tree and B-tree to index the trajectory data with different granularities, i.e., dividing the data into $n = 6,889$ (7k), $n = 13,410$ (13k), $n = 23,481$ (23k) index leaf nodes, respectively. For each granularity, we perform ES and RIS to estimate the total number of distinct trajectories, where we change the sampling budget ratio $a = B/n$ from 0.1% to 25.6%, i.e., the ratio between the number of sampled index leaf nodes and the total number of leaf nodes. Given a randomly generated query, we perform RIS sampling and estimation 200 times for each sampling budget ratio.

To evaluate the estimation accuracy of random index sampling, Figure 5(a) shows the normalized mean square error (NMSE) between our estimation results using RIS and the ground truth. NMSE [26] is a normalized measure of the dispersion of the estimates, defined as

$$NMSE(\hat{N}) = \frac{\sqrt{E[(\hat{N} - N)^2]}}{N}. \tag{8}$$

From Equation (8), an estimation with NMSE larger than 1 is not acceptable. From Figure 5(a), we observe that as the sampling budget increases, the average NMSE decreases quickly. For the same sampling budget ratio, smaller index leaf nodes (i.e., with larger n) lead to smaller NMSE, because smaller index leaf nodes lead to smaller variances of the number of distinct trajectories among index leaf nodes. Define the relative error ratio of an estimation as the normalized difference from the ground-truth, i.e., $b = (\hat{N} - N)/N$. Figure 5(b) shows the box plot of the relative error ratios. For each sampling budget ratio, three boxes are drawn for different granularities. Box plots display differences between populations, where the spacing between the different parts of the box helps indicate the degree of dispersion (spread) and skewness in the data, and identify outliers. The bottom and top of the box are always the first and third quartiles, and the band inside the box is always the second quartile (the median). The lowest datum is still within 1.5 interquartile range (IQR) of the lower quartile, and the highest datum is still within 1.5 IQR of the upper quartile [10]. Any data not included between the whiskers should be plotted as an outlier with a marker "+". We observe that the estimation converges to the ground truth as the sampling budget increases. Note that when the sampling budget ratio reaches 1%, the estimation error ratios become lower than 10%. Moreover, the dispersion of the estimated numbers validates the unbiasedness of the designed estimator (Equation (1)).

To evaluate the time efficiency of our RIS algorithm, Figure 5(c) shows the processing time of using ES and RIS. When ES is used, the processing time is more than 110 seconds (with a slight difference for different granularities), where RIS only needs on average 2 to 17 seconds, with two orders of magnitude time reduction. ***The total time reduction ratio is defined as a ratio of the reduced processing time to ES's processing time.*** Figure 5(d) shows the total time reduction ratio of RIS, which indicates the power of RIS, namely, a reduction ratio from 85% to 98%.

6.3 Concurrent Trajectory Aggregate Queries

To evaluate the performance of CRIS, we randomly generate concurrent queries and compare the time-efficiency and estimation accuracy with RIS and ES algorithms. Our results demonstrate that CRIS improves the performance significantly over that of ES and running RIS independently.

We generate three concurrent queries $\{q_1, q_2, q_3\}$ for 500 times with the following configuration. The spatial side lengths of q_1, q_2, and q_3 are 18 miles, 15 miles, and 12 miles, respectively. In time dimension, they all span for four days, i.e., from day 1 to day 4 for q_1, from day 3 to day 6 for q_2, and from day 5 to day 8 for q_3. We only consider a single index granularity as $n = 23,481$ (23k) index leaf nodes using Quad-tree and B-tree. To answer q_1, q_2, and q_3, we perform ES, RIS, and CRIS, with the sampling budget ratio $a = B/N$ varying from 0.1% to 25.6%, and compare their performance, in terms of the estimation accuracy, processing time, and time reduction ratio. Again, given three randomly generated concurrent queries, we run 200 times for RIS and CRIS for each sampling budget ratio.

Figure 6(a) presents the average normalized mean square error (NMSE) of our estimations using RIS and CRIS. CRIS indicates lower NMSE values for all concurrent queries q_1, q_2, and q_3. Moreover, as the sampling budget ratio increases, NMSE decreases for both RIS and CRIS. The box plots in Figure 6(b) show the distributions of the relative error ratios for q_1, q_2, and q_3. Clearly, the estimations by both RIS and CRIS algorithms converge to the ground-truth when the sampling budget ratio increases. In addition, given the same sampling budget ratio, CRIS has higher estimation accuracy than that of RIS. When the sampling budget ratio reaches 1%, the estimation error ratios are within 10%.

Moreover, Table 2 provides the numbers of sampled index leaf nodes collected by RIS and CRIS for different sampling budget ratios. We observe that CRIS requires much smaller number of samples than RIS by applying the overlapping sample reuse. Thus, the query processing time of CRIS is much smaller than that of RIS. As shown in Figure 6(c), comparing to ES (taking 226 seconds), RIS needs 5 to 26 seconds and CRIS only needs 4 to 17 seconds on average. Hence, CRIS reduces the processing time over RIS

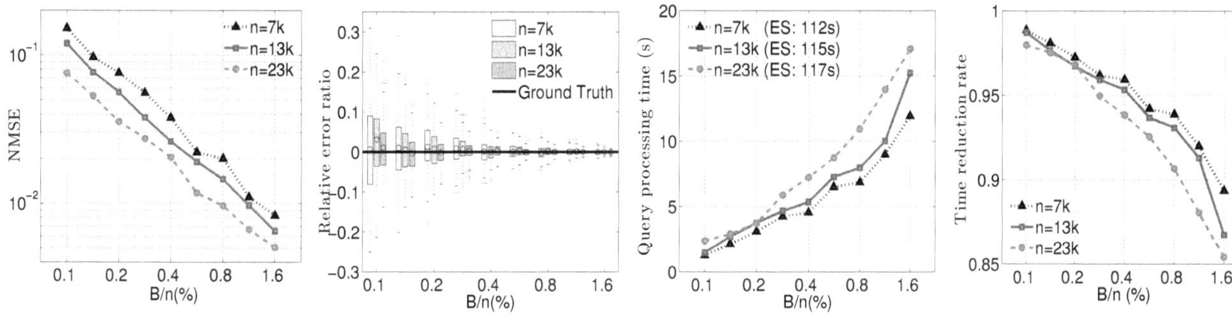

(a) NMSE (b) Relative error (c) Processing time (d) Time reduction rate

Figure 5: Performance comparison between RIS and exhaustive search (ES) algorithm

Table 2: Numbers of sampled indices required by RIS vs CRIS.

Sample Rate (%)	0.1	0.2	0.4	0.8	1.6	3.2	6.4	12.8	25.6
Samples (RIS)	35	69	139	278	555	1,111	2,221	4,443	8,885
Samples (CRIS)	21	42	84	167	334	669	1,337	2,675	5,350

by 20% to 34.6%. When considering the time reduction rate, Figure 6(d) shows that RIS and CRIS reduce the processing time over exhaustive search by 88% to 97% and 92% to 98%, respectively.

7. DISCUSSIONS AND EXTENSIONS

Throughout this paper, we take counting distinct trajectories in a spatio-temporal region as an example of trajectory aggregate queries. Our RIS and CRIS algorithms are in fact generic to other trajectory aggregate queries, such as sum and average. We briefly discuss how our sampling and estimation algorithms can be applied to these queries by adjusting the mapping function on an index leaf node. Due to the limited space, we introduce the unbiased estimators and omit the detailed proof and convergence analysis.

Sum. A typical sum aggregation query is "the total length of all trajectories with speed greater than 5 miles per hour in New York City during 2013". Let ℓ_r denote the length (in miles) of a trajectory r. Given an index leaf node R_i^q with $1 \leq i \leq n$, define $h_q(R_i^q) = \sum_{r \in R_i^q} \ell_r / k_r^q$. Then, the exact total length of trajectories is $\ell_q = \sum_{i=1}^n h_q(R_i^q)$. By following similar proof in Theorem 2, it is easy to prove that $\hat{\ell}_q$ in Equation (9) is the asymptotically unbiased estimator of ℓ_q.

$$\hat{\ell}_q = \frac{n}{B} \sum_{t=1}^{B} h_q(\hat{R}_t^q). \tag{9}$$

Average. An average query is "the average trajectory length of all trajectories with speed greater than 5 miles per hour in New York City during 2013". $L_q = \ell_q / N_q$ is thus the exact answer, where N_q is the number of distinct trajectories with speed greater than 5 miles per hour in New York City during 2013. The asymptotically unbiased estimator $\hat{L}_q$ is presented in Equation (10), which can be proven by the ratio form of the law of large numbers (Theorem 17.2.1 on p.426 in [22]).

$$\hat{L}_q = \frac{\sum_{t=1}^{B} h_q(\hat{R}_t^q)}{\sum_{t'=1}^{B} f_q(\hat{R}_{t'}^q)}. \tag{10}$$

8. CONCLUSION

Large-scale trajectory data create challenges in processing trajectory aggregate queries with stringent response-time constraints. Exhaustively brute-forcing the query space to get an exact answer is usually too time-consuming. Given a well-indexed trajectory database, in this paper, we develop random index sampling (RIS) algorithm that randomly samples a small number of index leaf nodes and the associated trajectories to estimate the answer to the trajectory aggregate query, with guaranteed estimation error bounds. Moreover, for concurrent trajectory aggregate queries with overlapping spatio-temporal query regions, we design concurrent random index sampling (CRIS) algorithm using stratified sampling and overlapping sample reuse that achieves higher estimation accuracy with less sampling budgets than that of using RIS algorithm independently. We evaluated our RIS and CRIS algorithms using a large-scale user trajectory dataset (with 3TB data) collected from a cellular service provider in China. Our extensive evaluation results show that RIS and CRIS algorithms outperform the exhaustive search algorithm for single and concurrent trajectory aggregate queries by two orders of magnitude in terms of processing time, while preserving a relative error ratio lower than 10%, with only 1% search cost of the exhaustive search algorithm.

9. ACKNOWLEDGEMENT

Yanhua Li and Zhi-Li Zhang were supported in part by NSF grants CNS-1117536, CRI-1305237, CNS-1411636, DoD DTRA grant HDTRA1-14-1-0040 and ARO MURI Award W911NF-12-1-0385. Jia Zeng was supported in part by NSFC grants No. 61373092 and 61033013, Natural Science Foundation of the Jiangsu Higher Education Institutions of China No. 12KJA520004, and Collaborative Innovation Center of Novel Software Technology and Industrialization.

10. REFERENCES

[1] J. L. Bentley. Multidimensional binary search trees used for associative searching. *Communications of the ACM*, 18(9):509–517, 1975.

[2] K. Beyer, P. J. Haas, B. Reinwald, Y. Sismanis, and R. Gemulla. On synopses for distinct-value estimation under multiset operations. In *ACM SIGMOD*, 2007.

[3] C. Böhm, S. Berchtold, and D. A. Keim. Searching in high-dimensional spaces: Index structures for improving the performance of multimedia databases. *ACM Computing Surveys*, 33(3):322–373, 2001.

[4] Y. Cai, K. A. Hua, G. Cao, and T. Xu. Real-time processing of range-monitoring queries in heterogeneous mobile databases. *IEEE TMC*, 5(7):931–942, 2006.

[5] V. P. Chakka, A. Everspaugh, and J. M. Patel. Indexing Large Trajectory Data Sets With SETI. In *CIDR*, 2003.

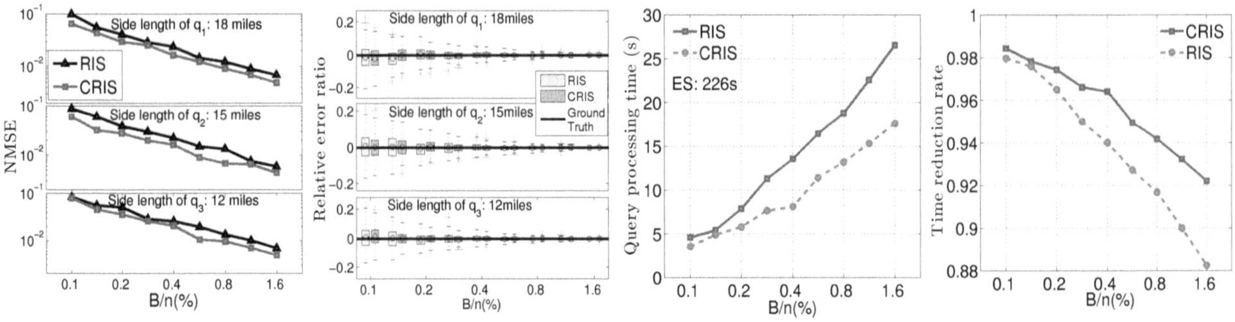

(a) NMSE (b) Relative error (c) Processing time (d) Time reduction rate

Figure 6: Performance comparison between CRIS, RIS and exhaustive search (ES) algorithms for continuous queries

[6] M. Charikar, S. Chaudhuri, R. Motwani, and V. Narasayya. Towards estimation error guarantees for distinct values. In *ACM PODS*, 2000.

[7] S. Chaudhuri, R. Motwani, and V. Narasayya. Random sampling for histogram construction: How much is enough? In *ACM SIGMOD*, 1998.

[8] K. Deng, K. Xie, K. Zheng, and X. Zhou. Trajectory indexing and retrieval. In *Computing with Spatial Trajectories*, pages 35–60. 2011.

[9] R. A. Finkel and J. L. Bentley. Quad trees a data structure for retrieval on composite keys. *Acta informatica*, 4(1):1–9, 1974.

[10] M. Frigge, D. C. Hoaglin, and B. Iglewicz. Some implementations of the boxplot. *The American Statistician*, 43(1):50–54, 1989.

[11] V. Gaede and O. Günther. Multidimensional access methods. *ACM Computing Surveys*, 30(2):170–231, 1998.

[12] P. B. Gibbons. Distinct sampling for highly-accurate answers to distinct values queries and event reports. In *VLDB*, 2001.

[13] R. H. Güting, T. Behr, and J. Xu. Efficient k-nearest neighbor search on moving object trajectories. *The VLDB Journal*, 19(5):687–714, 2010.

[14] P. J. Haas, J. F. Naughton, S. Seshadri, and L. Stokes. Sampling-based estimation of the number of distinct values of an attribute. In *VLDB*, 1995.

[15] Y. Huang, F. Zhu, M. Yuan, K. Deng, Y. Li, B. Ni, W. Dai, Q. Yang, and J. Zeng. Telco churn prediction with big data. In *ACM SIGMOD*, 2015.

[16] H. Jeung, M. L. Yiu, X. Zhou, C. S. Jensen, and H. T. Shen. Discovery of convoys in trajectory databases. In *VLDB*, 2008.

[17] D. M. Kane, J. Nelson, and D. P. Woodruff. An optimal algorithm for the distinct elements problem. In *ACM PODS*, 2010.

[18] J.-G. Lee, J. Han, and K.-Y. Whang. Trajectory clustering: A partition-and-group framework. In *ACM SIGMOD*, 2007.

[19] Y. Li, J. Luo, C.-Y. Chow, K.-L. Chan, Y. Ding, and F. Zhang. Growing the charging station network for electric vehicles with trajectory data analytics. In *IEEE ICDE*, 2015.

[20] Y. Li, M. Steiner, J. Bao, L. Wang, and T. Zhu. Region sampling and estimation of geosocial data with dynamic range calibration. In *IEEE ICDE*, 2014.

[21] Z. Li, B. Ding, J. Han, and R. Kays. Swarm: Mining relaxed temporal moving object clusters. In *VLDB*, 2010.

[22] S. Meyn and R. L. Tweedie. *Markov Chains and Stochastic Stability*. Cambridge University Press, New York, NY, USA, 2nd edition, 2009.

[23] F. Olken. *Random sampling from databases*. PhD thesis, University of California, 1993.

[24] D. Pfoser, C. S. Jensen, and Y. Theodoridis. Novel approaches to the indexing of moving object trajectories. In *VLDB*, 2000.

[25] I. Psaroudakis, M. Athanassoulis, and A. Ailamaki. Sharing data and work across concurrent analytical queries. In *VLDB*, 2013.

[26] B. Ribeiro and D. Towsley. Estimating and sampling graphs with multidimensional random walks. In *ACM IMC*, 2010.

[27] T. K. Sellis. Multiple-query optimization. *ACM TODS*, 13(1):23–52, 1988.

[28] S. Shalev-Shwartz and S. Ben-David. *Understanding Machine Learning: From Theory to Algorithms*. Cambridge University Press, 2014.

[29] H. Tan, W. Luo, and L. M. Ni. Clost: a hadoop-based storage system for big spatio-temporal data analytics. In *ACM CIKM*, 2012.

[30] Y. Tao and D. Papadias. Efficient historical r-trees. In *SSDBM*, 2001.

[31] Y. Tao and D. Papadias. MV3R-Tree: A spatio-temporal access method for timestamp and interval queries. In *VLDB*, 2001.

[32] C. Xu, Y. Gu, L. Chen, J. Qiao, and G. Yu. Interval reverse nearest neighbor queries on uncertain data with Markov correlations. In *IEEE ICDE*, 2013.

[33] J. Yuan, Y. Zheng, L. Zhang, X. Xie, and G. Sun. Where to find my next passenger? In *ACM UbiComp*, 2011.

[34] M. Yuan, K. Deng, J. Zeng, Y. Li, B. Ni, X. He, F. Wang, W. Dai, and Q. Yang. OceanST: A distributed analytic system for large-scale spatiotemporal mobile broadband data. In *VLDB Demo*, 2014.

[35] M. Zaharia, M. Chowdhury, M. J. Franklin, S. Shenker, and I. Stoica. Spark: cluster computing with working sets. In *HotCloud*, 2010.

[36] Y. Zheng, Y. Liu, J. Yuan, and X. Xie. Urban computing with taxicabs. In *ACM UbiComp*, 2011.

[37] P. Zhou, D. Zhang, B. Salzberg, G. Cooperman, and G. Kollios. Close pair queries in moving object databases. In *ACM SIGSPATIAL GIS*, 2005.

[38] J. Zobel, A. Moffat, and K. Ramamohanarao. Inverted files versus signature files for text indexing. *ACM TODS*, 23(4):453–490, 1998.

EsdRank: Connecting Query and Documents through External Semi-Structured Data

Chenyan Xiong
Language Technologies Institute
Carnegie Mellon University
Pittsburgh, PA 15213, USA
cx@cs.cmu.edu

Jamie Callan
Language Technologies Institute
Carnegie Mellon University
Pittsburgh, PA 15213, USA
callan@cs.cmu.edu

ABSTRACT

This paper presents EsdRank, a new technique for improving ranking using external semi-structured data such as controlled vocabularies and knowledge bases. EsdRank treats vocabularies, terms and entities from external data, as objects connecting query and documents. Evidence used to link query to objects, and to rank documents are incorporated as features between query-object and object-document correspondingly. A *latent listwise* learning to rank algorithm, Latent-ListMLE, models the objects as latent space between query and documents, and learns how to handle all evidence in a unified procedure from document relevance judgments. EsdRank is tested in two scenarios: Using a knowledge base for web search, and using a controlled vocabulary for medical search. Experiments on TREC Web Track and OHSUMED data show significant improvements over state-of-the-art baselines.

Keywords

Ranking, Learning to Rank, Semi-Structured Data, Controlled Vocabulary, MeSH, Knowledge Base, Freebase

1. INTRODUCTION

Prior research has produced many effective unsupervised retrieval models (e.g., BM25, language models, DPH) [9] and supervised learning to rank (LeToR) models (e.g., RankSVM, ListMLE) [19]. Unsupervised retrieval models successfully model relevance using information such as the terms in the query, the terms in the documents, and term level statistics such as term frequency (*tf*), inverse document frequency (*idf*), and document length. Learning to rank research derives new models and training methods to incorporate the rich information provided by unsupervised retrieved models, together with other evidence such as PageRank and spam score, as document ranking features, and provide state-of-the-art ranking performance.

Sometimes the information in the query and corpus alone is not sufficient to rank documents effectively. For example, query terms may be an incomplete description of a well-known concept, or there may be a *vocabulary mismatch* between queries and relevant documents. If the search engine relies solely on evidence from the query and corpus, its accuracy is limited.

One solution is to incorporate evidence that is *external* to the corpus, for example, from a controlled vocabulary, a thesaurus, WordNet, Wikipedia, or more recently, a knowledge base such as Freebase or DBpedia. Usually such resources are constructed manually or by carefully-designed information extraction systems and thus have different characteristics and greater consistency. The rich *semi-structured* information that they provide, for example, synonyms, ontologies, entities, and relationships, gives the search engine a different perspective for understanding the relationship between a query and a document, and provides opportunities for improving retrieval accuracy.

There is a long history of using *external semi-structured data* to improve full-text search [2, 10, 18, 20, 22, 29]. Prior research demonstrates that such resources can improve search accuracy. Many options have been proposed for various types of external resources, however there is little guidance about how to integrate new resources in a general manner. Prior work mainly focuses on how to better represent the query using external data, for example, how to select good expansion terms [29] and how to link to good entities [10]. The query representation formulated from external data provides useful enrichment of the original query. Then the ranking is produced by either an unsupervised retrieval model or an existing learning to rank model that combines multiple query representations. We strive to further boost ranking performance by developing a new learning to rank model that reasons jointly over query, external data, and documents.

This paper describes EsdRank, a new method for improving ranking using external, semi-structured data. EsdRank treats the vocabularies, terms and entities from external data as objects. The information from external data used for better query representation are used as features between the query and external objects. The document ranking evidence used in LeToR research is used as features between objects and documents. Instead of treating the features about query-objects and features about object-document individually, EsdRank uses a *latent-listwise* LeToR model, Latent-ListMLE, which treats the external objects as latent layer between query and documents, and learns how to handle the features between query, objects, and documents in one unified procedure directly from document relevance judgments.

Permission to make digital or hard copies of all or part of this work for personal or classroom use is granted without fee provided that copies are not made or distributed for profit or commercial advantage and that copies bear this notice and the full citation on the first page. Copyrights for components of this work owned by others than ACM must be honored. Abstracting with credit is permitted. To copy otherwise, or republish, to post on servers or to redistribute to lists, requires prior specific permission and/or a fee. Request permissions from Permissions@acm.org.
CIKM'15, October 19–23, 2015, Melbourne, Australia.
© 2015 ACM. ISBN 978-1-4503-3794-6/15/10 ...$15.00.
DOI: http://dx.doi.org/10.1145/2806416.2806456.

One major challenge in using external data is to find related objects for a query and documents. Several methods have been used by prior research [10, 29], but it is not clear how each of them contributes to final performance. This research explores three popular methods to select related objects from external data, including query annotation, object search, and document annotation. To investigate their effectiveness, we apply EsdRank with related objects generated by these methods on one newer type of external data, the Freebase knowledge base [3], and one classic type of external data, the MeSH controlled vocabulary[1], in web search and medical search respectively. Experiments on TREC Web Track and OHSUMED datasets show EsdRank's significant effectiveness over state-of-the-art ranking baselines, especially when using related objects from query annotations. Experiments also show that the effectiveness not only comes from the additional information from external data, but also our Latent-ListMLE model that uses it properly.

The next section describes related research. Section 3 discusses EsdRank, its Latent-ListMLE ranking model, related objects selection, and features. The experimental methodology and evaluation results are described in Sections 4 and 5 respectively. The last section summarizes the paper's contributions and discusses future work.

2. RELATED WORK

There is a long history of research on using information that is external to the document corpus to improve retrieval. The earliest information retrieval systems represented queries and documents using terms that were selected manually from controlled vocabularies. Controlled vocabulary representations required more effort to create during indexing and search, but were less susceptible to vocabulary mismatch between queries and documents, and required less sophisticated retrieval models.

As full-text search became popular, controlled vocabularies continued to be used in some systems. The use of controlled vocabularies is almost a necessity in medical search engines because queries are often about diseases, treatments or genes, whose special meanings may not be covered by their names. Typical procedures include using controlled vocabularies as alternative representations for matching query and document [22, 25], and expanding queries using synonyms [21]. However, the mixed results of systems participating in the TREC Genomics Track illustrate the difficulty of using controlled vocabularies in medical search; most systems require human efforts to be successful [26].

There is a rich literature on using dictionaries, thesauruses, and lexical resources such as WordNet to overcome vocabulary mismatch between queries and documents by adding synonyms and related concepts to queries and documents [18]. These approaches can be effective in enterprise search and domain-specific search environments [14], or improving recall of relevant documents in general search environments [18].

Recently a new type of semi-structured data, knowledge bases, has emerged. Examples include Wikipedia, its structured version DBpedia, Freebase [3] and the NELL KB [6]. Knowledge bases encode human knowledge about real world entities, such as names, aliases, descriptions, attributes, categories and relationships to other entities, in a semi-structured representation that is easily processed. Knowledge bases are a new path for search engines to better 'understand' queries and documents, but new techniques are required to use their novel and heterogeneous data types.

One intuitive method is to use the names and descriptions of knowledge base entities to expand the query. Xu et al. use pseudo relevance feedback in the Wikipedia corpus to obtain expansion terms that can be used to search other corpora [29]. Supervised methods have been used to pick better expansion terms from Wikipedia [4]. Wikipedia and other resources can be combined using both query concept weighting and query expansion for a better query representation [1]. Pan et al. use names of Freebase entities to expand queries [24]. Xiong et al. select expansion terms from Freebase entities retrieved by the query or discovered in its top retrieved documents [28]. Liu et al. had the best results in the TREC 2014 Web Track ad-hoc task using Freebase with manual labeling [20]. They pick entities textually similar with manually identified query entities, and rank documents by KL-divergence with these entities' descriptions.

A recent success in using Freebase is EQFE by Dalton et al. [10]. They study several ways to link Freebase entities to a query using query annotation, textual similarity, entity context model, and annotations from top retrieved documents. The name, alias and type fields of these entities are considered as possible expansion candidates. The combination of different linking methods, expansion fields, and hyper parameters in expansion are enumerated to get various expanded queries. These enumerated expansion queries are then used to calculate ranking scores for each document using a query likelihood or sequential dependency model. A learning to rank model uses these ranking scores as features for each document and produces final document rankings. EQFE provides a thorough exploration of information available to introduce entities between a query and documents, and is a major inspiration for EsdRank.

3. ESDRANK

EsdRank is intended to be a general technique for using external semi-structured data to improve ranking. External data elements are modeled as *objects*. An object could be a controlled vocabulary term, a term from another corpus, or a knowledge base entity. The evidence from the query, external data, and corpus is incorporated as features to express the relationship between query, object and document. A ranking model is then learned to rank documents with these objects and evidence.

In the first part of this section, we propose a novel latent listwise learning to rank model, Latent-ListMLE, as our ranking model. Latent-ListMLE handles the objects as a latent space between query and documents. The evidence between query-object, and object-document is naturally expressed as features connecting the query to the latent space, and then connecting latent space to documents.

Prior research found that a major challenge in using external data is to find related objects [7, 10, 29]. In the second part of this section, we explore three popular related object selection methods used in prior research. In the final part of this section, we describe the features used to connect query, objects and documents.

[1]http://www.nlm.nih.gov/mesh/meshhome.html

3.1 Latent-ListMLE

Given a query q and an initial set of retrieved documents D, a set of objects $O = \{o_1, ..., o_j, ..., o_m\}$ related to q and D is produced by one of the related object selection methods as described in Section 3.2. Features that describe relationships between query q and object o_j are denoted as vector v_j. Features that describe relationships between object o_j and document d_i are denoted as u_{ij}. The goal of Latent-ListMLE, like other learning to rank methods, is to re-rank D, but with the help of the related objects O and feature vectors $U = \{u_{11}, ..., u_{ij}, .., u_{nm}\}$ and $V = \{v_1, ..., v_j, ..., v_m\}$.

Latent-ListMLE treats O as the latent space between q and D and uses V, U as features to describe the relationships between query-object, and object-document. We will first revisit ListMLE [27], the listwise learning to rank model which Latent-ListMLE is built upon. Then we discuss the construction, learning, and ranking of Latent-ListMLE.

3.1.1 ListMLE Revisited

ListMLE defines the probability of a ranking (a list) being generated by a query in a parametric model. Maximum likelihood estimation (MLE) is used to find parameters that maximize the likelihood of the best ranking(s). However, the sample space of all possible rankings is the permutation of all candidate documents D, which is too large. One contribution of ListMLE is that it reduces the sample space by assuming the probability of a document being ranked at position i is independent of those ranked at previous positions.

Specifically, with a likelihood loss and a linear ranking model, ListMLE defines the probability of a document d_i being ranked at position i as:

$$p(d_i|q, S_i) = \frac{\exp(w^T x_i)}{\sum_{k=i}^{n} \exp(w^T x_k)}, \tag{1}$$

where $S_i = \{d_i \dots d_n\}$ are the documents that were not ranked in positions $1 \dots i-1$, x_i is the query-document feature vector for d_i, and w is the parameter vector to learn.

Equation 2 defines the likelihood of a given ranking $\vec{D}$ of candidate documents.

$$p(\vec{D}|q; w) = \prod_{i=1}^{n} \frac{\exp(w^T x_i)}{\sum_{k=i}^{n} \exp(w^T x_k)}. \tag{2}$$

The parameter vector w is learned by maximizing the likelihood for all given queries q_k and their best rankings $\vec{D}_k^*$ given document relevance judgments:

$$\hat{w} = \arg\max_{w} \prod_{k} p(\vec{D}_k^*|q_k; w). \tag{3}$$

This is an unconstrained convex optimization problem that can be solved efficiently by gradient methods.

3.1.2 Latent-ListMLE Construction

Latent-ListMLE extends ListMLE by adding a latent layer in the ranking generation process. The latent layer contains related objects O as possible representations of the original query q.

With the latent layer O, the ideal generation process of a ranking $\vec{D}$ is to first sample a ranking of objects $\vec{O}$, and then sample document ranking $\vec{D}$ based on $\vec{O}$. However, this process is also impractical due to the huge sampling space. Similarly to ListMLE, we assume that the probabilities of picking objects and documents at each position are independent with those at previous positions. Thus, the generative process is redefined to be:

For each position from 1 to N:

1. Sample o_j from multinomial distribution $Multi(O|q)$, with probability $p(o_j|q)$; and
2. Sample d_i from multinomial distribution $Multi(S_i|o_j)$, with probability $p(d_i|o_j, S_i)$.

We further define:

$$p(o_j|q) = \frac{\exp(\theta^T v_j)}{\sum_{k=1}^{m} \exp(\theta^T v_k)} \tag{4}$$

$$p(d_i|o_j, S_i) = \frac{\exp(w^T u_{ij})}{\sum_{k=i}^{n} \exp(w^T u_{kj})}, \tag{5}$$

where v_j is the query-object feature vector for o_j; u_{ij} is the object-document feature vector between d_i and o_j; m is the number of objects; and θ and w are the model parameters.

In this generative process, the latent layer is the sampled objects produced by query q, and the document ranking probability is conditioned on the sampled objects instead of the query. With this extension, the probability of picking d_i at position i is:

$$p(d_i|q, S_i) = \sum_{j=1}^{m} p(d_i|o_j, S_i) p(o_j|q) \tag{6}$$

$$= \sum_{j=1}^{m} \frac{\exp(w^T u_{ij})}{\sum_{k=i}^{n} \exp(w^T u_{kj})} \frac{\exp(\theta^T v_j)}{\sum_{k=1}^{m} \exp(\theta^T v_k)} \tag{7}$$

and the probability of ranking $\vec{D}$ given q is:

$$p(\vec{D}|q; w, \theta) = \prod_{i=1}^{n} \sum_{j=1}^{m} p(d_i|o_j, S_i) p(o_j|q). \tag{8}$$

Latent-ListMLE also uses query-document features by adding a 'query node' o_0 to O that represents query q. The features relating query q to o_0 are set to 0, thus o_0 is the 'origin point' for related objects. The features relating o_0 to documents are typical LeToR query-document features. The combination of query-document features and object-document features is done by treating them as individual dimensions in U, and setting missing feature dimensions' values to zero. So the dimensions referring to object-document similarities for the query node are set to zero, and vice versa.

Our idea of representing the query via related objects ($p(o|q)$) is similar to query expansion. In fact, if we use expansion terms as our related objects, and discard the document ranking part, Latent-ListMLE becomes a supervised query expansion method. On the other hand, if we only use the query node as related object, Latent-ListMLE is exactly the same as ListMLE. The difference is that, in Latent-ListMLE, the connections from query to latent layer, and from latent layer to documents are learned together in one unified procedure, which finds the best combination of query representation ($p(o|q)$) and document ranking ($p(d|o)$) together, instead of only focusing on one of them.

3.1.3 Learning

The parameters w and θ are learned using MLE with given queries and their best rankings. To keep the notation clear, we present the derivation with one training query q, without loss of generality.

For a training query q and its best ranking $\vec{D^*}$ derived from relevance labels, their log likelihood is:

$$l(\vec{D^*}|q;w,\theta) = \log p(\vec{D^*}|q;w,\theta) \tag{9}$$

$$= \sum_{i=1}^{n} \log \sum_{j=1}^{m} \Big(\frac{\exp(w^T u_{ij})}{\sum_{k=i}^{n} \exp(w^T u_{kj})} \times \tag{10}$$

$$\frac{\exp(\theta^T v_j)}{\sum_{k=1}^{m} \exp(\theta^T v_k)} \Big).$$

The goal of MLE is to find parameters w^*, θ^* such that:

$$w^*, \theta^* = \arg\max_{w,\theta} l(\vec{D^*}|q;w,\theta). \tag{11}$$

Directly maximizing Equation 10 is difficult due to the summation of the latent variables inside the log, thus we use the EM algorithm to solve this optimization problem.

The **E step** finds the posterior distribution of hidden variable o_j for each ranking position given the current parameters θ_{old} and w_{old}.

$$\pi(o_j|d_i,q) = p(o_j|d_i,q;\theta_{old},w_{old})$$
$$= \frac{p(d_i|o_j,S_i;w_{old})p(o_j|q;\theta_{old})}{\sum_{k=1}^{m} p(d_i|o_k,S_i;w_{old})p(o_k|q;\theta_{old})}.$$

The **M step** maximizes the expected log complete likelihood.

$$E(\tilde{l}) = E_{\pi(\vec{O}|\vec{D^*},q)} \log p(\vec{D^*},\vec{O}|q;w,\theta)$$
$$= \sum_{i=1}^{n}\sum_{j=1}^{m} \pi(o_j|d_i,q) \log p(d_i|o_j,S_i)p(o_j|q)$$
$$= \sum_{i,j} \pi(o_j|d_i,q) \log \frac{\exp(w^T u_{ij})}{\sum_{k=i}^{n} \exp(w^T u_{kj})} \frac{\exp(\theta^T v_j)}{\sum_{k=1}^{m} \exp(\theta^T v_k)}.$$

We use gradient ascent to maximize the expectation. The gradients are:

$$\frac{\partial E(\tilde{l})}{\partial w} = \sum_{i,j} \pi(o_j|d_i,q) \{u_{ij} - \frac{\sum_{k=i}^{n} u_{kj} \exp w^T u_{kj}}{\sum_{k=i}^{n} \exp w^T u_{kj}}\} \tag{12}$$

$$\frac{\partial E(\tilde{l})}{\partial \theta} = \sum_{i,j} \pi(o_j|d_i,q) \{v_j - \frac{\sum_{k=1}^{m} v_k \exp(\theta^T v_k)}{\sum_{k=1}^{m} \exp(\theta^T v_k)}\}. \tag{13}$$

The E step is very efficient with the closed form solution. The M step is an easy convex optimization problem. Intuitively, the E step finds the best assignment of object probabilities under current parameters and best document rankings, thus transferring document relevance information to latent objects. The M step learns the best parameters that fit the object probabilities provided by the E step. EM iterations are guaranteed to improve the likelihood until convergence. However, the overall optimization is not convex and has local optima. In practice the local optima problem can be suppressed by repeating the training several times with random initial w and θ, and using the result that converges to the largest likelihood.

3.1.4 Ranking

Given a learned model, a query, and an initial ranking, a new ranking is constructed by picking the document that has the highest probability $p(d_i|q,S_i)$ at each position from 1 to n. The complexity of picking one document is $O(nm)$, thus the total cost of ranking n documents with m related objects is $O(n^2m)$, which is slower than ListMLE's $O(n \log n)$ ranking complexity. We can restrict the number of documents n (e.g. 100) and related objects m (e.g. < 5) to maintain reasonable efficiency.

3.2 Related Objects

How to find related objects O given query q and documents D is important for using external data. Many options have been proposed by prior research [10, 20, 24, 29], but it is not clear which is the most reliable. This research studies the following three popular automatic methods to find related objects.

Query Annotation selects the objects that directly appear in the query. Based on specific object types in the external data, one can choose corresponding techniques to 'annotate' them to the query, for example, entity linking techniques [7] to find entities that appear in the query, or all query terms when the objects are terms from an external corpus.

Object Search selects the objects that are textually similar to the query. Search engines can be used to find such objects. We can build an index for all the objects in external data, in which each document is the textual data about the object, for example, name, alias, description and context words of an entity. Then textually similar objects can be retrieved by running the query to the index.

Document Annotation selects the objects that appear in retrieved documents D. The terms in retrieved documents have been widely used in query expansion. The entities that are annotated to D were also useful in prior work [10]. This method introduces objects that are more indirectly related to the query, such as 'President of United States' for the query 'Obama family tree'. A typical method to score and select objects from retrieved documents is the RM3 pseudo relevance feedback model [17].

3.3 Features

Representing the relationship between query and related objects is the major focus of prior research in using external data. We explore the following query-object features in EsdRank; most of them are inspired by Dalton et al. [10].

3.3.1 Features between Query and Objects

Object Selection Score features are the scores produced by the object selection step: Annotator confidence, object ranking score, and RM3 model score $s(q,o)$.

Textual Similarity features cover the similarities between the query and the object's textual fields. For example, one can use coordinate matches, BM25 scores, language model scores, and sequential dependency model (SDM) scores between the query and the object's textual fields, such as name, alias (if any) and descriptions if using entities.

Ontology Overlap features use the ontology, a common type of information for some external semi-structured datasets. When an ontology is available, one can build a multiclass classifier that classifies the query into the ontology, and use the overlaps with the object's ontology as features.

Object Frequency is the number of documents in the corpus the object appears in (e.g. term) or is annotated to (e.g. entity). This feature is query independent and distinguishes frequent objects from infrequent ones.

Similarity with Other Objects are the max and mean similarity of this object's name with the other related objects'. These features distinguish objects that have similar names with other related objects from those that do not.

3.3.2 Features between Objects and Documents

In learning to rank, rich query-document ranking features, such as multiple retrieval algorithms on different document fields, have been shown very important for ranking performance [19]. Our object-document features are similar to query-document features widely used in LeToR research. But objects may have richer contents than queries, enabling a larger set of features.

Textual Similarity features measure the similarity of a document and an object's textual fields. BM25, language model, SDM, coordinate match, and cosine similarity in the vector space model are used to calculate similarities between all combinations of an object's textual fields and a document's fields. These retrieval models are applied by using the object to 'retrieve' the document. The fusion of these similarity features provides multiple ways to express the object-document similarities for EsdRank.

Ontology Overlap features are the same as the ontology overlap features between query and object. The same multiclass classifier can be used to classify documents, and overlaps in the object's and document's top categories can be used as features.

Graph Connection features introduce information about the relationships in the external data and document annotations. If such graph-like information is available, one can start from the object, traverse its relations, and record the number of annotated objects reached at each step (usually within 2 steps) as features. These features model the 'closeness' of the object and the document's annotations in the external data's relationship graph.

Document Quality features are commonly used in learning to rank. We use classic document quality features such as document length, URL length, spam score, number of inlinks, stop word fraction, and whether the document is from Wikipedia (web corpus only).

3.4 Discussion

EsdRank provides general guidance about how to use external semi-structured data in ranking. When an external dataset is available, to use it in ranking, one can first use object selection methods to find related objects for each query, and then extract query-object and object-document features. Although the detailed object selection methods and features may vary for different datasets, we list some common related object selection methods and features that have been used widely in prior research to start with. One can also derive new related object selection methods and features based on other available information.

Related objects and features are handled by our latent listwise LeToR model, Latent-ListMLE. It models the objects as the latent space. As a result, evidence is decoupled into a query-object part and an object-document part, which is easier to learn than mixed together (as shown in Section 5.2). Instead of solely focusing on the query-object part, or the document ranking part, Latent-ListMLE learns them together using EM. Our experiments show that the additional evidence from external data and Latent-ListMLE are both necessary for EsdRank's effectiveness.

4. EXPERIMENTAL METHODOLOGY

EsdRank is intended to be a general method of using external semi-structured data, thus experiments test it with two types of semi-structured data and search tasks: Web search using the Freebase knowledge base, and medical search using the MeSH controlled vocabulary. The former uses a newer type of semi-structured data, a noisy corpus, and queries from web users; the latter uses a classic form of semi-structured data, a clean corpus, and queries from domain experts. Datasets and ranking features are determined by these two choices, as described below.

Data: Experiments on web search using Freebase were conducted with ClueWeb09-B and ClueWeb12-B13, two web corpora used often in IR research. Each corpus contains about 50 million English web documents. The 2009-2013 TREC Web Tracks provided 200 queries with relevance assessments for ClueWeb09 and 50 queries with relevance assessments for ClueWeb12. We used a snapshot of Freebase provided by Google on Oct 26th, 2014.[2]

Experiments on medical search using the MeSH controlled vocabulary were conducted with the OHSUMED corpus, a medical corpus used often in IR research. It contains abstracts of medical papers that are manually annotated with MeSH terms. The OHSUMED dataset includes 106 queries with relevance assessments. We used the 2014 MeSH dump provided by the U.S. National Libarary of Medicine (NIH).[3]

Indexing and Base Retrieval Model: The ClueWeb and OHSUMED corpora were indexed by the Indri search engine, using default stemming and stopwords. ClueWeb documents contain title, body and inlink fields. OHSUMED documents contain title and body fields.

Freebase and MeSH also were indexed by Indri, with each object (entity, controlled vocabulary term) treated as a document containing its associated text fields (name, alias, description). Objects without descriptions were discarded. Retrieval was done by Indri using its default settings.

Spam filtering is important for ClueWeb09, thus we removed the 70% spammiest documents using Waterloo spam scores [8]. Prior research questions the value of spam filtering for ClueWeb12 [10], thus we did not filter that dataset.

Related Objects: We implement three related generation methods as described in Section 3.2.

Query annotation (`AnnQ`) was done by TagMe [12], one of the best systems in the Short (Query) Track at the ERD14 workshop competition [7]. TagMe annotates the query with Wikipedia page ids. Wikipedia page ids were mapped to Freebase objects using their Wikipedia links and to MeSH controlled vocabulary terms using exact match.

Object search (`Osrch`) was done with the Indri search engine for both external semi-structured datasets. We investigated using Google's Freebase Search API to search for Freebase objects and PubMed's MeSH query annotations to annotate MeSH objects. Neither was significantly better than Indri search or TagMe annotation, thus we only report results with public solutions.

Google's FACC1 dataset provided annotations of Freebase entities in ClueWeb documents[4] [13]. The OHSUMED dataset contains MeSH annotations for each document. Document annotation (`AnnD`) objects are generated by first

---

[2]https://developers.google.com/freebase/data
[3]http://www.nlm.nih.gov/mesh/filelist.html
[4]http://lemurproject.org/clueweb09/

Table 1: Query-object features. 'Web' and 'Medical' indicate the number of features in each corpus.

Feature	Web	Medical
Score from Query Annotation	1	1
Score from Object Search	1	1
Score from Document Annotation	1	1
Language model of object's description	1	1
SDM of object's description	1	1
BM25 of object's description	1	1
Coordinate match of object's text fields	3	3
Top 3 categories overlap	1	1
Object's idf in corpus's annotation	1	1
Similarity with other objects	2	2
Total Dimensions	13	13

Table 2: Object-document features. 'Web' and 'Medical' indicate the number of features in each corpus. 'Field combinations' refers to combinations of an object's and a document's fields. An object's fields include name, alias, description, query minus name, query minus alias, and query minus description. ClueWeb documents (for Fb) contain title, body and inlink fields. OSHUMED documents (for MeSH) contain title and body fields.

Feature	Web	Medical
Language model of field combinations	18	12
SDM of field combinations	18	12
Cosine correlation of field combinations	18	12
Coordinate match of field combinations	18	12
BM25 of field combinations	18	12
Top 3 cateogories overlap	1	1
Is annotated to document	1	1
Connected in graph at 1,2 hop	2	0
Total Dimensions	94	62

retrieving documents from the ClueWeb or OHSUMED corpus, and then using the RM3 relevance model [17] to select annotated objects from these documents.

Thus, the experiments consider query annotation (`EsdRank-AnnQ`), object search (`EsdRank-Osrch`) and document annotation (`EsdRank-AnnD`) methods to select related objects.

Feature Extraction: We extract features described in Section 3.3. Our feature lists are shown in Tables 1–3.

For object-document text similarity features, each object field is dynamically expanded with a virtual field that contains any query terms that the field does not contain. For example, given an object with name 'Barack Obama' and query 'Obama family tree', the text 'family tree' is added to the object as a virtual field called 'query minus name'. Similar expansion is performed for 'query minus alias' and 'query minus description' fields. As a result, Latent-ListMLE also knows which part of the query is not covered by an object. This group of features is very important for long queries, in order to make sure documents only related to a small fraction of the query are not promoted too much.

The ontology features use the linear multiclass SVM implementation of SVMLight [15] as the classifier. The Freebase classes are the 100 most frequent (in FACC1 annotation) bottom categories in Freebase's two-level ontology tree. The classes for MeSH are all of the top level categories in

Table 3: Query-document and document quality features used by EsdRank and learning to rank baselines. 'Web' and 'Medical' indicate the number of features in each corpus.

Feature	Web	Medical
Language model of doc's fields	3	2
SDM of doc's fields	3	2
Cosine correlation of doc's fields	3	2
Coordinate match of doc's fields	3	2
BM25 of doc's fields	3	2
Spam Score	1	0
Number of inlinks	1	0
Stop word fraction	1	1
URL length	1	0
Document length	1	1
Is Wikipedia	1	0
Total Dimensions	21	12

MeSH's ontology. The training data is the descriptions from objects of each class. Objects are classified by their descriptions. Documents are classified by their texts. Queries are classified using voting by the top 100 documents that Indri retrieves for them [5]. The accuracy of Multiclass SVM in cross-validating on training data is above 70%.

The graph connection features between Freebase entities and ClueWeb documents are calculated using Freebase's knowledge graph. We treat all edges the same, leaving further exploration of edge type to future work. We only use the reachable at zero hop for OHSUMED, that is whether the MeSH term is annotated to the document.

Evaluation Metrics: We use ERR@20 and NDCG@20, which are the main evaluation metrics in the TREC Web Track ad hoc task. Besides these two metrics that focus on the top part of ranking, we also use MAP@100, which considers the quality over the entire reranked section.

Statistical significance was tested by the permutation test (Fisher's randomization test) with p-value < 0.05, which is a common choice in IR tasks.

Hyper-Parameters and Training: We follow standards in prior work to set hyper-parameters. The number of documents retrieved and re-ranked is set to 100. The same set of documents is used to generate document annotation `AnnD`. All supervised ranking models are evaluated on the testing folds in 10-fold cross validation. Cross-validation partitioning is done randomly and kept the same for all experiments. To suppress the local optima problem, in each cross-validation fold Latent-ListMLE is trained ten times with random initialization. The training result with the largest likelihood on training data is used for testing. In order to maintain reasonable ranking efficiency and avoid too many noisy objects, the number of related objects from `AnnD` and `Osrch` are restricted to at most 3. This restriction does not change `AnnQ` as none of our queries has more than 3 annotations.

Baselines: The first baseline is the Sequential Dependency Model (`SDM`) [23] approach which is widely recognized as a strong baseline. For ClueWeb datasets, we find that Dalton et al's SDM results obtained with Galago[5] are stronger than our SDM results obtained with Indri, thus we use their SDM results as a baseline. We also use `EQFE` rankings provided by them as second baseline on ClueWeb data

[5]http://ciir.cs.umass.edu/downloads/eqfe/runs/

sets. On OHSUMED we use the Indri query language to obtain SDM results. EQFE is not included for OHSUMED as it is specially designed for knowledge bases. The third and fourth baselines are two state-of-the-art learning to rank baselines: RankSVM (pairwise) [16] and ListMLE (listwise) [27]. Their features are shown in Table 3 and are trained and tested exactly the same as EsdRank.

Three of our baseline algorithms were used widely in prior research; the fourth (EQFE) is included because it has important similarities to EsdRank. We could have included other methods that use external data, for example, Wikipedia for query expansion [4, 29], Wikipedia as one resource for query formulations [1], and MeSH as an alternate document representation [22]. These methods mainly focus on using external data to better represent the query; they rank documents with unsupervised retrieval models. In recent TREC evaluations, supervised LeToR systems that use rich ranking features have shown much stronger performance than unsupervised retrieval systems. Thus we mainly compare with LeToR models with document ranking features, e.g., those in Table 3, which we believe are the strongest baselines available now.

5. EVALUATION RESULTS

This section first presents experiment results about EsdRank's overall accuracy. Then it investigates the effectiveness of our Latent-ListMLE model, together with the influence of related object quality on EsdRank's performance.

5.1 Overall Performance

Tables 4a, 4b, and 4c show the retrieval accuracy of several baseline methods and three versions of EsdRank on ClueWeb09, ClueWeb12, and OHSUMED datasets. The three variants of EsdRank differ only in how related objects are selected. †, ‡, § and ¶ indicate statistical significance over SDM, RankSVM, ListMLE and EQFE. The change relative to ListMLE is shown in parentheses. Win/Tie/Loss is the number of queries improved, unchanged or damaged as compared to ListMLE by ERR@20. The best performing method according to each evaluation metric is marked **bold**.

On all three data sets, the best EsdRank methods outperform all baselines on all metrics. The gain over ListMLE varies from 3.33% (OHSUMED, MAP@100) to 21.85% (ClueWeb09, ERR@20), with 5–7% being typical. We note that ListMLE is a very strong baseline; there is little prior work that provides statistically significant gains of this magnitude over ListMLE on the ClueWeb datasets. These improvements show the effectiveness of external data in ranking, which is EsdRank's only difference with ListMLE.

On ClueWeb data sets, all three versions of EsdRank outperform EQFE, and the best performing version improves over EQFE by 10%-30%. Both EQFE and EsdRank use Freebase as external data and learning to rank models to rank documents. The features between query and object in EsdRank are very similar with those used in EQFE. Why does EsdRank perform better than EQFE?

One difference is in the object-document features. EQFE uses the language model or SDM score between an entity's textual fields and the whole document to connect the entity to the document, while EsdRank uses a much larger feature set (Table 2). The object-document features in Table 2 provide multiple different views of object-document relevancy, which has been shown very effective in LeToR research [19]. More object-document features also better propagate document relevance judgments to latent objects in Latent-ListMLE's EM training procedure, and help it learn better weights for query-object features. We have tried EsdRank with only language model scores between an object's textual fields and the document as object-document features, however, results with this smaller feature set are no better than EQFE. In Section 5.2, our second experiment also shows that our Latent-ListMLE model is another essential factor for EsdRank's performance with its ability to handle features in the two parts properly.

On ClueWeb09 and OHSUMED, query annotation (EsdRank-AnnQ) performs the best with statistically significant improvements on almost all evaluations over all baselines, indicating query annotation is still the most effective in finding reliable objects. On ClueWeb12, EsdRank-AnnQ also outperforms all baselines, although less statistical significance is observed due to fewer training queries (only 50). It is interesting to see that EsdRank-AnnD performs better than EsdRank-AnnQ on ClueWeb12. This is consistent with results of EQFE [10], showing that FACC1 annotation might be of better quality for ClueWeb12 queries than ClueWeb09 queries. EsdRank-Osrch performs the worst on all three data sets. The reason is that object search provides related objects that might be textually similar to the query, but are actually noise. The ranking models designed to rank document use assumptions that may not be suitable for objects, leaving room for improvement in future research.

The different effectiveness of EsdRank with different related object selection methods shows the importance of related object quality. It is also well recognized as one of the most essential factors in determining the usefulness of external data in prior research [7, 11, 20, 28]. In Section 5.3, our third experiment studies the correlation between related objects' quality and EsdRank's performance.

5.2 Effectiveness of Latent-ListMLE

To investigate the effectiveness of Latent-ListMLE, in this experiment, we compare it with ListMLE, using the same external evidence, but with features generated by feature engineering techniques similar to those in Dalton et al. [10].

Formally, for each query q and document d_i pair, we have objects $\{o_1, ..., o_j, ..., o_m\}$, query-object features $V = \{v_1, ..., v_j, ..., v_m\}$ and object-document features $U_i = \{u_{i1}, ..., u_{ij}, ..., u_{im}\}$. Let $|u|$ and $|v|$ be the feature dimensions for query-object features and object-document features. We generate $|u| \times |v|$ features $x_i = \{x_i(1,1), ..., x_i(k_1,k_2), ..., x_i(|u|,|v|)\}$ by enumerating all combination of features in U_i and V. The combination of k_1-th feature in V and k_2-th feature U_i is defined as: $x_i(k_1,k_2) = \sum_j v_j(k_1) \times u_{ij}(k_2)$, the summation of corresponding features over all possible related objects. One may notice that if we only use language model scores as object-document features, this set up is exactly the same as EQFE. We name these 'flat' features in comparison with Latent-ListMLE's latent space model.

We put these 'flat' features into ListMLE and use the same training-testing procedure to evaluate them on our datasets. Evaluation results are shown in Table 5. ListMLE-AnnQ, ListMLE-Osrch and ListMLE-AnnD refer to the flat model with features from related objects selected by query annotation, object search and document annotation respectively. Relative performance (in brackets) and Win/Tie/loss

Table 4: Performance of EsdRank. AnnQ, Osrch and AnnD refer to object selection methods: Query annotation, object search and document annotation. Relative changes compared to ListMLE are shown in parentheses. Win/Tie/Loss is the number of queries improved, unchanged or hurt compared to ListMLE. †, ‡, § and ¶ show statistic significance ($p < 0.05$ in permutation test) over SDM, RankSVM, ListMLE and EQFE. The best method for each evaluation metric is marked **bold**.

(a) ClueWeb09

Method	MAP@100		NDCG@20		ERR@20		Win/Tie/Loss
SDM	0.375	(−8.54%)	0.214	(−2.92%)	0.135	(−13.52%)	75/30/95
EQFE	0.364	(−11.14%)	0.213	(−3.73%)	0.139	(−11.21%)	77/27/96
RankSVM	0.352†	(−14.14%)	0.193†	(−12.54%)	0.147	(−6.10%)	59/37/104
ListMLE	0.410†,‡,¶	–	0.221†,‡	–	0.156†	–	–
EsdRank-AnnQ	**0.437**†,‡,§,¶	**(6.59%)**	**0.237**†,‡,§,¶	**(7.17%)**	**0.190**†,‡,§,¶	**(21.85%)**	88/42/70
EsdRank-Osrch	0.397†,‡,¶	(−3.16%)	0.219†,‡	(−0.68%)	0.155†	(−0.75%)	71/47/82
EsdRank-AnnD	0.403†,‡,¶	(−1.69%)	0.221†,‡	(0.19%)	0.167†,¶	(6.70%)	75/36/89

(b) ClueWeb12

Method	MAP@100		NDCG@20		ERR@20		Win/Tie/Loss
SDM	0.293	(−26.19%)	0.126	(−27.53%)	0.091	(−25.66%)	18/7/25
EQFE	0.319	(−19.74%)	0.146†	(−16.02%)	0.106	(−13.61%)	17/7/26
RankSVM	0.383†	(−3.66%)	0.161†	(−7.29%)	0.114	(−7.48%)	16/13/21
ListMLE	0.397†,¶	–	0.174†,¶	–	0.123†	–	–
EsdRank-AnnQ	0.410†,¶	(3.12%)	0.181†,¶	(3.78%)	**0.133**†,‡,§,¶	**(8.39%)**	20/12/18
EsdRank-Osrch	0.391†,¶	(−1.51%)	0.167†	(−3.88%)	0.121†	(−1.26%)	22/10/18
EsdRank-AnnD	**0.440**†,‡,§,¶	**(10.69%)**	**0.186**†,‡,§,¶	**(7.15%)**	0.132†,¶	(7.67%)	24/14/12

(c) OHSUMED

Method	MAP@100		NDCG@20		ERR@20		Win/Tie/Loss
SDM	0.413	(−0.27%)	0.332	(−2.96%)	0.453	(−6.14%)	38/11/57
RankSVM	0.396	(−4.31%)	0.336	(−1.89%)	0.453	(−6.12%)	43/14/49
ListMLE	0.414	–	0.343	–	0.483	–	–
EsdRank-AnnQ	**0.428**‡,§	**(3.33%)**	**0.355**†,‡,§	**(3.54%)**	**0.511**†,‡,§	**(5.77%)**	56/16/34
EsdRank-Osrch	0.427‡,§	(3.22%)	0.347	(1.40%)	0.489‡	(1.29%)	44/17/45
EsdRank-AnnD	0.416	(0.62%)	0.342	(−0.16%)	0.500†,‡	(3.59%)	44/20/42

values are compared with ListMLE, which uses the same model but query-document features. ▽ indicates significantly worse performance than ListMLE in the permutation test ($p < 0.05$). ▼ indicates significantly worse performance compared to the corresponding version of EsdRank. For example, ListMLE-AnnQ is significantly worse than EsdRank-AnnQ if marked by ▼.

Most times these flat features hurt performance, with significant drops compared to ListMLE and corresponding EsdRank versions. Even on ClueWeb09, where the most training data is available, it is typical for flat features to perform more than 10% worse than EsdRank. These results demonstrate the advantage of using a latent space learning to rank model instead of a flat model to handle external evidence: By modeling related objects as hidden variables in latent space, Latent-ListMLE naturally separates query-object and object-document evidence, and uses the EM algorithm to propagate document level training data to the object level. As a result, Latent-ListMLE avoids feature explosion or confusing machine learning algorithms with highly correlated features, while still only requiring document relevance judgments.

5.3 Influence of Related Object Quality

Prior research [7, 11, 20, 28] and our evaluation results on EsdRank with different related objects all indicate the great influence of selected objects' quality on ranking accuracy. The third experiment further studies its influence on EsdRank's performance. Although directly measuring the quality is hard due to the lack of object level labels, we can indirectly characterize the quality by comparing the related objects selected by different methods, with the hypothesis that objects selected by multiple object selectors are more likely to have higher quality.

For each variant of EsdRank, queries were divided into two groups (Agree, Differ) based on whether the query had at least one related object in common with another variant. The two groups were compared using the same methodology reported earlier. The results are summarized in Table 6. Each row is the performance of one variant (first column), divided by overlaps with another variant (second column). Relative gains, Win/Tie/Loss, and statistical significance (§) are calculated based on comparison with ListMLE. Results for ClueWeb09, ClueWeb12 and OSHUMED queries are combined due to space limitations and because their trends are similar.

The two groups clearly perform differently. On queries with common objects (Agree), EsdRank is much more effective. For example, when the less effective AnnD and Osrch object selectors agree with the more effective AnnQ selector, they both outperform ListMLE with statistical significance. When they differ, they may be worse than ListMLE.

Table 5: Performance of `ListMLE` with flat features derived from external data. `AnnQ`, `Osrch` and `AnnD` refer to object selection methods: Query annotation, object search and document annotation. Relative changes and Win/Tie/Loss are compared to `ListMLE`. ▽ and ▼ indicate statistic significantly weaker performance compared to `ListMLE` and `EsdRank` (which uses the same information but `Latent-ListMLE`).

Data Set	Method	MAP@100	NDCG@20	ERR@20	Win/Tie/Loss
ClueWeb09	ListMLE-AnnQ	0.389▼ (−4.96%)	0.208▼ (−5.88%)	0.170▼ (8.99%)	73/35/92
	ListMLE-Osrch	0.331▽,▼ (−19.33%)	0.168▽,▼ (−23.79%)	0.127▽,▼ (−18.34%)	47/42/111
	ListMLE-AnnD	0.357▽,▼ (−12.79%)	0.197▽,▼ (−10.63%)	0.155 (−0.61%)	64/38/98
ClueWeb12	ListMLE-AnnQ	0.355▼ (−10.71%)	0.137▽,▼ (−21.04%)	0.098▽,▼ (−20.37%)	14/11/25
	ListMLE-Osrch	0.368 (−7.43%)	0.154 (−11.32%)	0.105 (−14.39%)	16/11/23
	ListMLE-AnnD	0.337▽,▼ (−15.06%)	0.149▽,▼ (−14.38%)	0.098▽,▼ (−20.65%)	14/10/26
OHSUMED	ListMLE-AnnQ	0.388▽,▼ (−6.13%)	0.323▽,▼ (−5.64%)	0.444▽,▼ (−7.94%)	39/15/52
	ListMLE-Osrch	0.400▼ (−3.37%)	0.323▽,▼ (−5.58%)	0.445▽,▼ (−7.84%)	38/15/53
	ListMLE-AnnD	0.397▽,▼ (−4.12%)	0.339 (−1.14%)	0.494 (2.43%)	40/16/50

Although `AnnQ` is the most effective individual method, its performance is further improved when it agrees with `AnnD`, outperforming `ListMLE` by more than 10% on all metrics. This level of improvement is close to the gains reported by Liu et al. [20] with *manual* query annotations.

The results also show that `EsdRank` behaves predictably. When simple object selectors agree, `EsdRank` is more likely to improve retrieval quality; when they disagree, the search engine can simply retreat to `ListMLE`.

Finding related objects for query and document is still an open problem in the literature. In the SIGIR ERD'14 workshop [7] many teams built their query annotators upon TagMe and obtained about 60% accuracy. It is still not clear how to adapt full text retrieval models to perform better object search. Document annotation can be done with very high precision but there is still room to improve recall, even in the widely used Google FACC1 annotations. Some prior research questions whether current Freebase query annotation is too noisy to be useful [11, 20]. With the help of features between query, object and document, `Latent-ListMLE` is able to improve retrieval accuracy even when object selection is noisy. As researchers improve the quality of object search and annotation, producing less noisy objects, we would expect `Latent-ListMLE`'s ranking accuracy to improve further.

6. CONCLUSION AND FUTURE WORK

EsdRank is a general method of using external semi-structured data in modern LeToR systems. It uses objects from external data, such as vocabularies and entities, as an interlingua between query and documents. Query-object and object-document relationships are expressed as features. Latent-ListMLE treats objects as latent layers between query and document, and learns how to use evidence between query, objects and documents in one unified procedure. This general method can be applied to a variety of semi-structured resources, and is easily trained using ordinary query-document relevance judgments.

Experiments with two rather different types of external semi-structured data – a classic controlled vocabulary and a newer knowledge base – and three well-known datasets show that EsdRank provides statistically significant improvements over several state-of-the-art ranking baselines.

Experiments with the single-layer LeToR model, which uses exactly the same information but expressed by 'flat' features, show much weaker performance than Latent-ListMLE. This result confirms the advantage of separating evidence about query-object and object-document relationships with the latent space, instead of mixing them together. The single-layer approach may result in a large and highly correlated feature space, which is hard for machine learning models to deal with.

Finding related objects for query and documents is a very important step for using external data in ranking. EsdRank is tested with three popular related object selection methods: query annotation, object search and document annotation. The evaluation results demonstrate the essential effect of related object quality on final ranking accuracy, and suggest that query annotation is the most reliable source for related objects under current techniques.

EsdRank is a general approach in which to explore the use of different types of semi-structured data in search. As better methods are developed for retrieving objects from semi-structured data and annotating objects in queries and documents, they can be used in EsdRank to improve retrieval and to cover a broader set of queries. Its use of objects as a latent space between queries and documents provides richer opportunities for feature and model development than seen so far in most learning to rank research. Thus, the implementation of EsdRank presented here can be seen as just a beginning.

7. ACKNOWLEDGMENTS

We thank Laura Dietz and the anonymous reviewers of a previous draft of this paper for comments that improved the paper. This research was supported by National Science Foundation (NSF) grant IIS-1422676 and a Google Research Award. Any opinions, findings, conclusions, and recommendations expressed in this paper are the authors' and do not necessarily reflect those of the sponsors.

8. REFERENCES

[1] M. Bendersky, D. Metzler, and W. B. Croft. Effective query formulation with multiple information sources. In *Proceedings of the fifth ACM International Conference on Web Search and Data Mining*, pages 443–452. ACM, 2012.

[2] A. Berger and J. Lafferty. Information retrieval as statistical translation. In *Proceedings of the 22nd Annual International ACM SIGIR Conference on Research and Development in Information Retrieval*, pages 222–229. ACM, 1999.

[3] K. Bollacker, C. Evans, P. Paritosh, T. Sturge, and J. Taylor. Freebase: a collaboratively created graph database for structuring human knowledge. In *Proceedings*

Table 6: The performances of **EsdRank**'s variants when they agree or differ with other variants, combined from three data sets. 'Agree' is defined by at least one overlap in related objects. Relative gain, Win/Tie/Loss and statistical significance § are compared with **ListMLE** on corresponding queries. The best relative gains for each variant are marked **bold**.

Method	Compare With	Group	MAP@100	NDCG@20	ERR@20	Win/Tie/Loss	Queries
AnnQ	AnnD	Agree	$0.541^{\S}$(**14.80%**)	$0.299^{\S}$(**12.89%**)	$0.254^{\S}$(**24.18%**)	54/14/26	94
		Differ	0.390 (0.90%)	0.252 (2.45%)	$0.286^{\S}$ (8.14%)	110/56/96	262
	Osrch	Agree	$0.495^{\S}$ (7.10%)	$0.328^{\S}$ (6.69%)	$0.347^{\S}$ (7.53%)	74/17/39	130
		Differ	0.393 (3.75%)	$0.227^{\S}$ (4.28%)	$0.238^{\S}$ (15.31%)	90/53/83	226
Osrch	AnnD	Agree	0.490 (1.81%)	0.287 (1.66%)	0.210 (0.08%)	29/9/21	59
		Differ	0.388 (−1.70%)	0.243 (−0.56%)	0.258 (0.45%)	108/65/124	297
	AnnQ	Agree	$0.482^{\S}$ (**4.41%**)	$0.320^{\S}$ (**4.02%**)	$0.340^{\S}$ (**5.37%**)	72/16/42	130
		Differ	0.361 (−4.81%)	0.210 (−3.53%)	0.198 (−4.08%)	65/58/103	226
AnnD	Osrch	Agree	0.504 (4.71%)	0.292 (3.49%)	$0.233^{\S}$ (11.41%)	30/7/22	59
		Differ	0.394 (−0.28%)	0.244 (0.09%)	0.267 (3.92%)	113/63/121	297
	AnnQ	Agree	$0.527^{\S}$(**11.69%**)	$0.285^{\S}$ (**7.74%**)	$0.248^{\S}$(**21.19%**)	50/12/32	94
		Differ	0.371 (−4.12%)	0.241 (−1.99%)	0.266 (0.47%)	93/58/111	262

of the 2008 ACM SIGMOD International Conference on Management of Data, pages 1247–1250. ACM, 2008.

[4] W. C. Brandão, R. L. Santos, N. Ziviani, E. S. Moura, and A. S. Silva. Learning to expand queries using entities. *Journal of the Association for Information Science and Technology (JASIST)*, 65(9):1870–1883, 2014.

[5] A. Z. Broder, M. Fontoura, E. Gabrilovich, A. Joshi, V. Josifovski, and T. Zhang. Robust classification of rare queries using web knowledge. In *Proceedings of the 30th Annual International ACM SIGIR Conference on Research and Development in Information Retrieval*, pages 231–238. ACM, 2007.

[6] A. Carlson, J. Betteridge, B. Kisiel, B. Settles, E. R. Hruschka Jr, and T. M. Mitchell. Toward an architecture for never-ending language learning. In *AAAI*, volume 5, page 3, 2010.

[7] D. Carmel, M.-W. Chang, E. Gabrilovich, B.-J. P. Hsu, and K. Wang. ERD'14: Entity recognition and disambiguation challenge. In *SIGIR '14: Proceedings of the 37th International ACM SIGIR Conference on Research and Development in Information Retrieval*. ACM, 2014.

[8] G. V. Cormack, M. D. Smucker, and C. L. Clarke. Efficient and effective spam filtering and re-ranking for large web datasets. *Information Retrieval*, 14(5):441–465, 2011.

[9] W. B. Croft, D. Metzler, and T. Strohman. *Search engines: Information Retrieval in practice*. Addison-Wesley Reading, 2010.

[10] J. Dalton, L. Dietz, and J. Allan. Entity query feature expansion using knowledge base links. In *Proceedings of the 37th Annual International ACM SIGIR Conference on Research and Development in Information Retrieval*, pages 365–374. ACM, 2014.

[11] L. Dietz and P. Verga. Umass at TREC 2014: Entity query feature expansion using knowledge base links. In *Proceedings of The 23st Text Retrieval Conference*, page To Appear. NIST, 2014.

[12] P. Ferragina and U. Scaiella. Fast and accurate annotation of short texts with wikipedia pages. *arXiv preprint arXiv:1006.3498*, 2010.

[13] E. Gabrilovich, M. Ringgaard, and A. Subramanya. FACC1: Freebase annotation of ClueWeb corpora, Version 1 (Release date 2013-06-26, Format version 1, Correction level 0), June 2013.

[14] G. Grefenstette and L. Wilber. *Search-Based Applications: At the Confluence of Search and Database Technologies*. 2010.

[15] T. Joachims. Making large-scale svm learning practical. LS8-Report 24, Universität Dortmund, LS VIII-Report, 1998.

[16] T. Joachims. Optimizing search engines using clickthrough data. In *Proceedings of the 8th ACM SIGKDD International Conference on Knowledge Discovery and Data Mining*, pages 133–142. ACM, 2002.

[17] V. Lavrenko and W. B. Croft. Relevance based language models. In *Proceedings of the 24th Annual International ACM SIGIR Conference on Research and Development in Information Retrieval*, pages 120–127. ACM, 2001.

[18] H. Li and J. Xu. Semantic matching in search. *Foundations and Trends in Information Retrieval*, 8:89, 2014.

[19] T.-Y. Liu. Learning to rank for information retrieval. *Foundations and Trends in Information Retrieval*, 3(3):225–331, 2009.

[20] X. Liu, P. Yang, and H. Fang. Entity came to rescue - leveraging entities to minimize risks in web search. In *Proceedings of The 23st Text Retrieval Conference, (TREC 2014)*, page To Appear. NIST, 2014.

[21] Y. Lu, H. Fang, and C. Zhai. An empirical study of gene synonym query expansion in biomedical information retrieval. *Information Retrieval Journal*, 12(1):51–68, 2009.

[22] Z. Lu, W. Kim, and W. J. Wilbur. Evaluation of query expansion using mesh in pubmed. *Information Retrieval Journal*, 12(1):69–80, 2009.

[23] D. Metzler and W. B. Croft. Latent concept expansion using markov random fields. In *Proceedings of the 30th Annual International ACM SIGIR Conference on Research and Development in Information Retrieval*, pages 311–318. ACM, 2007.

[24] D. Pan, P. Zhang, J. Li, D. Song, J.-R. Wen, Y. Hou, B. Hu, Y. Jia, and A. De Roeck. Using dempster-shafer's evidence theory for query expansion based on freebase knowledge. In *Information Retrieval Technology*, pages 121–132. Springer, 2013.

[25] T. Rajashekar and B. W. Croft. Combining automatic and manual index representations in probabilistic retrieval. *Journal of the American society for Information science*, 46(4):272–283, 1995.

[26] N. Stokes, Y. Li, L. Cavedon, and J. Zobel. Exploring criteria for successful query expansion in the genomic domain. *Information Retrieval*, 12(1):17–50, 2009.

[27] F. Xia, T.-Y. Liu, J. Wang, W. Zhang, and H. Li. Listwise approach to learning to rank: theory and algorithm. In *Proceedings of the 25th International Conference on Machine learning*, pages 1192–1199. ACM, 2008.

[28] C. Xiong and J. Callan. Query expansion with Freebase. In *Proceedings of the fifth ACM International Conference on the Theory of Information Retrieval*. ACM, 2015. To appear.

[29] Y. Xu, G. J. Jones, and B. Wang. Query dependent pseudo-relevance feedback based on wikipedia. In *Proceedings of the 32nd Annual International ACM SIGIR Conference on Research and Development in Information Retrieval*, pages 59–66. ACM, 2009.

A Probabilistic Framework for Temporal User Modeling on Microblogs

Jitao Sang[1,3], Dongyuan Lu[2], Changsheng Xu[1,3]
[1] Institute of Automation, Chinese Academy of Sciences
[2] School of Information Technology & Management, University of International Business and Economics
[3] China-Singapore Institute of Digital Media
jtsang@nlpr.ia.ac.cn, ludy@uibe.edu.cn, csxu@nlpr.ia.ac.cn

ABSTRACT

In social media, users have contributed enormous behavior data online which can be leveraged for user modeling and conduct personalized services. Temporal user modeling, which incorporates the timestamp of these behavior data and understands users' interest evolution, have attracted attention recently. With the recognition that user interests are vulnerable to transient events, many current temporal user modeling solutions propose to first identify the transient events and then consider the identified events into user behavior modeling. In this work, in the context of microblogs, we propose a unified probabilistic framework to simultaneously model the process of transient event detection and temporal user tweeting. The outputs of the framework include: (1) one long-term topic space spanning over general categories, (2) one short-term topic space for each time interval corresponding to the transient events, and (3) users' interest distributions over the long- and short-term topic spaces. Qualitative and quantitative experimental evaluation are conducted on a large-scale Twitter dataset, with more than 2 million users and 0.3 billion tweets. The promising results demonstrate the advantage of the proposed topic models.

Categories and Subject Descriptors

H.4 [**Information Systems Applications**]: Miscellaneous

General Terms

Algorithms, Experimentation

Keywords

temporal user modeling, topic model, event detection, microblogs

1. INTRODUCTION

The huge amount of User Generated Content (UGC) online has made the exploration and discovery of interesting resources extremely difficult. Traditional "one-to-all" strategy is no more adequate towards users' customized demands. Understanding the customized interests by building user profiles has stood out for solutions, and enabled "one-to-one" personalized information services. One of the most critical issues in building user profiles is the dynamicity problem, i.e., users' interests vary over time and should be reflected in their profiles [1]. Modeling users' temporal profiles can help providing more qualified services, e.g., recommending timely news to users by capturing their temporal interest shifting [2, 3], providing the right ad at the right time by analyzing users' recent shopping-related activities [4, 5].

One fundamental solution for temporal user modeling is based on the assumption that users' dynamic preferences are affected by both the long-term and the short-term interests [6, 2, 7, 8, 9, 10]. Long-term interests indicate users' stable preferences and distribute over general topic, e.g., the intrinsic interests in politics and sports. While short-term interests are generally consistent with long-term interests, they usually distribute over more specific topics and are changeable over time, e.g., the focuses on "Crimean crisis" at March, 2014, and "FIFA World Cup" around July, 2014. Successfully capturing the short-term interest evolvement will facilitate user preference understanding both in a timely fashion and at a fine-grained level, which is critical for personalized information services.

On microblogging websites, such as Twitter and Weibo, users' temporal behaviors are recognized to be affected by transient events [11], such as new product release and social breaking news. The dominant solutions conduct short-term interest modeling by investigating the interplay between users' temporal behaviors with the transient events detected in advance. For example, [2] first recognizes trending entities at specific periods and then represent users' short-term interests over these trending entities; [12] models user posting behavior as a generative process influenced by the breaking news, which are identified in advance by examining the bursty keywords. The current solutions separating the transient event detection and temporal user modeling suffer from two problems: (1) As illustrated from the example in Figure 1, the transient events and users' temporal behaviors are mutually influenced [13]: on one hand, transient events are identified from aggregated user behaviors; on the other hand, users' temporal behaviors are largely affected by the transient events, which results in the short-term interest evolvement. It is difficult to say influence in which direction happens first and is more significant. (2) The identified transient events beforehand are not well compatible with the task of temporal user modeling. For example, in [2, 12], transient events are represented by a set of bursty entities/keywords at each time interval. Different events mix with each other if they happen within the same time interval. However, for short-term interest modeling, users' interplay with the respective transient events is desired. Moreover, independently performing event detection will lead to loss of transient events which are important to understand

Permission to make digital or hard copies of all or part of this work for personal or classroom use is granted without fee provided that copies are not made or distributed for profit or commercial advantage and that copies bear this notice and the full citation on the first page. Copyrights for components of this work owned by others than ACM must be honored. Abstracting with credit is permitted. To copy otherwise, or republish, to post on servers or to redistribute to lists, requires prior specific permission and/or a fee. Request permissions from Permissions@acm.org.
CIKM'15, October 19–23, 2015, Melbourne, Australia.
© 2015 ACM. ISBN 978-1-4503-3794-6/15/10 ...$15.00.
DOI: http://dx.doi.org/10.1145/2806416.2806470.

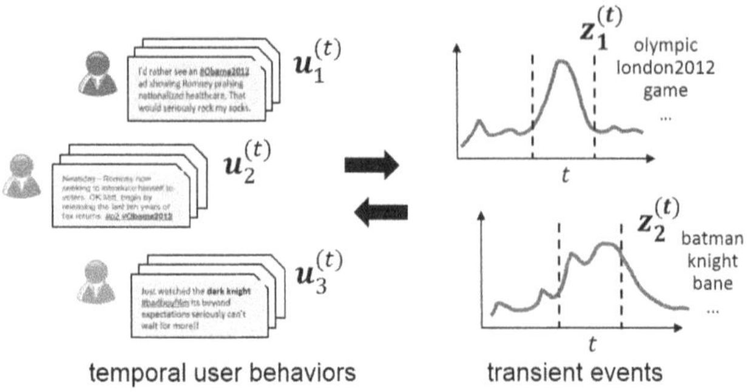

Figure 1: The interplay between users' temporal behaviors and the transient events.

short-term interest evolvement. For example, a local event, though significantly affecting the online behaviors of local users, will be drowned in a global fashion and thus cannot be identified to facilitate the task of temporal user modeling.

To address the above problems, in this paper, we propose a probabilistic framework for temporal user modeling on microblogs, where transient event detection and user tweeting modeling are conducted simultaneously. The user tweets are modeled in a fully generative way: one tweet by a specific user at a specific timestamp is generated either from his/her long-term interest or from his/her short-term interest at this time interval. The long-term interest is expected to distribute over the general topics in a global timeline. While, the short-term interest distributes over the temporal topics discovered at each corresponding time interval, which basically indicates the transient events. The model operates in a unified way, by inputting the user tweets attached with the posted timestamps, and outputting one long-term topic space, N short-term topic spaces [1], and users' long-term and short-term interest distributions. The advantages of this framework include: (1) Event detection and user modeling are conducted simultaneously in a unified topic-based framework. The simultaneity is consistent with the event-user behavior interplay that happened in real world. (2) The unified framework makes it possible to describe events and model users at the topic level. From the perspective of event detection, multiple transient events within one time interval are allowed and the compactness for each event representation is guaranteed. From the perspective of user modeling, both user interests over the general topics and user responses to the transient events are obtained.

The remainder of this paper is organized as follows: section 2 provides a brief review of related work on temporal user modeling, section 3 formally presents the proposed probabilistic topic models and elaborates the model learning and update solutions, followed by the experimental results and analysis in section 4. Finally in section 5, we conclude this work with future directions.

2. RELATED WORK

The goal of temporal user modeling is to capture the dynamic characteristics of users' interests over time. Researchers have proposed many solutions towards this goal. One straightforward idea is to record users' behaviors in time order and build user profiles at each time interval for temporal information services. For example, Zimdars [14] conducted an early work by extending the traditional collaborative filtering (CF) with time order information. With the aim to predict future user behaviors based on the history temporal data, this research line is much promoted by the famous Netflix Prize competition. The Netflix award winning algorithm *timeSVD++* [15] records the history user ratings in a factorization model and conducts prediction by setting bias at each specific time interval. Another popular temporal solution on the Netflix dataset is a Bayesian Probabilistic Tensor Factorization (BPTF) model [16], where users, items and time are represented in three-order tensors, and prediction is conducted in the shared low-dimensional factor space. In the context of microblogs, Abel et al. [17] proposed to represent temporal Twitter user profiles as a set of weighted concepts at each time interval, and conducted personalized website recommendation directly based on the cosine similarity. A recent work on Weibo incorporates the time factor into the matrix factorization model, SocialMF [18], and expresses user dynamic interests as a series of temporal matrices [11].

Another line for temporal user modeling is to analyze the user interest evolvement. The basic idea in most of the work is to emphasize on the new data and reduce the data's importance by time. In [19], a modified collaborative filtering algorithm weighted by time is proposed for temporal recommendation. An exponential time decay function is designed to calculate the time weights for different history user behaviors. A similar temporal user modeling solution is introduced in [20], where the interests' weights are reduced by time if they are not involved by the user until they disappear. Michlmayr and Cayzer [21] modeled user interest evolvement from two perspectives. They added evaporation and reinforcement operations to reduce the weight of old tagging data and increase the weight of repeated tagging data, respectively. An online evolutionary collaborative filtering model is proposed in [22], where temporal information is incorporated into an incremental updating algorithm to track the user interest evolvement over time. Recently, Ceren et al. [23] introduced their user interest inference work from microblogs. For modeling the interest evolution over time, a Markov like assumption is made: the current user interest is a function of the interests in previous time intervals and the estimate of interest at the current time interval.

Our work belongs to the third research line, which explicitly separates the dynamic component of user interests and build temporal user profiles from both long- and short-term interests. Xiang et al. [6] proposed a session-based temporal graph model to capture users' dynamic preferences on the social bookmarking websites, where all items viewed by a user construct his/her long-term interests and the items viewed at a given time interval construct the short-term interests. In [7], regarding history queries and clicked documents, the interaction between short- and long-term behaviors is investigated. An effective hybrid model is proposed for search personalization. Yang et al. [8] proposed a local implicit feedback model for temporal music recommendation, where local and global information are represented by implicit feedback and combined to capture users' stable and local changeable preferences.

As mentioned in *Introduction*, users' temporal behaviors are largely affected by the transient events, especially in the context of microblogs. In [2], the interaction between user dynamic interests and public trends on Twitter are investigated. The public trend at a given time interval is identified as a set of weighted entities in advance. Similarly in [12], the authors first detected the breaking news on Twitter from emerging bursty keywords, and then model the user tweeting behavior as influenced by the detected breaking news. Recently, Deng et al. [10] presented a cross-network solution to model the short-term interests, by discovering user-specific transient events on Twitter and conducting personalized

[1] N is the number of time intervals. Each short-term topic space corresponds to the identified temporal topics (transient events) within this time interval. In the rest of this paper, we will mix using "temporal topics" and "transient events" when no ambiguity is caused.

video recommendation on YouTube. These work largely ignore the mutual influence between transient events and users' temporal behaviors. This leads to the mixed and biased events towards the task of temporal user modeling. The most related work to this paper is [9], which models the fully generative process of user ratings as influenced both by the user-oriented topics and the time-oriented topics. The user- and time-oriented topics generally correspond to the long- and short-term interests. However, in their proposed topic model: (1) The proposed topic model in [9] is designed and evaluated on the bookmarking websites, e.g., MovieLens, Digg, Douban Movie, etc. The rating behaviors from all time shared the same time-oriented topic space, making it difficult to identify the real transient events at each time interval, especially in the context of noisy microblogs. For example, some long-standing words will be mixed into time-oriented topics and disturb the short-time interest modeling; (2) Within certain time interval, all users share the same temporal context, i.e., time-oriented topic distribution, and no user-specific temporal topic distribution is obtained. This actually assumes that all users take unique responses to the discovered transient events. In this paper, we obtain topic spaces for different time intervals and short-term topic distribution is assumed for each user: the derived short-term topics indicates the transient events at each time interval, and the user-specific topic distribution over the discovered short term topics reflects user's response/interest to the transient events.

3. THE APPROACH

3.1 Preliminaries

To model the generation of user' tweets, the proposed generative model is based on the standard topic model, or Latent Dirichlet Allocation (LDA [24]). Fig. 2(a) shows the graphical model of LDA. The generative process is assumed in a corpus-document-word structure, where the corpus consists of D documents and document d has N_d words. α and β are fixed parameters of symmetric Dirichlet priors for the D document-topic multinomials θ and the K topic-word multinomials ϕ. For each document d, the N_d words are generated by drawing a topic k from the document-topic distribution $p(z|\theta_d)$ and then drawing a word w from the topic-word distribution $p(w|z = k, \phi_k)$.

Since we intend to model the generation of user' tweets as influenced by alternative sources, an important extension to the standard topic model, LDA with switch variable is also introduced (as shown in Fig. 2(b)). The latent variable x acts as a switch: if $x = 1$, the previously described standard topic mechanism is used to generate the word, whereas if $x = 0$, words are sampled from a background distribution specific for the corpus [25]. The corpus-specific background distribution can be viewed as a general topic consisting of words that are commonly used across a broad range of documents in the corpus. The full generation process is described in Table 1. The conditional probability of generating a word w given a document d can be written as:

$$p(w|d) = \lambda_d \cdot \psi_w + (1 - \lambda_d) \cdot \sum_{k=1}^{K} \theta_{d,z_k} \phi_{z_k,w} \quad (1)$$

where $\lambda_d = p(x = 0|d)$, $1 - \lambda_d = p(x = 1|d)$, ψ_w is the probability of generating w from the background distribution, $\theta_{d,z_k} = p(z_k|\theta_d)$ is the document-topic distribution that document d selects the kth topic, and $\phi_{z_k,w} = p(w|z_k)$ is the topic-word distribution that generates w from the kth topic. By sampling the switch variable x for each word token, the common words can be identified (with sampled switch variable $x = 0$) and separated to construct the background topic, making the K other topics focused on specific aspects of the corpus. We can see that, by introducing the switch variable, topic model is able to explain the observed words in alternative ways. Extensive work have exploited this potential of switch variable with topic models to discover the broader structure of data [26, 27, 25].

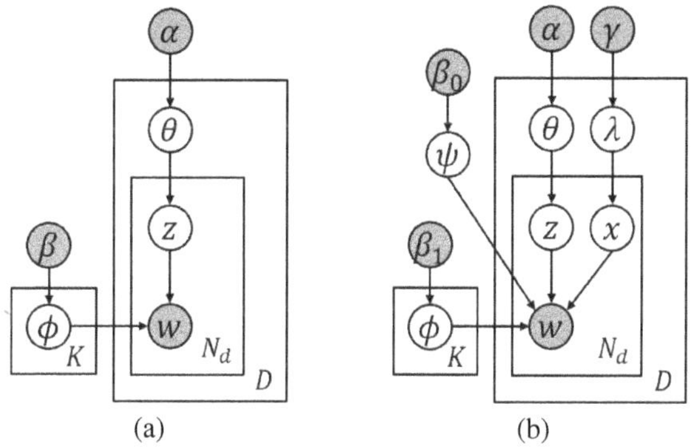

Figure 2: Graphical models for (a) the standard LDA topic model; and (b) topic model with switch variable enabling alternative generation sources.

Table 1: The generation process of LDA with switch variable.

1. Draw background multinomial distribution $\psi \sim \text{Dir}(\beta_0)$.
2. For each topic $k = 1, \cdots, K$:
   (a) draw topic-word multinomial distribution $\phi_k \sim \text{Dir}(\beta_1)$.
3. For each document d:
   (a) draw document-topic multinomial distribution $\theta_d \sim \text{Dir}(\alpha)$;
   (b) draw bernoulli distribution $\lambda_d \sim \text{Dir}(\gamma)$;
   (c) for each word $w_{d,i}$ in document d:
      i. draw a topic $z_{d,i} \sim \text{Multi}(\theta_d)$;
      ii. draw a switch variable $x \sim \text{Bernoulli}(\lambda_d)$;
      iii. draw $w_{d,i} \sim \text{Multi}(\psi)$ if $x = 0$, and $w_{d,i} \sim \text{Multi}(\phi_{z_{d,i}})$ if $x = 1$.

3.2 The Proposed Topic Model

This subsection introduces the proposed probabilistic topic model for temporal user modeling on microblogs. Specifically, we take tweets from Twitter as running example for elaboration. We follow the notations used in the standard LDA when possible.

3.2.1 *Temporal User Modeling (TUM) model*

As mentioned in *Introduction*, we explain users' temporal profiles as decomposed into long-term interests and short-term interests. From a generative perspective, user tweets can be assumed as an aggregated result from users' long-term and short-term interests. Inspired by the above introduced topic model, we realize this assumption by setting a similar binary switch variable x to control the generation source of the observed words w, i.e., either from a long-term topic z^L or from a short-term topic z^S. Since short-term interests should distribute over different time intervals, an observed variable t is further introduced to record the posted timestamp of the tweet. That is, once the switch variable of generation source is sampled as short-term interest, the short-term topic spaces ψ_t of

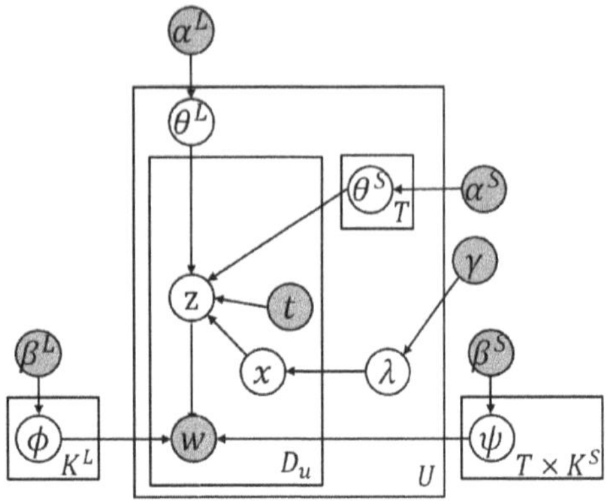

Figure 3: Probabilistic generative model of TUM.

the specific time interval t that the tweet was posted is selected to generate the word. In this case, since the topic spaces obtained for different time intervals are expected to indicate the transient events, users' short-term interests actually distribute over the transient events at the corresponding time intervals, i.e., the responses to the transient events reflect users' short-term preferences and affect their temporal tweeting behaviors.

Fig. 3 illustrates the graphical structure of the proposed Temporal User Modeling (TUM) model. The full generation process is described in Table 2. This model includes three sets of variables, i.e., the parameters $\{\Phi, \Psi, \Theta^L, \Theta^S, \boldsymbol{\lambda}\}$, the latent variables $\{X, Z\}$, and the observation W. We use Gibbs Sampling to generate samples for the latent variables and then calculate the desired parameters. Given the graphical model and generative process, it is straightforward to derive the full conditional probability of the latent variables for each word token $w_{u,i}$:

$$p(x_{u,i} = 0, z_{u,i} = k | X_{u,\neg i}, Z_{u,\neg i}, W; \cdot) \propto \frac{C_{U,X}(u,0) + \gamma}{C_U(u) + 2\gamma} \cdot \frac{C_{U,X,Z}(u,0,k) + \alpha^L}{C_{U,X}(u,0) + K^L\alpha^L} \cdot \frac{C_{X,Z,W}(0,k,w_{u,i}) + \beta^L}{C_{X,Z}(0,k) + |\mathcal{V}|\beta^L} \quad (2)$$

$$p(x_{u,i} = 1, z_{u,i} = k | X_{u,\neg i}, Z_{u,\neg i}, W; \cdot) \propto \frac{C_{U,X}(u,1) + \gamma}{C_U(u) + 2\gamma} \cdot \frac{C_{U,X,T,K^S}(u,1,t_{u,i},k) + \alpha^S}{C_{U,X,T}(u,1,t_{u,i}) + K^S\alpha^S} \cdot \frac{C_{X,T,K^S,W}(1,t_{u,i},k,w_{u,i}) + \beta^S}{C_{X,T,K^S}(1,t_{u,i},k) + |\mathcal{V}|\beta^S} \quad (3)$$

where $|\mathcal{V}|$ denotes the size of the word vocabulary, $t_{u,i}$ denotes the time interval when the word $w_{u,i}$ was posted, and $C(\cdot)$ stores the number of samples satisfying certain requirements during the iterative sampling process. For example, $C_{U,X,T,K^S}(u,1,t_{u,i},k)$ indicates the number of words for user u that are supposed to be generated from the short-term topic z^k at time interval $t_{u,i}$. Note that for model derivation simplification, we assume all parameters follow symmetric Dirichlet priors [2].

After a sufficient number of Gibbs sampling iterations, the approximate posterior can be used to obtain estimates of the desired parameters of topic spaces and user-topic distributions, by examining the counts of sampled latent variables of Z, X.

[2] The assumption for symmetric prior is easy to relax [28].

Table 2: The full generation process of TUM.

1. For each long-term topic $k = 1, \cdots, K^L$:
   (1) draw topic-word multinomial distribution $\boldsymbol{\phi}_k \sim \text{Dir}(\boldsymbol{\beta}^L)$.
2. For each time interval $t = 1, \cdots, T$:
   (1) for each short-time topic $k = 1, \cdots, K^S$ at the tth time interval:
      a. draw topic-word multinomial distribution $\boldsymbol{\psi}_{t,k} \sim \text{Dir}(\boldsymbol{\beta}_S)$.
3. For each user $u = 1, \cdots, U$:
   (1) draw long-term user-topic multinomial distribution $\boldsymbol{\theta}^L_u \sim \text{Dir}(\boldsymbol{\alpha}^L)$;
   (2) for each time interval $t = 1, \cdots, T$:
      a. draw short-term user-topic multinomial distribution $\boldsymbol{\theta}^S_{u,t} \sim \text{Dir}(\boldsymbol{\alpha}^S)$.
   (3) draw bernoulli distribution $\lambda_u \sim \text{Dir}(\gamma)$;
   (4) for each word $i = 1, \cdots, D_u$:
      a. draw a switch variable $x_{u,i} \sim \text{Bernoulli}(\lambda_u)$;
      b. if $x_{u,i} = 0$, first draw a topic $z_{u,i} \sim \text{Multi}(\boldsymbol{\theta}^L_u)$, then draw $w_{u,i} \sim \text{Multi}(\boldsymbol{\phi}_{z^L_{u,i}})$;
      c. if $x_{u,i} = 1$, first draw a topic $z_{u,i} \sim \text{Multi}(\boldsymbol{\theta}^S_{u,t})$, then draw $w_{u,i} \sim \text{Multi}(\boldsymbol{\psi}_{t,z^S_{u,i}})$. t is the time interval that the word $w_{u,i}$ was posted.

Specifically, the MAP estimates are as follows:

$$\begin{aligned}
\phi_{k,w} &= \frac{C_{X,Z,W}(0,k,w) + \beta^L}{C_{X,Z}(0,k) + |\mathcal{V}|\beta^L}, \\
\psi_{t,k,w} &= \frac{C_{X,T,K^S,W}(1,t,k,w) + \beta^S}{C_{X,T,K^S}(1,t,k) + |\mathcal{V}|\beta^s}, \\
\theta^L_{u,k} &= \frac{C_{U,X,Z}(u,0,k) + \alpha^L}{C_{U,X}(u,0) + K^L\alpha^L}, \\
\theta^S_{u,t,k} &= \frac{C_{U,X,T,K^S}(u,1,t,k) + \alpha^S}{C_{U,X,T}(u,1,t) + K^S\alpha^S}
\end{aligned} \quad (4)$$

3.2.2 *TwitterTUM model*

We also pursued a variant of TUM. In the context of microblogs, e.g., Twitter, single tweet is recognized to usually involve with one single topic [29]. In the above TUM model, the words in the same tweet are sampled separately from different topics. In practical implementation, it is reasonable to assume that users express unique interest in the same tweet. Therefore, we modify the TUM model by introducing an additive tweet plate and assuming that one tweet can be generated from only one long-term and one short-term topic. For example, user posted a tweet about the semifinal match between Germany and Brazil expressing his/her long-term interest in sports and short-term interest in 2014 FIFA World Cup.

Specifically, in the generative process, one long-term topic $z^L_{u,e}$ and one short-term topic $z^S_{u,e}$ are firstly sampled for the tweet e_u. The words in e_u are then generated from either $z^L_{u,e}$ or $z^S_{u,e}$ according to the sampling of switch variable x. This constraint is consistent with user tweeting behavior and improves the compactness of the derived topics, which helps discover more meaningful transient events. The modified model is referred to as TwitterTUM, whose graphical structure is shown in Fig. 4.

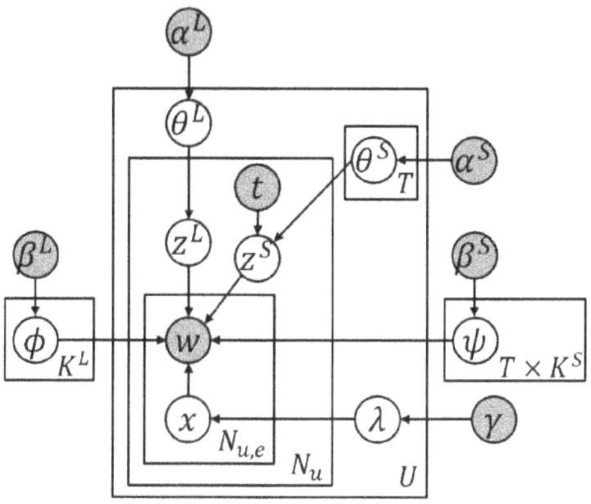

Figure 4: Probabilistic generative model of TwitterTUM.

Table 3: The generation process of one user in TwitterTUM.

For each user $u = 1, \cdots, U$:

(1) (2) (3): same with *TUM* in Table 2;

(4) for each tweet $e = 1, \cdots, N_u$:

a. draw long-term topic $z^L_{u,e} \sim \text{Multi}(\boldsymbol{\theta}^L_u)$;

b. draw short-term topic $z^S_{u,e} \sim \text{Multi}(\boldsymbol{\theta}^S_{u,t})$. t is the time interval that the tweet e was posted.

c. for each word $i = 1, \cdots, N_{u,e}$:

i. draw a switch variable $x_{u,e,i} \sim \text{Bernoulli}(\lambda_u)$;

ii. draw $w_{u,e,i} \sim \text{Multi}(\boldsymbol{\phi}_{z^L_{u,e}})$ if $x_{u,e,i} = 0$, and $w_{u,e,i} \sim \text{Multi}(\boldsymbol{\psi}_{t,z^S_{u,e}})$ if $x_{u,e,i} = 1$.

Since the generation of the long-term and short-term topics remain unchanged, we only summarize the generation process within the user and tweet plates in Table 3. The following equations list the main update rules in the Gibbs Sampling for TwitterTUM:

$$p(x_{u,e,i} = 0 | X_{u,e,\neg i}, Z^L, W; \cdot) \propto \frac{C_{U,X}(u,0) + \gamma}{C_U(u) + 2\gamma} \cdot \frac{C_{Z^L,W}(z^L_{u,e}, w_{u,e,i}) + \beta^L}{C_{Z^L}(z^L_{u,e}) + |\mathcal{V}|\beta^L};$$

$$p(x_{u,e,i} = 1 | X_{u,e,\neg i}, Z^S, W; \cdot) \propto \frac{C_{U,X}(u,1) + \gamma}{C_U(u) + 2\gamma} \cdot \frac{C_{T,Z^S,W}(t_{u,i}, z^S_{u,e}, w_{u,e,i}) + \beta^S}{C_{T,Z^S}(z^S_{u,e}) + |\mathcal{V}|\beta^S};$$

$$p(z^L_{u,e} = k | X, Z^L_{u,\neg e}, W; \cdot) \propto \frac{C_{U,Z^L}(u,k) + \alpha^L}{C_U(u) + K^L\alpha^L} \cdot \prod_{i=1}^{N_{u,e}} \left(\frac{C_{Z^L,W}(k, w_{u,e,i}) + \beta^L}{C_{Z^L}(k) + |\mathcal{V}|\beta^L} \right)^{1 - x_{u,e,i}};$$

$$p(z^S_{u,e} = k | X, Z^S_{u,\neg e}, W; \cdot) \propto \frac{C_{U,Z^S}(u,k) + \alpha^S}{C_U(u) + K^S\alpha^S} \cdot \prod_{i=1}^{N_{u,e}} \left(\frac{C_{T,Z^S,W}(t_{u,i}, k, w_{u,e,i}) + \beta^S}{C_{T,Z^S}(k) + |\mathcal{V}|\beta^S} \right)^{x_{u,e,i}}.$$

3.3 Batch Training v.s. Incremental Update

In the above introduced model learning, we assume the user tweets at all time intervals are observed simultaneously, and the long- and short-term parameters are estimated from all the observed data. We refer to this learning strategy as *batch training*. While, in practical implementation, data arrive in a stream. Moreover, the addressed temporal user modeling task needs the capability to update model continuously. These all necessitate the introduction of an incremental learning strategy to the proposed topic models. To this end, in this subsection, using TUM as example, we present an incremental learning strategy to scan new data on the basis of time interval, which is referred to as *incremental update*.

In the incremental update learning strategy, batch training is initially run on data of the first T_0 time intervals, and the model parameters are initialized as $\{\Phi^{(T_0)}, \Psi_{1:T_0}, \Theta^{L(T_0)}, \Theta^S_{1:T_0}\}$ according to Eqn. (4). Here the superscript $\cdot^{(T_0)}$ indicates the parameter value after observing T_0 time intervals, and the subscript $\cdot_{1:T_0}$ denotes the parameters from the first to the $T_0{}^{th}$ time intervals. Henceforth, with the arrival of data $W^{(t+1)}$ in every new time interval, fixing the value of old switch and topic latent variables $\{X_{1:t}, Z_{1:t}\}$, we sample $\{X_{(t+1)}, Z_{(t+1)}\}$ for each new word token by applying Eqn. (2) and Eqn. (3) conditioning on the words observed so far. We can see that for long-term topics, all the three components in Eqn. (2) are vulnerable to the samples in the previous time intervals, while for short-term topics the second and third components in Eqn. (3) are only decided by the analyzed samples at the current time intervals.

Subsequently, the MAP estimates of the parameters are updated using the sampled assignments of topic and switch variables to the data at the new time interval. According to the generative process described in Table 2, the short-term topics $\Psi_{1:t}$ and users' short-term interest distribution $\Theta^S_{1:t}$ at the previous t time intervals are not dependent on the incoming data, and thus should be fixed during update. This is easy to understand as $\Psi_{1:t}$ corresponds the occurred transient events and $\Theta^S_{1:t}$ indicates users' responses to these events. Therefore, after Gibbs sampling on the data at $t+1$ time interval, the model updates $\Phi^{(t)} \to \Phi^{(t+1)}$, $\Theta^{L(t)} \to \Theta^{L(t+1)}$ and estimates $\Psi_{t+1}, \Theta^S_{t+1}$.

Note that the sampled latent variables at the previous time intervals actually add up to the counts on the number of times words are sampled under certain conditions [3]. This plays the same role as hyper-parameters. Therefore, the generated model at the previous time intervals can be interpreted as a prior for the model at the successive time intervals. Specifically, users' long-term topic distribution is modified as follows:

$$\begin{aligned} \phi^{(t+1)}_{k,w} &\sim Dir(\beta^L_w + \beta^{L(t)}_w), \\ \theta^{L(t+1)}_{u,k} &\sim Dir(\alpha^L_k + \alpha^{L(t)}_k) \end{aligned} \tag{5}$$

where $\beta^{L(t)}_w \triangleq C^{1:t}_{X,K^L,W}(0,k,w), \alpha^{L(t)}_k \triangleq C^{1:t}_{U,X,K^L}(u,0,k)$ denote at the previous t time intervals the number of times that word w are generated from the kth long-term topic, and the number of words for user u that are generated from the kth long-term topic, respectively. To modify the contribution of history samples in computing the priors for the incoming data, a time decay term can be further added to define $\beta^{L(t)}_w$ and $\alpha^{L(t)}_k$ as follows:

$$\begin{aligned} \beta^{L(t)}_w &\triangleq \sum_{i=1}^{t} (1 - e^{-\frac{t-i}{\delta}}) \cdot C^{(i)}_{X,K^L,W}(0,k,w), \\ \alpha^{L(t)}_k &\triangleq \sum_{i=1}^{t} (1 - e^{-\frac{t-i}{\delta}}) \cdot C^{(i)}_{U,X,K^L}(u,0,k) \end{aligned} \tag{6}$$

[3] Since the vocabulary enlarges over time due to the new words from the incoming time intervals, we assume these words have zero count for all topics at the previous time intervals.

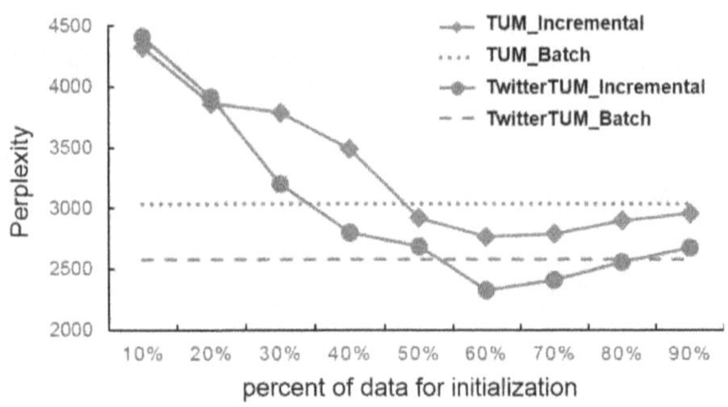

Figure 5: Perplexities for different learning strategies.

Table 4: Runtimes of different learning strategies (in seconds).

	Batch Training	Incremental Update		
		20%	50%	80%
TUM	9,325	4,658	6,525	8,621
TwitterTUM	14,772	6,639	9,383	12,199

where $C^{(i)}_{X,K^L,W}(0,k,w)$ denotes the number of times that word w are generated from the kth long-term topic at the ith time interval, δ is a tuning parameter to control the time decay speed [4].

In batch training, to simplify the learning process, we assume the short-term topic spaces of different time intervals share the same topic number K^S. In incremental update, respective short-term topic numbers are selected for each time interval by Bayesian model selection [30]. Specifically, for each time interval t, the likelihood $p(W^{(t)}|K^{S(t)})$ is calculated with different short-term topic number $K^{S(t)}$. The $K^{S,(t)}$ that obtains the largest likelihood is considered to best account for the structure of the data and thus set as the short-term topic number for this time interval [?].

Different from the short-term topics, the long-term topic structure is fixed in the initialization stage, i.e., the number of long-term topics has been decided after the first T_0 time intervals, and only the topic-word distributions are modified during incremental update. For this reason, the model performance depends critically on the accuracy of the topics inferred during the initialization stage. To compare the performance with different time intervals for initialization, we evaluate the held-out perplexity on a separate validation set from the collected 10-month Twitter dataset. By splitting the data from one month as one time interval, different number of initialization time intervals $T_0 = 1, \cdots, 9$ is examined, using the best short- and long-term topic number settings. Figure 5 shows the results for both TUM and TwitterTUM. The perplexity of the batch training strategy is also examined.

It is shown that the perplexity of incremental update learning strategy initially decreases as a function of the data utilized for initialization. This is due to the fact that more initialization time intervals will lead to more accurate long-term topic structure. The perplexity reaches the lowest point around 60% initialization data and then increases thereafter. With the increase of initialization time intervals, the flexibility in optimizing short-term topic number reduces. Therefore, a balance between the long- and short-term topic structures is critical to the final model performance. The results suggest that, by setting proper percent of data for initialization, the incremental update strategy can find a solution as good as the batch training strategy. Moreover, we can see that, by introducing an extra tweet plate, TwitterTUM generally obtains lower perplexity than TUM, showing its ability to find better topic structure. Table 4 summarizes the total runtimes before converge for different learning strategies. We can see that the batch training strategy generally converges slower than the incremental learning strategy, by costing more computation time on resampling all the latent variables in each iteration. For similar reason, TwitterTUM is slower than TUM in sampling additive latent variables.

[4] In our experiments on a 10-month Twitter dataset, we set $\delta \to \infty$ to remove the temporal difference.

4. EXPERIMENTS

4.1 Data Set

Twitter API is used to collect the dataset for the experiments. We started from a random Twitter user and crawled his followees using Breadth First Search. All the examined users' public tweets from Feb.1, 2012 to Nov.30, 2012 are collected. After removing non-English tweets, this results in 852,800 Twitter users with 599,818,231 tweets. To focus on the active Twitter users for temporal modeling, we further removed Twitter users with less than 1,000 tweets within the examined 10 month period. The final dataset contains 228,921 Twitter users and 362,217,995 tweets, with an average of 40 tweets for each user per week.

4.2 Perplexity Results

We first examine the performance of the proposed topic modesl in terms of perplexity. The perplexity in the context of this study measures the accuracy in predicting the coming of new tweets, which can be calculated over all test tweets:

$$\text{Perplexity}(\mathcal{D}_{test}) = \exp\left(-\frac{\sum_{d\in\mathcal{D}_{test}}\sum_{i=1}^{N_d}\log p_\Theta(w_{d,i})}{\sum_{d\in\mathcal{D}_{test}} N_d}\right) \tag{7}$$

where $\mathcal{D}_{test}$ is the test tweet set, $p_\Theta(w_{d,i})$ is the predictive probability of a word according to the derived model parameters. We randomly split the tweets of each user per month into 90% training tweets and 10% test tweets.

We compare the perplexities of the proposed TUM and TwitterTUM with two non-temporal and two temporal user modeling methods:

- **Author-Topic model (AT)** [31]: assuming the tweets are generated considering the authorship, i.e., the user static interests.
- **TwitterLDA** [29]: adding an additional tweet plate to the *AT* model, and constraining that only one topic is allowed within the same tweet.
- **Mixture Latent Topic model (Mixture)** [12]: a temporal user modeling solution assuming user posting is influenced by breaking news, social friends, as well as users' intrinsic interests. Since social influence is not the focus of this paper, we implemented a modified version of *Mixture* for comparison that removes the social friend influence.
- **TTCAM** [9]: a temporal user modeling solution that integrates the discovery of long-term and short-term topics in a unified model.

To simplify the performance comparison, we learned the proposed TUM and TwitterTUM using the batch training strategy. The examined topic models are run ten times and the obtained perplexity is averaged over the ten times and shown in Fig. 6. Time intervals for the temporal user modeling methods are changed from $T = 1$ day to $T = 2$ month. It is shown that: (1) The perplexities remain unchanged for the *AT* and *TwitterLDA* models. Basically, considering the temporal characteristics, the four temporal user modeling methods obtain better predictive performances than the

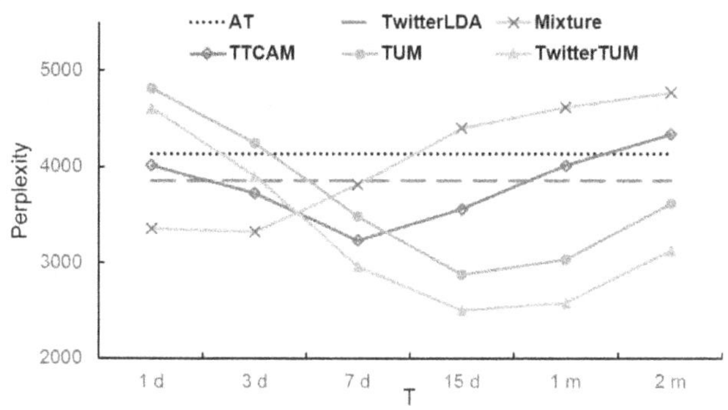

Figure 6: Perplexity with different time interval settings.

Table 5: Examples of discovered long-term topics by *TwitterTUM*.

Topic No.	Top words
Long 3	app apple google android kinect
Long 7	film movie festival films trailer
Long 14	game team live cup sports
Long 19	social twitter marketing search brand

non-temporal user modeling methods in terms of perplexity. (2) *Mixture* obtains the best predictive performance when the time interval is relative short ($T = 1 - 3\,\text{day}$). This is due to that when T becomes longer, the breaking news identified by *Mixture* are more likely to be the mixtures of several transient events. (3) When T increases, the perplexity of *TTCAM* first decreases, obtains the lowest value when $T = 7\,\text{day}$, and then increases. The reason for the early decreasing perplexity is that longer time intervals contribute to adequate user data and improved topic discovery. As the time interval gets longer, the reduced temporal influence leads to the increasing perplexity. (4) The proposed *TUM* and *TwitterTUM* follow the similar trend with *TTCAM*, and obtain the lowest perplexities when $T = 15\,\text{day}$. However, by setting respective short-term topics at each time interval and allowing users to have different responses to the short-term topics, *TUM* and *TwitterTUM* achieve even lower perplexities than *TTCAM*. This demonstrates that the proposed topic models are more consistent with the users' temporal tweeting behaviors on microblogs.

4.3 Discovered Topic Results

4.3.1 Long-term Topics

We first examine the discovered long-term topics using the proposed topic models. In the following, unless specified, the results of *TUM* and *TwitterTUM* are obtained with time interval $T = 15\,\text{day}$ and using the batch training strategy. Therefore, the number of time interval is 20. The number of long-term and short-term topics is selected by Bayesian model selection, that $K^L = 25$, $K^S = 10$.

Table 5 shows four of the discovered 25 long-term topics by *TwitterTUM*, with each topic represented by the five most probable words. We can see that within each topic, the probable words are semantic-consistent with each other. The discovered long-term topics basically describe some general topics like *digital goods*, *movie*, *sports*, *social marketing*, etc, which is consistent with our understanding and expectations.

To analyze the steadiness of long-term topics, we examine the popularity of the discovered long-term topics at different time intervals. The popularity of a long-term topic k at time interval

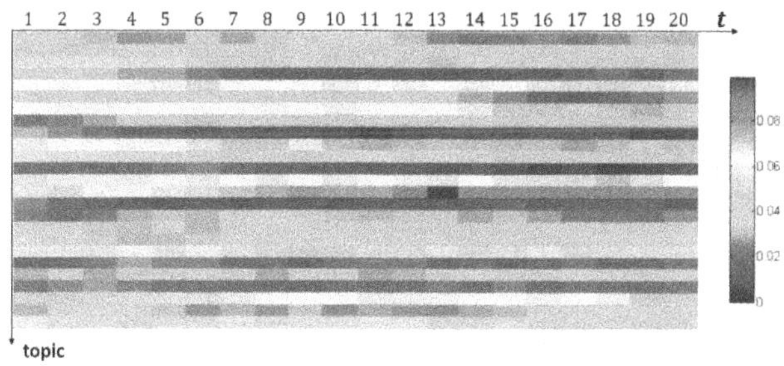

Figure 7: The popularity of long-term topics over time.

t is measured by the proportion of words that sampled from this topic, i.e., $C_{T,Z^L,X}(t,k,0)/C_{T,X}(t,0)$. Fig. 7 visualizes the popularity evolvement of the long-term topics. The colorbar on the right shows the corresponding popularity values. We can see that users' macro interests over the long-term topics are generally steady, with slight fluctuation at some time intervals. For example, the interest over the *topic* 14 increases at time interval 12 and 13, which is possibly due to the 2012 London Olympics between July 27 to August 12. This inter-relationship between the long-term and short-term topics will also be reflected and discussed in the later experiments.

For individual user's long-term topical interest evolvement, we examine into the results from *incremental update* learning with three month (30%) for initialization and 15 day as one time interval for update. Therefore, for each user, we obtained 15 long-term topic distributions, one derived from initialization and the other 14 derived at each update time interval. 3,000 users who have posted more than 100 tweets at each of the examined time intervals, are randomly selected to construct an active test user set $\mathcal{U}_{active}$. For each of the active users, we fitted his/her 15 topical distribution vectors with a multivariate normal distribution. The long-term topic distribution variance is defined as follows:

$$\text{Long-term interest variance}(u) = \frac{\sum_{i=1}^{15} d(\mathbf{u}_i^L, \boldsymbol{\mu}_u)}{15} \quad (8)$$

where $d(\cdot,\cdot)$ is the Euclidean distance, $\mathbf{u}_i^L$ is user u's i^{th} topical distribution vector over the long-term topics, $\boldsymbol{\mu}_u$ is the mean vector of u's fitted multivariate normal distribution. The results find that over 85% users have a long-term interest variance less than 0.002. This demonstrates that most users hold stable long-term interests and validates the steadiness of the long-term topic distribution at micro user level.

4.3.2 Short-term Topics

We then investigate into the discovered short-term topics. At each time interval t, a short-term topic space with $K^S = 10$ topics are obtained. These topics are ranked by their popularity, which is defined as the proportion of words that sampled from the topic, i.e., $C_{T,Z^S,X}(t,k,1)/C_{T,X}(t,1)$. The most popular short-term topics are expected to represent the transient events. Table 6 presents the three most popular short-term topics at time interval 12, with each topic represented by the five most probable words. It is easy to see that three transient events are identified and well described, i.e., "2012 London Olympics", "The Dark Knight Rises", "Syrian civil war". The identified short-term topics derive from the co-burst usage of tweet words and reflect users' increasing interests during this period.

For comparison, Table 7 presents the bursty words detected by *Mixture* at the same time interval, which is derived by examining the word frequency. The first row shows the top bursty words

Table 6: Examples of discovered short-term topics by *TwitterTUM* at time interval 12: from July 16 to July 31.

Topic No.	Top words
Short 3	olympic london2012 game ceremony beijing
Short 4	batman knight bane dark nolan
Short 7	syrian war bomb arab uprising

Table 7: Busty words by *Mixture* at the time interval 12.

Time interval	Top words
July 16-31	olympic london2012 vincente sports batman
July 27	london2012 game olympic heywood sports

between July 16-31, the same time span with the results from Table 6. It is shown that the words representative of different events are mixed, due to the fact that multiple transient events happen during the 15-day time interval. The second row shows the detected bursty words on July 27, when the opening ceremony of 2012 London Olympics took place. We can see, even reduce the time interval to one day, the top words detected by *Mixture* still have a very loose structure that different events mix with each other. The reason for this result is that, the word frequency is considered independent and the word-word co-occurrence in tweet usage is ignored. Moreover, without the separation from long-term topics, some general words also emerges as the bursty words, e.g., "game", "sports", which limits the capability to represent the transient events.

We further quantitatively evaluate the effectiveness of the discovered short-term topics in identifying transient events. Specifically, from the trending searches revealed by Google Zeitgeist 2012 [5], we selected 20 transient events with different categories happened from Feb.1, 2012 to Nov.30, 2012. By examining the top probable words, we found that 19 out of the 20 transient events were successfully identified from the top three ranked short-term topics at different time intervals. Table 8 shows four of the transient events and the corresponding short-term topics. We can see that the top probable words are consistent with each other and together serve as good indication for the transient events. In addition to the global events, we also found some local transient events. For example, at time interval 2 a short-term topic is discovered with the top words of "NUS, dog, singaporean, china, scholarship", which indicates the event of "NUS student insulting Singaporean" happened at Singapore on Feb.18, 2012. We examined the users who have high topical probability on this topic and found that many of them come from Singapore. The configuration of short-term topic spaces at each time intervals make it possible to identify the transient events popular in local users. This type of local events are neglected in a global scale by the methods of *Mixture* and *TTCAM*.

4.4 User Modeling Results

4.4.1 Personalized Information Recommendation

One significant application of user modeling on microblogs is to recommend users with interested information. On Twitter, retweet is the behavior to broadcast users' interested tweets to their followers and therefore can serve as the ground-truth for users' interests. In this subsection, we evaluate the different user modeling methods in the context of predicting whether a tweet will be retweeted by a test user.

[5] https://www.google.com/zeitgeist/2012.

Table 8: Transient events and the corresponding short-term topics.

Transient events	Time interval /Topic No.	Top words
Whitney Houston's death	1/3	whitneyhouston, whitney, drug, bobby, tragic
Gangnam Style upsurge	15/3	gangnamstyle, gangnam, spy, korean, youtube
Hurricane Sandy	18/1	sandy, hurricane, cyclone, pacific, victim
US presidential election 2012	19/5	obama, election, romney, democratic, immigration

Specifically, two experimental settings are conducted. (1) In the first setting, for each user in every time interval t, five random tweets that were retweeted by this user are assumed as relevant documents and construct the positive testing set. Since we focus on modeling the tweet content and ignore the social structure, the selected tweets are required to contain at least 50 characters. In this way, we identified 19,271 test users. For each test user, the selected five retweets at each time interval are removed from the topic model learning. 20 other tweets that were not retweeted at the same time interval are added as the negative test samples. (2) In the second setting, the goal is to simulate the process of personalized news recommendation. Within the collected tweet dataset, we identified 90,883 retweets to 75 tweets that (a) were originally posted by the official accounts of BBC or CNN, (b) were retweeted totally more than 10,000 times, and (c) contain more than 50 characters. These identified tweets are more likely in reporting some transient events, and the retweets from the examined users indicate the interest/response to the events. We selected 500 users who have retweeted at least five out of the 75 tweets to construct the test user set for the second setting. The average number of relevant tweets for each test user is 6.6.

Therefore, the tasks for the first (denoted as *retweet prediction*) and the second (denoted as *news recommendation*) settings, are to retrieve the five and on average 6.6 relevant retweets from the tweet collection consisting of 25 and 75 tweets, respectively. The predictive probability of user u retweeting d is estimated as:

$$p(d) = \frac{1}{N_d} \sum_{i=1}^{N_d} p_{\Theta_u}(w_{d,i})$$

where $p_{\Theta_u}(w_{d,i})$ is the probability of seeing word $w_{d,i}$ according to the learned model parameters for user u. The tweets are ranked according to the above predictive probability. We use Average Precision (AP) for evaluation, which is calculated as:

$$AP = \frac{\sum_{i=1}^{N^+ + N^-} (\sum_{j=1}^{i} \frac{rel(j)}{i} \times rel(i))}{N^+} \tag{9}$$

where N^+, N^- are the number of positive and negative tweets, i, j are the rank of the tweet, $rel(i)$ equalizes 1 if the tweet at rank i is relevant and 0 otherwise. The final result is shown in mean Average Precision (mAP), which is averaged over 500 users (for *news recommendation*), or 19,271 users and 20 time intervals (for *retweet prediction*).

The comparison results with the four baseline methods of the two experimental settings are shown in Fig. 8. It is easy to have the following observations: (1) The experimental results in terms of mAP are consistent with that of perplexity. The four temporal user modeling methods generally outperforms the two non-temporal

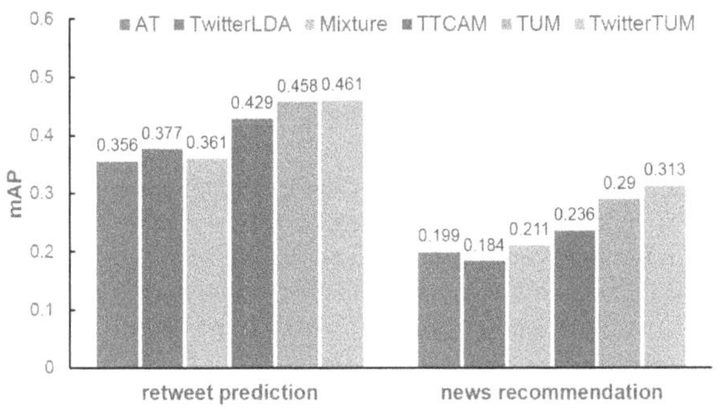

Figure 8: mAP of personalized information recommendation.

user modeling methods. The proposed two topic models obtain the best performance in both settings with a fixed time interval of 15 day. (2) The improvement over the baseline methods is more significant in *news recommendation* than *retweet prediction*. In the task of *news recommendation*, users' responses to the transient events are expected to contribute more to the final recommendation accuracy. However, *Mixture* mixes different transient events, and *TTCAM* assumes all users share the same interest distribution over time-oriented topics. This significant improvement shows the advantage of the proposed topic models in capturing users' responses to respective transient events.

4.4.2 Long-term and Short-term Interests

In this subsection, to understand the advantage in personalized information recommendation, we further investigated into the results of users' long-term and short-term interests. As shown in the previous experimental results, the discovered long-term and short-term topics are in different granularities and thus may semantically mix with each other. We invited three graduate students who are very familiar with Twitter to match each of the discovered 20*10=200 short-term topics to one of the 25 long-term topics, according to the most probable words of the topic. The final short-term and long-term topic matching pairs are obtained by aggregating the three labelers' votes, and recorded as $\text{Long}(z_i^{S(t)})$. For example, the short-term topic 12/3 and 12/4 (shown in Table 5) are labeled as matching the long-term topic 14 and 7 (shown in Table 4), respectively. These matching pairs are recorded as $\text{Long}(z_3^{S(12)}) = 14$, $\text{Long}(z_3^{S(12)}) = 7$.

In the proposed *TwitterTUM*, for each tweet, only one long-term topic and one short-term topic are allowed. We first examined the consistency of the sampled long- and short-term topics within the same tweet. We randomly selected 1,000,000 tweets and found that 74.4% were sampled with matched long- and short-term topics according to the labeled matching pairs. We then examined this consistency at user level. For each test user $u \in \mathcal{U}_{active}$, we investigated how his/her most significant short-term interest at each time interval matches the significant long-term interests. *Top-k accuracy* is utilized as the evaluation metric, which is calculated as follows:

$$\text{Top-k accuracy} = \frac{\sum_{t=1}^{20} \mathbf{I}(\tau_u(Long(\mathbf{u}^{S(t)}.max)) \leq k)}{20} \quad (10)$$

where $\mathbf{u}^{S(t)}.max$ denotes user u's maximum short-term topic at time interval t, $\tau_u(z^L)$ denotes the ranking position of z^L in user u's long-term topic distribution, $\mathbf{I}(\cdot)$ is indicator function returning 1 if it is true and 0 otherwise.

The final results are averaged over all the test users and shown in Fig. 9. We can see that for both proposed topic models,

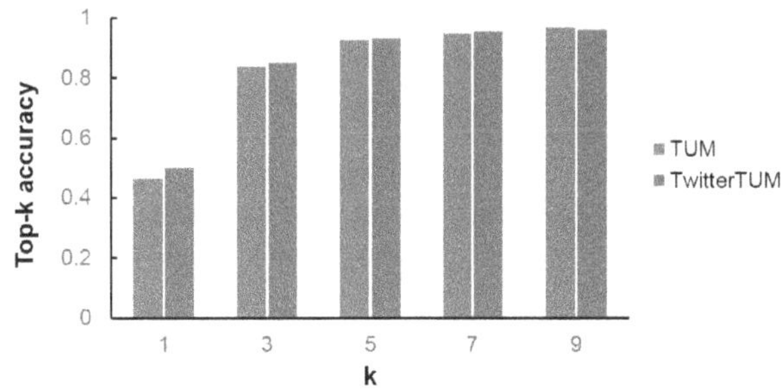

Figure 9: Consistency between long- and short-term interests.

about half of the users/time intervals have consistent short-term and long-term interests, i.e., the most significant short-term topic exactly matches the most significant long-term topic. Over 80% of users/time intervals have the matched long-term interest within the top-3 ranks. This indicates that users do not equally follow all the transient events as assumed by *TTCAM*, but choose to concern more about those consistent with their long-term interests. This result also interprets the phenomenon that long-term topic popularity fluctuates with the short-term topics as shown in Fig. 7. Moreover, one limitation for the proposed topic models is that, the accurate short-term topic distribution is conditioned on the adequate tweeting behavior at each time interval. This observation can be leveraged to make up for this limitation. For example, if users' tweeting behavior at one time interval is sparse, the discovered short-term topic distribution will be modified by its matching relation with the discovered long-term topic distribution.

5. CONCLUSION AND FUTURE WORK

In this paper, we have proposed a probabilistic framework to model the mutual interaction between users' temporal behavior and the transient events. At each time interval, a short-term topic space is discovered from users' co-burst tweeting patterns, which corresponds to the transient events popular during this period. We evaluated the performance of the proposed framework from three perspectives: perplexity, the discovered topic investigation, and the user modeling performance in personalized information recommendation. In the future, we will be working on: (1) addressing the limitation of requiring adequate behavior data within each time interval by leveraging the observed long- and short-term interest consistency, and (2) implementing the incremental learning strategy in real applications and exploring the potentials in transient event tracking.

6. ACKNOWLEDGEMENT

This work is supported in part by National Basic Research Program of China (No. 2012CB316304), National Natural Science Foundation of China (No. 61225009, 61332016, 61303176, 61432019, 61272256), and Beijing Natural Science Foundation (No. 4131004).

7. REFERENCES

[1] Ahmad Abdel-Hafez and Yue Xu. A survey of user modelling in social media websites. *Computer and Information Science*, 6(4):59–71, 2013.

[2] Qi Gao, Fabian Abel, Geert-Jan Houben, and Ke Tao. Interweaving trend and user modeling for personalized news recommendation. In *Web Intelligence*, pages 100–103, 2011.

[3] Ming Yan, Jitao Sang, and Changsheng Xu. Mining cross-network association for youtube video promotion. In *ACM Multimedia*, pages 557–566, 2014.

[4] Amr Ahmed, Yucheng Low, Mohamed Aly, Vanja Josifovski, and Alexander J. Smola. Scalable distributed inference of dynamic user interests for behavioral targeting. In *KDD*, pages 114–122, 2011.

[5] Jitao Sang, Tao Mei, and Changsheng Xu. Activity sensor: Check-in usage mining for local recommendation. *ACM Transactions on Intelligent Systems and Technology (TIST)*, 6(3):41, 2015.

[6] Liang Xiang, Quan Yuan, Shiwan Zhao, Li Chen, Xiatian Zhang, Qing Yang, and Jimeng Sun. Temporal recommendation on graphs via long- and short-term preference fusion. In *KDD*, pages 723–732, 2010.

[7] Paul N. Bennett, Ryen W. White, Wei Chu, Susan T. Dumais, Peter Bailey, Fedor Borisyuk, and Xiaoyuan Cui. Modeling the impact of short- and long-term behavior on search personalization. In *The 35th International ACM SIGIR conference on research and development in Information Retrieval, SIGIR '12, Portland, OR, USA, August 12-16, 2012*, pages 185–194, 2012.

[8] Diyi Yang, Tianqi Chen, Weinan Zhang, Qiuxia Lu, and Yong Yu. Local implicit feedback mining for music recommendation. In *RecSys*, pages 91–98, 2012.

[9] Hongzhi Yin, Bin Cui, Ling Chen, Zhiting Hu, and Zi Huang. A temporal context-aware model for user behavior modeling in social media systems. In *SIGMOD Conference*, pages 1543–1554, 2014.

[10] Zhengyu Deng, Ming Yan, Jitao Sang, and Changsheng Xu. Twitter is faster: Personalized time-aware video recommendation from twitter to youtube. *ACM Trans. Multimedia Comput. Commun. Appl.*, 2014.

[11] Hongyun Bao, Qiudan Li, Stephen Shaoyi Liao, Shuangyong Song, and Heng Gao. A new temporal and social pmf-based method to predict users' interests in micro-blogging. *Decision Support Systems*, 55(3):698–709, 2013.

[12] Zhiheng Xu, Yang Zhang, Yao Wu, and Qing Yang. Modeling user posting behavior on social media. In *SIGIR*, pages 545–554, 2012.

[13] Jitao Sang, Changsheng Xu, and Jing Liu. User-aware image tag refinement via ternary semantic analysis. *TMM*, 14(3):883–895, 2012.

[14] Andrew Zimdars, David Maxwell Chickering, and Christopher Meek. Using temporal data for making recommendations. In *UAI*, pages 580–588, 2001.

[15] Yehuda Koren. Collaborative filtering with temporal dynamics. In *KDD*, pages 447–456, 2009.

[16] Liang Xiong, Xi Chen, Tzu-Kuo Huang, Jeff G. Schneider, and Jaime G. Carbonell. Temporal collaborative filtering with bayesian probabilistic tensor factorization. In *SDM*, pages 211–222, 2010.

[17] Fabian Abel, Qi Gao, Geert-Jan Houben, and Ke Tao. Analyzing temporal dynamics in twitter profiles for personalized recommendations in the social web. In *WebSci*, page 2, 2011.

[18] Mohsen Jamali and Martin Ester. A matrix factorization technique with trust propagation for recommendation in social networks. In *RecSys*, pages 135–142, 2010.

[19] Yi Ding and Xue Li. Time weight collaborative filtering. In *Proceedings of the 14th ACM international conference on Information and knowledge management*, pages 485–492, 2005.

[20] Eugene Santos Jr and Hien Nguyen. Modeling users for adaptive information retrieval by capturing user intent. *Collaborative and Social Information Retrieval and Access: Techniques for Improved User Modeling. IGI Global*, pages 88–118, 2009.

[21] Elke Michlmayr and Steve Cayzer. Learning user profiles from tagging data and leveraging them for personal (ized) information access. In *Proceedings of the Workshop on Tagging and Metadata for Social Information Organization, 16th International World Wide Web Conference (WWW2007)*, pages 1–7, 2007.

[22] Nathan N Liu, Min Zhao, Evan Xiang, and Qiang Yang. Online evolutionary collaborative filtering. In *Proceedings of the fourth ACM conference on Recommender systems*, pages 95–102, 2010.

[23] Ceren Budak, Anitha Kannan, and Rakesh Agrawal Jan Pedersen. Inferring user interests from microblogs. 2014.

[24] David M Blei, Andrew Y Ng, and Michael I Jordan. Latent dirichlet allocation. *the Journal of machine Learning research*, 3:993–1022, 2003.

[25] Jitao Sang and Changsheng Xu. Right buddy makes the difference: An early exploration of social relation analysis in multimedia applications. In *Proceedings of the 20th ACM international conference on Multimedia*, pages 19–28, 2012.

[26] Michael Paul and Roxana Girju. Cross-cultural analysis of blogs and forums with mixed-collection topic models. In *Proceedings of the 2009 Conference on Empirical Methods in Natural Language Processing: Volume 3-Volume 3*, pages 1408–1417, 2009.

[27] Liangjie Hong, Byron Dom, Siva Gurumurthy, and Kostas Tsioutsiouliklis. A time-dependent topic model for multiple text streams. In *Proceedings of the 17th ACM SIGKDD international conference on Knowledge discovery and data mining*, pages 832–840, 2011.

[28] Hanna M. Wallach, David M. Mimno, and Andrew McCallum. Rethinking LDA: why priors matter. In *Advances in Neural Information Processing Systems*, pages 1973–1981, 2009.

[29] Wayne Xin Zhao, Jing Jiang, Jianshu Weng, Jing He, Ee-Peng Lim, Hongfei Yan, and Xiaoming Li. Comparing twitter and traditional media using topic models. In *Advances in Information Retrieval*, pages 338–349. 2011.

[30] Thomas L Griffiths and Mark Steyvers. Finding scientific topics. *Proceedings of the National academy of Sciences of the United States of America*, 101(Suppl 1):5228–5235, 2004.

[31] Michal Rosen-Zvi, Thomas Griffiths, Mark Steyvers, and Padhraic Smyth. The author-topic model for authors and documents. In *Proceedings of the 20th conference on Uncertainty in artificial intelligence*, pages 487–494, 2004.

Deriving Intensional Descriptions for Web Services

Maria Koutraki
University of Versailles
45 Av. des États Unis
78000, Versailles
France
kom@prism.uvsq.fr

Dan Vodislav
University of Cergy-Pontoise
2 Av. Adolphe-Chauvin
95302, Cergy-Pontoise
France
dan.vodislav@u-cergy.fr

Nicoleta Preda
University of Versailles
45 Av. des États Unis
78000, Versailles
France
preda@prism.uvsq.fr

ABSTRACT

Many data providers make their data available through Web service APIs. In order to unleash the potential of these sources for intelligent applications, the data has to be combined across different APIs. However, due to the heterogeneity of schemas, the integration of different APIs remains a mainly manual task to date. In this paper, we model an API method as a view with binding patterns over a global RDF schema. We present an algorithm that can automatically infer the view definition of a method in the global schema. We also show how to compute transformation functions that can transform API call results into this schema. The key idea of our approach is to exploit the intersection of API call results with a knowledge base and with other call results. Our experiments on more than 50 real Web services show that we can automatically infer the schema with a precision of 81%-100%.

Categories and Subject Descriptors

H.4 [**Information Systems Applications**]: Miscellaneous

General Terms

Algorithms

Keywords

Schema mapping, web services, views

1. INTRODUCTION

Web Services (WS). In recent years, several important content providers such as *Amazon*, *musicbrainz*, *IMDB*, *geonames*, *Google*, and *Twitter* have chosen to export their data through Web services. These services cover a large variety of domains: books, music, movies, geographic databases, transportation networks, social media, even personal data. This trend gained momentum thanks to the Open Data Initiative, the success of mash-up applications, and new initiatives that grant users programmatic access to their personal data. Users can access the data by invoking services, but they can hardly copy the entire content of the remote source. Hence, a Web service seems to be a sweet-spot in the trade-off between sharing the data and protecting it.

Permission to make digital or hard copies of all or part of this work for personal or classroom use is granted without fee provided that copies are not made or distributed for profit or commercial advantage and that copies bear this notice and the full citation on the first page. Copyrights for components of this work owned by others than ACM must be honored. Abstracting with credit is permitted. To copy otherwise, or republish, to post on servers or to redistribute to lists, requires prior specific permission and/or a fee. Request permissions from Permissions@acm.org.
CIKM'15, October 19–23, 2015, Melbourne, Australia.
© 2015 ACM. ISBN 978-1-4503-3794-6/15/10 ...$15.00.
DOI: http://dx.doi.org/10.1145/2806416.2806447.

```
http://www.last.fm/api/getAlbums?query=artist
Parameters:
    artist (Required): The artist name
```

Figure 2: A REST Web Service

The wealth of data exported by Web services is an opportunity for the development of new intelligent applications. For instance, it is possible to develop an application that proposes a trip to a concert. This application could gather concert recommendations from a social Web service such as *Facebook*'s or *Twitter*'s, retrieve offers for concert tickets from a ticketing Web service, check the user's calendar through a Web service from Google Calendar, load train stations from Geonames, and plan the trip through a travel Web service. The central challenge to such an endeavor is that the application has to join data across different services. This is difficult, because each Web service operates under its own local schema.

Modeling Web Services. A Web service is essentially a parameterized query over a remote source. In this paper, we concentrate on REST Web services. These services work by accessing a parameterized URL. For example, Last.fm offers a Web Service which, given an artist as input entity, returns the birthdate, the gender, and the albums of the artist. Figure 2 shows how this service is presented on the Last.fm Web page. We say that *artist* is the *input type* of this Web Service. In order to *call* this Web service, we replace the string "artist" by an *input entity*, says "Frank Sinatra", and access the URL. The server responds by sending the results of the request, which are usually in XML or JSON. Figure 3 shows the result of our example call. It contains the albums of Sinatra with their title, and all their singers, including Sinatra himself. The challenge is now to make this output interoperable with the results from other Web services.

Global Schemas. In order to make the service interoperable with other services, the state of art solution [15] is to assume a common global schema. Then, the Web services are represented as parameterized conjunctive queries (i.e., views with binding patterns) over this global schema. In our example, the global schema could contain relations such as *created* (for an artist who released an album) or *label* (for the relationship between an entity and its name). Expressed

$$getAlbumsByArtist^{ioooo}(y_4, y_1, y_2, y_3, y_5) \leftarrow label(x, y_4), birthdate(x, y_3), gender(x, g), label(g, y_5)$$
$$created(x, z), label(z, y_1), date(z, y_2)$$

Figure 1: View with binding patterns for the Web service getAlbumsByArtist.

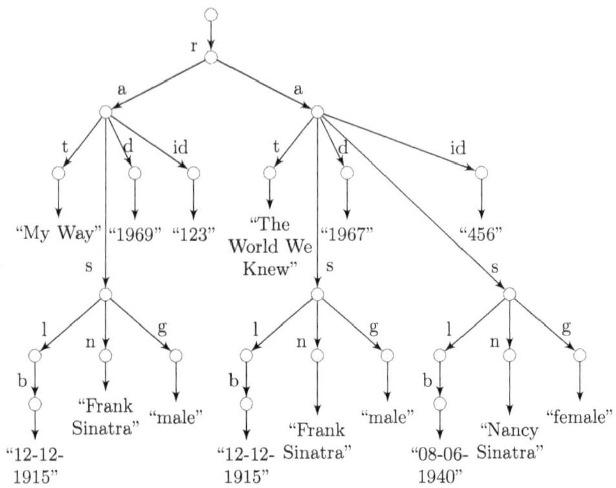

Figure 3: A call result for getAlbumsByArtist

in this global schema, the service becomes the query shown in Figure 1. Such a view is essentially a *parameterized conjunctive query*, where y_4 is the *input parameter* (the name of the artist) and all the other arguments are *output parameters* (the birthdate, the gender, the album, and the release date of the album). It is common to distinguish between an entity and its name. For example, while the g will be some internal identifier for a gender, the y_5 will be the label of that gender, such as, e.g., "female". The goal is to have all Web services expressed as views over the same global schema. This way, applications can uniformly reason about Web services in the terms of the global schema.

Problem Description. The central challenge with global schemas is that each Web service has to be mapped into this global schema. While the orchestration of Web services has received much attention lately, the transformation of services into the global schema is often done manually. Our goal is to deduce the schema fully automatically. More precisely, our goal is

Given:
- the URL and the input type of a Web service (Fig. 2)
- a global schema

Compute:
- the view of the Web service in the global schema (Fig. 1)

The URL of the Web Service and the input type can be found by a non-expert user on the Web page of the Web service (as in Figure 2). No knowledge of the output schema of the Web service is required. On the contrary, our goal is to deduce this output schema automatically.

This problem is challenging for several reasons. First, the node labels in the call results are usually vacuous and do not give away any semantics. In the example (Figure 3), they are just "r", "a", and "t". Second, it is not clear which nodes in the call result correspond to entities in the global schema. In the example, one can guess that the nodes labeled with "s" correspond to singers. However, the nodes labeled with "l" correspond to nothing in particular. Third, relations in the global schema can correspond to paths of different length in the call result. For example, the gender of an "s" node is 1 hop away, but the birth date is 2 hops away. Finally, the challenge is to transform a call result (Figure 3) into tuples in the global schema.

Our Approach. Our idea is to build upon existing knowledge bases (KBs). KBs such as YAGO [27] or DBpedia [3] provide a schema, a taxonomy of classes with their instances, and a several million facts in that schema. The instances can be used for probing the Web service. The facts can be used to guess the schema of the Web service. Our contributions are as follows:

- An algorithm that, given the URL and the input type of a Web service, computes the view in the global schema fully automatically.
- A method to compute a transformation function from the call results into the global schema.
- A variant of our algorithm that can be used to discover hidden input types for Web services.
- Experiments on more than 50 real-world Web services, showing that we can automatically create views with a precision between 81% and 100%, and discover hidden input types with a precision of more than 80%.

The rest of this paper is structured as follows: Section 2 discusses related work and Section 3 describes our data model. Sections 4 and 5 provide more details on the different parts of our method. Section 6 shows a baseline approach to our subject. Section 7 describes our algorithm for mining hidden input types. Section 8 presents experimental results, before Section 9 concludes.

2. RELATED WORK

To the best of our knowledge, no existing work can automatically infer views with binding patterns from Web services. However, our problem shares similarities with schema matching, query discovery, and Web service discovery.

Schema Matching. Determining the description of a Web service in terms of a global schema can be seen as a special case of schema mapping or ontology alignment. This is the problem of matching the concepts and the relations of one schema to the concepts and relations of another schema. Several approaches have been developed to this end.

(*i*) Approaches such as [4, 19] align the schemas of two KBs. In our scenario, we have only one KB, and the other "KB" is the Web service with no formal schema. Even when we call the service, we do not necessarily get information about its schema. This is because the output of the service usually contains only vacuous node labels and no concept names (as in Figure 3). Therefore, schema based approaches cannot be applied in our setting.

(*ii*) Several approaches use the overlap of instances to compute the alignment between two KBs [26, 16]. For us, the instances of the one "KB" is a tree (the call result of the WS) in which some nodes may correspond to entities, and other nodes are just intermediate nodes. The tree does not tell us which nodes are entities and which are not. One solution is to convert every possible path of the tree into a fact. However, as we will see in Section 8, this solution does not work well for Web services. The reason is twofold: First, a node in the tree may actually combine the properties of several entities, which leads the approach ad absurdum. Second, a fact from the call result may correspond to a join of several relations in the KB. State-of-the-art approaches for KB alignment, however, expect a one-to-one mapping.

(*iii*) Other approaches use machine learning to determine a mapping [9, 18]. They require training data, which is either provided by experts [9] or learned from pre-defined mappings [18]. In contrast, our solution requires no such input. We assume no human assistance during the mapping process. The user has no knowledge of the schema of the output.

(*iv*) Works such as [25, 31] aim to bootstrap a global schema. In [25] e.g., the authors show how the schema of a new ontology can be bootstrapped by using as input the WSDL schema descriptions of the Web Services using the SOAP protocol. In our scenario, we target the REST protocol, which provides no such information. Rather, our goal is to map services into an existing schema.

(*v*) We differentiate our work from works that map HTML tables to KBs (e.g. [17, 30]). For tables it is clear that columns are mapped to class entities and pairs of columns to relations. In our case, in contrast, the encoding of relations is unknown.

Query Discovery. Query discovery is concerned with the actual translation of data from one source to another. The state of art solution [19] exploits schema constraints, which are not available for Web services. Closest to our work, [28] derives intensional descriptions for WSs. However, the approach is semi-automatic, and requires the user's assistance during the process. Furthermore, it assumes an implicit translation of call results into tables. It can only deal with WSs that return properties for one class of entities. Our approach, in contrast, can deal with the general case where WSs return nested descriptions of entities of different types.

Web Service Discovery. The approaches of [10, 24] annotate a Web service with the concepts for which it returns instances. Our work goes beyond that. We compute views with binding patterns that map the entire call results to the KB. We also compute transformation functions that enable a uniform access to different Web services and which can be directly used for orchestrating Web services.

Orchestration and Mash-ups. Web service orchestration is concerned with joining several Web services in order to reply to a query [5, 23]. This work does not map services to a common schema. On the contrary, it requires that mapping as input. Other work proposes a new semantic model for representing Web services or mash-ups [22, 29]. Our work, in contrast, aims to represent Web services in the standard model of views with binding patterns [15].

Wrapper induction. Wrapper induction algorithms [8, 12] are concerned with automatically constructing information extraction rules ("wrappers") for Web pages. However, wrapper induction does not map the sources to a global target schema. Our work, in contrast, translates the schema of the WS into the classes and the relations of the KB.

Data Fusion. Given a schema mapping, data fusion [11] is concerned with aligning the instances from several sources. In contrast, our goal is to compute the schema mapping.

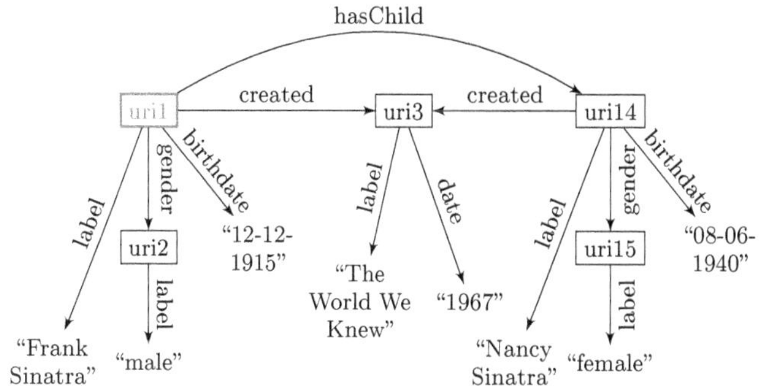

Figure 4: RDF (fragment).

3. PRELIMINARIES

3.1 Knowledge Bases

RDF Knowledge Bases. RDF is the standard of knowledge representation on the Semantic Web. The RDF model assumes a set of URIs, a set of literals, a set of classes, and a set of binary relations. A *URI* is an identifier of a real-world entity such as an organisation, a person or an abstract concept. These entities typically have a *name*, i.e., a human-readable string that identifies the entity. A *literal* is a string, a date, or a number. A *class* corresponds to a set of entities, such as the class of singers or the class of cities. A *relation* holds between two entities or between an entity and a literal. An element of a relation is called a *fact*, and we write $r(x, y)$ to say that the entity with URI x stands in the relation r with the entity with URI y. A *knowledge base* (KB) is a collection of facts. The *domain* of a relation is the class from which all first arguments of its facts are taken. Analogously, the *range* is the class of the second arguments. A relation is called the *inverse* of a relation r, written r^{-1}, if $\forall x, y : r(x, y) \Leftrightarrow r^{-}(y, x)$. We assume that the KB contains all inverse relations and their corresponding facts. This extension results in facts that have literals as their first argument, a minor digression from the standard. It is common to depict a KB as a labeled directed graph, where the nodes are entities or literals and the edges denote facts. Figure 4 shows a snippet of a KB. The entities are shown in boxes while literals are shown in quotation marks.

A relation is called *functional*, if there are no two distinct facts that share the relation and the first argument. Real life KBs may be noisy, and contain distinct facts for relations that should be functional (such as *bornIn*). Therefore, we make use of the functionality [26]:

$$fun(r) := \frac{\#x : \exists y : r(x, y)}{\#x, y : r(x, y)}$$

Here, $\#x : \Phi$ is the number of values for x for which Φ holds. Perfect functional relations will have a functionality of 1.

We assume that the KB schema contains the standard relations *type* (connecting an entity to a class), *subclassOf* (connecting a class to a more general class), and *label* (connecting an entity to a literal representing its name). If the KB contains the facts *type(e, c)* and *subclassOf(c, g)*, then by inference, it also contains the fact *type(e, g)*. We assume that all such inferences have been materialized.

KB Paths. In all of the following, we assume a given KB. We will write $r_1, ..., r_n(x, y)$ to mean that there is a *path* $r_1, ..., r_n$ from x to y that does not visit any node twice:

$$\exists x_1, ..., x_{n-1} : r_1(x, x_1) \wedge ... \wedge r_n(x_{n-1}, y) \wedge |\{x_1, ..., x_{n-1}\}| = n-1$$

We write $r_1, ..., r_n(x)$ to mean all entities reachable by that path from x, i.e., $r_1, ..., r_n(x) := \{y : r_1, ..., r_n(x, y)\}$. For simplicity, we also use p for a path of one or several relation names.

3.2 Web Services

Web Services. A Web service API provides several *Web services* (WS). A WS can be *called* by accessing a parameterized URL and by retrieving the *call result* document from the server. This document is typically in XML or JSON. For uniformity, we assume that call results in JSON are transformed to XML. This can be done by standard tools. In line with the XML standard, we represent an XML document as a rooted, unordered, labeled tree. We call the elements or the attributes of an XML tree *structure nodes*, and the values of the attributes or the contents of the elements *text nodes*. In Figure 3, structure nodes are depicted as circles while text nodes are shown in quotation marks.

WS Paths. Given a WS f, we refer to the root of the call result for x by $\lambda_f(x)$. We will omit the subscript f if it is clear from the context. We label an edge in the call result with the label of the target node of the edge. In Figure 3, e.g., the topmost edge will be labeled with "r". If an edge leads to a text node, we label the edge with the generic label τ. As for KBs, we write $l_1/.../l_n(x, y)$ to say that there is a *path* $l_1/.../l_n$ with edge labels $l_1, ..., l_n$ between node x and node y. In the example, $r/a/id/\tau(\lambda(FrankSinatra), 456)$. As before, we write p for $l_1/.../l_n$ and we define $p(x) := \{y : p(x, y)\}$.

This gives us a simple language that can express paths both in the call result and in the KB. This language is compatible with SPARQL [1] (the language for querying KBs), with XPath (the language for querying XML documents), and with XSLT [2] (the language used for our transformation functions). To distinguish paths in the call result from paths in the KB, we use "/" for XML and "." for RDF data.

Views With Binding Patterns. We abstract a WS as a *view with binding patterns*. Formally, a view with binding patterns is a conjunctive query of the form

$$q^{\bar{a}}(\bar{x}) \leftarrow r_1(\bar{x}_1), r_2(\bar{x}_2), \ldots, r_n(\bar{x}_n)$$

where $r_1, \ldots, r_n$ are relation names from the global KB and q is a new relation name. The tuples $\bar{x}_1, \bar{x}_2, \ldots \bar{x}_n$ contain either variables or constants. The query must be *safe*, *i.e.* $\bar{x} \subseteq \bar{x}_1, \bar{x}_2, \ldots \bar{x}_n$ (every variable in the head must appear also in the body). Every variable is adorned in $\bar{a}$ with a letter. We use i for input-output variables, and o for output variables. By input-output variable we mean that the result might return new bindings for that variable.

3.3 Observations

A Web service returns information about the input entity. The problem is that this information can be expressed in a multitude of ways in the call results. However, we have noticed that in practice, the call results follow a number of common sense principles.

I. The KB and the WS overlap. If the WS and the KB are from the same thematic domain (or if the KB is a general purpose KB), then we expect to see some overlap between the entities that the KB knows and the entities that the WS knows.

II. The call result is connected to the input entity. A Web service call always contains data related to its input entities. Hence, we expect that the entities contained in the call result appear in the KB and that they are connected to the input entities by paths that do not exceed a certain length. In practice, this length is not larger than three [21].

III. An injective mapping from entities to nodes. Whenever a call result contains an entity, this entity is usually represented as a structured node with sub-nodes. For example, in Figure 3, every album is represented by a subtree that is rooted in an a-node. Hence, we assume that for every entity in call result, there is at least one structured node that is shared by no other entity of the same class. We call this node an *entity node*.

IV. Relations correspond to linear path queries. We observed that typically, a relation between two entities is encoded as a path between the entity nodes and that the sequence of path labels is used consistently, i.e., it always expresses the same relation.

V. Text nodes map to literals in the KB. We have noticed that text nodes typically correspond to literals in the KB. Using a simple string similarity function, we can map a text node to an equivalent literal in the KB in the vast majority of cases.

4. SCHEMA DISCOVERY

Our algorithm for discovering the schema of a WS requires as input (1) a KB, (2) the URL of the WS, and (3) the input type of the WS. We assume that the input type is given as a class of the KB. Our algorithm proceeds in 4 steps:

1. Probing: We call the WS with several entities from the KB and obtain some sample call results (Section 4.1).
2. Path Discovery: We discover paths in the call results from the root to literals (Section 4.2).
3. Path Alignment: We align the paths in the call results with paths in the KB (Section 4.3).
4. View & Transformation Function Construction: Based on the aligned paths, we build the view and the transformation function (Section 5).

We will now detail these steps.

4.1 Probing

Our schema discovery algorithm requires a number of sample call results from the WS. To generate these, we make use of the input type of the WS: We can call the WS with instances of the input type from the KB. For example, if the input type is given as *singer*, we call the WS with instances of the class *singer* from the KB.

Not every instance of the input type in the KB will return a valid call result from the WS. The WS may not know all instances. However, it is likely that the WS stores data for known entities such as famous actors, acclaimed books, or big cities. Our intuition is that the KB, on the other hand, will likely contain more facts about such "important" entities. Therefore, we rank the entities of the input type by the descending number of facts about them, and call the WS with the top k of them. In our experiments (Section 8), we show that a number of $k = 100$ samples is usually sufficient. This corresponds to less than 0.01% of the data that the tested APIs contain.

Some WSs have more than one input. If we encounter a WS with input types $t_1, ..., t_n$, we find "important" entities of t_1. Then we find in the KB the entities of $t_2, ..., t_n$ that are connected to the entity for t_1. Finally, we probe the WS with these n entities. In what follows, we treat the call results as if they were call results about the single input entity from t_1. This will not hurt our mapping algorithm, since the other input entities are connected in the KB. If they are present in the call results, they will be discovered.

The probing gives us a set of input entities for which the calls have been executed and the results have been materialised. We call to such entities *samples*.

4.2 Path Discovery

Given a sample x, our goal is to align paths in the call result that originate at the root $\lambda(x)$ with paths in the KB that originate at the input entity x. For example, for the call result in Figure 3, we want to find that the path $r/a/t/\tau$ connects the root to the title of a song. So we want to align the path $r/a/t/\tau$ in the call result with the path *created.label* in the KB. In the following, we assume a fixed sample input entity x, and we write $(r/a/t/\tau, created.label)$ for our path alignment. To find these path alignments, we first generate all paths in the call result from the root to a literal, and all paths in the KB from the input entity x to a literal, and then align these paths.

Generating XML Paths. We first enumerate the paths from the root $\lambda(x)$ to text nodes. The result is a set of pairs of a path p and a text node y, (p, y), *s.t.* $y \in p(\lambda(x))$. This set is easily computed in a depth first traversal of the XML tree. Hence, the computation is linear in the size of the call result.

Generating KB Paths. Next, we generate the paths in the KB from x to literals. We compute the pairs of a path p' and a KB node y' (p', y'), *s.t.* $y \in p'(x)$ and y' is a literal. As per Observation *II*, we limit the search to paths of length smaller or equal to three. Hence, the results can be computed in a depth first traversal of the KB graph originating at x.

However, even short paths may lead to a huge number of results. For instance, *livesIn.hasNationality*$^-$ connects a person to all the other persons who have the nationality of the country where the person lives. Hence, the path connects "unrelated" entities via the very general concept *country*. Our goal is to exclude relationships with an absurdly high number of outgoing edges such as *hasNationality*$^-$, *hasYearOfBirth*$^-$, *hasGender*$^-$. For this purpose, we discard paths with relations whose functionality is smaller than $\alpha = 0.1$. In practice, this value proved to be safe as no results were lost.

Path Pairs. The next step generates path pairs that are candidates for the alignment. Two paths are candidates if they select *at least* one value in common. Given the results of the previous steps for the sample, it computes pairs of form

$$(p, p') \ s.t. \ \exists y \in p(\lambda(x)), y' \in p'(x) : y = y' \qquad (1)$$

This means that we implicitly align the input entity x with the root $\lambda(x)$ (Observation *II*).

String normalization. Note that we need to check the equality of two strings ($y = y'$). However, caution is needed when comparing text values extracted from the XML result to literals in the KB, because the two sources may use different writings. For example, the XML result may contain the string "Sinatra, Frank", while the KB may contain the string "Frank Sinatra". The alignment of strings across such differences is a well-studied field of research. In our implementation, we considered two strings equal if they share the same words, independent of punctuation signs, word ordering, and case. For this purpose, we normalise the values by lowercasing the string, reordering the words in alphabetical order, and omitting punctuation. Let *norm* be the normalisation function. Hence, in Equation (1), the equality $y = y'$ is replaced by $norm(y) = norm(y')$.

Aligning Paths with Common Values. A simple pairwise comparison of text nodes in the call result to literals in the KB can be highly inefficient. The number of pairs can easily exceed one thousand. Thanks to our normalisation, however, a pairwise comparison for similarity is no longer necessary: two strings are either identical or not considered similar. Therefore, we can use a merge-join algorithm. We sort each of the two sets of tuples produced in the previous steps by the normalised value of the second component. Then we can merge the two lists in order to produce the results. The complexity is $n \times log(n)$ where n is the cumulated size of the two lists. This yields a set of pairs of the form (p, p'), where p is a path from the call result and p' is a path from the KB and both lead to the same value. These are our candidates for the path alignment.

4.3 Path Alignment

For a set of samples S, and a candidate pair of paths (p, p'), we need to compute a confidence score for the alignment of p and p' with respect to S. We present two strategies to this end.

Overlapping

Method. The simplest method to align an XML path p with a KB path p' (which works best in practice) is to use the overlapping of the results. We say that p' *overlaps with* p, if

$$\forall x \in S \ \exists y : p(\lambda(x), y) \wedge p'(x, y)$$

For simplicity, we use y to denote a literal and a text node with the same (normalised) value. An overlap can be stronger or weaker, depending on the proportion of samples that overlap. We compute the *confidence* of the overlap as the number of samples for which their results overlap, divided by the total number of samples:

$$conf(\ (p, p')\ ) := \frac{\#x : \exists y : p(\lambda(x), y) \wedge p'(x, y)}{|S|}$$

Weaknesses of the Method. Although this simple method leads to remarkably good results, some alignments are lost. For instance, consider the alignment: $(r/a/s/l/e/\tau$, *diedOnDate*). If the living singers represent more than half of the input entities selected for sampling, then this alignment is lost. Hence, we also experimented with a second strategy for path alignment, which is based on subsumption.

Subsumption

Method. The subsumption strategy aligns two paths if the results of one are included in the results of the other. We are interested in mining KB paths subsumed by XML paths and vice-versa, XML paths subsumed by KB paths. Let p and p' two paths. We say that p' *subsumes* p, if

$$\forall x, y : p(x, y) \Rightarrow p'(x, y)$$

For instance, consider the path pair $(/r/a/s/n/\tau$, *label*). The XML path selects the name of the input entity for which albums are returned as well as the names of the other persons who released the respective albums. However, the KB path selects only the name of the input entity. Hence we have: *label* $\rightarrow /r/a/s/n/\tau$.

Confidence. There are different ways to compute the confidence of such rules [20, 7, 13]. The problem in our case is that our data on both sides is incomplete: When the KB does not contain a certain fact, the WS can still return it, and vice versa. Hence, we opted to use the *PCA confidence*, a measure developed for AMIE [13]. This measure is particularly suited for incomplete relations. The measure assumes that a source knows either *all* or *none* of the p-attributes of some x. Under this assumption, the formula counts as counter-examples for a rule $p(x, y) \rightarrow p'(x, y)$ only those instances x for which the query paths p return an answer, but where y is not among these answers. This yields the following confidence measure:

$$pcaconf(\ (p, p')\ ) := \frac{\#(x, y) : p(x, y) \wedge p'(x, y)}{\#(x, y) : \exists y' : p(x, y) \wedge p'(x, y')}$$

where $\#(x, y) : \mathcal{A}$ is the number of pairs (x, y) that fulfill $\mathcal{A}$.

This formula gives high confidence even if the alignments have small overlap. For instance, in our experiments, we found that the alignment *diedOnDate* $\rightarrow r/a/s/l/e/\tau$ achieves the highest confidence (*pcaconf*= 1). Hence, we can use *pcaconf* to spot possible alignments even if there is very small overlap. In such cases, the alignment is very risky. Hence, we have to validate such alignments through more probing. This works as follows: Whenever a path alignment achieves high PCA confidence, we select for probing, entities for which the newly discovered KB property is defined. Then we re-probe the WS with these entities.

The result of the path alignment is a set of pairs of the form (p, p'), where p is a path in the call result and p' is a path in the KB. Figure 5 shows the alignment for our running example.

$/r/a^*/t/\tau$	*created*.label*
$/r/a^*/d/\tau$	*created*.date*
$/r/a^*/s^*/l/b/\tau$	*birthdate*
$/r/a^*/s^*/n/\tau$	*label*
$/r/a^*/s^*/g/\tau$	*gender.label*

Figure 5: Results of the path alignment step for *getAlbumsByArtist*

$(r/a^*$, *created*$)$	z
$(r/a^*/s^*,)$	x
$(r/a^*/t/\tau$, *created*label*$)$	y_1
$(r/a^*/d/\tau$, *created*date*$)$	y_2
$(r/a^*/s^*/l/b/\tau$, *birthdate*$)$	y_3
$(r/a^*/s^*/n/\tau$, *label*$)$	y_4
$(r/a^*/s^*/g/\tau$, *gender.label*$)$	y_5

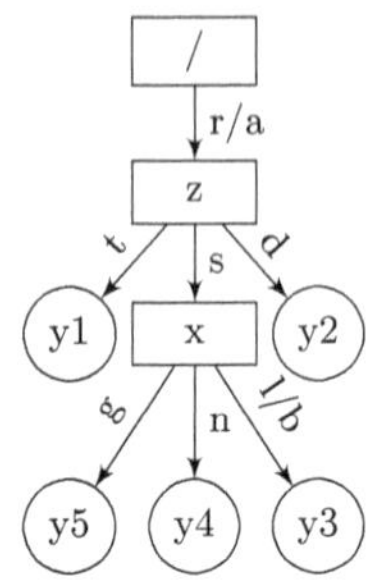

Figure 6: New path alignments and their associated variables for *getAlbumsByArtist* (left) and the tree-like hierarchy of paths in XML (right).

5. VIEW AND TRANSFORMATION

Branching Points. Our next step is to indicate *branching points* in the XML paths and the KB paths. These are denoted by the "*" in Figure 5. A branching point in a path means that there are several outgoing edges in the graph starting from that point of the path that are labeled with the same name. For example, following the path $r/a/t/\tau$ in the call result of Figure 3, we encounter several edges labeled with a. Hence, a is a branching point. Formally, we say that l_i is a branching point for the XML path $/l_1/l_2 \cdots /l_{i-1}/l_i \cdots /l_n$ *iff*

$$\exists x \in S, z, y_1, y_2\ :\ /l_1 \ldots /l_{i-1}(\lambda(x), z) \wedge \\ \wedge\, l_i(z, y_1) \wedge l_i(z, y_2) \wedge y_1 \neq y_2$$

We use a path summary in the form of a DataGuide tree [14] to keep track of all possible paths in the samples and of their branching points. Its construction requires only a depth first traversal of each sample tree and its size is small because we do not need to store the text nodes.

For the KB paths, we insert branching points whenever a relation is not a function. Some KBs explicitly declare their functions. If that is not the case, we compute the functionality for each relation (Section 3). Since KBs may contain some noise, we insert branching points at a relation only if its functionality is lower than $\beta = 0.9$.

Cut and Align. We now want to align also sub-portions of the paths. Our input are the path alignments produced by the previous step, annotated with branching points, and our output will be more path alignments. The clue of our algorithm is the insight that if we have a path of functional relations on the KB side, then this path has to be aligned to a (sub-)path with no branching points on the XML side. This means that the rightmost $*$ annotation of one path is aligned with the right most $*$ of the other path in the pair. Let us write $P * p$ to denote a path such that $P*$ ends in a branching point or it is the empty path, and p has no branching points. Then we generate new path alignments by recursively applying the following rule:

$$(P * p, P' * p') \rightsquigarrow (P, P')$$

For the path alignments in Figure 5, this gives rise to the new alignments in the Figure 6 (left).

Weakness of the Method. The annotation with branching points on the XML paths is biased by the set of XML call result samples. For example, if all call results return only singers that have released a single album, then our method will not annotate $/s$ as a branching point.

Duplicate Elimination. The previous step may result in associating the same KB path to different XML paths. This means that the same relationship appears multiple times in the call result. If this happens, we select the alignment that was generated from the pair with the highest confidence. Also, it may happen that several KB paths map to the same XML path. If the KB paths select literals, we use the same approach. If not, then they concern relationships between complex entities. For instance, we may have as candidates *created* and *bornIn.producedIn*$^-$. In that case, we select the path where the maximal functionality of its relations is minimal.

View Definition. We now want to deduce the view definition from our path alignments. We introduce a new variable for each path alignment (shown in the middle in Figure 6). Now, the view definition is simply the join of the KB paths with the appropriate variables. More precisely, let us write $P' \rightarrow v$, if some alignment (P, P') is associated to a variable

v. Then, we construct the body of the view definition with the following rules:

$$\left.\begin{array}{l} P* \rightarrow v_1 \\ P*p \rightarrow v_2 \end{array}\right\} \rightsquigarrow p(v_1, v_2)$$

$$\left.\begin{array}{l} P* \rightarrow v_1 \\ P*P'* \rightarrow v_2 \\ \nexists P''* \rightarrow v, P''' : P*P''*P''' = P*P'* \end{array}\right\} \rightsquigarrow P'(v_1, v_2)$$

The resulting atoms are added to the body of the view definition. The head atom of the view definition is the name of the WS. It contains only the variables that correspond to literals. This is because the entity identifiers used by the KB cannot be obtained by calling the WS. For our running example, we obtain exactly the view definition of Figure 1.

Transformation Function. We have shown how to derive automatically the view definition of a WS in the global schema. Now, we turn to the question of how we can transform a concrete call result into tuples of this view definition. Our idea is to use an XSLT script for this purpose. Given a call result of a WS, the script will extract bindings for the variables in the head of the view definition of the WS. We now explain how to derive this script automatically from our path alignments.

We first organise the XML paths of the path alignment as a tree. The root of the tree is labeled with "/", and the other nodes represent variables. Edges are labeled with path queries. In the example of Figure 6 (left), this leads to the tree shown in Figure 6 (right).

Algorithm 1 transforms such a tree into an XSLT script. It requires as input the root node of the tree. We assume that the functions *isRoot()*, *isLeaf()*, *getChildren()*, and *pathFromParent()* are available for every node. Let *pathFromParent()* return the path query on the edge between the node and its parent. For leaf nodes, the function omits the last part "text()" (τ). For instance, y_1*.pathFromParent()=t*. Our algorithm performs a depth-first search on the tree, and outputs a variable assignment for each edge of the tree.

Algorithm 1 makeXSLT(TreeNode v)

```
if v.isRoot() then
  print <xsl:template match="/">
  for v' : v.getChildren() do makeXSLT(v') end for
  print </xsl:template>
end if
if v.isLeaf() then
  print {v:<xsl:for-each select="v.pathFromParent()">
  {<xsl:value select="." >} </xsl:for-each>}
else
  print {<xsl:for-each select="v.pathFromParent()">
  for v' : v.getChildren() do makeXSLT(v') end for
  print </xsl:for-each>}
end if
```

The output of this algorithm is an XSLT script. This script is generated only once per WS. Each time a client calls the WS, the client has to execute the XSLT script on the call results, which will yield tuples in the view definition of the WS. We remark that this gives us an end-to-end solution for integrating Web services into a global schema: Given a schema and a WS, we can automatically derive a view definition of the WS, and a method to map the call results into that view definition.

6. BASELINE APPROACH

We have presented an end-to-end solution for the mapping of a Web service into a global schema. We will now present a baseline solution to this problem, which is based on wrapper induction. We adopt the approach that [21] has developed for mapping Deep Web forms into a KB. The approach creates a wrapper that extracts a pseudo-KB on the result pages of the Deep Web form. This pseudo-KB is then aligned with the reference KB using the PARIS ontology alignment algorithm [26]. A similar approach has been presented in [6] for mapping XML documents to RDF ontologies.

In the spirit of wrappers, we construct entities for repetitive structures. In our case, these are subtrees rooted at nodes that can have sibling nodes labeled with the same name. In our running example (Figure 3), these are the nodes labeled with a and s. We use an XSLT script to implement this wrapper. Conveniently, we can use Algorithm 1 to generate this script. As input, we use the DataGuide that we computed for our samples. The branching points and the leaf nodes are annotated with variables. Two XML paths with the same labels are mapped to the same relation in the pseudo-KB. Running this script on the call results will yield a pseudo-KB, much like in [21]. Then, we use PARIS to align this pseudo-KB with the reference KB.

Although this solution may seem reasonable, our experimental evaluation shows that it does not lead to good results. One problem with this approach is that two entities in the reference KB may map to the same entity node in the pseudo-KB. Another problem is that a single relation in the pseudo-KB may correspond to an entire path of relations in the reference KB. This derails KB alignment approaches such as PARIS, which assume that a single relation in one KB corresponds to a single relation in the other KB.

7. DISCOVERING HIDDEN INPUT TYPES

For some WSs the type of the input can be hidden - is defined locally by the Web service. Many API providers use internal ids rather than names to identify entities. Since ids are internal to the API, they can almost never be obtained from external sources (such as the KB). However, if they are contained in the result of some WS of the same API, they can be inferred by joining the data of the two WSs. While some Web services may be joinable, others may be incompatible. For example, it does not make sense to use the output of a WS that delivers albums id as inputs to a WS that expects movies id. We will now show that our approach for mapping Web services into a global schema can also be used to determine which Web services are joinable.

Let ρ_f be a function that maps a variable in the view of a WS f to its bindings in our samples of f. We consider the following problem: Given a WS f_O that has been mapped to the KB, and given another WS f_I with only one input of unknown type, compute join dependencies of the form:

$$(f_O, x, p, f_I)$$

Here, x is variable in the view of f_O. p is an XML path such that $\forall x' \in \rho_{f_O}(x)$, $p(x')$ has values for the input of f_I and f_I returns data relevant to x'.

EXAMPLE 1. Let f_O=*getAlbumsByArtist* and let f_I be a WS that returns songs by album-id. We aim to discover the following join dependency: $(f_O, z, id/\tau, f_I)$. Here, z is the variable used for album entities in the view in Figure 1. In the call result depicted in Figure 3, z had as bindings the two nodes labeled with a. Note that the path id/τ selects exactly the ids of the respective albums.

Mini-KB Extraction. The interesting aspect of our example join dependency is that it concerns paths in f_O that were not yet mapped to KB relations (namely id/τ). Our goal is now to extend our view definition and our transformation function to these unmapped paths. For each variable x in the view of f_O, and for each XML path p' s.t. $\exists x' \in \rho_{f_O}(x) \wedge p'(x') \neq \emptyset$, we add a new relation name to the schema of the KB, and we map p' to that new relation name. The XSLT script for f_O is updated accordingly. Let *mini-KB(x)* be a KB computed by applying the updated XSLT script to every call result in our sample for f_O.
Generating candidates. A candidate join dependency of the form (f_O, x, p, f_I) is computed for every variable x from the view of f_O and every path p in f_O where

$$\#x' : (x' \in \rho_{f_O}(x) \wedge p(x') \neq \emptyset) > \theta$$

In our experiments, we set $\theta = 20$. For probing f_I, we extract from *mini-KB(x)* tuples of the form:

$$(x^k, l) : \exists x' \in \rho_{f_O}(x) \wedge \sigma'_{f_O}(x') = x^k \wedge p(x', l)$$

where l serves to call f_I, but we see x^k as the input entity of that respective call. We now discuss when we keep a candidate join dependency (f_O, x, p, f_I).
Step 1: Catch Error Messages. If f_I returns systematically an error message, we discard the candidate. However, some WSs will not return an error message if fed with a bad input entity. Instead they will return results for all entities whose names or other attributes are similar to the input entity. Therefore, our first step cannot filter out all bad candidate join dependencies.
Step 2: Checking Input's Position in the Output. If the call is valid, then it should return information about the input value. This value should consistently appear under the same path(s) from the root (Observation *IV*). Assume that we discover that the input value occurs *always* under the path p_i in the call results of f_I. Then, we can filter out every candidate $(f"_O, x", p", f_I)$ that did not discover p_i as being the path with the inputs.
Step 3: Align f_I and the mini-KB. Finally, we use the path alignment algorithm from Section 4 to align label paths in the outputs of f_I with path relations in *mini-KB*(x). We rank the candidates between f_I and f_O according to the number of paths produced by the alignment. We select as solution the top candidate. The intuition is that f_I should return some of the properties of x returned also by f_O. For instance, for our example, we expect that the second WS recalls the singer of the album in its results, which in turn appears also in the output of *getAlbumsByArtist*.
Discovering Types for WS Inputs. Let our candidate (f_O, x, p, f_I) be a join dependency. Hence, f_I returns data relevant to x. Thus, we can say that the input of f_I has as type the class of x^k (or x) in the KB. However, the relation that links x^k to l in the KB might not be the default relation *label*. Hence, the input of f_I is annotated with the class of x^k (its input entity) and the (new) relation to which p is mapped to. With this, f_I is now ready to be mapped to the target KB.

8. EXPERIMENTS

Our algorithms are fully implemented in a system called *DORIS* (Discovering Ontological Relations In Services).
Data Sources. We have tested DORIS on more than 50 real WSs provided by more than 10 APIs. The data exported by the WSs cover four domains: music, movies, books, and geographic data. Table 1 shows the WS APIs that we considered, grouped by thematic domain. The first column shows the APIs. The third column shows the WSs offered by these APIs. Several APIs can provide the same WS. For example, both book APIs support *getAuthorInfoByName*. Therefore, the second column shows how many APIs support a given WS.

We have conducted experiments for three target KBs: YAGO [27] and DBpedia [3] (which are extracted from Wikipedia), and BNF (bnf.fr) (a KB from the domain of books curated by the National Library of France). We probed each Web Service for 100 samples.
Platform. Our system is implemented in Java (JVM 1.7). We use standard Java libraries to parse the XML and JSON call results. We use the Jena 2.11 library to store the KBs, and the Jena SPARQL functionality to query them. We ran all experiments on a personal laptop (2,9 GHz Intel Core i7, 8GB). Our method takes roughly 2 minutes to derive the schema of a WS (Path Alignment and Class & Atom Alignment).

Path Alignment

Our first series of experiments concerns the path alignment (Section 4). We probed each WS with instances of the input domain from the YAGO KB. As a gold standard, we designed the correct path alignments manually for each WS of each API.

Our first goal is to determine the right threshold for the overlapping algorithm. We examine the performance of our method with respect to different threshold values. Table 2 shows the average F-measure across all WSs for the alignment under different thresholds. The threshold 0.5 produces the best results, hence we use it for what follows.

Table 2: Average performance of Path Alignment

Threshold:	0.3	0.4	**0.5**	0.6	0.7
F-measure:	0.762	0.88	**0.89**	0.88	0.81

Then, we ran experiments for both alignment strategies: the overlapping and the subsumption strategy. For the subsumption, we checked whether the results of the KB path are subsumed by the results of the XML path ($KB \rightarrow WS$), and vice-versa ($WS \rightarrow KB$). Table 1 shows the precision and the recall for each WS (averaged over the APIs that provide the WS).

Our experiments show that the overlapping strategy (Overlap columns) can align paths with a precision (P) of 57%-100%. In the vast majority of cases, the precision is over 80%. Recall (R), likewise, is well over 90% in the majority of cases.

The subsumption strategy performs less well. The main reason is that the PCA confidence does not penalise alignments that have the support of a small number of samples. This yields many spurious matches. On the other

Table 1: **Path Alignment and Class & Atom Alignment on the YAGO KB.**

API	No	WS	Path Alignment Overlap P	R	KB→WS P	R	WS→KB P	R	Classes DORIS P	R	Atoms DORIS P	R	*PARIS* P	R
GeoData { geonames	1	getCityByName (*City*)	**1**	**0.73**	0.17	0.33	0.0	0.0	1	1	1	**0.67**	0.31	0.67
	1	getCountryByName (*Country*)	**0.62**	**0.71**	0.25	0.2	0.0	0.0	1	1	1	1	0.1	0.33
Books { isbndb, library_thing	2	getAuthorInfoById (*Id*)	**1**	1	0.29	0.49	0.35	0.89	1	1	1	1	0.33	0.37
	2	getAuthorInfoByName (*Author*)	**0.97**	**0.97**	0.32	0.48	0.23	0.5	1	1	1	1	0.41	0.62
	2	getBookInfoByTitle (*Book*)	0.84	1	0.85	0.72	0.5	0.5	1	1	1	1	0.29	0.5
Movies { themoviedb	1	getActorInfoById (*Id*)	**1**	**0.8**	0.33	0.8	0.23	1	1	1	1	**0.67**	0.4	0.67
	1	getActorInfoByName (*Actor*)	**1**	1	0.33	0.67	0.25	1	1	1	1	1	0.33	1
	1	getMoviesByActorId (*Id*)	0.88	1	0.27	0.43	1	0.57	1	1	1	1	0.25	0.67
Music { music_brainz, musixmatch, last_fm, echonest, deezer, discogs	6	getArtistInfoById (*Id*)	**0.82**	**0.89**	0.32	0.49	0.33	0.81	**0.89**	**0.78**	**0.83**	0.73	0.38	0.72
	1	getArtistInfoByMBID (*Id*)	**0.57**	1	0.2	0.5	0.19	0.75	1	1	1	1	0.33	1
	6	getArtistInfoByName (*Singer*)	**0.9**	**0.97**	0.33	0.49	0.46	0.31	**0.89**	**0.94**	**0.84**	0.9	0.28	0.72
	4	getAlbumByTitle (*Album*)	0.84	**0.75**	0.87	0.17	0.2	0.12	1	1	1	1	0.09	0.15
	4	getAlbumsByArtistId (*Id*)	**0.94**	**0.99**	0.22	0.2	0.46	0.57	1	1	1	1	0.29	0.37
	1	getAlbumsByArtistMBID (*Id*)	**1**	1	0.33	0.2	0.5	0.6	1	1	1	1	0.5	0.5
	2	getAlbumsByArtist (*Singer*)	**0.85**	**0.91**	0.29	0.31	0.67	0.38	**0.88**	1	**0.88**	1	0.24	0.33
	1	getTopTracksByArtistId (*Id*)	**1**	**0.93**	0.33	0.13	0.6	0.6	1	1	1	1	0.33	0.25
	4	getTrackByTitle (*Song*)	0.81	1	0.94	0.53	0.25	0.12	**0.79**	1	**0.86**	1	0.3	0.32
	2	getTracksByArtistId (*Id*)	**0.88**	1	0.17	0.22	0.17	0.33	**0.88**	1	**0.88**	1	0.25	0.66
	4	getTracksByArtist (*Singer*)	**0.91**	**0.94**	0.29	0.29	0.52	0.41	**0.83**	1	**0.81**	0.95	0.23	0.32

hand, this allows aligning paths with incomplete relations such as *diedOnDate*, *wasCreatedOnDate*, *hasLongintude*, and *hasLatitude*. In order to find these alignments also with the overlapping method, more samples would be needed.

Class and Atom Alignment

We refer to the bindings of a variable in the view using the term class. By atom we mean an atom of the view. We say that a class or an atom are correctly aligned if the transformation function extracts correct values for them. In order to evaluate the class and atom alignment, we first generated the ideal class and atom alignment manually. Then, we ran our alignment algorithm and compared the results to this gold standard. As input, we used the path alignments computed by the overlapping strategy.

Duplicate Removal. We first wanted to see whether duplicate removal helps precision and recall for the class and atom alignment (see Section 5). Hence, we ran the alignment with and without duplicate removal and measured precision and recall. Our experiments show that the technique helps: By removing the duplicates, the average precision across all Web services for YAGO relations rises from 45% to 91%. At the same time, recall is almost the same. It decreases from 95% for the algorithm that allows duplicates to 93% for the one that removes them. The precision and recall for classes remains unchanged. Therefore, we decided to remove duplicates in what follows.

YAGO. The results of aligning the Web services to the YAGO KB are presented in Table 1 on the right. We are happy to report that our system achieves a perfect precision and a perfect recall on nearly all WSs. Only very few WSs could not be mapped entirely correctly. We reckon that this is the first time that the result of WSs can be mapped fully automatically to the schema of a target KB.

Other KBs. We have also tested our algorithm on DBpedia and BNF. For DBpedia, we used all 50 WSs. For BNF, which is a domain-specific KB, we ran only the WSs from the Books domain. We present an average of the precision and recall of our class and atom alignment in Table 3. Since the BNF contains data that overlaps a lot with the WS, we obtain a perfect precision and recall for this KB. The other alignments are also of very respectable quality, with recall and precision values well over 90%.

Table 3: Average Performance of Alignments

	Precision Classes	Precision Atoms	Recall Classes	Recall Atoms
YAGO	0.92	0.91	0.96	0.93
DBpedia	0.91	0.92	0.98	0.95
BNF	1	1	1	1

Comparison to Baseline. In Section 6, we introduced a baseline approach to the problem of WS alignment. This approach transforms the WS call results into a pseudo-KB, and uses a state-of-the-art alignment approach (PARIS [26]) to align the pseudo-KB to the reference KB.

We ran PARIS with exactly the same data as DORIS. PARIS computes a confidence score for each alignment. We used a threshold of 0.6 on this score to determine the final output, which was the value for which PARIS performed best. The results of this approach are shown in the last two columns of Table 1. As we see, DORIS outperforms PARIS by a huge margin. DORIS achieves near-perfect alignment, while the precision and recall for PARIS are more in the area of 30%-60%. The reason is that PARIS performs very well when the schemas of the two ontologies are similar. This is not the case at all in our problem. Moreover, PARIS cannot discover complex relations alignments like *hasGender.label*, while DORIS discovered them.

Discovering Hidden Input Types

Our next experiment evaluates our algorithm for discovering join dependencies for WSs whose input type is hidden (Section 7). For each API, we determined the joins manually. Then, we ran our algorithm for each API, and compared the results to the true ones. Table 4 shows the precision and the recall for several variants of the algorithm: S1 and S2 implement Step 1 and Step 2 respectively. S23 implements Steps 2 and 3 together. We find that Step 1 sometimes excludes good answers, which leads to a drop in recall. The good news is that all strategies have a very high recall, which is almost perfect for S2 and S23. Furthermore, S23 achieves a precision that is consistently over 80%. Hence, our method is able to discover join dependencies and input types fully automatically with high accuracy.

Table 4: Join Dependencies Discovery

API	Precision			Recall		
	S1	S2	S23	S1	S2	S23
deezer	0.21	0.67	0.95	0.77	1	1
discogs	0.27	0.83	0.81	1	1	1
echonest	0.78	1	1	1	1	1
isbndb	0.48	0.82	0.82	1	1	1
last_fm	0.24	1	1	1	1	1
library_thing	0.57	0.6	1	1	1	1
music_brainz	0.1	0.84	0.84	0.93	0.93	0.93
musixmatch	0.11	0.55	0.83	1	1	1
themoviedb	0.19	0.78	0.89	1	1	1

9. CONCLUSION

In this paper, we have shown how to map the results of a Web service fully automatically into the schema of a knowledge base. Our approach aligns the call results of the Web service to relations of the KB, it derives a view definition of the service in the schema of the KB, and it discovers join dependencies between different WSs. Our experiments show that our approach produces near-perfect results on over 50 real Web services in a variety of domains. We hope that our techniques can provide a bridge between different data providers, and thus help the rise of tomorrow's knowledge-centric applications.

Acknowledgments. This work is supported by the research projects EDOP (PATRIMA LabEx) and ALODIS (PEPS FASCIDO 2015 - CNRS).

10. REFERENCES

[1] Sparql: `http://www.w3.org/TR/rdf-sparql-query/`.

[2] Xslt: `http://www.w3.org/TR/xslt20/`.

[3] S. Auer, C. Bizer, G. Kobilarov, J. Lehmann, R. Cyganiak, and Z. G. Ives. DBpedia: A nucleus for a Web of open data. In *ISWC*, 2007.

[4] D. Aumueller, H. H. Do, S. Massmann, and E. Rahm. Schema and ontology matching with coma++. In *SIGMOD Conference*, 2005.

[5] V. Bárány, M. Benedikt, and P. Bourhis. Access patterns and integrity constraints revisited. In *ICDT*, 2013.

[6] I. F. Cruz, H. Xiao, and F. Hsu. Peer-to-peer semantic integration of xml and rdf data sources. In *AP2PC*, 2004.

[7] L. Dehaspe and H. Toivonen. Discovery of frequent datalog patterns. *Data Min. Knowl. Discov.*, 3(1), 1999.

[8] N. Derouiche, B. Cautis, and T. Abdessalem. Automatic extraction of structured web data with domain knowledge. In *ICDE*, 2012.

[9] A. Doan, P. Domingos, and A. Y. Halevy. Reconciling schemas of disparate data sources: A machine-learning approach. In *SIGMOD Conference*, 2001.

[10] X. Dong, A. Y. Halevy, J. Madhavan, E. Nemes, and J. Zhang. Simlarity search for web services. In *VLDB*, 2004.

[11] X. L. Dong, E. Gabrilovich, G. Heitz, W. Horn, K. Murphy, S. Sun, and W. Zhang. From data fusion to knowledge fusion. *CoRR*, 2015.

[12] T. Furche, G. Gottlob, G. Grasso, X. Guo, G. Orsi, C. Schallhart, and C. Wang. Diadem: Thousands of websites to a single database. *PVLDB*, 2014.

[13] L. Galárraga, C. Teflioudi, K. Hose, and F. M. Suchanek. Amie: association rule mining under incomplete evidence in ontological knowledge bases. In *WWW*, 2013.

[14] R. Goldman and J. Widom. DataGuides: Enabling query formulation and optimization in semistructured databases. In *VLDB*, 1997.

[15] A. Y. Halevy. Answering queries using views: A survey. *VLDB J.*, 2001.

[16] T. Kirsten, A. Thor, and E. Rahm. Instance-based matching of large life science ontologies. In *DILS Workshop*, 2007.

[17] G. Limaye, S. Sarawagi, and S. Chakrabarti. Annotating and searching web tables using entities, types and relationships. *PVLDB*, 2010.

[18] J. Madhavan, P. A. Bernstein, A. Doan, and A. Y. Halevy. Corpus-based schema matching. In *ICDE*, 2005.

[19] R. J. Miller, L. M. Haas, and M. A. Hernández. Schema mapping as query discovery. In *VLDB*, 2000.

[20] S. Muggleton. Learning from positive data. In *ILP*, 1996.

[21] M. Oita, A. Amarilli, and P. Senellart. Cross-fertilizing deep web analysis and ontology enrichment. In *VLDS Workshop*, 2012.

[22] D. L. Phuoc, A. Polleres, M. Hauswirth, G. Tummarello, and C. Morbidoni. Rapid prototyping of semantic mash-ups through semantic web pipes. In *WWW*, 2009.

[23] N. Preda, F. M. Suchanek, W. Yuan, and G. Weikum. Susie: Search using services and information extraction. In *ICDE*, 2013.

[24] S. Quarteroni, M. Brambilla, and S. Ceri. A bottom-up, knowledge-aware approach to integrating and querying web data services. *TWEB*, 7(4):19, 2013.

[25] A. Segev and Q. Z. Sheng. Bootstrapping ontologies for web services. *IEEE T. Services Computing*, 5(1), 2012.

[26] F. M. Suchanek, S. Abiteboul, and P. Senellart. PARIS: Probabilistic alignment of relations, instances, and schema. *PVLDB*, 5(3), 2011.

[27] F. M. Suchanek, G. Kasneci, and G. Weikum. YAGO: A core of semantic kknowledge. In *WWW*, 2007.

[28] M. Taheriyan, C. A. Knoblock, P. A. Szekely, and J. L. Ambite. Rapidly integrating services into the linked data cloud. In *ISWC*, 2012.

[29] P. Traverso and M. Pistore. Automated composition of semantic web services into executable processes. In *ISWC*, 2004.

[30] P. Venetis, A. Y. Halevy, J. Madhavan, M. Pasca, W. Shen, F. W. 0003, G. Miao, and C. Wu. Recovering semantics of tables on the web. *PVLDB*, 2011.

[31] J. Wang, J. Wen, F. H. Lochovsky, and W. Ma. Instance-based schema matching for web databases by domain-specific query probing. In *VLDB*, 2004.

An Optimization Framework for Propagation of Query–Document Features by Query Similarity Functions

Maxim Zhukovskiy Tsimafei Khatkevich Gleb Gusev Pavel Serdyukov
Yandex
16 Leo Tolstoy St., Moscow, 119021 Russia
{zhukmax, tsimkha, gleb57, pavser}@yandex-team.ru

ABSTRACT

It is well known that a great number of query–document features which significantly improve the quality of ranking for popular queries, however, do not provide any benefit for new or rare queries since there is typically not enough data associated with those queries that is required to reliably compute the values of those features. It is a common practice to propagate the values of such features from popular to tail queries, if the queries are similar according to some predefined query similarity functions. In this paper, we propose new algorithms that facilitate and increase the effectiveness of this propagation. Given a query similarity function and a query–document relevance feature, we introduce two different approaches (linear weighting approach and tree-based approach) to learn a function of values of the similarity function and values of the feature for the similar queries w.r.t. the given document. The propagated value of the feature equals the value of the obtained function for the given query–document pair. For the purpose of finding the most effective method of propagating query–document features, we measure the effectiveness of different approaches to features propagation by performing experiments on a large dataset of labeled queries.

1. INTRODUCTION

Modern web search engines use a large number of relevance signals that are typically combined in a complex fashion via learning a ranking function. Using these features, popular commercial search engines can generally respond to most frequently asked queries (or *head queries*) with excellent results. However, providing answers of similarly high quality for tail queries, infrequently issued or previously unseen, is more difficult due the fact that the quality of some features [1] highly depends on the amount of the data available for calculation of those features that in turn is influenced by the query popularity. Previous studies [36] even reported that the quality of web page ranking for head queries is nearly the same for different search engines, while tail queries contribute to the major differences among search engines. Therefore, improving the performance of these queries by overcoming the sparseness of the data associated with them is one of the most critical challenges faced by search engines.

This problem is usually solved by propagating statistics between query–document pairs sharing the same document on the basis of query *similarity*, which can be determined via a *similarity function* [2, 5, 13, 21, 32, 34, 35, 38]. There is more than one way to define query similarity, which can be based on characteristics of user behavior ([13, 21, 26, 28, 32, 35]), semantic and syntactic properties of the queries [5, 17, 34, 38], and values of different features for different documents with respect to the considered queries [32]. Our motivation for this work is to understand how different similarities and other properties of queries can be incorporated in the most optimal way for solving the problem of propagating query–document features. For this purpose, we propose a general framework for learning a web page ranking function based on propagation of features via queries' similarities. The learning part of our framework allows to compare different propagating methods by evaluating ranking quality of trained rankers. Given two propagating methods, a set of regular query–document features, a set of query–document features that are computed by propagation, and an algorithm for learning a ranking function, we learn two different ranking functions, which are trained by using the same learning algorithm. The learning process differs only in the sets of propagated features that, in each process, are computed with a different propagation method (both sets of features contain the considered regular features). The first propagating method outperforms the second one, if the first ranking function outperforms the second one in terms of a considered measure of retrieval quality.

The effectiveness of propagating query–document features, as we demonstrate in this paper, depends on a variety of aspects that need to be considered by a propagating method, but that were overlooked by the state-of-the-art methods. Assume we are provided with a collection of queries Q, values of a feature f for query–document pairs (q, d) over all q from Q, and a collection of query similarity functions. The common approach to obtain the propagated value of the feature f for a target query–document pair (q, d) is the following [2, 13, 35]. The propagated feature value $\tilde{f}(q, d)$ equals

$$\sum_{\tilde{q} \in Q_q} w(\tilde{q}, q) f(\tilde{q}, d) \quad (1)$$

Permission to make digital or hard copies of all or part of this work for personal or classroom use is granted without fee provided that copies are not made or distributed for profit or commercial advantage and that copies bear this notice and the full citation on the first page. Copyrights for components of this work owned by others than ACM must be honored. Abstracting with credit is permitted. To copy otherwise, or republish, to post on servers or to redistribute to lists, requires prior specific permission and/or a fee. Request permissions from Permissions@acm.org.
CIKM'15, October 19–23, 2015, Melbourne, Australia.
© 2015 ACM. ISBN 978-1-4503-3794-6/15/10 ...$15.00.
DOI: http://dx.doi.org/10.1145/2806416.2806487.

taken over the queries $\tilde{q}$ which are similar to query q. The weights $w(\tilde{q}, q)$ and the set Q_q of similar queries are defined in some way on the basis of one of the existing query similarity functions $s(\tilde{q}, q)$.

So far, the values of the query similarity functions (sometimes, normalized) were used directly as the weights in Equation 1, without regard to their different nature and scale. Besides, there have been no comparison of the weighted mean as a function to aggregate the feature values for similar queries with any other function that could be taken over them. Also the state-of-the-art propagating method described by Equation 1 was not previously compared [2, 13, 35] with methods utilizing some more statistics about the distribution of the feature values over similar queries besides its linearly weighted mean.

The major contributions of this paper are the following.

First, we investigate different approaches to learn a function of similarity values which is used to compute the weights in the linear combination of the feature values in Equation 1. Moreover, we consider another approach to propagate (aggregate) query–document feature values based on the decision trees instead of taking the weighted sum and compare the performances of the approaches.

Second, when using different propagating methods, some important data associated with similar queries $\tilde{q}$ is currently neglected. We show that some properties of similar queries can help the ranker to use those similar queries more effectively for propagating. Our learning framework allows utilizing any query features to increase the contribution of propagated features to the quality of the ranking function.

To the best of our knowledge, we are the first to address the above-mentioned aspects of propagating query–document relevance features of a ranking model via a collection of query similarities of different types.

Third, we provide experiments on a large data set of labeled queries, compare performances of the state-of-the-art and proposed approaches and distinguish their combination that gives the best quality and advances the state-of-the-art. Moreover, our experimental results show that the best method of propagation significantly outperforms the state-of-the-art even if the features values are propagated in the case of the queries of high or moderate frequency. However, the relative quality of the final ranking functions is much greater for the tail queries.

The remainder of the paper is organized as follows. Section 2 contains a review of the methods of propagating query–document features and the ways of defining queries' similarity functions. In Section 3, we propose a classification of similarity functions. We describe our framework of propagating the features in Section 4. In Section 5, we introduce a method of exploiting some statistics about the distribution of the feature values over similar queries to use similar queries more effectively for the propagation algorithms from Section 4. The experimental results are reported in Section 6. In Section 7, we summarize the outcomes of our study, discuss its potential applications and directions of future work.

2. RELATED WORK

The problem of query–document features (especially, click-through data) sparseness has been reported in many studies [1, 11, 13]. The lack of implicit feedback for tail (new or rare) queries affects the quality of web search, and is known [36] to affect the quality of results for tail queries most negatively. The common approach to this problem is to propagate features from head to tail queries. It is ordinarily done by considering a query similarity function [2, 13], which, in general case, can be defined in different ways [5, 21, 32, 34, 35, 38].

Evaluating a high-quality query similarity function itself is an important task in web search, because it is helpful in such problems as query suggestion [20, 21], query reformulation [19, 31], and query expansion [30, 33]. We distinguish the following four types of similarity functions: text similarity functions (semantic and syntactic similarities), query–document features-based similarity functions, query-level user-based similarity functions and session-level user-based similarity functions.

Semantic similarity functions are typically computed based on the following intuition. Each query is associated with its n-gram vector. The closer two query n-gram vectors in the n-gram space are to each other (in accordance with some metrics), the more similar the queries are. This intuition was used to define a query similarity in [34, 38]. Syntactic similarity functions measure the distance between queries as term sequences. The most common syntactic function is the Levenshtein distance [5, 17, 18]. Query-document features-based similarities measure the distance between vectors of query–document features values for a pair of queries [32]. A query-level user-based similarity is computed on a click graph [13, 21, 32, 35]. Usually, a few steps of a random walk is used for this computation [13, 21, 26, 35]. A session-level user-based similarity is computed by using the information about co-occurrence of different queries in user search sessions [5]. In [26, 28], a random walk on a query-flow graph is exploited for similarity computation.

Query–document feature values can be propagated among queries (usually, from head to tail queries, but not always) after one or several similarity functions are defined. Despite the obvious practical importance of the research on the propagation of query–document relevance features by using similarity functions, its history is rather short. Given a similarity function, the most common approach is to define propagated feature values by Equation 1 (see [2, 13, 35]). For instance, Aktolga and Allan [2] use a query similarity function for the purpose of click-through data propagating. The resulting ranking score of a document with respect to a query q in their framework equals to a linear combination of the default ranking score, the original value of the click-through feature and the propagated value of the feature. The latter propagated value is the weighted sum of the values of the feature over all queries similar to the query q as in Equation 1 (the weights are equal to the respective outcomes of the similarity function). In their experiments, they consider only a small set of 2400 popular queries, among which they propagate click-through data (a query is considered popular, if it has at least 500 clicks).

In [13], the authors propagate click-through feature values as well. A query similarity function is used to expand the clickthrough streams of a document. The propagated features values are computed on the basis of these expanded clickthrough streams. The authors constrain the set of similar queries utilized to propagate click-through features by tuning a threshold on the value of the similarity function (for the purpose of propagating they use only those similar queries whose similarity value w.r.t. the target query exceeds the threshold). For any propagated feature $\tilde{f}$ from the paper there exists a query–document feature f such that for any query–document pair (q, d) and a clickthrough stream w of a document d the feature value $\tilde{f}(q, d)$ equals sum of $f(\tilde{q}, d)$ over all $\tilde{q}$ in w. Therefore, the propagated values in this method equal the linear combination of feature values with the binary weights (so, essentially are defined by Equation 1).

Unfortunately, both papers do not propose any method for optimizing the weights in the linear combinations of the feature values given ad-hoc similarity functions that define those weights. Our work elaborates the idea of query-document feature value propagation via query similarity functions proposed in these papers further. We experiment with several implementations of that idea and, most importantly, advance it by solving the problems posed in Section 1, thus aiming to make this approach worth taking more seriously for search engine development.

3. SIMILARITY FUNCTIONS

In this section, we introduce our classification of query similarity functions investigated in previous papers. Essentially, such a function should be computed on the basis of the following intuition: similar queries (in terms of this function) represent similar information needs. The similarity of these needs can be evaluated using the statistics of different nature. In particular, the computation of similarity might utilize some a priori data (lexical properties of the queries) or a posteriori data (shows of documents to the queries or clicks on documents shown to the queries). Therefore, our classification is based on the type of the data utilized for the computation of similarity functions. Specifically, we distinguish the following 4 classes: query–document features-based similarity (depending on the feature type it utilizes either a priori data or a posteriori data), query-level user-based similarity (utilizes a posteriori data), session-level user-based similarity (utilizes a posteriori data) and text similarity (semantic and syntactic similarity), which utilizes a priori data. We list several similarity functions of each class, which were commonly used in previous studies.

In what follows, we consider a set of queries Q and define all the similarities for a pair of queries from this set.

3.1. Features-based similarity. The computation of a *query–document features-based similarity* s of queries q_1 and q_2 [32] utilizes any type of data, which is used for measuring relevance of documents with respect to the queries. Let f be any nonnegative feature of a query–document pair. Let $D = \{d_j\}_{j=1}^N$ be a collection of documents. Consider two vectors $\mathbf{f}^{q_i} = (f(q_i, d_1), \ldots, f(q_i, d_N))$, $i \in \{1, 2\}$, of the feature values for all the documents with respect to queries q_1 and q_2 respectively.

Consider a function $g : \mathbb{R}_+^N \times \mathbb{R}_+^N \to \mathbb{R}_+$ chosen in such a way that, if two queries q_1 and q_2 are naturally similar, then the output value $g(\mathbf{f}^{q_1}, \mathbf{f}^{q_2})$ is likely to be high. *Query–document features-based similarity* s between q_1 and q_2 equals $s(q_1, q_2) = g(\mathbf{f}^{q_1}, \mathbf{f}^{q_2})$. We choose g from the set of two functions, scalar product and cosine, which provide the following two similarity functions:

$$\mathrm{SFS}^f(q_1, q_2) = \langle \mathbf{f}^{q_1}, \mathbf{f}^{q_2} \rangle, \;\; \mathrm{CFS}^f(q_1, q_2) = \cos(\mathbf{f}^{q_1}, \mathbf{f}^{q_2}),$$

for the given feature f.

Popular search engines store the anonymized information describing user behavior (visited pages, times of visiting, submitted queries etc.) in the query logs. In the next two sections, we consider queries' similarities mined from user search behavior data from the query logs.

3.2. Query-level user-based similarity. The similarity of the second type is based on properties of one of the bipartite graphs constructed by using user search behavior data and described in what follows. It is a common practice to compute such similarities (which are called *query-level user-based* similarities) using random walks on these graphs (see [13, 21, 27, 35]), because random walks model the user behavior. We consider two graphs: a click graph and a graph of shows. *Click graph* is a bipartite unoriented graph $G(Q, D, E)$, where Q is a set of queries, D is a set of documents and an edge $\{q, d\} \in E$ is weighted by the number cl_{qd} of clicks on document d shown to query q. *Graph of shows* is defined in a similar way, the weight of an edge $\{q, d\}$ in the graph of shows equals the number sh_{qd} of shows of document d to query q. Consider a random walk on a bipartite graph $G(Q, D, E)$ (either a click graph or a graph of shows), where the probability of transition by an edge $\{q, d\}$ is proportional to its weight w_{qd} (either $w_{qd} = \mathrm{cl}_{qd}$ or $w_{qd} = \mathrm{sh}_{qd}$). Let $q_1, q_2 \in Q$, $k \in \mathbb{N}$. Usually, query-level user-based similarities $\mathrm{QUS}_k^{\mathrm{cl}}(q_1, q_2)$ and $\mathrm{QUS}_k^{\mathrm{sh}}(q_1, q_2)$ [13] are defined as the probabilities of arriving at query q_2 after $2k$ steps of the random walks on the click graph and the graph of shows respectively, which have started from query q_1.

3.3. Session-level user-based similarity. User search sessions extracted from the query logs can serve as another source of information about similar queries. Indeed, users often reformulate queries in the same search session. Such reformulations often represent similar information needs. We call a similarity function *session-level user-based similarity*, if the input data for computing this function is extracted from the query log.

Particularly, we consider the similarity functions that were proposed in [5]. Using sessions extracted from query logs, the authors get the estimations $\mathsf{P}(q)$ and $\mathsf{P}(q_1, q_2)$, the probability of a query q to appear in an arbitrary search session and the probability of queries q_1, q_2 to appear in one search session respectively, which are utilized for computing four similarity functions: PMI, PMIJ, PMIS and PMIG. Apart from these functions, we consider a simple similarity function, which estimates the probability of the query q_1 to appear in a session under the condition that the query q_2 appears in that session: $\mathrm{CP}(q_1, q_2) = \mathsf{P}(q_1, q_2)/\mathsf{P}(q_2)$.

3.4. Text similarities (semantic and syntactic). There can be too little important data for computing similarities of new or rare queries which exploit some noise-prone query–document features or are based on users search behavior. Instead, the texts of such queries can be used for the estimation of their similarity. So, both semantic and syntactic similarities are computed by utilizing texts of the queries only. Therefore, we do not divide this class into two different subclasses.

Each query q can be represented by a vector v_q in the *n-gram vector space* [10, 34, 38], where each dimension corresponds to an n-gram (a sequence of n consecutive terms of a query from Q). To define v_q, one first defines nonnegative weights of the n-grams occurring in the query. These weights are the components of v_q that correspond to the n-

grams of the query. The other components of the vector are zero.

Similarly to the feature-based approach, we consider two functions, scalar product and cosine. Note that these functions are nonnegative-valued, because their arguments are nonnegative. Thereby, two *semantic similarities*,

$$\mathrm{SSS}_n(q_1, q_2) = \langle v_{q_1}, v_{q_2} \rangle, \ \mathrm{CSS}_n(q_1, q_2) = \cos(v_{q_1}, v_{q_2}),$$

are considered for a given value of n chosen for construction of the n-gram space.

As it was done in previous studies [34, 38], for any n-gram, term frequency *tf* or the feature *tf*×*idf* (see [6], we compute these features on the queries' corpus) are considered to be the weight w of the n-gram.

For any two queries q^1, q^2, *syntactic similarity* measures the distance between the queries q^1 and q^2 as sequences of terms. The most common syntactic similarity function is the *Levenshtein similarity* $s(q_1, q_2)$, which is defined by using the *Levenshtein distance* $\mathrm{dis}(q_1, q_2)$ [18] with the deletion, the insertion and the substitution costs which are equal to 1. The Levenshtein similarity equals $1 - \frac{\mathrm{dis}(q_1,q_2)}{\max\{|q_1|,|q_2|\}}$, where $|q|$ is the number of terms in q. In [5], the deletion and the insertion costs equal 1, and the substitution cost of x_1 for x_2 equals the normalized original Levenshtein distance $\frac{\mathrm{dis}(x_1,x_2)}{\max\{|x_1|,|x_2|\}}$ between terms x_1 are x_2, which are considered as sequences of characters. We call the similarity function between queries based on this modified Levenshtein distance *weighted Levenshtein similarity* (WLS). The value of this function depends on the orders of the terms in the queries. Alternatively, the authors of [5] introduce the weighted Levenshtein similarity, which avoids this effect. In order to calculate this similarity, we should sort the terms in each query in the alphabetical order. Then the weighted Levenshtein similarity computed for the reordered term sequences is called *ordered weighted Levenshtein similarity* (OWLS).

4. METHODS OF PROPAGATION

In this section, we introduce the state-of-the-art and a number of novel methods of propagating query–document features via query similarity functions. We consider two different propagating principles: linear weighting and tree-based. The first method is a generalization of the state-of-the-art propagating method which was proposed in the previous studies [2, 13, 35].

Let Q and D be a set of queries and a set of documents respectively. We consider a query–document feature $f\colon Q \times D \to \mathbb{R}$ and similarity functions $s_1, \dots, s_m : Q \times Q \to \mathbb{R}_+$. We assume that, for any query q and any $j \in \{1, \dots, m\}$, a set $Q_q = Q_q^j$ of queries, which are similar to q, can be obtained on the basis of the similarity function $s = s_j(\cdot, q)$. Sections 4.1–4.3 focus on propagating feature f to queries q based on Q_q and s.

4.1 State-of-the-art propagation and the problem statement

We start with a description of the standard way to propagate feature values across similar queries [2, 35]. It is based on the equation

$$\tilde{f}_w(q, d) := \sum_{\tilde{q} \in Q_q} w(\tilde{q}, q) f(\tilde{q}, d), \tag{2}$$

which defines the propagated feature value $\tilde{f}(q, d)$ as a weighted average of the feature values over similar queries $\tilde{q} \in Q_q$. The weights $w(\tilde{q}, q)$ reflect the importance of queries $\tilde{q}$ for query q and are defined on the basis of query similarities $s(\tilde{q}, q)$. In the state-of-the-art approach [2, 35], the weight function w is defined by

$$w(\tilde{q}, q) = s^{\sim}(\tilde{q}, q) := \frac{s(\tilde{q}, q)}{\sum_{\hat{q} \in Q_q} s(\hat{q}, q)}, \tag{3}$$

which is theoretically unfounded and may be suboptimal in practice.

Intuitively, we assume that the actual purpose of Equation 2 is to obtain a (more reliable) estimate

$$f(q, d) \sim \tilde{f}_w(q, d) \tag{4}$$

of unreliable or noisy feature value $f(q, d)$. In contrast to Equation 2 which, in fact, defines $\tilde{f}_w(q, d)$ in an ad-hoc unsupervised way, we propose to *learn* the weight function $w = w(\tilde{q}, q)$ in order to optimize the quality of estimation, i.e we directly minimize the mean squared deviation of the right-hand side of Equation 4 from its left-hand side:

$$\min_w \mathsf{E}(f(q, d) - \tilde{f}_w(q, d))^2. \tag{5}$$

Appendix A provides a theoretical foundation of Equation 4 and optimization Problem 5 in more precise and detailed terms. In Section 4.2, we propose novel methods of learning the weights $w(\tilde{q}, q)$ in the described optimization setting. In Section 4.3, we consider another approach to propagate query–document features as an alternative to the linear weighting approach defined by Equation 2.

4.2 Linear weighting

In this section, we introduce a method of learning the weighting function $w(\tilde{q}, q)$ used in Equation 2. We look for a solution w to Problem 5 of the form

$$w(\tilde{q}, q) = g(s^{\sim}(\tilde{q}, q)), \tag{6}$$

where g belongs to a parameterized class of nonnegative valued functions $\mathcal{G} = \{g_\gamma : \mathbb{R} \to \mathbb{R}, \gamma \in \Gamma\}$, and Γ denotes the parameter space[1].

We consider two different approaches to define class $\mathcal{G}$ further in this paper: 1) to choose a particular family of functions; 2) to divide segment $[0, 1]$ into N disjoint subsets $D_1, \dots, D_N$ and set $\mathcal{G}$ to be the space of step functions that are constant on each D_i, i.e. $g_\gamma(x) = \sum_{i=1}^N \gamma_i I_{D_i}(x)$, where N is a fixed natural number, $\gamma = (\gamma_1, \dots, \gamma_N) \in \mathbb{R}^N$ is the set of parameters, and I_{D_i} is the indicator function of D_i.

In the described setting, the optimization Problem 5 can be expressed as follows:

$$\sum_{(q,d) \in \mathcal{D}} h\left(f(q, d), \sum_{\tilde{q} \in Q_q} g_\gamma(s^{\sim}(\tilde{q}, q)) f(\tilde{q}, d)\right) \to \min_\gamma, \tag{7}$$

where $\mathcal{D}$ is a training set of query–document pairs and $h = h(x, y)$ (particularly, we consider the squared loss function $h(x, y) = (x - y)^2$).

4.2.1. Parametric family of functions. Let $\mathcal{G}$ be any parameterized class of functions g_γ w.r.t. the parameter (a vector of parameters) γ. For many classes of functions g_γ

[1] In our experiments, we consider $\Gamma \subset \mathbb{R}^N$.

(e.g., $\mathcal{G} = \{\gamma^x, \gamma \in \mathbb{R}\}$), Problem 7 does not have a closed-form solution. Consider an alternative optimization problem

$$\sum_{(q,d)\in\mathcal{D}} h\left(f(q,d), g_\gamma\left(\sum_{\tilde{q}\in Q_q} s^\sim(\tilde{q},q)f(\tilde{q},d)\right)\right) \to \min_\gamma, \quad (8)$$

which is obtained by interchanging the order of taking g_γ and summation over Q_q in the optimization Problem 7. It is easy to see that, for some classes $\mathcal{G}$, Problem 8 has a closed-form solution (e.g., a solution for a polynomial regression model with $\mathcal{G} = \{a_k x^k + \ldots + a_1 x + a_0, \gamma = (a_0, a_1, \ldots, a_k) \in \mathbb{R}^{k+1}\}$, $h = (x-y)^2$). Obviously, if $g_\gamma(\cdot)$ is not a linear homogeneous function, then Problems 7 and 8 are not equivalent or necessarily have similar solutions, as long as the values of $g_1^*(q) = g_\gamma(\sum_{\tilde{q}\in Q_q} s^\sim(\tilde{q},q)f(\tilde{q},d))$ and $g_2^*(q) = \sum_{\tilde{q}\in Q_q} g_\gamma(s^\sim(\tilde{q},q))f(\tilde{q},d)$ are not the same. However, if, for any $(q,d) \in \mathcal{D}$, we replace the values $f(\tilde{q},d)$ with their normalized modifications $f_q^\sim(\tilde{q},d) := f(\tilde{q},d)/\sum_{\hat{q}\in Q_q} f(\hat{q},d)$ in $g_1^*(q)$ and $g_2^*(q)$, then the obtained values (we denote them by $g_1^\sim(q)$ and $g_2^\sim(q)$) are close and hence we can arrive at the solution of the modification of Problem 7

$$\sum_{(q,d)\in\mathcal{D}} h\left(f^\sim(q,d), \sum_{\tilde{q}\in Q_q} g_\gamma(s^\sim(\tilde{q},q))f_q^\sim(\tilde{q},d)\right) \to \min_\gamma \quad (9)$$

by solving the modification of Problem 8

$$\sum_{(q,d)\in\mathcal{D}} h\left(f_q^\sim(q,d), g_\gamma\left(\sum_{\tilde{q}\in Q_q} s^\sim(\tilde{q},q)f_q^\sim(\tilde{q},d)\right)\right) \to \min_\gamma \quad (10)$$

Indeed, for linear functions $g_{(a_0,a_1)}(x) = a_0 + a_1 x$, the exact equality $g_1^\sim(q) = g_2^\sim(q)$ holds. For a convex function g_γ, $g_1^\sim(q)$ is slightly smaller than $g_2^\sim(q)$. For a concave function g_γ, $g_1^\sim(q)$ is slightly larger than $g_2^\sim(q)$. If g_γ is neither convex nor concave differentiable function, then, intuitively, the difference between is $g_1^\sim(q)$ and $g_2^\sim(q)$ is far less. Moreover, in Appendix B, for two classes $\mathcal{G}$, polynomial functions and power functions (the two classes we consider in our experiments, see Section 6.3) and Q_q large enough, we prove that

$$g_1^\sim(q) \sim g_2^\sim(q) \quad (11)$$

Therefore, in order to consider modifications of Problems 7 and 8 that have similar solutions, we, first, normalize the values of f and consider the optimization Problem 9 instead of Problem 7. Under our assumptions, Problem 9 reduces to Problem 10. Moreover, in Section 6.3, we show that the propagating method which is based on solving Problem 10 outperforms the state-of-the-art propagating method.

As we mentioned above, in Section 6.3, we consider a class of polynomial functions with degree 3 and a class of power functions. In the first case, Problem 10 with $h(x,y) = (x-y)^2$ is solved by ordinary least squares estimation for a polynomial regression model $\mathsf{E}(y \mid x)$, where $\sum_{\tilde{q}\in Q_q} s^\sim(\tilde{q},q) \cdot f_q^\sim(\tilde{q},d)$ is the explanatory variable x and $f_q^\sim(q,d)$ is the response variable y. In the second case, we change the loss function h, because, for the class of power functions, Problem 10 cannot be solved by ordinary least squares estimation (the iterative Gauss-Newton algorithm for a non-linear least squares optimization problem [14] can be used, but we avoid it because of its computational complexity). To motivate a choice of function h in this case, we study the dependency of $f_q^\sim(q,d)$ on $\sum_{\tilde{q}\in Q_q} s^\sim(\tilde{q},q)f_q^\sim(\tilde{q},d)$ in Section 6.3. As we show, the dependency of $\log f_q^\sim(q,d)$ on $\log \sum_{\tilde{q}\in Q_q} s^\sim(\tilde{q},q)f_q^\sim(\tilde{q},d)$ is approximately linear. Therefore, in this particular case we choose $h(x,y) = (\log x - \log y)^2$.

4.2.2. Step weighting functions. Assumption 11 is well-reasoned far not for any class of functions $\mathcal{G}$ and distributions $(f_q^\sim(\tilde{q},d),\ \tilde{q} \in Q_q)$. Fortunately, we do not need it in the case of the second approach to define $\mathcal{G}$, where $g_\gamma \in \mathcal{G}$ are step functions

$$g_\gamma(x) = \sum_{i=1}^{N} \gamma_i I_{D_i}(x) \quad (12)$$

and $D_1, \ldots, D_N \subset [0,1]$ are disjoint subsets. We learn parameters $\gamma = (\gamma_1, \ldots, \gamma_N) \in \mathbb{R}^N$ by minimizing the mean squared error (MSE) (Problem 7, where $h(x,y) = (x-y)^2$) exploiting the linear regression algorithm:

$$\gamma^T = (F^T F)^{-1} F^T \mathbf{f},$$

where $F = (F_{(q,d),i})_{(q,d)\in\mathcal{D}}^{i\in\{1,\ldots,N\}}$,

$$F_{(q,d),i} = \sum_{\tilde{q}\in Q_q} I_{D_i}(s^\sim(\tilde{q},q))f(\tilde{q},d), \quad (13)$$

$\mathbf{f} = (f(q,d),\ (q,d) \in \mathcal{D})^T$ is the vector of the values of the feature f, which are ordered in the same way as the elements of each column of matrix F.

4.3 Decision trees

In Sections 4.1 and 4.2, for a given query–document pair (q,d), we define the propagated feature value $\tilde{f}(q,d)$ by Equation 2. It defines a function, which linearly depends on the values of $f(\tilde{q},d)$ with coefficients $w(\tilde{q},q)$ calculated on the basis of similarities $s^\sim(\tilde{q},q)$. Certainly, this linear prediction method might be not the best performing among all the prediction principles, as linear learning models are known to be suboptimal in a variety of learning tasks. So, in the general case, a predicted feature value $\tilde{f}(q,d)$ equals a value of some function of feature values $f(\tilde{q},d)$ and similarity values $s^\sim(\tilde{q},q)$ ($\tilde{q} \in Q_q$). By this reason, we compare the linear approach described in Section 4.2 with the "tree-based approach", were a function of the same arguments $f(\tilde{q},d), s^\sim(\tilde{q},q)$ is learned using gradient boosted decision trees [12, 23, 29]). In this section, we consider this alternative approach to propagate query–document feature values.

For a query–document pair (q,d), the input of a tree-based model is a feature vector $X_1(q,d), \ldots, X_N(q,d)$ of dimension N, which is a parameter of the algorithm. We consider two ways to define features $X_1, \ldots, X_N$.

1. We simply take $(f(\tilde{q},d), s^\sim(\tilde{q},d) \mid \tilde{q} \in Q'_q)$, where $Q'_q \subset Q_q$ is the subset of queries $\tilde{q} \in Q_q$ with the $N/2$ largest values of $s^\sim(\tilde{q},q)$. The value of N is even in this case.

2. Given a partition $D_1, \ldots, D_N$ of $[0,1]$, we set $X_i(q,d) = F_{(q,d),i}$ (see Equation 13).

The second approach is motivated by the second optimization algorithm from Subsection 4.2.2, where we learn, in fact, a linear model predicting $\tilde{f}(q,d)$ using the same features $F_{(q,d),1}, \ldots, F_{(q,d),N}$.

The components of feature vectors $(f(\tilde{q},d), s^\sim(\tilde{q},q) \mid \tilde{q} \in Q_q)$ in the first approach should be ordered on the basis of some principle common across different pairs (q, d). We use the following ordering:

$$f(q_1, d), \dots, f(q_{N/2}, d), s^{\sim}(q_1, q), \dots, s^{\sim}(q_{N/2}, q),$$

where $Q_q = \{q_1, q_2, \dots\}$ is ordered in such a way that $s(q_1, q) \geqslant s(q_2, q) \geqslant \dots$. Here we set $f(q_i, d) = s^{\sim}(q_i, q) = 0$ for $i \in \{|Q_q| + 1, |Q_q| + 2, \dots, N/2\}$, if $|Q_q| < N/2$.

Our goal is to learn a function $g : \mathbb{R}^N \to \mathbb{R}$ such that the predicted values

$$\tilde{f}(q, d) = g(X_1(q, d), \dots, X_N(q, d)) \quad (14)$$

are close to the target values $f(q, d)$ for $(q, d) \in \mathcal{D}$, where $\mathcal{D}$ is a training set of query–document pairs (as in the previous section). We solve this problem by minimizing the squared loss function $\sum_{(q,d)\in\mathcal{D}}(\tilde{f}(q, d) - f(q, d))^2$ using gradient boosted decision trees [12]. We use the obtained function g to compute the propagated feature value $\tilde{f}(q, d)$ defined by Equation 14.

5. QUANTILES

In Section 1 we ask, if some statistics of the distributions of the feature values over similar queries besides the average value can help the ranker to use those similar queries more effectively. To answer this question, we use quantiles of four different distributions: the distribution of query frequencies, the distribution of the numbers of characters in queries (*character lengths* of queries), the distribution of the numbers of terms in queries (*term lengths* of queries), and the distribution of values of the similarity function in the following way. For each similarity s and query $q \in Q$, we divide the set Q_q of queries similar to q (which is obtained on the basis of the similarity function s), into 5 subsets $Q_q(1), \dots, Q_q(5)$ (see Equation 15) with respect to the values of quantiles and calculate the average value of query–document feature CTR (that we exploit in our experiments, see Section 6.2) over queries $\tilde{q} \in Q_q(i)$ and all pairs (q, d). We represent the dependency of the obtained values on quantile i in Figure 1 for 4 different similarities, one from each similarity type (see Section 3) and two types of distributions whose quantiles define $Q_q(i)$: the distribution of query frequencies and the distribution of the values of the similarity function. For most of these similarities, the dependencies are monotone. This means that the values of the feature for similar queries is lesser, on average, for greater quantiles of query frequency (similarity to initial query q). This observation suggests that the average values of the feature over queries from each $Q_q(i)$ may carry more information than the average value of the feature over all queries from Q_q alone. In our experiments, we show that these values provide useful information for improving the quality of ranking (see Section 6.3). In what follows, we describe how we use quantiles in detail.

As in Section 4, we consider a query–document feature f, a similarity function $s := s_j$, $j \in \{1, \dots, m\}$, and, for each $q \in Q$, a set $Q_q := Q_q^j$ of queries in Q, which are similar to q.

Let P be a distribution on $\mathbb{R}_+$. Consider a sample $X_1, \dots, X_n$ of the distribution P and an increasing sequence of numbers $\alpha_1, \dots, \alpha_r \in [0, 1]$. Let $\mu_1, \dots, \mu_r$ be the empirical $\alpha_1, \dots, \alpha_r$-quantiles of distribution P respectively. We construct the sample $X_1, \dots, X_n$ in two different ways: either it depends on q or it does not. The first way is to build the sample by using all the queries from Q_q for the frequency distribution and the distributions of lengths (i.e., $(X_1, \dots, X_n) = (y(\tilde{q}), \tilde{q} \in Q_q)$, where $y(\tilde{q})$ is either the frequency or a length of $\tilde{q}$) and all the pairs $(\tilde{q}, q)$, where $\tilde{q} \in Q_q$, for the similarity distribution (i.e., $(X_1, \dots, X_n) = (s(\tilde{q}, q), \tilde{q} \in Q_q)$). So, the quantiles depend on $q \in Q$. The second way is to take all the queries from Q for the frequency distribution and the distributions of lengths and all the pairs from $Q \times Q$ for the similarity distribution (the quantiles are the same for all the queries $q \in Q$).

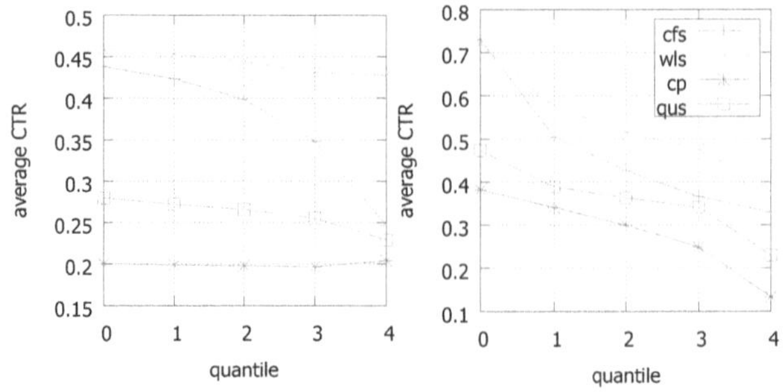

Figure 1: The dependencies of an average value of query–document feature CTR over queries from $Q_q(i)$ and all pairs (q, d) of the number of quantile i (4 similarity functions: $\mathrm{CFS}^{\mathrm{CTR}}$, WLS, CP, $\mathrm{QUS}_2^{\mathrm{cl}}$; frequency distribution (left), similarity distribution (right)).

We use the quantiles $\mu_1, \dots, \mu_r$ for dividing queries into disjoint subsets and propagating the values of feature f for each subset in the following way. For each $i \in \{1, \dots, r\}$, we define the propagated feature value $\tilde{f}^i(q, d)$ for the pair $(q, d) \in Q \times D$ either by Equation 2 in the linear weighting approach or by Equation 14 in the tree-based approach using

$$Q_q(i) := \{\tilde{q} \in Q_q : X_{l(\tilde{q})} \in (\mu_{i-1}, \mu_i]\} \quad (15)$$

instead of Q_q for learning the function g, where $\mu_0 = -\infty$ and $X_{l(\tilde{q})}$ is the element of the sample which corresponds either to the query $\tilde{q}$ (for the frequency distribution and the distributions of lengths) or to the pair $(\tilde{q}, q)$ (for the similarity distribution).

6. EXPERIMENTAL RESULTS

We compare the performance of different propagating techniques described in Section 4 by learning ranking functions using propagated query–document features. In the next section, we describe the details of learning to rank framework. In Section 6.1 and Section 6.2, we describe the dataset and the similarity functions we exploit in our experiments. Finally, we compare the performances of different propagating methods in Sections 6.3 and 6.4. First, we compute average values of ranking quality metrics on a test set of queries. Second, as we expect that our methods are especially useful for tail queries, Section 6.4 presents a closer look a the methods' performance on a subset of infrequent queries.

We consider the classical problem of ranking documents according to their relevance to a query [8]. It was shown that regression with gradient boosted decision trees, while computationally more efficient, is only marginally worse than the most advanced list-wise learning to rank methods [8], so, given the amount of calculations in our experiments and the fact that our methods are agnostic w.r.t. to a specific ranking method, we solve the ranking problem by minimizing MSE using a proprietary implementation of gradient boosted decision trees [12].

6.1 Data

For ranking evaluation, a random sample of queries Q_0 issued by the users of the European country under study was selected from the query logs of one of the most popular commercial web search engines. We selected 66.6% of the queries as our training set Q_1, 16.7% as the validation set Q_2 and the remaining 16.7% as the test set Q_3. The set Q_1 was divided into two subsets Q_1^1 and Q_1^2 of equal size, the first one is for learning to propagate query–document features, the second one is for learning to rank (see Table 1). For each query $q \in Q_0 \setminus Q_1^1$ (we do not need relevance labels for learning to propagate features), the relevance of each of the top ranked documents was judged by professional assessors hired by the search engine (we denote the set of these documents by $D(q)$). In our experiments, we consider only documents from the union $D := \bigcup_{q \in Q_0 \setminus Q_1^1} D(q)$ of judged documents over all queries in the dataset. The relevance labels were assigned using a popular graded relevance scale with labels: *perfect, excellent, good, fair, bad*. The data we use contains $\approx$ 1.9M query–document pairs and $\approx$ 90K unique queries (around 21 judged documents per query). We compare the methods on the test set in terms of average NDCG@3 and NDCG@5 metrics (see [7]), which were the primary measures in [2, 13].

Q (all queries)				
	Q_0 (ranking evaluation set)			
$\tilde{Q}$ (propagation set)	Q_1 (train)		Q_2 (validation)	Q_3 (test)
	Q_1^1 (predict.)	Q_1^2 (ranking)		
52.6M	30K	30K	15K	15K

Table 1: Sets of queries.

While our framework is not specific to a particular type of query-document features, in this paper, we experiment with click-through features for the sake of consistency with the previous papers [2, 11, 13]. One of the most widely used feature of that kind is CTR, another one is nCTR proposed in [2]. As the reliability of click-through feature values for query–document pairs (q, p) depends on the number of shows of p in response to q and the numbers of clicks on p shown to q, we construct a set $Q = Q_0 \cup \tilde{Q}$ of queries (see Table 1), which we use to propagate query–document features from in the following way. We add a query q to $\tilde{Q}$, if either the total number of shows of documents to q recorded in the query log (all the records were made from 1 January 2014 to 31 March 2014) is greater than 70 or the number of clicks on documents shown in response to q is greater than 6. For each labeled document d from the data set, we create top-1000 list of queries from $Q_0 \cup \tilde{Q}$, which have the largest number of shows of document d in response to them. We remove a query from $\tilde{Q}$, if it is not in such a top-1000 list for at least one document.The final set Q contains $\approx$ 52.7M queries.

For the purpose of evaluating features-based and query-level user-based similarities and for propagating click-through features, we consider all query–document pairs ($\approx$ 254.2M pairs) from the query logs, where all queries are from Q and the documents are from D.

6.2 Similarities and similar queries

In our experiments, we consider 30 query similarity functions. We exploit 6 features-based similarities (see Section 3.1): $\mathrm{SFS}^f, \mathrm{CFS}^f$, where f is one of the features BM25, CTR, nCTR (normalized CTR [2]); 9 query-level user-based similarities (see Section 3.2): $\mathrm{QUS}_1^{\mathrm{cl}}, \ldots, \mathrm{QUS}_6^{\mathrm{cl}}$ and $\mathrm{QUS}_1^{\mathrm{sh}}$, $\mathrm{QUS}_2^{\mathrm{sh}}$, $\mathrm{QUS}_3^{\mathrm{sh}}$; 5 session-level user-based similarities (see Section 3.3): PMI, PMIJ, PMIS, PMIG, CP, 8 semantic similarities (see Section 3.4): SSS_2, CSS_2, SSS_3, CSS_3, where w is either *tf* or *tf×idf*; 2 syntactic similarities (see Section 3.4): WLS and OWLS.

For each query q from the set Q_0, each similarity type $y \in \{1, \ldots, 4\}$ (we enumerate them in the same way as in Section 3), and each similarity function s of type y, we define a set of similar queries $Q_q(s) \subset Q$ by removing from the set Q queries $\tilde{q}$ with small values of similarity $s(\tilde{q}, q)$ (to avoid too outlying feature values for these queries $\tilde{q}$ w.r.t. a given document, which are used for propagation) in the following way. First, independently on q, we define a threshold $t(s)$ on the similarity values in such a way that there are 10%[2] of the values of s which are less than $t(s)$ and, for the query q, remove from Q all queries $\tilde{q}$ such that $s(\tilde{q}, q) \leqslant t(s)$. Second, we define a threshold $n(y)$ on the size of a set of top queries in set $Q_q(s)$ ranked by their similarity to q. The value of $n(y)$ was chosen from segment $[50, 2000]$ with step 50 by maximizing NDCG@3 on the part Q_1^2 of the training set (we exploit 5 regular query–document relevance features PageRank, BM25, Query Frequency, CTR, nCTR (apart from the features obtained via propagation) and 60 propagated CTR and nCTR by the linear weighting approach (each of these two features is propagated by using each of the considered similarity functions), where the weights for propagating are defined by Equation 3). It was also compared with the quality of the ranking function, which was learned without the threshold $n(y)$: the quality of the function which was learned by utilizing the threshold was better for all the similarity types. From this point, we consider only top $n(y)$ queries from $Q_q(s)$ for each similarity type y.

Finally, we filter out those similarity functions from the initial set, which do not influence the effectiveness of the propagation significantly (which is expected as many of them strongly correlated with each other). Let $y \in \{1, 2, 3, 4\}$ be a similarity type, $s_{y,1}, \ldots, s_{y,m(y)}$ be all the considered similarities of type y (we denote by $m(y)$ the number of similarity functions of type y). First, we train the ranking functions on the set Q_1^2 with 5 regular features and two sets of features $\tilde{f}_1, \ldots, \tilde{f}_{m(y)}$ defined by Equation 2 and Equation 3, where f is either CTR or nCTR. Further, for each $i \in \{1, \ldots, m(y)\}$, we remove two features $\tilde{f}_i$ (one for CTR and one for nCTR) at a time and train the ranking function. If the quality of the ranking function does not change statistically significantly (according to paired t-test with $p < 0.05$) on the validation set, we no longer exploit the similarity $s_{y,i}$ in our experiments.

After this procedure, the following 15 similarity functions remain: all the 6 features-based similarities, 3 query-level user-based similarities: $\mathrm{QUS}_2^{\mathrm{cl}}, \mathrm{QUS}_6^{\mathrm{cl}}$ and $\mathrm{QUS}_1^{\mathrm{sh}}$, 2 session-level user-based similarities (PMIJ, CP), 2 semantic similarities ($\mathrm{SSS}_3, \mathrm{CSS}_3$, where w is tf×idf), 2 syntactic similarities (WLS and OWLS).

[2]The maximal portion of queries which can be removed without a significant change in the ranking quality.

6.3 Propagation

All the ranking functions in this section were trained on the set Q_1. The meta-parameters for each ranking function were tuned by maximizing the respective quality measures on the set Q_2. We trained the ranking functions by exploiting the set of 5 regular features. Moreover, we learn 8 ranking functions by exploiting different sets of features which are described in what follows (see Table 2).

Rank. function	Features	NDCG@3	@5
Regular	Regular features only	0.61637	0.62757
State-of-the-art	Regular + 30 prop. features (Eq. 2,3)	0.63086	0.6463
Power	Regular + 30 prop. features (Eq. 2,6 g — pow. function)	0.63257	0.6478
Polynomial	Regular + 30 prop. features (Eq. 2,6, g — polynom)	0.63223	0.64749
Uniformly discrete	Regular + 30 prop. features (Eq. 2,6,12, uniform partition)	0.63293	0.64851
Equivalently discrete	Regular + 30 prop. features (Eq. 2,6,12, equal card. of sets)	0.63491	0.64978
Point-based tree-based	Regular + 30 prop. features (Eq. 14, features 1), § 4.3)	0.6288	0.6422
Interval-b. tree-based	Regular + 30 prop. features (Eq. 14, features 2), § 4.3)	0.63254	0.647
Equivalently discrete with quantiles	Reg. + 150 prop. feat. (equal card. of sets, similarity distrib.)	**0.63749**	**0.6521**

Table 2: Performances of the ranking functions for different sets of features on the test set.

For learning functions g used by propagation methods of Section 4.2 (Equation 6) and Section 4.3 (Equation 12) with each of the considered similarity functions, we set $Q = Q_1^1$. We construct the set $\mathcal{D}$ in the following way: pair (q, d) is in $\mathcal{D}$ if and only if the number of shows sh_{qd} of the document d to query q is greater than 25 and the number of shows of all documents to the query q is greater than 500. Let s be any of the considered similarity functions.

First, we assume that the continuous function g for the linear weighting propagating method (see Section 4.2.1) is a power function and study the dependency of $f_q^{\sim}(q,d)$ on $\hat{f}_q^{\sim}(q,d) = \sum_{\tilde{q}\in Q_q^j} s_j^{\sim}(\tilde{q},q) f_q^{\sim}(\tilde{q},d)$ for all pairs (q,d) such that $q \in Q_1^1$. To prove the choice of the function h (see Section 4.2.1), we interpret this dependency in the following way. For each value of $f_q^{\sim}(q,d)$, we find the mean value $\mathsf{E}\hat{f}_q^{\sim}(q,d)$ of $\hat{f}_{q_0}^{\sim}(q_0,d_0)$ over all pairs (q_0,d_0) such that $\hat{f}_{q_0}^{\sim}(q_0,d_0) \approx \hat{f}_q^{\sim}(q,d)$. On Figure 2 (for illustration purposes, we consider only two similarities here), we represent the dependency of $f_q^{\sim}(q,d)$ on $\mathsf{E}\hat{f}_q^{\sim}(q,d)$ and approximation $f^{\sim} = b\mathsf{E}\hat{f}^{\sim} + a$ using linear regression on the log-log scale plot (red line). As the dependency is approximately linear, we suppose that $\mathcal{G} = \{ax^b, \gamma = (a,b) \in \Gamma\}$, $\Gamma = \mathbb{R}^2$ and $h(x,y) = (\log x - \log y)^2$. We find the optimal γ in Problem 10 using the linear regression algorithm in the log-log scale for each similarity function (Figure 2, blue line) and, therefore, obtain 30 propagated features. Finally, we train the ranking function on the set Q_1^2 with 5 baseline features and the obtained 30 propagated features (see Table 2).

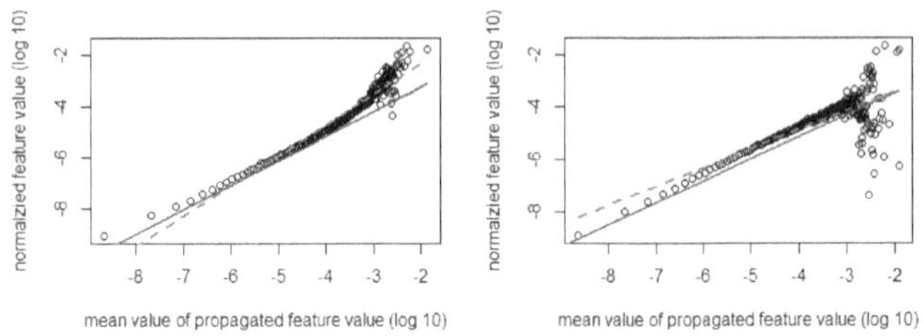

Figure 2: The dependency of $f^{\sim}$ from $\mathsf{E}\hat{f}^{\sim}$ and approximation of this dependency using linear regression on the log-log scale plot (red line) for two similarities, $\mathrm{CFS}^{\mathrm{CTR}}$ and PMIJ. For comparison, the blue line with learned parameters (a,b).

Second, we suppose that g is a polynomial function with degree 3 (see footnote 2), i.e. $\mathcal{G} = \{a_3x^3 + a_2x^2 + a_1x + a_0, \gamma = (a_3,a_2,a_1,a_0) \in \Gamma\}$, $\Gamma = \mathbb{R}^4$, and $h(x,y) = (x-y)^2$. We find the optimal γ in Equation 10 using the linear regression algorithm for each similarity function, obtain 30 propagated features and train the ranking function on the set Q_1^2 with 5 baseline features and the obtained 30 propagated features (see Table 2).

For learning the discrete function g we set $N = 100$ (see Section 4.2)[3]. We divide the segment $[0,1]$ into N intervals $D_1 = [0,d_1)$, $D_2 = [d_1,d_2), \ldots, D_{100} = [d_{99},1]$ in two different ways. Firstly, we exploit the uniform division: $d_i = \frac{i}{100}$, $i \in \{0,\ldots,99\}$, learn the parameters $\gamma_1,\ldots,\gamma_{100}$ (see Section 4.2) and obtain 30 propagated features (see Table 2). Secondly, we choose a random sample $\hat{Q}_1^1$ of 20% queries from Q_1^1 and let $d_1,\ldots,d_{99}$ be the empirical $0.01,\ldots,0.99$–quantiles of distribution of s when the second argument is in $\hat{Q}_1^1$. For learning the parameters $\gamma_1,\ldots,\gamma_{100}$ we remove the sample $\hat{Q}_1^1$ from the set Q_1^1. As the result, we also obtain 30 propagated features (see Table 2).

For each of the two ways of constructing sets of features in the tree-based approach (see Section 4.3) we consider three choices of the parameter M ($M = 100$, $M = 200$ and $M = 400$). The optimal values of M were chosen by maximizing NDCG@3 on Q_1^2 (see Section 6.1)[4].

We compare the effectiveness of all the methods of propagating in each class of propagating methods on the test set: continuous weights-based, discrete weights-based and tree-based (we consider 2 ranking functions from each class of methods) in Table 2. The best methods are *Power* in the continuous weighting class, *Equivalently discrete* in the discrete weights-based and *Interval-based tree-based* in the tree-based class. The best method of propagating is *Equivalently discrete*. The NDCG@3 and NDCG@5 gains of this method in comparison with *State-of-the-art* equal $\approx 0.6\%$ and $\approx 0.5\%$ respectively. The NDCG@3 and NDCG@5

[3]The value of N was chosen from $\{10, 100, 1000\}$ by maximizing NDCG@3 on Q_1^2 (see Section 6.1).

[4]For the point-based tree-based ranking function we chose $M = 200$ and for the interval-based tree-based ranking function we chose $M = 100$.

gains of this method in comparison with *Regular* equal $\approx 3\%$ and $\approx 3.5\%$ respectively. All the differences in metrics values are significant according to Paired Bootstrap Hypothesis Test [25] with $p < 0.01$.

For the best propagating method (*Equivalently discrete*), we use the quantiles (see Section 5) for dividing similarity scores into intervals and propagating the features for each interval. We consider 5 quantiles, $\alpha_1 = 0.2$, $\alpha_2 = 0.4$, $\alpha_3 = 0.6$, $\alpha_4 = 0.8$, $\alpha_5 = 1$ (see Section 5), for 4 different distributions (the distribution of frequencies, the distribution of character lengths, the distribution of term lengths and distribution of values of the respective similarity function). Moreover, we evaluate the quantiles by constructing samples by two methods (either each sample is constructed for each query or one sample is constructed for all the pairs of queries, see Section 5). We compare the performance of the obtained 8 ranking functions. Quantiles for the similarity distributions with one sample which is constructed for all the pairs of queries outperforms all the other propagating methods on the validation set with both NDCG@3 and NDCG@5 metrics. The NDCG@3 and NDCG@5 gains of *Equivalently discrete ranking function with quantiles* in comparison with simple *Equivalently discrete* ranking function equal $\approx 0.4\%$ for both ranking metrics on the test data (see Table 2). The NDCG@3 and NDCG@5 gains of this ranking function in comparison with *State-of-the-art* equal $\approx 1.1\%$ and $\approx 0.9\%$ respectively. The NDCG@3 and NDCG@5 gains of this method in comparison with *Regular* equal $\approx 3.4\%$ and $\approx 3.9\%$ respectively. All the differences of qualities are significant according to Paired Bootstrap Hypothesis Test with $p < 0.01$.

6.4 Performance on tail queries

We test our algorithm on the set of tail queries (see Figure 3). For the queries infrequently issued by users (with frequencies at most 5) the NDCG@3 and NDCG@5 gains of the *Equivalently discrete ranking function with quantiles* in comparison with *State-of-the-art* (*Regular*) equals $\approx 3.0\%$ ($\approx 13.7\%$) and $\approx 3.9\%$ ($\approx 13.8\%$) respectively. These gains decrease up to $\approx 1.9\%$ ($\approx 6.2\%$) and $\approx 2.2\%$ ($\approx 7.4\%$) respectively as frequencies grow up to 30.

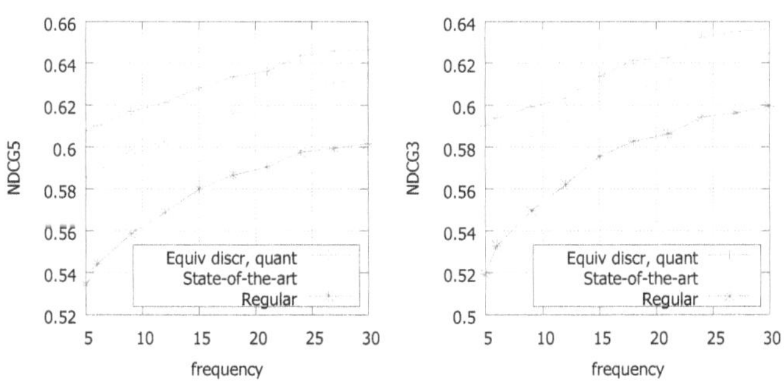

Figure 3: Comparison of our algorithm, *State-of-the-art* and *Regular* ranking functions for the tail queries.

7. CONCLUSIONS

In this paper, we consider different methods of propagating query–document relevance features for the purpose of improving the quality of page ranking. Given a similarity function and a query–document feature, we investigate different approaches to learn a function of similarity values and values of the feature for similar queries w.r.t. a given document. This function is further used to compute the propagated values of the features.

We also consider the statistics associated with distributions of character and term lengths of queries, queries' frequencies and queries' similarities and prove that it helps the ranker to use similar queries more effectively. Moreover, we choose the most effective type of the distribution and the most effective way of exploiting it.

Our experimental results show that the proposed propagating algorithms significantly outperform the state-of-the-art propagating algorithm. Moreover, as expected, the effectiveness of propagation by our method in comparison with the state-of-the-art approach depends heavily on the frequencies of queries which are supplemented with the features obtained via propagation. We observe that our methods are especially useful for rare (tail) queries.

It would be interesting to continue to study the properties and applicability of the propagating methods. We plan to determine in more detail, which properties of queries define whether they would benefit from propagation by different methods. Moreover, we are going to apply the propagating methods for different tasks besides web ranking.

8. REFERENCES

[1] E. Agichtein, E. Brill, S. Dumais, *Improving web search ranking by incorporating user behavior information*, Proc. SIGIR'06, pp. 19-26, 2006.

[2] E. Aktolga, J. Allan, *Reranking Search Results for Sparse Queries*, Proc. CIKM'11, pp. 173–182, 2011.

[3] R.M. Bell, Y. Koren, *Scalable Collaborative Filtering with Jointly Derived Neighborhood Interpolation Weights*, Proc. ICDM'07, pp. 43–52, 2007.

[4] M. Bilenko, R. W. White, *Mining the Search Trails of Surfing Crowds: Identifying Relevant Websites From User Activity*, Proc. WWW'08, pp. 51–60, 2008.

[5] F. De Bona, S. Reizler, K. Hall, M. Ciaramita, A. Herdağdelen, M. Holmqvist, *Learning Dense Models of Query Similarity from User Click Logs*, Proc. NAACL-HLT'10, pp. 474–482, 2010.

[6] C. Buckley, G. Salton, *Term-weighting approaches in automatic text retrieval*, Information Processing and Management, Elsevier, Vol. 24, No. 5, pp. 513–523, 1988.

[7] C. Calauzènes, N. Usunier, P. Gallinari, *On the (Non-)existence of Convex, Calibrated Surrogate Losses for Ranking*, NIPS'12, pp. 197–205, 2012.

[8] O. Chapelle, Y. Chang, *Yahoo! Learning To Rank Challenge Overview*, JMLR: Workshop and Conference Proceedings 14, pp. 1–24, 2011.

[9] O. Chapelle, D. Metzler, *Expected Reciprocal Rank for Graded Relevance*, CIKM'09, pp. 621-630, 2009.

[10] S. F. Chen, J. Goodman, *An Empirical Study of Smoothing Techniques for Language Modeling*, Technical Report TR-10-98, Computer Science Group, Harvard University, 1998.

[11] N. Craswell, M. Szummer, *Random walks on the click graph*, Proc. SIGIR'07, pp. 239–246, 2007.

[12] J. Friedman, *Greedy function approximation: a gradient boosting machine*, Ann. Statist., 29, pp. 1189–1232, 2001.

[13] J. Gao, W. Yuan, X. Li, K. Deng, J.-Y. Nie, *Smoothing Clickthrough Data for Web Search Ranking*, Proc. SIGIR'09, pp. 355–362, 2009.

[14] Greene, H. William, *Econometric analysis*, Prentice Hall, 4th ed, 1999.

[15] J. Guo, X. Cheng, G. Xu, X. Zhu, *Intent-Aware Query Similarity*, Proc. CIKM'11, pp. 259–268, 2011.
[16] T. Hastie, R. Tibshirani, J. Friedman, *The elements of statistical learning*, Springer, 2nd ed., 2009.
[17] R. Jones, B. Rey, O. Madani, W. Greiner, *Generating query substitutions*, Proc WWW'06, pp. 387–396, 2006.
[18] V.I. Levenshtein, *Binary codes capable of correcting deletions, insertions, and reversals*, Soviet Physics Doklady, 10(8): pp. 707–710, 1966.
[19] M. Li, Y. Zhang, M. Zhu, M. Zhou, *Exploring distributional similarity based models for query spelling correction*, In ACL–44, pp. 1025–1032, 2006.
[20] H. Ma, H. Yang, I. King, M. R. Lyu, *Learning latent semantic relations from clickthrough data for query suggestion*, Proc. CIKM'08, pp. 709–718, 2008.
[21] Q. Mei, D. Zhou, K. Church, *Query Suggestion Using Hitting Time*, Proc. CIKM'08, pp. 469–478, 2008.
[22] D. Metzler, S. Dumais, C. Meek, *Similarity Measures for Short Segments of Text*, Proc. ECIR'07, pp. 16–27, 2007.
[23] A. Mohan, Zh. Cheng, K. Weinberger, *Web-Search Ranking with Initialized Gradient Boosted Regression Trees*, In Yahoo! Learning to Rank Challenge, pp. 77–89, 2011.
[24] M. Sahami, T. D. Heilman, *A web-based kernel function for measuring the similarity of short text snippets*, Proc. WWW'06, pp. 377–386, 2006.
[25] T. Sakai, *Evaluating Evaluation Metrics based on the Bootstrap*, Proc. SIGIR'06, pp. 525–532, 2006.
[26] D. Sheldon, M. Shokouhi, M. Szummer, N. Craswell, *LambdaMerge: Merging the Results of Query Reformulations*, WSDM'11, pp. 795–804, 2011.
[27] Y. Song, L. He, *Optimal Rare Query Suggestion With Implicit User Feedback*, Proc. WWW'10, pp. 901–910, 2010.
[28] I. Szpektor, A. Gionis, Y. Maarek , *Improving Recommendation for Long-tail Queries via Templates*, Proc. WWW'11, pp. 47–56, 2011.
[29] S. Tyree, K. Q. Weinberger, K. Agrawal, *Parallel Boosted Regression Trees for Web Search Ranking*, WWW'11, pp. 387–396, 2011.
[30] E. M. Voorhees, *Query expansion using lexical-semantic relations*, Proc. SIGIR'94, pp. 61–69, 1994.
[31] X. Wang, C. Zhai, *Mining term association patterns from search logs for effective query reformulation*, Proc. CIKM'08, pp. 479–488, 2008.
[32] W. Wu, H. Li, J. Xu, *Learning Query and Document Similarities from Click-through Bipartite Graph with Metadata*, Proc. WSDM'13, pp. 687–696, 2013.
[33] J. Xu, W. B. Croft, *Query expansion using local and global document analysis*, Proc. SIGIR'96, pp. 4–11, 1996.
[34] J. Xu, G. Xu, *Learning Similarity Function for Rare Queries*, WSDM'11, pp. 615–624, 2011.
[35] X. Yi, J. Allan, *Discovering Missing Click-through Query Language Information for Web Search*, Proc. CIKM'11, pp. 153–162, 2011.
[36] H. Zaragoza, B. B. Cambazoglu, R. Baeza-Yates, *Web search solved?: all result rankings the same?*, Proc. CIKM'10, p. 529, 2010.
[37] C. Zhai, J. Lafferty, *A study of smoothing methods for language models applied to information retrieval*, ACM Transactions on Information Systems (TOIS), Vol. 22, No 2, pp. 179–214, 2004.
[38] Z. Zhang, O. Nasraoui, *Mining Search Engine Query Logs for Query Recommendation*, Proc. WWW'06 , pp. 1039–1040, 2006.

APPENDIX

A. PROBABILISTIC INTERPRETATION OF PROPAGATION APPROACHES

The optimization Problem 5 defined in Section 4.1 can be theoretically justified in the following assumptions. Let d be a fixed document. Consider a query as a random event $\mathbf{q}$ and a feature as a random variable $\mathbf{f}$. We assume that Q is a random sample of the distribution of $\mathbf{q}$, and the feature value $f(q,d)$ available in the dataset is an observation of conditional distribution $\mathsf{P}_{\mathbf{f}|\mathbf{q}}$. We assume that the conditional expectation $\mathsf{E}(\mathbf{f} \mid \mathbf{q}=q)$ carries more information on the relevance of d to q than the noisy observation $f(q,d)$. Since $\mathsf{E}(\mathbf{f} \mid \mathbf{q}=q)$ is not directly observed in the data, our task is to provide its estimation based on observed values $f(\tilde{q},d)$ for different $\tilde{q} \in Q_q$.

For example, consider $\mathbf{f} = CTR$ (click-through rate). In this case, the observed value $f(q,d) = CTR(q,d)$ is the number of clicks on d divided by the number of its shows to q and can be viewed as the observed success rate in a Bernoulli process, where a trial corresponds to a show. The value of $CTR(q,d)$ is an estimation of the success probability, which is the probability of a click on the document d shown to query q. When the number of shows is low, CTR can deviate from the true value of this probability significantly, thus providing an inaccurate estimation.

Our propagation approach is based on the intuition that conditional distribution $\mathsf{P}_{\mathbf{f}|\mathbf{q}=\tilde{q}}$ is similar to conditional distribution $\mathsf{P}_{\mathbf{f}|\mathbf{q}=q}$, if $\tilde{q}$ is similar to q. Relying on this, we consider the values $f(\tilde{q},d)$, $\tilde{q} \in Q_q$, as independent observations of $\mathsf{P}_{\mathbf{f}|\mathbf{q}=q}$. We substitute conditional distribution $\mathsf{P}_{\mathbf{f}|\mathbf{q}=q}$ by discrete empirical distribution of values $f(\tilde{q},d)$, $\tilde{q} \in Q_q$, taken with probabilities $w(\tilde{q},q)$, which decrease as similarity of $\tilde{q}$ to q decreases. We use expectation $\tilde{f}_w(q,d)$ of this surrogate distribution (see Equation 2) as a *propagated* estimate of $\mathsf{E}(\mathbf{f} \mid \mathbf{q}=q)$. This approach is similar to the technique of Nadaraya-Watson kernel-weighted estimation of conditional expectation [16, Section 2.8.2]. The main difference is that our observed events are queries, not quantitative variables, therefore, we cannot rely on Euclidean distance used by conventional kernel functions. Instead, we define weighting function $w(\tilde{q},q)$ on the basis of similarity function $s(\tilde{q},q)$.

We further argue that the weights $w(\tilde{q},q)$ should be tuned to directly minimize the mean squared deviation of the right-hand side of Equation 4 from its left-hand side. In fact, we have

$$\mathsf{E}\left((\mathsf{E}(\mathbf{f} \mid \mathbf{q}) - \tilde{f}_w(\mathbf{q},d))^2 \mid \mathbf{q}=q\right) =$$
$$\mathsf{E}\left(\left[(\mathbf{f} - \mathsf{E}(\mathbf{f} \mid \mathbf{q})) + (\mathsf{E}(\mathbf{f} \mid \mathbf{q}) - \tilde{f}_w(\mathbf{q},d))\right]^2 \mid \mathbf{q}=q\right) -$$
$$\mathsf{E}\left((\mathbf{f} - \mathsf{E}(\mathbf{f} \mid \mathbf{q}))^2 \mid \mathbf{q}=q\right) =$$
$$\mathsf{E}\left((\mathbf{f} - \tilde{f}_w(\mathbf{q},d))^2 \mid \mathbf{q}=q\right) - \mathsf{E}\left((\mathbf{f} - \mathsf{E}(\mathbf{f} \mid \mathbf{q}))^2 \mid \mathbf{q}=q\right).$$

Therefore, the optimization problem $\min_w \mathsf{E}(\mathsf{E}(\mathbf{f} \mid \mathbf{q}) - \tilde{f}_w(\mathbf{q},d))^2$ is equivalent to the optimization problem $\min_w \mathsf{E}(\mathbf{f} - \tilde{f}_w(\mathbf{q},d))^2 - \mathsf{E}(\mathbf{f} - \mathsf{E}(\mathbf{f} \mid \mathbf{q}))^2$ that is equivalent to Problem 5.

B. PROOF OF EQUATION 11

We rely on a hypotheses that $f(\tilde{q},d)$ are independent observations of $\mathsf{P}_{\mathbf{f}|\mathbf{q}=q}$ and on an additional hypothesis that $s(\tilde{q},d)$ are independent observations of some probability distribution $\mathsf{P}_{\mathbf{s}|\mathbf{q}=q}$ as well. Let $\xi_1,\ldots,\xi_n$ be independent nonnegative and identically distributed random variables such that for all $t \in \mathbb{Z}$ the inequality $\mathsf{E}\xi_1^t < \infty$ holds. By the law of large numbers and Markov's inequality, for any $\delta, \epsilon, \varepsilon > 0$ and n large enough,

$$\mathsf{P}(\exists i \in \{1,\ldots,n\} : \ \xi_i(\xi_1 + \ldots + \xi_n)^{-1} > n^{\epsilon-1}) <$$
$$n\mathsf{P}(\xi_1 > n^{\epsilon}(\mathsf{E}\xi_1 + \varepsilon)) + \mathsf{P}(\xi_1 + \ldots + \xi_n \geqslant (\mathsf{E}\xi_1 + \varepsilon)n) < \delta,$$
$$\mathsf{P}(\forall i \in \{1,\ldots,n\} \ \xi_i(\xi_1 + \ldots + \xi_n)^{-1} > n^{-\epsilon-1}) >$$
$$(\mathsf{P}(\xi_1 > n^{-\epsilon}(\mathsf{E}\xi_1 - \varepsilon), \xi_1 + \ldots + \xi_n > (\mathsf{E}\xi_1 - \varepsilon)n))^n > 1 - \delta$$

So, if k is the exponent of a power function g_γ, then $g_i^{\sim}(q) = |Q_q|^{-k(1+o(1))}$, $\ i \in \{1,2\}$. If $g_\gamma(x) = a_0 + \ldots + a_k x^k$, $a_0 \neq 0$, then $g_i^{\sim}(q) = a_0(1 + |Q_q|^{-1+o(1)})$, $\ i \in \{1,2\}$. If $g_\gamma(x) = a_s x^s + \ldots + a_k x^k$, then $g_i^{\sim}(q) = |Q_q|^{-s(1+o(1))}$, $\ i \in \{1,2\}$.

Rank Consistency based Multi-View Learning: A Privacy-Preserving Approach

Han-Jia Ye, De-Chuan Zhan, Yuan Miao, Yuan Jiang, Zhi-Hua Zhou
National Key Laboratory for Novel Software Technology, Nanjing University
Collaborative Innovation Center of Novel Software Technology and Industrialization
Nanjing, 210023, China
{yehj, zhandc, miaoy, jiangy, zhouzh}@lamda.nju.edu.cn

ABSTRACT

Complex media objects are often described by multi-view feature groups collected from diverse domains or information channels. Multi-view learning, which attempts to exploit the relationship among multiple views to improve learning performance, has drawn extensive attention. It is noteworthy that in some real-world applications, features of different views may come from different private data repositories, and thus, it is desired to exploit view relationship with data privacy preserved simultaneously. Existing multi-view learning approaches such as subspace methods and pre-fusion methods are not applicable in this scenario because they need to access the whole features, whereas late-fusion approaches could not exploit information from other views to improve the individual view-specific learners. In this paper, we propose a novel multi-view learning framework which works in a hybrid fusion manner. Specifically, we convert predicted values of each view into an Accumulated Prediction Matrix (APM) with low-rank constraint enforced jointly by the multiple views. The joint low-rank constraint enables the view-specific learner to exploit other views to help improve the performance, without accessing the features of other views. Thus, the proposed RANC framework provides a privacy-preserving way for multi-view learning. Furthermore, we consider variants of solutions to achieve *rank consistency* and present corresponding methods for the optimization. Empirical investigations on real datasets show that the proposed method achieves state-of-the-art performance on various tasks.

Categories and Subject Descriptors

H.2.8 [**Database Management**]: [Database Applications – Data Mining]; I.2.6 [**Artificial Intelligence**]: [Learning]

General Terms

Algorithms, Applications, Experimentation

Keywords

Multi-View Learning; Rank Consistency; Privacy-Preserving

Permission to make digital or hard copies of all or part of this work for personal or classroom use is granted without fee provided that copies are not made or distributed for profit or commercial advantage and that copies bear this notice and the full citation on the first page. Copyrights for components of this work owned by others than ACM must be honored. Abstracting with credit is permitted. To copy otherwise, or republish, to post on servers or to redistribute to lists, requires prior specific permission and/or a fee. Request permissions from Permissions@acm.org.
CIKM'15, October 19–23, 2015, Melbourne, Australia.
© 2015 ACM. ISBN 978-1-4503-3794-6/15/10 ...$15.00.
DOI: http://dx.doi.org/10.1145/2806416.2806552.

1. INTRODUCTION

With the rapid development of the Internet, a huge number of rich media objects can be collected from various information channels, e.g., nowadays a piece of news can be naturally described using text, audio, video clip and hyperlink[17][35]. In this paper, we focus on problems where data are gathered from multiple private information channels, i.e., features cannot be shared during processing. This problem occurs frequently in many scenarios, e.g., knowledge management/analysis on database with different views/tables whose access are prohibited from different users; multi-view data analysis when *cooperation-competition* relationship exists among enterprises or researchers. In a more concrete case of image analysis, researchers can extract their own features of images as well as get the retrieval results from Google. Nevertheless they cannot obtain the image features used by Google, i.e., the features of researchers or Google are information from different private channels.

In order to analyze complex information from multiple channels, multi-view learning has attracted extensive attention [21] [24] [34]. Various multi-view learning approaches can be classified into four groups: multi-view subspace learning algorithms aim at obtaining a common subspace shared by multiple views and then learn models in that shared subspace [13] [27]; pre fusion methods like multiple kernel learning [11] mainly fuse feature information by weighted combination of kernels produced separately on each view; late fusion methods combine outputs of the models constructed from different view-specific features but leave the classifiers training phase unimproved [36]; disagreement-based methods focus on how to use unlabeled data to enhance the performance of learners via the compatibility between two views [5] [31] [39].

The aforementioned methods have achieved great success in various tasks, except scenarios with cooperation competition where access to multi-view features is restricted. Subspace style and pre-fusion approaches have to interact with view features, so they could not protect the privacy of different information channels. Late fusion methods only build a combined model based on outputs from each view, and therefore, the information from other information channels could not help improve learning ability of view-specific classifiers. Most existing disagreement-based multi-view learning approaches, such as co-training [5], rely on strong assumptions like redundant and independent views; though recent theoretical studies [32] [33] disclosed that weaker assumption is sufficient, new effective algorithms are still in design.

In this paper, we propose a novel framework working in a hybrid fusion manner. This framework, RANC (RANk Consistency), can be easily applied to the cooperation-competition multi-view learning scenarios, because each view-specific learner is able to exploit the information from other views to improve the performance without accessing features of these views; in other words, the RANC framework provides a way to privacy-preserving multi-view learning. The defined *rank consistency* is a criterion for seeking consistent predictions on multiple views. We formulate it by introducing an Accumulated Prediction Matrix (APM) which is stacked by predicted values/labels of each view. It is notable that in the ideal case, the predicted results of multi-view models should be consistent on each view so the rank of APM should be equal to $C-1$, where C is the number of classes. However, the rank of APM is usually larger than $C-1$ in practice for the potential inconsistency among multi-view predictions. Practically, lower rank of APM implies more view consistency. Fig. 1 is an illustration of APM on a multi-view dataset Reuters, which gives a spectrum plot on singular values of APM. The x-axis are singular values sorted in descending order. The spectrum is long-tail distributed started from the $(C-1)$th singular value, which implies low rank property of APM. There are two obvious knee points (KP) in Fig. 1. KP_1 may be caused by the ambiguities among C classes in Reuters. Note that KP_1 can be vanished for separable problems. KP_2 at $C-1$ clearly reveals the rank consistency property in multi-view problems. Motivated by this observation from Fig. 1, RANC reduces the long tail components of APM to leverage predictions close to the ideal case, and apparently is naturally designed for applications with two or more views. Since those properties mentioned above can be estimated on the outputs from each view instead of directly using their features, the data privacy can be maintained to a greatest extent.

In our proposed framework, *rank consistency* criterion can be transformed into a rank regularizer term. Specifically, we use the truncated nuclear norm [15] to model it which can be incorporated with many different losses. Solving this framework leads to enhance the classification ability of view-specific predictor. RANC constructs a hybrid fusion paradigm combining advantages of both pre-fusion and late-fusion methods. In this paper, we demonstrate this framework with square loss in detail and the implementation can be optimized effectively with both Proximal Gradient (PG) and Alternative Direction Method of Multipliers (ADMM) techniques. Furthermore, the paper also presents an accelerated version with rank-one update which can also get satisfying results. We empirically validate the effectiveness of our framework and our model achieves significantly better performance on various tasks. The main contributions of this paper can be summarized as follows:

- A novel *rank consistency* criterion based multi-view learning framework (RANC), which preserves data privacy of multiple channels, i.e., the learner on each view will access to the corresponding view features only and its interactions with other views are limited.
- RANC can naturally handle data with more than two views. Besides, it can help improve the learning ability of the individual predictor during the training phase.
- Our solutions to RANC are rendered effective. Meanwhile, an accelerated implementation is also presented.

Section 2 gives the related work. The main proposed framework together with detailed solutions is presented in section 3. In section 4, empirical investigations on real datasets are discussed. Finally, we conclude in section 5.

2. RELATED WORK

How to exploit relationship among multiple views is fundamental to multi-view learning approaches. As mentioned above, there are 4 categories of multi-view learning methods, and their strategies of exploiting view relationship are of diversity to improve performance. Subspace approaches seek correlations between views, and subsequent tasks like classification will be performed in the learned subspace. E.g., CCA [13] finds a linear projection for each of two views and generates a shared subspace where the correlation between two views is maximized. Some others, such as MvDA [18] and MvLPP [27], are of similar intuitions. Pre-fusion methods consider fusing features or feature derivations (e.g., kernels [11], distances [37]) before the training phase. It is typical that they represent the features as multiple kernel matrices and then combine them in a kernel space. Multiple kernel learning, one of the widely used pre-fusion methods, learns a linear [9] or nonlinear [10] combination of kernels for classification. These two types of methods, however, both require access to features of all views.

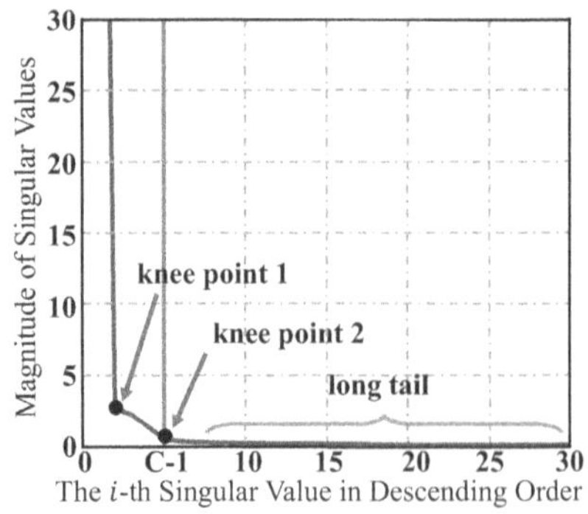

Figure 1: A typical singular value spectrum plot of APM on Reuters (5 views and 6 classes). APM is obtained with linear SVM on each view separately.

Late fusion strategies like RLF [36], aim at fusing the predicted values of each view while leaving multi-view features untouched. Nevertheless, the fusion process is not involved in classifier training phase, which makes late fusion not helpful in enhancing learners of each view. Moreover, it is required to retrain the whole late fusion model when the predictions on any of the views are changed, and this makes late fusion methods expensive and lack of flexibility.

Disagreement-based methods, such as Co-Training [5], focus on exploiting unlabeled data in semi-supervised learning scenarios. Traditional Co-Training enhances the performance of learners via the compatibility between views, but can hardly deal with multiple views [39].

By comprehensively considering the advantages and drawbacks of existing multi-view learning approaches, the proposed framework RANC defines a new criterion named *rank consistency* to characterize the consistency of predictions among multiple views. Rank consistency is implemented with matrix rank minimization regularizer. Rank minimization for a matrix is usually used in multi-class [12] or multi-label [22] problem, where different labels (output) are related to uniform input space (single input). In multi-label learning, rank based regularization is often used for reflecting the correlation between labels. However, in multi-view settings, classifiers are functional mappings which stretches across different views (input) and a single output. Consequently, it is required to define the rank consistency regularizer with a different data structure, namely, the accumulated prediction matrix (APM). Formulated on prediction matrix APM, RANC can protect features of individual view from being accessed by learners built on other views. Besides, RANC is fully incorporated in training of individual classifier on each view to refining the classifiers with updated predictions.

3. RANK CONSISTENCY BASED MULTI-VIEW LEARNING

In multi-view learning, an instance is characterized by multiple groups of features while they are only with one unified label. Without loss of generality, we suppose there are K views and each view has n instances, where the first l of n instances are labeled, and the rest $n-l$ are unlabeled. The ith instance $\mathbf{x}_i$ can be represented as a collection of view-specific vectors $\mathbf{x}_{i,k} \in \mathbb{R}^{d_k}$, where d_k is the dimension of the kth view. For labeled examples, instance $\mathbf{x}_i$ has label $y_i \in \{0,1\}$ in binary classification problem. In multi-class cases with C classes, the label y_i for instance $\mathbf{x}_i$ is expanded to a vector with C elements, where $y_{i,j}=1$ indicates the ith instance is with label j, otherwise, $y_{i,j}=0$. The whole data for kth view can be expressed as $X_k = [\mathbf{x}_{1,k}^\top; \mathbf{x}_{2,k}^\top; \cdots; \mathbf{x}_{n,k}^\top] \in \mathbb{R}^{n\times d_k}$, and the corresponding labels can be expressed as $Y \in \{0,1\}^{l\times C}$. Classifier on each view is denoted as $f_k : \mathbf{x}_{i,k} \to \hat{y}$, where $\mathbf{x}_{i,k} \in \mathbb{R}^{d_k}$, $\hat{y} \in \mathbb{R}^C$, and loss of instance i on view k is defined as $\ell(f_k(\mathbf{x}_{i,k}), y_i)$. Then the prediction of X_k on the kth view is combined into $F_k = [f_k(\mathbf{x}_{1,k})^\top; f_k(\mathbf{x}_{2,k})^\top; \cdots; f_k(\mathbf{x}_{n,k})^\top] \in \mathbb{R}^{n\times C}$, and predictions from all views can be stacked into an Accumulated Prediction Matrix (APM), which can be defined as $F = [F_1, F_2, \cdots, F_K] \in \mathbb{R}^{n\times CK}$.

Ideal multi-view classifiers f_k, $k=1,\cdots,K$, give identical outputs for a binary classification problem and consequently make the rank of APM F equal to one. Yet in practice, the rank of APM could not be exactly equal to one. As Fig. 1 shows, in a six-class problem, the singular values of APM in descending order reveal an "exponential like" decay with a long tail in the right part of Fig. 1. In particular, the second knee point appears at the 5th singular value. This is obviously consistent with our assumption that in practical cases, the rank of APM should be equal to the freedom degree of class number $C-1$. This phenomenon implies the predictions from all views tend to be with low rank when multi-view classifiers are not exactly identical. To induce consistency among multiple classifiers in multi-view learning, the *rank consistency* therefore can be defined as:

Definition 1. Rank consistency for predictions on multiple views on a certain data collection is an operator $RC(\cdot) : \mathbb{R}^{n\times CK} \to \mathbb{R}$, which defined on the APM F, and we define $RC(F) = \text{rank}(F)$.

We can summarize two fundamental properties of the defined rank consistency operator as follows:

Property 1. $RC(F)$ reflects the prediction compatibility among views. A large value of $RC(F)$ implies imperfection of prediction consistency, and a small value indicates predictions from all views are aligned well. (*Qualitative property*)

Property 2. The expected rank consistency is $C-1$, which is the freedom degree of label assignments in all views for concerned dataset. In particular, for a binary problem it is equal to 1. (*Quantitative property*)

Rank consistency can be easily used as a regularizer in a learning framework, which is helpful to achieve compatible and consistent predictions upon all views and can generate better classifier on each view. In next subsections, we first propose the whole RANC framework based on the defined rank consistency. After implementing concrete classifiers for each view, we show the proposed framework with rank consistency as a regularizer can be effectively solved with different techniques.

3.1 Rank Consistency Framework

The key to the proposed method is the use of the *rank consistency*, which boosts performance of view-specific learner by seeking for prediction consistency. Benefitted from the rank consistency as a regularizer, we can bridge the maximization of label consistency among multiple views and the part of the classification task together. We define the RANC framework as:

$$\min_F \sum_{k=1}^{K} L_k(F_k, Y) + \lambda \text{RC}(F). \quad (1)$$

There are K views and F is the APM. The first term L_k depicts the objective functions according to the property of the kth view. Furthermore, L_i and L_j can be different while the predictor on each view is self-adaptive. The second term, $RC(\cdot)$, is the rank consistency operator on APM, which leverages the prediction consistency to enhance learner on each view. $\lambda > 0$ is a balance parameter reflects the weights between view-specific objective and rank consistency regularizer.

Specifically, objective function L_k on the kth view in Eq. 1 is generally with the form of a regularized empirical loss:

$$\min_{F_k} L_k(F_k, Y) = \ell(F_k, Y) + \gamma r(F_k),$$

here $r(\cdot)$ is the regularizer for view-specific classifier. $\gamma > 0$ is a scalar coefficient to balance the weights of the two terms. Here the loss term $\ell(\cdot)$ can take several forms, e.g., square loss or hinge loss for both linear and nonlinear problems. Eq. 1 indicates the classifier in $\ell(\cdot)$ and the prediction results F_k for instances are connected, which provides the possibilities of refining predictions with rank consistency by optimizing them simultaneously. To simplify the discussion, here we use the regularized square loss as the basic objective function for each view, with linear classifiers $W_1, \cdots, W_K$:

$$\begin{aligned} \min_{W_k, b_k, F_k} \quad & \|X_k W_k + \mathbf{1}\boldsymbol{b}_k^\top - F_k\|_F^2 + \gamma \|W_k\|_F^2 \\ s.t. \quad & F_k \in \mathcal{D} : F_k^{1,\cdots,l} = Y,\ 0 \le F_k \le 1. \end{aligned} \quad (2)$$

The feasible domain of F_k is $\mathcal{D}$. Constraint $F_k^{1,\cdots,l} = Y$ restricts the prediction on labeled data the same as the ground truth to avoid collapsing of predictions, where $F_k^{1,\cdots,l}$ is the first l rows of the prediction matrix F_k. In addition, it constrains predicted values into the same range as true labels by $0 \le F_k \le 1$ to avoid trivial solutions. In Eq. 2, $\boldsymbol{b}_k \in \mathbb{R}^C$ is the bias for current predictor. By centralizing both instances and predictions, the objective can be rewritten as follows:

$$\ell(W_k, F_k) = \|H X_k W_k - H F_k\|_F^2 + \gamma \|W_k\|_F^2, \quad (3)$$

$H = I - \frac{1}{n}\mathbf{1}\mathbf{1}^\top$ is the centralization matrix, where I is the identity matrix and $\mathbf{1}$ is a vector with all the elements equal to one. Without loss of generality, we can assume the data matrix X is centralized so that $HX_k = X_k$. Furthermore, by taking derivative of Eq. 3 w.r.t. W_k and setting it to zero, we have:

$$W_k = (X_k^\top X_k + \gamma I)^{-1} X_k^\top F_k. \quad (4)$$

Combining Eq. 3 and Eq. 4, we simplify the rank consistency framework in Eq. 1 into a form only relying on the predicted values F_k of each view, i.e., the APM F, as follows:

$$\min_{F_k \in \mathcal{D}} \sum_{k=1}^{K} \text{Tr}(F_k^\top (H - X_k (X_k^\top X_k + \gamma I)^{-1} X_k^\top) F_k) + \lambda \text{RC}(F), \quad (5)$$

here $\text{Tr}(\cdot)$ is the matrix trace operator.

3.2 Directional Rank Consistency Optimization with Truncated Nuclear Norm

Rank norm minimization is NP-hard and nuclear norm (or trace norm) [7] usually acts as a convex surrogate. For a matrix $X \in \mathbb{R}^{m\times n}$, we assume its singular values σ_i, $i = 1, \cdots, \min(m, n)$, are ordered from large to small. The nuclear norm is defined as $\|X\|_* = \sum_{i=1}^{\min(m,n)} \sigma_i$. Nuclear norm has been widely used in various scenarios where rank norm minimization is required [12].

However, the quantitative property of *rank consistency* indicates consistent predictions of learners constructed on each view respectively always have $C-1$ freedom degree on sufficient large dataset. Blindly minimizing the rank of APM will break the natural structure of multi-view predictions and may lead to degeneration of classification performance. Therefore, a directional optimization approach, which can conduct the RC(F) until converging to $C - 1$ during the minimization procedure, is desired in our task. Inspired by [15], we use *truncated nuclear norm* as a surrogate function of the RC($\cdot$) operator:

Definition 2. Given a matrix $X \in \mathbb{R}^{m\times n}$, the truncated nuclear norm $\|X\|_r$ is defined as the sum of $min(m, n) - r$ minimum singular values, i.e., $\|X\|_r = \sum_{i=r+1}^{min(m,n)} \sigma_i(X)$.

Different from traditional nuclear norm minimization with all singular values preserved, truncated nuclear norm minimizes singular values with first r largest ones unchanged, which is more close to the true rank definition. If $\|X\|_r = 0$, there are only r non-zero singular values for X, and this explicitly indicates rank of X is less than or equals to r. Practically, in order to impel the RC(F) directional to the freedom degree of the APM, it is clear to set $r = C - 1$ in multi-view learning scenarios.

The truncated nuclear norm can be formulated as the equivalent form by the following theorem [15]:

THEOREM 1. *Given a matrix $X \in \mathbb{R}^{m\times n}$ and any non-negative integer $r (r \le min(m, n))$, for any matrix $A \in \mathbb{R}^{r\times m}$ and $B \in \mathbb{R}^{r\times n}$ such that $AA^\top = I_r, BB^\top = I_r$, where $I_r \in \mathbb{R}^{r\times r}$ is identity matrix. Truncated nuclear norm can be reformulated as:*

$$\|X\|_r = \|X\|_* - \max \mathrm{Tr}(AXB^\top).$$

If the singular value decomposition of matrix X is $X = U\Sigma V^\top$ where Σ is the diagonal matrix of singular values sorted in descending order and $U \in \mathbb{R}^{m\times n}$, $V \in \mathbb{R}^{n\times n}$. The optimal solution for the trace term in the above equation has a closed form solution: $A = (\mathbf{u}_1, \mathbf{u}_2, \cdots, \mathbf{u}_r)^\top$ and $B = (\mathbf{v}_1, \mathbf{v}_2, \cdots, \mathbf{v}_r)^\top$, corresponds to the first r columns of left and right singular vectors.

With Theorem 1, we can reformulate our objective function as:

$$\begin{aligned} F = \quad & \operatorname*{argmin}_{F_k \in \mathcal{D}} \sum_{k=1}^{K} L_k(F_k) + \|F\|_r \\ = \quad & \operatorname*{argmin}_{F_k \in \mathcal{D}} \sum_{k=1}^{K} L_k(F_k) + \|F\|_* - \max \mathrm{Tr}(AFB^\top), \\ & s.t.\ AA^\top = I,\ BB^\top = I. \end{aligned} \tag{6}$$

Because of the non-convexity of truncated nuclear norm, alternative approaches can be utilized for the optimization. A simple solution to Eq. 6 is alternating descent method. We can fix F and optimize A, B via SVD on F first, and then fix A and B to optimize F. When A and B are fixed, the subproblem is convex. The whole procedure is summarized in Algorithm 1.

In step 2, A and B can be obtained by SVD on F, which are the left and right singular vectors corresponding to the maximum $C-1$ singular values. As the number of actually required singular vectors is rather small, partial SVD can be used for more of efficient [3]. The most computational cost step, however, is the subproblem for solving F in Eq. 7. We will give a detailed investigation on employing Accelerate Proximal Gradient Descent Method (APG) [2] and Alternative Direction Method of Multipliers (ADMM) [6] for solving this subproblem in the following subsections.

Algorithm 1 The pseudo code of RANC

Require: training instances X_k for each view, parameters λ and γ, ϵ, initialize F using true label matrix;

1: **while** True **do**

2: Use F to solve A and B as Theorem 1;

3: Solve F with fixed A and B, i.e.,

$$F^{t+1} = \operatorname*{argmin}_{F_k \in \mathcal{D}} \sum_{k=1}^{K} L_k(F_k) + \|F\|_* - \mathrm{Tr}(AFB^\top) \tag{7}$$

4: **if** $\|F^{t+1} - F^t\|_F \le \epsilon$ **then**

5: Break;

6: **end if**

7: **end while**

8: Solve W_k from F using Eq. 4.

9: **return** W_k, classifier for each view.

It is noteworthy that the whole training procedure enhances the view-specific classifier only based on alternative updates of the prediction matrix F_k and its singular vectors. After each round of updating F_k, updated view-specific prediction will be passed back to corresponding learner of each view for model refinements. So RANC restricts interactions among multiple views within predictions without the access to original features of other views.

3.3 Solving RANC with APG

Note that when A and B are fixed, the problem is composed of two convex parts, i.e., a smooth loss term $P_1(F)$ and a non-smooth trace norm $P_2(F)$:

$$P_1(F) = \sum_{k=1}^{K} L_k(F_k) - \mathrm{Tr}(AFB^\top),\ P_2(F) = \|F\|_* \tag{8}$$

APG is suitable for solving Eq. 8 [16], which optimizes on a linearized approximation version of the original problem. In the tth iteration, if we denote the current optimization variable as F^t, then we can linearize the smooth part $P_1(\cdot)$ at F^t as:

$$\begin{aligned} Q(F) =& P_1(F^t) + \mathrm{Tr}(\langle \nabla P_1(F^t), F - F^t \rangle) \\ &+ \frac{L}{2}\|F - F^t\|_F^2 + P_2(F) \\ =& \sum_{k=1}^{K} L_k(F_k^t) - \mathrm{Tr}(AF^tB^\top) + \mathrm{Tr}(\langle \nabla P_1(F^t), F - F^t \rangle) \\ &+ \frac{L}{2}\|F - F^t\|_F^2 + \lambda\|F\|_*, \end{aligned}$$

where $\nabla P_1(F^t) = 2[E_1F_1^t, E_2F_2^t, \cdots, E_kF_k^t] - \lambda A^\top B$, where $E_k = H - X_k(X_k^\top X_k + \gamma I)^{-1}X_k^\top$, $k = 1, \cdots, K$. Here L is the Lipschitz coefficient, which can be estimated by line search strategy [2]. Minimizing $Q(F)$ w.r.t. F is equivalent to solving:

$$\hat{F} = \arg\min_F \lambda\|F\|_* + \frac{L}{2}\|F - (F^t - \frac{1}{L}\nabla P_1(F^t))\|_F^2. \tag{9}$$

Algorithm 2 The pseudo code for solving Eq. 7 with APG

Require: $\gamma, \alpha_1 = 1$, initialize Z^1 and F^1 using true label matrix;

```
while Stop criterion doesn't meet do
    Line search for best step-size L
    F̂^t = 𝔇_L(Z^t),  F^t = Proj_𝒟(F̂^t)
    α_{t+1} = (1+√(1+4α_t^2))/2
    Z^{t+1} = F^t + ((α_t − 1)/α_{t+1})(F^t − F^{t−1})
end while
return F_k.
```

APG updates using the optimal solution in Eq. 9 at each iteration. Given the following theorem [7] about the proximal operator for nuclear norm:

THEOREM 2. *For each $\tau \geq 0$ and $Y \in \mathbb{R}^{m\times n}$, we have*

$$D_\tau(Y) = \arg\min_X \frac{1}{2}\|X - Y\|_F^2 + \tau\|X\|_*$$

Here, $D_\tau(Y)$ is a matrix shrinkage operator for matrix Y, which can be calculated by SVD of Y. If SVD of Y is $Y = U\Sigma V^T$, then

$$D_\tau(Y) = UD_\tau(\Sigma)V^T, D_\tau(\Sigma) = diag(max(\sigma_i - \tau, 0)).$$

we can solve Eq. 9 in a closed form:

$$\hat{F} = \mathfrak{D}_L(F^t) \stackrel{\text{def}}{=} D_{\frac{\lambda}{L}}(F^t - \frac{1}{L}\nabla P_1(F^t)).$$

Note that the SVD approach in proximal projection is also time efficient, since it will only be applied to a thin matrix. The computation of F acquires the gradient of P_1, blocks of which are constructed using view feature information. Note that the k blocks are view-independent, we can distribute updated view-specific prediction in updated F_k back to each view and compute the $E_k F_k^t$ within the corresponding view. Then only K computation results with the same size of the prediction matrix F_k are returned, through which feature privacy is maintained. After we get $\hat{F}$ from Eq. 9, the feasible F can be obtained by projecting $\hat{F}$ into the $\mathcal{D}$ as in [8], which can be denoted as $\text{Proj}_\mathcal{D}(\hat{F})$. As a consequence, we have the RANC framework with APG in Algorithm 2.

3.4 Solving RANC with ADMM

Considering the diversity between representation among different views, the prediction of classifier on each view may has its own bias. So it is more reasonable to learn an optimal bias for each view, combined with which the last prediction matrix among views can be more comparable. It is notable that the introduced biases here are different from the classifier bias on each view. Let $\mathbf{b} \in \mathbb{R}^{KC\times 1}$ be the biases vector, where each element is the individual bias for the corresponding view. Together with learned optimal biases, we therefore can assume low rank property for the biased APM. Then the subproblem of Eq. 7 can be further formulated with defined E_k:

$$\min_{F\in\mathcal{D}} \sum_{k=1}^{K} \text{Tr}(F_k^\top E_k F_k) + \lambda\|F - \mathbf{1}\mathbf{b}^\top\|_* - \lambda\text{Tr}(A[F - \mathbf{1}\mathbf{b}^\top]B^\top). \tag{10}$$

To solve the problem of Eq. 10, an equality constraint $U = F - \mathbf{1}\mathbf{b}^\top$ is further introduced and the problem becomes:

$$\min_F \sum_{k=1}^{K} \text{Tr}(F_k^\top E_k F_k) + \lambda\|U\|_* - \lambda\text{Tr}(AUB^\top)$$
$$s.t.\ U = F - \mathbf{1}\mathbf{b}^\top,$$

which can be solved with augmented Lagrange dual form by maximizing the dual variable Λ:

$$L_\beta = \sum_{k=1}^{K} \text{Tr}(F_k^\top E_k F_k) + \lambda\|U\|_* - \lambda\text{Tr}(AUB^\top) \tag{11}$$
$$- \langle \Lambda, U - (F - \mathbf{1}\mathbf{b}^\top)\rangle + \frac{\beta}{2}\|U - (F - \mathbf{1}\mathbf{b}^\top)\|_F^2,$$

$\beta > 0$ is a scalar for the augmented term. The problem in Eq. 11 is similar to those problems which can be solved with ADMM [6]. However, here we have three blocks of variables in Eq. 11, namely blocks with U, $\mathbf{b}$ and F, which is with very different properties rather than the ordinary ADMM problems. Using ADMM directly can hardly get converged [29], consequently we employ a variant augmented Lagrange dual optimization technique [14] for our problem, which is a splitting variant of ADMM. After letting $Q = \mathbf{1}\mathbf{b}^\top$, we can solve an optimal candidate of Q^{t+1} by taking derivative of Eq. 11 w.r.t. Q and set it to zero, thus we have:

$$Q^{t+1} = \frac{1}{\beta}\Lambda^t - U^t + F^t. \tag{12}$$

Then the dual variable can be updated as:

$$\Lambda^{t+\frac{1}{2}} = \Lambda^t + \beta(Q^{t+1} + U^t - F^t). \tag{13}$$

With the updated Λ, the remaining variable U can be updated with an added proximal term:

$$\min_U \lambda\|U\|_* - \lambda\text{Tr}(AUB^\top) - \langle\Lambda^{t+\frac{1}{2}}, U\rangle + \frac{\mu\beta}{2}\|U - U^t\|_F^2.$$

According to Theorem 2, the optimal value has closed solution:

$$U^{t+1} = D_{\frac{\lambda}{\mu\beta}}(U^t + \frac{1}{\mu\beta}\Lambda^{t+\frac{1}{2}} + \frac{\lambda}{\mu\beta}A^\top B). \tag{14}$$

Similarly, the last block of variable F updates iteratively with:

$$\min_{F\in\mathcal{D}} \sum_{k=1}^{K} \text{Tr}(F_k^\top E_k F_k) + \langle\Lambda^{t+\frac{1}{2}}, F\rangle + \frac{\mu\beta}{2}\|F - F^t\|_F^2,$$

where the scalar $\mu > 2$ [14] and $\hat{F}_k$ has a closed form solution:

$$\hat{F}_k^{t+1} = (2E_k + \mu\beta I)^{-1}(\mu\beta F^t - \Lambda^{t+\frac{1}{2}})_k, \tag{15}$$

the subscript k of $(\mu\beta F^t - \Lambda^{t+\frac{1}{2}})$ means the kth block corresponding to the kth view. Similarly, each prediction $\hat{F}_k^{t+1}$ can be updated within its own view, i.e., each view receives the temporary result $(\mu\beta F^t - \Lambda^{t+\frac{1}{2}})_k$ and combines its feature transformation E_k to compute $\hat{F}_k^{t+1}$ in their own view respectively. The view independence of Eq. 15 ensures no interaction among views, which protects the data privacy. After obtained $\hat{F}_k^{t+1}$, we also need to project it into feasible domain as in last subsection by $F^{t+1} = \text{Proj}_\mathcal{D}(\hat{F})$. Update iterations for U and F are separated and consequently can be implemented in a parallel paradigm. After that a renewal of the dual variable should be carried out:

$$\Lambda^{t+1} = \Lambda^{t+\frac{1}{2}} + \beta(U^t - U^{t+1}) - \beta(F^t - F^{t+1}). \tag{16}$$

Algorithm 3 gives the sketch of this procedure. Following [14] [29], the whole procedure can be proved to be converged.

3.5 Rank-One Acceleration

RANC can be solved with APG or ADMM effectively together with truncated nuclear norm regularizer. In this section, an accelerated variation of RANC denoted as RANC_1 is proposed to restrict the rank of APM with rank-one update. Recall that in the ideal

Algorithm 3 The pseudo code for solving Eq. 7 with ADMM

Require: γ, μ, initialize F using true label matrix;
1: **while** Stop criterion doesn't meet **do**
2: Solve Q as Eq. 12
3: Update Λ as Eq. 13
4: Solve U as Eq. 14
5: Solve $\hat{F}$ by Eq. 15 and $F = \text{Proj}_{\mathcal{D}}(\hat{F})$
6: Update Λ as Eq. 16
7: **end while**
8: **return** F_k.

case, APM in C-class problem should be with rank $C-1$, i.e., for binary problems, rank of APM should be restrained to one, which provides facilitation for designing efficient rank-one approximation approach to RANC.

To simplify the discussion, we demonstrate the implementation in binary case where each view only gets a vector prediction value output, i.e., $F_k \in \mathbb{R}^{n\times 1}$ and the APM $F \in \mathbb{R}^{n\times K}$. For multi-class problem, the classification can be carried out with one-vs-rest strategies. The rank-one acceleration is brought forward based on the following property: $\text{rank}(X) = 1$, where $X \in \mathbb{R}^{m\times n}$, if and only if there are two vectors $\mathbf{u} \in \mathbb{R}^{m\times 1}$ and $\mathbf{v} \in \mathbb{R}^{n\times 1}$ that X can be decomposed into the outer product of $\mathbf{u}$ and $\mathbf{v}$, i.e., $X = \mathbf{u}\mathbf{v}^\top$.

Consequently, we can reduce the rank consistency of APM to one for binary case simply by using two vectors to approximate APM, i.e., we define $RC(F) = \|F - \mathbf{u}\mathbf{v}^\top\|_F^2$, where the error is estimated using Frobenius norm. Note that there are diversities between different views, we add biases $\mathbf{b} \in \mathbb{R}^K$ for view predictors to further facilitate the rank reduction of APM, i.e., we can redefine $RC(F) = \|F - \mathbf{1}\mathbf{b}^\top - \mathbf{u}\mathbf{v}^\top\|_F^2$. Unique solution of $\mathbf{u}$ and $\mathbf{v}$ can be obtained by restricting $\mathbf{u}$ and $\mathbf{v}$ orthogonal. We therefore can reformulate the original problem in Eq. 5 as follows:

$$\min_{F\in\mathcal{D},\mathbf{u}\mathbf{u}^\top=I,\mathbf{v}\mathbf{v}^\top=I} \sum_{k=1}^{K} L_k(F_k) + \|F - \mathbf{1}\mathbf{b}^\top - \mathbf{u}\mathbf{v}^\top\|_F^2. \quad (17)$$

The rank-one approximation formulation in Eq. 17 can be solved by alternative optimization. We first fix F for solving $\mathbf{u}$, $\mathbf{v}$ and $\mathbf{b}$, i.e., solving the following problem:

$$\min_{\mathbf{u}\mathbf{u}^\top=I,\mathbf{v}\mathbf{v}^\top=I} \|F - \mathbf{1}\mathbf{b}^\top - \mathbf{u}\mathbf{v}^\top\|_F^2.$$

Bias term $\mathbf{b}$, which aims at finding an optimal mean for individual prediction, can be solved as [23], i.e., $\mathbf{b}$ can be solved by $\mathbf{b} = F^\top\mathbf{1}/\mathbf{n}$, and then we can solve $\mathbf{u}$ and $\mathbf{v}$ with eigenvalue decomposition:

$$\begin{aligned} \mathbf{u} &= \arg\min_{\mathbf{u}} \text{Tr}(\mathbf{u}^\top F^\top H F \mathbf{u}), \quad (18)\\ \mathbf{v} &= (F - \mathbf{b}\mathbf{1}^\top)\mathbf{u}. \end{aligned}$$

It is notable that in Eq. 18, only the eigenvector of the largest eigenvalue is needed, which can alleviate the computation burden greatly [3]. In the second step, with the fixed approximate rank-one matrix, we can update F in a closed form. In particular, with the fixed rank-one approximation, we can update the view-specific predictors as:

$$\hat{F}_k = \lambda(E_k + \lambda I)^{-1}(\mathbf{u}\mathbf{v}^\top + \mathbf{1}\mathbf{b}^\top)_k, \quad (19)$$

where $(\mathbf{u}\mathbf{v}^\top + \mathbf{1}\mathbf{b}^\top)_k$ gives the kth column of matrix $\mathbf{u}\mathbf{v}^\top + \mathbf{1}\mathbf{b}^\top$. Each $\hat{F}_k$ can be updated on each view separately using a similar strategy as aforementioned. $F = \text{Proj}_{\mathcal{D}}(\hat{F})$ is executed to project $\hat{F}$ into the feasible domain. The above procedure should be iterated until convergence, which can be summarized in Algorithm 4.

Algorithm 4 The pseudo code of RANC_1

Require: γ, λ, initialize F using true label matrix;
1: **while** Stop criterion doesn't meet **do**
2: Solve $\mathbf{u}$ and $\mathbf{v}$ as in Eq. 18 and Eq. 19
3: Update F using Eq. 19 and $F = \text{Proj}_{\mathcal{D}}(\hat{F})$
4: **end while**
5: **return** F_k.

Table 1: Brief dataset description. Datasets with two views and more than two views are separated with a horizontal line.

Datasets	C	n	K	d_k ($k = 1, \cdots, K$)
Course	2	1051	2	66, 5
Citeseer	6	3264	2	3703, 3264
Cora	7	2708	2	1433, 2708
Cornell	5	195	2	1703, 195
Texas	5	185	2	1703, 185
Washington	5	217	2	1703, 217
Wisconsin	5	262	3	1703, 262
Advertise	2	983	5	457, 495
News-M2	2	1200	3	2000, 2000, 2000
News-M5	5	500	3	2000, 2000, 2000
News-M10	10	500	3	2000, 2000, 2000
News-NG1	2	500	3	2000, 2000, 2000
News-NG2	5	400	3	2000, 2000, 2000
News-NG3	8	1000	3	2000, 2000, 2000
Reuters	6	1600	5	2000, 2000, 2000, 2000, 2000

4. EXPERIMENT

We conduct extensive experiments on 15 real-world datasets with multiple views. We first give the general configurations. Then we comprehensively demonstrate effectiveness of our proposed framework (with three variants of solutions) in comparison with the state-of-the-art multi-view learning methods.

4.1 General Experiment Settings

Data used in experiments are consisted of two-view and multiple views (more than 2 views) datasets. Description sketches of datasets are summarized in Table 1. The Course dataset [5] describes web pages and the goal is to predict whether the given web page is a course page or not. The Citeseer dataset [26] is originally made of 4 views, i.e., content, inbound, outbound, cites, on the same documents. We follow [4] to choose the content and cites view in our experiment. In the content view, the documents are characterized by 3703 words. The Cora dataset [26] has the same structure as Citeseer. Following [4] the content view and the cites view are used in our experiment as well. The WebKB dataset [26] contains webpages collected from four universities: Cornell, Texas, Wisconsin and Washington which have 5 categories, i.e., student, project, course, stuff and faculty. Data in WebKB are described with two views: content and citation. We treat WebKB in 4 separate datasets grouped by universities. The Advertise dataset [20] [40] has 5 views, i.e., caption and alt features in html description together with base url, destination url and image url. Each example describes an image on the web, and the task of the dataset is to determine whether a given image may be an advertisement. The NewsGroup dataset [4] is of 6 groups extracted from the 20-Newsgroup dataset, i.e., M2, M5, M10, NG1, NG2, NG3. Every group contains 10 sample sets, and we choose the first set for all 6

Table 2: Classification accuracies (average value ± std.) compared with fusion and baseline methods. RANC_{PG} and RANC_{ADM} represent for the APG or ADMM solutions to RANC. RANC_1 denotes for the accelerated RANC version. Last three rows list the win/tie/lose counts on all datasets with t-test against other methods at significance level 95%. The best performance on each dataset is bolded.

	Our Methods			Pre-Fusion Methods					Late Fusion	Baseline	
Dataset	RANC_{PG}	RANC_{ADM}	RANC_1	CABMKL	MKL	SimpleMKL	GLMKL	LMKL	RLF	WNH	LS
Course	.893±.017	.899±.014	**.901±.017**	**.901±.018**	.893±.015	.893±.015	.898±.018	.834±.030	.866±.015	.875±.035	.887±.016
Citeseer	.694±.009	.704±.010	.671±.019	.692±.011	.689±.011	.685±.012	**.707±.008**	.681±.011	.693±.010	.650±.013	.694±.010
Cora	.784±.013	**.785±.013**	.653±.019	.748±.015	.733±.022	.731±.020	.762±.014	.675±.018	.782±.014	.648±.017	.716±.015
Cornell	**.730±.055**	.729±.055	.652±.045	.629±.068	.621±.069	.620±.067	.600±.055	.641±.055	.624±.060	.529±.070	.689±.056
Texas	**.738±.045**	.737±.050	.730±.046	.557±.006	.556±.003	.556±.003	.558±.007	.556±.000	.658±.038	.591±.082	.701±.047
Washington	**.776±.033**	.745±.050	.736±.041	.684±.031	.675±.034	.674±.033	.686±.027	.719±.029	.655±.032	.691±.058	.731±.047
Wisconsin	.641±.061	**.819±.031**	.688±.044	.727±.030	.727±.036	.725±.038	.702±.029	.740±.027	.637±.052	.719±.050	.545±.057
Advertise	.898±.020	.887±.024	.880±.096	.861±.003	.860±.000	.860±.000	.862±.004	.860±.000	.805±.028	**.918±.028**	.786±.080
News-M2	.963±.015	**.974±.013**	.963±.016	.849±.069	.779±.050	.779±.050	.930±.025	.818±.064	.964±.012	.700±.208	.963±.015
News-M5	.918±.033	.921±.019	.903±.024	.864±.033	.881±.030	.877±.028	.912±.025	.802±.036	**.924±.021**	.820±.145	.869±.023
News-M10	.788±.023	.787±.023	**.791±.026**	.656±.051	.667±.034	.657±.033	.756±.026	.555±.030	.741±.026	.700±.072	.735±.026
News-NG1	**.936±.031**	**.936±.032**	.906±.033	.904±.041	.865±.090	.865±.090	.901±.042	.879±.046	.928±.025	.894±.112	.885±.026
News-NG2	**.928±.012**	**.928±.012**	.922±.015	.896±.027	.908±.019	.907±.021	**.928±.015**	.862±.013	.922±.014	.461±.178	.875±.016
News-NG3	.923±.012	.923±.012	**.928±.010**	.910±.017	.887±.018	.887±.020	.926±.013	.852±.016	.911±.010	.385±.046	.884±.012
Reuters	.696±.022	.706±.020	**.715±.021**	.682±.023	.680±.024	.679±.022	.682±.018	.659±.022	.706±.019	.559±.028	.633±.025
W / T / L	RANC_{PG} vs. others			13 / 1 / 1	14 / 0 / 1	14 / 0 / 1	10 / 3 / 2	14 / 0 / 1	8 / 6 / 1	13 / 0 / 2	14 / 1 / 0
W / T / L	RANC_{ADM} vs. others			15 / 0 / 0	15 / 0 / 0	15 / 0 / 0	11 / 3 / 1	15 / 0 / 0	11 / 3 / 1	14 / 0 / 1	14 / 1 / 0
W / T / L	RANC_1 vs. others			9 / 3 / 3	11 / 1 / 3	11 / 1 / 3	7 / 6 / 2	9 / 3 / 3	9 / 2 / 4	11 / 3 / 1	11 / 1 / 3

groups in our experiment. There are 3 views in this dataset, which are made by different preprocessing methods for texts, namely using Partitioning Around Medoids, Supervised Mutual Information and Unsupervised Mutual Information [4]. In our experiments, we will denote these types of data as News-M2, News-M5, News-M10, News-NG1, News-NG2 and News-NG3. The Reuters dataset [4] is built from the Reuters RCV1/RCV2 Multilingual test collection, multi-view information is created from different languages, i.e., English, French, German, Italian and Spanish [4].

We run each method 30 times for 15 datasets. 70% of the data are randomly picked up for training and the remaining are for test. In the training set, we randomly choose 30% as the labeled data, and the left 70% as unlabeled ones. Parameters are selected by 5CV from $\{10^{-5}, 10^{-4}, \cdots, 10^{5}\}$ in the first split and fixed.

Since RANC leverages advantages of above four different types of multi-view learning paradigms, we should compare it with approaches from these four approaches.

4.2 Comparing With Fusion Methods

RANC framework is first compared with fusion approaches since it is a hybrid fusion method with advantages of pre-fusion and late fusion. In detail, we compare with 5 multiple kernel learning (MKL) methods in pre-fusion and the state-of-the-art late fusion method RLF (Robust Late Fusion method) [36]. The MKL methods are Centered Alignment-Based MKL algorithms [9], original SOCP formulated MKL algorithm from [1], Simple MKL method proposed by [25], Group Lasso-based MKL method from [19] and Localized MKL algorithm [10], which are denoted as CABMKL, MKL, SimpleMKL, GLMKL, LMKL in the following contexts and tables respectively. In RLF, we use the best tuned classifier with least square loss as initialized predictor [36]. Furthermore, the ensemble of least square classifier (LS) is listed as a baseline. WNH method [30] which combines all views data together and then uses $l_{2,1}$-norm to perform view selection is also listed as a baseline.

It is notable that fusion methods can output only one classification result for multi-view data, so we compare the integrated result (mean accuracy and std.) of RANC with them. Win/tie/lose counts with t-test at significance level 95% are also recorded in table 2, where the highest accuracy on each dataset is bolded. Probability voting is used for RANC to obtain the final fusion results. Three variants of RANC solutions in subsection 3.3, 3.4 and 3.5 are denoted as RANC_{PG}, RANC_{ADM} and RANC_1 respectively.

In Table 2, it can be clearly found that RANC gets better results on most datasets. The RANC_{ADM} returns more stable results. RANC_1, the accelerated solver, can also outperform all compared methods from the win/tie/lose counts on most datasets. As to the statistical test results, the RANC framework outperforms fusion methods in most cases, which validates the superiority of RANC. In general, RANC_{PG} achieves better results on two-view datasets while RANC_{ADM} performs better on datasets with more than two views. This may be due to the bias term introduced in RANC_{ADM} works when the number of views is large.

To investigate the efficiency of RANC_1, we conduct more experiments on a linux cluster with 2.53GHz 12 cores and 48Gb memory. The average training time costs (in seconds) of all RANC series methods, late fusion method RLF and a baseline method WNH are recorded in Table 3. Six datasets are picked up for this time costs test. Table 3 evidently verifies the efficiency of RANC_1, i.e., 9.85, 65.95, 80.41, 161.52 times faster than RANC_{PG}, RANC_{ADM}, RLF and WNH respectively in average. It is noteworthy that for those compared methods, training time of base classifiers build on each view is not included in RLF, and the implementation of WNH is only with 10 trials. In other words, the superiority of RANC_1 on speed can be further enlarged in a fair play.

4.3 Comparing with Subspace Approaches

Subspace multi-view learning approaches can provide classification results on individual view. In this section, we compare RANC with multi-view learning method in subspace learning paradigms. WNH [30] is also listed since it can provide predictions on each single view. In this part of experiments, multi-view Linear Discriminant Analysis, multi-view Canonical Correlation Analysis, multi-

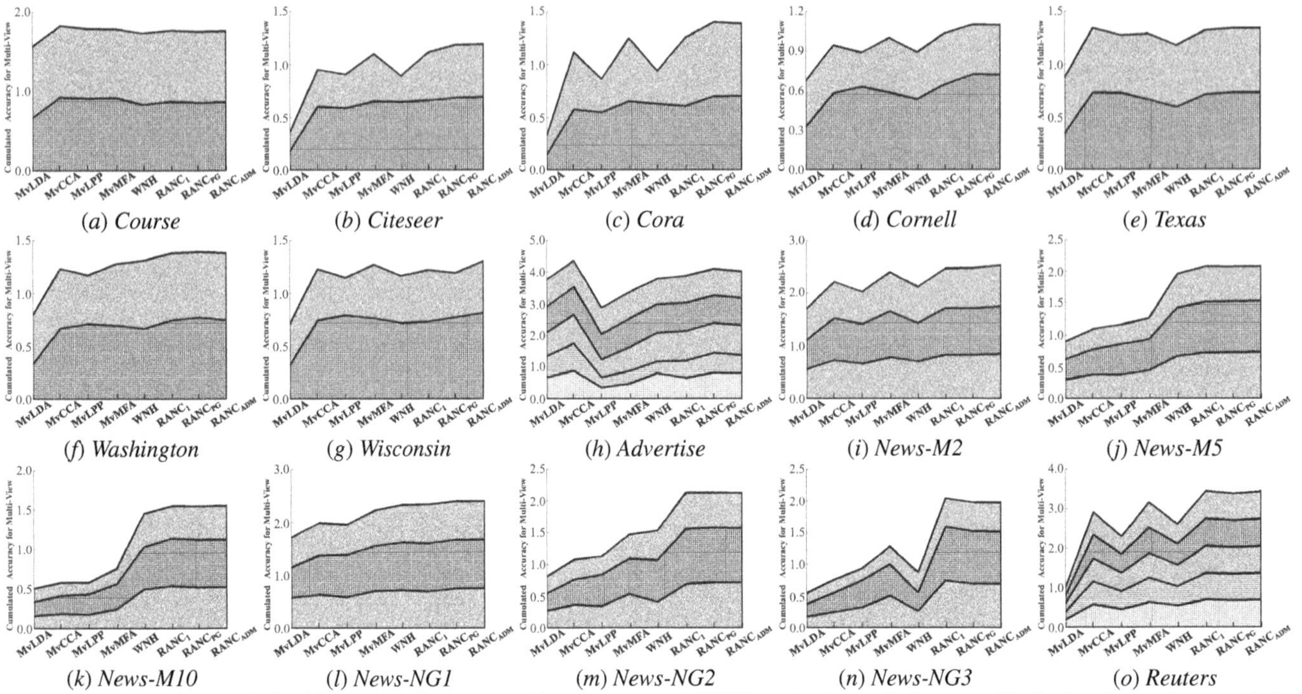

Figure 2: Comparisons of classification performance with subspace and WNH methods on all datasets. Each plot shows the cumulative classification accuracy results of each view on certain datasets and different views are plotted in different shadow styles. RANC_{PG} and RANC_{ADM} represent for solving RANC with PGM or ADMM. RANC_1 corresponds to the acceleration method.

Table 3: Average training time on 6 datasets (in seconds). Late fusion and baseline methods are compared. Pre-fusion methods, however, highly depend on classifiers invoked, so are not compared.

Time	RANC_1	RANC_{PG}	RANC_{ADM}	RLF	WNH
News-M2	1.983	29.913	107.923	146.920	935.517
News-NG3	20.350	259.153	1398.123	1676.290	1372.167
Reuters	17.383	222.730	1206.193	803.263	3724.660
Citeseer	64.870	277.717	4700.440	6494.440	1489.923
Cora	34.590	201.727	3080.983	4817.303	537.353
Wisconsin	0.580	2.677	24.157	23.450	102.797

view Locality Preserving Projections, multi-view Marginal Fisher Analysis (which are denoted as MV-LDA, MV-CCA, MV-LPP and MV-MFA) [27] are compared.

The Cumulative Accuracies Plots (CAP) on each view are shown in Fig. 2 for each compared method. In a CAP, there are K lines. The bottom line in each CAP gives the average accuracy on the first view. While the kth line provide the cumulative accuracy from the first view to the kth view, i.e., the cumulative accuracies equal to the summation of accuracies on all previous views. Therefore, the top line gives the overall accuracies of all views and the gap (marked with different style of shadows) between any adjacent lines describes the classification accuracy of different views. From the results in Fig. 2, RANC achieves best performance on most datasets, and RANC_{ADM} appears more stable than RANC_{PG} and RANC_1. Especially on some text datasets such as News-NG2 or Reuters, all of RANC method are significantly better than other compared methods.

4.4 Disagreement-based Methods Comparison

It is notable that during the training phase, multi-view learning approaches in fusion style and subspace learning style require to repeatedly access to the features from all views, thus those approaches are actually inappropriate for multi-view scenarios with private information channels. RANC and disagreement-based approaches, however, have the ability of boosting performance only with the predictions rather than directly reading the original features in other views.

We compare RANC with multi-view disagreement-based methods. Since most methods of this type are only applicable to two-view scenario, here comparisons on only two-view data are made in this section. Disagreement-based approaches can provide results on each view as well as an ensemble of two view's results. In this experiment, we conduct comparisons with classical Co-Training [5], CoTrade (Confident Co-Training with data editing) [38] and Co-Lap (Co-Regularized Laplacian SVM) [28]. The detailed results of KCCA (Kernel CCA) [13] are also reported. In KCCA, RBF kernel is used with default parameters.

The detailed results are listed in Table 4 where the classical Co-Training is denoted as CoTrain for short. From Table 4, it can be clearly found that RANC series methods achieve the best performance either on view-specific predictions or the final ensemble results. The t-test is also performed at 95% significance level, which shows the significant superiorities of RANC framework.

Although both RANC framework and disagreement-based methods can preserve the privacy of different information channels, the interactions of predictions are required in the training stage for both types of methods, which increases the chance of feature exposure from channels. Therefore this type of interactions should also be restricted during the training. To investigate the number of interactions during training, we conduct more experiments on the convergence of RANC_1 and Co-Training with results shown in Fig. 3. Due to the page limits, Fig. 3 gives the convergence plot on two datasets of two-views, i.e., Course and Texas, in one run. From the Fig. 3, it is notable that RANC_1 converges rapidly on these datasets, i.e., 5 iterations on Course and Texas for the final result.

Table 4: Classification accuracies (average value ± std.) compared with disagreement-based methods and Kernel CCA on two-view datasets. $RANC_{PG}$ and $RANC_{ADM}$ represent for the PGM or ADMM solutions to RANC. $RANC_1$ denotes for the accelerated RANC version. There are three parts separated with horizontal lines, each of which shows classification results on different views or the final integrated classification results. The last three rows on each sub-table list the win/tie/lose counts on the compared datasets with t-test against other methods at significance level 95%. The best performance on each dataset and each view is bolded.

View	dataset	$RANC_{PG}$	$RANC_{ADM}$	$RANC_1$	CoTrain	CoTrade	CoLap	KCCA
View 1	Course	.864±.016	.870±.016	**.878±.014**	.754±.237	.784±.212	.781±.000	.882±.020
	Citeseer	.687±.009	**.695±.010**	.663±.020	.208±.000	.208±.000	.210±.001	.236±.006
	Cora	.702±.013	**.703±.013**	.609±.018	.302±.000	.302±.000	.302±.001	.312±.004
	Cornell	**.724±.057**	.722±.058	.649±.065	.419±.018	.433±.012	.418±.000	.418±.009
	Texas	.731±.052	**.733±.049**	.712±.056	.567±.012	.570±.011	.556±.000	.562±.009
	Washington	**.768±.049**	.741±.051	.741±.039	.446±.013	.477±.012	.473±.000	.486±.019
	Wisonsin	.770±.042	**.813±.031**	.729±.030	.449±.011	.473±.017	.445±.003	.454±.012
	W / T / L	$RANC_{PG}$ vs. others			7 / 0 / 0	7 / 0 / 0	7 / 0 / 0	6 / 0 / 1
	W / T / L	$RANC_{ADM}$ vs. others			7 / 0 / 0	7 / 0 / 0	7 / 0 / 0	6 / 0 / 1
	W / T / L	$RANC_1$ vs. others			7 / 0 / 0	7 / 0 / 0	7 / 0 / 0	6 / 1 / 0
View 2	Course	.889±.014	.891±.014	.890±.015	.850±.028	.832±.122	.880±.015	**.901±.014**
	Citeseer	**.497±.016**	.494±.015	.447±.038	.209±.000	.209±.000	.314±.022	.222±.026
	Cora	**.698±.021**	.683±.021	.645±.018	.301±.001	.300±.001	.326±.005	.322±.034
	Cornell	.377±.066	.378±.067	.387±.068	**.429±.010**	.423±.007	.418±.000	.209±.057
	Texas	**.605±.041**	.603±.042	**.605±.042**	.566±.010	.562±.008	.556±.000	.521±.061
	Washington	.623±.038	**.639±.031**	.638±.032	.480±.007	.480±.007	.478±.008	.411±.085
	Wisonsin	.421±.084	**.492±.054**	.487±.036	.449±.006	.449±.006	.448±.006	.362±.065
	W / T / L	$RANC_{PG}$ vs. others			5 / 1 / 1	5 / 1 / 1	5 / 1 / 1	6 / 0 / 1
	W / T / L	$RANC_{ADM}$ vs. others			6 / 0 / 1	6 / 0 / 1	6 / 0 / 1	6 / 0 / 1
	W / T / L	$RANC_1$ vs. others			6 / 0 / 1	6 / 0 / 1	6 / 0 / 1	6 / 0 / 1
Final	Course	.893±.017	.899±.014	**.901±.017**	.824±.116	.813±.192	.787±.008	.901±.015
	Citeseer	.694±.009	**.704±.010**	.671±.019	.208±.000	.208±.000	.290±.019	.228±.024
	Cora	.784±.013	**.785±.013**	.653±.019	.302±.000	.302±.000	.305±.002	.334±.025
	Cornell	**.730±.055**	.729±.055	.652±.045	.418±.000	.418±.000	.418±.000	.243±.059
	Texas	**.738±.045**	.737±.050	.730±.046	.588±.014	.567±.010	.556±.000	.539±.069
	Washington	**.776±.033**	.745±.050	.736±.041	.473±.000	.473±.000	.473±.000	.507±.068
	Wisonsin	.641±.061	**.819±.031**	.688±.044	.444±.000	.446±.006	.444±.000	.435±.039
	W / T / L	$RANC_{PG}$ vs. others			7 / 0 / 0	7 / 0 / 0	7 / 0 / 0	6 / 0 / 1
	W / T / L	$RANC_{ADM}$ vs. others			7 / 0 / 0	7 / 0 / 0	7 / 0 / 0	6 / 1 / 0
	W / T / L	$RANC_1$ vs. others			7 / 0 / 0	7 / 0 / 0	7 / 0 / 0	6 / 1 / 0

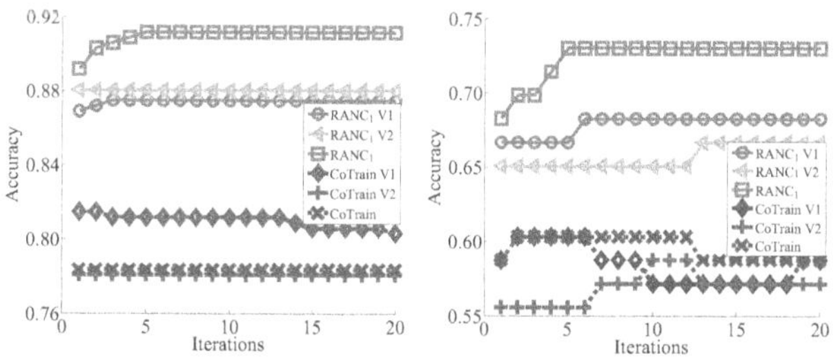

(a) *Course* (b) *Texas*

Figure 3: Classification performance vs. number of interactions. $RANC_1$ V1 and V2 denotes for the changes of classification performance on the first and second view respectively. The same naming scheme is applied to CoTrain.

As to individual views, $RANC_1$ gets converged after 4 iterations on Course and 12 iterations on Texas. While for Co-Training, the results are unstable in iterations. Furthermore, the performance of $RANC_1$ is superior to Co-Training to a great extent. It is noteworthy that in each iteration only predictions rather than raw features are exchanged, which preserves the data privacy.

5. CONCLUSION

This paper presents a novel multi-view privacy-preserving framework RANC (RANk Consistency multi-view learning) to boost performance of the predictor constructed on each view by exploiting the relationship among features from multiple private channels. In this scenario, information of one view cannot be shared with others'. We put forward the *rank consistency* defined on the accumulated prediction matrix (APM) via stacking multi-view predictions, and integrate the rank consistency in a regularizer for improving the classification performance. Properties of RANC suggest employing truncated nuclear norm to control the APM rank into an appropriate range. In our framework, view-specific learner can be enhanced without access to features of other views, therefore the data privacy is well-preserved. Three effective solutions for RANC are provided together including an accelerated variant. Extensive experiments in comparison with the state-of-the-art multi-view approaches are conducted on real datasets, which demonstrates the superiority of RANC in handling multi-view data. Incorporating with different loss functions in RANC framework will be further investigated, and theoretical studies on effects of RANC in multi-view scenario where feature importance varies will also be carried out in future.

Acknowledgments

The authors want to thank reviewers for helpful comments. This work was supported by 973 Program (2014CB340501) and NSFC (61273301, 61333014).

6. REFERENCES

[1] F. R. Bach, G. R. Lanckriet, and M. I. Jordan. Multiple kernel learning, conic duality, and the smo algorithm. In *Proceedings of the 21st International Conference on Machine Learning*, pages 6–13, Banff, Canada, 2004.

[2] A. Beck and M. Teboulle. A fast iterative shrinkage-thresholding algorithm for linear inverse problems. *SIAM Journal on Imaging Sciences*, 2(1):183–202, 2009.

[3] P. Berkhin. A survey on pagerank computing. *Internet Mathematics*, 2(1):73–120, 2005.

[4] G. Bisson and C. Grimal. Co-clustering of multi-view datasets: A parallelizable approach. In *Proceedings of the IEEE 12th International Conference on Data Mining*, pages 828–833, Brussels, Belgium, 2012.

[5] A. Blum and T. Mitchell. Combining labeled and unlabeled data with co-training. In *Proceedings of the 11th Annual Conference on Computational Learning Theory*, pages 92–100, Madison, WI., 1998.

[6] S. Boyd, N. Parikh, E. Chu, B. Peleato, and J. Eckstein. Distributed optimization and statistical learning via the alternating direction method of multipliers. *Foundations and Trends in Machine Learning*, 3(1):1–122, 2011.

[7] J.-F. Cai, E. J. Candès, and Z. Shen. A singular value thresholding algorithm for matrix completion. *SIAM Journal on Optimization*, 20(4):1956–1982, 2010.

[8] X. Chang, F. Nie, Y. Yang, and H. Huang. A convex formulation for semi-supervised multi-label feature selection. In *Proceedings of the 28th AAAI Conference on Artificial Intelligence*, pages 1171–1177, Quebec, Canada, 2014.

[9] C. Cortes, M. Mohri, and A. Rostamizadeh. Two-stage learning kernel algorithms. In *Proceedings of the 27th International Conference on Machine Learning*, pages 239–246, Haifa, Israel, 2010.

[10] M. Gönen and E. Alpaydin. Localized multiple kernel learning. In *Proceedings of the 25th International Conference on Machine Learning*, pages 352–359, Helsinki, Finland, 2008.

[11] M. Gönen and E. Alpaydın. Multiple kernel learning algorithms. *Journal of Machine Learning Research*, 12:2211–2268, 2011.

[12] Z. Harchaoui, M. Douze, M. Paulin, M. Dudik, and J. Malick. Large-scale image classification with trace-norm regularization. In *Proceedings of the IEEE Computer Society Conference on Computer Vision and Pattern Recognition*, pages 3386–3393, Providence, RI., 2012.

[13] D. Hardoon, S. Szedmak, and J. Shawe-Taylor. Canonical correlation analysis: An overview with application to learning methods. *Neural Computation*, 16(12):2639–2664, 2004.

[14] B. He, M. Tao, and X. Yuan. A splitting method for separable convex programming. *IMA Journal of Numerical Analysis*, 35(1):394–426, 2015.

[15] Y. Hu, D. Zhang, J. Ye, X. Li, and X. He. Fast and accurate matrix completion via truncated nuclear norm regularization. *IEEE Transactions on Pattern Analysis and Machine Intelligence*, 35(9):2117–2130, 2013.

[16] S. Ji and J. Ye. An accelerated gradient method for trace norm minimization. In *Proceedings of the 26th International Conference on Machine Learning*, pages 457–464, Montreal, Canada, 2009.

[17] X. Jin, F. Zhuang, H. Xiong, C. Du, P. Luo, and Q. He. Multi-task multi-view learning for heterogeneous tasks. In *Proceedings of the 23rd ACM International Conference on Information and Knowledge Management*, pages 441–450, Shanghai, China, 2014.

[18] M. Kan, S. Shan, H. Zhang, S. Lao, and X. Chen. Multi-view discriminant analysis. In *Proceedings of the 12th European Conference on Computer Vision*, pages 808–821, Florence, Italy, 2012.

[19] M. Kloft, U. Brefeld, S. Sonnenburg, and A. Zien. Non-sparse regularization and efficient training with multiple kernels. *arxiv preprint arXiv:1003.0079*, 2010.

[20] N. Kushmerick. Learning to remove internet advertisements. In *Proceedings of the 3rd Annual Conference on Autonomous Agents*, pages 175–181, Seattle, WA., 1999.

[21] X. Li, J. Gao, H. Li, L. Yang, and R. K. Srihari. A multimodal framework for unsupervised feature fusion. In *Proceedings of the 22nd ACM International Conference on Information and Knowledge Management*, pages 897–902, Burlingame, CA., 2013.

[22] J. Liu, S. Ji, and J. Ye. Multi-task feature learning via efficient l2,1-norm minimization. In *Proceedings of the 25th conference on Uncertainty in Artificial Intelligence*, pages 339–348, Montreal, Canada, 2009.

[23] F. Nie, J. Yuan, and H. Huang. Optimal mean robust principal component analysis. In *Proceedings of the 31st International Conference on Machine Learning*, pages 1062–1070, Beijing, China, 2014.

[24] M. Qian and C. Zhai. Unsupervised feature selection for multi-view clustering on text-image web news data. In *Proceedings of the 23rd ACM International Conference on Information and Knowledge Management*, pages 1963–1966, Shanghai, China, 2014.

[25] A. Rakotomamonjy, F. Bach, S. Canu, and Y. Grandvalet. SimpleMKL. *Journal of Machine Learning Research*, 9:2491–2521, 2008.

[26] P. Sen, G. M. Namata, M. Bilgic, L. Getoor, B. Gallagher, and T. Eliassi-Rad. Collective classification in network data. *AI Magazine*, 29(3):93–106, 2008.

[27] A. Sharma, A. Kumar, H. Daume, and D. W. Jacobs. Generalized multiview analysis: A discriminative latent space. In *Proceedings of the IEEE Computer Society Conference on Computer Vision and Pattern Recognition*, pages 2160–2167, Providence, RI., 2012.

[28] V. Sindhwani, P. Niyogi, and M. Belkin. A co-regularization approach to semi-supervised learning with multiple views. In *Proceedings of ICML workshop on Learning With Multiple Views*, pages 74–79, Bonn, Germany, 2005.

[29] M. Tao and X. Yuan. Recovering low-rank and sparse components of matrices from incomplete and noisy observations. *SIAM Journal on Optimization*, 21(1):57–81, 2011.

[30] H. Wang, F. Nie, and H. Huang. Multi-view clustering and feature learning via structured sparsity. In *Proceedings of the 30th International Conference on Machine Learning*, pages 352–360, Atlanta, GA., 2013.

[31] W. Wang and Z.-H. Zhou. Multi-view active learning in the non-realizable case. In *Advances in Neural Information Processing Systems 23*, pages 2388–2396. Cambridge, MA.: MIT Press, 2010.

[32] W. Wang and Z.-H. Zhou. A new analysis of co-training. In *Proceedings of the 27th International Conference on Machine Learning*, pages 1135–1142, Haifa, Israel, 2010.

[33] W. Wang and Z.-H. Zhou. Co-training with insufficient views. In *Proceedings of the 5th Asian Conference on Machine Learning*, pages 467–482, Canberra, Australia, 2013.

[34] C. Xu, D. Tao, and C. Xu. A survey on multi-view learning. *arXiv preprint arXiv:1304.5634*, 2013.

[35] Y. Yang, C. Lan, X. Li, B. Luo, and J. Huan. Automatic social circle detection using multi-view clustering. In *Proceedings of the 23rd ACM International Conference on Information and Knowledge Management*, pages 1019–1028, Shanghai, China, 2014.

[36] G. Ye, D. Liu, I.-H. Jhuo, and S.-F. Chang. Robust late fusion with rank minimization. In *Proceedings of the IEEE Computer Society Conference on Computer Vision and Pattern Recognition*, pages 3021–3028, Providence, RI., 2012.

[37] D. Zhai, H. Chang, S. Shan, X. Chen, and W. Gao. Multiview metric learning with global consistency and local smoothness. *ACM Transactions on Intelligent Systems and Technology*, 3(3):Article 53, 2012.

[38] M.-L. Zhang and Z.-H. Zhou. Cotrade: Confident co-training with data editing. *IEEE Transactions on Systems, Man, and Cybernetics, Part B: Cybernetics*, 41(6):1612–1626, 2011.

[39] Z.-H. Zhou and M. Li. Semi-supervised learning by disagreement. *Knowledge and Information Systems*, 24(3):415–439, 2010.

[40] Z.-H. Zhou, D.-C. Zhan, and Q. Yang. Semi-supervised learning with very few labeled training examples. In *Proceedings of the 22nd AAAI conference on Artificial Intelligence*, pages 675–680, Vancouver, Canada, 2007.

Differentially Private Histogram Publication For Dynamic Datasets: An Adaptive Sampling Approach

Haoran Li
Emory University
Atlanta, GA
hli57@emory.edu

Li Xiong
Emory University
Atlanta, GA
lxiong@emory.edu

Xiaoqian Jiang
University of California, San Diego
La Jolla, CA
x1jiang@ucsd.edu

Jinfei Liu
Emory University
Atlanta, GA
jinfei.liu@emory.edu

ABSTRACT

Differential privacy has recently become a de facto standard for private statistical data release. Many algorithms have been proposed to generate differentially private histograms or synthetic data. However, most of them focus on "one-time" release of a static dataset and do not adequately address the increasing need of releasing series of dynamic datasets in real time. A straightforward application of existing histogram methods on each snapshot of such dynamic datasets will incur high accumulated error due to the composibility of differential privacy and correlations or overlapping users between the snapshots. In this paper, we address the problem of releasing series of dynamic datasets in real time with differential privacy, using a novel adaptive distance-based sampling approach. Our first method, DSFT, uses a fixed distance threshold and releases a differentially private histogram only when the current snapshot is sufficiently different from the previous one, i.e., with a distance greater than a predefined threshold. Our second method, DSAT, further improves DSFT and uses a dynamic threshold adaptively adjusted by a feedback control mechanism to capture the data dynamics. Extensive experiments on real and synthetic datasets demonstrate that our approach achieves better utility than baseline methods and existing state-of-the-art methods.

Categories and Subject Descriptors

H.2.7 [**Database Administration**]: [Security, integrity, and protection]; H.2.8DatabaseApplications[Data mining]

General Terms

Theory, Performance, Experimentation

Keywords

Differential privacy; adaptive sampling; dynamic dataset release

Permission to make digital or hard copies of all or part of this work for personal or classroom use is granted without fee provided that copies are not made or distributed for profit or commercial advantage and that copies bear this notice and the full citation on the first page. Copyrights for components of this work owned by others than ACM must be honored. Abstracting with credit is permitted. To copy otherwise, or republish, to post on servers or to redistribute to lists, requires prior specific permission and/or a fee. Request permissions from Permissions@acm.org.

CIKM'15, October 19-23, 2015, Melbourne, VIC, Australia.

© 2015 ACM. ISBN 978-1-4503-3794-6/15/10...$15.00.

DOI: http://dx.doi.org/10.1145/2806416.2806452.

1. INTRODUCTION

Sharing dynamic private data while providing privacy guarantee enables many important data mining and knowledge discovery applications. Consider the examples below:

Medical research: A hospital gathers data from individual patients every day. The dynamic datasets, e.g. the daily datasets of individual patients with fevers, coughs, and different demographic attributes can be shared with researchers for cohort discovery, medical research, and seasonal epidemic outbreak monitoring.

Traffic Monitoring: A GPS service provider gathers data from individual users about their locations, speeds, mobility, etc. The dynamic datasets, e.g., the numbers of users at different regions during each time period, can be mined for commercial interest, such as congestion patterns on the roads.

A common scenario of such applications is that a trusted server gathers data from a large number of individual subscribers. The aggregated data can be then continuously shared with other untrusted entities for various purposes. The trusted server, i.e. publisher, therefore must ensure that releasing the data does not compromise the privacy of any individual who contributed data. The goal of our work is to enable publishers to share a series of dynamic private datasets over individual users while guaranteeing their privacy.

The current state-of-the-art standard for privacy preserving data publishing is differential privacy [9, 27], which requires that the output released by a data provider be perturbed by a randomized algorithm $\mathcal{A}$, so that the output of $\mathcal{A}$ remains roughly the same even if any individual tuple in the input data is arbitrarily modified. Given the output of $\mathcal{A}$, an adversary will not be able to infer much about any individual tuple in the input, and thus privacy is protected.

Most existing works on differentially private data release focus on "one-time" release of static data (e.g. [20, 29, 26, 7, 17], etc). In this paper, we study the problem of releasing histograms for dynamic datasets while guaranteeing user-level differential privacy, i.e., protecting the presence of a user in the entire series of dynamic datasets. In the worst case, a user may be present in all datasets in the series. A straight-forward application of the standard differential privacy mechanism or existing histogram method to each snapshot of the dataset will lead to a very high perturbation error $O(N)$ in the order of the number of datasets or snapshots N in the series, due to the composition theorem [22].

A set of related works have studied the problem of releasing aggregate time series and stream statistics. The works in [12, 6] proposed differentially private continual counters over a binary stream. However, both works adopt an event-level differential privacy, which protects the presence of an individual event, i.e. a user's contribution to the data stream at a single time point, rather than her presence or contribution to the entire series. The works in [25, 13, 14] studied the problem of releasing aggregate time-series with user-level differential privacy. Both works consider temporal correlations of the time-series. The paper [25] uses a Discrete Fourier Transform approach and is not applicable to real-time applications when data needs to be released at each time point. Other works [13, 14] take a model based approach which assumes original data is generated by an underlying process and uses the model based prediction to improve the accuracy of the released data. The limitation is that the model needs to be assumed or learned from public data with similar patterns and the method may not be effective when the real data deviates from the model.

The recent work [18] studies the problem similar to ours and represents the state-of-the-art. It proposed a novel w-event privacy framework by combining user-level and event-level privacy, which essentially guarantees user-level privacy within any window of w timestamps. When w is set to the number of time points in the series of data, or infinity for infinite data streams, it converges to user-level privacy. In addition, it proposed a sampling approach with various privacy budget allocation schemes to release data. However, in their schemes, privacy budgets may be exhausted prematurely or not fully utilized, still leading to suboptimal utility of the released data.

Our contributions. In this paper, we present a novel and principled adaptive distance-based sampling approach for releasing multiple histograms for a series of dynamic datasets in real time. We summarize the contributions and features of our approach below.

1). We propose a distance-based sampling approach to address the dynamics of evolving datasets under user-level differential privacy. Instead of generating a differentially private (DP) histogram at each time stamp, we only compute new histograms when the update is significant, i.e., the distance between the current dataset and the latest released dataset is higher than a threshold. Both the distance computation and threshold comparison are designed to guarantee differential privacy. The key observation is that datasets may be subject to small updates at times. Distance-based sampling allows us to release a new histogram only when the datasets have significant updates, hence saving the privacy budget and reducing the overall error of released histograms. In contrast to [18], we use an explicit threshold to determine the sampling points, inspired by the sparse vector technique [15] originally proposed for releasing DP counts only when the counts are greater than a threshold. The explicit threshold based sampling provides two advantages: 1) we can predefine a threshold based on the expected update rate of the data if there is prior domain knowledge, 2) we can dynamically adjust the threshold in a principled way based on data dynamics. Another important feature of our approach is that it is orthogonal to the histogram method used for each time point, i.e. it can use any of the state-of-the-art static differentially private histogram release method (e.g. [9, 28, 7, 26, 7, 17, 24, 20, 21, 30]) as a black box, which is efficient and effective for generating "one time" histograms.

2). We present two methods for defining the threshold. The first method, DSFT (*Distance*-based *Sampling* with *Fixed Threshold*), uses a predefined threshold T. The second improved method, DSAT (*Distance*-based *Sampling* with *Adaptive Threshold*), applies a feedback control mechanism to adaptively adjust the threshold T. Real world dynamic datasets may exhibit varying update behaviors across different settings. The adaptive threshold mechanism allows us to dynamically adjust the threshold T without having to rely on prior knowledge to tune the threshold. We use a PID (Proportional, Integral, and Derivative) controller [2] to detect the dynamics and adaptively adjust the threshold such that the privacy budget is not depleted prematurely due to high update and sampling rates or insufficiently utilized due to low update and sampling rates.

3). We present formal analysis of differential privacy guarantees, complexity, and utility for DSFT and DSAT. In our approach, each released DP histogram has either a perturbation error $O(C)$ at sampling points, where C is the maximum number of released DP histograms ($C << N$) or an update error with an upper bound (see Section 6). We also show a formal analysis of how to select optimal algorithmic parameters given a required utility guarantee.

4). In addition to standard user-level differential privacy, we further extend our methods under the framework of w-event privacy [18], so it can work with infinite series of evolving datasets.

5). Finally, we present extensive experiments using both synthetic and real datasets. Experiment results demonstrate that our methods significantly outperform the baseline approaches and existing state-of-the-art techniques [18].

We state the problem setting of releasing dynamic datasets under differential privacy in Section 3 and introduce w-event privacy and existing state-of-the-art solutions. We present our methods DSFT and DSAT while provide formal privacy analysis in Section 4, then follow by the utility analysis in Section 5. We extend our techniques to w-event privacy framework in Section 6. We include detailed experimental evaluation of our algorithms in Section 7 and conclude in Section 8.

2. RELATED WORK

Several mechanisms (e.g. [12, 6], etc) focus on event-level privacy in releasing counters, i.e. in publishing the number of event occurrences at every time point since the commencement of the system. These mechanisms consider the data stream as a bit string and at each time point they release the number of 1's seen so far. A set of related work focus on releasing aggregate time series or stream statistics under differential privacy as we discussed earlier [25, 13, 14]. The work in [25, 13] releases aggregate time-series with user-level differential privacy. Both works have some limitations as we discussed earlier. [31] releases dynamic transaction data under user-level privacy, and set an upper bound to limit the maximum number of updates to handle infinite updates. But it can only handle insertions updates.

The most recent work that is closely related to our work is Kellaris et al. [18] which deals with differentially private release of events or histograms for infinite stream. It proposes a w-event privacy framework by combining user-level and event-level privacy, which protects any event sequence occurring within any window of w timestamps. It is event-privacy with w = 1 and converges to user- level privacy with w = infinity. They also proposed two mechanisms, Budget Distribution (BD) and Budget Absorption (BA), to allocate the budget within one w-timestamp window. The key difference between our work and [18] is that our methods detect the data dynamics and adaptively adjust the distance threshold for sampling such that the privacy budget is not depleted prematurely due to high update and sampling rates or insufficiently utilized due to low update and sampling rates. In [18], privacy budgets may be depleted prematurely, especially when w is very large, or not fully utilized during the w timestamps. In addition, our method is independent of the histogram method used for each time point and can utilize any state-of-the-art histogram methods designed for static data release as a blackbox. In our experiments, we compare our methods with BD and BA in [18], since they represent the state-of-the-art and have been shown to perform better than other existing work.

Our distance threshold based sampling builds on top of the sparse vector technique [15] originally proposed for releasing differentially private counts only when the counts are greater than a threshold. The sparse vector technique has also been used in [19] for releasing top-k frequent itemsets given a static transaction dataset and a threshold derived from the kth frequent itemsets. In our work, we use the sparse vector technique in a novel way to enable differentially private distance based sampling for releasing dynamic datasets while adaptively adjusting the distance threshold.

3. PRELIMINARIES

In this section, we formally define the problem of releasing series of real-time dynamic histograms or datasets and introduce definitions on user-level differential privacy and w-event privacy. We summarize all frequently used notations in Table 1.

Table 1: Frequently used notations

Notation	Discription
$\mathbf{D}$	A series of original dynamic datasets
$\tilde{\mathbf{D}}$	A set of released DP datasets for $\mathbf{D}$
D_i or $\tilde{D}_i$	Snapshot of $\mathbf{D}$ or $\tilde{\mathbf{D}}$ at time point t_i
$\mathbf{H}$	A series of original dynamic histograms
$\tilde{\mathbf{H}}$	A set of released DP histograms for $\mathbf{H}$
H_i or $\tilde{H}_i$	Snapshot of $\mathbf{H}$ or $\tilde{\mathbf{H}}$ at time point t_i
N	Number of time points
C	Cutoff point (i.e. the upper bound of the number of released DP datasets)
U	Domain universe or number of histogram bins
ϵ	Overall privacy budget
ϵ_1	Privacy budget for the decision step
ϵ_2	Privacy budget for the sampling step
$d(D_i, \tilde{D}_j)$	The distance between D_i and $\tilde{D}_j$
Δ	The sensitivity of L_1 distance

3.1 Problem definition

Let N denote the total number of time points. Let $\mathbf{D}$ denote a series of original dynamic datasets and D_i be a dataset snapshot at time stamp t_i. We assume all snapshots have the same domain universe U, the product of domains of all attributes. For every t_i, we are to release a private dataset $\tilde{D}_i$. Over the N time stamps, the series of privately released dynamic datasets $\tilde{\mathbf{D}} = \{\tilde{D}_i : 1 \leq i \leq N\}$ should guarantee user-level ϵ-differential privacy.

In this paper, we call $\mathbf{H}$ as a series of original dynamic histograms (corresponding to $\mathbf{D}$) with H_i as a snapshot at t_i, and $\tilde{\mathbf{H}}$ as a series of released private dynamic histograms with $\tilde{H}_i$ as a private snapshot at t_i. Since a dataset can be transformed to a histogram, and a synthetic dataset can be constructed from a histogram, $\mathbf{D}$ and $\mathbf{H}$ are interchangeable in this paper.

3.2 Differential Privacy

Intuitively, a randomized mechanism $\mathcal{A}$ is differentially private if its outcome is not significantly affected by the removal or addition of any record. ϵ-differential privacy is formally defined as $Pr[\mathcal{A}(D) \in \mathcal{O}] \leq e^{\epsilon} Pr[\mathcal{A}(D') \in \mathcal{O}]$, where $\mathcal{O}$ is any arbitrary set of possible outputs of $\mathcal{A}$, D and D' are two neighbouring datasets differing in at most one record (i.e. D can be obtained from D' by adding or removing at most one record). In our problem definition, an adversary should learn approximately the same information about any individual user given $\tilde{\mathbf{D}}$, irrespective of its presence or absence in $\mathbf{D}$, and one individual can be present in up to N snapshots in $\mathbf{D}$. Two series of dynamic datasets $\mathbf{D}$ and $\hat{\mathbf{D}}$ are user-level neighbors if one can be obtained by adding or removing one individual (including all its occurrences in the snapshots) from the other. Then user-level ϵ-differential privacy is defined as below.

DEFINITION 3.1 (USER-LEVEL ϵ-DIFFERENTIAL PRIVACY). *Let $\mathcal{A}$ be a randomized mechanism over two user-level neighbors $\mathbf{D}$, and $\hat{\mathbf{D}}$ which differ in one user's presence in the entire series, and let $\mathcal{O}$ be any arbitrary set of possible outputs of $\mathcal{A}$. Algorithm $\mathcal{A}$ satisfies ϵ-differential privacy iff the following holds*

$$Pr[\mathcal{A}(\mathbf{D}) \in \mathcal{O}] \leq e^{\epsilon} Pr[\mathcal{A}(\hat{\mathbf{D}}) \in \mathcal{O}]$$

Laplace Mechanism. Dwork et al. [11] show that ϵ-differential privacy can be achieved by adding i.i.d. Laplace noise to query result $q(D)$, where D is a dataset. Formally, $\tilde{q}(D) = q(D) + (\nu_1, \ldots, \nu_M)'$, where $\nu_i \sim Lap(0, \frac{GS(q)}{\epsilon})$, for $i = 1, \ldots, M$, and M is the dimension of $q(D)$. ν_i follows a Laplace distribution with mean zero and scale $\frac{GS(q)}{\epsilon}$, where $GS(q)$ denotes the global sensitivity [11] of the query q. The global sensitivity is the maximum L_1 distance between the results of q from any two neighbouring datasets D and D', formally defined as $GS(q) = max_{D,D'}||q(D) - q(D')||_1$. In our problem setting, the global sensitivity of any two user-level neighbors $\mathbf{D}$ and $\hat{\mathbf{D}}$ is formally defined as

$$GS(q) = max_{\mathbf{D},\hat{\mathbf{D}}}||q(\mathbf{D}) - q(\hat{\mathbf{D}})||_N.$$

For a sequence of DP mechanisms, the sequential composition theorem [22] guarantees its overall privacy as follows:

THEOREM 3.1 (SEQUENTIAL COMPOSITION [22]). *For a sequence of n mechanisms $M_1, \ldots, M_n$ and each M_i provides ϵ_i-differential privacy, the sequence of M_i will provide $(\sum_{i=1}^{n} \epsilon_i)$ differential privacy.*

Hence, one way to achieve epsilon-differential privacy for the entire series of $\mathbf{D}$ is to apply Laplace mechanism for each D_i with noise $Lap(\frac{N}{\epsilon})$, which leads to $O(N)$ noise.

(α, σ)**-usefulness.** We use a formal utility metric (α, σ)-usefulness [3] to analyze the utility of each snapshot $\tilde{D}_i$ in $\tilde{\mathbf{D}}$.

DEFINITION 3.2 ((α, σ)-USEFULNESS). *A randomized mechanism $\mathbf{A}$ is (α, σ)-useful for queries in class $\mathcal{C}$ if with probability $1 - \sigma$, for every query $Q \in \mathcal{C}$ and a dataset D, $\mathbf{A}(D) = \tilde{D}$, $|Q(D) - Q(\tilde{D})| \leq \alpha$.*

3.3 w-event privacy

W-event privacy [18] is proposed as an extension of differential privacy to address release of infinite streams. It guarantees user-level ϵ-differential privacy for every sub sequence of length w (or over w timestamps) **anywhere** (i.e. it can start from any timestamp) in the original series of dynamic datasets. w-neighboring series of dynamic datasets, $\mathbf{D}_w$, and $\hat{\mathbf{D}}_w$, can be defined as the user-level neighbors under any sub sequence of length w anywhere. w-event privacy can be formally given as below:

DEFINITION 3.3 (W-EVENT ϵ-DIFFERENTIAL PRIVACY). *Let $\mathcal{A}$ be a randomized mechanism over two w-neighboring series of dynamic datasets $\mathbf{D}_w$, and $\hat{\mathbf{D}}_w$, and let $\mathcal{O}$ be any arbitrary set of possible outputs of $\mathcal{A}$. Algorithm $\mathcal{A}$ satisfies w-event ϵ-differential privacy (or, w-event privacy) iff the following holds*

$$Pr[\mathcal{A}(\mathbf{D}_w) \in \mathcal{O}] \leq e^{\epsilon} Pr[\mathcal{A}(\tilde{\mathbf{D}}_w) \in \mathcal{O}]$$

3.4 Baseline and Existing State-of-the-Art Solutions

Given our problem of releasing dynamic datasets under user-level privacy, we review some baseline and existing state-of-the-art methods which will motivate our approach. We will also compare our approach with these methods in the experiment section.

Baseline method. A baseline method is to apply existing "one time" DP histogram release methods to the dataset at every time point. If each released DP histogram preserves $\frac{\epsilon}{N}$-differential privacy, the series of N dynamic datasets guarantee ϵ-differential privacy by sequential composition theorem. This results in an overall noise of $O(N)$ which can be extremely large for large N. In an unbounded setting with N being infinite, this method will not be useful.

Fixed-sampling method. Another potential solution is to release $\frac{N}{I}$ DP histograms periodically given a sampling interval I. Privacy budget $\epsilon/\frac{N}{I}$ is allocated to each dataset at the sampling time point, and the entire private dataset series preserve ϵ-differential privacy. Unfortunately, the pre-defined sampling interval may not accurately capture the update pattern in the original series of dynamic datasets, leading to either high perturbation errors if sampling too frequently or large update errors if sampling not frequently enough or at wrong time points.

Approaches in w-event privacy. [18] proposes a sampling approach which computes the noisy distance between the dataset at the current time point and the original dataset at the latest sampling point, and then compares the noisy distance with the perturbation noise to be added if current dataset is to be released. If the distance is greater than the perturbation noise, a noisy dataset is released at current time stamp. The perturbation noise is determined by their privacy budget allocation schemes, Budget Distribution (BD) and Budget Absorption (BA), that allocate the budget to different timestamps in the w-event window. BD allocates the privacy budget in an exponentially decreasing fashion, in which earlier timestamps obtain exponentially more budget than later ones. BA starts by uniformly distributing the budget to all w timestamps, and accumulates the budget of non-sampling timestamps, which can be allocated later to the sampling timestamps. A main drawback of their approach is that the privacy budget may be exhausted prematurely (sampling too frequently in the beginning) or not fully utilized during all w timestamps (sampling not frequent enough), leading to suboptimal utility of the released data.

4. ADAPTIVE SAMPLING APPROACH

We propose an adaptive distance-based sampling approach to address the dynamics of evolving datasets under user-level differential privacy. Instead of generating a differentially private histogram at each time stamp, we only compute new histograms when the update is significant, i.e., the distance between the current dataset and the latest released dataset is higher than a threshold. The key observation is that datasets may be subject to small updates at times. Distance-based sampling allows us to release a new histogram only when the datasets have significant updates, hence saving the privacy budget and reducing the overall error of released histograms. In contrast to [18], we use an explicit threshold for distance comparison to determine the sampling points, which provides two advantages: 1) we can predefine a threshold based on the expected update rate of the data if there is prior domain knowledge, 2) we can dynamically adjust the threshold in a principled way based on data dynamics.

In this section, we first present the basic method, DSFT, which uses a predefined fixed threshold. This will allow us to analyze its privacy property which also applies to our adaptive method and facilitate our description of the adaptive method. We then introduce our adaptive method, DSAT, which dynamically adjusts the threshold in a principled way to adapt to the data dynamics.

4.1 DSFT

DSFT (Distance-based Sampling with Fixed Threshold) uses a fixed threshold and is divided into two steps at each time point ti: decision and sampling. The decision step computes a noisy distance between the original dataset H_i at current time stamp and the latest released histogram $\tilde{H}_j$ and determines if it is larger than a noisy threshold $\tilde{T}$. If yes, the sampling step generates a new DP histogram $\tilde{H}_i$, otherwise it outputs the previous $\tilde{H}_j$. The overall privacy budget is divided between the decision (ϵ_1) and sampling (ϵ_2) steps which are designed to guarantee differential privacy as we will analyze later.

Algorithm 1 presents DSFT. Line 1-4 initializes the privacy budget for the two steps, computes the noisy threshold, and releases a DP histogram at the first time stamp. Line 5-11 carry out the decision (line 7-8) and sampling (line 8-9) steps for each time point t_i if the number of released histograms is below the cutoff point C, and releases the last histogram with all remaining budget. For the distance $d(H_i, \tilde{H}_j)$, we use the L_1 distance in our implementation and other distance metrics (e.g. KL divergence) can be also used.

Algorithm 1 Distance-based Sampling with Fixed Threshold Algorithm (DSFT)

Input: $\mathbf{D} = \{D_i | 1 \leq i \leq N, i \in Z\}, T, C$ and ϵ.
Output: $\tilde{\mathbf{D}} = \{\tilde{D}_i | 1 \leq i \leq N, i \in Z\}$

1: Set $\epsilon_1 = k\epsilon$, $\epsilon_2 = \epsilon - \epsilon_1$, k is computed due to theorem 5.4;
2: Set $\tilde{T} = T + Lap(\frac{2\Delta}{\epsilon_1})$, Δ is computed due to lemma 4.1;
3: For D_1, release a DP dataset $\tilde{D}_1$ with $\frac{\epsilon_2}{C}$ privacy budget;
4: Set *count* $= 1$, and $j = 1$;
5: **for** each time point t_i with $i \geq 2$ **do**
6: **if** *count* $\geq C$, **then** set $\tilde{D}_i = \tilde{D}_j$ **continue**;
7: Set $\tilde{d}(D_i, \tilde{D}_j) = d(D_i, \tilde{D}_j) + Lap(\frac{2C\Delta}{\epsilon_1})$
8: **if** $\tilde{d}(D_i, \tilde{D}_j) \geq \tilde{T}$, **then** release $\tilde{D}_i$ at t_i with $\frac{\epsilon_2}{C}$ budget, and set *count* $=$ *count* $+ 1$, and $j = i$;
9: **else** use $\tilde{D}_j$ as the release of D_i;
10: **if** $i == N$ and *count* $< C$, **then** release $\tilde{D}_N$ with all remaining privacy budget;
11: **end for**

4.2 DSAT

In DSFT, a prior knowledge on $\mathbf{D}$ is needed for the user to determine an appropriate value T. Suppose there exists an optimal value of T which can enable the algorithm to exactly generate C DP histograms. If the threshold T is higher than the optimal value, there will be remaining privacy budgets that are not utilized. On the contrary, if T is smaller than the optimal value, the privacy budget will be exhausted prematurely, resulting in update errors for remaining time points. In this section, we present DSAT, Distance-based Sampling with Adaptive Threshold, that releases a series of DP dynamic histograms while adaptively adjusting the threshold T_i for each time point, based on data dynamics. With DSAT, we do not have to find an optimal value of T, which may be difficult in practice.

Figure 1 illustrates the framework of DSAT. Intuitively, we wish to have C sampling points over N time points, hence our target sampling rate is $\frac{C}{N}$. Suppose we have released C_i histograms at t_i. If $\frac{C_i}{i} < \frac{C}{N}$, we need to decrease the threshold to allow more sampling time points, and vice versa. For each t_i, we adjust the threshold based on the feedback error between the update ratio $\frac{C_i}{i}$ at t_i and the target ratio $\frac{C}{N}$, which is formally defined below.

DEFINITION 4.1 (FEEDBACK ERROR). *We define the feedback*

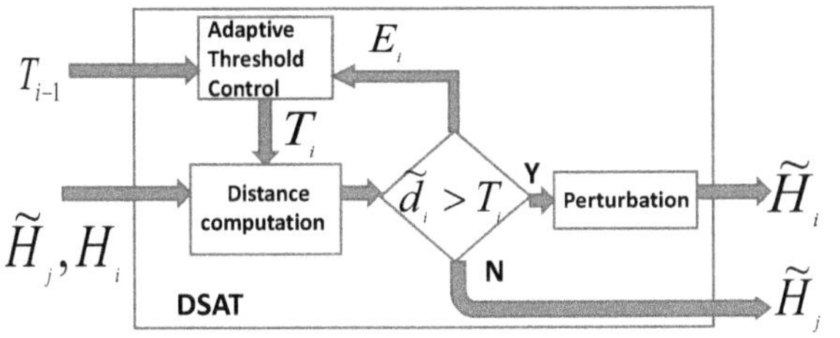

Figure 1: DSAT Framework

error E_i at t_i as follows:

$$E_i = |\frac{C_i}{i} - \frac{C}{N}| \quad (1)$$

where C_i means the number of sampling time points till t_i, C is the cutoff point, and N is the total number of time points.

DSAT adopts a PID (Proportional-Integral-Derivative) [2], a generic control loop feedback mechanism, to dynamically adjust the threshold T over time. Under our problem setting, we redefine the three correcting terms, *Proportional*, *Integral*, and *Derivative*, with the feedback error defined in Equation (1). These three terms are summed to compute the output u_i of PID controller at t_i. The final PID algorithm is defined as:

$$u_i = \underbrace{\theta_P \times e_i}_{proportional \quad term} + \underbrace{\theta_I \times \sum_{\tau=t_i-w+1}^{t_i} e_\tau}_{integral \quad term} + \underbrace{\theta_D \times \frac{e_i - e_j}{t_i - t_j}}_{derivative \quad term} \quad (2)$$

where $\theta_P, \theta_I, \theta_D$ are respectively the proportional gain, the integral gain, and the derivative gain, e_τ is the error at t_τ, t_i is the current time point, t_j is the latest sampling time point.

Proportional term: The first proportional term produces an output value that is proportional to the current error e_i. The proportional term can be amplified by the *proportional gain* θ_P. In our context, the error e_i at the current time point t_i is calculated by

$$e_i = \frac{|E_i - \delta|}{\delta} \quad (3)$$

where E_i is the feedback error defined in equation (1), parameter δ is the set point for E_i. We assume δ is 5% in our empirical studies, i.e. the maximum tolerance for the feedback error is 5%. It can be determined by users according to specific applications. The proportional term is defined as $\theta_P \times e_i$.

Integral term: The integral term is to eliminate the cumulated offset through multiplying the sum of the instantaneous error over time by the integral gain. We define the integral term as $\theta_I \times \sum_{\tau=t_i-w+1}^{t_i} e_\tau$, where θ_I is the *integral gain* and w represents the integral time window denoting how many recent errors are taken.

Derivative term: The derivative term determines the slope of error over time and changes the PID output in proportion to this rate of change via the *derivative gain* θ_D. It is defined as $\theta_D \times \frac{e_i - e_j}{t_i - t_j}$.

Given the PID error u_i, a new threshold T_i produced at the current time point t_i can be determined as follows:

$$T_i = T_{i-1} + sign(\frac{C_i}{i} - \frac{C}{N}) \times \theta \times u_i \quad (4)$$

T_{i-1} is the threshold produced at the previous time point t_{i-1}. Parameter θ determines the magnitude of impact of PID error on the T_i. $sign(.)$ is a sign function, indicating that if the update ratio $\frac{C_i}{i}$ is larger than the target ratio $\frac{C}{N}$, we need to increase T_j to generate less DP histograms and reduce the update ratio, and vice versa. Our DSAT uses only the proportional term in equation 2 in our experiment setting, for simplicity. That means, we set $\theta_P = 1$, $\theta_I = 0$, $\theta_D = 0$, and u_i is the same with e_i as defined in equation (3).

Algorithm 2 Distance-based Sampling with Adaptive Threshold Algorithm (DSAT)

Input: $\mathbf{D} = \{D_i | 1 \le i \le N, i \in Z\}, T, C$ and ϵ.
Output: $\tilde{\mathbf{D}} = \{\tilde{D}_i | 1 \le i \le N, i \in Z\}$
1: Run step 1,2,3,4 in Algorithm 1;
2: Skip the first M timestamps;
3: **for** each time point t_i with $i > M$ **do**
4:   **if** $count \ge C$, **then** set $\tilde{D}_i = \tilde{D}_j$
5:   Set $\tilde{d}(D_i, \tilde{D}_j) = d(D_i, \tilde{D}_j) + Lap(\frac{2C\Delta}{\epsilon_1})$
6:   Set $E_i = |\frac{count}{i} - \frac{C}{N}|$, $e_i = \frac{|E_i - \delta|}{\delta}$, and $u_i = \theta e_i$;
7:   **if** $\frac{count}{t} - \frac{C}{N} \le 0$, **then** set $\tilde{T}_i = max\{0, \tilde{T}_{i-1} - u_i\}$
8:   **else** set $\tilde{T}_i = min\{2, \tilde{T}_{i-1} + u_i\}$;
9:   **if** $\tilde{d}(D_i, \tilde{D}_j) \ge \tilde{T}_i$ **then**
10:     release a DP dataset $\tilde{D}_i$ at t_i with $\frac{\epsilon_2}{C}$ budget, and set $count = count + 1, j = i$;
11:   **else**
12:     release $\tilde{D}_j$;
13:   **end if**
14:   **if** $i == N$ and $count < C$ **then**
15:     release $\tilde{D}_N$ with all remaining privacy budget;
16:   **end if**
17: **end for**

Algorithm 2 presents DSAT. We use T_i to denote the produced threshold at t_i and other notations are the same as Algorithm 1. In Line 1, T_1 is set to be $T + Lap(\frac{\Delta}{\hat{\epsilon}_1})$. Different from Algorithm 1, $\hat{\epsilon}_1$ is a tiny privacy budget because the initial value T_1 is not significant in DSAT. We only need to bound it between 0 and 2, which is the domain of the L1 distance. Line 2 uses $\tilde{D}_1$ for the first M time points where M is a small integer number to allow a burn-in period and enough discrepancy to be accumulated, avoiding frequent updating of T_i during the beginning time periods. M can be user-specified and is not a sensitive parameter besides that it is much smaller than N. The algorithm from Line 3 to Line 12 is similar to Algorithm 1 except Line 6 to Line 8 which use the PID control to adaptively adjust and generate a new threshold T_i.

4.3 Privacy Analysis

Sensitivity analysis of L_1 Distance. In the sensitivity analysis, we use n_p (n_q) to denote the sum of all histogram bin counts of the histograms H_p (H_q). U is the number of histogram bins. Since the L_1 distance of Algorithm 1 and Algorithm 2 is computed using one private histogram and one original histogram, we only need to protect privacy for the original histogram.

LEMMA 4.1. *The sensitivity of L_1 distance $d(\tilde{H}_p, H_q)$ is $\Delta = \frac{2}{n_q - 1}$, where $\tilde{H}_p$ (H_q) is a DP histogram with the sum of all histogram bin counts as n_p (n_q). (Proof omitted due to space limitation)*

Privacy guarantee. Inspired by Hardt et al. [15], we formally provide the proof of privacy guarantee for the decision stage below. The intuition behind theorem 4.1 is that, the noises on both sides of $d(D_i, \tilde{D}_j) + Lap(\frac{2C\Delta}{\epsilon_1}) \ge T + Lap(\frac{2\Delta}{\epsilon_1})$ are necessary for the decision stage to be differentially private, even though T is publicly known.

THEOREM 4.1. *In algorithm 1, the decision stage guarantees ϵ_1-differential privacy.*

PROOF. $\mathbf{D}$ is a series of dynamic datasets with $\mathbf{D} = (D_1, \ldots, D_N)$ over N time points. $\hat{\mathbf{D}}$ is the user-level neighbor of $\mathbf{D}$, which is

$\hat{\mathbf{D}} = (\hat{D}_1, \ldots, \hat{D}_N)$. We say $\hat{\mathbf{D}}$ is the user-level neighbour of $\mathbf{D}$ if we can obtain $\hat{\mathbf{D}}$ by removing or adding only one individual user from $\mathbf{D}$ by the definition in section 3.2.

Let d_i denote $d(D_i, \tilde{D}_j)$ for every $i, j \in [N]([N] = \{1, \ldots, N\})$ beginning with $i = 2$, which is the true distance between D_i ad $\tilde{D}_j$, where $\tilde{D}_j$ is the private dataset released in the latest sampling time point t_j. Let $\tilde{d}_i$ denote $\tilde{d}(D_i, \tilde{D}_j)$, which is the DP L_1 distance.

For all pairs of user-level neighbours $\mathbf{D}$ and $\hat{\mathbf{D}}$, and the corresponding L_1 distance vectors $\mathbf{d} = (d_1, \ldots, d_N)$, we need to prove:

$$\log(\frac{\Pr_{\mathbf{D}}[d = \tilde{d}]}{\Pr_{\hat{\mathbf{D}}}[d = \tilde{d}]}) = \sum_{i=1}^{N} \log(\frac{\Pr_{\mathbf{D}}[d_i = \tilde{d}_i|\tilde{d}_{i-1}]}{\Pr_{\hat{\mathbf{D}}}[d_i = \tilde{d}_i|\tilde{d}_{i-1}]}) \leq \epsilon_1.$$

Because d_i is affected only by d_{i-1} at the previous time point, we have $\Pr_{\mathbf{D}}[d_i = \tilde{d}_i|\tilde{d}_{i-1}] = \Pr_{\hat{\mathbf{D}}}[d_i = \tilde{d}_i|\tilde{d}_{i-1}, \ldots, \tilde{d}_1]$. Let $S = \{i : \tilde{d}_i \geq \tilde{T}\}$ be the set of indices of $\tilde{d}_i$ at all sampling time points, and $S^C = \{i : \tilde{d}_i \leq \tilde{T}\}$ be the set of indices of $\tilde{d}_i$ at all non-sampling time points, we have $\log(\frac{\Pr_{\mathbf{D}}[d=\tilde{d}]}{\Pr_{\hat{\mathbf{D}}}[d=\tilde{d}]}) =$
$\sum_{i \in S} \log(\frac{\Pr_{\mathbf{D}}[d_i=\tilde{d}_i|\tilde{d}_{i-1}]}{\Pr_{\hat{\mathbf{D}}}[d_i=\tilde{d}_i|\tilde{d}_{i-1}]}) + \sum_{i \in S^C} \log(\frac{\Pr_{\mathbf{D}}[d_i=\emptyset|\tilde{d}_{i-1}]}{\Pr_{\hat{\mathbf{D}}}[d_i=\emptyset|\tilde{d}_{i-1}]})$.

Now we need to bound the two sums respectively. For the first sum, we can see that (1) independent Laplace noise with $Lap(\frac{2C\Delta}{\epsilon_1})$ is added to each distance with $\frac{\epsilon_1}{2C}$ differential privacy, (2) the computation of each L_1 distance needs to access the original histogram once, and (3) $|S| \leq C$ due to the algorithm, so we can obtain the following equation due to sequential composition theorem:

$$\sum_{i \in S} \log(\frac{\Pr_{\mathbf{D}}[d_i = \tilde{d}_i|\tilde{d}_{i-1}]}{\Pr_{\hat{\mathbf{D}}}[d_i = \tilde{d}_i|\tilde{d}_{i-1}]}) = \sum_{i \in S} \log(\frac{\Pr_{\mathbf{D}}[\nu_i = \tilde{d}_i - d_i]}{\Pr_{\hat{\mathbf{D}}}[\nu_i = \tilde{d}_i - d_i]}) \leq \frac{\epsilon_1}{2}$$

For the second sum, let $A_Z(\mathbf{D})$ be the set of all values of the noise variables $(\nu_1, \ldots, \nu_{N-1})$ that cause $\tilde{d}_i \leq \tilde{T}$ for all $i \in S^C$, when the mechanism runs on $\mathbf{D}$, conditioning on $\tilde{T} = Z$ and $d_i = \tilde{d}_i$ for all $i \in S$. Since from $\mathbf{D}$ to $\hat{\mathbf{D}}$, all distances may be increased by at most Δ (i.e. $\Delta = \frac{2}{n-1}$ for the L_1 distance due to lemma 4.1), which will cause each distance to remain less than $\tilde{T}$ if we increase $\tilde{T}$ by Δ. But the distances larger than $\tilde{T}$ may become less than $\tilde{T} + \Delta$, so $A_{\tilde{T}+\Delta}(\hat{\mathbf{D}}) \subseteq A_{\tilde{T}}(\mathbf{D}) \subseteq A_{\tilde{T}+\Delta}(\hat{\mathbf{D}})$. Thus, we have: $\frac{\Pr_{\mathbf{D}}\{\tilde{T}=T+\nu_1\}}{\Pr_{\hat{\mathbf{D}}}\{\tilde{T}=T+\Delta+\nu_2\}} \leq \exp(\frac{\epsilon_1}{2})$. Therefore, let $Z_1 = T + \nu_1$ and $Z_2 = T + \Delta + \nu_2$, we have:

$$\begin{aligned}
&\prod_{i \in N^C} \Pr_{\mathbf{D}}(d_i = \emptyset|\tilde{d}_{i-1}) \\
&= \int_{-\infty}^{\infty} \Pr(\hat{d} = Z_1) \Pr((\nu_1, \ldots, \nu_k) \in A_Z(D))dZ \\
&\leq \exp(\frac{\epsilon_1}{2}) \int_{-\infty}^{\infty} \Pr(\tilde{T} = Z_1) \Pr((\nu_1, \ldots, \nu_k) \in A_{Z_1}(D))dZ \\
&\leq \exp(\frac{\epsilon_1}{2}) \int_{-\infty}^{\infty} \Pr(\hat{T} = Z_2) \Pr((\nu_1, \ldots, \nu_k) \in A_{Z_2}(D'))dZ \\
&= \exp(\frac{\epsilon_1}{2}) \int_{-\infty}^{\infty} \Pr(\tilde{T} = Z_1) Pr((\nu_1, \ldots, \nu_k) \in A_{Z_1}(D'))dZ \\
&= \exp(\frac{\epsilon_1}{2}) \prod_{i \in N^C} \Pr_{\hat{\mathbf{D}}}(d_i = \emptyset|\tilde{d}_{i-1})
\end{aligned}$$

Therefore, we have $\frac{\prod_{i \in N^C} \Pr_{\mathbf{D}}(d_i=\emptyset|\tilde{d}_{i-1})}{\prod_{i \in N^C} \Pr_{\hat{\mathbf{D}}}(d_i=\emptyset|\tilde{d}_{i-1})} \leq \frac{\epsilon_1}{2}$ □

THEOREM 4.2. *Algorithm 1 and 2 preserve ϵ-differential privacy.*

PROOF. For Algorithm 1, the decision stage preserves ϵ_1-differential privacy due to theorem 4.1. Since releasing at most C DP histograms guarantees ϵ_2-differential privacy, algorithm 1 preserves $\epsilon_1 + \epsilon_2 = \epsilon$-differential privacy due to theorem 3.1. For Algorithm 2, since adaptively adjusting threshold (Line 6 to Line 8) uses no raw data, it does not influence differential privacy guarantee, thus Algorithm 2 guarantees ϵ-differential privacy. □

5. UTILITY ANALYSIS

We analyze the utility of DSFT and DSAT using (α, σ)-usefulness in definition 3.2 and show the conclusions in theorem 5.1 and 5.2. Since we assume LPA as the DP histogram release method, the conclusions can be heuristically used as the upper bound when new methods better than LPA are employed. Here $d(H_i, H_j)$ denotes L_1 distance between H_i and H_j.

Error quantification of DSFT. The utility of released datasets at sampling time points are analyzed based on lemma 5.1. The error of datasets at non-sampling time points are obtained via the error bound of the decision stage in lemma 5.2.

LEMMA 5.1. *(Sum of Independent Laplace variables [6]) Suppose that $X_1, \ldots, X_n$ are independent Laplace random variables, with each X_i following a $Lap(b_i)$ distribution. Denote $Z = \sum_{i=1}^{n} X_i$ and $b_M = max_i b_i$. Then for all $\gamma \geq \sqrt{\sum_{i=1}^{n} b_i^2}$ and $0 < \lambda < \frac{2\sqrt{2}\gamma^2}{b_M}$, we have $Pr[Z > \lambda] \leq exp(-\frac{\lambda^2}{8\gamma^2})$.*

LEMMA 5.2. *In Algorithm 1, for any $0 < \sigma < 1$, we can obtain*

$$Pr\{d(H_i, \tilde{H}_j) \leq T + \frac{4\sqrt{2}\Delta(1 - log\sigma)}{\epsilon_1}\} \geq 1 - \sigma \quad (5)$$

This means, with probability greater than $1 - \sigma$, we can set t_i as non-sampling time points. (Proof omitted due to space limitation.)

THEOREM 5.1. *For a range count query covering m histogram bins on $\tilde{H}_k$, and $0 < \sigma < 1$, if k is a sampling time point, we have that $Pr\{|A_k - \tilde{A}_k| \leq -\frac{2\sqrt{2}Clog(\frac{\sigma}{2})}{n\epsilon_2}\} \geq 1 - \sigma$, and if k is a non-sampling time point, we have that $Pr\{|A_k - \tilde{A}_k| \leq T + \frac{4\sqrt{2}\Delta[1-log(1-\sigma)]}{\epsilon_1} - \frac{2\sqrt{2}Clog(\frac{\sigma}{2})}{\epsilon_2}\} \geq (1 - \sigma)^2$, where A_k and $\tilde{A}_k$ are the query answers on the original histogram H_k and the DP histogram $\tilde{H}_k$. Therefore, each released histogram $\tilde{H}_k$ of our algorithms maintains (α, σ)-usefulness for range count queries.*

Error quantification of DSAT. We analyze the utility of DSAT based on theorem 5.2, and give the conclusion as below.

THEOREM 5.2. *For a range count query covering m histogram bins on $\tilde{H}_k$, and $0 < \sigma < 1$, if k is a sampling time point, the conclusion is the same as theorem 5.1 and if k is a non-sampling time point, we have $Pr\{|A_k - \tilde{A}_k| \leq T_k + \sum_{i=1}^{k} I_i u_i - \frac{2\sqrt{2}Clog(\frac{\sigma}{2})}{n\epsilon_2}\} \geq (1 - \sigma)^2$, where I_i is a value being 1 or -1, and dependent on the data, and u_i is defined in equation (2). Therefore, each released histogram $\tilde{H}_k$ of our algorithms maintains (α, σ)-usefulness for range count queries. (The conclusion can be obtained via equation (5) and we omitted the full proof.)*

Lower bound of the data cardinality. Since the injected noise in the decision stage is related with data cardinality, we analyze the lower bound of data cardinality to guarantee a relatively small injected noise compared to the true L_1 distance. This lower bound can be used to maintain a high accuracy at the decision stage.

THEOREM 5.3. *In DSFT, in order to satisfy (α, σ)-usefulness and guarantee the utility of the decision stage, it requires that $n \geq \frac{16\sqrt{2}\alpha(1-log(1-\sigma))}{T\epsilon_1}$, where σ is defined in lemma 5.2. (Proof can be deducted from lemma 5.2)*

Select the value of k in DSFT. Our algorithm requires ϵ to be divided between ϵ_1 and ϵ_2 with $\epsilon_1 = k\epsilon$. We now analyze how to select k. Assume $\mathbf{H} = (H_1, \ldots, H_N)$ corresponds to $\mathbf{D}$. For each i, we analyze the incurred noise variance of L_1 distance between H_i and $\tilde{H}_i$ when i is (1) a sampling time point and (2) a non-sampling time point.

LEMMA 5.3. *The noise variance of the L_1 distance between H_j and $\tilde{H}_j$, is $\hat{\sigma}_1 = O(\frac{UC^2}{n^2\epsilon_2^2})$ for a sampling time point, and $\hat{\sigma}_2 = O(\frac{8\Delta^2}{\epsilon_1^2} + \frac{32C^2\Delta^2}{\epsilon_1^2} + \frac{UC^2}{n^2\epsilon_2^2})$ for a non-sampling time point.*

PROOF. We skip this proof due to space limitation. □

THEOREM 5.4. *If we use L_1 distance and LPA, the k value can be obtained as $k = min\{\sqrt[3]{\frac{n^2(8\Delta^2+32C^2\Delta^2)}{UC^2}}, 1 - \frac{C}{N}\}$*

PROOF. Since k is only used when analyzing the distance at non-sampling time points, we can obtain the upper bound of noise variance at a non-sampling time point due to lemma 5.3 with $\epsilon_1 = \frac{k\epsilon}{k+1}$ and $\epsilon_2 = \frac{\epsilon}{k+1}$ by $\hat{\sigma}_2 = \frac{8\Delta^2+32C^2\Delta^2}{\epsilon^2}\frac{(k+1)^2}{k^2} + \frac{UC^2}{n^2\epsilon^2}(k+1)^2$. Let $f(k) = \hat{\sigma}_2$, then the first-order derivative of $f(k)$ is as follows: $\nabla_k f(k) = -\frac{2(k+1)}{k^3}\frac{8\Delta^2+32C^2\Delta^2}{\epsilon^2} + 2(k+1)\frac{UC^2}{n^2\epsilon^2}$. By setting $\nabla_k f(k) = 0$, we can obtain the value of k as: $k = \sqrt[3]{\frac{(8\Delta^2++32C^2\Delta^2)n^2}{UC^2}}$. Since the second-order derivative of $f(k)$ with respect to k is no less than 0, $k = \sqrt[3]{\frac{(8\Delta^2++32C^2\Delta^2)n^2}{UC^2}}$ is the value of k when $f(k)$ arrives at the minimum. Simultaneously, we must require the privacy budget of each sampling time point to be no less than that of each time point in the baseline method, which leads to $\frac{\epsilon_2}{C} \geq \frac{\epsilon}{N}$, and $k \leq 1 - \frac{C}{N}$. Therefore, we can obtain that $k = min\{\sqrt[3]{\frac{n^2(8\Delta^2+32C^2\Delta^2)}{UC^2}}, 1 - \frac{C}{N}\}$. □

6. EXTENSIONS TO INFINITE STREAMS

DSAT under w-event privacy. Algorithm 3 presents DSAT under w-event privacy. For the first w time points, we run DSAT normally and record the privacy budget $\epsilon_{2,i}$ for every time point i, i.e. $\epsilon_{2,i} = \frac{\epsilon_2}{C}$ if i is a sampling point and $\epsilon_{2,i} = 0$ otherwise. For time points $w+1$ to N, if the remaining privacy budget ϵ_{rm} for the current w-window is larger than zero, we compare the distance between H_i and $\tilde{H}_j$, modify the threshold and release a private histogram when the private distance is larger than the threshold; if no privacy budget is left, we skip the current time point and go to the next one.

Privacy guarantee. The first w time points guarantees ϵ-differential privacy. The condition in Line 4 of Algorithm 3 guarantees that if there is no remaining privacy budget (i.e. $\epsilon_{rm} \leq 0$) for the current w window from time point t_{i-1} to t_{i-w+1}, no new private datasets will be released. Therefore, for any w-length window beginning with any time point, at most ϵ privacy budget will be used. This leads to the conclusion that Algorithm 3 satisfies w-event privacy.

7. EXPERIMENT

We implemented our methods on top of two static histogram methods, LPA in Matlab and PSD [7] in Python. All the experiments are performed on a PC with a 2.9GHz CPU and a 8GB memory. Table 2 summarizes the parameters and their default values in the experiments.

Algorithm 3 DSAT under w-event privacy

Input:
$\mathbf{D} = \{D_i | 1 \leq i \leq N, i \in Z\}$, T, C and ϵ.
Output:
$\tilde{\mathbf{D}} = \{\tilde{D}_i | 1 \leq i \leq N, i \in Z\}$

1: Run DSAT for the first w time points;
2: **for** $i = (w+1)$ to N **do**
3: $\epsilon_{rm} = \epsilon_2 - \sum_{m=i-w+1}^{m=i-1} \epsilon_{2,m}$
4: **if** $\epsilon_{rm} \leq 0$ **then**
5: Set $\tilde{D}_i := D_j$, where j is the time point of last release;
6: **else**
7: Set $count = \frac{\sum_{m=i-w+1}^{m=i-1} \epsilon_{2,m}}{\epsilon_2/C}$
8: Compute $\tilde{d}(D_i, \tilde{D}_j) = d(D_i, \tilde{D}_j) + Lap(\frac{2C\Delta}{\epsilon_1})$;
9: Compute $E_i = |\frac{count}{i} - \frac{C}{w}|$, $e_i = \frac{|E_i - \delta|}{\delta}$, and $u_i = \theta \times e_i$;
10: **if** $\frac{count}{i} - \frac{C}{w} \leq 0$, **then** $\tilde{T}_i = max\{0, T_{i-1} - u_i\}$;
11: **else** set $\tilde{T}_i = min\{2, T_{i-1} + u_i\}$;
12: **if** $\tilde{d}(D_i, \tilde{D}_j) \geq \tilde{T}_i$, **then** set $\epsilon_{2,i} = \epsilon_2/C$, $\tilde{D}_i := D_i + \langle Lap(1/\epsilon_{2,i}) \rangle^U$, and $j = i$;
13: **else** set $\tilde{D}_i := D_j$;
14: **end if**
15: **end for**

Table 2: Experiment Parameters

Parameter	Description	Default value
N	Number of time points	500
d	Number of data dimensions	6
n	Number of tuples in D_i	500K
ϵ	Privacy budget	1.0
C	Cutoff point	$0.01 \times N$
r	Update rate	0.5
δ	Deviation tolerance	0.05
θ	Proportional gain	0.5

7.1 Experiment Setup

Datasets. We conducted our experiments with three datasets: the US census (`http://ipums.org`), the Taxi-Drive trajectory data (`http://research.microsoft.com/apps/`) and the Oldenburg traffic data [5].

The **US census dataset** contains six attributes, *Age*, *Gender*, *Education*, *Health insurance*, *Marital status* and *Income* with 3M tuples and domain sizes of 96, 2, 12, 2, 2, 3. Each tuple represents an individual user. In order to avoid the sparsity of histograms, we convert *Income* into a categorical attribute: values smaller than 0 (mapped to 1), values between 0 and 28K (mapped to 2), and values larger than 28K (mapped to 3). 28K is a median value. Values smaller than 0 means the tuples have ages smaller than 20. The number of histogram bins are the product of the domain sizes of all attributes.

We generate a series of dynamic datasets as follows. D_i is the original dataset at t_i. D_1 has 500K tuples randomly sampled from the original 3M tuples. A public pool is initiated using the remaining tuples. D_i ($i \geq 2$) is obtained by deleting m tuples from D_{i-1} while inserting m tuples randomly selected from the public pool to simulate the user updates. m is sampled from $N(\mu, \sigma^2)$, where μ is $\frac{r \times |D_{i-1}|}{2}$, and σ^2 is set to $100K$. Here, r is the *update rate*, $|D_i|$ is the data cardinality of D_i and datasets at all time points have the same data cardinality. The time points are partitioned into 10 periods with different values of m to simulate varying update patterns. All experiments use US census data by default since we can generate various datasets under different parameter settings.

The **Taxi trajectory dataset** has a one_week trajectories of $10,357$ taxis during the period of Feb. 2 to Feb. 8, 2008 within Beijing. We transfer the time dimension to 168 time points with 24×7. The total number of points in this dataset is about 15 million and the total distance of the trajectories reaches 9 million kilometers. We partition the longitude and latitude into 10×10 grids. We amplify the number of taxis to $110,357$ by sampling dummy points on extremely sparse time points and geographical areas while still keeping the patterns of original data.

We generated **Oldenburg traffic data** with the Brinkhoff generator [5]. The input of the generator is the road map of Oldenburg in Germany, and the output is a set of moving objects on the road network. We created the data set with 1000 discrete timestamps, with 500,000 objects at the beginning. A 2D grid with 1024×1024 cells is used to record the locations of the moving objects.

Comparison. We evaluate the utility of the private DP histograms of dynamic datasets by answering random range count queries. The query accuracy of DSAT is compared with three solutions described in Section 3: the baseline Laplace mechanism, the fixed-sampling method, and the state-of-the-art w-event privacy methods. LPA and PSD [7] are used to generate DP histograms at sampling time points. We note that our proposed sampling framework can utilize any state-of-the-art static histogram method at each sampling point. Here we just use, as an example, the standard LPA method as well as the PSD method [7] which is a state-of-the-art static histogram method that uses spatial partitioning. The goal is to compare our proposed methods and the three solutions. We also include the non-private methods to compare the update errors of DSAT and fixed-sampling.

Metrics. For the US census dataset, we generated random range-count queries with random query predicates on each attribute defined in the SQL format as "Select COUNT(*) from D, Where $A_1 \in I_1$ and $A_2 \in I_2$ and...and $A_m \in I_m$". I_i is a random interval generated from the domain of attribute A_i. For the traffic data, query rectangles with various sizes are randomly generated. In each experiment run, 5000 random queries are generated and the average absolute error over 10 runs is reported, which is defined as $E^a = \frac{1}{M \times N} \sum_{k=1}^{M} \sum_{i=1}^{N} |\tilde{A}_i^k - A_i^k|$, A_i^k is the true answer and $\tilde{A}_i^k$ is the noisy answer. Here we use the range-count query to measure the utility since it composes data histograms, and the range counts can be used for many significant mining tasks, e.g. dynamic stream clustering, outlier detection of time-series data, etc.

7.2 Results on user level privacy

In all experiments, we compare our methods with the baseline and fixed-sampling methods, which are denoted by "baseline" and "fixed" in figures. Unless specified, we use LPA by default as the underlying histogram method for the sampling point. We also use "DSAT-true" and "fixed-true" to denote the non-private versions of DSAT and fixed-sampling.

Absolute error vs. k. Figure 2 investigates how utility changes with various k values, which specify the budget allocation ratio between ϵ_1 and ϵ_2 for the decision and sampling stages respectively. With the value of C being 10, we compute k to be 0.0532 due to theorem 5.4. From Figure 2, we can observe that the empirical result matches the theoretical result well and the utility reaches the optimal value with k between 0.01 and 0.1. The error increases as k becomes larger or smaller than 0.1 or or 0.01, respectively. This is reasonable because larger k may lead to more perturbation error while smaller k values result in more update error.

DSFT and DSAT. In this experiment, we compare our proposed two methods DSFT and DSAT. From figure 3, we can observe that the error of DSFT is very sensitive to the threshold value T. As T

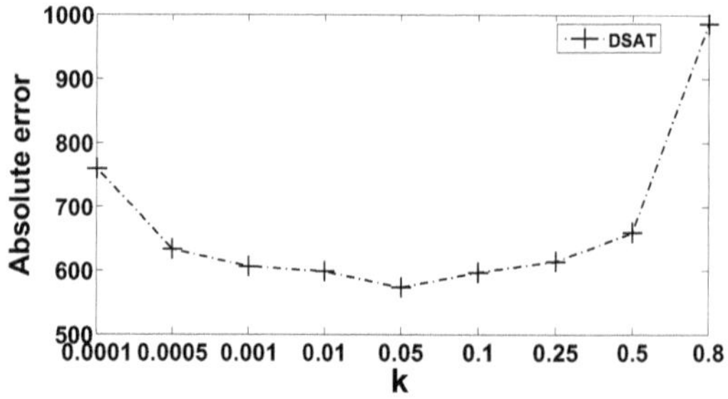

Figure 2: Absolute error vs. k

initially increases, the error decreases thanks to the decreased perturbation error. As T further increases, the error increases back up due to the increased sampling error which becomes the dominant error. Without prior knowledge, it is difficult to determine the optimal T. However, the average absolute error of DSAT is close to the lowest error of DSFT with the optimal threshold T value being around 0.025. Here the initial value of T for DSAT can be arbitrarily selected. Thus, the DSAT method with the PID control can effectively adjust T to an optimal one. In the remaining experiments, we only use DSAT to compare with other methods.

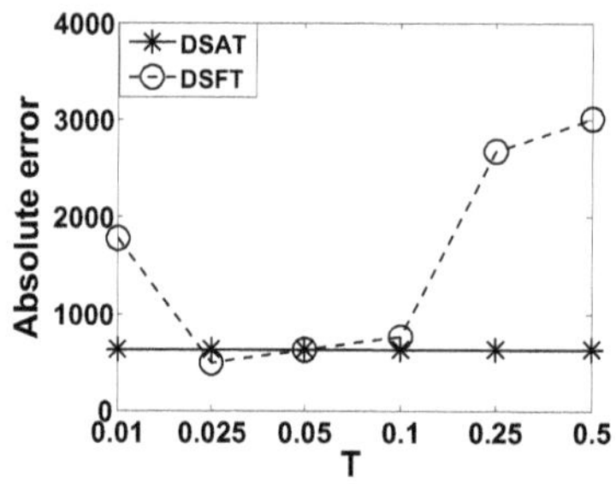

Figure 3: Absolute error vs. threshold value T

Absolute error vs. differential privacy. Figure 4 compares DSAT with other methods under various privacy budgets. The larger the privacy budget is, the closer the query accuracy is to non-private versions. Since the baseline performs one order of magnitude worse than other methods in most experiments, we do not include them for better readability of the graphs. The perturbation errors for fixed-sampling and DSAT are almost similar as the number of released DP histograms are the same. DSAT outperforms fixed-sampling because DSAT has much less update error, which can be seen from the comparison of non-private versions. Figure 4(b) uses the taxi trajectory dataset and Figure 4(c) uses PSD to release DP histograms with 3D US data. We can see that by using PSD, errors are generally improved compared to the ones using LPA. This further confirms that our methods can take advantage of any state-of-the-art static histogram methods for each sampling point.

Absolute error vs. update rate. We study the impact of the update rate r (defined in section 7.1) on the query accuracy for different methods, as shown in Figure 5. All methods remain stable for various update rates. The DSAT performs better than both non-private and private fixed-sampling methods. This is because the update error of non-private DSAT is much less than non-private fixed-sampling. This further verifies that our DSAT with PID controller succeeds in adaptively adjusting the threshold and the location of the sampling time point, leading to better performance.

Absolute error vs. dimensionality. Figure 6 examines the absolute error with various numbers of dimensions in the US dataset. DSAT again outperforms both non-private and private fixed-sampling

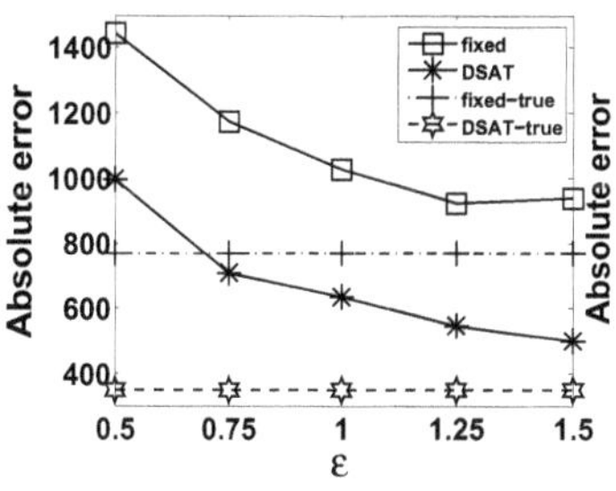

(a) US data

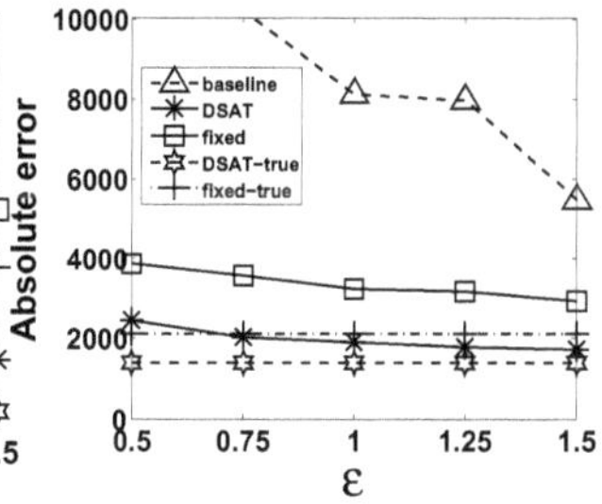

(b) Taxi-drive data

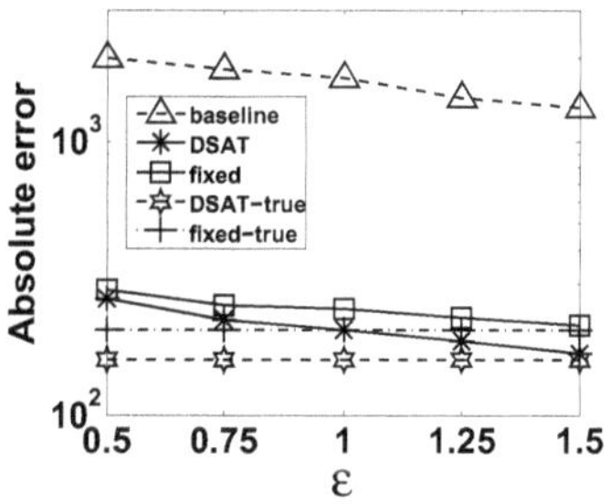

(c) US data (log-scale) with PSD

Figure 4: Accuracy vs. differential privacy budget

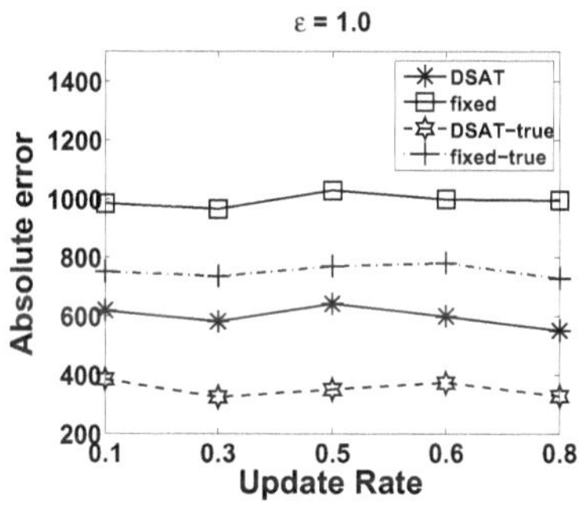

Figure 5: Absolute error vs. update rate

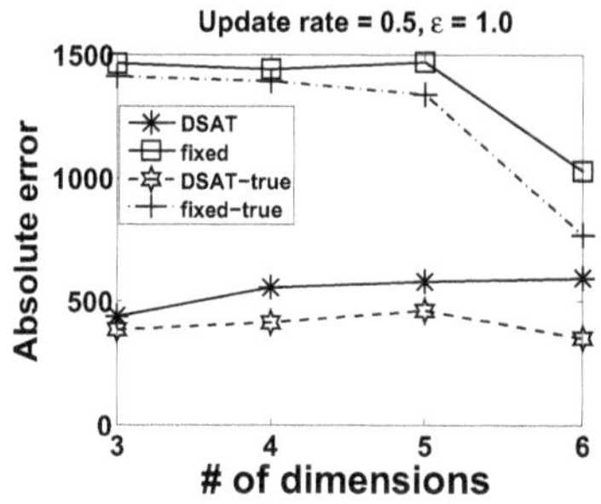

Figure 6: Absolute error vs. # of dimensions

methods with the dimensionality from 3 to 6. One interesting phenomena we observe is that the performances of non-private and private fixed-sampling methods improve sharply after five dimensions. This can be explained by the fact that a higher dimensionality results in a larger number of histogram bins. Given a threshold T, if the L_1 distance between two datasets D_i and D_{i-1} is below T, the previously released histogram will be used which incurs an update error. Given the same L_1 distance between two histograms, a larger number of bins would result in a smaller measured update error since the average difference for each histogram bin is smaller. Hence the fixed sampling methods show a dramatic drop in the error which is dominated by the update error. The DSAT methods are less sensitive to the number of dimensions because they already mitigate the update error by tuning the threshold adaptively. Hence the non-private DSAT shows a slight drop in the update error while the private DSAT shows a slight increase due to the dominating perturbation error.

Query accuracy vs. query range size. We study the impact of the query range size on the query accuracy for different methods. For each query range size, we randomly generated queries such that the product of the query ranges on each dimension equals the given size. Figure 7 presents the impact of various query range sizes on query accuracy in terms of relative error and absolute error. The relative error is defined as $E^r = \frac{1}{M \times N} \sum_{k=1}^{M} \sum_{i=1}^{N} \frac{|\tilde{A}_i^k - A_i^k|}{max(s, A_i^k)}$, where s is the sanity bound to mitigate the effect for $A_i^k = 0$. DSAT outperforms the private fixed-sampling method. The difference of relative errors between all methods is not obvious because of the large data cardinality in the US data. For all methods, the relative error gradually degrades as the query range size increases while the absolute error has the opposite trend. The reason is that when the query size is small, the true answer A_i^k is also small which may incur a small absolute error but large relative error. In this experiment, the sanity bound s is set to 1.

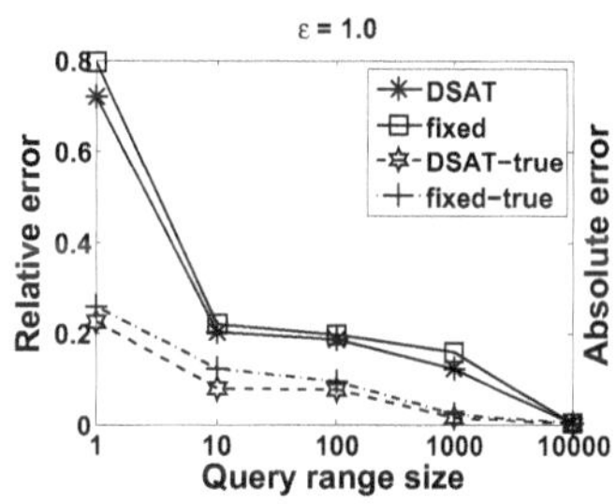

(a) Relative error

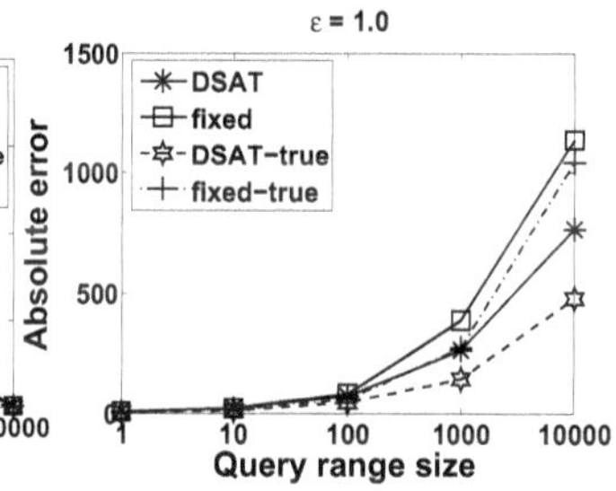

(b) Absolute error

Figure 7: Query accuracy vs. query range size

7.3 Results on w-event privacy

Query accuracy vs. parameter w. We use the Oldenburg traffic data in this experiment, since it contains 1000 timestamps that is sufficient to investigate the impact of w. We compare DSAT with BD and BA in [18] under w-event privacy framework while varying w values. BD and BA are implemented by using column partitioning technique and setting $\epsilon_1 = \frac{\epsilon}{U}$ as recommended in [18]. From figure 8, we can see that the gap between DSAT and BD or BA expands greatly as w increases. This is because our technique adaptively adjusts the threshold and allocates the privacy budget more appropriately. In contrast, BA and BD may not fully utilize or in advance exhaust most budget during w timestamps.

Query accuracy vs. differential privacy. In this experiment, we set w to be 800 using Oldenburg traffic data with 1000 timestamps. Figure 9 compares DSAT with BA and BD under various privacy budgets. We can see that BA degrades dramatically and the gap between BA and DSAT greatly expands as we reduce the privacy budget ϵ. This is because BA starts by uniformly distributing the budget to all w timestamps, and more perturbation error will be incurred when ϵ is small and w is large. Our DSAT performs well since the perturbation error of released datasets depends only on C.

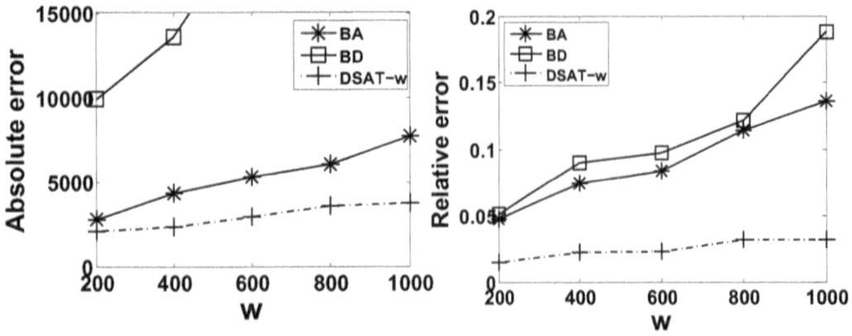

(a) Absolute error (b) Relative error

Figure 8: Query accuracy vs. w

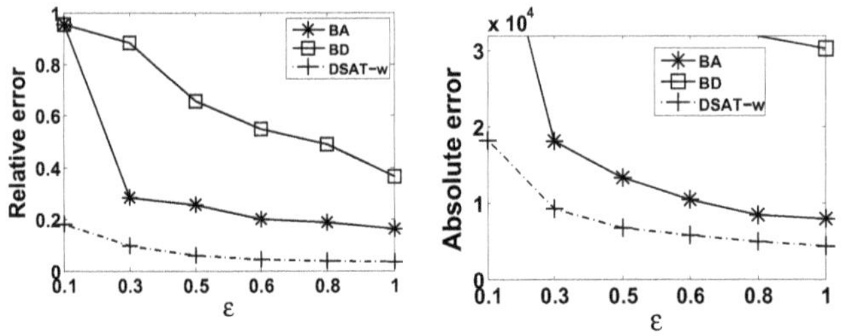

(a) Relative error (b) Absolute error

Figure 9: Query accuracy vs. differential privacy

8. CONCLUSIONS

In this paper, we have proposed an adaptive distance-based sampling approach to address the challenges of releasing a series of differentially private dynamic datasets in real time. With an upper bound to limit the number of DP data releases, our methods incur much smaller errors. We apply an adaptive control mechanism to dynamically adjust the threshold value. We also provide privacy and utility analysis for our method. Experiments on real and synthetic datasets show that our algorithm outperforms the baseline and existing state-of-the-art techniques. As future work, we would like to study update models and incorporate them into our sampling framework. We are also interested in applying the adaptive sampling framework for releasing other types of dynamic data with differential privacy, e.g. frequent patterns for dynamically changing transactional data and dynamic graph patterns in social networks.

Acknowledgment

This work is supported by the National Institute of Health (NIH) under award number R01GM114612, the Patient-Centered Outcomes Research Institute (PCORI) under award number ME-1310-07058, and the National Science Foundation (NSF) under award number 1117763, and partly supported by NLM (R00LM011392), NLM (R21LM012060), and NHLBI (U54HL108460). The content is solely the responsibility of the authors and does not necessarily represent the official views of the funding agencies.

9. REFERENCES

[1] G. Ács, C. Castelluccia, and R. Chen. Differentially private histogram publishing through lossy compression. In *ICDM*, 2012.

[2] K. H. Ang, G. Chong, and Y. Li. Pid control system analysis, design, and technology. *IEEE Trans. Contr. Sys. Techn.*, 13(4):559–576, 2005.

[3] K. L. Avrim Blum and A. Roth. A learning theory approach to non-interactive database privacy. In *STOC*, 2008.

[4] B. Barak, K. Chaudhuri, C. Dwork, S. Kale, F. McSherry, and K. Talwar. Privacy, accuracy, and consistency too: a holistic solution to contingency table release. In *PODS*, 2007.

[5] T. Brinkhoff. A framework for generating network-based moving objects. In *Geoinformatica*, pages 6(2), 153Ð180, 2002.

[6] T.-H. H. Chan, E. Shi, and D. Song. Private and continual release of statistics. *ACM Trans. Inf. Syst. Secur.*, 14(3):26, 2011.

[7] G. Cormode, C. M. Procopiuc, D. Srivastava, E. Shen, and T. Yu. Differentially private spatial decompositions. In *ICDE*, 2012.

[8] G. Cormode, C. M. Procopiuc, D. Srivastava, and T. T. L. Tran. Differentially private summaries for sparse data. In *ICDT*, pages 299–311, 2012.

[9] C. Dwork. Differential privacy. *Automata, Languages and Programming, Pt 2*, 4052, 2006.

[10] C. Dwork. A firm foundation for private data analysis. *Commun. ACM.*, 2011.

[11] C. Dwork, F. Mcsherry, K. Nissim, and A. Smith. Calibrating Noise to Sensitivity in Private Data Analysis. *Theory of Cryptography*, pages 1–20.

[12] C. Dwork, M. Naor, T. Pitassi, and G. N. Rothblum. Differential privacy under continual observation. In *STOC*, pages 715–724, 2010.

[13] L. Fan, L. Bonomi, L. Xiong, and V. Sunderam. Monitoring web browsing behaviors with differential privacy. In *WWW Conference*, 2014.

[14] L. Fan and L. Xiong. An adaptive approach to real-time aggregate monitoring with differential privacy. *IEEE TKDE*, 26(9):2094–2106, 2014.

[15] M. Hardt and G. N. Rothblum. A multiplicative weights mechanism for privacy-preserving data analysis. In *FOCS*, pages 61–70, 2010.

[16] M. Hayy, V. Rastogiz, G. Miklauy, and D. Suciu. Boosting the accuracy of differentially-private histograms through consistency. *VLDB*, 2010.

[17] G. Kellaris and S. Papadopoulos. Practical differential privacy via grouping and smoothing. In *VLDB*, 2013.

[18] G. Kellaris, S. Papadopoulos, X. Xiao, and D. Papadias. Differentially private event sequences over infinite streams. *PVLDB*, 7(12):1155–1166, 2014.

[19] J. Lee and C. W. Clifton. Top-k frequent itemsets via differentially private fp-trees. In *SigKDD, 2014*, pages 931–940, 2014.

[20] H. Li, L. Xiong, and X. Jiang. Differentially private synthesization of multi-dimensional data using copula functions. In *EDBT*, pages 475–486, 2014.

[21] H. Li, L. Xiong, L. Zhang, and X. Jiang. Dpsynthesizer: Differentially private data synthesizer for privacy preserving data sharing. *PVLDB*, 7(13):1677–1680, 2014.

[22] McSherry. Privacy integrated queries: an extensible platform for privacy-preserving data analysis. In *SIGMOD*, New York, NY, USA, 2009. ACM.

[23] W. H. Qardaji, W. Yang, and N. Li. Differentially private grids for geospatial data. In *ICDE*, 2013.

[24] W. H. Qardaji, W. Yang, and N. Li. Understanding hierarchical methods for differentially private histograms. *PVLDB*, 6(14):1954–1965, 2013.

[25] V. Rastogi and S. Nath. Differentially private aggregation of distributed time-series with transformation and encryption. In *SIGMOD*, pages 735–746, 2010.

[26] X. Xiao, G. Wang, and J. Gehrke. Differential privacy via wavelet transforms. In *ICDE*, pages 225–236, 2010.

[27] Y. Xiao and L. Xiong. Protecting locations with differential privacy under temporal correlations. In *CCS*, 2015.

[28] Y. Xiao, L. Xiong, L. Fan, S. Goryczka, and H. Li. Dpcube: Differentially private histogram release through multidimensional partitioning. *Transactions on Data Privacy*, 7(3):195–222, 2014.

[29] J. Xu, Z. Zhang, X. Xiao, Y. Yang, G. Yu, and M. Winslett. Differentially private histogram publication. *VLDB J.*, 2013.

[30] J. Zhang, G. Cormode, C. M. Procopiuc, D. Srivastava, and X. Xiao. Privbayes: private data release via bayesian networks. In *SIGMOD*, pages 1423–1434, 2014.

[31] X. Zhang, X. Meng, and R. Chen. Differentially private set-valued data release against incremental updates. In *DASFAA (1)*, 2013.

WaveCluster with Differential Privacy

Ling Chen [#1], Ting Yu [#1,2], Rada Chirkova [#1]
[#1] Department of Computer Science, North Carolina State University, Raleigh, NC, USA
[#2] Qatar Computing Research Institute, Doha, Qatar
[1] lchen10@ncsu.edu, [1,2] tyu@{ncsu.edu,qf.org.qa}, [1] rychirko@ncsu.edu

ABSTRACT

WaveCluster is an important family of grid-based clustering algorithms that are capable of finding clusters of arbitrary shapes. In this paper, we investigate techniques to perform WaveCluster while ensuring differential privacy. Our goal is to develop a general technique for achieving differential privacy on WaveCluster that accommodates different wavelet transforms. We show that straightforward techniques based on synthetic data generation and introduction of random noise when quantizing the data, though generally preserving the distribution of data, often introduce too much noise to preserve useful clusters. We then propose two optimized techniques, PrivTHR and PrivTHR$_{EM}$, which can significantly reduce data distortion during two key steps of WaveCluster: the quantization step and the significant grid identification step. We conduct extensive experiments based on four datasets that are particularly interesting in the context of clustering, and show that PrivTHR and PrivTHR$_{EM}$ achieve high utility when privacy budgets are properly allocated, conforming to our theoretical analysis.

Categories and Subject Descriptors

H.2.7 [**Database Administration**]: [Security, integrity, and protection]; H.2.8 [**Database Applications**]: [Data mining]

General Terms

Data mining, Privacy

Keywords

Differential Privacy, Wavelet Transform, Clustering

1. INTRODUCTION

Clustering is an important class of data analysis, which allows data analysts to gain valuable insights into data distribution when it is challenging to make hypotheses on raw data. Among various clustering techniques, a grid-based clustering algorithm called WaveCluster [33, 34] is famous for detecting clusters of arbitrary shapes. WaveCluster relies on wavelet transforms, a family of convolutions with appropriate kernel functions, to convert data into a transformed space, where the natural clusters in the data become more distinguishable.

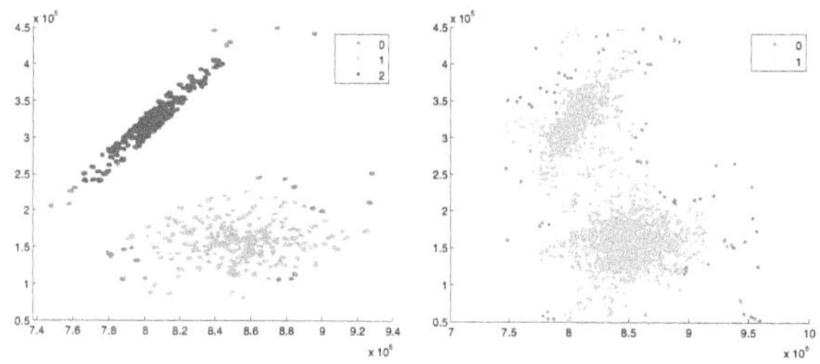

(a) Original (b) Baseline

Figure 1: Inaccurate clustering result produced by Baseline. (a) shows the WaveCluster results on the original data and (b) shows the WaveCluster results of Baseline, which leverages the adaptive-grid [31] approach to generate the synthetic data. Points in different clusters are shown in different colors, and the points marked by *red* are considered as noises.

In many data-analysis scenarios, when the data being analyzed contains personal information and the result of the analysis needs to be shared with the public or untrusted third parties, sensitive private information may be leaked, e.g., whether certain personal information is stored in a database or has contributed to the analysis. For example, the participation of one record may causes two clusters to be merged as one in the WaveCluster results. Thus, merely from the number of clusters returned (rather than which data points belong to which cluster), an adversary may infer a user's participation. Due to such potential leak of private information, data holders may be reluctant to share the original data or data-analysis results with each other or with the public.

In this paper, we develop techniques to perform WaveCluster with differential privacy [12, 14]. Differential privacy provides a provable strong privacy guarantee that the output of a computation is insensitive to any particular individual. In other words, based on the output, an adversary has limited ability to make inference about whether an individual is present or absent in the dataset. Differential privacy is often achieved by the perturbation of randomized algorithms, and the privacy level is controlled by a parameter ϵ called "privacy budget". Intuitively, the privacy protection via differential privacy grows stronger as ϵ grows smaller.

WaveCluster provides a framework that allows any kind of wavelet transform to be plugged in for data transformation, such as the Haar transform [3] and Biorthogonal transform [26]. There are various wavelet transforms that are suitable for different types of applications, such as image compression and signal processing [4]. Plugged in different wavelet transforms, WaveCluster can leverage different properties of the data, such as frequency and location, for

Permission to make digital or hard copies of all or part of this work for personal or classroom use is granted without fee provided that copies are not made or distributed for profit or commercial advantage and that copies bear this notice and the full citation on the first page. Copyrights for components of this work owned by others than ACM must be honored. Abstracting with credit is permitted. To copy otherwise, or republish, to post on servers or to redistribute to lists, requires prior specific permission and/or a fee. Request permissions from Permissions@acm.org.
CIKM'15, October 19–23, 2015, Melbourne, Australia.
© 2015 ACM. ISBN 978-1-4503-3794-6/15/10 ...$15.00.
DOI: http://dx.doi.org/10.1145/2806416.2806546.

finding the dense regions as clusters. Thus, in this paper, we aim to develop a general technique for achieving differential privacy on WaveCluster that accommodates different wavelet transforms.

We first consider a general technique, Baseline, that adapts existing differentially private data-publishing techniques to WaveCluster through synthetic data generation. Specifically, we could generate synthetic data based on any data model of the original data that is published through differential privacy, and then apply WaveCluster using any wavelet transform over the synthetic data. Baseline seems particularly promising as many effective differentially private data-publishing techniques have been proposed in the literature, all of which strive to preserve some important properties of the original data. Therefore, hopefully the "shape" of the original data is also preserved in the synthetic data, and consequently could be discovered by WaveCluster. Unfortunately, this synthetic data-generation technique often cannot produce accurate results, and the reasons are as follows. Differentially private data-publishing techniques such as spatial decompositions [10], adaptive-grid [31], and Privelet [37], output noisy descriptions of the data distribution and often contain negative counts for sparse partitions due to random noise. These negative counts do not affect the accuracy of large range queries (which is often one of the main utility measures in private data publishing) since zero-mean noise distribution smooths the effect of negative counts. However, in the synthetic dataset, negative counts cannot be smoothed away, which are typically set to zero counts. Thus, such synthetic data generation significantly distorts the data distribution and reduces the accuracy of the WaveCluster results, such as the example shown in Figure 1.

Motivated by the above challenge, we propose three techniques that enforce differential privacy on the key steps of WaveCluster, rather than relying on synthetic data generation. WaveCluster accepts as input a set of data points in a multi-dimensional space, and consists of the following main steps. First, in the quantization step WaveCluster quantizes the multi-dimensional space by dividing the space into grids, and computes the count of the data points in each grid. These counts of grids form a count matrix M. Second, in the wavelet transform step WaveCluster applies a wavelet transform on the count matrix M to obtain the approximation of the multi-dimensional space. Third, in the significant grid identification step WaveCluster identifies significant grids based on the pre-defined density threshold. Fourth, in the cluster identification step WaveCluster outputs as clusters the connected components from these significant grids [21].

To enforce differential privacy on WaveCluster, we first propose a technique, PrivQT, that introduces Laplacian noise to the quantization step. However, such straightforward privacy enforcement cannot produce usable private WaveCluster results, since the noise introduced in this step significantly distorts the number of significant grids (k) in the output. To address this issue, we further propose two techniques, PrivTHR and PrivTHR$_{EM}$, which enforce differential privacy on both the quantization step and the significant grid identification step. These two techniques differ in how to accurately determine k', the private version of k. To quantify the proposed techniques' utility, we present theoretical bounds for k' and the noise magnitude introduced in the quantization step, which allow a theoretical comparison between different techniques.

Traditionally, the effectiveness of WaveCluster is evaluated through visual inspection by human experts (i.e., visually determining whether the discovered clusters match those reflected in the user's mind) [33, 34]. Unfortunately, visual inspection is not quantitative, and thus it is inappropriate to systematically compare the impact of different techniques through visual inspection. Generally, researchers use quantitative measures to assess the utility of differentially private results, such as relative or absolute errors for range queries and accuracy for classification. But there is no existing utility measures for density-based clustering algorithms with differential privacy.

To mitigate this problem, we propose two types of utility measures. The first is to measure the dissimilarity between true and private WaveCluster results by measuring the differences of significant grids and clusters, which correspond to the outputs of the two key steps (the significant grid identification and the cluster identification) in WaveCluster. To more intuitively understand the usefulness of discovered clusters, our second utility measure considers one concrete application of cluster analysis, i.e., to build a classifier based on discovered clusters, and then use that classifier to predict future data. Thus, the prediction accuracy of the classifier from one aspect reflects the actual utility of private WaveCluster.

To evaluate the proposed techniques, our experiments use four datasets containing different data shapes that are interesting in the context of clustering [1, 9]. Our results show that PrivTHR and PrivTHR$_{EM}$ achieve high utility for both types of utility measures, and are superior to Baseline and PrivQT. The results also indicate that PrivTHR and PrivTHR$_{EM}$ can accurately estimate k' when proper budgets are allocated in the quantization and significant grid identification steps, which conforms to our theoretical analysis.

2. RELATED WORK

The syntactic approaches for privacy preserving clustering [18] is to output k-anonymous clusters. Friedman et al. [17] presented an algorithm to output k-anonymous clusters by using minimum spanning tree. Karakasidis et al. [22] created k-anonymous clusters by merging clusters so that each cluster contains at least k key values of the records. However, these approaches only satisfy syntactic privacy notions such as k-anonymity, and cannot provide formal guarantees of privacy as differential privacy.

In this work, our goal is to perform WaveCluster under differential privacy. The focus of initial work on differential privacy [12–15, 23] concerned the theoretical proof of its feasibility on various data analysis tasks, e.g., histogram and logistic regression. More recent work has focused on practical applications of differential privacy for privacy-preserving data publishing. An approach proposed by Barak et al. [6] encoded marginals with Fourier coefficients and then added noise to the released coefficients. Hay et al. [20] exploited consistency constraints to reduce noise for histogram counts. Xiao et al. [37] proposed *Privelet*, using wavelet transforms to reduce noise for histogram counts. Cormode et al. [10] indexed data by *kd*-trees and *quad*-trees, building the noisy trees with effective budget allocation strategies. Qardaji et al. [31] proposed uniform-grid and adaptive-grid methods to derive appropriate partition granularity in differentially private synopsis publishing. Xu et al. [38] proposed the *NoiseFirst* and *StructureFirst* techniques for constructing optimal noisy histograms, using dynamic programming and Exponential mechanism. These differentially private data publishing techniques are specifically crafted for answering range queries. However, synthesizing the dataset and applying WaveCluster on top of it often render WaveCluster results useless, since these techniques do not capture the essence of WaveCluster and introduce too much unnecessary noise.

Another important line of prior work focuses on integrating differential privacy into other practical data analysis tasks, such as regression analysis, model fitting, classification and etc. Chaudhuri et al. [7] proposed a differentially private regularized logistic regression algorithm that balances privacy with learnability. Zhang et al. [40] proposed a differentially private approach for logistic and linear regressions that involve perturbing the objective function of the regression model, rather than simply introducing noise into the results. Friedman et al. [16] incorporated differential privacy into several types of decision trees and subsequently demonstrated the tradeoff among privacy, accuracy and sample size. Using decision trees as an example application, Mohammed et al. [29] investigated a generalization-based algorithm for achieving differential privacy for classification problems.

Differentially private cluster analysis has also been studied in prior work. Zhang et al. [39] proposed differentially private model fitting based on genetic algorithms, with applications to k-means clustering. McSherry [27] introduced the PINQ framework, which has been applied to achieve differential privacy for k-means clustering using an iterative algorithm [36]. Nissim et al. [30] proposed the sample-aggregate framework that calibrates the noise magnitude according to the smooth sensitivity of a function. They showed that their framework can be applied to k-means clustering under the assumption that the dataset is well-separated. These research efforts primarily focus on centroid-based clustering, such as k-means, which is most suited for separating convex clusters and presents insufficient spatial information to detect clusters with complex shapes, e.g. concave shapes. In contrast to these research efforts, we propose techniques that enforce differential privacy on WaveCluster, which is not restricted to well-separated datasets, and can detect clusters with arbitrary shapes.

3. PRELIMINARIES

3.1 Differential Privacy

Differential privacy [12] is a recent privacy model, which guarantees that an adversary cannot infer an individual's presence in a dataset from the randomized output, despite having knowledge of all remaining individuals in the dataset.

DEFINITION 1. (**ϵ-differential privacy**): *Given any pair of neighboring databases D and D' that differ only in one individual record, a randomized algorithm A is ϵ-differentially private iff for any $S \subseteq Range(A)$:*

$$Pr[A(D) \in S] \leq Pr[A(D') \in S] * e^{\epsilon}$$

The parameter ϵ indicates the level of privacy, and we refer to it as the *privacy budget*. Appropriate allocation of the privacy budget for a computational process is important for reaching a favorable trade-off between privacy and utility. The most common strategy to achieve ϵ-differential privacy is to add noise to the output of a function. The magnitude of introduced noise is calibrated by the privacy budget ϵ and the sensitivity of the query function. The sensitivity of a query function is defined as the maximum difference between the outputs of the query function on any pair of neighboring databases:

$$\Delta f = \max_{D,D'} \parallel f(D) - f(D') \parallel_1$$

There are two common approaches for achieving ϵ-differential privacy: Laplace mechanism [14] and Exponential mechanism [28].

Laplace Mechanism: The output of a query function f is perturbed by adding noise from the Laplace distribution with probability density function $f(x|b) = \frac{1}{2b}\exp(-\frac{|x|}{b})$, $b = \frac{\Delta f}{\epsilon}$. The following randomized mechanism A_l satisfies ϵ-differential privacy:

$$\mathcal{A}_l(D) = f(D) + Lap(\frac{\Delta f}{\epsilon})$$

Exponential Mechanism: This mechanism returns an output that is close to the optimum, with respect to a quality function. A quality function $q(D,r)$ assigns a score to all possible outputs $r \in R$, where R is the output range of f, and better outputs receive higher scores. A randomized mechanism A_e that outputs $r \in R$ with probability

$$Pr[\mathcal{A}_e(D) = r] \propto exp(\frac{\epsilon q(D,r)}{2S(q)})$$

satisfies ϵ-differential privacy, where $S(q)$ is the sensitivity of the quality function.

Differential privacy has two properties: sequential composition and parallel composition. Sequential composition is that given n independent randomized mechanisms $A_1, A_2, \ldots, A_n$ where A_i ($1 \leq i \leq n$) satisfies ϵ_i-differential privacy, a sequence of A_i over the dataset D satisfies ϵ-differential privacy, where $\epsilon = \sum_1^n(\epsilon_i)$. Parallel composition is that given n independent randomized mechanisms $A_1, A_2, \ldots, A_n$ where A_i ($1 \leq i \leq n$) satisfies ϵ-differential privacy, a sequence of A_i over a set of disjoint data sets D_i satisfies ϵ-differential privacy.

3.2 WaveCluster

WaveCluster is an algorithm developed by Sheikholeslami et al. [33, 34] for the purpose of clustering spatial data. It works by using a wavelet transform to detect the boundaries between clusters. A wavelet transform allows the algorithm to distinguish between areas of high contrast (high frequency components) and areas of low contrast (low frequency components). The motivation behind this distinction is that within a cluster there should be low contrast and between clusters there should be an area of high contrast (the border). WaveCluster has the following steps:

Quantization: Quantize the feature space into grids of a specified size, creating a count matrix M.

Wavelet Transform: Apply a wavelet transform to the count matrix M, such as Haar transform [3] and Biorthogonal transform [26], and decompose M to the average subband that gives the approximation of the count matrix (W) and the detail subband that has the information about the boundaries of clusters.

Significant Grid Identification: Identify the significant grids from the average subband W. WaveCluster constructs a sorted list L of the positive wavelet transformed values obtained from W and compute the pth percentile of the values in L. The values that are below the pth percentile of L are non-significant values, and their corresponding grids are considered as non-significant grids. The data points in the non-significant grids are considered as noise.

Cluster Identification: Identify clusters from the significant grids using connected component labeling algorithm [21] (two grids are connected if they are adjacent), map the clusters back to the original multi-dimensional space, and label the data points based on which cluster the data points reside in.

Parameters. WaveCluster has four parameters to specify:

num_grid ($g_1, g_2, \ldots, g_n$): the number of grids that the n-dimensional space is partitioned into along each dimension. For the brevity of description, we simply use g to refer to the partitions of the n-dimensional space ($g_1, g_2, \ldots, g_n$).

densitythreshold (p): a percentage value p that specifies p% of the values in L are non-significant values. For ease of presentation, we use $k = (1-p)|L|$ to represent the top k values in L and their corresponding grids are considered as significant grids.

level: a wavelet decomposition level, which indicates how many times a wavelet transform is applied. The larger the level is, the more approximate the result is. In our techniques, we set level to 1 since a smaller level value provides more accurate results [34].

wavelet: a wavelet transform to be applied. Haar transform [3] is one of the simplest wavelet transforms and widely used, which is computed by iterating difference and averaging between odd and even samples of a signal (or a sequence of data points). Other commonly used wavelet transforms include Biorthogonal transform [26], Daubechies transform [11], and so on.

3.3 Differentially Private WaveCluster

Motivating Scenario. Consider a scenario with two participants: the data owner (e.g. hospitals) and the querier (e.g. data miner). The data owner holds raw data and has the legal obligation to protect individuals' privacy while the querier is eager to obtain cluster analysis results for further exploration. The goal of our work is to enable the data owner to release cluster analysis results using WaveCluster while not compromising the privacy of any individual. The data owner has a good knowledge of the raw data and it is not difficult for her to choose the appropriate parameters (e.g. num_grid, $densitythreshold$) for non-private WaveCluster. The parameters chosen for the non-private setting are directly used for the private setting, and thus the data owner does not need to infer another set of parameters for the private setting.

Problem Statement. Given a raw data set D, appropriate WaveCluster parameters for D and a privacy budget ϵ, our goal is to investigate an effective approach A such that A (1) satisfies ϵ-differential privacy, and (2) achieves high utility of the private WaveCluster results with regard to the utility metrics U.

4. APPROACHES

In this section, we present four techniques for achieving differential privacy on WaveCluster.

4.1 Baseline Approach (Baseline)

A straightforward technique to achieve differential privacy on WaveCluster is as follows: (1) adapt an existing ϵ-differential privacy preserving data publishing method to get the noisy description of the data distribution, such as a set of contingency tables or a spatial decomposition tree [10,31,37,38]; (2) generate a synthetic dataset according to the noisy description; (3) apply WaveCluster on the synthetic dataset. We refer to this technique as Baseline and its pseudocode can be found in [8].

Discussion. Baseline achieves differential privacy on WaveCluster through the achievement of differential privacy on data publishing. The adapted ϵ-differential privacy preserving data publishing method is designed for answering range queries. The noisy descriptions of the data distribution may contain negative counts for certain partitions since the noise distribution is Laplacian with zero mean. These negative counts do not affect the range query accuracy too much since zero-mean noise distribution smooths the effect of noise. However, when the method is used for generating a synthetic dataset, the noisy negative counts are reset as zero counts, causing the data distribution to change radically and further leading to the severe deviation in differentially private WaveCluster results.

4.2 Private Quantization (PrivQT)

To address the challenge faced by Baseline, we propose techniques that enforce differential privacy on the key steps of WaveCluster. Our first approach, called Private Quantization (PrivQT), introduces independent Laplacian noise in the quantization step to achieve differential privacy. In the quantization step, the data is divided into grids and the count matrix M is computed. To ensure differential privacy in this step, we rely on the Laplace mechanism that introduces independent Laplacian noise to M. Clearly, if we change one individual in the input data, such as adding, removing or modifying an individual, there is at most one change in one entry of M. According to the parallel composition property of differential privacy, the noise amount introduced to each grid is $Lap(\frac{1}{\epsilon})$, given a privacy budget ϵ. Since the following steps of WaveCluster

Algorithm 1 PrivTHR

Input: Dataset D, num_grid g, density threshold p, wavelet transform w, differential privacy budget ϵ, allocation percentage α
Output: A set of differentially private clusters
1: **procedure** $PrivTHR(D, g, p, w, \epsilon, \alpha)$
2: M' = PrivQuantization(D, g, $\alpha\epsilon$)
3: W' = WaveletTransform(M',w)
4: L' = ConvertToPosSortedArray(W')
5: $|Z|'$ = NoisyCountOfNonPosValues($D, g, w, (1-\alpha)\epsilon$)
6: L'' = RemoveFrom(L',0,$\frac{|Z|'}{2}$)
7: $k' = (1-p)|L''|$
8: d' = Top(k',L'')
9: **return** ConnCompLabel(W', d')
10: **end procedure**
11: **procedure** NoisyCountOfNonPosValues(D, g, w, ϵ)
12: M = Quantization(D, g)
13: W = WaveletTransform(M,w)
14: $|Z|$ = CountOfNonPos(W)
15: $|Z|' = |Z| + Lap(\frac{Sensitivity(|Z|)}{\epsilon})$
16: **return** $|Z|'$
17: **end procedure**

are carried on using the differentially private count matrix M', the clusters derived from these steps are also differentially private. The pseudocode of PrivQT can be found in [8].

Discussion. Although PrivQT achieves differential privacy, the noisy count matrix M' significantly distorts the number of noisy positive values in M' and consequently the clustering results. As Laplacian distribution is symmetric and has zero-mean, approximately half of the zero-count grids become noisy positive-count grids due to positive noise. These noisy positive-count grids may cause their corresponding wavelet transformed values in W' to become positive (depending on the targeted wavelet transform), which will inappropriately participate in the computation of k', the private version of k. Due to the significant distortion of k', the utility of PrivQT improves marginally even for a large privacy budget.

4.3 Private Quantization with Refined Noisy Density Threshold (PrivTHR)

The limitation of PrivQT lies in the severe distortion of k' by Laplacian noise introduced into count matrix M'. To mitigate the distortion, we propose a technique, PrivTHR, which prunes a portion of noisy positive values in W' to refine the computation of k'. Algorithm 1 shows the pseudocode of PrivTHR.

PrivTHR first introduces random noise to the count matrix M, similar to PrivQT, and obtains a noisy count matrix M' (Line 2). PrivTHR then applies a wavelet transform on M' to obtain W' (Line 3). W' is then turned into a list L' that keeps only positive values and the values in L' is sorted in ascending order (Line 4). Thus, only the positive values in W' will be used for computing k' based on the specified density threshold p. To reduce the distortion of k', starting from the smallest noisy positive values in L', PrivTHR discards the first $\frac{|Z|'}{2}$ values (Line 6), where Z represents the non-positive (negative or zero) values in the W and $|Z|'$ is a noisy estimate of $|Z|$ (Line 5). The reason why PrivTHR removes $\frac{|Z|'}{2}$ values from L' is based on the utility analysis (in Section 5.2) that approximately $\frac{|Z|}{2}$ non-positive values in W are turned into positive values due to the randomness of Laplacian noise. Since $|Z|$ partially describes the data distribution and releasing $|Z|$ without protection may leak private information, PrivTHR also introduces Laplacian noise to $|Z|$, ensuring the whole process correctly enforces differentially privacy (Lines 11-17). The noise introduced to $|Z|$ depends on the wavelet transform used to compute W. For example, if we use Haar transform for n-dimensional data, a value in W is computed by applying average for two neighboring elements along each dimension. Since any single change in the input only causes one entry of the count matrix M to change by 1, the change of M causes at maximum one value in W to change, and thus causes $|Z|$ to change by 1 at maximum, i.e., the sensitivity of $|Z|$ is 1[1]. Finally, PrivTHR obtains d' as the top k'th value in L'' (Line 8), where any value in L'' greater than d' is considered as a significant value, and applies the connected component labeling algorithm to identify clusters of significant grids (Line 9).

Budget Allocation. PrivTHR first introduces Laplacian noise in the quantization step using a privacy budget $\epsilon_1 = \alpha\epsilon$, where $0 < \alpha < 1$. In the significant grid identification step, PrivTHR further introduces Laplacian noise to $|Z|$ using the remaining privacy budget $\epsilon_2 = (1 - \alpha)\epsilon$. Based on utility analysis in Section 5.2.2, ϵ_2 should be allocated with a smaller amount of budget than ϵ_1. Our empirical results in Section 7 further show the impact of α on clustering accuracy.

4.4 Private Quantization with Noisy Threshold using Exponential Mechanism (PrivTHR$_{EM}$)

Besides pruning noisy positive values in W', we propose an alternative technique that employs Exponential mechanism for deriving k' from the sorted list of L. Algorithm 2 shows the pseudocode of PrivTHR$_{EM}$.

PrivTHR$_{EM}$ first introduces Laplacian noise to the count matrix M, which is similar to PrivQT and PrivTHR. After that, we obtain a noisy count matrix M' (Line 2) and the corresponding W' (Line 3). Different from the previous two techniques that compute k' from W', PrivTHR$_{EM}$ derives k' from W using Exponential mechanism (Lines 7-15). In this case, although the sorted list derived from W' is severely distorted in PrivTHR$_{EM}$, the derivation of k' from W is not affected by the distorted W'. Given sufficient privacy budget, k' derived from W using Exponential mechanism is reasonably accurate, compared to the case when k' is derived from W'.

The quality function fed into the Exponential mechanism is [10]:

$$q(L, X) = -|rank(x) - k|,$$

where L represents the sorted positive values in W with Min and Max values (Line 10), and X represents the possible output space, i.e., all the possible values in the range of $(0, Max]$. Given a W with m positive values and their relationships are $W_1 \geq W_2 \geq \ldots \geq W_m$, these m values divide the range $(0, Max]$ into m partitions: $(0, W_m], (W_m, W_{m-1}], \ldots, (W_2, W_1]$, and the ranks for these partitions are $m, m-1, \ldots, 2, 1$. For any $x \in (W_{i-1}, W_i]$, its rank is $rank(W_i)$. For example, if $x \in (W_2, W_1]$, $rank(x) = rank(W_1) = 1$. Similar to PrivTHR, when using Haar transform, any single change in the input causes only one value in W to change. Thus, at maximum one value will be added into or removed from L, causing the outcome of $q(L, X)$ to be changed by 1, i.e., the sensitivity of $q(L, X)$ is 1[2].

Plugging in the above quality function into Exponential mechanism, we obtain the following algorithm: for any value $x \in (0, Max]$, the Exponential mechanism (EM) returns x with probability $Pr[EM(L) = x] \propto exp(-\frac{\epsilon|rank(x)-k|}{2})$ (Line 12). Since all the values in a partition have the same probability to be chosen, a random value from the partition $Pt_i = (W_{i-1}, W_i]$ will be chosen with the probability proportional to $|Pt_i| * exp(-\frac{\epsilon}{2}|i - k|)$. In other words, once k' is chosen, PrivTHR$_{EM}$ further computes a uniform random value d' from Pt_i (Line 13), and any value in L' greater than d' is considered as a significant value.

Budget Allocation. Similar to PrivTHR, the privacy budget is split between two steps: introduction of Laplacian noise in quantization and obtaining k' using Exponential mechanism. Previous empirical experiments [10] on splitting budgets between obtaining noisy median and noisy counts suggest that, 30% vs. 70% budget allocation strategy performs best. Specifically, 70% of budget is allocated for obtaining noisy count matrix M' (Line 2) and the remaining budget is allocated for computing k' (Line 4).

Algorithm 2 PrivTHR$_{EM}$

Input: Dataset D, num_grid g, density threshold p, wavelet transform w, differential privacy budget ϵ, allocation percentage α
Output: A set of differentially private clusters

```
1:  procedure PrivTHR_EM(D, g, p, w, ε, α)
2:      M' = PrivQuantization(D, g, αε)
3:      W' = WaveletTransform(M',w)
4:      d' = NoisyDensityThreshold(D, g, p, w, (1 − α)ε)
5:      return ConnCompLabel(W', d')
6:  end procedure
7:  procedure NoisyDensityThreshold(D, g, p, w, ε)
8:      M = Quantization(D, g)
9:      W = WaveletTransform(M,w)
10:     L = ConvertToPosSortedArray(W)
11:     k = (1 − p)|L|
12:     k' = ExponentialMechanism(L,k,ε)
13:     d' = UniformRandom(L, k' )
14:     return d'
15: end procedure
```

5. PRIVACY AND UTILITY ANALYSIS

In this section, we present the privacy analysis and utility analysis of the proposed techniques PrivQT, PrivTHR and PrivTHR$_{EM}$.

5.1 Privacy Analysis

PrivQT introduces independent Laplacian noise $Lap(\frac{1}{\epsilon})$ to grid counts, which are computed on disjoint datasets. According to the parallel composition property of differential privacy described in Section 3.1, the privacy cost depends only on the worst guarantee of all computations over disjoint datasets. Therefore, PrivQT is ϵ-differentially private.

PrivTHR splits privacy budget into two parts. First, for private quantization, adding Laplacian noise $Lap(\frac{1}{\alpha\epsilon})$ achieves strict $\alpha\epsilon$-differential privacy. The proof is same as PrivQT. Second, PrivTHR introduces Laplacian noise $Lap(\frac{1}{(1-\alpha)\epsilon})$ to the true count of non-positive values in W, which achieves $(1-\alpha)\epsilon$-differential privacy. Using the composition property of differential privacy, PrivTHR achieves ϵ-differentially private since $\epsilon = \alpha\epsilon + (1 - \alpha)\epsilon$.

Similar to PrivTHR, PrivTHR$_{EM}$ has two steps of randomization: private quantization and obtaining k'. Private quantization achieves $\alpha\epsilon$-differential privacy according to Laplace mechanism and parallel composition property. Sampling k' by Exponential mechanism consumes budget of $(1-\alpha)\epsilon$, which achieves $(1-\alpha)\epsilon$-differential privacy. According to the composition property of differential privacy, PrivTHR$_{EM}$ is ϵ-differentially private.

5.2 Utility Analysis

In this section, we present utility guarantees of PrivQT, PrivTHR and PrivTHR$_{EM}$ with theoretical analysis. In the private results

[1]For other wavelet transforms that use circular convolutions, such as Biorthogonal transform, the sensitivity of $|Z|$ depends on the count of positive values and the count of negative values in the matrix computed by the coefficient vector [26].

[2]Similar to PrivTHR, for other wavelet transforms that use circular convolutions, the sensitivity of $q(L, X)$ depends on the count of positive values and the count of negative values in the matrix computed by the coefficient vector [26].

of WaveCluster, PrivQT, PrivTHR and PrivTHR$_{EM}$ return a list of noisy significant grids. To quantify the utility of PrivQT, PrivTHR and PrivTHR$_{EM}$, we consider finding significant grids whose wavelet transformed values surpass a threshold to be similar to finding the top-k frequent itemsets whose frequencies surpass a threshold. In significant grid identification, L is the list of positive wavelet transformed values from W sorted in ascending order, Z represents the set of non-positive values from W, and all the top-k values in L correspond to significant grids, where $k = (1-p)|L|$.

5.2.1 *Utility Analysis for* PrivQT.

We first provide the analysis of difference between k and k' in PrivQT. In PrivQT, the difference between k' and k depends on two factors: (1) a set of non-positive values in Z becoming noisy positive, $Z'_p = \{W'_Z | W'_Z = W_Z + Noise, W_Z \in Z, W'_Z > 0\}$, where W'_Z is the noisy value of zero value in Z, and (2) a set of positive values in L becoming noisy non-positive, $L'_n = \{W'_L | W'_L = W_L + Noise, W_L \in L, W'_L \leq 0\}$, where W'_L is the noisy value of positive value in L. That is, $k' = (1-p)(|L| + |Z'_p| - |L'_n|)$.

Analysis of $|Z'_p|$. In PrivQT, since we are adding $Lap(\frac{1}{\epsilon})$ noise to each grid count and the Haar transform computes the average from four adjacent grids, the noise added into a wavelet transformed value is the sum of four i.i.d. samples from the Laplace distribution. The sum of h i.i.d. Laplace distributions with mean 0 is the difference of two i.i.d. Gamma distributions [24], referred to as distribution T. Distribution T is a polynomial in $|x|$ divided by $e^{|x|}$, which is a symmetric function and thus the probability for distribution T to produce positive values is $\frac{1}{2}$. Thus, the events of values in Z adding positive noise from distribution T conform to the Binominal Distribution with parameters $|Z|$ and $\frac{1}{2}$, and its expected value is $\frac{|Z|}{2}$.

Analysis of $|L'_n|$. For L'_n, each value is added the noise conforming to the symmetric distribution T. The probability density function of $|L'_n|$ is $f_{|L'_n|}(x) = \binom{|L|}{x} \prod_{i=1}^{x} f_T(y \leq -W_i) \prod_{i=x+1}^{|L|} f_T(y > -W_i), W_i \in L$, and its expected value $E[|L'_n|]$ is $\sum_{n=1}^{|L|} f_T(y \leq -W_i)$. $E[|L'_n|]$ is large when W_i is small and there is limited privacy budget. The datasets that are interesting for clustering always have high-density cluster centers and low-density cluster borders. Only those values corresponding to border grids are possible to become noisy non-positive and the size of border grids is relatively small. Therefore, $E[|L'_n|]$ is a small constant. We refer to the value of $|L'_n|$ as θ in the following analysis.

Analysis of $k'-k$. In PrivQT, $E[k'-k] = (1-p)(\frac{|Z|}{2} - \theta)$. For those datasets that are interesting in the context of clustering, $|Z|$ is pretty large compared to the whole space since Z is used to separate different clusters. What is more, dense areas within clusters are typically larger than the space of cluster borders with low density, i.e. θ is far smaller than $\frac{|Z|}{2}$. In PrivQT, $\frac{|Z|}{2}$ dominates the difference between $k'-k$, which increases false positive rate. In PrivTHR and PrivTHR$_{EM}$, we use different strategies to minimize the difference between k' and k.

THEOREM 1. *In PrivQT with Haar transform, given* $0 < \omega < 1$, *let* $\eta_1 = \frac{|Z|}{2} - \sqrt{\frac{|Z|\ln(\frac{1}{\omega})}{2}}$, $\eta_2 = \frac{|Z|}{2} + \sqrt{\frac{|Z|\ln(\frac{1}{\omega})}{2}}$, *and* $\gamma = \frac{8}{\epsilon}\ln(\frac{4(|L|+|Z|)}{\omega})$, *then with probability at least* $(1-\omega)^2$, *(1) all value in L greater than* $W_{k'_{min}} + \gamma$ *are output, where* $k'_{min} = k + (1-p)(\eta_1 - \theta)$, *and (2) no values in L less than* $W_{k'_{max}} - \gamma$ *are output, where* $k'_{max} = k + (1-p)(\eta_2 - \theta)$.

PROOF. In PrivQT, $k' = (1-p)(|L| + |Z'_p| - |L'_n|)$. Since $|Z'_p|$ follows Binominal distribution with parameters $|Z|$ and $\frac{1}{2}$ and $|L'_n|$ is noted as a small value θ, k' follows the Binomial distribution and decides the number of values in L that become output. Let $1 - \omega = Pr(k' \geq k'_{min}) = Pr(|Z'_p| \geq \eta_1)$. As $Pr(|Z'_p| \geq \eta_1) =$ 1 - $Pr(|Z'_p| \leq \eta_1)$ and $Pr(|Z'_p| \leq \eta_1) \leq e^{(-2\frac{(\frac{|Z|}{2}-\eta_1)^2}{|Z|})}$ [5], we have $\eta_1 = \frac{|Z|}{2} - \sqrt{\frac{|Z|\ln(\frac{1}{\omega})}{2}}$. For constant ω, $\eta_1 = O(\frac{|Z|}{2} - \sqrt{\frac{|Z|}{2}})$ will suffice.

We can also derive the bound of γ, i.e., the noise added to each value in $L \cup Z$ based on ω. For Haar wavelet transform, each value in $L \cup Z$ is added the noise that is the sum of 4 Laplacian random variables divided by 2 (i.e., $\frac{4Lap(\frac{1}{\epsilon})}{2}$). For values in $L \cup Z$, let all $4(|L| + |Z|)$ Laplacian random variables generate noise within $[-\frac{\gamma}{4}, \frac{\gamma}{4}]$. The probability that no Laplacian random variable' value is outside $[-\frac{\gamma}{4}, \frac{\gamma}{4}]$ is $1 - Pr(A)$, where A is that at least one Laplacian random variable's value is outside $[-\frac{\gamma}{4}, \frac{\gamma}{4}]$. By union bound, $Pr(A) \leq \sum_{i=1}^{4(|L|+|Z|)} Pr(B_i)$, where B_i is that ith Laplacian random variable's noise is outside $[-\frac{\gamma}{4}, \frac{\gamma}{4}]$ and $Pr(B_i) = e^{-\frac{\epsilon\gamma}{8}}$. Thus, we can derive that with at least the probability $1 - 4(|L| + |Z|)e^{-\frac{\epsilon\gamma}{8}}$, no Laplacian random variable' value is outside $[-\frac{\gamma}{4}, \frac{\gamma}{4}]$, and each value in $L \cup Z$ has their noise amount within $[-\frac{\gamma}{2}, \frac{\gamma}{2}]$. Let $\omega = 4(|L| + |Z|)e^{-\frac{\epsilon\gamma}{8}}$, then we have $\gamma = \frac{8}{\epsilon}\ln(\frac{4(|L|+|Z|)}{\omega})$. For constant ω, $\gamma = O(\frac{ln(4(|L|+|Z|))}{\epsilon})$.

Subclaim (1) can be derived based on (a) with probability at least $1-\omega$, $k' \geq k'_{min}$ and (b) with probability at least $1-\omega$, the noise of each value in L being within $[-\frac{\gamma}{2}, \frac{\gamma}{2}]$. Detailed proof can be found in [8]. Subclaim (1) requires both conditions (a) and (b) to hold, and thus the probability is at least $(1-\omega)^2$.

Similar as k'_{min}, we can derive the upper bound k'_{max} of k' given ω. Let $1 - \omega = Pr(k' \leq k'_{max}) = Pr(|Z'_p| \leq \eta_2)$. Recall that $|Z'_p|$ follows Binomial distribution $(|Z|, \frac{1}{2})$, which is symmetric with respect to $\frac{|Z|}{2}$. Thus, the probability of sampling a value from the range $[0, \eta_2]$ is the same as sampling a value from the range $[\eta_1, |Z|]$, and we have $\eta_2 = |Z| - \eta_1 = \frac{|Z|}{2} + \sqrt{\frac{|Z|\ln(\frac{1}{\omega})}{2}}$. For constant ω, $\eta_2 = O(\frac{|Z|}{2} + \sqrt{\frac{|Z|}{2}})$ will suffice.

Subclaim (2) can be proved based on (c) with probability at least $1-\omega$, $k' \leq k'_{max}$ and (b) with probability at least $1-\omega$, the noise of each value in L being within $[-\frac{\gamma}{2}, \frac{\gamma}{2}]$. As subclaim (2) requires both conditions (c) and (b) to hold, the probability is at least $(1-\omega)^2$. □

For other wavelet transforms that use circular convolutions, such as Biorthogonal transform, the derivation for the bounds of k' with η_1 and η_2 remains the same since $|Z'_p|$ following Binomial distribution is independent of any wavelet transform being adapted. Thus, our framework is extensible to other wavelet transforms, and the bound of noise magnitude γ depends on the amount of adjacent grid counts involved in computing a wavelet transformed value.

5.2.2 *Utility Analysis for* PrivTHR.

THEOREM 2. *In PrivTHR with Haar transform, given* $0 < \omega < 1$, *let* $\eta_1 = \frac{|Z|}{2} - \sqrt{\frac{|Z|\ln(\frac{1}{\omega})}{2}}$, $\eta_2 = \frac{|Z|}{2} + \sqrt{\frac{|Z|\ln(\frac{1}{\omega})}{2}}$, $\gamma = \frac{8}{\epsilon_1}\ln(\frac{4(|L|+|Z|)}{\omega})$ *and* $\beta = \frac{2}{\epsilon_2}\ln(\frac{1}{\omega})$, *then with probability at least* $(1-\omega)^3$, *(1) all values in L greater than* $W_{k'_{min}} + \gamma$ *are output, where* $k'_{min} = k + (1-p)(\eta_1 - \theta - \frac{|Z|}{2} - \beta)$, *and (2) no values in L less than* $W_{k'_{max}} - \gamma$ *are output, where* $k'_{max} = k + (1-p)(\eta_2 - \theta - \frac{|Z|}{2} + \beta)$.

PROOF. In PrivTHR, we allocate ϵ_1 for private quantization and ϵ_2 for obtaining $|Z|'$, which makes $k' = (1-p)(|L| + |Z'_p| - \theta - \frac{|Z|}{2} + Lap(\frac{1}{\epsilon_2}))$. With the probability at least $1 - e^{-\frac{\epsilon_2\beta}{2}}$, $Lap(\frac{1}{\epsilon_2})$

has the noise amount within β. Let $1-\omega = 1-e^{-\frac{\epsilon_2 \beta}{2}}$, then we get $\beta = \frac{2}{\epsilon_2}\ln(\frac{1}{\omega})$. For constant ω, $\beta = O(\frac{1}{\epsilon_2})$ will suffice. The proofs of η_1, η_2, γ and subclaims (1) and (2) are the same as THEOREM 4, and $\gamma = O(\frac{\ln(4(|L|+|Z|))}{\epsilon_1})$ for constant ω. $\square$

Difference between PrivTHR and PrivQT: PrivTHR removing $\frac{|Z|}{2} \pm \beta$ positive values from L', and thus provides better utility guarantee than PrivQT. The reason is the difference between k' and k becomes $O(\sqrt{\frac{|Z|}{2}}) \pm (\beta+\theta)$ by THEOREMs 4 and 5, where θ is a small constant and β is small when sufficient budget is provided.

5.2.3 Utility Analysis for PrivTHR$_{EM}$.

THEOREM 3. *In PrivTHR$_{EM}$ with Haar transform, given $0 < \omega < 1$, let $\eta_1 = |L| - k - 1 + \frac{2}{\epsilon_2}\ln(\frac{|W_{max}-W_k|}{|W_k|\omega})$, $\eta_2 = k - 2 + \frac{2}{\epsilon_2}\ln(\frac{|W_k|}{|W_{max}-W_k|\omega})$, and $\gamma = \frac{8}{\epsilon_1}\ln(\frac{4(|L|+|Z|)}{\omega})$, then with probability at least $(1-\omega)^2$, (1) all values in L greater than $W_{k'_{min}}+\gamma$ are output, where $k'_{min} = k - \eta_1$, and (2) no values in L less than $W_{k'_{max}} - \gamma$ are output, where $k'_{max} = k + \eta_2$.*

PROOF. In PrivTHR$_{EM}$, we allocate ϵ_2 for deriving k' from W by employing Exponential Mechanism, a general method proposed in [28]. The probability of selecting a rank i is $|Pt_i| * exp(-\frac{\epsilon_2}{2}|i-k|)$, where Pt_i is the range $(W_{i-1}, W_i]$ decided by the $i-1$th and ith wavelet transformed values.

Let $1-\omega$ be the probability of sampling a k' where $k - k' \leq \eta_1$, then

$$\Leftrightarrow \omega < \frac{|W_{max} - W_k| * e^{-\frac{\epsilon_2}{2}(\eta_1+1)}}{|W_k| * e^{-\frac{\epsilon_2}{2}(|L|-k)}}$$

$$\Leftrightarrow \eta_1 < |L| - k - 1 + \frac{2}{\epsilon_2}\ln(\frac{|W_{max}-W_k|}{|W_k|\omega})$$

For constant ω, $\eta_1 = O(|L| - k + \frac{1}{\epsilon_2}\ln(\frac{|W_{max}-W_k|}{|W_k|})$ will suffice.

Let $1-\omega$ be the probability of sampling a k' where $k' - k \leq \eta_2$, then

$$\Leftrightarrow \omega < \frac{|W_k| * e^{-\frac{\epsilon_2}{2}(\eta_2+1)}}{|W_{max} - W_k| * e^{-\frac{\epsilon_2}{2}(k-1)}}$$

$$\Leftrightarrow \eta_2 < k - 2 + \frac{2}{\epsilon_2}\ln(\frac{|W_k|}{|W_{max}-W_k|\omega})$$

For constant ω, $\eta_2 = O(k + \frac{1}{\epsilon_2}\ln(\frac{|W_k|}{|W_{max}-W_k|})$ will suffice. The proof of γ and subclaims (1) and (2) are the same as THEOREM 4. $\square$

Analysis of PrivTHR and PrivTHR$_{EM}$. By THEOREMs 5 and 6, the accuracy for sampling k' in PrivTHR is dominated by $\frac{1}{\epsilon_2}$ while in PrivTHR$_{EM}$ the accuracy is dominated by $\frac{1}{\epsilon_2}\ln(\frac{|W_k|}{|W_{max}-W_k|})$. Depending on the data distribution, PrivTHR$_{EM}$ may present better or worse utility guarantee than PrivTHR: $\ln(\frac{|W_k|}{|W_{max}-W_k|})$ is positive when $\frac{|W_k|}{|W_{max}-W_k|} > 1$, and the accuracy for sampling k' in PrivTHR$_{EM}$ becomes more sensitive to ϵ_2 than PrivTHR; $\ln(\frac{|W_k|}{|W_{max}-W_k|})$ becomes negative when $\frac{|W_k|}{|W_{max}-W_k|}$ is less than 1, and the utility guarantee for PrivTHR$_{EM}$ becomes better.

6. QUANTITATIVE MEASURES

To quantitatively assess the utility of differentially private WaveCluster, we propose two types of measures for measuring the dissimilarity between true and differentially private WaveCluster results. The first type, DSG_C, measures the dissimilarity of the significant grids and the clusters between true and private results. The second type focuses on observing the usefulness of differentially private WaveCluster results for further data analysis. The reason is that a slight difference in the significant grids or clusters may cause a significant difference when using the WaveCluster results. In this paper, we choose a typical application of further data analysis: building a classifier from the clustering results to predict unlabeled data [19]. The classifier built from true WaveCluster results is called the true classifier clf_t while the classifier built from differentially private WaveCluster results is called the private classifier clf_p. To measure the dissimilarity between clf_t and clf_p, we propose two metrics: OCM and $2CE$.

6.1 Dissimilarity of Significant Grids and Clusters

DSG_C considers the dissimilarities of significant grids and clusters. Assume that there are t clusters of true significant grids and s clusters of differentially private significant grids. t might not be equal to s, and the cluster labels in t true clusters and s private clusters are completely arbitrary. To accommodate these differences, we adopt the Hungarian method [25], a combinatorial optimization algorithm, to solve the matching problem between t true clusters and s private clusters while minimizing the matching difference.

When cluster C_i matches to cluster C_j, we define that the distance d between cluster C_i and cluster C_j is $max\{|C_i \backslash C_j|, |C_j \backslash C_i|\}$. Consider a cluster $C_i = \{g_1, g_3, g_5\}$ and a cluster $C_j = \{g_1, g_5, g_7, g_9\}$. The distance d between clusters C_i and C_j is $max\{|\{g_3\}|, |\{g_7, g_9\}|\}$ $= 2$. Given t true clusters, s private clusters, and $t \geq s$, a matching $M_{t,s}$ of t true clusters and s private clusters is a set of cluster pairs, where each private cluster is matched with a true cluster. We then define the cost of a matching (M_{cost}) as the sum of all the distances between each cluster pair in the matching $M_{t,s}$ plus the count of significant grids in the non-matched clusters:

$$M_{cost} = \sum_{1 \leq i_x \leq t, 1 \leq j_y \leq s} max\{|C_{i_x} \backslash C_{j_y}|, |C_{j_y} \backslash C_{i_x}|\} + \sum_{1 \leq z \leq t} |C_z|$$

Here, i_x and j_y indicate the subscripts of clusters in a matched pair. $|C_z|$ represents the count of significant grids in the non-matched true clusters. Among all the possible matchings of clusters, we use the Hungarian method to find the optimal matching with the minimum M_{cost}, and computed DSG_C as:

$$DSG_C = \frac{M_{cost}}{|T|}$$

Here T denotes the set of significant grids in the true WaveCluster results.

6.2 Dissimilarity of Classifier Prediction

OCM and $2CE$ measure the dissimilarity between clf_t and clf_p. We name this way of evaluation as "clustering-first-then-classification": given a set of unlabeled data points, we use a portion of the data points (e.g., 90%) to compute WaveCluster results, where each cluster is a set of significant grids. Using the significant grids with cluster labels as training data, we build classifiers clf_t and clf_p, and use them to predict the classes for the remaining data points (e.g., 10%).

Dissimilarity of Classifiers based on Optimal Class Matching (OCM). OCM measures the dissimilarity between the two sets of classes predicted by clf_t and clf_p for the same test samples. We use L_t to denote the set of classes predicted by clf_t and L_p to denote the set of classes predicted by clf_p. Since L_t and L_p are completely arbitrary, we exploit the Hungarian method to find the optimal matching between L_t and L_p.

Assume that a class $L_{t,i}$ predicted by clf_t is matched to a class $L_{p,j}$ predicted by clf_p, forming a class pair. We compute the count of common test samples in the class $L_{t,i}$ and the class $L_{p,j}$, and

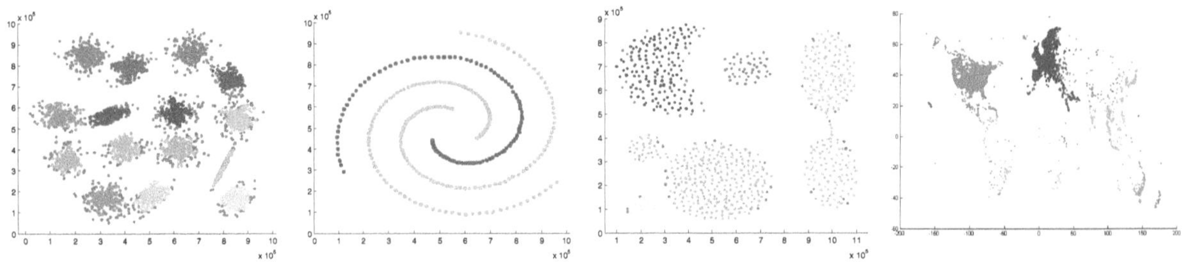

(a) *DS1*, $g = 64, p = 58$ (b) *DS2*, $g = 40, p = 10$ (c) *DS3*, $g = 36, p = 23$ (d) *Gowalla*, $g = 80, p = 31$

Figure 2: Illustration of datasets and their WaveCluster results.

sum the common test samples in each class pair to compute CT:

$$CT = \sum_{1 \leq i \leq c_1, 1 \leq j \leq c_2} |L_{t,i} \cap L_{p,j}|$$

Here c_1 is the count of classes in L_t and c_2 is the count of classes in L_p, and we assume $c_1 \geq c_2$. Since there are many possible mappings from the classes in L_t to the classes in L_p, we use the Hungarian method to find the optimal mapping that maximizes CT. Based on CT and the total count of the test samples TT, we derive the dissimilarity OCM:

$$OCM = 1 - \frac{CT}{TT}$$

When the dissimilarity is smaller, the differentially private WaveCluster results are more similar to the true WaveCluster results and maintain high utility for classification use.

Dissimilarity of Classifiers based on 2-Combination Enumeration ($2CE$). $2CE$ measures the dissimilarity between clf_t and clf_p based on relationships of every pair of test samples, i.e., whether two samples are in the same class. Essentially, given a pair of test samples A and B, we say A and B are classified consistently either (1) $clf_t(A) = clf_t(B)$ and $clf_p(A) = clf_p(B)$ or (2) $clf_t(A) \neq clf_t(B)$ and $clf_p(A) \neq clf_p(B)$. $2CE$ is the ratio of the count of test sample pairs that are not classified consistently over the total number of test sample pairs, which is the set of 2-combination of the test samples. $2CE$ uses pairs of test samples to eliminate the need of finding the optimal matching between the classes predicted by clf_t and clf_p.

7. EXPERIMENTS

We evaluate the proposed techniques using three datasets that are widely used in previous clustering algorithms [1], and one large scale dataset derived from the check-in information in Gowalla[3] geo-social networking website [9], which was used to evaluate grid-based clustering algorithms in [35].

7.1 Experiment Setup

In our experiments, we compare the performances of the four techniques, Baseline, PrivQT, PrivTHR, and PrivTHR$_{EM}$, on the four datasets using two types of measures proposed in Section 6. We use Haar transform as the wavelet transform and set the wavelet decomposition level to 1 for the four techniques. Baseline uses the adaptive-grid method [31] for synthetic data generation. The classification algorithm used for measuring OCM and $2CE$ is C4.5 decision tree algorithm [32]. We conduct experiments with privacy budgets ranging from 0.1 to 2.0; for each budget and each metric, we apply the techniques on each dataset for 10 times and compute their average performances. All experiments were conducted on a machine with Intel 2.67GHz CPU and 8GB RAM.

[3]https://snap.stanford.edu/data/loc-gowalla.html.

Datasets. The four clustering datasets contain different data shapes that are specially interesting for clustering. Figures 2 shows the WaveCluster results on the four datasets under certain parameter settings of grid size g and density threshold p. Any two adjacent clusters are marked with different colors. The points in red color are identified as noise, which fall into the non-significant grids. $DS1$ is a dataset containing 15 Gaussian clusters in convex shapes. It contains 30000 data points. The center area of each cluster has higher density and is resistant to noise. However, the overlapped area of two adjacent clusters has lower density and is prone to be affected by noise, which might turn the corresponding non-significant grids into significant grids and further connect two separate clusters. $DS2$ is a dataset with 3 spiral clusters. It contains 31200 data points. Some noisy significant grids are very likely to bridge the gap between adjacent spirals and merge them into one cluster. $DS3$ is a data dataset with 5 various shapes of clusters, including concave shapes. It contains 31520 data points. There are two clusters that both contain two sub components and a narrow line-shape area that bridges those two sub components. The narrow bridging area has low density and might be turned into non-significant grids, causing a cluster to split into two clusters. *Gowalla* is the check-in dataset resembling the world map, which records time and location information of users' check-ins. We use only the location information for evaluation. There are about 6.4M records. Such large size makes it infeasible to run experiments with C4.5 and Baseline due to memory constraints. Thus, similar to [31], we sampled 1M records from the dataset for evaluation.

7.2 Comparing Private k' With True k

We first measure the differences between the true k and private k's on each dataset with ϵ ranging from 0.1 to 2.0. Detailed results can be found in [8]. Our results show that for all datasets, when $\epsilon \geq 0.5$, the relative errors of k', i.e., $\frac{|k'-k|}{k}$, in PrivQT and PrivTHR$_{EM}$ are less than 4.7% on average, while the relative errors of k' in Baseline and PrivQT range from 32.2% to 150.5%. For example, in $DS2$, the true k is 144. When ϵ is 1, the average private k' is 141.0 (2.1%) for PrivTHR and 142.8 (0.8%) for PrivTHR$_{EM}$, while Baseline and PrivQT obtain 284.0 (97.2%) and 249.2 (73.1%) for the average k' respectively. Note that $|Z|$ is 241 in $DS2$, and the difference between the average k' and k is 105.2 for PrivQT, which is quite close to the theoretical bound $(1-p)\frac{|Z|}{2} = 108.45$ derived from our utility analysis in Section 5.2.1. When ϵ is 0.1, the k' in PrivTHR$_{EM}$ deviates from k more significantly than the k' in PrivTHR, indicating that PrivTHR$_{EM}$ is more sensitive to ϵ than PrivTHR as discussed in Section 5.2.3. For example, in $DS2$, the average k' in PrivTHR$_{EM}$ is 82.8 (42.5%) while the average k' in PrivTHR is 131.2 (8.9%).

7.3 Results of DSG_C

Figure 3 (a)-(d) show the results of DSG_C for the four techniques when the privacy budget ranges from 0.1 to 2.0. As shown in

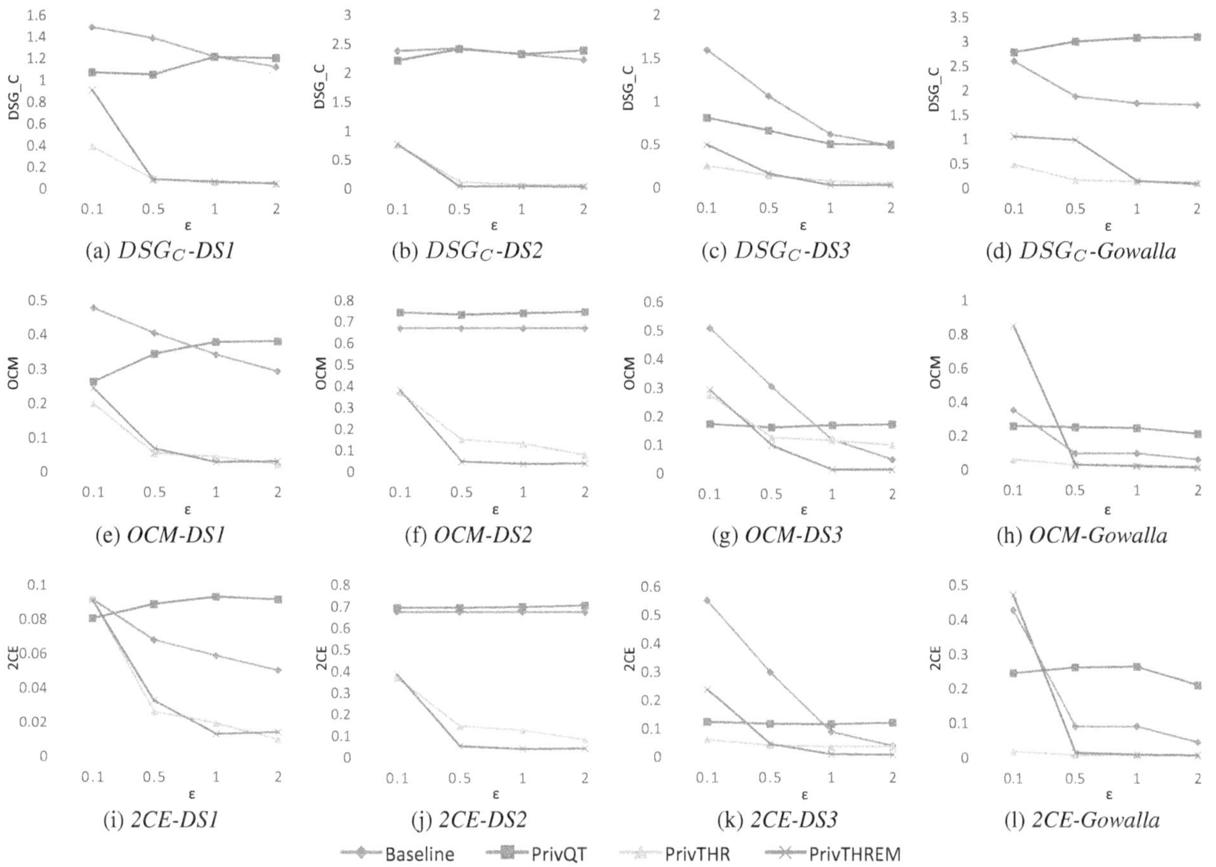

(a) DSG_C-*DS1* (b) DSG_C-*DS2* (c) DSG_C-*DS3* (d) DSG_C-*Gowalla*

(e) *OCM-DS1* (f) *OCM-DS2* (g) *OCM-DS3* (h) *OCM-Gowalla*

(i) *2CE-DS1* (j) *2CE-DS2* (k) *2CE-DS3* (l) *2CE-Gowalla*

Figure 3: Comparing DSG_C, OCM and $2CE$ of 4 techniques on $DS1$, $DS2$, $DS3$ and $Gowalla$ with increasing ϵ.

the results, both PrivTHR and PrivTHR$_{EM}$ achieve smaller DSG_C values than Baseline and PrivQT on all four datasets for all budgets. The reason is that though the noisy significant grids generated by Baseline and PrivQT may be similar to the true significant grids, these noisy significant grids result in very different shapes of clusters and thus a large value of DSG_C, while PrivTHR and PrivTHR$_{EM}$ preserve more accurate cluster shapes. For example, in $DS3$, the narrow line-shape areas and the gap between two adjacent clusters are sensitive to noise. If some noisy significant grids appear in these areas, two clusters may be merged into one; if some significant grids disappear due to noise, one cluster might be split into two. Such changes cause DSG_C to increase significantly.

Unlike the other techniques, PrivQT benefits little from the increased privacy budgets. For PrivQT, the difference between k' and k in PrivQT is dominated by $\frac{|Z|}{2}$. Increasing privacy budgets can only reduce noise magnitude and cannot smooth such difference.

Comparison to F-Measure Results. Clustering analysis usually uses F-measure as a representative external validations to measure the similarity between the ground truth (known class labels) and the clustering results [2]. In our experiments, we consider the true WaveCluster results as the ground truth. The detailed results can be found in [8]. Our results show that PrivQT and Baseline achieve high F-measure scores (more than 0.8) for almost all budgets in $DS1$, even though the private results produced by PrivQT and Baseline are quite different from the true results. For example, when $\epsilon = 0.1$, the private results of PrivQT and Baseline have more than 30 clusters while the true results have only 15 clusters. On the contrary, Figure 3 (a) shows that DSG_C is able to clearly differentiate the performances of the four techniques. The reason is that unlike DSG_C that allows only one-to-one mapping between true and private clusters, F-measure allows one-to-many or many-to-one mapping between true and private clusters. If the size of true clusters is larger than that of private clusters, F-measure allows many to one mapping, and vice versa. Thus, DSG_C presents more strict evaluation than F-measure in computing similarity/dissimilarity.

7.4 Results of OCM and $2CE$

Results of OCM. Figure 3 (e)-(h) show the results of OCM for the four techniques. As shown in the results, PrivTHR and PrivTHR$_{EM}$ achieve smaller OCM values than Baseline and PrivQT for all datasets when ϵ ranges from 0.5 to 2.0. When ϵ is greater than 0.5, the OCM values of PrivTHR and PrivTHR$_{EM}$ are less than 0.15 on $DS1$, $DS3$, and $Gowalla$, indicating the private classifier clf_p maintains highly similar prediction results as the true classifier clf_t. On $DS2$ that contains 3 spirals, PrivTHR$_{EM}$ still maintains a very low OCM value (< 0.1) when ϵ is greater than 0.5 while PrivTHR has a slightly worse OCM value (ranging from 0.1 to 0.2). Such results show that PrivTHR$_{EM}$ is more resilient to noise for concave-shaped data than PrivTHR.

Results of $2CE$. Figure 3 (i)-(l) show the results of $2CE$ for the four techniques. As shown in the results, PrivTHR and PrivTHR$_{EM}$ achieve smaller $2CE$ values than Baseline and PrivQT for all datasets when ϵ ranges from 0.5 to 2.0.

In general, all four techniques exhibit similar trends of $2CE$ as their trends in OCM. On $DS1$, all four techniques have very low $2CE$ values (< 0.1) though their corresponding OCM values are much higher (ranging from 0.05 to 0.5). The reason is that $2CE$ captures the relationships between data points while OCM focuses on the mappings of classes. If there are k test samples out of N total samples having different prediction results in the true and private results, $2CE$ expresses the differences as $C(k, 2) + k(N - k)$ over the total combinations of test samples $C(N, 2)$, while OCM

expresses the differences as k over N. On $DS1$, the k test samples are predicted to be in the same cluster in the private results and $C(k, 2)$ becomes close to 0. In this case, only $k(N-k)$ matters in the computation of $2CE$. Given that $C(N, 2)$ is much larger than N and $k(N-k)$ when N of $DS1$ is about 30,000, $2CE$ has a smaller value than OCM for measuring the differences, and thus is less sensitive to the noise on $DS1$.

Budget Allocation for PrivTHR. Based on the utility analysis Section 5.2.2, ϵ_1 for private quantization affects the accuracy of γ, and ϵ_2 for obtaining $|Z|'$ affects the accuracy of β. As the constant factor of γ, $\frac{8}{\epsilon_1} \ln\left(\frac{4(|L|+|Z|)}{\omega}\right)$, is larger than the constant factor of β, $\frac{2}{\epsilon_2} \ln\left(\frac{1}{\omega}\right)$, more budget should be allocated for ϵ_1 to achieve better utility. We evaluate the values of DSG_C of PrivTHR on $DS1$ under different budget allocation strategies, ranging from 1% for ϵ_1 to 99% for ϵ_1. Based on the results, the budget allocation strategy with 90% for ϵ_1 and 10% for ϵ_2 performs the best. The results of other measures on $DS1$ show the similar results, and the results of all the two types of measures on other datasets also show the similar results.

8. CONCLUSION

In this paper we have addressed the problem of cluster analysis with differential privacy. We take a well-known effective clustering algorithm called WaveCluster, and propose several ways to introduce randomness in the computation of WaveCluster. We also devise several new quantitative measures for examining the dissimilarity between the non-private and differentially private results and the usefulness of differentially private results in classification. In the future, we will investigate under differential privacy other categories of clustering algorithms, such as hierarchical clustering.

Acknowledgments. This work is supported in part by the National Science Foundation under the awards CNS-1314229.

9. REFERENCES

[1] Clustering datasets. http://cs.joensuu.fi/sipu/datasets/.
[2] E. Achtert, S. Goldhofer, H.-P. Kriegel, E. Schubert, and A. Zimek. Evaluation of clusterings - metrics and visual support. In *ICDE*, 2012.
[3] A. N. Akansu and R. A. Haddad. *Multiresolution Signal Decomposition: Transforms, Subbands, and Wavelets.* Academic Press, Inc., 1992.
[4] A. N. Akansu, W. A. Serdijn, and I. W. Selesnick. Emerging applications of wavelets: A review. *Phys. Commun.*, 3(1), 2010.
[5] N. Alon and J. H. Spencer. *The Probabilistic Method.* Wiley, 1992.
[6] B. Barak, K. Chaudhuri, C. Dwork, S. Kale, F. McSherry, and K. Talwar. Privacy, accuracy, and consistency too: A holistic solution to contingency table release. 2007.
[7] K. Chaudhuri and C. Monteleoni. Privacy-preserving logistic regression. In *NIPS*, 2008.
[8] L. Chen, T. Yu, and R. Chirkova. Wavecluster with differential privacy. *CoRR*, abs/1508.00192, 2015.
[9] E. Cho, S. A. Myers, and J. Leskovec. Friendship and mobility: User movement in location-based social networks. In *KDD*, 2011.
[10] G. Cormode, C. Procopiuc, D. Srivastava, E. Shen, and T. Yu. Differentially private spatial decompositions. In *ICDE*, 2012.
[11] I. Daubechies. *Ten Lectures on Wavelets.* Society for Industrial and Applied Mathematics, 1992.
[12] C. Dwork. Differential privacy: A survey of results. In *TAMC*, 2008.
[13] C. Dwork and J. Lei. Differential privacy and robust statistics. In *STOC*, 2009.
[14] C. Dwork, F. McSherry, K. Nissim, and A. Smith. Calibrating noise to sensitivity in private data analysis. In *TCC*, 2006.
[15] D. Feldman, A. Fiat, H. Kaplan, and K. Nissim. Private coresets. In *STOC*, 2009.
[16] A. Friedman and A. Schuster. Data mining with differential privacy. In *KDD*, 2010.
[17] A. Friedman, R. Wolff, and A. Schuster. Providing k-anonymity in data mining. *The VLDB Journal*, 17(4), July 2008.
[18] B. C. M. Fung, K. Wang, R. Chen, and P. S. Yu. Privacy-preserving data publishing: A survey of recent developments. *ACM Comput. Surv.*, 42(4), 2010.
[19] P. Green, F. J. Carmone, and S. M. Smith. Multidimensional scaling, section five: Dimension reducing methods and cluster analysis. 1989. Addison Wesley.
[20] M. Hay, V. Rastogi, G. Miklau, and D. Suciu. Boosting the accuracy of differentially private histograms through consistency. *PVLDB*, 3(1-2), 2010.
[21] B. K. P. Horn. *Robot Vision.* The MIT Press, 1988.
[22] A. Karakasidis and V. S. Verykios. Reference table based k-anonymous private blocking. In *SAC*, 2012.
[23] S. P. Kasiviswanathan, H. K. Lee, K. Nissim, S. Raskhodnikova, and A. Smith. What can we learn privately? In *FOCS*, 2008.
[24] S. Kotz, T. Kozubowski, and K. Podgórski. *The Laplace distribution and generalizations : a revisit with applications to communications, economics, engineering, and finance.* Birkhäuser, 2001.
[25] H. W. Kuhn. Variants of the hungarian method for assignment problems. *Naval Research Logistics Quarterly*, 3, 1956.
[26] S. G. Mallat. *A Wavelet Tour of Signal Processing. Academic Press.* Academic Press, Inc., 1999.
[27] F. McSherry. Privacy integrated queries: an extensible platform for privacy-preserving data analysis. *Commun. ACM*, 53(9), 2010.
[28] F. McSherry and K. Talwar. Mechanism design via differential privacy. In *FOCS*, 2007.
[29] N. Mohammed, R. Chen, B. C. Fung, and P. S. Yu. Differentially private data release for data mining. In *KDD*, 2011.
[30] K. Nissim, S. Raskhodnikova, and A. Smith. Smooth sensitivity and sampling in private data analysis. In *STOC*, 2007.
[31] W. H. Qardaji, W. Yang, and N. Li. Differentially private grids for geospatial data. In *ICDE*, 2013.
[32] J. R. Quinlan. *C4.5: Programs for Machine Learning.* Morgan Kaufmann Publishers Inc., San Francisco, CA, USA, 1993.
[33] G. Sheikholeslami, S. Chatterjee, and A. Zhang. Wavecluster: A multi-resolution clustering approach for very large spatial databases. In *VLDB*, 1998.
[34] G. Sheikholeslami, S. Chatterjee, and A. Zhang. Wavecluster: A wavelet-based clustering approach for spatial data in very large databases. *VLDB J.*, 8(3-4), 2000.
[35] J. Shi, N. Mamoulis, D. Wu, and D. W. Cheung. Density-based place clustering in geo-social networks. In *SIGMOD*, 2014.
[36] M. Winslett, Y. Yang, and Z. Zhang. Demonstration of damson: Differential privacy for analysis of large data. *ICPADS, IEEE Computer Society*, 2012.
[37] X. Xiao, G. Wang, and J. Gehrke. Differential privacy via wavelet transforms. *TKDE*, 23(8), 2011.
[38] J. Xu, Z. Zhang, X. Xiao, Y. Yang, G. Yu, and M. Winslett. Differentially private histogram publication. *VLDB J.*, 22(6), 2013.
[39] J. Zhang, X. Xiao, Y. Yang, Z. Zhang, and M. Winslett. Privgene: Differentially private model fitting using genetic algorithms. In *SIGMOD*, 2013.
[40] J. Zhang, Z. Zhang, X. Xiao, Y. Yang, and M. Winslett. Functional mechanism: Regression analysis under differential privacy. *PVLDB*, 5(11), 2012.

Process-Driven Data Privacy

Weiyi Xia
Vanderbilt University
Nashville, TN, USA

Murat Kantarcioglu
University of Texas at Dallas
Dallas, TX, USA

Zhiyu Wan
Vanderbilt University
Nashville, TN, USA

Raymond Heatherly
Vanderbilt University
Nashville, TN, USA

Yevgeniy Vorobeychik
Vanderbilt University
Nashville, TN, USA

Bradley Malin
Vanderbilt University
Nashville, TN, USA

ABSTRACT

The quantity of personal data gathered by service providers via our daily activities continues to grow at a rapid pace. The sharing, and the subsequent analysis of, such data can support a wide range of activities, but concerns around privacy often prompt an organization to transform the data to meet certain protection models (e.g., k-anonymity or ε-differential privacy). These models, however, are based on simplistic adversarial frameworks, which can lead to both under- and over-protection. For instance, such models often assume that an adversary attacks a protected record exactly once. We introduce a principled approach to explicitly model the attack process as a series of steps. Specifically, we engineer a factored Markov decision process (FMDP) to optimally plan an attack from the adversary's perspective and assess the privacy risk accordingly. The FMDP captures the uncertainty in the adversary's belief (e.g., the number of identified individuals that match the de-identified data) and enables the analysis of various real world deterrence mechanisms beyond a traditional protection model, such as a penalty for committing an attack. We present an algorithm to solve the FMDP and illustrate its efficiency by simulating an attack on publicly accessible U.S. census records against a real identified resource of over 500,000 individuals in a voter registry. Our results demonstrate that while traditional privacy models commonly expect an adversary to attack exactly once per record, an optimal attack in our model may involve exploiting none, one, or more individuals in the pool of candidates, depending on context.

Categories and Subject Descriptors

K.4.1 [**Computing Milieux**]: Computers and Society—*Privacy*; K.6.0 [**Computing Milieux**]: General—*Economics*

General Terms

Algorithms; Security; Theory

Permission to make digital or hard copies of all or part of this work for personal or classroom use is granted without fee provided that copies are not made or distributed for profit or commercial advantage and that copies bear this notice and the full citation on the first page. Copyrights for components of this work owned by others than ACM must be honored. Abstracting with credit is permitted. To copy otherwise, or republish, to post on servers or to redistribute to lists, requires prior specific permission and/or a fee. Request permissions from Permissions@acm.org.
CIKM'15, October 19–23, 2015, Melbourne, Australia.
© 2015 ACM. ISBN 978-1-4503-3794-6/15/10 ...$15.00.
DOI: http://dx.doi.org/10.1145/2806416.2806580.

Keywords

Privacy; Re-identification; Planning

1. INTRODUCTION

The quantity, quality, and diversity of personal data we shed through our daily activities continues to grow at a rapid pace. This data is collected by a wide range of organizations to assist in the optimization and refinement of the services they provide [1, 13]. At the same time, it is increasingly recognized that personal data has substantial worth beyond its initial use, such that it can be repurposed for a variety of endeavors, ranging from transparency in operations to basic research [23]. Despite the recognized value of personal data, organizations worry about how best to protect the rights of their constituents while maximizing the benefits [29].

One such right that our society tends to focus on is personal privacy. While privacy is an overloaded term that takes on many different forms [25], one quantitative, broadly concerned definition centers on the notion of anonymity. There are various regulations that encourage organizations to suppress identifying information from personal data prior to its dissemination. Several examples of regulations with explicit identity protections include the Privacy Rule of the Health Insurance Portability and Accountability Act of 1996 (HIPAA) in the United States and the Data Protection Directive in the European Union. However, there is growing evidence that the resulting data is susceptible to intrusions [19]. One major type of intrusion is the re-identification attack, which happens when an adversary combines de-identified records with external resources to determine the identity of the corresponding individuals (e.g., [12, 18, 26, 27]).

While such attacks are possible, it is unclear if they are probable. This is important because laws and regulations do not require perfect protection, but rather that data be shared in a manner that makes it difficult to ascertain an individual's identity. Organizations are thus afforded an opportunity to achieve data protection using risk management techniques, but they are hampered from accomplishing this goal for several reasons. First, there is little historical data on re-identification attacks [6]. This may be due to the rareness of such events or that they transpired behind closed doors. Second, prior investigations assume privacy risks can only be managed by perturbing data according to a formal model (e.g., k-anonymity [24] or ϵ-differential privacy [4]). Yet, there are many other elements that contribute to privacy risks, such as deterrence mechanisms (e.g., data user agreements, the time and effort to gather the external information necessary to compromise the data, or penalties

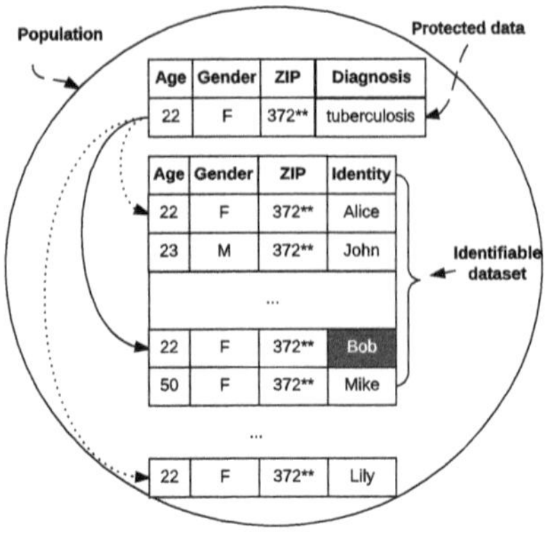

Figure 1: An example of a re-identification scenario.

for misusing data), that influence an adversary. Third, the typical adversarial model invoked in this setting assumes an attack is perpetrated in a pre-defined manner. For instance, under a k-anonymity framework it is assumed the adversary exploits an individual at random, with an expected success rate of $1/k$. Yet, an adversary could attempt to exploit all of the individuals in this group in the hopes that one will be the correct corresponding person. Under the ε-differential privacy framework, the publisher limits the number of times an adversary can query a statistical database to satisfy the given privacy budget.

To overcome these limitations, we introduce a principled approach to assess re-identification risk using a process framework that incorporates data- and penalty-based disincentives. This approach is based on a stochastic model, yielding a quantitative evaluation of the re-identification risk.

1.1 An Orienting Example

For context, Figure 1 depicts an example of the type of attack our re-identification risk framework is designed to handle. Here, Bob corresponds to the de-identified data. Now, there is a probability he is in the external dataset that contains identifying information and a set of attributes in common with the de-identified data. In the event the adversary accesses the external dataset, he will find that the record with a diagnosis of tuberculosis might correspond to Alice, Bob or neither (because the corresponding individual may not be in the dataset). The adversary will be successful if he exploits Bob; however, it is possible the adversary is not sufficiently motivated to start the attack and the adversary may choose to terminate his attack at any point in the process (because of insufficient expected payoffs). Our framework explicitly models the decisions the adversary must make and computes the probability that the adversary will reach a successful re-identification.

1.2 Contributions

The specific contributions of this paper include:

1. Re-identification Risk Model. This research proposes a novel re-identification risk framework that formalizes incentive and deterrence mechanisms (e.g., potential penalties and information uncertainty) that are present in the real world environments where a de-identified dataset is made available. This framework explicitly models the adversary as an optimal planning agent using a factored Markov decision process (FMDP). Given that the state space of the FMDP grows rapidly, we introduce a two-level linear programming algorithm to efficiently solve it.

2. Case Study. We evaluate risk in the scenario where an adversary attempts to leverage a public voter registry in a specific U.S. State to attack de-identified Census records. Under the traditional adversarial model, the adversary is assumed to randomly choose an individual from the group of indistinguishable individuals in the external dataset that matches the targeted record under attack. However, our findings illustrate that the adversary's behavior is highly dependent on the deterrence mechanism set in place. In particular, if the adversary's expectation of the probability of being detected for each exploitation of an individual remains constant across attempts and he will always be penalized if detected, he will choose to either attack 1) all the individuals in the correspond group or 2) none of the individuals. This result illustrates how traditional beliefs about risk can either underprotect or overprotect the data.

3. Sensitivity Analysis. We conduct a detailed sensitivity analysis on the parameters of the model to illustrate how the environment and policy decisions can influence the adversary's behavior. Specifically, we demonstrate how changes in the costs in each stage of the attack, penalty-based deterrence mechanism, and the probability of detection influences when the adversary will cease their attack. Our result demonstrates that the adversary's threshold is highly dependent on the deterrence mechanisms that are in place. This result is notable because it suggests that adversaries may be sufficiently deterred with a small amount of data manipulation, provided appropriate detection and penalization policies are instantiated.

We stress that our framework focuses on the application scenarios where record-level data needs to be shared. For example, in health care research setting, data sets containing patient information may need to be shared. In such scenarios, generalizing the data may be acceptable (e.g., instead of reporting exact birthday of individuals, we can only disclose the birth year) but adding noise may not be acceptable due to the semantic errors that may be introduced. Therefore, our proposed approach can be seen as complementary to recent developments in ϵ-differential privacy where synthetic data sets could be generated for preserving privacy and it is applicable for scenarios where differential privacy based approaches are not appropriate.

The remainder of this paper is organized as follows. In Section 2, we review related work on adversarial modeling and re-identification risk assessment approaches. In Section 3, we introduce the re-identification risk quantification framework. In Section 4 and 5, we present the FMDP and algorithms to solve it and compute the re-identification probability from the Markov process efficiently. In Section 6 and 7, we present an empirical analysis. In Section 8, we discuss the limitations of this work and provide future directions.

2. RELATED WORK

To provide context for our study, we discuss research in privacy preserving data publishing and adversarial modeling areas with a focus on where our work diverges.

2.1 Data Privacy Views

There are many different views on what constitutes a privacy violation when considering data publishing. These views argue that privacy can be compromised when a record is linked to the individual from whom it was derived (often referred to as *identity disclosure*) [10], the inference of a sensitive value associated with the corresponding individual (often referred to as *attribute disclosure*) [16], the ability to detect if someone is a member of a dataset (often referred to as the presence/absence problem) [9, 20], or the degree to which viewing an individual's contribution to a dataset permits an adversary to gain knowledge about them (the basis of models like ε-differential privacy) [2, 5, 8].

In this research, we focus on the identity disclosure problem because this is the primary focus of current regulation. We note, however, that our framework is applicable to any of the above scenarios because we are not introducing a new method for manipulating data. Rather, we are showing how to reason about pressures (e.g., penalties for misuse) that are beyond the scope of what such data manipulation techniques offer.

2.2 Disclosure Risk Management

It has been suggested that assessing disclosure risk requires a holistic modeling of different types of adversaries [7]. Such models should account for the motivation, means, opportunity cost, consequence of attempt, and likelihood of success. In this vein, a recent study [17] presented the concept of a data environment that is composed of data, agents and infrastructure. However, such investigations have not provided a formal approach to risk quantification that accounts for the elements in the data environment. Rather, existing disclosure risk measures mainly focus on the uniqueness of records in the dataset and in the population. For instance, three popular disclosure risk metrics (prosecutor, journalist and marketer) [14] assume that the adversary is always motivated to attack and the extra information required for re-identification is always available. As a consequence, the risk level is only dependent on the data itself.

Our disclosure risk measure explicitly formalizes the three elements of the data environment around the adversary's decision making. We note that there have been several other investigations in applying game theoretic frameworks to analyze the adversary's best course of action and the corresponding disclosure risk [28, 31]. For instance, the adversary in Wan et al. [31] is formalized as an opponent of the data publisher in a Stackelberg game. To maximize payout, the adversary decides if they should attack by comparing the potential gain against the cost of committing an attack. Yet, this model oversimplifies the adversary's decision process of gathering, linking, and exploiting data. Moreover, in their formalization, there were no explicitly modeled penalties for detecting the misuse of the data.

To mitigate the disclosure risk, the publisher can adopt various protection methods (e.g., randomization and generalization) according to given formal protection models. To apply these formal protection models in practice, a protection threshold (e.g., the k value for $k$anonymity [24]) needs to be selected and supported by risk and utility analysis. A method based on Pareto-optimality has been proposed to find the solutions with an optimal utility at different levels of k [3]. However, the risk metric used in such methods to determine the threshold is based solely on the protected data. By contrast, our framework can assist in determining what the threshold should be based on both the data set and other elements in the data environment.

2.3 Adversarial Modeling and MDPs

To the best of our knowledge, MDPs have not been used to

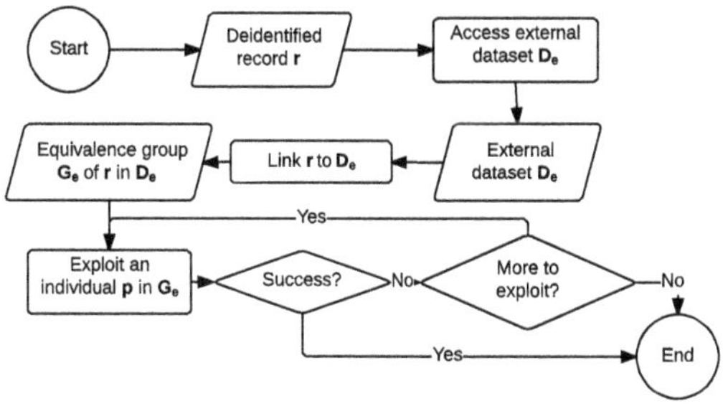

Figure 2: The re-identification attack process.

model adversaries in the privacy preserving data publication setting. Yet it has been proven to be a useful tool in modeling adversary's optimal planning in security problems. This is because the MDP representation captures an adversary's uncertainty on the outcome of a security related action [15]. Similarly, the adversary focused on privacy also exhibits uncertainty. For example, when the adversary chooses to exploit an individual, he is uncertain about whether or not he will be detected and pulished. Also, before the adversary chooses to access the external dataset, he may not be certain about number of identified individuals to which the de-identified record may be related. An important difference between our adversarial model and the one in Letchford and Vorobeychik [15] is that in the security scenario, the adversary terminates once he is caught, whereas in our model, the adversary may only pay a fine and continue to attack.

3. RE-IDENTIFICATION RISK QUANTIFICATION FRAMEWORK

Our framework quantifies the re-identification risk of publishing each record in a de-identified dataset. We assume the dataset is composed of person-level records in a relational form. We define re-identification risk as the composite of the probability that an adversary re-identifies a record and the harm it causes:

$$risk = P_{reid} \times L_{reid} \quad (1)$$

where P_{reid} is the re-identification probability and L_{reid} is the associated publisher loss. We assume L_{reid} is a predefined input, and focus on P_{reid}.

The re-identification probability is derived from the adversary's sequential decision process, outlined in Figure 2. The adversary begins with a de-identified record r. The adversary's first decision is to access an external table D_e or not. His second decision is whether to conduct a linkage attack, which yields an equivalence group of records G_e. This corresponds to the set of individuals with the same value as the target's published quasi-identifier (QI). At this point, each individual $\alpha \in G_e$ has a probability that they actually correspond to the targeted record r. This translates into a probability that an attack (e.g., confirmation of the patient's identity) on α will be successful. If the attack fails, the adversary can choose to exploit another individual from G_e. This process can repeat until the adversary decides to stop or he exhausts all of the records in G_e.

There are several notable aspects of this attack process. First, it should be recognized that this is a stochastic process. For example, the adversary may not know if the individual to whom the target record corresponds is in D_e. Therefore, the outcome of accessing the external dataset is

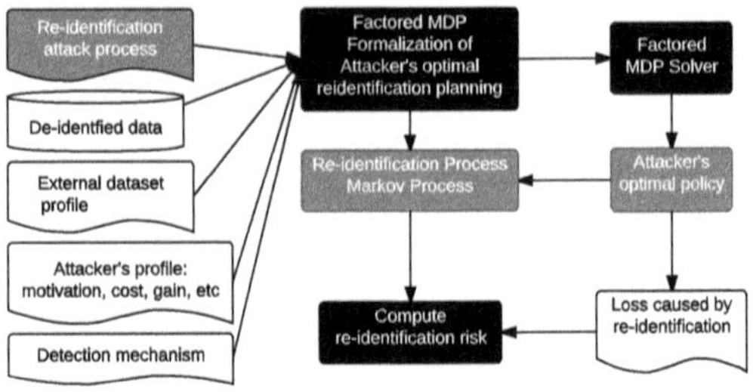

Figure 3: A general architecture of the re-identification risk quantification framework.

uncertain. Furthermore, the result of exploiting an individual is stochastic, with outcomes ranging from success to failure to being detected and punished. A second notable aspect of the attack process is that there is a cost and a reward associated with each action, for instance, the reward for a success, the cost of accessing D_e and the penalty if an attack is detected all determine the adversary's utility.

More precisely, we model the adversary as a planner using a factored Markov decision process (FMDP) [11]. In a FMDP, a state of the world is characterized by a collection of random variables (or factors). The adversary is modeled as a rational agent computing an optimal policy; i.e., an optimal action to choose in each state of the FMDP. Given such a policy, we can compute risk according to Equation 1.

In Figure 3, we show the general architecture of the re-identification risk quantification framework. The framework is composed of three modules (the black rectangles in Figure 3): 1) the FMDP formalization of the adversary's decision process, 2) the FMDP solver, and 3) the re-identification risk computation module. The FMDP formalization module takes four inputs: i) the attack decision process, ii) the de-identified data, iii) the external dataset profile, and iv) the adversary's profile. The factored MDP model is then solved by the FMDP solver module to determine the adversary's optimal policy. Finally, the risk computation module computes the quantified risk value given optimal attack policy and associated probability of successful re-identification attack. In the following sections, we dive into the details of each of the three modules.

4. RE-IDENTIFICATION AS AN FMDP

The FMDP model is a 4-tuple (X, A, R, P), where $X = \{X_0, ..., X_m\}$ is a finite set of random variables, each with a finite domain. In this model, A is a finite set of actions; R is the reward function $R(x, a)$, representing the reward for each action a taken in state $X = x$; and P is a Markovian transition function $P(X_i'|X_i^{parent}, a)$, which represents the probability distribution of the state variable X_i' in the next state given the value of a subset of state variables X_i^{parent} and action a (X_i^{parent} is the set of variables that X_i' is dependent on given the action is a). We denote the value of a state variable X_i in state x as $x[X_i]$. We assume that the FMDP has an infinite horizon, and time is exponentially discounted with a discount factor γ.

4.1 State variables

As summarized in Table 1, the FMDP model is based on eight state variables. Here, we take a moment to provide intuition into each of these variables. First, X_t is a binary variable that represents the termination of an attack. When $X_t = T$ (true), the corresponding state is absorbing, effectively ending the decision process. Next, we assume the existence of an attack detection mechanism, and the state of detection is indicated by a binary variable X_d. The following variable, X_s, indicates whether the exploit is successful (in which case the adversary obtains a positive reward). The next two variables are associated with data manipulation. X_a is a binary indicator of whether the external dataset D_e has been accessed, while X_l is a binary indicator of whether it has been linked to the published target record r. X_p maintains the number of times the exploitation has been detected and penalized. The final two variables, X_g and X_r keep track of the size of the equivalence group and the remaining unexploited individuals in the group. Thus, as the adversary attempts (unsuccessful) attacks on matched records, X_r decreases while X_g remains constant. This is because the original group size associated with linking is fixed. To keep our presentation compact, we represent each state x as a vector $[x_0, ..., x_m]$ in the FMDP model, where x_i denotes the value of the ith variable in the list $[X_t, X_d, X_p, X_s, X_a, X_l, X_g, X_r]$.

Table 1: The state variables of the FMDP model.

Variable	Explanation
X_t, binary	If **T**, attack is terminated
X_d, binary	If **T**, exploit of an individual is detected
X_p, integer	Number of previous exploits penalized
X_s, binary	If **T**, target record r is successfully re-identified
X_a, binary	If **T**, external dataset D_e has been accessed
X_l, binary	If **T**, target record r has been linked to the external dataset D_e
X_g, integer	The size of the equivalence group of target record r in external dataset D_e
X_r, integer	The remaining number of unexploited individuals in the equivalence group for record r in external dataset D_e

Table 2: The actions of the FMDP model.

Action	Explanation
terminate	Abort the attack
access	Access the external dataset D_e
link	Link the de-identified record r_i to the external dataset D_e
exploit	Exploit a random individual in the equivalence group of record r in the external dataset D_e

4.2 Action set

There are four classes of actions in our system, which are summarized in Table 2. The adversary has the option of aborting the attack at any time by choosing the *terminate* action. The other three actions represent the adversary's operation in three different phases of the attack. The *access* action represents the accessing of the external dataset D_e. The *link* action represents the linking of the de-identified record r to the external dataset D_e. The *exploit* action represents a potentially harmful exploitation of an individual that is deemed to be related to the record r under attack. The particular type of exploitation may differ under various circumstances. For example, if the adversary's goal is to demonstrate the vulnerability of the system, the exploit may be to prove they can contact the individual and confirm the record is really associated with them [30]. Or, the adversary's goal may be to conduct direct marketing to the individual based on the sensitive information in the record (e.g., for a particular pharmaceutical). Regardless, an exploit is assumed to be successful if it is conducted against the individual to whom the record corresponds.

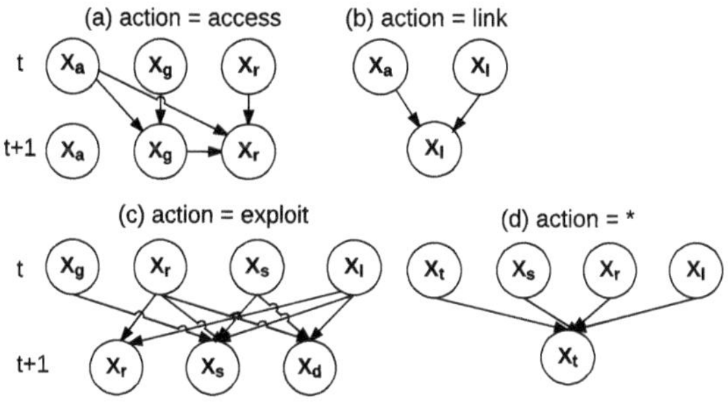

Figure 4: The dynamic Bayesian network (DBN) for each action of our FMDP model.

4.3 Reward

Reward functions are determined by several factors: the cost of taking an action, the loss to the adversary from detection (both negative rewards), and the gain from a successful attack. We formally define the reward function as:

$$R(x, a) = R_g(x[X_s], x[X_t]) + R_p(x[X_d], x[X_p]) - C_a \quad (2)$$

where C_a is the cost of action a (denoted by C_d, C_c, and C_e for *access*, *link*, and *exploit* actions, respectively). $C_a = 0$ for the *terminate* action. $R_g(x[X_s], x[X_t])$ represents the gain from a succussful exploitation. $R_g(x[X_s], x[X_t]) = G$, if $X_s = T$ and $X_t = F$ and 0 otherwise.

We assume there is a maximum number of times, n_f, that the adversary will be subject to a penalty (e.g., a fine for law or contract violation) if he is detected. Note that this permits an analysis on the special case of $n_f = 1$, where the adversary is only penalized once. This is notable because it represents the real scenario where a data user is penalized for violating a contract, but is not prevented from continuing to exploit the data they have already received. We denote the cost related to the fine as $R_p(x[X_d], x[X_p])$. $R_p(x[X_d], x[X_p]) = -C_p$, if $X_d = T \wedge X_p < n_f$ and 0 otherwise.

4.4 State transition dynamics

We use a dynamic Bayesian network (DBN) $\tau_a = \langle G_a, P_a \rangle$ for each action a (except action *terminate*), as shown in Figure 4, to represent the transition function $P(X_i | X_i^{parent}, a)$. We denote the current state and the next state as x and x', respectively. If the action is to *terminate*, $x'[X_t] = T$.

If the action is to access, as the DBN shows in Figure 4(a), there are 3 state variables that may change in the following step: X_a, X_g and X_r. We highlight that if the external dataset D_e has not yet been accessed (i.e., $x[X_a] = F$), the adversary's belief of the equivalence group size in the next state $x'[X_g]$ is a probability distribution over a set of values, represented as $P(G_{r,D_e})$. Our experiments simulate $P(G_{r,D_e})$ under different levels of certainty and its influence on the adversary's behavior and re-identification risk.

In Figure 4(b), the *link* action sets $x'[X_l] = T$ when $x[X_a] = T$ (i.e., external dataset is available for linkage).

The prerequisite condition for the *exploit* action is $x[X_l] = T$, $x[X_s] = F$, and $x[X_r] > 0$. In other words, we can only exploit a record if 1) the equivalence group is non-empty, 2) the dataset has been linked to the record, and 3) the record has not already been re-identified. In this case, the number of remaining candidates in the equivalence group is decremented ($x'[X_r] = x[X_r] - 1$).

Moreover, the probability that the exploited individual is associated with the record is the probability of selecting an individual at random from the set of individuals in the population (with the same quasi-identifier) who have not been exploited. The number of individuals with the same quasi-identifier in the population who have not been exploited is the sum of the number of individuals outside (i.e., $\frac{1-prior_{r,D_e}}{prior_{r,D_e}} \times x[X_g]$) and inside (i.e.,$x[X_r]$) the external dataset d_e. Thus, the success probability of an exploitation can be formally represented as:

$$P_{suc}(x[X_g], x[X_r], prior_{r,D_e}) = \Big(\frac{1 - prior_{r,D_e}}{prior_{r,D_e}} \times x[X_g] + x[X_r]\Big)^{-1} \quad (3)$$

where $prior_{r,D_e}$ is the probability that the individual corresponding to the data is in the external dataset D_e.

$P(x'[X_d] = T)$ (i.e., the probability of being caught) denoted as P_{det} can be modeled in a number of ways. Since the probability an exploit is detected is very likely to increase with repeated attempts due to various factors (e.g., increased vigilance), we model the detection probability using a sigmoid function:

$$P_{det} = (1 + e^{-(h_0 + h_1 \times (x[X_g] - x[X_r]))})^{-1} \quad (4)$$

where $x[X_g] - x[X_r]$ corresponds to the number of exploit attempts the adversary has committed against records in the equivalence group. Note that this formulation allows us to model the special case, where the probability of detection does not increase over time by setting $h_1 = 0$.

Finally, regardless of the action, the transition of variable X_t is determined as follows (see Figure 4(d)): $x'[X_t] = T$ if $x[X_t] = T \vee x[X_s] = T \vee (x[X_l] = T \wedge x[X_r] = 0)$.

5. ALGORITHMS

5.1 Solving the MDP

Solving an infinite-horizon discounted MDP amounts to computing an optimal policy, $\pi(x)$, which prescribes an optimal action to take in each state [22]. Equivalently, it suffices to compute a value function, $V(x)$, which is the optimal discounted sum of rewards of an optimal policy.

A number of methods exist for solving an MDP. Linear programming (LP) is one such method, which computes the value function, $V(x)$, for every state x. An important limitation of the standard methods, including LP, is scalability. In particular, if we do not take advantage of problem structure, the runtime is polynomial in the number of states, which itself grows exponentially in the number of state variables. Approaches exist that leverage the structure of the factored MDP, but they are approximate, and require the pre-specification of a fixed set of basis functions over the state space. Next, we present a special-purpose method, which we call Two-Level LP, that takes advantage of our problem structure (including the factored state) and reports an exact answer.

5.1.1 Two-level Linear Programming

We designed the Two-level LP algorithm under the principle of removing all the "well-known" parts from the FMDP structure to save space and runtime. The algorithm constructs a two-level structure from the state space. The states in the FMDP model form a *sink cluster* sub-structure, which satisfies the following properties: a) there is no outbound and b) there is only one inbound state (i.e., x_{start} has only one inbound edge). Based on the property of the FMDP, each sink cluster can be solved independently. The bottom-level of the Two-Level LP algorithm solves a LP and stores the value of the state x_{start} for each sink cluster. The top-level algorithm then constructs and solves a LP of the entire state space by replacing each sink state with its corresponding x_{start} and assigns the pre-computed $V(x_{start})$ to it.

Specifically, each sink cluster contains the descendant states of a state x_{start} in which the adversary has taken the action of access and link, but has not yet started exploitation, i.e., $x_{start} = [F, F, 0, F, T, T, s_i, s_i]$, $s_i \in (0, \max(G_{r,D_e}))$. Given two different group sizes s_1 and s_2, the two sink clusters with $x_{start} = [F, F, 0, F, T, T, s_1, s_1]$ and $x_{start} = [F, F, 0, F, T, T, s_2, s_2]$ do not overlap because the value X_g remains constant when $X_a = T$ and $X_l = T$. The resulting values of all the x_{start} states are used in the top-level LP to solve the values for the remaining states, such as the state in which the adversary is attempting to access the external dataset (i.e., $x = [F, F, 0, F, F, F, 0, 0]$).

We make two performance improvements for Two-Level LP. First, we introduce a pruning strategy which leverages the fact that the value of the starting states for each cluster (i.e., $V(x_{start} = [F, F, 0, F, T, T, s, s])$) decreases as the size of the equivalence group $X_g = s$ increases. We omit the proof of this property due to brevity.

Thus, we sort the sink cluster by the value of $x_{start}[X_g]$ in ascending order. Specifically, if $V(x_{start}) = 0$ given $x_{start}[X_g] = s$, then all of the sink clusters with $x_{start}[X_g] > s$ will be pruned. Second, we use a result caching strategy. In doing so, the result from the bottom-level LP is cached and reused with multiple records. This happens when there is an overlap in the adversary's belief of the probability distribution interval of the equivalence group size X_g.

5.2 Computing Re-identification Probability

The re-identification probability P_{reid} is the sum of the probability of reaching each of the states with $x[X_s] = T$ and $x[X_t] = F$ in 1 to t_{max} time steps. Formally, P_{reid} is computed as:

$$P_{reid} = \sum_{t=0}^{t=t_{max}} \sum_{x \in x_{suc}} M^t[x_0, x] \tag{5}$$

In equation 5, $x_0 = [F, F, 0, F, F, F, 0, 0]$ represents the state in which the adversary has not accessed the external dataset yet, x_{suc} is the set of states with $x[X_s] = T$ and $x[X_t] = F$, x is an arbitrary state. M is the state transition $N \times N$ matrix of a Markov chain, where N is the number of states.

The state transition matrix M is obtained by replacing the action a in the transition dynamics function of the FMDP with $policy(x)$, i.e., $P(X'_i | X_i^{parent}, policy(x))$. However, there is one exception. Given the current state is x_0, in the FMDP model, $x'[X_g]$ is a probability distribution over a range of values due to the uncertainty of the adversary's belief, while, in the risk computation Markov chain, $P(x'[X_g] = g_{r,D_e}) = 1$, g_{r,D_e} is the actual group size in D_e. This is because the Markov chain already embed's the adversary's optimal policy, and consequently the adversary's belief in the group size no longer matters. Instead, what matters is the actual group size. We assume that g_{r,D_e} is an input to the risk framework.

The value t_{max} is the maximum number of time steps it takes for all the states to transit into a state where $X_t = T$ (i.e., an absorbing sink state). Formally: $\exists t_{max} > 0$ $\forall x_i, x_j \in x_i, i \in [0, N], \text{if } x_j[X_t] \neq 0, M^{t_{max}}[x_i, x_j] = 0$.

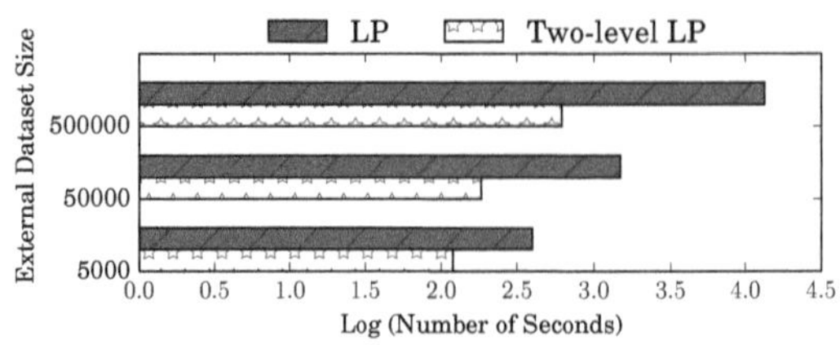

Figure 5: Runtime (log_{10}) of the FMDP solving algorithms for a dataset of 5000 de-identified records.

6. EXPERIMENTS

6.1 Dataset

Our experiments make use of three resources. First, we use the freely available North Carolina voter registration (NCVR) list [21] as the identified external dataset. This consists of 6,018,999 records without missing values over 18 fields. These include explicit identifiers (e.g., personal name and phone number), as well as quasi-identifiers (e.g., age, gender, race, and ethnic group). For the purposes of this study, we restricted the dataset to a set of four quasi-identifying attributes, {*Age*, *Race*, *Gender*, *5-Digit ZIP Code*}.

Second, we use the Adult dataset from the UCI Machine Learning Repository, as the de-identified dataset. This consists of 32,561 records with 14 fields each, based on a sample of the U.S. Census, without missing values. This dataset contains *Age*, *Race*, and *Gender*, but not *5-Digit ZIP Code*. As such, for each record in the Adult dataset, we synthesize and append a 5-digit NC ZIP code based on the population distribution in the US Census Bureau's 2010 Census Tables PCT12A-G. We also replaced a topcoded age value [90+] by a random value in the range of [90, 120].

Third, we assume that both the de-identified and identified datasets are sampled from the entire population of NC. In this case, it should be noted that the total size of the NC population, according to the census is 9,553,967.

6.2 Equivalence Group Size Distribution

In the experiments, the probability distribution of the value X_g after the adversary takes the action to access the dataset $P(G_{r,D_e})$ is derived from the adversary's knowledge about the external dataset D_e or the population statistics. Here, we consider two scenarios. In the first scenario the adversary knows the target's equivalence group size when starting the attack. Specifically, $P(G_{r,D_e} = g_{r,D_e}) = 1$. We refer to this scenario as the *known group* model.

However, the adversary may not have such knowledge before accessing D_e. In this case, we assume the adversary knows only the total size of the external dataset, n, and the probability density of the target's record, i.e., the joint probability of the target's quasi-identifying values $P(r[QI])$, in the population. Assuming that the external dataset is sampled uniformly at random from the population, $P(G_{r,D_e})$ can be represented as a binomial distribution defined in Equation 6:

$$P(G_{r,D_e} = k) = B(k, n, P(r[QI])) \tag{6}$$

We refer to this mechanism as the *unknown group* model.

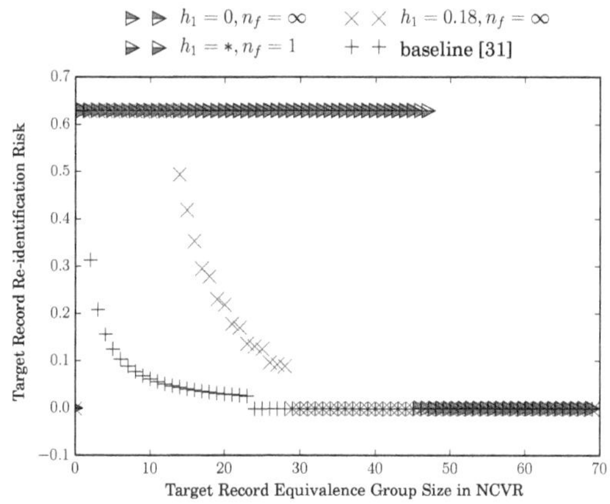

Figure 6: The equivalence group size for the target record in the NCVR dataset and the re-identification risk under the *known group scenario.*

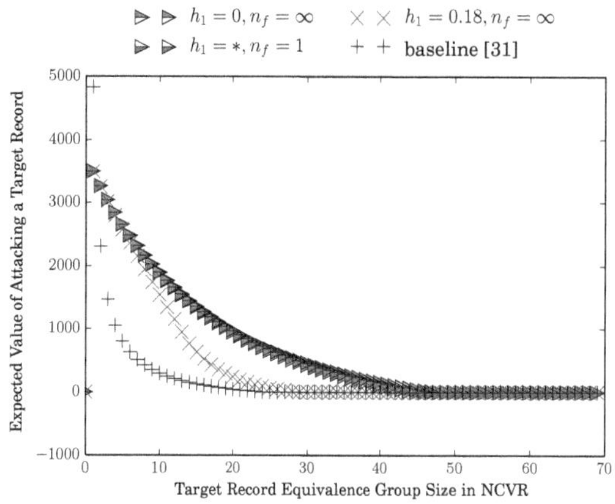

Figure 7: The equivalence group size of of the target record in the NCVR dataset and the adversary's expected payoff under the *known group scenario.*

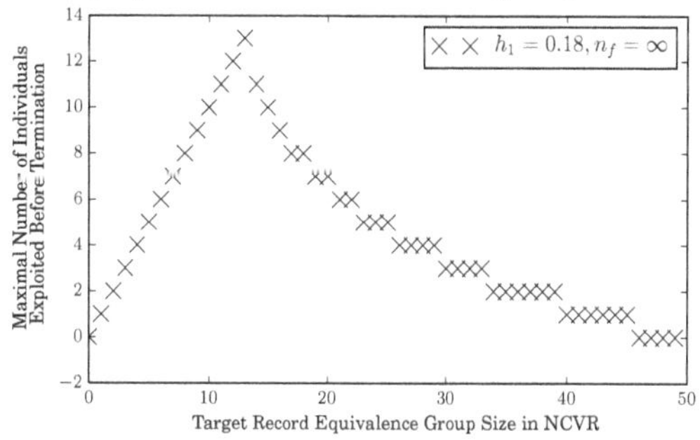

Figure 8: The size of the equivalence group of the target record in the NCVR dataset and the actual number of individuals the adversary exploits before terminating under the *known group* scenario.

7. RESULTS

7.1 Performance Analysis

We evaluated the runtime of the framework with 5000 randomly selected Adult records. In this analysis, we consider the *unknown group* scenario with a $P(G_{r,D_e})$ computed as Equation 6 in which the size of the external dataset is set to 3 different values: 5K, 50K, and 500K. We present the result of the *unknown group* scenario because the *known group* scenario yield FMDP with constant size state space, while *unknown group* scenario leads to increasing state space when the external dataset size n increases simply because of the interval of $P(G_{r,D_e})$ increase with n. The detection and penalty mechanism is set to $h_0 = -4.59$, $h_1 = *, n_f = 1$ (i.e., penalize only once and the probability of detection is 0.01 based on equation 4). The other parameters of the model were set to $prior_{r,D_e} = 0.63$, $C_d = 100$, $C_e = 10$, $G = 8000$ and $C_p = 10000$.

The algorithms were implemented in Python and all experiments were run on an Ubuntu server with 24 Intel(R) Xeon(R) CPUs at 2.4 GHz and 64 GB of RAM. The LP solver was the IBM ILOG CPLEX optimizer.

Figure 5 reports the runtime for the LP and Two-level LP algorithms. It can be seen that, as expected, the Two-level LP is always faster than the standard LP algorithm. The difference in speed is accentuated as the size of the external dataset grows. By the time there are 500K records in the external dataset, the runtime of the Two-level LP is approximately 21x faster (616 seconds vs. 13,444 seconds).

7.2 Case study

To perform a case study, we assume the Adult and NCVR records are random samples of the NC population. Thus, the prior probability that the individual corresponding to an Adult record is in the NCVR is the sample ratio, or $prior_{r,D_e} = 6,018,999/9,553,967 = 0.63$. The NCVR data is free; however, considering the effort to obtain it, we set the cost of accessing the external dataset C_d to \$100.

The cost to exploit, gain and penalty values were set to $C_e = \$10$, $G = \$8000$ and $C_p = \$10000$ for each record, respectively. We acknowledge these values may vary in practice. The goal is to simulate a case in which the adversary will attack at least a subset of the records. This allows us to examine how different deterrence mechanisms and uncertainty about the equivalence in the external datasets affects the adversary's behavior and the re-identification risk. Therefore, these parameters are selected from a range in which the adversary will attack some of the records.

7.2.1 Known Group Model

We compare the *known group* model to the risk model in [31]. This is the only available model for re-identification based on an adversary's optimal decision. In the baseline, the adversary makes a single decision on when to attack based on the total payoff:

$$Payoff_{baseline} = G * (\frac{prior_{r,D_e}}{G_{r,D_e}}) - p_{det} * C_p - C_d - C_l - C_e \quad (7)$$

If $Payoff_{baseline} > 0$, the adversary exploits a random individual and the risk of re-identification is $prior_{r,D_e}/G_{r,D_e}$. Otherwise, the risk is 0. The FMDP is configured under three detection and penalty settings: a) a constant detection probability with repeated penalties (i.e., $h_1 = 0$ and $n_f = \infty$), b) a one-time penalty (i.e., $h_1 = *$ and $n_f = 1$)[1] and c) an increasing rate of detection with repeated penalties (i.e., $h_1 = 0.18$ and $n_f = \infty$). In each setting, we set $h_0 = -4.59$. This yields a 0.01 detection rate for the first exploit, an increase to 0.012 for the next exploit, and so on.

The results are illustrated in Figure 6. There are three notable findings to highlight.

[1]The $*$ indicates that h_1 can be anything because only a single penalty is assigned.

Finding 1: The baseline risk never exceeds the FMDP models. This is because the baseline assumes that the adversary can only select one random individual, which is suboptimal. Thus, as can be seen in Figure 7, the baseline adversary's expected value drops at a faster rate than the adversary who acts according to the FMDP. Moreover, the adversary's success rate is also lower for the baseline. This is because the adversary only exploits one random individual from the equivalence group. This indicates that the baseline model often underestimates the re-identification risk.

Finding 2: When the detection probability is constant (i.e., $h_1 = 0$) and there is no upper bound on the number of times a penalty is levied on the adversary (i.e., $n_f = \infty$), the adversary either exploits 1) all records in the equivalence group or 2) no records.

Finding 3: When the probability of detection grows with repeated attempts (i.e., $h_1 > 0$) or there is an upper bound on the number of times a penalty is levied on the adversary (i.e., n_f is a finite value), the adversary exploits a subset of the equivalence group. In the scenario represented by Finding 2, the adversary chooses not to issue an attack when the equivalence group size is $\geq$ a threshold k, but the adversary exploits all the individuals in the equivalence group otherwise. Thus, the re-identification risk is either equal to the prior probability $prior_{r,D_e}$ or 0. This is because when the optimal action is to attack one individual in the NCVR equivalence group the subsequent optimal action is always to continue to exploit each of the remaining individuals provided that each exploitation has the same probability of being detected and the adversary will always be fined if detected.[2]

In the scenario of Finding 3, the adversary may terminate the attack before exhausting the candidates in the equivalence group. Thus, the risk can be any value between 0 and the prior probability $prior_{r,D_e}$. This is due to two possible reasons. First, if $h_1 > 0$, both the likelihood of detection and a successful re-identification are increasing when more individuals are exploited. Thus, the adversary stops when the increment in the expected penalty exceeds the increment in the expected payout, which can happen before the adversary exhausts all the candidates. Second, if n_f is finite, and the adversary was not detected in the previous exploitations, the expected payout can decrease when the number of the remaining cadidates reduces.

Similar to Finding 2, if the group size is $< k$, the adversary exploits all the individuals in the equivalence group. By contrast, if the group size is $\geq k'$, the adversary stops issuing an attack. For the group size in the range of (k, k'), the adversary's optimal action is to stop before reaching the last candidate in the group. The actual number of candidates the adversary will exploit before termination is shown in Figure 8. In this case, $k = 14$ and $k' = 29$.

These two findings are contradictory to what is expected by the baseline model. In particular, the records with equivalence group size $< k$ all have the same level of risk according to the FMDP model, while the records with smaller equivalence groups have more risk than those with larger equivalence groups according to the baseline model. The indication of this finding from the data protection perspective is that applying mechanisms, such as generalization, to increase the equivalence group size can only effectively reduce risk if the equivalence group size $\geq k$. In other words, increasing the equivalence group size to any value $< k$ will only harm the utility of the data without reducing the risk.

[2]We omit a proof of this claim due to brevity, but will make it available in a longer technical report upon acceptance.

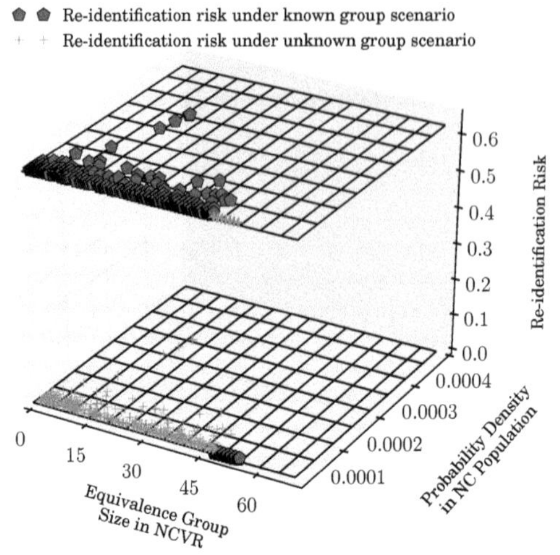

Figure 9: The equivalence group size, population probability density and the re-identification risk of the record with inconsistent risk values in the *known and unknown group* scenarios ($n_f = 1$).

7.2.2 *Unknown group Model*

The FMDP enables us to evaluate risk when the adversary is uncertain in the equivalence group size; i.e., the *unknown group* scenario. We assume that the adversary's belief of the group size is as in equation 6 with $n = 6018999$, with $p_{r[QI]}$ equal to the probability density of the corresponding target record in the NC census population. The other parameters are the same as defined in the *known group* model. Our result illustrates the following findings.

Finding 4: The unknown group scenario can yield *lower risk* than the known group scenario.

Finding 5: The unknown group scenario can yield *higher risk* than the known group scenario. These findings illustrate that uncertainty in the group size can change the action of the adversary. To make this observation more concrete, Figure 9 depicts the risk for the 1920 records that have exhibited different risk scores. 1118 of these records (or 58%) have a risk of 0.63 under the *known group* scenario and 0 under the *unknown group* scenario. The remaining 802 (or 42%) records have the exact opposite result. The former is due to the fact that the adversary underestimates the payoff by using the probability distribution of the equivalence group size. As a result, the adversary does not access D_e, while the actual group size is $<$ the threshold $k = 48$ and in the *known group* scenario the adversary will access D_e and attack. The latter is, on the other hand, due to adversary's overestimation of the expected payoff based on their inaccurate belief about the equivalence group size. These cases are counterintuitive because one may argue that even if the adversary decides to access D_e, he or she will not exploit and there is no risk because the actual equivalence group size is $\geq k = 48$. However, this is not always true because after the adversary obtains D_e, the cost C_d (i.e., the cost of accessing the external dataset) became a sunk cost. As a consequence, the payoff is computed without considering C_d and the threshold the adversary can tolerate increases from 48 to 51. If the actual equivalence group size is between the two thresholds, the adversary with less knowledge (i.e., in the *unknown group* scenario) may be able to cause greater risk, even though the adversary does not necessarily obtain a higher payoff than the *known group* adversary.

Records resulting in different risk levels in the *known* and *unknown group* scenarios are not very common in this experiment setting. A majority of the records lead to the same risk (94%, or 30641 in total). The is due primarily to the fact that this analysis is dominated by records whose corresponding equivalence group size is larger than 55. Specifically, 64%, or 20891 in total, satisfy this situation. This is notable because, even if a positive payoff expected from $P(G_{r,D_e})$ leads the *unknown group* adversary to access the external dataset, the adversary never chooses to exploit such records, yielding a risk of 0.

7.3 Sensitivity Analysis

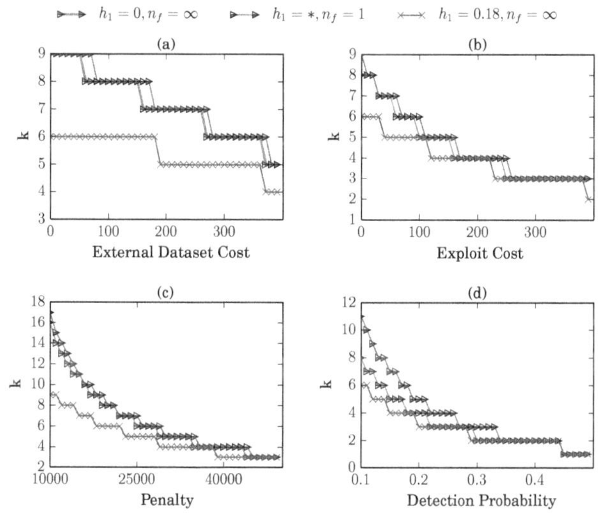

Figure 10: Sensitivity analysis on group size threshold (k) as a function of (a) external dataset cost C_a; (b) exploit cost C_e; (c) *Penalty*; and (d) detection probability P_{det}.

In this section, we investigate how the deterrence parameters influence the threshold k of the size of the equivalence group when the adversary walks away, such that the risk is 0 when equivalence group size is $\geq k$ under the three scenarios studied above. For this analysis, we assume a *known group* scenario and both the de-identified and external datasets cover the entire population, such that $prior_{r,D_e} = 1$. We vary 1) the cost to access data, 2) the cost to exploit the targeted individual, 3) the penalty levied when re-identification attempts are detected, and 4) the detection probability. In the analysis, we vary one variable at a time while holding all other variables constant to: C_p = \$20000, G = \$1000, C_e = \$10, C_l = \$0, C_a = \$100.

The result is unsurprising, but notable. Specifically, as illustrated in Figure 10, as the deterrence mechanism is ramped up, the expected payout is lower and the adversary tolerates less risk. For example, when the penalty is set to \$10,000, the adversary always attacks when the group size is smaller than 9 individuals. By the time the penalty is raised to \$50000, the adversary will only risk an attack if there is one individual in the group. This result clearly indicates that penalties and costs for access to data can quickly deter an adversary from committing an attack.

8. DISCUSSION AND CONCLUSIONS

This research provides a formal process-based approach to characterize the privacy risks for published data and opens a novel direction in the field of data privacy. It also introduces a scalable algorithm based on linear programming to solve the attacker's optimal planning problem. A core contribution of this approach is that it accounts for deterrence mechanisms beyond data manipulation methods. We demonstrated the feasibility through a case study in a real world scenario, where an adversary uses a publicly available population registry (with over 6,000,000 individuals) to attack a record subject to a data obfuscation mechanism.

Our results reveal that a broadly accepted adversarial model in which the adversary will randomly choose one individual that matches the record to attack can be suboptimal, and an adversary may try and exploit every individual in the corresponding equivalence class. In addition to penalization mechanism, our result demonstrated that the adversary's optimal decision depends on the information about the external resources they may use (e.g., voter registration lists) before they access them to mount an attack. This work provides strong evidence that the risk to such systems in the real world is heavily dependent on the amount of effort an adversary needs to exert and the expected payout they can receive based on their attack. This investigation further provides intuition into how data perturbation techniques can be complemented by alternative disincentive strategies (e.g., charging for access to data or levying fines for malicious behavior) to lower the risk inherent in data sharing.

Our approach has several limitations which can provide directions for future research in this area. First, if such a risk estimation procedure is to be put into practice, policy makers will need information about the nature of deterrence mechanisms, the existence and costs of external data resources, as well as the adversary's potential gain. Moreover, our work shows that knowing the prior probability that the corresponding target is in an external resource is critical to the model. Our model assumes that the external dataset is a random sample from a large population that also covers the protected data. Such information is not always readily available to the data publisher when evaluating risk. In the event the publisher believes they could underestimate such parameters, they may lobby for larger fines on misuse, thus deterring users with legitimate interests from accessing their resource. Thus, a future direction for research is in the development of approaches to estimate such parameters of the attack process. This may be possible, for example, by building a model for the detection rate based on existing detection mechanisms.

Second, there are limitations in the scope of the adversary's goals. Consider, the process model assumed an adversary targets only one record in the protected dataset at a time. It also assumes that the adversary has access to only one external resource to mount an attack. Perhaps more significantly, we assume that the success of an exploit will be confirmed. Yet, certain adversaries may be interested in multiple records in the protected data (or even the entire dataset) and may have access to multiple resources. Removing any of these assumptions will lead to an increase in the complexity of the adversary's decision problem. We note that the process model can be extended to account for these scenarios by introducing more state variables and actions. However, this will lead to an explosion in the state space.

Therefore, a future direction of research is to generalize the FMDP model while improving the scalability of the solver algorithm.

Finally, our empirical analysis was conducted on a specific type of data, namely the demographic information within the publicly available population registry. Such a process-based approach to privacy risk assessments is applicable to other types of data where the attack is not a linkage-based exploit, but focuses rather on other definitions of privacy, such as inferential disclosure. The adaptation of such a technique will depend on the extent to which the adversary's process for realizing their exploit can be represented.

9. ACKNOWLEDGMENTS

This work was sponsored by grants from the NIH (R01-HG006844, R01-LM009989, U01-HG006478, U01-HG006385), the NSF (CCF-0424422), the AFRL (FA8785-14-2-0180), and Sandia National Lab (contract 2191).

10. REFERENCES

[1] A. Bharadwaj, O. El Sawy, P. Pavlou, et al. Digital business strategy: toward a next generation of insights. *MIS Quarterly*, 37(2):471–482, 2013.

[2] L. Bonomi and L. Xiong. A two-phase algorithm for mining sequential patterns with differential privacy. In *Proc. 22nd ACM Int'l Conf. on Inform. and Knowl. Management*, pages 269–278, 2013.

[3] R. Dewri, I. Ray, I. Ray, et al. POkA: Identifying pareto-optimal k-anonymous nodes in a domain hierarchy lattice. In *Proc. 18th ACM Conf. on Inform. and Knowl. Management*, pages 1037–1046, 2009.

[4] C. Dwork. Differential privacy. In *Proc. Int'l Colloquium on Automata, Languages, and Programming*, pages 1–12. Springer, 2006.

[5] C. Dwork. The promise of differential privacy: A tutorial on algorithmic techniques. In *Proc. IEEE Annual Symp. on Foundations of Computer Science*, pages 1–12, 2011.

[6] K. El Emam, E. Jonker, L. Arbuckle, and B. Malin. A systematic review of re-identification attacks on health data. *PLoS ONE*, 6(12):e28071, 2010.

[7] M. Elliot and A. Dale. Scenarios of attack: the data intruder's perspective on statistical disclosure risk. *Netherlands Official Statistics*, 14:6-10, 1999.

[8] L. Fan and L. Xiong. Real time aggregate monitoring with differential privacy. In *Proc. 21st ACM Int'l Conf. on Inform. and Knowl. Management*, pages 2169–2173, 2012.

[9] D. Freni, C. Ruiz Vicente, S. Mascetti, et al. Preserving location and absence privacy in geo-social networks. In *Proc. 19th ACM Int'l Conf. on Inform. and Knowl. Management*, pages 309–318, 2010.

[10] B. C. M. Fung, K. Wang, R. Chen, and P. S. Yu. Privacy-preserving data publishing: A survey of recent developments. *ACM Computing Surveys*, 42(4), 2010.

[11] C. Guestrin, D. Koller, R. Parr, and S. Venkataraman. Efficient solution algorithms for factored MDPs. *CoRR*, abs/1106.1822, 2011.

[12] R. Jones, R. Kumar, B. Pang, and A. Tomkins. "I know what you did last summer": query logs and user privacy. In *Proc. 16th ACM Conf. on Inform. and Knowl. Management*, pages 909–914, 2007.

[13] O. Kwon, N. Lee, and B. Shin. Data quality management, data usage experience and acquisition intention of big data analytics. *Int'l Journal of Inform. Management*, 34(3):387–394, 2014.

[14] D. Lambert. Measures of disclosure risk and harm. *Journal of Official Statistics*, 9:313–331, 1993.

[15] J. Letchford and Y. Vorobeychik. Optimal interdiction of attack plans. In *Proc. Int'l Conf. on Autonomous Agents and Multi-agent Systems*, pages 199–206, 2013.

[16] A. Machanavajjhala, D. Kifer, J. Gehrke, et al. l-diversity: Privacy beyond k-anonymity. *ACM Trans. on Knowl. Discovery in Data*, 1(1), 2007.

[17] E. Mackey and M. Elliot. Understanding the data environment. *XRDS*, 20(1):36–39, Sept. 2013.

[18] A. Narayanan and V. Shmatikov. De-anonymizing social networks. In *Proc. 30th IEEE Symp. on Security and Privacy*, pages 173–187, 2009.

[19] A. Narayanan and V. Shmatikov. Myths and fallacies of "personally identifiable information". *Communications of the ACM*, 53(6):24–26, 2010.

[20] M. E. Nergiz, M. Atzori, and C. Clifton. Hiding the presence of individuals from shared databases. In *Proc. ACM SIGMOD Int'l Conf. on Management of Data*, pages 665–676, 2007.

[21] North Carolina Voter Registration Database, `ftp://alt.ncsbe.gov/data/`. Last accessed 4 Aug 2015.

[22] M. L. Puterman. *Markov Decision Processes: Discrete Stochastic Dynamic Programming*. John Wiley & Sons, Inc., New York, NY, USA, 1st edition, 1994.

[23] L. Roderick. Discipline and power in the digital age: the case of the US consumer data broker. *Critical Sociology*, 40(5):729–746, 2014.

[24] P. Samarati and L. Sweeney. Protecting privacy when disclosing information: k-anonymity and its enforcement through generalization and suppression. Technical Report SRI-CSL-98-04, SRI Computer Science Laboratory, 1998.

[25] D. Solove. A taxonomy of privacy. *University of Pennsylvania Law Review*, 154(3):477–560, 2006.

[26] M. Srivatsa and M. Hicks. Deanonymizing mobility traces: using social network as a side-channel. In *Proc. ACM Conf. on Computer and Communications Security*, pages 628–637, 2012.

[27] L. Sweeney. Uniqueness of simple demographics in the U.S. population. *Technical report, Carnegie Mellon University*, 2000.

[28] P. Tallon. An application of game theory to understanding statistical disclosure events. *UNECE/Eurostat Work Session on Data Confidentiality*, 2009.

[29] P. Tallon. Corporate governance of big data: perspectives on value, risk, and cost. *IEEE Computer*, 46(6):32–38, 2013.

[30] A. Tanner. Harvard professor re-identifies anonymous volunteers in DNA study. *Forbes*, 4 Apr 2013.

[31] Z. Wan, Y. Vorobeychik, W. Xia, et al. A game theoretic framework for analyzing re-identification risk. *PLoS ONE*, 10:e0120592, 2015.

Unsupervised Feature Selection on Data Streams

Hao Huang
GE Global Research
haohuanghw@gmail.com

Shinjae Yoo
Computational Science Center, Brookhaven National Laboratory
shinjae@gmail.com

Shiva Prasad Kasiviswanathan*
Samsung Research America
kasivisw@gmail.com

ABSTRACT

Massive data streams are continuously being generated from sources such as social media, broadcast news, etc., and typically these datapoints lie in high-dimensional spaces (such as the vocabulary space of a language). Timely and accurate feature subset selection in these massive data streams has important applications in model interpretation, computational/storage cost reduction, and generalization enhancement. In this paper, we introduce a novel unsupervised feature selection approach on data streams that selects important features by making only one pass over the data while utilizing limited storage. The proposed algorithm uses ideas from matrix sketching to efficiently maintain a low-rank approximation of the observed data and applies regularized regression on this approximation to identify the important features. We theoretically prove that our algorithm is close to an expensive offline approach based on global singular value decompositions. The experimental results on a variety of text and image datasets demonstrate the excellent ability of our approach to identify important features even in presence of concept drifts and also its efficiency over other popular scalable feature selection algorithms.

Categories and Subject Descriptors

I.5.2 [**Pattern Recognition**]: Design Methodology—*Feature Evaluation and Selection*

Keywords

Feature Selection; Unsupervised; Streaming Algorithms

1. INTRODUCTION

The *curse of dimensionality* plagues many complex learning tasks. A popular approach for overcoming this problem is by reducing the dimensionality of the feature space as that directly results in a faster computation time. At the same time, it is appealing to have *feature interpretability*, which some of the popular dimensionality reduction methods (e.g., PCA, spectral embeddings) do not possess because of their lack of direct connection to the observed feature space. In our work, we propose a novel approach to unsupervised feature selection, which is the problem of choosing a subset of important (original) features without any label information. The selected feature subset minimizes a very intuitive evaluation criterion while accounting for noise and redundancy. This in turn could lead to better: 1) model interpretation, 2) computational efficiency, and 3) generalization ability for the learning task.

One of the most important characteristic for any good feature selection approach is the ability to handle huge volumes of data. Most modern data such as documents, images, multimedia from the web naturally arrives in a streaming fashion. However, detecting an informative feature subset in a large volume of data stream is also a difficult problem due to the following reasons: 1) the data stream could be infinite, so any off-line algorithm that attempts to store the entire stream for analysis will eventually run out of memory, 2) the feature importance's change dynamically over time due to *concept-drift*, important features may become insignificant and vice-versa, and 3) for various online applications, it is important to obtain the feature subset in close to real-time.

Although there is considerable amount of previous literature on feature selection both in the batch [4, 14] and online setting [31, 23, 17], none of them handles large volume data stream effectively, given limited memory and CPU time, without any prior knowledge about labels. In practice, streams often contain inherently correlated data [19], so it is possible to reduce a large volume numerical stream into just a handful of hidden basis that compactly describe the key patterns of the data. We exploit this idea to reduce the complexity of streaming feature selection analysis.

Our Techniques. In this paper, we propose a streaming feature selection approach that easily adapts to the concept/topic drift arising in the data stream, and at every timestep provides a feature importance score (weight). Our streaming feature selection algorithm uses ideas from matrix sketching[1] to maintain a *low-rank approximation* of the entire observed data at every timestep, and this approximation is continually updated as new data arrives. For matrix sketching, we modify a recent algorithm (called *Frequent Directions*) proposed by Liberty [15, 2]. The *Frequent Di-*

*Part of this work done while the author was at GE Global Research.

[1]A sketch of a matrix Z is another matrix Z' that is much smaller than Z, but still approximates it well [15].

Permission to make digital or hard copies of part or all of this work for personal or classroom use is granted without fee provided that copies are not made or distributed for profit or commercial advantage and that copies bear this notice and the full citation on the first page. Copyrights for third-party components of this work must be honored. For all other uses, contact the Owner/Author(s). Copyright is held by the owner/author(s).
CIKM '15, October 19-23, 2015, Melbourne, VIC, Australia
ACM 978-1-4503-3794-6/15/10.
DOI: http://dx.doi.org/10.1145/2806416.2806521.

rections algorithm operates in a streaming model and constructs a sketch matrix using a simple idea of "shrinking" a few orthogonal vectors. However, just the low-rank approximation cannot by itself provide feature weighting. In our research this low-rank approximation is exploited and at every timestep the feature importance score is generated by performing a regression analysis. A regularization is added to prevent overfitting to the data (we explain the choice of regularization in Section 3.3). The idea of using regularized regression for feature selection in an unsupervised setting was recently proposed by Cai *et al.* [4], who empirically showed that it leads to a better choice of features for clustering and classification applications. Their main idea is to obtain feature importance using a regularized regression where the spectral embedding of the dataset is used as the regression target. However, the formulation presented in Cai *et al.* [4] operates in a batch setting and requires access to the entire affinity matrix for the regression step, which is not possible in a streaming setup. Our algorithm on the other hand, requires just *one pass* over the data, which is an essential requirement for any "true" streaming algorithm.

Our Contributions. To the best of our knowledge, ours is **the first unsupervised feature selection algorithm operating in a true data streaming setting**. Our feature selection algorithm is effective and efficient in the following ways:

(a) It is space and time efficient while requiring only one pass over the data. For a stream at time t consisting of n_t (≥ 1) datapoints in an m-dimensional space, our algorithm requires only $O(mn_t)$ space (linear in the size of the input) and $O(mn_t\ell)$ time, where the sketch matrix is of size $m \times \ell$. In practice, it suffices to set ℓ much smaller compared to m and n_t. Therefore, both the memory and computation requirements are almost linear in the input size (as the input at time t is an $m \times n_t$ matrix).

(b) It easily adapts to unseen patterns on the data stream and provides at every timestep an updated identification of the informative feature subset (i.e., at every timestep t it provides a feature ranking based on all the data that have arrived till time t), which gives it the ability of handling concept drift[2] (related experiments in Section 5.4).

(c) We provide theoretical support for our algorithm (Section 3.4), and show that it has a comparable performance to an expensive offline approach that uses singular value decompositions.

Empirical studies show that our streaming approach is efficient in terms of both space and time, while approaching the performance of popular batch algorithms on a wide array of datasets from both the text and the image domains.

2. PRELIMINARIES

Notation. We denote $[n] = 1 : n$. Vectors are always in column-wise fashion and are denoted by boldface letters. For a vector $\mathbf{v}$, $\mathbf{v}^\top$ denotes its transpose and $\|\mathbf{v}\|$ denotes its Euclidean norm. For a vector $(a_1, \dots, a_m) \in \mathbb{R}^m$, $diag(a_1, \dots, a_m) \in \mathbb{R}^{m \times m}$ denotes a diagonal matrix with $a_1, \dots, a_m$ as its diagonal entries. Let $\mathbb{I}_m$ denote an identity matrix of dimension $m \times m$. We use $rank(Z)$ to denote the rank of Z. For a matrix $Z \in \mathbb{R}^{m \times n}$, we use $z_{i,j}$ to denote its (i,j)th element. Spectral norm is defined as $\|Z\| = \sup\{\|Z\mathbf{v}\| : \|\mathbf{v}\| = 1\}$. We also use entry-wise norms denoted by $\|Z\|_p$, where $p = 2$ gives (Frobenius norm) $\|Z\|_F^2 = \sum_{ij} z_{i,j}^2$, $p = 1$ gives $\|Z\|_1 = \sum_{i,j} |z_{ij}|$, and $p = \infty$ gives $\|Z\|_\infty = \max_{i,j} |z_{i,j}|$. We use $Z \succeq 0$ if Z is a positive semidefinite (PSD) matrix and $Z \succeq Y$ if $Z - Y \succeq 0$. Given a set of matrices, $Z_1, \dots, Z_t$, we use the notation $Z_{[t]}$ to denote the matrix obtained by horizontally concatenating $Z_1, \dots, Z_t$, i.e., $Z_{[t]} = [Z_1 | \dots | Z_t]$.

We use $\textsc{Svd}(Z)$ to denote the singular value decomposition of Z, i.e., $\textsc{Svd}(Z) = U\Sigma V^\top$. Here U is an $m \times m$ orthogonal matrix, Σ is an $m \times n$ diagonal matrix, and V is an $n \times n$ orthogonal matrix. The diagonal entries of Σ, where $\sigma_1 \geq \sigma_2 \geq \dots \geq \sigma_m$ (given $m \leq n$), are known as the singular values of Z. We follow the common convention to list the singular values in non-increasing order. For a symmetric matrix $S \in \mathbb{R}^{m \times m}$, we use $\textsc{Eig}(S)$ to denote its eigenvalue decomposition, i.e., $U\Lambda U^\top = \textsc{Eig}(S)$. Here U is an $m \times m$ orthogonal matrix and Λ is an $m \times m$ diagonal matrix whose (real) entries are $\lambda_1, \dots, \lambda_m$ are known as the eigenvalues of S (again listed in non-increasing order).

The best rank-k approximation (in both the spectral and Frobenius norm sense) to a matrix $Z \in \mathbb{R}^{m \times n}$ is $Z_{(k)} = \sum_{i=1}^k \sigma_i \mathbf{u}_i \mathbf{v}_i^\top$, where σ_i ($i \leq k$) are the top-k singular values of Z, with associated left and right singular vectors $\mathbf{u}_i \in \mathbb{R}^m$ and $\mathbf{v}_i \in \mathbb{R}^n$, respectively. We use $\textsc{Svd}_k(Z)$ to denote the truncated singular value decomposition of $Z_{(k)}$, i.e., $Z_{(k)} = \textsc{Svd}_k(Z) = U_{(k)}\Sigma_{(k)}V_{(k)}^\top$. Here $\Sigma_{(k)} = diag(\sigma_1, \dots, \sigma_k) \in \mathbb{R}^{k \times k}$, $U_{(k)} = [\mathbf{u}_1, \dots, \mathbf{u}_k] \in \mathbb{R}^{m \times k}$, and $V_{(k)} = [\mathbf{v}_1, \dots, \mathbf{v}_k] \in \mathbb{R}^{n \times k}$. The following well-known theorem bounds the approximation error of the best rank-k approximation.

THEOREM 2.1. *[Golub* et al. *[8]] Let $Z \in \mathbb{R}^{m \times n}$ with $n > m$, and let $\sigma_1 \geq \dots \geq \sigma_m$ be the singular values of Z. Let $\textsc{Svd}_k(Z) = U_k\Sigma_k V_k^\top$. Then*

$$\min_{rank(X) \leq k} \|Z - X\|_F = \|Z - U_{(k)}\Sigma_{(k)}V_{(k)}^\top\|_F = \sqrt{\sum_{j=k+1}^{m} \sigma_{k+1}^2}.$$

3. FEATURE SELECTION ON STREAMS

In this section, we propose an online feature selection algorithm that operates in a streaming setting. We start by describing the problem of feature selection on data streams. Due to space constraints, we omit detailed proofs here.

3.1 Problem Formulation

We assume that the data items arrive in streams. Let $\{Y_t \in \mathbb{R}^{m \times n_t}, t = 1, 2, \dots\}$ denote a sequence of streaming items, where Y_t represents the data items introduced at timestep t. Here m is the size of feature space, and $n_t \geq 1$ is the number of data items arriving at time t.[3] We normalize Y_t such that each column in Y_t has a unit L_2-norm. Under this setup, feature selection aims at selecting the most informative feature subset based on certain evaluation criteria.

[2]As we discuss later, in some feature selection applications, one might wish to reweigh the points to emphasize more on the recent points than the older points, which can also be easily handled in our framework.

[3]One could consider, a setting where only one point comes at a time (i.e., $n_t = 1$), but by allowing $n_t \geq 1$, we allow more flexibility in our setup.

3.2 Our Motivation and Framework

Our main idea is based on maintaining, at each timestep t, a low-rank approximation of all the seen (till time t) data stream. By using a regression analysis on this low rank-matrix, we can weigh each feature with an up-to-date importance score.

In case of unsupervised feature selection, the evaluation criteria for selecting the feature subset is not provided explicitly, and the general idea is that we want to capture the most important characteristics of dataset without losing too much information. To this end, we perform a spectral decomposition on the affinity matrix to obtain a "flat" embedding of the datapoints. the intuition being that it is much easier to capture the global trends of the stream in this embedded space than in the original space. Let $Y_{[t]} = [Y_1|\dots|Y_t] = U_t\Sigma_t V_t^\top$. Since $Y_{[t]}$ is column-wise normalized to have unit Euclidean norm, $Y_{[t]}^\top Y_{[t]} = V_t\Sigma_t^2 V_t^\top$ forms the *cosine affinity matrix* of $Y_{[t]}$.

Cai *et al.* [4] proposed an unsupervised feature selection approach using V_t as the target variable in regression. The resulting regression problem can be stated as:

$$\min_X \|Y_{[t]}^\top X - V_t\|_F^2, \tag{1}$$

where each column in $X \in \mathbb{R}^{m\times n_t}$ contains the combination coefficient for different features in approximating the eigenvectors of $Y_{[t]}^\top Y_{[t]}$ (or equivalently the right singular vectors of $Y_{[t]}$). Intuitively, X measures each feature's contribution for representing the different clusters (obtained from the columns in V_t) in the data. Note that the solution for (1) is $X_t = U_t\Sigma_t^{-1}$ (assuming all the singular values in Σ_t are non-zero).

Now consider a rank-k approximation of $Y_{[t]}$ as defined by Theorem 2.1 (for an appropriately chosen parameter[4] k), let

$$Y_{[t]_{(k)}} = \textsc{Svd}_k(Y_{[t]}) = U_{t_{(k)}}\Sigma_{t_{(k)}}V_{t_{(k)}}^\top.$$

Given the low-rank approximation of $Y_{[t]}$, instead of using V_t as the regression target, we could use $V_{t_{(k)}}$ in (1). This yields the following (least-squares) regression problem:

$$\min_X \|Y_{[t]}^\top X - V_{t_{(k)}}\|_F^2. \tag{2}$$

Note that the solution for (2) is $X_t = U_{t_{(k)}}\Sigma_{t_{(k)}}^{-1}$ (assuming the top-k singular values of Σ_t are non-zero).

However, simply using (2) may lead to an unstable solution (if the input matrix is ill-conditioned) and also overfitting to the data [4]. Therefore, we add a regularization term, and define:

$$X_t = \operatorname{argmin}_{X=(x_{i,j})}\|Y_{[t]}^\top X - V_{t_{(k)}}\|_F^2 + \alpha\sum_{i,j}|x_{i,j}|^p, \tag{3}$$

where α is the regularization parameter that controls the trade-off between the loss function and the p-norm ($p \in \{1,2\}$). Generally, a regression formulation with L_1- ($p = 1$) and L_2-norm ($p = 2$) regularization are referred to as lasso and ridge regression respectively. The general formula of (3) was first concretized by Cai *et al.* [4] for the case of $p = 1$, who referred to it as *Multi-Cluster Feature Selection (MCFS)*.

[4]We defer the discussion on setting of k to later. Readers could think of k as a small number $k \ll \min(m, n_t)$.

After we obtain $X_t = (x_{t_{i,j}})$ from (3), we can assign feature importance score $\mathbf{w}_t = (w_{t_1}, \dots, w_{t_m}) \in \mathbb{R}^m$ (with the interpretation that the higher the score, the more important the feature is). One of the simplest way is by using the following equation introduced in [4]:

$$\forall i \in [m], w_{t_i} = \max_{1\le h\le k}|x_{t_{i,h}}|, \tag{4}$$

The aforementioned prototype algorithm for feature weighting is documented in Algorithm 1. The subsequent feature selection process can be done by ranking the $\mathbf{w}$ vector (in non-increasing order) and choosing the top-h features with the largest score (given that h features are needed).

Algorithm 1: GenFeatWeight (prototype algorithm for feature weighting)

Input: $Y_{[t]} \in \mathbb{R}^{m\times n_{[t]}}$, k, and $p \in \{1,2\}$
Output: Feature importance score $\mathbf{w}_t \in \mathbb{R}^m$ at time t
1 $U_{t_{(k)}}\Sigma_{t_{(k)}}V_{t_{(k)}}^\top \leftarrow \textsc{Svd}_k(Y_{[t]})$
(with $\Sigma_{t_{(k)}} = diag(\sigma_{t_1}, \dots, \sigma_{t_k})$)
2 $X_t \leftarrow \operatorname{argmin}_{X=(x_{i,j})}\|Y_{[t]}^\top X - V_{t_{(k)}}\|_F^2 + \alpha\sum_{i,j}|x_{i,j}|^p$
3 $\forall i \in [m]$, $w_{t_i} \leftarrow \max_{1\le h\le k}|x_{t_{i,h}}|$

Other Kernels. Although we concentrate on the cosine kernel, the above framework can be generalized to other kernel functions. One approach would be to use the random feature map transformations known for all radial-basis function kernels [21]. For instance, a Gaussian kernel can be approximated using random Fourier features [21] such that Gaussian kernel evaluation between a pair of datapoints can be approximated by the Euclidean inner product between the transformed pair. Using this randomized feature map one could, in a streaming fashion, transform all the datapoints, and then work exclusively with these transformed datapoints in a framework similar to detailed above.

Windowed Inputs. In our above problem formulations, all data till time t is used for selecting the top features at time t. However, some applications might require features to be selected based on a rolling window of inputs or by providing higher weights on the recent inputs, etc. Our algorithm could be easily adapted to these scenarios by modifying the matrix sketch construction. For simplicity, we ignore these aspects in this paper.

3.3 Lasso ($p = 1$) vs. Ridge ($p = 2$) Regression

The first efficiency issue in using (3) is due to the regularization type. It is well-known that the ridge regression penalizes regression coefficients, rather than accomplishing variable/feature selection, while the lasso regression to some extent automatically sets insignificant coefficients to be zero. However, there is no previous analysis in the framework of Algorithm 1 about the performance difference obtained by using either the lasso or ridge regressions. In this subsection, we investigate this important topic.

A simpler situation arises when the design matrix of the regression problem consists of *orthogonal columns*. In this case, it is easy to show theoretically that the lasso and ridge regressions select almost the same features (Corollary 3.2).

Lemma 3.1 (Restated from [35]). *Let $\hat{X}$ denote the simple least squares coefficients, or in other words, $\hat{X} \leftarrow$*

argmin$_X \|Y^\top X - A\|_F^2$. *Let* $\tilde{X}^R$ *and* $\tilde{X}^L$ *denote the estimators obtained from the lasso and ridge regressions, respectively. If* $Y^\top$ *has orthogonal columns, then* $\hat{X} = YA$, *and we have the following closed-form expressions:*

$$\forall i \in [m], j \in [k], \ \tilde{X}^L_{i,j} = sign(\hat{X}_{i,j})\{|\hat{X}_{i,j}| - \alpha/2\}_+,$$
$$\tilde{X}^R = \hat{X}/(1+\alpha),$$

where for any scalar z, z_+ *denotes the positive part, which is* z *if* $z > 0$ *and* 0 *otherwise.*

Let $\mathbf{w}^R$ and $\mathbf{w}^L$ be the feature importance score calculated from $\tilde{X}^R$ and $\tilde{X}^L$ using (4). The following corollary follows because $\tilde{X}^L$ and $\tilde{X}^R$ are based on thresholding or scaling $\hat{X}$.

COROLLARY 3.2. *If* $\mathbf{w}^L$ *has* h *non-zero weight features, then under the assumption of Lemma 3.1, the ranking of the top-h features in* $\mathbf{w}^L$ *coincides with the ranking of the top-h features in* $\mathbf{w}^R$.

The above corollary implies, under the column orthogonality constraint on the design matrix, the performances of the lasso and ridge regressions in Algorithm 1 (especially, for the important features), are almost the same. Therefore, we can potentially use the more computationally cheaper regularization without any significant loss in performance.

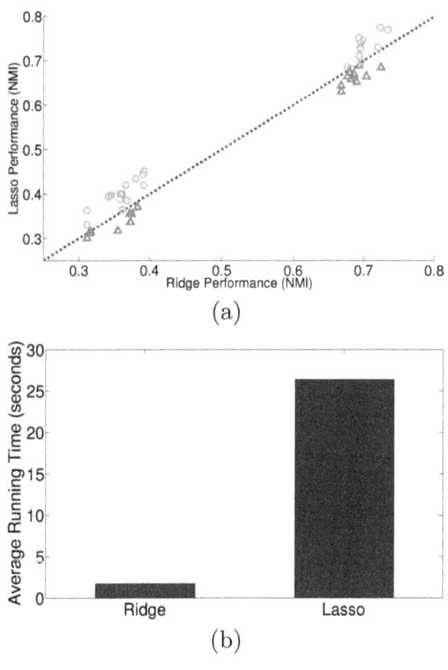

Figure 1: Performance comparison between the ridge ($p = 2$) and the lasso ($p = 1$) regression in the framework of (3). The top 1000 features are picked using (4). In Figure 1(a), red triangles show the tests when ridge outperforms lasso, while green circles show the tests when lasso outperforms ridge. These results indicate that the lasso regression is slightly better than the ridge regression, however the running times in Figure 1(b) show that the ridge regression is far more computationally efficient than the lasso regression. The parameter α was manually tuned here (we will further analyze the setting of α in Section 5).

Note that the orthogonality of the design matrix is a very rigid constraint. However, as we will see later (Algorithm STREAMFEATWEIGHT) in our setting, the design matrix will be of form $(U\Sigma)^\top$, where U is a matrix with orthogonal columns and Σ is a diagonal matrix (in our case, matrix of singular values). Since such a design matrix may not be *too far* from having orthonormal columns, we have a much higher chance of observing similar results from lasso and ridge regressions (as in Corollary 3.2) than in a general regression setting.[5] We conducted the following experiments to verify this hypothesis. We randomly sampled 45 datapoints from three text datasets ("20 Newsgroup", "RCV1", and "Reuters21578", refer to Section 5.1 for details about these datasets). For both cases of $p = 1$ and $p = 2$ in Algorithm GENFEATWEIGHT, we generated the top 1000 feature set from $\mathbf{w}^L$ and $\mathbf{w}^R$ respectively. We then used a simple K-means algorithm on these selected features to evaluate their effectiveness in identifying the (true) document classes (the reasoning behind performing such an evaluation is explained in Section 5). Figure 1(a) shows the clustering result under the Normalized Mutual Information (NMI) measure, and the results suggest that both the lasso and ridge regressions have comparable performances. However, in terms of running time (Figure 1(b)), ridge regression is substantially better than the lasso regression.[6] Since our goal is to handle large streaming datasets, ridge regression appears as a better choice[7], since it generates results very similar to the lasso regression in the framework of Algorithm GENFEATWEIGHT, but with far lesser running time. Therefore, we concentrate on the ridge regression from here on.

The simple closed form solution for (3) with $p = 2$ is as shown in the following lemma.

LEMMA 3.3. *Consider the ridge regression solution,*

$$X_t = argmin_{X=(x_{i,j})} \|Y_{[t]}^\top X - V_{t_{(k)}}\|_F^2 + \alpha \sum_{i,j} x_{i,j}^2.$$

Then we have the following:

$$X_t = U_{t_{(k)}} diag(\sigma_{t_1}/(\sigma_{t_1}^2 + \alpha), \ldots, \sigma_{t_k}/(\sigma_{t_k}^2 + \alpha)),$$

where $\sigma_{t_1}, \ldots, \sigma_{t_k}$ *are the top-k singular values in* $Y_{[t]_{(k)}}$.

Even though Algorithm GENFEATWEIGHT is quite simple, in a streaming environment the number of data items in $Y_{[t]}$ could become extremely large, which could lead to both computational and memory bottlenecks in running the algorithm. For example, the computational complexity of computing a truncated rank-k SVD is $O(mn_{[t]}k)$ [8] (given $Y_{[t]} \in \mathbb{R}^{m \times n_{[t]}}$), which is prohibitive when the number of columns in $Y_{[t]}$ becomes very large ($n_{[t]} \to \infty$). Our goal in the next section is to propose and analyze an efficient approach that has similar effectiveness as Algorithm GENFEATWEIGHT in identifying top features but does so by utilizing limited storage and just one pass over the data in a streaming setting.

[5]Note that if U has orthogonal columns and Σ is a diagonal matrix, then $(U\Sigma)^\top$ has orthogonal rows but depending on the singular values in Σ, the columns in $(U\Sigma)^\top$ may not exactly be orthogonal.

[6]For the lasso regression, we use the algorithm proposed by Cai *et al.* [4].

[7]Again note that this is not to be misconstrued as a general statement on the effectiveness of ridge vs. lasso regressions in other settings.

3.4 Matrix Sketching for Feature Weighting

As mentioned above the main bottleneck in Algorithm GENFEATWEIGHT is in generating a low-rank approximation of $Y_{[t]}$. To overcome this problem, we propose an approach based on matrix sketching that we outline next.

In his recent paper, Liberty [15] showed that by adapting the Misra-Gries approach for approximating frequency counts in a stream, one could obtain additive error bounds for matrix sketching. More formally, in the setting of [15], the input is a matrix $Z \in \mathbb{R}^{p \times d}$. In each step, one row of Z is processed by the algorithm (called *Frequent Directions*) in a streaming fashion, and the algorithm iteratively updates a matrix $Q \in \mathbb{R}^{q \times d}$ ($q \ll p$) such that for any unit vector $\mathbf{x} \in \mathbb{R}^d$, $\|Z\mathbf{x}\|^2 - \|Q\mathbf{x}\|^2 \leq 2\|Z\|_F^2/q$.

Recently, Ghashami and Philips [7], reanalyzed the *Frequent Directions* algorithm of Liberty [15], to show that it provides relative error bounds for low-rank matrix approximation. Instead of Q, their algorithm return Q_k (a rank-k approximation of Q) and their main result shows that $\|Z\|_F^2 - \|Q_k\|_F^2 \leq q/(q-k) \cdot \|Z - Z_k\|_F^2$.

Our approach for constructing a low-rank approximation of $Y_{[t]}$ (outlined between Steps 1-4 in Algorithm STREAMFEATWEIGHT) is based on extending the *Frequent Directions* algorithm of [15] to a more general setting where in every timestep, we add $n_t \geq 1$ new columns.[8] As in *Frequent Directions*, our algorithm requires just one pass over the data stream. Here, $B_t \in \mathbb{R}^{m \times \ell}$ is the matrix sketch. The parameter $\ell \geq k$, but is generally much smaller than m or n_t. We discuss more on the setting of ℓ later. The Step 5 in Algorithm STREAMFEATWEIGHT is obtained by using Lemma 3.3 to solve the following ridge regression problem (note that the SVD of $B_t = \tilde{U}_{t_{(\ell)}} \breve{\Sigma}_{t_{(\ell)}} \mathbb{I}_\ell$, so the identity matrix $\mathbb{I}_\ell$ represents the right singular vectors of B_t):

$$\tilde{X}_t = \operatorname{argmin}_{X=(x_{i,j})} \|B_t^\top X - [\mathbf{e}_1, \ldots, \mathbf{e}_k]\| + \alpha \sum_{i,j} x_{i,j}^2, \quad (5)$$

where $\mathbf{e}_i \in \mathbb{R}^\ell$ is a vector with 1 at location i, and 0 elsewhere (i.e., standard basis vector).

Algorithm 2: STREAMFEATWEIGHT (streaming update of feature weights at time t)

Input: $Y_t \in \mathbb{R}^{m \times n_t}$, $B_{t-1} \in \mathbb{R}^{m \times \ell}$, and $\alpha \in R$
Output: Feature importance score $\tilde{\mathbf{w}}_t \in \mathbb{R}^m$ and matrix sketch B_t at time t

1 $C_t \leftarrow [B_{t-1} | Y_t]$
2 $\tilde{U}_{t_{(\ell)}} \tilde{\Sigma}_{t_{(\ell)}} \tilde{V}_{t_{(\ell)}}^\top \leftarrow \mathrm{SVD}_\ell(C_t)$
(with $\tilde{\Sigma}_{t_{(\ell)}} = diag(\tilde{\sigma}_{t_1}, \ldots, \tilde{\sigma}_{t_\ell})$)
3 $\breve{\Sigma}_{t_{(\ell)}} \leftarrow$
$diag\left(\sqrt{\tilde{\sigma}_{t_1}^2 - \tilde{\sigma}_{t_\ell}^2}, \sqrt{\tilde{\sigma}_{t_2}^2 - \tilde{\sigma}_{t_\ell}^2}, \ldots, \sqrt{\tilde{\sigma}_{t_{\ell-1}}^2 - \tilde{\sigma}_{t_\ell}^2}, 0\right)$
4 $B_t \leftarrow \tilde{U}_{t_{(\ell)}} \breve{\Sigma}_{t_{(\ell)}}$
5 $\tilde{D}_{t_{(k)}} \leftarrow diag(\breve{\sigma}_{t_1}/(\breve{\sigma}_{t_1}^2 + \alpha), \ldots, \breve{\sigma}_{t_k}/(\breve{\sigma}_{t_k}^2 + \alpha))$
(where $\breve{\sigma}_{t_i}$ is the ith diagonal element in $\breve{\Sigma}_{t_{(\ell)}}$)
6 $\tilde{X}_t \leftarrow \tilde{U}_{t_{(k)}} \tilde{D}_{t_{(k)}}$
7 $\forall i \in [m], \tilde{w}_{t_i} \leftarrow \max_{1 \leq p \leq k} |\tilde{x}_{t_{i,p}}|$, where $\tilde{X}_t = (\tilde{x}_{t_{i,p}})$

[8]A similar sketching based low-rank matrix approximation approach was recently used in an entirely different context of anomaly detection by Hao and Kasiviswanathan [10]

At any time t, the running time of Algorithm STREAMFEATWEIGHT is $O(\max\{mn_t\ell, m\ell^2\})$ ($= O(mn_t\ell)$ if we assume $\ell \leq n_t$) by using power-iteration or rank-revealing QR decomposition for SVD [8] in Step 2. This computational complexity is much smaller than the $O(mn_{[t]}k)$ time complexity of Algorithm STREAMFEATWEIGHT (since $n_t\ell \ll n_{[t]}$). Between iterations, the algorithm only maintains the B_t matrix which takes $O(m\ell)$ storage. The overall space complexity of Algorithm STREAMFEATWEIGHT is linear in the size of the input (i.e., $O(mn_t)$) at every time t, compared to Algorithm GENFEATWEIGHT for which, at time t, the space complexity is $O(mn_{[t]})$

The major focus of the rest of this section is to provide theoretical support for Algorithm STREAMFEATWEIGHT, by showing that the $\tilde{\mathbf{w}}_t$ from Algorithm STREAMFEATWEIGHT is a good approximation of $\mathbf{w}_t$ obtained from Algorithm GENFEATWEIGHT (with $p = 2$).

3.4.1 *Theoretical Comparison (Bounding $\|\mathbf{w}_t - \tilde{\mathbf{w}}_t\|$)*

We start with observation that,

$$\begin{aligned}
\|\mathbf{w}_t - \tilde{\mathbf{w}}_t\| &\leq \|U_{t_{(k)}} D_{t_{(k)}} - \tilde{U}_{t_{(k)}} \tilde{D}_{t_{(k)}}\|_F \\
&= \|U_{t_{(k)}} D_{t_{(k)}} - \tilde{U}_{t_{(k)}} D_{t_{(k)}} + \tilde{U}_{t_{(k)}} D_{t_{(k)}} - \tilde{U}_{t_{(k)}} \tilde{D}_{t_{(k)}}\|_F \\
&\leq \|U_{t_{(k)}} D_{t_{(k)}} - \tilde{U}_{t_{(k)}} D_{t_{(k)}}\|_F + \|\tilde{U}_{t_{(k)}} D_{t_{(k)}} - \tilde{U}_{t_{(k)}} \tilde{D}_{t_{(k)}}\|_F \\
&\leq \|U_{t_{(k)}} - \tilde{U}_{t_{(k)}}\|_F \|D_{t_{(k)}}\| + \|\tilde{U}_{t_{(k)}}\| \|D_{t_{(k)}} - \tilde{D}_{t_{(k)}}\|_F \\
&\leq \|U_{t_{(k)}} - \tilde{U}_{t_{(k)}}\|_F \|D_{t_{(k)}}\| + \sqrt{k} \|D_{t_{(k)}} - \tilde{D}_{t_{(k)}}\|_\infty. \quad (6)
\end{aligned}$$

Therefore, a bound on $\|\mathbf{w}_t - \tilde{\mathbf{w}}_t\|$ follows from respective bounds on $\|U_{t_{(k)}} - \tilde{U}_{t_{(k)}}\|_F$ and $\|D_{t_{(k)}} - \tilde{D}_{t_{(k)}}\|_\infty$. Note that since the columns in $\tilde{U}_{t_{(k)}}$ are orthonormal, $\|\tilde{U}_{t_{(k)}}\| \leq 1$.

Bounding $\|\mathbf{U}_{t_{(k)}} - \tilde{\mathbf{U}}_{t_{(k)}}\|_F$. Here we use a recent result by Huang and Kasiviswanathan [10], who established an upper bound on $\|U_{t_{(k)}} - \tilde{U}_{t_{(k)}}\|_F$ by modifying the analysis of *Frequent Directions* by Ghashami and Philips [7] and combining it with some recent matrix perturbation results. To formally state their result we need few more definitions. Let

$$\kappa = \kappa_k(Y_{[t]}) = \sigma_{t_1}/\sigma_{t_k},$$

where σ_{t_i} is the ith singular value of $Y_{[t]}$.

1. Define Γ_a as,

$$\Gamma_a = \frac{\kappa^2 \|Y_{[t]_{(k)}}\|_F^2 - \|B_{t_{(k)}}\|_F^2}{\|Y_{[t]_{(k)}}\|_F^2 - \|B_{t_{(k)}}\|_F^2}. \quad (7)$$

It is easy to establish that for all t, $\|Y_{[t]_{(k)}}\|_F^2 \geq \|B_{t_{(k)}}\|_F^2$ (using an analysis from [10]), and by definition $\kappa \geq 1$, therefore $\Gamma_a \geq 1$. Furthermore, for small k's (as in our setting), typically κ is bounded, yielding $\Gamma_a = O(1)$.

2. Define Γ_b as,

$$\Gamma_b = 1 + \frac{2}{\kappa^2 - \|B_t\|^2/\|Y_{[t]}\|^2}. \quad (8)$$

Again it is easy to establish that $Y_{[t]} Y_{[t]}^\top \succeq B_t B_t^\top$ [15], and therefore, $\|B_t\|^2 \leq \|Y_{[t]}\|^2$. Typically κ is also bounded away from 1, yielding $\Gamma_b = O(1)$.

PROPOSITION 3.4 (HUANG AND KASIVISWANATHAN [10]). *Let λ_i denote the ith eigenvalue of $Y_{[t]} Y_{[t]}^\top$ and $L = \min_{i \neq j} |\lambda_i -$*

$\lambda_j| > 0$. *If*

$$\ell = \Omega\left(\frac{\sqrt{m}\kappa^2\|Y_{[t]}\|^2\Gamma_a\Gamma_b k\|Y_{[t]} - Y_{[t]_{(k)}}\|_F^2}{L^2}\right),$$

for Γ_a, Γ_b *defined in* (7), (8) *respectively, then*

$$\|U_{t_{(k)}} - \tilde{U}_{t_{(k)}}\|_F \leq \frac{\sqrt{2}L}{\sqrt{L + 8\kappa^2\|Y_{[t]}\|^2\sqrt[4]{L^2 + 16\kappa^4\|Y_{[t]}\|^4}}}.$$

Remark: For small k's, and assuming $1 < \kappa \leq O(1)$ (implying $\Gamma_a = O(1)$ and $\Gamma_b = O(1)$), the above bound on ℓ could be simplified to,

$$\ell = \Omega\left(\frac{\sqrt{m}\|Y_{[t]}\|^2\|Y_{[t]} - Y_{[t]_{(k)}}\|_F^2}{L^2}\right).$$

The assumption of $L > 0$ is also something that is commonly satisfied in practice, especially if m is reasonably smaller than the number of datapoints in $Y_{[t]}$.

Bounding $\|\mathbf{D}_{\mathbf{t}_{(\mathbf{k})}} - \tilde{\mathbf{D}}_{\mathbf{t}_{(\mathbf{k})}}\|_\infty$. Let σ_{t_i} and $\breve{\sigma}_{t_i}$ be the ith singular value of $Y_{[t]}$ and B_t respectively. We have,

$$\begin{aligned}\|D_{t_{(k)}} - \tilde{D}_{t_{(k)}}\|_\infty &= \max_{i\in[k]}\left|\frac{\sigma_{t_i}}{\sigma_{t_i}^{\ 2} + \alpha} - \frac{\breve{\sigma}_{t_i}}{\breve{\sigma}_{t_i}^2 + \alpha}\right| \\ &\leq \max_{i\in[k]}\left(\frac{|\sigma_{t_i} - \breve{\sigma}_{t_i}|}{\breve{\sigma}_{t_i}^2 + \alpha}\right).\end{aligned}$$

A standard application of Weyl's inequality [8], along with a bound on $\|\kappa^2 Y_{[t]}Y_{[t]}^\top - B_t B_t^\top\|$ provides the following proposition.

PROPOSITION 3.5.

$$\|D_{t_{(k)}} - \tilde{D}_{t_{(k)}}\|_\infty \leq \frac{\|Y_{[t]} - Y_{[t]_{(k)}}\|_F}{\breve{\sigma}_{t_k}^2 + \alpha}\sqrt{\frac{\Gamma_a\Gamma_b k}{\ell - k}}.$$

Putting it all Together (Bounding $\|\mathbf{w_t} - \tilde{\mathbf{w}}_\mathbf{t}\|$). The following theorem follows by combining (6) with Propositions 3.4 and 3.5.

THEOREM 3.1. *Let* $Y_1, \ldots, Y_t$ *be a sequence of matrices with* $Y_{[t]} = [Y_1|\ldots|Y_t]$. *Let* $Y_{[t]_{(k)}} = U_{t_{(k)}}\Sigma_{t_{(k)}}V_{t_{(k)}}^\top$ *be the best rank-k approximation of* $Y_{[t]}$. *Let* σ_{t_k} *and* $\breve{\sigma}_{t_k}$ *be the kth singular value of* $Y_{[t]}$ *and* B_t *respectively. Then* $\mathbf{w}_t$ *(generated by the Algorithm* GENFEATWEIGHT*) and* $\tilde{\mathbf{w}}_t$ *(generated by Algorithm* STREAMFEATWEIGHT*), under conditions from Proposition 3.4, satisfy:*

$$\begin{aligned}\|\mathbf{w}_t - \tilde{\mathbf{w}}_t\| \leq &\frac{k\|Y_{[t]} - Y_{[t]_{(k)}}\|_F}{\breve{\sigma}_{t_k}^2 + \alpha}\sqrt{\frac{\Gamma_a\Gamma_b}{\ell - k}} \\ &+ \frac{\sigma_{t_k}}{\sigma_{t_k}^2 + \alpha}\frac{\sqrt{2}L}{\sqrt{L + 8\kappa^2\|Y_{[t]}\|^2\sqrt[4]{L^2 + 16\kappa^4\|Y_{[t]}\|^4}}}.\end{aligned}$$

The above theorem shows that, under reasonable assumptions and setting of ℓ, both Algorithms GENFEATWEIGHT and STREAMFEATWEIGHT generate very identical feature vector weights at every timestep t. But as we discussed earlier, Algorithm STREAMFEATWEIGHT is far more efficient both in space and time consumptions. A point to note is that the Algorithm STREAMFEATWEIGHT can be used *with any value* of ℓ, the above bound on ℓ only guarantees that its feature selection results are similar to that of Algorithm GENFEATWEIGHT.

3.5 Discussion on Normalization

We generate $V_{t_{(k)}}$ using a cosine affinity matrix from L_2-norm column normalized $Y_{[t]}$. If we follow the same construction with a slightly different normalization, $Y_{[t]}$ to be zero mean and unit variance, then we obtain as regression target, the principal components (PCA) of $Y_{[t]}$. Each principal component captures different view of Pearson correlation coefficient matrix, and these principal components might be another good choice for the regression target. However, it is unclear how to construct this zero mean and unit variance normalization of $Y_{[t]}$ in a strict streaming fashion which is desired in this paper. The works of [16, 11] use $N^{-1}Y_{[t]}^\top Y_{[t]}$ for building random walk normalized cosine affinity matrix where the diagonal matrix $N_{i,i} = \sum_j (Y_{[t]}^\top Y_{[t]})_{i,j}$. Since we did not use the random walk normalization, $V_{t_{(k)}}$ is not approximating the normalized graph cut any more. However, in our case, $V_{t_{(k)}}$ is not directly used for clustering, but just an intermediate step to select the important feature subset. In our experiments (Section 5), we achieve quite similar results to the MCFS approach [4], where the affinity matrix is normalized in a batch setting.

4. RELATED WORK

We now justify the utility of our proposed approach by briefly comparing it with a few existing methods.

Our basic idea is to use regression analysis for feature selection. Many feature selection algorithms based on this idea have been proposed in the past decade. These algorithms operate by minimizing some appropriately defined objective function. Weston *et al.* [26] added an ℓ_0-norm constraint on the solution to enforce sparsity, which naturally leads to a natural variable (feature) selection. But minimizing with ℓ_0-regularization is NP-hard, therefore ℓ_1-norm, as a convex relaxation to ℓ_0-norm, was utilized in [27, 4]. Other norms on the regularization term such as ℓ_2-norm [6] and $\ell_{2,1}$-norm [33, 14] have also been explored for feature selection. One of the latest work in this area, proposed by Zhu *et al.* [34], performs feature selection by transferring models learnt on external (auxiliary) data sources, but it requires the dimensionality of target data to be high and the number of datapoints to be small, which usually is not the case in data streaming. Few other recently proposed approaches in this area include [32, 12]. Although these methods are effective and robust to some degree, they are extremely inefficient, in both time and space, to be applicable in a streaming setting.

Feature selection algorithms operating in an online setting were proposed in [31, 23, 17], but they all require multiple passes over the data to converge to a stable model, and hence are not *pass-efficient.* Few other efficient feature selection methods such as [9, 29, 30] seem not well-suited to operate in a streaming environment. In this paper, we propose a streaming algorithm that at every timestep efficiently assigns each feature an importance score (weight) that can be subsequently used to rank (or select) the (top) features.

Also in the streaming setting, the approach of *projected clustering* [1, 18] can be viewed as a technique for "local" feature selection. The idea here is to have each cluster specific to a particular feature subset that optimizes a quality criterion for that cluster. However, the feature subsets could be quite different across different clusters, therefore it leads to a complicated interpretation of clustering. Moreover, it is also very difficult to compare different clusters since their op-

	Dataset	#instances	#features	#clusters
1	Reuter21578	8,293	18,933	65
2	TDT2	9,394	36,771	30
3	20Newsgroup	18,846	26,214	20
4	RCV1	193,844	47,236	103
5	USPS	9,298	256	10
6	MNIST	70,000	784	10
7	Tiny	1,000,000	3,072	75,062

Table 1: Statistics of the experimental datasets.

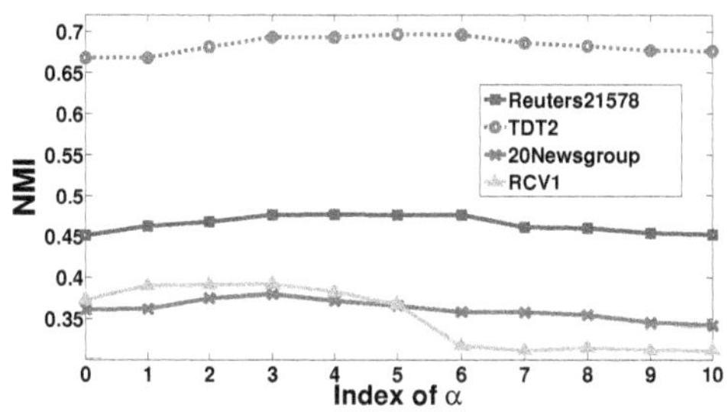

Figure 2: The effect of α on four text datasets. For each dataset, we randomly generate 30 subsets and record the average K-means (NMI) result on the top 1000 features. The x-axis is the index i of $\alpha = 2^i\sigma_k$ (where k is number of clusters in each dataset). It can be observed that the NMI results show smooth changes across different α, and $i = 3, 4, 5$ are reasonable choices.

timized subspaces are not in the same domain. On the other hand, our proposed approach provides a single comprehensive feature subset that covers all the clusters. Thereby, it gives an easy interpretation for clustering different classes.

In a somewhat orthogonal setting, online feature selection operating on *feature streams*[9] (instead of data streams as considered in this paper) have been investigated in [20, 28, 25].

5. EXPERIMENTAL ANALYSIS

In this section, we experimentally demonstrate that our proposed Algorithm StreamFeatWeight is highly scalable, while still providing almost similar quantitative results to other expensive batch feature selection approaches.

5.1 Experiment Setup

It would be the best to evaluate feature selection results based on ground truth feature importance. But in real world applications, we cannot easily find such ground truth because: 1) it is highly subjective to select candidate features because there are many similar features/terms, and 2) feature selection is typically an intermediate step for the rest of data analysis pipeline. However, we do have many datasets with ground truth cluster labels. This can be utilized to evaluate the quality of selected feature subset, by performing an unsupervised clustering on the feature-reduced dataset. If the selected feature subset is "good", then clustering the data restricted to just this subset of features should yield a "good" clustering result. Therefore, we evaluate the unsupervised feature selection algorithms by performing an unsupervised K-means clustering on the selected feature space. We used the popular Normalized Mutual Information (NMI) as our evaluation metric.

[9]Roughly, in this setting, feature vectors are streamed over time, e.g., one new feature is introduced at every timestep t.

Baselines. From now on, we refer to Algorithm StreamFeatWeight as **FSDS** (Feature Selection on Data Streams). To the best of our knowledge there is no other streaming unsupervised feature selection algorithm. We chose the following unsupervised batch feature selection approaches as baseline methods: Multi-Cluster Feature Selection (**MCFS**) [4], **LaplacianScore** [9], and Algorithm GenFeatWeight with $p = 2$ (henceforth, referred to as **GFW-p2**). MCFS (based on lasso regression) and LaplacianScore (based on finding local manifold structure) are both batch feature selection algorithms and were selected for comparison because they capture the essence of two popular ideas for feature selection.

Since we used clustering to measure the performance of feature selection, we also included for comparison the classical K-means (**Kmeans**) and a recent streaming variant of K-means (**StreamKM**) [22]. Both these K-means algorithms are operated on the whole feature set (unlike other compared approaches).

Datasets and Preprocessing. We evaluated the above algorithms on four popular text datasets (Reuter21578, TDT2, 20Newsgroup, and RCV1) and three image datasets (USPS, MNIST, and Tiny), whose statistics are summarized in Table 5.1. 20Newsgroup is a balanced dataset that covers 20 news topics. Reuters21578, TDT2, RCV1 are unbalanced datasets with quite different sizes of clusters. All these datasets can be found in [3]. Both the USPS and MNIST datasets have 10 classes of handwritten digits. Tiny is a large web-image collection for non-parametric object and scene recognition (downloaded from [24]). Among 80 million images, we randomly selected 1 million images and evaluated the result on 60,000 labeled images that cover 100 classes (from [13]). We directly performed experiments on the Tiny images with all the 3,072 raw features, which are 32 × 32 color images in RGB color channels.

MCFS and LaplacianScore algorithms are space and time inefficient due to computations of normalized Laplacian matrix or eigenvalue decomposition (also solving lasso regression for MCFS). We cannot evaluate such algorithms on large benchmark datasets. Therefore the majority of datasets were selected to compare the effectiveness of all the baselines. For the three image datasets, we used the approximation of Gaussian kernel using random feature maps [21]. For every timestep t, we used the same random projection basis and offset setting (refer to [11] for more details about implementing these random feature maps).

Parameter Settings. The number of selected features, h, was set from 200 to 2400 (in increments of 200) for text datasets, and from 25 to 200 (in increments of 25) for image datasets (since the number of meaningful features in raw images is usually small). In our streaming setting, the number of singular vectors k was set to be the same as the number of clusters in the dataset, which was assumed to be *a priori* known as in prior works [9, 4], and the size of each data stream (n_t's) as 1000 (we will further analyze stability against n_t in Section 5.4). Our proposed algorithm has two specific parameters: the size of matrix sketch ℓ (which is set as the square root of the feature size as suggested by the analysis in Section 3.4) and the regularization parameter α. There are prior works in deciding the best regularization parameter α [5]. However, given the target problem is unsupervised and the dataset is big, we performed the following experiments on sampled datasets to select α. We randomly generated 30 subsets from four text datasets respectively, and evaluated the average quality of the top-1000 selected features using Lemma 3.3 with various values of α. Since the singular value distributions (σ_j's) of most datasets usually decay rapidly, we set α as $2^i\sigma_k$ for $i \in \mathbb{R}$. The average NMI result is presented in Figure 2. It can be seen that the best results appear when i is around 3 to 5. Therefore we set $i = 3$ by default, and set $\alpha = 2^3\sigma_k$ for all our experiments. For the random feature maps using Gaussian kernel, we set bandwidth-scale as 5000 and the projected dimension as $\lceil n/k \rceil$ (following [11]).

For MCFS and LaplacianScore, we followed [4, 9] for their respective parameter settings. For the NMI evaluation step, we utilized the standard *within-cluster sum of squares K-means* (with 100 inner loops and 100 outer loops) to obtain stable cluster assignments.

5.2 General Performance Comparison

We make the following observations based on Figure 3.

(1) Compared with Kmeans/StreamKM on the whole features space, feature selection can indeed improve clustering performance on these high dimensional datasets. This is an argument in favor of performing feature selection (similar observations have been made elsewhere).

(2) In general, the regression-based algorithms (FSDS, GFW-p2, and MCFS) perform much better than the LaplacianScore algorithm. It is because LaplacianScore evaluates features individually, so that the selected feature subset may come from similar global patterns. On the other hand, the other three algorithms have more comprehensive views due to their use of regression-based feature selection w.r.t. different global patterns (eigenvectors).

(3) GFW-p2 has very comparable result with MCFS (which can be seen as further evidence supporting the lasso vs. ridge argument in Section 3.3), although the latter performs better than the former in some specific spots (e.g., with smaller number of features in the TDT2 dataset).

(4) On average, FSDS achieves more than 99% NMI of GFW-p2 on the text datasets. It confirms our theoretical proof (Theorem 3.1) that feature weight vectors produced by Algorithms GenFeatWeight and StreamFeatWeight are close to each other.

(5) Typically, FSDS achieves about 97% $\sim$ 99% NMI of M-CFS on the text datasets. This observation shows that in our problem setting (Sections 3.2 and 3.3), a streaming ridge-based method is capable of obtaining similar performance as that of a batch lasso-based method (MCFS). The FSDS performs worse than MCFS when the number of features is small (TDT2 dataset). It could probably be because the regression target of MCFS that comes from normalized spectral analysis may boost the quality of the small number of the selected features. However, if the number of features is large enough, FSDS and MCFS have very comparable performances.

(6) For the experiments on the image datasets (with approximated Gaussian kernel), FSDS has similar or even better performance than MCFS (Figures 3(e) and 3(f)).

(7) On large datasets, such as RCV1 (Figure 3(d)) and Tiny (Figure 3(g)), MCFS and LaplacianScore algorithms ran out of memory since they require constructing the affinity matrix (which takes $O(n^2)$ space). Memory troubles also prevented GFW-p2 from completion on the Tiny dataset.

5.3 Scalability Comparison

Figure 4 shows the scalability comparison between the feature selection algorithms using the Tiny dataset (k is set as 10 here). MCFS requires solving lasso while LaplacianScore needs full-matrix operations, therefore both of them are far less scalable than GFW-p2. FSDS is designed for a streaming setting and the computations in it happen without using any historical data, therefore it is the most efficient technique among all the compared approaches.

We observed that FSDS is on average about 10 times faster than LaplacianScore and about 50 times faster than MCFS. Also FSDS outperforms GFW-p2 when the dataset size is above $10,000$ and the difference between their running times will grow as the dataset size increases. On the 20Newsgroup dataset, FSDS takes about 23 seconds, and is about $3, 35$, and 100 times faster than GFW-p2, LaplacianScore, and MCFS respectively. Similarly, on the MNIST dataset, FSDS takes about 4 seconds, and is about $4, 64$, and 400 times faster than GFW-p2, LaplacianScore, and MCFS respectively.

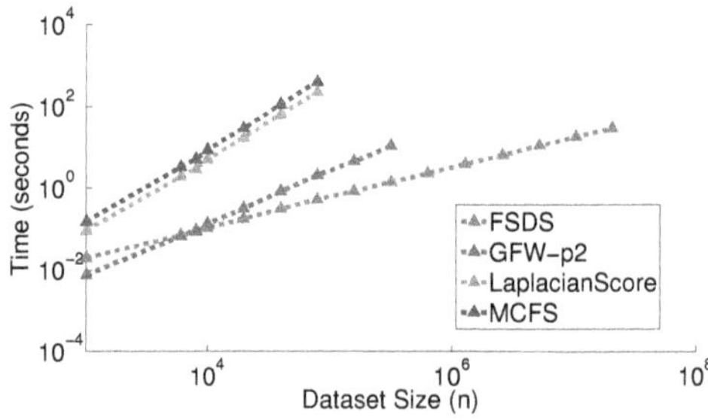

Figure 4: Scalability experiments on the Tiny dataset. Except our proposed FSDS, none of the other compared approaches could scale beyond $\approx 10^5$ points (failing because of their extremely high memory overhead).

5.4 Stability under Concept Drift, Batch Sizes

It is well-known that streaming algorithms are generally sensitive to the order of data, or concept drift. To test the performance of FSDS in such scenarios, we used the data stream sorted by timestamps as input. The performance of FSDS in this realistic testing environment is shown in Figure 5, with different sizes of feature set. We also compared against a scheme where we just used a static feature subset (with 200 features) without adapting to concept drift. This static feature subset was determined by FSDS using only the first $2,000$ samples. For the two unbalanced datasets Reuters21578 and TDT2, the larger clusters appear in the very beginning. Therefore, initially the approach based on static feature subset performs quite close to FSDS. However, as time goes on and concept drift becomes more prominent, FSDS continues maintaining a good stable performance across all the three datasets, which demonstrates that FSDS is capable of quickly adapting to concept drifts.

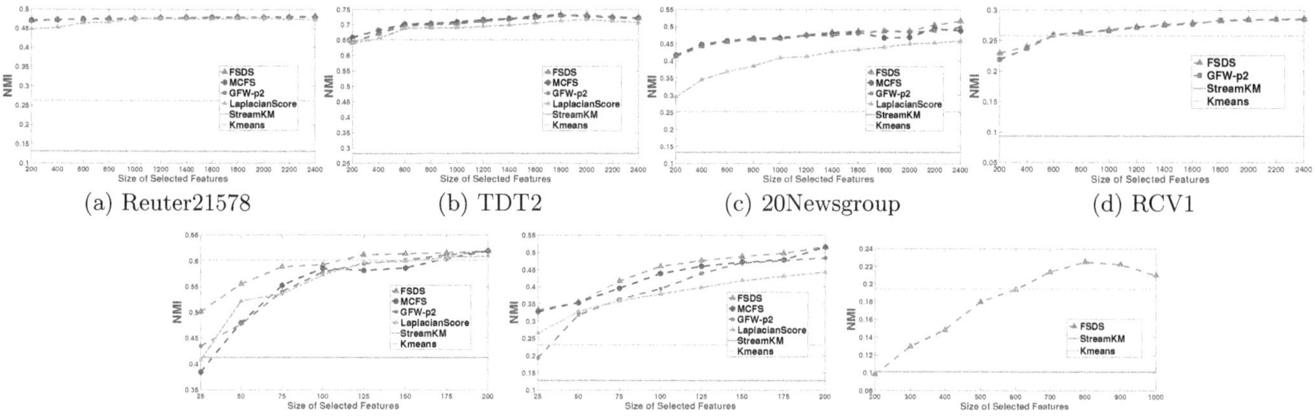

(a) Reuter21578 (b) TDT2 (c) 20Newsgroup (d) RCV1

(e) USPS (f) MNIST (g) Tiny

Figure 3: Performance of the compared algorithms on different datasets. A randomly shuffled data stream is used for the online algorithms. Kmeans and StreamKM algorithms were executed on the whole feature set (hence they always have horizontal lines). For all other approaches, the quality of feature selection methods is measured by executing K-means clustering on the selected feature subset. For the RCV1 and Tiny datasets, MCFS and LaplacianScore experiments ran into memory issues as they require storing the quadratic sized affinity matrix. Memory issues also prevented the completion of GFW-p2 on Tiny. Our proposed approach (FSDS) achieves at least 97% NMI of MCFS while operating in a highly scalable streaming setting.

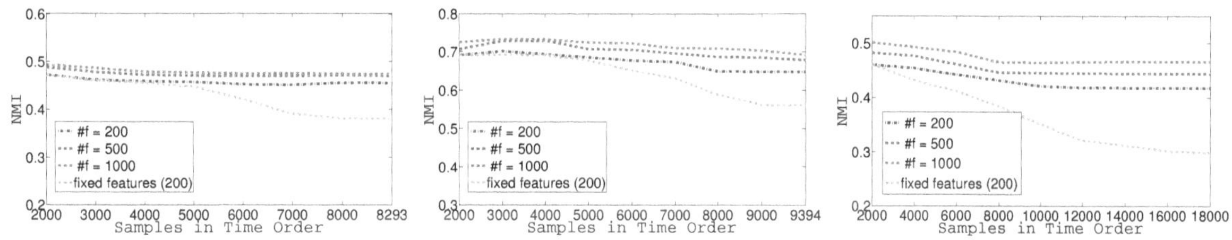

(a) Reuter21578 (b) TDT2 (c) 20Newsgroup

Figure 5: Concept drift test across time for FSDS. The results show that FSDS provides a stable performance even in the presence of inherent concept drift in the data stream.

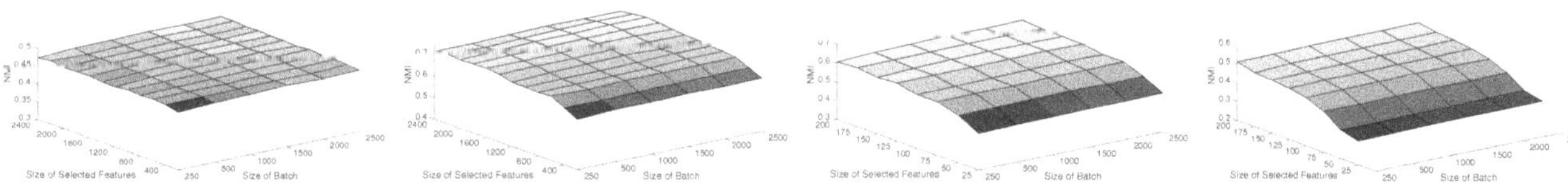

(a) Reuter21578 (b) TDT2 (c) USPS (d) MNIST

Figure 6: Stability test for FSDS across different batch sizes and feature subset sizes.

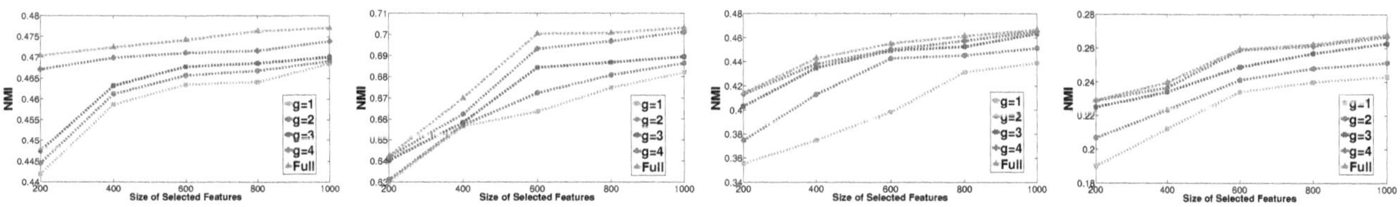

(a) Reuter21578 (b) TDT2 (c) 20Newsgroup (d) RCV1

Figure 7: Performance comparison of FSDS with different values of g.

FSDS tests across different batch sizes (n_t's) and feature subset sizes indicate its very stable behavior (Figure 6).

5.5 Efficient Storage

For many streaming applications, we not only want to identify the top-h features in the data but also want to store the data restricted to these top-h features at any time, to enable some further data mining analyses. In general, such analysis in streaming setting would require storing the whole data at each timestep as the set of the top-h features dynamically changes over time. However, using FSDS, we empirically noticed that storing the data stream restricted to top $g \times h$ features at each intermediate timestep, and a final selection of only those features which appear in the top $g \times h$ features for each of the intermediate timestep, suffices to get good results, even when g is a small number (i.e., 4). The results are shown in Figure 7. The number of features tested in these experiments are $h = \{200, 400, 600, 800, 1000\}$ with $g = \{1, 2, 3, 4\}$. We also report FSDS results where we store the entire data, and then use the data to obtain the final top h features (we call this strategy Full). Even setting $g = 1$, we already achieve about 91% NMI compared to the Full (FSDS) at $h = 200$. As we increase g, the results get better and it suggests that it could be enough to store data restricted to the top $O(h)$ features at each timestep to enable further analyses.

6. CONCLUSION

We proposed an unsupervised feature selection algorithm for handling high dimensional data points arriving in a streaming fashion. Our algorithm uses ideas from matrix sketching to generate a continuous low-rank approximation of the input, which is then used in a regularized regression framework to obtain the individual feature weights. The algorithm only requires one-pass over the data, utilizes limited storage, and operates in near-real time. Theoretical results and experimental validation confirm that our proposed algorithm is efficient in both space and time for the task of streaming unsupervised feature selection.

Acknowledgments

This research was supported in part by BNL PD 15-025, Center for Data Driven Discovery (C3D).

7. REFERENCES

[1] C. C. Aggarwal, J. Han, J. Wang, and P. S. Yu. A framework for projected clustering of high dimensional data streams. In *VLDB*, 2004.

[2] C. Boutsidis, D. Garber, Z. Karnin, and E. Liberty. Online principal components analysis. In *SODA*. SIAM, 2015.

[3] D. Cai. Datasets. http://bit.ly/1IpMnAy.

[4] D. Cai, C. Zhang, and X. He. Unsupervised feature selection for multi-cluster data. *SIGKDD*, 2010.

[5] S. Chatterjee and A. S. Hadi. *Regression Analysis by Example*. John Wiley & Sons, 2013.

[6] A. Dasgupta, P. Drineas, B. Harb, V. Josifovski, and M. W. Mahoney. Feature selection methods for text classification. In *SIGKDD*, pages 230–239, 2007.

[7] M. Ghashami and J. M. Phillips. Relative errors for deterministic low-rank matrix approximations. In *SODA*, pages 707–717, 2014.

[8] G. H. Golub and C. F. Van Loan. *Matrix Computations*, volume 3. JHU Press, 2012.

[9] X. He, D. Cai, and P. Niyogi. Laplacian score for feature selection. In *NIPS*, pages 507–514, 2005.

[10] H. Huang and S. Kasiviswanathan. Streaming anomaly detection using randomized matrix sketching. http://bit.ly/1FaDw6S.

[11] H. Huang, S. Yoo, D. Yu, and H. Qin. Diverse power iteration embeddings and its applications. In *ICDM*, 2014.

[12] H. Huang, S. Yoo, D. Yu, and H. Qin. Noise-resistant unsupervised feature selection via multi-perspective correlations. In *ICDM*, 2014.

[13] A. Krizhevsky, V. Nair, and G. Hinton. Cifar-100 dataset. http://bit.ly/1chapl0.

[14] Z. Li, Y. Yang, J. Liu, X. Zhou, and H. Lu. Unsupervised feature selection using nonnegative spectral analysis. *AAAI*, 2012.

[15] E. Liberty. Simple and deterministic matrix sketching. In *SIGKDD*, pages 581–588, 2013.

[16] F. Lin and W. W. Cohen. A very fast method for clustering big text datasets. In *ECAI*, 2010.

[17] C. Maung and H. Schweitzer. Pass-efficient unsupervised feature selection. In *NIPS*, 2013.

[18] I. Ntoutsi, A. Zimek, T. Palpanas, P. Kröger, and H.-P. Kriegel. Density-based projected clustering over high dimensional data streams. In *SDM*, 2012.

[19] S. Papadimitriou, J. Sun, and C. Faloutsos. Streaming pattern discovery in multiple time-series. *VLDB*, 2005.

[20] S. Perkins and J. Theiler. Online feature selection using grafting. In *ICML*, 2003.

[21] A. Rahimi and B. Recht. Random features for large-scale kernel machines. In *NIPS*, 2007.

[22] M. Shindler, A. Wong, and A. W. Meyerson. Fast and accurate k-means for large datasets. In *NIPS*, 2011.

[23] Q. Song, J. Ni, and G. Wang. A fast clustering-based feature subset selection algorithm for high-dimensional data. *TKDE*, 25(1), 2013.

[24] A. Torralba, R. Fergus, and W. T. Freeman. 80 million tiny images: A large data set for nonparametric object and scene recognition. *TPAMI*, 2008.

[25] J. Wang, P. Zhao, S. Hoi, and R. Jin. Online feature selection and its applications. *TKDE*, 26(3), 2014.

[26] J. Weston, A. Elisseeff, B. Scholkopf, and M. Tipping. Use of the zero norm with linear models and kernel methods. *JMLR*, 2003.

[27] D. M. Witten and R. Tibshirani. A framework for feature selection in clustering. *JASA*, 2010.

[28] X. Wu, K. Yu, H. Wang, and W. Ding. Online streaming feature selection. In *ICML*, 2010.

[29] S. Xiang, X. Shen, and J. Ye. Efficient sparse group feature selection via nonconvex optimization. In *ICML*, 2013.

[30] S. Xiang, T. Yang, and J. Ye. Simultaneous feature and feature group selection through hard thresholding. In *SIGKDD*, pages 532–541, 2014.

[31] H. Yang, M. R. Lyu, and I. King. Efficient online learning for multitask feature selection. *TKDD*, 2013.

[32] S. Yang, L. Yuan, Y. C. Lai, X. Shen, P. Wonka, and J. Ye. Feature grouping and selection over an undirected graph. In *SIGKDD*, 2012.

[33] Y. Yang, H. T. Shen, Z. Ma, Z. Huang, and X. Zhou. $l_{2,1}$-norm regularized discriminative feature selection for unsupervised learning. *IJCAI*, 2011.

[34] X. Zhu, Z. Huang, Y. Yang, T. H. Shen, C. Xu, and J. Luo. Self-taught dimensionality reduction on the high-dimensional small-sized data. *Pattern Recognition*, 46(1), 2013.

[35] H. Zou and T. Hastie. Regularization and variable selection via the elastic net. *Journal of the Royal Statistical Society*, 67(2), 2005.

Unsupervised Streaming Feature Selection in Social Media

Jundong Li†, Xia Hu‡, Jiliang Tang◇ and Huan Liu†
†Computer Science and Engineering, Arizona State University, Tempe, AZ, USA
‡Department of Computer Science and Engineering, Texas A&M University, College Station, TX, USA
◇Yahoo! Labs, Yahoo! Inc, Sunnyvale, CA, USA
{jundong.li, huan.liu}@asu.edu, hu@cse.tamu.edu, jlt@yahoo-inc.com

ABSTRACT

The explosive growth of social media sites brings about massive amounts of high-dimensional data. Feature selection is effective in preparing high-dimensional data for data analytics. The characteristics of social media present novel challenges for feature selection. First, social media data is not fully structured and its features are usually not predefined, but are generated dynamically. For example, in Twitter, slang words (features) are created everyday and quickly become popular within a short period of time. It is hard to directly apply traditional batch-mode feature selection methods to find such features. Second, given the nature of social media, label information is costly to collect. It exacerbates the problem of feature selection without knowing feature relevance. On the other hand, opportunities are also unequivocally present with additional data sources; for example, link information is ubiquitous in social media and could be helpful in selecting relevant features. In this paper, we study a novel problem to conduct unsupervised streaming feature selection for social media data. We investigate how to exploit link information in streaming feature selection, resulting in a novel unsupervised streaming feature selection framework USFS. Experimental results on two real-world social media datasets show the effectiveness and efficiency of the proposed framework comparing with the state-of-the-art unsupervised feature selection algorithms.

Categories and Subject Descriptors

D.2.8 [**DATABASE MANAGEMENT**]: Database Applications—*Data Mining*

Keywords

Unsupervised Feature Selection; Streaming Features; Social Media Data

Permission to make digital or hard copies of all or part of this work for personal or classroom use is granted without fee provided that copies are not made or distributed for profit or commercial advantage and that copies bear this notice and the full citation on the first page. Copyrights for components of this work owned by others than ACM must be honored. Abstracting with credit is permitted. To copy otherwise, or republish, to post on servers or to redistribute to lists, requires prior specific permission and/or a fee. Request permissions from Permissions@acm.org.
CIKM'15, October 19–23, 2015, Melbourne, Australia.
© 2015 ACM. ISBN 978-1-4503-3794-6/15/10 ...$15.00.
DOI: http://dx.doi.org/10.1145/2806416.2806501.

1. INTRODUCTION

The rapid growth and popularity of social media services such as Twitter[1], Facebook[2] provide a platform for people to perform online social activities by sharing information and communicating with others. Massive amounts of high-dimensional data (blogs, posts, images, etc.) are user generated and quickly disseminated. It is desirable and of great importance to reduce the dimensionality of social media data for many learning tasks due to the curse of dimensionality. One way to resolve this problem is feature selection [17, 20], which aims to select a subset of relevant features for a compact and accurate representation.

Traditional feature selection assumes that all features are static and known in advance. However, this assumption is invalid in many real-world applications especially in social media which is imbued with high-velocity streaming features. In social media, features are generated dynamically, new features are sequentially added and the size of features is unknown in most cases. For example, Twitter produces more than 320 millions of tweets everyday and a large amount of slang words (features) are continuously being user generated. These slang words promptly grab users' attention and become popular in a short time. It is not practical to wait until all features are available before performing feature selection. Another example is that after earthquakes, topics (features) like "Nepal" emerge as hot topics in social media shortly, traditional batch-mode feature selection can hardly capture and select such features timely. Therefore, it could be more appealing to perform *streaming feature selection* (SFS) [37] to rapidly adapt to the changes.

In SFS, the number of instances is considered to be constant while candidate features arrive one at a time, the task is to timely select a subset of relevant features from all features seen so far [37]. Instead of searching for the whole feature space which is costly, SFS processes a new feature upon its arrival. A general framework of streaming feature selection is presented in Figure 1. At each time step, a typical SFS algorithm first determines whether to accept the most recently arrived feature; if the feature is added to the selected feature set, it then determines whether to discard some existing features from the selected feature set. The process repeats until no new features show up anymore. The vast majority of existing streaming feature selection algorithms are supervised which utilize label information to guide feature selection process [27, 33, 37]. However, in social media, it is easy to amass vast quantities of unlabeled

[1] https://twitter.com/
[2] https://www.facebook.com/

data, while it is time and labor consuming to obtain labels. To deal with large-scale unlabeled data in social media, we propose to study unsupervised streaming feature selection. Unsupervised streaming feature selection is particularly difficult and challenging: (1) without any label information, it is difficult to assess the importance of features; and (2) features are usually not predefined but are generated dynamically, hence it cannot be carried out by directly applying traditional unsupervised feature selection algorithms.

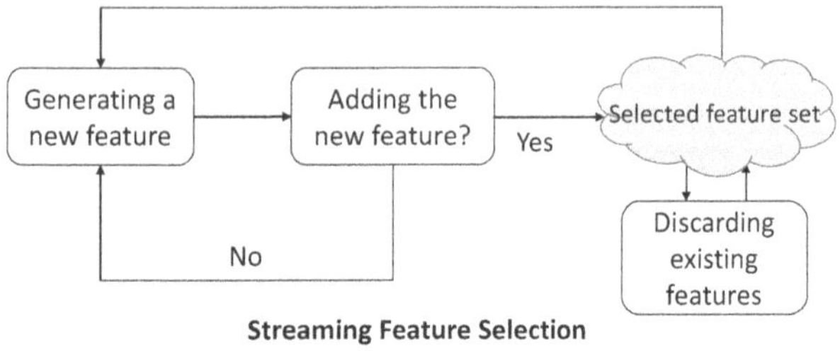

Figure 1: A framework of streaming feature selection. It consists of two phases: testing newly arrived features and testing existing features.

On the other hand, link information is abundant in social media. As observed by homophily [21] from social sciences, linked instances are likely to share similar features (or attributes). Therefore, as label information for supervised streaming feature selection, link information could provide helpful constraints to enable unsupervised streaming feature selection. However, linked social media data is inherently not independent and identically distributed (*i.i.d.*) while existing streaming feature selection are based on the data *i.i.d.* assumption, it is challenging to exploit link information for streaming feature selection.

In this work, we investigate: (1) how to exploit link information for feature selection; and (2) how to perform streaming feature selection in unsupervised scenarios. Our solutions to these two questions lead to a novel unsupervised streaming feature selection framework USFS. The main contributions of this paper are outlined as follows:

- Providing a principled approach to utilize link information to enable unsupervised streaming feature selection in social media;
- Proposing an unsupervised streaming feature selection framework, USFS, which exploits link and feature information simultaneously to select features dynamically and efficiently; and
- Evaluating the efficacy and efficiency of the proposed USFS framework on real-world social media datasets.

The rest of this paper is organized as follows. We formally define the problem of unsupervised streaming feature selection in Section 2. In Section 3, we introduce the proposed framework of unsupervised streaming feature selection. Empirical evaluation on real-world social media datasets is presented in Section 4 with discussion. In Section 5, we briefly review related work. The conclusion and future work are presented in Section 6.

2. PROBLEM STATEMENT

We first summarize some notations used in this paper. We use bold uppercase characters to denote matrices, bold lowercase characters to denote vectors, normal lowercase characters to denote scalars. For an arbitrary matrix $\mathbf{A} \in \mathbb{R}^{n \times d}$, $\mathbf{a}_i$ and $\mathbf{a}^j$ mean the i-th row and j-the column of matrix $\mathbf{A}$, respectively. $\mathbf{A}_{ij}$ or $\mathbf{a}_i^j$ denotes the (i, j)-th entry of matrix $\mathbf{A}$. $\mathbf{A}^{(t)}$ denotes the matrix of $\mathbf{A}$ at time step t, $(\mathbf{a}^{(t)})_i$ and $(\mathbf{a}^{(t)})^j$ represent i-th row and j-th column of matrix $\mathbf{A}^{(t)}$, respectively. $Tr(\mathbf{A})$ is the trace of matrix $\mathbf{A}$ if it is square, the Frobenius norm of the matrix $\mathbf{A} \in \mathbb{R}^{n \times d}$ is defined as $||\mathbf{A}||_F = \sqrt{\sum_{i=1}^{n} \sum_{j=1}^{d} \mathbf{A}_{ij}^2}$.

Let $\mathcal{U} = \{u_1, u_2, ..., u_n\}$ denote a set of n linked data instances. We assume features are dynamically generated and one feature arrives at each time step, thus, at time step t, each linked data instance is associated with a set of t features $\mathcal{F}^{(t)} = \{f_1, f_2, ..., f_t\}$. Then at the next time step $t+1$, each linked instance is tied with a new feature set $\mathcal{F}^{(t+1)} = \{f_1, f_2, ..., f_t, f_{t+1}\}$. The data representation at time step t and $t+1$ can be represented as $\mathbf{X}^{(t)} = [\mathbf{f}_1, \mathbf{f}_2, ..., \mathbf{f}_t]$ and $\mathbf{X}^{(t+1)} = [\mathbf{f}_1, \mathbf{f}_2, ..., \mathbf{f}_t, \mathbf{f}_{t+1}]$, where $\mathbf{f}_1, ..., \mathbf{f}_t, \mathbf{f}_{t+1}$ are the feature vectors corresponding to features $f_1, ..., f_t, f_{t+1}$. We denote the link information between instances in a matrix $\mathbf{M} \in \mathbb{R}^{n \times n}$, where $\mathbf{M}_{ij} = 1$ if u_i and u_j are linked, otherwise $\mathbf{M}_{ij} = 0$. The link information can either be a directed or an undirected graph. Note that in this paper, we do not consider the dynamics of link information and the reason is that link information does not change as fast as feature information; for example, the friend circles of most users are often stable once they are established.

With these notations, the task of *unsupervised streaming feature selection in social media* focuses on finding a subset of most relevant features $\mathcal{S}^{(t)} \subseteq \mathcal{F}^{(t)}$ at each time step t to facilitate clustering by utilizing both the feature information $\mathcal{F}^{(t)}$ and the link information $\mathbf{M}$.

3. UNSUPERVISED STREAMING FEATURE SELECTION IN SOCIAL MEDIA

The work flow of the proposed framework USFS is shown in Figure 2. We can observe that it consists of three components. The first component shows the representation of data. We have a set of linked instances (for example $u_1, u_2, ..., u_5$); for each linked instance, its features arrive through a streaming fashion, for example, $u_1, u_2, ..., u_5$ are associated with features $f_1, f_2..., f_t$ at time step t; are associated with features $f_1, f_2, ..., f_{t+i}$ at time step $t+i$. The second component shows the process of the algorithm, we will first talk about how to model link information via extracting social latent factors and how to use them as a constraint through a regression model in Section 3.1. Then we will introduce how to model feature information to make it consistent with social latent factors in Section 3.2. At last, we will show how to efficiently test new feature and existing features in Section 3.3. After that, as shown in the third component, we obtain a subset of relevant features at each time step (for example, $\mathcal{S}^{(t)}$ at time step t).

3.1 Modeling Link Information

Social media users connect to each other due to different factors such as movie fans, football enthusiasts, colleagues and each factor should be related to certain features (or at-

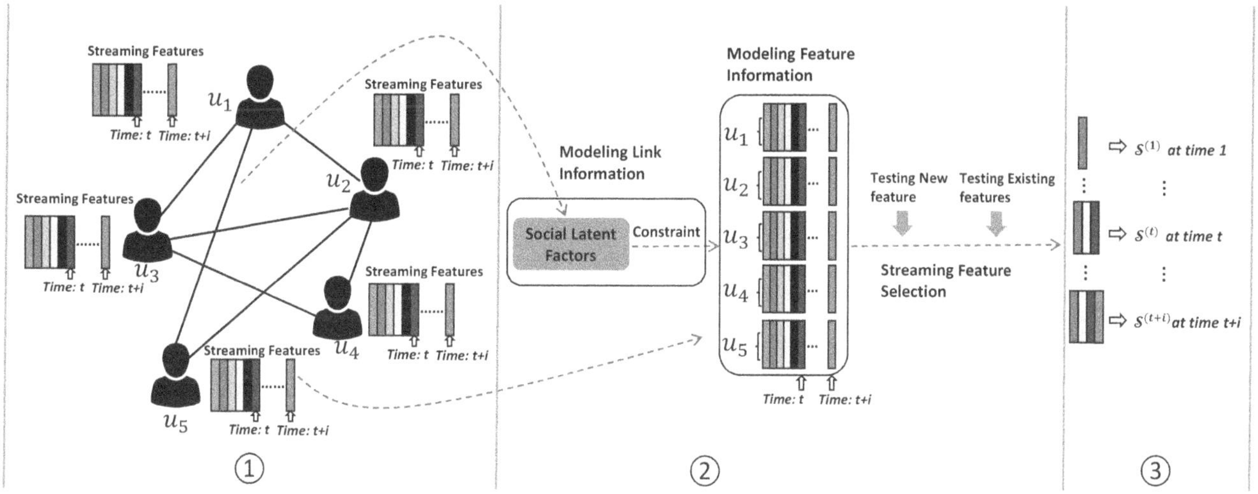

Figure 2: A framework of unsupervised streaming feature selection in social media.

tributes) of users [19]. Therefore, extracting these factors from link information should be very useful to steer the unsupervised streaming feature selection. However, in most cases, these hidden factors are not explicitly available in social media data.

Uncovering hidden social factors has been extensively studied [2, 22, 30]. In this work, we extract the social latent factors for each instance based on the mixed membership stochastic blockmodel [2]. In the blockmodel, it assumes that there exists a number of latent factors, and these latent factors interact with each other with certain probabilities to form social relationships. More specially, each instance is associated with a k-dimensional latent factor vector $\boldsymbol{\pi}_i \in \mathbb{R}^k$, where $\boldsymbol{\pi}_{ig}$ denotes the probability of u_i in factor g. This means that each instance can simultaneously be sided with multiple latent factors with different affiliation strength. For each instance, the indicator vector $\mathbf{z}_{i\to j}$ denotes the latent factor membership of u_i when it links to u_j and $\mathbf{z}_{i\leftarrow j}$ denotes the latent factor membership of u_i when it is linked from u_j. The interaction strength between different latent factors is encoded in a $k \times k$ stochastic matrix $\mathbf{B}$, in which each element is between 0 and 1. Then the observed link information is generated according to the following process:

1. For each linked instance u_i,
   - Draw a k dimensional vector $\boldsymbol{\pi}_i \sim \text{Dirichlet}(\theta)$.
2. For each pair of linked instance $(i, j) \in \mathcal{U} \times \mathcal{U}$,
   - Draw indicator vector $\mathbf{z}_{i\to j} \sim \text{Multinomial}(\boldsymbol{\pi}_i)$.
   - Draw indicator vector $\mathbf{z}_{i\leftarrow j} \sim \text{Multinomial}(\boldsymbol{\pi}_j)$.
   - Draw the relationship between u_i and u_j, $\mathbf{M}_{i,j} \sim \text{Bernoulli}(\mathbf{z}_{i\to j}\mathbf{B}\mathbf{z}_{i\leftarrow j})$.

Motivated by [12], we use a scalable inference algorithm to obtain the social latent factors $\mathbf{\Pi} = [\boldsymbol{\pi}_1, \boldsymbol{\pi}_2, ..., \boldsymbol{\pi}_n]^T \in \mathbb{R}^{n\times k}$ for all n instances efficiently.

As we obtain the social latent factors for each linked instances, we take advantage of them as a constraint to perform feature selection through a regression model. We measure the importance of each feature by its ability to differentiate different social latent factors. At time step t, given each social latent factor $\boldsymbol{\pi}^i$ (a column of $\mathbf{\Pi}$) for all instances, we are able to find a subset of most relevant features by the following minimization problem:

$$\begin{aligned}\min_{\mathbf{W}^{(t)}} \mathcal{J}(\mathbf{W}^{(t)}) &= \frac{1}{2}\sum_{i=1}^{k} ||\mathbf{X}^{(t)}(\mathbf{w}^{(t)})^i - \boldsymbol{\pi}^i||_2^2 + \alpha \sum_{i=1}^{k} ||(\mathbf{w}^{(t)})^i||_1 \\ &= \frac{1}{2}||\mathbf{X}^{(t)}\mathbf{W}^{(t)} - \mathbf{\Pi}||_F^2 + \alpha \sum_{i=1}^{k} ||(\mathbf{w}^{(t)})^i||_1,\end{aligned} \quad (1)$$

where $\mathbf{X}^{(t)} \in \mathbb{R}^{n\times t}$, $\mathbf{W}^{(t)} \in \mathbb{R}^{t\times k}$ is a mapping matrix which assigns each instance a k-dimensional social latent vector at time step t. Each column of $\mathbf{W}^{(t)}$, i.e., $(\mathbf{w}^{(t)})^i \in \mathbb{R}^t$ contains coefficients of t different features in approximating the i-th social latent vector of $\mathbf{\Pi}$. α is a parameter which controls the trade-off between the loss function and the ℓ_1-norm. One main advantage of ℓ_1-norm regression (Lasso) [31] is that it leads some coefficients of $(\mathbf{w}^{(t)})^i$ to be exact zero. This property makes it to be suitable for feature selection, as we can select features with corresponding non-zero coefficients.

In Lasso, the number of selected features is usually bounded by the number of data instances, which is unrealistic in many applications. Besides, features in social media usually have strong pairwise correlations, such as synonyms or antonyms words in text data. Lasso tends to randomly select features from a group and discards the others. Therefore, we employ the elastic net [38] on the basis of Eq. (1):

$$\begin{aligned}\min_{\mathbf{W}^{(t)}} \mathcal{J}(\mathbf{W}^{(t)}) &= \frac{1}{2}||\mathbf{X}^{(t)}\mathbf{W}^{(t)} - \mathbf{\Pi}||_F^2 + \alpha \sum_{i=1}^{k} ||(\mathbf{w}^{(t)})^i||_1 \\ &+ \frac{\beta}{2}||\mathbf{W}^{(t)}||_F^2,\end{aligned} \quad (2)$$

where the regularization term $\frac{\beta}{2}||\mathbf{W}^{(t)}||_F^2$ controls the robustness of the learned model.

3.2 Modeling Feature Information

In Twitter, if two users post similar contents (features), they are more likely to share similar social latent factors, like hobbies, education background, etc. The similarity of social latent factors reflects the correlation of two linked instances in the feature space. In other words, social latent factors of two instances are more likely to be consistent when their feature similarity (like textual similarity) is high. To model the feature information, we first construct a graph $\mathcal{G}$ to represent the feature similarity between different data instances. The adjacency matrix $\mathbf{A} \in \mathbb{R}^{n\times n}$ of the graph $\mathcal{G}$ at time step t is defined as:

$$\mathbf{A}_{ij}^{(t)} = \begin{cases} 1 & \text{if } (\mathbf{x}^{(t)})_i \in \mathcal{N}_p((\mathbf{x}^{(t)})_j) \text{ or } (\mathbf{x}^{(t)})_j \in \mathcal{N}_p((\mathbf{x}^{(t)})_i) \\ 0 & \text{otherwise} \end{cases}$$

where $(\mathbf{x}^{(t)})_i$ indicates the feature information of u_i, $\mathcal{N}_p((\mathbf{x}^{(t)})_i)$ represents p-nearest neighbors of $(\mathbf{x}^{(t)})_i$. Then feature information can be modeled by minimizing the following term:

$$\begin{aligned} &\frac{1}{2}\sum_{i=1}^{n}\sum_{j=1}^{n}\mathbf{A}_{ij}^{(t)}||(\mathbf{X}^{(t)}\mathbf{W}^{(t)})_i - (\mathbf{X}^{(t)}\mathbf{W}^{(t)})_j||_2^2 \\ &= Tr((\mathbf{X}^{(t)}\mathbf{W}^{(t)})^T(\mathbf{D}^{(t)} - \mathbf{A}^{(t)})(\mathbf{X}^{(t)}\mathbf{W}^{(t)})) \\ &= Tr((\mathbf{X}^{(t)}\mathbf{W}^{(t)})^T\mathbf{L}^{(t)}(\mathbf{X}^{(t)}\mathbf{W}^{(t)})), \end{aligned} \tag{3}$$

where $\mathbf{D}^{(t)} \in \mathbb{R}^{n\times n}$ is a diagonal matrix with $\mathbf{D}_{ii}^{(t)} = \sum_{j=1}^{n}\mathbf{A}_{ij}^{(t)}$, $\mathbf{L}^{(t)} = \mathbf{D}^{(t)} - \mathbf{A}^{(t)}$ is the Laplacian matrix. Since the Laplacian matrix in Eq. (3) is positive-semidefinite, Eq. (3) can also be written as:

$$\begin{aligned} &Tr((\mathbf{X}^{(t)}\mathbf{W}^{(t)})^T\mathbf{L}^{(t)}(\mathbf{X}^{(t)}\mathbf{W}^{(t)})) \\ &= ||(\mathbf{X}^{(t)}\mathbf{W}^{(t)})^T(\mathbf{L}^{(t)})^{\frac{1}{2}}||_F^2. \end{aligned} \tag{4}$$

The optimization formulation, which integrates feature information, is defined as:

$$\begin{aligned} \min_{\mathbf{W}^{(t)}} \mathcal{J}(\mathbf{W}^{(t)}) &= \frac{1}{2}||\mathbf{X}^{(t)}\mathbf{W}^{(t)} - \mathbf{\Pi}||_F^2 + \alpha\sum_{i=1}^{k}||(\mathbf{w}^{(t)})^i||_1 \\ &+ \frac{\beta}{2}||\mathbf{W}^{(t)}||_F^2 + \frac{\gamma}{2}||(\mathbf{X}^{(t)}\mathbf{W}^{(t)})^T(\mathbf{L}^{(t)})^{\frac{1}{2}}||_F^2, \end{aligned} \tag{5}$$

where γ is the regularization parameter to balance link information and feature information.

3.3 Streaming Feature Selection Framework

The objective function in Eq. (5) at time step t is parameterized by a transformation matrix $\mathbf{W}^{(t)}$. It can be further decomposed into a series of k sub-problems which correspond to k social latent factors:

$$\begin{aligned} \min_{(\mathbf{w}^{(t)})^i} \mathcal{J}((\mathbf{w}^{(t)})^i) &= \frac{1}{2}||\mathbf{X}^{(t)}(\mathbf{w}^{(t)})^i - \boldsymbol{\pi}^i||_2^2 + \alpha||(\mathbf{w}^{(t)})^i||_1 \\ &+ \frac{\beta}{2}||(\mathbf{w}^{(t)})^i||_2^2 + \frac{\gamma}{2}||(\mathbf{X}^{(t)}(\mathbf{w}^{(t)})^i)^T(\mathbf{L}^{(t)})^{\frac{1}{2}}||_2^2, \end{aligned} \tag{6}$$

where $i = 1, ..., k$. By solving each sub-problem in Eq. (6), we can select a subset of features at time t. Next we introduce how to efficiently perform feature selection when a new feature f_{t+1} is generated at a new time step $t + 1$. Following common steps of supervised streaming feature selection [33], the proposed framework will test: (1) whether we should select the new feature; and (2) whether we should discard some existing features.

3.3.1 Testing New Features

It can be observed from Eq. (6) that at time step $t + 1$, incorporating a new feature feature f_{t+1} involves adding a new non-zero weight value $(\mathbf{w}^{(t+1)})_{t+1}^i$ to the model, which incurs a penalty increasing $\alpha||(\mathbf{w}^{(t+1)})_{t+1}^i||_1$ on the ℓ_1 regularization term. The addition of the new feature f_{t+1} reduces the overall objective function value in Eq. (6) only when the overall reduction from the first, third, and forth term outweighs the increase of ℓ_1 penalty $\alpha||(\mathbf{w}^{(t)})_{t+1}^i||_1$.

Motivated by [26, 27], we adopt a stagewise way to check newly arrived features. Let $\mathcal{J}((\mathbf{w}^{(t+1)})^i)$ denotes the objective function of Eq. (6) at time step $t + 1$:

$$\begin{aligned} \min_{(\mathbf{w}^{(t+1)})^i} \mathcal{J}((\mathbf{w}^{(t+1)})^i) &= \frac{1}{2}||\mathbf{X}^{(t+1)}(\mathbf{w}^{(t+1)})^i - \boldsymbol{\pi}^i||_2^2 \\ &+ \alpha||(\mathbf{w}^{(t+1)})^i||_1 + \frac{\beta}{2}||(\mathbf{w}^{(t+1)})^i||_2^2 \\ &+ \frac{\gamma}{2}||(\mathbf{X}^{(t+1)}(\mathbf{w}^{(t+1)})^i)^T(\mathbf{L}^{(t+1)})^{\frac{1}{2}}||_2^2, \end{aligned} \tag{7}$$

then the derivative of $\mathcal{J}((\mathbf{w}^{(t+1)})^i)$ with respect to $(\mathbf{w}^{(t+1)})_{t+1}^i$ is as follows:

$$\begin{aligned} &\frac{\partial\mathcal{J}((\mathbf{w}^{(t+1)})^i)}{\partial(\mathbf{w}^{(t+1)})_{t+1}^i} \\ &= [(\mathbf{X}^{(t+1)})^T(\mathbf{X}^{(t+1)}(\mathbf{w}^{(t+1)})^i - \boldsymbol{\pi}^i) + \beta(\mathbf{w}^{(t+1)})^i \\ &+ \gamma(\mathbf{X}^{(t+1)})^T\mathbf{L}^{(t+1)}\mathbf{X}^{(t+1)}(\mathbf{w}^{(t+1)})^i]_{t+1} + \alpha\text{sign}((\mathbf{w}^{(t+1)})_{t+1}^i) \\ &= [(\mathbf{X}^{(t+1)})^T(\mathbf{X}^{(t+1)}(\mathbf{w}^{(t+1)})^i - \boldsymbol{\pi}^i) + \beta(\mathbf{w}^{(t+1)})^i \\ &+ \gamma(\mathbf{X}^{(t+1)})^T\mathbf{L}^{(t+1)}\mathbf{X}^{(t+1)}(\mathbf{w}^{(t+1)})^i]_{t+1} \pm \alpha. \end{aligned} \tag{8}$$

In Eq. (8), the derivative of ℓ_1-norm term $\alpha||(\mathbf{w}^{(t+1)})^i||_1$ w.r.t $(\mathbf{w}^{(t+1)})_{t+1}^i$ is not smooth. Here we discuss the sign of the derivative, i.e., $\text{sign}(\mathbf{w}^{(t+1)})_{t+1}^i$. When the new feature f_{t+1} arrives, we first set its feature coefficient $(\mathbf{w}^{(t+1)})_{t+1}^i$ to be zero and add it to the model, if:

$$\begin{aligned} &[(\mathbf{X}^{(t+1)})^T(\mathbf{X}^{(t+1)}(\mathbf{w}^{(t+1)})^i - \boldsymbol{\pi}^i) + \beta(\mathbf{w}^{(t+1)})^i \\ &+ \gamma(\mathbf{X}^{(t+1)})^T\mathbf{L}^{(t+1)}\mathbf{X}^{(t+1)}(\mathbf{w}^{(t+1)})^i]_{t+1} - \alpha > 0, \end{aligned} \tag{9}$$

it is easy to verify that:

$$\frac{\partial\mathcal{J}((\mathbf{w}^{(t+1)})^i)}{\partial(\mathbf{w}^{(t+1)})_{t+1}^i} > 0. \tag{10}$$

In order to reduce the objective function value $\mathcal{J}((\mathbf{w}^{(t+1)})^i)$, we need to slightly reduce the value of $(\mathbf{w}^{(t+1)})_{t+1}^i$ to make it negative, and then the sign of $(\mathbf{w}^{(t+1)})_{t+1}^i$ will be negative. For the same reason, if:

$$\begin{aligned} &[(\mathbf{X}^{(t+1)})^T(\mathbf{X}^{(t+1)}(\mathbf{w}^{(t+1)})^i - \boldsymbol{\pi}^i) + \beta(\mathbf{w}^{(t+1)})^i \\ &+ \gamma(\mathbf{X}^{(t+1)})^T\mathbf{L}^{(t+1)}\mathbf{X}^{(t+1)}(\mathbf{w}^{(t+1)})^i]_{t+1} + \alpha < 0, \end{aligned} \tag{11}$$

then:

$$\frac{\partial\mathcal{J}((\mathbf{w}^{(t+1)})^i)}{\partial(\mathbf{w}^{(t+1)})_{t+1}^i} < 0, \tag{12}$$

the sign of $(\mathbf{w}^{(t+1)})_{t+1}^i$ will be positive. If both of previous conditions are not satisfied, it is impossible to reduce the objective function value $\mathcal{J}((\mathbf{w}^{(t+1)})^i)$ by making $(\mathbf{w}^{(t+1)})_{t+1}^i$ as a small disturbance around 0. In other words, for the new feature f_{t+1}, we need to check:

$$\begin{aligned} &|[(\mathbf{X}^{(t+1)})^T(\mathbf{X}^{(t+1)}(\mathbf{w}^{(t+1)})^i - \boldsymbol{\pi}^i) + \beta(\mathbf{w}^{(t+1)})^i \\ &+ \gamma(\mathbf{X}^{(t+1)})^T\mathbf{L}^{(t+1)}\mathbf{X}^{(t+1)}(\mathbf{w}^{(t+1)})^i]_{t+1}| > \alpha. \end{aligned} \tag{13}$$

As the condition in Eq. (13) is satisfied, it indicates that the addition of the new feature f_{t+1} will reduce the objective function value $\mathcal{J}((\mathbf{w}^{(t+1)})^i)$, therefore the new feature is included in the model described in Eq. (7).

3.3.2 *Testing Existing Features*

In social media, when new features are continuously being generated, they may take place of some existing features since new features can better reflect the interests of users, etc. Old features become outdated as a result, therefore, in the proposed unsupervised streaming feature selection framework USFS, we also investigate if it is necessary to remove any existing selected features.

After a new feature is accepted and added to the model, we optimize Eq. (7) with respect to existing feature weights, the optimization may force some feature weights to be zero. If the feature weight obtains a zero value, it indicates that the existence of the feature is not likely to reduce the objective function value and the feature can be removed. Here we discuss how to solve the optimization problem in Eq. (7). The objective function in Eq. (7) is convex and the gradient with respect to $(\mathbf{w}^{(t+1)})^i_{t+1}$ can be easily obtained as Eq. (8), then a global optimum solution can be achieved. We choose to use a Broyden-Fletcher-Goldfarb-Shanno (BFGS) quasi-newton method [3] to solve the optimization problem. Unlike traditional Newton's method which requires the calculation of second derivatives (the Hessian), BFGS only needs the gradient of the objective function to be computed at each iteration. Therefore, it is more efficient than Newton's methods especially when Hessian evaluation is slow.

The minimization problem in Eq. (7) can be generalized to the following form:

$$\min f(\mathbf{x}), \quad \mathbf{x} \in \mathbb{R}^n. \tag{14}$$

At each iteration, the optimal solution $\mathbf{x}$ is updated as:

$$\mathbf{x}_{m+1} = \mathbf{x}_m - \delta_m \mathbf{H}_m \mathbf{g}_m, \tag{15}$$

where $\mathbf{H}_m = \mathbf{B}_m^{-1}$, $\mathbf{B}_m$ is an approximation to the Hessian matrix ($\mathbf{B}_m \approx [\nabla^2 f(\mathbf{x}_m)]$), $\mathbf{g}_m = \nabla f(\mathbf{x}_m)$ is the gradient and δ_m is the step size that can be determined by line search. Let the vectors $\mathbf{s}_m$ and $\mathbf{c}_m$ be:

$$\mathbf{s}_m = \mathbf{x}_{m+1} - \mathbf{x}_m, \ \mathbf{c}_m = \mathbf{g}_{m+1} - \mathbf{g}_m, \tag{16}$$

the next Hessian approximation has to meet the secant equation:

$$\mathbf{B}_{m+1}\mathbf{s}_m = \mathbf{c}_m. \tag{17}$$

By pre-multiplying the secant equation $\mathbf{s}_m^T$ at both sides, we obtain the curvature condition:

$$\underbrace{\mathbf{s}_m^T \mathbf{B}_{m+1} \mathbf{s}_m}_{>0} = \mathbf{s}_m^T \mathbf{c}_m > 0. \tag{18}$$

If the curvature condition is satisfied, $\mathbf{B}_{m+1}$ in the secant equation has at least one solution, which can be updated by the following way:

$$\mathbf{B}_{m+1} = \mathbf{B}_m + \frac{\mathbf{c}_m \mathbf{c}_m^T}{\mathbf{c}_m^T \mathbf{s}_m} - \frac{\mathbf{B}_m \mathbf{s}_m \mathbf{s}_m^T \mathbf{B}_m}{\mathbf{s}_m^T \mathbf{B}_m \mathbf{s}_m}. \tag{19}$$

Its inverse, i.e., $\mathbf{H}_{m+1}$, can be updated efficiently by Sherman-Morrison formula [10]:

$$\mathbf{H}_{m+1} = \mathbf{H}_m - \frac{\mathbf{s}_m \mathbf{c}_m^T \mathbf{H}_m + \mathbf{H}_m \mathbf{c}_m \mathbf{s}_m^T}{\mathbf{s}_m^T \mathbf{c}_m} + \left(1 + \frac{\mathbf{c}_m^T \mathbf{H}_m \mathbf{c}_m}{\mathbf{s}_m^T \mathbf{c}_m}\right) \frac{\mathbf{s}_m \mathbf{s}_m^T}{\mathbf{s}_m^T \mathbf{c}_m}. \tag{20}$$

With these, the BFGS algorithm to solve Eq. (7) is illustrated in Algorithm 1.

Algorithm 1 BFGS to optimize Eq. (7)

Input: Starting point $\mathbf{x}_0$, convergence threshold ϵ, initial inverse Hessian approximation $\mathbf{H}_0$
Output: Optimal solution $\mathbf{x}^*$

$m \leftarrow 0$
$\mathbf{g}_m = \nabla f(\mathbf{x}_m)$
while $||\mathbf{g}_m|| > \epsilon$ **do**
  Obtain a direction $\mathbf{p}_m = -\mathbf{H}_m \mathbf{g}_m$
  Compute $\mathbf{x}_{m+1} = \mathbf{x}_m + \delta_m \mathbf{p}_m$, where δ_m is chosen by line search to meet curvature condition
  $\mathbf{g}_{m+1} = \nabla f(\mathbf{x}_{m+1})$
  $\mathbf{s}_m = \mathbf{x}_{m+1} - \mathbf{x}_m$
  $\mathbf{c}_m = \mathbf{g}_{m+1} - \mathbf{g}_m$
  $\mathbf{H}_{m+1} = \mathbf{H}_m - \frac{\mathbf{s}_m \mathbf{c}_m^T \mathbf{H}_m + \mathbf{H}_m \mathbf{c}_m \mathbf{s}_m^T}{\mathbf{s}_m^T \mathbf{c}_m} + (1 + \frac{\mathbf{c}_m^T \mathbf{H}_m \mathbf{c}_m}{\mathbf{s}_m^T \mathbf{c}_m}) \frac{\mathbf{s}_m \mathbf{s}_m^T}{\mathbf{s}_m^T \mathbf{c}_m}$
  $m \leftarrow m + 1$
end while
return $\mathbf{x}_m$

3.3.3 *Feature Selection by USFS*

By solving all k sub-problems at time step $t+1$, we obtain the sparse coefficient matrix $\mathbf{W} = [(\mathbf{w}^{(t+1)})^1, ..., (\mathbf{w}^{(t+1)})^k]$. Since we solve each sub-problem separately, the number of non-zero weights in each $(\mathbf{w}^{(t+1)})^i (i = 1, ..., k)$ is not necessarily to be the same. For each feature f_j, if any of the k corresponding feature weight coefficients $(\mathbf{w}^{(t+1)})^i_j (i = 1, 2, ..., k)$ is nonzero, the feature is included in the final model, otherwise the feature is not selected. If f_j is selected, its feature score at time step $t+1$ is defined as:

$$FScore(j)^{(t+1)} = \max((\mathbf{w}^{(t+1)})^1_j, ..., (\mathbf{w}^{(t+1)})^k_j) \tag{21}$$

The selected features are then sorted according to their feature scores in a descending order, the higher the feature score, the more important the feature is.

The pseudo code of the proposed unsupervised streaming feature selection algorithm for social media data is illustrated in Algorithm 2. It efficiently performs unsupervised feature selection when a new feature f_{t+1} arrives. In line 1, we obtain the social latent factor matrix $\mathbf{\Pi}$ using the link information $\mathbf{M}$. The algorithm to check new feature and existing features is illustrated in lines 2-8. More specifically, for each sub-problem, we first check the gradient condition, this step decides whether we accept the new feature (line 3). If the condition is satisfied (line 4), the new feature is included in the model (line 5) and the model is re-optimized with respect to all existing feature weights (line 6). At last, when the new feature is included in the model, it updates the Laplacian matrix (line 10), calculates the feature scores, and updates the selected feature set (lines 11-12).

3.4 Time Complexity Analysis

3.4.1 *Time Complexity for All Streaming Features*

The mixed membership stochastic model to extract social latent factors has a time complexity of $O(n^2k^2)$. Assuming the total number of streaming features is t and the number of obtained features is s, the time complexity of updating

Algorithm 2 Unsupervised streaming feature selection framework (USFS)

Input: New feature f_{t+1} at time $t+1$, feature weight matrix $\mathbf{W}^{(t)}$ at previous time step t, link information $\mathbf{M}$, parameters α, β, γ, number of social latent factors k, number of nearest neighbors p

Output: Selected feature subset $\mathcal{S}^{(t+1)}$ at time step $t+1$

Obtain social latent factors $\mathbf{\Pi}$ from $\mathbf{M}$
for each social latent factor $\pi^l (l = 1, ..., k)$ **do**
  compute gradient g for f_{t+1} according to Eq. (8)
  if abs$(g) > \alpha$ **then**
    add feature f_{t+1} to the model
    optimize the model via BFGS in Algorithm 1
  end if
end for
if feature f_{t+1} is accepted **then**
  update Laplacian matrix $\mathbf{L}^{(t+1)}$
  obtain feature scores according to Eq. (21)
  sort features by scores and update $\mathcal{S}^{(t+1)}$
end if
return $\mathcal{S}^{(t+1)}$

Laplacian matrix is bounded by $O(n^2st)$. At each time step, we check the gradient condition in Eq. (13). The time complexity upper bound of the gradient checking over all t time steps is $O(n^2kst)$. Since we optimize the model in Eq. (7) when the new feature is accepted, the total time of optimization with BGFS is $O(n^2s^2t)$ in the worst case when the selected s features are the latest arrived s features.

Overall, the total time complexity of the proposed USFS is $O(n^2k^2) + O(n^2st) + O(n^2kst) + O(n^2s^2t)$. Since $k \ll t$ and $s \ll t$, the upper bound of the overall time complexity is $O(n^2s^2t)$. However, it only provides an upper bound, in real-world applications, the time complexity could be much lower than this upper bound. We will empirically show the efficiency of the proposed framework in the experiments.

3.4.2 *Time Complexity for An Individual Feature*

For the newly generated feature, suppose there are already s features in the model, if its previous feature is added in the model, the time complexity of gradient test is $O(n^2ks)$, otherwise the time complexity is only $O(n)$. To test existing features via BFGS, the time complexity is $O(n^2s^2)$.

4. EXPERIMENTS

In this section, we conduct experiments to evaluate the performance of the proposed framework USFS. In particular, we evaluate the following: 1) How is the quality of selected features by USFS compared with the state-of-the-art unsupervised feature selection algorithms? 2) How efficient is the proposed USFS framework? Before introducing the details of experiments, we first introduce the datasets and experimental settings.

4.1 Datasets

We use two real-world social media datasets BlogCatalog and Flickr for experimental evaluation. Some statistics of the datasets are listed in Table 1.

BlogCatalog: BlogCatalog[3] is a social blog directory which manages bloggers and their blogs. Bloggers are associated with sets of tags, which provide feature information. Users in blogcatalog follow each other which form the social link information. Bloggers can also register their blogs under predefined categories, which are used as ground truth for validation in our work.

Flickr: Flickr[4] is an image hosting and sharing website, the key features in flickr are tags, user can specify the list of tags to reflect their interests. Similar to blogcatalog, users in flickr can interact with others. Photos are organized under prespecified categories, which are used as the ground truth.

	BlogCatalog	Flickr
# of Users	5,196	7,575
# of Features	8,189	12,047
# of Links	171,743	239,738
# of Ave Degree	66.11	63.30
# of Classes	6	9

Table 1: Detailed information of datasets.

4.2 Experimental Settings

Following a standard way to assess unsupervised feature selection [4, 18, 29, 35], we use the clustering performance to evaluate the quality of selected features. Two commonly used clustering performance evaluation metrics, i.e., *accuracy* (ACC) and *normalized mutual information* (NMI) [4] are used in this paper.

To the best of our knowledge, we are the first to study streaming feature selection in social media. To investigate the effectiveness and the efficiency of the proposed framework, we choose the following state-of-the-art unsupervised feature selection algorithms as baseline methods:

- **LapScore**: Laplacian score [16] evaluates feature importance by its ability to preserve the local manifold structure of data.
- **SPEC**: Features are selected by spectral analysis [36] and SPEC can be considered as an extension of Laplacian score method.
- **NDFS**: Nonnegative Discriminative Unsupervised Feature Selection [18] which selects features via a joint nonnegative spectral analysis as well as a $\ell_{2,1}$-norm regularization.
- **LUFS**: LUFS utilizes both content information and link information to perform feature selection in an unsupervised scenario [29].

For LapScore, NDFS and USFS, we follow previous work [4, 16] to specify the number of neighborhood size to be 5 to construct the Laplacian matrix on the data instances. NDFS and LUFS have different regularization parameters, we set these regularization parameters according to the suggestions from the original papers. For USFS, we set the number of social latent factors as the number of clusters. There are three important regularization parameters α, β and γ in USFS. α controls the sparsity of the model, β is the parameter for elastic net which controls the robustness of the model, and γ balances the contribution of the link information and feature information. In the experiments, we empirically set $\alpha = 10$,

[3]http://www.blogcatalog.com/

[4]https://www.flickr.com/

$\beta = 0.1$, $\gamma = 0.1$ and more details about the effects of these parameters on the proposed framework will be discussed in Section 4.5.

All experiments are conducted on a machine with 16GB RAM and Intel Core i7-4770 CPU.

4.3 Quality of Selected Features

Following streaming feature selection settings that assume features arrive one at a time [37], we divide all features into 9 groups where we choose the first $\{20\%, ..., 90\%, 100\%\}$ as streaming features. In each group, we perform feature selection with traditional unsupervised feature selection algorithm as well as the proposed USFS algorithm. We record how many features USFS selects and specify the same number as that of selected features by traditional unsupervised feature selection algorithms for a fair comparison.

After obtaining the feature selection results, K-means clustering is performed based on the chosen features. We repeat the K-means algorithm 20 times and report average results because K-means may converge to local minima. The clustering results are evaluated by both *accuracy* (ACC) and *normalized mutual information* (NMI). The higher the ACC and NMI values are, the better feature selection performance is. The comparison results are shown in Table 2 and Table 3 for BlogCatalog and Flickr, respectively. Note that the number in parentheses in the table indicates the number of selected features determined by USFS. We make the following observations:

- USFS tends to accept new features at the very beginning, then it becomes increasingly difficult for newly generated features to alternate previous decisions since existing features already provide us enough information. For example, no new features are accepted anymore after the number of selected features reach 275 and 670 in BlogCatalog and Flickr, respectively.
- USFS consistently outperforms all baseline methods on both datasets with significant performance gain in most cases. The reason is that traditional unsupervised feature selection algorithms are based on the *i.i.d.* assumption which is invalid in linked social media data. USFS takes advantage of link information to guide the unsupervised streaming feature selection. It can also be observed that when feature information is scarce (for example 20%), link information could better complement feature information for feature selection. We also perform pair-wise wilcoxon signed-rank test [7] between USFS and other baseline methods on different proportions of streaming features and the test results show that USFS is significantly better (with both 0.01 and 0.05 significance level).
- For baseline methods, clustering performance gradually decreases when features are continuously generated. While for USFS, the clustering performance is relatively more stable when the proportion of streaming features varies from 20% to 100%. The number of selected features by USFS is also very stable, which varies from 236 to 275 in BlogCatalog and 562 to 670 in Flickr, respectively. It demonstrates the effectiveness of streaming feature selection, with a large amount of streaming features, we can only dynamically maintain a small set of relevant features without deteriorating the performance.

4.4 Efficiency Performance Comparison

To evaluate the efficiency of the proposed USFS algorithm, we compare the running time of different methods in Figure 3. As LapScore, SPEC, NDFS and LUFS are not designed for dealing with streaming features, we rerun the feature selection process at each time step. For both datasets, we set the cumulative running time threshold to be around 10^4 seconds since all methods except USFS take more than 50 hours. As can be observed, the proposed USFS algorithm is significantly faster than other baseline methods, the average processing time for each feature in BlogCatalog and Flickr is only 0.62 seconds and 1.37 seconds, respectively.

We also record the cumulative running time of USFS when the cumulative running time of other methods arrive the threshold (10^4 seconds), the results show that in BlogCatalog, USFS is 7×, 20×, 29×, 76× faster than LapScore, LUFS, NDFS, SPEC, respectively; in Flickr, USFS is 5×, 11×, 20×, 75× faster than LapScore, LUFS, NDFS, SPEC, respectively. The difference is becoming larger as the curve of USFS in Figure 3 is getting more smooth when streaming features continuously arrive.

4.5 Effects of Parameters

As discussed in Section 3, USFS has four important parameters: the number of social latent factors k, and parameters α, β, and γ in Eq. (6). To investigate the effects of these parameters, we vary one parameter each time and fix the other three to see how the parameter affects the feature selection performance in terms of clustering with different number of selected features. We only perform the parameter study on BlogCatalog dataset to save space since we have similar observations on the Flickr dataset.

First, we vary the number of social latent factors k from 5 to 10 while fix the other three parameters ($\alpha = 10$, $\beta = 0.1$, $\gamma = 0.1$). The clustering performance in terms of Accuracy and NMI is illustrated in Figure 4. The clustering performance is the best when the number of social latent factors is close to the number of clusters, which is 6 in BlogCatalog.

To assess the effect of parameter α which controls the model sparseness, we vary α as {0.001, 0.01, 0.1, 1, 10, 100, 1000} while fix $k = 6$, $\beta = 0.1$, $\gamma = 0.1$, performance variance between α and number of selected features is presented in Figure 5. With the increase of α, the clustering performance rises rapidly and then keeps stable between the range of 10 to 1000. A high value of α indicates that it is not easy for new features to pass the gradient test in Eq. (13), thus the accepted features are more relevant and meaningful.

We study the effect of parameter β which makes the model more robust. Similar to the setting of α, β is also in the range of {0.001, 0.01, 0.1, 1, 10, 100, 1000} and $k = 6$, $\alpha = 10$, $\gamma = 0.1$. The results are shown in Figure 6. We can see that clustering performance is much more sensitive to the number of selected features than to β. The performance is relatively higher when β is between 0.1 and 10.

At last, we evaluate the trade-off between link information and feature information by varying γ in {0.001, 0.01, 0.1, 1, 10, 100, 1000} while fix $k = 6$, $\alpha = 10$, $\beta = 0.1$. The results are presented in Figure 7. As shown in the figure, in most cases, the clustering performance first increases, reaches its peak and then it gradually decreases. The best performance achieves when γ is around 0.1. These observations suggest the importance of both link information and feature information in unsupervised streaming feature selection.

	Accuracy								
	20%(259)	30%(266)	40%(270)	50%(271)	60%(272)	70%(272)	80%(274)	90%(275)	100%(275)
LapScore	37.36	25.60	22.88	23.00	23.36	26.96	26.33	26.73	26.06
SPEC	30.10	29.50	24.79	21.48	18.88	19.63	18.34	18.30	18.01
NDFS	35.89	25.37	23.67	26.44	25.42	26.00	23.69	23.85	23.73
LUFS	24.65	24.11	22.27	22.84	22.50	20.71	21.61	20.71	20.48
USFS	**40.65**	**39.61**	**40.57**	**40.61**	**40.67**	**40.67**	**40.78**	**40.84**	**40.84**
	NMI								
	20%(259)	30%(266)	40%(270)	50%(271)	60%(272)	70%(272)	80%(274)	90%(275)	100%(275)
LapScore	0.1451	0.0600	0.0474	0.0510	0.0507	0.0743	0.0675	0.0793	0.0652
SPEC	0.0606	0.0765	0.0397	0.0143	0.0051	0.0098	0.0032	0.0029	0.0019
NDFS	0.1475	0.1250	0.1193	0.1092	0.1234	0.1006	0.1125	0.1130	0.1150
LUFS	0.0674	0.0533	0.0465	0.0490	0.0462	0.0492	0.0462	0.0345	0.0287
USFS	**0.2028**	**0.1861**	**0.2028**	**0.2026**	**0.2042**	**0.2042**	**0.2059**	**0.2072**	**0.2072**

Table 2: Clustering results with different feature selection algorithms on BlogCatalog dataset.

	Accuracy								
	20%(645)	30%(666)	40%(670)	50%(670)	60%(670)	70%(670)	80%(670)	90%(670)	100%(670)
LapScore	25.06	19.30	21.27	17.52	15.27	13.58	13.53	12.73	12.07
SPEC	25.52	20.26	17.50	15.46	13.53	14.11	13.94	13.52	13.07
NDFS	22.30	**29.50**	26.79	25.29	25.64	28.01	25.97	**29.08**	20.45
LUFS	27.13	22.11	19.19	24.00	24.79	19.97	18.22	19.24	23.99
USFS	**27.22**	**29.50**	**28.37**	**28.37**	**28.37**	**28.37**	**28.37**	28.37	**28.37**
	NMI								
	20%(645)	30%(666)	40%(670)	50%(670)	60%(670)	70%(670)	80%(670)	90%(670)	100%(670)
LapScore	0.1072	0.0629	0.0786	0.0521	0.0308	0.0143	0.0172	0.0100	0.0040
SPEC	0.0854	0.0546	0.0328	0.0245	0.0117	0.0152	0.0118	0.0109	0.0083
NDFS	0.0676	0.1260	0.1073	0.0876	0.0853	0.1207	0.1236	0.1152	0.0663
LUFS	0.1129	0.0958	0.0550	0.1015	0.1023	0.0602	0.0535	0.0524	0.0913
USFS	**0.1235**	**0.1368**	**0.1262**	**0.1262**	**0.1262**	**0.1262**	**0.1262**	**0.1262**	**0.1262**

Table 3: Clustering results with different feature selection algorithms on Flickr dataset.

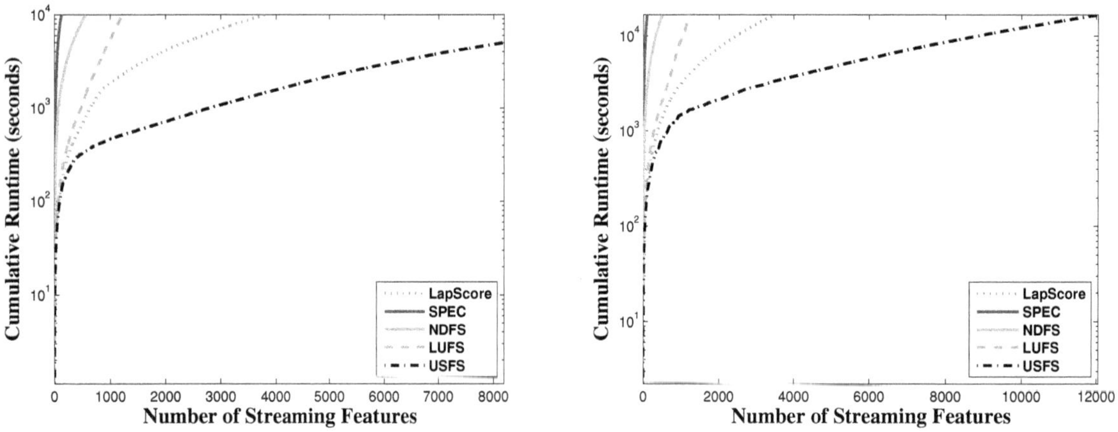

(a) BlogCatalog

(b) Flickr

Figure 3: The cumulative runtime on BlogCatalog dataset and Flickr dataset. The Y axes are in log scale.

5. RELATED WORK

In this section, we first briefly review some related work in traditional feature selection, then we introduce existing work on supervised streaming feature selection.

5.1 Traditional Feature Selection

Feature selection algorithms can be broadly grouped into three categories: filter methods, wrapper methods as well as embedded methods. Filter methods are independent of any learning algorithms and are thereby very efficient, they rely on some data characteristics such as distance, consistency, dependency, information, and correlation to measure the strength of each feature individually [13, 16, 25, 28]. Wrapper methods use the prediction power of a predefined learning algorithm to evaluate the quality of selected features. They are inevitably computational expensive since the search space grows exponentially with the number of features [9]. Embedded methods is a tradeoff between these two models which combines feature selection and model con-

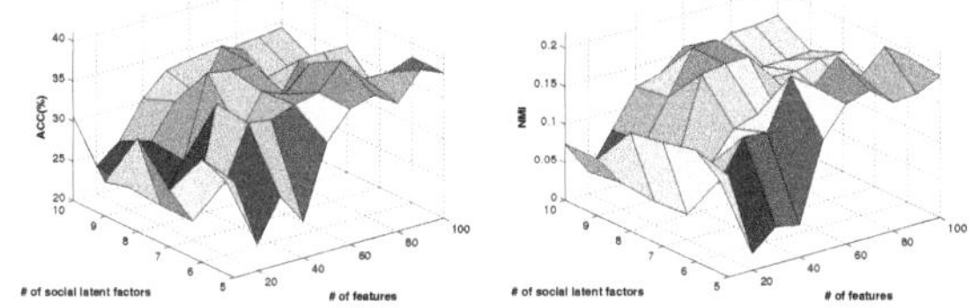

(a) Accuracy (b) NMI

Figure 4: Effect of # social latent factors.

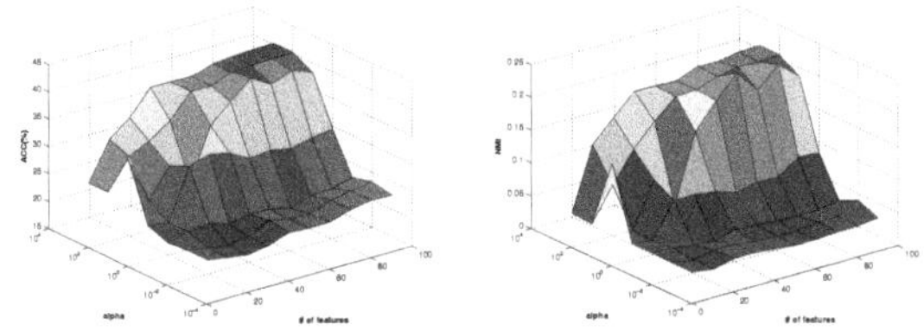

(a) Accuracy (b) NMI

Figure 5: Effect of α.

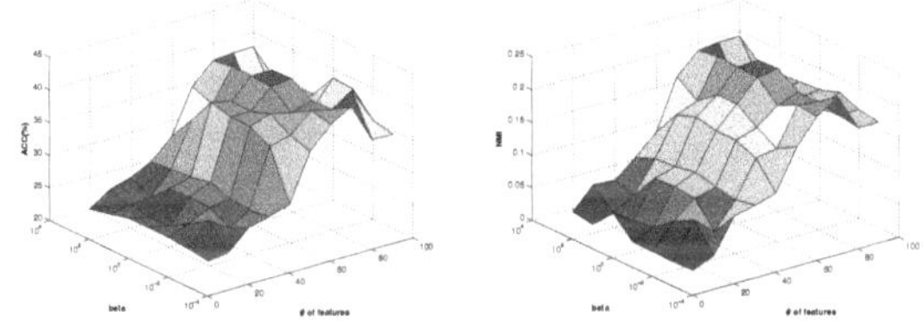

(a) Accuracy (b) NMI

Figure 6: Effect of β.

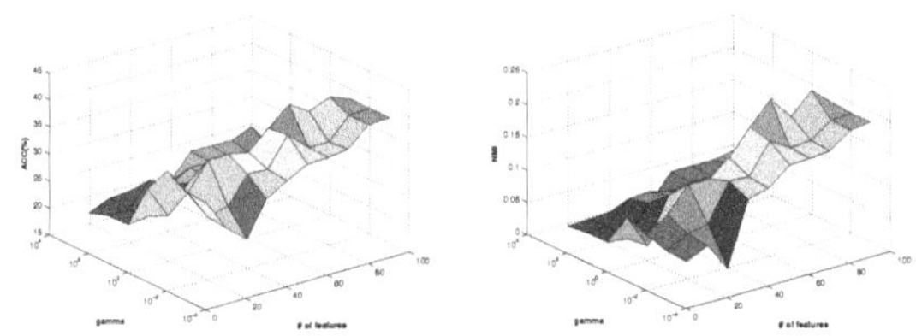

(a) Accuracy (b) NMI

Figure 7: Effect of γ.

struction [4, 15, 23]. Therefore, they are usually comparably efficient to filters and are comparably accurate to wrappers.

According to the availability of labels, feature selection methods consist of supervised methods and unsupervised methods. Supervised methods take advantage of the discriminative information encoded in class labels to select the subset of features that are able to distinguish instances from different classes [8, 23, 24]. Since real-world data is usually unlabeled and collecting labeled data is particular expensive requiring both time and effort, unsupervised feature selection receives more and more attention recently. Due to the lack of label information, unsupervised feature selection algorithms exploit different criteria to define the relevance of features such as data similarity [4, 16, 36] and local discriminative information [18, 35].

5.2 Streaming Feature Selection

Previous mentioned methods can only handle static dataset without considering the dynamic properties of features. Sometimes, it is difficult to obtain the whole feature space. Streaming feature selection, provides a solution to this problem. The first attempt to perform streaming feature selection is credited to Perkins and Theiler [27]. They adopted a stagewise gradient descent technique to dynamically update selected feature set. Alpha-investing calculates the p-value of new feature in a regression model to determine if it should be included. In Alpha-investing [37], once a feature is added, it will never be discarded in the future. OSFS [33] finds an optimal subset of features based on online feature relevance and feature redundancy analysis. At each time step, new candidate feature is accepted if it is strongly or weakly relevant to existing features; then existing but redundant features will be removed by redundancy analysis. In contrast to traditional streaming feature selection, Wang et al. [32] studied the problem of group streaming feature selection in which features continuously arrive in groups, the setting is more realistic in real-world applications. Guo et al. [14] proposed a node classification algorithm for streaming network. They consider the changes of network structure and node contents for node classification via feature selection techniques. All previous mentioned methods, focus on supervised scenarios, unsupervised streaming feature selection, however, is not well studied yet.

It should be noted that streaming feature selection differs from the task of feature selection/extraction on data streams, such as [1, 5, 6, 11, 34], in which feature sets are predefined while data are generated dynamically.

6. CONCLUSION AND FUTURE WORK

The prevalence of unlabeled, high-dimensional and high-velocity social media data presents new challenges for feature selection. Meanwhile, the unique characteristics of link information in social media bring about new opportunities as we might be able to leverage them to dynamically select relevant features efficiently. In this work, we study a novel problem, unsupervised streaming feature selection for social media data. In particular, we investigate how to take advantage of link information to perform unsupervised streaming feature selection. Also, we propose a stagewise algorithm to solve the optimization problem at each time step. Therefore, the model has the power to decide whether to add a newly arrived feature and whether to remove existing features promptly. Theoretical time complexity analysis and empirical experimental results on real-world social media datasets demonstrate that the proposed USFS framework works effectively and efficiently.

Future work can be focused on two aspects: First, in this work, we assume that the link information is relative stable compared with dynamic feature information. However, sometimes, the network structure is also continuously changing, how to perform streaming feature selection on dynamic network is a challenging problem and is unsolved yet. Second, in social media, we have features from multiple sources, like image features, text features, video features, etc. We will investigate how to fuse heterogeneous feature sources in the streaming feature selection task in the future.

Acknowledgments

This material is, in part, supported by National Science Foundation (NSF) under grant number IIS-1217466.

7. REFERENCES

[1] C. C. Aggarwal, J. Han, J. Wang, and P. S. Yu. A framework for projected clustering of high dimensional data streams. In *VLDB*, pages 852–863. VLDB Endowment, 2004.

[2] E. M. Airoldi, D. M. Blei, S. E. Fienberg, and E. P. Xing. Mixed membership stochastic blockmodels. In *NIPS*, pages 33–40, 2009.

[3] S. Boyd and L. Vandenberghe. *Convex Optimization.* Cambridge University Press, 2004.

[4] D. Cai, C. Zhang, and X. He. Unsupervised feature selection for multi-cluster data. In *KDD*, pages 333–342. ACM, 2010.

[5] X. Chen and K. S. Candan. Gi-nmf: Group incremental non-negative matrix factorization on data streams. In *CIKM*, pages 1119–1128. ACM, 2014.

[6] X. Chen and K. S. Candan. Lwi-svd: low-rank, windowed, incremental singular value decompositions on time-evolving data sets. In *KDD*, pages 987–996. ACM, 2014.

[7] J. Demšar. Statistical comparisons of classifiers over multiple data sets. *The Journal of Machine Learning Research*, 7:1–30, 2006.

[8] C. Ding and H. Peng. Minimum redundancy feature selection from microarray gene expression data. *Journal of bioinformatics and computational biology*, 3(02):185–205, 2005.

[9] J. G. Dy and C. E. Brodley. Feature subset selection and order identification for unsupervised learning. In *ICML*, pages 247–254, 2000.

[10] G. H. Golub and C. F. Van Loan. *Matrix computations*, volume 3. JHU Press, 2012.

[11] L. Gong, J. Zeng, and S. Zhang. Text stream clustering algorithm based on adaptive feature selection. *Expert Systems with Applications*, 38(3):1393–1399, 2011.

[12] P. K. Gopalan, S. Gerrish, M. Freedman, D. M. Blei, and D. M. Mimno. Scalable inference of overlapping communities. In *NIPS*, pages 2249–2257, 2012.

[13] Q. Gu, Z. Li, and J. Han. Generalized fisher score for feature selection. In *UAI*, pages 266–273, 2012.

[14] T. Guo, X. Zhu, J. Pei, and C. Zhang. Snoc: streaming network node classification. In *ICDM*, pages 150–159. IEEE, 2014.

[15] I. Guyon, J. Weston, S. Barnhill, and V. Vapnik. Gene selection for cancer classification using support vector machines. *Machine learning*, 46(1-3):389–422, 2002.

[16] X. He, D. Cai, and P. Niyogi. Laplacian score for feature selection. In *NIPS*, pages 507–514, 2005.

[17] G. H. John, R. Kohavi, K. Pfleger, et al. Irrelevant features and the subset selection problem. In *ICML*, 1994.

[18] Z. Li, Y. Yang, J. Liu, X. Zhou, and H. Lu. Unsupervised feature selection using nonnegative spectral analysis. In *AAAI*, pages 1026–1032, 2012.

[19] H. Liu, E.-P. Lim, H. W. Lauw, M.-T. Le, A. Sun, J. Srivastava, and Y. Kim. Predicting trusts among users of online communities: an epinions case study. In *EC*, pages 310–319. ACM, 2008.

[20] H. Liu and H. Motoda. *Computational Methods of Feature Selection.* CRC Press, 2007.

[21] M. McPherson, L. Smith-Lovin, and J. M. Cook. Birds of a feather: Homophily in social networks. *Annual Review of Sociology*, pages 415–444, 2001.

[22] M. E. Newman and M. Girvan. Finding and evaluating community structure in networks. *Physical review E*, 69(2):026113, 2004.

[23] F. Nie, H. Huang, X. Cai, and C. H. Ding. Efficient and robust feature selection via joint l2, 1-norms minimization. In *NIPS*, pages 1813–1821, 2010.

[24] F. Nie, S. Xiang, Y. Jia, C. Zhang, and S. Yan. Trace ratio criterion for feature selection. In *AAAI*, pages 671–676, 2008.

[25] H. Peng, F. Long, and C. Ding. Feature selection based on mutual information criteria of max-dependency, max-relevance, and min-redundancy. *IEEE Transactions on Pattern Analysis and Machine Intelligence*, 27(8):1226–1238, 2005.

[26] S. Perkins, K. Lacker, and J. Theiler. Grafting: Fast, incremental feature selection by gradient descent in function space. *The Journal of Machine Learning Research*, 3:1333–1356, 2003.

[27] S. Perkins and J. Theiler. Online feature selection using grafting. In *ICML*, pages 592–599, 2003.

[28] M. Robnik-Šikonja and I. Kononenko. Theoretical and empirical analysis of relieff and rrelieff. *Machine Learning*, 53(1-2):23–69, 2003.

[29] J. Tang and H. Liu. Unsupervised feature selection for linked social media data. In *KDD*, pages 904–912. ACM, 2012.

[30] L. Tang and H. Liu. Relational learning via latent social dimensions. In *KDD*, pages 817–826. ACM, 2009.

[31] R. Tibshirani. Regression shrinkage and selection via the lasso. *Journal of the Royal Statistical Society: Series B*, pages 267–288, 1996.

[32] J. Wang, Z.-Q. Zhao, X. Hu, Y.-M. Cheung, M. Wang, and X. Wu. Online group feature selection. In *IJCAI*, pages 1757–1763. AAAI Press, 2013.

[33] X. Wu, K. Yu, H. Wang, and W. Ding. Online streaming feature selection. In *ICML*, pages 1159–1166, 2010.

[34] W. Yang, H. Xu, and A. Theorem. Streaming sparse principal component analysis. In *ICML*, pages 494–503, 2015.

[35] Y. Yang, H. T. Shen, Z. Ma, Z. Huang, and X. Zhou. l2, 1-norm regularized discriminative feature selection for unsupervised learning. In *IJCAI*, pages 1589–1594, 2011.

[36] Z. Zhao and H. Liu. Spectral feature selection for supervised and unsupervised learning. In *ICML*, pages 1151–1157. ACM, 2007.

[37] J. Zhou, D. Foster, R. Stine, and L. Ungar. Streaming feature selection using alpha-investing. In *KDD*, pages 384–393. ACM, 2005.

[38] H. Zou and T. Hastie. Regularization and variable selection via the elastic net. *Journal of the Royal Statistical Society: Series B*, 67(2):301–320, 2005.

Weighted Similarity Estimation in Data Streams

Konstantin Kutzkov
NEC Laboratories Europe
Heidelberg, Germany
konstantin.kutzkov@neclab.eu

Mohamed Ahmed
NEC Laboratories Europe
Heidelberg, Germany
mohamed.ahmed@neclab.eu

Sofia Nikitaki
NEC Laboratories Europe
Heidelberg, Germany
sofia.nikitaki@neclab.eu

ABSTRACT

Similarity computation between pairs of objects is often a bottleneck in many applications that have to deal with massive volumes of data. Motivated by applications such as collaborative filtering in large-scale recommender systems, and influence probabilities learning in social networks, we present new randomized algorithms for the estimation of weighted similarity in data streams.

Previous works have addressed the problem of learning binary similarity measures in a streaming setting. To the best of our knowledge, the algorithms proposed here are the first that specifically address the estimation of weighted similarity in data streams. The algorithms need only one pass over the data, making them ideally suited to handling massive data streams in real time.

We obtain precise theoretical bounds on the approximation error and complexity of the algorithms. The results of evaluating our algorithms on two real-life datasets validate the theoretical findings and demonstrate the applicability of the proposed algorithms.

Categories and Subject Descriptors

H.2.8 [**Database Management**]: Database Applications—*Data mining*

General Terms

Theory; Algorithms; Experiments

Keywords

Recommender systems; Viral marketing; Collaborative filtering; Sketching; Streaming algorithms

1. INTRODUCTION

Similarity computation is a basic primitive in many data mining algorithms, ranging from association rule mining to clustering. However, for many Big data applications, similarity computation can be prohibitively expensive, hence necessitating the need for scalable methods for similarity estimation in massive datasets. As such the streaming model of computation has become extremely popular over the last decade, because it can handle massive data through sequentially processing the input. Further, streaming algorithms that need only one pass over the input open the door to real-time stream processing which considerably extends the applications domain. For example, Locality-sensitive hashing [17] techniques have found application in numerous research areas, see [11, 28, 30] for concrete examples.

Somewhat surprisingly however, similarity estimation in streams has received less attention for cases when the underlying similarity measures are weighted. Motivated by applications in recommender systems and viral marketing, in this work we consider how to estimate the *weighted* similarity between real vectors revealed in a streaming setting.

Related work.

Modern recommendation systems work with huge volumes of data which necessitates the scalable processing of the input. As such, traditional algorithms that work in an offline fashion are often not applicable since we cannot afford to load the full input in memory. Similarly, in online social networks, users activity results in huge amounts of data that needs to be processed efficiently. In the following we review previous work on stream processing for applications in recommender systems and viral marketing.

Collaborative filtering is widely applied in recommender systems. The basic idea is to recommend an item i to a user u if i has been highly ranked by users who have similar preferences to u. The similarity between users is defined based on their rating history, and is represented as a (sparse) vector whose dimensionality is the total number of items.

Several different similarity measures have been proposed in the literature, e.g. Jaccard and Cosine similarity, Euclidean distance and Pearson correlation. In a series of papers [3, 4, 5, 6], Bachrach et al. proposed sketching algorithms to estimate the Jaccard similarity between users using min-wise independent hashing [7]. Since Jaccard similarity only applies to unweighted sets, this is a simplication of the problem, whereby we are only interested which items users have rated, not how they have rated them. It is argued that rating itself is an indication of interest in a given product. However since user ratings indicate the level of interest,

Permission to make digital or hard copies of all or part of this work for personal or classroom use is granted without fee provided that copies are not made or distributed for profit or commercial advantage and that copies bear this notice and the full citation on the first page. Copyrights for components of this work owned by others than ACM must be honored. Abstracting with credit is permitted. To copy otherwise, or republish, to post on servers or to redistribute to lists, requires prior specific permission and/or a fee. Request permissions from Permissions@acm.org.
CIKM'15, October 19–23, 2015, Melbourne, Australia.
© 2015 ACM. ISBN 978-1-4503-3794-6/15/10 ...$15.00.
DOI: http://dx.doi.org/10.1145/2806416.2806514.

i.e. two users may provide conflicting ratings on the same item, in practice, weighted similarity is commonly used [23]. The state-of-the-art result is [5], which details how to combine the compact *bit-sketches* from [24] with the method proposed in [16] that achieve an exponential speed-up of the evaluation time of a "random enough" hash function. Finally, in [4], an extension of Jaccard similarity to ranking estimation is proposed. (Note however that the extension does not achieve the improved time and space complexity of [5].)

Influence propogation is widely studied in the context of viral marketing in social networks. Based on the observation that influence propagates through the network, the goal is to detect the influential users that are most likely to determine the overall behavior of the network. Such users may then be targeted during advertisement campaigns or used to predict the success of a campaign before launch. In a seminal work Kempe et al. [21] introduced the *independent cascade* model and presented approximation algorithms for influence maximization in social networks. Under this model, a user u influences a neighbor of hers v with a certain probability p_{uv}, however, the authors assume that propagation probabilities p_{uv} are known in advance.

Goyal et al. [18] present methods for inferring influence probabilities. Informally, they define different measures of influence probability, whereby a user u is said to have influenced a user v if an action performed by u is later performed by v within τ time units, for a suitably defined τ. Note that this approach does not distinguish between how actions are performed. Building upon this work, Kutzkov et al. [22] have presented streaming algorithms capable of estimating the influence probability between users using only a small amount of memory per user. In [22], the influence probability is defined as an extension of Jaccard similarity with time constraints, and the algorithm extends min-wise independent hashing to handle time constraints.

Finally, another thread of works has analyzed user behavior in online social networks, in terms of social and correlational influence [2, 14, 19, 20]. In particular, Jamali et al. [19, 20] have studied the problem of influence propagation in Social Rating Networks (SRN). The correlational influence between users is computed as a Pearson correlation between the rating vectors.

Our contribution.

- Similarity estimation in data streams for collaborative filtering. A simple extension of AMS sketching for inner product estimation yields new sketching algorithms for cosine similarity and Pearson correlation between real vectors revealed in a streaming fashion.
- We extend cosine similarity and Pearson correlation to also consider time constraints in order to model influence propagation in viral marketing and predict users behavior. Building upon the STRIP algorithm from [22], we design new algorithms for the estimation of the considered similarity measures. The algorithm is particularly suitable for input vectors with entries from a small discrete domain, a common situation in rating networks.

We obtain precise theoretical bounds on the complexity of the presented algorithms. An experimental evaluation on real datasets confirms the theoretical findings.

Organization of the paper.

In Section 2 we present necessary notation and formal definitions. In Section 3 we present and analyze a weighted similarity estimation algorithm for collaborative filtering in data streams. We extend the considered similarity measures to model influence propagation and present streaming algorithms for their estimation in Section 4. Results from experimental evaluation on real data are reported in Section 5. The paper is concluded in Section 6.

2. PRELIMINARIES

Notation.

The k-norm of a vector $x \in \mathbb{R}^n$ is defined as $\|x\|_k = (\sum_{i=1}^n |x_i|^k)$ The 2-norm of x will be denoted as $\|x\|$, and the 1-norm as $|x|$. Let U be a set of m users and I a set of n items. A rating given by user $u \in U$ on an item $i \in I$ is denoted as r_{ui}. A user is described by an n-dimensional real vector. For the i-th entry in u it holds $u_i = r_{ui}$, thus we will also use u_i instead of r_{ui} to denote u's rating on i. The set of items rated by user u is denoted by $I_u \subseteq I$. We will denote by $[n]$ the set $\{0, 1, \ldots, n-1\}$.

Similarity measures.

We consider following measures for the similarity between two vectors.

1. Jaccard similarity computes the probability that an item $i \in I_u \cup I_v$ is also contained in $I_u \cap I_v$:
$$jaccard(I_u, I_v) = \frac{|I_u \cap I_v|}{|I_u \cup I_v|}.$$
2. Cosine similarity.
$$cos(u, v) = \frac{\sum_{i \in I_u \cap I_v} u_i v_i}{\|u\|\|v\|}$$
where $\|u\| = (\sum_{i \in I_u} u_i^2)^{\frac{1}{2}}$.
3. Pearson correlation.
$$\rho(u, v) = \frac{\sum_{i \in I_u \cap I_v} (u_i - \tilde{u})(v_i - \tilde{v})}{\|\hat{u}\|\|\hat{v}\|}$$
where $\tilde{u} = \frac{1}{|I_u|}\sum_{i \in I_u} u_i$, $\|\hat{u}\| = (\sum_{i \in I_u} (u_i - \tilde{u})^2)^{\frac{1}{2}}$.

Hashing, Probability and Approximation guarantees.

We assume familiarity with basic probability theory notation. In the analysis of the algorithm we use Chebyshev inequality defined as follows. Let X be a random variable with expectation $\mathbf{E}[X]$ and variance $\mathbf{V}[X]$. Then
$$\Pr[|X - \mathbf{E}[X]| \geq \lambda] \leq \frac{\mathbf{V}[X]}{\lambda^2}.$$
A family $\mathcal{F}$ of functions from V to a finite set S is k*-wise independent* if for a function $f : V \to S$ chosen uniformly at random from $\mathcal{F}$ it holds
$$\Pr[f(v_1) = c_1 \wedge f(v_2) = c_2 \wedge \cdots \wedge f(v_k) = c_k] = \frac{1}{s^k}$$
for $s = |S|$, distinct $v_i \in V$ and any $c_i \in S$ and $k \in \mathbb{N}$.

A family $\mathcal{H}$ of functions from V to a finite totally ordered set S is called (ε, k)*-min-wise independent* if for any $X \subseteq V$

and $Y \subseteq X$, $|Y| = k$ for a function h chosen uniformly at random from $\mathcal{H}$ it holds

$$\Pr[\max_{y \in Y} h(y) < \min_{z \in X \setminus Y} h(z)] = (1 \pm \varepsilon) \frac{1}{\binom{|X|}{k}}$$

we will refer to a function chosen uniformly at random from a k-wise independent family as a k-wise independent function.

Finally, we will say that an algorithm computes an ε-approximation of a given quantity q if it returns a value $\tilde{q}$ such that $q - \varepsilon \leq \tilde{q} \leq q + \varepsilon$. In the theoretical analysis of the algorithms, we will show results stating that certain approximation guarantee is obtained with probability 2/3. Using the Chernoff inequality this probability can be amplified to $1 - \delta$ for any $\delta \in (0, 1)$ by running $O(\log \frac{1}{\delta})$ independent copies of the algorithm in parallel, c.f. [26]. Note that 2/3 can be replaced by any constant $c > 1/2$.

Problem statement.

Let $\mathcal{S}$ be a stream of triples (u, r_i, t_u) where u is the user identifier, r_i is the rating the user gives to item i, and t_u is the timestamp of the rating. We assume that each user rates an item at most once. Throughout the paper we will often represent the rating given by u on i as u_i instead of (u, r_{ui}).

We will consider the following two problems:

1. Collaborative filtering: Given users u and v, what is the similarity between u's and v's ratings for a given similarity measure? (Note that we disregard the timestamps of the ratings.)

2. Influence propagation: Given users $u, v \in U$, compute $sim_\Omega(u, v)$, i.e., the similarity between the ratings of u and v under a given similarity measure that satisfies given time constraint Ω. In particular, when a social graph $G = (V, E)$ is given, what is the probability that u influences a friend of hers v, i.e., $sim_\Omega(u, v)$ for $(u, v) \in E$. (Note that we present concrete examples for sim_Ω in Section 3.)

3. WEIGHTED SIMILARITY ESTIMATION IN DATA STREAMS

Before formally describing the proposed algorithms, we first provide an overview of our reasoning. We assume that we can store a sketch for each user's activity. Sketches are compact representations of a user's rating history. We observe that if we can estimate the inner product of uv, then we can also estimate $cos(u, v)$. This is achieved by computing $\|u\|$ and $\|v\|$ in a streaming setting by simply maintaining a counter to record the current value of the squared 2-norm of u and v. Utilising AMS sketches for the estimation of the inner product, as proposed in [12], we obtain an ε-approximation of $cos(u, v)$.

The Pearson correlation can be rewritten as $cos(u - \tilde{u}, v - \tilde{v})$, where $u - \tilde{u}$ is the vector obtained from u by replacing u_i with $u_i - \tilde{u}$, $\tilde{u}$ being the mean of u. Therefore, if two passes over the data are allowed, we can compute in the first pass the values $\tilde{u}$ and in a second pass we can run the cosine similarity estimation algorithm on the updated vectors $u - \tilde{u}$. We will show that the *linearity* of AMS sketches enables us to compute a sketch $u - \tilde{u}$ in a single pass without knowing $\tilde{u}$ in advance.

3.1 Algorithm

Before presenting our algorithm, we briefly present how AMS sketching works:

AMS sketching

AMS sketches were originally designed as an efficient technique for estimating the second moment of a data stream's frequency vectors [1]. For an (unweighted) stream $\mathcal{S} = i_1, i_2, i_3, \ldots$ over a set of items I, let f_i denote the frequency of item i, i.e., the number of occurrences of i in $\mathcal{S}$. Then the second moment of the stream $\mathcal{S}$ is defined as $F_2 = \sum_{i \in I} f_i^2$.

AMS sketching works as follows: Let $s : I \to \{-1, 1\}$ be a 4-wise independent function. We maintain a variable X, and for each incoming item i, we update X as X += $s(i)$. After processing the stream it holds that $X = \sum_{i \in I} s(i) f_i$, and we can show that $\mathbf{E}[X^2] = F_2$ since $\mathbf{E}[s(i)s(j)] = 0$ for $i \neq j$ and $s(i)^2 = 1$. Using that s is 4-wise independent, the variance of the estimator can be bounded by $\mathbf{V}[X^2] \leq \mathbf{E}[X^4] = F_2^2$. Since for a constant c, it holds that $\mathbf{V}(X/c) = \mathbf{V}(X)/c^2$, the average of $O(1/\varepsilon^2)$ random variables X, is an unbiased estimator of F_2 and has variance $\varepsilon^2 F_2^2$. A standard application of Chebyshev inequality yields that we obtain an ε-approximation from the average of $O(1/\varepsilon^2)$ AMS sketches. Finally, it was first observed in [12] that AMS sketching can be also used to estimate the inner product uv of vectors $u, v \in \mathbb{R}^m$. To do so, we maintain random variables $X = \sum_{i=1}^n s(i) u_i$ and $Y = \sum_{i=1}^n s(i) v_i$, then $\mathbf{E}[XY] = uv$ and, as we see next, the variance is bounded by $\mathbf{V}[XY] \leq (\|u\| \|v\|)^2$. From this, an estimate of $cos(u, v)$ easily follows.

A drawback of AMS sketching is that for each new item in the stream, we need to update all AMS sketches. The COUNT-SKETCH algorithm helps to overcome this by improving the update time [10]. Instead of working with many different AMS sketches, COUNT-SKETCH works with a single hash table. For a new entry u_i, one updates the hash table as $H_u[j]$ += $s(i) u_i$ where $j = h(i)$ for a suitably defined hash function $h : [n] \to [k]$. After processing the vectors u, v, their inner product can be estimated as $\sum_{j \in [k]} H_u[j] H_v[j]$. Intuitively, the larger hash table we use, the better estimates we obtain because we have less collisions between items.

Pseudocode

A weighted similarity estimation algorithm is presented in Figure 1. We assume that the input is a stream $\mathcal{S}$ of pairs (u, r_i) denoting that user u rated item i with a rating r_i. For each user, we keep a hash table H_u and we run the Count-Sketch algorithm. We process an incoming pair (u, r_i) by updating H_u with r_i. In addition to the sketches H_u, we keep the following arrays: C – counting the number of items rated by each user u, N – for computing the squared 2-norm of u and S – for computing $\sum_{i \in I_u} u_i$. We also extend the sketch H_u as follows: in the j-th cell we store an array $Sign_u$ such that $Sign_u[j] = \sum_{i \in I_u : h(i) = j} s(i)$, we will need $Sign_u$ for the estimation of Pearson correlation.

After processing the stream, an inner product uv is estimated from the sketches H_u and H_v. The estimation of cosine similarity follows directly from the respective definition. As we show in the theoretical analysis we compute Pearson correlation $\rho(u, v)$ as if we computed $cos(u - \tilde{u}, v - \tilde{v})$. We show in the proof of Theorem 2 that after processing the stream, using $C[u], S[u], N[u], Sign_u$ we can update the sketches H_u such that we obtain an estimate of the Pearson correlation $\rho(u, v)$.

ProcessRatings

Input: stream of user-rating pairs $\mathcal{S}$, pairwise independent function $h : \mathbb{R} \to [k]$, 4-wise independent $s : \mathbb{N} \to \{0, 1\}$

for each $(u_i) \in \mathcal{S}$ **do**
    $\text{Update}(u_i, h, s)$

Update

Input: rating u_i, k-wise independent function $h : \mathbb{N} \to [k]$, 4-wise independent $s : \mathbb{N} \to \{0, 1\}$

$H_u[h(i)] \mathrel{+}= s(i)u_i$
$N[u] \mathrel{+}= {u_i}^2$
$S[u] \mathrel{+}= u_i$
$C[u] \mathrel{+}= 1$
$Sign_u[h(i)] \mathrel{+}= s(i)$

EstimateCosine

Input: users u, v, sketches H, array N

$inner\_product = 0$
for $i = 1$ to k **do**
    $inner\_product \mathrel{+}= H_u[i]H_v[i]$
return $inner\_product/\sqrt{N[u]N[v]}$

EstimatePearson

Input: users u, v, sketches H, arrays N, S, C, $Sign$

$mean_u = S[u]/C[u]$
$mean_v = S[v]/C[v]$
$inner\_product = 0$
for $i = 1$ to k **do**
    $H_u[i] \mathrel{-}= Sign_u[i]mean_u$
    $H_v[i] \mathrel{-}= Sign_v[i]mean_v$
    $inner\_product \mathrel{+}= H_u[i]H_v[i]$
$norm_u = N[u] - 2mean_u S[u] + C[u]mean_u^2$
$norm_v = N[v] - 2mean_v S[v] + C[v]mean_v^2$
return $inner\_product/\sqrt{norm_u norm_v}$

Figure 1: Weighted similarity estimation through sketching.

3.2 Theoretical analysis

Cosine similarity.

Theorem 1. *Let $u, v \in \mathbb{R}^n$ be revealed in a streaming fashion. There exists a one-pass algorithm that returns an ε-approximation of $cos(u, v)$ with probability 2/3 and needs $O(\frac{1}{\varepsilon^2})$ space. Each vector entry u_i and v_i can be processed in $O(1)$ time. The estimation can be computed in $O(\frac{1}{\varepsilon^2})$ time.*

Proof. Assume for u and v we keep hash tables H_u and H_v recording k values, for k to be specified later. We also keep a counter N that will record the squared 2-norm of each vector u. Let $h : \mathbb{R} \to [k]$ and $s : \mathbb{N} \to \{-1, 1\}$. For a new arrival u_i we then update $H_u[h(i)] \mathrel{+}= s(i)u_i$. Simultaneously, we update $N[u] \mathrel{+}= u_i^2$. After processing the stream, we return $\frac{\sum_{i=1}^k H_u[i]H_v[i]}{\sqrt{N[u]N[v]}}$ as an estimate of $cos(u, v)$.

Clearly, after processing the stream $\|u\| = \sqrt{N[u]}$ and $\|v\| = \sqrt{N[v]}$. Therefore, an $\varepsilon\|u\|\|v\|$-approximation of uv will yield an ε-approximation of $cos(u, v)$. Let I_{ij} be an indicator variable for the event that $h(i) = h(j)$. For a pairwise independent h it holds $\Pr[I_{ij} = 1] = 1$ if $i = j$ and $\Pr[I_{ij} = 1] = 1/k$ for $i \neq j$. Note that $\mathbf{E}(I_{ij}) = \mathbf{E}(I_{ij}^2)$. Let $Z = \sum_{i=1}^k H_u[i]H_v[i] = \sum_{i,j\in[n]} s(i)s(j)u_iv_jI_{ij}$. By linearity of expectation it holds that $\mathbf{E}(Z) = uv$. For a 4-wise independent s the variance of the estimator can be upper bounded as follows:

$$\mathbf{V}(Z) = \mathbf{E}((\sum_{i,j\in[n]} s(i)s(j)u_iv_jI_{ij})^2) - \mathbf{E}(Z)^2$$

$$= \sum_{i,j,k,l\in[n]} \mathbf{E}(s(i)s(j)s(k)s(l)I_{ij}I_{kl})u_iu_kv_jv_l - \sum_{i,j\in[n]} u_iv_iu_jv_j$$

$$= \sum_{i,j\in[n]} E(I_{ii}I_{jj}u_iv_iu_jv_j) + \sum_{i,j\in[n]} E(I_{ij}u_i^2v_j^2) - \sum_{i,j\in[n]} u_iv_iu_jv_j$$

$$= \sum_{i,j\in[n]} u_i^2v_j^2/k = (\|u\|\|v\|)^2/k.$$

The above follows from linearity of expectation and from observing that for 4-wise independent s, $\mathbf{E}(s(i)s(j)s(k)s(l)) = 1$ if and only if there are two pairs of identical indices. By Chebyshev's inequality we have

$$\Pr[|Z - \mathbf{E}(Z)| \geq \varepsilon\|u\|\|v\|] \leq \frac{\mathbf{V}(Z)}{\varepsilon^2(\|u\|\|v\|)^2} \leq \frac{1}{\varepsilon^2 k}.$$

Therefore, for $k = O(1/\varepsilon^2)$ we can show that Z is an ε-approximation of uv with probability 2/3. □

Pearson correlation.

For Pearson correlation it holds $\rho(u, v) = cos(u - \tilde{u}, v - \tilde{v})$. Therefore, if we are able to perform two passes over the data, in the first pass we can compute $\tilde{u}, \tilde{v}$, and in a second pass update each component as $u_i - \tilde{u}$ and estimate the cosine similarity between the vectors. Next, we adjust AMS sketching to estimate $cos(u - \tilde{u}, v - \tilde{v})$ in a single pass, without knowing $\tilde{u}, \tilde{v}$ in advance.

Theorem 2. *Let $u, v \in \mathbb{R}^m$ be revealed in a streaming fashion. There exists a one-pass algorithm that returns an ε-approximation of $\rho(u, v)$ with probability 2/3. The algorithm needs $O(\frac{1}{\varepsilon^2})$ space. Each vector entry u_i, v_i can be processed in $O(1)$ time.*

Proof. Assume we know $\tilde{u}$ in advance. Let H_u be the sketch for $u - \tilde{u}$. Then, $H_u[k] = \sum_{i\in I_u:h(i)=k} s(i)(u_i - \tilde{u}) = \sum_{i\in I_u:h(i)=k} s(i)u_i - \sum_{i:h(i)=k} s(i)\tilde{u}$. After processing the stream it holds that $Sign_u[j] = \sum_{i\in I_u:h(i)=j} s(i)$, $S[u] = \sum_{i\in I_u} u_i$ and $C[u] = |I_u|$. Let $mean_u = S[u]/C[u]$. We thus update $H_u[j] \mathrel{-}= Sign_u[j]mean_u$. The squared norm $\|u - \tilde{u}\|^2$ is computed as $\|u\|^2 - 2S[u]mean_u + C[u]mean_u^2$. Thus, in each H_u we have exactly the same values if we had sketched the vector $u - \tilde{u}$. The complexity and approximation guarantee of the algorithm follow directly from the proof of Theorem 1 and the pseudocode. □

3.3 Comparison to previous work

In a series of papers Bachrach et al. presented sketching algorithms for Jaccard similarity estimation [3, 4, 5, 6]. The state-of-the-art result is presented in [5]. The authors present a min-wise independent hashing algorithm that combines *b*-bit min-wise hashing [24], and yields optimal space complexity, with the min-wise independent sampling approach [16] that achieves the best known processing time per update.

Inner product estimation using AMS sketching was presented in [12] but, to the best of our knowledge, extensions to similarity estimation have not been considered in the literature. This appears to be surprising since LSH based approaches might not be suitable when applied to high-speed streams. Consider for example cosine similarity. The LSH algorithm proposed in [9] needs space and update time $O(\frac{1}{\Theta(u,v)\varepsilon^2})$ for a relative $(1 \pm \varepsilon)$-approximation of the angle $\Theta(u,v)$, (the algorithm thus estimates $arccos(u,v)$)). From Theorem 1, we need space $O(\frac{1}{cos^2(u,v)\varepsilon^2})$, but the processing time per update is constant.

4. WEIGHTED SIMILARITY ESTIMATION WITH TIME CONSTRAINTS

We consider the problem of similarity estimation in data streams where an additional time constraint is introduced. In particular, we consider

$$\Omega(u_i, v_i) = \begin{cases} 1 & \text{if } 0 \le t(v_i) - t(u_i) \le \tau \\ 0 & \text{otherwise,} \end{cases}$$

i.e., $\Omega(u_i, v_i)$ is the binary constraint that evaluates whether user v has rated items i within τ time units after user u has rated item i. When clear from the context, we will write Ω instead of $\Omega(u_i, v_i)$. This allows to model propagation and influence as discussed in the introduction. Note that the approach presented in the previous section does not seem to apply here. AMS sketching is a linear transformation of the stream, i.e., the order in which we sketch the items does not affect the final result. However, when sketching the stream of ratings we have to also record information about the time when items were rated. We will thus present a different solution building upon the STRIP algorithm [22] that estimates Jaccard similarity with time constraints. In the following we extend the considered similarity measures to also include time constraints, briefly present the STRIP approach and discuss how to generalize it to weighted similarity measures estimation.

Similarity measures with time constraint.

We extend the considered similarity measures as follows:

- **Cosine similarity.**

$$cos_\Omega(u,v) = \frac{\sum_{i \in I_u \cap I_v} u_i v_i \Omega(u_i, v_i)}{\|u\| \|v\|}$$

- **Pearson correlation.**

$$\rho_\Omega(u,v) = \frac{\sum_{i \in I_u \cap I_v} (u_i - \tilde{u})(v_i - \tilde{v}) \Omega(u_i, v_i)}{\|\hat{u}\| \|\hat{v}\|}$$

The STRIP algorithm.

Assume we are given a social graph and a stream of user-action pairs (u, a_i) denoting that user u performed action a_i. Actions can denote any activity like liking a photo, sharing a video or rating an item. For a possible set of n actions, user's activity is represented by a (sparse) binary vector where the i-th entry denotes whether a user has performed the action a_i. In our context an action corresponds to rating an item, whereby we are not interested in the exact rating but only in the fact that the item was rated. We want to detect users that appear to have high influence on their neighbors. Since we are only interested *which* items a user has rated, we can assume that the items rated by user u correspond to an n-dimensional binary vector r^u such that $r_i^u = 1$ iff user u has rated item i. Following the definition from [18], the influence probability is defined as

$$p_{uv} = \frac{|A_{u2v}^\tau|}{|A_{u|v}|},$$

where A_{u2v}^τ is the set of actions that have propagated from u to v within τ time units, i.e., u has done the action within τ time units before v. $A_{u|v}$ is the set of actions performed by either u or v, independent of time. In our setting actions correspond to item ratings without distinguishing how the item is rated.

The STRIP algorithm works by extending min-wise independent hashing [7]. Let $h : \mathcal{A} \to [0,1]$ be a random hash function that maps actions to values in the interval $[0,1]$. (As shown in [22], we can assume that h is injective with high probability.) A user-action-timestamp triple (u, a_i, t_i) is then processed as follows: For each user u we keep a sample H_u that records the k action-timestamp pairs with the smallest hash values. If $h(a_i)$ is smaller than the largest entry in H_u, or H_u contains less than k entries, we add (a_i, t_i) to H_u and remove the $(k+1)$-th largest entry, if any. Implementing H_u as a priority queue guarantees fast update. Once the stream has been processed, the influence probability p_{uv} of user u on user v is estimated as

$$\frac{\Omega_\tau(H_u, H_v)}{k}$$

where $\Omega_\tau(H_u, H_v)$ denotes the set of actions in *both* H_u and H_v which satisfy the time constraint Ω.

The new approach.

Assume that ratings are small integer numbers. (Clearly, such an assumption is justified in practice, users usually rate items on a 5- or 10-scale.) We extend the STRIP approach to handle weighted similarity measures by treating each rating as being composed by r_{max} binary ratings, r_{max} being the maximum rating. More precisely, a rating r_u can be expressed as $r^u = \sum_{i=1}^{r_{max}} c_i^u$, where $c_i^u \in \{0,1\}$. The product of two ratings r^u, r^v can thus be written as

$$r^u r^v = \sum_{k=1}^{r_{max}} c_k^u \sum_{k=1}^{r_{max}} c_k^v = \sum_{k=1}^{r_{max}} \sum_{\ell=1}^{r_{max}} c_k^u c_\ell^v.$$

For example, let $r^u = 1$, $r^v = 3$ and $r_{max} = 3$. Then, $r_u = 1 + 0 + 0$, $r_v = 1 + 1 + 1$ and $r^u r^v = (1 \times 1 + 1 \times 1 + 1 \times 1) + (0 \times 1 + 0 \times 1 + 0 \times 1) + (0 \times 1 + 0 \times 1 + 0 \times 1)$.

Let $c_k^u \in \{0,1\}^n$ be the binary vector that corresponds to the k-th position of u's ratings. For example, assume $n = 5$, $r_{max} = 5$ and a user u has given following ratings: $r_{u1} = 3$, $r_{u4} = 5, r_{u5} = 1$, items 2 and 3 have not been rated by u. We have $c_1^u = (1,0,0,1,1)$, $c_2^u = (1,0,0,1,0)$, $c_3^u = (1,0,0,1,0)$, $c_4^u = (0,0,0,1,0)$ and $c_5^u = (0,0,0,1,0)$.

We can rewrite an inner product uv as the sum of r_{max}^2 inner products of binary vectors:

$$uv = \sum_{i=1}^{n} u_i v_i = \sum_{i=1}^{n} \sum_{k=1}^{r_{max}} c_k^{u_i} \sum_{\ell=1}^{r_{max}} c_\ell^{v_i} =$$

PROCESSSTREAM

Input: stream of user-rating-timestamp triples $\mathcal{S}$, pairwise independent function $h : \mathbb{N} \to [k]$

- **for** each $(u, r_{ui}, t_u) \in \mathcal{S}$ **do**
  - Let $c = (c_1, \ldots, c_{r_{max}})$ such that $c_\ell = 1$ for $1 \le \ell \le r_{ui}$ and $c_\ell = 0$ for $r_{ui}+1 \le \ell \le r_{max}$.
  - **for** $j = 1$ to r_{ui} **do**
    - STRIPUPDATE(u, i, t_u, j, h)
  - $N[u] \mathrel{+}= r_{ui}^2$
  - $S[u] \mathrel{+}= r_{ui}$
  - $C[u] \mathrel{+}= 1$

STRIPUPDATE

Input: user u, item i, timestamp t_u, sample number j, hash function $h : I \to (0, 1]$.

- **if** $h(i) < H_u^j.getMax()$ **then**
  - $H_u^j.pop()$
  - $H_u^j.add(h(i), t_u)$

MINWISEESTIMATE

Input: sketches H_u^k, H_v^ℓ, constraint Ω

- Let Min_s be the s pairs $(h(i), t)$ with the smallest hash value in $H_u^k \cup H_v^\ell$
- **return** $\frac{|\Omega(Min_s)|}{s}$

ESTIMATESUM

Input: user u, user v, sketches H, constraint Ω

- $sum_u = 0$
- **for** $k = 1$ to r_{max} **do**
  - $sum_u \mathrel{+}= MinWiseEstimate(H_u^k, H_v^1, \Omega)$
- **return** sum_u

ESTIMATEINNERPRODUCT

Input: users u, v, sketches H, constraint Ω

- $ip = 0$
- **for** $k = 1$ to r_{max} **do**
  - **for** $\ell = 1$ to r_{max} **do**
    - $ip \mathrel{+}= MinWiseEstimate(H_u^k, H_v^\ell, \Omega)$
- **return** ip

ESTIMATECOSINE

Input: users u, v, sketches H constraint Ω

- $ip = \text{EstimateInnerProduct}(u, v, H, \Omega)$
- **return** $ip/\sqrt{N[u]N[v]}$

ESTIMATEPEARSON

Input: users u, v, sketches H, arrays N, S, C, constraint Ω

- $ip = \text{ESTIMATEINNERPRODUCT}(u, v, H, \Omega)$
- $nnz_{\Omega(u,v)} = \text{MINWISEESTIMATE}(H_u^1, H_v^1, \Omega)$
- $sum_\Omega^u = \text{ESTIMATESUM}(H, u, v, \Omega)$
- $sum_\Omega^v = \text{ESTIMATESUM}(H, v, u, \Omega)$
- $m_u = S[u]/C[u]$, $m_v = S[v]/C[v]$
- $norms_u = N[u] - 2m_u S[u] + C[u]m_u^2$
- $norms_v = N[v] - 2m_v S[v] + C[v]m_v^2$
- $ip \mathrel{-}= m_u sum_\Omega^v + m_v sum_\Omega^u - nnz_{\Omega(u,v)} m_u m_v$
- **return** $ip/\sqrt{norms_u norms_v}$

Figure 2: Similarity estimation with time constraint.

$$= \sum_{k=1}^{r_{max}} \sum_{\ell=1}^{r_{max}} \sum_{i=1}^{n} c_k^{u_i} c_\ell^{v_i} = \sum_{k=1}^{r_{max}} \sum_{\ell=1}^{r_{max}} c_k^u c_\ell^v.$$

The above suggests the following algorithm. For each user we maintain r_{max} sketches. Thus, for each user we can consider r_{max} separate binary substreams. For each such stream we will run the STRIP algorithm and maintain a min-wise independent sample. Let (u_i, t_{ui}) be an incoming rating-timestamp tuple. We have to update u's k-th min-wise sample, $1 \le k \le r_{max}$, iff $r_{ui} \le k$. Once the stream has been processed, the inner product $uv_{\Omega(\tau)}$ can be estimated as $\sum_{k=1}^{r_{max}} \sum_{\ell=1}^{r_{max}} est(c_k^u c_{\ell}^v{}_{\Omega(\tau)})$ where $est(c_k^u c_\ell^v{}_{\Omega(\tau)})$ is the estimated constrained inner product of the binary vectors c_k^u and c_ℓ^v. A pseudocode based on the above discussion is presented in Figure 2.

Pearson correlation. Clearly, an estimation of uv_Ω results in an estimation of $cos_{\Omega(u,v)}$. However, for Pearson correlation we need to estimate $(u - \tilde{u})(v - \tilde{v})_\Omega$. Let $sum_{\Omega(u,v)}^u = \sum_{i \in I : \Omega(u_i, v_i)} u_i$, i.e., we sum over the u_i for which $\Omega(u_i, v_i)$ is satisfied. Let $nnz_{\Omega(u,v)} = \sum_{i \in \mathcal{I} : \Omega(u_i, v_i)} 1$, i.e., the number of entries in uv_Ω. By rewriting the inner product we obtain $(u - \tilde{u})(v - \tilde{v})_\Omega = uv_\Omega - \tilde{u} sum_{\Omega(u,v)}^u - \tilde{v} sum_{\Omega(u,v)}^v + nnz_{\Omega(u,v)} \tilde{u}\tilde{v}$. Thus, we need to estimate $sum_{\Omega(u,v)}^u$, $sum_{\Omega(u,v)}^v$ and the number of nonzero entries in uv_Ω. We observe that we can rewrite $sum_{\Omega(u,v)}^u$ as $\sum_{i=1}^{n} \sum_{k=1}^{r_{max}} c_k^{u_i} c_1^v{}_{\Omega(u,v)}$. This can be easily verified: we consider exactly those u_i for which $\Omega(u_i, v_i)$ and for each of them we add up exactly u_i 1's. The number of nonzero entries in uv_Ω is exactly the number of indices i for which $\Omega(u_i, v_i)$ is true, i.e., $c_1^u c_1^v$.

LEMMA 1. *Let $z \ge 0$, $x \ge 1$ and $0 < \varepsilon < 1/2$. Then $\frac{z}{x+\varepsilon} \ge (1 - \varepsilon)\frac{z}{x}$ and $\frac{z}{x-\varepsilon} \le (1 + 2\varepsilon)\frac{z}{x}$.*

PROOF. For $\varepsilon > 0$ it holds $\frac{z}{x+\varepsilon} \ge \frac{z}{(1+\varepsilon)x} = \frac{z}{x} - \frac{\varepsilon z}{(1+\varepsilon)x} \ge \frac{z}{x} - \frac{\varepsilon z}{x} = (1 - \varepsilon)\frac{z}{x}$.

Similarly, for $\varepsilon < 1/2$ we have $\frac{z}{x-\varepsilon} \le \frac{z}{(1-\varepsilon)x} = \frac{z}{x} + \frac{\varepsilon z}{(1-\varepsilon)x} \le \frac{z}{x} + \frac{2\varepsilon z}{x} = (1 + 2\varepsilon)\frac{z}{x}$ □

We first show that an inner product can be approximated using min-wise independent hashing.

THEOREM 3. *Let $\mathcal{S}$ be a stream of vector entries u_i, $1 \le i \le m$ arriving in arbitrary order for different vectors $u \in \mathbb{N}^n$. Let $u_i \le r_{max}$ for all vector entries. There exists a one-pass algorithm that computes a sketch of the user activity using $O(\frac{r_{max}}{\varepsilon^2} \log r_{max})$ space per user and $O(r_{max} \log r_{max} \log^2(\frac{1}{\varepsilon}))$ processing time per pair. For a vector pair $u, v \in \mathbb{R}^n$, after preprocessing the sketches of u and v in time $O(\frac{r_{max}}{\varepsilon^2} \log(\frac{r_{max}}{\varepsilon}))$ we obtain an $\varepsilon r_{max}(|u| + |v|)$-approximation of the inner product uv with probability 2/3 in time $O(\frac{r_{max}^2}{\varepsilon^2})$.*

PROOF. Consider an incoming entry u_i. We update all H_u^k for which it holds $u_i \ge k$. In H_u^k we keep the s pairs $(h(i), t_u)$ with smallest hash values. (Under the assumption that h is injective, the s pairs are well-defined.) We assume h is implemented as $(1/c, s)$-min-wise independent function [16], thus $h(i)$ can be stored in space $O(s)$ and evaluated in time $O(\log^2 s)$. Implementing H_u^k as a priority queue, the total processing time is $O(r_{max} \log^2 s)$.

We next show the quality of the estimate in terms of the sample size s. Let $A, B \subseteq [n]$ be two subsets. Let $\alpha = J(A, B)$ denote the Jaccard similarity between A and B. We first show how to obtain an ε-approximation of α. Let

$\min_s^h(A \cup B)$ denote the s smallest elements in $A \cup B$ under h. Let X be a random variable counting the number of attributes from $A \cap B$ in $\min_s^h(A \cup B)$. Clearly, it holds $E[X] = \alpha s$. The number of attributes from $A \cap B$ in size-s subsets follows hypergeometric distribution with s samples from a set of size n and αn successes. Thus, for $s > 1$ we have

$$V[X] = \alpha(1-\alpha)s\frac{n-s}{n-1} < \alpha s.$$

By Chebyshev's inequality we thus have

$$\Pr[|X - E[X]| \geq \varepsilon s] \leq \frac{V[X]}{\varepsilon^2 s^2} < \frac{\alpha}{\varepsilon^2 s}.$$

For $s = O(1/\varepsilon^2)$ we thus can bound the probability to $1/c$ for arbitrary fixed c. For h being $(1/c, k)$-wise independent we will thus obtain ε-approximation of α for $s = O(1/\varepsilon^2)$ with probability $\frac{2}{3}$.

We obtain an approximation of $|A \cup B|$ as follows. It holds $\alpha = \frac{|A \cap B|}{|A \cup B|} = \frac{|A \cap B|}{|A|+|B|-|A \cap B|}$. Thus, $|A \cap B| = \frac{\alpha(|A|+|B|)}{1+\alpha}$.

Consider an ε-approximation of α. For the approximation error of $|A \cap B|$ we obtain

$$\frac{(\alpha \pm \varepsilon)(|A|+|B|)}{1+\alpha \pm \varepsilon} = \frac{\alpha(|A|+|B|)}{1+\alpha \pm \varepsilon} \pm \frac{\varepsilon(|A|+|B|)}{1+\alpha \pm \varepsilon}.$$

By Lemma 1 and using $\alpha \in [0, 1]$ we can thus bound the approximation error by $O(\varepsilon(|A| + |B|))$.

The total approximation error for estimating an inner product uv is then bounded by

$$\sum_{k=1}^{r_{max}} \sum_{\ell=1}^{r_{max}} c_k^u c_\ell^v \pm \varepsilon(|c_k^u| + |c_\ell^v|) =$$

$$uv \pm \varepsilon(\sum_{\ell=1}^{r_{max}} \sum_{k=1}^{r_{max}} |c_k^u| + \sum_{k=1}^{r_{max}} \sum_{\ell=1}^{r_{max}} |c_\ell^v|) = uv \pm \varepsilon r_{max}(|u|+|v|).$$

In order to guarantee the ε-approximation error with probability $2/3$, we work with $t = O(\log r_{max})$ independent hash functions and sketches. By taking the median of the estimates from the t sketches, by Chernoff bounds each binary inner product $c_l^u c_\ell^v$ is approximated with probability $\frac{2}{3r_{max}^2}$. By the union bound we obtain an ε-approximation of uv with probability $2/3$.

The s smallest elements in the intersection of two sets with $O(s)$ elements each can be found in $O(s)$ time after presorting the sets in time $O(s \log s)$. Thus, from the sketches H_u and H_v the inner product uv can be estimated in time $O(\frac{r_{max}^2}{\varepsilon^2})$. The time and space bounds follow directly from the above discussion. □

We next extend the above result to estimate time constrained inner product uv_Ω.

THEOREM 4. *Let $\mathcal{S}$ be a stream of entry-timestamp pairs (u_i, t_{ui}) arriving in arbitrary order for different vectors $u \in \mathbb{N}^n$ such that $u_i \leq r_{max}$. There exists a one-pass algorithm that computes a sketch of the user activity using $O(\frac{r_{max}}{\varepsilon^2})$ space and $O(r_{max} \log^2(\frac{1}{\varepsilon}) \log r_{max})$ processing time per pair. Let Ω be an appropriately defined time constraint. For any two users u, v, from the sketches of u and v we obtain an $\varepsilon(|u|+|v|)$-approximation of the inner product uv_Ω with probability 2/3 in time $O(\frac{r_{max}^2}{\varepsilon^2})$.*

Source	# users	# items	# ratings
MovieLens[1]	71,567	10,681	10M
Flixster[2]	1M	49000	8.2M

Table 1: Evaluation datasets. Both ratings sets are for movies, and in 5-scale with half-star increments.

PROOF. Consider the estimation of the time constrained inner product of two binary vectors $c_k c_{\ell\Omega}$. As in the proof of Theorem 3, we consider two sets A, B and apply minwise independent hashing in order to estimate $\alpha_\Omega = \frac{|A \cap B_\Omega|}{|A \cup B|}$ ($A \cap B_\Omega$ are the elements in $A \cap B$ that satisfy Ω). Let $\alpha = \frac{|A \cap B|}{|A \cup B|}$. By the very same reasoning as in the proof of Theorem 3 we obtain an ε-approximation of α_Ω using $O(1/\varepsilon^2)$ space and $O(\log^2(\frac{1}{\varepsilon}))$ processing time.

Assume we have computed an $\varepsilon(|A| + |B|)$-approximation of $|A \cap B|$. (By Theorem 3 we need again $O(1/\varepsilon^2)$ space and $O(\log^2(\frac{1}{\varepsilon}))$ processing time.) It holds

$$|A \cap B|_\Omega = \alpha_\Omega |A \cup B| = \alpha_\Omega(|A| + |B| - |A \cap B|).$$

With some simple algebra we can bound the approximation error to $O(\varepsilon(|A|+|B|))$. The claimed time and space bounds follow directly from the above and the discussion in the proof of Theorem 3. □

The above two theorems yield following approximation guarantees for the considered similarity measures.

COROLLARY 1. *Let $u, v \in \mathbb{N}^n$ be revealed in a streaming fashion. Let $u_i, v_i \leq r_{max}$. There exists a one-pass streaming algorithm processing each entry in time $O(r_{max} \log r_{max} \log^2(\frac{1}{\varepsilon}))$ and returning a sketch for each vector using $O(\frac{r_{max}}{\varepsilon^2})$ space. After preprocessing each sketches in time $O(\frac{r_{max}}{\varepsilon^2} \log(\frac{r_{max}}{\varepsilon}))$ we compute $\varepsilon r_{max} cos(u, v)$-approximation of $cos_\Omega(u, v)$ and $\rho_\Omega(u, v)$ in time $O(\frac{r_{max}^2}{\varepsilon^2})$.*

PROOF. Observe that for $u, v \in \mathbb{N}^n$ it holds

$$|u|+|v| = \sum_{i=1}^{n}(u_i+v_i) \leq 2\sum_{i=1}^{n} \max(u_i, v_i) \leq 2\sum_{i=1}^{n} u_i v_i = 2uv.$$

(The last inequality follows from $u_i, v_i \geq 1$.) Thus, for $q \geq uv - \varepsilon r_{max}(|u| + |v|)$ we have

$$\frac{q}{\|u\|\|v\|} \geq \frac{uv - \varepsilon r_{max}(|u| + |v|)}{\|u\|\|v\|} \geq \frac{(1 - 2\varepsilon r_{max})uv}{\|u\|\|v\|} =$$

$$(1 - 2\varepsilon r_{max})cos(u, v).$$

Similarly, for $q \leq uv + \varepsilon r_{max}(|u| + |v|)$ we obtain

$$\frac{q}{\|u\|\|v\|} \leq (1 + 2\varepsilon r_{max})cos(u, v).$$

Rescaling ε, we obtain the claimed bound for cosine similarity.

Consider now Pearson correlation. As shown in the proof of Theorem 3, we obtain an $\varepsilon(|c_1^u + c_1^v|)$-approximation of the inner product $c_1^u c_{1\Omega}^v \leq uv_\Omega$, and an $\varepsilon r_{max}(c_1^u + |v|)$-approximation of $c_1^u \sum_{k=1}^{r_{max}} c_k^v \leq uv$ and $nnz_{\Omega(u,v)}$, within the claimed time and space bounds. Since $|c_1^u| \leq |u|$ for any $u \in \mathbb{N}^n$, we obtain an $O(\varepsilon r_{max}(|u| + |v|))$-approximation of $(u - \tilde{u})(v - \tilde{v})_\Omega$. Dividing by $\|u\|\|v\|$ yields the claimed approximation bounds. □

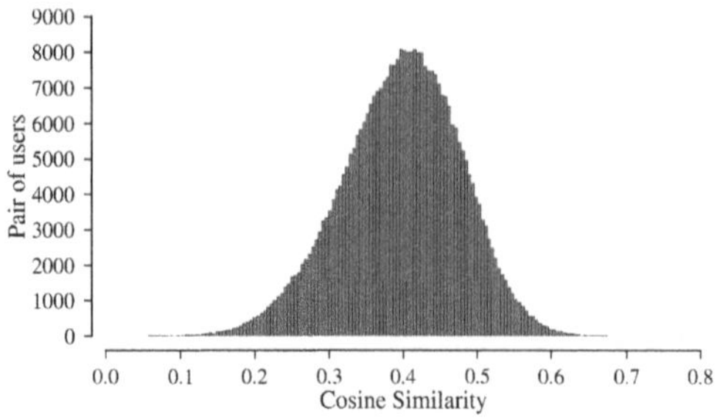

(a) Cosine similarity.

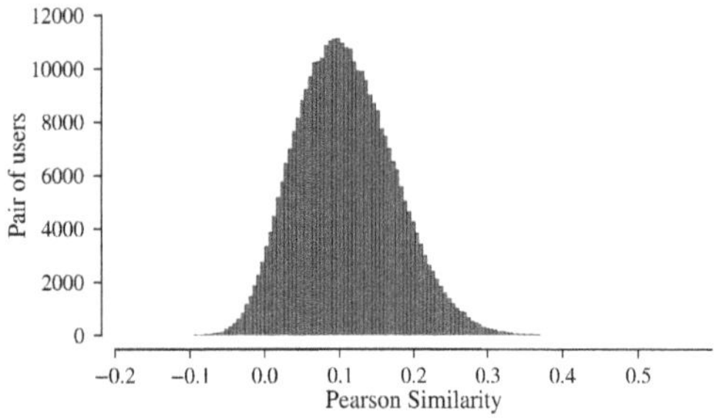

(b) Pearson correlation

Figure 3: Similarity distribution for the MovieLens dataset.

5. EXPERIMENTAL EVALUATION

In this section, we present experimental evaluation of the algorithms presented in Sections 3 and 4. The main purpose of the evaluation is to validate the theoretical findings on real data. Note that the approximation quality does not depend on the dataset size. Therefore, for larger dataset the space saving becomes more pronounced. We use two publicly available datasets, MovieLens and Flixtser detailed in Table 1. The two datasets consist of movie ratings on a 5-star scale, with half-star increments. In Figure 3 we plot the distribution of cosine similarity and Pearson correlation for the MovieLens dataset. In addition, the Flixster dataset contains a who-trusts-whom social network containing links between users. For more details on the properties of the two datasets we refer to [20, 29].

Implementation: The algorithms are implemented in the Python programming language using its standard data structures for the hash tables and priority queues. All experiments were performed on commodity hardware. We worked with a single hash function implemented using tabulation hashing [8]. Even if tabulation hashing is only 3-wise independent, it is known to simulate the behavior of a truly random hash function, see Pătraşcu and Thorup [27] for Chernoff-like concentration bounds for the randomness of tabulation hashing. (Note that working with several hash functions in parallel and returning the median of the estimates results in more accurate approximation. However, this comes at the price of slower processing time and increased space usage.)

Assume all keys come from a universe $\mathcal{U}$ of size n. With tabulation hashing, we view each key $r \in \mathcal{U}$ as a vector consisting of c characters, $r = (r_1, r_2, \ldots, r_c)$, where the i-th character is from a universe $\mathcal{U}_i$ of size $n^{1/c}$. (W.l.o.g. we assume that $n^{1/c}$ is an integer). For each universe $\mathcal{U}_i$, we initialize a table T_i and for each character $r_i \in \mathcal{U}_i$ we store a random value v_{r_i} obtained from the Marsaglia Random Number CDROM [3]. Then the hash value is computed as:

$$h_0(r) = T_1[r_1] \oplus T_2[r_2] \oplus \ldots \oplus T_c[r_c]$$

where $\oplus$ denotes the bit-wise XOR operation. Thus, for a small constant c, the space needed is $O(n^{1/c} \log n)$ bits and the evaluation time is $O(1)$. In our setting keys are 32-bit integers (the item ids), and we set $c = 4$. Clearly, this yields a very compact representation of the hash function.

[3]http://www.stat.fsu.edu/pub/diehard/cdrom/

	Cosine			Pearson		
s	aae	1-dev	2-dev	aae	1-dev	2-dev
100	0.0727	0.7282	0.9706	0.0818	0.6694	0.9482
200	0.0522	0.7184	0.9696	0.0568	0.679	0.9539
300	0.0426	0.7184	0.9694	0.0459	0.6818	0.9552
400	0.0421	0.6528	0.9442	0.0404	0.6761	0.9512
500	0.0338	0.7079	0.9646	0.0362	0.6747	0.9525
600	0.031	0.7059	0.9651	0.0322	0.686	0.9572
700	0.0382	0.5557	0.8941	0.0308	0.6694	0.9505
800	0.0345	0.5636	0.9035	0.0305	0.6417	0.9377

(a) MovieLens dataset.

	Cosine			Pearson		
s	aae	1-dev	2-dev	aae	1-dev	2-dev
100	0.0795	0.687	0.9514	0.081	0.6801	0.9492
200	0.0518	0.7382	0.9734	0.0577	0.6683	0.9480
300	0.0451	0.6906	0.9582	0.0463	0.6779	0.9559
400	0.0376	0.7088	0.9691	0.0394	0.6861	0.9573
500	0.0346	0.7067	0.9652	0.0347	0.6946	0.9559
600	0.0342	0.6534	0.9431	0.0325	0.6795	0.9542
700	0.0265	0.7425	0.9769	0.0297	0.6874	0.9572
800	0.0281	0.6614	0.958	0.0277	0.6908	0.9588

(b) Flixster dataset.

Table 2: Quality of the similarity approximation for varying sketch sizes.

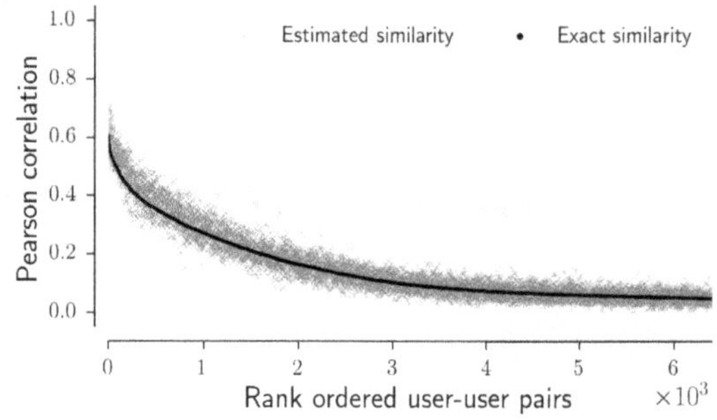

(a) Cosine similarity.

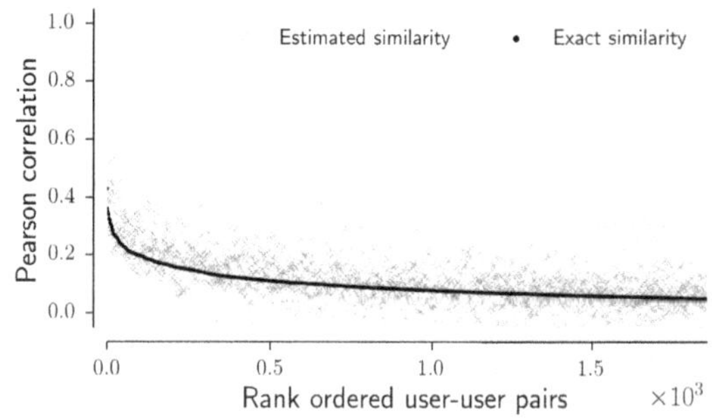

(b) Pearson correlation.

Figure 4: MovieLens approximation for sketch size $s = 200$, for pairs with similarity at least 0.1.

Evaluation: After sketching the activity for each user, we consider only users that have rated at least 1,000 movies. In MovieLens there are 840 such users and 1,204,445 ratings, and in Flixster there are 1,231 such users and 2,050,059 ratings. For the quality of approximation, we report i) the average approximation error (*aae*): $\sum_{i=1}^{n} \frac{|r_i - \tilde{r}_i|}{n}$, where $\tilde{r}$ is the approximated value of a rating r. ii) Given an approximation parameter ε, we report the quality of approximation in terms of the number of estimates $\tilde{r}_i$ that are within $[r_i - \varepsilon, r_i + \varepsilon]$ (denoted as *1-dev*), and within $[r_i - 2\varepsilon, r_i + 2\varepsilon]$ (*2-dev*). Finally, for all experiments we compute 1-dev and 2-dev w.r.t. $\varepsilon = 1/\sqrt{s}$[4], and not the more complicated form of the approximation guarantee we showed in Theorem 3. Note that the approximation guarantees in Section 4 also depend on r_{max} and the cosine similarity between users. Since the approximation quality scales with s, we present the approximation guarantees in terms of the sketch size per position, i.e., the total space usage is sr_{max}.

For the scalability of the algorithms, we report the memory requirements in terms of the sketch size (s) used, i.e., the number of entries stored in the sketch. Finally, we briefly report the run times of the algorithms on the datasets. The precise run times and actual space used highly depend on low-level technical details that are beyond the scope of the paper; we refer to [13] for a discussion on the evaluation of different implementations of streaming algorithms.

5.1 Weighted similarity estimation using AMS sketches

Having run the algorithms described in Section 3 on the datasets, we evaluated the impact of varying the sketch size (s) from 200 to 800 in increments of 100. The processing time varied between 90 - 110 seconds for MovieLens and 80-100 seconds for Flixster when varying sketch sizes.

To evaluate the approximation error (aae) and the percentage of good estimates (1-dev and 2-dev), we randomly sampled two separate groups of 300 users for each dataset and computed the similarity for every pair of users. In both MovieLens and Flixtser there are almost 90,000 pairs with cosine at least 0.1, while in MovieLens there are about 48,000 pairs with Pearson at least 0.1, and in Flixster – less than 10,000 pairs. Table 2 summarizes the results for MovieLens (Table 2a) and Flixster (Table 2b) respectively.

We observe as expected, the estimation error falls in response to increasing the sketch size (s). From the values 1-dev and 2-dev, we observe that the quality approximation is very high; the 2-dev ranges between 0.89 - 0.97 across both measures and data sets. Furthermore, the average error is always smaller than the ε-approximation given in Theorem 1 and Theorem 2. Figure 4 plots the exact alongside the approximated cosine similarity (Figure 4a), and Pearson correlation (Figure 4b) for MovieLens, with $s = 500$. As we see, despite working with a single hash function there are no outliers in the estimates.

5.2 Influence propagation probability estimation

We evaluated the algorithm listed in Section 4 on the two data sets, and tracked the influence probability between users for a period of 6 months. In order to speed up the processing time, we discretized the rating to be in a 5-star scale using ceiling r_{ui} to $\lceil r_{ui} \rceil$. However, we compute the exact similarity using the original 10-scale ratings. Because the social graph of the Flixster network is very sparse, to demonstrate statistical significance, we have increased the density of links. This is achieved by adding a new link between a pair of users u and v if $d(u) \cdot d(v) \geq 1/r$ for a random number in $(0, 1]$, where $d(u)$ is the number of neighbors of u in the network. Note that there is no social graph in the

[4]For example, for a sketch size $s = 400$ we have $\varepsilon = 0.05$

	Cosine			Pearson		
s	aae	1-dev	2-dev	aae	1-dev	2-dev
50	0.0562	0.9347	0.999	0.0842	0.8207	0.9767
100	0.0394	0.9341	0.9981	0.0711	0.748	0.9563
150	0.0271	0.967	0.9995	0.0489	0.8206	0.991
200	0.0243	0.9565	0.9987	0.0439	0.8036	0.9735
250	0.0256	0.9159	0.9924	0.0431	0.7698	0.9595
300	0.0201	0.9508	0.9975	0.0428	0.7264	0.9536
350	0.0227	0.8938	0.9826	0.0369	0.7815	0.9658
400	0.0183	0.9367	0.994	0.0331	0.779	0.9742

(a) MovieLens dataset.

	Cosine			Pearson		
s	aae	1-dev	2-dev	aae	1-dev	2-dev
50	0.0453	0.9794	0.9992	0.109	0.7194	0.9387
100	0.0394	0.9398	0.9991	0.0867	0.6644	0.9187
150	0.0365	0.9432	0.9868	0.0586	0.7551	0.9633
200	0.033	0.8911	0.9964	0.0508	0.7592	0.9529
250	0.0291	0.9154	0.9957	0.0448	0.7439	0.9727
300	0.0254	0.9091	0.9967	0.0419	0.7139	0.9384
350	0.0245	0.8861	0.9952	0.0408	0.6926	0.92658
400	0.0241	0.8824	0.994	0.0395	0.6319	0.8995

(b) Flixster dataset.

Table 3: Quality of approximation of the influence probability for varying sketch sizes.

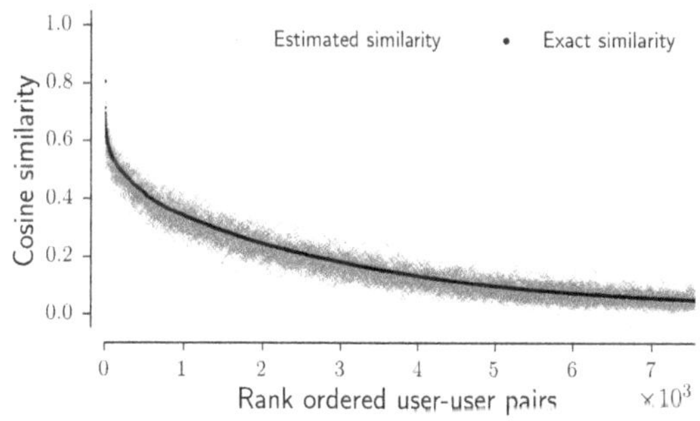

(a) Cosine similarity.

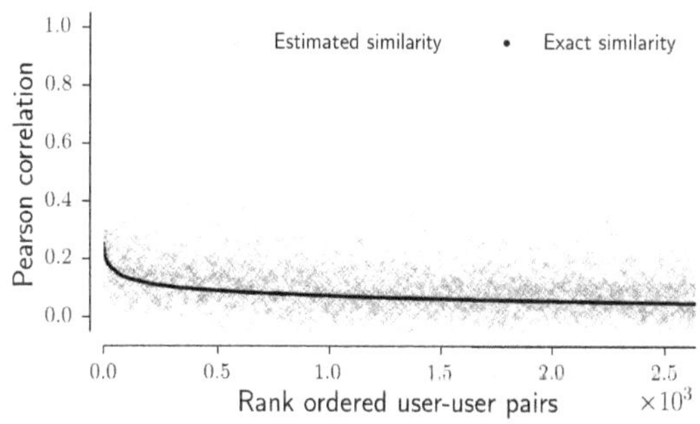

(b) Pearson correlation.

Figure 5: Approximation of the influence probability for Flixster dataset for sketch size $s = 200$.

MovieLens dataset. As discussed in the introduction, we are interested in users whose behaviour is a good predictor for the behaviour of other users and we consider all user pairs.

Table 3 again reports approximation error when varying the sketch size (s). We observe very precise estimates for cosine similarity for both datasets; Table 3a for MovieLens and Table 3b for Flixster. In fact these numbers are considerably better than what the theoretical analysis suggests. This is not very surprising, in [3] the authors also report a gap between theoretical and empirical approximation.

Furthermore, from Table 3 we observe that unsurprisingly, the approximation error for the Pearson correlation is higher than the corresponding Cosine similarity error. This is due to the fact that we need to estimate four different quantities which makes inaccurate estimates more likely. However, again the results show a lower error than the bounds we would expect from Theorem 3.

In Figure 5 we plot the approximation error for the Flixster dataset for sketch size 200. As evident, the approximation of the Pearson correlation is not so precise and there are a few significant outliers.

With respect to the datasets considered, space savings are made for smaller sketch sizes. For example, for a sketch size of 200 and ratings on a 5-scale, in the MovieLens dataset we need to store 840,000 samples, while for Flixster we need more than 1,2 million samples. (The pre-processed MovieLens and Flixster datasets contain 1,204,445 and 2,050,059 ratings respectively.) Finally, we observe higher running time compared to the AMS-sketch based algorithm, for MovieLens it varies between 170 and 190 seconds and for Flixster between 160 and 180. (However, this might be due to different time formats in the two datasets.)

6. CONCLUSIONS

We presented the first streaming algorithms for handling weighted similarity measures in data streams. The algorithms extend state-of-the-art techniques for scalable stream processing and are shown to be applicable to real-world domains. A few remarks are in place here. In [22] the algorithms were extended to min-wise independent hashing from sliding windows [15] where we are interested only in more recent user activity and to sublinear space usage where we are only interested in users whose activity is above certain threshold, i.e., have rated a certain amount of items. It is straightforward to extend the influence probability learning algorithm from Section 4 to also consider these extensions. However, it does not appear easy to extend the AMS sketch based algorithm from Section 3 to similarity estimation over sliding windows and active user mining. Finally, we note that it is easy to extend the here presented algorithms to the estimation of Euclidean distance, but due to lack of space we omit this result.

7. REFERENCES

[1] N. Alon, Y. Matias, M. Szegedy. The Space Complexity of Approximating the Frequency Moments. *J. Comput. Syst. Sci.* 58(1): 137–147 (1999)

[2] A. Anagnostopoulos, R. Kumar, M. Mahdian. Influence and correlation in social networks. *KDD 2008*: 7–15

[3] Y. Bachrach, R. Herbrich. Fingerprinting Ratings for Collaborative Filtering - Theoretical and Empirical Analysis. *SPIRE 2010*: 25–36

[4] Y. Bachrach, R. Herbrich, E. Porat. Sketching Algorithms for Approximating Rank Correlations in Collaborative Filtering Systems. *SPIRE 2009*: 344–352

[5] Y. Bachrach, E. Porat. Sketching for Big Data Recommender Systems Using Fast Pseudo-random Fingerprints. *ICALP (2) 2013*: 459–471

[6] Y. Bachrach, E. Porat, J. S. Rosenschein. Sketching Techniques for Collaborative Filtering. *IJCAI 2009*: 2016–2021

[7] A. Z. Broder, M. Charikar, A. M. Frieze, M. Mitzenmacher. Min-Wise Independent Permutations. *STOC 1998*: 327–336

[8] L. Carter, M. N. Wegman. Universal Classes of Hash Functions. *J. Comput. Syst. Sci. 18(2)*: 143–154 (1979)

[9] M. Charikar. Similarity estimation techniques from rounding algorithms. *STOC 2002*: 380–388

[10] M. Charikar, K. Chen, M. Farach-Colton. Finding frequent items in data streams. *Theor. Comput. Sci. 312(1)*: 3–15 (2004)

[11] E. Cohen, M. Datar, S. Fujiwara, A. Gionis, P. Indyk, R. Motwani, J. D. Ullman, C. Yang. Finding Interesting Associations without Support Pruning. *IEEE Trans. Knowl. Data Eng. 13(1)*: 64–78 (2001)

[12] G. Cormode, M. N. Garofalakis. Sketching Streams Through the Net: Distributed Approximate Query Tracking. *VLDB 2005*: 13–24

[13] G. Cormode, M. Hadjieleftheriou. Finding the frequent items in streams of data. *Commun. ACM 52(10)*: 97–105 (2009)

[14] D. J. Crandall, D. Cosley, D. P. Huttenlocher, J. M. Kleinberg, S. Suri. Feedback effects between similarity and social influence in online communities. *KDD 2008*: 160–168

[15] M. Datar, A. Gionis, P. Indyk, and R. Motwani. Maintaining stream statistics over sliding windows. *SIAM J. Comput., 31(6)*:1794 – 1813, 2002.

[16] G. Feigenblat, E. Porat, A. Shiftan. Exponential time improvement for min-wise based algorithms. *Inf. Comput. 209(4)*: 737–747 (2011)

[17] A. Gionis, P. Indyk, R. Motwani. Similarity Search in High Dimensions via Hashing. *VLDB 1999*: 518–529

[18] A. Goyal, F. Bonchi, L. V. S. Lakshmanan. Learning influence probabilities in social networks. *WSDM 2010*: 241–250

[19] M. Jamali, G. Haffari, M. Ester. Modeling the temporal dynamics of social rating networks using bidirectional effects of social relations and rating patterns. *WWW 2011*: 527–536

[20] M. Jamali, M. Ester. TrustWalker: a random walk model for combining trust-based and item-based recommendation. *KDD 2009*: 397–406

[21] D. Kempe, J. M. Kleinberg, E. Tardos. Maximizing the spread of influence through a social network. *KDD 2003*: 137–146

[22] K. Kutzkov, A. Bifet, F. Bonchi, A. Gionis. STRIP: stream learning of influence probabilities. *KDD 2013*: 275–283

[23] Y. Kwon. Improving top-n recommendation techniques using rating variance. *RecSys 2008*: 307–310

[24] P. Li, A. C. König. b-Bit minwise hashing. *WWW 2010*: 671–680

[25] P. Massa, P. Avesani. Trust-aware recommender systems. *RecSys 2007*: 17–24

[26] R. Motwani and P. Raghavan. *Randomized Algorithms.* Cambridge University Press, 1995.

[27] M. Pătraşcu, M. Thorup. The Power of Simple Tabulation Hashing. *J. ACM 59(3)*: 14 (2012)

[28] D. Ravichandran, P. Pantel, E.H. Hovy. Randomized Algorithms and NLP: Using Locality Sensitive Hash Functions for High Speed Noun Clustering. *ACL 2005*

[29] A. Said, B. J. Jain, S. Albayrak. Analyzing weighting schemes in collaborative filtering: cold start, post cold start and power users. *SAC 2012*: 2035–2040

[30] A. Shrivastava, P. Li. Asymmetric LSH (ALSH) for Sublinear Time Maximum Inner Product Search (MIPS). *NIPS 2014*: 2321–2329

Private Analysis of Infinite Data Streams via Retroactive Grouping

Rui Chen
Samsung Research America
Mountain View, CA, USA
rui.chen1@samsung.com

Yilin Shen
Samsung Research America
Mountain View, CA, USA
yilin.shen@samsung.com

Hongxia Jin
Samsung Research America
Mountain View, CA, USA
hongxia@acm.org

ABSTRACT

With the rapid advances in hardware technology, data streams are being generated daily in large volumes, enabling a wide range of real-time analytical tasks. Yet data streams from many sources are inherently sensitive, and thus providing continuous privacy protection in data streams has been a growing demand. In this paper, we consider the problem of private analysis of infinite data streams under differential privacy. We propose a novel data stream sanitization framework that periodically releases histograms summarizing the event distributions over sliding windows to support diverse data analysis tasks. Our framework consists of two modules, a sampling-based change monitoring module and a continuous histogram publication module. The monitoring module features an adaptive Bernoulli sampling process to accurately track the evolution of a data stream. We for the first time conduct error analysis of sampling under differential privacy, which allows to select the best sampling rate. The publication module features three different publishing strategies, including a novel technique called retroactive grouping to enjoy reduced noise. We provide theoretical analysis of the utility, privacy and complexity of our framework. Extensive experiments over real datasets demonstrate that our solution substantially outperforms the state-of-the-art competitors.

Categories and Subject Descriptors

H.2.7 [**DATABASE ADMINISTRATION**]: Security, integrity & protection

Keywords

Differential privacy, data stream, sampling-based monitoring, retroactive grouping

1. INTRODUCTION

With the rapid advances in hardware technology, there have been numerous applications that create and/or consume data streams in real time. Examples include public health surveillance, IoT device data, mobile data, GPS data, call detail records (CDRs), etc. Sharing such streams enables a wide spectrum of data analysis tasks in a real-time manner. However, streaming data from many sources are inherently sensitive, making privacy protection an increasingly important demand [17].

One notable privacy risk of sanitizing streaming data is that individually sanitized data could jointly compromise privacy. Fortunately, this risk can be gracefully addressed by the differential privacy model [8], which provides composable privacy guarantees for continuous data publishing over time. In the context of data streams, there are two instantiations of differential privacy providing different extents of privacy protection: *event-level* differential privacy and *user-level* differential privacy [9]. Event-level differential privacy hides any single event of any user from attackers, while user-level differential privacy hides all events of any user. In this paper, we follow the conventional use of event-level differential privacy [3, 5, 6, 9] mainly due to its ability to support private analysis of *infinite* data streams with reasonable accuracy. Infinite monitoring/analysis is a practical requirement in many applications. Meanwhile, we stress that event-level differential privacy still provides strong and meaningful privacy protection in that it provides *any* individual *plausible deniability* for *any* event in the published results.

While there have been a few existing works [3–6, 9–11, 13] on applying differential privacy to data streams, our problem setting is different from theirs and is oriented toward practical applications. We consider a more realistic data stream model that is widely used in real-world applications: periodically releasing synopsis structures (e.g., histograms) of sliding windows over practical infinite data streams (not simplified 0/1 strings as in some previous papers) [2]. Due to the consideration of practical usefulness, we advocate the *data-dependent* paradigm, which has been shown to be able to obtain significantly better utility in many cases [14]. The general idea of the data-dependent paradigm is to adaptively make use of the properties of the underlying data to guide private operations that lead to lower error.

More specifically, our solution is inspired by the power of grouping- or clustering-based approaches on *static* histogram publication [1, 18, 19]. These approaches group or cluster the bins of a histogram with similar counts to enjoy Laplace noise reduction proportional to the sizes of the groups or clusters. In the context of data streams, it is natural to attempt a similar idea to the time dimension: group time units with similar trends to improve utility. However,

Permission to make digital or hard copies of all or part of this work for personal or classroom use is granted without fee provided that copies are not made or distributed for profit or commercial advantage and that copies bear this notice and the full citation on the first page. Copyrights for components of this work owned by others than ACM must be honored. Abstracting with credit is permitted. To copy otherwise, or republish, to post on servers or to redistribute to lists, requires prior specific permission and/or a fee. Request permissions from Permissions@acm.org.
CIKM'15, October 19-23, 2015, Melbourne, VIC, Australia.
© 2015 ACM. ISBN 978-1-4503-3794-6/15/10 ...$15.00.
DOI: http://dx.doi.org/10.1145/2806416.2806454.

applying this idea to a data stream faces several non-trivial technical challenges: (1) The data elements (or events) arrive in real time. At the time of publication, we do not have knowledge about future trends. (2) It is required to release the histogram of the current sliding window at each timestamp. We cannot postpone publication to collect a batch of histograms to analyze their similarity. (3) Grouping with previously published histograms might increase the sensitivity and thus the magnitude of noise. In view of these challenges, we design a data stream sanitization framework equipped with novel sampling and publishing techniques to improve utility.

Contributions. In this paper, we consider a practical setting for continuously analyzing infinite data streams with the differential privacy guarantee. In addressing the problem, we first propose two first-cut solutions, accompanied with formal utility analysis, and then propose a novel data stream sanitization framework that is composed of two major modules: a sampling-based change monitoring module and a continuous histogram publication module.

The novelty of the monitoring module lies in an adaptive Bernoulli sampling process that accurately detects changes of the data stream even with a small privacy budget. While allowing to reduce Laplace error, sampling itself introduces a new source of sampling error, which is neglected in previous research. However, it needs to be carefully studied to properly adjust the sampling rate so as to improve accuracy. We for the first time quantify the sampling error and identify the best sampling rate as an optimization problem. Such analysis is useful for many sampling-based algorithms under differential privacy.

The publication module features three different publishing strategies, including a novel technique called *retroactive grouping*. It sophisticatedly selects time units to passively publish (i.e., approximate their statistics without explicitly using the Laplace mechanism) and then retroactively groups these units with later time units to enjoy reduced noise. We formally prove that retroactive grouping satisfies differential privacy. We theoretically analyze the accuracy of each released histogram and the space and time complexity of our solution to demonstrate its suitability for processing large-scale real-time data streams. We stress that while we focus on histograms in this paper, our general framework can easily accommodate other synopsis structures.

We have conducted an extensive experimental study over real datasets. The results confirm that our solution achieves substantially better utility than different competitors.

2. RELATED WORK

Applying differential privacy to data streams is a very recent topic. The first research papers [6, 9] consider computing the running sum of 1's (i.e., the number of 1's seen so far) over a simplified stream of 0's and 1's whose length is T. They independently present similar results. The proposed schemes encode the partial sums in terms of a full binary tree, where each node stores a partial sum plus noise with scale logarithmic in T, and answer the running sum by using the minimum number of nodes in the binary tree. Bolot et al. [3] extends the previous papers by considering decayed sum. A dyadic tree structure is maintained in a non-uniform manner. Our solution is orthogonal to these methods, but they can be combined to enhance each other.

Fan et al. [10] consider user-level differential privacy on *finite* streams. They present the FAST framework whose key idea is to adaptively sample the timestamps and take different publishing strategies for sampled and non-sampled timestamps in order to increase the privacy budget allocated to sampled timestamps. For sampled timestamps FAST releases their perturbed values by using the Laplace mechanism, while for non-sampled timestamps FAST releases their predicted counts instead. FAST is not directly beneficial to our problem setting because not sampling a timestamp does not increase other timestamps' privacy budgets. Also, the prediction accuracy could be low sometimes.

Kellaris et al. [13] propose a variant of event-level differential privacy called w-event differential privacy. It hides the presence/absence of any consecutive event sequence of size w. They introduce two privacy budget allocation schemes, Budget Distribution (BD) and Budget Absorption (BA), to achieve w-event differential privacy over infinite streams. Their contributions are orthogonal to ours. We aim at developing techniques to improve accuracy, which could be seamlessly incorporated into the w-event differential privacy framework.

Friedman et al. [11] study the problem of privately monitoring arbitrary *threshold* functions over *distributed* finite streams. This is achieved by the concept of Safe Zones, within which local vectors are guaranteed to satisfy the global privacy condition. Compared to theirs, our problem is more challenging in that we need to publish data, not merely signaling the exceeding of a given threshold. Similar to the distributed setting in [11], Chan et al. [5] study the problem of continual monitoring of heavy hitters from distributed streams by an untrusted aggregator.

A different problem setting on data streams is studied in [4]. Cao et al. consider to answer a given set of correlated sliding window aggregate queries. They propose to first sample a subset of representative queries, which will be answered by adding Laplace noise, and then estimate the answers to the remaining queries from the answers to the representatives.

As mentioned earlier, our work is motivated by studies on *static* histogram publication [1,18,19]. Xu et al. [18] propose to differentially privately group a histogram's bins based on the traditional histogram construction technique. One disadvantage of their solution is the requirement of knowing the number of groups in advance. Acs et al. [1] circumvent this drawback by proposing a bisection-based grouping strategy that automatically finds a good number of groups. Zhang et al. [19] argue that global clustering can achieve better utility than the local grouping schemes in [1, 18] and consequently propose a clustering framework that carefully balances the approximation error and the Laplace error. Unfortunately, such a global clustering scheme does not apply to data streams due to the challenges mentioned in the previous section.

3. PROBLEM FORMULATION

In this section, we first introduce the data stream model and the privacy notion in use and then give our problem statement.

3.1 Data Stream Model

In this paper, we consider an *infinite* data stream $\mathcal{S}$ consisting of an infinite number of events that arrive in real

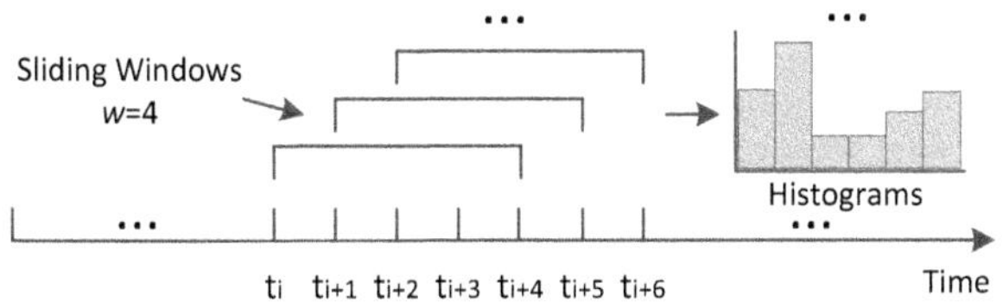

Figure 1: A sample data stream

time. Each event belongs to a user and is associated with an attribute value. The data publisher (e.g., the online recommender system in Example 1) continuously monitors the stream and publishes histograms summarizing the event distributions in the latest sliding windows at discrete timestamps. We consider publishing histograms as they have wide applications in a broad spectrum of problems [2]. Each bin B_i in a histogram $\mathbf{H}$ corresponds to an attribute value, and its count H_i is the number of events falling into B_i within the sliding window. We denote the total number of bins in $\mathbf{H}$ by $|\mathbf{H}|$. We call the time duration between two consecutive timestamps a *time unit*. The size of a sliding window is the number of time units it covers, which is denoted by ω. We denote the segment of $\mathcal{S}$ between timestamps t_i and t_j by $\mathcal{S}_{t_i}^{t_j}$, where $i < j$. Such a data stream model corresponds to many real-life applications, as illustrated below.

EXAMPLE 1. *For an online recommender system (e.g., Yelp), it is a business routine to continuously monitor and analyze users' events (e.g., users' visits to different types of restaurants). Periodically releasing histograms summarizing user events in the latest sliding windows (e.g., the distribution of restaurant types being visited in the past two weeks) is beneficial in many aspects, most importantly as a building block for recommendations. Such a scenario is illustrated in Figure 1, where the recommender system publishes the histograms of visits to different types of restaurants within the past 4 time units at every discrete timestamp. Each bin in a histogram corresponds to a restaurant type and has a count equal to the number of visits within the sliding window.*

3.2 Privacy Model

In the context of data streams, differential privacy rests on the notion of indistinguishability between two *neighboring* streams. In this paper, we follow the previous studies [3, 5, 6, 9] to define two data streams $\mathcal{S}$ and $\mathcal{S}'$ as neighbors if $\mathcal{S}$ can be obtained from $\mathcal{S}'$ by adding or removing at most a single event. Intuitively, differential privacy guarantees that an attacker with arbitrary background knowledge will not be able to (statistically) distinguish any computational result from $\mathcal{S}$ and $\mathcal{S}'$. This definition is formalized below.

Definition 1. (Event-Level Differential Privacy [9]) A randomized algorithm $\mathcal{K}$ gives event-level ϵ-differential privacy, if for any two neighboring streams $\mathcal{S}$ and $\mathcal{S}'$, and for any $O \subseteq Range(\mathcal{K})$,

$$P[\mathcal{K}(\mathcal{S}) \in O] \leq \exp(\epsilon) \cdot P[\mathcal{K}(\mathcal{S}') \in O],$$

where the probability is over the coin flips of $\mathcal{K}$.

Since two neighboring streams differ in a single event, it follows that an attacker is not able to distinguish the presence or absence of any event. Therefore, this privacy notion entitles *any* individual *plausible deniability* for *any* event in the published results. The privacy level is controlled by the parameter ϵ, also known as *privacy budget*. The smaller ϵ is, the more privacy we gain.

A standard technique to achieve differential privacy is the *Laplace mechanism* [8]. It injects properly calibrated Laplace noise into a function's output to mask the impact of any single tuple. The maximal impact of a tuple to the output of a function f is called its *sensitivity*.

Definition 2. (Sensitivity [8]) For a function $f : \mathcal{S} \rightarrow \mathbb{R}^d$, the sensitivity of f is $\Delta f = \max_{\mathcal{S},\mathcal{S}'} \|f(\mathcal{S}) - f(\mathcal{S}')\|_1$ for all neighboring streams $\mathcal{S}$ and $\mathcal{S}'$.

The Laplace noise needed to satisfy differential privacy is precisely calibrated by a function's sensitivity and the given privacy parameter, leading to the Laplace mechanism as follows.

THEOREM 1. [8] *For any function $f : \mathcal{S} \rightarrow \mathbb{R}^d$, the mechanism $\mathcal{K}$,*

$$\mathcal{K}(\mathcal{S}) = f(\mathcal{S}) + \left\langle \mathtt{Lap}_1(\frac{\Delta f}{\epsilon}), \ldots, \mathtt{Lap}_d(\frac{\Delta f}{\epsilon}) \right\rangle$$

gives ϵ-differential privacy, where $\mathtt{Lap}_i(\frac{\Delta f}{\epsilon})$ are i.i.d Laplace variables with scale parameter $\frac{\Delta f}{\epsilon}$.

For data streams, the graceful *composition properties* of differential privacy are particularly important for continuous privacy protection. The *sequential composition* property states that when combined differentially private subroutines still provide differential privacy guarantees.

THEOREM 2. [8] *Let each mechanism $\mathcal{K}_i$ provide ϵ_i-differential privacy. A sequence of $\mathcal{K}_i(D)$ over the database D provide $\sum \epsilon_i$-differential privacy.*

A special case is when the mechanisms are applied to *disjoint* databases, leading to the *parallel composition* property.

THEOREM 3. [8] *Let $\mathcal{K}_i$ provide ϵ_i-differential privacy. A sequence of $\mathcal{K}_i(D_i)$ over a set of disjoint databases D_i provides* $\max(\epsilon_i)$*-differential privacy.*

3.3 Problem Statement

In this paper, we consider the following problem: *Given an infinite data stream, at each discrete timestamp we would like to publish an accurate histogram that summarizes the event distribution in the current sliding window while satisfying event-level differential privacy.*

Following the convention in [18, 19], the accuracy (or utility) of a sanitized histogram is measured in terms of the expected *sum of squared error* (SSE). Given an original histogram $\mathbf{H}$ and its sanitized version $\widetilde{\mathbf{H}}$, the expected SSE is

$$\mathbb{E}(\mathtt{SSE}(\mathbf{H}, \widetilde{\mathbf{H}})) = \mathbb{E}\left(\sum_{i=1}^{|\mathbf{H}|} \left(H_i - \widetilde{H}_i\right)^2\right),$$

where H_i and $\widetilde{H}_i$ are the true and perturbed counts in $\mathbf{H}$ and $\widetilde{\mathbf{H}}$, respectively, and $|\mathbf{H}|$ is the number of bins. Accordingly, the error of a bin is measured by its expected squared error. In our problem, we publish a sanitized histogram at each timestamp summarizing the event distribution in the current sliding window, and therefore our utility goal is to minimize either the *average* or the *total* expected SSE of all published histograms.

4. TWO FIRST-CUT SOLUTIONS

In this section, we provide two first-cut solutions that help better understand the problem and motivate our solution.

4.1 Sliding Window Based Perturbation

To publish T histograms over a data stream[1], we can directly perturb the histograms of the sliding windows by the Laplace mechanism. The most straightforward approach is to make use of the sequential composition property to divide the total privacy budget ϵ into T portions, each being used for sanitizing a histogram. Since a single event can change exactly one bin's count by 1, the expected SSE of a histogram introduced by this approach is

$$\mathbb{E}(\texttt{SSE}(\mathbf{H}, \widetilde{\mathbf{H}})) = \mathbb{E}\sum_{i=1}^{|\mathbf{H}|}\left(H_i - H_i - \mathsf{Lap}\left(\frac{T}{\epsilon}\right)\right)^2 = \frac{2|\mathbf{H}|T^2}{\epsilon^2}.$$

For an infinite data stream, we need to publish an infinite number of histograms (i.e., $T \to \infty$), and therefore the above method can barely provide useful results. However, if we observe that a single event can affect *at most* ω sliding windows that cover it, where ω is the sliding window size, we can do better. The sensitivity of all count queries needed to build all the histograms is ω because a single event can affect at most ω bin counts by 1. Therefore, the expected SSE of a histogram becomes $\frac{2|\mathbf{H}|\omega^2}{\epsilon^2}$, where $\omega \ll T$.

4.2 Time Unit Based Perturbation

Another alternative is to add Laplace noise to the counts of each time unit and generate the histogram of a sliding window by summing the counts of all time units it covers. Since a single event can affect *at most* one bin's count in *at most* one time unit by 1 (irrespective of the fact that the data stream is infinite), the sensitivity of all count queries is 1. Thus the expected SSE of the histogram corresponding to a time unit is $\frac{2|\mathbf{H}|}{\epsilon^2}$, leading to an expected SSE of $\frac{2|\mathbf{H}|\omega}{\epsilon^2}$ for a histogram of a sliding window with size ω. It can be seen that this method is strictly better than the sliding window based perturbation approach. Therefore, we consider the time unit based perturbation as the baseline approach (referred to as `Baseline` in the sequel) and propose novel techniques to further improve its utility.

5. OUR SOLUTION

In this section, we first provide an overview of our data stream sanitization framework and then elaborate its two key components.

5.1 Overview

Our retroactive-grouping-based framework (referred to as `RG`) consists of two novel modules: a sampling-based change monitoring module and a continuous histogram publication module. The former adaptively determines the best sampling rates to learn the underlying stream's evolution, based on which the latter takes proper publishing strategies to improve utility.

We first summarize the notations that are most frequently used in the sequel. We denote a time duration starting at timestamp t_i and ending at t_j by $[t_i, t_j]$, where $i < j$. The segment of the data stream $\mathcal{S}$ in $[t_i, t_j]$ is then denoted by $\mathcal{S}_{t_i}^{t_j}$. We denote the histogram corresponding to the time duration $[t_i, t_j]$ by $\mathbf{H}_{t_i,t_j}$ and the count of a bin B_l in $\mathbf{H}_{t_i,t_j}$ by H_{t_i,t_j}^l. The histogram published at time t_i for its sliding window's duration $[t_{i-\omega}, t_i]$ is written as $\mathbf{H}_{t_i}$ for short, and its count of a bin B_l is written as $H_{t_i}^l$. When the context is clear, we may omit some subscripts or superscripts. We use tilded versions to denote differentially private variables.

[1]Here we introduce the parameter T just for the theoretical analysis. Our solution supports infinite streams.

Algorithm 1 Private histogram publication at time t_i

Input: Data Stream $\mathcal{S}$
Input: Current timestamp t_i
Input: Privacy budgets ϵ_1 and ϵ_2 s.t. $\epsilon_1 + \epsilon_2 = \epsilon$
Input: Sliding window size ω
Input: Histograms $\widetilde{\mathbf{H}}_{t_{k-1},t_k}$ with $i - \omega + 1 \le k \le i - 1$
Output: Sanitized histogram $\widetilde{\mathbf{H}}_{t_i}$

1: Calculate the difference vector $\mathbf{d}$ between $[t_{i-1}, t_i]$ and $[t_{i-2}, t_{i-1}]$ using ϵ_1; //see Algorithm 2
2: **for** each bin B_j **do**
3:   **if** $\mathbf{d}[j] \ge \frac{2}{\epsilon_2^2}$ **then** //see Section 5.3 for the use of $\frac{2}{\epsilon_2^2}$
4:     $\widetilde{H}_{t_{i-1},t_i}^j = H_{t_{i-1},t_i}^j + \mathsf{Lap}\left(\frac{1}{\epsilon_2}\right)$;
5:     $\mathcal{G}(B_j) = \varnothing$;
6:   **else**
7:     Add H_{t_{i-1},t_i}^j to $\mathcal{G}(B_j)$;
8:     **if** $|\mathcal{G}(B_j)| \ge m$ **then** //see Section 5.3 for m
9:       $\widetilde{H}_{t_{i-1},t_i}^j = \frac{\sum_{H_k \in \mathcal{G}(B_j)} H_k}{|\mathcal{G}(B_j)|} + \mathsf{Lap}\left(\frac{1}{|\mathcal{G}(B_j)|\epsilon_2}\right)$;
10:       $\mathcal{G}(B_j) = \varnothing$;
11:     **else**
12:       $\widetilde{H}_{t_{i-1},t_i}^j = \widetilde{H}_{t_{i-2},t_{i-1}}^j$;
13:   $\widetilde{H}_{t_i}^j = \sum_{k=i-\omega+1}^{i} \widetilde{H}_{t_{k-1},t_k}^j$;
14: **return** $\widetilde{\mathbf{H}}_{t_i}$;

At a timestamp t_i, Algorithm 1 presents how our framework releases a sanitized histogram for the current sliding window. Since we concern with event-level differential privacy, it is helpful to consider the events within different time units as *disjoint* databases. According to the parallel property, this allows us to use the full privacy budget on each time unit and offers us much flexibility in algorithm design. In Line 1, the monitoring module decides a proper sampling rate and calculates the difference vector $\mathbf{d}$ that measures the count differences of all bins between the current time unit and the previous time unit in terms of squared error. Since the monitoring module operates on the raw data, it needs to be guarded by differential privacy. For this purpose, the privacy budget ϵ_1 is assigned to it. Instead of comparing the SSE of the histograms in whole, we observe that the counts of different bins may change at different rates and therefore process each bin individually. Each element in $\mathbf{d}$ records the difference of the counts of a bin.

If the count difference of a bin is larger than the error introduced by the Laplace mechanism ($\frac{2}{\epsilon_2^2}$, see Section 5.3 for explanation), the best strategy is to employ the Laplace mechanism to generate the bin's noisy count (Line 4). Otherwise, there is room to improve. A natural idea is to approximate the current count with the previous (noisy) count, a method used in [13], which we call *passive publishing*. Unfortunately, in our setting passive publishing alone may not be able to improve accuracy. In [13], passive publishing benefits by saving on the privacy budget for future time units, while in our case each time unit can use the privacy budget in full. This implies that we can always use the Laplace mechanism to generate a noisy count with error no more than that of passive publishing, which is the sum of the Laplace error of the same magnitude and the approximation error (i.e., the actual difference between the current and the previous counts).

Here our key insight is that while not able to save on privacy budget, the time unit passively released (referred to as *passive time unit*) does help reduce sensitivity. To gain this benefit, we deliberately select some time units to passively publish and later group them with the time units with close counts, which we call *retroactive grouping*. At timestamp t_i, if we can find a retroactive group with a size $\geq m$ (a threshold determined by error analysis later) for a bin, we add *reduced* Laplace noise to the count (Line 9); otherwise we use passive publication (Line 12) to approximate the count. Finally, the noisy count of a bin in the current sliding window is the sum of the noisy counts of all time units in the window (Line 13).

5.2 Sampling-based Monitoring

Monitoring the evolution of a data stream is key to taking the proper publishing strategy in our framework. At each timestamp, we compute the differences between the counts of the current time unit and those of the previous time unit. *Sampling* is a common tool used on data streams mainly for the reason of efficiency. In the context of differential privacy, sampling also has an impact on the utility aspect. Previous research [15] has indicated the amplification effect of sampling on the privacy budget, which is formalized below.

THEOREM 4. [15] *Let $\mathcal{K}$ be an ϵ-differentially private algorithm. Let $\mathcal{K}_\gamma$ be another algorithm that first samples each tuple independently in its input dataset with probability γ and then applies $\mathcal{K}$ to the sampled dataset. $\mathcal{K}_\gamma$ satisfies $\ln(1+\gamma(e^\epsilon-1))$-differential privacy.*

Theorem 4 suggests that if the sample generated is *representative* (i.e., the statistics obtained over it are approximately the same as those of the original data), it is possible to obtain more accurate results over the sample by taking advantage of reduced Laplace noise. However, since sampling itself introduces a new source of error, *sampling error*, sampling may not always be helpful. To make a wise decision on whether or not to employ sampling (and the proper sampling rate), we need to carefully quantify the sampling error. While sampling has been used in previous research on differential privacy [12, 15], to our best knowledge, the sampling error was never quantified before. In this paper, we provide theoretical analysis on the sampling error.

Algorithm 2 presents the pseudocode of our sampling-based monitoring module. At each timestamp t_i, for each bin B_j, we estimate the difference between its counts in the current time unit $[t_{i-1}, t_i]$ and the previous time unit $[t_{i-2}, t_{i-1}]$. The first step is to determine the proper sampling rate γ_j for B_j (Line 2 of Algorithm 2). The sampling technique used in Theorem 4 is *Bernoulli sampling* [16]: For each coming event (of the population), perform a Bernoulli trial with the success probability $0 < \gamma_j \leq 1$, which is the sampling rate. If a success occurs, include the trial event as part of the sample; otherwise discard the event. Under Bernoulli sampling, given a sample size n_j, the population size N_j (i.e., B_j's true count in time unit $[t_{i-1}, t_i]$) can be

Algorithm 2 Sampling-based monitoring at time t_i

Input: Data stream $\mathcal{S}$
Input: Current timestamp t_i
Input: Privacy parameter ϵ_1
Input: Histogram $\widetilde{\mathbf{H}}_{t_{i-2},t_{i-1}}$
Output: Difference vector $\mathbf{d}$

1: **for** each bin B_j **do**
2: Compute the sampling rate γ_j;
3: Generate S_j by sampling events of B_j in $\mathcal{S}_{t_{i-1}}^{t_i}$ with rate γ_j;
4: $\widetilde{N}_j = \frac{|S_j| + \mathrm{Lap}\left(\frac{1}{\ln(e^{\epsilon_1}-1+\gamma_j)-\ln\gamma_j}\right)}{\gamma_j}$;
5: $\mathbf{d}[j] = \left(\widetilde{H}^j_{t_{i-2},t_{i-1}} - \widetilde{N}_j\right)^2$;
6: **return** $\mathbf{d}$;

estimated by $\hat{N}_j = \frac{n_j}{\gamma_j}$. $\hat{N}_j$ is an unbiased estimator of N_j. Since we use squared error to measure the utility of sanitized histograms, here we use mean squared error (MSE) to quantify the sampling error. Since the sample size n_j is a binomial variable, we have

$$\mathbb{E}(\mathtt{MSE}(N_j, \hat{N}_j)) = \sum_{i=0}^{N_j} P(n_j = i)\left(\frac{n_j}{\gamma_j} - N_j\right)^2, \qquad (1)$$

where $P(n_j = i) = \binom{N_j}{i}\gamma_j^i(1-\gamma_j)^{N_j-i}$ is the probability of having a sample size i. By solving Equation 1, we obtain $\mathbb{E}(\mathtt{MSE}(N_j, \hat{N}_j)) = \frac{N_j(1-\gamma_j)}{\gamma_j}$. This is the sampling error introduced in our monitoring module.

On the other hand, due to sampling, we enjoy reduced Laplace noise (see its construction in Line 4 of Algorithm 2), whose error can be quantified as per Theorem 4 as

$$\frac{2\gamma_j^2}{(\ln(e^{\epsilon_1}-1+\gamma_j)-\ln\gamma_j)^2}.$$

The total error is the sum of the sampling error and the Laplace error. Thus, we can express the total error as a function of γ_j and are interested in identifying the sampling rate γ_j that minimizes the total error, as formulated below:

$$\begin{aligned} \underset{\gamma_j}{\text{minimize}} \quad & \frac{N_j(1-\gamma_j)}{\gamma_j} + \frac{2\gamma_j^2}{(\ln(e^{\epsilon_1}-1+\gamma_j)-\ln\gamma_j)^2} \\ \text{subject to} \quad & 0 < \gamma_j \leq 1 \end{aligned}$$

Since γ_j is confined to the range $(0, 1]$, we can easily find the best rate by discretizing the range and applying the brute force method[2]. The above formulation is general to capture both the cases of sampling and *not* sampling. If $\gamma_j = 1$ is chosen, it means that no sampling should be applied. Therefore, our solution is general to make a decision on whether or not to apply sampling at all. Now the only unsolved problem is that in practice the population size N_j (and even its noisy version) is unknown before choosing γ_j. Here we estimate N_j by the noisy count in the previous time unit due to the fact that the statistics of a data stream may not change substantially in successive time units, a key assumption made in previous research [13]. Our experiments confirm that our foregoing error analysis precisely identifies

[2]In the experiments, we set the granularity to 1%.

the best sampling rate. In general, we observe that the benefit of sampling is more visible when the population size is relatively small or the privacy budget is small. This allows us to use a very small ϵ_1 (e.g., 0.1ϵ) to accurately monitor the evolution of a data stream.

For each bin B_j, after determining its sampling rate γ_j, we generate the sample S_j by including each event associated with B_j in the stream segment $\mathcal{S}_{t_{i-1}}^{t_i}$ with probability γ_j. We add reduced Laplace noise $\mathsf{Lap}\left(\frac{1}{\ln(e^{\epsilon_1}-1+\gamma_j)-\ln\gamma_j}\right)$ to the true sample size $|S_j|$, estimate the count by the unbiased estimator introduced before, and record the squared error between this estimation and the noisy count of the previous time unit in the difference vector $\mathbf{d}$. Since we keep track of the changes of bins independently, the same procedure needs to be applied to all bins.

5.3 Continuous Histogram Publication

As analyzed in Section 4, the time unit based perturbation method achieves strictly better accuracy than the sliding window based perturbation method. Thus we design our continuous histogram publication module based on this conclusion. Depending on the output of the monitoring module, our framework takes three different strategies to calculate the bins' noisy counts in the current time unit $[t_{i-1}, t_i]$.

We first quantify the error of the Laplace mechanism and use it as the sentinel to indicate which strategy to take. Since any single event can affect only one bin's count by exactly 1 (i.e., the sensitivity of the corresponding count queries is 1) and ϵ_2 is reserved for publication, for any count H_j, the squared error of its noisy version generated by the Laplace mechanism is

$$\mathbb{E}\left(H_j + \mathsf{Lap}\left(\frac{1}{\epsilon_2}\right) - H_j\right)^2 = \mathbb{E}\left(\mathsf{Lap}\left(\frac{1}{\epsilon_2}\right)\right)^2 = \frac{2}{\epsilon_2^2}.$$

This explains the threshold used in Line 3 of Algorithm 1. If the difference of a bin B_j's counts between the current time unit and the previous unit is $\geq \frac{2}{\epsilon_2^2}$, it is clear that using the standard Laplace mechanism to perturb the current count H_{t_{i-1},t_i}^j is the best strategy. Recall that we can use ϵ_2 to perturb the count and that the sensitivity is 1, and thus the Laplace noise is generated with scale parameter $\frac{1}{\epsilon_2}$. We will formally analyze the privacy guarantee of our solution in Section 6.2.

If the difference is $< \frac{2}{\epsilon_2^2}$, we examine whether it is possible to benefit from retroactive grouping and take the corresponding strategies. In the context of data streams, *the grouping must be done in a way that does not increase the sensitivity*; otherwise its benefit will be canceled out due to the increased sensitivity. It follows that the count of a bin in a time unit that has been previously released by the Laplace mechanism (using ϵ_2[3]) should never be asked again. For this reason, we deliberately choose some time units for passive publishing (and thus their counts have not been answered by the Laplace mechanism using ϵ_2) and later group a bin's current time unit with its previously passively published time units for reduced error.

We denote the retroactive group of a bin B_j by $\mathcal{G}(B_j)$ and its size by $|\mathcal{G}(B_j)|$. It contains the counts of the preceding passive time units up to (but not including) the most recent non-passive time unit. After each non-passive release, we empty $\mathcal{G}(B_j)$ (Lines 5 and 10 of Algorithm 1). It can be seen that such a construction does not increase the sensitivity. As a result, the counts of the first $|\mathcal{G}(B_j)|-1$ members in $\mathcal{G}(B_j)$ are approximated by the noisy count of the most recent non-passive time unit, and the last member, the count of the current time unit H_{t_{i-1},t_i}^j, will enjoy reduced Laplace noise. More specifically, H_{t_{i-1},t_i}^j is estimated by adding $\mathsf{Lap}\left(\frac{1}{|\mathcal{G}(B_j)|\epsilon_2}\right)$ to the count average of the retroactive group, that is

$$\widetilde{H}_{t_{i-1},t_i}^j = \frac{\sum_{H_k\in\mathcal{G}(B_j)} H_k}{|\mathcal{G}(B_j)|} + \mathsf{Lap}\left(\frac{1}{|\mathcal{G}(B_j)|\epsilon_2}\right).$$

We give the sensitivity of the group average here and prove its privacy guarantee later.

THEOREM 5. *The sensitivity of* $\frac{\sum_{H_k\in\mathcal{G}(B_j)} H_k}{|\mathcal{G}(B_j)|}$ *is* $\frac{1}{|\mathcal{G}(B_j)|}$.

PROOF. Since a single event can change a bin's count in at most one time unit by 1, it can change $\sum_{H_k\in\mathcal{G}(B_j)} H_k$ by at most 1, and therefore can change the average by at most $\frac{1}{|\mathcal{G}(B_j)|}$. This establishes the proof. □

For static histograms, we always prefer a larger group provided that the approximation error is low (i.e., all counts in the group are close) because the Laplace noise reduction of *every* member in the group is proportional to the group size. Unfortunately, this is not the case for a data stream. We need more sophisticated design. For a data stream, it is mandatory to release a histogram at each timestamp and the histogram is consumed in real time. The previously published counts (i.e., the first $|\mathcal{G}(B_j)|-1$ members in $\mathcal{G}(B_j)$) cannot benefit from the reduced Laplace noise due to retroactive grouping. This fact requires to carefully select the retroactive group size, the parameter m in Line 8 of Algorithm 1.

As per the problem definition, for a bin B_j, our goal is to minimize the average expected squared error of its retroactive group. To this end, we would like to express the average error as a function of m in order to identify the best m value. Here we need to first understand the squared error of a passive publication. Let H_i be a count from which H_j is approximated by a passive publication. Note that H_i and H_j do not have to belong to two consecutive time units because if the data stream evolves very slowly, H_j could be well approximated by the count of a time unit long ago. In a passive publication, we approximate H_j with the noisy version $\widetilde{H}_i$ of H_i and thus the expected error is

$$\begin{aligned}\mathbb{E}\left((H_j-\widetilde{H}_i)^2\right) &= \mathbb{E}\left((H_j-H_i-\mathsf{Lap}(\lambda))^2\right)\\ &= \underbrace{(H_j-H_i)^2}_{\text{Approximation error}} + \underbrace{2\lambda^2}_{\text{Laplace error}}\end{aligned}$$

where λ is the scale parameter of the Laplace noise added to $\widetilde{H}_i$. λ may not always be $\frac{1}{\epsilon_2}$ as $\widetilde{H}_i$ may be generated with reduced Laplace noise by retroactive grouping. The first item $(H_j-H_i)^2$ represents the *approximation error*, while the second item $2\lambda^2$ represents the *Laplace error*. The trade-off between these two types of errors lies at the core of our approach: *we would like to trade a small approximation error for a large reduction of Laplace error.* If the standard

[3]There is no need to worry about the queries issued using ϵ_1. This point will be made clear in Section 6.2.

Laplace mechanism is applied to H_i (in this case $\lambda = \frac{1}{\epsilon_2}$), passive publishing cannot perform better than directly applying the Laplace mechanism to H_j because $(H_j - H_i)^2 \geq 0$. Now we are ready to present the average expected squared error of noisy counts in a retroactive group.

THEOREM 6. *For a retroactive group $\mathcal{G}(B_j)$ of size m, its average expected squared error is*

$$\frac{\sum_{i=1}^{m-1}(H_i - H_0)^2 + (H_m - \bar{H})^2}{m} + \frac{2(m-1)\lambda^2}{m} + \frac{2}{(m\epsilon_2)^2},$$

where H_i with $1 \leq i \leq m$ is the ith element in $\mathcal{G}(B_j)$, $\bar{H}$ is the average of H_i's , H_0 is the true count from which the first $m-1$ members in $\mathcal{G}(B_j)$ are approximated, and λ is the scale of the Laplace noise added to H_0.

PROOF. Since the first $m-1$ members are passively released, all their noisy counts are approximated by $H_0 + \mathsf{Lap}(\lambda)$. Then, by definition, the average expected squared error of a retroactive group is

$$\mathbb{E}\left(\frac{\sum_{i=1}^{m}(\widetilde{H}_i - H_i)^2}{m}\right)$$
$$=\frac{1}{m}\mathbb{E}\left(\sum_{i=1}^{m-1}(\widetilde{H}_i - H_i)^2 + \left(H_m - \frac{\sum_{i=1}^{m} H_i}{m} - \mathsf{Lap}\left(\frac{1}{m\epsilon_2}\right)\right)^2\right)$$
$$=\frac{1}{m}\left(\sum_{j=1}^{m-1}(H_j - H_0)^2 + 2(m-1)\lambda^2 + (H_m - \bar{H})^2 + \frac{2}{m\epsilon_2^2}\right)$$
$$=\frac{\sum_{j=1}^{m-1}(H_j - H_0)^2 + (H_m - \bar{H})^2}{m} + \frac{2(m-1)\lambda^2 + \frac{2}{m\epsilon_2^2}}{m},$$

where the first item represents the approximation error and the second item represents the Laplace error. □

If we only consider the Laplace error, it is easy to derive the best value of m:

$$m = \underset{k \in \mathbb{N}^+ \backslash \{1\}}{\operatorname{argmin}} \left(\frac{2(k-1)\lambda^2}{k} + \frac{2}{(k\epsilon_2)^2}\right),$$

which gives $m = \frac{2}{(\lambda\epsilon_2)^2}$. However, with the increase of m, the approximation error often also increases, which requires to select a smaller m value. Since the approximation error is data-dependent and difficult to quantify, we empirically choose $m = \frac{2}{\lambda\epsilon_2}$ to account for the approximation error, which works well for all experimental datasets. Since λ is a variable that changes with the data stream, the value of m also changes.

We illustrate how to apply different publishing strategies in the following example.

EXAMPLE 2. *Consider the data stream in Figure 2. We focus on a single bin with its counts given on top of the time units. At timestamp t_2, since it is the first time unit, its true count 5 is perturbed by the Laplace mechanism. At t_3, let the difference between 75 and 5 detected by the monitoring module is $\geq \frac{2}{\epsilon_2^2}$, the true count 75 is released by the Laplace mechanism. Let the differences calculated from t_4 to t_9 be all $< \frac{2}{\epsilon_2^2}$. At t_4, the true count 74 in $[t_3, t_4]$ is passively released because the current retroactive group size is $< m = 2$. At t_5, the true count 73 is published using retroactive grouping and the group is then emptied. After that, the counts at t_6, t_7 and t_8 are passively released because now $m = 4$. Finally the true count 75 in $[t_8, t_9]$ is released using retroactive grouping.*

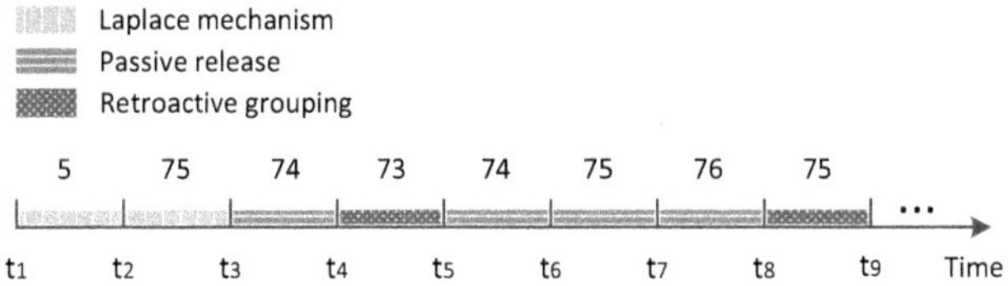

Figure 2: An illustration of continuous histogram publication

After obtaining a bin's noisy count in the current time unit using one of the publishing strategies, its noisy count in the current sliding window is the sum of the noisy counts of the time units covered by the sliding window (Line 13 of Algorithm 1). We repeat this procedure for all bins to produce the histogram to publish at t_i.

6. THEORETICAL ANALYSIS

In this section, we provide the theoretical analysis of RG.

6.1 Utility Analysis

We give the major utility result in the following theorem.

THEOREM 7. *For (a segment of) a data stream with T time units, if $T = 2^{l+1} - 1$ for some $l \in \mathbb{N}^+$, the minimum average expected SSE of the histograms published by* RG *is*

$$\frac{\omega|\mathbf{H}|}{3\epsilon_2^2} \cdot \frac{28(T+1)^2 - 60T - 28}{(T+1)^3 - (T+1)^2};$$

otherwise its minimum average expected SSE is

$$\frac{2\omega|\mathbf{H}|}{3T\epsilon_2^2} \cdot \left(14 - \frac{42}{2^{k+1}} + \frac{16 + 12T}{2^{2k+2}} + \frac{3}{T - 2^{k+1} + 1}\right),$$

where $k = \lfloor \log_2(T+1) - 1 \rfloor$.

PROOF. It is easy to see that the minimum average expected SSE is achieved when the events in each bin arrive at a fixed speed. In this case, the approximation error is 0 and the SSE solely comes from the Laplace error. By design, for any bin, its first time unit's count will be published by the Laplace mechanism with the Laplace error $\frac{2}{\epsilon_2^2}$. After that, if $T = 2^{l+1} - 1$ for some $l \in \mathbb{N}^+$, the retroactive group sizes are $2^1, 2^2, \cdots, 2^l$; otherwise, the retroactive group sizes are $2^1, 2^2, \cdots, 2^k, T - \sum_{i=0}^{k} 2^i$, where $k = \lfloor \log_2(T+1) - 1 \rfloor$. For both cases, the λ value of the ith group is $\frac{2}{2^i\epsilon_2}$. For space reasons, we only prove the latter case. The former is a simplified case of the latter and can be similarly proved. By Theorem 6, the Laplace error of the ith retroactive group is $\frac{2 \cdot 2^2(2^i - 1)}{(2^i\epsilon_2)^2} + \frac{2}{2^i\epsilon_2^2}$, where $1 \leq i \leq k$, and the Laplace error of the last group is $\frac{2 \cdot 2^2(T - \sum_{i=0}^{k} 2^i - 1)}{(2^{k+1}\epsilon_2)^2} + \frac{2}{(T - \sum_{i=0}^{k} 2^i)\epsilon_2^2}$. Then we can express the minimum average expected squared error of a bin in a time unit as

$$\frac{\sum_{i=0}^{k}\left(\frac{2 \cdot 2^2(2^i-1)}{(2^i\epsilon_2)^2} + \frac{2}{2^i\epsilon_2^2}\right) + \frac{2 \cdot 2^2(T - \sum_{i=0}^{k} 2^i - 1)}{(2^{k+1}\epsilon_2)^2} + \frac{2}{(T - \sum_{i=0}^{k} 2^i)\epsilon_2^2}}{T}$$
$$=\frac{2}{T\epsilon_2^2} \cdot \left(5\sum_{i=0}^{k}\frac{1}{2^i} - 4\sum_{i=0}^{k}\frac{1}{2^{2i}} + \frac{4(T - 2^{k+1})}{2^{2k+2}} + \frac{1}{T - 2^{k+1} + 1}\right)$$
$$=\frac{2}{3T\epsilon_2^2} \cdot \left(14 - \frac{42}{2^{k+1}} + \frac{16 + 12T}{2^{2k+2}} + \frac{3}{T - 2^{k+1} + 1}\right)$$

Since each histogram covers ω time units and has $|\mathbf{H}|$ bins, the minimum average expected SSE becomes

$$\frac{2\omega|\mathbf{H}|}{3T\epsilon_2^2}\cdot\left(14-\frac{42}{2^{k+1}}+\frac{16+12T}{2^{2k+2}}+\frac{3}{T-2^{k+1}+1}\right).$$

This completes the proof. □

Theorem 7 can be used to analyze the utility of not only an entire data stream (even an infinite stream by setting $T\to\infty$), but also a segment of a data stream. Since the minimum SSE is achieved when the approximation error is 0, Theorem 7 helps to identify the maximum Laplace error reduction that can be achieved by RG. For example, when $T=63$, the minimum Laplace error is $0.14\cdot\frac{\omega|\mathbf{H}|}{\epsilon_2^2}$. When $\epsilon_2=0.9\epsilon$, which is our experimental setting, the minimum Laplace error is just 8.6% of the Laplace error introduced by Baseline (which is $\frac{2\omega|\mathbf{H}|}{\epsilon^2}$).

When analyzing the utility of RG, we cannot ignore the approximation error, which is another source of error in RG. Due to the data-dependent nature of RG, it is very difficult to precisely quantify the approximation error. But it is helpful to consider the Laplace error reduction as the tolerance of RG for the approximation error. As long as the approximation error is less than the reduction, it is beneficial to use RG. In Section 7, we experimentally show that this is often the case on real-life data.

6.2 Privacy Analysis

To establish the privacy guarantee of RG, we mainly rely on the two composition properties of differential privacy. Now we give the formal privacy guarantee of RG.

THEOREM 8. *RG is ϵ-differentially private.*

PROOF. By sequential composition property, to prove that RG is ϵ-differentially private, it suffices to independently prove that the sampling-based change monitoring module satisfies ϵ_1-differential privacy and that the continuous histogram publication module satisfies ϵ_2-differential privacy, where $\epsilon=\epsilon_1+\epsilon_2$.

For the sampling-based change monitoring module, since any single event can appear in exactly one time unit, by definition of event-level differential privacy, we can consider the events within different time units as *disjoint* databases no matter how many time units there are in the data stream. By the parallel composition property, if the procedure for processing each time unit is ϵ_1-differentially private, the monitoring module for the entire data stream is still ϵ_1-differentially private. For any time unit, since an event is associated with exactly one bin, we can again apply the parallel composition property, which requires to prove that the noisy count of each bin in the time unit is ϵ_1-differentially private. Note that since the output of the monitoring module is based on raw data, it needs to be properly sanitized even though it does not directly publish its output.

For any bin B_j, we first prove that without sampling adding $\mathtt{Lap}\left(\frac{1}{\ln(e^{\epsilon_1}-1+\gamma_j)-\ln\gamma_j}\right)$ satisfies $(\ln(e^{\epsilon_1}-1+\gamma_j)-\ln\gamma_j)$-differential privacy. This directly follows the fact that the sensitivity of the count query is 1. Note that our method of learning γ_j does not consume any privacy budget as it is based on differentially private results. Now by Theorem 4, we learn that the sampling-based mechanism satisfies ϵ_1-differential privacy because

$$\ln(1+\gamma_j(e^{\ln(e^{\epsilon_1}-1+\gamma_j)-\ln\gamma_j}-1))=\epsilon_1.$$

Table 1: Dataset statistics

Dataset	Event no.	$\lvert\mathbf{H}\rvert$	Timestamp no.
World Cup	1,352,804,107	88,762	[176, 2112]
Traffic	8,107,643	342	[168, 1008]

Next we prove that the continuous histogram publication module is ϵ_2-differentially private. Establishing the privacy guarantee of the publication module is more tricky as we issue queries that span over several time units, and therefore we cannot treat the events in different time units as disjoint databases. But the fact that an event can fall into exactly one bin still holds. Therefore, by parallel composition, it suffices to prove that all noisy answers to all queries over any bin gives ϵ_2-differential privacy. We establish the proof by transforming all these queries into a standard Laplace mechanism. For each bin, we ask two types of queries: in Line 4 of Algorithm 1, we issue a count query to obtain the noisy count in the current time unit; in Line 9, we issue a query to obtain the noisy average of a retroactive group. By Theorem 5, the latter is equivalent to a sum query: what is the sum of the counts in a retroactive group, as the group size can be learned from the differentially private results. By design, no event can be involved in more than one of these queries because no time unit is involved in more than one query. It can be verified that for all these count and sum queries, a single event can change only one of the answers by exactly 1. Therefore, due to Theorem 1, the publication module is ϵ_2-differentially private. □

6.3 Space and Time Complexity

For real-time stream processing, the space complexity and time complexity of an algorithm are very important factors to consider. For the space complexity, RG never requires to store the entire data stream. At any timestamp, it only needs to store the events in the current time unit, the noisy counts of the past $\omega-1$ time units and the retroactive groups for all bins. Let n be the number of events in the current time unit and m_{max} be the maximum group size over the data stream. It is easy to verify that the space complexity is $O(n+(m_{max}+\omega)|\mathbf{H}|)$. In practice, m_{max} and ω are normally small numbers (compared to n and $|\mathbf{H}|$).

The time complexity of RG for each publication can be derived from Algorithm 1. In the monitoring module, for each bin, we calculate its sampling rate, where the runtime cost is $O(1)$. For each coming event we perform a Bernoulli trial to decide whether to include it in the sample. Therefore, the time complexity of the monitoring module is $O(n+|\mathbf{H}|)$, where n is the number of events arriving in the current time unit and $|\mathbf{H}|$ is the number of bins. In the publication module, in the worst case, for each bin, we need to sum all elements in its retroactive group and sum the noisy counts of the ω time units in the sliding window. The time complexity of processing all bins is $O\left((m_{max}+\omega)|\mathbf{H}|\right)$. The total time complexity is then $O\left(n+(m_{max}+\omega+1)|\mathbf{H}|\right)$.

As such, our sanitization framework introduces only a small space and time overhead and is suitable for processing large-scale real-time data streams.

7. EXPERIMENTAL EVALUATION

In this section, we empirically study the utility and scalability of our solution RG. For comparison reasons, we adapt the state-of-the-art techniques to our problem setting, including FAST [10] and BA [13]. We also implement Baseline

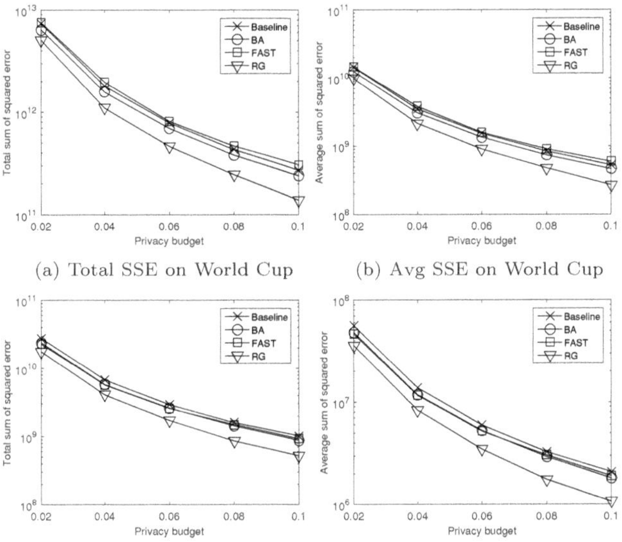

(a) Total SSE on World Cup (b) Avg SSE on World Cup

(c) Total SSE on Traffic (d) Avg SSE on Traffic

Figure 3: Error vs. privacy budget

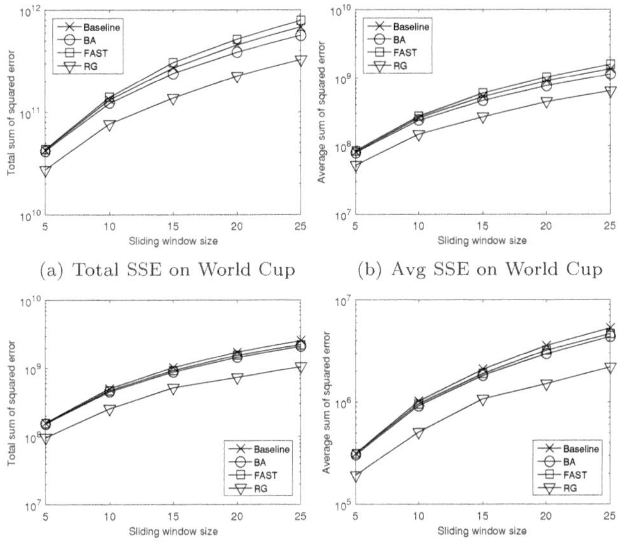

(a) Total SSE on World Cup (b) Avg SSE on World Cup

(c) Total SSE on Traffic (d) Avg SSE on Traffic

Figure 4: Error vs. sliding window size

introduced in Section 4.2. All methods are implemented in Java and tested on a machine with an Intel i7 2.40GHz CPU and 8GB RAM. In each experiment, every algorithm is executed 10 times, and the average is reported.

We use two real datasets in our experiments. The World Cup dataset[4] contains 1,352,804,107 requests made to the 1998 World Cup Web site in 88 consecutive days. After removing some irregular URLs, it contains 88,762 unique URLs, each being considered a bin. The Traffic dataset [7] contains passengers' 8,107,643 visits to 342 stations in the Montreal transportation system within one week. Similar to [13], we consider the number of timestamps as a variable parameter for investigation. The statistics of the datasets are summarized in Table 1. Unless explicitly specified, the default values of the parameters are set as follows: $\epsilon = 0.1$, $\epsilon_1 = 0.1\epsilon$, $\epsilon_2 = 0.9\epsilon$, $w = 15$, and the numbers of timestamps are 528 for World Cup and 504 for Traffic, respectively.

7.1 Utility Results

In our first set of experiments, we study the effect of privacy budget on all approaches. The total and average SSEs under different privacy budgets are reported in Figure 3. Note that the y-axis has a logarithmic scale. In general, the error decreases with the increase of privacy budget. As can be observed, RG substantially outperforms all competitors in all cases. RG can improve the accuracy of the second best approach by up to 43%.

Figure 4 presents the errors under different sliding window sizes. With the increase of the sliding window size, the error increases. Since all these approaches are essentially time unit based perturbation, including more time units in a sliding window results in a larger error. Also for this reason, the improvement of RG becomes more obvious with the increase of the sliding window size.

In the next set of experiments, we study the effect of the number of timestamps in Figure 5. This is equivalent to examining the effect of the magnitude of changes over time.

[4]Publicly available at: `http://ita.ee.lbl.gov/html/contrib/WorldCup.html`

Since more timestamps means more publications, the total SSE increases accordingly. More interesting observations are from the average SSE. The average SSE of `Baseline` is quite stable under different numbers of timestamps. This is because the Laplace noise injected by `Baseline` is independent of the underlying data (i.e., it is calibrated by the sensitivity and the privacy budget, not the underlying data). In contrast, the other approaches all benefit from the increase of the number of timestamps or equivalently the reduced changes between consecutive time units. In particular, for RG, having more timestamps implies a slower evolution, which in turn entitles more chances of applying retroactive grouping to reduce noise. Again, in all cases, RG performs significantly better than the other approaches.

7.2 Scalability Results

According to our theoretical analysis, the space complexity of RG is very small. Due to the space limit, we only report the results on the time complexity. We study the runtime of RG w.r.t the two dominating factors, namely the number of events and the number of bins. Figure 6 shows the runtimes of different approaches under different numbers of events. To form the test datasets, we uniformly select a percentage of total events at random. The runtime of `Fast` is too large to fit into the figures and therefore is omitted. The units of the y-axis are *millisecond* and *microseconds* in Figure 6(a) and (b), respectively. While larger than `Baseline` and `BA`, the runtime of RG is in general negligible: in the worst case the runtime per publication is less than 700 milliseconds on World Cup and less than 1 millisecond on Traffic. Also, the runtime of RG grows linearly with the number of events, conforming to our theoretical analysis. The runtimes for different bin numbers are shown in Figure 7. Again the results of `FAST` are omitted for the same reason. Similarly, we generate the test datasets by randomly extracting a percentage of bins. We can observe the expected trends on both World Cup and Traffic: the runtime is very small and increases linearly with the number of bins.

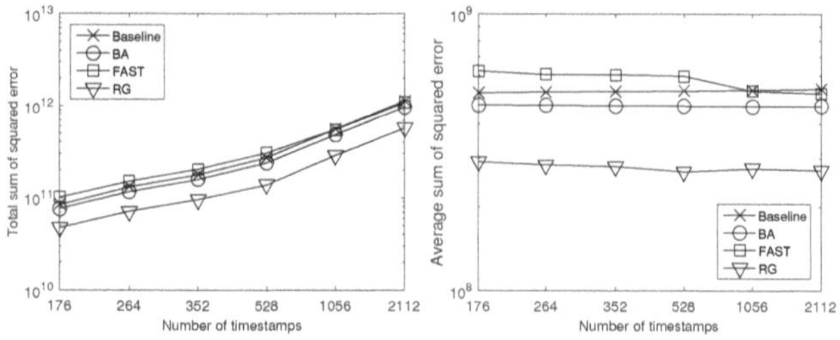

(a) Total SSE on World Cup (b) Avg SSE on World Cup

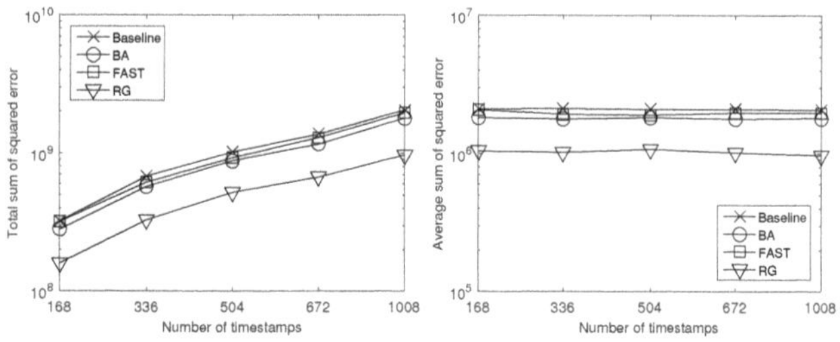

(c) Total SSE on Traffic (d) Avg SSE on Traffic

Figure 5: Error vs. number of timestamps

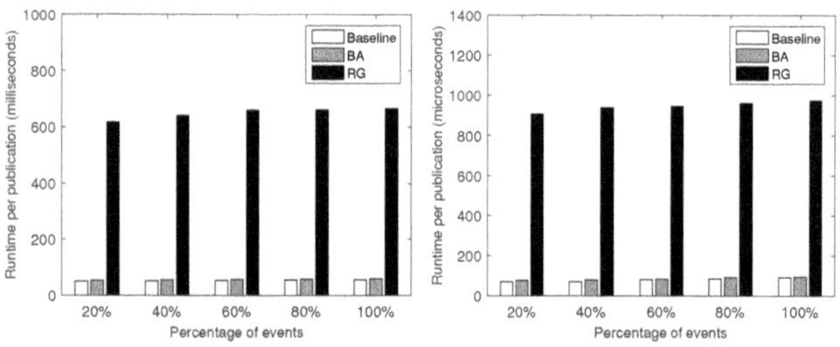

(a) Runtime on World Cup (b) Runtime on Traffic

Figure 6: Runtime vs. number of events

Finally, we would also like to note that since RG processes each bin independently, we can easily and substantially improve its runtime by parallel computing techniques.

8. CONCLUSION

In this paper, we consider the problem of continuously publishing histograms over an infinite data stream while satisfying differential privacy. We propose a novel sanitization framework consisting of two modules. The sampling-based monitoring module performs Bernoulli sampling by carefully quantifying the sampling error; the continuous publication module is equipped with a novel retroactive grouping technique to effectively reduce error. Our solution incurs a very small space and time overhead. Experiments over real datasets show that our framework outperforms the state-of-the-art competitors.

9. REFERENCES

[1] G. Acs, C. Castelluccia, and R. Chen. Differentially private histogram publishing through lossy compression. In *ICDM*, 2012.

[2] C. C. Aggarwal. *Data Streams: Models and Algorithms*. Springer, 2007.

[3] J. Bolot, N. Fawaz, S. Muthukrishnan, A. Nikolov, and N. Taft. Private decayed predicate sums on streams. In *ICDT*, 2013.

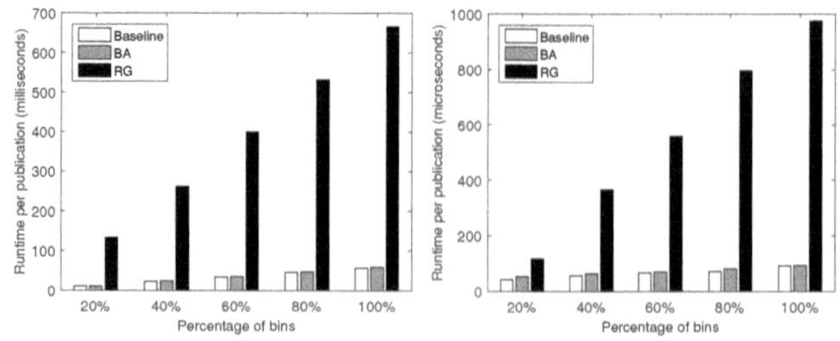

(a) Runtime on World Cup (b) Runtime on Traffic

Figure 7: Runtime vs. number of bins

[4] J. Cao, X. Qian, G. Ghinita, N. Li, E. Bertino, and K.-L. Tan. Efficient and accurate strategies for differentially-private sliding window queries. In *EDBT*, 2013.

[5] T.-H. H. Chan, M. Li, E. Shi, and W. Xu. Differentially private continual monitoring of heavy hitters from distributed streams. In *PETS*, 2012.

[6] T.-H. H. Chan, E. Shi, and D. Song. Private and continual release of statistics. *TISSEC*, 14(3):6, 2011.

[7] R. Chen, G. Acs, and C. Castelluccia. Differentially private sequential data publication via variable-length n-grams. In *CCS*, 2012.

[8] C. Dwork, F. McSherry, K. Nissim, and A. Smith. Calibrating noise to sensitivity in private data analysis. In *TCC*, 2006.

[9] C. Dwork, M. Naor, T. Pitassi, and G. N. Rothblum. Differential privacy under continual observation. In *STOC*, 2010.

[10] L. Fan and L. Xiong. An adaptive approach to real-time aggregate monitoring with differential privacy. *TKDE*, 26(9):2094–2106, 2014.

[11] A. Friedman, I. Sharfman, D. Keren, and A. Schuster. Privacy-preserving distributed stream monitoring. In *NDSS*, 2014.

[12] G. Kellaris and S. Papadopoulos. Practical differential privacy via grouping and smoothing. *PVLDB*, 6(5):301–312, 2013.

[13] G. Kellaris, S. Papadopoulos, X. Xiao, and D. Papadias. Differentially private event sequences over infinite streams. *PVLDB*, 7(12):1155–1166, 2014.

[14] C. Li, M. Hay, G. Miklau, and Y. Wang. A data- and workload-aware query answering algorithm for range queries under differential privacy. *PVLDB*, 7(5):341–352, 2014.

[15] N. Li, W. H. Qardaji, and D. Su. On sampling, anonymization, and differential privacy or, k-anonymization meets differentail privacy. In *ASIACCS*, 2012.

[16] C.-E. Sarndal, B. Swensson, and J. Vretman. *Model Assisted Survey Sampling*. Springer, 2003.

[17] N. Wang, J. Grossklags, and H. Xu. An online experiment of privacy authorization dialogues for social applications. In *CSCW*, 2013.

[18] J. Xu, Z. Zhang, X. Xiao, Y. Yang, and G. Yu. Differentially private histogram publication. In *ICDE*, 2012.

[19] X. Zhang, R. Chen, J. Xu, X. Meng, and Y. Xie. Towards accurate histogram publication under differential privacy. In *SDM*, 2014.

Parallel Lazy Semi-Naive Bayes Strategies for Effective and Efficient Document Classification

Felipe Viegas, Marcos André Gonçalves
Univ. Federal de Minas Gerais
Computer Science Dep.
Belo Horizonte, Brazil
{frviegas, mgoncalv}@dcc.ufmg.br

Wellington Martins
Univ. Federal de Goiás
Instituto de Informática
Goiânia, Brazil
wellington@inf.ufg.br

Leonardo Rocha
Univ. Federal de São João Del Rei
Computer Science Dep.
São João Del Rei, Brazil
lcrocha@ufsj.edu.br

ABSTRACT

Automatic Document Classification (ADC) is the basis of many important applications such as spam filtering and content organization. Naive Bayes (NB) approaches are a widely used classification paradigm, due to their simplicity, efficiency, absence of parameters and effectiveness. However, they do not present competitive effectiveness when compared to other modern statistical learning methods, such as SVMs. This is related to some characteristics of real document collections, such as class imbalance, feature sparseness and strong relationships among attributes. In this paper, we investigate whether the relaxation of the NB feature independence assumption (aka, Semi-NB approaches) can improve its effectiveness in large text collections. We propose four new Lazy Semi-NB strategies that exploit different ideas for alleviating the NB independence assumption. By being *lazy*, our solutions focus only on the most important features to classify a given test document, overcoming some Semi-NB issues when applied to ADC such as bias towards larger classes and overfitting and/or lack of generalization of the models. We demonstrate that our Lazy Semi-NB proposals can produce superior effectiveness when compared to state-of-the-art ADC classifiers such as SVM and KNN. Moreover, to overcome some efficiency issues of combining Semi-NB and lazy strategies, we take advantage of current manycore GPU architectures and present a massively parallelized version of the Semi-NB approaches. Our experimental results show that speedups of up to 63.36 times can be obtained when compared to serial solutions, making our proposals very practical in real-situations.

Categories and Subject Descriptors

H.3.3 [**Information Search and Retrieval**]: Information Search and Retrieval; I.5.4 [**Applications**]: Text processing;

Keywords

Text Classification; Semi-Naive Bayes; Parallelization

Permission to make digital or hard copies of all or part of this work for personal or classroom use is granted without fee provided that copies are not made or distributed for profit or commercial advantage and that copies bear this notice and the full citation on the first page. Copyrights for components of this work owned by others than ACM must be honored. Abstracting with credit is permitted. To copy otherwise, or republish, to post on servers or to redistribute to lists, requires prior specific permission and/or a fee. Request permissions from Permissions@acm.org.
CIKM'15, October 19–23, 2015, Melbourne, Australia
© 2015 ACM. ISBN 978-1-4503-3794-6/15/10 ...$15.00.
DOI: http://dx.doi.org/10.1145/2806416.2806565.

1. INTRODUCTION

The amount of data created and shared nowadays in all types of platforms reached unprecedented levels, making the organization and the extraction of useful knowledge from this huge amount of data one of the biggest challenges in Computer Science. Machine learning techniques, such as automatic document classification (ADC), have demonstrated to be a viable path towards this goal. Particularly, ADC techniques aim at building effective models capable of associating documents with well-defined semantic categories in an automated way. ADC techniques are the core component of many important applications such as spam filtering [11], organization of topic directories [7], identification of writing styles or authorship [29], among many others.

ADC methods usually exploit a supervised learning paradigm [22], i.e., a classification model is first "learned" using previously labeled documents (training set), and then used to classify unseen documents (the test set). There is a plethora of supervised ADC algorithms available in the literature, such as nearest-neighbor classifiers [27], support vector machines [8], boosting [21] and Bayesian models [17]. In this paper, we focus on the latter approach, due to its simplicity, efficiency, and effectiveness in several scenarios. In particular, we focus on Naive Bayes approaches, the most widely used Bayesian paradigm for text classification.

Although a widely used classification paradigm in ADC, other statistical learning methods, such as SVMs, have presented superior effectiveness when compared to NB approaches. This is related to some characteristics present in real document collections, such as class imbalance, feature sparseness and strong relationship among attributes, that can compromise some of the Naive Bayes premises [19, 14]. The class imbalance problem [18] happens when the number of documents of one or few classes covers most of the documents in a dataset. This naturally introduces a bias in the trained classifier towards assigning most unseen documents to the largest classes, incurring in a poor classification effectiveness in the minority classes, the most important ones in many applications (e.g. email spam, vandalism). The sparseness problem is related to the low frequency of certain features (i.e., terms/words) in some documents [18]. In NB, the conditional probability of a term a_j given a class c_i is estimated using all training documents from c_i in which a_j occurs. Such conditional probabilities may be negatively affected if a_j occurs in only a few documents of a given class, especially in smaller ones (i.e., those with few documents). The NB assumes that each attribute is independent, which actually is a false assumption in most of scenarios. It is unrealistic to expect that this assumption will hold in the real world, as correlations among attributes are common but not captured as dependencies in the NB model, decreasing its classification effectiveness.

There are some proposals in the literature that try to improve the NB effectiveness known as the *Semi-Naive Bayes* methods, which relax the NB attribute independence assumption [17], by reduction of data [5] or, mainly, by means of extensions of the structure of the learning model to represent feature dependencies [9, 12]. These strategies have produced some interesting gains in small datasets, such as those related to bioinformatics [9], but due to their high computational costs, implied by the complexity of representing the term dependencies, they cannot scale to ADC or other large classification tasks. Thus, investigating whether the relaxation of the NB attribute independence assumption is effective in large ADC tasks is still an open problem.

In this context, we introduce four original lazy Semi-NB strategy proposals which exploit the information of the document to be classified to reduce the complexity of the Semi-NB learned model. Our experimental results point out that further improvements can be obtained with these models, depending on some dataset characteristics. Furthermore, in order to make our proposals capable of running in large text collections, all of them are parallelized using graphics processing units (GPUs). Our implementation, exploiting intrinsic aspects of this type of architecture is a novel contribution.

In summary, the main research questions we address in this paper are: (Q1) Are our new Semi-NB proposals capable of improving a robust implementation of NB model? (Q2) Are these proposals competitive with state-of-the-art ADC classifiers such as SVMs? (Q3) Can we design an efficient Semi-NB implementation that allows testing interesting, but very costly, proposals that relax the NB independence assumption in large ADC tasks?

Overall, our main contributions include: (i) the proposal of four new lazy Semi-Naive Bayes approaches specially designed for ADC; (ii) the implementation of well structured GPU-based parallelization of the Semi-NB solutions; (iii) an investigation on the real impact of the NB attribute independence assumption in real text collections using our proposed Semi-NB approaches, thanks to the scalability offered by our GPU-based implementation; (iv) a large experimental evaluation considering many state-of-the-art baselines and representative datasets. Besides the originality of our proposals and investigations, our extensive experimental study is by itself a substantial contribution, as Semi-NB models have not been evaluated in the ADC scenarios we exploit.

The remainder of this paper is organized as follows. Section 2 covers related work. Section 3 describes the traditional NB and its variants, the baseline Semi-NB approaches and basic concepts of parallelism and GPU. Section 4 presents our Semi-NB proposals. Section 5 details our GPU-based Semi-NB implementations. Section 6 describes our experimental evaluations and Section 7 closes the paper.

2. RELATED WORK

The Naive Bayes is one of the most popular machine learning methods. Its simplicity, combined with its efficiency, makes it a very attractive method in various classification scenarios. However, this simplicity in the construction of the classification model can significantly compromise the effectiveness of this method in some scenarios, such as textual document classification. In [19] the authors argue that some characteristics of document collections such as imbalance among classes and data sparsity, significantly compromise the learning model proposed by the traditional NB model (the Multinomial one [17]). The authors also propose a simple heuristic that is based on data transformations and simple adjustments in the construction of the learning model, which was called Transformed Weight-normalized Complement Naive Bayes (TWCNB). The main idea of this heuristic is to perform a number of feature frequency transformations to improve the NB modeling text classification. Following this line, [28] presents another proposal for the construction of the model that combines Multinomial NB with the technique one-versus-all [28], widely used in multiclass classification scenarios. One more recent study shows that smoothing NB may improve the classification performance [1]. The authors applied the concept of linear interpolation smoothing to Naive Bayes Spam Classification. Another research line proposed to make the NB algorithm more effective in ADC is the use of different feature weighting strategies. In [13] the authors propose a per-document length normalization approach by introducing multivariate Poisson model for NB text classification. In addition, the authors propose a weighting method that can improve the effectiveness of the Naive Bayes classification in rare classes. Although not an explicit goal of this paper, we conducted a large investigation on the combination of different models and weighting strategies (described further below) aiming at defining a strong baseline NB baseline to compare with our Semi-NB proposals.

As mentioned earlier, NB is based on the premise that feature occurrences in documents of different classes are independent [17]. The main reason for the adoption of this premise is the time complexity, since the construction of a complete and optimal Bayesian network is an NP-hard problem [6]. Thus, a strategy that has being considered (called semi-Naive Bayes) is based on heuristics that relax the assumption of independence without ensuring the optimal model. The main group of Semi-NB techniques seeks to extend the structure of the NB, approximating it as much as possible to a Bayesian network, either by some latent variables to connect correlated features [9] or by explicitly representing feature dependencies [12]. Interdependencies among features are also allowed, being usually modeled by the z-dependence concept, introduced in [20], in which each feature is considered dependent on the class and on other z features, making possible the construction of Bayesian networks. The Naive Bayes establishes a 0-dependence while most existing methods of this group works with a 1-dependence, such as Tree Augmented Naive Bayes (TAN) [9]. In the case of this latter work, learning is performed using a conditional mutual information of each pair of features, keeping the pairs that increment quality classification the most. The Super Parent TAN (SP-TAN) [12] is a heuristic that extends TAN. The heuristic is greedy and optimizes the search space by correlated features. According to experimental results conducted by the authors, the strategy is more effective than traditional NB. However, due to its high computational cost, in both time and memory consumption, all these strategies have been evaluated only in small datasets, such as small bioinformatics databases. As far as we know, the evaluation of the effectiveness of suppressing this premise in large ADC tasks has not yet been investigated.

In order to make this evaluation computationally feasible, we also present as a contribution of this work a parallelized version of the Naive Bayes method on a many core GPU. GPU-based parallel implementations of classification algorithms have recently called attention of many researchers [16], since these implementations are able to achieve high levels of parallelism and lower power consumption [24]. A first GPU-based parallel implementation of the Naive Bayes was presented in [2], however, despite the good results achieved, it lacked the full exploitation of important GPU resources, such as coalesced memory access and shared memory. Unlike this proposal, the parallel implementation presented in this study achieves high levels of parallelism through better use of GPU memory hierarchy, multiprocessor occupancy and coalesced memory access. In addition, the implementation deals with the semi-Naive Bayes strategies that impose new challenges. In particular, we present new semi-Naive Bayes approaches constituting *lazy* extensions of the work presented in [12], aimed at efficiency and scalability. This allows us to evaluate how the assumption of independence between features limits the effectiveness of the NB algorithm in large ADC tasks.

3. BACKGROUND

For a better understanding of our proposals, in this section we briefly describe the original Naive Bayes algorithm and some of its extensions to better deal with ADC tasks. After, we present details of Semi-NB methods that constitute the basis for our work. And finally, we briefly describe some concepts of parallelism and GPU to facilitate understanding of our parallel strategies.

3.1 Naive Bayes and its Extensions for ADC

The Naive Bayes [17] algorithm is based on probabilistic models. It calculates the "score" of a class c_i as the probability of a document d_t being assigned to class c_i. Based on this score, a class ranking is created and NB assigns d_t to the class in the top of the ranking. More formally, let $P(c_i|d_t)$ be the probability of a test document $d_t(a_1, a_2, \ldots, a_j)$ to belong the the c_i class, where $(a_1, a_2, \ldots, a_j)$ is a feature vector (binary or weighted) representing the term set of document d_t. This probability is calculated using the Bayes Theorem. However, the calculation of $P(c_i|d_t)$ has a high computational cost, given that the number of possible vectors d_t is very high due to the potential number of term dependencies. To attenuate this problem, the NB algorithm assumes that the occurrence of all terms is independent from each other (the NB independence assumption), a simplification that makes the classification problem computationally viable. Thus, $P(c_i|d_t)$ is defined as $P(c_i|d_t) = \frac{P(c_i)\prod_{\forall j \in d_t} P(a_j|c_i)}{P(d_t)}$. By observing the Equation, we see that the fundamental question in the $P(c_i|d_t)$ definition is how to estimate $P(a_j|c_i)$. Thus, we define $P(a_j|c_i) = \frac{Tc_i(a_j)+\alpha}{\sum_{v \in V} Tc_i(v)+\alpha\cdot|\mathbb{V}|}$, where $Tc_i(a_j)$ is the number of occurrences of term a_j in class c_i; $\sum_{v \in V} Tc_i(v)$ is the summation of the occurrences of all terms in documents belonging to c_i and $|\mathbb{V}|$ is the vocabulary size. To avoid inconsistencies (e.g., division by zero), a weighted Laplace smoothing is usually applied, consisting of an addition of an α parameter to the numerator and as a multiplication factor to the vocabulary size in the denominator.

In ADC, the goal is to find the "best" class for d_t, usually defined as the one with the highest conditional probability. To avoid computational precision losses (e.g., due to floating point underflow), it is usually more adequate to add the log of the probabilities instead of performing the previously defined multiplication. Thus, this maximization, in most NB implementations is defined as $c_{NB}(d) = \underset{c_i \in C}{argmax}\left[logP(c_i) + \sum_{j=1}^{|\mathbb{V}|} logP(a_j|c_i)\right]$.

The NB model is the basis of Semi-NB strategies, since most of these strategies initialize their prediction model from the NB. So it is very important to have a robust NB model in order to build effective Semi-NB model. So we re-visit in the literature some strategies that propose adjustments in the NB model, making it more robust for text classification. These strategies are briefly described below:

Interpolated Naive Bayes (INB) [1] combines the Jelinek-Mercer smoothing method with the NB classifier. This smoothing method corresponds to a linear interpolation aimed at balancing two estimates using a *lambda* parameter. The interpolation can balance the estimates of terms given a class c_i along with the estimates of this term in the collection. Thus, we substitute the original formula by

$$c_{INB}(d) = \underset{c_i \in C}{argmax}\left[logP(c_i)\sum_{j=1}^{|\mathbb{V}|} \omega_{j,i}\right], \text{ where} \quad (1)$$
$$\omega_{j,i} = \lambda \cdot logP(a_j) + (1-\lambda)\cdot logP(a_j|c_i)$$

One-versus-All Naive Bayes (OVA NB) [28] combines the *One versus All* (OVA) strategy with the traditional NB classifier. To adapt the OVA strategy to the NB classifier, the complement of the probability for a given class c_i, is used. The complement of the probability of a term a_j in a given class c_i is the information contained in all classes but c_i, i.e., $P(a_j|\bar{c}_i) = \frac{T\bar{c}_i(a_j)+\alpha}{\sum_{v \in V} T\bar{c}_i(v)+\alpha\cdot|\mathbb{V}|}$, where, $T\bar{c}_i(a_j)$ is the number of occurrences of term a_j in all classes but c_i and $\sum_{v \in V} T\bar{c}_i(v)$ is the summation of the number of occurrences of all terms in the documents of all classes, but c_i. Due to imbalance issues, which may be exacerbated by the union of the "negative" classes, the apriori estimate of the class is not used in this model. The OVA-NB classification model is summarized as $c_{OVA}(d) = \underset{c_i \in C}{argmax}\left[\sum_{j=1}^{|\mathbb{V}|} logP(a_j|c_i) - logP(a_j|\bar{c}_i)\right]$.

Complement Naive Bayes (CNB) learning model, exploited in the TWCNB [19] proposal, utilizes only the complement of the probability $P(d_t|c_i)$, instead of using the information from c_i. This complement balances the information used in the learning model, not favoring the majority classes. The formula is : $c_{CNB}(d) = \underset{c_i \in C}{argmax}\left[\sum_{j=1}^{|\mathbb{V}|} -logP(a_j|\bar{c}_i)\right]$.

3.2 Semi-Naive Bayes

Over the years various techniques have been proposed to relax the independence assumption of the original NB models. In [9], the authors compared the Naive Bayes algorithm with Bayesian networks, which are more robust models to represent probability dependencies, since they have no restrictions. Surprisingly in some scenarios, Bayesian networks degraded the quality of classification. Thus, the authors proposed a restricted Bayesian model that combines the ability of Bayesian networks to represent dependencies between attributes and the simplicity of Naive Bayes.

This representation, called *Tree Augmented Naive Bayes* (TAN) [9], is defined by a main constraint: attributes may depend on only one other attribute in addition to the class. This restriction makes feasible the probabilistic calculations, since it is computationally very costly to compute multiple dependencies for any given attribute[1]. The classification model can be represented by the following maximization: $c_{TAN}(d) = \underset{c_i}{argmax}\left(P(c_i)\prod_{j=1}^{|\mathbb{V}|} P(a_j|c_i, \pi(a_j))\right)$, where $\pi(a_j)$ is the parent attribute of the attribute a_j.

The Super Parent TAN (SP-TAN) [12] is a variant of TAN, adopting the same representation. However, in order to add dependencies to the NB model, it uses a greedy search method (Hill Climbing Search). The construction of the SP-TAN network is given by the concepts of Super Parent and Favorite Child.

- Super Parent (SP): Given a Bayesian network, if we create a dependency to an attribute x for all the orphans attributes, it is called a Super Parent. Orphans attributes are the attributes that have only the class as a parent.
- Favorite Child (FC): If we extend a dependency of a Super Parent for each orphan and evaluate the quality of each dependence individually, the attribute that improves accuracy the most is the Favorite Child.

The choice of SP and FC attributes are conducted using a validation set, since the heuristic uses a prediction metric for evaluating the classification quality of the networks built by each candidate as SP. Thus, all dependencies are selected through this validation set and subsequently evaluated on the test set.

SP-TAN produced some gains compared with the traditional NB [12] in small datasets. However, when applied to real-world scenarios, such as large ADC datasets, this technique tends to lose performance due to overfitting issues caused by the strong dependencies found only in the validation set. Moreover, the two strategies (TAN and SP-TAN) are extremely costly in terms of computation time, preventing the execution of these heuristics in large datasets. Despite presenting different approaches to find dependencies between attributes, both strategies have the same time complexity, $O([\mathbb{D}_{train} \times |\mathbb{C}| + \mathbb{D}_{test} \times |\mathbb{C}| + |\mathbb{V}| \times |\mathbb{C}|] \times |\mathbb{V}|^2)$, with $\mathbb{D}_{train}$ being the density[2] of training documents, $\mathbb{D}_{test}$ being the density of test documents, $|\mathbb{C}|$ the number of classes, and $|\mathbb{V}|$ the number of attributes. Although the SP-TAN and TAN heuristics present the same complexity in the worst case, the SP-TAN heuristic has an average case less complex, since its complexity varies according to the number of selected dependencies. Thus, the heuristic only reaches the same complexity of the TAN if $V - 1$ dependencies are found, which is actually difficult to happen, since the SP-TAN tends to select fewer dependencies than TAN, keeping the effectiveness [12].

In here, we propose a heuristic, called *Lazy Super Parent Tree Augmented Naive Bayes* (LSPTAN) that seeks to solve the problems discussed above, enabling the application of a semi-NB techniques in large ADC tasks. Thus, we can evaluate whether the premise of independence among attributes, assumed by NB, impacts effectiveness in large ADC tasks, an open research problem.

[1]We will use the terms *attribute* and *feature* interchangeably, from now on.

[2]density is the sum of length of all documents, i.e. $\sum_{d=1}^{\mathbb{D}} V_d$

3.3 Parallelism and the GPU

Over the last years, the computer industry has shifted from pushing clock frequency to parallelism. Rather than increasing the speed of its individual processor cores, traditional CPUs (Central Processing Units) have increased the number of cores (multi-core processors) as the primary basis for increasing system performance. This trend has also been followed by many core GPU (Graphics Processing Unit) chips which have now thousands of processing cores. The general perception is that processors are not getting faster, but instead are getting wider, and the only way to improve performance is through the exploitation of parallelism.

CPUs are optimized for low-latency access and excel in running single-threaded processes whereas GPUs are optimized for high throughput and can deal with massive multi-threaded parallelism. GPUs can handle massive amounts of data, which is critical for Information Retrieval (IR), however its different architecture and memory hierarchy requires the design of novel algorithms and new implementation approaches. This situation has hampered the exploitation of this opportunity by the IR community. However, recent works on Database Scalability, Document Clustering and Learning to Rank [4, 23, 26] have produced some encouraging results.

GPUs are specialized architectures originally intended for graphics computations. However since mid-2000s they became a powerful accelerator for general purpose computing (GPGPU). Due to their high computation power and improved programmability, they became increasingly used for high performance scientific computing and, more recently, for big data analytics.

The GPU architecture has two levels of parallelism, wherein the first level there are P streaming multiprocessors (SMs) and within each multiprocessor there are p streaming processors (SPs). Thus a parallel program can be first divided into blocks of computation that can run independently on the P SMs (fat cores), without communicating with each other. These blocks, in turn, have to be further divided into smaller tasks (threads) that execute on the SPs (thin cores), but with each thread being able to communicate with other threads in the same block. Each of these threads has access to a larger global memory as well as to a small but fast shared memory and registers.

The GPU supports thousands of light-weight concurrent threads and, unlike the CPU threads, the overhead of creation and switching is negligible. To hide the high latency of the global memory, it is important to have more threads than the number of SPs and to have threads accessing consecutive memory addresses that can be easily coalesced. Another important data movement channel is the PCIExpress connection, whereby CPU and GPU can exchange data between each one's address space but in a much slower speed. The GPU programming model requires that part of the application runs on the CPU while the computationally-intensive part is accelerated by the GPU.

A GPU program exposes parallelism through a data-parallel SPMD (Single Program Multiple Data) special function, called kernel function. During implementation, the programmer can configure the number of threads to be used. Threads execute data parallel computations of the kernel and are organized in groups (thread blocks) that are further organized into a grid structure. When a kernel is launched, the blocks within a grid are distributed on idle SMs while the threads are mapped to the SPs.

4. LAZY SUPER PARENT TREE AUGUMENTED NAIVE BAYES (LSPTAN)

Our Lazy Super Parent TAN (LSPTAN) heuristic is a *postergated* version of the SP-TAN that constructs a *Tree Augmented Naive Bayes* for each test example. Dependencies between attributes are generated based on information from the example that is being classified. To build this version we adapted the method of evaluation and the selection of candidates for Super Parents and Favorite Children.

The SP-TAN algorithm exploits accuracy to select a candidate to SP (a_{sp}). In our strategy, we select the candidate a_{sp} whose classification model generates the highest probability $P(d_t|c_i, a_{sp})$ for the document d_t. Thus, each candidate a_{sp} builds its own model and classifies the document d_t, returning the predicted class c_i and its respective score $P(d_t|c_i, a_{sp})$. Based on the best scores for each candidate a_{sp}, we build a prediction score rank. This heuristic selects as best a_{sp} the attribute that holds the first position of this rank using the information of the (test) document being classified. This helps to reduce the number of candidates to SP and Favorite Child, scaling the overall classification process.

Building a Tree Augmented Naive Bayes for each test example is computationally expensive. Therefore, the LSPTAN builds a simpler network than SP-TAN. We select only the best SP to a test document. But there is no limitation for the choice of the Favorite Children. Thus, all the children attributes that increment the probability that the document belongs to a class, are included in the classification model.

The LSPTAN heuristic initially builds the model based on NB and initializes a set of orphans O, inserting into O all the attributes of the vocabulary. For each test document, the technique evaluates each attribute as a SP and, in the end, it selects as a_{sp} the attribute that has the highest probability $P(d_t|c_i, a_{sp})$. The next step is to find the Favorite Children of the SP attribute. Each attribute a_j is individually evaluated given the a_{sp} and subsequently selected as FC considering if the possible dependence of a_{sp} for a_j $(sp \neq j)$ increases the probability of the document belonging to class c_i.

We also propose three novel strategies that exploit different ideas for building a LSPTAN model. These strategies are described below:

The **LSPTAN**$_{SP}$ is a simpler strategy that does not select the Favorite Children. The idea is to analyze the impact of only selecting the best candidate to SP of all attributes without their children. This strategy has the potential to be much more efficient and scalable, although less effective in theory, since it captures less information in the model.

The **LSPTAN**$_{Class}$ is very similar to the strategy presented previously. So it uses the same method of evaluation and selection of candidates of the LSPTAN, however, this strategy selects a SP for each class. There is no limitation for the number of Favorite Children selected. The idea of this strategy is to capture the dependencies between attributes in each class. Thus, we give a chance to other SP candidates to increase their relevance when related only to their Favorite Children. The **LSPTAN**$_{class}$ heuristic initially builds the model based on NB and initializes a set of orphans O, inserting into O all the attributes of the vocabulary. Then, for each test document, the technique evaluates each attribute as a SP and, in the end, for each class c_i it selects as a_{sp} the attribute that has the highest probability $P(d_t|c_i, a_{sp})$ for the class c_i. In the end of this step, $|\mathbb{C}|$ a_{sp} attributes will be selected. The next step is to find the Favorite Children of each SP attribute. Each attribute is individually evaluated given the a_{sp} $(P(a_j|c_i, a_{sp}))$ and subsequently selected as FC considering if the possible dependence of a_{sp} for a_j $(sp \neq i)$ increases the probability of the document belonging to class c_i.

The **LSPTAN**$_{Restricted}$ is a more efficient version of LSPTAN, in which the SP candidates are evaluated with their Favorite Children. In this strategy, Favorite Children are the attributes that have $P(a_j|c_i, a_{sp})$ higher than the probability $P(a_j|c_i)$. Therefore, the SP candidates are associated with their Favorite Children rather than being associated with all orphans attributes. So, only the dependencies between attributes that increase the probability of a document belonging to a class c_i are included in the classification model. The SP candidates also have a restriction: they must exist in the test document in order to be chosen as the best SP. Thus, we limit the search space of candidates, avoiding that a very informative candidate (probably belonging of a majority class) is chosen.

The **LSPTAN**$_{Restricted}$ heuristic initially builds the model based on NB and initializes a set of orphans O, inserting into O all the attributes of the vocabulary. For each test document, the technique evaluates each attribute which belongs to the test document as a SP and it selects as a_{sp} the attribute that has the highest probability $P(d_t|c_i, a_{sp})$ for the class c_i. The next step is to find the Favorite Children of each SP attribute. Each attribute is individually evaluated given the a_{sp} $(P(a_j|c_i, a_{sp}))$ and subsequently selected as FC considering if the possible dependence of a_{sp} for a_j $(sp \neq j)$ respect the condition of $P(a_j|c_i, a_{sp}) > P(a_j|c_i)$.

5. PROPOSED IMPLEMENTATION

The Semi-NB (LSPTAN) heuristic presents many opportunities for a highly parallel GPU implementation. Since the LSPTAN is an extension of the Naive Bayes, the terms of a document can be processed independently, both the model generation and the classification task phases can take advantage of the high computational power of GPUs. The LSPTAN strategy opens up new opportunities for exploiting parallelism in a massive multi-threaded way. In this section we present our proposal of a new version of Semi-NB parallelized using Graphics Processors Units (GPU), which corresponds to another contribution of this paper.

5.1 Indexing Data

Given that document collections are usually sparse, with terms occurring in a few documents, we chose to represent the documents by a compact data structure. For this, we used four vectors: $docIndexVector$ representing the documents; $docAttributeVector$ that stores the attributes of each document; $docValueVector$ that stores the weights of the attributes for each document; and finally, $docClass$ that stores the classes of all documents. At $docIndexVector$ the index represents the document, and in each position of this vector we store the position where the list of terms of the document begins in vector $docAttributeVector$ and the frequency in the vector $docValueVector$. At $docClass$ each index also represents a document, and each position stores the respective document class.

Figure 1 shows an example of the data structure used. As can be seen, the document 0 of the database, starts its list of terms at the index 0 of the vector *docAttributeVector* and has two terms (terms 0 and 1), each of which has frequency equal to 1 as can be seen in vector *docValueVector*. In turn, the document 4 begins its list of terms in the position 8 of the vectors *docAttributeVector* and *docValueVector* and has only the term 1, with frequency also equal to 3. The document classes are in the vector *docClass*, where the documents 0 and 4 have classes 0 and 1 respectively.

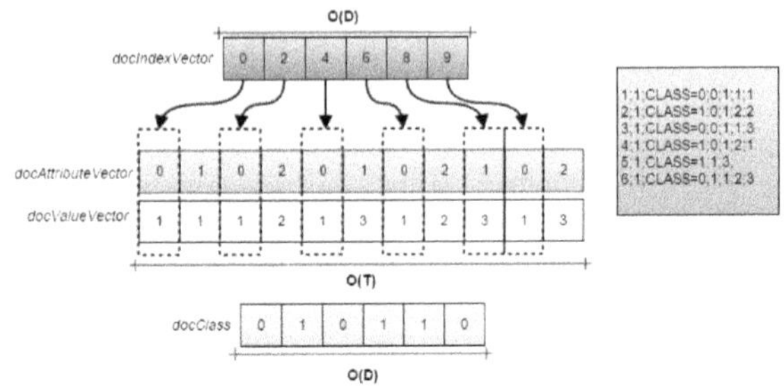

Figure 1: Data structure to represent the documents

5.2 LSPTAN GPU Implementation

Our parallelization proposal for the LSPTAN strategy is based on eight kernels implemented using the C language in CUDA. Kernel is the name given to the functions that run on the GPU. These kernels exploit the maximum possible parallelism, minimizing data dependencies between threads. It also focuses on maximizing the amount of computation performed by each thread. Since the computation of each SP and FC candidates can be done independently (as well as the actual classification) for each test document, the problem takes full advantage of the GPU parallelism. The following describes the parallelization strategy used to implement the eight kernels on the GPU:

1. Naive Bayes model: Given the frequencies of the terms occurred in the classes and the test documents data, the classification of the test documents can be performed in parallel. Thus, given a test document, each thread is responsible for calculating the conditional probability $P(a_j|c_i)$ of an attribute a_j for each class c_i, cooperating to produce the INB model described in Section 3.1.

2. Cumulative frequency of the attributes give the SP candidates within the classes: This kernel is responsible for computing the summation of occurrences of all terms in documents that occur together with the respective SP candidate in each class, i.e., $\sum_{v\in|\mathbb{V}|} Tc_i, a_{sp}(v)$. Since there is no dependency between the SP candidates, this kernel can take full advantage of the GPU parallelism. While reading the training documents data, each thread is associated with a SP candidate. Thus, each thread computes the cumulative frequency for each class.

3. Finding the documents having SP candidates: In text collections, usually (basically always) the documents do not have all the vocabulary words. Thus, this kernel is responsible for selecting the training documents data that have the SP candidates. While reading the training documents data, each thread is responsible for checking the respective term as a SP candidate. If one of the threads finds the SP candidate, the training document is tagged. These tagged documents will be used in the next kernel.

4. Computing the frequency of the attributes given the SP candidate: Once a candidate attribute is selected as a SP, this kernel computes the frequency of the attributes given the SP for each class, i.e., $Tc_i, a_{sp}(a_j)$.

5. Calculation of the probabilities of the terms in the classes given a SP: It calculates the conditional probability of the attributes given the SP for each class. Thus, each thread is responsible for computing the conditional probability of an attribute a_j given the SP candidate a_{sp} for each class, $P(a_j|c_i, a_{sp})= \frac{Tc_i, a_{sp}(a_j)+\alpha}{\sum_{v\in V} Tc_i, a_{sp}(v)+\alpha\cdot|\mathbb{V}|}$.

6. Construction of the classification model given the SP: Given the probability matrix built in the previous kernel for the SP candidate, this kernel works in the same way that the Naive Bayes kernel does. Thus, given a test document each thread is responsible for calculating the conditional probability $(P(a_j|c_i, a_{sp}))$ of an attribute a_j for each class given the SP candidate and thus cooperating to produce the LSPTAN model. The classification model can be represented by the maximization:

$$
\begin{aligned}
c_{sp}(d) &= \underset{c_i\in C}{argmax}\left[logP(c_i)+\sum_{j=1}^{|\mathbb{V}|}\omega_{j,i,sp}\right], \text{ where}\\
\omega_{j,i,sp} &= \lambda\cdot logP(a_j)+(1-\lambda)\cdot logP(a_j|c_i,a_{sp})
\end{aligned}
$$

7. Construction of the classification model given the SP and the FC: After selecting the best SP, the classification of documents for each Favorite Child can be performed in parallel. Each thread represents a FC candidate. Thus, each thread is responsible for classifying all test documents for a FC candidate for each class given the best SP. The classification model for a FC can be represented by the maximization:

$$
\begin{aligned}
c_{fc}(d) &= \underset{c_i\in C}{argmax}\left[logP(c_i)+\sum_{j=1}^{|\mathbb{V}|}\omega_{j,i,sp}+\omega_{fc,i,sp}\right], \text{ where}\\
\omega_{j,i,sp} &= \lambda\cdot logP(a_j)+(1-\lambda)\cdot logP(a_j|c_i,a_{sp})\\
\omega_{fc,i,sp} &= \lambda\cdot logP(a_{fc})+(1-\lambda)\cdot logP(a_{fc}|c_i,a_{sp})
\end{aligned}
$$

8. Updating of the classification model: After calculating the probabilities of the Favorite Children given the best SP for a test document data, this kernel has the function of updating the model built by NB, adding the probability of the FC given the best SP that increased the model probability. Each thread is responsible for an attribute and only the thread corresponding to a Favorite Child adds its probability to the LSPTAN model.

Figure 2 shows the sequence of execution of the LSPTAN strategies through the kernels. Thus, the LPSTAN_{SP} and $\text{LPSTAN}_{Restricted}$ strategies are faster than the other LSPTAN strategies because they only execute until the kernel 6.

5.3 Kernel Optimizations

In this section we present the optimizations applied in the kernels, in order to exploit the maximum parallelism possible, minimizing the dependence of data between threads. It also focuses on maximizing the amount of computation performed by each thread.

The kernels 1 and 6 exploit two levels of parallelism. In the first, it associates a block of threads with each test document and, at the second level, each of these threads is associated with a term of the same document. Thus, each block is responsible for classifying a specific test document while each thread of the block is responsible for calculating the probability of an attribute for each class, cooperating to produce the NB model. If the number of attributes is greater than the number of threads of a block, the document is split into k parts, where k is the rounded up ratio between the number of attributes of the document and the number of threads in the block. Then, each k part is calculated one at a time, in a round robin fashion, and the results are accumulated. As for the calculation of the logarithmic summation of the classification model, we implemented a binary tree parallel reduction using shared memory. Therefore, we allocated an array in shared memory whose size is equal to the number of threads in the block. Then, each thread stores the conditional probability in its respective position in the shared memory vector. The vector is divided into two sub vectors and then these sub-vectors are added. The process is repeated until the first position of the vector contains the total sum of the logarithms.

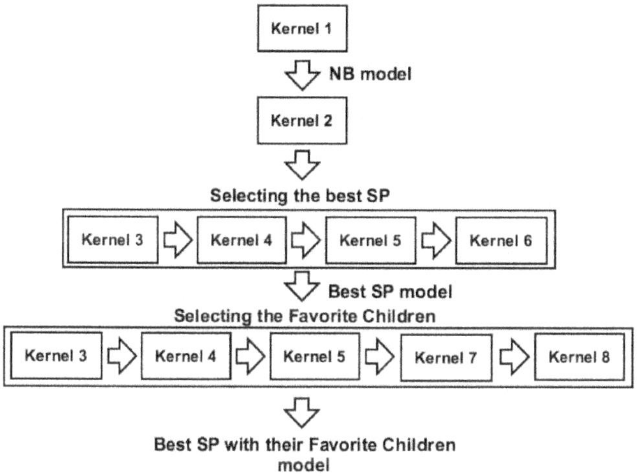

Figure 2: Execution of the kernels

The kernels 3 and 4 also exploit two levels of parallelism: the first associates a block of threads to training documents and, at the second level, each of the thread is associated with a term of the same document. Thus, in the second level, each kernel performs their respective roles, as described previously. In the kernel 4 as we are calculating the overall frequency of the attributes given the SP candidate in each class, we use the *atomicAdd* CUDA function to prevent access conflicts.

5.4 Complexity Analysis of the Solution

In this section we analyze the amount of time used to learn and evaluate the SP candidates, and then the amount of time used to select the Favorite Children of the best selected SP. The first step of learning a model given the SP candidate is based on computing the attribute frequencies in order to build the probability table for each class given the candidate. These frequencies are obtained in kernels 2 and 4. During the execution of these kernels, the training documents data D_{train} are read in parallel, while each thread block is responsible for a document. However, as described in section 3.3, the GPU has only a few (P) multiprocessors (SMs) and so there will be more thread blocks than SMs. Although the GPU does the block scheduling automatically, the parallelism is limited to P multiprocessors. In addition, inside each SM there are only p processors (SPs) which again limits the second level of parallelism, inside each SM, to a total of p processors. Therefore, the time spent in the kernels 3 and 4 is given by $\delta_3 = \delta_4 = O(\sum_{d=1}^{\frac{D_{train}}{P}} \frac{V_d}{p})$, where V_d is the document vocabulary whose terms are processed in as many steps of p threads as needed. The time spent in the kernel 2 is given by $\delta_2 = O(\frac{V}{P \times p} \times \sum_{d=1}^{D_{test}} V_d^2 \times C)$. This kernel must perform two passes over the vocabulary, first to check if the SP candidate belongs in the document and, if so, to compute the attribute frequencies.

After computing all the frequencies, the next step is to build the probability table given the SP candidate. This probability table is two-dimensional: vocabulary by class ($V \times C$). The time spent to build this table is $\delta_5 = O(\frac{V}{P \times p} \times C)$, because each thread is responsible for an attribute. Since we are working with real collections, it is not feasible in terms of memory space to build a three-dimensional table ($SP \times V \times C$), that stores the probability of all the SP candidates. We have a trade-off between space and time. So we have to update this probability table and the respective attribute frequencies (kernel4) whenever the strategy needs to evaluate a new candidate.

The next step consists in building the classification model (Bayesian network) for each test document given the SP candidate for each class. The time spent to build the classification model for the test documents is very similar to the time spent to compute the attribute frequencies given the SP candidate in the kernels 3 and 4, because we use the same two-level parallelism strategy. However, in this case test documents data D_{test} are read (instead of training documents data) for each class. The time[3] spent in this step is $\delta_1 = \delta_6 = O(\sum_{d=1}^{\frac{D_{test}}{P}} \frac{V_d}{p} \times C)$.

Once all the SP candidates are evaluated and the best SP is selected, the Favorite Children must be selected. For this, we must compute the attribute frequencies and build the probability table for the best SP. Then, the classification models are built considering only the dependencies between a FC attribute and its respective SP. Thus the time spent to evaluate all Favorite Children candidates is $\delta_7 = O(\frac{V}{P \times p} \times \sum_{d=1}^{D_{test}} V_d \times C)$, with each thread being responsible for each Favorite Child candidate. When a FC candidate is selected, the classification model must be updated. So the time spent to update the model is $\delta_8 = O(\frac{V_d}{P \times p})$.

The complexity of LSPTAN$_{SP}$ and LSPTAN$_{Restricted}$ is summarized by the time spent in finding the best SP attribute which is $O([\delta_3 + \delta_4 + \delta_5 + \delta_6] \times |\mathbb{V}|)$. The LSPTAN and LSPTAN$_{Class}$ are a bit slower with total time corresponding to $O(\delta_3 + \delta_4 + \delta_5 + \delta_7 + |\mathbb{V}| \times \delta_8)$ to select the FC attributes.

6. EXPERIMENTAL EVALUATION

6.1 Datasets

In order to evaluate the proposed combinations, we consider five real-world textual datasets, namely, 20 Newsgroups, Four Universities, Reuters, ACM Digital Library and RCV1 datasets. For all, we performed a traditional reprocessing task: we removed stop-words, using the standard SMART list, and applied a simple feature selection by removing terms with low "document frequency (DF)"[4]. Next, we give a brief description of each dataset.

4 Universities (4UNI), a.k.a, WebKB this dataset contains Web pages collected from Computer Science departments of four universities by the Carnegie Mellon University (CMU) text learning group. There is a total of 8,277

[3]The kernels 1 and 6 have the same complexity, because they exploit the same parallelism strategy, the only difference lies on the probabilities used to build the learning model.

[4]We removed all terms with DF ≤ 2

web pages, classified in 7 categories (such as student, faculty, course and project web pages).

Reuters (REUT90) this is a classical text dataset, composed by news articles collected and annotated by Carnegie Group, Inc. and Reuters, Ltd. We consider here a set of 13,327 articles, classified into 90 categories.

ACM-DL (ACM) a subset of the ACM Digital Library with 24,897 documents containing articles related to Computer Science. We considered only the first level of the taxonomy adopted by ACM, whereas each document is assigned to one of 11 classes.

20 Newsgroups (20NG) this dataset containing 18,805 newsgroup documents, partitioned almost evenly across 20 different newsgroups categories. 20NG has become a popular dataset for experiments in text applications of machine learning techniques.

RCV1 Uni The Reuters Corpus Volume 1 (RCV1) is a dataset with 804,427 English language news stories. We considered the complete topics taxonomy comprised of 103 classes. However, the original RCV1 is a multilabel dataset with the multilabel cases needing special treatment, such as score thresholding, etc. (see [15] for details). As our current focus is on unilabel tasks, to allow a fair comparison among the other datasets (which are also unilabel) and all baselines (which also focus on unilabel tasks), we decided to transform all multilabel cases into unilabel ones. In order to this fairly, we randomly selecting,among all documents with more than one label, a single label to be attached to that document. This procedure was applied in about 20% of the documents of RCV1 which happened to be multilabel.

Collections	Classes	# Attributes	# Documents	Density
4UNI	7	40,195	8,277	139.275
REUT90	90	19,590	13,327	77.1646
20NG	20	61,050	18,805	129.511
ACM	11	56,449	24,897	27.687
RCV1 Uni	103	134,932	804,427	78.1334

Table 1: General information on the data collections.

6.2 Experimental Setup

The LSPTAN strategies were compared using micro averaged F_1 (MicF_1) and macro averaged F_1 (MacF_1), standard information retrieval measures [27]. While the MicF_1 measures the classification effectiveness over all decisions (i.e., the pooled contingency tables of all classes), the MacF_1 measures the classification effectiveness for each individual class and averages them. All experiments were executed using a 5−fold cross-validation [3] procedure. The parameters were set via cross-validation on the training set[5], and the effectiveness of the algorithms, running with distinct types of features, were measured in the test partition. All experiments were run on a Quad-Core Intel Xeon E5620, running at 2.4GHz, with 16Gb RAM. The GPU experiments were run on a GeForce GTX TITAN Black, with 6Gb RAM.

We would like to point out that some of the results obtained in some datasets may differ from the ones reported in other works for the same datasets (e.g., [13, 19, 10]). Such discrepancies may be due to several factors such as differences in dataset preparation[6], the use of different splits of the datasets (e.g., some datasets have "default splits" such as REUT and RCV1[7]), the application of some score thresholding, such as SCUT, PCUT, etc., which, besides being an important step for multilabel problems, also affects classification performance by minimizing class imbalance effects, among other factors. We would like to stress that we ran all alternatives under the same conditions in all datasets, using standardized and well accepted cross-validation procedures that optimize parameters for each alternatives, and applying the proper statistical tools for the analysis of the results. All our datasets are available for others to replicate our results and test different configurations.

In order to evaluate the performance of our LSPTAN approaches, we compare then with SVM and KNN classifiers. Regarding SVM classifier, we adopt the LIBLINEAR [8] implementation on which the regularization parameter was chosen among eleven values from 2^{-5} to 2^{15} by using 5−fold cross-validation on each training dataset. In the KNN classifier, the size of neighborhood was set via cross-validation in the training set.

We also conduct controlled experiment to evaluate the effectiveness of classifiers combined with four different feature weighting schemes. We perform this investigation because previous works have demonstrated that the weighting schemes may have a profound influence in the NB performance [19] .The names and the descriptions of each feature weighting are given as follows: (1) **Term Frequency** measures the number of occurrences of a term in a text document [18]; (2) **Log of Term Frequency** – in collections in which the documents vary widely in size, the use of the logarithm of tf ($log(tf)$), instead of tf, is usually a better option, since the logarithm smoothies the frequency of occurrence of the terms; (3) **TF-IDF** penalizes terms by their document frequency [18]; (3) **Relative Frequency (RF)** is a length normalization method that normalizes the term frequency by dividing it by a normalization factor given by the maximum frequency of a term occurring in any text document of the collection [13], i.e., $RF = \frac{tf_i}{\alpha \cdot avdu + (1-\alpha) \cdot du_j}$, where $avdu$ indicate the average number of unique terms in a document over the collection and du_j means the number of tokens and unique terms in a document d_j. This linear interpolation smooths the length of each document using the characteristics of document collection. As mentioned earlier, the value of the α parameter is obtained with cross-validation in the training set.

6.3 Experimental Evaluation

6.3.1 Effectiveness

We start by demonstrating the effectiveness of the feature weighting schemes combined with the ADC classifiers. For each dataset, we tested the four described feature weighting schemes with KNN, SVM and the four discussed NB variants: the traditional one and its adaptations for the ADC idiosyncrasies. Table 3 presents the best obtained results.

In general, for the NB strategies, either the traditional or its variants, the best weighting scheme was RF. Regarding the NB variants the best one was INB + RF, which surpassed the results of traditional NB with the same weighting scheme. Therefore, as this combination of INB with the RF weighting scheme produced the best results, this will be the "strongest" version of Naive Bayes (hereafter called

[5]In other words, a portion of the training set was separated, as a type of validation set, to be used for parameterization.

[6]For instance, some works do exploit complex feature weighting schemes or feature selection mechanisms that do favor some algorithms in detriment to others.

[7]In fact, we do believe that running experiments only in the default splits is not the best experimental procedure as it does not allow a proper statistical treatment of the results.

Improved-NB) that we will use as the basis to build our lazy Semi-NB strategies. The best overall results for SVM and KNN were obtained using the $log(TF)-IDF$ weighting scheme, therefore these versions will be used as baselines.

We can see in Table 3 that the Improved NB version outperforms or ties with KNN in eight out of ten cases . When compared to SVM, the Improved-NB ties or outperforms this classifier also in eight out of ten cases, loosing in other two (regarding Mic$F$1). In fact, if we look at the Mac$F$1 results, Improved-NB outperformed or tied SVM and KNN in all five datasets. This is consistent with the fact that most of the learning models and weighting scheme adaptations were designed to deal with the class imbalance issue, which tends to favor Mac$F$1.

We present next the experiments performed to evaluate the effectiveness of our Semi-NB strategies. As mentioned before, the original SP-TAN proposal does not scale to the size of the datasets we experiment with, therefore we can not present results for this proposal.

Table 4 shows the results of our four LSPTAN strategies applied on the five real-world textual datasets. We compare our Semi-Naive Bayes strategies with Improved-NB , as we want to know if theses strategies are capable of extending this already strong baseline, improving its classification effectiveness. For comparison purposes, we select the best results of Naive Bayes (Improved-NB). In the $LSPTAN$ column is the strategy that selects the SP attribute and their Favorite Children in a lazy fashion, while the other columns contain the results of the proposed variants. As mentioned before, we initialize the LSPTAN network using the INB model with the RF feature weighting scheme, since this model generated the best results. INB is also the simplest model to be extended when compared to CNB and OVA NB, because it has fewer likelihoods to calculate, besides being the closest to the Multinomial version.

We can see in Table 4 that the best overall strategy was $LSPTAN_{SP}$, tying or improving the Improved-NB results in all ten results. In fact, some MicF1 and specially MacF1 results for 4UNI and RCV1[8] are among the best results ever reported for these datasets, with gains of up to 6.7% in MacroF1 in 4UNI and 12% in MicroF1 for this same dataset. The results of $LSPTAN_{SP}$ over $LSPTAN$ also show that the costly process of selecting the Favorite Children is unnecessary in most cases, helping to scale the technique. We also can observe that the $LSPTAN_{Class}$ reach the best results observed for the LSPTAN for the REUT90 dataset, tying with the Improved-NB. The best results for ACM and 20NG were obtained with for $LSPTAN_{Restricted}$, also with gains over Improved-NB.

We can observe in Table 5 that in nine out of ten cases we find a LSPTAN strategy equal or better than SVM (two ties and seven wins). When compared to KNN, the LSPTAN ties or outperforms this classifier in eight out of ten cases (one tie and seven wins). Overall, we can conclude that taking into account "some" dependencies (e.g., based on Super Parents and Favorite Children) may help to improve effectiveness in (large) datasets, depending on their characteristics. However, we were not able to choose the best LSPTAN strategy, since three of the four strategies have proven effective in different datasets.

[8]For RCV1 only, due to its size and high dimensionality, we reduced the training set in about 40% and adopted a constraint applied in [25], in which only features occurring in more than 30 documents are candidates for SP. Even with these limitations, we were able to obtain improvements.

6.4 Efficiency of LSPTAN

Table 2 shows the average time (seconds) to evaluate a SP candidate using our CPU and GPU implementations. Note that the evaluation of the SP candidate includes the building of the predictive model and the actual classification of all test documents. More precisely, we measure the execution time of kernels 1 to 6, where the kernels 3 to 6 are executed for each SP candidate. Since the whole vocabulary (large number of attributes) is evaluated for finding SP candidates, we measure the time to evaluate each candidate in a test fold. Notice that the average time to evaluate a SP candidate is practically the time to compute the attribute frequencies, build the probability table given the candidate and classify all test examples. As can be seen in Table 2, our GPU implementation shows significant speedup, ranging from 8.34 to 63.36 when compared to the sequential implementation.

Collections	CPU	GPU	Speedup
4UNI	0.081 ± 0.0019	0.0038 ± 0.00018	21.45
REUT90	0.96 ± 0.041	0.046 ± 0.0005	20.85
20NG	0.52 ± 0.025	0.0081 ± 0.00004	63.36
ACM	0.079 ± 0.0034	0.0094 ± 0.012	8.34
RCV1 Uni	93.82 ± 3.27	2.36 ± 0.046	39.8

Table 2: Efficiency of the GPU-based implementation in select the best Super Parent - time in seconds.

7. CONCLUSIONS AND FUTURE WORK

In this paper we have provided answers for important research questions regarding the relaxation of the NB attribute independence assumption. The answers for these research questions were mostly positive in the sense that, (i) we were able to propose four original lazy Semi-NB techniques capable to outperform in all the cases a strong implementation of NB, robust to ADC tasks. We also showed that (ii) our four LSPTAN solutions were able to tie or outperform the state-of-the-art textual classifiers: SVM and KNN. In fact, gains of more than 18.5% (MacF1 in REUT90) can be obtained by some of our strategies. Reminding that with our code availability, it is easy to check the best alternatives in a validation set. We also proposed a GPU-based parallel implementation of the LSPTAN strategies. In our proposal, we exploit a very compact data structure to index the documents aiming at minimizing memory consumption, as well as maximizing the opportunities for massive parallelization of the algorithm in GPUs. In our GPU-based implementation we exploit massive parallelism, minimizing data dependence between threads and maximizing the amount of computation performed by each thread. Thus, (iii) our Semi-NB approaches were able to take full advantage of the proposed parallel implementation since these approaches require intensive computation once the dataset has been transferred to the GPU.

As future work, we intend to investigate more deeply factors that affect the potential gains of using our lazy Semi-NB strategies, depending on the dataset characteristics. We believe this characterization will allow us to propose new improvements in the model structure. We also intend to expand our experimental evaluation adding other popular text classification methods, both eager and lazy, to see how they measure up when compared to our LSPTAN strategies. Finally, we will investigate how Feature Selection may affect the proposed Semi-NB methods, as they may remove dependencies among attributes while increasing efficiency.

Collections	SVM		KNN		RF_u + Traditional NB		Improved NB	
	Mac$F1$	Mic$F1$	Mac$F1$	Mic$F1$	Mac$F1$	Mic$F1$	Mac$F1$	Mic$F1$
4UNI	**56.02 ± 2.02**	70.91 ± 1.9	**58.24 ± 2.92**	**73.78 ± 0.7**	55.84 ± 1.51	63.14 ± 1.37	**57.57 ± 1.54**	64.07 ± 1.11
REUT90	30.38 ± 2.04	65.09 ± 0.21	29.95 ± 1.14	**68.04 ± 0.62**	32.64 ± 2.28	66.03 ± 0.82	**36.02 ± 2**	66.17 ± 0.76
20NG	84.92 ± 0.54	85.1 ± 0.6	88.41 ± 0.27	88.69 ± 0.67	86.6 ± 0.65	87.05 ± 0.63	**89.64 ± 0.6**	**90 ± 0.54**
ACM	58.00 ± 1.33	69.67 ± 0.45	59.75 ± 1.72	71.6 ± 0.46	57.49 ± 0.53	72.89 ± 0.25	**61.57 ± 1.6**	**74.61 ± 0.5**
RCV1 Uni	47.05 ± 0.35	**75.85 ± 0.08**	46.32 ± 0.72	68.23 ± 0.16	51.65 ± 0.89	69.28 ± 0.07	**51.68 ± 0.85**	69.28 ± 0.08

Table 3: Best results of Naive Bayes compared with ADC classifiers

Collections	Improved NB		LSPTAN		$LSPTAN_{SP}$		$LSPTAN_{Class}$		$LSPTAN_{Restricted}$	
	Mac$F1$	Mic$F1$	Mac$F1$	Mic$F1$	Mac$F1$	Mic$F1$	Mac$F1$	Mic$F1$	Mac$F1$	Mic$F1$
4UNI	57.58 ± 1.54	64.07 ± 1.11	**59.91 ± 1.45**	67.38 ± 0.96	**61.48 ± 1.68**	**71.99 ± 1.01**	57.87 ± 1.68	64.08 ± 1.19	59.92 ± 0.89	68.14 ± 1.72
REUT90	**36.02 ± 2**	**66.17 ± 0.76**	31.37 ± 1.39	64.2 ± 0.77	30.86 ± 0.74	63.97 ± 0.77	**36.21 ± 2.11**	**66.57 ± 0.57**	31.41 ± 1.62	63.4 ± 0.68
20NG	**89.64 ± 0.6**	**90 ± 0.54**	**89.66 ± 0.59**	**89.91 ± 0.58**	**89.01 ± 0.38**	**89.25 ± 0.39**	88.95 ± 0.58	89.35 ± 0.5	**90.24 ± 0.56**	**90.42 ± 0.56**
ACM	**61.57 ± 1.6**	74.61 ± 0.5	60.28 ± 0.92	**75.06 ± 0.57**	58.71 ± 0.92	**74.4 ± 0.57**	59.91 ± 0.6	**74.43 ± 0.68**	**63.05 ± 1.47**	**75.65 ± 0.33**
RCV1 Uni	51.68 ± 0.85	69.28 ± 0.08	–	–	**55.33 ± 0.72**	**73.41 ± 0.14**	–	–	52.83 ± 0.61	70.16 ± 0.12

Table 4: Results of the LSTAN strategies considering the Super Parent and Favorite Children.

Collections	SVM		KNN		Best-LSPTAN		Best-LSPTAN (Source)
	Mac$F1$	Mic$F1$	Mac$F1$	Mic$F1$	Mac$F1$	Mic$F1$	
4UNI	56.02 ± 2.02	70.91 ± 1.9	**58.24 ± 2.92**	**73.78 ± 0.7**	**61.48 ± 1.68**	71.99 ± 1.01	$LSPTAN_{SP}$
REUT90	30.38 ± 2.04	65.09 ± 0.21	29.95 ± 1.14	**68.04 ± 0.62**	**36.21 ± 2.11**	66.57 ± 0.57	$LSPTAN_{Class}$
20NG	84.92 ± 0.54	85.1 ± 0.6	88.41 ± 0.27	88.69 ± 0.67	**90.24 ± 0.56**	**90.42 ± 0.56**	$LSPTAN_{Restricted}$
ACM	58.00 ± 1.33	69.67 ± 0.45	59.75 ± 1.72	71.6 ± 0.46	**63.05 ± 1.47**	**75.65 ± 0.33**	$LSPTAN_{Restricted}$
RCV1 Uni	47.05 ± 0.35	**75.85 ± 0.08**	46.32 ± 0.72	68.23 ± 0.16	**55.33 ± 0.72**	73.41 ± 0.14	$LSPTAN_{SP}$

Table 5: Best results compared with SVM and KNN.

8. ACKNOWLEDGEMENTS

This work was partially supported by the Brazilian National Institute of Science and Technology for Web Research (MCT/CNPq/INCT Web Grant Number 573871/2008-6), and by the authors' individual grants from CNPq, CAPES, FINEP, FAPEMIG and FAPEG. We thank NVIDIA Corporation for equipment donations.

9. REFERENCES

[1] A. P. Adewole, O. J. Fakorede, and S. O. N. Akwuegbo. Evaluation of linear interpolation smoothing on naive bayes spam classifier, 2014.

[2] G. Andrade, F. Viegas, G. S. Ramos, J. Almeida, L. Rocha, M. Goncalves, and R. Ferreira. Gpu-nb: A fast cuda-based implementation of naive bayes. *SBAC'13*, 0:168–175, 2013.

[3] L. Breiman and P. Spector. Submodel Selection and Evaluation in Regression. The X-Random Case. *Int. Stat. Rev.*, 60(3), 1992.

[4] Y.-S. Chang, R.-K. Sheu, S.-M. Yuan, and J.-J. Hsu. Scaling database performance on gpus. *Information Systems Frontiers*, 14(4):909–924, 2012.

[5] L. Chen and S. Wang. Automated feature weighting in naive bayes for high-dimensional data classification. In *CIKM'12*, pages 1243–1252, 2012.

[6] G. F. Cooper. *Probabilistic inference using belief networks is NP-hard*. Knowledge Systems Laboratory, Computer Science Department, Univ., 1988.

[7] I. Fahmi. Examining learning algorithms for text classification in digital libraries. In *Master's thesis*, University of Groninge, Netherland, 2004.

[8] R.-E. Fan, K.-W. Chang, C.-J. Hsieh, X.-R. Wang, and C.-J. Lin. Liblinear: A library for large linear classification. *JMLR*, 9:1871–1874, 2008.

[9] N. Friedman, D. Geiger, and M. Goldszmidt. Bayesian network classifiers. *Mach. Learn.*, 29(2-3):131–163, Nov. 1997.

[10] S. Godbole and S. Sarawagi. Discriminative methods for multi-labeled classification. In *In Pacific-Asia KDD*, pages 22–30. Springer, 2004.

[11] J. Hovold. Naive bayes spam filtering using word-position-based attributes. In *CEAS*, 2005.

[12] E. J. Keogh and M. J. Pazzani. Learning augmented bayesian classifiers: A comparison of distribution-based and classification-based approaches, 1999.

[13] S.-B. Kim, K.-S. Han, H.-C. Rim, and S. H. Myaeng. Some effective techniques for naive bayes text classification. *IEEE TKDE*, 18(11):1457 -1466, nov. 2006.

[14] P. Langley and S. Sage. Induction of selective bayesian classifiers. In *Uncertainty in Artificial Intelligence*, pages 399–406. Morgan Kaufmann, 1994.

[15] D. Lewis, Y. Yang, T. Rose, and F. Li. RCV1: a new benchmark collection for text categorization research. *The Journal of Machine Learning Research*, 5:361–397, 2004.

[16] T.-K. Lin and S.-Y. Chien. Support vector machines on gpu with sparse matrix format. In *Machine Learning and Applications (ICMLA)*, pages 313–318, 2010.

[17] C. D. Manning, P. Raghavan, and H. Schütze. *Introduction to Information Retrieval*, chapter 13, pages 234–265. Cambridge University Press, 2008.

[18] L. Matthijssen. Automatic indexing and abstracting of document texts. *Artificial Intelligence and Law*, 8(4):343–347, 2000.

[19] J. D. M. Rennie, L. Shih, J. Teevan, and D. R. Karger. Tackling the poor assumptions of naive bayes text classifiers. In *ICML'03*, pages 616–623, 2003.

[20] M. Sahami. Learning limited dependence bayesian classifiers. In *In KDD-96*, pages 335–338. AAAI Press, 1996.

[21] R. E. Schapire and Y. Singer. Boostexter: A boosting-based system for text categorization. In *Machine Learning*, pages 135–168, 2000.

[22] F. Sebastiani. Machine learning in automated text categorization. *ACM Computing Surveys*, 34(1):1–47, 2002.

[23] B. E. Teitler, J. Sankaranarayanan, H. Samet, and M. D. Adelfio. Online document clustering using gpus. In *New Trends in DBs and Inf. Sys.*, pages 245–254. Springer, 2014.

[24] C. Timm, A. Gelenberg, P. Marwedel, and F. Weichert. *Reducing the Energy Consumption of Embedded Systems by Integrating General Purpose GPUs*. Technical reports in computer science. TU, Department of Computer Science, 2010.

[25] G. I. Webb, J. R. Boughton, and Z. Wang. Not so naive bayes: Aggregating one-dependence estimators. In *Machine Learning*, pages 5–24, 2005.

[26] A. S. (Yandex). Using gpus to accelerate learning to rank. In *NVIDIA GTC-GPU Technology Conference-2014*, 2014.

[27] Y. Yang. An evaluation of statistical approaches to text categorization. *Inf. Retr.*, 1(1-2):69–90, May 1999.

[28] T. Zhang and F. J. Oles. Text categorization based on regularized linear classification methods. *Inf. Ret.*, 4:5–31, 2000.

[29] R. Zheng, J. Li, H. Chen, and Z. Huang. A framework for authorship identification of online messages: Writing-style features and classification techniques. *JASIST*, 57(3):378–393, 2006.

A Novel Class Noise Estimation Method and Application in Classification

Lin Gui[1], Qin Lu[2], Ruifeng Xu[1*], Minglei Li[2], Qikang Wei[1]
1.Laboratory of Network Oriented Intelligent Computation,
Shenzhen Graduate School, Harbin Institute of Technology, Shenzhen, China
2.Department of Computing, the Hong Kong Polytechnic University, Hong Kong, China
guilin.nlp@gmail.com; csluqin@comp.polyu.edu.hk; xuruifeng@hitsz.edu.cn;
csmli@comp.polyu.edu.hk; weiqikang@hotmail.com

ABSTRACT
Noise in class labels of any training set can lead to poor classification results no matter what machine learning method is used. In this paper, we first present the problem of binary classification in the presence of random noise on the class labels, which we call class noise. To model class noise, a class noise rate is normally defined as a small independent probability of the class labels being inverted on the whole set of training data. In this paper, we propose a method to estimate class noise rate at the level of individual samples in real data. Based on the estimation result, we propose two approaches to handle class noise. The first technique is based on modifying a given surrogate loss function. The second technique eliminates class noise by sampling. Furthermore, we prove that the optimal hypothesis on the noisy distribution can approximate the optimal hypothesis on the clean distribution using both approaches. Our methods achieve over 87% accuracy on a synthetic non-separable dataset even when 40% of the labels are inverted. Comparisons to other algorithms show that our methods outperform state-of-the-art approaches on several benchmark datasets in different domains with different noise rates.

Categories and Subject Descriptors
I.5.1 [**PATTERN RECOGNITION**]: Models--- Statistical;

General Terms
Algorithms, Design, Experimentation.

Keywords
Class Noise, Learning with Noise, Noise Elimination.

1. INTRODUCTION
A typical machine learning method uses a classifier learned from a labeled dataset (i.e., the training data) to predict the class labels of new samples (i.e., the testing data). In most of the classification applications, the labels of the training data are assumed correct. However, real-world datasets often contain noise which may occur either in the feature set of the data, referred to as the **attribute noise**, or in the labels of the data, referred to as the **class noise**.

Permission to make digital or hard copies of all or part of this work for personal or classroom use is granted without fee provided that copies are not made or distributed for profit or commercial advantage and that copies bear this notice and the full citation on the first page. Copyrights for components of this work owned by others than ACM must be honored. Abstracting with credit is permitted. To copy otherwise, or republish, to post on servers or to redistribute to lists, requires prior specific permission and/or a fee. Request permissions from Permissions@acm.org
CIKM'15, October 19-23, 2015, Melbourne, VIC, Australia
© 2015 ACM. ISBN 978-1-4503-3794-6/15/10…$15.00
DOI: http://dx.doi.org/10.1145/2806416.2806554

Many studies have focused on dealing with attribute noise since it is quite common in data mining applications and machine learning tasks. Researchers such as [1, 2] have indicated that class noise can potentially be more detrimental than attribute noise. The importance of addressing the class noise problem is not limited to its adverse impact on classification performance [1]. We must point out that class noise is unavoidable in many real world applications including disease prediction in medical applications [3], food labeling for the food industry [4], and manual data labeling in many natural language processing applications [5]

To handle class noise in learning algorithms, the first issue is how to estimate the probability of class noise, referred to as the **class noise rate.** The second issue is how to train a classifier knowing that the training data contains class noise.

Generally speaking, there are two types of strategies to deal with class noise. The first entails learning with noise data and the second is based on noise elimination. In the **learning with noise method,** each training sample is assigned a weight based on an estimated probability of class noise, that is, the class noise rate. The learning algorithm will consider the class noise probability while learning from the original noisy training data [6]. Unfortunately, this method requires a priori knowledge of the class noise rate in the training data.

In the **noise elimination method**, attempts are first made to detect and remove erroneous data from the training set [7, 8, 9]. While this method can reduce the rate of class noise in the training data, it can also lead to the overall reduction of training samples. Because of the reduced training data, this method may lead to even worse results than when it is used for small training sets.

The performance of both methods relies on an appropriate estimation of class noise rate. In this paper, we first propose a novel method to estimate the noise rate of the training data at the level of individual samples and the estimation is done based on the sum of the Rademacher distribution [10] using k-Nearest Neighbors (k-NN) graphs. We then present two general methods to incorporate our proposed class noise estimation method into the two types of class noise handling strategies to reduce the impact of noisy data. Lastly, in the elimination based strategy, we introduce a sampling-based method to select high quality training data rather than to identify low quality data for elimination.

The rest of the paper is organized as follows. Section 2 provides a review of related works and basic definitions. Section 3 presents the problem setup and some background information. Section 4 presents our proposed class noise estimation method. Section 5 describes the methods to incorporate the proposed estimation into learning with noise strategy and the class noise elimination strategy. Section 6 presents performance evaluations based on both synthetic and real-world public datasets in different domains. Section 7 provides the conclusion and future work.

2. Related work and Basic Definitions

Identifying class noise is an important subject in machine learning. Previous work covers both the theoretical [11] and the application aspects [12, 13] of this topic. In this section, we briefly introduce these works from three perspectives: the source of class noise, the handling of class noise, and the application of class noise.

Class noises exist for different reasons. When used for disease prediction in medical applications [3], training data contains a probability of false positive or negative because data comes from medical experiments. In other words, class noises naturally exist and cannot be avoided. Food labeling for the food industry [4] also faces class noise problem. As shown by [4], because some food has high price than others, such as beef has a higher price than mutton, miss-labeling is an aforethought to achieve more benefit. The manual labeling of data in many natural language processing applications [5] naturally contains class noise because there is always a possibility of inter-annotator inconsistency.

Given an x, being the set of features of a sample, $\tilde{y}$ is the observed label of x; y is the true label of the sample of x and p is the probability to flip the true label into a noise label (thus p is the class noise rate, or **noise rate** for short). For any training algorithm, only x and $\tilde{y}$ can be observed. In general, class noises can be categorized into three different models based the dependency of noise to y and p [14]. The most common model used is the *Noise Completely at Random Model* [11, 15, 16]. In this model, class noise rate of a sample is completely random and independent of the labels and the feature set. Thus, an observed label $\tilde{y}$ is only determined by the true label and class noise rate. The other models assume dependency to either x or y [17-21].

The theoretical discussion about class noise and learning was first proposed by Angluin and Laird in 1988 [11]. In their work, all instances of the labeled data for binary classification have a uniform probability $p \in [0,1/2)$ of being inverted. This is referred to as the random classification noise.

Class noises are typically assumed to be stochastic in algorithms that can handle class noises. The work by [6] assumes a learned noise rate from prior knowledge and every sample is given the same probability, a simple assumption that may not be reasonable in all scenarios. The Cut Edge Weight statistic [8] also requires a prior assumed noise rate. This method uses the prior probability as a hypothesis to test if the training sample satisfies the null hypothesis. The method also requires the neighbors of a training sample to follow the central limit theorem, which is not reasonable because the set of neighbors are too small. Other works simply did not consider noise rate [5, 7, 9, 22].

There are two basic categories of strategies to dealing with class noise in training data: learning with class noise [5, 6, 16] and class noise elimination [7, 8, 9]. The learning with noise strategy approximates a distribution of noiseless training data using the distribution of the original training data with class noise and a priori knowledge about the class noise [6]. The problem, however, is that a priori knowledge of the class noise is not generally available, limiting the applicability of this method. Li [16] use the Kernel Fisher method to estimate the class noise. Then the estimation is used to achieve a robust algorithm to tolerate noise.

The class noise elimination strategy attempts to detect the samples with high noise probabilities and remove them from the training set. There are different methods to detect class noise that can be categorized as classification-based methods and graph-based methods. The classification-based method was first proposed by Brodley in 1999 [7]. He used K-fold cross-validation to split the training set into K subsets, and used any K-1 sets as the training data to classify the remaining data. If the classification result for a sample is different from the original label, that sample is considered class noise and is removed. Zhu et al. proposed a more efficient algorithm using the same ideal and made it suitable for large datasets [22]. Zhu also proposed a cost-sensitive approach based on K-fold cross-validation [1]. Sluba employed a 10-fold cross-validation to detect class noise [9] for their elimination. There are two major problems with the elimination approach. First, some correctly labeled training data can be lost because of potentially inaccurate class noise identification. Second, the number of samples in the training data will be reduced, potentially leading to an adverse effect on the learning algorithm performance. In elimination-based methods, reliable noise estimation crucial and inaccurate estimations can potentially degrade performance compared to using the original noisy dataset.

The graph-based method, known as the Cut Edge Weight statistic method, was proposed by Zighed [8]. The principal idea is based on the manifold assumption and a Bernoulli distribution assumption on the consistency of the labels. A similar approach was proposed by Jiang and Zhou, who used a k-NN graph to detect class noise without the need to consider noise rate as probabilities [23].

Problem Setup and Background

Let D denotes the clean distribution with no class noise, and (x_1, y_1), (x_2, y_2),..., (x_n, y_n) denote n training samples from D with true binary label y_i ($y_i = \pm 1, i = 1,2, \ldots, n$). When there are class noises, $\tilde{D}$ denotes the observed distribution which contains class noise, and the training sample from a noisy distribution $\tilde{D}$ are $(x_1, \tilde{y}_1)$, $(x_2, \tilde{y}_2)$,..., $(x_n, \tilde{y}_n)$, where the label $\tilde{y}_i$ may be different from the true label y_i. In this paper, we want to estimate noise rate at the level of the individual samples rather than for the whole collection of training data. Thus, we give definition of class noise rate as follows:

Definition.1: Let $(x_i, \tilde{y}_i) \in \tilde{D}$ be a sample from the noisy distribution, the class noise rate is the probability of the observed label different from the true label of x_i, denoted by $P(\tilde{y}_i \neq y_i | x_i)$.

According this definition, class noise rate is defined on individual data samples. Thus, the first issue we need to address is how to estimate the class noise rate for each training sample. The main challenge, however, is that a learner can only see the noisy data $(x_i, \tilde{y}_i) \in \tilde{D}$, and there is no a priori knowledge about the class noise rate and the clean distribution D.

Assuming that we can find a reasonably good estimation method, the second issue we need to address is how to make use of the estimated result to train a classifier on the noisy distribution.

Before we address the second issue, we need to know how to measure the performance of a classifier. Generally speaking, the objective of a classifier is to minimize a given loss function on a given set of training data. However, in this paper, the observed training data contains class noise. Thus, the minimized loss function on noisy training data may not be the minimized loss function on the clean data. So our objective is to find the estimation of the class noise rate for each individual sample such that the loss function on the noisy distribution can be modified.

Furthermore, the modified loss function can also minimize the loss on the clean distribution.

In order to address the problem in a formal way, we give some definitions below.

Definition.2. Let $f: X \to \mathbb{R}$ be a real-value decision function, defined as $f(x) = P(y = 1 \mid x) - 1/2$. The **risk** of f for each sample on clean distribution is 0-1 loss given by $R_D(f) = E_{(x,y)\sim D}(1_{sign(f(x))\neq y})$.

Let $l(f(x), y)$ denote a loss function with a real-value prediction, for the clean distribution where $y = \pm 1$ is the true label of x. Let the hat $\tilde{}$ denoted the modified loss function. We can then use $\tilde{l}(f(x), \tilde{y})$ to denote the modified loss function of the noisy distribution because the loss function is defined under the noisy distribution $\tilde{D}$. We can then use the estimation of the class noise rate for each individual sample and modify the loss function on the noisy distribution with an observed label. Three related risks are then defined as follows:

Definition.3.1: the **Expectation of *l*-risk** under the clean distribution D is defined as: $R_{l,D}(f) = E_{(x,y)\sim D}(l(f(x), y))$.

Definition.3.2: the **Expectation of $\tilde{l}$ -risk** under the noisy distribution $\tilde{D}$ is defined as: $R_{\tilde{l},\tilde{D}}(f) = E_{(x,\tilde{y})\sim\tilde{D}}(\tilde{l}(f(x), \tilde{y}))$.

Definition.3.3: the **Empirical $\tilde{l}$-risk** is defined on the training data as: $\hat{R}_{\tilde{l}}(f) = \frac{1}{n}\sum_{i=1}^{n} \tilde{l}(f(x_i), \tilde{y}_i)$.

Note that in the above definitions, the tilted hat $\tilde{}$ means that the noisy label will influence the marked object. The capped hat $\hat{}$ means that the marked object is an estimated result.

3. Class Noise Estimation

In this section, we first introduce our class noise model and the estimation method.

3.1 Class noise modeling

For training data without any priori knowledge on the noise rate, previous works on class noise modeling gives uniform noise rate on the entire training dataset. That is, the class noise rate is defined on the entire dataset as $p \in [0, 1/2)$. In this work, we drop this assumption and propose noise estimation performed on individual data samples.

According to **Definition.1**, class noise rate requires the estimation of the clean distribution $P(y_i|x_i)$ for each individual sample, which is generally impossible because the observed data is noisy. So, in this work, we model the class noise $P(\tilde{y}_i \neq y_i|x_i)$ by looking at the k nearest neighbors of x_i using the k-NN graph on the noisy data by a hypothesis testing method.

For any sample $(x_i, \tilde{y}_i)$ from the training set with the true label y_i, we first assume that the probability of $P(x_i, y_i)$ and $P(x_i)$ are continuous without any noisy label and all samples are independent of each other. Thus, $\forall\varepsilon > 0$, $\exists\delta > 0$, such that $d(x_i, x_j) < \varepsilon$, and $|P(x_i, y_i) - P(x_j, y_j)| < \delta$ and $|P(x_i) - P(x_j)| < \delta$.

Then, we can build a k-NN graph for noisy data $(x_i, \tilde{y}_i)$ to link the top k nearest samples $(x_j, \tilde{y}_j)$ in a graph. So, the distances between $(x_i, \tilde{y}_i)$ to its k nearest samples should also be small enough. Thus, we consider them to share the same probability, $P(y_i|x_i) \approx P(y_j|x_j)$ on the clean distribution.

The problem here is that we neither have clean data nor prior knowledge about the clean distribution. This means that we cannot estimate $P(y_i|x_i)$ for each individual sample. On the other hand, it is reasonable to assume that the true label of an individual sample should be similar to its nearest sample. Let $(x_i, \tilde{y}_i)$ denote the candidate sample whose class noise rate needs to be estimated and the k nearest samples as $(x_j, \tilde{y}_j)$, here j = 1,2,..,k.

We can then define a sign function on the candidate sample $(x_i, \tilde{y}_i)$ and its k nearest samples $(x_j, \tilde{y}_j)$:

$$I_{ij} = \begin{cases} 1, & if\ \tilde{y}_i \neq \tilde{y}_j \\ -1, & if\ \tilde{y}_i = \tilde{y}_j \end{cases} \tag{1}$$

I_{ij} can indicate the difference between an individual sample and its nearest label. Even though, $\tilde{y}_j$ can contain noise with some probability, the noise level of $\tilde{y}_i$ should be similar to that of $\tilde{y}_j$. The idea is that if the label of a candidate sample is different to its nearest sample, it should have a higher probability to be a noisy label. Based on this, we introduce a similarity function here, normalized over [0,1], denoted by $w_{ij} = sim(x_i, x_j)$.

Then, for each candidate sample, we define a statistic factor, S_i, referred to as the sum of noisy similarity, which can be used to measure the total noise level.

Definition.4: For any individual sample $(x_i, \tilde{y}_i) \in \tilde{D}$ and the top k nearest sample $(x_j, \tilde{y}_j)$, j = 1,2,..,k. under Formula (1) and a normalized similarity w_{ij}, the **sum of noisy similarity** is:

$$S_i = \sum_{j=1}^{k} I_{ij}\, w_{ij}. \tag{2}$$

The idea of similarity is only a hypothesis. Since the nearest samples may also contain noise, the sum of noisy similarity S_i is not a constant. Rather, it should follow some distribution. Let us refer to this distribution as the *Sum of Random Noise (SRN)*. For a sample $(x_i, \tilde{y}_i)$, let c denotes the number of k nearest neighbors whose labels are different from $\tilde{y}_i$. Then, the distribution of *SRN* with any specific c is known and shown as the 6 distributions on background in Fig.1. Obviously, the larger c is, the higher *SRN* should be for an individual sample. From the definition of S_i, we know that the distribution of S_i is dependent on $P(I_{ij})$ only. Since we cannot use the observed label to estimate $P(I_{ij})$, and we assume that $P(I_{ij} = 1) = 1/2$ here, which is based on the **Principle of Entropy Maximum (PEM).** That is, when there is no a priori knowledge, the best assumption for label difference is that they share the same probability. Under the principle of entropy maximum, the distribution of S_i is shown as the yellow shadow on the foreground in Fig.1, labeled as *SRN*.

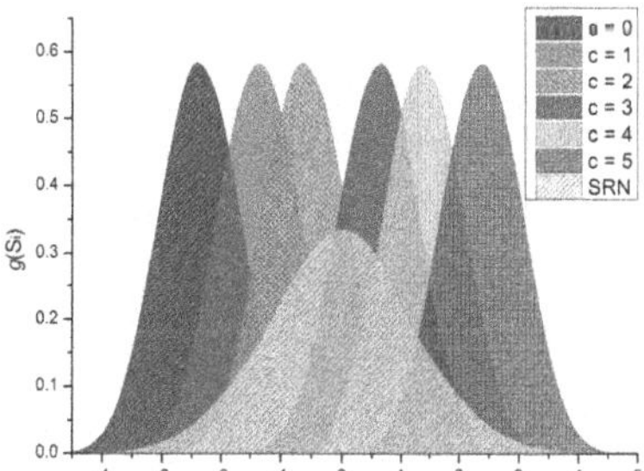

Fig. 1. The Sum of Random Noise (*SRN*) Distribution

Now, we can define the class noise rate for $(x_i, \tilde{y}_i)$ as the probability of S_i being opposite from *SRN*. Because $I_{ij} = 1$

indicates that the sample x_i has different label to its nearest neighbor and the similarity metric is between 0 to 1, the larger S_i is, the higher probably it should be that x_i has a noisy label. So, we should consider only the upper quantile of *SRN* here. Now, we can give the class noise rate under Definition.5.

Definition.5: For any individual sample $(x_i, \tilde{y}_i) \in \tilde{D}$ and the sum of noisy similarity S_i, the probability of *SRN* noted as P_{SRN}, the **class noise rate** $P(\tilde{y}_i \neq y_i|x_i)$ of $(x_i, \tilde{y}_i)$, is the probability of $1 - P_{SRN}(s \geq S_i)$.

If the principle of entropy maximum reveals a best guessing result, the upper quantile of *SRN* is the probability of the candidate sample being "worse" than a guessing result. So Definition.5 can be presented as a descriptive definition: *the class noise rate of a sample is defined as the probability of the observed label being worse than a guessed label.*

It should be noted that the 6 curves on the background in Fig.1 may easily be mistaken as a normal distribution. In fact, the curve will only approximate the normal distribution when the *k* in the k-NN graph is large enough, usually larger than 25 at least. However, a large *k* will lead to poor accuracy for kNN. [8, 12] actually used normal distribution in their work for noise estimation. Normal distribution is used as a compared estimation method in our experiment in Section 6. We think *SRN* is a more realistic estimation because in practice, *k* is much smaller than 25.

3.2 Class Noise Estimation

In this section, we introduce a method to estimate the class noise rate for individual samples under Definition.5.

We first need to find the estimation of $P(y_i|x_i)$. Since the observed label contains noise, and there is no prior knowledge about the distribution of class noise, the best estimation of $P(y_i = 1|x_i)$, denoted by $\hat{P}(y_i = 1|x_i)$ should minimize the risk of $\hat{P}(y_i = 1|x_i)$:

$$risk(\hat{P}(y_i = 1|x_i)) = \frac{1}{2}(P(y_i = 1|x_i) - \hat{P}(y_i = 1|x_i))^2$$

Since there is no prior distribution about $P(y_i = 1|x_i)$, we assume that $P(y_i = 1|x_i)$ follows a uniform distribution. That is, $P(y_i = 1|x_i)$ is completely random. Therefore,

$$\hat{P}(y_i = 1|x_i) = \operatorname*{argmin}_p \int_0^1 \frac{1}{2}(P(y_i = 1|x_i) - p)^2 dP(y_i = 1|x_i)$$

It can easily calculated that $\hat{P}(y_i = 1|x_i) = 1/2$, which means the best assumption for $P(y_i = 1|x_j)$ is $P(y_i = 1|x_i) = P(y_i = -1|x_i)$ when there is no prior knowledge about the clean distribution. This can also be explained by the **Principle of Entropy Maximum**. Under this assumption, the top *k* nearest samples of (x_j, y_j) have the same probability $P(y_i|x_i) \approx P(y_j|x_j)$, which implies that $P(I_{ij} = 1) = P(I_{ij} = -1) = 1/2$. Now, we can use this result to estimate the class noise rate under Definition.5.

Theorem.1.(*main result*) The **estimated class noise rate** of $(x_i, \tilde{y}_i) \in \tilde{D}$ denoted by $P_c(x_i)$, is:

$$P_c(x_i) \geq 1 - 0.5 \times \exp\left(-\frac{\left(\sum_{j=1}^{k} w_{ij} \cdot I_{ij}\right)^4}{2(\|w_i\|_1 \|w_i\|_2)^2}\right) \qquad (3)$$

The proof of Theorem.1 is based on Lemma.1 to be introduced below.

Lemma.1. Let $I_{i1}, I_{i2}, \ldots, I_{ik}$ be independent Bernoulli random variables ($P(I_{ij} = 1) = P(I_{ij} = -1) = 1/2$.), $w_{i1}, w_{i2}, \ldots, w_{ik}$ be a sequence of real number such that $w_i = (w_{i1}, w_{i2}, \ldots, w_{ik}) \in l_2$ and $t > 0$. We can then conclude that

$$P\left(\sum_{j=1}^{k} I_{ij} w_{ij} > K_{1,2}(w_i, t)\right) \leq e^{-\frac{t^2}{2}}$$

where $K_{1,2}(w_i, t)$ is defined as:

$$K_{1,2}(w_i, t) = \inf\{\|w'_i\|_1 + t\|w''_i\|_2\}$$

Here, $\|\cdot\|_1$ and $\|\cdot\|_2$ are the l_1 and l_2 norms; and $w'_i + w''_i = w_i$. This formula of $K_{1,2}(w_i, t)$ is well known as the *K*-method of real interpolation for Banach Space [24]. The proof of Lemma.1. was given by [10] in details which we will not repeat here.

The issue in is the calculation of $K_{1,2}(w_i, t)$ is quite complex and high cost. Here, we give Lemma.2 below which provides a simple sub-optimal solution of $K_{1,2}(w_i, t)$.

Lemma.2. Let $I_{i1}, I_{i2}, \ldots, I_{ik}$ be independent Bernoulli random variables ($P(I_{ij} = 1) = P(I_{ij} = -1) = 1/2$.), $w_{i1}, w_{i2}, \ldots, w_{ik}$ be a sequence of real number such that $w_i = (w_{i1}, w_{i2}, \ldots, w_{ik}) \in l_2$ and $t > 0$, we have:

$$P\left(\sum_{j=1}^{k} I_{ij} w_{ij} > \sqrt{t\|w_i\|_1 \|w_i\|_2}\right) \leq e^{-\frac{t^2}{2}}$$

where, $\|\cdot\|_1$ and $\|\cdot\|_2$ are the l_1 and l_2 norms.

Proof: First, let $w'_i = \alpha w_i$ and $w''_i = \beta w_i$, where α and β are two real numbers.

$$\inf\{\|w'_i\|_1 + t\|w''_i\|_2\} = \sqrt{t\|w_i\|_1 \|w_i\|_2}$$

Then, there is a subspace of the interpolation in the Banach space and the optimal result on the subspace is greater than the norm. Thus:

$$\sqrt{t\|w_i\|_1 \|w_i\|_2} \geq K_{1,2}(w_i, t) \qquad (4)$$

Assuming the **Probability Density Function** (PDF) of the *SRN* $P(S_i)$ is $g(x)$. Such that

$$P\left(S_i \geq K_{1,2}(w_i, t)\right) = \int_{K_{1,2}(w_i,t)}^{+\infty} g(x)dx$$

based on Formula(4),

$$\int_{K_{1,2}(w_i,t)}^{+\infty} g(x)dx \geq \int_{\sqrt{t\|w_i\|_1 \|w_i\|_2}}^{+\infty} g(x)dx$$

So,

$$e^{-\frac{t^2}{2}} \geq P\left(S_i \geq K_{1,2}(w_i, t)\right) \geq P(S_i > \sqrt{t\|w_i\|_1 \|w_i\|_2})$$

This will lead to the result of Lemma 2.

According to Definition.4, the estimated class noise rate $P_c(x_i)$ for $(x_i, \tilde{y}_i) \in \tilde{D}$ is the probability of $(x_i, \tilde{y}_i)$ not following *SRN*. According to Lemma.3, the probability of $(x_i, \tilde{y}_i)$ from *SRN* is less than $\exp\left(-\frac{\left(\sum_{j=1}^{k} w_{ij} \cdot I_{ij}\right)^4}{2(\|w_i\|_1 \|w_i\|_2)^2}\right)$ when $t > 0$.

Due to I_{ij} is a Rademacher random variable in our assumption, the probability of $t > 0$ and $t < 0$ are equal. Thus the estimated class noise rate is:

$$P_c(x_i) \geq 1 - 0.5 \times \exp(-\frac{\left(\sum_{j=1}^{k} w_{ij} \cdot l_{ij}\right)^4}{2(\|w_i\|_1 \|w_i\|_2)^2}) \square$$

For noise detection, the lower boundary is more significant since it pertains to the minimum noise rate of a labeled training sample. In practice, we can use

$$P_c(x_i) = 1 - 0.5 \times e^{(-r(x_i)/2)} \quad (5)$$

as the estimation for each training sample. Here,

$$r(x_i) = \frac{\left(\sum_{j=1}^{k} w_{ij} \cdot l_{ij}\right)^4}{(\|w_i\|_1 \|w_i\|_2)^2}$$

$P_c(x_i)$ can either be incorporated in the learning algorithms to weigh the importance of a training sample or be used to identify samples for elimination. It should be noted that $r(x_i)$ is symmetrical on S_i. It means that when S_i is less than 0, the upper quantile of *SRN* needs to be solved by the lower quantile of *SRN* which is introduced by the opposite sign function. In another word, when S_i is less than 0, $P_c(x_i)$ should be:

$$P_c(x_i) = 0.5 \times e^{(-r(x_i)/2)}$$

This inference can be easily proven by the symmetry of $r(x_i)$.

4. Learning in Noisy Data

In this section, we introduce our learning with noise strategy and class noise elimination method.

4.1 Learning with Noise Strategy

Based on the class noise estimation given in Formula (5), we propose a method using the learning with noise strategy. The fundamental idea is to use the estimated class noise rate to weigh a risk-of-loss function. The key is to ensure that the weighted loss function can adequately approximate the loss function for the clean training data. The loss function on the observed distribution is defined as

$$\tilde{l}(f(x_i), \tilde{y}_i) = \frac{(1-P_c(x_i))l(f(x_i), \tilde{y}_i) - P_c(x_i)l(f(x_i), -\tilde{y}_i)}{1-2(\frac{\sum_i P_c(x_i)}{n})} \quad (6)$$

where the numerator is formed by two parts. The first part is the original loss function with the observed labels weighted by their label correctness probabilities. The second is a penalty for the loss function with an inverted label (i.e., the probability of the observed label is incorrect) weighted by the class noise rate. The denominator is based on the average class noise rate to ensure that the noisy training data's loss function approximates the clean training data's loss function. This loss function is an updated version of the original loss function on noisy data. We are interested to know whether the minimum risk of the proposed loss function on the noisy training data can approximate the minimum risk of the loss function on the clean data. Let us assume that the training data is clean. Then, the risk of the loss function on the clean distribution and noisy distribution are defined according to Definition 3.1 to Definition 3.3.

As mentioned earlier in Section 3, we need to address two issues here. Will the empirical risk $\hat{R}_{\tilde{l}}(f)$ converge to the expected risk $R_{\tilde{l},\tilde{D}}(f)$ under the noisy distribution when n grows? Will the expected risk $R_{\tilde{l},\tilde{D}}(f)$ converge to $R_{l,D}(f)$ under the clean distribution? If the answer to both questions is yes, the empirical risk then converges to the clean distribution. Thus, we can train a classifier for the cleaning distribution by the noisy data without any prior knowledge.

Theorem.2. The empirical $\tilde{l}$-risk on the training data $\hat{R}(f)$ will converge to the risk $R_{\tilde{l},\tilde{D}}(f)$ of the loss function on the noise data with n independent and identically distributed training samples denote as $(x_1, \tilde{y}_1)$, $(x_2, \tilde{y}_2)$,…, $(x_n, \tilde{y}_n) \in \tilde{D}$, $(\tilde{y}_i = \pm 1, i = 1,2, \dots, n)$ when n grows.

Proof: Given n independent $(x_i, \tilde{y}_i)$, $P_c(x_i)$ denotes the class noise rate estimate by Formula (5) with the expectation $E(P_c(x_i))$. According to the Chebyshev law of large numbers, $\forall \varepsilon > 0$, $\exists \delta > 0$, and $N > 0$, such that when $n > N$,

$$\left|\sum_i \frac{P_c(x_i)}{n} - E(P_c(x_i))\right| \leq \varepsilon$$

is true with a probability of at least $1 - \delta$.

For the same reason, $\forall \varepsilon > 0$, $\exists \delta > 0$, and $N > 0$, when $n > N$,

$$\left|\frac{1}{n}\sum_{i=1}^{n} l(f(x_i), \tilde{y}_i) - E(l(f(x), \tilde{y}))\right| \leq \varepsilon$$

is true with a probability of at least $1 - \delta$.

Then, the risk on $\tilde{D}$ and the empirical $\tilde{l}$-risk on the training data satisfies

$$|\hat{R}(f) - R_{\tilde{l},\tilde{D}}(f)| \leq 2\varepsilon$$

With probability of at least $1 - \delta$. □

In other words, the empirical $\tilde{l}$-risk on the training data $\hat{R}(f)$ will converge to the risk $R_{\tilde{l},\tilde{D}}(f)$ of the loss function on the noise data when the size of training data is large enough.

If we have a perfectly correct estimation of the class noise rate, it is true that

$$E_{\tilde{y}}[\tilde{l}(f(x), \tilde{y})] = l(f(x), y).$$

Under this assumption, $R_{\tilde{l},\tilde{D}}(f)$ will converge to $R_{l,D}(f)$ under clean distribution. In order to distinguish the perfect estimation result and the estimation by our method, let f_p denote the perfect estimation.

Theorem.3. The minimum result of risk $R_{l,D}(f_p)$ will converge to the minimum risk $R_{l,D}(f)$ on the clean distribution when there is a perfect estimation of class noise rate.

The proof of Theorem.3 is given in detail by [6], which will not repeated here. Based on the proof, the following inequality holds

$$|R_{l,D}(\hat{f}_p) - R_{l,D}(f_*)| < 2\Re(\tilde{l} \circ \mathcal{F}) + 2\sqrt{\frac{\log(1/\delta)}{2n}} \quad (7)$$

with a probability of at least $1 - \delta$.

Here, f_* is the minimizer of $R_{l,D}(f)$ on the clean distirbution, $\hat{f}_p$ is the minimizer of $R_{l,D}(f_p)$ on the clean distribution and

$$\Re(\tilde{l} \circ \mathcal{F}) = \mathbb{E}_{x_i, \tilde{y}_i, \epsilon_i}[\sup_{f \in \mathcal{F}} = \frac{1}{n}\sum_{i=1}^{n} \epsilon_i \tilde{l}(f(x_i), \tilde{y}_i)]$$

where ϵ_i is an independent and identically distributed Rademacher random variable.□

The right side of the inequality in Formula (7) is bound by the richness of the function family $\mathcal{F}$ and the sample size of n. In other words, the class noise estimation method indeed ensures the optimality of $\hat{f}_p$ with the class noise distribution approximating the risk of the clean distribution.

Thus the risk of our estimation method $R_{l,D}(\hat{f})$ satisfy:

$$|R_{l,D}(\hat{f}) - R_{l,D}(f_*)| < |R_{l,D}(\hat{f}) - R_{l,D}(\hat{f}_p)| + |R_{l,D}(\hat{f}_p) - R_{l,D}(f_*)|$$

Because the second item is bound, the risk of our estimate is determined by the first item which is related to the estimation result. This can be interpreted as that when the size of the training set grows, the performance of the classifier trained on the noisy data is determined by the estimation result given in Formula (5).

4.2 Class noise Elimination Strategy

Existing class noise elimination strategies attempt to detect and eliminate noisy samples. In this work, we propose a sampling based method which focuses on selecting only high quality samples to form the training dataset rather than focusing on noisy samples. The quality of a training sample is defined based on its class-noise rate: the lower the class-noise rate, the higher the quality. We refer to this as a sampling-based method. The idea is to use an ensemble learning algorithm as a group of aggregate classifiers, each working on a subset of the training data. Even if a sample is considered noise in one classifier, it may still be used as correct data in other sampling rounds. Generally speaking, an ensemble learning algorithm can use either bagging or boosting (e.g., Adaboost). In this work, we use only the bagging strategy for evaluation.

Each training sample $(x_i, \tilde{y}_i)$ is assigned a weight $p_i = 1 - P_c(x_i)$. We use this weight to select samples in the training dataset. We deploy a bagging algorithm based on the sampling results to obtain a stable classifier on the training data. Any basic classifier can be used in this framework. To ensure the effectiveness of this strategy, we need to confirm that the learning algorithm approximates the learner on a clean distribution.

Let S_i denote the i-th sampling result with $h_i \in \mathcal{H}$ signifying the optimal hypothesis on S_i. Assume an optimal hypothesis on the clean distribution S' exists and is denoted by $h^* \in \mathcal{H}$. According to the Hoeffding boundary from Angluin and Laird [11], the difference between h_i and h^* is bound by:

$$d(h_i, h^*) \leq \sqrt{2\ln\left(\frac{2N}{\delta}\right)/[|S_i|(1-2\eta)]^2} \quad (8)$$

with a probability of at least $1 - \delta$. Here, N is a constant related to the feature space and η is the class-noise rate of S_i. Since the class-noise rate is bound by the result of each sampling, the distance from the optimal hypothesis on S_i to the optimal hypothesis on the clean distribution approaches zero as the size of S_i increases. The bagging strategy allows error correction in the sampling to achieve a superior and more stable result.

4.3 Computational complexity

From the introduction above, we can see that any learning algorithm should be composed by two parts. The first part is for noise estimation, the second part is for training. The training parts are dependent on the learning algorithms. Thus, the complexity discussed here is on the noise estimation part only.

Since the estimation is based on a k-NN graph, usually the computational complexity of kernel based method such as kNN is $O(n^2 d)$. Here, n is the size of the training set and d is the dimension of the feature space. There are some methods to speed up kNN as done in [28, 29] by reducing d for sparse data. However, the computational complexity is still $O(n^2)$. The next step is the estimation. According to Formula (5), the complexity is $O(kd)$. Thus, the computational complex of our estimation method is $O(n^2 d + kd)$. As k is fixed, and not related to data size, complexity is basically $O(n^2 d)$.

5. Performance Evaluation

5.1 Experimental Setup

Our experiments evaluate the estimation performance and show its utility in improving learning performance for both online and offline learning algorithms. In principle, we can use any learning algorithm for this evaluation. For demonstration purpose, we use a simple linear algorithm using perceptron-based online learning to avoid complex parameter tuning. This is referred to as *LiC* (Linear Classification). For offline learning, we use bagged non-linear SVMs with polynomial kernels, referred to as *SaC* (Sampling Classification). The pseudo code for the *LiC* algorithm is given below

Algorithm I: *LiC*

Input:
S: The training dataset with n samples;
$(x_i, \tilde{y}_i)$: The training sample, $(x_i, \tilde{y}_i) \in S$
λ: Learning rate for perceptron learning
a_0: Initialized weight of perceptron features
Training:
For each $(x_i, \tilde{y}_i)$ in S, build a k-NN graph and calculate $P_c(x_i)$ according to Formula (5)
For i=1 to n:
Compute the inner product: $\langle a_{i-1}, x_i \rangle$
Update: $a_i \leftarrow a_{i-1} - \lambda \frac{\partial \tilde{l}(\langle a_{i-1}, x_i \rangle, \tilde{y}_i)}{\partial a_{i-1}} x_i$
Output: a_n

For the *SaC* algorithm, the class noise rate estimation given in Formula (5) serves as the weight for each training sample during sampling. The pseudo code of the *SaC* algorithm is given below.

Algorithm II: *SaC*

Input:
S: The training dataset with n samples;
$(x_i, \tilde{y}_i)$: The training sample, $(x_i, \tilde{y}_i) \in S$
T: Number of iterations
Training:
For each $(x_i, \tilde{y}_i)$ in S, built a k-NN graph and calculate $P_c(x_i)$ according to formula (5)
For j=1 to T:
Sampling based on $1 - P_c(x_i)$ for each $(x_i, \tilde{y}_i)$, the result is S_j
Use the learner on S_j to train the classifier C_j
Output:
An ensemble classifier: $C = \sum_j C_j / \mathrm{T}$

Based on the two algorithms, we conduct two sets of experiments: one for *LiC* and *SaC* on a 2-D synthetic dataset and the other on public datasets with comparisons to other well-known methods.

5.2 Evaluation on Synthetic Data

We prepared one linearly separable dataset and one non-linearly separable set, each has 500 samples, to serve as the clean data as shown in Fig. 2. The corresponding testing datasets have similar distributions. The feature values are real numbers between 0 and 1 and the labels are binary (red circles and blue crosses represent positive and negative labels, respectively). The ratio of positive and negative samples is 1:1. Stochastic class noise is introduced into the clean training data to invert some labels. Experiments on linearly separable data with 20% and 40% noise levels are shown in Fig.3(a) and Fig.3(b) respectively.

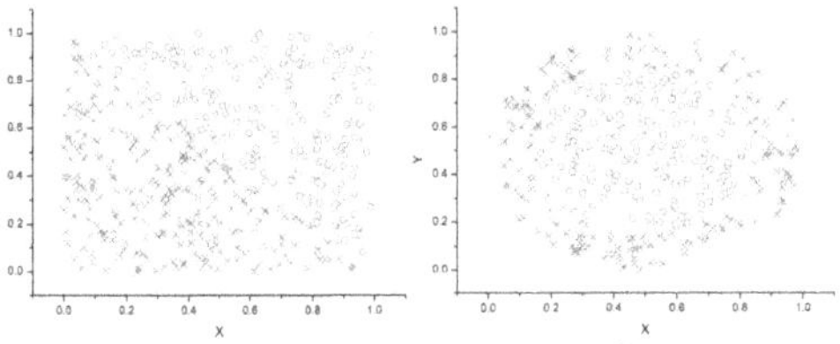

(a) (b)

Fig. 2. Linearly(a) and Non-Linearly(b) Separable Data

Fig. 3(c) and 3(d) show the respective result of *LiC* on the testing data and Table 1 shows the accuracy of both *LiC* and the Perceptron algorithm without noise estimation. Comparing Fig. 3(c) and 3(d), we can see that the decrease in accuracy is attributed to the shift of the linear separation boundary as the noise level increases (particularly evident at the bottom right corner). Table.1 indicates that noise estimation can make an obvious difference in performance. This is more apparent at higher noise level of 40%. *LiC* can achieve the improvement of 3.62% compared to the Perceptron algorithm.

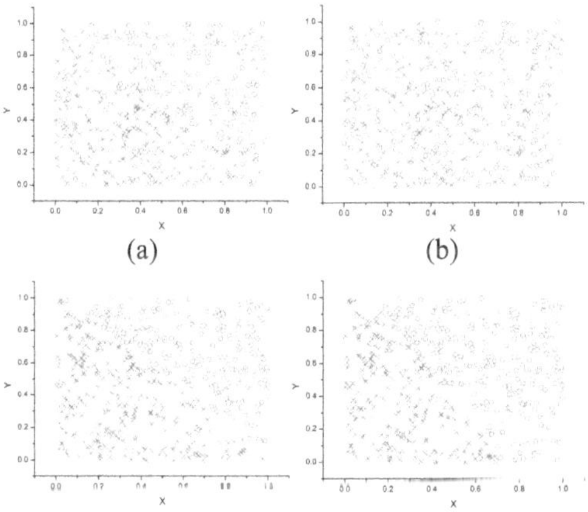

(a) (b)

(c) (d)

Fig. 3. Experiment on Linearly Separable Data

Table. 1. Experiment on Linearly Separable Data

Data	Noise rate	Method	Accuracy
(a)	20%	*LiC*	**97.19%**
(a)	20%	Perceptron	96.19%
(b)	40%	*LiC*	**91.78%**
(b)	40%	perceptron	88.57%

Fig. 4(a) and Fig. 4(b) show the non-linearly separable data with 20% and 40% noise levels, respectively, and Fig. 4(c) and Fig. 4(d) show the result of *SaC*. Table 2 shows the accuracy of *SaC* compared to RBF kernel based SVMs. Note that the improvement of 2.54%, when the class noise rate is 20%, is larger than *LiC* because non-linearly separable problem is more sensitive to class noise. However, when the class noise rate is 40%, the improvements of two algorithms are similar.

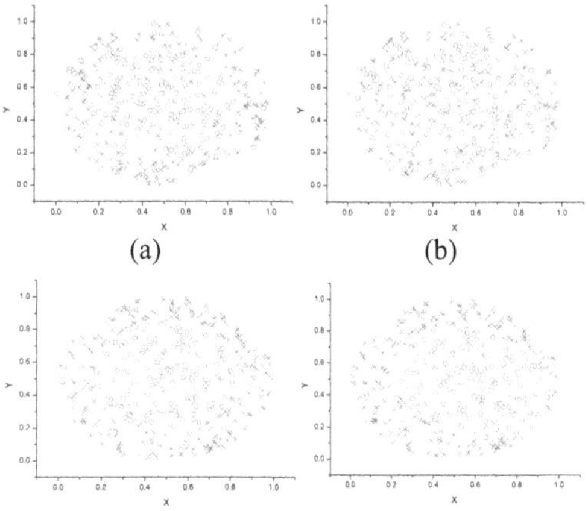

(a) (b)

(c) (d)

Fig. 4. Experiment on Non-Linearly Separable Data

Table. 2. Experiment on Non-Linearly Separable Data

Data	Noise rate	Method	Accuracy
(a)	20%	*SaC*	94.02%
(a)	20%	SVMs(RBF)	91.69%
(b)	40%	*SaC*	87.00%
(b)	40%	SVMs(RBF)	84.16%

5.3 Evaluation on Public Datasets

In this set of experiments, we evaluate the performance of our proposed methods using seven public datasets for binary classification with different class-noise rates: (1) the LEU [23] set of cancer data; (2) the Splice dataset for DNA sequence splice-junction classification; (3) the UCI Adult dataset collection containing seven subsets (referred to as a1a to a7a according to original naming of the data) of independent training and testing data [26]; (4) the DBWorld e-mails DataSet in English (in short, DB), which consists of 64 e-mails manually collected from DBWorld mailing list as binary labels of either "announces of conferences" or "everything else"; (5) the Farm Ads DataSet in English (in short, FADS), which is collected from text ads found on twelve websites that deal with various farm animal related topics with binary labels based on whether the content owner approves of the ad or not; (6) the Twitter Dataset for Arabic Sentiment Analysis Dataset (in short, TDA) with the class labels being opinion polarity; (7) the Product Reviews from Amazon in three categories, Book, DVD and Music (in short, PRA). The class labels are opinion polarity. The datasets (1) and (2) can be downloaded from the website of LibSVM[1]. The datasets (3) to (6) are from UCI[2] and (7) is from the NLPCC 2013 cross lingual opinion analysis evaluation task[3]. Datasets (4)-(7) are text data. The size, class ratio, types and dimensions of the datasets are listed in Table 3.

Table. 3. Overview of Datasets

Data	Type	Dimension	Training size(+/-)	Testing size(+/-)
LEU	Cancer	7129	38(0.71/0.29)	34(0.59/0.41)
Splice	DNA	60	1000(0.52/0.48)	2175(0.52/0.48)
UCI.a1a	Adult	123	1605(0.37/0.63)	30956(0.24/0.76)
UCI.a2a	Adult	123	2265(0.25/0.75)	30296(0.24/0.76)

[1] http://www.csie.ntu.edu.tw/~cjlin/libsvmtools/datasets

[2] http://www.ics.uci.edu

[3] http://tcci.ccf.org.cn/conference/2013/dldoc/evdata03.zip

UCI.a3a	Adult	123	3185(0.24/0.76)	29376(0.24/0.76)
UCI.a4a	Adult	123	4781(0.25/0.75)	27780(0.24/0.76)
UCI.a5a	Adult	123	6414(0.24/0.76)	26147(0.24/0.76)
UCI.a6a	Adult	123	11220(0.24/0.76)	21341(0.24/0.76)
UCI.a7a	Adult	123	16100(0.24/0.76)	16461(0.24/0.76)
DB	English	4698	64(0.45/0.55)	-------
FADS	English	54877	4143(0.51/0.49)	-------
TDA	Arabic	7415	2000(0.50/0.50)	-------
PRA_{Book}	Chinese	74643	4000(0.50/0.50)	-------
PRA_{DVD}	Chinese	74638	4000(0.50/0.50)	-------
PRA_{Music}	Chinese	74638	4000(0.50/0.50)	-------

To introduce the class noise into the training set, we stochastically invert the binary labels of training samples with a probability of 10%, 20%, and 30%, respectively. For the datasets (1) to (3), we train the binary classification algorithm on the noisy data. The algorithm is tuned on a development set before being used on the testing set. We use svm[light 4] as the basic classifier for this experiment. We choose two kind of similarity measures, the cosine similarity for text data, and the Euclidean Distance based similarity for all other data. The *k* in k-NN graph is 7 for *LiC*, *SaC* and CEWS. For the datasets (4) to (7), due to the lack of testing data, the result is based on 5-folds cross-validation.

We compare the performance of *LiC* with two state-of-the-art learning algorithms for noisy data: (1) the widely used open source robust method NHERD [27] and (2) the class noise log loss method, ℓ_{log} [6] which uses the same loss function as *LiC*. We also compare *SaC* with two state-of-the-art noise elimination systems: (3) Identifying Mislabeled Training Data (IMTD) [7] and (4) Cut Edge Weight Statistics (CEWS) [8]. Both ℓ_{log} and CEWS require prior knowledge of the class-noise for the training data. Thus, they are more appropriate for use as benchmarks rather than direct comparison to other algorithms, and should be discussed separately. Table 4 shows the accuracy of the six systems.

Table. 4. Performance of the Six Systems

Data	Noise rate	Learning with noise			Noise elimination		
		LiC	NHERD	ℓ_{log}*	***SaC***	IMTD	CEWS*
LEU	10%	87.88	81.62	**90.91**	**73.53**	58.82	**73.53**
	20%	**90.91**	76.62	84.85	**70.59**	58.82	67.65
	30%	**78.79**	58.68	57.58	58.82	58.82	58.82
Splice	10%	**84.67**	72.14	83.99	**85.17**	83.42	83.15
	20%	**83.05**	66.63	83.02	**83.34**	82.91	82.39
	30%	**79.53**	61.14	78.31	79.54	**80.83**	73.54
UCI.a1a	10%	**83.40**	81.23	83.33	83.25	**83.40**	82.86
	20%	81.40	79.30	**81.85**	82.78	79.79	**82.95**
	30%	**77.30**	74.78	77.10	**81.42**	78.39	81.31
UCI.a2a	10%	**84.24**	82.25	83.92	**84.14**	83.79	83.71
	20%	**83.16**	79.34	82.72	**83.12**	82.32	81.54
	30%	**80.66**	74.13	76.22	**81.81**	76.58	81.05
UCI.a3a	10%	**84.17**	82.79	83.93	83.54	**83.96**	83.07
	20%	**83.49**	81.14	82.23	**83.36**	78.02	82.83
	30%	**81.02**	77.52	80.23	**81.96**	79.28	81.35
UCI.a4a	10%	**84.28**	83.48	84.05	83.53	**83.95**	83.37
	20%	**84.10**	82.34	82.90	83.42	82.70	**83.51**
	30%	**81.81**	80.05	81.54	**82.46**	78.09	82.31
UCI.a5a	10%	**84.45**	83.57	83.78	**84.05**	84.03	83.87
	20%	**84.20**	82.88	83.06	83.47	**83.55**	83.23
	30%	79.20	**80.42**	74.71	**82.32**	80.30	82.22
UCI.a6a	10%	**84.77**	83.97	83.20	84.31	83.83	**84.44**
	20%	**83.38**	82.45	80.37	**83.49**	78.00	81.48
	30%	**81.83**	80.22	77.83	**82.21**	78.00	78.00
UCI.a7a	10%	**85.65**	84.58	82.93	**84.66**	84.45	83.14
	20%	**84.27**	82.87	80.43	**83.83**	78.17	81.65
	30%	**83.49**	80.28	78.67	**82.71**	79.33	80.86
DB	10%	**91.66**	**91.66**	87.98	**91.66**	66.67	73.53
	20%	**91.66**	75.00	84.50	58.33	58.33	**67.65**
	30%	**81.82**	58.33	80.52	58.33	58.33	58.33
FADS	10%	82.81	86.44	**90.91**	**90.28**	75.15	60.74
	20%	**84.38**	81.27	81.82	**86.07**	73.47	53.78
	30%	**85.58**	78.42	63.64	**82.59**	71.07	49.58
TDA	10%	**84.06**	82.92	82.35	**84.84**	71.88	47.68
	20%	**79.66**	76.81	77.70	**80.19**	65.28	45.97
	30%	**77.94**	68.70	76.23	**77.75**	58.92	47.19
PRA_{Book}	10%	77.72	75.65	**78.02**	**78.42**	63.38	64.36
	20%	75.55	74.31	**76.29**	**75.22**	61.65	56.97
	30%	**77.03**	69.52	76.97	**73.86**	59.43	70.04
PRA_{DVD}	10%	**80.42**	79.21	79.55	**81.44**	69.24	80.20
	20%	**79.43**	74.33	79.30	**80.32**	73.10	69.86
	30%	**78.96**	70.16	77.55	**76.71**	62.39	71.98
PRA_{Music}	10%	78.83	71.39	**79.35**	**77.84**	72.16	52.06
	20%	**79.84**	77.27	76.25	**79.25**	68.30	52.45
	30%	**75.23**	69.78	72.13	**74.10**	71.26	70.75
Macro Average	10%	83.62	81.53	**83.88**	**83.38**	76.54	74.65
	20%	**83.23**	78.17	81.15	**79.79**	73.63	71.59
	30%	**80.01**	72.14	75.28	**77.11**	71.40	71.16
Macro Average		**82.39**	77.28	80.10	**80.09**	73.85	72.47
Micro Average	10%	**83.63**	82.23	83.02	**83.72**	80.16	77.66
	20%	**82.70**	80.51	80.53	**82.59**	76.59	75.05
	30%	**80.99**	77.04	76.67	**80.77**	75.04	75.62
Micro Average		**82.44**	79.92	80.07	**82.36**	77.26	76.11

[4] http://svmlight.joachims.org

Comparison to Other Methods

Table 4 shows that our proposed algorithms *LiC* and *SaC* outperform the other the algorithms in most of the cases. In terms of both the macro average and the micro average which is weighted over the size of the different class labels, our algorithms clearly outperform all other methods. Even though the class-noise rate of the training data is provided to ℓ_{log} and CEWS, they only outperform *LiC* and *SaC* for the 10% and 20% noise levels of two and three datasets, respectively. This is because ℓ_{log} and CEWS require that all samples have the same class-noise rate for the probability weighting.

Fort the small training set, such as LEU, which has only 37 training samples, and DB, which has only 64 samples for training, the size effect is quite prominent. Intuitively, the noisy data elimination based method should not work well in these data. Results show that when the class noise rate increase to 20% and 30%, the high percentage of noise obviously have a big effect on the training data. Most methods have a big performance decrease for these two datasets, but *LiC* performs well and shows a significant advantage over other methods. This is because in the small training set, the size of training data is more important than the quality. *LiC* keeps the size of the training data. Due to the class noise estimation, *LiC* can also show a higher performance than ℓ_{log} even though ℓ_{log} also has the same size of training data.

When the training set grows, such as Splice which has 1,000 samples or TDA which has 2,000 samples, the quality of training samples becomes much more important. For these datasets, both *LiC* and *SaC* show better performance than the other methods. When the training set size becomes larger, the advantages of our methods become even more obviously for UCI Adult with 16,100 samples and the review text from Amazon with 4,000 samples. When the noise level is at the 30% level, *LiC* and *SaC* can achieve a 5% higher micro average accuracy than other methods.

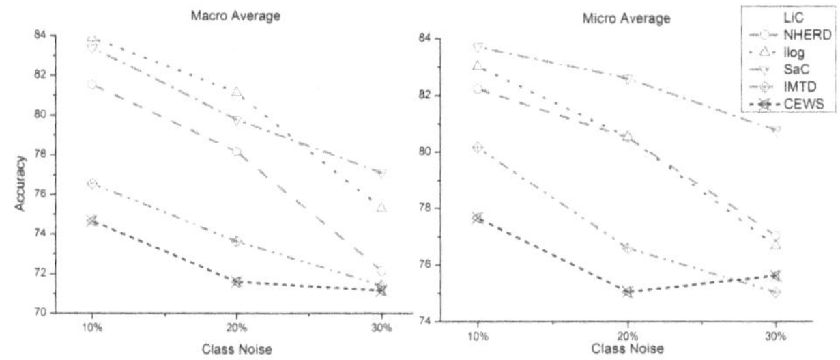

Fig. 5. Comparison between six methods

Generally speaking, both *LiC* and *SaC* show a more stable and more accurate performance in most cases as shown in Fig.5. For the cases which *LiC* and *SaC* cannot achieve the best performance, they are at least as competitive as the other methods. Thus, our proposed method is the overall best performer.

Comparison between *LiC* and *SaC*

We now compare the performance of the two proposed algorithms *LiC* and *SaC*. *LiC* is a learning with noise algorithm. Therefore, it should be more sensitive to the percentage of class noise in the training sample. On the other hand, *SaC* is a class noise elimination based method. It should be more sensitive to the size of training data. Take the small training dataset LEU as an example, it has only 37 samples. Thus any elimination on the training data will lead to degradation of performance. In this dataset, *LiC* is definitely a better choice than *SaC*. In general, we are more interested in the suitability of the two proposed strategies with respect to training data size. To eliminate the extremely small training datasets, we use "small" to means the size of training data at around 1,000 or so. For training set size at around 100 or so, we called them as "tiny training set".

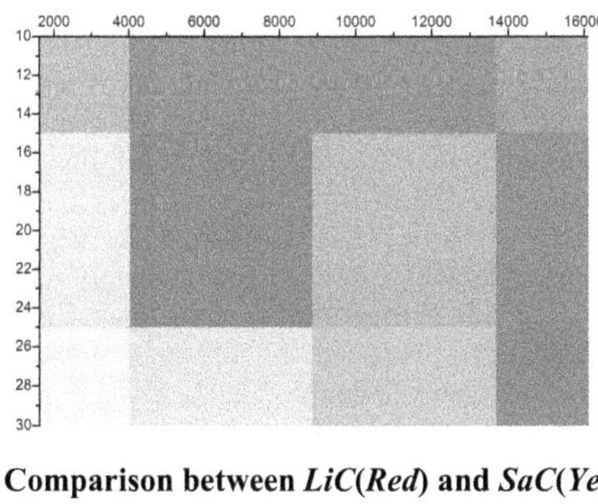

Fig. 6. Comparison between *LiC*(*Red*) and *SaC*(*Yellow*)

To examine the relationship between training set size and algorithm performance, we further analyze performance in more details for the UCI Adult dataset because the subsets are ordered by increasing size and all are from the same distribution and feature space. Fig. 6 shows the comparison of *LiC*(*Red*) to *SaC*(*Yellow*) for different dataset sizes and noise rates using color spectrum. The different shades indicate the relative suitability of the two algorithms. Here, the abscissa is the training set size and the ordinate is the class noise rate. We observe the following facts:

1. *LiC* is inefficient for small training sets(Indicated by pure yellow) and *SaC* is suitable for small data size.

2. Irrespective of the training size, *LiC* outperforms *SaC* for low class-noise (the color is more red than yellow). But when noise increase, *SaC* performs better (more yellow than red).

3. When the training size is relatively large, both *LiC* and *SaC* show similar performance and both are stable.

For text classification, because n-gram models are used to extract features, the feature space can be quite sparse and the elimination of noisy data may reduce the performance of classifier sharply. So, for tiny training sets such as DB, the size effect is very prominent. Note that *LiC* achieves an acceptable performance for DB even when the class-noise rate is 30%, whereas, all noise elimination based algorithms including *SaC* show very poor performance at higher noise levels. It is similar to the comparison on LEU dataset. Fig. 7 shows the performance for text classification which tend to have sparseness problem in the feature space. Here, the abscissa is the training set size and the ordinate is the class-accuracy.

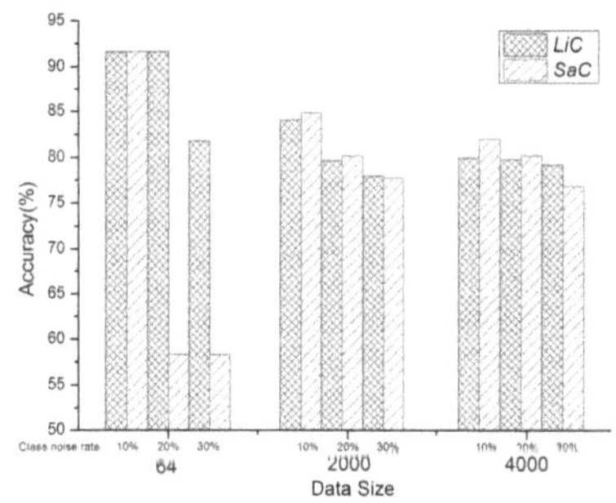

Fig.7 Comparison between *LiC* and *SaC* on text data

We observe the following from Fig. 7:

1. For the tiny training set, *SaC* is not acceptable and *LiC* achieves reasonably good performance.

2. For the small training set, *SaC* outperforms *LiC* when the class noise rate is low. But when noise rate increases, the gap between the two methods narrows.

3. Irrespective of the training size, *SaC* outperforms *LiC* for low class-noise rates. But when noise rate increases, *LiC* performs better.

4. When the training size is relatively large, *LiC* and *SaC* show similarly performance.

The performance of *SaC* is better than *LiC* when the class noise is low. The reason behind is that SVMs shows a higher performance than perceptron based algorithm when the feature space is large and sparse. So *SaC* is more suitable algorithm text classification.

In conclusion, *LiC* is more robust on data size and *SaC* is more robust on class noise rate. When the training set is relatively large, both algorithms perform similarly well and converge to a consistent result. This is proven through both the theoretical boundary analysis and the experimental results.

6. Conclusion and Future Work

In this paper, we present a novel class noise estimation method. We apply our method to both the learning with noise strategy and the class noise elimination strategy with calculated theoretic bounds for proof of accuracy. Both algorithms are competitive with state-of-the-art techniques and show superior performance on real datasets. We analyze the algorithm performance on different training dataset sizes and class-noise rates. Results conform to the learning theorem provided in Equation (7). In future work, we will investigate noise handling in semi-supervised tasks such as semi-supervised classification, transductive transfer learning, and also look into the domain adaptation problem. We will also consider different noise rate for different classes since label noise rates are often class-conditional in practice.

Acknowledgements

This work was supported by the National Natural Science Foundation of China (No. 61370165, 61203378), National 863 Program of China 2015AA015405, Natural Science Foundation of Guangdong Province S2013010014475, Shenzhen Development and Reform Commission Grant No.[2014]1507, Shenzhen Peacock Plan Research Grant KQCX20140521144507925, Baidu Collaborate Research Funding, and Hong Kong Polytechnic University Project Z0EP.

7. REFERENCES

[1] Zhu, X., and Wu, X "Class noise vs. attribute noise: A quantitative study." In Artificial Intelligence Review. 22(3): 177-210, 2004.

[2] Sáez, J. A., Galar, M, Luengo, J, and Herrera, F. "Analyzing the presence of noise in multi-class problems: alleviating its influence with the One-vs-One decomposition." In Knowledge and Information Systems. 38(1): 179-206, 2014.

[3] Joseph, L., Gyorkos, T. W., and Coupal, L.. "Bayesian estimation of disease prevalence and the parameters of diagnostic tests in the absence of a gold standard." In American Journal of Epidemiology. 3: 263-272, 1995.

[4] Cawthorn, D. M., Steinman, H. A., and Hoffman, L. C.. "A High Incidence of Species Substitution and Mislabelling Detected in Meat Products Sold in South Africa." In Food Control. 32(2): 440-449, 2013.

[5] Beigman, E. and Klebanov, B. B.. "Learning with Annotation Noise". In Proceedings of the 47th Annual Meeting of the ACL and the 4th IJCNLP of the AFNLP, 280–287, 2009.

[6] Natarajan, N., Dhillon, I. S., and Ravikumar, P.. "Learning with Noisy Labels". In Proceeding of Advances in Neural Information Processing Systems. 2013.

[7] Brodley, C. E., and Friedl, M. A.. "Identifying mislabeled training data." In Journal of Artificial Intelligence Research. 11: 131-167, 1999.

[8] Zighed, D.A., Lallich, S., Muhlenbach, F.. "A Statistical Approach to Class Separability". In Applied Stochastic Models in Business and Industry, Wiley-Blackwell, 21 (2): 187-197, 2005.

[9] Sluban, B., Gamberger, D., and Lavrac, N.. "Advances in Class Noise Detection." In Proceeding of European Conference on Artificial Intelligence, 1105-1106. 2010.

[10] Montgomery-Smith, S. J. "The distribution of Rademacher Sums." In Proceeding of the American Mathematical Society. 109(2): 517-522, 1990.

[11] Angluin, D., and D.Laird, P. "Learning from Noisy Examples." In Machine Learning 2(4): 343-370, 1988

[12] Zhang, M. L., and Zhou, Z. H.. "CoTrade: Confident Co-Training with Data Editing." In Systems, Man, and Cybernetics, Part B: Cybernetics, IEEE Transactions. 41(6): 1612-1626, 2011.

[13] Gui, L., Xu, R. F., Lu, Q., et al. "Cross-lingual Opinion Analysis via Negative Transfer Detection." In Proceedings of the 52th Annual Meeting of the ACL. 860-865, 2014.

[14] Frénay, B., and Verleysen, M.. "Classification in the Presence of Label Noise: a Survey". In IEEE Transactions on Neural Networks and Learning Systems, Vol. 25, 5, 2014.

[15] Heskes, T. "The use of being Stubborn and Introspective," In Studies in Cognitive Systems. 2000.

[16] Li, Y., Wessels, L. F. A., Ridder, D., and Reinders, M. J. T.. "Classification in the presence of class noise using a probabilistic Kernel Fisher method". In Pattern Recognition, Volume 40, Issue 12, December 2007, Pages 3349–3357.

[17] Scott, C., Blanchard. G., and Handy, G.. "Classification with Asymmetric Label Noise: Consistency and Maximal Denoising". In Journal of Machine Learning Research: Workshop and Conference Proceedings vol 30 (2013) 1–23

[18] Lawrence, N. D., and Schölkopf, B.. "Estimating a Kernel Fisher Discriminant in the Presence of Label Noise," In Proceeding of International Conference on Machine Learning. 306–313, 2001.

[19] Perez, C. J., Giron, F. J., Martin, J., Ruiz, M., and Rojano, C.. "Misclassified Multinomial Data: A Bayesian Approach," Revista De La Real Academia De Ciencias Exactas Físicas Y Naturales Serie A Matemáticas, vol. 101, no. 1, 71–80, 2007.

[20] Klebanov, B. B., and Beigman, E.. "From Annotator Agreement to Noise Models," In Computational. Linguistics, vol. 35, no. 4, 495–503, 2009..

[21] Kolcz, A., and Cormack, G. V.. "Genre-based Decomposition of Email Class Noise," In Proceeding of 15th ACM SIGKDD Conference on Knowledge Discovery and Data Mining, 427–436, 2009.

[22] Zhu, X., Wu, X., and Chen, Q. J.. "Eliminating Class Noise in Large Datasets." In Proceeding of International Conference on Machine Learning, vol. 3, 920-927. 2003.

[23] Jiang, Y., and Zhou, Z. H.. "Editing Training Data for k-NN Classifiers with Neural Network Ensemble." In Advances in Neural Networks, 356-361. Springer Berlin Heidelberg, 2004.

[24] Bennett, C., and Sharpley, M.. "Interpolation of Operators". Vol. 129. Academic press, 1988.

[25] Golub, T. R., Donna K. S., Pablo Tamayo, C. H., Michelle G., Jill, P. M., Hilary C.. "Molecular Classification of Cancer: Class Discovery and Class Prediction by Gene Expression Monitoring." Science. 286(5439): 531-537, 1999.

[26] Platt, J. C. "Fast Training of Support Vector Machines using Sequential Minimal Optimization". In Advances in Kernel Methods - Support Vector Learning, Cambridge, MA, 1998.

[27] Crammer, K., and Lee, D.. "Learning via Gaussian Herding." In Proceeding of Advances in Neural Information Processing Systems, 451-459. 2010.

[28] Cui, B., Ooi, B. C., Su, J., and Tan, K. L. "Contorting high dimensional data for efficient main memory KNN processing". In Proceeding of International Conference on Management of Data - SIGMOD , pp. 479-490, 2003.

[29] Hui, J., Ooi, B.C., Shen, H., Yu, C., Zhou, A.: An adaptive and efficient dimensionality reduction algorithm for high-dimensional indexing. In: Proc. 19th ICDE Conference, p. 87 2003.

Learning Task Grouping using Supervised Task Space Partitioning in Lifelong Multitask Learning

Meenakshi Mishra
Department of Electrical Engineering
and Computer Science
University of Kansas
mmishra@ku.edu

Jun Huan
Department of Electrical Engineering
and Computer Science
University of Kansas
jhuan@ku.edu

ABSTRACT

Lifelong multitask learning is a multitask learning framework in which a learning agent faces the tasks that need to be learnt in an online manner. Lifelong multitask learning framework may be applied to a variety of applications such as image annotation, robotics, automated machines etc, and hence, may prove to be a highly promising direction for further investigation. However, the lifelong learning framework comes with its own baggage of challenges. The biggest challenge is the fact that the characteristics of the future tasks which might be encountered by the learning agents are entirely unknown. If all the tasks are assumed to be related, there may be a risk of training from unrelated task resulting in negative transfer of information. To overcome this problem, both batch and online multitask learning algorithms learn task relationships. However, due to the unknown nature of the future tasks, learning the task relationships is also difficult in lifelong multitask learning. In this paper, we propose learning functions to model the task relationships as it is computationally cheaper in an online setting. More specifically, we learn partition functions in the task space to divide the tasks into cluster. Our major contribution is to present a global formulation to learn both the task partitions and the parameters. We provide a supervised learning framework to estimate both the partition function and the model. The current method has been implemented and compared against other leading lifelong learning algorithms using several real world datasets, and we show that the current method has a superior performance.

Keywords

Lifelong Multitask Learning, Online Learning, Feature Selection, Partition Models

1. INTRODUCTION

Lifelong multitask learning is a multitask learning framework where a learning agent transfers the knowledge from the already learnt tasks to the new tasks which it encounters for learning during its lifetime. Lifelong multitask learning can be viewed as a subset of online multitask learning problem where the framework is online in terms of the tasks. The inspiration for lifelong multitask learning comes from the natural process used by human beings for learning [23], as they have a natural tendency to transfer the knowledge from previously learnt tasks to new tasks. The lifelong multitask learning setting is of great utility for many real world problems where one needs to make predictions related to new tasks regularly. Examples of such applications may arise in online image annotation where new images are constantly being added by the users and new objects that need to be identified are repeatedly added to the list, or in the autonomous robots sent on exploratory mission in outer space or under water to explore and identify a new surrounding.

Lifelong multitask learning has been primarily studied by Eaton et al [7], where the authors develop an algorithm which can handle new tasks as they are faced by the learning agent during its lifetime of training. The authors assume that all the tasks are related in a sub-dimensional space which can be represented by a set of basis vectors. The authors aim to learn these basis vectors and the coefficients of these basis vectors for each task. This work has been extended by the authors in multiple ways as in [1, 15, 16, 17]. These methods only suffer from one inefficiency, and that is entire basis vector needs to updated when a new task arrives. Also, this method cannot do feature selection while learning the tasks.

In this paper, we focus on learning the structure of the tasks in lifelong multitask learning along with feature selection. Learning the task structure is especially hard in lifelong learning setting because there is no previous knowledge of the nature of new tasks that may be arriving. Thus, the task learning mechanism needs to be dynamic and able to evolve with changing nature of the task sets. For this purpose, we propose learning partition functions rather than task structure matrix for learning the task relationships. In this paper, we learn the task clusters by imposing a series of partitions on the task space in a supervised manner. We also assume that the similar tasks depend on the similar features. Therefore, we incorporate feature selection in our model as well.

Our main contribution in this paper is to present a global formulation for learning both partition models in task space and the task models using novel supervised learning formu-

Permission to make digital or hard copies of all or part of this work for personal or classroom use is granted without fee provided that copies are not made or distributed for profit or commercial advantage and that copies bear this notice and the full citation on the first page. Copyrights for components of this work owned by others than ACM must be honored. Abstracting with credit is permitted. To copy otherwise, or republish, to post on servers or to redistribute to lists, requires prior specific permission and/or a fee. Request permissions from Permissions@acm.org.
CIKM'15, October 19–23, 2015, Melbourne, Australia.
© 2015 ACM. ISBN 978-1-4503-3794-6/15/10 ...$15.00.
DOI: http://dx.doi.org/10.1145/2806416.2806570.

lation. This formulation partitions the task space such that the similar tasks remain in the same region using supervised learning and enforces similar tasks to depend on similar features. Learning both the task parameters and relationships is done in a supervised manner. We present the solution of this formulation using dual averaging technique for regularized stochastic gradient methods to solve for the sparsity constraints.

2. RELATED WORK

This paper is essentially a framework for multitask learning in a lifelong learning framework. The core idea of the present approach is to learn both the task relationships and task models using supervised learning in a lifelong learning framework.

The literature related to lifelong learning is very limited. The idea of lifelong learning has been known since 1996 when Thrun [23, 24] introduced the concept first in the machine learning community. Since then multiple authors have contributed to lifelong multitask learning in supervised setting [20, 21, 22]. These papers are about methods to incorporate previously learnt neural network so that the knowledge learnt may be used for future tasks and do not deal with identifying the task relationships. Recently, Eaton et al [7] published a study on lifelong multitask learning which assumes that the tasks are related in a sub dimensional latent space. This study is based on [13]. The authors learn the basis of the latent space in which the tasks are related along with the coefficients of the basis for each tasks. Since the authors assume sparse coefficients, an implicit task relationship is assumed in their algorithm, but the explicit task relationships may not be identified using this algorithm. Even though learning task relationships is a new concept in lifelong learning, it has been much explored in multitask learning algorithms.

In the traditional multitask learning algorithms, where all the tasks were initially assumed to be related to each other [2, 3, 4, 8], researchers observed that training unrelated tasks together may lead to negative transfer of information, which results in degradation of generalization error [12, 13]. To avoid this problem, researchers investigated learning task relationships such that the information is only transferred among the related tasks. The most common approach for solving this problem is to learn a positive semi-definite matrix to represent the task relationships [28, 9]. This positive semidefinite matrix is often the task covariance matrix or task kernel matrix [28], or Laplacian matrix or indicator matrix mapping each task to other related tasks [9]. Although task relationships are learnt using these fixed sized matrices, there are inherent problems in extending this method to lifelong learning. When a new task arrives, the knowledge learnt regarding existing task relationships is not directly transferrable to the new task. Also, each time a new task arrives, a new row and column needs to be added to task relationship matrix which is computationally expensive. Another method for learning task relationships is to use k nearest neighbors to identify the task clusters [11, 30, 29]. These methods use an unsupervised step to learn the task relationships. Some authors assume that the tasks are related in sub dimensional latent space, and learn the relationships in that latent space [13, 14, 10]. This method does not learn the explicit task relationships in the physical space. Kang et al learn an indicator matrix whose element in i^{th} row and j^{th} column takes the value 1 if the task in row i belongs to the group in column j otherwise 0. This algorithm does an explicit task relationship modeling, and does feature selection as well while learning the task parameters and thus bears closest resemblance to our algorithm. However, the information learnt regarding task relationships is non-transferable to the new tasks. All of the above algorithms learn the task relationship using an unsupervised step.

In this paper, we propose using supervised learning to learn explicit task relationship modeling. More specifically, we learn a global formulation for learning partition functions in a supervised fashion to group the tasks together and then learn the task models. Learning functions in the task space which divide the tasks into clusters are easier to learn in terms of optimization, and they provide an easy transfer of information from previously learnt task to the new task. Using a global formulation to learn the task clusters and task model ensures maximum coupling between the two learning assignments ensuring higher accuracy.

3. METHODOLOGY

In this paper, we learn a model for lifelong multitask learning scenario which learns the cluster of tasks as well as does feature selection. Before we give a description of our model, we would first like to describe the notation used, followed by a brief overview of our work. Proceeding which, we provide the details of our algorithm.

3.1 Notation Used

Throughout this text, we represent the matrices by capital letter, the vectors by bold faced lowercase letters and scalar values by lowercase letters. Given a matrix X, its jth column is represented by $\boldsymbol{x}_{*,j}$. For the same matrix X, the element at the ith row and j^{th} column is $x_{i,j}$.

The dataset being provided is represented by $\boldsymbol{D}$, which consists of the input features $\boldsymbol{x}_{i,t}$ and the output label $y_{i,t}$, where i ranges from $1...N_t$ and t ranges from $1...T$. N_t represents the number of samples in task t and T represents the total number of tasks. In a lifelong multitask setting, the values of N_t and T are undetermined.

The given dataset $\boldsymbol{D}$ consists of 2-tuple elements, where each entry $\boldsymbol{x}_{i,t}$ belongs to a d dimensional real valued vector, $\boldsymbol{x}_{i,t} \in \mathbb{R}^d$. The values of outputs depend on the tasks. For regression problems, the values of $y_{i,t}$ is a real number, $y_{i,t} \in \mathbb{R}$. For classification problems, $y_{i,t}$ is either 1 or 0, $y_{i,t} \in \{0,1\}$. We assume linear models for prediction throughout. Thus, the objective of the algorithm would be to learn the vector $\boldsymbol{w}_t$, where $\hat{y}_{i,t} = \boldsymbol{x}_{i,t}\boldsymbol{w}_t$ for linear regression and $\hat{y}_{i,t} = \sigma(\boldsymbol{x}_{i,t}\boldsymbol{w}_t)$ for classification problem. σ represents any monotonic function.

Given the above framework, the average empirical risk for all the tasks in this case may be given as

$$R = \frac{1}{T}\sum_{t=1}^{T}\frac{1}{N_t}\sum_{i=1}^{N_t} l(\boldsymbol{w_t}, \boldsymbol{x}_{i,t}, y_{i,t}) \quad (1)$$
$$= \frac{1}{T}\sum_{t=1}^{T} l(\boldsymbol{w}_t, D)$$

Here, l is the loss function used. Usually, l belongs to the sigmoid family of functions for classification problems and squared loss function for regression problems. If we minimize the above equation to solve for $\boldsymbol{w}_t$, then the tasks are not regularized and the objective is same as learning each task separately. Therefore, for multitask learning problems, a regularization term is added to the empirical risk to ensure that the tasks lie close together.

$$R = \frac{1}{T}\sum_{t=1}^{T} l(\boldsymbol{w}_t, D) + \lambda F(W) \quad (2)$$

where λ is a regularization constant, and F is a positive monotonic function of W. The common choices of F are L_1 norm, L_2 norm and trace norm.

3.2 Supervised Partitioning of the Task Space

In most multitask learning formulations, all the tasks are regularized together under the assumption that they are related similarly. There are multiple applications where all the tasks are not related to each other and it is beneficial to identify the related tasks. The existing multitask learning approaches alternate between unsupervised step and supervised step to learn the task relationships and task models. We introduce a new method to learn both the task relationships and task models in a supervised manner which may also be used in lifelong multitask setting.

In this paper, we propose learning partition functions to divide the task space into regions. As a result, the tasks in the same region are effectively clustered together. There are multiple benefits of using partition functions instead of indicator matrices to learn task relationships. Functions are easier to update in an online setting as opposed to indicator matrices. Therefore, learning functions results in more adaptive algorithm to lifelong learning setting. Second benefit of using function is that it is easier to transfer knowledge of previously learnt tasks to the new incoming tasks. The learnt function can easily provide rules for clustering the new incoming task. Third benefit lies in the fact that learning a discrete valued binary matrix using optimization techniques is much harder than learning a real valued continuous function. Therefore, we present this novel idea of learning partition functions in a supervised manner to cluster the task.

Let us first describe our algorithm for including a single partition function, and then we later extend the idea for creating multiple partition functions for creating r groups of tasks. Let us assume a function $g(X, \boldsymbol{y})$ which divides the task space or the model space into two regions, region 1 and region 2. Also, we assume that the task parameters, $\boldsymbol{w}_t$ can be given as either $\boldsymbol{u}_1 + \boldsymbol{v}_t$ or $\boldsymbol{u}_2 + \boldsymbol{v}_t$ depending on if the given task belongs to the region 1 or 2. Here, $\boldsymbol{u}_1$ is the common model for all the tasks which lie in region 1, and $\boldsymbol{u}_2$ is the model common for all the tasks in region 2. $\boldsymbol{v}_t$ are task specific models.

In this case, the empirical loss function can be written as

$$R = \min \frac{1}{T}\sum_{t=1}^{T} \mathbb{I}(g(\theta_t(X_t, \boldsymbol{y}_t)) = 0)\frac{1}{N_t}\sum_{i=1}^{N_t} l(\boldsymbol{u}_1, \boldsymbol{v}_t, \boldsymbol{x}_{i,t}, y_{i,t})$$
$$+ \frac{1}{T}\sum_{t=1}^{T} \mathbb{I}(g(\theta_t(X_t, \boldsymbol{y}_t)) = 1)\frac{1}{N_t}\sum_{i=1}^{N_t} l(\boldsymbol{u}_2, \boldsymbol{v}_t, \boldsymbol{x}_{i,t}, y_{i,t}) \quad (3)$$

Here, $\mathbb{I}$ is the indicator function and θ_t is a function that maps the input data X_t to the output $\boldsymbol{y}_t$ for a given task t, and thus, can be seen as the representative of the task t. Henceforth, we will represent $g(\theta_t(X_t, \boldsymbol{y}_t))$ as simply g. The function $l(\boldsymbol{u}_1, \boldsymbol{v}_t, \boldsymbol{x}_{i,t}, y_{i,t})$ is the loss function and measures the mean squared error between $\boldsymbol{x}_{i,t}(\boldsymbol{u}_1 + \boldsymbol{v}_t)$ and $y_{i,t}$. For classification problems, the loss function may belong to either zero-one loss function or sigmoidal family of functions.

Also, let us assume

$$l_t^1 = \frac{1}{N_t}\sum_{i=1}^{N_t} l(\boldsymbol{u}_1, \boldsymbol{v}_t, \boldsymbol{x}_{i,t}, y_{i,t})$$

and

$$l_t^2 = \frac{1}{N_t}\sum_{i=1}^{N_t} l(\boldsymbol{u}_2, \boldsymbol{v}_t, \boldsymbol{x}_{i,t}, y_{i,t})$$

Thus, the empirical risk described in equation 3 is

$$R = \min \frac{1}{T}\sum_{t=1}^{T} \mathbb{I}(g = 0) l_t^1 + \frac{1}{T}\sum_{t=1}^{T} \mathbb{I}(g = 1) l_t^2 \quad (4)$$

Now, let us consider the case where there are more than one partitions of the task space. Since, each partition function divides the task space into two regions, we adapt the framework of using a series of partition functions which recursively partition the task space hierarchically. In other words, we establish a tree structure in the task space with a partition function g^k at each node k of the tree. The function g^k divides the region at that node of the task space into two more regions. There is no partition function at the leaf nodes. Thus, each leaf node is associated with a region of the task space which is not partitioned any further. For each leaf node r, there exists a common task specific model $\boldsymbol{u}_r$ which is common for all the tasks that belong in the region associated with leaf node r. As mentioned before, there also exists task specific model $\boldsymbol{v}_t$, thus, the task model is given by $\boldsymbol{w}_t = \boldsymbol{u}_r + \boldsymbol{v}_t$, assuming task t belongs to region or leaf node r.

Let the left child of kth node of the partition tree be k_L and right node be k_R. For any node k, the value of empirical loss for a task t would then be

$$L_t^k = \begin{cases} \mathbb{I}(g_k = 0)L_t^{k_L} + \mathbb{I}(g_k = 1)L_t^{k_R} & \text{if } k \notin \text{leaf node} \\ l_t^k & \text{if } k \in \text{leaf node} \end{cases} \tag{5}$$

This formulation of the loss function is recursive. Thus, the loss function of the entire tree may be given by the loss function of the root node. The loss function of the root node is the sum of the total loss of its left child and right child. The left child loss and right child loss may further be broken down in the same way till we reach the leaf node. Thus, the loss function of the root node is same as the loss functions of the sum of leaf nodes. Therefore, if the root node is 1, the cumulative empirical risk is

$$R = \frac{1}{T}\sum_{t=1}^{T} L_t^1 \tag{6}$$

Additionally, we also impose the models to be sparse. That is, the common model in region r, $\boldsymbol{u}_r$ should only select some features relevant to all the tasks in the region. Similarly, the task specific models, $\boldsymbol{v}_t$ are assumed to be sparse too. Sparsity assumption is especially useful for tasks with large dimensionality. The empirical loss function is regularized using L_1 norm on regional and task specific models. Thus, the empirical loss function may be written as

$$R = \frac{1}{T}\sum_{t=1}^{T} L_t^1 + \lambda_1 \frac{1}{T}\sum_{t=1}^{T} \|\boldsymbol{v}_t\|_1 + \lambda_2 \sum_{r=1}^{p_l} \|\boldsymbol{u}_r\|_1 \tag{7}$$

assuming there are p_l leaf nodes. We need to solve for the values of $\boldsymbol{u}_r$, $\boldsymbol{v}_t$ and g_k. Henceforth, we will refer to all g_k as partition functions, $\boldsymbol{u}_r$ as region specific models and $\boldsymbol{v}_t$ as task specific model. We use alternative minimization to solve for each of the values. First, let us discuss how we can solve for a single partition function. Later, we will show how the same framework is extended for multiple partition functions.

3.2.1 Finding Single Partition Function

To find the solution for g for a single partition case, let us assume that the values of $\boldsymbol{u}_1$, $\boldsymbol{u}_2$ and $\boldsymbol{v}_t$ is fixed. Then, the risk function is

$$R = \min \frac{1}{T}\sum_{t=1}^{T} \mathbb{I}(g = 0) l_t^1 + \frac{1}{T}\sum_{t=1}^{T} \mathbb{I}(g = 1) l_t^2 \tag{8}$$

The regularization terms need not be included as the values of $\boldsymbol{u}_1$, $\boldsymbol{u}_2$ and $\boldsymbol{v}_t$ are fixed. Also, because $\boldsymbol{u}_1$, $\boldsymbol{u}_2$ and $\boldsymbol{v}_t$ are fixed, the values of l_t^1 and l_t^2 can be easily computed.

Theorem 1. *For a fixed values of vectors $\boldsymbol{u}_1$ and $\boldsymbol{u}_2$, the solution for finding the optimal partition function g which minimizes Equation 8 is same as finding the optimal classifier which minimizes the following empirical loss*

$$\frac{1}{T}\sum_{t=1}^{T} |l_t^1 - l_t^2| \mathbb{I}(g = (l_t^1 < l_t^2)) \tag{9}$$

PROOF. Let us define a set S consisting of all the indices t, where $l_t^1 < l_t^2$. Also let us define operator $>$, such that for $a > b$, the result is 1 if a is greater than b and 0 otherwise. We can rewrite equation 8 as.

$$\begin{aligned} R =& \frac{1}{T}\Big[\sum_{t\in S} \mathbb{I}(g = 0) l_t^1 + \sum_{t\notin S} \mathbb{I}(g = 0) l_t^1 \\ &+ \sum_{t\in S} \mathbb{I}(g = 1) l_t^2 + \sum_{t\notin S} \mathbb{I}(g = 1) l_t^2\Big] \\ =& \frac{1}{T}\Big[\sum_{t\in S} \mathbb{I}(g = (l_t^1 > l_t^2)) l_t^1 + \sum_{t\notin S} \mathbb{I}(g = (l_t^1 < l_t^2)) l_t^1 \\ &+ \sum_{t\in S} \mathbb{I}(g = (l_t^1 < l_t^2)) l_t^2 + \sum_{t\notin S} \mathbb{I}(g = (l_t^1 > l_t^2)) l_t^2\Big] \end{aligned}$$

Since, for all $t \in S$, the value of $l_t^1 > l_t^2$ is 0. Similar argument holds for other terms. Rearranging terms,

$$\begin{aligned} R =& \frac{1}{T}\Big[\sum_{t\in S} \mathbb{I}(g = (l_t^1 > l_t^2)) l_t^1 + \sum_{t\notin S} \mathbb{I}(g = (l_t^1 > l_t^2)) l_t^2 \\ &+ \sum_{t\in S} \mathbb{I}(g = (l_t^1 < l_t^2)) l_t^2 + \sum_{t\notin S} \mathbb{I}(g = (l_t^1 < l_t^2)) l_t^1\Big] \\ =& \frac{1}{T}\Big[\sum_{t=1}^{T} \mathbb{I}(g = (l_t^1 > l_t^2)) \min(l_t^1, l_t^2) \\ &+ \sum_{t=1}^{T} \mathbb{I}(g = (l_t^1 < l_t^2)) \max(l_t^1, l_t^2)\Big] \\ =& \frac{1}{T}\Big[\sum_{t=1}^{T} \mathbb{I}(g \neq (l_t^1 < l_t^2)) \min(l_t^1, l_t^2) \\ &+ \sum_{t=1}^{T} \mathbb{I}(g = (l_t^1 < l_t^2)) \max(l_t^1, l_t^2)\Big] \\ =& \frac{1}{T}\Big[\sum_{t=1}^{T} \mathbb{I}(g = (l_t^1 < l_t^2)) \max(l_t^1, l_t^2) \\ &+ \sum_{t=1}^{T} \big[1 - \mathbb{I}(g = (l_t^1 < l_t^2))\big] \min(l_t^1, l_t^2)\Big] \\ =& \frac{1}{T}\Big[\sum_{t=1}^{T} \mathbb{I}(g = (l_t^1 < l_t^2)) \max(l_t^1, l_t^2) \\ &- \sum_{t=1}^{T} \mathbb{I}(g = (l_t^1 < l_t^2)) \min(l_t^1, l_t^2) + \sum_{t=1}^{T} \min(l_t^1, l_t^2)\Big] \end{aligned} \tag{10}$$

Here, the last term is a constant and does not depend on function g. Minimization of R with respect to g will not be effected by the third term, and hence, can be removed. Thus, empirical risk may be given by

$$\begin{aligned} R &= \frac{1}{T}\sum_{t=1}^{T} \mathbb{I}(g = (l_t^1 < l_t^2))(\max(l_t^1, l_t^2) - \min(l_t^1, l_t^2)) \\ &= \frac{1}{T}\sum_{t=1}^{T} |l_t^1 - l_t^2| \mathbb{I}(g = (l_t^1 < l_t^2)) \end{aligned} \tag{11}$$

From theorem 1, it can be deduced that the optimal partition of the task space is obtained when each task is given the label 0, if model in partition 0 gives a lower error, and 1, if model in partition 1 gives a lower error. The empirical risk is then the weighted error of classifying these tasks, with weights for each error given as $|l_t^1 - l_t^2|$. The partition function in the task space, g, can be obtained by using any cost sensitive classifier. Here, we assume that the classifier g is a linear classifier. The value of θ_t used here is the single task learners obtained from solving logistic regression or linear regression problem. The details for θ_t are provided in section 3.2.3.

To compute the weights of linear classifier $\boldsymbol{g}$, we use the cost sensitive classifier developed by Zhang and Garcia [27]. For each incoming task t, the classifier $\boldsymbol{g}$ may be updated as

$$\boldsymbol{g}_t = \boldsymbol{g}_{t-1} + \tau_t \text{label } \theta_t \tag{12}$$

Here, the value of label is the label given to task t according to previous paragraph. The value of τ_t is defined as

$$\tau_t' = \frac{1 - \text{label } \boldsymbol{g}_{t-1}^T \theta_t}{\theta_t^T \theta_t}$$
$$\tau_t = \begin{cases} 0 & \text{if } \tau_t' < 0 \\ \tau_t' & \text{if } 0 < \tau_t' \le \alpha c_t \\ \alpha c_t & \text{if } \tau_t' > \alpha c_t \end{cases} \tag{13}$$

Here, α is a constant determining the size of step, and c_t is the weight associated with each task. Here, the value of c_t is $|l_t^1 - l_t^2|$.

3.2.2 Multiregion-Partitioned Task Space

The above theorem can be easily extended to a multi-region partitioned task space as well. For a given node k in the partition tree and a given task t, the empirical loss and the global empirical risk is given in equations 5 and 7.

In order to solve for each of the $\boldsymbol{g}_k$ for fixed task and model specific models in equation 7, we use alternate minimization. Thus, for each task, we first fix all the $\boldsymbol{u}_r$ and $\boldsymbol{g}_k$ for k in all nodes of the partition tree. Then, we pick one partition function g_k at a time and solve for that. Therefore, for each node k not in leaf node, the values of g_k is given by minimizing

$$\boldsymbol{g}_k = \min \frac{1}{T} \sum_{t=1}^{T} \mathbb{I}(g_k = 0) L_t^{k_L} + \mathbb{I}(g_k = 1) L_t^{k_R} \tag{14}$$

Minimizing the above equation is same as minimizing

$$\boldsymbol{g}_k = \min -\frac{1}{T} \sum_{t=1}^{T} |L_t^{k_L} - L_t^{k_R}| \mathbb{I}(g_k = (L_t^{k_L} > L_t^{k_R}) \tag{15}$$

This is a direct extension of Theorem 1. It is also easy to infer from theorem 1 that the value of $L_t^{k_L}$ is the smallest value of $l_t^{r_{kL}}$ where r_{kL} represents all the leaf nodes under the left child of node k. Similarly, $L_t^{k_R}$ is the minimum value of $l_t^{r_{kR}}$. Since, all other partition functions and region models are fixed, the value of $L_t^{k_L}$ and $L_t^{k_R}$ may easily be computed. Thus, the value of each partition function may be computed using any online cost sensitive classifier. After updating the partition functions, we solve for each $\boldsymbol{u}_r$ and $\boldsymbol{v}_t$ as described in the next section.

3.2.3 Predicting Regional and Task Specific Models

Given the value of the partition function, we know the region a given task belongs to. Let this region be depicted by r, and the indices of all tasks in this region belong to set S. The equation 7 then reduces to

$$R = \frac{1}{T} \sum_{t \in S} \frac{1}{N_t} \sum_{i=1}^{N_t} L(\boldsymbol{x}_{i,t}(\boldsymbol{u}_r + \boldsymbol{v}_t), y_{i,t}) + \lambda_1 \frac{1}{T} \sum_{t \in S} \|\boldsymbol{v}_t\|_1 + \lambda_2 \|\boldsymbol{u}_r\|_1 \tag{16}$$

The major inefficiency in the above equation is that it depends on all the samples from previous data owing to the inner summation in the equation. In order to overcome this efficiency, we use the trick used in [7]. We expand the inner summation term, $\frac{1}{N_t} \sum_{i=1}^{N_t} L(\boldsymbol{x}_{i,t}(\boldsymbol{u}_r + \boldsymbol{v}_t), y_{i,t})$, around $\theta_t = \min \frac{1}{N_t} \sum_{i=1}^{N_t} L(f(\boldsymbol{x}_{i,t}, \theta), y_{i,t})$. In other words, θ_t is the single task learner of task t. Using second order Taylor series expansion and ignoring all the constant terms, we get

$$R = \frac{1}{T} \sum_{t \in S} \|\theta_t - (\boldsymbol{u}_r + \boldsymbol{v}_t)\|_{D_t} + \lambda_1 \frac{1}{T} \sum_{t \in S} \|\boldsymbol{v}_t\|_1 + \lambda_2 \|\boldsymbol{u}_r\|_1 \tag{17}$$

where,

$$D_t = \nabla_{\theta,\theta} \frac{1}{N_t} \sum_{i=1}^{N_t} L(f(\boldsymbol{x}_{i,t}, \theta), y_{i,t})|_{\theta=\theta_t}$$
$$\theta_t = \min \frac{1}{N_t} \sum_{i=1}^{N_t} L(f(\boldsymbol{x}_{i,t}, \theta), y_{i,t})$$

and, $\|K\|_D$ is defined as $K^T DK$.

We can obtain the value of θ_t using linear or logistic regression. The value of θ_t may be easily updated online as well.

In order to find $\boldsymbol{v}_t$ and $\boldsymbol{u}_r$, we first fix $\boldsymbol{u}_r$ and solve for $\boldsymbol{v}_t$. The solution for $\boldsymbol{v}_t$ can be obtained by solving the following equation

$$R = \|\theta_t - (\boldsymbol{u}_r + \boldsymbol{v}_t)\|_{D_t} + \lambda_1 \|\boldsymbol{v}_t\|_1 \tag{18}$$

This equation can be solved using any off the shelf algorithm for solving L_1 norm regularization.

Then, we keep the values of $\boldsymbol{v}_t$ fixed, and find the value of $\boldsymbol{u}_r$. Therefore, we minimize the following equation

$$R = \frac{1}{T} \sum_{t \in S} \|\theta_t - (\boldsymbol{u}_r + \boldsymbol{v}_t)\|_{D_t} + \lambda_2 \|\boldsymbol{u}_r\|_1 \tag{19}$$

The above equation depends on all the tasks in the given region. In this case, using simple stochastic gradient algorithm to find the values of $\boldsymbol{u}_r$ in an online fashion may be used. However, it is very difficult to find the sparse solution in online framework because it is hard to find summation of different values which add to zero. For this purpose, we base our solution to find $\boldsymbol{u}_r$ on Lin Xiao's regularized dual averaging method [25].

The regularized dual averaging method updates the parameters by the average sub gradient of the function. Here, the value of the sub gradient d_t is

$$d_t = -2(\theta_t - \boldsymbol{v}_t - \boldsymbol{u}_r)tr(D_t) \tag{20}$$

where $tr(D_t)$ is the trace of matrix D_t. Then, the average sub gradient is computed as

$$\bar{d}_t = \frac{t-1}{t}\bar{d}_{t-1} + \frac{1}{t}d_t \tag{21}$$

Thus, the value of $\boldsymbol{u}_r$ is updated as

$$u_{r,j} = \begin{cases} 0, & \text{if } \|\bar{d}_{t,j}\| \leq \lambda_t^{RDA} \\ -\frac{\sqrt{t}}{\gamma}\left(\bar{d}_{t,j} - \lambda_t^{RDA} sign(\bar{d}_{t,j})\right) & \text{otherwise} \end{cases} \tag{22}$$

The value of $\lambda_t^{RDA} = \lambda_2 + \frac{\rho}{\sqrt{t}}$ and γ and ρ are regularizing parameters, $u_{r,j}$ is the jth element of vector $\boldsymbol{u}_r$.

3.2.4 Online Partitioning of Task Space

There is one more inefficiency that needs to be discussed. Since this algorithm is online algorithm, the number of partitions or the size of the partition tree is not fixed. Infact, we start out with the entire task space and partition the task space recursively as we encounter more and more tasks. There are two conditions that still need to be discussed. When do we decide to split a given region into two parts, and when do we stop growing the partition tree. The answer to the second question is to choose a maximum depth of the tree and do not grow the partition tree beyond the maximum depth. To evaluate the criteria for deciding when to split a region, we use a common intuition. All the tasks in a given region r share the same model $\boldsymbol{u}_r$. Thus, the loss function of the models in the same region will be in similar range. If a new task comes in, and the resulting loss l_t^r of new task t is significantly different in value than losses of other tasks, then new task t probably belongs to a separate group. Hence, the region must be split.

In order to detect the significant difference in values of losses, we use theory from change point detection. Change point detection estimation is a problem in machine learning which is associated with detecting change of events in a given signal. More specifically, we implement Shewart Control Chart [18, 5] to decide if change point has occurred and given region needs to be split. Here, we assume that the losses of the tasks in a given region are the samples belonging to gaussian distribution with mean m and variance σ. The values of m and σ can easily be estimated. Let us assume that the new task t belongs to a gaussian distribution with mean l_t^r and variance σ. Then the value of decision function for Shewhart Control Chart is given by $df = (m - l_t^r)^2/(2\sigma)$. Refer to [5] for derivation of decision function in Shewhart Control Chart for two gaussian functions. If df is greater than a constant h, then the region is split.

The summary of the entire algorithm is described in Algorithm 1.

Algorithm 1 Supervised Clustering in Lifelong Multitask Learning

Require: Data $\{X_t, \boldsymbol{y}_t$, λ_1, λ_2, Maximum depth of partition tree p, ρ
  Initialize values of $\boldsymbol{u}$, $\boldsymbol{v}$ and $\boldsymbol{g}$ as $\mathbf{0}$
  for all incoming task t **do**
    Get the next batch of data for task t
    Update value of θ_t using any single task regression or classification
    if Task t belongs to existing task **then**
      s = number of task in region r where task t belongs
      $\bar{d}_{t-1} = s\bar{d}_t - \frac{1}{t-1}d_t$
      $u_{r,j} = -\frac{\sqrt{s-1}}{\gamma}\left(\bar{d}_{t-1,j} - \lambda_t^{RDA} sign(\bar{d}_{t-1,j})\right)$ for all $\|\bar{d}_{t,j}\| \leq \lambda_t^{RDA}$
    end if
    Update the partition functions as in Algorithm 2
    Update the values of $\boldsymbol{v}$ by minimizing equation 18
    Update the values of $\boldsymbol{u}$ given the partition functions using equation 22
  end for

4. EXPERIMENTAL STUDIES

In this paper, we developed a lifelong multitask learning algorithm which learns groups of tasks and selects a common set of features for each group of tasks. The description of the algorithm has been provided in the previous section. Now, we demonstrate the performance of our algorithm with respect to other state of the art similar algorithms. We name our algorithm SUPART (Supervised partitioning of Tasks) and show that SUPART performs better than or equivalent to other methods. The list of the different methods to which we compare our algorithm is provided below:

BatchMTL: This algorithm is a multitask learning algorithm developed by Kang et al [12]. Kang et al also developed an algorithm for clustering the tasks in multitask learning framework and using feature selection to enforce that similar tasks depend on the similar features. BatchMTL is the closest multitask learning algorithm to our framework, except that BatchMTL is implemented in batch setting where entire data is available. Therefore, we use Kang et al's method to compare the performance of our algorithm.

ELLA: Efficient Lifelong Learning Algorithm, or ELLA, is a lifelong multitask learning algorithm [7]. In this algorithm, the authors assume that all the tasks are related in a sub dimensional space, and learn a set of basis functions representing the sub dimensional space in which the tasks are related. For each task, the coefficients for the basis function are also learnt. Since the coefficients are assumed to be sparse, sometimes an overlapping clustering effect on the tasks is also observed. We pick this algorithm for comparison because it is based in lifelong setting. We would like to thank the authors for providing us their code.

TREE: This algorithm is a baseline method. Here, we build the clustering structure of the tasks using hierarchical clustering and enforce that the tasks at each node remain close to each other by using a gaussian prior around the mean of the tasks belonging to that node.

Algorithm 2 Update the partition functions

Require: θ_t, t, h, p
  if t is the first task **then**
    Assign task t to first node of tree G which is the root
    Set the root node as the leaf node as well
  else
    g = partition function at root node of tree G
    while leaf node is not reached **do**
      Update partition g according to equation 13
      Set value of g as partition function of the next child of tree G
    end while
    if leaf node reached **then**
      m = mean of loss of all tasks in current region
      σ = variance of loss of all tasks in current region
      l = loss of task t
      if $(m-l)^2/(2*\sigma) > h$ and maximum depth of tree p is not reached **then**
        Split node
        Place all tasks in left child
        Place the task t in right child
        Compute the partition function g for this node
      end if
    end if
  end if

Table 1: Summary of each of the dataset

Dataset	# of tasks	# of features	# of samples
MNIST	10	87	20,000
USPS	10	64	20,000
LANDMINE	29	9	14,820
STOCK Market	25	16	24,452

STL: The single task learning algorithm which we use to compare our algorithm with bayesian online regression and classification methods as described in [6].

SUPART: This is the algorithm described in current paper. In this paper, we propose a global formulation for simultaneously partitioning and learning the tasks. In this way, both the task partitions and task parameters are learnt in a supervised setting.

4.1 Dataset Used

In order to evaluate the performance of our dataset, we use several real world datasets. The description of the dataset is provided below.

MNIST Dataset: The MNIST dataset is a collection of handwritten digits. We have downloaded this dataset from Kang's webpage [12]. This dataset is basically a subset of the original MNIST dataset which has already been preprocessed. In this dataset, principal component analysis was used to extract the top 64 features of each image. The data has been provided for only 2,000 image, and each image needs to be classified into one of the digits between 0 and 9. We binarize the tasks, and thus, each task description includes identification of a single digit out of the ten digits. Thus, there are 10 tasks, and all of the 2,000 images serve as the samples for each task. Therefore, there are effectively 20,000 samples belonging to the total of 10 tasks. The dimensionality of each of the samples is 64.

Table 3: The performance comparison of SUPART with Batch Method. The mean accuracies are reported here. The performance of batch algorithms are often seen as the maximum performance which an online algorithm may reach. Here, SUPART has a performance almost equivalent to the Batch Multitask Learning.

Dataset	Batch MTL	SUPART
MNIST	0.9000 ± 0.0001	0.8960 ± 0.0189
USPS	0.9000 ± 0.0001	0.8998 ± 0.0001
LANDMINE	0.7181 ± 0.0103	0.7308 ± 0.0107
STOCK	0.9249 ± 0.0101	0.9388 ± 0.0026

USPS Dataset: This dataset is also downloaded for Kang's webpage [12]. It is also a handwritten digit dataset which has been preprocessed using a similar procedure as the MNIST dataset. In USPS dataset, top 87 features were used. The task was again to identify the digit between 0 and 9 in the image. Again, we binarized the task, and thus, each task was to identify if an image contains a particular digit or not. The number of samples were 2,000 for each of the 10 task, making the effective number of samples to be 20,000, and the number of features in each sample was 87.

Stock Market Dataset: Stock market dataset is a compilation of the stock market prices which we compiled from Yahoo's financial services website. We selected 25 different companies from various market domains such as oil and gas industries, computers and electronics industries, pharmaceutical industries and finance. The weekly stock market prices from the period of December 1994 to December 2014 were obtained. Each task consisted of predicting the current stock market prices of each of the company based on the stock market prices of past sixteen weeks. There were a total of 25 tasks and 24,452 samples, and each sample having 16 features.

Landmine Detection Dataset: This dataset is about predicting the presence of a mine based on the radar images of the location. Originally, this dataset is from [26], however, we obtain the data from [7]. The dataset was available with the software for ELLA. The radar images were preprocessed and 9 features were extracted from the images, out of which 4 features were moment-based, 3 correlation-based, one energy-ratio feature and one spatial variance feature. The problem formulated as binary classification having 29 tasks, nine features and 14,820 samples.

Table 1 presents a summary of all the datasets.

4.2 Evaluation Protocol

All the models selected consisted of some hyper-parameters which need to be fixed by the user. The hyper-parameters were chosen using five fold crossvalidation on around fifty percent of the dataset. We also use a greedy search procedure if the algorithm has multiple hyper-parameters which need to be selected. Thus, we first fix all the hyper parameters to a constant value, and vary one at a time. We pick the value of the hyper parameter which minimizes the cross

Table 2: The performance comparison of SUPART with other methods. The mean accuracies are reported here. SUPART almost always produced best accuracies. For Stock Dataset, even though ELLA has the best performance the improvement is not statistically significant.

Dataset	STL	TREE	ELLA	SUPART
MNIST	0.5561 ± 0.0294	0.5691 ± 0.0286	0.8179 ± 0.0651	$\mathbf{0.8960 \pm 0.0189}$
USPS	0.5217 ± 0.0379	0.5269 ± 0.0399	0.8016 ± 0.0786	$\mathbf{0.8998 \pm 0.0001}$
LANDMINE	0.5535 ± 0.0173	0.5658 ± 0.0181	0.6515 ± 0.0313	$\mathbf{0.7308 \pm 0.0107}$
STOCK	0.9356 ± 0.0019	0.9372 ± 0.0018	$\mathbf{0.9399 \pm 0.0022}$	0.9388 ± 0.0026

validation error. The values of the hyper parameters thus selected are kept constant across all the experiments.

For Kang et al's method, the hyper parameters which needed to be selected were the number of groups to use, the regularization coefficient for the task parameters and task correlation matrix. The value of the number of groups were chosen from a pool of $\{2, 3, 4, 5\}$ and the values of regularization parameters were picked from $\{10^{-3}, 10^{-2}, 10^{-1}, 1, 10, 100\}$.

In ELLA, there were five different parameters which needed to be selected, namely, the number of basis selected, the regularization parameter for the basis, λ_1, regularization parameter for sparsity constraint of the basis coefficients in each task, μ, the ridge term for single task learner, λ_2, and the L_2 regularization component for the single task specific components, μ_2. The values of the number of basis function were chosen from a pool of $\{2, 4, 6, 8, 10\}$. The values of λ_1, μ and λ_2 were chosen from the pool of {exp(-12), exp(-8), exp(-4), exp(0), exp(4)}. The value of μ_2 was also selected from the same pool except the value of infinity was added to the pool according the author's guidelines.

In the TREE algorithm, the online bayesian methods for classification and regression were used as single task learners. The single task parameters were clustered using online top-down hierarchical clustering, and the mean of the tasks at each node was applied as the prior of each task. The same online single task learners were used for predicting online STL algorithm. There were two parameters used for online single task learners, the variance of the noise in the data, α, and the variance of the zero mean gaussian prior, β. The values of α and β were chosen from the pool of {0.001, 0.01, 0.1, 0, 1, 10, 100}. The gaussian prior was again used on each node of the hierarchical structure to regularize the related tasks together. The mean of all the tasks belonging to the node was used as the mean of the prior. The variance of the prior is chosen as the variance of the prior of its child node times the decay factor. The decay factor was picked from the pool of {1, 2, 5, 10, 20}.

Finally, in the current algorithm, SUPART, there were five parameters which needed to be selected, namely, the maximum depth of the tree, p, regularization constant of task specific parameters, λ_1, regularization constant for regional classifier, λ_2, the sparsity constraint, ρ and parameter dictating the step size, γ. The number of reject classifiers was picked from {2, 3, 4, 5}, and the values of λ_1, γ and ρ were picked from {0.001, 0.01, 0.1, 1, 0, 10, 100}, and λ_2 from $\{10^{-6}, 10^{-5}, 10^{-4}, 10^{-3}\}$. For deciding when to split the nodes, we need to choose the value of constant h. The value of h was picked from a pool of $\{0.05, 0.1, 0.15, 0.2\}$.

4.2.1 Performance Comparison

For all the algorithms tested, datasets were randomly divided into training and testing. All the algorithms were trained on the training dataset and evaluated on the testing dataset. For the MNIST and USPS dataset, 1000 samples from each tasks were picked for training and remaining for testing. Similarly, for Landmine Dataset, 300 samples and for Stock Market Dataset, 100 samples from each task were kept for training. The splits were consistent across all the models. The hyper parameters were fixed to the values that minimized the cross-validation error as found previously. The division of the dataset into training and testing was repeated 100 times. The samples from each task were fed into the algorithm one at a time and their performance on the test samples was measured. The order of the tasks were randomized between each run. The values of the hyper parameters were used based on cross-validation for all the algorithms and the task specific, region specific and the partition parameters were initialized with values of zeros. The test samples were only used for testing the model and did not contribute to the training. The results reported are on test dataset.

The results recorded are the average accuracy obtained from each randomization. The accuracy for the regression task is defined as $1 - nmse$, where $nmse$ is the normalized mean squared error. For the classification tasks, we define the accuracy as the ratio of the correctly classified samples to the total number of samples. The results are reported in Table 2.

As can be seen in the Table 2, the performance of SUPART is superior to all other algorithms, except for stock market dataset, where there is not significant difference in the performance of SUPART versus others.

We also compare SUPART with a batch multitask learning algorithm. We use Kang's method [12], Batch MTL, as the batch multitask method as this algorithm groups the tasks explicitly into groups and does feature selection as well. The comparison of SUPART with Batch MTL is provided in Table 3. Usually, online algorithms do not have as good performance as the batch algorithms and batch algorithms are often viewed as the maximum performance that may be achieved by any online algorithm. However, our algorithm performs almost as good as the Batch MTL. In Landmine and Stock Market data, it performs even better. The reason may be that both Landmine and Stock Market data have few number of features, and hence, do not benefit by the feature selection.

Figure 1: The average time taken in seconds to train plus test each algorithm. The vertical axis is the time in seconds on logarithmic scale and the horizontal axis represents the dataset. SUPART performs orders of magnitude faster than the batch MTL and significantly faster than other online algorithms.

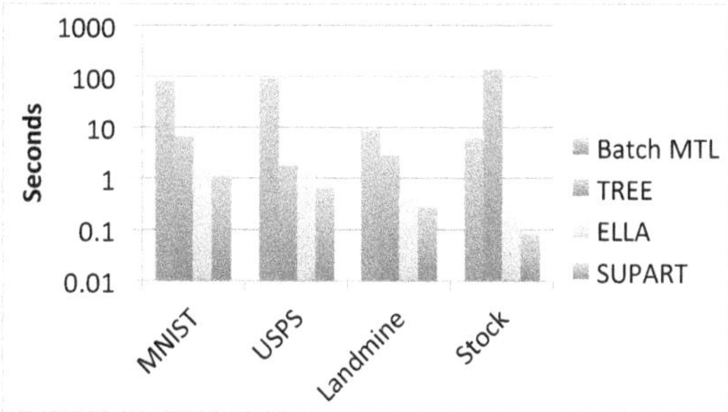

4.2.2 *Time comparison*

The time taken for training and testing each of the model was also recorded. We present the average time taken for each of the 100 randomizations along with the standard deviation. All the experiments were conducted on Intel(R) Xeon(TM) 3.2 GHz Linux Machine. The time is measured in seconds. The results are reported in Figure 1. Thus, it can be observed that SUPART has significantly faster performance than other methods and even faster than ELLA. The major reason for our model to be faster than ELLA is that in ELLA, all the basis vectors needs to be updated each time a new task arrives. In our model, we only update the vectors associated with the region the task belongs to.

4.2.3 *Comparison with online k-mean partitions*

In the current paper, the major contribution is to develop the framework to learn the task relationship modeling in a lifelong learning setting. In our framework, we partitioned the task space using supervised learning. We could have also chosen to partition the task space using unsupervised learning by learning linear functions such that tasks closest to each other are grouped together. Most common formulation would be to use of k-means to find the partition function. In order to show that supervised learning is better for partitioning task space, we use two methods to partition the task space in the current framework. The first method is using k-means algorithm to cluster the tasks into two groups at each node of the partition tree being developed in this algorithm and then defining the partition function as the line bisecting the line joining the mean of the two groups. We use the online k-mean algorithm presented by Shindler [19]. This algorithm is both fast as it requires only one pass of the dataset and has shown a good performance in unsupervised learning. The second method is to use our supervised learning approach to partition the task space as described in section 3.2.1. All other parameters were kept exactly the same in both the methods. The data was divided into training and testing and the performance was recorded 100 times. The same division of the data as used in previous sections were used here as well. The performance of using k-means versus the current algorithm is shown in table 4. The time comparison of the two methods is shown in table 5. As can be seen, the current method is faster and has similar performance than using k-means to partition the tasks.

Table 4: The performance comparison of using supervised learning versus using k-means to learn partition function. Results reported are average accuracies.

Dataset	k-Means	Supervised
MNIST	0.8863 ± 0.0245	$\mathbf{0.8960 \pm 0.0189}$
USPS	0.8972 ± 0.0128	$\mathbf{0.8998 \pm 0.0001}$
LANDMINE	0.7301 ± 0.0110	$\mathbf{0.7308 \pm 0.0107}$
STOCK	0.9317 ± 0.0027	$\mathbf{0.9388 \pm 0.0026}$

Table 5: The time comparison of using supervised learning versus using k-means to learn the partition functions. Results reported are average time in seconds.

Dataset	k-Means (sec)	Supervised (sec)
MNIST	1.1583 ± 0.0530	$\mathbf{1.1326 \pm 0.0573}$
USPS	0.6819 ± 0.0437	$\mathbf{0.6637 \pm 0.0543}$
LANDMINE	0.4766 ± 0.0206	$\mathbf{0.2768 \pm 0.0320}$
STOCK	0.1184 ± 0.0170	$\mathbf{0.0865 \pm 0.0256}$

It is observed that the k-means algorithm takes significantly more time for datasets with larger number of tasks such as landmine and stock dataset. We would like to make a note here that both the algorithms tested here are two different forms of the algorithm presented in this paper. In one algorithm, we use supervised method to learn partition functions whereas in other, we use k-means to learn partition function.

4.2.4 *Validation against Negative Transfer of Information*

The last experiment which we conducted was to measure the error as a function of task. For this experiment, we plot the average error on existing tasks over 100 runs, each time a new task is made available. The tasks were randomized in each of the 100 runs. The errors were plotted against the position of the task in the sequence in which it was encountered. We also plot the best exponential fit curve. The figure is shown in Figure 2. As can be seen in the figure, the overall trend of the error is decreasing in all the tasks. This shows that negative transfer does not occur in general as new tasks arrive and the new tasks arriving improve the overall performance.

Figure 2: The decrease in the overall error as a function of position in task sequence. The red line indicates best exponential fitting curve.

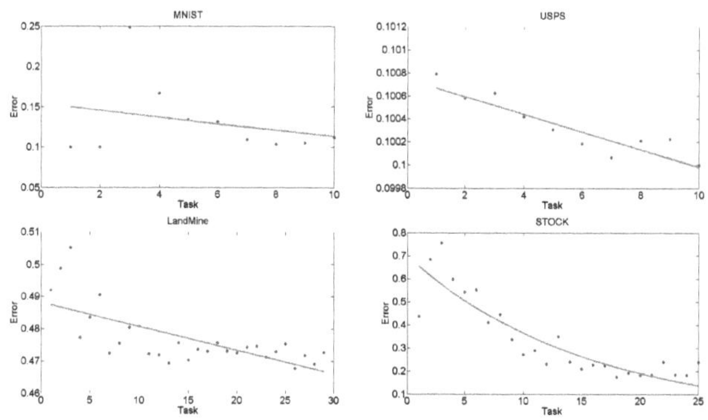

5. CONCLUSION

In this paper, we develop a novel algorithm for lifelong multitask learning in which we use partition functions to cluster the related tasks and learn the task parameters. We present a global formulation which partitions the task space and learns the task models using supervised learning. We also assume that the related tasks depend on similar set of features, and thus, regularize the similar tasks together using L_1 norm to implement feature selection.

The current algorithm, SUPART, is implemented and its performance is compared against leading lifelong learning algorithm. We observe that SUPART performs better than the leading algorithms in terms of both speed and accuracy.

6. REFERENCES

[1] H. B. Ammar, E. Eaton, P. Ruvolo, and M. Taylor. Online multi-task learning for policy gradient methods. In *Proceedings of the 31st International Conference on Machine Learning (ICML-14)*, pages 1206–1214, 2014.

[2] C. Archembeau, S. Guo, and O. Zoeter. Sparse bayesian multi-task learning. In *Advances in Neural Information Processing Systems*, volume 1, page 41, 2011.

[3] A. Argyriou, T. Evgeniou, and M. Pontil. Multi-task feature learning. In *Advances in Neural Information Processing Systems 19: Proceedings of the 2006 Conference*, volume 19, page 41. The MIT Press, 2007.

[4] B. Bakker and T. Heskes. Task clustering and gating for bayesian multitask learning. *The Journal of Machine Learning Research*, 4:83–99, 2003.

[5] M. Basseville, I. V. Nikiforov, et al. *Detection of abrupt changes: theory and application*, volume 104. Prentice Hall Englewood Cliffs, 1993.

[6] C. M. Bishop et al. *Pattern recognition and machine learning*, volume 4. springer New York, 2006.

[7] E. Eaton and P. L. Ruvolo. Ella: An efficient lifelong learning algorithm. In *Proceedings of the 30th International Conference on Machine Learning (ICML-13)*, pages 507–515, 2013.

[8] T. Evgeniou and M. Pontil. Regularized multi–task learning. In *Proceedings of the tenth ACM SIGKDD international conference on Knowledge discovery and data mining*, pages 109–117. ACM, 2004.

[9] H. Fei and J. Huan. Structured feature selection and task relationship inference for multi-task learning. *Knowledge and information systems*, 35(2):345–364, 2013.

[10] S. Gupta, D. Phung, and S. Venkatesh. Factorial multi-task learning: A bayesian nonparametric approach. In *Proceedings of the 30th International Conference on Machine Learning (ICML-13)*, pages 657–665, 2013.

[11] L. Jacob, F. Bach, and J.-P. Vert. Clustered multi-task learning: A convex formulation. *arXiv preprint arXiv:0809.2085*, 2008.

[12] Z. Kang, K. Grauman, and F. Sha. Learning with whom to share in multi-task feature learning. In *Proceedings of the 28th International Conference on Machine Learning (ICML-11)*, pages 521–528, 2011.

[13] A. Kumar and H. Daume III. Learning task grouping and overlap in multi-task learning. *arXiv preprint arXiv:1206.6417*, 2012.

[14] A. Passos, P. Rai, J. Wainer, and H. Daume III. Flexible modeling of latent task structures in multitask learning. *arXiv preprint arXiv:1206.6486*, 2012.

[15] P. Ruvolo and E. Eaton. Active task selection for lifelong machine learning. In *Proceedings of the 27th AAAI Conference on Artificial Intelligence (AAAI-13)*, July 2013.

[16] P. Ruvolo and E. Eaton. Scalable lifelong learning with active task selection. In *AAAI Spring Symposium: Lifelong Machine Learning*, 2013.

[17] P. Ruvolo and E. Eaton. Online multi-task learning via sparse dictionary optimization. In *Twenty-Eighth AAAI Conference on Artificial Intelligence (AAAI-14)*, 2014.

[18] W. A. Shewhart. *Economic control of quality of manufactured product*, volume 509. ASQ Quality Press, 1931.

[19] M. Shindler, A. Wong, and A. W. Meyerson. Fast and accurate k-means for large datasets. In *Advances in neural information processing systems*, pages 2375–2383, 2011.

[20] D. L. Silver and R. Poirier. *Sequential consolidation of learned task knowledge*. Springer, 2004.

[21] D. L. Silver, R. Poirier, and D. Currie. Inductive transfer with context-sensitive neural networks. *Machine Learning*, 73(3):313–336, 2008.

[22] R. J. Solomonoff. A system for incremental learning based on algorithmic probability. In *Proceedings of the Sixth Israeli Conference on Artificial Intelligence, Computer Vision and Pattern Recognition*, pages 515–527, 1989.

[23] S. Thrun. Learning to learn: Introduction. In *In Learning To Learn*. Citeseer, 1996.

[24] S. Thrun. Lifelong learning algorithms. In *Learning to learn*, pages 181–209. Springer, 1998.

[25] L. Xiao. Dual averaging method for regularized stochastic learning and online optimization. In *Advances in Neural Information Processing Systems*, pages 2116–2124, 2009.

[26] Y. Xue, X. Liao, L. Carin, and B. Krishnapuram. Multi-task learning for classification with dirichlet process priors. *The Journal of Machine Learning Research*, 8:35–63, 2007.

[27] J. Zhang and J. García. Online classifier adaptation for cost-sensitive learning. *Neural Computing and Applications*, pages 1–9, 2015.

[28] Y. Zhang and J. G. Schneider. Learning multiple tasks with a sparse matrix-normal penalty. In *Advances in Neural Information Processing Systems*, pages 2550–2558, 2010.

[29] W. Zhong and J. Kwok. Convex multitask learning with flexible task clusters. *arXiv preprint arXiv:1206.4601*, 2012.

[30] J. Zhou, J. Chen, and J. Ye. Clustered multi-task learning via alternating structure optimization. *Advances in Neural Information Processing Systems*, 25, 2011.

KSGM: Keynode-driven Scalable Graph Matching

Xilun Chen, K. Selçuk Candan
Arizona State University
Tempe, AZ, USA
{xilun.chen, candan}@asu.edu

Maria Luisa Sapino
University of Torino
Torino, Italy
marialuisa.sapino@unito.it

Paulo Shakarian
Arizona State University
Tempe, AZ, USA
shak@asu.edu

ABSTRACT

Understanding how a given pair of graphs align with each other (also known as the *graph matching* problem) is a critical task in many search, classification, and analysis applications. Unfortunately, the problem of *maximum common subgraph isomorphism* between two graphs is a well known NP-hard problem, rendering it impractical to search for exact graph alignments. While there are several heuristics, most of these analyze and encode global and local structural information for every node of the graph and then rank pairs of nodes across the two graphs based on their structural similarities. Moreover, many algorithms involve a post-processing (or refinement) step which aims to improve the initial matching accuracy. In this paper [1] we note that the expensive refinement phase of graph matching algorithms is not practical in any application where scalability is critical. It is also impractical to seek structural similarity between all pairs of nodes. We argue that a more practical and scalable solution is to seek structural *keynodes* of the input graphs that can be used to limit the amount of time needed to search for alignments. Naturally, these *keynodes* need to be selected carefully to prevent any degradations in accuracy during the alignment process. Given this motivation, in this paper, we first present a structural *keynode* extraction (SKE) algorithm and then use structural keynodes obtained during off-line processing for keynode-driven scalable graph matching (KSGM). Experiments show that the proposed keynode-driven scalable graph matching algorithms produce alignments that are as accurate as (or better than) the state-of-the-art algorithms, with significantly faster online executions.

1. INTRODUCTION

Graphs have been used to represent a large variety of complex data, from multimedia objects, social networks, hypertext/Web, knowledge graphs (RDF), mobility graphs,to protein interactions. Let D be a set of entities of interest, a graph, $G(V, E)$, defined over $V = D$ describes the relationships between pairs of objects in D. The elements in the set V are referred to as the nodes or vertices of the graph. The elements of the set E are referred to as the edges and they represent the pairwise relationships between the nodes of the graph. Edges can be directed or undirected, meaning that the relationship can be non-symmetric or symmetric, respectively. Nodes and edges of the graph can also be labeled or non-labeled. The label of an edge, for example, may denote the name of the relationship between the corresponding pair of nodes or may represent other meta-data, such as the certainty of the relationship or the cost of leveraging that relationship within an application.

[1]This work is supported by NSF Grants #1339835 and #1318788. This work is also supported in part by NSF grant #0856090.

Permission to make digital or hard copies of all or part of this work for personal or classroom use is granted without fee provided that copies are not made or distributed for profit or commercial advantage and that copies bear this notice and the full citation on the first page. Copyrights for components of this work owned by others than ACM must be honored. Abstracting with credit is permitted. To copy otherwise, or republish, to post on servers or to redistribute to lists, requires prior specific permission and/or a fee. Request permissions from Permissions@acm.org.

CIKM'15, October 19–23, 2015, Melbourne, Australia.
© 2015 ACM. ISBN 978-1-4503-3794-6/15/10 ...$15.00.
DOI: http://dx.doi.org/10.1145/2806416.2806577.

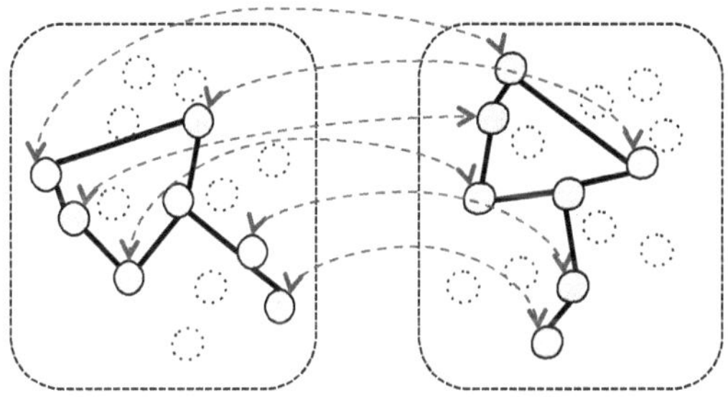

Figure 1: Graph matching/alignment problem seeks a *maximum common subgraph isomorphism* between two input graphs

Due to the success of the graph model as a powerful and flexible data representation, graph analysis and search tasks are also increasingly critical in many application domains. In particular, understanding how a given set of graphs align with each other (also known as the *graph matching/alignment* problem, Figure 1) forms the core task in many search, classification, and analysis applications. Unfortunately, the problem of *maximum common subgraph isomorphism* between two graphs is a well known NP-hard problem [24], making it impractical to search for exact or maximal graph alignments. As a result, while there are some attempts to improve the performance of exact maximum common subgraph matching solutions [23], most of the recent efforts in the area have focused on seeking approximate/inexact graph alignments [3, 18, 22, 19, 29].

While these algorithms differ in their specific techniques, most of them rely on a four phase process:

1. First, the matching algorithm analyzes and encodes the global structural information (for example a spectral signature [23]) corresponding to the nodes of the graph.
2. Secondly, the algorithm analyzes and encodes the local structural information (such as neighborhood degree distribution [29]) for the nodes of the graph.
3. Once these global and local signatures are encoded, the matching algorithm compares the signatures of pairs of nodes across the given graphs to rank these pairs of nodes (for example using a stable matching algorithm, like the Hungarian algorithm [16]) based on their overall structural similarities.

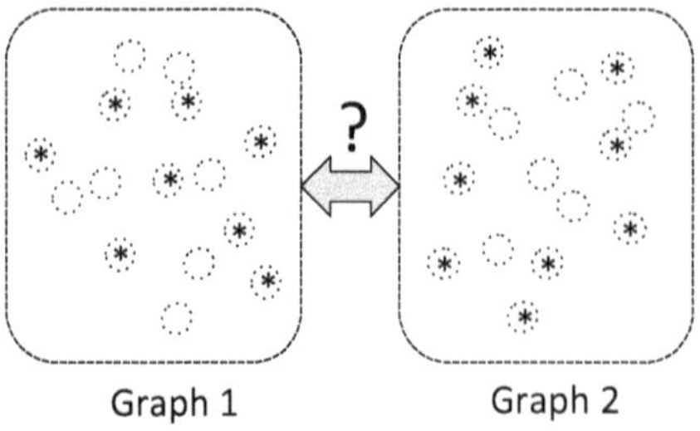

Figure 2: Keynode selection problem for scalable graph matching: the nodes marked with "*" are *keynodes* of the input graphs that can be used to reduce the amount of time needed to search for alignments

4. Finally, a post-processing, or refinement, step (involving, for example, a *vertex cover* operation) is used to improve the accuracy of the initial matching [29].

Unfortunately, many of these steps result in significant scalability challenges in terms of the matching time needed to compare the pairs of nodes:

- In particular, the expensive refinement phase of graph matching algorithms is not practical in applications where scalability of the graph matching operation is critical.
- Moreover, especially in very large graphs, it is also impractical to seek pairwise structural similarities for all node pairs during the graph matching process.

1.1 Contributions of this Paper

Based on these observations, in this paper, we argue that a more practical and scalable solution would be to seek structural *keynodes* of the input graphs that can be used to reduce the amount of time needed to search for alignments (Figure 2). Of course, these keynodes must be selected carefully to prevent any degradations in accuracy during the alignment process, especially because, as mentioned above, refinement post-processes are detrimental to scalability of matching algorithms.

Given this motivation, in this paper, we first present a highly efficient and effective *structural keynode extraction* (SKE) algorithm. The SKE algorithm, which is executed off-line, relies on a 3-step process:

1. In the first step, a PageRank algorithm [7] is ran to associate a structural score to each node in the graph.
2. In the second step, a scale-space (based on a difference-of-Gaussians (DoG) function defined over different scales of the graph) is constructed.
3. In the third step, keynode candidates are extracted by analyzing the resulting scale-space for extrema of the DoG function and a subset of these candidates are selected as structural keynodes.

We then propose a graph matching algorithm that uses these structural keynodes (obtained during off-line processing) for *keynode-driven scalable graph matching* (KSGM). In particular, KSGM extracts only *local* signatures and relies on the structural keynodes for fast node-to-node similarity searching. In addition, we also show that this keynode-driven approach not only reduces the number of comparisons that need to be performed online, but it also enables effective matching, even without having to rely on an expensive assignment algorithm, like the Hungarian algorithm (with $O(|V|^3)$ complexity). Experiment results show that the proposed structural keynode extraction and keynode-driven scalable graph matching algorithms produce alignments that are as accurate as (or better than) the state-of-the-art algorithms, while requiring significantly less online execution time without refinement.

1.2 Organization of this Paper

The paper is organized as follows: in the next section, we first introduce basic concepts and review existing graph matching algorithms. In Section 3, we provide overviews of the general graph matching process as well as the proposed keynode-driven scalable graph matching (KSGM) algorithm. Then, in Section 4, we present our structural keynode extraction (SKE) algorithm. In Sections 5 and 6, we discuss how to use these structural keynodes for obtaining graph alignments. We discuss the complexity of the proposed algorithms and parallelization opportunities in Section 7. We present experimental evaluations with various real and synthetic data sets in Section 8. These confirm that the proposed approximate graph matching algorithm is highly effective and efficient. Finally, we conclude the paper in Section 9.

2. BACKGROUND AND RELATED WORK

In this section, we review key concepts related to the graph matching problem and discuss the existing algorithms.

Graph Isomorphism: Given two graphs G and H, G is isomorphic to H if there exists a bijective mapping from the nodes of G to the nodes H that preserves the edge structure [13]: for any two vertices that are adjacent on G, the vertices they are mapped to are also adjacent on H, and vice versa.

Subgraph Isomorphism: Subgraph isomorphism seeks a bijective function, f, such that there is a subgraph G' of G and a subgraph H' of H, such that G' is isomorphic to H', with respect to f.

Maximum Common Subgraph Isomorphism: Maximum common subgraph isomorphism seeks the largest subgraph of G isomorphic to a subgraph of H [24]. Intuitively, the larger the maximum common subgraph of two graphs is, the more similar the graphs are to each other.

One of the first exact graph matching algorithms was proposed by Ullman [24]. An alternative way to search for a matching between two graphs is to rely on *graph edit distance* algorithms: given two graphs the corresponding graph edit distance is the least cost sequence of edit operations that transforms G_1 into G_2. Commonly used graph edit operations include *substitution*, *deletion*, and *insertion* of graph nodes and edges. Unfortunately, the graph edit distance problem is also known to be NP-complete [24]. In fact, even approximating graph-edit distance is very costly; the edit distance problem is known to be APX-hard [8]. [8] shows that graph isomorphism, subgraph isomorphism, and maximum common subgraph problem are special instances of the graph edit distance computation problem. Many subgraph isomorphism search algorithms have been developed, such as [15, 29, 14].

Approximate Graph Matching: In order to be applicable to large graphs, many heuristic and approximate graph matching algorithms have been proposed.

While, as we discussed above, graph matching through edit distance computation is an expensive task, there are various heuristics that have been developed to perform this operation more efficiently. `GraphGrep` [14] is one such technique, relying on a path-based representation of graphs. `GraphGrep` takes an undirected, node-labeled graph and for each node in the graph, it finds all paths that start at this node and have length up to a given, small upper bound, l_p. Given a path in the graph, the corresponding *id-path* is the list of the ids of the nodes on the path. The corresponding *label-path* is the list of the labels of the nodes on the path. The fingerprint of the graph, then, is a hash table, where each row contains the hash of the label-path and the corresponding number of id-paths in the graph. Irrelevant graphs are filtered out by comparing the numbers of id-paths for each matching hash key and by discarding those graphs which have at least one value in its fingerprint less than the corresponding value in the fingerprint of the query. Matching sub-graphs are found by focusing on the parts of the graph which correspond to the label-paths in the query. After, the relevant id-path sets are selected and overlapping id-paths are found and concatenated to build matching sub-graphs.

A common method to obtain an approximate graph matching is to use the eigenvectors derived from the adjacency matrix of the graph [23]: intuitively, two similar graphs should have similar eigenvectors; moreover, if we construct a $|V| \times |V|$ matrix (for example the Laplacian of the graph or a matrix encoding node distances) and decompose it into three matrices of $|V| \times c$, $c \times c$, and $c \times |V|$ elements using an eigen-decomposition technique like SVD, the c-length vector corresponding the node $v \in V$ can be used as a global-signature corresponding to node v. Once node-to-node similarities are computed, an assignment is usually found using an assignment algorithm, such as the Hungarian algorithm [16], which uses a primal-dual strategy to solve this problem in $O(|V|^3)$ time. This simple observation, led to several works leveraging different global-signatures for identifying node matches across different graphs [3, 18, 22, 19, 29]. [28] formulates the labeled weighted graph matching problem in the form of a convex-concave program, which searches for appropriate permutation matrices by solving a least-square problem. In addition, feature selection techniques are used for more accurate calculation [11, 12, 20]. In order to improve matching accuracy, [29] proposes to enrich the global-signatures associated to the graph nodes with local-signatures, encoding the properties of the immediate neighborhood of each node.

3. OVERVIEW OF KEYNODE-DRIVEN GRAPH MATCHING

Given a set $\mathcal{G} = \{G_1, G_2, ..., G_g\}$ of graphs and a query graph $G_q \in \mathcal{G}$, in this paper, we seek the maximum graph matching between G_q and all $G_i \in \mathcal{G}$ $(i \neq q)$. Note that the exact solution for this problem is NP-hard [24]. Since we treat *scalability* as a key constraint, we consider inexact solutions and rely on the *matching quality measure* proposed in [29] to evaluate the accuracies of the resulting alignments: Let $G_q(V_q, E_q)$ be a query graph and let $G_i(V_i, E_i)$ be a graph in $\mathcal{G}$. Let $M_{q,i}(V_{q,i}, E_{q,i})$ be a subgraph of both G_q and G_i, returned by an inexact subgraph search algorithm. [29] defines the *matching quality* function as follows:

$$quality(M_{q,i}) = \frac{|E_{q,i}|}{\min(|E_q|, |E_i|)},$$

Intuitively, the quality function describes how similar the given query graph G_q and known graph G_i are by using the ratio of matched edges and the maximum number of edges that can be possibly matched, which is equal to the minimum number of edges between two graphs. In other words, the larger the number of edges in the graph $M_{q,i}$, the better is the *quality* of the matching (or the more similar the two graphs are).

3.1 Challenges

Given a query graph G_q, our goal is to rank the graphs in $\mathcal{G}$ according to their matching similarities against G_q (and eventually return the top few matches to the user). [29] solves this problem by relying on a 6-step process, common to many graph search algorithms:

1. [29], first, analyzes the global structure of each graph through eigen-decomposition of the graph Laplacian matrix and encodes this in the form of a c-length vector associated to each node in the graph.
2. Secondly, [29] encodes the structural information local to each node, v_j, in the form of an s_j-length degree distribution vector, where s_j is the number of nodes in the k-neighborhood of the node.
3. Given the global and local signatures of all nodes in G_q and G_i, [29] then computes the global and local similarities for each pair of nodes from the two graphs, in $O(|V_q| \times |V_i| \times c)$ and $O(|V_q| \times |V_i| \times max_{v_j}(s_j))$ time, respectively. It then combines (by multiplying) the global and local similarities of each pair of nodes into a single value, thereby quantifying the overall similarity of the pair.
4. Once the overall similarities for $|V_q| \times |V_i|$ pairs of nodes are computed, [29] drops node pairs with small degrees and, then, expands the remaining set of *anchor* pairs by adding, in an iterative manner, immediate good nearby pairs to this anchor set.
5. When no more pairs can be added to the *anchor* set, [29] uses the Hungarian algorithm to identify an initial node matching in $O(max\{|V_q|, |V_i|\}^3)$ time.
6. Finally, as a post-processing step, [29] applies a vertex cover based refinement, which explores different subsets of the nodes and searches for better alignments than the one initially identified. In particular, the algorithm seeks *small vertex covers*, which are likely to give the mismatched nodes additional chances to be refined. Note that since the minimum vertex cover problem is known to be NP-hard, the algorithm searches for *minimal* vertex covers in $O(m \times n^3)$ time, where $m = min\{|E_q|, |E_i|\}$ and $n = max\{|V_q|, |V_i|\}$.

Algorithm 1 Overview of keynodes based graph matching

Input:
A set $\mathcal{G} = \{G_1, G_2, ...G_g\}$ of graphs
A query graph $G_q \in \mathcal{G}$.
Output:
Rank $G_i \in \mathcal{G}$ in terms of matching quality
Offline process:
for all $G_i \in \mathcal{G}$ (including G_q) **do**
  Perform *structural keynode extraction* (SKE) for G_i
  Extract local-signatures for all nodes in G_i
  (Optional) Extract global-signatures for all nodes in G_i
end for
Online process:
for all $G_i \in \mathcal{G}$ **do**
  Compute local similarities for keynode pairs from G_i and G_q.
  (Optional) Compute global similarities for keynode pairs from G_i and G_q and combine these with local similarities.
  Select anchors to obtain a base matching
  Expand the base matching to obtain $M_{q,i}$
  Compute matching quality, $quality(M_{q,i})$
end for
Rank $G_i \in \mathcal{G}$ in terms of $quality(M_{q,i})$

This process includes a number of very expensive steps: The first two steps, involving global and local analysis are expensive, but can be performed off-line and indexed for later reuse assuming that the graphs are available ahead of time. The last four steps, however, need to be performed on-line, yet they consist of operations that are quadratic or higher. In particular, the last refinement step, with $O(m \times n^3)$ time cost is impractical for most large data graphs.

In this paper, we note that Step 3 can be significantly sped up if the similarity computations are limited to only a small subset of the vertices in V_q and V_i (which we refer to as *keynodes* of V_q and V_i). However, the use of keynodes for node similarity computation is not sufficient to reduce the overall complexity as, once the keynodes are identified and the keynode pairs set is expanded, solving the assignment problem needed to return the matching would still take $O(max\{|V_q|, |V_i|\}^3)$ time, if we were to apply the Hungarian algorithm on the extracted keynodes. Therefore, we also need to reduce the time complexity of this step significantly. It is especially important that the initial keynode based similarity computation is accurate as we cannot afford a cubic algorithm like Hungarian algorithm to return a high-quality matching.

3.2 Outline of KSGM

Algorithm 1 illustrates an overview of the *keynode-driven scalable graph matching* (KSGM) process. In the rest of the paper, we study each step in detail. First, in the next two sections, we focus on the offline steps of KSGM, which involve identifying keynodes and extracting local-signatures. The online steps of the KSGM algorithm are discussed in Section 6.

4. STRUCTURAL KEYNODE EXTRACTION

In this section, we propose an off-line *structural keynode extraction* (SKE) algorithm which identifies $\Theta\%$ (where Θ is a user provided parameter) of the nodes in V as the keynode set, K, of a given graph, $G(V, E)$ to support scalable graph matching. The proposed SKE algorithm has a number of advantages: (a) First of all, the identified keynodes are robust against noise, such as random edge insertion/removal; and (b) the identified nodes represent structural features of the graph of different sizes and complexities (i.e., correspond to neighborhoods of different sizes).

4.1 Naive Solution - Selecting Structural Keynodes based on Node Significance

As described above, the keynodes of the graph need to *represent* the structural properties of the graph well (i.e., extracted keynodes need to be structurally *significant* in the graph) to support effective matching. Therefore, the first alternative is to rely on traditional node significance measures.

Measures like *betweenness* [26] and the *centrality/cohesion* [5], help quantify how *significant* any node is on a given graph based on the underlying graph topology. The *betweenness* measure [26], for example, quantifies the number of shortest paths that pass through a given node. The *centrality/cohesion* [5] measures quantify how close to a clique the given node and its neighbors are. Other *authority*, *prestige*, and *prominence* measures [4, 7, 5] quantify the significance of the node in the graph through eigen-analysis or random walks, which help measure how reachable a node is in the graph. PageRank [7] is one of the most widely-used random-walk based methods for measuring node significance and has been used in a variety of application domains, including web search, biology, and social networks. The basic thesis of PageRank is that a node is important if it is pointed to by other important nodes – it takes into account the connectivity of nodes in the graph by defining the score of the node $v_i \in V$ as the amount of time spent on v_i in a sufficiently long random walk on the graph. Given a graph $G(V, E)$, the PageRank scores are represented as $\vec{r}$, where

$$\vec{r} = \alpha \mathbf{T}_G \vec{r} + (1 - \alpha)\vec{t}$$

where $\mathbf{T}_G$ is a transition matrix corresponding to the graph G, $\vec{t}$ is a teleportation vector (such that $\vec{t}[i] = \frac{1}{|V|}$), and α if the residual probability (or equivalently, $(1 - \alpha)$ is the so-called teleportation probability). Unless the graph is weighted, the transition matrix, $\mathbf{T}_G$, is constructed such that for a node v with k (outgoing) neighbors, the transition probability from v to each of its (outgoing) neighbors will be $1/k$. If the graph is weighted, then the transition probabilities are adjusted in a way to account for the relative weights of the edges.

Therefore, as the first alternative, we consider a PageRank based keynode selection scheme: in this scheme, given a graph $G(V, E)$, we would (a) first identify the PageRank scores, $p(v_i)$, of all $v_i \in V$, then (b) we would rank the nodes in non-increasing order of PageRank scores, and finally, (c) we would return the top $\Theta\%$ of the nodes in V as the keynode set, K.

4.2 Proposed Solution - Robust Keynode Extraction through Scale Space Analysis

We note that the above alternative has a number of disadvantages:

- First of all, many of the structural significance measures, such as PageRank, are not entirely robust against modifications in the graph. The PageRank score of a node, for example, can jump significantly, if a new edge connects the sub-graph in which the node is contained to a high PageRank node in the graph.
- Secondly, common structural significance measures, like PageRank, capture the significance of a node in the whole graph and favor nodes that are *overall central*. However, this may be disadvantageous as there is a possibility that smaller scale, but distinct (and, therefore, useful for matching) structural features of the graph may be missed.

We therefore argue that we need a better alternative, which is both *robust* and *multi-scale*. We build the proposed SKE algorithm based on three key insights:

- *Robustness:* Even when the PageRank scores of the nodes themselves vary due to graph transformations, such as edge insertions and removals, a given node's PageRank score relative to the scores of the nodes in its neighborhood is likely to be stable.
- *Structural distinctiveness:* A node is structurally distinctive in its neighborhood, if "the relationship between its PageRank score to the PageRank scores of its neighbors" is different from the "relationships between the node's neighbors' PageRank scores and the PageRank scores of their own neighbors".
- *Multi-scale:* Since we do not know the scale of the structurally distinctive features of the graph, we need to search for features of potentially different sizes.

It is important to note that similar requirements also exist in other application domains. For example, algorithms for extracting such robust, local features have been developed for 2D images (SIFT [21]), uni-variate time series [9], and multi-variate time series [25]. In this paper, we argue that a similar process can be used to identify keynodes (corresponding to robust, multi-scale structural features) of a graph, if the nodes are annotated with PageRank scores ahead of the time. Let $G(V, E, p)$ be a PageRank-labeled graph, where $p()$ is a mapping from the nodes to the corresponding PageRank scores. What makes the problem of extracting local features from *PageRank*-labeled graphs challenging is that the concepts of *neighborhood*, *gradient*, and *smoothing* are not well-defined for graphs.

Therefore, before we describe the keynode extraction process, we describe how to smooth a PageRank-labeled graph. Intuitively, smoothing the graph with respect to the scores associated to the graph nodes creates versions of the given graph at different resolutions and, thus, helps identify features with different amounts of details.

4.2.1 *Gaussian Smoothing of a PageRank-Labeled Graph*

1D or 2D data are commonly smoothed by applying a convolution operation with a Gaussian window. For example, if $Y = \langle t_0, t_1, \ldots, t_l \rangle$ is a time series data and σ is a smoothing parameter, its smoothed version, $\tilde{Y}(t, \sigma)$, is obtained through $\mathcal{G}(t, \sigma) * Y(t)$ where $*$ is the convolution operation in t and $\mathcal{G}(t, \sigma)$ is the Gaussian function

$$\mathcal{G}(t, \sigma) = \frac{1}{\sqrt{2\pi}\sigma} e^{\frac{-t^2}{2\sigma^2}}.$$

Essentially, the Gaussian smoothing process takes a weighted average of values of the points in the vicinity of a given point, t.

The closer a point to t, the higher is the weight. Therefore, in order to implement a similar Gaussian smoothing of the given graph, we first need to define a distance function to measure how close different nodes are to each other. Common applicable definitions of node distance include the hop distance (determined by the shortest edge distance between the nodes on the given graph) or hitting distance [10]. In this paper, we use hop distance to measure how far nodes are to each other:

DEFINITION 1 (NODE DISTANCE MATRIX). Let us be given a graph $G(V, E)$ with n nodes. The ordering among the nodes is described through a set of node distance matrices, $\mathbf{N_j}$, where

- $\mathbf{N_j}$, for $j \geq 0$, is an $n \times n$ 0, 1-valued matrix, where for a given node v_i in the graph, G, the ith row in the matrix, $\mathbf{N_j}$ is 1 only for nodes that have node distance exactly j from the node v_i, and
- $\mathbf{N_j}$, for $j \leq 0$, is an $n \times n$ 0, 1-valued matrix, where for a given node v_i, the ith column in the matrix, $\mathbf{N}(j, G) = 1$ only for nodes that have distance exactly j on the inverted graph, where all edges are inverted. ◇

Intuitively, the cell $\mathbf{N_j}[v_1, v_2] = 1$ if the node v_2 is exactly j hops from v_1. When j is positive the hop-distance is measured following outgoing edges, whereas when j is negative, incoming edges are followed. Given this, we construct multiple scales of the given graph G by using a Gaussian graph smoothing function defined as follows.

DEFINITION 2 (GAUSSIAN GRAPH SMOOTHING FUNCTION). Let us be given a labeled graph $G(V, E, x)$ and let

- σ be a smoothing parameter.
- $X = \langle x(v_1), x(v_2), ..., x(v_n)\rangle$ be a vector encoding the labels associated with the nodes, $v_i \in V$.

Then, if G is a directed graph, the *non-normalized Gaussian graph smoothing function*, $S^{\oslash}_{G,\sigma}()$ is defined as

$$S^{\oslash}_{G,\sigma}(X) = \mathcal{G}(0, \sigma)\mathbf{I}X + \sum_{j=1}^{n} \mathcal{G}(j, \sigma)\mathbf{N_j}X + \sum_{j=1}^{n} \mathcal{G}(j, \sigma)\mathbf{N_j}X,$$

where $\mathcal{G}(0, \sigma)$ is a Gaussian function with zero mean and σ standard deviation. If, on the other hand, G is an undirected graph, then the *non-normalized Gaussian graph smoothing function* is

$$S^{\oslash}_{G,\sigma}(X) = \mathcal{G}(0, \sigma)\mathbf{I}X + \sum_{j=1}^{n} 2\mathcal{G}(j, \sigma)\mathbf{N_j}X.$$

Intuitively, $S^{\oslash}$ applies Gaussian-based weighted averaging to the entries of vector X based on the hop-distances[2]. However, unlike the basic Gaussian smoothing, during (non-normalized) relationship smoothing, there may be more than one node at the same distance and all such nodes have the same degree of contribution. As a consequence, the sum of all contributions may exceed 1.0. Therefore, the *normalized Gaussian graph smoothing function*, $S(G, \sigma)$, discounts weights based on the number of nodes at a given distance:

$$S_{G,\sigma}(X) = \left(S^{\oslash}_{G,\sigma}X\right) \div \left(S^{\oslash}_{G,\sigma}1_{(n)}\right),$$

where $1_{(n)}$ is an n-vector such that all values are 1 and "$\div$" is a pairwise division operation. ◇

[2]In practice, since the Gaussian function drops fast as we move away from the mean, we need to consider only a small window, w, of hops

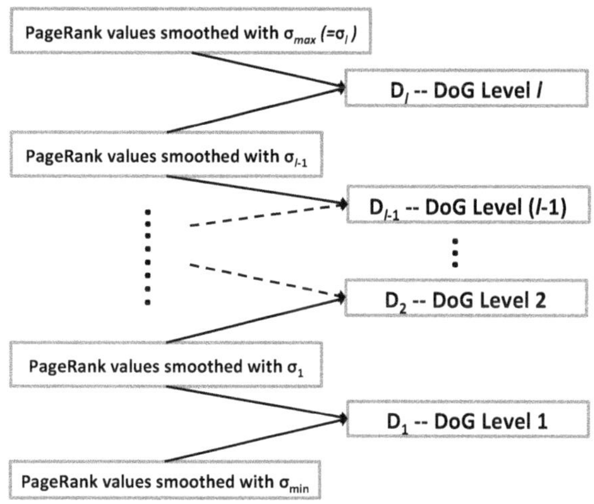

Figure 3: Computing the Difference-of-Gaussian (DoG) series of the PageRank values of a graph

Intuitively, the smoothing function S applies Gaussian smoothing on the X values (associated with the nodes, $v_i \in V$) based on the hop-distances between nodes and returns a vector

$$S_{G,\sigma}(X) = \langle \tilde{x}(v_1), \tilde{x}(v_2), \ldots, \tilde{x}(v_n)\rangle$$

encoding the smoothed X values associated with the graph nodes. Note that, since at a given hop distance there may be more than one node, all the nodes at the same distance have the same degree of contribution and the degree of contribution gets progressively smaller as we get further away from the node for which the smoothing is performed.

Therefore, given a PageRank-labeled graph, $G(V, E, p)$, and a corresponding PageRank vector, $P = \langle p(v_1), p(v_2), ..., p(v_n)\rangle$, encoding PageRank scores associated with the nodes, $v_i \in V$, the vector

$$S_{G,\sigma}(P) = \langle \tilde{p}(v_1), \tilde{p}(v_2), \ldots, \tilde{p}(v_n)\rangle,$$

encodes the σ-smoothing of the PageRank-annotated graph, $G(V, E, p)$. We also say that $S_{G,\sigma}(P)$ encodes the PageRank scores of G at scale σ.

We next describe how to construct a scale-space for the given graph through an iterative smoothing process leveraging the PageRank vector and the structure of the graph.

4.2.2 Graph Scale-Space Construction

The first step in identifying robust graph features is to generate a scale-space representing versions of the given graph with different amounts of details. In particular, building on the observation that features are often located where the differences between neighboring regions (also in different scales) are large, we seek structural features of the given graph at the extrema of the scale space defined by the difference-of-the-Gaussian (DoG) series. More specifically, given

- a PageRank-labeled graph, $G(V, E, p)$,
- the corresponding vector, $P = \langle p(v_1), p(v_2), ..., p(v_n)\rangle$ encoding the scores associated with the nodes, $v_i \in V$,
- a minimum smoothing scale, σ_{min},
- a maximum smoothing scale, σ_{max},
- the number, l, of levels of the scale space,

then, we compute a difference-of-Gaussians (DoG) series, $\mathbb{D}(G, P, \sigma_{min}, \sigma_{max}, l) = \{D_1, D_2, ..., D_l\}$, where each D_i encodes the differences of two nearby scales separated by a multiplicative factor k:

$$D_i = S_{G,k^i\sigma_{min}}(P) - S_{G,k^{i-1}\sigma_{min}}(P),$$

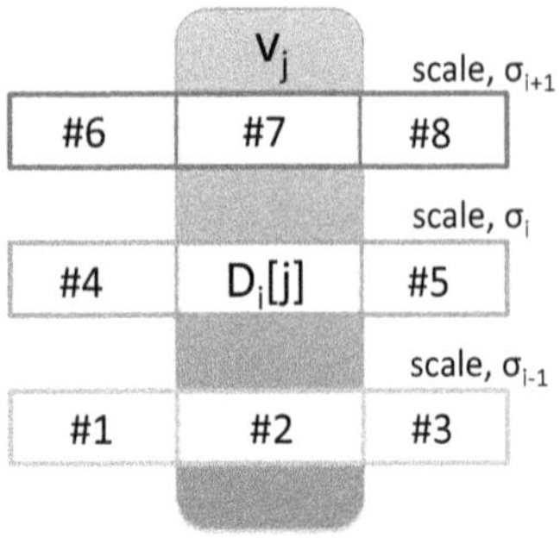

Figure 4: Extrema detection

where $k = \sqrt[l]{\frac{\sigma_{max}}{\sigma_{min}}}$. Figure 3 visualizes the process:

- On the left hand side of the figure, we have the incrementally smoothed versions of the PageRank vector, P. Here, the lowest level, $S_{G,\sigma_{min}}(P)$, corresponds to the most detailed version of the graph (with the least amount of smoothing), whereas $S_{G,\sigma_{max}}(P)$ corresponds to the least detailed (most smoothed) version of the graph. In other words, σ_{min} determines the sizes of the smallest structural features we can locate and $\sigma_{max} = k^l\sigma_{min}$ determines the sizes of the largest structural features we can identify. In particular, since under Gaussian smoothing, a diameter of 6σ would cover $\sim 99.73\%$ of the weights, the diameter of the smallest structural feature that can be identified using SKE is $\sim 6\sigma_{min}$ hops, whereas the diameter of the largest feature would be $\sim 6\sigma_{max}$ hops.

  The number of levels, l, denotes the number of detail levels (or scales) we explore between σ_{min} and σ_{max}. Intuitively, each of these levels corresponds to a different target size for the structural features of the graph.

- On the right hand side of the figure, we have the resulting Difference-of-Gaussian (DoG) series, consisting of vectors, D_1 through D_l.

Note that, intuitively, $D_i[j]$ measures how different the PageRank values of the neighborhood around v_j at scale $\sigma_{i-1}(= k^{i-1}\sigma_{min})$ are from the PageRank values of the neighborhood around v_j at scale $\sigma_i(= k^i\sigma_{min})$.

Therefore, a large $D_i[j]$ value would indicate a major structural change when neighborhoods of different size around v_j are considered (e.g., a node with a high PageRank score is included when considering a neighborhood of larger scale). In contrast, a small $D_i[j]$ indicates that there is minimal structural change when considering neighborhoods of different scales.

4.2.3 *Identifying Keynode Candidates*

As we mentioned earlier, our intuition is that a graph node is structurally distinctive in its neighborhood, if "the relationship between its PageRank score to the PageRank scores of its neighbors" is different from the "relationships between the node's neighbors' PageRank scores and the PageRank scores of their own neighbors, at multiple scales". Therefore, to locate the keynode candidates, we focus on the local extrema of the difference-of-Gaussian (DoG) series $\mathbb{D}$. More specifically, we identify $\langle v_j, \sigma_i\rangle$ pairs where the DoG value for node v_j at scale, $\sigma_i = k^i\sigma_{min}$, is an extremium (maximum and/or minimum) with respect to the neighbors of v_j in the same scale as well as neighbors in the previous and next levels of the scale space.

In order to verify if the pair $\langle v_j, \sigma_i\rangle$ is an extremium or not, we compare $D_i[j]$ with the values corresponding to eight DoG-neighbors in the scale-space, as visualized in Figure 4:

- DoG-neighbors numbered #2 and #7 correspond to the DoG values of the same node at the previous and next levels of the scale space. Therefore, we have

$$N_{\langle v_i,\sigma_j\rangle}[2] = D_{i-1}[j] \text{ and } N_{\langle v_i,\sigma_j\rangle}[7] = D_{i+1}[j].$$

- In contrast, DoG-neighbors #3, #5, and #8 correspond to the (average) DoG values of the forward neighbors of the node v_j, at the previous, current, and next levels of the scale space, respectively. Therefore, we have

$$N_{\langle v_i,\sigma_j\rangle}[3] = (\mathbb{F}D_{i-1})[j],$$
$$N_{\langle v_i,\sigma_j\rangle}[5] = (\mathbb{F}D_i)[j], \quad N_{\langle v_i,\sigma_j\rangle}[8] = (\mathbb{F}D_{i+1})[j],$$

  where, $\mathbb{F}$ is a row-normalized adjacency matrix accumulating the (averaged) contributions of the nodes to their neighbors along the forward edges.

- Similarly, DoG-neighbors #1, #4, and #6 correspond to the (average) DoG values of the backward neighbors at the previous, current, and next levels of the scale space. Therefore, we have

$$N_{\langle v_i,\sigma_j\rangle}[1] = (\mathbb{B}D_{i-1})[j],$$
$$N_{\langle v_i,\sigma_j\rangle}[4] = (\mathbb{B}D_i)[j], \quad N_{\langle v_i,\sigma_j\rangle}[6] = (\mathbb{B}D_{i+1})[j],$$

  where, $\mathbb{B}$ is a row-normalized backward-adjacency matrix (where all edges are reversed) accumulating the (averaged) contributions of the nodes to their neighbors along the backward direction of the edges.

Given these, the pair $\langle v_j, \sigma_i\rangle$ is an extremum (i.e., v_j is a keynode candidate at scale σ_i), iff $D_i[j]$ is a local maximum

$$D_i[j] \geq \underset{1\leq h\leq 8}{MAX}\, N_{\langle v_j,\sigma_i\rangle}[h]$$

or it is a local minimum

$$D_i[j] \leq \underset{1\leq h\leq 8}{MIN}\, N_{\langle v_j,\sigma_i\rangle}[h].$$

Intuitively, since $D_i[j]$ measures how different *the PageRank values of the neighborhood around* v_j *at scale* σ_i are from *the PageRank values of the neighborhood around* v_j *at scale* σ_{i-1}, a local maximum corresponds to a *highly scale-sensitive* region (amidst relatively *scale-insensitive* regions), whereas a local minimum corresponds to a *scale-insentive* region (amidst more *scale-sensitive* regions), of the graph.

4.2.4 *Selecting the Best Keynodes*

In the final step, we need to rank the keynode candidates and return the top $\frac{\Theta}{100} \times |V|$ of them, where Θ is a user provided parameter, as the keynode set, K. We propose *Extremum Ranking* to select the best keynodes.

Since keynodes are located at the local extrema of the DoG series, we can rank the keynode candidates based on their *extremum score* defined as follows: Let the pair $\langle v_j, \sigma_i\rangle$ be a local extremum. The corresponding extremum score, $\xi(\langle v_j, \sigma_i\rangle)$, is defined as

$$\begin{cases} D_i[j] - \left(\underset{1\leq h\leq 8}{MAX}\, N_{\langle v_j,\sigma_i\rangle}[h]\right) & \text{if } \langle v_j,\sigma_i\rangle \text{ is max.} \\ \left(\underset{1\leq h\leq 8}{MIN}\, N_{\langle v_j,\sigma_i\rangle}[h]\right) - D_i[j] & \text{if } \langle v_j,\sigma_i\rangle \text{ is min.} \end{cases}$$

Intuitively, the higher the extremum score is, the better local extremum (and, thus, a better keynode) is $\langle v_j, \sigma_i\rangle$.

5. LOCAL NODE SIGNATURES

The next step in the process is to extract the local signatures (to be used to compute local node similarities) for the nodes in the graph. Note that this process is also offline.

While there are different local signatures proposed in the literature, in our work we build on the k-neighborhood degree distribution based local signature proposed in [29] (both because it is simple and effective and also because this helps us compare our keynode-driven approach to the approach proposed in [29] more directly). Briefly, for each node $v_j \in V$ and for a user provided k, [29] first identifies the set, $N_k(v_j) \subseteq V$, of nodes that are at most k hops from v_j and extracts a subgraph, $G_k(v_j) \subseteq G$, induced by v_j and its k-hop neighbors. Then the degree sequence,

$$\kappa_j = [d_{j,1}, d_{j,2}, \ldots, d_{j,|N_k(v_j)|}]$$

consisting of the degrees of nodes in $G_k(v_j)$ (excluding v_j), sorted in non-increasing order, along with the degree of the node v_j and the numbers of vertices and edges in its k-hop neighborhood, form the local signature of node v_j:

$$local\_signature(v_j) = \langle \kappa_j, degree(v_j), \nu_j, \varepsilon_j \rangle,$$

where $\nu_j = |N_k(v_j) \cup \{v_j\}|$ is the number of nodes in $G_k(v_j)$ and $\varepsilon_j = |E_k(v_j)|$ is the number of edges.

Note that, while we use a local signature similar to that proposed in [29], we extend the node pair ranking function to better account for the node degrees as discussed later in Section 6.1.1. As we see in Section 8, this extension provides a significant boost in accuracy.

6. (KEYNODE-BASED) GRAPH MATCHING

As discussed in Section 3 and outlined in Algorithm 1, once the keynodes are extracted and local signatures are computed offline, the next steps of the algorithm are to

- compare the signatures of pairs of nodes across the given graphs to rank these pairs of nodes,
- select a set of pairs of keynodes (we refer it as anchor set) that serve as the base matching, and
- expand this base matching to obtain $M_{q,i}$.

We now describe how these steps are implemented in the keynode-driven scalable graph matching (KSGM) algorithm.

6.1 Anchor Set Selection

Let $G_1(V_1, E_1)$ and $G_2(V_2, E_2)$ be two graphs and let $K_1 \subseteq V_1$ and $K_2 \subseteq V_2$ be the corresponding keynodes identified by the SKE algorithm proposed in Section 4. The next step is to select a subset, A, of the pairs of nodes in $K_1 \times K_2$ as the anchor set of alignments based on a ranking function (a) evaluating how structurally similar a pair of nodes are and (b) how likely they are to lead to an effective expansion process to discover other alignments.

6.1.1 Node Similarity Matching and Node Pair Ranking

As we discussed in Section 5, KSGM uses a local node signature similar to the one proposed by [29]: $\langle \kappa_j, degree(v_j), \nu_j, \varepsilon_j \rangle$, where ν_j is the number of nodes in the neighborhood of v_j, ε_j is the number of neighborhood edges, and $\kappa_j = [d_{j,1}, d_{j,2}, \ldots, d_{j,|N_k(v_j)|}]$ consists of the degrees of nodes in the k-neighborhood of v_j (excluding v_j), sorted in non-increasing order.

Local Neighborhood Similarity.

Let v_i and v_j be two nodes (from two different graphs) and let $G_k(v_i)$ and $G'_k(v_j)$ be the corresponding induced $k-$neighborhood graphs. Then, local similarity function $nbhd\_sim(v_i, v_j)$ proposed by [29] accounts for the alignment between the degree distributions in these neighborhood graphs[3]:

$$nbhd\_sim(v_i, v_j) = \frac{n_{min} + D(v_i, v_j)}{(\nu_i + \varepsilon_i)(\nu_j + \varepsilon_j)},$$

where

$$d_{min} = min\{degree(v_i), degree(v_j)\}$$
$$n_{min} = min\{\nu_i, \nu_j\}$$
$$D(v_i, v_j) = \frac{d_{min} + \sum_{h=1}^{n_{min}-1} min\{d_{i,h}, d_{j,h}\}}{2}.$$

Node Pair Ranking with Extended Similarity.

While the local neighborhood similarity computation we use is similar to the one proposed in [29], we rank pairs of nodes differently. Let v_i and v_j be two nodes (from two different graphs). In particular, [29] ranks the pair $\langle v_i, v_j \rangle$ of nodes based on their neighborhood similarities, $nbhd\_sim(v_i, v_j)$. We, however, argue that neighborhood similarity is not sufficient for accounting for how effective the node pair is in supporting expansion. More specifically, we observe that a pair, $\langle v_i, v_j \rangle$, is likely to be a better anchor for expansion than the pair $\langle v_a, v_b \rangle$ if not only (a) the neighborhoods of v_i and v_j are more similar to each other than the pair, v_a and v_b, but also (b) if v_i and v_j have degrees that are more aligned with each other than v_a and v_b. Based on this observation, instead of applying a degree threshold, we propose that the pair $\langle v_i, v_j \rangle$ should be ranked based on the ranking function

$$\rho(v_i, v_j) = nbhd\_sim(v_i, v_j) \times \frac{min\{degree(v_i), degree(v_j)\}}{max\{degree(v_i), degree(v_j)\}}.$$

Note that [29] simply drops node pairs where the minumum of the two node degrees is smaller than the larger average degree of the two input graphs. We, however, argue that such node pairs may be useful, especially if the degrees in the graph are not uniformly distributed and the maximum matching occurs at the sparse portions of the graph. Therefore, we keep such pairs as long as they rank highly based on $\rho()$. We evaluate this ranking function in Section 8.

6.1.2 Keynode pair Selection

[29] uses the Hungarian algorithm to identify an initial node matching in $O(n^3)$ time, where $n = max\{|V_1|, |V_2|\}$. To reduce the execution time, [29] prunes those node pairs for which the similarity is ≤ 0.5. Since, instead of considering the node pairs in $V_1 \times V_2$, we only need to consider pairs of nodes in $K_1 \times K_2$, and since $|K_1| \ll |V_1|$ and $|K_2| \ll |V_2|$, keynode-driven processing is likely to be faster even without using the threshold. However, the cubic time of the Hungarian algorithm is still prohibitive and impractical for scalable graph matching. Therefore, we propose a greedy anchor selection algorithm, which (as we see in Section 8) performs very well when used along with keynodes selected in Section 4 and the proposed ranking function, $\rho()$. In particular, we first include all keynode pairs in $K_1 \times K_2$ into a queue in the order of their ranks based on $\rho()$, then, until the queue is empty, we remove and consider the keynode pair, $\langle v, u \rangle$ at the head of the queue. If neither v nor u has been marked `anchored`, we include $\langle v, u \rangle$ as an anchor and we mark v and u as `anchored`, otherwise, we drop the pair, $\langle v, u \rangle$.

Note that this process has $O((|K_1| \times |K_2|) \times log(|K_1| \times |K_2|))$ time cost (instead of the cubic cost of the Hungarian algorithm) and,

[3] In addition to using local similarities, [29] also extracts global signatures along with the local-signatures to compute node similarities. As we see in Section 8, the proposed keynode-driven graph matching algorithm achieves good results without having to rely on such global-signatures.

as we see in Section 8, performs very well in practice. Furthermore, the nature of Hungarian algorithm, which forces to pair all possible nodes to produce the optimal bipartite matching for the given two sets of nodes, is not guaranteed to provide a better matching in this case. Since the extracted keynodes are not all necessarily perfectly paired with each other, some keynodes can be a unique feature of the given graph, which does not align with other graphs, by forcing them to pair with other keynodes, it in fact introduces a bad initial base matching, and thus expand into an even worse matching. The proposed greedy matching algorithm, however, only consider the highly aligned keynodes, which in practice provides better results than the optimal bipartite matching.

6.2 Matching List Expansion

Because keynodes are inherently sparsely localized, the anchor set, A, is not necessarily a good final matching for graphs G_1 and G_2. We therefore need to expand this anchor list. Here, we follow [29]'s recommendation and expand the list incrementally by considering the neighbors (and their neighbors) until no effective expansion is possible (but we use the ranking function $\rho()$ instead of the node similarity function):

1. we first include all node pairs in A into a ranked queue (i.e., max-heap) in the order of their ranks based on the ranking function, $\rho()$,
2. then, for each node pair $\langle v, u\rangle \in A$, we also include the node pairs in $neighbors(u) \times neighbors(v)$ in the same ranked queue
3. then, until the ranked queue is empty, we remove and consider the node pair, $\langle v, u\rangle$ at the head of the ranked queue
   (a) if either v or u has not yet been marked `matched`, then
      i. we include the pair, $\langle v, u\rangle$, in the expanded matching list, L,
      ii. we mark both v and u as `matched`, and
      iii. then, the pairs in $neighbors(u) \times neighbors(v)$ are included in the ranked queue
   (b) otherwise, we drop the pair, $\langle v, u\rangle$

Once the anchor list is expanded, [29] relies on a post-process, with time complexity, $O(m \times n^3)$, where $m = min\{|E_1|, |E_2|\}$ and $n = max\{|V_1|, |V_2|\}$. This step is not scalable due to its prohibitive time complexity. Therefore, the proposed keynode-driven scalable graph matching (`KSGM`) algorithm omits this refinement post-process, due to its high time complexity[4]. Instead, the set, L, of node pairs remaining after the expansion process is directly returned as the aligned nodes of the matching, $M_{1,2}$, for the input graphs, G_1 and G_2.

7. TIME COMPLEXITY ANALYSIS

7.1 Offline Time Complexity

Let $G(V, E)$ be a graph to be indexed in the database.

7.1.1 *Structural Keynode Extraction*

The first step in structural keynode extraction is to obtain the PageRank scores for the nodes of the two graphs. While, this is an expensive operation (involving a matrix inversion with $O(|V|^{2.373})$ complexity for a graph with $|V|$ nodes), there are many efficient, approximate implementations of PageRank, including sublinear approximations [6].

The second step is the creation of an l-layer scale-space for G. To construct the scale space, we first construct a node distance matrix, which requires an all-pairs shortest path computation, with complexity $O(|V|^3)$ for a graph with $|V|$ nodes, but more efficient randomized algorithms exist [27]. Once the node distances have been computed, we construct the scale-space in $O(l \times |V| \times max\_w\_nbhd\_size)$, as for each of the l scales, the score of each node needs to be smoothed considering the scores of the vertices in its w-hop neighborhood (w is the Gaussian window size and $max\_w\_nbhd\_size$ is the size of the largest w-hop neighborhood in G).

Once the scale-space is constructed, next, we identify the keynode candidates. This involves $O(l \times |V|)$ time, because for each of the l scales, each node needs to be compared with a constant number (8) of DoG-neighbors in the scale-space.

Finally, we rank the keynode candidates to select the top $K = \frac{\Theta}{100}V$ many as the keynodes to bootstrap the online matching process. Let there be C many keynode candidates. Computing the ranking scores for these takes $O(C)$ time, because each keynode candidate needs to be compared with a constant number of DoG-neighbors and obtaining the top K takes $O(C \times log(K))$ time.

7.1.2 *Local Signature Extraction*

Since the local signature extraction process needs to extract the k-hop neighborhoods around the nodes, the complexity of this step is $O(|V| \times max\_k\_nbhd\_size)$, where $max\_k\_nbhd\_size$ is the size of the largest k-hop neighborhood in G. Note that this step can also leverage the node distance matrix constructed during the offline keynode extraction process.

7.2 Online Time Complexity

Let $G_1(V_1, E_1)$ and $G_2(V_2, E_2)$ be two graphs. The online process includes the following operations.

7.2.1 *Local Similarity Computation for Keynodes*

This process has $O(|K_1| \times |K_2| \times compare\_length)$ complexity, where
$compare\_length = min\{max\_k\_nbhd\_size_1, max\_k\_nbhd\_size$
since signatures (of length are compared for each pair of nodes in the keynode sets K_1 and K_2.

7.2.2 *Anchor Set Selection*

This greedy process has $O((|K_1| \times |K_2|) \times log(|K_1| \times |K_2|))$ time cost as each pair off nodes among the keynode sets need to be considered only once in ranked order.

7.2.3 *Anchor Set Expansion*

This has $O((|V_1| \times |V_2|) \times log(|V_1| \times |V_2|))$ worst case time cost, as in the worst case, all pairs of vertices across the two graphs may need to be considered for expansion in ranked order.

8. EXPERIMENTS

In this section, we present experimental evaluations of the proposed *keynode-driven scalable graph matching* (`KSGM`) algorithm. In particular, we compare `KSGM` to the graph matching algorithm presented in [29] in terms of efficiency and accuracy.

8.1 Data Sets

8.1.1 *Facebook Data Graph*

The first data set we used is the Facebook social circles data graph obtained from the Stanford Large Network Dataset Collection [2]. This is a connected graph with 4039 nodes and 88234 edges. The graph has a diameter of 8 and a 90-percentile effective diameter of 4.7. For the experiments, we constructed 10 subgraphs by uniformly sampling connected subsets, containing $60 - 70\%$ of the original graph nodes. Once the subgraphs are obtained, each of the subgraphs is used as a query against the rest. We report the averages of execution time and accuracy.

8.1.2 *Synthetic Graph Data Sets*

In addition to the Facebook graph, we also used synthetic graphs, where we controlled the topology, size, and node degree to explore

[4]Though, in cases where scalability is not critical, this refinement can be implemented without any change in the rest of the algorithm.

Table 1: Synthetic graph topologies and configurations

Graph topology	Number of nodes	Average degree
Erdos-Renyi (ER)	5000, 7500 (plus 1 to 10%)	4, 8, 16
Power law (PL)	5000, 7500 (plus 1 to 10%)	4, 8, 16

the advantages and disadvantages of the algorithms under different scenarios.

We generated the synthetic graphs using the well known random graph generating tool, NetworkX [1]. We consider two common graph topologies: the Erdos-Renyi (ER) model and the power law topology (PL) under the Barabasi-Albert model. Table 1 lists the number of nodes and average degree settings that we used for assessing our algorithms. For each configuration, we generated 10 graphs. Note that, in addition to the base sizes (of 5000 and 7500), we randomly created an additional 1 to 10% more nodes to ensure that the different graphs in the data set have slightly different numbers of nodes. As before, once the 10 graphs are obtained for each configuration, each of the subgraphs is used as query against the rest. We report the averages of execution time and accuracy.

8.2 Evaluation Criteria

All experiments were conducted using a 4-core Intel Core i5-2400, 3.10GHz, machine with 8GB memory, running 64-bit Windows 7 Enterprise. The codes were executed using Matlab 2013b and Visual Studio 2012. To evaluate accuracy, we use the matching quality defined in Section 3.

8.2.1 Execution Time

We report both offline and online execution times. As shown in Algorithm 1 in Section 3, for KSGM, the offline execution includes structural keynode and local-signature extraction steps. Online execution includes similarity computation, anchor selection, and expansion steps. [29] does not perform structural keynode extraction; instead, offline execution includes eigen-decomposition for global signatures.

For both KSGM and [29], we omit the refinement step as its complexity is prohibitive for scalable graph matching. For instance, for the Facebook graph for which KSGM takes $\sim$ 6 seconds for online processing for a pair of graphs, refinement takes $\sim$ 30 minutes – i.e., it causes a $\sim$ 260$\times$ slowdown[5].

8.3 Experiment Parameters

The default parameters for the structural keynode extraction (SKE) algorithm are as follows:

- PageRank teleportation probability $(1-\alpha) = 0.15$ (as is commonly assumed),
- least smoothing factor (σ_{min}) = 0.275, corresponding to $\sim$ 2-hop neighborhoods,
- maximum smoothing factor (σ_{max}) = 0.777, corresponding to $\sim$ 5-hop neighborhoods, and
- number (l) of smoothing levels = 6.

In addition, for KSGM, the default percentage (Θ) of keynodes selected from the graph was set to 3%. Also, for all algorithms, local signatures were extracted from 2-hop neighborhoods (i.e., $k = 2$), as recommended by the authors of [29].

8.4 Results for the Facebook Graph

8.4.1 Default Configuration

Table 2 lists the online and offline processing times and accuracy for the Facebook graph under the default parameter settings. As we see here, while KSGM spends more time in one-time, offline

[5]For this data configuration, when using expensive refinement post-processing, KSGM and [29]'s accuracies are 0.72 and 0.696, respectively.

Table 2: Experiment results for the Facebook Graph (default parameters)

	[29]	KSGM	PR	Random
Matching time (online, sec.)	19.2	**6.4**	7.25	6.0
Accuracy	35.4%	**38.0%**	34.12%	15.4%
Extraction time (offline, sec.)	11.5	110.4	0.39	-

Table 3: Impact of the keynode percentage, Θ, for the Facebook Graph

	2%	3%	4%	6%	8%
Matching time (online, sec.)	6.5	6.4	6.3	6.4	7.2
Accuracy	37.6%	38.0%	38.7%	36.4%	33.2%

Table 4: Impact of the node-pair ranking function, $\rho()$, for the Facebook Graph

	$\rho()$	w/o Degree	with Global
Matching time (online sec.)	6.4	6.0	4.0
Accuracy	38.0%	31.8%	22.9%

Table 5: Impact of the local-signature neighborhood size, k, for the Facebook Graph

	2 hops (default)	3 hops	4 hops
Matching time (online, sec.)	6.4	5.5	4.3
Accuracy	38.0%	33.9%	23.3%

processing, its online matching time is 3$\times$ faster than that of [29]. Moreover, the matching accuracy of KSGM is 1.2$\times$ better than that of the competitor, through it does not use global signatures, nor it relies on the optimal Hungarian algorithm for anchor selection.

The table also lists the performance of KSGM when using top PageRank (PR) scored nodes instead of those returned by the SKE algorithm. As we see here, while the offline process is faster when using PageRank scoring nodes, the runtime performance (both in terms of execution time and accuracy) is worse when using SKE keynodes. In addition, to see whether it is possible to achieve a competitive accuracy if we were to select a similar percentage of node randomly, in Table 2, we also include results where random keynodes are used in the matching online phase. As we can see, the accuracy drops significantly when we use random keynodes instead of using robust structural keynodes extracted by the proposed SKE algorithm[6]. These indicate that SKE is indeed effective in extracting structurally distinct and useful keynodes.

8.4.2 Impact of the Keynode Percentage

Table 3 studies the impact of the percentage, Θ, of the nodes used as keynodes. As we see, up to a point, the more keynodes we use, the more accurate and faster the matching becomes. Beyond that point, however, additional keynodes become disadvantageous. This indicates that top keynodes are the most effective in serving as good starting points and, as expected, below a certain rank they loose distinctiveness, resulting in increased cost and loss in accuracy.

8.4.3 Impact of the Node-Pair Ranking Function

Table 4 studies the impact of the node-pair ranking function, $\rho()$. In particular, we compare the performance of the ranking function proposed in Section 6.1.1, to the ranking function without degree extension and ranking function including additional global-signature similarity as proposed in [29]. As we see here, the proposed node-pair ranking function provides the best expansion opportunities (and thus provides the highest accuracy, with slight expansion time overhead). Also, the "with Global" optional provides a much worse matching. Thus, while the algorithm allows, we encourage the users not to use "with Global" option.

[6]The slight time gain when using random keynodes is due to the fact that random keynodes are not good starting points for expansion and, thus, the expansion process ends earlier.

Table 6: Experiment results for the synthetic data sets (avg. degree=4, varying models and number of nodes)

	PL(5000)	PL(7500)	ER(5000)	ER(7500)
KSGM *Online time (sec.)*	6.9	13.9	6.5	14.5
[29] Online time (sec.)	99.3	223.7	746.7	745.1
KSGM *Accuracy*	45.3%	45.1%	45.7%	51.2%
[29] Accuracy	42.9%	42.8%	46.3%	53.0%
KSGM *Offline time (sec.)*	130.0	284.7	134.8	270.8
[29] Offline time (sec.)	23.8	82.8	24.9	84.5

Table 7: Impact of the average node degree (number of nodes=5000, power law model)

	degree=4	degree=8	degree=16
KSGM *Online time (sec.)*	6.9	7.5	9.3
[29] Online time (sec.)	99.3	116.7	141.2
KSGM *Accuracy*	45.3%	25.2%	13.9%
[29] Accuracy	42.9%	25.1%	14.1%
KSGM *Offline time (sec.)*	130.0	199.1	396.7
[29] Offline time (sec.)	23.8	27.9	53.2

8.4.4 *Impact of the Neighborhood Size, k, for Local-Signatures*

Table 5 studies the impact of the neighborhood size, k, for local-signature extraction. As we see in the table, the highest accuracy is at 2 hops[7], increasing the neighborhood size negatively affects the accuracy, indicating that unless locally meaningful signatures are used, the resulting node-pair ranking is not effective for expansion. This shows the keynode matching process is more accurate when keynodes are easy to localize and this requires them to be distinct and locally representative. Large neighborhoods potentially violate both. Note that this is in line with the observation in Table 4.

8.5 Results for the Synthetic Data Sets

In this subsection, we consider the impacts of graph topology, size, and node degree using ER and PL topologies. We omit discussions of the impacts of the other parameters, as they mirror those presented in Tables 3 through 5.

8.5.1 *Default Configurations*

Table 6 lists the performances of KSGM and [29] for synthetic graphs for different topologies and numbers of nodes under the default parameter settings. As we see here, the online execution time of KSGM is significantly (10× to 115×) faster than that of [29], especially for the ER topology. Moreover, on both Erdos-Renyi (ER) and power law (PL) topologies, the accuracy is highly competitive, with KSGM providing non-negligible accuracy gains for the PL model (where it is relatively easier to identify effective keynodes).

8.5.2 *Impact of Average Node Degree*

Table 6 studies the impact of average node degree on matching accuracies for the power law graph. As we see in the table, both algorithms see a drop in the matching accuracy with larger node degrees. However, KSGM stays competitive in terms of accuracy, whereas it provides more gains in terms of online execution time.

9. CONCLUSIONS

Noticing that existing solutions to the graph matching problem face major scalability challenges, we argue that it is impractical to seek alignment among all pairs of nodes. Given these observations, in this paper, we first presented an offline *structural keynode extraction* (SKE) algorithm and then discussed how to use these structural keynodes in a novel *keynode-driven scalable graph matching* (KSGM) algorithm. *Keynodes* are selected carefully especially because a post refinement step is not feasible due to scalability requirements. Experiment results show that the proposed KSGM algorithm works faster than the state-of-the-art algorithms without refinement, yet produces alignments that are as good or better.

Acknowledgments

We thank the authors of [29] for sharing their source code and data.

10. REFERENCES

[1] http://networkx.github.io/
[2] http://snap.stanford.edu/index.html
[3] X. Bai, H. Yu, and E. R. Hancock. Graph matching using spectrament. ICPR 2004.
[4] A. Balmin, et al. ObjectRank: Authority-based keyword search in databases. VLDB, 2004.
[5] M.G. Borgatti, et al. Network measures of social capital. Connections 21(2):27-36, 1998.
[6] C. Borgs, M. Brautbar, J. T. Chayes, S.-H. Teng. Multiscale Matrix Sampling and Sublinear-Time PageRank Computation. Internet Mathematics 10(1-2): 20-48, 2014.
[7] S. Brin, et al. The anatomy of a large-scale hypertextual Web search engine. Computer Networks and ISDN Systems 30: 107-117, 1998.
[8] H. Bunke. Error correcting graph matching: On the influence of the underlying cost function. IEEE TPAMI, 21(9):917–922, 1999.
[9] K. S. Candan, R. Rossini, M. L. Sapino, X. Wang. sDTW: Computing DTW Distances using Locally Relevant Constraints based on Salient Feature Alignments. PVLDB, 1519-1530, 2012.
[10] M. Chen, J. Liu, and X. Tang. Clustering via random walk hitting time on directed graphs. AAAI 2008.
[11] Xilun Chen, K. Selcuk Candan. LWI-SVD: Low-rank, Windowed, Incremental Singular Value Decompositions on Time-Evolving Data Sets. KDD 2014.
[12] Xilun Chen, K. Selcuk Candan. GI-NMF: Group Incremental Non-Negative Matrix Factorization on Data Streams. CIKM 2014.
[13] T. H. Cormen, C. E. Leiserson, R. L. Rivest, and C. Stein. Introduction to Algorithms. 2001.
[14] R. Giugno and D. Shasha. Graphgrep: A fast and universal method for querying graphs. ICPR, pp. 112-115, 2002.
[15] W. S. Han, J. Lee, and J. H. Lee. TurboISO: Towards ultrafast and robust subgraph isomorphism search in large graph databases. SIGMOD 2013
[16] R. Jonker and T. Volgenant.Improving the Hungarian assignment algorithm. Oper. Res. 171-175. 1986.
[17] G. Karypis and V. Kumar "A fast and high quality multilevel scheme for partitioning irregular graphs". SIAM Journal on Scientific Computing 20 (1), 1999.
[18] D. Knossow, A. Sharma, D. Mateus, and R. Horaud. Inexact matching of large and sparse graphs using laplacian eigenvectors. GbRPR, 2009.
[19] W.-J. Lee and R. P. W. Duin. An inexact graph comparison approach in joint eigenspace. In SSPR/SPR, 35-44, 2008.
[20] Jundong Li, Xia Hu, Jiliang Tang, Huan Liu. Unsupervised Streaming Feature Selection in Social Media. CIKM 2015
[21] D. G. Lowe. Distinctive Image Features from Scale-Invariant Keypoints. Int. Journal of Computer Vision, 60, 2, 2004.
[22] K. Riesen, X. Jiang, and H. Bunke. Exact and inexact graph matching: Methodology and applications. Managing and Mining Graph Data, pages 217-247, 2010.
[23] S. Umeyama. An eigen decomposition approach to weighted graph matching problems. IEEE TPAMI, 10(5):695-703, 1988.
[24] J. R. Ullman. An algorithm for subgraph isomorphism, JACM Vol. 23, No. 1, pp. 31-42. 1976
[25] X. Wang, K. S. Candan, M. L. Sapino: Leveraging metadata for identifying local, robust multi-variate temporal (RMT) features. ICDE, 2014.
[26] White D.R., et al. Betweenness centrality measures for directed graphs. Social Networks, 16, 335-346,1994.
[27] R. Williams. Faster all-pairs shortest paths via circuit complexity. STOC, 664-673. 2014.
[28] M. Zaslavskiy, F. R. Bach, and J.-P. Vert. A path following algorithm for the graph matching problem. IEEE Trans. Pattern Anal. Mach. Intell., 31(12):2227-2242, 2009.
[29] Y. Zhu, L. Qin, J. X. Yu, et al. High Efficiency and Quality: Large Graphs Matching. CIKM, pp. 1755-1764. 2011.

[7]Coincidentally, this also is the scale at which the SKE algorithm located an overwhelming majority of the keynodes for this graph.

Protecting Your Children from Inappropriate Content in Mobile Apps: An Automatic Maturity Rating Framework

Bing Hu
Samsung Research America
binghu2006@gmail.com

Bin Liu
Rutgers University
binben.liu@rutgers.edu

Neil Zhenqiang Gong
ECpE, Iowa State University
neilgong@iastate.edu

Deguang Kong
Samsung Research America
doogkong@gmail.com

Hongxia Jin
Samsung Research America
hongxia.jin@samsung.com

ABSTRACT

Mobile applications (Apps) could expose children or adolescents to mature themes such as sexual content, violence and drug use, which harms their online safety. Therefore, mobile platforms provide rating policies to label the maturity levels of Apps and the reasons why an App has a given maturity level, which enables parents to select maturity-appropriate Apps for their children. However, existing approaches to implement these maturity rating policies are either costly (because of expensive manual labeling) or inaccurate (because of no centralized controls). In this work, we aim to design and build a machine learning framework to automatically predict maturity levels for mobile Apps and the associated reasons with a high accuracy and a low cost.

To this end, we take a multi-label classification approach to predict the mature contents in a given App and then label the maturity level according to a rating policy. Specifically, we extract novel features from App descriptions by leveraging *deep learning* techniques to automatically capture the semantic similarity between words and adapt Support Vector Machine to capture label correlations with *pearson correlation* in a multi-label classification setting. Moreover, we evaluate our approach and various baseline methods using datasets that we collected from both App Store and Google Play. We demonstrate that, with only App descriptions, our approach already achieves 85% Precision for predicting mature contents and 79% Precision for predicting maturity levels, which substantially outperforms baseline methods.

Categories and Subject Descriptors

H.2.8 [**Database Management**]: Database Applications—*Data mining*; H.4 [**Information Systems Applications**]: Miscellaneous

General Terms

Algorithms, Measurement, Experimentation

Permission to make digital or hard copies of all or part of this work for personal or classroom use is granted without fee provided that copies are not made or distributed for profit or commercial advantage and that copies bear this notice and the full citation on the first page. Copyrights for components of this work owned by others than ACM must be honored. Abstracting with credit is permitted. To copy otherwise, or republish, to post on servers or to redistribute to lists, requires prior specific permission and/or a fee. Request permissions from Permissions@acm.org.

CIKM'15, October 19–23, 2015, Melbourne, VIC, Australia.
© 2015 ACM. ISBN 978-1-4503-3794-6/15/10 ...$15.00.
DOI: http://dx.doi.org/10.1145/2806416.2806579.

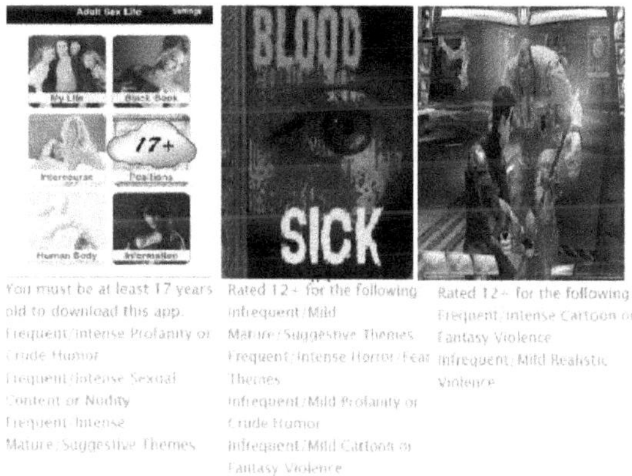

Figure 1: The mature contents and maturity levels of three Apps on App Store.

Keywords

Mobile Apps; Content Rating; Text Mining; Deep Learning; Pearson correlation.

1. INTRODUCTION

Mobile devices are becoming more and more popular in the past few years. However, Apps could expose children or adolescents to mature themes such as sexual content, violence, and drug use, which are harmful to their growth and development. Indeed, research from psychology has long established that teenagers who are exposed to content that glamorizes drug use, sex, or violence tend to engage in those activities themselves [27, 13, 28].

Therefore, similar to the conventional video game and movie industry, mobile platforms provide mechanisms to rate the maturity levels of Apps, which enables parents to select maturity-appropriate mobile Apps for their children. For instance, App Store has a maturity rating policy, which consists of four maturity levels, i.e., *4+*, *9+*, *12+*, and *17+*. Apps with different maturity levels are suitable for users with different ages, e.g., Apps with 17+ maturity level are appropriate for users who are at least 17 years old. In addition to the maturity level, App Store also identifies the detailed mature contents which make an App be rated as a specific maturity level. These mature contents are helpful for users to better understand the App, and to guide developers to modify their Apps in order to increase their audience population. For instance, Figure 1 shows the mature

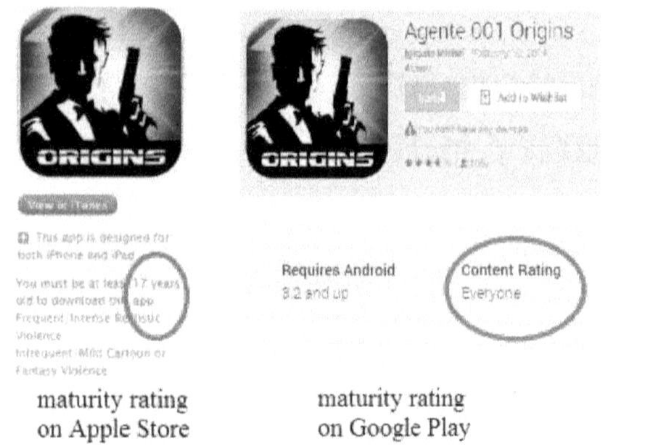

Figure 2: Inconsistency of maturity ratings for the same app in App Store and Google Play.

contents and maturity levels of three Apps on App Store. Google Play also establishes a rating policy that includes four maturity levels, i.e., *Everyone, Low Maturity, Medium Maturity,* and *High Maturity,* and they are corresponding to the four maturity levels on App Store.

Existing approaches to implement these maturity rating policies are either costly or inaccurate. Specifically, Apple Inc. hires employees to manually examine each submitted App in order to identify its maturity level and the associated reasons. Given the large amount of new Apps, e.g., 20,000 new Apps were submitted to App Store per month as of 2014 [2], this manual labeling approach is very costly and time-consuming. Unlike the centralized rating service provided by App Store, Google Play requires developers to label the maturity levels for their own Apps according to the Google Play's rating policy. These self-reported maturity levels are determined at the time when developers submit their Apps to Google Play and remain unchanged until users report inappropriateness. Although Google Play's strategy is scalable and less costly, the maturity ratings reported by developers could be inaccurate. Moreover, various reports [15, 25] have shown growing concerns among parents who have experienced inaccurate maturity ratings of Apps. Figure 2 shows an example of the mislabelling of the maturity ratings by the Android developers. Chen et al. [5] rated the maturity of apps using a keyword matching method through manual identification of the sensitive words that are highly correlated with apps' maturity in App descriptions. Their method achieves limited labeling accuracy because it does not consider the semantic meanings of words. Moreover, their method cannot produce evidences about why an App has a worse rating than another one.

In this work, we aim to design a scalable framework that automatically labels App maturity level and the associated reasons accurately. Our framework, called *Automatic App Maturity Rating (AAMR),* takes a rating policy and the description of an App as input, and predicts the mature content in the App and the maturity level of the App. We choose App description because it describes the content and functionality of an App, and thus it is a good indicator of the mature content (if any) in the App. However, App description based rating analysis faces several challenges:

⊙ Apps often have *short* and *concise* descriptions in order for users to quickly understand the Apps.

⊙ Natural languages are *ambiguous,* i.e., the same word or phrase has different meanings at different contexts; and natural languages have *synonyms,* i.e., the same mature theme can be expressed with different words or phrases.

⊙ Mature contents are correlated, i.e., some mature contents are likely to co-occur in Apps while some mature contents are mutually exclusive.

To address these challenges, we propose a two-stage machine learning approach to first predict the mature contents and then label the maturity levels. Specifically, we extract novel features from App descriptions. In particular, we use *word to vector model* [23, 24], which leverages *deep learning* technique to automatically capture the semantic similarity between words; to mitigate the language ambiguity, we use the bag-of-words feature to capture the context and global word distributions. With these features, we map the mature-content prediction to be a multi-label classification problem and we adapt SVM to capture label correlations. We choose Support Vector Machine (SVM) [7] for rating prediction since it was shown to outperform other classifiers for short text analysis [11]. We evaluate our approach and various baseline methods using large-scale datasets that we collected from both App Store and Google Play. We demonstrate that, using only App descriptions, our approach can already achieve 85% Precision on maturity content prediction and 79% Precision on maturity level prediction, and our approach substantially outperforms baseline methods including both automatic and human-labeling approaches.

The key contributions are summarized as follows:

- We propose a machine learning framework, called Automatic App Maturity Rating (AAMR), to automatically predict mature contents and label maturity levels accurately. To the best of our knowledge, this is the *first* systematic study about automatic maturity rating for mobile Apps.
- We extract novel features from App descriptions by leveraging *deep learning* techniques. Moreover, we adapt standard SVM as a *multi-label* classifier to capture label correlations using *pearson correlation.*
- We comprehensively evaluate our approach and other baseline methods using *large-scale real-world* datasets that we collected from both App Store and Google Play, and we show that our approach substantially outperforms baseline methods.

2. BACKGROUND AND DESIGN GOALS

In this section, we first introduce the maturity rating policies adopted by App Store and Google Play, and then we discuss the limitations of current approaches to implement the policies, which is followed by our design goals of our automatic App maturity rating system.

2.1 Two Maturity Rating Policies

App Store's Rating Policy: Table 1 shows the rating policy of App Store [16]. In this policy, Apps are classified into four categories, i.e., *4+*, *9+*, *12+*, and *17+*. Apps with the maturity level of *17+* are appropriate for users who are at least 17 years old. The maturity level of an App is related to the following mature contents: violence, sexual/maturity, profanity/humor, alcohol/drug/tobacco,etc. Moreover, different intensity of mature contents results in different maturity levels. For example, an App is rated as *9+* if it contains

Table 1: App Store Maturity Rating Policy

Content	Level	Rating	#
realistic violence	Infrequent/mild	9+	1
	Frequent/intense	12+	2
cartoon/fantasy violence	Frequent/intense	9+	3
horror-themed content	Infrequent/mild	9+	4
	Frequent/intense	12+	5
profanity/crude humor	Infrequent/mild	9+	6
	Frequent/intense	12+	7
sexual content/nudity	Infrequent/mild	12+	8
	Frequent/intense	17+	9
mature/suggestive content	Frequent/intense	17+	10
alcohol/tobacco/drug	Infrequent/mild	12+	11
	Frequent/intense	17+	12
gambling/contests	—	17+	13
simulated gambling	—	12+	14
treatment-focused content	Infrequent/mild	12+	15
	Frequent/intense	17+	16
unrestricted web access	—	17+	17
—	—	4+	

Table 2: Google Play Maturity Rating Policy

Content	Level	Rating	#
violence	mild cartoon	low	1
	fictional violence	low	2
	realistic	medium	3
	intense fictional	medium	4
	graphic	high	5
profanity/crude humor	frequent/intense	medium	6
hate	inflammatory cont.	medium	7
sexual/suggestive	include	medium	8
	focus	high	9
alcohol/tobacco/drug	reference	medium	10
	focus	high	11
gambling themes	—	medium	12
simulated gambling	—	medium	13
location	access	low	14
	publish/share	medium	15
UGC/social	host	medium	16
	focus	medium	17
—	—	everyone	

infrequent or *mild* "realistic violence", but it is rated as *12+* if the realistic violence is *frequent* or *intense*.

Google Play's Rating Policy: Similar to App Store, Google Play's policy also consists of four maturity levels. However, unlike App Store's policy whose maturity levels are directly related to numeric ages, Google Play's four levels are *everyone*, *low maturity*, *medium maturity*, and *high maturity* [1]. Table 2 illustrates Google Play's rating policy.

Comparing the two policies: We note that the two policies are equivalent under some conditions [5], i.e., some Apps have the same maturity level under the two rating policies. For instance, an App with only frequent profanity is labeled as *12+* by the App Store's policy and *medium* by the Google Play's policy, respectively. Thus, *12+* in the App Store's policy is equivalent to *medium* in the Google Play's policy for this App. Table 3 shows the mappings between Google Play's maturity levels and the App Store's maturity levels. The conditions for such mappings were discussed and obtained by Chen et al. [5]. However, App Store and Google Play treat different content as mature. For example, Google Play adopts "hate" and "location" as mature, but these content is not considered by App Store. Moreover, Google Play also considers the intensity of mature content when labeling maturity levels, but the definition of intensity is a slightly different from that of App Store. In our experiments, we will use these conditions to obtain groundtruth mature contents and maturity levels of Google Play Apps.

2.2 Limitations of Existing Rating Policy Implementations

An implementation of a policy is to label the maturity level of an App according to the rating policy. Existing implementations adopted by App Store and Google Play are either costly or inaccurate. On App Store, Apple Inc. hires trained employees to comprehensively evaluate each submitted App to label its maturity level, and such evaluations could include meta-data (e.g., App description, icon, and screenshots of the App) analysis and code analysis. Given the large amount of new Apps, e.g., 20,000 new Apps were submitted to App Store per month as of 2013 [2], this manual labeling approach is very costly and time-consuming.

Table 3: Mappings between maturity levels in Google Play and App Store

Maturity Levels	Google Play	App Store
1	Everyone	4+
2	Low Maturity	9+
3	Medium Maturity	12+
4	High Maturity	17+

Unlike the centralized rating service provided by App Store, Google Play requires developers to label the maturity levels for their own Apps according to the Google Play's rating policy. Although Google Play's strategy is scalable and less costly, the maturity ratings reported by developers could be inaccurate. For instance, in our dataset collected from Google Play, 45% Apps have incorrect developer-provided maturity levels.

2.3 Design Goals

To overcome the limitations of existing policy implementations, we propose an automatic App maturity rating framework. We have the following design goals for such a framework.

Policy Independent: Different platforms could have different rating policies. For instance, although Google Play's policy and App Store's policy are equivalent in some cases, they are different in general. Therefore, we aim to design our framework independent of policies. In other words, the input of our framework includes the specifications of a policy, and our framework produces the maturity level of an App under this policy.

Mature Contents to Support Maturity Levels: Predicting the mature contents in an App help users better understand the App and guide developers to modify their Apps in order to increase the number of potential users. For instance, an App is labeled as *17+* by App Store because of *frequent* sexual content. The developer could decrease the number of dirty words so that it is labeled as *12+*, which makes people whose ages are between 12 and 17 years old

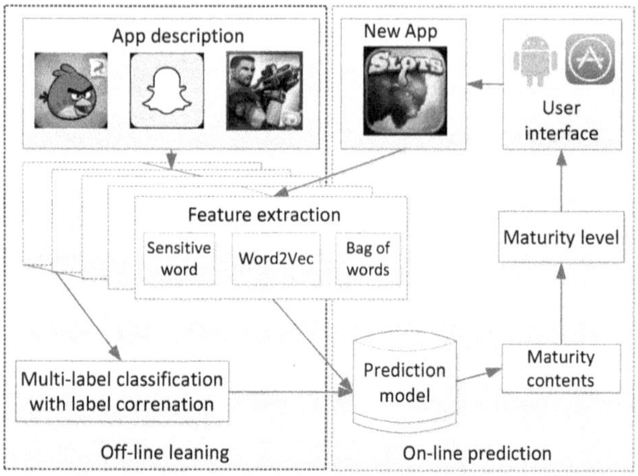

Figure 3: Overview of Automatic App Maturity Rating (AAMR) framework.

potential users of this App. Therefore, we aim to design our framework to give both the maturity levels and also the maturity words that support our rating.

Scalable and Accurate: Given the large number of new submitted Apps per month, we aim to design our framework to be scalable. In particular, our framework should produce maturity analysis results for Apps immediately after they are submitted. Moreover, our framework should produce the maturity analysis results with a high accuracy.

3. AUTOMATIC APP MATURITY RATING (AAMR) FRAMEWORK

3.1 Overview

Figure 3 illustrates the machine learning framework for automatic App maturity rating. In the off-line learning phase, we extract features from App descriptions and learn a multi-label classifier to predict the *mature content* in a given App. In the on-line prediction phase, our framework performs maturity rating in a two-stage approach, i.e., we first use the learned multi-label classifier to predict mature content in a new App and then label the maturity level according to the given rating policy.

We extract our features from *sensitive words* in maturity rating policies that directly refer to mature content, *augmented sensitive words* that are semantically similar to sensitive words, and bag-of-words model. Natural languages have synonyms, e.g., different words could represent the same mature content. Thus, we use augmented sensitive words that are synonyms of sensitive words to enrich our features. We obtain augmented sensitive words via recent *word-to-vector* techniques [24][23]. Specifically, a word-to-vector algorithm learns a vector representation for each word from a corpus of text, and two words are semantically similar if they have close vector representations. Moreover, natural languages are ambiguous, e.g., a sensitive word in an App description might not indicate that the App has mature content. Therefore, we use bag-of-words model to capture the *context* of sensitive words to mitigate the ambiguity issue.

We find that mature contents are correlated, i.e., some mature contents have very high co-occurrences in App descriptions. Therefore, we adapt multi-label Support Vector Machine (SVM) [7] to capture such correlations. We choose SVM because App descriptions are short and previous work [6] showed that SVM outperforms other classifiers for short text classification.

In the next few subsection, we will illustrate each component in more details.

3.2 Feature Engineering and Learning

We extract features from sensitive words in rating policies, augmented sensitive words that are semantically similar to sensitive words.

3.2.1 Extracting Sensitive Words

A maturity rating policy has clear definitions on maturity content. Therefore, we extract *sensitive words* from a rating policy that directly refer to mature content. For instance, the list of sensitive words we extract from the App Store's rating policy shown in Table 1 include *violence, horror, humor, profanity, sex, nudity, mature, alcohol, tobacco, drug, gambling*, and *treatment, etc.* We note that the list of sensitive words could be different for different rating policies because they could treat different contents as mature. For instance, Google Play also defines *hate* as mature content while App Store does not. We use binary features to represent sensitive words. Specifically, a feature has a value of 1 if the corresponding sensitive word appears in an App description, otherwise the feature has a value of 0.

Chen et al. [5] proposed to take these sensitive words as features and use them to directly learn a classifier to predict the maturity levels of Apps. The keyword-matching method, however, suffers from two limitations. First, natural languages have synonyms, e.g., *battle* is semantically similar to *violence*. Keyword-matching will miss these synonyms, which results in high false negatives. Second, natural languages are ambiguous, e.g., that a sensitive word appears in an App's description does not necessarily mean the App contains the corresponding mature content, which results in false positives. To address these limitations, we leverage feature augmentation to consider words that are semantically similar to sensitive words to capture the context.

3.2.2 Augmenting Features via Deep Learning

We first show an example to illustrate the issues introduced by synonyms. The following is a part of the description of an App named "Injustice: Gods Among Us":

> *Build an epic roster of DC heroes and villains and get ready for* ***battle****! INJUSTICE: GODS AMONG US is a free-to-play collectible card game where you build a roster of characters, moves,* ***powers****, and gear and enter the arena in touch-based 3-on-3 action* ***battle****. fight: Use the touch screen mechanics of your mobile device to* ***combat*** *your enemies in 3-on-3 action...*

In the above description, there are several words (shown in bold) strongly indicating *violence* content which is not suitable for children under a certain age. However, the sensitive words cannot represent such mature content. To address this problem, we leverage *word-to-vector (word2vec)* techniques developed by Google [24, 23] to augment sensitive words with semantically similar words.

Table 4: **Top-10 words that have the highest similarities with the sensitive word *sex*.**

word	cosine similarity
offend	0.4686
nudity	0.4333
intimate	0.4023
flirt	0.3612
wanted	0.3593
men	0.3326
adult	0.3323
hot	0.2974
confession	0.2898
position	0.2859

A word2vec algorithm learns a vector representation for each word from a corpus of texts in an unsupervised setting. These vector representations capture a large number of precise semantic word relationships. Specifically, two words are treated as semantically similar if they have close vector representations. As a word embedding technique, word2vec, can be viewed as a representational layer in a *deep learning* [4] architecture which transforms a word into a positional representation of the word relative to other words in the training dataset, where the position is represented as a data point in the new vector space.

In experiment, in order to get "*semantic*" meaning of words, we run the word2vec tool [32] using the app descriptions from more than 350,000 Apps in Google and App Store. For instance, Table 4 shows the top-10 words that have the highest similarities with the sensitive word *sex*. The similarity between two words is defined as the cosine similarity of the two corresponding vector representations.

For each sensitive word, we choose the top-200 words that have the highest cosine similarities, and we call these words *augmented sensitive words*. Note that some words might appear more than once in our augmented sensitive words because they might be similar to more than one sensitive word. Suppose we have n augmented sensitive words, we extract a feature vector with length n for each App. Specifically, if an augmented sensitive word appears in an App's description, the corresponding feature has a value that equals the cosine similarity between the augmented sensitive word and the corresponding sensitive word, otherwise the corresponding feature has a value of 0.

3.2.3 Bag-of-words

Given that the text data is very sparse, in some cases, App descriptions do not contain any sensitive word or augmented sensitive word. Moreover, whether a sensitive or an augmented sensitive word really indicates mature content depends on the context. Therefore, we further extract bag-of-words features from App descriptions.

We adopt *term frequency-inverse document frequency (TF-IDF)* to weight each word. TF-IDF is widely used in information retrieval and text mining [22, 30, 33]. The TF-IDF weights evaluate how important a word is to a document in a corpus of documents. Specifically, the TF-IDF weight of a word is composed by two parts. The first part computes the normalized Term Frequency (TF) and the second part is the Inverse Document Frequency (IDF). Formally, the TF-IDF weight of a word is calculated as follows, $w_{i,j} = TF_{i,j} \times log(\frac{N}{DF_i})$, where $TF_{i,j}$ is the term frequency of t_i in document d_j, N is the total number of documents in the corpus, and DF_i is the total number of documents that contain t_i.

3.2.4 Feature Concatenation

We concatenate the features extracted from sensitive words, augmented sensitive words, and bag-of-words model. For the sensitive word features, we extract twelve sensitive words from the App Store policy and thirteen sensitive words from the Google Play policy. For each sensitive word, we have the top-200 words with the highest cosine similarity. We use the most frequent 2000 words for the bag-of-words features. In total, we have 4,412 features for Apps on App Store and 4,613 features for Apps on Google Play.

3.3 Multi-label Classification

After feature extraction and feature learning from apps' descriptions, the next step is to build a machine learning classifier that can automatically classify an app into its corresponding maturity level.

More formally, let $\mathbf{x}_i \in \Re^p$ be the p-dimensional feature vector carried by each App i. Let $\mathbf{y}_i \in \{0,1\}^C$ be the C-dimensional binary vector denoting the maturity contents for App i. Then $\mathbf{Y} = [\mathbf{y}_1, \mathbf{y}_2, ...\mathbf{y}_n]$ corresponds to the maturity contents for all the apps. Furthermore, let $\mathbf{z} \in \Re^n$ be the set of the maturity levels of the mobile Apps, where $\mathbf{z} = [z_1, z_2, ...z_n]$ and z_i is the maturity level for each App i. More specifically, the mature content is defined by a maturity rating policy. For instance, both App Store and Google Play define 17 different mature contents, which are shown in Table 1 and Table 2, respectively, and $\mathbf{y}_i$ indicates what kind of mature content among the 17 contents the App i contains.

3.3.1 Key Idea

In the off-line training phase, we have a set of training mobile App data $\mathbf{L} = (\mathbf{x}_1, \mathbf{y}_1, z_1), (\mathbf{x}_2, \mathbf{y}_2, z_2), ...(\mathbf{x}_n, \mathbf{y}_n, z_n)$ where $\mathbf{x}_i$ is a feature vector extracted from an App description, $\mathbf{y}_i$ is the binary label vector indicating the maturity content, and $\mathbf{z}_i$ is the label of the maturity level, where $1 \leq i \leq n$.

In the on-line prediction phase, we perform maturity analysis in a *two-stage* approach, i.e.,

$$\text{App description}(\mathbf{x}) \rightarrow \text{maturity content}(\mathbf{y}) \rightarrow \text{maturity level}(z),$$

where in the first stage, the maturity contents is inferred from the app feature vectors, and in the second stage, the maturity level is predicted by combining maturity content based on the rating policy. For instance, if every element in $\mathbf{y}$ is zero, then the App has the lowest maturity level (i.e., *4+* on App Store and *Everyone* on Google Play).

Note in this procedure, an app is generally assigned to *multiple* (i.e., one or more) maturity content tags. This is known as "multi-label learning" in machine learning. Fortunately, we develop a method that can automatically adapt SVM to support multi-label classification by incorporating label correlations, with minimum efforts.

3.3.2 Multi-label Classification Using Linear SVM

As is illustrated before, to support multi-label classification task, we need to develop a method that is fast, scalable, and accurate. Linear classification method is a good fit to achieve these goals given the large number of new Apps and

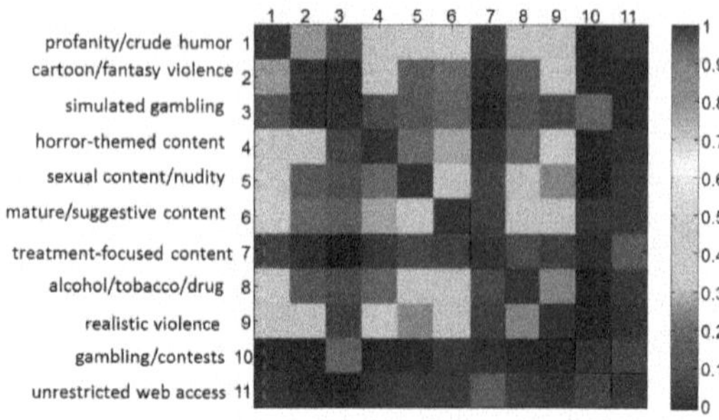

Figure 4: Correlation matrix for 11 types of maturity content, where (k, ℓ) element indicates the correlations between the tag k and ℓ. For illustration purpose, *infrequent/mild* and *frequent/intensive* are grouped together.

their meta data. Hence, in the context of app maturity level prediction, we use linear SVM as our method due to its strong capability in handling *short* text classification tasks such as [34, 29, 35, 11]. This is also further confirmed by our experiments.

Recall that in standard multi-class SVM problem, it finds the maximum-margin hyperplane [8] that has the largest separation (margin) among data points from different classes. To be exact, it optimizes:

$$\begin{aligned} \min_{\mathbf{w}_k, \xi_i} \quad & \frac{1}{2}\sum_{k=1}^{K} \mathbf{w}_k^T \mathbf{w}_k + C\sum_{i=1}^{n} \xi_i \\ s.t. \quad & \mathbf{w}_{y_i}^T \mathbf{x}_i - \mathbf{w}_k^T \mathbf{x}_i \geq 1 - \xi_i, \\ & \sum_{i=1}^{n} \xi_i \leq C, \;\; \xi_i \geq 0, \end{aligned} \tag{1}$$

where $\mathbf{w}_k$ is the decision hyperplane for k-th class ($1 \leq k \leq K$), y_i is the label for data $\mathbf{x}_i$, ξ_i is the slack variable, and C is the constant. According to "Loss + Regularization" format, Eq.(1) can be written as a sum over of a hinge loss and ℓ_2 regularization, *i.e.*,

$$\min_{\mathbf{W}} \sum_{i=1}^{n} (1 - \mathbf{w}_{y_i}^T \mathbf{x}_i + \max_{k \neq y_i} \mathbf{w}_k^T \mathbf{x}_i)_+ + \alpha \sum_{k=1}^{K} \|\mathbf{w}_k\|_2^2, \tag{2}$$

where $(x)_+ = \max\{x, 0\}$, $\mathbf{W} = [\mathbf{w}_1 \mathbf{w}_2 \cdots \mathbf{w}_K]$ is the hyperplane matrix. Let $\Omega(\mathbf{W}) = \sum_{k=1}^{K} \|\mathbf{w}_k\|_2^2$, Eq.(2) is equivalent to:

$$\min_{\mathbf{W}} f(\mathbf{W}; \mathbf{X}, \mathbf{Y}) + \alpha\Omega(\mathbf{W}), \tag{3}$$

where $f(\mathbf{W}; \mathbf{X}, \mathbf{Y}) = \sum_{i=1}^{n} (1 - \mathbf{w}_{y_i}^T \mathbf{x}_i + \max_{k \neq y_i} \mathbf{w}_k^T \mathbf{x}_i)_+$.

3.3.3 Adapting SVM for Label Correlations

To support multi-label classification, the idea is to transform the multi-label classification problem into multi-class problem by considering label correlations. The key observation is that many tags always co-occur together. The intuition is that the elimination of label correlations can help improve the performance, which is also confirmed in past researches [9][36][19].

In the context of maturity content rating, the two rating policies, which are shown in Table 1 and Table 2, both consider seventeen maturity content for maturity rating. Figure 4 shows the correlations among the maturity content considered by the App Store's rating policy. The figure was plotted based on the statistics from the real-world app dataset used in experiments. For illustration purpose, we combine the *infrequent/mild* and *frequent/intense* levels for the same maturity content together. However, we still treat the *infrequent/mild* and *frequent/intense* as two labels in our experiments.

We observe that there exists high correlations among some maturity content. For example, the *profanity or crude humor* and the *mature/suggestive themes* are highly positively correlated. Another example is that the *cartoon or fantasy violence* and *horror/fear theme* are highly positively correlated. In addition to the highly positive correlations, some maturity content are negatively correlated. In particular, the two levels of a maturity content are exclusive (i.e., perfectly negatively correlated). For instance, for the App shown in Figure 1.*left*, one of its maturity content is ***infrequent/mild*** *sexual content and nudity*, and thus ***frequent/intense*** *sexual content and nudity* will not be a maturity content of this App. The above observations motivate us to utilize correlations between maturity content to improve the accuracy of classification.

We adapt the standard multi-label SVM to capture label correlations. In particular, we use *pearson correlation coefficient* $\mathbf{R} = [R_{k\ell}] \in \Re^{K \times K}$ to capture the label co-occurrence, *i.e.*,

$$R_{k\ell} = \frac{\sum_{i=1}^{n} (Y_{ik} - \overline{Y_{:k}})(Y_{i\ell} - \overline{Y_{:\ell}})}{\sqrt{\sum_{i=1}^{n} (Y_{ik} - \overline{Y_{:k}})^2} \sqrt{\sum_{i=1}^{n} (Y_{i\ell} - \overline{Y_{:\ell}})^2}}, \quad 1 \leq k, \ell \leq K,$$

where $\mathbf{Y} \in \Re^{n \times K}$ is the class label matrix for maturity content, and

$$\overline{Y_{:k}} = \frac{1}{n}\sum_{i=1}^{n} Y_{ik}, \quad \overline{Y_{:\ell}} = \frac{1}{n}\sum_{i=1}^{n} Y_{i\ell}.$$

The label correlation matrix $\mathbf{R}$ measures the linear correlation (dependence) between each pair of classes k and ℓ, each entry of which is a number in the interval [-1, +1]. Positive number indicates positive correlation, 0 indicates no correlation, and negative indicates negative correlation. We would like to emphasize here that without the centering of the values corresponding to each label, it is impossible to capture the negative correlations.

Then the class label matrix is modified to:

$$\tilde{\mathbf{Y}} = \mathbf{Y}\mathbf{R}, \tag{5}$$

and finally we solve the following optimization problem Eq.(6) using the same method as in Eq. (3):

$$\min_{\mathbf{W}} f(\mathbf{W}; \mathbf{X}, \tilde{\mathbf{Y}}) + \alpha\Omega(\mathbf{W}). \tag{6}$$

Please note that our method can be applied to any generic loss functions such as logistic loss, LASSO, *etc*, but not limited to hinge loss shown in Eq.(6). The *pearson correlation* is indeed a generic method to eliminate both the label correlations and the feature correlations, which can be easily adapted to solve many other correlation problems emerged in data mining and machine learning communities.

Here, we give an example to illustrate how $\mathbf{Y}$ looks like. Suppose we have the class label corresponding to app i, $Y_{i:} = [0, 1, 0, ...0, 0, 1]$. After multiplying the correlation matrix $\mathbf{R} \in \Re^{k \times k}$, $Y_{i:}$ becomes $\tilde{Y}_{i:} = [0.1, 0.75, 0.6...0.2, 0.5, -0.9]$. Using the threshold calibration in [36], we obtain a threshold t in the training phase for mapping the continuous $\tilde{Y}_{ik}$ to

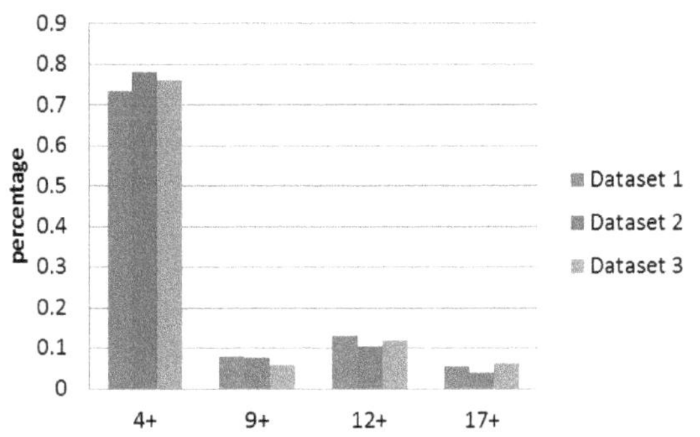

Figure 5: The distribution of ground truth maturity levels of Apps in our three datasets.

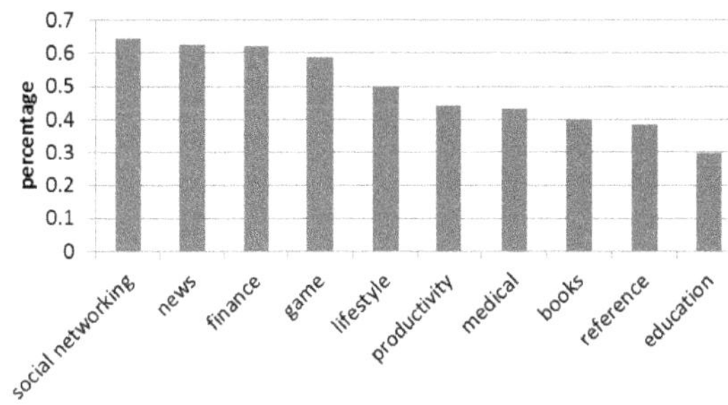

Figure 6: Top-10 categories of Google Play Apps in the Dataset 3 that have the most incorrect developer-provided maturity levels.

the binary label. In particular, if $\tilde{Y}_{ik} \leq t$, then $\tilde{Y}_{ik}$ is 0, otherwise $\tilde{Y}_{ik}$ is 1. In the training phase, we obtain $\mathbf{W}$ via solving Eq.(6) with $\mathbf{X}_{train}$ and $\tilde{\mathbf{Y}}_{train}$. In the testing phase, we first get $\tilde{\mathbf{Y}}_{test}$ with $\mathbf{W}$ and $\mathbf{X}_{test}$, and then we use t to map $\tilde{\mathbf{Y}}_{test}$ to $\mathbf{Y}$. In our experiments, we use the widely used package LibSVM [6] to implement adapted multi-label SVM classification with label correlations.

4. EXPERIMENTS

Recall that our automatic App maturity rating system not only predicts the maturity level for a given App but also provides the reasons why the App has the specific maturity level. Therefore, we evaluate both the maturity level prediction performance and the reason prediction performance. In the following, we introduce the datasets that we collected from both App Store and Google Play, evaluation metrics we adopt, training and testing, and compared approaches.

4.1 Experimental Setup

4.1.1 Data Collection

Crawling App Store and Google Play: We wrote crawlers in python to collect 105,108 free iOS Apps and 105,287 paid iOS Apps from App Store, and 261, 947 Android Apps from Google Play. Our crawls include the description and maturity level of each App. App Store also labels the mature contents that makes an App be rated as a specific maturity level. So we also crawl the mature contents for App Store Apps. We crawled our datasets between July 2014 and September 2014.

Obtaining groundtruth: Apple Inc. hires trained employees to manually perform maturity analysis for each submitted App. Therefore, for Apps from App Store, we take the maturity levels and the associated mature contents crawled from App Store as their groundtruth. Google Play Apps are rated by App developers, so their labels are not accurate. Chen et al. [5] characterized the conditions when the App Store's maturity rating policy and the Google Play's policy are equivalent, and we leverage their results to locate Apps whose Android version and iOS version have the same maturity levels and mature contents. Then, we take the maturity levels and mature contents of the iOS version as the groundtruth of the corresponding Android Apps. In summary, we have the following three datasets with groundtruth maturity information:

- **Dataset 1** consists of 105,108 free Apps in App Store.
- **Dataset 2** consists of 105,287 paid Apps in App Store.
- **Dataset 3** consists of 14,000 Apps in Google Play.

We distinguish between free Apps and paid Apps for App Store because we find that predicting their maturity levels achieves substantially different performances. However, most of Google Play Apps that have groundtruth maturity information are free, and thus we do not further classify them into free Apps and paid Apps.

Figure 5 shows the distribution of groudtruth maturity levels of Apps in our three datasets. We observe imbalanced distributions. For instance, 73% of Apps in the Dataset 1 have a maturity level of 4+, but only 5% of Apps in the Dataset 1 have a maturity level of 17+.

Unreliable Google Play ratings: A Google Play App is said to have an inaccurate maturity level if the maturity level provided by the developer does not match the groundtruth. Overall, we find that 45% of Apps in the Dataset 3 have inaccurate maturity levels. Figure 6 shows the fraction of Google Play Apps in the Dataset 3 that have inaccurate developer-provided maturity levels for top-10 App categories. We observe that Apps in the *social networking* category are most likely to be incorrectly rated by developers.

4.1.2 Evaluation Metrics

Since we classify both the maturity levels and the associated reasons, we evaluate various approaches in two aspects: 1) mature content classification, which is a multi-label task, and 2) maturity level classification, which is a multi-class task. Due to the extremely imbalanced label distributions as we show in Figure 5, we do not compare the algorithms in terms of accuracy. For instance, a classifier that always predicts 4+ as the maturity level can already achieve accuracies of more than 0.70.

Mature content classification: The mature content prediction is a multi-label classification problem. Thus, we adopt the metrics Precision, Recall, and F1-value [37], which are widely used to evaluate multi-label classification systems. Specifically, we denote by C the labels (possible mature contents). For each label $\ell \in C$, we denote by TP_ℓ, FP_ℓ, TN_ℓ, FN_ℓ the number of true positives, false positives, true negatives, and false negatives, respectively. Then, for each label $\ell \in C$, we have its precision, recall, and F1-value as $P_\ell = \frac{TP_\ell}{TP_\ell+FP_\ell}$, $R_\ell = \frac{TP_\ell}{TP_\ell+FN_\ell}$, and $F_\ell = \frac{2P_\ell R_\ell}{P_\ell+R_\ell}$, respectively. Then we compute the overall Precision, Recall, and F1-value by averaging the precisions, recalls, and F1-values over all labels, respectively.

Maturity level prediction: For maturity level prediction, we also use Precision, Recall, and F1-value as our evaluation metrics. More formally, let $TP_k, FP_k, TN_k, andFN_k$ be true positives, false positives, true negatives, and false negatives for Apps with maturity level k, respectively. Then for each level k, we have precision as $P_k = \frac{TP_k}{TP_k+FP_k}$, recall as $R_k = \frac{TP_k}{TP_k+FN_k}$, and F1-value as $F1_k = \frac{2P_k R_k}{P_k+R_k}$. The overall Precision, Recall, and F1-value are computed by averaging over all the maturity levels.

4.1.3 Training and Testing

For each of the three datasets, we sample 50% of it uniformly at random and treat them as the training data, and the rest of it is treated as the testing data. We repeat the experiments for 10 trials and average all metrics over them.[1]

4.1.4 Compared Approaches

We describe compared approaches for mature content prediction and maturity level prediction separately.

Mature content prediction: Recall that we extract features from sensitive words, augmented sensitive words, and bag-of-words model. Moreover, we consider label correlations. We aim to study the impact of each part. To this end, we add each part to our framework incrementally. Specifically, we compare the following methods:

- **AAMR-I**: Our framework AAMR with only features from bag-of-words. Label correlations are not considered.
- **AAMR-II**: Our framework AAMR with features from bag-of-words and sensitive words. Label correlations are not considered.
- **AAMR-III**: Our framework AAMR with features from sensitive words, augmented sensitive words, and bag-of-words model. Label correlations are not considered.
- **AAMR-IV**: Our framework AAMR with features from sensitive words, augmented sensitive words, and bag-of-words model. Label correlations are considered.

Maturity level prediction: We compare the following approaches to perform maturity level predictions:

- **Human Labeling (HL):** We asked 3 users (they are our colleagues) to manually label an App. Given a maturity rating policy, the users rated an App based on their experiences and their understanding of the App description. The ratings of the 3 users are aggregated in a majority voting way to get the final maturity level of the App. If majority voting does not agree upon a maturity level, we don't consider the App any more.
- **Developer Report (DR):** Google Play requires developers to report the maturity levels of their developed apps. For Apps in the Dataset 3, we compute the evaluation metrics for the ratings reported by App developers.
- **ALM [5]:** To the best of our knowledge, only Chen et al. [5] studied automatic App maturity level prediction. So we will adopt their method ALM as one baseline for comparisons. Note that the ALM method does not predict maturity contents, and thus we do not compare ALM with mature content prediction approaches.
- **Multi-Class Classification (MCC):** The multi-class classification method learns a multi-class classifier which directly maps our features extracted from App descriptions to the maturity levels. We use linear multi-class SVM as the classifier. Note that this method cannot identify mature contents in an App.
- **AAMR**: Our two-stage approach first predicts the mature contents in an App using adapted multi-label SVM with label correlations, and then labels the maturity level according to the rating policy.

[1]We find that the standard deviations of our metrics over the 10 trials are very small, and thus we do not show them for simplicity.

Table 5: Comparisons against human-based maturity rating approaches.

dataset	HL	DR	AAMR
Precision	0.43	0.68	0.77
Recall	0.34	0.57	0.76
F1_value	0.38	0.62	0.76

4.2 Results

4.2.1 Mature Content Prediction

Figure 7 shows the Precision, Recall, and F-value of the four methods AAMR-I, AAMR-I, AAMR-III, and AAMR-IV on the three datasets. We observe that feature augmentation, bag-of-words feature, and label correlation all improve mature content prediction.

4.2.2 Maturity Level Prediction

We report results for automatic maturity level prediction approaches and human labelling approaches separately.

Comparing automatic prediction approaches: Figure 8 shows the maturity level prediction performances among the three automatic approaches, i.e., ALM, MCC, and AAMR. We observe that both MCC and AAMR achieve much better performances than ALM. Specifically, MCC achieves around 0.44 larger F-value than ALM on average, and AAMR achieves 0.39 larger F-value than ALM on average. These observations indicate that our features are much better than sensitive words which are used by ALM. MCC achieves slightly better performances than our two-stage AAMR method. This is because our AAMR makes some incorrect predictions about mature contents, which are subsequently used to label maturity levels. The two-stage approach enlarges the impact of the incorrect mature content predictions. However, MCC method cannot identify the mature contents in an App.

Comparing with human-based methods: We compare our method AAMR with two human-based manually labelling approaches, i.e., HL and DR. Due to the limited human resources we have, we sample 500 Apps from the Dataset 3. For each sampled App, we ask three users (our colleagues) to rate the maturity level via reading the App description. The final maturity level of an App is determined by majority voting among the labels of the three users. If the three human labels do not agree upon a maturity level, we do not consider the App. After majority voting, we obtained 441 Apps that have agreed human labels. We also predict the maturity levels for these Apps using our learned AAMR model.

Table 5 shows the Precision, Recall, and F_value of human labelling (HL), developer report (DR), and our proposed automatic method AAMR. We observe that our method AAMR achieves much more accurate results than DR (14%

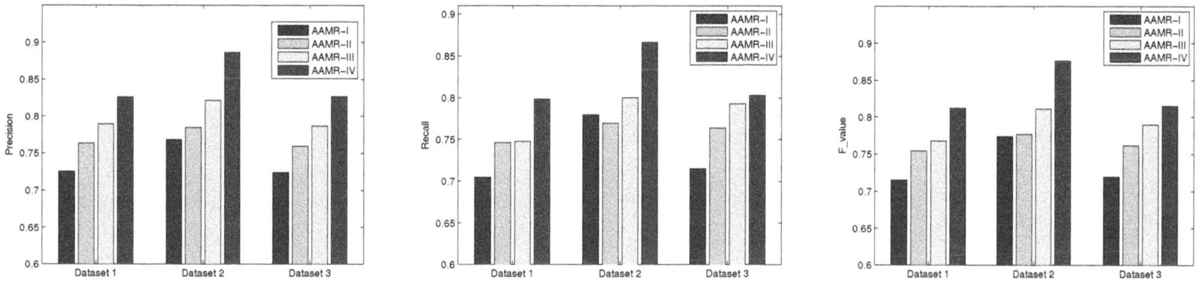

(a) Precision (b) Recall (c) F1_value

Figure 7: Impact of feature augmentation, bag-of-words feature, and label correlation. We find that these parts are complementary, i.e., adding each part incrementally improves the performance of our framework.

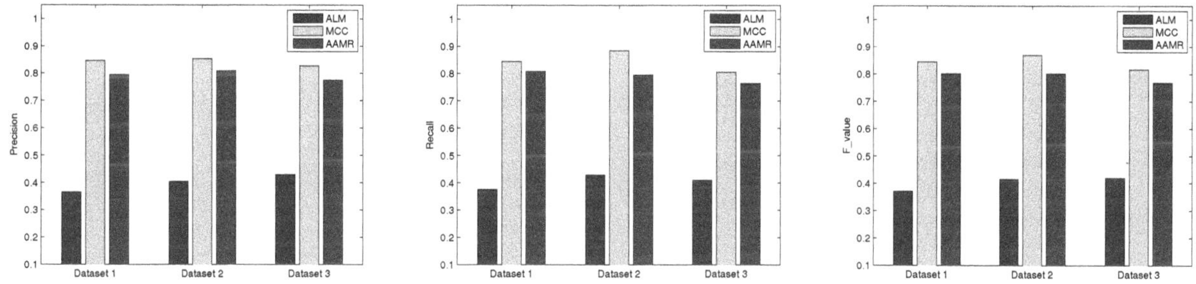

(a) Precision (b) Recall (c) F1_value

Figure 8: Results for the three compared automatic maturity level prediction approaches. We observe that MCC and AAMR substantially outperform ALM, which indicates the effectiveness of our novel features.

improvement in terms of F_value) and HL (38% improvement in terms of F_value). Human users can hardly achieve satisfactory accuracy in rating maturity levels. In our experiments, human users only achieve 38% F_values. We speculate the reason is that developers mainly describe functionality in App descriptions, and humans might not be able to correlate non-sensitive words to maturity levels. Moreover, DR achieves better performances than HL. We speculate the reason is that App developers have better understanding about their Apps and thus could provide more accurate maturity levels.

We further study how users and Android developers label maturity levels incorrectly. An App is *underrated* if the provided maturity level is lower than its groundtruth, otherwise an App is *overrated*. We find that App developers are more likely to underrate the maturity levels. Specifically, around 80% of incorrect labels provided by App developers are underrated while 46% of users-provided incorrect labels are underrated. We speculate the reason is that App developers underrated their Apps so that more people could become their users.

4.2.3 Summary

We demonstrate that feature learning (augmentation), bag-of-words features, and label correlations are all necessary, i.e., incorporating them increases the performances of our framework. Moreover, our approach substantially outperforms previous automatic approaches and human-based manual labelling approaches.

5. RELATED WORK

We review related work on mobile App maturity rating, text analysis, and other App-related studies.

Maturity rating: To the best of our knowledge, little research has been conducted for App maturity rating. Chen et al. [5] studied the severity of unreliable maturity ratings for mobile Apps on Google Play. By comparing the maturity ratings of such Apps on Google Play and App Store, they measured the severity of inaccurate maturity ratings of Google Play apps. The reason is that Google Play requires developers themselves to rate their own Apps and developers tend to underclaim the maturity level in order to attract a boarder range of users.

Text analysis: The bag-of-words model was first documented by Harris [14] and has been widely used for documentation classification [17]. Google developed the word to vector technique [23, 24], which learns a vector representation for each word to capture the syntactic and semantic word relationships. The algorithm takes a text corpus as input and produces the word vectors as output. Fan et al. [11] demonstrated that linear SVM [7] outperforms other classifiers for short text classification. Kong et al. [20] predicted the permission required by mobile apps from app descriptions using structure feature learning technique.

Other App-related studies: Many recent app-related work focus on security and privacy issues. Specifically, they either reveal the potential security risks in the Android platform [12, 3, 18] or enhance the overall Android security via retrofitting the android platform or adding more features into it [26, 10, 31]. In addition, users privacy preference can also be utilized in personalized mobile app recommendation [21]. These work are orthogonal to ours.

6. CONCLUSION AND FUTURE WORK

The *scope* of this work is to propose a framework that automatically predicts mature contents and maturity levels for mobile Apps from app descriptions. We map the mature content prediction to a multi-label classification problem and then use the predicted mature contents to label the maturity levels. First, we extract novel features from App descriptions using deep learning techniques by considering the semantics of words. Second, we adapt SVM to capture label correlations in a multi-label setting. The experiment results on real-world datasets demonstrate that our approach can achieve relatively high accuracies with only App descriptions, and that our approach substantially outperforms baseline methods,.

A few interesting directions include incorporating more features from information sources such as user comments, UI screenshots, and dynamic running behaviors of Apps into our framework, which makes our system more robust to attacks such as app description obfuscations, as well as rating maturity levels of dynamic contents such as advertisements in Apps.

Acknowledgment: We thank reviewers for their valuable comments.

7. REFERENCES

[1] Andriod App Ratings 2014. `https://support.google.com/googleplay/android-developer/answer/188189`, 2014.
[2] Apple Store new Apps. http://goo.gl/ojrhp2.
[3] L. Cen, D. Kong, H. Jin, and L. Si. Mobile app security risk assessment: A crowdsourcing ranking approach from user comments. In *SDM*, pages 658–666, 2015.
[4] H. Chang, Y. Zhou, P. Spellman, and B. Parvin. Stacked predictive sparse coding for classification of distinct regions in tumor histopathology. In *ICCV*, December 2013.
[5] Y. Chen, H. Xu, Y. Zhou, and S. Zhu. Is this app safe for children?: A comparison study of maturity ratings on android and ios applications. WWW '13, pages 201–212, 2013.
[6] C.-J. L. Chih-Chung Chang. Libsvm: A library for support vector machines. In *ACM Transactions on Intelligent Systems and Technology*, 2011.
[7] C. Cortes and V. Vapnik. Support-vector networks. *Machine Learning*, 1995.
[8] K. Crammer and Y. Singer. On the algorithmic implementation of multiclass kernel-based vector machines. *J. Mach. Learn. Res.*, 2, Mar. 2002.
[9] A. C. P. L. F. de Carvalho and A. A. Freitas. A tutorial on multi-label classification techniques. In *Foundations of Computational Intelligence (5)*, volume 205. 2009.
[10] M. Dietz, S. Shekhar, Y. Pisetsky, A. Shu, and D. S. Wallach. Quire: Lightweight provenance for smart phone operating systems. In *Usenix Security*, 2011.
[11] R. Fan, K. Chang, C. Hsieh, X. Wang, and C. Lin. Liblinear: A library for large linear classification. *Journal of Machine Learning Research*, 9, 2008.
[12] A. P. Felt, H. J. Wang, A. Moshchuk, S. Hanna, and E. Chin. Permission re-delegation: Attacks and defenses. In *Usenix Security*, 2011.
[13] D. M. Fergusson, J. M. Boden, and L. J. Horwood. Exposure to childhood sexual and physical abuse and adjustment in early adulthood. *Child abuse & neglect*, 32(6), 2008.
[14] Z. S. Harris. Distributional structure. *Word*, 1954.
[15] Inappropriate content making its way to mobile apps. http://goo.gl/dqilcg.
[16] iOS App Ratings 2014. `https://developer.apple.com/library/ios/documentation/LanguagesUtilities/Conceptual/iTunesConnect_Guide/iTunesConnect_Guide.pdf`, 2014.
[17] T. Joachims. *Learning to classify text using support vector machines: Methods, theory and algorithms.* Kluwer Academic Publishers, 2002.
[18] D. Kong, L. Cen, and H. Jin. AUTOREB: Automatically understanding the review-to-behavior fidelity in android applications. In *CCS*, 2015.
[19] D. Kong, C. H. Q. Ding, H. Huang, and H. Zhao. Multi-label relieff and f-statistic feature selections for image annotation. In *CVPR*, pages 2352–2359, 2012.
[20] D. Kong and H. Jin. Towards permission prediction on mobile apps via structure feature learning. In *SDM*, pages 604–612, 2015.
[21] B. Liu, D. Kong, L. Cen, N. Z. Gong, H. Jin, and H. Xiong. Personalized mobile app recommendation: Reconciling app functionality and user privacy preference. In *WSDM*, pages 315–324, 2015.
[22] C. Manning and H. Schutze. Foundation of statistical natural language processing. 1999.
[23] T. Mikolov, K. Chen, G. Corrado, and J. Dean. Efficient estimation of word representations in vector space. *CoRR*, abs/1301.3781, 2013.
[24] T. Mikolov, I. Sutskever, K. Chen, G. S. Corrado, and J. Dean. Distributed representations of words and phrases and their compositionality. In *NIPS*, 2013.
[25] Mobile Apps for Kids: Current Privacy Disclosures are Disappointing. http://goo.gl/xr1udt.
[26] D. Octeau, P. McDaniel, S. Jha, A. Bartel, E. Bodden, J. Klein, and Y. L. Traon. Effective inter-component communication mapping in android withepicc: An essential step towards holistic security analysis. In *Usenix Security*, 2013.
[27] R. E. O'Hara, F. X. Gibbons, M. Gerrard, Z. Li, and J. D. Sargent. Greater exposure to sexual content in popular movies predicts earlier sexual debut and increased sexual risk taking. *Psychological science*, 23(9), 2012.
[28] Overexposed and Under-Prepared: The Effects of Early Exposure to Sexual Content. http://goo.gl/x2whgr.
[29] A. Sadilek, S. P. Brennan, H. A. Kautz, and V. Silenzio. nemesis: Which restaurants should you avoid today? In *HCOMP 2013*, 2013.
[30] K. Spärck-Jones. A statistical interpretation of term specificity and its application in retrieval. pages 11–21, 1972.
[31] N. Wang, B. Zhang, B. Liu, and H. Jin. Investigating effects of control and ads awareness on android users' privacy behaviors and perceptions. In *MobileHCI 2015*. ACM, 2015.
[32] Word2Vec Tool for Computing Continuous Distributed Representations of Words. `https://code.google.com/p/word2vec/`.
[33] Y. Yang and J. O. Pedersen. A comparative study on feature selection in text categorization. In *ICML 1997*, 1997.
[34] H.-F. Yu, C.-H. Ho, P. Arunachalam, M. Somaiya, and C.-J. Lin. Product title classification versus text classification. 2012.
[35] G. Yuan, C. Ho, and C. Lin. Recent advances of large-scale linear classification. *Proceedings of the IEEE*, 100(9):2584–2603, 2012.
[36] M. Zhang and Z. Zhou. A review on multi-label learning algorithms. *IEEE TKDE*, 26(8), 2014.
[37] M.-L. Zhang and Z.-H. Zhou. A review on multi-label learning algorithms. *Knowledge and Data Engineering, IEEE Transactions on*, 26(8):1819–1837, Aug 2014.

The Role of Query Sessions in Interpreting Compound Noun Phrases

Marius Paşca
Google Inc.
1600 Amphitheatre Parkway
Mountain View, California 94043
mars@google.com

ABSTRACT

The meaning of compound noun phrases can be approximated in the form of lexical interpretations extracted from text. The interpretations hint at the role that modifiers play relative to heads within the noun phrases. In a study examining the role of query sessions in explaining compound noun phrases, candidate interpretations of compound noun phrases are extracted from pairs of queries that belong to the same query session. Experimental results over multiple evaluation sets of noun phrases show a higher accuracy of the interpretations when extracted from query sessions rather than from individual queries.

Categories and Subject Descriptors

I.2.7 [**Artificial Intelligence**]: Natural Language Processing; H.3.1 [**Information Storage and Retrieval**]: Content Analysis and Indexing; H.3.3 [**Information Storage and Retrieval**]: Information Search and Retrieval; I.2.6 [**Artificial Intelligence**]: Learning

General Terms

Algorithms, Experimentation

Keywords

Compound noun phrases, compositional concepts, open-domain information extraction, knowledge acquisition

1. INTRODUCTION

Motivation: A necessary step towards understanding the meaning of compound noun phrases (e.g., *"beatles songs"*, *"french macarons"*, *"ayurvedic medicinal plants"*) is to understand the roles that modifiers (*beatles*, *french*, *ayurvedic*) play within the noun phrases. Often, the roles can be approximated lexically, in the form of string interpretations (*"composed by"*, *"from"*, *"used in"*) that serve as connectors within what are effectively paraphrases (*"songs composed by beatles"*, *"macarons from france"*, *"medicinal plants used in ayurveda"*) of the compound noun phrases.

Evidence available within, and collected from, large text collections should be helpful in the analysis of compound noun phrases, and allow for the extraction of relevant interpretations. Indeed, textual document collections are a useful source for extracting paraphrases of compound noun phrases [19, 36]. As an alternative to using document collections, collections of Web search queries produce interpretations that may be more accurate [28] than when extracted from documents, even if the source queries are available simply as a set of queries that are independent from one another.

Contributions: Expanding upon [28], the experiments reported in this paper examine the role of Web search queries vs. query sessions in uncovering the semantics of open-domain class labels in particular; and of compound noun phrases in general. Queries and query sessions are the source for candidate lexical interpretations of compound noun phrases. The interpretations turn implicit properties or subsuming roles (*"composed by"*, *"from"*, *"used in"*) that modifiers (*beatles*, *french*, *ayurvedic*) play within longer noun phrases (*"beatles songs"*, *"french macarons"*, *"ayurvedic medicinal plants"*) into concrete strings. The roles of modifiers relative to heads of noun phrase compounds cannot be characterized in terms of a finite list of possible compounding relationships [10]. Hence, the interpretations are not restricted to a closed, pre-defined set. In experiments comparing query sessions and independent queries, over evaluation sets of noun phrases from multiple sources, more accurate interpretations are extracted from query sessions.

Permission to make digital or hard copies of all or part of this work for personal or classroom use is granted without fee provided that copies are not made or distributed for profit or commercial advantage and that copies bear this notice and the full citation on the first page. Copyrights for components of this work owned by others than the author(s) must be honored. Abstracting with credit is permitted. To copy otherwise, or republish, to post on servers or to redistribute to lists, requires prior specific permission and/or a fee. Request permissions from Permissions@acm.org.
CIKM'15, October 19–23, 2015, Melbourne, VIC, Australia
Copyright is held by the owner/author(s). Publication rights licensed to ACM.
ACM 978-1-4503-3794-6/15/10$15.00
DOI: http://dx.doi.org/10.1145/2806416.2806571 .

2. INTERPRETING NOUN PHRASES

Compounds: Let N be a compound noun phrase, containing a head H preceded by modifiers M. Each of H and M may contain one or multiple tokens. Being a compound, the sequence of modifiers and head in N act as a single noun [10, 16], which refers to a concept whose meaning is based on the semantics of its components [24, 35].

Hypothesis 1: If N is relevant and of interest to Web users, then in a sufficiently large corpus it will eventually be referred to in relatively more verbose search queries, which reveal the implicit role that modifiers M play relative to the head H.

Hypothesis 2: If N is relevant and of interest to Web users, then in a sufficiently large corpus it will eventually be referred to in the same query session [34] as more verbose search queries, which reveal the implicit role that modifiers M play relative to the head H.

Extraction from Queries: Figure 1 gives an overview of the role of queries and query sessions in extracting interpretations of compound noun phrases. The compound noun phrases to be interpreted are available as an input vocabulary of noun phrases. For example, the vocabulary might include the noun phrases *"beatles songs"* and *"ayurvedic medicinal plants"*. The source of candidate interpretations takes the form of anonymized queries, from which possible interpretations of the noun phrases must be extracted. The queries are available as a set of pairs of anonymized queries submitted

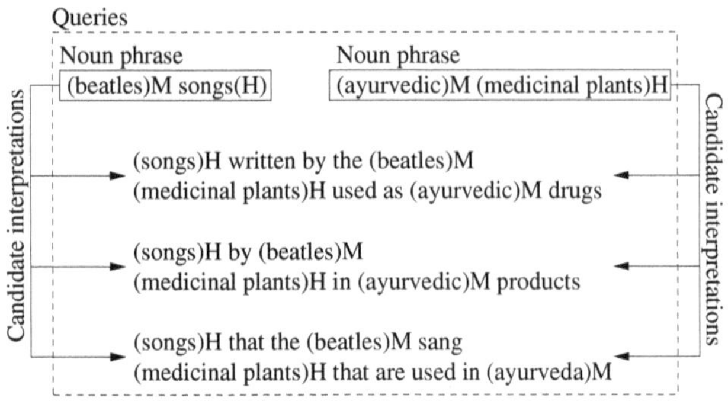

Figure 1: Extraction of interpretations of noun phrases from queries (H, M=head and modifier)

within the same query sessions, and also as a set of independent anonymized queries, collected from the queries that form the pairs. For example, the set of queries may include *"songs written by the beatles"* and *"medicinal plants in ayurvedic products"*. Optionally, if the queries are available as query sessions rather than merely as a set of queries, the queries *"beatles songs"* and *"songs written by the beatles"*, or *"ayurvedic medicinal plants"* and *"medicinal plants in ayurvedic products"*, may be pairs that belong to the same query sessions.

The extraction consists of several steps [28]: (1) the selection of a subset of queries that may be candidate interpretations of some yet-to-be-specified noun phrases; (2) the matching of the selected queries to the noun phrases to interpret; and (3) the aggregation of matched queries into candidate interpretations extracted for a noun phrase.

Selecting Candidate Interpretations: As a pre-requisite, the noun phrases to interpret and queries are both part-of-speech tagged [5]. A query is deemed to be a candidate interpretation of a hypothetical compound noun phrase that might consist in a modifier M immediately followed by a head H (e.g., *"(ayurvedic)$_M$ (medicinal plants)$_H$"*), if the query matches one of the following patterns [28]:

• passive constructs, for example *"(medicinal plants)$_H$ used as (ayurvedic)$_M$ drugs"*;

• prepositional constructs, for example *"(medicinal plants)$_H$ in (ayurvedic)$_M$ products"*;

• relative pronoun constructs, e.g., *"(medicinal plants)$_H$ that are used in (ayurveda)$_M$"*.

The patterns effectively split matching queries into four consecutive sequences of tokens Q=[Q_1 Q_2 Q_3 Q_4], where H and M correspond to Q_1 and Q_3, and Q_4 may be empty. For example, in the lower portion of Figure 1, one of the patterns matches the query *"(medicinal plants)$_H$ in (ayurvedic)$_M$ products"*, thus splitting the query into *"medicinal plants"* as Q_1, *"in"* as Q_2, *"ayurvedic"* as Q_3 and *"products"* as Q_4.

Mapping Noun Phrases to Interpretations: Each noun phrase to interpret is split into all possible decompositions of two consecutive sequences of tokens N=[N_1 N_2], where the two sequences correspond to a hypothetical modifier and a hypothetical head of the noun phrase. For example, the noun phrase *"ayurvedic medicinal plants"* is split into [*"ayurvedic medicinal"*, *"plants"*] and separately into [*"ayurvedic"*, *"medicinal plants"*]. If N_1 and Q_3, and N_2 and Q_1 respectively, match, then the matching query Q (e.g., *"(medicinal plants)$_H$ in (ayurvedic)$_M$ products"*) is retained as a candidate interpretation of the noun phrase N (*"(ayurvedic)$_M$ (medicinal plants)$_H$"*), as shown in the middle portion of Figure 1. If the noun phrases are interpreted using query sessions instead of independent queries, the matching query Q and the noun phrase N must satisfy an additional constraint, namely to be one of the pairs of queries that are available as part of the same query session. Otherwise, the matching query Q is discarded.

Mapping via Modifier Variants: At its simplest, the matching of the hypothetical modifier relies on strict string matching. Alternatively, original modifiers in the noun phrases to interpret may be matched to queries via expansion variants. Variants are phrases that likely play the same role, and therefore share interpretations, as modifiers relative to the head in a noun phrase. Variants allow for the extraction of candidate interpretations that may otherwise not be available in the input data. For example, the variant *rolling stones* available for *beatles* allows for the matching of *beatles* in the noun phrase *"(beatles)$_M$ (songs)$_H$"*, with *rolling stones* in the query *"(songs)$_H$ played by (rolling stones)$_M$"*. The candidate interpretation *"(songs)$_H$ played by (beatles)$_M$"* is extracted for the noun phrase *"(beatles)$_M$ (songs)$_H$"*, even though the query *"songs played by beatles"* might not be present among the input queries.

Possible sources of variants include, among others, distributionally similar phrases [21], where the phrases most similar to a modifier would act as its variants. Mappings from adjectival modifiers in noun phrases (e.g., *ayurvedic* in *"ayurvedic medicinal plants"* in Figure 1) into the nominal counterparts (e.g., *ayurveda*) that are likely to occur in interpretations (e.g., *"(medicinal plants)$_H$ that are used in (ayurveda)$_M$"*) are also useful. Concretely, as described later in the experimental setting, variants are generated using WordNet [12], distributional similarities and Wikipedia [33].

Aggregation of Candidate Interpretations: Candidate interpretations of a noun phrase are aggregated from source queries that matched the noun phrase. The frequency score of a candidate interpretation is the weighted sum of the frequencies of source queries from which the candidate interpretation is collected, possibly via variants of modifiers. In the weighted sum, the weights are similarity scores between the original modifier from the noun phrase, on one hand, and the variant from the source query into which the modifier was mapped, on the other hand [28]. The weights for the variants *beatles* and *rolling stones* relative to the original modifier *beatles* are 1.0 (identity) and within [0.0, 1.0] (distributional similarity), whereas the weights of adjectival modifiers such as *ayurveda* for *ayurvedic* are 1.0. Separately from the frequency score, a penalty score is computed that penalizes interpretations containing extraneous tokens. Specifically, the penalty counts the number of nouns or adjectives located outside the modifier and head. For example, the penalty scores assigned to the interpretations *"(songs)$_H$ by (beatles)$_M$"* and *"(medicinal plants)$_H$ that are used in (ayurveda)$_M$"* are 0. In comparison, the penalty scores for the interpretations *"(songs)$_H$ that (beatles)$_M$ play"* and *"(medicinal plants)$_H$ in (ayurvedic)$_M$ products"* are 1. From among candidate interpretations extracted for a noun phrase, interpretations whose penalty score is higher than 1 are discarded. Candidate interpretations extracted for a noun phrase are ranked in increasing order of their penalty scores or, in case of ties, in decreasing order of their frequency scores.

3. EXPERIMENTAL SETTING

Sources of Textual Data: The experiments rely on a random sample **S** of around 3 billion unique pairs of fully-anonymized Web search queries in English. The sample is drawn from pairs of queries within the same query session(s), as submitted to a general-purpose Web search engine. A session contains queries submitted in relatively quick succession by the same anonymized user [34]. The queries from the query pairs in the sample S are separately organized as a sample **Q** of around 1.5 billion unique queries. Each

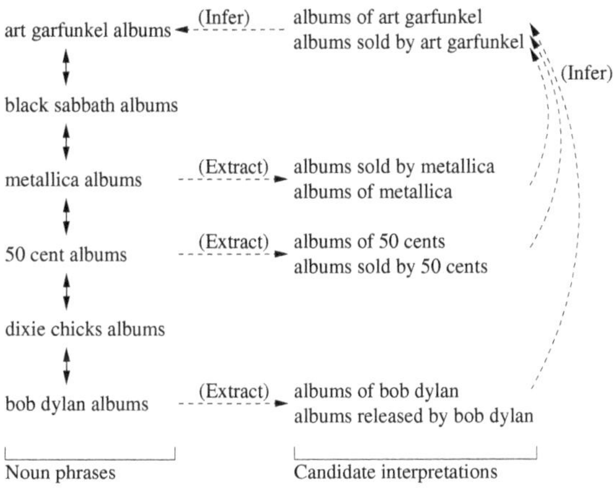

Figure 2: Acquisition of interpretations of compound noun phrases via wiki-templ variants

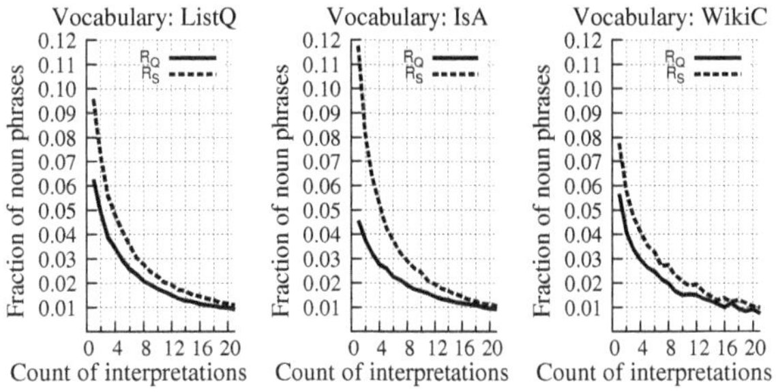

Figure 3: Distribution of the number of interpretations extracted per noun phrase, over noun phrases with some extracted interpretation(s). Computed over various vocabularies of noun phrases

query in Q is available independently from other queries, and is accompanied by its frequency of occurrence in the query logs. In this setup, each query in Q also appears as a query in some query pair in S. Conversely, each query in a query pair in S also appears as a query in Q.

Experimental Runs: The experiments consist in extracting interpretations from the independent queries Q, in the case of run $\mathbf{R}_Q$, as introduced in [28]; or from the query sessions S, in the case of run $\mathbf{R}_S$, as proposed here.

Sources of Variants: The original form of the modifiers is denoted as **orig-phrase**. Three types of variant phrases are collected for the purpose of matching modifiers within noun phrases to interpret, with phrases from queries. Relations encoded as Value-Of, Related-Noun and Derivationally-Related relations in WordNet [12] are the source of **adj-noun** variants. They map around 6,000 adjectives into one or more nouns (e.g., (*french*→*france*), (*electric*→*electricity*), (*aquatic*→*water*)). A repository of distributionally similar phrases, collected in advance [21, 29] from a sample of around 200 million Web documents in English, is the source of **dist-sim** variants. For each of around 1 million phrases, the variants consist of their 50 most similar phrases (e.g., *art garfunkel*→ {*carly simon*, *melissa manchester*, *aaron neville*, ..}). A snapshot of all Wikipedia [33] articles in English, as available in June 2014, is the source of **wiki-templ** variants. For each of around 50,000 phrases, their wiki-templ variants are collected from Wikipedia categories sharing a common parent Wikipedia category (e.g., *"albums by artist"*) and having a common head (*"art garfunkel albums"*, *"black sabbath albums"*, *"metallica albums"*). The different modifiers (*art garfunkel*, *black sabbath*, *metallica*) that accompany the shared head are collected as variants of one another. Among the four types of variants, wiki-templ variants are applied only when the noun phrase to interpret, and the source Wikipedia category names from which the variants were collected, have the same head. For example, *X=art garfunkel*→{*black sabbath*, *metallica*, *50 cent*, ..} is applied only in the context of the noun phrase *"X albums"*. As shown in Figure 2, the extraction of interpretations via some of the variants allows for effectively inferring interpretations via other variants, as long as the noun phrases share the same head. When computing the frequency score of a candidate interpretation as the weighted sum of the frequencies of source queries, the weights assigned are 1.0, for orig-phrase, adj-noun and wiki-templ variants; and the available distributional similarity scores within [0.0, 1.0], for dist-sim variants.

Vocabularies of Noun Phrases: The experiments acquire interpretations from queries, for noun phrases from three vocabularies. **ListQ** is a set of phrases *X* (e.g., *"aramaic words"*) from queries in the form [*list of X*], where the frequency of the query [*X*] is at most 100 times higher than the frequency of the query [*list of X*], and the frequency of the latter is at least 5. **IsA** is a set of class labels (e.g., *"academy award nominees"*), originally extracted from Web documents via Hearst patterns [15], and associated with at least 25 instances each (e.g., *zero dark thirty*). **WikiC** is a set of Wikipedia categories that contain some tokens in lowercase beyond prepositions and determiners, and whose heads are plural-form nouns (e.g., *"french fiction writers"*). Only phrases that are one of the full-length queries from the input set of Web search queries are retained in the respective sets, as vocabularies of noun phrases to interpret; other phrases are discarded.

4. EVALUATION RESULTS

Relative Coverage: Because it is not feasible to manually compile the exhaustive sets of all string forms of valid interpretations of all (or many) noun phrases, we compute relative instead of absolute coverage. At least one interpretation is extracted from query sessions and independent queries for more than 500,000 of the noun phrases from all input vocabularies. Considering only that subset, Figure 3 shows the distribution of the number of candidate interpretations extracted per noun phrase. Given a count of extracted candidate interpretations fixed between 1 and 20, run R_S consistently extracts that number of interpretations for a higher fraction of the noun phrases from the input vocabularies than R_Q does. The apparent advantage of run R_S over R_Q in fact reflects its inability to extract as many candidate interpretations as R_Q does. Indeed, although not shown in the graphs, more than 100 interpretations are extracted per noun phrase for 14.5% (R_Q) vs. 5.5% (R_S) of the noun phrases in ListQ, 24.8% (R_Q) vs. 5.6% (R_S) in IsA, and 16.7% (R_Q) vs. 7.1% (R_S) in WikiC.

Precision of Interpretations: From an input vocabulary, an initial weighted sample of 150 noun phrases with some interpretations extracted in both runs $\mathbf{R}_Q$ and $\mathbf{R}_S$ is manually inspected. The sampling weight is the frequency of the noun phrases as queries. A noun phrase from the selected sample is either retained, or discarded if deemed to be a non-interpretable phrase. A noun phrase is not interpretable if it is in fact an instance (*"new york"*, *"alicia keys"*) rather than a class; or it is not a properly formed noun phrase (*"watch movies"*); or does not refer to a meaningful class (*"3 significant figures"*). The manual inspection ends, once a sample of 100 noun phrases has been retained. The procedure gives weighted random samples of 100 noun phrases, drawn from each

Eval Set	Sample of Noun Phrases
ListQ	ayurvedic medicinal plants, black history people, good short stories, health care reform issues, hypoallergenic makeup brands, jive songs, male celebrities, periodic functions, plumbing snakes, simple carbs
IsA	automotive parts, casual shirts, classic rock bands, literature review, louis vuitton outlet, pc solutions, pdf reader, private equity firms, unix command, wordpress plugins
WikiC	carnivorous plants, differentiation rules, free online games, language tests, online games, time zones, toy dogs, viz characters, wedding dresses, wii accessories

Table 1: Samples from evaluation sets of noun phrases in each vocabulary

Examples of Correctness Annotations	
Noun Phrase	Interpretation
Correctness label: correct generic (numeric value: 1.0):	
final cut pro 7 shortcuts	shortcuts of final cut pro 7
military ranks	ranks in the military
pain assessment tool	assessment tool of pain
stephen king book	book by stephen king
Correctness label: correct specific (numeric value: 1.0):	
android tablet	tablet with android os
ayurvedic medicinal plants	medicinal plants used in ayurveda
flash games	games made with flash
omega 3 foods	foods that provide omega 3
Correctness label: okay (numeric value: 0.5):	
green technology	technology used for green building
lenovo laptops	laptops of lenovo company
nursery rhymes	rhymes for kids in nursery
toy dogs	dogs that are toy size
Correctness label: incorrect (numeric value: 0.0):	
cartoon characters	characters in cartoon network
flash games	games designed by flash
mexican films	films about mexican culture
omega watches	watches that look like omega

Table 2: Examples of interpretations manually annotated with each correctness label

of the ListQ, IsA and WikiC vocabularies. The samples, shown in Table 1, constitute the evaluation sets of phrases ListQ, IsA and WikiC, over which precision of interpretations is computed.

Following evaluation methodology introduced for other open-domain information extraction tasks, the top 20 interpretations extracted in an experimental run for each evaluation phrase are manually annotated with correctness labels. As shown in Table 2, an interpretation is annotated as: correct and generic, or correct and specific, if relevant; okay, if useful but containing non-essential information; or wrong. To compute the precision score over an evaluation set of phrases, the correctness labels are converted to numeric values. Precision of a ranked list of extracted interpretations is the average of the correctness values of the interpretations in the list.

Table 3 provides a comparison of precision scores at various ranks in the extracted lists of interpretations, as an average over all phrases from an evaluation set. Several conclusions can be drawn from the results. First, at a given rank, the average precision of a run varies from one evaluation set to another, since the evaluation sets are selected from vocabularies from different sources. Second, precision levels are encouraging for all runs. Third, with the exception of precision at rank 1 for the IsA evaluation set, run R_S produces more accurate interpretations than R_Q across all ranks and across all evaluation sets. In particular, when considering the top 20 interpretations extracted for all phrases from the union of all evaluation

Eval Set	Run	Precision@N				
		@1	@3	@5	@10	@20
ListQ	R_Q	0.824	0.742	0.656	0.541	0.443
	R_S	0.886	0.795	0.726	0.639	0.549
IsA	R_Q	0.790	0.636	0.533	0.429	0.336
	R_S	0.772	0.691	0.631	0.541	0.443
WikiC	R_Q	0.747	0.649	0.586	0.448	0.336
	R_S	0.801	0.717	0.662	0.568	0.478
Union of all	R_Q	0.787	0.676	0.592	0.473	0.372
	R_S	0.820	0.734	0.673	0.583	0.490
	+vs.R_Q	**+4.2%**	**+8.6%**	**+13.7%**	**+23.3%**	**+31.7%**

Table 3: Average precision, at various ranks in the ranked lists of interpretations extracted for noun phrases from various sets of evaluation phrases. Computed for each run, as an average over each evaluation set, and as an average over the union of all evaluation sets

Run: Eval Phrase (P@5) → [Ranked Candidate Interpretations]
R_Q: atm card (0.00) → [card stuck in atm, card retained by atm, card retained in atm, card captured by atm, card eaten by atm, ..]
R_S: atm card (1.00) → [card used in atm, card for atm]
R_Q: ayurvedic medicinal plants (1.00) → [medicinal plants in ayurveda, medicinal plants used in ayurveda, medicinal plants of ayurveda, medicinal plants used by ayurveda, medicinal plants used in ayurvedic medicines, ..]
R_S: ayurvedic medicinal plants (1.00) → [medicinal plants in ayurveda, medicinal plants used in ayurveda, medicinal plants of ayurveda, medicinal plants used by ayurveda, medicinal plants used in ayurvedic medicines, ..]
R_Q: chemical processes (0.40) → [processes of chemical weathering, processes in chemistry, processes involved in chemical weathering, processes of chemistry, processes in chemical weathering, ..]
R_S: chemical processes (1.00) → [processes in chemistry, processes of chemistry, processes that involve chemistry, processes involved in chemistry, processes related to chemistry, ..]
R_Q: michael jackson song (0.90) → [song by michael jackson, song of michael jackson, song from michael jackson, song sung by michael jackson, song written by michael jackson, ..]
R_S: michael jackson song (0.80) → [song by michael jackson, song of michael jackson, song from michael jackson, song sung by michael jackson, song for michael jackson, ..]
R_Q: special diet (0.10) → [diet with special k, diet of special k, diet for special forces, diet for special needs, diet before a special event, ..]
R_S: special diet (0.75) → [diet for special needs, diet for special conditions, ..]
R_Q: uk record companies (0.60) → [record companies in the uk, record companies in uk, record companies of uk, record companies in london uk, ..]
R_S: uk record companies (0.75) → [record companies in the uk, record companies in uk, record companies of uk, record companies in london uk]

Table 4: Top candidate interpretations extracted in the experimental runs for a sample of noun phrases from the ListQ evaluation set (P@5=precision at rank 5 in the ranked list of extracted interpretations)

sets, about half of the interpretations are correct, for R_S; vs. slightly over a third, for R_Q. At rank 1, the precision of R_S is higher than 0.8. Within an evaluation set, the accuracy of extracted interpretations varies between the experimental runs, as well as from one evaluation phrase to another, as illustrated in Table 4.

Presence of Relevant Interpretations: Since sometimes it is difficult to even manually enumerate as many as 20 distinct, relevant

Eval Set	Run	Average presence of any interpretations annotated as correct				
		@1	@3	@5	@10	@20
Correctness label: correct generic, or correct specific:						
ListQ	R_Q	0.795	0.875	0.898	0.920	0.932
	R_S	0.852	0.909	0.920	0.932	0.943
IsA	R_Q	0.765	0.852	0.852	0.876	0.901
	R_S	0.753	0.864	0.876	0.889	0.889
WikiC	R_Q	0.711	0.831	0.904	0.940	0.940
	R_S	0.771	0.879	0.940	0.964	0.964
Correctness label: correct specific only:						
ListQ	R_Q	0.034	0.284	0.386	0.545	0.614
	R_S	0.068	0.307	0.420	0.568	0.614
IsA	R_Q	0.086	0.210	0.309	0.506	0.593
	R_S	0.086	0.247	0.346	0.531	0.568
WikiC	R_Q	0.084	0.217	0.398	0.530	0.639
	R_S	0.133	0.241	0.410	0.590	0.651

Table 5: Average of scores indicating the presence or absence of any interpretations annotated as correct. Computed over interpretations extracted up to various ranks in the ranked lists of extracted interpretations

string forms of interpretations of a given noun phrase, measuring precision at a particular rank (e.g., 20) in a ranked list of interpretations may be too conservative. Table 5 summarizes a different type of scoring metric, namely the presence of any relevant interpretation, among the interpretations extracted up to a particular rank. Relevance is flexibly defined, by requiring the interpretations to have been assigned a certain correctness label, then computing the average number of evaluation phrases for which such interpretations are present up to a particular rank. Intuitively, the resulting scores at a given rank may be lower for R_S than for R_Q. Indeed, as R_S effectively attempts to discard incorrect interpretations that R_Q would otherwise produce, it may occasionally discard relevant interpretations. Especially when few interpretations are extracted in the first place, discarding relevant interpretations may adversely affect the scores measuring the presence of any relevant interpretations. However, even as they are affected by this phenomenon, the scores in Table 5 are still competitive for R_S relative to R_Q. The scores indicate that at least one of the top 5 interpretations is correct and specific for about 1 out of 3 noun phrases in the evaluation sets on average.

Popular Heads, Modifiers and Interpretations: The most frequent heads induced by interpretations extracted in R_S are shown in Figure 4. Although the incorrect head *wikipedia* is present in the upper graph, most of the heads and modifiers seem plausible, suggesting that the input vocabulary does contain reasonably clean compound noun phrases. In the lower graph, the prominence of location-related phrases (e.g., *uk*, *indian*) among the most popular modifiers for the ListQ vocabulary is not unexpected, but is not characteristic for all vocabularies. For example, in the case of the IsA vocabulary, the most popular modifiers are *business*, *social*, *good*, *human*, *famous*, with the earliest location-related modifier *american* being only the 24th most popular modifier.

Figure 5 illustrates the most popular interpretations extracted for noun phrases in the ListQ vocabulary. For example, if interpretations are restricted to those containing more than just prepositions and determiners, the ninth most popular interpretation is *"(H) written by (M)"*, where H and M stand for the induced heads and modifiers respectively.

Impact of Variants: Variants of modifiers provide alternatives in identifying and extracting candidate interpretations, even when the modifiers from the noun phrases are not present in their original

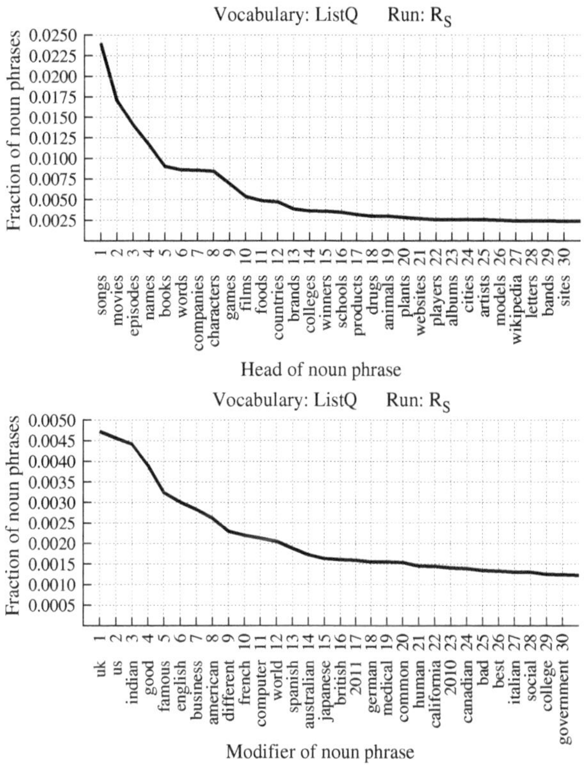

Figure 4: Most frequent heads and modifiers induced by interpretations extracted in run R_S for noun phrases from the ListQ vocabulary. Computed as the fraction of noun phrases with some extracted interpretation(s), which have a particular head (first graph) or modifier (second graph) induced by at least one of their top 10 interpretations

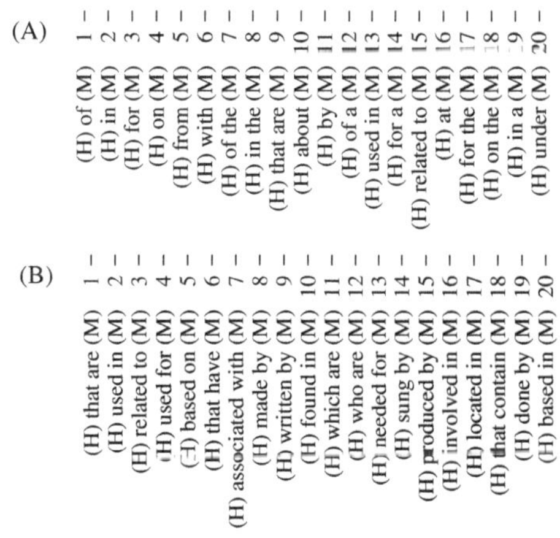

Figure 5: Most frequent interpretations extracted in run R_S for noun phrases from the ListQ vocabulary. Computed over the top 10 interpretations of noun phrases with some extracted interpretation(s). Collected interpretations are either unrestricted (A) or required (B) to include at least a token that is neither a preposition nor a determiner (second graph). (H) and (M) stand for portions of an interpretation that correspond to the head and modifier of the interpreted noun phrase

form in the interpretations. For illustration, the adj-noun variant *ethiopia* of the modifier *ethiopian* leads to the extraction of the in-

Vocab	Run	Variant Type			
		orig-phrase	adj-noun	dist-sim	wiki-templ
Interpretations produced by variant type (not exclusive):					
ListQ	R_Q	0.563	0.069	0.642	0.017
	R_S	0.543	0.069	0.680	0.019
IsA	R_Q	0.526	0.087	0.595	0.004
	R_S	0.475	0.085	0.670	0.005
WikiC	R_Q	0.373	0.074	0.672	0.423
	R_S	0.360	0.073	0.689	0.449
Interpretations produced only by variant type (exclusive):					
ListQ	R_Q	0.308	0.044	0.370	0.003
	R_S	0.270	0.043	0.389	0.004
IsA	R_Q	0.343	0.058	0.397	0.001
	R_S	0.273	0.053	0.450	0.001
WikiC	R_Q	0.128	0.044	0.284	0.137
	R_S	0.106	0.042	0.281	0.144

Table 6: Impact of various types of variants of modifiers, on the coverage of noun phrase interpretations. Computed as the fraction of the top 10 extracted interpretations produced by a particular variant type, and possibly by other variant types (upper portion); or produced only by a particular variant type, and by no other variant types (lower portion) (Vocab=vocabulary of noun phrases)

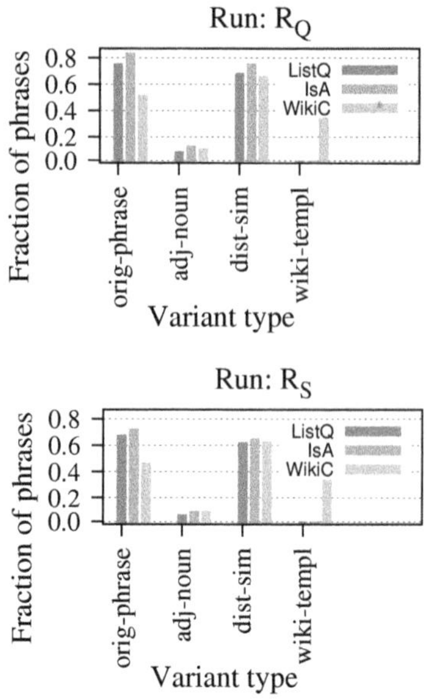

Figure 6: Impact of various types of variants of modifiers, on the coverage of noun phrase interpretations. Computed as the fraction of the noun phrases whose top 10 interpretations include some interpretation(s) produced only by a particular variant type, and by no other variant types

terpretation *"runners from ethiopia"* for the noun phrase *"ethiopian runners"*. Similarly, wiki-templ variants *metallica* and *50 cent* of the modifier *art garfunkel*, in the context *"X albums"*, allow for the extraction of the interpretation *"albums sold by art garfunkel"* for the noun phrase *"art garfunkel albums"*, via the interpretations *"albums sold by metallica"* and *"albums sold by 50 cent"*.

Table 6 quantifies the impact of various types of variants, on the coverage of noun phrase interpretations. The scores provided for each variant type correspond to either non-exclusive (upper portion of the table) or exclusive (lower portion) contribution of that variant type towards some extracted interpretations. In other words, in the lower portion, the scores capture the fraction of the top 10 interpretations that are produced only by that particular variant type. The results illustrate four phenomena. First, all variant types contribute to increasing coverage, relative to using only orig-phrase variants. Second, dist-sim variants have a particularly strong impact. Third, wiki-templ variants have a strong impact, but only when the contexts from which they were collected match the context of the noun phrase being interpreted. On the WikiC vocabulary in the lower portion of Table 6, the scores for wiki-templ illustrate the potential that contextual variants have for extracting additional interpretations. Fourth, the relative impact of the types of variants is comparable between runs R_Q and R_S.

Figure 6 quantifies the impact of various types of variants, on the coverage of noun phrase interpretations, and thus provides an alternative view to the lower portion of Table 6. The results illustrate several phenomena. First, dist-sim variants have a particularly strong impact. Second, wiki-templ variants have a strong impact, but only when the contexts from which they were collected match the context of the noun phrase being interpreted. On the WikiC vocabulary, the scores for wiki-templ illustrate the potential of contextual variants in extracting additional interpretations. Third, beyond inherent variations, the relative impact of the types of variants is consistent between runs R_Q and R_S.

Impact of Size of Textual Data: When more input queries or query sessions are available, better interpretations for more compound noun phrases may be extracted from the queries. Conversely, a reduction in the amount of textual data available in the form of queries may lead to interpretations of lower quality extracted for fewer compound noun phrases. Ablation experiments, whose results are summarized in Table 7, quantify the impact of the size of the textual data on the extracted interpretations. To this effect, the run R_S is applied to incrementally smaller input textual data. The input query session data is organized as a set of unique pairs of queries that are available as part of the same query session. From the entire query data of 100% of the query pairs, a series of iteratively smaller query data are created, in the form of random samples of 25%, 10% etc. of the original set of query pairs.

Query Data Size	E	Precision@N				
		@1	@3	@5	@10	@20
Over all evaluation phrases from ListQ:						
1%	42	0.324	0.278	0.260	0.242	0.236
5%	70	0.540	0.472	0.429	0.382	0.356
10%	76	0.608	0.534	0.483	0.433	0.379
25%	88	0.699	0.631	0.570	0.492	0.427
100%	100	0.886	0.795	0.726	0.639	0.549
Over subsets of evaluation phrases from ListQ that have some some extracted interpretation(s):						
1%	42	0.648	0.557	0.520	0.484	0.473
5%	70	0.731	0.638	0.581	0.517	0.481
10%	76	0.764	0.671	0.608	0.544	0.477
25%	88	0.788	0.712	0.643	0.555	0.482
100%	100	0.886	0.795	0.726	0.639	0.549

Table 7: Average precision of interpretations extracted in run R_S for noun phrases from the ListQ evaluation set, at various ranks in the ranked lists of interpretations extracted for noun phrases, when changing the size of the input query data from which interpretations are extracted. The input query data is reduced from the original data (100%) to iteratively smaller data. Computed as an average over the entire set of 100 evaluation phrases from ListQ (upper portion); and as an average over (variable) subsets E of the 100 evaluation phrases from ListQ that have some extracted interpretation(s) (lower portion)

Query Data Size	Average presence of any interpretations annotated as correct				
	@1	@3	@5	@10	@20
Over subsets of evaluation phrases from ListQ that have some some extracted interpretation(s):					
1%	0.591	0.659	0.659	0.659	0.659
5%	0.661	0.754	0.754	0.754	0.754
10%	0.714	0.829	0.843	0.843	0.843
25%	0.705	0.833	0.833	0.846	0.846
100%	0.852	0.909	0.920	0.932	0.943

Table 8: Average of scores indicating the presence or absence of any interpretations annotated as correct (i.e., correct generic or correct specific). Computed for run R_S over the ListQ evaluation set, when changing the size of the input query data from which interpretations are extracted. The input query data is reduced from the original data (100%) to iteratively smaller data. Computed over interpretations extracted up to various ranks in the ranked lists of extracted interpretations, as an average over (variable) subsets of the 100 evaluation phrases from ListQ that have some extracted interpretation(s)

As expected, there is a clear impact of the size of the input textual data, on interpretations extracted in run R_S over the ListQ evaluation set. The second column in Table 7 measures coverage. More precisely, it shows the number of evaluation phrases, out of the 100 evaluation phrases available in the ListQ evaluation set, for which some interpretations are extracted from query data of a particular size. When extracting from a quarter or a tenth of the original query data, some interpretations are extracted for 88 and 76 respectively of the 100 evaluation phrases.

The precision scores in the upper portion of Table 7 are computed as an average over all 100 evaluation phrases in ListQ. The scores quantify how precision increases, when the size of the input query data increases. But the scores are affected by both precision and coverage, rather than just precision. Indeed, when less input data is used, some of the decrease in scores can be attributed to the lack of any interpretations being extracted, for some of the evaluation phrases. Such evaluation phrases are effectively penalized, as they contribute zeros to the averages computed in the upper portion of the table. In contrast, no penalty is given to such evaluation phrases in the lower portion of Table 7. For a given input query data, the scores in the lower portion are computed over the subset of evaluation phrases with some extracted interpretations. Therefore, the scores in the lower portion of the table are a better indicator of the effect of a reduction in the size of the query data, on the quality of extracted ranked lists of interpretations. As the size of the textual data increases, the accuracy of the ranked lists of extracted interpretations also increases. Table 8 illustrates the same phenomenon, when considering the presence of any relevant interpretation, among the interpretations extracted up to a particular rank. As the size of the textual data increases, the interpretations extracted up to a particular rank include a relevant interpretation for more of the evaluation phrases, from among the subsets of evaluation phrases from ListQ for which run R_S extracts some interpretations for a given data size.

Interpretations from Queries <u>and</u> Sessions: An additional, hybrid run $\mathbf{R}_H$ merges the ranked candidate interpretations produced by R_S and R_Q. More precisely, a ranked list of candidate interpretations in R_H is the concatenation of the ranked list from R_S, if any, followed by the ranked list from R_Q. Only the earliest occurrence of any duplicate interpretation is retained in the merged list. Thus, run R_H re-ranks interpretations that are extracted from query

Vocab	Noun Phrases Have Interpretation(s)?					
	Yes			No		
	Count	Query Freq		Count	Query Freq	
	I	A_I	M_I	¬I	$A_{\neg I}$	$M_{\neg I}$
ListQ	243,662	$4.3 \times x_A$	$4.3 \times x_M$	33,657	x_A	x_M
IsA	171,938	$8.0 \times y_A$	$11.5 \times y_M$	12,655	y_A	y_M
WikiC	39,432	$3.6 \times z_A$	$8.4 \times z_A$	1,172	z_A	z_M

Table 9: Correlation between coverage of run R_S, measured as the presence of some extracted interpretation(s) for a noun phrase, on one hand; and frequency of the noun phrase as a query, on the other hand (Vocab=vocabulary; I=subset of noun phrases that are queries and have some extracted interpretation(s); ¬I=subset of noun phrases that are queries and do not have any extracted interpretation(s); A=average query frequency of noun phrases as queries; M=median query frequency of noun phrases as queries)

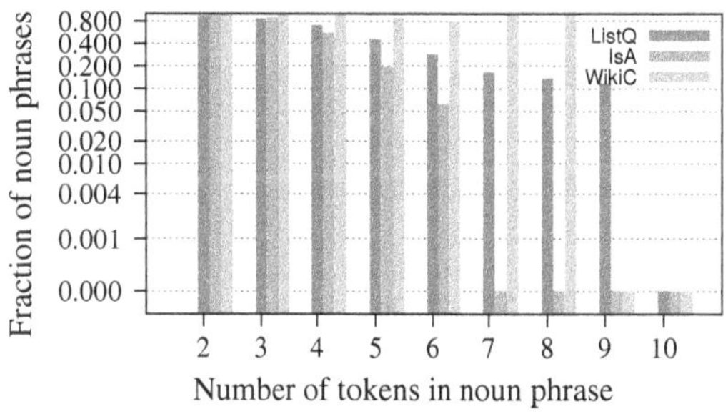

Figure 7: Ability of run R_S to extract interpretations for noun phrases, as a function of the length of (i.e., number of tokens in) noun phrases. Computed as the fraction of noun phrases from an input vocabulary with a particular number of tokens, for which there are some extracted interpretation(s)

sessions ahead of interpretations extracted only from independent queries, but otherwise keeps all interpretations extracted from independent queries as well. The precision at rank 1 is the same for R_H as for R_S, over each evaluation set and also over their union. At other ranks, R_H preserves the advantage (or disadvantage) in accuracy that R_S has over R_Q, but to a lesser degree. For example, when compared to earlier results in Table 3, the precision scores at ranks 5 and 20 for run R_H are 0.707 and 0.502 over the ListQ set, 0.619 and 0.396 over IsA, and 0.640 and 0.410 over WikiC.

Discussion: Independently of the source of queries (e.g., independent queries or query sessions) from which interpretations are extracted, a noun phrase is intuitively more difficult to interpret if it is relatively more rare or more complex (i.e., longer). Additional experiments quantify the effect in run R_S, by measuring the correlation between the presence of some extracted interpretations for an input noun phrase, on one hand; and the frequency of the noun phrase as a query (in Table 9), on the other hand. In Table 9, the effect is visible in that query frequency is higher for noun phrases with some extracted interpretations (in the left portion of the table) vs. noun phrases with none (in the right portion). For example, for the ListQ vocabulary, the average query frequency is 4.3 higher for noun phrases with some extracted interpretations. Similarly, in Figure 7, a larger fraction of the input noun phrases with a particular number of tokens have some extracted interpretations, when the number of tokens is lower rather than higher. The effect is somewhat less pronounced for, but still applicable to, the WikiC vocabulary. That a larger fraction of the longer noun phrases can be interpreted in the WikiC vocabulary is attributed to the role of wiki-templ variants in extracting interpretations that would otherwise not be available.

5. RELATED WORK

A large body of work addresses the more general task of open-domain information extraction from text [2, 6, 38, 11, 23, 17, 41]. Extracted relations are tuples of an argument (*yellow submarine*), a text fragment acting as the lexicalized relation (*composed by*), and another argument (*beatles*) (cf. [11, 22]). A particular type of extracted relations are IsA relations, linking instances (*yellow submarine*) with their class labels (*"beatles songs"*) [2, 8, 37, 20, 7, 39, 32, 13].

Interpretations extracted from queries act as a potential bridge between facts, on one hand, and class labels, on the other hand, available for instances. The former might be inferred from the latter and vice versa. There are two previous studies that are relevant to the task of extracting facts from existing noun phrases. First, [40] extract facts for attributes of instances, without requiring the presence of the verbal predicates usually employed [11] in open-domain information extraction. Second, in [26], relations encoded implicitly within Wikipedia categories are converted into explicit relations. As an example, the explicit relation *<deconstructing harry, directed, woody allen>* is obtained from the fact that *deconstructing harry* is listed under *"movies directed by woody allen"* in Wikipedia. The method in [26] relies on massive, manually-compiled knowledge, and does not attempt to interpret compound noun phrases.

Relevant interpretations (*"songs composed by beatles"*) represent alternative class labels of instances (*yellow submarine*) that may be originally associated with the class labels being interpreted (*"beatles songs"*). They may be beneficial in typed search [9] or entity search [1, 32]. In that case, class labels submitted as queries may be answered by instances available for the class labels.

In previous work on the acquisition of paraphrases of compound noun phrases, most methods [19, 36] operate over documents, and may rely on text analysis tools including syntactic parsing [25]. In contrast to [28], the experiments reported here extract interpretations from query sessions, and show that the interpretations are more accurate than from independent queries. The interpretations are further related to paraphrase acquisition in that, similarly to output of other open-domain information extraction methods, they would benefit from grouping together extractions that are lexically distinct but semantically equivalent.

Queries are used as a textual data source in other tasks in open-domain information extraction [18, 31, 14]. In particular, query sessions are shown to be useful in paraphrase acquisition [42], ranking class labels extracted for instances [27] or instances extracted for class labels [3] and the disambiguation of instances mentioned in queries relative to entries in external knowledge repositories [30, 4].

6. CONCLUSION

The experiments described in this paper quantify the extent to which interpretations better explain the roles that modifiers play within longer noun phrases, when the interpretations are extracted from query sessions rather than independent queries.

Future work explores the role of human-curated resources such as dictionaries and encyclopedias, in guiding the acquisition of interpretations from documents and queries; and alternatives for combining interpretations from queries and from query sessions.

7. REFERENCES

[1] K. Balog, M. Bron, and M. de Rijke. Category-based query modeling for entity search. In *Proceedings of the 32nd European Conference on Information Retrieval (ECIR-10)*, pages 319–331, Milton Keynes, United Kingdom, 2010.

[2] M. Banko, M. J. Cafarella, S. Soderland, M. Broadhead, and O. Etzioni. Open information extraction from the Web. In *Proceedings of the 20th International Joint Conference on Artificial Intelligence (IJCAI-07)*, pages 2670–2676, Hyderabad, India, 2007.

[3] B. Billerbeck, G. Demartini, C. Firan, T. Iofciu, and R. Krestel. Ranking entities using Web search query logs. In *Proceedings of the 14th European Conference on Research and Advanced Technology for Digital Libraries (ECDL-10)*, pages 273–281, Glasgow, Scotland, 2010.

[4] R. Blanco, G. Ottaviano, and E. Meij. Fast and space-efficient entity linking in queries. In *Proceedings of the 8th ACM Conference on Web Search and Data Mining (WSDM-15)*, pages 179–188, Shanghai, China, 2015.

[5] T. Brants. TnT - a statistical part of speech tagger. In *Proceedings of the 6th Conference on Applied Natural Language Processing (ANLP-00)*, pages 224–231, Seattle, Washington, 2000.

[6] M. Cafarella, A. Halevy, D. Wang, E. Wu, and Y. Zhang. WebTables: Exploring the power of tables on the Web. In *Proceedings of the 34th Conference on Very Large Data Bases (VLDB-08)*, pages 538–549, Auckland, New Zealand, 2008.

[7] B. Dalvi, W. Cohen, and J. Callan. Websets: Extracting sets of entities from the Web using unsupervised information extraction. In *Proceedings of the 5th ACM Conference on Web Search and Data Mining (WSDM-12)*, pages 243–252, Seattle, Washington, 2012.

[8] D. Davidov and A. Rappoport. Enhancement of lexical concepts using cross-lingual Web mining. In *Proceedings of the 2009 Conference on Empirical Methods in Natural Language Processing (EMNLP-09)*, pages 852–861, Singapore, 2009.

[9] G. Demartini, T. Iofciu, and A. de Vries. Overview of the INEX 2009 Entity Ranking track. In *INitiative for the Evaluation of XML Retrieval Workshop*, pages 254–264, Brisbane, Australia, 2009.

[10] P. Downing. On the creation and use of English compound nouns. *Language*, 53:810–842, 1977.

[11] A. Fader, S. Soderland, and O. Etzioni. Identifying relations for open information extraction. In *Proceedings of the 2011 Conference on Empirical Methods in Natural Language Processing (EMNLP-11)*, pages 1535–1545, Edinburgh, Scotland, 2011.

[12] C. Fellbaum, editor. *WordNet: An Electronic Lexical Database and Some of its Applications*. MIT Press, 1998.

[13] T. Flati, D. Vannella, T. Pasini, and R. Navigli. Two is bigger (and better) than one: the Wikipedia Bitaxonomy project. In *Proceedings of the 52nd Annual Meeting of the Association for Computational Linguistics (ACL-14)*, pages 945–955, Baltimore, Maryland, 2014.

[14] M. Gamon, T. Yano, X. Song, J. Apacible, and P. Pantel. Identifying salient entities in web pages. In *Proceedings of the 22nd International Conference on Information and Knowledge Management (CIKM-13)*, pages 2375–2380, Burlingame, California, 2013.

[15] M. Hearst. Automatic acquisition of hyponyms from large

text corpora. In *Proceedings of the 14th International Conference on Computational Linguistics (COLING-92)*, pages 539–545, Nantes, France, 1992.

[16] I. Hendrickx, Z. Kozareva, P. Nakov, D. Ó Séaghdha, S. Szpakowicz, and T. Veale. SemEval-2013 task 4: Free paraphrases of noun compounds. In *Proceedings of the 7th International Workshop on Semantic Evaluation (SemEval-13)*, pages 138–143, Atlanta, Georgia, 2013.

[17] J. Hoffart, F. Suchanek, K. Berberich, and G. Weikum. YAGO2: a spatially and temporally enhanced knowledge base from Wikipedia. *Artificial Intelligence Journal. Special Issue on Artificial Intelligence, Wikipedia and Semi-Structured Resources*, 194:28–61, 2013.

[18] A. Jain and M. Pennacchiotti. Open entity extraction from Web search query logs. In *Proceedings of the 23rd International Conference on Computational Linguistics (COLING-10)*, pages 510–518, Beijing, China, 2010.

[19] N. Kim and P. Nakov. Large-scale noun compound interpretation using bootstrapping and the Web as a corpus. In *Proceedings of the 2011 Conference on Empirical Methods in Natural Language Processing (EMNLP-11)*, pages 648–658, Edinburgh, Scotland, 2011.

[20] Z. Kozareva, K. Voevodski, and S. Teng. Class label enhancement via related instances. In *Proceedings of the 2011 Conference on Empirical Methods in Natural Language Processing (EMNLP-11)*, pages 118–128, Edinburgh, Scotland, 2011.

[21] D. Lin and X. Wu. Phrase clustering for discriminative learning. In *Proceedings of the 47th Annual Meeting of the Association for Computational Linguistics (ACL-IJCNLP-09)*, pages 1030–1038, Singapore, 2009.

[22] Mausam, M. Schmitz, S. Soderland, R. Bart, and O. Etzioni. Open language learning for information extraction. In *Proceedings of the 2012 Joint Conference on Empirical Methods in Natural Language Processing and Computational Natural Language Learning (EMNLP-CoNLL-12)*, pages 523–534, Jeju Island, Korea, 2012.

[23] F. Mesquita, J. Schmidek, and D. Barbosa. Effectiveness and efficiency of open relation extraction. In *Proceedings of the 2013 Conference on Empirical Methods in Natural Language Processing (EMNLP-13)*, pages 447–457, Seattle, Washington, 2013.

[24] J. Mitchell and M. Lapata. Composition in distributional models of semantics. *Cognitive Science*, 34(8):1388–1429, 2010.

[25] P. Nakov and M. Hearst. Semantic interpretation of noun compounds using verbal and other paraphrases. *ACM Transactions on Speech and Language Processing*, 10(3):1–51, 2013.

[26] V. Nastase and M. Strube. Decoding Wikipedia categories for knowledge acquisition. In *Proceedings of the 23rd National Conference on Artificial Intelligence (AAAI-08)*, pages 1219–1224, Chicago, Illinois, 2008.

[27] M. Paşca. Ranking class labels using query sessions. In *Proceedings of the 49th Annual Meeting of the Association for Computational Linguistics (ACL-11)*, pages 1607–1615, Portland, Oregon, 2011.

[28] M. Paşca. Interpreting compound noun phrases using Web search queries. In *Proceedings of the 2015 Conference of the North American Association for Computational Linguistics (NAACL-HLT-15)*, Denver, Colorado, 2015.

[29] P. Pantel, E. Crestan, A. Borkovsky, A. Popescu, and V. Vyas. Web-scale distributional similarity and entity set expansion. In *Proceedings of the 2009 Conference on Empirical Methods in Natural Language Processing (EMNLP-09)*, pages 938–947, Singapore, 2009.

[30] P. Pantel and A. Fuxman. Jigs and lures: Associating web queries with structured entities. In *Proceedings of the 49th Annual Meeting of the Association for Computational Linguistics (ACL-11)*, pages 83–92, Portland, Oregon, 2011.

[31] P. Pantel, T. Lin, and M. Gamon. Mining entity types from query logs via user intent modeling. In *Proceedings of the 50th Annual Meeting of the Association for Computational Linguistics (ACL-12)*, pages 563–571, Jeju Island, Korea, 2012.

[32] P. Pasupat and P. Liang. Zero-shot entity extraction from Web pages. In *Proceedings of the 52nd Annual Meeting of the Association for Computational Linguistics (ACL-14)*, pages 391–401, Baltimore, Maryland, 2014.

[33] M. Remy. Wikipedia: The free encyclopedia. *Online Information Review*, 26(6):434, 2002.

[34] C. Silverstein, H. Marais, M. Henzinger, and M. Moricz. Analysis of a very large Web search engine query log. *SIGIR Forum*, 33(1):6–12, 1999.

[35] R. Socher, J. Bauer, C. Manning, and A. Ng. Parsing with compositional vector grammars. In *Proceedings of the 51st Annual Meeting of the Association for Computational Linguistics (ACL-13)*, pages 455–465, Sofia, Bulgaria, 2013.

[36] T. Van de Cruys, S. Afantenos, and P. Muller. MELODI: A supervised distributional approach for free paraphrasing of noun compounds. In *Proceedings of the 7th International Workshop on Semantic Evaluation (SemEval-13)*, pages 144–147, Atlanta, Georgia, 2013.

[37] R. Wang and W. Cohen. Automatic set instance extraction using the Web. In *Proceedings of the 47th Annual Meeting of the Association for Computational Linguistics (ACL-IJCNLP-09)*, pages 441–449, Singapore, 2009.

[38] F. Wu and D. Weld. Open information extraction using Wikipedia. In *Proceedings of the 48th Annual Meeting of the Association for Computational Linguistics (ACL-10)*, pages 118–127, Uppsala, Sweden, 2010.

[39] W. Wu, H. Li, H. Wang, and K. Zhu. Probase: a probabilistic taxonomy for text understanding. In *Proceedings of the 2012 International Conference on Management of Data (SIGMOD-12)*, pages 481–492, Scottsdale, Arizona, 2012.

[40] M. Yahya, S. Whang, R. Gupta, and A. Halevy. ReNoun: Fact extraction for nominal attributes. In *Proceedings of the 2014 Conference on Empirical Methods in Natural Language Processing (EMNLP-14)*, pages 325–335, Doha, Qatar, 2014.

[41] X. Yao and B. Van Durme. Information extraction over structured data: Question Answering with Freebase. In *Proceedings of the 52nd Annual Meeting of the Association for Computational Linguistics (ACL-14)*, pages 956–966, Baltimore, Maryland, 2014.

[42] S. Zhao, H. Wang, and T. Liu. User behaviors lend a helping hand: Learning paraphrase query patterns from search log sessions. In *Proceedings of the 24th International Conference on Computational Linguistics (COLING-12)*, pages 3137–3152, Mumbai, India, 2012.

Deep Semantic Frame-based Deceptive Opinion Spam Analysis

Seongsoon Kim
Korea University
Seoul, Korea
seongkim@korea.ac.kr

Hyeokyoon Chang
Korea University
Seoul, Korea
hyeokyoon@korea.ac.kr

Seongwoon Lee
Korea University
Seoul, Korea
seongwoon@korea.ac.kr

Minhwan Yu
Korea University
Seoul, Korea
minhwan90@korea.ac.kr

Jaewoo Kang*
Korea University
Seoul, Korea
kangj@korea.ac.kr

ABSTRACT

User-generated content is becoming increasingly valuable to both individuals and businesses due to its usefulness and influence in e-commerce markets. As consumers rely more on such information, posting deceptive opinions, which can be deliberately used for potential profit, is becoming more of an issue. Existing work on opinion spam detection focuses mainly on linguistic features such as n-grams, syntactic patterns, or LIWC. However, deep semantic analysis remains largely unstudied. In this paper, we propose a frame-based deep semantic analysis method for understanding rich characteristics of deceptive and truthful opinions written by various types of individuals including crowdsourcing workers, employees who have expert-level domain knowledge about local businesses, and online users who post on Yelp and TripAdvisor. Using our proposed semantic frame feature, we developed a classification model that outperforms the baseline model and achieves an accuracy of nearly 91%. Also, we performed qualitative analysis of deceptive and truthful review datasets and considered their semantic differences. Finally, we successfully found some interesting features that existing methods were unable to identify.

Categories and Subject Descriptors

H.3.3 [**Information Storage and Retrieval**]: Information Search and Retrieval—*Information filtering*

General Terms

Algorithms, Experimentation

*Corresponding author.

Permission to make digital or hard copies of all or part of this work for personal or classroom use is granted without fee provided that copies are not made or distributed for profit or commercial advantage and that copies bear this notice and the full citation on the first page. Copyrights for components of this work owned by others than ACM must be honored. Abstracting with credit is permitted. To copy otherwise, or republish, to post on servers or to redistribute to lists, requires prior specific permission and/or a fee. Request permissions from Permissions@acm.org.
CIKM'15, October 19–23, 2015, Melbourne, Australia.
© 2015 ACM. ISBN 978-1-4503-3794-6/15/10 ...$15.00.
DOI: http://dx.doi.org/10.1145/2806416.2806551.

Keywords

Deceptive Opinion Spam, FrameNet, Semantic Analysis

1. INTRODUCTION

With the rapid growth of social network services and internet media, online review communities receive a significant amount of attention from both individuals and businesses. Online users increasingly rely on such reviews when making decisions. Recent surveys report that over 79% of users trust reviews written by others and consult them before making a purchase decision [1]. Naturally, there is also a growing concern about the potential for deceptive opinion spam or false reviews—fictitious opinions that are deliberately written to sound authentic to deceive readers for potential monetary gain [15]. Human readers usually cannot detect this kind of opinion spam because most opinion spam is carefully designed to avoid being identified by users or review content providers.

Since Jindal et al. introduced the first deceptive opinion spam problem to the research community [9], much significant work has been done on identifying deceptive opinion spam contents [4, 11, 15], individual spammers [10, 12] and spamming groups [13]. Recently, the research community as well as businesses have been concerned about the opinion spam issue. Yelp[1] may be one of the few top local business review hosting sites in the U.S. that takes this opinion spam issue seriously. It has been working on its own spam filtering method for over 10 years, and its spam filtering algorithm is still trade secret. Mukherjee et al. investigated the characteristics of real-life dataset collected from Yelp [14]. Even though the simple linguistic feature-based (such as n-gram) classification model is highly accurate in identifying crowdsourced deceptive opinion spam datasets [15], their study showed that it was no longer useful for the Yelp dataset. They used behavioral features of the users along with n-grams to classify Yelp's "filtered" and "non-filtered" reviews. The model that used behavioral features outperformed the baseline model that used only linguistic features. Mukherjee et al. assume that Yelp uses primarily the behavioral patterns of users with many internal metrics that are unavailable to the public.

[1]http://www.yelp.com

However, even though behavioral features can be used to identify deceptive opinions, they are ineffective at times. Suppose we used spammers' activity patterns to successfully find and block them from a site. If the spammers change their account name or make a new account (cold start), blocking spammers' access is no longer a useful filtering method. This scenario illustrates that content level review analysis still needs to be considered with individuals' behavioral patterns. Hence, the scope of this work also focuses on content level review analysis.

The majority of existing work focuses on review (or content) level classification tasks that are based on supervised learning approaches that use linguistic features. Linguistic features can be used as simple, yet powerful features in most classification tasks. However, we hardly know why specific features are highly weighted in trained models. Linguistic features do not convey semantic information that can help humans intuitively understand data. To gain insight into texts using linguistic features such as part-of-speech (POS) tags or n-grams, we need further analysis to interpret the characteristics of those features.

For example, Li et al. found that truthful reviews tend to include more nouns, adjectives, prepositions, and determiners (N, JJ, IN, and DT, respectively), while deceptive reviews tend to include more verbs, adverbs, and personal pronouns (V, RB, and PRP, respectively) [11]. The authors argue that domain experts tend to include more details about a local business using nouns, adjectives, preposition or determiners. However, the presence of particular linguistic features such as part-of-speech tags, LIWC categories, or n-gram tokens still cannot be solid evidence of truthful review contents. Also, Feng et al. showed that deep syntactic features driven from context free grammar (CFG) can improve opinion spam detection performance [4]. Their production rule is based on the CFG parse tree (e.g., NP^S $\rightarrow$ NN, NP^PP $\rightarrow$ DT NNP) which also does not carry meaningful semantic information.

In this paper, we view deceptive opinion analysis as a problem of understanding natural language. To overcome the limitations of the existing linguistic features mentioned above, we introduce a novel frame-based semantic feature based on FrameNet [5], a knowledge base in both human and machine-readable format. While there have been many studies on linguistic features such as n-gram, part-of-speech and syntactic structure, semantic analysis that uses frame features remains unstudied. Our contributions in this paper are four-fold:

- To the best of our knowledge, this is the first study to analyze deceptive opinion spam from a deep semantic level perspective.
- We propose two statistical analysis methods which we call Normalized Frame Rate (NFR) and Normalized Bi-frame Rate (NBFR) for the study of semantic frames.
- Using semantic frame features, we successfully improved the classification accuracy by 4.3% compared to the baseline.
- Last, we qualitatively analyzed the characteristics of all the truthful reviews and deceptive reviews in terms of their semantic differences.

We have found that truthful reviewers are more likely to focus on spatial details, which is consistent with previous studies [11, 15]. Moreover, truthful reviewers usually include exact dates or dimensions of objects to describe their real experience. Another interesting observation is that even though employees had expert-level knowledge of their specific business location and are able to include details in their review, the employees failed to mention details about their travel experience, itinerary, or travel activities. We also found different sentiment expression patterns in deceptive reviews and truthful reviews in terms of linguistic theory-based sentiment word categorization.

The rest of this paper is organized as follows. In Section 2, we briefly discuss previous opinion spam research trends. In Section 3, we describe our proposed Normalized Frame Rate (NFR) and Normalized Bi-frame Rate (NBFR) methods and their statistical validation. In Section 4, we qualitatively analyze semantic frame features. In Section 5, we report our own implementation of the baseline model in [15] and our classification results using semantic frame features with and without n-gram features. We conclude the paper and discuss future work in Section 6.

2. RELATED WORK AND BACKGROUND

Previous studies on spam detection. The opinion spam issue was first introduced by Jindal et al. [9] and was investigated after studies on web or email spam were published [2, 3, 8, 17]. The authors categorized review spam into several different types (untruthful opinions, reviews on brands only, and non-reviews) by characteristics, and proposed detection techniques using review centric, reviewer centric, and product centric features. In [12], target and deviation based spamming behavioral patterns were used to detect spammers. To support human evaluators' decision making, they also developed review spammer evaluation software that provides a visualization interface for reviews. The interface contains information about review duplication, review ratings, other recent ratings, and multiple reviews on the same products. Wang et al. proposed a review graph-based approach for finding fake reviewers [18]. They introduced three concepts regarding the trustiness of reviewers, the honesty of reviews, and the reliability of stores and their interrelationships. The experimental results and human participants confirmed that the proposed method can identify subtle spamming activities.

An in-depth study about deceptive opinion spam was conducted by Ott et al. [15]. They used Amazon Mechanical Turk[2] (AMT) to solicit fake reviews (which will be referred to as AMT dataset in this paper) about hotels in the Chicago area. Their model achieved high accuracy (89.8%) using simple n-gram-based features. Feng et al. introduced syntactic structures of review sentences and thus further boosted classification accuracy [4]. Li et al. developed multi-domain deceptive datasets (which will be referred to as Employee dataset) that include reviews by domain experts to establish general rules for identifying deceptive opinions in reviews [11]. Their Employee dataset compensates for the lack of experience of Turkers who also do not put much effort into faking reviews. Li et al. found that a lack of spatial details may not be a universal cue for deception. They also proposed general linguistic cues of deceptive opinion spam as different usage of part-of-speech tags, LIWC categories [16], and first-person singular pronouns.

[2]https://www.mturk.com/mturk/welcome

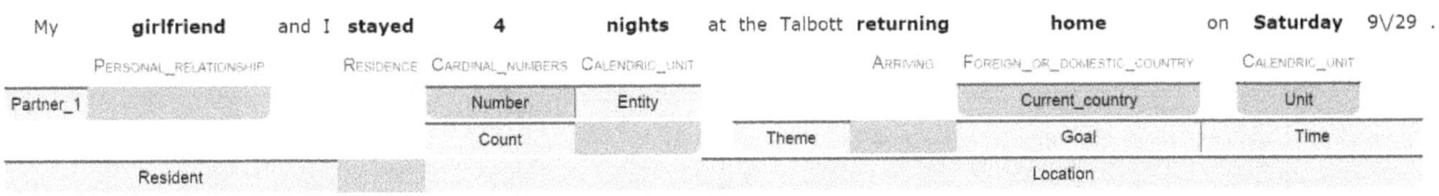

Figure 1: FrameNet parsing example from CMU's ARK syntactic & semantic parsing demo page (http://demo.ark.cs.cmu.edu/parse)

Although some studies focused mainly on identifying opinion spam content, some existing studies have used consumers' behavioral patterns to detect individual fake reviewers and fake review groups. For instance, Jindal et al. captured unusual review patterns using domain-independent rules [10]. Mukherjee et al. proposed several spamming behavioral indicators of spamming activities [13].

Semantic Frame Theory and FrameNet. FrameNet [5] is a lexical resource for English with semantic representations in combination of word sense disambiguation and semantic role labeling and is based on frame semantics [6]. Frames are cognitively founded and formally explored devices that represent knowledge about objects and categories by means of their attributes and values [7]. A word (or a lexical unit (LU)) in a sentence evokes a frame of semantic knowledge and the frame describes prototypical situations spoken in natural language. The frame contains a set of semantic roles that correspond to the participants (Frame Elements (FEs)) of a described event or situation. Many NLP researches use FrameNet especially for semantic role labeling, word sense disambiguation and question-answering.

In this work, we use FrameNet as our core analysis tool. In FrameNet, the machine processes all review content using semantic frame units. Unlike linguistic features, output results that are based on frames are also in human-readable and understandable format, which helps us understand the data more efficiently. We use a simple example to explain frame-based analysis.

Suppose we have the following sentence: *"My girlfriend and I stayed 4 nights at the Talbott returning home on Saturday 9/29."*[3] The FrameNet parsing result of the above sentence is described in Figure 1. In this example, a total of seven frames are identified. The darker gray box represents a frame that was evoked by a lexical unit and the successive lighter gray boxes represent their frame units (and frame range). Note that the verbs *stayed* and *returning* evoke their dedicated Residence and Arriving frames respectively, and the nouns *girlfriend* and *home* evoke Personal_relationship and Foreign_or_domestic_country frames, respectively. By analyzing these extracted frames, we can figure out that the reviewer would like to convey some sense of his or her relationships, travel schedule, and duration of stay.

We hypothesize that the frame occurrence may be different because of the different mindsets or experiences of truthful users and spammers. On this basis, we propose metrics for measuring the prevalence of frames for each dataset in the following subsection.

[3]This sentence is borrowed from the opinion spam dataset of [15].

3. METHODOLOGY

In this section, we present our methodology of using semantic frames for analyzing user-generated content. We first define measures of the difference between frame proportions for each dataset. We then obtain frames that have high discriminative power and explore their interesting characteristics.

3.1 Discriminative Frame Selection

Although there are many, not every frame that appears in a sentence is useful. To select the most effective frames for an analysis, we propose Normalized Frame Rate (NFR) and Normalized Bi-frame Rate (NBFR), both of which quantitatively measure the discriminative power of a frame and frame pairs, respectively. We will explain each metric using examples in Table 1.

3.1.1 Normalized Frame Rate (NFR)

We define Normalized Frame Rate (NFR) to compute the frame distribution differences between truthful reviews and deceptive opinion spam. The NFR value of a specific frame indicates the number of times the frame occurred compared with the total number of occurrences of frames in a dataset. Before we count each frame occurrence from the dataset, we first investigate whether there is a statistically significant difference of frame proportion between the deceptive opinion spam dataset and the truthful review dataset using a two-proportion z-test. The test result successfully rejects the null hypothesis. ($H0$: sample proportions of each frame are equal on both datasets in significant level $p < 0.01$)

Now, let us explain how to calculate the NFR value for each class. The *Personal_relationship* frame (f_1) occurred twice in the deceptive class but did not occur in the truthful class. Since the total sum of frame occurrence of the deceptive class is 11, the NFR value of f_1 is 2/11 or 0.18 for the deceptive class and 0 for the truthful class. Similarly, the *Calendric_unit* frame (f_4) occurred three times in the truthful class and twice in the deceptive class. The NFR value of f_4 for the truthful class is 0.33 and 0.18 for the deceptive class. Then we calculate the difference between two NFR values of a frame by subtracting the NFR value for the truthful class from the NFR value for the deceptive class. The difference between two NFR values for a specific frame f_m is calculated as below:

$$\Delta NFR_{f_m} = NFR_{D_{deceptive}} f_m - NFR_{D_{truthful}} f_m \quad (1)$$

For example, the ΔNFR_{f_4} value is -0.15 (0.18 - 0.3); it is negative because the *Calendric_unit* frame (f_4) is more likely to appear in the truthful class.

Table 1: Example with frame and bi-frame in the sentences

Class	Example Sentences	Bi-frame(s)
Deceptive	s_1: My **girlfriend**(f_1) and I **stayed**(f_2) **4**(f_3) **nights**(f_4) at the Talbott on **Saturday**(f_4) 9/29.	(f_1, f_2), (f_2, f_3), (f_3, f_4), (f_4, f_4)
	s_2: The Talbott **Hotel**(f_7) is **fantastic**(f_8).	(f_7, f_8)
	s_3: Me and my **husband**(f_1) **stayed**(f_2) at the Hyatt and I **satisfied**(f_9) with this **hotel**(f_7).	(f_1, f_2), (f_2, f_9), (f_9, f_7)
Truthful	s_4: We **stayed**(f_2) **2**(f_3) **nights**(f_4) in a cosy **bedroom**(f_{10}).	(f_2, f_3), (f_3, f_4), (f_4, f_{10})
	s_5: We **visited**(f_5) Chicago on the 4th of **July**(f_4) **weekend**(f_4) .	(f_5, f_4), (f_4, f_4)
	s_6: Breakfast **starts**(f_{11}) at 7 am and it was only **20**(f_3) $.	(f_{11}, f_3)
Frame Index	f_1: Personal_relationship f_2: Residence f_3: Cardinal_numbers f_4: Calendric_unit f_5: Arriving f_6: Foreign_or_domestic_country f_7: Buildings f_8: Desirability f_9: Experiencer_focus f_{10}: Building_subparts f_{11}: Process_start f_{12}: Sole_instance	

3.1.2 *Normalized Bi-frame Rate ($NBFR$)*

A bi-frame refers to a pair of successively occurring frames in a sentence. While bigram catches context of a text in n-gram-based approach, a bi-frame also conveys semantic context of a given sentence. Furthermore, we consider the frame sequence as the latent writing style of a reviewer.

We use Table 1 again to explain NBFR. In a sentence s_3, f_1, f_2, f_9 and f_7 frames are identified. We obtain bi-frame pairs by grouping successive frames into two such as (f_1, f_2), (f_2, f_9), and (f_9, f_7). We calculate NBFR value in the exact same way as we calculate NFR, but now we count two frames as one counting unit. For example, the bi-frame *Personal_relationship* (f_1) $\rightarrow$ *Residence* (f_2) occurred twice in the deceptive class but did not occur in the truthful class. Therefore, the NBFR value of the bi-frame *Personal_relationship* (f_1) $\rightarrow$ *Residence* (f_2) in the deceptive class is 2/7 (0.29). In general, ΔNBFR for frame f_i and f_j is calculated as below:

$$\Delta NBFR_{f_i f_j} = NBFR_{D_{deceptive} f_i f_j} - NBFR_{D_{truthful} f_i f_j} \quad (2)$$

Hence, $\Delta NBFR_{f_1 f_2}$ is a positive value of 0.29 which means that this bi-frame is more likely to appear in the deceptive class.

4. QUALITATIVE EVALUATION OF FRAME FEATURES

This section presents a qualitative analysis of frame features. We first introduce the dataset that was used in this paper in Section 4.1. Then, we investigate the individual frame characteristics that appeared in each dataset and look into bi-frames in Section 4.2.

4.1 Dataset

Table 2 shows the statistics of the datasets used in this paper. For the truthful opinion reviews, we used the TripAdvisor dataset from Ott et al. [15]. Details about the deceptive opinion spam datasets solicited from crowdsource, employees, and real-life screened reviews are described in what follows.

Table 2: Statistics of datasets

Class	Dataset	#of docs	#of unique words	size (in kB)
Deceptive	AMT	400	4,180	254
	Employee	140	1,856	62
	"not-recommended" (Yelp)	3,361	18,466	2,177
Truthful	TripAdvisor	400	4,934	265
	"recommended" (Yelp)	3,869	20,259	2,747

4.1.1 *AMT and Employee Dataset*

Gathering quality and reliable gold-standard deceptive opinion datasets is a challenging task in opinion spam analysis research. Ott et al. employed a crowdsourcing framework provided by Amazon to generate gold-standard deceptive opinion spam datasets [15]. However, Li et al. pointed out that the AMT dataset is only representative of a specific type of deception that is generated by people who do not have particular experience with a target local business [11]. The reviewers' lack of experience is complemented by hiring real employees and allowing them to write deceptive opinion reviews based on their higher-level domain knowledge.

For the experiment, we explore the gold-standard deceptive opinion datasets from [15], [11] and our own real-life dataset collected from Yelp. Since the AMT dataset contains only hotel reviews, we also only use the hotel employee dataset in [11]. We will investigate the characteristics of each dataset in relation to semantic frames, and not just linguistic differences which were already studied in previous work [4, 11, 15].

4.1.2 *Dataset from Yelp*

We gathered 3,869 "recommended" reviews and 3,361 "not currently recommended"[4] reviews for 265 hotels in the Chicago area from Yelp. We collected only 5-star reviews to constantly maintain the sentiment polarity. We mixed popular and unpopular hotels based on the number of reviews but we used only reviews of hotels whose overall ratings were over 3.5. The number of unique unigrams in the Yelp dataset was almost 4 times larger than that in the AMT dataset due to the different size of the dataset (~20,000 compared with ~5,000).

4.2 Frame-based Semantic Analysis

4.2.1 *Frame-by-frame Analysis*

The goal of our analysis is to understand how frames are distributed in different datasets. Figure 2 and Figure 3 illustrate the top 50 frames that were sorted by their ΔNFR value, which were differentially expressed in the deceptive class and the truthful class from each of the two datasets. The NFR value of each frame is ranged from -1.0 to 1.25 in the AMT dataset, and from -2.0 to 1.6 in the Employee dataset. By the definition of ΔNFR, if a frame's ΔNFR

[4] Yelp recently changed its review filtering service name from "filtered" to "not currently recommended". The word "currently" would give the sense that its review recommendation policy continues to change, so that blocked reviews are temporary.

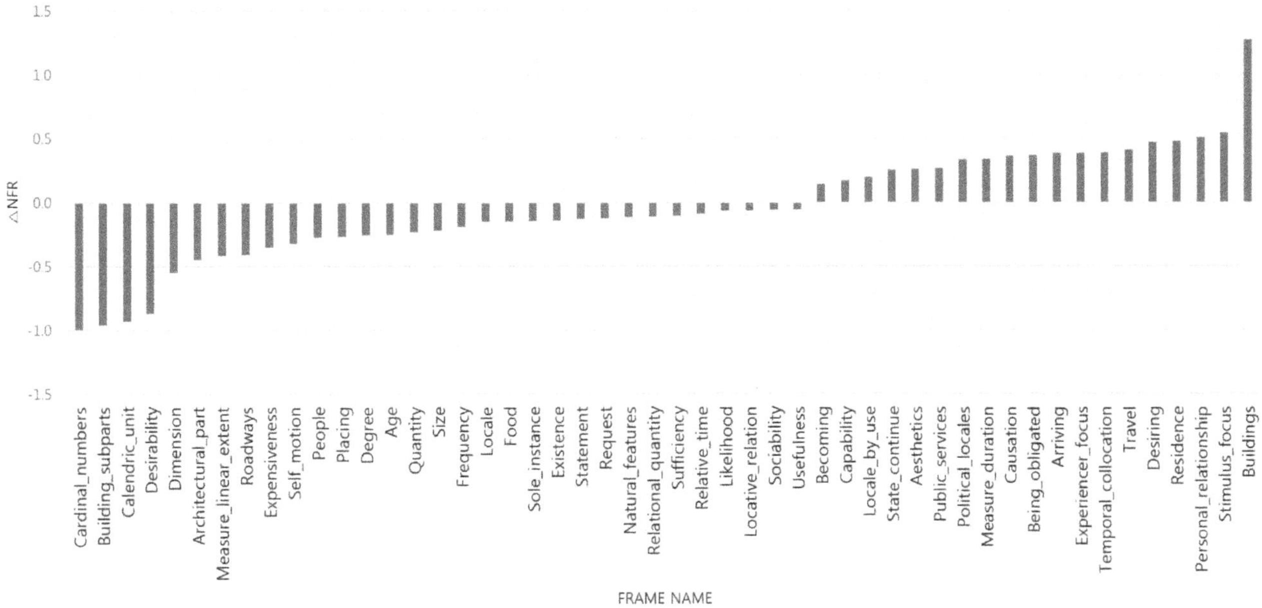

Figure 2: Top 50 differentially expressed frames sorted by ΔNFR in AMT dataset

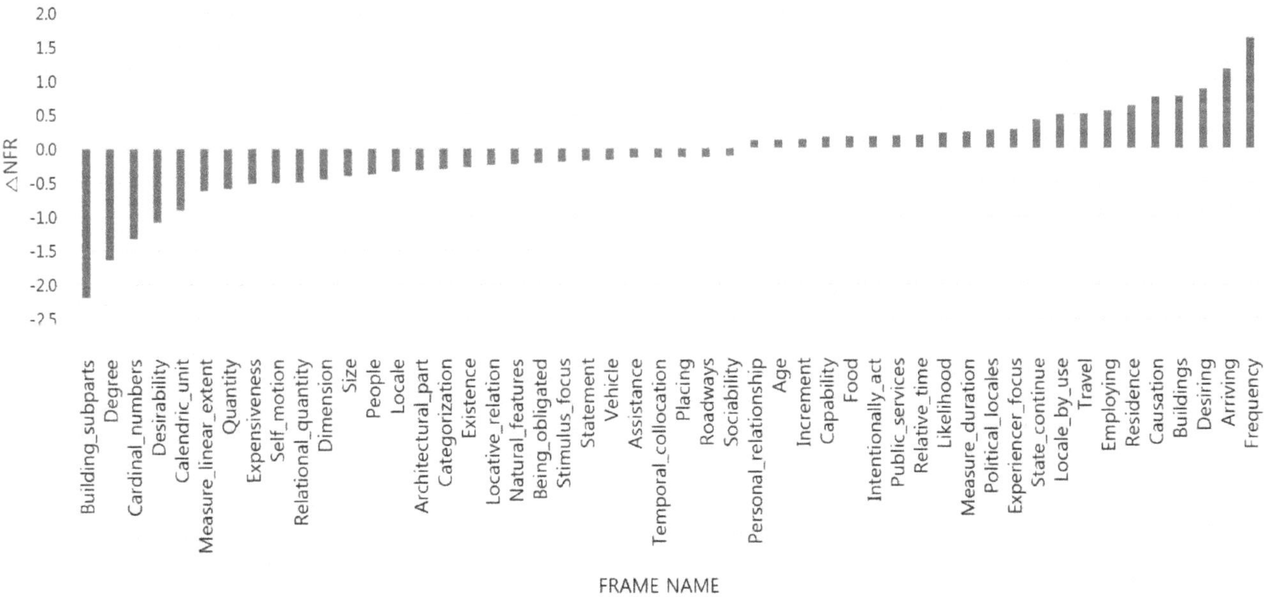

Figure 3: Top 50 differentially expressed frames sorted by ΔNFR in Employee dataset

value is negative, the frame is more likely to occur in the truthful dataset than in the deceptive class and vice-versa.

In this analysis, we found that the nature of the frames detected by our method is also largely consistent with previous deceptive opinion spam studies.

Spatial and business detail-related frames. We observed that frames such as Cardinal_numbers, Building_subparts, Calendric_unit, Dimension, Expensiveness, which are used to described the spatial details about a business are conspicuous in the truthful dataset. For example, the Cardinal_numbers and Calendric_unit frames express a specific date of travel or arrival, duration of stay, and so on. The Building_subparts frame evoked by lexical units such as *room, floor, bathroom,* and *lobby* is frequently used in both truthful datasets showing strong negative ΔNFR value for describing spatial details. These building parts are explained using specific measurements (Cardinal_number and Dimension). Furthermore, we can see that the truthful reviewers frequently commented on the price of a hotel (negative ΔNFR value of Expensiveness frame in both datasets).

This observation is consistent with previous studies that truthful reviewers are more likely to include spatial details mentioned above [11, 13, 15]. On the other hand, frames that have positive ΔNFR values (e.g., Buildings, Residence, Travel, etc.) are rather general and do not contain much detailed information.

Personal relationship-related frames. We found that the spammers deliberately emphasize relationship keywords to convince the reader that their review is based on real experience. For example, the Personal_relationship frame that is evoked by the lexical units *wife, husband, friend* is highly ranked in Table 4 which is also confirms the previous studies. In Ott et al., The highest weighted truthful and deceptive lexical features learned by the supervised model contain the word *husband* [15]. Similarly, the highly weighted LIWC feature list contains the word *family* in the study of Li et al. [11]. Unlike the previous studies, instead of capturing each individual word as a feature, our approach captures a semantic group of a word as a feature.

Comparison of our top-ranked lexical units and top-weighted terms in previous work. We observed that some of our top-k lexical units in Table 4 were also reported in previous studies [11, 14, 15]. For example, in the study of Li et al., the top weighted LIWC feature list contains the category word *number* in the truthful class. This corresponds to our ΔNFR negative Cardinal_numbers frame [11]. Furthermore, the lexical units *small, hotel,* and *husband* of the Dimension, Buildings, and Personal_relationship frames, respectively, are in the top-weighted lexical features list in [15]. The verb *felt* as well as nouns, which were captured by Mukherjee et al., would correspond to the lexical unit *felt like* of the Desiring frame [14].

Sentiment expression pattern analysis. Interestingly, we discovered that there are different sentiment expression patterns between deceptive Turkers and truthful reviewers. Table 3 shows that the Stimulus_focus frame is used more in the deceptive reviews while the Desirability frame is used more in the truthful review dataset even though both frames are related to sentiment expression. According to the FrameNet, the Stimulus evokes a particular emotion or experience in the Experiencer. For example, in the following sentence, *"The movie was quite fascinating."*[5] the stimulus *the movie* brings out positive emotions in the reviewer. On the other hand, the Desirability frame describes the event of judging the gradable attribute Evaluee for its quality. For the given sentence, *"The view was astonishing."*[6] the reviewer judges the goodness of the *view* aspect. We assume that Turkers tend to fabricate their emotions, and that truthful reviewers tend to evaluate a target using their real experience. Human readers may not be able to differentiate two sentiment words in spoken language. However, when machines read and process sentences, they capture subtle differences using the linguistic knowledge provided by the FrameNet lexical database.

4.2.2 Bi-frame Co-occurrence Matrix Similarity

Table 5 and Table 6 are the lists of the top differentially expressed bi-frames from the AMT dataset and the Employee dataset, respectively. Each table illustrates the top 15 and the bottom 15 bi-frames, all of which were ranked according to their ΔNBFR values. To investigate how bi-frame co-occurrence patterns of two datasets are different, we use their co-occurrence pattern similarity.

[5]Example sentence of Stimulus_focus frame in FrameNet.
[6]Example sentence of Desirability frame in FrameNet.

Table 3: Top 5 frame list of two datasets

Dataset	Deceptive	Truthful
AMT	Buildings	Cardinal_numbers
	Stimulus_focus	Building_subparts
	Personal_relationship	Calendric_unit
	Residence	Desirability
	Desiring	Dimension
Employee	Frequency	Building_subparts
	Arriving	Degree
	Desiring	Cardinal_numbers
	Buildings	Desirability
	Causation	Calendric_unit

Let L be the union of the top bi-frames in Table 5 and Table 6 where $|L|$=42. Then, we define $n \times n$ matrices M_d and M_t for the deceptive and the truthful dataset, respectively, where n is the number of frames in set L. Each cell of matrix M represents the NBFR value of bi-frame. By comparing the co-occurrence matrices of the two datasets, we can see how spammers and non-spammers write reviews differently in terms of semantic flow. The similarity between the two matrices M_d and M_t is calculated as follows.

$$sim(M_d, M_t) = \frac{vec(M_d) \cdot vec(M_t)}{\|vec(M_d)\|\|vec(M_t)\|} \tag{3}$$

Table 7 shows the similarity values computed between dataset pairs. To compare the similarity values, we needed a threshold value to make a decision whether two datasets show different bi-frame co-occurrence patterns. So we randomly divided a single dataset into two subsets and calculated their within-set similarity. We repeated this procedure 10 times and reported the averages in Table 7.

As we can see in Table 7, the similarity value of AMT (deceptive) and TripAdvisor (truthful) is less than the within-set similarity value (0.86 < 0.92). This means that the bi-frame patterns of deceptive and truthful reviews are different. There are also differences between AMT and Employee even though they are in the deceptive category. Li et al. also mentioned these characteristics and reported that their two-class classifier achieves an accuracy over 0.76 in distinguishing between Turker and Employee reviews [11]. Note that the similarity between Employee and TripAdvisor is almost equal to that of the Employee-within set. This implies that employees put more effort into writing fake reviews to try to sound authentic.

4.2.3 Qualitative Analysis of Bi-frame Occurring Patterns

In Table 5 and Table 6, we also observe a similar pattern in the top ΔNFR list. We see that in the truthful group (the negative value of ΔNBFR), the reviewers include details about the business. For instance, a bi-frame Building_subparts→Dimension appeared in both datasets and was most likely used to describe the interior of the hotel. The Self_motion frame evoked by the lexical unit *walk* or

Table 4: The most used frame lexical units of the top 5 frames

Class	Deceptive (AMT)					Truthful				
Frame Name	Buildings	Stimulus_focus	Personal_relationship	Residence	Desiring	Cardinal_numbers	Building_subparts	Calendric_unit	Desirability	Dimension
Lexical Unit	hotel	nice	husband	stay	wanted	one	room	night	great	large
	hotels	amazing	wife	stayed	want	2	rooms	nights	excellent	small
	home	relaxing	friends	staying	felt like	two	bathroom	day	wonderful	larger
	bar	relax	friend	living	feel like	3	lobby	weekend	good	high
	house	pleasant	couple	live	wish	4	bathrooms	morning	best	dark
Class	Deceptive (Employee)					Truthful				
Frame Name	Frequency	Arriving	Desiring	Buildings	Causation	Building_subparts	Degree	Cardinal_numbers	Desirability	Calendric_unit
Lexical Unit	always	get	feel like	hotel	made	room	very	one	great	night
	every	return	want	home	make	rooms	totally	2	excellent	nights
	never	visit	felt like	bar	making	bathroom	somewhat	two	good	day
	frequently	arrived	wanted	living	makes	lobby	fairly	3	wonderful	weekend
	rate	come	hope	pavilion	brought	bathrooms		4	best	morning

Table 5: The top and the bottom 15 most differentially expressed bi-frames in the AMT dataset

Top 15 Bi-frames	$\Delta NBFR$	Bottom 15 Bi-frames	$\Delta NBFR$
Residence Buildings	0.00354	Cardinal_numbers Calendric_unit	-0.004083
Building_subparts Public_services	0.00186	Desirability Locale	-0.002952
Locative_relation Measure_duration	0.00177	Building_subparts Dimension	-0.002282
Businesses Travel	0.00170	Calendric_unit Calendric_unit	-0.002097
Direction Buildings	0.00153	Dimension Building_subparts	-0.001859
Buildings Buildings	0.00140	Cardinal_numbers Measure_linear_extent	-0.001818
Buildings Inclusion	0.00136	Residence Locative_relation	-0.001796
Experiencer_focus Residence	0.00134	Building_subparts Desirability	-0.001756
Locale State_continue	0.00124	Locale Desirability	-0.001441
Buildings Residence	0.00120	Building_subparts Degree	-0.001294
Temporal_collocation Residence	0.00118	Self_motion Range	-0.001292
Arriving Buildings	0.00104	Desirability Frequency	-0.001191
Measure_duration Buildings	0.00103	Relational_quantity Cardinal_numbers	-0.001057
Desirability Expertise	0.00096	Age Buildings	-0.001057
Aesthetics Buildings	0.00093	Cardinal_numbers Measure_duration	-0.001049

Table 6: The top and the bottom 15 most differentially expressed bi-frames in the Employee dataset

Top 15 Bi-frames	$\Delta NBFR$	Bottom 15 Bi-frames	$\Delta NBFR$
Buildings Buildings	0.00357	Cardinal_numbers Calendric_unit	-0.00551
Capability Waiting	0.00250	Building_subparts Degree	-0.00476
Measure_duration Arriving	0.00248	Residence Locative_relation	-0.00449
Waiting Arriving	0.00248	Degree Stimulus_focus	-0.00303
Frequency Residence	0.00217	Calendric_unit Calendric_unit	-0.00263
Food Desirability	0.00204	Building_subparts Dimension	-0.00258
Capability Statement	0.00198	Building_subparts Desirability	-0.00247
Locative_relation Desirability	0.00191	Desirability Locale	-0.00237
Causation Residence	0.00188	Locale Desirability	-0.00219
Physical_artworks Building_subparts	0.00188	Desirability Measure_linear_extent	-0.00209
Locale State_continue	0.00172	Cardinal_numbers Measure_linear_extent	-0.00203
Ordinal_numbers Roadways	0.00167	Self_motion Range	-0.00192
Memory Being_named	0.00167	Degree Desirability	-0.00190
Activity_ongoing Locative_relation	0.00161	Degree Sociability	-0.00184
Personal_relationship Arriving	0.00161	Buildings Building_subparts	-0.00170

hike explains that the Self_mover[7] moves under its own direction along a path. Accordingly, the Self_motion→Range bi-frame was categorized in the truthful group and thus can be interpreted as a situation where the reviewer describes his or her activity around the hotel.

However, bi-frames in the deceptive group are mostly not notable and unspecific, compared with those in the truthful group. The Businesses→Travel bi-frame in the AMT dataset may indicate the reason of travel that fake reviewers fabricate for their reviews. This may be because paid Turkers need to quickly fabricate plausible reasons to try to sound authentic and pick a general topic such as business. On the other hand, employees are more likely to comment on the quality of a food (Food→Desirability).

[7]This is a core frame element of Self_motion frame in FrameNet.

Physical_artworks→Building_subparts well represent employees' detailed knowledge about the business. Personal_relationship→Arriving is also a conspicuous bi-frame which is more like a cliché in deception. Note that the Cardinal_numbers→Calendric_unit bi-frame is top ranked in both Tables 5 and 6 and has lowest ΔNBFR values, which means this bi-frame is more likely to appear in truthful reviews. Although employees can write details about the business (such as Physical_artwork), we can assume that they cannot fabricate details about an activity-based experience such as a specific date (Calendric_unit, Self_motion, etc.).

5. FRAME FEATURE VALIDATION ON CLASSIFICATION TASKS

We perform machine learning-based classification tasks to distinguish truthful reviews from deceptive reviews. In Section 5.1, we explain the pre-processing procedure used in the experiment. In Section 5.2, we report the classification results of varying features on different classification models.

5.1 Data Pre-processing and Frame Extraction

We set a default analysis unit as a single sentence for frame analysis. Since both datasets do not annotate sentence boundaries, we divide each review document into multiple sentences using OpenNLP Sentence Detector[8]. Then, each sentence is analyzed for dependency parsing and n-gram tokenization using Stanford Parser[9]. The parsed results are passed to SEMAPHORE V2.1, an automatic frame-semantic annotation[10] system for frame extraction.

Table 8 shows the statistics of the frame extraction results. The truthful dataset contains more frames than the deceptive dataset, but both datasets contain almost same number of unique frames. Due to the difficulties of gathering datasets from the real employees, the size of the Employee dataset is smaller than that of the AMT dataset.

Table 7: Bi-frame co-occurrence matrix similarity

Settings	Dataset	Similarity
Cross set	AMT&TripAdvisor	0.86
	AMT&Employee	0.78
	Employee&TripAdvisor	0.68
Within set	TripAdvisor	0.92
	AMT	0.91
	Employee	0.66

Table 8: Frame extraction statistics obtained from two datasets

Doc / Frame	Deceptive		Truthful
	AMT	Employee	
#of docs	400	140	400
#of frames	17131	3641	19153
#of unique frames	467	322	463

Table 9: Our implementation of the baseline

System	Feature	Acc	Deceptive			Truthful		
			Prec	Rec	F1	Prec	Rec	F1
Ott'11 [15]	Uni	0.884	0.870	0.903	0.886	0.899	0.865	0.882
	Bi$^+$	0.896	0.891	0.903	0.897	0.901	0.890	0.896
Our Impl.	Uni	0.870	0.868	0.873	0.870	0.872	0.868	0.870
	Bi$^+$	0.876	0.873	0.880	0.877	0.879	0.873	0.876

5.2 Classification Task

For a reliable comparison, we also report our own implementation[11] of [15] for the AMT dataset (Table 9). We use SVM (SVM^{light}, Joachim, 1999) and Naive Bayes classifiers as classification models. To find the separating hyperplane for SVM, a linear kernel is used. Each model is validated based on a nested 5-fold cross validation scheme which was also done by Ott et al. [15].

Nested cross-validation works in the following way. There is an inner CV loop where we search for optimal parameters using the parameter search algorithm (e.g., grid search). At the end of this process, we end up with k models (k being the number of folds in the outer loop) that gives the best accuracy within the inner CV. Note that the performance results of our implementation are slightly different from those of the original results reported in [15]. It is due to the different experimental settings such as model parameter, n-gram tokenization, and so on, which were not provided in the original paper.

Table 10: Classification result using frame feature-only

Dataset	Feature	Acc	Deceptive			Truthful		
			Prec	Rec	F1	Prec	Rec	F1
AMT vs. Truthful	Frm3	0.660	0.639	0.735	0.684	0.688	0.585	0.632
	Frm5	0.710	0.688	0.768	0.726	0.737	0.653	0.692
	Frm10	0.737	0.716	0.788	0.750	0.764	0.688	0.724
	Frm$_{full}$	0.774	0.753	0.815	0.783	0.798	0.733	0.764
Employee vs. Truthful	Frm3	0.824	0.727	0.514	0.603	0.846	0.933	0.887
	Frm5	0.856	0.763	0.643	0.698	0.882	0.930	0.905
	Frm10	0.878	0.803	0.700	0.748	0.900	0.940	0.919
	Frm$_{full}$	0.870	0.773	0.707	0.739	0.900	0.928	0.914

Table 11: Classification result varying the number of bi-frames with a fixed number of frame features

Feature	Bi-frm50	Bi-frm100	Bi-frm200	Bi-frm500	Bi-frm1000
AMT vs. Truthful	0.785	0.791	0.791	0.796	0.796
Employee vs. Truthful	0.876	0.878	0.876	0.870	0.872

5.2.1 *Frame-only Feature*

We report the classification result of using only frame feature and investigate how frame features are effective for differentiating spam and non-spam. Frm-k, (k = 1, 2 ...n) in Table 10 represents the number of k frames from the top and bottom in the frame list sorted by ΔNFR values.

First, we trained a SVM model using only frame features. Interestingly, we obtained a much higher classification accuracy when we used only six frame features (Frm3 setting in Table 10) than random guess of 50% (0.660 and 0.824) for both the AMT dataset and the Employee dataset. Adding more frame features gradually increases the accuracy. As we can see in Table 10, the model that uses the Frm5 feature yields almost the same accuracy as the model using the Frm$_{full}$ feature. This proves that the top-k frames can be used as discriminative features for training supervised classification models. The top 5 frames from both datasets are listed in Table 3.

5.2.2 *Frame and Bi-frame Features*

We also use bi-frames along with frame features. To compare the results of using only frame features reported in Table 10, we mixed the bi-frame feature onto the frame feature. Instead of using every combination of frames, we take only the top 1000 and the bottom 1000 bi-frame features in the bi-frame list which were sorted by their ΔNBFR value.

Figure 4 shows that the classification accuracy is gradually improved by adding bi-frame features to the model

[8]https://opennlp.apache.org/

[9]http://nlp.stanford.edu/software/stanford-dependencies.shtml

[10]http://www.ark.cs.cmu.edu/SEMAFOR/

[11]We were not able to obtain the original implementation from the authors.

Table 12: Classification result using frame features with n-grams

Dataset	Features	Acc	Deceptive			Truthful		
			Prec	Rec	F1	Prec	Rec	F1
AMT	Frm5+Uni_500$_{svm}$	0.877	0.866	0.892	0.879	0.889	0.862	0.876
	Frm15+Bi-Frm160+Uni_150$_{svm}$	0.881	0.877	0.888	0.882	0.886	0.875	0.881
	Frm30+Bi-Frm10+Bi$^+$_100$_{svm}$	0.887	0.880	0.897	0.889	0.895	0.877	0.886
	Frm5+Bi-Frm20+Bi$^+$_full$_{NB}$	0.914	0.903	0.928	0.915	0.925	0.900	0.913
	Our impl. of [15] Uni	0.870	0.868	0.873	0.870	0.872	0.868	0.870
	Our impl. of [15] Bi$^+$	0.876	0.873	0.880	0.877	0.879	0.873	0.876
Employee	Frm5+Uni_100$_{svm}$	0.900	0.830	0.771	0.800	0.921	0.945	0.933
	Frm5+Bi-Frm15+Uni_full$_{svm}$	0.924	0.872	0.829	0.850	0.941	0.958	0.949
	Frm5+Bi-Frm40+Bi$^+$_100$_{svm}$	0.917	0.852	0.824	0.836	0.938	0.950	0.944
	Frm5+Bi-Frm10+Bi$^+$_full$_{NB}$	0.867	0.746	0.736	0.741	0.908	0.913	0.910
	Same setting in [15] Uni$_{svm}$	0.916	0.857	0.814	0.835	0.936	0.953	0.944
	Same setting in [15] Bi$^+$$_{svm}$	0.894	0.837	0.736	0.783	0.911	0.950	0.930

compared to the model that used frame-only feature in both datasets. The semantic context delivered by bi-frames can be useful for detecting deceptive opinions. Next, we investigate how the number of bi-frames affects classification performance when the number of bi-frame features varies and when the number of frame features is fixed to "full". In this setting, the classification result did not change significantly.

In the AMT vs. Truthful setting in Table 11, the classification accuracy improved from 0.785 to 0.796 as a result of increasing the number of bi-frames. However, in the Employee vs. Truthful setting, the performance improvement was not as large as that in the AMT vs. Truthful setting. The accuracy did not improve even though we increased the number of bi-frames. From this result, we can assume that the more frame and bi-frame features we used, the more likely the performance will improve.

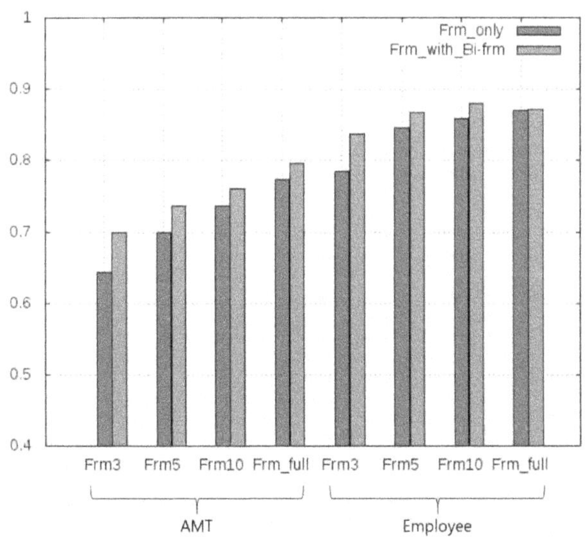

Figure 4: Classification accuracy using frame and bi-frame feature together

5.2.3 *Frame with Lexico-syntactic Features*

In this experiment, we train Naive Bayes and SVM classifiers using individual frame and bi-frame features in combination with lexical n-grams and the result is reported in Table 12. To address the question about the power of lexical n-grams, we vary the number of n-grams. We have evaluated every combination of features with various numbers of n-grams. However, we report only the meaningful results due to the limit of space. Likewise Frm-k, Uni-k indicates the top-k unigrams that were selected using the same ΔNFR method that we used to obtain the top-k frames. The superscript$^+$ of Bi$^+$ feature indicates that the bigram feature subsumes the unigram feature set.

In Table 12, the feature combination of Frm5 and Uni500 achieved an accuracy of 0.877 whereas the baseline result achieved an accuracy of 0.870 (using unigram-only features in our implementation of Ott et al. [15]). After various tries, we obtained the highest classification accuracy of 0.914 in the AMT dataset using the feature combination of Frm5, Bi-Frm20 and full Bi$^+$ with a Naive Bayes model (a 4.34% increase compared with our baseline implementation). In the Employee dataset, Frm5, Bi-Frm15 and Uni_full features obtained an accuracy of 0.924 using an SVM model (a 0.87% increase compared with the baseline).

5.2.4 *Classification on Yelp*

In Table 13, we also report an SVM classification result on the Yelp dataset. First, the classification experiments that use an n-gram feature on the Yelp data yielded an accuracy of 0.625. This result is consistent with [14] that simple linguistic features are hardly effective for real-life datasets (an accuracy of 0.676 was obtained from their Yelp dataset). Next, we added frame and bi-frame features (Frm5 and Bi-Frm20) to n-grams, which improved the performance of the previous classification task. However, the semantic frame feature did not improve classification performance. We assume that Yelp's review recommendation system does not consider the semantic features of review contents but utilizes other non-content features such as users' behavioral patterns, which were investigated by Mukherjee et al. [14].

Table 13: SVM 5-fold CV result on our Yelp dataset

Feature	Acc	Not recommended			Recommended		
		Prec	Rec	F1	Prec	Rec	F1
Uni	0.625	0.594	0.608	0.601	0.653	0.640	0.646
Bi$^+$	0.624	0.589	0.628	0.608	0.657	0.620	0.638
Frm+Uni_full	0.620	0.590	0.597	0.593	0.646	0.640	0.643
Frm+Bi$^+$_full	0.619	0.585	0.618	0.601	0.651	0.620	0.635

6. CONCLUSIONS

In this paper, we investigate deceptive opinion spam and truthful reviews using semantic frames. We also propose an analysis method for measuring the proportion of frame in a sentence. To the best of our knowledge, this is the first study to perform semantic frame analysis of customer reviews.

Our experimental results show that the classification model that used frame features outperformed the baseline model by 4.34% for the AMT dataset. Furthermore, using new semantic frame features, we successively captured some interpretable differences between fake and real reviews in terms of their unique semantic features, which cannot be done by other existing methods. For example, even though employees who have expert-level domain knowledge attempt to write a seemingly truthful review, they cannot fabricate specific details about an activity-based experience. We also captured subtle differences of sentiment expression patterns in deceptive and truthful review contents using a linguistic theoretical method. Looking at other domains such as restaurants or medical services using our proposed semantic analysis method remains for the future work in this area.

7. ACKNOWLEDGEMENTS

This work was supported by the National Research Foundation of Korea(NRF) grant funded by the Korea government(MSIP) (NRF-2014R1A2A1A10051238).

8. REFERENCES

[1] 2013 study: 79% of consumers trust online reviews as much as personal recommendations, "http://searchengineland.com/2013-study-79-of-consumers-trust-online-reviews-as-much-as-personal-recommendations-164565". Accessed: 2015-04-05.

[2] A. A. Benczur, K. Csalogany, T. Sarlos, and M. Uher. Spamrank–fully automatic link spam detection work in progress. In *Proceedings of the first international workshop on adversarial information retrieval on the web*, AIRWeb '05, Chiba, Japan, 2005.

[3] C. Castillo, D. Donato, A. Gionis, V. Murdock, and F. Silvestri. Know your neighbors: Web spam detection using the web topology. In *Proceedings of SIGIR*, Amsterdam, Netherlands, July 2007. ACM.

[4] S. Feng, R. Banerjee, and Y. Choi. Syntactic stylometry for deception detection. In *Proceedings of the 50th Annual Meeting of the Association for Computational Linguistics*, 2012.

[5] C. Fillmore, C. Johnson, and M. Petruck. Background to framenet. *International journal of lexicography*, 16(3):235, 2003.

[6] C. J. Fillmore. Frame semantics and the nature of language. In *Origins and Evolution of Language and Speech, 280*, 1976.

[7] T. Gamerschlag, D. Gerland, R. Osswald, and W. Petersen. *Frames and Concept Types: Applications in Language and Philosophy*, volume 94 of *0924-4662*. Springer International Publishing, 1 edition, 2014.

[8] Z. Gyöngyi, H. Garcia-Molina, and J. Pedersen. Combating web spam with trustrank. In *Proceedings of the Thirtieth international conference on Very large data bases-Volume 30*, VLDB '04, pages 576–587, 2004.

[9] N. Jindal and B. Liu. Opinion spam and analysis. In *Proceedings of the 2008 International Conference on Web Search and Data Mining*, WSDM '08, 2008.

[10] N. Jindal, B. Liu, and E.-P. Lim. Finding unusual review patterns using unexpected rules. In *Proceedings of the 19th ACM International Conference on Information and Knowledge Management*, CIKM '10, pages 1549–1552, New York, NY, USA, 2010. ACM.

[11] J. Li, M. Ott, C. Cardie, and E. Hovy. Towards a general rule for identifying deceptive opinion spam. In *Proceedings of the 52th Annual Meeting of the Association for Computational Linguistics*, 2014.

[12] E.-P. Lim, V.-A. Nguyen, N. Jindal, B. Liu, and H. W. Lauw. Detecting product review spammers using rating behaviors. In *Proceedings of the 19th ACM International Conference on Information and Knowledge Management*, CIKM '10, 2010.

[13] A. Mukherjee, B. Liu, and N. S. Glance. Spotting fake reviewer groups in consumer reviews. In *Proceedings of the 21st World Wide Web Conference, WWW 2012, Lyon, France, April 16-20, 2012*, pages 191–200.

[14] A. Mukherjee, V. Venkataraman, B. Liu, and N. S. Glance. What yelp fake review filter might be doing? In *Proceedings of the Seventh International Conference on Weblogs and Social Media, ICWSM 2013, Cambridge, Massachusetts, USA, July 8-11, 2013.*

[15] M. Ott, Y. Choi, C. Cardie, and J. T. Hancock. Finding deceptive opinion spam by any stretch of the imagination. In *Proceedings of the 49th Annual Meeting of the Association for Computational Linguistics*, 2011.

[16] J. W. Pennebaker, C. K. Chung, M. Ireland, A. Gonzales, and R. J. Booth. The Development and Psychometric Properties of LIWC2007. Austin, TX, USA LIWC. Net.

[17] N. Spirin and J. Han. Survey on web spam detection: principles and algorithms. *ACM SIGKDD Explorations Newsletter*, 13(2):50–64, 2012.

[18] G. Wang, S. Xie, B. Liu, and P. S. Yu. Review graph based online store review spammer detection. In *Proceedings of the 2011 IEEE 11th International Conference on Data Mining*, ICDM '11, pages 1242–1247, Washington, DC, USA, 2011. IEEE Computer Society.

Topic Modeling in Semantic Space with Keywords

Xiaojia Pu[1], Rong Jin[2,3], Gangshan Wu[1], Dingyi Han[3], Gui-Rong Xue[3]
[1]State Key Laboratory for Novel Software Technology, Nanjing University, Nanjing, China
[2]Department of Computer Science and Engineering, Michigan State University, East Lansing, USA
[3]Alibaba Group, Hangzhou, China
puxiaojia@gmail.com, gswu@nju.edu.cn,
{jinrong.jr,dingyi.han,grxue}@alibaba-inc.com

ABSTRACT

A common and convenient approach for user to describe his information need is to provide a set of keywords. Therefore, the technique to understand the need becomes crucial. In this paper, for the information need about a topic or category, we propose a novel method called TDCS(Topic Distilling with Compressive Sensing) for explicit and accurate modeling the topic implied by several keywords. The task is transformed as a topic reconstruction problem in the semantic space with a reasonable intuition that the topic is sparse in the semantic space. The latent semantic space could be mined from documents via unsupervised methods, e.g. LSI. Compressive sensing is leveraged to obtain a sparse representation from only a few keywords. In order to make the distilled topic more robust, an iterative learning approach is adopted. The experiment results show the effectiveness of our method. Moreover, with only a few semantic concepts remained for the topic, our method is efficient for subsequent text mining tasks.

Categories and Subject Descriptors

I.2.7 [**Artificial Intelligence**]: Natural Language Processing—*Text Analysis*; H.3.3 [**INFORMATION STORAGE AND RETRIEVAL**]: Information Search and Retrieval

Keywords

text mining, semantic space, compressive sensing

1. INTRODUCTION

With the rapid growth of Web data, there is an increasing need to get information on some interesting topics or categories. Due to the volume and velocity of Web data, it becomes crucial to provide an efficient and convenient way for users to get the information.

The interesting topic is often dynamic and differs a lot for various users. For example, one may be interested in 'food', while the other one is interested in 'sports'. It could be different in granularity. For example, compared with 'soccer', 'sports' is more coarse and 'world cup' is more fine. Moreover, the topic is often dynamic, which is context dependent. Therefore, it's almost impossible to define topic's categories and organize them in advance. It's essential to provide a flexible approach for user to acquire the information.

A common and convenient approach is that users describe the topic with several keywords, then an information system tries to understand the request and provide corresponding information service. The more accurately users describe the topic, the more precise service the information system could provide. In the usual manner of people's expressions, the system usually requires sufficient information to supply good service. However, in practice, a series of keywords are possible for indicating a topic if the user really has a clear information need. For example, the keywords, 'car, automobile, engine, sedan, bmw' probably imply an interest on the topic 'auto'. It's particularly attractive for the prompt need, since humans can quickly give keywords.

In such settings, given several keywords, the accurate understanding and modeling of the topic becomes an important and essential problem. The problem is not that easy, because sometimes the provided keywords are not sufficient. The complexity of the text representation and the randomness of provided keywords also increase the difficulty.

To address the problem, there are two kinds of existing methods. One is to tackle in the word space, such as bag of words(BOW) based method, e.g. VSM. The other kind of methods is to tackle in the semantic space.

VSM[23] is a purely term based method, in which the topic is represented as a bag of words, accounting for the number of occurrences of each term. This method is not sufficient for the problem, since there are many other words also beneficial to the topic.

Different with VSM, some methods try to exploit the semantic concepts or topics behind the documents or words, e.g. LSI, PLSI, LDA. Take example for LSI, through matrix decomposition, it builds a semantic space which, by intent, represents the semantic concepts in the dataset, and then projects both documents and words into the semantic dimensional space[6]. The most simple and natural approach is to model the topic in the semantic space by a projection from word space. However, it's still not accurate enough. Essentially, these methods construct semantic concepts by the exploitation of correlations among the co-occurring words. For a word, even it's strongly relevant with a topic, it's very likely to appear with the words

Permission to make digital or hard copies of all or part of this work for personal or classroom use is granted without fee provided that copies are not made or distributed for profit or commercial advantage and that copies bear this notice and the full citation on the first page. Copyrights for components of this work owned by others than ACM must be honored. Abstracting with credit is permitted. To copy otherwise, or republish, to post on servers or to redistribute to lists, requires prior specific permission and/or a fee. Request permissions from Permissions@acm.org.
CIKM'15, October 19–23, 2015, Melbourne, Australia.
© 2015 ACM. ISBN 978-1-4503-3794-6/15/10 ...$15.00.
DOI: http://dx.doi.org/10.1145/2806416.2806584.

mainly about other topics. Thus, the simple projection will inevitably introduce irrelevant semantic concepts which affects the precision of the topic.

Usually, a well specified topic should be cohesive in the semantic space[13][5]. In other words, the topic is sparse in the semantic space, which makes it possible to approximate the real semantic distribution of a topic with a few semantic concepts. In practice, utilizing only a few components of the semantic space to represent a topic could also lead to the computational efficiency in the following tasks, which is very beneficial especially for the big data. This is another important issue to motivate us to build a sparse model.

For our topic modeling problem, we try to construct a sparse topic in the semantic space with core semantic concepts. It's challenging because the number of keywords is too small. To this end, we propose a novel method called TDCS(Topic Distilling with Compressive Sensing), which aims to distill the topic in the semantic space from the keywords. The theory of compressive sensing(CS)[7][8] demonstrates that many natural signals are sparse or compressible in a transformed basis. Thus, we take advantage of CS to establish a sparse solution in the semantic space from only a few keywords. To make the result more robust, an iterative learning approach is adopted. Our proposed method is simple yet effective. Moreover, with only a few semantic concepts remained for the topic representation, our method is efficient for subsequent tasks, e.g. text classification.

The contributions of our paper can be summarized as follows:

1) To the best of our knowledge, we are the first one to use CS for topic modeling. We propose an effective method to distill the topic from only a few keywords which exploits and utilizes the sparsity of the semantic space.

2) Our method is very efficient, with less semantic components remained for topic representation, it can significantly reduce computational complexity for subsequent tasks.

3) Our method is flexible, which could be easily extended into other semantic spaces.

The rest of this paper is organized as follows. Firstly, the preliminaries are introduced in section 2. Then, our proposed method will be are described in detail in section 3 and 4. The experiments and results in section 5 demonstrate the effectiveness of our method. Some related works are discussed in section 6. Finally, we conclude our paper in section 7.

2. PRELIMINARIES

In this section, we give introduction on LSI and compressive sensing. Though we take LSI as the method for build the semantic space, our method could be easily extended into the semantic space built by other methods.

2.1 Latent Semantic Indexing

Latent semantic indexing(LSI) uses a standard matrix factorization technique, i.e. single value decomposition(SVD) to construct a latent semantic space.

Given the document-term matrix X of a corpus D, the d-th row X_d represents a document d in the corpus D. Supposing D is corpus of M documents, indexed by d. There are W distinct terms in the vocabulary.

Let the SVD of X be $X = U\Sigma V^T$, where the matrix U and V are orthogonal, and Σ is diagonal. The values $\sigma_1, \sigma_2, \ldots, \sigma_{min}\{W, M\}$ are the singular values of X.

For LSI, the matrix X is approximated by a rank-K approximation $\hat{X}$. This is usually done with a partial SVD using the singular vectors corresponding to the K largest singular values[1].

$$\hat{X} = \hat{U}\hat{\Sigma}\hat{V}^T \tag{1}$$

We can observe from Equation 1 that each term can be represented by the K-dimensional vector $\hat{T}_v$ which is the v-th row of the matrix $\hat{V}$. Similarly, the document also can be represented by the K-dimensional vector. Thus, LSI projects both terms and documents into a K-dimensional latent semantic space which could be utilized for some tasks, e.g. information retrieval.

Supposing we are given a query q which contains several terms, the query could be viewed as a short document and be projected into the latent semantic space using

$$\hat{q} = \Sigma^{-1}\hat{V}^T q. \tag{2}$$

From the practical perspective, LSI persists the principle semantic concepts in the dataset.

2.2 Compressive Sensing

Compressive sensing(CS) is an emerging technique to efficiently acquire and reconstruct a signal from a small number of non-adaptive linear measurements. The number of measurements are usually smaller than the dimension of the signal. [7][3].

The theory of CS is based on the observation that many natural signals are sparse or compressible. In other words, they have concise representations or structures when expressed in a transformed basis.

More precisely, as shown in Figure 1, let $x \in R^L$ denote a target signal in compressible basis Ψ, and $y \in R^n$ denote $n < L$ measurements of x, where $\Theta \in R^{n*L}$ is a measurement matrix, and we wish to recover the sparse signal $x \in R^L$ such that

$$y = \Theta x.$$

In the earliest studies of compressive sensing, the sparse signal recovery is cast into a linear programming problem:

$$\min_x |x|_1 \quad s.t. \quad |\Theta x - y|_2 \leq \epsilon, \tag{3}$$

where $|.|_1$ is the l_1 penalty function.

The sparse signal recovery could also be relaxed like LASSO, which aims to solve the following unconstrained l_1 regularized minimization problem by a non-linear procedure:

$$\min_x 1/2|\Theta x - y|_2^2 + \lambda|x|_1, \tag{4}$$

where λ is a regularization parameter.

When Θ satisfies the restricted isometry property (RIP)[4], one can reconstruct x by solving the above l_1 minimization problem[3][8]. The standard CS theory indicates that, an $s-$sparse vector in R^L can be recovered efficiently using $m = O(s\log(L/s))$ measurements[4].

3. OUR PROPOSED METHOD-TDCS

For our topic modeling problem, we want to build a topic representation upon the low level semantic concepts, and the training data are the keywords and the unlabeled text data.

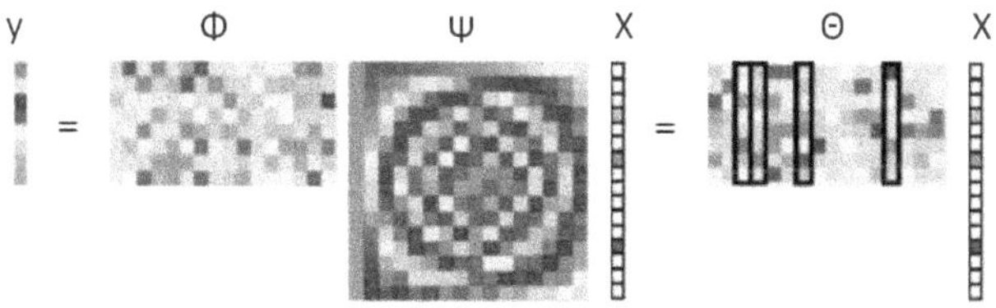

Figure 1: Illustration of Compressive Sensing.

3.1 Problem Definition

Previous topic modeling methods such as PLSA and LDA, model the documents as a mixture of hidden topics/latent semantic concepts, and each topic is usually a probability distribution over the words, w.r.t. $p(w|z)$, where z is the given topic, and w is the words in the vocabulary.

We aim to build a topic representation from several keywords upon the low level semantic concepts with the exploitation of semantic sparsity.

Specifically, given a dataset $D = \{d_1, ..., d_N\}$, and the keywords set $KS = \{keyword_1, ..., keyword_m\}$, we try to learn a topic T_{ks}, which is a distribution over low level semantic concepts/topics z, w.r.t. $p(z|T_{ks})$. T_{ks} is the topic described by the user provided keywords set KS, and z is the lower topics or semantic concepts mined from the documents via a unsupervised approach, e.g. LSI. Under the hypothesis of sparsity, most of the elements of the $p(z|T_{ks})$ are 0. Essentially, we want to refine the semantic concepts for the topic.

3.2 TDCS Framework

The reasonable hypothesis is that the topic is sparse in the semantic space. With the exploitation of the sparsity, we aim to obtain a more concise topic representation. That not only just means a more accurate topic, but also a significant improvement in computation efficiency. The challenging is that the number of keywords is usually very small and random.

We propose a TDCS(Topic Distilling with Compressive Sensing) framework for the problem. In the framework, the keywords are taken as the measurements, and the topic is constructed in the transformed semantic space. One-hot representation is used for each keyword's representation in word space, and they are projected into semantic space to build the measurement matrix. The value of the measurement is the probability or the confidence about the keyword's relevance with the target topic.

Though CS has excellent properties for this kind of task, there still exists the theoretical guideline. Ideally, based on the sparsity hypothesis, if the provided keywords are accurate and sufficient enough, the topic could be reconstructed efficiently. In practice, there are two crucial issues needed to care about. Firstly, the provided keywords may not be accurate enough. Secondly, the number of provided keywords may be smaller than the theoretical bound, though the bound is not very tight. Both the two issues could result in not reliable results. Therefore, an iterative learning approach is adopted to make the result more robust in our method.

The detailed framework and procedure is shown in Figure 2. A unsupervised method e.g. LSI is used to build the original latent semantic space. The keywords are taken as the training data. Firstly, the keywords in word space are projected into semantic space. Compressive sensing is utilized to construct the initial topic representation from them. After the initial topic representation generated, the topic will be reflected into word space in the feedback stage. In feedback stage, we choose the words most likely relevant with the topic to enrich the keywords set, i.e. updating the training data. Then with new keywords set, the learning procedure is conducted once again. The process will be repeated several times. If the stop criteria is satisfied, the iteration will be terminated.

For the convenience to understand the formulation and our proposed method, we list the detailed notation of each variables in Table 1.

Table 1: Notation of the Variables

variable	describtion
D	the dataset
X	document-term representation of the dataset
d	the document
Voc	the vocabulary of the dataset
N	the size of the vocabulary
KS	the set of keywords
m	number of keywords
K	the dimension of LSI's semantic space
L	the dimension of original signal space
s	the dimension of sparse signal
y	corresponding measurement values
A	the measurement matrix
T_{ks}	the topic implied by KS
$p(z\|T_{ks})$	the topic representation of T_{ks}
z	the semantic concepts/topics mined from data

4. TDCS_LSI

In this paper, we take the LSI to build the latent semantic space, so we call the method TDCS_LSI here. Our method could be easily extended into the semantic space built by other methods.

4.1 Latent Semantic Space Building

LSI is used to build the latent semantic space from the document-term matrix X. Ideally, a larger dataset could obtain a better semantic space. The common used term representation method is TFIDF[18], however, for some tasks, there are other better methods.

Through LSI, the term document matrix X will be decomposed into three components. For matrix V, each dimension v of $V = (v_1, ..., v_K)$ corresponds to a particular semantic concept and they are orthogonal with each other. The dimension v of V could be viewed as the semantic concept/topic z described in Section 3.1.

Since the matrix V is orthogonal, according to CS theory[4], the RIP criteria will be surely satisfied. V will be taken as the semantic basis, which corresponds to matrix Ψ in Figure 1.

The matrix size of X is usually very large and sparse for large data set, so we use an approximated algorithm PSVD[1] for LSI, which pursuits the singular vectors corresponding to the K largest singular values. K is an empirical value and should be carefully set.

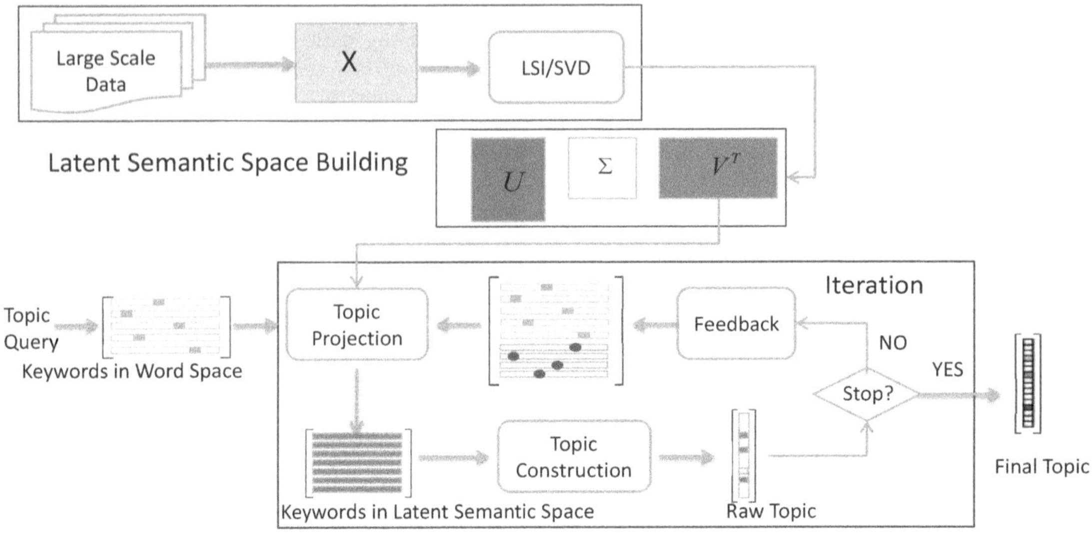

Figure 2: Procedure of the proposed TDCS method.

4.2 Keywords Projection to Semantic Space

The keywords are taken as the measurements, in this section, we will explain in detail how to build the measurement matrix through projecting keywords from word space to semantic space.

To represent the keyword of KS in word space, common used one-hot representation method is utilized. Specifically, for $keywrod_i$, the corresponding representation is

$$e_{idx_i} = (0 \dots, 1, \dots, 0)^T,$$

where idx_i is the index of the $keyword_i$ in the vocabulary Voc, and the corresponding element is 1 while others are 0.

All the keywords will compose the matrix

$$e = (e_{idx_1}, e_{idx_2}, \dots, e_{idx_m})^T, \tag{5}$$

where m denotes the number of keywords, and each row corresponds to a keyword.

For $keyword_i$, the projection from word space to semantic space will be

$$a_i = e^T_{idx_i} V,$$

a_i is the semantic distribution of $keyword_i$. Since each row of matrix V could be viewed as a words' semantic distribution in the latent semantic space, the projection essentially selects the corresponding semantic distribution of $keyword_i$.

The full projection of the keywords e will be

$$A = eV, \tag{6}$$

where each row of A i.e. a_i corresponds to a keyword's semantic distribution.

Under the CS framework, keywords are taken as the measurements, so the matrix e corresponds to Φ in Figure 1 and the matrix A corresponds to the measurement matrix Θ in Figure 1. The measurement values could be written as the vector below

$$y = (y_1, y_2, \dots, y_m)^T, \tag{7}$$

where $y_i = pro\_relevance(keyword_i, T_{ks}) \in (0, 1]$, which is the confidence or probability of the relevance between the keyword and the interesting topic.

Ideally, the user should provide the confidence value to each keyword, in practice, we take 1 as the default value which means all the keywords user provided are strongly relevant with the topic.

The training data KS could be written as a set of pairs, e.g. $\{keyword_i, y_i\}$.

4.3 Topic Construction with CS

The intuition is that the topic is sparse in the latent semantic space. Therefore, we try to find a subspace in V that can best construct and approximate the topic.

The distribution of topic T_{ks} is $p(z|T_{ks})$, for convenience, here we use α instead.

$$\alpha = (\alpha_1, \dots, \alpha_K)^T,$$

α_i measures how important the corresponding semantic concept v_i contributes to the target topic.

For each pair $\{keyword_i, y_i\}$ in the keywords set KS, the equation below should be satisfied.

$$a_i \alpha \approx y_i \tag{8}$$

Thus, for all pairs $\{keyword_i, y_i\} (i = 1, \dots, m)$, we need to find a α, such that,

$$A\alpha \approx y, \tag{9}$$

where $m << K$.

This is a standard compressive sensing problem. The matrix A is the measurement matrix, corresponding to Θ, and the y is the measurement value. α corresponds to the x in Figure 1.

Following compressive sensing approach, the optimization problem will be

$$\alpha_* = arg\ \min_{\alpha} |A\alpha - y|_2^2 + \lambda|\alpha|_1, \tag{10}$$

where y is set as 1 for all keywords in default as we described in last section. λ is the regularization parameter, which controls the degree of the sparsity. A larger λ always means a more sparse result.

The above problem is a sparse optimization problem because of the l_1 term, and in order to solve it efficiently, the package SLEP[1] is facilitated. The details of the package are described in [16] which implements several state-of-art methods for this kind of optimization problem.

λ is a very common parameter for LASSO as well as other sparse models, it's usually tuned in an interval via cross validation in the development set. We will give more detailed description about the parameter tuning in the experiments session.

This approach guarantees that α_* is sparse, i.e., most elements of $\alpha*$ is zero. That's consistent with our previous assumption that only a few latent semantic concepts contribute to a topic.

4.4 Iterative Learning Approach

Though the compressive sensing has excellent properties in many applications. However, in practice, sometimes, the number of keywords is too small to yield reliable results since the robust reconstruction needs sufficient measurements according to compressive sensing theory. The quality of the provided keywords is also an important issue for the topic construction.

Thus, an iterative approach is adopted to make the compressive sensing algorithm more robust for our task. This is a heuristic method to approximate a more stable topic representation.

To be specific, as shown in Figure 2, when an initial topic is generated through compressive sensing, we reflect the topic into word space in the feedback stage. For the reflection, the equation below is utilized,

$$\omega_* = V\alpha_*, \tag{11}$$

the parameter ω_* is the weight of words.

In feedback stage, we choose the words highly relevant with the topic as incremental keywords, w.r.t. IKS. The measurement value y_j of $keyword_j$ in IKS is set as the weight of the $keyword_j$ in ω_* after normalization.

IKS is added into the original keywords set KS to compose a new training set.

$$KS' = KS \cup IKS \tag{12}$$

where $IKS = \{\{keyword_j, y_j\} \dots\}$.

Through several rounds of compressive sensing and feedback, the topic will tend to stable.

During the iteration, an important factor is the size of the IKS, w.r.t. δ.

$$\delta = |IKS|_0 \tag{13}$$

If it's too small, the iteration will be too slow, however, if it's too large, the iteration will shock and lead to the deviation of real topic. The size is fine tuned in experiments by cross validation.

Another important issue is when to terminate the iteration. We could calculate the difference value between the last two topic's distribution, if the differ is small than a predefined threshold value, a converged solution is obtained. This method is sensitive to the threshold value which should be carefully tuned. An alternative strategy is to measure the difference in the word space, if the IKS no longer brings in new keywords for KS, we could consider to stop the iteration. It's usually equal with former one, and more practical, therefore we utilize this strategy in our method.

[1] http://yelab.net/software/SLEP/

Through our TDCS method, we get a sparse topic representation, i.e. α_* from the keywords KS, which captures the core semantic concepts and assign suitable weights(values) to them.

The detailed algorithm of our TDCS method is shown in Algorithm 1.

Algorithm 1 The detailed TDCS algorithm

input:
  document-term matrix X
  initial keyword list KS
output:
  topic representation: α_*
  w of vocabulary
% latent semantic space building
D is decomposed into $U\Sigma V^T$
repeat
    for each keyword in KS **do**
        generate the corresponding e_i
    end for
    generate the matrix e
    % topic projection
    $A = e * V$;
    % topic α
    find the α_* s.t. $min \quad |A\alpha - y|_2^2 + \lambda|\alpha|_1$
    % topic feedback
    $w = V * \alpha_*$;
    choose the words with highest weight
    form an incremental keyword list IKS
    $KS' = KS \cup IKS$;
    % update the training data
    $KS = KS'$
until $IKS - KS \approx NULL$

4.5 TDCS for Text Mining Tasks

With our TDCS method, the topic $p(z|T_{ks})$ i.e. α_* is learnt from the keywords KS, which could be used for many subsequent text mining tasks with the benefits both in accuracy and efficiency, for example, text classification, information retrieval. In this section, we give an introduction of the detailed usage.

4.5.1 Text Mining Tasks

Text Classification

For text classification, the interesting topic will be the category(class) in a dataset. Given a list of keywords to representing different categories, the objective is to learn a model to classify the documents. It becomes the problem called text classification by labeling words [15][11], existing methods are all tackling in the word space.

Usually, a linear classification model could be written as $g(f_w(x_i))$, where

$$f_w(x_i) = \omega^T x_i, \tag{14}$$

and $g(.)$ could be 0/1 function, sigmoid function, etc.

The loss function of for training the linear classification could be

$$J(w) = \sum_i L(y_i, f_w(x_i)) + \lambda R(w)$$

where the L could be square loss, log loss, hinge loss, etc. The $R(w)$ is the regularization term.

$f_w(x_i)$ is the most important part for these kinds of classifiers, which is the product of the parameter w and x_i, measuring the similarly between an instance and target class. For text classification, usually, x_i is the BOW representation of a document d_i, the classifiers try to learn a optimal w_* from the training data for $f_w(x_i)$.

Here, the training data is the keywords, different with existing methods, our method could skillfully transform the problem into semantic space. For one class classification, by projecting documents x into a K-dimensional semantic space, w.r.t. x', the w' will be learnt in the K-dimensional semantic space. The α_* learnt by our method is a very good choice as the w'_* for $f_{w'}(.)$.

Information Retrieval

For information retrieval, the keywords KS are treated as the query, w.r.t. q, the VSM[23] model will represent the query q and document d in word space, and then calculate the similarity between them with

$$sim(q, d) = q \cdot d. \tag{15}$$

For LSI, both the query and document in word space are projected into semantic space w.r.t. q' and d' following Equation 2, and then $sim(q', d')$ is calculated similar with VSM by Equation 15.

With our method, the query q is refined in the semantic space, a more accurate and concise q'' i.e. α_* could be used for the similarity calculation as below.

$$sim(q, d) = \alpha_* \cdot d' \tag{16}$$

4.5.2 *Computational Efficiency*

The main computation for text classification or information retrieval is the product between Q and $R(d)$, w.r.t. $Q \cdot R(d)$, here Q stands for w in $f_w(.)$ or q in $sim(q, d)$, $R(d)$ stands for x_i in $f_w(.)$ or d in $sim(q, d)$.

The original dimension of Q and $R(d)$ is N, N is the size of vocabulary. After the projection, N will be reduced to K. With our method, the effective dimension of Q for product calculation will be s, $s < K$. Usually, s is one order smaller than K. That means a great gain in computational complexity.

With our method, the theoretical time complexity for production will decrease from $O(N * M)$ or $O(K * M)$ to $O(s * M)$, where M is the size of dataset.

5. EXPERIMENTS

The topic representation is hard to evaluate directly, instead, we evaluate it in an indirect way. It will be utilized for concrete text mining tasks, here we choose text classification as the task and we will verify the effectiveness of our method through the performance of classification.

The evaluation metric AUC(Area under the Curve of ROC) is adopted to measure the performance[9]. A larger AUC indicates better performance.

Since the users are used to provide positive keywords for a target category which is similar with information retrieval, our task here is one class text classification, aiming to identity target category documents from unlabeled set.

The keywords generation process will be given in the experiments setting section. We will learn from each keywords set respectively.

All the experiments are performed on a PC with two Intel Xeon E5-2620 @ 2.0GHz CPUs and 8GB memory.

5.1 Datasets

We use the following datasets in our experiments, i.e. **20 Newsgroups**[2], **WebKB**[3] and **Movie Reviews**[4].

- **20 Newsgroups** The 20 Newsgroups data set is a collection of newsgroup documents and organized into 20 different newsgroups, each corresponding to a topic. Some of the newsgroups are very closely related to each other, while others are highly unrelated.
- **WebKB** The WebKB dataset contains web pages gathered from university computer science departments. The web pages are composed of 4 categories: *student*, *course*, *faculty* or *project*.
- **Movie Reviews** This dataset is a collection of movie reviews from IMDB. The movies are labeled with their overall sentiment polarity (positive or negative)[22].

All datasets were processed using lowercased stemmed unigram words, with HTML tags, stop-words and words with length less than three removed.

Table 2 summarizes the datasets statistics after these processing. For each dataset, we randomly select 1/5 of the dataset as the testing data, and use the rest of the dataset as training set.

Table 2: Dataset

data set	instances	categories	words
20 Newsgroups	18828	20	19789
WebKB	4199	4	7770
Movie Reviews	2000	2	13843

5.2 Methods for Comparison

The task here is one class text classification, . The labeled training data will be keywords other than documents. Existing standard methods for one class classification, such as one-class SVM[17] and PU learning[12] are not appropriate for the task , since they require sufficient labeled documents, so they .

GE/SWIRL

Since this task is to learn a classifier from keywords, we take GE/SWIRL[11] as the method for comparison, which is a state-of-the-art method for learning from features(words). GE/SWIRL is developed from GE(Generalized Expectation) which seeks a distribution that matches a set of given reference distribution over corresponding label if the feature(word) is given and utilizes the sequence information of the words. In this paper, for simplicity, the sequence is not considered.

Generalized Expectation (GE) with logistic regression is an existing framework for training classifiers with labeled features. The framework is designed for multi-class classification with multiple keywords sets, for convince, we modify it for one class classification by set the target class value of each keyword as 0.99 while the value of other classes as 0.01.

[2]http://people.cs.umass.edu/m̃ccallum/data.html
[3]http://www.cs.cmu.edu/w̃ebkb
[4]http://www.cs.cornell.edu/people/pabo/movie-review-data/

VSM and LSI

If we take the documents which belong to the target category as the relevant documents for the user provided keywords. This task could be viewed as a coarse-granularly information retrieval. Therefore, we also take the VSM and LSI as the methods for comparison.

For our TDCS method, the classifier is the $g(f_w(x))$, where $g(.)$ is 0/1 function, and $f_w(x) = \alpha_* \cdot x$.

For all the methods, one keywords set is trained each time as well as our TDCS method.

5.3 Experiment Settings

5.3.1 Topic Description(Keywords) Generation

user provided approach

Some real user provided keyword lists[11] are utilized for **WebKB** and **Movie Reviews**. In [11], the labeled keywords are formatted as list of {keyword,label} pairs. The labels are the categories. We extract the keywords from the list as the user generated keywords.

oracle approach

Ideally, a keyword should be highly predictive of the topic. In practice, we assume there exists an oracle that can reveal the keywords. We then select keyword according to their predictive power measured by TFIDF score of the given category. This is applied for **20 Newsgroups** because there're no public human labeled keywords for this dataset.

We created a keywords pool for each topic(category) of the datasets, the keywords are collected with above approaches. During the experiments, the keywords for a topic are randomly selected from the pool.

5.3.2 Implementation Details

All documents are represented by the vector of words. For term weighting method, **20 Newsgroups** and **WebKB** is tfidf , and **Movie Reviews** is 0/1, i.e. the occurrence of a word or not. There have been some works shown that for sentiment classification, the 0/1 representation is better than tfidf upon most of classification models[14].

Once the document-term matrices of training data generated, LSI is applied to build the semantic space. The dimension of the semantic space, i.e. K is empirically set as 200, which is a commonly used value[18].

The parameter λ in Equation 10 and δ in Equation 13 are fine tuned via cross validation. We randomly select 1/10 of the training data as the development set and conduct the parameter tuning in the development set. The parameter λ is tuned firstly without iteration, and then the δ is tuned.

The tuning procedure is simple, several keywords sets are chosen to build the models with different parameter values. The models will be utilized in the development dataset, after the evaluation of their performance, the parameter value of the best model is set as the final value.

The parameter λ is tuned in $[1e-5, 1e-4, 1e-3, 1e-2, 1e-1, 1]$, and δ is tuned in the interval $[1, \frac{m}{2}]$. After tuning, the value of λ used in the experiments is 0.01, and the value of δ is $\lfloor \frac{m}{2} \rfloor$.

5.4 Experiment Results

We evaluate the performance with different topic descriptions as well as different number of keywords, and give detailed analysis of the iterative approach.

For each category of the datasets, we repeated the experiments 100 times. In order to investigate general influence by the number of keywords, we randomly choose 5 and 10 keywords respectively each time to describe the topic in Movie Reviews. For 20 Newsgroups, we randomly choose 5 keywords as the topic description each time. For WebKB, we randomly choose keywords with variable-length from 5 to 10 each time. Table 3 summarizes the keyword numbers for each dataset.

The average results in three benchmark datasets is shown in Table 4[5]. The corresponding keywords setup is shown in Table 3. The only difference between Movie Reviews(k1) and Movie Reviews(k2) is the number of keywords provided.

Table 3: number of keywords for each dataset

dataset	number of keywords
Movie Reviews (k1)	5
Movie Reviews (k2)	10
20 Newsgroups	5
WebKB	5-10

Table 4: average results of three datasets

dataset	VSM	LSI	GE/SWIRL	TDCS
Movie Rev. (k1)	0.528	**0.545**	0.540	**0.596***
Movie Rev. (k2)	0.561	0.572	**0.584**	**0.619***
20 Newsgroups	0.578	**0.918**	0.891	**0.944***
WebKB	0.705	0.784	**0.802**	**0.825***

5.4.1 General Results

We can observe that in all the datasets and with different keyword setups, our TDCS method outperforms the other methods[6], which demonstrates the effectiveness and robustness of our method, and reveals that the distilled topic is more precise for text classification.

We can also find that when number of keywords is small, e.g. 5 in **Movie Reviews** and **20 Newsgroups**, the LSI is better than GE/SWIRL. However, GE/SWIRL will be better when the number increases, e.g. 10 in **Movie Reviews** and 5-10 in **WebKB**. A possible reason is that the LSI is superior in improving the recall especially when the number of keywords is too small. However, when the number of keywords increase, the impact of this aspect will be not obvious.

Essentially, in comparison with LSI, our method not only takes advantage of the semantic space to improve the recall, but also utilizes the semantic sparsity to distill important semantic components from the semantic space which lead to the improvement of precision.

The general results in **Movie Reviews** are not very good compared with the other two datasets, a possible reason is that the latent semantic space built by LSI is not ideal for sentiment classification. It's hard to guess what the basis vectors in the LSI space may correspond to. However, from the experiment results, it seems that there should be some

[5]The best and second best results are bold in text.

[6]* The improvement is statistically significant, since the p value < 0.05 according to t test.

semantic concepts highly relevant with sentiments since our method could get better results than others. With a better semantic space for sentiment analysis, the results of our method will be surely better.

In **20 Newsgroups**, we can find that LSI, GE/SWIRL and our TDCS method all get good results compared with the other datasets. The main reason is the generation approach of the keywords. We choose the keywords with high tfidf values as the topic descriptions, they are representative for the category and discriminative with other categories.

5.4.2 General Quantitative Analysis

From the results of **Movie Reviews** in Table 4, we can find that, roughly, when the number of keywords grows, the performance grows. The average result with 10 keywords is better than that with only 5 keywords. This suggests that for a robust topic construction with CS, sufficient measurements are needed.

Less Wins More: From Table 4 we can also find that our method can get better results with 5 keywords than VSM, LSI and GE/SWIRL with 10 keywords. This shows the advantage of our method especially when training data is small. With less training data, here is the 1/2 of the training data, our method could still get comparable and even better results. This very useful, since people are used to provide as few keywords as possible for a topic.

5.4.3 Detailed Results on Movie Reviews

In Table 5, we illustrate some detailed examples from the results in movie data. The detailed topic descriptions are shown in Table 6. These topic descriptions are all generated for the 'positive' category.

Table 5: results of examples on Movie Reviews

index	VSM	LSI	GE/SWIRL	TDCS
TD_1	0.508	0.502	**0.510**	**0.627**
TD_2	**0.514**	0.506	0.510	**0.518**
TD_3	0.580	**0.671**	0.647	**0.803**
TD_4	0.611	0.626	**0.642**	**0.743**
TD_5	0.551	0.564	**0.610**	**0.664**
TD_6	0.550	0.568	**0.594**	**0.647**

Table 6: keyword examples of the Movie Reviews

index	topic desc.
TD_1	talent, cool, alwai, laugh, great
TD_2	heartfelt, high, esteem, worth, provoc
TD_3	oscar, uniqu, easili, touch, esteem
TD_4	worth, inspir, entertain, great, amaz, uniqu, emot, success, astound, imagin
TD_5	love, modern, interest, nice, award, cclaim, top, success, excruciatingli, captiv
TD_6	heartwarm, must, incred, adventur, touch, special, represent, excel, provoc, funni

We can observe that the results are sensitive to the keywords provided, even though the number of keywords are the same with each other. For example, the keyword 'high' in TD_2 is not very good to indicate the positive sentiment, so the result is worse than others. Though TD_3 only has 5 keywords, it could even get the better result than those with 10 keywords. This reveals that the quality of the keywords is also an important factor for our method, i.e. the provided keywords should be representative for the topic.

The performance of topic TD_1 (5 keywords) with our method, is better than TD_4, TD_5 and TD_6 (10 keywords) with SVM or LSI method. This also demonstrates the effectiveness of our method, with 1/2 of training data, our method can get better results than those with full data.

5.4.4 Detailed Results on WebKB

Table 7 shows some detailed results on WebKB for 'faculty' category. The topic descriptions are given with variable size.

The result is not strictly in proportion to the number of keywords. That's reasonable, take example for TD_1 and TD_2, they are better than TD_3. The word 'depart' and 'email' in TD_3 are also possible in the 'student' category. This also suggests that good quality of the keywords is essential.

Table 7: keyword examples of the WebKB data

index	topic desc.	TDCS
TD_1	teacher, staff, professor, ta, teach	0.843
TD_2	advisori, editori, profession, director, coauthor	0.851
TD_3	teach, experi, educ, depart, email, graduat	0.712
TD_4	teacher, professor, career, job, faculti, depart, staff	0.860

5.4.5 Impact of Iteration

We give an example in 20 Newsgroups to show the impact of our iterative learning approach. The topic description T_1 and T_2 in Table 8 are both generated for the 'auto' category. Figure 3 shows the performance of text classification after each iteration. In general, the performance increases along with the increase of iteration numbers.

Table 8: keyword examples of the 20 Newsgroups

index	topic description
T_1	gear, bumper, chrysler, mazda, overpass
T_2	sedan, clutch, jetta, ferrari, dealer

Keywords Expansion: We also list the keywords which are mostly relevant with the topic description T_1 and T_2 respectively in Table 9. The keywords are picked from the final expanded set KS, and for each topic, we choose the top 20 keywords. We can find that if the user really have an interest on this topic, and give accurate descriptions, though the initial given keywords are different, the final expanded relevant keywords are very close. This gives an insight for better keyword recommendation.

Ideally, for a topic, if the descriptions are accurate enough, after the iteration, the constructed topic representations in semantic space will tend to be close. In practice, due to the semantic diversity of the keywords provided by different users, the difference between the distilled topic representations is unavoidable. The iterative learning approach could reduce the difference.

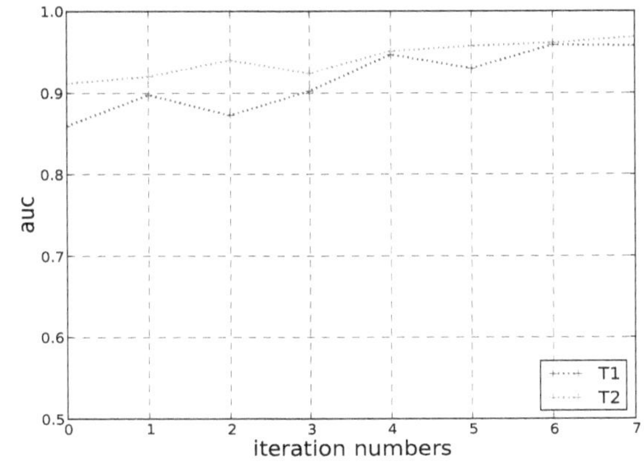

Figure 3: Classification performance along iteration

Table 9: Expanded Keywords on 20 Newsgroups

topic desc.	T_1	T_2
relevant keywords	car, opel, detector, owner, version, price, clutch, engin, color, nissan, auto, dealer, manual, ford, widget, model, drive, oil, toyota, speed	car, version, detector, engin, clutch, nissan, drive, auto, opel, ford, dealer, oil, honda, model, mile, bmw, toyota, speed, insur, audi

5.4.6 *Computation Cost for Text Classification*

Table 10 shows the average classification time for each dataset. The time duration is measured in seconds. We can see that with our method, the computation cost is smaller in a order of magnitude.

The computation is conducted with Matlab, which optimizes the matrix computation in memory, and datasets used in our experiments are tiny in comparison with real world datasets, therefore the total computation time is little. However, for real web data, which contains millions of documents, the difference will absolutely become larger, e.g. 1 hour vs. 10 hours.

Table 10: Classification Time

Data Set	VSM	LSI	TDCS
20 Newsgroups	7.45e-2	8.96e-4	1.29e-4
WebKB	9.6e-3	2.30e-4	5.69e-5
Movie Reviews	9.0e-3	1.78e-4	4.61e-5

Another issue for big data is that it's impossible to load all the data once a time. The frequent data throughput is essential, which is usually time-consuming. With the effective dimension reduction through our method, more data could be loaded into the memory for computation each time which is efficient and beneficial for text classification, information retrieval, etc.

Summary: We have presented comprehensive experiments using three different text collections to evaluate the effectiveness of the proposed TDCS method. In general, with more keywords, the result will be more accurate. The quality of the keywords is also an important issue. Moreover, with the reduction in the topic representation space, the computation complexity significantly reduces.

6. RELATED WORK

Our work focuses on the topic construction in the latent semantic space, in this paper, we take LSI to build the semantic space, and surely our method could be extended to other semantic spaces. Meanwhile, there have been arising works on the utilization of semantic sparsity in text mining recently.

6.1 Semantic Representation

There have been other methods for construct latent semantic concepts/topics, for example, PLSA[10] and LDA[2]. They are the typical techniques aiming to find useful latent semantic structure in the unstructured collection. They assume that each document exhibits multiple topics, yet ignores the correlation between topics. PLSA could be formulated a generation process including the document topic distribution and topic word distribution. It's highly sensitive to task domain, which is continuously changing in real documents. Different with PLSA, LDA uncovers the underlying semantic structure based on a hierarchical Bayesian analysis of the original texts. Thus, it becomes computationally very expensive on large data sets.

Word2Vec has emerged as a new technique to learn the distributed representation of words. The neural language model is used to represent the documents, and the learning algorithm is a combination of neural networks and softmax model[19]. It's a popular word embedding method, and was previously better than LSI for preserving linear regularities among words. [21] tells us that word2vec is essentially equivalent with the implicit matrix decomposition with some mathematical explanations.

These works give us a probability to extend our method into semantic representation space built by other methods.

6.2 Semantic Sparsity

In [5], a sparse latent semantic analysis model is proposed for text analysis, in which, the keyword distribution of each topic is sparse. In [20], they decompose the topic into low-rank principle component and sparse document component. The work is conducted on the assumption that each document has its own specific keywords which is sparse in comparison with other documents. In [25], a regularized LSI was proposed to obtain sparse semantic concepts(topics) belong to a document, aiming to scale up LSI for large document sets. In [24], a variation model of PLSI and LDA is proposed to fully leverage the sparsity of topics belonging to a document, which is efficient for large scale data.[13] propose a dual-sparse topic model with the hypothesis that in real-world scenarios, individual documents usually concentrate on several salient topics instead of covering a wide variety of topics. A real topic also adopts a narrow range of terms instead of a wide coverage of the vocabulary.

All these works are tackling the sparsity on documents or topics or words, and building models from the document data set. Our work is different with these works. Firstly, our mission is to construct a more concise topic upon the latent semantic space with the sparsity assumption. Secondly, we need to build the topic from only several keywords rather than documents.

7. CONCLUSION

In this paper, we propose a method called TDCS to distill the topic from dynamically provided keywords. The sparsity of the topic is exploited and utilized, and CS is skillfully applied to establish a sparse structure in the semantic space for the topic. With our method, a more precise topic could be obtained. Besides, our method is efficient for subsequent tasks with the significant reduction of computation.

The experiments on several benchmark datasets demonstrate the effectiveness of our method. Besides text classification, the TDCS method could be used for many other applications, for example, information retrieval, query understanding, keywords recommendation, since which could provide more accurate semantic information.

Our approach and results give promising future research direction towards the investigation of sparsity in text analysis. We would like to extend our work using other semantic representation methods in the future, and further explore the theoretical perspectives about this method.

8. ACKNOWLEDGMENTS

This work is supported by the National Science Foundation of China(No.61321491, No.61202320), National Social Science Foundation of China(No.11AZD121), and Natural Science Foundation of Jiangsu Province(No.BK2012304). It was also partially supported by Collaborative Innovation Center of Novel Software Technology and Industrialization.

9. REFERENCES

[1] M. W. Berry. Large scale sparse singular value computations. *International Journal of Supercomputer Applications*, 6:13–49, 1992.

[2] D. M. Blei, A. Y. Ng, and M. I. Jordan. Latent dirichlet allocation. *J. Mach. Learn. Res.*, 3:993–1022, Mar. 2003.

[3] E. J. Candes, J. Romberg, and T. Tao. Robust uncertainty principles: Exact signal reconstruction from highly incomplete frequency information. *IEEE Transactions on Information Theory*, 52(2):489–509, Feb. 2006.

[4] E. J. Candes, J. K. Romberg, and T. Tao. Stable signal recovery from incomplete and inaccurate measurements. *Communications on pure and applied mathematics*, 59(8):1207–1223, 2006.

[5] X. Chen, Y. Qi, B. Bai, Q. Lin, and J. G. Carbonell. Sparse latent semantic analysis. In *Proceedings of the 2011 SIAM International Conference on Data Mining*, pages 474–485, 2011.

[6] S. C. Deerwester, S. T. Dumais, T. K. Landauer, G. W. Furnas, and R. A. Harshman. Indexing by latent semantic analysis. *JASIS*, 41(6):391–407, 1990.

[7] D. L. Donoho. Compressed sensing. *IEEE Transactions on Information Theory*, 52:1289–1306, 2006.

[8] D. L. Donoho. For most large underdetermined systems of linear equations the minimal l1-norm solution is also the sparsest solution. *Communications on Pure and Applied Mathematics*, 59(6):797–829, 2006.

[9] J. A. Hanley and B. J. McNeil. The meaning and use of the area under a receiver operating characteristic (roc) curve. *Radiology*, 143(1):29–36, 1982.

[10] T. Hofmann. Probabilistic latent semantic indexing. In *Proceedings of the 22Nd Annual International ACM SIGIR Conference on Research and Development in Information Retrieval*, SIGIR '99, pages 50–57, New York, NY, USA, 1999. ACM.

[11] K.-S. Jun, J. Zhu, B. Settles, and T. Rogers. Learning from human-generated lists. In *Proceedings of the 30th International Conference on Machine Learning*, ICML'13, pages 181–189, 2013.

[12] X. Li and B. Liu. Learning to classify texts using positive and unlabeled data. In *IJCAI*, volume 3, pages 587–592, 2003.

[13] T. Lin, W. Tian, Q. Mei, and H. Cheng. The dual-sparse topic model: mining focused topics and focused terms in short text. In *Proceedings of the 23rd international conference on World wide web*, pages 539–550. International World Wide Web Conferences Steering Committee, 2014.

[14] B. Liu. Sentiment analysis and opinion mining. *Synthesis Lectures on Human Language Technologies*, 5(1):1–167, 2012.

[15] B. Liu, X. Li, W. S. Lee, and P. S. Yu. Text classification by labeling words. In *AAAI*, volume 4, pages 425–430, 2004.

[16] J. Liu, S. Ji, and J. Ye. *SLEP: Sparse Learning with Efficient Projections*. Arizona State University, 2009.

[17] L. M. Manevitz and M. Yousef. One-class svms for document classification. *the Journal of machine Learning research*, 2:139–154, 2002.

[18] C. D. Manning, P. Raghavan, and H. Schütze. *Introduction to Information Retrieval*. Cambridge University Press, New York, NY, USA, 2008.

[19] T. Mikolov, K. Chen, G. Corrado, and J. Dean. Efficient estimation of word representations in vector space. *arXiv preprint arXiv:1301.3781*, 2013.

[20] K. Min, Z. Zhang, J. Wright, and Y. Ma. Decomposing background topics from keywords by principal component pursuit. In *Proceedings of the 19th ACM International Conference on Information and Knowledge Management*, CIKM '10, pages 269–278, New York, NY, USA, 2010. ACM.

[21] Y. G. Omer Levy. Neural word embedding as implicit matrix factorization. In *Advances in Neural Information Processing Systems 27*. Curran Associates, Inc., 2014.

[22] B. Pang and L. Lee. A sentimental education: Sentiment analysis using subjectivity summarization based on minimum cuts. In *Proceedings of the ACL*, 2004.

[23] G. Salton, A. Wong, and C. S. Yang. A vector space model for automatic indexing. *Commun. ACM*, 18(11):613–620, Nov. 1975.

[24] K. Than and T. B. Ho. Fully sparse topic models. In *Machine Learning and Knowledge Discovery in Databases*, pages 490–505. Springer, 2012.

[25] Q. Wang, J. Xu, H. Li, and N. Craswell. Regularized latent semantic indexing. In *Proceedings of the 34th International ACM SIGIR Conference on Research and Development in Information Retrieval*, SIGIR '11, pages 685–694, New York, NY, USA, 2011. ACM.

F1: Accelerating the Optimization of Aggregate Continuous Queries

Anatoli U. Shein, Panos K. Chrysanthis, Alexandros Labrinidis
Department of Computer Science
University of Pittsburgh
(aus, panos, labrinid)@cs.pitt.edu

ABSTRACT

Data Stream Management Systems performing on-line analytics rely on the efficient execution of large numbers of Aggregate Continuous Queries (*ACQs*). The state-of-the-art *WeaveShare* optimizer uses the *Weavability* concept in order to selectively combine *ACQs* for partial aggregation and produce high quality execution plans. However, *WeaveShare* does not scale well with the number of *ACQs*. In this paper we propose a novel closed formula, *F*1, that accelerates *Weavability* calculations, and thus allows *WeaveShare* to achieve exceptional scalability in systems with heavy workloads. In general, *F*1 can reduce the computation time of any technique that combines partial aggregations within composite slides of multiple *ACQs*. We theoretically analyze the *Bit Set* approach currently used by *WeaveShare* and show that *F*1 is superior in both time and space complexities. We show that *F*1 performs $\sim 10^{62}$ times less operations compared to *Bit Set* to produce the same execution plan for the same input. We experimentally show that *F*1 executes up to 60,000 times faster and can handle 1,000,000 *ACQs* in a setting where the limit for the current technique is 550.

1. INTRODUCTION

Nowadays more and more applications are becoming available to wider audiences, resulting in an increase in the amount of data produced. In order to cope with the sheer volume of information, enterprises move to *Cloud* Infrastructures to minimize the purchase and maintenance cost of machinery, and be able to scale their services including on-line analytics.

On-line data analytics have gained momentum in many applications that need to ingest data fast and apply some form of computation. Data streams are part of this broader category of data management, where Data Stream Management Systems (*DSMS*) [1, 19, 3, 2, 14] have been proposed as suitable systems for handling large amounts of data, arriving with high velocity.

A representative example of on-line analytics can be found in stock market web applications, where multiple clients monitor price fluctuations of stocks. In these settings, a system needs to be able to answer analytical queries (i.e. average stock revenue, profit margin per stock, etc.) for different clients, each one with (possibly) different relaxation levels in terms of accuracy.

In *DSMS*, clients register their analytics queries on incoming data streams. Since these queries continuously aggregate streaming data to produce answers, they are called Aggregate Continuous Queries (*ACQs*). The accuracy of an *ACQ* can be thought of as the window in which the aggregation takes place, and the period at which the answer is re-calculated. Periodic properties that are often used to describe *ACQs* are *range* (**r**) and *slide* (**s**) (sometimes also referred to as *window* and *shift* [9]). A slide denotes the period at which an *ACQ* updates its answer; a range is the time window for which the statistics are calculated. For example, if a stock monitoring application has a slide of 3 sec and a range of 5 sec, it means that the application needs an updated result every 3 sec, and the result should be derived from data accumulated over the past 5 sec. An *ACQ* requires the *DSMS* to keep state over time, while performing aggregations. Often, it is useful to run partial aggregations on the data while accumulating it, and then produce the answer by performing the final aggregation over the partial results [6, 11, 12, 13]. It is clear that the greater the range and the smaller the slide of the *ACQ*, the higher its cost is to maintain (memory) and process (CPU).

Problem Statement In this work we focus on environments where a large number of long-running *ACQs* with different periodic properties (accuracies) are operating on the same data stream, calculating similar aggregate operations. Example of such an environment can be a *DSMS* deployed to *Cloud* Infrastructure, which results in a multitentant setting, where muliple *ACQs* with a wide range of different periodic features are executed on the same hardware. Since the *ACQs* are executed periodically (unlike one-shot queries), the opportunity to reduce the long-term overall processing costs by sharing final and partial results arises. For instance, assume that two *ACQs* monitor an average stock value over the same data stream. Both have a slide of 3 sec. The first one has a range of 5 sec, whereas the second one has a range of 10 sec. In this setting, it is beneficial to keep calculating the results for the first query and combine the last two for generating the results for the second query. This should take place every 3 sec, which is the common slide among those *ACQs*. Partial results sharing is applicable for all matching aggregate operations, such as *max*, *count*, *sum*, *average*, etc., and for different but com-

Permission to make digital or hard copies of all or part of this work for personal or classroom use is granted without fee provided that copies are not made or distributed for profit or commercial advantage and that copies bear this notice and the full citation on the first page. Copyrights for components of this work owned by others than ACM must be honored. Abstracting with credit is permitted. To copy otherwise, or republish, to post on servers or to redistribute to lists, requires prior specific permission and/or a fee. Request permissions from Permissions@acm.org.
CIKM'15, October 19–23, 2015, Melbourne, VIC, Australia
Copyright is held by the owner/author(s). Publication rights licensed to ACM.
ACM 978-1-4503-3794-6/15/10 ...$15.00.
DOI: http://dx.doi.org/10.1145/2806416.2806450.

patible aggregate operations, for example *sum*, *count* and *average* can share results by treating *average* as *sum/count*.

Typically, the number of *ACQs* with similar aggregation types can be overwhelming in on-line systems [3]. Therefore, it is crucial to be able to make decisions quickly on combining different *ACQs* into execution plans that would benefit the system. Unfortunately, the former has been proven to be NP-hard [24], and currently only approximation algorithms can produce acceptable execution plans.

The state-of-the-art *WeaveShare* algorithm produces very high quality execution plans by utilizing the *Weavability* concept [8], which is used to decide which *ACQs* are similar enough to be combined. *WeaveShare* is theoretically guaranteed to approximate the optimal cost-savings to within a factor of four for practical variants of the problem [4]. However, when we tried to implement it in a multiple-tenant *DSMS*, we observed that the current approach of calculating Weavability using *Bit Set* is very computationally expensive.

This motivated us to explore a more efficient algorithm to accelerate the calculation process in order to make the *WeaveShare* algorithm more scalable for systems with heavy workloads. Towards this, in this paper we propose a mathematical solution *Formula 1* (or $F1$), which reduces the number of operations needed to produce the efficient execution plan by $\sim 10^{62}$ times for the same set of 500 queries, and speeds up the plan generation time in our experiments by up to 60,000 times. $F1$ also eliminates concerns over the amount of system memory as it does not need to store any large data during its operation. In fact, $F1$ acceleration has enabled us to explore additional cost savings that can be achieved by utilizing the distributed nature of the *Cloud* Infrastructure by intelligently colocating *ACQs* on different computing nodes [17]. In general, $F1$ can reduce the computation time of any technique that combines partial aggregations within composite slides of multiple *ACQs*.

Contributions We make the following contributions:

- We propose a novel closed formula, $F1$, for calculating the number of overlapping partial result calculations between the *ACQs*, and show that $F1$ is applicable for all cases (with and without fragments).
- We theoretically evaluate the state-of-the-art *Weavability* calculation approach against $F1$ and provide a mathematical proof that $F1$ improves the time complexity from **at least e^n** to **at most 2^n**, and the space complexity correspondingly from **at least e^n** to **constant**.
- We experimentally evaluate $F1$ and show that we can achieve a speed increase of up to 60,000 times over the state-of-the-art techniques, which makes the processing of *ACQs* much more effective in an on-line *DSMS*.
- We show experimentally that $F1$ allows significantly better scalability in terms of the number of *ACQs*, input rate, and diversity of the *ACQ*'s time properties. We show that $F1$ is able to successfully process 1,000,000 *ACQs* when the limit of the current technique is 550.

Roadmap In the next section, we provide the background of our work. We introduce our new formula, $F1$, for the *Weavability* calculation and its additional optimization in Section 3. The complexity analysis on it is presented in Section 4. The evaluation platform and the experiments are discussed in Section 5. We summarize related work in Section 6 and conclude in Section 7.

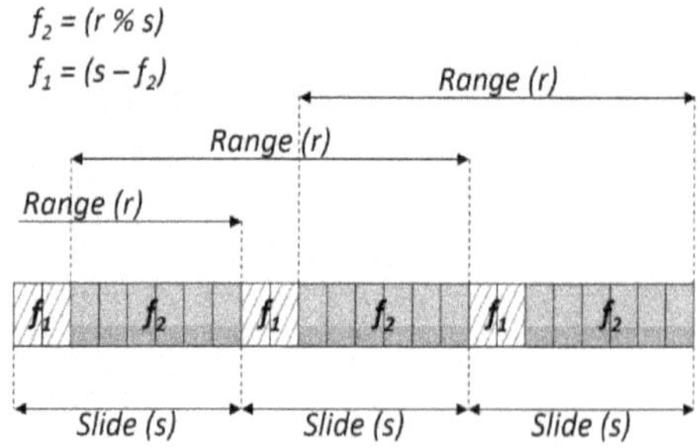

Figure 1: Paired Window Technique

2. BACKGROUND

In this paper, without a loss of generality, we target *ACQs* installed on the same data stream. Specifically, we scale the *WeaveShare* algorithm that has been shown to produce high quality execution plans of multiple *ACQs* by intelligently sharing partial aggregations.

Partial aggregation was proposed to improve the processing of *ACQs* [6, 11, 12, 13]. The idea behind partial aggregation is that we assemble the final answer from partial aggregates by performing a final aggregation over partials. For example, if an *ACQ* needs to calculate the maximum value over a specific time period, it can compute the maximum on each separate partition of streaming data, and then perform the final maximum operation on all obtained partial answers in order to get the result. Therefore, if the data set for the operation is split into n partitions, the system needs to perform n partial aggregations and one final aggregation to obtain the answer.

The question that immediately arises is how many partial aggregations are beneficial to perform before each final aggregation for a specific *ACQ*. This depends on the time properties of the *ACQ*.

- *The* ACQ *slide is greater or equal to the* ACQ *range.* In this case, partial aggregations are not beneficial. Only one aggregation is performed.
- *The* ACQ *slide is less than the* ACQ *range, and it divides the range evenly.* In this case it is beneficial to perform a partial aggregation every time period equal to the length of the slide.
- *The* ACQ *slide is less than the* ACQ *range, and it does not divide the range evenly.* In this case, it is beneficial to use the *Paired Window Technique* [11]. As can be seen from Figure 1, to use this approach one needs to calculate two fragment lengths f_1 and f_2. The second fragment can be found by performing range *mod* slide, and the first fragment by subtracting the second fragment from the slide. Partial aggregations should be computed at periods of fragment one and fragment two interchangeably.

Shared Processing of ACQs Several shared processing schemes as well as multiple *ACQs* optimizers utilize the *Paired Window Technique* [11, 8]. To show the benefits of sharing partial aggregations consider the following example:

Example 1 There are two *ACQs* that perform the *count* aggregate operation on the same data stream. The first *ACQ* has a slide of 2 sec and a range of 6 sec, the second one has a slide of 4 sec and a range of 8 sec. Therefore, the first *ACQ* is

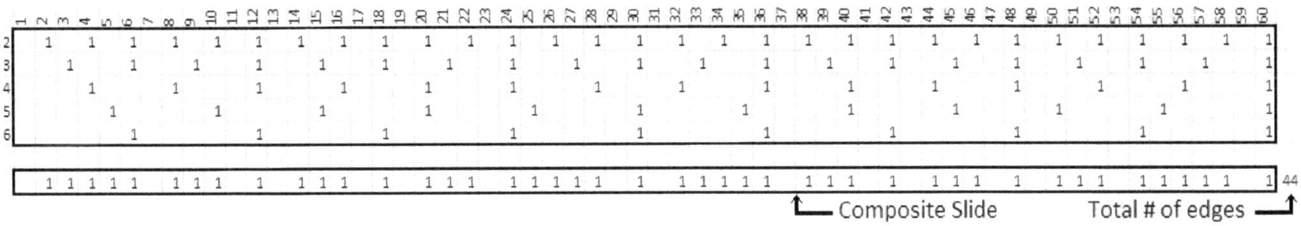

Figure 2: Marking edges produced by five different $ACQs$ with NO fragments in the composite slide, represented by a Bit Set

computing partial aggregates every 2 sec, and the second is computing the same partial aggregates every 4 sec. Clearly, the calculation producing partial aggregates only needs to be performed once every 2 sec, and both $ACQs$ can use these partial aggregates for their corresponding final aggregations. The first ACQ then will run each final aggregation over the last three partial aggregates, and the second ACQ will run each final aggregation over the last 4 partial aggregates.

The procedure to determine how many partial aggregations is needed after combining n $ACQs$ using a *Bit Set* is formalized as follows:

- Find the length of the new combined (composite) slide, which is the *Least Common Multiple* (LCM) of all the slides of the combined $ACQs$.
- Each slide is then repeated $LCM/slide$ times to fit the length of the new composite slide. All partial aggregations happening within each slide are also repeated and marked in the composite slide as *edges*.
- If the location is already marked, it cannot be marked again. If two $ACQs$ mark the same location, it means that location is a common *edge*.

Weavability is a metric that measures the benefit of sharing partial aggregations between any number of $ACQs$. If it is beneficial to share computations between these $ACQs$, then these $ACQs$ are known to *weave* well together. Intuitively, two $ACQs$ weave perfectly when their combined LCM contains only common edges. The following formula can be used to calculate the cost (C) of the execution plan before and after combining $ACQs$ from their own trees into shared trees. The difference between these costs tells us if the combination was a good choice or not.

$$C = m\lambda + \sum_{i=1}^{m} E_i \Omega_i \quad (1)$$

Note that m is the number of the trees in the plan, λ is input rate in tuples per second, E_i is edge rate of tree i, and Ω_i is the overlap factor of tree i. Edge rate is the number of partial aggregations performed per second, and the overlap factor is the total number of final-aggregation operations performed on each fragment.

The **WeaveShare** optimizer utilizes the concept of *Weavability* to produce an execution plan for a number of $ACQs$. It selectively partitions the $ACQs$ into multiple disjoint execution trees (i.e., groups), resulting in a dramatic reduction in the total processing costs of the query plan. *WeaveShare* starts with a no share plan where each ACQ has its own individual execution tree. Then, it iteratively considers all possible pairs of execution trees, and combines those which reduce the total plan cost the most, into a single tree. *WeaveShare* produces a final execution plan when it cannot find a pair that would reduce the total plan cost further.

The most complex part of the calculation occurs when the system is scheduling each partial aggregation operation (*edge*) and is tracking these operations using a *Bit Set* as mentioned above. The size of the *Bit Set* increases rapidly if the $ACQs$' time properties differ. For each ACQ added to the execution tree, *WeaveShare* needs to traverse the whole *Bit Set* to make sure that all partial aggregations necessary for this ACQ are marked in a *Bit Set* for future execution. Since the size of a *Bit Set* increases exponentially with the increase of the input size, traversing it becomes prohibitively time-consuming as we show in Section 4. Additionally, the exponential increase of the size of the *Bit Set* puts a hard limit on a system's capabilities, based on the amount of memory available.

3. FORMULA 1 (F1)

In this section, we describe our new formula $F1$ that significantly speeds up the edge rate calculation in a composite slide. We target two scenarios for $ACQs$ with matching or compatible aggregate operations: 1) when all ACQ slides are factors of their corresponding ranges, and 2) when some of the ranges are not multiples of their corresponding slides.

3.1 Case with *NO Fragments*

In the case when all of the ranges of the $ACQs$ that are being installed onto the *DSMS* are divisible by their corresponding slides, we can store partial aggregates at every slide. For example, if we have an ACQ with a slide of 3 sec and a range of 9 sec, we can store partial results every 3 sec, and perform the final aggregations on the 3 last saved partial aggregations to get the answer for the last 9 sec. In order to calculate the edge rate in *WeaveShare* after *weaving* together n $ACQs$, we need a *Bit Set* of the length equal to the LCM of all n slides. At first, the *Bit Set* is populated with zeros. For each one of n $ACQs$ we traverse the whole *Bit Set* and mark all bits whose indexes are divisible by the corresponding ACQ's slide with ones. If the bit was already marked, the algorithm does nothing and just moves to the next bit.

Example 2 Consider five stock monitoring $ACQs$ with the following slides: 2, 3, 4, 5, and 6. Their LCM is 60, therefore we need a *Bit Set* of size 60. First, we traverse the *Bit Set* and mark all indexes divisible by 2 (all even numbers up to 60). Now the *Bit Set* has 30 bits marked. Next we mark all indexes that are divisible by 3. The *Bit Set* already has 40 bits marked (10 overlapped with already marked ones). Next we mark all indexes that are divisible by 4. The *Bit Set* still has 40 bits marked since all of the bits we were trying to mark were already marked by a slide of 2. After repeating the same for slides of 5 and 6, we calculate how many bits we have in our *Bit Set*, and the answer is 44. This method is illustrated in the Figure 2.

To accelerate this calculation process we propose the *Formula 1* (or ***F*1**):

$$LCM_n \sum_{i=1}^{n} [(-1)^{i+1} G_1(n,i)] \quad (2)$$

Where $LCM_n = LCM(s_1, s_2, \ldots, s_n)$, and function $G_1(n,i)$ is a sum of the inversed LCMs of all possible groups of slides of size i from a set of size n. For example:

$$G_1(3,2) = \frac{1}{LCM(s_1,s_2)} + \frac{1}{LCM(s_1,s_3)} + \frac{1}{LCM(s_2,s_3)}$$

$F1$ can be expanded as follows:

$$LCM_n[G_1(n,1) - G_1(n,2) + \ldots \pm G_1(n,n-1) \mp G_1(n,n)] \quad (3)$$

Equation 3 is composed of an alternating series of function G_1 multiplied by the LCM_n. $LCM_n \cdot G_1(n,1)$ and represents the number of all edges produced by all $ACQs$ and therefore includes all overlapping edges. The goal of the calculation is to count every edge only once, even if it overlaps multiple times in different $ACQs$. Therefore, the rest of the elements of the series will eliminate all of the overlapping edges from the current result. $LCM_n \cdot G_1(n,2)$ represents the number of edges that overlap in all different pairs of slides and after subtracting it, we get a smaller number than the number we are looking for, because there are potentially some edges where more than two slides overlap at the same time. For example, if slides a, b, and c overlap at some specific edge e, we add it three times: for pairs (a,b), (a,c), and (b,c). The following element $LCM_n \cdot G_1(n,3)$ compensates for these cases by adding back all edges that overlap in each set of three slides. After adding it, we have again a larger number than the sought-after number, because we might have four or more slides overlapping at the same edge. Therefore, each element compensates for the previous ones' inaccuracies up to the point when we add/subtract the final edge of the composite slide, which clearly occurs only once, since $LCM_n \cdot G_1(n,n) = \frac{LCM_n}{LCM_n} = 1$. The last added/subtracted edge has an index equal to the LCM_n.

Equation 3 is an alternating series and we know in advance that the number of elements is always equal to the number of $ACQs$ in the execution tree and is a finite number. Therefore, by definition, the sequence always converges.

The following is an example of using $F1$ to calculate the number of edges:

Example 3 Consider the same set of stock monitoring $ACQs$ as we had in Example 1: slides are $2, 3, 4, 5$, and 6. As a first step of our algorithm we calculate the LCM_n of the whole set of slides. $LCM_n = LCM(2,3,4,5,6) = 60$. Next we substitute our values into Equation 11:

$$60 \cdot G_1(5,1) - 60 \cdot G_1(5,2) + 60 \cdot G_1(5,3) - 60 \cdot G_1(5,4) + 1$$

Every element is expanded as shown above. For example, the expansion of element $60 \cdot G_1(5,2)$ is as follows. (Note that LCM_{ab} denotes $LCM(a,b)$).

$$60 \cdot G_1(5,2) = \frac{60}{LCM_{23}} + \frac{60}{LCM_{24}} + \frac{60}{LCM_{25}} + \\ + \frac{60}{LCM_{26}} + \frac{60}{LCM_{34}} + \frac{60}{LCM_{35}} + \frac{60}{LCM_{36}} + \\ + \frac{60}{LCM_{45}} + \frac{60}{LCM_{46}} + \frac{60}{LCM_{56}} = 70$$

Finally we have: $87 - 70 + 36 - 10 + 1 = 44$
This answer matches the solution from Example 1.

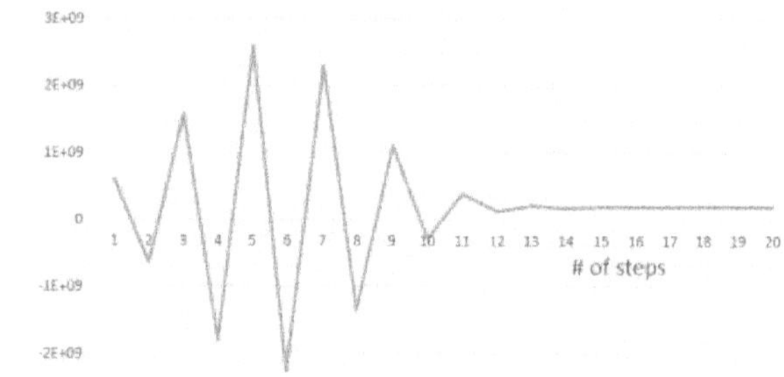

Figure 3: $F1$ converging to the solution for 20 $ACQs$ in 20 steps

Notice that the elements of the alternating series are interchangeably increasing and decreasing the solution as we approach the end of the calculation. For 20 different $ACQs$, the calculation of overlapping edges using $F1$ consists of 20 addition operations, causing the total number to change as depicted in Figure 3.

3.2 Case *WITH Fragments*

In case some of the ranges of the $ACQs$ that are being installed onto the *DSMS* are not divisible by their corresponding slides, according to the *Paired Window* approach, the slides should be broken into fragments. This enables us to store partial aggregates for every fragment. For example, if we have an ACQ with slide 5 sec and range 7 sec, the slide is split into two fragments: $f_2 = 7 \pmod 5 = 2$ and $f_1 = 5 - 2 = 3$. Now we can store partial results for first 3 sec, then for following 2 sec, then again for the following 3 sec and so on.

In the original *WeaveShare* [8], in order to calculate the edge rate after *weaving* together n $ACQs$ with fragments, we again need to work with a *Bit Set* of the length equal to the LCM of all n slides. The Bit Set is pre-populated with zeros again. For each ACQ we traverse the whole Bit Set and mark bits corresponding to the times when partial aggregations will happen with ones. If the bit was already marked, the algorithm does nothing and just moves to the next location.

Example 4 Consider four stock monitoring $ACQs$ with the following slides: $3, 4, 6$, and 9. $ACQs$ with slides of 4 and 6 consist of fragments $(3,1)$ and $(2,4)$ respectively. $ACQs$ 3 and 9 do not have fragments. The overall LCM of all slides together is 36, therefore we need a *Bit Set* of size 36. First, we traverse the *Bit Set* and mark all indexes that are divisible by 3 for the ACQ with a slide of 3 and no fragments. Now the *Bit Set* has 12 bits marked. Next consider an ACQ with a slide of 4 and fragments $(3,1)$. We traverse the *Bit Set* by starting from 0 and adding fragment 3 followed by fragment 1 repeatedly. Thus, the *Bit Set* will be marked at

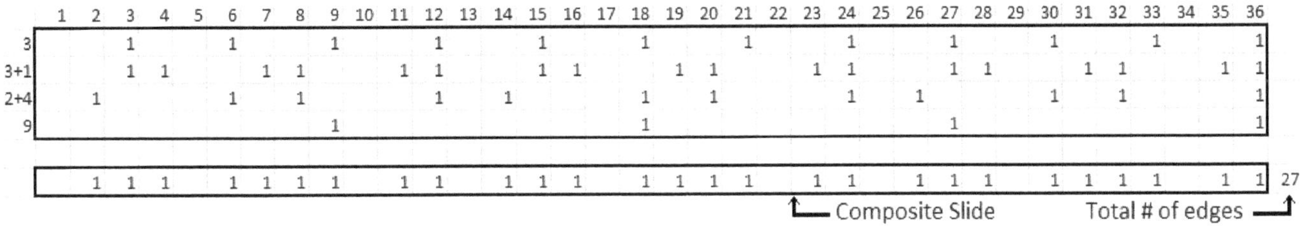

Figure 4: Marking edges produced by four different $ACQs$ WITH fragments in the composite slide, represented by a Bit Set

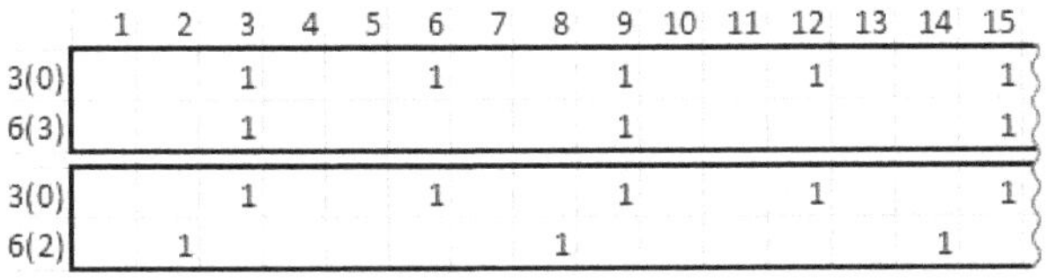

Figure 5: (slide 3, shift 0) and (slide 6, shift 3) **DO overlap**, but (slide 3, shift 0) and (slide 6, shift 2) **DO NOT**

indexes $3, 4, 7, 8, 11, 12$, etc. Now there are 24 marked bits. Next we continue to an ACQ with a slide of 6 and fragments $(2, 4)$. Again, we start at 0 and by adding 2 and 4 repeatedly we mark the following bits: $2, 6, 8, 12, 14$, etc., marking 27 bits in total. For the last ACQ with a slide of 9 and no fragments, we traverse the *Bit Set* at increments of size 9 and mark each 9th bit with one. The total number of set bits stays 27, because the last ACQ did not add any new bits, therefore our answer is 27. This method is illustrated in Figure 4.

To **generalize** $F1$ for both cases (if we do have $ACQs$ with fragments and if we do not) we introduce the notion of *shifts*. Each ACQ that does not have fragments has a *shift* of zero. Each ACQ that does have fragments must be presented as two $ACQs$ with the same slides, but different *shifts*. First one has a shift of zero, and the second one has a *shift* equal to the first fragment of the original ACQ.

When counting overlapping edges of $ACQs$, and when at least one of their shifts is not zero, we can encounter two different cases:

- $ACQs$ overlap, and the number of common edges is the same, as it would be if all of the $ACQs$' shifts were zeros.
- $ACQs$ do not overlap at all. Since the shifts are not compatible, the number of common edges is zero.

Example 5 Assume two $ACQs$ with slides of 3 and 6. If their corresponding shifts are 0 and 3, there is an overlapping edge every 6 time units. However, if the corresponding shifts are 0 and 2, there are no overlapping edges. This is illustrated in Figure 5.

To decide whether two $ACQs$ q_1 and q_2 (if at least one of them has non-zero shift) will overlap, we propose the following **Overlap Check Formula** based on GCD (*Greatest Common Divisor*):

$$|q_1.shift - q_2.shift| \mod GCD(q_1.slide, q_2.slide) \quad (4)$$

- If the *Overlap Check Formula* resolves to *zero* then the $ACQs$ **DO** overlap
- *Otherwise* the $ACQs$ **DO NOT** overlap

Proof of the **Overlap Check Formula** (by contradiction) Assume that we have two $ACQs$ q_1 and q_2, with corresponding slides s_1 and s_2, and shift difference h. Assume further that $h \ mod \ GCD(s_1, s_2) \neq 0$ and (for the sake of contradiction) the $ACQs$ *DO* overlap. Let us denote all edges produced by q_1 as $\{e_{1-1}, e_{1-2}, \ldots, e_{1-n}\}$, and edges of q_2 as $\{e_{2-1}, e_{2-2}, \ldots, e_{2-n}\}$. Let us first look at the two $ACQs$ separately. Since every edge produced by q_1 is divisible by s_1, and every edge produced by q_2 is divisible by s_2, and both s_1 and s_2 are divisible by $GCD(s_1, s_2)$ (by definition of GCD), every edge produced by q_1 and q_2 is divisible by $GCD(s_1, s_2)$. Therefore, all edges that are not divisible by $GCD(s_1, s_2)$ cannot possibly overlap any of the edges produced by either q_1 or q_2. Without loss of generality, let us consider q_2 from the standpoint of q_1. Then, all edges of q_2 are shifted by h with respect to edges of q_1, and they can be written as follows: $\{e_{2-1} + h, e_{2-2} + h, \ldots, e_{2-n} + h\}$. These edges should be divisible by $GCD(s_1, s_2)$ in order for them to overlap the edges of q_1: $\{e_{1-1}, e_{1-2}, \ldots, e_{1-n}\}$. We know that the edges $\{e_{2-1}, e_{2-2}, \ldots, e_{2-n}\}$ are divisible by $GCD(s_1, s_2)$. However, by the initial assumption, the shift h that is being added to them is not divisible by $GCD(s_1, s_2)$. Thus, edges $\{e_{2-1} + h, e_{2-2} + h, \ldots, e_{2-n} + h\}$ cannot possibly be divisible by $GCD(s_1, s_2)$. Therefore, none of the edges of q_2 can possibly overlap with the edges of q_1. In the case that h would actually be divisible by $GCD(s_1, s_2)$, all shifted edges of q_2 that are divisible by s_1 would overlap with the edges of q_1. However, the initial assumption states that h is not divisible by $GCD(s_1, s_2)$, which leads us to the conclusion that the $ACQs$ q_1 and q_2 do not overlap, which is a contradiction. Hence, the initial formula is correct. ■

Next we generalize our formula $F1$ for use in cases when $ACQs$ have fragments, and cases when none of the $ACQs$ have fragments. The **general F1** is:

$$LCM_n \sum_{i=1}^{n} [(-1)^{i+1} G_2(n, i)] \quad (5)$$

Where again $LCM_n = LCM(s_1, s_2, \ldots, s_n)$, and function G_2 is the same as function G_1, however all elements produced by G_2 have to be checked with the *Overlap Check Formula* for redundancy as described below. Prior to using this formula, for each ACQ that has fragments, we create two new $ACQs$: one of them has a shift of zero, another one has a shift equal to the first fragment of the original ACQ. All new $ACQs$ are added back to the set of the original $ACQs$ replacing the originals. To calculate each G_2 we find all possible groups of size x from the new set of $ACQs$ just like in the case with no fragments. Some of these groups are redundant because they do not have overlapping edges (because of the shifts). To remove all redundant groups, we check all possible pairs within each group using the *Overlap*

Check Formula, and if any of the pairs return a non-zero value, then the whole group is discarded. Otherwise, G_2 is calculated and used the same way as in the case with *NO* fragments. The generalized formula $F1$ still converges, which can be proven using the same strategy as in the case with no fragments.

Equation 5 expands into an alternating series likewise:

$$LCM_n[G_2(n,1) - G_2(n,2) + \ldots \pm G_2(n,n-1) \mp G_2(n,n)] \quad (6)$$

We show how Equation 6 works with the following example.

Example 6 Assume the same set of stock monitoring $ACQs$ as in Example 4: slides are 3, 4, 6, and 9, and $ACQs$ with slides of 4 and 6 consist of fragments $(3,1)$ and $(2,4)$ respectively. As a first step of our algorithm we calculate the LCM_n of the whole set of slides. $LCM_n = LCM(3,4,6,9) = 36$. Next we replace the $ACQs$ that have fragments with the $ACQs$ that have corresponding shifts. In our set we now have two $ACQs$ with a slide of 4 (shifts 0 and 3), and two $ACQs$ with a slide of 6 (shift 0 and shift 2). The rest of the $ACQs$ stay the same. We can substitute our values into the generalized formula $F1$:

$$36 \cdot G_2(6,1) - 36 \cdot G_1(6,2) + 36 \cdot G_1(6,3) - 36 \cdot G_1(6,4)$$

The calculation is almost identical to the case with no fragments, except every group produced by G_2 has to be checked with the *Overlap Check Formula* to see if it is redundant or not. For example, the expansion of the second group is shown below. Note that $3_0 4_3$ denotes a group of $ACQs$ with slides of 3 and 4 and shifts of 0 and 3, respectively. The fractions that have been crossed out did not pass the test with the *Overlap Check Formula*.

$$36 \cdot G_1(6,2) = \frac{36}{LCM_{3_0 4_3}} + \cancel{\frac{36}{LCM_{3_0 6_2}}} + \frac{36}{LCM_{3_0 9_0}} + \frac{36}{LCM_{3_0 4_0}} + \frac{36}{LCM_{3_0 6_0}} + \cancel{\frac{36}{LCM_{4_3 6_2}}} + \frac{36}{LCM_{4_3 9_0}} + \cancel{\frac{36}{LCM_{4_3 4_0}}} + \cancel{\frac{36}{LCM_{4_3 6_0}}} + \cancel{\frac{36}{LCM_{6_2 9_0}}} + \frac{36}{LCM_{6_2 4_0}} + \cancel{\frac{36}{LCM_{6_2 6_0}}} + \frac{36}{LCM_{9_0 4_0}} + \frac{36}{LCM_{9_0 6_0}} + \frac{36}{LCM_{4_0 6_0}} = 26$$

Finally we have: $46 - 26 + 8 - 1 = 27$
This solution matches the solution from Example 4.

3.3 *F1 Optimization*

Since we are using the Euclidean GCD algorithm for all of our LCM calculations, we found that we can achieve a significant additional speed up by utilizing the technique of memorization. We adopted this technique by preloading a table of GCDs into main memory before the execution begins. If the user is willing to allocate b bytes of memory to store the GCD table and each GCD takes g bytes of memory, we can store in memory GCDs of all the possible pairs of numbers up to $\sqrt{2b/g}$. In our implementation we are using 8 byte numbers of the Long type for calculations, so if we want to allocate 4 GB of main memory to store $GCDs$, we can fit GCDs of all the pairs of numbers up to 32,768. If we calculate the GCD for numbers that are larger than the above limit, the GCD table still save us some time by taking advantage of the recursive nature of the Euclidean algorithm. The effects of the optimization are shown in Section 5.

4. COMPLEXITY ANALYSIS

In this section, we calculate the difference between the complexities of *Bit Set* calculation and our $F1$ method.

Time Complexities To compare the time complexities we start by identifying the initial calculations needed by both algorithms. We denote the number of $ACQs$ as n, and the max slide as max. The following steps need to be done at the beginning of both algorithms.

- Remove all duplicate slides, since the same slides produce the same edges, and we do not want to repeat the same calculation for every duplicate. This is done by sorting slides with duplicate removal in $n \cdot logn$ time.
- Precalculate the LCM_n, which is the LCM of all slides and store it in the main memory. This operation takes $(n-1) \cdot log(max)$ at worst, since we need to perform LCM operation pairwise $n-1$ times, and each $LCM(a,b)$ needs at worst $log(min(a,b))$ operations [21].
- Remove all slides that are multiples of other slides included in the set. We do this because all edges produced by such slides are already produced by their factors. This can be done in $n \cdot (n-1)/2$ operations since our slide set is sorted, and for each subsequent slide we need to do a number of comparisons that equals the number of comparisons performed by the previous slide minus one.

Therefore, precalculation takes $n \cdot logn + (n-1) \cdot log(max) + n \cdot (n-1)/2$ operations, however since it is performed by both algorithms, we can ignore it for the matter of comparison.

After completing the initial computation, we now have LCM_n stored in main memory, and a set of slides which does not contain any duplicates or multiples. Therefore, the set can now only have either prime numbers or numbers for which their multiples do not appear in the set.

To better illustrate differences in complexity we utilize two different sets of slides:

- Working Set (S_w) is a set of slides that includes only prime numbers and numbers that do not have their multiples in this set. This is a set produced after the initial preparation and it is used in real working scenarios. An example of a valid working set: $S_w = 3, 5, 8, 14, \ldots, max$. $|Sw| = n$, and the maximum element is denoted as max.
- Auxiliary set (S_a) is a set of slides, that consists of sequential numbers. $Sa = 1, 2, \ldots, n$. $|Sa| = n$, and the maximum value max equals n. Note that this set contains all natural numbers from one to n, including multiples of other numbers from this set. It is still a valid set for our computation, and can be obtained by skipping the preliminary optimization that removes all multiples.

Next we show that the lower bound of the *Bit Set* calculation is higher than the upper bound of the $F1$ computation.

The complexity of the *Bit Set* calculation is:

$$\sum_{i=1}^{n} \frac{LCM_n}{s_i} \quad (7)$$

Where $LCM_n = LCM(s_1, s_2, \ldots, s_n)$. The complexity holds since for each of n $ACQs$ we would need to traverse the whole *Bit Set*, whose length is equal to the LCM of all slides of all $ACQs$, with a step equal to each ACQ's slide. We can expand the Equation 7 to the following:

$$LCM_n \cdot \left(\frac{1}{s_1} + \frac{1}{s_2} + \ldots + \frac{1}{s_n}\right) \quad (8)$$

First, we perform complexity analysis using the Auxiliary set S_a. Let us focus on the first part of the product in Equation 8: LCM_n. We know that the LCM of all numbers in this set is the product of the highest prime powers occurring in the set. The log of the LCM is therefore the sum of the $logs$ of the prime powers in the set:

$$log(LCM_n) = \sum_{i=2}^{n} f(i) \tag{9}$$

$$where f(i) = \begin{cases} log(p) & if\, i = p^m,\, where\, m \geq 1 \,\&\, p\, is\, prime \\ 0 & Otherwise \end{cases}$$

This sum has significance in the *Prime Number Theorem* and it is well known to be asymptotically equal to e^n [23].

Next we focus on the second part of the product in Equation 8: $(\frac{1}{s_1} + \frac{1}{s_2} + \ldots + \frac{1}{s_n})$. Since our set only has sequential numbers from one to n, this part will look like: $(\frac{1}{1} + \frac{1}{2} + \ldots + \frac{1}{n})$, which is a classic example of a diverging harmonic series $\sum_{n=1}^{\infty} \frac{1}{n}$. For any n, this series can be calculated as follows: $\sum_{n=1}^{\infty} \frac{1}{n} = ln(k) + \gamma + \epsilon_k$, where γ is the Euler-Mascheroni constant ($\gamma \approx 0.577$) and $\epsilon_k \sim \frac{1}{2k}$, which approaches zero as k goes to infinity[22]. For our purposes, since γ is a constant and ϵ_k is negligible, they are ignored. Also, we can say that time complexity $e^n \cdot ln(n)$ is asymptotically equal to e^n, therefore we can assume asymptotical time complexity of the *Bit Set* computation for set S_a is e^n.

When we use set S_w, the time complexity for LCM_n is larger than when using set S_a. This is true because we replace n sequential numbers that start from 1 with n non-duplicate primes and non-multiples, which are larger and have a larger total LCM. The time complexity for the part $\sum_{i=1}^{n} \frac{1}{s_i}$ becomes smaller, because we are increasing numbers in the denominator, however it is still insignificant, because even in the worst case we can lower bound it with $ln(max) - ln(max - n)$. Thus, the time complexity of the *Bit Set* computation for the working set S_w is at least e^n.

To calculate the complexity of $F1$, we need to determine the number of operations that need to be performed based on the size of the input. First, we know that the number of elements in our alternating series is equal to the number of $ACQs$ in the set. Let us take Equation 3 and expand LCM_n into the parentheses:

$$\begin{gathered} LCM_n \cdot G_1(n,1) - LCM_n \cdot G_1(n,2) + \ldots \\ \pm LCM_n \cdot G_1(n,n-1) \mp LCM_n \cdot G_1(n,n) \end{gathered} \tag{10}$$

As we previously mentioned, $LCM_n \cdot G_1(n,n) = 1$, therefore:

$$\begin{gathered} LCM_n \cdot G_1(n,1) - LCM_n \cdot G_1(n,2) + \ldots \\ \pm LCM_n \cdot G_1(n,n-1) \mp 1 \end{gathered} \tag{11}$$

To determine how many groups will be produced by each one of these elements we use binomial coefficients. Each element of type $LCM_n \cdot G_1(n,k)$ therefore produces $\binom{n}{k}$ of distinct k-element groups of type $\frac{LCM_n}{LCM_k}$, where $LCM_k = LCM(s_1, s_2, \ldots s_k)$. Therefore, the total number of all of these groups is: $\binom{n}{1} + \binom{n}{2} + \binom{n}{3} + \ldots + \binom{n}{n-1} + \binom{n}{n}$. By the additive property of binomial coefficients, this sum equals $2^n - 1$. Next we determine how many calculations are performed in each group. The numerator of all groups is LCM_n and since it is kept in main memory, we do not need to recalculate it every time. The denominator is LCM_k, and it is determined by calculating the LCM of the first two elements, and then iteratively calculating the $LCMs$ of the resulting number with the rest of the elements in the group. Therefore, for each group we need to perform $k-1$ LCM calculations, and one calculation to add the group to the total number, which makes k calculations total. Since each group with k elements needs k calculations, the total number of calculations needed for all groups becomes: $1\binom{n}{1} + 2\binom{n}{2} + 3\binom{n}{3} + \ldots + (n-1)\binom{n}{n-1} + n\binom{n}{n}$. This resolves to $2^{n-1} \cdot n$, which can be calculated by taking the generalization of binomial series: $(1+x)^a = \sum_{k=0}^{\infty} \binom{a}{k} \cdot x^k$ and differentiating it with respect to x and then substituting $x = 1$ [20]. Due to the use of the Euclidean algorithm to calculate the LCM, the complexity of each LCM calculation is $log(min(a,b))$ at most [21]. Therefore, at worst $F1$ has a time complexity of $2^{n-1} \cdot n \cdot log(max)$, which asymptotically equals 2^n.

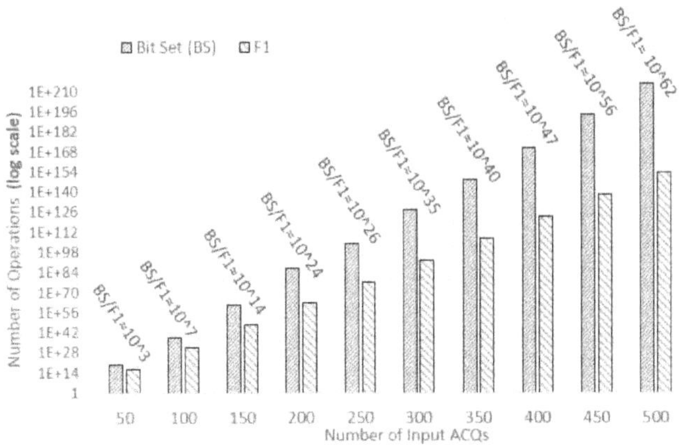

Figure 6: Number of operations needed by Bit Set and $F1$ for plan generation. Top labels show BitSet/$F1$ ratio

Thus, we have determined that the *Bit Set* calculation has a time complexity of **at least e^n**, and $F1$ has a time complexity of **at worst 2^n**. Clearly, when n goes to infinity, it is increasingly beneficial to use $F1$ versus *Bit Set*.

Additionally, since we have calculated the formulas for determining the exact number of operations done by both *Bit Set* and $F1$, we can compare the increase in the amount of operations performed by *Bit Set* and $F1$ with the increase of the number of input $ACQs$. The comparison is shown in Figure 6. $ACQs$ for this comparison were sequentially drawn from the Auxiliary set (S_a) introduced above. Note that since the difference between *Bit Set* and $F1$ operation numbers is drastic and grows exponentially we had to use a logarithmic scale to still see the operations of $F1$. This comparison shows that $F1$ is much more scalable than *Bit Set* in terms of the number of operations required.

Space Complexities The space complexity of the *Bit Set* calculation is LCM_n, since we have already shown that the *Bit Set* grows at the rate of e^n. The space complexity of the $F1$ calculation is $O(1)$ (*constant*) since it does not require storing edges. Edge overlaps are calculated strictly mathematically. Since $F1$ expands into a sum, we only need to keep one number in memory, which is increased or decreased by the elements of the alternating series sequentially. The improvement in space complexity is extremely important for the *WeaveShare* algorithm, since the leading cause of its failures with large workloads is "out of memory" errors.

5. EXPERIMENTAL EVALUATION

In this section, we summarize the results of our experimental evaluation of the scalability of $F1$ in terms of the size of the input set of the $ACQs$, the diversity of their time properties, and the input rate of the data stream.

5.1 Experimental Testbed

In order to show the significance of our *Weavability* calculation optimization we built an experimental platform in Java. Specifically, we implemented the *WeaveShare* optimizer as described in [8] with different options for calculating *Weavability*. Our workload is composed of a number of $ACQs$ with different characteristics. We are generating our workload synthetically in order to be able to fine-tune system parameters and get a more detailed sensitivity analysis of the optimizer's performance. Moreover, it allows us to target possible real-life scenarios and analyze them.

Our system's **experimental parameters** are:

[***Algorithm***] specifies which technique is used for *Weavability* calculations. The available techniques are: (a) Bit Set (BS), (b) Formula 1 ($F1$), and (c) Formula 1 + Optimization ($F1 + Opt$). The $F1 + Opt$ technique uses a 4 GB table for keeping $GCDs$ in main memory.

[$\boldsymbol{Q_{num}}$] Number of $ACQs$. We assume that all $ACQs$ are installed on the same data stream and their aggregate functions allow them to share partial aggregations among them. The actual function does not have any effect on performance other than the ability to share partial aggregations.

[$\boldsymbol{S_{max}}$] Maximum slide length, which provides an upper bound on how large slides of our $ACQs$ can be. The minimum slide allowed by the system always equals one.

[$\boldsymbol{\lambda}$] The input rate, which describes how fast tuples arrive through the input stream in our system.

[$\boldsymbol{Z_{skew}}$] Zipf distribution skew, which depicts the popularity of each slide length in the final set of $ACQs$. A Zipf skew of zero produces uniform distribution, and a greater Zipf skew is skewed towards large slides (for more realistic examples).

[$\boldsymbol{\Omega_{max}}$] Maximum overlap factor, which defines the upper bound for the overlap factor. The overlap factor of each ACQ is drawn from a uniform distribution between one and the maximum overlap factor.

[***Gen***] Generator type, which defines whether our workload is normal (Nrm) and includes any slides, or diverse (Div) and includes only prime slides.

5.2 Experimental Results

To test the scalability of our approaches $F1$ and $F1+Opt$ versus BS in terms of the parameters Q_{num}, S_{max}, λ, Z_{skew}, and Ω_{max}, we ran five experiments, where we varied each one of these parameters while keeping the rest of them fixed. The parameters were selected separately for each experiment in a way that would highlight the differences in the scalabilities of the three approaches the best. The experimental parameters are specified in the Table 1.

All results are taken as averages of running each experiment five times. Please note that since $F1$ and $F1 + Opt$ showed to have significantly smaller runtimes compared to BS, we had to use **logarithmic scale** to be able to display all techniques' performances in the same graphs.

We ran all our experiments on a dual Intel(R) Xeon(R) CPU E5-2650 v2 @ 2.60GHz server with 96 GB of RAM.

Exp 1: Number of ACQs Scalability (Figure 7)
In this test we varied the Q_{num} from 100 to 1,000,000.

Table 1: Experiment Parameters

#	Q_{num}	S_{max}	λ	Z_{skew}	Ω	Gen
1	*100 - 1M*	1K	0.002	0.5	10	Nrm
2	1K	*100-10K*	1	3	100	Div
3	1K	100	*100-1M*	1	1K	Nrm
4	50	500	0.1	*0-100*	100	Nrm
5	1K	600	1	3	*100-1*	Div

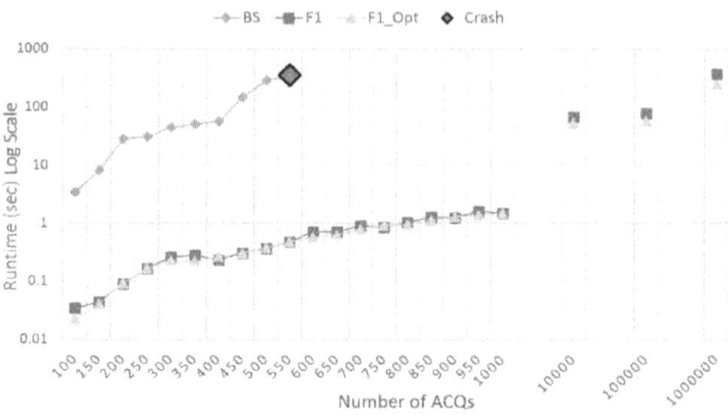

Figure 7: **Exp 1** Scalability of the number of ACQs

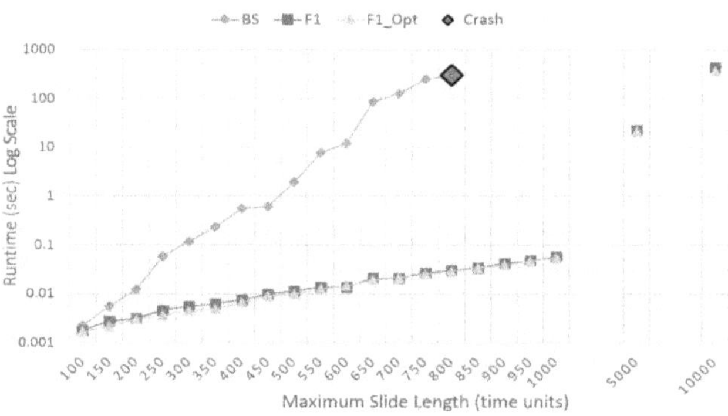

Figure 8: **Exp 2** Scalability of the maximum slide length

Clearly, increasing the Q_{num} also increases the amount of required calculations, causing higher runtimes for all three algorithms. The results are depicted in Figure 7. The *Bit Set* approach did not finish execution, because after we crossed Q_{num} of 550 it started running out of memory (on a 96GB RAM machine) and eventually crashed (on all runs). Otherwise, the growth rates of these techniques are similar to what we expected from the theoretical analysis of the time complexities of their underlying algorithms. The statistics show that our techniques' runtimes are on average 350 times faster than runtimes of BS with a maximum of 790 times, and our techniques are able to scale up to 1,000,000 $ACQs$ on this setting without running out of memory. Also, the $F1 + Opt$ plan outperformed the $F1$ plan by approximately 28% on average, validating our optimization expectations.

Exp 2: Max Slide Scalability (Figure 8)
In this test we varied the S_{max} from 100 to 10,000. Similarly to Exp 1, increasing the S_{max} also increases the amount of required calculations. This happens because with a higher max slide parameter, the generated $ACQs$ have longer slides, which results in higher $LCMs$ and fewer overlapping edges. In Figure 8 we see that the BS approach did not finish execution again after we crossed S_{max} of 800 because of the

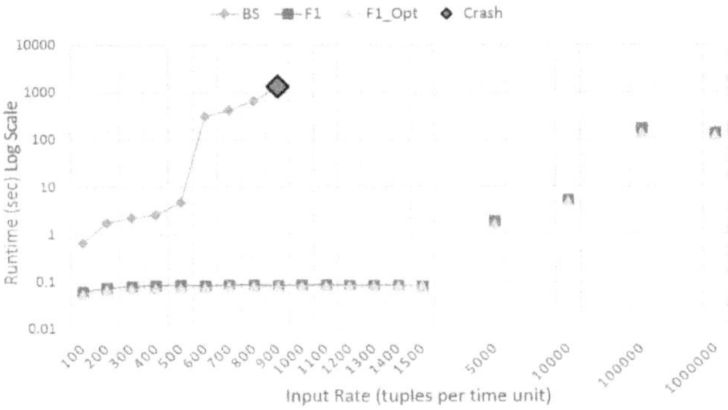

Figure 9: **Exp 3** Scalability of the input rate

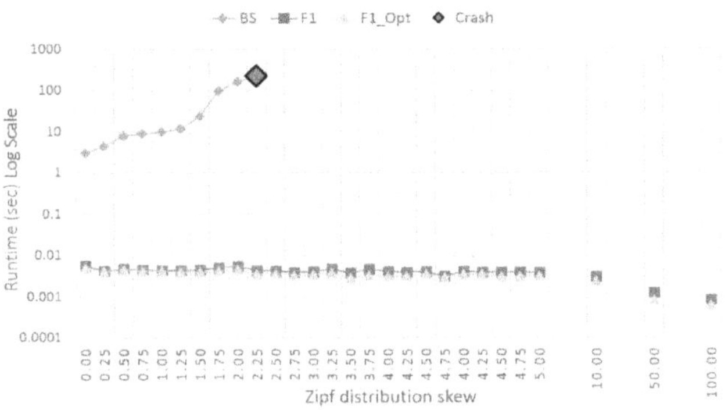

Figure 10: **Exp 4** Sensitivity to the zipf distribution skew

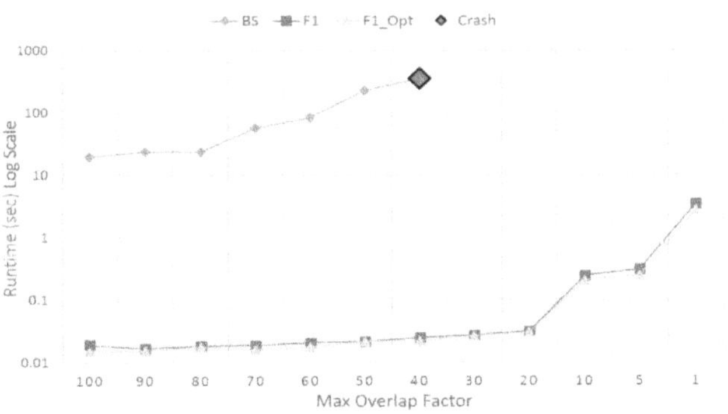

Figure 11: **Exp 5** Sensitivity to the maximum overlap factor

"out of memory" error. The growth rates of our techniques however are again similar to what we expected from our theoretical analysis of their time complexities. Our proposed techniques' runtimes in this experiment are on average 2,200 times faster than runtimes of *BS* with a maximum of 10,000 times, and our techniques are able to scale up to the S_{max} of 10,000 *ACQs* on this setting and finish the plan generation successfully. The $F1 + Opt$ plan outperformed the $F1$ plan by an average of 18%.

Exp 3: Input Rate Scalability (Figure 9)
In this test we varied λ from 100 to 100,000. Increasing λ also increases the amount of required calculations because with higher input rates, according to the Equation 1, it becomes more beneficial to combine more execution trees. This forces *WeaveShare* to combine some trees with different time properties that would not have been combined if the input rate was lower. Thus, increasing λ leads to higher LCMs and higher runtimes. The average number of execution trees formed at the end of the plan generation is 71 when $\lambda = 100$, 29 when $\lambda = 400$, 15 when $\lambda = 900$, 4 when $\lambda = 10,000$ and 1 when $\lambda = 100,000$ or 1,000,000. The fact that at some λ all trees get merged into one explains why runtimes stop increasing after this λ. In this setting it happened at $\lambda = 100,000$ (see Figure 9). In this experiment the *BS* approach crashed when λ reached 900, and the average number of trees at that point was 15. Our approaches demonstrated good scalability again and were able to increase input rate to the point where all trees are *Weaved* into one. On average our techniques ran 3,800 times faster than *BS* with a maximum of 16,000. The $F1 + Opt$ plan outperformed the $F1$ plan by the average of 19%.

Exp 4: Slide Skew Sensitivity (Figure 10)
In this test we varied the Z_{skew} from 0 to 100. This experiment is similar to the max slide scalability experiment, because in both experiments we are gradually increasing the amount of *ACQs* with large slides and therefore increasing the amount of required calculations. The difference is that, when skewing all slides drawn from the same set to the larger side, at some point they start repeating, which then reduces the amount of the required calculations. In our experiment (see Figure 10) we first observe the initial increase in the amount of computation, which leads the *BS* approach to crash with an "out of memory" error (at $Z_{skew} = 2.25$), and then we see gradual decrease in computation, because there are many repeating slides in the input set. In this setting our proposed techniques' runtimes are on average 14,000 times faster than runtimes of *BS* with a maximum of 60,000 times, and our techniques are able to scale up to the Z_{skew} of 100 and finish the plan generation successfully. The $F1 + Opt$ plan outperformed the $F1$ plan by the average of 18% again.

Exp 5: Overlap Factor Sensitivity (Figure 11)
In this test we varied the Ω from 100 to 1. We did it in reverse order since its value is inversely proportional to the amount of computation required to generate an execution plan using *WeaveShare*. Based on Equation 1 we can see that smaller Ωs benefit the total cost if their corresponding *ACQs* are combined to fewer execution trees, which causes *WeaveShare* to *Weave* more trees with different time properties together. In our experiment (see Figure 11) the *BS* approach crashed when Ω reached 40. Our approaches again demonstrated good scalability and were able to finish the plan generation successfully even with the minimum value of $\Omega = 1$. On average our techniques ran 5,600 times faster than *BS* with a maximum of 16,000. The $F1 + Opt$ plan outperformed the $F1$ plan by the average of 26%.

Experimental Results Summary Clearly, the above experimental results show that our techniques $F1$ and $F1+Opt$ deliver the best performance in terms of plan generation runtimes and scalability, while producing same high quality execution plans as the original *WeaveShare* optimizer. The results of our experiments are summarized in Table 2.

6. RELATED WORK

Techniques for the efficient processing of *ACQs* could be broadly classified into techniques for: 1) the *implementation* of the continuous aggregation operator, and 2) the *multi-query optimization* of multiple continuous aggregate queries.

Under the operator implementation techniques, *partial aggregation* has been proposed to minimize the repeated pro-

Table 2: Experimental Results

Experiment #	Param	Best Achieved BS	$F1$	Runtime: $BS/F1$ Avg	Max	$F1$ vs $F1+Opt$
1	Q_{num}	550*	1M	350	790	28%
2	S_{max}	800*	10K	2,200	10,000	18%
3	λ	900*	1M	3,800	16,000	19%
4	Z_{skew}	2.25*	100	14,000	60,000	18%
5	Ω	40*	1	5,600	16,000	26%

*Execution stopped with "out of memory" exception

cessing of overlapping data windows within a single aggregate (e.g., [12, 13, 6, 11, 24, 25, 18]) by processing each input tuple only once. As discussed in Section 2, *ACQ* processing is typically modeled as a two-level (i.e., two-operator) query execution plan. In order to minimize the cost of final aggregation, *TriOps* [7] uses intermediate function levels to pipeline partial aggregates to final-aggregate functions.

Under the multi-query optimization techniques, the general principle is to minimize the repeated processing of overlapping operations across multiple aggregate queries. This repetition occurs when queries exhibit an overlap in at least one of the following specifications: 1) predicate conditions, 2) group-by attributes, or 3) window settings.

Techniques leveraging overlaps in predicates and group-by attributes across *ACQs* are similar to classical multi-query optimization [16] that detects common subexpressions.

Techniques leveraging shared processing of overlapping windows across *ACQs* emerged with the paradigm shift for continuous queries. *Shared time slices* (*SLS*) [11] is one such a technique, which was also extended into *shared data shards* in order to share the processing of varying predicates, in addition to varying windows. Orthogonally, [15] extends classical subsumption-based multi-query optimization techniques towards sharing the processing of multiple *ACQs* with varying group-by attributes and similar windows.

Like *SLS*, *WeaveShare* [8] optimizes the shared processing of *ACQs* with varying windows by selectively partitioning them into execution trees resulting in a dramatic reduction in total processing costs. *WeaveShare* was also applied in distributed environments [17].

In [5], a demonstration of implementing event monitoring applications using the modified Hadoop framework was presented. Along the same lines are schemes for scaling operators/queries out when nodes get overloaded [9, 10].

7. CONCLUSIONS

The main contribution of this paper is a novel closed formula, $F1$, for accelerating *Weavability* calculations required for determining the best execution plans for sharing partial aggregations of *ACQs*. Our approach replaces the counting of the edges within a *Bit Set* with mathematical computation. We proved theoretically that $F1$ significantly decreases the number of operations required for the execution plan generation while reducing the algorithm's space consumption to the bare minimum. We showed experimentally that the $F1$ approach achieves up to 60,000 times faster plan generation times compared to the current state of the art, and is able to achieve much better scalability in terms of the number of input *ACQs*, their diversity, and the input rate of the data stream. It should be noted that $F1$ can reduce the computation time of any optimization technique that requires scheduling partial aggregations within composite slides of multiple *ACQs*.

Acknowledgments We would like to thank Profs. K. Pruhs, J. Sorenson, and E. Bach for their help with our theoretical analysis and C. Thoma and the anonymous reviewers for the insightful feedback. This work was supported in part by NSF award CBET-1250171 and a gift from EMC/Greenplum.

8. REFERENCES

[1] D. J. Abadi et al. Aurora: a new model and architecture for data stream management. *VLDBJ*, 2003.
[2] D. J. Abadi et al. The design of the borealis stream processing engine. In *CIDR*, 2005.
[3] T. Akidau et al. Millwheel: Fault-tolerant stream processing at internet scale. In *VLDB*, 2013.
[4] C. Chung, S. Guirguis, and A. Kurdia. Competitive cost-savings in data stream management systems. In *COCOON*. 2014.
[5] T. Condie, N. Conway, P. Alvaro, J. Hellerstein, J. Gerth, J. Talbot, K. Elmeleegy, R. Sears. Online aggregation and continuous query support in mapreduce. In *SIGMOD*, 2010.
[6] T. M. Ghanem, M. A. Hammad, M. F. Mokbel, W. G. Aref, and A. K. Elmagarmid. Incremental evaluation of sliding-window queries over data streams. *TKDE*, 2007.
[7] S. Guirguis, M. Sharaf, P. K. Chrysanthis, and A. Labrinidis. Three-level processing of multiple aggregate continuous queries. In *ICDE*, 2012.
[8] S. Guirguis, M. A. Sharaf, P. K. Chrysanthis, and A. Labrinidis. Optimized processing of multiple aggregate continuous queries. In *CIKM*, 2011.
[9] V. Gulisano, R. Jimenez-Peris, M. Patino-Martinez, C. Soriente, and P. Valduriez. Streamcloud: An elastic and scalable data streaming system. *IEEE TPDS*, 2012.
[10] N. R. Katsipoulakis, C. Thoma, E. A. Gratta, A. Labrinidis, A. J. Lee, and P. K. Chrysanthis. Confidential elastic processing of data streams. In *SIGMOD*, 2015.
[11] S. Krishnamurthy, C. Wu, and M. Franklin. On-the-fly sharing for streamed aggregation. In *SIGMOD*, 2006.
[12] J. Li, D. Maier, K. Tufte, V. Papadimos, and P. A. Tucker. No pane, no gain: efficient evaluation of sliding-window aggregates over data streams. *SIGMOD*, 2005.
[13] J. Li, D. Maier, K. Tufte, V. Papadimos, and P. A. Tucker. Semantics and evaluation techniques for window aggregates in data streams. In *SIGMOD*, 2005.
[14] R. Motwani, J. Widom, A. Arasu, B. Babcock, S. Babu, M. Datar, G. Manku, C. Olston, J. Rosenstein, , and R. Varma. Query processing, approximation, and resource management in a data stream management system. In *CIDR*, 2003.
[15] K. Naidu, R. Rastogi, S. Satkin, and A. Srinivasan. Memory-constrained aggregate computation over data streams. In *ICDE*, 2011.
[16] P. Roy, S. Seshadri, S. Sudarshan, and S. Bhobe. Efficient and extensible algorithms for multi query optimization. In *SIGMOD*, 2000.
[17] A. U. Shein, P. K. Chrysanthis, and A. Labrinidis. Processing of aggregate continuous queries in a distributed environment. In *BIRTE*. 2015.
[18] K. Tangwongsan, M. Hirzel, S. Schneider, K-L. Wu. General incremental sliding-window aggregation. *VLDB*, 2015.
[19] A. Toshniwal et al. Storm@twitter. In *SIGMOD*, 2014.
[20] E. Weisstein. Binomial series. Wolfram MathWorld.
[21] E. Weisstein. Euclidean algorithm. Wolfram MathWorld.
[22] E. Weisstein. Harmonic number. Wolfram MathWorld.
[23] E. Weisstein. Prime number theorem. Wolfram MathWorld.
[24] R. Zhang, N. Koudas, B. C. Ooi, D. Srivastava. Multiple aggregations over data streams. In *SIGMOD*, 2005.
[25] R. Zhang, N. Koudas, B. C. Ooi, D. Srivastava, and P. Zhou. Streaming multiple aggregations using phantoms. *VLDBJ*, 2010.

Fast Distributed Correlation Discovery Over Streaming Time-Series Data

Tian Guo
EPFL, Switzerland
tian.guo@epfl.ch

Saket Sathe
IBM Research – Australia
ssathe@au.ibm.com

Karl Aberer
EPFL, Switzerland
karl.aberer@epfl.ch

ABSTRACT

The dramatic rise of time-series data in a variety of contexts, such as social networks, mobile sensing, data centre monitoring, etc., has fuelled interest in obtaining real-time insights from such data using distributed stream processing systems. One such extremely valuable insight is the discovery of correlations in *real-time* from large-scale time-series data. A key challenge in discovering correlations is that the number of time-series pairs that have to be analyzed grows quadratically in the number of time-series, giving rise to a quadratic increase in both computation cost and communication cost between the cluster nodes in a distributed environment. To tackle the challenge, we propose a framework called AEGIS. AEGIS exploits well-established statistical properties to dramatically prune the number of time-series pairs that have to be evaluated for detecting interesting correlations. Our extensive experimental evaluations on real and synthetic datasets establish the efficacy of AEGIS over baselines.

Categories and Subject Descriptors

H.3 [**INFORMATION STORAGE AND RETRIEVAL**]: Information Search and Retrieval; H.3.4 [**Distributed systems**]; G.3 [**PROBABILITY AND STATISTICS**]: Correlation and regression analysis

Keywords

Time Series Analysis; Stream Processing; Distributed Computing; Approximate Algorithm

1. INTRODUCTION

Time-series data is dramatically increasing [4, 13]. This trend is observed since the devices producing time-series data have exploded. This has, obviously, led to a demand for accommodating more and more data for efficiently producing answers to diverse problems. One such important problem, which is the focus of this paper, is to discover correlations in real-time from massive-scale time-series data. Different correlation measures, such as the Pearson correlation coefficient, cosine similarity, extended Jaccard coefficient, etc., could be employed for this task.

Permission to make digital or hard copies of all or part of this work for personal or classroom use is granted without fee provided that copies are not made or distributed for profit or commercial advantage and that copies bear this notice and the full citation on the first page. Copyrights for components of this work owned by others than ACM must be honored. Abstracting with credit is permitted. To copy otherwise, or republish, to post on servers or to redistribute to lists, requires prior specific permission and/or a fee. Request permissions from Permissions@acm.org.
CIKM'15, October 19-23, 2015, Melbourne, VIC, Australia.
Copyright 2015 ACM. ISBN 978-1-4503-3794-6/15/10 $15.00.
DOI: http://dx.doi.org/10.1145/2806416.2806440

Real-time correlation detection from large-scale time series data plays an important role in diverse applications. In data center monitoring, correlations between performance counters (e.g. CPU, memory usage, etc.) across large number of servers are typically continuously queried for recognizing the servers with correlated performance patterns [8]. In financial applications, timely discovery of correlations among stock prices can lead stock traders to spot investment opportunities [20]. In online recommendation systems, correlation mining is used to find customers with similar shopping patterns and to provide dynamic recommendations based on how a given customer's behavior correlates with other customers.

Traditional real-time data processing systems [3] designed for this task run on a standalone machine, which cannot handle the rapidly increasing amounts of time series data. This has led to the development of many distributed, fault-tolerant, and real-time computation systems [2, 4, 9, 18]. One such popular system is Apache Storm [2]. Even though these systems exist, using them for efficiently discovering correlations in time-series is still a challenging problem. Such a trend is analogous to the trend observed in map-reduce systems (e.g., Apache Hadoop); where efficiently performing database operations, like joins, using map-reduce continues to remain a challenging problem [6, 12, 15].

Distributed real-time computation.
The problem of real-time correlation discovery has been well-studied in the centralized setting [5, 7, 8, 11, 13, 16, 17, 19, 20], where the assumption is that the time series can be stored and queried on a single machine. But when this assumption does not hold, the correlation discovery methods proposed in the centralized context have to be completely re-designed for the distributed environment.

Before we deep dive into the technical details of our approaches, in the following paragraphs let us briefly understand the operation of a distributed realtime computation system. The core idea of most distributed realtime computation systems is the notion of a **topology** [2, 9]. A topology is a directed graph where the vertexes are known as **processing elements**. A processing element transforms the incoming data according to its programmed operation and transmits it to neighbouring processing element(s) as defined by the topology. In the distributed environment, one or many instances of the processing elements are executed on the nodes of a cluster, where the inter-node communication is dictated by the topology. In addition to the above processing principles, below we describe useful concepts related to time series processing:

- **Stream** is an unbounded sequence of tuples, where each tuple is a key-value(s) pair. The key or any of the values could be a number, string or a generic object. We denote a tuple as $\tau = (\tau_k, \tau_v)$ where τ_k is the key and τ_v is the value.

- **Source element** is a source of the streaming data. It can be used for reading data from a file, REST, JSON, etc., and converting it to tuples. We denote a source element by $\mathcal{S}$.
- **Action element** is a processing element that consumes tuples it receives from a source element or another action element, processes them according to the defined logic, and transmits tuples to other action elements that have subscribed to it; we denote an action element by $\mathcal{B}$.
- **Task** is an instance of either a source or action element. One or more tasks are executed in a cluster. The time series streams processed by a task are referred to as its **local streams**. A source task and action task are denoted as $\bar{\mathcal{S}}$ and $\bar{\mathcal{B}}$ respectively.
- **Parallelism** of a given action or source element is the number of its respective tasks executed in the cluster. This is a user-defined parameter. The parallelism of action element $\mathcal{B}^{(x)}$ is denoted as $\mathcal{P}^{(x)}$.
- **Shuffling function** is a function defined for each edge of the topology. It determines the task(s) of the subsequent processing elements to which a tuple emitted from a task of the preceding action element should be sent. For example, if action element $\mathcal{B}^{(shf)}$ is connected to $\mathcal{B}^{(cmp)}$ in the topology, then the shuffling function between them is denoted as $\mathcal{H}(\tau_k; \mathcal{B}^{(shf)}, \mathcal{B}^{(cmp)})$. It is popular to use a **key-based shuffling function**. It computes the hash value of a tuple key and decides to which task(s) the tuple should be sent using this hash value.

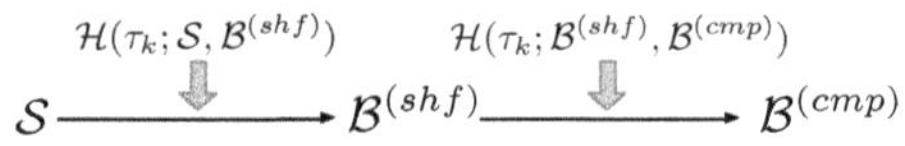

(a) Toy example of a topology.

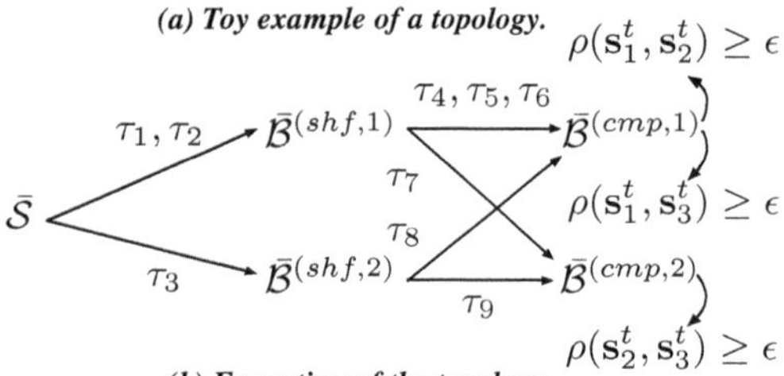

(b) Execution of the topology.

$\tau_1 = (\langle 1 \rangle, s_{1,k})$	$\tau_4 = (\langle 1, 2 \rangle, \mathbf{s}_1^t)$	$\tau_7 = (\langle 2, 3 \rangle, \mathbf{s}_2^t)$
$\tau_2 = (\langle 2 \rangle, s_{2,k})$	$\tau_5 = (\langle 1, 2 \rangle, \mathbf{s}_2^t)$	$\tau_8 = (\langle 1, 3 \rangle, \mathbf{s}_3^t)$
$\tau_3 = (\langle 3 \rangle, s_{3,k})$	$\tau_6 = (\langle 1, 3 \rangle, \mathbf{s}_1^t)$	$\tau_9 = (\langle 2, 3 \rangle, \mathbf{s}_3^t)$

(c) Communicated tuples.

Figure 1: A toy example of a topology.

Distributed correlation discovery.
Given n time-series data streams, we are interested in discovering the pairs of time series that are correlated beyond a threshold ϵ over a sliding window of size h. We refer to such time-series pairs as **ϵ-correlated** pairs. Consider a toy example where we have three time-series streams $\boldsymbol{s}_1$, $\boldsymbol{s}_2$, $\boldsymbol{s}_3$ and suppose we have the topology shown in Figure 1(a). This topology performs the **naïve pair-wise correlation computation** to obtain the correlations of all the time series pairs and then filter out the unqualified pairs. Similar to performing Cartesian product using MapReduce, we use two action elements, of which the first one is responsible for annotating the tuples and the second one performs the correlation computation.

Concretely, time series are read by the source task $\bar{\mathcal{S}}$. $\bar{\mathcal{S}}$ produces tuples of the form $(i, s_{i,k})$, where $i = (1, \ldots, 3)$ and k is the timestamp of the tuple at time instant k. The tuples are then distributed to action tasks $\bar{\mathcal{B}}^{(shf,1)}$ and $\bar{\mathcal{B}}^{(shf,2)}$ using the shuffling function $\mathcal{H}(\tau_k; \mathcal{S}, \mathcal{B}^{(shf)})$, which sends tuples of time series $\boldsymbol{s}_1$, $\boldsymbol{s}_2$ are to $\bar{\mathcal{B}}^{(shf,1)}$ and time series $\boldsymbol{s}_3$ to task $\bar{\mathcal{B}}^{(shf,2)}$. Each task of $\mathcal{B}^{(shf)}$ performs two steps. First, it maintains a sliding window for each local stream. For time series i, the **sliding window** ending at time stamp t is denoted by $\boldsymbol{s}_i^t = (s_{i,t}, \ldots, s_{i,t-h+1})$ and $\boldsymbol{s}_i^t \in \mathbb{R}^h$. We use t to represent the current ending timestamp of the sliding window.

Second, tasks of $\mathcal{B}^{(shf)}$ modify the keys of the local tuples assigned to them and create output tuples of the form $(\langle i, j \rangle, \boldsymbol{s}_i^t)$ if $j > i$ and $j \neq i$, (or $(\langle j, i \rangle, \boldsymbol{s}_i^t)$ if $i > j$) for each $j = (1, \ldots, 3)$. For example, task $\bar{\mathcal{B}}^{(shf,2)}$ will emit tuples τ_8 and τ_9 as shown in Figure 1(b) and Figure 1(c). In the final phase, each task $\bar{\mathcal{B}}^{(cmp,1)}$ or $\bar{\mathcal{B}}^{(cmp,2)}$ receives two tuples for a specific time series pair, where each tuple contains the sliding window of one of the two time series that the key refers to. For example, $\bar{\mathcal{B}}^{(cmp,2)}$ will receive τ_7 and τ_9, both of them have the same key $\langle 2, 3 \rangle$. The tasks of $\mathcal{B}^{(shf)}$ modify the keys because this allows tasks of $\mathcal{B}^{(cmp)}$ to utilize the tuples having same keys to perform pair-wise correlation computation and check the threshold ϵ.

Observe that the above approach has a major shortcoming: for large number of time series (larger n), $\mathcal{B}^{(shf)}$ generates and communicates an exceptionally large number ($\mathcal{O}(n^2)$) of tuples and $\mathcal{B}^{(cmp)}$ performs quadratic correlation computation. Thus this tremendously limits its scalability. In an attempt to ameliorate this situation, we propose the **AEGIS (Affine Time-Series Grouping with Partition-Aware Shuffling)** approach. To our best knowledge, this is the first work that proposes a truly distributed and scalable solution to the continuous and distributed correlation discovery problem. Overall, this paper makes the following concrete contributions.

- We define the streaming threshold correlation (or STCOR) query, and identify the necessity of optimizing the communication and computation cost involved in processing it (cf. Section 3) .
- For reducing AEGIS's communication overhead, we propose methods for sliding window grouping and approximation, such that communicating groups becomes highly efficient than communicating individual sliding window (cf. Section 4 and 5).
- Built into AEGIS is a novel shuffling technique called **PAS (Partition-Aware Shuffling)** that has the ability to determine and shuffle sliding window groups that could contain ϵ-correlated sliding windows to the *same* action tasks. This results in localized processing within an action task and dramatic reduction in communication overhead (cf. Section 4.2).
- We propose novel pruning techniques that operate on sliding window groups. Our pruning techniques can efficiently prune the groups that do not contain ϵ-correlated sliding window pairs, and therefore can quickly eliminate the need of examining a large number of pairs (cf. Section 5).
- We implement AEGIS and competitor baselines on an open-source fully-distributed realtime computation system called Apache Storm [2], and experimentally demonstrate that AEGIS delivers orders of magnitude improved performance (cf. Section 6).

2. RELATED WORK

Numerous systems [2, 3, 9, 18] have been developed to process data in an high-speed environment. Storm [2] is a widely-used platform, which provides fault tolerance and tuple processing guarantees. Unlike Storm, some systems like S4 [9] cannot guarantee that each tuple will be processed. Zaharia *et al.* [18] proposed a new model using micro-batches for distributed stream processing.

Their approach abandons the classical topology structure in stream processing. However, such models have larger processing latency compared to the one-tuple-at-a-time model of [2, 3, 9]. However, they do not support operators for performing correlation queries.

Various indexing techniques for querying the correlations of static time-series data stored in a centralized system have been proposed in [7, 8, 13, 17]. Such techniques are not suitable for our dynamic and distributed environment. Computing real-time correlations using a standalone machine has been a key focus of [5, 11, 16, 19], however these techniques are ineffective in a distributed environment. The StatStream system [20] specializes in discovering correlations using a grid structure, but it incurs prohibitive communication cost in a distributed environment. Recently, partitioning-based approaches have attracted attention for batch distributed data processing [6, 12, 15]. However, such approaches are data-dependent and need an aprori data pre-processing step to estimate the data distribution. Scanning the entire data to update the data distribution is impossible in a streaming environment. In summary, this paper is the first work that efficiently discovers correlations from massive time-series data in a scalable distributed environment.

3. FOUNDATION

We concretely define the problem of discovering streaming correlations in streaming time-series data with the help of the **streaming threshold correlation (STCOR) query**. In this paper, we have used the Pearson correlation coefficient (henceforth, correlation coefficient) to illustrate our techniques, however, our methods can be used for computing many other correlation measures (refer Section 5 for details).

3.1 Problem statement

The correlation coefficient $\rho(\boldsymbol{s}_i^t, \boldsymbol{s}_j^t)$ between sliding windows $\boldsymbol{s}_i^t$ and $\boldsymbol{s}_j^t$ is defined as follows:

$$\rho(\boldsymbol{s}_i^t, \boldsymbol{s}_j^t) = \frac{(\boldsymbol{s}_i^t - \overline{s}_i^t\mathbb{1})^T(\boldsymbol{s}_j^t - \overline{s}_j^t\mathbb{1})}{(h-1)\sigma_i^t\sigma_j^t}, \quad (1)$$

where σ_i^t and $\overline{s}_i^t$ (or σ_j^t and $\overline{s}_j^t$) are the sample standard deviation and mean of sliding window $\boldsymbol{s}_i^t$ (or $\boldsymbol{s}_j^t$), respectively. Another important concept is that of a **normalized sliding window**. A normalized sliding window of $\boldsymbol{s}_i^t$ is denoted as $\hat{\boldsymbol{s}}_i^t = (\hat{s}_{i,t}, \cdots, \hat{s}_{i,t-h+1})$ and is defined as [20],

$$\hat{\boldsymbol{s}}_i^t = \frac{\boldsymbol{s}_i^t - \overline{s}_i^t\mathbb{1}_h}{\sigma_i^t\sqrt{(h-1)}}, \quad (2)$$

where $\mathbb{1}_h$ is an all ones vector of size h. The vector $\hat{\boldsymbol{s}}_i^t$ is of unit length and therefore $(\hat{\boldsymbol{s}}_i^t)^\top\hat{\boldsymbol{s}}_i^t = 1$. The correlation coefficient can also be written using the normalized sliding windows as follows: $\rho(\boldsymbol{s}_i^t, \boldsymbol{s}_j^t) = (\hat{\boldsymbol{s}}_i^t)^\top\hat{\boldsymbol{s}}_j^t$. Since $\hat{\boldsymbol{s}}_i^t$ is a unit length vector, each of its entries $\hat{s}_{i,k}$ varies between $-1 \leq \hat{s}_{i,k} \leq 1$. Thus, the range of variation of the normalized sliding window is known apriori, and is independent of the variation in the original sliding window $\boldsymbol{s}_i^t$. We shall later exploit this important observation to create partitions over the space of normalized sliding windows.

Additionally, there exists an important relationship between the correlation coefficient and the Euclidean distance between normalized sliding windows [20],

$$\mathcal{D}(\hat{\boldsymbol{s}}_i^t, \hat{\boldsymbol{s}}_j^t) = \sqrt{2(1-\rho(\boldsymbol{s}_i^t, \boldsymbol{s}_j^t))}, \quad (3)$$

where $\mathcal{D}(\hat{\boldsymbol{s}}_i^t, \hat{\boldsymbol{s}}_j^t)$ is the Euclidean distance between $\hat{\boldsymbol{s}}_i^t$ and $\hat{\boldsymbol{s}}_j^t$. The correlation coefficient between two normalized sliding windows increases as the Euclidean distance between them decreases.

Next, suppose the total number of time-series pushed into the system is denoted by n and the set of all the sliding windows at time t is denoted by $\mathbf{S}^t$, then the STCOR query is defined as follows:

DEFINITION 3.1 (STCOR QUERY). *Given $\mathbf{S}^t$ continuously find the set of ϵ-correlated sliding window pairs for a given value of $0 < \epsilon \leq 1$. This query is formally written as:*

$$QC_\epsilon(\mathbf{S}^t) = \{\langle i,j\rangle | i \neq j, \rho(\boldsymbol{s}_i^t, \boldsymbol{s}_j^t) \geq \epsilon, \boldsymbol{s}_i^t \in \mathbf{S}^t, \boldsymbol{s}_j^t \in \mathbf{S}^t\}. \quad (4)$$

Alternatively, the STCOR query can be defined using the Euclidean distance between two normalized sliding windows, and is written as follows:

$$QD_\delta(\hat{\mathbf{S}}^t) = \{\langle i,j\rangle | i \neq j, \mathcal{D}(\hat{\boldsymbol{s}}_i^t, \hat{\boldsymbol{s}}_j^t) \leq \delta, \hat{\boldsymbol{s}}_i^t \text{ and } \hat{\boldsymbol{s}}_j^t \in \hat{\mathbf{S}}^t\}, \quad (5)$$

where δ is related to ϵ as $\delta = \sqrt{2(1-\epsilon)}$.

As ϵ decreases, δ increases and vice versa. ϵ is always assumed to be greater than zero, however, in practice it could be negative. In such cases it can be shown that if the entries in one of the sliding windows are reversed, then the negative ϵ can be treated as positive [20]. Thus, without loss of generality, henceforth we only focus on the positive threshold ϵ.

3.2 δ–Hypercube Structure

We partition the space of normalized sliding windows $\hat{\mathbf{S}}^t$ into h-dimensional orthogonal regular hypercubes called **δ-hypercubes**, where each hypercube has edges of length δ. The hypercube in which a normalized sliding window $\hat{\boldsymbol{s}}_i^t$ is contained is identified by its **coordinate vector**, which is given as follows:

$$\boldsymbol{c}_i^t = \left(\left\lceil\frac{\hat{s}_{i,t}}{\delta}\right\rceil, \ldots, \left\lceil\frac{\hat{s}_{i,t-h+1}}{\delta}\right\rceil\right). \quad (6)$$

Given an hypercube $\boldsymbol{c}_i^t$, the set of its neighbouring hypercubes is denoted as $\mathcal{N}(\boldsymbol{c}_i^t)$. For instance, Figure 2(*a*) shows a three-dimensional δ-hypercube structure for sliding window $\boldsymbol{s}_i^t$ of length 3; thus, dimensions t, $t-1$, and $t-2$ are shown. A normalized sliding window $\hat{\boldsymbol{s}}_i^t$ is mapped to the red δ-hypercube whose coordinate vector is $\boldsymbol{c}_i^t$. Figure 2(*b*) shows the set of the neighbouring hypercubes $\mathcal{N}(\boldsymbol{c}_i^t)$ around $\boldsymbol{c}_i^t$. The number of neighbouring hypercubes of $\boldsymbol{c}_i^t$, $|\mathcal{N}(\boldsymbol{c}_i^t)|$ grows exponentially w.r.t. h ($|\mathcal{N}(\boldsymbol{c}_i^t)| = 3^h$).

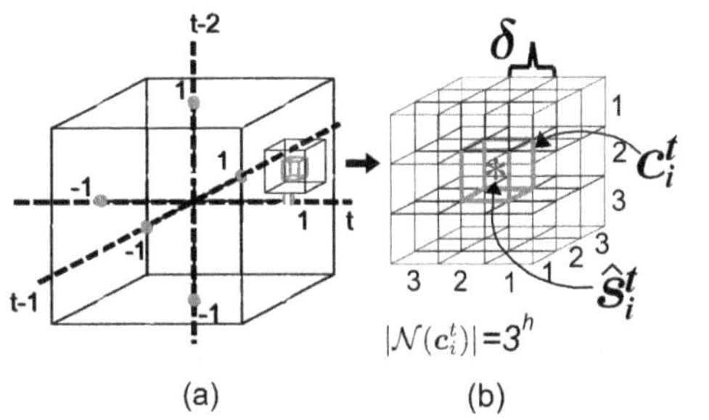

Figure 2: (a) δ–hypercube structures over the space of all normalized sliding windows. (b) $\mathcal{N}(\boldsymbol{c}_i^t)$.

An important property of such a hypercube structure is that given a $\hat{\boldsymbol{s}}_i^t$ and its $\boldsymbol{c}_i^t$, all the ϵ-correlated sliding windows are either contained in the hypercube $\boldsymbol{c}_i^t$ or in any of the hypercubes in $\mathcal{N}(\boldsymbol{c}_i^t)$. This property is due to relationship between ϵ and δ given in Definition 3.1. This property can be used for designing a shuffling strategy where an action task processing sliding window $\hat{\boldsymbol{s}}_i^t$, could emit tuples of the form $(\boldsymbol{c}_k^t, \hat{\boldsymbol{s}}_i^t)$ for all $\boldsymbol{c}_k^t \in \boldsymbol{c}_i^t \cup \mathcal{N}(\boldsymbol{c}_i^t)$. This strategy, although simplistic, does not work when $|\mathcal{N}(\boldsymbol{c}_i^t)|$ is large, which is typically the case. In such cases it leads to an exponential increase in communication cost and heavily constrained scalability [6].

4. REDUCING COMMUNICATION COST

This section introduces our core contribution – the **AEGIS approach**. As we shall experimentally demonstrate in Section 6, AEGIS exhibits orders of magnitude lower communication overhead as compared to baselines. The topology of AEGIS is depicted in Figure 3. As compared to topology of the naïve strategy from Section 1, AEGIS's topology differs in three aspects. First, for efficient shuffling and transmission of sliding windows, the first action element $\mathcal{B}_A^{(shf)}$ approximates and groups sliding windows (details will be discussed in Section 4.1). Second, action element $\mathcal{B}_A^{(cmp)}$ computes the correlation coefficients and removes both false negatives and false positives that could be introduced by $\mathcal{B}_A^{(shf)}$ (refer Section 5 for details). Third, the tuples between $\mathcal{B}_A^{(shf)}$ and $\mathcal{B}_A^{(cmp)}$ are shuffled using a novel approach refereed to as partition-aware shuffling (PAS) approach, which essentially shuffles a sliding window group from $\mathcal{B}_A^{(shf)}$ *only to those* action tasks of $\mathcal{B}_A^{(cmp)}$ containing correlated sliding windows (refer Section 4.2).

4.1 Grouping and Approximation

Each task of action element $\mathcal{B}_A^{(shf)}$ is assigned a subset of sliding windows $\mathbf{Z}^t \subset \mathbf{S}^t$ by a source task. When a new tuple is received from a source task at timestamp t, a action task of $\mathcal{B}_A^{(shf)}$ updates the normalized sliding windows that are present in its local sliding windows. This normalization is performed by incrementally updating all the quantities on the right-hand side of Eq. (2) [20]. The normalized sliding windows corresponding to $\mathbf{Z}^t$ are denoted as $\hat{\mathbf{Z}}^t$.

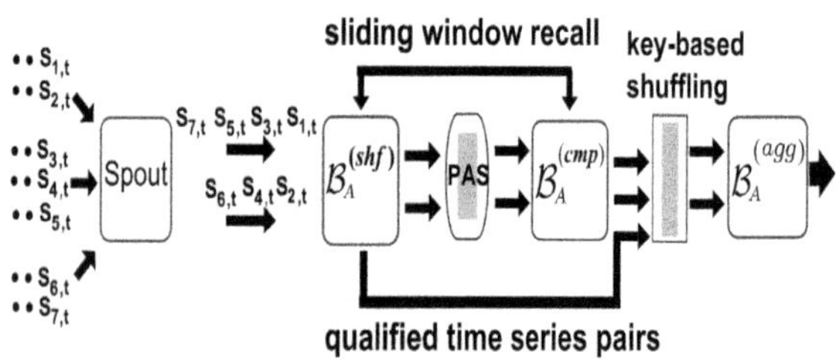

Figure 3: Topology architecture of the AEGIS approach.

Sliding window grouping: The second step that a action task of $\mathcal{B}_A^{(shf)}$ performs is to divide the sliding windows $\hat{\mathbf{Z}}^t$ into non-overlapping groups $\mathcal{G}_1^t, \ldots, \mathcal{G}_f^t$ known as **sliding window groups**. A leader is selected for each group, which is called the **pivot sliding window**. The pivot sliding window is selected such that the non-pivot sliding windows in a group can be accurately approximated using the pivot sliding window. The boundary of a sliding window group is represented by a **constant bounding hypercube (CBH)**. A CBH is a bounding hypercube constructed such that it includes the δ-hypercubes of all sliding windows in a sliding window group. For discovering the sliding window groups we propose an algorithm called **Local-Correlation Graph Based Grouping (LAP)**. LAP has two desirable properties: 1) it uses a greedy strategy to create a minimal number of groups, 2) the groups created by LAP are small, i.e., the length of each side of their CBH is at most a constant times δ. The second property is extremely important for shuffling sliding window groups only to those action tasks of $\mathcal{B}_A^{(cmp)}$ that contain ϵ-correlated pairs.

Since all the action tasks of $\mathcal{B}_A^{(shf)}$ execute the same LAP algorithm we explain this algorithm for a single task. First, correlation computation over the local sliding windows $\hat{\mathbf{Z}}^t$ is performed. This process generates an un-directed graph $L = \{V, E\}$ referred to as the **local-correlation graph**. Each vertex $v_i \in V$ ($i = 1, \ldots, |\hat{\mathbf{Z}}^t|$) represents a normalized sliding window in $\hat{\mathbf{Z}}^t$. An edge $e_{i,j} \in E$ is inserted between vertexes v_i and v_j if $\mathcal{D}(\hat{\boldsymbol{s}}_i^t, \hat{\boldsymbol{s}}_j^t) \leq \delta$. In practice, the overhead of computing the local-correlation graph is controlled by making sure that only a small number of sliding windows are assigned to each task of element $\mathcal{B}_A^{(shf)}$. This can be done by increasing the parallism of element $\mathcal{B}_A^{(shf)}$ as the number of time-series n increases.

Then, LAP algorithm is executed on the local-correlation graph for finding the sliding window groups and pivot sliding windows. The objective function minimized by LAP is as follows:

$$\begin{aligned} &\underset{x_i}{\text{minimize}} \sum_{i=1}^{|\hat{\mathbf{Z}}^t|} \mathbf{I}_{\{x_i=1\}} \\ &\text{subject to} \sum_{e_{i,j}\in E} x_j \geq 1, \forall\, i = 1, \ldots, |\hat{\mathbf{Z}}^t| \\ &\qquad x_i \in \{0,1\}, \forall\, i = 1, \ldots, |\hat{\mathbf{Z}}^t| \end{aligned} \tag{7}$$

where $x_i = 1$ indicates that a vertex v_i is chosen as the pivot sliding window. The constraint ensures that each non-pivot sliding window is assigned to at least one group. The optimization problem of Eq. (7) can be reduced to a set-cover problem, which is known to be NP-complete.

Therefore, we propose a greedy version of LAP called Greedy-LAP that efficiently finds a feasible solution and has a provable near-optimality guarantee. Greedy-LAP starts by finding the set of vertexes N_{v_i} that are connected to the vertex $v_i \in L$, then it executes the following steps. STEP 1: Choose the vertex with the highest degree, let that vertex be denoted as $\bar{v}$. STEP 2: A sliding window group $\mathcal{G}_{\bar{v}}^t$ is created by making the sliding window associated with $\bar{v}$ the pivot sliding window and the sliding windows associated with the vertexes $N_{\bar{v}}$ as non-pivot sliding windows. STEP 3: This group of vertexes is removed from the graph L and STEP 1 is executed until there are no vertexes left in L. It can be shown that the above steps greedily minimize the optimization function in Eq. (7). These steps can be efficiently implemented using BFS (breadth-first-search), where we keep track of the vertexes that the algorithm is not allowed to use.

It can be proved that Greedy-LAP is a $\ln(|\hat{\mathbf{Z}}^t|)$ approximation to LAP (refer [1] for the proof). Moreover, the Greedy-LAP algorithm guarantees that the length of each side of the CBH, which contains a sliding window group, is bounded by 3δ. We call this the **3δ property** of Greedy-LAP. A proof of this property can be found in [1]. The 3δ property is heavily used in the PAS shuffling phase discussed in Section 4.2.

Sliding window approximation: This step approximates each non-pivot sliding window with its pivot. We use a particular method known as the **affine transformation** to perform this approximation [13]. Given a non-pivot sliding window $\hat{\boldsymbol{s}}_i^t$ and a pivot sliding window $\hat{\boldsymbol{s}}_m^t$, the affine transformation between $\hat{\boldsymbol{s}}_i^t$ and $\hat{\boldsymbol{s}}_m^t$ is defined as:

$$\hat{\boldsymbol{s}}_i^t = w_{i,1}\hat{\boldsymbol{s}}_m^t + w_{i,0}\mathbb{1}_h = (\hat{\boldsymbol{s}}_m^t, \mathbb{1}_h)\boldsymbol{w}_i, \tag{8}$$

where matrix $(\hat{\boldsymbol{s}}_m^t, \mathbb{1}_h)$ is of size h-by-2. Since $h \gg 2$, Eq. (8) is an over-determined system, and we use the least-squares method to obtain an approximate affine transformation $\tilde{\boldsymbol{w}}_i$ of $\boldsymbol{w}_i$ as:

$$\hat{\boldsymbol{s}}_i^t = (\hat{\boldsymbol{s}}_m^t, \mathbb{1}_h)\begin{pmatrix} \tilde{w}_{i,1} \\ \tilde{w}_{i,0} \end{pmatrix} + \boldsymbol{e}_i, \tag{9}$$

where $\boldsymbol{e}_i$ is the residual error. The advantage of using affine transformations is twofold: (a) the size of the affine transformation is not dependent on the length of the sliding window, (b) the affine transformation and the pivot sliding window can be used for estimating certain statistical measures (including the correlation coefficient). Thus, a group can be effectively represented by the pivot sliding window plus the affine transformations for approximating the non-pivot sliding windows. In the subsequent sections, we will discuss how to shuffle a sliding window group and compute the correlations between inter-group and intra-group sliding windows.

Integration with dimensionality reduction techniques: Even though dimensionality reduction methods are not the focus of this paper, we briefly discuss how our framework can incorporate such techniques. Orthonormal transformation based dimensionality reduction (e.g., discrete Fourier transformation (DFT), random projections, etc.) can be seamlessly performed in the action element $\mathcal{B}_A^{(shf)}$. It is noteworthy that the aforementioned sliding window grouping works on such dimension-reduced sliding windows. In addition, due to the distance-preserving nature of dimensionality reduction techniques, the subsequent correlation computation can be performed on lower-dimensional sliding windows [8] without any modification.

Emitting sliding window group tuples: Lastly, each sliding window group is used for forming a output tuple of $\mathcal{B}_A^{(shf)}$. This tuple is constructed as follows. For a group $\mathcal{G}_j^t$, the *key* of the output tuple is the coordinate vector $\boldsymbol{c}_j^t$ corresponding to this group's pivot sliding window $\hat{\boldsymbol{s}}_j^t$. An action task of $\mathcal{B}_A^{(cmp)}$ uses $\boldsymbol{c}_j^t$ to locate the position and distribution of the sliding windows in $\mathcal{G}_j^t$. The *value* of the output tuple contains the pivot sliding window $\hat{\boldsymbol{s}}_j^t$ and the approximate solution $\tilde{\boldsymbol{w}}_i$ and error norm $\|\boldsymbol{e}_i\|$ for each non-pivot sliding window $\hat{\boldsymbol{s}}_i^t$ in $\mathcal{G}_j^t$. It is noteworthy that this information can be used to sufficiently reconstruct the non-pivot windows, such that correlation coefficients (and other measures) can be computed with acceptable accuracy. If the LAP algorithm, in the process of constructing the local-correlation graph, finds that a sliding window pair is already ϵ-correlated, then that pair is directly sent to a task of $\mathcal{B}_A^{(agg)}$ as shown in Figure 3.

4.2 Partition-Aware Shuffling

The naïve key-based shuffling function, discussed in Section 1 is communication inefficient due to the quadratic data replication. On the other hand, the way of shuffling sliding windows among δ-hypercubes, discussed in Section 3 makes the communication inefficiency even more severe, as the sliding window size h increases. Therefore, we propose an enhanced partition-aware shuffling function that (a) restricts the number of shuffling dimensions, thereby replicating sliding window groups independent of h and n, and (b) shuffles and replicates groups only to those tasks that could contain other groups with ϵ-correlated sliding windows.

The idea of PAS is to create coarse-grained partitions as compared to the ones created by the δ-hypercube structure of Section 3.2. The δ-hypercubes were created from the query threshold ϵ, on the contrary the PAS partitions are created based on the parallelism $\mathcal{P}_A^{(cmp)}$ of the second action element $\mathcal{B}_A^{(cmp)}$ in the topology. In PAS three things are ensured: 1) groups that lie in a particular PAS partition are consistently assigned to the same partition, which cannot be guaranteed in key-based shuffling, 2) each partition is handled by an unique action task of $\mathcal{B}_A^{(cmp)}$, 3) the sliding window groups that are not fully contained in a PAS partition are replicated and shuffled only to the neighbouring partitions, such that the replication of a sliding window group is bounded by $\mathcal{P}_A^{(cmp)}$ and communication overhead is drastically minimized.

Partitioning: The partitioning function f_{PAS} of PAS maps each normalized sliding window $\hat{\boldsymbol{s}}_i^t$ into a vector called the **partition**

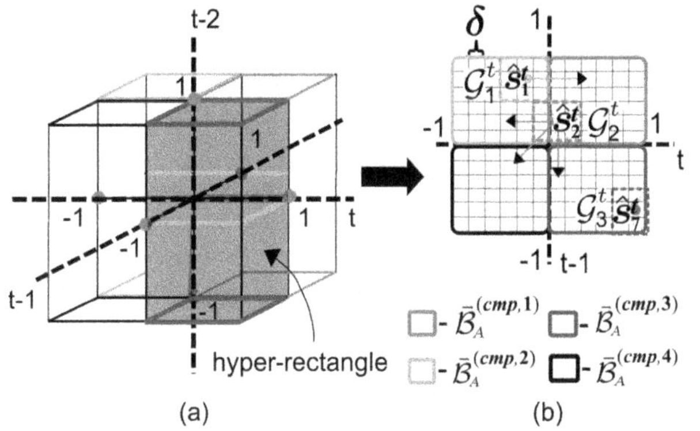

Figure 4: Illustration of PAS shuffling: (a) Parallelism $\mathcal{P}_A^{(cmp)}$ based hypercube partitioning; (b) Controlled sliding window group replication and shuffling amongst the partitions.

vector $\boldsymbol{p}_j^t$. Concretely, $f_{PAS} : \hat{\boldsymbol{s}}_i^t \mapsto \boldsymbol{p}_i^t$ and is written as:

$$\boldsymbol{p}_i^t = f_{PAS}(\hat{\boldsymbol{s}}_i^t) = (\text{sgn}(\hat{s}_{i,t})\lceil|\hat{s}_{i,t}|\rceil, ..., \text{sgn}(\hat{s}_{i,t-h+1})\lceil|\hat{s}_{i,t-h+1}|\rceil), \quad (10)$$

where $\text{sgn}(x)$ extracts the sign of its argument. Since $-1 \leq \hat{s}_{i,t} \leq 1$, each entry of the partition vector $\boldsymbol{p}_i^t$ is either -1 or 1. Next, the number of partitions created by the partition vector is matched to the user-defined parameter $\mathcal{P}_A^{(cmp)}$ as follows: compute $\bar{h} = \log_2(\mathcal{P}_A^{(cmp)})$, and if $\bar{h} \leq h$ the dimensionality of the partition vector is reduced by retaining only the first $\bar{h}$ entries of the partition vector. In case after computing $\bar{h}$ we find that $\bar{h} > h$, we simply keep all the entries in the partition vector.

An example of this operation is demonstrated in Figure 4(a) for 3D sliding windows. Suppose, $\mathcal{P}_A^{(cmp)} = 4$ then we have $\bar{h} = 2$. Since, $\bar{h} < 3$, only dimensions t and $t-1$ are used for partitioning in Figure 4(b). Thus, normalized sliding windows lying in the blue-grey hyper-rectangle are assigned to the blue partition (and to the $\bar{\mathcal{B}}_A^{(cmp,3)}$ action task) in Figure 4(b), similarly sliding windows in the red partition are assigned to task $\bar{\mathcal{B}}_A^{(cmp,1)}$, so on and so forth.

Controlled group replication and shuffling: There could be more than one partition to which a sliding window group has to be assigned in order to find ϵ-correlated pairs. The partitions to which a group should be assigned are determined as follows. Let $\bar{h}_s \subset (1, \ldots, \bar{h})$ be a subset of dimensions referred to as the **dimension subset**. Given a dimension subset $\bar{h}_s$, the **sub-permutation set** $R_j^{\bar{h}_s}$ of a partition vector $\boldsymbol{p}_j^t$ is defined as the set of all the permutations of $\boldsymbol{p}_j^t$, such that *only* the entries corresponding to the dimensions present in the dimension subset $\bar{h}_s$ are permuted and the remaining are held constant. For example, if $\boldsymbol{p}_j^t = (-1, 1, 1)$ and $\bar{h}_s = \{2, 3\}$, then only the 2nd and 3rd dimension of $\boldsymbol{p}_j^t$ are permuted to form $R_j^{\bar{h}_s}$ as follows: $R_j^{\bar{h}_s} = \{(-1,-1,-1), (-1,-1,1), (-1,1,-1), (-1,1,1)\}$. If a dimension subset could be found such that its sub-permutation set contains only the partitions that could potentially have ϵ-correlated sliding windows with one or more sliding windows from group $\mathcal{G}_j^t$, then $\mathcal{G}_j^t$ should be assigned to all the partitions present in the sub-permutation set. Such a dimension subset could be found using the following lemma:

LEMMA 4.1 (DIMENSION SUBSET GENERATION). *Given a sliding window group $\mathcal{G}_j^t$ with a pivot $\hat{\boldsymbol{s}}_j^t$ and $\boldsymbol{c}_j^t$ in partition $\boldsymbol{p}_j^t$, a dimension $k = (1, \cdots, \bar{h})$ is added to the set $\bar{h}_s$ if $\delta \cdot (c_{j,k} - 2 \cdot sgn(c_{j,k})) \cdot p_{j,k}^t < 0$, otherwise it is irrelevant.*

PROOF. The proof heavily relies on the 3δ property. Refer [1] for details. □

Embedded in Lemma 4.1 is also an algorithm for group replication. We essentially scan the vectors $\boldsymbol{c}_j^t$ and $\boldsymbol{p}_j^t$ of group $\mathcal{G}_j^t$ and check the condition given by Lemma 4.1 to generate the dimension subset $\bar{h}_s$, which is used for creating the sub-permutation set $R_j^{\bar{h}_s}$.

Intuitively, the replication condition given in Lemma 4.1 can be explained as follows: a sliding window group is relevant to a partition if the group's CBH is (a) fully contained in the partition, (b) overlaps with the partition, or (c) shares a boundary with the partition. For example, consider Figure 4(*b*), the group $\mathcal{G}_3^t$ (in blue) is fully contained in the partition $(1, -1)$, therefore it is only replicated and shuffled to that partition. $\mathcal{G}_1^t$ (in green) is contained in partition $(-1, 1)$ and shares a boundary with $(1, 1)$, therefore it is replicated to those two partitions. Likewise, $\mathcal{G}_2^t$ is replicated to partitions $(1, 1)$, $(-1, 1)$, $(-1, 1)$, and $(-1, -1)$.

5. COMPUTING CORRELATION MEASURES

Since all the action tasks of $\mathcal{B}_A^{(cmp)}$ perform the same function, in the following paragraphs we only describe the actions performed by a single task. Recall that each action task of $\mathcal{B}_A^{(cmp)}$ is responsible for processing all the sliding window groups assigned to a single PAS partition. Suppose, if exactly one group is shuffled to a task of $\mathcal{B}_A^{(cmp)}$, then this task has no action to perform. This is because even if there were ϵ-correlated pairs in that group, the LAP algorithm would have already detected and communicated them to tasks of the final action element $\mathcal{B}_A^{(agg)}$.

If more than one groups are shuffled to an action task, then for each group pair, the task judges whether it is necessary to examine the contents of these groups in detail or the pair can be pruned using a simple criterion. It turns out that it is indeed possible to derive a pruning criterion that only uses the pivot sliding windows of the groups to decide whether further examination is required. The following lemma discusses this criteria:

LEMMA 5.1 (PRUNING CRITERION). *Given two sliding window groups $\mathcal{G}_j^t$ and $\mathcal{G}_v^t$ respectively with pivot sliding windows $\hat{\boldsymbol{s}}_j^t$ and $\hat{\boldsymbol{s}}_v^t$, if there exists a dimension k such that $(c_{j,k} + 2) < (c_{v,k} - 1)$ (or $(c_{j,k} - 2) > (c_{v,k} + 1)$), where $k \in \{t, \cdots, h-t+1\}$, then the sliding windows in $\mathcal{G}_j^t$ and $\mathcal{G}_v^t$ are not correlated above ϵ. Otherwise, we have to compute the correlation coefficient between each pair of sliding windows in $\mathcal{G}_j^t$ and $\mathcal{G}_v^t$ and verify whether they are ϵ-correlated.*

PROOF. Refer [1]. □

Intuitively, Lemma 5.1 works as follows. A sliding window group pair requires further examination if (a) the CBH of the groups in the pair overlap with each other, or (b) they share a boundary with each other. For instance, in Figure 4(*b*) the CBHs of groups $\mathcal{G}_1^t$ and $\mathcal{G}_2^t$ share a boundary with each other, therefore further examination is required for these groups. On the contrary, the CBH of $\mathcal{G}_3^t$ in the blue partition does not overlap with that of $\mathcal{G}_2^t$, and therefore this group pair can be pruned. Next, using Lemma 5.1, only the sliding window group pairs that require further examination are selected. Then, for each group pair the sliding window pairs are formed by considering all the sliding windows in both groups together. Now, for each sliding window pair, three possibilities could occur: **(1)** both the sliding windows in the pair are non-pivot windows, **(2)** the pair has one pivot and one non-pivot windows. **(3)** both the sliding windows in the pair are pivot windows.

Recall that in a group the non-pivot sliding windows can only be reconstructed approximately. Naturally, if such approximately reconstructed sliding windows are used for correlation computation, the final query answer could contain sliding window pairs that are either false positives or false negatives. In the following paragraphs, we derive both upper and lower bounds for cases **(1)** and **(2)**, such that we can detect and delete any potential false positives or negatives in the query answer. Let us begin with the first case.

(1) Given two non-pivot sliding windows $\hat{\boldsymbol{s}}_i^t$ and $\hat{\boldsymbol{s}}_u^t$ that are approximated respectively by pivot sliding windows $\hat{\boldsymbol{s}}_j^t$ and $\hat{\boldsymbol{s}}_v^t$ as:

$$\hat{\boldsymbol{s}}_i^t = (\hat{\boldsymbol{s}}_j^t, \mathbb{1}_h)\tilde{\boldsymbol{w}}_i + \boldsymbol{e}_i, \ \hat{\boldsymbol{s}}_u^t = (\hat{\boldsymbol{s}}_v^t, \mathbb{1}_h)\tilde{\boldsymbol{w}}_u + \boldsymbol{e}_u. \tag{11}$$

We have,

$$\begin{aligned}\mathcal{D}(\hat{\boldsymbol{s}}_i^t, \hat{\boldsymbol{s}}_u^t) &= \|\hat{\boldsymbol{s}}_i^t - \hat{\boldsymbol{s}}_u^t\| \\ &= \|(\tilde{w}_{i,1} \cdot \hat{\boldsymbol{s}}_j^t - \tilde{w}_{u,1} \cdot \hat{\boldsymbol{s}}_v^t) + \mathbb{1}_h(\tilde{w}_{i,0} - \tilde{w}_{u,0}) + \boldsymbol{e}_i - \boldsymbol{e}_u\|.\end{aligned}$$

Let $\pi_{jv} = (\tilde{w}_{i,1} \cdot \hat{\boldsymbol{s}}_j^t - \tilde{w}_{u,1} \cdot \hat{\boldsymbol{s}}_v^t) + \mathbb{1}_h(\tilde{w}_{i,0} - \tilde{w}_{u,0})$. Using the triangular inequality, we can derive,

$$-\mathcal{D}(\hat{\boldsymbol{s}}_i^t, \hat{\boldsymbol{s}}_u^t) \leq \|\pi_{jv}\| - \|\boldsymbol{e}_i - \boldsymbol{e}_u\| \leq \mathcal{D}(\hat{\boldsymbol{s}}_i^t, \hat{\boldsymbol{s}}_u^t). \tag{12}$$

Since $\|\boldsymbol{e}_i - \boldsymbol{e}_u\| \leq \|\boldsymbol{e}_i\| + \|\boldsymbol{e}_u\|$, the second inequality of Eq. (12) is transformed to,

$$\mathcal{D}(\hat{\boldsymbol{s}}_i^t, \hat{\boldsymbol{s}}_u^t) \geq \|\pi_{jv}\| - (\|\boldsymbol{e}_i\| + \|\boldsymbol{e}_u\|).$$

Similarly, applying $\|\boldsymbol{e}_i - \boldsymbol{e}_u\| \geq | \ \|\boldsymbol{e}_i\| - \|\boldsymbol{e}_u\| \ |$ to the first inequality of Eq. (12), we can write the **lower bound** between two non-pivot sliding windows:

$$\begin{aligned}\mathcal{D}(\hat{\boldsymbol{s}}_i^t, \hat{\boldsymbol{s}}_u^t) \geq \max\{&\|\pi_{jv}\| - (\|\boldsymbol{e}_i\| + \|\boldsymbol{e}_u\|), \\ &| \ \|\boldsymbol{e}_i\| - \|\boldsymbol{e}_u\| \ | - \|\pi_{jv}\|\}.\end{aligned} \tag{13}$$

Let us denote the above lower bound as $\mathcal{L}_1$. Similarly, the **upper bound** is derived as follows:

$$\mathcal{D}(\hat{\boldsymbol{s}}_i^t, \hat{\boldsymbol{s}}_u^t) = \|\pi_{jv} + \boldsymbol{e}_i - \boldsymbol{e}_u\| \leq \|\pi_{jv}\| + \|\boldsymbol{e}_i\| + \|\boldsymbol{e}_u\|. \tag{14}$$

Let us denote the above upper bound as $\mathcal{U}_1$.

(2) Suppose the pair under consideration contains one pivot sliding window and one non-pivot sliding window. Let $\hat{\boldsymbol{s}}_j^t$ be the pivot sliding window and $\hat{\boldsymbol{s}}_u^t$ be the non-pivot sliding window, then the **lower bound** is given as follows:

$$\mathcal{D}(\hat{\boldsymbol{s}}_u^t, \hat{\boldsymbol{s}}_j^t) \geq | \ \|\pi_{uv}\| - \|\boldsymbol{e}_u\| \ |, \tag{15}$$

where $\pi_{uv} = \tilde{w}_{u,1} \cdot \hat{\boldsymbol{s}}_v^t - \hat{\boldsymbol{s}}_j^t + \tilde{w}_{u,0}\mathbb{1}_h$. Let us denote this lower bound as $\mathcal{L}_2$. Similarly, the **upper bound** is given as,

$$\mathcal{D}(\hat{\boldsymbol{s}}_u^t, \hat{\boldsymbol{s}}_j^t) \leq \|\pi_{uv}\| + \|\boldsymbol{e}_u\|. \tag{16}$$

Let us denote this upper bound as $\mathcal{U}_2$.

(3) In this case, since both the sliding windows are pivot windows, which are not approximated, we compute the Euclidean distance between them and verify whether it satisfies the threshold δ.

Observe that for computing the above upper and lower bounds only the pivot sliding windows, affine transformations, and norm of the residual error are required. Therefore, in PAS only these quantities are emitted as tuples. As is shown above, even the approximated sliding windows are sufficient to derive effective accuracy bounds. Finally, given two normalized sliding windows, if both the sliding windows are non-pivot then bounds $\mathcal{L}_1$ and $\mathcal{U}_1$ are computed, otherwise if one window is a pivot sliding window and the other is non-pivot, then $\mathcal{L}_2$ and $\mathcal{U}_2$ are computed. Then these bounds are used for eliminating false positives as follows:

- **True Positive:** If $\mathcal{U}_k < \delta$, then the sliding window pair is qualified and is reported to the last action element.

- **False Positive**: If $\mathcal{L}_k \leq \delta \leq \mathcal{U}_k$, then sliding window pair could be a false positive. In this case, $\mathcal{B}_A^{(cmp)}$ requests $\mathcal{B}_A^{(shf)}$ to send the original sliding windows for this pair and then it verifies whether the pair is qualified by computing precise correlation coefficient. $\mathcal{B}_A^{(shf)}$ retains the original sliding windows of a particular time instant, until $\mathcal{B}_A^{(cmp)}$ has finished processing them.
- **True Negative**: If $\mathcal{L}_k > \delta$, then pair is not qualified and is dropped.

The value of k can be 1 or 2 depending on whether case **(1)** or **(2)** is valid. In the final step all the sliding window pairs that are emitted by the tasks of $\mathcal{B}_A^{(cmp)}$ are aggregated by tasks of $\mathcal{B}_A^{(agg)}$, and the results are continuously returned to the user as shown in Figure 3.

Computing alternative correlation measures: The proposed AEGIS approach can seamlessly handle diverse correlation (or similarity) measures, such as cosine similarity, extended Jaccard similarity and Euclidean distance by adopting a measure-specific normalization processes for different measures. In the interest of space, we refer the interested reader to [1].

5.1 Cost Analysis

Here, we analyze the cost incurred by the AEGIS approach. The computational cost of the element $\mathcal{B}_A^{(shf)}$ includes (a) the cost of updating the normalized sliding windows, which can be performed in constant time, and (b) the cost of local-correlation graph construction and Greedy-LAP, which is significantly low as each task is assigned only a very small number of sliding windows.

The cost of communicating between $\mathcal{B}_A^{(shf)}$ and $\mathcal{B}_A^{(cmp)}$ can be decomposed as a product of the number of replicas performed by PAS and the cost of communicating each replica. The number of replicas for a sliding window group in PAS does not depend on n and h. And due to our advanced grouping and approximation methods the size (and therefore the communication cost) of each replica is typically low, and only increases extremely slowly. Next, the computation cost incurred by each task of action element $\mathcal{B}_A^{(cmp)}$ depends on the number of sliding window groups assigned to it. Again, the number of groups assigned to each task of $\mathcal{B}_A^{(cmp)}$ is typically very small. The communication between action elements $\mathcal{B}_A^{(cmp)}$ and $\mathcal{B}_A^{(agg)}$ depends on the number of qualified sliding window pairs. Since the number of such pairs is unknown apriori, we have to omit the analysis for $\mathcal{B}_A^{(agg)}$.

6. EXPERIMENTAL EVALUATION

In this section, we perform extensive experimental evaluation comparing AEGIS with baseline approaches. First, we describe the baselines in Section 6.1. Then, we introduce the parameters and metrics used for the experimental evaluation, the datasets and the cluster setup. The implementation of AEGIS and the baselines is done using Apache Storm. We choose Storm here, because Storm has lower processing latency compared to other distributed realtime computation system (e.g, S4, Spark Streaming) due to the one-at-a-time data processing model. Action and source elements are respectively implemented as bolts and spouts in Storm. Bolts and spouts in Storm have user-specified number of tasks (i.e., parallelism) that execute in parallel in the cluster. We implement the PAS shuffling using a *custom grouping function* provided by Storm.

6.1 Baselines

NAIVE: This is the naïve approach described in Section 1, but is improved to incrementally compute correlations [7].

DFTCQ: This is a DFT (discrete Fourier Transform) based approach proposed in [20], but we have adapted it to the distributed setting. It has a topology consisting of three action elements. The first action element shuffles a DFT-reduced sliding window in the way similar to NAIVE. The second action element computes the correlation measure and forwards qualified pairs to the last element, where duplicate removal is performed. For removing false-positives a sliding window recall phase, similar to AEGIS, is performed in the second action element.

LSHCQ: LSHCQ is based on locality sensitive hashing (LSH) [14]. LSH constructs multiple hash tables to find ϵ-correlated pairs. If two normalized sliding windows are correlated, they lie closer to each other in the Euclidean space. LSHCQ uses this property to replicate and shuffle potential qualified sliding window to the same task. The topology of LSHCQ consists of three action elements. The first element computes the hash value of the normalized sliding windows for each hash table. Sliding windows that are mapped to a bucket in each hash table are shuffled to the same task of the second action element, where the correlation computation is performed over the sliding windows in each bucket per hash table. LSH parameters are chosen to minimize the processing latency while ensuring the failure probability (i.e., the probability of not reporting a certain qualified pair) at 5% [14].

6.2 Parameters and Metrics

We use four evaluation parameters to establish the efficacy of AEGIS: sliding window size h, query threshold ϵ, parallelism of $\mathcal{B}_A^{(cmp)}$ denoted $\mathcal{P}_A^{(cmp)}$, and the time interval Δ between tuples in the spout $\mathcal{S}$ known as the **injection interval**. Δ is set by adjusting the data emitting frequency of the spout $\mathcal{S}$. For other parameters, we have a **basic setup** where: $\Delta = 1$sec, $h = 100$, $\epsilon = 0.95$ and $\mathcal{P}_A^{(cmp)} = 4$.

We use three performance metrics: communication cost, processing latency, and peak capacity. **Communication cost** is measured by the amount of data units communicated between the bolt tasks of $\mathcal{B}_A^{(shf)}$ and $\mathcal{B}_A^{(cmp)}$. Here, a data unit is a basic data type, which could be float, integer, etc. For AEGIS, the communication cost incurred during PAS and sliding window recalling during correlation computation is also included. **Processing latency** is the average processing time for each task of elements $\mathcal{B}_A^{(shf)}$ and $\mathcal{B}_A^{(cmp)}$ considered together. The processing time of $\mathcal{B}_A^{(agg)}$ is not included since it is insignificant, due to the use of hash-sets for duplicate removal. As before, for AEGIS, the time spent on recalling sliding windows is also included in the processing latency. The **peak capacity** is the maximum number of time series that an approach can simultaneously process without causing bottlenecks [2, 20]. A **bottleneck** is caused when sliding windows from the current time instant have to wait (in memory), for the sliding windows from a previous time instant to finish processing [2, 20]. Bottlenecks caused by any bolt tasks are detected and reported by the Storm cluster UI [2]. All the performance metrics reported in this section are computed by averaging every 20 seconds for 10 times, after the cluster reaches a stable state.

6.3 Datasets and Cluster Details

We use one synthetic and one real dataset for evaluating all the approaches. The **synthetic dataset** is generated as follows. Given the required number of time series n, we first generate $\frac{n}{\alpha}$ seed time series. Each seed time series is generated using a random walk model [20]. From each seed time series $\boldsymbol{s}_i$, we produce α dataset as follows:

$$s_{j,t} = \gamma_{j,t} + \beta_j \cdot s_{i,t},$$

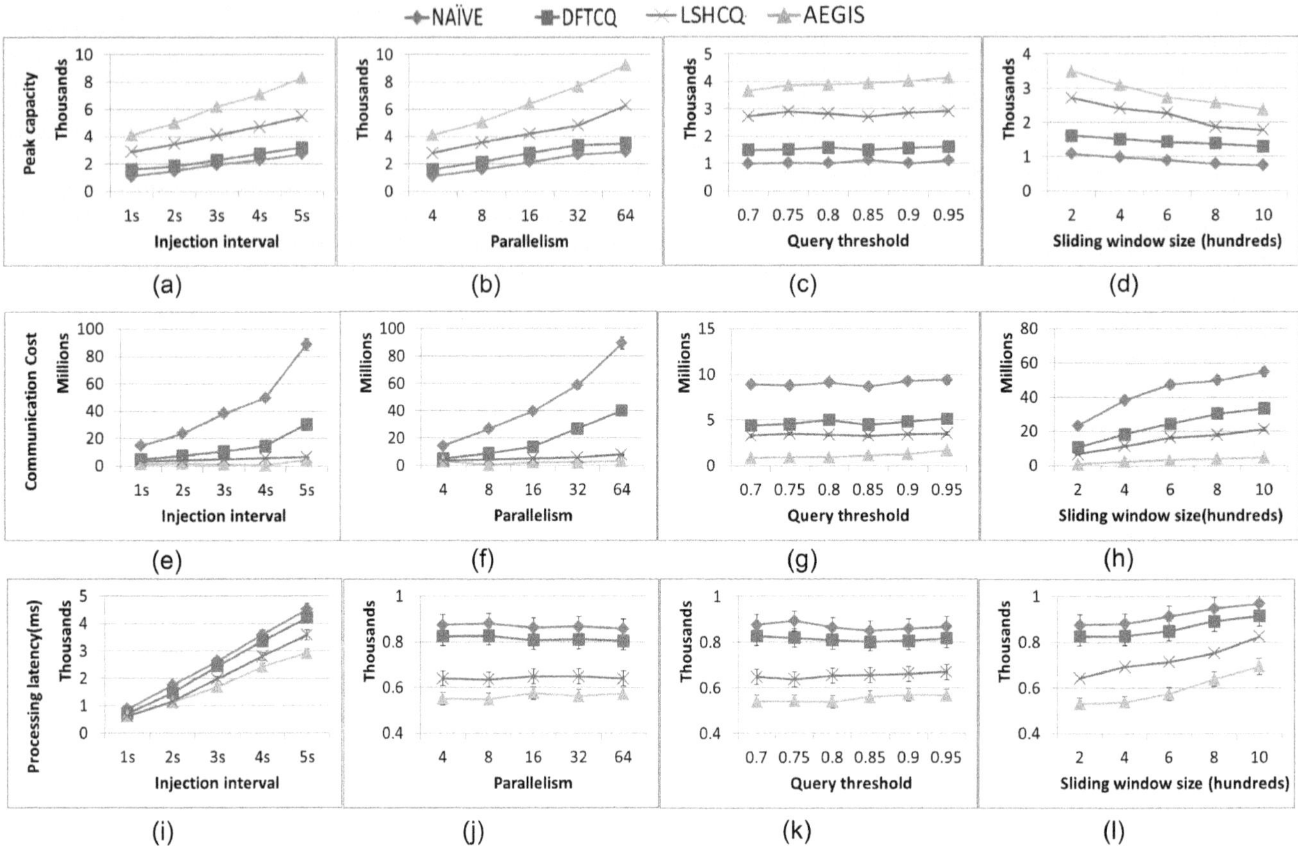

Figure 5: The performance metrics as a function of the parameters shown at peak capacity. (a)-(d) the peak capacity itself, (e)-(h) communication cost at above corresponding peak capacities and (i)-(l) processing latency at above corresponding peak capacities.

where $\gamma_{j,t}$ and β_j are real random numbers between $[0, 100]$, and β_j is sampled once for each time series $\boldsymbol{s}_j$, while $\gamma_{j,t}$ is sampled once for *each entry* in the dataset time series $\boldsymbol{s}_j$. In our experiments, we set $\alpha = 100$ and $n = 10000$.

The **real dataset** is the *Google Cluster Usage* [10] data. It records extensive activities of 12K cluster nodes from a data center over a span of 29 days. We extract three parameters: CPU usage, memory usage and disk space usage for each cluster node. The total number of time series extracted is 36K. For both datasets, the source element $\mathcal{S}$ reads the data files stored in the local file system and then continuously pushes the data to Storm at a given injection interval.

Cluster Setup: The experiments are performed using a cluster consisting of 1 master and 8 slaves. The master node has 64GB RAM, 4TB disk space (4 x 1TB disks in RAID5) and 12 x 2.30 GHz (Intel Xeon E5-2630) cores. Each slave node has 6 x 2.30 GHz (Intel Xeon E5-2630) cores, 32GB RAM and 6TB disk space (3 x 2TB disks). All the nodes are connected via 1GB Ethernet.

6.4 Measuring Peak Performance

Peak performance is the performance measured when the cluster is at peak capacity. The results shown in these set of experiments are for real data. The results for synthetic data exhibit similar trends in [1] and are omitted due to space limitations. The aim of this set of experiments is to demonstrate how each metric (communication cost, processing latency, or peak capacity) varies as a function of one parameter, while the other parameters are set to their basic setup values, *and the cluster is processing time series at peak capacity.*

For instance, assume we are interested in studying the effect of injection interval, we start by setting the other parameters to their basic setup values (i.e., $\mathcal{P}_A^{(cmp)} = 4$, $\epsilon = 0.95$, $h = 100$). Then as we start to increase the injection interval, the cluster is able to handle more and more time series, since now it has more time to process each one of them. Therefore, we start injecting more time series into the cluster until it reaches peak capacity. Then at peak capacity we note and report the values of the metrics

Peak Capacity: The peak capacity increases as a function of the injection interval and parallelism (refer Figure 5(a) and (b)). This is because more resources and processing time becomes available in the cluster thereby improving peak capacity. Therefore, at the highest level of parallelism and injection interval, AEGIS and LSHCQ exhibit 3x and 2x more peak capacity than NAIVE. In addition, the increase of query threshold has very little effect on the peak capacities of NAIVE, DFTCQ and LSHCQ approaches (refer Figure 5(c)). However, the peak capacity of AEGIS presents an increasing trend, since increasing query correlation threshold (ϵ) leads to the decrease of the distance threshold (δ), which leads to lower replication and improved communication efficiency. For maximum level of query threshold, AEGIS exhibits 3x more peak capacity than NAIVE. AEGIS achieves about 1.5x improvement over LSHCQ because LSHCQ requires a large number of hash tables to achieve high recall rate [14], and maintaining a large number of hash tables incurs high communication overhead.

On the other hand, the sliding window size affects the peak capacity adversely (refer Figure 5(d)) for all approaches. This is because when sliding window size increases approaches like DFTCQ typically need more DFT coefficients to retain the same amount of energy, and LSHCQ takes more time for computing the hash values. And since the parallelism (or available resources) of all the action elements is fixed in this experiment the peak capacity drops to keep the system bottleneck free. However, in practice peak capacity can be maintained by increasing parallelism. Concretely, at maximum value of the sliding window size AEGIS shows a 2.5x improvement over NAIVE.

Communication Cost: As peak capacity increases with injection interval and parallelism, the communication cost increases (refer Figure 5(e) and (f)) as well. The reason is that more communication is required for maintaining that peak capacity. Even with increased communication costs, at the highest level of the injection interval, AEGIS requires 12x and 4x lower communication than NAIVE and DFTCQ respectively, at maximum level of parallelism it needs 12x less communication over NAIVE, and at most selective query threshold it needs 4x less than NAIVE. Observe that with the increase of the query threshold, the communication costs are largely stable for all approaches (refer Figure 5(g)). While the communication cost significantly increases with the sliding window size for NAIVE, DFTCQ, and LSHCQ (refer Figure 5(h)). At the highest value of sliding window size, AEGIS needs 9x, 6x, and 4x lower communication than NAIVE, DFTCQ, and LSHCQ respectively.

Processing Latency: Since peak capacity increases with increase in injection interval, the processing latency increases because more number of time series need to be processed (refer Figure 5(i)). In particular, for injection interval the lowest latencies shown by AEGIS are 1.5x better as compared to NAIVE. In Figure 5(j), the processing latency of all approaches is relatively stable when parallelism increases. This is because the amount of sliding windows distributed to each task is relatively stable due to the increase of parallelism. In addition, the processing latencies of all approaches varies little when query threshold increases (refer Figure 5(k)). On the other hand, the processing latency increases with increase in sliding window size (refer Figure 5(l)) since action elements spend more time on processing and parsing communicated long sliding windows. For sliding window size the maximum improvement in latency obtained is 1.5x as compared to NAIVE.

6.5 Analysing Sensitivity

In this set of experiments we will study how sensitive the metrics are to the changes in the parameters, while the cluster is not operating at peak capacity, but is processing a constant ($n = 8000$) number of time series. Since the cluster is only processing a constant number of time series, here we only consider two metrics: communication cost and processing latency. The **sensitivity** of a given performance metric (communication cost or processing latency) to a given parameter is measured by varying the parameter within a pre-defined range, while setting the other parameters to their basic setup values, and computing the mean and standard deviation of the variation observed in the performance metric.

For instance, say we are interested to measure the sensitivity of the communication cost to the sliding window size h. Then we vary the sliding window size in a pre-defined range and then compute the sample mean and standard deviation of the communication cost we obtained for each sliding window size. The sample mean and standard deviation are the numbers reported as sensitivity. The results for communication cost and processing latency are shown in Table 1 and Table 2 respectively. We have highlighted the last row of both tables, since communication cost and processing latency exhibit significant variation with respect to h. Due to limited

Table 1: Mean communication cost (in millions of data units) as a function of the parameters for synthetic data. Numbers in parenthesis are standard deviations. Significant variation of the communication cost is shown in boldface.

	NAIVE	DFTCQ	LSHCQ	AEGIS
Δ (10-15 secs)	640 ($\pm$12)	123 ($\pm$8)	9.7 ($\pm$0.5)	2.8 ($\pm$0.7)
$\mathcal{P}_A^{(cmp)}$ (4-64 tasks)	632 ($\pm$ 16)	134 ($\pm$11)	11.1 ($\pm$0.9)	3.5 ($\pm$1.8)
ϵ (0.7-0.95)	624 ($\pm$23)	117 ($\pm$7)	10 ($\pm$1.2)	3.2 ($\pm$1.1)
h (100-1000)	**840 ($\pm$128)**	**213 ($\pm$67)**	**43.3 ($\pm$8.9)**	**29 ($\pm$6.3)**

Table 2: Mean processing latency (in seconds) as a function of the parameters for synthetic data. Numbers in parenthesis are standard deviations. Significant variation of the processing latency is shown in boldface.

	NAIVE	DFTCQ	LSHCQ	AEGIS
Δ (10-15 secs)	8.6 ($\pm$1.1)	8.3 ($\pm$1.1)	6.7 ($\pm$1.2)	4.5 ($\pm$0.8)
$\mathcal{P}_A^{(cmp)}$ (4-64 tasks)	7.5 ($\pm$1.3)	6.8 ($\pm$1.2)	5.3 ($\pm$1.3)	4.0 ($\pm$0.6)
ϵ (0.7-0.95)	8.2 ($\pm$1.5)	8.7 ($\pm$1.5)	7.1 ($\pm$1.7)	4.4 ($\pm$1.1)
h (100-1000)	**11.6 ($\pm$ 6.4)**	**9.1 ($\pm$ 5.8)**	**8.2 ($\pm$4.9)**	**7.3 ($\pm$4.2)**

space, we show the results only for the synthetic dataset, as the trends exhibited by real dataset are similar (refer [1]).

Communication Cost: In Table 1, it can be observed that for all the parameters the mean communication cost of AEGIS is relatively stable and orders of magnitude lower as compared to the others. For the sliding window size h, AEGIS has nearly 20x, 10x and 2x lower cost as compared to NAIVE, DFTCQ and LSHCQ. Similarly, for the query threshold ϵ, AEGIS is nearly 60x, 10x and 3x more efficient than NAIVE, DFTCQ and LSHCQ. The injection interval Δ and the parallelism of $\mathcal{P}_A^{(cmp)}$ show similar trends. Thus, AEGIS is highly effective in managing the communication cost when dealing with significantly large variations of the parameters. This is because PAS in AEGIS robustly mitigates changes to the communication cost arising from different values of the parameters.

Processing Latency: The latency of AEGIS is lower and more robust as compared to NAIVE, DFTCQ and LSHCQ. Concretely, for the injection interval Δ, AEGIS approach has nearly 2x lower latency as compared to NAIVE. For the query threshold ϵ, average improvement in the latency of AEGIS *w.r.t.* to NAIVE and DFTCQ is approximately 2x. When sliding window length increases, the processing latencies of all the approaches increase and thus present larger mean and standard errors. Specifically, the latency of AEGIS is about 50% lower as compared to NAIVE. Overall, AEGIS exhibits orders of magnitude improvement in communication cost and processing latency, and is significantly robust to changes in the parameters.

6.6 Analysing Pruning Power

This set of experiments evaluate the pruning power of AEGIS against LSHCQ. **Pruning power** is defined as the ratio of the number of pairs that are pruned (without having to compute the correlation measure) to the total number of time-series pairs. Higher values of pruning power are considered better. Since the pruning

Table 3: Pruning power of AEGIS and LSHCQ as a function of query threshold ϵ and sliding-window length h for real data. The upper value in each cell corresponds to AEGIS, while the lower value corresponds to LSHCQ.

ϵ \ h	200	400	600	800	1000
0.7	**0.858**	0.836	0.819	0.764	**0.717**
	0.552	0.574	0.599	0.542	**0.583**
0.75	0.861	0.862	0.811	0.778	0.757
	0.582	0.584	0.579	0.532	0.563
0.8	0.864	0.870	0.832	0.761	0.777
	0.612	0.604	0.588	0.599	0.602
0.85	0.881	0.862	0.831	0.837	0.776
	0.653	0.638	0.669	0.644	0.631
0.9	0.884	0.872	0.832	0.812	0.701
	0.663	0.628	0.667	0.658	0.641
0.95	**0.907**	0.865	0.836	0.798	**0.736**
	0.713	0.735	0.714	0.705	**0.716**

power is directly affected by the query threshold ϵ and sliding-window length h, in Table 3 we present pruning power as a function of these two parameters. The results in Table 3 are on the real dataset (refer [1] for results on synthetic data). In this experiment Δ and $\mathcal{P}_A^{(shf)}$ are set to their basic set-up values.

Here we only compare AEGIS with LSHCQ, because NAIVE and DFTCQ approaches do not perform pruning and always evaluate all sliding window pairs. In each cell of Table 3, the upper value is for AEGIS, while the lower value is for LSHCQ. In AEGIS, PAS only shuffles together the sliding window groups that could potentially contain ϵ-correlated pairs, therefore many pairs are pruned during the data shuffling phase. Furthermore, higher values of ϵ and shorter sliding windows (lower h) lead to insignificant residual errors while approximating the non-pivot sliding windows in the sliding window groups (refer Section 4), and lead to tighter bounds on the derived correlation (refer Section 5); thereby significantly increasing the pruning power.

It is observed that pruning power of AEGIS decreases as h increases and increases as ϵ increases. AEGIS achieves the maximum pruning power 0.907 at the maximum $\epsilon = 0.95$ and minimum $h = 200$. The pruning power of LSHCQ is largely affected only by ϵ, while varying little under different sliding window sizes. Overall, AEGIS achieves a maximum of 50% improvement over LSHCQ when $\epsilon = 0.7$ and $h = 200$.

7. CONCLUSION

In this paper, we proposed approaches for real-time correlation discovering in large time-series data. Our main proposal the AEGIS approach, uses intelligent time series grouping, approximation, and partition-aware data shuffling methods to dramatically improve performance. We demonstrated that AEGIS significantly reduces the communication cost and can easily operate on a large number of time series through extensive experiments.

8. ACKNOWLEDGMENTS

This work was supported by Nano-Tera.ch through the OpenSenseII project.

9. REFERENCES

[1] Tech. report – `http://infoscience.epfl.ch/record/210363`.

[2] Storm. `http://storm-project.net/`.

[3] D. Abadi, D. Carney, U. Cetintemel, M. Cherniack, C. Convey, S. Lee, M. Stonebraker, N. Tatbul, and S. Zdonik. Aurora : A new model and architecture for data stream management. *VLDB Journal*, pages 120–139, 2003.

[4] L. Abraham, J. Allen, O. Barykin, V. Borkar, B. Chopra, C. Gerea, D. Merl, J. Metzler, D. Reiss, S. Subramanian, et al. Scuba: diving into data at facebook. *PVLDB*, 6(11):1057–1067, 2013.

[5] R. Cole, D. Shasha, and X. Zhao. Fast window correlations over uncooperative time series. In *ACM SIGKDD*, pages 743–749. ACM, 2005.

[6] S. Fries, B. Boden, G. Stepien, and T. Seidl. Phidj: Parallel similarity self-join for high-dimensional vector data with mapreduce. In *ICDE*, pages 796–807. IEEE, 2014.

[7] Y. Li, M. L. Yiu, Z. Gong, et al. Discovering longest-lasting correlation in sequence databases. *PVLDB Endowment*, 6(14):1666–1677, 2013.

[8] A. Mueen, S. Nath, and J. Liu. Fast approximate correlation for massive time-series data. In *SIGMOD*, pages 171–182, 2010.

[9] L. Neumeyer, B. Robbins, A. Nair, and A. Kesari. S4: Distributed stream computing platform. In *ICDMW*, pages 170–177. IEEE, 2010.

[10] C. Reiss, J. Wilkes, and J. L. Hellerstein. Google cluster-usage traces: format+ schema. *Google Inc., White Paper*, 2011.

[11] Y. Sakurai, S. Papadimitriou, and C. Faloutsos. Braid: Stream mining through group lag correlations. In *ACM SIGMOD*, pages 599–610. ACM, 2005.

[12] A. D. Sarma, Y. He, and S. Chaudhuri. Clusterjoin: A similarity joins framework using map-reduce. In *PVLDB*, 2014.

[13] S. Sathe and K. Aberer. AFFINITY: Efficiently querying statistical measures on time- series data. In *ICDE*, pages 841–852, 2013.

[14] N. Sundaram, A. Turmukhametova, N. Satish, T. Mostak, P. Indyk, S. Madden, and P. Dubey. Streaming similarity search over one billion tweets using parallel locality-sensitive hashing. *PVLDB*, 6:1930–1941, 2013.

[15] Y. Wang, A. Metwally, and S. Parthasarathy. Scalable all-pairs similarity search in metric spaces. In *19th ACM SIGKDD*, pages 829–837. ACM, 2013.

[16] D. Wu, Y. Ke, J. X. Yu, S. Y. Philip, and L. Chen. Leadership discovery when data correlatively evolve. *World Wide Web*, 14(1):1–25, 2011.

[17] Q. Xie, S. Shang, B. Yuan, C. Pang, and X. Zhang. Local correlation detection with linearity enhancement in streaming data. In *ACM CIKM*, pages 309–318. ACM, 2013.

[18] M. Zaharia, T. Das, H. Li, S. Shenker, and I. Stoica. Discretized streams: an efficient and fault-tolerant model for stream processing on large clusters. In *4th USENIX HotCloud*, pages 10–10. USENIX, 2012.

[19] T. Zhang, D. Yue, Y. Gu, and G. Yu. Boolean representation based data-adaptive correlation analysis over time series streams. In *CIKM*, pages 203–212. ACM, 2007.

[20] Y. Zhu and D. Shasha. Statstream: Statistical monitoring of thousands of data streams in real time. In *VLDB*, pages 358–369, 2002.

Time Series Analysis of Nursing Notes for Mortality Prediction via a State Transition Topic Model

Yohan Jo
Carnegie Mellon University
yohanj@cs.cmu.edu

Natasha Loghmanpour
Carnegie Mellon University
nloghman@cmu.edu

Carolyn Penstein Rosé
Carnegie Mellon University
cprose@cs.cmu.edu

ABSTRACT

Accurate mortality prediction is an important task in intensive care units in order to channel prompt care to patients in the most critical condition and to reduce nurses' alarm fatigue. Nursing notes carry valuable information in this regard, but nothing has been reported about the effectiveness of temporal analysis of nursing notes in mortality prediction tasks.

We propose a time series model that uncovers the temporal dynamics of patients' underlying states from nursing notes. The effectiveness of this information in mortality prediction is examined for mortality prediction for five different time spans ranging from one day to one year. Our experiments show that the model captures both patient states and their temporal dynamics that have a strong correlation with patient mortality. The results also show that incorporating temporal information improves performance in long-term mortality prediction, but has no significant effect in short-term prediction.

Categories and Subject Descriptors

J.3 [**Computer Applications**]: Life and Medical Sciences—*Medical information system*; I.2.1 [**Artificial Intelligence**]: Applications and Expert Systems—*Medicine and Science*; H.2.8 [**Database Management**]: Database Applications—*Data mining*; G.3 [**Mathematics of Computing**]: Probability and Statistics—*Time series analysis*

General Terms

Algorithms, Human Factors, Languages

Keywords

Healthcare, Medical Data Mining, Nursing Notes, Mortality Prediction, Hidden Markov Model, Latent Dirichlet Allocation, State Transition Topic Model

1. INTRODUCTION

Predicting a patient's risk of mortality and taking appropriate action are important activities in intensive care units (ICUs). High accuracy in mortality prediction helps nurses manage patient care by placing patients in different priority queues. It also enhances nurses' efficiency by reducing the number of false alarms, which cause them alarm fatigue and desensitize them to real alarms [6]. In this respect, nursing notes contain valuable information to inform more accurate prediction models. This information includes nurses' observations and intuitions that do not fit into the accompanying recorded structured data. Nursing notes have the potential to uncover hidden clues about a patient's health and mental state as they change over time, such as the factors of family support and mental fitness (Figure 1).

```
PROB: S/P AVR FUNCTIONAL HEALTH PATTERNS AND HISTORY COMPLETED IN CHART.
NEURO: PT AWAKE, FOLLOWING COMMANDS. MAE, NODS APPROPRIATELY. PERL.
CV: SR NO VEA NOTED. CONT ON MILRINONE AND NEO. CO/CI [**7-26**]. K
REPLACED MULTIPLE TIMES. CT DRAINING S/S DRAINAGE. PACER OFF. MORPHINE
FOR PAIN X3 WITH GOOD EFFECT.
RESP: PT WEANING. LUNGS WITH WHEEZES, CLEARED WITH COMBIVENT INHALER.
SUCTION FOR THICK CLEAR/YELLOW SPUTUM. PT STILL ACIDOTIC, IMV 16, TV 700.
GI: NGT TO LOW CONT SUCTION, NO DRAINAGE,
ENDO: INITIAL BS ELEVATED AND TREATED PER PROTOCOL.
GU: ADEQUATE AMOUNT OF CLEAR YELLOW URINE. PLACEMENT CHECKED-GOOD.
SOCIAL: FAMILY HERE TO VISIT.
ASSESSMENT: WEANING SLOWLY
PLAN: RECHECK ABGS, LYTES. SUCTION PRN. MED FOR PAIN. CONT VENT WEAN.
```

Figure 1: Example Nursing Note

However, the potential of nursing notes in informing mortality prediction has started to be investigated only recently [8, 14]. Furthermore, there is no previous work on temporal analysis of nursing notes and its use for mortality prediction, while time series analysis of patient signals and clinical data has shown a lot of benefits in patient outcome prediction [5, 23, 13, 18]. Hence, this paper offers the following contributions to this important research field.

- Proposes and evaluates a model to uncover the temporal dynamics of underlying patient states from nursing notes.
- Evaluates the effectiveness of the identified temporal dynamics for improving mortality prediction.
- Offers qualitative insight into different types of textual features regarding their roles in mortality prediction.

We propose a novel and intuitive model that combines a hidden Markov model (HMM) and latent Dirichlet allocation (LDA) [4]. This model assumes that there are a set of underlying patient states, and every pair of states has a meaningful transition probability. Each state is represented by a topic distribution, from which nursing notes are generated. The model, when applied to nursing notes, learns topics embedded in nursing notes, the topic distribution of each state and each nursing note, and state transition prob-

Permission to make digital or hard copies of all or part of this work for personal or classroom use is granted without fee provided that copies are not made or distributed for profit or commercial advantage and that copies bear this notice and the full citation on the first page. Copyrights for components of this work owned by others than ACM must be honored. Abstracting with credit is permitted. To copy otherwise, or republish, to post on servers or to redistribute to lists, requires prior specific permission and/or a fee. Request permissions from Permissions@acm.org.
CIKM'15, October 19–23, 2015, Melbourne, Australia.
© 2015 ACM. ISBN 978-1-4503-3794-6/15/10 ...$15.00.
DOI: http://dx.doi.org/10.1145/2806416.2806541.

abilities. We can also estimate a sequence of states each patient is identified as having transitioned through, which is then used for mortality prediction. This model is general enough to be applied for the purpose of identifying temporal dynamics in any text stream. Our simple and general model shows effectiveness in uncovering latent patient states in nursing notes and improving mortality prediction. The model is described in detail in Section 4.

Three tasks are evaluated in order to validate the learned temporal information and its benefit for mortality prediction. In Task 1 (Section 6.1), we qualitatively describe the learned topics, underlying patient states, and state transition patterns revealed from ICU nursing notes. In Task 2 (Section 6.2), we perform mortality prediction and show that including the temporal information achieves a significant improvement for long-term predictions, but little effect in short-term prediction. In Task 3 (Section 6.3), we examine individual textual features more in detail. Along with the temporal information, we investigate two other types of textual features—n-grams and standard topics—with respect to their roles and limitations in mortality prediction. To the best of our knowledge, this article is the most comprehensive treatment of the use of textual features for mortality prediction to date.

We first introduce related work (Section 2) and formally define the problem (Section 3). Next, we explain our model in detail (Section 4). For experiments, we first describe the experimental settings (Section 5), and perform the three tasks aforementioned (Section 6). Finally, we conclude the paper by summarizing the findings and discuss limitations (Section 7).

2. RELATED WORK

This section describes previous work on *patient mortality prediction based on free-text medical documents* and *joint models of topics and time.* Only recently did free-text medical documents—nursing notes, discharge summaries, laboratory test reports, radiology reports, etc.— start to be employed for mortality prediction [14, 8]. These studies used medical notes from MIMIC II Clinical Database and employed topic modeling approaches. Specifically, Lehman et al. [14] extracted topics from nursing notes using the hierarchical Dirichlet process [19] and used the learned topic distributions as input to logistic linear regression for predicting each patient's mortality. Ghassemi et al. [8], whose work is the most related work with ours, took a similar approach, except that they learned topics using latent Dirichlet allocation and used a support vector machine for mortality prediction. These studies showed the promise of nursing notes, with which they achieved higher accuracy in mortality prediction than with admission-time patient information such as ages and Simplified Acute Physiology Scores. Our work adopts these approaches as baselines.

This paper presents the first work to model the temporal dynamics of patients' states from nursing notes and apply this information to mortality prediction. The work by Ghassemi et al. [8] and our work are different in several aspects. Their work used nursing notes, laboratory test results, and radiology reports, but our work focuses only on nursing notes. Also, they excluded NICU (neonatal ICU) patients, but we include all types of patients. This actually reveals an interesting pattern of NICU patients in their state transitions. Their work made prediction for in-hospital and post-discharge mortality, but our work predicts 1-day, 1-week, 1-month, 6-month, and 1-year mortality, which may be of more interest to patients, families, and nurses and doctors for taking appropriate action.

There have been a lot of efforts to incorporate temporal aspects into topic models for other types of text. One big category of prior approaches attempts to model topic evolution over time [2, 7, 11, 15]. Under the assumption that the language models of topics change over time, these models discover topic dynamics from time-stamped documents. Our work is not aiming at modeling topic evolution. Some other models instead assume that topic popularity changes over time [10, 21]. In these models, the probability of a topic being manifested depends on the timestamp of the document. This trend, however, is too general to apply to different conditions of individual patients, and these models do not assume any underlying states of patients. There is also a set of segment-level time-aware topic models [3, 9, 20, 26]. These models suppose that the topic of a segment or word is affected by the topic of the previous segment or word within the document. This assumption is effective in modeling topic consistency within a segment of text and topic transition between segments. However, this topic transition can hardly represent the transition of patient states.

Not as popular as the previous categories, a few topic models consider the inter-dependency of topic distributions between documents. These models can again be categorized into two subgroups. In the first subgroup, the topic distribution of a document directly determines the next document's topic distribution usually via a transition matrix [17, 22, 25]. This assumption may be too strong for nursing notes since the topics of a nursing note are dependent on the complex details of a patients' condition, rather than being unambiguously determined by the previous note's topic distribution. Indeed, the mixed membership Markov model [17] did not produce interpretable state sequences and performed poorly in mortality prediction.

The second subgroup of models, to which our model belongs, assumes hidden underlying states, and each state is associated with a topic distribution from which documents are generated [24]. The state of a document is probabilistically determined by the previous document's state. In our task, this type of model is reasonable in that a patient's state is probabilistically determined by the previous state, and each state generates documents with certain topics. Also, the finite set of underlying states, unlike the infinite state space of the first subgroup, makes it straightforward to draw a state transition diagram such as Figure 4. Although the other model in this group [24] has a similar generative process, it assumes a set of independent state sequences, and each sequence has no branch factors. That is, slightly different state paths can be made only by independent sets of states and state sequences, which makes it nontrivial to compare the states of different patients. This is the main difference from our model, which assumes a shared set of states and branch factors.

3. MORTALITY PREDICTION

We define mortality prediction as the prediction of a patient's mortality or survival from a reference time within a given timeframe (e.g., one day, one month, etc.) on the basis of the patient's nursing notes up to the reference time. The prediction task will be used to validate our model (Section 4), which gives visibility to sequences of patients' latent

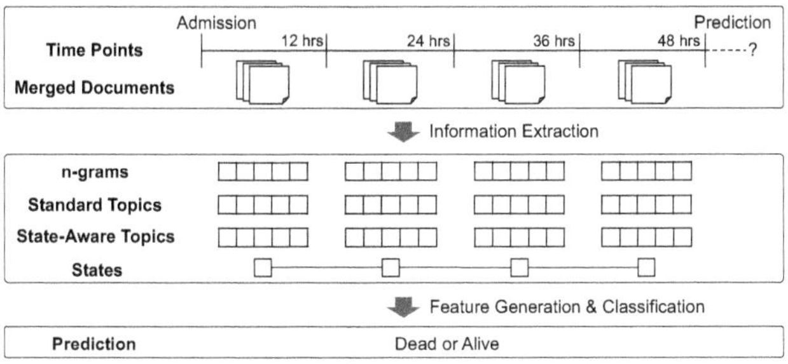

Figure 2: Process of Mortality Prediction

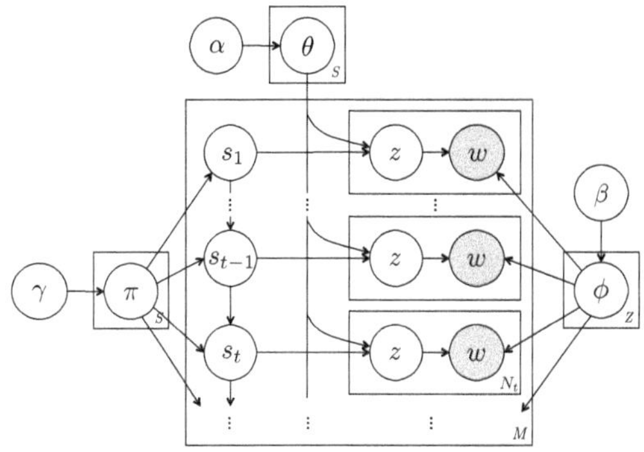

Figure 3: Graphical Representation of STTM.

states through the interpretation of the topic distributions of their nursing notes. The improvement over baseline in the prediction task using this representation validates that the patterns identified from nursing notes say something important about the experience of patients over time.

We perform predictions in the short-term (one day and one week) and in the long-term (one month, six months, and one year). Figure 2 illustrates the overall prediction process. For an ICU stay of a patient, we consider every 12 hours as one time point. Since some notes are too short or focus only on a single topic, all nursing notes in the same time point are merged into one document for analysis so that the merged document can reflect the overall topics at that time point. In this way, one sequence of composite documents is obtained for each patient. The task then is, given a sequence of documents of a patient, to predict the patient's mortality or survival within a given term from the time of the last document in the series, e.g., one week. One classifier is made for each time point. The classifier of the i-th time point makes prediction based on the nursing notes written until the i-th time point. The i-th classifier is trained on the nursing notes of all patients written during their first i time points. In training, the document sequences of the patients who died within the given term are counted as positive instances, and the other sequences negative instances.

4. STATE TRANSITION TOPIC MODEL

To extract the temporal dynamics of patients' underlying states from nursing notes, we propose an intuitive model called the State Transition Topic Model (STTM). STTM is a joint model integrating a hidden Markov model (HMM) and latent Dirichlet allocation (LDA). Different from the standard LDA, our model assumes latent underlying states and transition probabilities between them. Each state is represented by a probability distribution over topics from which a document is generated. STTM thus models hidden states and topics simultaneously. Consider the following scenario. A patient moves between states as time elapses according to the Markovian assumption, i.e., following state transition probability distributions. When a patient enters a state, a document is generated from the state's topic distribution according to the LDA assumption. When applied on a set of sequences of documents, STTM can learn a set of topics that constitute the documents, the topic distribution of each state and each document, and state transition probabilities. Based on this, we can estimate a patient's state at each time point, producing a sequence of states for the entire ICU stay. Note that this model is general enough to be applied not only to nursing notes, but any streams of data points. In the following sections, we formally describe the model and an inference method based on Gibbs sampling.

Table 1: Meanings of Notations

d_t^m	the t-th document in sequence m
$w_{t,i}^m$	the i-th word in d_t^m
$z_{t,i}^m$	the topic assigned to $w_{t,i}^m$
s_t^m	the state of d_t^m
$\mathbf{w}_t^m$	all words in d_t^m
$\mathbf{z}_{t,-i}^m$	the topics of all words in d_t^m except for $w_{t,i}^m$
$\mathbf{s}_{-(m,t)}$	the states of all documents except for d_t^m
$N_{m,t,j}^{MTZ}$	the number of words in d_t^m assigned topic j
$N_{j,w}^{ZW}$	the number of words w assigned topic j
$N_{c,j}^{SZ}$	the number of words assigned topic j in state c
$N_{c,c'}^{SS}$	the number of states c followed by state c'

4.1 Formal Definition

Suppose that there are S states, Z topics, and W unique words. The probability distribution over words for topic j is denoted by ϕ_j, which is a W-dimensional vector, and the probability distribution over topics at state c is denoted by θ_c, which is a Z-dimensional vector. The transition probability distribution of state c is denoted by π_c, which is an S-dimensional vector. We assume that all initial states come from the "0th" state, a special state that has no incoming edges. Thus, $\pi_{0,c}$ represents the probability of state c being an initial state. We take the full Bayesian approach, assuming Dirichlet priors γ, α, and β for π_c, θ_c, and ϕ_j, respectively. The graphical representation is shown in Figure 3, and the meanings of notations are listed in Table 1. The generative process is as follows.

1. For each state $c = 0, ..., S$,
   - (a) Draw a transition distribution $\pi_c \sim \text{Dirichlet}(\gamma)$
   - (b) Draw a topic distribution $\theta_c \sim \text{Dirichlet}(\alpha)$
2. For each topic $j = 1, ..., Z$,
   - (a) Draw a word distribution $\phi_j \sim \text{Dirichlet}(\beta)$
3. For each document at time point $t = 1, 2, ...$,
   - (a) Choose a state $s_t \sim \text{Categorical}(\pi_{s_{t-1}})$
   - (b) For each word,
     - i. Choose a topic $z \sim \text{Categorical}(\theta_{s_t})$
     - ii. Choose a word $w \sim \text{Categorical}(\phi_z)$

4.2 Inference

Gibbs sampling is used for inference. Each iteration samples $z_{t,i}^m$ and s_t^m according to the following conditional probabilities.

$$p(z_{t,i}^m = j | \mathbf{z}_{t,-i}^m, \mathbf{w}_t^m, s_t^m) \propto (N_{m,t,j}^{MTZ} + \alpha) \frac{N_{j,w_{t,i}^m}^{ZW} + \beta}{\sum_j (N_{j,w_{t,i}^m}^{ZW} + \beta)},$$

$$p(s_t^m = c | \mathbf{s}_{-(m,t)}, \mathbf{z}_t^m) \propto$$

$$\left(\prod_j \frac{\Gamma\left(N_{c,j}^{SZ} + \alpha + N_{m,t,j}^{MTZ}\right)}{\Gamma\left(N_{c,j}^{SZ} + \alpha\right)}\right) \frac{\Gamma\left(\sum_{j'} (N_{c,j'}^{SZ} + \alpha)\right)}{\Gamma\left(\sum_{j'} (N_{c,j'}^{SZ} + \alpha) + |\mathbf{z}_t^m|\right)} \times$$

$$(N_{s_{t-1}^m,c}^{SS} + \gamma) \frac{N_{c,s_{t+1}^m}^{SS} + \mathbf{1}(s_{t-1}^m = c = s_{t+1}^m) + \gamma}{\sum_{s_{t+1}^m} \left(N_{c,s_{t+1}^m}^{SS} + \mathbf{1}(s_{t-1}^m = c = s_{t+1}^m) + \gamma\right)}.$$

Based on the sampling results, we can estimate ϕ_j, θ_c, and π_c as follows.

$$\phi_{j,w} = \frac{N_{j,w}^{ZW} + \beta}{\sum_w (N_{j,w}^{ZW} + \beta)}, \theta_{c,j} = \frac{N_{c,j}^{SZ} + \alpha}{\sum_j (N_{c,j}^{SZ} + \alpha)},$$

$$\pi_{c,c'} = \frac{N_{c,c'}^{SS} + \gamma}{\sum_{c'} (N_{c,c'}^{SS} + \gamma)}, \theta_{t,j}^m = \frac{N_{c,c'}^{MTZ} + \alpha}{\sum_{c'} (N_{c,c'}^{MTZ} + \alpha)},$$

where θ_t^m is the document-wise topic distribution of d_t^m. A more detailed derivation process and the source code are available on our website[1].

5. EXPERIMENTAL SETTINGS

This section describes our experimental settings in detail.

5.1 Data

We use MIMIC II Clinical Database[2], which contains comprehensive clinical data of ICU patients collected between 2001 and 2008. This database contains information such as the demographics of de-identified patients, the records of their ICU and hospital admissions, nursing notes and reports, laboratory test results, and medications. Among this information, we use nursing notes for mortality prediction (Figure 1). The content usually includes the patient's neurological state, laboratory test results, medications, descriptions of facial expressions, social activities, and the nurse's impression and plans. We exclude radiology reports to make clear the impact of nursing notes, which are yet to be fully investigated for mortality prediction; however, in a real world application of the technology, those reports could be used as well to enhance the performance. Radiology reports are different from nursing notes in that they are grounded results of radiology tests but exist only for certain types of patients. Like the study by Ghassemi et al. [8], discharge summaries are also excluded since they include patient outcomes, though again, in a real world application these could be included for long term predictions. The purpose of our evaluation here is to evaluate one specific source of prediction, not to achieve the highest possible performance that could be achieved by including all available indicators.

Mortality prediction is meant to be performed during the first ICU stays of patients. We thus retrieve all nursing notes of patients written in their first ICU stay. Nursing notes are constrained to be longer than 100 characters excluding spaces (shorter notes are discarded). Nursing notes from the same time point (12 hour segment) are merged into a single document. Table 2(a) shows the statistics of the generated sequences, and Table 2(b) shows the characteristics of patients by different ICU types. The list of subject_id's is available on our website.

Nursing notes are preprocessed as follows. First, in order to reduce the sparsity of de-identified information, the de-identified pieces of text, e.g., patient names, are normalized to their category name. For example, "[**Female First Name (un) 978**]" is normalized to "PHI_FEMALEFIRSTNAME". Second, to distinguish whether a situation is positive or negative, simple negation rules are applied. That is, a word and its prefix "no", "not", or "without" are combined to one word with the prefix "no_". For example, "without spits" is changed to "no_spits". Third, words without any alphabet are removed. Fourth, the 21 most frequent words are removed because they are function words with little meaning and would othersise take the top positions of learned topics. Lehman et al.'s work [14] used only Unified Medical Language System codes. This enhances the interpretability of the result, but loses valuable information such as patients' social aspects.

Table 2: Data Statistics

(a) Statistics of retrieved nursing notes

# of sequences (=# of patients)	8,808
# of notes	187,808
# of merged documents	97,769
Avg length of merged documents	1,548 chars (Stddev=904)
Avg length of sequences	11 (Stddev=23)

(b) Characteristics of ICU types

	NICU	*CSRU*	*MICU*	*CCU*	*FICU*	*SICU*
# of patients	2332	2244	1918	1358	711	245
Avg. stay	10	4	5	4	5	3

(c) Percentages of patients who died within certain periods of time after admission

Died within	*1 day*	*1 week*	*1 month*	*6 months*	*1 year*
%	0.03	0.08	0.14	0.19	0.22

5.2 Classifiers

We use cost-sensitive SVMs to handle the imbalance between positive and negative instances (Table 2(c)). Weka[3]'s CostSensitiveClassifier along with SMO configured to return a probability distribution is used in this work. Because of the time-sensitive nature of treatments in an ICU, missing patients in a critical condition may compromise their chances of recovery. In cost-sensitive SVMs, false negatives can be assigned a larger cost than false positives, so that the classifiers are trained not to over-predict negative instances. An alternative to cost-sensitive classifiers could be to resample

[1] http://cs.cmu.edu/~yohanj/research/CIKM15
[2] http://www.physionet.org
[3] http://www.cs.waikato.ac.nz/ml/weka/

negative instances in order to balance them with positive instances. However, this technique suffers from huge variance in effectiveness depending on the resampling result, and we would also miss the opportunity to take advantage of all instances. In contrast, cost-sensitive SVMs can make use of the entire data while providing stable performance scores.

We use 10-fold cross-validation for evaluation. Each fold consists of a training set (81%), a validation set (9%), and a test set (10%). The cost of false positives is fixed to 1, and the training phase explores the space of false negative costs in two rounds to find the best cost using the validation set. The first round explores from 10 to 150 with an interval of 10, finding the cost c with the highest score. The second round searches from $c-9$ to $c+9$ with an interval of 1. The cost that performs the best across the two rounds is selected for the final test. This method has several advantages over searching the entire cost space with an interval of 1. Since performance scores make a unimodal shape in terms of costs, it finds the optimal point faster, and it can circumvent an outlier peak, which may lead to overfitting.

Our evaluation makes use of the Mann-Whitney U test score for comparison, also known as Area Under ROC Curve (AUC). AUC measures how well a trained classifier discriminates positive instances and negative instances and is widely used in this domain.

5.3 Features

Four types of textual features are explored in this work: n-grams, standard topics (i.e., not time sensitive), state-aware topics, and state transitions. These features are associated with different levels of abstractions; n-grams are directly observed, whereas topics and states are inferred.

n-grams: For each patient, unigrams and bigrams are extracted from nursing notes. We empirically decided to use 200 and 100 top n-grams for the mortality group and the survival group, respectively, in terms of pointwise mutual information (PMI). The PMI was calculated on the training data. The decision to use different sizes of n-grams for the two groups comes from the fact that the mortality group, which is much smaller than the survival group, requires more n-grams for high recall. The selected n-grams are merged into the final vocabulary. This process is performed for each prediction term. For each patient, a vocabulary-sized feature vector is made such that each element is set to 1 if the corresponding n-gram appears in the patient's nursing notes written until the prediction time.

Standard topics: Topic distributions learned by LDA are used, using the classification method suggested by Ghassemi et al. [8]. For each patient, topic distributions are extracted from individual nursing notes (not merged notes) written until the prediction time. The extracted topic distributions are averaged and aggregated into one feature vector, whose dimension is equal to the number of topics.

State-aware topics: Document-wise topic distributions ($\theta^m_{t,j}$) learned by STTM are used. STTM estimates one state per time point, thus generating one topic distribution for each time point. The topic distributions of all documents written until the prediction time are aggregated into one feature vector as for standard topics.

State transitions: For each patient, a sequence of states is estimated by STTM. The relative frequencies of states and those of state transitions (pairs of states) are represented as a feature vector. Therefore, if there are S states, the dimension of the feature vector is $S + S^2$. For making this feature, only the latest four time points (i.e., two days) are considered; otherwise, longer sequences tend to include more states and have lower element values. The number four has been chosen empirically.

To simulate the real world prediction task, where topics and states should be estimated as nursing notes are obtained, we estimate the LDA model only on the training set, and the topic distributions of the validation and test data are inferred from the learned topics, using Gibbs sampling. Similarly, we run STTM only on the training set, and a Viterbi algorithm is used to infer an unseen document's state based on the state transition distribution and topic distribution of each state. Once states are finalized, the document's topic distribution is estimated using maximum likelihood estimation.

5.4 Model Parameters

For both LDA and STTM, symmetric Dirichlet priors are used such that α is set to 0.1 and β to 0.001, which fosters sparse distributions over topics and words. γ is set to 1 so that any probability distribution is equally probable for π_c. Gibbs sampling is run for 2000 iterations. The numbers of topics and states are different for each task.

6. EXPERIMENTS

In this section, we first demonstrate the information extracted from the nursing notes by STTM (Task 1). Then, we show improvement in mortality prediction when the extracted temporal information is used (Task 2). Lastly, we evaluate individual features in order to interpret the result of Task 2 and gain insights into the strengths and weaknesses of the individual features (Task 3).

6.1 TASK 1: TEMPORAL INFORMATION EXTRACTION BY STTM

This section is to illustrate and interpret state-aware topics and state transitions learned by STTM over nursing notes on one fold, which will be used for mortality prediction in the tasks evaluated later in the paper. We also demonstrate the kinds of insights STTM is capable of offering. The number of topics and states are set to 10 for the sake of interpretability. Note that interpretability is critical in the medical domain [12], and too many topics and states may make the model hard to interpret. Table 3 and Figure 4 show learned topics and state transitions, respectively.

Table 3 shows the learned topics with manually assigned labels, topical words, and example snippets from nursing notes. Topical words are the words with the highest mutual information with each of the learned topics. These state-aware topics show some differences from standard topics learned by LDA over the same data with the same parameter settings, i.e., on merged nursing notes with 10 topics (not listed here for space). First, there are cases where STTM dedicates two topics that correspond to one standard topic as follows. The admission topics for general patients (T3) and infants (T0) capture the fact that general patients and infants usually follow different state sequences (as seen in Figure 4). Newborn jaundice (T4) and sepsis (T8) can also be explained by different state paths on which they appear. Family visiting (T2) and social activities (T5) share many overlapping words, but family visiting is one of the most critical indicators of patient mortality when it involves discussion of a patient's death. On the other hand, general social activities appear in nursing

Table 3: State-Aware Topics Learned From Nursing Notes

T0. Infant admission	**T5. Social activities**
infant, nicu, delivery, cbc, normal, sepsis, maternal, born, admission, risk, baby, gbs, PHI_DATE, apgars, pregnancy	he, she, that, her, his, have, been, but, had, very, also, will, PHI_LASTNAME, if, need, would, after, about, did, they, it
Admit/transfer note Infant admitted from l&D for sepsis eval. [**Name8 (MD) 63**] MD/NNP note for hx and physical.	NPN Pt left AMA, he felt that he needed to get home to help take care of his daughters
T1. Stability	**T6. Summary**
feeds, cares, infant, well, voiding, continue, parents, feeding, active, stable, support, cc, ra, far, crib, swaddled, mom, fen	am, social, place, blood, progress, due, care, up, time, pm, fluid, npn, per, noted, cxr, id, area, cc, pain, urine, site, currently
continue to encourage po feeds. 4: G/D temps stable in an open crib. alert and active with cares. sleeps well inbetween.	NURSING PROGRESS NOTE 11 PM - 7 AM NO COMPLAINTS HR 80'S...SBP 90-100'S..
T2. Family visiting	**T7. Respiratory support**
family, patient, but, today, pts, sats, team, placed, iv, mg, bp, mask, off, afternoon, night, started, status, able, day, continues	thick, vent, secretions, peep, coarse, sputum, abg, suctioned, yellow, goal, tube, trach, remains, gtt, eyes, amts, skin
npn Pt expired at 7:40pm. Family at bedside with pt. Emotional support given to family at this very difficult time.	Resp Care: Pt continues trached and on ventilatory support with simv 600x14/+5 peep/5 psv/fio2 .4 with acceptable abg
T3. Admission	**T8. Sepsis**
ccu, micu, PHI_DATE, cath, s/p, c/o, PHI_HOSPITAL, admitted, admission, sob, floor, arrival, hct, arrived, ns, wife	npo, settings, fio2, pn, infusing, secretions, cbg, rate, vent, amp, coarse, respiratory, gas, lytes, received, ett, white, simv, cloudy
Pt transfered to [**Hospital1 22**] for ERCP which was done on arrival to MICU.	Respiratory Care Note Pt.continues on SIMV 22/5 R 34 and FIO2 33-44%. BS are coarse. Pt. sx'd for mod.
T4. Newborn jaundice	**T9. Laboratory tests**
bili, infant, cpap, baby, isolette, caffeine, servo, nested, phototherapy, enteral, mom, feeds, cc/kg/day, cc/k/d, will	pain, sbp, gtt, neuro, clear, cough, intact, oob, mg, pulses, foley, neo, bs, effect, ct, bases, given, activity, mae, lopressor, po
#6-O: under single phototherapy, bili pending this am. sl jaundiced. #4-O; temp stable in servo isolette, active and alert	7p-7a Neuro: a+ox3. Pain controlled with Percocet. CV: sbp initially 140's, 2.5mg iv with effect. SR with long PR, rate 80's.

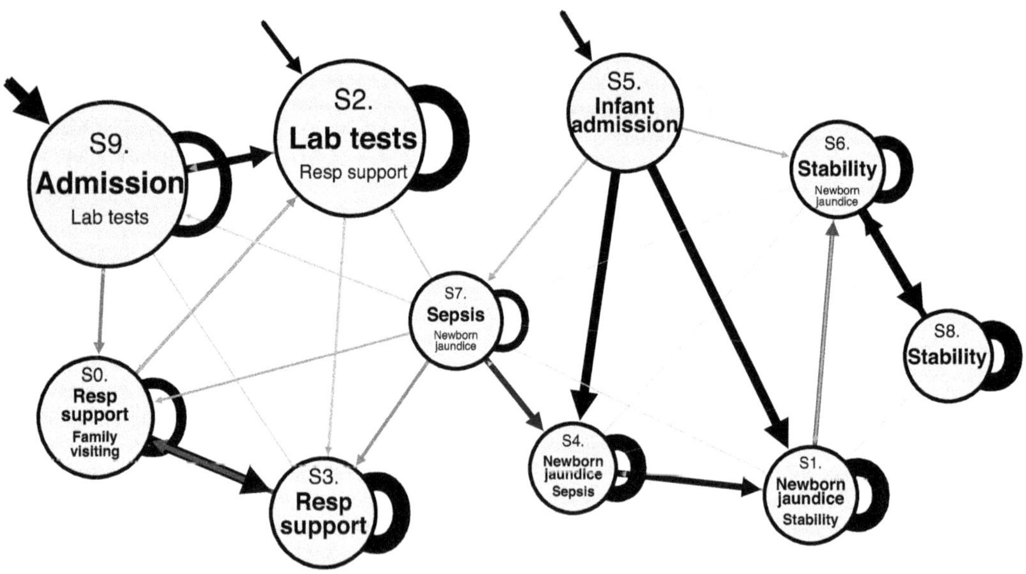

Figure 4: State Transitions Learned From Nursing Notes

notes at anytime. These examples show that STTM splits topics if they appear in different stages of patients. There are opposite cases, too. Stability topic (T1) corresponds to two similar standard topics. Drainage and sounds in organs are topics that appear only in standard topics. These topics may distinguish different symptoms better than state-aware topics do. However, many of these symptoms appear simultaneously in one stage of a patient's journey, and STTM tends to combine them into one topic. For instance, there may be many different outcomes of a patient's stability, but STTM counts all of them as one topic that appears when a patient's condition becomes stable, and dedicates other topics to explain different stages.

Figure 4 is the state transition graph constructed by the learned transition probabilities. Nodes are states and arrows are transitions. Since a state is represented by a topic distribution, node labels reflect the relative proportions of topics. Yet, the labels should not be overemphasized as if each state covers only those topics in the label. Node sizes reflect the number of patients that are assigned to those states at least once. The thickness of an arrow reflects the transition probability. The arrows coming into S9, S2, and S5 without a source state indicate the probabilities of these states being initial states. Transitions with too small probabilities are not shown in the graph for clarity.

The most notable characteristic is the two big components bridged by S7. The states in the left component are more descriptive of general patients, whereas the states in the right have a large proportion of infant issues. Stability prevails in the right component, which is consistent with the data, wherein neonates are likely to end up being stable in ICUs. The states S9, S2, and S5 are found to be initial states in most sequences. This is reflected by their constituting topics as well, that is, large proportions of general admission (T3) and infant admission (T0). State 2 represents various laboratory tests, which are also common in patients' initial stages. It is interesting that only the infant admission state (S5) is in the right component, indicating the different patterns of NICU patients from other patients. Data analysis confirms that State 5 and thus its connected states capture neonatal patients well; 1725 out of 1727 patients who start from State 5 are neonatal patients, and this accounts for 92% of the entire neonatal patients in the training set.

In summary, STTM captures topics with unique characteristics by taking into account time and state transition. Also, it may not be as straightforward to use other time-aware topic models described in Section 2 to draw a diagram like Figure 4 that provides the whole picture of patient states and state transitions.

6.2 TASK 2: MORTALITY PREDICTION WITH TEMPORAL INFORMATION

This section examines mortality prediction performance meant to validate the insights offered in Task 1. We examine whether temporal information conveyed by state-aware topics and state transitions add any predictive power over standard topics in mortality prediction. The following four combinations of features are compared.

GT: Baseline 50 standard topics. This corresponds to the state-of-the-art method used by Ghassemi et al. [8].

GT+ST: 50 standard topics plus state transitions trained with 10 topics and 10 states.

GT+SA: 50 standard topics plus state transitions and state-aware topics trained with 10 topics and 10 states.

GT+SA+: This feature is the same as GT+SA except that for time points 11-20, it uses state transitions trained on longer sequences. Since most sequences are very short (the median is 2.03 days), STTM is hindered from obtaining good prediction performance for patients with long ICU stays. We therefore train STTM on a subset of training data that includes only those sequences longer than five time points. For prediction at time points 1-10, the original state transitions are used, and at time points 11-20, the newly trained state transitions are used. Therefore, GT+SA and GT+SA+ make the same performance until time point 10.

Table 4 shows the AUC scores averaged across time points. Best scores are in bold, and scores higher than the baseline (GT) are marked with an asterisk if it is statistically significant. Paired t-tests were used for significance tests, and p-values < 0.05 are considered significant as in common mortality prediction tasks [16]. For short-term predic-

Table 4: Performance of Mortality Prediction with Combined Features

	GT	*GT+ST*	*GT+SA*	*GT+SA+*
1-Day	**0.7325**	0.7218	0.7224	0.7235
1-Week	0.7781	0.7772	**0.7811**	0.7784
1-Month	0.7820	*0.7860	*0.7866	***0.7871**
6-Month	0.7882	0.7884	***0.7921**	*0.7912
1-Year	0.7905	0.7912	0.7930	***0.7939**

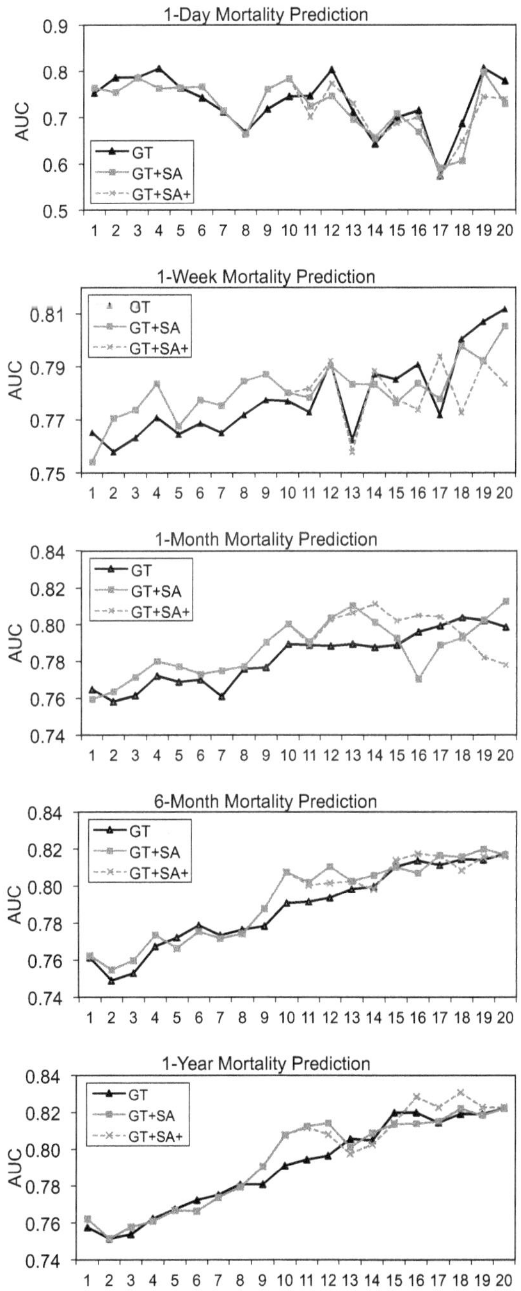

Figure 5: Performance of Mortality Prediction by Prediction Terms and Time Points

tions (1-day and 1-week), incorporating temporal information does not significantly enhance performance. However, for long-term predictions (1-month, 6-months, and 1-year), the temporal information achieves a statistically significant improvement. Training STTM on long sequences turns out to be effective for performance improvement. Figure 5 shows the performance by terms and time points.

Short Term (1-day & 1-week): For 1-day prediction, incorporating temporal information very slightly harms performance, although the effect is not statistically significant. We found no difference in the diversity of states or the frequency of state change between patients who died within one day and those surviving longer. Hence, this result is rooted in the difficulty of predicting patient outcome in the very near future. For instance, it is very hard to tell whether a patient would die today or tomorrow. For 1-week prediction, temporal information starts to help achieve higher performance, although it is not statistically significant yet. There exists a big gap in average scores between 1-day and 1-week. This reflects the difficulty of predicting very short-term consequences. Intuitively, for a patient who is fighting against death right now, clinical measures could be more helpful. This supports the result of previous research that included laboratory and radiology reports [8], which shows higher prediction accuracies for shorter terms.

Long Term (1-month, 6-month & 1-year): For long-term predictions, GT+SA and GT+SA+ outperform the baseline with statistical significance. Training on long sequences is helpful to achieve higher accuracies for 1-month and 1-year predictions. As expected, it enhances prediction performance for later time points, because long sequences help STTM to be trained well for patients who stay in ICUs for a long time. Interestingly, all the combined models (GT+ST, GT+SA, GT+SA+) outperform the baseline for 1-month prediction, but their statistical significance decreases for longer terms. This indicates that temporal information during an ICU stay loses its prediction power as the target future becomes further. This task proves the effectiveness of the temporal information extracted from nursing notes in mortality prediction tasks.

6.3 TASK 3: MORTALITY PREDICTION BY INDIVIDUAL FEATURES

This section measures mortality prediction performance based on each of the four types of textual features: n-grams, standard topics, state-aware topics, and state transitions. The purpose of this task is to take a closer look at what information each feature type captures in mortality prediction. These word-level, topic-level, and state-level features can be seen as being associated with different levels of abstraction. To the best of our knowledge, there is no article that provides a comprehensive view of different types of textual features in mortality prediction tasks. The number of states is fixed to 10 in our experiments.

Table 5 shows the mortality prediction performance of the four individual feature types. Best scores are in bold, and an asterisk is marked if a score is higher than the baseline (StandTopic) or a baseline score is higher than any other scores with statistical significance. N-grams perform poorly compared to topics and state transitions. For 10 topics, state-aware topics perform better than standard topics in most cases, and even state transitions alone are competitive with standard topics. This shows that the learned temporal information is correlated with patient mortality. For 50 topics, the performance of standard topics improves a lot because increasing the number of topics enables to capture more various topics related to mortality. On the other hand, the performance of state-aware topics and state transitions remains almost the same. This is probably because the number of possible topic distributions is restricted to the number of states, preventing documents from having a variety of topic distributions. Although state-related features do not beat standard topics on their own, recall that they enhance performance when used together as shown in Task 2. The performance of state-related features may improve if the number of states is increased at the expense of interpretability. Replacing state parameters θ's with Dirichlet priors α's may also give more freedom to topic distributions.

The rest of this section discusses the performance of individual features. The high markers of mortality and error cases are examined to identify their limitations and possible directions for improvement. For illustration, we pick the classifier at time point 4 (e.g., two days after admission), which is near median of all ICU stays (=2.03 days).

n-grams: To see indicative n-grams, enrichment [8] has been calculated for each n-gram w as $\frac{\sum_n q_{nw} * \mathbf{1}(n)}{\sum_n q_{nw}}$, where n is a patient index, q_{nw} is the feature value, and $\mathbf{1}(n)$ is equal to 1 if patient n died. The enrichment of an n-gram represents the relative frequency of positive instances who have that n-gram, so higher enrichment indicates higher likelihood of mortality. Table 6(a) shows n-grams with the highest and lowest enrichment on average across different terms. Only those n-grams that occur in at least 1% of the entire nursing notes are shown to filter out overfitted n-grams. High mortality markers include descriptions about patient conditions (e.g., "neuro unresponsive" and "mottled"), nurses' actions (e.g., "cmo (comfort measures only)" and "dnr (do not resuscitate)"), medications (e.g., "levophed" and "vasopressin"), and family responses (e.g., "priest" and "meeting held"). High survival markers include a lot of patient conditions such as "no_spits", "active alert", and "ad lib".

Table 5: Performance of Mortality Prediction with Individual Features

		10 Topics				50 Topics			
	n-grams	*StandTopic*	*StateTopic*	*StateTrans*	*StateAll*	*StandTopic*	*StateTopic*	*StateTrans*	*StateAll*
1-Day	0.563	0.709	**0.711**	0.709	0.708	***0.733**	0.705	0.703	0.691
1-Week	0.651	0.746	**0.749**	0.746	0.747	***0.778**	0.749	0.737	0.751
1-Month	0.691	0.753	0.759	0.758	***0.762**	***0.782**	0.758	0.749	0.763
6-Month	0.726	0.766	0.767	0.766	***0.771**	***0.788**	0.769	0.757	0.769
1-Year	0.732	0.772	0.771	0.769	**0.773**	***0.790**	0.776	0.760	0.775

Table 6: n-gram Features

(a) High markers of mortality

cmo, neuro unresponsive, poor prognosis, prognosis, priest, fixed, dnr, comfort measures, wishes, dnr/dni, brain, levophed

(b) n-grams with high error contribution

afib, afebrile, nl, will continue, labs, tlc, distended bs, cardiac, abd, code status, right, rate, meds, distended, only,

Table 7: Standard Topic Features

(a) High markers of mortality

T16. Unresponsiveness	neuro, pupils, mm, eyes, left, right, head, drain, sbp, icp
T10. Heart failure medicine	gtt, dr, PHI_LASTNAME, fluid, levophed, bolus, levo, aware, map, started
T29. Pain reliever	propofol, sedated, sedation, fentanyl, versed, peep, gtt, cc/hr, vent, secretions

(b) Topics with high error contribution

T41. Infant delivery	nicu, delivery, infant, cbc, maternal, sepsis, born, admission, gbs, risk
T28. Respiratory infection	settings, fio2, vent, gas, rate, secretion, cbg, map, npo, ett, lytes
T17. TSICU	per, t/sicu, skin, id, tsicu, systems, review, endo, prophylaxis, fx

To examine the reason for the poor performance of n-grams, each n-gram's error contribution has been calculated as $f_w(N_w^{\mathrm{P}} - N_w^{\mathrm{N}})$, where f_w is the feature weight of n-gram w learned by SVM, and N_w^{P} and N_w^{N} are the fractions of positive instances and negative instances who have this n-gram, respectively. Since features that contribute to mortality (survival) have negative (positive) feature weights, the lower the error contribution the better. Table 6(b) shows the n-grams with the highest error contribution. The list includes apparently neutral terms such as "will continue", "labs", "right", and "rate", whose polarity depends on the context. Most of these terms are also very frequent, which significantly harms the prediction performance of n-grams.

Standard Topics (50 topics): We calculated the enrichment of each topic across different terms (Table 7). In this case, the feature values are real numbers between 0 and 1. Unresponsiveness (T16) and taking heart failure medicines (T10) and pain relievers (T29) turn out to be significant signs across all prediction terms. These topics and the n-gram high markers capture similar themes. However, the reduced dimension and the lower sparsity of standard topics significantly improves performance.

The error contribution of the topics shows that infant delivery (T41), respiratory infection (T28), and TSICU (trauma surgical ICU) (T17) contribute to classification error the most. This is reasonable because these topics are not fine-grained enough to the extent that their existence directly leads to mortality. This is the limitation of unsupervised topic models, and splitting these topics may improve performance significantly.

State-Aware Topics (10 topics): Figure 6(a) shows the enrichment of each state-aware topic. Respiratory support (T7), family visiting (T2), summary (T6), and admission (T3) are always in top for all terms. Laboratory tests (T9) are slightly lower. Stability (T1), newborn jaundice (T4), infant admission (T0), and sepsis (T8) have very low enrichment. These topics are reliably indicative of survival.

State Transitions (10 topics): Figure 6(b) shows the enrichment of each state. Interestingly, states have higher variance in enrichment than state-aware topics, indicating that states do reflect different mortality possibilities. The state about respiratory support and family visiting (S0) has the highest enrichment, followed by the state about respiratory support without family visiting (S3).

Figure 6(c) shows the average enrichment of state transitions over all terms. Rows are source states and columns are target states. The first five are the states in the left component in Figure 4, and the last five are in the right component. Red and green indicate high and low enrichment, respectively, and black represents no transition found. Patients who move from respiratory problems (S3) to sepsis (S7) and who are admitted (S9) and moved to respiratory support (S0) show the highest enrichment. In contrast, patients who move from respiratory problems (S3) to general lab tests (S2) show relatively low enrichment. State transitions centered around S7 (sepsis) show moderate enrichment. This is consistent with the recent report that mortality rates can be significantly reduced when sepsis is well controlled [1].

Note that high markers differ across time points. For example, high marker topics after five days from admission comprise a lot of neonate-related topics, because most adult patients have been discharged by this time (see Table 2(c)).

7. CONCLUSION

This paper proposes and evaluates a novel approach to mortality prediction using latent temporal information in nursing notes. Our joint model of an HMM and LDA reveals the temporal dynamics of patients' underlying states latent

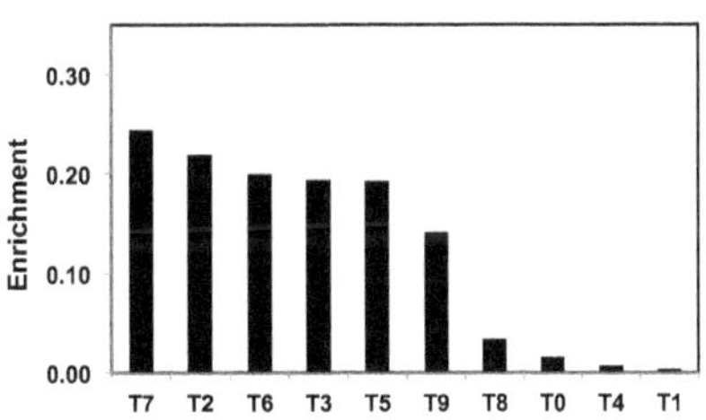

(a) Enrichment of state-aware topics

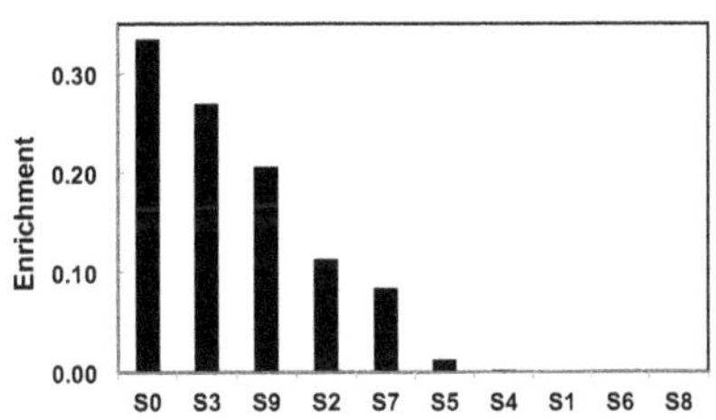

(b) Enrichment of states

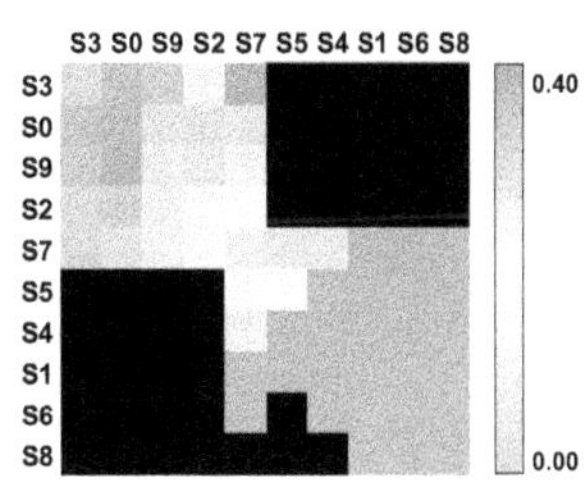

(c) Enrichment of state transitions

Figure 6: State-Related Features

within nursing notes. The information—state-aware topics and state transitions—is then leveraged to improve mortality prediction performance. Task 1 shows that the model finds a meaningful trend of patients' state transitions and topics from nursing notes. Task 2 shows that the learned temporal information is beneficial for long term mortality prediction, but not much in short-term prediction. Task 3 suggests that the learned states indeed have different levels of enrichment indicating that the states are related with mortality and survival. In addition, four types of text features are examined both quantitatively and qualitatively, providing a comprehensive view of the roles and limitations of the textual features in mortality prediction tasks.

There are limitations as well. The current version of STTM shows no improvement in mortality prediction when the number of topics is increased from 10 to 50. This may be partly because the number of possible topic distributions is restricted to the number of states. However, we need to try STTM on other data and evaluate in different aspects as well in order to better understand the scalability of STTM. Another limitation is that our approach has no improvement when applied to NICUs and the others separately. This might be due to the reduced data size and the sparsity of the feature space (e.g., 100 possible state transitions). For example, the number of NICU patients is only a fourth of the entire patient population, and the other ICU patients have very short stays (Table 2(c)). More sophisticated approaches are desirable to use temporal information for different ICU types.

8. ACKNOWLEDGMENTS

This research was supported by the Naval Research Laboratory under grant number N00173-09-F-0237.

9. REFERENCES

[1] J. R. Beardsley, C. M. Jones, J. Chou, M. Currie-Coyoy, T. Jackson, and A. Orsborn. Code Sepsis: Improving Sepsis Care; Saving Patients' Lives. *ASHP Best Practices Award*, 2014.

[2] D. M. Blei and J. D. Lafferty. Dynamic topic models. In *ICML '06*, pages 113–120, 2006.

[3] D. M. Blei and P. J. Moreno. Topic segmentation with an aspect hidden Markov model. In *ACM SIGIR '01*, pages 343–348, 2001.

[4] D. M. Blei, A. Y. Ng, and M. I. Jordan. Latent dirichlet allocation. *JMLR*, 3:993–1022, 2003.

[5] C.-c. Chia, Z. Syed, and A. Arbor. Scalable Noise Mining in Long-Term Electrocardiographic Time-Series to Predict Death Following Heart Attacks. *KDD '14*, pages 125–134, 2014.

[6] M. Cvach. Monitor alarm fatigue: an integrative review. *Biomedical instrumentation & technology*, 46(4):268–77, 2012.

[7] Z. J. Gao, Y. Song, S. Liu, H. Wang, H. Wei, Y. Chen, and W. Cui. Tracking and Connecting Topics via Incremental Hierarchical Dirichlet Processes. In *IEEE ICDM '11*, pages 1056–1061, 2011.

[8] M. Ghassemi, T. Naumann, F. Doshi-Velez, N. Brimmer, R. Joshi, A. Rumshisky, and P. Szolovits. Unfolding Physiological State : Mortality Modelling in Intensive Care Units. *KDD '14*, pages 75–84, 2014.

[9] A. Gruber, M. Rosen-Zvi, and Y. Weiss. Hidden topic Markov models. *AISTATS '07*, pages 163–170, 2007.

[10] L. Hong, B. Dom, S. Gurumurthy, and K. Tsioutsiouliklis. A time-dependent topic model for multiple text streams. In *KDD '11*, page 832, 2011.

[11] L. Hong, D. Yin, J. Guo, and B. D. Davison. Tracking trends: incorporating term volume into temporal topic models. In *KDD '11*, page 484, 2011.

[12] A. Kalogeratos, V. Chasanis, G. Rakocevic, A. Likas, Z. Babovic, and M. Novakovic. Mining Clinical Data. In G. Rakocevic, T. Djukic, N. Filipovic, and V. Milutinović, editors, *Computational Medicine in Data Mining and Modeling SE - 1*, pages 1–34. 2013.

[13] L.-W. Lehman, R. Adams, L. Mayaud, G. Moody, A. Malhotra, R. Mark, and S. Nemati. A physiological time series dynamics-based approach to patient monitoring and outcome prediction. *IEEE journal of biomedical and health informatics*, PP(99):1, 2014.

[14] L.-w. Lehman, M. Saeed, W. Long, J. Lee, and R. Mark. Risk stratification of ICU patients using topic models inferred from unstructured progress notes. *AMIA Annual Symposium proceedings*, 2012:505–11, 2012.

[15] Q. Mei and C. Zhai. Discovering evolutionary theme patterns from text. In *KDD '05*, page 198, 2005.

[16] R. Menéndez, R. Martínez, S. Reyes, J. Mensa, X. Filella, M. A. Marcos, A. Martínez, C. Esquinas, P. Ramirez, and A. Torres. Biomarkers improve mortality prediction by prognostic scales in community -acquired pneumonia. *Thorax*, 64(7):587–91, 2009.

[17] M. J. Paul. Mixed Membership Markov Models for Unsupervised Conversation Modeling. In *EMNLP-CoNLL '12*, pages 94–104, 2012.

[18] Z. Syed, B. M. Scirica, S. Mohanavelu, P. Sung, E. L. Michelson, C. P. Cannon, P. H. Stone, C. M. Stultz, and J. V. Guttag. Relation of death within 90 days of non-ST-elevation acute coronary syndromes to variability in electrocardiographic morphology. *The American journal of cardiology*, 103(3):307–11, 2009.

[19] Y. W. Teh, M. I. Jordan, M. J. Beal, and D. M. Blei. Hierarchical Dirichlet Processes. *Journal of the American Statistical Association*, 101(476):1566–1581, 2006.

[20] H. Wang, D. Zhang, and C. Zhai. Structural Topic Model for Latent Topical Structure Analysis. *ACL '11*, pages 1526–1535, 2011.

[21] X. Wang and A. McCallum. Topics over time: a non-Markov continuous-time model of topical trends. In *KDD '06*, page 424, 2006.

[22] Y. Wang, E. Agichtein, and M. Benzi. Tm-lda: Efficient online modeling of latent topic transitions in social media. In *KDD '12*, pages 123–131, 2012.

[23] J. Wiens, E. Horvitz, and J. V. Guttag. Patient Risk Stratification for Hospital-Associated C. diff as a Time-Series Classification Task. In *Advances in Neural Information Processing Systems*, pages 467–475, 2012.

[24] J. Yang, J. McAuley, J. Leskovec, P. LePendu, and N. Shah. Finding progression stages in time-evolving event sequences. In *WWW '14*, pages 783–794, 2014.

[25] J. Zhang, Y. Song, C. Zhang, and S. Liu. Evolutionary hierarchical dirichlet processes for multiple correlated time-varying corpora. In *KDD '10*, page 1079, 2010.

[26] J. Zhu and E. P. Xing. Conditional topic random fields. *ICML '10*, pages 1239–1246, 2010.

Learning Relative Similarity from Data Streams: Active Online Learning Approaches

Shuji Hao†, Peilin Zhao‡, Steven C.H. Hoi§, Chunyan Miao¶
†Interdisciplinary Graduate School,Nanyang Technological University, NTU, Singapore
‡Data Analytics Department, Institute for Infocomm Research, A*STAR, Singapore
§School of Information Systems, Singapore Management University, Singapore
¶School of Computer Engineering, Nanyang Technological University, Singapore
haos0001@e.ntu.edu.sg, zhaop@i2r.a-star.edu.sg, chhoi@smu.edu.sg, ascymiao@ntu.edu.sg

ABSTRACT

Relative similarity learning, as an important learning scheme for information retrieval, aims to learn a bi-linear similarity function from a collection of labeled instance-pairs, and the learned function would assign a high similarity value for a similar instance-pair and a low value for a dissimilar pair. Existing algorithms usually assume the labels of all the pairs in data streams are always made available for learning. However, this is not always realistic in practice since the number of possible pairs is quadratic to the number of instances in the database, and manually labeling the pairs could be very costly and time consuming. To overcome the limitation, we propose a novel framework of active online similarity learning. Specifically, we propose two new algorithms: (i) PAAS: Passive-Aggressive Active Similarity learning; (ii) CWAS: Confidence-Weighted Active Similarity learning, and we will prove their mistake bounds in theory. We have conducted extensive experiments on a variety of real-world data sets, and we find encouraging results that validate the empirical effectiveness of the proposed algorithms.

Categories and Subject Descriptors

H.4 [**Information Systems Applications**]: Miscellaneous; D.2.8 [**Information Retrieval**]: Online Learning—*Active Learning*

Keywords

Image Retrieval, Active Learning, Online Learning

1. INTRODUCTION

Similarity learning, also known as distance learning, has been widely studied in machine learning and data mining communities. It plays a critical role in a wide range of real-world applications, such as ranking[4], recommendation system[1], image retrieval [21, 26, 2, 30, 17] and text information retrieval [9], etc. In previous research, a variety of machine learning approaches have been proposed for learning distance or similarity functions from training data [31, 29, 14]. One of the most notable schemes is the Distance Metric Learning (DML) approach, which aims to learn a Mahalanobis distance [31] and requires the distance metric satisfying the Positive Semi-Definiteness (PSD) property. However, imposing the PSD requirement often makes the DML task computationally challenging, particularly when handling large-scale training data in high dimensional spaces, although various approximate techniques have been proposed to improve computational efficiency. Another strong assumption of DML approaches is that the exact distances of all pairs of instances should be obtained, which are usually costly and time consuming.

Instead of learning the Mahalanobis distance, another technique is to explore the relative similarity learning [4], which aims to learn a bilinear similarity model for measuring the similarity of any instance pair (two instances) by eliminating the PSD requirement, which is thus much more computationally efficient and scalable. More importantly, only relative similarities among any two pairs of instances are needed, which greatly alleviates the requirement of exact distances among all instances. In literature, several online learning algorithms have been proposed for learning relative similarity from data streams. Most existing studies generally assume that the data streams of instance pairs are fully labeled. However, we argue this may not be a realistic setting since the number of instance pairs is quadratic with respect to the number of instances, and labeling such a massive pool of instance pairs could be extremely costly and time consuming for large-scale applications, especially when the labeling task has to explicitly involve human in the loop in an early stage of deploying a new system.

Unlike the existing relative similarity learning approaches, in this paper, we investigate a novel scheme of active online learning of relative similarity from unlabeled data streams without requiring labeling every instance pair. Specifically, we propose two efficient and scalable online learning algorithms to tackle the new problem: (i) PAAS: Passive-Aggressive Active Similarity learning and (ii) CWAS: Confidence-Weighted Active Similarity learning. We then analyze the theoretical bounds of the proposed online learning algorithms, and further validate their empirical performances via an extensive set of experiments on various real datasets. The encouraging results show that the proposed online active relative similarity learning algorithms can achieve highly competitive performance while significantly reducing the amount of labeling costs.

The rest of this paper is organized as follows. We first review related work, and then present the formulation of the proposed two algorithms as well as their theoretical analysis. Further, we empirically validate the proposed algorithms in terms of effectiveness and efficiency, and finally conclude this paper and discuss the future work.

Permission to make digital or hard copies of all or part of this work for personal or classroom use is granted without fee provided that copies are not made or distributed for profit or commercial advantage and that copies bear this notice and the full citation on the first page. Copyrights for components of this work owned by others than ACM must be honored. Abstracting with credit is permitted. To copy otherwise, or republish, to post on servers or to redistribute to lists, requires prior specific permission and/or a fee. Request permissions from Permissions@acm.org.
CIKM'15, October 19–23, 2015, Melbourne, Australia.
© 2015 ACM. ISBN 978-1-4503-3794-6/15/10 ...$15.00.
DOI: http://dx.doi.org/10.1145/2806416.2806464.

2. RELATED WORK

This paper is mainly related to two major categories of studies in literature: similarity learning, and active learning. We briefly review each of them below.

Similarity learning has been extensively studied in machine learning and data mining communities. Most existing works have been focused on DML [31] for learning a Mahalanobis distance through a PSD matrix [16, 22, 24]. Weinberger et al. [28] proposed a large margin nearest-neighbor classifier to address the DML problem in the context of ranking. Globerson and Roweis [11] proposed to address the positive constraints in a supervised setting. Based on LogDet-regularization with different loss functions, Davis et al. [8] proposed online metric learning algorithms. All these algorithms aim to learn a PSD matrix $\mathbf{M}$, based on which the dissimilarity of two images $\mathbf{x}_1$ and $\mathbf{x}_2$ is measured by computing $(\mathbf{x}_1 - \mathbf{x}_2)^\top \mathbf{M}(\mathbf{x}_1 - \mathbf{x}_2)$. However, it is computationally costly to impose the PSD constraint on $\mathbf{M}$, which makes these algorithms inappropriate for large-scale problems. To overcome this limitation, the bilinear form similarity function $\mathbf{x}_1^\top \mathbf{M}\mathbf{x}_2$ is proposed, where $\mathbf{M}$ is not required to be PSD. Along this direction, Chechik et al. [4] proposed the first-order relative similarity learning algorithm "OASIS" based on the first-order based online learning algorithm [6, 35, 15]. Recently, Crammer and Chechik [5] proposed a second-order relative similarity learning algorithm "AROMA" based on second-order based online learning algorithm [7, 33]. However, all these algorithms require a large set of labeled data to train the similarity models, which is not always realistic in many real-world applications due to the expensive labeling cost.

Active learning is a learning technique for reducing labeling cost by querying the most informative examples for labeling, which has been extensively studied in machine learning literature [3]. Existing active learning algorithms could be generally classified into four categories: uncertainty-based [18, 27, 34], searching through the hypothesis space [10], minimizing the expected error and variance on the pool of unlabeled instances [20, 13], and exploiting the structure information [25] among the instances. More can be found in the comprehensive survey [23]. Our strategy is more related to the work in the first two categories. Specifically, we adopt the typical active learning strategy in the work [3, 32, 19], where the algorithm maintains a Bernoulli random variable $Z_t \in \{0,1\}$ with probability $\delta/(\delta + |p_t|)$, and p_t is the margin of the similarity function on the t-th triplet. The algorithm will query the label and update the model only when $Z_t = 1$.

Despite being extensively studied [23], most of the active strategies are proposed for the classification or regression tasks. To our knowledge, there is no previous work exploring the active strategy on the relative similarity learning problem. To alleviate the cost in labeling, we explore the idea of active learning algorithms for overcoming the limitation of conventional relative similarity learning approaches.

3. ACTIVE ONLINE LEARNING OF RELATIVE SIMILARITY FROM DATA STREAMS

In this section, we first introduce the problem setting for active online learning of relative similarity from data streams, and then present the details of the proposed Active Online Similarity Learning algorithms.

3.1 Problem Formulation

Following [4], we would study the problem of online learning a relative similarity function $S(\mathbf{x}, \mathbf{x}'), \forall \mathbf{x}, \mathbf{x}' \in \mathbb{R}^d$, which measures the similarity between $\mathbf{x}$ and $\mathbf{x}'$. Formally, let

$$\{(\mathbf{x}_t, \mathbf{x}_t^1, \mathbf{x}_t^2; y_t) \in \mathbb{R}^d \times \mathbb{R}^d \times \mathbb{R}^d \times \{-1, +1\} | t \in [T]\}$$

be a sequence of triplets (where $[T] = \{1, \ldots, T\}$) . For the t-th triplet, $y_t = 1$ indicates $\mathbf{x}_t$ instance is more similar with $\mathbf{x}_t^1$ than $\mathbf{x}_t^2$, while $y_t = -1$ implies $\mathbf{x}_t$ is less similar with $\mathbf{x}_t^1$ than $\mathbf{x}_t^2$. Our goal is to learn a similarity function $S(\mathbf{x}, \mathbf{x}')$ that assigns a higher similarity score to the similar pair and a lower similarity score to the non-similar pair. Formally, given a triplet$(\mathbf{x}_t, \mathbf{x}_t^1, \mathbf{x}_t^2; y_t)$, the learned similar function should satisfy:

$$y_t[S(\mathbf{x}_t, \mathbf{x}_t^1) - S(\mathbf{x}_t, \mathbf{x}_t^2)] \geq 0, \quad \forall t \in [T].$$

For the similarity function, we specifically adopt a linear similarity function that has a bi-linear form,

$$S(\mathbf{x}, \mathbf{x}') = \mathbf{x}^\top \mathbf{M}\mathbf{x}', \tag{1}$$

where $\mathbf{M} \in \mathbb{R}^{d \times d}$. To note, it is possible to learn a $\mathbf{M} \in \mathbb{R}^{d \times d'}$, where $d \neq d'$, as similarity function between two different spaces, however we will assume $d = d'$ for simplicity.

To learn the parameter $\mathbf{M}$, we could introduce some loss functions to measure its performance on the t-th triplet, for example, the hinge loss is defined as

$$\ell(M; (\mathbf{x}_t, \mathbf{x}_t^1, \mathbf{x}_t^2; y_t)) = \Big[1 - y_t[S(\mathbf{x}_t, \mathbf{x}_t^1) - S(\mathbf{x}_t, \mathbf{x}_t^2)]\Big]_+, \tag{2}$$

where the hinge loss $[\cdot]_+ = \max(0, \cdot)$ encourages $y_t[S(\mathbf{x}_t, \mathbf{x}_t^1) - S(\mathbf{x}_t, \mathbf{x}_t^2)] \geq 1$. It is also possible to define other loss functions, e.g. logistic loss. In this article, we adopt the hinge loss for simplicity.

To solve this online relative similarity learning task, we can adopt those existing methods including Perceptron, Online Gradient Descent, Online Passive Aggressive, etc. Although these online learning algorithms can achieve a cumulative loss comparable with the one attained by any fixed hypothesis, one major limitation is that they require all the labels of the instances while labeling instances might be very expensive or time consuming. To solve this problem, we would study active online similarity learning, which will try to only query the labels of a few informative instances so that the number of queried labels is reduced while the performance dose not degrade too much.

3.2 PAAS: Passive-Aggressive Active Similarity learning

To solve Active Online Similarity Learning, we propose to adopt the selective sampling technique used in [3]. Specifically we will use a stochastic sampling scheme to decide whether it is necessary to query the label of the current instance. This scheme maintains a Bernoulli random variable $Z_t \in \{0,1\}$, where $Z_t = 1$ indicates the label should be queried at the t-th step. More specifically, this scheme employs the following sampling probability

$$\Pr(Z_t = 1) = \frac{\delta}{\delta + |p_t|}, \tag{3}$$

where $\delta > 0$ is a parameter to tune the number of queried labels and

$$p_t = \mathbf{x}_t^\top \mathbf{M}_t(\mathbf{x}_t^1 - \mathbf{x}_t^2) \tag{4}$$

is the margin of similarities between $\mathbf{x}_t^\top \mathbf{M}\mathbf{x}_t^1$ and $\mathbf{x}_t^\top \mathbf{M}\mathbf{x}_t^2$. Intuitively, the smaller the value of $|p_t|$, the lower the confidence of the model on the current prediction; as a consequence, we should query the label with a higher probability of $\Pr(Z_t = 1)$. Once

Algorithm 1 PAAS: The proposed algorithm of Passive-Aggressive Active Similarity learning

Input: smooth parameters $\delta > 0, C > 0$
Initialize: $\mathbf{M}_1 = 0$
for $t = 1, 2, \dots, T$ **do**
  Receive $(\mathbf{x}_t, \mathbf{x}_t^1, \mathbf{x}_t^2)$ and compute $X_t = \mathbf{x}_t(\mathbf{x}_t^1 - \mathbf{x}_t^2)^\top$;
  Compute $p_t = \mathrm{Tr}(\mathbf{M}_t \mathbf{X}_t^\top)$ and $\hat{y}_t = \mathrm{sign}(p_t)$;
  Sample $Z_t \in \{0, 1\}$ with $\Pr(Z_t = 1) = \frac{\delta}{\delta + |p_t|}$;
  if $Z_t = 1$ **then**
    Query y_t and compute $\ell_t(\mathbf{M}_t) = \max(0, 1 - y_t p_t)$;
    Update: $\mathbf{M}_{t+1} = \mathbf{M}_t + \tau_t y_t \mathbf{X}_t$;
    where $\tau_t = \min\left\{C, \frac{\ell_t(\mathbf{M}_t)}{\|\mathbf{X}_t\|_F^2}\right\}$.
  else
    $\mathbf{M}_{t+1} = \mathbf{M}_t$;
  end if
end for
Output: $\mathbf{M}_{T+1}$

the label is queried, the algorithm will update the model using the online Passive Aggressive strategy, i.e.,

$$\mathbf{M}_{t+1} = \arg\min_{\mathbf{M}} \left\{\frac{1}{2}\|\mathbf{M} - \mathbf{M}_t\|_F^2 + C\ell_t(M)\right\},$$

where $\ell_t(M) = \ell(M; (\mathbf{x}_t, \mathbf{x}_t^1, \mathbf{x}_t^2; y_t))$ and $C > 0$ is a trade-off between minimizing the adjustment of the model and minimizing the loss of the new model on the current example. This will produce a first-order update method [4, 6], i.e.,

$$\mathbf{M}_{t+1} = \mathbf{M}_t + \tau_t y_t \mathbf{X}_t,$$

where $\tau_t = \min\left\{C, \frac{\ell_t(\mathbf{M}_t)}{\|\mathbf{X}_t\|_F^2}\right\}$, and $\mathbf{X}_t = \mathbf{x}_t(\mathbf{x}_t^1 - \mathbf{x}_t^2)^\top$. Finally, the proposed Passive-Aggressive Active Similarity learning (PAAS) algorithm is summarized in Algorithm 1.

3.3 CWAS: Confidence-Weighted Active Similarity learning

To improve the learning performance, a second order similarity learning algorithm AROMA is proposed [5], which does not only use the first order information but also the second-order information, i.e., the covariance matrix for all the features, to update the model. Compared to the first-order algorithm OASIS, the effectiveness of AROMA has been theoretically and empirically verified. However, directly combining AROMA with query strategy in Equation (3) makes the theoretical analysis challenging.

Following the similar idea of AROMA, we assume the model maintains a Gaussian distribution, $\mathcal{N}(\mathbf{M}, \mathbf{\Sigma})$, where $\mathbf{M} \in \mathbb{R}^{d\times d}$ and $\mathbf{\Sigma} \in \mathbb{R}^{d^2\times d^2}$ encode the model's knowledge of and confidence of the model. At the t-th round, when receiving $(\mathbf{x}_t, \mathbf{x}_t^1, \mathbf{x}_t^2)$, we firstly decide whether it is necessary to query the true label based on Equation (3). If $Z_t = 1$, we query the label and update the distribution by minimizing the following objective function

$$f_t(\mathbf{M}, \mathbf{\Sigma}) = D_{KL}(\mathcal{N}(\mathrm{vec}(\mathbf{M}), \mathbf{\Sigma})\|\mathcal{N}(\mathrm{vec}(\mathbf{M}_t), \mathbf{\Sigma}_t)) + \eta\mathrm{Tr}(\mathbf{G}_t^\top \mathbf{M}) + \frac{1}{2\gamma}\mathrm{vec}(\mathbf{X}_t)^\top \mathbf{\Sigma}\mathrm{vec}(\mathbf{X}_t),$$

where

$$D_{KL}(\mathcal{N}(\mu, \mathbf{\Sigma})\|\mathcal{N}(\mu_t, \mathbf{\Sigma}_t)) = \frac{1}{2}\left[\ln(\frac{|\mathbf{\Sigma}_t|}{|\mathbf{\Sigma}|}) + \mathrm{Tr}(\mathbf{\Sigma}_t^{-1}\mathbf{\Sigma}) + (\mu_t - \mu)^\top \mathbf{\Sigma}_t^{-1}(\mu_t - \mu) - d\right],$$

is the Kullback-Leibler divergence of two distributions, $\mathbf{G}_t = \partial\ell_t(\mathbf{M}_t) = -y_t\mathbf{X}_t$, where $\mathbf{X}_t = \mathbf{x}_t(\mathbf{x}_t^1 - \mathbf{x}_t^2)^\top$ and $\mathrm{vec}(\mathbf{X}) = [\mathbf{X}_{11}, \dots, \mathbf{X}_{1d}, \dots, \mathbf{X}_{d1}, \dots, \mathbf{X}_{dd}]^\top$. The first term is to keep the new distribution not far away from the old one. The second term is a first order approximation of the current loss function at the current model, which is used to minimize the loss of the new model on the current example. The final term is to update the confidence of the model, since a new triplet is observed. η and γ are two positive parameters to trade off these objectives.

Algorithm 2 CWAS: The proposed algorithm of Confidence-Weighted Active Similarity learning

Input: learning rate η; regularization parameter γ
Initialize: $\mathbf{\Sigma}_1 = I^{d^2\times d^2}$, $\mathbf{M}_1 = 0^{d\times d}$
for $t = 1, 2, \dots, T$ **do**
  Receive $(\mathbf{x}_t, \mathbf{x}_t^1, \mathbf{x}_t^2)$ and compute $\mathbf{X}_t = \mathbf{x}_t(\mathbf{x}_t^1 - \mathbf{x}_t^2)^\top$;
  $p_t = \mathrm{Tr}(\mathbf{M}_t^\top \mathbf{X}_t)$, and $\hat{y}_t = \mathrm{sign}(p_t)$;
  Sample $Z_t \in \{0, 1\}$ with $\Pr(Z_t = 1) = \frac{\delta}{\delta + |p_t|}$;
  if $Z_t = 1$ **then**
    Query y_t, and compute $\ell_t(\mathbf{M}_t) = [1 - y_t p_t]_+$;
    if $\ell_t(\mathbf{M}_t) > 0$ **then**
      $\mathbf{\Sigma}_{t+1} = \mathbf{\Sigma}_t - \frac{\mathbf{\Sigma}_t \mathrm{vec}(\mathbf{X}_t)\mathrm{vec}(\mathbf{X}_t)^\top \mathbf{\Sigma}_t}{\gamma + \mathrm{vec}(\mathbf{X}_t)^\top \mathbf{\Sigma}_t \mathrm{vec}(\mathbf{X}_t)}$;
      $\mathbf{G}_t = \partial\ell_t(\mathbf{M}_t) = -y_t\mathbf{X}_t$;
      $\mathbf{M}_{t+1} = \mathrm{mat}\left[\mathrm{vec}(\mathbf{M}_t) - \eta\mathbf{\Sigma}_{t+1}\mathrm{vec}(\mathbf{G}_t)\right]$;
    else
      $\mathbf{\Sigma}_{t+1} = \mathbf{\Sigma}_t$, $\mathbf{M}_{t+1} = \mathbf{M}_t$;
    end if
  else
    $\mathbf{\Sigma}_{t+1} = \mathbf{\Sigma}_t$, $\mathbf{M}_{t+1} = \mathbf{M}_t$;
  end if
end for
Output: $\mathbf{M}_{T+1}$

To solve this optimization problem, we can set the derivatives $\partial_{\mathbf{M}} f_t(\mathbf{M}_{t+1}, \mathbf{\Sigma})$ and $\partial_{\mathbf{\Sigma}} f_t(\mu, \mathbf{\Sigma}_{t+1})$ as zeros, respectively to get the following updating rules:

$$\mathbf{M}_{t+1} = \mathrm{mat}\left[\mathrm{vec}(\mathbf{M}_t) - \eta\mathbf{\Sigma}_t\mathrm{vec}(\mathbf{G}_t)\right], \quad (5)$$

$$\mathbf{\Sigma}_{t+1} = \mathbf{\Sigma}_t - \frac{\mathbf{\Sigma}_t\mathrm{vec}(\mathbf{X}_t)\mathrm{vec}(\mathbf{X}_t)^\top\mathbf{\Sigma}_t}{\gamma + \mathrm{vec}(\mathbf{X}_t)^\top\mathbf{\Sigma}_t\mathrm{vec}(\mathbf{X}_t)}, \quad (6)$$

where $\mathrm{mat}(\cdot)$ is the inverse function of $\mathrm{vec}(\cdot)$.

Finally, we summarize the proposed CWAS in Algorithm 2.

Remark One key drawback of this algorithm is that the dimension of $\mathbf{\Sigma}_t$ is $d^2 \times d^2$, which will result in very high memory and computational complexities. In practice, we can use diagonal $\mathbf{\Sigma}_t$ to reduce these complexities. Or equivalently, we can store a matrix $\mathbf{\Sigma}_t \in \mathbb{R}^{d\times d}$, and change the Equations (5) and (6) into

$$\mathbf{M}_{t+1} = \mathbf{M}_t - \eta\mathbf{\Sigma}_t \odot \mathbf{G}_t, \quad (7)$$

$$\mathbf{\Sigma}_{t+1} = \mathbf{\Sigma}_t - \frac{\mathbf{\Sigma}_t \odot \mathbf{X}_t \odot \mathbf{X}_t \odot \mathbf{\Sigma}_t}{\gamma + \sum_{ij}(\mathbf{X}_t \odot \mathbf{\Sigma}_t \odot \mathbf{X}_t)_{ij}}, \quad (8)$$

where $\odot$ is element-wise product.

3.4 Theoretical Analysis

Denote $m_t = \mathbb{I}(y_t \neq \hat{y}_t)$, we would analyze the performance of the proposed two algorithms in terms of expected mistake bounds $\mathbb{E}[\sum_{t=1}^T m_t]$. We will provide all the detailed proofs in the appendix. Firstly, we have the following theorem for the first-order algorithm PAAS.

THEOREM 1. *If the PAAS algorithm is run with a sequence of triplets* $(\mathbf{x}_t, \mathbf{x}_t^1, \mathbf{x}_t^2; y_t)$, $t \in [T]$, *with* $D_X = \max\|X_t\|_F$, *then* *for any $T > 0$, and $\mathbf{M} \in \mathbb{R}^{d \times d}$, we have*

$$\mathbb{E}[\sum_{t=1}^{T} m_t] \le \frac{\beta}{\delta}\Big\{(\frac{\delta+1}{2})^2\|\mathbf{M}\|_F^2 + (\delta+1)CL_T(\mathbf{M})\Big\},$$

where $\beta = \max(1/C, D_X^2)$, and $L_T(\mathbf{M}) = \sum_{t=1}^{T} \ell_t(\mathbf{M})$. In addition, the expected number of labels queried equals to $\sum_{t=1}^{T} \mathbb{E}[\frac{\delta}{\delta+|p_t|}]$.

Remark: The above bound depends on the choice of parameter δ. Generally, δ could be viewed as a parameter to rule the extent to which the learning model fits the present data [3]. Minimizing the right hand side over δ, we can observe that setting $\delta = \sqrt{1 + 4CL_T(\mathbf{M})/\|\mathbf{M}\|_F^2}$ in the above theorem gives the following upper bound for $\mathbb{E}[\sum_{t=1}^{T} m_t]$

$$\beta\{\frac{1}{2}\|\mathbf{M}\|_F^2 + CL_T(\mathbf{M}) + \frac{1}{2}\|\mathbf{M}\|_F\sqrt{\|\mathbf{M}\|_F^2 + 4CL_T(\mathbf{M})}\}.$$

Under the same assumptions as in the above theorem, we have the following theoretical guarantee for the second-order algorithm CWAS.

THEOREM 2. *If the algorithm CWAS is run with a sequence of examples $(\mathbf{x}_t, \mathbf{x}_t^1, \mathbf{x}_t^2; y_t)$, $t \in [T]$, then for any $T > 0$, and $\mathbf{M} \in \mathbb{R}^{d \times d}$, we have*

$$\mathbb{E}\sum_{t=1}^{T}[m_t] \le \sum_{t=1}^{T} Z_t \ell_t(\mathbf{M})$$
$$+\frac{1}{\eta\delta}(D_M + |1-\delta|\|\mathbf{M}\|)^2 Tr(\mathbf{\Sigma}_{T+1}^{-1}) + \frac{\eta\gamma}{2\delta}\ln(|\mathbf{\Sigma}_{T+1}^{-1}|).$$

Setting $\eta = (D_M + |1-\delta|\|\mathbf{M}\|)\sqrt{\frac{2}{\gamma}Tr(\mathbf{\Sigma}_{T+1}^{-1})/\ln(|\mathbf{\Sigma}_{T+1}^{-1}|)}$, the following bound holds for CWAS

$$\mathbb{E}[\sum_{t=1}^{T} m_t]$$
$$\le L_T(\mathbf{M}) + \frac{|1-\delta|\|\mathbf{M}\|_F^2 + D_M}{\delta}\sqrt{2\gamma Tr(\mathbf{\Sigma}_{T+1}^{-1})\ln|\mathbf{\Sigma}_{T+1}^{-1}|},$$

where $D_M = \max_t \|\mathbf{M}_t - \mathbf{M}\|_F^2$.

Remark By optimizing over δ, and setting $\delta = 1$, we will have

$$\mathbb{E}[\sum_{t=1}^{T} m_t] \le L_T(\mathbf{M}) + D_M\sqrt{2\gamma \mathrm{Tr}(\mathbf{\Sigma}_{T+1}^{-1})\ln|\mathbf{\Sigma}_{T+1}^{-1}|}.$$

4. EXPERIMENTS

In this section, we conduct experiments to evaluate the efficacy of the proposed algorithms for online similarity learning from data streams on several benchmark datasets.

4.1 Datasets

To examine the performance, we conduct extensive experiments on a variety of benchmark datasets from web machine learning repositories. Table 1 shows the details of five datasets used in our experiments. Caltech256 [12] is a standard dataset for the image classification and ranking problem [1]. We use the same classes with [4] to generate the *caltech50* and *caltech249*. The other datasets are standard machine learning datasets publicly available at LIBSVM [2] and UCI Machine Learning Repository [3].

[1]http://www.vision.caltech.edu/Image_Datasets/Caltech256/

[2]http://www.csie.ntu.edu.tw/~cjlin/libsvmtools/datasets/

[3]https://archive.ics.uci.edu/ml/datasets.html

Table 1: Datasets used in the following experiments

Dataset	# Classes	# Instances	# Features	# Triplets
caltech249	249	16185	1000	1200000
caltech50	50	3250	1000	250000
covtype	7	455	54	10000
letter	26	1690	16	10140
pendigits	10	650	16	16848
satimage	6	390	36	18000
segment	7	455	19	25000
shuttle	7	458	9	4000

We evaluated the performance of all algorithms using precision-at-top-k, a standard ranking precision measure based on nearest neighbors. For each query instance in the test set, all other test instances were ranked according to their similarity to the query instance based on Equation (1), and the number of same-class instances among the top k instances (the k nearest neighbors) is computed, and then averaged across test instances. This measure is short named as AP. We also calculated the mean Average Precision (mAP), a measure that is widely used in the information retrieval community. For both of the AP and mAP measures, we set $k = 10$.

On all datasets, we used standard 5-fold cross validation and report both the AP and the mAP on test set. In Table 1, *# Triplets* represents the number of triplets $(\mathbf{x}_t, \mathbf{x}_t^1, \mathbf{x}_t^2)$ constructed based on the training set in each fold.

4.2 Comparison Schemes

To examine the efficacy, we compare the proposed algorithms with the state-of-the-art relative similarity learning algorithms, where they have to query every triplet's label during training stage.

- **OASIS:** the state-of-the-art first-order online similarity learning algorithm [4]. It should be noted that this algorithm is also the passive version of our proposed PAAS algorithm;
- **AROMA:** the state-of-the-art second-order online similarity learning algorithm [5], and **AROMA-d** represents its diagonal version.

To our knowledge, there is no work on exploring active learning on the relative similarity learning, so we compare our proposed algorithms with their random versions, where they randomly decide whether to query the label of t-th triplet.

- **PAAS:** the proposed first-order Passive Aggressive Active online Similarity Learning as shown in Algorithm 1;
- **PARS:** a variant of the proposed algorithm PAAS, where we use a uniform distribution to randomly query labels and keep the query ratio same as PAAS;
- **CWS:** the passive version of the algorithm CWAS, where we query each triplet in the training phrase.
- **CWAS:** the proposed Confidence-Weighted Active online Similarity Learning as shown in Algorithm 2. **CWAS-d** is the diagonal version with Equation (7) and (8) as updating rules.
- **CWRS:** a variant of the algorithm CWAS, where we use a uniform distribution to randomly query labels and keep the query ratio same as CWAS. **CWRS-d** is the diagonal version with Equation (7) and (8) as updating rules;

Table 2: Performance of algorithms on different datasets with the query ratio fixed to about 20%

	cotype				letter			
Alg.	Query(%)	AP@10	mAP@10	Time(s)	Query(%)	AP@10	mAP@10	Time(s)
PARS	20.620 ± 0.955	0.446 ± 0.036	0.334 ± 0.035	0.006 ± 0.008	20.6 ± 0.827	0.198 ± 0.024	0.127 ± 0.025	0.007 ± 0.000
PAAS	20.710 ± 0.336	0.512 ± 0.035	0.409 ± 0.027	0.006 ± 0.008	20.6 ± 0.667	0.233 ± 0.020	0.158 ± 0.023	0.007 ± 0.000
CWRS	20.960 ± 0.670	0.585 ± 0.027	0.476 ± 0.040	11.860 ± 1.741	19.4 ± 1.078	0.362 ± 0.019	0.276 ± 0.021	0.104 ± 0.005
CWAS	20.890 ± 0.677	**0.624 ± 0.038**	**0.515 ± 0.043**	22.390 ± 1.448	19.4 ± 0.507	**0.385 ± 0.012**	**0.298±0.012**	0.134 ± 0.005
	pendigits				satimage			
Alg.	Query(%)	AP@10	mAP@10	Time(s)	Query(%)	AP@10	mAP@10	Time(s)
PARS	22.2 ± 0.378	0.527 ± 0.056	0.418 ± 0.063	0.010 ± 0.001	20.4 ± 0.387	0.493 ± 0.044	0.408 ± 0.040	0.046 ± 0.001
PAAS	22.2 ± 0.526	0.554 ± 0.027	0.452 ± 0.024	0.010 ± 0.001	20.5 ± 0.274	0.509 ± 0.031	0.423 ± 0.022	0.050 ± 0.001
CWRS	19.3 ± 1.068	0.673 ± 0.020	0.588 ± 0.032	0.181 ± 0.016	19.6 ± 0.860	0.643 ± 0.010	0.560 ± 0.013	4.476 ± 0.257
CWAS	19.3 ± 0.925	**0.700 ± 0.010**	**0.619 ± 0.018**	0.287 ± 0.021	19.5 ± 0.517	**0.657 ± 0.008**	**0.574 ± 0.011**	9.390 ± 0.446
	segment				shuttle			
Alg.	Query(%)	AP@10	mAP@10	Time(s)	Query(%)	AP@10	mAP@10	Time(s)
PARS	21.2 ± 0.366	0.361 ± 0.034	0.253 ± 0.041	0.020 ± 0.001	21.07 ± 0.898	0.435 ± 0.058	0.313 ± 0.054	0.001 ± 0.000
PAAS	21.2 ± 0.607	0.436 ± 0.029	0.316 ± 0.031	0.021 ± 0.000	20.64 ± 0.807	0.513 ± 0.027	0.403 ± 0.042	0.001 ± 0.000
CWRS	19.2 ± 0.817	0.690 ± 0.074	0.575 ± 0.103	0.297 ± 0.024	20.25 ± 1.117	0.502 ± 0.037	0.417 ± 0.059	0.006 ± 0.001
CWAS	19.2 ± 0.781	**0.787 ± 0.019**	**0.729±0.039**	0.573± 0.036	20.84 ± 0.873	**0.561 ± 0.024**	**0.493±0.017**	0.009± 0.001

For all algorithms, the parameters are searched within the space $10^{[-5:1:5]}$ using cross validation. For both PAAS and CWAS algorithms, we evaluate their performances on 10 different query ratios which are achieved by setting the sampling threshold $\delta = 2^{[-10:2:10]}$. The query ratio represents the ratio of queried labels over the total number of triplets in the data stream. PARS and CWRS are also evaluated on 10 query ratios by setting the random sampling parameters according to the query ratios in PAAS and CWAS, respectively.

4.3 Evaluation of Fixed Query Ratio

In this experiment, we evaluate the performance of the proposed algorithms with some fixed query ratios. Table 2 shows the experimental results on different datasets.

First of all, with the same query ratio, the proposed active similarity learning algorithms (CWAS and PAAS) consistently outperform their random versions (CWRS and PARS), respectively. Besides, CWAS greatly outperforms PAAS over all the datasets. Moreover, both CWAS and PAAS also achieve smaller variances as compared to their random algorithms (PARS and CWRS), respectively. These observations further confirm the effectiveness and robustness of the proposed algorithms.

Secondly, on all the datasets, the proposed second-order active online similarity learning algorithm CWAS always achieves the best performance and the smallest variance. This is consistent with the previous results as shown in Figure 1 and 3, which further confirms the effectiveness of exploiting the second-order information.

Thirdly, by examining the running time cost, PAAS and CWAS spent slightly more time cost as compared to their random variants, respectively, mainly due to the cost of computing the query strategies.

In addition, CWAS in general spends more time than PAAS due to the computation of the second order information. However, the extra time cost could almost be ignored considering the high efficiency of the online learning scheme. In practice, for the higher dimensional datasets, we could adopt the diagonal version algorithm "CWAS-d" to further reduce the running time cost, as shown in subsequent experiments.

4.4 Evaluation of Varied Query Ratios

In this section, we evaluate the performance of the proposed algorithms with varied query ratios as shown in Figure 1. Several observations could be drawn from the results.

Firstly, we can observe that the proposed active online learning algorithms can consistently outperform their random versions, respectively. This observation is consistent with the one in Table 2 and confirms the effectiveness of the proposed algorithms on selecting informative instances. More importantly, with around 30% query ratio, the proposed algorithm CWAS could achieve the similar performance as CWS which queries all. This means that the proposed second-order active algorithm CWAS could save us around 70% effort compared to the traditional passive algorithms. For the proposed first-order active algorithm, PAAS could save us around 50% effort compared to the passive algorithm OASIS.

Secondly, the proposed second-order algorithm CWAS can outperform the first-order algorithm PAAS. From Figure1, we can observe CWAS could outperform PAAS on most of the datasets from the very small query ratio. The same result also could be observed on the CWRS compared to the PARS. These findings confirmed the effectiveness of introducing the second-order information. From the figure, we also could observe that the baseline second-order algorithm AROMA could achieve a little higher performance than our proposed algorithm CWS, on some datasets. One possible reason may be that the learning rate η is fixed in our algorithm in the Equation (5), while it is adaptive in the algorithm AROMA [7]. However, CWS in general is comparable with AROMA, while its active version is much easier to be theoretically analyzed.

4.5 Evaluation of Parameter Sensitivity

In this section, we evaluate the sensitivity of the parameters both in Algorithm 1 and 2, respectively. However, it is difficult to evaluate the algorithms with active query strategies. Thus, we evaluate their passive versions OASIS and CWS, respectively. Figure 2 shows the varied performances corresponding to different parameters on four of the datasets. For each dataset, the left figure shows the performance (Y-axis) corresponding to the parameter C (X-axis) in OASIS, and the right figure shows the performance (different color) corresponding to parameter γ (X-axis) and η (Y-axis)

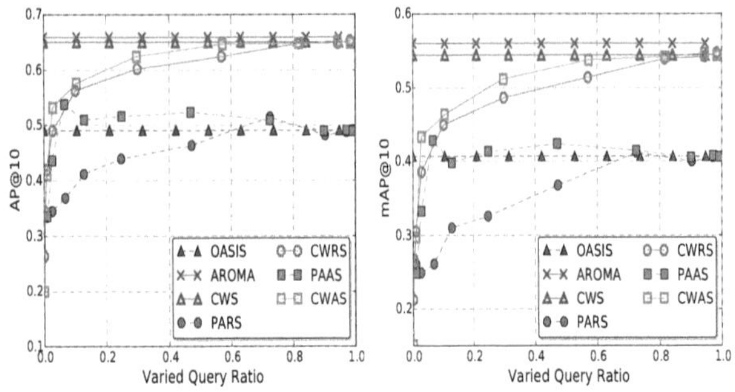

(a) AP (b) mAP

covtype

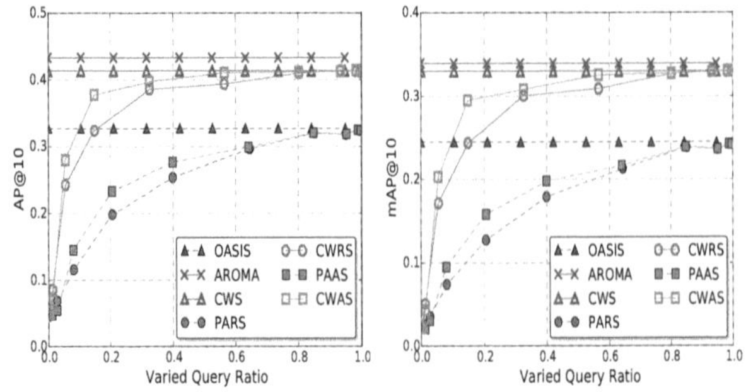

(a) AP (b) mAP

letter

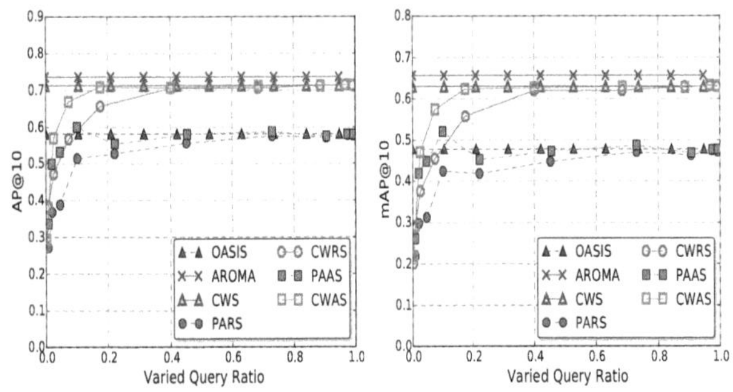

(a) AP (b) mAP

pendigits

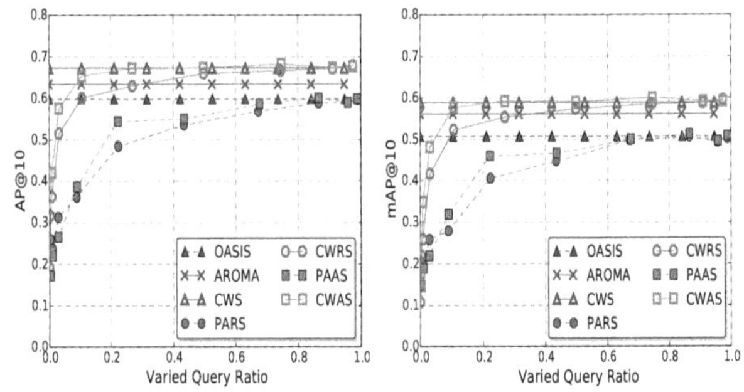

(a) AP (b) mAP

satimage

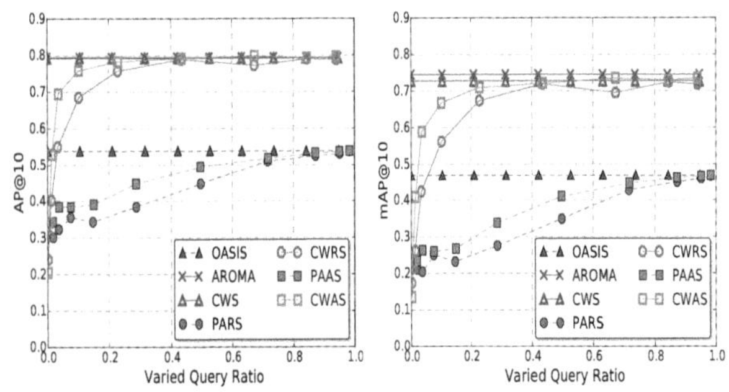

(a) AP (b) mAP

segment

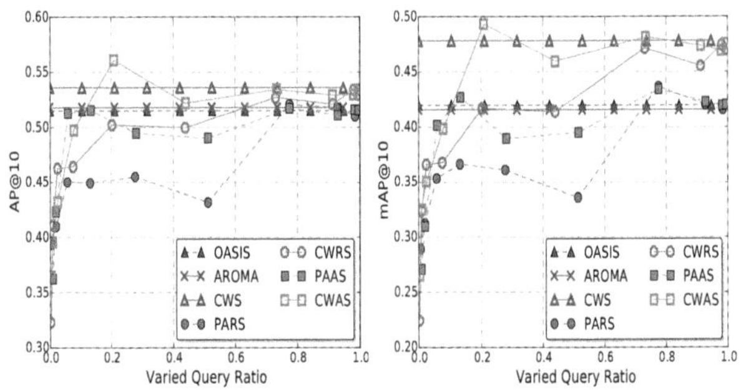

(a) AP (b) mAP

shuttle

Figure 1: Performance with varied query ratios on the test datasets, where AP@10 denotes Average Precision at 10, and mAP@10 denotes mean Average Precision at 10.

in CWS, where bright color corresponds to higher performance in terms of Average Precision at 10 than the dark color.

For the parameter C, we can see it greatly affects the results of OASIS, on all of the datasets, which could be explained using our mistake bound in Theorem 1. Specifically, the mistake bound could be divided into two terms, and the parameter C divides the first term and multiplies the second term. When C is too small, the first term will dominate the mistake bound, and the second term will dominate the mistake bound when C is too large. This is consistent with the results shown in Figure 2. For most of the datasets, $C = 1$ would present a promising result.

For algorithm CWS, the relationship between the performance and the parameters is relatively complex. From Figure 2, we can observe that the learning rate parameter η should be not too small in general. And the regularization parameter γ should be search around 1.

4.6 Evaluation of Efficiency and Scalability

Although the second-order algorithm CWAS greatly outperforms the first-order algorithm PAAS, it is costly to maintain the covariance matrix when the number of features is large. To reduce the complexity, we can use their diagonal versions by Equations (7) and (8). To test the diagonal algorithm CWAS-d, we carried out experiments on large-scale datasets *caltech50* and *caltech249* shown in Figure 3, where we can observe similar results as the one in Figure 1. In addition, the increase of performance of CWAS-d over PAAS is not as large as CWAS in Figure 1 as expected, since only part of the second-order information is used.

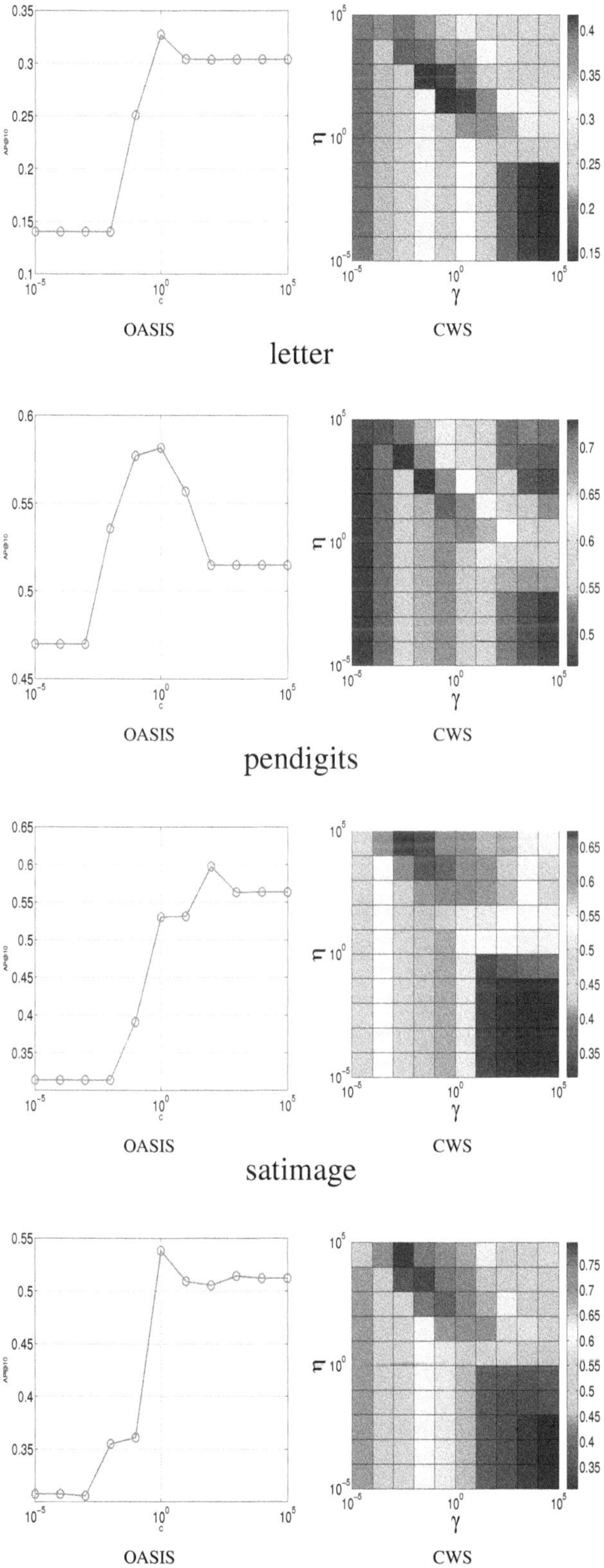

Figure 2: Sensitivity of the parameters

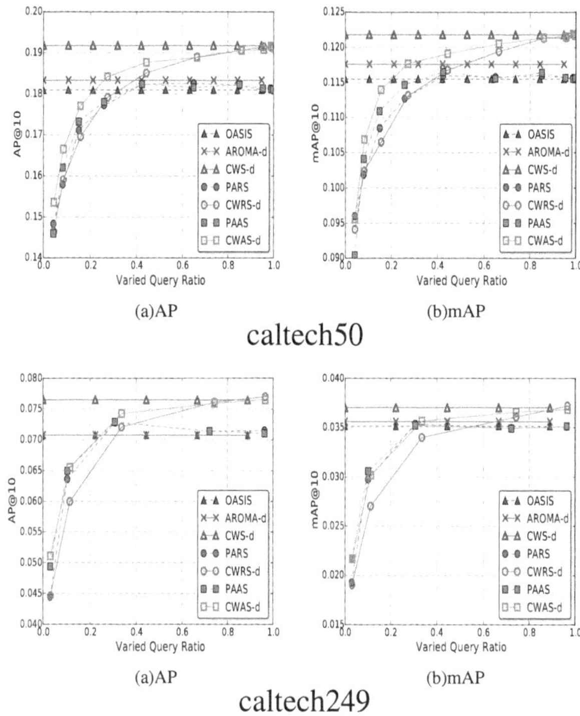

Figure 3: Performance on the large-scale datasets

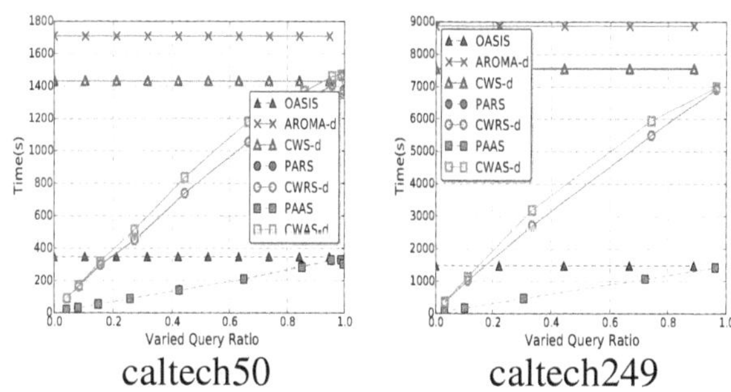

Figure 4: Time cost corresponding to varied querying ratio on large-scale datasets

In Figure 4, we evaluate the relationship between the querying ratio and the time-cost of our proposed algorithms. From the figure, we can see that the time cost of the proposed algorithms is lineally increasing with respect to the increasing querying ratio. Besides, CWAS-d cost a little extra time than its random version CWRS-d due to the computation of the query strategy, and PAAS costs almost the same as its random version PARS. What's more, the second-order algorithm CWAS-d cost more than the first-order algorithm PAAS due to the computation of the second-order information, this is consistent with the finding in Table 2. More importantly, in Figure 3, we can observe that with around 30% query ratio, the proposed algorithm PAAS and CWAS-d could obtain similar performances as their passive versions OASIS and CWS-d, respectively. Meanwhile, when the query ratio is around 30%, in Figure 4, PAAS and CWAS-d only spends around 30% of the time spent by OASIS and CWS-d , respectively. These observations illustrate that our proposed algorithms can save a lot effort in labeling and training the model without sacrificing performance compared to the passive algorithms which query the labels of all the triplets.

5. CONCLUSIONS

To overcome the critical limitation of traditional passive online similarity learning from data streams, in this paper, we proposed a novel framework of active online learning for relative similarity learning. Specifically, we proposed two active online similarity learning algorithms for reducing the number of queried labels in the learning process. We theoretically analyzed the bounds of the proposed algorithms and conducted extensive experiments to examine the effectiveness of their empirical performance. The encouraging empirical results validate the effectiveness and efficiency of the proposed algorithms.

There are several aspects we are interested to explore in future. Firstly, it would be more interesting to design an automatic method to assign the parameter δ to control the query ratio, currently, it is manually assigned.

Secondly, for the proposed second-order based algorithm CWAS, it would be more effective to consider the second-order information when designing the query strategy, such as the covariance information contained in $\mathbf{\Sigma}$.

Thirdly, we are interested to design a real online active relative similarity learning where the labels of instance come from several noisy online workers, such as from the crowdsourcing platforms.

6. ACKNOWLEDGEMENT

This research is supported by the National Research Foundation, Prime Minister's Office, Singapore under its IDM Futures Funding Initiative and administered by the Interactive and Digital Media Programme Office. This research is also partially supported by Singapore MOE tier 1 research grant (C220/MSS14C003).

Appendix

In this appendix, we provide the proofs of the theorems in the section 3.4.

Theoretical Analysis on PAAS

To prove the Theorem 1, we need the following lemma.

LEMMA 1. *Let $(\mathbf{x}_t, \mathbf{x}_t^1, \mathbf{x}_t^2; y_t)$, $t \in [T]$ be a sequence of input triplets, where $\mathbf{x}_t, \mathbf{x}_t^1, \mathbf{x}_t^2 \in \mathbb{R}^d$ and $y_t \in \{-1, +1\}$ for all t. Let τ_t be the step size parameter for PAAS as given in the algorithm. Then the following bound holds for any $\mathbf{M} \in \mathbb{R}^{d\times d}$:*

$$\sum_{t=1}^{T} 2\tau_t Z_t \left[l_t(\alpha - |p_t|) + m_t(\alpha + |p_t|)\right]$$
$$\le \alpha^2 \|\mathbf{M}\|_F^2 + \sum_{t=1}^{T} \tau_t^2 \|\mathbf{X}_t\|_F^2 + \sum_{t=1}^{T} 2\alpha\tau_t \ell_t(\mathbf{M}),$$

where $l_t = \mathbb{I}(\ell_t(\mathbf{M}_t) > 0$ and $\mathrm{sign}(p_t) = y_t)$, $m_t = \mathbb{I}(\mathrm{sign}(p_t) \neq y_t)$, $\mathbb{I}$ is the indicator function, $\alpha > 0$ and $\mathbf{X}_t = \mathbf{x}_t(\mathbf{x}_t^1 - \mathbf{x}_t^2)^\top$.

Lemma 1 can be proved using similar techniques in [3].Given Lemma 1, Theorem 1 can be proven as follows:

PROOF. According to Lemma 1, we have

$$\alpha^2\|\mathbf{M}\|_F^2 + \sum_{t=1}^{T} 2\alpha\tau_t\ell_t(\mathbf{M}_t)$$
$$\ge \sum_{t=1}^{T} 2\tau_t Z_t[l_t(\alpha - |p_t|) + m_t(\alpha + |p_t|)] - \sum_{t=1}^{T} \tau_t^2\|\mathbf{X}_t\|_F^2$$
$$= \sum_{t=1}^{T} 2\tau_t Z_t[l_t(\alpha - |p_t| - \frac{\tau_t}{2}\|\mathbf{X}_t\|_F^2) + m_t(\alpha + |p_t| - \frac{\tau_t}{2}\|\mathbf{X}_t\|_F^2)]$$
$$\ge \sum_{t=1}^{T} 2\tau_t Z_t[l_t(\alpha - |p_t| - \frac{\ell_t(\mathbf{M}_t)}{2}) + m_t(\alpha + |p_t| - \frac{\ell_t(\mathbf{M}_t)}{2})]$$
$$= \sum_{t=1}^{T} l_t Z_t 2\tau_t(\alpha - \frac{1 + |p_t|}{2}) + \sum_{t=1}^{T} m_t Z_t 2\tau_t(\alpha - \frac{1 - |p_t|}{2}).$$

Plugging $\alpha = \frac{\delta+1}{2}$, $\delta \ge 1$ into the above inequality will result in

$$(\frac{\delta+1}{2})^2\|\mathbf{M}\|_F^2 + \sum_{t=1}^{T}(\delta+1)\tau_t\ell_t(M)$$
$$\ge \sum_{t=1}^{T} m_t Z_t \tau_t(\delta + |p_t|).$$

Since $\tau_t \ge \min(C, 1/D_X^2)$, the above inequality implies:

$$(\frac{\delta+1}{2})^2\|\mathbf{M}\|_F^2 + \sum_{t=1}^{T}(\delta+1)\tau_t\ell_t(M)$$
$$\ge \min(C, 1/D_X^2)\sum_{t=1}^{T} m_t Z_t(\delta + |p_t|).$$

Taking expectation with the above inequality, plugging the equality $\mathbb{E}Z_t = \delta/(\delta + |p_t|)$ and re-arranging the result conclude this theorem. □

Theoretical Analysis on CWAS

In this subsection we will abuse $\mathbf{M}_t$, G_t, $\mathbf{X}_t$ to denote vec(M_t), vec$(\mathbf{G}_t)$, and vec(X_t), respectively. To prove Theorem 2, we need the following lemma.

LEMMA 2. *Let $(\mathbf{x}_t, \mathbf{x}_t^1, \mathbf{x}_t^2; y_t)$, $t \in [T]$ be a sequence of input triplets, where $\mathbf{x}_t, \mathbf{x}_t^1, \mathbf{x}_t^2 \in \mathbb{R}^d$ and $y_t \in \{-1, +1\}$ for all t. If the CWAS is run on this sequence of triplets, then the following bound holds for any $\mathbf{M} \in \mathbb{R}^{d\times d}$,*

$$Z_t[m_t(\delta + |p_t|) + l_t(\delta - |p_t|)]$$
$$\le \frac{Z_t}{2\eta}\Big[\|\mathbf{M}_t - \delta\mathbf{M}\|_{\mathbf{\Sigma}_{t+1}^{-1}}^2 - \|\mathbf{M}_{t+1} - \delta\mathbf{M}\|_{\mathbf{\Sigma}_{t+1}^{-1}}^2$$
$$+ \|\mathbf{M}_t - \mathbf{M}_{t+1}\|_{\mathbf{\Sigma}_{t+1}^{-1}}^2\Big] + \delta Z_t\ell_t(\mathbf{M}_t),$$

where $l_t = \mathbb{I}(\ell_t(\mathbf{M}_t) > 0$ and $\mathrm{sign}(p_t) = y_t)$, $m_t = \mathbb{I}(\mathrm{sign}(p_t) \neq y_t)$, $\mathbb{I}$ is the indicator function, $\delta > 0$ and $\|\mathbf{M}_t - \delta\mathbf{M}\|_{\mathbf{\Sigma}_{t+1}^{-1}}^2$ actually denotes $\|vec(\mathbf{M}_t) - vec(\delta\mathbf{M})\|_{\mathbf{\Sigma}_{t+1}^{-1}}^2$.

PROOF. When $Z_t = 0$, it is easy to verify the inequality in the theorem.

When $Z_t = 1$, it is easy to observe that

$$\mathbf{M}_{t+1} = \arg\min_{\mathbf{M}} f_t(\mathbf{M}),$$

where

$$f_t(\mathbf{M}) = \frac{1}{2}\|\mathbf{M}_t - \mathbf{M}\|_{\mathbf{\Sigma}_{t+1}^{-1}}^2 + \eta\mathbf{G}_t^\top\mathbf{M}.$$

Because f_t is convex, we have the following inequality $\forall \mathbf{M}$,

$$\begin{aligned} 0 &\le \partial f_t(\mathbf{M}_{t+1})^\top(\mathbf{M} - \mathbf{M}_{t+1}) \\ &= [\mathbf{\Sigma}_{t+1}^{-1}(\mathbf{M}_{t+1} - \mathbf{M}_t) + \eta\mathbf{G}_t]^\top(\mathbf{M} - \mathbf{M}_{t+1}). \end{aligned}$$

Re-arranging the above inequality will result in

$$\begin{aligned} &\eta\mathbf{G}_t^\top(\mathbf{M}_{t+1} - \mathbf{M}) \\ &\le (\mathbf{M}_{t+1} - \mathbf{M}_t)^\top\mathbf{\Sigma}_{t+1}^{-1}(\mathbf{M} - \mathbf{M}_{t+1}) \\ &= \frac{1}{2}[\|\mathbf{M}_t - \mathbf{M}\|^2_{\mathbf{\Sigma}_{t+1}^{-1}} - \|\mathbf{M}_{t+1} - \mathbf{M}\|^2_{\mathbf{\Sigma}_{t+1}^{-1}} \\ &\quad -\|\mathbf{M}_t - \mathbf{M}_{t+1}\|^2_{\mathbf{\Sigma}_{t+1}^{-1}}]. \end{aligned}$$

Now, we would provide a lower bound for $\mathbf{G}_t^\top(\mathbf{M}_{t+1} - \mathbf{M})$,

$$\begin{aligned} &\mathbf{G}_t^\top(\mathbf{M}_{t+1} - \mathbf{M}) - \mathbf{G}_t^\top(\mathbf{M}_t - \mathbf{M}) + \mathbf{G}_t^\top(\mathbf{M}_{t+1} - \mathbf{M}_t) \\ &= (l_t + m_t)(-y_t X_t^\top \mathbf{M}_t) + (l_t + m_t) y_t X_t^\top \mathbf{M} \\ &-\frac{1}{\eta}\|\mathbf{M}_t - \mathbf{M}_{t+1}\|^2_{\mathbf{\Sigma}_{t+1}^{-1}}, \end{aligned}$$

where the second inequality used the facts $\mathbf{G}_t = (l_t + m_t)(-y_t\mathbf{X}_t)$ and $\partial f_t(\mathbf{M}_{t+1}) = 0$, i.e.,

$$\mathbf{\Sigma}_{t+1}^{-1}(\boldsymbol{\mu}_{t+1} - \mu_t) + \eta\mathbf{G}_t = 0.$$

Combining the above equality with the facts

$$m_t(-y_t\mathbf{X}_t^\top\mathbf{M}_t) = M_t|p_t|, l_t(-y_t\mathbf{X}_t^\top\mathbf{M}_t) = -l_t|p_t|$$

and

$$y_t\mathbf{X}_t^\top\mathbf{M}_t + \delta\ell_t(\mathbf{M}/\delta) \ge y_t p_t + \delta(1 - y_t p_t/\delta) = \delta,$$

we get the following bound for $\mathbf{G}_t^\top(\mathbf{M}_{t+1} - \mathbf{M})$,

$$\begin{aligned} &\mathbf{G}_t^\top(\mathbf{M}_{t+1} - \mathbf{M}) \\ &\ge (m_t|p_t| - l_t|p_t|) + (l_t + m_t)[\delta - \delta\ell_t(\mathbf{M}/\delta)] \\ &\quad -\frac{1}{\eta}\|\mathbf{M}_t - \mathbf{M}_{t+1}\|^2_{\mathbf{\Sigma}_{t+1}^{-1}} \\ &= [m_t(\delta + |p_t|) + l_t(\delta - |p_t|)] - (l_t + m_t)\delta\ell_t(\mathbf{M}/\delta) \\ &\quad -\frac{1}{\eta}\|\mathbf{M}_t - \mathbf{M}_{t+1}\|^2_{\mathbf{\Sigma}_{t+1}^{-1}}. \end{aligned}$$

Combining the previous inequalities, will give the following important inequality

$$\begin{aligned} &[m_t(\delta + |p_t|) + l_t(\delta - |p_t|)] \\ &\le \frac{1}{2\eta}[\|\mathbf{M}_t - \delta\mathbf{M}\|^2_{\mathbf{\Sigma}_{t+1}^{-1}} - \|\mathbf{M}_{t+1} - \delta\mathbf{M}\|^2_{\mathbf{\Sigma}_{t+1}^{-1}} \\ &\quad -\|\mathbf{M}_t - \mathbf{M}_{t+1}\|^2_{\mathbf{\Sigma}_{t+1}^{-1}}] + \frac{1}{\eta}\|\mathbf{M}_t - \mathbf{M}_{t+1}\|^2_{\mathbf{\Sigma}_{t+1}^{-1}} + \delta\ell_t(\mathbf{M}/\delta) \\ &- \frac{1}{2\eta}[\|\mathbf{M}_t - \delta\mathbf{M}\|^2_{\mathbf{\Sigma}_{t+1}^{-1}} - \|\mathbf{M}_{t+1} - \delta\mathbf{M}\|^?_{\mathbf{\Sigma}_{t+1}^{-1}} \\ &\quad +\|\mathbf{M}_t - \mathbf{M}_{t+1}\|^2_{\mathbf{\Sigma}_{t+1}^{-1}}] + \delta\ell_t(\mathbf{M}/\delta). \end{aligned}$$

Replacing $\mathbf{M}$ with $\delta\mathbf{M}$ concludes the proof. □

Given Lemma 2, the theorem 2 can be proven as follows:

PROOF. Firstly, according to the update rule

$$\mathbf{M}_{t+1} = \text{mat}[\text{vec}(\mathbf{M}_t) - \eta\mathbf{\Sigma}_t\text{vec}(G_t)],$$

we can derive the following equality

$$\begin{aligned} &\|\mathbf{M}_t - \mathbf{M}_{t+1}\|^2_{\mathbf{\Sigma}_{t+1}^{-1}} = \eta^2\mathbf{G}_t^\top\mathbf{\Sigma}_{t+1}\mathbf{G}_t \\ &= \eta^2(m_t + l_t)\mathbf{X}_t^\top\mathbf{\Sigma}_{t+1}\mathbf{X}_t = \eta^2\gamma(1 - \frac{|\mathbf{\Sigma}_t^{-1}|}{|\mathbf{\Sigma}_{t+1}^{-1}|}), \end{aligned}$$

where, we used the fact $A = B + \mathbf{x}\mathbf{x}^\top$ implies $\mathbf{x}^\top A^{-1}\mathbf{x} = 1 - \frac{|B|}{|A|}$. Plugging the above equality into the inequality in the Lemma 2, and re-arranging it will gives

$$\begin{aligned} &Z_t[m_t(\delta + |p_t|) + l_t(\delta - |p_t|)] \\ &\le \frac{Z_t}{2\eta}\left[\|\mathbf{M}_t - \delta\mathbf{M}\|^2_{\mathbf{\Sigma}_{t+1}^{-1}} - \|\mathbf{M}_{t+1} - \delta\mathbf{M}\|^2_{\mathbf{\Sigma}_{t+1}^{-1}}\right] \\ &\quad + \frac{Z_t\eta\gamma}{2}(1 - \frac{|\mathbf{\Sigma}_t^{-1}|}{|\mathbf{\Sigma}_{t+1}^{-1}|}) + \delta Z_t\ell_t(\mathbf{M}_t). \end{aligned}$$

Summing the above inequality over $t = 1, 2, \ldots, T$ can give

$$\begin{aligned} &\sum_{t=1}^T Z_t[m_t(\delta + |p_t|) + l_t(\delta - |p_t|)] \le \sum_{t=1}^T \delta Z_t\ell_t(\mathbf{M}_t) \\ &+ \sum_{t=1}^T \frac{Z_t}{2\eta}\left[\|\mathbf{M}_t - \delta\mathbf{M}\|^2_{\mathbf{\Sigma}_{t+1}^{-1}} - \|\mathbf{M}_{t+1} - \delta\mathbf{M}\|^2_{\mathbf{\Sigma}_{t+1}^{-1}}\right] \\ &+ \sum_{t=1}^T \frac{Z_t\eta\gamma}{2}(1 - \frac{|\mathbf{\Sigma}_t^{-1}|}{|\mathbf{\Sigma}_{t+1}^{-1}|}). \end{aligned}$$

Now, we would like to bound the right hand side of the above inequality. Firstly, we bound the first term as

$$\begin{aligned} &\sum_{t=1}^T Z_t\left[\|\mathbf{M}_t - \delta\mathbf{M}\|^2_{\mathbf{\Sigma}_{t+1}^{-1}} - \|\mathbf{M}_{t+1} - \delta\mathbf{M}\|^2_{\mathbf{\Sigma}_{t+1}^{-1}}\right] \\ &\le \|\mathbf{M}_1 - \delta\mathbf{M}\|^2_{\mathbf{\Sigma}_2^{-1}} + \sum_{t=2}^T[\|\mathbf{M}_t - \delta\mathbf{M}\|^2_{\mathbf{\Sigma}_{t+1}^{-1}} - \|\mathbf{M}_t - \delta\mathbf{M}\|^2_{\mathbf{\Sigma}_t^{-1}}] \\ &\le \|\mathbf{M}_1 - \delta\mathbf{M}\|^2\text{Tr}(\mathbf{\Sigma}_2^{-1}) + \sum_{t=2}^T\|\mathbf{M}_t - \delta\mathbf{M}\|^2\text{Tr}(\mathbf{\Sigma}_{t+1}^{-1} - \mathbf{\Sigma}_t^{-1}) \\ &= \max_{t\le T}\|\mathbf{M}_t - \delta\mathbf{M}\|^2\text{Tr}(\mathbf{\Sigma}_{T+1}^{-1}) \\ &\le 2(D_M + |1 - \delta|\|\mathbf{M}\|)^2\text{Tr}(\mathbf{\Sigma}_{T+1}^{-1}), \end{aligned}$$

where $D_M = \max_{t\le T}\|\mathbf{M}_t - \mathbf{M}\|^2$. Combining the above two inequalities, result in

$$\begin{aligned} &\sum_{t=1}^T Z_t[m_t(\delta + |p_t|)] \le \delta\sum_{t=1}^T Z_t\ell_t(\mathbf{M}) \\ &\quad + \frac{1}{\eta}(D_M + (1 - \delta)^2\|\mathbf{M}\|^2)\text{Tr}(\mathbf{\Sigma}_{T+1}^{-1}) + \sum_{t=1}^T \frac{Z_t\eta\gamma}{2}(1 - \frac{|\mathbf{\Sigma}_t^{-1}|}{|\mathbf{\Sigma}_{t+1}^{-1}|}) \\ &\le \delta\sum_{t=1}^T Z_t\ell_t(\mathbf{M}) + \frac{1}{\eta}(D_M + |1 - \delta|\|\mathbf{M}\|)^2\text{Tr}(\mathbf{\Sigma}_{T+1}^{-1}) \\ &\quad + \frac{\eta\gamma}{2}\ln(|\mathbf{\Sigma}_{T+1}^{-1}|), \end{aligned}$$

where we used the fact $(1 - \frac{|A|}{|B|}) \le \ln\frac{|B|}{|A|}$, since $1 - x \le -\ln x$ for all $x > 0$.

Taking expectation with the above inequality and using the fact $\mathbb{E}[Z_t] = \frac{\delta}{\delta + |p_t|}$ gives

$$\begin{aligned} &\delta\mathbb{E}\sum_{t=1}^T[m_t] \le \delta\sum_{t=1}^T Z_t\ell_t(\mathbf{M}) \\ &+ \frac{1}{\eta}(D_M + |1 - \delta|\|\mathbf{M}\|)^2\text{Tr}(\mathbf{\Sigma}_{T+1}^{-1}) + \frac{\eta\gamma}{2}\ln(|\mathbf{\Sigma}_{T+1}^{-1}|). \end{aligned}$$

Dividing the above inequality with δ concludes the proof. □

7. REFERENCES

[1] G. Adomavicius and A. Tuzhilin. Toward the next generation of recommender systems: A survey of the state-of-the-art and possible extensions. *Knowledge and Data Engineering, IEEE Transactions on*, 17(6):734–749, 2005.

[2] Q. Cao, Y. Ying, and P. Li. Similarity metric learning for face recognition. In *Computer Vision (ICCV), 2013 IEEE International Conference on*, pages 2408–2415. IEEE, 2013.

[3] N. Cesa-Bianchi, C. Gentile, and L. Zaniboni. Worst-case analysis of selective sampling for linear classification. *The Journal of Machine Learning Research*, 7:1205–1230, Dec. 2006.

[4] G. Chechik, V. Sharma, U. Shalit, and S. Bengio. Large scale online learning of image similarity through ranking. *Journal of Machine Learning Research*, 11:1109–1135, 2010.

[5] K. Crammer and G. Chechik. Adaptive regularization for similarity measures. In *Proceedings of the 29th International Conference on Machine Learning, ICML, Edinburgh, Scotland, UK, June 26 - July 1*, 2012.

[6] K. Crammer, O. Dekel, J. Keshet, and S. Shalev-shwartz. Online passive-aggressive algorithms. *The Journal of Machine ...*, 7:551–585, 2006.

[7] K. Crammer, A. Kulesza, and M. Dredze. Adaptive regularization of weight vectors. In *Advances in Neural Information Processing Systems*, pages 414–422, 2009.

[8] J. V. Davis, B. Kulis, P. Jain, S. Sra, and I. S. Dhillon. Information-theoretic metric learning. In *Proceedings of the 24th international conference on Machine learning*, pages 209–216. ACM, 2007.

[9] W. B. Frakes and R. Baeza-Yates, editors. *Information Retrieval: Data Structures and Algorithms*. Prentice-Hall, Inc., Upper Saddle River, NJ, USA, 1992.

[10] Y. Freund and Y. Mansour. Learning under persistent drift. In *Computational Learning Theory*, pages 109–118, 1997.

[11] A. Globerson and S. T. Roweis. Metric learning by collapsing classes. In *Advances in neural information processing systems*, pages 451–458, 2005.

[12] G. Griffin, A. Holub, and P. Perona. Caltech-256 object category dataset. 2007.

[13] Y. Guo and D. Schuurmans. Discriminative batch mode active learning. In *Advances in neural information processing systems*, pages 593–600, 2008.

[14] S. C. Hoi, W. Liu, M. R. Lyu, and W.-Y. Ma. Learning distance metrics with contextual constraints for image retrieval. In *Proceedings of IEEE Conference on Computer Vision and Pattern Recognition (CVPR2006)*, New York, US, 2006.

[15] S. C. Hoi, J. Wang, and P. Zhao. Libol: A library for online learning algorithms. *The Journal of Machine Learning Research*, 15(1):495–499, 2014.

[16] R. Jin, S. Wang, and Y. Zhou. Regularized distance metric learning: Theory and algorithm. In *Advances in neural information processing systems*, pages 862–870, 2009.

[17] D. D. Lewis. Learning in intelligent information retrieval. In *Machine Learning: Proceedings of the Eighth International Workshop*, pages 235–239, 2014.

[18] D. D. Lewis and J. Catlett. Heterogenous uncertainty sampling for supervised learning. In *ICML*, volume 94, pages 148–156, 1994.

[19] J. Lu, P. Zhao, and S. C. Hoi. Online passive aggressive active learning and its applications. In *Journal of Machine Learning Research - Proceedings Track (ACML2014)*, 2014.

[20] N. Roy, A. Mccallum, and M. W. Com. Toward optimal active learning through sampling estimation of error reduction. In *ICML*, Williamstown, 2001.

[21] Y. Rui, T. S. Huang, and S.-F. Chang. Image retrieval: Current techniques, promising directions, and open issues. *Journal of visual communication and image representation*, 10(1):39–62, 1999.

[22] M. Schultz and T. Joachims. Learning a distance metric from relative comparisons. *Advances in neural information processing systems (NIPS)*, page 41, 2004.

[23] B. Settles. Active learning literature survey. *University of Wisconsin, Madison*, 52:55–66, 2010.

[24] S. Shalev-Shwartz, Y. Singer, and A. Y. Ng. Online and batch learning of pseudo-metrics. In *Proceedings of the twenty-first international conference on Machine learning*, page 94. ACM, 2004.

[25] V. S. Sheng, F. Provost, and P. G. Ipeirotis. Get another label? improving data quality and data mining using multiple, noisy labelers. In *Proceedings of the 14th ACM SIGKDD international conference on Knowledge discovery and data mining*, pages 614–622. ACM, 2008.

[26] L. Si, R. Jin, S. C. Hoi, and M. R. Lyu. Collaborative image retrieval via regularized metric learning. *ACM Multimedia Systems Journal (MMSJ)*, 12(1):34–44, 2006.

[27] S. Tong and D. Koller. Support vector machine active learning with applications to text classification. *The Journal of Machine Learning Research*, pages 45–66, 2002.

[28] K. Q. Weinberger, J. Blitzer, and L. K. Saul. Distance metric learning for large margin nearest neighbor classification. In *Advances in neural information processing systems*, pages 1473–1480, 2005.

[29] L. Wu, R. Jin, S. C. Hoi, J. Zhu, and N. Yu. Learning bregman distance functions and its application for semi-supervised clustering. In Y. Bengio, D. Schuurmans, J. Lafferty, C. K. I. Williams, and A. Culotta, editors, *Advances in Neural Information Processing Systems 22*, pages 2089–2097, 2009.

[30] W. Wu, H. Li, and J. Xu. Learning query and document similarities from click-through bipartite graph with metadata. In *Proceedings of the sixth ACM international conference on Web search and data mining*, pages 687–696. ACM, 2013.

[31] L. Yang and R. Jin. Distance metric learning: A comprehensive survey. *Michigan State Universiy*, 2, 2006.

[32] P. Zhao and S. C. Hoi. Cost-sensitive online active learning with application to malicious url detection. In *Proceedings of the 19th ACM SIGKDD international conference on Knowledge discovery and data mining - KDD '13*, page 919, New York, New York, USA, 2013. ACM Press.

[33] P. Zhao, S. C. Hoi, and R. Jin. Double updating online learning. *The Journal of Machine Learning Research*, 12:1587–1615, 2011.

[34] P. Zhao, S. C. Hoi, and J. Zhuang. Active learning with expert advice. In *UAI2013*. AUAI Press, Corvallis, Oregon, 2013.

[35] P. Zhao, R. Jin, T. Yang, and S. C. Hoi. Online auc maximization. In *Proceedings of the 28th International Conference on Machine Learning (ICML-11)*, pages 233–240, 2011.

Ad Hoc Monitoring of Vocabulary Shifts over Time

Tom Kenter[†] tom.kenter@uva.nl
Melvin Wevers[‡] m.j.h.f.wevers@uu.nl
Pim Huijnen[‡] p.huijnen@uu.nl
Maarten de Rijke[†] derijke@uva.nl

[†]University of Amsterdam, Amsterdam, The Netherlands
[‡]University of Utrecht, Utrecht, The Netherlands

ABSTRACT

Word meanings change over time. Detecting shifts in meaning for particular words has been the focus of much research recently. We address the complementary problem of monitoring shifts in vocabulary over time. That is, given a small seed set of words, we are interested in monitoring which terms are used over time to refer to the underlying concept denoted by the seed words.

In this paper, we propose an algorithm for monitoring shifts in vocabulary over time, given a small set of seed terms. We use distributional semantic methods to infer a series of semantic spaces over time from a large body of time-stamped unstructured textual documents. We construct semantic networks of terms based on their representation in the semantic spaces and use graph-based measures to calculate saliency of terms. Based on the graph-based measures we produce ranked lists of terms that represent the concept underlying the initial seed terms over time as final output.

As the task of monitoring shifting vocabularies over time for an ad hoc set of seed words is, to the best of our knowledge, a new one, we construct our own evaluation set. Our main contributions are the introduction of the task of ad hoc monitoring of vocabulary shifts over time, the description of an algorithm for tracking shifting vocabularies over time given a small set of seed words, and a systematic evaluation of results over a substantial period of time (over four decades). Additionally, we make our newly constructed evaluation set publicly available.

Categories and Subject Descriptors

H.3.1 [**Content Analysis and Indexing**]: Linguistic processing; H.3.3 [**Information Search and Retrieval**]: Retrieval models

Keywords

Vocabulary shift; distributional semantics

1. INTRODUCTION

Word meanings change over time [11, 27]. Detecting shifts in meaning for particular words has been the focus of much research recently [11, 13, 14, 18, 19, 29]. In this paper we address the complementary problem of monitoring shifts in vocabulary over time.

Permission to make digital or hard copies of all or part of this work for personal or classroom use is granted without fee provided that copies are not made or distributed for profit or commercial advantage and that copies bear this notice and the full citation on the first page. Copyrights for components of this work owned by others than the author(s) must be honored. Abstracting with credit is permitted. To copy otherwise, or republish, to post on servers or to redistribute to lists, requires prior specific permission and/or a fee. Request permissions from Permissions@acm.org.
CIKM'15, October 19–23, 2015, Melbourne, Australia.
Copyright is held by the owner/author(s). Publication rights licensed to ACM.
ACM 978-1-4503-3794-6/15/10 ...$15.00.
DOI: http://dx.doi.org/10.1145/2806416.2806474.

Rather than taking a word as an anchor to monitor its (shifts in) meaning over time, we take the meaning as an anchor, and monitor the evolving set of words that are used to denote it. As an example, consider music storage media. Nowadays, we carry music with us on iPods and mp3 players. Before that there were compact discs. Prior to cds there were records, and music cassettes. Few of the words that were used in, say, the 1950s to describe the media used for storing music are still in use today. Following this example, the question we set ourselves to answer is "what words were used previously, where nowadays the words 'mp3 player' and 'iPod' are used?" An algorithm for monitoring vocabulary shifts over time has the words "iPod" and "mp3 player" as its input; as output it produces ranked lists of words per time period, e.g., every 5 years, of the words in that period that represent the concept underlying the initial input words. In what follows, we refer to such ranked lists of words per time period as *vocabularies*. The initial set of input terms we call *seed terms*.

Not all concepts evolve as dramatically as the sound carrier example above does, where the entire vocabulary changes in the course of a few decades. Often, many terms in the vocabulary remain relevant over time. A successful system for monitoring vocabulary shifts over time should strike a balance between an adaptive strategy that responds to changes in vocabulary, and a more conservative approach that keeps the vocabulary stable.

The problem setting we address is inspired by collaborations with digital humanities scholars in the field of history. Changes in discourse over time are a popular topic of studies in the humanities [10, 12, 15, 23]. Lists of keywords are usually maintained manually. However, "[f]inding the right keywords demands expert knowledge of the field of study and a great deal of perseverance and creativity" [15]. The methods for finding shifts in vocabulary over time that we propose in this paper are aimed at automating this task in a time-aware fashion. The resulting vocabularies are returned to the humanities scholars, as an indication of changes in discourse in the underlying corpus. They may be used for exploratory ends, to discover unfamiliar relevant historical terms. Additionally, as discussed in our future work section §6, if the vocabularies are of sufficient quality, they can be used for time-aware query expansion in an document retrieval setting for an historical corpus.

There has been extensive work on the related but different problem of concept drift in the context of ontologies and taxonomies; see, e.g., [27]. Any semantic ontology of terms should adapt over time in order to keep up with changes in meaning of the terms it contains. In this paper, however, we approach concept drift from a user perspective and not from an ontology perspective. This means that we do not assume pre-defined ontologies to be available and we do not aim to infer ontologies. Our primary motivation is to track evolving vocabularies over time for a user-provided topic of interest. This motivation leads to the following set of requirements:

1. **Words as retrieval unit** – Rather than outputting documents, as in a classic information retrieval scenario, an algorithm for monitoring shifts in vocabulary over time should, given a set of seed terms and a corpus, outputs words for a sequence of periods in time.
2. **Ad hoc** – An algorithm for monitoring shifts in vocabulary over time should work ad hoc. I.e., it should not be dependent on a predefined ontology or a fixed set of topics. The user should be able to provide ad hoc input at runtime. This requirement entails that very limited input of the user should be enough. Typically, one or two initial terms should suffice as an initial seed set.
3. **Broad time coverage** – An algorithm for monitoring shifts in vocabulary over time should be able to cover a substantial amount of time, at least multiple decades, long enough for interesting changes in discourse to occur.
4. **Comprehensible outcome** – The output produced by an algorithm for monitoring shifts in vocabulary over time should be easy to consume by humans. This means that the vocabularies that an algorithm yields should be limited in size, typically consisting of only a few words.

We note that an additional implication of the ad hoc requirement (requirement 2 in the list) is that no in-depth historical or domain knowledge of a user should be necessary. I.e., a user should not be required to have extensive knowledge of the concepts the input words are about nor of the underlying corpus. Rather, an effective method for monitoring shifts in vocabulary over time should provide new insights about the concepts and the corpus.

The comprehensible outcome requirement (requirement 4) entails that an optimal rate should be found for emitting vocabularies, regardless of a method's internals. If the rate is too low, too many vocabularies are produced, which leads to too much repetition. A rate that is too high would cause interesting shifts to go unnoticed. Precursory discussions with domain experts in the area of the history of ideas revealed that five years periods were deemed optimal.[1]

We propose an algorithm for monitoring shifts in vocabularies over time given a small user-provided set of seed terms and a period of reference. We note that this task is related to, but different from, tracking topics over time [9, 28], where topic models such as LDA and PLSA are used to monitor changes in a predefined number of topics. A crucial difference between topic modelling approaches and the method we propose is that, rather than relying on a predefined number of fixed topics, we allow for ad hoc queries.

Briefly, our proposed algorithm proceeds as follows. We first use distributional semantic models to infer a series of semantic spaces over time from a large body of time-stamped textual documents. We then construct semantic networks of terms based on their representation in the semantic spaces and use graph-based measures to calculate saliency of terms. Finally, we output shifting vocabularies over time—i.e., for a small set of seed words we output ranked lists of terms for a consecutive series of periods in time. The words in the vocabularies are meant to denote the same concept as the seed words do. As there is, to the best of our knowledge, no evaluation set available that allows for the intrinsic evaluation of monitoring shifts in vocabularies over time, we construct our own.

Our main contributions are:

- We introduce of the task of ad hoc monitoring of vocabulary shifts over time;
- We describe an algorithm for monitoring shifts in vocabularies over time, given a small, ad hoc set of seed words;
- We perform a systematic intrinsic evaluation of results of our proposed algorithm over a substantial time period (over four decades);
- We share our evaluation data, which can be downloaded from `http://ilps.science.uva.nl/resources/shifts`.

In the next section, §2, we discuss related work. In §3 we describe our method of tracking vocabularies over time. Our experimental setup is detailed in §4 while the results of the experiments are presented and analysed in §5. In §6 we conclude.

2. RELATED WORK

In this section we describe previous research related to the various aspects of our method of monitoring shifts in vocabularies over time.

2.1 Change in vocabulary over time with topic models

Topic models, like LDA and PLSA have been used extensively to monitor topics over time, starting with seminal work in [6, 28]. In [12] topic models are used to model the history of scientific ideas through time. The setting is similar, but different to the one addressed here, as word distributions of topics are inferred from the entire dataset and vocabulary shift is not modelled directly. Rather, the changes over time are modelled as shifts in the probability distribution of topics over the years. A related setting is addressed in [9] where topics and vocabulary are monitored over time.

The most important difference between topic model-based approaches, such as the ones discussed above, and the method we present in this paper is that our approach allows for an ad hoc setting. Topic models aim to infer a fixed set of latent topics from a corpus. This is the case even when non-parametric methods are employed [7], for which the number of topics is not fixed but inferred from the data. The non-parametric models allow for more flexibility, but once the algorithm has ran, there is a fixed set of topics it inferred. The inferred topics can be investigated to see interesting patterns over time, but if the topic of interest to the user is not in the inferred set of topics, there is no way around this.

Evaluation, from the perspective of the topics, is typically extrinsic, rather than intrinsic. The top-10 words for a selection of topics is shown in [12] but not evaluated. In [9] perplexity of the inferred topics is used as evaluation metric.

2.2 History of ideas

In the humanities, changing vocabularies are researched as well, in the field of intellectual history or the "history of ideas". In the context of the history of ideas, a distinction is made between the *intension* of an idea and its *extension* in [4]. The intension is the meaning of a concept, the extension comprises its mentions: "The extension of [a] concept differs through time. When confronted with certain changes in extension in the data, one likely conjecture is that the meaning of the concept [...] has changed" [4]. In this paper we regard the words used to denote this meaning as its extension, rather than sentences or entire articles as in, e.g., [27]. Although the intension of a concept changes as its extension changes,

[1]We note that alternatively, the optimal rate of emitting vocabularies could be determined programmatically. In theory, it could even differ between sets of seed words. The evaluation of such an approach would require extra, non-trivial annotator effort and we consider it outside the scope of the present paper.

we assume that the intension changes gradually over time (e.g., the intension of the concept of nuclear weapons is relatively stable over time, while the names of particular instances, and the words used to refer to nuclear weapons might change over time as the techniques involved evolve). By monitoring shifts in vocabularies over time, we aim to monitor shifts in the extension of a concept. We assume that the intension of a concept is continuous enough over time to allow for such monitoring. By adhering to this assumption we follow e.g. Kuukkanen who introduces a distinction between the core of a concept and its margins when discussing conceptual change: "the main idea is that conceptual continuity requires the stability of the core of the concept, but not necessarily that of the margin, which is something that enables a description of context-specific features" [20]. While we do not explicitly model the core or margin of concepts, we do assume conceptual continuity.

2.3 Topic detection and tracking

The goal of topic tracking systems, given a stream of documents, is to extract documents from the stream which are relevant to a set of topics of interest. Topics, in this setting, are typically events [1] or entities [8]. As events and entities may evolve over time, many adaptive document filtering algorithms have been proposed [3, 16, 25]. A sliding window approach is used on a stream of documents in [25], a component we also use in our method of monitoring shifting vocabularies over time in §3.

Document filtering algorithms typically contain a profile of the events or entities they monitor in the form of a (weighted) list of words which can adapt over time. Maintaining such a profile is clearly analogous to the task addressed in this paper, although we aim to track the words that are used to describe the meaning of a concept, rather than events or entities. Furthermore, it is important to note that in our present setting of vocabulary tracking the aim is to list terms that are semantically very similar to one another, while in the document filtering case it is beneficial for a filtering profile to cover a range of aspects as diverse as possible concerning the event or entity in question.

2.4 Change of word semantics over time

Research on detecting semantic shifts for words has seen a surge of interest recently. In [18] word vectors are trained on a corpus spanning over more than a century, with word2vec [21]. The vectors are trained on an incrementally growing time window, rather than a sliding window as we propose to do here. Several examples are shown to illustrate that dramatic semantic changes over time can be detected by monitoring the distance between the word vector of word in the initial model, that contains the least recent documents, and the vector from models trained on the windows including more recent material. Similarly, in [29] words are monitored over centuries. A number of examples is presented that show that changes in meaning as well as additional meanings of words can be detected. In [11] semantic change between words is measured with a distributional semantics method. The Google Books Ngram corpus is used to construct co-occurrence vectors of words in two decades (the 1960s and the 1990s, which is roughly the same time frame we use in our experiments). The task is to detect whether or not words have undergone a drastic semantic change, and human annotators were asked to annotate for a hundred words whether or not their meaning changed over the decades. In [13, 14] co-occurrence statistics are used to find related words to a specific term, which are monitored to find the sudden shifts in meaning.

We should note that, though monitoring the shifts in meanings of words over time is very related to the setting in these papers, there is a key difference in what we are trying to achieve. To illustrate, consider the main example used in [18]: the word "gay". The meaning of this word shifted considerably over the last century. Rather than focussing on the word "gay" itself to monitor its shift in meaning, the question we ask is: what words came in its place? Apparently, the meaning of the word "gay" evolved, and it now (largely) means something else from what it used to mean. So, which terms took its place? Which terms were used in a later time frame, to denote the meaning that was previously referred to by "gay?" Our aim is to track the *concept underlying a particular set of seed words* (of which there can be more than one). Crucially, in our adapative approach for monitoring vocabulary shifts over time, we allow the original seed words to disappear completely. However, as the task in this work is related to the one addressed in, e.g. [13, 14], we construct our baseline accordingly.

2.5 Distributional semantics

Distributional semantic approaches are based on the intuition that words appearing in similar contexts tend to have similar meanings. Words are typically represented as vectors where the vectors incorporate information about the context. Recent advances in neural network language models have led to new ways of computing word vectors, where more training material can be leveraged than was previously feasible. In our experiments in §4 we use word2vec [21] to infer word vectors. Word vectors, also referred to as word embeddings, embed words in a semantic space. This means that the word vectors for words with a similar meaning are close in the semantic space they are embedded in.

We note that using word2vec is not the only way to get distributional semantic word representations. Methods based on co-occurrence have been used for tasks similar to ours as described above. An alternative more similar to word2vec is the GloVe algorithm [24]. We use word2vec in our experiments as it has proven to yield high-quality word embeddings [2, 22]. The same goes for the GloVe algorithm but it needs considerably more resources in terms of training time and memory consumption, which is a drawback given the large size of our corpus. There is no theoretical restriction, however, on the choice of distributional semantic model in the algorithms we propose in §3.

2.6 Methods of evaluation

The evaluation used to assess the quality of the approaches discussed above is frequently based on small number of positive examples [12–14, 18, 19, 29]. Following [11] we perform explicit intrinsic evaluation, where we ask human annotators to judge the quality of the output of our algorithms directly.

The research presented in this paper extends previous work in a number of ways. Firstly, rather than focussing on monitoring the change in meaning of particular words over time, as in e.g. [11, 13, 14], we monitor the underlying concept, by monitoring the set of words that is used to denote it over time. We describe an algorithm for constructing a semantic network of related terms and for maintaining this network over time. Secondly, we do not rely on a fixed set of topics or pre-defined ontologies, but allow for ad hoc input: a small set of input words, specified by the user. Thirdly, we perform systematic intrinsic evaluation of our methods for generating shifting vocabularies over time.

3. MONITORING SHIFTING VOCABULARIES THROUGH TIME

In this section we describe our algorithm for monitoring shifts in vocabulary over time. By *vocabulary* we mean a ranked list of unique terms.

3.1 Overview

Our algorithms for monitoring shifts in vocabulary over time use three components: *sliding time windows*, *generation algorithm* and *aggregation algorithm*.

We use time windows of multiple years in length (we experiment with 5 and 10 year time windows in our experiments in §5) and extract documents out of our corpus that were published within the time window. The window length is in years and every next window starts one year later than the previous window. If we use, e.g., ten-year windows, and the overall time period starts in 1950, we have a 1950–1959 window, a 1951–1960 window, etc. From the documents published within a time window we compute a semantic model (see §2.5). So we have one semantic model for each sliding window in time. The computation of the semantic models is a pre-processing step. It is done only once for a given corpus.

As mentioned in §1 when discussing requirement 4, the optimal period for outputting vocabularies is five years. However, the sliding windows are one year apart. Because of this, our method for constructing vocabularies over time comprises two algorithms. The first algorithm, which we refer to as the *generation algorithm*, outputs a series of vocabularies, one for each sliding time window, using a semantic network from the semantic model constructed from the documents in the time window. The second algorithm, which we refer to as the *aggregation algorithm*, aggregates over the vocabularies generated by the generation algorithm to produce the final vocabularies for the desired time period.

The generation algorithm uses graph-based measures to extract the most salient words from a semantic network for a given time window. The salient words are used as input to the next iteration of the algorithm. In short, the generation algorithm takes the original user-provided words as its input and *adaptively* updates this seed set by iterating over the sliding time windows.

Our algorithms for generating shifting vocabularies over time are completely unsupervised. No labelled training data is needed. Furthermore, no pre-defined ontologies are necessary. Only a large amount of unlabelled data is needed to derive word vectors from.

In what follows we describe three methods of generating shifting vocabularies over time. The *adaptive* method uses both the generation algorithm and the aggregation algorithm. The *non-adaptive* only uses the aggregation algorithm to aggregate over vocabularies generated from the sliding time windows. The *hybrid* method combines the vocabularies produced by the adaptive and non-adaptive methods. As the sliding time windows are used by all three methods, we first turn to discussing these.

3.1.1 Sliding time windows

As detailed in §2.2 the intuition underlying our model for monitoring shifts in vocabulary over time is that word meanings, and the semantic relations between words, shift gradually and continuously over time [4, 20, 27]. To make use of this continuum when constructing semantic models, we split the time period we are monitoring in multiple time windows, and calculate a semantic model from each of these windows. I.e., we extract all documents from the corpus that were published in the desired time window and train a word2vec model on their text contents.

To be sensitive to rapid changes, it would be beneficial to have short time windows. However, previous research has proven that the quality of the semantic models inferred by word2vec is higher when more training data is used [21]. We solve this conflict in requirements on the size of the training data for the semantic models by using *overlapping* time windows. By taking an extended period of time, we obtain a sufficient amount of data for constructing high-quality semantic models. As the windows are only one year apart from each other, changes in the semantic relations between words can be detected between subsequent models, while the vast majority of relations will remain stable, due to the overlap.

3.2 Adaptive method for generating shifting vocabularies over time

In this section we describe the generation algorithm and the aggregation algorithm, for our adaptive method of monitoring shifting vocabularies over time.

3.2.1 Generation algorithm; generating shifting vocabularies over time

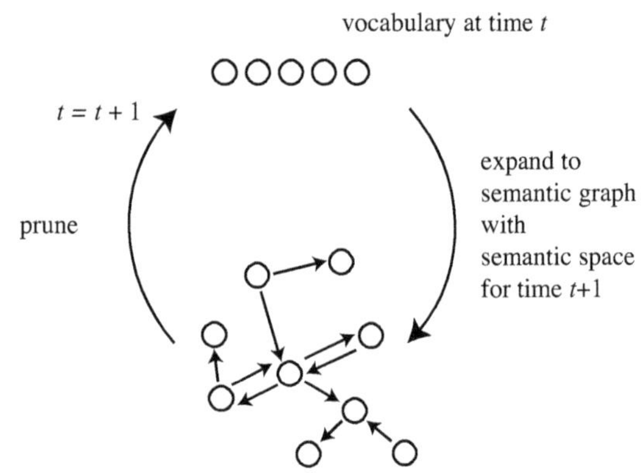

Figure 1: Schematic representation of the generation algorithm for generating vocabularies over time.

In Figure 1 a schematic overview is given of the generation algorithm for generating vocabularies over time from sliding windows. Every iteration consists of an expansion step and a pruning step. In the expansion step, a semantic graph is constructed from a list of seed terms and a semantic space. In the pruning step, the top terms, according to a graph-based measure, are extracted from the graph. This vocabulary is the input to the next iteration. As can be seen from this schematic overview, the original input words do not necessarily end up in the vocabulary one (or more) iterations later.

In Algorithm 1 the pseudocode for the generation algorithm is provided. At the very first iteration, the input consists of the seed set as provided by the user (Algorithm 1, line 1). As a key requirement of our method is limited effort by the user, we use only a few terms (typically one or two) as input. In the outer loop is carried out K times (line 2), once for every semantic model, derived from the K sliding time windows. In the expansion step (line 4–8), we construct a weighted, directed, partial semantic graph from the set of seed terms, given the semantic space from the next time window. To do this, we obtain the related terms for every word in the seed set, with a minimum similarity ς (line 5). Per seed set term we take at most n related terms. The terms obtained in this manner are the vertices of our graph. Form these vertices we construct a semantic graph (line 9). The edges in the graph are directed and weighted. We draw an edge from vertex w_i to w_j if w_j is in the list of related words of w_i. The weight on the edge is determined by the strength of the association between w_i and w_j in the semantic space. The network is partial as we do not construct an extensive network of all possible vertices (i.e., all word types in the corpus), but rather extract the part of the network in the vicinity of the seed terms. In the pruning step the top-n terms are selected relative to their degree centrality in the semantic network (line 10).

We use elementary variants of degree centrality: in-degree and out-degree. More involved measures like PageRank can be considered as well, especially when larger parts of the graph are extracted.

Required: $W = [w_1 \dots w_{|W|}]$: a set of seed terms
Required: Series of semantic spaces $S = [sem_1 ... sem_K]$, ordered by time
Required: ς: minimum similarity
Required: n: maximum number of terms to return
Result: List of vocabularies $v_1 \dots v_{|K|}$
1 $v_0 = W$;
2 **for** $k \leftarrow 1 \dots |K|$ **do**
3   vertices = [];
    /* expand */
4   **foreach** $w \in v_{k-1}$ **do**
5   **foreach** $w_{related} \in related\_words(w, sem_k, \varsigma, n)$ **do**
6   vertices = vertices $\cup$ $w_{related}$;
7   **end**
8   **end**
9   semanticNetwork = drawEdges(vertices);
    /* prune */
10   v_k = top-n nodes from semanticNetwork w.r.t. degree centrality
11 **end**

Algorithm 1: Generation algorithm: adaptively generating vocabularies from sliding time windows

e.g. by finding related words of related words, and so on. However, preliminary experiments showed that the relation between the original seed terms and related terms of related terms can quickly become arbitrary. A method relying on such terms would run a considerable risk of topic drift.

We compute four measures of degree centrality: number of inlinks, weighted sum of inlinks, number of outlinks and weighted sum of outlinks. The choice of degree centrality measure is a parameter of our model. We discuss the effect of this parameter on the results of our experiments in §5.2.

Direction in time. In this section we describe a forward pass, where we start with the oldest time window and progress towards the future. The same method can be applied the other way around, as would, e.g., be appropriate for the iPod example in §1. In Algorithm 1 this means that we start with $v_{|K|}$ in line 1, range over $k \leftarrow |K| \dots 1$ in line 2 and iterate over $w \in v_{k+1}$ in line 4.

3.2.2 Aggregation algorithm: Producing the final output vocabularies

For each semantic space, generated from documents in overlapping time windows one year apart, the generation algorithm generates a vocabulary. If we monitor, e.g., a period of four decades, 40 vocabularies are generated, one for every overlapping window. The final output presented to the user, however, should be one vocabulary for every 5 year period, so 8 vocabularies, in the example case. To generate the final output vocabularies, we aggregate over the vocabularies generated by the generation algorithm.

The aggregation step producing the final vocabularies is distinct from the principal underlying method of generating vocabularies for all overlapping time windows. If the final vocabularies should be generated for periods of 4 or 6 years, rather than 5, the output of the generation algorithm could be used unaltered, and only one parameter needs to be changed in the aggregation algorithm.

Algorithm 2 lists the pseudocode of our method for aggregating over the vocabularies output by Algorithm 1 to produce the final output vocabularies. The first step in each iteration (line 2) is to select a set of vocabularies relevant to the time period at hand τ_t. We select all vocabularies constructed from time windows that have an overlap with τ_t. This step is needed as the length of the time windows is a parameter of the model and might not be the same as the length of τ_i. We can, e.g., use 10-year windows in the generation algorithm, while we output vocabularies for 5-year periods in the final step (i.e. the length of every period τ_t is 5).

Required: List of vocabularies $V = v_1 \dots v_{|K|}$
Required: List of time frames $T = [\tau_1 \dots \tau_{|T|}]$ for which to output vocabularies
Required: n: maximum number of terms to return
Result: List of vocabularies $v_{\tau_1} \dots v_{|T|}$
1 **for** $t \leftarrow 1 \dots |T|$ **do**
2     $V' = [v \in V \mid v$ relevant to $\tau_t]$;
3   **foreach** $v \in V'$ **do**
4   **foreach** $w \in v$ **do**
5             $score_w {+}{=} f_{weight}(v, \tau_t) * score_{w,v}$;
6   **end**
7   **end**
8   v_{τ_t} = top-n terms w sorted by $score_w$;
9 **end**

Algorithm 2: Aggregation algorithm: Aggregating vocabularies output by the generation algorithm to produce the final output vocabularies.

In the inner loops of Algorithm 2 we iterate over the words in the selected vocabularies (line 3–7). We compute a score for all words, which consists of their score in vocabulary v (their degree centrality, see previous section) weighted by a weight function $f_{weight}(v, \tau)$ that assigns a weight to a vocabulary v for a time frame τ.

Vocabulary weighting function. As described above, each vocabulary v_{τ_t} is constructed from a semantic space, derived from the texts of documents published in a time window, spanning a number of years. The time window has an overlap with time period τ_t that we want to output a vocabulary for. Therefore, a weighting is needed which expresses how much vocabulary v should contribute to v_{τ_t}, the final vocabulary we output for τ_t.

The most straightforward way of weighting is to weight all vocabularies equally (i.e., apply no weighting at all). However, the central years in the period the vocabulary is derived from are most likely to best capture its semantics (e.g., if we look at the decade 1970–1979, the documents in the early 1970s might still have echoes of the late sixties, while in the late 1970s, the 1980s might already become apparent; the middle years will define the vocabulary most clearly). We implement this intuition by assuming that the probability of the contribution of years to a vocabulary v is given by a Gaussian distribution, where the mean of the distribution is the centre of the period, and we assume a standard deviation of 1.0. We model the distribution of the years in τ in a similar fashion, where the mean is the central year of τ. Given these two distributions we can use the Jensen-Shannon divergence as a proxy for the weight of v with respect to τ:

$$f_{JSD}(v, \tau) = JSD(\mathcal{N}(\mu_v, \sigma_v^2) \parallel \mathcal{N}(\mu_\tau, \sigma_\tau^2)),$$

where we have $\sigma_v^2 = \sigma_\tau^2 = 1$.

We note that simple overlap metrics, like, e.g.. Jaccard distance, do not measure what we want, as a the Jaccard distance between two periods, where one period overlaps completely with the other, is always the same, regardless whether they overlap in the central region of the longer period or not.

3.3 Non-adaptive method for generating shifting vocabularies over time

Using the adaptive method for generating vocabularies, it is well possible that none of the words in the original seed set are present after a few iterations. This is a desired effect, but it also introduces the risk of topic drift. I.e., the adaptive algorithm might focus on an aspect of meaning that was not intended by the user, which can cause the vocabularies being generated to drift in the wrong direction. To counter this effect, we also include runs in our experiments where the initial seed set is kept static. That is, we omit Algorithm 1, and instead output the n words most related to the words in the original seed set for every sliding time window. To generate the final vocabularies we do employ Algorithm 2.

We refer to this method, that follows a static seed set for generating shifting vocabularies over time as *non-adaptive* method.

3.4 Hybrid runs

To combine the exploratory effect of the adaptive approach with the more conservative approach of the non-adaptive approach, we combine the runs of both methods of producing shifting vocabularies over time to produce *hybrid* runs. In particular, we replace the least central terms of the vocabularies produced by the non-adaptive method by the top i vocabulary terms produced by the adaptive method with respect to degree centrality. In §5 we report results for different values of i.

4. EXPERIMENTAL SETUP

To measure the quality of the different methods of generating vocabularies over time we perform a systematic, intrinsic evaluation. Our research questions are:

RQ1 Given that we have an exploratory, adaptive approach and a conservative, non-adaptive approach for generating shifting vocabularies over time, can we combine the two in such a way that performance is gained over the components?

RQ2 How do the parameters of the generation algorithm and the aggregation algorithm affect performance?

The first research question, RQ1, concerns the balance between an exploratory response to change in vocabularies, which introduces the risk of topic drift, and a static, conservative approach, which does not allow for substantial evolution of vocabularies. In §5.1 we report on the results for our experiments regarding this question.

The second research question, RQ2, concerns our algorithms for generating vocabularies over time more specifically. As detailed in §3 we construct semantic networks to find salient terms in specific time periods. We are interested in evaluating whether, e.g., the weighting of edges is beneficial or not, or whether selecting nodes based on in-degree yields better results than using out-degree.

We analyse the performance regarding all parameters of our algorithms of generating shifting vocabularies over time in §5.2. In the remainder of this section we detail the aspects of our experimental setup.

4.1 Ground truth data

The natural ground truth data for our task of monitoring shifting vocabularies over time are the shifting vocabularies themselves. We make use of human annotators to obtain this ground truth data. The annotators' task is, given all unique words occurring in a corpus of timestamped documents, to indicate which words are relevant to a particular topic of interest in a certain time period. As it is not feasible for annotators to judge all word types in a corpus, we employ a pooling approach, which we detail below. Below, we also provide the characteristics of the seed terms.

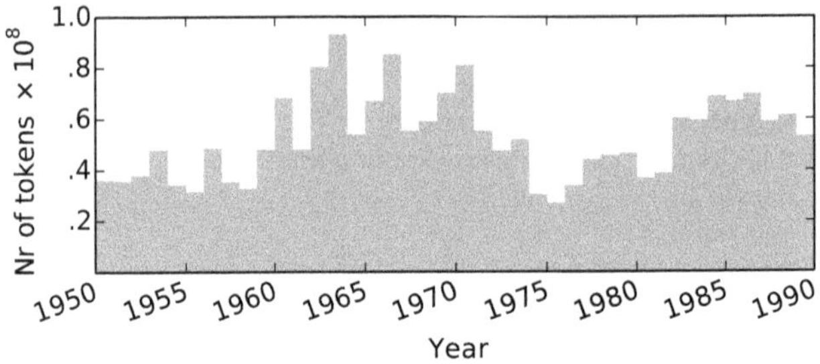

Figure 2: Number of tokens per year

Given a small number of seed terms, and a short text describing the underlying information need, the annotators were asked to judge terms per period on a 3 point scale: *irrelevant*, *related* and *perfect*. The *related* category is used for borderline cases in which a result is not completely off the mark, but is not exactly right either.

There were 6 annotators in total, all of whom are academic historians, well-acquainted with both the corpus and the evaluation time period. None of the authors took part in the annotation effort.

Following, e.g., [11] we use the pairwise Pearson correlation to determine inter-annotator agreement. The Pearson correlation coefficient is .555 with a p-value $< 10^{-5}$. It shows that the judgements are highly correlated between annotators and that the averaged judgements can reliably be used to evaluate our experiments.

The sets of seed terms and the ground truth annotations are publicly available. The material can be downloaded from `http://ilps.science.uva.nl/resources/shifts`.

Pooling. We produce output using each of the methods for generating vocabularies over time that we consider, and all combinations of parameters. We pool these results, similar to how the runs of IR systems are pooled in a classical TREC-style evaluation [26]. In our setting, however, the unit of retrieval is a word for a given time period, rather than a document. Annotators are presented with the aggregated results of all runs combined.

Corpus. Our corpus is a collection of Dutch newspapers, digitised by the Royal Library of the Netherlands.[2] We use four decades, 1950 up until 1990, as our evaluation period as this period is long enough for interesting changes to occur and modern enough for the OCR quality to be reasonable.[3]

The corpus contains 26 614 346 documents (newspaper articles) in the four decades we consider. Together, they comprise 1 940 841 unique words and 2 141 992 571 tokens. Figure 2 gives an overview of the numbers of tokens per year. As can be observed from this figure, the tokens are not evenly distributed across the years, but there is no bias towards either modern or historical documents. We used the Python NLTK Punkt Sentence Tokenizer [5] and remove additional unicode non-word characters.

Seed terms. There are 21 sets of seed terms in our experiments, which are provided by Dutch historians, who are familiar with the corpus and the time period selected. The terms are inspired by their own, real-life, research questions and by observations they

[2]The full newspaper corpus, and more, can be queried at `http://www.delpher.nl`.

[3]No official numbers concerning the OCR quality throughout this corpus are available. Anecdotal evidence suggests though that modern material is of higher quality.

Table 1: Overview of the Dutch seed set words

Seed words	English explanation	Direction
cd, compactdisc	cd, compact disc	backwards
computer	computer	backwards
doping	drugs (sports-related)	backwards
efficiency, efficiëntie	efficiency	backwards
gastarbeider, gastarbeiders, immigranten	immigrants	backwards
geboortebeperking, geboorteregeling	birth control	forwards
holocaust	holocaust	backwards
internet	internet	backwards
jodenvervolging, deportatie, deportaties	persecution of Jews (in WWII)	forwards
marxisme	marxism	forwards
multinational	multinational	backwards
neger, negers, negerin, kleurling	negro, coloured people	forwards
quiz	quiz	backwards
supermarkt	supermarket	backwards
waterstofbom, atoombommen waterstofbommen, atoombom	hydrogen bomb	forwards
zelfbedieningswinkel, zelfbedieningszaak, kruidenier	self-service shop	forwards
amsterdam, rotterdam, utrecht	large Dutch cities	forwards
boek, boeken, boekje	books	forwards
koe, koeien	cows	forwards
mozart, beethoven, brahms	classical composers	forwards
viool, violen	classical instruments	forwards

made from the corpus. As discussed in §3, an algorithm for generating vocabularies over time can run either forwards or backwards in time. It was left up to the historians to decide on the most natural direction in time, per set of seed terms. In Table 1 we present an overview of the seed sets, together with the direction in time. The bottom 5 rows in Table 1 list 5, so-called, a-historical seed sets. The concepts denoted by these seed sets are assumed, by the historians, to stay relatively stable over the entire evaluation period. We include the a-historical seed sets for two reasons. Firstly, we want to avoid a bias in the test set towards changing concepts, i.e., we do not want the test set to only consist of examples of which it is apparent that they evolve over time, as this would put the non-adaptive methods at an unfair disadvantage. Secondly, we want to check for over-generating, by which we mean, in this context, generating changing vocabularies while there is in fact no change. A method that is too exploratory might always find new terms and might show evolving list of words erroneously. To be able to measure such behaviour, we add the a-historical seed term sets.

On average the seed term lists are 2.1 words in length. The ground truth vocabularies (i.e. the list of relevant words per time period) are 9.32 words in length on average.

4.2 Evaluation

Our algorithms for generating shifting vocabularies over time produce ranked lists of words. The Cranfield-style evaluation setting allows us to use traditional IR evaluation metrics suitable for evaluating ranked lists, NDCG and MAP, in addition to the standard F_1 metric.

4.3 Parameters and settings

For the generation algorithm, we use 5-year and 10-year sliding time windows to compute semantical spaces from. Preliminary experiments showed that values between .6 and .7 are reasonable values for ς. Hence we experiment with $\varsigma \in [.6, .65, .7]$. For degree centrality we use 4 variants, as described in §3.2.1: sum of inlinks, weighted sum of inlinks, sum of outlinks, weighted sum of outlinks.

The aggregation algorithm has only one parameter: the vocabulary weighting function. We experiment with a uniform weighting function (i.e., no weighting), and the JSD-weighting function, described in §3.2.2.

As discussed in §2.5 we use word2vec [21] to generate word vectors for every time window. We employ default settings; Skip-gram architecture, with hierarchical softmax and no negative sampling, vector dimensionality of 300, window size of 5, and minimum word frequency of 5.

In all experiments, the vocabulary size n is set to 10.

4.4 Baseline

As noted in §2, the work described in [13, 14] is related to our present setting. Following this work, we construct our baseline by using a time slice approach. However, we use neural network language models to construct semantic models to derive semantic proximity from, rather than co-occurrence measures as in [13, 14], as the computation of a full co-occur-rence matrix on the corpus used in our experiments is intractable, due to its size. For every time window τ_t our baseline methods outputs the top-n most related words derived from a semantic model trained on the documents published in time window τ_t.

5. RESULTS AND ANALYSIS

We begin by answering our research questions and proceed by contrasting the adaptive approach and the non-adaptive approach, described in §3.2 and §3.3, respectively.

5.1 Hybrid vs. Non-hybrid approaches

To answer RQ1 we conduct experiments with all methods described above and all parameter settings. Table 2 contains an overview of the results yielded by the best parameter setting.[4]

Table 2: Results for JSD weighting with 10-year periods, $\varsigma = .65$, in-degree over weighted edges. Statistically significant differences from the baseline, measured with a two-tailed paired t-test, is marked for $p < .02^{\dagger}$ and $p < 10^{-6\ddagger}$

Method	F_1	p	r	NDCG	MAP
hybrid ($i = 1$)	$.384^{\ddagger}$	$.537^{\ddagger}$	$.406^{\ddagger}$	$.646^{\ddagger}$	$.343^{\ddagger}$
hybrid ($i = 2$)	$.391^{\ddagger}$	$.544^{\ddagger}$	$\mathbf{.414}^{\ddagger}$	$.650^{\ddagger}$	$\mathbf{.346}^{\ddagger}$
hybrid ($i = 3$)	$\mathbf{.392}^{\ddagger}$	$\mathbf{.548}^{\ddagger}$	$.411^{\ddagger}$	$\mathbf{.653}^{\ddagger}$	$.345^{\ddagger}$
hybrid ($i = 4$)	$.389^{\ddagger}$	$.545^{\ddagger}$	$.405^{\ddagger}$	$.651^{\ddagger}$	$.343^{\ddagger}$
hybrid ($i = 5$)	$.385^{\ddagger}$	$.541^{\ddagger}$	$.399^{\ddagger}$	$.649^{\ddagger}$	$.339^{\ddagger}$
adaptive	.344	$.551^{\ddagger}$	.298	$.514^{\dagger}$	$.237^{\dagger}$
non-adaptive	$.367^{\ddagger}$	$.521^{\ddagger}$	$.389^{\ddagger}$	$.630^{\ddagger}$	$.332^{\ddagger}$
baseline	.303	.450	.296	.554	.266

The key observation from Table 2 is that the hybrid approach outperforms both the baseline, and the adaptive method and non-adaptive method separately, on all metrics, regardless of the value of i. It is important to note that the parameter setting reported in Table 2 consistently yields the highest results on all metrics for the hybrid method, regardless of the value of i.

5.1.1 *Adaptive vs. non-adaptive*

The non-adaptive method outperforms the baseline by itself. The adaptive method only does so in terms of F_1. As is clear from Table 2, though, the adaptive method can add valuable information

[4]Note that due to macro-averaging, the macro-F_1 scores can and do end up lower than the individual macro-precision and macro-recall scores.

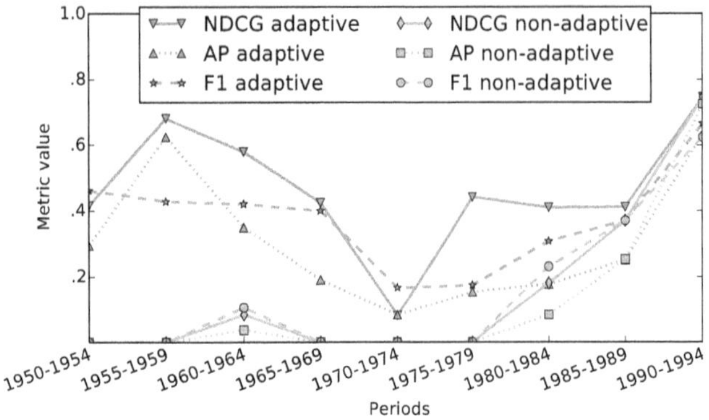

Figure 3: Comparison of results between the adaptive and non-adaptive run for the seed words "cd, compact disc." Direction is backwards in time.

to the non-adaptive method. In this section we present a number of examples to illustrate the difference between the two. To highlight the difference, we only show examples of the non-hybrid runs in this section. These runs contributed to the results in the rows labeled 'adaptive' and 'non-adaptive' in Table 2.

In Figure 3 the results are displayed for the non-adaptive run and the adaptive run for the seed words "cd, compactdisc." The direction for this example is backward, i.e., we start with the seed words in the 1990–1994 period and go backward in time.

As we can clearly see from the figure, the performance of the non-adaptive run quickly degrades over time (recall that we are going backward in time). Interestingly, the adaptive run, after a glitch in the 1970–1974 period, manages to pick up to get decent performance again for the time periods in the 1950s and 1960s. This indicates that the network approach, in which a network of related terms is promoted, can be beneficial.

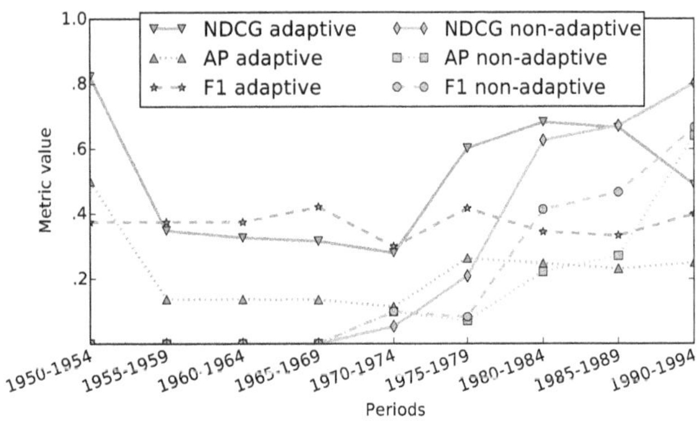

Figure 4: Comparison of results between the adaptive and non-adaptive run for the seed word "holocaust." Direction is backward in time.

We see a similar pattern in the results for the seed word "holocaust" in Figure 4. Again, we are going backward in time for this example. The performance of the non-adaptive run steadily degrades as we go back in time. This can be explained by the fact that the word "holocaust" barely occurs in the corpus prior to 1978.[5] The term was introduced in Dutch discourse by an American television series by that name. Initially, the term was used primarily to refer to the series, but gradually it became a more general term that now means the same as it does in English.

In Figure 5 the results are displayed for the seed word "multinational." The word "multinational" rarely occurs in the 1950s and

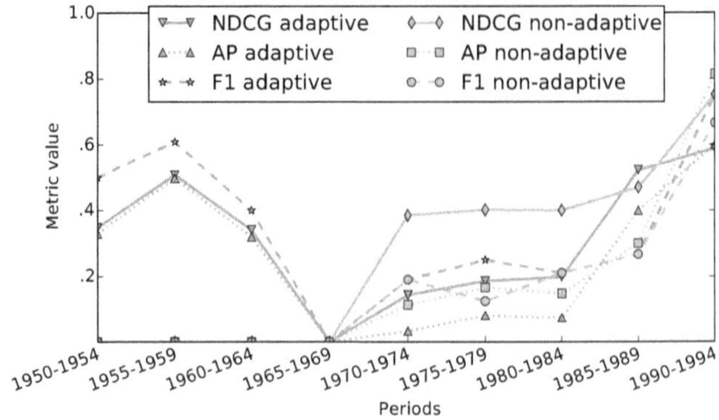

Figure 5: Comparison of results between the adaptive and non-adaptive run for the seed word "multinational." Direction is backward in time.

1960s in the Dutch digitised newspapers.[6] This is clearly reflected in Figure 5 and both the adaptive and the non-adaptive method suffer from this. Close inspection of the documents in which the word does occur in this period reveal that it is used in a political context (where it means international) rather than in a business context as later on. Importantly, the adaptive run is able to recover its drop in performance, while the non-adaptive run is unable to do so, and keeps getting zero performance.

The examples in this section clearly show the limitations of non-adaptive approach that simply follows a static set of words and the words related to them over time. If the words in the seed set simply do not exist in the period of interest (as in the "cd" example), change in meaning (the "multinational" example), or are not used throughout the entire period of interest (the "holocaust" example), a static approach can only fail.

5.1.2 Overgeneration

As discussed in §4.1 the evaluation set contains 5 a-historical seed term sets to check for overgenerating. In Table 3 we display the results on the a-historical subset of the ground truth seed sets, based on the same parameter settings used for Table 2.

Table 3: Results for adaptive and non-adaptive method on a-historical seed sets only

Method	F_1	NDCG	MAP
adaptive	.395	.849	.254
non-adaptive	.387	.872	.254

As we can observe from Table 3 the results between the adaptive and non-adaptive runs are comparable. None of the differences is statistically significant for $\alpha = .05$ for a two-tailed paired t-test. We conclude from these results that our adaptive method for generating shifting vocabularies over time does not overgenerate. That is, if no changes occur in a vocabulary concerning a particular topic, none are in fact picked up by the adaptive method.

5.2 Parameter analysis

To answer research question RQ2 we analyse the effect of the parameters of the generation algorithm and the aggregation algorithm. For the generation algorithm the parameters are the length of the sliding time window, minimal semantic distance ς and the method of computing degree centrality. For the aggregation algorithm we have one parameter, the vocabulary weighting function.

[5]See: http://kbkranten.politicalmashup.nl/#q/holocaust

[6]See: http://kbkranten.politicalmashup.nl/#q/multinational

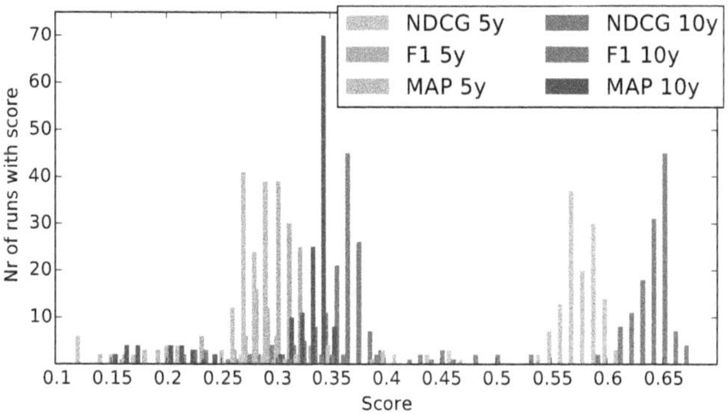

Figure 6: Comparison of results per metric, grouped by time window length. (Best viewed in color.)

Length of sliding time windows. The length of the sliding time windows affects both the adaptive method and the non-adaptive method. In Figure 6 performance of all runs — adaptive, non-adaptive and hybrid, all parameter settings — is plotted, grouped by window length. As is clear from the figure, using 10 year sliding windows yields better results in a vast majority of cases, for all metrics. In Table 4 the t-statistics and p-values are listed per metric for a paired t-test between the results per window length (the results are paired per parameter setting).

Table 4: Results of two-tailed paired t-test between the performance of all results per window length, paired by parameter setting

Metric	t-statistic	p-value
NDCG	-20.8	5.34×10^{-19}
MAP	-24.0	1.08×10^{-20}
F_1	-19.6	2.73×10^{-18}

From these findings we conclude that using a longer time window to train a semantic model yields better performance for our current task, which supports the claim made in [21] that more training data yields better semantic models. Do note, though, that, due to the adaptive nature of our task, we can not use arbitrarily long time windows, as the changes in meaning and vocabulary we are interested in might go unnoticed that way.

Minimum distance. As discussed in §3.2.1 the ς parameter controls which related words are taken into account for constructing semantic networks. In Table 5 the results across different levels of ς are displayed for all methods of generating shifting vocabularies over time, that use the generation algorithm (the non-adaptive method only uses the aggregation algorithm). The results are consistently lower than the results in Table 2, regardless of the method. This clearly indicates that a value of $\varsigma = .65$ is to be preferred for all methods, adaptive, non-adaptive or hybrid.

Table 5: Top results for different settings of minimum similarity ς, all other settings as in Table 2

Method	ς	F_1	p	r	NDCG	MAP
hybrid ($i = 1$)	.7	.367	.521	.389	.630	.332
	.6	.376	.530	.398	.637	.338
hybrid ($i = 2$)	.7	.368	.523	.385	.630	.332
	.6	.378	.534	.395	.636	.338
hybrid ($i = 3$)	.7	.372	.530	.388	.634	.335
	.6	.370	.526	.385	.632	.332
hybrid ($i = 4$)	.7	.370	.529	.381	.632	.333
	.6	.365	.521	.376	.627	.329
hybrid ($i = 5$)	.7	.366	.525	.372	.628	.331
	.6	.358	.515	.365	.622	.323
adaptive	.7	.316	.678	.241	.485	.220
	.6	.292	.442	.273	.442	.206

Degree centrality. Regarding the different ways of calculating degree centrality we observe a very consistent pattern: choosing in-degree always yields better results than choosing out-degree. The best performance with out-degree, in terms of F_1, other settings as in Table 2 is yielded by the hybrid method, with $i = 1$. It yields an F_1 of .370, NDCG of .632 and MAP of .333, all of which is lower than the scores of the best performing hybrid runs.

Putting weights on the edges consistently leads to performance superior to unweighted edges. The best performance, in terms of F_1, without weighted edges, and other settings as in Table 2 is yielded by the hybrid method with $i = 1$, which yields an F_1 of .369, NDCG of .632 and MAP of .333.

Vocabulary weighting function. In case of the non-adaptive method, not weighting the vocabularies leads to a small increase in performance: F_1 .368, NDCG .632 and MAP .333, regardless of the value for minimum similarity ς. These differences, however, are not statistically significant for $\alpha = .5$ for a two-tailed paired t-test. Furthermore, for the hybrid method, applying weighting for generating vocabularies over time nearly always yields better results when $i > 1$. These findings suggest that weighting of vocabularies is beneficial for generating shifting vocabularies over time.

5.3 Error analysis

In 9 cases of the 21, merging adaptive and non-adaptive runs for the hybrid runs led to performance that was less than the best performing of the two. In this section we will discuss three such examples. Typically, the decrease in performance was small (~1%).

Table 6: Results of the hybrid run ($i = 3$) for seed set "marxism," for the last time period (the direction in time is forward). Words occurring in the ground truth set are marked with a *.

Period	Vocabulary[7]
1990–1994	communism*, marxism*, capitalism, humanism, christianity, socialism*, imperialism, atheism, militarism *(in two different spelling variants)*

Table 6 shows the vocabulary output for the hybrid run ($i = 3$) with seed set "marxism" for the 1990–1994 period. The direction is forward in time. This means that we start with the concept of marxism in 1950 and follow it as time progresses. As we can see from the results, the adaptive run has picked up on related terms and has become too general (the concepts, though they are related, are mainstream socio-economical movements, ideologies and isms). Much more on-topic words, like, e.g., "leninism" and "stalinism," which were used in the late 1990s in the newspaper corpus are picked up by the non-adaptive run.

We see a different pattern for the run with the seed set "hydrogen bomb" in Table 7. Here, the adaptive run nearly loses track of the nuclear weapons completely, and rather focusses on missiles.[8]

The examples in this section show that the adaptive method for monitoring shifting vocabularies over time can be susceptible to

[7] The original words are in Dutch, translations by the authors

[8] The term "atomic warheads" was not annotated as correct, even though it means the same as "nuclear warhead," because it was hardly ever used, while "nuclear warhead" was used abundantly.

Table 7: Results of the hybrid run ($i = 3$) for seed set "hydrogen bomb" for the last time period (forward direction in time). Words occurring in the ground truth set are marked with a *.

Period	Vocabulary
1990–1994	launching facilities, rockets, ballistic, launching pads, nuclear warheads*, nuclear submarines, atomic warheads, nuclear payload*, multi-headed, bomber

topic drift. It can loose specificity (the "marxism" example) or it can drift in the wrong direction (the "hydrogen bomb" example). Especially in cases like this, a combination with a more conservative, non-adaptive approach is beneficial.

6. CONCLUSIONS AND FUTURE WORK

We introduced the task of ad hoc monitoring of vocabulary shifts over time. We presented several algorithms for monitoring vocabularies over time and perform systematic, intrinsic evaluation of their results. Our results show that our approach of combining an exploratory method of generating shifting vocabularies over time with a conservative approach consistently and significantly beats a baseline inspired by related research, and that it consistently performs better than the two approaches it combines.

Intrinsic evaluation of semantic methods is difficult. Constructing a manually labelled dataset as we did is costly and labour-intensive. We hope that disclosing the full evaluation set is beneficial to research in this area.

High-quality, on-topic vocabularies over time can beneficial in many cases both in IR and in digital humanities research. The vocabularies can be used as a way of exploring data, as is the underlying scenario in this paper. Furthermore however, they could be used for time-aware query expansion, where the query expansion depends on the timestamps of documents in a corpus.

Future work should focus on longer evaluation periods, e.g. a century of material. Furthermore, additional graph-based measures could be taken into account. Moreover, different types of shift in vocabulary might be discerned. Similar to how document ranking systems are tailored towards query intent, systems for monitoring shifting vocabularies over time could be optimised in terms of optimal parameter settings or choice of algorithm, depending on the type of vocabulary shift they aim to monitor.

The performance of an adaptive method for monitoring shifting vocabularies may degrade or improve over time. However, traditional evaluation metrics like NDCG or MAP are time-agnostic. Additional insights could be obtained when a time-aware evaluation metric, such as, e.g., proposed in [17] in the context of document filtering systems, would be applied to the present setting.

Acknowledgments.

This research was supported by Amsterdam Data Science, the Dutch national program COMMIT, Elsevier, the European Community's Seventh Framework Programme (FP7/2007-2013) under grant agreement nr 312827 (VOX-Pol), the ESF Research Network Program ELIAS, the HPC Fund the Royal Dutch Academy of Sciences (KNAW) under the Elite Network Shifts project, the Microsoft Research Ph.D. program, the Netherlands eScience Center under project number 027.012.105, the Netherlands Institute for Sound and Vision, the Netherlands Organisation for Scientific Research (NWO) under project nrs 727.011.005, 612.001.116, HOR-11-10, 640.006.-013, 612.066.930, CI-14-25, SH-322-15, the Yahoo! Faculty Research and Engagement Program, and Yandex.

7. REFERENCES

[1] J. Allan. *Topic detection and tracking: event-based information organization.* Springer Science & Business Media, 2002.

[2] M. Baroni, G. Dinu, and G. Kruszewski. Don't count, predict! a systematic comparison of context-counting vs. context-predicting semantic vectors. In *ACL 2014*, 2014.

[3] R. Berendsen, E. Meij, D. Odijk, M. de Rijke, and W. Weerkamp. The university of amsterdam at trec 2012. In *TREC 2012*, 2012.

[4] A. Betti and H. van den Berg. Modelling the history of ideas. *British Journal for the History of Philosophy*, 2014.

[5] S. Bird, E. Klein, and E. Loper. *Natural language processing with Python.* O'Reilly Media, Inc., 2009.

[6] D. M. Blei and J. D. Lafferty. Dynamic topic models. In *Proceedings of the 23rd international conference on Machine learning*, 2006.

[7] D. M. Blei, T. L. Griffiths, and M. I. Jordan. The nested chinese restaurant process and bayesian nonparametric inference of topic hierarchies. *J. ACM*, 2010.

[8] J. R. Frank, S. J. Bauer, M. Kleiman-Weiner, D. A. Roberts, N. Tripuraneni, C. Zhang, C. Ré, E. Voorhees, and I. Soboroff. Evaluating stream filtering for entity profile updates for TREC 2013. In *TREC 2013 Working Notes*. NIST, 2013.

[9] A. Gohr, A. Hinneburg, R. Schult, and M. Spiliopoulou. Topic evolution in a stream of documents. In *SDM*, 2009.

[10] J. Guldi. The history of walking and the digital turn: Stride and lounge in london, 1808–1851. *The Journal of Modern History*, 2012.

[11] K. Gulordava and M. Baroni. A distributional similarity approach to the detection of semantic change in the google books ngram corpus. In *GEMS*, 2011.

[12] D. Hall, D. Jurafsky, and C. D. Manning. Studying the history of ideas using topic models. In *EMNLP*, 2008.

[13] G. Heyer, F. Holz, and S. Teresniak. Change of topics over time-tracking topics by their change of meaning. *KDIR*, 2009.

[14] F. Holz and S. Teresniak. Towards automatic detection and tracking of topic change. In *Computational linguistics and intelligent text processing*. 2010.

[15] P. Huijnen, F. Laan, M. de Rijke, and T. Pieters. A digital humanities approach to the history of science. In *Social Informatics*. 2014.

[16] T. Kenter. Filtering documents over time for evolving topics. In *TREC 2013*, 2013.

[17] T. Kenter, K. Balog, and M. de Rijke. Evaluating document filtering systems over time. *Information Processing & Management*, 2015.

[18] Y. Kim, Y.-I. Chiu, K. Hanaki, D. Hegde, and S. Petrov. Temporal analysis of language through neural language models. In *LACSS*, 2014.

[19] V. Kulkarni, R. Al-Rfou, B. Perozzi, and S. Skiena. Statistically significant detection of linguistic change. *CoRR*, 2014.

[20] J. Kuukkanen. Making sense of conceptual change. *History and theory*, 2008.

[21] T. Mikolov, K. Chen, G. Corrado, and J. Dean. Efficient estimation of word representations in vector space. *arXiv preprint arXiv:1301.3781*, 2013.

[22] T. Mikolov, I. Sutskever, K. Chen, G. S. Corrado, and J. Dean. Distributed representations of words and phrases and their compositionality. In *NIPS 2013*, 2013.

[23] F. Moretti and D. Pestre. Bankspeak. *New Left Review*, 2015.

[24] J. Pennington, R. Socher, and C. D. Manning. Glove: Global vectors for word representation. *EMNLP 2014*, 2014.

[25] A. Saha and V. Sindhwani. Learning evolving and emerging topics in social media: a dynamic nmf approach with temporal regularization. In *WSDM*, 2012.

[26] K. Sparck Jones and van Rijsbergen C. Report on the need for and provision of an" ideal" information retrieval test collection. *British Library Research and Development Report 5266*, 1975.

[27] S. Wang, S. Schlobach, and M. Klein. Concept drift and how to identify it. *Web Semantics*, 2011.

[28] X. Wang and A. McCallum. Topics over time: a non-markov continuous-time model of topical trends. In *SIGKDD*, 2006.

[29] D. T. Wijaya and R. Yeniterzi. Understanding semantic change of words over centuries. In *DETECT*, 2011.

Balancing Novelty and Salience: Adaptive Learning to Rank Entities for Timeline Summarization of High-impact Events

Tuan Tran, Claudia Niederée, Nattiya Kanhabua, Ujwal Gadiraju, and Avishek Anand

L3S Research Center / Leibniz Universität Hannover, Germany

{ttran, niederee, kanhabua, gadiraju, anand}@L3S.de

ABSTRACT

Long-running, high-impact events such as the Boston Marathon bombing often develop through many stages and involve a large number of entities in their unfolding. Timeline summarization of an event by key sentences eases story digestion, but does not distinguish between what a user remembers and what she might want to re-check. In this work, we present a novel approach for timeline summarization of high-impact events, which uses entities instead of sentences for summarizing the event at each individual point in time. Such entity summaries can serve as both (1) important memory cues in a retrospective event consideration and (2) pointers for personalized event exploration. In order to automatically create such summaries, it is crucial to identify the "right" entities for inclusion. We propose to learn a ranking function for entities, with a dynamically adapted trade-off between the in-document salience of entities and the informativeness of entities across documents, i.e., the level of new information associated with an entity for a time point under consideration. Furthermore, for capturing collective attention for an entity we use an innovative soft labeling approach based on Wikipedia. Our experiments on a real large news datasets confirm the effectiveness of the proposed methods.

Categories and Subject Descriptors H.3.3 [Information Storage and Retrieval]: Information Search and Retrieval

General Terms Algorithms, Experimentation

Keywords Entity Retrieval, Timeline Summarization, Wikipedia, Learning to Rank, News, Temporal Ranking

1. INTRODUCTION

High-impact, real-world events often unfold in an unexpected way, dynamically involving a variety of entities. This is especially true for long-running events when full information about the event and its development becomes available only in the course of days after the happening, as in the case of a recent Germanwings airplane crash. In this paper,

Figure 1: Entity Timeline for the 2015 Germanwings Plane Crash Event

we study event timeline summarization and present a novel method which shows key entities at different time points of an event thus capturing this dynamic event unfolding. In contrast to other work in event summarization [34, 23], our *entity timelines* use entities instead of sentences as main units of summarization as depicted in the case of the 2015 Germanwings plan crash (Figure 1). Such summaries can be easily digested and used both as starting points for personalized exploration of event details, and for retrospective revisiting. The latter can be triggered by a new similar event, or by a new twist in the story. For example, the testimonial of the captain in the Costa Concordia trial in late 2014 triggered a revisiting of the disaster in 2012.

From a cognitive perspective, for event revisiting, we rather create "memory cues" to support remembering the unfolded events than summaries for rehearsing the details. In fact, memory cues can be regarded as "a circumstance or piece of information which aids the memory in retrieving details not re-called spontaneously" (Oxford online dictionary, 2015). In this sense, our work is related to the idea of designing or creating memory cues for real-life remembering [29]. Entities such as persons and locations have been identified as very effective external memory cues [2]. In addition, the importance of entities in event summarization has also been shown in recent work [24, 25].

For creating an entity timeline,the entities to be used in the summary have to be chosen carefully. They should 1) be characteristic for a respective time point of the event, 2) not be repetitive (if nothing new happened with respect to the entities), 3) be associated to relevant event information, and 4) be interesting to the reader. For this purpose, we propose an approach to entity summarization, which dynamically combines *entity salience* with the *informativeness* of entities at a considered point in time. Entity salience, on

Permission to make digital or hard copies of all or part of this work for personal or classroom use is granted without fee provided that copies are not made or distributed for profit or commercial advantage and that copies bear this notice and the full citation on the first page. Copyrights for components of this work owned by others than ACM must be honored. Abstracting with credit is permitted. To copy otherwise, or republish, to post on servers or to redistribute to lists, requires prior specific permission and/or a fee. Request permissions from permissions@acm.org.
CIKM'15, October 19-23, 2015, Melbourne, VIC, Australia.
Copyright 2015 ACM 978-1-4503-3794-6/15/10 ...$15.00
http://dx.doi.org/10.1145/2806416.2806486.

the one hand, considers the property of being in the focus of attention in a document has been studied in previous work [5, 12, 10]. In [5], Boguraev and Kennedy use salient text phrases for the creation of so-called *capsule overviews*, whereas recently methods for the identification of salient entities, e.g., in Web pages [12] and news articles [10], have been developed. Informativeness, on the other hand, assesses the level of new information associated with an entity in a text and can be computationally measured using features derived from statistical and linguistic information [33].

In more detail, we aim at optimizing a trade-off between the in-document salience of entities and the informativeness of entities across documents describing the unfolding of an event. Our contributions are:

- We are the first to propose an entity timeline for novel user experience in event exploration and digestion.
- We propose a novel entity ranking model that dynamically learns a trade-off between entity salience and informativeness.
- For training our ranking model, we propose a method for gathering soft labels (or ground truths) by mining collective attention in Wikipedia.

We validate our contributions with experiments on a large real-world news dataset covering various types of events. The rest of the paper is organized as follows. Section 2 discusses the related work. Sections 3 and 4 detail our proposed method. Section 5 discusses features used in learning framework. Section 6 presents the experiments and results. Finally, Section 7 concludes our paper.

2. RELATED WORK

News Summarization. The task of news summarization has been already studied in various contexts, which range from focusing on multi-document summarization [5, 11] to generating a timeline summary for a specific news story [34, 23, 28, 35]. News stories can be complex, having a non-linear structure and associated to multiple aspects. Shahaf et al. [27] propose a novel method for summarizing complex stories using metro maps that explicitly capture the relations among different aspects and display a temporal development of the stories. Instead of using documents or sentences as a information units, we provide a set of entities, as *memory cues*, for supporting event exploration and digestion at each individual point in time. To the best of our knowledge, none of the previous work provides a trade-off solution that balances between content-based and collective attention-based approaches, in supporting the entity-centric summarization.

Entity Ranking and Entity Salience. In recent years, entity retrieval and ranking have gained interest from the IR community moving beyond traditional document retrieval to more specific information about entities in response to a query, e.g., [24, 25]. Although a lot of interesting work on entity ranking has already been proposed, most of previous works have focused on static collections, thus ignoring the temporal dynamics of queries and documents. The relevant work closest to ours in this respect is by Demartini et al. [8], where the task tackled is to identify the entities that best describe the documents for a given query. The entities are identified by analyzing the top-k retrieved documents at the time when the query was issued as well as relevant documents in the past. In IR, salient entities in news documents help improving the performance of document retrieval [25]. There is a body of work in identifying salient entities in general Web [12] and in news domain [10], but the existing work does not take into account the time dimension. Our work targets a different question, using entities as a pivot, and it considers the global context (timeline of the event) as a new dimension of entity salience determination.

Learning to Rank Multiple Criteria. In our work, we apply a learning to rank (L2R) technique to generate timeline summaries in a similar way as done in [28, 23]. In contrast to the previous work, we propose a novel joint learning method, which optimizes different aspects of an event. The model is able to distinguish the aspects semantically. We also incorporate the time effect (i.e., decay) into the joint model, making our learning to rank time-sensitive and suitable for timeline summarization.

3. OVERVIEW

3.1 Preliminaries

Long-running Event. Following [23], we define a long-running event as "a newsworthy happening in the world that is significant enough to be reported on over multiple days". Each event is represented by a short textual description or a set of keywords q, where we will use q to denote the event in the rest of this paper. For example, the bombing incident during Boston Marathon in April 2013 can be described by the terms "boston marathon bombing". We assume that the relevant time frame is split into a sequence of consecutive non-overlapping, equal-sized time intervals $T = \{t_1, \ldots, t_n\}$ in a chronological order, in our case individual days. Furthermore, for a given event q, there is a set of timestamped documents D_q (each with a publication date) reporting on the event. We define a *reporting timeline* $T_q = \{t_{k_1}, \ldots, t_{k_j}\}$ as an ordered list of (not necessarily consecutive) those time periods t_{k_i} in T, which contain the publication date of at least document in D_q. Finally, we denote the set of all documents about q published within a time period t_{k_i} as $D_{q,i}$.

Entity. We are interested in named entities mentioned in documents, namely, persons, organizations, locations. An entity e can be identified by a canonical name, and can have multiple terms or phrases associated with e, called **labels**, which refer to the entity. We call an appearance of an entity label in a document, a **mention** of e, denoted by m. We define E_q as the set of all entities mentioned in D_q. Furthermore, we define the text snippet surrounding m (e.g., sentence or phrases) as the **mention context**, denoted $c(m)$.

Entity Salience and Informativeness. Similarly to [10], we define the entity salience as the quality of "being in the focus of attention" in the corresponding documents. Another relevant aspect considered for selecting entities to be included in an event timeline is *informativeness* [12], which imposes that selected entities in an evolving event should also deliver novel information when compared to the past information. For example, although the airline "Germanwings" stays relevant for many articles reporting on the plane crash, it will only be considered as informative, if new information about the airline becomes available.

Problem. Given a long-running event q, a time interval t_i in its reporting timeline T_q, and the set of entities E_q, we aim to identify the top-k salient and informative entities for supporting the exploration and digestion of q at t_i.

3.2 Approach Overview

We tackle this problem by learning a function for ranking entities, which is aimed at optimizing the trade-off between in-document entity salience and the informativeness of entities across documents:

$$y_t^{(q)} = f(\mathbf{E}, \omega_{\text{s}}, \omega_{\text{i}}), f \in \mathcal{F} \tag{1}$$

where $y_t^{(q)}$ is the vector of ranking scores for entities in E_q at time interval t, $\mathbf{E}$ is a matrix composed from feature vectors of entities in E_q extracted from their mention contexts. $\omega_{\text{s}}, \omega_{\text{i}}$ are the unknown parameter vectors for ranking entities based on salience and informativeness, respectively.

In our work, a ranking function is based on a learning-to-rank technique [19]. A general approach for learning-to-rank is to optimize a defined loss function L given manual annotation or judgments $\mathbf{y}_j^{(q)}$ of entities for a set of training events $\mathcal{Q}$ within the time intervals T_q:

$$\hat{f} = \arg\min_{f \in \mathcal{F}} \sum_{q \in \mathcal{Q}} \sum_{t_j \in T_q} L(f(\mathbf{E}_j^{(q)}, \omega_{\text{s}}, \omega_{\text{i}}), \mathbf{y}_j^{(q)}) \tag{2}$$

Two major challenges must be taken into account when learning a ranking function defined in Equation 2. First, we need a reliable source for building judgments (ground truths) for annotating entities by considering their salience with respect to a given event. In addition, the judgments must be dynamically adapted to the evolving of entities along the unfolding event, i.e., bearing of novel information. Second, the models of our two aspects $\omega_{\text{s}}, \omega_{\text{i}}$ must be unified to produce a joint learned function for ranking entities. In the subsequent sections, we will explain our proposed method for these challenges in more detail.

3.3 Framework

Figure 2 gives an overview of our entity ranking framework covering both the training and the application/testing phase.

Given one event q, its reporting timeline, and the set of documents D_q (in practice, D_q can be given a priori, or can be retrieved using different retrieval models) we identify the entity set E_q using our entity extraction, which consists of named entity recognition, co-reference and context extraction (Section 4.1).

When the event is used for training (training phase), we link a subset of E_q to Wikipedia concepts, which comprises the popular and emerging entities of the event. To facilitate the learning process, these entities are softly labeled using view statistics from Wikipedia (Section 4.2), serving as training instances. Although we use popular entities for training, we design the features such that it can be generalized to arbitrary entities, independent from Wikipedia.

The next component in our framework is the adaptive learning that jointly learns the salience and informativeness models, taking into account the diverse nature of events and their evolution. (Section 4.4).

In the application phase, entity and feature extraction are applied the same as in training phase. First, the input event and time interval is examined against the joint models to return the adaptive scores (details in Section 4.5). Then, entities are put into an ensemble ranking, using the adapted models, to produce the final ranks for the summary.

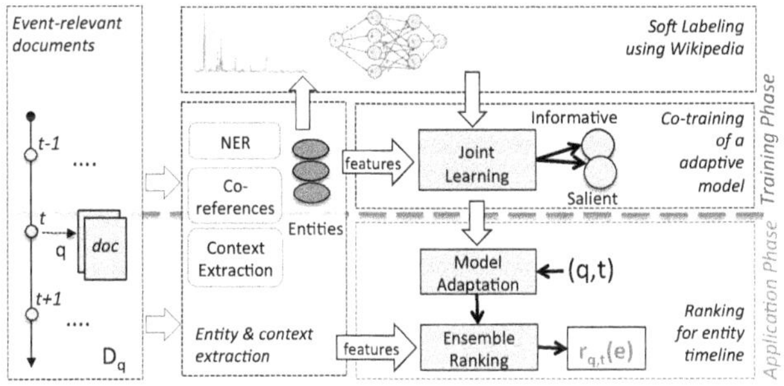

Figure 2: Overview of the Entity-centric Summarization Framework

4. METHODOLOGY

4.1 Entity Extraction

First, we discuss how we can extract entities, the key units in our framework. For each document in the set, , we employ a named entity recognizer to identify mentions of entities in three categories (persons, locations and organizations). For each mention, we include the containing sentences as the context. Mentions that do not contain any alphabetical characters or only stop words are removed.

We additionally use intra- and cross-document co-reference to track mentions pertaining to the same entity. First, an intra-document co-reference system is employed to identify all co-reference chains for entity mentions within a document. We include each reference in the chain together with its sentence to the set of mention contexts of the entity. Second, to identify mentions that potentially refer to the same real-world entity across documents, we adapt the state-of-the-art cross-document co-reference method proposed by Lee et al.[22]. This method first clusters documents based on their content using an Expectation Maximization (EM) algorithm, then iteratively merges references (verbal and nominal) to entities and events in each cluster.

Speeding up co-reference resolution. To speed up the computation, we do not use EM clustering as [22], but employ a set of heuristics, which have proven to be effective in practice. First, we only consider cross-document co-references from documents of the same day. Second, instead of clustering an entire document set, we use mentions with their contextual sentences (kept in the order of their appearance in the original documents) as "pseudo-documents" for the clustering. Third, we assume that mentions to the same entity have similar labels. Hence, we represent entity mention labels as vectors using two-grams (for instance, "Obama" becomes "ob", "ba", "am", "ma") and apply LSH clustering [15] to group similar mentions. LSH has been proven to perform well in entity disambiguation tasks [17], and it is much faster than the standard EM-based clustering.

Finally, for each entity mention, we merge its contextual sentences with those of all other references of the same co-reference chain to obtain the event-level context for an entity , which will be used as inputs for constructing the entity features. We note that while we are aware of other methods to increase the quality of entity extraction by linking them to a knowledge base such as YAGO or DBpedia, we choose not to limit our entities to such knowledge bases, so as to be able to identify and rank more entities in the "long tail".

4.2 Mining Wikipedia for Soft Labeling

In the following, we explain how the training data is generated. Specifically, given an event q, an interval t and an entity e, we aim to automatically generate the score $y_j^{(q)}$ such that $y_j^{(q)}(e) > y_j^{(q)}(e')$ if the entity e is more prominent than the entity e' with respect to the event q at time t. This score can be used as a soft labelling to learn the ranking functions mentioned in Equation 2. The use of soft labeling for entities' salience has already been proposed in [12], where user click behaviour in query logs is used as an indicator for entity salience scores. Dunnietz et al. [10] proposed treating entities in news headlines as salient, and propagate those salience scores to other entities via the PageRank algorithm. The limitation of these measures is that they restrict the assessment of salience to the scope of individual documents, and do not consider the temporal dimension. In contrast, our soft labels are evolving, i.e., an entity can have different labels for one event at different time intervals.

The soft labeling is based on the assumption that for globally trending news event, prominence of related entities can be observed by the collective attention paid to resources representing the entities. For instance, during the Boston marathon bombing, Wikipedia pages about the bomber *Tsarnaev* were created and viewed 15,000 times after one day, indicating their strong salience driven by the event. For soft labeling, we exploit the page view statistic of Wikipedia articles, which reflects the interest of users in an entity: Most obviously, Wikipedia articles are viewed for currently popular entities indicating entity salience. However, taking the encyclopedic character of Wikipedia into account, Wikipedia articles are also viewed in expectation of new information about an entity indicating its (expected) informativeness, especially in the context of an ongoing event. Actually, Wikipedia has gained attention in recent years as a source of temporal event information [32]. Event-triggered bursts in page views, as they are for example used in [7] for event detection, are thus a good proxy for the interestingness of an event-related entity at a considered point in time, which is influenced both by the salience and the informativeness of the event.

Therefore, we propose a new metric called *View Outlier Ratio* or VOR to approximate the soft labels for a combined measure of entity salience and informativeness as follows. For each entity e and for a given time interval t_i, we first construct the time series of view count from the corresponding Wikipedia page of e in the window of size w:

$$T_e = [v_{e,i-w}, v_{e,i-w+1}, \dots v_{e,i}, v_{e,i+1}, \dots v_{i+w}]$$

where each $v_{e,j}$ is the view count of the Wikipedia page of e at t_j. From T_e we calculate the median $m_{e,i}$ and define VOR as follows.

DEFINITION 1. *The View Outlier Ratio is the ratio of difference between the entity view and the median:*

$$vor(e_i) = \frac{|v_{e,i} - m_{e,i}|}{\max(m_{e,i}, m_{min})} \quad (3)$$

where m_{min} is a minimum threshold to regularize entities with too low view activity.

4.3 Unified Ranking Function

We now turn our attention to defining the ranking function in Equation 1. The intuition is that for each event q and time t_i, we rank an entity e higher than others if: (1) e is more relevant to the central parts of documents in $D_{q,i}$ where it appears (salience); and (2) the context of e is more diverse to other contexts (of e or other entities) at $D_{q,i-1}$. Moreover, these two criteria should be unified in an adaptive way that depends on the query, that is, event and time. For example, users interested in a festival might wish to know more about salient entities of the event, while those that follow a breaking story prefer entities with more fresh information. Even for one event, the importance of salience and informativeness might vary over time. For instance, informativeness is more important at the beginning when the event is updated frequently. Based on this intuition, we propose the following ranking function:

$$\mathbf{y_t^{(q)}} = S(q,t)\, \omega_s^T \mathbf{E}_s \; + \; \gamma(t)\, I(q,t) \omega_i^T \mathbf{E}_i \quad (4)$$

where $\mathbf{E}_s$ is the $|E_q| \times M$ matrix representing the M dimensional feature vectors of entities used to learn the salience score (M is the number of salience features), and $\mathbf{E}_i$ is the $|E| \times N$ is the matrix of N dimensional informativeness feature vectors (N is the number of informativeness features). $S(q,t)$ and $I(q,t)$ represent the scores of salience and informativeness tendency for an event q at t. Here we introduce another factor, $\gamma(t)$, which is the decay function of time t, controlling how much the informativeness should have impact on the overall ranking. The rationale of γ is that when the distance between two time intervals t_i and t_{i-1}[1] is long, informativeness has less impact on the overall ranking. For example, if there are only reports about the news after one year (anniversary of a past event), the changes of entities in that long time period should not contribute much to the informativeness criterion.

4.4 Multi-criteria Learning Model

We now discuss how to learn the above ranking function using Equation 2. A straightforward way is to learn the two models ω_s and ω_i separately, and assign values to S, I in a pre-defined manner, then aggregate into Equation 4. However, this is not desirable, since it requires to build two sets of training data for salience and informativeness at the same time, which is expensive. Secondly, previous work has pointed out that a "hard" classification of query based on intent itself is a difficult problem, and can harm the ranking performance [14]. In this work, we exploit the *divide and conquer* (DAC) learning framework in [3] as follows. We define $\mathbf{E}^*$ as the $|E| \times (M+N)$ matrix of $(M+N)$ dimensional *extension vectors* from the corresponding vectors of $\mathbf{E}_s$ and $\mathbf{E}_i$ matrices. Similarly, we define ω_s^* as the $(M+N)$ extension vectors of zero vector $\mathbf{0}$, and the vectors ω_s, and ω_i^* as the $(N+M)$ extension vector of ω_i and $\mathbf{0}$. With this transformation, Equation 4 can be written as:

$$y_t^{(q)} = S(q,t)\, g(\mathbf{E}^*, \omega_s^*) \; + \; \gamma(t)\; I(q,t) g(\mathbf{E}^*, \omega_i^*) \quad (5)$$

where $g(\mathbf{E}^*, \omega) = \omega^T \mathbf{E}^*$ is a linear function. Incorporating Equations 2 and 5, we can co-learn the models ω_s^*, ω_i^* (and thus ω_s, ω_s) simultaneously, using any loss functions. For instance, if we use hinge loss as in [3], we can then adapt the RankSVM [19], an algorithm that seeks to learn the linear function g in (5) by minimizing the number of misordered

[1] note that news events are not always reported on consecutive time intervals

document pairs. For completeness, we describe here the traditional objective function of RankSVM:

$$\min_{\omega,\xi_{q,t,a,b}} \frac{1}{2}\|\omega\|^2 + c \sum_{q,t,a,b} \xi_{q,t,a,b} \text{ , } s.t. \tag{6}$$

$$\omega^T \mathbf{E}^{*(q)}_{t,a} \geq \omega^T \mathbf{E}^{*(q)}_{t,b} + 1 - \xi_{q,t,a,b} \forall \mathbf{E}^{*(q)}_{t,a} \succ \mathbf{E}^{*(q)}_{t,b}, \xi_{q,t,a,b} \geq 0$$

where $\mathbf{E}^{*(q)}_{t,a} \succ \mathbf{E}^{*(q)}_{t,b}$ implies that entity a is ranked higher than entity b for the event q at time t, $\xi_{q,t,a,b}$ denotes slack variables, and c sets the trade-off between the training error and model complexity. If we change the linear function g to f, we can adapt (2) into (6) to obtain the following objective function:

$$\min_{\omega,\xi_{q,t,a,b}} \frac{\|\omega_{\mathrm{s}}\|^2 + \|\omega_{\mathrm{i}}\|^2}{2} + c \sum_{q,t,a,b} \xi_{q,t,a,b} \quad \text{s.t.}$$

$$S(q,t)g(\mathbf{E}^{*(q)}_{t,a}, \omega^*_{\mathrm{s}}) + \gamma(t)I(q,t)g(\mathbf{E}^{*(q)}_{t,a}, \omega^*_{\mathrm{i}}) \geq \tag{7}$$

$$S(q,t)g(\mathbf{E}^{*(q)}_{t,b}, \omega^*_{\mathrm{s}}) + \gamma(t)I(q,t)g(\mathbf{E}^{*(q)}_{t,b}, \omega^*_{\mathrm{i}}) + 1 - \xi_{q,t,a,b},$$

$$\forall \mathbf{E}^{*(q)}_{t,a} \succ \mathbf{E}^{*(q)}_{t,b}, \xi_{q,t,a,b} \geq 0$$

4.5 Event-based Models Adaptation

The adaptive scores $S(q,t), I(q,t)$ and the decay function $\gamma(t)$ is critical to adapting the salience and informativeness models. A naïve supervised approach to pre-define the categories for event (S, I) is impractical and detrimental to ranking performance if the training data is biased. Instead, previous work on query-dependent ranking [14, 3] often exploit the "locality property" of query spaces, i.e., features of queries of the same category are more similar than those of different categories. Bian et al.[3] constructed query features using top-retrieved documents, and clustered them via a mixture model. However, the feature setting is the same for all clusters, making it hard to infer the semantics of the query categories.

In this work, we inherit and adjust the approach in [3] as follows. For each event q and time t, we obtain all entities appearing in $D_{q,t}$ to build the "pseudo-feedback" for the query (q,t). We then build the query features from the pseudo-feedback as follows. From each matrix $\mathbf{E}_{\mathrm{s}}, \mathbf{E}_{\mathrm{i}}$, we take the *mean* and *variance* of the feature values of all entities in the pseudo feedback. As a result, each pair (q,t) is mapped into two feature vectors (with $2M$ and $2N$ dimensions) corresponding to the salience and informativeness spaces. In each space, we use Gaussian Mixture model to calculate the centroid of the training queries, and use the distance of the query feature vector to the centroid as its corresponding adaptive score:

$$C(q,t) = 1 - \frac{\|\mathbf{x}^{q,t}_C - \mathbf{x}^C\|^2}{\max_{q' \in \mathcal{Q}, t' \in T_{q'}} \|\mathbf{x}^{q',t'}_C - \mathbf{x}^C\|^2} \tag{8}$$

where $C \in \{I, S\}$ indicates the event categories, $\mathbf{x}^{q,t}_C$ is the query feature in the feature space of C, and $\mathbf{x}^C$ is the centroid of feature vectors in training set $\mathcal{Q}$ in the corresponding space. The scores are scaled between 0 and 1.

Decayed Informativeness. The decay function $\gamma(t_i)$ adjusts the contribution of informativeness into the adaptive model and is defined by:

$$\gamma(t_i) = \alpha^{\lambda \frac{|t_i - t_{i-1}|}{\mu}} \tag{9}$$

where λ, α are parameters ($0 < \alpha < 1, \lambda > 0$), and μ is the interval unit distance. Equation 9 represents the time impact onto the informativeness of entities: When the time lag between two intervals is high, the difference in contexts of entities between them is less likely to correlate with the informativeness quality of entities.

5. ENTITY RANKING FEATURES

We now discuss the salience and informativeness features for entity ranking. Ranking features are extracted from event documents where the entity appears as follows. These features, called *individual features*, are extracted two different levels. First, at **context** level, features are extracted independently from each mention and its contexts. Features of this level include mention word offset, context length, or importance scores of the context within the document using summarization algorithms (SumBasic or SumFocus features). Second, at **label** level, features are extracted from all mentions, for instance aggregated term (document) frequencies of mentions.

Based on the individual features, the entity features are constructed as follows. For each entity and feature dimension, we have the list of feature values $(z_1, z_2, \ldots, z_n)$, where z_i is the individual feature of label or mention categories. For label level, we simply take the average of z_i's over all entity labels. For mention level, each z_i is weighted by the the confidence score of the document containing the corresponding mention and context. Such confidence score can be calculated by several ways, for instance by a reference model (e.g., BM25) when retrieving the document, or by calculating the authority score of the document in the collection (e.g., using PageRank algorithm). For all features, we apply quantile normalization, such that all individual features (and thus entity aggregated features) are scaled between $[0, 1]$. Below we describe the most important features.

5.1 Salience Features

Context Importance Features. One important evidence of entity salience is context of the entity mentions. It is well-known that text at the beginning of document contains more salient information [12, 10]. Besides position, the content of sentences, per se or in relations with other sentences, also indicates the salience of entities. We apply SumBasic [26] and LexRank [11] summarization algorithms to obtain the scores of contexts (features Sum-B and PR, respectively).

Human-perceived Salience Features. Entity salience can be assessed by reader's intentions or interests [12], and recent study suggests that user interest in entities can be attracted via serendipity in texts [6]. We follow this direction and apply features presented in[6], namely setimentality, attitudes, and readability scores of each mention context. For readability, we also include two other standard metrics, Gunning Fog index [16] and Fleisch-Kincaid index [20].

Query-related Features. Another class of salience features involves ones that are dependent on the event queries. Following [31], we use the overlap between contexts and the event query at the unigram, bigram levels, and at bigram where tokens are tolerable to have 4 words in between (Bi4 feature). We also compute the query-focused SumFocus [30] score of contexts as another feature. It is worth noting that for all of these features, the event queries used are the ones that have been extended using the query expansion (see Event Document and Timelines, Section 6.1).

Salience features		Informativeness features	
Feature(s)	**Description**	**Feature(s)**	**Description**
Tf / Df (M)	Term / Doc. frequency of mention in $D_{q,i}$	PTf / Pdf (M)	Term / Doc. frequency of mention in $D_{q,i-1}$
WO / SO (C)	Word / sent. offset of mention in context	CoEntE (M)	Number of co-occurring entities in $D_{q,i-1}$
SentLen (C)	Context length with/without stopwords	CTI(C)	CTI score of mention given its context in $D_{q,i}$ and $D_{q,i-1}$ [33]
Sent-5 /-10 (C)	Context length with/without stopwords > 5/10 ?		
1- / 2- / 3-Sent (C)	Is context among 1/3/5 first sentences ?	TDiv (C,M)	Topic diversity of context in $D_{q,i}$, $D_{q,i-1}$
TITLE (M)	Is the mention in titles of any $d \in D_{q,i}$?	CosSim (C)	Cosine similarity of context in $D_{q,i}$, $D_{q,i-1}$
CoEntM (M)	No. of entities in same context as mention	DisSim (C)	Distributional similarity of context in $D_{q,i}$, $D_{q,i-1}$
Sum-B / -F (C)	SumBasic / SumFocus score of context		
Uni / Bi / Bi4 (C)	Uni-/Bi-/skip-Bigram overlap with query	EntDif (M)	Entity difference of context in $D_{q,i}$, $D_{q,i-1}$
Att / Sent (C)	Attitude / Sentimentality score of context	TITLEP (M)	Is the mention in titles of any $d \in D_{q,i-1}$?
Read-1 / -2 / -3 (C)	Fleisch / Fog / Kincaid readability scores	NewsFracP (M)	Frac. of news-specific terms in $D_{q,i-1}$
PR (C)	Sentence centrality score (PageRank)		
POS (C)	POS-tag of mention in context		
NewsFrac (M)	Fraction of news-specific terms co-occurring with mention		

Table 1: Selected Informativeness and Salience Features for Entity Ranking at Label (M) and Context (C) Level

5.2 Informativeness Features

Informativeness for words has been studied extensively in linguistics community. We adapt the state-of-the-art measure [33], which incorporates the context of mentions. Given a mention m of entity e, the context-aware informativeness score of m for event q at t_i is defined by:

$$inf(m,i) = \begin{cases} 1 & U_{q,i-1} = \emptyset \\ \frac{\sum_{c' \in U_{q,i-1}} \kappa(c',c(m)) s(d_{c'},q,i-1)}{|U_{q,i-1}|} & U_{q,i-1} \neq \emptyset \end{cases}$$

where $U_{q,i-1}$ is the set of mention contexts of e in $D_{q,i-1}$, $d_{c'}$ is the document consisting the context c', $\kappa(c', c(m))$ is the sentence dis-similarity, and $s(d_{c'}, q, i-1)$ is the retrieval score of $d_{c'}$. We normalize the metric to $[0, 1]$, and set it to 1, when the entity first appears in $D_{q,i}$. To measure $\kappa(c', c(m))$, we can employ different strategies, leading to different features:

CTI. The most straightforward strategy is to employ a lexicon for the sentence similarity. We use the NESim method [9] for this strategy.

Topic Diversity. Besides lexicon-based, we also calculate the informativeness on a higher level by representing contexts by latent topics, using latent Dirichlet Allocation model [4]. Topic diversity of a context c w.r.t other context c' of the same entity on previous time interval is defined as

$$\kappa(c', c(m)) = \sqrt{\sum_{k=1}^{\tau} (p(\psi_k|c(m)) - p(\psi_k|c'))^2}$$

where τ is the number of topics and ψ_k is the topic index.

Distributional Similarity. Another strategy uses Kullback-Leibler divergence for the dissimilarity:

$$DisSim(c', c(m)) = -KL(\theta_{c(m)}, \theta_{c'}) = \quad (10)$$

$$-\sum_{w_i} P(w_i|\theta_{c(m)}) \log \frac{P(w_i|\theta'_c))}{P(w_i|\theta_c(m))} \quad (11)$$

where θ_d and θ_c are the language models for contexts c', c. We use Dirichlet smoothing method for scarce words.

Label Level. Besides context level, we also calculate a number of features at label level, by aggregating the mention features over $D_{q,i-1}$ for event q at time t_i (Table 1). For label-level topic diversity, we use the same metric, but using concatenated contexts instead of individual ones. Additionally, we also calculate the entity difference between two context sets of the same entity in $D_{q,i-1}$ and $D_{q,i}$:

$$EntDif(e) = \|CoEnt_i(e) \cap \overline{CoEnt_{i-1}(e)}\|$$

where $CoEnt_i(e)$ is set of co-occurring entities of e in $D_{q,i}$.

6. EXPERIMENTS AND EVALUATIONS

6.1 Setup

Datasets. For our experiments, we work with a real-world, large-scale news dataset. Specifically, we use KBA 2014 Filtered Stream Corpus (SC14) dataset, which is used for TREC 2014 Temporal Summarization track[2]. We extract news and mainstream articles from the dataset, consisting of 7,592,062 documents. The dataset covers 15 long-running news events from December 2012 to April 2013. All events are high-impact, discussed largely in news media, and have their own Wikipedia pages. Each event has a predefined time span (ranging from 4 to 18 days), and is represented by one textual phrase that is used as the initial event query. Based on the event type (available in the dataset), we group the events into 4 categories: Accident, riot and protest, natural disaster, crime (shooting, bombing).

Event Documents. To construct the event document set for the study, we firstly group the documents into individual days by their publication timestamps, and index documents for each day. In total, this results in 126 different indices. For each index, we remove boilerplate texts from document using Boilerpipe [21], skip stop words, and lemmatize the terms. Then we use the pre-defined textual phrases of the events, issue it as a query to the corresponding indices (indices of days within the event period), retrieving from each the top 10 documents using BM25 weighting model. We improve the results using Kullback-Leibler query expansion [18], and add top 30 expanded terms to construct the event query q used for query-related features computation.

Timelines. To build the reporting timeline T_q, for each event, we manually go through all the days of the event pe-

[2] `http://s3.amazonaws.com/aws-publicdatasets/trec/kba/index.html`

riod, check the content of the top-retrieved document, and remove the day from the timeline if this top-ranked documents is not about the event. In total, we have 153 pairs (*event,day*) for all event reporting timelines.

Entities. We use Stanford parser to recognize named entities from the boilerplated content of the documents, and match them with the entities detected by BBN's Serif tool (provided in SC14 corpus) to reduce noise. For the matching entities, we use the in-document co-reference chains, which are available in SC14, and apply the cross-document coreference (Section 4.1) to group mentions to entities. We use the sentences as the mention contexts. In total, we detect 72,267 named entities from the corpus, with an average of 5.04 contexts per each.

Training Data. From 153 (*event,day*) pairs, we randomly choose 4 events belonging to 4 different categories mentioned above as a training data, resulting in 39 pairs. To build training entities (i.e. to identify subset of entities to Wikipedia concepts, see Section 4.1), we apply two named entity disambiguation softwares, WikipediaMiner and Tagme. These are the supervised machine learning tools to identify named entities from natural language texts and link them to Wikipedia. We train the models of both the tools from a Wikipedia dump downloaded in 2014 July, so as to cover all possible entities in the SC14 corpus. We only use entities co-detected by both the tools, resulting in 402 distinct entities and 665 training tuples (*entity,event,day*). We use the Wikipedia page view dataset, which is publicly available, to build the soft labels for these entities.

Parameter Settings. We modify RankSVM for our joint learning tasks. Features are normalized using the Standard scaling. We tune parameters via grid search with 5-fold cross validation and set trade-off parameter $c = 20$. WikipediaMiner and Tagme tools are used with default parameter settings. For the decay parameters, given the rather small time range of events in our dataset, we empirically set $\lambda = 2, \alpha = 0.5, \mu =$ 1day, and leave more advance tuning for future work. For soft labeling, we set the window size w to 10 days, which is the average length of reporting timelines. The threshold m_{min} is tuned as followed. For each training pair, a human expert knowing the 4 training events well is presented with the entities, their mention contexts and content of the corresponding document. The expert is asked to put the labels on the entity from "falsely detected", "non-salient entity", "salient but not informative" to "salient and informative". Based on this judgement, we compute VOR scores with m_{min} from 1 to 100, and optimize the rank of entities based on VOR scores using NDCG metric. We find that $m_{min} = 12$ yields the best performance.

6.2 Evaluation

Baselines. We compare our approach with the following competitive baselines.

TAER: Dermatini et al. [8] proposed a learning framework to retrieve the most salient entities from the news, taking into consideration information from documents previously published. This approach can be considered as "salience-pro", since the entity salience is measured within a document, although it implicitly complements the informativeness via history documents. We train the model on the same annotated data provided by the author.

IUS[23]: This work represents the "informativeness-pro" approach, it attempts to build update summaries for events by incrementally selecting sentences, maximizing the gain and coverage with respect to summaries on previous days. Since we are not interested in adaptively determining the cutoff values for the summary, we implement only the learning-to-rank method reported in [23] to score the sentences. We adapt IUS into entity summarization by extracting named entities from each sentence. Then, the ranking score of the entity is calculated as the average of scores of all of its sentences across all documents.

In addition, we evaluate three other variants of our approach. The first two variants involve only salience and informativeness features for learning. We denote these as *SAL* and *INF*. The third variant linearly combines all salience and informativeness features, denoted as *No-Adapt*. All are trained and predicted using the traditional RankSVM.

Evaluation Metrics. We consider the traditional information retrieval performance metrics: precisions, NDCG and MAP. Besides, we also aim to evaluate the performance of ranking in timeline summarization context, where effective systems do not just introduce relevant, but also novel and interesting results compared to the past. This was inspired by recent work in user experience of entity retrieval [13, 6]. One popular metric widely adopted in existing work to measure such user-perceived quality is the *serendipity*, which measures degree to which results are "not highly relevant but interesting" to user taste [1]. Traditional serendipity metric was proposed to contrast the retrieval results with some obvious baseline [6]. In our case, we propose to use serendipity to measure the informativeness and salience by contrasting the results of one day to previous day of the same event:

$$SRDP = \frac{\sum_{e \in UNEXP} rel(e)}{|UNEXP|} \tag{12}$$

where $UNEXP$ is the set of entities not appearing on the previous day, and rel is the human relevance judgment of the entity. The relevance part ensures the salience of the entity, while the $UNEXP$ part ensures the informativeness of the entity over the event reporting timeline.

Assessment Setup.

We exclude the 39 training pairs from the overall 153 (*event,day*) pairs to obtain 114 pairs for testing. For each of these pairs, we pooled the top-10 entities returned by all methods. In total, this results in 3,336 tuples (*entity, event, day*) to be assessed. To accommodate the assessment, we contextualize the tuples as follows. For each tuple, we extract one sentence containing the entity from the document with the highest retrieval score (BM25), using the event as the query and on the index corresponding to the day. If there are several sentences, we extract the longest one. Next, we describe our two assessments setup, expert-based and crowdsource-based.

Expert Assessment. To evaluate the quality of the systems, we employ an expert-based evaluation as follows. 5 volunteers who are IT experts and work on temporal and event analysis were asked to assess on one or several events of their interest. For each event, the assessors were encouraged to check the corresponding Wikipedia page beforehand to gain sufficient knowledge. Then, for each tuple, we add one more contextualizing sentence, extracted from the previous date of the event. If there is no such sentence, a "NIL" string will be presented. We asked the assessors to check the tuple and the two sentences, and optionally, to use search engines to look for more event information on the questioned date. Then, the assessors were asked to assess the importance of the entity with respect to the event and date, in four following scales. **1**: Entity is obviously not relevant to the event; **2**: Entity is relevant to the event, but it has no new information compared to the previous day; **3**: Entity is relevant to the event and linked to new information, but it does not play a salient role in the sentence; **4**: Entity is relevant to the event, has new information, and is salient in the presented sentence. The inter-assessor agreement score for this task is $\kappa = 0.4$ under the Cohen's Kappa score.

Crowdsourced Assessment. In addition, we also set up a larger-scale assessment based on crowdsourcing. We use `Crowdflower.com` platform to deploy the evaluation tasks. Each tuple presented to workers consists of date, short description of the event, entity, and the sentence. Instead of direct asking for salience and informativeness of entities to event and date we decide for a simpler task: Asking the workers to assess entities in two steps: (1) Assessing whether the sentence is obviously relevant to the event (workers assess on a 3-point Likert scale,from "1-Not Relavant" to "3-Obviously Relevant"); and (2) assessing whether the entity is important in the sentence (by virtue of being a subject or object of the sentence, binary feedback).

Tasks are delivered such that tuples of the same *(event,day)* pair go into one Crowdflower job, thus the worker has a chance to gain knowledge about event on the day and respond faster and more reliably. We pay USD 0.03 for each tuple. To maintain the quality, we follow state-of-the-art guidelines and recommendations, and receive 5 independent responses for each tuple. We create a gold standard for 311 tuples, and discard responses from workers who fail to maintain an agreement of above 70% against the gold standard. In total, we received 20 760 responses, 8 940 from which were qualified. The inter-worker agreement was 98.67% under Pairwise Percent Agreement, with average variance of 42%, indicating a reasonably good quality given the fairly high complexity of the task.

6.3 Results and Discussion

The upper part of Table 2 summarizes the main results of our experiments from the expert evaluation. The results show the performance of the two baselines (*TAER* and *IUS*) and of the consideration of Salience and Informativeness features in isolation with respect to precision. In general, all performances are low, indicating the relatively high complexity of this new task. In addition, as can be seen from this part of the table, even the approach relying on our salience features or informativeness features in isolation already outperforms the two baselines. This is due to the fact that our approach does not consider documents in isolation as the baselines do. Rather, we take a more comprehensive view considering event level instead of document level features via feature aggregation. In more details, the first baseline (*TAER*) employs a quite restricted features for entity ranking (e.g. document frequency), and thus fails to identify important entities event-wise.

Furthermore, the results also show the performance of the non-adaptive combination of salience and informativeness (*No-Adapt*) as well as our approach (*AdaptER*), which uses an adaptive combination of informativeness and saliency. It becomes clear that an improvement by combining the salience and the informativeness features over the use of the isolated features can only be achieved by fusing the two features in a more sophisticated way: *No-Adapt* does not perform better than the maximum of *SAL* and *INF* ($MAX(S,I)$), it even performs worse in under some metrics such as P@10. In contrast, *AdaptER* clearly outperforms the maximum of *SAL* and *INF* as well as its non-adaptive version for most metrics. For instance, we achieve 16% improvement of MAP scores as compared with the $MAX(S,I)$.

Besides precision, we also consider serendipity (SRDP) as a complementary measure in our experiments, as discussed above. This metric measures how likely the approach brings unseen and interesting results to the user. Under SRDP, our approach outperforms significantly both the baseline and the maximum of *SAL* and *INF*. We achieve 14% improvement of serendipity at top-1 entities, and 29% at top-3 entities. Thus, our top-retrieved entities do not only cover relevance, but are also more interesting, often unseen on the previous day (contributing to more informative results).

The lower part of the Table 2 shows the same results for the crowdsourced assessment. The same trends of performance can be observed, where our approach outperforms in all the metrics. In comparison to the expert evaluation, the results are overall lower. A possible reason for this is the complexity of the crowdsourcing task, which requires knowledge about the considered event in order to give high quality feedback (see Expert Assessment setup, Section 6.1). Nevertheless, the adaptive model is still able to achieve significant gain, especially under the serendipity measurement.

		P@10	MAP
No-Adapt	Soft-labeled	0.32	0.225
	Supervised	0.346	0.247
AdaptER	Soft-labeled	0.368	0.264
	Supervised	0.357	0.259

Table 3: Performance of systems with(-out) soft labeling

Next, we evaluate the effectiveness of soft labeling in covering salience and informativeness. For this purpose, we manually annotate entities obtained from the reporting timeline of 4 training events, with respect to the salience and informativeness (see Parameter settings, Section 6.1). We then re-train both non-adaptive and adaptive models using this annotated data (supervised approach). Table 3 shows the precision and MAP scores of the supervised approach in comparison to our soft labelling-based approach. The similarity in performance between them, regardless of the models they have been used for, confirms that our soft labelling properly captures both salience and informativeness.

Feature Analysis. Analysing the influence of different feature groups (see Section 5) can give insights into what factors contribute to the entity ranking performance. To study the feature impacts, we do an ablation study and remove incrementally a group of features, and re-evaluate the performance using the expert assessment. Since reducing the feature dimensions directly affects the query features and its adaptive scores, to ensure the fair comparison, we perform the study for the non-adaptive setting. Table 4 shows the MAP scores of ablated models. The symbol ▼ indicates a significant decrease with respect to *No-Adapt* model (with full features), and thus implies the high influence of the corresponding feature group. From the table, we can see that

Method	P@1	P@3	P@10	MAP	SRDP@1	SRDP@3	SRDP@10
Ranking performance from expert assessment							
TAER	0.436	0.315	0.182	0.109	0.315	0.210	0.121
IUS	0.395	0.325	0.236	0.141	0.335	0.217	0.176
SAL	0.493▲	0.423	0.338▲	0.217▲	0.421	0.320	0.240▲
INF	0.480▲	0.436	0.354▲	0.227▲	0.441▲	0.340	0.256▲
MAX(S,I)	0.493	0.436	0.354	0.227	0.441	0.340	0.256
No-Adapt	0.503	0.461	0.320	0.225	0.396	0.338	0.215
AdaptER	**0.546**	**0.485**	**0.368**	**0.264**	**0.507▲**	**0.440▲**	**0.275**
Ranking performance from crowdsourced assessment							
TAER	0.229	0.183	0.106	0.066	0.201	0.146	0.079
IUS	0.258	0.202	0.154	0.092	0.197	0.165	0.119
SAL	0.320	0.279	0.207	0.139	0.279	0.218	0.154
INF	0.313	0.283	0.214	0.146	0.306	0.229▲	0.160
MAX(S,I)	0.320	0.283	0.214	0.146	0.306	0.229	0.160
No-Adapt	0.271	0.252	0.181	0.123	0.236	0.208	0.144
AdaptER	**0.388▲**	**0.340**	**0.237**	**0.178**	**0.361**	**0.361▲**	**0.315▲**

Table 2: Entity-ranking performance using different assessment settings. In each setting, significance is tested against line 1, TAER (within the first group), and line 5, MAX(S,I) (within the second group). Symbol ▲ indicates cases with confirmed significant increase

the most influential feature groups include context importance feature (salience features) and informativeness feature group of context level.

Ablated feature set	MAP
Context importance	0.086▼
Human-perceived	0.097
Informativeness, context level	0.06▼
Informativeness, label level	0.120

Table 4: MAP of No-Adapt when feature groups are ablated (full-feature MAP score: 0.225)

Anecdotic Example. In table 5, we show one example of top-selected entities for the event "Boston marathon bombing 2013". Additionally, we show some selected sentences covering the entities, to enable the understanding of the entities' roles within the event on the presented days. As can be seen, the timeline corresponding to *TAER* approach (upper part) gives more salience credits to entities frequently mentioned throughout the news (such as Boston marathon), keeping them in high ranks throughout the timeline. The approach is not responsive to less salient but interesting entities (such as Pop Francis, a rather unrelated entity to the event, but get involved via his condolecence and activities to victims of the bombing). On the other hand, using an adaptive ranking with informativeness incorporated, the resulting entities are not just more diverse (including related events such as Marathon Bruins), but also expose more new and emerging information.

7. CONCLUSIONS

In this paper, we have presented a novel approach for timeline summarization of high-impact news events, using entities as the main unit of summary. We propose to dynamically adapt between entity salience and informativeness for improving the user experience of the summary. Furthermore, we introduce an adaptive learning to rank framework that jointly learns the salience and informativeness features in a unified manner. To scale the learning, we exploit Wikipedia page views as an implicit signal of user interest towards entities related to high-impact events. Our experiments have shown that the introduced methods considerably improve the entity selection performance, using both small-scale expert-based and large-scale crowdsourced assessments. The evaluation also confirms that integrating salience and informativeness can significantly improve the user experience of finding surprisingly interesting results.

As the problem discussed in the paper is new, there are several promising directions to explore for future work. We aim to investigate further the impact of adaptation in different types of events, using larger and more diverse sets of events. Furthermore, we plan to study more advanced ways to mine Wikipedia temporal information as signals of collective attention towards public events. We are planning to use this for further improving our VOR measure for the soft labeling approach. Other direction includes investigating deeper models to improve the performances of current entity timeline summarization systems, which are quite low.

Acknowledgements. This work was partially funded by the European Commission for the FP7 project ForgetIT (under grant No. 600826) and the ERC Advanced Grant ALEXANDRIA (under grant No. 339233).

8. REFERENCES

[1] P. André, J. Teevan, and S. T. Dumais. From x-rays to silly putty via uranus: serendipity and its role in web search. In *CHI*, 2009.

[2] D. Berntsen. *Involuntary autobiographical memories: An introduction to the unbidden past.* Cambridge University Press, 2009.

[3] J. Bian, X. Li, F. Li, Z. Zheng, and H. Zha. Ranking specialization for web search: a divide-and-conquer approach by using topical ranksvm. In *WWW*, 2010.

[4] D. M. Blei, A. Y. Ng, and M. I. Jordan. Latent dirichlet allocation. *J. Mach. Learn. Res.*, 2003.

April 15	*April 16*	*April 17*
Boston Marathon **Mass General Hospital** **Boston.com**	**Boston** **Boston Marathon** **Vatican**	**Boston Marathon** **Boston** **Boston University**
- Two bombs exploded near the finish of the Boston Marathon on Monday, killing two people, injuring 22 others - At least four people are in the emergency room at Mass General Hospital	Deeply grieved by news of the loss of life and grave injuries caused by the act of violence perpetrated last evening in Boston, His Holiness Pope Francis wishes me to assure you of his sympathy ...	- FBI confirmed that pressure cookers may have been used as explosive devices at the Boston Marathon. - The third victim was identified Wednesday as Boston University graduate student Lingzi Lu.
Boston Marathon **Marathon Bruins** **New York City**	**Pope Francis** **Vatican** **Boston Marathon**	**FBI** **Boston University** **Lingzi Lu**
- Two bombs exploded near the finish of the Boston Marathon on Monday, killing two people, injuring 22 others - The NHL postponed the Boston Bruins' Monday hockey game due to the bombing	The Vatican sent a telegram to Boston Cardinal on Tuesday, in which Pope Francis expresses sympathy for the victims of the marathon bombings...	- FBI confirmed that pressure cookers may have been used as explosive devices at the Boston Marathon. - The third victim was identified Wednesday as Boston University graduate student Lingzi Lu.

Table 5: Examples of top-3 entities on Boston Marathon Bombing 2013 using TAER (top) and AdaptER(bottom) for April 15, 16 and 17

[5] B. Boguraev and C. Kennedy. Salience-based content characterisation of text documents. *ACL*, 1997.

[6] I. Bordino, Y. Mejova, and M. Lalmas. Penguins in sweaters, or serendipitous entity search on user-generated content. In *CIKM*, 2013.

[7] M. Ciglan and K. Nørvåg. Wikipop: Personalized event detection system based on wikipedia page view statistics. In *CIKM*, 2010.

[8] G. Demartini, M. M. S. Missen, R. Blanco, and H. Zaragoza. Taer: time-aware entity retrieval-exploiting the past to find relevant entities in news articles. In *CIKM*, 2010.

[9] Q. Do, D. Roth, M. Sammons, Y. Tu, and V. Vydiswaran. Robust, light-weight approaches to compute lexical similarity. *Computer Science Research and Technical Reports, University of Illinois*, 2009.

[10] J. Dunietz and D. Gillick. A new entity salience task with millions of training examples. *EACL*, 2014.

[11] G. Erkan and D. R. Radev. Lexrank: Graph-based lexical centrality as salience in text summarization. *J. Artif. Intell. Res.(JAIR)*, 22(1):457–479, 2004.

[12] M. Gamon, T. Yano, X. Song, J. Apacible, and P. Pantel. Identifying salient entities in web pages. In *CIKM*, 2013.

[13] M. Ge, C. Delgado-Battenfeld, and D. Jannach. Beyond accuracy: evaluating recommender systems by coverage and serendipity. In *RecSys*, 2010.

[14] X. Geng, T.-Y. Liu, T. Qin, A. Arnold, H. Li, and H.-Y. Shum. Query dependent ranking using k-nearest neighbor. In *SIGIR*, 2008.

[15] A. Gionis, P. Indyk, R. Motwani, et al. Similarity search in high dimensions via hashing. In *VLDB*, volume 99, 1999.

[16] R. Gunning. Judges scold lawyers for bad writing, 1952.

[17] J. Hoffart, S. Seufert, D. B. Nguyen, M. Theobald, and G. Weikum. Kore: keyphrase overlap relatedness for entity disambiguation. In *CIKM*, 2012.

[18] H. Imran and A. Sharan. Improving effectiveness of query expansion using information theoretic approach. In *Trends in Applied Intelligent Systems*. 2010.

[19] T. Joachims. Optimizing search engines using clickthrough data. In *KDD*, 2002.

[20] J. P. Kincaid, R. P. Fishburne Jr, R. L. Rogers, and B. S. Chissom. Derivation of new readability formulas (automated readability index, fog count and flesch reading ease formula) for navy enlisted personnel. Technical report, DTIC Document, 1975.

[21] C. Kohlschütter, P. Fankhauser, and W. Nejdl. Boilerplate detection using shallow text features. In *WSDM*. ACM, 2010.

[22] H. Lee, M. Recasens, A. Chang, M. Surdeanu, and D. Jurafsky. Joint entity and event coreference resolution across documents. In *EMNLP*, 2012.

[23] R. McCreadie, C. Macdonald, and I. Ounis. Incremental update summarization: Adaptive sentence selection based on prevalence and novelty. In *CIKM*, 2014.

[24] X. Meng, F. Wei, X. Liu, M. Zhou, S. Li, and H. Wang. Entity-centric topic-oriented opinion summarization in twitter. In *KDD*, 2012.

[25] Y. Moshfeghi, M. Matthews, R. Blanco, and J. M. Jose. Influence of timeline and named-entity components on user engagement. In *ECIR*. 2013.

[26] A. Nenkova and R. Passonneau. Evaluating content selection in summarization: The pyramid method. In *NAACL-HLT*, 2004.

[27] D. Shahaf, C. Guestrin, and E. Horvitz. Trains of thought: Generating information maps. In *WWW*, 2012.

[28] G. B. Tran, T. Tran, N.-K. Tran, M. Alrifai, and N. Kanhabua. Leverage learning to rank in an optimization framework for timeline summarization. In *TAIA Workshop at SIGIR*, 2013.

[29] E. van den Hoven and B. Egge. The cue is key - design for real-life remembering. *Zeitschrift für Psychologie.*, 222(2):110–117, 2014.

[30] L. Vanderwende, H. Suzuki, C. Brockett, and A. Nenkova. Beyond sumbasic: Task-focused summarization with sentence simplification and lexical expansion. *Information Processing & Management*, 43(6), 2007.

[31] L. Wang, H. Raghavan, V. Castelli, R. Florian, and C. Cardie. A sentence compression based framework to query-focused multi-document summarization. In *ACL*, 2013.

[32] S. Whiting, J. Jose, and O. Alonso. Wikipedia as a time machine. In *WWW*, pages 857–862, 2014.

[33] Z. Wu and C. L. Giles. Measuring term informativeness in context. In *NAACL-HLT*, 2013.

[34] R. Yan, X. Wan, J. Otterbacher, L. Kong, X. Li, and Y. Zhang. Evolutionary timeline summarization: a balanced optimization framework via iterative substitution. In *SIGIR*, 2011.

[35] X. W. Zhao, Y. Guo, R. Yan, Y. He, and X. Li. Timeline generation with social attention. In *SIGIR*, 2013.

Location-Based Influence Maximization in Social Networks

Tao Zhou, Jiuxin Cao*, Bo Liu, Shuai Xu, Ziqing Zhu, Junzhou Luo
Key Laboratory of Computer Network and Information Integration of MoE of China(No.93k-9)
School of Computer Science and Engineering
Southeast University, Nanjing, China
{zhoutao, jx.cao, bliu, xushuai7, zzqxztc, jluo}@seu.edu.cn

ABSTRACT

In this paper, we aim at the product promotion in O2O model and carry out the research of location-based influence maximization on the platform of LBSN. As offline consuming behavior exists under the O2O environment, the traditional online influence diffusion model could not describe the product acceptance accurately. Moreover, the existing researches of influence maximization tend to only concern on the online network of relationships but rarely take the offline part into consideration. This paper introduces the location property into the influence maximization to accord with the characteristic of O2O model. Firstly, we propose an improved influence diffusion model called TP Model which could accurately describe the process of accepting products under the O2O environment. Meanwhile, the definition of location-based influence maximization is presented. Then the user mobility pattern is analyzed and the calculation method of offline probability is designed. Considering the influence ability, a location-based influence maximization algorithm named TPH is proposed. Experiments prove TPH algorithm has general advantage. Finally, focusing on the performance of TPH algorithm under special circumstances, MR algorithm is designed as complement and experiments also verify its high effectiveness.

Categories and Subject Descriptors

J.4 [**Social and Behavioral Sciences**]: Sociology; H.2.8 [**Database Management**]: Database Application—*Data Mining*

General Terms

Algorithms, Experimentation, Performance

Keywords

Diffusion model, influence maximization, LBSN, O2O, social networks

*Contact Author

Permission to make digital or hard copies of all or part of this work for personal or classroom use is granted without fee provided that copies are not made or distributed for profit or commercial advantage and that copies bear this notice and the full citation on the first page. Copyrights for components of this work owned by others than ACM must be honored. Abstracting with credit is permitted. To copy otherwise, or republish, to post on servers or to redistribute to lists, requires prior specific permission and/or a fee. Request permissions from Permissions@acm.org.
CIKM'15, October 19–23, 2015, Melbourne, VIC, Australia.
© 2015 ACM. ISBN 978-1-4503-3794-6/15/10 ...$15.00.
DOI: http://dx.doi.org/10.1145/2806416.2806462.

1. INTRODUCTION

In recent years, social networks become increasingly popular providing important platform for people to share their ideas, activities and interests. Messages and ideas propagate fast through social networks, making it an outstanding environment for the promotion of products and services. Influence maximization is one of the major problems in social networks. It comes from the viral marketing which takes advantage of "word-of-mouth" effect to promote products. Influence maximization could be described as an algorithm problem of determining a certain number of initial users in social network to maximize the spread of influence through the word-of-mouth effect [1].

Existing researches on influence maximization have made significant achievement. However, they tend to focus only on the online social network, against the trend that the business model becomes more likely to connect the online and offline aspects together. The concept of a new business model called O2O draws increasingly more attention of the whole industry. O2O stands for Online to Offline, which means to conduct online promotion and purchasing in order to drive the offline marketing and consuming. The key point is to bring the online consumers to the offline shops. Rather than the physical goods in the traditional B2C model, the transaction subject in O2O model is the life service product such as catering and entertainment.

O2O model brings new challenges to the influence maximization. As we mentioned above, the traditional influence maximization problem lacks the concern about the offline parts of the product promotion and the traditional online influence diffusion model could not offer accurate description about the process of product acceptance any more. The factors that affect the diffusion process are not only the online features like the network topology, but also the offline user properties, because the daily activity area and consuming location preference will greatly affect the probability of accepting the life service product which has location property as the same. Meanwhile, the target of the influence maximization is altered, since the promotion needs to pay attention to the users who are more likely to carry out the consuming behavior in the aspect of the geography for gaining higher benefit. To sum up, the offline phase of the marketing should be regarded as important content when it comes to the O2O environment and we need to consider the influence diffusion model and the influence maximization problem in a location-based way.

O2O model has a close relation with the location-based social network (LBSN). Being different from the traditional one, LBSN could track and share user location information in addition to providing communication approach for the user. There is a new kind of social structure generated by the user location in LBSN [2]. Carrying plenty of information of both social network and location-based behavior, LBSN becomes a nonnegligible platform for the product promotion in O2O model. So for the location-based influence maximization, LBSN would be an important research environment.

In this paper, we will focus on the influence maximization in O2O model based on the real data of LBSN. A new diffusion model for O2O will be designed combining the online and offline parts and the definition of location-based influence maximization problem will be given. We will consider the user location property and make use of historical location information to explore the location preference of user offline consuming behavior. Finally two algorithms called TPH and MR will be presented and the experiments prove the algorithms effective in solving the location-based influence maximization problem.

The remainder of the paper is organized as follows. In Section 2, the related work is presented. The dataset we use in this paper is introduced in Section 3. A new influence diffusion model is proposed and the location-based influence maximization problem based on the model is defined in Section 4. In Section 5, online probability, an important parameter in the model and the problem, is discussed and the calculation method is introduced. Two algorithms for the problem are designed in Section 6 and the performance of them is evaluated. Finally, Section 7 concludes the paper.

2. RELATED WORKS

Influence maximization was first described as an algorithm problem by Domingos and Richardson [1], and was first formulated as a discrete optimization problem by Kempe, Kleinberg and Tardos [3]. Kempe et al. proved that it is an NP-hard problem and gave a greedy optimization algorithm with provable approximation guarantee. However, the greedy algorithm executes monte carlo simulation [4] to obtain the approximated solution of the influenced set size, which faces the shortage of high time complexity.

Some researches aim to improve the greedy algorithm. Leskovec et al. proposed the CELF (Cost-effective Lazy Forward Selection) algorithm [5]. It takes the advantage of submodularity property of influence maximization and greatly reduces the calculation of approximation. Goyal et al. [6] presented CELF++ algorithm which is an improvement of CELF, further decreasing the amount of calculation. Chen et al. [7] proposed two improvements of greedy algorithm: NewGreedy and MixedGreedy algorithms. The former one removes the edges which have no contribution to the influence diffusion to get a smaller graph and the latter one combines CELF with NewGreedy.

Another direction of research is the heuristic algorithm. Compared with greedy algorithm, it has the huge advantage in speed. Basic heuristic algorithms include Max Degree algorithm (selecting nodes according to the degree), distance centrality algorithm (selecting nodes according to the average distance to the other nodes) and so on. In [7], Chen et al. designed the Degree Discount Heuristic algorithm which makes discount to the degree of the neighbors when a node is selected into initial set. Beside the heuristic algorithm using network structure, there are other methods introducing the web search approach into node selecting, such as PageRank [8] and HITS [9] algorithms.

The influence maximization related with location is still a domain remaining to be researched. Li et al. [10] worked on the location-aware influence maximization. In their problem, each user has geographical location and the target users should be located in a given region. The paper proposed two greedy algorithms with 1-1/e approximation ratio and another two algorithms to meet the instant-speed requirement. The existing work considering location information in influence maximization only regards location as a simple user property and has not analyzed the user mobility behaviors. But in the real O2O environment, the influence spreading is closely related with the user location preference. Analysis on the user historical behaviors should be taken and the problem based on the mobility behavior is worthy to be solved.

The existing researches mainly concern about the single aspect of online social network and regard location as a simple property. It is needed to consider the influence maximization problem which describe the real O2O promotion and makes full use of location information. How to model the real problem in O2O environment and design the solution for the proposed problem is the important content of this paper.

3. DATASET

A significant feature and novelty of our research is to describe the objective fact, so we would like to carry out our research on the basis of real data.

LBSN is an important platform for influence diffusion in O2O environment. It contains both user social network and geographic information which could provide conditions for our research. We conduct our research on the dataset of Foursquare, the biggest and the most popular LBSN at present.

As our problem is associated with both the online and offline information, we need to retrieve both the user network and user check-ins at the same time. Because of the API restriction, the user historical check-ins could not be crawled directly. To solve the problem, we make use of the interaction of Foursquare and Twitter. Since users of Foursquare could bind their Twitter account and share their check-ins as tweets on Twitter, we could retrieve the historical tweets of a user and further manipulate the tweets to get the historical check-ins. By this way, we obtain the complete dataset consisting of online social network and offline historical check-ins.

The final dataset we use includes users living in New York and check-ins made in New York, as only the check-ins occurred in the living city of a user could be the reference to determine his or her daily geographic preference. Meanwhile, to a seller who provides life service product, people in the same city would be the main target that might bring long-term and stable benefit, while people out of the same city must be restricted by space and time to conduct the consuming behavior for the product. We extract the New York dataset based on the property of the users and check-ins. In the other aspect, we only concentrate on the consuming check-ins as we are interested in the geographic preference of user consuming behavior. Therefore the data is further filtered according to the category information offered by Foursquare to get the consuming check-in dataset

Table 1: Dataset parameters

Users	10901
Edges	170048
Average degree	15.599
Network diameter	9
Average path length	3.761
Check-ins	764328
Average check-ins	70.115

in New York which contains a variety of consuming behavior types. The basic parameters of the final dataset are listed in Table 1.

4. TWO PHASE MODEL AND LOCATION-BASED INFLUENCE MAXIMIZATION

4.1 Two Phase Model

The influence diffusion process under the O2O environment contains transition between online behavior and offline behavior. When users are influenced by others online, they would take the offline experience first before determining whether to accept the product or not. However, in traditional diffusion model such as Linear Threshold Model (LT) [11] and Independent Cascade Model (IC)[12, 13], only the online diffusion process exists while the offline part is always missing. So a new influence diffusion model is needed to describe the product acceptance considering both online and offline sections.

Whether a user would take an offline experience after being influenced online lies on the location property of both the user and the promoted product, because the consuming behavior of a user is affected by his or her consuming location preference which reflects the daily activity area. The further the product is away from the user daily activity area, the lower the probability is for the user to try out the product offline. Thus for a given product location L, each user has a probability to consume there, which is also the probability to accept the product offline. To introduce the new diffusion model, we first give the following definitions.

Definition 1. **Online Probability** $p_{i,j}^{on}$ The probability that user i successfully influences user j through edge $< i,j >$, which corresponds to the probability in the traditional influence diffusion model. This is a property on edge $< i,j >$.

Definition 2. **Offline probability** $p_{i,L}^{off}$ The probability that user i goes to location L for consuming, which is the probability that user accepts the product offline. This is a property of node i.

There are two phases in our diffusion model: online phase and offline phase, which reflects the process of accepting a product under the O2O circumstances. The model defines four states of a user:

Definition 3. **Inactive state** In this state, the user has not been online influenced by the neighbor.

Definition 4. **Online-active state** In this state, the user has been influenced by the neighbor and accepted the product online, but the offline experience has not been conducted.

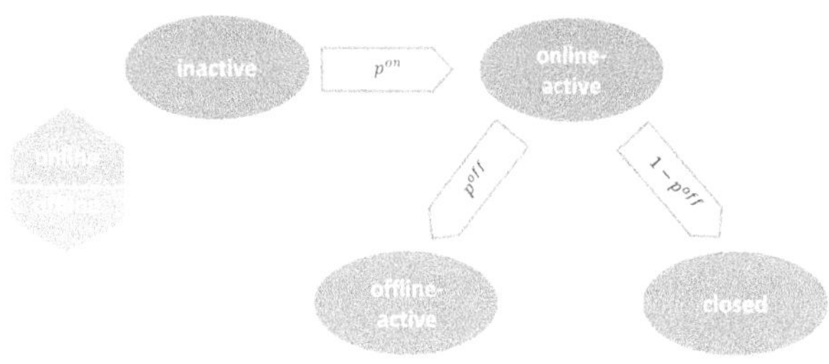

Figure 1: User state transition diagram

Definition 5. **Offline-active state** After transiting into the online-active state, the user steps into the offline phase. The offline-active state means the user has accepted the product offline.

Definition 6. **Closed state** After stepping into the offline phase, the user does not accept the product and moves into the closed state. Thereafter the user could not be influenced anymore and will never transit into any active states.

The user state transition diagram is shown in Fig. 1.

We propose the **Two Phase Model (TP model)** on the basis of the IC model, describing the process of product promotion involving the geographic property. Given a product to be promoted locating in L, and an initial node set A_0 in which the users has already been in the offline-active state, the procedure of the influence diffusion in TP model unfolds in the following discrete steps:

In step t, if node v first becomes offline-active, it will have a chance to activate each currently inactive neighbor w to make w transit into online-active state. The activate attempt succeeds with the online probability $p_{v,w}^{on}$. If v succeeds, w will become online-active in step $t+1$, and then enter into the offline phase. In the offline phase, w may transit into offline-active state with the offline probability $p_{w,L}^{off}$; otherwise it will switch to closed state. No matter whether the activate attempt of v succeeds or not, v cannot try to activate w in the following rounds. If w has more than one neighbor that transit into online-active state in step t, then these neighbors could try to activate w in arbitrary order, but all the attempts must happen in step t. The diffusion process is terminated when there are no more nodes that could get into the offline-active state.

Connections exist between the two phases and four states in TP model. Inactive state and online-active state belong to the online phase, while offline active state and closed state belong to offline phase. The transition from online phase to offline phase starts at the online-active state, which means the user starts an offline experience, and in turn the offline-active state brings the offline behavior back to the online diffusion, which means the user gets back online and continues to activate other users.

In TP model, the offline probability $p_{w,L}^{off}$ is related to the product location L and the consuming location preference of user w, and we will discuss the details in Section 5. On the other hand, the online probability $p_{v,w}^{on}$ could be set or calculated according to the manner of traditional online model, e.g. set the equal value for all the edges or calculate the different probability of each edge according to certain rules. This separation of online and offline probabilities brings relatively high universality and flexibility to TP model.

4.2 Location-based influence maximization

The location-based influence maximization problem under the O2O circumstances is different from the traditional one in multiple aspects. Firstly, the traditional models are not proper anymore and TP model which aims at the O2O model should be adopted instead. Moreover, the target of influence maximization is more specific. As different users have different offline probability to carry out the consuming behavior for the same product, the target users of the promotion should be those who are more likely to conduct the actual consuming behavior. Thus the purpose of this new problem is to have the most target users influenced when the diffusion completes.

The **location-based influence maximization problem** could be formally described as following:

Given a directed graph $G(V, E)$, in which V is the node set representing the users in the social networks, and E is the edge set representing the relations between users. $\forall v_i \in V(1 \leqslant i \leqslant |V|)$, C_i denotes its consuming check-in set, and given a location $L = (lat, lon)$, v_i has the offline probability $p^{off}_{v_i,L}$ representing the probability with which v_i will consume in location L.

Given a TP Model, the initial nodes number k and the product location $L = (lat, lon)$, the location-based influence maximization problem is to find a set of initial nodes $S \subseteq V$, $|S| = k$, and after the diffusion completes according to the TP model, the final influenced target nodes could be the most. Here, the target nodes satisfies $p^{off}_{v_i,L} > \theta$, where θ is a given threshold.

The threshold θ could be set according to the real situation. It reflects the expectation of the promoter on the target users. Targeting on the users who have the higher possibility to consume could create more promotion benefits, because those users are more likely to become repeat customers. Even though the users out of the target set may have nonzero offline probability, obviously their activity areas are too far that they could not bring the long-term and stable benefit. This consideration also emphasizes the locality, which is an important feature of O2O model.

5. OFFLINE PROBABILITY

Offline probability is an important parameter to describe the offline behavior of a user. It is the probability for a user to head for a given location and consume there, which is essentially a representation of the user mobility pattern. The existing researches have revealed that the probability with which a user moves from one location to another has certain relation with the distance between the two locations. In the other aspect, the historical check-ins could be the real and explicit reflection of user mobility behavior. A single check-in shows a user appears in a certain location, while multiple check-ins could indicate the daily activity area of the user, making the historical consuming check-in record useful in the offline probability calculation. This section will combine the mobility pattern of single movement and the historical check-in record to propose calculation method of the offline probability.

5.1 User mobility pattern analysis

The displacement behavior of human beings follows certain pattern. Existing researches have discussed the relationship between displacement distance and probability.

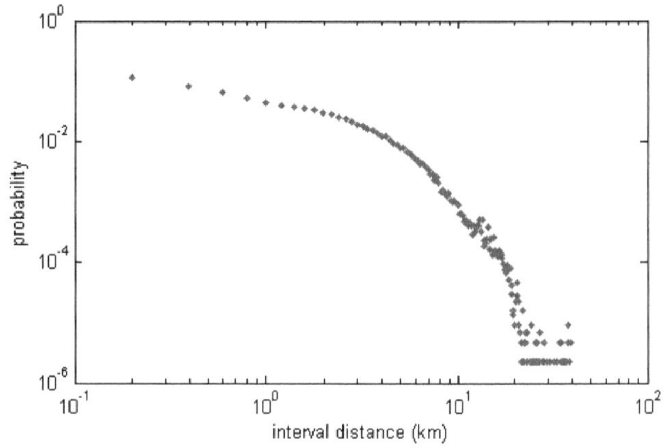

Figure 2: Displacement distribution of NY users

Some of them studied the behavior of animals and claimed that the trajectory of animals could be estimated by Lévy flight [14, 15]. In [16], authors looked into the mobility data collected from cellphones which could indicate the human trajectory and analyzed human mobility pattern. They found that the distribution of displacement distance could be approximated by a truncated power-law:

$$P(\Delta r) = (\Delta r + \Delta r_0)^{-\beta} exp(-\frac{\Delta r}{k}) \quad (1)$$

where Δr denotes the displacement distance of a user, Δr_0 and β are the parameters in power-law, and k is the cutoff value.

Inspired by the distribution, we conduct the statistics on the displacement distribution of New York users based on the Foursquare check-in dataset. We sort the check-in set C_u of user u according to the check-in time and get the check-in sequence $S_u = (c_1, c_2, ..., c_i)$. A single displacement distance d_i could be calculated as the distance of two adjacent check-ins from the sequence, which is $|c_i - c_{i-1}|$. We calculate the displacement distance of New York users and draw the displacement distribution as shown in Fig. 2.

As Fig. 2 indicates, the displacement distribution of New York users could also be approximated by a truncated power-law described in Eq.1. We use Eq.1 to fit the displacement data of New York users and get the parameter value in the equation. For users in New York, $\Delta r_0 = 1.69856$, $\beta = 2.41922$ and $k = 7.05365$.

5.2 Calculation of offline probability

Based on the user mobility pattern, we could calculate the offline probability of a user utilizing the historical check-in record. For a single user in New York whose consuming check-in set is C, given a product location L, the offline probability with which the user consumes in location L after it transits into online-active state could be calculated as:

$$P^{off}_L = 1 - \prod_{all\ c_i \in C} (1 - p_i) \quad (2)$$

$$p_i = (dis_i + \Delta dis)^{-\beta} exp(-\frac{dis_i}{k}) \quad (3)$$

where dis_i denotes the distance from historical consuming check-in c_i to location L, $\Delta dis = 1.69856$, $\beta = 2.41922$ and

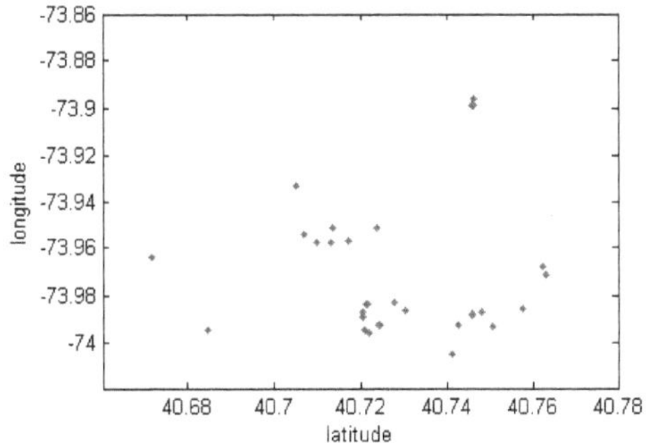

(a) Consuming check-in of a user

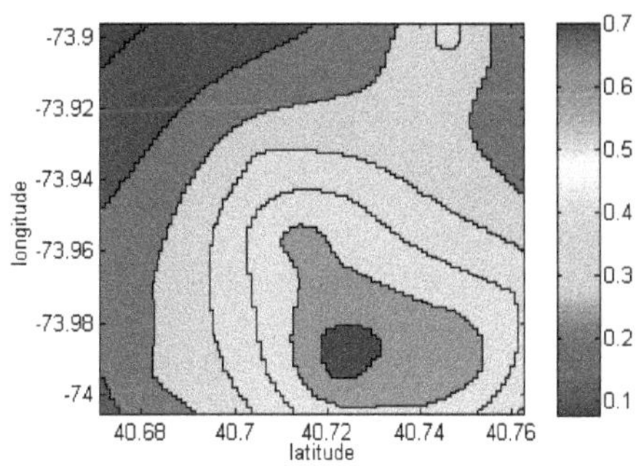

(b) Contour map of its offline probability

Figure 3: Example of offline probability

$k = 7.05365$. Eq.3 comes from Eq.1. p_i means for each historical consuming check-in c_i , the probability with which the user leaves from the position of c_i to location L for consuming.

The consuming check-in of a user is the reflection of his or her daily activity area. If a user has a check-in in location A, it implies the user appears in location A so that A is a possible activity position of the user. So we could assume the user may start from location A and head to location L for consuming and further assume each historical consuming check-in location is a possible starting point for the consuming behavior.

In Eq.2, the physical meaning of $\prod_{all\ c_i \in C}(1 - p_i)$ is the probability that no matter which historical consuming check-in location the user departs from , he or she will not conduct any consuming behavior in location L. Thus the probability that this situation does not occur will be P_L^{off} , which could be calculated by Eq.2. Its physical meaning is that departing from any of the historical consuming check-in locations, the user would get to location L and conduct consuming behavior for at least one time, which is actually the offline probability in our problem.

Fig. 3 (a) plots the consuming check-ins of a randomly selected user in the longitude and latitude coordinate system. Fig. 3 (b) is the contour map of its offline probability. Fig. 3 shows the consistency of offline probability distribution and historical consuming behavior. The distribution tends to spread from several centers. The central parts with higher probability correspond to the areas with denser check-ins, which are actually the daily activity centers of the user. Obviously, it is relatively more possible for the user to have consuming behavior in these areas. In another aspect, the further the location is apart from the center, which means it has fewer check-ins around, the lower the probability is for the user to go consuming there. So in general the distribution is consistent with the practical situation. What should be emphasized is that although only a few check-in locations appear in the upper-right part, the check-in times in these locations are relatively more, so a small center is formed in the contour map there, showing that it is still an activity area of the user. This proves the comprehensiveness of the calculation method on reflecting the consuming location preference.

Based on Eq.2 and Eq.3, given any product location L, for each user i in the social network, the offline probability could be calculated and be utilized in the TP model and location-based influence maximization.

6. LOCATION-BASED INFLUENCE MAXIMIZATION ALGORITHM AND EXPERIMENT EVALUATION

6.1 Two-Phase Heuristic Algorithm

In this section, we would propose a heuristic algorithm to solve the location-based influence maximization problem. In TP model, each node has its own offline probability for a given product, so the consideration on the location-based influence maximization cannot only focus on the network topology, but also the offline property of each node. We first propose a heuristic parameter H based on TP model, which takes both network topology and online-offline probability into account, to measure the influence of each node.

Given a location L, the value of H could be calculated with Eq.4.

$$H_i = \sum_{each\ neighbor\ j\ of\ i} p_{i,j}^{on} p_{j,L}^{off} \tag{4}$$

Here, $p_{i,j}^{on}$ is the probability that user i influences user j though edge $< i, j >$, namely the online probability on edge $< i, j >$, while $p_{j,L}^{off}$ is the probability that user j has consuming behavior in location L, namely the offline probability of user j.

The definition of H combines the influence propagation ability and propagation range of a user at the same time. For a user i who has a neighbor j, $p_{i,j}^{on} p_{j,L}^{off}$ describes the ability user i has to push user j into offline-active state. The larger the value is, the more possible it is for the influence to propagate from user i to user j. So this value could outline the propagation ability. Adding the values of all the neighbors together, in the other aspect, considers the network topology. A user with more neighbors has more chances to influence others. So the addition process outlines the propagation range. In general, the heuristic parameter H could serve as a synthesized indicator to measure the user influence.

Based on the heuristic parameter, we propose the Two-Phase Heuristic Algorithm (TPH algorithm) to solve the location-based influence maximization problem. TPH algorithm calculates the value of H_i for each user node i, and select k nodes with largest H value as initial nodes. It is summarized in Algorithm 1.

Algorithm 1 Two-Phase Heuristic Algorithm (TPH)

Input: Social network $G(V, E)$, TP model, initial nodes number k, product location L
Output: initial nodes set S (with the size of k)
1: initialize $S = \varnothing$;
2: calculate the value of heuristic parameter H for all of the nodes in V;
3: **for** $i = 1$ to k **do**
4: select node u in $V \backslash S$ with the largest H value;
5: $S = S \cup \{u\}$;
6: **end for**
7: **return** S;

For a given product location L, each node in social network G has a corresponding offline probability.

In Algorithm 1, line 2 calculates the value of H for each node according to Eq.4. Line 3 to line 6 select k nodes with largest H value and add them into the initial node set. As the calculation of H for each node needs to process all of its neighbors, the time complexity of line 2 is $O(m)$, in which m denotes the number of edges in the network. The complexity of the selection procedure from line 3 to line 6 is $O(klogn)$, where n denotes the number of nodes in the network. So the total time complexity of TPH algorithm is $O(klogn + m)$.

6.2 Experiment Evaluation of TPH

In order to evaluate the performance of TPH Algorithm, this section compares it with several common heuristic algorithms. The experiment runs in the PC machine with Intel Core i5 2.80GHz processor, 2G memory and 64 bit Windows 7 operating system. The experiment program is coded in C++.

As explained in Section 4, TP model offers more accurate description for influence diffusion in O2O environment. The experiment will execute all the algorithms based on TP model to prove the effectiveness of TPH algorithm on location-based influence maximization problem. According to the definition of the problem in Section 4, the evaluation criterion of the experiment is the number of the influenced target users. The algorithm that obtains more influenced target users has the better performance in influence diffusion.

6.2.1 *Experiment setup*

The dataset adopted in the experiment is the real one in Foursquare introduced in Section 3, consisting of the user network in New York and the historical consuming check-ins located in New York. Considering the compatibility with our problem, we choose three common and representative heuristic algorithms to make comparison: Max Degree algorithm (Degree), Degree Discount algorithm (DD) and PageRank algorithm (PR). Max Degree algorithm selects k nodes with largest degree as initial seeds. DD algorithm makes certain discount on the neighbor degree of selected seed node. Here, we use the online probability in the discount calculation. PR algorithm is the core search algorithm of Google and could be used in ranking process. Here, we set the damping ratio in PR algorithm as 0.85. Besides, random algorithm is executed as a reference.

Table 2: Experiment parameters

Product location L	Popular	Normal	Unpopular
Target user threshold θ	0.3	0.5	
Online probability p_{on}	0.01	0.05	0.1

When we set the location-based influence maximization problem, the product location L and the target user threshold θ should be given. A single user will have different offline probability for different location L and different threshold would determine different target user group. So in order to provide a comprehensive evaluation on the algorithm performance, the experiment generates specific influence maximization problems with different L and threshold. Besides, as the experiment set the same online probability p_{on} for each edge in TP model according to the traditional manner and the value of p_{on} will affect the diffusion result, different online probability would be set to make an exhaustive analysis. The choices of the three parameters L, θ and p_{on} are shown in Table 2.

We have defined three location types based on the popularity. People are more likely to consume in the popular locations but much less in the unpopular location. Normal locations are the non-extreme ones between popular and unpopular locations. According to the definition, it is obvious that the general offline probabilities of the user group to consume in a popular location are relatively high, while those to consume in an unpopular location are relatively low. Thus, the average offline probability of all the users, denoting as $AVG(p_{off})$, could be utilized as the criterion to classify the locations. We analyze a large number of samples and set the following rules:

$$location\ L\ is \begin{cases} popular & if\ AVG(p_{off}) \geqslant 0.4 \\ normal & if\ 0.04 \leqslant AVG(p_{off}) < 0.4 \\ unpopular & if\ AVG(p_{off}) < 0.04 \end{cases}$$

To avoid overfitting, we randomly select 10 locations for each location type, and the final experiment result is the average of the 10 cases for each configuration setting.

The target user threshold θ is set to 0.3 or 0.5, respectively representing a lower and a higher expectation on the target user. If θ is higher, the target users would be extremely few when L is not popular, which is not suitable for experiment analysis. Moreover, the promoters in real life would not set excessively harsh criteria for target user. So the higher threshold here is 0.5. The online probability p_{on} is set to 0.01, 0.05 or 0.1. If the offline probabilities are generally low, then a relatively high online probability would be chosen to make the result clear.

6.2.2 *Experiment result and analysis*

When L is a normal location, the experiment result is illustrated in Fig. 4. The horizontal axis shows the number of initial nodes and the vertical axis shows the number of influenced target nodes after the diffusion terminates. Fig. 4 illustrates significant superiority of TPH algorithm over the others when L locates in normal area. The three compared algorithms have similar performance among which the DD algorithm performs a little better. The values of online probability and threshold have effect on the final number of influenced target users, but they do not change the overall trend of the experiment data. TPH algorithm outperforms

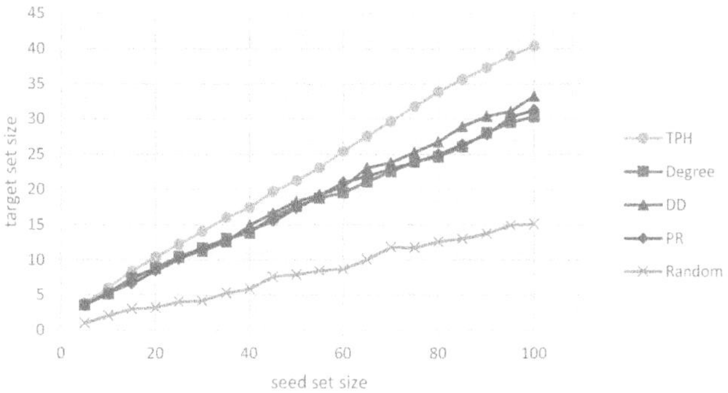

(a) p_{on}=0.01 threshold=0.3

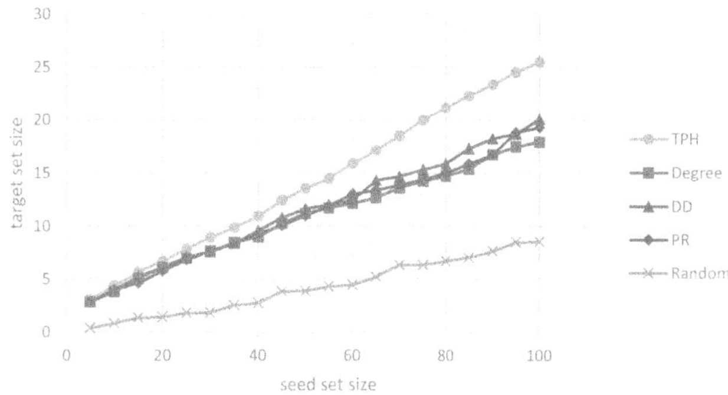

(b) p_{on}=0.01 threshold=0.5

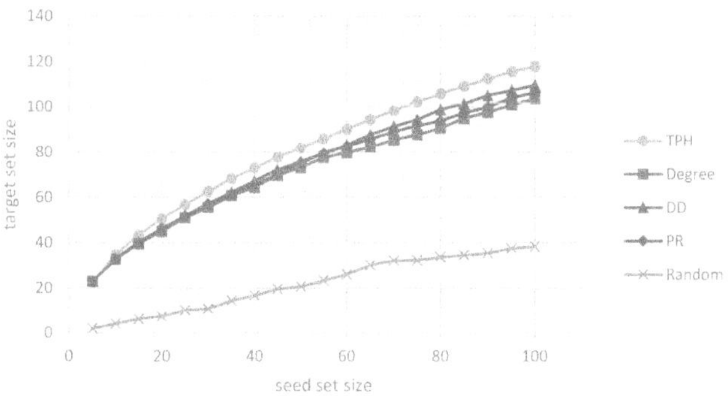

(c) p_{on}=0.05 threshold=0.3

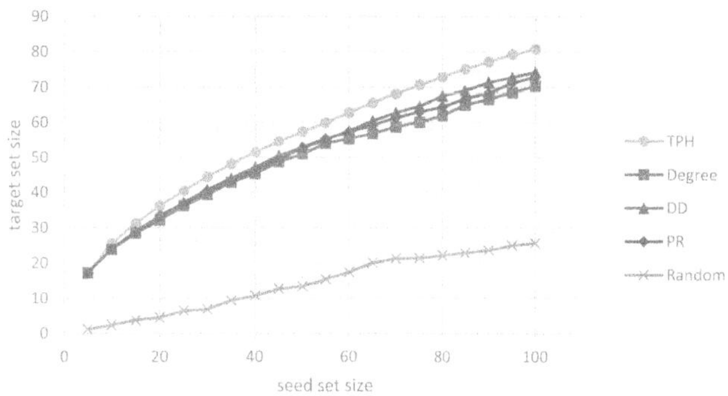

(d) p_{on}=0.05 threshold=0.5

Figure 4: Performance of different algorithm when L a normal location

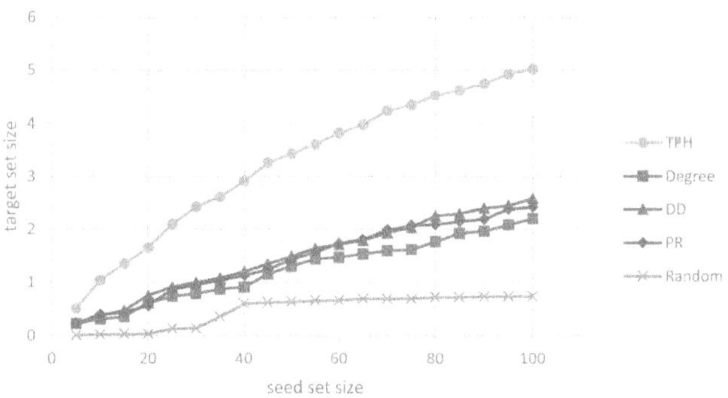

(a) p_{on}=0.05 threshold=0.3

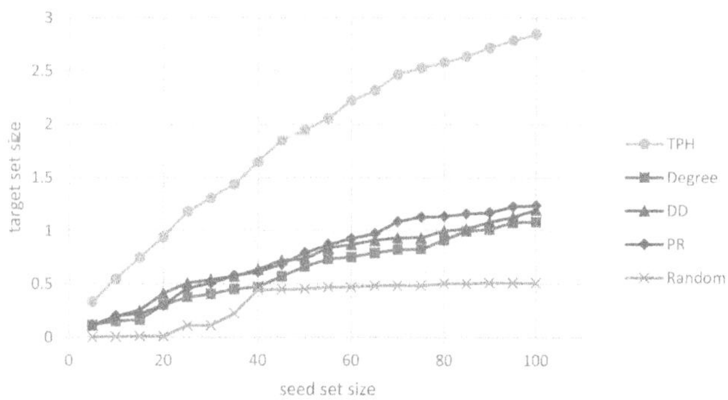

(b) p_{on}=0.05 threshold=0.5

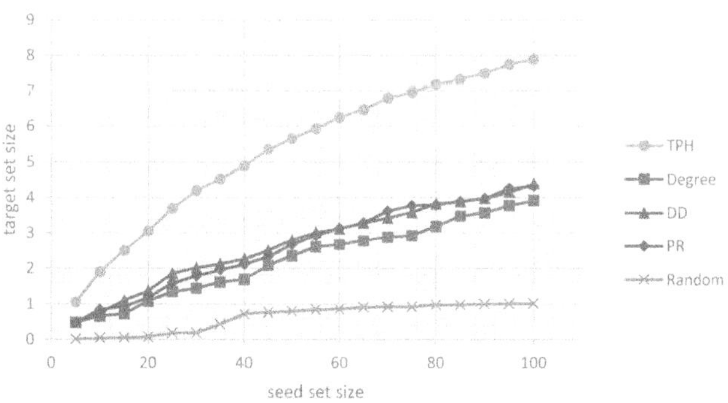

(c) p_{on}=0.1 threshold=0.3

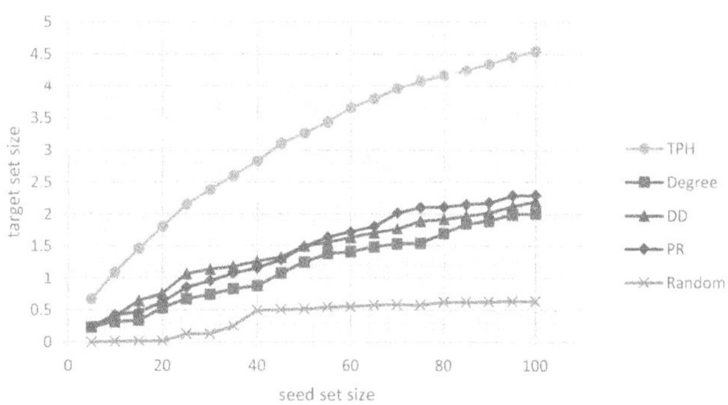

(d) p_{on}=0.1 threshold=0.5

Figure 5: Performance of different algorithm when L is an unpopular location

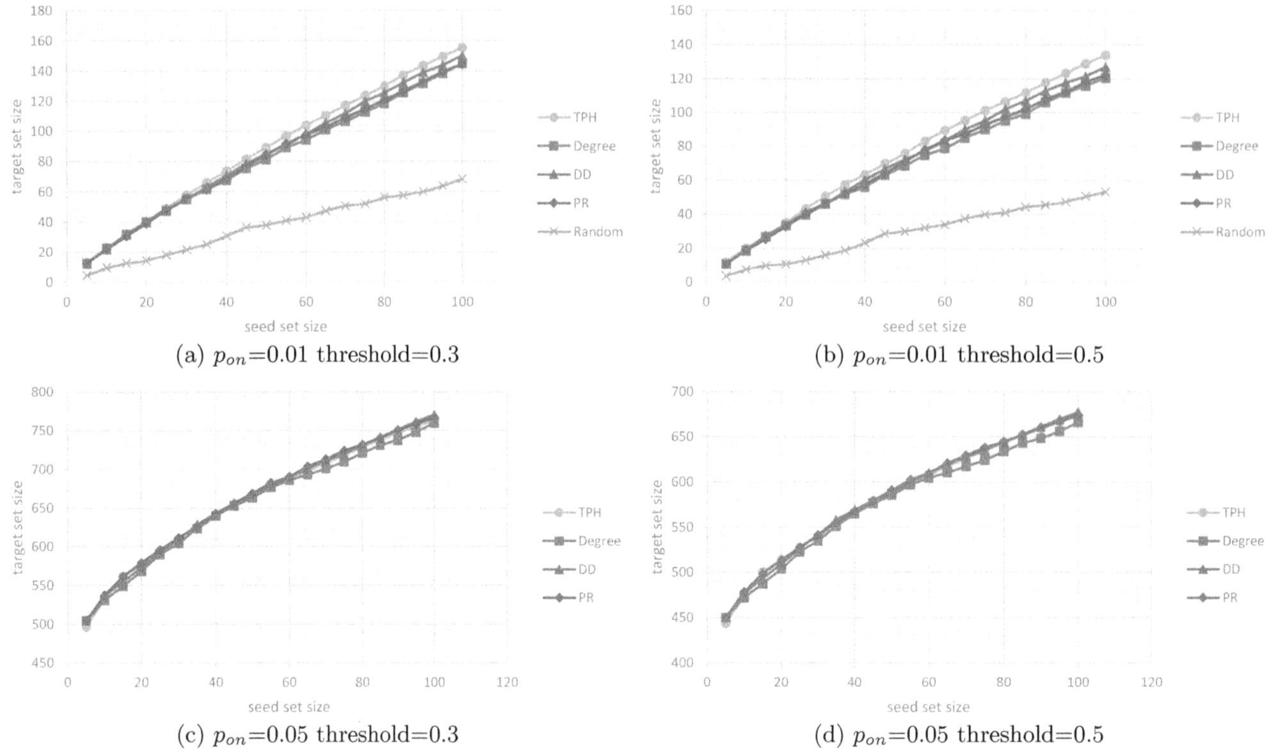

(a) p_{on}=0.01 threshold=0.3

(b) p_{on}=0.01 threshold=0.5

(c) p_{on}=0.05 threshold=0.3

(d) p_{on}=0.05 threshold=0.5

Figure 6: Performance of different algorithm when L is a popular location

the other algorithms in all cases when online probability and threshold are different.

When L is an unpopular location, the experiment result is shown in Fig. 5. It again shows the better performance of TPH algorithm. Similarly, the change of online probability and threshold has no significant influence on the trend of experiment data and TPH algorithm performs better in each case.

When L is a popular location, the experiment result is shown in Fig. 6. The performance of random algorithm is far behind the others while others have similar results in Figs. 6(c) (d), so we do not illustrate the curve of random algorithm in the graph. Fig. 6 indicates a relatively big effect of the online probability on the diffusion result when L is popular. When online probability is 0.01, TPH algorithm again shows superiority in diffusion result and the performance of Degree Discount algorithm is close to TPH. However, when the online probability comes to 0.05, TPH loses its advantage and all the algorithms have similar diffusion results and increasing trend. This phenomenon is related to both online and offline probability. As L being popular, the offline probabilities of most users will be generally high. When the online probability is further set to a relatively high value, the overall influence diffusion ability of the network becomes strong and a large number of users could be influenced. Each algorithm tries to choose the nodes with higher influence indicator it defines, but when the diffusion ability of the network itself is already quite strong, the difference between different selection methods is relatively slight. It is because the seed nodes chosen by one algorithm may be covered during the diffusion process of another algorithm, which will decrease the dissimilarity of individual algorithms. Unlike online probability, threshold has little effect on the general diffusion trend.

6.2.3 *Experiment conclusion*

Among the three experiment parameters, the effect of target user threshold is insignificant on the performance trend of the algorithms. The product location L significantly affects the experiment result and when L is a popular location, the online probability also has influence on the algorithm performance.

In general, TPH algorithm has outstanding advantage over the other ones. When L is not popular, this advantage is more significant, while in the special case where L is popular and online probability is high, the performance of TPH algorithm is similar with other ones.

6.3 Multi-Rank Algorithm

TPH algorithm is not satisfying when product location L is popular and online probability is relatively high. In order to make a complement, we propose the Multi-Rank algorithm (MR algorithm) which could improve the diffusion result in this situation.

The main idea of MR algorithm is to take the activation accessibility into account, which reflects whether a user is easy to be activated (to transit into offline-active state). The algorithm will select the nodes which are more likely to influence others from those with low activation accessibility.

Looking into the initial nodes selected by TPH algorithm in the last case of the experiment, we notice that as the influence diffusion ability of the network is strong, there is high possibility for those selected nodes to have high activation accessibility, which means even if we do not select them as initial nodes, the influence may spread to them later. However, once the influence propagates to the nodes with low activation accessibility, the diffusion process may be terminated and the influence could not cover the other areas which are connected by these nodes, making the diffusion performance stuck. So we consider the problem in a brand new way, selecting the initial nodes from those with low activation accessibility, which could activate the areas that are formerly difficult to be covered. Moreover, as the general diffusion ability is strong, some nodes with high activation accessibility which are selected by TPH but not by MR could also be covered in the diffusion process.

When selecting from the nodes with low activation accessibility, we also apply the idea of TPH algorithm. The heuristic parameter H in TPH algorithm is adopted to guarantee the influence diffusion ability carried by the initial nodes themselves is relatively high.

In order to measure the activation accessibility, we first define a ranking basis R. It is utilized to rank the node to distinguish whether it is easy to transit into offline-active state. Given a user i and product location L, the value of R_i could be calculated as:

$$R_i = R_i^{neighbor} + R_i^{self} \tag{5}$$

$$R_i^{neighbor} = 1 - \prod_{each\ neighbor\ j\ of\ i} (1 - p_{j,L}^{off}) \tag{6}$$

$$R_i^{self} = p_{i,L}^{off} \tag{7}$$

The larger R_i is, the easier user i is to be activated. When we say a user has high activation accessibility, first of all, he or she should be easy to switch to offline-active state, and meanwhile the neighbors of this user should also be easy to be activated. If none of the neighbors are activated, the user could never be activated at all. So the definition of R_i has two parts, in which $R_i^{neighbor}$ denotes the activation accessibility of neighbors of user node i and R_i^{self} denotes the activation accessibility of user node i itself. With regard to $R_i^{neighbor}$, $p_{j,L}^{off}$ in Eq.6 is the offline probability of user j. The physical meaning of multiplying all the $(1 - p_{j,L}^{off})$ is to calculate the probability that none of the neighbors of user node i would transit into offline-active state. So the physical meaning of $R_i^{neighbor}$ is the probability that at least one of these neighbors become offline-active from online-active state. The higher $R_i^{neighbor}$ is, the higher activation accessibility the neighbors have in general. For R_i^{self}, its value is the offline probability of user node i. The higher R_i^{self} is, the higher activation accessibility i itself has. The value of R_i is the sum of $R_i^{neighbor}$ and R_i^{self}.

MR algorithm first calculates the ranking basis R for all the nodes, and then ranks each node according to the value of R. The method of ranking is to sort the nodes by a descending order of R, and the former half are defined as high-ranking nodes while the latter half are defined as low-ranking nodes. High-ranking nodes are those with high activation accessibility and low-ranking nodes are the opposite. At last, MR algorithm selects k nodes with largest influence from the low-ranking node set as the initial nodes applying TPH algorithm. Its process is summarized in Algorithm 2.

As the same as TPH algorithm, for a given product location L, each node in social network G has a corresponding offline probability. In Algorithm 2, line 2 calculates the value of R for each node according to Eq.5. Line 3 to line 6 rank the nodes and create the low-ranking node set. Line 7 to line 11 apply TPH algorithm to choose the initial nodes from the low-ranking node set. The time complexity of calculating the value of R and H is $O(m)$ and the complexity of ranking user nodes is $O(nlogn)$, in which m and n denote to the number of edges and nodes in the network respectively. The complexity of selecting k initial nodes is $O(klogn)$. So the total time complexity of MR algorithm is $O(nlogn + m)$.

Algorithm 2 Multi-Rank Algorithm (MR)

Input: Social network $G(V, E)$, TP model, initial nodes number k, product location L

Output: initial nodes set S (with the size of k)

```
1: initialize S = ∅, LS = ∅ ; // LS is the set of low-ranking nodes
2: calculate the ranking basis R for all the nodes in V;
3: sort the nodes in V by the descending order of R and obtain the node sequence (v1, v2, ..., vn);
4: for i = n/2 to n do
5:     LS = LS ∪ {vi};
6: end for
7: calculate the value of heuristic parameter H for all of the nodes in LS;
8: for j = 1 to k do
9:     select node u in LS\S with the largest H value;
10:    S = S ∪ {u};
11: end for
12: return S;
```

6.4 Experiment Evaluation of MR

In order to prove the effectiveness of MR algorithm, we run the comparison experiment together with the former algorithms. As MR algorithm is a complement for TPH algorithm when product location L is popular and online probability is high, we set the experiment according to the third case in section 6.2.2, where L is popular and the online probability is 0.05. Again, 10 popular locations are randomly selected to calculate the average data. The result in Fig. 7 shows the outstanding performance of MR algorithm and also proves its steady advantage. While other algorithms have similar diffusion results, MR algorithm brings a large improvement in the range of diffusion. MR algorithm is proved to be an effective complement for TPH algorithm when L is popular and online probability is high.

7. CONCLUSION

This paper aims at the product promotion in O2O model and carries out the study of location-based influence maximization on the platform of LBSN. We first propose the Two Phase Model, a new diffusion model which could be adopted under the O2O environment. Then the location-based influence maximization problem is defined and the calculation method of offline probability is present by analyzing the user mobility pattern. Next, the TPH algorithm is proposed for location-based influence maximization and MR algorithm is designed as the complement. At last, experiments prove TPH and MR algorithm has significant effectiveness. In the future work, we would further consider the semantic information of consuming location and analyze user location preference of different semantic categories. Moreover, we would introduce the temporal property of user consuming behavior

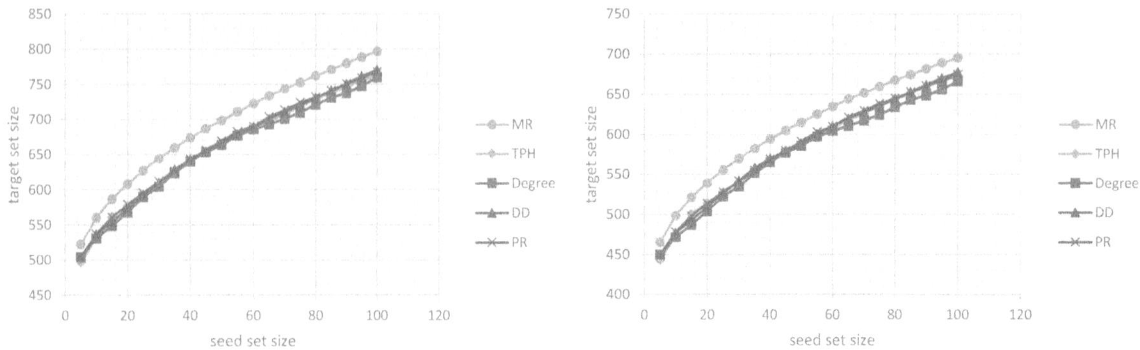

(a) p_{on}=0.05 threshold=0.3 (b) p_{on}=0.05 threshold=0.5

Figure 7: Performance of MR algorithm

to study the influence diffusion with time restriction so that the more general solution could be raised.

8. ACKNOWLEDGMENTS

This work is supported by National Natural Science Foundation of China (61272531, 61202449, 61272054, 61370207, 61370208, 61300024, 61320106007 and 61472081), China high technology 863 program (2013AA013503), Jiangsu Technology Planning Program (SBY2014021039-10), Jiangsu Provincial Key Laboratory of Network and Information Security under Grant No.BM2003201 and Key Laboratory of Computer Network and Information Integration of Ministry of Education of China under Grant No.93k-9.

9. REFERENCES

[1] Pedro Domingos and Matt Richardson. Mining the network value of customers. In *Proceedings of the seventh ACM SIGKDD international conference on Knowledge discovery and data mining*, pages 57–66. ACM, 2001.

[2] Yu Zheng and Xiaofang Zhou. *Computing with spatial trajectories*. Springer Science & Business Media, 2011.

[3] David Kempe, Jon Kleinberg, and Éva Tardos. Maximizing the spread of influence through a social network. In *Proceedings of the ninth ACM SIGKDD international conference on Knowledge discovery and data mining*, pages 137–146. ACM, 2003.

[4] David JC MacKay. Introduction to monte carlo methods. In *Learning in graphical models*, pages 175–204. Springer, 1998.

[5] Jure Leskovec, Andreas Krause, Carlos Guestrin, Christos Faloutsos, Jeanne VanBriesen, and Natalie Glance. Cost-effective outbreak detection in networks. In *Proceedings of the 13th ACM SIGKDD international conference on Knowledge discovery and data mining*, pages 420–429. ACM, 2007.

[6] Amit Goyal, Wei Lu, and Laks VS Lakshmanan. Celf++: optimizing the greedy algorithm for influence maximization in social networks. In *Proceedings of the 20th international conference companion on World wide web*, pages 47–48. ACM, 2011.

[7] Wei Chen, Yajun Wang, and Siyu Yang. Efficient influence maximization in social networks. In *Proceedings of the 15th ACM SIGKDD international conference on Knowledge discovery and data mining*, pages 199–208. ACM, 2009.

[8] Sergey Brin and Lawrence Page. The anatomy of a large-scale hypertextual web search engine. *Computer networks and ISDN systems*, 30(1):107–117, 1998.

[9] Jon M Kleinberg. Authoritative sources in a hyperlinked environment. *Journal of the ACM (JACM)*, 46(5):604–632, 1999.

[10] Guoliang Li, Shuo Chen, Jianhua Feng, Kian-lee Tan, and Wen-syan Li. Efficient location-aware influence maximization. In *Proceedings of the 2014 ACM SIGMOD international conference on Management of data*, pages 87–98. ACM, 2014.

[11] H Peyton Young. The diffusion of innovations in social networks. *The Economy As an Evolving Complex System III: Current Perspectives and Future Directions*, 267, 2006.

[12] Duncan J Watts. A simple model of global cascades on random networks. *Proceedings of the National Academy of Sciences*, 99(9):5766–5771, 2002.

[13] Jacob Goldenberg, Barak Libai, and Eitan Muller. Talk of the network: A complex systems look at the underlying process of word-of-mouth. *Marketing letters*, 12(3):211–223, 2001.

[14] Joseph Klafter, Michael F Shlesinger, and Gert Zumofen. Beyond brownian motion. *Physics today*, 49(2):33–39, 1996.

[15] Rosario N Mantegna and H Eugene Stanley. Stochastic process with ultraslow convergence to a gaussian: the truncated lévy flight. *Physical Review Letters*, 73(22):2946–2949, 1994.

[16] Marta C Gonzalez, Cesar A Hidalgo, and Albert-Laszlo Barabasi. Understanding individual human mobility patterns. *Nature*, 453(7196):779–782, 2008.

Location and Time Aware Social Collaborative Retrieval for New Successive Point-of-Interest Recommendation

Wei Zhang[†] Jianyong Wang[†♮]

[†]Department of Computer Science and Technology, Tsinghua University, Beijing 100084, China

[♮]Jiangsu Collaborative Innovation Center for Language Ability, Jiangsu Normal University, Xuzhou 221009, China

zwei11@mails.tsinghua.edu.cn, jianyong@tsinghua.edu.cn

ABSTRACT

In location-based social networks (LBSNs), new successive point-of-interest (POI) recommendation is a newly formulated task which tries to regard the POI a user currently visits as his POI-related query and recommend new POIs the user has not visited before. While carefully designed methods are proposed to solve this problem, they ignore the essence of the task which involves retrieval and recommendation problem simultaneously and fail to employ the social relations or temporal information adequately to improve the results.

In order to solve this problem, we propose a new model called location and time aware social collaborative retrieval model (LTSCR), which has two distinct advantages: (1) it models the location, time, and social information simultaneously for the successive POI recommendation task; (2) it efficiently utilizes the merits of the collaborative retrieval model which leverages weighted approximately ranked pairwise (WARP) loss for achieving better top-n ranking results, just as the new successive POI recommendation task needs. We conducted some comprehensive experiments on publicly available datasets and demonstrate the power of the proposed method, with 46.6% growth in Precision@5 and 47.3% improvement in Recall@5 over the best previous method.

Categories and Subject Descriptors

H.3.3 [**Information Storage and Retrieval**]: Information Search and Retrieval—*Information Filtering, Retrieval Models*

General Terms

Algorithms, Experimentation

Keywords

Collaborative Retrieval, Location based Social Networks, Successive Location Recommendation

Permission to make digital or hard copies of all or part of this work for personal or classroom use is granted without fee provided that copies are not made or distributed for profit or commercial advantage and that copies bear this notice and the full citation on the first page. Copyrights for components of this work owned by others than ACM must be honored. Abstracting with credit is permitted. To copy otherwise, or republish, to post on servers or to redistribute to lists, requires prior specific permission and/or a fee. Request permissions from Permissions@acm.org.

CIKM'15, October 19-23, 2015, Melbourne, VIC, Australia.

© 2015 ACM. ISBN 978-1-4503-3794-6/15/10 ...$15.00.

DOI: http://dx.doi.org/10.1145/2806416.2806564.

1. INTRODUCTION

With the popularity of location-based social networks (LBSNs) allowing users to share their location-embedded information or attend location-aware activities at given time, more and more researchers pay attention to research tasks in this field, such as event-related recommendation [14, 27, 26], location prediction [12, 1], and location-aware information retrieval [21], etc.

In these studies, successive POI recommendation [4] is a newly emerging task which tries to treat users' current POIs as POI-related queries and recommend new POIs users have not visited before. Hence, it can be regarded as a hybrid task involving both retrieval and recommendation. It is important for real-time location-aware recommender systems. For example, it is extremely common that when a user visited one location just now, he may not be clear where to go next. The recommender system can treat the current location of the user as his location-aware query and automatically recommend new POIs, which is beneficial for both users and businesses.

Compared with traditional POI recommendation task which also tries to recommend new POIs for users [3, 25, 13, 7, 10, 9], the essential difference is that the performance of successive POI recommendation task is largely influenced by users' current visiting locations. To be more specific, the location which a user will visit next is usually near his current visiting POI. Besides, the shift from one specified location to another specific location may be very common. One example is the popular travel route in a tourist city, in which the transition from one POI to another is usually fixed. Without explicitly modeling the users' current visiting POIs, the approaches of traditional POI recommendation cannot capture the localization of successive visiting and the frequent shift patterns. Thus, it will result in poor performance by directly applying the models designed for traditional POI recommendation to successive POI recommendation task.

Existing approaches for successive POI recommendation task [17, 4] consider users' current locations to generate recommendation results. Nevertheless, they ignore to utilize the social relations between users or temporal information of visiting adequately, which can influence users' final decisions to a certain extent. On the one hand, social relations indicate that users may visit locations their friends have been to, which is reasonable as friends have similar interests. On the other hand, users and locations both have their own temporal characteristics. Different users may have various visiting patterns in the same period which are determined by their own habits. POIs also have different probability of being visited in different time periods. For example, restaurants are more likely to be visited in lunch and dinner time. In later data analysis, we verify that check-in patterns of users and POIs over timelines are indeed diverse through correlation analysis. Besides, the characteristic of hybrid retrieval and recommendation involved in this task still needs to be studied, especially when modeling the top-k ranking results of recommendations which is significant for successive POI recommendation, as for each user the number of successive POIs visited for specific location-aware query is small.

To tackle the above issues, we propose a new model called *location and time aware social collaborative retrieval model (LTSCR)*. It is a natural extension of the recently proposed collaborative retrieval model (CRM) [20] which models query, user, and item in a unified model and first employs the loss function called weighted approximate rank pairwise (WARP) loss [18, 19] in collaborative filtering to gain better top k recommendation results and is more suitable for bybrid task involving retrieval and recommendation task simultaneously, which is similar to our successive POI recommendation task. In order to better model the users' successive check-in behaviors in LBSNs, LTSCR considers users' current visiting locations, visiting time, and user himself as implicit queries. Each candidate location is composed of three types of latent factors: (1) the first kind of factor captures transition patterns between successive check-in POIs, (2) the second models preference between users and locations, (3) and the third reveals locations' popularity over time. Besides, social relations are utilized to regularize the degree of interest similarity between friends, and the localization property is employed to constrain candidate POIs to be within the near regions of the query POI.

In summary, our major contributions in this paper are summarized as follows:

- We consider users' current visiting locations, visiting time, social relations, and the localization of successive check-ins simultaneously for successive POI recommendation task.
- We propose a complete model called *Location and Time Aware Social Collaborative Retrieval (LTSCR)* which incorporates the above information into a unified model and utilizes the merits of standard collaborative retrieval model to the successive POI recommendation task in LBSNs.
- We have conducted experiments on publicly available data sets from LBSNs. The results demonstrate that LTSCR performs better than several other methods.

The rest of the paper is organized as follows: we first discuss the related works in Section 2. Section 3 gives necessary preliminaries for successive modeling. In Section 4, we formulate our model in detail. Section 5 presents the experimental results and analysis. Finally, we conclude this paper in Section 6.

2. RELATED WORK

In this section, we briefly introduce three lines of researches related to our task: (a) traditional POI recommendation; (b) successive POI recommendation; and (c) collaborative retrieval.

Traditional POI Recommendation. Traditional POI recommendation task has been extensively studied in the last several years. Many researches hold a central assumption that nearer locations will be more likely to be visited by users. Based on this, a series of works incorporate distance influence factor into diverse traditional recommendation models [23, 3, 11]. Ye et al. [23] first combined distance influence factor with user-based collaborative filtering method. Then Cheng et al. [3] blended probabilistic matrix factorization with a gaussian mixture model to capture the influence of distance. More recently, Kurashima [11] proposed a geo topic model to integrate distance factor with latent Dirichlet allocation [2]. Another research direction is to utilize temporal information check-ins to improve location recommendation results [25, 7, 10]. Similar to the evolutional trend of researches for integrating distance factor, they also incorporate temporal information into user-based collaborative filtering, matrix factorization and topic model successively. The above works demonstrate the advantages of considering location distance information and temporal information in traditional POI recommendation, which can motivate the research in successive POI recommendation.

Successive POI Recommendation. Lately, a few successive POI recommendation works [17, 4] have been conducted. Snag et al. [17] proposed a probabilistic model to integrate category transition probability and POI popularity to solve this problem. However, their method relies on categories of POIs and user attributes such as gender and residence information, which might not be easy to get due to privacy concern. Thus their method cannot be directly used in this paper. Cheng et al. [4] extended the state-of-the-art context-aware recommendation method, i.e., factorized personalized Markov chain (FPMC) [15], to provide a new model called FPMC with localized region constraint for successive POI recommendation. They divided the geographical space into grids, and the candidate recommendation locations for a user should be within the grid the user currently stays in or its surrounding eight grids. This condition is called localized region constraint. The experimental results indicated the effectiveness of their method. As they ignore to utilize the social relations between users and temporal information of visiting, our works first propose two extensions based on their model to incorporate these useful information and then we propose a new model called LTSCR to combine the extensions with the standard collaborative model, which makes our works largely different from theirs. Two recent works [5, 22] try to predict the next user movement based on users' previous sequential movements. Yet our problem is obviously different from theirs in two aspects. First, they consider which place users will move to and when they will reach while we concentrate on recommending new POIs which users have not visited before. Second, they need to utilize multiple recent check-ins of each user to construct sequential model for location transfer and time information prediction while we only regard each user's current visiting location as a query for collaborative retrieval. Besides, Yin et. al. [24] proposed a location-content-aware recommender system which recommends items given a query location from users. However, their problem setting is different from ours as the query locations in theirs are regions (e.g. cities) and they want to recommend spatial items within those regions while our queries include all locations and we try to recommend POIs near those query locations.

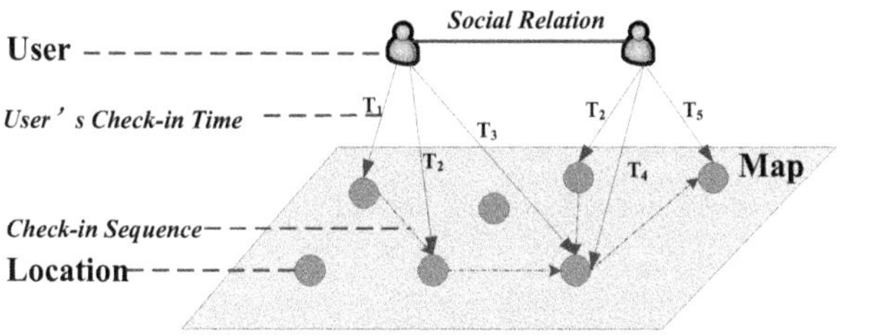

Figure 1: Basic Overview of Location-based Social Network.

Collaborative Retrieval. Collaborative retrieval task was first proposed by Weston et al. [20]. It blends traditional information retrieval and personalized recommendation tasks. In order to solve this problem, they proposed a latent collaborative retrieval model, which could be roughly divided into two parts. The first part modeles the relation among query, user, and item for solving retrieval problem. The second part captured the relation between user and item for dealing with the recommendation problem. Besides, the model adoptes the WARP loss function to train the model in order to gain better top k results. Upon this model, Hsiao et al. [9] incorporated social relation information to regularize user latent factors and achieved better results. More details about collaborative retrieval model can be referred in the next section. In this paper, we propose a new model called LTSCR based on the standard collaborative model to solve our problem.

3. PRELIMINARIES

In this section, we first analyze properties of the datasets from LBSNs. Then we formulate the successive POI recommendation problem in our setting. After that, the standard method for this task is presented. Finally, the collaborative retrieval model is introduced at last as the cornerstone of the subject of the next section.

3.1 Data Analysis

Location-based social networks are common in current social networks. Almost all LBSNs and their variations share the following basic data attributes: user set $\mathcal{U}$, POI set $\mathcal{P}$, social relation set $\mathcal{S}$, and temporal information set $\mathcal{T}$. Their primary relations are shown in Figure 1. Basically, for a user u, when he visits a POI p at time t, he can share this check-in record with others, such as his friend set $S(u)$. In this work, we adopt two publicly available datasets published by [6] to test our proposed models. The first one was crawled from Brightkite and the other was from Gowalla. Thus, we denominate the first data set as Brightkite and the second as Gowalla for convenience.

In order to compute the distance distribution of successive check-in pairs, we first mine the successive check-in pairs. Inspired by the methods mentioned in [20, 4], we determine a maximal time interval T_{max}. For any two successive check-in POIs from the same user, the check-in time difference can not exceed T_{max}. After we collect enough consecutive check-in pairs, we calculate the cumulative distribution of distance between successive check-in locations. Figure 2 shows that in Gowalla dataset, 90.1% check-in pairs lie within 5 miles and only less than 6% pairs' distances surpass 10 miles. This phenomenon about localization of successive check-ins is less

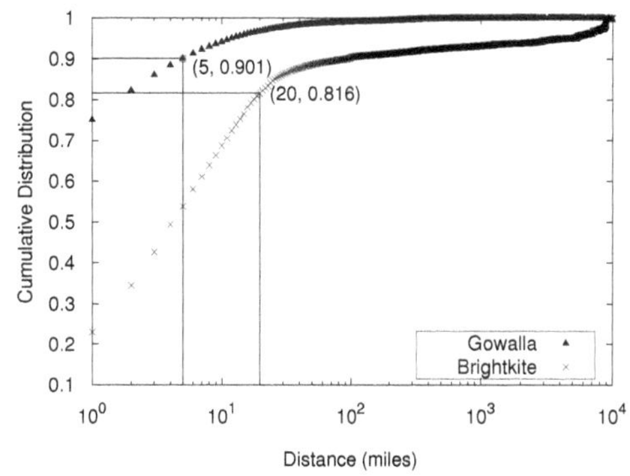

Figure 2: Distance Between Successive Check-in POIs.

visible in Brightkite dataset. However, there are still more than half check-in pairs' distances within 5 miles and more than eighty percents pairs' distances less than 20 miles. In summary, users' next POI choices are constrained in local regions near their current visiting POIs.

Besides, we also want to check whether temporal information may influence the successive POI recommendation results. It is intuitive that for different users, their own habits may cause very different visiting patterns as time goes on. And for specific POI, its check-in patterns should be different from other POIs belonging to different categories. For example, parks are usually visited by users in daytime, while restaurants are preferred by users at dinner time. To verify this, we utilize Pearson correlation to measure the correlation of users' temporal check-in patterns in the same location region to ensure the local time consistency and the same as for POIs. More specifically, we first filter users or locations with few check-in records. We use a 24 dimensional vector to represent the temporal check-in pattern of each user or item, with each dimension corresponding to an hour and each value denoting the total check-in count belonging to that hour. Then for users (or POIs) in the same geographical region, we calculate their Pearson correlation in pair and average the results finally for all pairs in all regions. The results for both datasets are shown in Figure 3. We can see that all of them lies in the interval $[+0.22, +0.32]$, which means the temporal check-in patterns have low positive correlation. Another phenomenon is that the correlation of locations' temporal check-in patterns is a little lower than users' on both datasets. In all, the check-in patterns of users and POIs over time are indeed diverse. The above analysis suggests us to utilize the temporal information of visiting to help successive POI recommendation.

3.2 Problem Formulation

Based on the above data analysis, we formulate the successive POI recommendation task below. Given a user $u\,(u \in \mathcal{U})$, his already visited POI set $P(u)$, his current visiting POI $i\,(i \in \mathcal{P})$, and the corresponding visiting timestamp $t\,(t \in \mathcal{T})$, the task is to recommend a new POI $c\,(c \notin P(u))$ for user to visit successively. Generally, top k new POIs are delivered to user u which are ranked according the score gotten from a defined score function $f(u, t, i, c)$.

In the collaborative retrieval setting, i and t can be considered as a location and time aware query of user u. The user wants to know which successive POI he can visit in the near

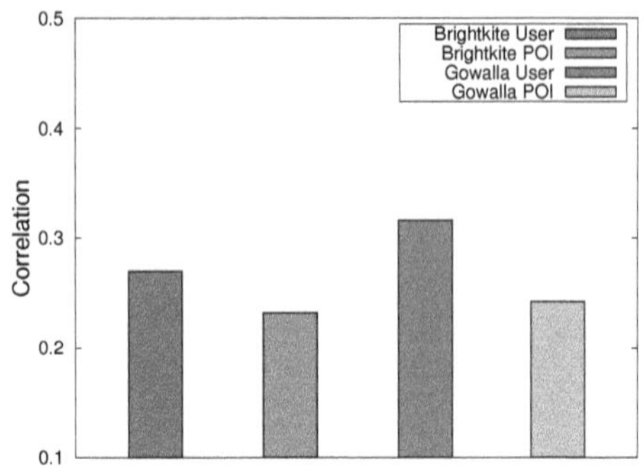

Figure 3: Average Correlation of Temporal Check-in Patterns of Users/POIs.

future. Hence, the above task can be regarded as one kind of collaborative retrieval task. However, there is no need to consider all POIs as candidate results as the works [20, 9] do because of the localization property of successive check-ins. Thus, we only need to search near POIs according to i to determine the final results, which is supported by the previous data analysis.

3.3 Collaborative Retrieval Modeling

The central idea of collaborative retrieval is to capture the relation among users, queries, and items in a unified model to calculate the possibility score $f(u,q,i)$ of user u preferring item i under the query q. Assume $\mathcal{I}$ and $\mathcal{Q}$ denote the item set and query set, respectively. $\mathcal{K}$ is the dimension of latent factors, $\mathbf{U} \in \mathbb{R}^{\mathcal{K}\times|\mathcal{U}|}$ are user factors, $\mathbf{V} \in \mathbb{R}^{\mathcal{K}\times|\mathcal{I}|}$ are item factors, $\mathbf{Q} \in \mathbb{R}^{\mathcal{K}\times|\mathcal{Q}|}$ are query factors, $\mathbf{U}_u \in \mathbb{R}^{\mathcal{K}}$ is the latent factor of user u, $\mathbf{V}_i \in \mathbb{R}^{\mathcal{K}}$ is the latent factor of item i, and $\mathbf{Q}_q \in \mathbb{R}^{\mathcal{K}}$ is the latent factor of query q. Then for a user u, given a query $q (q \in \mathcal{Q})$ and an item i, the score function is formally expressed as follows,

$$f(u,q,i) = \mathbf{Q}_q^{\mathrm{T}}\mathbf{T}_u\mathbf{V}_i + \mathbf{U}_u^{\mathrm{T}}\mathbf{V}_i \tag{1}$$

where $\mathbf{T}_u \in \mathbb{R}^{\mathcal{K}\times\mathcal{K}}$ is a user dependent transform matrix. We can see that the first part of the equation is to capture the relation among query, user, and item, while the second part is to model the relation between user and item. Thus, the first part corresponds to the retrieval model and the second part corresponds to the recommendation model.

The collaborative retrieval model utilizes weighted approximate rank pairwise (WARP) [18] loss to complement traditional pairwise loss functions. Unlike previous pairwise loss functions which treat all training pairs equally, the WARP loss actively learns more from training pairs where positive items have high ranking positions and thus can achieve better top k ranking results (see [19] for more explanations). The rank for each positive item i is defined as below,

$$r(i) = \sum_{j\neq i} \mathbb{I}\big((1 + f(u,q,j)) > f(u,q,i)\big) \tag{2}$$

where $\mathbb{I}(\cdot)$ is an indicator function. It is clear that if $f(u,q,i)$ gets larger value, less items will satisfy $\big((1 + f(u,q,j)) > f(u,q,i)\big)$ and item i should get lower rank.

Computing the scores of all items to get ranks is not efficient. Hence, an approximate method is proposed. For a given positive item i, it draws a negative item j without replacement and terminates until item j satisfies the margin-based comparison $1 + f(u,q,j) > f(u,q,i)$. Suppose the number of sampling step to get j for i is N_i. Then the approximate rank is calculated below,

$$\widetilde{r}(i) \approx \left\lfloor \frac{|\mathcal{I}| - 1}{N_{s,i}} \right\rfloor \tag{3}$$

where $\lfloor\cdot\rfloor$ means the floor function, $|\mathcal{I}|$ is the total number of items.

After getting the approximate rank, the rank loss for the positive item i is defined as follows,

$$L(\widetilde{r}(i)) = \sum_{n=1}^{\widetilde{r}(i)} \omega_n, \qquad with \quad \omega_1 \geq \omega_2 \geq \cdots \geq 0. \tag{4}$$

where ω_n is the weight of position n in the ranked list and often defined to be $1/n$.

To optimize the loss function, efficient learning algorithms such as stochastic gradient descent (SGD) require that it is derivable for model parameters. Following the idea from [19], the margin function $\max(0, 1 + f(u,q,j) - f(u,q,i))$ can be added to meet the requirement. During the learning process, all the training pairs are weighed in every iteration according to the above two equations.

In summary, the collaborative retrieval model has two main characteristics: (1) it computes both query dependent and independent preference score through the retrieval model and recommendation model respectively, and jointly learn query, user, and item factors in a unified model; (2) it utilizes WARP loss function for optimization to get better top-k ranking recommendation results. Inspired by the above two ideas, we design our model for better modeling users' successive check-in behaviors and further achieve superior recommendation results.

4. METHODS

In this section, we first discuss the method to handle social relations and temporal information. Based on this, we then introduce the integrated new model we proposed and the corresponding model parameter learning approach.

4.1 Social Relation

Social relations are basic elements in social networks, which cover friendship, following relationship, trust relationship, etc. These relations could be one-way or two-way relation. Usually, users with social relations tend to have similar preferences and affect each other in some activities. Intuitively, these are also suitable for successive POI recommendation task, since users have more possibility of visiting the POIs their friends have visited.

Social regularization is an elegant approach to integrating social relations with the latent factor model (Ma et al. 2011). It encourages users who are socially connected to have similar latent factors. Assume the original objective function is $\mathcal{L}_o$, the objective function of social regularization corresponds to $\mathcal{L}_s$, then the hybrid objective function becomes their blending, i.e., $\mathcal{L}_o + \alpha\mathcal{L}_s$ with a relative weight α.

We define the objective function of social regularization as follows,

$$\mathcal{L}_s = \sum_{u\in\mathcal{U}} ||\mathbf{U}_u - \frac{1}{\sum_{u'\in S(u)} \mathbf{B}_{u,u'}} \sum_{u'\in S(u)} \mathbf{B}_{u,u'}\mathbf{U}_{u'}||_2 \tag{5}$$

where $S(u)$ means the friend set of user u, $\beta_{u,u'}$ is the similarity value of user u and his friend u', $||\cdot||_2$ is the L2-norm. Thus, the central problem becomes how to compute the similarity value β_{u,u_f}. Using binary social relation directly cannot capture the different degrees of similarity between user u and his different friends. To address this issue, we define the following formula to compute the similarity degree,

$$\mathbf{B}_{u,u'} = \begin{cases} \frac{\sum_{i=1}^{|\mathcal{U}|} S_{u,i} S_{u',i}}{\sqrt{\sum_{i=1}^{|\mathcal{U}|}(S_{u,i})^2}\sqrt{\sum_{i=1}^{|\mathcal{U}|}(S_{u',i})^2}} & \text{if } u' \in S(u) \\ 0 & \text{else} \end{cases} \quad (6)$$

where $S_{u,i}$ equals 1 if user u and i are friends. We only keep their friends who rank within top k by the similarity degree to save computation cost for later parameter learning in Equation 9. In the experiments, we set k to be 10.

4.2 Temporal Information

To model temporal information of users' check-ins, we first segment the continuous temporal space into fixed-sized time periods. For example, we can just treat one hour of a day as one time period, which means the number of time periods $|\mathcal{T}|$ is 24. Then for any timestamp, it will belong to one time period uniquely. This could be easily determined by the hour value of the timestamp. In addition to constructing time periods based on hours, we can also consider weekday, month, and season information. There is a trade-off between time granularity and model complexity. In other words, too many periods will result in the overfitting problem, and further influence the final results. In this paper, we find that dividing 24 hours of each day into 6 time periods and meanwhile differentiating weekdays and weekends can get a little better results. Thus the number of time periods is set to be 12 ($|\mathcal{T}| = 2 \times 6$) in experiments.

Based on previous data analysis, incorporating the time period information into the new model for both users and POIs is promising. To reflect the diverse preference of users in different time periods, we extend the user latent factor $\mathbf{U}_u \in \mathbb{R}^{\mathcal{K}}$ to the user temporal latent matrix $\mathbf{U}_u \in \mathbb{R}^{\mathcal{K}\times|\mathcal{T}|}$, where $\mathbf{U}_{u,t} \in \mathbb{R}^{\mathcal{K}}$ denotes the temporal latent factor in time period t for user u. Besides, in order to reveal the popularity of each location changed over time periods, we add a temporal popularity factor $\mathbf{T}_i \in \mathbb{R}^{|\mathcal{T}|}$ for each POI i.

One concern for the operations is that the user temporal matrix $\mathbf{U}_u$ has $\mathcal{K} \times |\mathcal{T}|$ parameters to be learned. Thus it is more likely to suffer from overfitting than without considering temporal information. To overcome this issue, we can further add temporal regularization term to the objective function to control user temporal matrix in addition to social regularization term. In this work, we suppose that the change of factors of near time periods may be smooth. We calculate the similarity degree between near time periods based on the check-in behaviors of each user through cosine similarity. For each time period t, there are two near time periods, i.e., t_{-1} and t_{+1}. The first time period is near to the last due to periodicity. We denote the two similarity values as $\mathbf{A}_{t,t_{-1}}$ and $\mathbf{A}_{t,t_{+1}}$, respectively. Assume $P(u,t)$ denotes the POI set user u has visited in time period t, then the similarity degree $\mathbf{A}_{t,t_{-1}}$ can be computed as follows,

$$\mathbf{A}_{t,t_{-1}} = \frac{\sum_{i=1}^{|\mathcal{P}|} P_{u,t,i} P_{u,t_{-1},i}}{\sqrt{\sum_{i=1}^{|\mathcal{P}|}(P_{u,t,i})^2}\sqrt{\sum_{i=1}^{|\mathcal{P}|}(P_{u,t_{-1},i})^2}} \quad (7)$$

Analogously, $\mathbf{A}_{t,t_{+1}}$ can be calculated in the same way.

4.3 Model Construction and Learning

Inspired by the above results and the collaborative retrieval model introduced in Section 3.3, we formulate our new model (LTSCR). For a user u, $\mathbf{U}_{u,t} \in \mathbb{R}^{\mathcal{K}}$ denotes his temporal latent factor. For a POI i, it has three types of latent factors: 1) $\mathbf{P}_i \in \mathbb{R}^{\mathcal{K}}$ captures the transition patterns between successive check-in POIs. It can be regarded as the retrieval part in the collaborative retrieval model. Adding additional user dependent transformation matrix like CRM for this task does not improve the final results significantly and increase the computation cost through our experiments. Thus we leave them out in our approach; 2) $\mathbf{V}_i \in \mathbb{R}^{\mathcal{K}}$ models the preference between users and locations. It can be considered as the recommendation part in CRM; 3) $\mathbf{T}_i \in \mathbb{R}^{|\mathcal{T}|}$ denotes the popularity of the location changed over time periods.

Given the above statement, the recommendation ranking score can be calculated as follows. For a user u, assume the current POI he is visiting is i and the corresponding time period is t, which means the input query of user u is constituted by a POI-time pair (i,t). The preference to the next candidate POI c he may visit is measured by the following score function,

$$f(u,t,i,c) = (1-\alpha-\beta)\mathbf{P}_i^{\mathrm{T}}\mathbf{P}_c + \alpha\mathbf{U}_{u,t}^{\mathrm{T}}\mathbf{V}_c + \beta\mathbf{T}_{c,t} \quad (8)$$

where α and β control the relative strength of each part above and should meet the constraints: $\alpha \in \mathbb{R}_+$, $\beta \in \mathbb{R}_+$, and $\alpha + \beta \leq 1$. The setting of these two parameters will be discussed in Section 5.4.2. We should emphasize that we adopt $\mathbf{P}_i^{\mathrm{T}}\mathbf{P}_c$ instead of $\mathbf{P}_i^{\mathrm{T}}\mathbf{V}_c$ in the above equation as it can achieve better experimental results. This may be explained by the fact that the first one can directly learn the transition patterns from data.

In order to utilize the localized region constraint, we constrain the candidate recommendation location c should be within the grid the user currently stays in (the grid i belongs to) or its surrounding eight grids, which is the same as (Cheng et al. 2013). More details about the grid size setting can be referred in the later dataset preprocessing section.

We incorporate the social regularization term and the temporal regularization term mentioned before into our new model for learning from users' real check-in behaviors by expanding the standard WARP loss function. Given a user u and his current visiting POI i, we denote his true successive visiting POI as c. The learning process should first sample one negative POI c' to construct the training pair (u,t,i,c,c'). Under the localized region constraint, all the negative POIs should also be within the grid covering i or its surrounding eight grids. We use $\Omega_{tr}(u)$ to denote all the training pairs related to user u. With this spirit, LTSCR solves the following learning problem,

$$\begin{aligned} \min_{\mathbf{U},\mathbf{P},\mathbf{V},\mathbf{T}} & \sum_{u\in\mathcal{U}}\sum_{\Omega_{tr}(u)} L(\tilde{r}(c))\cdot\max\left(0, 1+f(u,t,i,c')-f(u,t,i,c)\right) \\ & + \frac{\sigma}{2}\sum_{u\in\mathcal{U}}\sum_{t\in|\mathcal{T}|}||\mathbf{U}_{u,t} - \frac{1}{\sum_{u'\in S(u)}\mathbf{B}_{u,u'}}\sum_{u'\in S(u)}\mathbf{B}_{u,u'}\mathbf{U}_{u',t}||_2 \\ & + \frac{\gamma}{2}\sum_{u\in\mathcal{U}}\sum_{t\in|\mathcal{T}|}\mathbf{A}_{t,t_{-1}}||\mathbf{U}_{u,t}-\mathbf{U}_{u,t_{-1}}||_2 + \mathbf{A}_{t,t_{+1}}||\mathbf{U}_{u,t}-\mathbf{U}_{u,t_{+1}}||_2 \\ & + \frac{\lambda}{2}\sum_{i\in\mathcal{P}}\left(||\mathbf{V}_i||_2 + ||\mathbf{P}_i||_2 + ||\mathbf{T}_i||_2\right) \end{aligned} \quad (9)$$

where the sampled negative POI c' for query POI i with positive POI c in LTSCR should satisfy the margin-based comparison $1 + f(u,t,i,c) > f(u,t,i,c')$. The last terms of the above optimization target are regularization terms which control the overfitting problem and are often employed in latent facor models. The number of sampling step for finding the adequate negative POI determines the approximate rank $\widetilde{r}(c)$ according to Equation 3. σ, γ, and λ are regularization parameters for the model which can be tuned on validation datasets.

The SGD algorithm is leveraged to optimize the above objective function. The central idea of SGD is to randomly scan all training pairs and update parameters though the gradient descent direction of the target function for each training pair. Each update is done by the following equation,

$$\Theta \leftarrow \Theta - \eta \cdot \frac{\partial Obj(\Theta)}{\partial \Theta} \tag{10}$$

where η corresponds to the learning rate. Θ denotes all model parameters, and Obj denotes the objective function shown in Equation 9.

Given a training pair (u,t,i,c,c') from the whole training data, the key gradients of all related parameters are computed as follows,

$$\begin{aligned}
\frac{\partial Obj(\mathbf{U}_{u,t,k})}{\partial \mathbf{U}_{u,t,k}} &= \alpha(\mathbf{V}_{c',k} - \mathbf{V}_{c,k})L(\widetilde{r}(c)) \\
&+ \sigma(\mathbf{U}_{u,t,k} - \frac{1}{\sum_{u' \in S(u)} \mathbf{B}_{u,u'}} \sum_{u' \in S(u)} \mathbf{B}_{u,u'}\mathbf{U}_{u',t,k}) \\
&+ \gamma(\mathbf{A}_{t,t_{-1}}(\mathbf{U}_{u,t,k} - \mathbf{U}_{u,t_{-1},k}) + \mathbf{A}_{t,t_{+1}}(\mathbf{U}_{u,t,k} - \mathbf{U}_{u,t_{+1},k})) \\
\frac{\partial Obj(\mathbf{P}_{i,k})}{\partial \mathbf{P}_{i,k}} &= (1-\alpha-\beta)(\mathbf{P}_{c',k} - \mathbf{P}_{c,k})L(\widetilde{r}(c)) + \lambda \mathbf{P}_{i,k} \\
\frac{\partial Obj(\mathbf{P}_{c,k})}{\partial \mathbf{P}_{c,k}} &= (1-\alpha-\beta)(-\mathbf{P}_{i,k})L(\widetilde{r}(c)) + \lambda \mathbf{P}_{c,k} \\
\frac{\partial Obj(\mathbf{V}_{c,k})}{\partial \mathbf{V}_{c,k}} &= -\alpha \mathbf{U}_{u,t,k} L(\widetilde{r}(c)) + \lambda \mathbf{V}_{c,k} \\
\frac{\partial Obj(\mathbf{T}_{c,t})}{\partial \mathbf{T}_{c,t}} &= -\beta L(\widetilde{r}(c)) + \lambda \mathbf{T}_{c,t}
\end{aligned} \tag{11}$$

We only list the gradients related to the positive location c. However, it is easy to derivate the similar gradients related to the negative location c'. After the gradients are calculated, we can update the parameters through Equation 10 uniformly. In summary, the complete learning algorithm for LTSCR is described in Algorithm 1.

Algorithm 1: The Learning Algorithm

Input: Training records $\mathcal{TR}$, Social similarities $\mathcal{SS}$, Temporal similarities $\mathcal{TS}$, Geographical grids $\mathcal{GG}$

Output: Optimal user factors $\mathbf{U}$, POI factors $W = \{\mathbf{P}, \mathbf{V}, \mathbf{T}\}$.

```
tt=0;
Initialize hyper-parameters;
Randomly initialize U, P, V, T;
while Obj(U, P, V, T) not converged and tt ≤ T_max do
    Randomly shuffle the training records TR;
    foreach training record k do
        Get (u, t, i, c) from record k;
        Sampling desirable negative POI c';
        Compute all gradients through Equation 11;
        Update model parameters by Equation 10;
        tt = tt + 1;
```

5. EXPERIMENTAL STUDY

To demonstrate the effectiveness and efficiency of our proposed models, we conducted experiments on two real datasets. We first describe the data preprocessing procedure in Section 5.1 and then give a simple introduction to the evaluation metrics we used in this task. We explain all the methods we compare in the experiments in Section 5.3. Lastly, we compare the results of all methods and analyze the possible reasons. All the algorithms were implemented using C++ and we conducted all the experiments on a server (four 3.00GHz CPU cores, 20GB memory) with 64-bit Linux system. In this paper, we exploit the same ordinary data structures for all the algorithms and do not consider any parallel computation.

5.1 Datasets Preprocessing

We employ two public datasets, i.e., Brightkite and Gowalla in the experiments, just as mentioned in Section 3.1. As stated in Section 3.2, we address the problem of successive POI recommendation problem. When a user specifies a POI and its corresponding visiting time, the algorithms should recommend new POIs the user prefers to visit in the near future. In order to evaluate the results of all methods, we should extract reasonable successive check-in records from the same user to simulate the process. In the experiments, we regard two successive check-ins within $T = 2\,(hour)$ as a valid successive check-in pair. This strategy is similar to [20, 4]. To filter noisy data, we further select users who have at least 10 records and POIs which have at least 5 records in all check-in pairs gotten from the previous step. After finishing the preprocessing, we gain the ultimate experimental datasets. The details of the two datasets are shown in Table 1.

Table 1: Basic Statistics of Location-based Social Network Data.

Dataset	User	POI	Check-in Pair	Edge
Brightkite	4930	14393	126160	64504
Gowalla	34113	146544	1138971	283570

In order to utilize the localized region constraint motivated by the data analysis in Section 3.1, we divide the geographical space into nearly equally-sized grids whose areas are $0.05(longitude) \times 0.05(latitude)$, which can include most successive check-in pairs. We randomly divide the two datasets into training, validation, and test datasets according to the ratio $7:1:2$, meanwhile, assure that each user and POI occur at least one time in the training data. All the models are trained on the training datasets and all the hyper-parameters are tuned on the validation datasets. Finally, we compare all the models on the test datasets.

5.2 Evaluation Measures

To evaluate the successive POI recommendation results, we adopt two types of standard evaluation metrics: (1) Pre-

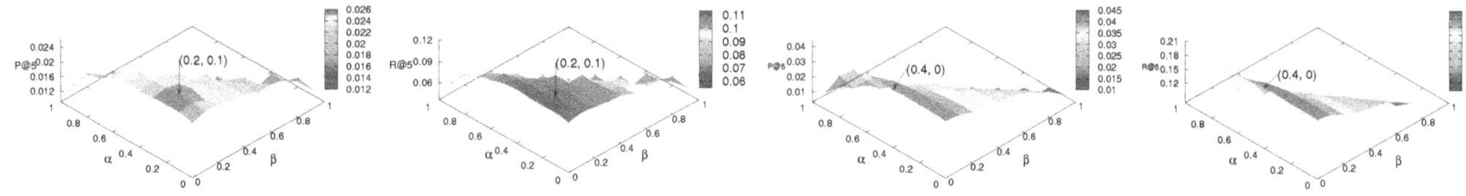

(a) Precision@5 in Brightkite. (b) Recall@5 in Brightkite. (c) Precision@5 in Gowalla. (d) Recall@5 in Gowalla.

Figure 4: Impact of Different Settings of α and β.

cision@n (Precision at Position n) and Recall@n (Recall at Position n), and (2) MRR(Mean Reciprocal Rank).

Precision and recall are mainly used in previous recommendation tasks [20, 4] which relate to our work. Generally, it is computed by the following formula,

$$R@n = \frac{N_{tr}}{N_t}, \qquad P@n = \frac{N_{tr}}{n} \tag{12}$$

where N_{tr} denotes the number of truly recommended items, and N_t represents the number of total true items.

We should emphasize that for each query POI, the number of true recommendation results is small for collaborative retrieval task. Therefore, the precision of results may be relative low as long as k is not small. That's also why the works [20, 9] do not use metric Precision@n. As a complementary, we adopt MRR metric that concentrates on measuring positions of the first correct recommendation results. In our problem setting, MRR is calculated as

$$MRR = \frac{1}{|\mathcal{U}|}\sum_{u}^{|\mathcal{U}|}\frac{1}{|Q_u|}\sum_{i}^{|Q_u|}\frac{1}{rank_i} \tag{13}$$

where $|Q_u|$ is the number of implicit location queries each user u has and $rank_i$ specifies the position of the first correct successive POI the user will visit based on the query i.

5.3 Comparison Methods and Components

We adopt the following five methods in the experiments. Among them, the first two are popularity based methods and the middle two are model based methods. The main targets of the experiments are to demonstrate that our proposed method outperforms these methods.

- **POP**: Pure popularity based method is simple with only considering the total check-in count of each POI for this task. Thus it can be regarded as the baseline for our later comparisons.
- **POP+LR**: It briefly extends POP by additional incorporating localized region constraint for POI candidates generation. In other words, for each query POI, the successive POIs to be recommended should have large total check-in count and meanwhile be located in its surrounding grids.
- **PMF+LR**: Probabilistic matrix factorization (PMF) is a standard approach for recommendation tasks [16], which can be extended by incorporating distance factor for traditional POI recommendation task [3]. We adapt this model to the successive POI recommendation task by additionally considering localized region constraint. Thus, it can be treated as a direct adaptation of traditional POI recommendation approach to successive POI recommendation task.
- **FPMC+LR**: FPMC+LR is the statc-of-the-art method for successive POI recommendation task [4]. Compared to PMF+LR, it utilizes the users' current visiting POI information.
- **LTSCR**: Location and time aware social collaborative retrieval model is the perfect model we proposed which integrates social relation, location information, temporal information with collaborative retrieval framework. We hope to verify its superiority.

Besides, it is also necessary to verify the effectiveness of the main components of LTSCR. To achieve this, we adopt the strategy similar to the forward selection method which is frequently employed in feature selection task [8]. Specifically, starting from the basic model (FPMC+LR), we add one more component that we intend to test each time and compare them in an incremental fashion. Here, we conclude the two partial methods to be adopted in later comparison as follows,

- **FPMC+LR+S**: The approach incorporates social relations into FPMC+LR. If the results show that this model outperforms FPMC+LR, then it can demonstrate users indeed prefer to visit POIs that their friends have visited empirically.
- **FPMC+LR+ST**: This model further considers temporal information of visiting. We adopt the same way as LTSCR used to model temporal information. If it behaves better than the previous method, the benefit of temporal information is experimentally verified.

Based on the results of the above partial methods of LTSCR, we can also demonstrate the advantage of utilizing the merits of CRM by comparing LTSCR with FPMC+LR+ST.

5.4 Parameter Settings

In this part, we mainly describe the hyper-parameters we tuned for LTSCR on the validation datasets. The other adopted comparison methods are also tuned to ensure to achieve their good results.

5.4.1 Learning Rate and Factor Dimension

There is a tradeoff between learning speed and convergence guarantee for learning rate setting. Without specific mention, we set learning rate η to be 0.01 for all models. The dimension of all latent factors are set to be 20 for Brightkite

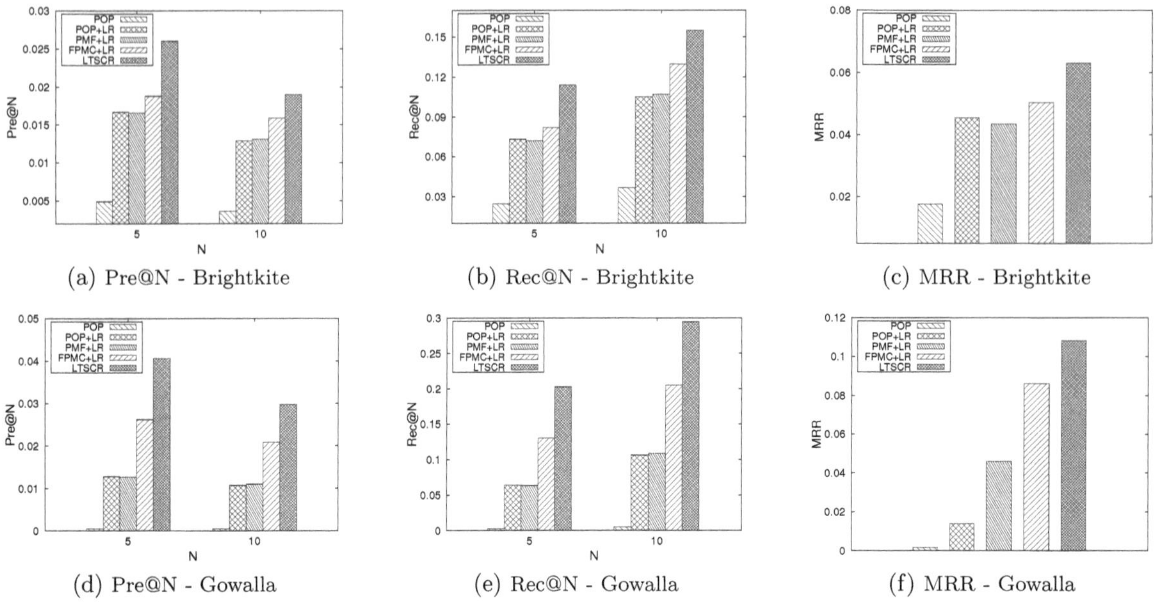

(a) Pre@N - Brightkite (b) Rec@N - Brightkite (c) MRR - Brightkite

(d) Pre@N - Gowalla (e) Rec@N - Gowalla (f) MRR - Gowalla

Figure 5: Comparisons of Different Methods on Recall@k, Precision@k, and MRR Metric.

dataset and 40 for Gowalla in our most experiments. This is inspired by the analysis of dimension influence on recommendation performance in Section 5.5.3.

5.4.2 *Tuning of Parameter α and β*

As shown in Equation 8, α and β control the relative influence of different parts on preference score computation. Here, we determine them based on the performances of Precision@5 and Recall@5 on validation datasets which coincide with the recommendation objective. Specifically, we employ the grid search method to get optimal setting by configuring α and β with different combinations. As Figure 4 shows, temporal factors of POIs play a minor role in optimal results compared with the other two parts. The optimal parameter configurations are pointed out in both figures and it is evident that the variations of results near the optimal point are relatively smooth. Without loss of generality, we set $\alpha = 0.2, \beta = 0.1$ for Brightkite data and $\alpha = 0.4, \beta = 0$ for Gowalla data, respectively.

5.4.3 *Regularization Parameters*

The regularization terms λ for all latent factors are set to be 0.1 across all the models based on the results on validation dataset after several trials on $\{10^{-3}, 10^{-2}, \cdots, 10^{3}\}$. It is intuitive that γ and σ should be larger than λ as they capture additional knowledge to constrain the latent factors. We experimented many combinations for γ and σ. Experimentally, we find that the results continue to grow slowly with increase of γ and σ as long as they are larger than 1 and not too large. Empirically, we set them to be 10 which can ensure good results.

5.5 Experimental Results

5.5.1 *Comparison Study*

We start with discussing the results reported in Figure 5. Firstly, we compare the two POI popularity based methods, i.e., POP with POP+LR. From the table, we can see that POP+LR performs consistently better than POP in both datasets. The phenomenon is rational since POP+LR utilizes the localization property of successive check-ins and ranks POIs only in local regions.

Then we analyze the results of the basic model based approach PMF+LR. Actually, we find the results of PMF+LR shows no improvements over POP+LR's, except the result corresponding to MRR metric in Gowalla dataset. Knowledge gotten from the above comparison is two-folds. It reflects that PMF+LR is not very suited for the successive POI recommendation task. Besides, popularity based method is not very robust when the size of candidate POIs is large as their performance drops significantly in the large Gowalla dataset. By comparing FPMC+LR with the above methods, we can conclude that the incorporation of users' current visiting locations is crucial for the successive POI recommendation task. This can be explained by that the current location each user stays in can be regarded as an implicit query which is an indicative for his successive check-in choice.

Finally, we contrast LTSCR with all other models. As the results show, LTSCR behaves vastly superior to both PMF+LR and FPMC+LR, which reveals that our proposed approach improves the state-of-the-art results significantly. The analysis of the key components of LTSCR is introduced subsequently. As we mentioned before, for each location and time aware query, the number of true recommendation results is small for successive POI recommendation task. Therefore, the precision of results may be relative low as long as n in Precision@n is not small. However, the relative improvements on Precision@n are significant. For example, LTSCR achieves 38.3% and 54.9% relative improvements over FPMC+LR on metric Precision@5 for datasets Brightkite and Gowalla, respectively.

5.5.2 *Effectiveness of Main Components*

We verify the effectiveness of utilizing social relation, temporal information, and collaborative retrieval framework in LTSCR through an incremental comparison strategy using the results shown in Figure 6.

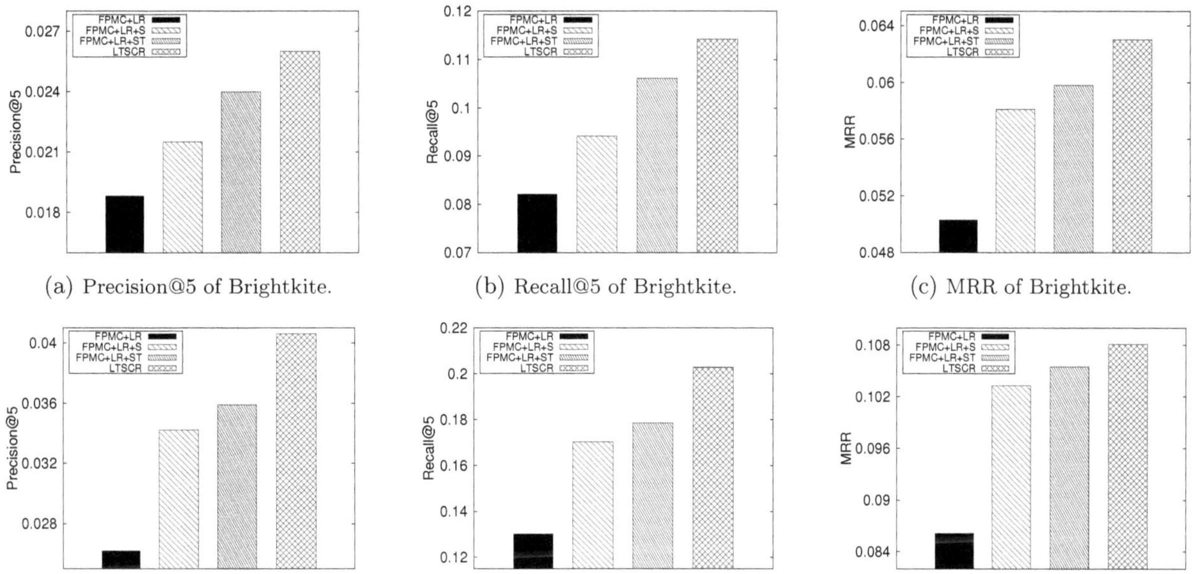

(a) Precision@5 of Brightkite. (b) Recall@5 of Brightkite. (c) MRR of Brightkite.

(d) Precision@5 of Gowalla. (e) Recall@5 of Gowalla. (f) MRR of Gowalla.

Figure 6: Performance of Different Components of LTSCR.

First, FPMC+LR+S consistently outperforms FPMC+LR in the two datasets notably. This indicates the effectiveness of using social relation for our task. Based on FPMC+LR+S, FPMC+LR+ST is further provided which is a direct extension of FPMC+LR+S by incorporating temporal information in the model, just as we mentioned in Section 5.3. The comparison between FPMC+LR+ST and FPMC+LR+S fits in with our expectation, as FPMC+LR+ST achieves better results. Thus, considering temporal information can benefit the task. Finally, to demonstrate the superiority of collaborative retrieval framework, we make a comparison between LTSCR and FPMC+LR+ST. As expected, LTSCR behaves the best among all the methods and outperforms FPMC+LR+ST.

In summary, through the above incremental comparisons, we can conclude that the main components we utilized are suited for the successive POI recommendation task.

5.5.3 *Dimension Influence*

In this section, we will briefly discuss how the dimension of latent factors influences the results. We conduct experiments on Precision@5 and Recall@5 on two datasets separately with different dimension setting changing from 5 to 100. The results are reported in Figure 8.

Clearly, the variation trend of the results on Brightkite dataset is not very stable. Although almost all the methods increase monotonously before reaching dimension 10, PMF+LR encounters an inflection point at this dimension. Purely increasing the dimension of latent factors may cause the overfitting problem, especially on the Brightkite dataset which is not very large. From a whole perspective, setting dimension to be 20 for Brightkite is an acceptable choice.

On the other hand, the curves drawn in Figure 8(c) and 8(d) are much clearer to reflect how the change of the dimension influences the results on Gowalla dataset. When the dimension is small, i.e., less than 30, the growth rate is fast. Then they start to converge after the dimension surpass 30 and retain pretty stable after 40.

From the two figures, we can also conclude that our proposed method consistently outperforms the other two model-based approaches, no matter how large the dimension is.

5.5.4 *Learning Cost Analysis*

Under the SGD learning framework, the total time of learning for LTSCR is mainly dominated by the cost of each learning iteration and the number of iterations.

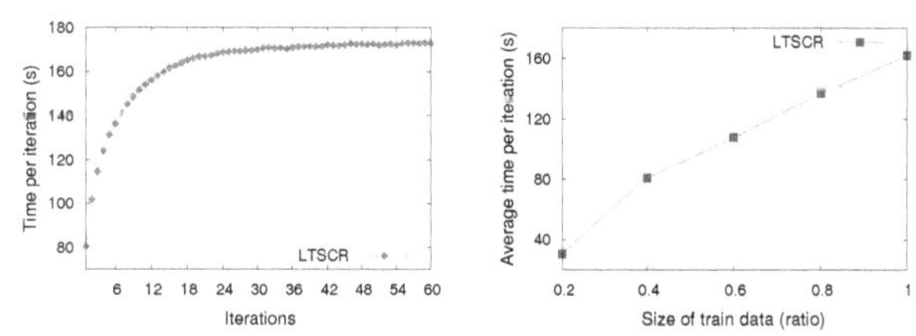

(a) Change of Time Cost (b) Data Size Influence

Figure 7: Time Cost of LTSCR on Gowalla.

In each iteration, the time cost depends on the size of training instances and learning speed for each instance. As we introduced in Section 3.3, the sampling process for WARP loss could only be terminated when a sampled item satisfies the margin-based comparison. Thus, At the beginning of learning, the time cost for each instance is small as it is rapid to sample a negative item which satisfies the requirement. As the optimization process proceeds, the time cost will increase. Theoretically, the maximal number of sampling step for a training pair is $|\mathcal{P}| - 1$. However, when the optimization converges, the time cost of sampling will also be bounded. We tested the LTSCR's learning time cost of each iteration on the large Gowalla dataset, which has nearly one million training pairs. As shown in Figure 7(a), when the time cost reaches a stable state, it is only slightly over 2 times as large as the time cost of the beginning, which is acceptable for model learning.

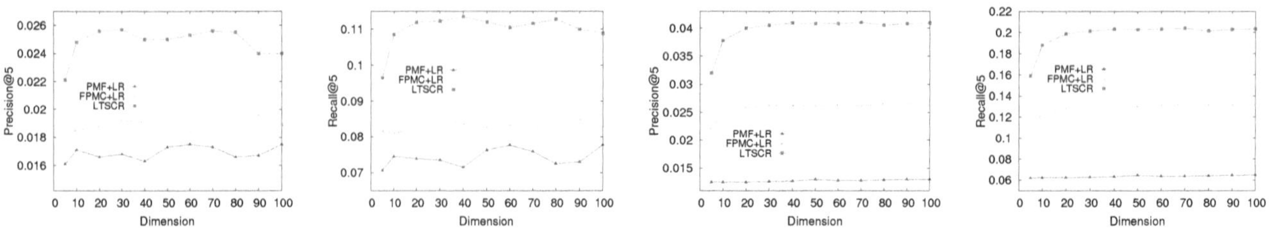

(a) Precision@5 of Brightkite. (b) Recall@5 of Brightkite. (c) Precision@5 of Gowalla. (d) Recall@5 of Gowalla.

Figure 8: Results with Varying Dimension.

Besides, we tested how the data size affects the time cost of the learning of LTSCR on the large Gowalla dataset. From the results shown in Figure 7(b), we can estimate the average time cost of one iteration grows about linearly with the size of the dataset.

6. CONCLUSION

In this paper, we have proposed a new latent factor model called LTSCR for successive POI recommendation task. The new model not only considers users' current visiting locations, temporal information of visiting, social relations, and the localization of successive check-ins simultaneously, but also utilizes the merits of collaborative retrieval model. We validate the model on two real datasets. The experimental results have shown that 1) social and temporal information are indeed beneficial for this task, and 2) LTSCR outperforms the several other methods.

Acknowledgments

We thank the anonymous reviewers for their valuable and constructive comments. This work was supported in part by National Basic Research Program of China (973 Program) under Grant No. 2011CB302206, National Natural Science Foundation of China under Grant No. 61272088, and Tsinghua University Initiative Scientific Research Program.

7. REFERENCES

[1] A. Ahmed, L. Hong, and A. J. Smola. Hierarchical geographical modeling of user locations from social media posts. In *WWW*, pages 25–36, 2013.

[2] D. M. Blei, A. Y. Ng, and M. I. Jordan. Latent dirichlet allocation. *J. Mach. Learn. Res.*, 3:993–1022, Mar. 2003.

[3] C. Cheng, H. Yang, I. King, and M. R. Lyu. Fused matrix factorization with geographical and social influence in location-based social networks. In *AAAI*, 2012.

[4] C. Cheng, H. Yang, M. R. Lyu, and I. King. Where you like to go next: Successive point-of-interest recommendation. In *IJCAI*, 2013.

[5] H. Cheng, J. Ye, and Z. Zhu. What's your next move: User activity prediction in location-based social networks. In *SDM*, pages 171–179, 2013.

[6] E. Cho, S. A. Myers, and J. Leskovec. Friendship and mobility: user movement in location-based social networks. In *KDD*, pages 1082–1090, 2011.

[7] H. Gao, J. Tang, X. Hu, and H. Liu. Exploring temporal effects for location recommendation on location-based social networks. In *RecSys*, pages 93–100, 2013.

[8] I. Guyon and A. Elisseeff. An introduction to variable and feature selection. *J. Mach. Learn. Res.*, 3:1157–1182, Mar. 2003.

[9] K.-J. Hsiao, A. Kulesza, and A. O. H. III. Social collaborative retrieval. In *WSDM*, pages 293–302, 2014.

[10] B. Hu, M. Jamali, and M. Ester. Spatio-temporal topic modeling in mobile social media for location recommendation. In *ICDM*, pages 1073–1078, 2013.

[11] T. Kurashima, T. Iwata, T. Hoshide, N. Takaya, and K. Fujimura. Geo topic model: joint modeling of user's activity area and interests for location recommendation. In *WSDM*, pages 375–384, 2013.

[12] R. Li, S. Wang, H. Deng, R. Wang, and K. C.-C. Chang. Towards social user profiling: unified and discriminative influence model for inferring home locations. In *KDD*, pages 1023–1031, 2012.

[13] B. Liu, Y. Fu, Z. Yao, and H. Xiong. Learning geographical preferences for point-of-interest recommendation. In *KDD*, pages 1043–1051, 2013.

[14] X. Liu, Q. He, Y. Tian, W.-C. Lee, J. McPherson, and J. Han. Event-based social networks: linking the online and offline social worlds. In *KDD*, pages 1032–1040, 2012.

[15] S. Rendle, C. Freudenthaler, and L. Schmidt-Thieme. Factorizing personalized markov chains for next-basket recommendation. In *WWW*, pages 811–820, 2010.

[16] R. Salakhutdinov and A. Mnih. Probabilistic matrix factorization. In *NIPS*, 2007.

[17] J. Sang, T. Mei, J.-T. Sun, C. Xu, and S. Li. Probabilistic sequential pois recommendation via check-in data. In *SIGSPATIAL*, pages 402–405, 2012.

[18] N. Usunier, D. Buffoni, and P. Gallinari. Ranking with ordered weighted pairwise classification. In *Proceedings of the 26th Annual International Conference on Machine Learning*, ICML '09, pages 1057–1064, New York, NY, USA, 2009. ACM.

[19] J. Weston, S. Bengio, and N. Usunier. Large scale image annotation: Learning to rank with joint word-image embeddings. *Mach. Learn.*, 81(1):21–35, Oct. 2010.

[20] J. Weston, C. Wang, R. J. Weiss, and A. Berenzweig. Latent collaborative retrieval. In *ICML*, 2012.

[21] D.-N. Yang, C.-Y. Shen, W.-C. Lee, and M.-S. Chen. On socio-spatial group query for location-based social networks. In *KDD*, pages 949–957, 2012.

[22] N. Yang, X. Kong, F. Wang, and P. S. Yu. When and where: Predicting human movements based on social spatial-temporal events. In *SDM*, pages 515–523, 2014.

[23] M. Ye, P. Yin, W.-C. Lee, and D.-L. Lee. Exploiting geographical influence for collaborative point-of-interest recommendation. In *SIGIR*, pages 325–334, 2011.

[24] H. Yin, Y. Sun, B. Cui, Z. Hu, and L. Chen. Lcars: A location-content-aware recommender system. In *KDD*, pages 221–229, New York, NY, USA, 2013. ACM.

[25] Q. Yuan, G. Cong, Z. Ma, A. Sun, and N. Magnenat-Thalmann. Time-aware point-of-interest recommendation. In *SIGIR*, pages 363–372, 2013.

[26] W. Zhang and J. Wang. A collective bayesian poisson factorization model for cold-start local event recommendation. In *KDD*, Sydney, Australia, 2015.

[27] W. Zhang, J. Wang, and W. Feng. Combining latent factor model with location features for event-based group recommendation. In *KDD*, pages 910–918, Chicago, IL, USA, 2013.

Where you Instagram? Associating Your Instagram Photos with Points of Interest

Xutao Li[+] Tuan-Anh Nguyen Pham[+] Gao Cong[+]
Quan Yuan[+] Xiao-Li Li[#] Shonali Krishnaswamy[#]
[+]School of Computer Engineering, Nanyang Technological University, Singapore.
{lixutao@, pham0070@e., gaocong@, qyuan1@e.}ntu.edu.sg
[#]Institute for Infocomm Research(I2R), A*STAR, Singapore.
{xlli, spkrishna}@i2r.a-star.edu.sg

ABSTRACT

Instagram, an online photo-sharing platform, has gained increasing popularity. It allows users to take photos, apply digital filters and share them with friends instantaneously by using mobile devices. Instagram provides users with the functionality to associate their photos with points of interest, and it thus becomes feasible to study the association between points of interest and Instagram photos. However, no previous work studies the association. In this paper, we propose to study the problem of mapping Instagram photos to points of interest. To understand the problem, we analyze Instagram datasets, and report our findings, which also characterize the challenges of the problem. To address the challenges, we propose to model the mapping problem as a ranking problem, and develop a method to learn a ranking function by exploiting the textual, visual and user information of photos. To maximize the prediction effectiveness for textual and visual information, and incorporate the users' visiting preferences, we propose three subobjectives for learning the parameters of the proposed ranking function. Experimental results on two sets of Instagram data show that the proposed method substantially outperforms existing methods that are adapted to handle the problem.

Categories and Subject Descriptors

H.3.3 [**Information Storage and Retrieval**]: Information Filtering

Keywords

Photo Mapping; Ranking; Point of Interest

1. INTRODUCTION

Instagram, a mobile based photo-sharing system, allows users to share their photos with friends instantaneously on various social networking platforms, e.g., Facebook, Twitter, etc. It provides users with many digital filters for creating magic visual effects on their photos, and users can express their sentiments/opinions and give comments on uploaded photos. Launched in October 2010, Instagram has gained popularity rapidly over the past several years. As of December 2014, it had over 300 million active users who shared more than 20 billion photos.[1] The Instagram community is still growing at a rapid speed and on average more than 40 million photos are uploaded per day.

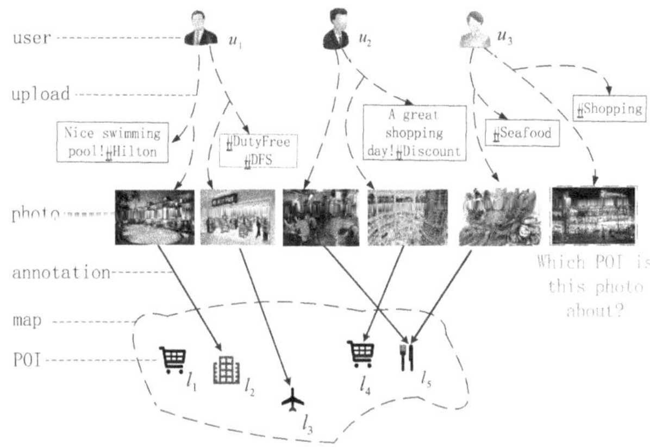

Figure 1: A graph representation of the interactions in Instagram.

One interesting functionality of Instragram is that it allows users to associate photos with Points of Interest (POIs), which offers an exciting opportunity to study the association between photos and POIs. In Figure 1, we give an example to show how users, photos and POIs interplay with each other. In Instagram a user can upload photos with textual descriptions and hashtags. For example, user u_1 submitted a photo with the description "Nice swimming pool!" and meanwhile the hashtag "#Hilton" was used. Users can also associate the uploaded photos with POIs, e.g., user u_1 annotated the two pictures he uploaded to the POIs ℓ_2 and ℓ_3, respectively.

Knowing the association between photos and POIs has important applications. First, it provides both visual and textual annotations about POIs for users to explore. For example, when we are interested in visiting a POI, we can browse the photos associated with it to see the POI and it-

Permission to make digital or hard copies of all or part of this work for personal or classroom use is granted without fee provided that copies are not made or distributed for profit or commercial advantage and that copies bear this notice and the full citation on the first page. Copyrights for components of this work owned by others than ACM must be honored. Abstracting with credit is permitted. To copy otherwise, or republish, to post on servers or to redistribute to lists, requires prior specific permission and/or a fee. Request permissions from Permissions@acm.org.

CIKM'15, October 19 - 23, 2015, Melbourne, VIC, Australia

© 2015 ACM. ISBN 978-1-4503-3794-6/15/10...$15.00

DOI: http://dx.doi.org/10.1145/2806416.2806463 .

[1] http://www.statista.com/statistics/253577/number-of-monthly-active-instagram-users/

s environment; meanwhile, we can read the corresponding textual information to find interesting aspects or social activities related to the POI. Second, the association is a fundamental data preprocessing task, which is a prerequisite for other mining tasks. Third, associating photos and POIs will help to understand users' preferences over POIs. Recently, Silva et al. have studied the Instagram data [22], compared Instagram photos with the check-ins on Foursquare [23], and shown that photos can be mimicked as check-ins at POIs.

When users upload photos, they need manually associate photos with POIs, which can be tedious. In Instagram, only less than 30% pictures are annotated to POIs by users. Thus, studying how to automatically map Instagram photos to POIs is an important problem. However, to the best of our knowledge, no existing work has considered the problem.

In this paper, we propose to study the problem of mapping the Instagram photos to POIs. Specifically, given the photos that have been associated with POIs as training set, we learn a mapping function to annotate a photo that is not associated with POI. The problem is challenging because of two reasons. First, as we will see in Section 3.2, we find that the number of photos associated with each POI follows a power law distribution. That is, a great number of POIs have very few photos and thus it is difficult to train an effective mapping model for them due to the data scarcity problem. Second, we have not only visual and textual information, but also user visiting information to explore. The visiting preferences of users over POIs, as an important type of information, should be exploited, which is also a way to overcome the data scarcity problem. As we will see in Section 3.2, however, we find that users tend to take photos at POIs that are new to them, and this makes it difficult to exploit users' visiting preferences.

Note that our problem differs from previous studies on mapping Flickr photos to the earth. Previous work on Flickr photos can be classified into two types. One type is associating photos to some landmarks [5, 14, 3], and the other is dividing the world map into grids and then predicting which grid a photo belongs to [20, 18, 11, 16]. For the first type, the landmarks usually refer to popular places and thus there are enough photos in each landmark to train a model. In our case, as aforementioned we lack photos for the majority of POIs due to the power law distribution. Furthermore, in these approaches [5, 14], the number of landmarks considered is limited, and it is unclear how to effectively scale these approaches coping with many POIs when the training samples are scarce. For the second type, a grid region usually contains multiple POIs and mapping photos to a grid level is insufficient to annotate POIs. Another major difference is these previous studies do not exploit the visiting preferences of users to POIs. However, Instagram data reveals users' visiting preferences over POIs [23], and thus it is important to exploit user information in our problem.

To solve the photo mapping problem, we first explore the characteristics of Instagram data. We make three interesting observations: (1) most of POIs have fewer than 10 photos; (2) users in general associate fewer than 50 photos with POIs in one year and the number of users who associate more than 50 photos decreases in a power law fashion; (3) users tend to take photos at POIs that are new to them. These findings are reported for the first time, and also characterize the challenges of our problem (to be analyzed in Section 3.2). Second, we model the mapping problem as a ranking problem, and define a function to score POIs in terms of the textual context, visual content and user information for a given photo. In particular, we propose a new multi-task model to combine the textual, visual and user information for learning the scoring function. In the proposed model, we maximize prediction abilities of the combined (textual, visual and user) information as the main objective, and maximize prediction effectiveness of textual and visual information as two subobjectives. As a result, the most informative features from textual context and visual content can be effectively combined into the function. Moreover, we effectively incorporate the visiting preferences of users into the scoring function by designing another weighted matrix factorization subobjective. The contributions of this paper can be summarized as follows.

- We define the new problem of associating Instagram photos with POIs. We make interesting observations on Instagram and report new findings on Instagram for the first time. To the best of our knowledge, we are the first to propose and study the problem.

- We propose a method, Ranking with Textual, Visual and User information for Photos to POIs, called Rank-TVU_P2P, which is able to combine not only the textual and visual information but also users' visiting preferences for mapping Instagram photos to POIs. In the proposed method, we develop a subtask to maximize the prediction effectiveness for each type of information (textual context, visual content and user). In particular, a weighted matrix factorization subtask is developed for modeling the visiting preferences of users. As a result, the most effective information is combined into our scoring function for POIs.

- Extensive experiments on two sets of Instagram data, namely, New York City and Singapore, are conducted, and the results show that our proposed method outperforms baseline methods significantly. Moreover, the experimental results demonstrate the usefulness of each type of information, and the importance of our developed subobjectives (subtasks).

The rest of the paper is organized as follows. In Section 2, we briefly review related work. In Section 3, we explore the Instagram data and present some interesting patterns we find. Our proposed model is introduced in Section 4 and experimental results are presented in Section 5. Finally, we conclude the paper with some future research directions in Section 6.

2. RELATED WORK

2.1 Geolocating Images

Previous work on geolocating images can be categorized into two types. One type is dividing the concerned region into grids and predicting the grid where an image resides, and the other type is identifying from a set of candidates the landmark that an image refers to.

Grid Prediction. Hays and Efros [6] propose a data driven approach to calibrating Flickr images to grids on the earth. In the approach, they first filter Flickr images by some specific geo-related and some obviously geo-unrelated tags, and then place the images onto $200km \times 200km$ grids by employing K-nearest neighbors algorithm with some predefined visual features. Instead of leveraging visual features, Serdyukov et al. [20] adopt textual features, i.e., user-generated tags, to map the Flickr photos to grids. They build a Language Model (LM) for each grid in terms of its associated tags, and place the photos according to the probability calculated by the LMs. Liu et al. [16] propose to build LM for a user in terms of the tags he/she used, and then combine it with grid-based LM for mapping Flickr images to grids. In this approach, only textual features are considered.

Our problem differs from these previous studies [6, 20, 16] mainly in two aspects. First, we aim to associate Instagram photos with POIs, instead of grids. A grid usually contains multiple POIs and mapping photos to grid level is insufficient to annotate POIs. Nevertheless, we adapt the approach in the work [16] for our problem, and compare with it in our experiments. Second, previous studies do not consider the visiting preferences of users. However, the photos uploaded in Instagram resemble check-ins [23], which are very useful to characterize users' preferences over POIs and should not be overlooked for our problem.

Landmark Identification. Crandall et al. [5] combine both visual (Scale Invariant Feature Transform–SIFT features [17]) and textual (tag features) information to place Flickr photos onto landmarks, which is a representative work on landmark identification. In their work, they focus on identifying which of 10 landmarks in a city an image belongs to. Their solution is considering the problem as a multi-class classification problem. In particular, they build Support Vector Machine (SVM) and Naive Bayesian (NB) based on visual and textual features, respectively, and then combine the classification results of them to produce final prediction. Other example studies on landmark identification include [14], [3], [25] and [1].

Our work differs from these studies in two aspects. First, the landmarks often refer to popular places and thus there exit sufficient photos to train a classification model. However, in our problem, we lack training photos because most of POIs have only a few photos. Moreover, the number of landmark candidates considered in previous studies is very small , e.g., 10 landmarks [5], while the number of POIs is much larger, e.g., more than one thousand. It is not very effective to train a classification model for our problem where the training samples are scarce, as we will see in the experiments. Second, these studies do not consider the users' preferences over POIs.

2.2 Geolocating Tweets or Users

As a vast amount of tweets and online information are generated by users, several studies have been conducted for predicting locations of tweets or users [2, 4, 12, 24]. For example, based on user-supplied home address information and social friendship information in Facebook, Backstrom et al. [2] propose to predict the locations of users by measuring and using their social and spatial proximity. Cheng et al. [4] develop a probabilistic approach to estimating the city-level location of a Twitter user, which purely relies on the content of his/her tweets. In their approach, a classification model is first built to identify the geoscope word in tweets for estimating users' locations, and then a lattice-based neighborhood smoothing model is proposed to refine the estimations. Recently, Li et al. [12] study a similar problem to identify the cities of residence for Twitter users. They propose a unified discriminative influence model based on the assumption that Twitter users tend to follow users living close to them. However, these approaches focus on a city-level granularity and cannot solve our problem because city-level accuracy is too coarse to associate photos with POIs. Moreover, users' visiting preferences over POIs and visual features of photos are not explored in the approaches. Yuan et al. [24] develop a spatio-temporal topic model based on Twitter data, which can also be used for estimating users' locations or tweets' locations given a time.

Table 1: Data statistics of NYC and SG.

Statistics	NYC	SG
# of photos	21,910,375	13,168,666
# of POIs	602,604	372,104
# of users	126,543	87,281
% of photos annotated to POIs	29	26
% of photos with textual info.	92	94

3. INSTAGRAM EXPLORATION

3.1 Data Description

We crawled two sets of Instagram data from 13 Nov 2013 to 13 Nov 2014, which were from users in New York City (NYC) and Singapore (SG), respectively. When crawling the data, a user was considered from NYC or SG if more than a half of his/her Instagram photos were taken in the region of NYC or SG. We refer to the two datasets as NYC and SG, respectively. NYC comprises 602,604 POIs and 21,910,375 photos taken by 126,543 users, and SG comprises 372,104 POIs and 13,168,666 photos taken by 87,281 users. 92% and 94% of NYC and SG photos are accompanied with textual information, respectively. When users upload photos, they need manually associate photos with POIs. We find that 29% and 26% photos have been already annotated to POIs by users for both data, respectively. In other words, more than 70% of photos in Instagram are not mapped to POIs. The basic statistics of both data are summarized in Table 1.

3.2 Data Analysis

Observation 1: Number of photos per POI. We show in Figures 2(a) and 2(b) the empirical Complementary Cumulative Distribution Function (CCDF) of number of photos per POI, for NYC and SG data, respectively. We observe that both CCDFs follow the power law distribution, i.e., $P[X \geq x] = x^{\alpha}$, where X is a random variable for the number of photos and α is a coefficient. By fitting the empirical distribution, we obtain the coefficient $\alpha = -0.96$ and $\alpha = -0.99$ for NYC and SG, respectively.

Given a power law distribution, we can compute $x \approx \lfloor \exp(\frac{\ln P}{\alpha}) \rfloor$ if we know the probability $P[X \geq x]$. For example, when $P[X \geq x] = 10\%$, we have $x \approx 11$ and $x \approx 10$ for NYC and SG, respectively.[2] This means only 10% of POIs have at least 11 or 10 photos for NYC and SG, respectively, and the other 90% of POIs have no more than 11 or 10 photos. Due to this issue, it would not be effective to train a

[2]This is in accordance with the empirical distribution we computed, where $P[X \geq 11] = 9.82\%$ and $P[X \geq 10] = 10.2\%$ for NYC and SG, respectively.

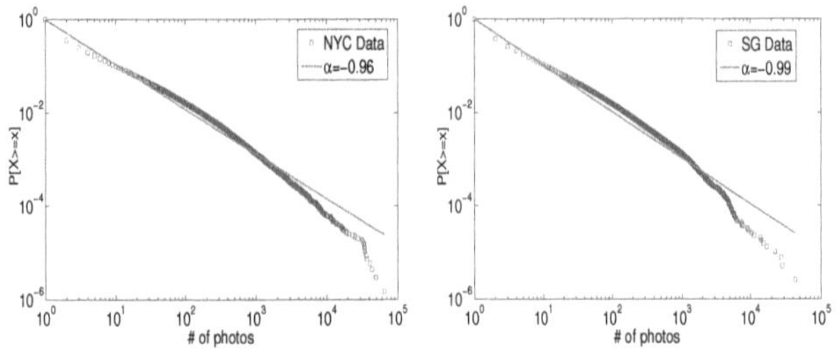

(a) NYC (b) SG

Figure 2: Distribution of number of photos per POI.

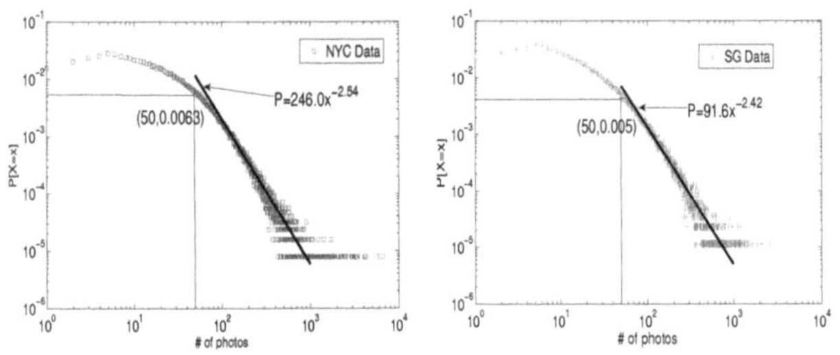

(a) NYC (b) SG

Figure 3: Distribution of number of photos associated with POIs per user.

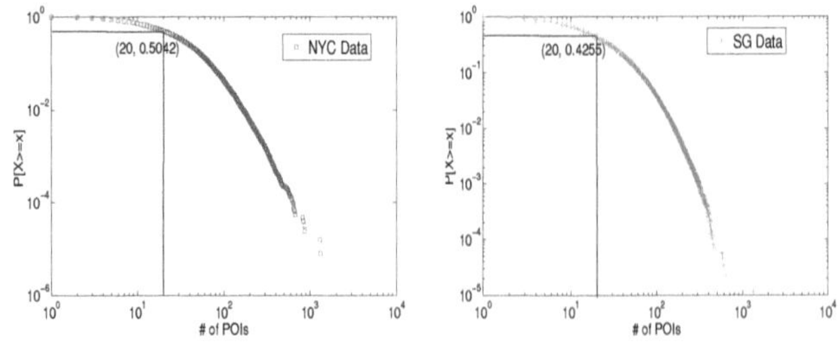

(a) NYC (b) SG

Figure 4: Distribution of number of POIs per user.

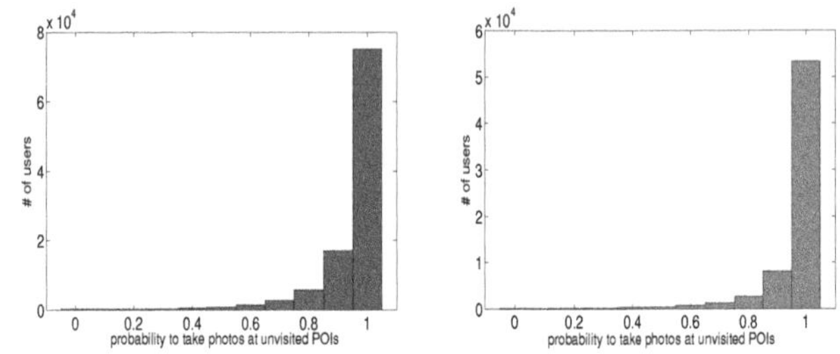

(a) NYC (b) SG

Figure 5: Histogram of the probability to take photos at POIs that are new to users.

classifier for POIs as the previous methods [14, 5] for Landmark identification do (as we will see in the experiments), because most of POIs will lack training samples.

Observation 2: Number of photos per user. We show in Figures 3(a) and 3(b) the empirical Probability Density Function (PDF) of number of photos associated with POIs per user. We can see from both figures that the probability first slightly increases, peaks when the number of photos is around 5, and then decreases rapidly after 50, which is not a power law distribution.[3] However, the righthand part after the peak has a heavy tail, which can be modeled with a power law distribution, as shown in the figures. This observation indicates that Instagram users in general associate fewer than 50 photos with POIs in one year (recall that both datasets are for one year period), and the number of users who associate more than 50 photos decreases with a power law probability. This observation suggests that we have only a few annotated training samples for each user.

Observation 3: Behaviors of users. First, we study the number of POIs where a user took photos. We plot the empirical CCDF of number of POIs per user in Figures 4(a) and 4(b) for NYC and SG data, respectively. We observe that 50.42% of users in NYC and 42.55% of users in SG have visited and taken photos at more than 20 POIs. This indicates we cannot easily determine which POI a photo is associated with based on users' visiting information, because users take photos at many POIs.

Another interesting finding about users' behaviors is that they incline to take photos at POIs that are new to them. To observe this, we calculate the probability that a user takes photos at newly-visited POIs by the following three steps: (i) for each user, we sort his/her photos taken at (associated with) POIs by time; (ii) we employ the first five POIs as initial visited set for each user, and then iterate through his/her sorting list to count whether a photo is taken at a new POI or a visited POI; meanwhile, we update the visited POI set by including the POI for each checked photo; (iii) according to the counting results, we can compute the probability P_u for user u to take a photo at new POIs as:

$$P_u = \frac{n_u}{n_u + o_u} \tag{1}$$

where n_u counts the number of new POIs for user u in step (ii) and o_u counts the number of visited POIs. Finally, we depict a histogram with the probabilities of all the users. The histograms are shown in Figures 5(a) and 5(b) for NYC and SG, respectively.

We can see that a greater portion of users have high probability (say 0.8 to 1.0) to take photos at newly-visited POIs (or we call previously-unvisited POIs for a user). This can be explained by the intuition that new POIs are usually more attractive for users to take photos than the visited ones; for previously visited POIs, users rarely take photos and annotate them again within the period of our data collection (1 year). The finding further indicates the difficulty in exploiting users' visiting behaviors to associate photos with POIs.

4. PROBLEM DEFINITION AND PROPOSED METHOD

In this section, we first define the problem of associating Instagram photos with POIs, and then present our proposed approach to solving the problem.

4.1 Notations and Problem Definition

Notations. Let $\mathcal{U}$ be a set of users $\{u_1, u_2, \cdots, u_{|\mathcal{U}|}\}$, $\mathcal{P}$ denote a set of photos $\{p_1, p_2, \cdots, p_{|\mathcal{P}|}\}$ and $\mathcal{L}$ denote

[3]It resembles a Double Pareto Lognormal Distribution [21].

Table 2: A list of notations

symbols	meanings
$\mathcal{U}$	the set of users: $\{u_1, u_2, \cdots, u_{\lvert\mathcal{U}\rvert}\}$
$\mathcal{P}$	the set of photos: $\{p_1, p_2, \cdots, p_{\lvert\mathcal{P}\rvert}\}$
$\mathcal{L}$	the set of POIs: $\{\ell_1, \ell_2, \cdots, \ell_{\lvert\mathcal{L}\rvert}\}$
$\mathbf{x}_p$	textual feature vector of photo p
$\mathbf{y}_p$	visual feature vector of photo p
$\mathcal{D}$	training set $\mathcal{D} \subset \mathcal{P}$, where $p \in \mathcal{D}$ has $p.u$ and $p.\ell$
$\mathbf{w}_\ell$	textual factor of POI ℓ interacting with photos
$\mathbf{v}_\ell$	visual factor of POI ℓ interacting with photos
$\mathbf{u}_u$	latent factor of user u interacting with POIs
$\mathbf{l}_l$	latent factor of POI ℓ interacting with users
$h(z)$	the hinge-loss function: $max(0, 1 - z)$

a set of POIs $\{\ell_1, \ell_2, \cdots, \ell_{|\mathcal{L}|}\}$ in an Instagram database. As photos are associated with textual context, we employ the bag-of-word model to represent each photo p as an m-dimensional vector $\mathbf{x}_p$, where x_{pi} denotes the frequency of word i for photo p. We note that $\mathbf{x}_p$ is a zero vector if a photo does not have textual description. However, this does not take place usually because more than 90% photos have the textual information as aforementioned in Table 1. For visual content, we extract visual words to construct features [5]. Specifically, for each photo, we first use the standard computer vision technique Scale Invariant Feature Transform (SIFT) [17][4] to produce a set of keypoints, where each keypoint is represented as a 128-dimensional vector. Subsequently, the keypoints from all the photos are clustered into n-clusters to create a "visual vocabulary", where each cluster is considered as a "visual word". Finally, we assign each keypoint in a photo to its closest cluster, and then represent each photo as a n-dimensional vector which indicates how many times each "visual word" appears in the photo. That is, for each photo p, we form a n-dimensional vector $\mathbf{y}_p$, where y_{pi} denotes the frequency of "visual word" i appearing in photo p. For clarity, we summarize the notations used in this paper in Table 2.

Associating photos with POIs: *Based on the set of photos that are associated with POIs by Instagram users, we aim at learning a function for mapping a photo to a POI. Formally, given a training set $\mathcal{D} \subset \mathcal{P}$, where each $p \in \mathcal{D}$ has two attributes $p.u$ and $p.\ell$: $p.u$ denoting the user who uploads photo p and $p.\ell$ denoting the POI that photo p is associated with, we learn a mapping function $f : \{(u, p, \mathbf{x}_p, \mathbf{y}_p)\} \rightarrow \mathcal{L}$ which is used to predict the POI for a photo that is not associated with a POI.*

According to **Observation** 1 in Section 3.2, the number of training samples for most of POIs is small. Hence, building a classifier for POIs in $\mathcal{L}$ based on textual and visual features may not yield good accuracy for mapping. To learn the mapping function we propose a new approach that effectively exploits not only the visual and textual information of photos, but also the information of the users who upload them. Next, we present our proposed method.

4.2 Proposed Method

We approach the mapping problem by treat it as a ranking problem. We develop an approach to learning a function from the training set $\mathcal{D}$ to score each POI for a given photo to be associated, and then rank the POIs based on their scores. The textual context, visual content, and user information of a photo are taken into account in learning the ranking function. Since there are multiple types of information, we design a subtask for each type to maximize its predicting effectiveness. As a result, the most effective information of each type can be combined into the scoring function.

Next, we present how we embody this idea in details. We first embody our method by only considering textual context and visual content, and then introduce how our method exploits the user information.

4.2.1 Combining Textual Context and Visual Content

In this subsection, we present an approach to combining textual contexts and visual contents of photos to learn a scoring function for mapping a photo to a POI. We first introduce two factors $\mathbf{w}_\ell$ and $\mathbf{v}_\ell$ of m-dimension and n-dimension for each POI ℓ, and then use them to model the interactions with textual and visual features of photos, respectively. The scoring function is defined as follows:

$$s_{p\ell} = \mathbf{w}_\ell \cdot \mathbf{x}_p + \mathbf{v}_\ell \cdot \mathbf{y}_p \tag{2}$$

where $s_{p\ell}$ denotes the interaction score between photo p and POI ℓ, and operator $\cdot$ represents the inner product. Clearly, the score $s_{p\ell}$ is computed by a sum of textual interaction score $\mathbf{w}_\ell \cdot \mathbf{x}_p$ and visual interaction score $\mathbf{v}_\ell \cdot \mathbf{y}_p$ between POI ℓ and photo p.

Next, our objective is to learn $\{\mathbf{w}_\ell\}_{\ell\in\mathcal{L}}$ and $\{\mathbf{v}_\ell\}_{\ell\in\mathcal{L}}$ such that for each photo p its correct POI is expected to be ranked higher than the other POIs. In particular, we extend *a pairwise classification* approach that is used in RankSVM [9] for this objective. That is, given each training sample $p \in \mathcal{D}$, we compare pairwisely the scores of POIs $p.\ell$ and ℓ' ($\ell' \in \mathcal{L}$ and $\ell' \neq p.\ell$) to check whether they are ranked correctly; if $p.\ell$ is ranked higher than ℓ', there is no loss; otherwise a loss is produced. Specifically, we have the following objective function to minimize:

$$\mathcal{O}_{main} = \sum_{\substack{p\in\mathcal{D},\\ \ell=p.\ell}} \sum_{\substack{\ell'\in\mathcal{L},\\ \ell'\neq\ell}} h(s_{p\ell} - s_{p\ell'}) \tag{3}$$

where $h(z) = max(0, 1 - z)$ is the hinge-loss for converting the score difference between two POIs into a penalty. We note that the hinge-loss is nonzero only if $z < 1$.

In Eq. (3) the two types of information, i.e., the textual context and the visual content, are combined directly and the objective function might not exploit the most informative features from each type of information. For overcoming this issue, we design two subtasks for assistance, namely, to rank the correct POI higher than the other POIs when only a single type of information is presented. By following the idea of Eq. (3), we write another subobjective function to minimize for each subtask:

$$\mathcal{O}_1 = \sum_{\substack{p\in\mathcal{D},\\ \ell=p.\ell}} \sum_{\substack{\ell'\in\mathcal{L},\\ \ell'\neq\ell}} h(\mathbf{w}_\ell \cdot \mathbf{x}_p - \mathbf{w}_{\ell'} \cdot \mathbf{x}_p) \tag{4}$$

and

$$\mathcal{O}_2 = \sum_{\substack{p\in\mathcal{D},\\ \ell=p.\ell}} \sum_{\substack{\ell'\in\mathcal{L},\\ \ell'\neq\ell}} h(\mathbf{v}_\ell \cdot \mathbf{y}_p - \mathbf{v}_{\ell'} \cdot \mathbf{y}_p). \tag{5}$$

When minimizing $\mathcal{O}_1$, the factor $\mathbf{w}_\ell$ will encode the most discriminative textual features for POI ℓ, as $\mathcal{O}_1$ aims at ranking POIs correctly by only utilizing textual features; similarly, minimizing $\mathcal{O}_2$ will push $\mathbf{v}_\ell$ exploit the most discriminative visual features.

[4]We use the software provided by http://koen.me/research/downloads/

Putting $\mathcal{O}_{main}$, $\mathcal{O}_1$ and $\mathcal{O}_2$ together, we thus have a new objective function for minimizing as:

$$\mathcal{J} = \mathcal{O}_{main} + \alpha_1\mathcal{O}_1 + \alpha_2\mathcal{O}_2 + \frac{\lambda_W}{2}\sum_{\ell\in\mathcal{L}}||\mathbf{w}_\ell||_2^2 + \frac{\lambda_V}{2}\sum_{\ell\in\mathcal{L}}||\mathbf{v}_\ell||_2^2 \quad (6)$$

where α_1 and α_2 are two parameters for balancing between the main objective and two subobjectives; $\frac{\lambda_W}{2}\sum_{\ell\in\mathcal{L}}||\mathbf{w}_\ell||_2^2$ and $\frac{\lambda_V}{2}\sum_{\ell\in\mathcal{L}}||\mathbf{v}_\ell||_2^2$ are two regularization terms to prevent from over-fitting; λ_W and λ_V are regularization parameters. We have tried ℓ_1-norm as regularization terms to make the solutions of $\{\mathbf{w}_\ell\}_{\ell\in\mathcal{L}}$ and $\{\mathbf{v}_\ell\}_{\ell\in\mathcal{L}}$ sparse, but it turns out the performance is not good. The reason may be the discriminative terms for POIs are usually infrequent textual (or visual) words. These words are forced to be zeros in the solution of $\{\mathbf{w}_\ell\}_{\ell\in\mathcal{L}}$ (or $\{\mathbf{v}_\ell\}_{\ell\in\mathcal{L}}$) when ℓ_1-norm is used, which thus deteriorates the performance.

When minimizing $\mathcal{J}$, the objective $\mathcal{O}_{main}$ is in charge of ranking the target POI correctly by combining textual context and visual content of photos, and the subobjectives $\mathcal{O}_1$ and $\mathcal{O}_2$ will push $\{\mathbf{w}_\ell\}_{\ell\in\mathcal{L}}$ and $\{\mathbf{v}_\ell\}_{\ell\in\mathcal{L}}$ to exploit the informative textual and visual features, respectively.

4.2.2 Incorporating User Preference

In this subsection, we discuss how to incorporate the user information of photos to make prediction. Intuitively, we aim at exploring users' visiting preferences over POIs, i.e., how likely a user visits a POI, which is useful for inferring where his/her photo is taken. According to **Observation** 3 in Section 3.2, however, users tend to take photos at previously unvisited POIs. Therefore, it is insufficient to model the visiting preference of a user based on his/her visited POIs. A good solution should be able to model the preferences of users over both visited and unvisited POIs. This makes exploiting users' visiting preferences in ranking POIs a non-trivial task.

To address the challenge, we propose a new approach based on factorization model to incorporate the user information. Factorization model has been proven to be a promising tool for capturing users' preferences, which has been applied in recommendation systems [10, 19, 15, 13]. As both users and POIs do not have explicit feature representations in our problem, we learn to embed users and POIs into a latent space for modeling their interactions. Specifically, we introduce a latent factor $\mathbf{u}_u$ of k-dimension for each user u and a latent factor $\mathbf{l}_\ell$ of k-dimension for each POI ℓ. By using them, we extend the scoring function in Eq. (2) as:

$$s_{up\ell} = \mathbf{w}_\ell \cdot \mathbf{x}_p + \mathbf{v}_\ell \cdot \mathbf{y}_p + \mathbf{u}_u \cdot \mathbf{l}_\ell \quad (7)$$

where $s_{up\ell}$ represents the interaction score among user u, photo p and POI ℓ. We incorporate the user preference in the ranking function by including the term $\mathbf{u}_u \cdot \mathbf{l}_\ell$. Different from textual and visual information, where $\mathbf{x}_p$ and $\mathbf{y}_p$ are predefined explicit representations in the terms $\mathbf{w}_\ell \cdot \mathbf{x}_p$ and $\mathbf{v}_\ell \cdot \mathbf{y}_p$, respectively, both $\mathbf{u}_u$ and $\mathbf{l}_\ell$ are unknown and require to be solved.

Replacing $s_{p\ell}$ with $s_{up\ell}$ in Eq. (3), the objective function can be extended as:

$$\mathcal{O}_{main'} = \sum_{\substack{p\in\mathcal{D},\\ \ell=p.\ell,u=p.u}} \sum_{\substack{\ell'\in\mathcal{L},\\ \ell'\neq\ell}} h(s_{up\ell} - s_{up\ell'}) \quad (8)$$

and the objective function $\mathcal{J}$ in Eq. (6) can also be updated by replacing $\mathcal{O}_{main}$ with $\mathcal{O}_{main'}$ here.

When minimizing the objective function $\mathcal{J}$, the latent factors of users and POIs will be optimized to encode users' visiting preferences. However, the optimization is a combined effect of textual, visual and user information, and the users' visiting preferences might not be effectively utilized. To address this issue, we design a subobjective for solely modeling the visiting preferences of users.

Our subobjective is performing matrix factorization on user-POI interaction data. Based on the training set $\mathcal{D}$, we can construct a $|\mathcal{U}| \times |\mathcal{L}|$ matrix $\mathbf{A}$, where $a_{u\ell}$ denote the frequency of user u takes photos at POI ℓ. Note that we use a transformation by setting $\tilde{a}_{u\ell} = \frac{1}{2}(\log(a_{u\ell})+1)$ in our implementation, because a small number of POIs may have very large frequency. Then we compute the latent factors of users and POIs, such that the user-POI interactions, modeled as inner product of users' latent factors and POIs' latent factors, are a good approximation of the matrix $\mathbf{A}$. However, approximating the matrix directly will over-highlight the users' preferences on visited POIs, because unvisited POIs have zero frequencies and directly approximating them will lead users' preferences over unvisited POIs close to zero, which is not reasonable for our problem since users tend to take photos at unvisited POIs and thus their preferences to unvisited POIs should not be too small. On the other hand, we cannot only approximate the non-zero entries in matrix $\mathbf{A}$, because the data is too sparse according to **Observation** 2 in Section 3.2. As a trade-off, we consider using weighted matrix factorization. In particular, we construct a $|\mathcal{U}| \times |\mathcal{L}|$ weighted matrix $\mathbf{B}$ by assigning larger weights for non-zero entries and smaller weights for zero entries as:

$$b_{u\ell} = \begin{cases} 1 & \text{if } a_{u\ell} > 0 \\ \varepsilon & \textit{otherwise} \end{cases}$$

where $\varepsilon = 0.001$ is used in this paper. Because we give smaller weights for zero entries (corresponding to unvisited POIs), which is a relaxation for fitting zero entries, the users' preferences over unvisited POIs thus will not be very close to zero. The subobjective function of the task is written as:

$$\mathcal{O}_3 = \frac{1}{2}\sum_{u\in\mathcal{U}}\sum_{\ell\in\mathcal{L}} b_{u\ell}(\tilde{a}_{u\ell} - \mathbf{u}_u \cdot \mathbf{l}_l)^2 \quad (9)$$

The final objective function is thus changed into:

$$\mathcal{J}' = \mathcal{O}_{main'} + \alpha_1\mathcal{O}_1 + \alpha_2\mathcal{O}_2 + \alpha_3\mathcal{O}_3 + \frac{\lambda_W}{2}\sum_{\ell\in\mathcal{L}}||\mathbf{w}_\ell||_2^2 + \frac{\lambda_V}{2}\sum_{\ell\in\mathcal{L}}||\mathbf{v}_\ell||_2^2 + \frac{\lambda_{UL}}{2}\left(\sum_{u\in\mathcal{U}}||\mathbf{u}_u||_2^2 + \sum_{\ell\in\mathcal{L}}||\mathbf{l}_\ell||_2^2\right) \quad (10)$$

where α_3 is a parameter for controlling the importance of the user preference subtask; $\frac{\lambda_{UL}}{2}\left(\sum_{u\in\mathcal{U}}||\mathbf{u}_u||_2^2 + \sum_{\ell\in\mathcal{L}}||\mathbf{l}_\ell||_2^2\right)$ is a regularization term to prevent over-fitting problem and λ_{UL} is a regularization parameter. Here we use one regularization parameter for the latent factors of users and POIs, because only their inner product values matter to our objective function.

4.2.3 Optimization and Learning Algorithm

In this subsection, we discuss how we optimize the objective function $\mathcal{J}'$ to learn the prediction model. Let $\theta \in \{\mathbf{u}_u, \mathbf{l}_\ell, \mathbf{w}_\ell, \mathbf{v}_\ell\}$, where $u \in \mathcal{U}$ and $\ell \in \mathcal{L}$, denote the parameters of our model. We adopt the Stochastic Gradient Descent (SGD) method for learning them. As $\mathcal{J}'$ is composed of one main objective $\mathcal{O}_{main'}$ and three subobjectives $\alpha_1\mathcal{O}_1$, $\alpha_2\mathcal{O}_2$ and $\alpha_3\mathcal{O}_3$, we perform the SGD updates alternatively for these objectives. That is, in each iteration, we sample one training instance $p \in \mathcal{D}$ and then update parameters as follows for each objective:

$$\textit{main objective}: \quad \theta \leftarrow \theta - \gamma \frac{\partial \mathcal{O}_{main'}}{\partial \theta} \tag{11}$$

$$\textit{subobjective 1}: \quad \theta \leftarrow \theta - \gamma \frac{\partial \alpha_1 \mathcal{O}_1}{\partial \theta} \tag{12}$$

$$\textit{subobjective 2}: \quad \theta \leftarrow \theta - \gamma \frac{\partial \alpha_2 \mathcal{O}_2}{\partial \theta} \tag{13}$$

$$\textit{subobjective 3}: \quad \theta \leftarrow \theta - \gamma \frac{\partial \alpha_3 \mathcal{O}_3}{\partial \theta} \tag{14}$$

where γ is the learning rate.

Next, we show how to calculate the corresponding gradients used in above updating formulae. As the main objective, subobjective 1 and subobjective 2 are similar, we derive the gradients for the main objective here as an example:

$$-\frac{\partial \mathcal{O}_{main'}}{\partial \theta} = \begin{cases} \mathbf{l}_\ell - \mathbf{l}_{\ell'} - \lambda_{UL}\mathbf{u}_u & \text{if } \theta = \mathbf{u}_u, \\ \mathbf{u}_u - \lambda_{UL}\mathbf{l}_\ell & \text{if } \theta = \mathbf{l}_\ell, \\ -\mathbf{u}_u - \lambda_{UL}\mathbf{l}_{\ell'} & \text{if } \theta = \mathbf{l}_{\ell'}, \\ \mathbf{x}_p - \lambda_W \mathbf{w}_\ell & \text{if } \theta = \mathbf{w}_\ell, \\ -\mathbf{x}_p - \lambda_W \mathbf{w}_{\ell'} & \text{if } \theta = \mathbf{w}_{\ell'}, \\ \mathbf{y}_p - \lambda_V \mathbf{v}_\ell & \text{if } \theta = \mathbf{v}_\ell, \\ -\mathbf{y}_p - \lambda_V \mathbf{v}_{\ell'} & \text{if } \theta = \mathbf{v}_{\ell'}, \\ 0 & \textit{otherwise}. \end{cases}$$

We note that only if $s_{up\ell} - s_{up\ell'} < 1$, the hinge-loss is nonzero and we use the above gradient calculations for updating parameters; otherwise, the hinge-loss is zero and we do not need to update parameters. Moreover, the corresponding regularization terms are incorporated into the calculations. For subobjectives 1 and 2, $\frac{\partial \alpha_1 \mathcal{O}_1}{\partial \theta}$ and $\frac{\partial \alpha_2 \mathcal{O}_2}{\partial \theta}$ can be computed in the similar way. The gradients for subobjective 3 are derived as follows:

$$-\frac{\partial \alpha_3 \mathcal{O}_3}{\partial \theta} = \begin{cases} \alpha_3 \sum_{\ell \in \mathcal{L}} b_{u\ell}(a_{u\ell} - \mathbf{u}_u \cdot \mathbf{l}_\ell)\mathbf{l}_\ell - \alpha_3 \lambda_{UL}\mathbf{u}_u & \text{if } \theta = \mathbf{u}_u, \\ \alpha_3 \sum_{u \in \mathcal{U}} b_{u\ell}(a_{u\ell} - \mathbf{u}_u \cdot \mathbf{l}_\ell)\mathbf{u}_u - \alpha_3 \lambda_{UL}\mathbf{l}_\ell & \text{if } \theta = \mathbf{l}_\ell, \\ 0 & \textit{otherwise}. \end{cases}$$

We note that when deriving the gradients for each subobjective, the corresponding regularization terms should be incorporated.

The proposed method, Ranking with Textual, Visual and User information for Photos to POIs, called RankTVU_P2P, can thus be summarized as Algorithm 1. In the algorithm, we iteratively update the model parameters based on the main objective and three subobjectives until the performance on validation set is stable and does not increase. After obtaining the model parameters, the mapping score of a photo to a POI is calculated as Eq. (7). The larger the score is, the better the photo is mapped to the corresponding POI.

5. EXPERIMENTS

In this section, we conduct extensive experiments to evaluate our proposed technique with the existing three state-of-the-arts, based on two Instagram datasets that we have crawled from the users in New York City (NYC) and Singapore (SG), respectively.

Algorithm 1: RankTVU_P2P

input : training set $\mathcal{D}$, validation set $\mathcal{V}$, learning rate γ, parameters α_1, α_2 and α_3
output: model parameters θ

Initialize θ with Normal distribution $\mathcal{N}(0, 0.01)$;
repeat
  for $p \in \mathcal{D}$ **do**
    $\theta \leftarrow \theta - \gamma \frac{\partial \mathcal{O}_{main'}}{\partial \theta}$;
    $\theta \leftarrow \theta - \gamma \frac{\partial \alpha_1 \mathcal{O}_1}{\partial \theta}$;
    $\theta \leftarrow \theta - \gamma \frac{\partial \alpha_2 \mathcal{O}_2}{\partial \theta}$;
    $\theta \leftarrow \theta - \gamma \frac{\partial \alpha_3 \mathcal{O}_3}{\partial \theta}$;
until *the performance on validation set $\mathcal{V}$ does not increase*;
return θ

5.1 Experimental Setup

5.1.1 Data Preprocessing

For NYC and SG datasets we crawled, we use the most recent three months data, i.e., from 13 Aug 2014 to 13 Nov 2014, in our experiments to evaluate the performance of different algorithms. For data preprocessing, we remove POIs with less than 5 photos and users who visited less than 10 and 5 POIs in NYC and SG, respectively.[5] As our aim is to test the performance of photo mapping, we only use the photos that have already been associated with POIs by Instagram users. We construct the textual representation of photos by keeping the words with frequency larger than 10 into textual vocabulary. Note that we employ the word frequency in the bag-of-word model as discussed in Section 4.1. For the visual representation, we construct 1000 visual words as vocabulary by using the method introduced in Section 4.1. After preprocessing, NYC dataset comprises 2,049 POIs and 74,758 photos from 3,556 users, and SG dataset comprises 1,363 POIs and 58,072 photos from 5,717 users. Each photo is represented as a 1000-dimensional visual feature vector, and represented as a 8217-dimensional and a 6696-dimensional textual feature vector for NYC and SG, respectively. Then, for each user, we mark off 20% of his/her most recent photos to build the test set and mark off another 10% earlier photos as tuning/validation set. The remaining (the earliest) 70% photos are employed as training set for building the prediction models. The datasets are available at http://www.ntu.edu.sg/home/gaocong/data/Instagram.zip

5.1.2 Evaluation Metrics

We employ two standard metrics to evaluate the performance of photo associating results as in [20], namely, Mean Reciprocal Rank and Accuracy within top N, denoted by MRR and Acc@N, respectively, where N is the number of candidate POIs produced by algorithms. MRR is the average of the reciprocal ranks of the results produced for all the photos in test set. Specifically, it is computed as follows:

$$MRR = \frac{1}{|\mathcal{P}_{test}|} \sum_{p \in \mathcal{P}_{test}} \frac{1}{rank_{p,\ell}} \tag{15}$$

[5]We perform the preprocessing to reduce noises. We note that after the preprocessing the data is still very sparse, where 51.7% and 47.9% POIs have less than 10 photos in NYC and SG, respectively.

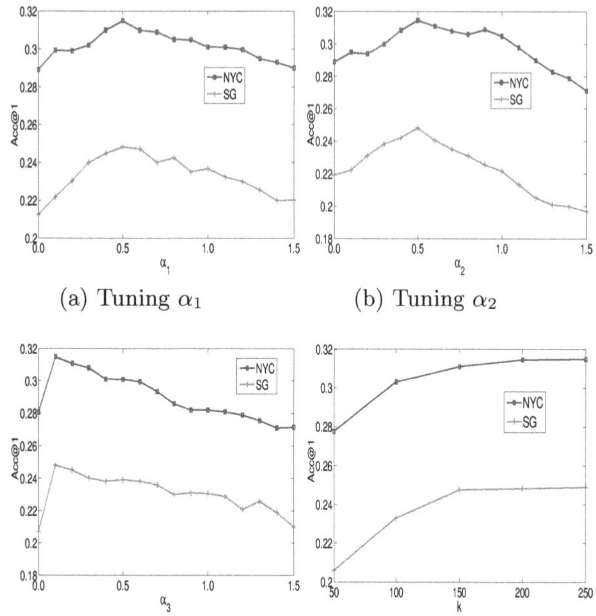

(a) Tuning α_1 (b) Tuning α_2

(c) Tuning α_3 (d) Tuning k.

Figure 6: Parameter tuning.

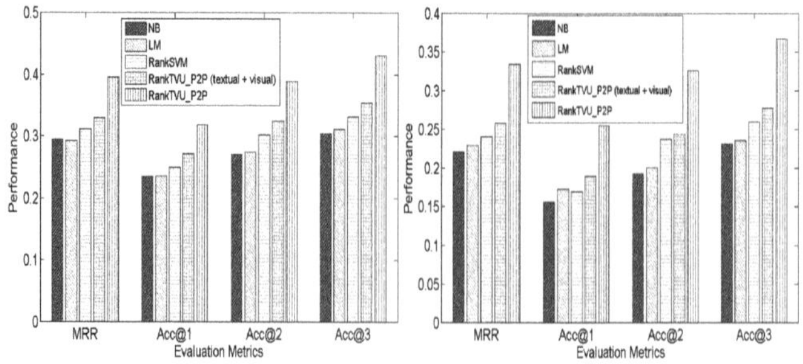

(a) NYC (b) SG

Figure 7: Performance comparisons.

where $rank_{p.\ell}$ is the position of target POI $p.\ell$ in the ranking list produced by algorithms for the test photo p; $\mathcal{P}_{test}$ denotes the test set. Clearly, a bigger MRR indicates the target POI is highly ranked and thus a better result. Acc@N is computed as:

$$Acc@N = \frac{1}{|\mathcal{P}_{test}|} \sum_{p \in \mathcal{P}_{test}} |Top(N,p) \cap \{p.\ell\}| \tag{16}$$

where $Top(N,p)$ denotes the set of top-N candidate POIs produced by algorithms for the test photo p. Acc@N considers a mapping is correct as long as the target POI $p.\ell$ for photo p is ranked within top-N positions. For N, we use the values of 1, 2 and 3 ($N = 1$ is the default value) in the experiments, respectively, as the accuracies of those top predicted results are definitely more important for our problem.

5.1.3 Baseline Algorithms

The following three related methods are utilized as the baselines.

- NB: This is the Naive Bayesian method, which has been used in the landmark identification task [5]. We build an NB model for textual and visual content individually, and subsequently use the optimal linear combination of the two models to make a prediction.
- LM: This is the Language Model. As shown in Section 2, it is proposed for placing photos onto grids [20, 16]. Similarly, for combining visual and textual information, we build a LM for each of them, and then adopt a linear combination of both models for associating photos with POIs.
- RankSVM: As our proposed method is ranking based method, we also employ state-of-the-art ranking technique RankSVM [9] as a baseline.

All the existing methods cannot leverage user information to infer users' visiting preferences to unvisited POIs. Different from them, our approach has a weighted matrix factorization subobjective $\mathcal{O}_3$, which acts as a recommender component and is capable of exploiting such information. For a fair comparison, we use our tuning set to find the optimal parameters for all the baseline methods, and then use them to evaluate the performance on test set.

5.2 Experimental Results

5.2.1 Parameter Setting and Tuning

In the experiments, we set the regularization parameters $\lambda_V = \lambda_{UL} = 0.1$ and $\lambda_W = 0.001$, and set the learning rate γ as a small value 0.01 in our experiments to ensure the generalization accuracy. Next, we tune the parameters α_1, α_2 and α_3 used in three subobjectives, and the dimension k of latent factors of users and POIs, based on tuning set, to show how they affect the performance of the proposed method. For parameters α_1, α_2 and α_3, we first perform grid search to find the optimal combination of them, and then tune each parameter by fixing the other twos to demonstrate their individual impact on the performance.

Figure 6(a) shows how the performance of the proposed method changes when we tune the parameter α_1, which controls the weight of textual subojective $\mathcal{O}_1$. We can see from this figure the proposed method performs the best at $\alpha_1 = 0.5$ on both NYC and SG datasets. We show the effect of parameter α_2, controlling the weight of visual subobjective $\mathcal{O}_2$, in the Figure 6(b). It can be seen that the best performance is delivered at $\alpha_2 = 0.5$ on the two datasets. Figure 6(c) shows how the parameter α_3, used for combining user preference subobjective $\mathcal{O}_3$, affects the performance of the proposed method. We observe that the performance first increases and then decreases as α_3 is increased, and the best performance is yielded at $\alpha_3 = 0.1$ for both datasets. We note that although α_1 and α_2 are larger than α_3, we cannot conclude that the textual and visual subobjectives are more important than user preference subobjective, because the subojective functions $\mathcal{O}_1$, $\mathcal{O}_2$ and $\mathcal{O}_3$ may be in different scales. We will analyze how the three subobjectives affect the performance in the next subsection. Finally, we show the effect of dimension k of latent factors on performance in Figure 6(d). We find that the performance increases as the dimension k is increased. After k exceeding 200, the performance does not change significantly and thus we use k=200 in our experiments.

5.2.2 *Performance Comparison and Analysis*

Performance Comparison. Figure 7 presents the performance comparison results of different algorithms. RankTVP_P2P (textual + visual) denotes our approach utilizing only textual and visual content. We can see from the figure that the proposed method RankTVU_P2P performs the best, in terms of two evaluation metrics, namely MRR and Acc@N. It outperforms RankSVM, LM and NB, in terms of Acc@1, by more than 27.25% and 41.75% on NYC and SG, respectively. This is because RankTVU_P2P exploits the users' visiting preferences over POIs (but RankSVM, LM and NB cannot leverage), which is an important information source for handling the sparsity problem of training data. When only utilizing the textual and visual content, we observe that our approach still delivers better performance than the baseline algorithms. In terms of Acc@1, the improvements are more than 12.5% and 11.7% on the two datasets, respectively. Moreover, we can see that RankSVM outperforms the other two baseline methods, which are all classifier based approaches. This may be attributed to that RankSVM, as a ranking based method, is more suitable to address the mapping problem when training samples are scarce. Finally, we observe that the Acc@N increases as N increases for all the methods. This is because the evaluation metric Acc@N considers a mapping is correct as long as the target POI for a test photo is ranked within top-N positions. We find that the proposed RankTVU_P2P method consistently performs better than the baselines for different values of N.

Impact of Different Types of Information. Next, we analyze how different types of information affect our results. We incorporate the information one by one into our proposed RankTVU_P2P to test how the performance changes. Figure 8 shows the detailed results on both datasets. We observe the performance of our model increases when textual, visual and user information are incorporated one by one in terms of both MRR and Acc@N. When combing textual context with visual content, the performance improves, in terms of Acc@1, 11.0% and 14.1% on NYC and SG, respectively. When we further incorporate the user information, in terms of Acc@1 the performance boost 17.2% and 34.4% on both datasets, respectively. Finally, we find our model with only textual context achieves 76.9% and 65.2% of the best performance with all the three types of information incorporated, on NYC and SG, respectively. The observations demonstrate the usefulness of each type of information. As the three types of information are from different views, they may contain complementary information to enhance each other for identifying the target POIs, which is a key reason that we obtain substantial improvements when combining them. According to the results, we also find that although visual content is important for associating photos with POIs, textual and user information have greater contributions to the final results.

Impact of Subobjectives. Finally, we study how our designed subobjectives in RankTVU_P2P help us obtain a better performance. To determine their individual effects on our proposed RankTVU_P2P performance, we take apart the subobjective functions from RankTVU_P2P one by one, and check their impacts on the performance. Figure 9 presents the results on both datasets, where we use the suffix "$-\mathcal{O}_i$" to denote the result obtained by removing subjective $\mathcal{O}_i$ (i=1, 2 and 3) from RankTVU_P2P.

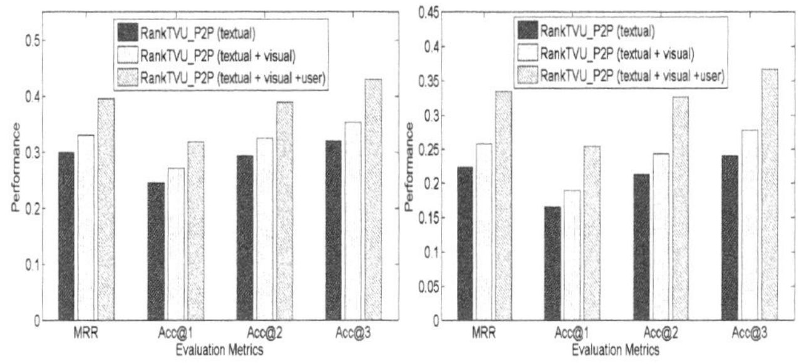

(a) NYC (b) SG

Figure 8: Impact of different types of information.

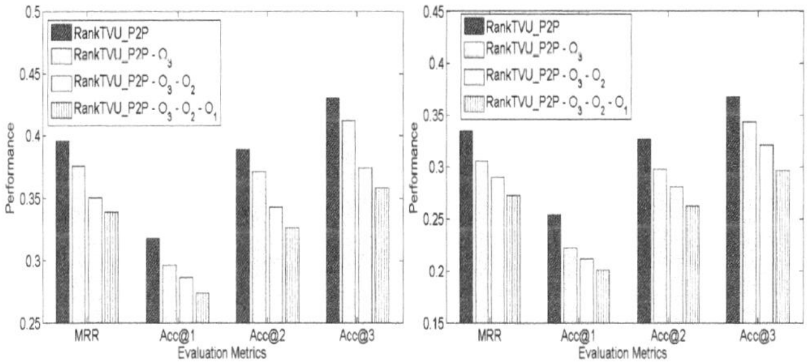

(a) NYC (b) SG

Figure 9: Impact of subojectives.

We observe that the performance of RankTVU_P2P decreases when we remove the subojectives $\mathcal{O}_3$, $\mathcal{O}_2$ and $\mathcal{O}_1$ one by one. Comparing RankTVU_P2P with RankTVU_P2P-$\mathcal{O}_3$, we find that incorporating the subobjective $\mathcal{O}_3$ improves the performance, in terms of Acc@1, 7.2% and 14.2% on NYC and SG, respectively. Moreover, by checking the results for RankTVU_P2P-$\mathcal{O}_3$ and RankTVU_P2P-$\mathcal{O}_3$-$\mathcal{O}_2$, we can see that 3.6% and 5.1% improvements, in terms of Acc@1, are obtained with the incorporation of the subojective $\mathcal{O}_2$ on both datasets, respectively. Finally, studying the results of RankTVU_P2P-$\mathcal{O}_3$-$\mathcal{O}_2$ and RankTVU_P2P-$\mathcal{O}_3$-$\mathcal{O}_2$-$\mathcal{O}_1$, we observe that the subojective $\mathcal{O}_1$ leads to 4.7% and 5.5% improvements in terms of Acc@1 on NYC and SG, respectively.

The results demonstrate these three designed subojectives play crucial roles for helping RankTVU_P2P obtain better performance. The reason is that the subojectives ($\mathcal{O}_1$, $\mathcal{O}_2$ and $\mathcal{O}_3$) will push the scoring function for POIs to exploit the most useful information from textual context, visual content and user information of photos.

6. CONCLUSIONS

In this paper, we define and study the problem of associating Instagram photos with POIs. To address the problem, we first find some interesting patterns contained in Instagram by data analysis, and then propose a ranking based mapping method, called RankTVU_P2P. In the proposed method, a new multi-task objective function is developed, where the main objective is to score POIs with the three types of information, namely, textual context, visual content, and user, and the other subobjectives are to maximize the prediction effectiveness for each type of information. In particular, we design a weighted matrix factorization subobjective to learn the visiting preferences of users over POIs. A stochastic gradient descent based algorithm is developed to optimize the objective function for learning parameters of our model. Extensive experiments are conducted on two sets of Instagram data, namely, NYC and SG, and the results show that our model outperforms the baseline methods substantially.

Although Instagram has gained increasing popularity, little research has been conducted on it [8, 23, 7]. We propose a new research problem based on Instagram in this paper. Based on our work, several interesting problems can be investigated or studied in the future. First, we only consider the Instagram photos that can be associated with POIs in our work such that we just focus on how to solve the mapping problem. However, it would be interesting to study whether a photo from Instagram is really related to POIs or not in the future. Second, there are other types of information that could be investigated in Instagram, e.g., time stamps of photos, coordinates of photos (only available for the photos taken when GPS is enabled) and category information of POIs, etc.

7. ACKNOWLEDGEMENT

This work is supported in part by a grant awarded by a Singapore MOE AcRF Tier 2 Grant (ARC30/12) and a grant awarded by Microsoft Research Asia.

8. REFERENCES

[1] Y. Avrithis, Y. Kalantidis, G. Tolias, and E. Spyrou. Retrieving landmark and non-landmark images from community photo collections. In *Proceedings of ICM*, pages 153–162. ACM, 2010.

[2] L. Backstrom, E. Sun, and C. Marlow. Find me if you can: improving geographical prediction with social and spatial proximity. In *Proceedings of WWW*, pages 61–70. ACM, 2010.

[3] W.-C. Chen, A. Battestini, N. Gelfand, and V. Setlur. Visual summaries of popular landmarks from community photo collections. In *The Forty-Third Asilomar Conference on Signals, Systems and Computers*, pages 1248–1255. IEEE, 2009.

[4] Z. Cheng, J. Caverlee, and K. Lee. You are where you tweet: a content-based approach to geo-locating twitter users. In *Proceedings of CIKM*, pages 759–768. ACM, 2010.

[5] D. J. Crandall, L. Backstrom, D. Huttenlocher, and J. Kleinberg. Mapping the world's photos. In *Proceedings of WWW*, pages 761–770. ACM, 2009.

[6] J. Hays and A. A. Efros. Im2gps: estimating geographic information from a single image. In *CVPR*, pages 1–8. IEEE, 2008.

[7] N. Hochman and L. Manovich. Zooming into an instagram city: Reading the local through social media. *First Monday*, 18(7), 2013.

[8] Y. Hu, L. Manikonda, S. Kambhampati, et al. What we instagram: A first analysis of instagram photo content and user types. In *Proceedings of ICWSM*, AAAI, 2014.

[9] T. Joachims. Training linear SVMs in linear time. In *Proceedings of SIGKDD*, pages 217–226. ACM, 2006.

[10] Y. Koren, R. Bell, and C. Volinsky. Matrix factorization techniques for recommender systems. *Computer*, (8):30–37, 2009.

[11] D. Leung and S. Newsam. Proximate sensing: Inferring what-is-where from georeferenced photo collections. In *CVPR*, pages 2955–2962. IEEE, 2010.

[12] R. Li, S. Wang, H. Deng, R. Wang, and K. C.-C. Chang. Towards social user profiling: unified and discriminative influence model for inferring home locations. In *Proceedings of SIGKDD*, pages 1023–1031. ACM, 2012.

[13] X. Li, G. Cong, X. Li, T. A. N. Pham, and S. Krishnaswamy. Rank-GeoFM: A ranking based geographical factorization method for point of interest recommendation. In *Proceedings of SIGIR*, ACM, 2015.

[14] Y. Li, D. J. Crandall, and D. P. Huttenlocher. Landmark classification in large-scale image collections. In *ICCV*, pages 1957–1964. IEEE, 2009.

[15] D. Lian, C. Zhao, X. Xie, G. Sun, E. Chen, and Y. Rui. GeoMF: joint geographical modeling and matrix factorization for point-of-interest recommendation. In *Proceedings of SIGKDD*, pages 831–840. ACM, 2014.

[16] B. Liu, Q. Yuan, G. Cong, and D. Xu. Where your photo is taken: Geolocation prediction for social images. *JASIST*, 65(6):1232–1243, 2014.

[17] D. G. Lowe. Distinctive image features from scale-invariant keypoints. *IJCV*, 60(2):91–110, 2004.

[18] F. O. Ostermann, M. Tomko, and R. Purves. User evaluation of automatically generated keywords and toponyms for geo-referenced images. *JASIST*, 64(3):480–499, 2013.

[19] S. Rendle. Factorization machines. In *ICDM*, pages 995–1000. IEEE, 2010.

[20] P. Serdyukov, V. Murdock, and R. Van Zwol. Placing flickr photos on a map. In *Proceedings of SIGIR*, pages 484–491. ACM, 2009.

[21] M. Seshadri, S. Machiraju, A. Sridharan, J. Bolot, C. Faloutsos, and J. Leskove. Mobile call graphs: beyond power-law and lognormal distributions. In *Proceedings of SIGKDD*, pages 596–604. ACM, 2008.

[22] T. H. Silva, P. O. Melo, J. M. Almeida, J. Salles, and A. A. Loureiro. A picture of instagram is worth more than a thousand words: Workload characterization and application. In *DCOSS*, pages 123–132. IEEE, 2013.

[23] T. H. Silva, P. O. Vaz de Melo, J. M. Almeida, J. Salles, and A. A. Loureiro. A comparison of foursquare and instagram to the study of city dynamics and urban social behavior. In *Proceedings of SIGKDD International Workshop on Urban Computing*, page 4. ACM, 2013.

[24] Q. Yuan, G. Cong, Z. Ma, A. Sun, and N. M. Thalmann. Who, where, when and what: discover spatio-temporal topics for twitter users. In *Proceedings of SIGKDD*, pages 605–613. ACM, 2013.

[25] Y.-T. Zheng, M. Zhao, Y. Song, H. Adam, U. Buddemeier, A. Bissacco, F. Brucher, T.-S. Chua, and H. Neven. Tour the world: building a web-scale landmark recognition engine. In *CVPR*, pages 1085–1092. IEEE, 2009.

Gradient-based Signatures for Efficient Similarity Search in Large-scale Multimedia Databases

Christian Beecks Merih Seran Uysal Judith Hermanns Thomas Seidl
Data Management and Data Exploration Group
RWTH Aachen University
Germany
{beecks, uysal, hermanns, seidl}@cs.rwth-aachen.de

ABSTRACT

With the continuous rise of multimedia, the question of how to access large-scale multimedia databases efficiently has become of crucial importance. Given a multimedia database comprising millions of multimedia objects, how to approximate the content-based properties of the corresponding feature representations in order to carry out similarity search efficiently and with high accuracy? In this paper, we propose the concept of gradient-based signatures in order to aggregate content-based features of multimedia objects by means of generative models. We provide theoretical insights into our approach including closed-form expressions for the computation of gradient-based signatures with respect to Gaussian mixture models and additionally investigate different binarization methods for gradient-based signatures in order to query databases comprising millions of multimedia objects with high accuracy in less than one second.

Categories and Subject Descriptors

H.3.3 [**Information Storage and Retrieval**]: Information Search and Retrieval; H.2.4 [**Database Management**]: Systems—*Multimedia databases*

General Terms

Theory, Performance, Experimentation

Keywords

Gradient-based Signature, Gaussian Mixture Model, Similarity Search, Multimedia Databases

1. INTRODUCTION

With the continuous rise of multimedia, the question of how to access large-scale multimedia databases efficiently has become of crucial importance. The extensive spread of mobile devices and the rapid expansion of the internet allow users to generate, process, store, and share multimedia data in everyday situations. As an example, the majority of social networking sites such as *Facebook*[1], *Twitter*[2], *Tumblr*[3], and *Instagram*[4] comprise millions of users that create multimedia data at billion-scale every single day.

The multitude of data and the versatility of information access challenge todays' multimedia databases. In many application areas including information retrieval, data mining, and computer vision, users are no longer satisfied with keyword-based access but want to search, browse, explore, and analyze multimedia databases by content-based characteristics of the multimedia objects. One fundamental operation underlying this content-based information access is similarity search which aims at retrieving the most similar multimedia objects with respect to a query.

In order to carry out similarity search for query-like multimedia objects, the way of modeling similarity is of major significance due to its impact on efficiency and effectiveness. In fact, similarity search requires a formal definition of a similarity model that provides methods for modeling and comparing content-based properties of multimedia objects. The need for effective and efficient similarity models is inherently given in the fields of content-based image retrieval [16, 56], video retrieval [26], and audio retrieval [41] and in many other research fields, such as data mining [13, 22, 46, 66], information retrieval [39], pattern recognition [18], and computer vision [57].

A generic approach to model similarity between multimedia objects consists in representing their content-based properties by individual-binning feature signatures [4, 52], which can be compared by means of distance-based similarity measures [4, 8] such as the Earth Mover's Distance [52], the Signature Quadratic Form Distance [10], and the Signature Matching Distance [6]. One advantage of these similarity models is the user-customizable applicability in various domains. By comparing object-specific feature quantizations with distance-based similarity measures, these approaches can be tailored to individual multimedia objects and adapted to the users' notions of perceptual similarity.

Similarity search in multimedia databases by feature signatures and distance-based similarity measures requires efficient query processing and indexing approaches since the computation time complexity of a single distance computation is at least quadratic in the number of individual bins of the corresponding feature signatures [4]. Processing queries

[1]http://facebook.com
[2]http://twitter.com
[3]http://tumblr.com
[4]http://instagram.com

Permission to make digital or hard copies of all or part of this work for personal or classroom use is granted without fee provided that copies are not made or distributed for profit or commercial advantage and that copies bear this notice and the full citation on the first page. Copyrights for components of this work owned by others than the author(s) must be honored. Abstracting with credit is permitted. To copy otherwise, or republish, to post on servers or to redistribute to lists, requires prior specific permission and/or a fee. Request permissions from Permissions@acm.org.
CIKM'15, October 19–23, 2015, Melbourne, Australia.
Copyright is held by the owner/author(s). Publication rights licensed to ACM.
ACM 978-1-4503-3794-6/15/10 ...$15.00.
DOI: http://dx.doi.org/10.1145/2806416.2806459.

in million-scale multimedia databases still remains one of the major challenges.

In this paper, we address the problem of efficient and accurate k-nearest-neighbor query processing in multimedia databases comprising millions of feature signatures. To this end, we propose and investigate the concept of *gradient-based signatures* which approximate the information contained in a feature signature with respect to a common generative model. Moreover, by binarizing gradient-based signatures, we show that our proposal is able to process k-nearest-neighbor queries in a multimedia database comprising 5 million images with high accuracy in approximately 0.5 seconds. Our main contributions are summarized as follows:

- We propose and investigate gradient-based signatures as a compact feature signature approximation.
- We present different binarization methods leading to binary gradient-based signatures.
- We conduct an extensive performance analysis on different benchmark databases indicating the high efficiency and accuracy of our approach.

The remainder of this paper is structured as follows: Section 2 presents preliminary information and outlines related work. Section 3 introduces gradient-based signatures while Section 4 provides further theoretical insights. The binarization methods for gradient-based signatures are investigated in Section 5. The results of the performance analysis are given in Section 6 before we conclude the paper with an outlook on future work in Section 7.

2. PRELIMINARIES AND RELATED WORK

2.1 Feature Signature Model

The content-based properties of multimedia objects are frequently described by means of features $f_1, \dots, f_k \in \mathbb{F}$ in a feature space $(\mathbb{F}, \delta)$ that is additionally endowed with a function $\delta : \mathbb{F} \times \mathbb{F} \to \mathbb{R}$ for comparing two individual features. By indicating the relevance of each feature, a multimedia object is mathematically modeled by a *feature representation* $X : \mathbb{F} \to \mathbb{R}$. Thus, a feature representation X is a function which relates each feature $f \in \mathbb{F}$ with a *weight* $X(f) \in \mathbb{R}$, where the weight of zero is designated for features which are not relevant for the representation of the corresponding multimedia object. Those features which are assigned non-zero weights are named as *representatives* and are defined for a feature representation X by the set $\mathrm{R}_X = \{f \in \mathbb{F} | X(f) \neq 0\} \subseteq \mathbb{F}$. Restricting a feature representation X to a finite set of representatives $\mathrm{R}_X \subseteq \mathbb{F}$ yields a *feature signature*, whose formal definition is given below.

Definition 1. (Feature signature)
Let $(\mathbb{F}, \delta)$ be a feature space. A *feature signature* $X \in \mathbb{R}^{\mathbb{F}}$ is defined as:

$$X : \mathbb{F} \to \mathbb{R} \text{ subject to } |\{f \in \mathbb{F} | X(f) \neq 0\}| < \infty$$

A feature signature X allows us to define a finite set of contributing features, i.e. features with a weight unequal to zero, individually for each multimedia object. In the remainder of this paper, we assume that the weights of the feature signatures are non-negative, i.e. $\forall X \in \mathbb{R}^{\mathbb{F}}, f \in \mathbb{F} : X(f) \geq 0$.

In order to elucidate the idea of a feature signature, we depict two example images and their corresponding feature signatures in Figure 1. The representatives of the feature signatures are visualized by colored circles with diameters indicating their weights and are based on position, color, and texture information. As can be seen in this example, feature signatures are able to visually approximate image content by utilizing individual representatives of contributing features. More theoretical details regarding this feature representation model can be found in [4].

(a) original image (b) feature signature

(c) original image (d) feature signature

Figure 1: Two example images and visualizations of the corresponding feature signatures.

2.2 Distance-based Similarity Measures

One well-known approach for the comparison of feature signatures is the Earth Mover's Distance [52], which is a transformation-based approach that measures the cost of transforming one feature signature into another one. The Earth Mover's Distance between two feature signatures $X, Y \in \mathbb{R}^{\mathbb{F}}$ is defined as a minimum-cost flow of all possible flows $F = \{f | f : \mathbb{F} \times \mathbb{F} \to \mathbb{R}\}$ as $\mathrm{EMD}_\delta(X,Y) = \min_{f \in F} \left\{ \frac{\sum_{x \in \mathbb{F}} \sum_{y \in \mathbb{F}} f(x,y) \cdot \delta(x,y)}{\min\{\sum_{x \in \mathbb{F}} X(x), \sum_{y \in \mathbb{F}} Y(y)\}} \right\}$, subject to the constraints of non-negativity, i.e. $\forall x, y \in \mathbb{F} : \; f(x,y) \geq 0$, source, i.e. $\forall x \in \mathbb{F} : \; \sum_{y \in \mathbb{F}} f(x,y) \leq X(x)$, target, i.e. $\forall y \in \mathbb{F} : \sum_{x \in \mathbb{F}} f(x,y) \leq Y(y)$, and total flow, i.e. $\sum_{x \in \mathbb{F}} \sum_{y \in \mathbb{F}} f(x,y) = \min\{\sum_{x \in \mathbb{F}} X(x), \sum_{y \in \mathbb{F}} Y(y)\}$.

The Perceptually Modified Hausdorff Distance [45] and the Signature Matching Distance [6] are matching-based approaches. They define a distance value between two feature signatures $X, Y \in \mathbb{R}^{\mathbb{F}}$ by making use of a matching $\mathrm{m} \subseteq \mathbb{F} \times \mathbb{F}$ and a cost function $\mathrm{c} : 2^{\mathbb{F} \times \mathbb{F}} \to \mathbb{R}$. While the Signature Matching Distance is defined for any matching and any cost function as $\mathrm{SMD}_\delta(X,Y) = \mathrm{c}(\mathrm{m}_{X \to Y}) + \mathrm{c}(\mathrm{m}_{Y \to X}) - 2\lambda \cdot \mathrm{c}(\mathrm{m}_{X \leftrightarrow Y})$ for $0 \leq \lambda \leq 1$, the Perceptually Hausdorff Distance is defined as $\mathrm{PMHD}_\delta(X,Y) = \max\{\mathrm{c}(\mathrm{m}^{\delta/w^*}_{X \to Y}), \mathrm{c}(\mathrm{m}^{\delta/w^*}_{Y \to X})\}$, with cost function $\mathrm{c}(\mathrm{m}^{\delta/w^*}_{X \to Y}) = \frac{\sum_{(x,y) \in \mathrm{m}^{\delta/w^*}_{X \to Y}} X(x) \cdot \frac{\delta(x,y)}{\min\{X(x), Y(y)\}}}{\sum_{(x,y) \in \mathrm{m}^{\delta/w^*}_{X \to Y}} X(x)}$ and distance weight ratio matching $\mathrm{m}^{\delta/w^*}_{X \to Y} = \{(x,y) \,|\, x \in \mathrm{R}_X \wedge y = \mathrm{argmin}_{y' \in \mathrm{R}_Y} \frac{\delta(x,y')}{\min\{X(x), Y(y')\}}$

The Signature Quadratic Form Distance [10] is a correlation-based approach which adapts the generic concept of correlation to feature signatures. The Signature Quadratic Form Distance is defined based on the similarity correlation $\langle X, Y\rangle_s = \sum_{x,y\in\mathbb{F}} X(x)\cdot Y(y)\cdot s(x,y)$ between two feature signatures with respect to a similarity function $s:\mathbb{F}\times\mathbb{F}\rightarrow\mathbb{R}$ as $\text{SQFD}_s(X,Y) = \left(\langle X,X\rangle_s - 2\cdot\langle X,Y\rangle_s + \langle Y,Y\rangle_s\right)^{\frac{1}{2}}$.

Depending on the type of multimedia data and the intended notion of similarity, different types of distance-based similarity measures can thus be used.

2.3 Efficient Query Processing and Indexing

Similarity search in large-scale multimedia databases by feature signatures and distance-based similarity measures remains a challenging issue. If the distance-based similarity measure satisfies the metric postulates, metric access methods [15, 24, 65] are able to avoid a time-consuming sequential scan and to process k-nearest-neighbor queries efficiently.

A fundamental approach underlying many access methods is the multi-step approach which has been investigated and extended in [1, 20, 25, 32, 33, 55].

In addition to metric access methods, many efficient query processing and indexing approaches have been proposed for the Earth Mover's Distance [2, 3, 51, 53, 58, 59, 60, 62, 64] and the Signature Quadratic Form Distance [7, 9, 11, 12, 36, 37] including the utilization of multi-core CPU and many-core GPU architectures [34, 35].

Except for the latter, none of the aforementioned approaches is able to process k-nearest-neighbor queries in multimedia databases comprising millions of feature signatures with a query response time of less than one second.

2.4 Fisher Framework

The idea of our proposal is akin to that of Fisher scores derived from generative probability models. Given a generative probability model $p(x|\theta)$ with parameters θ over a multidimensional Euclidean space $\mathbb{R}^d$, the Fisher score with respect to a set $\{x_1, x_2, \ldots, x_n\}\subset\mathbb{R}^d$ of pairwise disjoint Euclidean vectors is defined as $U_x = \nabla_\theta \log p(\{x_1, x_2, \ldots, x_n\}|\theta)$. Intuitively, the Fisher score U_x describes how the parameters of the generative probability model have to be adapted in order to better fit the set $\{x_1, x_2, \ldots, x_n\}$. The similarity between two Fisher scores U_x and U_y is defined in [28] via a Gaussian Kernel as $k(U_x, U_y) = e^{-\frac{1}{2}(U_x-U_y)^T\cdot F^{-1}\cdot(U_x-U_y)}$ and further simplified to the Fisher kernel [29] as $k(U_x,U_y) = U_x^T\cdot F^{-1}\cdot U_y$, where F^{-1} denotes the inverted Fisher information matrix that is frequently approximated by the identity matrix.

The Fisher framework described above provides a model which handles variable length data that is represented by sets of pairwise disjoint Euclidean vectors and concerns the global dependencies within the data. It thus combines the advantages of both discriminative and generative models and has been applied to various domains such as speech recognition [42], text mining [19], DNA analysis [29], handwritten word-spotting [50], image classification [54], image categorization [48], image retrieval [49], web audio classification [43], and relevance feedback-based video retrieval [40].

The application of the Fisher framework is restricted to sets of pairwise disjoint Euclidean vectors. In this work, we advance the concept of the Fisher framework and propose its application to feature signatures of multimedia objects.

3. GRADIENT-BASED SIGNATURES

Given a large-scale multimedia database comprising millions of multimedia objects, how to approximate the content-based properties of the corresponding feature signatures in order to carry out similarity search efficiently and with high accuracy? We propose to address this issue by means of *gradient-based signatures.*

Gradient-based signatures aggregate feature signatures with respect to a generative model. Instead of explicitly modeling the content-based properties of a multimedia object via the representatives and weights of the corresponding feature signature, we propose to implicitly model these properties via the gradients of the log-likelihood function of the model parameters with respect to the given feature signature. To this end, we suppose that any generative model $p\in\mathbb{R}^{\mathbb{F}}$ over a feature space $\mathbb{F}$ is completely characterized by its parameters θ. For instance, a Gaussian mixture model, which is defined for all $x\in\mathbb{R}^d$ as $g(x|\theta) = \sum_{k=1}^{n}\pi_k\cdot\mathcal{N}(x|\mu_k,\Sigma_k)$, is characterized by the parameters $\theta = \{\pi_k, \mu_{k_{[i]}}, \sigma_{k_{[i,j]}} | 1\leq k\leq n \wedge 1\leq i,j\leq d\}$. For the sake of convenience, we denote the parameter space of all possible parameters by Θ.

Given a generative model $p\in\mathbb{R}^{\mathbb{F}}$, we introduce the likelihood of the parameters θ with respect to a given feature signature $X\in\mathbb{R}^{\mathbb{F}}$ based on the probabilities of the corresponding features from the feature space $\mathbb{F}$. The formal definition is shown below.

Definition 2. (Likelihood of parameters with respect to a given feature signature)
Let $(\mathbb{F},\delta)$ be a multi-dimensional Euclidean feature space, i.e. $\mathbb{F}=\mathbb{R}^d$, and θ be the parameters characterizing a generative model $p\in\mathbb{R}^{\mathbb{F}}$. The *likelihood of parameters θ with respect to a given feature signature* $X\in\mathbb{R}^{\mathbb{F}}$ is defined as:

$$\mathcal{L}(\theta|X) = \prod_{f\in\mathbb{F}} p(f|\theta)^{X(f)}$$

As can be seen in the definition above, the likelihood $\mathcal{L}(\theta|X)$ of the parameters θ for a given feature signature X is determined by multiplying the density values $p(f|\theta)^{X(f)}$ of all features $f\in\mathbb{F}$. More precisely, the likelihood can be restricted to the representatives $\mathrm{R}_X\subseteq\mathbb{F}$ of the corresponding feature signature X and can thus be computed in linear time complexity $\mathcal{O}(|\mathrm{R}_X|)$ as $\mathcal{L}(\theta|X) = \prod_{f\in\mathrm{R}_X} p(f|\theta)^{X(f)}$, provided a constant time complexity for evaluating the generative model and the exponentiation.

Intuitively, the likelihood $\mathcal{L}(\theta|X)$ describes how likely a feature signature X is generated by a generative model p with respect to a certain parameterization θ. The value of the likelihood function, however, is not a suitable means of aggregation in order to express and compare the content-based properties of multimedia objects. Instead of using this single figure, we propose to take into account the gradients of the logarithm of the likelihood function for a given feature signature of a multimedia object. By assigning each model parameter $\lambda\in\theta$ to its gradient, i.e. its partial derivative, we define a gradient-based signature as a function from the parameter space Θ to the real numbers $\mathbb{R}$. In this way, we facilitate the definition of gradient-based signatures with respect to any generative model as shown below.

Definition 3. (Gradient-based signature)
Let $(\mathbb{F},\delta)$ be a multi-dimensional Euclidean feature space, i.e. $\mathbb{F}=\mathbb{R}^d$, and $X\in\mathbb{R}^{\mathbb{F}}$ be a feature signature. Given the

parameters $\theta \subset \Theta$ characterizing a generative model $p \in \mathbb{R}^{\mathbb{F}}$, the *gradient-based signature* $X_\nabla : \Theta \to \mathbb{R}$ is defined for all $\lambda \in \Theta$ as:

$$X_\nabla(\lambda) = \begin{cases} \nabla_\lambda \log \mathcal{L}(\theta|X) & ,\lambda \in \theta \\ 0 & ,otherwise \end{cases}$$

A gradient-based signature $X_\nabla \in \mathbb{R}^\Theta$ aggregates the representatives of a feature signature $X \in \mathbb{R}^{\mathbb{F}}$ according to the parameters θ of the underlying generative model p and describes how to adapt the model parameters θ in order to better fit the feature signature X. In this way, the complexity in terms of storage space of a gradient-based signature X_∇ is bounded by the model parameters and it holds for the representatives R_{X_∇} of a gradient-based signature X_∇ that $R_{X_\nabla} \subseteq \theta$. If two gradient-based signatures are defined based on the same parameters θ, i.e. if they are defined with respect to a common generative model, their comparison can be carried out in linear time complexity $\mathcal{O}(|\theta|)$, as shown in the following section.

3.1 (Dis)similarity Measures

Given two gradient-based signatures that are defined with different parameterizations $\theta, \theta' \subset \Theta$, their comparison can be carried out via any signature-based similarity measure, cf. Section 2.2, in an at least quadratic computation time complexity $\mathcal{O}(|\theta| \cdot |\theta'|)$. To this end, the parameter space Θ has to be endowed with an appropriate ground distance $\delta : \Theta \times \Theta \to \mathbb{R}$ that models the dissimilarity between any two parameters.

In order to avoid a quadratic computation time complexity for a single comparison, we assume a common generative model with parameters θ underlying the gradient-based signatures. In this case, all gradient-based signatures share the same parameters $\lambda \in \theta$ which can be aligned prior to query processing and compared in a bin-by-bin manner. In fact, two gradient-based signatures X_∇ and Y_∇ can be thought of as vectors $\mathbf{x}_\nabla = [\nabla_{\lambda_1} \log \mathcal{L}(\theta|X), \ldots, \nabla_{\lambda_{|\theta|}} \log \mathcal{L}(\theta|X)] \in \mathbb{R}^{|\theta|}$ and $\mathbf{y}_\nabla = [\nabla_{\lambda_1} \log \mathcal{L}(\theta|Y), \ldots, \nabla_{\lambda_{|\theta|}} \log \mathcal{L}(\theta|Y)] \in \mathbb{R}^{|\theta|}$ in a multi-dimensional Euclidean space $\mathbb{R}^{|\theta|}$ which can be compared by means of classic vector space approaches such as the cosine similarity and the Minkowski distance.

Definition 4. (Cosine similarity)
Let $(\mathbb{F}, \delta)$ be a feature space and $X_\nabla, Y_\nabla \in \mathbb{R}^\Theta$ be two gradient-based signatures. The *cosine similarity* $cos : \mathbb{R}^\Theta \times \mathbb{R}^\Theta \to \mathbb{R}$ between X_∇ and Y_∇ is defined as:

$$cos(X_\nabla, Y_\nabla) = \frac{\sum_{\lambda \in \Theta} X_\nabla(\lambda) \cdot Y_\nabla(\lambda)}{\sqrt{\sum_{\lambda \in \Theta} X_\nabla(\lambda)^2} \cdot \sqrt{\sum_{\lambda \in \Theta} Y_\nabla(\lambda)^2}}$$

Definition 5. (Minkowski distance)
Let $(\mathbb{F}, \delta)$ be a feature space and $X_\nabla, Y_\nabla \in \mathbb{R}^\Theta$ be two gradient-based signatures. The *Minkowski distance* $L_p : \mathbb{R}^\Theta \times \mathbb{R}^\Theta \to \mathbb{R}$ between X_∇ and Y_∇ is defined for $p \in \mathbb{R}^{\geq 0}$ as:

$$L_p(X_\nabla, Y_\nabla) = \left(\sum_{\lambda \in \Theta} |X_\nabla(\lambda) - Y_\nabla(\lambda)|^p \right)^{\frac{1}{p}}$$

As can be seen from the definitions above, both cosine similarity $cos(X_\nabla, Y_\nabla)$ and Minkowski distance $L_p(X_\nabla, Y_\nabla)$ between two gradient-based signatures X_∇ and Y_∇ show different properties. While the similarity value defined by the cosine similarity is attributed to the angle between the corresponding vectors $\mathbf{x}_\nabla$ and $\mathbf{y}_\nabla$, the dissimilarity value defined by the Minkowski distance depends on the parameter-wise differences $X_\nabla(\lambda) - Y_\nabla(\lambda) = \nabla_\lambda \log \mathcal{L}(\theta|X) - \nabla_\lambda \log \mathcal{L}(\theta|Y)$. The computation time complexity of both approaches is linear in the number of parameters and thus lies in $\mathcal{O}(|\theta|)$.

The combination of gradient-based signatures and Minkowski distances epitomizes an efficient and indexable similarity model for similarity search in large-scale multimedia databases. Before we study the performance of the proposal, we give some theoretical insights in the following section.

4. THEORETICAL INSIGHTS

Modeling the content-based characteristics of multimedia objects by means of gradient-based signatures inevitably leads to the question of which generative model to be chosen. In the remainder of this section, we thus provide closed-form expressions for mixture models with a particular focus on Gaussian mixture models. In addition, we deepen our knowledge by investigating the Euclidean distance on gradient-based signatures.

4.1 Closed-form Expressions

A frequently encountered generative model in the context of multimedia data and in particular for modeling the content-based features of images is the Gaussian mixture model [5, 21, 23, 31, 38, 47, 61, 63]. A Gaussian mixture model comprises a finite linear combination of normal distributions and thus provides an expressive yet compact way of generatively describing a distribution in a feature space $\mathbb{F}$. There are many reasons for utilizing normal distributions [14]: First, they are very tractable analytically. Second, they have familiar symmetrical bell shapes. Third, they approximate a large variety of probability distributions according to the central limit theorem. The formal definition of a Gaussian mixture model is given below.

Definition 6. (Gaussian mixture model)
Let $(\mathbb{F}, \delta)$ be a multi-dimensional Euclidean feature space, i.e. $\mathbb{F} = \mathbb{R}^d$. A *Gaussian mixture model* $g \in \mathbb{R}^{\mathbb{F}}$ *with parameters* $\theta = \{\pi_k, \mu_{k_{[i]}}, \sigma_{k_{[i,j]}} | 1 \leq k \leq n \wedge 1 \leq i, j \leq d\}$ is defined for all $f \in \mathbb{F}$ as:

$$g(f|\theta) \quad = \quad \sum_{k=1}^{n} \pi_k \cdot \mathcal{N}(f|\mu_k, \Sigma_k),$$

where the normal distribution $\mathcal{N}(f|\mu_k, \Sigma_k) \in \mathbb{R}^{\mathbb{F}}$ is defined as $\mathcal{N}(f|\mu_k, \Sigma_k) = \frac{1}{\sqrt{(2\pi)^d |\Sigma_k|}} e^{-\frac{1}{2}(f-\mu_k)\Sigma_k^{-1}(f-\mu_k)^T}$.

Any Gaussian mixture model over a multi-dimensional Euclidean feature space $\mathbb{F} = \mathbb{R}^d$ is completely described by the parameters $\theta = \{\pi_k, \mu_{k_{[i]}}, \sigma_{k_{[i,j]}} | 1 \leq k \leq n \wedge 1 \leq i, j \leq d\}$ reflecting the prior probabilities $\pi_k \in \mathbb{R}^+$ such that $\sum_{k=1}^{n} \pi_k = 1$, the means $\mu_k \in \mathbb{R}^d$, and covariance matrices $\Sigma_k \in \mathbb{R}^{d \times d}$ for $1 \leq k \leq n$.

Before we propose closed-form expressions for computing the gradients with respect to the means and variances of a Gaussian mixture model for a given feature signature, we first show that the computation of the gradients for any mixture model is in general attributed to its components.

Theorem 1. (Gradients for mixture models)
Let $(\mathbb{F}, \delta)$ be a multi-dimensional Euclidean feature space,

i.e. $\mathbb{F} = \mathbb{R}^d$, $X \in \mathbb{R}^{\mathbb{F}}$ be a feature signature, and $\theta = \bigcup_{k=1}^{n} \theta_k$ be the parameters of a mixture model $p \in \mathbb{R}^{\mathbb{F}}$ with $n \in \mathbb{N}$ components. For all parameters $\lambda \in \theta$ it holds that:

$$\nabla_\lambda \log \mathcal{L}(\theta|X) = \sum_{f \in \mathbb{F}} X(f) \cdot \frac{\sum_{k=1}^{n} \nabla_\lambda \pi_k \cdot p(f|\theta_k)}{p(f|\theta)}$$

PROOF.

$$\begin{aligned}
\nabla_\lambda \log \mathcal{L}(\theta|X) &= \nabla_\lambda \log \prod_{f \in \mathbb{F}} p(f|\theta)^{X(f)} \\
&= \nabla_\lambda \sum_{f \in \mathbb{F}} \log p(f|\theta)^{X(f)} \\
&= \sum_{f \in \mathbb{F}} X(f) \cdot \nabla_\lambda \log p(f|\theta) \\
&= \sum_{f \in \mathbb{F}} X(f) \cdot \frac{\nabla_\lambda p(f|\theta)}{p(f|\theta)} \\
&= \sum_{f \in \mathbb{F}} X(f) \cdot \frac{\nabla_\lambda \sum_{k=1}^{n} \pi_k \cdot p(f|\theta_k)}{p(f|\theta)} \\
&= \sum_{f \in \mathbb{F}} X(f) \cdot \frac{\sum_{k=1}^{n} \nabla_\lambda \pi_k \cdot p(f|\theta_k)}{p(f|\theta)}
\end{aligned}$$

□

The theorem above provides a formal means of deriving the gradient $\nabla_\lambda \log \mathcal{L}(\theta|X)$ of each parameter $\lambda \in \theta$ by adding the gradients $\nabla_\lambda \pi_k \cdot p(f|\theta_k)$ of all mixture components $1 \leq k \leq n$ for each feature $f \in \mathbb{F}$. As an example, for a Gaussian mixture model g with parameterization $\theta = \bigcup_{k=1}^{n} \{\pi_k, \mu_k, \Sigma_k\}$, the gradient $\nabla_\lambda \log \mathcal{L}(\theta|X)$ is thus attributed to the gradients $\nabla_\lambda \pi_k \cdot \mathcal{N}(f|\mu_k, \Sigma_k)$ of the normal distributions of the mixture components. The following lemma is finally devoted to the closed-form expressions of gradients with respect to the means and variances of Gaussian mixture models with diagonal covariance matrices.

Lemma 1. (Gradients for Gaussian mixture models) Let $(\mathbb{F}, \delta)$ be a multi-dimensional Euclidean feature space, i.e. $\mathbb{F} = \mathbb{R}^d$, $X \in \mathbb{R}^{\mathbb{F}}$ be a feature signature, and $\theta = \{\pi_k, \mu_{k_{[i]}}, \sigma_{k_{[i,j]}} | 1 \leq k \leq n \wedge 1 \leq i, j \leq d\}$ be the parameters characterizing a Gaussian mixture model $g \in \mathbb{R}^{\mathbb{F}}$ with diagonal covariance matrices, i.e. $\forall i \neq j : \sigma_{k_{[i,j]}} = 0$. It holds for all parameters $\mu_{k_{[i]}}, \sigma_{k_{[i,i]}} \in \theta$ that:

$$\begin{aligned}
\nabla_{\mu_{k_{[i]}}} \log \mathcal{L}(\theta|X) &= \sum_{f \in \mathbb{F}} X(f) \cdot \gamma(k|f) \cdot \left(\frac{f_{[i]} - \mu_{k_{[i]}}}{\sigma^2_{k_{[i,i]}}} \right), \\
\nabla_{\sigma_{k_{[i,i]}}} \log \mathcal{L}(\theta|X) &= \\
\sum_{f \in \mathbb{F}} X(f) \cdot \gamma(k|f) \cdot &\left(\left(\frac{f_{[i]} - \mu_{k_{[i]}}}{\sigma^2_{k_{[i,i]}}} \right)^2 - \frac{1}{\sigma_{k_{[i,i]}}} \right),
\end{aligned}$$

where the responsibility $\gamma(k|f)$ of mixture component k for a given feature $f \in \mathbb{F}$ is defined as $\gamma(k|f) = \frac{\pi_k \cdot \mathcal{N}(f|\mu_k, \Sigma_k)}{g(f|\theta)}$.

PROOF. By making use of Theorem 1, one can show that $\nabla_{\mu_{k_{[i]}}} \log \mathcal{L}(\theta|X) = \sum_{f \in \mathbb{F}} X(f) \cdot \frac{\sum_{k=1}^{n} \nabla_{\mu_{k_{[i]}}} \pi_k \cdot \mathcal{N}(f|\mu_k, \Sigma_k)}{g(f|\theta)}$. Differential calculus yields that $\nabla_{\mu_{k_{[i]}}} \pi_k \cdot \mathcal{N}(f|\mu_k, \Sigma_k) = \mathcal{N}(f|\mu_k, \Sigma_k) \cdot \left(\frac{f_{[i]} - \mu_{k_{[i]}}}{\sigma^2_{k_{[i,i]}}} \right)$ and thus the first statement. The second statement can be shown analogously. □

Lemma 1 finally provides a way of computing gradient-based signatures by means of closed-form expressions. The computation of the gradients $\nabla_{\mu_{k_{[i]}}} \log \mathcal{L}(\theta|X)$ and $\nabla_{\sigma_{k_{[i,i]}}} \log \mathcal{L}(\theta|X)$ for a given feature signature $X \in \mathbb{R}^{\mathbb{F}}$ can be restricted to the corresponding representatives $\mathrm{R}_X \subseteq \mathbb{F}$. Therefore, the time complexity of a single gradient computation lies in $\mathcal{O}(|\mathrm{R}_X| \cdot \zeta)$ where ζ denotes the computation time complexity of evaluating the responsibility $\gamma(k|f)$.

Computing gradient-based signatures prior to query processing makes sense for very large multimedia databases. If the multimedia database is updated frequently and/or the generative model changes dynamically, interrupting query processing for the sake of databasing gradient-based signatures inevitably leads to the problem of high query latency. In order to counteract this issue, we show how to compute the Euclidean distance between two gradient-based signatures in an ad-hoc manner by means of the Signature Quadratic Form Distance between the corresponding feature signatures in the following section.

4.2 On the Euclidean Distance

The Euclidean distance $\mathrm{L}_2(X_\nabla, Y_\nabla)$ between two gradient-based signatures $X_\nabla, Y_\nabla \in \mathbb{R}^\Theta$ with respect to the parameters $\theta \subset \Theta$ of a generative model $p \in \mathbb{R}^{\mathbb{F}}$ is equivalent to the Signature Quadratic Form Distance $\mathrm{SQFD}_{s_\nabla}(X, Y)$ between the corresponding feature signatures $X, Y \in \mathbb{R}^{\mathbb{F}}$ by utilizing the similarity function $s_\nabla(f, g) = \sum_{\lambda \in \theta} \nabla_\lambda \log p(f|\theta) \cdot \nabla_\lambda \log p(g|\theta)$. This is formally shown in the theorem below.

Theorem 2. (Equivalence of L_2 *and* SQFD*)* Let $(\mathbb{F}, \delta)$ be a feature space and $\theta \subset \Theta$ be the parameters characterizing a generative model $p \in \mathbb{R}^{\mathbb{F}}$. It holds for all feature signatures $X, Y \in \mathbb{R}^{\mathbb{F}}$ and corresponding gradient-based signatures $X_\nabla, Y_\nabla \in \mathbb{R}^\Theta$ with respect to the parameters θ of p that:

$$\mathrm{L}_2(X_\nabla, Y_\nabla) = \mathrm{SQFD}_{s_\nabla}(X, Y),$$

where the similarity function $s_\nabla : \mathbb{F} \times \mathbb{F} \to \mathbb{R}$ is defined for all $f, g \in \mathbb{F}$ as $s_\nabla(f, g) = \sum_{\lambda \in \theta} \nabla_\lambda \log p(f|\theta) \cdot \nabla_\lambda \log p(g|\theta)$.

PROOF.

$$\begin{aligned}
&\mathrm{L}_2(X_\nabla, Y_\nabla)^2 \\
= &\sum_{\lambda \in \Theta} (X_\nabla(\lambda) - Y_\nabla(\lambda))^2 \\
= &\sum_{\lambda \in \theta} (\nabla_\lambda \log \mathcal{L}(\theta|X) - \nabla_\lambda \log \mathcal{L}(\theta|Y))^2 \\
= &\sum_{\lambda \in \theta} \left(\sum_{f \in \mathbb{F}} (X(f) - Y(f)) \cdot \frac{\sum_{k=1}^{n} \nabla_\lambda \pi_k \cdot p(f|\theta_k)}{p(f|\theta)} \right)^2 \\
= &\sum_{\lambda \in \theta} \left(\sum_{f \in \mathbb{F}} (X(f) - Y(f)) \cdot \nabla_\lambda \log p(f|\theta) \right)^2 \\
= &\sum_{\lambda \in \theta} \left(\sum_{f \in \mathbb{F}} \sum_{g \in \mathbb{F}} (X(f) - Y(f)) \cdot (X(g) - Y(g)) \cdot \right. \\
&\left. \nabla_\lambda \log p(f|\theta) \cdot \nabla_\lambda \log p(g|\theta) \right) \\
= &\sum_{f \in \mathbb{F}} \sum_{g \in \mathbb{F}} (X(f) - Y(f)) \cdot (X(g) - Y(g)) \cdot \\
&\left(\sum_{\lambda \in \theta} \nabla_\lambda \log p(f|\theta) \cdot \nabla_\lambda \log p(g|\theta) \right)
\end{aligned}$$

$$= \sum_{f\in\mathbb{F}}\sum_{g\in\mathbb{F}}(X(f)-Y(f))\cdot(X(g)-Y(g))\cdot s_{\nabla}(f,g)$$
$$= \text{SQFD}_{s_{\nabla}}(X,Y)^2$$

Consequently, the statement is shown. □

The similarity function $s_{\nabla}(f,g)$ is a dot product evaluated according to the parameters $\lambda \in \theta$ between the gradients $\nabla_{\lambda}\log p(f|\theta)$ and $\nabla_{\lambda}\log p(g|\theta)$ of the corresponding features $f,g \in \mathbb{F}$. The similarity function $s_{\nabla}(f,g)$ yields a large positive value if the gradients of both features f and g point into the same direction for many parameters $\lambda \in \theta$, i.e. if the adaption of parameters in order to maximize the log-likelihood function is similar for both features f and g. The more gradients point into different directions, the smaller the value of the similarity function $s_{\nabla}(f,g)$.

To summarize, the similarity function $s_{\nabla}(f,g)$ utilized within the Signature Quadratic Form Distance is less influenced by the distance between the features f and g but their relationship to the parameters of the underlying generative model.

5. BINARY GRADIENT-BASED SIGNATURES

Binarizing gradient-based signatures leads to compact content-based feature representations of multimedia objects. Consider for instance a feature signature $X \in \mathbb{R}^{\mathbb{F}}$ with $n = |\text{R}_X|$ representatives over a d-dimensional Euclidean feature space $\mathbb{F} = \mathbb{R}^d$. Storing this feature signature requires $n + (n \cdot d)$ floating point values which typically comprise 4 bytes each. In contrast, if we consider a generative model with parameters θ, the number of floating point values of the corresponding gradient-based signature $X_{\nabla} \in \mathbb{R}^{\Theta}$ is reduced to $|\theta|$. Binarizing this gradient-based signature X_{∇} will further significantly reduce the storage space from $|\theta|$ floating point values to $|\theta|$ bits.

The most intuitive approach to binarize a gradient-based signature consists in substituting positive weights by a value of one and non-positive weights by a value of zero. We denote this approach as *natural binarization* which is defined for a gradient-based signature $X_{\nabla} \in \mathbb{R}^{\Theta}$ and for all parameters $\lambda \in \Theta$ as follows:

$$X_{\nabla}^{b^{\pm}}(\lambda) = \begin{cases} 1 & ,X_{\nabla}(\lambda) > 0 \\ 0 & ,X_{\nabla}(\lambda) \leq 0 \end{cases}$$

The natural binarization exploits the fact that the gradient-based signature X_{∇} describes how to adapt the model parameters θ in order to maximize the likelihood $\mathcal{L}(\theta|X)$. The increase or decrease of a single parameter $\lambda \in \theta$ can thus be easily expressed by means of a binary notation.

The individual data distribution within each single parameter λ, however, is completely ignored by the natural binarization. To this end, we further propose to binarize gradient-based signatures according to the expectation values $\text{E}[\lambda|\mathbb{X}] = \frac{1}{|\mathbb{X}|}\cdot\sum_{X_{\nabla}\in\mathbb{X}} X_{\nabla}(\lambda)$ of the parameters $\lambda \in \theta$ for a given training data set $\mathbb{X} \subset \mathbb{R}^{\Theta}$. We denote this approach as *expectation binarization* which is defined for a gradient-based signature $X_{\nabla} \in \mathbb{R}^{\Theta}$ and for all parameters $\lambda \in \Theta$ as follows:

$$X_{\nabla}^{b^{\text{E}}}(\lambda) = \begin{cases} 1 & ,X_{\nabla}(\lambda) > \text{E}[\lambda|\mathbb{X}] \\ 0 & ,X_{\nabla}(\lambda) \leq \text{E}[\lambda|\mathbb{X}] \end{cases}$$

A binary gradient-based signature $X_{\nabla}^{b^{\text{E}}}$ describes how each single parameter λ deviates from the expectation value $\text{E}[\lambda|\mathbb{X}]$ based on the training data set $\mathbb{X}$. Since this approach may be sensitive to outliers in the training data set $\mathbb{X}$, we additionally propose to replace the expectation value by the median value. We denote this approach as *median binarization* which is defined for a gradient-based signature $X_{\nabla} \in \mathbb{R}^{\Theta}$ and for all parameters $\lambda \in \Theta$ as follows:

$$X_{\nabla}^{b^{\text{M}}}(\lambda) = \begin{cases} 1 & ,X_{\nabla}(\lambda) > \text{M}[\lambda|\mathbb{X}] \\ 0 & ,X_{\nabla}(\lambda) \leq \text{M}[\lambda|\mathbb{X}] \end{cases}$$

where $\text{M}[\lambda|\mathbb{X}]$ is defined as the median of parameter λ with respect to the training set $\mathbb{X}$.

The dissimilarity between two binary gradient-based signatures is evaluated by the logical operation XOR, i.e. by counting the number bit differences. The question of which binarization method will lead to the highest retrieval performance is evaluated in the following section.

6. PERFORMANCE ANALYSIS

6.1 Experimental Setup

Evaluating the performance of distance-based similarity search approaches is a highly empirical discipline. It is nearly unforeseeable which approach will provide the best results with respect to the qualities of accuracy and efficiency. To this end, we evaluated the proposed (binary) gradient-based signatures on different benchmark image databases.

The **Holidays database** [30] comprises 1,491 holiday photos corresponding to a large variety of scene types. It was designed to test the robustness, for instance, to rotation, viewpoint, and illumination changes. The **UKBench database** [44] consists of 10,200 images showing different objects or scenes that are photographed from four different viewpoints. Both databases provide ground truth information including queries that are used to evaluate the accuracy of the approaches. The **ImageNet database** [17] is a large-scale image database with more than 14 million heterogenous images. We use this database to evaluate the scalability of our approach in terms of accuracy and efficiency. Finally, the **MIRFlickr database** [27] includes 1 million images crawled from *Flickr*[5] and is used for training the generative models and binarization methods.

We computed feature signatures for each image of the aforementioned databases by first extracting local feature descriptors, denoted by PCT, describing the relative spatial information of a pixel, its CIELAB color value, and its coarseness and contrast values as described in [6] and then clustering the extracted feature descriptors by the k-means algorithm. In this way, we obtained feature signatures with 10 up to 100 representatives over a 7-dimensional feature space $\mathbb{F} = \mathbb{R}^7$. In addition, we trained Gaussian mixture models with diagonal covariance matrices comprising 10 up to 50 components over the aforementioned feature space by utilizing features from the MIRFlickr database. Based on these Gaussian mixture models and feature signatures, we computed gradient-based signatures with resect to the parameters $\theta_{\mu} = \{\mu_k\}_{k=1}^{n}$ of the Gaussian mixture models, since these parameters indicate superior quality in terms of accuracy within preliminary investigations in comparison to other parameters.

[5]`http://flickr.com`

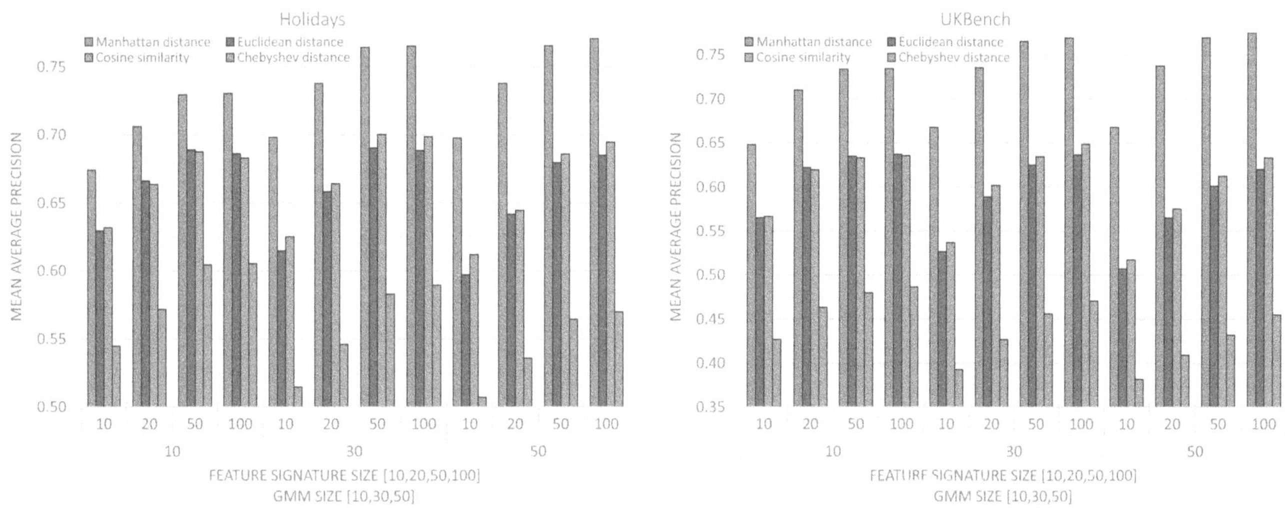

Figure 2: Mean average precision values for gradient-based signatures with respect to different (dis)similarity measures as a function of feature signature size and GMM size for the Holidays and UKBench databases.

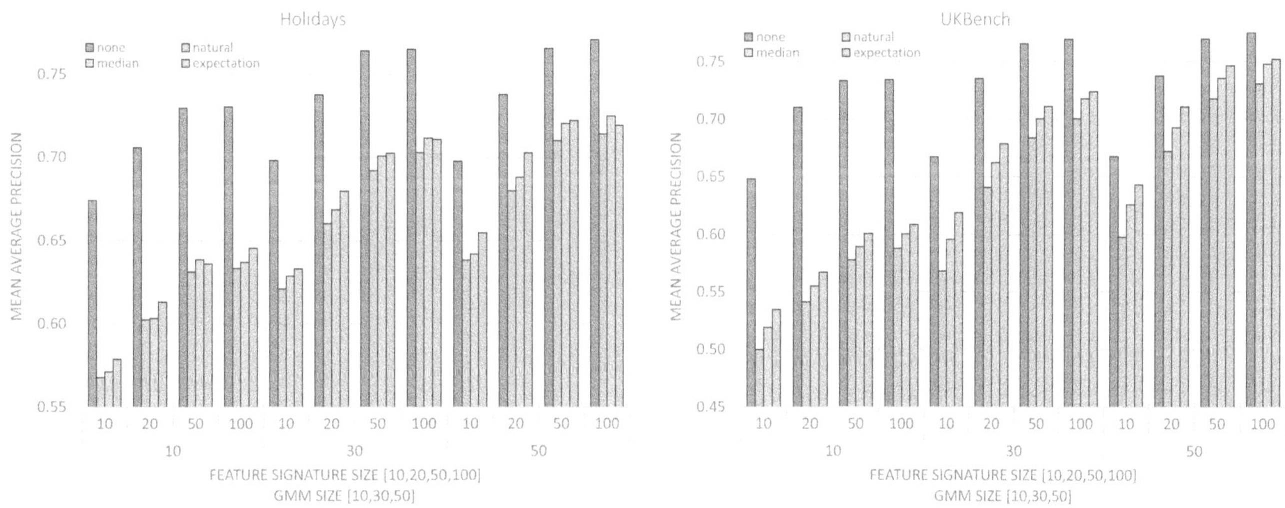

Figure 3: Mean average precision values for gradient-based signatures with respect to different binarization methods as a function of feature signature size and GMM size for the Holidays and UKBench databases.

We implemented all approaches in Java 1.8 and conducted the experiments on a single-core 3.4 GHz machine equipped with 16 GB of main memory.

6.2 Experimental Results

In the first series of experiments, we investigated the performance of gradient-based signatures in terms of accuracy by means of the mean average precision measure, which provides a single-figure measure of quality across all recall levels [39]. The mean average precision measure is evaluated on the 500 and 2,550 selected queries of the Holidays and UKBench databases for gradient-based signatures based on Gaussian mixture models of sizes 10, 30, and 50 and feature signatures of sizes 10, 20, 50, and 100. The results with respect to different (dis)similarity measures are shown in Figure 2. As can be seen in this figure, the combination of gradient-based signatures and Manhattan distance achieves the highest mean average precision values for both databases. On average, increasing the number of components of the Gaussian mixture model and the size of the underlying feature signatures results in higher retrieval accuracy. On the Holidays database, the maximum mean average precision value of 0.77 is achieved with gradient-based signatures obtained from a Gaussian mixture model of size 40 and feature signatures of size 90. On the UKBench database, the maximum mean average precision value of 0.78 is achieved with gradient-based signatures obtained from a Gaussian mixture model of size 50 and feature signatures of size 100. By additionally weighting the parameters of the gradient-based signatures with the approximation of the Fisher in-

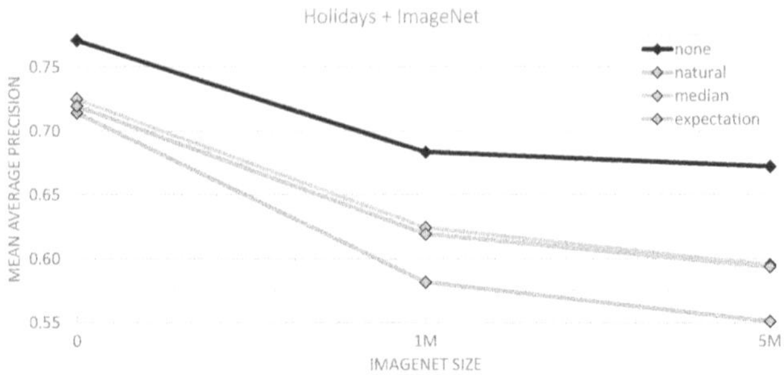

Figure 4: Mean average precision values for gradient-based signatures with respect to different binarization methods as a function of the size of the ImageNet database.

formation matrix as proposed in [48], the performance increases to mean average precision values of 0.78 and 0.82 on the Holidays and UKBench database, respectively.

In the second series of experiments, we evaluated the performance of binary gradient-based signatures. To this end, we compared the different binarization methods natural $X_\nabla^{b^\pm}$, expectation $X_\nabla^{b^E}$, and median $X_\nabla^{b^M}$, as proposed in Section 5, with non-binarized gradient-based signatures and the Manhattan distance. The results in terms of mean average precision values are depicted in Figure 3. Binary gradient-based signatures show the same tendency as gradient-based signatures. Increasing the number of components of the Gaussian mixture model and the size of the underlying feature signatures results in higher retrieval accuracy. The highest mean average precision values of 0.73 and 0.75 on the Holidays and UKBench databases are achieved with the expectation binarization method and Gaussian mixture models of size 40 and 50 and feature signatures of size 80 and 100, respectively.

We furthermore evaluated the scalability in terms of accuracy of binary gradient-based signatures by increasing the Holidays database with additional images from the ImageNet database. The corresponding mean average precision values are shown in Figure 4. As can be seen in the figure, the loss of accuracy by utilizing binary gradient-based signatures instead of gradient-based signatures is approximately 10%. By increasing the Holidays database with 5 million images, gradient-based signatures endowed with the Manhattan distance achieve a mean average precision value of 0.67 while the corresponding binary gradient-based signatures achieve a mean average precision value of 0.59.

The performance in terms of accuracy of (binary) gradient-based signatures in comparison to the state-of-the-art signature-based approaches is summarized in Table 1. In particular, we compare different variants of our approach to the Earth Mover's Distance (EMD), the Perceptually Modified Hausdorff Distance (PMHD), the Signature Matching Distance (SMD), and the Signature Quadratic Form Distance (SQFD). We report the highest mean average precision values and the corresponding signature size as well as as the size of the Gaussian mixture model where appropriate. According to Table 1, gradient-based signatures (X_∇, L_1) in combination with the Manhattan distance are able to outperform the well-known Earth Mover's Distance and the Signature Quadratic Form Distance. The Earth Mover's Distance is

Table 1: Comparison to the state-of-the-art signature-based approaches on the Holidays and UKBench databases.

	Holidays		UKBench	
	MAP	sig./gmm	MAP	sig./gmm
EMD	0.72	90	0.74	50
PMHD	0.80	80	0.87	90
SMD	0.81	100	0.85	60
SQFD	0.76	40	0.77	60
X_∇, L_1	0.77	90/40	0.78	100/50
X_∇, L_1, FIM	0.78	90/40	0.82	100/50
$X_\nabla^{b^\pm}$, XOR	0.72	80/40	0.73	100/50
$X_\nabla^{b^E}$, XOR	0.73	80/40	0.75	100/50
$X_\nabla^{b^M}$, XOR	0.73	100/50	0.75	100/50

Table 2: Average query response times in milliseconds for the Holidays + ImageNet database comprising 5 million gradient-based signatures.

	GMM size		
	10	30	50
X_∇, L_1	419.1ms	1297.6ms	1617.6ms
$X_\nabla^{b^\pm}$, XOR	400.8ms	476.8ms	588.7ms

even outperformed by making use of binary gradient-based signatures ($X_\nabla^{b^E}$, XOR) and the logical operation XOR. The highest performance in terms of accuracy is reached by the Signature Matching Distance on the Holidays database and the Perceptually Modified Hausdorff Distance on the UKBench database.

Summarizing, the performance results reported above show that gradient-based signatures are able to outperform state-of-the-art signature-based approaches in terms of accuracy. The suitability of gradient-based signatures for efficient similarity search in multimedia databases comprising millions of feature signatures is indicated by means of Table 2, where we summarize the average query response times for 100-nearest-neighbor queries in a multimedia database comprising 5 million gradient-based signatures. The queries are processed via a sequential scan, i.e. without any additional indexing structure.

While the query response times for gradient-based signatures (X_∇, L_1) endowed with the Manhattan distance significantly increase from approximately 0.4 seconds to 1.6 seconds when increasing the size of the underlying Gaussian mixture model, the query response times for binary gradient-based signatures ($X_\nabla^{b^\pm}$, XOR), which are compared via the logical operation XOR, increase only marginally and approximately stay around a value of 0.5 seconds.

The query response times show that gradient-based signatures are orders of magnitude faster than conventional signature-based approaches. According to [6], the Signature Matching Distance is one of the most efficient signature-based distance function that performs 1 million distance computations for feature signatures of size 10 in approximately 1.4 seconds. For a feature signature size of 100, the Signature Matching Distance requires approximately 82.2 seconds.

To conclude, our extensive performance analysis shows that the problem of similarity search in large-scale multimedia databases comprising millions of feature signatures can be solved efficiently and with high accuracy by means of gradient-based signatures. Moreover, by making use of binary gradient-based signatures, we are able to process k-nearest-neighbor queries with a sequential scan in a multimedia database comprising 5 million images with high accuracy in approximately 0.5 seconds on a single-core machine without any additional indexing structure.

7. CONCLUSIONS AND FUTURE WORK

In this paper, we have addressed the problem of efficient and accurate similarity search in multimedia databases comprising millions of feature signatures. Since query processing and indexing based on the feature signature approach remains one of the major challenges for large-scale multimedia databases, we have proposed and theoretically investigated the concept of gradient-based signatures which approximate the content-based properties of multimedia objects that are represented by feature signatures with respect to a common generative model. We have shown that gradient-based signatures are able to outperform state-of-the-art signature-based approaches in terms of accuracy and efficiency.

As future work, we intend to investigate indexing and query processing approaches for gradient-based signatures.

Acknowledgments

This work is funded by DFG grant SE 1039/7-1.

8. REFERENCES

[1] R. Agrawal, C. Faloutsos, and A. N. Swami. Efficient similarity search in sequence databases. In *FODO*, pp. 69–84, 1993.

[2] I. Assent, A. Wenning, and T. Seidl. Approximation techniques for indexing the earth mover's distance in multimedia databases. In *ICDE*, page 11, 2006.

[3] I. Assent, M. Wichterich, T. Meisen, and T. Seidl. Efficient similarity search using the earth mover's distance for large multimedia databases. In *ICDE*, pp. 307–316, 2008.

[4] C. Beecks. *Distance-based similarity models for content-based multimedia retrieval.* PhD thesis, RWTH Aachen University, 2013.

[5] C. Beecks, A. M. Ivanescu, S. Kirchhoff, and T. Seidl. Modeling image similarity by gaussian mixture models and the signature quadratic form distance. In *ICCV*, pp. 1754–1761, 2011.

[6] C. Beecks, S. Kirchhoff, and T. Seidl. Signature matching distance for content-based image retrieval. In *ICMR*, pp. 41–48, 2013.

[7] C. Beecks, J. Lokoč, T. Seidl, and T. Skopal. Indexing the signature quadratic form distance for efficient content-based multimedia retrieval. In *ICMR*, pp. 24:1–8, 2011.

[8] C. Beecks, M. S. Uysal, and T. Seidl. A comparative study of similarity measures for content-based multimedia retrieval. In *ICME*, pp. 1552–1557, 2010.

[9] C. Beecks, M. S. Uysal, and T. Seidl. Efficient k-nearest neighbor queries with the signature quadratic form distance. In *ICDEW*, pp. 10–15, 2010.

[10] C. Beecks, M. S. Uysal, and T. Seidl. Signature quadratic form distance. In *CIVR*, pp. 438–445, 2010.

[11] C. Beecks, M. S. Uysal, and T. Seidl. Similarity matrix compression for efficient signature quadratic form distance computation. In *SISAP*, pp. 109–114, 2010.

[12] C. Beecks, M. S. Uysal, and T. Seidl. L2-signature quadratic form distance for efficient query processing in very large multimedia databases. In *MMM*, pp. 381–391, 2011.

[13] C. Bhatt and M. Kankanhalli. Multimedia data mining: state of the art and challenges. *Multimedia Tools and Applications*, 51:35–76, 2011.

[14] G. Casella and R. Berger. *Statistical Inference.* Duxbury Press, 2001.

[15] E. Chávez, G. Navarro, R. A. Baeza-Yates, and J. L. Marroquín. Searching in metric spaces. *ACM Computing Surveys*, 33(3):273–321, 2001.

[16] R. Datta, D. Joshi, J. Li, and J. Z. Wang. Image retrieval: Ideas, influences, and trends of the new age. *ACM Computing Surveys*, 40(2):5:1–5:60, 2008.

[17] J. Deng, W. Dong, R. Socher, L. Li, K. Li, and F. Li. Imagenet: A large-scale hierarchical image database. In *CVPR*, pp. 248–255, 2009.

[18] R. O. Duda, P. E. Hart, and D. G. Stork. *Pattern classification.* Wiley-Interscience, 2001.

[19] C. Elkan. Deriving tf-idf as a fisher kernel. In *String Processing and Information Retrieval*, pp. 295–300. Springer, 2005.

[20] C. Faloutsos, M. Ranganathan, and Y. Manolopoulos. Fast subsequence matching in time-series databases. In *SIGMOD*, pp. 419–429, 1994.

[21] J. Goldberger, S. Gordon, and H. Greenspan. An efficient image similarity measure based on approximations of kl-divergence between two gaussian mixtures. In *ICCV*, pp. 487–493, 2003.

[22] J. Han, M. Kamber, and J. Pei. *Data Mining, Second Edition: Concepts and Techniques.* Data Mining, the Morgan Kaufmann Ser. in Data Management Systems Series. Elsevier Science, 2006.

[23] J. Hershey and P. Olsen. Approximating the kullback leibler divergence between gaussian mixture models. In *ICASSP*, pp. 317–320, 2007.

[24] M. Hetland. The basic principles of metric indexing. In *Swarm Intelligence for Multi-objective Problems in Data Mining*, pp. 199–232, 2009.

[25] M. E. Houle, X. Ma, M. Nett, and V. Oria. Dimensional testing for multi-step similarity search. In *ICDM*, pp. 299–308, 2012.

[26] W. Hu, N. Xie, L. Li, X. Zeng, and S. J. Maybank. A survey on visual content-based video indexing and retrieval. *IEEE Transactions on Systems, Man, and Cybernetics, Part C*, 41(6):797–819, 2011.

[27] M. J. Huiskes and M. S. Lew. The mir flickr retrieval evaluation. In *MIR*, pp. 39–43, 2008.

[28] T. Jaakkola, M. Diekhans, and D. Haussler. A discriminative framework for detecting remote protein homologies. *JCB*, 7(1-2):95–114, 2000.

[29] T. Jaakkola, D. Haussler, et al. Exploiting generative models in discriminative classifiers. *Advances in neural information processing systems*, pp. 487–493, 1999.

[30] H. Jegou, M. Douze, and C. Schmid. Hamming embedding and weak geometric consistency for large scale image search. In *ECCV*, pp. 304–317, 2008.

[31] S. Jeong, C. S. Won, and R. M. Gray. An adaptive color image retrieval framework using gauss mixtures. In *ICIP*, pp. 945–948, 2008.

[32] F. Korn, N. Sidiropoulos, C. Faloutsos, E. L. Siegel, and Z. Protopapas. Fast nearest neighbor search in medical image databases. In *VLDB*, pp. 215–226, 1996.

[33] H.-P. Kriegel, P. Kröger, P. Kunath, and M. Renz. Generalizing the optimality of multi-step k-nearest neighbor query processing. In *SSTD*, pp. 75–92, 2007.

[34] M. Kruliš, J. Lokoč, C. Beecks, T. Skopal, and T. Seidl. Processing the signature quadratic form distance on many-core gpu architectures. In *CIKM*, pp. 2373–2376, 2011.

[35] M. Kruliš, T. Skopal, J. Lokoč, and C. Beecks. Combining cpu and gpu architectures for fast similarity search. *Distributed and Parallel Databases*, 30(3-4):179–207, 2012.

[36] J. Lokoc. Approximating the signature quadratic form distance using scalable feature signatures. In *MMM*, pp. 86–97, 2014.

[37] J. Lokoč, M. L. Hetland, T. Skopal, and C. Beecks. Ptolemaic indexing of the signature quadratic form distance. In *SISAP*, pp. 9–16, 2011.

[38] M. Luszczkiewicz-Piatek. Which color space should be chosen for robust color image retrieval based on mixture modeling. In *Image Processing and Communications Challenges 5*, pp. 55–64, 2014.

[39] C. Manning, P. Raghavan, and H. Schutze. *Introduction to information retrieval*, volume 1. Cambridge University Press Cambridge, 2008.

[40] I. Mironica, B. Ionescu, J. Uijlings, and N. Sebe. Fisher kernel based relevance feedback for multimodal video retrieval. In *ICMR*, pp. 65–72, 2013.

[41] D. Mitrovic, M. Zeppelzauer, and C. Breiteneder. Features for content-based audio retrieval. *Advances in Computers*, 78:71–150, 2010.

[42] P. J. Moreno and R. Rifkin. Using the fisher kernel method for web audio classification. In *ICASSP*, pp. 2417–2420, 2000.

[43] P. J. Moreno and R. Rifkin. Using the fisher kernel method for web audio classification. In *ICASSP*, pp. 2417–2420, 2000.

[44] D. Nistér and H. Stewénius. Scalable recognition with a vocabulary tree. In *CVPR*, pp. 2161–2168, 2006.

[45] B. G. Park, K. M. Lee, and S. U. Lee. Color-based image retrieval using perceptually modified hausdorff distance. *EURASIP Journal of Image and Video Processing*, 2008:4:1–4:10, 2008.

[46] N. Patel and I. Sethi. Multimedia data mining: An overview. In *Multimedia Data Mining and Knowledge Discovery*, pp. 14–41, 2007.

[47] H. H. Permuter, J. M. Francos, and I. H. Jermyn. Gaussian mixture models of texture and colour for image database retrieval. In *ICASSP*, pp. 569–572, 2003.

[48] F. Perronnin and C. Dance. Fisher kernels on visual vocabularies for image categorization. In *CVPR*, pp. 1–8, 2007.

[49] F. Perronnin, Y. Liu, J. Sánchez, and H. Poirier. Large-scale image retrieval with compressed fisher vectors. In *CVPR*, pp. 3384–3391, 2010.

[50] F. Perronnin and J. A. Rodríguez-Serrano. Fisher kernels for handwritten word-spotting. In *ICDAR*, pp. 106–110, 2009.

[51] Y. Rubner, C. Tomasi, and L. J. Guibas. A metric for distributions with applications to image databases. In *ICCV*, pp. 59–66, 1998.

[52] Y. Rubner, C. Tomasi, and L. J. Guibas. The earth mover's distance as a metric for image retrieval. *IJCV*, 40(2):99–121, 2000.

[53] B. E. Ruttenberg and A. K. Singh. Indexing the earth mover's distance using normal distributions. *PVLDB*, 5(3):205–216, 2011.

[54] J. Sánchez, F. Perronnin, T. Mensink, and J. J. Verbeek. Image classification with the fisher vector: Theory and practice. *IJCV*, 105(3):222–245, 2013.

[55] T. Seidl and H.-P. Kriegel. Optimal multi-step k-nearest neighbor search. In *SIGMOD*, pp. 154–165, 1998.

[56] A. W. M. Smeulders, M. Worring, S. Santini, A. Gupta, and R. Jain. Content-based image retrieval at the end of the early years. *IEEE TPAMI*, 22(12):1349–1380, 2000.

[57] R. Szeliski. *Computer Vision: Algorithms and Applications*. Texts in computer science. Springer London, 2010.

[58] Y. Tang, L. H. U, Y. Cai, N. Mamoulis, and R. Cheng. Earth mover's distance based similarity search at scale. *PVLDB*, 7(4):313–324, 2013.

[59] M. S. Uysal, C. Beecks, J. Schmücking, and T. Seidl. Efficient filter approximation using the earth mover's distance in very large multimedia databases with feature signatures. In *CIKM*, pp. 979–988, 2014.

[60] M. S. Uysal, C. Beecks, J. Schmücking, and T. Seidl. Efficient similarity search in scientific databases with feature signatures. In *SSDBM*, pp. 30:1–30:12, 2015.

[61] N. Vasconcelos. On the complexity of probabilistic image retrieval. In *ICCV*, pp. 400–407, 2001.

[62] M. Wichterich, I. Assent, P. Kranen, and T. Seidl. Efficient emd-based similarity search in multimedia databases via flexible dimensionality reduction. In *SIGMOD*, pp. 199–212, 2008.

[63] X. Xing, Y. Zhang, and B. Gong. Mixture model based contextual image retrieval. In *CIVR*, pp. 251–258, 2010.

[64] J. Xu, Z. Zhang, A. K. H. Tung, and G. Yu. Efficient and effective similarity search over probabilistic data based on earth mover's distance. *VLDB J.*, 21(4):535–559, 2012.

[65] P. Zezula, G. Amato, V. Dohnal, and M. Batko. *Similarity Search - The Metric Space Approach*, volume 32 of *Advances in Database Systems*. Kluwer, 2006.

[66] Z. Zhang and R. Zhang. Multimedia data mining. In O. Maimon and L. Rokach, editors, *Data Mining and Knowledge Discovery Handbook*, pp. 1081–1109. Springer US, 2010.

Cross-Modal Similarity Learning : A Low Rank Bilinear Formulation *

Cuicui Kang
Institute of Information Engineering, Chinese Academy of Sciences
kangcuicui@iie.ac.cn

Shengcai Liao
Institute of Automation, Chinese Academy of Sciences
scliao@nlpr.ia.ac.cn

Yonghao He
Institute of Automation, Chinese Academy of Sciences
yhhe@nlpr.ia.ac.cn

Jian Wang
Institute of Automation, Chinese Academy of Sciences
jian.wang@nlpr.ia.ac.cn

Wenjia Niu
Institute of Information Engineering, Chinese Academy of Sciences
niuwenjia@iie.ac.cn

Shiming Xiang
Institute of Automation, Chinese Academy of Sciences
smxiang@nlpr.ia.ac.cn

ABSTRACT

The cross-media retrieval problem has received much attention in recent years due to the rapid increasing of multimedia data on the Internet. A new approach to the problem has been raised which intends to match features of different modalities directly. In this research, there are two critical issues: how to get rid of the heterogeneity between different modalities and how to match the cross-modal features of different dimensions. Recently metric learning methods show a good capability in learning a distance metric to explore the relationship between data points. However, the traditional metric learning algorithms only focus on single-modal features, which suffer difficulties in addressing the cross-modal features of different dimensions. In this paper, we propose a cross-modal similarity learning algorithm for the cross-modal feature matching. The proposed method takes a bilinear formulation, and with the nuclear-norm penalization, it achieves low-rank representation. Accordingly, the accelerated proximal gradient algorithm is successfully imported to find the optimal solution with a fast convergence rate $O(1/t^2)$. Experiments on three well known image-text cross-media retrieval databases show that the proposed method achieves the best performance compared to the state-of-the-art algorithms.

*This work was supported in part by the National Basic Research Program of China (Grant 2012CB316304), the National Natural Science Foundation of China (Grants 61272331, 91338202 and 91438105), the Strategic Priority Research Program of the Chinese Academy of Sciences Grant (XDA06030200), Beijing Key Lab of Intelligent Telecommunication Software and Multimedia (ITSM201502), Guangxi Key Laboratory of Trusted Software (KX201418).

Permission to make digital or hard copies of all or part of this work for personal or classroom use is granted without fee provided that copies are not made or distributed for profit or commercial advantage and that copies bear this notice and the full citation on the first page. Copyrights for components of this work owned by others than ACM must be honored. Abstracting with credit is permitted. To copy otherwise, or republish, to post on servers or to redistribute to lists, requires prior specific permission and/or a fee. Request permissions from Permissions@acm.org.

CIKM'15, October 19–23, 2015, Melbourne, Australia.

© 2015 ACM. ISBN 978-1-4503-3794-6/15/10 ...$15.00.

DOI: http://dx.doi.org/10.1145/2806416.2806469.

Categories and Subject Descriptors

H.3 [**Information Storage and Retrieval**]: Information Search and Retrieval

Keywords

Multimedia Retrieval; Cross-Modality; Similarity Learning; Nuclear Norm; Accelerated Proximal Gradient.

1. INTRODUCTION

A large amount of multimedia data has been released on the Internet during the past decade, and it is still rapidly increasing. From this big amount of media data, there exist some popular but different modalities, such as images, audios and documents. As a result, the requirement of cross-modal retrieval becomes a new problem to both researchers and the industry. Examples include the heterogenous face recognition (i.e. sketches and photos), cross-lingual retrieval, and the cross-media retrieval. Take the image-document cross retrieval as an example, given an image, the task is to find the documents that best describe it, or on the contrary, given several words, the task is to find the most related images.

Recently, Rasiwasia et al. [29] proposed a new approach to the multimedia information retrieval problem. In the research, the authors want to match features of different modalities directly, although the cross-modal data is in rather different feature spaces. The key problem to this research is to best reduce the heterogeneity among the different modal features, or find a common latent space in which the different modal features can be matched to each other.

Classical algorithms have been applied to solve the problem, such as the Canonical Correlation Analysis (CCA) [15, 29] and the Partial Least Squares (PLS) [30, 32]. Specifically, the CCA aims at learning a latent space where the correlations between the projected features of the two modalities have been mutually maximized. Similar to the CCA, the PLS also learns a latent space, but with different formulations to extract latent vectors [30]. In the work of [29, 8], Rasiwasia et al. proposed a semantic correlation matching (SCM) algorithm to deal with the problem. In the algorithm, a semantic level matching is suggested to combine with the linear correlations among the features. They also pointed out that, the correlation matching (such as CCA) is not enough for cross-modal matching, and the semantic level matching brings much benefit in working out the problem. This is consistent with that the class label information is very helpful to reduce the semantic gap, which is well known in the image retrieval field denoting the gap between the high level documents and low level images. Beyond these methods, there are some other algorithms to deal with the problem, such as the generalized multiview analysis (GMA) [32], the weakly paired maximum covariance analysis (WMCA) [23], the deep neural network [27, 34], etc. [4, 28, 19, 42, 43, 41, 13].

Recently, metric learning algorithms have been popularly studied. The target of metric learning is to find a distance metric by using the similar constraints and the dissimilar constraints [39]. Following the work of Xing et al. [39], there are some popular algorithms like the Large Margin Nearest Neighbor (LMNN) [37], the Information-Theoretic Metric Learning (ITML) [9], the Relevance Component Analysis (RCA) [2], and the Discriminative Component Analysis (DCA) which is based on the RCA [16]. Specifically, the LMNN was proposed to use a large margin setting to improve the kNN classification. The ITML algorithm proposed by Davis et al. aims at minimizing the differential relative entropy between two multivariate Gaussians. However, these traditional metric learning algorithms are designed for a single modality. They suffer the difficulty of learning the similarity/distance metrics between different modalities, especially with totaly different features.

Inspired by metric learning, we propose a novel logistic loss based cross-modality similarity function learning algorithm for the cross-media retrieval. The similarity formulation is in a bilinear form of two modalities, and a fast optimization algorithm is imported to find the optimal solution with a convergence rate of $O(1/t^2)$, where t is the number of iterations. Besides, the nuclear-norm regularization is imported in the formulation to explore the structures of the different modalities for robust learning. The proposed algorithm is applied to multimedia information retrieval on three popularly used multimedia databases for experiments, namely the Pascal VOC2007 database [12, 32], the NUS-WIDE database [7], and the Wikipedia database [29]. Experimental results show that the proposed algorithm is effective for cross-media retrieval. Especially, on the Wikipedia database the proposed algorithm outperforms the second best one for more than 6%.

The rest of the paper is organized as following. In Section 2, a concise review is given for the related works in the cross-modal information retrieval field and the metric learning field. Then, in Section 3, after a brief introduction of the Metric Learning problem, the formulation of the proposed algorithm and how to find the optimal solution are introduced in detail. The experiments are described in Section 4 to validate the effectiveness of the proposed algorithm. Finally, Section 5 gives the conclusion of the paper.

2. RELATED WORK

Information Retrieval (IR) is an important problem in the multimedia field. However, many traditional methods to the problem belong to the unimodal algorithms, such as the document retrieval and the content based image retrieval. Due to the rapid development of Internet applications, the cross-modality information retrieval becomes a common scene. To retrieve an image, the query terms may be of various different modalities, such as paragraphs, sketches and audios. Thus, cross-modal matching and learning algorithms which can match different modality data directly become a new research interest in the IR field.

Among these cross-modal matching algorithms, the CCA algorithm is the most widely used method in the multimedia field [15, 17, 29, 24]. The target of CCA is to learn a latent space by maximizing the correlating relationships between two modality features. Thus the different modal features can be projected to the latent space for similarity computation. The algorithm is also used as the correlation matching (CM) method by Rasiwasia et al. [29]. Beyond CCA, the PLS algorithm is another classical method for cross-modal data [30, 31, 32]. The core idea of it is very similar with that of CCA, which is to extract the latent vectors with maximal correlations.

In [29] where the cross-modal IR was suggested, Rasiwasia et al. proposed a supervised algorithm for the image-text cross-modal retrieval problem, namely the SCM algorithm. The SCM is one of the most famous and the current state-of-the-art algorithm. To reduce the semantic gap between images and documents, the sematic level matching is developed based on the learned maximal correlation latent space by CCA. Thus, the algorithm can be separated into two steps. The correlational matching between different modalities by CCA is done in the first step. Then, based on it a semantic space is learned in the second step. As indicated in [29, 8], the class information is an important information to reduce the semantic gap. Thus, in order to use the class labels, Sharma et al. proposed a GMA algorithm to learn a discriminative latent space for cross-modal data and treat it as an eigenvalue problem. The algorithm shows great performance to the pose and lighting invariant face recognition and cross-modal retrieval problems.

In fact, some methods targeting to the heterogenous face recognition problem are available to deal with the cross-modality IR problem, such as the Multiview Discriminant Analysis (MvDA) method [20]. The MvDA algorithm aims at learning a common space where the between-class variations from both inter-view and intra-view are maximized, and the within-class variations from both inter-view and intra-view are minimized. In the transfer learning field, some algorithms are also related [11, 22, 23, 33]. Such as in [23], Lampert and Krömer proposed a weakly-paired maximum covariance analysis method to deal with the not fully paired (not one-by-one paired) training data. Besides, Wang et al. [36] proposed an iterative algorithm based on sparsity to learn the coupled feature spaces for the different modalities. The work in [41] also proposed a greedy dictionary construction approach to select dictionary atoms for constructing a modality-adaptive dictionary pair. In the deep learning field, the works [27] and [34] both used the restricted boltzmann machine for the cross-modal feature learning.

In the literature of the metric learning field, Chechik et al. [6] imported an online similarity function learning for large-scale images. But the algorithm is designed for single-modality in a triplet ranking formulation. Kulis et al. also proposed to learn an asymmetric transformation matrix for domain adaption [22]. Besides, a metric learning algorithm for different modalities was also realized by Wu et al. [38]. The objective function in their work learns the projections for the different modalities, respectively, to best separate the similar points set and the dissimilar points set. However, the pair-wise information is ignored in the algorithm. In [40] and [25], the authors also proposed to learn two projections for each modality to minimize the distances of the two modalities in the target feature space. Zhai et al. also used the semantic information in the second step based on a unified k-NN graph. However, both of the algorithms are not convex, thus the optimal solution is not guaranteed. In contrast, the proposed formulation in this paper is a strict convex problem, and the optimal solution is achieved by the accelerated proximal gradient (APG) algorithm [26, 35, 3].

3. SIMILARITY LEARNING FOR CROSS MODALITIES

3.1 Traditional Metric Learning

In this section, we give a brief review of the traditional metric learning problem, which was firstly studied by Xing et al. [39] to learn a distance metric according to the similar points and dissimilar points.

Suppose that there is a set of m data points $\{\mathbf{x}_i \in \mathbb{R}^d\}_{i=1}^m$, where each data point is with a d dimensional feature. Besides, we are also given the binary similarity information indicating whether two data points are similar or not. Specifically, there are two sets of paired points, which can be described as follows:

$$\begin{cases} \mathcal{S} = \{(\mathbf{x}_i, \mathbf{x}_j) \mid \mathbf{x}_i \text{ and } \mathbf{x}_j \text{ are in the same class}\}, \\ \mathcal{D} = \{(\mathbf{x}_i, \mathbf{x}_j) \mid \mathbf{x}_i \text{ and } \mathbf{x}_j \text{ are not in the same class}\}, \end{cases} \tag{1}$$

where $\mathcal{S}$ is called the must-link set containing the similar pairs and the $\mathcal{D}$ is called the cannot-link set containing the dissimilar pairs.

Given the two sets, the task of metric learning is to learn a distance metric in the following form,

$$d(\mathbf{x}_i, \mathbf{x}_j)_{\mathbf{M}} = \|\mathbf{x}_i - \mathbf{x}_j\|_{\mathbf{M}} = \sqrt{(\mathbf{x}_i - \mathbf{x}_j)^T \mathbf{M} (\mathbf{x}_i - \mathbf{x}_j)}, \tag{2}$$

where $\mathbf{M} \in \mathbb{R}^{d \times d}$ is a Mahalanobis distance metric that should be learned. It can be easily found that $\mathbf{M}$ is symmetric. Furthermore, to be a valid metric, $\mathbf{M}$ must satisfy the non-negativity and the triangle inequality. Thus $\mathbf{M}$ is required to be positive semi-definite, namely $\mathbf{M} \succeq 0$.

Inspired by the metric learning formulation, we want to learn a similarity function to evaluate two modality features which are in different dimensions, for example the $\langle image, text \rangle$ pairs. In this way, the different modality features can be matched directly with the learned similarity function. The proposed formulation is introduced as follows.

3.2 Problem Definition and Formulation

Suppose that there is a multimedia database $\mathcal{A} = \{(\mathbf{x}_1, l_1^x), (\mathbf{x}_2, l_2^x), \ldots, (\mathbf{x}_m, l_m^x), (\mathbf{z}_1, l_1^z), \ldots, (\mathbf{z}_n, l_n^z)\}$ constructed from two-modality data sets $\mathcal{X}$ and $\mathcal{Z}$. Sample $\mathbf{x}_i \in \mathbb{R}^{d_1}$ is from the modal $\mathcal{X}$, such as the image, document, or audio, and $\mathbf{z}_i \in \mathbb{R}^{d_2}$ belongs to the modality $\mathcal{Z}$ which is different from the modality $\mathcal{X}$, where d_1 and d_2 are dimensions of the two modality features, respectively. The l_i^x and l_j^z are the class labels of the samples $\mathbf{x}_i$ and $\mathbf{z}_j$ respectively. The connection between the two modalities is that they share c classes, for example, dog, shoes and buildings. The cross matching problem is how to match the cross-modal samples $\mathbf{x}_i$ and $\mathbf{z}_j$ directly.

Similar with the metric learning, we also define two pairwise sets on the cross-modal samples,

$$\begin{cases} \mathcal{S} = \{(\mathbf{x}_i, \mathbf{z}_j) \mid l_i^x = l_j^z\}, \\ \mathcal{D} = \{(\mathbf{x}_i, \mathbf{z}_j) \mid l_i^x \neq l_j^z\}, \end{cases} \tag{3}$$

where $\mathcal{S}$ is the must-link set with similar pairs from the two different modalities, and $\mathcal{D}$ is the cannot-link set with dissimilar pairs from the two modalities.

Based on these definitions, we want to learn a similarity function which can measure the similarity between any two different modal features. The formulation of the proposed algorithm is

$$\min_{\mathbf{M}} \sum_{i,j=1}^{m,n} w_{ij} \log(1 + \exp(-y_{ij} S_{\mathbf{M}}(\mathbf{x}_i, \mathbf{z}_j))) + \lambda \|\mathbf{M}\|_*, \tag{4}$$

where $S_{\mathbf{M}}(\mathbf{x}_i, \mathbf{z}_j)$ is the similarity function parameterized by a matrix $\mathbf{M} \in \mathbb{R}^{d_1 \times d_2}$, which is to be learned in a bilinear form,

$$S_{\mathbf{M}}(\mathbf{x}_i, \mathbf{z}_j) = \mathbf{x}_i^T \mathbf{M} \mathbf{z}_j. \tag{5}$$

The formulation in Eqn.(4) contains a loss function item and a regularization item. The loss function is based on the logistic sigmoid function [14], $\delta(x) = 1/(1 + \exp(-x))$, which is often integrated in $-\log(\delta(x))$ to approximate the hinge loss function to avoid the discontinuity of the gradient. Here, $y_{ij} \in \{+1, -1\}$ is a sign indicating whether the pair is similar (positive) or dissimilar (negative). Specifically,

$$y_{ij} = \begin{cases} +1 & (\mathbf{x}_i, \mathbf{z}_j) \in \mathcal{S}, \\ -1 & (\mathbf{x}_i, \mathbf{z}_j) \in \mathcal{D}. \end{cases} \tag{6}$$

For w_{ij} in the formulation, it stands for the weight of the $(\mathbf{x}_i, \mathbf{z}_j)$ pair, which is used to deal with unbalanced positive and negative samples. In our experiments, we set the weights for positive (negative) pairs to be the reciprocal of the number of positive (negative) pairs.

As for the regularization term in Eqn.(4), the nuclear norm $\|\cdot\|_*$ is used, which is defined as the sum of the singular values of a matrix. The functions of the nuclear norm in the proposed formulation lie in two folds. On one fold, the constraint can be treated as a scale regularization of $\mathbf{M}$. It makes the solution to Eqn.(4) in a constrained domain. On the other fold, the nuclear norm can make the learned metric matrix $\mathbf{M}$ with a low rank, which is a desirable property and has been widely used in the machine learning field. In the problem Eqn.(4), the nuclear norm may help to discover the connections between the two modalities and result in a robust learning.

3.3 Optimization

In this subsection, the accelerated proximal gradient algorithm (APG) [26, 35] is utilized to find the optimal solution of Eqn.(4). The APG algorithm is a kind of first order gradient descent method [3, 18, 26, 35], which has received popular attentions in recent years due to its fast convergence rate of $O(1/t^2)$ when dealing with the problem of convex and smooth loss function regularized by non-smooth constraints.

For convenience, the formulation in Eqn.(4) can be rewritten as

$$\min_{\mathbf{M}} f(\mathbf{M}) = l(\mathbf{M}) + \lambda \|\mathbf{M}\|_*, \tag{7}$$

where

$$l(\mathbf{M}) = \sum_{i,j=1}^{m,n} w_{ij} \log(1 + \exp(-y_{ij}\mathbf{x}_i^T \mathbf{M} \mathbf{z}_j)). \quad (8)$$

Note that $l(\mathbf{M})$ is a smooth and convex function, and the objective function is convex. Accordingly, the APG algorithm can be used to solve the proposed formulation.

To find the optimal minimizer, we first construct a proximal operator of the Eqn. (7), which is

$$\begin{aligned} \min_{\mathbf{M}} g(\mathbf{M}) &= l(\mathbf{Q}_t) + \langle l'(\mathbf{Q}_t), \mathbf{M} - \mathbf{Q}_t \rangle \\ &+ \frac{1}{2\eta_t}\|\mathbf{M} - \mathbf{Q}_t\|_2^2 + \lambda\|\mathbf{M}\|_*, \end{aligned} \quad (9)$$

where $\{\mathbf{Q}_t\}$ is a sequence of the search points, $l'(\mathbf{Q}_t)$ is the gradient of $l(\cdot)$ at the $\mathbf{Q}_t$ point, and η_t is the update step size at the t-th iteration. The $l'(\mathbf{Q}_t)$ is

$$\frac{\partial l(\mathbf{M})}{\partial \mathbf{M}}|_{\mathbf{Q}_t} = -\sum_{i,j=1}^{m,n} \frac{w_{ij} y_{ij}}{1 + \exp(y_{ij}\mathbf{x}_i^T \mathbf{Q}_t \mathbf{z}_j)} \mathbf{x}_i \mathbf{z}_j^T, \quad (10)$$

By defining a matrix $\mathbf{T}$ with each entry T_{ij} as

$$T_{ij} = \frac{w_{ij} y_{ij}}{1 + \exp(y_{ij}\mathbf{x}_i^T \mathbf{Q}_t \mathbf{z}_j)}, \quad (11)$$

we can conveniently compute $\mathbf{T}$ as

$$\mathbf{T} = \mathbf{W} \odot \mathbf{Y} \odot \frac{1}{1 + \exp(\mathbf{Y} \odot \mathbf{X}^T \mathbf{Q}_t \mathbf{Z})}, \quad (12)$$

where $\odot$ is the element-wise product of two matrices. $\mathbf{W} \in \mathbb{R}^{m \times n}$ is the weight matrix with w_{ij} for each pair of the cross-modal samples, and $\mathbf{Y} \in \mathbb{R}^{m \times n}$ is the sign matrix with y_{ij} defined in Eqn.(6). The $\mathbf{X} \in \mathbb{R}^{d_1 \times m}$ is the data matrix containing the m samples of the modality $\mathcal{X}$, and $\mathbf{Z} \in \mathbb{R}^{d_2 \times n}$ consists of the n samples of the modality $\mathcal{Z}$.

With these definitions, Eqn.(10) can be simplified as

$$\begin{aligned} l'(\mathbf{Q}_t) = \frac{\partial l(\mathbf{M})}{\partial \mathbf{M}}|_{\mathbf{Q}_t} &= -\sum_{i=1}^{m}\sum_{j=1}^{n} T_{ij}\mathbf{x}_i \mathbf{z}_j^T \\ &= -\mathbf{X}\mathbf{T}\mathbf{Z}^T \end{aligned} \quad (13)$$

By removing the constant term $l(\mathbf{Q}_t)$ and adding another constant term $\eta_t\|l'(\mathbf{Q}_t)\|_2^2/2$ with respect to $\mathbf{M}$, the proximal operator of Eqn. (9) is equal to

$$\min_{\mathbf{M}} \frac{1}{2}\|\mathbf{M} \quad \tilde{\mathbf{M}}_t\|_F^2 + \lambda\eta_t\|\mathbf{M}\|_*, \quad (14)$$

where

$$\tilde{\mathbf{M}}_t = \mathbf{Q}_t - \eta_t l'(\mathbf{Q}_t). \quad (15)$$

According to [5], the minimization of the objective function Eqn.(14) can be solved by a soft-thresholding technique. Firstly, the singular value decomposition (SVD) is used to find the eigenvalues for the matrix $\tilde{\mathbf{M}}$. Then, a soft-thresholding is applied on the computed eigenvalues. In summary,

THEOREM 1. *Assume matrix $\mathbf{L} \in \mathbb{R}^{m \times n}$ and the SVD decomposition of it is $\mathbf{L} = \mathbf{U}\mathbf{\Sigma}\mathbf{V}^T$, where $\mathbf{U} \in \mathbb{R}^{d_1 \times r}$ and $\mathbf{V} \in \mathbb{R}^{d_2 \times r}$ are constructed by orthogonal vectors, and $\mathbf{\Sigma}$ is a diagonal matrix with diagonal values $\Sigma_{ii} \geq 0$ and rank$(\mathbf{\Sigma}) = r$. Then the following objective function [5]*

$$C_\gamma(\mathbf{M}) = \min_{\mathbf{M}} \frac{1}{2}\|\mathbf{M} - \mathbf{L}\|_F^2 + \gamma\|\mathbf{M}\|_* \quad (16)$$

has a closed-form solution $C_\gamma(\mathbf{M}) = \mathbf{U}\mathbf{\Sigma}_\gamma\mathbf{V}^T$, where $(\Sigma_\gamma)_{ii} = \max\{0, \Sigma_{ii} - \gamma\}$ is the soft-thresholding result of the matrix $\mathbf{\Sigma}$ by the regularization parameter γ .

Algorithm 1: Optimization for Eqn. (4).

Input: $\mathbf{X} \in \mathbb{R}^{d_1 \times m}$, $\mathbf{Z} \in \mathbb{R}^{d_2 \times n}$, and $\mathbf{Y} \in \mathbb{R}^{m \times n}$.
Output: $\mathbf{M} \in \mathbb{R}^{d_1 \times d_2}$
Initialization $\mathbf{Q}_t = \mathbf{0}, t = 1$;
repeat
  Compute $\tilde{\mathbf{M}}_t$ as in Eqn. (12) (13) (15);
  Decompose $\tilde{\mathbf{M}}_t = \mathbf{U}\mathbf{\Sigma}\mathbf{V}^T$;
  Update $\mathbf{M}_{t+1} = \mathbf{U}\mathbf{\Sigma}_{\lambda\eta_t}\mathbf{V}^T$;
  Update $\mathbf{Q}_{t+1}$ as in Eqn. (17).
until *convergence*;

The proof can be found in the Appendix. Accordingly, we get the $\mathbf{M}_{t+1} = \mathbf{U}\mathbf{\Sigma}_{\lambda\eta_t}\mathbf{V}^T$. Then, the APG algorithm accelerates the proximal gradient descent by updating $\mathbf{Q}_{t+1}$ with

$$\mathbf{Q}_{t+1} = \mathbf{M}_{t+1} + \frac{\alpha_t - 1}{\alpha_{t+1}}(\mathbf{M}_{t+1} - \mathbf{M}_t) \quad (17)$$

where $\alpha_{t+1} = (1 + \sqrt{1 + 4\alpha_t^2})/2$ and $\alpha_1 = 1$. In fact, the α_t can be updated in other ways if the certain conditions are satisfied [26, 35]. As for the step size η_t, it can be estimated in the algorithm by comparing the objective function and its proximal operator [3], whose derivation is omitted here due to the paper length.

It turns out that the APG algorithm updates $\mathbf{M}_t$ and $\mathbf{Q}_t$ iteratively to find the optimal solution, and the searching point $\mathbf{Q}_t$ is a linear combination of the latest two solutions of $\mathbf{M}_t$ and $\mathbf{M}_{t-1}$. The steps of the proposed algorithm is summarized in Algorithm 1.

4. EXPERIMENT

In this section, the proposed low rank bilinear similarity learning algorithm (denoted as LRBS) is compared with several popular and state-of-the-art algorithms by experiments on three famous image-text databases.

Compared Methods: To evaluate the performance of the proposed algorithm, several famous algorithms in the cross-media retrieval field were compared in the experiments, including the popular methods CCA [15, 29] and PLS [30, 31], and the state-of-the-art methods SCM [29], the Microsoft algorithm (MsAlg) [38], and the Generalized Multiview Analysis methods, including the GMLDA (Generalized Multiview Linear Discriminant Analysis) and the GMMFA (Generalized Multiview Marginal Fisher Analysis) [32]. A brief introduction of these algorithms can be found in the related work section.

Evaluation Metrics: For the evaluation, the mean average precision (MAP) and the precision-recall curve metrics were used in the experiments. In fact, both of them are popularly used in evaluation of information retrieval systems. Given one query and its N retrieved documents in a rank, the average precision is computed by AveP $= \frac{1}{T}\sum_{r=1}^{N} P(r)rel(r)$, where T is the number of the relevant documents in the retrieval, $P(r)$ is the precision of the top r retrieved documents, and $rel(r)$ is a binary function denoting whether the r-th retrieved document is relevant to the

Table 1: MAP (%) results on the Pascal VOC2007 database.

	Without PCA		
Methods	Image query	Text query	Average
CCA/SCM	–	–	–
PLS	47.55	45.69	46.62
MsAlg	58.43	59.40	58.91
GMLDA	39.95	35.95	37.95
GMMFA	37.97	33.17	35.57
LRBS	65.15	**68.74**	**66.95**
	With PCA		
Methods	Image query	Text query	Average
CCA	49.06	48.33	48.69
PLS	47.55	45.68	46.62
SCM	63.98	59.73	61.86
MsAlg	58.58	58.84	58.71
GMLDA	**65.62**	66.32	65.97
GMMFA	65.48	66.15	65.81
LRBS	65.10	68.69	66.90

Table 2: MAP (%) results on the Wikipedia database.

	Without PCA		
Methods	Image query	Text query	Average
CCA/SCM	–	–	–
PLS	30.54	28.05	29.30
MsAlg	37.28	32.70	34.99
GMLDA	24.93	18.18	21.55
GMMFA	24.03	16.51	20.27
LRBS	**44.48**	**37.70**	**41.09**
	With PCA		
Methods	Image query	Text query	Average
CCA	19.70	17.84	18.77
PLS	30.55	28.03	29.29
SCM	37.13	28.23	32.68
MsAlg	36.07	30.75	33.41
GMLDA	36.77	29.71	33.24
GMMFA	38.74	31.09	34.91
LRBS	44.41	**37.70**	41.06

Table 3: MAP (%) results on the NUS-WIDE database.

	Without PCA		
Methods	Image query	Text query	Average
CCA/SCM	–	–	–
PLS	13.66	13.45	13.55
MsAlg	20.70	19.43	20.07
GMLDA	10.37	8.47	9.42
GMMFA	9.80	8.00	8.90
LRBS	**21.75**	**20.79**	**21.27**
	With PCA		
Methods	Image query	Text query	Average
CCA	4.75	4.64	4.70
PLS	13.77	13.44	13.61
SCM	16.44	14.07	15.26
MsAlg	20.02	18.20	19.11
GMLDA	20.31	18.48	19.39
GMMFA	19.98	18.32	19.15
LRBS	21.73	20.73	21.23

query or not. Having the AveP calculated for each query, the MAP is computed as the average AveP score of all queries. Besides of the MAP and precision-recall curve, we also displayed the precision-scope curve for a better visualization, where the scope denotes the number of retrieved documents. Therefore, by the precision-scope curve it is more easily to see the precision of the top r documents presented to the users.

4.1 Databases

In the experiments, three famous images and texts databases in the multimedia retrieval field are used to evaluate the performance of the proposed algorithm, namely the Pascal VOC2007 database, the Wikipedia database, and the NUS-WIDE database.

The Pascal VOC2007 dataset consists of 9963 images from 20 categories [12], which was split into a training set with 5011 images and a test set with 4952 images. Since some of the images are with multi-labels, the images containing only one object were selected in the experiments [32]. As a result, there are 2808 images for the training set and 2841 images for the test set. For the features, the 399-dimensional word frequency feature [17] was used for the text, and the convolutional neural network (CNN) feature, which was trained on the ImageNet [21], was used as the image feature. The CNN source code, namely Decaf [10], can be freely downloaded on the web for research purpose[1]. In the experiments, only the outputs of the sixth layer were used as the image feature, resulting in 4096 dimensions.

The Wikipedia dataset[2] is constructed from the Wikipedia's "featured articles", which is a continually updated collection selected and reviewed by the Wikipedia's editors since 2009. Among the articles in the collection, Rasiwasia et al. built a dataset by selecting ten popular categories [29]. Each image in the dataset is associated with a section of at least 70 words. In total, the dataset consists of 2866 image-document pairs. In [29], the dataset was randomly split into a training set of 2173 image-document pairs and a test set of the remaining 693 pairs. The text feature was derived from the Latent Dirichlet Allocation model (LDA) with 200 topics [8]. Similar as on the Pascal VOC2007 database, the CNN feature was also used for the images on this dataset.

The NUS-WIDE dataset is a large-scale real-world database where the images were crawled from the "Flickr" website by the Media Search Lab in the National University of Singapore [7]. The database is constructed with 269,648 images associated with tags. The organizers has labeled the images with 81 concepts for evaluation. They also provided all the URLs of the images on the web to facilitate further research[3]. In the experiment, we used 40 concepts which contained the most uniquely labeled images, and 250 images per concept were randomly selected for evaluation. The selected images were further randomly separated into a training set and a test set, which contain 6000 images and 3630 images respectively. Again, the CNN feature for the images was used in the experiment. As for the text feature, the provided 1000-dimensional word frequency feature by the database organizers [7] was imported.

[1]http://daggerfs.com/

[2]http://www.svcl.ucsd.edu/projects/crossmodal/

[3]http://lms.comp.nus.edu.sg/research/NUS-WIDE.htm

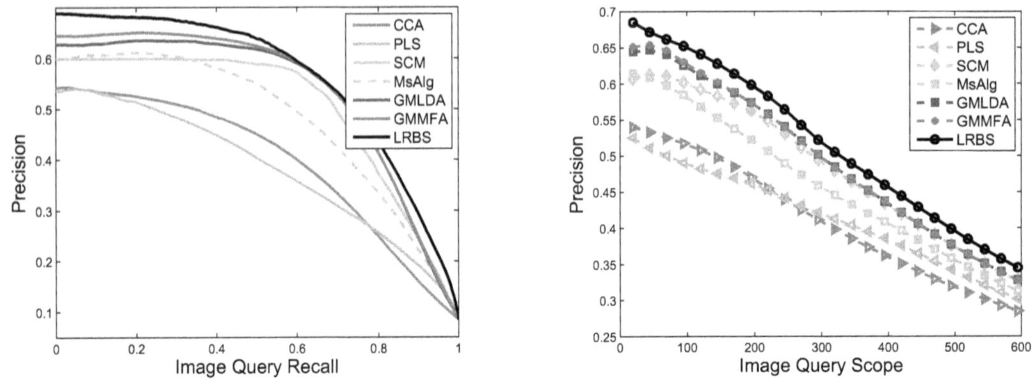

(a) Image-to-Text

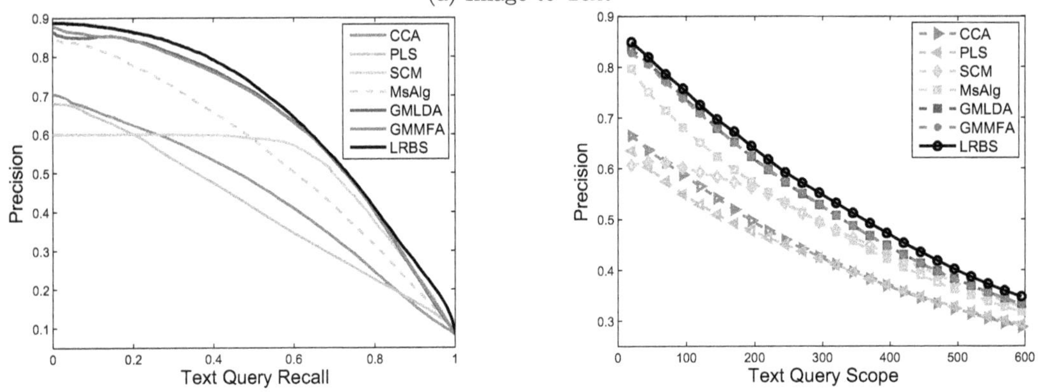

(b) Text-to-Image

Figure 1: Precision-recall and precision-scope curves on the Pascal VOC2007 database for the Image-to-Text retrieval experiment and the Text-to-Image retrieval experiment.

4.2 Experimental Results

In the experiments, we found that the CCA, PLS and G-MA algorithms all performed better with PCA dimensional reduction than without it. Thus, we displayed both the experimental results with PCA and without PCA for all the algorithms. With PCA, about 99% energy were preserved for the features. As a result, the dimension of the CNN image feature was reduced to 1000 on the three databases. As for the text feature, it was reduced to 200 on the Pascal VOC2007 database, 180 on the Wikipedia and 800 on the NUS-WIDE database. The MAPs of the experimental results are shown in Table 1, Table 2 and Table 3 for the VOC2007, the Wikipedia and the NUS-WIDE databases respectively, where the black bold numbers are the best performances, and the blue bold ones are the second best across the performances with PCA and not with PCA. The precision-recall and precision-scope curves are shown in Figure 1, 2 and Figure 3 for the three datasets, respectively.

From Table 1, Table 2 and Table 3 it can be observed that the proposed LRBS algorithm achieves the best performance on the three databases. On the Wikipedia dataset, no matter with PCA and without PCA, the proposed method performs about 6% higher than the second best algorithm (the GMMFA algorithm with PCA and the MsAlg algorithm without PCA). The followings are MsAlg with PCA, GMLDA with PCA and the SCM with PCA, which perform comparable to each other. This ranking is similar with that on the NUS-WIDE database. On the VOC2007 dataset, LRBS outperforms the second best one, the GMLDA algorithm with PCA, by 1%. The followings are the SCM with PCA and the MsAlg algorithms. It can be also observed that the GMMFA and the GMLDA perform closely to each other on the three datasets.

It should be noted that the CCA without dimensional reduction cannot be applied since the feature matrix is not with full rank. This is the same with the SCM which needs CCA as the first step for correlation matching. Obviously, the GMA methods with PCA dimensional reduction perform better than without PCA. In contrast, for the PLS, MsAlg, and LRBS algorithms, they perform almost the same with PCA dimensional reduction and without it. The reason may lie in that the PCA dimension reduction removes part of the redundant information and noises. However, PCA may also discard some useful information at the same time. This may be the reason that the performances of the MsAlg and LRBS algorithms do not improve with PCA.

Table 1, 2 and 3 also show that the supervised algorithms (the MsAlg, GMMFA, GMLDA, SCM and LRBS algorithms) clearly outperform unsupervised ones (the CCA and the PLS). It is because the class information used in supervised learning could partly reduce the semantic gap between low-level image features and high-level semantic meanings. The work in [8] also found that the combination of correlation matching and semantic matching can work better.

Figure 1, Figure 2 and Figure 3 display the precision-recall curves and the precision-scope curves of the compared algorithms for the image-text cross retrieval task. The per-

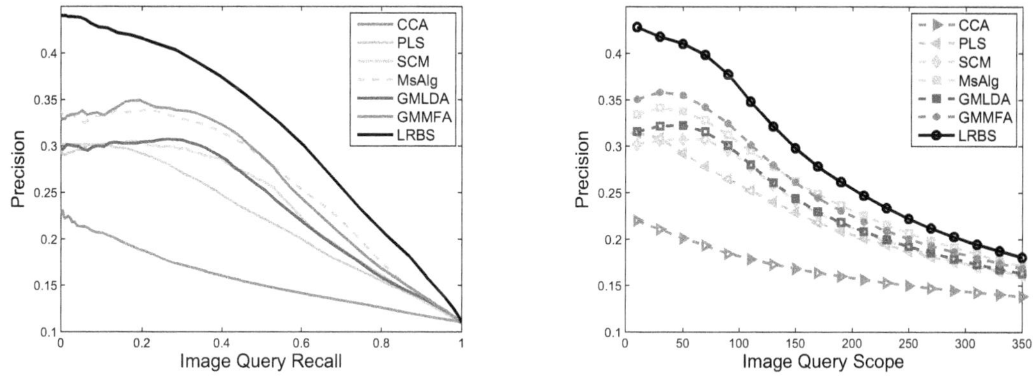

(a) Image-to-Text

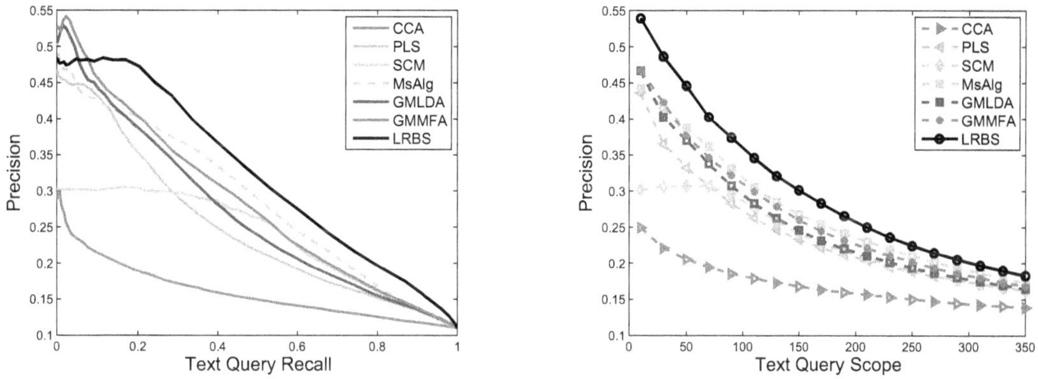

(b) Text-to-Image

Figure 2: Precision-recall and precision-scope curves on the Wikipedia database for the Image-to-Text retrieval experiment and the Text-to-Image retrieval experiment.

formances of the GMA methods without PCA dimensional reduction are not shown in the figures due to the low performances. Note that the figures on show the best performance of each compared algorithm. For example, since the performance of the MsAlg method with PCA is slightly lower than without PCA, the figures just display the performance of the MsAlg without PCA. In these figures, it is also observed that the proposed algorithm has the best performance on all databases, followed by GMLDA, GMMFA and MsAlg methods, which are comparable to each other. From the precision-recall figures, it is clearly that with the same recall rate, the proposed method gets the highest precision in all compared algorithms, especially on the Wikipedia dataset. This is similar with the precision-scope curves, which plot the precision under different numbers of the top r retrieved samples. In summary, the experimental results show that the proposed algorithm successfully learns a similarity function for cross-modal matching.

In Figure 6, the singular values of the learned similarity metric matrix are shown, which contains the top 80 singular values. From the figure we can see that the learned $\mathbf{M}$ has a low rank, indicating that the proposed LRBS algorithm succeeds to find the similar structures in the data. It can be seen that the similarity metric of the Wikipeda dataset has the lowest rank. This is partly because the Wikipedia dataset only contains 10 categories. In contrast, the NUS-WIDE dataset contains the most categories, thus its similarity metric has a relatively high rank. In Figure 4 and Figure 5, some retrieved samples by the proposed LRBS algorithm in the experiment are shown. The retrieved samples also indicate that the LRBS is an effective cross-modality information retrieval algorithm.

(a) (b) (c)

Figure 6: The singular values of the learned similarity function matrix M on the three databases, where the values are shown in gray, and the 1 of gray value is the most lightest. (a) On the Wikipedia database; (b) On the Pascal VOC2007 database; (c) On the NUS-WIDE database.

5. CONCLUSION

In this paper, we proposed a novel similarity function learning method inspired by metric learning algorithms. The similarity function is learned in a bilinear form of two different modality features, which can handle cross-modal features with different dimensions. The accelerated proximal gradient method is successfully imported to find the optimal solution with a fast convergence rate. Besides, we also im-

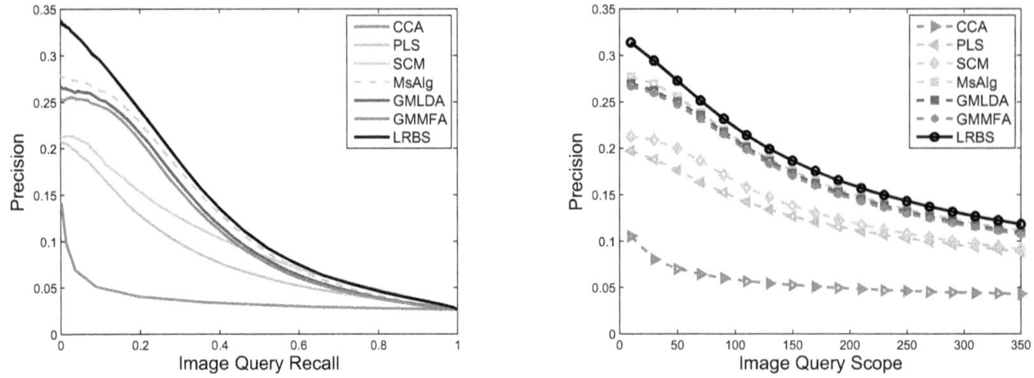

(a) Image-to-Text

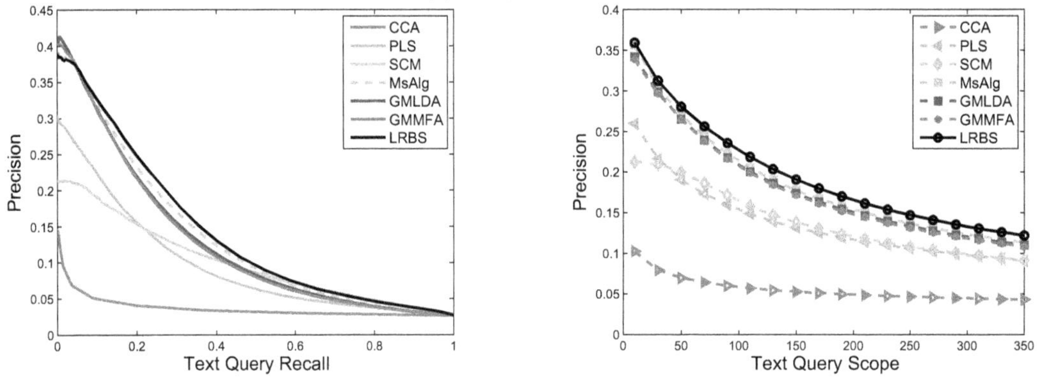

(b) Text-to-Image

Figure 3: Precision-recall and precision-scope curves on the NUS-WIDE database for the Image-to-Text retrieval experiment and the Text-to-Image retrieval experiment.

Query Tags	Top Retrieved Images
Boat Water Sky	
Bird, Eye feather leaves branch beak Grass	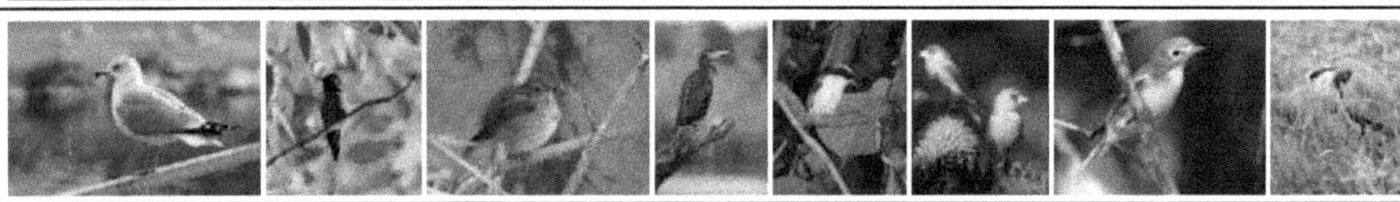
Bus, Sky Wheel Ground Antenna Window	
Tvmonitor Diningtable Keyboard Wire	

Figure 4: The retrieved samples from texts to images by the proposed LRBS algorithm on the Pascal VOC2007 database.

ported the nuclear-norm to explore the structures and connections of the two modalities. The experiments are evaluated on three famous multimedia databases for the image-text cross-modal information retrieval problem, showing that the proposed algorithm has the best performance compared to the state-of-the-art algorithms.

Figure 5: The retrieved samples from texts to images by the proposed LRBS algorithm on the Wikipedia database. The figure shows the probe paragraphs and the corresponding top retrieved images.

6. ADDITIONAL AUTHORS

Additional author: Chunhong Pan (Institute of Automation, Chinese Academy of Sciences, email: `chpan@nlpr.ia.ac.cn`).

7. REFERENCES

[1] F. R. Bach. Consistency of trace norm minimization. *Journal of Machine Learning Research*, 9:1019–1048, 2008.

[2] A. Bar-Hillel, T. Hertz, N. Shental, and D. Weinshall. Learning distance functions using equivalence relations. In *ICML*, pages 11–18, 2003.

[3] A. Beck and M. Teboulle. A fast iterative shrinkage-thresholding algorithm for linear inverse problems. *SIAM J. Imaging Sciences*, 2(1):183–202, 2009.

[4] M. Bronstein, A. Bronstein, F. Michel, and N. Paragios. Data fusion through cross-modality metric learning using similarity-sensitive hashing. In *CVPR*, pages 3594–3601, 2010.

[5] J.-F. Cai, E. J. Candès, and Z. Shen. A singular value thresholding algorithm for matrix completion. *SIAM Journal on Optimization*, 20(4):1956–1982, 2010.

[6] G. Chechik, U. Shalit, V. Sharma, and S. Bengio. An online algorithm for large scale image similarity learning. In *NIPS*, pages 306–314, 2009.

[7] T.-S. Chua, J. Tang, R. Hong, H. Li, Z. Luo, and Y.-T. Zheng. NUS-WIDE: A Real-World Web Image Database from National University of Singapore. In *ACM Conf. on Image and Video Retrieval*, 2009.

[8] J. Costa Pereira, E. Coviello, G. Doyle, N. Rasiwasia, G. Lanckriet, R. Levy, and N. Vasconcelos. On the role of correlation and abstraction in cross-modal multimedia retrieval. *TPAMI*, 36(3):521–535, 2014.

[9] J. V. Davis, B. Kulis, P. Jain, S. Sra, and I. S. Dhillon. Information-theoretic metric learning. In *ICML*, volume 227, pages 209–216, 2007.

[10] J. Donahue, Y. Jia, O. Vinyals, J. Hoffman, N. Zhang, E. Tzeng, and T. Darrell. Decaf: A deep convolutional activation feature for generic visual recognition. *arXiv preprint arXiv:1310.1531*, 2013.

[11] L. Duan, D. Xu, and I. W. Tsang. Learning with augmented features for heterogeneous domain adaptation. In *ICML*, pages 711–718, 2012.

[12] M. Everingham, L. Van Gool, C. K. I. Williams, J. Winn, and A. Zisserman. The PASCAL Visual Object Classes Challenge 2007 Results, 2007.

[13] Y. Gong, Q. Ke, M. Isard, and S. Lazebnik. A multi-view embedding space for modeling internet images, tags, and their semantics. *International Journal of Computer Vision*, 106(2):210–233, 2014.

[14] M. Guillaumin, J. J. Verbeek, and C. Schmid. Is that you? metric learning approaches for face identification. In *International Conference on Computer Vision*, pages 498–505, 2009.

[15] D. R. Hardoon, S. Szedmák, and J. Shawe-Taylor. Canonical correlation analysis: An overview with application to learning methods. *Neural Computation*, 16(12):2639–2664, 2004.

[16] S. C. H. Hoi, W. Liu, M. R. Lyu, and W.-Y. Ma. Learning distance metrics with contextual constraints for image retrieval. In *CVPR*, pages 2072–2078, 2006.

[17] S. J. Hwang and K. Grauman. Accounting for the relative importance of objects in image retrieval. In *BMVC*, pages 1–12, 2010.

[18] S. Ji and J. Ye. An accelerated gradient method for trace norm minimization. In *ICML*, pages 457–464, 2009.

[19] Y. Jia, M. Salzmann, and T. Darrell. Learning cross-modality similarity for multinomial data. In *International Conference on Computer Vision*, pages 2407–2414, 2011.

[20] M. Kan, S. Shan, H. Zhang, S. Lao, and X. Chen. Multi-view discriminant analysis. In *ECCV (1)*, volume 7572, pages 808–821, 2012.
[21] A. Krizhevsky, I. Sutskever, and G. E. Hinton. Imagenet classification with deep convolutional neural networks. In *NIPS*, pages 1106–1114, 2012.
[22] B. Kulis, K. Saenko, and T. Darrell. What you saw is not what you get: Domain adaptation using asymmetric kernel transforms. In *CVPR*, pages 1785–1792, 2011.
[23] C. H. Lampert and O. Krömer. Weakly-paired maximum covariance analysis for multimodal dimensionality reduction and transfer learning. In *ECCV*, pages 566–579, 2010.
[24] A. Li, S. Shan, X. Chen, and W. Gao. Face recognition based on non-corresponding region matching. In *International Conference on Computer Vision*, pages 1060–1067, 2011.
[25] A. Mignon and F. Jurie. CMML: a New Metric Learning Approach for Cross Modal Matching. In *Asian Conference on Computer Vision*, 2012.
[26] Y. Nesterov. *Introductory Lectures on Convex Optimization: A Basic Course*. Kluwer Academic Publishers, 2003.
[27] J. Ngiam, A. Khosla, M. Kim, J. Nam, H. Lee, and A. Y. Ng. Multimodal deep learning. In *ICML*, pages 689–696, 2011.
[28] Y. Pan, T. Yao, T. Mei, H. Li, C.-W. Ngo, and Y. Rui. Click-through-based cross-view learning for image search. In *ACM conference on Research and Development in Information Retrieval (SIGIR)*, 2014.
[29] N. Rasiwasia, J. C. Pereira, E. Coviello, G. Doyle, G. R. G. Lanckriet, R. Levy, and N. Vasconcelos. A new approach to cross-modal multimedia retrieval. In *ACM Multimedia*, pages 251–260, 2010.
[30] R. Rosipal and N. Krämer. Overview and recent advances in partial least squares. In *SLSFS*, pages 34–51. Springer, 2006.
[31] A. Sharma and D. W. Jacobs. Bypassing synthesis: PLS for face recognition with pose, low-resolution and sketch. In *CVPR*, pages 593–600, 2011.
[32] A. Sharma, A. Kumar, H. D. III, and D. W. Jacobs. Generalized multiview analysis: A discriminative latent space. In *CVPR*, pages 2160–2167, 2012.
[33] R. Socher, M. Ganjoo, C. D. Manning, and A. Y. Ng. Zero-shot learning through cross-modal transfer. In *NIPS*, pages 935–943, 2013.
[34] N. Srivastava and R. Salakhutdinov. Multimodal learning with deep boltzmann machines. In *NIPS*, pages 2231–2239, 2012.
[35] P. Tseng. On accelerated proximal gradient methods for convex-concave optimization. *submitted to SIAM Journal on Optimization*, 2008.
[36] K. Wang, R. He, W. Wang, L. Wang, and T. Tan. Learning coupled feature spaces for cross-modal matching. In *International Conference on Computer Vision*, pages 2088–2095, 2013.
[37] K. Weinberger, J. Blitzer, and L. Saul. Distance metric learning for large margin nearest neighbor classification. *NIPS*, pages 1473–1480, 2006.
[38] W. Wu, J. Xu, and H. Li. Learning similarity function between objects in heterogeneous spaces. Technical Report MSR-TR-2010-86, 2010.
[39] E. P. Xing, A. Y. Ng, M. I. Jordan, and S. J. Russell. Distance metric learning with application to clustering with side-information. In *NIPS*, pages 505–512, 2002.
[40] X. Zhai, Y. Peng, and J. Xiao. Heterogeneous metric learning with joint graph regularization for cross-media retrieval. In *AAAI*, pages 1198–1204, 2013.
[41] F. Zhu, L. Shao, and M. Yu. Cross-modality submodular dictionary learning for information retrieval. In *CIKM*, pages 1479–1488, 2014.
[42] J. Zhuang and S. C. H. Hoi. A two-view learning approach for image tag ranking. In *WSDM*, pages 625–634, 2011.
[43] Y. Zhuang, Y. F. Wang, F. Wu, Y. Zhang, and W. Lu. Supervised coupled dictionary learning with group structures for multi-modal retrieval. In *AAAI*, pages 1070–1076, 2013.

APPENDIX

A. PROOF OF THEOREM 1

PROOF. Considering that the objective function in Eqn. (16) is a strongly convex function, a unique solution exists. Thus we just need to prove that the optimal solution is equal to $C_\gamma(\mathbf{M})$ [5]. Considering that $\hat{\mathbf{M}}$ is the optimal solution of Eqn.(16) if and only if $\mathbf{0}$ is a subgradient of the function at the point $\hat{\mathbf{M}}$, we have

$$\mathbf{0} \in \hat{\mathbf{M}} - \mathbf{L} + \gamma\partial\|\hat{\mathbf{M}}\|_*, \tag{18}$$

where the $\partial\|\hat{\mathbf{M}}\|_*$ is the subgradient of the nuclear norm. Let the SVD decomposition of an arbitrary matrix $\mathbf{A} \in \mathbb{R}^{m\times n}$ is $\mathbf{A} = \mathbf{P}_1\mathbf{\Lambda}\mathbf{P}_2^T$, then the subgradient of its nuclear norm is [1, 5]

$$\begin{aligned}\partial\|\mathbf{A}\|_* = \{\mathbf{P}_1\mathbf{P}_2^T + \mathbf{S} : \mathbf{S} \in \mathbb{R}^{m\times n}, \mathbf{P}_1^T\mathbf{S} = 0, \\ \mathbf{S}\mathbf{P}_2 = 0, \|\mathbf{S}\|_2 \leq 1\}.\end{aligned} \tag{19}$$

Denote the SVD decomposition of $\mathbf{L}$ in Eqn.(16) as

$$\mathbf{L} = \mathbf{U}_0\mathbf{\Sigma}_0\mathbf{V}_0^T + \mathbf{U}_1\mathbf{\Sigma}_1\mathbf{V}_1^T,$$

where $\mathbf{U}_0\mathbf{\Sigma}_0\mathbf{V}_0^T$ is the part of SVD with singular values greater than γ, and the $\mathbf{U}_0\mathbf{\Sigma}_0\mathbf{V}_0^T$ corresponds to the remaining part. By denoting $\hat{\mathbf{M}} = C_\gamma(\mathbf{M})$, we have

$$\hat{\mathbf{M}} = \mathbf{U}_0(\mathbf{\Sigma}_0 - \gamma\mathbf{I})\mathbf{V}_0^T.$$

Therefore,

$$\mathbf{L} - \hat{\mathbf{M}} = \mathbf{L} - C_\gamma(\mathbf{M}) = \gamma(\mathbf{U}_0\mathbf{V}_0^T + \mathbf{S}),$$

where

$$\mathbf{S} = \gamma^{-1}\mathbf{U}_1\Sigma_1\mathbf{V}_1^T.$$

It turns out that $\mathbf{U}_0^T\mathbf{S} = 0$, $\mathbf{S}\mathbf{V}_0 = 0$, and $\|\mathbf{S}\|_2 \leq 1$ since Σ_1 is bounded by γ. Finally, we have proved that $\mathbf{L} - C_\gamma(\mathbf{M}) \in \gamma\partial\|C_\gamma(\mathbf{M})\|_*$, which shows that $C_\gamma(\mathbf{M})$ is the optimal solution of Eqn.(16).

□

Efficient Sparse Matrix Multiplication on GPU for Large Social Network Analysis

Yong-Yeon Jo
Dept. of Computer & Software
Hanyang University
Seoul, Korea
jyy0430@hanyang.ac.kr

Sang-Wook Kim*
Dept. of Computer & Software
Hanyang University
Seoul, Korea
wook@hanyang.ac.kr

Duck-Ho Bae
Dept. of Electronics & Computer Engineering
Hanyang University
Seoul, Korea
dhbae@agape.hanyang.ac.kr

ABSTRACT

As a number of social network services appear online recently, there have been many attempts to analyze social networks for extracting valuable information. Most existing methods first represent a social network as a *quite sparse* adjacency matrix, and then analyze it through matrix operations such as matrix multiplication. Due to the large scale and high complexity, efficient processing multiplications is an important issue in social network analysis. In this paper, we propose a GPU-based method for efficient sparse matrix multiplication through the parallel computing paradigm. The proposed method aims at balancing the amount of workload both at fine- and coarse-grained levels for maximizing the degree of parallelism in GPU. Through extensive experiments using synthetic and real-world datasets, we show that the proposed method outperforms previous methods by up to three orders-of-magnitude.

Categories and Subject Descriptors

H.4 [**Information Systems Applications**]: Miscellaneous

General Terms

Measurement, Algorithms

Keywords

Sparse matrix multiplication; social network analysis; GPU

1. INTRODUCTION

Recently, the amount of social networks data is rapidly growing with various kinds of social network services being widely used. Moreover, a huge number of mobile devices accelerate the growth of the volume of social networks data. Due to large scale and high complexity, there have been a lot of studies to analyze social networks to extract valuable information. They exploit the analysis results to address issues in ranking [1], similarity measure [2][3], and recommendation [4][5]. In general, a social network G can be represented as a set of nodes V and a set of edges E, i.e., $G =< V, E >$, where each edge can have its own weight. One of typical formats for representing such social networks is the *adjacency matrix* (shortly, matrix), where an *element* of a matrix means a weight of an edge. Most of social network analyses can be done through matrix-matrix multiplication or matrix-vector multiplication [1][2][5].

As the scale of social networks increases, the size of matrices increases as well. Thus, in order to compute multiplications of such *big matrices*, the following two kinds of approaches have been proposed: (1) a distributed computing approach and (2) a parallel computing approach. The distributed computing approach locates social network data over multiple machines and computes the multiplication through communications among machines. For example, a MapReduce based method [6] belongs to this approach. On the other hand, the parallel computing approach locates the data on a *single* machine and computes the multiplication with a large number of processors inside the machine. For example, a *Graphic Processor Unit* (GPU) based method [7] belongs to this approach. Between the two approaches, the distributed computing approach might be more scalable and flexible than the parallel computing one, but it requires high cost and high management overhead of distributed systems.

There have been many parallel computing methods based on GPU proposed for matrix multiplication [8][9]. *NVIDIA*, one of major manufacturers of GPU, has proposed various matrix multiplication methods based on GPU. Those methods can be categorized into three types depending on the *sparsity of matrices*: (1) multiplication for *two dense matrices*, (2) multiplication for a *spare matrix* and a *dense one*, and (3) multiplication for *two sparse matrices*. NVIDIA provides three different implementations (i.e., libraries) for those methods, *cuBlas*, *csrMM* [8], and *csrGEMM* [9], respectively. In addition to the NVIDIA's methods, Yang et. al. [7] have proposed a sparse matrix-vector multiplications (*spMV*) method. This method can be easily extended to support sparse matrix multiplication by performing spMV iteratively. Hereafter, we call this extended method *spMV-E*.

GPU has characteristics different from CPU. If a GPU-based method does not consider them, the performance of matrix multiplication using GPU can be significantly degraded [8][9]. First, GPU follows the *single instruction multiple threads* (SIMT) where multiple threads perform the *same instruction concurrently* [10]. Second, GPU has various kinds of memories having distinct characteristics. In particular, device memory is the largest, but the slowest one among them. It plays a role like main memory in CPU, and thus has all the data before GPU processing.

Besides, social networks have their own unique characteristics. If a GPU-based method for social network analysis does not take

*Corresponding author

Permission to make digital or hard copies of all or part of this work for personal or classroom use is granted without fee provided that copies are not made or distributed for profit or commercial advantage and that copies bear this notice and the full citation on the first page. Copyrights for components of this work owned by others than ACM must be honored. Abstracting with credit is permitted. To copy otherwise, or republish, to post on servers or to redistribute to lists, requires prior specific permission and/or a fee. Request permissions from Permissions@acm.org.
CIKM'15, October 19–23, 2015, Melbourne, Australia.
© 2015 ACM. ISBN 978-1-4503-3794-6/15/10 ...$15.00.
DOI: http://dx.doi.org/10.1145/2806416.2806445.

them into account, the performance of matrix multiplication could be degraded as well. First, social networks are *sparse*, that is, the number of edges is much smaller than that of all the possible edges (relationships) among nodes [11]. For example, the density of DBLP data is 0.001% ($|V|$=317k, $|E|$= 1,049k), and that of Youtube data is only 0.0002% ($|V|$=1,134k, $|E|$=2,987k). As a result, most elements of matrices for social networks are just zeros (i.e., empty). Second, social networks follow the *power-law* degree distribution [7][12]. That is, so-called *hub nodes* have a extremely high out-degree while ordinary nodes a low out-degree. In the matrices for social networks, some rows (or columns) might have a large number of non-zero elements, while other rows (or columns) have only few non-zero elements. That is, the distribution of non-zero elements tends to be highly skewed [7].

Existing GPU-based methods for matrix multiplication do not consider the above characteristics of social networks, leading to the following problems. First, it is difficult for the methods using the *dense matrices* such as cuBlas and csrMM[8] to handle even moderate-scale social networks (e.g., $|V|$=20,000) due to the limited size of device memory (e.g., 6GB) [13]. Since most of real-world social networks are much bigger than that size, they are not applicable in the analysis of real-world social networks. Second, the methods using the *matrix in sparse format* such as csrGEMM [9] and spMV-E tend to degrade the performance due to poor load balancing of computations in either the thread level or the Streaming Processor (SM) level. Because the distribution of non-zero elements tends to be highly skewed in a social network [7], in the inner and row-row products, some non-zero elements in a matrix could be matched, during a matrix multiplication, to a fairly large number of non-zero elements in the other matrix. That means some thread could spend much longer time to complete its own work than other threads. The overall computation time in GPU is determined by the slowest thread among all running threads in the SIMT model. The same phenomenon could occur at the SM level as well.

We propose an *efficient sparse matrix multiplication method* for social network analysis on GPU that improves the performance in orders-of-magnitude by good load balancing of computations at both the thread level and the SM level. The proposed method performs matrix multiplication based on the *outer product* scheme, that is, column-row vector multiplication. In the outer product, each element in a column vector is multiplied by all the elements in a row vector. The outer product is much less affected by the distribution of non-zero elements of a matrix, and so, the amount of workload tends to be evenly distributed over threads. The proposed method also rearranges the amount of workload at the SM level such that a heavier amount of workload is performed *before* a lighter amount of workload, where a heavier (lighter) one means a column-row vector multiplication having a more (less) number of pairs of non-zero elements matched. This rearrangement could reduce the total amount of computation time in a matrix multiplication.

The contributions of this paper can be summarized as follows:

- We propose an scheme based on the outer product for matrix multiplication on GPU that performs nice load balancing at the *fine-grained level*, i.e., at the thread level.

- We propose a load balancing strategy at the *coarse-grained level*, i.e., at the SM level, that rearranges the amount of workloads among SMs so as to make the whole multiplication process completed within a short time.

- Through extensive experiments using both synthetic and real-world datasets, we demonstrate that the proposed method outperforms the existing methods in up to two orders-of-magnitude.

The rest of this paper is organized as follows. Section 2 reviews CUDA and related work for matrix multiplication using GPU. Section 3 points out the problems that the existing methods suffer from. Section 4 proposes our method to solve these problems. Section 5 demonstrates and analyzes the results of experimental evaluation. Finally, Section 6 summarizes and concludes the paper.

2. RELATED WORK

2.1 CUDA

In this section, we present the characteristics of *compute unified device architecture* (CUDA) in accordance with the problem of matrix multiplication. CUDA is a technique based on the concept of *general purpose computing on graphic processing unit* (GPGPU) that is supported by NVIDIA [14][15]. Figure 1 shows the architecture of CUDA. CUDA consists of a set of *streaming multiprocessors* (SM), each of which is again composed of a set of *streaming processors* (SP). It follows the *single instruction multiple threads* (SIMT) model on which multiple threads execute the same instruction at one time. An execution of a CUDA program is partitioned into a grid of thread blocks that run logically in parallel. A *thread block* consists of *warps*, each of which usually consists of a set of 32 threads. *Threads* in a warp can run concurrently on an SM [10]. A user can make the scheduler of GPU assign a set of thread blocks to a specific SM in a specific order. Just for simplicity in our explanation (without loss of generality), we assume that a thread block consists of a warp.

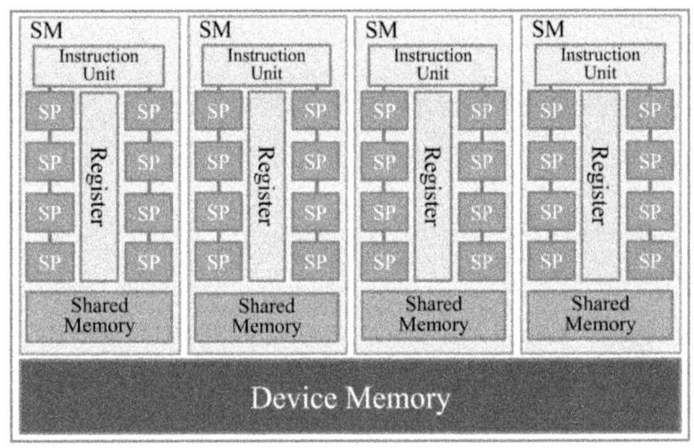

Figure 1: Example of CUDA.

There are various kinds of memories on CUDA such as device memory, shared memory, texture memory, constant memory, and register. Among them, we focus on the device memory and the shared memory, mainly used in a matrix multiplication. The *device memory* is very large (capacity: 500MB $\sim$ 6GB), but relatively slow (access latency: 400 $\sim$ 600 cycles), and is visible to all threads on the device [14]. The data processed in CUDA should be loaded into the device memory in advance. If the data is scattered over the device memory, a lot of accesses to the memory could occur in reading them. A lot of memory accesses lead to performance degradation due to the high latency of the device memory. Thus, it is preferred to store data consecutively and to access it in a coalesced fashion, which is called *coalesced memory access* [15]. Each SM is equipped with an on-chip memory, which is called the shared memory [10]. The *shared memory* is smaller (4KB $\sim$ 16KB), but faster (access latency: 20 $\sim$ 40 cycles) than the device memory. It is only visible to the threads of the same thread block. If multiple threads try to access the shared memory at the same time, they need to be serialized to avoid conflicts [16].

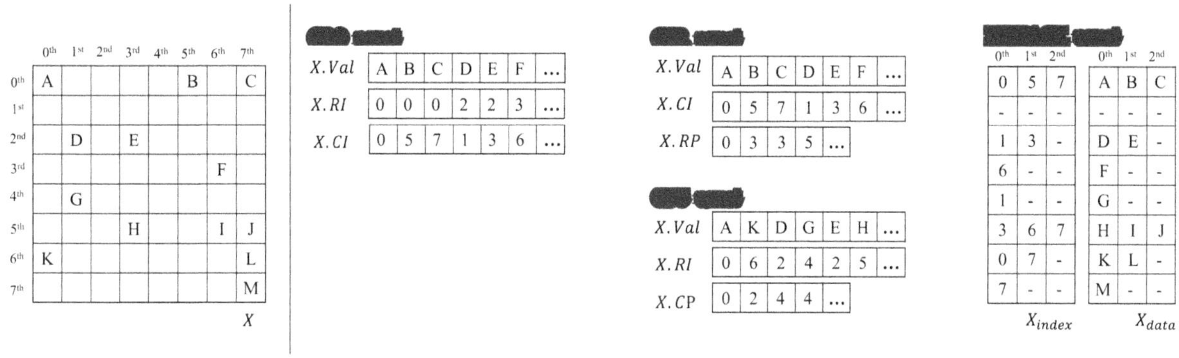

Figure 2: Sparse formats for a matrix.

2.2 Sparse Format for Matrix

There are different sparse formats representing a matrix. Among them, we present four sparse formats mainly used in this paper such as the coordinate list (COO) format, the compressed sparse column (CSC) format, the compressed sparse row (CSR) format, and the ELLPACK format [17][18].

The *COO format* consists of three arrays: an array storing non-zero element values (VAL), an array storing row indices (RI), and an array storing col indices (CI). The *CSC format* consists of three arrays: an array storing non-zero element values (VAL), an array storing row indices (RI), an array storing column pointers, each of which refers to the first element of each column (CP) [7]. The *CSR format* consists of three arrays: an array storing non-zero element values (VAL), an array storing column indices (CI), and an array storing row pointers, each of which refers to the first element of each row (RP) [17]. We can compute the number of non-zero elements in a row (or a column) by a difference between $RP[i+1]$ and $RP[i]$ (or $CP[i+1]$ and $CP[i]$) in the CSR (or CSC) format. The *ELLPACK format* stores all elements of the matrix in an n-by-k two-dimensional array if each row of an n-by-n matrix has up to k non-zero elements, where row vectors with fewer than k non-zero elements are zero-padded. A column index and a value of each element are stored in index and data arrays, respectively [18].

Figure 2 shows the COO, CSC, CSR, and ELLPACK formats. In the COO format, VAL normally stores element A (shortly, $\{A\}$), $\{B\}$, and $\{C\}$ in sequence in row major, from $X[0][]$ to $X[7][]$. RI stores row indeces of elements while CI does column indeces of elements. In the CSC format, VAL stores $\{A\}$, $\{K\}$, and $\{D\}$ in column major, from $X[][0]$ to $X[][7]$. RI stores row indeces of elements. $CP[1]$ stores 2 because $CP[1]$ refers to $\{D\}$ which is the 2nd element of X in the order based on column major (when $\{A\}$ is 0th). In the CSR format, VAL stores $\{A\}$, $\{B\}$, and $\{C\}$ in row major, from $X[0][]$ to $X[7][]$. CI stores column indeces of elements. $RP[1]$ stores 3 because $RP[1]$ refer to $\{D\}$ is the 3rd element in X. In the ELLPACK format, 8-by-8 X is represented by 8-by-3 X_{data} and 8-by-3 X_{index}. The first row of X_{data} stores $\{A\}$, $\{B\}$, and $\{C\}$ as elements of $X[0][]$. The first row of X_{index} stores 0, 5, and 7 as indices of elements in $X[0][]$.

2.3 Existing Matrix Multiplication on GPU

In this section, we briefly review existing methods of matrix multiplication on device memory in GPU.

2.3.1 Multiplication of dense-dense matrices (cuBlas)

We present a multiplication method of *dense-dense* matrices, called *cuBlas*, proposed by NVIDIA, which is based on the *inner product* of $Eq.(1)$ [8].

$$Z[i][j] = \sum_{k}^{n} X[i][k] \times Y[k][j] \quad (1)$$

cuBlas divides each matrix to multiple sub-matrices. A thread block performs the multiplications between a sub-matrix X_s of X and a sub-matrix Y_s of Y, and each thread performs the multiplication of $X_s[i][]$ with $Y_s[][j]$ of those sub-matrices. Since cuBlas uses the dense format where a zero element also occupies memory space, cuBlas is not suitable for social networks where most of elements are zeros within the dense matrix.

Figure 3 shows an example of cuBlas. For multiplying X and Y, each of which is an 8-by-8 matrix, each matrix is spilt into multiple 4-by-4 sub-matrices of $X_{1\sim4}$, $Y_{1\sim4}$, and $Z_{1\sim4}$, respectively. The thread block 1 performs multiplication of X_1 with Y_1, where thread 1 multiplies $X_1[0][]$ and $Y_1[][0]$ and stores the result in $Z_1[0][0]$.

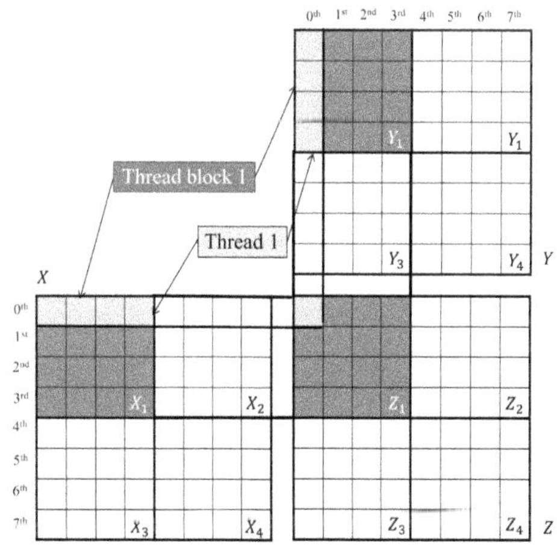

Figure 3: Example of cuBlas ($X \times Y = Z$).

2.3.2 Multiplication of sparse-dense matrices (csrMM)

We present a multiplication method of *sparse-dense* matrices, called *csrMM*, proposed by NVIDIA [8]. It is based on the CSR vector method which is a method for a sparse matrix and a vector multiplication (spMV). For multiplication of sparse-dense matrices, csrMM performs the CSR vector method iteratively for each vector of the dense matrix [8]. csrMM represents X as the CSR (sparse) format and other matrices, Y and Z, as the matrix in dense format. In the CSR vector method, a thread block performs the multiplication of $X[i][]$ and $Y[][j]$ and stores the result in $Z[i][j]$. Here, a thread performs the multiplication of one element of $X[i][]$ with $Y[i][j]$ [17].

Figure 4 shows the CSR vector method. Thread block 1 performs multiplications for the elements between $RP[0]$ and $RP[1] - 1$. Thread 1 multiplies $X[0][0]$ with $Y[0][0]$, then, stores the result in $Z[0][0]$.

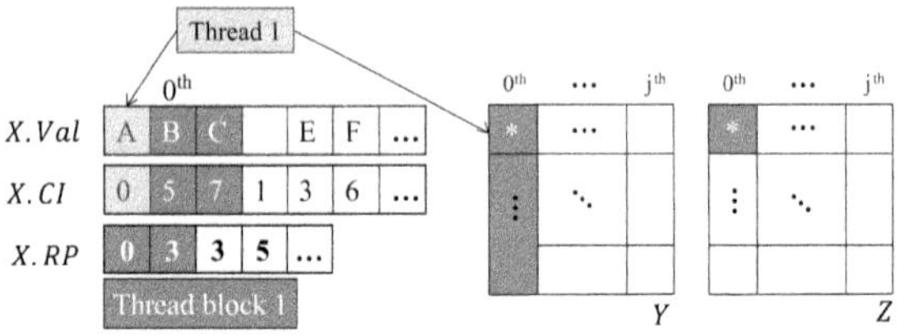

Figure 4: Example of the CSR vector method.

2.3.3 *Multiplication of sparse-sparse matrices (csrGEMM)*

We present a multiplication method of *sparse-sparse* matrices, called *csrGEMM* also proposed by NVIDIA [9]. In csrGEMM, all matrices are represented in the CSR format. csrGEMM is based on the *row-row product* of $Eq.(2)$.

$$Z[i][] = \sum_{j}^{n}(X[i][j] \times Y[j][]) \quad (2)$$

A thread block performs the multiplication of $X[i][]$ and rows of Y, and produces $Z[i][]$. Here, a thread multiplies $X[i][j]$ and $Y[j][k]$, where k means a element in Y[j] [9]. Figure 5 shows an example of csrGEMM. Thread block 1 multiplies $X[0][]$ with $Y[0][]$, $Y[5][]$ and $Y[7][]$. Threads 1 and 2 multiply $X[0][0]$ with $Y[0][0]$ and $Y[0][3]$, then store the result in $Z[0][0]$ and $Z[0][3]$, respectively. Threads 3, 4 and 5 multiply $X[0][5]$ with $Y[5][2]$, $Y[5][5]$, and $Y[5][6]$, then store the result in $Z[0][2]$, $Z[0][5]$, and $Z[0][6]$, respectively. As well, threads 6, 7, 8, 9 and 10 multiply $X[0][7]$ with non-zero elements of $Y[7][1]$, $Y[7][2]$, $Y[7][3]$, $Y[7][4]$, and $Y[7][7]$ then store the result in $Z[0][1]$, $Z[0][2]$, $Z[0][3]$, $Z[0][4]$, and $Z[0][7]$, respectively.

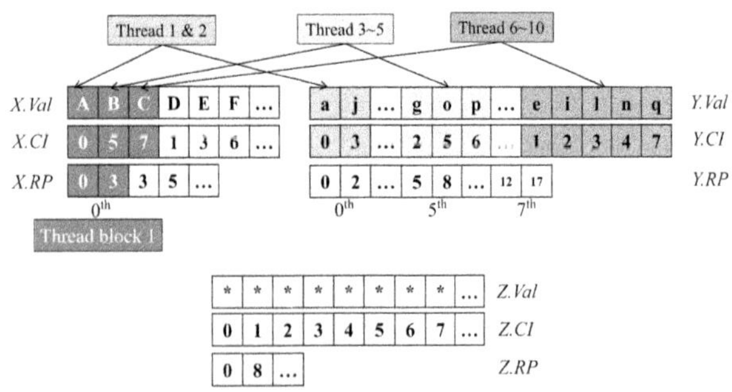

Figure 5: Example of csrGEMM.

2.3.4 *Extension of sparse matrix-vector multiplication (spMV-E)*

We present the most efficient spMV method proposed by Yang. et. al. In this method, a matrix is divided into sub-matrices. Here, the CSR vector method is employed when the row vectors of a sub-matrix are long and have similar lengths; Otherwise, the ELL method is employed [7]. As already mentioned in Section 2.3.2, the spMV method can be easily extended to support matrix multiplication by performing it iteratively. Thus we modify this method for two sparse matrix multiplication, which we call this modified one, spMV-E in this paper. In order to utilize the spMV method for two sparse matrices multiplication, we employ the CSC format for column vectors of matrix Y because spMV-E accesses these vectors in column major. Then, it performs multiplications only for a pair of non-zero elements.

We only present the ELL method [17] here because the CSR vector method has already been introduced in Section 2.3.2. In the ELL method, a thread block multiplies a set of rows in X as many as its threads with a column. Here, a thread multiplies $X[i][]$ with a column. Figure 6 shows an example of the ELL method. If thread block 1 consists of three threads, it performs the multiplications of $X[0][]$, $X[1][]$, and $X[2][]$ with $Y[][j]$. Here, thread 1 performs the multiplication of $X[0][]$ with $Y[][0]$, then stores the result in $Z[0][0]$ [17].

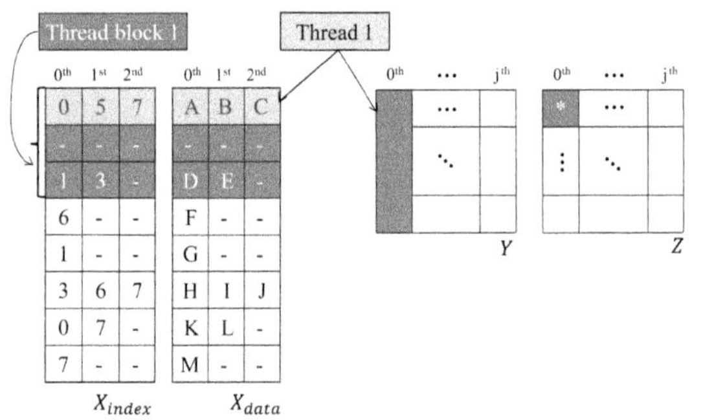

Figure 6: Example of the ELL method.

3. OBSERVATIONS

In this section, we present three observations on the problems that the existing methods have.

Observation 1: The kernel function having a conditional branch for a matrix multiplication causes the poor performance due to the waiting time. All the threads in a warp execute the same instruction concurrently due to the nature of the SIMT architecture of GPU. Thus, if a conditional branch appears, some threads in a warp execute necessary instructions while other threads in the same warp are just waiting (doing nothing).

For example, due to the inner product based on the CSR vector method in spMV-E, there can be no $Y[j][i]$ multiplied with $X[i][j]$. For multiplication of $X[i][j]$ with $Y[j][i]$, there are two steps of computation: confirm presence or absence of a pair of non-zero elements ($Chk(\cdot)$); multiply them ($Mul(\cdot)$).

Algorithm 1 shows the pseudo code of the two sparse matrix multiplication based on the CSR vector method using only sparse format. In the CUDA program, the thread block index and dimension ($blockIdx.x$ and $blockDim.x$) and thread index ($threadIdx.x$) are given. Here, num_thread represents the number of threads in a thread block. In the CSR vector method, a thread in a thread block performs checking the indices of elements (Line 8: $Chk(\cdot)$), and then multiplies two elements if row_index is the same as column_index (Line 9: $Mul(\cdot)$). Otherwise, a thread just waits for other threads to be completed in the same warp. That is, the *thread divergence* due to the conditional branch causes such waiting time over threads, which is a considerably time-consuming.

Observation 2: The skewed distribution of non-zero elements causes poor load balancing in a thread level. Figure 7 shows

Algorithm 1 Two sparse matrix multiplication based on CSR vector method

Input: X (CSR format), Y (CSC format)
Output: Z (COO format)

```
tid = blockDim.x * blockIdx.x + threadIdx.x;
warp_id = tid/ num_thread;
row = warp_id;
for i ∈ the size of Y.CP[] do
  if row < the size of X.RP[] then
    for col_index ∈ X.RP[row] to X.RP[row + 1] do
      for row_index ∈ Y.CP[row] to Y.CP[row + 1] do
        if row_index = col_index then
          val=X.VAL[row_index]*Y.VAL[col_index];
          After parallel sum reduction then store values;
        end if
      end for
    end for
  end if
end for
```

the power-law degree distribution found in a real-world social network[12]. The x-axis represents the number of nodes that have corresponding out-degrees, and the y-axis does count (i.e., the number of out-degree). This figure means that some nodes have a large number of edges while many ordinary nodes have a few edges. In other words, some rows (or columns) have a large number of non-zero elements while other rows (or columns) have only a few non-zero elements in a matrix. This leads to poor load balancing of computations in a thread level in the case of a method that assigns a thread to a row (or a column). The amount of workload for a matrix multiplication is considerably different with threads. The threads having a light amount of workload could wait for a long time until other threads having a heavy amount of workload are completed due to the nature of the SIMT architecture of GPU.

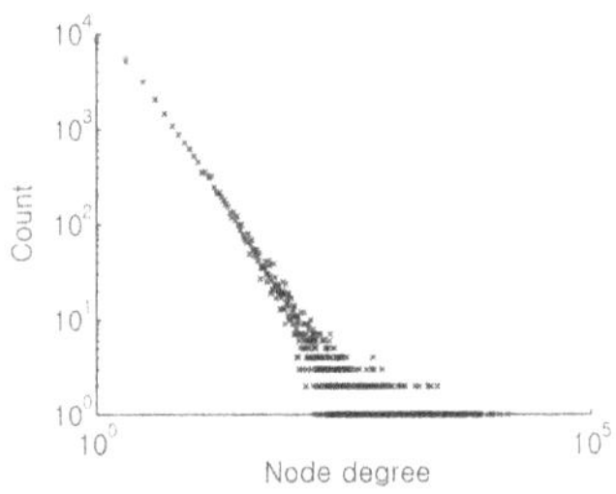

Figure 7: Power-law degree distribution in a social network.

Observation 3: A naive scheduling method for thread blocks incur poor load balancing in a thread block level due to the skewed distribution of non-zero elements. In the case of a method that assigns a thread block to a row (or a column), the amount of workload can be also significantly different over thread blocks due to the skewed distribution of social network data. Since a naive scheduling method would assign thread blocks to each SM in row major order, the amount of workload in SM could be different over SMs. This naive method might make the total execution time very long in case the thread block having the heavy amount of workload is assigned to an SM at the last moment. Therefore, it is very important to balance the amount of workloads among SMs evenly. Figure 8(a) shows a case that an SM waits for another SM, where *Block* denotes a thread block; *workload* does the amount of workload assigned to each block. Block 6 having the heaviest Workload is executed on SM1 at the end of the program. In this case, the completion of the program is delayed until block 6 finishes, while SM2 keeps waiting after its completion.

4. PROPOSED METHOD

4.1 Load Balancing Strategy at Fine-Grained Level

We propose *the outer product based scheme* for matrix multiplication on GPU. The the outer product based scheme for matrix multiplication is defined in Eq.(3) below [19]. All the schemes (based on the inner, outer, and row-row product) for matrix multiplication require the *exactly same amount of multiplications between elements (elements multiplication)*. However, unlike the inner and row-row product based schemes, outer product based scheme accesses only once a column and a row in two matrices X and Y, respectively. In other words, $X[][i]$ only is multiplied only with $Y[i][]$ for each i. In addition, every element of $X[][i]$ has the same amount of elements multiplication because it should be multiplied by all the elements of $Y[i][]$.

$$Z[][] = \sum_{i}^{n} X[j][i] \times Y[i][k] \qquad (3)$$

In order to solve the problems found in Observations 1 and 2 in Section 3, we use the characteristics of the outer product based scheme as follows.

First, the conditional branch over threads does not occur thanks to another characteristic of the outer product based scheme: $X[j][i]$ is multiplied with all the elements in $Y[i][]$ *without performing* $Chk(\cdot)$. If a thread performs the multiplications of $X[j][i]$ with all the elements in $Y[i][]$, it performs only $Mul(\cdot)$. This solves the problem mentioned in Observation 2. Second, we can solve the poor load balancing *in a thread level* with the the outer product based scheme. In a thread block, all the threads have the amount of workload as much as that proportional to the number of elements in $Y[i][]$. Therefore, each thread block should perform the multiplication of $X[][i]$ with $Y[i][]$, where each thread multiplies $X[j][i]$ with all the elements in $Y[i][]$, there by having the same workload. This solves the problem stated in Observation 2.

Here, thread blocks could face the confliction when they save the results of multiplications at the same time. It needs the *atomic operation* to avoid the confliction, leading to some performance degradation. However, we individually secure the result space of multiplications for thread blocks then merge the result sub-matrices into a result matrix on main memory. Due to the size limitation of device memory, we just need to divide matrices to sub-matrices, each of which fits in the device memory. It incurs transferring sub-matrices between the main memory and the device memory. This transferring cost is, however, not a big issue, considering we can reduce the computation time greatly.

Figure 9 shows the proposed method for $Z = X[][i] \times Y[i][]$. Thread block 1 takes responsibility for a part of matrix multiplication for $X[][0]$ and $Y[0][]$. As a result, thread 1 yields $Z[0][0]$ and $Z[0][3]$ by multiplying $X[0][0]$ with $Y[0][0]$ and $Y[0][3]$, respectively; thread 2 does $Z[6][0]$ to $Z[6][3]$ by multiplying $X[6][0]$ with $Y[6][0]$ and $Y[6][3]$, respectively.

4.2 Load Balancing Strategy at Coarse-Grained Level

As mentioned in Observation 3, the social network data represented by a matrix follows the power-law degree distribution. In the case of such matrices, the numbers of non-zero elements in different columns or rows could be significantly different [7]. This

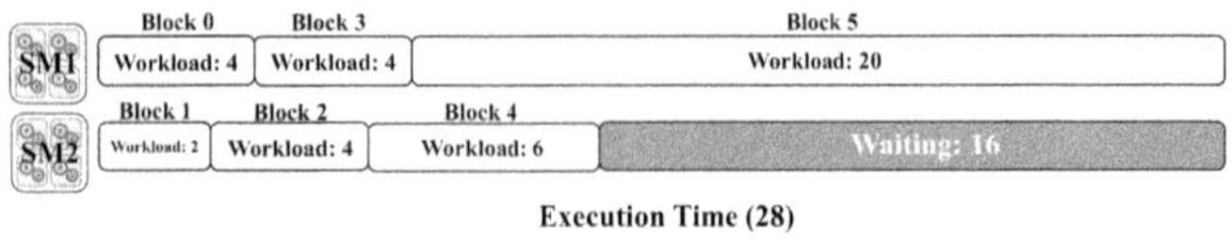

(a) Block assignments with unsorted WLT

Before sorting WLT

Index	0	1	3	5	6	7
Workload	4	2	4	4	6	20
	Block 0	Block 1	Block 2	Block 3	Block 4	Block 5

(b) Workload table without sorting

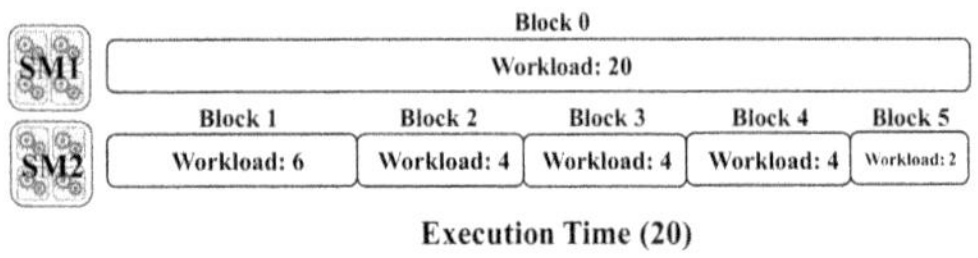

(c) Block assignments with sorted WLT

After sorting WLT

Index	7	6	3	5	0	1
Workload	20	6	4	4	4	2
	Block 0	Block 1	Block 2	Block 3	Block 4	Block 5

(d) Workload table with sorting

Figure 8: Result of load balancing in a SM level.

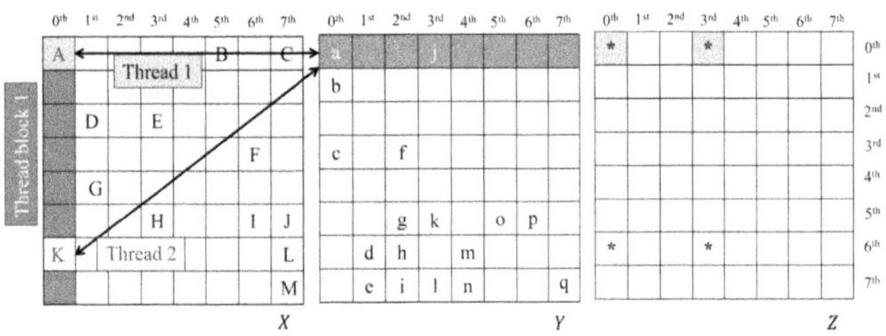

Figure 9: The outer product based scheme for matrix multiplication.

causes the amount of workload over thread blocks to be different greatly, which makes the amount of workload unevenly distributed over SMs, if thread blocks are arbitrary assigned to SMs. If a thread block having the largest workload is assigned to an SM at the end of the process, all other SMs wait until the thread block is done as Figure 8(a).

In order to solve this problem, the amount of workload needs to be evenly assigned over SMs independently of the number of thread blocks. For making the amount of workload balanced over SMs, we should first compute the number of elements multiplications occurring in multiplying every pair of a column and a row. Its time complexity is $O(1)$ due to a pointer array in the CSC (or CSR) format. In a thread block, the amount of actual workload is slightly different from that of the elements multiplications because multiple threads in a thread block are concurrently processed by different SPs. The amount of workload in the thread block can be computed as in Eq.(4) where $\#X[][i]$ (resp. $\#Y[i][]$) means the number of elements in a column in X(resp. a row in Y), $\#threads$ does the number of threads and TB does a thread block.

$$Workload_i = (\#X[][i] \ / \ \#threads \ in \ TB) \times \#Y[i][] \quad (4)$$

Then, we need to assign the amount of workload to SMs as evenly as possible. Making the amount of workload distributed over SMs evenly is the task to find combinatorial optimization of given thread blocks. It is similar to the well-known *knapsack problem* to find combinatorial optimization of a set of items given [20]. In particular, this is a 0-1 knapsack problem since a thread block cannot be performed on two or more SMs. Since our load balancing problem is a NP-hard problem, it is difficult to find the optimal solution within a reasonable time. Thus, we propose a heuristic method based on a greedy algorithm.

The proposed method sorts the pairs of column and row (assigned to thread blocks) in descending order by the amount of workload, and then assigns *the thread block having the heaviest amount of workload first* to an SM available. In order to sort the thread blocks according to their workload efficiently, the proposed method creates a data structure called *workload table* (WLT). WLT consists of two arrays WLT_{index} and $WLT_{workload}$ having the same size. Each entry in WLT_{index} stores the index of a pair of column and row (to be assigned to a thread block) and each entry in $WLT_{workload}$ stores the amount of workload of the pair.

The time complexity of generating WLT_{index} and $WLT_{workload}$ is $O(n)$ because Eq.(4) $O(1)$ complexity needs to be computed n times in n-by-n two matrices multiplications. The space complexity of WLT is $O(n)$ as well.

Figure 8(b) and 8(d) show WLT generated from X and Y presented in Figure 9. By sorting entries of WLT according to the amount of workload, we no longer need to sort the matrices of much larger sizes. We note that WLT has a much smaller number of elements than n because there are many columns and rows, X and Y, that have no non-zero elements inside. In Figure 8(c), WLT has only six entries because there are no elements in the 2nd and 4th columns of X, likewise, in the 2nd and 4th rows of Y.

If thread blocks are assigned to SMs according to the sorted indexes in WLT, some SMs execute the thread blocks having the heavy amount of workload while other SMs execute a more number of remaining (relatively lighter) thread blocks. As a result, the proposed method arranges the last thread blocks to complete their execution at the similar times, which alleviates poor load balancing in a SM level. The thread blocks are assigned to SMs according to the sorted entries in WLT in Figure 8(d). While SM1 performs the multiplication of block 0 having the heaviest amount of workload, SM2 performs the multiplication of other blocks (block $1 \sim 5$) having relatively smaller amount of workload than block 0. These blocks perform computations of multiplication on SM2. By using this strategy for load balancing in the SM level, we could improve the degree of parallelism of GPU considerably.

4.3 lbGEMM Algorithm

In order to further improve the performance of a matrix multiplication in GPU, we adopt two additional techniques: (T1) using the coalesced memory access and (T2) utilizing the shared memory. We adopt $T1$ by storing X and Y as the CSC and CSR formats, respectively, for accessing in X in column major and Y in row major, in the outer product based scheme. Since each thread in the same thread block performs the multiplication of one element of $X[][i]$ with all the element of $Y[i][]$, all the threads share all the elements of $Y[i][]$. Thus, we adopt $T2$ by loading $Y[i][]$, which is only accessed by $X[][i]$, to the *shared memory*.

Algorithm 2 shows the pseudo code of our method called lbGEMM (load balanced spGEMM). The input is a pair of X and Y in the CSC and CSR formats, respectively. The output is Z in the COO format. The matrices X, Y, and Z in these formats are loaded into the main memory, and then the sub-matrices of X', Y', and Z' are transferred to device memory. The size of sub-matrices needs to fit in that of device memory. The values of $Y'[i][]$ assigned to a thread block are loaded into shared memory. Then, *row_length* is computed by the number of elements in $Y'[i][]$ by referring to $Y'.RP$. Finally, the thread performs the multiplication of each element of the column in X' with the row in Y' on shared memory, and stores the result.

Algorithm 2 Fast sparse matrices multiplication on GPU

Input: X' (CSC format), Y' (CSR format)
Output: Z' (COO format)

tid =threadIdx.x;
tbid = blockDim.x × blockIdx.x + blockDim.y × blockIdx.y;
row_length = $Y'.RP[tbid+1]$ - $Y'.RP[tbid]$;
load values from $Y'.VAL$[tbid] to $Y'.VAL$[tbid] + row_length to the shared memory;
for i ∈ row_length **do**
  val= $X'.VAL[tid] \times Y'.VAL[i]$;
  x = $X'.CP[tid]$;
  y = $Y'.RP[i]$;
  $Z'.RI[]$ = x; $Z'.CI[]$ = y; $Z'.VAL[]$ = val;
end for

5. EXPERIMENTS

We evaluate the performance of the proposed method compared with previous methods for a matrix multiplication on GPU.

5.1 Experimental Environment

We conducted experiments using the server equipped with Intel i7 3.4GHz, 32GB main memory, and *GTX TITAN Black* [13] as GPU. This GPU has 2,880 SPs, each of which has the clock of 889MHz.

In our experiments, we used both synthetic and real-world social network datasets, loadable on main memory. Table 1 shows the basic statistics of them [11] where *#Mul.* indicates the number of elements multiplications occurring in a matrix multiplication. We observed that, in real-world Stanford social network datasets, as the number of nodes increases, the density tends to decrease. Thus, we divided the real-world social network datasets into two groups, Group S and Group L, according to the number of nodes included. Group S has relatively small networks consisting of less than 100,000 nodes and having relatively high density of more than 0.01% while Group L does relatively large networks consisting of more than 100,000 nodes and having the density of less than 0.001%. Since our social networks data consist of different numbers of nodes, we cannot multiply a pair of matrices for different social networks. So, in our experiments, we performed self-multiplications where X and Y are identical (i.e., $Z = X \times Y$).

Table 1: Stanford social network datasets

	Data	#Nodes	#Edges	Density (%)	#Mul.
S	EmailEnron	36k	367k	2.73e-02	0.05B
	Slashdot	82k	948k	1.40e-02	0.1B
L	Amazon	262k	1,234k	1.80e-03	0.006B
	DBLP	317k	1,049k	1.04e-03	0.007B
	Youtube	1,134k	2,987k	2.32e-04	0.2B
	Wiki-Talk	2,394k	5,021k	8.70e-05	1.3B
	LiveJournal	4,847k	68,993k	2.94e-04	5.4B

5.2 Implementations

For a matrix multiplication in GPU, the total size of matrices X, Y, and Z should be smaller than that of device memory in GPU. However, it often exceeds the size of the device memory in the case of a huge volume of real-world social networks. Thus, we load entire matrices X and Y first to main memory in host and divide them to smaller sub-matrices X' and Y' in such a way that each pair of sub-matrices can be multiplied on the device memory.

We discuss how to divide a matrix into smaller sub-matrices for each method in more detail. In the case of dense matrices, we determine the sizes of sub-matrices in the number of nodes (say n) loadable in the device memory, and then partition the whole matrices into their n-by-n sub-matrices. A matrix in sparse format stores only non-zero elements (indicating edges in a social network) in row major (or column major) order. In the case of sparse matrices, we determine the sizes of sub-matrices in the number of non-zero elements (say e) loadable in the device memory, and then partition the whole matrices into smaller sub-matrices having the sizes thus determined.

In the following, we present how to multiply sub-matrices X' and Y' to get Z' in GPU with each method. In the case of using cuBlas, we first determine the number of nodes (say n) for X', Y', and Z' loadable in the device memory. For multiplication of each pair of sub-matrices in GPU, we call cuBlas implemented in the NVIDIA Library [8].

csrMM uses sparse sub-matrix X' unlike dense sub-matrix X' of cuBlas. The size of space is dominantly determined by sub-matrices Y' and Z' since they are much larger than sub-matrix X'. Thus we first determine the sizes of Y' and Z' loadable in device memory, and partition X' according to the sizes of Y' or Z'. For multiplication of each pair of sub-matrices in GPU, we call csrMM implemented in the NVIDIA Library [8].

In multiplications of two sparse matrices (i.e., with csrGEMM, spMV-E, and lbGEMM), we first determine e that makes X', Y', and Z' loadable in device memory, partition the three matrices X, Y, and Z into smaller sub-matrices X', Y', and Z' according to e, and call each method for multiplying each pair of sub-matrices in GPU.

In csrGEMM of the NVIDIA Library [9], a thread block is in charge of a row of X' together with several rows of Y'. If non-zero elements within a row of X' exceeds the size of shared memory, its corresponding thread block could not run. To address this problem, we divide a row having a large number of non-zero elements in X' into smaller sub-rows, and make a thread block process the sub-rows *serially*. This makes the thread block executed multiple times while other concurrently running thread blocks are executed only once, which leads to *poor thread-block-level load balancing* in csrGEMM. Since, in real-world social networks, the number of non-zero elements in a row (i.e., number of edges to a node) could be significantly large owing to the *power-law*, this poor load balancing is likely to occur frequently in csrGEMM.

5.3 Experiments on Real-World Datasets

Table 2 shows the execution times for matrix multiplication with seven datasets obtained by different methods. The total execution time consists of (1) transmission time ($trans$) for transferring data between main memory in host and device memory in GPU and (2) computation time (com) spent for matrix multiplication in GPU. Table 3 indicates the portion of transmission and computation times to the total execution time.

In the case of dense matrices, the number of nodes is a dominant factor to determine the execution time because it determines the size of dense matrices. Thus, a social network with a large number of nodes increases both of the transmission and computation times.

In the case of sparse matrices, the number of non-zero elements (i.e., edges) and also the number of elements multiplications are two dominant factors to determine the execution time. The transmission time from main memory to device memory is determined by the number of non-zero elements in X and Y while the transmission time from device memory to main memory is determined by the number of non-zero elements in Z. We note that the number of non-zero elements in Z is dependent on the number of multiplications. These two factors affect the computation time differently depending on multiplication methods.

In cuBlas, the execution time increases as the number of nodes increases due to all dense matrices X, Y, and Z. The computation time occupies about 77% of the total execution time in all cases because cuBlas performs a large number of elements multiplications even for zero-elements.

As in cuBlas, the total execution time of csrMM tends to increase as the number of nodes grows. The transmission time is affected by the number of non-zero elements within X in sparse format and the number of nodes in two dense matrices Y and Z. The computation time is dependent on the number of non-zero elements in X to be multiplied to all the elements in Y. Compared with cuBlas, the computation time occupies a small portion (less than 20%) of the total execution time in csrMM since only the non-zero elements in X are involved in elements multiplications with csrMM. The transmission time occupies more than 80% of the execution time. Since dense matrices Y and Z are much larger than X in sparse format, the number of nodes in a social network dominates the execution time in csrMM.

The total execution time of spMV-E dramatically increases with the number of non-zero elements (i.e., edges in a social network). The transmission time depends on the number of non-zero elements within all sparse matrices X, Y and Z. The computation time is also dependent on the number of non-zero elements, rather than the number of multiplications, in spMV-E. This is because of the *thread divergence*, which is more likely to occur as the number of non-zero elements increases. The thread divergence leads to poor load balancing in GPU due to $Chk(\cdot)$ mentioned in Observation 2, thereby requiring much more computation time.

The total execution time of csrGEMM dramatically grows as the number of elements multiplications increases. this is mainly due to poor load balancing in the thread block level. There is no significant difference between the portions of the transmission and computation times in our datasets, except for the LiveJournal dataset. The resulting matrix Z normally determines the transmission time because it is much larger than both of X and Y. The computation time is dependent on the number of elements multiplications. There is an exceptional case that the portion of the transmission time is larger than that of the computation time in the LiveJournal dataset, which is the largest in our datasets. the LiveJournal dataset contains a large number of non-zero elements (i.e., edges), however, does not incur a large number of actual elements multiplications. This causes a large time for data transmission from main memory to device memory but a relatively small time for computations in GPU.

The total execution time of lbGEMM, our method, increases with the number of elements multiplications. We note that the execution time of lbGEMM does not dramatically increases thanks to good load balancing both in the thread level and the SM level (but not thread block level) unlike other methods for two sparse matrices (spMV-E and csrGEMM). There are some differences in ratios of transmission and computation times depending on social network data. We conjecture that the differences are due to different numbers of threads concurrently executed in GPU. lbGEMM allocates a thread block for elements multiplications between a column in X' and a row in matrix Y', and does a thread in the thread block for multiplications between an element in the column of X' and all the elements in the row of Y'. Because different numbers of non-zero elements exist inside columns, the numbers of threads used in thread blocks could be different. As a thread block employs a more number of threads, the computational parallelism in GPU gets higher, leading to shorter computation time. We note that all the threads in a thread block have an identical number of elements multiplications, which guarantees load balancing in a thread-level. For example, the number of multiplications for Youtube is twice as large as that for Slashdot while the execution time for Youtube is not twice as large as that for Slashdot. We observed that the number of threads in a thread block with Youtube was 32 on average while it was 64 with Slashdot.

Let us compare the execution times of all the methods. csrMM outperforms cuBlas five times by reducing the number of unnecessary multiplications involving zero-elements. Although spMV-E is for two matrices both in sparse format, it shows poor performance (even worse than csrMM) due to poor load balancing in the thread level (i.e., thread divergence) within GPU. csrGEMM and lbGEMM, which only adopt sparse format, outperform cuBlas, csrMM, and spMV-E significantly. In particular, our lbGEMM achieves a dramatic improvement in performance by 3 to 145 times, compared with csrGEMM, thanks to good load balancing in both the thread and SM levels. A performance gap in execution time between lbGEMM and csrGEMM increases with the number of elements multiplications.

5.4 Experiments on Synthetic Datasets

Now, we show the scalability of lbGEMM with synthetic datasets compared with existing ones. Following the characteristics of real-world datasets used, we generated the three types of synthetic datasets (*S1, L1,* and *L2*). $S1$ for relatively small networks and $L1$ & $L2$ for relatively large networks. *S1* has 20,000 nodes which are all loadable on device memory for running cuBlas. It has various densities of 0.1% $\sim$ 2%, and is similar to those in Group S in real-world network datasets. Here, we changed the density up to 2% (seams unrealistic) in order to do in-depth investigation on some cases not observed in real-world datasets; *L1* has 1,000,000 nodes with various densities of 0.001% $\sim$ 0.0001%. It imitates Group L of real-world datasets; *L2* consists of 1,000,000 $\sim$ 5,000,000 nodes of a fixed density of 0.0001%, which also imitates Group L of real-world datasets. We generated all the synthetic datasets in such a way that it follows the power-law distribution.

5.4.1 Synthetic datasets S1

Figure 10(a) shows the execution time obtained by changing the density on $S1$. The x-axis indicates the density of matrices and the y-axis does the execution time in *log scale*. We note that the execution time of cuBlas is identical regardless of density since

Table 2: Execution time of each method on real-world datasets (in seconds)

Datasets \ Methods	cuBlas	csrMM	spMV-E	csrGEMM	lbGEMM
EmailEnron	20.13	4.06	53.26	0.97	0.27
Slashdot	125.95	24.59	371.14	4.03	0.65
Amazon	990.98	161.86	999.38	0.51	0.05
DBLP	1290.95	412.90	970.35	1.13	0.05
Youtube	16,404.94	2,918.48	10,378.88	91.97	1.56
Wiki-Talk	72,654.67	14,135.74	30,864.14	1,047.41	7.98
LiveJournal	297,706.50	59,428.04	9,853,068.00	6,369.87	43.84

Table 3: Portion of transmission and computation time to the total execution time (%)

Methods	cuBlas		csrMM		spMV-E		csrGEMM		lbGEMM	
Datasets	tran	com	tran	com	tran	com	tran	com	tran	com
EmailEnron	23.07	76.92	81.69	18.30	0.1	99.9	56.46	43.53	68.58	31.41
Slashdot	22.75	77.24	81.75	18.24	0.1	99.9	54.52	45.47	65.12	34.87
Amazon	22.62	77.37	93.17	6.83	0.1	99.9	51.91	48.08	45.89	54.11
DBLP	22.52	77.47	93.08	6.91	0.1	99.9	51.29	48.70	50.35	49.64
Youtube	22.44	77.55	91.45	8.54	0.1	99.9	50.34	49.65	51.91	48.08
Wiki-Talk	22.61	77.38	80.38	19.61	0.1	99.9	50.25	49.74	56.85	43.14
LiveJournal	22.12	77.87	88.76	11.23	0.1	99.9	73.11	26.88	55.18	44.81

it is the method of dense-dense matrix multiplication and thus is not affected by the density. We observe that the performance of lbGEMM becomes worse than that of cuBlas in the density of 2%. We note that this high density of a social network is unrealistic in practice. However, we show this result just for indicating the cross-over point; csrMM performs worse than cuBlas from the density of 1%. In particular, spMV-E is the worst one except for the density of 0.1%. spMV-E has the overhead of checking whether an element of $X[i][]$ matches with some element of $Y[][i]$ (i.e., $Chk(\cdot)$). The overhead becomes larger as the number of non-zero elements increases. However, we note that real-world social networks do not have a chance to have such a high density as seen in Table 1.

5.4.2 *Synthetic datasets L1*

Figure 10(b) shows the execution time obtained by changing the density on $L1$. The x-axis indicates the density of matrices and the y-axis does the execution time in *log scale*. Similar to the result on $S1$, the execution time of all the methods except for cuBlas increases with the increase of density. lbGEMM is shown to outperform all other methods significantly. The performance of csrGEMM becomes worse due to the poor load balancing over threads and/or thread blocks. We observe the execution time of csrMM increases slightly with changing the density. spMV-E is the worst one in this experiment. It spends more execution time than other methods. So, we only show a part of the result of spMV-E.

5.4.3 *Synthetic datasets L2*

Figure 10(c) shows the execution time with different numbers of nodes on $L2$. The x-axis represents the number of nodes and the y-axis does the execution time in *log scale*. The execution time of all the methods increases as the number of nodes gets larger. We see that lbGEMM consistently outperforms all other methods. We know that the performance of spMV-E is greatly affected by the number of nodes as well as the density.

Summary: Through the experiments with synthetic datasets, we observe lbGEMM, significantly outperforms other methods (by up to 1,400 times compared with csrGEMM, the second best one) in situations where the datasets have low density and consist of a large number of nodes, indicating with the characteristics of real-world social networks. Therefore, we could expect lbGEMM outperforms others in real-world datasets. We also observe that the performance of csrGEMM becomes worse in datasets following the power-law due to its poor load balancing; spMV-E is significantly influenced by both the density and the number of nodes; csrMM tends to be more influenced by the number of nodes than the density; cuBlas is only influenced by the number of nodes.

5.5 SimRank: A Case Study

SimRank [2] is a well-known algorithm for link-based similarity computations. The SimRank computation consists of multiplications of three matrices and one addition of two matrices as shown in Eq.(5). The multiplications of three matrices can be subdivided into two separate steps (each of which involves a multiplication of two matrices) as in Eq.(6), where S^k denotes the similarity matrix obtained for the kth iteration, T does the matrix for temporary storage, W does the adjacency matrix, I does the identity matrix, and c represents a damping factor. The result of the SimRank computation can be obtained by performing Eq.(6) iteratively until it faces an equilibrium state.

$$S^k = cW^t S^{k-1} W + (1-c)I \tag{5}$$

$$\begin{cases} (1)\ \ T = cW^t \times S^{k-1} \\ (2)\ \ S^k = T \times W + (1-c)I \end{cases} \tag{6}$$

As a case study, we evaluate the performance of lbGEMM in comparison with csrGEMM (best among the existing ones) by applying them into the SimRank computation on the DBLP dataset. We tried to apply spMV-E, csrMM, and cuBlas as well, but failed to obtain their results because they spent a huge amount of time in computations. We observed that lbGEMM outperforms csrGEMM by about 970 times (lbGEMM: 8.8 seconds and csrGEMM: 8,626.2 seconds) in this experiment. This result indicates that lbGEMM

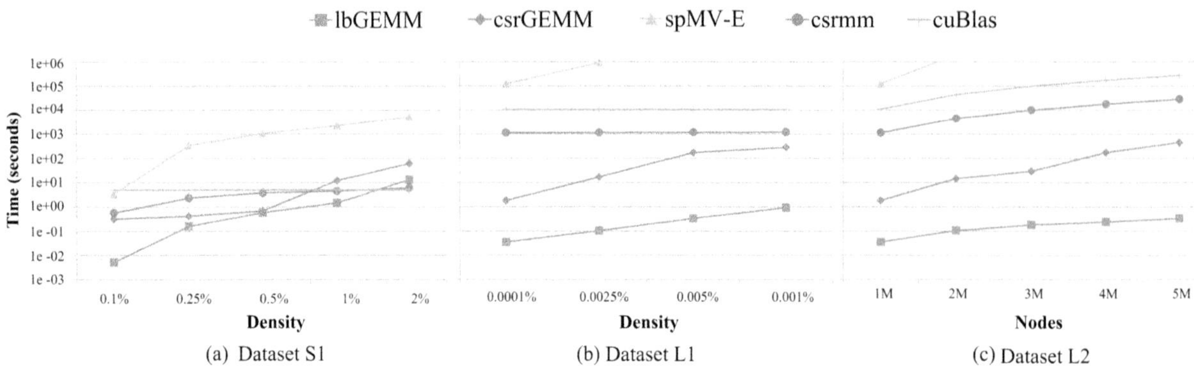

Figure 10: Performance comparisons with datasets.

is quite beneficial in real-world applications involved with matrix multiplication.

6. CONCLUSIONS

This paper proposed an efficient method for sparse matrix multiplications on GPU that is mainly targeted for analyzing large social networks.

We observed that real-world social networks usually have the characteristics of a very low density (e.g., 0.001%) following the power-law degree distribution. For such social networks, the existing methods based on the inner product or row-row product could degrade the performance due to poor load balancing in either the thread or SM levels.

Our lbGEMM performs sparse matrix multiplication based on the outer product scheme. It distributes the amount of workload evenly among threads. In order to fully utilize the ideal computing power of GPU, we need to balance the amount of workload over SMs. Towards this goal, we proposed a strategy based on a greedy algorithm by using the WLT data structure. In lbGEMM, while some SMs execute thread blocks having a large amount of workload, other SMs execute the rest of number of (relatively small) thread blocks. Thus, lbGEMM could make the last thread blocks completed at similar times, and so, could achieve good load balancing of computations in the SM level.

Finally, through extensive experiments using both synthetic and real-world datasets, we showed that lbGEMM dramatically outperforms existing methods based on GPU by up to three orders-of-magnitude. In addition, we evaluated the performance of lbGEMM in a real-world application, SimRank, as a case study and showed lbGEMM performs 970 times better than csrGEMM (the best one in existing ones). We believe that our method could be used as a very useful building block for developing a variety of algorithms to analyze a large real-world social networks.

7. ACKNOWLEDGMENTS

This work was supported by (1) Semiconductor Industry Collaborative Project between Hanyang University and Samsung Electronics Co. Ltd., (2) the National Research Foundation of Korea (NRF) grant funded by the Korea government (MSIP) (No. NRF-2014R1A2A1A10054151).

8. REFERENCES

[1] D. Bae, S. Hwang, and S. Kim, "Constructing Seminal Paper Genealogy," In *Proc. ACM Int'l Conf. on Information and Knowledge Management*, ACM CIKM, pp. 2101-2104, 2011.

[2] G. He et al., "Parallel SimRank Computation on Large Graphs with Iterative Aggregation," In *Proc. ACM Int'l Conf. on Knowledge Discovery and Data Mining*, ACM SIGKDD, pp. 543-552, 2010.

[3] Y. Cai et al., "Efficient algorithm for computing link-based similarity in real world networks," In *Proc. IEEE Int'l Conf. on Data Mining*, ICDM, pp. 734-739, 2009.

[4] Y. Dong et al., "Link Prediction and Recommendation across Heterogeneous Social Networks," In *Proc. IEEE Int'l Conf. on Data Mining*, ICDM, pp. 181-190, 2012.

[5] Koren et al., "Matrix Factorization Techniques for Recommender Systems," *Computer*, Vol. 42, No. 8, pp. 30-37, 2009.

[6] U. Kang et al., "PEGASUS: A Peta-Scale Graph Mining System Implementation and Observations," In *Proc. IEEE Int'l Conf. on Data Mining*, ICDM, p.229-238, 2009.

[7] X. Yang, S. Parthasarathy, and P. Sadayappan, "Fast Sparse Matrix-Vector Multiplication on GPUs: Implications for Graph Mining," *VLDB Endowment*, Vol. 4, No. 4, pp. 231-242, 2011.

[8] NVIDIA CUPARSE and CUBLAS libraries, https://developer.nvidia.com/gpu-accelerated-libraries

[9] csrGEMM library, http://on-demand.gputechconf.com/gtc/2012/presentations/S0285-GTC2012-Sparse-Matrix-Multiplication.pdf

[10] D. Kirk and W. Hwu, Programming Massively Parallel Processors, Morgan Kaufmann, 2010.

[11] Stanford Large Network Dataset Collection, http://snap.stanford.edu/data/

[12] J. Leskovec, J. Kleinberg, and C. Faloutsos, "Graph Evolution: Densification and Shrinking Diameters," *ACM Transactions on Knowledge Discovery from Data (TKDD)*, Vol. 1, No. 1, pp. 1-41, 2007.

[13] GTX Titan Black Specification, http://www.geforce.com/hardware/desktop-gpus/geforce-gtx-titan-black/specifications

[14] S. Ryoo et al., "Optimization Principles and Application Performance Evaluation of a Multithreaded GPU using CUDA," In *Proc. ACM Int'l Symp. on Principles and Practice of Parallel Programming*, ACM SIGPLAN, pp. 73-82, 2008.

[15] V. Volkov and J. Demmel, "Benchmarking GPUs to Tune Dense Linear Algebra," In *Proc. Int'l Conf. on Supercomputing*, SC, pp. 1-11, 2008.

[16] S. Ryoo et al., "Program Optimization Space Pruning for a Multithreaded GPU," In *Proc. Int'l Symp. on Code Generation and Optimization*, CGO, pp. 195-204, 2008.

[17] N. Bell and M. Garland, Efficient Sparse Matrix-Vector Multiplication on CUDA, NVIDIA Technical Report NVR-2008-2004, NVIDIA Corporation, 2008.

[18] J. W. Choi, et al., "Model-Driven Autotuning of Sparse Matrix-Vector Multiply on GPUs," In *Proc. ACM SIGPLAN Symp. on Principles and Practice of Parallel Programming*, PPoPP, pp. 115-126, 2010.

[19] Linear Algebra (4th Edition), S. Lipcshutz, M. Lipson, Schaum's Outlines, McGraw Hill (USA), 2009.

[20] O. Ibarra and C. Kim, "Fast Approximation Algorithms for the Knapsack and Sum of Subset Problems", *Journal of the ACM*, Vol. 22, No. 4, pp. 463-468, 1975.

The Role Of Citation Context In Predicting Long-Term Citation Profiles: An Experimental Study Based On A Massive Bibliographic Text Dataset

Mayank Singh, Vikas Patidar, Suhansanu Kumar, Tanmoy Chakraborty,
Animesh Mukherjee, Pawan Goyal
Department of Computer Science and Engineering
Indian Institute of Technology, Kharagpur, WB, India
mayank.singh@cse.iitkgp.ernet.in,vikaspatidar859@gmail.com
{suhansanu.kumar,its_tanmoy,animeshm,pawang}@cse.iitkgp.ernet.in

ABSTRACT

The impact and significance of a scientific publication is measured mostly by the number of citations it accumulates over the years. Early prediction of the citation profile of research articles is a significant as well as challenging problem. In this paper, we argue that features gathered from the **citation contexts** of the research papers can be very relevant for citation prediction. Analyzing a massive dataset of nearly 1.5 million computer science articles and more than 26 million citation contexts, we show that average **countX** (number of times a paper is cited within the same article) and average **citeWords** (number of words within the citation context) discriminate between various citation ranges as well as citation categories. We use these features in a stratified learning framework for future citation prediction. Experimental results show that the proposed model significantly outperforms the existing citation prediction models by a margin of 8-10% on an average under various experimental settings. Specifically, the features derived from the citation context help in predicting long-term citation behavior.

Categories and Subject Descriptors

H.2.8 [**Database Application**]: Data mining

Keywords

Long-Term Impact; Citation Prediction; Citation Context; Stratified Learning

1. INTRODUCTION

Citation count of a publication is among the most commonly accepted metric by the research community for evaluating the impact and quality of a research article. Citation count refers to the number of citations received by an article within a specified time-period [2]. Highly-cited works remain as one of the most important criteria for various organization (e.g. companies, universities and governments) to identify the best talents, especially at their initial stages.

Permission to make digital or hard copies of all or part of this work for personal or classroom use is granted without fee provided that copies are not made or distributed for profit or commercial advantage and that copies bear this notice and the full citation on the first page. Copyrights for components of this work owned by others than ACM must be honored. Abstracting with credit is permitted. To copy otherwise, or republish, to post on servers or to redistribute to lists, requires prior specific permission and/or a fee. Request permissions from Permissions@acm.org.
CIKM'15, October 19–23, 2015, Melbourne, VIC, Australia.
© 2015 ACM. ISBN 978-1-4503-3794-6/15/10 ...$15.00.
DOI: http://dx.doi.org/10.1145/2806416.2806566.

An early estimate would help in identification of promising articles that could accelerate research and dissemination of new knowledge. This has motivated the interest in the field of future citation prediction [17, 19].

Prediction of future citation counts, however, is difficult because of the nature and dynamics of citations [8, 10]. The citation ranges for the papers published by the same authors or the same venues show a lot of variation. The same can be said about the field of the papers as well. A very recent study [7] has shown that all the scientific papers do not follow the same trajectory and found 6 different citation patterns.

The existing works have used various venue and author centric features, along with the citation information from the initial years for the task of citation prediction. In this paper, we argue that the features extracted from the citation contexts can be extremely helpful for the future prediction. Citation context refers to textual descriptions of a given scientific paper found in other papers in the document collection which cites it [1]. A citation context is, in principle, a set of sentences where a paper is referred to. The intuition behind using the citation context features comes from the hypothesis that citation contexts reflect the opinion of the scientific community about the particular work. We show that even using some very simplistic features extracted from the citation context can boost the performance of a citation prediction system significantly.

Towards this objective, we use a massive dataset consisting of more than 26 million citation contexts for nearly 1.5 million research papers in the computer science domain, crawled from Microsoft Academic Search (MAS)[1]. We extract two features from the citation contexts – average countX (number of times a paper is cited within the same article, averaged over all the citing papers) and average citeWords (number of words within the citation context, averaged over all the citing papers). We show that these features are quite discriminative and exhibit different trends not only for different citation ranges but also for the citation categories identified in [7]. We then append these features along with various other features in an earlier framework based on *stratified learning* [6]. Experimental results show that addition of these two features gives an R^2-correlation of 0.84, 0.81 and 0.78 towards predicting the citation count at 5, 7 and 9 years after publication, improving the prediction accuracy by 8-10% on an average over the nearest baseline. Specifically, these features help in predicting the long term citation behavior of the research papers. We would like to stress here that this study brings forth the tremendous potential of

[1]http://academic.research.microsoft.com/

the content of a scientific article in predicting future citation counts; the huge success of only two very simple content related features proposed here makes the authors believe that deeper analysis of the content can lead to further significant improvements in the related areas of research.

The rest of the paper has been organized as follows. We discuss the related previous works in section 2. Section 3 describes the citation context dataset used for this experimental study. The two citation context features utilized for our study have been described in section 4. The citation prediction model has been described in section 5. The experiments to evaluate our system under different settings have been reported in section 6 along with a detailed comparison and feature analysis. Finally, conclusions and future works have been presented in section 7.

2. RELATED WORK

In recent years, several researchers have investigated the problem of future citation count prediction [17, 19, 20, 21]. Most of the past works have proposed a set of features and used a supervised learning model to predict the citation count at a later time point. Many works use only the information available at the time of publication to predict future citation count, while other works also use information available from the initial years after publication. For instance, Fu and Aliferis [9] predict citation count with the information available at the time of publication. They incorporate features like number of authors, number of articles for the first author, number of citations for the first author, number of affiliations, the journal impact factor, title, abstract, MeSH terms[2] etc. Support Vector Machines (SVM) have been used to predict citation count after 10 years of publication. Similarly, Livne et al. [14] use features like authors, author institutions, venue and references to train a Support vector regression (SVR). They observe that venue and the references are the most significant features for citation count prediction.

Callaham et al. [16] use decision trees to predict citation counts of 204 publications from emergency medicine specialty meeting. They use features like impact factor of journal, research design, number of subjects, rated subjectively for scientific quality, newsworthiness etc. Kulkarni et al. [11] use linear regression and achieve an R^2 of 0.2 for the prediction of citation count for five year ahead window using 328 medical articles. They use features like journal name, month of publication, study design, clinical category of the article etc.

Brody et al. [3] use information after the publication to forecast citation count. Download data within the first 6 months after publication is used as a predictive feature. Similarly, Lokker et al. [15] use features related to the article and journal, like number of authors, pages, references etc. for the prediction task. Castillo et al. [5] use the number of citations, authors' reputation and the source of paper citations as the predictive features.

Liangyue et al. [13] propose a joint predictive model to forecast the long-term scientific impact problem, formulated as a regularized optimization problem. Their work addresses four key algorithmic challenges, including the scholarly feature design, the non-linearity, the domain-heterogeneity and dynamics. Further, they propose a fast online update algorithm to adapt joint predictive model efficiently over time. They observe that citation history is a strong indicator of long-term impact and using additional contextual or content features brings little marginal benefits in terms of prediction performance. An analysis on 463,348 papers from Physical Review (PR) corpus suggests high heterogeneity in the citation histories [18]. They present three fundamental mechanisms that drive citation history, namely preferential attachment, aging and novelty, and importance of a discovery (fitness). Combining these mechanisms allows to collapse the citation histories of papers from different journals and disciplines into a single curve, indicating that all papers tend to follow a similar universal temporal pattern.

Yan et al. present two similar works on citation prediction problem [19, 20]. They have introduced features covering venue prestige, content novelty and diversity, and authors' influence and activity. Pobiedina and Ichise [17] introduce a new feature GERscore (Graph Evolution Rule score), based on frequent graph pattern mining techniques, for citation prediction. Yu et al. [21] propose a new data structure namely discriminative term buckets to capture both document similarity and potential citation relation. They also propose metapath based feature space to interpret structural information in citation prediction. Along with these novel ideas, they present an extensive analysis on differences between citation prediction problem and the related work, e.g., traditional link prediction solution.

One of the previous works [6] suggests that *stratified learning approach* leads to good prediction accuracy. They observe that there exist six different patterns of citation profiles of research papers based on the number and position of peaks in the citation profile. Further, a two-stage prediction model was proposed, which maps a query paper into one of the six categories in the first stage, and then in the second stage, a regression module is run only on the subpopulation corresponding to that category to predict the future citation count of the query paper. They achieve a superior performance just by using the features at the time of publication. Motivated by this study, we also use a stratified learning framework for citation prediction. However, since the prime objective of this work is to show the utility of citation context features which are available only after publication, we utilize the citation context features derived from the first two years after publication along with the publication time features to improve the prediction accuracy.

To the best of our knowledge, this is the first work that attempts to use citation context based features in the citation prediction problem. We use a massive dataset of more than 26 million citation contexts from computer science research articles towards this goal. The next section describes the dataset used in this study.

3. DATASET

In this paper, we use two computer science datasets, both crawled from Microsoft Academic Search (MAS)[3]. First dataset (bibliographic dataset) consists of bibliographic information of papers, the title of the paper, a unique index for the paper, its author(s), the affiliation of the author(s), the year of publication, the publication venue, references, citation contexts, the related field(s)[4] of the paper, the abstract and the keywords of the papers [6]. Second dataset (citation context dataset) consists of more than 26 million citation contexts pre-processed and annotated with cited and citing paper information.

Table 1 details various statistics for both the datasets.

Definition I: We will say that paper P *cites* paper C, if paper P refers to paper C in the text. P is termed as **citing paper** while C is termed as **cited paper**. P can refer to C at many places in the text. In our present work, we only consider the sentence as citation context where the reference to the paper is explicitly present.

[2]http://www.nlm.nih.gov/mesh/

[3]http://academic.research.microsoft.com

[4]Note that the different sub-branches like Algorithms, AI, Operating Systems etc. constitute different "fields" of computer science domain.

For an example, Chakraborty et al. [6] cites Yan et al. [19] as *Recently, Yan et al. conduct two similar experiments [**25**, 26], to study features covering venue prestige, content novelty and diversity and authors' influence and activity. They also account for the temporal dynamics by taking a recent version of each feature calculated on a limited time window. To the best of our knowledge, this is the latest and the most accurate future citation count prediction model, and therefore serves as the baseline system in this paper. We conduct an extended examination of all these factors related to citation counts, with many new features added.*

Although, the above context consists of four sentences, we only consider the first sentence as the citation context since it explicitly refers to Yan et al. [19].

Definition II: countX for a cited paper C with respect to a citing paper P is defined as the number of citation contexts, when a paper P cites paper C. Citation context count for a paper C denotes the sum of countX from all the citations for C.

Table 1: General information about the datasets

Dataset I	Year range	1960-2010
	Number of computer science fields	21
	Number of publications	1,359,338
	Number of authors	138,923
	Avg. number of papers per author	5.43
	Avg. number of authors per paper	2.40
Dataset II	Number of citation contexts	26,197,440
	Avg. number of citation contexts per paper	19.27
	Avg. number of words per citation context	26
	Number of papers having at least one citation context	1,279,104

Each paper has a specific citation context count. Figure 1 shows the distribution of papers having specific citation context count in our dataset. Long tail depicts that many papers have less number of citation context count while a small number of papers have high citation context count.

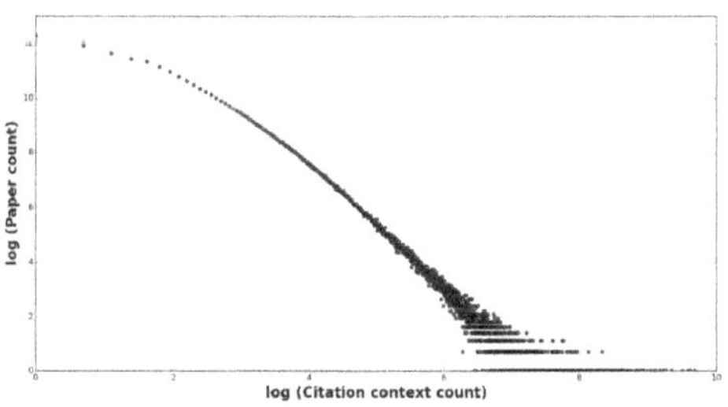

Figure 1: Distribution of citation context count in our dataset

Definition III: citeWords for a cited paper C with respect to a citing paper P is defined as the number of words in the citation context, when a paper P cites paper C. If multiple papers are cited within the same citation context, the number of words are equally divided among all the cited papers. If a paper is cited multiple times within the same paper, citeWords is computed by summing over the words in all the citation contexts.

In the next section, we discuss in detail how the average values of countX and citeWords behave for papers with various citation ranges.

4. AVERAGE COUNTX AND CITEWORDS

After identifying countX and citeWords as two features from the citation contexts, we study in detail as to whether these features are discriminative with respect to the number of citations. To normalize with respect to various ranges of citations, we only used the average values of countX and citeWords for a publication in each year starting from its publication.

To give a working example as to how these features are computed, Table 2 presents citation contexts for paper *P* titled as "*On Relaxed Dynamic Programming in Switching Systems*", published in 2005. The first column gives the citer_ids, which refer to MAS identifier for the papers citing paper *P*. Publication year of the citing paper is shown in column 2. Column 3 gives the exact citation context(s) in the citing paper for paper *P*. Below, we describe as to how the average countX and average citeWords features are computed for *P* over the years.

4.1 Average countX

For a citation edge from paper Q to paper P (i.e., Q citing P), countX denotes the number of times paper P is cited in paper Q. A high value of countX implies that paper P is cited multiple times by paper Q and thus, P might be quite relevant for paper Q. Possibly, Q has cited P for its different aspects. Our hypothesis is that if we consider all the papers citing paper P and find the average value of countX for P, it may serve as a very strong feature to measure the importance of P.

Let us assume that the papers $Q_1, Q_2, \ldots, Q_n$ are citing paper P for $N_1, N_2, \ldots, N_n$ times respectively in the tth year after publication of P. We define the average countX metric for paper P for the tth year as

$$average\ countX(P,t) = \frac{\sum_{j=1}^{n} N_j}{n} \quad (1)$$

Using the example in Table 2, average countX value for paper *P* for the first year after publication (year 2006) can be calculated as: $average\ countX(P,1) = \frac{2+1}{2} = 1.5$. This is because there are two citing papers in year 2006, one of which cites P twice within the same paper while the other cites it only once.

4.2 Average citeWords

For a citation edge from paper Q to paper P, citeWords denotes the number of words in the citation context(s), where P has been referred to. Since more than one paper might be cited within the same citation context, number of words are divided among all the cited papers. Similar to countX, a high value of citeWords implies that paper P has been discussed in more details by paper Q and therefore, paper P might be relevant for paper Q. Dividing by the number of papers cited within the citation context takes care of the fact that the words in citation contexts have been used to describe multiple papers. Similar to countX, our hypothesis is that finding the average number of words that other papers use to describe P could be indicative of the importance of paper P.

Let us assume that paper P is cited by another paper Q_i in m different citation contexts, $S_1, \ldots, S_m$. For this citation edge, citeWords is computed as

$$citeWords(P,Q_i) = \sum_{i=1}^{m} AW(S_i,P,Q_i) \quad (2)$$

where $AW(S_i,P,Q_i)$ denotes the average number of words used in sentence S_i to describe P. In general, if $k \geq 1$ papers are cited within the sentence S_i, the average words for each of these k papers (including P) is given by:

$$AW(S,P,Q_i) = \frac{Len(S)}{k} \quad (3)$$

where $Len(S)$ denotes the length of a sentence S and is simply computed by counting the number of words appearing in it. Now, assume that the papers $Q_1, Q_2, \ldots, Q_n$ are citing paper P in the tth year after publication of P. We define the average citeWords metric for paper P for the tth year as:

$$Average\ citeWords(P,t) = \frac{\sum_{j=1}^{n} citeWords(P, Q_i)}{n} \quad (4)$$

Using Table 2, average citeWords value for paper *P* for the third year after publication (year 2008) can be calculated as:

$(citeWords(P, 6413388) + citeWords(P, 5052733))/2$

To compute $citeWords(P, 5052733)$, we see that paper 5052733 cites P in one citation context when a total of two papers are cited. Thus

$citeWords(P, 5052733) = \frac{11}{2} = 5.5$, where 11 is the length of the citation context.

Similarly, paper 6413388 cites paper P twice but in both the citation contexts, two papers are cited. Therefore,

$$citeWords(P, 6413388) = \frac{25}{2} + \frac{16}{2} = 20.5$$

Thus, $Average\ citeWords(P, 3) = \frac{20.5+5.5}{2} = 13$.

4.3 Correlation between citation counts and citation content features over the years

We investigate whether the average countX and average citeWords values over the years are correlated with the number of citations a paper receives. We reiterate that both average countX and average citeWords are normalized with respect to the number of citations received by the paper. We divide the set of papers in our dataset into 6 buckets based on the following criterion on the number of citations.

Bucket 1: Top 0.1% papers – citations 389-7859

Bucket 2: Top 0.1 - 1% papers – citations 95-389

Bucket 3: Top 1 - 5% papers – citations 29-95

Bucket 4: Top 5 - 10% papers – citations 16-29

Bucket 5: Top 10 - 25% papers – citations 6-16

Bucket 6: Rest of the papers – citations 0-6

For each of the Citation buckets, we plot the temporal profile for the average countX values, averaged for all the papers within that bucket, in Figure 2. The $X-$axis denotes the year after publication for the paper, ranging from 0 (same year as publication) to 10 (10th year after publication). While averaging for a citation bucket for a particular year, we consider only those papers which have non-zero citations in that year. Minimum value of countX can be 1 for any citation edge. Interestingly, as per our hypothesis, various citation ranges show differences in terms of the average countX values. Some important observations from Figure 2 are:

1. There is an increase in value of countX in initial years irrespective of the citation bucket, and it further decreases continuously over the years. A slight increase is observed for the 10th year after publication.

2. Highly cited papers are cited more number of times in a single paper.

We clearly see a correlation between the number of citations and the average countX profiles of the papers. Further, we investigate whether the countX values can discriminate between the 6 citation categories identified in [7]. Accordingly, we divided the set of papers into 6 categories mentioned in [7]. For readability, the six categories are described below:

(i) PeakInit: Papers whose citation count peaks within 5 years of publication followed by an exponential decay.

(ii) PeakMul: Papers having multiple peaks in different time periods of the citation history.

(iii) PeakLate: Papers having very few citations at the beginning and then a single peak after at least 5 years of the publication followed by an exponential decay in citation count.

(iv) MonDec: Papers whose citation count peaks in the immediate next year of the publication followed by a monotonic decrease in the number of citations.

(v) MonIncr: Papers having a monotonic increase in the number of citations from the very beginning of the year of publication till the date of observation.

(vi) Oth: Papers not belonging to any of the above mentioned categories belong to this category.

Figure 3 presents the temporal profile of average countX values for each of these 6 categories. Again, we can see that the average countX values are the highest for the $MonIncr$ and $PeakLate$ categories, which have been identified as having the categories corresponding to high number of citations in [7]. Similarly, average countX values are the lowest for the $MonDec$ and $Others$, which have been identified as the categories corresponding to the low number of citations (see [7] for details).

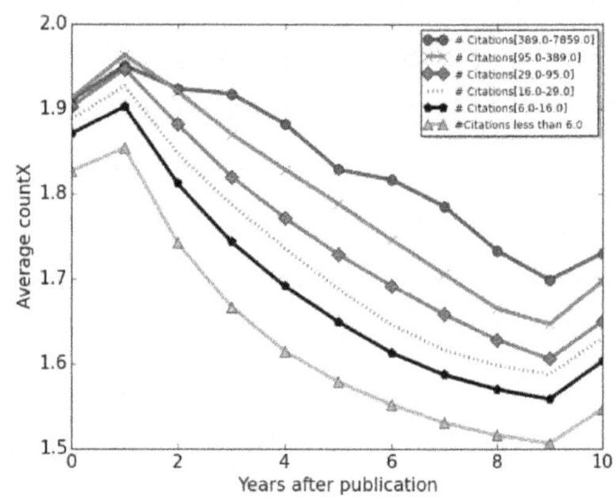

Figure 2: Average countX: temporal profiles for six citation buckets over the publication age

We now plot the temporal profile for the average citeWords values for the six citation buckets in Figure 4. Similar to average countX, while averaging for a citation bucket for a particular year, we consider only those papers which have a non-zero citation in that year. Average citeWords also shows a very similar trend as that seen with the average countX values, an initial increase and then a decreasing trend over the years. Interestingly, differences are observed between various citation ranges with the papers having the highest citations also earning a high number of average citeWords over the years.

We further use six citation categories to plot the temporal profiles in Figure 5. The trends are again very similar to those observed for the case of average countX values, with the MonIncr and PeakLate categories having a higher value of average citeWords than the other categories and MonDec category having the lowest values.

Table 2: Example citation contexts for paper (*P*) titled as *On Relaxed Dynamic Programming in Switching Systems*, published in 2005. Citer_id represents MAS identifier of the paper citing paper *P*. Publication year represents year of publication of citing paper. Finally, Context column contains the citing sentence. There are several instances where a paper is cited more than once in a citing paper. Also, a citing sentence might cite more than one paper. Citations are sorted in the descending order of the year of publication of citing paper. Bold face text represents cited paper reference.

citer_id	Publication year	Context
5330841	2010	Our approach relies on the following result from relaxed dynamic programming [**12**, 15], which is a straightforward generalization of proposition [5, Proposition 2.4], cf. [7] for a proof
6899965	2009	In [18, **19**] a relaxed dynamic programming procedure is proposed
		The existence of a solution is assumed in [18,**19**], which is different from the objective in this paper; to obtain a sub-optimal solution only when the minimum does not exist
5179891	2009	Recently, this has been studied by Lincoln and Rantzer in [**11**,17]
5977376	2009	The paper [**6**] (see also [5]) uses controllability conditions and techniques from relaxed dynamic programming [13, 18] in order to compute explicit estimates for the degree of suboptimality, which in particular lead to bounds on the stabilizing optimization horizon N which are, however, in general not optimal
6006644	2009	Our approach relies on results on relaxed dynamic programming [9], [**13**] already used in an MPC context in [7] which we adapt to our variable control horizon setting
6413388	2008	Inequalities of such type have been used frequently in the optimal control literature, however, a systematic study seems to have performed only recently in [**14**, 18]
		The approach we take in this paper relies on recently developed results on relaxed dynamic programming [**14**, 18]
5052733	2008	These general algorithms are also used to study switched systems in [**11**], [12]
5433268	2007	Some are based on a newly elaborated condition of optimality see e.g., [1], [**2**],[3], others are more related to semi-classical approaches see e.g., [4], [5], [6], [7]
4971068	2007	A novel approach to overcome some of the difficulties mentioned above was recently proposed in [**4**], [5], [3], see also [14] for examples from switching systems
12659162	2006	For further details on the theoretical foundations, the reader is referred to [**13**]]
		Further discussion of the implicit algorithm is given in [**13**]
50488928	2006	In a recent work, it is shown that the optimal control problem can be reformulated as an approximate linear-quadratic problem, whose complexity grows only polynomially [**10**]
2992574	2005	Konda and Tsitsiklis [KoT03], Marbach and Tsitsiklis [MaT01], **Rantzer [Ran05]**,
12894773	2005	In [16], This led some to develop relaxed DP techniques, e.g. (**Rantzer, 2005**)

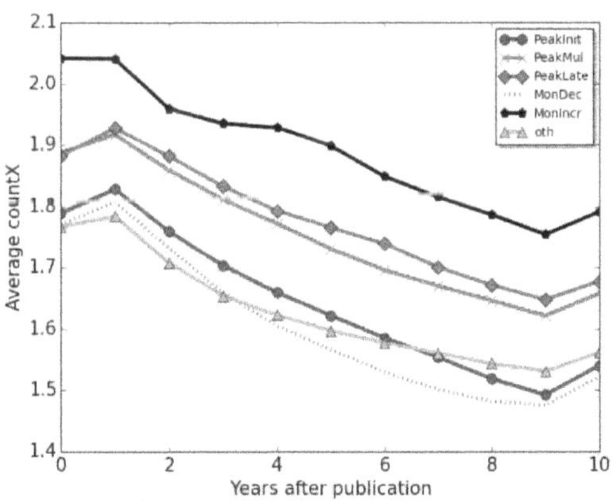

Figure 3: Average countX: temporal profiles for the six citation categories [7] over the publication age

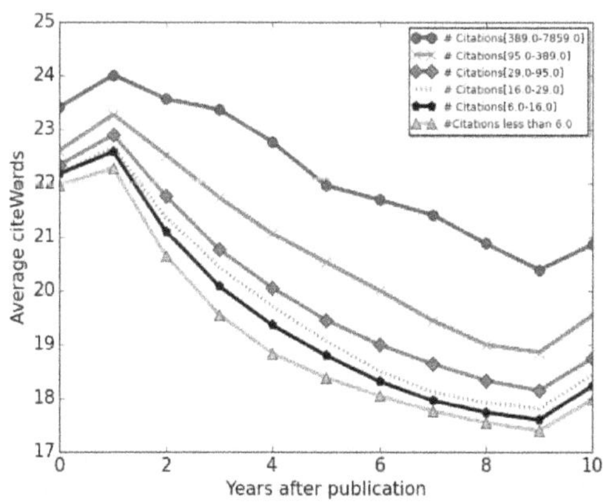

Figure 4: Average citeWords: temporal profiles for the six citation buckets over the first 10 years of publication age

4.4 Correlation between citation counts and citation context features for the initial years

To motivate the importance of average countX and citeWords as features for future citation prediction, Table 3 shows some specific examples of papers having the same citation count in the first two years after publication but different average countX and citeWords values. What we observe is that in both the cases, among the papers having the same citation count, the paper having a high countX (and citeWords) value in the initial two years receives a much higher citation count in the future. Thus, the average countX feature from the initial years of publication can serve as an important feature towards predicting future citations.

Table 3: Example paper-pairs having a similar citation count in the initial 2 years of publication but different countX values.

Paper ID	Initial citation count	Initial Avg. countX	Initial Avg. citeWords	Final Citation count
349111	4	1.75	41.75	140
25	4	1	10.58	47
1911	7	3.29	47.9	155
349954	7	1.42	16.35	38

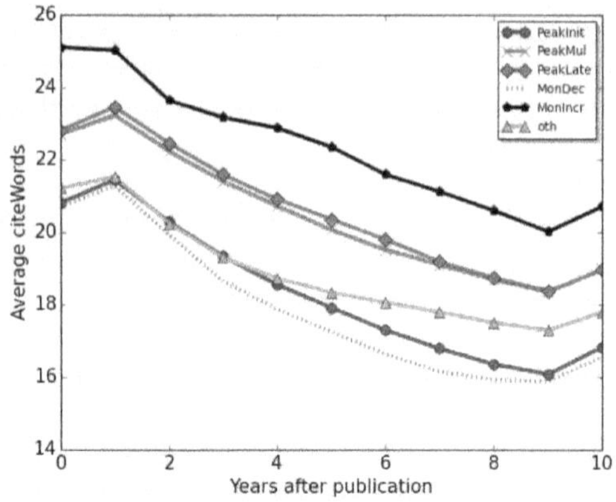

Figure 5: Average citeWords: temporal profiles for the six citation categories [7] over the first 10 years of publication age

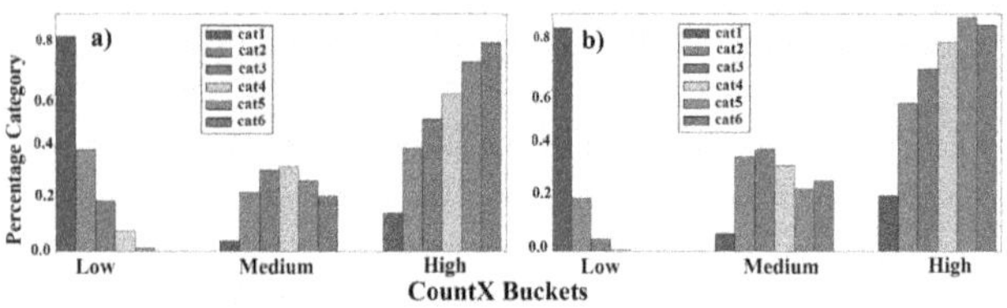

Figure 6: Correlating citation count and countX buckets. (a) Correlation at 5 years after publication; (b) Correlation at 9 years after publication

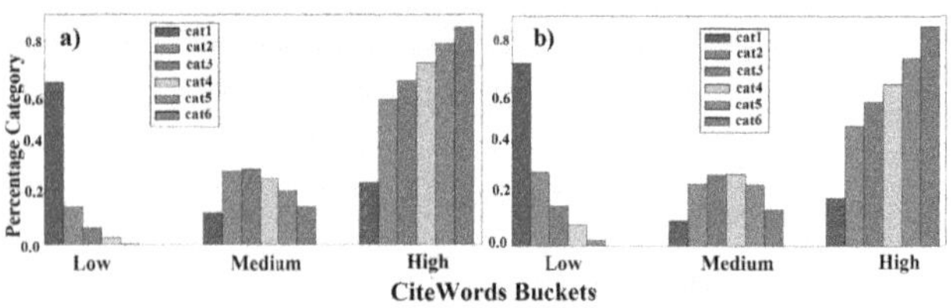

Figure 7: Correlating citation count and citeWords buckets. (a) Correlation at 5 years after publication; (b) Correlation at 9 years after publication

We further study whether the average countX and average citeWords values from the initial two years after publication can serve as discriminating features to predict citations at a later point of time. We, therefore, divide all the papers in 3 ranges as per the average countX values ($\{1\}$, $(1, 1.5]$ and $(1.5, -)$) and as per the average citeWords ($(0, 10.5]$, $(10.5, 16.5]$ and $(16.5, -)$ in the initial two years of publication. We call these ranges as low, medium and high respectively. We now take citation counts of the papers for the time points, corresponding to 5 and 9 years after publication. For each such time point, we create 6 different citation buckets (top 0.1% etc.) and plot the distribution of the papers falling into these 6 citation buckets on various countX and citeWords ranges. For example, 5 years after publication, 75% of the papers in the lowest citation category have an average countX value=1 (see Figure 6(a)). On the other hand, more than 75% of the papers in the top two categories (top 0.1% and top 0.1-1%) have a countX value ≥ 1.5. The trend becomes much more prominent for 9 years after publication (Figure 6(b)), with the probability of a paper having countX ≥ 1.5 increasing with increasing citation counts.

Very similar trends are observed for the average citeWords as well (see Figure 7). From these figures as well as examples in Table 3, it is clear that information from average countX and average citeWords in the initial years of publication acts as a discriminating factor for the future citation counts, such that most of the highly cited papers have high values of average countX and citeWords in the initial years, which is not true for the low-cited papers.

Motivated by these examples, we now use these citation context features for the task of future citation prediction. The model is described in the next section.

5. CITATION PREDICTION MODEL

We extend the two-stage stratified learning framework proposed in [6] with the addition of three features. In the first stage, a query paper is classified into one of the citation profile category using Support Vector Machine (SVM) learning model. Further, for each category, a Support Vector Regression (SVR) model is learned for predicting citation counts. Thus, given a query paper, we first classify it into one of the six citation profile categories. Post classification, category based SVR is used to predict citation count. Our citation prediction model uses features at the time of publication, along with the citation information from the first 2 years after publication. Features from the time of publication are the same as reported in [6]. These features can be divided into three categories: features based on the paper content, features based on author information and features based on venue information. For the sake of completeness, we describe these features in brief below. For more details, the reader is requested to look into [6].

5.1 Features based on paper content

We used five paper-centric features as proposed in [6]. Last three among these are entropy based features.

(a) Team-size (Team): The number of authors in a paper.

(b) Reference count (RefCount): The number of references mentioned in the reference section of a paper.

(c) Reference diversity (RDI): RDI measures the diversity in the fields of the referred papers. A paper citing papers of various fields has a high value of RDI.

(d) Keyword diversity (KDI): Keyword diversity refers to diversity in the keywords mentioned in the paper.

(e) Topic diversity (Topic): Each paper is assigned a set of probable topics inferred from LDA. Topic diversity gives a diversity over these probable topics.

5.2 Features based on Author information

The author of a publication plays an important role in its popularity. The following four author-centric features were used for citation prediction.

(a) Author h-index (HIndex): H-index is a standard measure for author productivity and impact. This feature measures average h-index of the authors at the time of publication.

(b) Author productivity (ProAuth): Author productivity refers to the count of his publications. A more productive author will produce more. The feature is an average of the productivity of the all the co-authors of a paper.

(c) Author diversity (AuthDiv): Author diversity refers to the diversity in the research fields of author publications. A highly diverse author will publish in different domains. The feature is an average of all the authors taken together.

(d) Sociality of author (NOCA): This feature counts the number of co-authors in all the publications of each author present in the paper.

5.3 Features based on venue information

We also used certain features based on the prestige as well as the diversity of the venue, where the paper has been published. These features are described in detail below.

(a) Short term venue prestige (VenPresS): Short term venue prestige measures the average number of citations for the papers published in a venue during the two preceding years.

(b) Long term venue prestige (VenPresL): Long term venue prestige measures the average number of citations for the papers published in a venue so far.

(c) Venue diversity (VenDiv): This feature measures the diversity in the research fields of the papers published in a venue.

5.4 Features after the publication year

In addition to these features, we also utilize the two features derived from the citation context, the average countX and average citeWords for the first 2 years after publication, as well citation count received after the first 2 years of publication.

In the next section, we report the experiments using our citation prediction model.

6. EXPERIMENTS

We perform experiments using the stratified learning framework for citation prediction. We selected papers having at least 10 years of history and published in between 1970 - 2005. We divided this dataset into training and testing sets. For training, we consider papers published in between 1970 - 2000. For testing purpose, we took the range as 2001 - 2005. First of all, we learn a stage-I classification model using our training dataset. We also learn separate regression models for each citation category, for each time point, for which the citation count is to be predicted. Given a query paper, first the classification model is used to assign a citation category (stratum) to it (stage I). In stage II, a regression model trained on the assigned category is used for citation count prediction for the specified time periods. We use all the features described in section 5. We have used three different time points $\Delta t = 5, 7,$ and 9 for prediction.

We evaluate our model on two baselines. The first baseline [19] is similar to our model except that it does not include the classification stage. Thus, all the features are directly used in a regression model for citation prediction. We use Chakraborty et al. [6] as the second baseline. While the authors conducted experiments both with and without the initial year of publication information, we use the citation count of first two years for their method for a fair comparison. Thus, this baseline is very similar to our model with the only difference being that we use two citation context features identified in this paper, average countX and average citeWords, for the tth year after publication, with $t = 0, 1, 2$.

6.1 Evaluation metrics

We use the following three metrics for evaluating our results.

6.1.1 Coefficient of determination (R^2)

Coefficient of determination (R^2) [4] is a number that indicates how well data fit a statistical model of future outcome prediction. It measures the variability introduced by the statistical model. It is defined as the proportionate reduction in uncertainty, measured by Kullback-Leibler divergence, due to the inclusion of regressors. Let d be the document in test document set D_T, we calculate R^2 as:

$$R^2 = \frac{\sum_{d \epsilon D_T} (C_{T_{ccp}}(d) - C_T(D_T))^2}{\sum_{d \epsilon D_T} (C_T(d) - C_T(D_T))^2} \quad (5)$$

Here, $C_{T_{ccp}}(d)$ denotes the predicted citation count for document d. $C_T(D_T)$ denotes the mean of observed citation counts for documents in D_T. ($C_T(d)$ denotes actual citation count for document d. R^2 values ranges from 0 to 1. A larger value indicates better performance.

6.1.2 Pearson correlation coefficient (ρ)

Pearson correlation co-efficient (ρ) [12] measures the degree of linear dependence between two variables. It is defined as the covariance of the two variables divided by the product of their standard deviations.

$$\rho_{X,Y} = \frac{cov(X,Y)}{\sigma_X \sigma_Y} \quad (6)$$

$$cov(X,Y) = E[(X - \mu_X)(Y - \mu_Y)] \quad (7)$$

Here, cov(X,Y) denotes covariance between X and Y, σ_X and σ_Y denote standard deviation values for X and Y respectively. Similarly, μ_X and μ_Y denote mean values for variables X and Y respectively. E represents the expected value. ρ ranges from -1 to 1, where $\rho = 1$ corresponds to a total positive correlation, 0 corresponds to no correlation, and -1 corresponds to total negative correlation. A larger value indicates better performance.

6.1.3 Mean squared error (θ)

Mean square error (θ) measures the expected value of the squared error loss in estimation. It is a risk function corresponding to the expected value of the squared error loss. For n number of observations, we define mean squared error as:

$$\theta = \frac{\sum_{i=1}^{n} (\hat{Y_i} - Y_i)^2}{n} \quad (8)$$

Here, $\hat{Y}$ and Y denote the vectors of predicted and actual values respectively. A smaller value indicates better performance.

6.2 Comparisons with the baseline models

Next, we compare the performance of the two baselines with our model. We also present performance statistics for stage I (classification) and stage II (prediction). Along with performance analysis, we compare categories and analyze results.

Table 4 compares the performance of these baselines with our model. Columns 2-4 in Table 4 show the predictive performance for baseline I using three metrics, while columns 5-7 show the predictive performance of baseline II. Columns 8-10 show the performance of our model.

We observe that for all the three systems, performance decreases with the increase in time period for prediction, with the best performance achieved for $\Delta t = 5$. While baseline I performs the worst among the three models, the R^2 value of 0.56 obtained for $\Delta t = 5$ is in itself significantly better that some previous works. For example, Kulkarni et al. [11] achieved an R^2 value of 0.2 using 328 medical articles. Baseline II performs better than baseline I for all of the three time-periods. This performance improvement can be credited to the stratified learning approach used in baseline II, as was established in [6]. Our model performs better than both the baselines for all the three time-periods. While the improvements over the first baseline are almost over 50% in terms of R^2, improvement of the order of 8-10% are achieved over baseline II as well. Improvement in terms of θ are of the order of 20-25% over the baseline II. Since the only difference between baseline II and our model are the average countX and average citeWords features identified in this paper, this improvement can be credited to the use of initial year information from the citation context of the paper.

Table 4: Performance comparison between Baseline I, Baseline II, and our model. Three evaluation metrics - θ, R^2 and ρ are used. A low value of θ and high values of R^2 and ρ represent an efficient model. Prediction is made over three time periods - $\Delta t = 5$, $\Delta t = 7$ and $\Delta t = 9$.

	Baseline I			Baseline II			Our Model		
	R^2	ρ	θ	R^2	ρ	θ	R^2	ρ	θ
Δ t=5	0.56	0.59	14.56	0.78	0.76	10.45	**0.84**	**0.79**	**7.86**
Δ t=7	0.54	0.57	15.90	0.74	0.72	12.57	**0.81**	**0.75**	**9.70**
Δ t=9	0.51	0.54	17.22	0.73	0.68	14.89	**0.78**	**0.74**	**12.43**

6.3 Category-wise performance analysis

Since we use the six categories as strata, we further analyze the prediction results for each of these categories. Table 5 presents category-wise performance metrics (except the category *Oth*) values for the three time-periods. Figure 8 gives the scatter plots for each category for the prediction task for the three time periods. $X-$axis denotes the actual citation count, while the $Y-$axis denotes the predicted citation count.

From Table 5, we observe that for $\Delta t = 5$, the performance is the best for the *PeakLate* category on all the three metrics. Figure 8 also confirms this observation with most of the points densely accumulated around $x = y$ line. For $\Delta t = 7$, *PeakLate* performs the best on ρ, while *MonDec* and *MonIncr* perform well on R^2 and θ respectively. For $\Delta t = 9$, *MonIncr* performs the best among all the categories for all the three evaluation metrics. Overall, *PeakLate* and *MonIncr* categories perform the best. This is very crucial for the citation prediction model, as these categories correspond to the highly cited papers [6].

From Figure 8, we observe that for $\Delta t = 5$, all categories show roughly the same pattern. Majority of the papers lie below the line, which denotes that in the initial years after publication our model slightly under-estimates the citation counts. The only cases of over-estimation are for the *PeakMul* category, $\Delta t = 9$ (majority papers above the line) and for the *MonIncr* category for $\Delta t = 7$.

6.4 SVM classification analysis

The first stage SVM model classifies each paper into one of the six categories. Table 6 presents the confusion matrix of SVM classification. Each entry in the first column represents a ground truth category of the paper. Similarly, each entry in the first row represents predicted category. We observe that around 50% of *Oth* category paper are wrongly classified into *PeakMul*. While *MonDec* has the highest accuracy (0.989), more than 29% *PeakInit* are classified into *MonDec*, which in turn decreases the accuracy for *PeakInit* category. As our dataset is highly biased towards *Oth* category (highest % of papers), SVM overestimates *Oth* category in the classification. Classification inaccuracy in the first stage decreases prediction accuracy in the second stage, with the *Oth* category playing a significant role in lowering the precision.

6.5 Paperwise analysis

Table 7 presents one best representative paper from each of the five categories. For each paper, we calculate the absolute difference between actual citation count and predicted citation count for our model, baseline I and baseline II for three time periods. As observed from Table 7, our model is closest to the actual values in terms of citations at any time instance.

6.6 Feature Analysis

We now study as to how various features correlate with the actual citation counts. Accordingly, we divide our features into 6 different sets and compute Spearman's correlation for the three time-periods in Table 8. We can see from the table that the last three features, namely average countX, average citeWords and 2-year citations, show a much higher correlation than the other three feature sets. While the correlation for 2-year citation feature is slightly higher than average countX for $\Delta t = 5$, correlation is the highest for average countX for $\Delta t = 9$. Thus, average countX serves as the most important feature for predicting the long term citation behavior of the papers.

Table 8: Average Spearman's rank correlation of each feature category (column 1) with the actual citation count without categorization for Δ t=5,7 and 9 years after publication

Feature category	Δ t=5	Δ t=7	Δ t=9
Author centric	0.387	0.342	0.317
Venue centric	0.343	0.309	0.285
Paper centric	0.429	0.417	0.392
Average countX	0.569	0.543	0.521
Average citeWords	0.512	0.499	0.481
2 year citation	0.571	0.543	0.502

6.7 Comparison with past works

The experimental results clearly confirm that the proposed method for citation prediction outperforms the other baselines for various time-periods. Further, we wanted to put this work in perspective of the previous related works for this problem. Table 9 lists five other works and compares them for the size of the dataset used for the study, year-ranges of the test papers, method used by the papers, as well a time period for which the R^2 values have been reported. Our dataset size is comparable to the other datasets reported in the literature. Also, we achieve a better R^2 value on this massive dataset than the ones reported earlier in the literature. Our prediction time period ($\Delta t = 9$) is the maximum among all these works.

7. CONCLUSION AND FUTURE WORK

In this paper, we have used a massive dataset of citation contexts to show that the features extracted from the citation contexts of the papers, in the immediate years after publication, play a vital role for the task of future citation prediction. We introduced two new features, average countX and average citeWords, and feature analysis showed that these citation context features are highly correlated with the actual citation counts, specifically for the long-range citation prediction.

For the citation prediction task, we used a stratified learning framework, similar to [6]. Experimental results confirm that including the citation context features significantly improves the accuracy over [6] under various experimental settings for different evaluation metrics.

In future, we plan to extend this work along many different dimensions. First, we only used two features from the citation context in this work. More features based on the textual analysis of citation contexts can be investigated. Also, we would like to investigate the classifier further to reduce the errors due to the classification stage. In addition, we plan to make the citation context dataset publicly available with additional insights and properties.

Table 5: Category-wise prediction accuracies using three metrics.

	PeakInit			PeakMul			PeakLate			MonDec			MonIncr		
	R^2	ρ	θ	R^2	ρ	θ	R^2	ρ	θ	R^2	ρ	θ	R^2	ρ	θ
Δ t=5	0.76	0.81	7.09	0.79	0.73	8.25	**0.89**	**0.83**	**1.96**	0.88	0.78	12.20	0.79	0.79	11.51
Δ t=7	0.77	0.72	9.91	0.78	0.76	9.78	0.81	**0.78**	9.88	**0.89**	0.77	9.86	0.80	0.76	**9.22**
Δ t=9	0.74	0.75	14.44	0.78	0.73	13.40	0.79	0.75	13.32	0.79	0.75	13.32	**0.79**	**0.79**	**12.61**

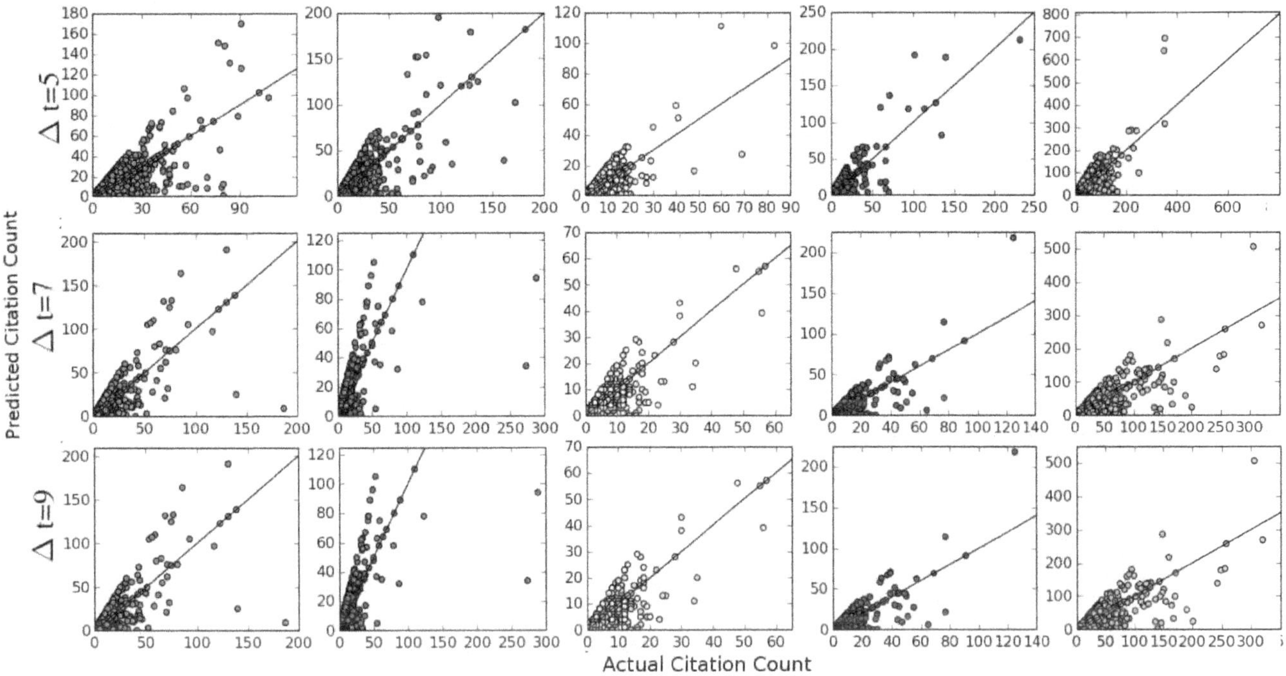

Figure 8: (Color online) Change in prediction over the time-periods for each category. Each scatter plot shows relation between actual citation count with predicted citation count. Here, from left to right, red color represents *PeakInit*, green color represents *PeakMul*, yellow color represents *PeakLate*, blue color represents *MonDec* and cyan color represents *MonIncr*. Black color line represents $x = y$ line passing through origin.

Table 6: SVM classification confusion matrix: Column 1 represents the ground truth categories, column 2 represents total number of papers in each of these categories, columns 3-8 represent the predicted categories and column 9 presents the accuracy values for each category. Correct classification results are highlighted in bold font from column 3-8. In column 9, highlighted bold font represents both the highest and lowest accuracy values

	No. of papers in category	PeakInit	PeakMul	PeakLate	MonDec	MonIncr	Oth	Accuracy
PeakInit	15178	**10987**	12	134	3245	43	757	0.724
PeakMul	30969	6	**27554**	1	1	0	3407	0.889
PeakLate	8946	49	0	**7298**	23	0	1665	0.815
MonDec	5263	1	22	0	**5207**	0	55	**0.989**
MonIncr	4010	1	64	1	0	**3005**	1003	0.749
Oth	142792	13	70618	23	1	0	**72138**	**0.494**

8. REFERENCES

[1] B. Aljaber, N. Stokes, J. Bailey, and J. Pei. Document clustering of scientific texts using citation contexts. *Information Retrieval*, 13(2):101–131, 2010.

[2] L. Bornmann and H.-D. Daniel. What do citation counts measure? a review of studies on citing behavior. *Journal of Documentation*, 64(1):45–80, 2008.

[3] T. Brody, S. Harnad, and L. Carr. Earlier web usage statistics as predictors of later citation impact. *Journal of the American Society for Information Science and Technology*, 57(8):1060–1072, 2006.

[4] A. C. Cameron and F. A. Windmeijer. An r-squared measure of goodness of fit for some common nonlinear regression models. *Journal of Econometrics*, 77(2):329–342, 1997.

[5] C. Castillo, D. Donato, and A. Gionis. Estimating number of citations using author reputation. In *String processing and information retrieval*, pages 107–117. Springer, 2007.

[6] T. Chakraborty, S. Kumar, P. Goyal, N. Ganguly, and A. Mukherjee. Towards a stratified learning approach to

Table 7: A best representative paper for each category: each paper is mapped to its MAS paper-id. Column 3 gives the actual citation count for the paper for 3 time points. Columns 4-6, 7-9 and 10-12 give the absolute difference between the actual citation count and the predicted citation count for the three systems for three different time-periods. Bold font represents the best predictions for each time period in each category. Values in parenthesis indicate predicted citation count.

Category	MAS Paper-id	Actual citation count (Δt =5,7,9)	Baseline I			Baseline II			Our Model		
			Δt= 5	Δt= 7	Δt= 9	Δ t= 5	Δt= 7	Δt= 9	Δt= 5	Δt= 7	Δt= 9
PeakInit	73939	35,20,5	7(28)	5(25)	14(19)	10(25)	**1(21)**	10(15)	**5(30)**	2(22)	**5(10)**
PeakMul	1447048	37,43,41	7(30)	11(22)	13(28)	9(48)	9(52)	14(55)	**5(42)**	**5(48)**	**3(38)**
PeakLate	837621	30,33,36	9(21)	8(25)	18(18)	8(38)	9(42)	19(55)	**5(35)**	**5(38)**	**9(45)**
MonDec	23419	8,6,3	7(1)	2(8)	7(10)	1(7)	1(7)	3(6)	**0(8)**	**1(7)**	**1(4)**
MonIncr	9871	18,20,26	6(12)	10(10)	10(16)	3(21)	3(23)	4(30)	**2(20)**	**1(21)**	**2(24)**

Table 9: Comparing related works in citation prediction: column 1 presents the title of the paper, column 2 presents the size of the dataset used in the paper, column 3 lists year range of test papers, column 4 presents the time periods used for prediction, column 5 lists the method/model used for prediction and column 6 presents the R^2 values reported in the paper for a time period, comparable across different methods. Papers are arranged in the increasing order of R^2 values.

Title of paper	Dataset Size	Year range	Time period(s)	Method	R^2(time period)
Prediction of citation counts for clinical articles at two years using data available within three weeks of publication: retrospective cohort study [15]	1274	2005	3.5	decision trees	0.14(3.5)
Characteristics Associated with Citation Rate of the Medical Literature [11]	328	1999 - 2000	5	linear regression	0.2(5)
Journal prestige, publication bias, and other characteristics associated with citation of published studies in peer-reviewed journals [16]	204	1991	2	multiple regression	0.60(2)
Towards a Stratified Learning Approach to Predict Future Citation Counts [6]	1,549,317	2001-2005	1,2,3,4,5	SVR	0.71(5)
		1996 - 2000	1,2,3,4,5	SVR	0.74(5)
Citation Count Prediction: Learning to Estimate Future Citations for Literature [20]	1,558,499	1960 - 2011	5	CART	0.752(5)
The role of citation context in predicting long-term citation profiles: an experimental study based on a massive bibliographic text dataset [our model]	1,359,338	2001-2005	5,7,9	SVR	0.84(5)

predict future citation counts. In *Proceedings of the 14th ACM/IEEE-CS Joint Conference on Digital Libraries*, JCDL '14, pages 351–360. IEEE Press, 2014.

[7] T. Chakraborty, S. Kumar, P. Goyal, N. Ganguly, and A. Mukherjee. On the categorization of scientific citation profiles in computer sciences. *CoRR*, abs/1503.06268, 2015.

[8] D. G. Feitelson and U. Yovel. Predictive ranking of computer scientists using citeseer data. *Journal of Documentation*, 60(1):44–61, 2004.

[9] L. D. Fu and C. Aliferis. Models for predicting and explaining citation count of biomedical articles. *PMC*, 2008:222–226, 2008.

[10] L. Getoor. Link mining: a new data mining challenge. *ACM SIGKDD Explorations Newsletter*, 5(1):84–89, 2003.

[11] A. V. Kulkarni, J. W. Busse, and I. Shams. Characteristics associated with citation rate of the medical literature. *PLoS ONE*, 2(5):e403, 05 2007.

[12] J. Lee Rodgers and W. A. Nicewander. Thirteen ways to look at the correlation coefficient. *The American Statistician*, 42(1):59–66, 1988.

[13] L. Li and H. Tong. The child is father of the man: Foresee the success at the early stage. *arXiv preprint arXiv:1504.00948*, 2015.

[14] A. Livne, E. Adar, J. Teevan, and S. Dumais. Predicting citation counts using text and graph mining. In *Proc. the iConference 2013 Workshop on Computational Scientometrics: Theory and Applications*, 2013.

[15] C. Lokker, K. McKibbon, R. J. McKinlay, N. L. Wilczynski, and R. B. Haynes. Prediction of citation counts for clinical articles at two years using data available within three weeks of publication: retrospective cohort study. *BMJ*, 336(7645):655–657, 2008.

[16] C. M, W. RL, and W. E. Journal prestige, publication bias, and other characteristics associated with citation of published studies in peer-reviewed journals. *JAMA*, 287(21):2847–2850, 2002.

[17] N. Pobiedina and R. Ichise. Predicting citation counts for academic literature using graph pattern mining. In *Modern Advances in Applied Intelligence*, pages 109–119. Springer, 2014.

[18] D. Wang, C. Song, and A.-L. BarabÃąsi. Quantifying long-term scientific impact. *Science*, 342(6154):127–132, 2013.

[19] R. Yan, C. Huang, J. Tang, Y. Zhang, and X. Li. To better stand on the shoulder of giants. In *Proceedings of the 12th ACM/IEEE-CS joint conference on Digital Libraries*, pages 51–60. ACM, 2012.

[20] R. Yan, J. Tang, X. Liu, D. Shan, and X. Li. Citation count prediction: learning to estimate future citations for literature. In *Proceedings of the 20th ACM international conference on Information and knowledge management*, pages 1247–1252. ACM, 2011.

[21] X. Yu, Q. Gu, M. Zhou, and J. Han. Citation prediction in heterogeneous bibliographic networks. In *SDM*, volume 12, pages 1119–1130. SIAM, 2012.

Discovering Canonical Correlations between Topical and Topological Information in Document Networks

Yuan He
Department of Computer Science
Tongji University, China
yaronhe@outlook.com

Cheng Wang
Department of Computer Science
Tongji University, China
chengwang@tongji.edu.cn

Changjun Jiang
Department of Computer Science
Tongji University, China
cjjiang@tongji.edu.cn

ABSTRACT

Document network is a kind of intriguing dataset which can provide both topical (textual content) and topological (relational link) information. A key point in viably modeling such datasets is to discover proper denominators beneath the two different types of data, text and link. Most previous work introduces the assumption that documents closely linked with each other share common latent topics. However, the heterophily (i.e., tendency to link to different others) of nodes is neglected, which is pervasive in social networks. In this paper, we simultaneously incorporate community detection and topic modeling in a unified framework, and appeal to Canonical Correlation Analysis (CCA) to capture the latent semantic correlations between the two heterogeneous latent factors, *community* and *topic*. Despite of the homophily (i.e., tendency to link to similar others) or heterophily, CCA can properly capture the inherent correlations which *fit* the dataset itself without any prior hypothesis. Logistic normal prior is also employed in modeling network to better capture the community correlations. We derive efficient inference and learning algorithms based on variational EM methods. The effectiveness of our proposed model is comprehensively verified on three different types of datasets which are namely hyperlinked networks of web pages, social networks of friends and coauthor networks of publications. Experimental results show that our approach achieves significant improvements on both topic modeling and community detection compared with the current state of the art. Meanwhile, our model is impressive in discovering correlations between extracted topics and communities.

Categories and Subject Descriptors

H.0 [**Information Systems**]: General; H.3.5 [**Information Storage and Retrieval**]: Online Information Services

General Terms

Algorithms, Experiments

Permission to make digital or hard copies of all or part of this work for personal or classroom use is granted without fee provided that copies are not made or distributed for prof t or commercial advantage and that copies bear this notice and the full citation on the f rst page. Copyrights for components of this work owned by others than ACM must be honored. Abstracting with credit is permitted. To copy otherwise, or republish, to post on servers or to redistribute to lists, requires prior specif c permission and/or a fee. Request permissions from Permissions@acm.org.
CIKM'15, October 19–23, 2015, Melbourne, Australia.
© 2015 ACM. ISBN 978-1-4503-3794-6/15/10 ...$15.00.
DOI: http://dx.doi.org/10.1145/2806416.2806518.

Keywords

Document Networks, Probabilistic Topic Model, Community Detection, CCA

1. INTRODUCTION

The prevalence of social media has strongly propelled the popularity of User Generated Content (UGC) online. Unlike the past websites, social networks thrive on relationships. The rich connectivity patterns make documents contain much more than a set of plain texts. Rather, they can be viewed as text-associated nodes in graphs, or we call them document networks. Previous studies have evolved to two trains of thoughts in modeling the heterogeneous sources, text and link, in document networks. The first kind tries to absorb link information into topic modeling [38, 18, 9, 31, 8, 22]. The emphasis of such models is to improve the topic quality. Link information is only treated as additional knowledge. Generally, these models are always extensions of traditional topic models, such as LDA [7]. Latent patterns beneath the massive links are neglected. The second kind of thought tries to absorb textual information to better decompose the network [20, 40, 44, 21]. Such work always focuses on community detection. Topic similarity is only considered as *latent links* to reinforce or supply the observed edges. Though very different in methods, the two thoughts share a common assumption that two nodes closely linked with each other have very similar topic distribution. However, we must challenge this intuition to its limitations. Homophily (i.e., tendency to link to similar others) is a ubiquitous attribute of nodes in networks. For example, users like to follow others with similar interests, and web pages tend to cite relevant sites. However, heterophily (i.e., tendency to link to different others) is also important and prevalent. In twitter, people like not only users that share similar topics but also ones who post interesting but unseen news or jokes. Creative and original content always draws more attention, which may have nothing in common with the past posts of an interested user. Meanwhile, it is not strange that friends in a social network have conflict interests. Only considering homophily may neglect or even wrongly model such information.

In this paper, we would like our model to inherently capture the latent correlations between text and link so that it can properly fit the dataset and has no strong prior hypothesis. To achieve better efficiency and more interpretable results, we first reduce text and link to lower dimensional representations, topic and community. Canonical Correlation Analysis (CCA) [3, 17] which is a well-known machine learning algorithm is then applied to capture the latent semantic association between them. CCA aims to maximize the covariance between two random sets, thus it builds a reasonable bridge for topic and community to interact with each other. This not only makes our model elegant in algebra but also totally unsupervised in implementation. On account of these advantages, we name our model Canonical Topical-Topological Analysis (CTTA). Specifically, it is an unified model which can simultaneously perform topic modeling and community detection, as well as discovering the correlations between them. Some previous work [42, 29] also aims at the same problem as we do, but it is a pity that they can not jump out of the *homophily* assumption mentioned above.

Discovering association between topic and community allows us to predict links when only given texts (or vise versa) [28, 4, 5]. Similarly, finding topic-topic (community-community) relations would enable us to predict similar content (links) when given specific content (links), which is also what we expect our model to achieve. It is feasible if we carefully select the topic modeling and community detection algorithms. Parametric topic models (i.e., LDA [7] and PLSA [19]) and nonparametric Bayesian methods (i.e., HDP [37]) have achieved great success in extracting meaningful topics from document collections. Correlated Topic Model (CTM), as a famous variation of LDA, replaces the Dirichlet prior with **normal** prior [2] so that it overcomes LDA's limitation in describing topic correlations. Coincidentally, in the probabilistic interpretation of CCA [3, 17], the two random sets are also drawn from **normal** distribution (Section 3.2). Thus we can naturally combine CTM and CCA by overlapping their sharing part. When it comes to community detection, probabilistic models [1, 24] also show great power in projecting nodes to low-dimensional communities. One of the state-of-the-art algorithms is Mixed Membership Stochastic Blockmodels (MMSB) [1]. Similar to LDA, MMSB also uses Dirichlet prior for the community membership of each node. Inspired by the improvement from LDA to CTM, we replace this prior with **normal** distribution as well. This operation also enhances the ability of MMSB in capturing the correlations between communities. Now we can take the same step to combine MMSB and CCA as we did for CTM and CCA. With CTM modeling topics, MMSB detecting communities, and CCA capturing mutual interactions, our model links everything together.

The experimental evaluation is comprehensively conducted on three different datasets, hyperlinked networks of web pages, social networks of friends and coauthor networks of publications. The results demonstrate not only the preponderance of our model in modeling topics and detecting communities, but also the capability in discovering correlations between them. The main contributions of this paper are as follows:

- It proposes a novel model CTTA, which is short for Canonical Topical-Topological Analysis. CTTA comprehensively captures community-community, topic-topic and community-topic correlations.

- The introduction of Canonical Correlation Analysis (CCA) makes our model properly fit the dataset and need no prior hypothesis, such as nodes closely linked with each other share common topics.

- We derive an efficient mean-field variational EM algorithm for approximate posterior inference, which also significantly remedies the computational burden.

- Comprehensive evaluations on three different datasets are conducted to compare the proposed model with state-of-the-art baselines. The results verify the excellent performance of CTTA.

The rest of this paper is organized as follows: Section 2 introduces the related work. Section 3 describes the details of our proposed CTTA model. Section 5 shows the demonstration and experiment results compared with baselines. Conclusions are given in Section 6.

2. RELATED WORK

Statical topic models such as LDA [7] and PLSA [19] use a set of topic distributions over a fixed vocabulary to describe a corpus of documents. The extracted topics can be considered as low-dimensional and semantic coherent representations for the massive document collection. The main improvement from PLSA to LDA is the introduction of Dirichlet prior for the multinomial distributions, which enables us to incorporate prior knowledge when modeling topics. Such attribute leads to many subsequent studies [25, 35, 32] which aim to improve the topic coherence by absorbing prior knowledge into the prior parameters. Mimno et al. [32] propose an extremely flexible model named Dirichlet-multinomial regression (DMR) which can encode arbitrary features of documents into the parameters of Dirichlet prior. A number of extensions [38, 18] of DMR demonstrate its effectiveness. Network structure can also be converted to proper document features and as well be modeled by DMR. Hefny et al. [18] use path-constrained random walks algorithm [27] to express complex relations and encode graph information into their DMR based topic model. Wahabzada et al. place Gaussian process (GP) prior for DMR to better incorporate node features. Specifically, the covariance function of GP is a function of document attributes and relations, in which p-steps random walk kernel [45] is selected to express the link structures. Another extension of LDA without applying DMR to model document networks is Relational Topic Model (RTM) [9]. In RTM, each document is first generated from topics as in LDA. The links between documents are then modeled as binary variables, one for each pair of documents. The similarity between a pair of documents is measured by the Hadamard (element-wise) product of their topic distributions. Though powerful, the Hadamard product only allows the-same-topic interactions. Chen et al. [11] overcome this limitation of RTM by replacing the Hadamard product with a full weight matrix which allows all pairwise topic interactions, which is also more suitable for asymmetric networks. Other than extensions of LDA, Mei et al. augment the PLSA objective function with a network harmonic regularization penalty that encourages topic mixtures of related documents to be similar. All the models mentioned above are general and can be applied to any document networks. However, their main concern is topic modeling.

On the other hand, researches also fall into a specific kind of dataset which is publications (writings) with coauthor or citation networks. Such kind of dataset is a special case of document networks. Researchers are concerned with not only the texts and links, but also the authors and contexts.

However, we can still gain much inspiration from them. The Author-Topic (AT) model [36] learns the topic of a document conditioned on the mixture of authors, which implicitly assumes that the distribution over topics of a certain author keeps the same for all his/her documents. Kataria et al. [23] model the influence of cited authors along with the interests of citing authors. They hypothesize that apart from the citations present in documents, the context surrounding the citation mention provides extra topical information about the cited authors. Zheng et al. [44] conduct community detection algorithm considering both the participations of authors and textual contents of documents. Mccallum et al. [30] propose the Topic-Author-Recipient model to consider sender and receiver information so that the distribution over topics is conditioned distinctly on both the sender and recipient.

When switching our emphasis from the textual content to the network structure in documents networks, we would gain another train of studies which aim to discover patterns hidden in the intricate edges. Mixture Membership Stochastic Blockmodel (MMSB) [1] is one of the state-of-the-art generative models, which can simultaneously factorize the network and infer the latent communities. Traditionally, community is a group of nodes with denser interactions amongst its members than those between its members and the remainder. Tremendous studies [34, 14, 26, 41] such as spectral clustering have paid much attention in discovering communities in massive networks. To achieve a tradeoff between analyzing documents and exploiting network, Yin et al. [42] handle topic modeling and community detection in the same framework. In their proposed model LCTA (Latent Community Topic Analysis), one community can correspond to multiple topics and multiple communities can share the same topic. Liu et al. [29] also consider that topic and community are inner-dependent. Whether a link exists between two documents follows a binomial distribution parameterized by the similarity between topic mixtures and community mixtures. Our proposed model is more powerful in both topic modeling and community detection. Meanwhile, it is also elegant in capturing the semantic relations between topics and communities compared to previous work.

3. MODELING DOCUMENT NETWORK

In this section, we give the instantiation of our proposed Canonical Topical-Topological Analysis (CTTA) model with Correlated Topic Model (CTM) [6], Mixed Membership Stochastic Blockmodels (MMSB) [1] and Canonical Correlation Analysis (CCA) [17], which are three main ingredients of our model. The model description that follows assumes the reader is familiar with these three basic models. However, what is still worth mentioning first would be the probabilistic interpretation of CCA.

3.1 Canonical Correlation Analysis

Given two random sets of variables x_1 and x_2, CCA is concerned with finding a pair of linear transformations so that one component within each set of transformed variables is correlated with a single component in the other set. Meanwhile, the correlation between x_1 and x_2 is maximized. Bach et al. [3] provide a probabilistic interpretation of CCA , which enables the use of local CCA models as components of a larger probabilistic model.

Suppose $x_1 \in \mathbb{R}^{m_1}$ and $x_2 \in \mathbb{R}^{m_2}$, both of which depend on the latent correlation factor $z \in \mathbb{R}^d$. The generative process of CCA can be described as follows:

$$z \sim \mathcal{N}(\mathbf{0}, \boldsymbol{I}_d), \quad min\{m_1, m_2\} \geqslant d \geqslant 1$$
$$x_1|z \sim \mathcal{N}(W_1 z + \mu_1, \Psi_1), \quad W_1 \in \mathbb{R}^{m_1 \times d}, \Psi_1 \succeq 0$$
$$x_2|z \sim \mathcal{N}(W_2 z + \mu_2, \Psi_2), \quad W_2 \in \mathbb{R}^{m_2 \times d}, \Psi_2 \succeq 0$$

A very important feature that CCA possesses is that it can measure the correlation between two sets in different dimensional spaces. In our CTTA model, this feature enables us to set different number of topics and communities in exploring the document network. Though word and link are heterogeneous, CCA captures the latent semantic association between their low-dimensional representations, namely topic and community.

3.2 Canonical Topical-Topological Analysis

In this section, we present the details of our proposed Canonical Topical-Topological Analysis (CTTA) model, which simultaneously explores the topical and topological factors in document networks. For the latent topic factor, we appeal to CTM, which improves LDA by replacing the Dirichlet prior with normal distribution to capture the topical correlations. By coincidence, both random sets x_1 and x_2 are drawn from normal distribution in the generative process of CCA. Thus we can naturally integrates CCA and CTM by fitting x_1 (or x_2) as the per-document topic proportion prior. The topical correlation is explicitly captured by the covariance matrix of the normal distribution. For the latent community factor, we employ MMSB to factorize the network and infer latent clusters. However, an intractable problem which we confront first is that the mixed community (block) membership for each node (document) is drawn from Dirichlet prior. Inspired by CTM, we also appeal to log normal distribution and generate the block membership from function $f(x_i) = exp(x_i)/\sum_j exp(x_j)$, where x is normally distributed. Now the integration of MMSB and CCA is the same as that of CTM and CCA. Topic modeling and community detection are elegantly coupled together with the help of CCA, and both do not loss their adept ability either.

The directed graphical model of CTTA is depicted in Fig. 1. Let D be the number of documents in the corpus where each document d has N_d words. The vocabulary size is denoted by V. K is the manually specified topic size. T is the number of communities. L is the dimension of latent correlation factor in CCA. $\beta_{1:K}$ are K multinomials over the word vocabulary. $Y(p,q)$ denotes the measurement taken on the pair of documents (p,q). In this paper, we consider the document network as a directed graph, where $Y(p,q) \in \{0,1\}$. If there is a link from document p to q, $Y(p,q)$ equals 1. $Y(p,q)$ also need not equal $Y(q,p)$. Each document d is associated with a topic proportion vector η_d and a community membership vector α_d, where $f(\eta_{d,k})$ denotes the probability of document d selecting topic k, and $f(\alpha_{d,t})$ denotes the probability of d belonging to community t. The probabilities of interactions between different communities are defined by a matrix $B_{(T \times T)}$, where $B(t_1, t_2)$ denotes the probability of having a connection from a node in community t_1 to a node in community t_2. For edge $Y(p,q)$, the vector $\overrightarrow{C}_{p \to q}$ represents the community membership of document p when it connects to q, and $\overleftarrow{C}_{q \leftarrow p}$ represents the community membership of document q when it is connected from p. We

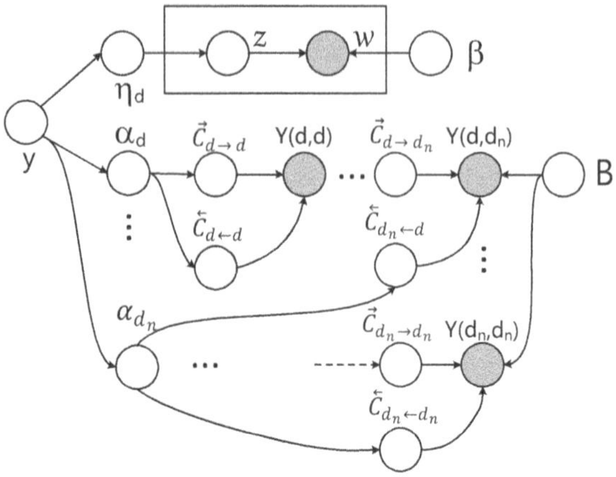

Figure 1: The graphical model of Canonical Topical-Topological Analysis

spare no efforts to keep the symbols similar to those in the original paper of CTM and MMSB so that the generative process could be more readable. The generative process of CTTA is as follows:

1. Draw a global L-dimensional Gaussian correlation factor: $y \sim \mathcal{N}(\mathbf{0}, \boldsymbol{I}_L)$. The dimension $L \leq min\{K, T\}$, where K is the number of topics in the documents and T is the number of communities in the network.
2. For each document $d \in \{1, ..., D\}$
   a) Draw K dimensional topic proportions: $\eta_d|y \sim \mathcal{N}(M_z y + \mu_z, \Sigma_z); M_z \in \mathbb{R}^{K \times L}, \Sigma_z \succeq 0$
   b) Draw T dimensional community proportions: $\alpha_d|y \sim \mathcal{N}(M_c y + \mu_c, \Sigma_c); M_c \in \mathbb{R}^{T \times L}, \Sigma_c \succeq 0$
3. For each document $d \in \{1, ..., D\}$
   a) For each word $w_{d,n}$, where $n \in \{1, ..., N_d\}$:
      i. Draw a topic $z_{d,n}|\eta_d \sim Mult(f(\eta_d))$
      ii. Emit word $w_{d,n}|\{z_{d,n}, \beta_{1:K}\} \sim Mult(\beta_{z_{d,n}})$
4. For each pair of documents $(p, q) \in D * D$:
   a) Draw membership indicator for the initiator: $\overrightarrow{C}_{p\rightarrow q}|\alpha_p \sim Mult(f(\alpha_p))$
   b) Draw membership indicator for the initiator: $\overleftarrow{C}_{q\leftarrow p}|\alpha_q \sim Mult(f(\alpha_q))$
   c) Sample the value of their interaction: $Y(p, q) \sim Bernoulli(\overrightarrow{C}^{\intercal}_{p\rightarrow q} B \overleftarrow{C}_{q\leftarrow p}); B \in \mathbb{R}^{T \times T}$

** The $f(x)$ function mentioned above refers to: $f(x_i) = exp(x_i)/\sum_j exp(x_j)$ for $i \in \{1, 2, ..., \lambda\}$, where λ is the dimension of x

We make the following notes for the Canonical Topical-Topological Analysis model:

(1) The generative steps (step 2a and 3) form the core of the Correlated Topic Model. In step 2a, the per-document topic proportion η_d is drawn from Gaussian prior which depends on the latent correlation factor y of CCA. Step 2b and 4 form the main body of Mixed Membership Stochastic Blockmodels. The Dirichlet prior in MMSB is replaced by Gaussian distribution in Step 2b. Then α_d is mapped to the topic simplex with function detailed in step **. The Gaussian distribution also reinforces the ability of MMSB in capturing the correlations between communities. Step 1 and 2 are the generative steps of CCA, from which we can easily find that communities and topics are closely coupled together and significantly interact with each other.

(2) The model parameters in CTTA comprise the set $\Theta = \{M_z, \mu_z, \Sigma_z, M_c, \mu_c, \Sigma_c, \beta, B\}$. For brevity, the two sets of latent community indicators are denoted by $\{\overrightarrow{C}_{p\rightarrow q}; p, q \in [1, D]\} = \overrightarrow{C}$ and $\{\overleftarrow{C}_{q\leftarrow p}; p, q \in [1, D]\} = \overleftarrow{C}$. Now the latent variables form the variable set $\Phi = \{y, \eta, \alpha, z, \overrightarrow{C}, \overleftarrow{C}\}$. Note that the parameters M_z and M_c are matrices with dimensions $K * L$ and $T * L$ respectively. They linearly transform topic and community from their own spaces to the space of y (step 2a and 2b). The observable variables are the documents $\boldsymbol{D}$ and links $\boldsymbol{Y}$.

The following equation gives the probability that $\boldsymbol{D}$ and $\boldsymbol{Y}$ arise from the CTTA model given the model parameters Θ:

$$P(\boldsymbol{D}, \boldsymbol{Y}|\Theta) =$$

$$\int_y \int_\eta \int_\alpha p(y) \prod_{d=1}^{D} p(\eta_d|y, M_z, \mu_z, \Sigma_z) \prod_{d=1}^{D} p(\alpha_d|y, M_c, \mu_c, \Sigma_c)$$

$$\times \prod_{p,q} \sum_{\overrightarrow{C}_{p\rightarrow q}, \overleftarrow{C}_{q\leftarrow p}} P(Y(p, q)|\overrightarrow{C}_{p\rightarrow q}, \overleftarrow{C}_{q\leftarrow p}, B) p(\overrightarrow{C}_{p\rightarrow q}|\alpha_p) p(\overleftarrow{C}_{q\leftarrow p}$$

$$\times \prod_{d=1}^{D} \prod_{n=1}^{N_d} \sum_{k=1}^{K} P(z_{d,n}|\eta_d) P(w_{d,n}|z_{d,n}, \beta) d_\eta d_\alpha d_y$$

Now our task turns to find the optimal model parameters Θ which can maximize the posterior probability given the observed documents and links:

$$\arg\max_{\Theta} \log P(\boldsymbol{D}, \boldsymbol{Y}|\Theta)$$

Unfortunately, it is computationally intractable to determine the true posterior distribution, because the normal (or the logistic normal when considering the $f(x)$ function) prior is not conjugate to the multinomial. Meanwhile, too many latent variables are coupled together. In this paper, we introduce the variational EM algorithm [39] which is widely applied by Blei et al [6, 7]. In many optimal problems, it is more computationally manageable than existing standard methods, such as Markov Chain Monte Carlo.

4. VARIATIONAL INFERENCE AND PARAMETER ESTIMATION

Though the unified CTTA model is elegant in simultaneously modeling documents and accompanied network, posterior inference is the central challenge to use it. In this paper, we make use of variational EM methods to efficiently obtain an approximation of the posterior distribution. The derivation is complicated, which however considerably remedies the computational burden when executing.

4.1 Variational Inference: E-step

During the E-step, we update the posterior distribution over the unobservable variables $\Phi = \{y, \eta, \alpha, z, \overrightarrow{C}, \overleftarrow{C}\}$. In mean-field variational methods, we posit a simple distribution of the latent variables with free parameters so that the approximation is close in the Kullback-Leibler divergence to the true posterior. In this paper, we introduce a factorized distribution $q(\Phi)$ in which the latent variables are independent of each other. The details of $q(\Phi)$ are listed as follows:

$$y \sim \mathcal{N}(\bar{y}, \Sigma_y) \qquad z \sim Mult(\phi_z)$$
$$\eta_{d,i} \sim \mathcal{N}(\bar{\eta}_{d,i}, \Sigma_{\eta d,i}) \qquad \overrightarrow{C} \sim Mult(\overrightarrow{\phi_c})$$
$$\alpha_{d,i} \sim \mathcal{N}(\bar{\alpha}_{d,i}, \Sigma_{\alpha d,i}) \qquad \overleftarrow{C} \sim Mult(\overleftarrow{\phi_c})$$

Note that η_d ($\eta_{d,i}$ where $i \in [1, K]$) is set as K independent univariate Gaussians, and α_d ($\alpha_{d,i}$ where $i \in [1, T]$) is set as T independent univariate Gaussians. It comes true since these variational parameters are fit using a single observed document d (In Eqs. 17-24, the sum of documents is removed from both sides of the equations). There is no advantage in introducing a non-diagonal variational covariance matrix. Now we have a set of free variational parameters

$$\upsilon = \{\bar{y}, \Sigma_y, \bar{\eta}_d, \Sigma_{\eta d}, \bar{\alpha}_d, \Sigma_{\alpha d}, \phi_z, \overrightarrow{\phi_c}, \overleftarrow{\phi_c}\}$$

Following Jordan et al. [39], we bound the log likelihood using Jensen's inequality. That is

$$\log P(\boldsymbol{D}, \boldsymbol{Y}|\Theta) \geqslant \mathbb{E}_q(\log P(\boldsymbol{D}, \boldsymbol{Y}, \Phi|\Theta, \upsilon)) + H(q)$$

where $\log P(\boldsymbol{D}, \boldsymbol{Y}, \Phi|\Theta, \upsilon)$ is the log likelihood function for the complete data set which contains both latent variables and observed document network. We expand the lower bound of the log likelihood as follows:

$$\begin{aligned}
\log P(\boldsymbol{D}, \boldsymbol{Y}|\Theta) \geqslant & \sum_{d=1}^{D} \mathbb{E}_q(\log P(\eta_d|y, \Theta)) + \sum_{d=1}^{D} \mathbb{E}_q(\log P(\alpha_d|y, \Theta)) \\
& + \sum_{d=1}^{D} \sum_{n=1}^{N_d} \mathbb{E}_q(\log P(z_{d,n}|\eta_d)) + \sum_{d=1}^{D} \sum_{n=1}^{N_d} \mathbb{E}_q(\log P(w_{d,n}|z_{d,n}, \beta)) \\
& + \sum_{p,q} \mathbb{E}_q(\log P(\overrightarrow{C}_{p\to q}|\alpha_p)) + \sum_{p,q} \mathbb{E}_q(\log P(\overleftarrow{C}_{q\leftarrow p}|\alpha_q)) \\
& + \sum_{p,q} \mathbb{E}_q(\log P(Y(p,q|\overrightarrow{C}_{p\to q}, \overleftarrow{C}_{q\leftarrow p}, B))) \\
& + \mathbb{E}_q(\log P(y)) + H(q)
\end{aligned}$$

Then we further expand the above equation in terms of the model parameters Θ and the variational parameters Φ. Each term on the right-hand side is shown below:

$$\mathbb{E}_q(\log P(y)) = -\frac{1}{2}\log(2\pi) - \frac{1}{2}tr(\Sigma_y) - \frac{1}{2}\bar{y}^\intercal \bar{y} \tag{1}$$

where $tr(\Sigma_y)$ is the trace of the covariance matrix Σ_y.

$$\begin{aligned}
\mathbb{E}_q(\log P(\eta_d|y, \Theta)) = & \frac{1}{2}\log(|\Sigma_z^{-1}|) - \frac{K}{2}\log(2\pi) \\
& - \frac{1}{2}tr(diag(\Sigma_{\eta,d})\Sigma_z^{-1}) - \frac{1}{2}tr(M_z\Sigma_y M_z{}^\intercal \Sigma_z^{-1}) \\
& - \frac{1}{2}tr(\bar{\eta}_d - M_z\bar{y} - \mu_z)(\bar{\eta}_d - M_z\bar{y} - \mu_z)^\intercal \Sigma_z^{-1}
\end{aligned} \tag{2}$$

This term is expanded utilizing the property of matrix normal distribution $X \sim \mathcal{MN}(M, U, V)$, of which $\mathbb{E}(X^\intercal BX) = V tr(UB^\intercal) + M^\intercal BM$. Similar expansion goes for

$$\begin{aligned}
\mathbb{E}_q(\log P(\alpha_d|y, \Theta)) = & \frac{1}{2}\log(|\Sigma_c^{-1}|) - \frac{T}{2}\log(2\pi) \\
& - \frac{1}{2}tr(diag(\Sigma_{\alpha,d})\Sigma_c^{-1}) - \frac{1}{2}tr(M_c\Sigma_y M_c{}^\intercal \Sigma_c^{-1}) \\
& - \frac{1}{2}tr(\bar{\alpha}_d - M_c\bar{y} - \mu_c)(\bar{\alpha}_d - M_c\bar{y} - \mu_c)^\intercal \Sigma_c^{-1}
\end{aligned} \tag{3}$$

$$\mathbb{E}_q(\log P(w_{d,n}|z_{d,n}, \beta)) = \sum_{k=1}^{K} \phi_{zd,n,k} \log(\beta_{kw_{d,n}}) \tag{4}$$

where $w_{d,n}$ denotes the nth word in document d. The per-document topic proportion η_d is drawn from Gaussian distribution, from which a topic z is sampled with the equation $P(z|\eta_{d,i}) = exp(\eta_{d,i})/\sum_j exp(\eta_{d,j})$. The nonconjugacy leads to the difficulty in computing the expected log probability of a topic assignment. We lower bound the expectation of the log likelihood with the Taylor expansion $\log(x) = \log(\zeta) + \zeta^{-1}(x - \zeta) + \mathcal{O}(x)$. Thus

$$\begin{aligned}
\mathbb{E}_q(\log P(z_{d,n}|\eta_d)) \geqslant & \sum_{k=1}^{K} \bar{\eta}_{d,k}\phi_{zd,n,k} + 1 - \log\zeta_{1d} \\
& - \zeta_{1d}{}^{-1}\sum_{k=1}^{K} exp(\bar{\eta}_{d,k} + \Sigma_{\eta d,k}/2)
\end{aligned} \tag{5}$$

where ζ_{1d} is an additional variational parameter. Similar derivations are conducted that

$$\begin{aligned}
\mathbb{E}_q(\log P(\overrightarrow{C}_{p\to q}|\alpha_p)) = & \sum_{t=1}^{T} \bar{\alpha}_{p,t}\overrightarrow{\phi}_{cp\to q,t} + 1 - \log\zeta_{2p} \\
& - \zeta_{2p}{}^{-1}\sum_{t=1}^{T} exp(\bar{\alpha}_{p,t} + \Sigma_{\alpha p,t}/2)
\end{aligned} \tag{6}$$

$$\begin{aligned}
\mathbb{E}_q(\log P(\overleftarrow{C}_{q\leftarrow p}|\alpha_q)) = & \sum_{t=1}^{T} \bar{\alpha}_{q,t}\overleftarrow{\phi}_{cq\leftarrow p,t} + 1 - \log\zeta_{3q} \\
& - \zeta_{3q}{}^{-1}\sum_{t=1}^{T} exp(\bar{\alpha}_{q,t} + \Sigma_{\alpha q,t}/2)
\end{aligned} \tag{7}$$

$$\begin{aligned}
\mathbb{E}_q(\log P(Y(p,q)|\overrightarrow{C}_{p\to q}, \overleftarrow{C}_{q\leftarrow p}, B)) = & \sum_{p=g,q=h} \overrightarrow{\phi}_{cp\to q,g}\overleftarrow{\phi}_{cq\leftarrow p,h} \\
& \times \log B(g,h)^{Y(p,q)}[1 - B(g,h)]^{1-Y(p,q)}
\end{aligned} \tag{8}$$

where $p = g$ (or $q = h$) refers to that document p (or q) belongs to the community g (or h).

$$\begin{aligned}
H(q) = & \frac{1}{2}\log det(\Sigma_y) + \sum_{d=1}^{D}\sum_{k=1}^{K}\frac{1}{2}\log\Sigma_{\eta_{d,k}} \\
& + \sum_{d=1}^{D}\sum_{t=1}^{T}\frac{1}{2}\log\Sigma_{\alpha_{d,t}} - \sum_{d=1}^{D}\sum_{n=1}^{N_d}\sum_{k=1}^{K}\phi_{zd,n,k}\log\phi_{zd,n,k} \\
& - \sum_{p,q}\sum_{t=1}^{T}\overrightarrow{\phi}_{cp\to q,t}\log\overrightarrow{\phi}_{cp\to q,t} - \sum_{p,q}\sum_{t=1}^{T}\overleftarrow{\phi}_{cq\leftarrow p,t}\log\overleftarrow{\phi}_{cq\leftarrow p,t}
\end{aligned} \tag{9}$$

We substitute Eqs. 1-9 into the log likelihood function, and maximize the lower bound by taking the partial derivatives with respect to the variational parameters υ and setting them to zero. The update equations are listed below:

$$\Sigma_y = (|D|M_z{}^\intercal\Sigma_z{}^{-1}M_z + |D|M_c{}^\intercal\Sigma_c{}^{-1}M_c + \boldsymbol{I}_L)^{-1} \tag{10}$$

$$y = \Sigma_y\sum_{d=1}^{D}(M_z^\intercal\Sigma_z{}^{-1}(\bar{\eta}_d - \mu_z) + M_c{}^\intercal\Sigma_c{}^{-1}(\bar{\alpha}_d - \mu_c)) \tag{11}$$

$$\zeta_{1d} = \sum_{k=1}^{K} exp(\bar{\eta}_{d,k} + \frac{1}{2}\Sigma_{\eta d,k}) \tag{12}$$

$$\zeta_{2d} = \zeta_{3d} = \sum_{t=1}^{T} exp(\bar{\alpha}_{d,t} + \frac{1}{2}\Sigma_{\alpha d,t}) \quad (13)$$

$$\phi_{zd,n,k} \propto \beta_{k,w_{d,n}} exp(\bar{\eta}_{d,k}) \quad (14)$$

$$\overrightarrow{\phi}_{cp\rightarrow q,g} \propto e^{\bar{\alpha}_{p,g}} \prod_{h} (B(g,h)^{Y(p,q)}[1-B(g,h)]^{1-Y(p,q)})^{\overleftarrow{\phi}_{cq\leftarrow p,h}} \quad (15)$$

$$\overleftarrow{\phi}_{cq\leftarrow p,h} \propto e^{\bar{\alpha}_{q,h}} \prod_{g} (B(g,h)^{Y(p,q)}[1-B(g,h)]^{1-Y(p,q)})^{\overrightarrow{\phi}_{cp\rightarrow q,g}} \quad (16)$$

For the variational parameters $\{\bar{\eta}_d, \Sigma_{\eta d}, \bar{\alpha}_d, \Sigma_{\alpha d}\}$, there is no analytic solution. Thus we apply the Newton-Raphson method. For $\bar{\eta}_d$, we have

$$\sum_{n=1}^{N_d} \Sigma_{zd,n} - \frac{N_d}{\zeta_{1d}} exp(\bar{\eta}_d + \Sigma_\eta/2) + {\Sigma_z}^{-1}(M_z\bar{y} + \mu_z - \bar{\eta}_d) = 0 \quad (17)$$

The second order derivative for η_d is

$$\nabla_{\eta_d^2} = diag(-\frac{N_d}{\zeta_{1d}} exp(\bar{\eta}_d + \Sigma_{\eta d}/2)) - {\Sigma_z}^{-1} \quad (18)$$

The $diag(v)$ function returns a diagnose matrix by placing the vector v on its diagnose. The derivative for each coordinate of $\Sigma_{\eta d}$ is

$$\nabla_{\Sigma_{\eta d,i}} = -\Sigma_{z(i,i)}^{-1} - \frac{N_d}{\zeta_{1d}} exp(\bar{\eta}_{d,i} + \Sigma_{\eta d,i}/2) + \frac{1}{\Sigma_{\eta d,i}} = 0 \quad (19)$$

$$\nabla_{\Sigma^2_{\eta d,i}} = -\frac{N_d}{2\zeta_{1d}} exp(\bar{\eta}_{d,i} + \Sigma_{\eta d,i}/2) - \frac{1}{{\Sigma_{\eta d,i}}^2} \quad (20)$$

Similarly, we can also derive the first and second derivatives for $\{\bar{\alpha}_d, \Sigma_{\alpha d}\}$ as follows:

$$\nabla_{\bar{\alpha}_d} = \Sigma_c^{-1}(M_c\bar{y} + \mu_c - \bar{\alpha}_d) + \sum_{d,q} \overrightarrow{\phi}_{cd\rightarrow q} + \sum_{p,d} \overleftarrow{\phi}_{cd\leftarrow p} - \frac{2N_d}{\zeta_{2d}} exp(\bar{\alpha}_d + \Sigma_{\alpha d}/2) = 0 \quad (21)$$

$$\nabla_{\bar{\alpha}_d^2} = diag(-\frac{2N_d}{\zeta_{2d}} exp(\bar{\alpha}_d + \Sigma_{\alpha d}/2)) - \Sigma_c^{-1} \quad (22)$$

$$\nabla_{\Sigma_{\alpha d,i}} = -\frac{1}{2}\Sigma_{c(i,i)}^{-1} - \frac{N_d}{\zeta_{2d}} exp(\bar{\alpha}_{d,i} + \Sigma_{\alpha d,i}/2) + \frac{1}{2\Sigma_{\alpha d,i}} = 0 \quad (23)$$

$$\nabla_{\Sigma^2_{\alpha d,i}} = -\frac{N_d}{2\zeta_{2d}} exp(\bar{\alpha}_{d,i} + \Sigma_{\alpha d,i}/2) - \frac{1}{2{\Sigma_{\alpha d,i}}^2} \quad (24)$$

Sparsity: In large networks such as Facebook, there are always a large amount of non-interactions. In other words, they are *sparse*. However, we can hardly say that people with no links between each other in Facebook are not friends in reality, or they have little in common. Analogically, we either can not say that web pages contain no mutual hyperlinks are irrelevant. Such nodes may just lack opportunity aware of each other's existence in the network. In these cases, treating the missing links as unobserved variables is more faithful to the underlying semantics of the data, which is also accepted in [9, 1]. Thus the $D * D$ pair-wise space of step 4 in the generative process is reduced to the space of all observed links. This operation can not only reflect our lack of knowledge about the relationship in the network but also considerably decrease the computational cost.

4.2 Parameter estimation: M-step

In the E-step, we update the *variational parameters* v to find the tightest lower bound on the log likelihood based on the observations of documents and accompanied network. In the M-step, we update the *model parameters* Φ to maximize the log likelihood based on the updated *variational parameters*. Similar to the process in the E-step, we calculate the partial derivatives with respect to each model parameter and set them to zero. The update equations are listed as follows:

$$M_z = \frac{1}{|D|}\sum_{d=1}^{D}(\bar{\eta}_d\bar{y}^\intercal - \mu_z\bar{y}^\intercal)(\Sigma_y + \bar{y}\bar{y}^\intercal)^{-1} \quad (25)$$

$$M_c = \frac{1}{|D|}\sum_{d=1}^{D}(\bar{\alpha}_d\bar{y}^\intercal - \mu_c\bar{y}^\intercal)(\Sigma_y + \bar{y}\bar{y}^\intercal)^{-1} \quad (26)$$

$$\mu_z = \frac{1}{|D|}\sum_{d=1}^{D}(\bar{\eta}_d - M_z\bar{y}) \quad (27)$$

$$\mu_c = \frac{1}{|D|}\sum_{d=1}^{D}(\bar{\alpha}_d - M_c\bar{y}) \quad (28)$$

$$\Sigma_z = \frac{1}{|D|}\sum_{d=1}^{D}(diag(\Sigma_{\eta d}) + M_z\Sigma_y M_z^\intercal + (\bar{\eta}_d - M_z\bar{y} - \mu_z)(\bar{\eta}_d - M_z\bar{y} - \mu_z)^\intercal) \quad (29)$$

$$\Sigma_c = \frac{1}{|D|}\sum_{d=1}^{D}(diag(\Sigma_{\alpha d}) + M_c\Sigma_y M_c^\intercal + (\bar{\alpha}_d - M_c\bar{y} - \mu_c)(\bar{\alpha}_d - M_c\bar{y} - \mu_c)^\intercal) \quad (30)$$

$$B(g,h) = \frac{\sum_{p,q} Y(p,q)\overrightarrow{\phi}_{cp\rightarrow q,g}\overleftarrow{\phi}_{cq\leftarrow p,h}}{\sum_{p,q}\overrightarrow{\phi}_{cp\rightarrow q,g}\overleftarrow{\phi}_{cq\leftarrow p,h}} \quad (31)$$

$$\beta_{k,v} \propto \sum_{d=1}^{D}\sum_{n}^{N_d}\phi_{zd,n,k}\delta(w_{d,n} = v) \quad (32)$$

where the $\delta(w_{d,n} = v)$ is the Kronecker delta function which returns 1 only when $w_{d,n}$ equals v. We iteratively execute the E-step with Eqs. 10 - 24 and M-step with Eqs.25 - 32 until the model parameters converge.

5. EXPERIMENTS

In this section, we present the quantity and quality evaluations for our proposed model with some state-of-the-art baselines from three aspects: *topic modeling*, *community detection* and *topic-community correlation analysis*. By jointly modeling documents and alongside network, we consider that the analysis of communities and topics would mutually enhance each other, and the quality of both would achieve a prominent improvement. On the other hand, CCA reveals the latent semantic correlations between community and topic. To better present the advantages brought by CCA, we visually construct a relational graph with the discovered associations as edges. Four different models are compared in the experiments:

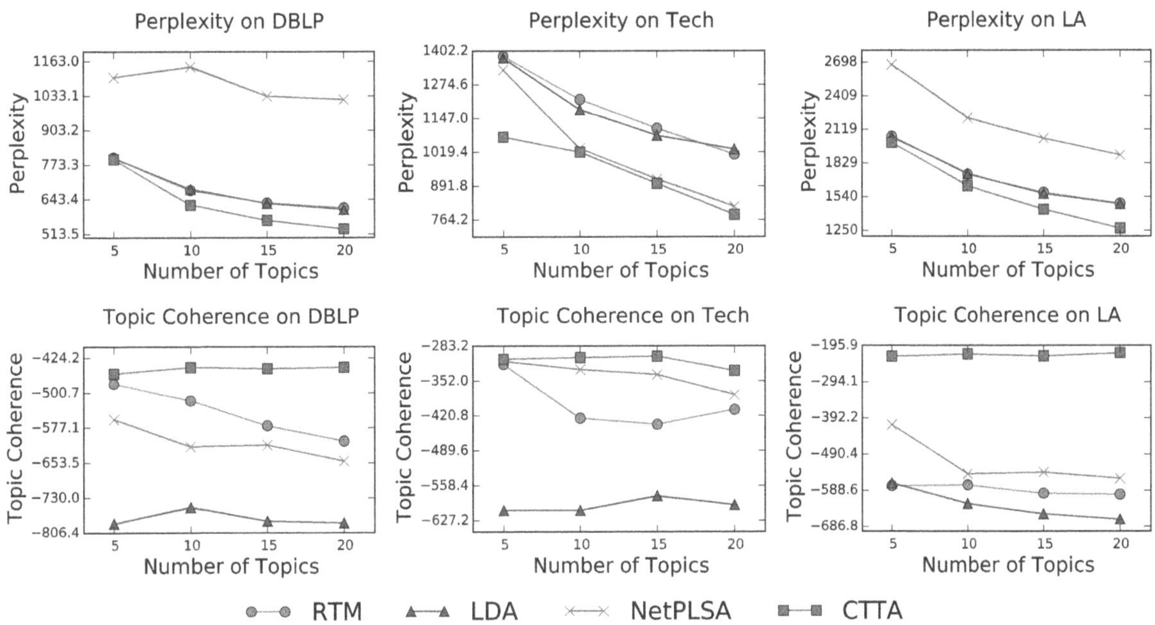

Figure 2: Perplexity and Topic Coherence scores of different models (Note that we ignore the results of LCTA since its perplexity scores reach ten thousands)

- **RTM**: Relational Topic Model (RTM) [9] is a famous extension of LDA in modeing document networks. It assumes that documents with similar topic distributions are more likely to have links. However, RTM can not discover communities.

- **NetPLSA**: NetPLSA [31] is designed adapted to any text collections with an associated network. It regularizes PLSA with a harmonic regularizer based on the graph structure. It is either unable to detect communities.

- **LCTA**: Latent Community Topic Analysis (LCTA) [42] simultaneously performs topic modeling and community detection as our model does. It outperforms many baseline methods such as LinkLDA [15] and SSNLDA [43].

- **Classic LDA**: LDA [7] is the basic knowledge-free unsupervised topic model. It is impressive in extracting semantic coherent topics.

5.1 Datasets and Settings

Datasets: We apply our model on three public datasets: Foursquare check-in dataset with friendship relations [1], blog posts with hyperlink network [2] and DBLP dataset with coauthor graph [3]. From the Foursquare dataset, we extract the check-ins of people registered at Los Angeles and aggregate all *tips* (texts posted by users to describe a location) of a person as a single document. In order to make a document contain certain number of words, we remove the users who post less than 30 tips. Then we link the documents according to the friendship relations between the corresponding users. The blog posts dataset contains technical blogs which cite others with hyperlinks. Since this dataset is of great quality, we take no more operations to remove noise. Dealing with the DBLP dataset is a little complicate. We first extract four different conferences, SIGIR, WWW, KDD and NIPS from the large xml file. For each paper, the title in text and all its authors are extracted. We then construct the coauthor network by linking two unique authors with an edge if they have coauthored in at least one paper. To make the coauthor network not so sparse, we remove authors who publish papers less than 7. The three datasets are denoted as LA, Tech and DBLP respectively in the following parts for brevity. The statistics of the three processed datasets are shown in Table 1.

Table 1: Datasets statistics

Dataset	Documents	Edges	Words
LA	715	3554	26230
Tech	567	2694	18043
DBLP	1118	7348	7098

Parameter Settings: We implement the LDA and RTM with Gibbs sampling methods. Both models are trained using 2000 Gibbs iterations to ensure convergence. We set the hyperpameters $\alpha = 50/K$ and $\beta = 0.01$ heuristically, which reports the best model quality in [16]. LCTA and NetPLSA are inferred by EM algorithm. We conduct the inference algorithm until the relative change in the log likelihood is less than 10^{-3}, which is also the threshold set in our model.

5.2 Topic Modeling

Many objective metrics have been applied to measure the quality of generated topics. In language modeling, the *Perplexity* is used in convention, which is algebraicly equivalent to the inverse of the geometric mean per-word likelihood. A lower perplexity score indicates better generalization performance. Thus we first compare the perplexity score to mea-

[1] `https://www.dropbox.com/s/4nwb7zpsj25ibyh/check-in data.zip`
[2] `http://www-bcf.usc.edu/~liu32/data/tech_blog.zip`
[3] `http://dblp.uni-trier.de/xml/`

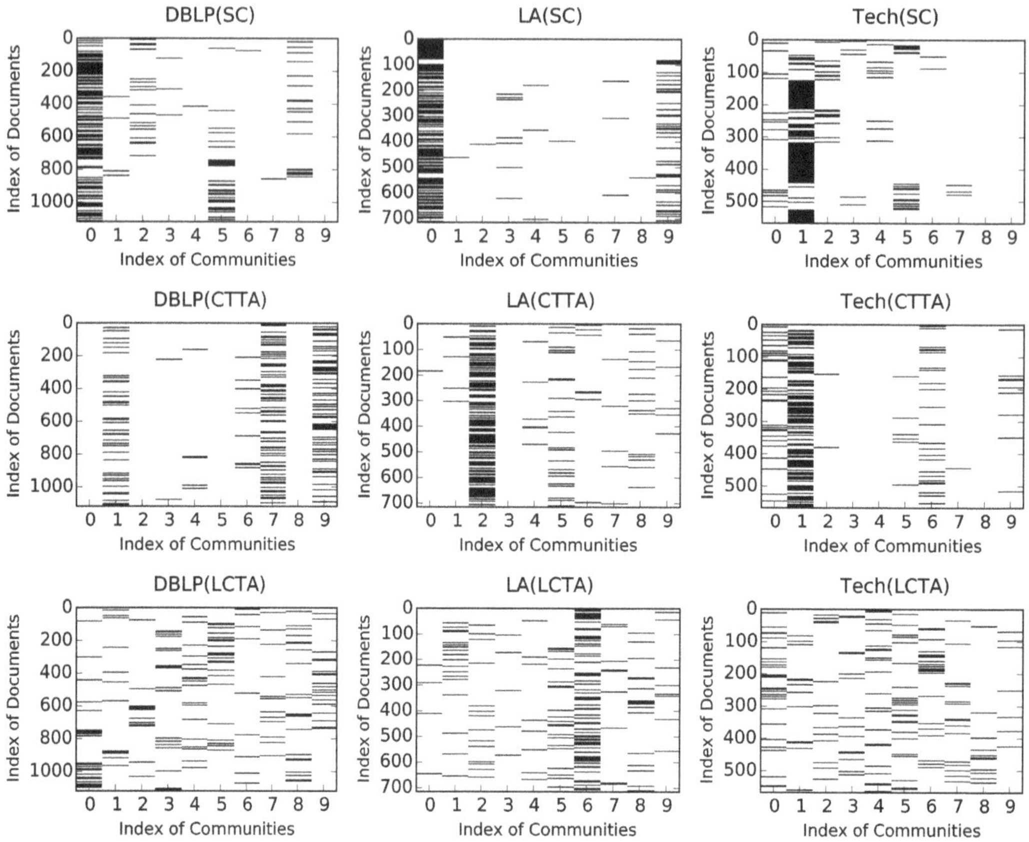

Figure 3: Grouping results of Spectral Clustering, CTTA and LCTA

sure how well our model fits the data. However, previous work also points out that human judgments are sometimes contrary to the perplexity measure [10, 13]. To better reflect the advantage of introducing network information, we secondly apply *Topic Coherence* metric [33] in this paper. This metric is firstly proposed by Mimno et al. [33]. They point out that the topic coherence score corresponds well with human coherence judgments. This metric is also widely used by Chen et al [12, 13]. Good model would generate coherent topics with accurate semantic clustering, and higher coherence score indicates higher quality of topics. In our experiment, 20 most probable words in each topic are used and the average coherence value is calculated for comparison. We fix the number of communities to $T = 10$ in LCTA and CTTA, which are the only two models capable to discover communities.

Figure 2 illustrates the perplexity and coherence scores on different number of topics. Note that the perplexity scores of LCTA incredibly reach ten thousands, which are much bigger than the other models. Thus we do not plot it in the figure for clarity. We can see that our proposed model achieves impressive improvement on all the three datasets. In Figure 5, we directly show three example topics of which the top 10 words are extremely coherent and interpretable. RTM yields very close perplexity scores to that of LDA, but it outperforms LDA in topic coherence with a large margin. NetPLSA performs extraordinarily well on Tech dataset. However, it gets much worse results on LA and DBLP. This may come from its assumption that topic similar documents tend to have a link, which is practical to webpages with hyperlinks, but friendship and coauthorship may not follow this hypothesis. Our model is elegant in capturing the latent semantic correlations between topics and communities. It aims to fit the observed data and relies on no prior hypothesis. Thus it is general for all the corpora with network structure.

5.3 Community Detection

An important advantage of CTTA model is its ability to simultaneously model topics and discover communities. However, it is always hard to intuitively depict the latent clusters beneath the network. Previous work [31] directly plots out the network with some standard graphs layout algorithm such as "*Spring Embedder*". However, when it comes to large graph with thousands of edges, this method loses its effectiveness. The generated figure is always a massive gather of nodes, and we can hardly detect any community visually. In this paper, we measure the *grouping result* and *cut edge weights* to evaluate the performance. We compare our model with LCTA and Spectral Clustering (SC). SC is a powerful tool in analyzing communities on large networks [41], which is widely applied by researchers all over the world.

Figure 3 depicts the grouping results. The number of communities is restricted to 10. We can see that our model yields similar clustering patterns as SC but has more balanced clusters. This means that CTTA correctly reveals the topological information in the datasets. But with incorporating topical information, we make the results better. LCTA outputs extremely balanced clusters which are totally different from those of SC. This is unacceptable. Fig 4

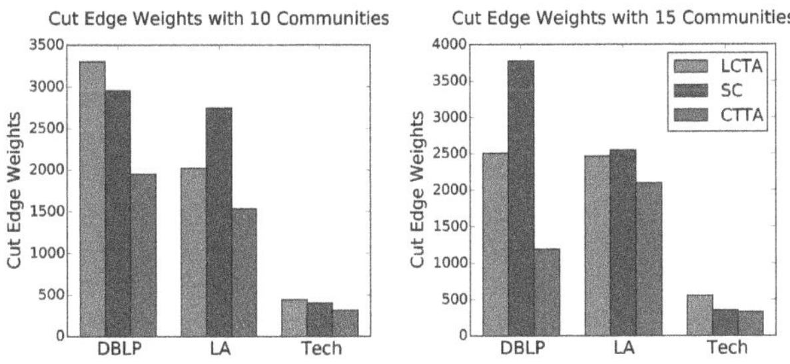

Figure 4: Cut edge weights on three datasets

shows the cut edge weights when the number of communities is set to 10 and 15. This metric presents the total weight of edges across different communities. Lower value indicates better clustering effect. On all the three datasets, CTTA gets much lower scores. The performance of LCTA is not so stable with the changing of community size. This may be partially caused by its assumption that two linked users are drawn from the same community. Generally, with the increase of community size, CTTA performs better.

5.4 Topic-community Correlation Analysis

In this part, we give a direct evaluation of the results generated by our model. With the topic-topic (T-T) correlations captured by CTM, the community-community (C-C) correlations captured by MMSB, and the topic-community (T-C) correlations captured by CCA, the CCTA model builds a complete graph that links every component together. Thus we visually depict the extracted topics and communities, as well as the edges (T-T, C-C, T-C correlations) amongst them. Note that only the pair which has prominently higher relevancy in the covariance matrix is connected with an edge. It is a pity that nodes in LA and Tech are common users and web pages, which makes it hard for readers to subjectively judge the performance without knowing the users' interests or carefully reading the whole web page content. While authors in the DBLP dataset are more familiar to readers. What's more, most authors only concentrate on their major research interests, which are also easy to access on the web. Thus the relational graph on DBLP is much easier to understand and judge. Here the 10 most probable words in the topic-word distribution are extracted to represent each research topic. Communities are labelled with the names of authors who publish the most papers in it.

From Figure 5 we can see that the *Bayesian Methods* topic is associated with all the extracted communities and topics, which may be on account of its popularity in different fields. The correlations between communities and corresponding topics are accurately captured by the latent correlation factors. We also find an edge connecting the communities of *Information Retrieval* and *Language Modeling* , which may be because the numerous overlapping algorithms applied by both. Meanwhile, the top 10 words in each topic are very coherent, and we can give very accurate semantic interpretation to label them.

6. CONCLUSIONS

This paper proposes a novel model CTTA which simultaneously performs topic modeling and community detection on document networks. The introduction of CCA makes our model capable to analyze correlations between the heterogeneous topic and community, as well better model the heterophily (i.e., tendency to link to different others) and homophily (i.e., tendency to link to similar others) attributes of nodes. Comprehensive evaluations on three different datasets show that CTTA outperforms state-of-the-art baselines with significant improvements. With increasing studies focusing on document networks, we believe that our proposed model is promising to advance the researches in this field. The application of CCA also offers inspirations for studies which would like to discover correlations between two sets of variables in other fields.

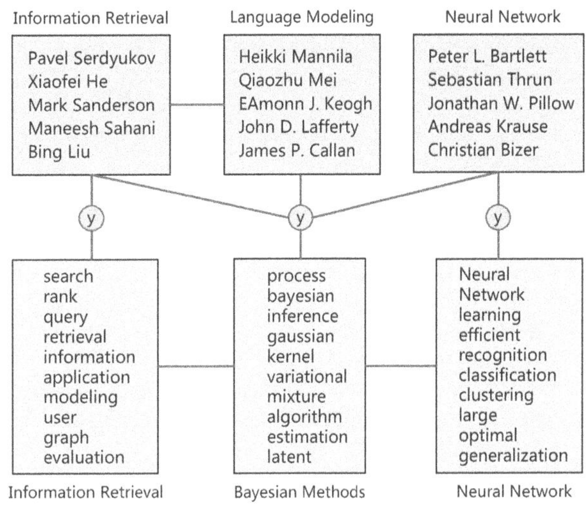

Figure 5: Correlations amongst topics and communities

7. ACKNOWLEDGMENTS

The research of authors is partially supported by the National Natural Science Foundation of China under Grant No. 91218301 and No. 61202383, HongKong, Macao and Taiwan Science & Technology Cooperation Program of China under Grant No. 2013DFM10100, the Program for New Century Excellent Talents in University (NCET) under Grant No. NCET-12-0414, and the Natural Science Foundation of Shanghai under Grant No. 12ZR1451200.

8. REFERENCES

[1] E. M. Airoldi, D. M. Blei, S. E. Fienberg, and E. P. Xing. Mixed membership stochastic blockmodels. In *Advances in Neural Information Processing Systems 21*. Curran Associates, Inc., 2009.

[2] J. Aitchison. The statistical analysis of compositional data. 1986.

[3] F. R. Bach and M. I. Jordan. A probabilistic interpretation of canonical correlation analysis. 2005.

[4] L. Backstrom and J. Leskovec. Supervised random walks: predicting and recommending links in social networks. In *WSDM '11*, 2011.

[5] N. Barbieri, F. Bonchi, and G. Manco. Who to follow and why: link prediction with explanations. In *SIGKDD '14*, 2014.

[6] D. Blei and J. Lafferty. Correlated topic models. *Advances in neural information processing systems*, 2006.

[7] D. M. Blei, A. Y. Ng, and M. I. Jordan. Latent dirichlet allocation. *the Journal of machine Learning research*, 2003.
[8] D. Cai, X. Wang, and X. He. Probabilistic dyadic data analysis with local and global consistency. In *ICML '09*. ACM, 2009.
[9] J. Chang and D. M. Blei. Relational topic models for document networks. In *AISTATS*, JMLR Proceedings, 2009.
[10] J. Chang, S. Gerrish, C. Wang, J. L. Boyd-graber, and D. M. Blei. Reading tea leaves: How humans interpret topic models. In *Advances in neural information processing systems*, pages 288–296, 2009.
[11] N. Chen, J. Zhu, F. Xia, and B. Zhang. Generalized relational topic models with data augmentation. AAAI Press, 2013.
[12] Z. Chen and B. Liu. Mining topics in documents: Standing on the shoulders of big data. In *SIGKDD '14*. ACM, 2014.
[13] Z. Chen, A. Mukherjee, B. Liu, M. Hsu, M. Castellanos, and R. Ghosh. Leveraging multi-domain prior knowledge in topic models. In *IJCAI '13*. AAAI Press, 2013.
[14] A. Clauset, M. E. J. Newman, and C. Moore. Finding community structure in very large networks. *Phys. Rev. E*, 2004.
[15] E. Erosheva, S. Fienberg, and J. Lafferty. Mixed-membership models of scientific publications. *Proceedings of the National Academy of Sciences*, 2004.
[16] T. L. Griffiths and M. Steyvers. Finding scientific topics. *Proceedings of the National Academy of Sciences*, 2004.
[17] J. F. Hair, W. C. Black, B. J. Babin, R. E. Anderson, and R. L. Tatham. *Multivariate data analysis*, volume 6. Pearson Prentice Hall Upper Saddle River, NJ, 2006.
[18] A. Hefny, G. Gordon, and K. Sycara. Random walk features for network-aware topic models. 2013.
[19] T. Hofmann. Probabilistic latent semantic indexing. In *SIGIR '99*. ACM, 1999.
[20] B. Hu and M. Ester. Social topic modeling for point-of-interest recommendation in location-based social networks. In *ICDM '14*. IEEE, 2014.
[21] B. Hu, M. Jamali, and M. Ester. Spatio-temporal topic modeling in mobile social media for location recommendation. In *ICDM '13*. IEEE, 2013.
[22] S. Huh and S. E. Fienberg. Discriminative topic modeling based on manifold learning. *TKDD*, 2012.
[23] S. Kataria, P. Mitra, C. Caragea, and C. L. Giles. Context sensitive topic models for author influence in document networks. In *IJCAI '11*, 2011.
[24] C. Kemp, J. B. Tenenbaum, T. L. Griffiths, T. Yamada, and N. Ueda. Learning systems of concepts with an infinite relational model. In *AAAI '06*, 2006.
[25] H. Kim, Y. Sun, J. Hockenmaier, and J. Han. Etm: Entity topic models for mining documents associated with entities. In *ICDM '12*, 2012.
[26] J. Kleinberg. The small-world phenomenon: An algorithmic perspective. In *Proceedings of the Thirty-second Annual ACM Symposium on Theory of Computing*, STOC. ACM, 2000.
[27] N. Lao, T. Mitchell, and W. W. Cohen. Random walk inference and learning in a large scale knowledge base. In *EMNLP '11*, 2011.
[28] D. Liben-Nowell and J. Kleinberg. The link-prediction problem for social networks. *Journal of the American society for information science and technology*, 2007.
[29] Y. Liu, A. Niculescu-Mizil, and W. Gryc. Topic-link lda: joint models of topic and author community. In *ICML '09*. ACM, 2009.
[30] A. McCallum, A. Corrada-Emmanuel, and X. Wang. Topic and role discovery in social networks. *Computer Science Department Faculty Publication Series*, 2005.
[31] Q. Mei, D. Cai, D. Zhang, and C. Zhai. Topic modeling with network regularization. In *WWW '08*. ACM, 2008.
[32] D. Mimno and A. McCallum. Topic models conditioned on arbitrary features with dirichlet-multinomial regression. *arXiv preprint arXiv:1206.3278*, 2012.
[33] D. Mimno, H. M. Wallach, E. Talley, M. Leenders, and A. McCallum. Optimizing semantic coherence in topic models. In *EMNLP '11*, 2011.
[34] A. B. N. Pathak and K. Erickson. Social topic models for community extraction. In *SNA-KDD '08*, 2008.
[35] D. Ramage, D. Hall, R. Nallapati, and C. D. Manning. Labeled lda: A supervised topic model for credit attribution in multi-labeled corpora. In *EMNLP '09*, 2009.
[36] M. Steyvers, P. Smyth, M. Rosen-Zvi, and T. Griffiths. Probabilistic author-topic models for information discovery. In *SIGKDD '04*. ACM, 2004.
[37] Y. W. Teh, M. I. Jordan, M. J. Beal, and D. M. Blei. Hierarchical dirichlet processes. *Journal of the american statistical association*, 2006.
[38] M. Wahabzada, Z. Xu, and K. Kersting. Topic models conditioned on relations. In *Machine Learning and Knowledge Discovery in Databases*. Springer, 2010.
[39] M. Wainwright and M. Jordan. A variational principle for graphical models. *New Directions in Statistical Signal Processing*, 2005.
[40] J. Weng, E.-P. Lim, J. Jiang, and Q. He. Twitterrank: finding topic-sensitive influential twitterers. In *WSDM '10*. ACM, 2010.
[41] L. Wu, X. Wu, A. Lu, and Z.-H. Zhou. A spectral approach to detecting subtle anomalies in graphs. *Journal of Intelligent Information Systems*, 2013.
[42] Z. Yin, L. Cao, Q. Gu, and J. Han. Latent community topic analysis: Integration of community discovery with topic modeling. *ACM Trans. Intell. Syst. Technol.*, 2012.
[43] H. Zhang, C. L. Giles, H. C. Foley, and J. Yen. Probabilistic community discovery using hierarchical latent gaussian mixture model. In *AAAI '07*, 2007.
[44] G. Zheng, J. Guo, L. Yang, S. Xu, S. Bao, Z. Su, D. Han, and Y. Yu. Mining topics on participations for community discovery. In *SIGIR '11*. ACM, 2011.
[45] X. Zhu, J. Kandola, J. Lafferty, and Z. Ghahramani. Graph kernels by spectral transforms. *Semi-Supervised Learning*, 2005.

Chronological Citation Recommendation with Information-Need Shifting

Zhuoren Jiang
[1]Institute of Computer Science & Technology
Peking University
Beijing, China, 100871
[2]College of Transportation Management
Dalian Maritime University
Dalian, China, 116026
jzr1986@gmail.com

Xiaozhong Liu
Department of Information and Library Science
Indiana University
Bloomington, IN, USA, 47405
liu237@indiana.edu

Liangcai Gao
Institute of Computer Science & Technology
Peking University
Beijing, China, 100871
glc@pku.edu.cn

ABSTRACT

As the volume of publications has increased dramatically, an urgent need has developed to assist researchers in locating high-quality, candidate-cited papers from a research repository. Traditional scholarly recommendation approaches ignore the chronological nature of citation recommendations. In this study, we propose a novel method called "Chronological Citation Recommendation" which assumes initial user information needs could shift while users are searching for papers in different time slices. We model the information-need shifts with two-level modeling: dynamic time-related ranking feature construction and dynamic evolving feature weight training. In more detail, we employed a supervised document influence model to characterize the content "time-varying" dynamics and constructed a novel heterogeneous graph that encapsulates dynamic topic-based information, time-decay paper/topic citation information, and word-based information. We applied multiple meta-paths for different ranking hypotheses which carried different types of information for citation recommendation in various time slices, along with information-need shifting. We also used multiple learning-to-rank models to optimize the feature weights for different time slices to generate the final "Chronological Citation Recommendation" rankings. The use of Chronological Citation Recommendation suggests time-series ranking lists based on initial user textual information need and characterizes the information-need shifting. Experiments on the ACM corpus show that Chronological Citation Recommendation can significantly enhance citation recommendation performance.

Categories and Subject Descriptors

H.3.3 [**Information Storage and Retrieval**]: Information Search and Retrieval

Permission to make digital or hard copies of all or part of this work for personal or classroom use is granted without fee provided that copies are not made or distributed for profit or commercial advantage and that copies bear this notice and the full citation on the first page. Copyrights for components of this work owned by others than ACM must be honored. Abstracting with credit is permitted. To copy otherwise, or republish, to post on servers or to redistribute to lists, requires prior specific permission and/or a fee. Request permissions from Permissions@acm.org.

CIKM'15, CIKM'15, October 19-23, 2015, Melbourne, VIC, Australia
© 2015 ACM. ISBN 978-1-4503-3794-6/15/10 ...$15.00.
DOI: http://dx.doi.org/10.1145/2806416.2806567.

Keywords

Chronological Citation Recommendation, Information-Need Shifting, Supervised Dynamic Topic Modeling, Heterogeneous Graph Mining, Learning to Rank

1. INTRODUCTION AND MOTIVATION

Finding and reading potential candidate articles for citation is essential to good research. Recent systematic efforts, such as Google Scholar and Microsoft Academic Search, exist to serve this need. Given the explosion of scientific papers, however, researchers are plagued by information overload, such as an overwhelming list of retrieved publications based on a textual query. To solve this problem, researchers have proposed a number of different solutions to effectively recommend high-quality papers to scholars. Alongside classic textual information retrieval and recommendation approaches, topic information and link information between papers, such as citation relationships, have been proven to enhance recommendation performance [4, 10, 13].

The important chronological nature of citation recommendation, however, has been ignored in previous studies. From a citation recommendation standpoint, an information need may feature different variations depending on varying time slices. For instance, as Figure 1 shows, if a scholar's query (initial information need) is related to *"Latent Dirichlet Allocation,"* he/she is most likely interested in the papers focusing on this theme that had been most recently published. However, the scholar's information need could implicitly shift if he/she needs to investigate earlier publications. For instance, given the same query, the scholar might be interested in publications focusing on *"Latent Semantic Indexing"* or *"Probabilistic Latent Semantic Indexing"* between 1990 and 2000, and *"Word Clustering"* or *"Probability Theory"* studies published before 1990. The information need can also be more complex than a static model based on a single method of feature representation and ranking fusion. The importance of the varying ranking features may also shift in different time slices. For example, for any given targeted text query, users may prefer classical readings published decades ago related to (but not necessarily similar as) the query (i.e., revealed by PageRank or random walk), and they may be interested in the more recent studies similar to the query (i.e., revealed by language model or topic model). No single existing model can cover this kind of shifting. In this study, we define this phenomenon as **"Information-Need Shifting."** It challenges most of the existing text- or citation-based search methods, which generate a general list of papers based on a static recommendation or retrieval model.

Figure 1: Diagrammatic sketch of information-need shifting

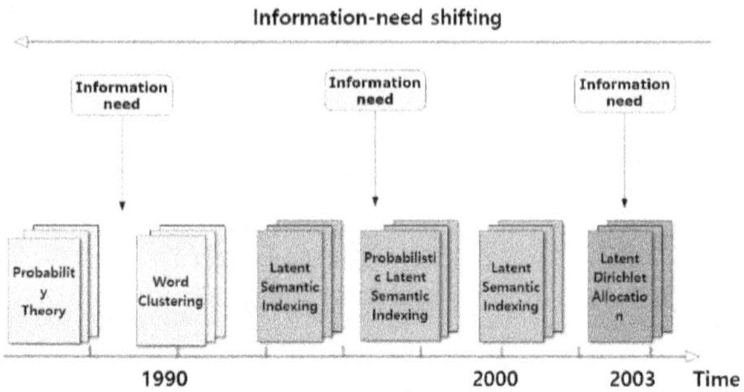

Modeling information-need shifting is significant for citation recommendation in that a large number of cited papers may not be similar or share the same topic as the citing article or textual query. Modeling information-need shifting can be especially important for junior scholars (exploratory tasks [15]), interdisciplinary studies, and review tasks. In this paper, we characterize the information-need shifting from two different viewpoints: (1) Dynamic chronological feature extraction and (2) Dynamic evolving feature weight training. With dynamic chronological feature extraction, we estimate the chronological information-need shifting based on the three indicators: *dynamic topic-based information*, e.g., scientific topic evolution, topic mixture proportion in a paper or a paper's topical influence; *citation relationships between papers or topics*; and *word information*, e.g., TFIDF. All of these indicators are conceptualized as the various meta-paths on an innovative heterogeneous chronological graph as time-related ranking features. With dynamic evolving feature weight training, after harvesting all the dynamic ranking features, the information-need shifting (chronological citation recommendation) problem is characterized by a number of learning-to-rank models (in which each model estimates an information need on a specific time slice) to optimize the feature weights for different time slices and capture the weight evolving trajectory. We estimated the effect of information-need shifting by evaluating the citation recommendation performance for different historical periods.

The contribution of this paper is twofold. First, we propose a novel chronological citation recommendation method to assist scholars in more effectively identifying and accessing the recommendation results, and better understanding the discipline's development (given a textual query). Chronological citation recommendation, unlike most existing efforts, considers information-need shifting and generates multiple lists of ranked papers for a given number of time slices. Second, we propose an innovative approach to characterize the information-need shifting by employing two-level modeling: (1) We construct the time-related ranking features from the time-decayed citation relations between papers/topics, dynamic topic-based information and word information. All of these indicators are addressed by a number of meta-path features, plus a random walk algorithm, on an innovative heterogeneous graph. (2) We apply learning-to-rank algorithms, plus dynamic graph-based feature integration, to optimize the feature weights and capture the feature importance evolution. Information-need shifting, then, is characterized as the time-series recommendation ranking models. Each ranking model will be utilized to optimize the publication ranking results for a distinct time slice. To the best of our knowledge, few prior studies addressed these problems.

In the remainder of this paper, we: (1) propose our novel method for chronological citation recommendation via supervised dynamic topic modeling, heterogeneous graph mining and learning-to-rank methods; (2) review relevant literature and methodology; (3) describe the experiment setting and evaluation results; and (4) discuss the findings and limitations of the study and identify subsequent research steps.

2. RESEARCH METHODS

In this section, we propose an innovative method for chronological citation recommendation by estimating user information-need shifting. In more detail, in section 2.1, we propose a supervised dynamic topic model for characterizing the publication topic dynamics and publication topical influence. We then construct a novel heterogeneous graph, in section 2.2, to integrate dynamic topic-based information, citation relationship, and word information for chronological citation recommendation. Twenty-three meta-path-based ranking features are employed on the graph along with random walk algorithm. In section 2.3, we estimate user information-need shifting by using learning-to-rank method, and generate chronological citation recommendation results.

2.1 Supervised Dynamic Topic Training

Publication content and its associated latent topics provide the first kind of important information for user information-need shifting estimation. Topic models are useful tools for analyzing the words of texts to discover the patterns of terms in document collections. In most previous studies, a topic, namely a term distribution, was always static. However, this assumption is oversimplified and is inappropriate for scholarly publication collections. For example, the content of a research paper discussing *"Information Retrieval"* in 1990 can be very different from a similar study from 2010. That motivates us to use a dynamic topic model that enables an algorithm to estimate topic change over time and characterize the content dynamics in a corpus. In this paper, we assume that scientific topics are evolving over time, and the evolving topics located in different time slices are interconnected in a historical trajectory.

Dynamic topic model (DTM) [1] has been demonstrated as a useful tool which can explicitly model the dynamics of the underlying topics. DTM introduces a Markov chain of term distributions to capture probabilities that drift over time. It models the documents of each time slice with a K-component topic model, where the topics associated with slice t evolve from the topics associated with previous slice t -*1*:

$$\beta_{t,k}|\beta_{t-1,k} \sim \mathbb{N}\left(\beta_{t-1,k}, \sigma^2 I\right)$$

The natural parameter $\beta_{t,k}$ is considered as the term distribution at time slice t for topic k, where σ^2 is the transition variance. Based on DTM, Gerrish and Blei [8] proposed the document influence model (DIM). In DIM, a normally distributed influence score $l_{d,k}$ is assigned to each article which is a scalar value that describes the influence that article d has on the topic k. Topic drift is similar as DTM, where DIM restricts attention to the influence score for that topic and to the words of each document that are assigned to it:

$$\beta_{t,k}|\beta_{t-1,k}, (w,l,z)_{t-1,1:D}$$
$$\sim \mathbb{N}\left(\beta_{t-1,k} + exp\left(-\beta_{t-1,k} \sum_d l_{d,k} \sum_n w_{d,n} z_{d,n,k}, \sigma^2 I\right)\right)$$

Here, $z_{d,n,k}$ is the indicator that the nth word in document d is assigned to topic k. DIM assumes that the higher the influence, the more the words of the article affect how the topic drifts.

Though DIM tracks the language dynamic successfully, it has some limitations. The topics learned from the model are hard to interpret, and the number setting of topics in a corpus is arbitrary (as are other unsupervised LDA methods). Meanwhile, DTM and DIM ignore the citation relations between scientific articles, which should be important to estimate information-need shifting. Scholarly publication collections, unlike other kinds of corpora, provide very rich metadata, i.e., author-provided keyword and citation metadata. This characteristic motivates us to use scientific metadata to enhance the dynamic topic evolution performance. As with DIM, we posit K topic trajectories, and the document set of each time slice is modeled with a supervised topic model Labeled LDA (LLDA) [18]. LLDA associates individual words in a document with their most appropriate labels (keywords). In this study, the labels are author-provided keywords (for each paper). The number of topics in LLDA is the number of unique keyword labels K in the corpus. This makes our model a "Supervised Document Influence Model" (SDIM). The graphical representation of the supervised document influence model is depicted in Figure 2.

Figure 2: Graphical representation of the supervised document influence model

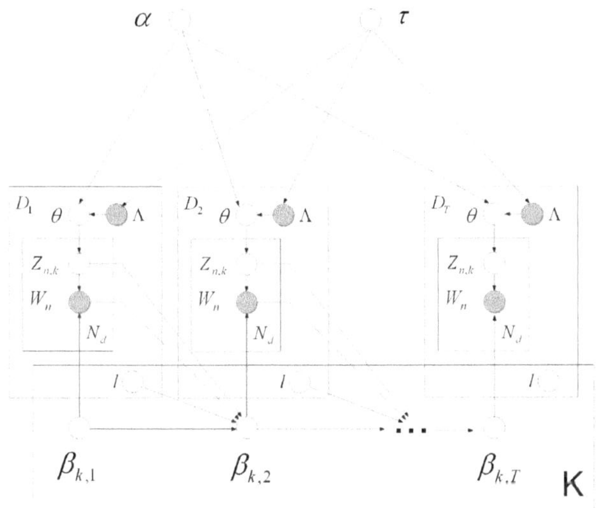

As Figure 2 shows, K is the number of topic labels in all time slices; T is the number of time slices; time slice T is the latest time slice; time slice 1 is the earliest; and D is the publication set. $D = \{D_1, D_2, ...D_T\}$, where D_i $(1 \leq i \leq T)$ is the papers published in time slice i; W represents the word; $V = \{W_1, W_2, ..., W_{|V|}\}$ represents the vocabulary of the corpus; N_d represents the word number of document d; $z_{n,k}$ is the word-topic assignment; θ is a multinomial distribution representing the topic mixture proportions; α is a Dirichlet prior distribution; $\beta_{t,k}$ is topic k associated with slice t; l represents the document's influences over topics; Λ is a binary vector of document's labels; τ represents a labeling prior probability.

For each document, the traditional DIM draws a multinomial mixture distribution θ over all K topics from a Dirichlet prior α. However, in SDIM, for each document d, we would like to restrict θ to be defined only over the topics that correspond to its labels (paper's keywords). Since the word-topic assignment $z_{n,k}$ is drawn from θ, this restriction ensures that all the topic assignments are limited to the document's keyword labels. To achieve this objective, we generate the document's labels Λ using a Bernoulli coin toss for each topic k, with a labeling prior probability τ. As keyword label is the metadata of the corpus, so Λ can be easily obtained by observation. For example, suppose we have three keywords in corpus; we use these keywords as the topic's labels, $K = 3$; paper d has $keyword_1$ and $keyword_3$, so $\Lambda = \{1, 0, 1\}$, that will restrict θ to be defined as $\theta = \{\theta_1, 0, \theta_3\}$, then all the topic assignments for d are exclusively limited to $keyword_1$ and $keyword_3$.

To use this model, we need to analyze a multi-labeled sequential scholarly publication collection (with keyword and publication date metadata) through posterior inference. This reveals a set of K dynamic changing topics and influence scores for each paper and each topic, which explicitly characterizes the "time-varying" dynamics of publication content, and overcomes the problem of traditional DIM. The detailed posterior inference is similar to DIM, which can be found in [8].

By pre-training the scholarly corpus using supervised document influence model, we can obtain three time-series distributions:

*(1) Time-series document-topic distributions (**TDTD**)*

$$\theta = \left\{ \begin{array}{cccc} \theta_{t_1,d_1^1,1:K}, & \theta_{t_2,d_1^2,1:K}, & \cdots & \theta_{t_T,d_1^T,1:K} \\ \theta_{t_1,d_2^1,1:K}, & \theta_{t_2,d_2^2,1:K}, & \cdots & \theta_{t_T,d_2^T,1:K} \\ \cdots & \cdots & \cdots & \cdots \\ \theta_{t_1,d_{D_1}^1,1:K}, & \theta_{t_2,d_{D_2}^2,1:K}, & \cdots & \theta_{t_T,d_{D_T}^T,1:K} \end{array} \right\}$$

Where, $\theta_{t_i,d_m^i,k}$ is k^{th} topic's $(1 \leq k \leq K)$ proportion in $d_m{}^{th}$ publication $(1 \leq d_m \leq |D_i|)$ published in time slice i $(1 \leq i \leq T)$. ***TDTD*** represents the proportions of historical topics in papers published in a specific time slice.

*(2) Time-series topic-word distributions (**TTWD**)*

$$\beta = \left\{ \begin{array}{cccc} \beta_{t_1,w_1,1:K}, & \beta_{t_2,w_1,1:K}, & \cdots & \beta_{t_T,w_1,1:K} \\ \beta_{t_1,w_2,1:K}, & \beta_{t_2,w_2,1:K}, & \cdots & \beta_{t_T,w_2,1:K} \\ \cdots & \cdots & \cdots & \cdots \\ \beta_{t_1,w_{|V|},1:K}, & \beta_{t_2,w_{|V|},1:K}, & \cdots & \beta_{t_T,w_{|V|},1:K} \end{array} \right\}$$

Where, $\beta_{t_i,w_n,k}$ is the probability of term w_n $(1 \leq n \leq |V|)$ appearing in k^{th} topic $(1 \leq k \leq K)$ in time slice i $(1 \leq i \leq T)$. ***TTWD*** represents the relevance between terms and historical topics in a specific time slice.

*(3) Time-series document-topic influence distributions (**TDTL**)*

$$L = \left\{ \begin{array}{cccc} l_{t_1,d_1^1,1:K}, & l_{t_2,d_1^2,1:K}, & \cdots & l_{t_{T-1},d_1^{T-1},1:K} \\ l_{t_1,d_2^1,1:K}, & l_{t_2,d_2^2,1:K}, & \cdots & l_{t_{T-1},d_2^{T-1},1:K} \\ \cdots & \cdots & \cdots & \cdots \\ l_{t_1,d_{D_1}^1,1:K}, & l_{t_2,d_{D_2}^2,1:K}, & \cdots & l_{t_{T-1},d_{D_{T-1}}^{T-1},1:K} \end{array} \right\}$$

Where, $l_{t_i,d_m^i,k}$ is the influence of $d_m{}^{th}$ document $(1 \leq d_m \leq |D_i|)$ on k^{th} topic $(1 \leq k \leq K)$ published in time slice i $(1 \leq i \leq T-1)$. ***TDTL*** represents the publication's influence on a historical topic in a specific time slice.

These three time-series topic-based distributions characterize the content dynamics on the topic level and will provide the dynamic topic-based information (dynamic topic mixture proportion, dynamic topic evolution and dynamic topical influence) in chronological citation recommendation. Unlike unsupervised approaches, these three distributions are more sparse and accurate. By using keyword metadata, we know the total number of topics, and we can observe if a keyword ever appears in a time slice. For instance, the keyword (topic) *"Latent Dirichlet Allocation (LDA)"* is first proposed in 2003; so the studies in the time slices prior to 2003 cannot contain this topic (i.e., $\beta_{\mathbf{t<2003,w,"LDA"}} = 0$).

2.2 Heterogeneous Graph Construction

Although SDIM can be potentially helpful for chronological citation recommendation by providing dynamic topic-based information, it also has two limitations for modeling the information-need shifting. First, SDIM doesn't utilize citation information, and the citation relations can be very important to characterize the information-need shifting. Second, SDIM, along with the three distributions, provides heterogeneous ranking information (features) which can hardly be represented as a unique ranking function. For instance, we can hardly propose a unique function to integrate topic inference, paper citation and topic evolution probabilities efficiently. To address these problems, we propose a heterogeneous graph mining approach where each kind of ranking information is conceptualized as a meta-path on the heterogeneous graph. The chronological citation recommendation with information-need shifting can then be estimated through learning-to-rank (by integrating different time-related meta-path based ranking features and feature weight training).

A heterogeneous graph, namely a heterogeneous information network, is a directed graph which contains multiple types of objects and links. In a heterogeneous graph, two different types of vertices can be connected via different paths that carry different types of information. A meta-path represents a composite relation over two vertices. For example, $W^* \stackrel{cons}{\leftarrow} T_{time} \stackrel{r}{\leftarrow} P^?$ denotes a meta-path between a query word (W^*) and a candidate cited paper ($P^?$) connected by a historical topic (T_{time}) that has the word and is related to the paper. Sun et al. [22] give the formal definition of "Heterogeneous information network," "Network schema" and "Meta-path."

We will construct a heterogeneous graph (Figure 3) with three types of vertices: (1) W, Word; (2) T_{time}, Historical Topic (with topic label); and (3) P_{time}, Paper published in specific time slice. The historical topic is time-slice dependent, which means even if different topics share the same keyword label, they are considered to be different topics if they belong to different time slices, i.e. $Language\ model_{(2000)}$ and $Language\ model_{(2006)}$ are two different topics (two vertices on the graph) in this study.

The input of chronological citation recommendation is a piece of text to briefly summarize the information need, i.e., paper abstract or research idea description. We use two types of starting vertices on the graph to represent the user textual query: (1) W^*, the word in the query; and (2) $T_{time}{}^*$, the query-related historical topics generated via dynamic topic inference (LDA inference [2] for each time slice). Note that given the same query, as demonstrated in the last section, different time slices may have different query-related topic distributions based on ***TTWD***.

The end vertex on the ranking meta-path is the candidate-cited paper, $P_{time}{}^?$, in a specific time slice. The output is several lists of ranked candidate papers in different time slices, which could potentially be cited given the user's query and reflect the user information-need shifting.

Table 1 presents the edges in the heterogeneous graph. Each edge carries one or more types of information, and it has its own weight. The sum of the weights (transitioning probability) of the edges of a specific type from the same vertex will be 1.

Table 1: Edges in the constructed heterogeneous graph

Edge	Description	Information Carrying
$P \stackrel{h}{\rightarrow} W$	Paper has word	Word-based information
$T_{time} \stackrel{cons}{\rightarrow} W$	Historical topic consists of words	Dynamic topic-based information
$T_{time} \stackrel{cite}{\rightarrow} T_{time}$	Historical topic cites historical topic	Time-decay topic citation information
$P_{time} \stackrel{cite}{\rightarrow} P_{time}$	Paper cites paper.	Time-decay paper citation information
$T_{time} \stackrel{cont}{\rightarrow} P_{time}$	Historical topic is contributed by paper	Time-decay paper citation information and dynamic topic-based information
$T_{time} \stackrel{infl}{\rightarrow} P_{time}$	Historical topic is influenced by paper	Dynamic topic-based information
$P_{time} \stackrel{r}{\rightarrow} T_{time}$	Paper is related to historical topic	Dynamic topic-based information

(1) The weight of $P_i \stackrel{h}{\rightarrow} W_n$ is the normalized TF-IDF value of

Figure 3: Constructed heterogeneous graph with textual query

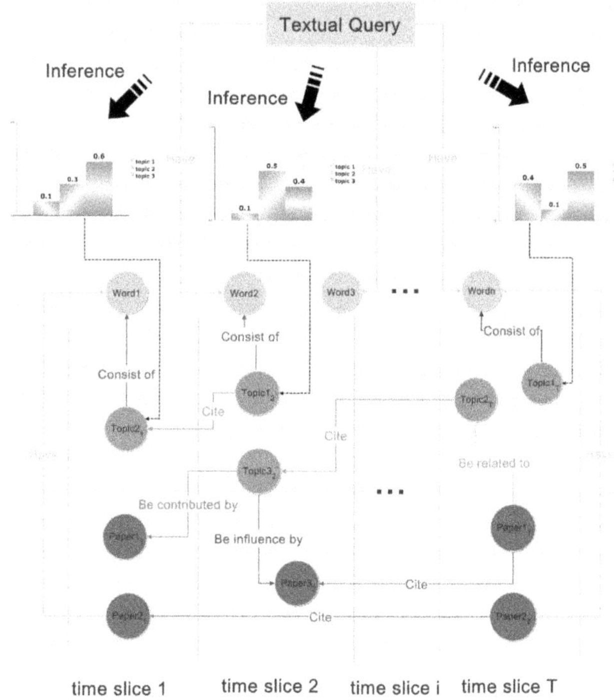

$word_n$ in $paper_i$.

(2) The weight of $T_k{}^{t_i} \stackrel{cons}{\rightarrow} W_n$ is the probability $\beta_{t_i,w_n,k}$ from ***TTWD***.

(3) The weight of $T_m{}^{t_i} \stackrel{cite}{\rightarrow} T_n{}^{t_j}$ is the time-decay topic citation probability $\frac{1}{out_{T_m{}^{t_i}} * \Psi_{T_m{}^{t_i}}} * \varepsilon_{t_i}$; $out_{T_m{}^{t_i}}$ is the number of outlinks of historical topic $T_m{}^{t_i}$; $\Psi_{T_m{}^{t_i}}$ is the normalization parameter, which is the sum of all the weights of outlinks of historical topic $T_m{}^{t_i}$; ε_{t_i} is the time decay factor, which ensures that the citation from historical topic in recent time slice has more weight [24], $\varepsilon_{t_i} = \frac{1}{log_2(2+T-i)}$.

(4) Similarly, the weight of $P_m{}^{t_i} \stackrel{cite}{\rightarrow} P_n{}^{t_j}$ is the time-decay paper citation probability $\frac{1}{out_{P_m{}^{t_i}} * \Psi_{P_m{}^{t_i}}} * \varepsilon_{t_i}$.

(5) The weight of $T_k{}^{t_i} \stackrel{infl}{\rightarrow} P_m{}^{t_i}$ is the influence score of $l_{t_i,d^i_m,k}$ from ***TDTL*** (topic influenced by paper).

(6) The weight of $P_m{}^{t_i} \stackrel{r}{\rightarrow} T_k{}^{t_i}$ is the proportion $\theta_{t_i,d^i_m,k}$ from ***TDTD*** (paper related to topic).

(7) The weight of $T_{time} \stackrel{cont}{\rightarrow} P_{time}$ is the contribution of each paper to a historical topic (topic contributed by a paper). In order to estimate this contribution, we calculate the paper's importance given a historical topic $T_n{}^{t_j}$ by using PageRank with Prior algorithm [25]. The normalized topical PageRank authority score is used for the weights of $T_k{}^{t_j} \stackrel{cont}{\rightarrow} P_m{}^{t_i}$. For this step, we use a classical homogeneous graph where the vertex is a paper. The citation relationship between the vertices is utilized to calculate the PageRank authority scores. Each vertex is also characterized by a topic prior vector which is $\theta_{t_i,d^i_m,1:K}$ from ***TDTD***. The result of PageRank (with prior) is the historical topic authority vector of the paper; i.e., for $P_m{}^{t_i}$, the result is a paper authority vector $Authority(P_m{}^{t_i}|T_{1:K}{}^{t_j})$, the authority score of $P_m{}^{t_i}$ given the historical topics $T_{1:K}{}^{t_j}$. Note that $T_k{}^{t_j}$ is contributed by $P_m{}^{t_i}$ ($T_k{}^{t_j} \stackrel{cont}{\rightarrow} P_m{}^{t_i}$) doesn't necessarily mean $P_m{}^{t_i}$ is related

to $T_k{}^{t_j}$ ($P_m{}^{t_i} \xrightarrow{r} T_k{}^{t_j}$). For example, some "topic modeling" papers published in the year 2003 can be important for the historical topic, $Information\ Retrieval_{(2006-2007)}$. Meanwhile, $T_{time} \overset{infl}{\rightarrow} P_{time}$ and $T_{time} \overset{cont}{\rightarrow} P_{time}$ are different because the former one is generated from content based dynamic topic modeling, while the latter one comes from citation relations.

We use meta-path plus random walk from starting vertices to candidate paper vertices in the heterogeneous graph as the ranking functions. In order to quantify the ranking score of the candidate paper vertices, we use random walk probability from starting (query) vertices to the target paper vertices following a meta-path:

$$r(v_i^{(1)}, v_j^{(l+1)}) = \sum_{t=v_i^{(1)} \rightsquigarrow v_j^{(l+1)}} RW(t)$$

Where t is a tour from $v_i^{(1)}$ to $v_j^{(l+1)}$ following the meta-path, and $RW(t)$ is the simulated random walk probability of the tour t. Suppose $t = (v_{i1}^{(1)}, v_{i2}^{(2)}, \ldots, v_{il+1}^{(l+1)})$, the random walk probability is then,

$$RW(t) = \prod_j w(v_{ij}^{(j)}, v_{i,j+1}^{(j+1)}) p(v_{ij}^{(j)})$$

where $w(v_{ij}^{(j)}, v_{i,j+1}^{(j+1)})$ is the weight of edge $v_{ij}^{(j)} \rightarrow v_{i,j+1}^{(j+1)}$, and $p(v_{ij}^{(j)})$ is the vertex prior probability. Note that we don't consider the direction of edges when we calculate the simulated random walk probability.

For example, given meta-path $W^* \overset{h}{\leftarrow} P^?$, the relevance score from $W_n{}^*$ to $P_{m,time}{}^?$ can be calculated by $p(W_n{}^*) * w(W_n{}^* \overset{h}{\leftarrow} P_{m,time}{}^?)$, where $p(W_n{}^*)$ is the normalized TF-IDF value of W_n in query and $w(W_n{}^* \overset{h}{\leftarrow} P_{m,time}{}^?)$ is the weight of edge which is the normalized TF-IDF value of W_n in candidate paper $P_{m,time}{}^?$.

The total ranking score from a set of starting vertices to a candidate paper's vertex can be defined as:

$$r(Q, v_j^{(l+1)}) = \sum_{v_i^{(1)} \subset Q} r(v_i^{(1)}, v_j^{(l+1)})$$

All meta-paths investigated in this study are listed in Table 2. All these meta-paths address different ranking hypotheses, and each meta-path carries one or more types of dynamic ranking information. We use these meta-paths as chronological ranking features, and the total ranking score of a publication for a specific meta-path is the ranking feature value for this publication. By constructing and calculating all these time-related meta-path based ranking features, we achieve the first level modeling of information-need shifting for chronological citation recommendation.

2.3 Modeling Information-Need Shifting via Learning to Rank

After obtaining the different dynamic ranking features, it's vital to characterize information-need shifting. In this study, we use learning-to-rank to integrate all the ranking features for each time slice and estimate the evolving feature weights in different time slices. As mentioned in section 1, user information need can vary in different time slices (information-need shifting). We train multi-ranking models, $\{\Phi_1, \Phi_2 ... \Phi_T\}$ (total T time slices), for different time slices. The information need in time slice t can be characterized as: $\Phi_t \cong L(\Re_{1,t}, \Re_{2,t}, \cdots, \Re_{c,t}, \cdots)$, which means the candidate cited paper recommendation ranking in time slice t, and $\Re_{c,t}$ represents the recommendation score for paper c published in time slice t. Each candidate paper is assigned different ranking scores via various meta-paths. We also assume the importance (feature weight) of different ranking features can be significantly different for different time slices. In this study, $\Re_{c,t}$ is calculated by:

$$\Re_{c,t} = \sum_{i=1}^{n} [\omega_i^t * r_i(Q^q, v_t^c)] = \sum_{i=1}^{n} \{\omega_i^t * \sum_{v_q \in Q^q} [r_i(v_q, v_t^c)]\}$$

given that n is the number of ranking features; ω_i^t is the weight for ranking feature i, it should be time evolving; Q^q is the starting vertices from the user initial textual query; v_t^c is the candidate publication vertex in time slice t; $r_i(Q^q, v_t^c)$ is the total feature ranking score for meta-path i.

We estimate the effect of information-need shifting by evaluating the recommendation performance for different historical periods. Following this strategy, we use learning-to-rank to train the time-evolving ω_i^t for ranking feature i in time slice t to optimize the recommendation performance. Learning-to-rank [12] optimizes ranking performance using machine learning techniques. In the learning-to-rank framework, documents are usually represented by ranking feature vectors. We use learning-to-rank to combine different meta-path based ranking features and model the information-need shifting while avoiding manual parameter tuning. Specifically, we train the ranking models by using a list-wise algorithm (Coordinate Ascent [16]) on the training data. A training metric (nDCG@k or MAP@k) needs to be applied, and the model that performs best is recorded for each time slice. Because nDCG is more sensitive on the order of the recommendation results – especially the top recommendation orders – compared with MAP, we choose nDCG@k as a training metric. We use a scientific candidate publication set and a set of testing paper for training and evaluation. The abstracts of testing papers are used as the experiment query, and the (author-provided) reference lists are employed as the judgment data. The cite time of different cited papers indicates the importance of each cited paper (for nDCG relevance score). A more detailed evaluation setting will be addressed in the experiment section. After training is complete, we evaluate the trained models on the test data in an evaluation metric (nDCG@k). N-fold cross-validation will be used in this study. Coordinate Ascent is a relatively simple algorithm which iteratively optimizes a multivariate objective ranking function for meta-path feature integration and algorithm evaluation. A more detailed algorithm description can be found in [16].

3. RELATED WORK

Citation Recommendation and Citation Relationship

Scientific recommendation occurs when a scientific publication, venue, or author is recommended to users based on the similarity between the recommended resource and user profiles or samples of in progress text. Similar to previous studies in text information retrieval and text mining, a number of studies employed text similarity approaches, such as paper/author content matching [3,4,6,9,10] and unsupervised topic modeling [1,14,26].

Scholarly or bibliographic networks, i.e., networks based on citation or co-authorship, are another important approach that has been used to recommend scientific resources. For instance, Shi, Leskovec, and McFarland [19] developed citation projection graphs by investigating citations among publications cited by a given paper. Unsupervised topic modeling was also used for citation analysis [26] where visible candidate citations, hidden scientific topics, and visible words were represented in different layers. A restricted Boltzmann machine model was used for building the relationship between user input and recommended citation ranking. In this study, we employed citation importance decay, which was

Table 2: All meta-paths for chronological citation recommendation

No.	Meta-Path	Publication Ranking Hypothesis
1	$W^* \xleftarrow{h} P^?$	The candidate paper is important, if the important word in query also is important to the candidate paper
2	$W^* \xleftarrow{h} P \xrightarrow{cite} P^?$	The candidate paper is important, if the candidate paper is cited by the papers have the important words in the query
3	$W^* \xleftarrow{cons} T_{time} \xleftarrow{r} P^?$	The candidate paper is important, if the candidate paper is related to the historical topics that consist of the words in the query
4	$W^* \xleftarrow{cons} T_{time} \xrightarrow{infl} P^?$	The candidate paper is important, if the candidate paper has enormous influence on the historical topics that consist of the words in the query
5	$W^* \xleftarrow{cons} T_{time} \xrightarrow{cont} P^?$	The candidate paper is important, if the candidate paper contributes to the historical topics that consist of the words in the query
6	${T_{time}}^* \xleftarrow{r} P^?$	The candidate paper is important, if the candidate paper is related to the related historical topics of query
7	${T_{time}}^* \xrightarrow{infl} P^?$	The candidate paper is important, if the related historical topics of query are influenced by the candidate paper
8	${T_{time}}^* \xrightarrow{cont} P^?$	The candidate paper is important, if the related historical topics of query are contributed by the candidate paper
9	${T_{time}}^* \xleftarrow{r} P \xrightarrow{cite} P^?$	The candidate paper is important, if the candidate paper is cited by the papers which are related to the related historical topics of query
10	${T_{time}}^* \xrightarrow{infl} P \xrightarrow{cite} P^?$	The candidate paper is important, if the candidate paper is cited by the papers which have influence on the related historical topics of query
11	${T_{time}}^* \xrightarrow{cont} P \xrightarrow{cite} P^?$	The candidate paper is important, if the candidate paper is cited by the papers contribute to the related historical topics of query
12	${T_{time}}^* \xrightarrow{cite} T_{time} \xleftarrow{r} P^?$	The candidate paper is important, if the candidate paper is related to the historical topics which are cited by the related historical topics of query
13	${T_{time}}^* \xrightarrow{cite} T_{time} \xrightarrow{infl} P^?$	The candidate paper is important, if the candidate paper has enormous influence on the historical topics which are cited by the related historical topics of query
14	${T_{time}}^* \xrightarrow{cite} T_{time} \xrightarrow{cont} P^?$	The candidate paper is important, if the candidate paper contributes to the historical topics which are cited by the related historical topics of query
15	$W^* \xleftarrow{h} P^? \xrightarrow{r} {T_{time}}^*$	The candidate paper is important, if the important word in the query is important to the candidate paper, and the candidate paper is also related to the related historical topics of query
16	$W^* \xleftarrow{h} P^? \xleftarrow{infl} {T_{time}}^*$	The candidate paper is important, if the important word in the query is important to the candidate paper, and the candidate paper also has enormous influence on the related historical topics of query
17	$W^* \xleftarrow{h} P^? \xleftarrow{cont} {T_{time}}^*$	The candidate paper is important, if the important word in the query is important to the candidate paper, and the candidate paper also contributes to the related historical topics of query
18	$W^* \xleftarrow{h} P \xrightarrow{cite} P^? \xrightarrow{r} {T_{time}}^*$	The candidate paper is important, if the candidate paper is cited by the papers have important word in the query and it is also related to the related historical topics of query
19	$W^* \xleftarrow{h} P \xrightarrow{cite} P^? \xleftarrow{infl} {T_{time}}^*$	The candidate paper is important, if the candidate paper is cited by the papers have important word in the query and it also has influence on the related historical topics of query
20	$W^* \xleftarrow{h} P \xrightarrow{cite} P^? \xleftarrow{cont} {T_{time}}^*$	The candidate paper is important, if the candidate paper is cited by the papers have important word in the query and it also contributes to the related historical topics of query
21	$W^* \xleftarrow{h} P^? \xleftarrow{cite} P \xrightarrow{r} {T_{time}}^*$	The candidate paper is important, if the candidate paper has important word in the query and is cited by the papers which are related to the related historical topics of query
22	$W^* \xleftarrow{h} P^? \xleftarrow{cite} P \xleftarrow{infl} {T_{time}}^*$	The candidate paper is important, if the candidate paper has important word in the query and is cited by the papers which have influence on the related historical topics of query
23	$W^* \xleftarrow{h} P^? \xleftarrow{cite} P \xleftarrow{cont} {T_{time}}^*$	The candidate paper is important, if the candidate paper has important word in the query and is cited by the papers which contribute to the related historical topics of query

word-based information   time-decay paper citation information   time-decay topic citation information   dynamic topic-based information

similar to CiteRank [24] (an enhanced ranking algorithm compared to PageRank), which enabled the ranking method to estimate the traffic $T_i(\tau_{dir}, \alpha)$ to a given $paper_i$. For this method, a recent paper was more likely to be selected with a probability that was exponentially discounted according to the age of the paper, τ_{dir}, at every step of the path, with probability α that the researcher was satisfied/saturated and halted his/her line of inquiry. Dietz et. al's citation Influence Model [5] was another effective method of weighing the importance of a citation relation which employed citing and cited paper topic distribution, and the compatibility-based citation weighting of two topic mixtures as measured by the Jensen-Shannon Divergence. Based on these works, Nallapati et. al. [17] proposed Pairwise-Link-LDA and Link-PLSA-LDA whose goal was to predict important unseen citation between papers by using topic-based graph models.

To the best of our knowledge, few existing studies have investigated the chronological citation recommendation problem. Intuitively, for citation recommendation, user information should shift for different time slices. In this study, we will address this problem.

Dynamic Topic Modeling

Topic dynamics has been recently investigated. Laura Dietz et al. [5], for example, devised a probabilistic topic model that explains the generation of documents. The model incorporates the aspects of topical innovation and topical inheritance via citations. Blei and Lafferty [1] proposed a dynamic topic model (DTM), which explicitly characterized the chronological nature of sequential corpora by utilizing a Markov chain of term distributions over time along with multiple LDA-based topic distributions. Based on [1], Gerrish and Blei proposed the document influence model (DIM) [8]. This model respected the ordering of the documents and not only tracked how underlying theme has changed over time, but also captured how past articles exhibit varying influence on future articles. Unfortunately, both DTM and DIM may not be an appropriate solution for the citation recommendation task for three reasons. First, given a textual information need, DTM or DIM alone cannot discover optimized dynamic topic chains in terms of user textual information needs. Second, scientific publications are interlinked by citation, which contains important information. DTM or DIM, however, assumes documents are independent of each other, and the number of topics, as other unsupervised LDA approaches, are not given. Liu et al., [14] found that the unsupervised LDA approach is not ideal for scientific publications, and scientific metadata, i.e., author assigned keywords, should be used to enhance the topic modeling performance.

In order to solve this problem, we utilized Labeled-LDA (LLDA) [18], which used corpus metadata, i.e., keywords and categories, to enhance the topic modeling process and constrained topic models by defining a one-to-one correspondence between latent topics and labels which solved the problems of topic number setting and topic interpretability. We proposed our work based on DIM, and added supervised technology into DIM by combining LLDA.

Heterogeneous Graph Mining

The concept of meta-path was first proposed in [22], which could systematically capture the semantic relation between objects in a heterogeneous information network scenario. Different meta-path-based mining tasks were studied, including similarity search [22], relationship prediction [20, 21], user-guided clustering [23], and recommendation [13]. It turned out the meta-path served as a very critical feature extraction tool for most of the mining tasks in a heterogeneous information network. In this paper, we employed meta-path-based approach as the ranking features, which were extracted from an innovative, dynamic scholarly heterogeneous network.

More recently, Lao and Cohen [11] used both supervised and unsupervised methods with the Random Walk with Restart (RWR) algorithm for citation, author, and venue recommendation. A similar approach was also used by [13]. It had been demonstrated that by using the heterogeneous link information in a network, mining functions, such as similarity search, ranking, clustering and classification could be significantly enhanced [27].

4. EXPERIMENT

In this section, we describe the experimental setting and results. Detailed analysis and conclusions are presented in the next section.

4.1 Data

We extracted 45,372 publications with 107,691 citation relations from 6,818 journals and 4,455 conference proceedings or workshops on computer science between 1951 and 2011 (from the *ACM digital library*). We used the title and the abstract information to represent the content of the paper. All the selected papers' contents featured more than 80 words after removing stop words and stemming each term to its root. The vocabulary size was 6,517. The most frequent 5% of terms and words occurring fewer than 15 times were removed. Author-provided keywords were used as topic labels for SDIM training. The initial number of labels was 1,082, regardless of time slice, and the total historical topic number was 8,072. To verify and compare different recommendation algorithms, we split the corpus into eight time slices: *pre-1990, 1990-1999, 2000-2002, 2003-2005, 2006-2007, 2008-2009, the year 2010* and *the year 2011*. Each time slice contained a similar number of papers. We generated 2,957,476 paper-has-word relations, 107,691 paper-cite-paper relations, 2,242,547 historical-topic-cite-historical-topic relations. After pre-training, we also found 165,970 historical-topic-influenced-by-paper relations, 174,009 paper-related-to-historical-topic relations, 2,171,771 historical-topic-consist-of-word relations (the top 300 words were kept). We then ran PageRank with historical topic prior and generated 1,634,365 historical-topic-contributed-by-paper relations (top 250 papers were kept).

For citation recommendation evaluation, we used a test collection of 274 papers. The selected papers met the following conditions: (1) the selected papers were excluded from the 45,372 publication candidate citation collection; (2) each selected paper featured more than 15 citations to the candidate citation collection, and (3) each paper's abstract featured at least 150 words. The abstract was used as a working context to represent information need, and we recommended citations from the candidate citation collection. In this research, we used an importance score, ranging from 0-4, as the candidate cited paper importance to calculate nDCG scores. For example, if a candidate cited paper was not cited by the target testing paper, the importance score was 0. If a citation was cited four or more times in the citing paper, then it was probably very important for the target citing publication, and its importance score was 4. Each testing paper's citations were partitioned into eight time slices according to the cited paper's publication date. By evaluating the recommendation performance in different time slices, we could estimate the effect of information-need shifting.

We then provided a set of ranked recommendation lists for chronological citation recommendation by learning-to-rank training and evaluation for different time slices. However, as the citation data for the two most recent time slices (year 2010 and 2011) were too sparse (total valid citations were fewer than 10), we only trained and evaluated the recommendation model for the first six time slices (until year 2009).

4.2 Meta-path ranking performance

In the experiment, we used the proposed meta-path as the ranking feature for chronological citation recommendation. Meanwhile, we needed to employ the baseline feature groups for comparison. However, chronological citation recommendation and information-need shifting is a newly proposed problem, and few existing algorithms address this problem. We chose five classic models as baseline feature groups. These models were widely used in practice and had proven to be very effective scholarly recommendation methods. Particularly, as chronological citation recommendation is designed for time-series citation recommendation, we need to compare it with other time-related algorithms. As mentioned in section 3, CiteRank [24] is an enhanced ranking algorithm based on PageRank, which is designed for citation network with time information. The baselines are listed as follows:

1. **PageRank**: Applied the classical PageRank algorithm in paper citation network (query independent).
2. **CiteRank**: Applied the CiteRank algorithm [24] in paper citation network with the default parameters ($\alpha = 0.50, \tau_{dir} = 2.6\ years$ [24]). This baseline is also query independent.
3. **BM25**: BM25 model for test query.
4. **Language Model with Dirichlet prior smoothing (LM-D)**: Language Model with Dirichlet smoothing for test query.
5. **Language Model with Jelinek-Mercer smoothing (LM-JM)**: Language Model with Jelinek-Mercer smoothing for test query.

For each baseline algorithm, we first generated the whole ranked paper list (time slice independent), then partitioned the list into a set of sub-lists based on the publication year.

As Table 3 shows, different features perform differently. There are two meta-path based features (Meta-Path 2 and 20, bold in the table) that outperform all the baseline algorithms with averaged MAP of all time slices. Meanwhile, there are three meta-path based features (Meta-Path 2, 20 and 21, bold in the table) that outperform all the baseline algorithms with averaged nDCG of all time slices.

Table 3: The Average MAP and nDCG Performance

	MAP10	MAP30	MAP50	MAP100	nDCG@10	nDCG@30	nDCG@50	nDCG@100
PageRank	0.0145	0.0251	0.0325	0.0462	0.0263	0.0302	0.0378	0.0480
CiteRank	0.0197	0.0310	0.0390	0.0537	0.0210	0.0280	0.0344	0.0490
BM25	0.0086	0.0108	0.0118	0.0135	0.0151	0.0181	0.0193	0.0235
LM-D	0.0073	0.0093	0.0103	0.0119	0.0150	0.0180	0.0207	0.0242
LM-JM	0.0083	0.0104	0.0114	0.0130	0.0150	0.0175	0.0189	0.0227
Meta-Path 1	0.0119	0.0156	0.0174	0.0200	0.0183	0.0218	0.0239	0.0286
Meta-Path 2	**0.0344***	**0.0527***	**0.0642***	**0.0828***	**0.0333***	**0.0420**	**0.0488**	**0.0646***
Meta-Path 3	0.0029	0.0052	0.0066	0.0088	0.0065	0.0105	0.0134	0.0179
Meta-Path 4	0.0021	0.0032	0.0039	0.0047	0.0023	0.0044	0.0055	0.0078
Meta-Path 5	0.0125	0.0230	0.0298	0.0415	0.0219	0.0279	0.0327	0.0439
Meta-Path 6	0.0024	0.0038	0.0045	0.0058	0.0070	0.0094	0.0115	0.0151
Meta-Path 7	0.0017	0.0026	0.0032	0.0044	0.0023	0.0038	0.0059	0.0100
Meta-Path 8	0.0042	0.0083	0.0110	0.0170	0.0077	0.0146	0.0180	0.0259
Meta-Path 9	0.0141	0.0219	0.0269	0.0359	0.0185	0.0264	0.0313	0.0429
Meta-Path 10	0.0071	0.0139	0.0188	0.0290	0.0114	0.0192	0.0246	0.0356
Meta-Path 11	0.0101	0.0186	0.0249	0.0362	0.0158	0.0235	0.0296	0.0407
Meta-Path 12	0.0011	0.0023	0.0033	0.0054	0.0018	0.0033	0.0048	0.0102
Meta-Path 13	0.0019	0.0030	0.0039	0.0056	0.0029	0.0057	0.0085	0.0140
Meta-Path 14	0.0126	0.0223	0.0282	0.0388	0.0223	0.0268	0.0323	0.0427
Meta-Path 15	0.0061	0.0087	0.0102	0.0122	0.0138	0.0166	0.0195	0.0235
Meta-Path 16	0.0041	0.0063	0.0074	0.0093	0.0082	0.0118	0.0143	0.0188
Meta-Path 17	0.0098	0.0153	0.0189	0.0251	0.0161	0.0213	0.0263	0.0342
Meta-Path 18	0.0174	0.0253	0.0294	0.0354	0.0260	0.0327	0.0371	0.0443
Meta-Path 19	0.0135	0.0193	0.0229	0.0289	0.0169	0.0234	0.0285	0.0369
Meta-Path 20	**0.0273**	**0.0450**	**0.0552**	**0.0715**	**0.0327**	**0.0422***	**0.0490***	**0.0623**
Meta-Path 21	0.0209	0.0305	0.0361	0.0463	**0.0277**	**0.0353**	**0.0397**	**0.0510**
Meta-Path 22	0.0141	0.0235	0.0292	0.0405	0.0182	0.0264	0.0330	0.0447
Meta-Path 23	0.0177	0.0282	0.0348	0.0467	0.0221	0.0304	0.0359	0.0476

*** the best result** word-based information time-decay paper citation information time-decay topic citation information dynamic topic-based information

However, Table 3 only indicates the averaged performance. In fact, even the best-performing ranking feature cannot always outperform the baseline algorithms in each time slice. For instance, Meta-Path 2 achieves the best averaged nDCG@10, but in the pre-1990 time slice, its ranking performance (nDCG@10 = 0.0927) is worse than PageRank's performance (nDCG@10 = 0.1279). In next step, the chronological citation recommendation method used learning-to-rank to integrate all the ranking features and trained the time-evolving model to enhance the recommendation performance. Note that each meta-path generates a ranking feature, and low performance features are not necessarily useless from a learning-to-rank perspective. Instead, some ranking features can be very useful if they can provide a distinct or novel ranking contribution [7].

4.3 Chronological Citation Recommendation

For Chronological Citation Recommendation, all the meta-paths proposed in Table 2 were used as features via learning-to-rank. To avoid evaluation bias, we applied five-fold cross-validation for each time slice. Specifically, for each time slice, we trained a Coordinate Ascent model on each fold that optimizes for nDCG@10; this model was evaluated on the corresponding test data for the current fold also using nDCG@10. The dynamic ranking feature weight for each time slice was the average value of 5-fold cross-validation learn-to-rank training results for this time slice.

As Figure 4 shows, the result of chronological citation recommendation (CCR) method is promising. We chose top two best meta-path based ranking features for averaged nDCG evaluation result of all time slices (Meta-Path 2 and 20) and five baseline algorithms for comparison. The chronological citation recommendation model achieves the best performance with all the average nDCG evaluation metrics (t-test, $p < 0.005$).

In different time slices, the chronological citation recommendation (CCR) model still achieved the best performance with all nDCG evaluation metrics (nDCG@10 - nDCG@100), except one metric (nDCG@50 for time slice of "2003-2005"). For this metric, CiteRank(nDCG@50 = 0.0237) outperforms CCR(nDCG@50 = 0.0213). In Figure 5, we present the nDCG@10 performance of chronological citation recommendation (CCR) model in different time slices comparing baseline algorithms.

Figure 4: The Average nDCG Performance of final rankings using Chronological Citation Recommendation

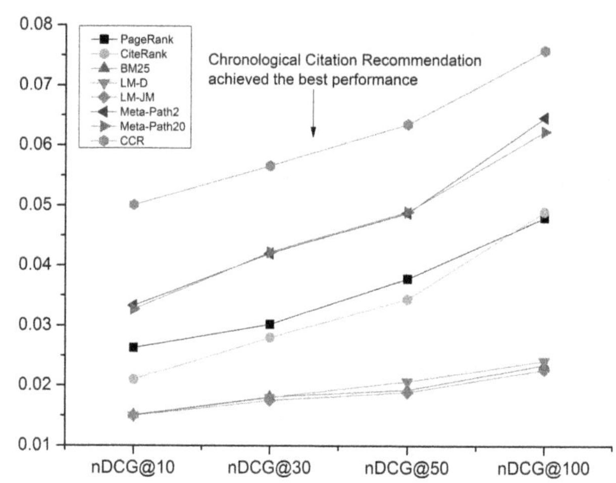

Each ranking feature received a time-evolving weight from the learning-to-ranking training, and the weight represented the ranking feature's contribution to the recommendation performance in a specific time slice. As Figure 6 shows, we present the weight evolution of four meta-path features in different time slices. The orange dotted line represents the linear trend line. These four meta-paths carry different types of information. Meta-Path 1 (carrying word-based information) and Meta-Path 4 (carrying dynamic topic-based

Figure 5: nDCG@10 performance comparison in different time slices

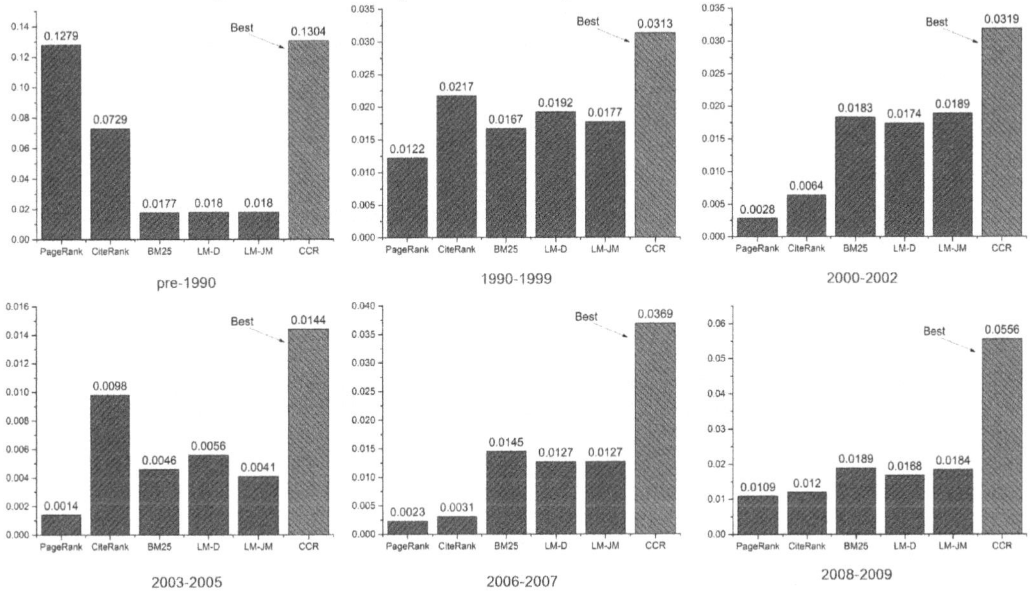

information) weights (contribution) are increasing from the oldest time slice to the newest time slice. Meta-Path 9 (carrying time-decay paper citation information and dynamic topic-based information) and Meta-Path 12 (carrying time-decay topic citation information and dynamic topic-based information) weights, on the contrary, contribute less to the newer time slices. We can generalize from this finding that: with the citation density getting lower in recent time slices, the content-based ranking features (word or topic) are increasingly important in recommending recent publications, while citation-based features are more important for recommending historical publications. We can also find that the absolute values of different ranking features are varying significantly. For instance, compared with the Meta-Path 4 (dynamic topic-based information) feature, the Meta-Path 1 (word-based information) feature is a "stronger" feature, which means Meta-Path 1 feature will provide more contribution in chronological citation recommendation along with information-need shifting.

Figure 6: Feature weight evolution in different time slices

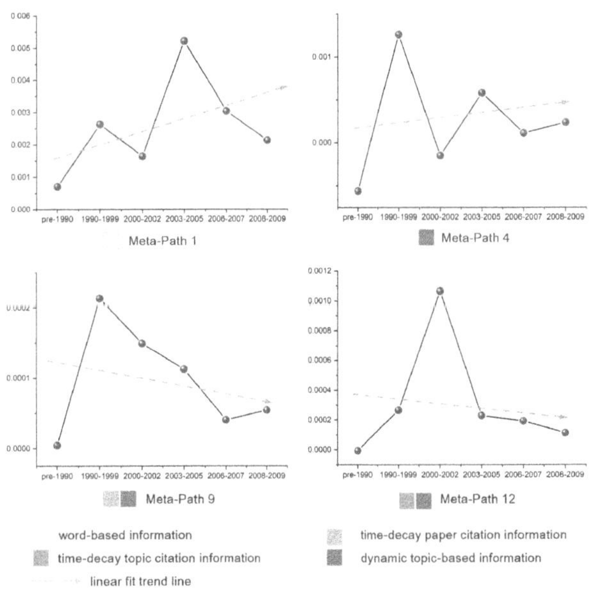

5. ANALYSIS AND CONCLUSION

In this study we propose "Chronological Citation Recommendation," which addresses the requirement of characterizing "information-need shifting." We characterize the information-need shifting with two-level modeling: (1) dynamic time-related ranking feature construction with supervised dynamic document influence model training, and meta-path-based ranking features on a novel heterogeneous graph along with random walk algorithm; (2) dynamic evolving feature weight training by applying learning-to-rank to train multi-ranking models in different time slices for optimizing the chronological citation recommendation performance. Experiment results with multi-labeled ACM sequential data show that the new method can significantly enhance the citation recommendation performance in different time slices. This result supports our hypothesis and demonstrates that chronological citation recommendation improves time-series citation recommendation performance compared to general paper ranking using classic models and time-related algorithms. In other words, the result proves that, given a textual query, the new method can better characterize the information-need shifting in different time slices and give better time-series recommendation lists.

In this study, different meta-paths reflect different ranking hypotheses. Whether they carry the same type of information or the information is totally different, the ranking performance differs. For instance, as Table 2 and Table 3 show, although Meta-Path 8 and Meta-Path 9 both contain time-decay paper citation information and dynamic topic-based information, the hypotheses are different, and the ranking performances are wide apart. Experiment also shows that in all the ranking features – Meta-Path 2, carrying word-based information, and time-decay paper citation information – achieves the best ranking performance with all averaged MAP evaluation metrics, averaged nDCG@10 and nDCG@100. Other well-performing meta-path rankings, such as Meta-Path 20 and 21, also contain these two types of information. In contrast, the rankings of meta-paths which only contain dynamic topic-based information or time-decay topic citation information, such as Meta-Path 3, 4, 6, 7, 12 and 13, perform less effectively in the experiment. These results demonstrate the importance of word-based information and time-decay paper citation information. They are indispensable in chronological citation recommendation and modeling the information-need shifting.

The chronological citation recommendation model in each time slice is a learned model via learning-to-rank, which contains all types of information and combines all the feature information optimally by training the feature weight in different time slices. Its ranking performance is promising. As Figure 4 and Figure 5 show, the chronological citation recommendation achieves the best in all time slices. Moreover, the chronological citation recommendation ranking in each time slice is most stable when compared with baseline algorithms. As Figure 6 shows, the feature weight is evolving over time. It not only reflects the different contributions of different time-related ranking features, but also captures the ranking feature time-evolving trajectory. These results indicate the new method can probably address the information-need shifting problem and enhance the citation recommendation performance.

The methodological limitations of this work are twofold. First, after splitting into different time slices, the citations of the test corpus were sparse in several time slices. More evaluation and model training methods should be applied in future work. Second, the title and abstract (along with pruning) limits experiment vocabulary to a relatively small set. More sophisticated text features could be extracted from full text data.

In future work, we will validate chronological citation recommendation in other multi-labeled sequential datasets, i.e., PubMed, and create more sophisticated learning-to-rank algorithms for characterizing information-need shifting.

6. ACKNOWLEDGMENTS

Special thanks to Prof. Yan Chen for her valuable suggestions during the planning and development of this research work. This work is supported by the Projects of National Natural Science Foundation of China (No.61202232 and No. 61472014).

7. REFERENCES

[1] David M Blei and John D Lafferty. Dynamic topic models. In *Proceedings of the 23rd international conference on Machine learning*, pages 113–120. ACM, 2006.

[2] David M Blei, Andrew Y Ng, and Michael I Jordan. Latent dirichlet allocation. *the Journal of machine Learning research*, 3:993–1022, 2003.

[3] Peter Brusilovsky, Oliviero Stock, and Carlo Strapparava. *Adaptive hypermedia and adaptive Web-based systems*. Springer, 2000.

[4] Kannan Chandrasekaran, Susan Gauch, Praveen Lakkaraju, and Hiep Phuc Luong. Concept-based document recommendations for citeseer authors. In *Adaptive Hypermedia and Adaptive Web-Based Systems*, pages 83–92. Springer, 2008.

[5] Laura Dietz, Steffen Bickel, and Tobias Scheffer. Unsupervised prediction of citation influences. In *Proceedings of the 24th international conference on Machine learning*, pages 233–240. ACM, 2007.

[6] Elena Erosheva, Stephen Fienberg, and John Lafferty. Mixed-membership models of scientific publications. *Proceedings of the National Academy of Sciences of the United States of America*, 101(Suppl 1):5220–5227, 2004.

[7] Xiubo Geng, Tie-Yan Liu, Tao Qin, and Hang Li. Feature selection for ranking. In *Proceedings of the 30th annual international ACM SIGIR conference on Research and development in information retrieval*, pages 407–414. ACM, 2007.

[8] Sean Gerrish and David M Blei. A language-based approach to measuring scholarly impact. In *Proceedings of the 27th International Conference on Machine Learning (ICML-10)*, pages 375–382, 2010.

[9] Qi He, Daniel Kifer, Jian Pei, Prasenjit Mitra, and C Lee Giles. Citation recommendation without author supervision. In *Proceedings of the fourth ACM international conference on Web search and data mining*, pages 755–764. ACM, 2011.

[10] Qi He, Jian Pei, Daniel Kifer, Prasenjit Mitra, and Lee Giles. Context-aware citation recommendation. In *Proceedings of the 19th international conference on World wide web*, pages 421–430. ACM, 2010.

[11] Ni Lao and William W Cohen. Relational retrieval using a combination of path-constrained random walks. *Machine learning*, 81(1):53–67, 2010.

[12] Tie-Yan Liu. Learning to rank for information retrieval. *Foundations and Trends in Information Retrieval*, 3(3):225–331, 2009.

[13] Xiaozhong Liu, Yingying Yu, Chun Guo, Yizhou Sun, and Liangcai Gao. Full-text based context-rich heterogeneous network mining approach for citation recommendation. In *Digital Libraries (JCDL), 2014 IEEE/ACM Joint Conference on*, pages 361–370. IEEE, 2014.

[14] Xiaozhong Liu, Jinsong Zhang, and Chun Guo. Full-text citation analysis: A new method to enhance scholarly networks. *Journal of the American Society for Information Science and Technology*, 64(9):1852–1863, 2013.

[15] Gary Marchionini. Exploratory search: from finding to understanding. *Communications of the ACM*, 49(4):41–46, 2006.

[16] Donald Metzler and W Bruce Croft. Linear feature-based models for information retrieval. *Information Retrieval*, 10(3):257–274, 2007.

[17] Ramesh M Nallapati, Amr Ahmed, Eric P Xing, and William W Cohen. Joint latent topic models for text and citations. In *Proceedings of the 14th ACM SIGKDD international conference on Knowledge discovery and data mining*, pages 542–550. ACM, 2008.

[18] Daniel Ramage, David Hall, Ramesh Nallapati, and Christopher D Manning. Labeled lda: A supervised topic model for credit attribution in multi-labeled corpora. In *Proceedings of the 2009 Conference on Empirical Methods in Natural Language Processing: Volume 1-Volume 1*, pages 248–256. Association for Computational Linguistics, 2009.

[19] Xiaolin Shi, Jure Leskovec, and Daniel A McFarland. Citing for high impact. In *Proceedings of the 10th annual joint conference on Digital libraries*, pages 49–58. ACM, 2010.

[20] Y. Sun, R. Barber, M. Gupta, C. Aggarwal, and J. Han. Co-author relationship prediction in heterogeneous bibliographic networks. In *Proc. 2011 Int. Conf. Advances in Social Network Analysis and Mining (ASONAM'11)*, Kaohsiung, Taiwan, 2011.

[21] Y. Sun, J. Han, C. C. Aggarwal, and N. Chawla. When will it happen? relationship prediction in heterogeneous information networks. In *Proc. 2012 ACM Int. Conf. on Web Search and Data Mining (WSDM'12)*, Seattle, WA, 2012.

[22] Y. Sun, J. Han, X. Yan, P. S. Yu, and T. Wu. PathSim: Meta path-based top-k similarity search in heterogeneous information networks. In *Proc. 2011 Int. Conf. Very Large Data Bases (VLDB'11)*, Seattle, WA, 2011.

[23] Y. Sun, B. Norick, J. Han, X. Yan, P. S. Yu, and X. Yu. Integrating meta-path selection with user guided object clustering in heterogeneous information networks. In *Proc. of 2012 ACM SIGKDD Int. Conf. on Knowledge Discovery and Data Mining (KDD'12)*, Beijing, China, 2012.

[24] Dylan Walker, Huafeng Xie, Koon-Kiu Yan, and Sergei Maslov. Ranking scientific publications using a model of network traffic. *Journal of Statistical Mechanics: Theory and Experiment*, 2007(06):P06010, 2007.

[25] Scott White and Padhraic Smyth. Algorithms for estimating relative importance in networks. In *Proceedings of the ninth ACM SIGKDD international conference on Knowledge discovery and data mining*, pages 266–275. ACM, 2003.

[26] Huan Xia, Juanzi Li, Jie Tang, and Marie-Francine Moens. Plink-lda: Using link as prior information in topic modeling. In *Database Systems for Advanced Applications*, pages 213–227. Springer, 2012.

[27] Xiao Yu, Quanquan Gu, Mianwei Zhou, and Jiawei Han. Citation prediction in heterogeneous bibliographic networks. In *SDM*, pages 1119–1130. SIAM, 2012.

Answering Questions with Complex Semantic Constraints on Open Knowledge Bases

Pengcheng Yin[†] Nan Duan[‡] Ben Kao[†] Junwei Bao[§] Ming Zhou[‡]
[†] The University of Hong Kong [‡] Microsoft Research Asia [§] Harbin Institute of Technology
[†] {pcyin, kao}@cs.hku.hk [‡§] {nanduan, v-jubao, mingzhou}@microsoft.com

ABSTRACT

A knowledge-based question-answering system (KB-QA) is one that answers natural language questions with information stored in a large-scale knowledge base (KB). Existing KB-QA systems are either powered by *curated KBs* in which factual knowledge is encoded in entities and relations with well-structured schemas, or by *open KBs*, which contain assertions represented in the form of triples (e.g., ⟨*subject; relation phrase; argument*⟩). We show that both approaches fall short in answering questions with *complex* prepositional or adverbial constraints. We propose using n-tuple assertions, which are assertions with an arbitrary number of arguments, and n-tuple open KB (nOKB), which is an open knowledge base of n-tuple assertions. We present TAQA, a novel KB-QA system that is based on an nOKB and illustrate via experiments how TAQA can effectively answer complex questions with rich semantic constraints. Our work also results in a new open KB containing 120M n-tuple assertions and a collection of 300 labeled complex questions, which is made publicly available[1] for further research.

1. INTRODUCTION

A question-answering (QA) system is one that automatically answers questions posed in natural languages (NLs). Many of these systems are powered by knowledge bases (KBs), whose information is often encoded as entities and relations with well-structured schemas. With a knowledge-based QA (KB-QA) system, a natural-language question is typically answered in two steps: (1) the free-form natural-language question is transformed into a structured query (e.g., SPARQL query [18]); and (2) answers are retrieved by executing the structured query against a KB [4, 5, 13, 12, 3, 18]. Most of existing research on KB-QA systems focuses on answering questions with *simple semantic constraints*, which are often expressed by the verb phrase of one or multiple binary relations, such as:

single relation: *Who* $[invented]_{rel}$ *the telephone?* [4]

multiple relations: *Who* $[was\ married\ to]_{rel1}$ *an actor that* $[played\ in]_{rel2}$ *Forrest Gump?* [18]

Relatively few efforts, however, have been spent on answering questions with rich semantic constraints, such as those that are expressed via prepositional or adverbial modifiers. As an example, consider the following question:

Question: *What was the currency of Spain before 2002?*
Correct Answer: *Peseta* **Incorrect Answer:** *Euro.*

In this example, the prepositional phrase *"before 2002"* imposes a temporal constraint of the question. As we will elaborate shortly, such constraints are not conveniently handled by QA systems built on existing KB models. Very often, such constraints are lost during the transformation of questions into KB queries, resulting in incorrect answers (e.g., the answer "Euro" is returned instead of "Peseta"). The objective of this paper is to study how questions with complex semantic constraints, particularly those expressed via prepositional or adverbial phrases, can be answered on a KB-QA system. For convenient, we call those questions with complex semantic constraints *"complex questions"*, while those without *"simple questions"*.

To understand the difficulties of existing KB-QA systems in answering complex questions, let us first briefly describe their underlying KBs. KB-QA systems can be categorized into *curated KB-QA systems* and *open KB-QA systems*. While the former has a longer history with a number of implementations (e.g., DEANNA [18] and PARASEMPRE [5]), the latter has been recently proposed by Fader et al. (PARALEX [13] and OQA [12]). A curated KB-QA system is built upon a curated KB (e.g., Freebase [6] and DBpedia [1]), which is collaboratively and manually created. Information is modeled as entities and relations that strictly follow a predefined schema. Figures 1(a) and 1(c) show two snippets taken from Freebase. Since a curated KB is manually edited, it is generally accurate and precise. There are, however, two aspects of it that weaken its ability in answering complex questions.

[Query transformation] An open question has to be first transformed into a structured query (such as SPARQL query) that is compatible with the KB schema, after which the query is executed against the KB to obtain answers. For example, Figure 1(b) shows a SPARQL query (Y_1) for the question Q_1: *"What was James K. Polk?"* This query is obtained by observing that `government_position` is an occupation relation that semantically matches the verb *"was"* in Q_1. The transformation from Q_1 to Y_1 is straightforward considering that Y_1 involves only one relation in the KB. Now consider a complex question Q_2: *"What was James K. Polk before he was president?"* The additional semantic

[1] `http://taqa.pcyin.me`

Permission to make digital or hard copies of all or part of this work for personal or classroom use is granted without fee provided that copies are not made or distributed for profit or commercial advantage and that copies bear this notice and the full citation on the first page. Copyrights for components of this work owned by others than ACM must be honored. Abstracting with credit is permitted. To copy otherwise, or republish, to post on servers or to redistribute to lists, requires prior specific permission and/or a fee. Request permissions from Permissions@acm.org.
CIKM'15, October 19–23, 2015, Melbourne, Australia.
© 2015 ACM. ISBN 978-1-4503-3794-6/15/10 ...$15.00.
DOI: http://dx.doi.org/10.1145/2806416.2806542.

constraint given in Q_2 leads to a much more complex query Y_2. Although the temporal information of the occupation that is needed to answer Q_2 has been encoded using Compound Value Types (CVTs) in Freebase, as denoted by two $\otimes$ nodes in Figure 1(a), existing curated KB-QA systems do not yet have the logic to leverage this information and correctly generate the required queries of complex questions in general. As a result, complex constraints (such as *"before he was president"*) of questions are often neglected and incorrect answers ensue.

[Incompleteness] Another problem faced by curated KB-QA systems is the often incomplete KB schema. This often results in insufficient knowledge to resolve the complex constraints posed in a question. For example, the question $Q3$: *"What was the currency of Spain before 2002?"* cannot be answered by the Freebase snippet shown in Figure 1(c) because the years of circulation of the currencies are not recorded in the KB.[2]

Recently, Fader et al. put forward open KB-QA systems as an alternative approach for KB-QA [12, 13]. An open KB [14] is a large collection of n-tuple assertions that are automatically extracted from web corpora by means of *open information extraction* (open IE) techniques [2, 11, 8, 17]. An assertion is a string n-tuple ($n \geq 3$) which contains one subject (*sbj*), one relation phrase (*rel*), and multiple arguments (*arg*) in the form:

$$\langle sbj; rel; Arg = \{arg_1, arg_2, \cdots, arg_{n-2}\}\rangle.$$

Each element in the tuple is called a *field*. Table 1 gives examples of such n-tuple assertions. The first assertion A_1, for example, is a 4-tuple: it consists of 1 subject (field), 1 relation phrase (field) and 2 arguments (fields). Since assertions in an open KB are automatically acquired from unstructured text, they are often unnormalized and noisy. Nevertheless, two unique features of open KB make it potentially more suitable for QA. First, as assertions are extracted from text, all of their fields are strings in a natural language. They can therefore naturally be used to answer NL questions by string matchings. In particular, unlike a curated KB, there is not a predefined schema and hence no complex query transformation is needed. Second, assertions in n-tuple form contain rich semantic information, which can be used to answer questions with complex semantic constraints. For example, Question Q_2, which is difficult to handle by a curated KB, can be easily answered by matching a derived *tuple query* ⟨*"James K. Polk"*; *"was"*; *?x*, *"before he was president"*⟩ against assertion A_1 in Table 1.

Although open KBs stand out in handling complex questions, the state-of-the-art open KB-QA system, OQA [12], is designed to operate on *triplet* assertions, each of which contains only one single argument (in addition to a subject and a relation phrase). In fact, the OQA system is powered by such an open KB of triples. This restricted model of assertions (triples instead of n-tuple) limits the ability of OQA in answering questions with complex semantic constraints. It is non-trivial to adapt the methodology of OQA to an n-tuple open KB for two reasons. First, questions with semantic modifiers exhibit a variety of syntactic forms. OQA, however, parses simple questions into tuple queries using a small number of hand-crafted Part-of-Speech (POS) templates. While this approach works very well with triples under a rigid subject-relation-argument format, it is difficult to extend those templates to cover questions with complex semantic constraints, especially those that require (n-tuple) assertions with multiple arguments (e.g., assertions A_1 and A_2) to derive answers. Second, the query language of OQA only supports querying triplet assertions. The query language needs to be extended to handle n-tuple open KB, whose assertions contain arbitrary numbers of arguments.

Considering the limitations of existing KB-QA systems in answering complex questions, our goal is to design and implement a novel open KB-QA system that can fully leverage the rich semantics of n-tuple assertions for answering questions with complex semantic constraints. To achieve this goal, two key components in an open KB-QA system, *question parsing* and *open KB querying*, have to be redesigned. As an overview, we propose a generic question parsing method that is based on dependency parsing. Our method is able to parse syntactically diverse questions with rich semantic constraints. Moreover, we put forward an alignment-based answer extraction approach, which is capable of efficiently answering tuple queries using assertions with an arbitrary number of arguments. Apart from these two contributions which focus on leveraging n-tuple open KBs, we also improve the general quality of KB-QA by designing a question paraphraser powered by rich *association features* [5]. Question paraphrasing has been proven important for open KB-QA in bridging the lexical/sytactic gap between user-issued questions and relevant KB assertions. Existing works employ shallow statistical features (e.g., PMI values) to evaluate each paraphrased question, which is unreliable when the dataset used for paraphrasing is noisy. To improve accuracy, we instead use rich association features to learn soft paraphrase rules.

In summary, the main contributions of our paper are:

[nOKB] Existing open KBs (such as OPEN IE [12], PROBASE [19] and NELL [7]) contain only triples. As we have explained, answering complex questions often require n-tuple assertions of multiple arguments because they are much richer in their semantic contents. Existing open KBs are thus inadequate. We fill this void by creating an n-tuple open KB (called nOKB) of 120M assertions together with an evaluation question set of 300 (and counting) complex questions with labeled reference answers, which is released to the public to facilitate further research.

[TAQA] We designed and implemented an n-Tuple-Assertion-based Question-Answering system (called TAQA) that operates on an nOKB for answering questions with complex semantic constraints. We detail the key features of all the major components of TAQA and discuss how they were designed to work with n-tuple assertions.

[Experiments] We conducted extensive experiments to compare TAQA against state-of-the-art open KB-QA and curated KB-QA systems. Our results show that TAQA outperforms other KB-QA systems in answering complex questions. This shows strong evidence that n-tuple assertions are indispensable in answering questions with rich semantic constraints.

The rest of the paper is organized as follows. Section 2 describes the workflow of TAQA and its major components. Section 3 shows our experimental results comparing TAQA against other state-of-the-art KB-QA systems. Section 4 further illustrates our proposed system by means of a case study. Section 5 discusses related works. Finally, Section 6 concludes the paper and discusses several future research directions.

[2]This could have been solved by introducing a CVT node.

Id	Subject	Relation Phrase	Arguments	Frequency	Confidence
A_1	James K. Polk	was	a governor, before he was president	2	0.94
A_2	the currency of Spain	was	the Peseta, before 2002	3	0.86
A_3	the Euro	is	national currency of Spain, since 2002	5	0.78
A_4	the Peseta	was	the currency of Spain	3	0.85
A_5	Spain	introduced	the Euro, as legal tender, in Jan. 2002	2	0.77
A_6	the Vatican Lira	was replaced	by Euro, as official currency, in 2002	1	0.90
A_7	the currency of France	was	the France Franc, before 2002	2	0.77
A_8	the Greek currency	was	the drachma, before 2002	4	0.94

Table 1: Example assertions in nOKB. Arguments fields are separated by commas.

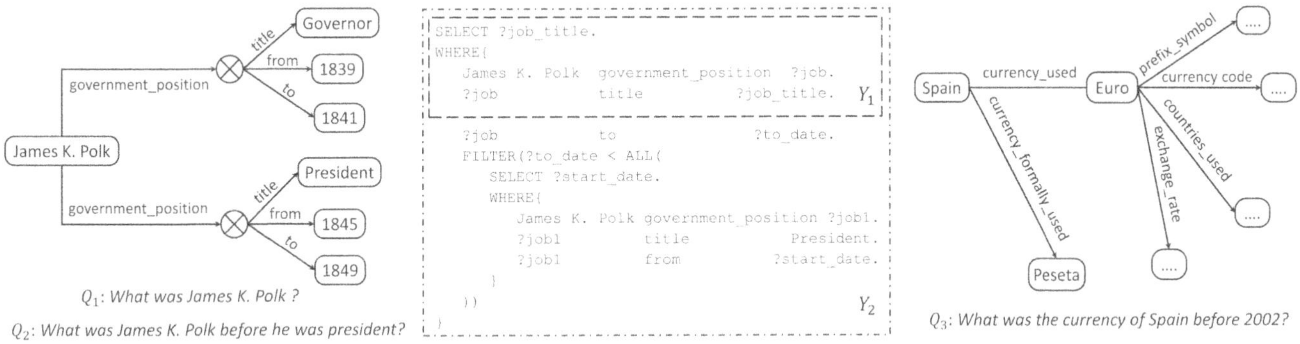

(a) (b) (c)

Figure 1: Freebase snippets and example SPARQL queries

2. SYSTEM

In this section we introduce our system TAQA. We first give an overview of TAQA's workflow, followed by implementation details of each major component.

2.1 Overview

Given a natural language question Q, TAQA processes the question and outputs a list of ranked candidate answers $\mathcal{A}$. Figure 2 gives an illustrative example that shows the various steps involved. There are four key components:

Question Paraphrasing (Section 2.2), which rewrites the original user-issued question into a set of paraphrased questions. Web users generally use informal and casual wordings and expressions in questions. These questions are difficult to parse and are hard to match with assertions in an open KB. Question paraphrasing reformulates original informal questions into formalized ones, which share similar grammatical structures and vocabulary with open KB assertions. Moreover, each paraphrased question derives tuple queries that are executed against the KB for answers. By rewriting the user's question into multiple paraphrased questions, multiple queries are generated. This enhances the recall of the QA system. To improve the quality of question paraphrasing, in TAQA, we employ rich *association features* to help find high-quality paraphrased questions.

Question Parsing (Section 2.3), which parses each paraphrased question into a set of *tuple queries*. A tuple query (e.g., ⟨*?x*; "*wrote*"; "*Harry Potter*"⟩) is similar to an n-tuple assertion except that one of its fields is unknown. TAQA employs a novel question parser that is able to identify rich semantic constraints expressed in the question by analyzing its dependency structure.

Open KB Querying (Section 2.4), which executes each tuple query against the open KB to obtain a list of candidate answers. In order to effectively answer tuple queries using semantically rich n-tuple assertions, we propose a novel alignment-based answer extraction approach that is capable of pinpointing answers from open KB assertions that have various numbers of arguments.

Answer Ranking (Section 2.5), which consolidates and ranks candidate answers derived from different tuple queries. Each candidate answer is associated with a set of features that are obtained through the various steps in the whole question-answering process. TAQA employs a log-linear model on the features to rank the candidate answers. Due to the large feature space (which consists of over $20,000$ sparse features), we use AdaGrad [10] to facilitate fast and effective learning of the ranking model.

2.2 Question Paraphrasing

We follow the approach taken by OQA [12] of paraphrasing a question using *paraphrasing templates*. A paraphrasing template (PT) has the form

$$PT : p_{src} \mapsto p_{tgt}$$

where p_{src} and p_{tgt} are the source and target templates, respectively. Each such template is a string with wildcard variables. The purpose of a PT is to map a syntactic pattern to an alternative one to facilitate the retrieval of relevant assertions in the open KB. The following is an example PT:

PT_1: *What kind of money did they use in* $*_{NP}$ $\mapsto$
What was the national currency of $*_{NP}$

where $*_{NP}$ is a wildcard variable that captures a noun phrase. A user-issued question Q that matches the source template of a PT is rewritten according to the target template of the PT. Complex semantic constraints expressed as prepositional/adverbial phrases in Q are left out in template matching. These phrases are retained in the rewritten questions in their original form. An example of applying PT_1 on question Q_4 is shown in Figure 2. Note that the rewritten question Q_5 allows a perfect match with assertion A_2 (Table 1), which provides the best answer to Q_4.

We use the WIKIANSWERS paraphrasing templates dataset released by [12], which contains 5 million templates created by mining related questions tagged by users on WIKIAN-

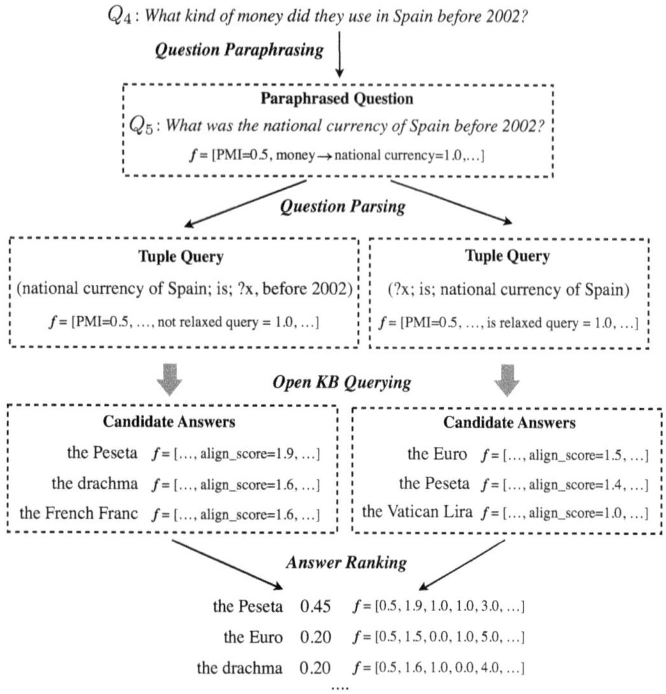

Figure 2: TAQA's workflow

Algorithm 1: question parsing algorithm

```
   input  : natural language question Q
   output: a set of tuple queries T_Q
1  T_Q = ∅, AnsType = null
2  DT_Q = dependency_parsing(Q)
3  rel = root = root_word(DT_Q)
4  S = {w ∈ Q | w <--nsubj,nsubjpass-- root}
5  foreach word s ∈ S do
6      if qword ∈ descendants(s) then sbj = ?x
7      else sbj = all words in descendants(s)
8      Arg = ∅
9      foreach w ∈ children(root), w ∉ rel, w ∉ sbj do
10         if qword ∈ descendants(w) then
11             if w is a preposition then arg = w ?x
12             else if qword = "where" or "when" then
13                 arg = in/on ?x
14             else arg = ?x
15         else arg = all words in descendants(w)
16         Arg = Arg ∪ {arg}
17     TQ = ⟨sbj; rel; Arg⟩
18     T_Q = T_Q ∪ {TQ}
19 AnsType = detect_answer_type(Q)
20 if AnsType! = null then
21     foreach query TQ_i ∈ T_Q do
22         TQ_i = [TQ_i ∧ ⟨?x; "is-a"; AnsType⟩]
23 return T_Q
```

SWERS. The dataset is large but noisy, containing many invalid *PTs*. Consider the following *PT*:

PT_2: *What kind of money did they use in* $*_{NP} \mapsto$
What is the economic system of $*_{NP}$

In [12], this problem is addressed by scoring each paraphrasing template using shallow features like its PMI value and Part-of-Speech (POS) tags. However, we found that using those shallow features alone is often inadequate. For example, PT_1 has identical POS tags as those of PT_2.

In this paper we propose using rich *association features* to identify high-quality question paraphrasing templates from noisy data. The intuition is that strong associations between elements in p_{src} and p_{tgt} often indicate good paraphrasing templates. For example, the association between *"money"* and *"national currency"* (PT_1, a good *PT*) is much stronger than that between *"money"* and *"economic system"* (PT_2, a bad *PT*). Although the idea of using association features has been explored in curated KB-QA systems [5] to rank generated queries, our work first applies it in the context of open KB-QA for measuring the quality of question paraphrasing.

Specifically, for each *PT*: $p_{src} \mapsto p_{tgt}$, we iterate through spans of text $s \in p_{src}$ and $t \in p_{tgt}$ to identify a set of *association phrases*, $\langle s, t \rangle$. For each $\langle s, t \rangle$, we generate a set of indicative association features using the feature templates listed in Table 3. These features are used in the answer ranker (Section 2.5) to measure the quality of the *PT*s used in deriving the answers. Following [5], we identify association phrases by looking-up a table that contains 1.3 million phrase pairs. For example, an indicator feature, $\mathbb{I}\{$*"money"* $\in p_{src} \wedge$ *"national currency"* $\in p_{tgt}\}$ is generated for the association phrases ⟨*"money"*, *"national currency"*⟩. During training, the answer ranker will learn each feature's weight based on its predictive power. Also, answers derived from high quality *PT*s will be given more credits. With our training data, the question paraphraser uses over 20,000 association features.

Besides the association features introduced above, we also use a set of statistical features such as the PMI value of the *PT*s, the log normalized frequency of p_{src} and p_{tgt}, etc. The full set of features used in paraphrasing is listed in Table 3.

2.3 Question Parsing

Each paraphrased question Q is parsed into a set of structured tuple queries (TQs): $\mathcal{T}_Q = \{TQ_1, TQ_2, \ldots, TQ_K\}$. Each tuple query TQ_i has the form: $TQ_i = \langle sbj; rel; Arg \rangle$, which is similar to that of an n-tuple assertion (see Section 1). For a TQ, either the subject field *sbj* or one of the arguments in *Arg* is a wildcard (denoted by $?x$), which indicates the hidden answer the question Q seeks for. We call that wildcard, $?x$, the *query focus* of Q, denoted by F_Q.

Existing open KB-QA systems employ a small number of hand-crafted POS templates to parse questions into tuple queries [12], which are limited in coverage and can only handle questions *without* complex semantic constraints. In this paper we propose a novel approach of parsing questions by *dependency analysis*. This approach is partially inspired by recent advances in open IE [17, 8] research, where dependency parsing has been used to extract open IE assertions, but never to parse questions into tuple queries. Algorithm 1 shows our question parsing algorithm.

Given a question Q, TAQA first applies the Stanford parser to construct a *dependency tree*, DT_Q (Line 2). The nodes in DT_Q are made up of words in Q. The root of DT_Q is usually the main verb of Q and each edge in DT_Q denotes a pairwise dependency relation between two words in Q. For example, in the sentence: *"Bell makes electronic products"*, the word *"Bell"* is a nominal subject (`nsubj`) of *"makes"*, and hence the dependency *"Bell"* $\xleftarrow{\texttt{nsubj}}$ *"makes"* is derived. Table 2 shows three example questions (Q_5, Q_6, Q_7) and their respective dependency trees. Given a dependency tree, TAQA analyzes the tree to identify the various fields of a tuple query (i.e., *sbj*, *rel*, and the arguments in *Arg*) as follows:

Table 2: **Examples of questions, dependency trees and generated tuple queries**

question and dependency tree	tuple queries
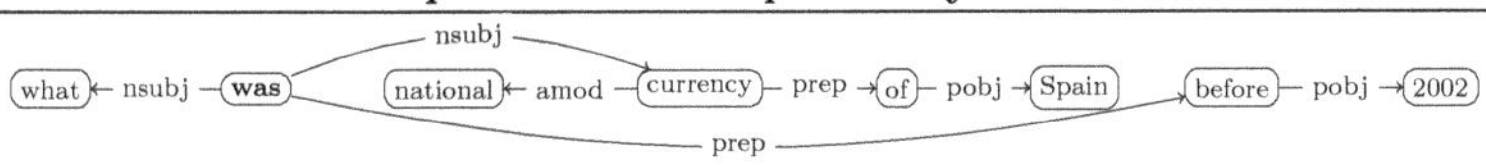 Q_5: *What was the national currency of Spain before 2002?*	TQ_1: ⟨*national currency of Spain; is; ?x, before 2002*⟩ TQ_2: ⟨*?x; is; national currency of Spain, before 2002*⟩ TQ_3(relaxed): ⟨*national currency of Spain; is; ?x*⟩ TQ_4(relaxed): ⟨*?x; is; national currency of Spain*⟩
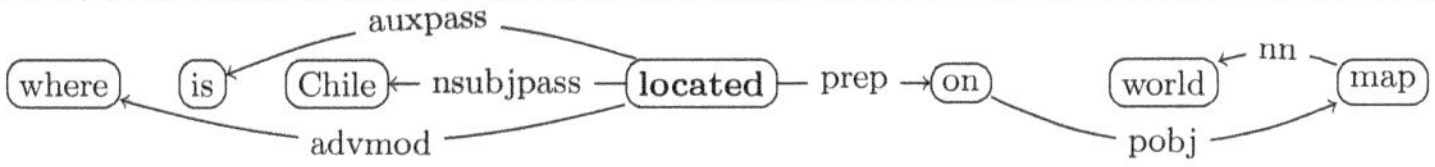 Q_6: *Where is Chile located on world map?*	TQ_5: ⟨*Chile; is located; in/on ?x, on world map*⟩ TQ_6(relaxed): ⟨*Chile; is located; in/on ?x*⟩
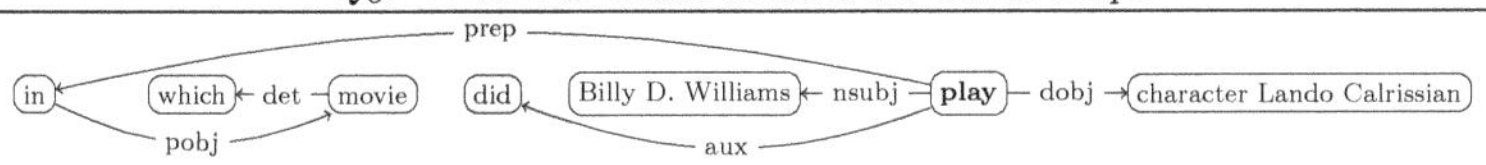 Q_7: *In which movie did Billy D. Williams play character Lando Calrissian?*	TQ_7: ⟨*Billy D. Williams; play; character Lando Calrissian, in ?x*⟩ ∧ ⟨*?x; is-a; movie*⟩ TQ_8(relaxed): ⟨*Billy D. Williams; play; in ?x*⟩ ∧⟨*?x; is-a; movie*⟩

[Identify Relation Phrase] (Line 3) The root word *root* of DT_Q is included in *rel* together with auxiliary words that are children of *root* and that satisfy certain dependency relations with *root*. These dependency relations include *copula* (`cop`), *auxiliary* (`aux`), *passive auxiliary* (`auxpass`), *phrasal verb particle* (`prt`), etc. For example, the relation phrase of question Q_6 in Table 2 is *"is located"* because *"located"* is the root verb and *"is"* is related to *"located"* by the dependency *"is"* $\xleftarrow{\text{auxpass}}$ *"located"*.

[Identify Subject] (Lines 6-7) First, all nodes that are nominal subjects (`nsubj`) or passive nominal subjects (`nsubjpass`) of *root* are collected in a set $\mathcal{S}$. Then, for each node $s \in \mathcal{S}$, if the question word[3], *qword*, is a descendant of s, the subject *sbj* is the query focus *?x*. Otherwise, *sbj* includes all the descendants of s. Note that there could be multiple nominal subjects in DT_Q. In this case, we generate one tuple query for each `nsubj`. For example, question Q_5 in Table 2 derives 2 tuple queries TQ_1 and TQ_2.

[Identify Arguments] (Lines 9-16) Any child node w of *root* that is not identified as a subject (*sbj*) or does not belong to the relation phrase (*rel*) in the previous step derives an argument in *Arg*. Specifically, if the question word is a descendant of w, we create an argument that includes a query focus *?x*; otherwise, the argument includes all the descendants of w.

[Compound Queries] (Lines 19-22) For each tuple query TQ_i obtained from the previous steps, we augment it by deducing an *answer type*, *AnsType*, forming a compound conjunctive query [TQ_i ∧ ⟨?*x*;"*is-a*"; *AnsType*⟩]. The purpose is to prune the search space for the answer (when the query is later executed against a KB) by restricting the scope of the query focus. For example, Question Q_7 in Table 2 derives the tuple query TQ_7. Note that the focus for this query can be restricted to the type *"movie"*, which is expressed by the augmenting tuple query ⟨*?x*; "*is-a*"; "*movie*"⟩. TAQA identifies the noun phrase between *qword* and the auxiliary[4] or root verb as *AnsType*.

[Generate Relaxed Queries] Finally, if the question Q is a complex question (with prepositional/adverbial constraints), TAQA will remove the complex constraints and additional objects of *root* (e.g., *"character Lando Calrissian"* in Q_7) and derives a *relaxed question* Q'. Algorithm 1 is then applied onto Q' to generate (relaxed) tuples queries. The reasons are twofold. First, some complex constraints are redundant and uninformative. For example, consider question Q_6 in Table 2. The constraint *"on world map"* is uninformative; Q_6 can be answered as well in its relaxed form. Second, using relaxed tuple queries can improve coverage, since there are likely assertions in the KB that do not mention the constraints given in the original question Q. TQ_6 in Table 2 is a relaxed tuple query of question Q_6. The use of relaxed tuple queries in answering questions is also illustrated in Figure 2 (see the right branch of the workflow).

[3]Question words are "*what*", "*who*", "*where*", "*when*" and "*which*".

[4]Auxiliary verbs include "*do*", "*did*", "*does*", "*is*", "*was*", "*are*", etc.

2.4 Open KB Querying

After obtaining the set of tuple queries $\mathcal{T}_Q$, the next task is to execute each query $TQ \in \mathcal{T}_Q$ against the open KB to obtain a set of candidate answers $\mathcal{A}_{TQ}$. This is carried out in two steps. First, a set of assertions, $\mathcal{R}_{TQ}$, in the open KB that are relevant to the query TQ is retrieved. In TAQA, assertions are indexed by Apache Solr[5], which retrieves a ranked list of assertions based on the terms mentioned in the assertions and those in the tuple query. We refine $\mathcal{R}_{TQ}$ by removing assertions that have fewer fields than TQ, and then retaining the top-50 of the remaining ones.

Next, we need to align the fields of TQ against those of each assertion $r \in \mathcal{R}_{TQ}$. This is done to identify the field in r that matches the query focus F_Q, which is then taken as the answer of TQ. Unlike OQA, for which queries and assertions are both triples, TAQA deals with n-tuple queries and assertions with an arbitrary number of arguments. The multiplicity of *Arg* fields involves a complex alignment problem. We put forward a novel answer extraction approach which models the alignment problem as a matching problem on a weighted bipartite graph. Figure 3 illustrates the alignment between a tuple query TQ_7 (mentioned in Table 2) against the assertion r : ⟨"*Billy Dee Williams*"; ...⟩ (shown in the figure). Specifically, in the bipartite graph G, fields in TQ form one type of nodes while fields in r form another. Let $TQ.i$ and $r.j$ denote the i-th field of TQ and the j-th field of r, respectively. The weight of the edge connecting $TQ.i$ and $r.j$ in G is given by the following similarity measure:

$$\begin{aligned} \textit{similarity}(TQ.i, r.j) &= \alpha \cdot \textit{text\_similarity}(TQ.i, r.j) \\ &+ (1-\alpha) \cdot \textit{pattern\_similarity}(TQ.i, r.j) \end{aligned}$$

where α is a tuning weight ($\alpha = 0.5$ in the experiment). *text_similarity* is the TF-IDF score of two lemmatized strings. *pattern_similarity* is the sum of three indicator functions that utilize POS/prefix/question patterns:

- $\mathbb{I}_1 = 1$ iff ($TQ.i$ is $?x$) ∧ ($r.j$ is a noun phrase).

[5]`http://lucene.apache.org/solr/`

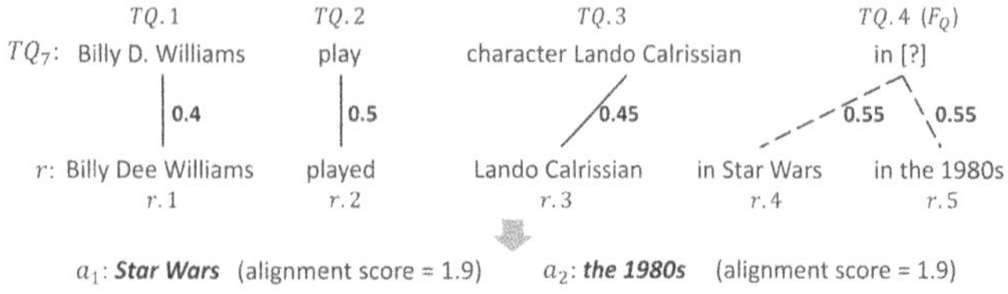

Figure 3: n-tuple alignment

- $\mathbb{I}_2 = 1$ iff (*qword* is *"when"*) $\wedge$ ($TQ.i$ is *"in/on" ?x*) $\wedge$ ($r.j$ is of the pattern *"in/on date_time_string"*).
- $\mathbb{I}_3 = 1$ iff ($TQ.i$ is F_Q) $\wedge$ (F_Q and $r.j$ start with the same preposition).

We then seek all optimal matchings for the following constrained optimization:

$$\max : \sum_i \sum_j x_{ij} \cdot similarity(TQ.i, r.j)$$

$$\text{subject to: } (x_{11} = 1),\ (x_{22} = 1),\ (x_{ij} \in \{0, 1\})$$
$$(0 \le \sum_i x_{ij} \le 1),\ \ (\sum_j x_{ij} = 1). \qquad (1)$$

where $x_{ij} = 1$ iff $TQ.i$ is aligned to $r.j$. The constraints $x_{11} = 1$ forces the alignment between two *sbj* fields. Likewise with $x_{22} = 1$ for the *rel* fields. The field of r that is aligned to the query focus field of TQ in each optimal matching is added to $\mathcal{A}_{TQ}$ as an answer. As an example, in Figure 3, there are two optimal matchings (the query focus field has equal weights with *"in Star Wars"* and *"in the 1980s"*), deriving two answers (a_1 and a_2).

The tuple query used in the illustration (Figure 3) is actually part of a compound query (TQ_7 in Table 2). For such cases, TAQA verifies the answer by querying the KB using the other part of the query. For example, TAQA evaluates the tuples ⟨*"Star Wars"*; *"is-a"*; *"movie"*⟩ and ⟨*"the 1980s"*; *"is-a"*; *"movie"*⟩ against the KB. Answer a_2 is eliminated because it is not supported by the assertions in the KB.

2.5 Answer Ranking

Generally, a question Q is paraphrased into multiple questions, each such question is parsed into multiple tuple queries and each tuple query can derive multiple answers. TAQA collects all these candidate answers into an answer set $\mathcal{A}$. The final stage of the QA process is to determine the best answer in $\mathcal{A}$. An answer $a \in \mathcal{A}$ is associated with many features as it is derived along the paraphrasing-parsing-querying process. We use $\boldsymbol{f}(a) = [f_1(a), f_2(a), \ldots, f_M(a)]$ to denote the feature vector of a. TAQA uses these features to rank the candidate answers. Table 3 lists the features used in TAQA.

The answer set $\mathcal{A}$ is first *consolidated*. In many cases, the same answers are derived via different paraphrasing-parsing-querying outputs. These answers have the same string value but different feature vectors, which should be combined. Specifically, if a_i, $a_j \in \mathcal{A}$ are same answers, then their feature vectors are combined by taking the *best* value for each individual feature. For example, if f_k represents the alignment score (Equation 1) of the assertion that derives an answer, then the combined feature value is $\max(f_k(a_i), f_k(a_j))$ because a higher alignment score indicates better answer quality. This simple approach of consolidating features has been proven useful in [15]. Furthermore, we add statistical features that measure the "popularity" of answers. These features include the occurrence frequency of an answer in $\mathcal{A}$, and the answer's n-gram correlation defined in [9].

KB	# assertions	# relation phrases
OPEN IE	458M	6M
PROBASE	170M	1
NELL	2M	300
nOKB	120M	4.6M

Table 4: Statistics of nOKB+ used by TAQA

WebQuestions	
▷ who played jacob black in twilight?	Taylor Lautner
▷ what timezone is nashville tn?	Central Time Zone
▷ who did roger federer married?	Mirka Federer
ComplexQuestions	
▷ what team did shaq play for before the lakers?	Orlando Magic
▷ what country gained its independence from britain in 1960?	Cyprus
▷ what did france lose to the british in the treaty of paris in 1763?	Dominica

Table 5: Sample questions from WEBQ and COMPQ

After consolidation, we apply a standard log-linear model to estimate the probability $p(a|Q)$ for each $a \in \mathcal{A}$:

$$p(a|Q) = \frac{exp\{\sum_{k=1}^{M} \lambda_k \cdot f_k(a)\}}{\sum_{a' \in \mathcal{A}} exp\{\sum_{k=1}^{M} \lambda_k \cdot f_k(a')\}}$$

where λ_k denotes the k-th feature's weight, and rank candidate answers accordingly. We limit the size of $\mathcal{A}$ to the top 200 candidates when calculating $p(a|Q)$.

We tune the feature weights $\boldsymbol{\lambda} = \{\lambda_k\}$ using a set of N question and gold-standard answer pairs $\mathcal{D} = \{(Q_t, a_t)\}$, by maximizing the log-likelihood of the training data:

$$\mathcal{L}(\mathcal{D}; \boldsymbol{\lambda}) = \sum_{t=1}^{N} \log p(a_t|Q_t; \boldsymbol{\lambda})$$

TAQA employs AdaGrad [10] to effectively learn the weights of over 20,000 sparse features.

3. EXPERIMENT

In this section we evaluate TAQA. We primarily address the following two questions: (1) How does TAQA's performance compare with the state-of-the-art open KB-QA and curated KB-QA systems, especially in answering complex questions? (2) How do the various components of TAQA impact the system's performance? We will first describe the open KB TAQA uses, the evaluating question sets, the performance metrics, and two other KB-QA systems, namely, OQA and PARASEMPRE, before presenting the results. We also present insightful case study in Section 4.

[Open KBs] There are three well known open KBs, namely, OPEN IE [12], PROBASE [19] and NELL [7]. OPEN IE is a large open KB built by performing open IE on CLUEWEB. PROBASE is an open KB of `is-a` assertions extracted from 1.68B web pages. NELL is a relatively small open KB which contains highly precise assertions. Assertions in the above three KBs are all triples. As we have explained, n-tuple assertions are richer in semantics, and are more suitable for answering complex questions. Hence, we build a new open KB of n-tuple assertions (called nOKB) using the latest open IE technique. Here, we briefly discuss how nOKB was built.

First, we need to collect a set of documents $\mathcal{D}$ from which assertions are extracted. We collect all English Wikipedia

Table 3: List of features used in TAQA

Question Paraphrasing, association feature templates ($\langle s, t \rangle$: association phrases)		
▷ $\mathbb{I}\{lemma(s) \in p_{src} \wedge lemma(t) \in p_{tgt}\}$, $lemma(\cdot)$ is the lemmatised text	▷ $\mathbb{I}\{pos(s) \in p_{src} \wedge pos(t) \in p_{tgt}\}$, $pos(\cdot)$ is POS tags	
▷ $\mathbb{I}\{lemma(s)$ and $lemma(t)$ are synonyms$\}$	▷ $\mathbb{I}\{lemma(s)$ and $lemma(t)$ are word-net derivations$\}$ [5]	
Question Paraphrasing, other features (Q_i: paraphrased question, p_{src}: source template, p_{tgt}: target template)		
▷ $\mathbb{I}\{Q_i$ is the original question$\}$	▷ $PMI(p_{src} \mapsto p_{tgt})$, PMI value of the paraphrase template	
▷ $\lvert$words captured by $*_{NP}\rvert / \lvert p_{src} \rvert$	▷ log normalized frequency of p_{src} and p_{tgt}	
Question Parsing (TQ: tuple query)		
▷ $\mathbb{I}\{TQ$ is relaxed query$\}$	▷ $\mathbb{I}\{TQ$ is not relaxed query$\}$	
Open KB Querying (r: assertion, a: candidate answer)		
▷ alignment score of TQ and r	▷ word count of the answer a	▷ ratio of capital words in a
▷ the average IDF value of words in a	▷ $\mathbb{I}\{a$ in a predefined entity list$\}$	▷ $\mathbb{I}\{a$ is a date time $\wedge$ $qword$ = "*when*"$\}$
▷ cosine similarity of fields in r and TQ	▷ extraction frequency and confidence of r	▷ the rank of $r \in \mathcal{R}_{TQ}$
▷ the source of r (cf. Table 4)	▷ $\mathbb{I}\{TQ$ is join query$\}$	▷ cosine similarity of join keys
Answer Ranking ($\mathcal{A}$: candidate answers set)		
▷ n-gram correlation score of a [9]	▷ occurrence frequency of a in $\mathcal{A}$	

documents into a set $\mathcal{D}_{wiki}$. Also, for each question Q in an evaluation question set $\mathcal{QS}$ (we will explain shortly how $\mathcal{QS}$ is obtained), we submit Q to a commercial search engine and retrieve top-200 documents. The retrieved documents for all the questions form the set $\mathcal{D}_{\mathcal{QS}}$. We get $\mathcal{D} = \mathcal{D}_{wiki} \cup \mathcal{D}_{\mathcal{QS}}$, which contains 5.7M web pages. We use OpenNLP[6] to extract sentences from documents, and filter out non-English sentences and those with more than 100 words. After that, we apply Open IE 4.1[7] to the sentences to obtain n-tuple assertions. We remove assertions whose subject or argument fields are either stop words or more than 10 words in length. The process results in 163M sentences and 120M n-tuple assertions. These 120M assertions form nOKB. TAQA operates on assertions provided by all 4 open KBs. We denote the combined KB, nOKB+. Table 4 summarizes these KBs.

[Question Sets] The experiments were conducted on two sets of questions, WebQuestions and ComplexQuestions. Each question set is a collection of (question, gold-standard-answer) pairs. Table 5 gives example pairs taken from the two sets.

WebQuestions [4] (abbrev. WEBQ) is the de facto question set used to evaluate curated KB-QA systems. It consists of 5,810 question-answer pairs. Questions are collected by the Google Suggest API and manually answered by AMT workers using Freebase. WEBQ is moderated for curated KB-QA systems in that all questions are answerable with Freebase (a curated KB). We observe that most of the questions in WEBQ are simple questions; only 80 (4%) of the questions in the test set of WEBQ (2,032 questions) come with complex semantic constraints.

ComplexQuestions (abbrev. COMPQ) is a new dataset created in this work, which focuses on open domain complex questions with prepositional/adverbial constraints. COMPQ consists of 300 complex questions obtained as follows: First, all 80 complex questions in WEBQ are added to COMPQ. Next, we follow the approach given in [4] to crawl questions using the Google Suggest API. We start with a seed question Q^*: *"Who did Tom Hanks play in Toy Story?"*. We google Q^* to obtain at most 10 suggested questions. We retain those suggested questions that begin with a *wh*-word and which contain at least one preposition. For each such question, we remove the entities mentioned in the question and submit the resulting string to google to obtain more suggested questions. The process is repeated in a breadth-first manner. Due to space limitation, readers are referred to [4] for the details of the procedure. We collected a total of 100,000 questions, and then randomly picked 220 complex questions out of the pool. Of all the questions in COMPQ, 20 of them have either 2 or 3 complex constraints, the rest have 1 complex constraint each.

[Metrics] WEBQ comes with a set of answers that are labeled as correct or incorrect [12]. For COMPQ, we manually label the answers returned by the QA systems we tested. Given a question, each QA system computes a ranked list of answers and returns the top-ranked one as the final answer. We measure the performance of a system by its accuracy:

$$acc = \frac{\text{number of correctly answered questions}}{\text{total number of questions}}.$$

[QA systems] We compare TAQA against the current state-of-the-art KB-QA systems: OQA [12], which is the latest open KB-QA system based on triple-form assertions, and PARASEMPRE [5], which is an advanced curated KB-QA system powered by Freebase. We use nOKB+ as the open KB for both OQA and TAQA. For OQA and PARASEMPRE, we use the trained models provided by their authors.[8] For TAQA, we train its feature weights $\boldsymbol{\lambda}$ on nOKB+ using the standard training set of WEBQ (3,778 questions).

3.1 Results

Table 6 shows the accuracy (acc) of the the three KB-QA systems when presented questions from the two question sets. Readers are reminded that PARASEMPRE uses a different KB (Freebase) from that of OQA and TAQA (nOKB+). The performance numbers of PARASEMPRE should not be compared directly with those of the other two systems. Nonetheless, these numbers provide interesting references.

We first compare OQA and TAQA in answering complex questions (COMPQ). From Table 6, we see that OQA had a hard time handling complex questions with an accuracy of only 2%. We studied how OQA handled each of the 300 questions in COMPQ. We make the following observations about its poor performance. First, OQA relies on a limited number of hand-crafted POS templates for question parsing. These templates are inadequate in parsing questions with complex semantic constraints (see Section 2.3). In fact, only about 10% of the questions in COMPQ are successfully parsed by OQA into tuple queries; the other 90% do not result in any tuple queries and thus are not answered by OQA. In sharp contrast, TAQA employs dependency analysis in ques-

[6]`http://opennlp.apache.org/`

[7]`http://knowitall.github.io/openie/`

[8]We also train OQA on nOKB+, but the provided model gives better results.

Systems	ComplexQuestions	WebQuestions
OQA	2.0%	22.9%
TAQA	**39.3%**	35.6%
PARASEMPRE	9.7%	**45.8%**

Table 6: Accuracies (*acc*) of systems

tion parsing, which allows it to successfully parse 98% of the questions. Second, OQA was designed to handle triplets assertions. In particular, only the first three fields (*sbj*, *rel*, and the first argument in *Arg*) of assertions in nOKB+ are used. OQA is therefore unable to fully utilize the rich semantic information that is often displayed in the additional argument fields of n-tuple assertions. TAQA, on the other hand, employs a matching approach to align complex tuple queries to n-tuple assertions. This allows TAQA to make full use of the assertions' argument fields, resulting in a very respectable accuracy of 39.3%.

We also used PARASEMPRE to answer COMPQ questions and registered a 9.7% accuracy. Given a question Q, PARASEMPRE first parses Q into a number of SPARQL queries. It then evaluates the queries and executes the top-ranked one against Freebase. We found that due to the complexity of questions in COMPQ, PARASEMPRE generates an average of 2,090 candidate queries for each question in COMPQ, in an attempt to cover all potential answers. It turns out that most of these queries are *false queries*, which lead to incorrect answers. The big pool of queries makes it very difficult for PARASEMPRE to identify the best query to obtain the correct answers with any less-than-perfect ranking method. In contrast, TAQA generates, on average, 25 tuple queries for each question in COMPQ. The small query pool makes it easier to identify (rank) the best query for a correct answer. Moreover, many of the SPARQL queries generated by PARASEMPRE fail in capturing the questions' complex constraints. For example, the query PARASEMPRE executed for the question: *"What character did Anna Kendrick play in Twilight?"* is without the underlined constraint. In contrast, for the same question, TAQA executes the tuple query ⟨*"Anna Kendrick"*; *"play"*; *?x*, *"in Twilight"*⟩∧⟨*?x*; *"is-a"*; *"character"*⟩ and extracts the correct answer from assertion ⟨*"Anna Kendrick"*; *"plays"*; *"Jessica Stanley"*, *"in Twilight"*⟩.

Another reason why PARASEMPRE gives a relatively low accuracy for COMPQ questions is the restricted coverage of Freebase (a curated KB). For example, PARASEMPRE fails to answer the question *"When did Canada gain independence from England?"* because Freebase does not contain the factual knowledge about the independence of countries.

Next, we consider questions from WEBQ. Recall that questions in WEBQ are predominately simple questions and that all are answerable with information on Freebase. PARASEMPRE is very effective in answering them, which is reflected by the very high (45.8%) accuracy.

Because of the simplicity of WEBQ questions, OQA does not encounter much problem in parsing questions or executing queries in triples form. Its gives a decent accuracy of 22.9% with WEBQ. Despite the fact that simple questions do not necessarily require the rich information provided by the additional argument fields in n-tuple assertions (which TAQA excels in manipulating), TAQA still outperforms OQA significantly (with an accuracy of 35.6%). Besides the sophisticated techniques TAQA employs in the paraphrasing, parsing, querying, and ranking, we found that another factor that contributes to the gap is the difference

Systems	ComplexQuestions	WebQuestions
TAQA (Full model)	39.3%	35.6%
No complex constraints	29.3% (-10.0%)	34.0% (-1.6%)
No relaxed queries	27.7% (-11.6%)	32.3% (-3.3%)
No association features	35.3% (-4.0%)	30.3% (-5.3%)
No answer consolidation	32.3% (-7.0%)	26.3% (-9.3%)

Table 7: Component ablation test for TAQA (*acc*)

in the style of the queries generated by the two systems. The POS templates used in OQA for question parsing is designed for generating REVERB style queries [11] (e.g., ⟨*?x*; *"is national currency of"*; *"Spain"*⟩) instead of OPENIE style queries (e.g., ⟨*?x*; *"is"*; *"national currency of Spain"*⟩), which are generated by the tool we use to build nOKB. In other words, assertions in nOKB, which are used in our experiment, match the tuple queries generated by TAQA better. This facilitates query execution and hence gives a higher accuracy. This observation leads to an interesting question of how open IE assertion styles impact QA systems, which we leave as a future work.

TAQA's performance on WEBQ is slightly lower than that on COMPQ. We note that this could be attributed to the fact that nOKB+ does not have adequate knowledge to support answering some questions in WEBQ that are tailored for Freebase. For example, TAQA makes a constant error in answering questions about tourist attractions like *"What to see in Paris?"*, a category of question that is not well covered by nOKB+. In contrast, PARASEMPRE can easily answer these questions using `tourist_attractions` relation in Freebase.

TAQA employs a number of techniques along the question-answering process. Our next set of experiments is to evaluate the effectiveness of each component. This is done by removing these components one at a time and observing the accuracy of the resulting system. Table 7 shows the results.

In the first test (labeled "No complex constraints"), we stripped all complex constraints (e.g., *"before 2002"*) from the tuple queries generated by the question parser. Each *TQ* is thus in the basic triple form. For COMPQ questions, we see that the accuracy drops by 10% points. This shows that the ability of TAQA's parser in composing queries in the n-tuple form has a significant impact in answering complex questions. One might expect *acc* to drop even lower than the 29.3% shown, considering that stripping the complex constraints would "destroy" the questions in COMPQ, which are all complex questions. The answer to this is twofold. First, sometimes complex constraints in questions are redundant and the questions can be answered by simpler triple queries. An example is *"Who plays Bilbo Baggins in The Hobbit?"*, which can be answered by the triple query ⟨*?x*; *"plays"*; *"bilbo baggins"*⟩. Second, for cases where dropping the constraints causes ambiguity in answers, sometimes, the correct answers can still be got simply because they happen to be the most popular answers among the assertions in the KB. For questions in WEBQ, stripping complex constraints had little effects, since questions are predominately simple questions.

In question parsing, relaxed queries (those with complex constraints removed) are generated in addition to the regular ones. The objective is to improve the coverage of queries (Section 2.3). In our next test, we suppressed relaxed query generation (labeled "No relaxed queries"). For COMPQ, we see an accuracy drop of 11.6% points, which is even more than that in the first test. This shows that considering all the constraints in questions (no relaxed queries) is no bet-

Rank:	1	2-5	6-10	11-20	>20
ComplexQuestions	59.9%	19.8%	8.1%	4.1%	8.1%
WebQuestions	62.7%	15.8%	6.4%	4.9%	10.2%

Table 8: Rank distribution of correct answers

ter than ignoring all of them (no constraints); the coverage of queries is indeed an important factor. TAQA (full model) is able to combine the scattered evidence of answers extracted from both relaxed and "complete" queries via answer consolidation (Section 2.5), which boosts the rank of the answers that are derived from both forms of queries. An example question is *"What book did Charles Darwin wrote in 1859?"*, which has a relevant assertion A: ⟨*"Charles Darwin"*; *"wrote"*; *"On the Origin of Species"*, *"in 1859"*⟩. Without relaxed queries, the correct answer was ranked only second because A has a low frequency in the KB. The full model correctly ranked the answer top-1 because it got more evidence for the answer from the relaxed query ⟨*"Charles Darwin"*; *"wrote"*; *?x*⟩ which is supported by a frequent assertion ⟨*"Darwin"*; *"wrote the book"*; *"On the Origin of Species"*⟩.

While OQA uses shallow features in question paraphrasing, TAQA uses 20,000 association features in addition to shallow statistical features (Section 2.2). Our next test removed all association features (labeled "No association features"). We observed an accuracy drop of 4.0% and 5.3% for CompQ and WebQ, respectively. This shows that association features are very useful in paraphrasing. Finally, TAQA performs answer consolidation in the answer ranking step (Section 2.5) — the same answers (but with different feature vectors) are consolidated into one by combining their feature vectors. The last test turned off answer consolidation (labeled "No answer consolidation"). In this case, we see significant drops in accuracy of 7.0% and 9.3% for CompQ and WebQ, respectively. Answer consolidation, which allows TAQA to ensemble scattered evidence in the KB for more confidence in answers, is seen as an important technique.

Our last experiment investigates the effectiveness of TAQA's answer ranker (Section 2.5). We say that a question Q is *answerable* by TAQA if it's correct answer appears in the ranked list of candidate answers generated for Q. Intuitively, for an answerable question, TAQA is capable of identifying the correct answer as a candidate. An effective ranker would rank the correct answer first in the list so that it is returned as the final answer. In our experiment, 65.7% of CompQ questions and 56.8% of WebQ questions are answerable. For those answerable questions, Table 8 shows the distribution of their ranks. From the table, we see that TAQA's ranker is very effective; the distribution is very skewed towards the top ranks. In particular, for both CompQ and WebQ questions, around 60% of correct answers were ranked top-1 and around 80% of them were ranked top-5. The distributions shown in Table 8 is indeed insightful. For example, for CompQ, 19.8% of correct answers were ranked top-2-to-5, which are about 1/3 of those top-1 ones (59.9%). These correct answers were so close to be picked as the final answers. If we can further improve TAQA's ranker such that all these correct answers are promoted to top-1, we would have effectively improve the accuracy of TAQA by 1/3. This discussion indicates that more effort should be spent on further improving the ranker.

4. CASE STUDY

In this section we present a few representative questions that illustrate successful and failed cases of TAQA (Table 9). Through these cases, we obtain insights into the key components of a good KB-QA system.

	Example 1
Question:	Q_9: What movies did Morgan Freeman star in?
Paraphrased:	Q'_9: What movies did Morgan Freeman play in?
	Q''_9: What movies did Morgan Freeman star in?
Queries:	TQ'_9: ⟨*Morgan Freeman; play; in ?x*⟩∧⟨*?x; is-a; movie*⟩
	TQ''_9: ⟨*Morgan Freeman; star; in ?x*⟩∧⟨*?x; is-a; movie*⟩
Assertions:	A_9: ⟨*Morgan Freeman; played; god, in Bruce Almighty*⟩
	A_{10}: ⟨*Morgan Freeman; starred; in Bruce Almighty*⟩
Answer:	**Bruce Almighty**
	Example 2
Question:	Q_{10}: Where did Barack Obama go to college in 1991?
Paraphrased:	Q'_{10}: Where did Barack Obama graduate from in 1991?
	Q''_{10}: Which university did Barack Obama attend in 1991?
Queries:	TQ'_{10}: ⟨*Barack Obama; graduate; from ?x, in 1991*⟩
	TQ''_{10}: ⟨*Barack Obama; attend; ?x*⟩∧⟨*?x; is-a; university*⟩
Assertions:	A_{11}: ⟨Barack Obama; graduated; *from Harvard Law School, in 1979 and 1991*⟩
	A_{12}: ⟨*Barack Obama; graduated; magna cum laude, from Harvard Law School, in 1991*⟩
	A_{13}: ⟨*Barack Obama; attended; Harvard Law School*⟩
Answer:	**Harvard Law School**
	Example 3
Question:	Q_{11}: Where Turkish people originate?
Paraphrased:	Q'_{11}: Where is Turkish people origin?
Queries:	TQ'_{11}: ⟨*Turkish people; is; origin, in ?x*⟩
Assertions:	A_{14}: ⟨*many Turkish Alevi; are; of Arab origin, in Syria*⟩
Answer:	**Syria**
	Example 4
Question:	Q_{12}: Who was the father of King George VI?
Queries:	TQ_{12}: ⟨*?x; was; father of King George VI*⟩
Assertions:	A_{15}: ⟨*Queen Elizabeth; was; wife of King George VI*⟩ (extracted from 10 relevant assertions)
	A_{16}: ⟨*George V; was; father of King George VI*⟩ (extracted from 1 relevant assertion)
Answer:	Queen Elizabeth

Table 9: Examples of successful and failed cases

Open KBs are noisy and unnormalized. A challenging problem is to bridge the lexical/syntactic gap between input questions and relevant assertions. When this gap is small, TAQA is very successful in finding the correct answer. Example 1 shows such a case. Question Q_9 is paraphrased into Q'_9 and Q''_9, which match perfectly the assertions A_9 and A_{10} in the KB, respectively. This results in a correct answer. When the lexical gap is large, paraphrasing is our hope in narrowing the gap. Example 2 shows such a case. Question Q_{10} uses informal expressions, which shares little lexical overlap with the relevant assertions (A_{11}, A_{12}, A_{13}). In this example, TAQA successfully paraphrases Q_{10} into formalized ones (Q'_{10}, Q''_{10}), which are parsed into tuple queries (TQ'_{10}, TQ''_{10}) that perfectly match the assertions.

While good paraphrasing can help bridge the lexical gaps, poor paraphrasing can adversely affect question parsing. TAQA's parser employs dependency analysis, which requires questions to follow correct grammatical rules. If the paraphrased questions are grammatically incorrect, the parsed tuple queries will be erroneous, resulting in incorrect answers. Example 3 shows such a case. Question Q_{11} is paraphrased as a grammatically ill-formed question (Q'_{11}), which is parsed into a malformed dependency tree, resulting in a meaningless tuple query (TQ'_{11}) and an incorrect answer.

Similarity measures (see Section 2.4), which are used to evaluate the relatedness between tuple queries and assertions play an important role in filtering incorrect candidate answers. In the current implementation, TAQA primarily employs cosine similarity on text, which is insufficient to measure the semantic relatedness between queries and assertions. This is illustrated by Example 4. For Question Q_{12}, TAQA returns the incorrect answer *"Queen Elizabeth"* instead of the correct one *"King George V"*. The reason is that although assertion A_{16} gives a larger cosine similarity with the tuple query TQ_{12} than does A_{15}, the difference in the similarity scores is marginal. The higher popularity of A_{15} in the KB over-offsets the similarity difference, giving *"Queen Elizabeth"* a higher rank. To improve, one needs to look into similarity measures that can discover deep semantic relatedness between short-texts, which has been recognized as a fundamental task in AI.

5. RELATED WORKS

There are two lines of research in KB-QA systems. One focuses on curated KBs and the key challenge is to transform the lexicon of NL questions to structured KB queries. SEMPRE [4] utilizes a set of REVERB extractions to map NL phrases to KB relations. Kwiatkowski et al. [16] proposed to learn intermediate semantic representations directly from NL questions, with which KB queries are derived on the fly using WIKTIONARY as synonymy features. Xu et al. [20] proposed to learn an alignment model between NL phrases and Freebase relations from large web corpora. They approached the task of finding corresponding Freebase relations given NL phrases via classification. Recently, Berant et al. [5] proposed PARASEMPRE, which applies an "over-generate and re-rank" strategy. The strategy is to enumerate possible KB queries and transform them to synthetic NL questions. They also applied a paraphrase model with rich association and embedding features to rank candidate queries based on the similarity between the input and the synthesized questions.

Another line of research focuses on open KB-QA. PARALEX [13] is the first open KB-QA system, which is based on learned lexicons from a corpus of question paraphrases. More recently, Fader et al. proposed OQA [12], a unified framework for open domain question answering on curated and open KBs. OQA processes questions using a cascaded pipeline of paraphrasing, question parsing, query rewriting and execution. Our work is similar with OQA in decomposing QA into different sub-components. However, we put forward a number of techniques which are essential in processing complex questions.

6. CONCLUSION AND FUTURE WORK

In this paper we presented a novel open KB-QA system, TAQA, that is able to answer questions with complex semantic constraints using n-tuple open KB, nOKB. We proposed new question parsing and answer extraction methods that are adapted to n-tuple assertions. Empirical evaluation showed that our system significantly outperformed state-of-the-art curated KB-QA and open KB-QA systems in answering questions with rich semantic constraints.

Through discussions, we have identified a number of key issues that have strong implications to the performance of TAQA. These include (1) question parsing that is robust to grammatical errors in questions, (2) similarity measures that can capture the deep semantic relatedness between queries and assertions, (3) answer ranking that can leverage more powerful features. In addition, efficient methods for cleaning and canonicalizing n-tuple assertions would greatly improve the quality of the open KB, and thus the QA accuracy.

Finally, we remark that TAQA and PARASEMPRE excel in handling complex questions and simple questions, respectively. In practice, user-issued questions can be of either kind. A natural extension to our work for handling a mixed question workload is ensembling. As an example, we trained an ensemble model using RankBoost with simple statistical features to re-rank the combined top-10 outputs from TAQA and PARASEMPRE. On a mixed question set of 30% complex questions and 70% simple questions, the ensemble model achieves an accuracy of 46.6%, which is better than running TAQA on COMPQ (39.3%) or PARASEMPRE on WEBQ (45.8%). This shows that ensembling is a promising approach for further explore.

Acknowledgments

This research is supported by Hong Kong Research Grants Council GRF grant HKU712712E. We would like to thank the anonymous reviewers for their insightful comments.

7. REFERENCES

[1] S. Auer et al. Dbpedia: A nucleus for a web of open data. In *ISWC/ASWC*, 2007.
[2] M. Banko, M. J. Cafarella, S. Soderland, M. Broadhead, and O. Etzioni. Open information extraction from the web. In *IJCAI*, 2007.
[3] J. Bao et al. Knowledge-based question answering as machine translation. In *ACL (1)*, 2014.
[4] J. Berant, A. Chou, R. Frostig, and P. Liang. Semantic parsing on freebase from question-answer pairs. In *EMNLP*, 2013.
[5] J. Berant and P. Liang. Semantic parsing via paraphrasing. In *ACL (1)*, 2014.
[6] K. D. Bollacker and C. Evans et al. Freebase: a collaboratively created graph database for structuring human knowledge. In *SIGMOD*, 2008.
[7] A. Carlson et al. Toward an architecture for never-ending language learning. In *AAAI*, 2010.
[8] L. D. Corro et al. Clausie: clause-based open information extraction. In *WWW*, 2013.
[9] N. Duan. Minimum bayes risk based answer re-ranking for question answering. In *ACL (2)*, 2013.
[10] J. C. Duchi, E. Hazan, and Y. Singer. Adaptive subgradient methods for online learning and stochastic optimization. In *JMLR*, 2011.
[11] A. Fader, S. Soderland, and O. Etzioni. Identifying relations for open information extraction. In *EMNLP*, 2011.
[12] A. Fader, L. Zettlemoyer, and O. Etzioni. Open Question Answering Over Curated and Extracted Knowledge Bases. In *KDD*, 2014.
[13] A. Fader, L. S. Zettlemoyer, and O. Etzioni. Paraphrase-driven learning for open question answering. In *ACL (1)*, 2013.
[14] L. Galarraga, G. Heitz, K. Murphy, and F. M. Suchanek. Canonicalizing open knowledge bases. In *CIKM*, 2014.
[15] D. Gondek and A. Lally et al. A framework for merging and ranking of answers in deepqa. *IBM Journal of Research and Development*, 2012.
[16] T. Kwiatkowski et al. Scaling semantic parsers with on-the-fly ontology matching. In *EMNLP*, 2013.
[17] Mausam, M. Schmitz, S. Soderland, R. Bart, and O. Etzioni. Open language learning for information extraction. In *EMNLP-CoNLL*, 2012.
[18] Y. Mohamed. Natural language questions for the web of data. In *EMNLP-CoNLL*, 2012.
[19] W. Wu et al. Probase: a probabilistic taxonomy for text understanding. In *SIGMOD*, 2012.
[20] X. Yao and B. V. Durme. Information extraction over structured data: Question answering with freebase. In *ACL (1)*, 2014.

Inducing Space Dirichlet Process Mixture Large-Margin Entity Relationship Inference in Knowledge Bases

Sotirios P. Chatzis
Department of Electrical Eng., Computer Eng., and Informatics
Cyprus University of Technology
33 Saripolou Str.
Limassol 3603, Cyprus
sotirios.chatzis@eecei.cut.ac.cy

ABSTRACT

In this paper, we focus on the problem of extending a given knowledge base by accurately predicting additional true facts based on the facts included in it. This is an essential problem of knowledge representation systems, since knowledge bases typically suffer from incompleteness and lack of ability to reason over their discrete entities and relationships. To achieve our goals, in our work we introduce an inducing space nonparametric Bayesian large-margin inference model, capable of reasoning over relationships between pairs of entities. Previous works addressing the entity relationship inference problem model each entity based on atomic entity vector representations. In contrast, our method exploits word feature vectors to directly obtain high-dimensional nonlinear inducing space representations for entity pairs. This way, we allow for extracting salient latent characteristics and interaction dynamics within entity pairs that can be useful for inferring their relationships. On this basis, our model performs the relations inference task by postulating a set of binary Dirichlet process mixture large-margin classifiers, presented with the derived inducing space representations of the considered entity pairs. Bayesian inference for this inducing space model is performed under the mean-field inference paradigm. This is made possible by leveraging a recently proposed latent variable formulation of regularized large-margin classifiers that facilitates mean-field parameter estimation. We exhibit the superiority of our approach over the state-of-the-art by considering the problem of predicting additional true relations between entities given subsets of the WordNet and FreeBase knowledge bases.

Categories and Subject Descriptors

G.3 [**Probability and Statistics**]: Nonparametric statistics; I.2.6 [**Learning**]: Induction

Permission to make digital or hard copies of all or part of this work for personal or classroom use is granted without fee provided that copies are not made or distributed for profit or commercial advantage and that copies bear this notice and the full citation on the first page. Copyrights for components of this work owned by others than ACM must be honored. Abstracting with credit is permitted. To copy otherwise, or republish, to post on servers or to redistribute to lists, requires prior specific permission and/or a fee. Request permissions from Permissions@acm.org.
CIKM'15, October 19–23, 2015, Melbourne, Australia.
© 2015 ACM. ISBN 978-1-4503-3794-6/15/10 ...$15.00.
DOI: http://dx.doi.org/10.1145/2806416.2806499.

Keywords

Knowledge bases; large-margin classifiers; mean-field inference; Dirichlet process.

1. INTRODUCTION

Knowledge bases are relational databases designed for knowledge management, collection, and retrieval. Recently, significant research effort has been devoted to building large web-based knowledge bases, which encompass a huge amount of data regarding general or specific-domain knowledge; WordNet [1], Freebase [2] and Yago [3] are just a few characteristic such examples. Each of these knowledge bases has been developed with the goal to address a specific problem, for instance producing an intuitively usable dictionary and thesaurus, and proposing a global on-line information resource for semantic web applications. Nevertheless, it is now widely accepted that such knowledge bases could be also leveraged to perform a large number of diverse data mining applications, e.g. question answering (Siri), query expansion [4], coreference resolution [5], and information retrieval [6].

Despite the potential of such systems, this kind of applications is greatly hindered by inherent inadequacies of knowledge bases, namely their incompleteness and the fact that they do not explicitly provide appropriate reasoning capabilities. To resolve these issues, several researchers have proposed approaches for knowledge base extension based on big text data inference and analysis methods. Nevertheless, the lack of adequate textual information to base the knowledge base extension procedure upon has rendered such attempts rather unsuccessful [7, 8, 9]. Inspired from these drawbacks, a complementary approach widely adopted in the related literature consists in predicting the likely truth of additional facts based on existing facts in the given knowledge bases.

To effect this task, existing approaches resort to representing the *entities* (objects or individuals) in the given knowledge bases as feature vectors; [10, 11, 12] are characteristic such works. In these methods, (optimal) vector representations *are learned* for the given entities and are subsequently used to train classification models for performing the relation inference task. In a recent modification of this paradigm, [13] represented the given entities as combinations of their constituent word vectors, with the latter being *learned* from the available data; the so-extracted representations are then presented to a neural network classifier suitable for classifying pairs of feature vectors to learned relation classes. Finally, several researchers have considered tensor factorization models to perform the entity relation inference task. Two characteristic such cases are: (i) the method presented in [14], where tensor factorization and nonparametric Bayesian clustering is utilized for learning relational structures, and inference is performed by means of Markov chain monte-carlo (MCMC) sampling; and (ii) the approach proposed in [15], which instead of MCMC inference yields point-estimates of the model parameters by resorting to the DEDICOM tensor decomposition [16].

In this work, *we propose a completely different feature extraction mechanism* for performing the entity pair relations inference procedure. Specifically, we introduce a *hierarchical* method for entity pair representation extraction comprising two subsequent stages: On the *first* stage, we perform feature representation for individual entities in the given knowledge bases. For this purpose, for each entity we compute the *average* of its word vectors, as discussed in [13]; these *word* vectors are *trained* on the available data. Further, on the *second* stage, *we postulate an inducing space projection model, that maps the individual feature vectors of an entity pair to a joint high-dimensional inducing space feature vector that is eventually used to perform the relation inference task.* The resulting *pairwise* inducing space feature vectors generated from the so-learned mapping encode both the salient characteristics of each entity in the pair, as well as the dynamics/correlations between them; this way, they are expected to yield much more useful entity pair representations for performing the relations inference task compared to existing techniques.

Turning to prediction generation, existing entity relations inference approaches typically resort to similarity-based score models [12, 10], simple bilinear classifiers [11], or more advanced single-layer neural network classifiers [13, 17], appropriately designed to allow for relating pairs of feature vectors to class labels. On the contrary, in this work *we propose utilization of large-margin classification techniques* to perform the relationship inference task. Large-margin methods, inspired from the literature of support vector machines (SVMs) [18, 19, 20], have attracted significant interest from the machine learning community due to their unparalleled performance in challenging classification tasks. Thus, we expect that leveraging the strengths of large-margin classifiers in the context of our method will yield significant performance advantages for the entity relationship inference algorithm.

Despite these advantages, a significant challenge that perplexes the utilization of large-margin classifiers in the context of our approach concerns the fact that the modeled entity pairs are represented as inducing space vectors, expressed as deterministic functions of unknown parameters that must be trained as part of the model learning procedure. To resolve these issues, and facilitate efficient training of our model under an elegant algorithmic framework, we resort to a recently proposed latent variable formulation of the objective function of regularized large-margin classifiers [21]. This latent variable formulation expresses the large-margin classification objective function as a variance-mean mixture of linear models with normal errors. This way, it allows for seamlessly integrating the inducing space feature representation component of our model into the overall parameter estimation procedure.

Finally, a significant problem the affects large-margin classification models concerns the fact that conventional large-margin classifiers are not capable of taking into account that the modeled data may comprise a set of multiple underlying structures (e.g., clusters), each of which might be better modeled by using a separate dedicated model component. To overcome such limitations, recent progress has been made on developing mixture-of-experts formulations of large-margin classifiers, which split the input space into a number of subregions and learn a separate classifier within each region (e.g., [22, 23]). Under such a model formulation, a problem that comes to the fore concerns data-driven determination of the most appropriate number of model components (underlying clusters). As a solution toward the amelioration of this issue, [20] recently proposed the exploitation of nonparametric Bayesian techniques, which offer a promising direction to bypass the model selection problem and automatically resolve the unknown number of experts.

Nonparametric Bayesian modeling techniques, especially Dirichlet process mixture (DPM) models, have become very popular in statistics over the last few years, for performing nonparametric density estimation [24, 25, 26]. Briefly, a realization of a DPM can be seen as an infinite mixture of distributions with given parametric shape (e.g., Gaussian). This theory is based on the observation that an infinite number of component distributions in an ordinary finite mixture model tends on the limit to a Dirichlet process (DP) prior [25, 27]. Eventually, as a part of the model fitting procedure, the nonparametric Bayesian inference scheme induced by a DPM model yields a posterior distribution on the proper number of model component densities (inferred clusters) [28], rather than selecting a fixed number of mixture components. Hence, the obtained nonparametric Bayesian formulation eliminates the need of doing inference (or making arbitrary choices) on the number of mixture components (clusters) necessary to represent the modeled data.

Inspired from these advances, our method postulates a nonparametric Bayesian model, based on the introduction of a DP prior over the space of possible large-margin classifiers defined in the whole space of inducing variables. This way, we allow for better dealing with tasks entailing multiple modes, which simple large-margin models often fail to successfully handle. We derive efficient model training and inference algorithms for our model, resorting to the mean-field framework [29, 28, 30, 31], and a truncated stick-breaking formulation of the DP [32, 33]. We dub our approach inducing space Dirichlet process mixture large-margin entity relationship inference (iDLER).

The remainder of this paper is organized as follows: In Section 2, we provide a brief introduction to the Dirichlet process and its function as a prior in nonparametric Bayesian models. In Section 3, we introduce our model and derive its inference and training algorithms. In Section 4, we perform the experimental evaluation of our approach by training on relationships in WordNet and Freebase, and evaluating model predictive performance on a held-out set of unseen relational triplets. As we show, our model outperforms previously introduced related models, such as the state-of-the-art approaches presented in [10, 11, 12, 13, 17]. Finally, in the concluding section of this paper, we summarize our results and discuss directions for future research.

2. THE DIRICHLET PROCESS

Dirichlet process models were first introduced by Ferguson [34]. A DP is characterized by a base distribution G_0 and a positive scalar γ, usually referred to as the innovation parameter, and is denoted as $\mathrm{DP}(\gamma, G_0)$. Essentially, a DP is a distribution placed over a distribution. Let us suppose we randomly draw a sample distribution G from a DP, and, subsequently, we independently draw M random variables $\{\Theta_m^*\}_{m=1}^M$ from G:

$$G|\gamma, G_0 \sim \mathrm{DP}(\gamma, G_0) \tag{1}$$

$$\Theta_m^*|G \sim G, \quad m = 1, \dots M \tag{2}$$

Integrating out G, the joint distribution of the variables $\{\Theta_m^*\}_{m=1}^M$ can be shown to exhibit a clustering effect. Specifically, given the first $M-1$ samples of G, $\{\Theta_m^*\}_{m=1}^{M-1}$, it can be shown that a new sample Θ_M^* is either (a) drawn from the base distribution G_0 with probability $\frac{\gamma}{\gamma+M-1}$, or (b) is selected from the existing draws, according to a multinomial allocation, with probabilities proportional to the number of the previous draws with the same allocation [35]. Let $\{\Theta_c\}_{c=1}^C$ be the set of distinct values taken by the variables $\{\Theta_m^*\}_{m=1}^{M-1}$. Denoting as ν_c^{M-1} the number of values in $\{\Theta_m^*\}_{m=1}^{M-1}$ that equal to Θ_c, the distribution of Θ_M^* given $\{\Theta_m^*\}_{m=1}^{M-1}$ can be shown to be of the form [35]

$$p(\Theta_M^*|\{\Theta_m^*\}_{m=1}^{M-1}, \gamma, G_0) = \frac{\gamma}{\gamma+M-1} G_0 + \sum_{c=1}^{C} \frac{\nu_c^{M-1}}{\gamma+M-1} \delta_{\Theta_c} \tag{3}$$

where δ_{Θ_c} denotes the distribution concentrated at a single point Θ_c. These results illustrate two key properties of the DP scheme. First, the innovation parameter γ plays a key-role in determining the number of distinct parameter values. A larger γ induces a higher tendency of drawing new parameters from the base distribution G_0; indeed, as $\gamma \to \infty$ we get $G \to G_0$. Conversely, as $\gamma \to 0$ all $\{\Theta_m^*\}_{m=1}^M$ tend to cluster to a single random variable. Second, the more often a parameter is shared, the more likely it will be shared in the future.

A characterization of the (unconditional) distribution of the random variable G drawn from a DP, $\mathrm{DP}(\gamma, G_0)$, is provided by the stick-breaking construction of Sethuraman [32]. Consider two infinite collections of independent random variables $\boldsymbol{v} = [v_c]_{c=1}^\infty$, $\{\Theta_c\}_{c=1}^\infty$, where the v_c are drawn from a Beta distribution, and the Θ_c are independently drawn from the base distribution G_0. The stick-breaking representation of G is then given by

$$G = \sum_{c=1}^{\infty} \varpi_c(\boldsymbol{v}) \delta_{\Theta_c} \tag{4}$$

where

$$v_c \sim \mathrm{Beta}(1, \gamma) \tag{5}$$

$$\varpi_c(\boldsymbol{v}) = v_c \prod_{j=1}^{c-1} (1 - v_j) \quad \in [0, 1] \tag{6}$$

and

$$\sum_{c=1}^{\infty} \varpi_c(\boldsymbol{v}) = 1 \tag{7}$$

Under the stick-breaking representation of the DP, the atoms Θ_c, drawn independently from the base distribution G_0, can be seen as the parameters of the component distributions of a mixture model comprising an unbounded number of component densities, with mixing proportions $\varpi_c(\boldsymbol{v})$.

3. PROPOSED APPROACH

3.1 Model Formulation

As already discussed, the problem addressed in this paper concerns extending existing knowledge bases that contain incomplete information. Specifically, our goal is to create a model capable of inferring relations between the entities in an existing knowledge base that are not already included in it due to its partial and incomplete nature.

Let us denote as (e_1, e_2) a pair of entities included in a given knowledge base. Let us also denote as $\mathcal{R} = \{1, \dots R\}$ the set of relation types encompassed in this knowledge base. Under this formulation, the addressed problem consists in creating a model capable of inferring for any pair of entities (e_1, e_2) from this knowledge base whether they satisfy each one of the encoded relationships; for instance, whether the pair $(e_1, e_2) =$ (snow leopard, head) satisfies the relationship $r =$ "has part."

As briefly reviewed in the previous section, existing approaches address this problem by obtaining feature vector representations for each entity, and presenting them to some appropriate classifier trained to correlate *pairs* of feature vectors with learned classes (relations). Specifically, most related works *learn* to *optimally* extract entity-level feature representations, which are subsequently used to perform a classification task, assigning pairs of entities to relationships (e.g., [10, 11, 12]). More recently, [13] proposed that entity-level feature representation be performed by learning feature vectors *on the word level*, and combining the feature vectors of the words that comprise each entity. This way, the extracted feature representations allow for sharing statistical strength between the words consisting the modeled entities, thus yielding better predictive accuracy compared to the previous approaches. The so-obtained feature vector representations of the modeled entities are eventually presented to suitable classifiers to effect the relationship inference (classification) task: neural network architectures [13, 17], distance-based models [12, 10], and bilinear classifiers [11, 14] are characteristic examples of classification models used for this task.

As discussed in Section 1, in this work we propose to address this problem by exploiting the merits of large-margin classifiers. Specifically, to effect the relationship inference task, we consider postulating DPM models comprising regularized large-margin binary classifiers, suitable for classification of pairs of feature vectors. Let us consider a modeled relationship type $r \in \mathcal{R}$. To create a model capable of inferring whether a pair of entities (e_1, e_2) in a given knowledge base satisfy this relationship, we postulate a DPM of L^α-norm regularized large-margin classifiers; the objective function of the cth model component classifier reads [18]:

$$d_\alpha(\boldsymbol{\beta}_c, \nu_c) = \sum_{n=1}^{N} \max\big(1 - y_n \boldsymbol{x}_n^T \boldsymbol{\beta}_c, 0\big) + \nu_c^{-\alpha} \sum_{k=1}^{K} \left| \frac{\beta_{ck}}{\sigma_k} \right|^\alpha \quad c = 1, \dots, \infty \tag{8}$$

where σ_k is the standard deviation of the kth element of the feature vectors $\boldsymbol{x}$, ν_c is a tuning hyperparameter of the cth postulated large-margin classifier, $\boldsymbol{\beta}_c = [\beta_{ck}]_{k=1}^K$ is the parameters vector of the cth model component, N is the number of training examples, the classification labels $y_n \in$

$\{-1, 1\}$ indicate whether the nth entity pair satisfies the relationship or not, and $\alpha \in (0, 2]$.

In our model, the feature vectors $\boldsymbol{x}_n$ correspond to *entity pairs,* and constitute joint inducing space projections of the feature vectors of each entity in the pair, that capture the salient characteristics of both each entity as well as of the dynamics of their interactions/correlation patterns. Specifically, we postulate the following nonlinear deterministic inducing space projection function:

$$\begin{aligned}\boldsymbol{x}_n &\triangleq \boldsymbol{x}(\boldsymbol{e}_{1n}, \boldsymbol{e}_{2n}) \\ &= h\left([\boldsymbol{e}_{1n}\boldsymbol{W}_k\boldsymbol{e}_{2n}]_{k=1}^{K} + \boldsymbol{V}_1\boldsymbol{e}_{1n} + \boldsymbol{V}_2\boldsymbol{e}_{2n} + \boldsymbol{\xi}\right)\end{aligned} \tag{9}$$

where $\boldsymbol{e}_{1n}, \boldsymbol{e}_{2n} \in \mathbb{R}^F$ are the individual feature vectors of each entity in the nth training pair; the *trainable* parameters $\boldsymbol{W}_k \in \mathbb{R}^{F\times F}$ are matrices designed for extracting the salient dynamics/correlations between entities in a pair, while the $\boldsymbol{V}_1, \boldsymbol{V}_2 \in \mathbb{R}^{K\times F}$ are *trainable* parameter matrices designed for capturing salient individual features of each entity in the pair, $\boldsymbol{\xi}$ is a bias parameter, and $h(\cdot)$ is a sigmoid nonlinearity. Note that, in the above postulated model, the size of the derived inducing space projections K is a model hyperparameter that can be heuristically selected to optimize model performance. The same holds for the dimensionality F of the feature vector representations $\boldsymbol{e}$ of each individual entity.

Turning to the individual feature vector representations of each entity, as we have already discussed, we elect to perform modeling and training on the *word* level *instead of* the *entity* level, similar to [13]. That is, we model each word as an F-dimensional vector, and compute entity feature vectors by composing their constituent word vectors. This way, we allow for sharing of statistical strength between the words describing each entity.

Note also that training word vectors instead of entity vectors as part of the model learning procedure has the additional advantage of allowing to leverage previously obtained unsupervised word vectors, capturing some salient syntactic and semantic distribution properties. This way, we obtain a proper model initialization scheme that enables faster convergence to good parameter estimates (much better than, e.g., having to resort to randomly initialized feature vectors, which is the solution usually adopted in the literature [10, 11, 12]).

3.2 Model Training

To allow for derivation of an elegant and computationally efficient training algorithm for our model, we resort to a recently proposed latent variable representation of regularized large-margin classifiers [21]. This formulation renders training of our model amenable to the mean-field inference paradigm, giving rise to expectation-maximization (EM)-style [36] algorithms with proved convergence [29, 31, 33].

Specifically, let us consider the model pertaining to the relationship type $r \in \mathcal{R}$. We introduce the set of variables $\{z_{cn}\}_{c,n=1}^{\infty,N}$, with $z_{cn} = 1$ if the nth training vector $\boldsymbol{x}_n$ belongs to the cth cluster formulated in the considered inducing space (modeled by the cth postulated model component), $z_{cn} = 0$ otherwise. Then, following [21], minimization of the objective function (8) of the DPM component classifiers of our model w.r.t. the parameters $\boldsymbol{\beta}_c$ and ν_c can be shown to be equivalent to finding the mode of the pseudo-posterior distribution

$$p(\boldsymbol{\beta}_c, \nu_c|\alpha; \boldsymbol{X}, Y, Z) \propto p(\boldsymbol{\beta}_c|\nu_c, \alpha; \boldsymbol{X}, Y, Z)p(\nu_c) \tag{10}$$

where $\boldsymbol{X} = [\boldsymbol{x}(\boldsymbol{e}_{1n}, \boldsymbol{e}_{2n})]_{n=1}^N$, $Y = \{y_n\}_{n=1}^N$,

$$p(\boldsymbol{\beta}_c|\nu_c, \alpha; \boldsymbol{X}, Y, Z) \propto C(\nu_c)\mathcal{L}(Y|\boldsymbol{\beta}_c; \boldsymbol{X}, Z)p(\boldsymbol{\beta}_c|\nu_c, \alpha) \tag{11}$$

$p(\nu_c)$ and $p(\boldsymbol{\beta}_c|\nu_c, \alpha)$ are appropriate prior distributions on the model parameters, $\mathcal{L}(Y|\boldsymbol{\beta}_c; \boldsymbol{X}, Z)$ is a pseudo-likelihood function of the cth model component of the form:

$$\mathcal{L}(Y|\boldsymbol{\beta}_c; \boldsymbol{X}, Z) = \prod_{n=1}^{N}\left[\exp\left\{-2\max\left(1 - y_n\boldsymbol{x}_n^T\boldsymbol{\beta}_c, 0\right)\right\}\right]^{z_{cn}} \tag{12}$$

and $C(\nu_c)$ is an appropriate normalization constant. In these derivations, both the pseudo-likelihood contribution of each training example, $\mathcal{L}(y_n|\boldsymbol{\beta}_c; \boldsymbol{x}_n, z_{cn} = 1)$, as well as the prior $p(\boldsymbol{\beta}_c|\nu_c, \alpha)$ can be expressed as *location-scale* mixtures of normals. Regarding the component-wise pseudo-likelihood contribution of each training example $\{\boldsymbol{x}_n, y_n\}$, the equivalent *location-scale* mixture of normals expression reads [21]:

$$\begin{aligned}\mathcal{L}(y_n|\boldsymbol{\beta}_c; \boldsymbol{x}_n, z_{cn} = 1) = &\int_0^\infty \frac{1}{\sqrt{2\pi\lambda_{cn}}} \\ &\times \exp\left(-\frac{1}{2}\frac{(1 + \lambda_{cn} - y_n\boldsymbol{x}_n^T\boldsymbol{\beta}_c)^2}{\lambda_{cn}}\right)\mathrm{d}\lambda_{cn}\end{aligned} \tag{13}$$

where the λ_{cn} are introduced latent variables (one for each training example) that characterize the derived location-scale mixture formulation. Similarly, the prior $p(\boldsymbol{\beta}_c|\nu_c, \alpha)$ can be shown to yield [21]

$$p(\boldsymbol{\beta}_c|\nu_c, \alpha) = \prod_{k=1}^{K} p(\beta_{ck}|\nu_c, \alpha) \tag{14}$$

where

$$p(\beta_{ck}|\nu_c, \alpha) = \int_0^\infty \phi(\beta_{ck}|0, \nu^2\omega_{ck}\sigma_k^2)p(\omega_{ck}|\alpha)\mathrm{d}\omega_{ck} \tag{15}$$

with the introduced latent variables ω_{ck} being imposed the prior

$$p(\omega_{ck}|\alpha) \propto \omega_{ck}^{-\frac{3}{2}}\mathrm{St}_{\frac{\alpha}{2}}^{+}(\omega_{ck}^{-1}) \tag{16}$$

where $\mathrm{St}_{\frac{\alpha}{2}}^{+}(\cdot)$ is the probability density function of a positive stable random variable of index $\frac{\alpha}{2}$, and $\phi(\cdot|\mu, s^2)$ is the cumulative distribution function of a normal with mean μ and variance s^2.

On this basis, we essentially yield a data augmentation scheme for our model [21], which can be straightforwardly exploited under the mean-field inference principle to obtain an elegant and computationally efficient iterative training algorithm. For this purpose, we proceed by utilizing the stick-breaking formulation of the DP prior, imposed over the postulated component classifiers of our model as described in Section 2. We have

$$p(z_{cn} = 1|\boldsymbol{v}) = \varpi_c(\boldsymbol{v}) \tag{17}$$

$$\varpi_c(\boldsymbol{v}) = v_c\prod_{j=1}^{c-1}(1 - v_j) \in [0, 1] \tag{18}$$

with

$$\sum_{c=1}^{\infty} \varpi_c(\boldsymbol{v}) = 1 \tag{19}$$

$$p(v_c) = \text{Beta}(v_c|1, \gamma) \tag{20}$$

This concludes the prior configuration of our model.

As usual with nonparametric Bayesian modeling techniques, a problem training algorithm derivation for our model is confronted with concerns the need to deal with a theoretically infinite number of parameters, which is clearly computationally intractable. In this work, to resolve this issue we resort to a common strategy in the literature of Bayesian nonparametrics, formulated on the basis of a *truncated* stick-breaking representation of the DP [33]. That is, *we fix a value C and we set $\varpi_c(\boldsymbol{v})$ equal to zero for $c > C$.* Note that, under this setting, the treated iDLER model involves a full DP prior; truncation is not imposed on the model itself, but only on the posterior distribution to allow for a tractable inference procedure.

Exploiting these results, we proceed to derive an alternating expectation-conditional maximization (AECM)-type algorithm for training of our iDLER model. AECM [37] is an extension of the EM algorithm [36] where *the specification of the complete data is allowed to be different on each algorithm step.* By utilizing the AECM framework, we are capable of *seamlessly* handling parameter estimation for the large-margin component classifiers, the nonlinear inducing space entity pair representation component of our model, and the word feature vector representations, under *computationally simpler* updating equations compared to conventional EM-type formulations.

On *each iteration*, our proposed model training algorithm comprises simple and computationally efficient conditional maximization steps, organized in *four* distinct cycles. *On the first cycle*, we update the estimates of the parameters of the large-margin component classifiers. For this purpose, we specify the complete data of the algorithm to comprise the latent variables Z, $\boldsymbol{\lambda}_c = [\lambda_{cn}]_{n=1}^{N}$, and $\boldsymbol{\omega}_c = [\omega_{ck}]_{k=1}^{K}$, $c \in \{1, \dots, C\}$, as well as the training labels set Y and the corresponding inducing space projections $\boldsymbol{X}$. Under this formulation, the maximized quantity on the *first cycle* of the AECM algorithm is the posterior expectation of the complete data log-posterior $Q(\{\boldsymbol{\beta}_c, \nu_c\}_{c=1}^{C} | \{\hat{\boldsymbol{\beta}}_c, \hat{\nu}_c\}_{c=1}^{C})$, evaluated at the current parameter estimates, which reads

$$Q(\{\boldsymbol{\beta}_c, \nu_c\}_{c=1}^{C} | \{\hat{\boldsymbol{\beta}}_c, \hat{\nu}_c\}_{c=1}^{C}) = \sum_{c=1}^{C} Q(\boldsymbol{\beta}_c, \nu_c | \hat{\boldsymbol{\beta}}_c, \hat{\nu}_c) \tag{21}$$

$$\begin{aligned} Q(\boldsymbol{\beta}_c, \nu_c | \hat{\boldsymbol{\beta}}_c, \hat{\nu}_c) = \int & \log p(\boldsymbol{\beta}_c, \nu_c | \boldsymbol{\lambda}_c, \boldsymbol{\omega}_c; \boldsymbol{X}, Y, \hat{Z}) \\ & \times p(\boldsymbol{\lambda}_c, \boldsymbol{\omega}_c | \hat{\boldsymbol{\beta}}_c, \hat{\nu}_c; \boldsymbol{X}, Y, \hat{Z}) \mathrm{d}\boldsymbol{\lambda}_c \mathrm{d}\boldsymbol{\omega}_c \end{aligned} \tag{22}$$

where the $\hat{Z}$ comprises the posterior expectations of the latent variables set Z, $\{\hat{\boldsymbol{\beta}}_c, \hat{\nu}_c\}$ are the current estimates of the parameters $\{\boldsymbol{\beta}_c, \nu_c\}$, $p(\boldsymbol{\lambda}_c, \boldsymbol{\omega}_c | \hat{\boldsymbol{\beta}}_c, \hat{\nu}_c; \boldsymbol{X}, Y, \hat{Z})$ is the posterior of the latent variables $\boldsymbol{\lambda}_c$ and $\boldsymbol{\omega}_c$, and we have (ignoring constant terms) [21]:

$$\begin{aligned} \log p(\boldsymbol{\beta}_c, \nu_c | \boldsymbol{\lambda}_c, \boldsymbol{\omega}_c; \boldsymbol{X}, Y, \hat{Z}) = & -\frac{1}{2\nu_c^2} \sum_{k=1}^{K} \frac{\beta_{ck}^2}{\sigma_k^2 \omega_{ck}} \\ & -\frac{1}{2} \sum_{n=1}^{N} \hat{z}_{cn} \frac{(1 + \lambda_{cn} - y_n \boldsymbol{x}_n^T \boldsymbol{\beta}_c)^2}{\lambda_{cn}} \end{aligned} \tag{23}$$

Following [37], to effect the first cycle of the proposed AECM-type algorithm, we first perform an E-step that calculates the value of the objective function $Q(\boldsymbol{\beta}_c, \nu_c | \hat{\boldsymbol{\beta}}_c, \hat{\nu}_c)$, and then proceed with an M-step, where new updates of the model parameter estimates $\hat{\boldsymbol{\beta}}_c$ and $\hat{\nu}_c$ are obtained by maximization of $Q(\boldsymbol{\beta}_c, \nu_c | \hat{\boldsymbol{\beta}}_c, \hat{\nu}_c)$. Specifically, assuming an inverse Gamma prior distribution over ν_c^{α}, i.e.

$$p(\nu_c | \alpha) = \mathcal{IG}(\nu_c^{\alpha} | a_\nu, b_\nu) \tag{24}$$

similar to [21], it can be shown that the *E-step of the first cycle* of the derived AECM-type algorithm reduces to computation of the *sufficient statistics* [21]

$$\hat{\boldsymbol{\lambda}}_c^{-1} = \left[\left| 1 - y_n \boldsymbol{x}_n^T \hat{\boldsymbol{\beta}}_c \right|^{-1} \right]_{n=1}^{N} \tag{25}$$

$$\hat{\boldsymbol{\Lambda}}_c^{-1} = \text{diag}(\hat{\boldsymbol{\lambda}}_c^{-1}) \tag{26}$$

$$\hat{\omega}_{ck}^{-1} = \alpha \left| \hat{\beta}_{ck} \right|^{\alpha - 2} (\hat{\nu}_c \sigma_k)^{2 - \alpha} \tag{27}$$

$$\hat{\boldsymbol{\Omega}}_c^{-1} = \text{diag}\left([\hat{\omega}_{ck}^{-1}]_{k=1}^{K} \right) \tag{28}$$

where $\text{diag}(\boldsymbol{\kappa})$ denotes a square diagonal matrix with the elements of vector $\boldsymbol{\kappa}$ on the main diagonal, as well as of the latent cluster assignment posteriors:

$$\hat{z}_{cn} \propto \exp\left(\mathbb{E}[\log \varpi_c(\boldsymbol{v})]\right) \exp\left(\varphi_{nc}\right) \tag{29}$$

where

$$\mathbb{E}[\log \varpi_c(\boldsymbol{v})] = \sum_{c'=1}^{c-1} \mathbb{E}[\log(1 - v_{c'})] + \mathbb{E}[\log v_c] \tag{30}$$

$\mathbb{E}[\cdot]$ denotes the posterior expectation of a quantity, and

$$\varphi_{nc} = -2\max\left(1 - y_n \boldsymbol{x}_n^T \hat{\boldsymbol{\beta}}_c, 0\right) \tag{31}$$

On the other hand, the *M-step* reduces to the *updates*

$$\hat{\boldsymbol{\beta}}_c = \left(\hat{\nu}_c^{-2} \boldsymbol{\Sigma}^{-1} \hat{\boldsymbol{\Omega}}_c^{-1} + \tilde{\boldsymbol{X}}_c^T \hat{\boldsymbol{\Lambda}}_c^{-1} \boldsymbol{X} \right)^{-1} \tilde{\boldsymbol{X}}_c^T (1 + \hat{\boldsymbol{\lambda}}_c^{-1}) \tag{32}$$

and

$$\hat{\nu}_c^{-\alpha} = \frac{b_\nu + \sum_{k=1}^{K} \left| \hat{\beta}_{ck} / \sigma_k \right|^{\alpha}}{K/\alpha + a_\nu - 1} \tag{33}$$

where $\boldsymbol{\Sigma} = \text{diag}([\sigma_k^2]_{k=1}^{K})$, and $\tilde{\boldsymbol{X}}_c = [\tilde{\boldsymbol{x}}_{cn}]_{c=1}^{c}$ with $\tilde{\boldsymbol{x}}_{cn} \triangleq \hat{z}_{cn} \boldsymbol{x}_n$.

On the second cycle of the derived AECM-type algorithm, we update the estimates of the parameters of the nonlinear projection component of the postulated models that yields the inducing space feature vectors $\boldsymbol{X}$. For this purpose, we specify the complete data of the algorithm to comprise the latent variables Z and $\{\boldsymbol{\lambda}_c\}_{c=1}^{C}$, as well as the training labels set Y and the corresponding entity pairs set $E = \{\boldsymbol{e}_{1n}, \boldsymbol{e}_{2n}\}_{n=1}^{N}$. Under this formulation, the maximized quantity on the *second cycle* of the AECM algorithm becomes

$$Q(\{\boldsymbol{W}_k\}_{k=1}^K, \boldsymbol{V}_1, \boldsymbol{V}_2, \boldsymbol{\xi} | \{\hat{\boldsymbol{W}}_k\}_{k=1}^K, \hat{\boldsymbol{V}}_1, \hat{\boldsymbol{V}}_2, \hat{\boldsymbol{\xi}}; \{\hat{\boldsymbol{\beta}}_c\}_{c=1}^C)$$
$$= \int \log p(\{\boldsymbol{W}_k\}_{k=1}^K, \boldsymbol{V}_1, \boldsymbol{V}_2, \boldsymbol{\xi} | \{\boldsymbol{\lambda}_c; \hat{\boldsymbol{\beta}}_c\}_{c=1}^C, E, Y, \hat{Z})$$
$$\times \prod_{c=1}^{C} p(\boldsymbol{\lambda}_c | \hat{\boldsymbol{\beta}}_c; \boldsymbol{X}, Y, \hat{Z}) \mathrm{d}\boldsymbol{\lambda}_c \tag{34}$$

where $\log p(\{\boldsymbol{W}_k\}_{k=1}^K, \boldsymbol{V}_1, \boldsymbol{V}_2, \boldsymbol{\xi} | \{\boldsymbol{\lambda}_c; \hat{\boldsymbol{\beta}}_c\}_{c=1}^C, E, Y, \hat{Z})$ yields (ignoring constant terms) [21]:

$$\log p(\{\boldsymbol{W}_k\}_{k=1}^K, \boldsymbol{V}_1, \boldsymbol{V}_2, \boldsymbol{\xi} | \{\boldsymbol{\lambda}_c; \hat{\boldsymbol{\beta}}_c\}_{c=1}^C, E, Y, \hat{Z})$$
$$= -\frac{1}{2} \sum_{c=1}^{C} \sum_{n=1}^{N} \hat{z}_{cn} \frac{(1 + \lambda_{cn} - y_n \boldsymbol{x}(\boldsymbol{e}_{1n}, \boldsymbol{e}_{2n})^T \hat{\boldsymbol{\beta}}_c)^2}{\lambda_{cn}} \tag{35}$$

with $\boldsymbol{x}(\boldsymbol{e}_{1n}, \boldsymbol{e}_{2n})$ being now considered a function of the unknown parameters $\{\boldsymbol{W}_k\}_{k=1}^K, \boldsymbol{V}_1, \boldsymbol{V}_2$, and $\boldsymbol{\xi}$, given by (9). On this basis, and similar to the first cycle of the algorithm, *the E-step on the second cycle* of the AECM algorithm reduces to computation of the *sufficient statistics* $\hat{\boldsymbol{\lambda}}_c^{-1}$ *and* $\hat{\boldsymbol{\Lambda}}_c^{-1}$, given by Eqs. (25)-(26), and the posterior expectations $\hat{z}_{cn}$, given by (29), while the *M-step reduces to* local execution of a gradient-based optimization algorithm to optimize (34). In our experiments, to effect these M-step updates, we resort to stochastic gradient ascent.

Further, the *third cycle* of the proposed AECM algorithm is focused on updating the learned feature representations of the words in the modeled knowledge bases. This procedure yields a complete data configuration similar to the second cycle of the AECM algorithm, with similar resulting E-step. The only difference consists in the fact that, on the M-step, instead of optimization of (34) w.r.t. $\{\boldsymbol{W}_k\}_{k=1}^K$, $\{\boldsymbol{V}_j\}_{j=1}^2$, and $\boldsymbol{\xi}$, we optimize it over the word vectors that constitute the entity feature representations $\{\boldsymbol{e}_{jn}\}_{j,n=1}^{2,N}$ of the modeled entities. For this latter purpose, we resort to optimization by means of stochastic gradient ascent, similar to the second cycle of the algorithm.

Finally, on the *fourth cycle* of the AECM-type training algorithm of our model, we consider the latent variables to comprise the latent cluster assignment variables, Z, and we effect the updating of the posteriors of the stick-variables $\{\boldsymbol{v}_c\}_{c=1}^C$. It can be shown that these updates are similar to the updates obtained in [33] for the case of a simple DPM comprising Gaussian distributions as its components. Specifically, on the E-step of the fourth cycle of the algorithm, we update the posterior expectations set $\hat{Z}$, given by (29), while the M-step comprises the updates of the stick-breaking posteriors; we have [33]:

$$p(v_c | \boldsymbol{X}, Y, Z) = \mathrm{Beta}(v_c | \epsilon_{c,1}, \epsilon_{c,2}) \tag{36}$$

where

$$\epsilon_{c,1} = 1 + \sum_{n=1}^{N} \hat{z}_{cn} \tag{37}$$

$$\epsilon_{c,2} = \gamma + \sum_{c'=c+1}^{C} \sum_{n=1}^{N} \hat{z}_{c'n} \tag{38}$$

whence

$$\mathbb{E}[\log v_c] = \psi(\epsilon_{c,1}) - \psi(\epsilon_{c,1} + \epsilon_{c,2}) \tag{39}$$

$$\mathbb{E}[\log(1 - v_c)] = \psi(\epsilon_{c,2}) - \psi(\epsilon_{c,1} + \epsilon_{c,2}) \tag{40}$$

In the above equations, $\psi(\cdot)$ denotes the Digamma function.

An outline of the AECM-type training algorithm of our model is provided in Table 1.

3.3 Prediction Generation

Once we have trained our model, inference for a pair of entities (e_1, e_2) w.r.t. a relationship type $r \in \mathcal{R}$ can be performed by computing the decision function value of the corresponding large-margin mixture-of-experts classifier. Specifically, under the proposed model configuration scheme, the decision function of the postulated models yields:

$$g(\boldsymbol{e}_1, \boldsymbol{e}_2) = \sum_{c=1}^{C} \mathbb{E}[\varpi_c(\boldsymbol{v})] \left(\boldsymbol{x}(\boldsymbol{e}_1, \boldsymbol{e}_2)^T \hat{\boldsymbol{\beta}}_c \right) \tag{41}$$

where $\boldsymbol{x}(\boldsymbol{e}_1, \boldsymbol{e}_2)$ is calculated based on (9), using the obtained model parameter estimates, and we have

$$\mathbb{E}[\varpi_c(\boldsymbol{v})] = \mathbb{E}[v_c] \prod_{j<c} (1 - \mathbb{E}[v_j]) \tag{42}$$

and

$$\mathbb{E}[v_c] = \frac{\epsilon_{c,1}}{\epsilon_{c,1} + \epsilon_{c,2}} \tag{43}$$

4. EXPERIMENTAL EVALUATION

In this section, we perform an extensive experimental evaluation of our method, and compare its performance to related state-of-the-art approaches. Specifically, we consider two popular knowledge bases, namely WordNet [1] and FreeBase [2], and use our model to predict whether some relations hold based on existing relations described therein. This way, we essentially attempt to mimic common sense reasoning in the context of an inferential procedure driven by our method. For instance, if some entity in a given knowledge base represents an individual born in London, our model should be capable of inferring that their nationality should be British. In a similar fashion, when it comes to a Bengal tiger, our model should be capable of both inferring that its natural habitat should be somewhere in India, and that it should be classified as a carnivorous mammal.

For comparative purposes, apart from evaluation of our method, we also cite the performance of two similarity-based score models, namely the distance-based model presented in [10] and the Hadamard model presented in [12], a bilinear classifier-based method, presented in [11], the method presented in [17], which is based on single-layer neural network classifiers, and the recently proposed neural tensor network (NTN) model [13], which is based on a single-layer neural network classifier that learns feature representations on the word level instead of the individual entity level, similar to our approach.

For reference purposes, we replicate the experimental setup of [13], setting the dimensionality of the feature vectors used to represent the modeled entities equal to $F = 100$. Model training is performed using a subset of the actual relations included in the used knowledge bases as positive examples; an *equal* number of negative examples are created by taking the true relationships in the used positive examples and replacing one of the two entities correlated therein with randomly selected irrelevant ones. The word feature vectors of

Table 1: Outline of the AECM-type training algorithm of iDLER.

- For *each* modeled relationship type $r \in \mathcal{R}$, do the following:

1. Set the iteration counter to $it := 0$.
2. Run the *first* cycle of the algorithm:
   E-step: Update the sufficient statistics $\hat{\boldsymbol{\lambda}}_c^{-1}$, $\hat{\boldsymbol{\Lambda}}_c^{-1}$, $\hat{\omega}_c^{-1}$, $\hat{\boldsymbol{\Omega}}_c^{-1}$, and $\hat{z}_{cn}$, using (25)-(29).
   M-step: Compute the parameter updates $\hat{\boldsymbol{\beta}}_c$ and $\hat{\nu}_c$, using (32)-(33).
3. Run the *second* cycle of the algorithm:
   E-step: Update the sufficient statistics $\hat{\boldsymbol{\lambda}}_c^{-1}$, $\hat{\boldsymbol{\Lambda}}_c^{-1}$, and $\hat{z}_{cn}$, using (25)-(26) and (29).
   M-step: Compute the parameter updates $\{\hat{\boldsymbol{W}}_k\}_{k=1}^K, \hat{\boldsymbol{V}}_1, \hat{\boldsymbol{V}}_2, \hat{\boldsymbol{\xi}}$, by optimizing (34) over them using stochastic gradient ascent.
4. Run the *third* cycle of the algorithm:
   E-step: Update the sufficient statistics $\hat{\boldsymbol{\lambda}}_c^{-1}$, $\hat{\boldsymbol{\Lambda}}_c^{-1}$, and $\hat{z}_{cn}$, using (25)-(26) and (29).
   M-step: Update the word feature vectors by optimizing (34) over them using stochastic gradient ascent.
5. Run the *fourth* cycle of the algorithm:
   E-step: Update the sufficient statistics $\hat{z}_{cn}$ using (29).
   M-step: Update the posterior expectations pertaining to the stick-variables v_c, using (36)-(40).
6. If not converged, increase the iteration counter, $it := it + 1$, and **goto** 2.
   Otherwise, **exit.**

our approach are initialized by adopting the method presented in [38]; this method essentially consists in exploiting unsupervised semantic word vectors, capturing some salient syntactic and semantic distribution properties, as discussed in Section 3.1. We set the innovation parameter of our model equal to a modest $\gamma = 1$ in all our experiments.

We developed our source codes in MATLAB R2014b. We executed our experiments as single-threaded processes on an Intel Xeon 2.5GHz Quad-Core CPU with 64GB RAM.

4.1 WordNet Experiments

4.1.1 Experimental setup

WordNet is a large lexical database of English, where nouns, verbs, adjectives, and adverbs are grouped into sets of cognitive synonyms (*synsets*), each expressing a distinct concept. Synsets are interlinked by means of conceptual-semantic and lexical relations. WordNet superficially resembles a thesaurus, in that it groups words together based on their meanings. However, there are some important distinctions. First, WordNet interlinks not just word forms—strings of letters—but specific senses of words. As a result, words that are found in close proximity to one another in the network are semantically disambiguated. Second, WordNet labels the semantic relations among words, whereas the groupings of words in a thesaurus does not follow any explicit pattern other than meaning similarity.

Table 2: WordNet: Prediction accuracy (%) of the evaluated methods (optimal model configuration).

Method	Accuracy (%)
Distance Model [10]	68.3
Hadamard Model [12]	80.0
Bilinear Classifier [11]	84.1
Neural Network [17]	76.0
NTN [13]	86.2
iDLER	87.5

WordNet contains a total of 38,696 unique entities that take part in 11 different types of relations. Based on these data, we construct 112,581 relational *triplets* for *training*, half of which contain actual relationships between entity pairs included in the knowledge base (positive examples), and half comprise negative examples created by random replacement of the entities in the positive examples, as described previously. Further, in order to allow for performing model selection, we create a *development* set. For this purpose, we use a small subset of the remainder of the actual entity pair relationships (positive examples), and we create an equal number of negative examples by randomly switching entities from actual relations. This way, we obtain a development set with 2,609 triplets in total.

Finally, to obtain a *testing* set for classification, we use the remainder of the actual relationship triplets in WordNet, and augment it by randomly switching entities from actual testing relations, resulting in a testing set with equal numbers of positive and negative examples. Note that, similar to [13], we filter out trivial triplets from our testing data, namely triplets both the entities of which also appear in the training set in a different relation or order. Finally, in the case of synsets containing multiple words, we pick only the first, most frequent one. This experimental setup eventually yields a total of 10,544 triplets used for testing. The final accuracy is based on how many triplets are classified correctly as relevant or irrelevant.

4.1.2 Comparative prediction accuracy

In Table 2, we provide the prediction accuracy obtained by both our iDLER method and its considered competitors. These results have been obtained for *optimal* model configuration, as deemed by exploiting the available *development* dataset. In the case of iDLER, this entails postulating models with different values of the regularization constant $\alpha \in (0, 2]$, and different dimensionalities of the inducing space (pairwise entity) projections, $\boldsymbol{x}(\boldsymbol{e}_1, \boldsymbol{e}_2) \in \mathbb{R}^K$, that our method inherently derives. As we observe from these results, iDLER offers an improved predictive performance compared to the state-of-the-art.

4.2 FreeBase Experiments

4.2.1 Experimental setup

Freebase is a large collaborative knowledge base consisting of metadata composed mainly by its community members. It is an online collection of structured data harvested from many sources, including individual, user-submitted wiki contributions. In our experiments, we use the relational triplets included in the *People* domain, out of which we extract 13 relation types that contain a total of 75,043 entities. Similar to [13], we use data from all of these relations for training, but retain only data from 7 of them for testing, discarding the remaining 6, namely *place of death, place of birth, location, parents, children, spouse*. We elect for this experimental setup since the omitted 6 relation types are very hard to predict, e.g., the name of somebody's spouse is hard to infer from other knowledge in the database.

On this basis, we obtain a training dataset that comprises 316,232 relational *triplets*, half of which contain actual relationships between entity pairs included in the knowledge base (positive examples), and half consist of negative examples created by random replacement of the entities in the positive examples, as in the previous experiments.

Model selection is performed by creating an appropriate *development* set from a fraction of the remaining data, similar to Section 4.1. Here, the used development set contains a total of 5,908 triplets of both positive and negative examples. Finally, to obtain a *testing* set for classification, we use the remainder of the actual relationship triplets in FreeBase, and augment it by randomly switching entities from actual testing relations, resulting in a testing set with equal numbers of positive and negative examples. We filter out trivial triplets from our testing data, similar to the experiments of Section 4.1.

Note that, similar to [13], in the context of the procedure of *development set* and *test set* formation, we constrain the entities from the possible answer set by allowing entities in a given position in the formed pairs *only* if they appeared in the same position in the training dataset. For example, given a correct pair (Pablo Picasso, Spain) w.r.t. the relationship "nationality," a potential negative example to include in our development and test sets is (Pablo Picasso, United States): Such a pair includes a country that is irrelevant to the nationality of Pablo Picasso; thus, correctly labeling this pair as negative requires that the evaluated model can infer subtle correlations from the used training datasets. On the other hand, a pair, e.g., of the form (Pablo Picasso, Van Gogh) would be much easier for a model to label as negative: Since neither of the entities included in this pair contain words pertaining to *countries*, correctly labeling it as irrelevant w.r.t. the "nationality" relationship can be performed merely on a word content basis. Hence, we elect to exclude such pairs, since they do not allow for assessing the performance of an evaluated model in the much more difficult task of inferring subtle correlations from the used training datasets, which is the ultimate goal of our approach.

4.2.2 Comparative prediction accuracy

In Table 3, we provide the prediction accuracy obtained by both our iDLER method and its considered competitors. These results have been obtained for *optimal* model configuration, as deemed by exploiting the available *development* dataset. In the case of iDLER, this entails postulating models with different values of the regularization constant $\alpha \in (0, 2]$, and different dimensionalities of the inducing space (pairwise entity) projections, $\boldsymbol{x}(\boldsymbol{e}_1, \boldsymbol{e}_2) \in \mathbb{R}^K$, that our method inherently derives. As we observe from these results, iDLER offers an improved predictive performance compared to the state-of-the-art.

Table 3: FreeBase: Prediction accuracy (%) of the evaluated methods (optimal model configuration).

Method	Accuracy (%)
Distance Model [10]	61.0
Hadamard Model [12]	68.8
Bilinear Classifier [11]	87.7
Neural Network [17]	85.3
NTN [13]	90.0
iDLER	90.8

Table 4: FreeBase: Computational complexity comparisons between iDLER and the second best performing method (time in seconds).

Method	iDLER	NTN
Training time (average time per iteration)	151.69	138.20
Prediction time (average time per entity pair)	0.000715	0.000579

4.3 Computational Complexity

To conclude, let us now turn our investigations to the computational complexity of our method, and how it compares to the competition. As we observe from the discussions of Sections 3.2 and 3.3, iDLER model training and inference do not entail computationally demanding calculations. As a result, training and inference using our model are not expected to impose significantly higher computational requirements compared to the second best performing method, i.e. NTN.

Indeed, let us focus on the FreeBase dataset; similar results can be also obtained for the WordNet dataset (since both datasets are of similar scale). As we illustrate in Table 4, one iteration of the training algorithm of iDLER in the case of the FreeBase dataset imposes only a slight computational overhead compared to the second best performing method, i.e. NTN (these results pertain to the model configuration that yields optimal accuracy). Similar is the case when it comes to prediction generation. Indeed, as also shown in Table 4, the time required by both iDLER and NTN for prediction generation on the FreeBase dataset is of the same order of magnitude, and very low in both cases. Thus, from these discussions we deduce that our approach offers a favorable accuracy-complexity tradeoff over the state-of-the-art.

5. CONCLUSIONS AND FUTURE WORK

In this paper, we presented a large-margin methodology for reasoning over relationships between pairs of entities in knowledge bases. Contrary to existing works, our proposed method relies on large-margin classification techniques to effect the entity relations inference task, based on an inducing space representation of entity pair feature vectors. These inducing space representations capture salient information of both the individual features of each entity and of the entity correlations in the context of the modeled pairs; thus, they allow for better performing the large-margin inference task for the modeled data. As we discussed, feature representation learning for the observed data is performed on the individual word level instead of the entity level, to allow for sharing statistical strength between the feature vector representations of entities with common words.

To allow for better dealing with data comprising multiple modes, we assumed that the postulated inducing space comprises a set of subspaces (clusters), each of which can be modeled by a separate large-margin classifier. This way, we essentially obtained a mixture-of-experts model formulation, over which we imposed a DP prior to allow for data-driven determination of the most appropriate number of component experts. To perform model training, we utilized a recently proposed data augmentation scheme that yields an elegant and computationally efficient model training algorithm under the AECM framework.

One issue our current work does not sufficiently address concerns appropriate data-driven selection of the number of inducing space dimensions. Indeed, as we have shown through our experimental evaluations, inducing space dimensionality is a factor that affects model performance in both the considered knowledge bases. Therefore, coming up with an appropriate model formulation allowing for automatic data-driven inducing space dimensionality selection would be a significant improvement of our model. Toward this end, one could consider adoption of techniques from the field of Bayesian nonparametrics, similar to the procedure we adopted in this work for automatic selection of the number of component classifiers. For instance, one could consider imposition of Indian buffet process priors [39, 40] to achieve this goal.

Another issue our approach does not explicitly address is the case of having to deal with *polysemous* words. In such cases, sharing statistical strength between entities with similar word content may yield misleading results. One possible way to remedy this limitation could be obtained by allowing for multiple feature vectors per word, similar to [38]. Examination of solutions to both the above problems, along the lines discussed here or other alternative approaches, is part of our ongoing and future research work.

6. REFERENCES

[1] G. Miller, "WordNet: A lexical database for English," *Communications of the ACM*, 1995.

[2] K. Bollacker, C. Evans, P. Paritosh, T. Sturge, and J. Taylor, "Freebase: a collaboratively created graph database for structuring human knowledge," in *Proc. ACM SIGMOD*, 2008.

[3] F. M. Suchanek, G. Kasneci, and G. Weikum, "Yago: a core of semantic knowledge," in *Proc. 16th international conference on World Wide Web*, 2007.

[4] J. Graupmann, R. Schenkel, and G. Weikum, "The SphereSearch engine for unified ranked retrieval of heterogeneous XML and web documents," in *Proc. VLDB*, 2005.

[5] V. Ng and C. Cardie, "Improving machine learning approaches to coreference resolution," in *Proc. ACL*, 2002.

[6] A. Yates, M. Banko, M. Broadhead, M. J. Cafarella, O. Etzioni, and S. Soderland, "Textrunner: Open information extraction on the web," in *Proc. HLT-NAACL*, 2007.

[7] R. Snow, D. Jurafsky, and A. Y. Ng, "Learning syntactic patterns for automatic hypernym discovery," in *Proc. NIPS*, 2005.

[8] A. Fader, S. Soderland, and O. Etzioni, "Identifying relations for open information extraction," in *Proc. EMNLP*, 2011.

[9] G. Angeli and C. D. Manning, "Philosophers are mortal: Inferring the truth of unseen facts," in *CoNLL*, 2013.

[10] A. Bordes, J. Weston, R. Collobert, and Y. Bengio, "Learning structured embeddings of knowledge bases," in *Proc. AAAI*, 2011.

[11] R. Jenatton, N. L. Roux, A. Bordes, and G. Obozinski, "A latent factor model for highly multi-relational data," in *Proc. NIPS*, 2012.

[12] A. Bordes, X. Glorot, J. Weston, and Y. Bengio, "Joint learning of words and meaning representations for open-text semantic parsing," in *Proc. AISTATS*, 2012.

[13] R. Socher, D. Chen, C. D. Manning, and A. Y. Ng, "Reasoning with neural tensor networks for knowledge base completion," in *Proc. NIPS*, 2014.

[14] I. Sutskever, R. Salakhutdinov, and J. B. Tenenbaum, "Modelling relational data using Bayesian clustered tensor factorization," in *Proc. NIPS*, 2009.

[15] M. Nickel, V. Tresp, and H. Kriegel, "A three-way model for collective learning on multi-relational data," in *Proc. ICML*, 2011.

[16] R. A. Harshman, "Models for analysis of asymmetrical relationships among n objects or stimuli," in *Proc. First Joint Meeting of the Psychometric Society and the Society for Mathematical Psychology*, 1978.

[17] R. Collobert and J. Weston, "A unified architecture for natural language processing: deep neural networks with multitask learning," in *Proc. ICML*, 2008.

[18] V. N. Vapnik, *Statistical Learning Theory*. New York: Wiley, 1998.

[19] Y. Altun, I. Tsochantaridis, and T. Hofmann, "Hidden Markov support vector machines," in *Proc. ICML*, 2004.

[20] J. Zhu, N. Chen, and E. P. Xing, "Infinite SVM: a Dirichlet process mixture of large-margin kernel machines," in *Proc. ICML*, 2011.

[21] N. G. Polson and S. L. Scott, "Data augmentation for support vector machines," *Bayesian Analysis*, vol. 6, no. 1, pp. 1–24, 2011.

[22] R. Collobert, S. Bengio, and Y. Bengio, "A parallel mixture of SVMs for very large scale problems," in *Proc. NIPS*, 2002.

[23] Z. Fu, A. Robles-Kelly, and J. Zhou, "Mixing linear SVMs for nonlinear classification," *IEEE Trans. on Neural Networks*, vol. 21, no. 2, pp. 1963 – 1975, 2010.

[24] S. Walker, P. Damien, P. Laud, and A. Smith, "Bayesian nonparametric inference for random distributions and related functions," *J. Roy. Statist. Soc. B*, vol. 61, no. 3, pp. 485–527, 1999.

[25] R. Neal, "Markov chain sampling methods for Dirichlet process mixture models," *J. Comput. Graph. Statist.*, vol. 9, pp. 249–265, 2000.

[26] P. Muller and F. Quintana, "Nonparametric Bayesian data analysis," *Statist. Sci.*, vol. 19, no. 1, pp. 95–110, 2004.

[27] C. Antoniak, "Mixtures of Dirichlet processes with applications to Bayesian nonparametric problems." *The Annals of Statistics*, vol. 2, no. 6, pp. 1152–1174, 1974.

[28] D. Blei and M. Jordan, "Variational methods for the Dirichlet process," in *21st Int. Conf. Machine Learning*, New York, NY, USA, July 2004, pp. 12–19.

[29] T. Jaakkola and M. Jordan, "Bayesian parameter estimation via variational methods," *Statistics and Computing*, vol. 10, pp. 25–37, 2000.

[30] H. Attias, "A variational Bayesian framework for graphical models," in *Proc. Ann. Conf. Neural Information Processing Systems*, 2000.

[31] J. Winn and C. Bishop, "Variational message passing," *J. Machine Learning Research*, vol. 6, pp. 661–694, 2005.

[32] J. Sethuraman, "A constructive definition of the Dirichlet prior," *Statistica Sinica*, vol. 2, pp. 639–650, 1994.

[33] D. M. Blei and M. I. Jordan, "Variational inference for Dirichlet process mixtures," *Bayesian Analysis*, vol. 1, no. 1, pp. 121–144, 2006.

[34] T. Ferguson, "A Bayesian analysis of some nonparametric problems," *The Annals of Statistics*, vol. 1, pp. 209–230, 1973.

[35] D. Blackwell and J. MacQueen, "Ferguson distributions via Pólya urn schemes," *The Annals of Statistics*, vol. 1, no. 2, pp. 353–355, 1973.

[36] A. Dempster, N. Laird, and D. Rubin, "Maximum likelihood from incomplete data via the EM algorithm," *Journal of the Royal Statistical Society, B*, vol. 39, no. 1, pp. 1–38, 1977.

[37] X. L. Meng and D. van Dyk, "The EM algorithm - an old folk song sung to a fast new tune (with discussion)," *Journal of the Royal Statistical Society, B*, vol. 59, pp. 511–567, 1997.

[38] E. H. Huang, R. Socher, C. D. Manning, and A. Y. Ng, "Improving word representations via global context and multiple word prototypes," in *Proc. ACL*, 2012.

[39] T. Griffiths and Z. Ghahramani, "Infinite latent feature models and the Indian buffet process," Gatsby Computational Neuroscience Unit, Tech. Rep. TR 2005-001, 2005.

[40] Y. W. Teh, D. Gorur, and Z. Ghahramani, "Stick-breaking construction for the Indian buffet process," in *Proc. AISTATS*, 2007.

Semi-Automated Exploration of Data Warehouses

Thibault Sellam
CWI
Amsterdam, the Netherlands
thibault.sellam@cwi.nl

Emmanuel Müller
KIT
Karlsruhe, Germany
emmanuel.mueller@kit.edu

Martin Kersten
CWI
Amsterdam, the Netherlands
martin.kersten@cwi.nl

ABSTRACT

Exploratory data analysis tries to discover novel dependencies and unexpected patterns in large databases. Traditionally, this process is manual and hypothesis-driven. However, analysts can come short of patience and imagination. In this paper, we introduce Claude, a hypothesis generator for data warehouses. Claude follows a 2-step approach: (1) It detects interesting views, by exploiting non-linear statistical dependencies between the dimensions and the measure. (2) To explain its findings, it detects local patterns in these views and describes them with SQL queries. Technically, we derive a model of interestingness from fundamental information theory. To exploit this model, we present aggressive approximations and heuristics, allowing Claude to be fast and more accurate than state-of-art view selection algorithms.

Categories and Subject Descriptors

H.2.8 [**Database Applications**]: Data mining

Keywords

Data exploration; Query recommendation; Feature selection; Subgroup discovery

1. INTRODUCTION

Businesses and scientists willing to extract knowledge from databases face a dilemma. On one hand, software editors have commercialized quantity of visual Business Intelligence tools, such as Tableau or Qlik. Yet, these rely almost entirely on users' expertise, intuition, and patience. In an exploratory scenario, when users know little about their data, such tools can involve time-consuming cycles of trial and error. On the other hand, automated, machine learning methods have gained much popularity, as shown by the recent success of industrial "data scientists". Nevertheless, at the time of writing this paper, these experts are still a rare and expensive resource. Can we find a middle way? Can we design a flexible, accessible method to automatically analyze data warehouses?

Consider the following scenario. A government analyst studies criminality in US cities. The database describes how a *measure*, the number of crimes, varies along several dozen *dimensions*, e.g., the population, unemployment rate, or location. Which cities are prone to crime? Can we identify causes, correlations, or patterns? For our analyst, inspecting how every possible combination of dimensions correlates with crime is close to impossible. But important observations could hide behind unexpected dependencies. Our aim is to automatically *generate hypotheses* about what influences the measure. We want to synthesize SQL queries which highlight what causes crime to vary, and how these variations occur. Given such queries, even lay users could explore their data and detect unexpected patterns.

We believe that this problem is extremely common in both business and science, where multi-dimensional data warehouses have been deployed for years. Addressing it with an automated method would allow analysts and researchers to make discoveries more quickly, focusing on interpretation rather than writing queries. Such a technique could also provoke serendipitous findings, e.g., highlighting a surprising correlation or confronting an ill-posed hypothesis. Besides, the problem is getting more pressing as data warehouses grow in size and complexity: manual exploration can turn out to be a painful exercise when dealing with hundreds of columns.

Automating data exploration is a difficult problem for two reasons. First, how do we recognize "interesting" queries? There is, to our knowledge, no universal measure of interestingness. The challenge is to devise a theoretically well-founded model, general enough to cover a wide range of use cases. The second problem is efficiency: given a measure of interest, how can we explore the space of all database queries quickly enough to support large datasets? We must design efficient methods to traverse all possible combinations of dimensions.

Several semi-automated exploration frameworks were proposed in the past, in the context of OLAP data cubes [17, 10]. They assumed that databases contained less than a dozen well-known dimensions. The whole challenge was to drill-in correctly, in order to locate "exceptions", e.g., local anomalies. We believe that many of these assumptions do not hold anymore. In our model, databases can contain more than a hundred dimensions with mixed types. Analysts have little to no knowledge about the effects of these dimensions, even less about their combination and their effect on a given

Permission to make digital or hard copies of all or part of this work for personal or classroom use is granted without fee provided that copies are not made or distributed for profit or commercial advantage and that copies bear this notice and the full citation on the first page. Copyrights for components of this work owned by others than ACM must be honored. Abstracting with credit is permitted. To copy otherwise, or republish, to post on servers or to redistribute to lists, requires prior specific permission and/or a fee. Request permissions from Permissions@acm.org.
CIKM'15, October 19–23, 2015, Melbourne, Australia.
© 2015 ACM. ISBN 978-1-4503-3794-6/15/10 ...$15.00.
DOI: http://dx.doi.org/10.1145/2806416.2806538.

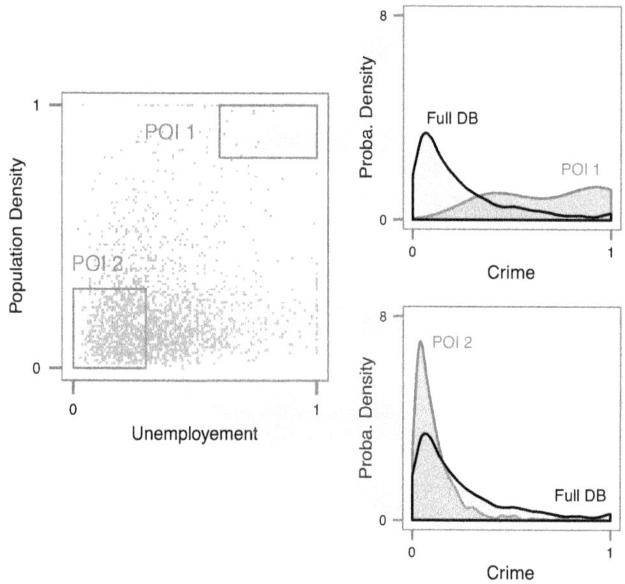

Figure 1: Example view, with two points of interest. All values are normalized.

measure. Therefore, our challenge is to depict a general picture of how the measure varies across any possible view on the database.

In this paper, we introduce *Claude*, a hypothesis generator for data warehouses. Claude's aim is to detect interesting views, i.e., interesting combination of dimensions, and highlight local patterns in these views. We make three contributions: (1) We derive a model of what makes a view "interesting" from fundamental information theory. (2) We present aggressive methods to detect good views in large databases, based on approximations and greedy search. (3) We apply our model to real-life situations, involving either humans (data exploration by subgroup discovery) or automatic predictors (classification algorithms).

The rest of this paper is organized as follows. Section 2 gives an overview of our model, which we refine in Section 3. Sections 4 describes how to compute the quality a view, Section 5 presents our view detection algorithm, and Section 6 introduces how to detect points of interest. We present our experiments in Section 7, related work in Section 8 and conclude in Section 9.

2. PROBLEM FORMULATION

Let us define our problem setting. We assume that the data is given in flat database table DB. This table contains two types of columns: the *dimensions* $X_0, \ldots, X_N$ and a *measure* (or *target*) T. This model is logical, we are oblivious to the physical structure of the data. Our aim is to describe how the measure varies across the dimensions. To do so, we want to detect **views**, i.e. *interesting* selections of dimensions. We also want to show *why* these views are interesting, by detecting **points of interests** (POI). A point of interest is a region in the view where the measure behaves unusually.

We demonstrate these notions with a running example. We want to understand what causes crime in US communities. We have a database of cities with several dozen socio-economic indicators (for instance, employment, age, or diplomas). For each city we also have the annual number of violent crimes: this is our target variable. Figure 1 presents an example view. The leftmost scatterplot pictures the dimensions `Unemployment` and `Population Density`. Why did Claude pick these two columns? The two POIs provide explanations. Cities with high densities and high unemployment rates have more crimes (cf. POI_1). In contrast, cities with low densities and lower employment rates tend to be safer (cf. POI_2).

In our example, `Unemployment` and `Population Density` are interesting because their combination influences the target `Crime`. We can measure this relationship with statistical dependence. This is the most basic assumption behind our study: a view is interesting if its dimensions are *jointly dependent* to the measure. We evaluate the degree of this dependence with our notion of **view strength**.

DEFINITION 1. *Consider a view $V = \{X_1, \ldots, X_D\}$, the target T, and measure of statistical dependence $\mathfrak{S}$. We define the strength of the view V as follows:*

$$\sigma(V) = \mathfrak{S}(\mathcal{X}_1, \ldots, \mathcal{X}_D; \mathcal{T}) \tag{1}$$

We assume that each database column X contains samples from a random variable $\mathcal{X}$ and measure the dependence accordingly.

Observe the two POIs in Figure 1. The measure's distribution in these regions differs from its distribution in the rest of the database: it is skewed to the right in POI_1, it is skewed to the left in POI_2. We name this property **POI divergence**. Intuitively, a region is divergent if the target behaves unexpectedly for its tuples. Consider a view based on the random variables $\mathcal{X}_1, \ldots, \mathcal{X}_D$, with respective sample spaces $\Omega_1, \ldots, \Omega_D$. The set $R \subset \Omega_1 \times \ldots \times \Omega_D$ represents a region in this view. The random variable $\mathcal{T}$ represents the target *for the whole database*. The random variable $[\mathcal{T}|(\mathcal{X}_1, \ldots, \mathcal{X}_D) \in R]$ represents the target *for the tuples within* R. We shorten this notation to $\mathcal{T}|R$. The region R is a good point of interest if $\mathcal{T}|R$ and $\mathcal{T}$ have large differences in distribution.

DEFINITION 2. *Let $R \subset \Omega_1 \times \ldots \times \Omega_D$ represent a region in the view $\{X_1, \ldots, X_D\}$, and let $\mathcal{T}$ represent our target variable. The function $\mathfrak{D}$ measures the dissimilarity between two probability distributions. We define R's* ***divergence****:*

$$\delta(R) = \mathfrak{D}(\mathcal{T}|R; \mathcal{T}) \tag{2}$$

Before we present our instantiation of strength and divergence in Section 3, we formulate our general problem statement:

PROBLEM 1. *Consider a dataset DB, a target column T, a measure of statistical dependence $\mathfrak{S}$ and a measure of distribution dissimilarity $\mathfrak{D}$. Find the top K strongest views with at most D columns. For each of these views, find the top P divergent POIs.*

To solve this problem, Claude operates in two steps. First, it detects K strong sets of columns. We call this step *column search*. Then, it extracts P POIs for each view. This is the *POI detection* step.

In the rest of this paper, we will illustrate Claude's views with mathematical notation or visualizations. In practice however, Claude expresses its recommendations with SQL queries. It returns points of interest as follows:

```
SELECT X1, ... , Xd, T
FROM DB
WHERE X1 BETWEEN [L1, H1]
  AND ...
  AND Xd BETWEEN [Ld, Hd]
```

In this query, X1, ..., Xd represent the variables of the view, [L1, H1] ... [Ln, Hn] represents the bounds of the POI, and T represents the target.

3. INTERESTINGNESS MODEL

We presented views and POIs without specifying any measure of dependence $\mathfrak{S}$ or dissimilarity $\mathfrak{D}$. In the following section, we instantiate these quantities using fundamental information theory.

3.1 View Strength

A set of dimensions is interesting if its columns are jointly dependent to the target. To quantify this dependence, we use *mutual information*. This measure presents many advantages: it is sensible to non-linear dependences, it can cope with any kind of variables, and it is practical to compute.

The *entropy* $H(\mathcal{X})$ of a variable $\mathcal{X}$ describes its variability [3]. If $\mathcal{X}$ has a constant value, then $H(\mathcal{X}) = 0$. In contrast, if $\mathcal{X}$ is highly unpredictable (e.g., $\mathcal{X}$ is the outcome of flipping a perfectly balanced coin) then $H(\mathcal{X})$ is maximal. Formally, if $\mathcal{X}$ is a discrete variable with sample space Ω, then we have:

$$H(\mathcal{X}) = -\sum_{x\in\Omega} P(\mathcal{X} = x) \cdot \log P(\mathcal{X} = x) \tag{3}$$

If $\mathcal{X}$ is continuous with density p, we define it as follows:

$$H(\mathcal{X}) = -\int_{-\infty}^{+\infty} p(x) \cdot \log p(x) \mathrm{d}x \tag{4}$$

We can use the entropy to describe how variables interact. If two variables are dependent, then conditioning (e.g., restricting the range of values) on one variable will affect the other. In our example, cities with high unemployment have high levels of crime. Therefore, conditioning on the variable `Unemployment` decreases the uncertainty of the variable `Crime`. This causes a loss in entropy, and the value of this loss is the mutual information. Formally, if $\mathcal{X}$ and $\mathcal{T}$ are two random variables, the expression $H(\mathcal{T}|\mathcal{X} = x)$ describes the entropy of $\mathcal{T}$ *given* $X = x$. If we average this expression over all possible values of x, we obtain the conditional entropy: $H(\mathcal{T}|\mathcal{X}) = \mathbb{E}_x[H(\mathcal{T}|\mathcal{X} = x)]$. We define the mutual information I as follows:

$$I(\mathcal{X}; \mathcal{T}) = H(\mathcal{T}) - H(\mathcal{T}|\mathcal{X}) \tag{5}$$

The mutual information is the loss in entropy between $\mathcal{T}$ and $\mathcal{T}|\mathcal{X}$. It is symmetric, and it is always positive or null. We can generalize this quantity to joint distributions, which gives us our new, refined version of view strength:

$$\boldsymbol{\sigma(V) = I(\mathcal{X}_1, \ldots, \mathcal{X}_D; \mathcal{T})} \tag{6}$$

A view is strong if the mutual information between the target and its dimensions is high.

In practice, we do not know the distributions of the variables $\mathcal{X}_n$, but we have access to the samples X_n. Therefore, we *estimate* the strength. If the variables are discrete, we set $\hat{P}(\mathcal{X}_n = x)$ to be the proportion of tuples with $X_n = x$.

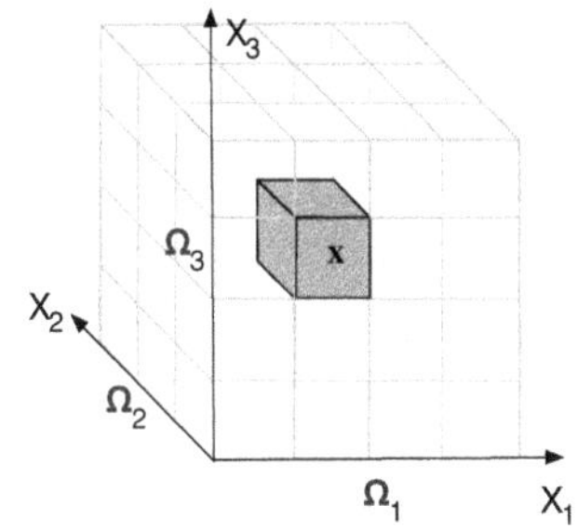

Figure 2: Example of view with three discrete variables $V = \{X_1, X_2, X_3\}$. The average divergence of the cells $\delta(\mathbf{x})$ equals the strength of the view $\sigma(V)$.

We "plug" this estimator in Equations 3, to obtain the estimated entropy $\hat{H}(\mathcal{X})$. We then use this approximation in Equation 5. Dealing with continuous vari'ables is more difficult, for two reasons. First, estimating the density function in Equation 4 is costly, especially with multivariate distributions. Second, it is not clear how to deal with mixed datasets, e.g. continuous and discrete dimensions, or discrete target and continuous dimensions. Therefore, Claude bins all the continuous variables, and treats them like discrete columns.

3.2 Points of Interest and Divergence

Let us now refine our definition of divergence. We established that the divergence of a POI is the dissimilarity between the target's distribution within this POI, and the target's distribution in the whole database. To measure this dissimilarity, we use the *Kullback-Leibler divergence* (KL). The KL divergence measures the difference between two probability distributions. It is null if the two distributions are similar, and it grows when the distributions differ. Formally, if $\mathcal{X}$ and $\mathcal{Y}$ are two discrete random variables with the same sample space Ω, we have:

$$KL(\mathcal{X} \parallel \mathcal{Y}) = \sum_{x\in\Omega} P(\mathcal{X} = x) \cdot \log \frac{P(\mathcal{X} = x)}{P(\mathcal{Y} = x)} \tag{7}$$

As Claude discretizes the continuous variables, we ignore the continuous case (cf. Section 3.1). Our region R is a good point of interest if $KL(\mathcal{T}|R \parallel \mathcal{T})$ is as large as possible:

$$\boldsymbol{\delta(R) = KL(\mathcal{T}|R \parallel \mathcal{T})} \tag{8}$$

In our model, view strength and POI divergence are closely related. Consider a view V, made of discrete variables. If we compute the divergence of each tuple and average the results, we obtain the V's strength. We illustrate this property with Figure 2. Therefore, strength and divergence are "two sides of the same coin". We formalize this property with the lemma below.

LEMMA 1. *If V is a view with d discrete variables and $\mathbf{x} \in \Omega_1 \times \ldots \Omega_D$ is a tuple from this view, then:*

$$\sigma(V) = \mathbb{E}_{\mathbf{x}}\left[\delta(\{\mathbf{x}\})\right] \tag{9}$$

PROOF. The random vector $\mathbf{X}$ describes the columns of V. Applying Bayes's theorem to Cover and Thomas, Equation 2.35 [3], we obtain $I(\mathbf{X}; \mathcal{T}) = \mathbb{E}_{\mathbf{x}}[KL(T|\{\mathbf{x}\} \parallel T)]$. Substituting the left side with Equation 6, and the right side with Equation 8, we obtain the lemma. □

Suppose that we obtained a view V by discretizing a set of continuous variables V^*. The average divergence of V's bins equals the strength of V, but not that of V^*. Fortunately, these quantities converge as the bins get small.

LEMMA 2. *The view V is a set of continuous variables, V^b is a discretized version of V in which each variable is binned with bin size b, and $\mathbf{x}^b$ is a tuple from V^b. We have $\mathbb{E}_{\mathbf{x^b}}[\delta(\{\mathbf{x^b}\})] \to \sigma(V)$ as $b \to 0$.*

PROOF. Let the D-dimensional random vector $\mathbf{X}$ describe the (continuous) variables of V, and $\mathbf{X}^b$ describe the (discrete) variables of V^b. By generalizing Cover and Thomas, Theorem 8.3.1 [3], we infer that $H(\mathbf{X}^b) + D \cdot \log b \to H(\mathbf{X})$ as $b \to 0$. Thus, using Equation 5, we have $I(\mathbf{X}^b, \mathcal{T}) \to I(\mathbf{X}, \mathcal{T})$. We conclude that $\sigma(V^b) \to \sigma(V)$. We apply Equation 9 to obtain the lemma. □

4. APPROXIMATE VIEW STRENGTH

We now have a functional definition of view strength. At this point, we could easily envision a greedy heuristic to detect the top K views in a database. We start with simple views, based on one dimension. We then add columns, one by one. To test if a column X is worth adding to a view V, we compute the strength $\sigma(V \cup \{X\})$. If the result is high enough, we keep the candidate. If not, we discard it. We will present such an algorithm in Section 5. However, we must first discuss how to compute $\sigma(V \cup \{X\})$.

Equations 6 and 9 describe several methods to compute the strength of a view. Nevertheless, none of these fit iterative algorithms. Suppose that we wish to compute the strength of a view V, then the strength of another view $V \cup \{X\}$. These equations give us no opportunity to share computations, we must obtain $\sigma(V)$ and $\sigma(V \cup \{X\})$ separately. Furthermore, both expressions are expensive, as they involve group-by queries over the whole database. Therefore, we need an alternative *recursive* formulation for the strength of a view:

LEMMA 3. *Consider a view $V = \{X_1, \ldots, X_i\}$, and a target T. For any column X_{i+1}:*

$$\sigma(V \cup \{X_{i+1}\}) = \sigma(V) + I(\mathcal{X}_{i+1}; \mathcal{T} | \mathcal{X}_1, \ldots, \mathcal{X}_i) \quad (10)$$

PROOF. This lemma is a consequence of the Mutual Information's chain rule, Cover and Thomas, Theorem 2.5.2 [3]. □

This lemma describes how adding a column impacts the strength of a view. For any random variables $\mathcal{X}_i, \mathcal{X}_j, \mathcal{T}$, the notation $I(\mathcal{X}_j; \mathcal{T}|\mathcal{X}_i)$ expresses the *conditional mutual information.* The conditional mutual information is a conditioned version of the mutual information: it describes the dependency between $\mathcal{X}_j$ and $\mathcal{T}$ *given restrictions on* $\mathcal{X}_i$. To obtain it, we compute the mutual information between $\mathcal{X}_j$ and $\mathcal{T}$ given all the possible values of $\mathcal{X}_i$, and average the results. Formally:

$$I(\mathcal{X}_j; \mathcal{T}|\mathcal{X}_i) = \mathbb{E}_{x_i}[I(\mathcal{X}_j; \mathcal{T})|\mathcal{X}_i = x_i)] \quad (11)$$

The influence of $\mathcal{X}_i$ can go either way: it can weaken the dependency between $\mathcal{X}_j$ and $\mathcal{T}$, or it can strengthen it. The conditional mutual information is positive or null, and it is bounded by the entropy of $\mathcal{X}_j$ and T.

Unfortunately, we cannot directly exploit Lemma 3 in our algorithm: estimating $I(\mathcal{X}_{i+1}; \mathcal{T}|\mathcal{X}_1, \ldots, \mathcal{X}_i)$ for every candidate $\{X_1, \ldots, X_{i+1}\}$ is as expensive as computing the strength directly. However, we can use an approximation. Recall that $V = \{X_1, \ldots, X_i\}$, we exploit the following observation:

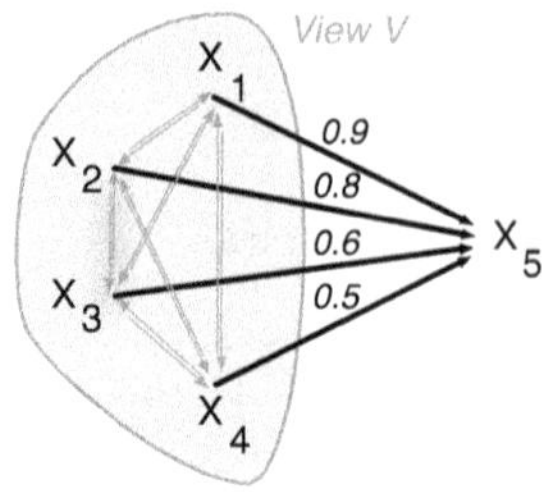

Figure 3: Example of co-dependency graph with 5 dimensions. To approximate the strength of $V \cup \{X_5\}$, we add the weight of edge (X_4, X_5) to V's strength - in this case 0.5.

$$\begin{aligned} \sigma(V \cup \{X_{i+1}\}) &= \sigma(V) + I(\mathcal{X}_{i+1}; \mathcal{T}|\mathcal{X}_1, \ldots, \mathcal{X}_i) \\ &\approx \sigma(V) + I(\mathcal{X}_{i+1}; \mathcal{T}|\mathcal{X}_i) \end{aligned} \quad (12)$$

The idea behind this approximation is naive: we assume that $I(\mathcal{X}_{i+1}; \mathcal{T}|\mathcal{X}_1, \ldots, \mathcal{X}_i) \approx I(\mathcal{X}_{i+1}; \mathcal{T}|\mathcal{X}_i)$. We simply ignore the high order dependencies. Thanks to this assumption, we can compute the strength of our candidates much faster.

Our new approach operates in two steps, an offline step and an online step. Offline, we compute the conditional mutual information $I(\mathcal{X}_j; \mathcal{T}|\mathcal{X}_i)$ between every pair of variable $(\mathcal{X}_i, \mathcal{X}_j)$. We call the resulting structure **co-dependency graph**. In this graph, the vertices represent the dimensions, and the edges represent the conditional mutual information. The co-dependency graph is oriented and weighted. Online, we run a greedy algorithm as described previously, but we use Equation 12 to evaluate new candidates. To compute the strength of a view $V \cup \{X_{i+1}\}$ with $V = \{X_1, \ldots, X_i\}$, we fetch the value of $I(\mathcal{X}_{i+1}; \mathcal{T}|\mathcal{X}_i)$ in the co-dependency graph and add it to V's strength. We illustrate this method in Figure 3. Previously, computing $\sigma(V \cup \{X_{i+1}\})$ involved heavy groupings and aggregations on the whole dataset. Now, we simply perform a lookup in a graph with N edges, where N is the number of columns in the database.

Note that our approximation has a drawback: it depends on the order in which we include the variables in the view. If we enrich a view by successively adding variables X_1, X_2 and X_3, then we obtain a different strength than if we incorporate X_3, X_2 then X_1. Similarly, in Equation 12, we obtain different approximations if we change the indexing of the dimensions $\mathcal{X}_1, \ldots, \mathcal{X}_i$. For more robustness, we introduce a "pessimistic" variant:

$$\sigma(V \cup \{X_{i+1}\}) \approx \min_{n \in [1,i]} \sigma(V) + I(\mathcal{X}_{i+1}; \mathcal{T}|\mathcal{X}_n) \quad (13)$$

Instead of adding the strength $I(\mathcal{X}_{i+1}; \mathcal{T}|\mathcal{X}_i)$, where $\mathcal{X}_i$ is the last variable inserted, we add $I(\mathcal{X}_{i+1}; T|\mathcal{X}_n)$, where $\mathcal{X}_n$ is the variable which weakens $\mathcal{X}_{i+1}$ the most. We will use this version in the rest of the paper.

5. PRACTICAL COLUMN SELECTION

This section presents our view search strategy. Our aim is to find the top K views with at most D columns. If our database includes N dimensions, our search space contains $\sum_{n \le N} \binom{N}{n} = 2^N$ combinations, which is clearly impractical. Therefore, we resort to a greedy, level-wise heuristic.

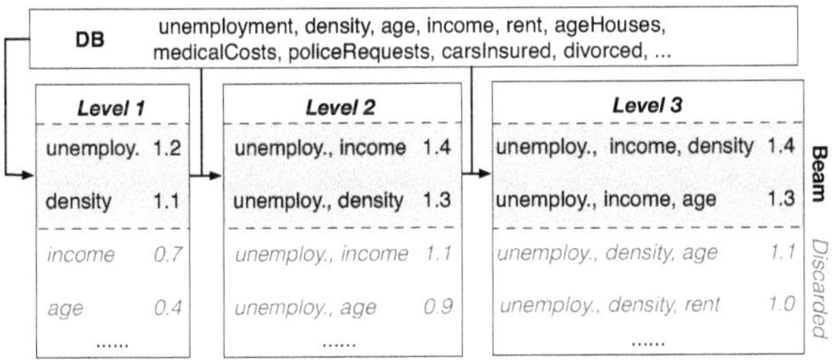

Figure 4: Example of Beam Search, with $D = 3$ and beam size $B = 2$

Algorithm 1 Beam Search for view selection

```
function TopViews(K, D, B, DB)
    Beam ← {}
    for i ∈ [1, D] do
        Cand ← {}, Scores ← {}
        for V ∈ Beam do
            for X ∈ columns(DB) do
                Cand ← Cand ∪ {V ∪ {X}}
                Scores ← Scores ∪ σ(V ∪ {X})
            end for
        end for
        Beam ← findTopK(Cand, Scores, B)
    end for
    return findTopK(Cand, Scores, K)
end function
```

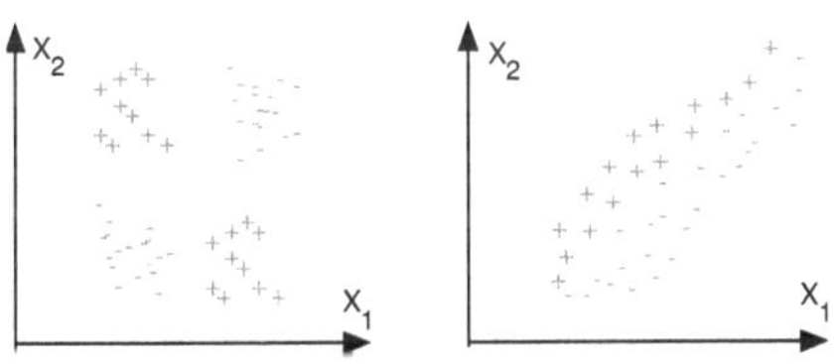

Figure 5: Limit cases of the beam search strategy. The variables X_1 and X_2 represent two dimensions. The symbol and color of the plots represent the value of the target.

5.1 Base algorithm

Our algorithm is based on *beam search*, illustrated in Figure 4. To initialize the algorithm, we compute the strength of each variable separately. We sort the candidates, and keep the top B elements. We call this set the *beam*, greyed in the figure. Then, we generate new candidates, by appending each variable of the database to each variable in the beam. We obtain views with two columns. We compute the strength of these views, keep the top B strongest and discard the others. This gives us a new beam. We repeat the procedure until the views in the beam contain D variables, or the views stop improving. Algorithm 1 presents the full procedure.

Thanks to our strategy, we avoid exploring an exponentially large search space. Instead, we compute the strengths of at most $N.B$ candidates at each level. The size of the beam lets us control the trade-off between accuracy and runtime. With a small beam, we evaluate less candidates, and thus terminate earlier. Oppositely, a large beam lets us explore more candidates. Let us explain why this is necessary.

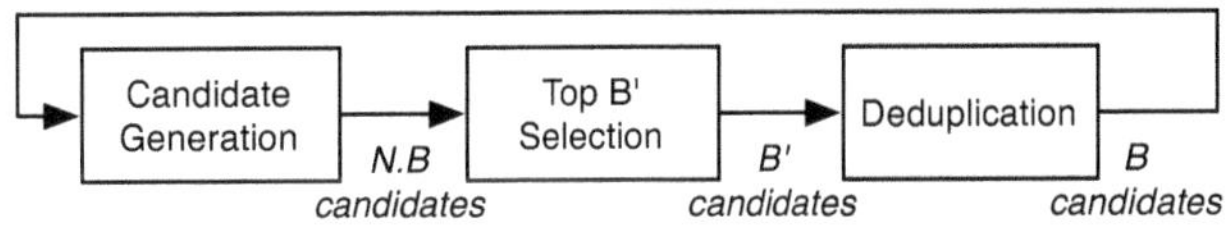

Figure 6: Beam search augmented with a deduplication step. We display in italic the size of the intermediate results. Note that $N \cdot B \geq B' \geq B$.

At each level of the algorithm, we discard the views which are too weak to reach the top B candidates. We assume that if a combination of columns is weak at level i, then it will be weak at all subsequent levels. Unfortunately, this assumption does *not* hold: we can form strong views by combining weak columns; there are "jumps" in the search space. Consider for instance the two classic scenarios pictured in Figure 5. The dimensions X_1 and X_2 taken in isolation are weak: we can infer no useful information about the target from either of them. However, their combination is very interesting. Equivalently, the views $\{X_1\}$ and $\{X_2\}$ have a very poor strength, but $\{X_1, X_2\}$ is an excellent candidate. If the beam is too tight, we may discard $\{X_1\}$ and $\{X_2\}$ early because of low scores. We lose the opportunity to discover $\{X_1, X_2\}$. Therefore, we recommend to set $B > K$. During our experiments, we obtained excellent results with $B \geq 2 \cdot K$ (cf. Section 7.3).

5.2 Approximations and Refinements

In total, we evaluate the strength of $B \cdot N$ candidates for the D levels of the beam search. To carry out this computation, we can either use the exact formulation of strength, as shown in Equation 6, or use the approximation scheme presented in Section 4. In Claude's implementation, we opted for a hybrid approach. We perform the first two levels of search with the exact strength (which is equivalent to building the co-dependency graph). Then, for all subsequent steps, we use the approximations. Finally, we revert to the exact strength for the top k ranking, at the very end of the procedure. Thanks to this method, we obtain significant speed gains at little accuracy cost.

5.3 Deduplication

Our algorithm seeks strong views. In some cases however, it may be preferable to have weaker but more diverse views. To deal with those cases, we introduce an optional *deduplication* step, during which we reduce the number of views with an algorithm from the literature. As pictured in Figure 6, we run this procedure at the end of each beam search iteration. By definition, deduplication reduces the number of candidates. Therefore, to obtain B views at the end of the algorithm, we must generate $B' > B$ views beforehand. A low B' yields more variety, while a high B' may lead to stronger views.

Authors have proposed quantity of methods to deduplicate itemsets in the pattern mining literature [25, 21]. We opted for a simple compression-based approach. First, we compute the dissimilarity between every pair of views with the Jaccard dissimilarity. Given two views V_i and V_j, it is defined as follows: $d_J(V_i, V_j) = |V_i \cap V_j| / |V_i \cup V_j|$. We then cluster the resulting matrix with Partitioning Around Medoids, an algorithm of type k-medoids. We refer the interested reader to the literature for more details [11].

Dataset	Columns	Rows	#Views	#Variables
MuskMolecules	167	6,600	22	18
Crime	128	1,996	20	17
BreastCancer	34	234	10	13
PenDigits	17	7,496	9	10
BankMarketing	17	45,213	11	8
LetterRecog	16	20,000	10	12
USCensus	14	32,578	10	7
MAGICTelescope	11	19,022	1	10

Table 1: Characteristics of the datasets. The last two columns are used for comparison with 4S, cf. Section 7.3.

View	Score (normalized)
Police.Overtime, Pct.Vacant.Boarded, Pct.Race.White	0.51
Pct.Families.2.Parents, Pct.Race.White, Police.Requests.Per.Officer	0.49
Pct.Police.White, Pct.Police.Minority, Pct.Vacant.House.Boarded	0.37
Pct.Empl.Profes.Services, Pct.Empl.Manual, Pct.Police.On.Patrol	0.37
Pct.Retired, Pct.Use.Public.Transports, Pct.Police.On.Patrol	0.35
Pct.Recently.Moved, Population.Density, Police.Cars	0.34

Table 2: Example of views generated by Claude for the US Crime dataset.

6. DETECTING POINTS OF INTEREST

We previously described how to find strong views. We now explain how to identify P points of interests for each of these views.

We instantiate POIs by a well-known analysis called *subgroup discovery* [13, 23], which can be formulated as follows: given a set of tuples, a target column and a measure of exceptionality, detect sets of tuples for which the target behaves exceptionally. In our case, we instantiate the exceptionality measure with divergence.

As pointed our by van Leeuwen and Knobbe [20], we can also solve the subgroup discovery problem with beam search. Let V represent the view to analyze. As the variables are binned, can form a grid over V, as shown in Figure 2. We denote by b the number of bins for each variable. To initialize the algorithm, we compute the divergence of each cell and keep the top B_{POI} most divergent. We obtain our beam. We then "drill" into each of these cells: we decompose them into smaller cells by splitting the edges into b bins. We evaluate the new candidates and keep the top B_{POI} most divergent. We reiterate until the algorithm converges. As shown in the subgroup discovery literature [23, 20], we can generalize this method to binary and nominal data. For each distinct level x_i of a variable X, we create two groups: tuples for which $X = x_i$, and tuples for which $X \neq x_i$.

In practice, KL-based approaches tends to favor smaller regions. Therefore, Beam Search may converge late, or not at all. A practical solution is to set a minimum count threshold. Alternatively, we can alter our model to take the size into account [20]. Let R represents a region with count $|R|$, and $|DB|$ represent the number of tuples in the database. We introduce the *weighted* deviation $\delta_w(R) = |R|/|DB| \times \delta(R)$. This new score introduces a penalty for small POIs.

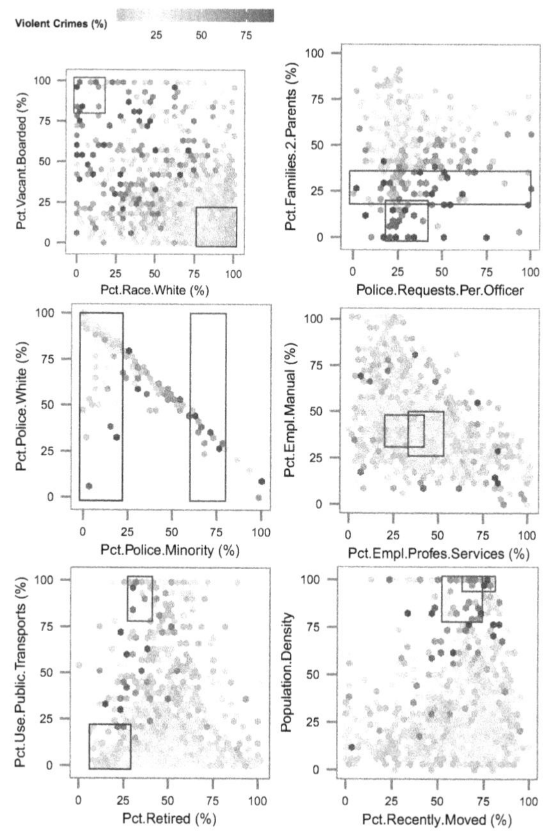

Figure 7: Heatmaps of the US Crime Dataset, based on Claude's output. Each box represents a Point of Interest.

7. EXPERIMENTS

We now present our experimental results. All our experiments are based on 8 datasets from the UCI Repository, described in Table 1. The files are freely available online[1]. In several experiments, we report the *normalized* view strength instead of the usual strength; if V is a view with entropy $H(V)$, we obtain it as follows: $\sigma_{norm}(V) = \sigma(V)/H(V)$.

7.1 Detailed Example: Crimes in the US

In this section, we showcase Claude with a real-life example: we analyze the Communities and Crime dataset form the UCI repository[2]. Our aim is to understand which US cities are subject to violent crimes. Our database compiles crime data and socio-economic indicators about 1994 communities, with a total of 128 variables. The data comes mostly from the 90's, and it was provided by official US sources - among others, the 1990 US census and the 1995 FBI Uniform Crime Report. All the variables are normalized to have a minimum of 0 and a maximum of 100.

We generated $K = 100$ views with up to $D = 3$ dimensions, both with and without deduplication. We present a selection of views in Table 2, along with 2-dimension heat maps in Figure 7. Observe that strong views have a visual signature: in the top two maps, the blue and red areas are neatly separated. In the bottom two views, the distinction is less clear.

[1]archive.ics.uci.edu/ml/

[2]archive.ics.uci.edu/ml/datasets/Communities+and+Crime

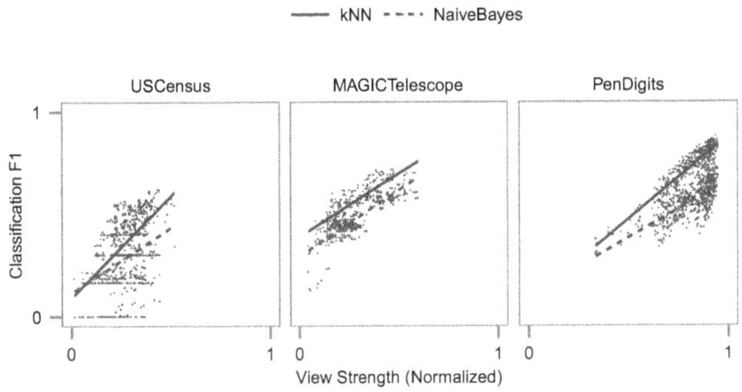

Figure 8: Strength vs. Classification accuracy for 500 random views. We obtained the blue and red lines with simple linear regression.

The first view of Table 2 is the best one we found: `Police.Overtime, Pct.Race.White, Pct.Vacant.Boarded`. It has a score of 0.51. which means that these three variables contain 51% of the target's information. The columns `Police.Overtime` and `Pct.White.Race` respectively describe the average time overworked by the police and the percentage of caucasian population. The third variable, `Pct.Vacant.Boarded` was surprising to us: it describes the percentage of vacant houses which are boarded up. How does this relate to crime? We could assume that boarded houses are associated with long term abandon, and thus, poverty. The top-left plot of Figure 7 shows the relation between race, boarded houses and crime. Observe that the variables complement each other: a high proportion of caucasians may or may not lead to low crime. However, a high proportion of caucasians *combined with* a low rate of boarded house correspond to safe areas, while little caucasians and many boarded houses correspond to more violent communities.

Our second view shows that cities with more monoparental families tend to be more violent: the correlation is clearly visible, and both POIs point to the bottom of the chart. However, close inspection also reveals surprises: a few communities have a relatively high number of two-parents families, but also high indicators of police requests and crime (in the top right corner of the chart). Manual queries reveals that many of these cities are located in the suburbs of Los Angeles, and contain a majority of Hispanics. Does this explain the peculiarity? We leave this question open for future investigations. We see that some findings come from the recommendations directly while others are serendipitous. But in both cases, Claude lets us discover "nuggets" with little prior knowledge and few assumptions.

7.2 View Strength and Prediction

In this section, we show experimentally that our notion of view strength "works", e.g. that strong views effectively provide information about the target column. To verify this assumption, we simulate users with statistical classifiers. Consider a view V over a database. If a classifier can predict the value of the target from V's columns, then V is informative. Oppositely, if the classifier fails, then V is potentially uninteresting. In a nutshell, we should observe a positive correlation between views strength and classification accuracy.

We now detail our experiment. We chose three datasets from the UCI repository. For each dataset, we generated 500 random views and measured their strengths. We then trained classifiers on each of these views, and measured their performance. We report the results in Figure 8. We chose two classification algorithms: Naive Bayes, and 5-Nearest Neighbors. We chose those because they contain no built-in mechanism to filter out irrelevant variables (as opposed to, e.g., decision trees). We measure classification performance with 5-fold validation, to avoid the effects of overfitting.

In all three cases, we observe a positive correlation between the strengths of the views and the accuracy of the predictions. We confirm these observations with statistical tests: the coefficients of determination (R^2) vary between 0.11 and 0.84, which indicates the presence of a trend (despite some variability). Furthermore, the p-values associated to the coefficients are all under 10^{-3}, this gives us excellent confidence that the strength influences positively the prediction accuracy. In conclusion, strong views are indeed more instructive.

7.3 View Selection

We now evaluate Claude's output and runtime in detail. In this section, we verify if Claude's algorithm produces good views in a short amount of time. To do so, we compare it to four methods, three of which come from the machine learning literature. Our first baseline, `Exact`, is similar to Claude, but we removed the approximation scheme presented in 4 - instead we compute the exact the mutual information, as in Equation 6 The method should be slower, but more accurate.

The second algorithm, `Clique`, is a top-down approach inspired by recent work on pattern mining [24]. We build a graph where each vertex i represents a column D_i, and each edge (i, j) represents the view $\{D_i, D_j\}$. We then eliminate all the edges except those which represent the top B views. To detect views with $D > 2$ columns, we seek cliques in this degenerated graph. We used the `igraph` package from R. We expect this algorithm to be very fast, but less accurate.

The third method, `Wrap 5-NN`, is a classic feature selection algorithm [9]. The idea is to train a 5-Nearest Neighbor classifier with increasingly large sets of variables. We first test each variable separately, and keep the column which led to the best prediction. Then we keep adding variables in a breadth-first manner, until the quality of the predictions stops increasing or we reach n variables. Our implementation is based on the `class` package from R. We modified the original algorithm to maintain and update q distinct sets of variables instead of just one. We chose the nearest neighbor algorithm because it is fast, and it gave us good performance, as shown in 7.2. We expect this algorithm to be very slow, but close to optimal.

Finally, the last method, `4S` is a state-of-the-art subspace search method from the unsupervised learning literature [14]. The aim of the algorithm is to detect "interesting" subspaces in large databases, independently of a target variable. To do so, it seeks groups of variables which are mutually correlated, with sketches and graph-based techniques. We used the author's implementation, written in Java. We expect the algorithm to be very fast and reasonably accurate.

We use 8 public datasets, presented in Section 7. For a fair comparison, we must ensure that each algorithm generates the same number of views (K) with the same number of variables (D). However, we have no way to specify these parameters a priori with 4S, because the algorithm has a

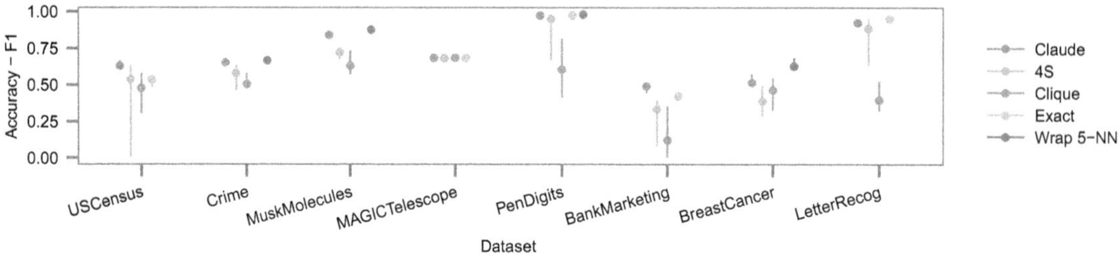

Figure 9: Performance of the View Selection algorithms. For each data set, we generate q views, train a 5-NN classifier over the columns of each view and report the classification accuracy (F1, 5-fold cross validation). The points represent median scores, the bars represent the lowest and greatest scores.

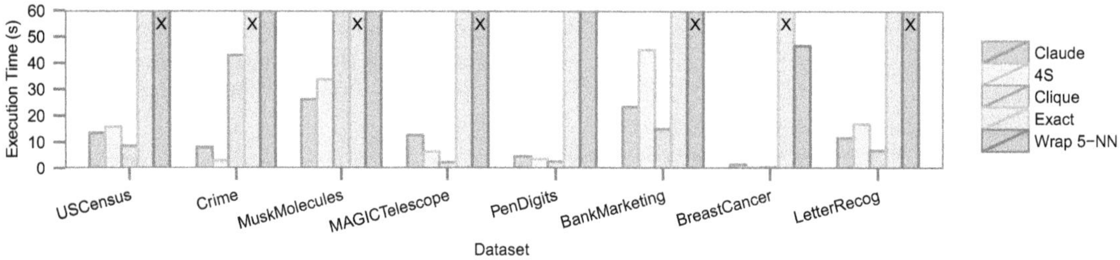

Figure 10: Execution time of the View Selection algorithms. A `X` symbol indicates that the experiment did not finish within 3,600 seconds.

built-in mechanism to pick optimal values. Therefore, we run 4S first on each dataset, we let it chose K and D, and we use these values for the remaining algorithms. We report the obtained parameters in Table 1.

We implemented Claude in R, except for some information theory primitives written in C. For practical reasons, we interrupted all the experiments which lasted more than 1 hour. Our test system is based on a 3.40 GHz Intel(R) Core(TM) i7-2600 processor. It is equipped with 16 GB RAM, but the Java heap space is limited to 8 GB. The operating system is Fedora 16.

Accuracy. In Figure 9, we compare the quality of the views returned by each algorithm. For each competitor, we generate q views with n variables, train a classifier on each view and measure the quality of the predictions. For the classification, we use both Naive Bayes and 5-Nearest Neighbors, and report the highest score. We measure accuracy with the F1 score on 5-fold cross validation; higher is better.

The method `Wrap 5-NN` comes first for all the datasets on which it completed. This is not surprising since the algorithm optimizes exactly what we measure: `Wrap 5-NN` is our "gold standard". Our two algorithms, **`Claude`** and **`Exhaustive`**, come very close. This indicates that both algorithms find good views, and that our approximation scheme works correctly. The algorithms `4S` and **`Clique`** come much lower. As 4S is completely unsupervised, we cannot expect it to perform as well as the other approaches. The assumptions behind **`Clique`** are apparently too naive.

Runtime. Figure 10 shows the runtime of our experiments. The algorithms `Exact` and `Wrap 5-NN` are orders of magnitude slower than the other approaches. The remaining three approaches are comparable: depending on the datasets, either **`Clique`** or `4S` come first. Claude comes first for `MuskMolecules`, and close second for all the other datasets. In conclusion, Claude is comparable to its competitors in terms of runtime, but it generates better views.

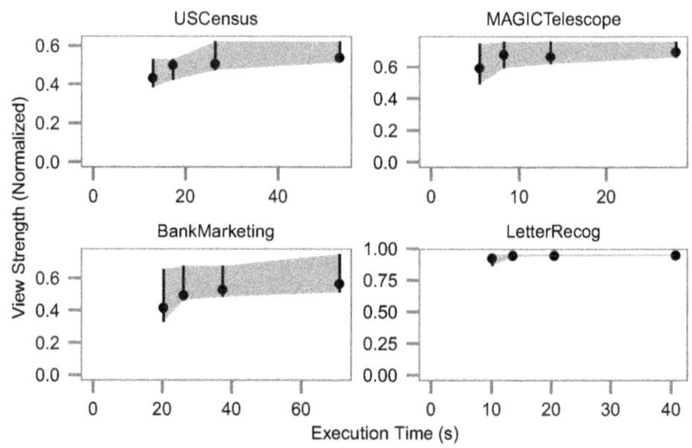

Figure 11: Impact of the beam size on the execution time and view strength. For each dataset, we generated 25 views with beam size 25, 50, 100 and 250. The points represent the medium scores, the bars represent the lowest and greatest scores.

Impact of the beam size. Figure 11 shows the impact of the beam size B on Claude's performance, for 4 databases. To obtain these plots, we ran Claude with $K = 25$ and $D = 5$, and varied B between 25 and 250. We observe that smaller beams lead to lower execution times, while larger beam lead to stronger views. However, the heuristic converges fast: we observe little to no improvement for B greater than 50.

Impact of the deduplication. We show the impact of our deduplication strategy in Figure 12. We ran Claude with $K = 25$ and $D = 5$ and increased the level of deduplication, i.e., varied the value of B' between B and $N.B$ (cf. Section 5.3). A level of 0% means that $B' = B$. A level of 100%

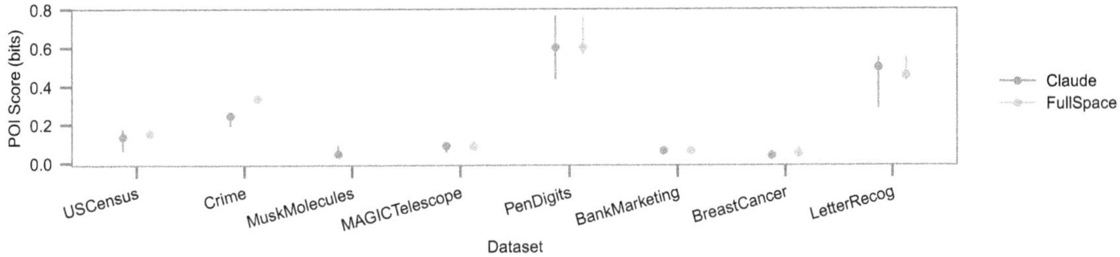

Figure 13: Quality of the Point of Interests. For each view, we detect $P = 10$ POIs. The points represent median scores, the bars represent the lowest and greatest scores.

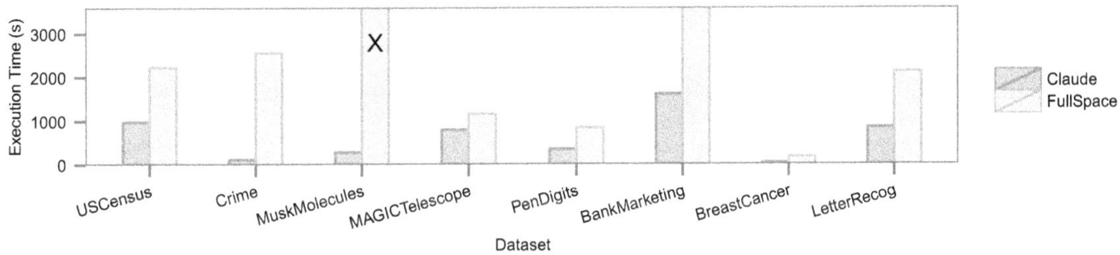

Figure 14: Execution time of the POI detection. A `X` symbol indicates that the experiment did not finish within 7,200 seconds.

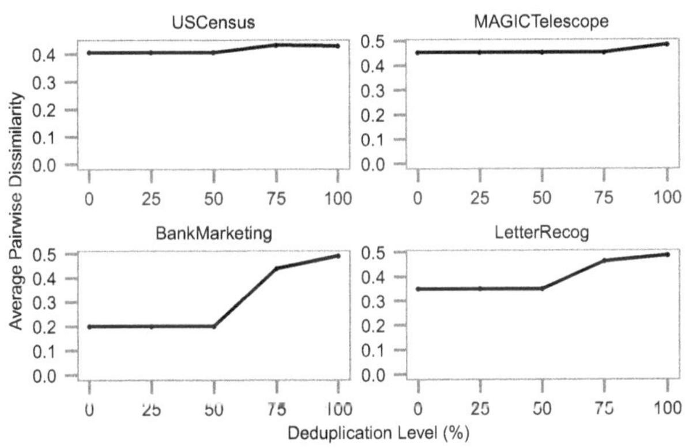

Figure 12: Impact of the deduplication. We generated 25 views for each dataset. The y-axis presents the average Jaccard dissimilarity between every pair of views.

means that $B' = N.B$. To measure the diversity of the views, we measured the Jaccard dissimilarity between every pair of views and averaged the results. We observe that the strategy works in all four cases, but with different levels of efficiency. In the **BankMarketing** case, our strategy almost doubles the pairwise dissimilarity of the views. The effect is much lighter on datasets with few columns, such as `USCensus` and `MAGICTelescope`.

7.4 POI Detection

In this section, we evaluate Claude's POI detection strategy. We compare two approaches. The first approach is the algorithm presented in the paper: first we search K views, then we return P POIs per view. The second approach, `FullSpace`, is the method used in much of the recent Subgroup Discovery literature [20, 7]. The idea is to apply Beam Search on the whole database directly. Instead of seeking P POIs in K projections, we seek $K.P$ selections from the full column space; we skip the view selection step. We use the same datasets as previously. Our default parameters are $K = 25$, $D = 5$, $B = 50$ and $P = 10$. To set the beam size, we use a rule of thumb: $B_{POI} = 2.k$ (B_{POI} is the beam used for POI detection, not for view search). To gather sufficient data, we raise our time limit to 2 hours.

Figure 13 compares the quality of the POIs found by both algorithms. The strategy `FullSpace` gives slightly better results on `Crime` and `PenDigits`, but the difference is close to null. The scores are similar on all the other datasets. We conclude that Claude's POIs are very close to those found by a state-of-the-art Subgroup Discovery approach. Figure 14 compares the runtimes of both approaches. We observe that Claude is much faster than `FullSpace`. The difference grows with the number of columns: the runtimes are almost similar for datasets with few columns (`MAGICTelescope`), but `Claude` is considerably faster for larger databases (more than an order of magnitude difference for `MuskMolecules`). This is a positive side-effect of our approach: decoupling view search and POI extraction allows us to find subgroups faster in high dimension datasets.

8. RELATED WORK

SQL Query Recommendation. We identify two types of approaches: *human-driven* systems and *data-driven* systems. Human-driven systems learn from user feedback. For instance, Chatzopoulou et al. make recommendations from query logs, similarly to search engines [2]. In Explore-by-Example, the system infers queries from examples provided by the user [5]. With Charles, the engine decomposes user queries into smaller queries, which can then be decomposed further [18]. Sarawagi's method builds a maximum entropy model over the database from the user's history [16]. Bonifati et al. propose a similar method to recommend joins [1]. Claude competes with neither of these approaches, since it uses the content of the database only.

Our work is closer data-driven data recommendation. The general idea is to build a statistical model of the database, and find regions which behave unexpectedly. Sarawagi et al.

have published seminal work on this topic [17]. Their system requires that the data is organized in an OLAP cube (with hierarchical dimensions), it supposes that the users know which variables to use, and it seeks thin-grained deviations. Oppositely, our system uses regular tables, it recommends views (not only selections) and it seeks large trends. Similarly, constrained gradient analysis [10, 6] focuses only on hierarchical data cubes. More recently, Dash et al. have proposed a method to reveal surprising subsets in a faceted search context [4]. This method is related to Claude, but it targets document search, it does not recommend views.

Projection Search. Authors from the data visualization literature have proposed methods to detect the "best" projections of multidimensional data sets, such as Projection Pursuit [8], Scagnostics [22], or Tatu et al.'s relevance measures [19]. Such methods would form excellent complements for Claude's recommendations. Nevertheless, most of them focus on 2-dimensional scatterplots, are limited to continuous variables, and involve materializing and analyzing every possible 2D projection of the data.

Feature Selection, Subspace Search. Choosing which variables to use for classification or regression is a crucial problem, for which dozens of methods were proposed [9]. Similarly to Claude, some of these methods rely on mutual information [15]. Nevertheless, the objective is different. A feature selection algorithm seeks *one* set of variables, on which a statistical predictor will perform optimally. Claude seeks several, small sets of variables, simple enough to be interpreted by a humans. In fact, Claude is halfway between inference and exploration. On the unsupervised learning side, our work is close to subspace search. The idea is detect subspaces where the data is clustered distinctly [12, 14]. We compare Claude to state-of-the-art methods in our Experiments section.

9. CONCLUSION

We formalized what makes a query "interesting", using the mutual information and the Kullback-Leibler divergence. We presented practical methods to detect these queries, using carefully designed approximations. Finally, we presented and evaluated Claude, a system based on these ideas. The methods we developed for this study have broader applications than the strict realm of query recommendation. Our column selection scheme competes with state-of-the-art feature selection methods. Also, the idea to decouple column selection selection from subgroup search could benefit a wide range of subgroup discovery algorithms.

We are genuinely excited about the possible extensions of this study. Future work includes dealing explicitly with the structure of the data, e.g., hierarchical dimensions and relational joins. We will study how to integrate Claude more tightly with visualizations, for a fully interactive experience. Finally, we will refine our framework with causation models.

10. ACKNOWLEDGEMENTS

This publication was supported by the Dutch national program COMMIT.

11. REFERENCES

[1] A. Bonifati, R. Ciucanu, and S. Staworko. Interactive inference of join queries. In *EDBT*, pages 451–462, 2014.

[2] G. Chatzopoulou, M. Eirinaki, and N. Polyzotis. Query recommendations for interactive database exploration. In *SSDBM*, pages 3–18, 2009.

[3] T. M. Cover and J. A. Thomas. *Elements of information theory*. John Wiley & Sons, 2012.

[4] D. Dash, J. Rao, N. Megiddo, A. Ailamaki, and G. Lohman. Dynamic faceted search for discovery-driven analysis. In *ACM CIKM*, pages 3–12, 2008.

[5] K. Dimitriadou, O. Papaemmanouil, and Y. Diao. Explore-by-example: An automatic query steering framework for interactive data exploration. In *ACM SIGMOD*, pages 517–528, 2014.

[6] G. Dong, J. Han, J. Lam, J. Pei, and K. Wang. Mining multi-dimensional constrained gradients in data cubes. In *VLDB*, pages 321–330, 2001.

[7] W. Duivesteijn, A. Knobbe, A. Feelders, and M. van Leeuwen. Subgroup discovery meets bayesian networks–an exceptional model mining approach. In *IEEE ICDM*, pages 158–167, 2010.

[8] J. Friedman and J. Tukey. A projection pursuit algorithm for exploratory data analysis. In *IEEE TC*, page 149, 1974.

[9] I. Guyon and A. Elisseeff. An introduction to variable and feature selection. *The Journal of Machine Learning Research*, pages 1157–1182, 2003.

[10] T. Imieliński, L. Khachiyan, and A. Abdulghani. Cubegrades: Generalizing association rules. *Data Mining and Knowledge Discovery*, pages 219–257, 2002.

[11] L. Kaufman and P. J. Rousseeuw. *Finding groups in data: an introduction to cluster analysis*. John Wiley & Sons, 2009.

[12] F. Keller, E. Muller, and K. Bohm. Hics: high contrast subspaces for density-based outlier ranking. In *ICDE*, pages 1037–1048, 2012.

[13] W. Klösgen. Explora: A multipattern and multistrategy discovery assistant. *AAAI Advances in Knowledge Discovery and Data Mining*, pages 249–271, 1996.

[14] H. V. Nguyen, E. Muller, and K. Bohm. 4s: Scalable subspace search scheme overcoming traditional apriori processing. In *IEEE Big Data*, pages 359–367, 2013.

[15] H. Peng, F. Long, and C. Ding. Feature selection based on mutual information criteria of max-dependency, max-relevance, and min-redundancy. In *IEEE PAMI*, pages 1226–1238, 2005.

[16] S. Sarawagi. User-adaptive exploration of multidimensional data. In *VLDB*, pages 307–316, 2000.

[17] S. Sarawagi, R. Agrawal, and N. Megiddo. Discovery-driven exploration of olap data cubes. In *EDBT*, 1998.

[18] T. Sellam and M. L. Kersten. Meet charles, big data query advisor. In *CIDR*, 2013.

[19] A. Tatu, G. Albuquerque, M. Eisemann, P. Bak, H. Theisel, M. Magnor, and D. Keim. Automated analytical methods to support visual exploration of high-dimensional data. In *IEEE TVCG*, pages 584–597, 2011.

[20] M. van Leeuwen and A. Knobbe. Non-redundant subgroup discovery in large and complex data. In *ECML PKDD*, pages 459–474. 2011.

[21] M. van Leeuwen, J. Vreeken, and A. Siebes. Compression picks item sets that matter. In *PKDD*, pages 585–592. 2006.

[22] L. Wilkinson, A. Anand, and R. L. Grossman. Graph-theoretic scagnostics. In *IEEE Infovis*, page 21, 2005.

[23] S. Wrobel. An algorithm for multi-relational discovery of subgroups. In *PKDD*, pages 78–87. 1997.

[24] Y. Xie and P. S. Yu. Max-clique: a top-down graph-based approach to frequent pattern mining. In *IEEE ICDM*, pages 1139–1144, 2010.

[25] D. Xin, J. Han, X. Yan, and H. Cheng. Mining compressed frequent-pattern sets. In *VLDB*, pages 709–720, 2005.

Large-scale Knowledge Base Completion: Inferring via Grounding Network Sampling over Selected Instances

Zhuoyu Wei[1,2], Jun Zhao[1], Kang Liu[1], Zhenyu Qi[2], Zhengya Sun[1] and Guanhua Tian[2]
[1] National Laboratory of Pattern Recognition, Institute of Automation, Chinese Academy of Sciences
[2] Interactive Digital Media Technology Research, Institute of Automation, Chinese Academy of Sciences
{zhuoyu.wei, zhenyu.qi, zhengya.sun, guanhua.tian}@ia.ac.cn, {jzhao, kliu}@nlpr.ia.ac.cn

ABSTRACT

Constructing large-scale knowledge bases has attracted much attention in recent years, for which Knowledge Base Completion (KBC) is a key technique. In general, inferring new facts in a large-scale knowledge base is not a trivial task. The large number of inferred candidate facts has resulted in the failure of the majority of previous approaches. Inference approaches can achieve high precision for formulas that are accurate, but they are required to infer candidate instances one by one, and extremely large candidate sets bog them down in expensive calculations. In contrast, the existing embedding-based methods can easily calculate similarity-based scores for each candidate instance as opposed to using inference, so they can handle large-scale data. However, this type of method does not consider explicit logical semantics and usually has unsatisfactory precision. To resolve the limitations of the above two types of methods, we propose an approach through Inferring via Grounding Network Sampling over Selected Instances. We first employ an embedding-based model to make the instance selection and generate much smaller candidate sets for subsequent fact inference, which not only narrows the candidate sets but also filters out part of the noise instances. Then, we only make inferences within these candidate sets by running a data-driven inference algorithm on the Markov Logic Network (MLN), which is called Inferring via Grounding Network Sampling (INS). In this process, we especially incorporate the similarity priori generated by embedding-based models into INS to promote the inference precision. The experimental results show that our approach improved Hits@1 from 32.911% to 71.692% on the FB15K dataset and achieved much better AP@n evaluations than state-of-the-art methods.

Categories and Subject Descriptors

E.1 [**Data**]: DATA STRUCTURES—*Graphs and networks*

Keywords

Knowledge Base Completion; Embedding; Inference

Permission to make digital or hard copies of all or part of this work for personal or classroom use is granted without fee provided that copies are not made or distributed for profit or commercial advantage and that copies bear this notice and the full citation on the first page. Copyrights for components of this work owned by others than ACM must be honored. Abstracting with credit is permitted. To copy otherwise, or republish, to post on servers or to redistribute to lists, requires prior specific permission and/or a fee. Request permissions from Permissions@acm.org.
CIKM'15 October 19-23, 2015, Melbourne, VIC, Australia
© 2015 ACM. ISBN 978-1-4503-3794-6/15/10 ...$15.00.
DOI: http://dx.doi.org/10.1145/2806416.2806513.

1. INTRODUCTION

Automatically extracting facts from texts and constructing large-scale knowledge bases (KB) have grown vigorously in recent years. As a result, several typical knowledge bases have been built, such as Freebase [2], Nell [6], YAGO [10], and Knowledge Vault [7]. However, these extracted repositories are far from completion. To complete the constructed KBs, according to the conclusion in [7], using an existing knowledge base to complete itself is an important supplement for automatic knowledge extraction to increase the number of facts in KBs and cannot be substituted by other techniques. Therefore, this paper focuses on the large-scale knowledge base completion (KBC) and is committed to predicting the missing links in the existing knowledge base.

In general, according to the process of KBC, there are two types of approaches: inference-based approaches and embedding-based approaches.

First, inference-based approaches [22, 16, 24] usually employ logic formulas to infer the missing links among existing entities in a KB. They manually or automatically construct various logic formulas and learn the weight of each formula by sampling or counting groundings from existing KBs. These weighted formulas are viewed as the long-range interactions across several relations. The biggest limitation of such approaches is the computation complexity. These methods need to infer knowledge one by one, which implies the computation complexity is linearly growing with the size of candidate sets. However, usually, there are extremely large candidate sets for some specific relations in large-scale KBC, and in each candidate set, only one or a few are actually correct. For example, *Barack Obama's mother* is missing in a KB, and we need to find out who *Barack Obama's mother* is. All persons or females in the KB are candidates, but only one is the correct selection. The huge candidate set brings inference-based approaches to an unacceptable running time. Although some methods have avoided this issue through simple operations, such as only adding a small part of false facts to testing sets [13, 23], this strategy is too coarse to obtain precise inference results. On the other hand, there are some noise candidates, which may violate formulas and mislead inference algorithms. Therefore, existing inference methods that rely on formulas cannot remove the noises by themselves, and the noises may result in the decrease of the performance.

In contrast, embedding-based methods [21, 5, 12, 4, 3, 26, 18] are not affected by huge candidate sets because they can easily calculate similarity-based scores for each candidate instance after learning representations of entities and rela-

Table 1: Several embedding approach results on FB15K

Embedding Model	Hits@1(%)	Hits@10(%)
Uns[4]	0.384	15.573
SE[5]	28.633	61.026
SME-lin[3]	29.807	68.386
SME-bil[3]	32.911	68.506
TransE[4]	29.401	73.71

tions. Unfortunately, embedding-based approaches do not consider explicit logical semantics and cannot capture the interaction between different relations well enough. Most of them simply model the direct interaction between relations by entity embeddings, apart from the long-range interaction across several relations. Thus, their results are universally unsatisfactory. Table 1 shows several typical embedding models' Hits@1 and Hits@10 evaluations[1] on the FB15K dataset [4]. Although many embedding-based methods could obtain high ratings in Top N results (N>1), they usually have low performance in Top 1 results (the more useful metric than Top N in KBC).

To resolve the limitations of the above two types of methods, we propose a novel approach by inferring via grounding network sampling over selected instances. We first employ an embedding-based model to perform instances selection. In specific, we employ TransE [4] to learn the representations of entities and relations in the KB. We calculate similarity scores between candidates and the input query, and we select Top-N instances to constitute a new smaller candidate set for subsequent fact inference. In this way, we not only filter out a part of the noise but also improve the efficiency of the inference algorithm. Meanwhile, the corresponding similarity scores are recorded and viewed as the prior to supervise the subsequent inference. We perform logical inference over selected instances by exploiting a data-driven inference algorithm on a Markov Logic Network (MLN), which is called Inferring via Grounding Network Sampling (**INS**). INS could consider the long-range interaction across several relations that were ignored in existing embedding-based methods. Moreover, we improve INS and propose a **INS-ES** algorithm (Inferring via ground Network Sampling Merging Embedding Similarity Priori), which could consider the probability of the transition between states when performing network sampling for inference. In this way, the recorded similarity scores can be incorporated naturally into our model and the inference process can be supervised in some way, which is beneficial for improving the inference precision. In general, our method is an comprehensive combination of two types of methods for knowledge inference, and it could not only avoid the disadvantage of inference-based methods (cannot handle large-scale knowledge bases) but also could improve the weakness of embedding-based methods (cannot obtain explicit logical semantics and cannot sufficiently capture the interaction between different relations). Experiments show that our approach has significant improvement compared with state-of-the-art methods, increasing Hits@1 from 32.911% to 71.692% on the FB15K.

The main contributions of this work are summarized as follows.

- We propose employing embedding-based methods to select instances and generate much smaller candidate sets for knowledge inference, which drastically reduces the running time of inferring on large-scale KBs.
- We employ MLN to model the large-scale KB and propose an inferring algorithm **INS** to infer overselected instances. In this way, the explicit semantics and long-range interaction across different relations could be captured.
- We specially incorporate the similarity scores generated by the embedding-based model into INS-ES to promote the inference precision.

[1]Hits@n means the proportion of correct entities ranked in the top N

2. PRELIMINARIES

Knowledge Base is a structural information storage system, e.g., Freebase, that usually contains entities, relations, and facts. A KB can be viewed as a directed graph $G(V, E, R)$. The vertex set V contains all entities in KB, and the edge set E contains all facts. R is the set of relations that can be viewed as edge labels. We only consider binary relation in this paper. $r(h, t)$ is an example of a fact, and there is an edge from h to t with label r.

Knowledge Base Completion is the prediction of additional true facts using only an existing database[23]. Given a KB, noted as $G(V, E, R)$, our goal is to predict a new fact set E' with high precision and recall, and V and R remain unchanged. For example, 93.8% of persons included in Freebase have no place of birth, and 78.5% of them have no nationality[20]; KBC is committed to predicting them.

Embedding means representing each entity in KB as a low-dimension numeric vector, and different dimensions of the vector may implicitly represent different aspects of an entity. Relations in KB usually have relevant representations, such as vectors, matrixes and tensors. Entities interact under a specific relation by performing arithmetical operations between entity embeddings and relation's representation.

3. FRAMEWORK

The sketch of our approach's framework is shown in Figure 1. In general, it contains two main parts: (a) selecting instances and (b) inferring instances.

Selecting instances ((a) in Figure 1). First, we choose an embedding-based model to learn distributed representations for both entities and relations in the existing knowledge base. For most of the existing embedding-based models, the objective is always to make $r(h, t)$ in the KB more similar than other $r(h, t')$ or $r(h', t)$ generated randomly. For example, if *BornIn(Barack Obama, Honolulu)* exists in KB but *BornIn(Barack Obama, Washington)* does not, *(Barack Obama, Honolulu)* should be more similar than *(Barack Obama, Washington)* under the relation *BornIn*. Second, we employ learned representations of entities and relations to calculate similarity scores for each instance and sort them in descending order to pick the Top N to form a new smaller candidate set. To the query *Mother(Barack Obama, ?)*, there is an entity set $\mathcal{X}$, and each $x \in \mathcal{X}$ can replace *?* in *Mother(Barack Obama, ?)*, where x can be any person or female. *Mother(Barack Obama,* $\mathcal{X}$*)* denotes the entire candidate set $\mathcal{S}$, and we calculate all similarity scores for each *Mother(Barack Obama, x)* to pick N instances with the highest similarity scores for subsequent fact inference.

Inferring instances ((b) in Figure 1). In this component, we employ MLN to model KB and infer selected

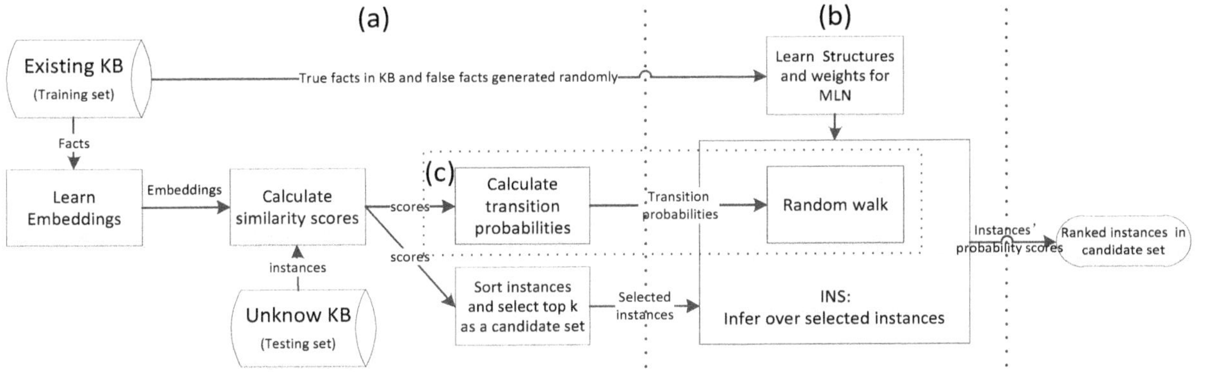

Figure 1: The sketch of the framework: (a) selecting instances; (b) inferring instances; (c) incorporating similarity priori generated by embedding-based methods.

instances on it. Before performing inference, we need to learn the structure and weights for MLN. Specifically, we employ the method in [24] to learn structure and weights simultaneously by performing random walks. Then, we propose an inferring algorithm, called Inferring via Ground Network Sampling or **INS** for short. INS performs random walks on the Partial Order Graph (POG) to generate paths and changes them to grounding formulas. For example, for *Mother(Barack Obama, Ann Dunham)*, we can obtain paths such as[*Barack Obama*] → [*Honolulu*] →[*Ann Dunham*] from random walks and turn it into a formula such as *BornIn(Barack Obama,Honolulu)* ∧ *LiveIn(Ann Dunham, Honolulu)* ⇒ *Mother(Barack Obama, Ann Dunham)*. For each selected instance, we count formulas in which the instance occurs and treat counts of formulas as the instance features. Then, instance features are used to calculate probabilities for each instance. These probabilities can be viewed as final predictions for outputting.

Furthermore, we replace the uniform transition probability in random walks with the function of similarities calculated by the embedding model for the purpose of improving precision ((c) in Figure 1). Originally, each state adjacent to the current state has an equal transition probability, so the inference is completely independent from the previous instance selection. However, the similarity scores obtained from the embedding-based method should not only contribute in building candidate sets but should also be used in the following inferring process as a priori. The improved method employs a function from the similarity score to the transition probability, noted as $p_{trans} = f(s_{sim})$, where p_{trans} means the probability of transition from one state to an adjacent state in random walks and s_{sim} means the similarity score. For example, for *Mother(Barack Obama, x)*, if an state contains a selected instance, e.g., *Ann Dunham*, we assign $f(s_{sim}(Mother(BarackObama, AnnDunham)))$ to this state; otherwise, a small default probability is assigned to the adjacent state.

4. SELECTING INSTANCES BY USING EMBEDDINGS

To narrow candidate sets for subsequent fact inference, we make instance selection for each entire candidate set $\mathcal{S}$, for example, *Mother(Barack Obama, X)*. We propose employing embedding-based methods to do selection and describe the process as follows.

We first choose an existing embedding-based model to learn distributed representations for both entities and relations in the KB. Almost all embedding-based models embed entities into a relatively low (e.g., 50) dimensional embedding vector space $\mathbb{R}^k$ while representing relations in different ways. Therefore, for a specific fact $r(h,t)$, we represent h and t as vectors E_h and E_t, respectively, and abstract the representation of r as E_r. Meanwhile, different embedding-based models design different similarity-score-functions $f_s(E_h, E_t, E_r)$ to measure the similarity of entities under a specific representation of relations. For example, SE [5] represents a relation as two matrixes $R_r^{lhs} \in \mathbb{R}^{k\times k}$ and $R_r^{rhs} \in \mathbb{R}^{k\times k}$ and employs a kernel density estimation following the Gaussian kernel as the similarity-score-function; SME [3] represents a relation as a matrix, and its similarity-score-function is merged into a neural network; TransE [4] represents a relation as a vector with the same dimension as the entities and simply employs the negative 1-norm of the vector $(E_h + E_r - E_t)$.

Most of the embedding-based models design their objectives to make $f_s(E_h, E_t, E_r)$ larger than other $f_s(E_h, E_{t'}, E_r)$ or $f_s(E_{h'}, E_t, E_r)$, where $r(h,t)$ exists in the KB but $r(h,t')$ or $r(h',t)$ does not. Formally, we can define a uniform pairwise loss function as follows:

$$\mathcal{L} = \sum_{r(h,t)\in KB} \sum_{r(h',t')\in KB'_{r(h,t)}} [\gamma + f_s(r(h',t')) - f_s(r(h,t))]_+ \quad (1)$$

where $[x]_+$ denotes the positive part of x. $KB'_{r(h,t)}$ is sampled randomly from $\{r(h,t')\} \cup \{r(h',t)\}$, and $\gamma > 0$ is a margin hyperparameter.

Specifically, we employ TransE as the embedding-based model, which has been proved to be effective for knowledge base embedding [4]. We mainly apply TransE to generate candidate sets for inference in our experiments. TransE [4] is a simple and practical model, and it embeds all entities and relations into the same k-dimensional vector space by viewing r in $r(h,t)$ as a translation. TransE thinks E_t should be the nearest neighbor of $E_h + E_r$ in the same vector space and designs the similarity-score-function as $f_s(E_h, E_t, E_r) = -|E_h + E_r - E_t|$. In essence, TransE replaces the complex matrix multiplications with a vector addition operation.

After the learning process, we obtain embeddings for entities and relations in KB that contain semantic similarities. For example, the embedding of *Barack Obama* is close to the embedding of *Ann Dunham* under *Mother* relation. We calculate similarity scores for each candidate $r(h,t)$ by employing the similarity-score-function $f_s(E_h, E_t, E_r)$, which is simple enough to be completed in a short running time. Then, we sort the candidate instances in descending order by their similarity scores and pick the Top N to form a new smaller candidate set. For example, for the query *Who is Barack Obama's mother*, we calculate all f_s(Mother(Barack Obama, x)) and pick the Top 10 persons as a new candidate set. We only require that *Ann Dunham* (the true answer) be in the Top 10 regardless of its place, which can be handled sufficiently by the existing embedding-based methods. In this way, the subsequent logical inference would be constrained by a smaller selected instance space, and the computational difficulty of inference-based methods is avoided.

5. INFERRING INSTANCES WITHIN CANDIDATE SET

The network structure and logical interaction in KBs make it natural to apply MLN to model KBs. Performing inference on MLN to predict missing links in KB is in accordance with KBC. In this section, we describe details of the inference approaches based on MLN, which includes two parts: 1) using MLN to model the exiting knowledge base for the task of KBC; 2) inferring overselected instances obtained from embedding-based methods. In terms of inference-based methods based on MLN, the huge candidate set is not the only reason that may cause the expensive calculation. The vast facts and the large grounding space also cause the unacceptable running time for both the learning and inferring process. In particular, learning structures for MLN suffer from a severe scale issue [15, 14, 13, 19, 11], which leads to the result that MLN-based approaches are scarcely applied to the task of large-scale KBC. We propose an inferring algorithm via grounding network sampling, noted as INS. INS employs the learning method in [24] to learn structure and weights for MLN simultaneously and performs random walks on the Partial Order Graph (POG) [1] instead of the original KB, which treats paths as POG nodes. INS is able to take all Horn clauses with the query at the place of both head and body, which can capture more logical factors and cover more useful formulas. As the INS extension, INS-ES, short for Inferring via ground Network Sampling Merging Embedding Similarity Priori, takes advantage of similarity priori obtained from previous embedding-based models to achieve a further promotion.

5.1 Modelling KBC by MLN

To obtain new knowledge from the existing KB, we regard all facts in the existing KB as evidences and regard candidate facts as queries. First of all, we need to model the existing KB and candidate facts in a MLN, and then rank candidates by their likelihood.

Markov logic can be viewed as a probabilistic extension of first-order logic by attaching weights to formulas. Each weight reflects the relative strength or importance of the corresponding formula. Higher weight indicates greater reward to a world that satisfies the formula. More formally, let X be the set of all true facts in KBs, F be the set of all first-order formulas in the MLN, w_i be the weight associated with formula $f_i \in F$, and G_{f_i} be the set of all possible groundings of formula f_i; then the probability of a possible world x is defined as:

$$\begin{aligned} P_w(X=x) &= \frac{1}{Z} exp(\sum_{f_i \in F} w_i \sum_{g \in G_{f_i}} g(x)) \\ &= \frac{1}{Z} exp(\sum_{f_i \in F} w_i n_i(x)) \end{aligned} \tag{2}$$

where $Z = \sum_{x' \in X} exp(\sum_{f_i \in F} w_i n_i(x'))$ is the normalizing constant, w represents a set of formula weights, $g(x)$ equals 1 if g is satisfied and 0 otherwise, and $n_i(x)$ denotes the number of true groundings of f_i in x.

To model a knowledge base by MLN, we first view the KB from the perspective of Markov Networks: Facts can be true or false, so we treat all facts in the existing KB as binary random variables. We add them to a Markov Network as nodes and set their truth values as true. All facts not in the KB are not added to the Markov Network explicitly, and only a small part of them are generated when necessary. To represent interdependence between random variables, we add undirected edges for each two facts that share one common entity. There are no hyperedges in Markov Networks. When more than two nodes share one common entity, we add edges for each two of them to represent the dependence between two variables and use cliques [2] to represent dependence between all of them. MLN simplifies the dependence between more than two facts by splitting cliques into logical formulas. MLN generalizes formulas by replacing entities with variables and replacing facts with relation types. Finally, MLN learns weights for each conceptualized formula by counting groundings and treats weight formulas as features to predict missing links.

To obtain useful formulas and precise weights for one specific query $\mathcal{Q}$, we discriminatively learn structures and weights of the MLN for $\mathcal{Q}$, which means only facts under $\mathcal{Q}$ are treated as queries. Therefore, we care about the probability of the possible world only containing the specific query facts and treat other facts as evidence. We note the query as Y and compute its conditional probability given evidence X as follows:

$$P_w(Y=y|X=x) = \frac{1}{Z_y} exp(\sum_{f_i \in F_Y} w_i n_i(x,y)) \tag{3}$$

Different from Equation (2), each f_i in F_Y must involve the query Y, and groundings of f_i are counted when the Y is set as true and false, respectively. The normalizing constant Z_y aggregates the probabilities for all possible y, and $Z_y = \sum_{y' \in Y} exp(\sum_{f_i \in F_Y} w_i n_i(x, y'))$.

For brevity, only non-recursive formulas are considered, and all queries become independent after evidence is given. The normalizing constant Z_y can be simplified as the sum of two parts when $Y=1$ and $Y=0$. Therefore, for one specific grounding query Y_j, its conditional probability is simplified as follows:

$$P_w(Y_j = y_j | X = x) = \frac{exp(\sum_{f_i \in F_{Y_j}} w_i n_i(x, y_{[Y_j=y_j]}))}{exp(\sum_{f_i \in F_{Y_j}} w_i n_i(x, y_{[Y_j=0]})) + exp(\sum_{f_i \in F_{Y_j}} w_i n_i(x, y_{[Y_j=1]}))} \tag{4}$$

[2]en.wikipedia.org/wiki/Clique_(graph_theory)

where $n_i(x, y_{[Y_j=y_j]})$ is the number of true groundings of the ith formula when all the evidence facts in X and the query Y_j are set to their truth values. Analogously, $n_i(x, y_{[Y_j=0]})$ and $n_i(x, y_{[Y_j=1]})$ are the numbers when Y_j is set as 0 and 1, respectively.

For each MLN model under a specific query relation $\mathcal{Q}$, we employ the algorithm described in [24] to learn structure and weights discriminatively. Algorithm [24] performs random walks starting from a number of initial nodes sampled randomly and collects paths constituted by linking entities during random walks. In this process, we generate grounding formulas by replacing each two adjacent nodes in a path with facts containing them in the existing KB. Therefore, one path obtained from random walks can be changed to various grounding formulas because there are possibly several facts under different relations between two adjacent entities.

After heuristic pruning, we only keep grounding formulas containing a true fact under $\mathcal{Q}$, and conceptualize them by replacing entities by variables. For example, the grounding formula *BornIn(Barack Obama,Honolulu)* $\wedge$ *LiveIn(Ann Dunham,Honolulu)* $\Rightarrow$ *Mother(Barack Obama, Ann Dunham)* is conceptualized to *BornIn*(x_1, x_2) $\wedge$ *LiveIn*(x_3, x_2) $\Rightarrow$ *Mother* (x_1, x_3). For one specific fact under $\mathcal{Q}$, all formulas attached to it are counted as its features, and the fact with counts of formulas are used to learn formula weights by Equation (4).

5.2 Inferring Over Selected Instances

For a specific query relation $\mathcal{Q}$, we have obtained candidate sets and an MLN learned under $\mathcal{Q}$. We exploit an inferring algorithm to independently calculate the probability of each selected instance being true, called **INS** (Inferring via ground Network Sampling). Additionally, we will describe its extension, **INS-ES** (Inferring via ground Network Sampling Merging Embedding Similarity Priori).

5.2.1 INS algorithm

INS is a data-driven algorithm and follows 4 steps: Performing random walks on POG; generating grounding formulas; counting formulas for instances; calculating probabilities for each instance. Algorithm 1 shows the detail of INS, where **KB** is the training set, **C** is the candidate fact set, $\mathcal{Q}$ is the query relation, **F** is the formula set with weights learned previously, **S** is the seed set, F_p is the grounding formula set, **q** is one query in **C**, and **QDI** is a map from query to data instance.

First, INS performs random walks on the POG to generate entity paths. We collect all entities occurring in selected instances under $\mathcal{Q}$ to form a set of initial nodes by employing each entity to build a single node path. Then, we perform random walks from each initial node to obtain paths of entities. There are formulas learned with a query at the place of body. For example, for *BornIn*(x_1,x_2) $\wedge$ *LiveIn*(x_3,x_2) $\Rightarrow$ *Mother*(x_1,x_3), when *BornIn* or *LiveIn* is treated as the query relation $\mathcal{Q}$, we regard it as a formula with the query in body. To obtain this type of formula, we assume all candidates are true and put them in the existing KB before performing random walks because the truth values of all candidates are unknown, and INS randomly walks to them only when they exist in the KB. The above process is presented in Line 1 to 7 of Algorithm 1; Line 5 to 7 is the core strategy of random walks which is detailed in Section 5.2.2.

Second, INS generates grounding formula bodies from each sampled path: We first transform adjacent nodes into grounding facts, which only occur in the existing KB. Then, to add heads to these formulas, we link the head and tail of the path with several possible relations, which can be true or false. After obtaining grounding formulas, all of them are conceptualized to generate a great deal of conceptualized formulas, which never have to be learned or pruned, and INS simply ignores them. Line 8 to 15 shows the generating and conceptualizing process.

Third, all formulas that remain are counted as features for a specific selected instance $r(h,t)$ that occurs in these formulas. INS travels all instances in the map of **QDI** and finally employs Equation (4) to calculate the probability for each candidate instance, which corresponds to Line 16 to 17. In particular, for some selected instance without any formulas, their scores are set to 0 directly.

Algorithm 1: INS (KB, C, $\mathcal{Q}$, F).

Input: **KB**, **C**, $\mathcal{Q}$, **F**
Output: Probabilities for each instance in **C**.
1: Set $\mathbf{q} \in \mathbf{C}$ to true, add them to **KB**.
2: **QDI** $\leftarrow$ building pairs <**q**, empty instance>
3: **S** $\leftarrow$ entities in **q**, $\mathbf{q} \in \mathbf{C}$.
4: Foreach $\mathbf{s} \in \mathbf{S}$:
5: Initialize Path State **p** from s.
6: Repeat Until MaxIterator:
7: **p** $\leftarrow$ RandomToNextPathState(**p**).
8: $F_p \leftarrow$ GenerateFormulas(**p**).
9: Foreach $f_p \in F_p$.
10: If **q** in f_p
11: Conceptualize f_p.
12: If $f_p \in \mathbf{F}$
13: Add f_p truth counting to **QDI(q)**
14: Else Ignore f_p.
15: Else Ignore f_p.
16: Foreach $\mathbf{q} \in \mathbf{C}$:
17: Calculate **P(q|KB,F)** by **q** and weights of **F** using Equation (4)

5.2.2 Grounding Network Sampling

We apply grounding network sampling to obtain entity paths uniformly and count formulas for each selected instance. To sample grounding network, we perform random walks on a POG.

POG is a directed graph and its nodes are subgraphs in the KB which is viewed as a graph. For KBC, we simplify it by only considering simple paths but not subgraphs. Edges in POG can be divided into three categories: super-edge, sub-edge and restart-edge. We take an example to explain them: There are two nodes, n_1 =[*Barack Obama*] $\rightarrow$[*Honolulu*] and n_2 = [*Ann Dunham*] $\rightarrow$ [*Barack Obama*] $\rightarrow$ [*Honolulu*]. The edge from n_1 to n_2 is a super-edge, while the edge from n_2 to n_1 is a sub-edge, and edges from n_1 or n_2 to the initial node are restart-edges, where the initial node can be [*Barack Obama*] or [*Honolulu*]. We make an further explanation for three types of edges, and they can be viewed as three operations: (1) Add one node to the existing path, e.g., add [*Ann Dunham*] to n_1 at the far left; (2) Remove one node from the existing path, e.g., remove [*Ann Dunham*] from n_2; (3) Restart from the initial node which is determined before the random walk starting, e.g., both n_1 and n_2 can restart from [*Barack Obama*] which is in query *Mother(Barack Obama,x)*.

To achieve a uniform distribution for all the simple paths, we exploit ideas from Metropolis-Hastings (MH) algorithm to perform random walks on the graph [1, 17]. Note the stationary distribution of node u as $\pi(u)$. At the current state $X_t = u$, the next state X_{t+1} is proposed with a proposal probability Q(u, v)(u $\neq$ v). The proposed transition to v is accepted with an acceptance probability $A(u, v)$, that is,

$$A(u,v) = min\{1, \frac{\pi(v)Q(v,u)}{\pi(u)Q(u,v)}\} \tag{5}$$

and rejected with probability $1 - A(u, v)$ in which case the state X_{t+1} remained unchanged.

The purpose of random walk on POG is to perform an unbiased graph sampling for MLN's structure and weight learning, so INS proposes that the target stationary distribution should be set to the uniform distribution $\pi = (1/n, 1/n, ..., 1/n)$, where $n = |N_{next}|$ represents the number of possible next states. Corresponding to super-edge and sub-edge, we also divide N_{next} into N_+ and N_-, and denote $d_+(u) = |N_+(u)|$ and $d_-(u) = |N_-(u)|$. Additionally, INS sets a fixed probability of restarting noted as γ. Exploring effect of adjusting γ to result is beyond focus of this paper, so we directly set $\gamma = 0.35$ in our experiment. The proposal probability is defined as follows:

$$Q(u,v) = \begin{cases} \gamma \quad , if\ restart \\ \frac{1-\gamma}{2d_+(u)}, if\ v \in N_+(u) \\ \frac{1-\gamma}{2d_-(u)}, if\ v \in N_-(u) \end{cases} \tag{6}$$

This process corresponds to the RandomToNextPathState(**p**) in Algorithm 1 (Line 7).

5.2.3 INS-ES algorithm

To incorporate the similarity a priori of candidates obtained from the previous embedding method, we exploit another inferring algorithm, noted as **INS-ES**. INS-ES replaces the uniform transition probability with the function of similarity scores obtained from the embedding-based method. It benefits from the framework of the MH algorithm, which employs a type of proposal probability $Q(u, v)$ to obtain a desired stationary distribution π for random walks. $Q(u, v)$ can be viewed as a state transition probability of an arbitrary irreducible Markov chain on the whole state space $\mathcal{N}$, with constraints: $Q(u, v) > 0$ if and only if $Q(v, u) > 0$, and $Q(u, v) = 0$ for all $(u, v) \notin \mathcal{E}(u \neq v)$, where $\mathcal{E}$ is the set of edges [17]. In INS, it assigns equal value to $Q(u, v), v \in N_{next}(u)$, which can achieve an unbiased graph sampling. However, now, we expect to utilize similarity a priori obtained from embedding-based methods in random walk process. We assign distinguishing $Q(u, v)$ to different adjacent nodes to break the unbiased graph sampling. This strategy can guide random walks to nodes containing selected instances with larger probabilities than others. More specifically, the instance, being at the more frontal position in the candidate set, is more likely to be visited.

In the previous step of making the instance selection, each selected instance has been assigned a similarity score for ranking. The embedding-based methods treat the similarity scores as the final results for KBC. Although Table 1 shows that these results are insufficient for the task of KBC, we believe there are still some priori knowledge that imply that one instance with a higher score is more likely to be true.

To replace the uniform probabilities by similarity priori, we just need to reassign transition probabilities only for super-edges and keep probabilities unchanged for sub-edges and restart-edges. During random walks, we use entities added to paths to represent candidate states for simplicity. When the current state is u and we expect to travel to the next state, $|N_+(u)|$ includes all entities adjacent to two marginal entities in the current path. For example, when the current state contains a path, $n_1 = [BarackObama] \rightarrow [Honolulu]$, $N_+(n_1)$ is composed of all entities adjacent to *[Barack Obama]* or *[Honolulu]*, and we assign diverse transition probabilities to states in $N_+(n_1)$. We split $N_+(n_1)$ into two parts: $N_{+_{cand}}(n_1)$ and $N_{+_{usal}}(n_1)$. $N_{+_{cand}}(n_1)$ represents the subset, in which nodes all come from selected instances, and other nodes form $N_{+_{usal}}(n_1)$. We assign distinguishing $Q(u, v)$ to entities in $N_{+_{cand}}(u)$ and assign default $Q(u, v)$ for $N_{+_{usal}}(u)$ as follows:

$$Q(u,v) = \begin{cases} \frac{(1-\gamma)f(score_v)}{2Z}, v \in N_{+_{cand}}(u) \\ \frac{1-\gamma}{2Z} \quad\quad , v \in N_{+_{usal}}(u) \end{cases} \tag{7}$$

where Z is a normalizing constant and $Z = |N_{+_{usal}}(u)| + \sum_{j \in N_{+_{cand}}(u)} f(score_v)$, $score_v$ is the similarity score of $\mathcal{Q}(u, v)$ and $f(score_v)$ is a function to map similarity to probability. We design a heuristic equation for $f(score_v)$:

$$f(score_v) = \lambda \cdot \frac{score_v}{|score|_{max}} + 1 \tag{8}$$

To normalize $score_v$, we first divide it by $|score|_{max}$, which is the maximum absolute value of the similarity score under $\mathcal{Q}$. Then, multiply by a coefficient λ, which can adjust the strength of the influence from the embedding priori. With the increase in λ, an adjacent node that occurs in a selected instance has larger and larger transition probability from the current state, which means the strength of the embedding similarity priori is stronger and stronger. However, an overlarge λ means that other nodes that never occur in any selected instance are ignored easily and are never visited when λ is infinite. We add 1 to the function as a base value, so that the candidate entity with $score_v = 0$ has the same transition probability as ordinary ones. When $\lambda = 1$, $f(score_v)$ is always 1, and INS-ES degrades into INS.

6. EXPERIMENTS AND EVALUATIONS

We perform all experiments on an FB15K dataset, which is sampled from Freebase [4]. It contains 592,213 true facts with 14,951 entities and 1345 relation types. It has been split randomly into training, validation, and testing sets. These sets only contain true facts. For the learning process, both embedding-based methods and inference-based methods have their own strategies to generate false facts. However, for testing, false facts are uniformly generated for all methods as described in [4]. For each true fact $r(h, t)$ in the testing set, the tail t is replaced by every entity in the existing KB, and these are mixed with the true one, forming the Left Testing Subset. Then, the head h is replaced in the same way, noted as the Right Testing Subset.

Two parts of experiments are performed:

- Explore the effectiveness of embedding-based methods on KBC and discuss which embedding-based method performs best on instance selection, which is important for subsequent logical inference based on our INS and INS-ES algorithms.

- Explore the effectiveness of INS-ES algorithm for KBC. We perform a comparison between our approaches and several state-of-the-art methods, including embedding-based methods and inference-based methods.

All following experiments are performed by a single thread on the servers with 24 Intel Xeon E5-2620 clocked at 2.00GHZ, with 64GB RAM, running Linux 2.6.32.

6.1 Instance Selection

We compare several embedding-based methods with a traditional approach to selecting different sizes of candidate sets. Hits@n can be viewed as the true facts coverage in n-size candidate sets because we believe that the more the true facts are covered, the better the selection is.

6.1.1 Compared Methods

BFS is a traditional approach based on an adjacent hypothesis, which means an entity t being adjacent or reachable via one skip from h implies $r(h,t)$ is more likely to be true. BFS is treated as a baseline.

Embedding-based methods described previously, **SE** [5], **SME**[3](linear and bilinear), **TransE** [4], are as compared. As a baseline for TransE, **Unstructured** (**Uns**, for short), which is a naive version of TransE that ignores the effect of various relations, is treated as a baseline as well.

6.1.2 Set up

We implement BFS in java by ourselves, but for Uns, SE, SME-lin, SME-bil and TransE, we use the codes on TransE's homepage[3] and keep the default setting for parameters. Similar to evaluation methods in [4, 26, 18], we evaluate Left Testing Subsets and Right Testing Subsets for each true fact $r(h,t)$ in testing KB. There may be other true facts in Left and Right Testing Subsets in addition to $r(h,t)$, but previous evaluation methods ignore them. For example, in the Left Testing Subset of $r(h,t)$, there is a true fact $r(h,t^{'})$ also occurring in testing the KB, and we should treat it the same as $r(h,t)$ when calculating Hits@n and AP@n. Our evaluation considers such $r(h,t^{'})$ in testing the KB, so that the Hits@10 value is different from those reported in [4, 26, 18].

6.1.3 Results

Figure 2 shows that, except for Uns, all embedding-based methods are better than BFS, the traditional approach. It indicates that most embedding-based methods have advantages on instance selection.

In Figure 2, the best Hits@1 is 32.911%, achieved by SME-bil, but after n increases to 10, TransE begins to outperform the other methods. In addition, TransE is the simplest method, and its running time is the shortest. Therefore, TransE is the most suitable method for generating smaller candidate sets for the subsequent logical inference.

TransE's Hits@50 has exceeded 90%, and Hits@100 is 94.568%, which is sufficient for subsequent fact inference. On the other hand, when n>100, all methods' Hits@n gradually approach 100%, and the performance of BFS starts to reach values that are close to the performance of embedding-based methods. The advantages of embedding-based methods disappear with the increase in n, and too large candidate sets would slow down the subsequent inferring algorithm. Therefore, we set the size of candidate set to 100 for subsequent experiments.

[3]https://everest.hds.utc.fr/doku.php?id=en:transe

6.2 Knowledge Base Completion

In this subsection, we compare our approaches with state-of-the-art methods including embedding-based methods and inference-based methods. Additionally, we explore the effect of similarity obtained a priori by the embedding-based method by comparing INS-ES with INS.

We employ Hits@n and AP@n as evaluations for the following experiments. Unlike instance selection, we employ Hits@1 as the most important metric because a good Hits@n with a large n cannot indicate that an approach has a good performance. AP@n is used as the other metric for the supplementary of Hits@n. AP@n can give a reasonable evaluation for $\mathcal{Q}(h,?)$, which has more than one true answer.

6.2.1 Compared Methods

Embedding-based methods We employ Uns, SE, SME-lin, SME-bil and TransE to represent embedding-based approaches in the same way as the methods in the experimental subsection of instance selection. However, we treat the output from embedding-based models as the final results.

Inference-based methods There are many methods that belong to this category. Most of them infer instances through logical formulas, but few of them can be used in KBC for their computation complexity. Here, we employ the INS algorithm to infer potential facts in the testing set and treat it as representative of inference-based methods.

Our approaches We apply the INS algorithm to infer overselected instances obtained from different embedding-based models. As **Embedding-based methods**, we choose Uns, SE, SME-lin, SME-bil and TransE to select instances and refer to the methods inferring over them as Uns-INS, SE-INS, SME-lin-INS, SME-bil-INS, TransE-INS, respectively.

Our approach with a priori We continue to expand TransE-INS by incorporating the similarity generated a priori by the embedding-based model into INS, noted as TransE-INS-ES. As an important super-parameter of TransE-INS-ES, λ in (in Equation 8) controls the strength of the effect of the similarity priori. We use TransE-INS-ES-λ to denote our method with different λ, where n denotes different λ.

6.2.2 Set up

We keep the default parameter setting for all embedding-based methods as in the instance selection. The number of selected instances is set to 100. For the INS algorithm, we set the maximum formula length as $l_f = 5$. The size of the initial node random walk starting from M_{random} is 500. The random walk times from one starting point T is 50 for learning and 1000 for inference. The restarting probability in random walk $P_{restart}$ is 0.35. The maximum number of iterations of the weight learner $M_{learner}$ is 100, and the L2-norm parameter C is 1. We employ the TransE-INS with 1000-size candidate sets to approximate INS because it cannot run completely to infer each instance directly, which is also the main reason that we make instance selection before inference. The implement is available online.[4]

[4]https://github.com/ZhuoyuWei/fpMLN

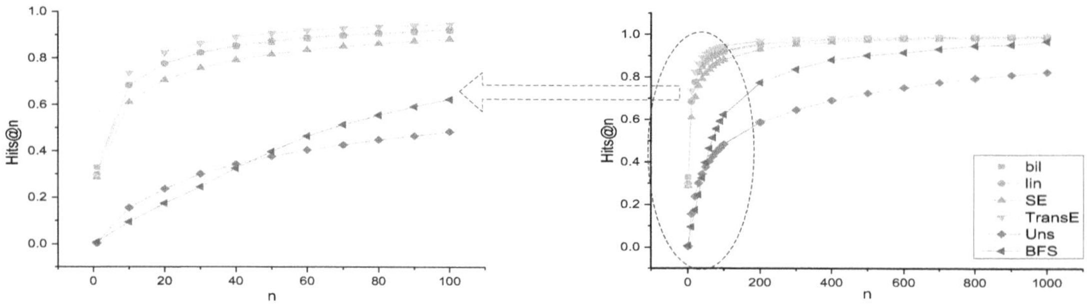

Figure 2: Hit curves of various methods for instance selection that generates candidate sets with different sizes. The range of n in the right graph is [0,1000], and the left graph is an enlarged view of the part at [0, 100].

Table 2: AP@n of various methods on FB15K

	Methods	Hits@1(AP@1)	Hits@10	AP@2	AP@3	AP@5	AP@7	AP@10
2.a	Uns	0.00384	0.15573	0.01305	0.01747	0.02128	0.02336	0.02571
	SME-bil	0.32911	0.68506	0.32119	0.3208	0.32655	0.32951	0.33348
	SME-lin	0.29807	0.68386	0.29136	0.29011	0.29426	0.29805	0.30102
	SE	0.28633	0.61026	0.28015	0.27996	0.28194	0.28480	0.28737
	TransE	0.29401	0.73710	0.30263	0.30835	0.31691	0.32099	0.32529
2.b	*INS**	0.32540	0.51917	0.30472	0.29668	0.28869	0.28519	0.28232
2.c	Uns-INS	0.32899	0.39388	0.30518	0.29349	0.28302	0.28102	0.28288
	SME-bil-INS	0.69212	0.83464	0.67224	0.66194	0.65233	0.65051	0.65483
	SME-lin-INS	0.68143	0.82478	0.65615	0.64645	0.63599	0.63568	0.64042
	SE-INS	0.67333	0.79938	0.65196	0.64158	0.63029	0.62823	0.63236
	TransE-INS	**0.69303**	**0.84894**	**0.67540**	**0.66566**	**0.65781**	**0.65550**	**0.66114**
2.d	TransE-INS-ES4.5	**0.71692**	**0.86633**	**0.70146**	**0.69320**	**0.68386**	**0.68100**	**0.68557**

6.2.3 Ours method vs. State-of-the-art methods

Table 2 shows the results of the comparison between our methods and state-of-the-art methods for KBC. From the results, we can obtain the following observations.

1) Our methods (except Uns-INS) in Table 2.c and 2.d achieve performance improvement over other methods in Table 2.a and 2.b. This indicates that our method based on Inferring via Grounding Network Sampling over Selected Instances is effective for the task of KBC.

2) Our methods, which perform inference after select instances by embedding-based methods in Table 2.c, all outperform only the corresponding embedding-based models in Table 2.a. For example, TransE's Hits@1 is 29.401%, which was the state-of-the-art method for KBC, while TransE-INS promotes Hits@1 to 69.303%, and TransE-INS also achieves much higher Hits@10 and AP@n. This proves the effectiveness of inferring instances following instance selection by embedding-based models, and the significant improvement is derived from the fact that our approaches consider explicit logical semantics and interaction between different relations, which is ignored in embedding-based models.

3) Our methods, which first make instances selection and generate small-scale candidate sets for INS in Table 2.c, outperform only INS in Table 2.b. The reason is that there are some noise instances, which may mislead the INS algorithm, but they are filtered by instance selection via embedding-based methods. It further indicates that embedding-based models can capture implicit factors that are ignored in inference methods, and both of these two methods cannot be substituted by each other.

4) Our extensional method, which incorporates the similarity generated a priori by the embedding-based model into INS in Table 2.d, outperforms our methods without the similarity priori in Table 2.c. This proves that the similarities obtained from embedding-based methods are helpful for promoting the inference precision as a priori.

6.2.4 Detailed Discussion

In this part, we engage in a detailed discussion on our proposed approaches.

Effect of the candidate set size We explore the effect of the number of instances for subsequent fact inference, and we employ TransE-INS as the experimental method. Figure 3 shows the results. The horizontal axis represents the number of selected instances, noted as N. The vertical axes of (a), (b) represent Hits@n, AP@n, respectively. Hits@1,Hits@10 and Hits@100 are presented in Figure 3.a. The best Hits@1 occurs at N=50, while the best Hits@10 and Hits@100 occur at N=200. When N>200, the performance keeps decreasing with an increasing N, and the AP@n in Figure 3.b has the similar appearance. This indicates that making instance selection before inferring to generate small-scale candidate sets is an effective mechanism, which not only narrows the inferring space but also filters out part of the noise.

Effect to running time Figure 3.c shows the running time of performing inference, which indicates the computation complexity of inference is linearly growing with the increase in the candidate set size. This proves that inference on large-scale KBs without first reducing candidates would take an extremely long period of time. Therefore, selecting instances to narrow the inferring space in our approach is necessary and ensures that the inferring algorithm is completed in a short time.

Effect of the similarity priori We are going to prove the effectiveness of incorporating the similarity priori generated by the embedding-based model into INS by comparing TransE-INS with several TransE-INS-ES with different λ. Figure 4 shows the results of INS and INS-ES over 100 se-

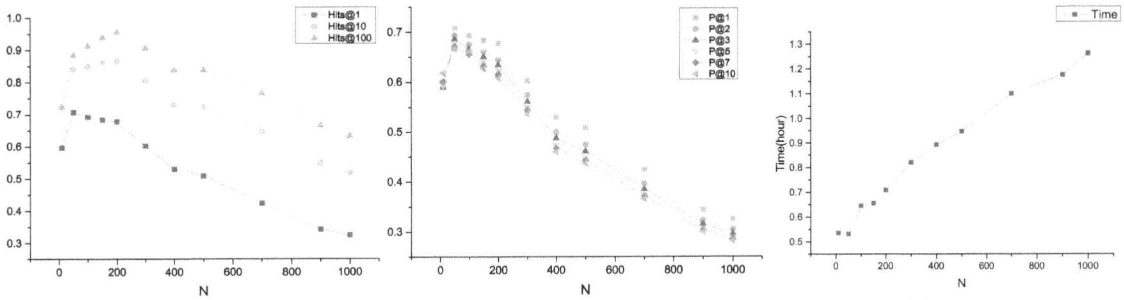

(a) Hits@n (b) AP@n (c) Times

Figure 3: Hits@n, AP@n and Time curves of TransE-INS with different size candidate sets.

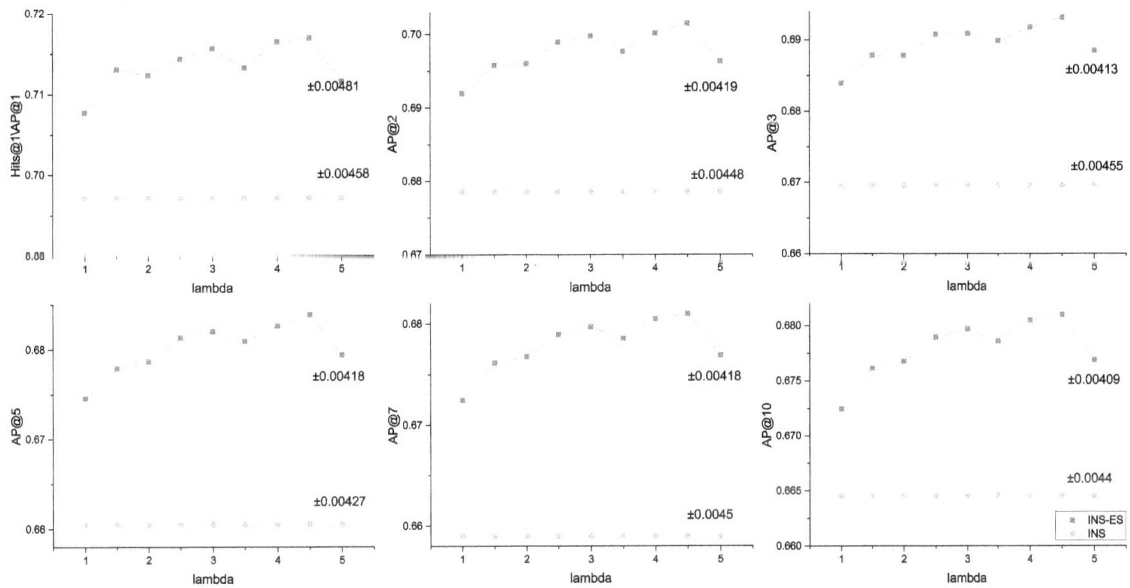

Figure 4: Comparing TransE-INS and TransE-INS-ES with different λ

lected instances generated by TransE. The horizontal axes represent λ, and the vertical axes in six sub-figures represent AP@1 (equal to Hits@1/100), AP@2, AP@3, AP@5, AP@7, AP@10. To reduce the randomness and highlight the effect of similarity priori, this experiment is repeated 5 times, and we report the mean and variance of AP@n. Regardless of the λ, INS-ES outperforms INS on Hits@1 and AP@n, and the best performance of INS-ES is achieved when $\lambda = 4.5$. This indicates that incorporating the similarity priori into a random walk process can achieve better performance. The curves also show that the performance is becoming better with the effect of similarity priori increase until $\lambda = 4.5$, and then the performance starts to become worse. The performance decrease may be caused by an excessively strong effect of similarity priori easily ignoring the nodes, which never occurs in selected facts, but these nodes may be accompanied by useful information.

7. RELATED WORK

Our work is related to two main categories of KBC methods: embedding-based approaches [21, 5, 12, 23, 4, 3, 26, 18] and inference-based approaches [22, 16, 24].

Nearly all embedding-based approaches represent entities as low dimensional vectors, but the representation for relations is multifarious. SE [5] represents each relation as two matrixes to capture the left and right interaction with one entity. RESCAL [21] represents relations as only one matrix and employs the product of three elements in a fact as similarity. SME[3] also represents relations as one matrix but employs an energy function to transform the interaction between the relation and entity. In the simplest way, TransE [4] represents relations in the same vector space as entities. The extensions of TransE, TransH [26] and TransR [18] also represent relations as low dimensional vectors, but there are differences between them: The former interprets a relation as a translating operation on a hyperplane to address one-to-many, many-to-one, and many-to-many relations, but the latter represents entities and relations in distinct spaces and projects entities from entity space to relation space. Tranc [9] and [12] take 2-way interactions between one entity and one relation into account. As a more complicated model, NTN [23] represents relations as tensors and matrixes simultaneously. However, these embedding-based methods do not consider explicit logical semantics and cannot sufficiently capture the interaction between different relations. Our approach applies a subsequent fact inference to overcome these shortages.

Inference-based methods usually view a KB as a graph, and seek, count or sample sub-structures (e.g., paths, subgraphs) to judge or calculate probability for a new fact. There are some typical inferring methods for KBC: ARM (association rule mining) [8], ILP (inductive logic programming) [25], and MLN [22]. They are all limited by the large size of the candidate sets, but our approach speeds up MLN and employs it as a subsequent inference model for its high precision. MLN is an appropriate model for KBC because it applies weighted formulas to capture long-range interaction across several relations. The main issue of MLN is the computation complexity of the learning structure and inferring; thus, the methods based on MLN cannot be extended to large-scale knowledge bases. [15, 14, 13, 19, 11] are all proposed methods to speed up the learning and inferring process, but most of them still need grounding facts or formulas, so that the issue of computation complexity has still not been adequately addressed. PRA [16] employs random walks, but unlike our approach, it simplifies MLN by only keeping the horn clause with the query at the place of head. A promising algorithm is proposed by Sun [24], which is also a data-driven algorithm based on random walks that learns structure and weights simultaneously. Our approach takes advantage of this and employs a similar mechanism for inference and replaces the uniform transition probability for promotion.

8. CONCLUSIONS

We proposed employing embedding-based models to make instance selection for subsequent fact inference and exploited INS and INS-ES (incorporating embedding a priori) algorithms to infer facts on MLN, which improved Hits@1 from 32.911% to 71.692% for the FB15K dataset.

9. ACKNOWLEDGMENTS

The authors are supported by the National High Technology Research and Development Program of China (No. 2015AA015402) and the National Natural Science Foundation of China (No. 61272332, 61202329, 61303179 and 613031 72).

10. REFERENCES

[1] M. Al Hasan and M. J. Zaki. Output space sampling for graph patterns. *In VLDB*, 2009.

[2] K. Bollacker, C. Evans, P. Paritosh, T. Sturge, and J. Taylor. Freebase: a collaboratively created graph database for structuring human knowledge. In *SIGMOD*, 2008.

[3] A. Bordes, X. Glorot, J. Weston, and Y. Bengio. A semantic matching energy function for learning with multi-relational data. *Machine Learning*, 2013.

[4] A. Bordes, N. Usunier, A. Garcia-Duran, J. Weston, and O. Yakhnenko. Translating embeddings for modeling multi-relational data. In *NIPS*, 2013.

[5] A. Bordes, J. Weston, R. Collobert, Y. Bengio, et al. Learning structured embeddings of knowledge bases. In *AAAI*, 2011.

[6] A. Carlson, J. Betteridge, B. Kisiel, B. Settles, E. R. Hruschka Jr, and T. M. Mitchell. Toward an architecture for never-ending language learning. In *AAAI*, 2010.

[7] X. L. Dong, K. Murphy, E. Gabrilovich, G. Heitz, W. Horn, N. Lao, T. Strohmann, S. Sun, and W. Zhang. Knowledge vault: A web-scale approach to probabilistic knowledge fusion. In *KDD*, 2014.

[8] L. A. Galárraga, C. Teflioudi, K. Hose, and F. Suchanek. Amie: association rule mining under incomplete evidence in ontological knowledge bases. In *WWW*, 2013.

[9] A. García-Durán, A. Bordes, and N. Usunier. Effective blending of two and three-way interactions for modeling multi-relational data. In *ECML/PKDD*. 2014.

[10] J. Hoffart, F. M. Suchanek, K. Berberich, and G. Weikum. Yago2: a spatially and temporally enhanced knowledge base from wikipedia. *Artificial Intelligence*, 2013.

[11] T. N. Huynh and R. J. Mooney. Discriminative structure and parameter learning for markov logic networks. In *ICML*, 2008.

[12] R. Jenatton, N. L. Roux, A. Bordes, and G. R. Obozinski. A latent factor model for highly multi-relational data. In *NIPS*, 2012.

[13] T. Khot, S. Natarajan, K. Kersting, and J. Shavlik. Learning markov logic networks via functional gradient boosting. In *ICDM*, 2011.

[14] S. Kok and P. Domingos. Learning the structure of markov logic networks. In *ICML*, 2005.

[15] S. Kok and P. Domingos. Learning markov logic networks using structural motifs. In *ICML*, 2010.

[16] N. Lao, T. Mitchell, and W. W. Cohen. Random walk inference and learning in a large scale knowledge base. In *EMNLP*, 2011.

[17] C.-H. Lee, X. Xu, and D. Y. Eun. Beyond random walk and metropolis-hastings samplers: why you should not backtrack for unbiased graph sampling. In *SIGMETRICS*, 2012.

[18] Y. Lin, Z. Liu, M. Sun, Y. Liu, and X. Zhu. Learning entity and relation embeddings for knowledge graph completion. In *AAAI*, 2015.

[19] L. Mihalkova and R. J. Mooney. Bottom-up learning of markov logic network structure. In *ICML*, 2007.

[20] B. Min, R. Grishman, L. Wan, C. Wang, and D. Gondek. Distant supervision for relation extraction with an incomplete knowledge base. In *HLT-NAACL*, 2013.

[21] M. Nickel, V. Tresp, and H.-P. Kriegel. A three-way model for collective learning on multi-relational data. In *ICML*, 2011.

[22] M. Richardson and P. Domingos. Markov logic networks. *Machine learning*, 2006.

[23] R. Socher, D. Chen, C. D. Manning, and A. Ng. Reasoning with neural tensor networks for knowledge base completion. In *NIPS*, 2013.

[24] Z. Sun, Z. Wei, J. Wang, and H. Hao. Scalable learning for structure in markov logic networks. In *AAAI 2014 Workshop on StarAI*, 2014.

[25] W. Y. Wang, K. Mazaitis, and W. W. Cohen. Programming with personalized pagerank: a locally groundable first-order probabilistic logic. In *CIKM*, 2013.

[26] Z. Wang, J. Zhang, J. Feng, and Z. Chen. Knowledge graph embedding by translating on hyperplanes. In *AAAI*, 2014.

Author Index

Aberer, Karl 1161
Ackermann, Hanno 1491
Ahmed, Mohamed 1051
Ahukorala, Kumaripaba 1703
Ai, Qingyao 303
Ai, Xusheng 1803
Ailem, Melissa 1807
Ainy, Eleanor 483
Akella, Ramakrishna 173
Alamoudi, Abdullah 3
Albakour, M-Dyaa 53
Aletras, Nikolaos 1953
Ali, Mohammed Eunus 931
Altingovde, Ismail Sengor 1947
Alyoubi, Khaled H. 1521
Amer-Yahia, Sihem 403, 1421, 1531
Anand, Avishek 323, 1201
Anastasiu, David C. 791
Andrzejak, Artur 93
Ang, Min-Hwee 723
Anwar, Adnan 1811
Anwar, Tarique 1671
Arapakis, Ioannis 1695
Ardon, Sebastien 1591
Arya, Dhruv 1699
Aslam, Javed A. 1391
Asudeh, Abolfazl 753
Azevedo, Leonardo Guerreiro . 1831
Azzopardi, Leif 313, 1787, 1943
Bae, Duck-Ho 1261
Bagdouri, Mossaab 593, 1707
Bailey, Peter 1759
Baldwin, Timothy 1863, 1953
Balog, Krisztian 1945
Bao, Junwei 1301
Barrio, Pablo 153
Barua, Sukarna 931
Bast, Hannah 1431
Beecks, Christian 1241
Bellarykar, Nikhil 1899
Belongie, Serge 183
Bengio, Yoshua 553
Bennett, Paul N. 1735
Berardi, Giacomo 1711
Berkovsky, Shlomo 1591
Bidoit, Nicole 713
Bing, Lidong 103
Bizid, Imen 1715
Björklund, Henrik 1541
Bonchi, Francesco 1851
Borcea, Cristian 413
Borkar, Vinayak 3
Botezatu, Mirela Madalina 1371
Bourhis, Pierre 483
Boursier, Patrice 1715
Braslavski, Pavel 1571
Büch, Lutz 93
Cai, Weidong 871
Cai, Weidong 1401
Callan, Jamie 951
Cambazoglu, B. Barla ... 1695, 1947
Candan, K. Selçuk 1101
Cao, Cheng 513
Cao, Jiuxin 1211
Cao, Shaosheng 891
Cao, Yanan 801
Carey, Michael J. 3
Carmel, David 283
Carterette, Ben 1795
Cautis, Bogdan 563
Caverlee, James 213, 513
Ceroni, Andrea 1815
Cetintas, Suleyman 203
Cha, Meeyoung 1879
Chae, Dong-Kyu 1819
Chakraborty, Tanmoy 1271
Chang, Hyeokyoon 1131
Chang, Yi 603
Chatzis, Sotirios P. 1311
Chen, Chen 1351
Chen, Fang 193
Chen, Gang 1891
Chen, Hongxiang 1891
Chen, Ke 1891
Chen, Ling 1011, 1687
Chen, Ming-Syan 163
Chen, Rui 1061
Chen, Tao 1661
Chen, Wei 1923
Chen, Xiao 1661
Chen, Xilun 1101
Chen, Ye 1581
Chen, Yi 413
Chen, Yongqiang 1719
Chen, Zheng 133
Cheng, Jian 1775
Cheng, Jianpeng 133
Cheng, Pu-Jen 1441
Cheng, Qiang 393
Cheng, Xueqi 901, 1799
Cheung, David 443
Chirkova, Rada 1011
Chitsaz, Mahsa 743
Cho, Seong-Je 1819
Choi, Byron 723
Choromanski, Krzysztof 1381
Chow, Chi-Yin 941, 1641
Christophides, Vassilis 1531
Chrysanthis, Panos K. 1151
Chung, Jinwook 513
Chung, Young-joo 1779
Cong, Gao 1231
Craswell, Nick 1755
Croft, W. Bruce 303
Cui, Yin 183
Cui, Zhiming 1803
Culpepper, J. Shane 293
da S. Torres, Ricardo 83
Dalton, Jeffrey 1945

Daudjee, Khuzaima 243
Davidson, Susan B. 483
Davtyan, Martin 783
De, Abir 223
de Bayser, Maira Gatti 1831
De Francisci Morales, Gianmarco 273
De Nies, Tom 1823
de Rijke, Maarten 1191, 1411
Deng, Ke 941
Deolalikar, Vinay 1767
Deshpande, Prasad M. 123
Deutch, Daniel 483
Deveaud, Romain 53
Develder, Chris 153
Dhillon, Inderjit S. 203
Dietz, Laura 1461
Dimou, Anastasia 1823
Ding, Wanying 1621
Doan, Minh Tuan 1827
Dou, Zhicheng 63
Doucet, Antoine 1715, 1945
Douzal-Chouakria, Ahlame 1531
Drutsa, Alexey 763
Du, Changying 1847
Du, Jianfeng 743
Du, Xiaoyong 861
Duan, Huizhong 333
Duan, Nan 1301
Dumais, Susan T. 1551
Dyreson, Curtis 723
Eickhoff, Carsten 783
Estrin, Deborah 183
Esuli, Andrea 1711
Faiz, Sami 1715
Fan, Feifan 573
Fang, Rui 1867
Fang, Xiu Susie 493, 503
Feng, Jianhua 693
Fetahu, Besnik 323
Fischer, Peter M. 1823
Fisichella, Marco 1815
Fu, Jinhua 1871
Fu, Xiaoqin 1931
Fu, Yun 811
Fujishiro, Hiroyuki 1859
Gadiraju, Ujwal 1201, 1815
Ganguly, Niloy 583
Gao, Hongchang 871
Gao, Liangcai 1291
Gao, Wei 1751
Gao, Xin 1915
Garcia-Alvarado, Carlos 1939
Garimella, Kiran 273
Gast, Nicolas 703
Gaussier, Eric 1421
Ge, Hancheng 513
Genevès, Pierre 1675
Ghosh, Kripabandhu 1723
Ghosh, Saptarshi 583
Ghosh, Subham 583
Gionis, Aristides 273
Giurgiu, Ioana 1371
Glowacka, Dorota 1703
Gonçalves, Marcos André ..83, 1071
Gong, Neil Zhenqiang 1111
Gong, Yeyun 533
Goyal, Pawan 583, 1271
Grauer, Lidia 1727
Gravano, Luis 153
Gribel, Daniel Lemes 1831
Grover, Raman 3
Grue Simonsen, Jakob 553
Gu, Quanquan 443
Gu, Xiaoyan 33
Gui, Lin 1081
Guido, Nicola 1675
Gullo, Francesco 1481, 1851
Guo, Jiafeng 1799
Guo, Li 801
Guo, Lifan 1621
Guo, Tian 1161
Guo, Weiyu 1731
Gurunath Kulkarni, Ranjitha 543
Gusev, Gleb 763, 981
Hagen, Matthias 1571
Halawi, Guy 283
Halkidi, Maria 1481
Han, Dingyi 1141
Han, Jiawei 443
Hanbury, Allan 1763
Hao, Shuji 1181
Hashem, Tanzima 931
Hassan, Naeemul 753, 1835
Hassan Awadallah, Ahmed 543, 1551
Ha-Thuc, Viet 1699
Haussmann, Elmar 1431
He, Jia 113
He, Jingrui 463
He, Jun 861
He, Qing 113, 1847
He, Ran 1911
He, Shizhu 623
He, Tingting 1621
He, Wei 861
He, Xiangnan 1661
He, Yonghao 1251
He, Yuan 1281
Heatherly, Raymond 1021
Helmer, Sven 1521
Hermanns, Judith 1241
Herschel, Melanie 713
Hofmann, Thomas 783
Hoi, Steven C.H. 1181
Hong, Dezhi 363
Hong, Liangjie 1895
Hsieh, Hsun-Ping 1839
Hsu, Wynne 523, 831
Hu, Bing 1111
Hu, Sha 63
Hu, Xia 1041
Hu, Xiaohua 1621
Huan, Jun 1091
Huang, Hao 1031
Huang, Heng 871, 1401
Huang, Jiajia 1611

Huang, Junming 901
Huang, Minlie 343
Huang, Pengtao 23
Huang, Weijing 1923
Huang, Xuanjing 533
Huang, Xuedong 1783
Huang, Yalou 1799
Huang, Yongfeng 1601
Huijnen, Pim 1191
Hwang, Heasoo 1883
Iacoboni, Giorgio 243
Ibrahim, Yusra 1945
Ilves, Kalle 1703
Islam, Md. Saiful 1671
Jagadish, Hosagrahar V. 1679
Jameel, Shoaib 103
Jamil, Hasan M. 1679
Järvelin, Kalervo 313
Jeong, Kyosung 1683
Ji, Guoliang 623
Jiang, Bo 1843
Jiang, Changjun 1281
Jiang, Jyun-Yu 1441
Jiang, Xiaoqian 1001
Jiang, Yuan 991
Jiang, Zhuoren 1291
Jie, Luo 603
Jin, Hongxia 1061, 1111
Jin, Rong 1141
Jin, Xin 113, 1847
Jo, Yohan 1171
Jo, Yong-Yeon 1261
Jones, Rosie 543
Jose, Joemon M. 1955
Jueng, Hoyoung 671
Kacimi, Mouna 233, 1951
Kafaar, Mohamed Ali 1591
Kalra, Achir 413
Kamali, Shahin 243
Kamps, Jaap 1561
Kan, Min-Yen 1661
Kang, Cuicui 1251
Kang, Jaewoo 1131
Kang, Ying 33
Kang, Zhao 393
Kanhabua, Nattiya 1201
Kantarcioglu, Murat 1021
Kantere, Verena 473
Kao, Ben 443, 1301
Karypis, George 791
Kasiviswanathan, Shiva Prasad 1031
Kawale, Jaya 811
Kawase, Yasushi 1471
Kementsietsidis, Anastasios 473
Kemkes, Philipp 1491
Kenter, Tom 1191, 1411
Kersten, Martin 1321
Keskustalo, Heikki 313
Khan, Arijit 1851
Kharitonov, Eugene 773
Khatkevich, Tsimafei 981
Kholghi, Mahnoosh 143
KhudaBukhsh, Ashiqur R. 1735
Kim, Jaewoo 1879
Kim, Sang-Wook . 1261, 1683, 1819
Kim, Seongsoon 1131
Kim, Yesol 1819
Kimura, Akisato 1859
King, Irwin 821, 851
Kiran, Uday 253
Kiseleva, Julia 1561
Kishore, Shaunak 73
Kitsuregawa, Masaru 253
Kleisarchaki, Sofia 1531
Kohjima, Masahiro 1855
Köhler, Henning 1361
Kong, Deguang 1111
Kourogi, Sawa 1859
Koutraki, Maria 971
Koutsopoulos, Iordanis 1481
Krishnaswamy, Shonali 1231
Kulik, Lars 931
Kulkarni, Vinay 1899
Kumar, Suhansanu 1271
Kutzkov, Konstantin 1051
Labrinidis, Alexandros 1151
Lagrée, Paul 563
Lakshminarasimhan, Sriram 123
Lam, Wai 103
Lan, Yanyan 1799
Lan, Yi-Feng 163
Latecki, Longin Jan 1903
Lau, Jey Han 1953
Lauw, Hady W. 1691
Lawlor, Matthew 73
Layaïda, Nabil 1675
Leckie, Christopher 1827
Lee, Chia-Jung 303
Lee, Doheon 1941
Lee, Kuang-Chih 203
Lee, Kyumin 513
Lee, Mong Li 523, 831
Lee, Sang-goo 1883
Lee, Seongwoon 1131
Lee, Wang-Chien 163
Lei, Kai 1923
Leiva, Luis A. 1695
Leroy, Vincent 1421
Lewin-Eytan, Liane 283
Lezina, Galina 1571
Li, Bin 193
Li, Chao 673
Li, Chengkai 753, 1835
Li, Cheng-Te 1839
Li, Gang 801
Li, Guo 1919
Li, Guoliang 693
Li, Haoran 1001, 1511
Li, Jundong 633, 1041
Li, Kang 1767
Li, Minglei 1081
Li, Peng 1401
Li, Qian 801
Li, Quanzhi 1867
Li, Sheng 811

Li, Tao 1907
Li, Xiang 443
Li, Xiao-Li 1231
Li, Xiu 23
Li, Xue 493, 503
Li, Xuhui 1611
Li, Xutao 1231
Li, Yanhua 941
Li, Zhao 1871, 1919
Li, Zhidong 193
Liang, Hongwei 911
Liang, Huizhi 1863
Liang, Jiguang 1843
Liang, Weifa 263
Liao, Shengcai 1251
Lim, Sungchae 1683
Limsopatham, Nut 1739
Lin, Chin-Yew 1441
Lin, Peng 193
Lin, Xuemin 921
Link, Sebastian 1361
Lioma, Christina 553
Liu, Bin 1111
Liu, Bo 1211
Liu, Chengfei 263, 1671
Liu, Hongyan 861
Liu, Huan 423, 1041, 1651
Liu, Jinfei 1511
Liu, Jing 1441
Liu, Kang 623, 1331
Liu, Lei 881
Liu, Qiang 613, 1743
Liu, Xi 881
Liu, Xiaomo 1867
Liu, Xiaozhong 1291
Liu, Yiqun 1581
Livingston, Mark 1955
Loghmanpour, Natasha 1171
Lomakina, Aleksandra 1727
Lu, Dongyuan 961
Lu, Hanqing 1775
Lu, Haokai 213
Lu, Qin 1081
Lu, Wei 891
Lu, Xiaolu 293
Lu, Yueming 1751
Luo, Hengliang 343
Luo, Jun 1511
Luo, Junzhou 1211
Luo, Ping 113, 453, 1847
Lv, Chao 573
Lv, Yuanhua 841, 1747
Ma, Jing 1751
Ma, Shaoping 1581
Maarek, Yoelle 283
Macdonald, Craig 53, 773, 1711, 1739, 1955
Madsen, Kasper Grud Skat 13
Mahanti, Anirban 1591
Mahmood, Abdun Naser 1811
Makarov, Nikita 1561
Malin, Bradley 1021
Man, Tong 901
Mannens, Erik 1823
Mao, Renxin 1871
Markert, Katja 323
Martens, Wim 1541
Martins, Wellington 1071
Massonnet, Guillaume 703
Matsubayashi, Tatsushi 1855
Maxwell, David 313
Mazumder, Sahisnu 1875
McAuley, Julian 821
McCann, Julie A. 1791
Medlar, Alan 1703
Mehta, Sameep 1875
Melo, Gerard de 223
Meng, Dan 33
Metrikov, Pavel 1391
Miao, Chunyan 1181
Miao, Yuan 991
Milo, Tova 483
Mirisaee, Hamid 1421
Mishra, Meenakshi 1091
Mitra, Bhaskar 1755
Miyauchi, Atsushi 1471
Moffat, Alistair 293, 1759
Moschitti, Alessandro 1451
Moshfeghi, Yashar 1955
Moshtaghi, Masud 1827
Mukherjee, Animesh 1271
Mukherjee, Subhabrata 353
Müller, Emmanuel 1321
Nadif, Mohamed 1807
Nagata, Masaaki 1927
Nam, Jiin 1879
Nandi, Animesh 123
Nayef, Nibal 1715
Nguyen, Anthony 143
Nie, Feiping 871
Nie, Jian-Yun 553
Niederée, Claudia 1201
Nikitaki, Sofia 1051
Nikulin, Vadim 1561
Nishikawa, Hitoshi 1859
Niu, Wei 213
Niu, Wenjia 801, 1251
Nourbakhsh, Armineh 1867
Nutt, Werner 233, 733
Oard, Douglas W. 593, 1707
Odijk, Daan 1551
Omidvar-Tehrani, Behrooz 403
Ordonez, Carlos 1939
Orfanoudakis, George 473
Ounis, Iadh 53, 773, 1711, 1739, 1955
Ozertem, Umut 543
Palanisamy, Balaji 673
Palotti, João 1763
Pan, Chunhong 1251
Pan, Sinno Jialin 1847
Paolo Ponzetto, Simone 1461
Paramonov, Sergey 733
Park, Jaram 1879
Park, Kunwoo 1879
Park, Youngki 1883

Parui, Swapan Kumar 1723
Pasca, Marius 1121
Patel, Dhaval 1875
Patidar, Vikas 1271
Paul, Saurabh 1887
Pavlu, Virgil 1391
Peng, Chong 393
Peng, Min 1611
Peng, Pai 1891
Perez, Yonathan 73
Petroni, Fabio 243
Pham, Tuan-Anh Nguyen 1231
Pickens, Jeremy 1943
Pollak, John P. 183
Pradhan, Neeraj 1767
Prasojo, Radityo Eko 233
Preda, Nicoleta 971, 1951
Preum, Sarah Masud 433
Pu, Xiaojia 1141
Qi, Yanjun 433
Qi, Zhenyu 1331
Qian, Mingjie 1895
Qiang, Runwei 573
Qin, Huazheng 463
Qin, Jianbin 1351
Querzoni, Leonardo 243
Rafiei, Davood 1949
Raghavan, Sriram 123
Rahman, Altaf 603
Rajan, Suju 1895
Rajasegarar, Sutharshan 1827
Ram, Nilam 1501
Ramanath, Maya 1951
Raviv, Ariel 283
Reijsbergen, Daniel 703
Rezvani, Mojtaba 263
Rhim, Eunhee 1879
Rocha, Leonardo 1071
Roisin, Cécile 1675
Role, François 1807
Rosé, Carolyn Penstein 1171
Rostamizadeh, Afshin 1381
Roychoudhury, Suman 1899
Rudra, Koustav 583
S Bhowmick, Sourav 723
Sadiq, Shazia 671, 1631
Sakai, Tetsuya 63, 1943
Salathe, Marcel 1501
Salehi, Mahsa 1827
Sang, Jitao 961
Sapino, Maria Luisa 1101
Sathe, Saket 1161
Savković, Ognjen 733
Sawada, Hiroshi 1855
Schockaert, Steven 103
Scholer, Falk 1759
Schueppert, Michael 73
Schuhmacher, Michael 1461
Sebastiani, Fabrizio 1711
Seidl, Thomas 1241
Sellam, Thibault 1321
Sellis, Timos 473
Serdyukov, Pavel 773, 981
Sha, Ying 1843
Shah, Sameena 1867
Shah, Zubair 1811
Shakarian, Paulo 1101
Shang, Haichuan 253
Shang, Yue 1621
Shao, Yingxia 1631
Shein, Anatoli U. 1151
Sheldon, Daniel 303
Shen, Chih-Ya 163
Shen, Huawei 901
Shen, Yilin 1061
Sheng, Quan Z. 493, 503
Sheng, Victor S. 1803, 1931
Shi, Chuan 453
Shi, Yue 1895
Shin, Donghyuk 203
Shou, Lidan 1891
Shu, Jinyun 1601
Shu, Le 1903
Shuai, Hong-Han 163
Siersdorfer, Stefan 1491
Sifer, Mark 1771
Singh, Mayank 1271
Sinha, Shakti 1699
Sitbon, Laurianne 143
Sohangir, Sahar 1907
Song, Chonggang 523, 831
Song, Dawei 1719
Song, Il-Yeol 1939
Song, Min 1941
Song, Qiang 1775
Sordoni, Alessandro 553
Soulier, Laure 43, 1943
Sozio, Mauro 273
Stankovic, John A. 433
Stein, Benno 1571
Stevenson, Mark 1953
Su, Hao 683
Subramanian, Suriya 123
Sudoh, Katsuhoto 1927
Sun, Jianling 911
Sun, Jiashen 343
Sun, Weiwei 683
Sun, Xuyang 533
Sun, Zhengya 1331
Swezey, Robin M.E, ...1779
Syed, Umar 1381
Tamine, Lynda 43, 1943
Tan, Jianlong 801
Tan, Pang-Ning 881
Tan, Tieniu 1731, 1911
Tanaka, Katsumi 1949
Tandon, Niket 223
Tang, Jiliang 1041, 1651
Tang, Shu 861
Tanin, Egemen 931
Taxidou, Io 1823
Teevan, Jaime 1
Termier, Alexandre 403
Thakuriah, Piyushimita 1955
Thomas, Paul 1759
Tian, Guanhua 1331

Timm, Thomas 1541
Tomkins, Andrew 1349
Tonellotto, Nicola 1947
Tran, Tuan 1201
Tremayne, Mark 1835
Triantafillou, Peter 1955
Tribastone, Mirco 703
Tsang, Ivor 1687
Tu, Chuanchuan 683
Tuarob, Suppawong 1501
Tucker, Conrad S. 1501
Tymoshenko, Kateryna 1451
Tzompanaki, Aikaterini 713
Ufliand, Anna 763
Uysal, Merih Seran 1241
Vahabi, Hossein 553, 563, 1481
Vallet, David 1591
Van de Walle, Rik 1823
Vargas, Javier A. 83
Verborgh, Ruben 1823
Verspoor, Karin 1941
Viegas, Felipe 1071
Vodislav, Dan 971
Völske, Michael 1571
Vorobeychik, Yevgeniy 1021
Vu, Hai L. 1671
Wan, Chang 443
Wan, Zhiyu 1021
Wang, Benyou 1719
Wang, Cheng 1281
Wang, Chong 413
Wang, Chunye 173
Wang, Dingding 1907
Wang, Dong 1911
Wang, Haishuai 1687
Wang, Haixun 653
Wang, Hao 1631
Wang, Hongning 363
Wang, Houfeng 1935
Wang, Hua 1611
Wang, Huaming 1783
Wang, Jian 1251
Wang, Jianyong 1221
Wang, Jim Jing-Yan 1915
Wang, Ke 911
Wang, Kewen 743
Wang, Liang 383, 613, 1731, 1743, 1911
Wang, Lihong 1843
Wang, Meng 1581
Wang, Peng 1919
Wang, Ruhui 1923
Wang, Suhang 1651
Wang, Tengjiao 1923
Wang, Wei 463, 683, 1351
Wang, Weiping 33
Wang, Xianzhi 493, 503
Wang, Xiaojie 63
Wang, Xiaoyang 921
Wang, Xun 1927
Wang, Yang 193
Wang, Yi 193
Wang, Zhe 743
Wang, Zhenghao 1783
Wang, Zhongyuan 133, 653
Wei, Qikang 1081
Wei, Zhongyu 1751
Wei, Zhuoyu 1331
Weikum, Gerhard 223, 353
Wen, Ji-Rong 63, 133, 653
Wevers, Melvin 1191
White, Ryen W. 1551, 1735
Whitehouse, Kamin 363
Wiesmann, Dorothea 1371
Wilkie, Colin 1787
Wohler, Thomas 1851
Wong, Kam-Fai 1751
Wood, Peter T. 1521
Wu, Bin 453
Wu, Fangzhao 1601
Wu, Gangshan 1141
Wu, Hao 683
Wu, Jian 1803, 1931
Wu, Shu 383, 613, 1731, 1743
Wu, Xindong 1931
Xia, Weiyi Xia 1021
Xiang, Shiming 1251
Xiao, Yanghua 463, 653
Xie, Maoqiang 1799
Xie, Sihong 603
Xiong, Chenyan 951
Xiong, Li 1001, 1511
Xu, Chang 1891
Xu, Changsheng 961
Xu, Jiajie 671
Xu, Jun 1799
Xu, Qiongkai 891
Xu, Ruifeng 1081
Xu, Shuai 1211
Xu, Wenzheng 263
Xu, Xiaofei 493, 503
Xue, Gui-Rong 1141
Yan, Jun 133
Yan, Rui 1621, 1839
Yan, Shengquan 1783
Yang, De-Nian 163
Yang, Deqing 463
Yang, Jianwu 573
Yang, Longqi 183
Yang, Peng 643
Yang, Qiang 941
Yang, Xiankai 343
Yao, Lina 493, 503
Yao, Yufeng 1803
Ye, Han-Jia 991
Ye, Tengyuan 1691
Yin, Hongzhi 1631
Yin, Pengcheng 1301
Yin, Qiyue 383, 1911
Yoo, Shinjae 1031
Yoon, Seunghyun 1879
Yu, Feng 1743
Yu, Minghe 693
Yu, Minhwan 1131
Yu, Philip S. 163, 453, 603, 841
Yu, Ting 1011

Yu, Weiren 1791
Yu, Xiao 443
Yuan, Bo 23
Yuan, Mingxuan 941
Yuan, Quan 1231
Yuan, Ting 1775
Yuan, Zhigang 1601
Yue, Yading 453
Zafarani, Reza 423
Zaiane, Osmar 633
Zaruba, Gergely V. 753
Zeng, Jia 941
Zengin, Mustafa 1795
Zerr, Sergej 1491
Zhai, ChengXiang 333
Zhan, De-Chuan 991
Zhan, Liming 921
Zhang, Bang 193
Zhang, Chengqi 1687
Zhang, Chenyi 911
Zhang, Fan 183
Zhang, Gensheng 753
Zhang, Haoyu 1511
Zhang, Jia-Dong 941, 1641
Zhang, Jiawei 841
Zhang, Jing 1931
Zhang, Jingyuan 603
Zhang, Min 1581
Zhang, Peng 1687, 1719, 1919
Zhang, Qi 533
Zhang, Qing 1935
Zhang, Wei 1221
Zhang, Wenjie 921
Zhang, Yanchun 1611
Zhang, Yaogong 1799
Zhang, Ying 921
Zhang, Zhi-Li 941
Zhang, Zhiqiang 453
Zhao, H.Vicky 851
Zhao, Jun 623, 1331
Zhao, Li 343
Zhao, Peilin 643, 1181
Zhao, Peixiang 373
Zhao, Pengpeng 1803
Zhao, Tong 821, 851
Zhao, Xiang 253
Zheng, Baihua 683
Zheng, Kai 671
Zheng, Yu 1641
Zhou, Chuan 1919
Zhou, Ke 1581
Zhou, Ming 1301
Zhou, Tao 1211
Zhou, Xiaofang 671, 1631
Zhou, Yongluan 13
Zhou, Zhi-Hua 991
Zhu, Jiahui 1611
Zhu, Xiaoyan 343
Zhu, Ziqing 1211
Zhuang, Fuzhen 113, 1847
Zhukovskiy, Maxim 981
Zuccon, Guido 143, 1763

www.ingramcontent.com/pod-product-compliance
Ingram Content Group UK Ltd.
Pitfield, Milton Keynes, MK11 3LW, UK
UKHW051419290926
15471UKWH00009B/1688

9 781450 34116